# Official 1984 National Football League

# Record & Fact Book

A National Football League Book.
Workman Publishing, New York.

# National Football League, 1984

410 Park Avenue, New York, N.Y. 10022    (212) 758-1500

Commissioner: Pete Rozelle
Executive Director: Don Weiss
Director of Administration: Joe Rhein
Treasurer: John Schoemer
Counsel to Commissioner: Jay Moyer
Special Assistant to Commissioner: Robert Woodrum
Director of Operations: Jan Van Duser
Director of Public Relations: Jim Heffernan
Director of Information: Joe Browne
Director of Broadcasting: Val Pinchbeck, Jr.
Director of Security: Warren Welsh
Assistant Director of Security: Charles R. Jackson
Director of Player Personnel: Joel Bussert
Supervisor of Officials: Art McNally
Assistant Supervisor of Officials: Jack Reader
Assistant Supervisor of Officials: Nick Skorich
Director of Special Events: Jim Steeg
Assistant Director of Special Events: Susan McCann
Controller: Tom Sullivan
Director of Personnel: Wayne Rosen

## American Football Conference
President: Lamar Hunt, Kansas City Chiefs
Assistant to President: Al Ward
Director of Information: Fran Connors

## National Football Conference
President: Wellington Mara, New York Giants
Assistant to President: Bill Granholm
Director of Information: Dick Maxwell

**Cover Photograph by Richard Mackson.**

Printed in the United States of America.

A National Football League Book.
Compiled by the NFL Public Relations Department
  and Seymour Siwoff.
Edited by Fran Connors, AFC Director of Information,
  Pete Abitante, NFL Public Relations, and
  Chuck Garrity, Jr., NFLP Creative Services.
Statistics by Elias Sports Bureau.
Produced by NFL Properties, Inc., Creative Services
  Division.

Workman Publishing Co.
1 West 39th Street, New York, N.Y. 10018
Manufactured in the United States of America.
First printing, July 1984.

10 9 8 7 6 5 4 3 2 1

# Contents

All times P.M. local daylight.
Nationally televised games in parentheses. CBS and NBC television
doubleheader games in the regular season to be announced.

## Preseason/First Week

| | | |
|---|---|---|
| **Saturday, July 28** | Seattle ___ vs. Tampa Bay ___ at Canton, Ohio | (ABC) 3:00 |
| **Friday, August 3** | New York Giants ___ at New England ___ | 7:30 |
| **Saturday, August 4** | Atlanta ___ at Minnesota ___ | 7:00 |
| | Buffalo ___ at Seattle ___ | 7:30 |
| | Cincinnati ___ at New York Jets ___ | 8:30 |
| | Colts ___ at Miami ___ | 8:00 |
| | Green Bay ___ at Dallas ___ | 8:00 |
| | Houston ___ at Tampa Bay ___ | 8:00 |
| | Los Angeles Raiders ___ at San Francisco ___ | 6:00 |
| | Los Angeles Rams ___ at San Diego ___ | 6:00 |
| | New Orleans ___ at Kansas City ___ | 7:30 |
| | Philadelphia ___ at Detroit ___ | 7:00 |
| | Pittsburgh ___ at Cleveland ___ | 7:30 |
| | St. Louis ___ at Chicago ___ | 6:00 |
| | Washington ___ at Denver ___ | 7:00 |

## Preseason/Second Week

| | | |
|---|---|---|
| **Friday, August 10** | Kansas City ___ at St. Louis ___ | 7:30 |
| | Los Angeles Raiders ___ at Washington ___ | 8:00 |
| **Saturday, August 11** | Atlanta ___ at New Orleans ___ | 7:00 |
| | Chicago ___ vs. Green Bay ___ at Milwaukee | 7:00 |
| | Cincinnati ___ at Tampa Bay ___ | 8:00 |
| | Dallas ___ at San Diego ___ | 6:00 |
| | Miami ___ at Minnesota ___ | 7:00 |
| | New England ___ at Buffalo ___ | 6:00 |
| | New York Giants ___ at Colts ___ | 7:00 |
| | New York Jets ___ at Houston ___ | 8:00 |
| | Philadelphia ___ at Pittsburgh ___ | 6:00 |
| | San Francisco ___ at Denver ___ | 7:00 |
| | Seattle ___ at Detroit ___ | 7:00 |
| **Monday, August 13** | Cleveland ___ at Los Angeles Rams ___ | 7:00 |

## Preseason/Third Week

| | | |
|---|---|---|
| **Thursday, August 16** | Pittsburgh ___ at Dallas ___ | (ABC) 8:00 |
| **Friday, August 17** | New England ___ at Washington ___ | (NBC) 8:00 |
| | St. Louis ___ at Seattle ___ | 7:30 |
| **Saturday, August 18** | Cincinnati ___ at Chicago ___ | 6:00 |
| | Cleveland ___ at Kansas City ___ | 7:30 |
| | Colts ___ at Denver ___ | 7:00 |
| | Detroit ___ at Buffalo ___ | 6:00 |
| | Green Bay ___ at Los Angeles Rams ___ | 7:00 |
| | New Orleans ___ at Houston ___ | 8:00 |
| | New York Jets ___ at New York Giants ___ | 8:00 |
| | Philadelphia ___ at Minnesota ___ | 7:00 |
| | San Francisco ___ at San Diego ___ | (CBS) 6:00 |
| | Tampa Bay ___ at Atlanta ___ | 8:00 |
| **Sunday, August 19** | Miami ___ at Los Angeles Raiders ___ | (NBC) 1:00 |

## Preseason/Fourth Week

**Thursday, August 23**
| | | |
|---|---|---|
| Cleveland ___ at Philadelphia ___ | | 7:00 |
| San Diego ___ at Los Angeles Rams ___ | | 7:00 |

**Friday, August 24**
| | | |
|---|---|---|
| Denver ___ at Atlanta ___ | | 8:00 |
| Detroit ___ at Cincinnati ___ | | 7:00 |
| Kansas City ___ at New England ___ | | 7:30 |
| Miami ___ at Tampa Bay ___ | | 8:00 |
| Minnesota ___ at St. Louis ___ | | 7:30 |
| New York Jets ___ at Los Angeles Raiders ___ | (NBC) | 6:00 |
| Seattle ___ at San Francisco ___ | | 6:00 |

**Saturday, August 25**
| | | |
|---|---|---|
| Colts ___ at Green Bay ___ | | 7:00 |
| Houston ___ at Dallas ___ | (CBS) | 8:00 |
| Pittsburgh ___ at New York Giants ___ | | 8:00 |
| Washington ___ at New Orleans ___ | (ABC) | 12:00 |

**Sunday, August 26**
| | | |
|---|---|---|
| Chicago ___ vs. Buffalo ___ at Indianapolis | (CBS) | 12:00 |

## First Week

**Sunday, September 2**
**(NBC-TV doubleheader)**
| | |
|---|---|
| Atlanta ___ at New Orleans ___ | 12:00 |
| Cincinnati ___ at Denver ___ | 2:00 |
| Cleveland ___ at Seattle ___ | 1:00 |
| Kansas City ___ at Pittsburgh ___ | 1:00 |
| Los Angeles Raiders ___ at Houston ___ | 3:00 |
| Miami ___ at Washington ___ | 1:00 |
| New England ___ at Buffalo ___ | 1:00 |
| New York Jets ___ at Colts ___ | 3:00 |
| Philadelphia ___ at New York Giants ___ | 1:00 |
| St. Louis ___ at Green Bay ___ | 12:00 |
| San Diego ___ at Minnesota ___ | 12:00 |
| San Francisco ___ at Detroit ___ | 1:00 |
| Tampa Bay ___ at Chicago ___ | 12:00 |

**Monday, September 3**
| | | |
|---|---|---|
| Dallas ___ at Los Angeles Rams ___ | (ABC) | 6:00 |

## Second Week

**Thursday, September 6**
| | | |
|---|---|---|
| Pittsburgh ___ at New York Jets ___ | (ABC) | 9:00 |

**Sunday, September 9**
**(NBC-TV doubleheader)**
| | |
|---|---|
| Buffalo ___ at St. Louis ___ | 12:00 |
| Cleveland ___ at Los Angeles Rams ___ | 1:00 |
| Colts ___ at Houston ___ | 3:00 |
| Dallas ___ at New York Giants ___ | 1:00 |
| Denver ___ at Chicago ___ | 12:00 |
| Detroit ___ at Atlanta ___ | 1:00 |
| Green Bay ___ at Los Angeles Raiders ___ | 1:00 |
| Kansas City ___ at Cincinnati ___ | 1:00 |
| Minnesota ___ at Philadelphia ___ | 1:00 |
| New England ___ at Miami ___ | 1:00 |
| San Diego ___ at Seattle ___ | 1:00 |
| Tampa Bay ___ at New Orleans ___ | 12:00 |

**Monday, September 10**
| | | |
|---|---|---|
| Washington ___ at San Francisco ___ | (ABC) | 6:00 |

## Third Week

**Sunday, September 16**
**(CBS-TV doubleheader)**
| | | |
|---|---|---|
| Atlanta ___ at Minnesota ___ | | 12:00 |
| Chicago ___ at Green Bay ___ | | 12:00 |
| Cincinnati ___ at New York Jets ___ | | 1:00 |
| Denver ___ at Cleveland ___ | (ABC) | 9:00 |
| Detroit ___ at Tampa Bay ___ | | 4:00 |
| Houston ___ at San Diego ___ | | 1:00 |
| Los Angeles Raiders ___ at Kansas City ___ | | 12:00 |
| Los Angeles Rams ___ at Pittsburgh ___ | | 4:00 |
| New Orleans ___ at San Francisco ___ | | 1:00 |
| New York Giants ___ at Washington ___ | | 4:00 |
| Philadelphia ___ at Dallas ___ | | 3:00 |
| St. Louis ___ at Colts ___ | | 12:00 |
| Seattle ___ at New England ___ | | 1:00 |

**Monday, September 17**
| | | |
|---|---|---|
| Miami ___ at Buffalo ___ | (ABC) | 9:00 |

## Fourth Week

| | | |
|---|---|---|
| **Sunday, September 23** <br> **(CBS-TV doubleheader)** | Chicago ___ at Seattle ___ | 1:00 |
| | Colts ___ at Miami ___ | 4:00 |
| | Green Bay ___ at Dallas ___ | 3:00 |
| | Houston ___ at Atlanta ___ | 1:00 |
| | Kansas City ___ at Denver ___ | 2:00 |
| | Los Angeles Rams ___ at Cincinnati ___ | 1:00 |
| | Minnesota ___ at Detroit ___ | 1:00 |
| | New York Jets ___ at Buffalo ___ | 1:00 |
| | Pittsburgh ___ at Cleveland ___ | 1:00 |
| | St. Louis ___ at New Orleans ___ | 12:00 |
| | San Francisco ___ at Philadelphia ___ | 1:00 |
| | Tampa Bay ___ at New York Giants ___ | 4:00 |
| | Washington ___ at New England ___ | 1:00 |
| **Monday, September 24** | San Diego ___ at Los Angeles Raiders ___ | (ABC) 6:00 |

## Fifth Week

| | | |
|---|---|---|
| **Sunday, September 30** <br> **(CBS-TV doubleheader)** | Atlanta ___ at San Francisco ___ | 1:00 |
| | Buffalo ___ at Colts ___ | 12:00 |
| | Cleveland ___ at Kansas City ___ | 12:00 |
| | Dallas ___ at Chicago ___ | 12:00 |
| | Detroit ___ at San Diego ___ | 1:00 |
| | Green Bay ___ at Tampa Bay ___ | 4:00 |
| | Los Angeles Raiders ___ at Denver ___ | 2:00 |
| | Miami ___ at St. Louis ___ | 12:00 |
| | New England ___ at New York Jets ___ | 1:00 |
| | New Orleans ___ at Houston ___ | 3:00 |
| | New York Giants ___ at Los Angeles Rams ___ | 1:00 |
| | Philadelphia ___ at Washington ___ | 4:00 |
| | Seattle ___ at Minnesota ___ | 12:00 |
| **Monday, October 1** | Cincinnati ___ at Pittsburgh ___ | (ABC) 9:00 |

## Sixth Week

| | | |
|---|---|---|
| **Sunday, October 7** <br> **(NBC-TV doubleheader)** | Atlanta ___ at Los Angeles Rams ___ | 1:00 |
| | Denver ___ at Detroit ___ | 1:00 |
| | Houston ___ at Cincinnati ___ | 4:00 |
| | Miami ___ at Pittsburgh ___ | 1:00 |
| | Minnesota ___ at Tampa Bay ___ | 1:00 |
| | New England ___ at Cleveland ___ | 1:00 |
| | New Orleans ___ at Chicago ___ | 12:00 |
| | New York Jets ___ at Kansas City ___ | 12:00 |
| | Philadelphia ___ at Buffalo ___ | 1:00 |
| | St. Louis ___ at Dallas ___ | 12:00 |
| | San Diego ___ at Green Bay ___ | 3:00 |
| | Seattle ___ at Los Angeles Raiders ___ | 1:00 |
| | Washington ___ at Colts ___ | 12:00 |
| **Monday, October 8** | San Francisco ___ at New York Giants ___ | (ABC) 9:00 |

## Seventh Week

| | | |
|---|---|---|
| **Sunday, October 14** <br> **(CBS-TV doubleheader)** | Buffalo ___ at Seattle ___ | 1:00 |
| | Chicago ___ at St. Louis ___ | 12:00 |
| | Cincinnati ___ at New England ___ | 1:00 |
| | Colts ___ at Philadelphia ___ | 1:00 |
| | Dallas ___ at Washington ___ | 4:00 |
| | Houston ___ at Miami ___ | 1:00 |
| | Los Angeles Rams ___ at New Orleans ___ | 12:00 |
| | Minnesota ___ at Los Angeles Raiders ___ | 1:00 |
| | New York Giants ___ at Atlanta ___ | 1:00 |
| | New York Jets ___ at Cleveland ___ | 1:00 |
| | Pittsburgh ___ at San Francisco ___ | 1:00 |
| | San Diego ___ at Kansas City ___ | 12:00 |
| | Tampa Bay ___ at Detroit ___ | 1:00 |
| **Monday, October 15** | Green Bay ___ at Denver ___ | (ABC) 7:00 |

## Eighth Week

| | | | |
|---|---|---|---|
| **Sunday, October 21** | Chicago ___ at Tampa Bay ___ | | 1:00 |
| **(NBC-TV doubleheader)** | Cleveland ___ at Cincinnati ___ | | 1:00 |
| | Denver ___ at Buffalo ___ | | 1:00 |
| | Detroit ___ at Minnesota ___ | | 12:00 |
| | Kansas City ___ at New York Jets ___ | | 4:00 |
| | Los Angeles Raiders ___ at San Diego ___ | | 1:00 |
| | Miami ___ at New England ___ | | 1:00 |
| | New Orleans ___ at Dallas ___ | | (ABC) 9:00 |
| | New York Giants ___ at Philadelphia ___ | | 1:00 |
| | Pittsburgh ___ at Colts ___ | | 12:00 |
| | San Francisco ___ at Houston ___ | | 3:00 |
| | Seattle ___ vs. Green Bay ___ at Milwaukee | | 12:00 |
| | Washington ___ at St. Louis ___ | | 12:00 |
| **Monday, October 22** | Los Angeles Rams ___ at Atlanta ___ | | (ABC) 9:00 |

## Ninth Week

| | | | |
|---|---|---|---|
| **Sunday, October 28** | Atlanta ___ at Pittsburgh ___ | | 4:00 |
| **(CBS-TV doubleheader)** | Buffalo ___ at Miami ___ | | 4:00 |
| | Cincinnati ___ at Houston ___ | | 12:00 |
| | Colts ___ at Dallas ___ | | 12:00 |
| | Denver ___ at Los Angeles Raiders ___ | | 1:00 |
| | Detroit ___ at Green Bay ___ | | 12:00 |
| | Minnesota ___ at Chicago ___ | | 12:00 |
| | New Orleans ___ at Cleveland ___ | | 1:00 |
| | New York Jets ___ at New England ___ | | 1:00 |
| | St. Louis ___ at Philadelphia ___ | | 1:00 |
| | San Francisco ___ at Los Angeles Rams ___ | | 1:00 |
| | Tampa Bay ___ at Kansas City ___ | | 12:00 |
| | Washington ___ at New York Giants ___ | | 4:00 |
| **Monday, October 29** | Seattle ___ at San Diego ___ | | (ABC) 6:00 |

## Tenth Week

| | | | |
|---|---|---|---|
| **Sunday, November 4** | Cincinnati ___ at San Francisco ___ | | 1:00 |
| **(NBC-TV doubleheader)** | Cleveland ___ at Buffalo ___ | | 1:00 |
| | Green Bay ___ at New Orleans ___ | | 12:00 |
| | Houston ___ at Pittsburgh ___ | | 1:00 |
| | Kansas City ___ at Seattle ___ | | 1:00 |
| | Los Angeles Raiders ___ at Chicago ___ | | 12:00 |
| | Los Angeles Rams ___ at St. Louis ___ | | 3:00 |
| | Miami ___ at New York Jets ___ | | 4:00 |
| | New England ___ at Denver ___ | | 2:00 |
| | New York Giants ___ at Dallas ___ | | 12:00 |
| | Philadelphia ___ at Detroit ___ | | 1:00 |
| | San Diego ___ at Colts ___ | | 1:00 |
| | Tampa Bay ___ at Minnesota ___ | | 12:00 |
| **Monday, November 5** | Atlanta ___ at Washington ___ | | (ABC) 9:00 |

## Eleventh Week

| | | | |
|---|---|---|---|
| **Sunday, November 11** | Buffalo ___ at New England ___ | | 1:00 |
| **(CBS-TV doubleheader)** | Chicago ___ at Los Angeles Rams ___ | | 1:00 |
| | Colts ___ at New York Jets ___ | | 1:00 |
| | Dallas ___ at St. Louis ___ | | 12:00 |
| | Denver ___ at San Diego ___ | | 1:00 |
| | Detroit ___ at Washington ___ | | 1:00 |
| | Houston ___ at Kansas City ___ | | 12:00 |
| | Minnesota ___ vs. Green Bay ___ at Milwaukee | | 12:00 |
| | New Orleans ___ at Atlanta ___ | | 1:00 |
| | New York Giants ___ at Tampa Bay ___ | | 4:00 |
| | Philadelphia ___ at Miami ___ | | 1:00 |
| | Pittsburgh ___ at Cincinnati ___ | | 1:00 |
| | San Francisco ___ at Cleveland ___ | | 1:00 |
| **Monday, November 12** | Los Angeles Raiders ___ at Seattle ___ | | (ABC) 6:00 |

## Twelfth Week

| | | |
|---|---|---|
| **Sunday, November 18** | Cleveland ___ at Atlanta ___ | 1:00 |
| **(NBC-TV doubleheader)** | Dallas ___ at Buffalo ___ | 1:00 |
| | Detroit ___ at Chicago ___ | 12:00 |
| | Kansas City ___ at Los Angeles Raiders ___ | 1:00 |
| | L.A. Rams ___ vs. Green Bay ___ at Milwaukee | 12:00 |
| | Miami ___ at San Diego ___ | 1:00 |
| | Minnesota ___ at Denver ___ | 2:00 |
| | New England ___ at Colts ___ | 1:00 |
| | New York Jets ___ at Houston ___ | 3:00 |
| | St. Louis ___ at New York Giants ___ | 1:00 |
| | Seattle ___ at Cincinnati ___ | 1:00 |
| | Tampa Bay ___ at San Francisco ___ | 1:00 |
| | Washington ___ at Philadelphia ___ | 1:00 |
| **Monday, November 19** | Pittsburgh ___ at New Orleans ___ | (ABC) 8:00 |

## Thirteenth Week

| | | |
|---|---|---|
| **Thursday, November 22** | Green Bay ___ at Detroit ___ | (CBS) 12:30 |
| **(Thanksgiving Day)** | New England ___ at Dallas ___ | (NBC) 3:00 |
| **Sunday, November 25** | Atlanta ___ at Cincinnati ___ | 1:00 |
| **(CBS-TV doubleheader)** | Buffalo ___ at Washington ___ | 1:00 |
| | Chicago ___ at Minnesota ___ | 3:00 |
| | Colts ___ at Los Angeles Raiders ___ | 1:00 |
| | Houston ___ at Cleveland ___ | 1:00 |
| | Kansas City ___ at New York Giants ___ | 1:00 |
| | Los Angeles Rams ___ at Tampa Bay ___ | 1:00 |
| | Philadelphia ___ at St. Louis ___ | 12:00 |
| | San Diego ___ at Pittsburgh ___ | 1:00 |
| | San Francisco ___ at New Orleans ___ | 3:00 |
| | Seattle ___ at Denver ___ | 2:00 |
| **Monday, November 26** | New York Jets ___ at Miami ___ | (ABC) 9:00 |

## Fourteenth Week

| | | |
|---|---|---|
| **Thursday, November 29** | Washington ___ at Minnesota ___ | (ABC) 9:00 |
| **Sunday, December 2** | Cincinnati ___ at Cleveland ___ | 1:00 |
| **(NBC-TV doubleheader)** | Colts ___ at Buffalo ___ | 1:00 |
| | Dallas ___ at Philadelphia ___ | 1:00 |
| | Denver ___ at Kansas City ___ | 12:00 |
| | Detroit ___ at Seattle ___ | 1:00 |
| | Los Angeles Raiders ___ at Miami ___ | 4:00 |
| | New Orleans ___ at Los Angeles Rams ___ | 1:00 |
| | New York Giants ___ at New York Jets ___ | 1:00 |
| | Pittsburgh ___ at Houston ___ | 12:00 |
| | St. Louis ___ at New England ___ | 1:00 |
| | San Francisco ___ at Atlanta ___ | 1:00 |
| | Tampa Bay ___ at Green Bay ___ | 12:00 |
| **Monday, December 3** | Chicago ___ at San Diego ___ | (ABC) 6:00 |

## Fifteenth Week

| | | |
|---|---|---|
| **Saturday, December 8** | Buffalo ___ at New York Jets ___ | (NBC) 12:30 |
| | Minnesota ___ at San Francisco ___ | (CBS) 1:00 |
| **Sunday, December 9** | Atlanta ___ at Tampa Bay ___ | 1:00 |
| **(CBS-TV doubleheader)** | Cincinnati ___ at New Orleans ___ | 12:00 |
| | Cleveland ___ at Pittsburgh ___ | 1:00 |
| | Green Bay ___ at Chicago ___ | 12:00 |
| | Houston ___ at Los Angeles Rams ___ | 1:00 |
| | Miami ___ at Colts ___ | 1:00 |
| | New England ___ at Philadelphia ___ | 1:00 |
| | New York Giants ___ at St. Louis ___ | 12:00 |
| | San Diego ___ at Denver ___ | 2:00 |
| | Seattle ___ at Kansas City ___ | 12:00 |
| | Washington ___ at Dallas ___ | 3:00 |
| **Monday, December 10** | Los Angeles Raiders ___ at Detroit ___ | (ABC) 9:00 |

## Sixteenth Week

**Friday, December 14**    Los Angeles Rams ___ at San Francisco ___    (ABC) 6:00

**Saturday, December 15**    Denver ___ at Seattle ___    (NBC) 1:00
New Orleans ___ at New York Giants ___    (CBS) 12:30

**Sunday, December 16**
**(NBC-TV doubleheader)**

Buffalo ___ at Cincinnati ___    1:00
Chicago ___ at Detroit ___    1:00
Cleveland ___ at Houston ___    12:00
Colts ___ at New England ___    1:00
Green Bay ___ at Minnesota ___    12:00
Kansas City ___ at San Diego ___    1:00
New York Jets ___ at Tampa Bay ___    1:00
Philadelphia ___ at Atlanta ___    4:00
Pittsburgh ___ at Los Angeles Raiders ___    1:00
St. Louis ___ at Washington ___    1:00

**Monday, December 17**    Dallas ___ at Miami ___    (ABC) 9:00

## First Round Playoff Games

**Sunday, December 23, 1984**

American Football Conference

_____ at _____ (NBC)

National Football Conference

_____ at _____ (CBS)

### Site Priorities

Two wild card teams (fourth- and fifth-best records) from each conference will enter the first round of the playoffs. The wild cards from the same conference will play each other. Home clubs will be the clubs with the best won-lost-tied percentage in the regular season. If tied in record, the tie will be broken by the tie-breaking procedure already in effect.

## Divisional Playoff Games

**Saturday, December 29, 1984**

American Football Conference

_____ at _____ (NBC)

National Football Conference

_____ at _____ (CBS)

**Sunday, December 30, 1984**

American Football Conference

_____ at _____ (NBC)

National Football Conference

_____ at _____ (CBS)

### Site Priorities

In each conference, the two division winners with the highest won-lost-tied percentage during the regular season will be the home teams. The division winner with the best percentage will be host to the wild card winner from the first round playoff, and the division winner with the second best percentage will be host to the third division winner, unless the wild card team is from the same division as the winner with the highest percentage. In that case, the division winner with the best percentage will be host to the third division winner and the second highest division winner will be host to the wild card.

## Conference Championship Games, Super Bowl XIX, and AFC-NFC Pro Bowl

**Sunday, January 6, 1985**

American Football Conference Championship Game

_____ at _____ (NBC)

National Football Conference Championship Game

_____ at _____ (CBS)

**Sunday, January 20, 1985**

Super Bowl XIX at Stanford Stadium, Palo Alto, California

_____ vs. _____ (ABC)

**Sunday, January 27, 1985**

AFC-NFC Pro Bowl at Honolulu, Hawaii

AFC _____ vs. NFC _____ (ABC)

### Site Priorities for Championship Games

The home teams will be the surviving divisional playoff winners with the best won-lost-tied percentage during the regular season. The wild card team will never be the home team, in either the divisional playoffs or the championship games. Any ties in won-lost-tied percentage will be broken by the tie-breaking procedures already in effect.

## Postseason Games

| | |
|---|---|
| Sunday, December 23 | AFC and NFC First Round Playoffs (NBC and CBS) |
| Saturday, December 29 | AFC and NFC Divisional Playoffs (NBC and CBS) |
| Sunday, December 30 | AFC and NFC Divisional Playoffs (NBC and CBS) |
| Sunday, January 6 | AFC and NFC Championship Games (NBC and CBS) |
| Sunday, January 20 | Super Bowl XIX at Stanford Stadium, Palo Alto, California (ABC) |
| Sunday, January 27 | AFC-NFC Pro Bowl, Honolulu, Hawaii (ABC) |

## Nationally Televised Games

(All games carried on CBS Radio Network.)

### Regular Season

| | |
|---|---|
| Monday, September 3 | Dallas at Los Angeles Rams (night, ABC) |
| Thursday, September 6 | Pittsburgh at New York Jets (night, ABC) |
| Monday, September 10 | Washington at San Francisco (night, ABC) |
| Sunday, September 16 | Denver at Cleveland (night, ABC) |
| Monday, September 17 | Miami at Buffalo (night, ABC) |
| Monday, September 24 | San Diego at Los Angeles Raiders (night, ABC) |
| Monday, October 1 | Cincinnati at Pittsburgh (night, ABC) |
| Monday, October 8 | San Francisco at New York Giants (night, ABC) |
| Monday, October 15 | Green Bay at Denver (night, ABC) |
| Sunday, October 21 | New Orleans at Dallas (night, ABC) |
| Monday, October 22 | Los Angeles Rams at Atlanta (night, ABC) |
| Monday, October 29 | Seattle at San Diego (night, ABC) |
| Monday, November 5 | Atlanta at Washington (night, ABC) |
| Monday, November 12 | Los Angeles Raiders at Seattle (night, ABC) |
| Monday, November 19 | Pittsburgh at New Orleans (night, ABC) |
| Thursday, November 22 | (Thanksgiving) Green Bay at Detroit (day, CBS) New England at Dallas (day, NBC) |
| Monday, November 26 | New York Jets at Miami (night, ABC) |
| Thursday, November 29 | Washington at Minnesota (night, ABC) |
| Monday, December 3 | Chicago at San Diego (night, ABC) |
| Saturday, December 8 | Buffalo at New York Jets (day, NBC) Minnesota at San Francisco (day, CBS) |
| Monday, December 10 | Los Angeles Raiders at Detroit (night, ABC) |
| Friday, December 14 | Los Angeles Rams at San Francisco (night, ABC) |
| Saturday, December 15 | Denver at Seattle (day, NBC) New Orleans at New York Giants (day, CBS) |
| Monday, December 17 | Dallas at Miami (night, ABC) |

## AFC-NFC Interconference Games

(Sunday unless noted; all times local)

| | | |
|---|---|---|
| September 2 | Miami at Washington | 4:00 |
| | San Diego at Minnesota | 12:00 |
| September 9 | Buffalo at St. Louis | 12:00 |
| | Cleveland at Los Angeles Rams | 1:00 |
| | Denver at Chicago | 12:00 |
| | Green Bay at Los Angeles Raiders | 1:00 |
| September 16 | Los Angeles Rams at Pittsburgh | 4:00 |
| | St. Louis at Colts | 12:00 |
| September 23 | Chicago at Seattle | 1:00 |
| | Houston at Atlanta | 1:00 |
| | Los Angeles Rams at Cincinnati | 1:00 |
| | Washington at New England | 1:00 |
| September 30 | Detroit at San Diego | 1:00 |
| | Miami at St. Louis | 12:00 |
| | New Orleans at Houston | 3:00 |
| | Seattle at Minnesota | 12:00 |
| October 7 | Denver at Detroit | 1:00 |
| | Philadelphia at Buffalo | 1:00 |
| | San Diego at Green Bay | 3:00 |
| | Washington at Colts | 12:00 |
| October 14 | Colts at Philadelphia | 1:00 |
| | Minnesota at Los Angeles Raiders | 1:00 |
| | Pittsburgh at San Francisco | 1:00 |
| October 15 | Green Bay at Denver (Monday night) | 7:00 |
| October 21 | San Francisco at Houston | 3:00 |
| | Seattle at Green Bay | 12:00 |
| October 28 | Atlanta at Pittsburgh | 4:00 |
| | Colts at Dallas | 12:00 |
| | New Orleans at Cleveland | 1:00 |
| | Tampa Bay at Kansas City | 12:00 |
| November 4 | Cincinnati at San Francisco | 1:00 |
| | Los Angeles Raiders at Chicago | 12:00 |

| | | |
|---|---|---|
| November 11 | Philadelphia at Miami | 1:00 |
| | San Francisco at Cleveland | 1:00 |
| November 18 | Cleveland at Atlanta | 1:00 |
| | Dallas at Buffalo | 1:00 |
| | Minnesota at Denver | 2:00 |
| November 19 | Pittsburgh at New Orleans (Monday night) | 8:00 |
| November 22 | New England at Dallas (Thanksgiving) | 3:00 |
| November 25 | Atlanta at Cincinnati | 1:00 |
| | Buffalo at Washington | 1:00 |
| | Kansas City at New York Giants | 1:00 |
| December 2 | Detroit at Seattle | 1:00 |
| | New York Giants at New York Jets | 1:00 |
| | St. Louis at New England | 1:00 |
| December 3 | Chicago at San Diego (Monday night) | 6:00 |
| December 9 | Cincinnati at New Orleans | 12:00 |
| | Houston at Los Angeles Rams | 1:00 |
| | New England at Philadelphia | 1:00 |
| December 10 | Los Angeles Raiders at Detroit (Monday night) | 9:00 |
| December 16 | New York Jets at Tampa Bay | 1:00 |
| December 17 | Dallas at Miami (Monday night) | 9:00 |

## Monday Night Games at a Glance

(All times local; televised by ABC and broadcast by CBS Radio.)

| | | |
|---|---|---|
| September 3 | Dallas at Los Angeles Rams | 6:00 |
| September 10 | Washington at San Francisco | 6:00 |
| September 17 | Miami at Buffalo | 9:00 |
| September 24 | San Diego at Los Angeles Raiders | 6:00 |
| October 1 | Cincinnati at Pittsburgh | 9:00 |
| October 8 | San Francisco at New York Giants | 9:00 |
| October 15 | Green Bay at Denver | 7:00 |
| October 22 | Los Angeles Rams at Atlanta | 9:00 |
| October 29 | Seattle at San Diego | 6:00 |
| November 5 | Atlanta at Washington | 9:00 |
| November 12 | Los Angeles Raiders at Seattle | 6:00 |
| November 19 | Pittsburgh at New Orleans | 8:00 |
| November 26 | New York Jets at Miami | 9:00 |
| December 3 | Chicago at San Diego | 6:00 |
| December 10 | Los Angeles Raiders at Detroit | 9:00 |
| December 17 | Dallas at Miami | 9:00 |

## Sunday, Thursday, & Friday Night Games at a Glance

(All times local; televised by ABC and broadcast by CBS Radio.)

| | | |
|---|---|---|
| Thursday, September 6 | Pittsburgh at New York Jets | 9:00 |
| Sunday, September 16 | Denver at Cleveland | 9:00 |
| Sunday, October 21 | New Orleans at Dallas | 8:00 |
| Thursday, November 29 | Washington at Minnesota | 8:00 |
| Friday, December 14 | Los Angeles Rams at San Francisco | 6:00 |

## Waivers

The waiver system is a procedure by which player contracts or NFL rights to players are made available by a club to other clubs in the League. During the procedure the 27 other clubs either file claims to obtain the players or waive the opportunity to do so—thus the term "waiver." Claiming clubs are assigned players on a priority based on the inverse of won-and-lost standing. The claiming period normally is 10 days during the offseason and 24 hours from early July through December. In some circumstances another 24 hours is added on to allow the original club to rescind its action (known as a recall of a waiver request) and/or the claiming club to do the same (known as withdrawal of a claim). If a player passes through waivers unclaimed and is not recalled by the original club, he becomes a free agent. All waivers from July through December are no-recall and no withdrawal. Under the Collective Bargaining Agreement, from February 1 through October 9, any veteran who has acquired four years of pension credit may, if about to be assigned to another club through the waiver system, reject such assignment and become a free agent.

## Active List

The Active List is the principal status for players participating for a club. It consists of all players under contract, including option, who are eligible for preseason, regular season, and postseason games. Clubs are allowed to open training camp with an unlimited number of players but thereafter must meet a series of mandatory roster reductions prior to the season opener. Teams will be permitted to dress up to 49 players for each regular season and postseason game during the 1984 season. The Active List maximums and dates for 1984 are:

August 14 . . . . . . . . . . . . . . . . . . . . . . 70 players
August 21 . . . . . . . . . . . . . . . . . . . . . . 60 players
August 27 . . . . . . . . . . . . . . . . . . . . . . 49 players

## Reserve List

The Reserve List is a status for players who, for reasons of injury, retirement, military service, or other circumstances, are not immediately available for participation with a club. Those players in the category of Reserve/Injured who were physically unable to play football for a minimum of four weeks from the date of going onto Reserve may be re-activated by their clubs upon clearing procedural recall waivers; in addition, each club will have five free re-activations for players meeting the four-week requirement who were placed on Reserve following the final cutdown. Clubs participating in postseason competition will be granted an additional free re-activation. Players not meeting the four-week requirement may not return in the same season to the Active List of the club which originally placed them on Reserve, but may be assigned through the waiver system to other clubs. Players in the category of Reserve/Retired may not be reinstated during the period from 30 days before the end of the regular season on through the postseason.

## Trades

Unrestricted trading between the AFC and NFC is allowed in 1984 through October 9, after which all trading will end until January 28, 1985.

## Annual Player Limits

**NFL**

| Year(s) | Limit |
|---------|-------|
| 1983 | 49 |
| 1982 | 45†–49 |
| 1978–81 | 45 |
| 1975–77 | 43 |
| 1974 | 47 |
| 1964–73 | 40 |
| 1963 | 37 |
| 1961–62 | 36 |
| 1960 | 38 |
| 1959 | 36 |
| 1957–58 | 35 |
| 1951–56 | 33 |
| 1949–50 | 32 |
| 1948 | 35 |
| 1947 | 35*–34 |
| 1945–46 | 33 |
| 1943–44 | 28 |
| 1940–42 | 33 |
| 1938–39 | 30 |
| 1936–37 | 25 |
| 1935 | 24 |
| 1930–34 | 20 |
| 1926–29 | 18 |
| 1925 | 16 |

†45 for first two games
*35 for first three games

**AFL**

| Year(s) | Limit |
|---------|-------|
| 1966–69 | 40 |
| 1965 | 38 |
| 1964 | 34 |
| 1962–63 | 33 |
| 1960–61 | 35 |

## Tie-Breaking Procedures

The following procedures will be used to break standings ties for postseason playoffs and to determine regular season schedules.

### To Break a Tie Within a Division

If, at the end of the regular season, two or more clubs in the same division finish with identical won-lost-tied percentages, the following steps will be taken until a champion is determined.

### Two Clubs

1. Head-to-head (best won-lost-tied percentage in games between the clubs).
2. Best won-lost-tied percentage in games played within the division.
3. Best won-lost-tied percentage in games played within the conference.
4. Best won-lost-tied percentage in common games, if applicable.
5. Best net points in division games.
6. Best net points in all games.
7. Strength of schedule.
8. Best net touchdowns in all games.
9. Coin toss.

### Three or More Clubs

(Note: If two clubs remain tied after a third club is eliminated during any step, tie-breaker reverts to step 1 of two-club format.)

1. Head-to-head (best won-lost-tied percentage in games among the clubs).
2. Best won-lost-tied percentage in games played within the division.
3. Best won-lost-tied percentage in games played within the conference.
4. Best won-lost-tied percentage in common games.
5. Best net points in division games.
6. Best net points in all games.
7. Strength of schedule.
8. Best net touchdowns in all games.
9. Coin toss.

### To Break a Tie for the Wild Card Team

If it is necessary to break ties to determine the two Wild Card clubs from each conference, the following steps will be taken.

1. If the tied clubs are from the same division, apply division tie-breaker.
2. If the tied clubs are from different divisions, apply the following steps.

### Two Clubs

1. Head-to-head, if applicable.
2. Best won-lost-tied percentage in games played within the conference.
3. Best won-lost-tied percentage in common games, minimum of four.
4. Best average net points in conference games.
5. Best net points in all games.
6. Strength of schedule.
7. Best net touchdowns in all games.
8. Coin toss.

### Three or More Clubs

(Note: If two clubs remain tied after other clubs are eliminated, tie-breaker reverts to step 1 of applicable two-club format.)

1. Head-to-head sweep. (Applicable only if one club has defeated each of the others, or if one club has lost to each of the others.)
2. Best won-lost-tied percentage in games played within the conference.
3. Best won-lost-tied percentage in common games, minimum of four.
4. Best average net points in conference games.
5. Best net points in all games.
6. Strength of schedule.
7. Best net touchdowns in all games.
8. Coin toss.

### Tie-Breaking Procedure for Selection Meeting

If two or more clubs are tied for selection order, the conventional strength of schedule tie-breaker will be applied, subject to the following exceptions for playoff teams.

1. The Super Bowl winner will be last and the Super Bowl loser will be next-to-last.
2. Any non-Super Bowl playoff team involved in a tie moves down in drafting priority as follows:
   A. Participation by a club in the playoffs without a victory adds one-half victory to the club's regular season won-lost-tied record.
   B. For each victory in the playoffs, one full victory will be added to the club's regular season won-lost-tied record.
3. Clubs with the best won-lost-tied records after these steps are applied will drop to their appropriate spots at the bottom of the tied segment. In no case will the above process move a club lower than the segment in which it was initially tied.

# Look for in 1984

**Things that could happen in 1984:**

• Either Franco Harris, Pittsburgh, or Walter Payton, Chicago—or both—could surpass Jim Brown as the NFL's all-time leader in rushing yardage. Brown gained 12,312 yards in his nine seasons in the NFL (1957-65). Harris, who begins his thirteenth year in 1984, starts 1984 with 11,950 yards, while Payton, in his tenth season, starts with 11,625 yards. (Harris already holds the record for career rushing attempts with 2,881.)

• The same two players, Payton and Harris, are in pursuit of another of Brown's career records, most combined yardage. (This category includes all yards gained via rushing, receiving, and various returns.) Brown's total was 15,459. Payton starts 1984 with a total of 15,252, while Harris begins the season with 14,449. (Harris already holds the record for combined career attempts, 3,212.)

• John Riggins, Washington, needs 564 yards rushing to become the fifth player in NFL history to accumulate 10,000 yards. In addition to Brown, Harris, and Payton, Riggins, now entering his thirteenth season, would join O.J. Simpson, who gained 11,236 yards in 11 years.

• Riggins needs six touchdowns to become the fifth player in NFL history to score 100 touchdowns. Brown (126), Lenny Moore (113), Don Hutson (105), and Harris (100) all have reached that mark. Payton starts the 1984 season 13 touchdowns shy of 100.

• Ken Anderson, Cincinnati, needs 48 pass completions to become the fourth quarterback in NFL history to reach 2,500 career completions. The only players to have reached that mark are Fran Tarkenton (3,686), Johnny Unitas (2,830), and Jim Hart (2,590), who will be playing his first year with Washington after 18 seasons in St. Louis. Dan Fouts, San Diego, needs 232 completions to reach the 2,500 mark.

• Three individuals have the opportunity to reach 600 career receptions. Charlie Joiner, San Diego (596), Harold Carmichael, a free agent (589), and Harold Jackson, Seattle (579), are all within striking distance not only of the 600 mark, but also the career record of 649 receptions held by Charley Taylor. Besides Taylor, only two others have caught 600 career passes: Don Maynard (633) and Raymond Berry (631).

• Joiner needs 19 more yards on receptions to become the fourth player in history to reach the 10,000-yard mark. Only Maynard (11,834), Jackson (10,372), and Lance Alworth (10,266) have reached this level.

• John James, Houston, needs five punts to become only the second player in NFL history to punt 1,000 times. Jerrel Wilson is the all-time record holder with 1,072.

# Active Coaches' Career Records

## Start of 1984 Season

| Coach | Team(s) | Yrs. | Regular Season Won | Lost | Tied | Pct. | Postseason Won | Lost | Tied | Pct. | Career Won | Lost | Tied | Pct. |
|---|---|---|---|---|---|---|---|---|---|---|---|---|---|---|
| Joe Gibbs | Washington Redskins | 3 | 30 | 11 | 0 | .732 | 6 | 1 | 0 | .857 | 36 | 12 | 0 | .750 |
| Don Shula | Baltimore Colts, Miami Dolphins | 21 | 213 | 80 | 6 | .722 | 13 | 11 | 0 | .541 | 226 | 91 | 6 | .709 |
| Tom Flores | Los Angeles Raiders | 5 | 47 | 26 | 0 | .644 | 8 | 1 | 0 | .888 | 55 | 27 | 0 | .670 |
| Tom Landry | Dallas Cowboys | 24 | 214 | 119 | 6 | .640 | 20 | 15 | 0 | .571 | 234 | 134 | 6 | .634 |
| Chuck Noll | Pittsburgh Steelers | 15 | 133 | 81 | 1 | .621 | 14 | 6 | 0 | .700 | 147 | 87 | 1 | .628 |
| Chuck Knox | Los Angeles Rams, Buffalo Bills, Seattle Seahawks | 11 | 100 | 58 | 1 | .632 | 6 | 8 | 0 | .429 | 106 | 66 | 1 | .616 |
| Don Coryell | St. Louis Cardinals, San Diego Chargers | 11 | 95 | 59 | 1 | .616 | 3 | 6 | 0 | .333 | 98 | 65 | 1 | .601 |
| John Robinson | Los Angeles Rams | 1 | 9 | 7 | 0 | .563 | 1 | 1 | 0 | .500 | 10 | 8 | 0 | .555 |
| O. A. (Bum) Phillips | Houston Oilers, New Orleans Saints | 9 | 71 | 60 | 0 | .542 | 4 | 3 | 0 | .571 | 75 | 63 | 0 | .543 |
| Forrest Gregg | Cleveland Browns, Cincinnati Bengals, Green Bay Packers | 7 | 50 | 48 | 0 | .510 | 2 | 2 | 0 | .500 | 52 | 50 | 0 | .510 |
| Sam Rutigliano | Cleveland Browns | 6 | 46 | 43 | 0 | .517 | 0 | 2 | 0 | .000 | 46 | 45 | 0 | .505 |
| Dan Reeves | Denver Broncos | 3 | 21 | 20 | 0 | .512 | 0 | 1 | 0 | .000 | 21 | 21 | 0 | .500 |
| Ron Meyer | New England Patriots | 2 | 13 | 12 | 0 | .520 | 0 | 1 | 0 | .000 | 13 | 13 | 0 | .500 |
| Kay Stephenson | Buffalo Bills | 1 | 8 | 8 | 0 | .500 | 0 | 0 | 0 | .000 | 8 | 8 | 0 | .500 |
| Bill Walsh | San Francisco 49ers | 5 | 34 | 39 | 0 | .466 | 4 | 1 | 0 | .800 | 38 | 40 | 0 | .487 |
| Monte Clark | San Francisco 49ers, Detroit Lions | 7 | 47 | 56 | 0 | .456 | 0 | 2 | 0 | .000 | 47 | 58 | 0 | .448 |
| Jim Hanifan | St. Louis Cardinals | 4 | 25 | 31 | 1 | .447 | 0 | 1 | 0 | .000 | 25 | 32 | 1 | .440 |
| Mike Ditka | Chicago Bears | 2 | 11 | 14 | 0 | .440 | 0 | 0 | 0 | .000 | 11 | 14 | 0 | .440 |
| Dan Henning | Atlanta Falcons | 1 | 7 | 9 | 0 | .438 | 0 | 0 | 0 | .000 | 7 | 9 | 0 | .438 |
| Joe Walton | New York Jets | 1 | 7 | 9 | 0 | .438 | 0 | 0 | 0 | .000 | 7 | 9 | 0 | .438 |
| John Mackovic | Kansas City Chiefs | 1 | 6 | 10 | 0 | .375 | 0 | 0 | 0 | .000 | 6 | 10 | 0 | .375 |
| John McKay | Tampa Bay Buccaneers | 8 | 38 | 78 | 1 | .329 | 1 | 3 | 0 | .250 | 39 | 81 | 1 | .326 |
| Frank Kush | Baltimore Colts | 2 | 7 | 17 | 1 | .300 | 0 | 0 | 0 | .000 | 7 | 17 | 1 | .300 |
| Marion Campbell | Atlanta Falcons, Philadelphia Eagles | 3 | 11 | 30 | 0 | .268 | 0 | 0 | 0 | .000 | 11 | 30 | 0 | .268 |
| Bill Parcells | New York Giants | 1 | 3 | 12 | 1 | .219 | 0 | 0 | 0 | .000 | 3 | 12 | 1 | .219 |
| Hugh Campbell | Houston Oilers | 0 | 0 | 0 | 0 | .000 | 0 | 0 | 0 | .000 | 0 | 0 | 0 | .000 |
| Les Steckel | Minnesota Vikings | 0 | 0 | 0 | 0 | .000 | 0 | 0 | 0 | .000 | 0 | 0 | 0 | .000 |
| Sam Wyche | Cincinnati Bengals | 0 | 0 | 0 | 0 | .000 | 0 | 0 | 0 | .000 | 0 | 0 | 0 | .000 |

# Coaches With 100 Career Victories

## Start of 1984 Season

| Coach | Team(s) | Yrs. | Regular Season Won | Lost | Tied | Pct. | Postseason Won | Lost | Tied | Pct. | Career Won | Lost | Tied | Pct. |
|---|---|---|---|---|---|---|---|---|---|---|---|---|---|---|
| George Halas | Chicago Bears | 40 | 319 | 148 | 31 | .672 | 6 | 3 | 0 | .667 | 325 | 151 | 31 | .672 |
| Tom Landry | Dallas Cowboys | 24 | 214 | 119 | 6 | .640 | 20 | 15 | 0 | .571 | 234 | 134 | 6 | .634 |
| Earl (Curly) Lambeau | Green Bay Packers, Chicago Cardinals, Washington Redskins | 33 | 231 | 133 | 23 | .627 | 3 | 2 | 0 | .600 | 234 | 135 | 23 | .626 |
| Don Shula | Baltimore Colts, Miami Dolphins | 21 | 213 | 80 | 6 | .722 | 13 | 11 | 0 | .541 | 226 | 91 | 6 | .709 |
| Paul Brown | Cleveland Browns, Cincinnati Bengals | 21 | 166 | 100 | 6 | .621 | 4 | 8 | 0 | .333 | 170 | 108 | 6 | .609 |
| Bud Grant | Minnesota Vikings | 17 | 151 | 87 | 5 | .633 | 10 | 12 | 0 | .455 | 161 | 99 | 5 | .617 |
| Steve Owen | New York Giants | 23 | 151 | 100 | 17 | .595 | 3 | 8 | 0 | .273 | 154 | 108 | 17 | .582 |
| Chuck Noll | Pittsburgh Steelers | 15 | 133 | 81 | 1 | .621 | 14 | 6 | 0 | .700 | 147 | 87 | 1 | .628 |
| Hank Stram | Kansas City Chiefs, New Orleans Saints | 17 | 131 | 97 | 10 | .571 | 5 | 3 | 0 | .625 | 136 | 100 | 10 | .573 |
| Weeb Ewbank | Baltimore Colts, New York Jets | 20 | 130 | 129 | 7 | .502 | 4 | 1 | 0 | .800 | 134 | 130 | 7 | .507 |
| Sid Gillman | Los Angeles Rams, San Diego Chargers, Houston Oilers | 18 | 122 | 99 | 7 | .550 | 1 | 5 | 0 | .167 | 123 | 104 | 7 | .541 |
| George Allen | Los Angeles Rams, Washington Redskins | 12 | 116 | 47 | 5 | .705 | 2 | 7 | 0 | .222 | 118 | 54 | 5 | .681 |
| John Madden | Oakland Raiders | 10 | 103 | 32 | 7 | .750 | 9 | 7 | 0 | .563 | 112 | 39 | 7 | .731 |
| Ray (Buddy) Parker | Chicago Cardinals, Detroit Lions, Pittsburgh Steelers | 15 | 104 | 75 | 9 | .577 | 3 | 1 | 0 | .750 | 107 | 76 | 9 | .581 |
| Chuck Knox | Los Angeles Rams, Buffalo Bills, Seattle Seahawks | 11 | 100 | 58 | 1 | .632 | 6 | 8 | 0 | .429 | 106 | 66 | 1 | .616 |
| Vince Lombardi | Green Bay Packers, Washington Redskins | 10 | 96 | 34 | 6 | .728 | 9 | 1 | 0 | .900 | 105 | 35 | 6 | .740 |

# AFC ACTIVE STATISTICAL LEADERS

## LEADING ACTIVE PASSERS, AMERICAN FOOTBALL CONFERENCE
1,000 or more attempts

| | Yrs. | Att. | Comp. | Pct. Comp. | Yards | Avg. Gain | TD | Pct. TD | Had Int. | Pct. Int. | Rate Pts. |
|---|---|---|---|---|---|---|---|---|---|---|---|
| Ken Anderson, Cin. | 13 | 4145 | 2452 | 59.2 | 30390 | 7.33 | 184 | 4.4 | 146 | 3.5 | 82.0 |
| Dan Fouts, S.D. | 11 | 3873 | 2268 | 58.6 | 30114 | 7.78 | 182 | 4.7 | 168 | 4.3 | 80.9 |
| Bill Kenney, K.C. | 4 | 1115 | 625 | 56.1 | 8065 | 7.23 | 45 | 4.0 | 42 | 3.8 | 76.7 |
| Terry Bradshaw, Pitt. | 14 | 3901 | 2025 | 51.9 | 27989 | 7.17 | 212 | 5.4 | 210 | 5.4 | 70.9 |
| Steve Grogan, N.E. | 9 | 2613 | 1357 | 51.9 | 19826 | 7.59 | 136 | 5.2 | 156 | 6.0 | 69.4 |
| Joe Ferguson, Buff. | 11 | 3822 | 1997 | 52.3 | 25599 | 6.70 | 169 | 4.4 | 173 | 4.5 | 69.4 |
| Jim Zorn, Sea. | 8 | 2973 | 1586 | 53.3 | 20042 | 6.74 | 107 | 3.6 | 131 | 4.4 | 68.3 |
| Jim Plunkett, Raiders | 12 | 3148 | 1631 | 51.8 | 21620 | 6.87 | 141 | 4.5 | 176 | 5.6 | 65.5 |

## TOP 10 ACTIVE RUSHERS, AFC
2,000 or more yards

| | Yrs. | Att. | Yards | TD |
|---|---|---|---|---|
| 1. Franco Harris, Pitt. | 12 | 2881 | 11950 | 91 |
| 2. Earl Campbell, Hou. | 6 | 1883 | 8296 | 69 |
| 3. Chuck Muncie, S.D. | 8 | 1547 | 6651 | 71 |
| 4. Mike Pruitt, Clev. | 8 | 1430 | 6034 | 41 |
| 5. Greg Pruitt, Raiders | 11 | 1188 | 5672 | 27 |
| 6. Pete Johnson, S.D. | 7 | 1402 | 5421 | 64 |
| 7. Sherman Smith, S.D. | 8 | 834 | 3520 | 28 |
| 8. Cullen Bryant, Sea. | 11 | 828 | 3204 | 20 |
| 9. Curtis Dickey, Colts | 4 | 660 | 2933 | 23 |
| 10. Tony Collins, N.E. | 3 | 587 | 2554 | 18 |

### Other Leading Rushers
| | | | | |
|---|---|---|---|---|
| Roosevelt Leaks, Buff. | 9 | 663 | 2406 | 28 |
| Terry Bradshaw, Pitt. | 14 | 444 | 2257 | 32 |
| Andra Franklin, Mia. | 3 | 602 | 2158 | 22 |
| Ken Anderson, Cin. | 13 | 385 | 2156 | 20 |
| Kenny King, Raiders | 5 | 496 | 2156 | 7 |
| Tony Nathan, Mia. | 5 | 440 | 2095 | 10 |
| Freeman McNeil, N.Y.J. | 3 | 448 | 2063 | 9 |
| Steve Grogan, N.E. | 9 | 370 | 2049 | 29 |
| Charles Alexander, Cin. | 5 | 572 | 2010 | 9 |

## TOP 10 ACTIVE PASS RECEIVERS, AFC
200 or more receptions

| | Yrs. | No. | Yards | TD |
|---|---|---|---|---|
| 1. Charlie Joiner, S.D. | 15 | 596 | 9981 | 50 |
| 2. Harold Jackson, Sea. | 16 | 579 | 10372 | 76 |
| 3. Cliff Branch, Raiders | 12 | 474 | 8284 | 67 |
| 4. Steve Largent, Sea. | 8 | 471 | 7608 | 60 |
| 5. Isaac Curtis, Cin. | 11 | 404 | 6966 | 53 |
| 6. Nat Moore, Mia. | 10 | 378 | 5841 | 54 |
| 7. Charle Young, Sea. | 11 | 357 | 4418 | 24 |
| 8. Ozzie Newsome, Clev. | 6 | 351 | 4569 | 29 |
| 9. Kellen Winslow, S.D. | 5 | 344 | 4513 | 35 |
| 10. Wes Chandler, S.D. | 6 | 341 | 5535 | 34 |

### Other Leading Pass Receivers
| | | | | |
|---|---|---|---|---|
| Greg Pruitt, Raiders | 11 | 326 | 3057 | 18 |
| John Stallworth, Pitt. | 10 | 307 | 5404 | 44 |
| Franco Harris, Pitt. | 12 | 306 | 2284 | 9 |
| Henry Marshall, K.C. | 8 | 281 | 4409 | 28 |
| Stanley Morgan, N.E. | 7 | 274 | 5732 | 37 |
| Wesley Walker, N.Y.J. | 7 | 271 | 5082 | 39 |
| Duriel Harris, Clev. | 8 | 266 | 4510 | 18 |
| Dave Logan, Den. | 8 | 262 | 4247 | 24 |
| Chuck Muncie, S.D. | 8 | 259 | 2285 | 3 |
| Mike Pruitt, Clev. | 8 | 250 | 1732 | 5 |
| Jerry Butler, Buff. | 5 | 222 | 3229 | 25 |
| Sherman Smith, S.D. | 8 | 217 | 2393 | 10 |
| Bruce Harper, N.Y.J. | 7 | 215 | 2338 | 12 |

## TOP 10 ACTIVE SCORERS, AFC
250 or more points

| | Yrs. | TD | FG | PAT | TP |
|---|---|---|---|---|---|
| 1. Pat Leahy, N.Y.J. | 10 | 0 | 141 | 268 | 691 |
| 2. Chris Bahr, Raiders | 8 | 0 | 126 | 281 | 659 |
| 3. Franco Harris, Pitt. | 12 | 100 | 0 | 0 | 600 |
| 4. Joe Danelo, Buff. | 9 | 0 | 125 | 223 | 598 |
| 5. Rolf Benirschke, S.D. | 7 | 0 | 113 | 246 | 585 |
| 6. Harold Jackson, Sea. | 16 | 76 | 0 | 0 | 456 |
| 7. Uwe von Schamann, Mia. | 5 | 0 | 92 | 171 | 447 |
| 8. Chuck Muncie, S.D. | 8 | 74 | 0 | 0 | 444 |
| 9. Pete Johnson, S.D. | 7 | 70 | 0 | 0 | 420 |
| 10. Matt Bahr, Clev. | 5 | 0 | 80 | 178 | 418 |

### Other Leading Scorers
| | | | | | |
|---|---|---|---|---|---|
| Earl Campbell, Hou. | 6 | 69 | 0 | 0 | 414 |
| Tony Franklin, N.E. | 5 | 0 | 80 | 172 | 412 |
| Nick Lowery, K.C. | 5 | 0 | 89 | 142 | 409 |
| Cliff Branch, Raiders | 12 | 67 | 0 | 0 | 402 |
| Jim Breech, Cin. | 5 | 0 | 74 | 165 | 387 |
| Steve Largent, Sea. | 8 | 61 | 0 | 0 | 366 |
| Nat Moore, Mia. | 10 | 55 | 0 | 0 | 330 |
| Isaac Curtis, Cin. | 11 | 53 | 0 | 0 | 318 |
| Charlie Joiner, S.D. | 15 | 50 | 0 | 0 | 300 |
| Greg Pruitt, Raiders | 11 | 47 | 0 | 0 | 282 |
| Mike Pruitt, Clev. | 8 | 46 | 0 | 0 | 276 |
| John Stallworth, Pitt. | 10 | 45 | 0 | 0 | 270 |

## TOP 10 ACTIVE INTERCEPTORS, AFC
20 or more interceptions

| | Yrs. | No. | Yards | TD |
|---|---|---|---|---|
| 1. Clarence Scott, Clev. | 13 | 39 | 407 | 2 |
| 2. Donnie Shell, Pitt. | 10 | 36 | 310 | 0 |
| 3. Steve Foley, Den. | 8 | 33 | 439 | 0 |
| 4. Lester Hayes, Raiders | 7 | 32 | 535 | 3 |
| 5. Dave Brown, Sea. | 9 | 31 | 348 | 1 |
| 6. Lyle Blackwood, Mia. | 11 | 30 | 546 | 2 |
| 7. Rod Perry, Clev. | 9 | 29 | 407 | 4 |
| Mike Haynes, Raiders | 8 | 29 | 393 | 1 |
| 9. John Harris, Sea. | 6 | 28 | 326 | 2 |
| Jack Lambert, Pitt. | 10 | 28 | 243 | 0 |

### Other Leading Interceptors
| | | | | |
|---|---|---|---|---|
| Mike Reinfeldt, Hou. | 8 | 26 | 375 | 0 |
| Ted Hendricks, Raiders | 15 | 26 | 332 | 1 |
| Mario Clark, Buff. | 8 | 25 | 438 | 0 |
| Terry Jackson, Sea. | 4 | 24 | 282 | 2 |
| Gerald Small, Mia. | 6 | 23 | 378 | 1 |
| Tim Fox, S.D. | 8 | 23 | 332 | 0 |
| Gregg Bingham, Hou. | 11 | 21 | 279 | 0 |
| Tom Jackson, Den. | 11 | 20 | 340 | 3 |

## TOP 10 ACTIVE PUNT RETURNERS, AFC
40 or more punt returns

| | Yrs. | No. | Yards | Avg. | TD |
|---|---|---|---|---|---|
| 1. Paul Johns, Sea. | 3 | 63 | 703 | 11.2 | 1 |
| 2. Tommy Vigorito, Mia. | 3 | 57 | 633 | 11.1 | 2 |
| 3. J. T. Smith, K.C. | 6 | 181 | 1990 | 11.0 | 4 |
| 4. Greg Pruitt, Raiders | 11 | 141 | 1534 | 10.9 | 1 |
| James Brooks, Cin. | 4 | 52 | 565 | 10.9 | 0 |
| 6. Mike Haynes, Raiders | 8 | 111 | 1159 | 10.4 | 2 |
| Stanley Morgan, N.E. | 7 | 92 | 960 | 10.4 | 1 |
| 8. Cullen Bryant, Sea. | 11 | 71 | 707 | 10.0 | 0 |
| 9. Ricky Smith, N.E. | 2 | 54 | 537 | 9.9 | 0 |
| 10. Bruce Harper, N.Y.J. | 7 | 183 | 1784 | 9.7 | 1 |
| Roland James, N.E. | 4 | 40 | 387 | 9.7 | 1 |

### Other Leading Punt Returners
| | | | | | |
|---|---|---|---|---|---|
| Mark Clayton, Mia. | 1 | 41 | 392 | 9.6 | 1 |
| Tony Nathan, Mia. | 5 | 51 | 484 | 9.5 | 1 |
| Butch Johnson, Hou. | 8 | 146 | 1313 | 9.0 | 0 |
| Paul Skansi, Pitt. | 1 | 43 | 363 | 8.4 | 0 |
| Larry Anderson, Colts | 6 | 48 | 400 | 8.3 | 0 |
| Dino Hall, Clev. | 5 | 111 | 901 | 8.1 | 0 |
| Nesby Glasgow, Colts | 5 | 72 | 572 | 7.9 | 1 |
| Carl Roaches, Hou. | 4 | 125 | 943 | 7.5 | 0 |
| Len Walterscheid, Buff. | 7 | 57 | 424 | 7.4 | 0 |
| Cle Montgomery, Raiders | 4 | 48 | 344 | 7.2 | 0 |
| Roland Hooks, Buff. | 7 | 43 | 302 | 7.0 | 0 |
| Wes Chandler, S.D. | 6 | 58 | 387 | 6.7 | 0 |
| Robb Riddick, Buff. | 2 | 46 | 289 | 6.3 | 0 |
| Lyle Blackwood, Mia. | 11 | 68 | 319 | 4.7 | 0 |

## TOP 10 ACTIVE KICKOFF RETURNERS, AFC
40 or more kickoff returns

| | Yrs. | No. | Yards | Avg. | TD |
|---|---|---|---|---|---|
| 1. Ray Clayborn, N.E. | 7 | 57 | 1538 | 27.0 | 3 |
| 2. Cullen Bryant, Sea. | 11 | 66 | 1760 | 26.7 | 3 |
| 3. Duriel Harris, Clev. | 8 | 56 | 1416 | 25.3 | 0 |
| 4. Fulton Walker, Mia. | 3 | 94 | 2327 | 24.8 | 1 |
| 5. Greg Pruitt, Raiders | 11 | 103 | 2498 | 24.3 | 1 |
| 6. Carlos Carson, K.C. | 4 | 51 | 1206 | 23.6 | 0 |
| 7. Butch Johnson, Hou. | 8 | 79 | 1832 | 23.2 | 0 |
| 8. Nesby Glasgow, Colts | 5 | 84 | 1904 | 22.7 | 0 |
| 9. Ricky Smith, N.E. | 2 | 66 | 1483 | 22.5 | 1 |
| 10. Bruce Harper, N.Y.J. | 7 | 243 | 5407 | 22.3 | 0 |

### Other Leading Kickoff Returners
| | | | | | |
|---|---|---|---|---|---|
| Larry Anderson, Colts | 6 | 167 | 3692 | 22.1 | 1 |
| James Brooks, Cin. | 4 | 105 | 2305 | 22.0 | 0 |
| Dwight Walker, Clev. | 2 | 42 | 922 | 22.0 | 0 |
| David Verser, Cin. | 3 | 58 | 1264 | 21.8 | 0 |
| Wes Chandler, S.D. | 6 | 47 | 1021 | 21.7 | 0 |
| Carl Roaches, Hou. | 4 | 120 | 2597 | 21.6 | 2 |
| Tony Nathan, Mia. | 5 | 53 | 1133 | 21.4 | 0 |
| Zachary Dixon, Sea. | 5 | 103 | 2188 | 21.2 | 1 |
| Dino Hall, Clev. | 5 | 151 | 3185 | 21.1 | 0 |
| Aundra Thompson, Colts | 6 | 52 | 1090 | 21.0 | 1 |
| Ray Griffin, Cin. | 6 | 40 | 833 | 20.8 | 0 |
| Cle Montgomery, Raiders | 4 | 99 | 2001 | 20.2 | 0 |
| Roland Hooks, Buff. | 7 | 48 | 969 | 20.2 | 0 |
| Anthony Hancock, K.C. | 2 | 56 | 1124 | 20.1 | 0 |
| Robb Riddick, Buff. | 2 | 42 | 825 | 19.6 | 0 |
| Kim Anderson, Colts | 4 | 40 | 779 | 19.5 | 0 |
| Steve Wilson, Den. | 5 | 58 | 1107 | 19.1 | 0 |

## TOP 10 ACTIVE PUNTERS, AFC
50 or more punts

| | Yrs. | No. | Avg. | LG |
|---|---|---|---|---|
| 1. Rohn Stark, Balt. | 2 | 137 | 45.0 | 68 |
| 2. Rich Camarillo, N.E. | 3 | 177 | 43.6 | 76 |
| 3. Maury Buford, S.D. | 2 | 84 | 43.2 | 71 |
| 4. Reggie Roby, Mia. | 1 | 74 | 43.1 | 64 |
| 5. Ray Guy, Raiders | 11 | 779 | 42.9 | 74 |
| 6. Pat McInally, Cin. | 8 | 576 | 41.8 | 67 |
| Luke Prestridge, Den. | 5 | 377 | 41.8 | 67 |
| 8. Craig Colquitt, Pitt. | 5 | 359 | 41.4 | 74 |
| 9. Steve Cox, Clev. | 3 | 116 | 41.0 | 66 |
| 10. John James, Hou. | 12 | 995 | 40.7 | 75 |

### Other Leading Punters
| | | | | |
|---|---|---|---|---|
| Chuck Ramsey, N.Y.J. | 7 | 479 | 40.1 | 79 |
| Jim Arnold, K.C. | 1 | 93 | 39.9 | 64 |
| Greg Cater, Buff. | 4 | 277 | 39.2 | 71 |
| Jeff West, Sea. | 8 | 515 | 38.2 | 62 |

# NFC ACTIVE STATISTICAL LEADERS

## LEADING ACTIVE PASSERS, NATIONAL FOOTBALL CONFERENCE
1,000 or more attempts

| | Yrs. | Att. | Comp. | Pct. Comp. | Yards | Avg. Gain | TD | Pct. TD | Had Int. | Pct. Int. | Rate Pts. |
|---|---|---|---|---|---|---|---|---|---|---|---|
| Joe Montana, S.F. | 5 | 1645 | 1045 | 63.5 | 11979 | 7.28 | 78 | 4.7 | 44 | 2.7 | 90.0 |
| Danny White, Dall. | 8 | 1710 | 1029 | 60.2 | 13174 | 7.70 | 98 | 5.7 | 79 | 4.6 | 84.2 |
| Vince Ferragamo, Rams | 6 | 1222 | 701 | 57.4 | 9059 | 7.41 | 68 | 5.6 | 63 | 5.2 | 77.8 |
| Joe Theismann, Wash. | 10 | 2824 | 1594 | 56.4 | 20041 | 7.10 | 128 | 4.5 | 109 | 3.9 | 77.7 |
| Ken Stabler, N.O. | 14 | 3723 | 2237 | 60.1 | 27599 | 7.41 | 192 | 5.2 | 217 | 5.8 | 75.9 |
| Steve Bartkowski, Atl. | 9 | 2950 | 1621 | 54.9 | 20574 | 6.97 | 138 | 4.7 | 130 | 4.4 | 74.2 |
| Ron Jaworski, Phil. | 10 | 2886 | 1525 | 52.8 | 20073 | 6.96 | 135 | 4.7 | 119 | 4.1 | 73.5 |
| Tommy Kramer, Minn. | 7 | 2144 | 1202 | 56.1 | 13953 | 6.51 | 91 | 4.2 | 92 | 4.3 | 72.2 |
| Gary Danielson, Det. | 7 | 1274 | 700 | 54.9 | 8809 | 6.91 | 52 | 4.1 | 56 | 4.4 | 72.0 |
| Richard Todd, N.O. | 8 | 2623 | 1433 | 54.6 | 18241 | 6.95 | 110 | 4.2 | 138 | 5.3 | 68.6 |
| Lynn Dickey, G.B. | 11 | 2410 | 1338 | 55.5 | 17921 | 7.44 | 101 | 4.2 | 143 | 5.9 | 68.6 |
| Archie Manning, Minn. | 12 | 3548 | 1959 | 55.2 | 23366 | 6.59 | 123 | 3.5 | 170 | 4.8 | 67.1 |
| Jim Hart, Wash. | 18 | 5069 | 2590 | 51.1 | 34639 | 6.83 | 209 | 4.1 | 247 | 4.9 | 66.6 |
| Steve DeBerg, T.B. | 6 | 1747 | 984 | 56.3 | 11039 | 6.32 | 59 | 3.4 | 84 | 4.8 | 66.6 |
| Bob Avellini, Chi. | 8 | 1057 | 530 | 50.1 | 6823 | 6.46 | 33 | 3.1 | 66 | 6.2 | 55.2 |

## TOP 10 ACTIVE RUSHERS, NFC
2,000 or more yards

| | Yrs. | Att. | Yards | TD |
|---|---|---|---|---|
| 1. Walter Payton, Chi. | 9 | 2666 | 11625 | 78 |
| 2. John Riggins, Wash. | 12 | 2413 | 9436 | 82 |
| 3. Tony Dorsett, Dall. | 7 | 1834 | 8336 | 53 |
| 4. Ottis Anderson, St.L. | 5 | 1401 | 6190 | 34 |
| 5. William Andrews, Atl. | 5 | 1263 | 5772 | 29 |
| 6. Wilbert Montgomery, Phil. | 7 | 1264 | 5749 | 43 |
| 7. Dexter Bussey, Det. | 10 | 1171 | 5014 | 18 |
| 8. Robert Newhouse, Dall. | 12 | 1160 | 4784 | 31 |
| 9. Joe Washington, Wash. | 7 | 1087 | 4437 | 10 |
| 10. Billy Sims, Det. | 4 | 1001 | 4419 | 37 |

### Other Leading Rushers

| | | | | |
|---|---|---|---|---|
| Wendell Tyler, S.F. | 7 | 896 | 4122 | 37 |
| Rickey Young, Minn. | 9 | 1011 | 3666 | 23 |
| Tony Galbreath, Minn. | 8 | 954 | 3653 | 34 |
| Ted Brown, Minn. | 5 | 863 | 3517 | 26 |
| Wayne Morris, St.L. | 8 | 894 | 3375 | 37 |
| Rob Carpenter, N.Y.G. | 7 | 860 | 3364 | 22 |
| George Rogers, N.O. | 3 | 756 | 3353 | 21 |
| Scott Dierking, T.B. | 7 | 731 | 2901 | 18 |
| Gerry Ellis, G.B. | 4 | 525 | 2329 | 14 |
| Archie Manning, Minn. | 12 | 373 | 2155 | 18 |
| Horace King, Det. | 9 | 549 | 2081 | 9 |

## TOP 10 ACTIVE PASS RECEIVERS, NFC
200 or more receptions

| | Yrs. | No. | Yards | TD |
|---|---|---|---|---|
| 1. Drew Pearson, Dall. | 11 | 489 | 7822 | 48 |
| 2. Rickey Young, Minn. | 9 | 408 | 3285 | 16 |
| 3. Dave Casper, Minn. | 10 | 374 | 5187 | 50 |
| 4. Sammy White, Minn. | 8 | 364 | 5925 | 49 |
| Pat Tilley, St.L. | 8 | 364 | 5470 | 26 |
| Tony Galbreath, Minn. | 8 | 364 | 2866 | 8 |
| 7. Alfred Jenkins, Atl. | 9 | 359 | 6258 | 40 |
| 8. Joe Washington, Wash. | 7 | 345 | 3011 | 17 |
| 9. James Lofton, G.B. | 6 | 335 | 6302 | 34 |
| 10. Walter Payton, Chi. | 9 | 328 | 3088 | 9 |

### Other Leading Pass Receivers

| | | | | |
|---|---|---|---|---|
| John Jefferson, G.B. | 6 | 322 | 5345 | 47 |
| Dwight Clark, S.F. | 5 | 315 | 4081 | 25 |
| Freddie Solomon, S.F. | 9 | 306 | 4850 | 37 |
| Tony Hill, Dall. | 7 | 295 | 5241 | 36 |
| Sam McCullum, Minn. | 10 | 274 | 4017 | 26 |
| David Hill, Rams | 8 | 273 | 3334 | 25 |
| William Andrews, Atl. | 5 | 272 | 2612 | 11 |
| Russ Francis, S.F. | 8 | 252 | 3631 | 34 |
| Ted Brown, Minn. | 5 | 248 | 2078 | 7 |
| Tony Dorsett, Dall. | 7 | 241 | 2080 | 7 |
| Billy Johnson, Atl. | 9 | 237 | 2869 | 17 |
| John Riggins, Wash. | 12 | 237 | 2029 | 12 |
| Paul Coffman, G.B. | 6 | 230 | 2995 | 24 |
| Mike Barber, Rams | 8 | 213 | 2709 | 17 |
| Jimmie Giles, T.B. | 7 | 211 | 3286 | 23 |
| Wilbert Mongomery, Phil. | 7 | 206 | 1946 | 12 |
| Earnest Gray, N.Y.G. | 5 | 205 | 3239 | 25 |

## TOP 10 ACTIVE SCORERS, NFC
250 or more points

| | Yrs. | TD | FG | PAT | TP |
|---|---|---|---|---|---|
| 1. Jan Stenerud, G.B. | 17 | 0 | 338 | 509 | 1523 |
| 2. Mark Moseley, Wash. | 13 | 0 | 242 | 378 | 1104 |
| 3. Ray Wersching, S.F. | 11 | 0 | 146 | 263 | 701 |
| 4. Rafael Septien, Dall. | 7 | 0 | 123 | 302 | 671 |
| 5. John Riggins, Wash. | 12 | 94 | 0 | 0 | 564 |
| 6. Bob Thomas, Chi. | 9 | 0 | 111 | 213 | 546 |
| 7. Walter Payton, Chi. | 9 | 87 | 0 | 0 | 522 |
| 8. Benny Ricardo, Minn. | 6 | 0 | 89 | 166 | 433 |
| 9. Neil O'Donoghue, St.L. | 7 | 0 | 79 | 173 | 410 |
| 10. Eddie Murray, Det. | 4 | 0 | 88 | 135 | 399 |

### Other Leading Scorers

| | | | | | |
|---|---|---|---|---|---|
| Tony Dorsett, Dall. | 7 | 61 | 0 | 0 | 366 |
| Rick Danmeier, Minn. | 6 | 0 | 70 | 154 | 364 |
| Wilbert Montgomery, Phil. | 7 | 56 | 0 | 0 | 336 |
| Dave Casper, Minn. | 10 | 51 | 0 | 0 | 306 |
| Drew Pearson, Dall. | 11 | 50 | 0 | 0 | 300 |
| Wendell Tyler, S.F. | 7 | 49 | 0 | 0 | 294 |
| Sammy White, Minn. | 8 | 49 | 0 | 0 | 294 |
| John Jefferson, G.B. | 6 | 47 | 0 | 0 | 282 |
| Freddie Solomon, S.F. | 9 | 45 | 0 | 0 | 270 |
| Tony Galbreath, Minn. | 8 | 42 | 2 | 1 | 259 |
| Mick Luckhurst, Atl. | 3 | 0 | 48 | 115 | 259 |
| Wayne Morris, St.L. | 8 | 42 | 0 | 0 | 252 |
| Billy Sims, Det. | 4 | 42 | 0 | 0 | 252 |

## TOP 10 ACTIVE INTERCEPTORS, NFC
20 or more interceptions

| | Yrs. | No. | Yards | TD |
|---|---|---|---|---|
| 1. Cedric Brown, T.B. | 8 | 28 | 579 | 2 |
| Mike Washington, T.B. | 8 | 28 | 418 | 3 |
| Herman Edwards, Phil. | 7 | 28 | 90 | 0 |
| 4. Mark Murphy, Wash. | 7 | 27 | 282 | 0 |
| 5. Dennis Thurman, Dall. | 6 | 26 | 460 | 2 |
| 6. Nolan Cromwell, Rams | 7 | 25 | 483 | 2 |
| Neal Colzie, T.B. | 9 | 25 | 412 | 1 |
| Gary Fencik, Chi. | 8 | 25 | 306 | 1 |
| Terry Schmidt, Chi. | 10 | 25 | 205 | 3 |
| 10. Gary Green, Rams | 7 | 24 | 330 | 1 |

### Other Leading Interceptors

| | | | | |
|---|---|---|---|---|
| Dwight Hicks, S.F. | 5 | 23 | 476 | 3 |
| Randy Logan, Phil. | 11 | 23 | 293 | 0 |
| Johnnie Gray, G.B. | 9 | 22 | 332 | 1 |
| Everson Walls, Dall. | 3 | 22 | 264 | 0 |
| Eric Harris, Rams | 4 | 21 | 329 | 1 |

## TOP 10 ACTIVE PUNT RETURNERS, NFC
40 or more punt returns

| | Yrs. | No. | Yards | Avg. | TD |
|---|---|---|---|---|---|
| 1. Billy Johnson, Atl. | 9 | 225 | 2802 | 12.5 | 6 |
| 2. Neal Colzie, T.B. | 9 | 170 | 1759 | 10.3 | 0 |
| 3. LeRoy Irvin, Rams | 4 | 135 | 1365 | 10.1 | 4 |
| 4. Jeff Fisher, Chi. | 3 | 63 | 633 | 10.0 | 1 |
| 5. Robbie Martin, Det. | 3 | 93 | 908 | 9.8 | 2 |
| 6. Mike Nelms, Wash. | 4 | 163 | 1520 | 9.3 | 2 |
| 7. Freddie Solomon, S.F. | 9 | 177 | 1614 | 9.1 | 4 |
| 8. Stump Mitchell, St.L. | 3 | 107 | 947 | 8.9 | 1 |
| 9. Jeff Groth, N.O. | 5 | 98 | 855 | 8.7 | 0 |
| 10. James Jones, Dall. | 3 | 87 | 736 | 8.5 | 0 |
| Phillip Epps, G.B. | 2 | 56 | 474 | 8.5 | 1 |

### Other Leading Punt Returners

| | | | | | |
|---|---|---|---|---|---|
| Theo Bell, T.B. | 7 | 185 | 1501 | 8.1 | 0 |
| Rich Mauti, N.O. | 6 | 75 | 610 | 8.1 | 0 |
| Leon Bright, N.Y.G. | 3 | 106 | 852 | 8.0 | 0 |
| Alvin Garrett, Wash. | 4 | 43 | 344 | 8.0 | 0 |
| Pete Shaw, N.Y.G. | 7 | 41 | 322 | 7.9 | 0 |
| Johnnie Gray, G.B. | 9 | 85 | 656 | 7.7 | 0 |
| Dwight Hicks, S.F. | 5 | 54 | 403 | 7.5 | 0 |
| Willard Harrell, St.L. | 9 | 123 | 854 | 6.9 | 2 |
| Ron Fellows, Dall. | 3 | 46 | 308 | 6.7 | 0 |

## TOP 10 ACTIVE KICKOFF RETURNERS, NFC
40 or more kickoff returns

| | Yrs. | No. | Yards | Avg. | TD |
|---|---|---|---|---|---|
| 1. Mike Nelms, Wash. | 4 | 133 | 3268 | 24.6 | 0 |
| 2. Billy Johnson, Atl. | 9 | 121 | 2902 | 24.0 | 2 |
| 3. Brian Baschnagel, Chi. | 8 | 89 | 2102 | 23.6 | 1 |
| 4. Roy Green, St.L. | 5 | 82 | 1899 | 23.2 | 1 |
| 5. Wayne Wilson, N.O. | 5 | 67 | 1542 | 23.0 | 0 |
| 6. Rich Mauti, N.O. | 6 | 123 | 2822 | 22.9 | 0 |
| 7. Stump Mitchell, St.L. | 3 | 107 | 2434 | 22.7 | 0 |
| 8. Alvin Hall, Det. | 3 | 64 | 1443 | 22.5 | 1 |
| Jarvis Redwine, Minn. | 3 | 50 | 1124 | 22.5 | 0 |
| 10. James Owens, T.B. | 5 | 119 | 2633 | 22.1 | 2 |

### Other Leading Kickoff Returners

| | | | | | |
|---|---|---|---|---|---|
| Mike McCoy, G.B. | 8 | 54 | 1187 | 22.0 | 0 |
| Jimmy Rogers, N.O. | 4 | 77 | 1678 | 21.8 | 0 |
| Rick Kane, Det. | 7 | 61 | 1327 | 21.8 | 0 |
| James Jones, Dall. | 3 | 61 | 1283 | 21.0 | 0 |
| Barry Redden, Rams | 2 | 41 | 860 | 21.0 | 0 |
| Ron Fellows, Dall. | 3 | 67 | 1384 | 20.7 | 0 |
| Michael Morton, T.B. | 2 | 51 | 1050 | 20.6 | 0 |
| Leon Bright, N.Y.G. | 3 | 50 | 1028 | 20.6 | 0 |
| Alvin Garrett, Wash. | 4 | 50 | 1013 | 20.3 | 0 |
| Dana McLemore, S.F. | 2 | 46 | 929 | 20.2 | 0 |
| Willard Harrell, St.L. | 9 | 84 | 1690 | 20.1 | 0 |
| Drew Hill, Rams | 4 | 145 | 2895 | 20.0 | 1 |
| Jeff Moore, S.F. | 5 | 40 | 784 | 19.6 | 0 |
| Beasley Reese, T.B. | 8 | 40 | 775 | 19.4 | 0 |
| Mark Lee, G.B. | 4 | 45 | 859 | 19.1 | 0 |
| Robbie Martin, Det. | 3 | 49 | 917 | 18.7 | 0 |
| Harlan Huckleby, G.B. | 4 | 56 | 1039 | 18.6 | 0 |

## TOP 10 ACTIVE PUNTERS, NFC
50 or more punts

| | Yrs. | No. | Avg. | LG |
|---|---|---|---|---|
| 1. Carl Birdsong, St.L. | 3 | 208 | 42.2 | 75 |
| 2. Frank Garcia, T.B. | 2 | 97 | 42.1 | 64 |
| 3. Dave Jennings, N.Y.G. | 10 | 841 | 41.8 | 73 |
| 4. Bucky Scribner, G.B. | 1 | 69 | 41.6 | 70 |
| 5. John Misko, Rams | 2 | 127 | 41.4 | 67 |
| 6. Mike Black, Det. | 1 | 71 | 41.0 | 60 |
| 7. Russell Erxleben, N.O. | 5 | 279 | 40.6 | 60 |
| 8. Jim Miller, Dall. | 4 | 219 | 40.5 | 80 |
| 9. Danny White, Dall. | 8 | 527 | 40.4 | 73 |
| 10. Max Runager, Phil. | 5 | 315 | 40.3 | 64 |
| Ralph Giacomarro, Atl. | 1 | 70 | 40.3 | 57 |

### Other Leading Punters

| | | | | |
|---|---|---|---|---|
| Greg Coleman, Minn. | 7 | 520 | 40.2 | 73 |
| Ray Stachowicz, Chi. | 3 | 136 | 40.2 | 72 |
| Tom Orosz, S.F. | 3 | 183 | 39.8 | 61 |
| Jeff Hayes, Wash. | 2 | 123 | 38.5 | 58 |
| Mike Wood, S.F. | 5 | 82 | 36.8 | 81 |

49th Annual NFL Draft, May 1-2, 1984

## Atlanta Falcons

1. Bryan, Rick—9, DT, Oklahoma
2. Case, Scott—32, DB, Oklahoma, from Philadelphia
   Benson, Thomas—36, LB, Oklahoma
3. McSwain, Rod—63, DB, Clemson
4. Malancon, Rydell—94, LB, Louisiana State
5. Choice to San Francisco
   Benson, Cliff—132, TE, Purdue, from Denver through San Francisco
6. Bennett, Ben—148, QB, Duke

   Ralph, Dan—163, DT, Oregon, from San Francisco
7. Dodge, Kirk—175, LB, Nevada-Las Vegas
8. Jackson, Jeff—206—LB, Auburn
9. Howe, Glen—233, T, Southern Mississippi
10. Franklin, Derrick—260, DB, Fresno State
11. Norman, Tommy—287, WR, Jackson State
12. Holmes, Don—318, WR, Mesa, Colo.

## Buffalo Bills

1. Choice to Miami
   Bell, Greg—26, RB, Notre Dame, from Miami
2. Richardson, Eric—41, WR, San Jose State
3. Choice to New Orleans
   Bellinger, Rodney—77, DB, Miami, from Cleveland
   McNanie, Sean—79, DE, San Diego State, from Pittsburgh through Miami
   Neal, Speedy—82, RB, Miami, from Miami

4. Brookins, Mitchell—95, WR, Illinois
5. Kidd, John—128, P, Northwestern
6. Slaton, Tony—155, C, Southern California
7. David, Stan—182, DB, Texas Tech
8. Rayfield, Stacy—209, DB, Texas-Arlington
9. Howell, Leroy—236, DE, Appalachian State
10. Azelby, Joe—263, LB, Harvard
11. White, Craig—299, WR, Missouri
12. Davis, Russell—322, WR, Maryland

## Chicago Bears

1. Marshall, Wilber—11, LB, Florida
2. Rivera, Ron—44, LB, California
3. Humphries, Stefan—71, G, Michigan
4. Andrews, Tom—98, G, Louisville
5. Choice to Washington through San Diego, Seattle, and New York Giants
6. Choice to Dallas
7. Robertson, Nakita—179, RB, Central Arkansas
8. Anderson, Brad—212, WR, Arizona
9. Choice to San Francisco

   Casale, Mark—244, QB, Montclair State, from Cleveland
10. Vestman, Kurt—266, TE, Idaho
    Gayle, Shaun—271, DB, Ohio State, from Cleveland
11. Choice to Los Angeles Rams
    Butkus, Mark—297, DT, Illinois, from Cleveland
12. Choice to Miami through San Francisco
    Jordan, Donald—330, RB, Houston, from Cleveland

## Cincinnati Bengals

1. Hunley, Ricky—7, LB, Arizona
   Koch, Pete—16, DE, Maryland, from New England
   Blados, Brian—28, T, North Carolina, from Los Angeles Raiders through New England
2. Esiason, Boomer—38, QB, Maryland
3. Jennings, Stanford—65, RB, Furman
4. Farley, John—92, RB, Cal State-Sacramento
5. Bussey, Barney—119, DB, South Carolina State

6. Kern, Don—150, TE, Arizona State
7. Barker, Leo—177, LB, New Mexico State
8. Reimers, Bruce—204, T, Iowa State
9. Kozerski, Bruce—231, C, Holy Cross
10. Jackson, Aaron—262, LB, North Carolina
    Ziegler, Brent—265, RB, Syracuse, from New England
11. McKeaver, Steve—289, RB, Central State, Okla.
12. Raquet, Steve—316, LB, Holy Cross

## Cleveland Browns

1. Rogers, Don—18, DB, UCLA
2. Rockins, Chris—48, DB, Oklahoma State, from Los Angeles Rams
   Davis, Bruce—50, WR, Baylor
3. Choice to Buffalo
4. Bolden, Rickey—96, TE, Southern Methodist, from New Orleans through Denver
   Brennan, Brian—104, WR, Boston College
5. Piepkorn, Dave—131, T, North Dakota State

6. Nugent, Terry—158, QB, Colorado State
7. Dumont, Jim—190, LB, Rutgers
8. Choice to New York Jets
9. Jones, Don—227, WR, Texas A&M, from Philadelphia
   Choice to Chicago
10. Choice to Chicago
    Byner, Earnest—280, RB, East Carolina, from Los Angeles Raiders
11. Choice to Chicago
12. Choice to Chicago

## Dallas Cowboys

1. Cannon, Billy, Jr.—25, LB, Texas A&M
2. Scott, Victor—40, DB, Colorado, from Minnesota through Houston
   Choice to Houston
3. Cornwell, Fred—81, TE, Southern California
4. DeOssie, Steve—110, LB, Boston College
5. Pelluer, Steve—113, QB, Washington, from Tampa Bay
   Granger, Norm—137, RB, Iowa

6. Lockhart, Eugene—152, LB, Houston, from Chicago
   Levelis, Joe—166, G, Iowa
7. Martin, Ed—193, LB, Indiana State
8. Revell, Mike—222, RB, Bethune-Cookman
9. Hunt, John—232, G, Florida, from Colts
   Maune, Neil—249, G, Notre Dame
10. Salonen, Brian—278, TE, Montana
11. Aughtman, Dowe—304, DT, Auburn
12. Lewis, Carl—334, WR, Houston

## Denver Broncos

1. Choice to Colts
2. Townsend, Andre—46, DE, Mississippi
3. Lilly, Tony—78, DB, Florida
4. Robbins, Randy—89, DB, Arizona, from San Diego through Tampa Bay
   Choice to New York Giants
5. Choice to Atlanta through San Francisco
6. Smith, Aaron—159, LB, Utah State

7. Kay, Clarence—186, TE, Georgia
8. Hood, Winford—207, T, Georgia, from Green Bay
   Garnett, Scott—218, DT, Washington
9. Brewer, Chris—245, RB, Arizona
10. Micho, Bobby—272, TE, Texas
11. Lang, Gene—298, RB, Louisiana State
12. Jarmin, Murray—326, WR, Clemson

## Detroit Lions

1. Lewis, David—20, TE, California
2. Mandley, Pete—47, WR, Northern Arizona
3. Williams, Eric—62, DT, Washington State, from San Diego through St. Louis
   Anderson, Ernest—74, RB, Oklahoma
   Baack, Steve—75, DE, Oregon, from Los Angeles Rams
4. D'Addio, Dave—106, RB, Maryland
5. Choice to Los Angeles Rams

6. Witkowski, John—160, QB, Columbia
7. Carter, Jimmie—178, LB, New Mexico, from Colts
   Atkins, Renwick—187, T, Kansas
8. Jones, David—214, C, Texas
9. Hollins, Rich—246, WR, West Virginia
10. Frizzell, William—259, DB, North Carolina Central, from Colts
    Thaxton, James—273, DB, Louisiana Tech
11. Saxon, Mike—300, P, San Diego State
12. Streno, Glenn—327, C, Tennessee

## Green Bay Packers

1. Carreker, Alphonso—12, DE, Florida State
2. Choice to New York Jets through San Diego
3. Humphrey, Donnie—72, DT, Auburn
4. Dorsey, John—99, LB, Connecticut
5. Flynn, Tom—126, DB, Pittsburgh
6. Wright, Randy—153, QB, Wisconsin

7. Jones, Daryll—181, DB, Georgia
8. Choice to Denver
9. Choice to Kansas City
10. Hoffman, Gary—267, T, Santa Clara
11. Cannon, Mark—294, C, Texas-Arlington
12. Taylor, Lenny—313, WR, Tennessee, from San Diego
    Emans, Mark—323, LB, Bowling Green

## Houston Oilers

1. Steinkuhler, Dean—2, T, Nebraska
2. Smith, Doug—29, DE, Auburn
   Eason, Bo—54, DB, Cal-Davis, from Dallas
3. Meads, Johnny—58, LB, Nicholls State
4. Studaway, Mark—85, DE, Tennessee
   Allen, Patrick—100, DB, Utah State, from Minnesota
5. Lyles, Robert—114, LB, Texas Christian
6. Grimsley, John—141, LB, Kentucky
   Mullins, Eric—161, WR, Stanford, from Los Angeles Rams

7. Joyner, Willie—170, RB, Maryland
8. Baugh, Kevin—197, WR, Penn State
9. Donaldson, Jeff—226, DB, Colorado
   Johnson, Mike—228, DE, Illinois, from New York Giants
   Russell, Mike—252, LB, Toledo, from Los Angeles Raiders
10. Choice to Los Angeles Rams
11. Choice to Los Angeles Raiders
12. Choice to Los Angeles Rams

## Indianapolis Colts

1. Coleman, Leonard—8, DB, Vanderbilt
   Solt, Ron—19, G, Maryland, from Denver
2. Winter, Blaise—35, DT, Syracuse
3. Scott, Chris—66, DT, Purdue
4. Curry, Craig—93, DB, Texas
   Wonsley, George—103, RB, Mississippi State, from Seattle
5. Tate, Golden—120, WR, Tennessee State

   Call, Kevin—130, T, Colorado State, from Seattle
6. Beverly, Dwight—147, RB, Illinois
7. Choice to Detroit
8. Daniel, Eugene—205, DB, Louisiana State
9. Choice to Dallas
10. Choice to Detroit
11. Stowe, Bob—290, T, Illinois
12. Hathaway, Steve—317, LB, West Virginia

## Kansas City Chiefs

1. Maas, Bill—5, DT, Pittsburgh
   Alt, John—21, T, Iowa, from Los Angeles Rams
2. Radecic, Scott—34, LB, Penn State
3. Heard, Herman—61, RB, Southern Colorado
4. Robinson, Mark—90, DB, Penn State
5. Holle, Eric—117, DE, Texas
   Paine, Jeff—134, LB, Texas A&M, from Los Angeles Rams

6. Stevens, Rufus—146, WR, Grambling
7. Ross, Kevin—173, DB, Temple
8. Clark, Randy—202, DB, Florida
9. Auer, Scott—229, T, Michigan State
   Hestera, Dave—240, TE, Colorado, from Green Bay
10. Wenglikowski, Al—258, LB, Pittsburgh
11. Johnson, Bobby—285, RB, San Jose State
12. Lang, Mark—314, LB, Texas

## Los Angeles Raiders

1. Choice to Cincinnati through New England
2. Jones, Sean—51, DE, Northeastern, from San Francisco
   Choice to San Francisco
3. McCall, Joe—84, RB, Pittsburgh
4. Choice to Tampa Bay
5. Parker, Andy—127, TE, Utah, from Minnesota
   Choice to Minnesota
6. Toran, Stacey—168, DB, Notre Dame

7. Willis, Mitch—183, DE, Southern Methodist, from New Orleans
   Choice to Minnesota
8. Seale, Sam—224, WR, Western State, Colo.
9. Choice to Houston
10. Choice to Cleveland
11. Williams, Gardner—282, DB, St. Mary's, Calif., from Houston
    Choice to Minnesota
12. Essington, Randy—336, QB, Colorado

## Los Angeles Rams

1. Choice to Kansas City
2. Choice to Cleveland
3. Choice to Detroit
4. Choice to Washington through Houston
5. Stephens, Hal—133, DE, East Carolina, from Detroit
   Choice to Kansas City
6. Choice to Houston
7. Radachowsky, George—188, DB, Boston College

8. Brady, Ed—215, LB, Illinois
9. Reynolds, George—242, P, Penn State
10. Vann, Norwood—253, TE, East Carolina, from Houston
    Dooley, Joe—274, C, Ohio State
11. Harper, Michael—293, RB, Southern California, from Chicago
    Love, Dwyane—301, RB, Houston
12. Fisher, Rod—309, DB, Oklahoma State, from Houston
    Bias, Moe—328, LB, Illinois

## Miami Dolphins

1. Shipp, Jackie—14, LB, Oklahoma, from Buffalo
   Choice to Buffalo
2. Brophy, Jay—53, LB, Miami
3. Choice to Buffalo
4. Carter, Joe—109, RB, Alabama
5. May, Dean—138, QB, Louisville
6. Tatum, Rowland—165, LB, Ohio State
7. Carvalho, Bernard—194, G, Hawaii
8. Landry, Ronnie—221, RB, McNeese State
9. Boyle, Jim—250, T, Tulane
10. Chesley, John—277, TE, Oklahoma State
11. Brown, Bud—305, DB, Southern Mississippi
12. Devane, William—320, DT, Clemson, from Chicago through San Francisco
    Weingrad, Mike—333, LB, Illinois

## Minnesota Vikings

1. Millard, Keith—13, DE, Washington State
2. Choice to Dallas through Houston
3. Anderson, Alfred—67, RB, Baylor
4. Choice to Houston
5. Choice to Los Angeles Raiders
   Rice, Allen—140, RB, Baylor, from Los Angeles Raiders
6. Collins, Dwight—154, WR, Pittsburgh
7. Haines, John—180, DT, Texas
   Lewis, Loyd—196, G, Texas A&I, from Los Angeles Raiders
8. Sverchek, Paul—208, DT, Cal Poly-SLO
9. Kidd, Keith—235, WR, Arkansas
10. Spencer, James—268, LB, Oklahoma State
11. Pickett, Edgar—295, LB, Clemson
    Thompson, Lawrence—308, WR, Miami, from Los Angeles Raiders
12. Jones, Mike—321, RB, North Carolina A&T

## New England Patriots

1. Fryar, Irving—1, WR, Nebraska, from Tampa Bay through Cincinnati
   Choice to Cincinnati
2. Williams, Ed—43, LB, Texas
3. Williams, Jon—70, RB, Penn State
4. Choice to New Orleans
5. Fairchild, Paul—124, G, Kansas
6. Gibson, Ernest—151, DB, Furman
7. Kallmeyer, Bruce—184, K, Kansas
   Williams, Derwin—192, WR, New Mexico, from San Francisco
8. Keyton, James—211, T, Arizona State
9. Bolzan, Scott—238, T, Northern Illinois
   Windham, David—251, LB, Jackson State, from Washington
10. Choice to Cincinnati
11. Flager, Charlie—292, G, Washington State
12. Howell, Harper—319, TE, UCLA

## New Orleans Saints

1. Choice to New York Jets
2. Geathers, James—42, DE, Wichita State
3. Hoage, Terry—68, DB, Georgia, from Buffalo
   Anthony, Tyrone—69, RB, North Carolina
4. Choice to Cleveland through Denver
   Hilgenberg, Joel—97, C, Iowa, from New England
5. Fields, Jitter—123, DB, Texas
6. Thorp, Don—156, DT, Illinois
7. Choice to Los Angeles Raiders
8. Terrell, Clemon—210, RB, Southern Mississippi
9. Hansen, Brian—237, P, Sioux Falls, S.D.
10. Gray, Paul—264, LB, Western Kentucky
11. Bourgeau, Michel—291, DE, Boise State
12. Nelson, Byron—324, T, Arizona

## New York Giants

1. Banks, Carl—3, LB, Michigan State
   Roberts, Bill—27, T, Ohio State, from Washington
2. Choice to Washington
3. Hostetler, Jeff—59, QB, West Virginia
4. Goode, Conrad—87, T, Missouri
   Reasons, Gary—105, LB, Northwestern Louisiana, from Denver
5. Harris, Clint—115, DB, East Carolina
6. Scott, Jim—143, DE, Clemson
7. Manuel, Lionel—171, WR, Pacific
8. Choice to San Diego
9. Choice to Houston
10. Jordan, David—255, G, Auburn
    Golden, Heyward—257, DB, South Carolina State, from San Diego
11. Cephous, Frank—283, RB, UCLA
12. Green, Lawrence—311, LB, Tennessee-Chattanooga

## New York Jets

1. Carter, Russell—10, DB, Southern Methodist
   Faurot, Ron—15, DE, Arkansas, from New Orleans
2. Sweeney, Jim—37, C, Pittsburgh
   Dennison, Glenn—39, TE, Miami, from Green Bay through San Diego
3. Clifton, Kyle—64, LB, Texas Christian
4. Bell, Bobby—91, LB, Missouri
5. Armstrong, Tron—122, WR, Eastern Kentucky
6. Paige, Tony—149, RB, Virginia Tech
7. Hamilton, Harry—176, DB, Penn State
8. Griggs, Billy—203, TE, Virginia
   Wright, Brett—217, P, Southeast Louisiana, from Cleveland
9. Baldwin, Tom—234, DT, Tulsa
10. Cone, Ronny—261, RB, Georgia Tech
11. Martin, Dan—288, T, Iowa State
12. Roberson, David—315, WR, Houston

## Philadelphia Eagles

1. Jackson, Kenny—4, WR, Penn State
2. Choice to Atlanta
3. Russell, Rusty—60, T, South Carolina
4. Cooper, Evan—88, DB, Michigan
5. Hardy, Andre—116, RB, St. Mary's, Calif.
6. Raridon, Scott—145, T, Nebraska
7. Hayes, Joe—172, RB, Central State, Okla.
8. Matsakis, Manny—200, K, Capital
9. Choice to Cleveland
10. Thomas, John—256, DB, Texas Christian
11. Robertson, John—284, T, East Carolina
12. McFadden, Paul—312, K, Youngstown State

## Pittsburgh Steelers

1. Lipps, Louis—23, WR, Southern Mississippi
2. Kolodziejski, Chris—52, TE, Wyoming
3. Choice to Buffalo through Miami
4. Thompson, Weegie—108, WR, Florida State
   Long, Terry—111, G, East Carolina, from Washington
5. Hughes, Van—135, DT, Southwest Texas State
6. Brown, Chris—164, DB, Notre Dame
7. Campbell, Scott—191, QB, Purdue
8. Rasmussen, Randy—220, C, Minnesota
9. Erenberg, Rich—247, RB, Colgate
10. McJunkin, Kirk—276, T, Texas
11. Veals, Elton—303, RB, Tulane
12. Gillespie, Fernandars—332, RB, William Jewell

## St. Louis Cardinals

1. Duncan, Clyde—17, WR, Tennessee
2. Dawson, Doug—45, G, Texas
3. Choice to San Francisco
   McIvor, Rick—80, QB, Texas, from San Francisco
4. Bayless, Martin—101, DB, Bowling Green
5. Leiding, Jeff—129, LB, Texas
   Goode, John—136, TE, Youngstown State, from San Francisco
6. Clark, Rod—157, LB, Southwest Texas State
7. Walker, Quentin—185, RB, Virginia
8. Noga, Falaniko—201, LB, Hawaii, from San Diego
   Paulling, Bob—213, K, Clemson
9. Walker, John—241, RB, Texas
10. Smythe, Mark—269, DT, Indiana
11. Mackey, Kyle—296, QB, East Texas State
12. Parker, Paul—325, G, Oklahoma

## San Diego Chargers

1. Cade, Mossy—6, DB, Texas
2. Guendling, Mike—33, LB, Northwestern
3. Choice to Detroit through St. Louis
4. Choice to Denver through Tampa Bay
5. James, Lionel—118, KR, Auburn
6. Guthrie, Keith—144, DT, Texas A&M
7. Bendross, Jesse—174, WR, Alabama
8. Woodard, Raymond—199, DT, Texas, from New York Giants
   Choice to St. Louis
   Craighead, Bob—219, RB, Northeast Louisiana, from San Francisco
9. Barnes, Zack—230, DT, Alabama State
10. Choice to New York Giants
11. McGee, Buford—286, RB, Mississippi
12. Choice to Green Bay
    Harper, Maurice—331, WR, La Verne, from San Francisco

## San Francisco 49ers

1. Shell, Todd—24, LB, Brigham Young
2. Choice to Los Angeles Raiders
   Frank, John—56, TE, Ohio State, from Los Angeles Raiders
3. McIntyre, Guy—73, G, Georgia, from St. Louis
   Choice to St. Louis
4. Choice to Tampa Bay through San Diego
5. Carter, Michael—121, DT, Southern Methodist, from Atlanta
   Choice to St. Louis
   Fuller, Jeff—139, LB, Texas A&M, from Washington through Los Angeles Raiders
6. Choice to Atlanta
7. Choice to New England
8. Choice to San Diego
9. Miller, Lee—239, DB, Cal State-Fullerton, from Chicago
   Harmon, Derrick—248, RB, Cornell
10. Moritz, Dave—275, WR, Iowa
11. Pendleton, Kirk—307, WR, Brigham Young
12. Choice to San Diego

## Seattle Seahawks

1. Taylor, Terry—22, DB, Southern Illinois
2. Turner, Daryl—49, WR, Michigan State
3. Young, Fred—76, LB, New Mexico State
   Hagood, Rickey—86, DT, South Carolina, from Tampa Bay through San Francisco
4. Choice to Colts
5. Choice to Colts
6. Kaiser, John—162, LB, Arizona
7. Slater, Sam—189, T, Weber State
8. Puzar, John—216, C, Long Beach State
9. Schreiber, Adam—243, G, Texas
10. Morris, Randall—270, RB, Tennessee
11. Gemza, Steve—302, T, UCLA
12. Windham, Theodis—329, DB, Utah State

## Tampa Bay Buccaneers

1. Choice to New England through Cincinnati
2. Browner, Keith—30, LB, Southern California
3. Acorn, Fred—57, DB, Texas
4. Choice to Seattle through San Francisco
   Gunter, Michael—107, RB, Tulsa, from San Francisco through San Diego
   Heller, Ron—112, T, Penn State, from Los Angeles Raiders
5. Choice to Dallas
6. Washington, Chris—142, LB, Iowa State
7. Carroll, Jay—169, TE, Minnesota
8. Robinson, Fred—198, DE, Miami
9. Mallory, Rick—225, G, Washington
10. Gallery, Jim—254, K, Minnesota
11. Kiel, Blair—281, QB, Notre Dame
12. Jemison, Thad—310, WR, Ohio State

## Washington Redskins

1. Choice to New York Giants
2. Slater, Bob—31, DT, Oklahoma, from New York Giants
   Hamilton, Steve—55, DE, East Carolina
3. Schroeder, Jay—83, QB, UCLA
4. Smith, Jimmy—102, RB, Elon, from Los Angeles Rams through Houston
   Choice to Pittsburgh
5. Pegues, Jeff—125, LB, East Carolina, from Chicago through San Diego, Seattle, and New York Giants
   Choice to San Francisco through Los Angeles Raiders
6. Singer, Curt—167, T, Tennessee
7. Smith, Mark—195, WR, North Carolina
8. Smith, Jeff—223, DB, Missouri
9. Choice to New England
10. Griffin, Keith—279, RB, Miami
11. Jones, Anthony—306, TE, Wichita State
12. Thomas, Curtland—335, WR, Missouri

# THE AFC

Buffalo Bills
Cincinnati Bengals
Cleveland Browns
Denver Broncos
Houston Oilers
Indianapolis Colts
Kansas City Chiefs
Los Angeles Raiders
Miami Dolphins
New England Patriots
New York Jets
Pittsburgh Steelers
San Diego Chargers
Seattle Seahawks

# BUFFALO BILLS

**American Football Conference
Eastern Division**

**Team Colors:** Royal Blue, Scarlet Red,
and White

**One Bills Drive
Orchard Park, New York 14127
Telephone: (716) 648-1800**

**Club Officials**

President: Ralph C. Wilson, Jr.
Executive-Vice President: Patrick J. McGroder, Jr.
Vice President-Administration and General
    Manager: Terry Bledsoe
Vice President: Richard O. Morrison
Vice President and Head Coach: Kay Stephenson
Vice President-Player Personnel: Norm Pollom
Vice President-Public Relations: L. Budd Thalman
Ticket Director: Jim Cipriano
Assistant Ticket Director: Adam Ziccardi
Assistant Public Relations Director: Dave Senko
Assistant Director of Player Personnel:
    Bruce Nicholas
Director of Purchasing and Marketing:
    Bill Munson
Trainers: Ed Abramoski, Bud Tice
Equipment Manager: Dave Hojnowski
Strength and Conditioning Coordinator:
    Jim Speros

**Stadium:** Rich Stadium • **Capacity:** 80,290
            One Bills Drive
            Orchard Park, New York 14127

**Playing Surface:** AstroTurf

**Training Camp:** Fredonia State University
                  College
                  Fredonia, New York 14063

## 1984 SCHEDULE

**Preseason**
| | | |
|---|---|---|
| Aug. 4 | at Seattle | 7:30 |
| Aug. 11 | **New England** | 6:00 |
| Aug. 18 | **Detroit** | 6:00 |
| Aug. 26 | vs. Chicago at Indianapolis | 12:00 |

**Regular Season**
| | | |
|---|---|---|
| Sept. 2 | **New England** | 1:00 |
| Sept. 9 | at St. Louis | 12:00 |
| Sept. 17 | **Miami** (Monday) | 9:00 |
| Sept. 23 | **New York Jets** | 1:00 |
| Sept. 30 | at Colts | 12:00 |
| Oct. 7 | **Philadelphia** | 1:00 |
| Oct. 14 | at Seattle | 1:00 |
| Oct. 21 | **Denver** | 1:00 |
| Oct. 28 | at Miami | 4:00 |
| Nov. 4 | **Cleveland** | 1:00 |
| Nov. 11 | at New England | 1:00 |
| Nov. 18 | **Dallas** | 1:00 |
| Nov. 25 | at Washington | 1:00 |
| Dec. 2 | **Colts** | 1:00 |
| Dec. 8 | at N.Y. Jets (Saturday) | 12:30 |
| Dec. 16 | at Cincinnati | 1:00 |

## BILLS COACHING HISTORY

**(152-188-8)**

| | | |
|---|---|---|
| 1960-61 | Buster Ramsey | 11-16-1 |
| 1962-65 | Lou Saban | 38-19-3 |
| 1966-68 | Joe Collier* | 13-17-1 |
| 1968 | Harvey Johnson | 1-10-1 |
| 1969-70 | John Rauch | 7-20-1 |
| 1971 | Harvey Johnson | 1-13-0 |
| 1972-76 | Lou Saban** | 32-28-1 |
| 1976-77 | Jim Ringo | 3-20-0 |
| 1978-82 | Chuck Knox | 38-38-0 |
| 1983 | Kay Stephenson | 8-8-0 |

*Released after two games in 1968
**Resigned after five games in 1976

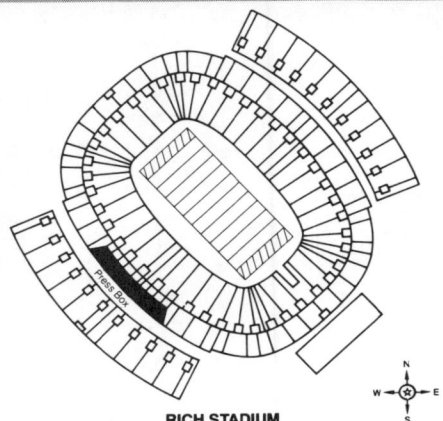

**RICH STADIUM**

## RECORD HOLDERS

### Individual Records—Career

| Category | Name | Performance |
|---|---|---|
| Rushing (Yds.) | O.J. Simpson, 1969-1977 | 10,183 |
| Passing (Yds.) | Joe Ferguson, 1973-1983 | 25,599 |
| Passing (TDs) | Joe Ferguson, 1973-1983 | 169 |
| Receiving (No.) | Elbert Dubenion, 1960-67 | 296 |
| Receiving (Yds.) | Elbert Dubenion, 1960-67 | 5,304 |
| Interceptions | George Byrd, 1964-1970 | 40 |
| Punting (Avg.) | Paul Maguire, 1964-1970 | 42.1 |
| Punt Return (Avg.) | Keith Moody, 1976-79 | 10.5 |
| Kickoff Return (Avg.) | Wallace Francis, 1973-74 | 27.2 |
| Field Goals | John Leypoldt, 1971-76 | 74 |
| Touchdowns (Tot.) | O.J. Simpson, 1969-1977 | 70 |
| Points | O.J. Simpson, 1969-1977 | 420 |

### Individual Records—Single Season

| Category | Name | Performance |
|---|---|---|
| Rushing (Yds.) | O.J. Simpson, 1973 | 2,003 |
| Passing (Yds.) | Joe Ferguson, 1981 | 3,652 |
| Passing (TDs) | Joe Ferguson, 1983 | 26 |
| Receiving (No.) | Frank Lewis, 1981 | 70 |
| Receiving (Yds.) | Frank Lewis, 1981 | 1,244 |
| Interceptions | Billy Atkins, 1961 | 10 |
| | Tom Janik, 1967 | 10 |
| Punting (Avg.) | Billy Atkins, 1961 | 44.5 |
| Punt Return (Avg.) | Keith Moody, 1977 | 13.1 |
| Kickoff Return (Avg.) | Ed Rutkowski, 1963 | 30.2 |
| Field Goals | Pete Gogolak, 1965 | 28 |
| Touchdowns (Tot.) | O.J. Simpson, 1975 | 23 |
| Points | O.J. Simpson, 1975 | 138 |

### Individual Records—Single Game

| Category | Name | Performance |
|---|---|---|
| Rushing (Yds.) | O.J. Simpson, 11-25-76 | 273 |
| Passing (Yds.) | Joe Ferguson, 10-9-83 | 419 |
| Passing (TDs) | Joe Ferguson, 9-23-79, 10-9-83 | 5 |
| Receiving (No.) | Glenn Bass, 12-3-61 | 12 |
| | Bill Miller, 10-5-63 | 12 |
| Receiving (Yds.) | Jerry Butler, 9-23-79 | 255 |
| Interceptions | Many times | 3 |
| | Last time by Jeff Nixon, 9-7-80 | |
| Field Goals | Pete Gogolak, 12-5-65 | 5 |
| Touchdowns (Tot.) | Cookie Gilchrist, 12-8-63 | 5 |
| Points | Cookie Gilchrist, 12-8-63 | 30 |

## 1983 TEAM STATISTICS

| | Buffalo | Opp. |
|---|---|---|
| Total First Downs | 309 | 332 |
| Rushing | 100 | 148 |
| Passing | 171 | 148 |
| Penalty | 38 | 36 |
| Third Down Efficiency | 71/212 | 81/221 |
| Third Down Percentage | 33.5 | 36.7 |
| Total Net Yards | 4823 | 5809 |
| Total Offensive Plays | 1023 | 1078 |
| Avg. Gain per Play | 4.7 | 5.4 |
| Avg. Gain per Game | 301.4 | 363.1 |
| Net Yards Rushing | 1736 | 2503 |
| Total Rushing Plays | 415 | 566 |
| Avg. Gain per Rush | 4.2 | 4.4 |
| Avg. Gain Rushing per Game | 108.5 | 156.4 |
| Net Yards Passing | 3087 | 3306 |
| Lost Attempting to Pass | 37/351 | 32/247 |
| Gross Yards Passing | 3438 | 3553 |
| Attempts/Completions | 571/317 | 480/286 |
| Percent Completed | 55.5 | 59.6 |
| Had Intercepted | 28 | 13 |
| Avg. Net Passing per Game | 192.9 | 206.6 |
| Punts/Avg. | 89/39.7 | 78/42.9 |
| Punt Returns/Avg. | 44/5.5 | 42/9.6 |
| Kickoff Returns/Avg. | 64/21.3 | 53/17.9 |
| Interceptions/Avg. Ret. | 13/11.8 | 28/11.8 |
| Penalties/Yards | 144/1094 | 128/1298 |
| Fumbles/Ball Lost | 24/12 | 32/18 |
| Total Points | 283 | 351 |
| Avg. Points per Game | 17.7 | 21.9 |
| Touchdowns | 36 | 39 |
| Rushing | 4 | 14 |
| Passing | 30 | 22 |
| Returns and Recoveries | 2 | 3 |
| Field Goals | 11/26 | 26/39 |
| Conversions | 34/36 | 39/39 |
| Safeties | 0 | 0 |
| Avg. Time of Possession | 28:24 | 31:36 |

## 1983 TEAM RECORD
### Preseason (1-3)

| Date | Buffalo | | Opponents |
|---|---|---|---|
| 8/6 | 17 | Chicago | 27 |
| 8/13 | 10 | *Cleveland | 27 |
| 8/20 | 17 | Detroit | 16 |
| 8/27 | 19 | *Washington | 27 |
| | 63 | | 97 |

### Regular Season (8-8)

| Date | Buffalo | | Opp. | Att. |
|---|---|---|---|---|
| 9/4 | 0 | *Miami | 12 | 78,683 |
| 9/11 | 10 | Cincinnati | 6 | 46,841 |
| 9/18 | 28 | *Baltimore | 23 | 40,937 |
| 9/25 | 30 | *Houston | 13 | 60,070 |
| 10/3 | 10 | *New York Jets | 34 | 79,933 |
| 10/9 | 38 | Miami (OT) | 35 | 54,482 |
| 10/16 | 30 | Baltimore | 7 | 38,565 |
| 10/23 | 0 | *New England | 31 | 60,424 |
| 10/30 | 27 | *New Orleans | 21 | 49,413 |
| 11/6 | 7 | New England | 21 | 42,604 |
| 11/13 | 24 | New York Jets | 17 | 48,513 |
| 11/20 | 24 | *Los Angeles Raiders | 27 | 72,393 |
| 11/27 | 17 | Los Angeles Rams | 41 | 48,246 |
| 12/4 | 14 | Kansas City | 9 | 27,104 |
| 12/11 | 10 | *San Francisco | 23 | 38,039 |
| 12/18 | 14 | Atlanta | 31 | 31,015 |
| | 283 | | 351 | 817,262 |

*Home Game     (OT) Overtime

### Score by Periods

| | | | | | | | |
|---|---|---|---|---|---|---|---|
| Buffalo | 28 | 87 | 55 | 110 | 3 | — | 283 |
| Opponents | 29 | 108 | 92 | 122 | 0 | — | 351 |

### Attendance
Home 479,892     Away 337,370     Total 817,262
Single game home record, 79,933 (10-3-83)
Single season home record, 601,138 (1981)

## 1983 INDIVIDUAL STATISTICS

### Rushing

| | Att. | Yds. | Avg. | LG | TD |
|---|---|---|---|---|---|
| Cribbs | 263 | 1131 | 4.3 | 45 | 3 |
| Moore | 60 | 275 | 4.6 | 21 | 0 |
| Leaks | 58 | 157 | 2.7 | 12 | 1 |
| Ferguson | 20 | 88 | 4.4 | 19 | 0 |
| Hunter | 2 | 28 | 14.0 | 24 | 0 |
| Kofler | 4 | 25 | 6.3 | 11 | 0 |
| Riddick | 4 | 18 | 4.5 | 12 | 0 |
| V. Williams | 3 | 11 | 3.7 | 5 | 0 |
| Franklin | 1 | 3 | 3.0 | 3 | 0 |
| Buffalo | 415 | 1736 | 4.2 | 45 | 4 |
| Opponents | 566 | 2503 | 4.4 | 50t | 14 |

### Passing

| | Att. | Comp. | Pct. | Yds. | TD | Int. | Tkld. | Rate |
|---|---|---|---|---|---|---|---|---|
| Ferguson | 508 | 281 | 55.3 | 2995 | 26 | 25 | 27/266 | 69.3 |
| Kofler | 61 | 35 | 57.4 | 440 | 4 | 3 | 10/85 | 81.3 |
| Cribbs | 2 | 1 | 50.0 | 3 | 0 | 0 | 0/0 | 56.3 |
| Buffalo | 571 | 317 | 55.5 | 3438 | 30 | 28 | 37/351 | 70.5 |
| Opponents | 480 | 286 | 59.6 | 3553 | 22 | 13 | 32/247 | 86.6 |

### Receiving

| | No. | Yds. | Avg. | LG | TD |
|---|---|---|---|---|---|
| Cribbs | 57 | 524 | 9.2 | 33t | 7 |
| Lewis | 36 | 486 | 13.5 | 27t | 3 |
| Hunter | 36 | 402 | 11.2 | 40t | 3 |
| Butler | 36 | 385 | 10.7 | 25 | 3 |
| Moore | 34 | 199 | 5.9 | 21 | 1 |
| Franklin | 30 | 452 | 15.1 | 43t | 4 |
| Brammer | 25 | 215 | 8.6 | 21 | 2 |
| Tuttle | 17 | 261 | 15.4 | 38 | 3 |
| Mosley | 14 | 180 | 12.9 | 35 | 3 |
| Dawkins | 11 | 123 | 11.2 | 28t | 1 |
| Barnett | 10 | 94 | 9.4 | 14 | 0 |
| Leaks | 8 | 74 | 9.3 | 12 | 0 |
| Riddick | 3 | 43 | 14.3 | 24 | 0 |
| Buffalo | 317 | 3438 | 10.8 | 43t | 30 |
| Opponents | 286 | 3553 | 12.4 | 72t | 22 |

### Interceptions

| | No. | Yds. | Avg. | LG | TD |
|---|---|---|---|---|---|
| Freeman | 3 | 40 | 13.3 | 29 | 0 |
| C. Williams | 3 | 6 | 2.0 | 4 | 0 |
| Sanford | 2 | 39 | 19.5 | 20 | 0 |
| Romes | 2 | 27 | 13.5 | 27 | 0 |
| Keating | 2 | 20 | 10.0 | 17 | 0 |
| Kennedy | 1 | 22 | 22.0 | 22t | 1 |
| Buffalo | 13 | 154 | 11.8 | 29 | 1 |
| Opponents | 28 | 330 | 11.8 | 60t | 2 |

### Punting

| | No. | Yds. | Avg. | In 20 | LG |
|---|---|---|---|---|---|
| Cater | 89 | 3533 | 39.7 | 24 | 60 |
| Buffalo | 89 | 3533 | 39.7 | 24 | 60 |
| Opponents | 78 | 3344 | 42.9 | 20 | 67 |

### Punt Returns

| | No. | FC | Yds. | Avg. | LG | TD |
|---|---|---|---|---|---|---|
| Riddick | 42 | 5 | 241 | 5.7 | 24 | 0 |
| Hurley | 1 | 0 | 0 | 0.0 | 0 | 0 |
| V. Williams | 1 | 0 | 0 | 0.0 | 0 | 0 |
| Buffalo | 44 | 5 | 241 | 5.5 | 24 | 0 |
| Opponents | 42 | 22 | 403 | 9.6 | 62 | 0 |

### Kickoff Returns

| | No. | Yds. | Avg. | LG | TD |
|---|---|---|---|---|---|
| V. Williams | 22 | 494 | 22.5 | 60 | 0 |
| Riddick | 28 | 568 | 20.3 | 49 | 0 |
| Mosley | 9 | 236 | 26.2 | 33 | 0 |
| B. Williams | 3 | 56 | 18.7 | 23 | 0 |
| Talley | 2 | 9 | 4.5 | 5 | 0 |
| Buffalo | 64 | 1363 | 21.3 | 60 | 0 |
| Opponents | 53 | 949 | 17.9 | 43 | 0 |

### Scoring

| | TD | TD R | TD P | TD Rt | PAT | FG | TP |
|---|---|---|---|---|---|---|---|
| Danelo | | | | | 33/34 | 10/20 | 63 |
| Cribbs | 10 | 3 | 7 | 0 | | | 60 |
| Franklin | 4 | 0 | 4 | 0 | | | 24 |
| Butler | 3 | 0 | 3 | 0 | | | 18 |
| Hunter | 3 | 0 | 3 | 0 | | | 18 |
| Lewis | 3 | 0 | 3 | 0 | | | 18 |
| Mosley | 3 | 0 | 3 | 0 | | | 18 |
| Tuttle | 3 | 0 | 3 | 0 | | | 18 |
| Brammer | 2 | 0 | 2 | 0 | | | 12 |
| Dawkins | 1 | 0 | 1 | 0 | | | 6 |
| Kennedy | 1 | 0 | 0 | 1 | | | 6 |
| Kilson | 1 | 0 | 0 | 1 | | | 6 |
| Leaks | 1 | 1 | 0 | 0 | | | 6 |
| Moore | 1 | 0 | 1 | 0 | | | 6 |
| Steinfort | | | | | 1/1 | 1/6 | 4 |
| Buffalo | 36 | 4 | 30 | 2 | 34/36 | 11/26 | 283 |
| Opponents | 39 | 14 | 22 | 3 | 39/39 | 26/39 | 351 |

## FIRST-ROUND SELECTIONS

(If Club had no first-round selection, first player drafted is listed with round in parentheses.)

| Year | Player, College, Position |
|---|---|
| 1960 | Richie Lucas, Penn State, QB |
| 1961 | Ken Rice, Auburn, T |
| 1962 | Ernie Davis, Syracuse, RB |
| 1963 | Dave Behrman, Michigan State, C |
| 1964 | Carl Eller, Minnesota, DE |
| 1965 | Jim Davidson, Ohio State, T |
| 1966 | Mike Dennis, Mississippi, RB |
| 1967 | John Pitts, Arizona State, S |
| 1968 | Haven Moses, San Diego State, WR |
| 1969 | O.J. Simpson, Southern California, RB |
| 1970 | Al Cowlings, Southern California, DE |
| 1971 | J. D. Hill, Arizona State, WR |
| 1972 | Walt Patulski, Notre Dame, DE |
| 1973 | Paul Seymour, Michigan, TE |
| | Joe DeLamielleure, Michigan State, G |
| 1974 | Reuben Gant, Oklahoma State, TE |
| 1975 | Tom Ruud, Nebraska, LB |
| 1976 | Mario Clark, Oregon, DB |
| 1977 | Phil Dokes, Oklahoma State, DT |
| 1978 | Terry Miller, Oklahoma State, RB |
| 1979 | Tom Cousineau, Ohio State, LB |
| | Jerry Butler, Clemson, WR |
| 1980 | Jim Ritcher, North Carolina State, C |
| 1981 | Booker Moore, Penn State, RB |
| 1982 | Perry Tuttle, Clemson, WR |
| 1983 | Tony Hunter, Notre Dame, TE |
| | Jim Kelly, Miami, QB |
| 1984 | Greg Bell, Notre Dame, RB |

# BUFFALO BILLS 1984 VETERAN ROSTER

| No. | Name | Pos. | Ht. | Wt. | Birth-date | NFL Exp. | College | Birthplace | Residence | Games in '83 |
|-----|------|------|-----|-----|-----------|----------|---------|-----------|-----------|--------------|
| 75 | Acker, Bill | NT | 6-3 | 255 | 11/7/56 | 5 | Texas | Freer, Tex. | Freer, Tex. | 11 |
| 84 | Barnett, Buster | TE | 6-5 | 235 | 11/24/58 | 4 | Jackson State | Brooksville, Miss. | Jackson, Miss. | 15 |
| 73 | Borchardt, Jon | G | 6-5 | 255 | 8/13/57 | 6 | Montana State | Minneapolis, Minn. | Orchard Park, N.Y. | 16 |
| 86 | Brammer, Mark | TE | 6-3 | 235 | 5/3/58 | 5 | Michigan State | Traverse City, Mich. | Orchard Park, N.Y. | 12 |
| 80 | Butler, Jerry | WR | 6-0 | 178 | 10/12/57 | 6 | Clemson | Greenwood, S.C. | East Amherst, N.Y. | 9 |
| 67 | Caldwell, Darryl | T | 6-5 | 245 | 2/2/60 | 2 | Tennessee State | Birmingham, Ala. | Birmingham, Ala. | 14 |
| 7 | Cater, Greg | P | 6-0 | 191 | 4/17/57 | 5 | Tennessee-Chattanooga | LaGrange, La. | Athens, Tenn. | 16 |
| 29 | †Clark, Mario | CB | 6-2 | 195 | 3/29/54 | 9 | Oregon | Pasadena, Calif. | Studio City, Calif. | 14 |
| 63 | Cross, Justin | T | 6-6 | 265 | 4/29/59 | 3 | Western State, Colo. | Montreal, Canada | Orchard Park, N.Y. | 15 |
| 18 | Danelo, Joe | K | 5-9 | 166 | 9/2/53 | 10 | Washington State | Spokane, Wash. | San Pedro, Calif. | 14 |
| 89 | Dawkins, Julius | WR | 6-1 | 196 | 1/4/61 | 2 | Pittsburgh | Monessen, Pa. | Monessen, Pa. | 11 |
| 70 | †Devlin, Joe | T | 6-5 | 250 | 2/23/54 | 8 | Iowa | Phoenixville, Pa. | Eden, N.Y. | 0* |
| 19 | Dufek, Joe | QB | 6-4 | 215 | 8/23/61 | 2 | Yale | Kent, Ohio | Hamburg, N.Y. | 16 |
| 12 | Ferguson, Joe | QB | 6-1 | 195 | 4/23/50 | 12 | Arkansas | Alvin, Tex. | Shreveport, La. | 16 |
| 28 | †Flint, Judson | S | 6-0 | 201 | 1/26/57 | 4 | Memphis State | Farrell, Pa. | Cleveland Heights, Ohio | 1 |
| 85 | Franklin, Byron | WR | 6-1 | 179 | 9/4/58 | 4 | Auburn | Florence, Ala. | Sheffield, Ala. | 15 |
| 22 | Freeman, Steve | S | 5-11 | 185 | 5/8/53 | 10 | Mississippi State | Lamesa, Tex. | Lamesa, Tex. | 16 |
| 53 | Grant, Will | C | 6-4 | 248 | 3/7/54 | 7 | Kentucky | Milton, Mass. | Boston, N.Y. | 16 |
| 55 | Haslett, Jim | LB | 6-3 | 232 | 12/9/55 | 6 | Indiana, Pa. | Pittsburgh, Pa. | Orchard Park, N.Y. | 5 |
| 49 | Holt, Robert | WR | 6-1 | 182 | 10/4/59 | 2 | Baylor | Dennison, Tex. | Grand Prairie, Tex. | 0* |
| 25 | †Hooks, Roland | RB | 6-0 | 195 | 1/2/53 | 8 | North Carolina State | Brooklyn, N.Y. | Westminster, Colo. | 0* |
| 87 | Hunter, Tony | TE | 6-3 | 237 | 5/22/60 | 2 | Notre Dame | Cincinnati, Ohio | Cincinnati, Ohio | 13 |
| 47 | Hurley, Bill | S | 5-11 | 185 | 5/16/57 | 3 | Syracuse | Depew, N.Y. | Bethel Park, Pa. | 14* |
| 90 | Hutchinson, Scott | DE | 6-4 | 255 | 4/27/56 | 6 | Florida | Winter Park, Fla. | Winter Park, Fla. | 5 |
| 91 | †Johnson, Ken | DE | 6-5 | 253 | 3/25/55 | 6 | Knoxville | Nashville, Tenn. | Nashville, Tenn. | 16 |
| 72 | Jones, Ken | T | 6-5 | 256 | 12/1/52 | 9 | Arkansas State | St. Louis, Mo. | Niagara Falls, N.Y. | 16 |
| 50 | Junkin, Trey | LB | 6-2 | 221 | 1/23/61 | 2 | Louisiana Tech | Little Rock, Ark. | Winnfield, La. | 16 |
| 52 | Keating, Chris | LB | 6-2 | 223 | 10/12/57 | 6 | Maine | Boston, Mass. | Hamburg, N.Y. | 16 |
| 21 | Kennedy, Mike | S | 6-0 | 195 | 2/26/59 | 2 | Toledo | Toledo, Ohio | Toledo, Ohio | 12 |
| 43 | Kilson, David | CB | 6-1 | 200 | 8/11/61 | 2 | Nevada-Reno | San Francisco, Calif. | Sacramento, Calif. | 16 |
| 10 | Kofler, Matt | QB | 6-3 | 192 | 8/30/59 | 3 | San Diego State | Kelso, Wash. | El Cajon, Calif. | 16 |
| 42 | Kush, Rod | S | 6-0 | 188 | 12/29/56 | 5 | Nebraska-Omaha | Omaha, Neb. | Gretna, Neb. | 4 |
| 48 | Leaks, Roosevelt | RB | 5-10 | 225 | 1/31/53 | 10 | Texas | Brenham, Tex. | Austin, Tex. | 12 |
| 59 | Lumpkin, Joey | LB | 6-2 | 230 | 2/19/60 | 3 | Arizona State | Ardmore, Okla. | Scottsdale, Ariz. | 14 |
| 61 | †Lynch, Tom | G | 6-5 | 250 | 5/24/55 | 8 | Boston College | Chicago, Ill. | Salem, N.H. | 15 |
| 54 | Marve, Eugene | LB | 6-2 | 230 | 8/14/60 | 3 | Saginaw Valley State | Flint, Mich. | Otisville, Mich. | 16 |
| 58 | Merrill, Mark | LB | 6-3 | 234 | 5/5/55 | 6 | Minnesota | Minneapolis, Minn. | New Brighton, Minn. | 12 |
| 34 | Moore, Booker | FB | 5-11 | 224 | 6/23/59 | 3 | Penn State | Flint, Mich. | East Aurora, N.Y. | 15 |
| 88 | †Mosley, Mike | WR | 6-2 | 192 | 6/30/58 | 3 | Texas A&M | Hillsboro, Tex. | Humble, Tex. | 7 |
| 38 | Nixon, Jeff | S | 6-3 | 190 | 10/13/56 | 5 | Richmond | Fursten Feldbruck, Ger. | Blasdell, N.Y. | 0* |
| 62 | Parker, Ervin | LB | 6-5 | 240 | 8/19/58 | 3 | South Carolina State | Georgetown, S.C. | Amherst, N.Y. | 16 |
| 40 | Riddick, Robb | RB | 6-0 | 195 | 4/26/57 | 3 | Millersville State, Pa. | Quakertown, Pa. | West Seneca, N.Y. | 16 |
| 51 | Ritcher, Jim | G | 6-3 | 251 | 5/21/58 | 5 | North Carolina State | Berea, Ohio | Raleigh, N.C. | 16 |
| 26 | Romes, Charles | CB | 6-1 | 190 | 12/16/54 | 8 | North Carolina Central | Durham, N.C. | Bolton, N.C. | 16 |
| 57 | Sanford, Lucius | LB | 6-2 | 216 | 2/14/56 | 7 | Georgia Tech | Atlanta, Ga. | Buffalo, N.Y. | 16 |
| 76 | Smerlas, Fred | NT | 6-3 | 270 | 4/8/57 | 6 | Boston College | Waltham, Mass. | Waltham, Mass. | 16 |
| 56 | Talley, Darryl | LB | 6-3 | 231 | 7/10/60 | 2 | West Virginia | East Cleveland, Ohio | East Cleveland, Ohio | 16 |
| | Taylor, Roger | T | 6-6 | 275 | 1/5/58 | 2 | Oklahoma State | Shawnee, Okla. | Blue Springs, Mo. | 0* |
| 24 | Thompson, Gary | CB | 6-0 | 180 | 2/23/59 | 2 | College of the Redwoods | Castro Valley, Calif. | San Jose, Calif. | 16 |
| | Tongue, Marco | S | 5-9 | 180 | 4/6/60 | 2 | Bowie State | Annapolis, Md. | Glen Burnie, Md. | 7* |
| 81 | Tuttle, Perry | WR | 6-0 | 178 | 8/2/59 | 3 | Clemson | Lexington, N.C. | Lexington, N.C. | 9 |
| 93 | Virkus, Scott | DE | 6-5 | 248 | 9/7/59 | 2 | San Francisco C.C. | Palo Alto, Calif. | Rochester, N.Y. | 15 |
| 65 | Vogler, Tim | C-G | 6-3 | 245 | 10/20/56 | 6 | Ohio State | Covington, Ohio | Hamburg, N.Y. | 16 |
| 45 | Walterscheid, Len | S | 5-11 | 190 | 9/13/54 | 8 | Southern Utah State | Gainesville, Tex. | Moab, Utah | 3 |
| 77 | Williams, Ben | DE | 6-3 | 245 | 9/1/54 | 9 | Mississippi | Yazoo City, Miss. | Jackson, Miss. | 16 |
| 27 | Williams, Chris | CB | 6-0 | 197 | 1/22/59 | 3 | Louisiana State | Alexander, La. | Williamsville, N.Y. | 16 |
| 23 | Williams, Van | RB | 6-0 | 208 | 3/15/59 | 2 | Carson-Newman | Johnson City, Tenn. | Johnson City, Tenn. | 16 |
| | Williams, Vince | RB | 6-0 | 231 | 10/24/59 | 2 | Oregon | Tacoma, Wash. | Edmonds, Wash. | 1* |

* Devlin, Holt, Hooks, and Nixon missed '83 season due to injuries; Hurley played 4 games with New Orleans, 10 with Buffalo in '83; Taylor last active with Kansas City in '81; Tongue played 7 games with Baltimore in '83; Vince Williams played 1 game with San Francisco in '83.

†Option playout; subject to developments.

Also played with Bills in '83—RB Joe Cribbs (16 games), WR Frank Lewis (11), NT Mark Roopenian (3), K Fred Steinfort (2), LB Phil Villapiano (4), DE Sherman White (8).

## COACHING STAFF

### Head Coach, Kay Stephenson

**Pro Career:** Guided Bills to 8-8 season and kept them in playoff contention until the final Sunday in his rookie season as an NFL head coach. Was the NFL's youngest head coach in 1983. Named to coach the North team in the 1983 Senior Bowl Classic. Promoted to head coach of the Bills on February 1, 1983. Served as the Bills' quarterback coach from 1978-82. Signed as a free agent with the San Diego Chargers in 1967 before being traded to the Bills in 1968. Injury riddled in 1968 and 1969 and was with Oakland and Atlanta briefly before retiring in 1970. Played one year with the Jacksonville Sharks of the WFL in 1974. Joined Jacksonville coaching staff as offensive coordinator and director of player personnel in 1975. Quarterback coach with the Los Angeles Rams in 1977 before joining the Bills in 1978.

**Background:** Attended Pensacola, Fla., High School and the University of Florida where he was backup quarterback to Steve Spurrier 1963-66. Assistant football coach at Rice University in 1971. Head coach and Athletic Director at Baker County, Fla., High School in 1973.

**Personal:** Born December 17, 1944, DeFuniak Springs, Fla. Kay and wife, Mary Jac, live in Orchard Park, New York. Has a daughter, Sheryl, 21.

### Assistant Coaches

**John Becker,** quarterbacks; born February 16, 1943, Alexandria, Va., lives in Orchard Park, N.Y. Cal State-Northridge 1965. No pro playing experience. College coach: UCLA 1970-71, New Mexico C.C. 1972-73, Los Angeles Valley J.C. 1974-76 (head coach), Oregon 1977-79. Pro coach: Philadelphia Eagles 1980-83, first year with Bills.

**Pete Carroll,** defensive backfield; born September 15, 1951, San Francisco, Calif., lives in Orchard Park, N.Y. Defensive back Pacific 1969-1972. No pro playing experience. College coach: Arkansas 1977, Iowa State 1978, Ohio State 1979, North Carolina State 1980-82, Pacific 1983. Pro coach: First year with Bills.

**Milt Jackson,** wide receivers; born October 16, 1943, Groesbeck, Tex., lives in Orchard Park, N.Y. Defensive back Tulsa 1966-67. Pro defensive back San Francisco 49ers 1967-68. College coach: Oregon State 1973, Rice 1974, California 1975-76, Oregon 1977-78, UCLA 1979. Pro coach: San Francisco 49ers 1980-82, joined Bills in 1983.

**Monte Kiffin,** linebackers; born February 29, 1940, Lexington, Neb., lives in Orchard Park, N.Y. Defensive end Nebraska 1961-63. Pro defensive end Winnipeg (CFL) 1965-66. College coach: Nebraska 1966-76, Arkansas 1977-79, North Carolina State 1980-82 (head coach). Pro coach: Green Bay Packers 1983, first year with Bills.

**Don Lawrence,** defensive coordinator-defensive line; born June 4, 1937, Cleveland, Ohio, lives in Orchard Park, N.Y. Tackle Notre Dame 1953-55. Pro tackle Washington Redskins 1956-61. College coach: Notre Dame 1963-67, Kansas State 1968-69, Cincinnati 1970, Virginia 1971-73 (head coach), Texas Christian 1974-75, Missouri 1976-77. Pro coach: British Columbia Lions (CFL) 1978-79, Kansas City Chiefs 1980-82, joined Bills in 1983.

**Andy MacDonald,** running backs; born January 2, 1930, Flint, Mich., lives in Orchard Park, N.Y. Quarterback Central Michigan 1950-51. No pro playing experience. College coach: Iowa 1961-64, Northern Arizona 1965-68, Tulsa 1969, Colorado State 1970-71, Michigan State 1973-75. Pro coach: Seattle Seahawks 1976-82, joined Bills in 1983.

**Miller McCalmon,** defensive assistant-special teams; born January 9, 1947, Denver, Colo., lives in Orchard Park, N.Y. Defensive back Tulsa 1968-69. No pro playing experience. College coach: Tulsa 1970, Colorado State 1971-72. Pro coach: Baltimore Colts 1978-79, joined Bills in 1980.

**Perry Moss,** tight ends; born August 4, 1926, Tulsa, Okla., lives in Orchard Park, N.Y. Quarterback Tulsa 1944, Illinois 1946-47. Pro quarterback Green Bay Packers 1948. College coach: Illinois 1949, Washington 1950-51, Louisiana State 1952-53, Miami 1954-56, Wisconsin 1957-58, Florida State 1959, Marshall 1969. Pro coach: Ottawa Roughriders (CFL) head coach 1960-63, Chicago Bears 1970-73, Green Bay Packers 1974, San Antonio (WFL) head coach 1975, joined Bills in 1983.

**Jim Niblack,** offensive line; born August 29, 1930, Americus, Ga., lives in Orchard Park, N.Y. Tackle Florida 1952-55. No pro playing experience. College coach: Florida 1976, Kentucky 1977-78. Pro coach: Jacksonville (WFL) 1974-75, joined Bills in 1983.

## BUFFALO BILLS 1984 FIRST-YEAR ROSTER

| Name | Pos. | Ht. | Wt. | Birth-date | College | Birthplace | Residence | How Acq. |
|------|------|-----|-----|-----------|---------|-----------|-----------|----------|
| Azelby, Joe | LB | 6-1 | 225 | 3/5/62 | Harvard | New York, N.Y. | Dumont, N.J. | D10 |
| Baldwin, Bruce (1) | S | 6-1 | 197 | 9/15/59 | Harding | Jacksonville, Ill. | Studio City, Calif. | FA |
| Barnett, Marty | QB | 6-2 | 183 | 8/12/61 | Buffalo | Buffalo, N.Y. | N. Tonawanda, N.Y. | FA |
| Bell, Greg | RB | 5-10 | 210 | 8/1/62 | Notre Dame | Columbus, Ohio | Columbus, Ohio | D1 |
| Bellinger, Rodney | CB | 5-8 | 181 | 6/4/62 | Miami | Miami, Fla. | Coral Gables, Fla. | D3 |
| Brookins, Mitchell | WR | 5-11 | 196 | 12/10/60 | Illinois | Chicago, Ill. | Chicago, Ill. | D4 |
| David, Stan | S | 6-3 | 210 | 2/17/62 | Texas Tech | North Platte, Neb. | Tucumcari, N.M. | D7 |
| Davis, Russell | TE | 6-4 | 217 | 6/16/60 | Maryland | Harrisburg, Pa. | Steelton, Pa. | D12 |
| Duncan, James (1) | WR | 6-0 | 165 | 2/7/60 | Ithaca | Buffalo, N.Y. | Elmira, N.Y. | FA |
| Gipson, Reggie (1) | RB | 6-2 | 205 | 7/27/60 | Alabama A&M | Birmingham, Ala. | Brighton, Ala. | FA |
| Howell, Leroy | DE | 6-4 | 235 | 11/4/62 | Appalachian State | Columbus, S.C. | Columbus, S.C. | D9 |
| Kidd, John | P | 6-3 | 201 | 8/22/61 | Northwestern | Findlay, Ohio | Findlay, Ohio | D5 |
| Marshall, Alford (1) | CB | 6-1 | 193 | 5/13/60 | Jackson State | Eufawa, Ala. | Middletown, Conn. | FA |
| McCray, Timmy (1) | RB | 5-11 | 193 | 8/20/60 | Tulane | Waycross, Ga. | Waycross, Ga. | FA |
| McNanie, Sean | DE | 6-5 | 252 | 9/9/61 | San Diego State | Mundelein, Ill. | Mundelein, Ill. | D3a |
| Morehead, Terence (1) | WR | 6-1 | 200 | 12/21/59 | UCLA | Waterloo, Iowa | Los Angeles, Calif. | FA |
| Neal, Robert | FB | 6-2 | 254 | 8/26/62 | Miami | Key West, Fla. | Key West, Fla. | D3b |
| Newton, Cecil (1) | CB | 6-2 | 210 | 8/18/60 | Savannah State | Atlanta, Ga. | College Park, Ga. | FA |
| Patterson, Darrell (1) | LB | 6-2 | 230 | 12/14/61 | Texas Christian | Canonsburg, Pa. | Canonsburg, Pa. | FA |
| Payne, Jimmy (1) | DE | 6-3 | 264 | 2/9/60 | Georgia | Athens, Ga. | Athens Ga. | D4a('83) |
| Rayfield, Stacy | S | 6-1 | 201 | 8/24/61 | Texas-Arlington | Texarkana, Ark. | Texarkana, Ark. | D8 |
| Richardson, Eric | WR | 6-1 | 183 | 4/18/62 | San Jose State | San Francisco, Calif. | Novato, Calif. | D2 |
| Riggitano, Frank | K | 5-10 | 205 | 4/10/61 | Susquehanna | Philadelphia, Pa. | Cape May, N.J. | FA |
| Slaton, Tony | C | 6-3 | 269 | 4/12/61 | Southern California | Merced, Calif. | Merced, Calif. | D6 |
| VandenBoom, Matt (1) | S | 6-3 | 201 | 4/18/60 | Wisconsin | Appleton, Wis. | Kimberly, Wis. | D5('83) |
| White, Craig | WR | 6-1 | 194 | 10/8/61 | Missouri | Fillmore, Mo. | Lawrence, Kan. | D11 |
| White, Larry (1) | NT | 6-5 | 270 | 10/11/61 | Jackson State | Tuscaloosa, Ala. | Tuscaloosa, Ala. | D11('83) |
| Whitfield, Calvin | CB | 5-9 | 180 | 8/16/60 | Rhode Island | New Rochelle, N.Y. | New Rochelle, N.Y. | FA |
| Williams, James (1) | TE | 6-2 | 228 | 4/18/61 | Wyoming | Tuscaloosa, Ala. | Syracuse, N.Y. | FA |
| Williams, Keith (1) | WR | 6-0 | 178 | 9/19/60 | Pittsburgh | Syracuse, N.Y. | Pittsburgh, Pa. | FA |

Players who report to an NFL team for the first time are designated on rosters as rookies (R). If a player reported to an NFL training camp in a previous year but was not on the active squad for three or more regular season or postseason games, he is listed on the first-year roster and designated by a (1). Thereafter, a player who is on the active squad for three or more regular season or postseason games is credited with an additional year of playing experience.

## NOTES

_____

_____

_____

_____

_____

_____

_____

_____

_____

_____

_____

# CINCINNATI BENGALS

**American Football Conference
Central Division**

**Team Colors:** Black, Orange, and White

**200 Riverfront Stadium
Cincinnati, Ohio 45202
Telephone:** (513) 621-3550

## Club Officials

President: John Sawyer
General Manager: Paul E. Brown
Assistant General Manager: Michael Brown
Business Manager: Bill Connelly
Consultant: John Murdough
Director of Public Relations: Allan Heim
Director of Player Personnel: Pete Brown
Ticket Manager: Paul Kelly
Trainer: Marv Pollins
Equipment Managers: Tom Gray, Al Davis

**Stadium:** Riverfront Stadium • **Capacity:** 59,754
200 Riverfront Stadium
Cincinnati, Ohio 45202

**Playing Surface:** AstroTurf

**Training Camp:** Wilmington College
Wilmington, Ohio 45177

## 1984 SCHEDULE

### Preseason
| | | |
|---|---|---|
| Aug. 4 | at New York Jets | 8:30 |
| Aug. 11 | at Tampa Bay | 8:00 |
| Aug. 18 | at Chicago | 6:00 |
| Aug. 24 | **Detroit** | 7:00 |

### Regular Season
| | | |
|---|---|---|
| Sept. 2 | at Denver | 2:00 |
| Sept. 9 | **Kansas City** | 1:00 |
| Sept. 16 | at New York Jets | 1:00 |
| Sept. 23 | **Los Angeles Rams** | 1:00 |
| Oct. 1 | at Pittsburgh (Monday) | 9:00 |
| Oct. 7 | **Houston** | 4:00 |
| Oct. 14 | at New England | 1:00 |
| Oct. 21 | **Cleveland** | 1:00 |
| Oct. 28 | at Houston | 12:00 |
| Nov. 4 | at San Francisco | 1:00 |
| Nov. 11 | **Pittsburgh** | 1:00 |
| Nov. 18 | **Seattle** | 1:00 |
| Nov. 25 | **Atlanta** | 1:00 |
| Dec. 2 | at Cleveland | 1:00 |
| Dec. 9 | at New Orleans | 12:00 |
| Dec. 16 | **Buffalo** | 1:00 |

## BENGALS COACHING HISTORY

### (115-120-1)
| | | |
|---|---|---|
| 1968-75 | Paul Brown | 55-59-1 |
| 1976-78 | Bill Johnson* | 18-15-0 |
| 1978-79 | Homer Rice | 8-19-0 |
| 1980-83 | Forrest Gregg | 34-27-0 |

*Resigned after five games in 1978

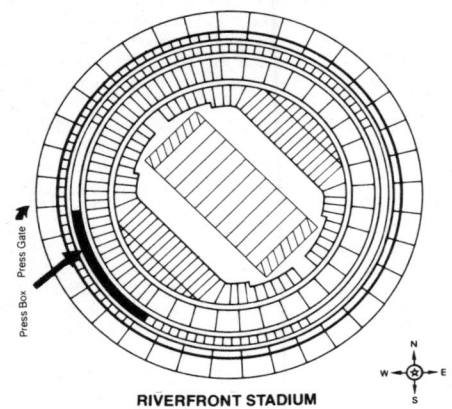

**RIVERFRONT STADIUM**

## RECORD HOLDERS

### Individual Records — Career
| Category | Name | Performance |
|---|---|---|
| Rushing (Yds.) | Pete Johnson, 1977-1983 | 5,421 |
| Passing (Yds.) | Ken Anderson, 1973-1983 | 30,396 |
| Passing (TDs.) | Ken Anderson, 1973-1983 | 184 |
| Receiving (No.) | Isaac Curtis, 1973-1983 | 408 |
| Receiving (Yds.) | Isaac Curtis, 1973-1983 | 6,971 |
| Interceptions (No.) | Ken Riley, 1969-1983 | 63 |
| Punting (Avg.) | Dave Lewis, 1970-73 | 43.9 |
| Punt Return (Avg.) | Lemar Parrish, 1970-78 | 9.2 |
| Kickoff Return (Avg.) | Lemar Parrish, 1970-78 | 24.7 |
| Field Goals | Horst Muhlmann, 1969-74 | 120 |
| Touchdowns (Tot.) | Pete Johnson, 1977-1983 | 70 |
| Points | Horst Muhlmann, 1969-74 | 549 |

### Individual Records — Single Season
| Category | Name | Performance |
|---|---|---|
| Rushing (Yds.) | Pete Johnson, 1981 | 1,077 |
| Passing (Yds.) | Ken Anderson, 1981 | 3,754 |
| Passing (TDs.) | Ken Anderson, 1981 | 29 |
| Receiving (No.) | Dan Ross, 1981 | 71 |
| Receiving (Yds.) | Cris Collinsworth, 1983 | 1,130 |
| Interceptions | Ken Riley, 1976 | 9 |
| Punting (Avg.) | Dave Lewis, 1970 | 46.2 |
| Punt Return (Avg.) | Lemar Parrish, 1974 | 13.1 |
| Kickoff Return (Avg.) | Lemar Parrish, 1980 | 30.2 |
| Field Goals | Horst Muhlmann, 1972 | 27 |
| Touchdowns (Tot.) | Pete Johnson, 1981 | 16 |
| Points | Jim Breech, 1981 | 115 |

### Individual Records — Single Game
| Category | Name | Performance |
|---|---|---|
| Rushing (Yds.) | Pete Johnson, 12-17-78 | 160 |
| Passing (Yds.) | Ken Anderson, 11-17-75 | 447 |
| Passing (TDs.) | Many times | 4 |
| | Last time by Ken Anderson, 11-29-81 | |
| Receiving (No.) | Many times | 10 |
| | Last time by Cris Collinsworth, 9-27-81 | |
| Receiving (Yds.) | Cris Collinsworth, 10-2-83 | 216 |
| Interceptions | Many times | 3 |
| | Last time by Ken Riley, 11-28-83 | |
| Field Goals | Horst Muhlmann, 11-8-70, 9-24-72 | 5 |
| Touchdowns (Tot.) | Many times | 3 |
| | Last time by Pete Johnson, 11-6-83 | |
| Points | Horst Muhlmann, 11-8-70, 12-17-72 | 19 |

## 1983 TEAM STATISTICS

| | Cincinnati | Opp. |
|---|---|---|
| Total First Downs | 327 | 276 |
| Rushing | 127 | 96 |
| Passing | 179 | 156 |
| Penalty | 21 | 24 |
| Third Down Efficiency | 97/212 | 94/216 |
| Third Down Percentage | 45.8 | 43.5 |
| Total Net Yards | 5287 | 4327 |
| Total Offensive Plays | 1036 | 973 |
| Avg. Gain per Play | 5.1 | 4.4 |
| Avg. Gain per Game | 330.4 | 270.4 |
| Net Yards Rushing | 2104 | 1499 |
| Total Rushing Plays | 542 | 430 |
| Avg. Gain per Rush | 3.9 | 3.5 |
| Avg. Gain Rushing per Game | 131.5 | 93.7 |
| Net Yards Passing | 3183 | 2828 |
| Lost Attempting to Pass | 40/309 | 41/335 |
| Gross Yards Passing | 3492 | 3163 |
| Attempts/Completions | 454/290 | 502/288 |
| Percent Completed | 63.9 | 57.4 |
| Had Intercepted | 18 | 23 |
| Avg. Net Passing per Game | 198.9 | 176.8 |
| Punts/Avg. | 69/40.6 | 76/42.3 |
| Punt Returns/Avg. | 49/8.4 | 41/7.6 |
| Kickoff Returns/Avg. | 54/20.3 | 68/19.1 |
| Interceptions/Avg. Ret. | 23/16.0 | 18/16.6 |
| Penalties/Yards | 99/837 | 100/871 |
| Fumbles/Ball Lost | 35/15 | 35/16 |
| Total Points | 346 | 302 |
| Avg. Points per Game | 21.6 | 18.9 |
| Touchdowns | 43 | 36 |
| Rushing | 24 | 16 |
| Passing | 14 | 17 |
| Returns and Recoveries | 5 | 3 |
| Field Goals | 16/23 | 17/22 |
| Conversions | 40/43 | 35/36 |
| Safeties | 0 | 0 |
| Avg. Time of Possession | 31:29 | 28:31 |

## 1983 TEAM RECORD

### Preseason (0-4)

| Date | Cincinnati | | Opponents |
|---|---|---|---|
| 8/6 | 7 | *Kansas City | 24 |
| 8/12 | 23 | Washington | 27 |
| 8/18 | 17 | *New York Jets (OT) | 20 |
| 8/27 | 7 | Detroit | 34 |
| | 54 | | 105 |

### Regular Season (7-9)

| Date | Cincinnati | | Opp. | Att. |
|---|---|---|---|---|
| 9/4 | 10 | *Los Angeles Raiders | 20 | 50,956 |
| 9/11 | 6 | *Buffalo | 10 | 46,841 |
| 9/15 | 7 | Cleveland | 17 | 79,574 |
| 9/25 | 23 | Tampa Bay | 17 | 56,023 |
| 10/2 | 31 | *Baltimore | 34 | 48,104 |
| 10/10 | 14 | *Pittsburgh | 24 | 56,086 |
| 10/16 | 17 | Denver | 24 | 74,305 |
| 10/23 | 28 | *Cleveland | 21 | 50,047 |
| 10/30 | 34 | *Green Bay | 14 | 53,349 |
| 11/6 | 55 | Houston | 14 | 39,706 |
| 11/13 | 15 | Kansas City | 20 | 41,711 |
| 11/20 | 38 | *Houston | 10 | 46,375 |
| 11/28 | 14 | Miami | 38 | 74,506 |
| 12/4 | 23 | Pittsburgh | 10 | 55,832 |
| 12/11 | 17 | *Detroit | 9 | 45,728 |
| 12/17 | 14 | Minnesota | 20 | 51,565 |
| | 346 | | 302 | 870,708 |

*Home Game     (OT) Overtime

### Score by Periods

| | | | | | | |
|---|---|---|---|---|---|---|
| Cincinnati | 102 | 140 | 54 | 50 | — | 346 |
| Opponents | 55 | 86 | 65 | 96 | — | 302 |

### Attendance

Home 397,486     Away 473,222     Total 870,708
Single game home record, 60,284 (10-17-71)
Single season home record, 422,430 (1981)

## 1983 INDIVIDUAL STATISTICS

### Rushing

| | Att. | Yds. | Avg. | LG | TD |
|---|---|---|---|---|---|
| Johnson | 210 | 763 | 3.6 | 16t | 14 |
| Alexander | 153 | 523 | 3.4 | 12 | 3 |
| S. Wilson | 56 | 267 | 4.8 | 18 | 1 |
| Kinnebrew | 39 | 156 | 4.0 | 17 | 3 |
| Anderson | 22 | 147 | 6.7 | 29 | 1 |
| Schonert | 29 | 117 | 4.0 | 15 | 2 |
| Tate | 25 | 77 | 3.1 | 13 | 0 |
| Verser | 2 | 31 | 15.5 | 29 | 0 |
| Martin | 2 | 21 | 10.5 | 15 | 0 |
| Collinsworth | 2 | 2 | 1.0 | 8 | 0 |
| Kreider | 1 | 2 | 2.0 | 2 | 0 |
| Christensen | 1 | −2 | −2.0 | −2 | 0 |
| Cincinnati | 542 | 2104 | 3.9 | 29 | 24 |
| Opponents | 430 | 1499 | 3.5 | 40 | 16 |

### Passing

| | Att. | Comp. | Pct. | Yds. | TD | Int. | Tkld. | Rate |
|---|---|---|---|---|---|---|---|---|
| Anderson | 297 | 198 | 66.7 | 2333 | 12 | 13 | 25/187 | 85.6 |
| Schonert | 156 | 92 | 59.0 | 1159 | 2 | 5 | 15/122 | 73.1 |
| Kreider | 1 | 0 | 0.0 | 0 | 0 | 0 | 0/0 | 39.6 |
| Cincinnati | 454 | 290 | 63.9 | 3492 | 14 | 18 | 40/309 | 81.1 |
| Opponents | 502 | 288 | 57.4 | 3163 | 17 | 23 | 41/335 | 68.3 |

### Receiving

| | No. | Yds. | Avg. | LG | TD |
|---|---|---|---|---|---|
| Collinsworth | 66 | 1130 | 17.1 | 63 | 5 |
| Curtis | 42 | 571 | 13.6 | 80t | 2 |
| Kreider | 42 | 554 | 13.2 | 54 | 1 |
| Ross | 42 | 483 | 11.5 | 30 | 3 |
| Alexander | 32 | 187 | 5.8 | 14 | 0 |
| Tate | 18 | 142 | 7.9 | 25 | 0 |
| Johnson | 15 | 129 | 8.6 | 18 | 0 |
| S. Wilson | 12 | 107 | 8.9 | 19 | 1 |
| Harris | 8 | 66 | 8.3 | 14 | 2 |
| Verser | 7 | 82 | 11.7 | 22 | 0 |
| Martin | 2 | 22 | 11.0 | 12 | 0 |
| Holman | 2 | 15 | 7.5 | 10 | 0 |
| Kinnebrew | 2 | 4 | 2.0 | 2 | 0 |
| Cincinnati | 290 | 3492 | 12.0 | 80t | 14 |
| Opponents | 288 | 3163 | 11.0 | 53 | 17 |

### Interceptions

| | No. | Yds. | Avg. | LG | TD |
|---|---|---|---|---|---|
| Riley | 8 | 89 | 11.1 | 42t | 2 |
| Horton | 5 | 121 | 24.2 | 55t | 1 |
| Kemp | 3 | 26 | 8.7 | 26 | 0 |
| Breeden | 2 | 47 | 23.5 | 39 | 0 |
| R. Griffin | 2 | 24 | 12.0 | 24 | 0 |
| Jackson | 2 | 21 | 10.5 | 15 | 0 |
| J. Griffin | 1 | 41 | 41.0 | 41t | 1 |
| Cincinnati | 23 | 369 | 16.0 | 55t | 4 |
| Opponents | 18 | 298 | 16.6 | 70t | 2 |

### Punting

| | No. | Yds. | Avg. | In 20 | LG |
|---|---|---|---|---|---|
| McInally | 67 | 2804 | 41.9 | 13 | 60 |
| Cincinnati | 69 | 2804 | 40.6 | 13 | 60 |
| Opponents | 76 | 3211 | 42.3 | 21 | 70 |

### Punt Returns

| | No. | FC | Yds. | Avg. | LG | TD |
|---|---|---|---|---|---|---|
| Martin | 23 | 3 | 227 | 9.9 | 19 | 0 |
| Simmons | 25 | 2 | 173 | 6.9 | 43 | 0 |
| Horton | 1 | 1 | 10 | 10.0 | 10 | 0 |
| Cincinnati | 49 | 6 | 410 | 8.4 | 43 | 0 |
| Opponents | 41 | 5 | 310 | 7.6 | 50 | 0 |

### Kickoff Returns

| | No. | Yds. | Avg. | LG | TD |
|---|---|---|---|---|---|
| Simmons | 14 | 317 | 22.6 | 36 | 0 |
| Tate | 13 | 218 | 16.8 | 23 | 0 |
| Verser | 13 | 253 | 19.5 | 29 | 0 |
| S. Wilson | 7 | 161 | 23.0 | 32 | 0 |
| Horton | 5 | 128 | 25.6 | 49 | 0 |
| Dinkel | 1 | 1 | 1.0 | 1 | 0 |
| Martin | 1 | 19 | 19.0 | 19 | 0 |
| Cincinnati | 54 | 1097 | 20.3 | 49 | 0 |
| Opponents | 68 | 1298 | 19.1 | 90 | 0 |

### Scoring

| | TD | TD R | TD P | TD Rt | PAT | FG | TP |
|---|---|---|---|---|---|---|---|
| Breech | | | | | 39/41 | 16/23 | 87 |
| Johnson | 14 | 14 | 0 | 0 | | | 84 |
| Collinsworth | 5 | 0 | 5 | 0 | | | 30 |
| Alexander | 3 | 3 | 0 | 0 | | | 18 |
| Kinnebrew | 3 | 3 | 0 | 0 | | | 18 |
| Ross | 3 | 0 | 3 | 0 | | | 18 |
| Curtis | 2 | 0 | 2 | 0 | | | 12 |
| Harris | 2 | 0 | 2 | 0 | | | 12 |
| Riley | 2 | 0 | 0 | 2 | | | 12 |
| Schonert | 2 | 2 | 0 | 0 | | | 12 |
| S. Wilson | 2 | 1 | 1 | 0 | | | 12 |
| Anderson | 1 | 1 | 0 | 0 | | | 6 |
| J. Griffin | 1 | 0 | 0 | 1 | | | 6 |
| Horton | 1 | 0 | 0 | 1 | | | 6 |
| Kreider | 1 | 0 | 1 | 0 | | | 6 |
| Williams | 1 | 0 | 0 | 1 | | | 6 |
| Browner | | | | | 1/1 | 0/0 | 1 |
| Cincinnati | 43 | 24 | 14 | 5 | 40/43 | 16/23 | 346 |
| Opponents | 36 | 16 | 17 | 3 | 35/36 | 17/22 | 302 |

## FIRST-ROUND SELECTIONS

(If Club had no first-round selection, first player drafted is listed with round in parentheses.)

| Year | Player, College, Position |
|---|---|
| 1968 | Bob Johnson, Tennessee, C |
| 1969 | Greg Cook, Cincinnati, QB |
| 1970 | Mike Reid, Penn State, DT |
| 1971 | Vernon Holland, Tennessee State, T |
| 1972 | Sherman White, California, DE |
| 1973 | Isaac Curtis, San Diego State, WR |
| 1974 | Bill Kollar, Montana State, DT |
| 1975 | Glenn Cameron, Florida, LB |
| 1976 | Billy Brooks, Oklahoma, WR |
| | Archie Griffin, Ohio State, RB |
| 1977 | Eddie Edwards, Miami, DT |
| | Wilson Whitley, Houston, DT |
| | Mike Cobb, Michigan State, TE |
| 1978 | Ross Browner, Notre Dame, DT |
| | Blair Bush, Washington, C |
| 1979 | Jack Thompson, Washington State, QB |
| | Charles Alexander, Louisiana State, RB |
| 1980 | Anthony Muñoz, Southern California, T |
| 1981 | David Verser, Kansas, WR |
| 1982 | Glen Collins, Mississippi State, DE |
| 1983 | Dave Rimington, Nebraska, C |
| 1984 | Ricky Hunley, Arizona, LB |
| | Pete Koch, Maryland, DE |
| | Brian Blados, North Carolina, T |

## CINCINNATI BENGALS 1984 VETERAN ROSTER

| No. | Name | Pos. | Ht. | Wt. | Birth-date | NFL Exp. | College | Birthplace | Residence | Games in '83 |
|---|---|---|---|---|---|---|---|---|---|---|
| 40 | Alexander, Charles | RB | 6-1 | 226 | 7/28/57 | 6 | Louisiana State | Galveston, Tex. | Baton Rouge, La. | 14 |
| 14 | Anderson, Ken | QB | 6-3 | 212 | 2/15/49 | 14 | Augustana, Ill. | Batavia, Ill. | Ft. Mitchell, Ky. | 13 |
| 61 | Boyarsky, Jerry | NT | 6-3 | 290 | 5/15/59 | 4 | Pittsburgh | Scranton, Pa. | Olyphant, Pa. | 15 |
| 10 | Breech, Jim | K | 5-6 | 161 | 4/11/56 | 6 | California | Sacramento, Calif. | Cincinnati, Ohio | 16 |
| 34 | Breeden, Louis | CB | 5-11 | 185 | 10/26/53 | 7 | North Carolina Central | Hamlet, N.C. | Cincinnati, Ohio | 14 |
|  | t-Brooks, James | RB | 5-9 | 177 | 12/28/58 | 4 | Auburn | Warner Robins, Ga. | Warner Robins, Ga. | 15 |
| 79 | Browner, Ross | DE | 6-3 | 261 | 3/22/54 | 7 | Notre Dame | Warren, Ohio | Atlanta, Ga. | 12 |
| 67 | Burley, Gary | DE | 6-3 | 282 | 12/8/52 | 9 | Pittsburgh | Urbancrest, Ohio | Cincinnati, Ohio | 14 |
| 50 | Cameron, Glenn | LB | 6-2 | 228 | 2/21/53 | 10 | Florida | Coral Gables, Fla. | Gainesville, Fla. | 16 |
| 11 | Christensen, Jeff | QB | 6-3 | 202 | 1/8/60 | 2 | Eastern Illinois | Gibson City, Ill. | Ft. Mitchell, Ky. | 1 |
| 76 | Collins, Glen | DE | 6-6 | 265 | 7/10/59 | 3 | Mississippi State | Jackson, Miss. | Jackson, Miss. | 16 |
| 80 | Collinsworth, Cris | WR | 6-5 | 192 | 1/27/59 | 4 | Florida | Dayton, Ohio | Titusville, Fla. | 14 |
| 85 | †Curtis, Isaac | WR | 6-1 | 192 | 10/20/50 | 12 | San Diego State | Santa Ana, Calif. | Cincinnati, Ohio | 16 |
| 73 | Edwards, Eddie | DE | 6-5 | 256 | 4/25/54 | 8 | Miami | Sumter, S.C. | Marietta, Ga. | 16 |
| 49 | Frazier, Guy | LB | 6-2 | 221 | 7/20/59 | 4 | Wyoming | Detroit, Mich. | Cincinnati, Ohio | 10 |
| 48 | Gibler, Andy | TE | 6-4 | 234 | 4/30/61 | 2 | Missouri | Independence, Mo. | Columbia, Mo. | 2 |
| 22 | Griffin, James | S | 6-2 | 197 | 9/7/61 | 2 | Middle Tennessee State | Camilla, Ga. | Pelham, Ga. | 16 |
| 44 | Griffin, Ray | CB | 5-10 | 186 | 6/29/56 | 7 | Ohio State | Columbus, Ohio | Columbus, Ohio | 16 |
| 66 | Hannula, Jim | T | 6-6 | 264 | 7/2/59 | 2 | Northern Illinois | Elgin, Ill. | Villa Hills, Ky. | 15 |
| 83 | Harris, M.L. | TE | 6-5 | 238 | 1/16/54 | 5 | Kansas State | Columbus, Ohio | Cincinnati, Ohio | 12 |
| 27 | †Hicks, Bryan | S | 6-0 | 192 | 1/24/57 | 4 | McNeese State | Lake Charles, La. | Lake Charles, La. | 0* |
| 82 | Holman, Rodney | TE | 6-3 | 232 | 4/20/60 | 3 | Tulane | Ypsilanti, Mich. | New Orleans, La. | 16 |
| 20 | Horton, Ray | CB | 5-11 | 190 | 4/12/60 | 2 | Washington | Tacoma, Wash. | Seattle, Wash. | 16 |
| 37 | Jackson, Robert | S | 5-10 | 186 | 10/10/58 | 3 | Central Michigan | Grand Rapids, Mich. | Hamilton, Ohio | 16 |
| 26 | Kemp, Bobby | S | 6-0 | 191 | 5/29/59 | 4 | Cal State-Fullerton | Oakland, Calif. | Cincinnati, Ohio | 16 |
| 28 | Kinnebrew, Larry | RB | 6-1 | 252 | 6/11/59 | 2 | Tennessee State | Rome, Ga. | Rome, Ga. | 16 |
| 86 | Kreider, Steve | WR | 6-3 | 192 | 5/12/58 | 6 | Lehigh | Reading, Pa. | Cincinnati, Ohio | 16 |
| 69 | Krumrie, Tim | NT | 6-2 | 262 | 5/20/60 | 2 | Wisconsin | Eau Claire, Wis. | Eau Claire, Wis. | 16 |
| 47 | Maidlow, Steve | LB | 6-2 | 234 | 6/6/60 | 2 | Michigan State | Lansing, Mich. | East Lansing, Mich. | 16 |
| 88 | Martin, Mike | WR-KR | 5-10 | 186 | 11/18/60 | 2 | Illinois | Washington, D.C. | Washington, D.C. | 10 |
| 87 | McInally, Pat | P | 6-6 | 212 | 5/7/53 | 9 | Harvard | Villa Park, Calif. | Villa Park, Calif. | 16 |
| 65 | Montoya, Max | G | 6-5 | 275 | 5/12/56 | 6 | UCLA | Alexander, Ala. | Cincinnati, Ohio | 16 |
| 60 | Moore, Blake | C | 6-5 | 267 | 5/8/58 | 5 | Wooster | Durham, N.C. | Cincinnati, Ohio | 16 |
| 78 | Muñoz, Anthony | T | 6-6 | 278 | 8/19/58 | 5 | Southern California | Ontario, Calif. | Cincinnati, Ohio | 16 |
| 68 | Obrovac, Mike | G | 6-6 | 275 | 10/11/55 | 4 | Bowling Green | Canton, Ohio | Florence, Ky. | 10 |
| 51 | Razzano, Rick | LB | 5-11 | 227 | 11/15/55 | 5 | Virginia Tech | New Castle, Pa. | Mason, Ohio | 16 |
| 64 | Rimington, Dave | C | 6-3 | 288 | 8/13/62 | 2 | Nebraska | Omaha, Neb. | Ft. Mitchell, Ky. | 12 |
| 15 | Schonert, Turk | QB | 6-1 | 190 | 1/15/57 | 5 | Stanford | Placentia, Calif. | Park Hills, Ky. | 9 |
| 59 | Schuh, Jeff | LB | 6-2 | 228 | 5/22/58 | 4 | Minnesota | Crystal, Minn. | Brooklyn Park, Minn. | 16 |
| 25 | Simmons, John | CB-KR | 5-11 | 192 | 12/1/58 | 4 | Southern Methodist | Little Rock, Ark. | Little Rock, Ark. | 16 |
| 56 | Simpkins, Ron | LB | 6-1 | 235 | 4/2/58 | 4 | Michigan | Detroit, Mich. | Hamilton, Ohio | 15 |
| 23 | Tate, Rodney | RB-KR | 5-11 | 190 | 2/14/59 | 3 | Texas | Okanulgee, Okla. | Austin, Tex. | 12 |
| 35 | Turner, Jimmy | CB | 6-0 | 187 | 6/15/59 | 2 | UCLA | Sherman, Tex. | Los Angeles, Calif. | 16 |
| 81 | Verser, David | WR-KR | 6-1 | 202 | 3/1/58 | 4 | Kansas | Kansas City, Kan. | Cincinnati, Ohio | 13 |
| 70 | Weaver, Emanuel | NT | 6-4 | 260 | 6/28/60 | 2 | South Carolina | New Orleans, La. | Columbia, S.C. | 0* |
| 57 | Williams, Reggie | LB | 6-0 | 228 | 9/19/54 | 9 | Dartmouth | Flint, Mich. | Cincinnati, Ohio | 16 |
| 77 | Wilson, Mike | T | 6-5 | 271 | 5/28/55 | 7 | Georgia | Norfolk, Va. | Gainesville, Ga. | 16 |
| 32 | Wilson, Stanley | RB | 5-10 | 210 | 8/23/61 | 2 | Oklahoma | Los Angeles, Calif. | Cincinnati, Ohio | 10 |

\* Hicks and Weaver missed '83 season due to injuries.

†Option playout; subject to developments.

t-Bengals traded for Brooks (San Diego Chargers).

Traded—Running back Pete Johnson to San Diego.

Retired—Ken Riley, 15-year cornerback, 14 games in '83.

Also played with Bengals in '83—LB Tom Dinkel (16 games), C Dave Lapham (16), LB Jim LeClair (14), NT Chris Lindstrom (1), TE Dan Ross (16).

## COACHING STAFF

### Head Coach, Sam Wyche

**Pro Career:** Became the fifth head coach in Cincinnati history when he was named to lead the Bengals on December 28, 1983. Played quarterback with Bengals 1968-70, Washington Redskins 1971-73, Detroit Lions 1974-75, St. Louis 1976, and Buffalo 1977. Quarterback coach with the San Francisco 49ers 1979-82.

**Background:** Attended North Fulton High School in Atlanta and Furman University where he was the quarterback from 1962-66. Assistant coach at South Carolina in 1967. Head coach at Indiana University in 1983.

**Personal:** Born January 5, 1945, in Atlanta, Ga. Sam and his wife, Jane, have two children—Zak and Kerry. They live in Cincinnati.

### Assistant Coaches

**Jim Anderson,** running backs; born March 27, 1948, Harrisburg, Pa., lives in Cincinnati. Linebacker-defensive end Cal Western (U.S. International) 1969-70. College coach Cal Western 1970-71, Scottsdale Community College 1973, Nevada-Las Vegas 1974-75, Southern Methodist 1977-80, Stanford 1981-83. Pro coach: First year with Bengals.

**Bruce Coslet,** wide receivers-passing game; born August 5, 1946, Oakdale, Calif., lives in Cincinnati. Tight end University of the Pacific 1967-69. Pro tight end Cincinnati Bengals 1969-76. Pro coach: San Francisco 49ers 1980, joined Bengals in 1981.

**Joe Faragalli,** quarterbacks-tight ends-offense; born April 18, 1929, Philadelphia, Pa., lives in Cincinnati. Villanova 1950-53. College coach Villanova 1962-66, Brown University 1970-73, Marshall 1973. Pro coach: Winnipeg Blue Bombers (CFL) 1967-69, 1974-77, Edmonton Eskimos (CFL) 1977-1980, Saskatchewan Rough Riders (CFL) 1980-82 (head coach), first year with Bengals.

**Dick LeBeau,** defensive coordinator-defensive backs; born September 9, 1937, London, Ohio, lives in Cincinnati, Ohio. Halfback Ohio State 1957-59. Pro defensive back Detroit Lions 1959-72. Pro coach: Philadelphia Eagles 1973-75, Green Bay Packers 1976-79, joined Bengals in 1980.

**Jim McNally,** offensive line-running game; born December 13, 1943, Buffalo, New York, lives in Cincinnati. Guard University of Buffalo 1961-65. No pro playing experience. College coach: Buffalo 1966-69, Marshall 1973-75, Boston College 1976-78, Wake Forest 1979. Pro coach: Joined Bengals in 1980.

**Dick Selcer,** linebackers; born August 22, 1937, Cincinnati, Ohio, lives in Cincinnati. Running back Notre Dame 1955-58. No pro playing experience. College coach: Xavier, Ohio 1962-64, 1970-71 (head coach), Cincinnati 1965-66, Brown 1967-69, Wisconsin 1972-74, Kansas State 1975-77, Southwestern Louisiana 1978-80. Pro coach: Houston Oilers 1981-83, first year with Bengals.

**Bill Urbanik,** defensive line; born December 27, 1946, Donora, Pa., lives in Cincinnati. Lineman Ohio State 1965-68. No pro playing experience. College coach: Marshall 1971-73, 1975, Northern Illinois 1976-78, Wake Forest 1978-83. Pro coach: First year with Bengals.

**Trent Walters,** defensive backfield; born November 20, 1943, lives in Cincinnati. Defensive back Indiana University 1963-65. Pro defensive back Edmonton Eskimos (CFL) 1966-67. College coach: Indiana 1968-71, 1973-80, Louisville 1972, Washington 1981-83. Pro coach: First year with Bengals.

**Kim Wood,** strength; born July 12, 1945, Barrington, Ill., lives in Cincinnati. Running back Wisconsin 1965-68. No pro playing experience. Pro coach: Joined Bengals in 1975.

## CINCINNATI BENGALS 1984 FIRST-YEAR ROSTER

| Name | Pos. | Ht. | Wt. | Birth-date | College | Birthplace | Residence | How Acq. |
|------|------|-----|-----|-----------|---------|-----------|-----------|----------|
| Achter, Rodney (1) | WR | 6-2 | 195 | 2/14/61 | Toledo | Toledo, Ohio | Toledo, Ohio | FA |
| Barker, Leo | LB | 6-1 | 221 | 11/7/59 | New Mexico State | Panama | Las Cruces, N.M. | D7 |
| Battle, Ralph | S | 6-2 | 205 | 6/15/61 | Jacksonville State | Huntsville, Ala. | Huntsville, Ala. | FA |
| Benson, Stephan | WR | 5-10 | 170 | 2/6/61 | Indiana | Lauderhill, Fla. | Bloomington, Ind. | FA |
| Blados, Brian | T-G | 6-4 | 308 | 1/11/62 | North Carolina | Arlington, Va. | Chapel Hill, N.C. | D1b |
| Esiason, Boomer | QB | 6-4 | 220 | 4/17/61 | Maryland | East Islip, N.Y. | College Park, Md. | D2 |
| Evans, Marlin | LB | 6-3 | 218 | 2/19/60 | Indiana | Cincinnati, Ohio | Cincinnati, Ohio | FA |
| Helton, Jack | TE | 6-3 | 239 | 11/3/58 | Kent State | Birmingham, Ala. | Columbus, Ohio | FA |
| Hunley, Ricky | LB | 6-1 | 237 | 11/11/61 | Arizona | Petersburg, Va. | Tucson, Ariz. | D1 |
| Jackson, Aaron | LB | 6-2 | 235 | 3/16/61 | North Carolina | Washington, D.C. | Chapel Hill, N.C. | D10 |
| Jennings, Stanford | RB | 6-1 | 205 | 3/12/62 | Furman | Summerville, S.C. | Greenville, S.C. | D3 |
| Jones, Jerry (1) | WR | 6-2 | 198 | 6/29/61 | Texas-El Paso | Laurel, Miss. | Houston, Tex. | FA |
| Kern, Don | TE | 6-4 | 225 | 8/25/62 | Arizona State | Los Gatos, Calif. | Tempe, Ariz. | D6 |
| Koch, Pete | NT | 6-6 | 265 | 1/23/62 | Maryland | Nassau County, N.Y. | College Park, Md. | D1a |
| Kozerski, Bruce | T-C | 6-4 | 275 | 4/2/62 | Holy Cross | Plains, Pa. | Worcester, Mass. | D9 |
| McKeaver, Steve | RB | 6-2 | 209 | 1/30/60 | Central State, Okla. | Altus, Okla. | Seattle, Wash. | D11 |
| Musgrave, Benn | T | 6-6 | 270 | 3/20/62 | Iowa State | Omaha, Neb. | Ames, Iowa | FA |
| Pickering, Clay | WR | 6-5 | 215 | 6/2/61 | Maine | Jacksonville, Fla. | Hyannis, Mass. | FA |
| Pillman, Brian | LB | 5-10 | 228 | 5/22/62 | Miami, Ohio | Cincinnati, Ohio | Cincinnati, Ohio | FA |
| Reimers, Bruce | T-G | 6-7 | 280 | 9/18/60 | Iowa State | Algona, Iowa | Ames, Iowa | D8 |
| Rico, John | WR | 5-10 | 180 | 1/25/60 | Cal State-Hayward | Newman, Calif. | Newman, Calif. | FA |
| Smith, Gary (1) | G | 6-2 | 265 | 1/27/60 | Virginia Tech | Bitburg, Germany | Blacksburg, Va. | FA |
| Swafford, Don (1) | T | 6-8 | 280 | 3/23/57 | Florida | Dayton, Ohio | Brooksville, Fla. | FA |
| Vernasco, John | QB | 6-2 | 200 | 2/8/61 | Evansville | Mishawaka, Ind. | Ft. Wayne, Ind. | FA |
| Williams, Gary (1) | WR | 6-2 | 215 | 9/4/59 | Ohio State | Wilmington, Ohio | Columbus, Ohio | D11 ('83) |
| Williams, Robert (1) | RB | 6-2 | 215 | 2/8/61 | Washington State | Los Angeles, Calif. | Compton, Calif. | FA |
| Zeigler, Brent | RB | 5-11 | 227 | 1/21/61 | Syracuse | West Islip, N.Y. | Syracuse, N.Y. | D10a |

Players who report to an NFL team for the first time are designated on rosters as rookies (R). If a player reported to an NFL training camp in a previous year but was not on the active squad for three or more regular season or postseason games, he is listed on the first-year roster and designated by a (1). Thereafter, a player who is on the active squad for three or more regular season or postseason games is credited with an additional year of playing experience.

## NOTES

# CLEVELAND BROWNS

**American Football Conference**
**Central Division**

**Team Colors:** Seal Brown, Orange,
and White

**Tower B**
**Cleveland Stadium**
**Cleveland, Ohio 44114**
**Telephone: (216) 696-5555**

### Club Officials

President: Arthur B. Modell
Executive Vice President-Legal and
    Administrative: Jim Bailey
Assistant to the President: Ernie Accorsi
Director of Player Relations: Paul Warfield
Vice President, Finance: Mike Poplar
Director of Player Personnel: Bill Davis
Director of Public Relations: Kevin Byrne
Director of Operations: Denny Lynch
Director of Advertising: John Minco
Director of Pro Personnel: Chip Falivene
Director of Security: Ted Chappelle
Area Scouts: Dom Anile, Dave Beckman,
    Tom Heckert, Tom Miner, Mike Nixon
Film Coordinator: Ed Ulinski
Ticket Director: Bill Breit
Head Trainer: Bill Tessendorf
Equipment Manager: Charley Cusick

**Stadium:** Cleveland Stadium • **Capacity:** 80,098
    West 3rd Street
    Cleveland, Ohio 44114

**Playing Surface:** Grass

**Training Camp:** Lakeland Community College
    Mentor, Ohio 44094

## 1984 SCHEDULE

### Preseason
| | | |
|---|---|---|
| Aug. 4 | **Pittsburgh** | 7:30 |
| Aug. 13 | at Los Angeles Rams | 7:00 |
| Aug. 18 | at Kansas City | 7:30 |
| Aug. 23 | at Philadelphia | 7:00 |

### Regular Season
| | | |
|---|---|---|
| Sept. 2 | at Seattle | 1:00 |
| Sept. 9 | at Los Angeles Rams | 1:00 |
| Sept. 16 | **Denver** | 9:00 |
| Sept. 23 | **Pittsburgh** | 1:00 |
| Sept. 30 | at Kansas City | 12:00 |
| Oct. 7 | **New England** | 1:00 |
| Oct. 14 | **New York Jets** | 1:00 |
| Oct. 21 | at Cincinnati | 1:00 |
| Oct. 28 | **New Orleans** | 1:00 |
| Nov. 4 | at Buffalo | 1:00 |
| Nov. 11 | **San Francisco** | 1:00 |
| Nov. 18 | at Atlanta | 1:00 |
| Nov. 25 | **Houston** | 1:00 |
| Dec. 2 | **Cincinnati** | 1:00 |
| Dec. 9 | at Pittsburgh | 1:00 |
| Dec. 16 | at Houston | 12:00 |

## BROWNS COACHING HISTORY

### (288-182-9)
| | | |
|---|---|---|
| 1950-62 | Paul Brown | 115-49-5 |
| 1963-70 | Blanton Collier | 79-38-2 |
| 1971-74 | Nick Skorich | 30-26-2 |
| 1975-77 | Forrest Gregg* | 18-23-0 |
| 1977 | Dick Modzelewski | 0-1-0 |
| 1978-83 | Sam Rutigliano | 46-45-0 |

*Released after 13 games in 1977

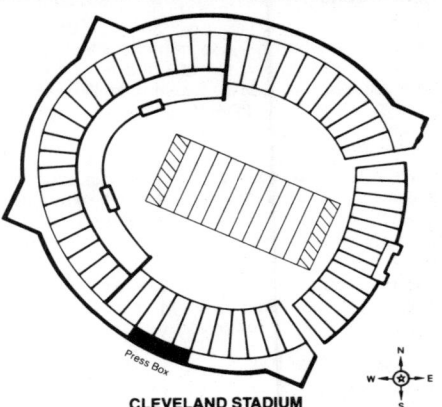

**CLEVELAND STADIUM**

## RECORD HOLDERS

### Individual Records—Career
| Category | Name | Performance |
|---|---|---|
| Rushing (Yds.) | Jim Brown, 1957-1965 | 12,312 |
| Passing (Yds.) | Brian Sipe, 1974-1983 | 23,713 |
| Passing (TDs) | Brian Sipe, 1974-1983 | 154 |
| Receiving (No.) | Ozzie Newsome, 1978-1983 | 351 |
| Receiving (Yds.) | Ray Renfro, 1952-1963 | 5,508 |
| Interceptions | Thom Darden, 1972-74, 1976-1981 | 45 |
| Punting (Avg.) | Horace Gillom, 1950-56 | 43.8 |
| Punt Return (Avg.) | Greg Pruitt, 1973-1981 | 11.8 |
| Kickoff Return (Avg.) | Greg Pruitt, 1973-1981 | 26.3 |
| Field Goals | Lou Groza, 1950-59, 1961-67 | 234 |
| Touchdowns (Tot.) | Jim Brown, 1957-1965 | 126 |
| Points | Lou Groza, 1950-59, 1961-67 | 1,349 |

### Individual Records—Single Season
| Category | Name | Performance |
|---|---|---|
| Rushing (Yds.) | Jim Brown, 1963 | 1,863 |
| Passing (Yds.) | Brian Sipe, 1980 | 4,132 |
| Passing (TDs) | Brian Sipe, 1980 | 30 |
| Receiving (No.) | Ozzie Newsome, 1983 | 89 |
| Receiving (Yds.) | Paul Warfield, 1968 | 1,067 |
| Interceptions | Thom Darden, 1978 | 10 |
| Punting (Avg.) | Gary Collins, 1965 | 46.7 |
| Punt Return (Avg.) | Leroy Kelly, 1965 | 15.6 |
| Kickoff Return (Avg.) | Bo Scott, 1969 | 28.9 |
| Field Goals | Lou Groza, 1953 | 23 |
| Touchdowns (Tot.) | Jim Brown, 1965 | 21 |
| Points | Jim Brown, 1965 | 126 |

### Individual Records—Single Game
| Category | Name | Performance |
|---|---|---|
| Rushing (Yds.) | Jim Brown, 11-24-57, 11-19-61 | 237 |
| Passing (Yds.) | Brian Sipe, 10-25-81 | 444 |
| Passing (TDs) | Frank Ryan, 12-12-64 | 5 |
| | Bill Nelsen, 11-2-69 | 5 |
| | Brian Sipe, 10-7-79 | 5 |
| Receiving (No.) | Mac Speedie, 11-9-52 | 11 |
| Receiving (Yds.) | Darrell Brewster, 12-6-53 | 182 |
| Interceptions | Many times | 3 |
| | Last time by Hanford Dixon, 12-19-82 | |
| Field Goals | Don Cockroft, 10-19-75 | 5 |
| Touchdowns (Tot.) | Dub Jones, 11-25-51 | 6 |
| Points | Dub Jones, 11-25-51 | 36 |

## 1983 TEAM STATISTICS

| | Cleveland | Opp. |
|---|---|---|
| Total First Downs | 327 | 309 |
| Rushing | 113 | 138 |
| Passing | 186 | 155 |
| Penalty | 28 | 16 |
| Third Down Efficiency | 99/223 | 82/204 |
| Third Down Percentage | 44.4 | 40.2 |
| Total Net Yards | 5583 | 5142 |
| Total Offensive Plays | 1065 | 1029 |
| Avg. Gain per Play | 5.2 | 5.0 |
| Avg. Gain per Game | 348.9 | 321.4 |
| Net Yards Rushing | 1922 | 2065 |
| Total Rushing Plays | 465 | 528 |
| Avg. Gain per Rush | 4.1 | 3.9 |
| Avg. Gain Rushing per Game | 120.1 | 129.1 |
| Net Yards Passing | 3661 | 3077 |
| Lost Attempting to Pass | 33/271 | 32/239 |
| Gross Yards Passing | 3932 | 3316 |
| Attempts/Completions | 567/324 | 469/280 |
| Percent Completed | 57.1 | 59.7 |
| Had Intercepted | 28 | 22 |
| Avg. Net Passing per Game | 228.8 | 192.3 |
| Punts/Avg. | 70/40.8 | 73/40.5 |
| Punt Returns/Avg. | 42/7.4 | 30/10.3 |
| Kickoff Returns/Avg. | 63/20.5 | 61/18.9 |
| Interceptions/Avg. Ret. | 22/13.5 | 28/18.1 |
| Penalties/Yards | 115/991 | 105/940 |
| Fumbles/Ball Lost | 21/10 | 30/10 |
| Total Points | 356 | 342 |
| Avg. Points per Game | 22.3 | 21.4 |
| Touchdowns | 42 | 42 |
| Rushing | 13 | 15 |
| Passing | 27 | 22 |
| Returns and Recoveries | 2 | 5 |
| Field Goals | 22/25 | 16/22 |
| Conversions | 38/40 | 40/42 |
| Safeties | 0 | 1 |
| Avg. Time of Possession | 30:50 | 29:10 |

## 1983 TEAM RECORD
### Preseason (3-1)

| Date | Cleveland | | Opponents |
|---|---|---|---|
| 8/6 | 21 | Green Bay | 20 |
| 8/13 | 27 | Buffalo | 10 |
| 8/20 | 10 | Denver | 19 |
| 8/26 | 20 | *Los Angeles Raiders | 17 |
| | 78 | | 66 |

### Regular Season (9-7)

| Date | Cleveland | | Opp. | Att. |
|---|---|---|---|---|
| 9/4 | 21 | *Minnesota | 27 | 70,087 |
| 9/11 | 31 | Detroit | 26 | 60,095 |
| 9/15 | 17 | *Cincinnati | 7 | 79,574 |
| 9/25 | 30 | San Diego (OT) | 24 | 49,482 |
| 10/2 | 9 | *Seattle | 24 | 75,446 |
| 10/9 | 10 | *New York Jets | 7 | 78,235 |
| 10/16 | 17 | Pittsburgh | 44 | 59,263 |
| 10/23 | 21 | Cincinnati | 28 | 50,047 |
| 10/30 | 25 | *Houston (OT) | 19 | 66,955 |
| 11/6 | 21 | Green Bay | 35 | 54,089 |
| 11/13 | 20 | *Tampa Bay | 0 | 56,091 |
| 11/20 | 30 | New England | 0 | 40,987 |
| 11/27 | 41 | *Baltimore | 23 | 65,812 |
| 12/4 | 6 | Denver | 27 | 70,912 |
| 12/11 | 27 | Houston | 34 | 29,746 |
| 12/18 | 30 | *Pittsburgh | 17 | 72,313 |
| | 356 | | 342 | 979,134 |

*Home Game    (OT) Overtime

### Score by Periods

| Cleveland | 76 | 120 | 82 | 66 | 12 | — | 356 |
|---|---|---|---|---|---|---|---|
| Opponents | 70 | 125 | 63 | 84 | 0 | — | 342 |

### Attendance

Home 564,513    Away 414,621    Total 979,134
Single game home record, 85,703 (9-21-70)
Single season home record, 619,683 (1980)

## 1983 INDIVIDUAL STATISTICS

### Rushing

| | Att. | Yds. | Avg. | LG | TD |
|---|---|---|---|---|---|
| Pruitt | 293 | 1184 | 4.0 | 27 | 10 |
| Green | 104 | 497 | 4.8 | 29 | 3 |
| Walker | 19 | 100 | 5.3 | 15 | 0 |
| Sipe | 26 | 56 | 2.2 | 9 | 0 |
| Davis | 13 | 42 | 3.2 | 16 | 0 |
| Jones | 1 | 19 | 19.0 | 19 | 0 |
| McDonald | 3 | 17 | 5.7 | 10 | 0 |
| Holt | 3 | 8 | 2.7 | 4 | 0 |
| Adams | 1 | 2 | 2.0 | 2 | 0 |
| Hall | 1 | 2 | 2.0 | 2 | 0 |
| Belk | 1 | −5 | −5.0 | −5 | 0 |
| Cleveland | 465 | 1922 | 4.1 | 29 | 13 |
| Opponents | 528 | 2065 | 3.9 | 40 | 15 |

### Passing

| | Att. | Comp. | Pct. | Yds. | TD | Int. | Tkld. | Rate |
|---|---|---|---|---|---|---|---|---|
| Sipe | 496 | 291 | 58.7 | 3566 | 26 | 23 | 27/233 | 79.1 |
| McDonald | 68 | 32 | 47.1 | 341 | 1 | 4 | 6/38 | 42.6 |
| Walker | 3 | 1 | 33.3 | 25 | 0 | 1 | 0/0 | 25.0 |
| Cleveland | 567 | 324 | 57.1 | 3932 | 27 | 28 | 33/271 | 73.9 |
| Opponents | 469 | 280 | 59.7 | 3316 | 22 | 22 | 32/239 | 77.4 |

### Receiving

| | No. | Yds. | Avg. | LG | TD |
|---|---|---|---|---|---|
| Newsome | 89 | 970 | 10.9 | 66t | 6 |
| Logan | 37 | 627 | 16.9 | 34 | 2 |
| Jones | 36 | 507 | 14.1 | 32t | 4 |
| Pruitt | 30 | 157 | 5.2 | 21 | 2 |
| Holt | 29 | 420 | 14.5 | 48t | 3 |
| Walker | 29 | 273 | 9.4 | 35 | 1 |
| Green | 25 | 167 | 6.7 | 33 | 1 |
| Adams | 20 | 374 | 18.7 | 59 | 2 |
| Feacher | 13 | 217 | 16.7 | 42t | 3 |
| Belk | 5 | 141 | 28.2 | 64t | 2 |
| Davis | 5 | 20 | 4.0 | 10 | 0 |
| Hall | 4 | 33 | 8.3 | 18 | 0 |
| Dieken | 1 | 14 | 14.0 | 14t | 1 |
| Stracka | 1 | 12 | 12.0 | 12 | 0 |
| Cleveland | 324 | 3932 | 12.1 | 66t | 27 |
| Opponents | 280 | 3316 | 11.8 | 80t | 22 |

### Interceptions

| | No. | Yds. | Avg. | LG | TD |
|---|---|---|---|---|---|
| Cousineau | 4 | 47 | 11.8 | 15 | 0 |
| Banks | 3 | 95 | 31.7 | 65t | 1 |
| Whitwell | 3 | 67 | 22.3 | 28 | 0 |
| Dixon | 3 | 41 | 13.7 | 35 | 0 |
| Burrell | 2 | 0 | 0.0 | 0 | 0 |
| L. Johnson | 2 | 0 | 0.0 | 0 | 0 |
| Scott | 2 | 0 | 0.0 | 0 | 0 |
| Perry | 1 | 21 | 21.0 | 21 | 0 |
| Gross | 1 | 18 | 18.0 | 18 | 0 |
| Golic | 1 | 7 | 7.0 | 7t | 1 |
| Cleveland | 22 | 296 | 13.5 | 65t | 2 |
| Opponents | 28 | 508 | 18.1 | 73t | 3 |

### Punting

| | No. | Yds. | Avg. | In 20 | LG |
|---|---|---|---|---|---|
| Gossett | 70 | 2854 | 40.8 | 17 | 60 |
| Cleveland | 70 | 2854 | 40.8 | 17 | 60 |
| Opponents | 73 | 2954 | 40.5 | 18 | 61 |

### Punt Returns

| | No. | FC | Yds. | Avg. | LG | TD |
|---|---|---|---|---|---|---|
| Hall | 39 | 12 | 284 | 7.3 | 19 | 0 |
| Walker | 3 | 0 | 26 | 8.7 | 13 | 0 |
| Cleveland | 42 | 12 | 310 | 7.4 | 19 | 0 |
| Opponents | 30 | 10 | 309 | 10.3 | 66 | 0 |

### Kickoff Returns

| | No. | Yds. | Avg. | LG | TD |
|---|---|---|---|---|---|
| Walker | 29 | 627 | 21.6 | 38 | 0 |
| Green | 17 | 350 | 20.6 | 30 | 0 |
| Hall | 11 | 237 | 21.5 | 28 | 0 |
| Ferguson | 2 | 36 | 18.0 | 27 | 0 |
| Nicolas | 2 | 29 | 14.5 | 15 | 0 |
| Contz | 1 | 3 | 3.0 | 3 | 0 |
| Davis | 1 | 8 | 8.0 | 8 | 0 |
| Cleveland | 63 | 1290 | 20.5 | 38 | 0 |
| Opponents | 61 | 1155 | 18.9 | 93t | 1 |

### Scoring

| | TD | TD R | TD P | TD Rt | PAT | FG | TP |
|---|---|---|---|---|---|---|---|
| Bahr | | | | | 38/40 | 21/24 | 101 |
| Pruitt | 12 | 10 | 2 | 0 | | | 72 |
| Newsome | 6 | 0 | 6 | 0 | | | 36 |
| Green | 4 | 3 | 1 | 0 | | | 24 |
| Jones | 4 | 0 | 4 | 0 | | | 24 |
| Feacher | 3 | 0 | 3 | 0 | | | 18 |
| Holt | 3 | 0 | 3 | 0 | | | 18 |
| Adams | 2 | 0 | 2 | 0 | | | 12 |
| Belk | 2 | 0 | 2 | 0 | | | 12 |
| Logan | 2 | 0 | 2 | 0 | | | 12 |
| Banks | 1 | 0 | 0 | 1 | | | 6 |
| Dieken | 1 | 0 | 1 | 0 | | | 6 |
| Golic | 1 | 0 | 0 | 1 | | | 6 |
| Walker | 1 | 0 | 1 | 0 | | | 6 |
| Cox | | | | | 0/0 | 1/1 | 3 |
| Cleveland | 42 | 13 | 27 | 2 | 38/40 | 22/25 | 356 |
| Opponents | 42 | 15 | 22 | 5 | 40/42 | 16/22 | 342 |

## FIRST-ROUND SELECTIONS

(If Club had no first-round selection, first player drafted is listed with round in parentheses.)

| Year | Player, College, Position |
|---|---|
| 1950 | Ken Carpenter, Oregon State, B |
| 1951 | Ken Konz, Louisiana State, B |
| 1952 | Bert Rechichar, Tennessee, DB |
| | Harry Agganis, Boston U., QB |
| 1953 | Doug Atkins, Tennessee, DE |
| 1954 | Bobby Garrett, Stanford, QB |
| | John Bauer, Illinois, G |
| 1955 | Kurt Burris, Oklahoma, C |
| 1956 | Preston Carpenter, Arkansas, B |
| 1957 | Jim Brown, Syracuse, B |
| 1958 | Jim Shofner, Texas Christian, DB |
| 1959 | Rich Kreitling, Illinois, DE |
| 1960 | Jim Houston, Ohio State, DE |
| 1961 | Bobby Crespino, Mississippi, TE |
| 1962 | Gary Collins, Maryland, WR |
| | Leroy Jackson, Western Illinois, RB |
| 1963 | Tom Hutchinson, Kentucky, WR |
| 1964 | Paul Warfield, Ohio State, WR |
| 1965 | James Garcia, Purdue, T (2) |
| 1966 | Milt Morin, Massachusetts, TE |
| 1967 | Bob Matheson, Duke, LB |
| 1968 | Marvin Upshaw, Trinity, Texas, DT-DE |
| 1969 | Ron Johnson, Michigan, RB |
| 1970 | Mike Phipps, Purdue, QB |
| | Bob McKay, Texas, T |
| 1971 | Clarence Scott, Kansas State, CB |
| 1972 | Thom Darden, Michigan, DB |
| 1973 | Steve Holden, Arizona State, WR |
| | Pete Adams, Southern California, T |
| 1974 | Billy Corbett, Johnson C. Smith, T (2) |
| 1975 | Mack Mitchell, Houston, DE |
| 1976 | Mike Pruitt, Purdue, RB |
| 1977 | Robert Jackson, Texas A&M, LB |
| 1978 | Clay Matthews, Southern California, LB |
| | Ozzie Newsome, Alabama, TE |
| 1979 | Willis Adams, Houston, WR |
| 1980 | Charles White, Southern California, RB |
| 1981 | Hanford Dixon, Southern Mississippi, DB |
| 1982 | Chip Banks, Southern California, LB |
| 1983 | Ron Brown, Arizona State, WR (2) |
| 1984 | Don Rogers, UCLA, DB |

# CLEVELAND BROWNS 1984 VETERAN ROSTER

| No. | Name | Pos. | Ht. | Wt. | Birth-date | NFL Exp. | College | Birthplace | Residence | Games in '83 |
|---|---|---|---|---|---|---|---|---|---|---|
| 80 | Adams, Willis | WR | 6-2 | 200 | 8/22/56 | 5 | Houston | Weimar, Tex. | Houston, Tex. | 16 |
| 52 | Ambrose, Dick | LB | 6-0 | 228 | 1/17/53 | 10 | Virginia | New Rochelle, N.Y. | North Olmsted, Ohio | 6 |
| 61 | Baab, Mike | C | 6-4 | 270 | 12/6/59 | 3 | Texas | Fort Worth, Tex. | Lakewood, Ohio | 15 |
| 9 | Bahr, Matt | K | 5-10 | 175 | 7/6/56 | 6 | Penn State | Philadelphia, Pa. | Pittsburgh, Pa. | 16 |
| 99 | Baldwin, Keith | DE | 6-4 | 250 | 10/13/60 | 3 | Texas A&M | Houston, Tex. | Middleburg Heights, Ohio | 16 |
| 56 | Banks, Chip | LB | 6-4 | 233 | 9/18/59 | 3 | Southern California | Fort Lawton, Okla. | Parma, Ohio | 16 |
| 88 | Belk, Rocky | WR | 6-0 | 187 | 6/20/60 | 2 | Miami | Alexandria, Va. | Parma, Ohio | 10 |
| 47 | Braziel, Larry | CB | 6-0 | 184 | 9/25/54 | 6 | Southern California | Fort Worth, Tex. | North Olmsted, Ohio | 13 |
| 97 | Brown, Thomas | DE | 6-4 | 255 | 7/8/57 | 4 | Baylor | Galveston, Tex. | North Olmsted, Ohio | 16 |
| 49 | Burrell, Clinton | S | 6-1 | 192 | 9/4/56 | 5 | Louisiana State | Franklin, La. | Middleburg Heights, Ohio | 12 |
| 96 | Camp, Reggie | DE | 6-4 | 264 | 2/28/61 | 2 | California | San Francisco, Calif. | Bratenahl, Ohio | 16 |
| 59 | Carver, Dale | LB | 6-2 | 225 | 3/5/61 | 2 | Georgia | Melbourne, Fla. | Middleburg Heights, Ohio | 16 |
| 75 | Contz, Bill | T | 6-5 | 260 | 12/5/61 | 2 | Penn State | Belle Vernon, Pa. | North Royalton, Ohio | 16 |
| 50 | Cousineau, Tom | LB | 6-3 | 225 | 5/6/57 | 3 | Ohio State | Bloomington, Ind. | Rocky River, Ohio | 16 |
| 15 | Cox, Steve | P-K | 6-4 | 195 | 5/11/58 | 4 | Arkansas | Shreveport, La. | Charleston, Ark. | 7 |
| 38 | Davis, Johnny | RB | 6-1 | 235 | 7/17/56 | 7 | Alabama | Montgomery, Ala. | Euclid, Ohio | 16 |
| 64 | DeLamielleure, Joe | G | 6-3 | 260 | 3/16/51 | 12 | Michigan State | Detroit, Mich. | Charlotte, N.C. | 16 |
| 54 | DeLeone, Tom | C | 6-2 | 254 | 8/13/50 | 13 | Ohio State | Kent, Ohio | Medina, Ohio | 16 |
| 73 | Dieken, Doug | T | 6-5 | 252 | 2/12/49 | 14 | Illinois | Streator, Ill. | Bay Village, Ohio | 16 |
| 29 | Dixon, Hanford | CB | 5-11 | 182 | 12/25/58 | 4 | Southern Mississippi | Mobile, Ala. | Lakewood, Ohio | 16 |
| 74 | Farren, Paul | T | 6-5 | 251 | 12/24/60 | 2 | Boston University | Cohasset, Mass. | Parma, Ohio | 16 |
| 83 | Feacher, Ricky | WR | 5-10 | 180 | 2/11/54 | 9 | Mississippi Valley | Crystal River, Fla. | Warrensville Hts., Ohio | 9 |
| 10 | Flick, Tom | QB | 6-3 | 190 | 8/30/58 | 3 | Washington | Patuxent River, Md. | Cleveland, Ohio | 0* |
| 94 | Franks, Elvis | DE | 6-4 | 265 | 7/9/57 | 5 | Morgan State | Doucette, Tex. | South Euclid, Ohio | 16 |
| 79 | Golic, Bob | NT | 6-2 | 260 | 10/26/57 | 5 | Notre Dame | Cleveland, Ohio | Mentor, Ohio | 16 |
| 30 | Green, Boyce | RB | 5-11 | 215 | 6/24/60 | 2 | Carson-Newman | Beaufort, S.C. | Parma, Ohio | 13 |
| 31 | Gross, Al | S | 6-1 | 186 | 1/4/61 | 2 | Arizona | Stockton, Calif. | Strongsville, Ohio | 16 |
| 78 | t-Hairston, Carl | DE | 6-4 | 260 | 12/15/52 | 9 | Maryland-Eastern Shore | Martinsville, Va. | Cleveland, Ohio | 16 |
| 26 | Hall, Dino | RB-KR | 5-7 | 165 | 12/6/55 | 6 | Glassboro State | Atlantic City, N.J. | Pleasantville, N.J. | 16 |
| 84 | Harmon, Michael | WR | 6-0 | 208 | 7/24/61 | 2 | Mississippi | Kosciusko, Miss. | Cleveland, Ohio | 9 |
|  | t-Harris, Duriel | WR | 5-11 | 184 | 11/27/54 | 9 | New Mexico State | Port Arthur, Tex. | Miami, Fla. | 12 |
| 81 | Holt, Harry | TE | 6-4 | 230 | 12/29/57 | 2 | Arizona | Harlingen Tex. | Mentor, Ohio | 15 |
| 70 | Hopkins, Thomas | T | 6-6 | 260 | 1/13/60 | 2 | Alabama A&M | Butler, Ala. | North Olmsted, Ohio | 2 |
| 68 | Jackson, Robert | G | 6-5 | 260 | 4/1/53 | 10 | Duke | Charlotte, N.C. | Bay Village, Ohio | 16 |
| 51 | Johnson, Eddie | LB | 6-1 | 215 | 2/3/59 | 4 | Louisville | Albany, Ga. | Brook Park, Ohio | 16 |
| 48 | Johnson, Lawrence | CB | 5-11 | 204 | 9/11/57 | 5 | Wisconsin | Gary, Ind. | Shaker Heights, Ohio | 16 |
| 89 | Jones, Bobby | WR | 5-11 | 185 | 7/12/55 | 7 | No College | Sharon, Pa. | Brookfield, Ohio | 15 |
| 86 | Manning, Wade | WR | 5-11 | 190 | 7/25/55 | 4 | Ohio State | Meadville, Pa. | Shaker Heights, Ohio | 0* |
| 57 | Matthews, Clay | LB | 6-2 | 230 | 3/15/56 | 7 | Southern California | Palo Alto, Calif. | Los Angeles, Calif. | 16 |
| 16 | McDonald, Paul | QB | 6-2 | 185 | 2/23/58 | 5 | Southern California | Montebello, Calif. | Newport Beach, Calif. | 16 |
| 82 | Newsome, Ozzie | TE | 6-2 | 232 | 3/16/56 | 7 | Alabama | Muscle Shoals, Ala. | Bratenahl, Ohio | 16 |
| 58 | Nicolas, Scott | LB | 6-3 | 226 | 8/7/60 | 3 | Miami | Wichita Falls, Tex. | Strongsville, Ohio | 16 |
| 40 | Perry, Rod | CB | 5-9 | 185 | 9/11/53 | 10 | Colorado | Fresno, Calif. | North Olmsted, Ohio | 16 |
| 43 | Pruitt, Mike | RB | 6-0 | 225 | 4/3/54 | 9 | Purdue | Chicago, Ill. | Westlake, Ohio | 15 |
| 72 | Puzzuoli, Dave | NT | 6-3 | 260 | 1/12/61 | 2 | Pittsburgh | Stamford, Conn. | Parma, Ohio | 16 |
| 63 | Risien, Cody | T | 6-7 | 270 | 3/22/54 | 6 | Texas A&M | Bryan, Tex. | Houston, Tex. | 16 |
| 22 | Scott, Clarence | S | 6-0 | 190 | 4/9/49 | 14 | Kansas State | Atlanta, Ga. | Decatur, Ga. | 16 |
| 87 | Stracka, Tim | TE | 6-3 | 225 | 9/27/59 | 2 | Wisconsin | Madison, Wis. | Parma, Ohio | 13 |
| 12 | †Trocano, Rick | QB | 6-0 | 188 | 4/4/59 | 4 | Pittsburgh | Cleveland, Ohio | Lakewood, Ohio | 0* |
| 42 | Walker, Dwight | RB-KR | 5-10 | 185 | 1/10/59 | 3 | Nicholls State | Metairie, La. | Parma, Ohio | 16 |
| 55 | Weathers, Curtis | LB | 6-5 | 230 | 9/16/56 | 6 | Mississippi | Memphis, Tenn. | Berea, Ohio | 16 |
| 25 | White, Charles | RB | 5-10 | 190 | 1/22/58 | 4 | Southern California | Los Angeles, Calif. | Strongsville, Ohio | 0* |
| 81 | Whitwell, Mike | S | 6-0 | 175 | 11/14/58 | 3 | Texas A&M | Kenedy, Tex. | North Royalton, Ohio | 16 |

\* Flick last active with New England in '82; Manning last active with Denver in '82; Trocano active for 16 games with Cleveland in '83 but did not play; White missed '83 season due to injury.

†Option playout; subject to developments.

t-Browns traded for Hairston (Philadelphia) and Harris (Miami).

Traded—Wide receiver Dave Logan to Denver.

Also played with Browns in '83—RB Vagas Ferguson (1 game), P Jeff Gossett (16), QB Brian Sipe (16).

## COACHING STAFF

### Head Coach, Sam Rutigliano

**Pro Career:** Starts his seventh season as an NFL head coach. His teams have produced records of 8-8 (1978), 9-7 (1979), 11-5 (1980), 5-11 (1981), 4-5 (1982) and 9-7 (1983). The 1980 Browns won first AFC Central title since 1971. Pro assistant for 11 years before taking over at Cleveland. Was receivers coach with the Denver Broncos 1967-70, offensive coordinator with the New England Patriots 1971-72 and receivers coach in 1973, defensive backfield coach with the New York Jets 1974-75, and receivers coach for the New Orleans Saints for two years prior to his present assignment with the Browns. Career record: 46-45. No pro playing experience.

**Background:** Played end at Tulsa from 1954-56. Earned master's degree at Columbia University. Coached on the college level at Connecticut 1964-65 and Maryland 1966.

**Personal:** Born July 1, 1932, Brooklyn, N.Y. Sam and his wife, Barbara, live in Cleveland and have three children — Paul, Alison, and Kerry.

### Assistant Coaches

**Dave Adolph,** linebackers; born June 6, 1937, Akron, Ohio, lives in Richfield. Guard-linebacker Akron University 1955-58. No pro playing experience. College coach: Akron 1963-64, Connecticut 1965-68, Kentucky 1969-72, Illinois 1973-76, Ohio State 1977-78. Pro coach: Joined Browns in 1979.

**Joe Daniels,** receivers; born November 15, 1942, Bethel Park, Pa., lives in Brecksville, Ohio. No pro playing experience. College coach: East Stroudsburg 1966, New Hampshire 1967-68, Boston College 1969-76, West Virginia 1977-79, Pittsburgh 1980-82. Pro coach: Joined Browns in 1983.

**Jim Garrett,** director of research and development; born June 19, 1930, Rutherford, N.J., lives in Cleveland Heights. Running back Utah State, 1949-52. Pro running back Philadelphia Eagles 1954, British Columbia Lions (CFL) 1955, New York Giants 1956, Ottawa Rough Riders (CFL) 1957. College coach: Coast Guard 1957-58, Lehigh 1959, Susquehanna 1960-66 (head coach). Pro coach: New York Giants 1970-73, Houston Texans (WFL) 1974 (head coach), New Orleans Saints 1976-77, joined Browns in 1978.

**Howard Mudd,** offensive line; born February 10, 1942, Midland, Mich., lives in Medina, Ohio. Guard Hillsdale 1961-64. Pro guard San Francisco 49ers 1964-69, Chicago Bears 1970-71. College coach: California 1972-73. Pro coach: San Diego Chargers 1974-76, San Francisco 49ers 1977, Seattle Seahawks 1978-82, joined Browns in 1983.

**John Petercuskie,** special teams; born January 31, 1925, Old Forge, Pa., lives in Strongsville, Ohio. Guard East Stroudsburg State 1947-49. No pro playing experience. College coach: Dartmouth 1966-68, Boston College 1969-72, Princeton 1973-77. Pro coach: Joined Browns in 1978.

**Tom Pratt,** defensive line; born June 21, 1935, Edgerton, Wis., lives in Medina, Ohio. Linebacker Miami 1954-56. No pro playing experience. College coach: Miami 1957-59, Southern Mississippi 1960-62. Pro coach: Kansas City Chiefs 1963-77, New Orleans Saints 1978-80, joined Browns in 1981.

**Dave Redding,** strength and conditioning; born June 14, 1952, North Platte, Neb., lives in Medina, Ohio. Defensive end Nebraska 1972-75. No pro playing experience. College coach: Nebraska 1976, Washington State 1977, Missouri 1978-81. Pro coach: Joined Browns in 1982.

**Joe Scannella,** offensive coordinator-running backs; born May 2, 1931, Passaic, N.J., lives in Strongsville, Ohio. Quarterback Lehigh 1947-50. Pro safety Saskatchewan Roughriders (CFL) 1951-52. College coach: Cornell 1960, C.W. Post 1963-68, Vermont 1970-71. Pro coach: Montreal Alouettes (CFL) 1969, 1978-81 (head coach); Oakland Raiders 1972-77, joined Browns in 1982.

**Marty Schottenheimer,** defensive coordinator-defensive backs; born September 23, 1943, Canonsburg, Pa., lives in Strongsville, Ohio. Linebacker Pittsburgh 1962-65. Pro linebacker Buffalo Bills 1965-68, Boston Patriots 1969-70. Pro coach: Portland Storm (WFL) 1974, New York Giants 1975-77, Detroit Lions 1978-79, joined Browns in 1980.

**Darvin Wallis,** special assistant; born February 14, 1949, Ft. Branch, Ind., lives in Middleburg Hts., Ohio. No pro playing experience. College coach: Adams State 1976-77, Tulane 1978-79, Mississippi 1980-81. Pro coach: Joined Browns in 1982.

## CLEVELAND BROWNS 1984 FIRST-YEAR ROSTER

| Name | Pos. | Ht. | Wt. | Birth-date | College | Birthplace | Residence | How Acq. |
|---|---|---|---|---|---|---|---|---|
| Agee, Timothy | S | 5-10 | 180 | 11/25/62 | West Virginia | Burlington, N.C. | Bethesda, Md. | FA |
| Ball, Bobby | WR | 6-1 | 190 | 11/12/62 | Kent State | Orange, N.J. | Verona, N.J. | FA |
| Banks, James (1) | RB | 6-2 | 210 | 4/20/61 | Indiana State | Cincinnati, Ohio | Cincinnati, Ohio | FA |
| Barnes, Duane | T | 6-5 | 280 | 8/1/60 | West Virginia | Pittsburgh, Pa. | Pittsburgh, Pa. | FA |
| Bolden, Rickey | TE | 6-6 | 250 | 9/8/61 | Southern Methodist | Dallas, Tex. | Dallas, Tex. | D4 |
| Brennan, Brian | WR | 5-9 | 178 | 2/15/62 | Boston College | Bloomfield, Mich. | Bloomfield, Mich. | D4a |
| Bridgman, Mark | S | 6-1 | 185 | 6/19/62 | Furman | San Angelo, Tex. | Marion, S.C. | FA |
| Byner, Earnest | FB | 5-10 | 215 | 9/15/62 | East Carolina | Milledgeville, Ga. | Milledgeville, Ga. | D10 |
| Currens, Lance | WR | 5-9 | 175 | 4/30/61 | Baldwin-Wallace | Medina, Ohio | Wadsworth, Ohio | FA |
| Davis, Bruce | WR | 5-8 | 160 | 2/25/63 | Baylor | Dallas, Tex. | Dallas, Tex. | D2a |
| Davis, Larry | FB | 6-1 | 230 | 7/7/62 | Luther | Chicago, Ill. | Chicago, Ill. | FA |
| Downing, Curtis | S | 6-0 | 197 | 10/12/60 | Wilmington | Cleveland, Ohio | Wilmington, Ohio | FA |
| Dumont, Jim | LB | 6-1 | 224 | 7/16/61 | Rutgers | Bristol, Pa. | Levittown, Pa. | D7 |
| Griffin, Stephen | NT | 6-4 | 263 | 4/10/61 | Kent State | Buffalo, N.Y. | Lancaster, N.Y. | FA |
| Ham, Robin (1) | C-G | 6-3 | 260 | 7/21/59 | West Texas State | Odessa, Tex. | Berea, Ohio | FA |
| Higgins, Scott | S | 5-11 | 180 | 2/28/62 | Westminster, Pa. | Pittsburgh, Pa. | Pittsburgh, Pa. | FA |
| Johnson, Brad | C | 6-3 | 261 | 8/18/59 | Nebraska | Harvard, Neb. | Harvard, Neb. | FA |
| Jones, Don | WR | 6-2 | 200 | 10/13/60 | Texas A&M | Los Angeles, Calif. | Nacogdoches, Tex. | D9 |
| Merritts, James | DE | 6-2 | 265 | 3/22/61 | Akron | Roaring Springs, Pa. | Hollidaysburg, Pa. | FA |
| Moore, David | G | 6-3 | 310 | 7/24/60 | Ohio University | Clairton, Pa. | Clairton, Pa. | FA |
| Morgan, Darren | CB-S | 5-10 | 173 | 3/27/62 | Akron | Warren, Ohio | Warren, Ohio | FA |
| Nease, Michael | G | 6-3 | 272 | 10/30/61 | Tenn.-Chattanooga | Parrottsville, Tenn. | Parrottsville, Tenn. | FA |
| Nowaske, Jim (1) | DE | 6-4 | 255 | 4/14/61 | Adrian | Detroit, Mich. | Lincoln Park, Mich. | FA |
| Nugent, Terry | QB | 6-4 | 218 | 12/5/61 | Colorado State | Merced, Calif. | Elk Grove, Calif. | D6 |
| Piepkorn, Dave | T-G | 6-6 | 270 | 11/16/60 | North Dakota State | Fargo, N.D. | Fargo, N.D. | D5 |
| Reynolds, James | RB | 6-1 | 200 | 12/15/60 | Akron | Annapolis, Md. | Wadsworth, Ohio | FA |
| Rockins, Chris | S | 6-0 | 195 | 5/18/62 | Oklahoma State | Sherman, Tex. | Sherman, Tex. | D2 |
| Rogers, Don | S | 6-1 | 206 | 9/17/62 | UCLA | Texarkana, Ark. | Sacramento, Calif. | D1 |
| Sigourney, Christopher | P | 6-2 | 205 | 4/22/61 | Illinois | Elgin, Ill. | Elgin, Ill. | FA |
| Smith, Darryl | CB | 5-10 | 173 | 6/13/58 | Lamar | La Marque, Tex. | Galveston, Tex. | FA |
| Washington, Edward | WR | 6-3 | 192 | 9/14/62 | Ohio University | Cleveland, Ohio | Cleveland, Ohio | FA |

Players who report to an NFL team for the first time are designated on rosters as rookies (R). If a player reported to an NFL training camp in a previous year but was not on the active squad for three or more regular season or postseason games, he is listed on the first-year roster and designated by a (1). Thereafter, a player who is on the active squad for three or more regular season or postseason games is credited with an additional year of playing experience.

## NOTES

**American Football Conference
Western Division**

**Team Colors:** Orange, Royal Blue,
and White

**5700 Logan Street
Denver, Colorado 80216
Telephone: (303) 296-1982**

**Club Officials**

President, Chief Executive Officer:
  Patrick D. Bowlen
Assistant General Manager: John Beake
Director of Administration: Sandy Waters
Coordinator of College Scouting: Reed Johnson
Coordinator of Combine Scouting: Carroll Hardy
Director of Public Relations: Charlie Lee
Publicity Director: Jim Saccomano
Treasurer: Robert M. Hurley
Ticket Manager: Gail Stuckey
Equipment Manager: Bill Harpole
Trainer: Steve Antonopulos

**Stadium:** Denver Mile High Stadium •
  **Capacity:** 75,100
  1900 West Eliot
  Denver, Colorado 80204

**Playing Surface:** Grass (PAT)

**Training Camp:** University of Northern Colorado
  Greeley, Colorado 80521

## 1984 SCHEDULE

**Preseason**

| | | |
|---|---|---|
| Aug. 4 | **Washington** | 7:00 |
| Aug. 11 | **San Francisco** | 7:00 |
| Aug. 18 | **Colts** | 7:00 |
| Aug. 24 | at Atlanta | 8:00 |

**Regular Season**

| | | |
|---|---|---|
| Sept. 2 | **Cincinnati** | 2:00 |
| Sept. 9 | at Chicago | 12:00 |
| Sept. 16 | at Cleveland | 9:00 |
| Sept. 23 | **Kansas City** | 2:00 |
| Sept. 30 | **Los Angeles Raiders** | 2:00 |
| Oct. 7 | at Detroit | 1:00 |
| Oct. 15 | **Green Bay** (Monday) | 7:00 |
| Oct. 21 | at Buffalo | 1:00 |
| Oct. 28 | at Los Angeles Raiders | 1:00 |
| Nov. 4 | **New England** | 2:00 |
| Nov. 11 | at San Diego | 1:00 |
| Nov. 18 | **Minnesota** | 2:00 |
| Nov. 25 | **Seattle** | 2:00 |
| Dec. 2 | at Kansas City | 12:00 |
| Dec. 9 | **San Diego** | 2:00 |
| Dec. 15 | at Seattle (Saturday) | 1:00 |

## BRONCOS COACHING HISTORY

### (145-193-9)

| | | |
|---|---|---|
| 1960-61 | Frank Filchock | 7-20-1 |
| 1962-64 | Jack Faulkner* | 9-22-1 |
| 1964-66 | Mac Speedie** | 6-19-1 |
| 1966 | Ray Malavasi | 4-8-0 |
| 1967-71 | Lou Saban*** | 20-42-3 |
| 1971 | Jerry Smith | 2-3-0 |
| 1972-76 | John Ralston | 34-33-3 |
| 1977-80 | Robert (Red) Miller | 42-25-0 |
| 1981-83 | Dan Reeves | 21-21-0 |

  *Released after four games in 1964
 **Resigned after two games in 1966
***Resigned after nine games in 1971

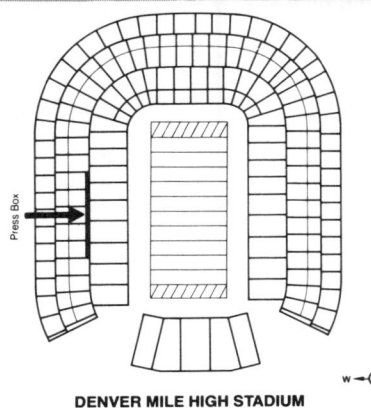

**DENVER MILE HIGH STADIUM**

## RECORD HOLDERS

### Individual Records—Career

| Category | Name | Performance |
|---|---|---|
| Rushing (Yds.) | Floyd Little, 1967-1975 | 6,323 |
| Passing (Yds.) | Craig Morton, 1977-1982 | 11,895 |
| Passing (TDs) | Craig Morton, 1977-1982 | 74 |
| Receiving (No.) | Lionel Taylor, 1960-66 | 543 |
| Receiving (Yds.) | Lionel Taylor, 1960-66 | 6,872 |
| Interceptions | Goose Gonsoulin, 1960-66 | 43 |
| Punting (Avg.) | Jim Fraser, 1962-64 | 45.2 |
| Punt Return (Avg.) | Rick Upchurch, 1975-1983 | 12.1 |
| Kickoff Return (Avg.) | Abner Haynes, 1965-66 | 26.3 |
| Field Goals | Jim Turner, 1971-79 | 151 |
| Touchdowns (Tot.) | Floyd Little, 1967-1975 | 54 |
| Points | Jim Turner, 1971-79 | 742 |

### Individual Records—Single Season

| Category | Name | Performance |
|---|---|---|
| Rushing (Yds.) | Otis Armstrong, 1974 | 1,407 |
| Passing (Yds.) | Craig Morton, 1981 | 3,195 |
| Passing (TDs) | Frank Tripucka, 1960 | 24 |
| Receiving (No.) | Lionel Taylor, 1961 | 100 |
| Receiving (Yds.) | Steve Watson, 1981 | 1,244 |
| Interceptions | Goose Gonsoulin, 1960 | 11 |
| Punting (Avg.) | Jim Fraser, 1963 | 46.1 |
| Punt Return (Avg.) | Floyd Little, 1967 | 16.9 |
| Kickoff Return (Avg.) | Bill Thompson, 1969 | 28.5 |
| Field Goals | Gene Mingo, 1962 | 27 |
| Touchdowns (Tot.) | Floyd Little, 1972, 1973 | 13 |
| | Steve Watson, 1981 | 13 |
| Points | Gene Mingo, 1962 | 137 |

### Individual Records—Single Game

| Category | Name | Performance |
|---|---|---|
| Rushing (Yds.) | Otis Armstrong, 12-8-74 | 183 |
| Passing (Yds.) | Frank Tripucka, 9-15-62 | 447 |
| Passing (TDs) | Frank Tripucka, 10-28-62 | 5 |
| Receiving (No.) | Lionel Taylor, 11-29-64 | 13 |
| | Bobby Anderson, 9-30-73 | 13 |
| Receiving (Yds.) | Lionel Taylor, 11-27-60 | 199 |
| Interceptions | Goose Gonsoulin, 9-18-60 | 4 |
| | Willie Brown, 11-15-64 | 4 |
| Field Goals | Gene Mingo, 10-6-63 | 5 |
| | Rich Karlis, 11-20-83 | 5 |
| Touchdowns (Tot.) | Many times | 3 |
| | Last time by Steve Watson, 9-20-81 | |
| Points | Gene Mingo, 12-10-60 | 21 |

## 1983 TEAM STATISTICS

| | Denver | Opp. |
|---|---|---|
| Total First Downs | 292 | 321 |
| Rushing | 99 | 119 |
| Passing | 155 | 185 |
| Penalty | 38 | 17 |
| Third Down Efficiency | 68/213 | 92/235 |
| Third Down Percentage | 31.9 | 39.1 |
| Total Net Yards | 4811 | 5609 |
| Total Offensive Plays | 1025 | 1099 |
| Avg. Gain per Play | 4.7 | 5.1 |
| Avg. Gain per Game | 300.7 | 350.6 |
| Net Yards Rushing | 1784 | 1938 |
| Total Rushing Plays | 471 | 509 |
| Avg. Gain per Rush | 3.8 | 3.8 |
| Avg. Gain Rushing per Game | 111.5 | 121.1 |
| Net Yards Passing | 3027 | 3671 |
| Lost Attempting to Pass | 55/439 | 38/317 |
| Gross Yards Passing | 3466 | 3988 |
| Attempts/Completions | 499/254 | 552/307 |
| Percent Completed | 50.9 | 55.6 |
| Had Intercepted | 22 | 27 |
| Avg. Net Passing per Game | 189.2 | 229.4 |
| Punts/Avg. | 87/41.6 | 77/44.2 |
| Punt Returns/Avg. | 38/11.1 | 55/9.5 |
| Kickoff Returns/Avg. | 56/19.2 | 46/17.9 |
| Interceptions/Avg. Ret. | 27/13.1 | 22/12.8 |
| Penalties/Yards | 100/804 | 138/1097 |
| Fumbles/Ball Lost | 34/19 | 46/20 |
| Total Points | 302 | 327 |
| Avg. Points per Game | 18.9 | 20.4 |
| Touchdowns | 34 | 36 |
| Rushing | 15 | 14 |
| Passing | 17 | 18 |
| Returns and Recoveries | 2 | 4 |
| Field Goals | 21/25 | 25/33 |
| Conversions | 33/34 | 34/36 |
| Safeties | 1 | 1 |
| Avg. Time of Possession | 29:31 | 30:29 |

## 1983 TEAM RECORD
### Preseason (3-1)

| Date | Denver | | Opponents |
|---|---|---|---|
| 8/5 | 10 | *Seattle | 7 |
| 8/13 | 21 | Atlanta | 10 |
| 8/20 | 19 | *Cleveland | 10 |
| 8/26 | 3 | Minnesota | 34 |
| | 53 | | 61 |

### Regular Season (9-7)

| Date | Denver | | Opp. | Att. |
|---|---|---|---|---|
| 9/4 | 14 | Pittsburgh | 10 | 58,233 |
| 9/11 | 17 | Baltimore | 10 | 51,482 |
| 9/18 | 10 | *Philadelphia | 13 | 74,202 |
| 9/25 | 7 | *Los Angeles Raiders | 22 | 74,289 |
| 10/2 | 14 | Chicago | 31 | 58,210 |
| 10/9 | 26 | Houston | 14 | 44,209 |
| 10/16 | 24 | *Cincinnati | 17 | 74,305 |
| 10/23 | 14 | *San Diego | 6 | 74,581 |
| 10/30 | 27 | *Kansas City | 24 | 74,640 |
| 11/6 | 19 | Seattle | 27 | 61,189 |
| 11/13 | 20 | Los Angeles Raiders | 22 | 51,945 |
| 11/20 | 38 | *Seattle | 27 | 74,710 |
| 11/27 | 7 | San Diego | 31 | 44,050 |
| 12/4 | 27 | *Cleveland | 6 | 70,912 |
| 12/11 | 21 | *Baltimore | 19 | 74,854 |
| 12/18 | 17 | Kansas City | 48 | 11,377 |
| | 302 | | 327 | 973,188 |

*Home Game

### Score by Periods

| | | | | | | |
|---|---|---|---|---|---|---|
| Denver | 41 | 80 | 39 | 142 | — | 302 |
| Opponents | 85 | 87 | 76 | 79 | — | 327 |

### Attendance
Home 592,493    Away 380,695    Total 973,188
Single game home record, 74,997 (10-7-79)
Single season home record, 598,402 (1981)

## 1983 INDIVIDUAL STATISTICS

### Rushing

| | Att. | Yds. | Avg. | LG | TD |
|---|---|---|---|---|---|
| Winder | 196 | 757 | 3.9 | 52 | 3 |
| Poole | 81 | 246 | 3.0 | 19 | 4 |
| Preston | 57 | 222 | 3.9 | 28 | 1 |
| Willhite | 43 | 188 | 4.4 | 24t | 3 |
| Elway | 28 | 146 | 5.2 | 23 | 1 |
| Parros | 30 | 96 | 3.2 | 13 | 1 |
| Myles | 8 | 52 | 6.5 | 16 | 0 |
| DeBerg | 13 | 28 | 2.2 | 11 | 1 |
| Upchurch | 6 | 19 | 3.2 | 9 | 0 |
| Kubiak | 4 | 17 | 4.3 | 8 | 1 |
| Watson | 3 | 17 | 5.7 | 10 | 0 |
| Prestridge | 1 | 7 | 7.0 | 7 | 0 |
| J. Wright | 1 | −11 | −11.0 | −11 | 0 |
| Denver | 471 | 1784 | 3.8 | 52 | 15 |
| Opponents | 509 | 1938 | 3.8 | 29 | 14 |

### Passing

| | Att. | Comp. | Pct. | Yds. | TD | Int. | Tkld. | Rate |
|---|---|---|---|---|---|---|---|---|
| DeBerg | 215 | 119 | 55.3 | 1617 | 9 | 7 | 25/201 | 79.9 |
| Elway | 259 | 123 | 47.5 | 1663 | 7 | 14 | 28/218 | 54.9 |
| Kubiak | 22 | 12 | 54.5 | 186 | 1 | 1 | 2/20 | 79.0 |
| Upchurch | 2 | 0 | 0.0 | 0 | 0 | 0 | 0/0 | 39.6 |
| Willhite | 1 | 0 | 0.0 | 0 | 0 | 0 | 0/0 | 39.6 |
| Denver | 499 | 254 | 50.9 | 3466 | 17 | 22 | 55/439 | 66.4 |
| Opponents | 552 | 307 | 55.6 | 3988 | 18 | 27 | 38/317 | 69.0 |

### Receiving

| | No. | Yds. | Avg. | LG | TD |
|---|---|---|---|---|---|
| Watson | 59 | 1133 | 19.2 | 78t | 5 |
| Upchurch | 40 | 639 | 16.0 | 40 | 2 |
| Winder | 23 | 150 | 6.5 | 17 | 0 |
| Egloff | 20 | 205 | 10.3 | 32 | 2 |
| Poole | 20 | 184 | 9.2 | 23 | 0 |
| Preston | 17 | 137 | 8.1 | 25 | 1 |
| Willhite | 14 | 153 | 10.9 | 26t | 1 |
| J. Wright | 13 | 134 | 10.3 | 23 | 0 |
| Thomas | 12 | 182 | 15.2 | 44 | 0 |
| Parros | 12 | 126 | 10.5 | 33t | 2 |
| Sampson | 10 | 200 | 20.0 | 49t | 3 |
| Myles | 7 | 119 | 17.0 | 33 | 1 |
| Odoms | 4 | 62 | 15.5 | 21 | 0 |
| Sawyer | 3 | 42 | 14.0 | 17 | 0 |
| Denver | 254 | 3466 | 13.6 | 78t | 17 |
| Opponents | 307 | 3988 | 13.0 | 72t | 18 |

### Interceptions

| | No. | Yds. | Avg. | LG | TD |
|---|---|---|---|---|---|
| L. Wright | 6 | 50 | 8.3 | 34 | 0 |
| Wilson | 5 | 91 | 18.2 | 36 | 0 |
| Foley | 5 | 28 | 5.6 | 16 | 0 |
| Harden | 4 | 127 | 31.8 | 48 | 0 |
| Smith | 4 | 39 | 9.8 | 23 | 0 |
| R. Jackson | 1 | 15 | 15.0 | 15 | 0 |
| Gradishar | 1 | 5 | 5.0 | 5 | 0 |
| T. Jackson | 1 | 0 | 0.0 | 0 | 0 |
| Denver | 27 | 355 | 13.1 | 48 | 0 |
| Opponents | 22 | 281 | 12.8 | 58t | 3 |

### Punting

| | No. | Yds. | Avg. | In 20 | LG |
|---|---|---|---|---|---|
| Prestridge | 87 | 3620 | 41.6 | 19 | 60 |
| Denver | 87 | 3620 | 41.6 | 19 | 60 |
| Opponents | 77 | 3406 | 44.2 | 18 | 68 |

### Punt Returns

| | No. | FC | Yds. | Avg. | LG | TD |
|---|---|---|---|---|---|---|
| Thomas | 33 | 9 | 368 | 11.2 | 70t | 1 |
| Upchurch | 4 | 1 | 52 | 13.0 | 17 | 0 |
| L. Wright | 1 | 0 | 0 | 0.0 | 0 | 0 |
| Denver | 38 | 10 | 420 | 11.1 | 70t | 1 |
| Opponents | 55 | 8 | 524 | 9.5 | 34 | 0 |

### Kickoff Returns

| | No. | Yds. | Avg. | LG | TD |
|---|---|---|---|---|---|
| Thomas | 28 | 573 | 20.5 | 42 | 0 |
| Wilson | 24 | 485 | 20.2 | 32 | 0 |
| Studdard | 2 | 8 | 4.0 | 8 | 0 |
| Harden | 1 | 9 | 9.0 | 9 | 0 |
| T. Jackson | 1 | 2 | 2.0 | 2 | 0 |
| Denver | 56 | 1077 | 19.2 | 42 | 0 |
| Opponents | 46 | 824 | 17.9 | 42 | 0 |

### Scoring

| | TD | TD R | TD P | TD Rt | PAT | FG | TP |
|---|---|---|---|---|---|---|---|
| Karlis | | | | | 33/34 | 21/25 | 96 |
| Watson | 5 | 0 | 5 | 0 | | | 30 |
| Poole | 4 | 4 | 0 | 0 | | | 24 |
| Willhite | 4 | 3 | 1 | 0 | | | 24 |
| Parros | 3 | 1 | 2 | 0 | | | 18 |
| Sampson | 3 | 0 | 3 | 0 | | | 18 |
| Winder | 3 | 3 | 0 | 0 | | | 18 |
| Egloff | 2 | 0 | 2 | 0 | | | 12 |
| Preston | 2 | 1 | 1 | 0 | | | 12 |
| Upchurch | 2 | 0 | 2 | 0 | | | 12 |
| Chavous | 1 | 0 | 0 | 1 | | | 6 |
| DeBerg | 1 | 1 | 0 | 0 | | | 6 |
| Elway | 1 | 1 | 0 | 0 | | | 6 |
| Kubiak | 1 | 1 | 0 | 0 | | | 6 |
| Myles | 1 | 0 | 1 | 0 | | | 6 |
| Thomas | 1 | 0 | 0 | 1 | | | 6 |
| Jones | | | (Safety) | | | | 2 |
| Denver | 34 | 15 | 17 | 2 | 33/34 | 21/25 | 302 |
| Opponents | 36 | 14 | 18 | 4 | 34/36 | 25/33 | 327 |

### FIRST-ROUND SELECTIONS

(If Club had no first-round selection, first player drafted is listed with round in parentheses.)

| Year | Player, College, Position |
|---|---|
| 1960 | Roger LeClerc, Trinity, Connecticut, C |
| 1961 | Bob Gaiters, New Mexico State, RB |
| 1962 | Merlin Olsen, Utah State, DT |
| 1963 | Kermit Alexander, UCLA, CB |
| 1964 | Bob Brown, Nebraska, T |
| 1965 | Dick Butkus, Illinois, LB (2) |
| 1966 | Jerry Shay, Purdue, DT |
| 1967 | Floyd Little, Syracuse, RB |
| 1968 | Curley Culp, Arizona State, DE (2) |
| 1969 | Grady Cavness, Texas-El Paso, DB (2) |
| 1970 | Bob Anderson, Colorado, RB |
| 1971 | Marv Montgomery, Southern California, T |
| 1972 | Riley Odoms, Houston, TE |
| 1973 | Otis Armstrong, Purdue, RB |
| 1974 | Randy Gradishar, Ohio State, LB |
| 1975 | Louis Wright, San Jose State, DB |
| 1976 | Tom Glassic, Virginia, G |
| 1977 | Steve Schindler, Boston College, G |
| 1978 | Don Latimer, Miami, DT |
| 1979 | Kelvin Clark, Nebraska, T |
| 1980 | Rulon Jones, Utah State, DE (2) |
| 1981 | Dennis Smith, Southern California, DB |
| 1982 | Gerald Willhite, San Jose State, RB |
| 1983 | Chris Hinton, Northwestern, G |
| 1984 | Andre Townsend, Mississippi, DE (2) |

# DENVER BRONCOS 1984 VETERAN ROSTER

| No. | Name | Pos. | Ht. | Wt. | Birth-date | NFL Exp. | College | Birthplace | Residence | Games in '83 |
|-----|------|------|-----|-----|------------|----------|---------|------------|------------|--------------|
| 74 | Baker, Jerry | NT | 6-2 | 297 | 3/6/60 | 2 | Tulane | Fort Meade, Fla. | Fort Meade, Fla. | 5 |
| 86 | Barnett, Dean | TE | 6-2 | 225 | 6/6/57 | 2 | Nevada-Las Vegas | La Habra, Calif. | Las Vegas, Nev. | 8 |
| 54 | Bishop, Keith | C-G | 6-3 | 260 | 3/10/57 | 4 | Baylor | San Diego, Calif. | Englewood, Colo. | 16 |
| | t-Blinka, Stan | LB | 6-2 | 230 | 4/29/57 | 6 | Sam Houston State | Columbus, Ohio | Rockdale, Tex. | 16 |
| 65 | Bowyer, Walt | DE | 6-4 | 245 | 9/8/60 | 2 | Arizona State | Pittsburgh, Pa. | Denver, Colo. | 14 |
| | t-Brunner, Scott | QB | 6-5 | 200 | 3/24/57 | 5 | Delaware | Sellersville, Pa. | Cranbury, N.J. | 16 |
| 64 | Bryan, Bill | C | 6-2 | 258 | 6/21/55 | 7 | Duke | Burlington, N.C. | Burlington, N.C. | 16 |
| 58 | Busick, Steve | LB | 6-4 | 227 | 12/10/58 | 4 | Southern California | Los Angeles, Calif. | Aurora, Colo. | 16 |
| 68 | Carter, Rubin | NT | 6-0 | 256 | 12/12/52 | 10 | Miami | Pompano Beach, Fla. | Aurora, Colo. | 16 |
| 79 | †Chavous, Barney | DE | 6-3 | 258 | 3/22/51 | 12 | South Carolina State | Aiken, S.C. | Aurora, Colo. | 15 |
| 59 | Comeaux, Darren | LB | 6-1 | 227 | 4/15/60 | 3 | Arizona State | Shawnee, Okla. | San Diego, Calif. | 14 |
| 63 | Cooper, Mark | T | 6-5 | 267 | 2/14/60 | 2 | Miami | Miami, Fla. | Miami, Fla. | 10 |
| 55 | Dennison, Rick | LB | 6-2 | 215 | 6/22/58 | 3 | Colorado State | Kalispel, Mont. | Louisville, Colo. | 16 |
| 21 | Dupree, Myron | CB | 5-11 | 180 | 10/15/61 | 2 | North Carolina Central | New York, N.Y. | Rocky Mount, N.C. | 16 |
| 85 | Egloff, Ron | TE | 6-5 | 227 | 10/2/55 | 8 | Wisconsin | Plymouth, Mich. | Englewood, Colo. | 16 |
| 7 | Elway, John | QB | 6-4 | 202 | 6/28/60 | 2 | Stanford | Port Angeles, Wash. | San Jose, Calif. | 11 |
| 43 | Foley, Steve | S | 6-2 | 190 | 11/11/53 | 9 | Tulane | New Orleans, La. | Independence, La. | 14 |
| 31 | Harden, Mike | S | 6-1 | 192 | 2/16/58 | 3 | Michigan | Memphis, Tenn. | Aurora, Colo. | 15 |
| 73 | Hollingsworth, Shawn | T | 6-2 | 260 | 12/4/61 | 2 | Angelo State | Brownwood, Tex. | Aurora, Colo. | 5 |
| 60 | †Howard, Paul | G | 6-3 | 260 | 9/12/50 | 11 | Brigham Young | San Jose, Calif. | Redding, Calif. | 16 |
| 28 | †Jackson, Roger | S | 6-0 | 186 | 2/28/59 | 3 | Bethune-Cookman | Macon, Ga. | Macon, Ga. | 16 |
| 57 | Jackson, Tom | LB | 5-11 | 220 | 4/4/51 | 12 | Louisville | Cleveland, Ohio | Aurora, Colo. | 12 |
| 75 | Jones, Rulon | DE | 6-6 | 260 | 3/25/58 | 5 | Utah State | Salt Lake City, Utah | Thornton, Colo. | 12 |
| 3 | Karlis, Rich | K | 6-0 | 180 | 5/23/59 | 3 | Cincinnati | Salem, Ohio | Denver, Colo. | 16 |
| 8 | Kubiak, Gary | QB | 6-0 | 192 | 8/15/61 | 2 | Texas A&M | Houston, Tex. | Houston, Tex. | 4 |
| 76 | Lanier, Ken | T | 6-3 | 269 | 7/8/59 | 4 | Florida State | Columbus, Ohio | Columbus, Ohio | 16 |
| | t-Logan, Dave | WR | 6-4 | 216 | 2/2/54 | 9 | Colorado | Fargo, N.D. | Strongsville, Ohio | 16 |
| 41 | Lytle, Rob | RB-TE | 5-11 | 195 | 11/12/54 | 8 | Michigan | Fremont, Ohio | Fremont, Ohio | 4 |
| 66 | Manor, Brison | DE | 6-4 | 235 | 8/10/52 | 8 | Arkansas | Bridgeton, N.J. | North Little Rock, Ark. | 16 |
| 77 | Mecklenburg, Karl | LB | 6-3 | 250 | 9/1/60 | 2 | Minnesota | Seattle, Wash. | Wheatridge, Colo. | 16 |
| 29 | Myers, Wilbur | S | 5-11 | 195 | 8/17/61 | 2 | Delta State | Bassfield, Miss. | Bassfield, Miss. | 16 |
| 39 | Myles, Jesse | RB | 5-10 | 210 | 9/28/60 | 2 | Louisiana State | New Orleans, La. | Gray, La. | 16 |
| 24 | Parros, Rick | RB | 5-11 | 200 | 6/14/58 | 4 | Utah State | Brooklyn, N.Y. | Denver, Colo. | 6 |
| 34 | Poole, Nathan | RB | 5-9 | 212 | 12/17/56 | 5 | Louisville | Alexander City, Ala. | Aurora, Colo. | 16 |
| 11 | Prestridge, Luke | P | 6-4 | 235 | 9/17/56 | 6 | Baylor | Houston, Tex. | Englewood, Colo. | 16 |
| | t-Ramson, Eason | TE | 6-2 | 234 | 4/30/56 | 6 | Washington State | Sacramento, Calif. | Foster City, Calif. | 16 |
| 50 | Ryan, Jim | LB | 6-1 | 215 | 5/18/57 | 6 | William & Mary | Bellmawr, N.J. | Englewood, Colo. | 15 |
| 84 | Sampson, Clint | WR | 5-11 | 183 | 1/4/61 | 2 | San Diego State | Los Angeles, Calif. | Los Angeles, Calif. | 16 |
| 83 | Sawyer, John | TE | 6-2 | 230 | 7/26/53 | 9 | Southern Mississippi | Baker, La. | Ethel, La. | 14* |
| 49 | Smith, Dennis | S | 6-3 | 200 | 2/3/59 | 4 | Southern California | Santa Monica, Calif. | Aurora, Colo. | 14 |
| 78 | Stachowski, Rich | NT | 6-4 | 245 | 3/29/61 | 2 | California | Los Angeles, Calif. | Burbank, Calif. | 14 |
| 70 | Studdard, Dave | T | 6-4 | 260 | 11/22/55 | 6 | Texas | San Antonio, Tex. | Littleton, Colo. | 16 |
| 51 | Swenson, Bob | LB | 6-3 | 225 | 7/1/53 | 8 | California | Stockton, Calif. | Longmont, Colo. | 2 |
| 82 | Thomas, Zach | WR | 6-0 | 182 | 9/8/60 | 2 | South Carolina State | Rockledge, Fla. | Cocoa, Fla. | 16 |
| 67 | Uecker, Keith | T | 6-5 | 260 | 6/29/60 | 3 | Auburn | Auburn, Ala. | Hollywood, Fla. | 16 |
| 81 | Watson, Steve | WR | 6-4 | 195 | 5/28/57 | 6 | Temple | Baltimore, Md. | Arvada, Colo. | 16 |
| 47 | Willhite, Gerald | RB | 5-10 | 200 | 5/30/59 | 3 | San Jose State | Sacramento, Calif. | Rancho Cordova, Calif. | 8 |
| 45 | Wilson, Steve | CB | 5-10 | 195 | 8/24/57 | 6 | Howard | Jacksonville, Fla. | Richardson, Tex. | 16 |
| 23 | Winder, Sammy | RB | 5-11 | 203 | 7/15/59 | 3 | Southern Mississippi | Madison, Miss. | Aurora, Colo. | 14 |
| 52 | Woodard, Ken | LB | 6-1 | 218 | 1/22/60 | 3 | Tuskegee Institute | Detroit, Mich. | Detroit, Mich. | 16 |
| 87 | Wright, Jim | TE | 6-3 | 240 | 9/1/56 | 7 | Texas Christian | Fort Hood, Tex. | Houston, Tex. | 6 |
| 20 | Wright, Louis | CB | 6-2 | 200 | 1/31/53 | 10 | San Jose State | Gilmer, Tex. | Bakersfield, Calif. | 16 |

* Sawyer played 7 games with Washington, 7 with Denver in '83.

†Option playout; subject to developments.

t-Broncos traded for Blinka (New York Jets), Brunner (New York Giants), Logan (Cleveland), Ramson (San Francisco).

Traded—Quarterback Steve DeBerg to Tampa Bay.

Retired—Tom Glassic, 8-year guard, 12 games in '83; Randy Gradishar, 10-year linebacker, 16 in '83; Rick Upchurch, 9-year wide receiver, 12 in '83.

Also played with Broncos in '83—TE Clay Brown (3 games), NT Don Latimer (12), TE Riley Odoms (2), RB Dave Preston (14), S Steve Trimble (5).

## COACHING STAFF

### Head Coach, Dan Reeves

**Pro Career:** Became ninth head coach in Broncos history on February 28, 1981, after spending entire pro career as both player and coach with Dallas Cowboys. Guided Broncos to 9-7 record and a playoff berth in 1983, following 10-6 mark in 1981 and 2-7 record in 1982. He joined the Cowboys as a free agent running back in 1965 and became a member of the coaching staff in 1970 when he undertook the dual role of player-coach for two seasons. Was Cowboys offensive backfield coach from 1972-76 and became offensive coordinator in 1977. Was an all-purpose running back during his eight seasons as a player, rushing for 1,990 yards and catching 129 passes for 1,693. Career record: 21-21.

**Background:** Quarterback at South Carolina from 1962-64 and was inducted into the school's Hall of Fame in 1978.

**Personal:** Born January 19, 1944, Rome, Ga. Dan and his wife, Pam, live in Denver and have three children—Dana, Laura, and Lee.

### Assistant Coaches

**Marvin Bass,** offensive line; born August 28, 1919, Norfolk, Va., lives in Denver. Tackle William & Mary 1940-42. No pro playing experience. College coach: William & Mary 1944-48, 1950-51 (head coach), North Carolina 1949, 1953-55, South Carolina 1956-59, 1961-65, Georgia Tech 1960, Richmond 1973. Pro coach: Washington Redskins 1952, Montreal Beavers (Continental League) 1966-67, Montreal Alouettes (CFL) 1968, Buffalo Bills 1969-71, Birmingham Americans (WFL) 1974-75, joined Broncos in 1982.

**Joe Collier,** assistant head coach, defense; born June 7, 1932, Rock Island, Ill., lives in Denver. End Northwestern 1950-53. No pro playing experience. College coach: Western Illinois 1957-59. Pro coach: Boston Patriots 1960-62, Buffalo Bills 1963-68 (head coach 1966-68), joined Broncos in 1969.

**Alex Gibbs,** offensive line; born February 11, 1941, Morganton, N.C., lives in Denver. Running back-defensive back Davidson 1959-63. No pro playing experience. College coach: Duke 1969-70, Kentucky 1971-72, West Virginia 1973-74, Ohio State 1975-78, Auburn 1979-81, Georgia 1982-83. Pro coach: First year with Broncos.

**Stan Jones,** defensive line; born November 24, 1931, Altoona, Pa., lives in Denver. Tackle Maryland 1950-53. Pro lineman Chicago Bears 1954-65, Washington Redskins 1966. Pro coach: Denver Broncos 1967-71, Buffalo Bills 1972-75, rejoined Broncos in 1976.

**Myrel Moore,** linebackers-special teams; born March 9, 1934, Sebastopol, Calif., lives in Denver. Receiver California-Davis 1955-57. Pro defensive back Washington Redskins 1958. College coach: Santa Ana J.C. 1959-62, California 1963-71. Pro coach: Denver Broncos 1972-77, Oakland Raiders 1978-79, rejoined Broncos in 1983.

**Nick Nicolau,** running backs; born May 5, 1933, New York, N.Y., lives in Denver. Running back Southern Connecticut 1957-59. No pro playing experience. College coach: Southern Connecticut 1960, Springfield 1961, Bridgeport 1962-69 (head coach 1965-69), Massachusetts 1970, Connecticut 1971-72, Kentucky 1973-75, Kent State 1976. Pro coach: Hamilton Tiger Cats (CFL) 1977, Montreal Alouettes (CFL) 1978-79, New Orleans Saints 1980, joined Broncos in 1981.

**Fran Polsfoot,** tight ends; born April 19, 1927, Montesano, Wash., lives in Denver. End Washington State 1946-49. Pro end Chicago Cardinals 1950-52, Washington Redskins 1953. College coach: Wisconsin State 1954-61. Pro coach: St. Louis Cardinals 1962-67, Houston Oilers 1968-71, 1975-76, Cleveland Browns 1972-74, joined Broncos in 1977.

**Mike Shanahan,** wide receivers; born August 24, 1952, Oak Park, Ill., lives in Denver. Quarterback Eastern Illinois 1970-73. No pro playing experience. College coach: Oklahoma 1975-76, Northern Arizona 1977, Eastern Illinois 1978, Minnesota 1979, Florida 1980-83. Pro coach: First year with Broncos.

**Charlie West,** defensive backs; born August 31, 1946, Big Spring, Tex., lives in Denver. Defensive back Texas El-Paso 1963-67. Pro defensive back Minnesota Vikings 1968-73, Detroit Lions 1974-78, Denver Broncos 1978-79. College coach: MacAlister 1981, California 1982. Pro coach: Joined Broncos in 1983.

## DENVER BRONCOS 1984 FIRST-YEAR ROSTER

| Name | Pos. | Ht. | Wt. | Birth-date | College | Birthplace | Residence | How Acq. |
|------|------|-----|-----|-----------|---------|-----------|-----------|----------|
| Brewer, Chris | RB | 6-1 | 192 | 1/23/62 | Arizona | Denver, Colo. | Tucson, Ariz. | D9 |
| Felknor, Bret (1) | DE | 6-4 | 245 | 4/26/61 | Hamline | Minneapolis, Minn. | Anoka, Minn. | FA |
| Gaines, Charles | LB | 6-2 | 225 | 12/7/58 | Wyoming | Ft. Carson, Colo. | Golden, Colo. | FA |
| Garnett, Scott | NT | 6-2 | 263 | 12/3/62 | Washington | Harrisburg, Pa. | Pasadena, Calif. | D8a |
| Harris, Weedy (1) | LB | 6-2 | 223 | 12/2/60 | Houston | Waco, Tex. | Waco, Tex. | FA |
| Higginbothan, John (1) | NT | 6-2 | 270 | 4/26/59 | Oklahoma | Hugo, Okla. | Hugo, Okla. | FA |
| Hood, Winford | TE | 6-3 | 240 | 3/29/62 | Georgia | Atlanta, Ga. | Atlanta, Ga. | D8 |
| Jarman, Murray | WR | 6-5 | 210 | 1/26/61 | Clemson | Birmingham, Ala. | Delray Beach, Fla. | D12 |
| Kay, Clarence | TE | 6-3 | 225 | 7/30/61 | Georgia | Seneca, S.C. | Seneca, S.C. | D7 |
| Lang, Gene | RB | 5-10 | 196 | 3/15/62 | Louisiana State | Gulfport, Miss. | Pass Christian, Miss. | D11 |
| Leary, Bill (1) | LB | 6-2 | 230 | 6/14/58 | Mesa | Denver, Colo. | Lakewood, Colo. | FA |
| Lilly, Tony | S | 6-0 | 199 | 2/15/62 | Florida | Alexandria, Va. | Woodbridge, Va. | D3 |
| Micho, Bobby | TE | 6-3 | 227 | 3/7/62 | Texas | Omaha, Neb. | Austin, Tex. | D10 |
| Niko, Maomao (1) | G | 6-3 | 290 | 3/31/60 | San Jose State | San Francisco, Calif. | Hayward, Calif. | FA |
| Raikes, Jeff (1) | WR | 6-1 | 189 | 7/1/60 | Colorado State | Denver, Colo. | Denver, Colo. | FA |
| Robbins, Randy | CB | 6-1 | 182 | 9/14/62 | Arizona | Casa Grande, Ariz. | Tucson, Ariz. | D4 |
| Russell, Marlin | LB | 6-1 | 230 | 9/12/61 | Toledo | Toledo, Ohio | Walbridge, Ohio | FA |
| Smith, Aaron | LB | 6-2 | 209 | 8/10/62 | Utah State | Los Angeles, Calif. | Logan, Utah | D6 |
| Smith, Darryl (1) | CB | 6-1 | 195 | 7/8/60 | Virginia | Hampton, Va. | Newport News, Va. | FA |
| Staff, Mike (1) | DE | 6-6 | 258 | 2/4/61 | Northern Colorado | Chicago, Ill. | Greeley, Colo. | FA |
| Townsend, Andre | NT | 6-2 | 253 | 10/8/62 | Mississippi | Chicago, Ill. | Oxford, Miss. | D2 |

Players who report to an NFL team for the first time are designated on rosters as rookies (R). If a player reported to an NFL training camp in a previous year but was not on the active squad for three or more regular season or postseason games, he is listed on the first-year roster and designated by a (1). Thereafter, a player who is on the active squad for three or more regular season or postseason games is credited with an additional year of playing experience.

## NOTES

_____

37

## American Football Conference
## Central Division

**Team Colors:** Columbia Blue, Scarlet, and White

**Box 1516**
**Houston, Texas 77001**
**Telephone: (713) 797-9111**

### Club Officials
President: K. S. (Bud) Adams, Jr.
Executive Vice President-General Manager:
   Ladd K. Herzeg
Vice President-Player Personnel: Mike Holovak
Director of Administration: Rick Nichols
Media Relations Director: Bob Hyde
Marketing/Media Relations: Gregg Stengel
Ticket Manager: David Fuqua
Head Trainer: Jerry Meins
Assistant Trainer: Joel Krekelberg
Equipment Manager: Gordon Batty

**Stadium:** Astrodome • **Capacity:** 50,496
   Loop 610, Kirby and Fannin Streets
   Houston, Texas 77054

**Playing Surface:** AstroTurf

**Training Camp:** Angelo State University
   San Angelo, Texas 76901

## 1984 SCHEDULE

### Preseason
| | | |
|---|---|---|
| Aug. 4 | at Tampa Bay | 8:00 |
| Aug. 11 | **New York Jets** | 8:00 |
| Aug. 18 | **New Orleans** | 8:00 |
| Aug. 25 | at Dallas | 8:00 |

### Regular Season
| | | |
|---|---|---|
| Sept. 2 | **Los Angeles Raiders** | 3:00 |
| Sept. 9 | **Colts** | 3:00 |
| Sept. 16 | at San Diego | 1:00 |
| Sept. 23 | at Atlanta | 1:00 |
| Sept. 30 | **New Orleans** | 3:00 |
| Oct. 7 | at Cincinnati | 4:00 |
| Oct. 14 | at Miami | 1:00 |
| Oct. 21 | **San Francisco** | 3:00 |
| Oct. 28 | **Cincinnati** | 12:00 |
| Nov. 4 | at Pittsburgh | 1:00 |
| Nov. 11 | at Kansas City | 12:00 |
| Nov. 18 | **New York Jets** | 3:00 |
| Nov. 25 | at Cleveland | 1:00 |
| Dec. 2 | **Pittsburgh** | 12:00 |
| Dec. 9 | at Los Angeles Rams | 1:00 |
| Dec. 16 | **Cleveland** | 12:00 |

## OILERS COACHING HISTORY
### (157-190-6)
| | | |
|---|---|---|
| 1960-61 | Lou Rymkus* | 12-7-1 |
| 1961 | Wally Lemm | 10-2-0 |
| 1962-63 | Frank (Pop) Ivy | 17-12-0 |
| 1964 | Sammy Baugh | 4-10-0 |
| 1965 | Hugh Taylor | 4-10-0 |
| 1966-70 | Wally Lemm | 28-38-4 |
| 1971 | Ed Hughes | 4-9-1 |
| 1972-73 | Bill Peterson** | 1-18-0 |
| 1973-74 | Sid Gillman | 8-15-0 |
| 1975-80 | O.A. (Bum) Phillips | 59-38-0 |
| 1981-83 | Ed Biles*** | 8-23-0 |
| 1983 | Chuck Studley | 2-8-0 |

*Released after five games in 1961
**Released after five games in 1973
***Released after six games in 1983

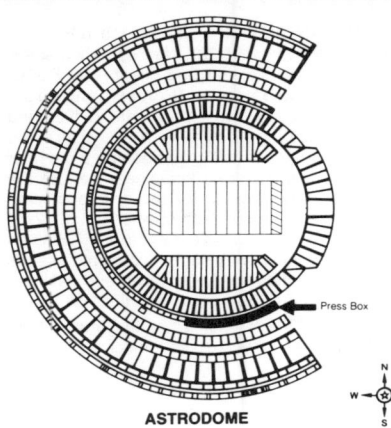

**ASTRODOME**

Press Box

N
W E
S

## RECORD HOLDERS
### Individual Records—Career
| Category | Name | Performance |
|---|---|---|
| Rushing (Yds.) | Earl Campbell, 1978-1983 | 8,296 |
| Passing (Yds.) | George Blanda, 1960-66 | 19,149 |
| Passing (TDs) | George Blanda, 1960-66 | 165 |
| Receiving (No.) | Charles Hennigan, 1960-66 | 410 |
| Receiving (Yds.) | Ken Burrough, 1971-1982 | 6,907 |
| Interceptions | Jim Norton, 1960-68 | 45 |
| Punting (Avg.) | Jim Norton, 1960-68 | 42.3 |
| Punt Return (Avg.) | Billy Johnson, 1974-1980 | 13.2 |
| Kickoff Return (Avg.) | Bobby Jancik, 1962-67 | 26.4 |
| Field Goals | George Blanda, 1960-66 | 91 |
| Touchdowns (Tot.) | Earl Campbell, 1978-1983 | 69 |
| Points | George Blanda, 1960-66 | 596 |

### Individual Records—Single Season
| Category | Name | Performance |
|---|---|---|
| Rushing (Yds.) | Earl Campbell, 1980 | 1,934 |
| Passing (Yds.) | George Blanda, 1961 | 3,330 |
| Passing (TDs) | George Blanda, 1961 | 36 |
| Receiving (No.) | Charles Hennigan, 1964 | 101 |
| Receiving (Yds.) | Charles Hennigan, 1961 | 1,746 |
| Interceptions | Fred Glick, 1963 | 12 |
| | Mike Reinfeldt, 1979 | 12 |
| Punting (Avg.) | Jim Norton, 1965 | 44.2 |
| Punt Return (Avg.) | Billy Johnson, 1977 | 15.4 |
| Kickoff Return (Avg.) | Ken Hall, 1960 | 31.2 |
| Field Goals | Toni Fritsch, 1979 | 21 |
| Touchdowns (Tot.) | Earl Campbell, 1979 | 19 |
| Points | George Blanda, 1960 | 115 |

### Individual Records—Single Game
| Category | Name | Performance |
|---|---|---|
| Rushing (Yds.) | Billy Cannon, 12-10-61 | 216 |
| Passing (Yds.) | George Blanda, 10-29-61 | 464 |
| Passing (TDs) | George Blanda, 11-19-61 | 7 |
| Receiving (No.) | Charles Hennigan, 10-13-61 | 13 |
| Receiving (Yds.) | Charles Hennigan, 10-13-61 | 272 |
| Interceptions | Many times | 3 |
| | Last time by Willie Alexander, 11-14-71 | |
| Field Goals | Skip Butler, 10-12-75 | 6 |
| Touchdowns (Tot.) | Billy Cannon, 12-10-61 | 5 |
| Points | Billy Cannon, 12-10-61 | 30 |

## 1983 TEAM STATISTICS

| | Houston | Opp. |
|---|---|---|
| Total First Downs | 295 | 332 |
| Rushing | 120 | 161 |
| Passing | 155 | 150 |
| Penalty | 20 | 21 |
| Third Down Efficiency | 87/223 | 85/205 |
| Third Down Percentage | 39.0 | 41.5 |
| Total Net Yards | 4900 | 5632 |
| Total Offensive Plays | 1033 | 1031 |
| Avg. Gain per Play | 4.7 | 5.5 |
| Avg. Gain per Game | 306.3 | 352.0 |
| Net Yards Rushing | 1998 | 2787 |
| Total Rushing Plays | 502 | 576 |
| Avg. Gain per Rush | 4.0 | 4.8 |
| Avg. Gain Rushing per Game | 124.9 | 174.2 |
| Net Yards Passing | 2902 | 2845 |
| Lost Attempting to Pass | 49/384 | 31/250 |
| Gross Yards Passing | 3286 | 3095 |
| Attempts/Completions | 482/260 | 424/252 |
| Percent Completed | 53.9 | 59.4 |
| Had Intercepted | 29 | 14 |
| Avg. Net Passing per Game | 181.4 | 177.8 |
| Punts/Avg. | 80/39.2 | 65/39.5 |
| Punt Returns/Avg. | 20/8.0 | 47/7.5 |
| Kickoff Returns/Avg. | 83/20.2 | 61/21.0 |
| Interceptions/Avg. Ret. | 14/9.6 | 29/13.5 |
| Penalties/Yards | 84/784 | 104/825 |
| Fumbles/Ball Lost | 26/18 | 34/15 |
| Total Points | 288 | 460 |
| Avg. Points per Game | 18.0 | 28.8 |
| Touchdowns | 34 | 54 |
| Rushing | 16 | 23 |
| Passing | 16 | 26 |
| Returns and Recoveries | 2 | 5 |
| Field Goals | 17/21 | 29/36 |
| Conversions | 33/34 | 49/54 |
| Safeties | 0 | 0 |
| Avg. Time of Possession | 29:40 | 30:20 |

## 1983 TEAM RECORD
### Preseason (0-4)

| Date | Houston | | Opponents |
|---|---|---|---|
| 8/4 | 0 | *Baltimore | 15 |
| 8/13 | 17 | *Tampa Bay | 23 |
| 8/20 | 13 | New Orleans | 20 |
| 8/27 | 31 | Dallas | 34 |
| | 61 | | 92 |

### Regular Season (2-14)

| Date | Houston | | Opp. | Att. |
|---|---|---|---|---|
| 9/4 | 38 | *Green Bay (OT) | 41 | 44,073 |
| 9/11 | 6 | Los Angeles Raiders | 20 | 37,526 |
| 9/18 | 28 | *Pittsburgh | 40 | 44,150 |
| 9/25 | 13 | Buffalo | 30 | 60,070 |
| 10/2 | 10 | Pittsburgh | 17 | 56,901 |
| 10/9 | 14 | *Denver | 26 | 44,209 |
| 10/16 | 14 | Minnesota | 34 | 58,910 |
| 10/23 | 10 | *Kansas City (OT) | 13 | 39,462 |
| 10/30 | 19 | Cleveland (OT) | 25 | 66,955 |
| 11/6 | 14 | *Cincinnati | 55 | 39,706 |
| 11/13 | 27 | *Detroit | 17 | 40,660 |
| 11/20 | 10 | Cincinnati | 38 | 46,375 |
| 11/27 | 24 | Tampa Bay | 33 | 38,625 |
| 12/4 | 17 | *Miami | 24 | 39,434 |
| 12/11 | 34 | *Cleveland | 27 | 29,746 |
| 12/18 | 10 | Baltimore | 20 | 20,418 |
| | 288 | | 460 | 707,220 |

*Home Game    (OT) Overtime

### Score by Periods

| Houston | 67 | 57 | 67 | 97 | 0 | — | 288 |
|---|---|---|---|---|---|---|---|
| Opponents | 100 | 157 | 81 | 110 | 12 | — | 460 |

### Attendance
Home 321,440    Away 385,780    Total 707,220
Single game home record, 55,293 (12-10-79)
Single season home record, 400,156 (1980)

## 1983 INDIVIDUAL STATISTICS

### Rushing

| | Att. | Yds. | Avg. | LG | TD |
|---|---|---|---|---|---|
| Campbell | 322 | 1301 | 4.0 | 42 | 12 |
| Moriarty | 65 | 321 | 4.9 | 80 | 3 |
| Craft | 55 | 147 | 2.7 | 8 | 0 |
| Luck | 17 | 55 | 3.2 | 17 | 0 |
| Walls | 5 | 44 | 8.8 | 14 | 0 |
| Nielsen | 8 | 43 | 5.4 | 20 | 0 |
| Edwards | 16 | 40 | 2.5 | 9 | 0 |
| Smith | 2 | 16 | 8.0 | 9 | 0 |
| Manning | 2 | 13 | 6.5 | 11 | 0 |
| Crutchfield | 3 | 7 | 2.3 | 5 | 0 |
| Allen | 1 | 5 | 5.0 | 5 | 0 |
| Dressel | 1 | 3 | 3.0 | 3 | 0 |
| Renfro | 1 | 3 | 3.0 | 3 | 0 |
| C. Brown | 3 | 0 | 0.0 | 1t | 1 |
| James | 1 | 0 | 0.0 | 0 | 0 |
| Houston | 502 | 1998 | 4.0 | 80 | 16 |
| Opponents | 576 | 2787 | 4.8 | 52 | 23 |

### Passing

| | Att. | Comp. | Pct. | Yds. | TD | Int. | Tkld. | Rate |
|---|---|---|---|---|---|---|---|---|
| Luck | 217 | 124 | 57.1 | 1375 | 8 | 13 | 16/138 | 63.4 |
| Nielsen | 175 | 90 | 51.4 | 1125 | 5 | 8 | 22/163 | 62.2 |
| Manning | 88 | 44 | 50.0 | 755 | 2 | 8 | 11/83 | 49.2 |
| Bryant | 1 | 1 | 100.0 | 24 | 1 | 0 | 0/0 | 158.3 |
| James | 1 | 1 | 100.0 | 7 | 0 | 0 | 0/0 | 95.8 |
| Houston | 482 | 260 | 53.9 | 3286 | 16 | 29 | 49/384 | 61.4 |
| Opponents | 424 | 252 | 59.4 | 3095 | 26 | 14 | 31/250 | 88.7 |

### Receiving

| | No. | Yds. | Avg. | LG | TD |
|---|---|---|---|---|---|
| Smith | 83 | 1176 | 14.2 | 47t | 6 |
| Dressel | 32 | 316 | 9.9 | 35t | 4 |
| Renfro | 23 | 316 | 13.7 | 38t | 2 |
| Campbell | 19 | 216 | 11.4 | 66 | 0 |
| Bryant | 16 | 211 | 13.2 | 26 | 0 |
| McCloskey | 16 | 137 | 8.6 | 20 | 1 |
| Holston | 14 | 205 | 14.6 | 43 | 0 |
| Walls | 12 | 276 | 23.0 | 48 | 1 |
| Arnold | 12 | 137 | 11.4 | 37 | 1 |
| Craft | 12 | 99 | 8.3 | 14 | 0 |
| Edwards | 9 | 79 | 8.8 | 20 | 1 |
| Casper | 7 | 79 | 11.3 | 17 | 0 |
| Moriarty | 4 | 32 | 8.0 | 12 | 0 |
| Kempf | 1 | 7 | 7.0 | 7 | 0 |
| Houston | 260 | 3286 | 12.6 | 66 | 16 |
| Opponents | 252 | 3095 | 12.3 | 74t | 26 |

### Interceptions

| | No. | Yds. | Avg. | LG | TD |
|---|---|---|---|---|---|
| Tullis | 5 | 65 | 13.0 | 44 | 0 |
| Kay | 2 | 31 | 15.5 | 27 | 0 |
| Bostic | 2 | 0 | 0.0 | 0 | 0 |
| Reinfeldt | 1 | 19 | 19.0 | 19 | 0 |
| S. Brown | 1 | 16 | 16.0 | 16 | 0 |
| Bingham | 1 | 4 | 4.0 | 4 | 0 |
| Abraham | 1 | 0 | 0.0 | 0 | 0 |
| Riley | 1 | 0 | 0.0 | 0 | 0 |
| Houston | 14 | 135 | 9.6 | 44 | 0 |
| Opponents | 29 | 392 | 13.5 | 71t | 2 |

### Punting

| | No. | Yds. | Avg. | In 20 | LG |
|---|---|---|---|---|---|
| James | 79 | 3136 | 39.7 | 12 | 53 |
| Houston | 80 | 3136 | 39.2 | 12 | 53 |
| Opponents | 65 | 2567 | 39.5 | 19 | 60 |

### Punt Returns

| | No. | FC | Yds. | Avg. | LG | TD |
|---|---|---|---|---|---|---|
| Roaches | 20 | 9 | 159 | 8.0 | 23 | 0 |
| Houston | 20 | 9 | 159 | 8.0 | 23 | 0 |
| Opponents | 47 | 15 | 354 | 7.5 | 43 | 0 |

### Kickoff Returns

| | No. | Yds. | Avg. | LG | TD |
|---|---|---|---|---|---|
| S. Brown | 31 | 795 | 25.6 | 93t | 1 |
| Roaches | 34 | 641 | 18.9 | 97t | 1 |
| Walls | 9 | 110 | 12.2 | 25 | 0 |
| Dressel | 4 | 40 | 10.0 | 13 | 0 |
| Moriarty | 2 | 25 | 12.5 | 16 | 0 |
| Hunt | 1 | 12 | 12.0 | 12 | 0 |
| McCloskey | 1 | 11 | 11.0 | 11 | 0 |
| Tullis | 1 | 16 | 16.0 | 16 | 0 |
| Riley | 0 | 26 | — | 26 | 0 |
| Houston | 83 | 1676 | 20.2 | 97t | 2 |
| Opponents | 61 | 1280 | 21.0 | 55 | 0 |

### Scoring

| | TD | TD R | TD P | TD Rt | PAT | FG | TP |
|---|---|---|---|---|---|---|---|
| Kempf | | | | | 33/34 | 17/21 | 84 |
| Campbell | 12 | 12 | 0 | 0 | | | 72 |
| Smith | 6 | 0 | 6 | 0 | | | 36 |
| Dressel | 4 | 0 | 4 | 0 | | | 24 |
| Moriarty | 3 | 3 | 0 | 0 | | | 18 |
| Renfro | 2 | 0 | 2 | 0 | | | 12 |
| Arnold | 1 | 0 | 1 | 0 | | | 6 |
| C. Brown | 1 | 1 | 0 | 0 | | | 6 |
| S. Brown | 1 | 0 | 0 | 1 | | | 6 |
| Edwards | 1 | 0 | 1 | 0 | | | 6 |
| McCloskey | 1 | 0 | 1 | 0 | | | 6 |
| Roaches | 1 | 0 | 0 | 1 | | | 6 |
| Walls | 1 | 0 | 1 | 0 | | | 6 |
| Houston | 34 | 16 | 16 | 2 | 33/34 | 17/21 | 288 |
| Opponents | 54 | 23 | 26 | 5 | 49/53 | 29/36 | 460 |

## FIRST-ROUND SELECTIONS
(If Club had no first-round selection, first player drafted is listed with round in parentheses.)

| Year | Player, College, Position |
|---|---|
| 1960 | Billy Cannon, Louisiana State, RB |
| 1961 | Mike Ditka, Pittsburgh, E |
| 1962 | Ray Jacobs, Howard Payne, DT |
| 1963 | Danny Brabham, Arkansas, LB |
| 1964 | Scott Appleton, Texas, DT |
| 1965 | Lawrence Elkins, Baylor, WR |
| 1966 | Tommy Nobis, Texas, LB |
| 1967 | George Webster, Michigan State, LB |
| | Tom Regner, Notre Dame, G |
| 1968 | Mac Haik, Mississippi, WR (2) |
| 1969 | Ron Pritchard, Arizona State, LB |
| 1970 | Doug Wilkerson, N. Carolina Central, G |
| 1971 | Dan Pastorini, Santa Clara, QB |
| 1972 | Greg Sampson, Stanford, DE |
| 1973 | John Matuszak, Tampa, DE |
| | George Amundson, Iowa State, RB |
| 1974 | Steve Manstedt, Nebraska, LB (4) |
| 1975 | Robert Brazile, Jackson State, LB |
| | Don Hardeman, Texas A&I, RB |
| 1976 | Mike Barber, Louisiana Tech, TE (2) |
| 1977 | Morris Towns, Missouri, T |
| 1978 | Earl Campbell, Texas, RB |
| 1979 | Mike Stensrud, Iowa State, DE (2) |
| 1980 | Angelo Fields, Michigan State, T (2) |
| 1981 | Michael Holston, Morgan State, WR (3) |
| 1982 | Mike Munchak, Penn State, G |
| 1983 | Bruce Matthews, Southern California, T |
| 1984 | Dean Steinkuhler, Nebraska, T |

## HOUSTON OILERS 1984 VETERAN ROSTER

| No. | Name | Pos. | Ht. | Wt. | Birth-date | NFL Exp. | College | Birthplace | Residence | Games in '83 |
|---|---|---|---|---|---|---|---|---|---|---|
| 56 | Abraham, Robert | LB | 6-1 | 215 | 7/13/60 | 3 | North Carolina State | Myrtle Beach, S.C. | Raleigh, N.C. | 14 |
| 87 | Arnold, Walt | TE | 6-3 | 234 | 8/31/58 | 5 | New Mexico | Galveston, Tex. | Albuquerque, N.M. | 13 |
| 80 | Bailey, Harold | WR | 6-2 | 196 | 4/12/57 | 3 | Oklahoma State | Houston, Tex. | Missouri City, Tex. | 0* |
| 75 | Baker, Jesse | DE | 6-5 | 272 | 7/10/57 | 6 | Jacksonville State | Conyers, Ga. | Stafford, Tex. | 16 |
| 54 | Bingham, Gregg | LB | 6-1 | 225 | 3/13/51 | 12 | Purdue | Chicago, Ill. | Missouri City, Tex. | 16 |
| 25 | Bostic, Keith | S | 6-1 | 212 | 1/17/61 | 2 | Michigan | Ann Arbor, Mich. | Houston, Tex. | 16 |
| 52 | Brazile, Robert | LB | 6-4 | 237 | 2/7/53 | 10 | Jackson State | Pineland, Ala. | Houston, Tex. | 16 |
| 24 | Brown, Steve | CB-KR | 5-11 | 188 | 5/20/60 | 2 | Oregon | Sacramento, Calif. | Houston, Tex. | 16 |
| 81 | Bryant, Steve | WR | 6-2 | 191 | 10/10/59 | 3 | Purdue | Los Angeles, Calif. | Houston, Tex. | 16 |
| 34 | Campbell, Earl | RB | 5-11 | 238 | 3/29/55 | 7 | Texas | Tyler, Tex. | Houston, Tex. | 14 |
| 58 | †Carter, David | C | 6-2 | 260 | 11/27/53 | 8 | Western Kentucky | Vincennes, Ind. | Sugar Land, Tex. | 16 |
| 40 | Craft, Donnie | RB | 6-0 | 205 | 11/19/59 | 3 | Louisville | Panama City, Fla. | Missouri City, Tex. | 15 |
| 88 | Dressel, Chris | TE | 6-4 | 231 | 2/7/61 | 2 | Stanford | Placentia, Calif. | Palo Alto, Calif. | 16 |
| 32 | Edwards, Stan | RB | 6-0 | 210 | 5/20/60 | 3 | Michigan | Detroit, Mich. | Detroit, Mich. | 14 |
| 78 | Foster, Jerome | DE | 6-2 | 258 | 7/25/60 | 2 | Ohio State | Detroit, Mich. | Warren, Mich. | 16 |
| 77 | France, Doug | T | 6-5 | 266 | 4/26/53 | 9 | Ohio State | Dayton, Ohio | Fountain Valley, Calif. | 13 |
| 90 | Hamm, Bob | DE | 6-4 | 248 | 4/24/59 | 2 | Nevada-Reno | Kansas City, Mo. | Sunnyvale, Calif. | 16 |
| 36 | Hartwig, Carter | S | 6-0 | 207 | 2/2/56 | 6 | Southern California | Culver City, Calif. | Missouri City, Tex. | 16 |
| 21 | Hatchett, Derrick | CB | 5-11 | 184 | 8/14/58 | 5 | Texas | Bryan, Tex. | Baltimore, Md. | 8* |
| 23 | Hill, Greg | CB | 6-1 | 189 | 2/12/61 | 2 | Oklahoma State | Orange, Tex. | Houston, Tex. | 14 |
| 84 | †Holston, Mike | WR | 6-3 | 188 | 1/8/58 | 4 | Morgan State | Washington, D.C. | Houston, Tex. | 16 |
| 66 | Howell, Pat | G | 6-6 | 260 | 3/12/57 | 6 | Southern California | Fresno, Calif. | Clovis, Calif. | 9* |
| 50 | Hunt, Daryl | LB | 6-3 | 235 | 11/3/56 | 6 | Oklahoma | Odessa, Tex. | Sugar Land, Tex. | 16 |
| 6 | James, John | P | 6-3 | 196 | 1/21/49 | 13 | Florida | Panama City, Fla. | Gainesville, Fla. | 16 |
| 86 | t-Johnson, Butch | WR | 6-1 | 187 | 5/28/54 | 9 | Cal-Riverside | Los Angeles, Calif. | Carrollton, Tex. | 16 |
| 57 | Joiner, Tim | LB | 6-4 | 224 | 1/7/61 | 2 | Louisiana State | Los Angeles, Calif. | Baton Rouge, La. | 15 |
| 22 | Kay, Bill | CB | 6-1 | 190 | 1/10/60 | 4 | Purdue | Detroit, Mich. | Houston, Tex. | 16 |
| 4 | †Kempf, Florian | K | 5-9 | 170 | 5/25/56 | 3 | Pennsylvania | Philadelphia, Pa. | Philadelphia, Pa. | 16 |
| 71 | Kennard, Ken | DE | 6-2 | 255 | 10/4/54 | 8 | Angelo State | Fort Worth, Tex. | Houston, Tex. | 0* |
| 10 | Luck, Oliver | QB | 6-2 | 193 | 4/5/60 | 3 | West Virginia | Cleveland, Ohio | Houston, Tex. | 7 |
| 74 | Matthews, Bruce | G-T | 6-4 | 269 | 8/8/61 | 2 | Southern California | Arcadia, Calif. | Sierra Madre, Calif. | 16 |
| 89 | McCloskey, Mike | TE | 6-5 | 240 | 2/2/61 | 2 | Penn State | Philadelphia, Pa. | Philadelphia, Pa. | 16 |
| 26 | Meadows, Darryl | S | 6-1 | 199 | 2/15/61 | 2 | Toledo | Cincinnati, Ohio | Cincinnati, Ohio | 16 |
| 30 | Moriarty, Larry | RB | 6-1 | 228 | 4/24/58 | 2 | Notre Dame | Santa Barbara, Calif. | San Luis Obispo, Calif. | 16 |
| 63 | Munchak, Mike | G | 6-3 | 275 | 3/5/60 | 3 | Penn State | Scranton, Pa. | Sugar Land, Tex. | 16 |
| 12 | Ransom, Brian | QB | 6-3 | 205 | 7/9/60 | 2 | Tennessee State | Omaha, Neb. | Houston, Tex. | 0* |
| 37 | Reinfeldt, Mike | S | 6-2 | 192 | 5/6/53 | 9 | Wisconsin-Milwaukee | Baraboo, Wis. | Missouri City, Tex. | 4 |
| 53 | Riley, Avon | LB | 6-3 | 225 | 2/10/58 | 4 | UCLA | Savannah, Ga. | Stafford, Tex. | 16 |
| 85 | Roaches, Carl | KR-WR | 5-8 | 170 | 10/2/53 | 5 | Texas A&M | Houston, Tex. | Missouri City, Tex. | 16 |
| 73 | Salem, Harvey | T | 6-6 | 264 | 1/15/61 | 2 | California | Berkeley, Calif. | Berkeley, Calif. | 16 |
| 62 | †Schuhmacher, John | G | 6-3 | 267 | 9/23/55 | 4 | Southern California | Salem, Ore. | Missouri City, Tex. | 1 |
| 83 | †Smith, Tim | WR | 6-2 | 203 | 3/20/57 | 5 | Nebraska | Tucson, Ariz. | Stafford, Tex. | 16 |
| 72 | Sochia, Brian | NT | 6-3 | 250 | 7/21/61 | 2 | Northwest Oklahoma | Massena, N.Y. | Brasher Falls, N.Y. | 12 |
| 67 | Stensrud, Mike | NT | 6-5 | 285 | 2/19/56 | 6 | Iowa State | Lake Mills, Iowa | Ames, Iowa | 16 |
| 68 | †Studdard, Les | C | 6-4 | 260 | 12/14/58 | 3 | Texas | El Paso, Tex. | Moore, Tex. | 6 |
| 51 | Thompson, Ted | LB | 6-1 | 219 | 1/17/53 | 10 | Southern Methodist | Atlanta, Tex. | Missouri City, Tex. | 16 |
| 76 | †Towns, Morris | T | 6-4 | 263 | 1/10/54 | 8 | Missouri | St. Louis, Mo. | Houston, Tex. | 14 |
| 20 | Tullis, Willie | CB | 6-0 | 193 | 4/5/58 | 4 | Troy State | Newville, Ala. | Houston, Tex. | 16 |
| 86 | Walls, Herkie | WR | 5-8 | 154 | 7/18/61 | 2 | Texas | Garland, Tex. | Garland, Tex. | 16 |
| 79 | Whitley, Wilson | NT | 6-3 | 265 | 4/28/55 | 7 | Houston | Brenham, Tex. | Houston, Tex. | 0* |
| 33 | Wilson, J.C. | CB-S | 6-0 | 184 | 3/11/56 | 7 | Pittsburgh | Cleveland, Ohio | Houston, Tex. | 13 |

* Bailey missed '83 season due to injury; Hatchett played 7 games with Baltimore, 1 with Houston in '83; Howell played 2 games with Atlanta, 7 with Houston; Kennard active for 5 games, but did not play; Ransom active for 12 games, but did not play; Whitley active for 1 game, but did not play.

†Option playout; subject to developments.

t-Oilers traded for Johnson (Dallas).

Traded—Running back Dwayne Crutchfield to L.A. Rams, wide receiver Mike Renfro to Dallas.

Retired—Elvin Bethea, 16-year defensive end, 7 games in '83; Gifford Nielsen, 6-year quarterback, 7 games in '83.

Also played with Oilers in '83—RB Gary Allen (1 game), RB Curtis Brown (2), TE Dave Casper (3), RB Vagas Ferguson (1), QB Archie Manning (3), CB Tate Randle (2), G Al Steinfeld (8), G Ralph Williams (1).

## COACHING STAFF

### Head Coach, Hugh Campbell

**Pro Career:** Named head coach of the Oilers January 3, 1984 after spending 1983 season as head coach with the Los Angeles Express of USFL where he compiled an 8-10 record. From 1977-1982, Campbell was head coach of the Edmonton Eskimos of the Canadian Football League. Was Western Division champion all six years in Edmonton and was five time winner of Grey Cup from 1978-1982. Campbell's .773 winning percentage as head coach is best in CFL history. Pro player with Saskatchewan Roughriders of the CFL from 1963-1967, and again in 1969. Still holds numerous Roughriders and CFL records in receiving. Originally a fourth-round draft pick of San Francisco 49ers as wide receiver.

**Background:** Wide receiver at Washington State University from 1959-1962. Named to several Bowl games after senior season. Assistant coach at Washington State from 1965-1969. Head Coach of Whitworth College in Spokane, Washington from 1970-1976.

**Personal:** Born May 21, 1941, San Jose, California. Hugh and wife, Louise, have four children—Robin, Jill, Rick, and Molly.

### Assistant Coaches

**Bill Allerheiligen,** weight and strength coordinator; born February 10, 1951, Concordia, Kan., lives in Sugar Land, Tex. Nebraska 1973. No college or pro playing experience. College Coach: Kearney State 1976, Nebraska 1977-78, Kansas State 1979-80, Notre Dame 1981. Pro coach: Joined Oilers in 1982.

**O. Kay Dalton,** offensive coordinator; born May 4, 1932, Moab, Utah, lives in Missouri City, Tex. Tight end Colorado State 1950-54. No pro playing experience. College Coach: Trinidad State 1958-60, Western State 1961-65, Colorado 1971-72. Pro coach: Montreal Alouettes (CFL) 1966-69 (head coach 1967-69), British Columbia Lions (CFL) 1970, Denver Broncos 1973-76, Buffalo Bills 1977, Kansas City Chiefs 1978-82, joined Oilers in 1983.

**John Devlin,** linebackers; born April 12, 1937, Norristown, Pa., lives in Houston, Tex. Tackle West Chester State 1956-58. No pro playing experience. College coach: Army 1963-65, Virginia Tech 1966-70, Florida State 1971-72, Maryland 1973-81, Kentucky 1982-83. Pro coach: First year with Oilers.

**Gene Gaines,** special teams; born June 26, 1938, Los Angeles, Calif., lives in Houston, Tex. Running back-defensive back UCLA 1958-60. Pro running back Ottawa Roughriders (CFL) 1962-69, Montreal Alouettes (CFL) 1961, 1970-76. Pro coach: Montreal Alouettes (CFL) 1976-81, Edmonton Eskimos (CFL) 1982, Los Angeles Express (USFL) 1983, first year with Oilers.

**Jerry Glanville,** defensive coordinator; born October 14, 1941, Detroit, Mich., lives in Houston, Tex. Guard-linebacker Northern Michigan 1961-63. No pro playing experience. College coach: Northern Michigan 1966, Western Kentucky 1967, Georgia Tech 1968-73. Pro coach: Detroit Lions 1974-76, Atlanta Falcons 1977-82, Buffalo Bills 1983, first year with Oilers.

**Kenny Houston,** defensive backfield; born November 12, 1944, Lufkin, Tex., lives in Kingwood, Tex. Linebacker Prairie View A&M 1962-1966. Pro defensive back Houston Oilers 1967-72, Washington Redskins 1973-1980. Pro coach: Joined Oilers in 1982.

**Bruce Lemmerman,** receivers; born October 4, 1945, Los Angeles, Calif., lives in Houston, Tex. Quarterback San Fernando Valley State 1965-67. Pro quarterback Atlanta Falcons 1968-70, Edmonton Eskimos (CFL) 1971-79, Hamilton Tiger Cats (CFL) 1980. Pro coach: Edmonton Eskimos 1981-82, Los Angeles Express (USFL) 1983, first year with Oilers.

**Bob Padilla,** defensive line; born February 11, 1936, Santa Ana, Calif., lives in Houston, Tex. Lineman Fresno State. No pro playing experience. College coach: Fresno State 1968-72, 1978-79, San Jose State 1973-75, Michigan State 1976-78, Washington State 1980-81, Arizona State 1982-83. Pro coach: First year with Oilers.

**Al Roberts,** running backs; born January 6, 1944, Fresno Calif., lives in Houston, Tex. Running back Puget Sound 1963-65. No pro playing experience. College coach: Washington 1977-82. Pro coach: Los Angeles Express (USFL) 1983, first year with Oilers.

**Bill Walsh,** offensive line; born September 8, 1927, Phillipsburg, N.J., lives in Houston, Tex. Center Notre Dame 1945-48. Pro center Pittsburgh Steelers 1949-54. College coach: Notre Dame 1955-58, Kansas State 1959. Pro coach: Kansas City Chiefs 1960-74, Atlanta Falcons 1975-82, joined Oilers in 1983.

## HOUSTON OILERS 1984 FIRST-YEAR ROSTER

| Name | Pos. | Ht. | Wt. | Birth-date | College | Birthplace | Residence | How Acq. |
|---|---|---|---|---|---|---|---|---|
| Allen, Patrick | CB | 5-10 | 180 | 8/26/61 | Utah State | Seattle, Wash. | Seattle, Wash. | D4a |
| Baugh, Kevin | WR-KR | 5-9 | 175 | 9/27/61 | Penn State | Deer Park, N.Y. | Deer Park, N.Y. | D8 |
| Coty, Paul | C | 6-2 | 252 | 5/4/61 | Washington | Duluth, Minn. | Centralia, Wash. | FA |
| Craver, Jon (1) | LB | 6-3 | 240 | 3/24/61 | James Madison | York, Pa. | Hagerstown, Md. | FA |
| Donaldson, Jeff | CB-S | 6-0 | 180 | 4/19/62 | Colorado | Ft. Collins, Colo. | Ft. Collins, Colo. | D9 |
| Eason, Bo | S | 6-2 | 205 | 3/10/61 | Cal-Davis | Walnut Grove, Calif. | Walnut Grove, Calif. | D2a |
| Gannon, Chuck | T | 6-5 | 274 | 3/7/61 | Indiana | Detroit, Mich. | Ypsilanti, Mich. | FA |
| Grimsley, John | LB | 6-2 | 225 | 2/25/62 | Kentucky | Canton, Ohio | Canton, Ohio | D6 |
| Jenkins, Melvin | RB | 5-10 | 203 | 10/15/58 | Morehouse | Colorado Spgs., Colo. | East Orange N.J. | FA |
| Johnson, Mike | DE | 6-5 | 225 | 4/24/62 | Illinois | Chicago, Ill. | Landover, Md. | D9a |
| Jones, Juan | LB | 6-2 | 220 | 9/6/61 | Morgan State | Dallas, Tex. | Dallas, Tex. | FA |
| Joyner, Willie | RB | 5-10 | 200 | 4/2/62 | Maryland | Brooklyn, N.Y. | Brooklyn, N.Y. | D7 |
| Ledbetter, Weldon | RB | 6-0 | 220 | 10/23/60 | Oklahoma | St. Louis, Mo. | St. Louis, Mo. | FA |
| Lindstrom, Chris (1) | DE | 6-7 | 245 | 4/3/60 | Boston University | Weymouth, Mass. | Weymouth, Mass. | FA |
| Lyday, Allen (1) | S | 5-10 | 180 | 9/16/60 | Nebraska | Wichita, Kan. | Lincoln, Neb. | FA |
| Lyles, Robert | LB | 6-1 | 210 | 3/21/61 | Texas Christian | Los Angeles, Calif. | Ft. Worth, Tex. | D5 |
| Meads, Johnny | LB | 6-2 | 220 | 6/25/61 | Nicholls State | Labadieville, La. | Labadieville, La. | D3 |
| Moon, Warren (1) | QB | 6-3 | 210 | 11/18/56 | Washington | Los Angeles, Calif. | Redmond, Wash. | FA |
| Mullins, Eric | WR | 5-11 | 175 | 7/30/62 | Stanford | Houston, Tex. | Houston, Tex. | D6a |
| Russell, Mike | LB | 6-1 | 230 | 9/12/61 | Toledo | Walbridge, Ohio | Walbridge, Ohio | D9b |
| Smith, Doug | DE | 6-4 | 301 | 6/6/60 | Auburn | Bayboro, N.C. | Bayboro, N.C. | D2 |
| Steinkuhler, Dean | T | 6-3 | 275 | 1/27/61 | Nebraska | Burr, Neb. | Lincoln, Neb. | D1 |
| Studaway, Mark | DE | 6-3 | 250 | 9/20/60 | Tennessee | Memphis, Tenn. | Memphis, Tenn. | D4 |
| Swoboda, Mark | TE | 6-3 | 230 | 11/17/59 | Wisconsin | Chippewa Falls, Wis. | Largo, Fla. | FA |
| Weeks, Louis | LB | 6-1 | 238 | 1/28/61 | Maryland | Baltimore, Md. | Pasadena, Md. | FA |

Players who report to an NFL team for the first time are designated on rosters as rookies (R). If a player reported to an NFL training camp in a previous year but was not on the active squad for three or more regular season or postseason games, he is listed on the first-year roster and designated by a (1). Thereafter, a player who is on the active squad for three or more regular season or postseason games is credited with an additional year of playing experience.

## NOTES

## American Football Conference
## Eastern Division

**Team Colors:** Royal Blue, White, and Silver

**P. O. Box 20000**
**Indianapolis, Indiana 46220**
**Telephone: (317) 252-2658**

### Club Officials

President-Treasurer: Robert Irsay
Vice President-General Manager: James Irsay
Vice President-General Counsel:
   Michael G. Chernoff
Assistant General Manager: Bob Terpening
Director of Player Personnel: Jack Bushofsky
Director of College Scouting: Clyde Powers
Controller: Joe Dezelan
Director of Operations: Pete Ward
Director of Public Relations: Bob Walters
Assistant Director of Public Relations: Bob Eller
Purchasing Administrator: David Filer
Equipment Manager: Jon Scott
Assistant Equipment Manager: John Starliper
Cinematographer: Marty Heckscher
Cheerleader Director: Meg Irsay

**Stadium:** Hoosier Dome • **Capacity:** 61,000
   100 South Capitol Avenue
   Indianapolis, Indiana 46225

**Playing Surface:** AstroTurf

**Training Camp:** Anderson College
   Anderson, Indiana 46011

### 1984 SCHEDULE

**Preseason**

| | | |
|---|---|---|
| Aug. 4 | at Miami | 8:00 |
| Aug. 11 | **New York Giants** | 7:00 |
| Aug. 18 | at Denver | 7:00 |
| Aug. 25 | at Green Bay | 7:00 |

**Regular Season**

| | | |
|---|---|---|
| Sept. 2 | **New York Jets** | 3:00 |
| Sept. 9 | at Houston | 3:00 |
| Sept. 16 | **St. Louis** | 12:00 |
| Sept. 23 | at Miami | 4:00 |
| Sept. 30 | **Buffalo** | 12:00 |
| Oct. 7 | **Washington** | 12:00 |
| Oct. 14 | at Philadelphia | 1:00 |
| Oct. 21 | **Pittsburgh** | 12:00 |
| Oct. 28 | at Dallas | 12:00 |
| Nov. 4 | **San Diego** | 1:00 |
| Nov. 11 | at New York Jets | 1:00 |
| Nov. 18 | **New England** | 1:00 |
| Nov. 25 | at Los Angeles Raiders | 1:00 |
| Dec. 2 | at Buffalo | 1:00 |
| Dec. 9 | **Miami** | 1:00 |
| Dec. 16 | at New England | 1:00 |

## COLTS COACHING HISTORY

### (229-201-7)

| | | |
|---|---|---|
| 1953 | Keith Molesworth | 3-9-0 |
| 1954-62 | Weeb Ewbank | 60-53-1 |
| 1963-69 | Don Shula | 73-25-4 |
| 1970-72 | Don McCafferty* | 26-11-1 |
| 1972 | John Sandusky | 4-5-0 |
| 1973-74 | Howard Schnellenberger** | 4-13-0 |
| 1974 | Joe Thomas | 2-9-0 |
| 1975-79 | Ted Marchibroda | 41-36-0 |
| 1980-81 | Mike McCormack | 9-23-0 |
| 1982-83 | Frank Kush | 7-17-1 |

*Released after five games in 1972
**Released after three games in 1974

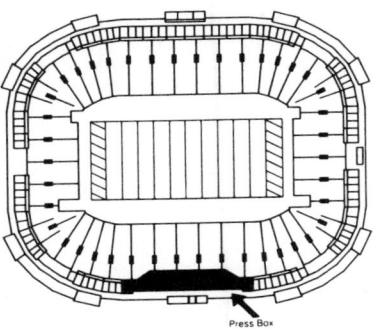

**HOOSIER DOME**

## RECORD HOLDERS

### Individual Records—Career

| Category | Name | Performance |
|---|---|---|
| Rushing (Yds.) | Lydell Mitchell, 1972-77 | 5,487 |
| Passing (Yds.) | Johnny Unitas, 1956-1972 | 39,768 |
| Passing (TDs) | Johnny Unitas, 1956-1972 | 287 |
| Receiving (No.) | Raymond Berry, 1955-1967 | 631 |
| Receiving (Yds.) | Raymond Berry, 1955-1967 | 9,275 |
| Interceptions | Bob Boyd, 1960-68 | 57 |
| Punting (Avg.) | Rohn Stark, 1982-83 | 45.0 |
| Punt Return (Avg.) | Wendell Harris, 1964 | 12.6 |
| Kickoff Return (Avg.) | Jim Duncan, 1969-1971 | 32.5 |
| Field Goals | Lou Michaels, 1964-69 | 107 |
| Touchdowns (Tot.) | Lenny Moore, 1956-1967 | 113 |
| Points | Lenny Moore, 1956-1967 | 678 |

### Individual Records—Single Season

| Category | Name | Performance |
|---|---|---|
| Rushing (Yds.) | Lydell Mitchell, 1976 | 1,200 |
| Passing (Yds.) | Johnny Unitas, 1963 | 3,481 |
| Passing (TDs) | Johnny Unitas, 1959 | 32 |
| Receiving (No.) | Joe Washington, 1979 | 82 |
| Receiving (Yds.) | Raymond Berry, 1960 | 1,298 |
| Interceptions | Tom Keane, 1953 | 11 |
| Punting (Avg.) | David Lee, 1966 | 45.6 |
| Punt Return (Avg.) | Wendell Harris, 1964 | 12.6 |
| Kickoff Return (Avg.) | Jim Duncan, 1970 | 35.4 |
| Field Goals | Raul Allegre, 1983 | 30 |
| Touchdowns (Tot.) | Lenny Moore, 1964 | 20 |
| Points | Lenny Moore, 1964 | 120 |

### Individual Records—Single Game

| Category | Name | Performance |
|---|---|---|
| Rushing (Yds.) | Norm Bulaich, 9-19-71 | 198 |
| Passing (Yds.) | Johnny Unitas, 9-17-67 | 401 |
| Passing (TDs) | Gary Cuozzo, 11-14-65 | 5 |
| Receiving (No.) | Lydell Mitchell, 12-15-74 | 13 |
| | Joe Washington, 9-2-79 | 13 |
| Receiving (Yds.) | Raymond Berry, 11-10-57 | 224 |
| Interceptions | Many times | 3 |
| | Last time by Lyle Blackwood, 11-20-77 | |
| Field Goals | Raul Allegre, 10-30-83 | 5 |
| Touchdowns (Tot.) | Many times | 4 |
| | Last time by Lydell Mitchell, 10-12-75 | |
| Points | Many times | 24 |
| | Last time by Lydell Mitchell, 10-12-75 | |

## 1983 TEAM STATISTICS

| | Baltimore | Opp. |
|---|---|---|
| Total First Downs | 272 | 321 |
| Rushing | 146 | 123 |
| Passing | 110 | 166 |
| Penalty | 16 | 32 |
| Third Down Efficiency | 78/226 | 87/219 |
| Third Down Percentage | 34.5 | 39.7 |
| Total Net Yards | 5018 | 5640 |
| Total Offensive Plays | 1025 | 1045 |
| Avg. Gain per Play | 4.9 | 5.4 |
| Avg. Gain per Game | 313.6 | 352.5 |
| Net Yards Rushing | 2695 | 2118 |
| Total Rushing Plays | 601 | 516 |
| Avg. Gain per Rush | 4.5 | 4.1 |
| Avg. Gain Rushing per Game | 168.4 | 132.4 |
| Net Yards Passing | 2323 | 3522 |
| Lost Attempting to Pass | 47/340 | 41/310 |
| Gross Yards Passing | 2663 | 3832 |
| Attempts/Completions | 377/188 | 488/281 |
| Percent Completed | 49.9 | 57.6 |
| Had Intercepted | 22 | 20 |
| Avg. Net Passing per Game | 145.2 | 220.1 |
| Punts/Avg. | 91/45.3 | 80/41.6 |
| Punt Returns/Avg. | 44/6.7 | 55/11.7 |
| Kickoff Returns/Avg. | 62/19.3 | 61/18.7 |
| Interceptions/Avg. Ret. | 20/15.7 | 22/5.3 |
| Penalties/Yards | 120/986 | 82/666 |
| Fumbles/Ball Lost | 32/11 | 29/16 |
| Total Points | 264 | 354 |
| Avg. Points per Game | 16.5 | 22.1 |
| Touchdowns | 25 | 45 |
| Rushing | 10 | 13 |
| Passing | 12 | 31 |
| Returns and Recoveries | 3 | 1 |
| Field Goals | 30/35 | 14/23 |
| Conversions | 22/24 | 42/45 |
| Safeties | 1 | 0 |
| Avg. Time of Possession | 29:26 | 30:34 |

## 1983 TEAM RECORD

### Preseason (2-2)

| Date | Baltimore | | Opponents |
|---|---|---|---|
| 8/4 | 15 | Houston | 0 |
| 8/13 | 10 | Minnesota | 7 |
| 8/20 | 14 | New York Giants | 27 |
| 8/26 | 7 | Atlanta | 10 |
| | 46 | | 44 |

### Regular Season (7-9)

| Date | Baltimore | | Opp. | Att. |
|---|---|---|---|---|
| 9/4 | 29 | New England (OT) | 23 | 45,526 |
| 9/11 | 10 | *Denver | 17 | 51,482 |
| 9/18 | 23 | Buffalo | 28 | 40,937 |
| 9/25 | 22 | *Chicago (OT) | 19 | 34,350 |
| 10/2 | 34 | Cincinnati | 31 | 48,104 |
| 10/9 | 12 | *New England | 7 | 35,618 |
| 10/16 | 7 | *Buffalo | 30 | 38,565 |
| 10/23 | 7 | *Miami | 21 | 32,343 |
| 10/30 | 22 | Philadelphia | 21 | 59,150 |
| 11/6 | 17 | New York Jets | 14 | 53,323 |
| 11/13 | 13 | *Pittsburgh | 24 | 57,319 |
| 11/20 | 0 | Miami | 37 | 54,482 |
| 11/27 | 23 | Cleveland | 41 | 65,812 |
| 12/4 | 6 | *New York Jets | 10 | 29,431 |
| 12/11 | 19 | Denver | 21 | 74,854 |
| 12/18 | 20 | *Houston | 10 | 20,418 |
| | 264 | | 354 | 741,714 |

*Home Game    (OT) Overtime

### Score by Periods

| Baltimore | 44 | 86 | 57 | 68 | 9 | — | 264 |
|---|---|---|---|---|---|---|---|
| Opponents | 62 | 136 | 54 | 102 | 0 | — | 354 |

### Attendance

Home 299,526    Away 442,188    Total 741,714
Single game home record, 60,763 (12-14-77)
Single season home record, 418,292 (1968)

## 1983 INDIVIDUAL STATISTICS

### Rushing

| | Att. | Yds. | Avg. | LG | TD |
|---|---|---|---|---|---|
| Dickey | 254 | 1122 | 4.4 | 56 | 4 |
| McMillan | 198 | 802 | 4.1 | 39t | 5 |
| Pagel | 54 | 441 | 8.2 | 33 | 0 |
| Moore | 57 | 205 | 3.6 | 13 | 1 |
| N. Williams | 28 | 77 | 2.8 | 13 | 0 |
| Reed | 2 | 27 | 13.5 | 18 | 0 |
| Dixon | 5 | 14 | 2.8 | 7 | 0 |
| Stark | 1 | 8 | 8.0 | 8 | 0 |
| Herrmann | 1 | 0 | 0.0 | 0 | 0 |
| Krauss | 1 | −1 | −1.0 | −1 | 0 |
| Colts | 601 | 2695 | 4.5 | 56 | 10 |
| Opponents | 516 | 2118 | 4.1 | 77 | 13 |

### Passing

| | Att. | Comp. | Pct. | Yds. | TD | Int. | Tkld. | Rate |
|---|---|---|---|---|---|---|---|---|
| Pagel | 328 | 163 | 49.7 | 2353 | 12 | 17 | 40/278 | 64.0 |
| Herrmann | 36 | 18 | 50.0 | 256 | 0 | 3 | 7/62 | 38.7 |
| Reed | 10 | 6 | 60.0 | 34 | 0 | 1 | 0/0 | 26.7 |
| J. Taylor | 2 | 1 | 50.0 | 20 | 0 | 1 | 0/0 | 45.8 |
| Stark | 1 | 0 | 0.0 | 0 | 0 | 0 | 0/0 | 39.6 |
| Colts | 377 | 188 | 49.9 | 2663 | 12 | 22 | 47/340 | 59.4 |
| Opponents | 488 | 281 | 57.6 | 3832 | 31 | 20 | 41/310 | 86.9 |

### Receiving

| | No. | Yds. | Avg. | LG | TD |
|---|---|---|---|---|---|
| Henry | 30 | 416 | 13.9 | 40t | 4 |
| T. Porter | 28 | 384 | 13.7 | 38 | 0 |
| Bouza | 25 | 385 | 15.4 | 26 | 0 |
| Sherwin | 25 | 358 | 14.3 | 30 | 0 |
| Dickey | 24 | 483 | 20.1 | 72t | 3 |
| McMillan | 24 | 195 | 8.1 | 27 | 1 |
| Butler | 10 | 207 | 20.7 | 60 | 3 |
| Oatis | 6 | 93 | 15.5 | 25 | 0 |
| Moore | 6 | 38 | 6.3 | 16 | 0 |
| Beach | 5 | 56 | 11.2 | 16 | 1 |
| N. Williams | 4 | 46 | 11.5 | 19 | 0 |
| Dixon | 1 | 2 | 2.0 | 2 | 0 |
| Colts | 188 | 2663 | 14.2 | 72t | 12 |
| Opponents | 281 | 3832 | 13.6 | 85t | 31 |

### Interceptions

| | No. | Yds. | Avg. | LG | TD |
|---|---|---|---|---|---|
| Hatchett | 4 | 36 | 9.0 | 25 | 0 |
| Glasgow | 3 | 35 | 11.7 | 18 | 0 |
| K. Anderson | 2 | 81 | 40.5 | 71t | 1 |
| Bracelin | 2 | 19 | 9.5 | 19 | 0 |
| Delaney | 2 | 16 | 8.0 | 11 | 0 |
| Burroughs | 2 | 8 | 4.0 | 8 | 0 |
| Randle | 1 | 41 | 41.0 | 41 | 0 |
| K. Williams | 1 | 32 | 32.0 | 18 | 0 |
| Maxwell | 1 | 31 | 31.0 | 31 | 0 |
| Cooks | 1 | 15 | 15.0 | 15 | 0 |
| L. Anderson | 1 | 0 | 0.0 | 0 | 0 |
| Colts | 20 | 314 | 15.7 | 71t | 1 |
| Opponents | 22 | 117 | 5.3 | 34 | 0 |

### Punting

| | No. | Yds. | Avg. | In 20 | LG |
|---|---|---|---|---|---|
| Stark | 91 | 4124 | 45.3 | 20 | 68 |
| Colts | 91 | 4124 | 45.3 | 20 | 68 |
| Opponents | 80 | 3329 | 41.6 | 27 | 64 |

### Punt Returns

| | No. | FC | Yds. | Avg. | LG | TD |
|---|---|---|---|---|---|---|
| L. Anderson | 20 | 4 | 138 | 6.9 | 20 | 0 |
| R. Porter | 14 | 5 | 104 | 7.4 | 50 | 0 |
| K. Williams | 9 | 4 | 43 | 4.8 | 13 | 0 |
| Glasgow | 1 | 1 | 9 | 9.0 | 9 | 0 |
| Colts | 44 | 14 | 294 | 6.7 | 50 | 0 |
| Opponents | 55 | 7 | 642 | 11.7 | 60t | 1 |

### Kickoff Returns

| | No. | Yds. | Avg. | LG | TD |
|---|---|---|---|---|---|
| K. Williams | 20 | 490 | 24.5 | 90 | 0 |
| R. Porter | 18 | 340 | 18.9 | 28 | 0 |
| L. Anderson | 18 | 309 | 17.2 | 26 | 0 |
| Dixon | 2 | 23 | 11.5 | 14 | 0 |
| Moore | 2 | 40 | 20.0 | 23 | 0 |
| Beach | 1 | 0 | 0.0 | 0 | 0 |
| Bouza | 1 | −4 | −4.0 | −4 | 0 |
| Colts | 62 | 1198 | 19.3 | 90 | 0 |
| Opponents | 61 | 1138 | 18.7 | 38 | 0 |

### Scoring

| | TD | TD R | TD P | TD Rt | PAT | FG | TP |
|---|---|---|---|---|---|---|---|
| Allegre | | | | | 22/24 | 30/35 | 112 |
| Dickey | 7 | 4 | 3 | 0 | | | 42 |
| McMillan | 6 | 5 | 1 | 0 | | | 36 |
| Henry | 4 | 0 | 4 | 0 | | | 24 |
| Butler | 3 | 0 | 3 | 0 | | | 18 |
| K. Anderson | 1 | 0 | 0 | 1 | | | 6 |
| L. Anderson | 1 | 0 | 0 | 1 | | | 6 |
| Beach | 1 | 0 | 1 | 0 | | | 6 |
| Cooks | 1 | 0 | 0 | 1 | | | 6 |
| Moore | 1 | 1 | 0 | 0 | | | 6 |
| D. Thompson | | | (Safety) | | | | 2 |
| Colts | 25 | 10 | 12 | 3 | 22/24 | 30/35 | 264 |
| Opponents | 45 | 13 | 31 | 1 | 42/45 | 14/23 | 354 |

## FIRST-ROUND SELECTIONS

(If Club had no first-round selection, first player drafted is listed with round in parentheses.)

| Year | Player, College, Position |
|---|---|
| 1953 | Billy Vessels, Oklahoma, B |
| 1954 | Cotton Davidson, Baylor, B |
| 1955 | George Shaw, Oregon, B |
| | Alan Ameche, Wisconsin, FB |
| 1956 | Lenny Moore, Penn State, B |
| 1957 | Jim Parker, Ohio State, G |
| 1958 | Lenny Lyles, Louisville, B |
| 1959 | Jackie Burkett, Auburn, C |
| 1960 | Ron Mix, Southern California, T |
| 1961 | Tom Matte, Ohio State, RB |
| 1962 | Wendell Harris, Louisiana State, S |
| 1963 | Bob Vogel, Ohio State, T |
| 1964 | Marv Woodson, Indiana, CB |
| 1965 | Mike Curtis, Duke, LB |
| 1966 | Sam Ball, Kentucky, T |
| 1967 | Bubba Smith, Michigan State, DT |
| | Jim Detwiler, Michigan, RB |
| 1968 | John Williams, Minnesota, G |
| 1969 | Eddie Hinton, Oklahoma, WR |
| 1970 | Norman Bulaich, Texas Christian, RB |
| 1971 | Don McCauley, North Carolina, RB |
| | Leonard Dunlap, North Texas State, DB |
| 1972 | Tom Drougas, Oregon, T |
| 1973 | Bert Jones, Louisiana State, QB |
| | Joe Ehrmann, DT, Syracuse |
| 1974 | John Dutton, Nebraska, DE |
| | Roger Carr, Louisiana Tech, WR |
| 1975 | Ken Huff, North Carolina, G |
| 1976 | Ken Novak, Purdue, DT |
| 1977 | Randy Burke, Kentucky, WR |
| 1978 | Reese McCall, Auburn, TE |
| 1979 | Barry Krauss, Alabama, LB |
| 1980 | Curtis Dickey, Texas A&M, RB |
| | Derrick Hatchett, Texas, DB |
| 1981 | Randy McMillan, Pittsburgh, RB |
| | Donnell Thompson, North Carolina, DT |
| 1982 | Johnie Cooks, Mississippi State, LB |
| | Art Schlichter, Ohio State, QB |
| 1983 | John Elway, Stanford, QB |
| 1984 | Leonard Coleman, Vanderbilt, DB |
| | Ron Solt, Maryland, G |

## INDIANAPOLIS COLTS 1984 VETERAN ROSTER

| No. | Name | Pos. | Ht. | Wt. | Birth-date | NFL Exp. | College | Birthplace | Residence | Games in '83 |
|-----|------|------|-----|-----|-----------|----------|---------|-----------|-----------|--------------|
| 74 | Abramowitz, Sid | T | 6-6 | 279 | 5/21/60 | 2 | Tulsa | Culver City, Calif. | Randallstown, Md. | 14 |
| 2 | Allegre, Raul | K | 5-9 | 165 | 6/15/59 | 2 | Texas | Torreon, Coaguila, Mex. | Austin, Tex. | 16 |
| 26 | Anderson, Kim | S | 5-11 | 189 | 6/19/57 | 5 | Arizona State | Pasadena, Calif. | Los Angeles, Calif. | 16 |
| 30 | Anderson, Larry | S | 6-1 | 192 | 9/25/56 | 7 | Louisiana Tech | Monroe, La. | Shreveport, La. | 9 |
| 72 | Baldischwiler, Karl | T | 6-5 | 267 | 1/19/56 | 7 | Oklahoma | Okmulgee, Okla. | Oklahoma City, Okla. | 14 |
| 97 | Ballard, Quinton | NT | 6-3 | 289 | 11/18/60 | 2 | Elon College | Ahoskie, N.C. | Gates, N.C. | 15 |
| 81 | Beach, Pat | TE | 6-4 | 243 | 12/28/59 | 3 | Washington State | Grant's Pass, Ore. | Pullman, Wash. | 16 |
| 90 | Bell, Mark | DE | 6-4 | 240 | 8/30/57 | 5 | Colorado State | Wichita, Kan. | Wichita, Kan. | 7 |
| 85 | Bouza, Matt | WR | 6-3 | 211 | 4/8/59 | 3 | California | San Jose, Calif. | Walnut Creek, Calif. | 11 |
| 52 | Bracelin, Greg | LB | 6-2 | 213 | 4/16/57 | 5 | California | Lawrence, Kan. | Littleton, Colo. | 16 |
| 45 | Burroughs, James | CB | 6-1 | 198 | 1/21/58 | 3 | Michigan State | Pahokee, Fla. | West Palm Beach, Fla. | 16 |
| 80 | Butler, Ray | WR | 6-3 | 206 | 6/28/56 | 5 | Southern California | Sweeney, Tex. | Lake Jackson, Tex. | 11 |
| 98 | Cooks, Johnie | LB | 6-4 | 234 | 11/23/58 | 3 | Mississippi State | Leland, Miss. | Randallstown, Md. | 16 |
| 33 | Dickey, Curtis | RB | 6-1 | 214 | 11/27/56 | 5 | Texas A&M | Madisonville, Tex. | Houston, Tex. | 16 |
| 53 | Donaldson, Ray | C | 6-3 | 269 | 5/18/58 | 5 | Georgia | Rome, Ga. | Rome, Ga. | 16 |
| 50 | Feasel, Grant | C | 6-8 | 267 | 6/28/60 | 2 | Abilene Christian | Barstow, Calif. | Garland, Tex. | 11 |
| 25 | Glasgow, Nesby | S | 5-10 | 187 | 4/15/57 | 6 | Washington | Los Angeles, Calif. | Randallstown, Md. | 16 |
| 88 | Henry, Bernard | WR | 6-0 | 179 | 4/9/60 | 3 | Arizona State | Los Angeles, Calif. | Los Angeles, Calif. | 15 |
| 9 | Herrmann, Mark | QB | 6-5 | 199 | 1/8/59 | 4 | Purdue | Cincinnati, Ohio | Englewood, Colo. | 2 |
| 75 | Hinton, Chris | G | 6-4 | 280 | 7/31/61 | 2 | Northwestern | Chicago, Ill. | Timonium, Md. | 16 |
| 57 | †Humiston, Mike | LB | 6-3 | 238 | 1/8/59 | 3 | Weber State | Oceanside, Calif. | Chico, Calif. | 0* |
| 51 | Jones, Ricky | LB | 6-2 | 227 | 3/9/55 | 8 | Tuskegee | Birmingham, Ala. | Birmingham, Ala. | 16 |
| 29 | †Kafentzis, Mark | S | 5-10 | 185 | 6/30/58 | 3 | Hawaii | Richland, Wash. | Richland, Wash. | 15 |
| 55 | Krauss, Barry | LB | 6-3 | 247 | 3/17/57 | 6 | Alabama | Pompano Beach, Fla. | Glen Arm, Md. | 16 |
| 56 | Maxwell, Vernon | LB | 6-2 | 219 | 10/25/61 | 4 | Arizona State | Birmingham, Ala. | Carson, Calif. | 16 |
| 32 | McMillan, Randy | FB | 6-1 | 220 | 12/17/58 | 4 | Pittsburgh | Havre de Grace, Md. | Timonium, Md. | 16 |
| 76 | Mills, Jim | T | 6-9 | 271 | 9/23/61 | 2 | Hawaii | Vancouver, Canada | Richmond, Canada | 7 |
| 23 | Moore, Alvin | RB | 6-0 | 194 | 5/3/59 | 2 | Arizona State | Randolph, Ariz. | Casa Grande, Ariz. | 15 |
| 84 | Oatis, Victor | WR | 6-0 | 177 | 1/6/59 | 2 | Northwestern Louisiana | Monroe, La. | Natchitoches, La. | 9 |
| 49 | Odom, Cliff | LB | 6-2 | 233 | 9/15/58 | 4 | Texas-Arlington | Beaumont, Tex. | Arlington, Tex. | 15 |
| 60 | Padjen, Gary | LB | 6-2 | 251 | 7/2/58 | 3 | Arizona State | Salt Lake City, Utah | Owings Mills, Md. | 16 |
| 18 | Pagel, Mike | QB | 6-2 | 201 | 9/13/60 | 3 | Arizona State | Douglas, Ariz. | Chandler, Ariz. | 15 |
| 78 | Parker, Steve | DE | 6-4 | 250 | 9/21/59 | 2 | Eastern Illinois | Evanston, Ill. | Towson, Md. | 16 |
| 20 | Porter, Rick | RB | 5-10 | 204 | 1/14/60 | 2 | Slippery Rock State | Baltimore, Md. | Baltimore, Md. | 14 |
| 87 | Porter, Tracy | WR | 6-1 | 196 | 6/1/59 | 4 | Louisiana State | Baton Rouge, La. | Baton Rouge, La. | 16 |
| 35 | Randle, Tate | CB | 6-0 | 202 | 8/15/59 | 3 | Texas Tech | Fredericksburg, Tex. | Lubbock, Tex. | 12* |
| 8 | Reed, Mark | QB | 6-3 | 204 | 2/21/59 | 3 | Moorhead State, Minn. | Moorhead, Minn. | Moorhead, Minn. | 1 |
| 83 | Sherwin, Tim | TE | 6-6 | 238 | 5/4/58 | 4 | Boston College | Watervliet, N.Y. | Cockeysville, Md. | 15 |
| 79 | Sinnott, John | T | 6-4 | 274 | 4/15/58 | 3 | Brown | Wexford, Ireland | Durham, Mass. | 0* |
| 86 | Smith, Phil | WR | 6-3 | 188 | 4/28/60 | 2 | San Diego State | Los Angeles, Calif. | Compton, Calif. | 1 |
| 3 | Stark, Rohn | P | 6-3 | 199 | 5/4/59 | 3 | Florida State | Minneapolis, Minn. | Tallahassee, Fla. | 16 |
| 12 | Taylor, Jim Bob | QB | 6-2 | 197 | 9/9/59 | 2 | Georgia Tech | San Antonio, Tex. | Somerset, Tex. | 8 |
| 21 | †Thompson, Aundra | WR | 6-1 | 186 | 1/2/53 | 8 | East Texas State | Dallas, Tex. | Dallas, Tex. | 0* |
| 99 | Thompson, Donnell | DE | 6-4 | 263 | 10/27/58 | 4 | North Carolina | Lumberton, N.C. | Chapel Hill, N.C. | 14 |
| 64 | Utt, Ben | G | 6-5 | 267 | 6/13/59 | 3 | Georgia Tech | Richmond, Calif. | Columbia, Md. | 16 |
| 71 | Waechter, Henry | DE | 6-6 | 270 | 2/13/59 | 3 | Nebraska | Dubuque, Iowa | Walton, Neb. | 11 |
| 44 | Williams, Kendall | CB | 5-9 | 189 | 2/7/59 | 2 | Arizona State | Long Beach, Calif. | Long Beach, Calif. | 16 |
| 39 | Williams, Newton | RB | 5-10 | 204 | 5/10/59 | 3 | Arizona State | Charlotte, N.C. | Charlotte, N.C. | 16 |
| 69 | Wisniewski, Leo | NT | 6-1 | 264 | 11/6/59 | 3 | Penn State | Hancock, Mich. | Tampa, Fla. | 15 |
| 73 | Wright, Steve | G | 6-5 | 263 | 4/8/59 | 4 | Northern Iowa | Wayzata, Minn. | Wayzata, Minn. | 13 |
| 86 | Young, Dave | TE | 6-5 | 240 | 2/9/59 | 3 | Purdue | Akron, Ohio | West Lafayette, Ind. | 1 |

* Humiston and Sinnott missed '83 season due to injuries; Randle played 2 games with Houston in '83, 10 with Baltimore.

†Option playout; subject to developments.

Also played with Colts in '83—NT Earnest Barnes (7 games), S Jeff Delaney (11), RB Zach Dixon (2), T Jeff Hart (14), CB Derrick Hatchett (7), T Lindsey Mason (5), LB Sanders Shiver (16), DE Hosea Taylor (4), CB Marco Tongue (7).

## COACHING STAFF

### Head Coach, Frank Kush

**Pro Career:** Became Colts tenth head coach on December 21, 1981. Baltimore finished 0-8-1 in 1982 and 7-9 in '83. Entered pro coaching ranks for first time in 1981 when he was named head coach of Hamilton Tiger-Cats of the Canadian Football League.Guided Hamilton to an 11-4-1 mark and a first-place finish in the Eastern Conference before being tabbed by the Colts. No pro playing experience. Career record: 7-17-1.

**Background:** In 1958, succeeded Dan Devine as head coach at Arizona State where he compiled 176-54-1 record in 22 seasons, including 6-1 mark in bowl competition. His 1975 team was 12-0 and ranked number two in both wire service polls. Kush began coaching career at Arizona State as defensive line coach in 1955. He played defensive guard at Michigan State from 1950-52 and was a consensus All-America in his senior year, helping the Spartans achieve a 9-0 record and capture the national championship.

**Personal:** Born January 20, 1929, Windber, Pa. Frank and his wife, Fran, have three sons—Dan, David, and Damian. They live in Indianapolis.

### Assistant Coaches

**Zeke Bratkowski,** offensive coordinator-quarterbacks; born October 20, 1931, Danville, Ill., lives in Indianapolis. Quarterback Georgia 1951-53. Pro quarterback Chicago Bears 1954, 1957-60, Los Angeles Rams 1961-63, Green Bay Packers 1963-68, 1971. Pro coach: Green Bay Packers 1969-70, 1975-81, Chicago Bears 1972-74, joined Colts in 1982.

**George Catavolos,** defensive backs; born May 8, 1945, Chicago, lives in Indianapolis. Defensive Back Purdue 1965-67. No pro playing experience. College coach: Purdue 1968-69, Middle Tennessee 1969, Louisville 1970, Purdue 1971-76, Kentucky 1977-81, Tennessee 1982-83. Pro coach: First year with Colts.

**Gunther Cunningham,** defensive line; born June 19, 1946, Munich, Germany, lives in Indianapolis. Linebacker Oregon 1965-67. No pro playing experience. College coach: Oregon 1969-71, Arkansas 1972, Stanford 1973-76, California 1977-80. Pro coach: Hamilton Tiger-Cats (CFL) 1981, joined Colts in 1982.

**Hal Hunter,** offensive line; born June 3, 1934, Canonsburg, Pa., lives in Indianapolis. Linebacker-guard Pittsburgh 1953-55. Pro guard Pittsburgh Steelers 1956. College coach: Richmond 1958-61, West Virginia 1962-63, Maryland 1964-65, Duke 1966-70, Kentucky 1971-72, Indiana 1973-76, California (Pa.) State 1977-80 (head coach). Pro coach: Hamilton Tiger-Cats (CFL) 1981, joined Colts in 1982.

**Richard Mann,** wide receivers; born April 20, 1947, Aliquippa, Pa., lives in Indianapolis. Wide receiver Arizona State 1966-68. No pro playing experience. College coach: Arizona State 1974-79. Louisville 1980-81. Pro coach: Joined Colts in 1982.

**Roger Theder,** running backs; born September 22, 1939, Watertown, Wis., lives in Indianapolis. Quarterback Western Michigan 1960-62. No pro playing experience. College coach: Bowling Green 1963, Northern Illinois 1964-67, Stanford 1968-71, California 1972-81 (head coach 1978-81). Pro coach: Joined Colts in 1982.

**Rick Venturi,** linebackers; born February 23, 1946, Taylorville, Ill., lives in Indianapolis. Quarterback Northwestern 1965-67. No pro playing experience. College coach: Northwestern 1968-72, 1978-80 (head coach), Purdue 1973-76, Illinois 1977. Pro coach: Joined Colts in 1982.

**Mike Westhoff,** tight ends-special teams-weight training; born January 10, 1948, Pittsburgh, Pa., lives in Indianapolis. Tight end Wichita State. No pro playing experience. College coach: Indiana 1974-75, Dayton 1976, Indiana State 1977, Northwestern 1978-80, Texas Christian 1981. Pro coach: Joined Colts in 1982.

## INDIANAPOLIS COLTS 1984 FIRST-YEAR ROSTER

| Name | Pos. | Ht. | Wt. | Birth-date | College | Birthplace | Residence | How Acq. |
|---|---|---|---|---|---|---|---|---|
| Bettis, James (1) | RB | 5-10 | 180 | 2/20/59 | Cincinnati | Cincinnati, Ohio | Cincinnati, Ohio | FA |
| Beverly, Dwight | RB | 6-0 | 200 | 12/5/61 | Illinois | Long Beach, Calif. | Champaign, Ill. | D6 |
| Call, Kevin | T | 6-7 | 289 | 11/13/61 | Colorado State | Boulder, Colo. | Ft. Collins, Colo. | D5a |
| Campbell, Jim (1) | TE | 6-3 | 230 | 11/9/59 | Kentucky | Winchester, Va. | Lexington, Ky. | FA |
| Coleman, Leonard | CB | 6-2 | 208 | 1/30/62 | Vanderbilt | Boynton Beach, Fla. | Nashville, Tenn. | D1 |
| Cook, Art (1) | LB | 6-3 | 220 | 8/24/58 | Morgan State | Richmond, Va. | Richmond, Va. | FA |
| Curry, Craig | S | 6-0 | 187 | 7/20/61 | Texas | Houston, Tex. | Austin, Tex. | D4 |
| Daniel, Eugene | CB | 6-0 | 181 | 5/4/61 | Louisiana State | Baton Rouge, La. | Baton Rouge, La. | D8 |
| Dumas, Marvin | WR | 5-11 | 184 | 2/21/60 | Nicholls State | Vacherie, La. | Thibodaux, La. | FA |
| Hambrick, Darrel (1) | WR | 6-4 | 210 | 12/20/60 | Nevada-Las Vegas | Los Angeles, Calif. | Cudahy, Calif. | FA |
| Hathaway, Steve | DE | 6-4 | 220 | 4/26/62 | West Virginia | Beaver, Pa. | Morgantown, W.Va. | D12 |
| Jones, Arrington (1) | RB | 6-1 | 230 | 2/16/59 | Winston-Salem | Richmond, Va. | Richmond, Va. | FA |
| Jones, Ken (1) | T | 6-5 | 275 | 9/12/60 | Tennessee | Nashville, Tenn. | Knoxville, Tenn. | FA |
| Joyner, Russ (1) | LB | 6-4 | 240 | 9/7/60 | Boston College | Bronx, N.Y. | Bronx, N.Y. | FA |
| Kennell, Lonnie (1) | NT | 6-2 | 270 | 12/8/61 | Wichita State | Crescent City, Fla. | Crescent City, Fla. | FA |
| Kurdyla, Kevin (1) | T-G | 6-4 | 265 | 6/14/59 | Rutgers | Newark, N.J. | Newark, N.J. | FA |
| Neely, Tony | CB-S | 6-2 | 200 | 6/10/59 | Arizona | Baltimore, Md. | Bridgeville, Pa. | FA |
| Poles, Junior (1) | DE | 6-5 | 270 | 2/24/61 | Boston College | Ft. Dixon, N.C. | Caledonia, N.Y. | FA |
| Reeves, Morgan | RB | 5-11 | 191 | 11/23/58 | Michigan State | Columbia, S.C. | Irmose, S.C. | FA |
| Scott, Chris | NT | 6-5 | 245 | 12/11/61 | Purdue | Berea, Ohio | West Lafayette, Ind. | D3 |
| Solt, Ron | G | 6-3 | 265 | 5/19/62 | Maryland | Wilkes-Barre, Pa. | College Park, Md. | D1a |
| Snow, Pat | WR | 6-0 | 190 | 1/29/60 | Akron | Dayton, Ohio | Leavittsburg, Ohio | FA |
| Stephanos, Bill (1) | G | 6-5 | 260 | 3/24/57 | Boston College | Lynn, Mass. | Lynn, Mass. | FA |
| Stowe, Bob | T | 6-4 | 265 | 7/1/62 | Illinois | Mt. Pleasant, N.J. | Champaign, Ill. | D11 |
| Tate, Ben (1) | FB | 6-1 | 238 | 8/29/61 | N. Carolina Central | Philadelphia, Pa. | Berlin, Md. | FA |
| Tate, Golden | WR | 6-3 | 190 | 7/5/60 | Tennessee State | Greenville, Miss. | Nashville, Tenn. | D5 |
| Wertz, Larry | LB | 6-3 | 230 | 2/28/58 | Jackson State | Newberry, S.C. | Newberry, S.C. | FA |
| Winters, Blaise | NT | 6-3 | 262 | 1/31/62 | Syracuse | Blauvelt, N.Y. | Syracuse, N.Y. | D2 |
| Wonsley, George | RB | 6-0 | 205 | 3/25/61 | Mississippi State | Moss Point, Miss. | Mississippi St., Miss. | D4a |

Players who report to an NFL team for the first time are designated on rosters as rookies (R). If a player reported to an NFL training camp in a previous year but was not on the active squad for three or more regular season or postseason games, he is listed on the first-year roster and designated by a (1). Thereafter, a player who is on the active squad for three or more regular season or postseason games is credited with an additional year of playing experience.

## NOTES

_____
_____
_____
_____
_____
_____
_____
_____
_____
_____
_____
_____
_____
_____
_____
_____
_____
_____
_____
_____
_____
_____
_____

# KANSAS CITY CHIEFS

## CHIEFS COACHING HISTORY

### Dallas Texans 1960-62
### (178-161-10)

| | | |
|---|---|---|
| 1960-74 | Hank Stram | 129-79-10 |
| 1975-77 | Paul Wiggin* | 11-24-0 |
| 1977 | Tom Bettis | 1-6-0 |
| 1978-82 | Marv Levy | 31-42-0 |
| 1983 | John Mackovic | 6-10-0 |

*Released after seven games in 1977

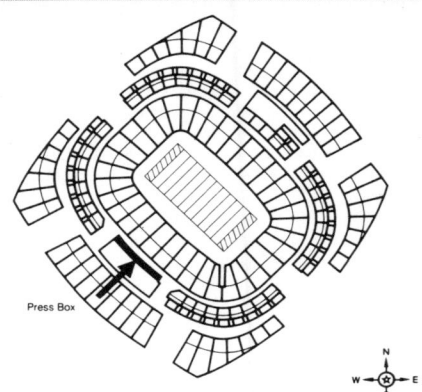

Press Box

ARROWHEAD

**American Football Conference
Western Division**

**Team Colors:** Red, Gold, and White

**One Arrowhead Drive
Kansas City, Missouri 64129
Telephone: (816) 924-9300**

**Club Officials**

Owner: Lamar Hunt
President: Jack Steadman
Vice President and General Manager: Jim Schaaf
Director of Player Personnel: Les Miller
Manager of Administration: Don Steadman
Treasurer: Randy Cooper
Secretary: Jim Seigfried
Stadium Manager: Bob Wachter
Ticket Manager: Joe Mazza
Public Relations Director: Bob Sprenger
Assistant Director of Public Relations: Gary Heise
Promotions Director: Mitch Wheeler
Director of Sales: David Smith
Manager of Information Systems: Andy Sawyer
Trainer: Dave Kendall
Equipment Coordinator: Jon Phillips

**Stadium:** Arrowhead Stadium • **Capacity:** 78,067
   One Arrowhead Drive
   Kansas City, Missouri 64129

**Playing Surface:** Tartan Turf

**Training Camp:** William Jewell College
   Liberty, Missouri 64068

## 1984 SCHEDULE

**Preseason**
| | | |
|---|---|---|
| Aug. 4 | **New Orleans** | 7:30 |
| Aug. 10 | at St. Louis | 7:30 |
| Aug. 18 | **Cleveland** | 7:30 |
| Aug. 24 | at New England | 7:30 |

**Regular Season**
| | | |
|---|---|---|
| Sept. 2 | at Pittsburgh | 1:00 |
| Sept. 9 | at Cincinnati | 1:00 |
| Sept. 16 | **Los Angeles Raiders** | 12:00 |
| Sept. 23 | at Denver | 2:00 |
| Sept. 30 | **Cleveland** | 12:00 |
| Oct. 7 | **New York Jets** | 12:00 |
| Oct. 14 | **San Diego** | 12:00 |
| Oct. 21 | at New York Jets | 4:00 |
| Oct. 28 | **Tampa Bay** | 12:00 |
| Nov. 4 | at Seattle | 1:00 |
| Nov. 11 | **Houston** | 12:00 |
| Nov. 18 | at Los Angeles Raiders | 1:00 |
| Nov. 25 | at New York Giants | 1:00 |
| Dec. 2 | **Denver** | 12:00 |
| Dec. 9 | **Seattle** | 12:00 |
| Dec. 16 | at San Diego | 1:00 |

## RECORD HOLDERS
### Individual Records—Career

| Category | Name | Performance |
|---|---|---|
| Rushing (Yds.) | Ed Podolak, 1969-1977 | 4,451 |
| Passing (Yds.) | Len Dawson, 1962-1975 | 28,507 |
| Passing (TDs) | Len Dawson, 1962-1975 | 237 |
| Receiving (No.) | Otis Taylor, 1965-1975 | 410 |
| Receiving (Yds.) | Otis Taylor, 1965-1975 | 7,306 |
| Interceptions | Emmitt Thomas, 1966-1978 | 58 |
| Punting (Avg.) | Jerrel Wilson, 1963-1977 | 43.5 |
| Punt Return (Avg.) | J.T. Smith, 1979-1983 | 11.0 |
| Kickoff Return (Avg.) | Noland Smith, 1967-69 | 26.8 |
| Field Goals | Jan Stenerud, 1967-1979 | 279 |
| Touchdowns (Tot.) | Otis Taylor, 1965-1975 | 60 |
| Points | Jan Stenerud, 1967-1979 | 1,231 |

### Individual Records—Single Season

| Category | Name | Performance |
|---|---|---|
| Rushing (Yds.) | Joe Delaney, 1981 | 1,121 |
| Passing (Yds.) | Bill Kenney, 1983 | 4,348 |
| Passing (TDs) | Len Dawson, 1964 | 30 |
| Receiving (No.) | Carlos Carson, 1983 | 80 |
| Receiving (Yds.) | Carlos Carson, 1983 | 1,351 |
| Interceptions | Emmitt Thomas, 1974 | 12 |
| Punting (Avg.) | Jerrel Wilson, 1965 | 46.0 |
| Punt Return (Avg.) | Abner Haynes, 1960 | 15.4 |
| Kickoff Return (Avg.) | Dave Grayson, 1962 | 29.7 |
| Field Goals | Jan Stenerud, 1968, 1970 | 30 |
| Touchdowns (Tot.) | Abner Haynes, 1962 | 19 |
| Points | Jan Stenerud, 1968 | 129 |

### Individual Records—Single Game

| Category | Name | Performance |
|---|---|---|
| Rushing (Yds.) | Joe Delaney, 11-15-81 | 193 |
| Passing (Yds.) | Len Dawson, 11-1-64 | 435 |
| Passing (TDs) | Len Dawson, 11-1-64 | 6 |
| Receiving (No.) | Ed Podolak, 10-7-73 | 12 |
| Receiving (Yds.) | Curtis McClinton, 12-19-65 | 213 |
| Interceptions | Bobby Ply, 12-16-62 | 4 |
| | Bobby Hunt, 12-4-64 | 4 |
| Field Goals | Jan Stenerud, 11-2-69, 12-7-69, 12-19-71 | 5 |
| Touchdowns (Tot.) | Abner Haynes, 11-26-61 | 5 |
| Points | Abner Haynes, 11-26-61 | 30 |

## 1983 TEAM STATISTICS

| | Kansas City | Opp. |
|---|---|---|
| Total First Downs | 314 | 319 |
| Rushing | 83 | 136 |
| Passing | 208 | 158 |
| Penalty | 23 | 25 |
| Third Down Efficiency | 93/233 | 85/221 |
| Third Down Percentage | 39.9 | 38.5 |
| Total Net Yards | 5595 | 5386 |
| Total Offensive Plays | 1074 | 1089 |
| Avg. Gain per Play | 5.2 | 4.9 |
| Avg. Gain per Game | 349.7 | 336.6 |
| Net Yards Rushing | 1254 | 2275 |
| Total Rushing Plays | 387 | 554 |
| Avg. Gain per Rush | 3.2 | 4.1 |
| Avg. Gain Rushing per Game | 78.4 | 142.2 |
| Net Yards Passing | 4341 | 3111 |
| Lost Attempting to Pass | 46/343 | 35/250 |
| Gross Yards Passing | 4684 | 3361 |
| Attempts/Completions | 641/369 | 500/261 |
| Percent Completed | 57.6 | 52.2 |
| Had Intercepted | 19 | 30 |
| Avg. Net Passing per Game | 271.3 | 194.4 |
| Punts/Avg. | 93/39.9 | 85/41.2 |
| Punt Returns/Avg. | 40/7.3 | 54/10.4 |
| Kickoff Returns/Avg. | 54/17.2 | 75/20.4 |
| Interceptions/Avg. Ret. | 30/16.1 | 19/17.0 |
| Penalties/Yards | 113/911 | 105/837 |
| Fumbles/Ball Lost | 31/19 | 35/21 |
| Total Points | 386 | 367 |
| Avg. Points per Game | 24.1 | 22.9 |
| Touchdowns | 45 | 44 |
| Rushing | 13 | 18 |
| Passing | 29 | 21 |
| Returns and Recoveries | 3 | 5 |
| Field Goals | 24/30 | 20/26 |
| Conversions | 44/45 | 43/44 |
| Safeties | 0 | 0 |
| Avg. Time of Possession | 28:53 | 31:07 |

## 1983 TEAM RECORD

### Preseason (2-2)

| Date | Kansas City | | Opponents |
|---|---|---|---|
| 8/6 | 24 | Cincinnati | 7 |
| 8/13 | 13 | *Detroit | 17 |
| 8/20 | 17 | *St. Louis | 16 |
| 8/27 | 17 | Chicago (OT) | 20 |
| | 71 | | 60 |

### Regular Season (6-10)

| Date | Kansas City | | Opp. | Att. |
|---|---|---|---|---|
| 9/4 | 17 | *Seattle | 13 | 42,531 |
| 9/12 | 14 | *San Diego | 17 | 62,150 |
| 9/18 | 12 | Washington | 27 | 52,610 |
| 9/25 | 6 | Miami | 14 | 50,785 |
| 10/2 | 38 | *St. Louis | 14 | 58,975 |
| 10/9 | 20 | Los Angeles Raiders | 21 | 40,492 |
| 10/16 | 38 | *New York Giants | 17 | 55,449 |
| 10/23 | 13 | Houston (OT) | 10 | 39,462 |
| 10/30 | 24 | Denver | 27 | 74,640 |
| 11/6 | 20 | *Los Angeles Raiders | 28 | 73,497 |
| 11/13 | 20 | *Cincinnati | 15 | 41,711 |
| 11/20 | 21 | Dallas | 41 | 64,103 |
| 11/27 | 48 | Seattle (OT) | 51 | 56,793 |
| 12/4 | 9 | *Buffalo | 14 | 27,104 |
| 12/11 | 38 | San Diego | 41 | 35,910 |
| 12/18 | 48 | *Denver | 17 | 11,377 |
| | 386 | | 367 | 787,589 |

*Home Game  (OT) Overtime

### Score by Periods

| | | | | | | | |
|---|---|---|---|---|---|---|---|
| Kansas City | 86 | 96 | 85 | 116 | 3 | — | 386 |
| Opponents | 57 | 89 | 88 | 130 | 3 | — | 367 |

### Attendance

Home 372,794    Away 414,795    Total 787,589
Single game home record, 82,094 (11-5-72)
Single season home record, 509,291 (1972)

## 1983 INDIVIDUAL STATISTICS

### Rushing

| | Att. | Yds. | Avg. | LG | TD |
|---|---|---|---|---|---|
| B. Jackson | 152 | 499 | 3.3 | 19 | 2 |
| Brown | 124 | 467 | 3.8 | 49t | 8 |
| J. Thomas | 44 | 115 | 2.6 | 11 | 0 |
| Kenney | 23 | 59 | 2.6 | 11 | 3 |
| K. Thomas | 15 | 55 | 3.7 | 28 | 0 |
| Ricks | 21 | 28 | 1.3 | 10 | 0 |
| Carson | 2 | 20 | 10.0 | 18 | 0 |
| Hadnot | 4 | 10 | 2.5 | 7 | 0 |
| Scott | 1 | 1 | 1.0 | 1 | 0 |
| Blackledge | 1 | 0 | 0.0 | 0 | 0 |
| Kansas City | 387 | 1254 | 3.2 | 49t | 13 |
| Opponents | 554 | 2275 | 4.1 | 60 | 18 |

### Passing

| | Att. | Comp. | Pct. | Yds. | TD | Int. | Tkld. | Rate |
|---|---|---|---|---|---|---|---|---|
| Kenney | 603 | 346 | 57.4 | 4348 | 24 | 18 | 41/284 | 80.8 |
| Blackledge | 34 | 20 | 58.8 | 259 | 3 | 0 | 4/50 | 112.3 |
| J. Thomas | 2 | 1 | 50.0 | 18 | 1 | 1 | 0/0 | 81.3 |
| Brown | 1 | 1 | 100.0 | 11 | 0 | 0 | 0/0 | 112.5 |
| Carson | 1 | 1 | 100.0 | 48 | 1 | 0 | 0/0 | 158.3 |
| Marshall | 0 | 0 | — | 0 | 0 | 0 | 1/9 | 0.0 |
| Kansas City | 641 | 369 | 57.6 | 4684 | 29 | 19 | 46/343 | 83.2 |
| Opponents | 500 | 261 | 52.2 | 3361 | 21 | 30 | 35/250 | 62.6 |

### Receiving

| | No. | Yds. | Avg. | LG | TD |
|---|---|---|---|---|---|
| Carson | 80 | 1351 | 16.9 | 50t | 7 |
| Marshall | 50 | 788 | 15.8 | 52 | 6 |
| Brown | 47 | 418 | 8.9 | 53 | 2 |
| Hancock | 37 | 584 | 15.8 | 50 | 1 |
| B. Jackson | 32 | 243 | 7.6 | 29 | 0 |
| Paige | 30 | 528 | 17.6 | 43 | 6 |
| Scott | 29 | 247 | 8.5 | 22 | 6 |
| K. Thomas | 28 | 236 | 8.4 | 25 | 1 |
| Beckman | 13 | 130 | 10.0 | 20 | 0 |
| J. Thomas | 10 | 51 | 5.1 | 9 | 0 |
| J. Smith | 7 | 85 | 12.1 | 18 | 0 |
| Ricks | 3 | 5 | 1.7 | 7 | 0 |
| Hadnot | 2 | 18 | 9.0 | 16 | 0 |
| Kenney | 1 | 0 | 0.0 | 0 | 0 |
| Kansas City | 369 | 4684 | 12.7 | 53 | 29 |
| Opponents | 261 | 3361 | 12.9 | 58 | 21 |

### Interceptions

| | No. | Yds. | Avg. | LG | TD |
|---|---|---|---|---|---|
| Cherry | 7 | 100 | 14.3 | 41 | 0 |
| Green | 6 | 59 | 9.8 | 25 | 0 |
| Roquemore | 4 | 117 | 29.3 | 42t | 1 |
| Burruss | 4 | 46 | 11.5 | 27 | 0 |
| Lewis | 4 | 42 | 10.5 | 34 | 0 |
| L. Smith | 3 | 99 | 33.0 | 58t | 1 |
| Bryant | 1 | 19 | 19.0 | 19 | 0 |
| Potter | 1 | 0 | 0.0 | 0 | 0 |
| Kansas City | 30 | 482 | 16.1 | 58t | 2 |
| Opponents | 19 | 323 | 17.0 | 48 | 2 |

### Punting

| | No. | Yds. | Avg. | In 20 | LG |
|---|---|---|---|---|---|
| Arnold | 93 | 3710 | 39.9 | 21 | 64 |
| Kansas City | 93 | 3710 | 39.9 | 21 | 64 |
| Opponents | 85 | 3500 | 41.2 | 17 | 60 |

### Punt Returns

| | No. | FC | Yds. | Avg. | LG | TD |
|---|---|---|---|---|---|---|
| J. Smith | 26 | 5 | 210 | 8.1 | 19 | 0 |
| Hancock | 14 | 9 | 81 | 5.8 | 18 | 0 |
| Kansas City | 40 | 14 | 291 | 7.3 | 19 | 0 |
| Opponents | 54 | 7 | 559 | 10.4 | 68t | 1 |

### Kickoff Returns

| | No. | Yds. | Avg. | LG | TD |
|---|---|---|---|---|---|
| Hancock | 29 | 515 | 17.8 | 33 | 0 |
| Brown | 15 | 301 | 20.1 | 46 | 0 |
| Roquemore | 3 | 36 | 12.0 | 13 | 0 |
| Cherry | 2 | 54 | 27.0 | 31 | 0 |
| Carson | 1 | 12 | 12.0 | 12 | 0 |
| Daniels | 1 | 0 | 0.0 | 0 | 0 |
| Lindstrom | 1 | 0 | 0.0 | 0 | 0 |
| J. Smith | 1 | 5 | 5.0 | 5 | 0 |
| K. Thomas | 1 | 6 | 6.0 | 6 | 0 |
| Burruss | 0 | 0 | — | 0 | 0 |
| Kansas City | 54 | 929 | 17.2 | 46 | 0 |
| Opponents | 75 | 1528 | 20.4 | 50 | 0 |

### Scoring

| | TD | TD R | TD P | TD Rt | PAT | FG | TP |
|---|---|---|---|---|---|---|---|
| Lowery | | | | | 44/45 | 24/30 | 116 |
| Brown | 10 | 8 | 2 | 0 | | | 60 |
| Carson | 7 | 0 | 7 | 0 | | | 42 |
| Marshall | 6 | 0 | 6 | 0 | | | 36 |
| Paige | 6 | 0 | 6 | 0 | | | 36 |
| Scott | 6 | 0 | 6 | 0 | | | 36 |
| Kenney | 3 | 3 | 0 | 0 | | | 18 |
| B. Jackson | 2 | 2 | 0 | 0 | | | 12 |
| Hancock | 1 | 0 | 1 | 0 | | | 6 |
| C. Jackson | 1 | 0 | 0 | 1 | | | 6 |
| Roquemore | 1 | 0 | 0 | 1 | | | 6 |
| L. Smith | 1 | 0 | 0 | 1 | | | 6 |
| K. Thomas | 1 | 0 | 1 | 0 | | | 6 |
| Kansas City | 45 | 13 | 29 | 3 | 44/45 | 24/30 | 386 |
| Opponents | 44 | 18 | 21 | 5 | 43/44 | 20/26 | 367 |

## FIRST-ROUND SELECTIONS

(If Club had no first-round selection, first player drafted is listed with round in parentheses.)

| Year | Player, College, Position |
|---|---|
| 1960 | Don Meredith, Southern Methodist, QB |
| 1961 | E.J. Holub, Texas Tech, C |
| 1962 | Ronnie Bull, Baylor, RB |
| 1963 | Buck Buchanan, Grambling, DT |
| | Ed Budde, Michigan State, G |
| 1964 | Pete Beathard, Southern California, QB |
| 1965 | Gale Sayers, Kansas, RB |
| 1966 | Aaron Brown, Minnesota, DE |
| 1967 | Gene Trosch, Miami, DE-DT |
| 1968 | Mo Moorman, Texas A&M, G |
| | George Daney, Texas-El Paso, G |
| 1969 | Jim Marsalis, Tennessee State, CB |
| 1970 | Sid Smith, Southern California, T |
| 1971 | Elmo Wright, Houston, WR |
| 1972 | Jeff Kinney, Nebraska, RB |
| 1973 | Gary Butler, Rice, TE (2) |
| 1974 | Woody Green, Arizona State, RB |
| 1975 | Elmore Stephens, Kentucky, TE (2) |
| 1976 | Rod Walters, Iowa, G |
| 1977 | Gary Green, Baylor, DB |
| 1978 | Art Still, Kentucky, DE |
| 1979 | Mike Bell, Colorado State, DE |
| | Steve Fuller, Clemson, QB |
| 1980 | Brad Budde, Southern California, G |
| 1981 | Willie Scott, South Carolina, TE |
| 1982 | Anthony Hancock, Tennessee, WR |
| 1983 | Todd Blackledge, Penn State, QB |
| 1984 | Bill Maas, Pittsburgh, DT |
| | John Alt, Iowa, T |

# KANSAS CITY CHIEFS 1984 VETERAN ROSTER

| No. | Name | Pos. | Ht. | Wt. | Birth-date | NFL Exp. | College | Birthplace | Residence | Games in '83 |
|---|---|---|---|---|---|---|---|---|---|---|
| 6 | Arnold, Jim | P | 6-2 | 212 | 1/31/61 | 2 | Vanderbilt | Dalton, Ga. | Kansas City, Mo. | 16 |
| 77 | Baldinger, Rich | T-G | 6-4 | 280 | 12/31/59 | 3 | Wake Forest | Camp Le Jeune, N.C. | Massapequa, N.Y. | 8* |
| 85 | Beckman, Ed | TE | 6-4 | 239 | 1/2/55 | 8 | Florida State | Key West, Fla. | Kansas City, Mo. | 15 |
| 99 | Bell, Mike | DE | 6-4 | 250 | 8/30/57 | 5 | Colorado State | Wichita, Kan. | Overland Park, Kan. | 16 |
| 14 | Blackledge, Todd | QB | 6-3 | 225 | 2/25/61 | 2 | Penn State | Canton, Ohio | Lee's Summit, Mo. | 4 |
| 57 | Blanton, Jerry | LB | 6-1 | 236 | 12/20/56 | 6 | Kentucky | Toledo, Ohio | Toledo, Ohio | 16 |
| 27 | Brown, Theotis | RB | 6-3 | 225 | 4/20/57 | 6 | UCLA | Chicago, Ill. | Bellevue, Wash. | 15* |
| 66 | Budde, Brad | G | 6-4 | 260 | 5/9/58 | 5 | Southern California | Detroit, Mich. | Overland Park, Kan. | 12 |
| 34 | Burruss, Lloyd | S | 6-0 | 202 | 10/31/57 | 4 | Maryland | Charlottesville, Va. | Charlottesville, Va. | 12 |
| 88 | Carson, Carlos | WR | 5-11 | 174 | 12/28/58 | 5 | Louisiana State | Lake Worth, Fla. | Grandview, Mo. | 16 |
| 20 | Cherry, Deron | S | 5-11 | 190 | 9/12/59 | 4 | Rutgers | Riverside, N.J. | Kansas City, Mo. | 16 |
| 65 | Condon, Tom | G | 6-3 | 275 | 12/26/52 | 11 | Boston College | Derby, Conn. | Kansas City, Mo. | 9 |
| 50 | Daniels, Calvin | LB | 6-3 | 236 | 12/26/58 | 3 | North Carolina | Morehead City, N.C. | Kansas City, Mo. | 16 |
| 75 | Gardner, Ellis | T-G | 6-4 | 263 | 9/16/61 | 2 | Georgia Tech | Chattanooga, Tenn. | Signal Mountain, Tenn. | 8 |
| 82 | Hancock, Anthony | WR-KR | 6-0 | 187 | 6/10/60 | 3 | Tennessee | Cleveland, Ohio | Kansas City, Mo. | 16 |
| 56 | Haynes, Louis | LB | 6-0 | 227 | 1/17/60 | 3 | North Texas State | New Orleans, La. | Grandview, Mo. | 5 |
| 60 | Herkenhoff, Matt | T | 6-4 | 272 | 4/2/51 | 9 | Minnesota | Melrose, Minn. | Kansas City, Mo. | 12 |
| 52 | †Howard, Thomas | LB | 6-2 | 215 | 8/18/54 | 8 | Texas Tech | Lubbock, Tex. | Lubbock, Tex. | 16 |
| 43 | Jackson, Billy | RB | 5-10 | 215 | 9/13/59 | 4 | Alabama | Phenix City, Ala. | Phenix City, Ala. | 16 |
| 51 | Jackson, Charles | LB | 6-2 | 222 | 3/22/55 | 7 | Washington | Berkeley, Calif. | Fairway, Kan. | 15 |
| 22 | Jakes, Van | CB | 5-11 | 185 | 5/10/61 | 2 | Kent State | Phenix City, Ala. | Buffalo, N.Y. | 14 |
| 9 | Kenney, Bill | QB | 6-4 | 211 | 1/20/55 | 6 | Northern Colorado | San Francisco, Calif. | Lee's Summit, Mo. | 16 |
| 64 | Kirchner, Mark | T-G | 6-3 | 261 | 10/19/59 | 2 | Baylor | Pasadena, Tex. | Waco, Tex. | 5* |
| 55 | Klug, Dave | LB | 6-4 | 230 | 5/17/58 | 3 | Concordia, Minn. | Litchfield, Minn. | Independence, Mo. | 1 |
| 91 | Kremer, Ken | NT | 6-4 | 252 | 7/16/57 | 6 | Ball State | Hammond, Ind. | Merriam, Kan. | 16 |
| 29 | Lewis, Albert | CB | 6-2 | 190 | 10/6/60 | 2 | Grambling | Mansfield, La. | Kansas City, Mo. | 16 |
| 71 | Lindstrom, Dave | DE | 6-6 | 255 | 11/16/54 | 7 | Boston University | Cambridge, Mass. | Overland Park, Kan. | 16 |
| 62 | Lingner, Adam | C-G | 6-4 | 240 | 11/2/60 | 2 | Illinois | Indianapolis, Ind. | Lee's Summit, Mo. | 16 |
| 8 | Lowery, Nick | K | 6-4 | 189 | 5/27/56 | 5 | Dartmouth | Munich, Germany | Lee's Summit, Mo. | 16 |
| 72 | Lutz, David | T | 6-5 | 280 | 12/30/59 | 2 | Georgia Tech | Monroe, N.C. | Atlanta, Ga. | 16 |
| 74 | Mangiero, Dino | NT | 6-2 | 264 | 12/19/58 | 5 | Rutgers | New York, N.Y. | Staten Island, N.Y. | 16 |
| 89 | Marshall, Henry | WR | 6-2 | 220 | 8/9/54 | 9 | Missouri | Broxton, Ga. | Kansas City, Mo. | 13 |
|  | McAlister, Ken | LB | 6-5 | 220 | 4/15/60 | 3 | San Francisco | Oakland, Calif. | Oakland, Calif. | 6* |
| 83 | Paige, Stephon | WR | 6-1 | 180 | 10/15/61 | 2 | Fresno State | Slidell, La. | Fresno, Calif. | 16 |
| 58 | Potter, Steve | LB | 6-3 | 235 | 11/6/57 | 4 | Virginia | Bradford, Pa. | Ft. Lauderdale, Fla. | 16 |
| 79 | Prater, Dean | DE | 6-5 | 245 | 9/29/58 | 2 | Oklahoma State | Altus, Okla. | Overland Park, Kan. | 16 |
| 42 | Ricks, Lawrence | RB | 5-9 | 194 | 6/4/61 | 2 | Michigan | Barberton, Ohio | Barberton, Ohio | 12 |
| 38 | Roquemore, Durwood | S | 6-1 | 180 | 1/19/60 | 3 | Texas A&I | Dallas, Tex. | Dallas, Tex. | 15 |
| 70 | Rourke, Jim | T-G | 6-5 | 263 | 2/10/57 | 5 | Boston College | Weymouth, Mass. | North Abington, Mass. | 11 |
| 53 | Rush, Bob | C | 6-5 | 264 | 2/27/55 | 7 | Memphis State | Santa Monica, Calif. | Germantown, Tenn. | 15 |
| 81 | Scott, Willie | TE | 6-4 | 245 | 2/13/59 | 4 | South Carolina | Newberry, S.C. | Columbia, S.C. | 16 |
| 86 | Smith, J.T. | WR-KR | 6-2 | 185 | 10/29/55 | 7 | North Texas State | Leonard, Tex. | Blue Springs, Mo. | 9 |
| 23 | Smith, Lucious | CB | 5-10 | 190 | 1/17/57 | 5 | Cal State-Fullerton | Columbus, Ga. | Anaheim, Calif. | 16 |
| 59 | Spani, Gary | LB | 6-2 | 228 | 1/9/56 | 7 | Kansas State | Satanta, Kan. | Lee's Summit, Mo. | 10 |
| 67 | Still, Art | DE | 6-7 | 245 | 12/5/55 | 7 | Kentucky | Camden, N.J. | Kansas City, Mo. | 15 |
| 35 | Thomas, Ken | RB | 5-9 | 211 | 2/11/60 | 2 | San Jose State | Hanford, Calif. | Hanford, Calif. | 14 |
| 54 | Walker, James | LB | 6-1 | 250 | 12/9/59 | 2 | Kansas State | Wichita, Kan. | Wichita, Kan. | 4 |
| 87 | Wetzel, Ron | TE | 6-5 | 242 | 11/10/60 | 2 | Arizona State | Pittsburgh, Pa. | Pittsburgh, Pa. | 16 |
| 92 | Yakavonis, Ray | NT | 6-4 | 250 | 1/20/57 | 4 | East Stroudsburg State | Wilkes-Barre, Pa. | Wilkes-Barre, Pa. | 4* |
| 61 | †Zamberlin, John | LB | 6-2 | 226 | 2/13/56 | 6 | Pacific Lutheran | Tacoma, Wash. | Tacoma, Wash. | 14 |

* Baldinger played 2 games with New York Giants in '83, 6 with Kansas City; Brown played 3 games with Seattle, 12 with Kansas City; Kirchner played 3 games with Pittsburgh, 5 with Kansas City; McAlister played 2 games with Seattle, 6 with San Francisco; Yakavonis played 2 games with Minnesota, 2 with Kansas City.

†Option playout; subject to developments.

Traded—Running back Jewerl Thomas to San Diego, cornerback Gary Green to Los Angeles Rams.

Also played with Chiefs in '83—CB Trent Bryant (16 games), QB Bob Gagliano (1), RB James Hadnot (5), G-T Bob Simmons (15).

## COACHING STAFF

### Head Coach,
### John Mackovic

**Pro Career:** Begins second season as Chiefs head coach. Compiled a 6-10 record in his first campaign in 1983. Came to the Chiefs after serving as quarterback coach with Dallas Cowboys in 1981-82. No pro playing experience.

**Background:** Played quarterback for Wake Forest 1961-64. Was freshman coach at Army in 1967-68 before coaching at San Jose State as offensive co-ordinator 1969-70. Returned to Army as an assistant 1971-72, then to Arizona 1973-76, and Purdue 1977. Became head coach at Wake Forest 1978-80 before going to the Cowboys.

**Personal:** Born October 1, 1943, Barberton, Ohio. John and his wife, Arlene, live in Kansas City, and have two children—Aimee and John III.

### Assistant Coaches

**Bud Carson,** defensive coordinator-defensive backs; born April 28, 1931, Brackenridge, Pa., lives in Kansas City. Defensive back North Carolina 1948-52. No pro playing experience. College coach: North Carolina 1957-64, South Carolina 1965, Georgia Tech 1966-71 (head coach). Pro coach: Pittsburgh Steelers 1972-77, Los Angeles Rams 1978-81, Baltimore Colts 1982, joined Chiefs in 1983.

**Walt Corey,** defensive line; born May 9, 1938, Latrobe, Pa., lives in Kansas City. Defensive end Miami 1957-59. Pro linebacker Kansas City Chiefs 1960-66. College coach: Utah State 1967-69, Miami 1970-71. Pro coach: Kansas City Chiefs 1971-74, Cleveland Browns 1975-77, rejoined Chiefs in 1978.

**Dan Daniel,** inside linebackers; born April 10, 1933, Huron, S.D., lives in Kansas City. Quarterback-defensive back Huron College 1958-62. No pro playing experience. College coach: MacAlister College 1965, Colorado State 1966-69, Navy 1970, Wyoming 1971, Houston 1972-77. Pro coach: Edmonton Eskimos (CFL) 1978-81, Calgary Stampeders (CFL) 1982, joined Chiefs in 1983.

**Doug Graber,** defensive backs and defensive quality control; born September 26, 1944, Detroit, Mich., lives in Kansas City. Defensive back Wayne State 1963-66. No pro playing experience. College coach: Michigan Tech 1969-71, Eastern Michigan 1972-75, Ball State 1976-77, Wisconsin 1978-81, Montana State 1982 (head coach). Pro coach: Joined Chiefs in 1983.

**J.D. Helm,** offensive assistant and quality control; born December 27, 1940, El Dorado Springs, Mo., lives in Overland Park, Kan. Running back Kansas 1959-60. No pro playing experience. College coach: Brigham Young 1969-75. Pro coach: Joined Chiefs in 1976.

**C.T. Hewgley,** offensive and defensive lines-coordinator of strength and conditioning program; born August 22, 1925, Nashville, Tenn., lives in Kansas City. Tackle Wyoming 1947-50. No pro playing experience. College coach: Miami 1968-70, Wyoming 1971-73, Nebraska-Omaha 1974 (head coach), Michigan State 1976-79, Arizona State 1980-82. Pro coach: Joined Chiefs in 1983.

**Rod Humenuik,** offensive line-running game; born June 17, 1938, Detroit, Mich., lives in Kansas City. Guard Southern California 1956-58. Pro guard Winnipeg Blue Bombers (CFL) 1960-62. College coach: Fullerton, Calif., J.C. 1964-65, Southern California 1966-70, Cal State-Northridge 1971-72 (head coach). Pro coach: Toronto Argonauts (CFL) 1973-74, Cleveland Browns 1975-82, joined Chiefs in 1983.

**Pete McCulley,** quarterbacks; born November 29, 1931, Franklin, Miss., lives in Kansas City. Quarterback Louisiana Tech 1954-56. No pro playing experience. College coach: Stephen F. Austin 1959, Houston 1960-61, Baylor 1963-69, Navy 1970-72. Pro coach: Baltimore Colts 1973-75, Washington Redskins 1976-77, San Francisco 49ers 1978 (head coach nine games), New York Jets 1979-82, joined Chiefs in 1983.

## KANSAS CITY CHIEFS 1984 FIRST-YEAR ROSTER

| Name | Pos. | Ht. | Wt. | Birth-date | College | Birthplace | Residence | How Acq. |
|------|------|-----|-----|-----------|---------|-----------|-----------|----------|
| Alt, John | T | 6-7 | 278 | 5/30/62 | Iowa | Stuttgart, Germany | Columbia, Minn. | D1a |
| Arterberry, Greg | WR | 6-2 | 199 | 3/8/62 | Texas Christian | Tyler, Tex. | Tyler, Tex. | FA |
| Auer, Scott | G-T | 6-4 | 255 | 10/4/61 | Michigan State | Ft. Wayne, Ind. | Ft. Wayne, Ind. | D9 |
| Bauer, Mark | T | 6-4 | 256 | 4/25/62 | Drake | St. Louis, Mo. | St. Louis, Mo. | FA |
| Booze, Bill | WR | 6-1 | 193 | 2/2/62 | Cincinnati | Vineland, N.Y. | Vineland, N.Y. | FA |
| Bracken, Don | P | 6-1 | 190 | 2/16/62 | Michigan | Thermopolis, Wyo. | Thermopolis, Wyo. | FA |
| Clark, Randy | S | 6-0 | 195 | 2/18/62 | Florida | Venice, Fla. | Venice, Fla. | D8 |
| Conway, John | P | 6-2 | 185 | 9/24/60 | Oklahoma State | Baytown, Tex. | Baytown, Tex. | FA |
| Dahl, Mike | G | 6-3 | 245 | 12/26/61 | Pittsburgh | Joppa, Md. | Joppa, Md. | FA |
| Davis, John | LB | 6-3 | 224 | 2/20/62 | Jackson State | Prichard, Ala. | Prichard, Ala. | FA |
| Denfeld, Philip (1) | TE | 6-5 | 235 | 7/31/61 | Wake Forest | Colorado Spgs., Colo. | Annandale, Va. | FA |
| Dorsey, Melvin | RB | 5-10 | 198 | 5/8/60 | Western Carolina | Sautee, Ga. | Sautee, Ga. | FA |
| Etzel, Scott | C | 6-4 | 272 | 7/6/62 | Northern Iowa | Hampton, Ill. | Hampton, Ill. | FA |
| Fletcher, Lafayette | WR-KR | 5-10 | 175 | 10/9/61 | Fresno State | Inglewood, Calif. | Inglewood, Calif. | FA |
| Fruehan, Mark | LB | 6-1 | 195 | 6/26/61 | Penn State | Moscow, Pa. | Moscow, Pa. | FA |
| Godfrey, Mike | QB | 6-1 | 200 | 7/18/61 | Montana State | Eugene, Ore. | Eugene, Ore. | FA |
| Goolsby, Ernie (1) | RB | 6-1 | 232 | 4/29/61 | Vanderbilt | Dodge City, Kan. | Blue Springs, Mo. | FA |
| Grogan, Tom | QB | 6-2 | 203 | 10/31/60 | Iowa | Kansas City, Kan. | Kansas City, Kan. | FA |
| Gwinn, Derek | G | 6-3 | 251 | 12/20/60 | Georgia Tech | Winter Park, Fla. | Winter Park, Fla. | FA |
| Hall, Glen | S | 6-2 | 210 | 7/27/61 | Grambling | Mansfield, La. | Mansfield, La. | FA |
| Heard, Herman | RB | 5-10 | 184 | 11/24/61 | Southern Colorado | Denver, Colo. | Denver, Colo. | D3 |
| Heckman, Dennis | K | 5-10 | 168 | 1/1/61 | Akron | Akron, Ohio | Akron, Ohio | FA |
| Hestera, Dave | TE | 6-3 | 240 | 5/15/61 | Colorado | Pamona, Wyo. | Berwynn, Ill. | D9a |
| Hodges, Steve | RB | 5-9 | 205 | 12/29/60 | William Jewell | Ferguson, Mo. | Ferguson, Mo. | FA |
| Hogan, Kedrick | LB | 6-3 | 232 | 10/22/61 | Southern | New Orleans, La. | New Orleans, La. | FA |
| Holle, Eric | DE | 6-4 | 250 | 9/5/60 | Texas | Austin, Tex. | Austin, Tex. | D5 |
| Howell, Wesley (1) | TE | 6-3 | 235 | 3/8/60 | California | Castro Valley, Calif. | Castro Valley, Calif. | FA |
| Jennings, Jarvis | FB | 5-11 | 212 | 10/12/61 | Richmond | Jefferson City, Tenn. | Jefferson City, Tenn. | FA |
| Johnson, Bobby | RB | 6-1 | 191 | 9/30/62 | San Jose State | Monterey, Calif. | Monterey, Calif. | D11 |
| Jones, Donald (1) | CB | 6-0 | 183 | 3/28/58 | Southern California | San Francisco, Calif. | Carson, Calif. | FA |
| Jones, E.J. | FB | 5-11 | 212 | 2/1/62 | Kansas | Chicago, Ill. | Chicago, Ill. | FA |
| Kalafat, Jim | LB | 5-11 | 219 | 2/21/62 | Montana State | Great Falls, Mont. | Great Falls, Mont. | FA |
| Lang, Mark | LB | 6-2 | 235 | 6/27/61 | Texas | Monahans, Tex. | Iraan, Tex. | D12 |
| Lee, Daniel | DE | 6-4 | 230 | 7/16/61 | Carthage College | Burlington, Wis. | Burlington, Wis. | FA |
| Ligon, Al | S | 6-1 | 170 | 10/14/61 | Nevada-Las Vegas | Gardena, Calif. | Gardena, Calif. | FA |
| McDade, Clarence | LB | 6-2 | 205 | 3/4/62 | Southern Methodist | Waco, Tex. | Waco, Tex. | FA |
| Mack, Eric | WR | 6-2 | 217 | 4/14/60 | Kansas State | Covington, Va. | Covington, Va. | FA |
| Maas, Bill | NT | 6-4 | 265 | 3/2/62 | Pittsburgh | Newton Square, Pa. | Newton Square, Pa. | D1 |
| Metcalf, Issac (1) | CB-S | 6-2 | 193 | 4/18/61 | Baylor | Waco, Tex. | Waco, Tex. | FA |
| Naumcheff, David | WR | 6-1 | 176 | 2/2/61 | Ball State | Muncie, Ind. | Muncie, Ind. | FA |
| Newman, Mike | CB | 5-10 | 165 | 10/25/61 | William Jewell | Kansas City, Mo. | Kansas City, Mo. | FA |
| Osiecki, John | QB | 6-5 | 202 | 5/18/60 | Arizona State | Ansonia, Conn. | Ansonia, Conn. | FA |
| Paffenroth, Dave (1) | LB | 6-1 | 240 | 2/5/61 | Penn State | Middletown, N.Y. | Kansas City, Mo. | FA |
| Paine, Jeff | LB | 6-2 | 224 | 8/19/61 | Texas A&M | Carland, Tex. | Richardson, Tex. | D5a |
| Parker, Kerry (1) | CB | 6-1 | 187 | 10/3/55 | Grambling | New Orleans, La. | New Orleans, La. | FA |
| Pearl, Ivan | CB | 5-8 | 185 | 12/31/61 | Kansas State | Parkville, Mo. | Parkville, Mo. | FA |
| Porter, Rob | S | 6-1 | 200 | 5/9/62 | Holy Cross | Mahwah, N.J. | Mahwah, N.J. | FA |
| Posey, Daryl (1) | RB | 6-0 | 209 | 5/13/60 | Mississippi College | Biloxi, Miss. | Kansas City, Mo. | D7a('83) |
| Radecic, Scott | LB | 6-2 | 240 | 6/14/62 | Penn State | Pittsburgh, Pa. | Pittsburgh, Pa. | D2 |
| Revis, Norm | TE | 6-4 | 234 | 9/12/61 | Southern Methodist | Diamond Bar, Calif. | Diamond Bar, Calif. | FA |
| Robinson, Mark | S | 5-10 | 206 | 9/13/62 | Penn State | Silver Spring, Md. | Silver Spring, Md. | D4 |
| Ross, Kevin | CB | 5-9 | 180 | 1/16/62 | Temple | Paulsboro, N.J. | Paulsboro, N.J. | D7 |
| Shaw, Jeff | S | 6-2 | 185 | 6/1/62 | Nevada-Reno | Las Vegas, Nev. | Las Vegas, Nev. | FA |
| Smith, Cary | T | 6-5 | 258 | 5/7/62 | Pacific | Walnut Creek, Calif. | Walnut Creek, Calif. | FA |
| Sorenson, Barry | CB | 5-10 | 180 | 5/5/62 | North Dakota State | Brainerd, Minn. | Brainerd, Minn. | FA |
| Stevens, Rufus | WR | 6-3 | 182 | 1/13/61 | Grambling | Monroe, La. | Monroe, La. | D6 |
| Tipton, Darryl | LB | 6-2 | 229 | 7/31/62 | Tulane | Ypsilanti, Mich. | Ypsilanti, Mich. | FA |
| Tootle, Jeff | LB | 6-1 | 203 | 8/29/62 | Mesa College, Colo. | Aurora, Colo. | Aurora, Colo. | FA |
| Waters, Dean | C | 6-3 | 248 | 5/19/61 | Georgia Tech | Augusta, Ga. | Augusta, Ga. | FA |
| Wenglikowski, Al | LB | 6-1 | 220 | 8/3/60 | Pittsburgh | Franklin, Ohio | Franklin, Ohio | D10 |
| Williams, Leonard | RB | 5-11 | 195 | 6/27/60 | Western Carolina | Greensboro, N.C. | Greensboro, N.C. | FA |
| Williams, Tom | CB | 6-0 | 172 | 1/11/62 | Drake | Clinton, Iowa | Clinton, Iowa | FA |
| Youst, Randy | WR | 5-11 | 186 | 4/23/61 | Taylor, Ind. | Loveland, Ohio | Loveland, Ohio | FA |

Players who report to an NFL team for the first time are designated on rosters as rookies (R). If a player reported to an NFL training camp in a previous year but was not on the active squad for three or more regular season or postseason games, he is listed on the first-year roster and designated by a (1). Thereafter, a player who is on the active squad for three or more regular season or postseason games is credited with an additional year of playing experience.

**Willie Peete,** offensive backs; born September 14, 1937, Mesa, Ariz., lives in Kansas City. Wide receiver Arizona 1956-59. No pro playing experience. College coach: Arizona 1970-82. Pro coach: Joined Chiefs in 1983.

**Jim Vechiarella,** outside linebackers-special teams; born February 20, 1937, Youngstown, Ohio, lives in Kansas City. Linebacker Youngstown State 1955-57. No pro playing experience. College coach: Youngstown State 1964-74, Southern Illinois 1976-77, Tulane 1978-80. Pro coach: Charlotte Hornets (WFL) 1975, Los Angeles Rams 1980-82, joined Chiefs in 1983.

**Richard Williamson,** receivers; born April 13, 1941, Fort Deposit, Ala., lives in Kansas City. Wide receiver Alabama 1959-62. No pro playing experience. College coach: Arkansas 1968-69, 1972-74, Alabama 1963-67, 1970-71, Memphis State 1975-80. Pro coach: Joined Chiefs in 1983.

# LOS ANGELES RAIDERS

**American Football Conference
Western Division**

**Team Colors:** Silver and Black

**332 Center Street
El Segundo, California 90245
Telephone:** (213) 322-3451

### Club Officials

Managing General Partner: Al Davis
Executive Assistant: Al LoCasale
Player Personnel: Ron Wolf
Business Manager: Ken LaRue
Senior Administrators: Tom Grimes, Irv Kaze
Marketing/Promotions: Mike Ornstein
Community Relations: Gil Hernandez,
    Calvin Peterson
Ticket Operations: Peter Eiges
Comptroller: Peggy Ferguson
Trainers: George Anderson, H. Rod Martin
Equipment Manager: Richard Romanski

**Stadium:** Los Angeles Memorial Coliseum •
    **Capacity:** 92,516
    3911 South Figueroa Street
    Los Angeles, California 90037

**Playing Surface:** Grass

**Training Camp:** El Rancho Tropicana
    Santa Rosa, California 95401

## 1984 SCHEDULE

### Preseason
| | | |
|---|---|---|
| Aug. 4 | at San Francisco | 6:00 |
| Aug. 10 | at Washington | 8:00 |
| Aug. 19 | **Miami** | 1:00 |
| Aug. 24 | **New York Jets** | 6:00 |

### Regular Season
| | | |
|---|---|---|
| Sept. 2 | at Houston | 3:00 |
| Sept. 9 | **Green Bay** | 1:00 |
| Sept. 16 | at Kansas City | 12:00 |
| Sept. 24 | **San Diego** (Monday) | 6:00 |
| Sept. 30 | at Denver | 2:00 |
| Oct. 7 | **Seattle** | 1:00 |
| Oct. 14 | **Minnesota** | 1:00 |
| Oct. 21 | at San Diego | 1:00 |
| Oct. 28 | **Denver** | 1:00 |
| Nov. 4 | at Chicago | 12:00 |
| Nov. 12 | at Seattle (Monday) | 6:00 |
| Nov. 18 | **Kansas City** | 1:00 |
| Nov. 25 | **Colts** | 1:00 |
| Dec. 2 | at Miami | 4:00 |
| Dec. 10 | at Detroit (Monday) | 9:00 |
| Dec. 16 | **Pittsburgh** | 1:00 |

## RAIDERS COACHING HISTORY

**Oakland 1960-81
(234-125-11)**

| | | |
|---|---|---|
| 1960-61 | Eddie Erdelatz* | 6-10-0 |
| 1961-62 | Marty Feldman** | 2-15-0 |
| 1962 | Red Conkright | 1-8-0 |
| 1963-65 | Al Davis | 23-16-3 |
| 1966-68 | John Rauch | 35-10-1 |
| 1969-78 | John Madden | 112-39-7 |
| 1979-83 | Tom Flores | 55-27-0 |

*Released after two games in 1961
**Released after five games in 1962

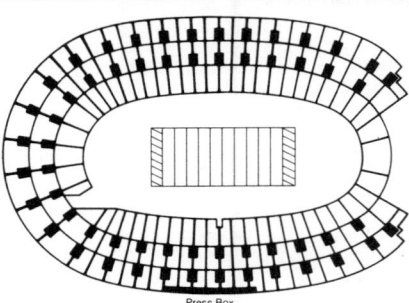

**MEMORIAL COLISEUM**

## RECORD HOLDERS
### Individual Records—Career
| Category | Name | Performance |
|---|---|---|
| Rushing (Yds.) | Mark van Eeghen, 1974-1981 | 5,907 |
| Passing (Yds.) | Ken Stabler, 1970-79 | 19,078 |
| Passing (TDs) | Ken Stabler, 1970-79 | 150 |
| Receiving (No.) | Fred Biletnikoff, 1965-1978 | 589 |
| Receiving (Yds.) | Fred Biletnikoff, 1965-1978 | 8,974 |
| Interceptions | Willie Brown, 1967-1978 | 39 |
| Punting (Avg.) | Ray Guy, 1973-1983 | 42.9 |
| Punt Return (Avg.) | Claude Gibson, 1963-65 | 12.6 |
| Kickoff Return (Avg.) | Jack Larscheid, 1960-61 | 28.4 |
| Field Goals | George Blanda, 1967-1975 | 156 |
| Touchdowns (Tot.) | Fred Biletnikoff, 1967-1978 | 77 |
| Points | George Blanda, 1967-1975 | 863 |

### Individual Records—Single Season
| Category | Name | Performance |
|---|---|---|
| Rushing (Yds.) | Mark van Eeghen, 1977 | 1,273 |
| Passing (Yds.) | Ken Stabler, 1979 | 3,615 |
| Passing (TDs) | Daryle Lamonica, 1969 | 34 |
| Receiving (No.) | Todd Christensen, 1983 | 92 |
| Receiving (Yds.) | Art Powell, 1964 | 1,361 |
| Interceptions | Lester Hayes, 1980 | 13 |
| Punting (Avg.) | Ray Guy, 1973 | 45.3 |
| Punt Return (Avg.) | Claude Gibson, 1963 | 14.4 |
| Kickoff Return (Avg.) | Harold Hart, 1975 | 30.5 |
| Field Goals | George Blanda, 1973 | 23 |
| Touchdowns (Tot.) | Art Powell, 1963 | 16 |
| | Pete Banaszak, 1975 | 16 |
| Points | George Blanda, 1968 | 117 |

### Individual Records—Single Game
| Category | Name | Performance |
|---|---|---|
| Rushing (Yds.) | Clem Daniels, 10-20-63 | 200 |
| Passing (Yds.) | Cotton Davidson, 10-25-64 | 427 |
| Passing (TDs) | Tom Flores, 12-22-63 | 6 |
| | Daryle Lamonica, 10-19-69 | 6 |
| Receiving (No.) | Dave Casper, 10-3-76 | 12 |
| Receiving (Yds.) | Art Powell, 12-22-63 | 247 |
| Interceptions | Many times | 3 |
| | Last time by Charles Phillips, 12-8-75 | |
| Field Goals | Many times | 4 |
| | Last time by Chris Bahr, 10-23-83 | |
| Touchdowns (Tot.) | Art Powell, 12-22-63 | 4 |
| Points | Art Powell, 12-22-63 | 24 |

## 1983 TEAM STATISTICS

| | L.A. Raiders | Opp. |
|---|---|---|
| Total First Downs | 356 | 285 |
| Rushing | 143 | 86 |
| Passing | 181 | 170 |
| Penalty | 32 | 29 |
| Third Down Efficiency | 100/223 | 72/225 |
| Third Down Percentage | 44.8 | 32.0 |
| Total Net Yards | 5686 | 4748 |
| Total Offensive Plays | 1101 | 1024 |
| Avg. Gain per Play | 5.2 | 4.6 |
| Avg. Gain per Game | 355.4 | 296.8 |
| Net Yards Rushing | 2240 | 1586 |
| Total Rushing Plays | 542 | 436 |
| Avg. Gain per Rush | 4.1 | 3.6 |
| Avg. Gain Rushing per Game | 140.0 | 99.1 |
| Net Yards Passing | 3446 | 3162 |
| Lost Attempting to Pass | 55/464 | 57/484 |
| Gross Yards Passing | 3910 | 3646 |
| Attempts/Completions | 504/301 | 531/282 |
| Percent Completed | 59.7 | 53.1 |
| Had Intercepted | 24 | 20 |
| Avg. Net Passing per Game | 215.4 | 197.6 |
| Punts/Avg. | 78/42.8 | 100/40.6 |
| Punt Returns/Avg. | 58/11.5 | 35/9.5 |
| Kickoff Returns/Avg. | 61/19.3 | 68/18.0 |
| Interceptions/Avg. Ret. | 20/11.9 | 24/15.9 |
| Penalties/Yards | 121/992 | 109/947 |
| Fumbles/Ball Lost | 46/25 | 31/16 |
| Total Points | 442 | 338 |
| Avg. Points per Game | 27.6 | 21.1 |
| Touchdowns | 54 | 40 |
| Rushing | 18 | 13 |
| Passing | 31 | 20 |
| Returns and Recoveries | 5 | 7 |
| Field Goals | 21/27 | 19/25 |
| Conversions | 51/54 | 39/40 |
| Safeties | 2 | 1 |
| Avg. Time of Possession | 30:58 | 29:02 |

## 1983 TEAM RECORD

### Preseason (1-3)

| Date | Los Angeles Raiders | | Opponents | |
|---|---|---|---|---|
| 8/6 | 26 | *San Francisco (OT) | 23 | |
| 8/13 | 17 | New York Jets | 20 | |
| 8/20 | 21 | *Chicago | 27 | |
| 8/26 | 17 | Cleveland | 20 | |
| | 81 | | 90 | |

### Regular Season (12-4)

| Date | Los Angeles Raiders | | Opp. | Att. |
|---|---|---|---|---|
| 9/4 | 20 | Cincinnati | 10 | 50,956 |
| 9/11 | 20 | *Houston | 6 | 37,526 |
| 9/19 | 27 | *Miami | 14 | 57,796 |
| 9/25 | 22 | Denver | 7 | 74,289 |
| 10/2 | 35 | Washington | 37 | 54,016 |
| 10/9 | 21 | *Kansas City | 20 | 40,492 |
| 10/16 | 36 | Seattle | 38 | 60,967 |
| 10/23 | 40 | Dallas | 38 | 64,991 |
| 10/30 | 21 | *Seattle | 34 | 49,708 |
| 11/6 | 28 | Kansas City | 20 | 73,497 |
| 11/13 | 22 | *Denver | 20 | 51,945 |
| 11/20 | 27 | Buffalo | 24 | 72,393 |
| 11/27 | 27 | *New York Giants | 12 | 41,473 |
| 12/1 | 42 | San Diego | 10 | 47,760 |
| 12/11 | 24 | *St. Louis | 34 | 32,111 |
| 12/18 | 30 | *San Diego | 14 | 57,325 |
| | 442 | | 338 | 867,245 |

*Home Game    (OT) Overtime

### Score by Periods

| | | | | | | |
|---|---|---|---|---|---|---|
| L.A. Raiders | 75 | 131 | 108 | 128 | — | 442 |
| Opponents | 61 | 85 | 54 | 138 | — | 338 |

### Attendance

Home 368,376    Away 498,869    Total 867,245
Single game home record, 78,939 (1-2-72; Oakland Stadium), 90,334 (1-1-84; LA Coliseum)
Single season home record, 557,881 (1972; Oakland Stadium), 368,376 (1983; LA Coliseum).

## 1983 INDIVIDUAL STATISTICS

### Rushing

| | Att. | Yds. | Avg. | LG | TD |
|---|---|---|---|---|---|
| Allen | 266 | 1014 | 3.8 | 19 | 9 |
| Hawkins | 110 | 526 | 4.8 | 32 | 6 |
| King | 82 | 294 | 3.6 | 16 | 1 |
| Pruitt | 26 | 154 | 5.9 | 18 | 2 |
| Wilson | 13 | 122 | 9.4 | 23 | 0 |
| Plunkett | 26 | 78 | 3.0 | 20 | 0 |
| Berns | 6 | 22 | 3.7 | 13 | 0 |
| Branch | 1 | 20 | 20.0 | 20 | 0 |
| Barnwell | 1 | 12 | 12.0 | 12 | 0 |
| Montgomery | 2 | 7 | 3.5 | 5 | 0 |
| Jensen | 1 | 5 | 5.0 | 5 | 0 |
| Willis | 5 | 0 | 0.0 | 4 | 0 |
| Humm | 1 | −1 | −1.0 | −1 | 0 |
| Guy | 2 | −13 | −6.5 | −3 | 0 |
| L.A. Raiders | 542 | 2240 | 4.1 | 32 | 18 |
| Opponents | 436 | 1586 | 3.6 | 80 | 13 |

### Passing

| | Att. | Comp. | Pct. | Yds. | TD | Int. | Tkld. | Rate |
|---|---|---|---|---|---|---|---|---|
| Plunkett | 379 | 230 | 60.7 | 2935 | 20 | 18 | 42/363 | 82.7 |
| Wilson | 117 | 67 | 57.3 | 864 | 8 | 6 | 10/75 | 82.0 |
| Allen | 7 | 4 | 57.1 | 111 | 3 | 0 | 3/26 | 141.4 |
| Pruitt | 1 | 0 | 0.0 | 0 | 0 | 0 | 0/0 | 39.6 |
| Raiders | 504 | 301 | 59.7 | 3910 | 31 | 24 | 55/464 | 84.8 |
| Opponents | 531 | 282 | 53.1 | 3646 | 20 | 20 | 57/484 | 71.8 |

### Receiving

| | No. | Yds. | Avg. | LG | TD |
|---|---|---|---|---|---|
| Christensen | 92 | 1247 | 13.6 | 45 | 12 |
| Allen | 68 | 590 | 8.7 | 36 | 2 |
| Branch | 39 | 696 | 17.8 | 99t | 5 |
| Barnwell | 35 | 513 | 14.7 | 41 | 1 |
| Hawkins | 20 | 150 | 7.5 | 28 | 2 |
| Williams | 14 | 259 | 18.5 | 50t | 3 |
| King | 14 | 149 | 10.6 | 34t | 1 |
| Muhammad | 13 | 252 | 19.4 | 45 | 2 |
| Montgomery | 2 | 29 | 14.5 | 15 | 0 |
| Hasselbeck | 2 | 17 | 8.5 | 13t | 2 |
| Pruitt | 1 | 6 | 6.0 | 6 | 0 |
| Jensen | 1 | 2 | 2.0 | 2t | 1 |
| L.A. Raiders | 301 | 3910 | 13.0 | 99t | 31 |
| Opponents | 282 | 3646 | 12.9 | 67 | 20 |

### Interceptions

| | No. | Yds. | Avg. | LG | TD |
|---|---|---|---|---|---|
| McElroy | 8 | 68 | 8.5 | 28 | 0 |
| Martin | 4 | 81 | 20.3 | 40t | 2 |
| Hayes | 2 | 49 | 24.5 | 28 | 0 |
| Millen | 1 | 14 | 14.0 | 14 | 0 |
| Watts | 1 | 13 | 13.0 | 13 | 0 |
| J. Davis | 1 | 10 | 10.0 | 10 | 0 |
| M. Davis | 1 | 3 | 3.0 | 3 | 0 |
| Haynes | 1 | 0 | 0.0 | 0 | 0 |
| McKinney | 1 | 0 | 0.0 | 0 | 0 |
| L.A. Raiders | 20 | 238 | 11.9 | 40t | 2 |
| Opponents | 24 | 381 | 15.9 | 44 | 0 |

### Punting

| | No. | Yds. | Avg. | In 20 | LG |
|---|---|---|---|---|---|
| Guy | 78 | 3336 | 42.8 | 17 | 67 |
| L.A. Raiders | 78 | 3336 | 42.8 | 17 | 67 |
| Opponents | 100 | 4060 | 40.6 | 20 | 62 |

### Punt Returns

| | No. | FC | Yds. | Avg. | LG | TD |
|---|---|---|---|---|---|---|
| Pruitt | 58 | 18 | 666 | 11.5 | 97t | 1 |
| L.A. Raiders | 58 | 18 | 666 | 11.5 | 97t | 1 |
| Opponents | 35 | 10 | 334 | 9.5 | 75t | 2 |

### Kickoff Returns

| | No. | Yds. | Avg. | LG | TD |
|---|---|---|---|---|---|
| Montgomery | 21 | 464 | 22.1 | 48 | 0 |
| Pruitt | 31 | 604 | 19.5 | 42 | 0 |
| Williams | 5 | 88 | 17.6 | 19 | 0 |
| Millen | 2 | 19 | 9.5 | 10 | 0 |
| Jensen | 1 | 0 | 0.0 | 0 | 0 |
| Martin | 1 | 0 | 0.0 | 0 | 0 |
| L.A. Raiders | 61 | 1175 | 19.3 | 48 | 0 |
| Opponents | 68 | 1227 | 18.0 | 50 | 0 |

### Scoring

| | TD | TD R | TD P | TD Rt | PAT | FG | TP |
|---|---|---|---|---|---|---|---|
| Bahr | | | | | 51/53 | 21/27 | 114 |
| Allen | 12 | 9 | 2 | 1 | | | 72 |
| Christensen | 12 | 0 | 12 | 0 | | | 72 |
| Hawkins | 8 | 6 | 2 | 0 | | | 48 |
| Branch | 5 | 0 | 5 | 0 | | | 30 |
| Pruitt | 3 | 2 | 0 | 1 | | | 18 |
| Williams | 3 | 0 | 3 | 0 | | | 18 |
| Hasselbeck | 2 | 0 | 2 | 0 | | | 12 |
| King | 2 | 1 | 1 | 0 | | | 12 |
| Martin | 2 | 0 | 0 | 2 | | | 12 |
| Muhammad | 2 | 0 | 2 | 0 | | | 12 |
| Townsend | 1 | 0 | 0 | 1 | | | 8 |
| Barnwell | 1 | 0 | 1 | 0 | | | 6 |
| Jensen | 1 | 0 | 1 | 0 | | | 6 |
| Alzado | | (Safety) | | | | | 2 |
| L.A. Raiders | 54 | 18 | 31 | 5 | 51/54 | 21/27 | 442 |
| Opponents | 40 | 13 | 20 | 7 | 39/40 | 19/25 | 338 |

## FIRST-ROUND SELECTIONS

(If Club had no first-round selection, first player drafted is listed with round in parentheses.)

| Year | Player, College, Position |
|---|---|
| 1960 | Dale Hackbart, Wisconsin, CB |
| 1961 | Joe Rutgens, Illinois, DT |
| 1962 | Roman Gabriel, North Carolina State, QB |
| 1963 | George Wilson, Alabama, RB (6) |
| 1964 | Tony Lorick, Arizona State, RB |
| 1965 | Harry Schuh, Memphis State, T |
| 1966 | Rodger Bird, Kentucky, S |
| 1967 | Gene Upshaw, Texas A&I, G |
| 1968 | Eldridge Dickey, Tennessee State, QB |
| 1969 | Art Thoms, Syracuse, DT |
| 1970 | Raymond Chester, Morgan State, TE |
| 1971 | Jack Tatum, Ohio State, S |
| 1972 | Mike Siani, Villanova, WR |
| 1973 | Ray Guy, Southern Mississippi, K-P |
| 1974 | Henry Lawrence, Florida A&M, T |
| 1975 | Neal Colzie, Ohio State, DB |
| 1976 | Charles Philyaw, Texas Southern, DT (2) |
| 1977 | Mike Davis, Colorado, DB (2) |
| 1978 | Dave Browning, Washington, DE (2) |
| 1979 | Willie Jones, Florida State, DE (2) |
| 1980 | Marc Wilson, Brigham Young, QB |
| 1981 | Ted Watts, Texas Tech, DB |
| | Curt Marsh, Washington, T |
| 1982 | Marcus Allen, Southern California, RB |
| 1983 | Don Mosebar, Southern California, T |
| 1984 | Sean Jones, Northeastern, DE (2) |

# LOS ANGELES RAIDERS 1984 VETERAN ROSTER

| No. | Name | Pos. | Ht. | Wt. | Birth-date | NFL Exp. | College | Birthplace | Residence | Games in '83 |
|---|---|---|---|---|---|---|---|---|---|---|
| 32 | Allen, Marcus | RB | 6-2 | 205 | 3/22/60 | 3 | Southern California | San Diego, Calif. | Brentwood, Calif. | 16 |
| 77 | Alzado, Lyle | DE | 6-3 | 260 | 4/3/49 | 14 | Yankton | Brooklyn, N.Y. | Manhattan Beach, Calif. | 15 |
| 10 | Bahr, Chris | K | 5-10 | 175 | 2/3/53 | 9 | Penn State | State College, Pa. | Cincinnati, Ohio | 16 |
| 56 | Barnes, Jeff | LB | 6-2 | 230 | 3/1/55 | 8 | California | Philadelphia, Pa. | San Leandro, Calif. | 16 |
| 80 | Barnwell, Malcolm | WR | 5-11 | 185 | 6/28/58 | 4 | Virginia Union | Charleston, S.C. | Midlothian, Va. | 16 |
| 40 | †Berns, Rick | RB | 6-2 | 215 | 2/5/56 | 5 | Nebraska | Okinawa, Japan | Lincoln, Neb. | 16 |
| 21 | Branch, Cliff | WR | 5-11 | 170 | 8/1/48 | 13 | Colorado | Houston, Tex. | Hermosa Beach, Calif. | 12 |
| 54 | Byrd, Darryl | LB | 6-1 | 220 | 9/3/60 | 2 | Illinois | San Diego, Calif. | Union City, Calif. | 16 |
| 57 | Caldwell, Tony | LB | 6-1 | 225 | 4/1/61 | 2 | Washington | Los Angeles, Calif. | Seattle, Wash. | 16 |
| 46 | Christensen, Todd | TE | 6-3 | 230 | 8/3/56 | 6 | Brigham Young | Bellefonte, Pa. | El Segundo, Calif. | 16 |
| 50 | Dalby, Dave | C | 6-3 | 250 | 8/19/50 | 13 | UCLA | Alexandria, Minn. | Castro Valley, Calif. | 16 |
| 79 | Davis, Bruce | T | 6-6 | 280 | 6/21/56 | 6 | UCLA | Rutherford, N.C. | Daly City, Calif. | 16 |
| 45 | Davis, James | CB | 6-0 | 195 | 6/12/57 | 3 | Southern | Los Angeles, Calif. | Baton Rouge, La. | 16 |
| 36 | Davis, Mike | S | 6-3 | 205 | 4/15/56 | 7 | Colorado | Los Angeles, Calif. | Playa Del Rey, Calif. | 16 |
|  | t-Golsteyn, Jerry | QB | 6-4 | 210 | 8/6/54 | 6 | Northern Illinois | West Allis, Wis. | Chula Vista, Fla. | 5 |
| 8 | Guy, Ray | P | 6-3 | 190 | 12/22/49 | 12 | Southern Mississippi | Swainsboro, Ga. | Hattiesburg, Miss. | 16 |
| 73 | Hannah, Charley | G | 6-5 | 260 | 7/26/55 | 8 | Alabama | Canton, Ga. | Tampa, Fla. | 16 |
| 87 | Hasselbeck, Don | TE | 6-7 | 245 | 4/1/55 | 8 | Colorado | Cincinnati, Ohio | Norfolk, Mass. | 15* |
| 27 | Hawkins, Frank | RB | 5-9 | 200 | 7/3/59 | 4 | Nevada-Reno | Las Vegas, Nev. | Las Vegas, Nev. | 16 |
| 37 | Hayes, Lester | CB | 6-0 | 200 | 1/22/55 | 8 | Texas A&M | Houston, Tex. | Alameda, Calif. | 16 |
| 22 | Haynes, Mike | CB | 6-2 | 190 | 7/1/53 | 9 | Arizona State | Dennison, Tex. | Redondo Beach, Calif. | 5 |
| 83 | Hendricks, Ted | LB | 6-7 | 240 | 11/1/47 | 16 | Miami | Guatemala City, Guat. | Orinda, Calif. | 16 |
| 48 | Hill, Kenny | S | 6-0 | 195 | 7/25/58 | 4 | Yale | Oak Grove, La. | Daly City, Calif. | 16 |
| 11 | †Humm, David | QB | 6-2 | 190 | 4/2/52 | 10 | Nebraska | Las Vegas, Nev. | Las Vegas, Nev. | 6 |
| 31 | Jensen, Derrick | TE-RB | 6-1 | 220 | 4/27/56 | 6 | Texas-Arlington | Waukegan, Ill. | Manhattan Beach, Calif. | 16 |
| 74 | Jordan, Shelby | T | 6-7 | 285 | 1/23/52 | 9 | Washington, Mo. | St. Louis, Mo. | El Segundo, Calif. | 13 |
| 33 | King, Kenny | RB | 5-11 | 205 | 3/7/57 | 6 | Oklahoma | Clarendon, Tex. | Alameda, Calif. | 15 |
| 62 | Kinlaw, Reggie | NT | 6-2 | 245 | 1/9/57 | 5 | Oklahoma | Miami, Fla. | Pacoima, Calif. | 16 |
| 70 | Lawrence, Henry | T | 6-4 | 270 | 9/26/51 | 11 | Florida A&M | Danville, Pa. | Palmetto, Fla. | 16 |
| 75 | Long, Howie | DE | 6-5 | 270 | 1/12/60 | 4 | Villanova | Sommerville, Mass. | Redondo Beach, Calif. | 16 |
| 60 | Marsh, Curt | G | 6-5 | 270 | 8/25/59 | 3 | Washington | Tacoma, Wash. | Snohomish, Wash. | 0* |
| 53 | Martin, Rod | LB | 6-2 | 220 | 4/7/54 | 8 | Southern California | Welch, W. Va. | Venice, Calif. | 16 |
| 65 | Marvin, Mickey | G | 6-4 | 265 | 10/5/55 | 8 | Tennessee | Hendersonville, N.C. | Etowah, N.C. | 14 |
| 26 | McElroy, Vann | S | 6-2 | 190 | 1/13/60 | 3 | Baylor | Birmingham, Ala. | Dallas, Tex. | 16 |
| 23 | McKinney, Odis | S | 6-2 | 190 | 5/19/57 | 7 | Colorado | Detroit, Mich. | Woodland Hills, Calif. | 16 |
| 55 | Millen, Matt | LB | 6-2 | 250 | 3/12/58 | 4 | Penn State | Hokendauqua, Pa. | Whitehall, Pa. | 16 |
| 28 | Montgomery, Cle | WR | 5-8 | 180 | 7/1/56 | 4 | Abilene Christian | Greenville, Miss. | Los Angeles, Calif. | 14 |
| 72 | Mosebar, Don | T | 6-6 | 270 | 9/11/61 | 2 | Southern California | Yakima, Wash. | El Segundo, Calif. | 14 |
| 82 | Muhammad, Calvin | WR | 5-11 | 190 | 12/10/58 | 3 | Texas Southern | Jacksonville, Fla. | El Segundo, Calif. | 15 |
| 76 | Muransky, Ed | T | 6-7 | 275 | 1/20/63 | 3 | Michigan | Youngstown, Ohio | Boardman, Ohio | 16 |
| 51 | Nelson, Bob | LB | 6-4 | 235 | 6/30/53 | 8 | Nebraska | Stillwater, Minn. | Wayzata, Minn. | 16 |
| 71 | Pickel, Bill | DE | 6-5 | 260 | 11/5/59 | 2 | Rutgers | Queens, N.Y. | Lomita, Calif. | 16 |
| 16 | Plunkett, Jim | QB | 6-2 | 215 | 12/5/47 | 14 | Stanford | San Jose, Calif. | Atherton, Calif. | 14 |
| 34 | Pruitt, Greg | RB | 5-10 | 190 | 8/18/51 | 12 | Oklahoma | Houston, Tex. | Shaker Heights, Ohio | 16 |
| 68 | Robinson, Johnny | NT-DE | 6-2 | 255 | 2/14/58 | 4 | Louisiana Tech | Jonesboro, La. | Ruston, La. | 4 |
| 52 | Romano, Jim | C | 6-3 | 255 | 3/4/53 | 3 | Penn State | Glen Cove, N.Y. | Forestville, Calif. | 1 |
| 58 | Squirek, Jack | LB | 6-4 | 225 | 2/16/59 | 3 | Illinois | Cleveland, Ohio | Marina Del Rey, Calif. | 16 |
| 66 | Sylvester, Steve | C-G | 6-4 | 260 | 3/4/53 | 10 | Notre Dame | Cincinnati, Ohio | Cincinnati, Ohio | 9 |
| 93 | Townsend, Greg | DE | 6-3 | 240 | 11/3/61 | 2 | Texas Christian | Los Angeles, Calif. | Culver City, Calif. | 16 |
| 20 | Watts, Ted | CB | 6-0 | 195 | 5/29/59 | 4 | Texas Tech | Tarpon Springs, Fla. | Oakland, Calif. | 16 |
| 85 | Williams, Dokie | WR | 5-11 | 180 | 8/25/60 | 2 | UCLA | Oceanside, Calif. | Los Angeles, Calif. | 16 |
| 38 | Willis, Chester | RB | 5-11 | 195 | 5/2/58 | 4 | Auburn | Elberton, Ga. | Gainesville, Ga. | 13 |
| 6 | Wilson, Marc | QB | 6-6 | 220 | 2/15/57 | 5 | Brigham Young | Bremerton, Wash. | Woodinville, Wash. | 10 |

\* Hasselbeck played 1 game with New England, 14 with Raiders in '83; Marsh missed '83 season due to injury.

†Option playout; subject to developments.

t-Raiders traded for Golsteyn (Tampa Bay).

Traded—Cornerback Irvin Phillips to Tampa Bay.

Also played with Raiders in '83—S Don Bessillieu (4 games), TE Derrick Ramsey (2), NT Archie Reese (10), NT Dave Stalls (6).

## COACHING STAFF

### Head Coach,
### Tom Flores

**Pro Career:** Begins sixth year as head coach. Guided Raiders to 38-9 victory over Redskins in Super Bowl XVIII and 27-10 win over Eagles in Super Bowl XV. Has been with Raiders organization as either a player or coach for 17 years. Played six years at quarterback for Raiders from 1960-66. After spending two years (1967-68) with the Buffalo Bills and two seasons (1969-70) with the Kansas City Chiefs, Flores returned to Oakland as receivers coach in February, 1972. Ranks as Raiders number-three all-time passer with 11,635 yards and 92 touchdowns. He also passed for a club record six touchdowns in one game in 1963. Career record: 55-27.

**Background:** Quarterback at Fresno J.C. 1954-55 and Pacific 1956-57. Coached at his alma mater in 1959 before joining Raiders as a quarterback in 1960.

**Personal:** Born March 21, 1937 in Fresno, Calif. Tom and his wife, Barbara, live in Los Angeles. They have twin sons, Mark and Scott, and a daughter, Kimberly.

### Assistant Coaches

**Sam Boghosian,** offensive line; born December 22, 1931, Fresno, Calif., lives in Los Angeles. Guard UCLA 1951-54. No pro playing experience. College coach: UCLA 1955-64, Oregon State 1965-73. Pro coach: Houston Oilers 1974-75, Seattle Seahawks 1976-77, joined Raiders in 1979.

**Willie Brown,** defensive backfield; born December 2, 1940, Yazu City, Miss., lives in Los Angeles. Defensive back Grambling 1959-62. Pro cornerback Denver 1963-66, Oakland Raiders 1967-78. Pro coach: Joined Raiders in 1979.

**Chet Franklin,** defensive backfield; born March 19, 1935, Ontario, Ore., lives in Los Angeles. Guard Utah 1954-56. No pro playing experience. College coach: Stanford 1959, Oklahoma 1960-62, Colorado 1963-70. Pro coach: San Francisco 49ers 1971-74, Kansas City Chiefs 1975-77, New Orleans Saints 1978-79, joined Raiders in 1980.

**Larry Kennan,** quarterbacks; born June 13, 1944, Pomona, Calif., lives in Los Angeles. Quarterback LaVerne College 1962-65. College coach: Colorado 1969-72, Nevada-Las Vegas 1973-75, SMU 1976-78, Lamar 1979-81. Pro coach: Joined Raiders in 1982.

**Earl Leggett,** defensive line; born May 5, 1933, Jacksonville, Fla., lives in Los Angeles. Tackle Hinds J.C. 1953-54, Louisiana State 1955-56. Pro defensive tackle Chicago Bears 1957-65, Los Angeles Rams 1966, New Orleans Saints 1967-68. College coach: Nicholls State 1971, Texas Christian 1972-73. Pro coach: Southern California Sun (WFL) 1974-75, Seattle Seahawks 1976-77, San Francisco 49ers 1978, joined Raiders in 1980.

**Bob Mischak,** tight ends, strength and conditioning; born October 25, 1932, Newark, N.J., lives in Los Angeles. Guard Army 1951-53. Pro guard New York Titans 1960-62, Oakland Raiders 1963-65. College coach: Army 1966-73. Pro coach: Joined Raiders in 1973.

**Steve Ortmayer,** football operations and special teams; born February 13, 1944, Painesville, Ohio, lives in Los Angeles. La Verne College 1966. No pro playing experience. College coach: Colorado 1967-73, Georgia Tech 1974. Pro coach: Kansas City Chiefs 1975-77, joined Raiders in 1978.

**Art Shell,** assistant; born November 26, 1946, Charleston, S.C., lives in Los Angeles. Tackle Maryland State 1965-67. Pro offensive tackle Oakland Raiders 1968-81, Los Angeles Raiders 1982. Pro coach: Joined Raiders in 1983.

**Tom Walsh,** receivers; born April 16, 1949, Vallejo, Calif., lives in Los Angeles. UC-Santa Barbara 1971. No college or pro playing experience. College coach: San Diego University 1972-76, U.S. International 1979, Murray State 1980, Cincinnati 1981. Pro coach: Joined Raiders in 1982.

**Ray Willsey,** offensive backfield; born September 30, 1929, Regina, Saskatchewan, lives in Los Angeles. Quarterback-defensive back California 1951-52. Pro back Edmonton Eskimos (CFL) 1953. College coach: California 1954-55, 1964-71 (head coach), Washington 1956, Texas 1957-59. Pro coach: St. Louis Cardinals 1960-61, 1973-77, Washington Redskins 1962-63, joined Raiders in 1978.

**Bob Zeman,** linebackers; born February 22, 1937, Wheaton, Ill., lives in Los Angeles. Fullback-halfback Wisconsin 1957-59. Pro defensive back Los Angeles-San Diego Chargers 1960-61, 1965-66, Denver Broncos 1962-63. College coach: Northwestern 1968-69, Wisconsin 1970. Pro coach: Oakland Raiders 1971-77, Denver Broncos 1978-82, Buffalo Bills 1983, rejoined Raiders in 1984.

## LOS ANGELES RAIDERS 1984 FIRST-YEAR ROSTER

| Name | Pos. | Ht. | Wt. | Birth-date | College | Birthplace | Residence | How Acq. |
|------|------|-----|-----|-----------|---------|-----------|-----------|----------|
| Adams, Stanley (1) | LB | 6-2 | 215 | 5/22/60 | Memphis State | Marion, Ark. | Memphis, Tenn. | FA |
| Bearden, Jerome (1) | S | 6-1 | 190 | 2/26/59 | San Jose State | Tacoma, Wash. | San Jose, Calif. | FA |
| Coley, Ray (1) | DE | 6-4 | 250 | 9/29/59 | Alabama A&M | Atmore, Ala. | Atmore, Ala. | FA |
| Dotterer, Mike (1) | RB | 5-11 | 195 | 12/4/60 | Stanford | Saskatoon, Sask. | New York, N.Y. | D8('83) |
| Elisara, Matt (1) | NT | 6-3 | 260 | 9/25/59 | Washington State | American Samoa | Walla Walla, Wash. | FA |
| Essington, Randy | QB | 6-3 | 205 | 9/22/61 | Colorado | Norwalk, Calif. | Brea, Calif. | D12 |
| Hopkins, Greg | QB | 6-1 | 200 | 12/22/59 | La Verne | Corona, Calif. | Long Beach, Calif. | FA |
| Jones, Sean | DE | 6-7 | 280 | 12/19/62 | Northeastern | Kingston, Jamaica | Montclair, N.J. | D2 |
| Kimble, Don (1) | LB | 6-2 | 230 | 10/31/60 | Texas-El Paso | Houston, Tex. | Houston, Tex. | FA |
| McCall, Jeff (1) | RB | 6-2 | 225 | 7/4/60 | Clemson | Fayetteville, N.C. | Culver City, Calif. | D7('83) |
| McCall, Joe | RB | 5-11 | 195 | 2/17/62 | Pittsburgh | Miami, Fla. | Miami, Fla. | D3 |
| Parker, Andy | TE | 6-5 | 235 | 9/8/61 | Utah | Redlands, Calif. | Laguna Hills, Calif. | D5 |
| Parrish, Jerry | WR | 6-1 | 185 | 9/27/59 | Eastern Kentucky | Auburndale, Fla. | Auburndale, Fla. | FA |
| Rogan, John (1) | QB | 6-1 | 200 | 1/30/60 | Yale | New York, N.Y. | East Meadow, N.Y. | FA |
| Seale, Sam | WR | 5-9 | 175 | 10/6/62 | Western St., Colo. | Barbados, W. Indies | Orange, N.J. | D8 |
| Simmons, Victor (1) | WR | 6-1 | 190 | 11/5/60 | Oregon State | Joilet, Ill. | Inglewood, Calif. | FA |
| Skillings, Vince (1) | CB | 5-11 | 180 | 5/3/59 | Ohio State | Latrobe, Pa. | Brenizer, Pa. | FA |
| Smith, Waddell (1) | WR | 6-1 | 180 | 8/24/55 | Kansas | New Orleans, La. | Los Angeles, Calif. | FA |
| Toran, Stacey | S | 6-2 | 200 | 11/10/61 | Notre Dame | Indianapolis, Ind. | Indianapolis, Ind. | D6 |
| Williams, Gardner | CB | 6-2 | 190 | 12/11/61 | St. Mary's, Calif. | Washington, D.C. | Moraga, Calif. | D11 |
| Willis, Mitch | DE | 6-7 | 265 | 3/16/62 | Southern Methodist | Dallas, Tex. | Arlington, Tex. | D7 |
| York, Jeff | WR | 6-0 | 185 | 8/20/60 | Cal State-Fullerton | Folkston, Ga. | Orange, Calif. | FA |

Players who report to an NFL team for the first time are designated on rosters as rookies (R). If a player reported to an NFL training camp in a previous year but was not on the active squad for three or more regular season or postseason games, he is listed on the first-year roster and designated by a (1). Thereafter, a player who is on the active squad for three or more regular season or postseason games is credited with an additional year of playing experience.

## NOTES

_____
_____
_____
_____
_____
_____
_____
_____
_____
_____
_____
_____
_____
_____
_____
_____
_____
_____

# MIAMI DOLPHINS

## American Football Conference
## Eastern Division

**Team Colors:** Aqua, Coral, and White

**4770 Biscayne Boulevard**
**Suite 1440**
**Miami, Florida 33137**
**Telephone: (305) 576-1000**

**Club Officials**

President: Joseph Robbie
Vice President/General Manager:
  J. Michael Robbie
Vice President/Head Coach: Don Shula
Vice President/Special Projects and
  Development: Donald Poss
Director of Pro Personnel: Charley Winner
Director of Player Personnel: Chuck Connor
Director of Publicity: Chip Namias
Director of Sales: Frank Buetel
Ticket Director: Steve Dangerfield
Controller: Howard Rieman
Trainer: Bob Lundy
Equipment Manager: Dan Dowe

**Stadium:** Orange Bowl • **Capacity:** 75,206
  1501 N.W. Third Street
  Miami, Florida 33125

**Playing Surface:** Grass

**Training Camp:** St. Thomas of Villanova
  16400-D NW 32nd Avenue
  Miami, Florida 33054

## 1984 SCHEDULE

**Preseason**

| | | |
|---|---|---|
| Aug. 4 | **Colts** | 8:00 |
| Aug. 11 | at Minnesota | 7:00 |
| Aug. 19 | at Los Angeles Raiders | 1:00 |
| Aug. 24 | at Tampa Bay | 8:00 |

**Regular Season**

| | | |
|---|---|---|
| Sept. 2 | at Washington | 1:00 |
| Sept. 9 | **New England** | 1:00 |
| Sept. 17 | at Buffalo (Monday) | 9:00 |
| Sept. 23 | **Colts** | 4:00 |
| Sept. 30 | at St. Louis | 12:00 |
| Oct. 7 | at Pittsburgh | 1:00 |
| Oct. 14 | **Houston** | 1:00 |
| Oct. 21 | at New England | 1:00 |
| Oct. 28 | **Buffalo** | 4:00 |
| Nov. 4 | at New York Jets | 4:00 |
| Nov. 11 | **Philadelphia** | 1:00 |
| Nov. 18 | at San Diego | 1:00 |
| Nov. 26 | **New York Jets** (Monday) | 9:00 |
| Dec. 2 | **Los Angeles Raiders** | 4:00 |
| Dec. 9 | at Colts | 1:00 |
| Dec. 17 | **Dallas** (Monday) | 9:00 |

## DOLPHINS COACHING HISTORY

**(168-105-4)**

| | | |
|---|---|---|
| 1966-69 | George Wilson | 15-39-2 |
| 1970-83 | Don Shula | 153-66-2 |

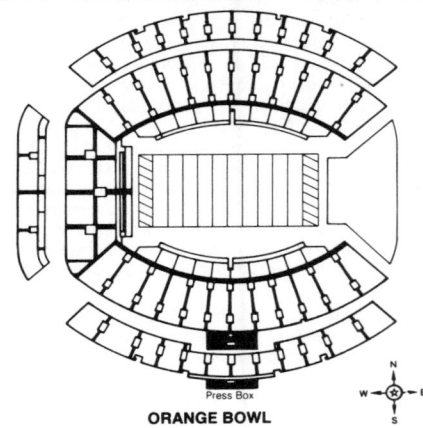

**ORANGE BOWL**

## RECORD HOLDERS

### Individual Records—Career

| Category | Name | Performance |
|---|---|---|
| Rushing (Yds.) | Larry Csonka, 1968-1974, 1979 | 6,737 |
| Passing (Yds.) | Bob Griese, 1967-1980 | 25,092 |
| Passing (TDs) | Bob Griese, 1967-1980 | 192 |
| Receiving (No.) | Nat Moore, 1974-1983 | 378 |
| Receiving (Yds.) | Nat Moore, 1974-1983 | 5,842 |
| Interceptions | Jake Scott, 1970-75 | 35 |
| Punting (Avg.) | Larry Seiple, 1967-1977 | 40.0 |
| Punt Return (Avg.) | Freddie Solomon, 1975-77 | 11.4 |
| Kickoff Return (Avg.) | Mercury Morris, 1969-1975 | 26.5 |
| Field Goals | Garo Yepremian, 1970-78 | 165 |
| Touchdowns (Tot.) | Larry Csonka, 1968-1974, 1979 | 57 |
| Points | Garo Yepremian, 1970-78 | 830 |

### Individual Records—Single Season

| Category | Name | Performance |
|---|---|---|
| Rushing (Yds.) | Delvin Williams, 1978 | 1,258 |
| Passing (Yds.) | Bob Griese, 1968 | 2,473 |
| Passing (TDs) | Bob Griese, 1977 | 22 |
| Receiving (No.) | Jack Clancy, 1967 | 67 |
| Receiving (Yds.) | Mark Duper, 1983 | 1,003 |
| Interceptions | Dick Westmoreland, 1967 | 10 |
| Punting (Avg.) | Reggie Roby, 1983 | 43.1 |
| Punt Return (Avg.) | Freddie Solomon, 1975 | 12.3 |
| Kickoff Return (Avg.) | Duriel Harris, 1976 | 32.9 |
| Field Goals | Garo Yepremian, 1971 | 28 |
| Touchdowns (Tot.) | Nat Moore, 1977 | 13 |
| | Larry Csonka, 1979 | 13 |
| Points | Garo Yepremian, 1971 | 117 |

### Individual Records—Single Game

| Category | Name | Performance |
|---|---|---|
| Rushing (Yds.) | Mercury Morris, 9-30-73 | 197 |
| Passing (Yds.) | David Woodley, 10-25-81 | 408 |
| Passing (TDs) | Bob Griese, 11-24-77 | 6 |
| Receiving (No.) | Duriel Harris, 10-28-79 | 10 |
| Receiving (Yds.) | Nat Moore, 10-4-81 | 210 |
| Interceptions | Dick Anderson, 12-3-73 | 4 |
| Field Goals | Garo Yepremian, 9-26-71 | 5 |
| Touchdowns (Tot.) | Paul Warfield, 12-15-73 | 4 |
| Points | Paul Warfield, 12-15-73 | 24 |

## 1983 TEAM STATISTICS

| | Miami | Opp. |
|---|---|---|
| Total First Downs | 314 | 288 |
| Rushing | 132 | 122 |
| Passing | 151 | 147 |
| Penalty | 31 | 19 |
| Third Down Efficiency | 81/212 | 78/205 |
| Third Down Percentage | 38.2 | 38.0 |
| Total Net Yards | 5195 | 5039 |
| Total Offensive Plays | 1033 | 989 |
| Avg. Gain per Play | 5.0 | 5.1 |
| Avg. Gain per Game | 324.7 | 314.9 |
| Net Yards Rushing | 2150 | 2037 |
| Total Rushing Plays | 568 | 460 |
| Avg. Gain per Rush | 3.8 | 4.4 |
| Avg. Gain Rushing per Game | 134.4 | 127.3 |
| Net Yards Passing | 3045 | 3002 |
| Lost Attempting to Pass | 23/190 | 49/363 |
| Gross Yards Passing | 3235 | 3365 |
| Attempts/Completions | 442/254 | 480/277 |
| Percent Completed | 57.5 | 57.7 |
| Had Intercepted | 11 | 26 |
| Avg. Net Passing per Game | 190.3 | 187.6 |
| Punts/Avg. | 75/42.5 | 90/40.8 |
| Punt Returns/Avg. | 55/10.6 | 32/7.2 |
| Kickoff Returns/Avg. | 47/23.1 | 54/19.0 |
| Interceptions/Avg. Ret. | 26/13.3 | 11/18.5 |
| Penalties/Yards | 64/567 | 95/837 |
| Fumbles/Ball Lost | 30/16 | 38/17 |
| Total Points | 389 | 250 |
| Avg. Points per Game | 24.3 | 15.6 |
| Touchdowns | 48 | 32 |
| Rushing | 16 | 11 |
| Passing | 28 | 19 |
| Returns and Recoveries | 4 | 2 |
| Field Goals | 18/27 | 9/15 |
| Conversions | 45/48 | 31/32 |
| Safeties | 1 | 0 |
| Avg. Time of Possession | 31:20 | 28:40 |

## 1983 TEAM RECORD

### Preseason (2-2)

| Date | Miami | | Opponents |
|---|---|---|---|
| 8/6 | 17 | Dallas | 20 |
| 8/13 | 17 | *New Orleans | 19 |
| 8/19 | 38 | Washington | 7 |
| 8/26 | 24 | New York Giants | 3 |
| | 96 | | 49 |

### Regular Season (12-4)

| Date | Miami | | Opp. | Att. |
|---|---|---|---|---|
| 9/4 | 12 | Buffalo | 0 | 78,683 |
| 9/11 | 34 | *New England | 24 | 59,343 |
| 9/19 | 14 | Los Angeles Raiders | 27 | 57,796 |
| 9/25 | 14 | *Kansas City | 6 | 50,785 |
| 10/2 | 7 | New Orleans | 17 | 66,489 |
| 10/9 | 35 | *Buffalo (OT) | 38 | 59,948 |
| 10/16 | 32 | New York Jets | 14 | 58,615 |
| 10/23 | 21 | Baltimore | 7 | 32,343 |
| 10/30 | 30 | *Los Angeles Rams | 14 | 72,175 |
| 11/6 | 20 | San Francisco | 17 | 57,832 |
| 11/13 | 6 | New England | 17 | 60,771 |
| 11/20 | 37 | *Baltimore | 0 | 54,482 |
| 11/28 | 38 | *Cincinnati | 14 | 74,506 |
| 12/4 | 24 | Houston | 17 | 39,434 |
| 12/10 | 31 | *Atlanta | 24 | 56,725 |
| 12/16 | 34 | *New York Jets | 14 | 59,975 |
| | 389 | | 250 | 939,902 |

*Home Game       (OT) Overtime

### Score by Periods

| | | | | | | | |
|---|---|---|---|---|---|---|---|
| Miami | 56 | 135 | 91 | 107 | 0 | — | 389 |
| Opponents | 62 | 68 | 44 | 73 | 3 | — | 250 |

### Attendance

Home 487,939     Away 451,963     Total 939,902
Single game home record, 78,939 (1-2-72)
Single season home record, 557,881 (1972)

## 1983 INDIVIDUAL STATISTICS

### Rushing

| | Att. | Yds. | Avg. | LG | TD |
|---|---|---|---|---|---|
| Franklin | 224 | 746 | 3.3 | 18 | 8 |
| Nathan | 151 | 685 | 4.5 | 40 | 3 |
| Overstreet | 85 | 392 | 4.6 | 44 | 1 |
| Bennett | 49 | 197 | 4.0 | 25 | 2 |
| Woodley | 19 | 78 | 4.1 | 15 | 0 |
| Marino | 28 | 45 | 1.6 | 15 | 2 |
| Hill | 2 | 12 | 6.0 | 10 | 0 |
| Clayton | 2 | 9 | 4.5 | 9 | 0 |
| Hardy | 1 | 2 | 2.0 | 2 | 0 |
| Harris | 1 | 0 | 0.0 | 0 | 0 |
| Strock | 6 | −16 | −2.7 | 0 | 0 |
| Miami | 568 | 2150 | 3.8 | 44 | 16 |
| Opponents | 460 | 2037 | 4.4 | 55 | 11 |

### Passing

| | Att. | Comp. | Pct. | Yds. | TD | Int. | Tkld. | Rate |
|---|---|---|---|---|---|---|---|---|
| Marino | 296 | 173 | 58.4 | 2210 | 20 | 6 | 10/80 | 96.0 |
| Woodley | 89 | 43 | 48.3 | 528 | 3 | 4 | 10/80 | 59.6 |
| Strock | 52 | 34 | 65.4 | 403 | 4 | 1 | 3/30 | 106.5 |
| Nathan | 4 | 3 | 75.0 | 46 | 0 | 0 | 0/0 | 112.5 |
| Clayton | 1 | 1 | 100.0 | 48 | 1 | 0 | 0/0 | 158.3 |
| Miami | 442 | 254 | 57.5 | 3235 | 28 | 11 | 23/190 | 91.2 |
| Opponents | 480 | 277 | 57.7 | 3365 | 19 | 26 | 49/363 | 70.0 |

### Receiving

| | No. | Yds. | Avg. | LG | TD |
|---|---|---|---|---|---|
| Nathan | 52 | 461 | 8.9 | 25 | 1 |
| Duper | 51 | 1003 | 19.7 | 85t | 10 |
| Moore | 39 | 558 | 14.3 | 66t | 6 |
| Rose | 29 | 345 | 11.9 | 37 | 3 |
| Johnson | 24 | 189 | 7.9 | 33 | 4 |
| Hardy | 22 | 202 | 9.2 | 25 | 0 |
| Harris | 15 | 260 | 17.3 | 64t | 1 |
| Overstreet | 8 | 55 | 6.9 | 20 | 2 |
| Clayton | 6 | 114 | 19.0 | 39 | 1 |
| Bennett | 6 | 35 | 5.8 | 9 | 0 |
| Vigorito | 1 | 7 | 7.0 | 7 | 0 |
| Woodley | 1 | 6 | 6.0 | 6 | 0 |
| Miami | 254 | 3235 | 12.7 | 85t | 28 |
| Opponents | 277 | 3365 | 12.1 | 80t | 19 |

### Interceptions

| | No. | Yds. | Avg. | LG | TD |
|---|---|---|---|---|---|
| Judson | 6 | 60 | 10.0 | 29 | 0 |
| Small | 5 | 60 | 12.0 | 28 | 0 |
| L. Blackwood | 4 | 77 | 19.3 | 45 | 0 |
| G. Blackwood | 3 | 0 | 0.0 | 0 | 0 |
| Kozlowski | 2 | 73 | 36.5 | 38t | 2 |
| Bokamper | 2 | 43 | 21.5 | 24t | 1 |
| Rhone | 1 | 15 | 15.0 | 15 | 0 |
| Lankford | 1 | 10 | 10.0 | 10 | 0 |
| Walker | 1 | 7 | 7.0 | 7 | 0 |
| Brown | 1 | 0 | 0.0 | 0 | 0 |
| Miami | 26 | 345 | 13.3 | 45 | 3 |
| Opponents | 11 | 203 | 18.5 | 45 | 1 |

### Punting

| | No. | Yds. | Avg. | In 20 | LG |
|---|---|---|---|---|---|
| Roby | 74 | 3189 | 43.1 | 26 | 64 |
| Miami | 75 | 3189 | 42.5 | 26 | 64 |
| Opponents | 90 | 3674 | 40.8 | 25 | 63 |

### Punt Returns

| | No. | FC | Yds. | Avg. | LG | TD |
|---|---|---|---|---|---|---|
| Clayton | 41 | 11 | 392 | 9.6 | 60t | 1 |
| Walker | 8 | 0 | 86 | 10.8 | 23 | 0 |
| Kozlowski | 2 | 10 | 12 | 6.0 | 11 | 0 |
| G. Blackwood | 1 | 2 | 10 | 10.0 | 10 | 0 |
| Heflin | 1 | 0 | 19 | 19.0 | 19 | 0 |
| Sowell | 1 | 0 | 0 | 0.0 | 0 | 0 |
| Vigorito | 1 | 0 | 62 | 62.0 | 62 | 0 |
| Miami | 55 | 23 | 581 | 10.6 | 62 | 1 |
| Opponents | 32 | 13 | 229 | 7.2 | 24 | 0 |

### Kickoff Returns

| | No. | Yds. | Avg. | LG | TD |
|---|---|---|---|---|---|
| Walker | 36 | 962 | 26.7 | 78 | 0 |
| Kozlowski | 4 | 50 | 12.5 | 23 | 0 |
| Nathan | 3 | 15 | 5.0 | 12 | 0 |
| Bennett | 1 | 6 | 6.0 | 6 | 0 |
| Brown | 1 | 0 | 0.0 | 0 | 0 |
| Clayton | 1 | 25 | 25.0 | 25 | 0 |
| Heflin | 1 | 27 | 27.0 | 27 | 0 |
| Miami | 47 | 1085 | 23.1 | 78 | 0 |
| Opponents | 54 | 1024 | 19.0 | 40 | 0 |

### Scoring

| | TD | TD R | TD P | TD Rt | PAT | FG | TP |
|---|---|---|---|---|---|---|---|
| von Schamann | | | | | 45/48 | 18/27 | 99 |
| Duper | 10 | 0 | 10 | 0 | | | 60 |
| Franklin | 8 | 8 | 0 | 0 | | | 48 |
| Moore | 6 | 0 | 6 | 0 | | | 36 |
| Johnson | 4 | 0 | 4 | 0 | | | 24 |
| Nathan | 4 | 3 | 1 | 0 | | | 24 |
| Overstreet | 3 | 1 | 2 | 0 | | | 18 |
| Rose | 3 | 0 | 3 | 0 | | | 18 |
| Bennett | 2 | 2 | 0 | 0 | | | 12 |
| Clayton | 2 | 0 | 1 | 1 | | | 12 |
| Kozlowski | 2 | 0 | 0 | 2 | | | 12 |
| Marino | 2 | 2 | 0 | 0 | | | 12 |
| Bokamper | 1 | 0 | 0 | 1 | | | 6 |
| Harris | 1 | 0 | 1 | 0 | | | 6 |
| Charles | | (Safety) | | | | | 2 |
| Miami | 48 | 16 | 28 | 4 | 45/48 | 18/27 | 389 |
| Opponents | 32 | 11 | 19 | 2 | 31/32 | 9/15 | 250 |

## FIRST-ROUND SELECTIONS

(If Club had no first-round selection, first player drafted is listed with round in parentheses.)

| Year | Player, College, Position |
|---|---|
| 1966 | Jim Grabowski, Illinois, RB |
| | Rick Norton, Kentucky, QB |
| 1967 | Bob Griese, Purdue, QB |
| 1968 | Larry Csonka, Syracuse, RB |
| | Doug Crusan, Indiana, T |
| 1969 | Bill Stanfill, Georgia, DE |
| 1970 | Jim Mandich, Michigan, TE (2) |
| 1971 | Otto Stowe, Iowa State, WR (2) |
| 1972 | Mike Kadish, Notre Dame, DT |
| 1973 | Chuck Bradley, Oregon, C (2) |
| 1974 | Donald Reese, Jackson State, DE |
| 1975 | Darryl Carlton, Tampa, T |
| 1976 | Larry Gordon, Arizona State, LB |
| | Kim Bokamper, San Jose State, LB |
| 1977 | A.J. Duhe, Louisiana State, DT |
| 1978 | Guy Benjamin, Stanford, QB (2) |
| 1979 | Jon Giesler, Michigan, T |
| 1980 | Don McNeal, Alabama, DB |
| 1981 | David Overstreet, Oklahoma, RB |
| 1982 | Roy Foster, Southern California, G |
| 1983 | Dan Marino, Pittsburgh, QB |
| 1984 | Jackie Shipp, Oklahoma, LB |

# MIAMI DOLPHINS 1984 VETERAN ROSTER

| No. | Name | Pos. | Ht. | Wt. | Birth-date | NFL Exp. | College | Birthplace | Residence | Games in '83 |
|---|---|---|---|---|---|---|---|---|---|---|
| 70 | Barnett, Bill | DE | 6-4 | 250 | 5/10/56 | 5 | Nebraska | St. Paul, Minn. | Lincoln, Neb. | 15 |
| 73 | Baumhower, Bob | NT | 6-5 | 265 | 8/4/55 | 8 | Alabama | Portsmouth, Va. | Fort Lauderdale, Fla. | 16 |
| 34 | †Bennett, Woody | FB | 6-2 | 222 | 3/24/55 | 6 | Miami | York, Pa. | York, Pa. | 16 |
| 78 | Benson, Charles | DE | 6-3 | 267 | 11/21/60 | 2 | Baylor | Houston, Tex. | Houston, Tex. | 8 |
| 75 | Betters, Doug | DE | 6-7 | 260 | 6/11/56 | 7 | Nevada-Reno | Lincoln, Neb. | Whitefish, Mont. | 16 |
| 47 | Blackwood, Glenn | S | 6-0 | 188 | 2/23/57 | 6 | Texas | San Antonio, Tex. | Miami, Fla. | 16 |
| 42 | Blackwood, Lyle | S | 6-1 | 195 | 5/24/51 | 12 | Texas Christian | San Antonio, Tex. | Austin, Tex. | 16 |
| 58 | Bokamper, Kim | DE | 6-6 | 250 | 9/25/54 | 8 | San Jose State | San Diego, Calif. | Fort Lauderdale, Fla. | 15 |
| 56 | Bowser, Charles | LB | 6-3 | 232 | 10/2/59 | 3 | Duke | Plymouth, N.C. | Washington, D.C. | 16 |
| 51 | Brown, Mark | LB | 6-2 | 218 | 7/18/61 | 2 | Purdue | Los Angeles, Calif. | Los Angeles, Calif. | 14 |
| 59 | Brudzinski, Bob | LB | 6-4 | 229 | 1/1/55 | 8 | Ohio State | Freemont, Ohio | Orange, Calif. | 16 |
| 81 | Cefalo, Jimmy | WR | 5-11 | 188 | 10/5/56 | 6 | Penn State | Pittston, Pa. | North Miami Beach, Fla. | 1 |
| 71 | Charles, Mike | NT | 6-4 | 283 | 9/23/62 | 2 | Syracuse | Newark, N.J. | East Orange, N.J. | 16 |
| 76 | †Clark, Steve | NT | 6-4 | 255 | 8/2/60 | 3 | Utah | Salt Lake City, Utah | Salt Lake City, Utah | 11 |
| 83 | Clayton, Mark | WR | 5-9 | 172 | 4/8/61 | 2 | Louisville | Indianapolis, Ind. | Hialeah, Fla. | 15 |
| 77 | Duhe, A.J. | LB | 6-4 | 240 | 11/27/55 | 8 | Louisiana State | New Orleans, La. | Miami Shores, Fla. | 15 |
| 85 | Duper, Mark | WR | 5-9 | 193 | 1/25/59 | 3 | Northwestern Louisiana | Pineville, La. | Mansura, La. | 16 |
| 61 | Foster, Roy | G-T | 6-4 | 272 | 5/24/60 | 3 | Southern California | Los Angeles, Calif. | Miami, Fla. | 16 |
| 37 | Franklin, Andra | FB | 5-10 | 228 | 8/22/59 | 4 | Nebraska | Anniston, Ala. | Lincoln, Neb. | 15 |
| 79 | †Giesler, Jon | T | 6-5 | 260 | 12/23/56 | 6 | Michigan | Toledo, Ohio | Cooper City, Fla. | 16 |
| 74 | Green, Cleveland | T | 6-3 | 262 | 9/11/57 | 6 | Southern | Bolton, Miss. | Miami, Fla. | 16 |
| 84 | Hardy, Bruce | TE | 6-4 | 232 | 6/1/56 | 7 | Arizona State | Murray, Utah | South Jordan, Utah | 15 |
| 88 | Heflin, Vince | WR | 6-2 | 185 | 7/7/59 | 3 | Central State, Ohio | Dayton, Ohio | Dayton, Ohio | 14 |
| 53 | Hester, Ron | LB | 6-1 | 226 | 5/26/59 | 2 | Florida State | Atlanta, Ga. | Hialeah, Fla. | 0* |
| 31 | Hill, Eddie | RB | 6-2 | 206 | 5/13/57 | 6 | Memphis State | Nashville, Tenn. | Plantation, Fla. | 16 |
| 11 | Jensen, Jim | WR | 6-4 | 215 | 11/14/58 | 4 | Boston University | Abington, Pa. | Pembroke Pines, Fla. | 16 |
| 87 | Johnson, Dan | TE | 6-3 | 240 | 5/17/60 | 2 | Iowa State | Minneapolis, Minn. | Pembroke Pines, Fla. | 16 |
| 49 | Judson, William | CB | 6-1 | 187 | 3/26/59 | 3 | South Carolina State | Detroit, Mich. | Atlanta, Ga. | 16 |
| 40 | Kozlowski, Mike | S | 6-0 | 198 | 2/24/56 | 5 | Colorado | Newark, N.J. | Plantation, Fla. | 16 |
| 67 | Kuechenberg, Bob | G | 6-2 | 255 | 10/14/47 | 15 | Notre Dame | Gary, Ind. | Miami Beach, Fla. | 16 |
| 68 | †Laakso, Eric | T | 6-4 | 265 | 11/29/56 | 7 | Tulane | New York, N.Y. | Cooper City, Fla. | 15 |
| 44 | Lankford, Paul | CB | 6-1 | 182 | 6/15/58 | 3 | Penn State | New York, N.Y. | Farmingdale, N.Y. | 16 |
| 13 | Marino, Dan | QB | 6-3 | 214 | 9/15/61 | 2 | Pittsburgh | Pittsburgh, Pa. | Pittsburgh, Pa. | 11 |
| 28 | McNeal, Don | CB | 5-11 | 192 | 5/6/58 | 4 | Alabama | Atmore, Ala. | Miami, Fla. | 0* |
| 89 | Moore, Nat | WR | 5-9 | 188 | 9/19/51 | 11 | Florida | Tallahassee, Fla. | Miami, Fla. | 16 |
| 22 | Nathan, Tony | RB | 6-0 | 206 | 12/14/56 | 6 | Alabama | Birmingham, Ala. | Birmingham, Ala. | 16 |
| 64 | Newman, Ed | G | 6-2 | 255 | 6/4/51 | 12 | Duke | Woodbury, N.Y. | Miami, Fla. | 16 |
| 55 | Rhone, Earnest | LB | 6-2 | 224 | 8/20/53 | 9 | Henderson, Ark. | Ogden, Ark. | Texarkana, Tex. | 12 |
| 4 | Roby, Reggie | P | 6-2 | 243 | 7/30/61 | 2 | Iowa | Waterloo, Iowa | Cedar Rapids, Iowa | 16 |
| 80 | Rose, Joe | TE | 6-3 | 230 | 6/24/57 | 5 | California | Marysville, Calif. | Pembroke Pines, Fla. | 16 |
|  | †Shull, Steve | LB | 6-1 | 224 | 3/27/58 | 4 | William & Mary | Philadelphia, Pa. | Cooper City, Fla. | 0* |
| 48 | Small, Gerald | CB | 5-11 | 192 | 8/10/56 | 7 | San Jose State | Washington, N.C. | Miami, Fla. | 15 |
| 45 | Sowell, Robert | CB-S | 5-11 | 175 | 6/23/61 | 2 | Howard | Columbus, Ohio | Columbus, Ohio | 16 |
| 57 | Stephenson, Dwight | C | 6-2 | 255 | 11/20/57 | 5 | Alabama | Murfreesboro, N.C. | Miami, Fla. | 16 |
| 10 | Strock, Don | QB | 6-5 | 220 | 11/27/50 | 11 | Virginia Tech | Pottstown, Pa. | Miami Springs, Fla. | 15 |
| 52 | Tautolo, Terry | LB | 6-2 | 227 | 8/30/54 | 9 | UCLA | Corona, Calif. | Long Beach, Calif. | 9 |
| 54 | Thomas, Rodell | LB | 6-2 | 225 | 8/2/58 | 4 | Alabama State | Quincy, Fla. | Quincy, Fla. | 16 |
|  | Tilley, Emmett | LB | 5-11 | 240 | 2/13/61 | 2 | Duke | Durham, N.C. | Durham, N.C. | 6 |
| 60 | Toews, Jeff | G | 6-3 | 255 | 11/4/57 | 6 | Washington | San Jose, Calif. | Pembroke Pines, Fla. | 8 |
| 32 | Vigorito, Tom | RB | 5-10 | 190 | 10/23/59 | 3 | Virginia | Passaic, N.J. | Pembroke Pines, Fla. | 1 |
| 5 | von Schamann, Uwe | K | 6-0 | 188 | 4/23/56 | 6 | Oklahoma | West Berlin, Germany | Norman, Okla. | 16 |
| 41 | Walker, Fulton | CB | 5-10 | 196 | 4/30/58 | 4 | West Virginia | Martinsburg, W. Va. | Martinsburg, W. Va. | 15 |

* Hester, McNeal, and Shull missed '83 season due to injuries.

†Option playout; subject to developments.

Traded—Center Mark Dennard to Philadelphia, wide receiver Duriel Harris to Cleveland, quarterback David Woodley to Pittsburgh.

Also played with Dolphins in '83—RB David Overstreet (14 games).

## COACHING STAFF

### Head Coach, Don Shula

**Pro Career:** Begins his twenty-second season as an NFL head coach, fifteenth with the Dolphins. Miami has won or shared first place in the AFC East in 11 of his 14 years there. Has highest winning percentage (.709) among active NFL coaches. He captured back-to-back NFL championships, defeating Washington 14-7 in Super Bowl VII and Minnesota 24-7 in Super Bowl VIII. Lost to Dallas 24-3 in Super Bowl VI and to Washington 27-17 in Super Bowl XVII. His 1972 17-0 club is considered NFL's greatest team ever. Started his pro playing career with Cleveland Browns as defensive back in 1951. After two seasons with Browns, spent 1953-56 with Baltimore Colts and 1957 with Washington Redskins. Joined Detroit Lions as defensive coach in 1960 and was named head coach of the Colts in 1963. Baltimore had a 13-1 record in 1968 and captured NFL championship before losing to New York Jets in Super Bowl III. Career record: 226-91-6.

**Background:** Outstanding offensive player at John Carroll University in Cleveland before becoming defensive specialist as a pro. His alma mater gave him doctorate in humanities, May 1973. Served as assistant coach at Virginia in 1958 and at Kentucky in 1959.

**Personal:** Born January 4, 1930, in Painesville, Ohio. Don and his wife, Dorothy, live in Miami Lakes and have five children—David, Donna, Sharon, Annie, and Mike.

### Assistant Coaches

**Tom Keane,** defensive backfield; born September 7, 1926, Bellaire, Ohio, lives in Miami. Back Ohio State 1944, West Virginia 1946-47. Pro back Los Angeles Rams 1948-51, Dallas Texans 1952, Baltimore Colts 1953-54, Chicago Cardinals 1957. Pro coach: Calgary Stampeders (CFL) 1960, Wheeling (UFL) 1961-64, Pittsburgh Steelers 1965, joined Dolphins in 1966.

**Bob Matheson,** special teams; born November 25, 1944, Boone, N.C., lives in Hollywood, Fla. Linebacker Duke 1964-66. Pro linebacker Cleveland Browns 1967-70, Miami Dolphins 1971-80. College coach: Duke 1981-82. Pro coach: Joined Dolphins in 1983.

**John Sandusky,** offense-offensive line; born December 28, 1925, Philadelphia, lives in Cooper City, Fla. Tackle Villanova 1946-49. Pro tackle Cleveland Browns 1950-55, Green Bay Packers 1956. College coach: Villanova 1957-58. Pro coach: Baltimore Colts 1959-72 (head coach 1972), Philadelphia Eagles 1973-75, joined Dolphins in 1976.

**Mike Scarry,** defensive line-run defense; born February 1, 1920, Duquesne, Pa., lives in Miami. Center Waynesburg 1939-41. Pro center Cleveland Rams 1944-45, Cleveland Browns (AAFC) 1946-47. College coach: Western Reserve 1948-49, Santa Clara 1950-52, Loras 1953, Washington State 1954-55, Cincinnati 1956-62, Waynesburg 1963-65 (head coach). Pro coach: Washington Redskins 1966-68, joined Dolphins in 1970.

**David Shula,** receivers coach; born May 28, 1959, Lexington, Ky., lives in Miami. Wide receiver Dartmouth 1977-80. Pro receiver Baltimore Colts 1981. Pro coach: Joined Dolphins in 1982.

**Chuck Studley,** defense; born January 17, 1929, Maywood Ill., lives in Miami Lakes. Guard Illinois 1949-51. No pro playing experience. College coach: Illinois 1955-59. Massachusetts 1960 (head coach), Cincinnati 1961-68 (head coach). Pro coach: Cincinnati Bengals 1969-78, San Francisco 49ers 1979-82, Houston Oilers 1983 (interim head coach), first year with Dolphins.

**Carl Taseff,** offensive backfield; born September 28, 1928, Cleveland, lives in Pembroke Pines, Fla. Back John Carroll 1947-50. Pro defensive back Cleveland Browns 1951, Baltimore Colts 1953-61, Philadelphia Eagles 1961, Buffalo Bills 1962. Pro coach: Boston Patriots 1964, Detroit Lions 1965-66, joined Dolphins in 1970.

**Junior Wade,** strength-flexibility; born February 2, 1947, Bath, S.C., lives in Hialeah. South Carolina State 1969. No college or pro football playing experience. Pro coach: Joined Dolphins in 1975.

## MIAMI DOLPHINS 1984 FIRST-YEAR ROSTER

| Name | Pos. | Ht. | Wt. | Birth-date | College | Birthplace | Residence | How Acq. |
|------|------|-----|-----|-----------|---------|-----------|-----------|----------|
| Blakley, Robert (1) | WR | 6-1 | 195 | 9/20/59 | North Dakota State | St. Paul, Minn. | St. Paul, Minn. | FA |
| Boyle, Jim | G-T | 6-5 | 273 | 7/27/61 | Tulane | Cincinnati, Ohio | New Orleans, La. | D9 |
| Brophy, Jay | LB | 6-3 | 227 | 7/27/60 | Miami | Akron, Ohio | Miami, Fla. | D2 |
| Brown, Bud | CB-S | 6-0 | 187 | 4/19/61 | So. Mississippi | DeKalb, Miss. | DeKalb, Miss. | D11 |
| Campbell, Todd (1) | NT | 6-2 | 255 | 1/28/61 | West Virginia | New Kensington, Pa. | New Kensington, Pa. | FA |
| Carter, Joe | RB | 5-11 | 198 | 6/23/62 | Alabama | Starkeville, Miss. | Starkeville, Miss. | D4 |
| Carvalho, Bernard | G-T | 6-3 | 252 | 9/29/61 | Hawaii | Kauai, Hawaii | Kauai, Hawaii | D7 |
| Chatman, Marvin | CB-S | 5-11 | 180 | 11/9/60 | Memphis State | Miami, Fla. | Miami, Fla. | FA |
| Chesley, John | TE | 6-5 | 225 | 7/2/62 | Oklahoma State | Washington, D.C. | Washington, D.C. | D10 |
| DeVane, William | NT | 6-2 | 275 | 5/28/62 | Clemson | Jacksonville, N.C. | Jacksonville, N.C. | D12 |
| Grier, Anthony | CB-S | 6-1 | 190 | 10/31/61 | Livingston | Kendall, Fla. | Florida City, Fla. | FA |
| Jones, Andra (1) | CB-S | 6-2 | 203 | 1/7/60 | Albany State | Macon, Ga. | Macon, Ga. | FA |
| Landry, Ronald | FB | 6-1 | 221 | 7/8/62 | McNeese State | Jennings, La. | Jennings, La. | D8 |
| Lewis, Charles | RB | 5-11 | 239 | 4/23/61 | Albany State | Meridian, Miss. | Cleveland, Ohio | FA |
| May, Dean | QB | 6-5 | 220 | 5/26/62 | Louisville | Tampa, Fla. | Louisville, Ky. | D5 |
| Muckle, Willie | G | 6-1 | 251 | 5/20/61 | Albany State | Middletown, Conn. | Statham, Ga. | FA |
| Nelson, David | RB | 6-2 | 230 | 11/23/63 | Heidelberg | Miami, Fla. | North Miami, Fla. | FA |
| Newby, Jonathan (1) | WR | 6-1 | 185 | 6/12/60 | Western Kentucky | McKeesport, Pa. | Clairton, Pa. | FA |
| Richt, Mark (1) | QB | 6-1 | 193 | 2/18/60 | Miami | Omaha, Neb. | Boca Raton, Fla. | FA |
| Shipp, Jackie | LB | 6-3 | 235 | 3/19/62 | Oklahoma | Stillwater, Okla. | Norman, Okla. | D1 |
| Tatum, Rowland | LB | 6-1 | 226 | 11/20/62 | Ohio State | Inglewood, Calif. | Inglewood, Calif. | D6 |
| Weingrad, Mike | LB | 6-2 | 232 | 7/2/60 | Illinois | Columbus, Ohio | Columbus, Ohio | D12a |

Players who report to an NFL team for the first time are designated on rosters as rookies (R). If a player reported to an NFL training camp in a previous year but was not on the active squad for three or more regular season or postseason games, he is listed on the first-year roster and designated by a (1). Thereafter, a player who is on the active squad for three or more regular season or postseason games is credited with an additional year of playing experience.

## NOTES

# NEW ENGLAND PATRIOTS

**American Football Conference
Eastern Division**

**Team Colors:** Red, White, and Blue

**Sullivan Stadium
Route 1
Foxboro, Massachusetts 02035
Telephone: (617) 543-7911, 262-1776**

### Club Officials

President: William H. Sullivan, Jr.
Executive Vice President: Charles W. Sullivan
Vice President: Francis J. (Bucko) Kilroy
General Manager: Patrick J. Sullivan
Director of Player Development: Dick Steinberg
Director of Pro Scouting: Bill McPeak
Director of College Scouting: Joe Mendes
Executive Director of Player Personnel:
  Darryl Stingley
Personnel Scouts: George Blackburn, Bobby
  Grier, Pat Naughton, Bob Teahan
Director of Public Relations/Sales: Tom Hoffman
Director of Promotions: Dave Wintergrass
Director of Publicity: Jim Greenidge
Director of Ticket Sales: Peter Thompson
Box Office Manager: Ken Sternfeld
Trainer: Ron O'Neil
Equipment Manager: George Luongo
Film Manager: Ken Deininger

**Stadium:** Sullivan Stadium • **Capacity:** 61,150
        Route 1
        Foxboro, Massachusetts 02035

**Playing Surface:** Super Turf

**Training Camp:** Bryant College
                Smithfield, Rhode Island 02917

## 1984 SCHEDULE

### Preseason
| | | |
|---|---|---|
| Aug. 3 | **New York Giants** | 7:30 |
| Aug. 11 | at Buffalo | 6:00 |
| Aug. 17 | at Washington | 8:00 |
| Aug. 24 | **Kansas City** | 7:30 |

### Regular Season
| | | |
|---|---|---|
| Sept. 2 | at Buffalo | 1:00 |
| Sept. 9 | at Miami | 1:00 |
| Sept. 16 | **Seattle** | 1:00 |
| Sept. 23 | **Washington** | 1:00 |
| Sept. 30 | at New York Jets | 1:00 |
| Oct. 7 | at Cleveland | 1:00 |
| Oct. 14 | **Cincinnati** | 1:00 |
| Oct. 21 | **Miami** | 1:00 |
| Oct. 28 | **New York Jets** | 1:00 |
| Nov. 4 | at Denver | 2:00 |
| Nov. 11 | **Buffalo** | 1:00 |
| Nov. 18 | at Colts | 1:00 |
| Nov. 22 | at Dallas (Thanksgiving) | 3:00 |
| Dec. 2 | **St. Louis** | 1:00 |
| Dec. 9 | at Philadelphia | 1:00 |
| Dec. 16 | **Colts** | 1:00 |

## PATRIOTS COACHING HISTORY

**Boston 1960-70
(155-182-9)**

| | | |
|---|---|---|
| 1960-61 | Lou Saban* | 7-12-0 |
| 1961-68 | Mike Holovak | 53-47-9 |
| 1969-70 | Clive Rush** | 5-18-0 |
| 1970-72 | John Mazur*** | 9-19-0 |
| 1972 | Phil Bengtson | 1-4-0 |
| 1973-78 | Chuck Fairbanks | 46-42-0 |
| 1979-81 | Ron Erhardt | 21-27-0 |
| 1982-83 | Ron Meyer | 13-13-0 |

*Released after five games in 1961
**Released after nine games in 1970
***Released after nine games in 1972

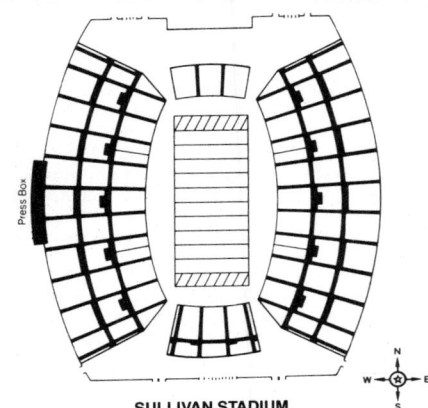

**SULLIVAN STADIUM**

## RECORD HOLDERS

### Individual Records—Career

| Category | Name | Performance |
|---|---|---|
| Rushing (Yds.) | Sam Cunningham, 1973-79, 1981-82 | 5,453 |
| Passing (Yds.) | Steve Grogan, 1975-1983 | 19,826 |
| Passing (TDs) | Steve Grogan, 1975-1983 | 136 |
| Receiving (No.) | Gino Cappelletti, 1960-1970 | 292 |
| Receiving (Yds.) | Stanley Morgan, 1977-1983 | 5,732 |
| Interceptions | Ron Hall, 1961-67 | 29 |
| Punting (Avg.) | Rich Camarillo, 1981-83 | 43.5 |
| Punt Return (Avg.) | Mack Herron, 1973-75 | 12.0 |
| Kickoff Return (Avg.) | Horace Ivory, 1977-1981 | 27.6 |
| Field Goals | Gino Cappelletti, 1960-1970 | 176 |
| Touchdowns (Tot.) | Sam Cunningham, 1973-79, 1981-82 | 49 |
| Points | Gino Cappelletti, 1960-1970 | 1,130 |

### Individual Records—Single Season

| Category | Name | Performance |
|---|---|---|
| Rushing (Yds.) | Jim Nance, 1966 | 1,458 |
| Passing (Yds.) | Vito (Babe) Parilli, 1964 | 3,465 |
| Passing (TDs) | Vito (Babe) Parilli, 1964 | 31 |
| Receiving (No.) | Stanley Morgan, 1983 | 58 |
| Receiving (Yds.) | Stanley Morgan, 1981 | 1,029 |
| Interceptions | Ron Hall, 1964 | 11 |
| Punting (Avg.) | Rich Camarillo, 1983 | 44.6 |
| Punt Return (Avg.) | Mack Herron, 1974 | 14.8 |
| Kickoff Return (Avg.) | Raymond Clayborn, 1977 | 31.0 |
| Field Goals | John Smith, 1980 | 26 |
| Touchdowns (Tot.) | Steve Grogan, 1976 | 13 |
| | Stanley Morgan, 1979 | 13 |
| Points | Gino Cappelletti, 1964 | 155 |

### Individual Records—Single Game

| Category | Name | Performance |
|---|---|---|
| Rushing (Yds.) | Tony Collins, 9-18-83 | 212 |
| Passing (Yds.) | Vito (Babe) Parilli, 10-16-64 | 422 |
| Passing (TDs) | Vito (Babe) Parilli, 11-15-64, 10-15-67 | 5 |
| | Steve Grogan, 9-9-79 | 5 |
| Receiving (No.) | Art Graham, 11-20-66 | 11 |
| Receiving (Yds.) | Stanley Morgan, 11-8-81 | 182 |
| Interceptions | Many times | 3 |
| | Last time by Roland James, 10-23-83 | |
| Field Goals | Gino Cappelletti, 10-4-64 | 6 |
| Touchdowns (Tot.) | Many times | 3 |
| | Last time by Mosi Tatupu, 12-11-83 | |
| Points | Gino Cappelletti, 12-18-65 | 28 |

## 1983 TEAM STATISTICS

| | New England | Opp. |
|---|---|---|
| Total First Downs | 284 | 326 |
|   Rushing | 130 | 129 |
|   Passing | 138 | 172 |
|   Penalty | 16 | 25 |
| Third Down Efficiency | 82/206 | 102/235 |
| Third Down Percentage | 39.8 | 43.4 |
| Total Net Yards | 5311 | 5576 |
|   Total Offensive Plays | 995 | 1102 |
|   Avg. Gain per Play | 5.3 | 5.1 |
|   Avg. Gain per Game | 331.9 | 348.5 |
| Net Yards Rushing | 2605 | 2281 |
|   Total Rushing Plays | 538 | 549 |
|   Avg. Gain per Rush | 4.8 | 4.2 |
|   Avg. Gain Rushing per Game | 162.8 | 142.6 |
| Net Yards Passing | 2706 | 3295 |
|   Lost Attempting to Pass | 45/334 | 39/270 |
|   Gross Yards Passing | 3040 | 3565 |
|   Attempts/Completions | 412/220 | 514/277 |
|   Percent Completed | 53.3 | 53.9 |
|   Had Intercepted | 18 | 17 |
|   Avg. Net Passing per Game | 169.1 | 205.9 |
| Punts/Avg. | 81/44.6 | 78/42.0 |
| Punt Returns/Avg. | 44/9.1 | 48/8.2 |
| Kickoff Returns/Avg. | 57/20.3 | 55/19.7 |
| Interceptions/Avg. Ret. | 17/11.9 | 18/20.1 |
| Penalties/Yards | 90/815 | 84/674 |
| Fumbles/Ball Lost | 47/20 | 30/19 |
| Total Points | 274 | 289 |
|   Avg. Points per Game | 17.1 | 18.1 |
|   Touchdowns | 36 | 31 |
|   Rushing | 19 | 9 |
|   Passing | 16 | 19 |
|   Returns and Recoveries | 1 | 3 |
|   Field Goals | 9/22 | 24/31 |
|   Conversions | 31/36 | 29/31 |
|   Safeties | 0 | 1 |
| Avg. Time of Possession | 29:21 | 30:39 |

## 1983 TEAM RECORD

### Preseason (0-4)

| Date | New England | | Opponents |
|---|---|---|---|
| 8/6 | 16 | Pittsburgh | 27 |
| 8/14 | 15 | San Francisco | 17 |
| 8/20 | 7 | Los Angeles Rams | 13 |
| 8/26 | 21 | Tampa Bay | 41 |
| | 59 | | 98 |

### Regular Season (8-8)

| Date | New England | | Opp. | * Att. |
|---|---|---|---|---|
| 9/4 | 23 | *Baltimore (OT) | 29 | 45,526 |
| 9/11 | 24 | Miami | 34 | 59,343 |
| 9/18 | 23 | *New York Jets | 13 | 43,182 |
| 9/25 | 28 | Pittsburgh | 23 | 58,282 |
| 10/2 | 13 | *San Francisco | 33 | 54,293 |
| 10/9 | 7 | Baltimore | 12 | 35,618 |
| 10/16 | 37 | *San Diego | 21 | 59,016 |
| 10/23 | 31 | Buffalo | 0 | 60,424 |
| 10/30 | 13 | Atlanta | 24 | 47,546 |
| 11/6 | 21 | *Buffalo | 7 | 42,604 |
| 11/13 | 17 | *Miami | 6 | 60,771 |
| 11/20 | 0 | *Cleveland | 30 | 40,987 |
| 11/27 | 3 | New York Jets | 26 | 48,620 |
| 12/4 | 7 | *New Orleans | 0 | 24,579 |
| 12/11 | 21 | Los Angeles Rams | 7 | 46,503 |
| 12/18 | 6 | Seattle | 24 | 59,688 |
| | 274 | | 289 | 786,982 |

*Home Game      (OT) Overtime

### Score by Periods

| | | | | | | | |
|---|---|---|---|---|---|---|---|
| New England | 53 | 71 | 40 | 110 | 0 | — | 274 |
| Opponents | 47 | 110 | 67 | 59 | 6 | — | 289 |

### Attendance

Home 370,958     Away 416,024     Total 786,982

Single game home record, 61,457 (12-5-71)

Single season home record, 475,081 (1978)

## 1983 INDIVIDUAL STATISTICS

### Rushing

| | Att. | Yds. | Avg. | LG | TD |
|---|---|---|---|---|---|
| Collins | 219 | 1049 | 4.8 | 50t | 10 |
| Tatupu | 106 | 578 | 5.5 | 55 | 4 |
| R. Weathers | 73 | 418 | 5.7 | 77t | 1 |
| van Eeghen | 95 | 358 | 3.8 | 11 | 2 |
| Grogan | 23 | 108 | 4.7 | 17 | 2 |
| Eason | 19 | 39 | 2.1 | 12 | 0 |
| C. Weathers | 1 | 28 | 28.0 | 28 | 0 |
| Kerrigan | 1 | 14 | 14.0 | 14 | 0 |
| Morgan | 1 | 13 | 13.0 | 13 | 0 |
| New England | 538 | 2605 | 4.8 | 77 | 19 |
| Opponents | 549 | 2281 | 4.2 | 29 | 9 |

### Passing

| | Att. | Comp. | Pct. | Yds. | TD | Int. | Tkld. | Rate |
|---|---|---|---|---|---|---|---|---|
| Grogan | 303 | 168 | 55.4 | 2411 | 15 | 12 | 29/195 | 81.4 |
| Eason | 95 | 46 | 48.4 | 557 | 1 | 5 | 16/139 | 48.4 |
| Kerrigan | 14 | 6 | 42.9 | 72 | 0 | 1 | 0/0 | 29.5 |
| New Eng. | 412 | 220 | 53.4 | 3040 | 16 | 18 | 45/334 | 72.1 |
| Opponents | 514 | 277 | 53.9 | 3565 | 19 | 17 | 39/270 | 74.4 |

### Receiving

| | No. | Yds. | Avg. | LG | TD |
|---|---|---|---|---|---|
| Morgan | 58 | 863 | 14.9 | 50t | 2 |
| Collins | 27 | 257 | 9.5 | 20 | 0 |
| Ramsey | 24 | 335 | 14.0 | 39 | 6 |
| R. Weathers | 23 | 212 | 9.2 | 19 | 0 |
| Jones | 20 | 323 | 16.2 | 30 | 1 |
| C. Weathers | 19 | 379 | 19.9 | 58t | 3 |
| Starring | 17 | 389 | 22.9 | 76t | 2 |
| van Eeghen | 10 | 102 | 10.2 | 23t | 0 |
| Tatupu | 10 | 97 | 9.7 | 17 | 1 |
| Dawson | 9 | 84 | 9.3 | 14 | 1 |
| Hasselbeck | 1 | 7 | 7.0 | 7 | 0 |
| B. Williams | 1 | 0 | 0.0 | 0 | 0 |
| Grogan | 1 | −8 | −8.0 | −8 | 0 |
| New England | 220 | 3040 | 13.8 | 76t | 16 |
| Opponents | 277 | 3565 | 12.9 | 68t | 19 |

### Interceptions

| | No. | Yds. | Avg. | LG | TD |
|---|---|---|---|---|---|
| Sanford | 7 | 24 | 3.4 | 16 | 0 |
| James | 5 | 99 | 19.8 | 46 | 0 |
| Marion | 2 | 4 | 2.0 | 4 | 0 |
| Blackmon | 1 | 39 | 39.0 | 39 | 0 |
| Nelson | 1 | 6 | 6.0 | 6 | 0 |
| McGrew | 1 | 3 | 3.0 | 3 | 0 |
| Weishuhn | 0 | 27 | — | 27t | 1 |
| New England | 17 | 202 | 11.9 | 46 | 1 |
| Opponents | 18 | 361 | 20.1 | 65t | 1 |

### Punting

| | No. | Yds. | Avg. | In 20 | LG |
|---|---|---|---|---|---|
| Camarillo | 81 | 3615 | 44.6 | 25 | 70 |
| New England | 81 | 3615 | 44.6 | 25 | 70 |
| Opponents | 78 | 3273 | 42.0 | 21 | 62 |

### Punt Returns

| | No. | FC | Yds. | Avg. | LG | TD |
|---|---|---|---|---|---|---|
| R. Smith | 38 | 12 | 398 | 10.5 | 55 | 0 |
| C. Weathers | 4 | 0 | 1 | 0.3 | 3 | 0 |
| Lee | 1 | 0 | 0 | 0.0 | 0 | 0 |
| Sanford | 1 | 2 | 0 | 0.0 | 0 | 0 |
| New England | 44 | 14 | 399 | 9.1 | 55 | 0 |
| Opponents | 48 | 6 | 392 | 8.2 | 22 | 0 |

### Kickoff Returns

| | No. | Yds. | Avg. | LG | TD |
|---|---|---|---|---|---|
| R. Smith | 42 | 916 | 21.8 | 53 | 0 |
| Jones | 4 | 63 | 15.8 | 23 | 0 |
| Lee | 4 | 40 | 10.0 | 19 | 0 |
| C. Weathers | 3 | 58 | 19.3 | 33 | 0 |
| R. Weathers | 3 | 68 | 22.7 | 29 | 0 |
| Golden | 1 | 10 | 10.0 | 10 | 0 |
| New England | 57 | 1155 | 20.3 | 53 | 0 |
| Opponents | 55 | 1082 | 19.7 | 60 | 0 |

### Scoring

| | TD | TD R | TD P | TD Rt | PAT | FG | TP |
|---|---|---|---|---|---|---|---|
| Collins | 10 | 10 | 0 | 0 | | | 60 |
| Ramsey | 6 | 0 | 6 | 0 | | | 36 |
| Steinfort | | | | | 16/17 | 6/15 | 34 |
| Tatupu | 5 | 4 | 1 | 0 | | | 30 |
| J. Smith | | | | | 12/15 | 3/6 | 21 |
| C. Weathers | 3 | 0 | 3 | 0 | | | 18 |
| Grogan | 2 | 2 | 0 | 0 | | | 12 |
| Morgan | 2 | 0 | 2 | 0 | | | 12 |
| Starring | 2 | 0 | 2 | 0 | | | 12 |
| van Eeghen | 2 | 2 | 0 | 0 | | | 12 |
| Dawson | 1 | 0 | 1 | 0 | | | 6 |
| Jones | 1 | 0 | 1 | 0 | | | 6 |
| R. Weathers | 1 | 1 | 0 | 0 | | | 6 |
| Weishuhn | 1 | 0 | 0 | 1 | | | 6 |
| Zendejas | | | | | | 3/4 | 0/1 | 3 |
| New England | 36 | 19 | 16 | 1 | 31/36 | 9/22 | 274 |
| Opponents | 31 | 9 | 19 | 3 | 29/30 | 24/31 | 289 |

## FIRST-ROUND SELECTIONS

(If Club had no first-round selection, first player drafted is listed with round in parentheses.)

| Year | Player, College, Position |
|---|---|
| 1960 | Ron Burton, Northwestern, RB |
| 1961 | Tommy Mason, Tulane, RB |
| 1962 | Gary Collins, Maryland, WR |
| 1963 | Art Graham, Boston College, WR |
| 1964 | Jack Concannon, Boston College, QB |
| 1965 | Jerry Rush, Michigan State, DE |
| 1966 | Karl Singer, Purdue, T |
| 1967 | John Charles, Purdue, S |
| 1968 | Dennis Byrd, North Carolina State, DE |
| 1969 | Ron Sellers, Florida State, WR |
| 1970 | Phil Olsen, Utah State, DE |
| 1971 | Jim Plunkett, Stanford, QB |
| 1972 | Tom Reynolds, San Diego State, WR (2) |
| 1973 | John Hannah, Alabama, G |
| | Sam Cunningham, Southern California, RB |
| | Darryl Stingley, Purdue, WR |
| 1974 | Steve Corbett, Boston College, G (2) |
| 1975 | Russ Francis, Oregon, TE |
| 1976 | Mike Haynes, Arizona State, DB |
| | Pete Brock, Colorado, C |
| | Tim Fox, Ohio State, DB |
| 1977 | Raymond Clayborn, Texas, DB |
| | Stanley Morgan, Tennessee, WR |
| 1978 | Bob Cryder, Alabama, G |
| 1979 | Rick Sanford, South Carolina, DB |
| 1980 | Roland James, Tennessee, DB |
| | Vagas Ferguson, Notre Dame, RB |
| 1981 | Brian Holloway, Stanford, T |
| 1982 | Kenneth Sims, Texas, DT |
| | Lester Williams, Miami, DT |
| 1983 | Tony Eason, Illinois, QB |
| 1984 | Irving Fryar, Nebraska, WR |

# NEW ENGLAND PATRIOTS 1984 VETERAN ROSTER

| No. | Name | Pos. | Ht. | Wt. | Birth-date | NFL Exp. | College | Birthplace | Residence | Games in '83 |
|---|---|---|---|---|---|---|---|---|---|---|
| 85 | †Adams, Julius | DE | 6-3 | 270 | 4/26/48 | 13 | Texas Southern | Macon, Ga. | Roberta, Ga. | 16 |
| 55 | Blackmon, Don | LB | 6-3 | 235 | 3/14/58 | 4 | Tulsa | Pompano Beach, Fla. | Sunrise, Fla. | 15 |
| 58 | Brock, Pete | C | 6-5 | 270 | 7/14/54 | 9 | Colorado | Portland, Ore. | Norfolk, Mass. | 13 |
| 3 | Camarillo, Rich | P | 5-11 | 191 | 11/29/59 | 4 | Washington | Whittier, Calif. | Foxboro, Mass. | 16 |
| 26 | Clayborn, Ray | CB | 6-0 | 186 | 1/2/55 | 8 | Texas | Ft. Worth, Tex. | Austin, Tex. | 16 |
| 33 | Collins, Tony | RB | 5-11 | 203 | 5/27/59 | 4 | East Carolina | Sanford, Fla. | Stoughton, Mass. | 16 |
| 91 | Crump, George | DE | 6-4 | 260 | 7/22/59 | 2 | East Carolina | Portsmouth, Va. | Mansfield, Mass. | 0* |
| 75 | Cryder, Bob | T | 6-4 | 282 | 9/7/56 | 7 | Alabama | East St. Louis, Ill. | Stoughton, Mass. | 14 |
| 87 | Dawson, Lin | TE | 6-3 | 240 | 6/24/59 | 4 | North Carolina State | Norfolk, Va. | Kinston, N.C. | 13 |
| 47 | Dombrowski, Paul | CB-S | 6-0 | 185 | 8/8/56 | 5 | Linfield College | Sumter, S.C. | Stoughton, Mass. | 7 |
| 11 | Eason, Tony | QB | 6-4 | 212 | 10/8/59 | 2 | Illinois | Walnut Grove, Calif. | Millis, Mass. | 16 |
|  | t-Franklin, Tony | K | 5-8 | 182 | 11/18/56 | 6 | Texas A&M | Big Spring, Tex. | San Antonio, Tex. | 16 |
| 59 | Golden, Tim | LB | 6-1 | 220 | 11/15/59 | 3 | Florida | Pahokee, Fla. | Gainesville, Fla. | 16 |
| 14 | Grogan, Steve | QB | 6-4 | 210 | 7/24/53 | 10 | Kansas State | San Antonio, Tex. | Foxboro, Mass. | 12 |
| 68 | Haley, Darryl | T | 6-4 | 265 | 2/16/61 | 3 | Utah | Gardena, Calif. | Salt Lake City, Utah | 16 |
| 73 | Hannah, John | G | 6-3 | 265 | 4/4/51 | 12 | Alabama | Canton, Ga. | Westwood, Mass. | 16 |
| 70 | Henson, Luther | NT | 6-0 | 275 | 3/25/59 | 3 | Ohio State | Sandusky, Ohio | Sandusky, Ohio | 4 |
| 76 | Holloway, Brian | T | 6-7 | 288 | 7/25/59 | 4 | Stanford | Omaha, Neb. | Stephentown, N.Y. | 16 |
| 51 | Ingram, Brian | LB | 6-4 | 235 | 10/31/59 | 3 | Tennessee | Memphis, Tenn. | Newport, Tenn. | 4 |
| 38 | James, Roland | S | 6-2 | 191 | 2/18/58 | 5 | Tennessee | Jamestown, Ohio | Rehoboth, Mass. | 16 |
| 83 | Jones, Cedric | WR | 5-11 | 184 | 6/1/60 | 3 | Duke | Norfolk, Va. | Norwood, Mass. | 15 |
| 19 | Kerrigan, Mike | QB | 6-3 | 205 | 4/27/60 | 2 | Northwestern | Chicago, Ill. | Chicago, Ill. | 1 |
| 22 | Lee, Keith | CB-S | 5-11 | 193 | 12/22/57 | 4 | Colorado State | San Antonio, Tex. | Westminster, Colo. | 15 |
| 42 | Lippett, Ronnie | CB | 5-11 | 180 | 12/10/60 | 2 | Miami | Melbourne, Fla. | Sebring, Fla. | 16 |
| 31 | Marion, Fred | S | 6-2 | 191 | 8/2/59 | 3 | Miami | Gainesville, Fla. | Mansfield, Mass. | 16 |
| 50 | McGrew, Larry | LB | 6-5 | 233 | 7/23/57 | 4 | Southern California | Berkeley, Calif. | Richmond, Calif. | 16 |
| 67 | Moore, Steve | T | 6-4 | 285 | 10/1/60 | 2 | Tennessee State | Memphis, Tenn. | Memphis, Tenn. | 4 |
| 86 | Morgan, Stanley | WR | 5-11 | 181 | 2/17/55 | 8 | Tennessee | Easley, S.C. | Germantown, Tenn. | 16 |
| 57 | Nelson, Steve | LB | 6-2 | 230 | 4/26/51 | 11 | North Dakota State | Farmington, Minn. | Norfolk, Mass. | 8 |
| 98 | Owens, Dennis | NT | 6-1 | 258 | 2/24/60 | 3 | North Carolina State | Clinton, N.C. | Hampton, Va. | 16 |
| 35 | Peoples, George | RB | 6-0 | 215 | 8/25/60 | 3 | Auburn | Tampa, Fla. | Seffner, Fla. | 16 |
| 88 | Ramsey, Derrick | TE | 6-5 | 235 | 12/23/56 | 7 | Kentucky | Hastings, Fla. | Oakland, Calif. | 16* |
| 52 | Rembert, Johnny | LB | 6-3 | 234 | 1/19/61 | 2 | Clemson | Hollandale, Miss. | Arcadia, Fla. | 15 |
| 95 | Reynolds, Ed | LB | 6-5 | 230 | 9/23/61 | 2 | Virginia | Stuttgart, Germany | Ridgeway, Va. | 12 |
| 65 | Rogers, Doug | DE | 6-5 | 260 | 6/23/60 | 3 | Stanford | Bakersfield, Calif. | Bakersfield, Calif. | 12* |
| 25 | Sanford, Rick | S | 6-1 | 192 | 1/9/57 | 6 | South Carolina | Rock Hill, S.C. | Foxboro, Mass. | 16 |
| 77 | Sims, Kenneth | DE | 6-5 | 271 | 10/31/59 | 3 | Texas | Kosse, Tex. | Austin, Tex. | 5 |
| 27 | Smith, Ricky | CB-S-KR | 6-0 | 182 | 7/20/60 | 3 | Alabama State | Quincy, Fla. | Pensacola, Fla. | 16 |
| 81 | Starring, Stephen | WR | 5-10 | 172 | 7/30/61 | 2 | McNeese State | Baton Rouge, La. | Lake Charles, La. | 15 |
| 30 | Tatupu, Mosi | RB | 6-0 | 227 | 4/26/55 | 7 | Southern California | Pago Pago, Amer. Samoa | San Diego, Calif. | 16 |
| 56 | Tippett, Andre | LB | 6-3 | 241 | 12/27/59 | 3 | Iowa | Birmingham, Ala. | Stoughton, Mass. | 15 |
| 82 | Weathers, Clarence | WR | 5-9 | 170 | 1/10/62 | 2 | Delaware State | Greens Pond, S.C. | Norwood, Mass. | 16 |
| 24 | Weathers, Robert | RB | 6-2 | 222 | 9/13/60 | 3 | Arizona | Westfield, N.Y. | Stoughton, Mass. | 15 |
| 53 | Weishuhn, Clayton | LB | 6-2 | 221 | 10/9/59 | 3 | Angelo State | San Angelo, Tex. | San Angelo, Tex. | 16 |
| 62 | Wheeler, Dwight | C | 6-3 | 274 | 1/13/55 | 6 | Tennessee State | Memphis, Tenn. | Nashville, Tenn. | 16 |
| 80 | †Williams, Brooks | TE | 6-4 | 226 | 12/7/54 | 7 | North Carolina | Baltimore, Md. | Virginia Beach, Va. | 13 |
| 72 | Williams, Lester | NT | 6-3 | 272 | 1/19/59 | 3 | Miami | Miami, Fla. | Stoughton, Mass. | 15 |
| 90 | Williams, Toby | DE | 6-3 | 254 | 11/19/59 | 2 | Nebraska | Washington, D.C. | Mansfield, Mass. | 16 |
| 48 | Wilson, Darryal | WR | 6-0 | 182 | 9/19/60 | 2 | Tennessee | Florence, Ala. | Bristol, Va. | 9 |
| 61 | Wooten, Ron | G | 6-4 | 273 | 6/28/59 | 3 | North Carolina | Cape Cod, Mass. | Norfolk, Mass. | 16 |

* Crump was active for 2 games with New England in '83, but did not play; Ramsey played 2 games with Los Angeles Raiders in '83, 14 with New England; Rogers played 2 games with Atlanta, 10 with New England in '83.

†Option playout; subject to developments.

t-Patriots traded for Franklin (Philadelphia).

Also played with Patriots in '83—DE Dave Browning (12 games), LB John Gillen (8), DE Marshall Harris (6), TE Don Hasselbeck (1), C Art Kuehn (2), K John Smith (5), DE Ron Spears (1), K Fred Steinfort (9), RB Mark van Eeghen (15).

## COACHING STAFF

### Head Coach,
### Ron Meyer

**Pro Career:** Begins third year in pro coaching ranks as head coach of the Patriots. Led New England to 5-4 record in 1982 and first postseason playoff berth since 1978. Made his first appearance in NFL as a personnel assistant with Dallas from 1971-72. Named New England head coach January 15, 1982. No pro playing experience. Career record: 13-13.

**Background:** Walk-on defensive back at Purdue 1959-62. Selected to the All-Big 10 Academic Team and recipient of Nobel Kizer Award for athletic and academic achievement in 1963. Assistant coach at Purdue 1965-70. Became head coach at Nevada-Las Vegas in 1973 and directed Rebels to a three-year record of 27-8, including an undefeated (11-0) regular season in 1974 before losing in the National Semifinals in NCAA Division II. Head coach at Southern Methodist 1976-81, where he led Mustangs to 1981 Southwest Conference title.

**Personal:** Born February 17, 1941, in Westerville, Ohio. He and his wife, Cindy, live in Westwood, Mass. with their four children—Ron, Jr., Ralph, Katryn, and Elizabeth.

### Assistant Coaches

**Tommy Brasher,** defensive line; born December 30, 1940, El Dorado, Ark., lives in Dover, Mass. Linebacker Arkansas 1961-63. No pro playing experience. College coach: Arkansas 1970, Virginia Tech 1971-73, Northeast Louisiana 1974, 1976, Southern Methodist 1977-81. Pro coach: Shreveport (WFL) 1975, joined Patriots in 1982.

**Cleve Bryant,** offensive backs; born March 27, 1947, Marrianna, Fla., lives in Norfolk, Mass. Quarterback Ohio University 1967-69. No pro playing experience. College coach: Miami, Ohio 1977, North Carolina 1978-81. Pro coach: Joined Patriots in 1982.

**LeBaron Caruthers,** strength and conditioning; born April 20, 1954, Nashville, Tenn., lives in Mansfield, Mass. Tackle East Carolina 1972-73. No pro playing experience. College coach: Auburn 1978-79, Southern Methodist 1980-81. Pro coach: Joined Patriots in 1982.

**Steve Endicott,** receivers; born December 27, 1950, Grants Pass, Ore., lives in Weymouth, Mass. Quarterback Oregon State 1969-71. No pro playing experience. College coach: Oregon State 1972, Miami 1973-75, Southern Methodist 1976-81. Pro coach: Winnipeg Blue Bombers (CFL) 1977, Toronto Argonauts (CFL) 1978, joined Patriots in 1982.

**Lew Erber,** offensive coordinator-quarterbacks; born May 27, 1934, Clifton, N.J., lives in Foxboro. Running back Montclair State 1954-55. No pro playing experience. College coach: Iowa State 1967-68, California Western 1969-72, San Diego State 1973, California 1974. Pro coach: San Francisco 49ers 1975, Oakland Raiders 1976-81, joined Patriots in 1982.

**Bill Muir,** offensive line; born October 26, 1942, Pittsburgh, Pa., lives in Plainville, Mass. Tackle Susquehanna 1963-65. No pro playing experience. College coach: Susquehanna 1965, Delaware Valley 1966-67, Rhode Island 1970-71, Idaho State 1972-73, Southern Methodist 1976-77. Pro coach: Orlando (Continental Football League) 1968-69, Houston-Shreveport (WFL) 1974-75, joined Patriots in 1982.

**Rod Rust,** defensive coordinator; born August 2, 1928, Webster City, Iowa, lives in Foxboro. Center-linebacker Iowa State 1947-50. No pro playing experience. College coach: New Mexico 1960-62, Stanford 1963-66, North Texas State 1967-72 (head coach). Pro coach: Montreal Alouettes (CFL) 1973-75, Philadelphia Eagles 1976-77, Kansas City Chiefs 1978-82, joined Patriots in 1983.

**Dante Scarnecchia,** special teams-tight ends; born February 15, 1948, Los Angeles, Calif., lives in Wrentham, Mass. Center California Western 1966-69. No pro playing experience. College coach: California Western 1970-72, Iowa State 1973-74, Southern Methodist 1975-76, 1980-81, Pacific 1977-78. Pro coach: Joined Patriots in 1982.

## NEW ENGLAND PATRIOTS 1984 FIRST-YEAR ROSTER

| Name | Pos. | Ht. | Wt. | Birth-date | College | Birthplace | Residence | How Acq. |
|------|------|-----|-----|-----------|---------|-----------|-----------|----------|
| Bolzan, Scott | T | 6-4 | 277 | 6/25/62 | Northern Illinois | Chicago, Ill. | Calumet City, Ill. | D9 |
| Botha, Naas (1) | K | 5-9 | 170 | 2/27/58 | Pretoria, So. Africa | Breyton, So. Africa | Dallas, Tex. | FA |
| Coash, Beau (1) | TE | 6-3 | 228 | 6/12/60 | Middlebury College | New York, N.Y. | Rye, N.Y. | FA |
| Creswell, Smiley (1) | DE | 6-4 | 251 | 12/11/59 | Michigan State | Everett, Wash. | Monroe, Wash. | D5('83) |
| Ekern, Andy (1) | T | 6-6 | 263 | 7/26/61 | Missouri | Columbia, Mo. | Mexico, Mo. | D12a('83) |
| Fairchild, Paul | G | 6-3 | 267 | 8/14/61 | Kansas | Carroll, Iowa | Glidden, Iowa | D5 |
| Flager, Charlie | G | 6-3 | 260 | 2/28/61 | Washington State | Spokane, Wash. | Chattaroy, Wash. | D11 |
| Fryar, Irving | WR | 5-11 | 198 | 9/28/62 | Nebraska | Mount Holly, N.J. | Mount Holly, N.J. | D1 |
| Gibson, Ernest | CB-S | 5-10 | 189 | 10/3/61 | Furman | Jacksonville, Fla. | Jacksonville, Fla. | D6 |
| Howell, Harper | TE | 6-3 | 227 | 7/20/61 | UCLA | Coral Gables, Fla. | Boulder, Colo. | D12 |
| James, Craig (1) | RB | 6-0 | 215 | 1/2/61 | Southern Methodist | Jacksonville, Fla. | Dallas, Tex. | D7 ('83) |
| Johnson, Vanclive | LB | 6-3 | 223 | 2/9/61 | So. Connecticut St. | Jamaica, West Indies | Brooklyn, N.Y. | FA |
| Kallmeyer, Bruce | K | 5-10 | 184 | 2/8/62 | Kansas | Kansas City, Kan. | Overland Park, Kan. | D7 |
| Keyton, James | T | 6-5 | 274 | 9/9/62 | Arizona State | Lansing, Mich. | Lansing, Mich. | D8 |
| Lee, Keith A. | LB | 6-4 | 230 | 5/11/60 | Virginia | Frederick, Md. | Charlottesville, Va. | FA |
| Lewis, Darryl (1) | TE | 6-6 | 226 | 4/16/61 | Texas | Mt. Pleasant, Tex. | Arlington, Tex. | D5a('83) |
| Seccareccia, Robert | T-G | 6-3 | 210 | 8/30/61 | Rhode Island | Providence, R.I. | Pawtucket, R.I. | FA |
| Wienke, David | QB | 6-1 | 190 | 4/18/61 | Rhode Island | Hinsdale, Ill. | Lisle, Ill. | FA |
| Windham, David | LB | 6-2 | 240 | 3/14/61 | Jackson State | Mobile, Ala. | Prichard, Ala. | D9a |
| Williams, Derwin | WR | 6-0 | 173 | 5/6/61 | New Mexico | Brownwood, Tex. | Brownwood, Tex. | D7 |
| Williams, Ed | LB | 6-3 | 244 | 8/9/61 | Texas | Odessa, Tex. | Odessa, Tex. | D2 |
| Williams, Jon | RB | 5-9 | 205 | 6/1/61 | Penn State | Somerville, N.J. | Somerville, N.J. | D3 |
| Zendejas, Joaquin (1) | K | 5-11 | 178 | 1/14/60 | La Verne | Mexico | Chino, Calif. | FA |

Players who report to an NFL team for the first time are designated on rosters as rookies (R). If a player reported to an NFL training camp in a previous year but was not on the active squad for three or more regular season or postseason games, he is listed on the first-year roster and designated by a (1). Thereafter, a player who is on the active squad for three or more regular season or postseason games is credited with an additional year of playing experience.

## NOTES

_____
_____
_____
_____
_____
_____
_____
_____
_____
_____
_____
_____
_____
_____
_____
_____
_____
_____
_____

**Steve Sidwell,** linebackers; born August 30, 1944, Winfield, Kan., lives in Wrentham, Mass. Center-linebacker Colorado 1963-66. No pro playing experience. College coach: Colorado 1968-73, Nevada-Las Vegas 1974, Southern Methodist 1976-81. Pro coach: Joined Patriots in 1982.

**Steve Walters,** defensive backs; born June 16, 1948, Jonesboro, Ark., lives in Wrentham, Mass. Defensive back Arkansas 1969-70. No pro playing experience. College coach: Tampa 1973, Northeast Louisiana 1974-75, Morehead State 1976, Tulsa 1977-78, Memphis State 1979, Southern Methodist 1980-81. Pro coach: Joined Patriots in 1982.

# NEW YORK JETS

**American Football Conference
Eastern Division**

**Team Colors:** Kelly Green and White

598 Madison Avenue
New York, New York 10022
Telephone: (212) 421-6600

**Club Officials**

Chairman of the Board: Leon Hess
President-Chief Operating Officer: Jim Kensil
Secretary and Administrative Manager:
 Steve Gutman
Director of Player Personnel: Mike Hickey
Pro Personnel Director: Jim Royer
Talent Scouts: Joe Collins, Don Grammer,
 Sid Hall, Marv Sunderland
Director of Public Relations: Frank Ramos
Assistant Director of Public Relations: Ron Cohen
Director of Operations: Tim Davey
Traveling Secretary: Mike Kensil
Ticket Manager: Bob Parente
Film Director: Jim Pons
Trainer: Bob Reese
Assistant Trainer: Pepper Burruss
Equipment Manager: Bill Hampton

**Stadium:** Giants Stadium • **Capacity:** 76,891
 East Rutherford, New Jersey 07073

**Playing Surface:** AstroTurf

**Training Center:** 1000 Fulton Avenue
 Hempstead, New York 11550
 516-538-6600

## 1984 SCHEDULE

**Preseason**
| | | |
|---|---|---|
| Aug. 4 | **Cincinnati** | 8:30 |
| Aug. 11 | at Houston | 8:00 |
| Aug. 18 | at New York Giants | 8:00 |
| Aug. 24 | at Los Angeles Raiders | 6:00 |

**Regular Season**
| | | |
|---|---|---|
| Sept. 2 | at Colts | 3:00 |
| Sept. 6 | **Pittsburgh** (Thursday) | 9:00 |
| Sept. 16 | **Cincinnati** | 1:00 |
| Sept. 23 | at Buffalo | 1:00 |
| Sept. 30 | **New England** | 1:00 |
| Oct. 7 | at Kansas City | 12:00 |
| Oct. 14 | at Cleveland | 1:00 |
| Oct. 21 | **Kansas City** | 4:00 |
| Oct. 28 | at New England | 1:00 |
| Nov. 4 | **Miami** | 4:00 |
| Nov. 11 | **Colts** | 1:00 |
| Nov. 18 | at Houston | 3:00 |
| Nov. 26 | at Miami (Monday) | 9:00 |
| Dec. 2 | **New York Giants** | 1:00 |
| Dec. 8 | **Buffalo** (Saturday) | 12:30 |
| Dec. 16 | at Tampa Bay | 1:00 |

## JETS COACHING HISTORY

**New York Titans 1960-62
(154-187-7)**

| | | |
|---|---|---|
| 1960-61 | Sammy Baugh | 14-14-0 |
| 1962 | Clyde (Bulldog) Turner | 5-9-0 |
| 1963-73 | Weeb Ewbank | 74-77-6 |
| 1974-75 | Charley Winner* | 9-14-0 |
| 1975 | Ken Shipp | 1-4-0 |
| 1976 | Lou Holtz** | 3-10-0 |
| 1976 | Mike Holovak | 0-1-0 |
| 1977-82 | Walt Michaels | 41-49-1 |
| 1983 | Joe Walton | 7-9-0 |

 *Released after nine games in 1975
**Resigned after 13 games in 1976

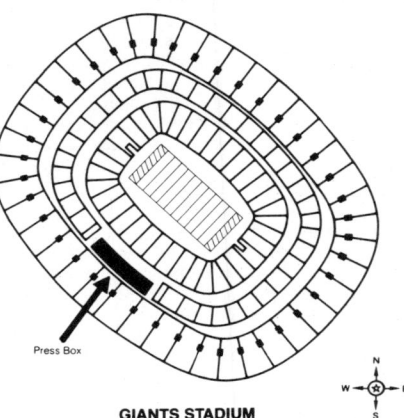

Press Box

**GIANTS STADIUM**

## RECORD HOLDERS
### Individual Records—Career

| Category | Name | Performance |
|---|---|---|
| Rushing (Yds.) | Emerson Boozer, 1966-1975 | 5,104 |
| Passing (Yds.) | Joe Namath, 1965-1976 | 27,057 |
| Passing (TDs) | Joe Namath, 1965-1976 | 170 |
| Receiving (No.) | Don Maynard, 1960-1972 | 627 |
| Receiving (Yds.) | Don Maynard, 1960-1972 | 11,732 |
| Interceptions | Bill Baird, 1963-69 | 34 |
| Punting (Avg.) | Curley Johnson, 1961-68 | 42.8 |
| Punt Return (Avg.) | Dick Christy, 1961-63 | 16.2 |
| Kickoff Return (Avg.) | Lou Piccone, 1974-76 | 24.9 |
| Field Goals | Jim Turner, 1964-1970 | 153 |
| Touchdowns (Tot.) | Don Maynard, 1960-1972 | 88 |
| Points | Jim Turner, 1964-1970 | 697 |

### Individual Records—Single Season

| Category | Name | Performance |
|---|---|---|
| Rushing (Yds.) | John Riggins, 1975 | 1,005 |
| Passing (Yds.) | Joe Namath, 1967 | 4,007 |
| Passing (TDs) | Joe Namath, 1967 | 26 |
| | Al Dorow, 1960 | 26 |
| Receiving (No.) | George Sauer, 1967 | 75 |
| Receiving (Yds.) | Don Maynard, 1967 | 1,434 |
| Interceptions | Dainard Paulson, 1964 | 12 |
| Punting (Avg.) | Curley Johnson, 1965 | 45.3 |
| Punt Return (Avg.) | Dick Christy, 1961 | 21.3 |
| Kickoff Return (Avg.) | Leon Burton, 1960 | 28.7 |
| Field Goals | Jim Turner, 1968 | 34 |
| Touchdowns (Tot.) | Art Powell, 1960 | 14 |
| | Don Maynard, 1965 | 14 |
| | Emerson Boozer, 1972 | 14 |
| Points | Jim Turner, 1968 | 145 |

### Individual Records—Single Game

| Category | Name | Performance |
|---|---|---|
| Rushing (Yds.) | Matt Snell, 10-17-64 | 180 |
| Passing (Yds.) | Joe Namath, 9-24-72 | 496 |
| Passing (TDs) | Joe Namath, 9-24-72 | 6 |
| Receiving (No.) | Clark Gaines, 9-21-80 | 17 |
| Receiving (Yds.) | Don Maynard, 11-17-68 | 228 |
| Interceptions | Dainard Paulson, 9-28-63 | 3 |
| | Bill Baird, 10-31-64 | 3 |
| | Rich Sowells, 9-23-73 | 3 |
| Field Goals | Jim Turner, 11-3-68 | 6 |
| | Bobby Howfield, 12-3-72 | 6 |
| Touchdowns (Tot.) | Many times | 3 |
| | Last time by Wesley Walker, 12-6-82 | |
| Points | Jim Turner, 11-3-68 | 19 |

## 1983 TEAM STATISTICS

| | N.Y. Jets | Opp. |
|---|---|---|
| Total First Downs | 313 | 298 |
| Rushing | 126 | 126 |
| Passing | 171 | 151 |
| Penalty | 16 | 21 |
| Third Down Efficiency | 80/214 | 83/220 |
| Third Down Percentage | 37.4 | 37.7 |
| Total Net Yards | 5493 | 5301 |
| Total Offensive Plays | 1076 | 1058 |
| Avg. Gain per Play | 5.1 | 5.0 |
| Avg. Gain per Game | 343.3 | 331.3 |
| Net Yards Rushing | 2068 | 2378 |
| Total Rushing Plays | 474 | 547 |
| Avg. Gain per Rush | 4.4 | 4.3 |
| Avg. Gain Rushing per Game | 129.3 | 148.6 |
| Net Yards Passing | 3425 | 2923 |
| Lost Attempting to Pass | 43/317 | 48/378 |
| Gross Yards Passing | 3742 | 3301 |
| Attempts/Completions | 559/330 | 463/269 |
| Percent Completed | 59.0 | 58.1 |
| Had Intercepted | 28 | 22 |
| Avg. Net Passing per Game | 214.1 | 182.7 |
| Punts/Avg. | 82/39.2 | 85/41.1 |
| Punt Returns/Avg. | 38/11.1 | 47/7.8 |
| Kickoff Returns/Avg. | 66/20.8 | 50/21.3 |
| Interceptions/Avg. Ret. | 22/15.5 | 28/13.3 |
| Penalties/Yards | 110/1059 | 96/784 |
| Fumbles/Ball Lost | 29/19 | 29/14 |
| Total Points | 313 | 331 |
| Avg. Points per Game | 19.6 | 20.7 |
| Touchdowns | 38 | 39 |
| Rushing | 11 | 13 |
| Passing | 21 | 22 |
| Returns and Recoveries | 6 | 4 |
| Field Goals | 16/24 | 20/28 |
| Conversions | 37/38 | 35/39 |
| Safeties | 0 | 1 |
| Avg. Time of Possession | 29:23 | 30:37 |

## 1983 TEAM RECORD
### Preseason (2-2)

| Date | New York Jets | | Opponents |
|---|---|---|---|
| 8/7 | 16 | New York Giants | 23 |
| 8/13 | 20 | *Los Angeles Raiders | 17 |
| 8/18 | 20 | Cincinnati (OT) | 17 |
| 8/27 | 10 | New Orleans | 17 |
| | 66 | | 74 |

### Regular Season (7-9)

| Date | New York Jets | Opp. | Att. |
|---|---|---|---|
| 9/4 | 41 | San Diego 29 | 51,004 |
| 9/11 | 10 | *Seattle 17 | 50,066 |
| 9/18 | 13 | New England 23 | 43,182 |
| 9/25 | 27 | *L.A. Rams (OT) 24 | 52,070 |
| 10/3 | 34 | Buffalo 10 | 79,933 |
| 10/9 | 7 | Cleveland 10 | 78,235 |
| 10/16 | 14 | *Miami 32 | 58,615 |
| 10/23 | 21 | *Atlanta 27 | 46,878 |
| 10/30 | 27 | San Francisco 13 | 54,796 |
| 11/6 | 14 | *Baltimore 17 | 53,323 |
| 11/13 | 17 | *Buffalo 24 | 48,513 |
| 11/21 | 31 | New Orleans 28 | 68,606 |
| 11/27 | 26 | *New England 3 | 48,620 |
| 12/4 | 10 | Baltimore 6 | 29,431 |
| 12/10 | 7 | *Pittsburgh 34 | 53,996 |
| 12/16 | 14 | Miami 34 | 59,975 |
| | 313 | 331 | 877,243 |

*Home Game   (OT) Overtime

### Score by Periods

| | | | | | | | |
|---|---|---|---|---|---|---|---|
| New York Jets | 28 | 101 | 75 | 106 | 3 | — | 313 |
| Opponents | 72 | 66 | 90 | 103 | 0 | — | 331 |

### Attendance

Home 412,081   Away 465,162   Total 877,243
Single game home record, 63,962 (11-5-72; Shea Stadium)
Single season home record, 441,099 (1971; Shea Stadium)

## 1983 INDIVIDUAL STATISTICS

### Rushing

| | Att. | Yds. | Avg. | LG | TD |
|---|---|---|---|---|---|
| McNeil | 160 | 654 | 4.1 | 19 | 1 |
| Crutchfield | 137 | 571 | 4.2 | 17 | 3 |
| Harper | 51 | 354 | 6.9 | 78t | 1 |
| Dierking | 28 | 113 | 4.0 | 31 | 3 |
| Todd | 35 | 101 | 2.9 | 17 | 0 |
| Hector | 16 | 85 | 5.3 | 42 | 0 |
| Barber | 15 | 77 | 5.1 | 13 | 1 |
| Augustyniak | 18 | 50 | 2.8 | 6 | 2 |
| Lewis | 5 | 25 | 5.0 | 7 | 0 |
| Ryan | 4 | 23 | 5.8 | 25 | 0 |
| Jones | 4 | 10 | 2.5 | 9 | 0 |
| Crosby | 1 | 5 | 5.0 | 5 | 0 |
| N.Y. Jets | 474 | 2068 | 4.4 | 78t | 11 |
| Opponents | 547 | 2378 | 4.3 | 85t | 13 |

### Passing

| | Att. | Comp. | Pct. | Yds. | TD | Int. | Tkld. | Rate |
|---|---|---|---|---|---|---|---|---|
| Todd | 518 | 308 | 59.5 | 3478 | 18 | 26 | 42/314 | 70.3 |
| Ryan | 40 | 21 | 52.5 | 259 | 2 | 2 | 1/3 | 68.6 |
| McNeil | 1 | 1 | 100.0 | 5 | 1 | 0 | 0/0 | 127.1 |
| N.Y. Jets | 559 | 330 | 59.0 | 3742 | 21 | 28 | 43/317 | 70.8 |
| Opponents | 463 | 269 | 58.1 | 3301 | 22 | 22 | 48/378 | 76.2 |

### Receiving

| | No. | Yds. | Avg. | LG | TD |
|---|---|---|---|---|---|
| W. Walker | 61 | 868 | 14.2 | 64t | 7 |
| Harper | 48 | 413 | 8.6 | 33 | 2 |
| Jones | 43 | 734 | 17.1 | 50t | 4 |
| Dierking | 33 | 275 | 8.3 | 19 | 0 |
| Barkum | 32 | 385 | 12.0 | 34 | 1 |
| Shuler | 26 | 272 | 10.5 | 28 | 1 |
| McNeil | 21 | 172 | 8.2 | 21 | 3 |
| Crutchfield | 19 | 133 | 7.0 | 15 | 0 |
| Gaffney | 17 | 243 | 14.3 | 35 | 0 |
| Augustyniak | 10 | 71 | 7.1 | 17 | 1 |
| Barber | 7 | 48 | 6.9 | 12 | 1 |
| Lewis | 6 | 62 | 10.3 | 23 | 0 |
| Hector | 5 | 61 | 12.2 | 22t | 1 |
| Harmon | 1 | 4 | 4.0 | 4 | 0 |
| Coombs | 1 | 1 | 1.0 | 1 | 0 |
| N.Y. Jets | 330 | 3742 | 11.3 | 64t | 21 |
| Opponents | 269 | 3301 | 12.3 | 66t | 22 |

### Interceptions

| | No. | Yds. | Avg. | LG | TD |
|---|---|---|---|---|---|
| Mehl | 7 | 57 | 8.1 | 34t | 1 |
| Holmes | 3 | 107 | 35.7 | 43t | 1 |
| Ray | 3 | 77 | 25.7 | 42 | 0 |
| Lynn | 3 | 70 | 23.3 | 42t | 1 |
| Jackson | 2 | 8 | 4.0 | 8 | 0 |
| Schroy | 2 | 6 | 3.0 | 4 | 0 |
| Buttle | 1 | 17 | 17.0 | 17 | 0 |
| Crable | 1 | 0 | 0.0 | 0 | 0 |
| N.Y. Jets | 22 | 342 | 15.5 | 43t | 3 |
| Opponents | 28 | 372 | 13.3 | 58 | 3 |

### Punting

| | No. | Yds. | Avg. | In 20 | LG |
|---|---|---|---|---|---|
| Ramsey | 81 | 3218 | 39.7 | 17 | 56 |
| N.Y. Jets | 82 | 3218 | 39.2 | 17 | 56 |
| Opponents | 85 | 3491 | 41.1 | 22 | 60 |

### Punt Returns

| | No. | FC | Yds. | Avg. | LG | TD |
|---|---|---|---|---|---|---|
| Springs | 23 | 4 | 287 | 12.5 | 76t | 1 |
| Harmon | 12 | 8 | 109 | 9.1 | 21 | 0 |
| Mullen | 2 | 3 | 13 | 6.5 | 9 | 0 |
| Schroy | 1 | 0 | 11 | 11.0 | 11 | 0 |
| N.Y. Jets | 38 | 15 | 420 | 11.1 | 76t | 1 |
| Opponents | 47 | 18 | 367 | 7.8 | 71t | 1 |

### Kickoff Returns

| | No. | Yds. | Avg. | LG | TD |
|---|---|---|---|---|---|
| Springs | 16 | 364 | 22.8 | 64 | 0 |
| Brown | 29 | 645 | 22.2 | 46 | 0 |
| Hector | 14 | 274 | 19.6 | 45 | 0 |
| Mullen | 3 | 57 | 19.0 | 26 | 0 |
| Barber | 1 | 9 | 9.0 | 9 | 0 |
| Harper | 1 | 16 | 16.0 | 16 | 0 |
| McElroy | 1 | 7 | 7.0 | 7 | 0 |
| Shuler | 1 | 3 | 3.0 | 3 | 0 |
| N.Y. Jets | 66 | 1375 | 20.8 | 64 | 0 |
| Opponents | 50 | 1063 | 21.3 | 78 | 0 |

### Scoring

| | TD | TD R | TD P | TD Rt | PAT | FG | TP |
|---|---|---|---|---|---|---|---|
| Leahy | | | | | 36/37 | 16/24 | 84 |
| W. Walker | 7 | 0 | 7 | 0 | | | 42 |
| Jones | 4 | 0 | 4 | 0 | | | 24 |
| McNeil | 4 | 1 | 3 | 0 | | | 24 |
| Augustyniak | 3 | 2 | 1 | 0 | | | 18 |
| Crutchfield | 3 | 3 | 0 | 0 | | | 18 |
| Dierking | 3 | 3 | 0 | 0 | | | 18 |
| Harper | 3 | 1 | 2 | 0 | | | 18 |
| Barber | 2 | 1 | 1 | 0 | | | 12 |
| Holmes | 2 | 0 | 0 | 2 | | | 12 |
| Barkum | 1 | 0 | 1 | 0 | | | 6 |
| Gastineau | 1 | 0 | 0 | 1 | | | 6 |
| Hector | 1 | 0 | 1 | 0 | | | 6 |
| Lynn | 1 | 0 | 0 | 1 | | | 6 |
| Mehl | 1 | 0 | 0 | 1 | | | 6 |
| Shuler | 1 | 0 | 1 | 0 | | | 6 |
| Springs | 1 | 0 | 0 | 1 | | | 6 |
| Ryan | | | | | 1/1 | 0/0 | 1 |
| N.Y. Jets | 38 | 11 | 21 | 6 | 37/38 | 16/24 | 313 |
| Opponents | 39 | 13 | 22 | 4 | 35/39 | 20/28 | 331 |

## FIRST-ROUND SELECTIONS

(If Club had no first-round selection, first player drafted is listed with round in parentheses.)

| Year | Player, College, Position |
|---|---|
| 1960 | George Izo, Notre Dame, QB |
| 1961 | Tom Brown, Minnesota, G |
| 1962 | Sandy Stephens, Minnesota, QB |
| 1963 | Jerry Stovall, Louisiana State, S |
| 1964 | Matt Snell, Ohio State, RB |
| 1965 | Joe Namath, Alabama, QB |
| | Tom Nowatzke, Indiana, RB |
| 1966 | Bill Yearby, Michigan, DT |
| 1967 | Paul Seiler, Notre Dame, T |
| 1968 | Lee White, Weber State, RB |
| 1969 | Dave Foley, Ohio State, T |
| 1970 | Steve Tannen, Florida, CB |
| 1971 | John Riggins, Kansas, RB |
| 1972 | Jerome Barkum, Jackson State, WR |
| | Mike Taylor, Michigan, LB |
| 1973 | Burgess Owens, Miami, DB |
| 1974 | Carl Barzilauskas, Indiana, DT |
| 1975 | Anthony Davis, Southern California, RB (2) |
| 1976 | Richard Todd, Alabama, QB |
| 1977 | Marvin Powell, Southern California, T |
| 1978 | Chris Ward, Ohio State, T |
| 1979 | Marty Lyons, Alabama, DE |
| 1980 | Johnny (Lam) Jones, Texas, WR |
| 1981 | Freeman McNeil, UCLA, RB |
| 1982 | Bob Crable, Notre Dame, LB |
| 1983 | Ken O'Brien, Cal-Davis, QB |
| 1984 | Russell Carter, Southern Methodist, DB |
| | Ron Faurot, Arkansas, DE |

# NEW YORK JETS 1984 VETERAN ROSTER

| No. | Name | Pos. | Ht. | Wt. | Birth-date | NFL Exp. | College | Birthplace | Residence | Games in '83 |
|---|---|---|---|---|---|---|---|---|---|---|
| 60 | Alexander, Dan | G | 6-4 | 260 | 6/17/55 | 8 | Louisiana State | Houston, Tex. | Houston, Tex. | 16 |
| 35 | Augustyniak, Mike | FB | 5-11 | 226 | 7/17/56 | 4 | Purdue | Fort Wayne, Ind. | Port Washington, N.Y. | 8 |
| 31 | Barber, Marion | FB | 6-3 | 224 | 12/6/59 | 3 | Minnesota | Ft. Lauderdale, Fla. | Minneapolis, Minn. | 14 |
| 78 | Bennett, Barry | DT-DE | 6-4 | 257 | 12/10/55 | 7 | Concordia | Long Prairie, Minn. | Buffalo, Minn. | 13 |
| 64 | Bingham, Guy | C-G-T | 6-3 | 255 | 2/25/58 | 5 | Montana | Koizumi Gumma Ken, Jap. | Aberdeen, Wash. | 16 |
| 89 | Brown, Preston | WR-KR | 5-11 | 187 | 3/2/58 | 4 | Vanderbilt | Nashville, Tenn. | Huntsville, Ala. | 16 |
| 83 | Bruckner, Nick | WR | 5-11 | 185 | 5/19/61 | 2 | Syracuse | Astoria, N.Y. | Selden, N.Y. | 7 |
| 51 | Buttle, Greg | LB | 6-3 | 232 | 6/20/54 | 9 | Penn State | Atlantic City, N.J. | Jericho, N.Y. | 9 |
| 88 | Coombs, Tom | TE | 6-3 | 227 | 5/31/59 | 3 | Idaho | Eureka, Calif. | Olympia, Wash. | 12 |
| 50 | Crable, Bob | LB | 6-3 | 232 | 9/22/59 | 3 | Notre Dame | Cincinnati, Ohio | Cincinnati, Ohio | 14 |
| 52 | Eliopulos, Jim | LB | 6-2 | 229 | 4/18/59 | 2 | Wyoming | Dearborn, Mich. | Cheyenne, Wyo. | 12* |
| 65 | Fields, Joe | C | 6-2 | 253 | 11/14/53 | 10 | Widener | Woodbury, N.J. | Moorestown, N.J. | 12 |
| 38 | Floyd, George | S-CB | 5-11 | 190 | 12/21/60 | 2 | Eastern Kentucky | Tampa, Fla. | Florence, Ky. | 0* |
| 81 | Gaffney, Derrick | WR | 6-1 | 182 | 5/24/55 | 7 | Florida | Jacksonville, Fla. | Jacksonville, Fla. | 16 |
| 99 | Gastineau, Mark | DE | 6-5 | 265 | 11/20/56 | 6 | East Central Oklahoma | Ardmore, Okla. | Huntington, N.Y. | 16 |
| 94 | Guilbeau, Rusty | DE | 6-4 | 260 | 11/20/58 | 3 | McNeese State | Sunset, La. | Sunset, La. | 16 |
| 42 | Harper, Bruce | RB-KR | 5-8 | 177 | 6/20/55 | 8 | Kutztown State | Englewood, N.J. | Norwood, N.J. | 9 |
| 34 | Hector, Johnny | RB | 5-11 | 197 | 11/26/60 | 2 | Texas A&M | Lafayette, La. | New Iberia, La. | 10 |
| 40 | Jackson, Bobby | CB | 5-10 | 180 | 12/23/54 | 7 | Florida State | Albany, Ga. | Westbury, N.Y. | 15 |
| 80 | Jones, Johnny (Lam) | WR | 5-11 | 180 | 4/4/58 | 5 | Texas | Lawton, Okla. | Austin, Tex. | 14 |
| 73 | Klecko, Joe | DT-DE | 6-3 | 263 | 10/15/53 | 8 | Temple | Chester, Pa. | West Chester, Pa. | 16 |
| 30 | Klever, Rocky | RB | 6-3 | 225 | 7/10/59 | 2 | Montana | Portland, Ore. | Missoula, Mont. | 5 |
| 5 | Leahy, Pat | K | 6-0 | 189 | 3/19/51 | 11 | St. Louis University | St. Louis, Mo. | St. Louis, Mo. | 16 |
| 22 | Lewis, Kenny | RB | 6-0 | 196 | 10/2/57 | 4 | Virginia Tech | Danville, Va. | Hempstead, N.Y. | 7 |
| 61 | Lilja, George | C | 6-4 | 250 | 3/3/58 | 3 | Michigan | Evergreen Park, Ill. | Orange, Calif. | 1 |
| 71 | Luscinski, Jim | T-G | 6-5 | 275 | 12/16/58 | 2 | Norwich | Arlington, Mass. | Hanover, Mass. | 0* |
| 29 | Lynn, Johnny | CB-S | 6-0 | 198 | 12/19/56 | 5 | UCLA | Los Angeles, Calif. | Altadena, Calif. | 16 |
| 93 | Lyons, Marty | DT | 6-5 | 265 | 1/15/57 | 6 | Alabama | Tokoma Park, Md. | Huntington Station, N.Y. | 16 |
| 68 | McElroy, Reggie | T | 6-6 | 270 | 3/4/60 | 2 | West Texas State | Beaumont, Tex. | Amarillo, Tex. | 16 |
| 24 | McNeil, Freeman | RB | 5-11 | 218 | 4/22/59 | 4 | UCLA | Jackson, Miss. | Dix Hills, N.Y. | 9 |
| 56 | Mehl, Lance | LB | 6-3 | 233 | 2/14/58 | 5 | Penn State | Bellaire, Ohio | Pt. Lookout, N.Y. | 16 |
| 20 | Mullen, Davlin | CB-KR | 6-1 | 177 | 2/17/60 | 2 | Western Kentucky | McKeesport, Pa. | Clairton, Pa. | 11 |
| 16 | O'Brien, Ken | QB | 6-4 | 210 | 11/27/60 | 2 | Cal-Davis | Rockville Center, N.Y. | Sacramento, Calif. | 0* |
| 62 | Pellegrini, Joe | C-G | 6-4 | 252 | 4/8/57 | 3 | Harvard | Boston, Mass. | Cedarhurst, N.Y. | 16 |
| 79 | Powell, Marvin | T | 6-5 | 260 | 8/30/55 | 8 | Southern California | Fort Bragg, N.C. | East Meadow, N.Y. | 16 |
| 15 | Ramsey, Chuck | P | 6-2 | 189 | 2/24/52 | 8 | Wake Forest | Rock Hill, S.C. | Knoxville, Tenn. | 16 |
| 28 | Ray, Darrol | S | 6-1 | 198 | 6/25/58 | 5 | Oklahoma | San Francisco, Calif. | Hempstead, N.Y. | 16 |
| 76 | Rudolph, Ben | DT-DE | 6-5 | 266 | 8/29/57 | 4 | Long Beach State | Evergreen, Ala. | Daphne, Ala. | 16 |
| 10 | Ryan, Pat | QB | 6-3 | 210 | 9/16/55 | 7 | Tennessee | Hutchinson, Kan. | Knoxville, Tenn. | 16 |
| 48 | Schroy, Ken | S | 6-2 | 198 | 9/22/52 | 8 | Maryland | Valley Forge, Pa. | Garden City, N.Y. | 16 |
| 82 | Shuler, Mickey | TE | 6-3 | 231 | 8/21/56 | 7 | Penn State | Harrisburg, Pa. | Marysville, Pa. | 0* |
| 87 | Sohn, Kurt | WR-KR | 5-11 | 180 | 6/26/56 | 3 | Fordham | Ithaca, N.Y. | Levittown, N.Y. | 16 |
| 21 | Springs, Kirk | S-CB | 6-0 | 192 | 8/10/58 | 4 | Miami, Ohio | Cincinnati, Ohio | Cincinnati, Ohio | 4 |
| 70 | Waldemore, Stan | G-T | 6-4 | 269 | 2/20/55 | 7 | Nebraska | Newark, N.J. | East Hanover, N.J. | 16 |
| 85 | Walker, Wesley | WR | 6-0 | 179 | 5/26/55 | 8 | California | San Bernardino, Calif. | Dix Hills, N.Y. | 16 |
| 72 | Ward, Chris | T | 6-3 | 269 | 12/16/55 | 7 | Ohio State | Cleveland, Ohio | Dix Hills, N.Y. | 14 |
| 57 | Woodring, John | LB | 6-2 | 232 | 4/4/59 | 4 | Brown | Philadelphia, Pa. | Port Washington, N.Y. | |

* Eliopulos played 4 games with St. Louis, 8 with Jets in '83; Floyd, Luscinski, and Sohn missed '83 season due to injuries; O'Brien active for 16 games in '83 but did not play.

Traded—Linebacker Stan Blinka to Denver, running back Scott Dierking to Tampa Bay, defensive end Kenny Neil and defensive tackle Abdul Salaam to San Diego, and quarterback Richard Todd to New Orleans.

Also played with Jets in '83—TE Jerome Barkum (15 games), LB Ron Crosby (16), FB Dwayne Crutchfield (11), WR Mike Harmon (9), CB Jerry Holmes (16), S Jesse Johnson (4).

## COACHING STAFF

### Head Coach, Joe Walton

**Pro Career:** Begins second year as head coach of the Jets. Entered pro coaching ranks as an assistant with the New York Giants in 1969-73. Joined the Washington Redskins' staff in 1974 and became the Redskins' offensive coordinator in 1978. Originally came to the Jets as the offensive coordinator in 1981. Career record: 7-9.

**Background:** Played tight end for the University of Pittsburgh 1953-56, before playing professionally for the Washington Redskins 1957-60 and the New York Giants 1961-63. Walton did some radio work before joining the Giants staff as a scout in 1967-68.

**Personal:** Born December 15, 1935, Beaver Falls, Pa. Joe and his wife, Ginger, have three children— Jodi, Stacy, and Joseph, Jr. They live in Long Island.

### Assistant Coaches

**Bill Baird,** defensive backs; born March 1, 1939, Lindsay, Calif., lives in New York City. Defensive back San Francisco State 1959-61. Pro defensive back New York Jets 1963-69. College coach: Stanford 1970, Fresno State 1973-75, 1979, Pacific 1980. Pro coach: Joined Jets in 1981.

**Ralph Baker,** linebackers; born August 25, 1942, Lewiston, Pa., lives in New York. Linebacker Penn State 1961-63. Pro linebacker New York Jets 1964-74. Pro coach: Joined Jets in 1980.

**Ray Callahan,** defensive line; born April 28, 1933, Lebanon, Ky., lives in Long Island. Guard-linebacker Kentucky 1952-56. No pro playing experience. College coach: Kentucky 1963-67, Cincinnati 1967-72 (head coach 1969-72). Pro coach: Baltimore Colts 1973, Florida Blazers (WFL) 1974, Chicago Bears 1975-77, Houston Oilers 1981-82, joined Jets in 1983.

**Mike Faulkiner,** special assistant to the head coach; born March 27, 1947, Cameron, W. Va., lives in Long Island. Quarterback-defensive back at West Virginia Tech 1967-70. No pro playing experience. College coach: Eastern Illinois 1981. Pro coach: Toronto Argonauts (CFL) 1979, New York Giants 1980, Montreal Alouettes (CFL) 1982, joined Jets in 1983.

**Joe Gardi,** assistant head coach-defensive coordinator; born March 2, 1929, Newark, N.J., lives in Sayville, N. Y. Offensive-defensive tackle Maryland 1956-59. No pro playing experience. College coach: Maryland 1970-74. Pro coach: Philadelphia Bell (WFL) 1974-75 (interim head coach one game in 1975), Portland Thunder (WFL) 1975 (head coach), joined Jets in 1976.

**Bobby Hammond,** running backs; born February 20, 1952, Orangeburg, S.C., lives in New York. Running back Morgan State 1973-75. Pro running back New York Giants 1976-79, Washington Redskins 1979-80. Pro coach: Joined Jets in 1983.

**Rich Kotite,** receivers-pass offense coordinator; born October 13, 1942, Brooklyn, lives in Long Island. End Wagner 1963-65. Pro tight end New York Giants 1967, 1969-72, Pittsburgh Steelers 1968. College coach: Tennessee-Chattanooga 1973-76. Pro coach: New Orleans Saints 1977, Cleveland Browns 1978-82, joined Jets in 1983.

**Larry Pasquale,** special teams; born April 21, 1941, New York, N.Y., lives in New York. Quarterback Bridgeport 1961-63. No pro playing experience. College coach: Slippery Rock State 1967, Boston University 1968, Navy 1969-70, Massachusetts 1971-75, Idaho State 1976. Pro coach: Montreal Alouettes (CFL) 1977-78, Detroit Lions 1979, joined Jets in 1980.

**Jim Ringo,** offensive line-run offense coordinator; born November 21, 1932, Orange, N.J. lives in Long Island. Center Syracuse 1950-52. Pro center Green Bay Packers 1953-63, Philadelphia Eagles 1964-66. Pro coach: Chicago Bears 1969-71, Buffalo Bills 1972-77 (1976-77 head coach), New England Patriots 1978-81, Los Angeles Rams 1982, joined Jets in 1983.

## NEW YORK JETS 1984 FIRST-YEAR ROSTER

| Name | Pos. | Ht. | Wt. | Birth-date | College | Birthplace | Residence | How Acq. |
|---|---|---|---|---|---|---|---|---|
| Allen, Mark | TE | 6-4 | 225 | 4/29/60 | Montclair State | Newark, N.J. | Livingston, N.J. | FA |
| Armstrong, Tron | WR | 6-1 | 200 | 8/18/61 | Eastern Kentucky | St. Petersburg, Fla. | St. Petersburg, Fla. | D5 |
| Baldwin, Tom | DT | 6-4 | 255 | 5/13/61 | Tulsa | Abergreen Park, Ill. | Lansing, Ill. | D9 |
| Banker, Ted (1) | C | 6-2 | 260 | 2/17/61 | Southeast Missouri | St. Louis, Mo. | Millstadt, Ill. | FA |
| Beauford, Daniel | LB | 6-2 | 230 | 7/19/60 | J.C. Smith | Baltimore, Md. | Baltimore, Md. | FA |
| Bell, Bobby | LB | 6-2 | 217 | 2/7/62 | Missouri | St. Paul, Minn. | Lee's Summit, Mo. | D4 |
| Blakey, Jonathan | TE | 6-4 | 234 | 1/29/61 | Detroit | Nashville, Tenn. | Detroit, Mich. | FA |
| Branch, Bruce | G | 6-4 | 265 | 8/15/61 | Arizona State | Camden, N.J. | Tempe, Ariz. | FA |
| Brown, Reginald | WR | 6-0 | 185 | 8/21/61 | Temple | Brooklyn, N.Y. | Brooklyn, N.Y. | FA |
| Buchla, Bruce | QB | 6-2 | 202 | 5/17/57 | Nebraska | Bridgeport, Conn. | Bridgeport, Conn. | FA |
| Carnes, Tom | G | 6-4 | 275 | 11/10/59 | East Carolina | Norfolk, Va. | Greenville, N.C. | FA |
| Carpentieri, Russ (1) | K | 5-10 | 195 | 10/3/61 | Syracuse | Bronxville, N.Y. | Valhalla, N.Y. | FA |
| Carter, Russell | CB-S | 6-2 | 195 | 2/10/62 | Southern Methodist | Ardmore, Pa. | Audubon, Pa. | D1 |
| Chachere, Gary (1) | DT | 6-3 | 258 | 9/14/58 | Oklahoma State | Houston, Tex. | Houston, Tex. | FA |
| Clifton, Kyle | LB | 6-3 | 230 | 8/23/62 | Texas Christian | Only, Tex. | Bridgeport, Tex. | D3 |
| Cone, Ronny | FB | 6-2 | 225 | 4/27/61 | Georgia Tech | Bulloch County, Ga. | Statesboro, Ga. | D10 |
| Conran, Patrick (1) | S | 6-1 | 185 | 10/29/60 | Yale | Mt. Clemens, Mich. | Brighton, Mass. | FA |
| Cooper, Chester (1) | WR | 6-2 | 200 | 8/13/59 | Minnesota | Camden, N.J. | Minneapolis, Minn. | FA |
| Corrigan, Pete | RB | 6-1 | 214 | 5/31/59 | Purdue | Bronxville, N.Y. | Deer Park, N.Y. | FA |
| Cowles, Christopher (1) | T | 6-6 | 286 | 6/25/59 | Kent State | Oberlin, Ohio | Kent, Ohio | FA |
| Cummings, Mack (1) | WR | 6-0 | 175 | 3/3/59 | E. Tennessee State | Gainesville, Fla. | Gainesville, Fla. | FA |
| Davidson, Chy (1) | WR | 5-11 | 175 | 5/9/59 | Rhode Island | Queens, N.Y. | Queens Village, N.Y. | FA |
| DeBose, Ronnie (1) | TE | 6-4 | 232 | 10/13/58 | UCLA | Los Angeles, Calif. | Carson, Calif. | FA |
| Delaney, Dino | S | 6-0 | 205 | 3/3/61 | Stony Brook | New York, N.Y. | W. Hempstead, N.Y. | FA |
| Dennison, Glenn | TE | 6-3 | 225 | 11/17/61 | Miami | Beaver Falls, Pa. | Beaver Falls, Pa. | D2a |
| Dorn, David (1) | WR | 6-1 | 195 | 7/25/59 | Rutgers | Elmer, N.J. | Glassboro, N.J. | FA |
| Evans, Raymond | TE | 6-3 | 238 | 12/4/59 | Ohio State | Queens, N.Y. | Jamaica, N.Y. | FA |
| Faurot, Ron | DE-DT | 6-7 | 260 | 1/27/62 | Arkansas | Wichita, Kan. | Hurst, Tex. | D1a |
| Fishback, Ricky (1) | CB | 5-10 | 204 | 3/26/60 | Arkansas State | Murfreesboro, Tenn. | Murfreesboro, Tenn. | FA |
| Fowler, Reggie (1) | LB | 6-2 | 222 | 2/4/60 | Wyoming | Birmingham, Ala. | Tucson, Ariz. | FA |
| George, Kelly (1) | LB | 6-3 | 230 | 5/21/60 | Ball State | Ft. Wayne, Ind. | Indianapolis, Ind. | FA |
| Giles, Gene (1) | WR | 6-2 | 180 | 3/16/59 | Minnesota-Duluth | Suffern, N.Y. | Spring Valley, N.Y. | FA |
| Griggs, Billy | TE | 6-2 | 230 | 8/4/62 | Virginia | Camden, N.J. | Pensauken, N.J. | D8 |
| Hamilton, Harry | S | 5-11 | 190 | 11/29/62 | Penn State | Jamaica, N.Y. | Wilkes-Barre, Pa. | D7 |
| Healy, Gerry | TE | 6-5 | 248 | 5/6/61 | New Hampshire | Greenwich, Conn. | Scituate, Mass. | FA |
| Horton, Ron | WR | 6-4 | 195 | 7/11/61 | Wichita State | Atlanta, Ga. | Wichita, Kan. | FA |
| Humphery, Bobby (1) | WR | 5-10 | 170 | 8/23/61 | New Mexico State | Lubbock, Tex. | Las Cruces, N.M. | D9('83) |
| Hunter, Jimmy (1) | LB | 6-2 | 217 | 4/10/60 | Indiana | Birmingham, Ala. | Bloomington, Ill. | FA |
| Inverso, Glen (1) | QB | 6-1 | 199 | 6/24/58 | Liberty Baptist | McKees Rocks, Pa. | Crystal Lake, Ill. | FA |
| Jehn, Mark (1) | P | 6-2 | 205 | 7/20/57 | Western Illinois | Wausau, Wis. | Sparks, Nev. | FA |
| Kent, John | G | 6-3 | 263 | 7/13/61 | James Madison | Levittown, Pa. | Levittown, Pa. | FA |
| Lashley, Robert (1) | S | 6-3 | 198 | 3/31/61 | Purdue | Mt. Clemens, Mich. | Mt. Clemens, Mich. | FA |
| Martin, Dan | T | 6-4 | 275 | 7/4/61 | Iowa State | Elkhorn, Wis. | William Bay, Wis. | D11 |
| Minter, Cedric | RB | 5-10 | 190 | 11/14/58 | Boise State | Charleston, S.C. | Boise, Idaho | FA |
| Morales, Marco | K | 5-11 | 177 | 1/7/62 | San Diego State | Mexicali, Mexico | Chula Vista, Calif. | FA |
| Oltman, Dennis | LB | 6-0 | 227 | 6/17/61 | Western Maryland | Baltimore, Md. | Pasadena, Md. | FA |
| O'Neil, Brian (1) | S | 6-3 | 195 | 11/12/61 | Alfred | Buffalo, N.Y. | Geneseo, N.Y. | FA |
| Paige, Tony | FB | 5-10 | 225 | 10/14/62 | Virginia Tech | Washington, D.C. | Washington, D.C. | D6 |
| Pipszynski, Joe (1) | G-T | 6-4 | 270 | 4/30/61 | Citadel | Riverhead, N.Y. | Riverhead, N.Y. | FA |
| Porter, Donald | WR | 6-1 | 190 | 3/5/59 | Presbyterian | Washington, D.C. | Washington, D.C. | FA |
| Reda, Lewis | S | 6-0 | 192 | 10/10/61 | Delaware | Bronx, N.Y. | Yonkers, N.Y. | FA |
| Reilly, Dan | DT | 6-1 | 255 | 3/23/61 | Missouri Valley | South Amboy, N.J. | Woodbridge, N.J. | FA |
| Roberson, Dave | WR | 6-0 | 200 | 5/8/62 | Houston | Dallas, Tex. | Dallas, Tex. | D12 |
| Ropella, Randy | C | 6-2 | 244 | 4/28/61 | Wisconsin-Oshkosh | Neenah, Wis. | Menasha, Wis. | FA |
| Schofield, Gary | QB | 6-2 | 209 | 6/8/61 | Wake Forest | Paoli, Pa. | Philadelphia, Pa. | FA |
| Scott, John | S | 6-4 | 210 | 9/30/60 | Virginia Tech | Charlottesville, Va. | Shipman, Va. | FA |
| Shed, Randy | RB | 5-11 | 220 | 2/26/62 | Missouri-Rolla | Kirkwood, Mo. | Rolla, Mo. | FA |
| Simmons, Ricky | S | 6-1 | 190 | 12/19/60 | S. Carolina State | East Meadow, N.Y. | Roosevelt, N.Y. | FA |
| Sweeney, Jim | G-C | 6-4 | 260 | 8/8/62 | Pittsburgh | Pittsburgh, Pa. | Pittsburgh, Pa. | D2 |
| Thompson, Del | RB | 6-0 | 203 | 2/21/58 | Texas-El Paso | Kermit, Tex. | Hamlin, Tex. | FA |
| Tucker, Tom | RB | 5-9 | 205 | 9/8/60 | Westchester C.C. | Mt. Kisco, N.Y. | Yorktown, N.Y. | FA |
| Walker, John (1) | DT | 6-6 | 270 | 9/12/61 | Nebraska-Omaha | Omaha, Neb. | Omaha, Neb. | D5('83) |
| Wright, Bret | P | 6-4 | 205 | 1/5/62 | S.E. Louisiana | Ponchatoula, La. | Denham Springs, La. | D8a |

Players who report to an NFL team for the first time are designated on rosters as rookies (R). If a player reported to an NFL training camp in a previous year but was not on the active squad for three or more regular season or postseason games, he is listed on the first-year roster and designated by a (1). Thereafter, a player who is on the active squad for three or more regular season or postseason games is credited with an additional year of playing experience.

# NOTES

# PITTSBURGH STEELERS

**American Football Conference
Central Division**

**Team Colors:** Black and Gold

**Three Rivers Stadium
300 Stadium Circle
Pittsburgh, Pennsylvania 15212
Telephone: (412) 323-1200**

**Club Officials**

Chairman of the Board: Arthur J. Rooney, Sr.
President: Daniel M. Rooney
Vice President: John R. McGinley
Vice President: Arthur J. Rooney, Jr.
Traveling Secretary: Jim Boston
Controller: Dennis P. Thimons
Publicity Director: Joe Gordon
Assistant Publicity Director: John Evenson
Director of Player Personnel: Dick Haley
Assistant Director of Player Personnel:
    William Nunn, Jr.
Pro Talent Scout: Tom Modrak
Talent Scout-West Coast: Bob Schmitz
College Talent Scout: Joe Krupa
Director of Ticket Sales: Geraldine R. Glenn
Trainer: Ralph Berlin
Equipment Manager: Anthony Parisi

**Stadium:** Three Rivers Stadium •
    **Capacity:** 59,000
    300 Stadium Circle
    Pittsburgh, Pennsylvania 15212

**Playing Surface:** AstroTurf

**Training Camp:** St. Vincent College
    Latrobe, Pennsylvania 15650

## 1984 SCHEDULE

**Preseason**

| | | |
|---|---|---|
| Aug. 4 | at Cleveland | 7:30 |
| Aug. 11 | **Philadelphia** | 6:00 |
| Aug. 16 | at Dallas | 8:00 |
| Aug. 25 | at New York Giants | 8:00 |

**Regular Season**

| | | |
|---|---|---|
| Sept. 2 | **Kansas City** | 1:00 |
| Sept. 6 | at New York Jets (Thursday) | 9:00 |
| Sept. 16 | **Los Angeles Rams** | 4:00 |
| Sept. 23 | at Cleveland | 1:00 |
| Oct. 1 | **Cincinnati** (Monday) | 9:00 |
| Oct. 7 | **Miami** | 1:00 |
| Oct. 14 | at San Francisco | 1:00 |
| Oct. 21 | at Colts | 12:00 |
| Oct. 28 | **Atlanta** | 4:00 |
| Nov. 4 | **Houston** | 1:00 |
| Nov. 11 | at Cincinnati | 1:00 |
| Nov. 19 | at New Orleans (Monday) | 8:00 |
| Nov. 25 | **San Diego** | 1:00 |
| Dec. 2 | at Houston | 12:00 |
| Dec. 9 | **Cleveland** | 1:00 |
| Dec. 16 | at Los Angeles Raiders | 1:00 |

## STEELERS COACHING HISTORY
### (308-342-20)

| | | |
|---|---|---|
| 1933 | Forrest (Jap) Douds | 3-6-2 |
| 1934 | Luby DiMelio | 2-10-0 |
| 1935-36 | Joe Bach | 10-14-0 |
| 1937-39 | Johnny Blood (McNally) | 6-19-0 |
| 1939-40 | Walter Kiesling | 3-13-3 |
| 1941 | Bert Bell | 0-2-0 |
| | Aldo (Buff) Donelli | 0-5-0 |
| 1941-44 | Walter Kiesling* | 13-20-2 |
| 1945 | Jim Leonard | 2-8-0 |
| 1946-47 | Jock Sutherland | 13-10-1 |
| 1948-51 | Johnny Michelosen | 20-26-2 |
| 1952-53 | Joe Bach | 11-13-0 |
| 1954-56 | Walter Kiesling | 14-22-0 |
| 1957-64 | Raymond (Buddy) Parker | 51-47-6 |
| 1965 | Mike Nixon | 2-12-0 |
| 1966-68 | Bill Austin | 11-28-3 |
| 1969-83 | Chuck Noll | 147-87-1 |

*Co-Coach with Earl (Greasy) Neale in Philadelphia-Pittsburgh merger in 1943 and with Phil Handler in Chicago Cardinal-Pittsburgh merger in 1944.

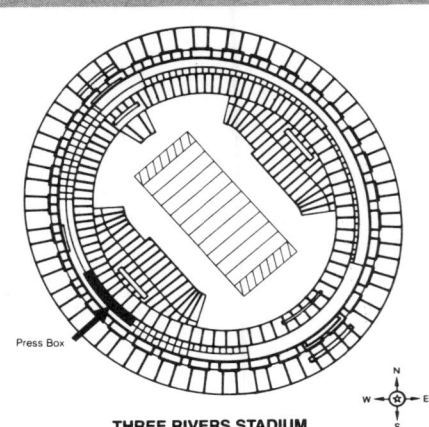

**THREE RIVERS STADIUM**

## RECORD HOLDERS
### Individual Records—Career

| Category | Name | Performance |
|---|---|---|
| Rushing (Yds.) | Franco Harris, 1972-1983 | 11,950 |
| Passing (Yds.) | Terry Bradshaw, 1970-1983 | 27,989 |
| Passing (TDs) | Terry Bradshaw, 1970-1983 | 212 |
| Receiving (No.) | Lynn Swann, 1974-1982 | 336 |
| Receiving (Yds.) | Lynn Swann, 1974-1982 | 5,462 |
| Interceptions | Mel Blount, 1971-1983 | 57 |
| Punting (Avg.) | Bobby Joe Green, 1960-61 | 45.7 |
| Punt Return (Avg.) | Bobby Gage, 1949-1950 | 14.9 |
| Kickoff Return (Avg.) | Lynn Chandnois, 1950-56 | 29.6 |
| Field Goals | Roy Gerela, 1971-78 | 146 |
| Touchdowns (Tot.) | Franco Harris, 1972-1983 | 100 |
| Points | Roy Gerela, 1971-78 | 731 |

### Individual Records—Single Season

| Category | Name | Performance |
|---|---|---|
| Rushing (Yds.) | Franco Harris, 1975 | 1,246 |
| Passing (Yds.) | Terry Bradshaw, 1979 | 3,724 |
| Passing (TDs) | Terry Bradshaw, 1978 | 28 |
| Receiving (No.) | John Stallworth, 1979 | 70 |
| Receiving (Yds.) | Buddy Dial, 1963 | 1,295 |
| Interceptions | Mel Blount, 1975 | 11 |
| Punting (Avg.) | Bobby Joe Green, 1961 | 47.0 |
| Punt Return (Avg.) | Bobby Gage, 1949 | 16.0 |
| Kickoff Return (Avg.) | Lynn Chandnois, 1952 | 35.2 |
| Field Goals | Roy Gerela, 1973 | 29 |
| Touchdowns (Tot.) | Franco Harris, 1976 | 14 |
| Points | Roy Gerela, 1973 | 123 |

### Individual Records—Single Game

| Category | Name | Performance |
|---|---|---|
| Rushing (Yds.) | John Fuqua, 12-20-70 | 218 |
| Passing (Yds.) | Bobby Layne, 12-3-58 | 409 |
| Passing (TDs) | Terry Bradshaw, 11-15-81 | 5 |
| Receiving (No.) | J.R. Wilburn, 10-22-67 | 12 |
| Receiving (Yds.) | Buddy Dial, 10-22-61 | 235 |
| Interceptions | Jack Butler, 12-13-53 | 4 |
| Field Goals | Many times | 4 |
| | Last time by Gary Anderson, 11-6-83 | |
| Touchdowns (Tot.) | Ray Mathews, 10-17-54 | 4 |
| | Roy Jefferson, 11-3-68 | 4 |
| Points | Ray Mathews, 10-17-54 | 24 |
| | Roy Jefferson, 11-3-68 | 24 |

## 1983 TEAM STATISTICS

| | Pittsburgh | Opp. |
|---|---|---|
| Total First Downs | 312 | 278 |
| Rushing | 156 | 100 |
| Passing | 141 | 151 |
| Penalty | 15 | 27 |
| Third Down Efficiency | 100/233 | 76/216 |
| Third Down Percentage | 42.9 | 35.2 |
| Total Net Yards | 5014 | 4732 |
| Total Offensive Plays | 1075 | 1006 |
| Avg. Gain per Play | 4.7 | 4.7 |
| Avg. Gain per Game | 313.4 | 295.8 |
| Net Yards Rushing | 2610 | 1833 |
| Total Rushing Plays | 614 | 509 |
| Avg. Gain per Rush | 4.3 | 3.6 |
| Avg. Gain Rushing per Game | 163.1 | 114.6 |
| Net Yards Passing | 2404 | 2899 |
| Lost Attempting to Pass | 52/350 | 50/361 |
| Gross Yards Passing | 2754 | 3260 |
| Attempts/Completions | 409/211 | 447/238 |
| Percent Completed | 51.6 | 53.2 |
| Had Intercepted | 23 | 28 |
| Avg. Net Passing per Game | 150.3 | 181.2 |
| Punts/Avg. | 80/41.9 | 88/41.1 |
| Punt Returns/Avg. | 51/8.3 | 44/9.5 |
| Kickoff Returns/Avg. | 59/18.1 | 65/23.2 |
| Interceptions/Avg. Ret. | 28/15.5 | 23/11.0 |
| Penalties/Yards | 99/836 | 96/782 |
| Fumbles/Ball Lost | 42/20 | 34/17 |
| Total Points | 355 | 303 |
| Avg. Points per Game | 22.2 | 18.9 |
| Touchdowns | 39 | 37 |
| Rushing | 17 | 14 |
| Passing | 15 | 19 |
| Returns and Recoveries | 7 | 4 |
| Field Goals | 27/31 | 15/20 |
| Conversions | 38/39 | 36/37 |
| Safeties | 1 | 0 |
| Avg. Time of Possession | 30:40 | 29:20 |

## 1983 TEAM RECORD
### Preseason (4-1)

| Date | Pittsburgh | | Opponents |
|---|---|---|---|
| 7/30 | 27 | New Orleans | 14 |
| 8/6 | 27 | New England | 16 |
| 8/12 | 13 | *New York Giants | 22 |
| 8/20 | 24 | Dallas | 7 |
| 8/25 | 10 | Philadelphia | 3 |
| | 101 | | 62 |

### Regular Season (10-6)

| Date | Pittsburgh | | Opp. | Att. |
|---|---|---|---|---|
| 9/4 | 10 | *Denver | 14 | 58,233 |
| 9/11 | 25 | Green Bay | 21 | 55,204 |
| 9/18 | 40 | Houston | 28 | 44,150 |
| 9/25 | 23 | *New England | 28 | 58,282 |
| 10/2 | 17 | *Houston | 10 | 56,901 |
| 10/10 | 24 | Cincinnati | 14 | 56,086 |
| 10/16 | 44 | *Cleveland | 17 | 59,263 |
| 10/23 | 27 | Seattle | 21 | 61,615 |
| 10/30 | 17 | *Tampa Bay | 12 | 57,648 |
| 11/6 | 26 | *San Diego | 3 | 58,191 |
| 11/13 | 24 | Baltimore | 13 | 57,319 |
| 11/20 | 14 | *Minnesota | 17 | 58,417 |
| 11/24 | 3 | Detroit | 45 | 77,724 |
| 12/4 | 10 | *Cincinnati | 23 | 55,832 |
| 12/10 | 34 | New York Jets | 7 | 53,996 |
| 12/18 | 17 | Cleveland | 30 | 72,313 |
| | 355 | | 303 | 941,174 |

*Home Game

### Score by Periods

| | | | | | | |
|---|---|---|---|---|---|---|
| Pittsburgh | 95 | 105 | 30 | 125 | — | 355 |
| Opponents | 80 | 78 | 72 | 73 | — | 303 |

### Attendance
Home 462,767    Away 478,407    Total 941,174
Single game home record, 59,263 (10-16-83)
Single season home record, 462,767 (1983)

## 1983 INDIVIDUAL STATISTICS

### Rushing

| | Att. | Yds. | Avg. | LG | TD |
|---|---|---|---|---|---|
| F. Harris | 279 | 1007 | 3.6 | 19 | 5 |
| Pollard | 135 | 608 | 4.5 | 32 | 4 |
| Stoudt | 77 | 479 | 6.2 | 23 | 4 |
| Abercrombie | 112 | 446 | 4.0 | 50t | 4 |
| Hawthorne | 5 | 47 | 9.4 | 20 | 0 |
| T. Harris | 2 | 15 | 7.5 | 10 | 0 |
| Odom | 2 | 7 | 3.5 | 4 | 0 |
| Bradshaw | 1 | 3 | 3.0 | 3 | 0 |
| Sweeney | 1 | −2 | −2.0 | −2 | 0 |
| Pittsburgh | 614 | 2610 | 4.3 | 50t | 17 |
| Opponents | 509 | 1833 | 3.6 | 30 | 14 |

### Passing

| | Att. | Comp. | Pct. | Yds. | TD | Int. | Tkld. | Rate |
|---|---|---|---|---|---|---|---|---|
| Stoudt | 381 | 197 | 51.7 | 2553 | 12 | 21 | 51/339 | 60.6 |
| Malone | 20 | 9 | 45.0 | 124 | 1 | 2 | 1/11 | 42.5 |
| Bradshaw | 8 | 5 | 62.5 | 77 | 2 | 0 | 0/0 | 133.9 |
| Pittsburgh | 409 | 211 | 51.6 | 2754 | 15 | 23 | 52/350 | 61.9 |
| Opponents | 447 | 238 | 53.2 | 3260 | 19 | 28 | 50/361 | 64.9 |

### Receiving

| | No. | Yds. | Avg. | LG | TD |
|---|---|---|---|---|---|
| Sweeney | 39 | 577 | 14.8 | 42 | 5 |
| Cunningham | 35 | 442 | 12.6 | 29 | 3 |
| F. Harris | 34 | 278 | 8.2 | 29t | 2 |
| Abercrombie | 26 | 391 | 15.0 | 51t | 3 |
| Hawthorne | 19 | 300 | 15.8 | 52 | 0 |
| Garrity | 19 | 279 | 14.7 | 38 | 1 |
| Pollard | 16 | 127 | 7.9 | 17 | 0 |
| Capers | 10 | 185 | 18.5 | 36 | 1 |
| Stallworth | 8 | 100 | 12.5 | 20 | 0 |
| Skansi | 3 | 39 | 13.0 | 21 | 0 |
| Rodgers | 2 | 36 | 18.0 | 25 | 0 |
| Pittsburgh | 211 | 2754 | 13.1 | 52 | 15 |
| Opponents | 238 | 3260 | 13.7 | 76t | 19 |

### Interceptions

| | No. | Yds. | Avg. | LG | TD |
|---|---|---|---|---|---|
| Woods | 5 | 53 | 10.6 | 31 | 0 |
| Shell | 5 | 18 | 3.6 | 18 | 0 |
| Blount | 4 | 32 | 8.0 | 21 | 0 |
| Woodruff | 3 | 85 | 28.3 | 47 | 0 |
| Johnson | 3 | 84 | 28.0 | 34t | 1 |
| Merriweather | 3 | 55 | 18.3 | 31t | 1 |
| Lambert | 2 | −1 | −0.5 | 0 | 0 |
| Clayton | 1 | 70 | 70.0 | 70t | 1 |
| Washington | 1 | 25 | 25.0 | 25 | 0 |
| Hinkle | 1 | 14 | 14.0 | 14t | 1 |
| Pittsburgh | 28 | 435 | 15.5 | 70t | 4 |
| Opponents | 23 | 252 | 11.0 | 70 | 2 |

### Punting

| | No. | Yds. | Avg. | In 20 | LG |
|---|---|---|---|---|---|
| Colquitt | 80 | 3352 | 41.9 | 20 | 58 |
| Pittsburgh | 80 | 3352 | 41.9 | 20 | 58 |
| Opponents | 88 | 3615 | 41.1 | 11 | 61 |

### Punt Returns

| | No. | FC | Yds. | Avg. | LG | TD |
|---|---|---|---|---|---|---|
| Skansi | 43 | 9 | 363 | 8.4 | 57 | 0 |
| Woods | 5 | 0 | 46 | 9.2 | 13 | 0 |
| T. Harris | 3 | 0 | 12 | 4.0 | 8 | 0 |
| Pittsburgh | 51 | 9 | 421 | 8.3 | 57 | 0 |
| Opponents | 44 | 6 | 418 | 9.5 | 81t | 1 |

### Kickoff Returns

| | No. | Yds. | Avg. | LG | TD |
|---|---|---|---|---|---|
| Odom | 39 | 756 | 19.4 | 35 | 0 |
| T. Harris | 18 | 289 | 16.1 | 32 | 0 |
| Bingham | 1 | 15 | 15.0 | 15 | 0 |
| Kohrs | 1 | 6 | 6.0 | 6 | 0 |
| Donnalley | 0 | 2 | — | 2 | 0 |
| Pittsburgh | 59 | 1068 | 18.1 | 35 | 0 |
| Opponents | 65 | 1507 | 23.2 | 97t | 1 |

### Scoring

| | TD | TD R | TD P | TD Rt | PAT | FG | TP |
|---|---|---|---|---|---|---|---|
| Anderson | | | | | 38/39 | 27/31 | 119 |
| Abercrombie | 7 | 4 | 3 | 0 | | | 42 |
| F. Harris | 7 | 5 | 2 | 0 | | | 42 |
| Sweeney | 5 | 0 | 5 | 0 | | | 30 |
| Pollard | 4 | 4 | 0 | 0 | | | 24 |
| Stoudt | 4 | 4 | 0 | 0 | | | 24 |
| Cunningham | 3 | 0 | 3 | 0 | | | 18 |
| Best | 1 | 0 | 0 | 1 | | | 6 |
| Blount | 1 | 0 | 0 | 1 | | | 6 |
| Capers | 1 | 0 | 1 | 0 | | | 6 |
| Clayton | 1 | 0 | 0 | 1 | | | 6 |
| Garrity | 1 | 0 | 1 | 0 | | | 6 |
| Hinkle | 1 | 0 | 0 | 1 | | | 6 |
| Johnson | 1 | 0 | 0 | 1 | | | 6 |
| Merriweather | 1 | 0 | 0 | 1 | | | 6 |
| Woods | 1 | 0 | 0 | 1 | | | 6 |
| Kohrs | | (Safety) | | | | | 2 |
| Pittsburgh | 39 | 17 | 15 | 7 | 38/39 | 27/31 | 355 |
| Opponents | 37 | 14 | 19 | 4 | 36/37 | 15/20 | 303 |

### FIRST-ROUND SELECTIONS

(If Club had no first-round selection, first player drafted is listed with round in parentheses.)

| Year | Player, College, Position |
|---|---|
| 1936 | Bill Shakespeare, Notre Dame, B |
| 1937 | Mike Basrak, Duquesne, C |
| 1938 | Byron (Whizzer) White, Colorado, B |
| 1939 | Bill Patterson, Baylor, B (3) |
| 1940 | Kay Eakin, Arkansas, B |
| 1941 | Chet Gladchuk, Boston College, C (2) |
| 1942 | Bill Dudley, Virginia, B |
| 1943 | Bill Daley, Minnesota, B |
| 1944 | Johnny Podesto, St. Mary's, California, B |
| 1945 | Paul Duhart, Florida, B |
| 1946 | Felix (Doc) Blanchard, Army, B |
| 1947 | Hub Bechtol, Texas, E |
| 1948 | Dan Edwards, Georgia, E |
| 1949 | Bobby Gage, Clemson, B |
| 1950 | Lynn Chandnois, Michigan State, B |
| 1951 | Butch Avinger, Alabama, B |
| 1952 | Ed Modzelewski, Maryland, B |
| 1953 | Ted Marchibroda, St. Bonaventure, B |
| 1954 | Johnny Lattner, Notre Dame, B |
| 1955 | Frank Varrichione, Notre Dame, T |
| 1956 | Gary Glick, Colorado A&M, B |
| | Art Davis, Mississippi State, B |
| 1957 | Len Dawson, Purdue, B |
| 1958 | Larry Krutko, West Virginia, B (2) |
| 1959 | Tom Barnett, Purdue, B (8) |
| 1960 | Jack Spikes, Texas Christian, RB |
| 1961 | Myron Pottios, Notre Dame, LB (2) |
| 1962 | Bob Ferguson, Ohio State, RB |
| 1963 | Frank Atkinson, Stanford, T (8) |
| 1964 | Paul Martha, Pittsburgh, S |
| 1965 | Roy Jefferson, Utah, WR (2) |
| 1966 | Dick Leftridge, West Virginia, RB |
| 1967 | Don Shy, San Diego State, RB (2) |
| 1968 | Mike Taylor, Southern California, T |
| 1969 | Joe Greene, North Texas State, DT |
| 1970 | Terry Bradshaw, Louisiana Tech, QB |
| 1971 | Frank Lewis, Grambling, WR |
| 1972 | Franco Harris, Penn State, RB |
| 1973 | J. T. Thomas, Florida State, DB |
| 1974 | Lynn Swann, Southern California, WR |
| 1975 | Dave Brown, Michigan, DB |
| 1976 | Bennie Cunningham, Clemson, TE |
| 1977 | Robin Cole, New Mexico, LB |
| 1978 | Ron Johnson, Eastern Michigan, DB |
| 1979 | Greg Hawthorne, Baylor, RB |
| 1980 | Mark Malone, Arizona State, QB |
| 1981 | Keith Gary, Oklahoma, DE |
| 1982 | Walter Abercrombie, Baylor, RB |
| 1983 | Gabriel Rivera, Texas Tech, DT |
| 1984 | Louis Lipps, Southern Mississippi, WR |

## PITTSBURGH STEELERS 1984 VETERAN ROSTER

| No. | Name | Pos. | Ht. | Wt. | Birth-date | NFL Exp. | College | Birthplace | Residence | Games in '83 |
|---|---|---|---|---|---|---|---|---|---|---|
| 34 | Abercrombie, Walter | RB | 5-11 | 210 | 9/26/59 | 3 | Baylor | Waco, Tex. | Waco, Tex. | 15 |
| 1 | Anderson, Gary | K | 5-11 | 156 | 7/16/59 | 3 | Syracuse | Parys, South Africa | Pittsburgh, Pa. | 16 |
| 65 | Beasley, Tom | DE-NT | 6-5 | 248 | 8/11/54 | 7 | Virginia Tech | Bluefield, W. Va. | Prosperity, Pa. | 16 |
| 25 | Best, Greg | S | 5-10 | 185 | 1/14/60 | 2 | Kansas State | New Brighton, Pa. | Beaver Falls, Pa. | 13 |
| 54 | Bingham, Craig | LB | 6-2 | 211 | 9/29/59 | 3 | Syracuse | Kingston, Jamaica | Pittsburgh, Pa. | 12 |
| 71 | Boures, Emil | G-C | 6-1 | 261 | 1/29/60 | 3 | Pittsburgh | Bridgeport, Pa. | Pittsburgh, Pa. | 16 |
| 12 | Bradshaw, Terry | QB | 6-3 | 210 | 9/2/48 | 15 | Louisiana Tech | Shreveport, La. | Grand Cane, La. | 1 |
| 79 | Brown, Larry | T | 6-4 | 270 | 6/6/49 | 14 | Kansas | Jacksonville, Fla. | Pittsburgh, Pa. | 8 |
| 80 | Capers, Wayne | WR | 6-2 | 193 | 5/17/61 | 2 | Kansas | Miami, Fla. | Miami, Fla. | 11 |
| 33 | Clayton, Harvey | CB | 5-9 | 170 | 4/4/61 | 2 | Florida State | Kendall, Fla. | Florida City, Fla. | 14 |
| 56 | Cole, Robin | LB | 6-2 | 220 | 9/11/55 | 8 | New Mexico | Los Angeles, Calif. | Washington, Pa. | 16 |
| 5 | Colquitt, Craig | P | 6-1 | 182 | 6/9/54 | 6 | Tennessee | Knoxville, Tenn. | Knoxville, Tenn. | 16 |
| 77 | Courson, Steve | G | 6-1 | 270 | 10/1/55 | 7 | South Carolina | Philadelphia, Pa. | Pittsburgh, Pa. | 9 |
| 89 | Cunningham, Bennie | TE | 6-5 | 260 | 12/23/54 | 9 | Clemson | Laurens, S.C. | Piedmont, S.C. | 16 |
| 45 | Davis, Russell | RB | 6-1 | 231 | 9/15/56 | 5 | Michigan | Millen, Ga. | Pittsburgh, Pa. | 5 |
| 55 | Donnalley, Rick | C-G | 6-2 | 257 | 12/11/58 | 3 | North Carolina | Wilmington, Del. | Pittsburgh, Pa. | 16 |
| 88 | Dunaway, Craig | TE | 6-2 | 233 | 3/27/61 | 2 | Michigan | Lake Charles, La. | Pittsburgh, Pa. | 11 |
| 67 | Dunn, Gary | NT | 6-3 | 260 | 8/24/53 | 8 | Miami | Miami, Fla. | Miami, Fla. | 13 |
| 20 | †French, Ernest | S | 5-11 | 195 | 9/5/59 | 2 | Alabama A&M | Tensaw, Ala. | Bay Minette, Ala. | 0* |
| 86 | Garrity, Gregg | WR | 5-10 | 171 | 11/24/60 | 2 | Penn State | Pittsburgh, Pa. | Pittsburgh, Pa. | 15 |
| 92 | Gary, Keith | DE | 6-3 | 255 | 9/14/59 | 2 | Oklahoma | Bethesda, Md. | Pittsburgh, Pa. | 16 |
| 95 | Goodman, John | DE | 6-6 | 250 | 11/12/58 | 4 | Oklahoma | Oklahoma City, Okla. | Garland, Tex. | 13 |
| 32 | Harris, Franco | RB | 6-2 | 225 | 3/7/50 | 13 | Penn State | Fort Dix, N.J. | Pittsburgh, Pa. | 16 |
| 43 | Harris, Tim | RB | 5-9 | 206 | 6/15/61 | 2 | Washington State | Compton, Calif. | Compton, Calif. | 14 |
| 27 | Hawthorne, Greg | WR-RB | 6-2 | 225 | 9/5/56 | 6 | Baylor | Fort Worth, Tex. | Pittsburgh, Pa. | 10 |
| 53 | Hinkle, Bryan | LB | 6-1 | 220 | 6/4/59 | 3 | Oregon | Long Beach, Calif. | Silverdale, Wash. | 16 |
| 62 | Ilkin, Tunch | T | 6-3 | 255 | 9/23/57 | 5 | Indiana State | Istanbul, Turkey | Pittsburgh, Pa. | 11 |
| 29 | Johnson, Ron | S | 5-10 | 200 | 6/8/56 | 7 | Eastern Michigan | Detroit, Mich. | Pittsburgh, Pa. | 12 |
| 90 | Kohrs, Bob | LB | 6-3 | 235 | 11/8/58 | 4 | Arizona State | Phoenix, Ariz. | Pittsburgh, Pa. | 9 |
| 58 | Lambert, Jack | LB | 6-4 | 220 | 7/8/52 | 11 | Kent State | Mantua, Ohio | Pittsburgh, Pa. | 15 |
| 50 | Little, David | LB | 6-1 | 220 | 1/3/59 | 4 | Florida | Miami, Fla. | Miami, Fla. | 16 |
| 16 | Malone, Mark | QB | 6-4 | 223 | 11/22/58 | 5 | Arizona State | El Cajon, Calif. | Pittsburgh, Pa. | 2 |
| 57 | Merriweather, Mike | LB | 6-2 | 215 | 11/26/60 | 2 | Pacific | Albans, N.Y. | Vallejo, Calif. | 16 |
| 64 | Nelson, Edmund | NT-DE | 6-3 | 270 | 4/3/60 | 3 | Auburn | Live Oak, Fla. | Tampa, Fla. | 16 |
| 44 | Odom, Henry | RB-KR | 5-10 | 200 | 2/12/59 | 2 | South Carolina State | Bamburg, S.C. | Olar, S.C. | 16 |
| 66 | Petersen, Ted | T | 6-5 | 245 | 2/7/55 | 7 | Eastern Illinois | Kankakee, Ill. | Pittsburgh, Pa. | 13 |
| 30 | Pollard, Frank | RB | 5-10 | 218 | 6/15/57 | 5 | Baylor | Meridian, Tex. | Meridian, Tex. | 16 |
| 87 | Rodgers, John | TE | 6-2 | 220 | 2/7/60 | 3 | Louisiana Tech | Omaha, Tex. | Daingerfield, Tex. | 15 |
| 31 | Shell, Donnie | S | 5-11 | 190 | 8/26/51 | 11 | South Carolina State | Whitmire, S.C. | Columbia, S.C. | 16 |
| 81 | Skansi, Paul | WR-KR | 5-11 | 190 | 1/11/60 | 2 | Washington | Tacoma, Wash. | Gig Harbor, Wash. | 15 |
| 82 | Stallworth, John | WR | 6-2 | 191 | 8/26/52 | 11 | Alabama A&M | Tuscaloosa, Ala. | Huntsville, Ala. | 4 |
| 85 | Sweeney, Calvin | WR | 6-2 | 190 | 1/12/55 | 5 | Southern California | Riverside, Calif. | Santa Monica, Calif. | 16 |
| 51 | Toews, Loren | LB | 6-3 | 220 | 11/3/51 | 12 | California | Dinuba, Calif. | Pittsburgh, Pa. | 16 |
| 41 | Washington, Sam | CB | 5-8 | 180 | 3/7/60 | 3 | Mississippi Valley State | Tampa, Fla. | Tampa, Fla. | 16 |
| 52 | Webster, Mike | C | 6-1 | 250 | 3/18/52 | 11 | Wisconsin | Tomahawk, Wis. | Pittsburgh, Pa. | 16 |
| 21 | Williams, Eric | S | 5-11 | 183 | 2/21/60 | 2 | North Carolina State | Raleigh, N.C. | Garner, N.C. | 3 |
| 93 | Willis, Keith | DE | 6-1 | 251 | 7/29/59 | 3 | Northeastern | Newark, N.J. | Pittsburgh, Pa. | 14 |
| 61 | Wingle, Blake | G | 6-2 | 267 | 4/17/60 | 2 | UCLA | Pottsville, Calif. | Canonsburg, Pa. | 16 |
| 73 | Wolfley, Craig | G | 6-1 | 265 | 5/19/58 | 5 | Syracuse | Buffalo, N.Y. | Pittsburgh, Pa. | 14 |
| | t-Woodley, David | QB | 6-2 | 202 | 10/25/58 | 5 | Louisiana State | Shreveport, La. | Ft. Lauderdale, Fla. | 5 |
| 49 | Woodruff, Dwayne | CB | 5-11 | 198 | 2/18/57 | 6 | Louisville | Bowling Green, Ky. | Pittsburgh, Pa. | 15 |
| 22 | Woods, Rick | S | 6-0 | 196 | 11/16/59 | 3 | Boise State | Boise, Idaho | Pittsburgh, Pa. | 15 |

* French missed '83 season due to injury.

†Option playout; subject to developments.

t-Steelers traded for Woodley (Miami).

Retired—Mel Blount, 14-year cornerback, 16 games in '83.

Also played with Steelers in '83—T Mark Kirchner (3 games), DT Gabe Rivera (6), QB Cliff Stoudt (16).

## COACHING STAFF

### Head Coach, Chuck Noll

**Pro Career:** Became first NFL coach to win four Super Bowls when Steelers defeated Los Angeles 31-19 in Super Bowl XIV. Has guided Steelers into postseason play 10 of last 12 years. Led Steelers to consecutive NFL championships twice (1974-75, 1978-79). Has fourth-highest won-lost percentage among active coaches (.628) and ranks eighth among the NFL's all-time winningest coaches with a career record of 147-87-1. Played pro ball as guard-linebacker for Cleveland Browns from 1953-59. At age 28, he started coaching career as defensive coach with Los Angeles (San Diego) Chargers in 1960. Left after 1965 season to become Don Shula's defensive backfield assistant in Baltimore. Remained with Colts until taking over Pittsburgh reins as head coach in 1969.

**Background:** Was an all-state star at Benedictine High in Cleveland. Captained the University of Dayton team, playing both tackle and linebacker. He was drafted by the Browns in 1953.

**Personal:** Born in Cleveland on January 5, 1932. He and wife, Marianne, live in Pittsburgh and have one son—Chris.

### Assistant Coaches

**Ron Blackledge,** offensive line-tackles/tight ends; born April 15, 1938, Canton, Ohio, lives in Pittsburgh. Tight end and defensive end Bowling Green 1957-59. No pro playing experience. College coach: Ashland 1968-69, Cincinnati 1970-72, Kentucky 1973-75, Princeton 1976, Kent State 1977-81 (head coach 1979-81). Pro coach: Joined Steelers in 1982.

**Tony Dungy,** defensive coordinator; born October 6, 1955, Jackson, Mich., lives in Pittsburgh. Quarterback Minnesota 1973-76. Pro safety Pittsburgh Steelers 1977-78, San Francisco 49ers 1979. College coach: Minnesota 1980. Pro coach: Joined Steelers in 1981.

**Dennis Fitzgerald,** inside linebackers; born March 13, 1936, Ann Arbor, Mich., lives in Pittsburgh. Running back Michigan 1958-60. No pro playing experience. College coach: Michigan 1961-68, Kentucky 1969-70, Kent State 1971-77 (head coach 1975-77), Syracuse 1978-80, Tulane 1981. Pro coach: Joined Steelers in 1982.

**Dick Hoak,** offensive backfield; born December 8, 1939, Jeannette, Pa., lives in Greenburg, Pa. Halfback-quarterback Penn State 1958-60. Pro running back Pittsburgh Steelers 1961-70. Pro coach: Joined Steelers in 1972.

**Jed Hughes,** outside linebackers; born November 14, 1947, New York, N.Y., lives in Pittsburgh. Tight end Gettysburg 1968-70. No pro playing experience. College coach: Stanford 1971-72, Michigan 1973-75, UCLA 1976-81. Pro coach: Minnesota Vikings 1982-83, first year with Steelers.

**Jon Kolb,** defensive line and conditioning; born August 30, 1947, Ponca City, Okla., lives in Pittsburgh. Center-linebacker Oklahoma State 1966-68. Pro tackle Pittsburgh Steelers 1969-81. Pro coach: Joined Steelers in 1982.

**Bill Meyers,** offensive line-guards/centers; born October 8, 1946, Chippewa Falls, Wis., lives in Pittsburgh. Tackle Stanford 1970-71. No pro playing experience. College coach: California 1972-73, 1977-78, Santa Clara 1974-76, Notre Dame 1979-81. Pro coach: Green Bay Packers 1982-83, first year with Steelers.

**Tom Moore,** offensive coordinator; born November 7, 1938, Owatonna, Minn., lives in Pittsburgh. Quarterback Iowa 1957-60. No pro playing experience. College coach: Iowa 1961-62, Dayton 1965-68, Wake Forest 1969, Georgia Tech 1970-71, Minnesota 1972-73, 1975-76. Pro coach: New York Stars (WFL) 1974, joined Steelers in 1977.

## PITTSBURGH STEELERS 1984 FIRST-YEAR ROSTER

| Name | Pos. | Ht. | Wt. | Birth-date | College | Birthplace | Residence | How Acq. |
|------|------|-----|-----|-----------|---------|-----------|-----------|----------|
| Brown, Chris | S-CB | 6-0 | 195 | 4/11/62 | Notre Dame | Owensboro, Ky. | Owensboro, Ky. | D6 |
| Campbell, Scott | QB | 5-11 | 201 | 4/15/62 | Purdue | Hershey, Pa. | Hershey, Pa. | D7 |
| Catano, Mark | G | 6-3 | 265 | 1/26/62 | Valdosta State | Yonkers, N.Y. | Peekskill, N.Y. | FA |
| Erenberg, Rich | RB | 5-10 | 200 | 4/17/62 | Colgate | Chappaqua, N.Y. | Chappaqua, N.Y. | D9 |
| Gillespie, Fernandars | RB | 5-10 | 178 | 2/26/62 | William Jewell | St. Louis, Mo. | St. Louis, Mo. | D12 |
| Hull, Jay (1) | G | 6-2 | 240 | 8/25/60 | Wichita State | Pittsburgh, Pa. | Pittsburgh, Pa. | FA |
| Kolodziejski, Chris | TE | 6-3 | 231 | 2/5/61 | Wyoming | Augsburg, Germany | Malibu, Calif. | D2 |
| Lawrence, Ben | G | 6-1 | 285 | 9/19/61 | Indiana, Pa. | Sparta, Wis. | Pittsburgh, Pa. | FA |
| Lipps, Louis | WR-KR | 5-10 | 190 | 8/9/62 | So. Mississippi | New Orleans, La. | Reserve, La. | D1 |
| Long, Terry | G | 5-11 | 272 | 7/21/59 | East Carolina | Columbia, S.C. | Greenville, N.C. | D4 |
| McJunkin, Kirk | G-T | 6-3 | 250 | 3/15/61 | Texas | Dallas, Tex. | Dallas, Tex. | D10 |
| Meyer, John (1) | T | 6-6 | 257 | 5/28/59 | Arizona State | Phoenix, Ariz. | Phoenix, Ariz. | D2('82) |
| Rash, Lou (1) | CB | 5-9 | 170 | 6/5/60 | Mississippi Valley | Cleveland, Miss. | Cleveland, Miss. | FA |
| Rasmussen, Randy | C-G | 6-2 | 253 | 9/27/60 | Minnesota | Minneapolis, Minn. | Minneapolis, Minn. | D8 |
| Rostosky, Pete (1) | T | 6-4 | 245 | 7/29/61 | Connecticut | Monongahela, Pa. | Monongahela, Pa. | FA |
| Seabaugh, Todd (1) | LB | 6-4 | 220 | 3/16/61 | San Diego State | Santa Paula, Calif. | Santa Paula, Calif. | D3('83) |
| Schifko, Scott | G | 6-1 | 259 | 11/12/62 | Waynesburg | Coraopolis, Pa. | Waynesburg, Pa. | FA |
| Thompson, Weegie | WR | 6-6 | 210 | 3/21/61 | Florida State | Pensacola, Fla. | Midlothian, Va. | D4 |
| Veals, Elton | RB | 5-11 | 223 | 3/26/61 | Tulane | Baton Rouge, La. | Baton Rouge, La. | D11 |

Players who report to an NFL team for the first time are designated on rosters as rookies (R). If a player reported to an NFL training camp in a previous year but was not on the active squad for three or more regular season or postseason games, he is listed on the first-year roster and designated by a (1). Thereafter, a player who is on the active squad for three or more regular season or postseason games is credited with an additional year of playing experience.

## NOTES

# SAN DIEGO CHARGERS

**American Football Conference
Western Division**

**Team Colors:** Royal Blue, Gold, and White

**San Diego Jack Murphy Stadium
P.O. Box 20666
San Diego, California 92120
Telephone: (619) 280-2111**

**Club Officials**

President: Eugene V. Klein
General Manager: John R. Sanders
Assistant General Manager: Paul (Tank) Younger
Assistant to the President: Jack Teele
Administrative Assistant, Player Personnel:
  John Trump
Chief Scout: Aubrey (Red) Phillips
Director of Public Relations: Rick Smith
Business Manager: Pat Curran
Director of Marketing: Rich Israel
Director of Ticket Operations: Joe Scott
Assistant Director of Public Relations:
  Bill Johnston
Controller: Frances Beede
Trainer: Ric McDonald
Equipment Manager: Sid Brooks

**Stadium:** San Diego Jack Murphy Stadium •
  **Capacity:** 60,100
  9449 Friars Road
  San Diego, California 92108

**Playing Surface:** Grass

**Training Camp:** University of California-
  San Diego
  La Jolla, California 92037

## 1984 SCHEDULE

**Preseason**

| | | |
|---|---|---|
| Aug. 4 | **Los Angeles Rams** | 6:00 |
| Aug. 11 | **Dallas** | 6:00 |
| Aug. 18 | **San Francisco** | 6:00 |
| Aug. 23 | at Los Angeles Rams | 7:00 |

**Regular Season**

| | | |
|---|---|---|
| Sept. 2 | at Minnesota | 12:00 |
| Sept. 9 | at Seattle | 1:00 |
| Sept. 16 | **Houston** | 1:00 |
| Sept. 24 | at L.A. Raiders (Monday) | 6:00 |
| Sept. 30 | **Detroit** | 1:00 |
| Oct. 7 | at Green Bay | 3:00 |
| Oct. 14 | at Kansas City | 12:00 |
| Oct. 21 | **Los Angeles Raiders** | 1:00 |
| Oct. 29 | **Seattle** (Monday) | 6:00 |
| Nov. 4 | at Colts | 1:00 |
| Nov. 11 | **Denver** | 1:00 |
| Nov. 18 | **Miami** | 1:00 |
| Nov. 25 | at Pittsburgh | 1:00 |
| Dec. 3 | **Chicago** (Monday) | 6:00 |
| Dec. 9 | at Denver | 2:00 |
| Dec. 16 | **Kansas City** | 1:00 |

## CHARGERS COACHING HISTORY

**Los Angeles 1960
(181-161-11)**

| | | |
|---|---|---|
| 1960-69 | Sid Gillman* | 83-51-6 |
| 1969-70 | Charlie Waller | 9-7-3 |
| 1971 | Sid Gillman** | 4-6-0 |
| 1971-73 | Harland Svare*** | 7-17-2 |
| 1973 | Ron Waller | 1-5-0 |
| 1974-78 | Tommy Prothro**** | 21-39-0 |
| 1978-83 | Don Coryell | 56-36-0 |

  *Retired after nine games in 1969
  **Released after 10 games in 1971
  ***Resigned after eight games in 1973
****Resigned after four games in 1978

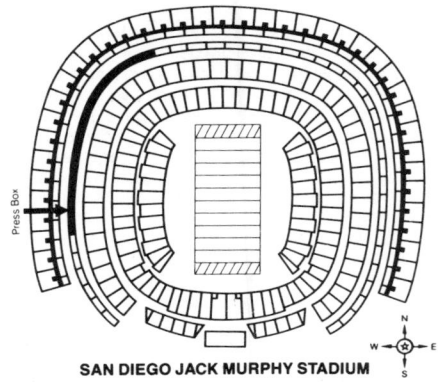

**SAN DIEGO JACK MURPHY STADIUM**

## RECORD HOLDERS

### Individual Records—Career

| Category | Name | Performance |
|---|---|---|
| Rushing (Yds.) | Paul Lowe, 1960-67 | 4,963 |
| Passing (Yds.) | Dan Fouts, 1973-1983 | 30,114 |
| Passing (TDs) | John Hadl, 1962-1972 | 201 |
| Receiving (No.) | Lance Alworth, 1962-1970 | 493 |
| Receiving (Yds.) | Lance Alworth, 1962-1970 | 9,585 |
| Interceptions | Dick Harris, 1960-65 | 29 |
| Punting (Avg.) | Dennis Partee, 1968-1975 | 41.2 |
| Punt Return (Avg.) | Leslie (Speedy) Duncan, 1964-1970 | 12.3 |
| Kickoff Return (Avg.) | Leslie (Speedy) Duncan, 1964-1970 | 25.2 |
| Field Goals | Rolf Benirschke, 1977-1983 | 113 |
| Touchdowns (Tot.) | Lance Alworth, 1962-1970 | 83 |
| Points | Rolf Benirschke, 1977-1983 | 585 |

### Individual Records—Single Season

| Category | Name | Performance |
|---|---|---|
| Rushing (Yds.) | Don Woods, 1974 | 1,162 |
| Passing (Yds.) | Dan Fouts, 1981 | 4,802 |
| Passing (TDs) | Dan Fouts, 1981 | 33 |
| Receiving (No.) | Kellen Winslow, 1980 | 89 |
| Receiving (Yds.) | Lance Alworth, 1965 | 1,602 |
| Interceptions | Charlie McNeil, 1961 | 9 |
| Punting (Avg.) | Dennis Partee, 1969 | 44.6 |
| Punt Return (Avg.) | Leslie (Speedy) Duncan, 1965 | 15.5 |
| Kickoff Return (Avg.) | Keith Lincoln, 1962 | 28.4 |
| Field Goals | Rolf Benirschke, 1980 | 24 |
| Touchdowns (Tot.) | Chuck Muncie, 1981 | 19 |
| Points | Rolf Benirschke, 1980 | 118 |

### Individual Records—Single Game

| Category | Name | Performance |
|---|---|---|
| Rushing (Yds.) | Keith Lincoln, 1-5-64 | 206 |
| Passing (Yds.) | Dan Fouts, 10-19-80, 12-11-82 | 444 |
| Passing (TDs) | Dan Fouts, 11-22-81 | 6 |
| Receiving (No.) | Kellen Winslow, 12-11-83 | 14 |
| Receiving (Yds.) | Wes Chandler, 12-20-82 | 260 |
| Interceptions | Many times | 3 |
| | Last time by Pete Shaw, 11-2-80 | |
| Field Goals | Many times | 4 |
| | Last time by Rolf Benirschke, 12-22-80 | |
| Touchdowns (Tot.) | Kellen Winslow, 11-22-81 | 5 |
| Points | Kellen Winslow, 11-22-81 | 30 |

## 1983 TEAM STATISTICS

| | San Diego | Opp. |
|---|---|---|
| Total First Downs | 361 | 347 |
| Rushing | 106 | 137 |
| Passing | 230 | 187 |
| Penalty | 25 | 23 |
| Third Down Efficiency | 93/215 | 109/231 |
| Third Down Percentage | 43.3 | 47.2 |
| Total Net Yards | 6197 | 5955 |
| Total Offensive Plays | 1086 | 1127 |
| Avg. Gain per Play | 5.7 | 5.3 |
| Avg. Gain per Game | 387.3 | 372.2 |
| Net Yards Rushing | 1536 | 2173 |
| Total Rushing Plays | 423 | 552 |
| Avg. Gain per Rush | 3.6 | 3.9 |
| Avg. Gain Rushing per Game | 96.0 | 135.8 |
| Net Yards Passing | 4661 | 3782 |
| Lost Attempting to Pass | 28/230 | 31/269 |
| Gross Yards Passing | 4891 | 4051 |
| Attempts/Completions | 635/369 | 544/330 |
| Percent Completed | 58.1 | 60.7 |
| Had Intercepted | 33 | 16 |
| Avg. Net Passing per Game | 291.3 | 236.4 |
| Punts/Avg. | 63/43.9 | 70/39.7 |
| Punt Returns/Avg. | 33/6.5 | 35/8.5 |
| Kickoff Returns/Avg. | 74/18.6 | 70/20.4 |
| Interceptions/Avg. Ret. | 16/9.6 | 33/11.4 |
| Penalties/Yards | 115/961 | 111/953 |
| Fumbles/Ball Lost | 42/22 | 26/17 |
| Total Points | 358 | 462 |
| Avg. Points per Game | 22.4 | 28.9 |
| Touchdowns | 45 | 57 |
| Rushing | 16 | 26 |
| Passing | 27 | 28 |
| Returns and Recoveries | 2 | 3 |
| Field Goals | 15/24 | 22/29 |
| Conversions | 43/45 | 54/57 |
| Safeties | 0 | 0 |
| Avg. Time of Possession | 28:04 | 31:56 |

## 1983 TEAM RECORD
### Preseason (2-2)

| Date | San Diego | | Opponents |
|---|---|---|---|
| 8/6 | 20 | Los Angeles Rams | 34 |
| 8/13 | 20 | *Philadelphia | 21 |
| 8/20 | 24 | *San Francisco | 7 |
| 8/26 | 27 | *Los Angeles Rams | 17 |
| | 91 | | 79 |

### Regular Season (6-10)

| Date | San Diego | | Opp. | Att. |
|---|---|---|---|---|
| 9/4 | 29 | *New York Jets | 41 | 51,004 |
| 9/12 | 17 | Kansas City | 14 | 62,150 |
| 9/18 | 31 | Seattle | 34 | 61,714 |
| 9/25 | 24 | *Cleveland (OT) | 30 | 49,482 |
| 10/2 | 41 | New York Giants | 34 | 73,892 |
| 10/9 | 28 | *Seattle | 21 | 49,132 |
| 10/16 | 21 | New England | 37 | 59,016 |
| 10/23 | 6 | Denver | 14 | 74,581 |
| 10/31 | 24 | *Washington | 27 | 46,414 |
| 11/6 | 3 | Pittsburgh | 26 | 58,191 |
| 11/13 | 24 | *Dallas | 23 | 46,192 |
| 11/20 | 14 | St. Louis | 44 | 40,644 |
| 11/27 | 31 | *Denver | 7 | 44,050 |
| 12/1 | 10 | *Los Angeles Raiders | 42 | 47,760 |
| 12/11 | 41 | *Kansas City | 38 | 35,910 |
| 12/18 | 14 | Los Angeles Raiders | 30 | 57,325 |
| | 358 | | 462 | 857,457 |

*Home Game  (OT) Overtime

### Score by Periods

| | | | | | | | |
|---|---|---|---|---|---|---|---|
| San Diego | 92 | 92 | 75 | 99 | 0 | — | 358 |
| Opponents | 83 | 137 | 95 | 141 | 6 | — | 462 |

### Attendance
Home 369,944   Away 487,513   Total 857,457
Single game home record, 54,611 (12-31-72)
Single season home record, 411,661 (1981)

## 1983 INDIVIDUAL STATISTICS

### Rushing

| | Att. | Yds. | Avg. | LG | TD |
|---|---|---|---|---|---|
| Muncie | 235 | 886 | 3.8 | 34t | 12 |
| Brooks | 127 | 516 | 4.1 | 61 | 3 |
| S. Smith | 24 | 91 | 3.8 | 20 | 0 |
| Jackson | 11 | 39 | 3.5 | 6 | 0 |
| Chandler | 2 | 25 | 12.5 | 23 | 0 |
| Cappelletti | 1 | 5 | 5.0 | 5 | 0 |
| Mathison | 1 | 0 | 0.0 | 0 | 0 |
| Fouts | 12 | −5 | −0.4 | 3 | 1 |
| Sievers | 1 | −7 | −7.0 | −7 | 0 |
| Luther | 9 | −14 | −1.6 | 8 | 0 |
| San Diego | 423 | 1536 | 3.6 | 61 | 16 |
| Opponents | 552 | 2173 | 3.9 | 49t | 26 |

### Passing

| | Att. | Comp. | Pct. | Yds. | TD | Int. | Tkld. | Rate |
|---|---|---|---|---|---|---|---|---|
| Fouts | 340 | 215 | 63.2 | 2975 | 20 | 15 | 14/107 | 92.5 |
| Luther | 287 | 151 | 52.6 | 1875 | 7 | 17 | 13/120 | 56.6 |
| Mathison | 5 | 3 | 60.0 | 41 | 0 | 1 | 0/0 | 46.7 |
| Buford | 1 | 0 | 0.0 | 0 | 0 | 0 | 0/0 | 39.6 |
| Holohan | 1 | 0 | 0.0 | 0 | 0 | 0 | 0/0 | 39.6 |
| S. Smith | 1 | 0 | 0.0 | 0 | 0 | 0 | 0/0 | 39.6 |
| Chandler | 0 | 0 | — | 0 | 0 | 0 | 1/3 | 0.0 |
| San Diego | 635 | 369 | 58.1 | 4891 | 27 | 33 | 28/230 | 75.1 |
| Opponents | 544 | 330 | 60.7 | 4051 | 28 | 16 | 31/269 | 88.6 |

### Receiving

| | No. | Yds. | Avg. | LG | TD |
|---|---|---|---|---|---|
| Winslow | 88 | 1172 | 13.3 | 46 | 8 |
| Joiner | 65 | 960 | 14.8 | 33t | 3 |
| Chandler | 58 | 845 | 14.6 | 44t | 5 |
| Muncie | 42 | 396 | 9.4 | 27 | 1 |
| Sievers | 33 | 452 | 13.7 | 28 | 3 |
| Brooks | 25 | 215 | 8.6 | 36 | 0 |
| Holohan | 23 | 272 | 11.8 | 35 | 2 |
| Duckworth | 20 | 422 | 21.1 | 59t | 5 |
| S. Smith | 6 | 51 | 8.5 | 21 | 0 |
| Jackson | 5 | 42 | 8.4 | 10 | 0 |
| Carr | 2 | 36 | 18.0 | 23 | 0 |
| Scales | 2 | 28 | 14.0 | 14 | 0 |
| San Diego | 369 | 4891 | 13.3 | 59t | 27 |
| Opponents | 330 | 4051 | 12.3 | 71t | 28 |

### Interceptions

| | No. | Yds. | Avg. | LG | TD |
|---|---|---|---|---|---|
| Walters | 7 | 55 | 7.9 | 33 | 0 |
| Young | 2 | 49 | 24.5 | 40t | 1 |
| Fox | 2 | 14 | 7.0 | 14 | 0 |
| King | 1 | 19 | 19.0 | 19 | 0 |
| Preston | 1 | 13 | 13.0 | 13 | 0 |
| Green | 1 | 3 | 3.0 | 3 | 0 |
| Byrd | 1 | 0 | 0.0 | 0 | 0 |
| McPherson | 1 | 0 | 0.0 | 0 | 0 |
| San Diego | 16 | 153 | 9.6 | 40t | 1 |
| Opponents | 33 | 377 | 11.4 | 39 | 2 |

### Punting

| | No. | Yds. | Avg. | In 20 | LG |
|---|---|---|---|---|---|
| Buford | 63 | 2763 | 43.9 | 13 | 60 |
| San Diego | 63 | 2763 | 43.9 | 13 | 60 |
| Opponents | 70 | 2780 | 39.7 | 27 | 55 |

### Punt Returns

| | No. | FC | Yds. | Avg. | LG | TD |
|---|---|---|---|---|---|---|
| Brooks | 18 | 4 | 137 | 7.6 | 30 | 0 |
| Chandler | 8 | 6 | 26 | 3.3 | 11 | 0 |
| Fortune | 4 | 0 | 16 | 4.0 | 9 | 0 |
| Scales | 2 | 0 | 34 | 17.0 | 30 | 0 |
| Laird | 1 | 0 | 0 | 0.0 | 0 | 0 |
| San Diego | 33 | 10 | 213 | 6.5 | 30 | 0 |
| Opponents | 35 | 5 | 299 | 8.5 | 28 | 0 |

### Kickoff Returns

| | No. | Yds. | Avg. | LG | TD |
|---|---|---|---|---|---|
| Brooks | 32 | 607 | 19.0 | 34 | 0 |
| Laird | 15 | 342 | 22.8 | 41 | 0 |
| Jackson | 11 | 201 | 18.3 | 32 | 0 |
| McPherson | 5 | 77 | 15.4 | 19 | 0 |
| Jodat | 3 | 45 | 15.0 | 18 | 0 |
| Young | 3 | 41 | 13.7 | 19 | 0 |
| S. Smith | 2 | 32 | 16.0 | 21 | 0 |
| B. Smith | 1 | 10 | 10.0 | 10 | 0 |
| Scales | 1 | 16 | 16.0 | 16 | 0 |
| Sievers | 1 | 6 | 6.0 | 6 | 0 |
| San Diego | 74 | 1377 | 18.6 | 41 | 0 |
| Opponents | 70 | 1426 | 20.4 | 64 | 0 |

### Scoring

| | TD | TD R | TD P | TD Rt | PAT | FG | TP |
|---|---|---|---|---|---|---|---|
| Benirschke | | | | | 43/45 | 15/24 | 88 |
| Muncie | 13 | 12 | 1 | 0 | | | 78 |
| Winslow | 8 | 0 | 8 | 0 | | | 48 |
| Chandler | 5 | 0 | 5 | 0 | | | 30 |
| Duckworth | 5 | 0 | 5 | 0 | | | 30 |
| Brooks | 3 | 3 | 0 | 0 | | | 18 |
| Joiner | 3 | 0 | 3 | 0 | | | 18 |
| Sievers | 3 | 0 | 3 | 0 | | | 18 |
| Holohan | 2 | 0 | 2 | 0 | | | 12 |
| Fouts | 1 | 1 | 0 | 0 | | | 6 |
| Nelson | 1 | 0 | 0 | 1 | | | 6 |
| Young | 1 | 0 | 0 | 1 | | | 6 |
| San Diego | 45 | 16 | 27 | 2 | 43/45 | 15/24 | 358 |
| Opponents | 57 | 26 | 28 | 3 | 54/56 | 22/29 | 462 |

## FIRST-ROUND SELECTIONS

(If Club had no first-round selection, first player drafted is listed with round in parentheses.)

| Year | Player, College, Position |
|---|---|
| 1960 | Monty Stickles, Notre Dame, E |
| 1961 | Earl Faison, Indiana, DE |
| 1962 | Bob Ferguson, Ohio State, RB |
| 1963 | Walt Sweeney, Syracuse, G |
| 1964 | Ted Davis, Georgia Tech, LB |
| 1965 | Steve DeLong, Tennessee, DE |
| 1966 | Don Davis, Cal State-Los Angeles, DT |
| 1967 | Ron Billingsley, Wyoming, DE |
| 1968 | Russ Washington, Missouri, DT |
| | Jimmy Hill, Texas A&I, DB |
| 1969 | Marty Domres, Columbia, QB |
| | Bob Bobich, Miami, Ohio, LB |
| 1970 | Walker Gillette, Richmond, WR |
| 1971 | Leon Burns, Long Beach State, RB |
| 1972 | Pete Lazetich, Stanford, DE (2) |
| 1973 | Johnny Rodgers, Nebraska, WR |
| 1974 | Bo Matthews, Colorado, RB |
| | Don Goode, Kansas, LB |
| 1975 | Gary Johnson, Grambling, DT |
| | Mike Williams, Louisiana State, DB |
| 1976 | Joe Washington, Oklahoma, RB |
| 1977 | Bob Rush, Memphis State, C |
| 1978 | John Jefferson, Arizona State, WR |
| 1979 | Kellen Winslow, Missouri, TE |
| 1980 | Ed Luther, San Jose State, QB (4) |
| 1981 | James Brooks, Auburn, RB |
| 1982 | Hollis Hall, Clemson, DB (7) |
| 1983 | Billy Ray Smith, Arkansas, LB |
| | Gary Anderson, Arkansas, RB |
| | Gill Byrd, San Jose State, DB |
| 1984 | Mossy Cade, Texas, DB |

## SAN DIEGO CHARGERS 1984 VETERAN ROSTER

| No. | Name | Pos. | Ht. | Wt. | Birth-date | NFL Exp. | College | Birthplace | Residence | Games in '83 |
|---|---|---|---|---|---|---|---|---|---|---|
| 91 | Ackerman, Richard | NT | 6-4 | 254 | 6/16/59 | 3 | Memphis State | La Grange, Ill. | San Diego, Calif. | 15 |
| 6 | Benirschke, Rolf | K | 6-1 | 179 | 2/7/55 | 8 | California-Davis | Boston, Mass. | San Diego, Calif. | 16 |
| 50 | Bradley, Carlos | LB | 6-0 | 226 | 4/27/60 | 4 | Wake Forest | Philadelphia, Pa. | San Diego, Calif. | 16 |
| 61 | †Brown, Don | T | 6-6 | 262 | 4/2/59 | 2 | Santa Clara | San Jose, Calif. | San Jose, Calif. | 13 |
| 7 | Buford, Maury | P | 6-0 | 185 | 2/18/60 | 3 | Texas Tech | Mt. Pleasant, Tex. | Mt. Pleasant, Tex. | 16 |
| 22 | Byrd, Gill | CB | 5-11 | 191 | 2/20/61 | 2 | San Jose State | San Francisco, Calif. | San Diego, Calif. | 14 |
| 89 | Chandler, Wes | WR | 6-0 | 183 | 8/22/56 | 7 | Florida | New Smyrna Beach, Fla. | New Orleans, La. | 16 |
| 77 | Claphan, Sam | T | 6-6 | 267 | 10/10/56 | 4 | Oklahoma | Tahlequah, Okla. | Norman, Okla. | 16 |
|  | t-Downing, Walt | C-G | 6-3 | 270 | 6/11/56 | 7 | Michigan | Coatesville, Pa. | Mountain View, Calif. | 12 |
| 82 | Duckworth, Bobby | WR | 6-3 | 197 | 11/27/58 | 3 | Arkansas | Crossett, Ark. | San Diego, Calif. | 16 |
| 78 | Ehin, Chuck | DE | 6-4 | 254 | 7/1/61 | 2 | Brigham Young | Marysville, Calif. | San Diego, Calif. | 9 |
| 72 | Elko, Bill | G | 6-5 | 277 | 12/28/59 | 2 | Louisiana State | New York, N.Y. | San Diego, Calif. | 11 |
| 56 | Evans, Larry | LB | 6-2 | 220 | 7/11/53 | 9 | Mississippi College | Biloxi, Miss. | Englewood, Colo. | 3 |
| 76 | Ferguson, Keith | DE | 6-5 | 241 | 4/3/59 | 4 | Ohio State | Miami, Fla. | San Diego, Calif. | 16 |
| 84 | Fortune, Hosea | WR | 6-0 | 176 | 3/4/59 | 2 | Rice | New Orleans, La. | Los Angeles, Calif. | 4 |
| 14 | Fouts, Dan | QB | 6-3 | 205 | 6/10/51 | 12 | Oregon | San Francisco, Calif. | Sisters, Ore. | 10 |
| 48 | Fox, Tim | S | 5-11 | 186 | 11/1/53 | 9 | Ohio State | Canton, Ohio | Foxboro, Mass. | 12 |
| 75 | Gissinger, Andrew | T | 6-5 | 277 | 7/4/59 | 3 | Syracuse | Barberton, Ohio | San Diego, Calif. | 16 |
| 69 | Gofourth, Derrel | G-C | 6-3 | 260 | 3/20/55 | 8 | Oklahoma State | Little Parsons, Kan. | Stillwater, Okla. | 15 |
| 58 | Green, Mike | LB | 6-0 | 226 | 6/29/61 | 2 | Oklahoma State | Port Arthur, Tex. | Stillwater, Okla. | 16 |
| 28 | Greene, Ken | S | 6-3 | 203 | 5/8/56 | 7 | Washington State | Lewiston, Idaho | Vancouver, Wash. | 16 |
| 43 | Gregor, Bob | S | 6-2 | 190 | 2/10/57 | 2 | Washington State | Riverside, Calif. | San Diego, Calif. | 5 |
| 20 | Henderson, Reuben | CB | 6-1 | 188 | 10/3/58 | 4 | San Diego State | Santa Monica, Calif. | San Diego, Calif. | 14 |
| 88 | Holohan, Pete | TE | 6-4 | 240 | 7/25/59 | 4 | Notre Dame | Albany, N.Y. | San Diego, Calif. | 16 |
| 41 | Jackson, Earnest | RB | 5-10 | 208 | 12/18/59 | 2 | Texas A&M | Needville, Tex. | Dallas, Tex. | 12 |
| 40 | Jodat, Jim | RB | 5-11 | 213 | 3/3/54 | 8 | Carthage | Milwaukee, Wis. | Huntington Beach, Calif. | 15 |
| 79 | Johnson, Gary | DE | 6-2 | 255 | 8/31/52 | 10 | Grambling | Shreveport, La. | San Diego, Calif. | 16 |
|  | t-Johnson, Pete | RB | 6-0 | 272 | 3/2/54 | 8 | Ohio State | Peach County, Ga. | Westerville, Ohio | 11 |
| 18 | †Joiner, Charlie | WR | 5-11 | 180 | 10/14/47 | 16 | Grambling | Many, La. | Houston, Tex. | 12 |
|  | t-Kelley, Brian | LB | 6-3 | 222 | 9/1/51 | 12 | California Lutheran | Dallas, Tex. | Upper Saddle River, N.J. | 16 |
| 57 | King, Linden | LB | 6-5 | 245 | 6/28/55 | 7 | Colorado State | Memphis, Tenn. | San Diego, Calif. | 16 |
| 64 | †Loewen, Chuck | G-T | 6-4 | 264 | 1/23/57 | 4 | South Dakota State | Mountain Lake, Minn. | San Diego, Calif. | 0* |
| 51 | Lowe, Woodrow | LB | 6-0 | 226 | 6/9/54 | 9 | Alabama | Columbus, Ga. | Seale, Ala. | 16 |
| 11 | Luther, Ed | QB | 6-3 | 210 | 1/2/57 | 5 | San Jose State | Gardena, Calif. | Carlsbad, Calif. | 16 |
| 62 | Macek, Don | C | 6-2 | 260 | 7/2/54 | 9 | Boston College | Manchester, N.H. | San Diego, Calif. | 11 |
| 12 | Mathison, Bruce | QB | 6-3 | 210 | 4/25/59 | 2 | Nebraska | Superior, Wis. | San Diego, Calif. | 1 |
| 60 | McKnight, Dennis | C-G | 6-3 | 260 | 9/12/59 | 3 | Drake | Dallas, Tex. | San Diego, Calif. | 16 |
| 24 | McPherson, Miles | CB | 6-0 | 183 | 3/30/60 | 3 | New Haven University | Brooklyn, N.Y. | San Diego, Calif. | 11 |
| 46 | Muncie, Chuck | RB | 6-2 | 228 | 3/17/53 | 9 | California | Uniontown, Pa. | San Diego, Calif. | 15 |
|  | t-Neil, Kenny | DE | 6-4 | 255 | 1/8/59 | 4 | Iowa State | Cincinnati, Ohio | Cincinnati, Ohio | 16 |
| 55 | †Nelson, Derrie | LB | 6-1 | 234 | 2/8/58 | 2 | Nebraska | York, Neb. | Fairmont, Neb. | 15 |
| 52 | Preston, Ray | LB | 6-0 | 220 | 1/25/54 | 9 | Syracuse | Lawrence, Mass. | San Diego, Calif. | 16 |
|  | t-Salaam, Abdul | NT | 6-3 | 269 | 2/12/53 | 9 | Kent State | New Brockton, Ala. | Cincinnati, Ohio | 1 |
| 66 | Shields, Billy | T | 6-8 | 284 | 8/23/53 | 10 | Georgia Tech | Vicksburg, Miss. | San Diego, Calif. | 16 |
| 85 | Sievers, Eric | TE | 6-4 | 233 | 11/9/58 | 4 | Maryland | Urbana, Ill. | San Diego, Calif. | 16 |
| 54 | Smith, Billy Ray | LB | 6-3 | 239 | 8/10/61 | 2 | Arkansas | Fayetteville, Ark. | Fayetteville, Ark. | 16 |
| 47 | Smith, Sherman | RB | 6-4 | 225 | 11/1/54 | 9 | Miami, Ohio | Youngstown, Ohio | Woodinville, Wash. | 13 |
|  | t-Thomas, Jewerl | RB | 5-10 | 228 | 9/10/57 | 5 | San Jose State | Hanford, Calif. | San Jose, Calif. | 10 |
| 59 | Thrift, Cliff | LB | 6-1 | 230 | 5/3/56 | 6 | East Central Oklahoma | Dallas, Tex. | San Diego, Calif. | 6 |
| 23 | Walters, Danny | CB | 6-1 | 187 | 11/4/60 | 2 | Arkansas | Prescott, Ark. | Chicago, Ill. | 16 |
| 67 | White, Ed | G | 6-2 | 279 | 4/4/47 | 16 | California | San Diego, Calif. | Carlsbad, Calif. | 16 |
| 63 | Wilkerson, Doug | G | 6-3 | 258 | 3/27/47 | 15 | North Carolina Central | Fayetteville, N.C. | Spring Valley, Calif. | 12 |
| 45 | Williams, Henry | CB | 6-0 | 180 | 12/2/56 | 3 | San Diego State | Greensboro, Ala. | Los Angeles, Calif. | 6* |
| 80 | Winslow, Kellen | TE | 6-5 | 251 | 11/5/57 | 6 | Missouri | St. Louis, Mo. | San Diego, Calif. | 16 |
| 49 | †Young, Andre | S | 6-0 | 203 | 11/22/60 | 3 | Louisiana Tech | West Monroe, La. | West Monroe, La. | 15 |

* Loewen missed '83 season due to injury; Williams played 5 games with Los Angeles Rams, 1 with San Diego in '83.

†Option playout; subject to developments.

t-Chargers traded for Downing (San Francisco), P. Johnson (Cincinnati), Kelley (New York Giants), Neil and Salaam (New York Jets), Thomas (Kansas City).

Traded—Running back James Brooks to Cincinnati, defensive tackle Louie Kelcher to San Francisco.

Retired—Roger Carr, 10-year wide receiver, 4 games in '83

Also played with Chargers in '83—FB John Cappelletti (1 game), DE Leroy Jones (12), S Bruce Laird (14), CB Darrell Pattillo (1), WR Dwight Scales (7).

## COACHING STAFF

### Head Coach, Don Coryell

**Pro Career:** Begins seventh year as San Diego's head coach. Became head coach of the Chargers after fourth game of 1978 season and led them to eight wins in final 12 games. Before coming to Chargers was St. Louis Cardinals head coach for five seasons, compiling a 42-29-1 record and leading Cardinals to the NFC East titles in 1974-75. Career record: 98-65-1.

**Background:** Played defensive back for University of Washington 1947-49. Assistant coach Punahou Academy, Honolulu, 1951. Head coach Farrington High School, Honolulu, 1952. Head coach University of British Columbia 1953-54. Head coach, Fort Ord, California, army team 1956. Head coach Whittier College 1957-59 (23-5-1). Offensive backfield coach at Southern California 1960. Head coach at San Diego State from 1961-72 where he compiled a 104-19-2 record.

**Personal:** Born October 17, 1924 in Seattle, Washington. Graduated from Lincoln High School, Seattle, in 1943. Served in United States Army 1943-46, released as first lieutenant. Don and his wife, Aliisa, live in San Diego and have two children —Mike and Mindy.

### Assistant Coaches

**Tom Bass,** defensive coordinator; born August 2, 1936, Riverside, Calif., lives in San Diego. Linebacker San Jose State 1955-57. No pro playing experience. College coach: San Jose State 1958-59, San Diego State 1960-62. Pro coach: San Diego Chargers 1964-67, Cincinnati Bengals 1968-69, Tampa Bay Buccaneers 1977-81, rejoined Chargers in 1982.

**Marv Braden,** special assistant; born January 25, 1938, Kansas City, Mo., lives in San Diego. Linebacker Southwest Missouri State 1956-59. No pro playing experience. College coach: Northeast Missouri State 1967-68 (head coach), U.S. International 1969-72, Iowa State 1973, Southern Methodist 1974-75, Michigan State 1976. Pro coach: Denver Broncos 1977-80, joined Chargers in 1981.

**Earnel Durden,** offensive backs; born January 24, 1937, Los Angeles, lives in La Mesa, Calif. Halfback Oregon State 1956-58. No pro playing experience. College coach: Compton, Calif., J.C., 1966-67, Long Beach State 1968, UCLA 1969-70. Pro coach: Los Angeles Rams 1971-72, Houston Oilers 1973, joined Chargers in 1974.

**Dave Levy,** offensive coordinator; born October 25, 1932, Carrollton, Mo., lives in Solana Beach, Calif. Guard UCLA 1953-54. No pro playing experience. College coach: UCLA 1954, Long Beach City College 1955, Southern California 1960-75. Pro coach: Joined Chargers in 1980.

**Al Saunders,** receivers; born February 1, 1947, London, Eng., lives in San Diego. Defensive back San Jose State 1966-68. No pro playing experience. College coach: Southern California 1970-71, Missouri 1972, Utah State 1973-75, California 1976-81, Tennessee 1982. Pro coach: Joined Chargers in 1983.

**Doug Shively,** defensive line; born March 18, 1938, Lexington, Ky., lives in San Diego. End Kentucky 1955-58. No pro playing experience. College coach: Virginia Tech 1961-66, Kentucky 1967-69, Clemson 1970-72, North Carolina 1973. Pro coach: New Orleans Saints 1974-76, Atlanta Falcons 1977-82, Arizona Wranglers (USFL, head coach) 1983, first year with Chargers.

**Jim Wagstaff,** defensive backfield; born June 12, 1936, American Falls, Idaho, lives in San Diego. Back Idaho State 1954-58. Pro defensive back Chicago Cardinals 1959, Buffalo Bills 1960-61. College coach: Boise State 1969-72. Pro coach: Los Angeles Rams 1973-77, Buffalo Bills 1978-80, joined Chargers in 1981.

## SAN DIEGO CHARGERS 1984 FIRST-YEAR ROSTER

| Name | Pos. | Ht. | Wt. | Birth-date | College | Birthplace | Residence | How Acq. |
|------|------|-----|-----|------------|---------|------------|-----------|----------|
| Baker, Tony | WR | 6-1 | 197 | 4/15/61 | Mississippi Valley | Louisville, Miss. | Louisville, Miss. | FA |
| Barnes, Zachary | DE | 6-6 | 254 | 11/9/60 | Alabama State | Dothan, Ala. | Dothan, Ala. | D9 |
| Bendross, Jesse | WR | 6-0 | 192 | 5/19/61 | Alabama | Hollywood, Fla. | Hollywood, Fla. | D7 |
| Cade, Mossy | CB | 6-0 | 180 | 12/26/61 | Texas | Eloy, Ariz. | Austin, Tex. | D1 |
| Craighead, Bob | RB | 6-1 | 200 | 6/7/61 | N.E. Louisiana | McComb, Miss. | Monroe, La. | D8a |
| Guendling, Mike | LB | 6-3 | 239 | 6/18/62 | Northwestern | Elk Grove, Ill. | Elk Grove, Ill. | D2 |
| Guthrie, Keith | NT | 6-4 | 264 | 8/17/62 | Texas A&M | Tyler, Tex. | Tyler, Tex. | D6 |
| Harper, Paine | WR | 5-11 | 188 | 5/30/61 | La Verne | Los Angeles, Calif. | Los Angeles, Calif. | D12 |
| James, Lionel | RB-KR | 5-6 | 171 | 5/25/62 | Auburn | Albany, Ga. | Albany, Ga. | D5 |
| Jenkins, Todd | WR | 6-2 | 194 | 12/22/61 | Northwestern | Chicago, Ill. | Evanston, Ill. | FA |
| Lang, Bee | WR | 5-7 | 165 | 9/11/62 | Florida | Tallahassee, Fla. | Miami, Fla. | FA |
| Marshall, Vincent | TE | 6-4 | 233 | 6/18/60 | Alabama State | Woodbury, Ga. | Thomasville, Ga. | FA |
| McGee, Buford | RB | 6-0 | 201 | 8/16/60 | Mississippi | Durant, Miss. | Durant, Miss. | D11 |
| Miller, Deron (1) | TE | 6-4 | 230 | 7/11/61 | Rice | Flemington, N.J. | Naples, Fla. | FA |
| Pleasant, Mike (1) | RB | 6-1 | 195 | 8/16/58 | Oklahoma | Muskogee, Okla. | Muskogee, Okla. | FA |
| Rome, Tag | WR | 5-8 | 173 | 8/13/61 | N.E. Louisiana | Donaldson, La. | Jonesboro, La. | FA |
| Taylor, Kerry | RB | 5-11 | 184 | 10/23/62 | So. Connecticut | Yonkers, N.Y. | Mt. Vernon, N.Y. | FA |
| Woodard, Ray | DE-NT | 6-6 | 267 | 8/20/61 | Texas | Lufkin, Tex. | Lufkin, Tex. | D8 |

Players who report to an NFL team for the first time are designated on rosters as rookies (R). If a player reported to an NFL training camp in a previous year but was not on the active squad for three or more regular season or postseason games, he is listed on the first-year roster and designated by a (1). Thereafter, a player who is on the active squad for three or more regular season or postseason games is credited with an additional year of playing experience.

# NOTES

_____

_____

_____

_____

_____

_____

_____

_____

_____

_____

_____

_____

_____

_____

**Chuck Weber,** linebackers; born March 26, 1930, Philadelphia, lives in San Diego. Linebacker West Chester State 1949-53. Pro linebacker Cleveland Browns 1955-56, Chicago Cardinals 1956-58, Philadelphia Eagles 1959-61. Pro coach: Boston Patriots 1964-67, San Diego Chargers 1968-69, Cincinnati Bengals 1970-75, St. Louis Cardinals 1976-77, Cleveland Browns 1978-79, Baltimore Colts 1980-81, rejoined Chargers in 1982.

**Ernie Zampese,** quarterbacks-passing game; born March 12, 1936, Santa Barbara, Calif., lives in San Diego. Halfback Southern California 1956-58. No pro playing experience. College coach: Hancock J.C. 1962-65, Cal Poly-SLO 1966, San Diego State 1967-75. Pro coach: San Diego Chargers 1976, rejoined Chargers in 1978.

# SEATTLE SEAHAWKS

**American Football Conference
Western Division**

**Team Colors:** Blue, Green, and Silver

**5305 Lake Washington Boulevard
Kirkland, Washington 98033
Telephone:** (206) 827-9777

**Club Officials**

President-General Manager: Mike McCormack
Assistant General Manager: Chuck Allen
Director of Player Personnel: Mike Allman
Public Relations Director: Gary Wright
Assistant Public Relations Director: Dave Neubert
Business Manager: Mickey Loomis
Ticket Manager: James Nagaoka
Trainer: Jim Whitesel
Equipment Manager: Walt Loeffler

**Stadium:** Kingdome • **Capacity:** 64,757
201 South King Street
Seattle, Washington 98104

**Playing Surface:** AstroTurf

**Training Camp:** Eastern Washington University
Cheney, Washington 99004

## 1984 SCHEDULE

**Preseason**

| | | |
|---|---|---|
| July 28 | vs. Tampa Bay at Canton. . . | 3:00 |
| Aug. 4 | **Buffalo** | 7:30 |
| Aug. 11 | at Detroit | 7:00 |
| Aug. 17 | **St. Louis** | 7:30 |
| Aug. 24 | at San Francisco | 6:00 |

**Regular Season**

| | | |
|---|---|---|
| Sept. 2 | **Cleveland** | 1:00 |
| Sept. 9 | **San Diego** | 1:00 |
| Sept. 16 | at New England | 1:00 |
| Sept. 23 | **Chicago** | 1:00 |
| Sept. 30 | at Minnesota | 12:00 |
| Oct. 7 | at Los Angeles Raiders | 1:00 |
| Oct. 14 | **Buffalo** | 1:00 |
| Oct. 21 | vs. Green Bay at Milwaukee | 12:00 |
| Oct. 29 | at San Diego (Monday) | 6:00 |
| Nov. 4 | **Kansas City** | 1:00 |
| Nov. 12 | **L.A. Raiders** (Monday) | 6:00 |
| Nov. 18 | at Cincinnati | 1:00 |
| Nov. 25 | at Denver | 2:00 |
| Dec. 2 | **Detroit** | 1:00 |
| Dec. 9 | at Kansas City | 12:00 |
| Dec. 15 | **Denver** (Saturday) | 1:00 |

## SEAHAWKS COACHING HISTORY

**(50-70-0)**

| | | |
|---|---|---|
| 1976-82 | Jack Patera* | 35-59-0 |
| 1982 | Mike McCormack | 4-3-0 |
| 1983 | Chuck Knox | 11-8-0 |

*Released after 2 games in 1982

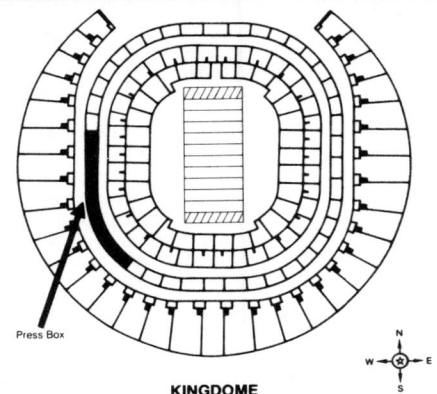

Press Box

**KINGDOME**

## RECORD HOLDERS

### Individual Records — Career

| Category | Name | Performance |
|---|---|---|
| Rushing (Yds.) | Sherman Smith, 1976-1982 | 3,429 |
| Passing (Yds.) | Jim Zorn, 1976-1983 | 20,042 |
| Passing (TDs) | Jim Zorn, 1976-1983 | 107 |
| Receiving (No.) | Steve Largent, 1976-1983 | 471 |
| Receiving (Yds.) | Steve Largent, 1976-1983 | 7,608 |
| Interceptions | Dave Brown, 1976-1983 | 31 |
| Punting (Avg.) | Herman Weaver, 1977-1980 | 40.0 |
| Punt Return (Avg.) | Paul Johns, 1981-83 | 11.2 |
| Kickoff Return (Avg.) | Zachary Dixon, 1983 | 23.4 |
| Field Goals | Efren Herrera, 1978-1981 | 64 |
| Touchdowns (Tot.) | Steve Largent, 1976-1983 | 61 |
| Points | Steve Largent, 1976-1983 | 366 |

### Individual Records — Single Season

| Category | Name | Performance |
|---|---|---|
| Rushing (Yds.) | Curt Warner, 1983 | 1,449 |
| Passing (Yds.) | Jim Zorn, 1979 | 3,661 |
| Passing (TDs) | Jim Zorn, 1979 | 20 |
| Receiving (No.) | Steve Largent, 1981 | 75 |
| Receiving (Yds.) | Steve Largent, 1979 | 1,237 |
| Interceptions | John Harris, 1981 | 10 |
| Punting (Avg.) | Herman Weaver, 1980 | 41.8 |
| Punt Return (Avg.) | Paul Johns, 1983 | 11.3 |
| Kickoff Return (Avg.) | Al Hunter, 1978 | 24.1 |
| Field Goals | Efren Herrera, 1980 | 20 |
| Touchdowns (Tot.) | David Sims, 1978 | 15 |
| | Sherman Smith, 1979 | 15 |
| Points | Norm Johnson, 1983 | 103 |

### Individual Records — Single Game

| Category | Name | Performance |
|---|---|---|
| Rushing (Yds.) | Curt Warner, 11-27-83 | 207 |
| Passing (Yds.) | Dave Krieg, 11-20-83 | 418 |
| Passing (TDs) | Many times | 4 |
| | Last time by Jim Zorn, 9-21-80 | |
| Receiving (No.) | David Hughes, 9-27-81 | 12 |
| Receiving (Yds.) | Sam McCullum, 12-16-79 | 173 |
| Interceptions | Many times | 2 |
| | Last time by John Harris, 11-1-81 | |
| Field Goals | Efren Herrera, 10-5-80 | 4 |
| Touchdowns (Tot.) | Many times | 3 |
| | Last time by Curt Warner, 11-27-83 | |
| Points | Many times | 18 |
| | Last time by Curt Warner, 11-27-83 | |

## 1983 TEAM STATISTICS

| | Seattle | Opp. |
|---|---|---|
| Total First Downs | 300 | 351 |
| Rushing | 131 | 128 |
| Passing | 153 | 195 |
| Penalty | 16 | 28 |
| Third Down Efficiency | 96/219 | 95/214 |
| Third Down Percentage | 43.8 | 44.4 |
| Total Net Yards | 5092 | 6029 |
| Total Offensive Plays | 1042 | 1075 |
| Avg. Gain per Play | 4.9 | 5.6 |
| Avg. Gain per Game | 318.3 | 376.8 |
| Net Yards Rushing | 2119 | 2198 |
| Total Rushing Plays | 546 | 511 |
| Avg. Gain per Rush | 3.9 | 4.3 |
| Avg. Gain Rushing per Game | 132.4 | 137.4 |
| Net Yards Passing | 2973 | 3831 |
| Lost Attempting to Pass | 47/343 | 43/351 |
| Gross Yards Passing | 3316 | 4182 |
| Attempts/Completions | 449/251 | 521/311 |
| Percent Completed | 55.9 | 59.7 |
| Had Intercepted | 18 | 26 |
| Avg. Net Passing per Game | 185.8 | 239.4 |
| Punts/Avg. | 79/39.5 | 68/40.5 |
| Punt Returns/Avg. | 34/10.8 | 36/5.1 |
| Kickoff Returns/Avg. | 71/22.2 | 59/16.1 |
| Interceptions/Avg. Ret. | 26/14.0 | 18/15.5 |
| Penalties/Yards | 102/890 | 91/725 |
| Fumbles/Ball Lost | 36/20 | 44/28 |
| Total Points | 403 | 397 |
| Avg. Points per Game | 25.2 | 24.8 |
| Touchdowns | 50 | 48 |
| Rushing | 19 | 14 |
| Passing | 25 | 33 |
| Returns and Recoveries | 6 | 1 |
| Field Goals | 18/25 | 20/26 |
| Conversions | 49/50 | 43/48 |
| Safeties | 0 | 3 |
| Avg. Time of Possession | 29:52 | 30:08 |

## 1983 TEAM RECORD
### Preseason (2-2)

| Date | Seattle | | Opponents |
|---|---|---|---|
| 8/5 | 7 | Denver | 10 |
| 8/12 | 38 | *Green Bay | 21 |
| 8/19 | 17 | *Minnesota | 19 |
| 8/27 | 20 | San Francisco | 6 |
| | 82 | | 56 |

### Regular Season (9-7)

| Date | Seattle | | Opp. | Att. |
|---|---|---|---|---|
| 9/4 | 13 | Kansas City | 17 | 42,531 |
| 9/11 | 17 | New York Jets | 10 | 50,066 |
| 9/18 | 34 | *San Diego | 31 | 61,714 |
| 9/25 | 17 | *Washington | 27 | 60,718 |
| 10/2 | 24 | Cleveland | 9 | 75,446 |
| 10/9 | 21 | San Diego | 28 | 49,132 |
| 10/16 | 38 | *Los Angeles Raiders | 36 | 60,967 |
| 10/23 | 21 | *Pittsburgh | 27 | 61,615 |
| 10/30 | 34 | Los Angeles Raiders | 21 | 49,708 |
| 11/6 | 27 | *Denver | 19 | 61,189 |
| 11/13 | 28 | St. Louis | 33 | 33,280 |
| 11/20 | 27 | Denver | 38 | 74,710 |
| 11/27 | 51 | *Kansas City (OT) | 48 | 56,793 |
| 12/4 | 10 | *Dallas | 35 | 63,352 |
| 12/11 | 17 | New York Giants | 12 | 48,942 |
| 12/18 | 24 | *New England | 6 | 59,688 |
| | 403 | | 397 | 909,851 |

*Home Game    (OT) Overtime

### Score by Periods

| | | | | | | | |
|---|---|---|---|---|---|---|---|
| Seattle | 67 | 99 | 102 | 132 | 3 | — | 403 |
| Opponents | 69 | 134 | 56 | 138 | 0 | — | 397 |

### Attendance
Home 486,036    Away 423,815    Total 909,851
Single game home record, 63,352 (12-4-83)
Single season home record, 487,881 (1979)

## 1983 INDIVIDUAL STATISTICS

### Rushing

| | Att. | Yds. | Avg. | LG | TD |
|---|---|---|---|---|---|
| Warner | 335 | 1449 | 4.3 | 60 | 13 |
| Hughes | 83 | 313 | 3.8 | 26 | 1 |
| Doornink | 40 | 99 | 2.5 | 9 | 2 |
| C. Bryant | 27 | 87 | 3.2 | 9 | 0 |
| Zorn | 30 | 71 | 2.4 | 18t | 1 |
| Krieg | 16 | 55 | 3.4 | 10t | 2 |
| Dixon | 4 | 18 | 4.5 | 6 | 0 |
| T. Brown | 6 | 14 | 2.3 | 6 | 0 |
| Johns | 2 | 12 | 6.0 | 26 | 0 |
| Lane | 3 | 1 | 0.3 | 7 | 0 |
| Seattle | 546 | 2119 | 3.9 | 60 | 19 |
| Opponents | 511 | 2198 | 4.3 | 37 | 14 |

### Passing

| | Att. | Comp. | Pct. | Yds. | TD | Int. | Tkld. | Rate |
|---|---|---|---|---|---|---|---|---|
| Krieg | 243 | 147 | 60.5 | 2139 | 18 | 11 | 38/279 | 95.0 |
| Zorn | 205 | 103 | 50.2 | 1166 | 7 | 7 | 9/64 | 64.8 |
| Largent | 1 | 1 | 100.0 | 11 | 0 | 0 | 0/0 | 112.5 |
| Seattle | 449 | 251 | 55.9 | 3316 | 25 | 18 | 47/343 | 81.3 |
| Opponents | 521 | 311 | 59.7 | 4182 | 33 | 26 | 43/351 | 85.6 |

### Receiving

| | No. | Yds. | Avg. | LG | TD |
|---|---|---|---|---|---|
| Largent | 72 | 1074 | 14.9 | 46t | 11 |
| Warner | 42 | 325 | 7.7 | 28 | 1 |
| Young | 36 | 529 | 14.7 | 47 | 2 |
| Johns | 34 | 486 | 14.3 | 30t | 4 |
| Doornink | 24 | 328 | 13.7 | 47 | 2 |
| Walker | 12 | 248 | 20.7 | 50t | 2 |
| Hughes | 10 | 100 | 10.0 | 33t | 1 |
| H. Jackson | 8 | 126 | 15.8 | 29 | 1 |
| Metzelaars | 7 | 72 | 10.3 | 17t | 1 |
| C. Bryant | 3 | 8 | 2.7 | 3 | 0 |
| Lane | 2 | 9 | 4.5 | 7 | 0 |
| Krieg | 1 | 11 | 11.0 | 11 | 0 |
| Seattle | 251 | 3316 | 13.2 | 50t | 25 |
| Opponents | 311 | 4182 | 13.4 | 78t | 33 |

### Interceptions

| | No. | Yds. | Avg. | LG | TD |
|---|---|---|---|---|---|
| Easley | 7 | 106 | 15.1 | 48 | 0 |
| D. Brown | 6 | 83 | 13.8 | 37 | 0 |
| Simpson | 4 | 39 | 9.8 | 14 | 0 |
| Harris | 2 | 15 | 7.5 | 10 | 0 |
| Green | 1 | 73 | 73.0 | 73t | 1 |
| Moyer | 1 | 19 | 19.0 | 19t | 1 |
| Robinson | 1 | 18 | 18.0 | 18 | 0 |
| Scholtz | 1 | 8 | 8.0 | 8 | 0 |
| Justin | 1 | 2 | 2.0 | 2 | 0 |
| Butler | 1 | 0 | 0.0 | 0 | 0 |
| Williams | 1 | 0 | 0.0 | 0 | 0 |
| Seattle | 26 | 363 | 14.0 | 73t | 2 |
| Opponents | 18 | 279 | 15.5 | 40t | 1 |

### Punting

| | No. | Yds. | Avg. | In 20 | LG |
|---|---|---|---|---|---|
| West | 79 | 3118 | 39.5 | 25 | 56 |
| Seattle | 79 | 3118 | 39.5 | 25 | 56 |
| Opponents | 68 | 2754 | 40.5 | 14 | 58 |

### Punt Returns

| | No. | FC | Yds. | Avg. | LG | TD |
|---|---|---|---|---|---|---|
| Johns | 28 | 5 | 316 | 11.3 | 75t | 1 |
| G. Johnson | 3 | 1 | 17 | 5.7 | 10 | 0 |
| Harris | 2 | 0 | 27 | 13.5 | 14 | 0 |
| Easley | 1 | 0 | 6 | 6.0 | 6 | 0 |
| Seattle | 34 | 6 | 366 | 10.8 | 75t | 1 |
| Opponents | 36 | 18 | 185 | 5.1 | 16 | 0 |

### Kickoff Returns

| | No. | Yds. | Avg. | LG | TD |
|---|---|---|---|---|---|
| Dixon | 49 | 1148 | 23.4 | 94t | 1 |
| Hughes | 12 | 282 | 23.5 | 35 | 0 |
| Lane | 4 | 58 | 14.5 | 18 | 0 |
| McAlister | 3 | 59 | 19.7 | 22 | 0 |
| Tice | 2 | 28 | 14.0 | 19 | 0 |
| Metzelaars | 1 | 0 | 0.0 | 0 | 0 |
| Seattle | 71 | 1575 | 22.2 | 94t | 1 |
| Opponents | 59 | 952 | 16.1 | 45 | 0 |

### Scoring

| | TD | TD R | TD P | TD Rt | PAT | FG | TP |
|---|---|---|---|---|---|---|---|
| N. Johnson | | | | | 49/50 | 18/25 | 103 |
| Warner | 14 | 13 | 1 | 0 | | | 84 |
| Largent | 11 | 0 | 11 | 0 | | | 66 |
| Johns | 5 | 0 | 4 | 1 | | | 30 |
| Doornink | 4 | 2 | 2 | 0 | | | 24 |
| Hughes | 2 | 1 | 1 | 0 | | | 12 |
| Krieg | 2 | 2 | 0 | 0 | | | 12 |
| Robinson | 2 | 0 | 0 | 2 | | | 12 |
| Walker | 2 | 0 | 2 | 0 | | | 12 |
| Young | 2 | 0 | 2 | 0 | | | 12 |
| Dixon | 1 | 0 | 0 | 1 | | | 6 |
| Green | 1 | 0 | 0 | 1 | | | 6 |
| H. Jackson | 1 | 0 | 1 | 0 | | | 6 |
| Metzelaars | 1 | 0 | 1 | 0 | | | 6 |
| Moyer | 1 | 0 | 0 | 1 | | | 6 |
| Zorn | 1 | 1 | 0 | 0 | | | 6 |
| Seattle | 50 | 19 | 25 | 6 | 49/50 | 18/25 | 403 |
| Opponents | 48 | 14 | 33 | 1 | 43/48 | 20/26 | 397 |

## FIRST-ROUND SELECTIONS

(If Club had no first-round selection, first player drafted is listed with round in parentheses.)

| Year | Player, College, Position |
|---|---|
| 1976 | Steve Niehaus, Notre Dame, DT |
| 1977 | Steve August, Tulsa, G |
| 1978 | Keith Simpson, Memphis State, DB |
| 1979 | Manu Tuiasosopo, UCLA, DT |
| 1980 | Jacob Green, Texas A&M, DE |
| 1981 | Ken Easley, UCLA, DB |
| 1982 | Jeff Bryant, Clemson, DE |
| 1983 | Curt Warner, Penn State, RB |
| 1984 | Terry Taylor, Southern Illinois, DB |

## SEATTLE SEAHAWKS 1984 VETERAN ROSTER

| No. | Name | Pos. | Ht. | Wt. | Birth-date | NFL Exp. | College | Birthplace | Residence | Games in '83 |
|-----|------|------|-----|-----|-----------|----------|---------|-----------|-----------|--------------|
| 76 | †August, Steve | T | 6-5 | 258 | 9/4/54 | 8 | Tulsa | Jeanette, Pa. | Redmond, Wash. | 15 |
| 65 | Bailey, Edwin | G | 6-5 | 265 | 5/15/59 | 4 | South Carolina State | Savannah, Ga. | Kirkland, Wash. | 16 |
| 22 | Brown, Dave | CB | 6-2 | 190 | 1/16/53 | 10 | Michigan | Akron, Ohio | Woodinville, Wash. | 16 |
| 32 | †Bryant, Cullen | FB | 6-1 | 236 | 5/20/51 | 12 | Colorado | Fort Sill, Okla. | Broomfield, Colo. | 10 |
| 77 | Bryant, Jeff | DE | 6-5 | 270 | 5/22/60 | 3 | Clemson | Atlanta, Ga. | Decatur, Ga. | 16 |
| 59 | Bush, Blair | C | 6-3 | 252 | 11/25/56 | 7 | Washington | Fort Hood, Tex. | Seattle, Wash. | 16 |
| 53 | Butler, Keith | LB | 6-4 | 225 | 5/16/56 | 7 | Memphis State | Anniston, Ala. | Bothell, Wash. | 16 |
| 83 | Castor, Chris | WR | 6-0 | 170 | 8/13/60 | 2 | Duke | Burlington, N.C. | Bellevue, Wash. | 8 |
| 31 | Dixon, Zachary | RB | 6-1 | 204 | 3/5/57 | 6 | Temple | Dorchester, Mass. | Owings Mills, Md. | 15* |
| 33 | Doornink, Dan | FB | 6-3 | 210 | 2/1/56 | 7 | Washington State | Wapato, Wash. | Kirkland, Wash. | 16 |
| 35 | Dufek, Don | S | 6-0 | 195 | 4/28/54 | 8 | Michigan | Ann Arbor, Mich. | Redmond, Wash. | 14 |
| 66 | Dugan, Bill | G | 6-3 | 271 | 6/5/59 | 4 | Penn State | Hornell, N.Y. | Hornell, N.Y. | 15 |
| 45 | Easley, Kenny | S | 6-3 | 205 | 1/15/59 | 4 | UCLA | Chesapeake, Va. | Kirkland, Wash. | 16 |
| 64 | Essink, Ron | T | 6-6 | 260 | 7/30/58 | 5 | Grand Valley State | Zeeland, Mich. | Kirkland, Wash. | 16 |
| 50 | Flones, Brian | LB | 6-1 | 228 | 9/1/59 | 3 | Washington State | Mt. Vernon, Wash. | Redmond, Wash. | 0* |
| 56 | Gaines, Greg | LB | 6-3 | 220 | 10/16/58 | 3 | Tennessee | Martinsville, Va. | Knoxville, Tenn. | 15 |
| 79 | Green, Jacob | DE | 6-3 | 255 | 1/21/57 | 5 | Texas A&M | Pasadena, Tex. | Bellevue, Wash. | 16 |
| 75 | †Hardy, Robert | NT | 6-2 | 250 | 7/3/56 | 5 | Jackson State | Tulsa, Okla. | Issaquah, Wash. | 0* |
| 44 | Harris, John | S | 6-2 | 200 | 6/13/56 | 7 | Arizona State | Fort Benning, Ga. | Woodinville, Wash. | 16 |
| 69 | Hernandez, Matt | T | 6-6 | 260 | 10/16/61 | 2 | Purdue | Detroit, Mich. | East Detroit, Mich. | 8 |
| 63 | Hicks, Mark | LB | 6-2 | 225 | 11/7/60 | 2 | Arizona State | Los Angeles, Calif. | Los Angeles, Calif. | 8 |
| 46 | Hughes, David | FB | 6-0 | 220 | 6/1/59 | 4 | Boise State | Honolulu, Hawaii | Kirkland, Wash. | 16 |
| 70 | Irvin, Darrell | DE | 6-4 | 255 | 1/21/57 | 5 | Oklahoma | Pawhuska, Okla. | Bellevue, Wash. | 16 |
| 29 | †Jackson, Harold | WR | 5-10 | 175 | 1/6/46 | 17 | Jackson State | Hattiesburg, Miss. | Los Angeles, Calif. | 15 |
| 55 | Jackson, Michael | LB | 6-1 | 220 | 7/15/57 | 6 | Washington | Pasco, Wash. | Bellevue, Wash. | 11 |
|  | t-Jackson, Terry | CB | 5-11 | 197 | 12/9/55 | 7 | San Diego State | Sherman, Tex. | Secaucus, N.J. | 12 |
| 85 | Johns, Paul | WR | 5-11 | 170 | 11/14/58 | 4 | Tulsa | Waco, Tex. | Redmond, Wash. | 11 |
| 9 | †Johnson, Norm | K | 6-2 | 193 | 5/31/60 | 3 | UCLA | Inglewood, Calif. | Redmond, Wash. | 16 |
| 62 | Kauahi, Kani | C | 6-2 | 260 | 9/6/59 | 3 | Hawaii | Kehaka, Hawaii | De Soto, Tex. | 10 |
| 17 | Krieg, Dave | QB | 6-1 | 185 | 10/20/58 | 5 | Milton | Iola, Wis. | Rothschild, Wis. | 9 |
| 37 | †Lane, Eric | RB | 6-0 | 195 | 1/6/59 | 4 | Brigham Young | Oakland, Calif. | Edmonds, Wash. | 16 |
| 80 | Largent, Steve | WR | 5-10 | 184 | 9/28/54 | 9 | Tulsa | Tulsa, Okla. | Sapulpa, Okla. | 15 |
| 67 | McKenzie, Reggie | G | 6-5 | 255 | 7/27/50 | 13 | Michigan | Detroit, Mich. | Kirkland, Wash. | 14 |
| 51 | Merriman, Sam | LB | 6-3 | 225 | 5/5/61 | 2 | Idaho | Tucson, Ariz. | Kirkland, Wash. | 16 |
| 88 | †Metzelaars, Pete | TE | 6-7 | 240 | 5/24/60 | 3 | Wabash | Three Rivers, Mich. | Woodinville, Wash. | 16 |
| 21 | Moyer, Paul | S | 6-1 | 201 | 7/26/61 | 2 | Arizona State | Anaheim, Calif. | Villa Park, Calif. | 16 |
| 72 | Nash, Joe | NT | 6-3 | 250 | 10/11/60 | 3 | Boston College | Boston, Mass. | West Roxbury, Mass. | 16 |
| 52 | †Norman, Joe | LB | 6-1 | 220 | 10/15/56 | 5 | Indiana | Millersburg, Ohio | Bellevue, Wash. | 11 |
| 61 | Pratt, Robert | G | 6-4 | 250 | 5/25/51 | 11 | North Carolina | Richmond, Va. | Richmond, Va. | 15 |
| 57 | Robinson, Shelton | LB | 6-2 | 233 | 9/14/60 | 3 | North Carolina | Goldsboro, N.C. | Kirkland, Wash. | 16 |
| 58 | Scholtz, Bruce | LB | 6-6 | 240 | 9/26/58 | 3 | Texas | La Grange, Tex. | Bellevue, Wash. | 16 |
| 42 | Simpson, Keith | CB | 6-1 | 195 | 3/9/56 | 7 | Memphis State | Memphis, Tenn. | Kirkland, Wash. | 14 |
| 86 | Tice, Mike | TE | 6-7 | 250 | 2/2/59 | 4 | Maryland | Bayshore, N.Y. | Woodinville, Wash. | 15 |
| 89 | Walker, Byron | WR | 6-4 | 190 | 7/28/60 | 3 | Citadel | Scott Base, Ill. | Warner Robins, Ga. | 16 |
| 28 | Warner, Curt | RB | 5-11 | 205 | 3/18/61 | 2 | Penn State | Wyoming, W. Va. | Pineville, W. Va. | 16 |
| 8 | †West, Jeff | P | 6-2 | 205 | 4/6/53 | 9 | Cincinnati | Ravenna, Ohio | Redmond, Wash. | 16 |
| 54 | Williams, Eugene | LB | 6-1 | 220 | 6/15/60 | 3 | Tulsa | Longview, Tex. | Longview, Tex. | 4 |
| 87 | †Young, Charle | TE | 6-4 | 234 | 2/5/51 | 12 | Southern California | Fresno, Calif. | Woodinville, Wash. | 12 |
| 10 | Zorn, Jim | QB | 6-2 | 200 | 5/10/53 | 9 | Cal Poly-Pomona | Whittier, Calif. | Mercer Island, Wash. | 16 |

* Dixon played 2 games with Baltimore, 13 with Seattle in '83; Flones and Hardy missed '83 season due to injuries.

†Option playout; subject to developments.

t-Seahawks traded for T. Jackson (New York Giants).

Traded—Nose tackle Manu Tuiasosopo to San Francisco.

Also played with Seahawks in '83—RB Theotis Brown (3 games), DE Sam Clancy (13), CB Greggory Johnson (16), CB Kerry Justin (16), S Ken McAlister (2), LB Gary Wimmer (3).

## COACHING STAFF

### Head Coach, Chuck Knox

**Pro Career:** Named head coach of Seahawks on January 26, 1983 after five seasons as head coach of Buffalo where he led Bills to AFC East title in 1980. Led Los Angeles Rams to five straight NFC West titles before taking over Bills in 1978. Pro assistant with New York Jets 1963-66, coaching offensive line, before moving to Detroit in 1967. Served Lions in same capacity until named head coach of Rams in 1973. No pro playing experience. Career record: 106-66-1.

**Background:** Played tackle for Juniata College in Huntington, Pa., 1950-53. Was assistant coach at his alma mater in 1954, then spent 1955 season as line coach at Ellwood City High School in Pennsylvania. Moved to Wake Forest as an assistant coach for 1959-60, then Kentucky in 1961-62.

**Personal:** Born April 27, 1932 in Sewickley, Pa. Chuck and his wife, Shirley, live in Bellevue and have four children—Chris, Kathy, Colleen, and Chuck.

### Assistant Coaches

**Tom Catlin,** assistant head coach-defensive coordinator-linebackers; born September 8, 1931, Ponca City, Okla., lives in Kirkland. Center-linebacker Oklahoma 1950-52. Pro linebacker Cleveland Browns 1953-54, 1957-58, Philadelphia Eagles 1959. College coach: Army 1956. Pro coach: Dallas Texans-Kansas City Chiefs 1960-65, Los Angeles Rams 1966-77, Buffalo Bills 1978-82, joined Seahawks in 1983.

**George Dyer,** defensive line; born May 4, 1940, Alhambra, Calif., lives in Redmond. Center-linebacker U.C. Santa Barbara 1961-63. No pro playing experience. College coach: Humboldt State 1964-66, Coalinga, Calif., J.C. 1967 (head coach), Portland State 1968-71, Idaho 1972, San Jose State 1973, Michigan State 1977-79, Arizona State 1980-81. Pro coach: Winnipeg Blue Bombers (CFL) 1974-76 (head coach), Buffalo Bills 1982, joined Seahawks in 1983.

**Chick Harris,** offensive backfield; born September 21, 1945, Durham, N.C., lives in Redmond. Running back Northern Arizona 1966-69. No pro playing experience. College coach: Colorado State 1970-72, Long Beach State 1973-74, Washington 1975-80. Pro coach: Buffalo Bills 1981-82, joined Seahawks in 1983.

**Ralph Hawkins,** defensive backfield; born May 4, 1935, Washington, D.C., lives in Redmond. Quarterback-defensive back Maryland 1953-55. Pro defensive back New York Titans (AFL) 1960. College coach: Maryland 1959-60, 1967, Southern Methodist 1961, Kentucky 1962-65, Army 1966, Cincinnati 1968. Pro coach: Buffalo Bills 1969-71, 1981-82, Washington Redskins 1973-77, Baltimore Colts 1978, New York Giants 1979-80, joined Seahawks in 1983.

**Ken Meyer,** quarterbacks; born July 14, 1926, Erie, Pa., lives in Bellevue. Quarterback Denison 1947-50. No pro playing experience. College coach: Denison 1952-57, Wake Forest 1958-59, Florida State 1960-62, Alabama 1963-67, Tulane 1981-82. Pro coach: San Francisco 49ers 1968, 1977 (head coach), New York Jets 1969-72, Los Angeles Rams 1973-76, Chicago Bears 1978-80, joined Seahawks in 1983.

**Steve Moore,** receivers; born August 19, 1947, Los Angeles, Calif., lives in Bellevue. Running back U.C. Santa Barbara 1968-69. No pro playing experience. College coach: U.C. Santa Barbara 1970-71, Army 1975, Rice 1976-77. Pro coach: Buffalo Bills 1978-82, joined Seahawks in 1983.

**Ray Prochaska,** offensive coordinator-offensive line; born August 9, 1919, Ulysses, Neb., lives in Redmond. End Nebraska 1939-40. Pro end Cleveland Rams 1941. College coach: Nebraska 1946-54. Pro coach: Edmonton (CFL) 1955-57, Chicago-St. Louis Cardinals 1958-65, Los Angeles Rams 1966-70, 1973-77, Cleveland Browns 1971-72, Buffalo Bills 1978-82, joined Seahawks in 1983.

**Rusty Tillman,** tight ends-special teams; born February 27, 1948, Beloit, Wis., lives in Kirkland. Linebacker Northern Arizona 1967-69. Pro linebacker Washington Redskins 1970-77. Pro coach: Joined Seahawks in 1979.

**Joe Vitt,** special assignments; born August 23, 1954, Camden, N.J., lives in Kirkland. Linebacker Towson State 1973-75. No pro playing experience. Pro coach: Baltimore Colts 1979-81, joined Seahawks in 1982.

## SEATTLE SEAHAWKS 1984 FIRST-YEAR ROSTER

| Name | Pos. | Ht. | Wt. | Birth-date | College | Birthplace | Residence | How Acq. |
|------|------|-----|-----|-----------|---------|-----------|-----------|----------|
| Gemza, Steve | T | 6-8 | 277 | 1/6/61 | UCLA | Dayton, Ohio | Los Angeles, Calif. | D11 |
| Hagood, Rickey | NT | 6-2 | 295 | 4/24/61 | South Carolina | Easley, S.C. | West Columbia, S.C. | D4 |
| Kaiser, John | LB | 6-3 | 221 | 6/6/62 | Arizona | Oconomowoc, Wis. | Tucson, Ariz. | D6 |
| Morris, Randall | RB | 6-0 | 183 | 4/22/62 | Tennessee | Anniston, Ala. | Knoxville, Tenn. | D10 |
| Puzar, John | C | 6-6 | 255 | 6/27/62 | Long Beach State | Los Angeles, Calif. | Long Beach, Calif. | D8 |
| Schreiber, Adam | G | 6-4 | 250 | 2/20/62 | Texas | Galveston, Tex. | Austin, Tex. | D9 |
| Slater, Sam | T | 6-8 | 277 | 6/8/62 | Weber State | Bronxville, N.Y. | Ogden, Utah | D7 |
| Taylor, Terry | CB | 5-10 | 175 | 7/18/61 | Southern Illinois | Warren, Ohio | Youngstown, Ohio | D1 |
| Turner, Daryl | WR | 6-3 | 198 | 12/15/61 | Michigan State | Wadley, Ga. | East Lansing, Mich. | D2 |
| Windham, Theo | CB | 6-1 | 195 | 5/22/61 | Utah State | Birmingham, Ala. | Logan, Utah | D12 |
| Young, Fred | LB | 6-1 | 220 | 11/14/61 | New Mexico State | Dallas, Tex. | Las Cruces, N.M. | D3 |

Players who report to an NFL team for the first time are designated on rosters as rookies (R). If a player reported to an NFL training camp in a previous year but was not on the active squad for three or more regular season or postseason games, he is listed on the first-year roster and designated by a (1). Thereafter, a player who is on the active squad for three or more regular season or postseason games is credited with an additional year of playing experience.

## NOTES

_____

_____

_____

_____

_____

_____

_____

_____

_____

_____

_____

_____

_____

_____

_____

_____

_____

_____

_____

_____

# THE NFC

Atlanta Falcons

Chicago Bears

Dallas Cowboys

Detroit Lions

Green Bay Packers

Los Angeles Rams

Minnesota Vikings

New Orleans Saints

New York Giants

Philadelphia Eagles

St. Louis Cardinals

San Francisco 49ers

Tampa Bay Buccaneers

Washington Redskins

## National Football Conference
## Western Division

**Team Colors:** Red, Black, White, and Silver

**Suwanee Road at I-85**
**Suwanee, Georgia 30174**
**Telephone: (404) 588-1111**

**Club Officials**

Chairman of the Board: Rankin M. Smith, Sr.
President: Rankin Smith, Jr.
Executive Vice President: Eddie LeBaron
General Manager: Tom Braatz
Corporate Secretary: Taylor Smith
Chief Financial Officer: Jim Hay
Director of Pro Personnel: Bill Jobko
Scouts: Bob Cegelski, John Jelacic, Bob Riggle,
  Bill Striegel
Ticket Manager: Ken Grantham
Public Relations Director: Charlie Dayton
Assistant Director of Public Relations:
  Bob Dickinson
Assistant Director of Community Affairs:
  Carol Henderson
Head Trainer: Jerry Rhea
Assistant Trainer: Billy Brooks
Equipment Manager: Whitey Zimmerman
Assistant Equipment Manager: Horace Daniel

**Stadium:** Atlanta-Fulton County Stadium •
  **Capacity:** 60,748
  521 Capitol Avenue, S.W.
  Atlanta, Georgia 30312
**Playing Surface:** Grass
**Training Camp:** Suwanee Road at I-85
  Suwanee, Georgia 30174

## 1984 SCHEDULE

**Preseason**

| | | |
|---|---|---|
| Aug. 4 | at Minnesota | 7:00 |
| Aug. 11 | at New Orleans | 7:00 |
| Aug. 18 | **Tampa Bay** | 8:00 |
| Aug. 24 | **Denver** | 8:00 |

**Regular Season**

| | | |
|---|---|---|
| Sept. 2 | at New Orleans | 12:00 |
| Sept. 9 | **Detroit** | 1:00 |
| Sept. 16 | at Minnesota | 12:00 |
| Sept. 23 | **Houston** | 1:00 |
| Sept. 30 | at San Francisco | 1:00 |
| Oct. 7 | at Los Angeles Rams | 1:00 |
| Oct. 14 | **New York Giants** | 1:00 |
| Oct. 22 | **L.A. Rams** (Monday) | 9:00 |
| Oct. 28 | at Pittsburgh | 4:00 |
| Nov. 5 | at Washington (Monday) | 9:00 |
| Nov. 11 | **New Orleans** | 1:00 |
| Nov. 18 | **Cleveland** | 1:00 |
| Nov. 25 | at Cincinnati | 1:00 |
| Dec. 2 | **San Francisco** | 1:00 |
| Dec. 9 | at Tampa Bay | 1:00 |
| Dec. 16 | **Philadelphia** | 4:00 |

## FALCONS COACHING HISTORY

### (104-153-4)

| | | |
|---|---|---|
| 1966-68 | Norb Hecker* | 4-26-1 |
| 1968-74 | Norm Van Brocklin** | 37-49-3 |
| 1974-76 | Marion Campbell*** | 6-19-0 |
| 1976 | Pat Peppler | 3-6-0 |
| 1977-82 | Leeman Bennett | 47-44-0 |
| 1983 | Dan Henning | 7-9-0 |

*Released after three games in 1968
**Released after eight games in 1974
***Released after five games in 1976

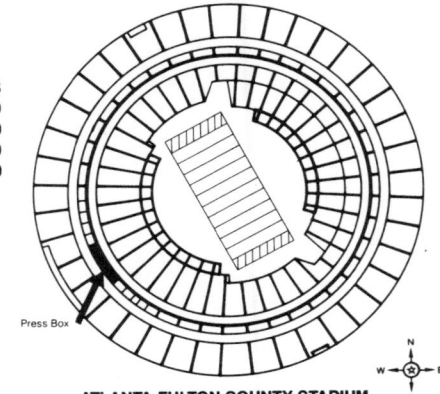

Press Box

**ATLANTA-FULTON COUNTY STADIUM**

## RECORD HOLDERS

### Individual Records—Career

| Category | Name | Performance |
|---|---|---|
| Rushing (Yds.) | William Andrews, 1979-1983 | 5,772 |
| Passing (Yds.) | Steve Bartkowski, 1975-1983 | 20,572 |
| Passing (TDs) | Steve Bartkowski, 1975-1983 | 138 |
| Receiving (No.) | Alfred Jenkins, 1975-1983 | 359 |
| Receiving (Yds.) | Alfred Jenkins, 1975-1983 | 6,257 |
| Interceptions | Rolland Lawrence, 1973-1981 | 39 |
| Punting (Avg.) | Billy Lothridge, 1966-1971 | 44.3 |
| Punt Return (Avg.) | Al Dodd, 1973-74 | 11.8 |
| Kickoff Return (Avg.) | Ron Smith, 1966-67 | 24.3 |
| Field Goals | Nick Mike-Mayer, 1973-77 | 56 |
| Touchdowns (Tot.) | Alfred Jenkins, 1975-1983 | 40 |
| | William Andrews, 1979-1983 | 40 |
| Points | Nick Mike-Mayer, 1973-77 | 270 |

### Individual Records—Single Season

| Category | Name | Performance |
|---|---|---|
| Rushing (Yds.) | William Andrews, 1983 | 1,567 |
| Passing (Yds.) | Steve Bartkowski, 1981 | 3,830 |
| Passing (TDs) | Steve Bartkowski, 1980 | 31 |
| Receiving (No.) | William Andrews, 1981 | 81 |
| Receiving (Yds.) | Alfred Jenkins, 1981 | 1,358 |
| Interceptions | Rolland Lawrence, 1975 | 9 |
| Punting (Avg.) | Billy Lothridge, 1968 | 44.3 |
| Punt Return (Avg.) | Gerald Tinker, 1974 | 13.9 |
| Kickoff Return (Avg.) | Dennis Pearson, 1978 | 26.7 |
| Field Goals | Nick Mike-Mayer, 1973 | 26 |
| Touchdowns (Tot.) | Alfred Jenkins, 1981 | 13 |
| Points | Mick Luckhurst, 1981 | 114 |

### Individual Records—Single Game

| Category | Name | Performance |
|---|---|---|
| Rushing (Yds.) | William Andrews, 9-2-79 | 167 |
| Passing (Yds.) | Steve Bartkowski, 11-15-81 | 416 |
| Passing (TDs) | Randy Johnson, 11-16-69 | 4 |
| | Steve Bartkowski, 10-19-80, 10-18-81 | 4 |
| Receiving (No.) | William Andrews, 11-15-81 | 15 |
| Receiving (Yds.) | Ken Burrow, 10-3-71, 12-19-71 | 190 |
| Interceptions | Many times | 2 |
| | Last time by Kenny Johnson, 11-27-83 | |
| Field Goals | Nick Mike-Mayer, 11-4-73 | 5 |
| | Last time by Tim Mazzetti, 10-30-78 | 5 |
| Touchdowns (Tot.) | Many times | 3 |
| | Last time by William Andrews, 12-18-83 | |
| Points | Many times | 18 |
| | Last time by William Andrews, 12-18-83 | |

## 1983 TEAM STATISTICS

| | Atlanta | Opp. |
|---|---|---|
| Total First Downs | 325 | 342 |
| Rushing | 118 | 139 |
| Passing | 190 | 187 |
| Penalty | 17 | 16 |
| Third Down Efficiency | 108/223 | 95/202 |
| Third Down Percentage | 48.4 | 47.0 |
| Total Net Yards | 5628 | 5826 |
| Total Offensive Plays | 1054 | 1023 |
| Avg. Gain per Play | 5.3 | 5.7 |
| Avg. Gain per Game | 351.8 | 364.1 |
| Net Yards Rushing | 2224 | 2309 |
| Total Rushing Plays | 492 | 499 |
| Avg. Gain per Rush | 4.5 | 4.6 |
| Avg. Gain Rushing per Game | 139.0 | 144.3 |
| Net Yards Passing | 3404 | 3517 |
| Lost Attempting to Pass | 55/389 | 31/217 |
| Gross Yards Passing | 3793 | 3734 |
| Attempts/Completions | 507/321 | 493/313 |
| Percent Completed | 63.3 | 63.5 |
| Had Intercepted | 10 | 15 |
| Avg. Net Passing per Game | 212.8 | 219.8 |
| Punts/Avg. | 71/39.8 | 67/42.0 |
| Punt Returns/Avg. | 46/10.6 | 34/5.3 |
| Kickoff Returns/Avg. | 67/18.8 | 60/20.2 |
| Interceptions/Avg. Ret. | 15/14.1 | 10/9.4 |
| Penalties/Yards | 90/806 | 81/710 |
| Fumbles/Ball Lost | 36/19 | 26/15 |
| Total Points | 370 | 389 |
| Avg. Points per Game | 23.1 | 24.3 |
| Touchdowns | 46 | 49 |
| Rushing | 17 | 20 |
| Passing | 24 | 28 |
| Returns and Recoveries | 5 | 1 |
| Field Goals | 17/22 | 17/26 |
| Conversions | 43/45 | 44/49 |
| Safeties | 0 | 0 |
| Avg. Time of Possession | 30:12 | 29:48 |

## 1983 TEAM RECORD
### Preseason (2-2)

| Date | Atlanta | | Opponents |
|---|---|---|---|
| 8/6 | 13 | *Washington (OT) | 10 |
| 8/13 | 10 | Denver | 21 |
| 8/20 | 6 | Tampa Bay | 17 |
| 8/26 | 10 | *Baltimore | 7 |
| | 39 | | 55 |

### Regular Season (7-9)

| Date | Atlanta | | Opp. | Att. |
|---|---|---|---|---|
| 9/4 | 20 | Chicago | 17 | 60,165 |
| 9/11 | 13 | *New York Giants (OT) | 16 | 52,850 |
| 9/18 | 30 | Detroit | 14 | 54,622 |
| 9/25 | 20 | San Francisco | 24 | 57,814 |
| 10/2 | 24 | *Philadelphia | 28 | 50,621 |
| 10/9 | 17 | *New Orleans | 19 | 51,654 |
| 10/16 | 21 | Los Angeles Rams | 27 | 50,404 |
| 10/23 | 27 | New York Jets | 21 | 46,878 |
| 10/30 | 24 | *New England | 13 | 47,546 |
| 11/6 | 10 | New Orleans | 27 | 67,062 |
| 11/14 | 13 | *Los Angeles Rams | 36 | 31,203 |
| 11/20 | 28 | *San Francisco | 24 | 32,782 |
| 11/27 | 47 | *Green Bay (OT) | 41 | 35,688 |
| 12/4 | 21 | Washington | 37 | 52,074 |
| 12/10 | 24 | Miami | 31 | 56,725 |
| 12/18 | 31 | *Buffalo | 14 | 31,015 |
| | 370 | | 389 | 779,103 |

*Home Game    (OT) Overtime

### Score by Periods

| | | | | | | | |
|---|---|---|---|---|---|---|---|
| Atlanta | 25 | 127 | 68 | 144 | 6 | — | 370 |
| Opponents | 69 | 113 | 99 | 105 | 3 | — | 389 |

### Attendance
Home 333,359    Away 445,744    Total 779,103
Single game home record, 59,257 (10-30-77)
Single season home record, 442,457 (1980)

## 1983 INDIVIDUAL STATISTICS

### Rushing

| | Att. | Yds. | Avg. | LG | TD |
|---|---|---|---|---|---|
| Andrews | 331 | 1567 | 4.7 | 27 | 7 |
| Riggs | 100 | 437 | 4.4 | 40t | 8 |
| B. Johnson | 15 | 83 | 5.5 | 36 | 0 |
| Cain | 19 | 63 | 3.3 | 10 | 1 |
| Bartkowski | 16 | 38 | 2.4 | 10 | 1 |
| Giacomarro | 2 | 13 | 6.5 | 13 | 0 |
| Moroski | 2 | 12 | 6.0 | 7 | 0 |
| Robinson | 3 | 9 | 3.0 | 7 | 0 |
| Williams | 1 | 5 | 5.0 | 5 | 0 |
| J. Miller | 1 | 2 | 2.0 | 2 | 0 |
| Bailey | 2 | -5 | -2.5 | 0 | 0 |
| Atlanta | 492 | 2224 | 4.5 | 40t | 17 |
| Opponents | 499 | 2309 | 4.6 | 78t | 20 |

### Passing

| | Att. | Comp. | Pct. | Yds. | TD | Int. | Tkld. | Rate |
|---|---|---|---|---|---|---|---|---|
| Bartkowski | 432 | 274 | 63.4 | 3167 | 22 | 5 | 51/348 | 97.6 |
| Moroski | 70 | 45 | 64.3 | 575 | 2 | 4 | 4/41 | 75.6 |
| Hodge | 2 | 1 | 50.0 | 28 | 0 | 1 | 0/0 | 56.3 |
| Andrews | 1 | 0 | 0.0 | 0 | 0 | 0 | 0/0 | 39.6 |
| Giacomarro | 1 | 1 | 100.0 | 23 | 0 | 0 | 0/0 | 118.8 |
| B. Johnson | 1 | 0 | 0.0 | 0 | 0 | 0 | 0/0 | 39.6 |
| Atlanta | 507 | 321 | 63.3 | 3793 | 24 | 10 | 55/389 | 93.6 |
| Opponents | 493 | 313 | 63.5 | 3734 | 28 | 15 | 31/217 | 92.8 |

### Receiving

| | No. | Yds. | Avg. | LG | TD |
|---|---|---|---|---|---|
| B. Johnson | 64 | 709 | 11.1 | 47t | 4 |
| Andrews | 59 | 609 | 10.3 | 40 | 4 |
| Bailey | 55 | 881 | 16.0 | 53 | 6 |
| Jenkins | 38 | 487 | 12.8 | 26 | 1 |
| Hodge | 25 | 280 | 11.2 | 76t | 4 |
| Riggs | 17 | 149 | 8.8 | 25 | 0 |
| J. Miller | 16 | 125 | 7.8 | 19 | 0 |
| Jackson | 13 | 220 | 16.9 | 54t | 3 |
| Robinson | 12 | 100 | 8.3 | 15 | 0 |
| Cox | 9 | 83 | 9.2 | 19 | 1 |
| Young | 6 | 74 | 12.3 | 19 | 1 |
| Matthews | 3 | 37 | 12.3 | 23 | 0 |
| Cain | 3 | 24 | 8.0 | 11 | 0 |
| Curran | 1 | 15 | 15.0 | 15 | 0 |
| Atlanta | 321 | 3793 | 11.8 | 76t | 24 |
| Opponents | 313 | 3734 | 11.9 | 61t | 28 |

### Interceptions

| | No. | Yds. | Avg. | LG | TD |
|---|---|---|---|---|---|
| Pridemore | 4 | 56 | 14.0 | 25 | 0 |
| Butler | 4 | 12 | 3.0 | 12 | 0 |
| Glazebrook | 3 | 30 | 10.0 | 25 | 0 |
| K. Johnson | 2 | 57 | 28.5 | 31t | 2 |
| Richardson | 1 | 38 | 38.0 | 38 | 0 |
| Jones | 1 | 19 | 19.0 | 19 | 0 |
| Atlanta | 15 | 212 | 14.1 | 38 | 2 |
| Opponents | 10 | 94 | 9.4 | 26 | 0 |

### Punting

| | No. | Yds. | Avg. | In 20 | LG |
|---|---|---|---|---|---|
| Giacomarro | 70 | 2823 | 40.3 | 18 | 57 |
| Atlanta | 71 | 2823 | 39.8 | 18 | 57 |
| Opponents | 67 | 2812 | 42.0 | 12 | 66 |

### Punt Returns

| | No. | FC | Yds. | Avg. | LG | TD |
|---|---|---|---|---|---|---|
| B. Johnson | 46 | 4 | 489 | 10.6 | 71t | 1 |
| Atlanta | 46 | 4 | 489 | 10.6 | 71t | 1 |
| Opponents | 34 | 12 | 179 | 5.3 | 22 | 0 |

### Kickoff Returns

| | No. | Yds. | Avg. | LG | TD |
|---|---|---|---|---|---|
| Williams | 23 | 461 | 20.0 | 34 | 0 |
| Riggs | 17 | 330 | 19.4 | 35 | 0 |
| K. Johnson | 11 | 224 | 20.4 | 28 | 0 |
| Cain | 11 | 200 | 18.2 | 24 | 0 |
| Curran | 2 | 26 | 13.0 | 16 | 0 |
| Glazebrook | 2 | 0 | 0.0 | 0 | 0 |
| Butler | 1 | 17 | 17.0 | 17 | 0 |
| Atlanta | 67 | 1258 | 18.8 | 35 | 0 |
| Opponents | 60 | 1212 | 20.2 | 73 | 0 |

### Scoring

| | TD | TD R | TD P | TD Rt | PAT | FG | TP |
|---|---|---|---|---|---|---|---|
| Luckhurst | | | | | 43/45 | 17/22 | 94 |
| Andrews | 11 | 7 | 4 | 0 | | | 66 |
| Riggs | 8 | 8 | 0 | 0 | | | 48 |
| Bailey | 6 | 0 | 6 | 0 | | | 36 |
| B. Johnson | 5 | 0 | 4 | 1 | | | 30 |
| Hodge | 4 | 0 | 4 | 0 | | | 24 |
| Jackson | 3 | 0 | 3 | 0 | | | 18 |
| K. Johnson | 2 | 0 | 0 | 2 | | | 12 |
| Bartkowski | 1 | 1 | 0 | 0 | | | 6 |
| Cain | 1 | 1 | 0 | 0 | | | 6 |
| Cox | 1 | 0 | 1 | 0 | | | 6 |
| Gaison | 1 | 0 | 0 | 1 | | | 6 |
| Jenkins | 1 | 0 | 1 | 0 | | | 6 |
| Rade | 1 | 0 | 0 | 1 | | | 6 |
| Young | 1 | 0 | 1 | 0 | | | 6 |
| Atlanta | 46 | 17 | 24 | 5 | 43/45 | 17/22 | 370 |
| Opponents | 49 | 20 | 28 | 1 | 44/49 | 17/26 | 389 |

## FIRST-ROUND SELECTIONS

(If Club had no first-round selection, first player drafted is listed with round in parentheses.)

| Year | Player, College, Position |
|---|---|
| 1966 | Tommy Nobis, Texas, LB |
| | Randy Johnson, Texas A&I, QB |
| 1967 | Leo Carroll, San Diego State, DE (2) |
| 1968 | Claude Humphrey, Tennessee State, DE |
| 1969 | George Kunz, Notre Dame, T |
| 1970 | John Small, Citadel, LB |
| 1971 | Joe Profit, Northeast Louisiana, RB |
| 1972 | Clarence Ellis, Notre Dame, DB |
| 1973 | Greg Marx, Notre Dame, DT (2) |
| 1974 | Gerald Tinker, Kent State, WR (2) |
| 1975 | Steve Bartkowski, California, QB |
| 1976 | Bubba Bean, Texas A&M, RB |
| 1977 | Warren Bryant, Kentucky, T |
| | Wilson Faumuina, San Jose State, DT |
| 1978 | Mike Kenn, Michigan, T |
| 1979 | Don Smith, Miami, DE |
| 1980 | Junior Miller, Nebraska, TE |
| 1981 | Bobby Butler, Florida State, DB |
| 1982 | Gerald Riggs, Arizona State, RB |
| 1983 | Mike Pitts, Alabama, DE |
| 1984 | Rick Bryan, Oklahoma, DT |

## ATLANTA FALCONS 1984 VETERAN ROSTER

| No. | Name | Pos. | Ht. | Wt. | Birth-date | NFL Exp. | College | Birthplace | Residence | Games in '83 |
|---|---|---|---|---|---|---|---|---|---|---|
| 31 | Andrews, William | RB | 6-0 | 213 | 12/25/55 | 6 | Auburn | Thomasville, Ga. | Duluth, Ga. | 16 |
| 82 | Bailey, Stacey | WR | 6-1 | 160 | 2/10/60 | 3 | San Jose State | San Rafael, Calif. | Duluth, Ga. | 14 |
| 10 | Bartkowski, Steve | QB | 6-4 | 218 | 11/12/52 | 10 | California | Des Moines, Iowa | Cumming, Ga. | 14 |
| 69 | Benish, Dan | DT | 6-5 | 265 | 11/21/61 | 2 | Clemson | Youngstown, Ohio | Lawrenceville, Ga. | 16 |
| 26 | Britt, James | S | 6-0 | 185 | 9/12/60 | 2 | Louisiana State | Minden, La. | Tucker, Ga. | 14 |
| 66 | Bryant, Warren | T | 6-7 | 270 | 11/11/55 | 8 | Kentucky | Miami, Fla. | Roswell, Ga. | 16 |
| 23 | Butler, Bobby | CB | 5-11 | 175 | 5/28/59 | 4 | Florida State | Boynton Beach, Fla. | Norcross, Ga. | 16 |
| 21 | Cain, Lynn | RB | 6-1 | 205 | 10/16/55 | 6 | Southern California | Los Angeles, Calif. | Dunwoody, Ga. | 16 |
| 88 | Cox, Arthur | TE | 6-3 | 245 | 2/5/61 | 2 | Texas Southern | Plant City, Fla. | Doraville, Ga. | 16 |
| 89 | Curran, William | WR | 5-10 | 175 | 12/30/59 | 3 | UCLA | Inglewood, Calif. | Ventura, Calif. | 16 |
| 50 | Curry, Buddy | LB | 6-4 | 228 | 6/4/58 | 5 | North Carolina | Danville, Va. | Norcross, Ga. | 16 |
| 51 | Dixon, Rich | LB | 6-2 | 235 | 8/6/59 | 2 | California | Roswell, N.M. | Berkeley, Calif. | 14 |
| 71 | Dufour, Dan | G | 6-5 | 280 | 10/18/60 | 2 | UCLA | Lynn, Mass. | Norcross, Ga. | 16 |
| 58 | Frye, David | LB | 6-2 | 205 | 6/21/61 | 2 | Purdue | Cincinnati, Ohio | Cincinnati, Ohio | 16 |
| 34 | Gaison, Blane | S | 6-1 | 188 | 5/13/58 | 4 | Hawaii | Kanehoe, Hawaii | Kanehoe, Hawaii | 16 |
| 1 | Giacomarro, Ralph | P | 6-0 | 190 | 1/17/61 | 2 | Penn State | Passaic, N.J. | Alpharetta, Ga. | 16 |
| 36 | Glazebrook, Bob | S | 6-1 | 200 | 3/7/56 | 7 | Fresno State | Fresno, Calif. | Lawrenceville, Ga. | 13 |
| 52 | Harper, John | LB | 6-3 | 230 | 6/12/60 | 2 | Southern Illinois | Memphis, Tenn. | Norcross, Ga. | 11 |
| 30 | Haworth, Steve | CB | 5-11 | 190 | 9/16/61 | 2 | Oklahoma | Clark AFB, Philippines | Norcross, Ga. | 12 |
| 83 | Hodge, Floyd | WR | 6-0 | 190 | 7/18/59 | 3 | Utah | Compton, Calif. | Duluth, Ga. | 4 |
| 85 | Jackson, Alfred | WR | 6-0 | 185 | 8/3/55 | 7 | Texas | Cameron, Tex. | Austin, Tex. | 11 |
| 84 | Jenkins, Alfred | WR | 5-9 | 155 | 1/25/52 | 9 | Morris Brown | Hogansville, Ga. | College Park, Ga. | 16 |
| 81 | Johnson, Billy | WR-KR | 5-9 | 170 | 1/27/52 | 9 | Widener | Bouthwyn, Pa. | Duluth, Ga. | 16 |
| 37 | Johnson, Kenny | CB | 5-11 | 172 | 1/7/58 | 5 | Mississippi State | Moss Point, Miss. | Moss Point, Miss. | 16 |
| 20 | Jones, Earl | CB | 6-1 | 175 | 7/19/57 | 5 | Norfolk State | Tuscaloosa, Ala. | Virginia Beach, Va. | 16 |
| 78 | Kenn, Mike | T | 6-7 | 255 | 2/9/56 | 7 | Michigan | Evanston, Ill. | Roswell, Ga. | 16 |
| 54 | Kuykendall, Fulton | LB | 6-4 | 228 | 6/10/53 | 10 | UCLA | Coronado, Calif. | Roswell, Ga. | 14 |
| 70 | Lee, Ron | G-T | 6-3 | 260 | 12/24/56 | 6 | Baylor | Pine Bluff, Ark. | Miami, Fla. | 12 |
| 55 | Levenick, Dave | LB | 6-3 | 220 | 5/29/59 | 2 | Wisconsin | Milwaukee, Wis. | Roswell, Ga. | 16 |
| 18 | Luckhurst, Mick | K | 6-0 | 180 | 3/31/58 | 4 | California | Redbourn, England | Buford, Ga. | 16 |
| 49 | Matthews, Allama | TE | 6-3 | 230 | 8/24/61 | 2 | Vanderbilt | Jacksonville, Fla. | Jacksonville, Fla. | 16 |
| 87 | Mikeska, Russ | TE | 6-3 | 222 | 9/10/55 | 5 | Texas A&M | Temple, Tex. | Alpharetta, Ga. | 0* |
| 62 | Miller, Brett | T | 6-7 | 275 | 10/2/58 | 2 | Iowa | Lynwood, Calif. | Alpharetta, Ga. | 16 |
| 80 | Miller, Junior | TE | 6-4 | 240 | 11/26/57 | 5 | Nebraska | Midland, Tex. | Lincoln, Neb. | 15 |
| 15 | Moroski, Mike | QB | 6-4 | 200 | 9/4/57 | 6 | Cal-Davis | Novato, Calif. | Cumming, Ga. | 16 |
| 53 | Musser, Neal | LB | 6-3 | 223 | 3/20/57 | 3 | North Carolina State | Elon, N.C. | Doraville, Ga. | 0* |
| 74 | Pitts, Mike | DE | 6-5 | 260 | 9/25/60 | 2 | Alabama | Pell City, Ala. | Tuscaloosa, Ala. | 16 |
| 27 | Pridemore, Tom | S | 5-11 | 186 | 4/29/56 | 7 | West Virginia | Ansted, W. Va. | Lawrenceville, Ga. | 16 |
| 72 | Provence, Andrew | DT | 6-3 | 265 | 3/8/61 | 2 | South Carolina | Savannah, Ga. | Duluth, Ga. | 16 |
| 59 | Rade, John | LB | 6-1 | 220 | 8/31/60 | 2 | Boise State | Ceres, Calif. | Modesto, Calif. | 16 |
| 56 | Richardson, Al | LB | 6-3 | 220 | 9/23/57 | 5 | Georgia Tech | Miami, Fla. | Stone Mountain, Ga. | 5 |
| 42 | Riggs, Gerald | RB | 6-1 | 230 | 11/6/60 | 3 | Arizona State | Tulluha, La. | Alpharetta, Ga. | 16 |
| 33 | Robinson, Bo | RB | 6-2 | 235 | 5/27/56 | 6 | West Texas State | LaMesa, Tex. | Norcross, Ga. | 12 |
| 67 | Sanders, Eric | T | 6-7 | 270 | 10/22/58 | 4 | Nevada-Reno | Reno, Nev. | Roswell, Ga. | 16 |
| 61 | Scully, John | G | 6-6 | 255 | 8/2/58 | 4 | Notre Dame | Long Island, N.Y. | Roswell, Ga. | 16 |
| 65 | Smith, Don | DT | 6-5 | 260 | 5/9/57 | 6 | Miami | Oakland, Calif. | Tarpon Springs, Fla. | 14 |
| 68 | Thielemann, R.C. | G | 6-4 | 252 | 8/12/55 | 8 | Arkansas | Houston, Tex. | Norcross, Ga. | 14 |
| 43 | Tutson, Tom | CB | 6-1 | 180 | 5/20/58 | 2 | South Carolina State | Jay, Fla. | Jay, Fla. | 10 |
| 57 | Van Note, Jeff | C | 6-2 | 250 | 2/7/46 | 16 | Kentucky | South Orange, N.J. | Roswell, Ga. | 16 |
| 22 | Williams, Richard | RB | 6-0 | 205 | 8/13/60 | 2 | Memphis State | Eustis, Fla. | Eustis, Fla. | 14 |
| 79 | Yeates, Jeff | DE | 6-3 | 252 | 8/3/51 | 11 | Boston College | Buffalo, N.Y. | Atlanta, Ga. | 16 |
| 86 | Young, Ben | TE | 6-4 | 225 | 1/13/60 | 2 | Texas-Arlington | Toledo, Ohio | Norcross, Ga. | 11 |
| 63 | Zele, Mike | DT | 6-4 | 250 | 7/13/56 | 6 | Kent State | Euclid, Ohio | Euclid, Ohio | 4 |

* Mikeska and Musser missed '83 season due to injuries.

Retired—Jeff Merrow, 9-year defensive end, 16 games in '83.

Also played with Falcons in '83—RB Reggie Brown (2 games), G Pat Howell (2), DE Doug Rogers (2).

## COACHING STAFF

### Head Coach, Dan Henning

**Pro Career:** Begins second season as Falcons head coach. Came from the Washington Redskins where he was assistant head coach under Joe Gibbs, helping the Redskins to a 20-9 record in 1981 and 1982 and a Super Bowl victory in 1983. Also was an assistant with Houston 1972, New York Jets 1976-78, and Miami Dolphins 1979-80. Played quarterback for the San Diego Chargers 1964-67. Career record: 7-9.

**Background:** Played quarterback for William and Mary 1960-63. Began college coaching career with Florida State 1968-70, 1974, Virginia Tech 1971, 1973.

**Personal:** Born June 21, 1942, Bronx, N.Y. Dan and his wife, Sandy, have five children—Mary K, Patty, Danny, Terry, and Mike. They reside in Roswell, Ga.

### Assistant Coaches

**Steve Crosby,** running backs; born July 3, 1950, Pawnee Rock, Kan., lives in Norcross, Ga. Running back Fort Hays (Kan.) College 1971-73. Pro running back New York Giants 1974-76. Pro coach: Miami Dolphins 1977-82, joined Falcons in 1983.

**George Dostal,** strength and conditioning; born October 25, 1934, Cleveland, Ohio, lives in Lawrenceville, Ga. Fullback-linebacker Kent State 1964-67. No pro playing experience. College coach: Clemson 1977-82. Pro coach: Joined Falcons in 1983.

**Sam Elliott,** administrative assistant; born August 3, 1946, Huntington, W. Va., lives in Norcross, Ga. Quarterback-defensive back Ohio State 1965-67. No pro playing experience. College coach: Ohio State 1968, Florida State 1969-70, 1974, Kent State 1971-73. Pro coach: Joined Falcons in 1983.

**Ted Fritsch,** special teams; born August 26, 1950, Green Bay, Wis., lives in Marietta, Ga. Center St. Norbert 1969-71. Pro center Atlanta Falcons 1972-75, Washington Redskins 1976-79. Pro coach: Joined Falcons in 1983.

**Bob Fry,** offensive coordinator-offensive line; born November 11, 1930, Cincinnati, Ohio, lives in Roswell, Ga. Tackle Kentucky 1949-52. Pro tackle Los Angeles Rams 1953-59, Dallas Cowboys 1960-64. Pro coach: Atlanta Falcons 1966-68, Pittsburgh Steelers 1969-73, New York Jets 1974-82, rejoined Falcons in 1983.

**Bob Harrison,** receivers; born September 9, 1941, Cleveland, Ohio, lives in Roswell, Ga. End Kent State 1961-64. No pro playing experience. College coach: Kent State 1969-70, Iowa 1971-73, Cornell 1974, North Carolina State 1975-76, Tennessee 1977-82. Pro coach: Joined Falcons in 1983.

**Bobby Jackson,** linebackers; born February 16, 1940, Forsyth, Ga., lives in Roswell, Ga. Linebacker-running back Samford 1959-62. No pro playing experience. College coach: Florida State 1965-69, Kansas State 1970-74, Louisville 1975-76, Tennessee 1977-82. Pro coach: Joined Falcons in 1983.

**John Marshall,** defensive coordinator; born October 2, 1945, Arroyo Grande, Calif., lives in Roswell, Ga. Oregon 1960. No pro playing experience. College coach: Oregon 1970-76, Southern California 1977-79. Pro coach: Green Bay Packers 1980-82, joined Falcons in 1983.

**Garry Puetz,** assistant offensive line; born March 14, 1952, Chicago, Ill., lives in Lithonia, Ga. Offensive line Valparaiso 1969-72. Pro offensive lineman New York Jets 1973-78, Tampa Bay Buccaneers 1978, Philadelphia Eagles 1979, New England Patriots 1979-81, Washington Redskins 1982. Pro coach: Joined Falcons in 1983.

**Dan Sekanovich,** assistant head coach-defensive line; born July 27, 1933, Hazleton, Pa., lives in Roswell, Ga. Defensive end Tennessee 1951-53. Pro defensive end Montreal Alouettes (CFL) 1955. College coach: Susquehanna 1961-63, Connecticut 1964-67, Pittsburgh 1968, Navy 1969-70, Kentucky 1971-72. Pro coach: Montreal Alouettes (CFL) 1973-76, New York Jets 1977-82, joined Falcons in 1983.

**Jack Stanton,** defensive backfield; born June 7, 1938 in Bridgeville, Pa., lives in Atlanta. Halfback North Carolina State 1958-60. Defensive back Toronto Argonauts (CFL) 1961, Pittsburgh Steelers 1961. College coach: George Washington 1967, North Carolina State 1968-72, Florida State 1973, 1976-83, North Carolina 1974-75. Pro coach: First year with Falcons.

## ATLANTA FALCONS 1984 FIRST-YEAR ROSTER

| Name | Pos. | Ht. | Wt. | Birth-date | College | Birthplace | Residence | How Acq. |
|---|---|---|---|---|---|---|---|---|
| Archer, David | QB | 6-1 | 200 | 2/15/62 | Iowa State | Fayetteville, N.C. | Soda Springs, Idaho | FA |
| Benson, Cliff | TE | 6-3 | 237 | 8/28/61 | Purdue | Chicago, Ill. | Robbins, Ill. | D5 |
| Benson, Thomas | LB | 6-2 | 235 | 9/6/61 | Oklahoma | Ardmore, Okla. | Ardmore, Okla. | D2a |
| Bryan, Rick | DT | 6-4 | 260 | 3/20/62 | Oklahoma | Coweta, Okla. | Coweta, Okla. | D1 |
| Case, Scott | CB-S | 6-0 | 178 | 5/17/62 | Oklahoma | Edmond, Okla. | Edmond, Okla. | D2 |
| Coleman, Chuck | RB | 5-9 | 180 | 8/14/61 | Tennessee | Humbolt, Tenn. | Louisville, Ky. | FA |
| Dodge, Kirk | LB | 6-1 | 231 | 6/4/62 | Nevada-Las Vegas | Whittier, Calif. | La Habra, Calif. | D7 |
| Franklin, Derrick | CB-S | 5-10 | 179 | 7/13/61 | Fresno State | Fresno, Calif. | Fresno, Calif. | D10 |
| Gay, Stan | CB-S | 5-9 | 176 | 2/6/60 | Alabama | Tuskegee, Ala. | Tuskegee, Ala. | FA |
| Green, Darren | WR | 5-9 | 164 | 3/19/62 | Kansas | Lawrence, Kan. | Lawrence, Kan. | FA |
| Harris, Roy | DE | 6-2 | 261 | 3/26/61 | Florida | Winter Garden, Fla. | Winter Garden, Fla. | FA |
| Henkowski, Nick | QB | 6-1 | 197 | 2/5/62 | Northern Colorado | St. Joseph, Mo. | Englewood, Colo. | FA |
| Howe, Glen | T | 6-6 | 265 | 10/18/61 | So. Mississippi | New Albany, Miss. | New Albany, Miss. | D9 |
| Jackson, Jeff | LB | 6-0 | 235 | 10/9/61 | Auburn | Shreveport, La. | Griffin, Ga. | D8 |
| Landrum, Mike | TE | 6-2 | 231 | 11/6/61 | So. Mississippi | Laurel, Miss. | Laurel, Miss. | FA |
| Malancon, Rydell | LB | 6-2 | 219 | 1/10/62 | Louisiana State | New Orleans, La. | Vacheria, La. | D4 |
| Matthews, John | T | 6-4 | 262 | 3/19/61 | Tennessee | Memphis, Tenn. | Memphis, Tenn. | FA |
| McSwain, Rodney | CB-S | 6-1 | 198 | 1/28/62 | Clemson | Caroleen, N.C. | Caroleen, N.C. | D3 |
| Ralph, Dan | DT | 6-4 | 268 | 3/9/61 | Oregon | Denver, Colo. | Northglenn, Colo. | D6a |
| Riggins, Clyde | S | 5-10 | 185 | 2/5/61 | Colorado | Brooksville, Fla. | Glen Cove, N.Y. | FA |
| Ryerson, Scott | K | 6-2 | 215 | 6/7/62 | Central Florida | Ft. Lee, Va. | Orlando, Fla. | FA |
| Smith, Carl | WR | 5-9 | 171 | 8/30/62 | Troy State | Tallahassee, Fla. | Tallahassee, Fla. | FA |
| Smith, Wayne | WR | 6-2 | 191 | 7/15/61 | Tulane | New Orleans, La. | New Orleans, La. | FA |
| Stamps, Sylvester | RB | 5-7 | 166 | 2/24/61 | Jackson State | Vicksburg, Miss. | Vicksburg, Miss. | FA |
| Sullivan, Ervin | WR | 5-9 | 154 | 10/25/60 | Miles | Birmingham, Ala. | Birmingham, Ala. | FA |
| Taylor, John | LB | 6-2 | 234 | 6/21/60 | Hawaii | Seattle, Wash. | Seattle, Wash. | FA |
| Thomas, Donald | CB | 6-1 | 181 | 4/12/61 | Tulane | New Orleans, La. | Donaldsonville, La. | FA |
| Tyrell, Tim | RB | 6-1 | 201 | 2/19/61 | Northern Illinois | Chicago, Ill. | Hoffman Estates, Ill. | FA |
| Weil, Jack | P | 5-10 | 170 | 3/16/62 | Wyoming | Denver, Colo. | Northglenn, Colo. | FA |
| Williams, Jimmie | WR | 6-0 | 172 | 10/23/61 | Texas A&M | Marshall, Tex. | Marshall, Tex. | FA |

Players who report to an NFL team for the first time are designated on rosters as rookies (R). If a player reported to an NFL training camp in a previous year but was not on the active squad for three or more regular season or postseason games, he is listed on the first-year roster and designated by a (1). Thereafter, a player who is on the active squad for three or more regular season or postseason games is credited with an additional year of playing experience.

## NOTES

_____
_____
_____
_____
_____
_____
_____
_____
_____
_____
_____
_____
_____
_____

# CHICAGO BEARS

**National Football Conference**
**Central Division**

**Team Colors:** Navy Blue, Orange, and White

**Corporate Headquarters and Ticket Offices:**
55 E. Jackson Blvd., Chicago, Illinois 60604
Telephone: (312) 663-5100 (Administrative), (312) 663-5408 (Tickets)
**Halas Hall (Coaching Staff, Personnel, Public Relations):**
250 North Washington, Lake Forest, Illinois 60045
Telephone: (312) 295-6600 (Halas Hall)

## Club Officials

Chairman of the Board: Edward W. McCaskey
President and Chief Executive Officer: Michael B. McCaskey
Vice President and General Manager, Treasurer: Jerome R. Vainisi
Vice President: Charles A. Brizzolara
Secretary: Virginia H. McCaskey
Dir., Player Personnel: Bill Tobin
Dir., Community Involvement: Pat McCaskey
Dir., Marketing/Communications: Bill McGrane
Coordinator of Media Relations: Ken Valdiserri
Ticket Manager: George Arneson
Trainer: Fred Caito
Strength Coordinator: Clyde Emrich
Equipment Manager: Ray Earley
Scouts: Jim Parmer, Rod Graves, Don King

**Stadium:** Soldier Field • **Capacity:** 65,790
425 McFetridge Place
Chicago, Illinois 60605

**Playing Surface:** AstroTurf

**Training Camp:** Halas Hall, 250 N. Washington, Lake Forest, Illinois 60045

## 1984 SCHEDULE

**Preseason**
| | | |
|---|---|---|
| Aug. 4 | **St. Louis** | 6:00 |
| Aug. 11 | vs. Green Bay at Milwaukee | 7:00 |
| Aug. 18 | **Cincinnati** | 6:00 |
| Aug. 26 | vs. Buffalo at Indianapolis | 12:00 |

**Regular Season**
| | | |
|---|---|---|
| Sept. 2 | **Tampa Bay** | 12:00 |
| Sept. 9 | **Denver** | 12:00 |
| Sept. 16 | at Green Bay | 12:00 |
| Sept. 23 | at Seattle | 1:00 |
| Sept. 30 | **Dallas** | 12:00 |
| Oct. 7 | **New Orleans** | 12:00 |
| Oct. 14 | at St. Louis | 12:00 |
| Oct. 21 | at Tampa Bay | 1:00 |
| Oct. 28 | **Minnesota** | 12:00 |
| Nov. 4 | **Los Angeles Raiders** | 12:00 |
| Nov. 11 | at Los Angeles Rams | 1:00 |
| Nov. 18 | **Detroit** | 12:00 |
| Nov. 25 | at Minnesota | 3:00 |
| Dec. 3 | at San Diego (Monday) | 6:00 |
| Dec. 9 | **Green Bay** | 12:00 |
| Dec. 16 | at Detroit | 1:00 |

## BEARS COACHING HISTORY

### Chicago Staleys 1921
### (479-321-42)

| | | |
|---|---|---|
| 1920-29 | George Halas | 85-31-19 |
| 1930-32 | Ralph Jones | 24-10-7 |
| 1933-42 | George Halas* | 88-25-4 |
| 1942-45 | Hunk Anderson-Luke Johnsos** | 24-12-2 |
| 1946-55 | George Halas | 77-42-2 |
| 1956-57 | John (Paddy) Driscoll | 14-10-1 |
| 1958-67 | George Halas | 75-53-6 |
| 1968-71 | Jim Dooley | 20-36-0 |
| 1972-74 | Abe Gibron | 11-30-1 |
| 1975-77 | Jack Pardee | 20-23-0 |
| 1978-81 | Neill Armstrong | 30-35-0 |
| 1982-83 | Mike Ditka | 11-14-0 |

*Retired November 1 to re-enter Navy
**Co-coaches

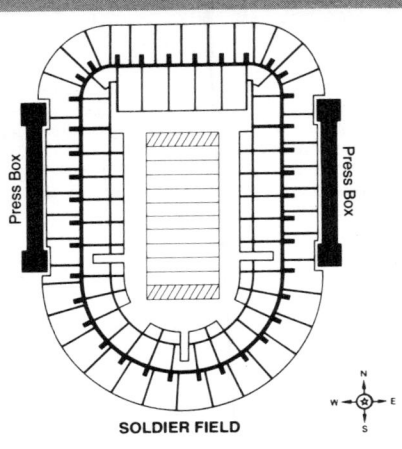

**SOLDIER FIELD**

## RECORD HOLDERS
### Individual Records—Career

| Category | Name | Performance |
|---|---|---|
| Rushing (Yds.) | Walter Payton, 1975-1983 | 11,625 |
| Passing (Yds.) | Sid Luckman, 1939-1950 | 14,686 |
| Passing (TDs) | Sid Luckman, 1939-1950 | 137 |
| Receiving (No.) | Johnny Morris, 1958-1967 | 356 |
| Receiving (Yds.) | Johnny Morris, 1958-1967 | 5,059 |
| Interceptions | Richie Petitbon, 1959-1968 | 37 |
| Punting (Avg.) | George Gulyanics, 1947-1952 | 44.5 |
| Punt Return (Avg.) | Ray (Scooter) McLean, 1940-47 | 14.8 |
| Kickoff Return (Avg.) | Gale Sayers, 1965-1971 | 30.6 |
| Field Goals | Bob Thomas, 1975-1983 | 106 |
| Touchdowns (Tot.) | Walter Payton, 1975-1983 | 87 |
| Points | George Blanda, 1948-1958 | 541 |

### Individual Records—Single Season

| Category | Name | Performance |
|---|---|---|
| Rushing (Yds.) | Walter Payton, 1977 | 1,852 |
| Passing (Yds.) | Bill Wade, 1962 | 3,172 |
| Passing (TDs) | Sid Luckman, 1943 | 28 |
| Receiving (No.) | Johnny Morris, 1964 | 93 |
| Receiving (Yds.) | Johnny Morris, 1964 | 1,200 |
| Interceptions | Roosevelt Taylor, 1963 | 9 |
| Punting (Avg.) | Bobby Joe Green, 1963 | 46.4 |
| Punt Return (Avg.) | Harry Clark, 1943 | 15.8 |
| Kickoff Return (Avg.) | Gale Sayers, 1967 | 37.7 |
| Field Goals | Mac Percival, 1968 | 25 |
| Touchdowns (Tot.) | Gale Sayers, 1965 | 22 |
| Points | Gale Sayers, 1965 | 132 |

### Individual Records—Single Game

| Category | Name | Performance |
|---|---|---|
| Rushing (Yds.) | Walter Payton, 11-20-77 | 275 |
| Passing (Yds.) | Johnny Lujack, 12-11-49 | 468 |
| Passing (TDs) | Sid Luckman, 11-14-43 | 7 |
| Receiving (No.) | Jim Keane, 10-23-49 | 14 |
| Receiving (Yds.) | Harlon Hill, 10-31-54 | 214 |
| Interceptions | Many times | 3 |
| | Last time by Ross Brupbacher, 12-12-76 | |
| Field Goals | Roger LeClerc, 12-3-61 | 5 |
| | Mac Percival, 10-20-68 | 5 |
| Touchdowns (Tot.) | Gale Sayers, 12-12-65 | 6 |
| Points | Gale Sayers, 12-12-65 | 36 |

## 1983 TEAM STATISTICS

| | Chicago | Opp. |
|---|---|---|
| Total First Downs | 308 | 286 |
| Rushing | 154 | 113 |
| Passing | 136 | 154 |
| Penalty | 18 | 19 |
| Third Down Efficiency | 79/229 | 73/217 |
| Third Down Percentage | 34.5 | 33.6 |
| Total Net Yards | 5830 | 5132 |
| Total Offensive Plays | 1083 | 1023 |
| Avg. Gain per Play | 5.4 | 5.0 |
| Avg. Gain per Game | 364.4 | 320.8 |
| Net Yards Rushing | 2727 | 2000 |
| Total Rushing Plays | 583 | 482 |
| Avg. Gain per Rush | 4.7 | 4.1 |
| Avg. Gain Rushing per Game | 170.4 | 125.0 |
| Net Yards Passing | 3103 | 3132 |
| Lost Attempting to Pass | 53/358 | 51/384 |
| Gross Yards Passing | 3461 | 3516 |
| Attempts/Completions | 447/255 | 490/249 |
| Percent Completed | 57.0 | 50.8 |
| Had Intercepted | 22 | 21 |
| Avg. Net Passing per Game | 193.9 | 195.8 |
| Punts/Avg. | 94/36.2 | 99/38.6 |
| Punt Returns/Avg. | 56/8.0 | 44/7.3 |
| Kickoff Returns/Avg. | 58/16.4 | 66/18.6 |
| Interceptions/Avg. Ret. | 21/10.2 | 22/13.2 |
| Penalties/Yards | 107/869 | 86/687 |
| Fumbles/Ball Lost | 25/14 | 37/17 |
| Total Points | 311 | 301 |
| Avg. Points per Game | 19.4 | 18.8 |
| Touchdowns | 39 | 36 |
| Rushing | 14 | 20 |
| Passing | 21 | 15 |
| Returns and Recoveries | 4 | 1 |
| Field Goals | 14/25 | 17/23 |
| Conversions | 35/39 | 34/36 |
| Safeties | 0 | 0 |
| Avg. Time of Possession | 32:11 | 27:49 |

## 1983 TEAM RECORD
### Preseason (3-1)

| Date | Chicago | | Opponents |
|---|---|---|---|
| 8/6 | 27 | *Buffalo | 17 |
| 8/13 | 24 | St. Louis (OT) | 27 |
| 8/20 | 27 | Los Angeles Raiders | 21 |
| 8/27 | 20 | *Kansas City (OT) | 17 |
| | 98 | | 82 |

### Regular Season (8-8)

| Date | Chicago | | Opp. | Att. |
|---|---|---|---|---|
| 9/4 | 17 | *Atlanta | 20 | 60,165 |
| 9/11 | 17 | *Tampa Bay | 10 | 58,186 |
| 9/18 | 31 | New Orleans (OT) | 34 | 64,692 |
| 9/25 | 19 | Baltimore (OT) | 22 | 34,350 |
| 10/2 | 31 | *Denver | 14 | 58,210 |
| 10/9 | 14 | *Minnesota | 23 | 59,632 |
| 10/16 | 17 | Detroit | 31 | 66,709 |
| 10/23 | 7 | Philadelphia | 6 | 45,263 |
| 10/30 | 17 | *Detroit | 38 | 58,764 |
| 11/6 | 14 | Los Angeles Rams | 21 | 53,010 |
| 11/13 | 17 | *Philadelphia | 14 | 47,524 |
| 11/20 | 27 | Tampa Bay | 0 | 36,816 |
| 11/27 | 13 | *San Francisco | 3 | 40,483 |
| 12/4 | 28 | Green Bay | 31 | 51,244 |
| 12/11 | 19 | Minnesota | 13 | 57,880 |
| 12/18 | 23 | *Green Bay | 21 | 35,807 |
| | 311 | | 301 | 828,735 |

*Home Game    (OT) Overtime

### Score by Periods

| | | | | | | | |
|---|---|---|---|---|---|---|---|
| Chicago | 55 | 104 | 40 | 112 | 0 | — | 311 |
| Opponents | 78 | 63 | 83 | 71 | 6 | — | 301 |

### Attendance
Home 418,771    Away 409,964    Total 828,735
Single game home record, 80,259 (11-24-66)
Single season home record, 511,541 (1981)

## 1983 INDIVIDUAL STATISTICS

### Rushing

| | Att. | Yds. | Avg. | LG | TD |
|---|---|---|---|---|---|
| Payton | 314 | 1421 | 4.5 | 49t | 6 |
| Suhey | 149 | 681 | 4.6 | 39 | 4 |
| McMahon | 55 | 307 | 5.6 | 32 | 2 |
| Evans | 22 | 142 | 6.5 | 27 | 1 |
| Gentry | 16 | 65 | 4.1 | 17 | 0 |
| Gault | 4 | 31 | 7.8 | 22 | 0 |
| Parsons | 1 | 27 | 27.0 | 27 | 0 |
| C. Thomas | 8 | 25 | 3.1 | 9 | 0 |
| Hutchison | 6 | 13 | 2.2 | 5 | 1 |
| Margerum | 1 | 7 | 7.0 | 7 | 0 |
| Moorehead | 5 | 6 | 1.2 | 5 | 0 |
| Baschnagel | 2 | 2 | 1.0 | 2 | 0 |
| Chicago | 583 | 2727 | 4.7 | 49t | 14 |
| Opponents | 482 | 2000 | 4.1 | 71 | 20 |

### Passing

| | Att. | Comp. | Pct. | Yds. | TD | Int. | Tkld. | Rate |
|---|---|---|---|---|---|---|---|---|
| McMahon | 295 | 175 | 59.3 | 2184 | 12 | 13 | 42/266 | 77.6 |
| Evans | 145 | 76 | 52.4 | 1108 | 5 | 7 | 11/92 | 69.0 |
| Payton | 6 | 3 | 50.0 | 95 | 3 | 2 | 0/0 | 95.8 |
| Suhey | 1 | 1 | 100.0 | 74 | 1 | 0 | 0/0 | 158.3 |
| Chicago | 447 | 255 | 57.0 | 3461 | 21 | 22 | 53/358 | 77.0 |
| Opponents | 490 | 249 | 50.8 | 3516 | 15 | 21 | 51/384 | 66.7 |

### Receiving

| | No. | Yds. | Avg. | LG | TD |
|---|---|---|---|---|---|
| Payton | 53 | 607 | 11.5 | 74t | 2 |
| Suhey | 49 | 429 | 8.8 | 52 | 1 |
| Moorehead | 42 | 597 | 14.2 | 36 | 3 |
| Gault | 40 | 836 | 20.9 | 87t | 8 |
| Margerum | 21 | 336 | 16.0 | 60 | 2 |
| McKinnon | 20 | 326 | 16.3 | 49t | 4 |
| Saldi | 12 | 119 | 9.9 | 16 | 0 |
| Dunsmore | 8 | 102 | 12.8 | 24 | 0 |
| Baschnagel | 5 | 70 | 14.0 | 24 | 0 |
| C. Thomas | 2 | 13 | 6.5 | 7 | 0 |
| Gentry | 2 | 8 | 4.0 | 6 | 0 |
| McMahon | 1 | 18 | 18.0 | 18t | 1 |
| Chicago | 255 | 3461 | 13.6 | 87t | 21 |
| Opponents | 249 | 3516 | 14.1 | 74 | 15 |

### Interceptions

| | No. | Yds. | Avg. | LG | TD |
|---|---|---|---|---|---|
| Frazier | 7 | 135 | 19.3 | 58 | 1 |
| Schmidt | 5 | 31 | 6.2 | 32t | 1 |
| Richardson | 5 | 9 | 1.8 | 6 | 0 |
| Fencik | 2 | 34 | 17.0 | 20 | 0 |
| Wilson | 1 | 6 | 6.0 | 6 | 0 |
| Singletary | 1 | 0 | 0.0 | 0 | 0 |
| Chicago | 21 | 215 | 10.2 | 58 | 2 |
| Opponents | 22 | 291 | 13.2 | 35 | 1 |

### Punting

| | No. | Yds. | Avg. | In 20 | LG |
|---|---|---|---|---|---|
| Parsons | 79 | 2916 | 36.9 | 21 | 54 |
| Stachowicz | 12 | 447 | 37.3 | 0 | 48 |
| McMahon | 1 | 36 | 36.0 | 0 | 36 |
| Chicago | 94 | 3399 | 36.2 | 21 | 54 |
| Opponents | 99 | 3821 | 38.6 | 25 | 60 |

### Punt Returns

| | No. | FC | Yds. | Avg. | LG | TD |
|---|---|---|---|---|---|---|
| McKinnon | 34 | 3 | 316 | 9.3 | 59t | 1 |
| Fisher | 13 | 3 | 71 | 5.5 | 11 | 0 |
| Gault | 9 | 1 | 60 | 6.7 | 12 | 0 |
| Chicago | 56 | 7 | 447 | 8.0 | 59t | 1 |
| Opponents | 44 | 14 | 322 | 7.3 | 34 | 0 |

### Kickoff Returns

| | No. | Yds. | Avg. | LG | TD |
|---|---|---|---|---|---|
| Hutchison | 17 | 259 | 15.2 | 28 | 0 |
| Gault | 13 | 276 | 21.2 | 38 | 0 |
| Gentry | 7 | 130 | 18.6 | 28 | 0 |
| Watts | 5 | 79 | 15.8 | 21 | 0 |
| Baschnagel | 3 | 42 | 14.0 | 19 | 0 |
| Duerson | 3 | 66 | 22.0 | 24 | 0 |
| Bell | 2 | 18 | 9.0 | 18 | 0 |
| Cabral | 2 | 11 | 5.5 | 6 | 0 |
| McKinnon | 2 | 42 | 21.0 | 25 | 0 |
| Rains | 2 | 11 | 5.5 | 11 | 0 |
| Janata | 1 | 2 | 2.0 | 2 | 0 |
| Richardson | 1 | 17 | 17.0 | 17 | 0 |
| Chicago | 58 | 953 | 16.4 | 38 | 0 |
| Opponents | 66 | 1229 | 18.6 | 61 | 0 |

### Scoring

| | TD | TD R | TD P | TD Rt | PAT | FG | TP |
|---|---|---|---|---|---|---|---|
| B. Thomas | | | | | 35/38 | 14/25 | 77 |
| Gault | 8 | 0 | 8 | 0 | | | 48 |
| Payton | 8 | 6 | 2 | 0 | | | 48 |
| McKinnon | 5 | 0 | 4 | 1 | | | 30 |
| Suhey | 5 | 4 | 1 | 0 | | | 30 |
| McMahon | 3 | 2 | 1 | 0 | | | 18 |
| Moorehead | 3 | 0 | 3 | 0 | | | 18 |
| Margerum | 2 | 0 | 2 | 0 | | | 12 |
| Evans | 1 | 1 | 0 | 0 | | | 6 |
| Frazier | 1 | 0 | 0 | 1 | | | 6 |
| Hartenstine | 1 | 0 | 0 | 1 | | | 6 |
| Hutchison | 1 | 1 | 0 | 0 | | | 6 |
| Schmidt | 1 | 0 | 0 | 1 | | | 6 |
| Chicago | 39 | 14 | 21 | 4 | 35/39 | 14/25 | 311 |
| Opponents | 36 | 20 | 15 | 1 | 34/36 | 17/23 | 301 |

## FIRST-ROUND SELECTIONS

(If Club had no first-round selection, first player drafted is listed with round in parentheses.)

| Year | Player, College, Position |
|---|---|
| 1936 | Joe Stydahar, West Virginia, T |
| 1937 | Les McDonald, Nebraska, E |
| 1938 | Joe Gray, Oregon State, B |
| 1939 | Sid Luckman, Columbia, B |
| | Bill Osmanski, Holy Cross, B |
| 1940 | C. (Bulldog) Turner, Hardin-Simmons, C |
| 1941 | Tom Harmon, Michigan, B |
| | Norm Standlee, Stanford, B |
| | Don Scott, Ohio State, B |
| 1942 | Frankie Albert, Stanford, B |
| 1943 | Bob Steuber, Missouri, B |
| 1944 | Ray Evans, Kansas, B |
| 1945 | Don Lund, Michigan, B |
| 1946 | Johnny Lujack, Notre Dame, B |
| 1947 | Bob Fenimore, Oklahoma A&M, B |
| | Don Kindt, Wisconsin, B |
| 1948 | Bobby Layne, Texas, B |
| | Max Baumgardner, Texas, E |
| 1949 | Dick Harris, Texas, C |
| 1950 | Chuck Hunsinger, Florida, B |
| | Fred Morrison, Ohio State, B |
| 1951 | Bob Williams, Notre Dame, B |
| | Billy Stone, Bradley, B |
| | Gene Schroeder, Virginia, E |
| 1952 | Jim Dooley, Miami, B |
| 1953 | Billy Anderson, Compton (Calif.) JC, B |
| 1954 | Stan Wallace, Illinois, B |
| 1955 | Ron Drzewiecki, Marquette, B |
| 1956 | Menan (Tex) Schriewer, Texas, E |
| 1957 | Earl Leggett, Louisiana State, T |
| 1958 | Chuck Howley, West Virginia, G |
| 1959 | Don Clark, Ohio State, B |
| 1960 | Roger Davis, Syracuse, G |
| 1961 | Mike Ditka, Pittsburgh, E |
| 1962 | Ronnie Bull, Baylor, RB |
| 1963 | Dave Behrman, Michigan State, C |
| 1964 | Dick Evey, Tennessee, DT |
| 1965 | Dick Butkus, Illinois, LB |
| | Gale Sayers, Kansas, RB |
| | Steve DeLong, Tennessee, T |
| 1966 | George Rice, Louisiana State, DT |
| 1967 | Loyd Phillips, Arkansas, DE |
| 1968 | Mike Hull, Southern California, RB |
| 1969 | Rufus Mayes, Ohio State, T |
| 1970 | George Farmer, UCLA, WR (3) |
| 1971 | Joe Moore, Missouri, RB |
| 1972 | Lionel Antoine, Southern Illinois, T |
| | Craig Clemons, Iowa, DB |
| 1973 | Wally Chambers, Eastern Kentucky, DE |
| 1974 | Waymond Bryant, Tennessee State, LB |
| | Dave Gallagher, Michigan, DT |
| 1975 | Walter Payton, Jackson State, RB |
| 1976 | Dennis Lick, Wisconsin, T |
| 1977 | Ted Albrecht, California, T |
| 1978 | Brad Shearer, Texas, DT (3) |
| 1979 | Dan Hampton, Arkansas, DT |
| | Al Harris, Arizona State, DE |
| 1980 | Otis Wilson, Louisville, LB |
| 1981 | Keith Van Horne, Southern California, T |
| 1982 | Jim McMahon, Brigham Young, QB |
| 1983 | Jimbo Covert, Pittsburgh, T |
| | Willie Gault, Tennessee, WR |
| 1984 | Wilber Marshall, Florida, LB |

# CHICAGO BEARS 1984 VETERAN ROSTER

| No. | Name | Pos. | Ht. | Wt. | Birth-date | NFL Exp. | College | Birthplace | Residence | Games in '83 |
|---|---|---|---|---|---|---|---|---|---|---|
| 51 | Atkins, Kelvin | LB | 6-3 | 235 | 7/3/60 | 2 | Illinois | Orlando, Fla. | Forest Park, Ill. | 13 |
| 7 | Avellini, Bob | QB | 6-2 | 210 | 8/28/53 | 10 | Maryland | Queens, N.Y. | Chicago, Ill. | 2 |
| 84 | Baschnagel, Brian | WR | 6-0 | 184 | 1/8/54 | 9 | Ohio State | Kingston, N.Y. | Chicago, Ill. | 16 |
| 79 | Becker, Kurt | G | 6-5 | 270 | 12/22/58 | 3 | Michigan | Aurora, Ill. | Chicago, Ill. | 16 |
| 25 | Bell, Todd | S | 6-0 | 207 | 11/28/58 | 4 | Ohio State | Middletown, Ohio | Middletown, Ohio | 15 |
| 62 | Bortz, Mark | G | 6-5 | 267 | 2/12/61 | 2 | Iowa | Pardeeville, Wis. | Vernon Hills, Ill. | 16 |
| 54 | Cabral, Brian | LB | 6-1 | 224 | 6/23/56 | 2 | Colorado | Ft. Benning, Ga. | Libertyville, Ill. | 16 |
| 74 | Covert, Jim | T | 6-4 | 271 | 3/22/60 | 2 | Pittsburgh | Conway, Pa. | Highland Park, Ill. | 16 |
| 95 | Dent, Richard | DE | 6-5 | 240 | 12/13/60 | 2 | Tennessee State | Atlanta, Ga. | Atlanta, Ga. | 16 |
| 22 | Duerson, Dave | S | 6-0 | 202 | 11/28/60 | 2 | Notre Dame | Muncie, Ind. | Muncie, Ind. | 16 |
| 88 | Dunsmore, Pat | TE | 6-2 | 230 | 10/2/59 | 2 | Drake | Duluth, Minn. | Arkeny, Iowa | 16 |
| 64 | Fada, Rob | G | 6-2 | 258 | 5/7/61 | 2 | Pittsburgh | Fairborn, Ohio | Fairborn, Ohio | 12 |
| 45 | Fencik, Gary | S | 6-1 | 197 | 6/11/54 | 9 | Yale | Chicago, Ill. | Libertyville, Ill. | 8 |
| 24 | Fisher, Jeff | CB | 5-10 | 195 | 2/25/58 | 4 | Southern California | Culver City, Calif. | Libertyville, Ill. | 8 |
| 21 | Frazier, Leslie | CB | 6-0 | 189 | 4/3/59 | 4 | Alcorn State | Columbus, Miss. | Vernon Hills, Ill. | 16 |
| 71 | Frederick, Andy | T | 6-6 | 265 | 7/25/54 | 8 | New Mexico | Oak Park, Ill. | Dallas, Tex. | 16 |
|  | t-Fuller, Steve | QB | 6-4 | 198 | 1/5/57 | 6 | Clemson | Enid, Okla. | Spartanburg, S.C. | 0* |
| 83 | Gault, Willie | WR | 6-0 | 178 | 9/5/60 | 2 | Tennessee | Griffin, Ga. | Lake Forest, Ill. | 16 |
| 29 | Gentry, Dennis | RB | 5-8 | 173 | 2/10/59 | 3 | Baylor | Lubbock, Tex. | Temple, Tex. | 15 |
| 99 | Hampton, Dan | DT | 6-5 | 270 | 9/19/57 | 6 | Arkansas | Oklahoma City, Okla. | Lake Bluff, Ill. | 11 |
| 90 | Harris, Al | LB | 6-5 | 250 | 12/31/56 | 6 | Arizona State | Bangor, Maine | Aurora, Colo. | 12 |
| 73 | Hartenstine, Mike | DE | 6-3 | 243 | 7/27/53 | 10 | Penn State | Allentown, Pa. | Lake Bluff, Ill. | 16 |
| 63 | Hilgenberg, Jay | C | 6-3 | 260 | 3/21/59 | 4 | Iowa | Iowa City, Iowa | Deerfield, Ill. | 16 |
| 32 | Hutchison, Anthony | RB | 5-10 | 180 | 2/4/61 | 2 | Texas Tech | Houston, Tex. | San Antonio, Tex. | 13 |
| 65 | Jackson, Noah | G | 6-2 | 265 | 4/14/51 | 10 | Tampa | Jacksonville, Fla. | Lake Forest, Ill. | 15 |
| 72 | Janata, John | T | 6-7 | 255 | 4/10/61 | 2 | Illinois | Chicago, Ill. | Chicago, Ill. | 14 |
| 98 | Keys, Tyrone | DE | 6-7 | 260 | 10/24/59 | 2 | Mississippi State | Brookhaven, Miss. | Jackson, Miss. | 15 |
| 82 | Margerum, Ken | WR | 6-0 | 180 | 10/5/58 | 4 | Stanford | Fountain Valley, Calif. | Stanford, Calif. | 16 |
| 85 | McKinnon, Dennis | WR | 6-2 | 185 | 8/22/61 | 2 | Florida State | Quitman, Ga. | Miami, Fla. | 14 |
| 9 | McMahon, Jim | QB | 6-0 | 187 | 8/21/59 | 3 | Brigham Young | Jersey City, N.J. | Northbrook, Ill. | 14 |
| 76 | McMichael, Steve | DT | 6-2 | 260 | 10/17/57 | 5 | Texas | Houston, Tex. | Lake Forest, Ill. | 16 |
| 87 | Moorehead, Emery | TE | 6-2 | 220 | 3/22/54 | 8 | Colorado | Evanston, Ill. | Broomfield, Colo. | 16 |
| 68 | Osborne, Jim | DT | 6-3 | 245 | 9/7/49 | 13 | Southern | Sylvania, Ga. | Lake Forest, Ill. | 16 |
| 34 | Payton, Walter | RB | 5-10 | 202 | 7/25/54 | 10 | Jackson State | Columbus, Miss. | Arlington Heights, Ill. | 16 |
| 20 | Potter, Kevin | S | 5-10 | 188 | 12/19/59 | 2 | Missouri | St. Louis, Mo. | St. Louis, Mo. | 5* |
| 53 | Rains, Dan | LB | 6-1 | 220 | 4/26/56 | 3 | Cincinnati | Rochester, Pa. | Aliquippa, Pa. | 16 |
| 27 | Richardson, Mike | CB | 6-0 | 188 | 5/23/61 | 2 | Arizona State | Compton, Calif. | Los Angeles, Calif. | 16 |
| 81 | Saldi, Jay | TE | 6-3 | 230 | 10/8/54 | 9 | South Carolina | White Plains, N.Y. | Richardson, Tex. | 13 |
| 44 | Schmidt, Terry | CB | 6-0 | 177 | 5/28/52 | 11 | Ball State | Columbus, Ind. | Lake Forest, Ill. | 13 |
| 57 | Simmons, David | LB | 6-4 | 225 | 1/19/57 | 4 | North Carolina | Goldsboro, N.C. | Lake Bluff, Ill. | 13 |
| 50 | Singletary, Mike | LB | 5-11 | 230 | 10/9/58 | 4 | Baylor | Houston, Tex. | Houston, Tex. | 16 |
| 19 | Stachowicz, Ray | P | 6-0 | 185 | 3/6/59 | 3 | Michigan State | Cleveland, Ohio | Broadview Heights, Ohio | 2 |
| 26 | Suhey, Matt | RB | 5-11 | 217 | 7/7/58 | 5 | Penn State | State College, Pa. | Highland Park, Ill. | 16 |
| 16 | Thomas, Bob | K | 5-10 | 175 | 8/7/52 | 9 | Notre Dame | Rochester, N.Y. | Naperville, Ill. | 16 |
| 33 | Thomas, Calvin | RB | 5-11 | 220 | 1/7/60 | 3 | Illinois | St. Louis, Mo. | Forest Park, Ill. | 13 |
| 78 | Van Horne, Keith | T | 6-6 | 265 | 11/6/57 | 4 | Southern California | Mt. Lebanon, Pa. | Deerfield, Ill. | 14 |
| 80 | Watts, Rickey | WR | 6-1 | 203 | 5/16/57 | 6 | Tulsa | Longview, Tex. | Wilmette, Ill. | 4 |
| 43 | Williams, Walt | CB | 6-1 | 185 | 7/10/56 | 8 | New Mexico | Port Arthur, Tex. | Las Cruces, N.M. | 15 |
| 55 | Wilson, Otis | LB | 6-2 | 222 | 9/15/57 | 5 | Louisville | New York, N.Y. | Gurnee, Ill. | 16 |

* Fuller active for 16 games with L.A. Rams in '83, but did not play; Potter played 1 game with Houston, 4 with Chicago in '83.

t-Bears traded for Fuller (Los Angeles Rams).

Also played with Bears in '83—LB Gary Campbell (6 games), QB Vince Evans (9), G Perry Hartnett (2), LB Jerry Muckensturm (1), C Dan Neal (8), P Bob Parsons (14), G Revie Sorie (3).

## COACHING STAFF

### Head Coach, Mike Ditka

**Pro Career:** Became tenth head coach in Bears 62-year history on January 20, 1982 after serving nine years as an offensive assistant with Dallas Cowboys. Led Bears to 8-8 mark in 1983, their best finish since 1979. Ditka is a 22-year veteran of the NFL as both a player and coach. Had 12-year playing career as a tight end with the Chicago Bears (1961-66), Philadelphia Eagles (1967-68), and Dallas Cowboys (1969-72). A first-round draft choice by Chicago in 1961, Ditka was NFL rookie of the year, all-NFL (1961-64), and played in five Pro Bowls (1962-66). He joined the Cowboys' coaching staff in 1973. In addition to working with the Dallas special teams, he coached the Cowboys' receivers. Career record: 11-14.

**Background:** Played at Pittsburgh from 1958-60 and was a unanimous All-America his senior year. A two-way performer, he played both defensive end and linebacker. He also was one of the nation's leading punters with a 40-plus yard average over three years.

**Personal:** Born October 18, 1939, Carnegie, Pa. Mike and his wife, Diana, live in Chicago and have four chidren—Michael, Mark, Megan, and Matt.

### Assistant Coaches

**Jim Dooley,** research and quality control; born February 8, 1930, Stoutsville, Mo., lives in Chicago. End Miami 1949-51. Pro receiver Chicago Bears 1952-61. Pro coach: Chicago Bears 1962-71 (head coach 1968-71), Buffalo Bills 1972, rejoined Bears in 1981.

**Dale Haupt,** defensive line; born April 12, 1929, Manitowic, Wis., lives in Chicago. Guard Wyoming 1951-53. Pro guard Green Bay Packers 1954. College coach: Tennessee 1960-63, Iowa State 1964-65, Richmond 1966-71, North Carolina State 1972-76, Duke 1977. Pro coach: Joined Bears in 1978.

**Ed Hughes,** offensive coordinator; born October 23, 1927, Buffalo, N.Y., lives in Chicago. Halfback Tulsa 1952-53. Pro defensive back Los Angeles Rams 1954-55, New York Giants 1956-58. Pro coach: Dallas Texans 1960-62, Denver Broncos 1963, Washington Redskins 1964-67, San Francisco 49ers 1968-70, Houston Oilers 1971 (head coach), St. Louis Cardinals 1972, Dallas Cowboys 1973-76, Detroit Lions 1977, New Orleans Saints 1978-80, Philadelphia Eagles 1981, joined Bears in 1982.

**Jim LaRue,** defensive backfield; born August 11, 1925, Clinton, Okla., lives in Chicago. Halfback Carson-Newman 1943, Duke 1944-45, Maryland 1947-49. No pro playing experience. College coach: Maryland 1950, Kansas State 1951-54, Houston 1955-56, Southern Methodist 1957-58, Arizona 1959-66 (head coach), Utah 1967-73, Wake Forest 1974-75. Pro coach: Buffalo Bills 1976-77, joined Bears in 1978.

**Ted Plumb,** receivers; born August 20, 1939, Reno, Nev., lives in Chicago. End Baylor 1959-61. No pro playing experience. College coach: Cerritos, Calif., J.C. 1966-67, Texas Christian 1968-70, Tulsa 1971, Kansas 1972-73. Pro coach: New York Giants 1974-76, Atlanta Falcons 1977-79, joined Bears in 1980.

**Johnny Roland,** offensive backs; born May 21, 1943, Corpus Christi, Tex., lives in Chicago. Running back Missouri 1963-65. Pro running back St. Louis Cardinals 1966-72, New York Giants 1973. College coach: Notre Dame 1975. Pro coach: Green Bay Packers 1974, Philadelphia Eagles 1976-78, joined Bears in 1983.

**Buddy Ryan,** defensive coordinator; born February 16, 1934, Frederick, Okla., lives in Chicago. Guard Oklahoma State 1952-55. No pro playing experience. College coach: Buffalo 1961-65, Vanderbilt 1966, University of Pacific 1967. Pro coach: New York Jets 1968-75, Minnesota Vikings 1976-77, joined Bears in 1978.

## CHICAGO BEARS 1984 FIRST-YEAR ROSTER

| Name | Pos. | Ht. | Wt. | Birth-date | College | Birthplace | Residence | How Acq. |
|------|------|-----|-----|-----------|---------|-----------|-----------|----------|
| Abbott, Vince (1) | K | 5-11 | 195 | 5/31/58 | Cal St.-Fullerton | London, England | Santa Ana, Calif. | FA |
| Anderson, Brad | WR | 6-3 | 196 | 1/21/61 | Arizona | Glendale, Ariz. | Glendale, Ariz. | D8 |
| Andrews, Tom | T-C | 6-4 | 250 | 1/11/62 | Louisville | Parma, Ohio | Louisville, Ky. | D4 |
| Bass, Michael (1) | K | 6-0 | 215 | 6/1/60 | Illinois | San Jose, Calif. | Fisher, Ill. | FA |
| Butkus, Mark | DT | 6-4 | 261 | 12/3/61 | Illinois | Lansing, Ill. | Lansing, Ill. | D11 |
| Carpenter, Dean | K | 5-10 | 175 | 10/6/59 | Chicago University | Chicago, Ill. | Schaumburg, Ill. | FA |
| Casale, Mark | QB | 6-2 | 225 | 9/17/62 | Montclair State | Union, N.J. | Union, N.J. | D9 |
| Gayle, Shaun | CB-S | 5-11 | 195 | 3/8/62 | Ohio State | Hampton, Va. | Columbus, Ohio | D10 |
| Humphries, Stefan | G | 6-4 | 248 | 1/20/62 | Michigan | Broward, Fla. | Ann Arbor, Mich. | D3 |
| Jordan, Donald | FB | 6-0 | 201 | 2/9/62 | Houston | Houston, Tex. | Houston, Tex. | D12 |
| Marshall, Wilber | LB | 6-1 | 230 | 4/18/62 | Florida | Titusville, Fla. | Gainesville, Fla. | D1 |
| Moy, Sylvester (1) | WR | 6-0 | 182 | 7/1/59 | Grambling | Monroe, La. | Monroe, La. | FA |
| Norman, Tim (1) | G | 6-6 | 270 | 7/10/59 | Illinois | Oak Park, Ill. | Winfield, Ill. | FA |
| Renner, William (1) | P | 6-0 | 192 | 5/23/59 | Virginia Tech | Quantico, Va. | Dublin, Va. | FA |
| Rivera, Ron | LB | 6-3 | 235 | 1/7/62 | California | Monterey, Calif. | Berkeley, Calif. | D2 |
| Robertson, Nakita | RB | 5-11 | 211 | 5/18/61 | Central Arkansas | West Memphis, Ark. | Conway, Ark. | D7 |
| Vestman, Kurt | TE | 6-3 | 235 | 7/5/60 | Idaho | Bainbridge Is., Wash. | Moscow, Idaho | D10 |

Players who report to an NFL team for the first time are designated on rosters as rookies (R). If a player reported to an NFL training camp in a previous year but was not on the active squad for three or more regular season or postseason games, he is listed on the first-year roster and designated by a (1). Thereafter, a player who is on the active squad for three or more regular season or postseason games is credited with an additional year of playing experience.

## NOTES

**Dick Stanfel,** offensive line; born July 20, 1927, San Francisco, Calif., lives in Chicago. Guard San Francisco 1948-51. Pro guard Detroit Lions 1952-55, Washington Redskins 1956-58. College coach: Notre Dame 1959-62, California 1963. Pro coach: Philadelphia Eagles 1964-70, San Francisco 49ers 1971-75, New Orleans Saints 1976-80 (head coach, 4 games in 1980), joined Bears in 1981.

# DALLAS COWBOYS

**National Football Conference
Eastern Division**

**Team Colors:** Royal Blue, Metallic Silver
Blue, and White

**6116 North Central Expressway
Dallas, Texas 75206
Telephone: (214) 369-8000**

### Club Officials

General Partner: H.R. Bright
President-General Manager: Texas E. Schramm
Vice President-Personnel Development:
  Gil Brandt
Vice President-Treasurer: Don Wilson
Vice President-Administration: Joe Bailey
Public Relations Director: Doug Todd
Business Manager: Dan Werner
Assistant Public Relations Director: Greg Aiello
Ticket Manager: Steve Orsini
Trainers: Don Cochren, Ken Locker
Equipment Manager: William T. (Buck) Buchanan
Cheerleaders Director: Suzanne Mitchell

**Stadium:** Texas Stadium • **Capacity:** 65,101
Irving, Texas 75062

**Playing Surface:** Texas Turf

**Training Camp:** California Lutheran College
Thousand Oaks, California
91360

## 1984 SCHEDULE

### Preseason
Aug. 4   **Green Bay** . . . . . . . . . . . . . . 8:00
Aug. 11  at San Diego. . . . . . . . . . . . . 6:00
Aug. 16  **Pittsburgh** . . . . . . . . . . . . . . 8:00
Aug. 25  **Houston** . . . . . . . . . . . . . . . . 8:00

### Regular Season
Sept. 3   at L.A. Rams (Monday). . . . . 6:00
Sept. 9   at New York Giants . . . . . . . 1:00
Sept. 16  **Philadelphia** . . . . . . . . . . . . 3:00
Sept. 23  **Green Bay** . . . . . . . . . . . . . . 3:00
Sept. 30  at Chicago . . . . . . . . . . . . . 12:00
Oct. 7   **St. Louis**. . . . . . . . . . . . . . 12:00
Oct. 14  at Washington . . . . . . . . . . . 4:00
Oct. 21  **New Orleans** . . . . . . . . . . . . 8:00
Oct. 28  **Colts** . . . . . . . . . . . . . . . . . 12:00
Nov. 4   **New York Giants** . . . . . . . 12:00
Nov. 11  at St. Louis . . . . . . . . . . . . . 12:00
Nov. 18  at Buffalo. . . . . . . . . . . . . . . . 1:00
Nov. 22  **New England** (Thanksgiving) 3:00
Dec. 2   at Philadelphia . . . . . . . . . . 1:00
Dec. 9   **Washington**. . . . . . . . . . . . . 3:00
Dec. 17  at Miami (Monday). . . . . . . . 9:00

## COWBOYS COACHING HISTORY

**(234-134-6)**
1960-83   Tom Landry . . . . . . . . . . . . . . 234-134-6

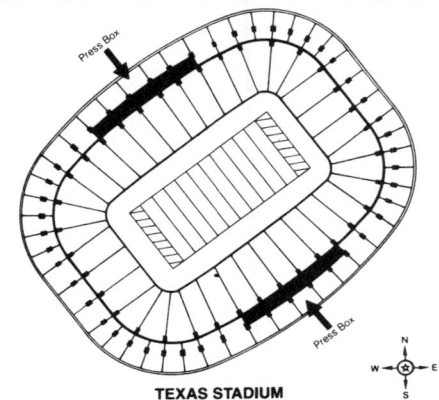

**TEXAS STADIUM**

## RECORD HOLDERS

### Individual Records — Career

| Category | Name | Performance |
|---|---|---|
| Rushing (Yds.) | Tony Dorsett, 1977-1983 | 8,336 |
| Passing (Yds.) | Roger Staubach, 1969-1979 | 22,700 |
| Passing (TDs) | Roger Staubach, 1969-1979 | 153 |
| Receiving (No.) | Drew Pearson, 1973-1983 | 489 |
| Receiving (Yds.) | Bob Hayes, 1965-1974 | 7,295 |
| Interceptions | Mel Renfro, 1964-1977 | 52 |
| Punting (Avg.) | Sam Baker, 1962-63 | 45.1 |
| Punt Return (Avg.) | Bob Hayes, 1965-1974 | 11.1 |
| Kickoff Return (Avg.) | Mel Renfro, 1964-1977 | 26.4 |
| Field Goals | Rafael Septien, 1978-1983 | 105 |
| Touchdowns (Tot.) | Bob Hayes, 1965-1974 | 76 |
| Points | Rafael Septien, 1978-1983 | 585 |

### Individual Records — Single Season

| Category | Name | Performance |
|---|---|---|
| Rushing (Yds.) | Tony Dorsett, 1981 | 1,646 |
| Passing (Yds.) | Danny White, 1983 | 3,980 |
| Passing (TDs) | Danny White, 1983 | 29 |
| Receiving (No.) | Ron Springs, 1983 | 73 |
| Receiving (Yds.) | Bob Hayes, 1966 | 1,232 |
| Interceptions | Everson Walls, 1981 | 11 |
| Punting (Avg.) | Sam Baker, 1962 | 45.4 |
| Punt Return (Avg.) | Bob Hayes, 1968 | 20.8 |
| Kickoff Return (Avg.) | Mel Renfro, 1965 | 30.0 |
| Field Goals | Rafael Septien, 1981 | 27 |
| Touchdowns (Tot.) | Dan Reeves, 1966 | 16 |
| Points | Rafael Septien, 1983 | 123 |

### Individual Records — Single Game

| Category | Name | Performance |
|---|---|---|
| Rushing (Yds.) | Tony Dorsett, 12-4-77 | 206 |
| Passing (Yds.) | Don Meredith, 11-10-63 | 460 |
| Passing (TDs) | Many times | 5 |
| | Last time by Danny White, 10-30-83 | |
| Receiving (No.) | Lance Rentzel, 11-19-67 | 13 |
| Receiving (Yds.) | Bob Hayes, 11-13-66 | 246 |
| Interceptions | Herb Adderley, 9-26-71 | 3 |
| | Lee Roy Jordan, 11-4-73 | 3 |
| | Dennis Thurman, 12-13-81 | 3 |
| Field Goals | Many times | 4 |
| | Last time by Rafael Septien, 9-21-81 | |
| Touchdowns (Tot.) | Many times | 4 |
| | Last time by Duane Thomas, 12-18-71 | |
| Points | Many times | 24 |
| | Last time by Duane Thomas, 12-18-71 | |

## 1983 TEAM STATISTICS

| | Dallas | Opp. |
|---|---|---|
| Total First Downs | 342 | 286 |
| Rushing | 109 | 82 |
| Passing | 205 | 181 |
| Penalty | 28 | 23 |
| Third Down Efficiency | 98/228 | 79/224 |
| Third Down Percentage | 43.0 | 35.3 |
| Total Net Yards | 5959 | 5427 |
| Total Offensive Plays | 1110 | 1025 |
| Avg. Gain per Play | 5.4 | 5.3 |
| Avg. Gain per Game | 372.4 | 339.2 |
| Net Yards Rushing | 2117 | 1499 |
| Total Rushing Plays | 519 | 410 |
| Avg. Gain per Rush | 4.1 | 3.7 |
| Avg. Gain Rushing per Game | 132.3 | 93.7 |
| Net Yards Passing | 3842 | 3928 |
| Lost Attempting to Pass | 37/314 | 57/437 |
| Gross Yards Passing | 4156 | 4365 |
| Attempts/Completions | 554/346 | 558/299 |
| Percent Completed | 62.5 | 53.6 |
| Had Intercepted | 25 | 27 |
| Avg. Net Passing per Game | 240.1 | 245.5 |
| Punts/Avg. | 83/39.4 | 84/41.8 |
| Punt Returns/Avg. | 51/9.0 | 53/11.1 |
| Kickoff Returns/Avg. | 71/19.0 | 78/23.2 |
| Interceptions/Avg. Ret. | 27/17.3 | 25/14.3 |
| Penalties/Yards | 99/847 | 100/873 |
| Fumbles/Ball Lost | 30/14 | 31/21 |
| Total Points | 479 | 360 |
| Avg. Points per Game | 29.9 | 22.5 |
| Touchdowns | 59 | 42 |
| Rushing | 21 | 12 |
| Passing | 31 | 27 |
| Returns and Recoveries | 7 | 3 |
| Field Goals | 22/27 | 22/30 |
| Conversions | 57/59 | 42/42 |
| Safeties | 1 | 0 |
| Avg. Time of Possession | 33:08 | 26:52 |

## 1983 TEAM RECORD

### Preseason (3-1)

| Date | Dallas | | Opponents |
|---|---|---|---|
| 8/6 | 20 | *Miami | 17 |
| 8/15 | 30 | Los Angeles Rams | 7 |
| 8/20 | 7 | *Pittsburgh | 24 |
| 8/27 | 34 | *Houston | 31 |
| | 91 | | 79 |

### Regular Season (12-4)

| Date | Dallas | | Opp. | Att. |
|---|---|---|---|---|
| 9/5 | 31 | Washington | 30 | 55,045 |
| 9/11 | 34 | St. Louis | 17 | 48,532 |
| 9/18 | 28 | *New York Giants | 13 | 62,347 |
| 9/25 | 21 | *New Orleans | 20 | 62,136 |
| 10/2 | 37 | Minnesota | 24 | 60,774 |
| 10/9 | 27 | Tampa Bay (OT) | 24 | 63,308 |
| 10/16 | 37 | *Philadelphia | 7 | 63,070 |
| 10/23 | 38 | *Los Angeles Raiders | 40 | 64,991 |
| 10/30 | 38 | New York Giants | 20 | 76,142 |
| 11/6 | 27 | Philadelphia | 20 | 71,236 |
| 11/13 | 23 | San Diego | 24 | 46,192 |
| 11/20 | 41 | *Kansas City | 21 | 64,103 |
| 11/24 | 35 | *St. Louis | 17 | 60,764 |
| 12/4 | 35 | Seattle | 10 | 63,352 |
| 12/11 | 10 | *Washington | 31 | 65,074 |
| 12/19 | 17 | San Francisco | 42 | 59,957 |
| | 479 | | 360 | 987,023 |

*Home Game     (OT) Overtime

### Score by Periods

| | | | | | | | |
|---|---|---|---|---|---|---|---|
| Dallas | 75 | 154 | 79 | 168 | 3 | — | 479 |
| Opponents | 120 | 84 | 70 | 86 | 0 | — | 360 |

### Attendance

Home 505,793     Away 481,230     Total 987,023
Single game home record, 80,259 (11-24-66)
Single season home record, 511,541 (1981)

## 1983 INDIVIDUAL STATISTICS

### Rushing

| | Att. | Yds. | Avg. | LG | TD |
|---|---|---|---|---|---|
| Dorsett | 289 | 1321 | 4.6 | 77 | 8 |
| Springs | 149 | 541 | 3.6 | 19t | 7 |
| Newsome | 44 | 185 | 4.2 | 20 | 2 |
| Newhouse | 9 | 34 | 3.8 | 8 | 0 |
| D. White | 18 | 31 | 1.7 | 22 | 4 |
| Pearson | 2 | 13 | 6.5 | 10 | 0 |
| T. Hill | 1 | 2 | 2.0 | 2 | 0 |
| Johnson | 1 | 0 | 0.0 | 0 | 0 |
| Hogeboom | 6 | −10 | −1.7 | −1 | 0 |
| Dallas | 519 | 2117 | 4.1 | 77 | 21 |
| Opponents | 410 | 1499 | 3.7 | 32 | 12 |

### Passing

| | Att. | Comp. | Pct. | Yds. | TD | Int. | Tkld. | Rate |
|---|---|---|---|---|---|---|---|---|
| D. White | 533 | 334 | 62.7 | 3980 | 29 | 23 | 37/314 | 85.6 |
| Hogeboom | 17 | 11 | 64.7 | 161 | 1 | 1 | 0/0 | 90.6 |
| Springs | 2 | 1 | 50.0 | 15 | 1 | 0 | 0/0 | 114.6 |
| Dorsett | 1 | 0 | 0.0 | 0 | 0 | 0 | 0/0 | 39.6 |
| Pearson | 1 | 0 | 0.0 | 0 | 0 | 1 | 0/0 | 0.0 |
| Dallas | 554 | 346 | 62.5 | 4156 | 31 | 25 | 37/314 | 85.2 |
| Opponents | 558 | 299 | 53.6 | 4365 | 27 | 27 | 57/437 | 75.3 |

### Receiving

| | No. | Yds. | Avg. | LG | TD |
|---|---|---|---|---|---|
| Springs | 73 | 589 | 8.1 | 80t | 1 |
| T. Hill | 49 | 801 | 16.3 | 75t | 7 |
| Pearson | 47 | 545 | 11.6 | 32 | 5 |
| Cosbie | 46 | 588 | 12.8 | 61t | 6 |
| Johnson | 41 | 561 | 13.7 | 46 | 3 |
| Dorsett | 40 | 287 | 7.2 | 24 | 1 |
| Donley | 18 | 370 | 20.6 | 47 | 2 |
| Newsome | 18 | 250 | 13.9 | 52t | 4 |
| DuPree | 12 | 142 | 11.8 | 28 | 1 |
| D. White | 1 | 15 | 15.0 | 15t | 1 |
| Rafferty | 1 | 8 | 8.0 | 8 | 0 |
| Dallas | 346 | 4156 | 12.0 | 80t | 31 |
| Opponents | 299 | 4365 | 14.6 | 83t | 27 |

### Interceptions

| | No. | Yds. | Avg. | LG | TD |
|---|---|---|---|---|---|
| Thurman | 6 | 49 | 8.2 | 34 | 0 |
| Fellows | 5 | 139 | 27.8 | 58t | 1 |
| Downs | 4 | 80 | 20.0 | 28 | 0 |
| Walls | 4 | 70 | 17.5 | 37 | 0 |
| Clinkscale | 2 | 68 | 34.0 | 68t | 1 |
| R. Hill | 2 | 12 | 6.0 | 12 | 0 |
| Bates | 1 | 29 | 29.0 | 29 | 0 |
| E. Jones | 1 | 12 | 12.0 | 12 | 0 |
| Dickerson | 1 | 8 | 8.0 | 8 | 0 |
| Breunig | 1 | 0 | 0.0 | 0 | 0 |
| Dallas | 27 | 467 | 17.3 | 68t | 2 |
| Opponents | 25 | 358 | 14.3 | 48t | 1 |

### Punting

| | No. | Yds. | Avg. | In 20 | LG |
|---|---|---|---|---|---|
| Warren | 39 | 1551 | 39.8 | 7 | 54 |
| D. White | 38 | 1543 | 40.6 | 6 | 50 |
| Miller | 5 | 178 | 35.6 | 1 | 43 |
| Dallas | 83 | 3272 | 39.4 | 14 | 54 |
| Opponents | 84 | 3515 | 41.8 | 23 | 59 |

### Punt Returns

| | No. | FC | Yds. | Avg. | LG | TD |
|---|---|---|---|---|---|---|
| R. Hill | 30 | 2 | 232 | 7.7 | 37 | 0 |
| Fellows | 10 | 3 | 75 | 7.5 | 14 | 0 |
| Allen | 9 | 1 | 153 | 17.0 | 68t | 1 |
| Donley | 1 | 0 | 1 | 1.0 | 1 | 0 |
| Newhouse | 1 | 0 | 0 | 0.0 | 0 | 0 |
| Dallas | 51 | 6 | 461 | 9.0 | 68t | 1 |
| Opponents | 53 | 9 | 588 | 11.1 | 56t | 1 |

### Kickoff Returns

| | No. | Yds. | Avg. | LG | TD |
|---|---|---|---|---|---|
| Fellows | 43 | 855 | 19.9 | 53 | 0 |
| R. Hill | 14 | 243 | 17.4 | 40 | 0 |
| Allen | 8 | 178 | 22.3 | 31 | 0 |
| Cosbie | 2 | 17 | 8.5 | 10 | 0 |
| Huther | 1 | 0 | 0.0 | 0 | 0 |
| McSwain | 1 | 17 | 17.0 | 17 | 0 |
| Newsome | 1 | 28 | 28.0 | 28 | 0 |
| Springs | 1 | 13 | 13.0 | 13 | 0 |
| Dallas | 71 | 1351 | 19.0 | 53 | 0 |
| Opponents | 78 | 1806 | 23.2 | 66 | 0 |

### Scoring

| | TD | TD R | TD P | TD Rt | PAT | FG | TP |
|---|---|---|---|---|---|---|---|
| Septien | | | | | 57/59 | 22/27 | 123 |
| Dorsett | 9 | 8 | 1 | 0 | | | 54 |
| Springs | 8 | 7 | 1 | 0 | | | 48 |
| T. Hill | 7 | 0 | 7 | 0 | | | 42 |
| Cosbie | 6 | 0 | 6 | 0 | | | 36 |
| Newsome | 6 | 2 | 4 | 0 | | | 36 |
| Pearson | 5 | 0 | 5 | 0 | | | 30 |
| D. White | 5 | 4 | 1 | 0 | | | 30 |
| Johnson | 3 | 0 | 3 | 0 | | | 18 |
| Donley | 2 | 0 | 2 | 0 | | | 12 |
| Fellows | 2 | 0 | 0 | 2 | | | 12 |
| Allen | 1 | 0 | 0 | 1 | | | 6 |
| Clinkscale | 1 | 0 | 0 | 1 | | | 6 |
| Downs | 1 | 0 | 0 | 1 | | | 6 |
| DuPree | 1 | 0 | 1 | 0 | | | 6 |
| Hegman | 1 | 0 | 0 | 1 | | | 6 |
| Thurman | 1 | 0 | 0 | 1 | | | 6 |
| Dickerson | | | (Safety) | | | | 2 |
| Dallas | 59 | 21 | 31 | 7 | 57/59 | 22/27 | 479 |
| Opponents | 42 | 12 | 27 | 3 | 42/42 | 22/30 | 360 |

### FIRST-ROUND SELECTIONS

(If Club had no first-round selection, first player drafted is listed with round in parentheses.)

| Year | Player, College, Position |
|---|---|
| 1960 | None |
| 1961 | Bob Lilly, Texas Christian, DT |
| 1962 | Sonny Gibbs, Texas Christian, QB (2) |
| 1963 | Lee Roy Jordan, Alabama, LB |
| 1964 | Scott Appleton, Texas, DT |
| 1965 | Craig Morton, California, QB |
| 1966 | John Niland, Iowa, G |
| 1967 | Phil Clark, Northwestern, DB (3) |
| 1968 | Dennis Homan, Alabama, WR |
| 1969 | Calvin Hill, Yale, RB |
| 1970 | Duane Thomas, West Texas State, RB |
| 1971 | Tody Smith, Southern California, DE |
| 1972 | Bill Thomas, Boston College, RB |
| 1973 | Billy Joe DuPree, Michigan State, TE |
| 1974 | Ed (Too Tall) Jones, Tennessee State, DE |
| | Charley Young, North Carolina State, RB |
| 1975 | Randy White, Maryland, LB |
| | Thomas Henderson, Langston, LB |
| 1976 | Aaron Kyle, Wyoming, DB |
| 1977 | Tony Dorsett, Pittsburgh, RB |
| 1978 | Larry Bethea, Michigan State, DE |
| 1979 | Robert Shaw, Tennessee, C |
| 1980 | Bill Roe, Colorado, LB (3) |
| 1981 | Howard Richards, Missouri, T |
| 1982 | Rod Hill, Kentucky State, DB |
| 1983 | Jim Jeffcoat, Arizona State, DE |
| 1984 | Billy Cannon, Jr., Texas A&M, LB |

# DALLAS COWBOYS 1984 VETERAN ROSTER

| No. | Name | Pos. | Ht. | Wt. | Birth-date | NFL Exp. | College | Birthplace | Residence | Games in '83 |
|---|---|---|---|---|---|---|---|---|---|---|
| 31 | Allen, Gary | RB | 5-10 | 183 | 4/23/60 | 3 | Hawaii | Baldwin Park, Calif. | Baldwin Park, Calif. | 7* |
| 62 | Baldinger, Brian | G | 6-4 | 253 | 1/7/59 | 3 | Duke | Massapequa, N.Y. | Dallas, Tex. | 16 |
| 40 | Bates, Bill | S | 6-1 | 195 | 6/6/61 | 2 | Tennessee | Knoxville, Tenn. | Knoxville, Tenn. | 16 |
| 53 | Breunig, Bob | LB | 6-2 | 225 | 7/4/53 | 10 | Arizona State | Inglewood, Calif. | Dallas, Tex. | 16 |
| 47 | Clinkscale, Dextor | S | 5-11 | 190 | 4/13/58 | 4 | South Carolina State | Greenville, S.C. | Dallas, Tex. | 15 |
| 61 | Cooper, Jim | T | 6-5 | 263 | 9/28/55 | 8 | Temple | Philadelphia, Pa. | Richardson, Tex. | 16 |
| 84 | Cosbie, Doug | TE | 6-6 | 232 | 2/27/56 | 6 | Santa Clara | Mountain View, Calif. | Plano, Tex. | 16 |
| 51 | Dickerson, Anthony | LB | 6-2 | 222 | 6/9/57 | 5 | Southern Methodist | Texas City, Tex. | Garland, Tex. | 16 |
| 83 | Donley, Doug | WR | 6-0 | 173 | 2/6/59 | 4 | Ohio State | Cambridge, Ohio | Garland, Tex. | 11 |
| 33 | Dorsett, Tony | RB | 5-11 | 192 | 4/7/54 | 8 | Pittsburgh | Aliquippa, Pa. | Dallas, Tex. | 16 |
| 26 | Downs, Michael | S | 6-3 | 203 | 6/9/59 | 4 | Rice | Dallas, Tex. | Dallas, Tex. | 16 |
| 78 | Dutton, John | DT | 6-7 | 275 | 2/6/51 | 11 | Nebraska | Evansville, Ind. | Dallas, Tex. | 16 |
| 27 | Fellows, Ron | CB | 6-0 | 174 | 11/7/58 | 4 | Missouri | South Bend, Ind. | Dallas, Tex. | 16 |
| 58 | Hegman, Mike | LB | 6-1 | 228 | 1/17/53 | 9 | Tennessee State | Memphis, Tenn. | Dallas, Tex. | 16 |
| 25 | Hill, Rod | CB | 6-0 | 182 | 3/14/59 | 3 | Kentucky State | Detroit, Mich. | Dallas, Tex. | 14 |
| 80 | Hill, Tony | WR | 6-2 | 198 | 6/23/56 | 8 | Stanford | San Diego, Calif. | Dallas, Tex. | 12 |
| 14 | Hogeboom, Gary | QB | 6-4 | 199 | 8/21/58 | 5 | Central Michigan | Grand Rapids, Mich. | Dallas, Tex. | 6 |
| 77 | Jeffcoat, Jim | DE | 6-5 | 264 | 4/1/61 | 2 | Arizona State | Long Branch, N.J. | Matawan, N.J. | 16 |
| 72 | Jones, Ed | DE | 6-9 | 272 | 2/23/51 | 10 | Tennessee State | Jackson, Tenn. | Dallas, Tex. | 16 |
| 23 | †Jones, James | RB | 5-10 | 202 | 12/6/58 | 4 | Mississippi State | Vicksburg, Miss. | Dallas, Tex. | 0* |
| 57 | King, Angelo | LB | 6-1 | 230 | 2/10/58 | 4 | South Carolina State | Columbia, S.C. | Dallas, Tex. | 16 |
| 52 | McLean, Scott | LB | 6-4 | 233 | 12/16/60 | 2 | Florida State | Clermont, Fla. | Dallas, Tex. | 4 |
| 35 | McSwain, Chuck | RB | 6-0 | 191 | 2/21/61 | 2 | Clemson | Rutherford, N.C. | Forest City, N.C. | 1 |
| 3 | Miller, Jim | P | 5-11 | 183 | 7/5/57 | 5 | Mississippi | Ripley, Miss. | Ripley, Miss. | 2 |
| 44 | †Newhouse, Robert | RB | 5-10 | 219 | 1/9/50 | 13 | Houston | Longview, Tex. | Dallas, Tex. | 16 |
| 30 | Newsome, Timmy | RB | 6-1 | 231 | 5/17/58 | 5 | Winston-Salem State | Ahoskie, N.C. | Dallas, Tex. | 16 |
| 88 | Pearson, Drew | WR | 6-0 | 193 | 1/12/51 | 12 | Tulsa | South River, N.J. | Dallas, Tex. | 14 |
| 65 | Petersen, Kurt | G | 6-4 | 268 | 6/17/57 | 5 | Missouri | St. Louis, Mo. | Carrollton, Tex. | 14 |
| 75 | Pozderac, Phil | T | 6-9 | 270 | 12/19/59 | 3 | Notre Dame | Cleveland, Ohio | Dallas, Tex. | 16 |
| 64 | Rafferty, Tom | C | 6-3 | 259 | 8/2/54 | 9 | Penn State | Syracuse, N.Y. | Dallas, Tex. | 16 |
|  | t-Renfro, Mike | WR | 6-0 | 188 | 6/19/55 | 7 | Texas Christian | Fort Worth Tex. | Missouri, Tex. | 9 |
| 70 | Richards, Howard | G | 6-6 | 258 | 8/7/59 | 4 | Missouri | St. Louis, Mo. | Richardson, Tex. | 16 |
| 50 | Rohrer, Jeff | LB | 6-3 | 232 | 12/25/58 | 3 | Yale | Manhattan Beach, Calif. | Dallas, Tex. | 16 |
| 66 | Schultz, Chris | T | 6-8 | 265 | 2/16/60 | 2 | Arizona | Burlington, Ontario | Dallas, Tex. | 5 |
| 68 | Scott, Herbert | G | 6-2 | 260 | 1/18/53 | 10 | Virginia Union | Virginia Beach, Va. | Lucas, Tex. | 16 |
| 1 | Septien, Rafael | K | 5-10 | 180 | 12/12/53 | 8 | Southwest Louisiana | Mexico City, Mex. | Dallas, Tex. | 16 |
| 82 | Simmons, Cleo | TE | 6-2 | 225 | 10/21/60 | 2 | Jackson State | Mobile, Ala. | Mobile, Ala. | 11 |
| 60 | Smerek, Don | DT | 6-7 | 257 | 12/20/57 | 3 | Nevada-Reno | Waterford, Mich. | Dallas, Tex. | 15 |
| 20 | Springs, Ron | RB | 6-1 | 210 | 11/1/56 | 5 | Ohio State | Williamsburg, Va. | Dallas, Tex. | 16 |
| 32 | Thurman, Dennis | CB | 5-11 | 183 | 4/13/56 | 7 | Southern California | Los Angeles, Calif. | Farmers Branch, Tex. | 16 |
| 63 | Titensor, Glen | C | 6-4 | 260 | 2/21/58 | 4 | Brigham Young | Westminster, Calif. | Dallas, Tex. | 15 |
| 71 | Tuinei, Mark | DT | 6-5 | 270 | 3/31/60 | 2 | Hawaii | Oceanside, Calif. | Honolulu, Hawaii | 10 |
| 24 | Walls, Everson | CB | 6-1 | 194 | 12/28/59 | 4 | Grambling | Dallas, Tex. | Dallas, Tex. | 16 |
| 58 | Walter, Mike | LB | 6-3 | 238 | 11/30/60 | 2 | Oregon | Salem, Ore. | Eugene, Ore. | 15 |
| 5 | Warren, John | P | 6-0 | 207 | 11/8/60 | 2 | Tennessee | Jesup, Ga. | Knoxville, Tenn. | 9 |
| 11 | White, Danny | QB-P | 6-2 | 196 | 2/9/52 | 9 | Arizona State | Mesa, Ariz. | Wylie, Tex. | 16 |
| 54 | White, Randy | DT | 6-4 | 263 | 1/15/53 | 10 | Maryland | Wilmington, Del. | Dallas, Tex. | 16 |

\* Allen played 1 game with Houston, 6 with Dallas in '83; J. Jones missed '83 season due to injury.

†Option playout; subject to developments.

t-Cowboys traded for Renfro (Oilers).

Traded—Wide receiver Butch Johnson to Houston.

Retired—Pat Donovan, 9-year tackle, 15 games in '83; Billy Joe DuPree, 11-year tight end, 16 games in '83; Harvey Martin, 11-year defensive end, 16 games in '83.

Also played with Cowboys in '83—DT Larry Bethea (14 games), QB Glenn Carano (16), LB Bruce Huther (11).

## COACHING STAFF

### Head Coach,
### Tom Landry

**Pro Career:** Last year's 12-4 season record boosted the Cowboys into the playoffs for an NFL record ninth consecutive year and the seventeenth time in the last 18 years. Landry has compiled 18 winning seasons in succession. Cowboys became the fourth team in NFL to win a second Super Bowl. They defeated Denver 27-10 in Super Bowl XII on January 15, 1978 at Louisiana Superdome. Dallas has played in four other Super Bowls (V, VI, X, and XIII), winning Game VI 24-3 over Miami. Cowboys only head coach in their 24-year history, Landry has compiled a 234-134-6 record. Pro defensive back with New York Yanks (AAFC) 1949, New York Giants 1950-55. Player-coach with Giants 1954-55, named all-pro in 1954. Defensive assistant coach with Giants 1956-59 before moving to Dallas as head coach in 1960.

**Background:** Halfback, University of Texas 1947-48, and played in Longhorns' victories over Alabama in 1948 Sugar Bowl and Georgia in 1949 Orange Bowl.

**Personal:** Born September 11, 1924 in Mission, Tex. A World War II bomber pilot. Tom and his wife, Alicia, live in Dallas and have three children—Tom Jr., Kitty, and Lisa.

### Assistant Coaches

**Neill Armstrong,** research and development; born March 9, 1926, Tishomingo, Okla., lives in Dallas. End Oklahoma State 1943-46. Pro end-defensive back Philadelphia Eagles 1947-51, Winnipeg Blue Bombers (CFL) 1951, 1953-54. College coach: Oklahoma State 1955-61. Pro coach: Houston Oilers 1962-63, Edmonton Eskimos (CFL) 1964-69 (head coach), Minnesota Vikings 1970-77, Chicago Bears 1978-81 (head coach), joined Cowboys in 1982.

**Al Lavan,** running backs; born September 13, 1946, Pierce, Fla., lives in Dallas. Defensive back Colorado State 1965-67. Pro defensive back Philadelphia Eagles 1968, Atlanta Falcons 1969-70. College coach: Colorado State 1972, Louisville 1973, Iowa State 1974, Georgia Tech 1977-78, Stanford 1979. Pro coach: Atlanta Falcons 1975-76, joined Cowboys in 1980.

**Alan Lowry,** special teams; born November 21, 1950, Irving, Tex., lives in Dallas. Defensive back-quarterback Texas 1970-72. No pro playing experience. College coach: Virginia Tech 1974, Wyoming 1975, Texas 1976-81. Pro coach: Joined Cowboys in 1982.

**Jim Myers,** assistant head coach-offensive line; born November 12, 1921, Madison, W. Va., lives in Dallas. Guard Tennessee 1941-42, 1946, Duke 1943. No pro playing experience. College coach: Wofford 1947, Vanderbilt 1948, UCLA 1949-56, Iowa State 1957 (head coach), Texas A&M 1958-61 (head coach). Pro coach: Joined Cowboys in 1962.

**Dick Nolan,** receivers; born March 26, 1932, Pittsburgh, Pa., lives in Dallas. Offensive-defensive back Maryland 1951-53. Pro defensive back New York Giants 1954-57, 1959-61, St. Louis Cardinals 1958, Dallas player-coach 1962. Pro coach: Dallas Cowboys 1963-67, San Francisco 49ers 1968-75 (head coach), New Orleans Saints 1977-80 (head coach), Houston Oilers 1981, rejoined Cowboys in 1982.

**Jim Shofner,** quarterbacks; born December 18, 1935, Grapevine, Tex., lives in Dallas. Running back Texas Christian 1955-57. Pro defensive back Cleveland Browns 1958-63. College coach: Texas Christian 1964-66, 1974-76 (head coach). Pro coach: San Francisco 49ers 1967-73, 1977, Cleveland Browns 1978-80, Houston Oilers 1981-82, joined Cowboys in 1983.

**Gene Stallings,** defensive backs; born March 2, 1935, Paris, Tex., lives in Dallas. End Texas A&M 1954-57. No pro playing experience. College coach: Texas A&M 1957, 1965-71 (head coach), Alabama 1958-64. Pro coach: Joined Cowboys in 1972.

**Ernie Stautner,** defensive coordinator-defensive line; born April 2, 1925, Kham, Bavaria, lives in Dallas. Tackle Boston College 1946-49. Pro defensive tackle Pittsburgh Steelers 1950-63. Pro coach: Pittsburgh Steelers 1963-64, Washington Redskins 1965, joined Cowboys in 1966.

**Jerry Tubbs,** linebackers; born January 23, 1935, Breckenridge, Tex., lives in Dallas. Center-linebacker Oklahoma 1954-56. Pro linebacker Chicago Cardinals 1957, San Francisco 49ers 1958-59, Dallas Cowboys 1960-67. Pro coach: Joined Cowboys in 1965.

**Bob Ward,** conditioning; born July 4, 1933, Huntington Park, Calif., lives in Dallas. Fullback-quarterback Whitworth College 1952-54. Doctorate in physical education, Indiana University. No pro playing experience. College coach: Fullerton, Calif. J.C. (track) 1965-75. Pro coach: Joined Cowboys in 1975.

## DALLAS COWBOYS 1984 FIRST-YEAR ROSTER

| Name | Pos. | Ht. | Wt. | Birth-date | College | Birthplace | Residence | How Acq. |
|------|------|-----|-----|-----------|---------|-----------|-----------|---------|
| Aughtman, Dowe | DT-DE | 6-2 | 272 | 1/28/61 | Auburn | Brewton, Ala. | Brewton, Ala. | D11 |
| Beautrow, Jim (1) | TE | 6-3 | 225 | 1/6/60 | San Diego State | Santa Barbara, Calif. | Santa Barbara, Calif. | FA |
| Bone, Rod (1) | S | 6-2 | 196 | 2/4/61 | Notre Dame | Las Cruces, N.M. | Las Cruces, N.M. | FA |
| Caldwell, Bryan (1) | DE | 6-4 | 248 | 5/6/60 | Arizona State | Oakland, Calif. | Mesa, Ariz. | D3('83) |
| Cannon, Billy | LB | 6-4 | 235 | 10/8/61 | Texas A&M | Baton Rouge, La. | Baton Rouge, La. | D1 |
| Cornwell, Fred | TE | 6-5 | 236 | 8/7/61 | Southern California | Osborne, Kan. | Saugus, Calif. | D3 |
| DeOssie, Steve | LB | 6-2 | 250 | 11/22/62 | Boston College | Tacoma, Wash. | Roslindale, Mass. | D4 |
| Granger, Norm | RB | 5-9 | 217 | 9/14/61 | Iowa | Newark, N.J. | Newark, N.J. | D5a |
| Hunt, John | T-G | 6-4 | 262 | 11/6/62 | Florida | Orlando, Fla. | Orlando, Fla. | D9 |
| Krenk, Mitch (1) | TE | 6-4 | 225 | 11/19/59 | Nebraska | Crete, Neb. | Lincoln, Neb. | FA |
| Langston, Mike (1) | DE | 6-4 | 255 | 1/17/61 | Arizona State | Beaver Falls, Pa. | Beaver Falls, Pa. | FA |
| Lewis, Carl | WR | 6-3 | 187 | 7/1/61 | Houston | Willingsboro, N.J. | Willingsboro, N.J. | D12 |
| Lockhart, Eugene | LB | 6-2 | 228 | 4/2/61 | Houston | Crockett, Tex. | Crockett, Tex. | D6 |
| Martin, Ed | LB | 6-3 | 218 | 5/29/62 | Indiana State | Atlanta, Ga. | Evanston, Ill. | D7 |
| Maune, Neal | T-G | 6-4 | 249 | 11/4/60 | Notre Dame | Washington, Mo. | Marthasville, Mo. | D9a |
| Pelluer, Steve | QB | 6-4 | 204 | 7/29/62 | Washington | Bellevue, Wash. | Yakima, Wash. | D5 |
| Phillips, Kirk (1) | WR | 6-1 | 195 | 7/31/60 | Tulsa | Poteau, Okla. | Spiro, Okla. | FA |
| Revell, Mike | RB | 5-11 | 197 | 1/23/62 | Bethune-Cookman | Brooksville, Fla. | Brooksville, Fla. | D8 |
| Salonen, Brian | TE | 6-2 | 227 | 7/29/61 | Montana | Glasgow, Mont. | Great Falls, Mont. | D10 |
| Scott, Victor | CB-S | 5-10 | 182 | 6/1/62 | Colorado | St. Louis, Mo. | East St. Louis, Ill. | D2 |
| Taylor, Dan (1) | T | 6-3 | 258 | 5/13/59 | Idaho State | Olympia, Wash. | Olympia, Wash. | D11('83) |
| Veldman, Gregg (1) | TE | 6-3 | 255 | 7/27/60 | Moorhead State | Minneapolis, Minn. | South St. Paul, Minn. | FA |

Players who report to an NFL team for the first time are designated on rosters as rookies (R). If a player reported to an NFL training camp in a previous year but was not on the active squad for three or more regular season or postseason games, he is listed on the first-year roster and designated by a (1). Thereafter, a player who is on the active squad for three or more regular season or postseason games is credited with an additional year of playing experience.

## NOTES

_____

_____

_____

_____

_____

_____

_____

_____

_____

_____

_____

_____

_____

_____

_____

_____

_____

_____

**National Football Conference
Central Division**

**Team Colors:** Honolulu Blue and Silver

**Pontiac Silverdome
1200 Featherstone Road — Box 4200
Pontiac, Michigan 48057
Telephone: (313) 335-4131**

**Club Officials**

President-Owner: William Clay Ford
Executive Vice President-General Manager:
  Russell Thomas
Director of Football Operations-Head Coach:
  Monte Clark
Director of Player Personnel: Tim Rooney
Controller: Charles Schmidt
College Scouts: Joe Bushofsky, Dirk Dierking,
  Ron Hughes, Jim Owen
Director of Public Relations: Don Kremer
Publicity Assistant: Brian Muir
Ticket Manager: Fred Otto
Trainer: Kent Falb
Strength and Conditioning: Gary Wade
Equipment Manager: Dan Jaroshewich

**Stadium:** Pontiac Silverdome • **Capacity:** 80,638
  1200 Featherstone Road
  Pontiac, Michigan 48057

**Playing Surface:** AstroTurf

**Training Camp:** Oakland University
  Rochester, Michigan 48063

## 1984 SCHEDULE

**Preseason**

| | | |
|---|---|---|
| Aug. 4 | **Philadelphia** | 7:00 |
| Aug. 11 | **Seattle** | 7:00 |
| Aug. 18 | at Buffalo | 6:00 |
| Aug. 24 | at Cincinnati | 7:00 |

**Regular Season**

| | | |
|---|---|---|
| Sept. 2 | **San Francisco** | 1:00 |
| Sept. 9 | at Atlanta | 1:00 |
| Sept. 16 | at Tampa Bay | 4:00 |
| Sept. 23 | **Minnesota** | 1:00 |
| Sept. 30 | at San Diego | 1:00 |
| Oct. 7 | **Denver** | 1:00 |
| Oct. 14 | **Tampa Bay** | 1:00 |
| Oct. 21 | at Minnesota | 12:00 |
| Oct. 28 | at Green Bay | 12:00 |
| Nov. 4 | **Philadelphia** | 1:00 |
| Nov. 11 | at Washington | 1:00 |
| Nov. 18 | at Chicago | 12:00 |
| Nov. 22 | **Green Bay** (Thanksgiving) | 12:30 |
| Dec. 2 | at Seattle | 1:00 |
| Dec. 10 | **L.A. Raiders** (Monday) | 9:00 |
| Dec. 16 | **Chicago** | 1:00 |

## LIONS COACHING HISTORY

**Portsmouth Spartans 1930-33
(343-325-31)**

| | | |
|---|---|---|
| 1930-36 | George (Potsy) Clark | 53-26-9 |
| 1937-38 | Earl (Dutch) Clark | 14-8-0 |
| 1939 | Gus Henderson | 6-5-0 |
| 1940 | George (Potsy) Clark | 5-5-1 |
| 1941-42 | Bill Edwards* | 4-9-1 |
| 1942 | John Karcis | 0-8-0 |
| 1943-47 | Charles (Gus) Dorais | 20-31-2 |
| 1948-50 | Alvin (Bo) McMillin | 12-24-0 |
| 1951-56 | Raymond (Buddy) Parker | 50-24-2 |
| 1957-64 | George Wilson | 55-45-6 |
| 1965-66 | Harry Gilmer | 10-16-2 |
| 1967-72 | Joe Schmidt | 43-35-7 |
| 1973 | Don McCafferty | 6-7-1 |
| 1974-76 | Rick Forzano** | 15-17-0 |
| 1976-77 | Tommy Hudspeth | 11-13-0 |
| 1978-83 | Monte Clark | 39-52-0 |

*Resigned after three games in 1942
**Resigned after four games in 1976

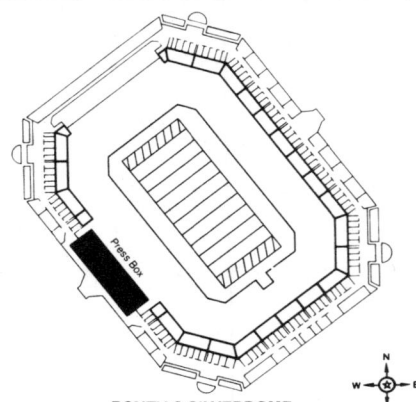

**PONTIAC SILVERDOME**

## RECORD HOLDERS

### Individual Records—Career

| Category | Name | Performance |
|---|---|---|
| Rushing (Yds.) | Dexter Bussey, 1974-1983 | 5,014 |
| Passing (Yds.) | Bobby Layne, 1950-58 | 15,710 |
| Passing (TDs) | Bobby Layne, 1950-58 | 118 |
| Receiving (No.) | Charlie Sanders, 1968-1977 | 336 |
| Receiving (Yds.) | Gail Cogdill, 1960-68 | 5,220 |
| Interceptions | Dick LeBeau, 1959-1972 | 62 |
| Punting (Avg.) | Yale Lary, 1952-53, 1956-1964 | 44.3 |
| Punt Return (Avg.) | Jack Christiansen, 1951-58 | 12.8 |
| Kickoff Return (Avg.) | Pat Studstill, 1961-67 | 25.7 |
| Field Goals | Errol Mann, 1969-1976 | 141 |
| Touchdowns (Tot.) | Billy Sims, 1980-83 | 42 |
| Points | Errol Mann, 1969-1976 | 636 |

### Individual Records—Single Season

| Category | Name | Performance |
|---|---|---|
| Rushing (Yds.) | Billy Sims, 1981 | 1,437 |
| Passing (Yds.) | Gary Danielson, 1980 | 3,223 |
| Passing (TDs) | Bobby Layne, 1951 | 26 |
| Receiving (No.) | Pat Studstill, 1966 | 67 |
| Receiving (Yds.) | Pat Studstill, 1966 | 1,266 |
| Interceptions | Don Doll, 1950 | 12 |
| | Jack Christiansen, 1953 | 12 |
| Punting (Avg.) | Yale Lary, 1963 | 48.9 |
| Punt Return (Avg.) | Jack Christiansen, 1952 | 21.5 |
| Kickoff Return (Avg.) | Tom Watkins, 1965 | 34.4 |
| Field Goals | Ed Murray, 1980 | 27 |
| Touchdowns (Tot.) | Billy Sims, 1980 | 16 |
| Points | Doak Walker, 1950 | 128 |

### Individual Records—Single Game

| Category | Name | Performance |
|---|---|---|
| Rushing (Yds.) | Bob Hoernschemeyer, 11-23-50 | 198 |
| Passing (Yds.) | Bobby Layne, 11-5-50 | 374 |
| Passing (TDs) | Gary Danielson, 12-9-78 | 5 |
| Receiving (No.) | Cloyce Box, 12-3-50 | 12 |
| Receiving (Yds.) | Cloyce Box, 12-3-50 | 302 |
| Interceptions | Don Doll, 10-23-49 | 4 |
| Field Goals | Garo Yepremian, 11-13-66 | 6 |
| Touchdowns (Tot.) | Cloyce Box, 12-3-50 | 4 |
| Points | Cloyce Box, 12-3-50 | 24 |

## 1983 TEAM STATISTICS

| | Detroit | Opp. |
|---|---|---|
| Total First Downs . . . . . . . . . . . . . . . . . | 315 | 324 |
| Rushing . . . . . . . . . . . . . . . . . . . . . | 136 | 133 |
| Passing . . . . . . . . . . . . . . . . . . . . | 156 | 161 |
| Penalty . . . . . . . . . . . . . . . . . . . . | 23 | 30 |
| Third Down Efficiency . . . . . . . . . . . | 97/224 | 80/213 |
| Third Down Percentage . . . . . . . . . | 43.3 | 37.6 |
| Total Net Yards . . . . . . . . . . . . . . . . . | 5136 | 5216 |
| Total Offensive Plays . . . . . . . . . . . . | 1061 | 1061 |
| Avg. Gain per Play . . . . . . . . . . . . . | 4.8 | 4.9 |
| Avg. Gain per Game . . . . . . . . . . . | 321.0 | 326.0 |
| Net Yards Rushing . . . . . . . . . . . . . . | 2181 | 2104 |
| Total Rushing Plays . . . . . . . . . . . . . | 513 | 503 |
| Avg. Gain per Rush . . . . . . . . . . . . | 4.3 | 4.2 |
| Avg. Gain Rushing per Game. . . . . | 136.3 | 131.5 |
| Net Yards Passing . . . . . . . . . . . . . . | 2955 | 3112 |
| Lost Attempting to Pass . . . . . . . . | 45/342 | 43/289 |
| Gross Yards Passing . . . . . . . . . . . | 3297 | 3401 |
| Attempts/Completions . . . . . . . . . . | 503/263 | 515/297 |
| Percent Completed . . . . . . . . . . . . | 52.3 | 57.7 |
| Had Intercepted . . . . . . . . . . . . . . . | 23 | 22 |
| Avg. Net Passing per Game . . . . . . | 184.7 | 194.5 |
| Punts/Avg. . . . . . . . . . . . . . . . . . . . | 72/40.4 | 79/40.1 |
| Punt Returns/Avg. . . . . . . . . . . . . . | 46/11.3 | 39/7.7 |
| Kickoff Returns/Avg. . . . . . . . . . . . | 61/19.5 | 71/16.1 |
| Interceptions/Avg. Ret. . . . . . . . . . | 22/8.4 | 23/10.5 |
| Penalties/Yards . . . . . . . . . . . . . . . | 118/988 | 117/1062 |
| Fumbles/Ball Lost . . . . . . . . . . . . . . | 41/16 | 33/15 |
| Total Points . . . . . . . . . . . . . . . . . . | 347 | 286 |
| Avg. Points per Game . . . . . . . . . . . | 21.7 | 17.9 |
| Touchdowns . . . . . . . . . . . . . . . . . | 38 | 33 |
| Rushing . . . . . . . . . . . . . . . . . . . | 18 | 11 |
| Passing . . . . . . . . . . . . . . . . . . . | 19 | 21 |
| Returns and Recoveries . . . . . . . . . | 1 | 1 |
| Field Goals . . . . . . . . . . . . . . . . . | 25/32 | 18/26 |
| Conversions . . . . . . . . . . . . . . . . | 38/38 | 32/33 |
| Safeties . . . . . . . . . . . . . . . . . . . | 3 | 1 |
| Avg. Time of Possession . . . . . . . . . . | 30:08 | 29:52 |

## 1983 TEAM RECORD
### Preseason (2-2)

| Date | Detroit | | Opponents |
|---|---|---|---|
| 8/5 | 17 | Philadelphia | 21 |
| 8/13 | 17 | Kansas City | 13 |
| 8/20 | 16 | *Buffalo | 17 |
| 8/27 | 34 | *Cincinnati | 7 |
| | 84 | | 58 |

### Regular Season (9-7)

| Date | Detroit | | Opp. | Att. |
|---|---|---|---|---|
| 9/4 | 11 | Tampa Bay | 0 | 62,154 |
| 9/11 | 26 | *Cleveland | 31 | 60,095 |
| 9/18 | 14 | *Atlanta | 30 | 54,622 |
| 9/25 | 17 | Minnesota | 20 | 58,254 |
| 10/2 | 10 | Los Angeles Rams | 21 | 49,403 |
| 10/9 | 38 | *Green Bay | 14 | 67,738 |
| 10/16 | 31 | *Chicago | 17 | 66,709 |
| 10/23 | 17 | Washington | 38 | 43,189 |
| 10/30 | 38 | Chicago | 17 | 58,764 |
| 11/7 | 15 | *New York Giants | 9 | 68,985 |
| 11/13 | 17 | Houston | 27 | 40,660 |
| 11/20 | 23 | Green Bay (OT) | 20 | 50,050 |
| 11/24 | 45 | *Pittsburgh | 3 | 77,724 |
| 12/5 | 13 | *Minnesota | 2 | 79,169 |
| 12/11 | 9 | Cincinnati | 17 | 45,375 |
| 12/18 | 23 | *Tampa Bay | 20 | 78,553 |
| | 347 | | 286 | 961,444 |

*Home Game          (OT) Overtime

### Score by Periods

| | | | | | | | |
|---|---|---|---|---|---|---|---|
| Detroit | 73 | 109 | 88 | 74 | 3 | — | 347 |
| Opponents | 54 | 122 | 37 | 73 | 0 | — | 286 |

### Attendance
Home 553,595     Away 407,849     Total 961,444
Single game home record, 80,444 (12-20-81)
Single season home record, 621,353 (1980)

## 1983 INDIVIDUAL STATISTICS

### Rushing

| | Att. | Yds. | Avg. | LG | TD |
|---|---|---|---|---|---|
| Sims | 220 | 1040 | 4.7 | 41 | 7 |
| Jones | 135 | 475 | 3.5 | 18 | 6 |
| Bussey | 57 | 249 | 4.4 | 26 | 0 |
| Hipple | 41 | 171 | 4.2 | 27 | 3 |
| V. Thompson | 40 | 138 | 3.5 | 10 | 1 |
| L. Thompson | 4 | 72 | 18.0 | 40t | 1 |
| Kane | 4 | 19 | 4.8 | 9 | 0 |
| Nichols | 1 | 13 | 13.0 | 13 | 0 |
| Danielson | 6 | 8 | 1.3 | 8 | 0 |
| King | 3 | 6 | 2.0 | 4 | 0 |
| Black | 2 | −10 | −5.0 | 0 | 0 |
| Detroit | 513 | 2181 | 4.3 | 41 | 18 |
| Opponents | 503 | 2104 | 4.2 | 42 | 11 |

### Passing

| | Att. | Comp. | Pct. | Yds. | TD | Int. | Tkld. | Rate |
|---|---|---|---|---|---|---|---|---|
| Hipple | 387 | 204 | 52.7 | 2577 | 12 | 18 | 37/274 | 64.7 |
| Danielson | 113 | 59 | 52.2 | 720 | 7 | 4 | 8/68 | 78.0 |
| Jones | 2 | 0 | 0.0 | 0 | 0 | 0 | 0/0 | 39.6 |
| Black | 1 | 0 | 0.0 | 0 | 0 | 1 | 0/0 | 0.0 |
| Detroit | 503 | 263 | 52.3 | 3297 | 19 | 23 | 45/342 | 66.5 |
| Opponents | 515 | 297 | 57.7 | 3401 | 21 | 22 | 43/289 | 73.5 |

### Receiving

| | No. | Yds. | Avg. | LG | TD |
|---|---|---|---|---|---|
| Jones | 46 | 467 | 10.2 | 46 | 1 |
| Sims | 42 | 419 | 10.0 | 54 | 0 |
| L. Thompson | 41 | 752 | 18.3 | 80t | 3 |
| Chadwick | 40 | 617 | 15.4 | 45 | 4 |
| Nichols | 29 | 437 | 15.1 | 46 | 1 |
| Norris | 26 | 291 | 11.2 | 41 | 7 |
| Rubick | 10 | 81 | 8.1 | 15 | 1 |
| King | 9 | 76 | 8.4 | 14 | 0 |
| Bussey | 8 | 49 | 6.1 | 14t | 1 |
| Scott | 5 | 71 | 14.2 | 25 | 1 |
| V. Thompson | 4 | 16 | 4.0 | 8 | 0 |
| Kane | 2 | 15 | 7.5 | 9 | 0 |
| McCall | 1 | 6 | 6.0 | 6 | 0 |
| Detroit | 263 | 3297 | 12.5 | 80t | 19 |
| Opponents | 297 | 3401 | 11.5 | 84 | 21 |

### Interceptions

| | No. | Yds. | Avg. | LG | TD |
|---|---|---|---|---|---|
| McNorton | 7 | 30 | 4.3 | 15 | 0 |
| Watkins | 4 | 48 | 12.0 | 31 | 0 |
| Cobb | 4 | 19 | 4.8 | 13 | 0 |
| Barnes | 2 | 70 | 35.0 | 70 | 0 |
| Hall | 2 | 18 | 9.0 | 18 | 0 |
| Fantetti | 2 | 0 | 0.0 | 0 | 0 |
| Latimer | 1 | 0 | 0.0 | 0 | 0 |
| Detroit | 22 | 185 | 8.4 | 70 | 0 |
| Opponents | 23 | 241 | 10.5 | 31 | 0 |

### Punting

| | No. | Yds. | Avg. | In 20 | LG |
|---|---|---|---|---|---|
| Black | 71 | 2911 | 41.0 | 17 | 60 |
| Detroit | 72 | 2911 | 40.4 | 17 | 60 |
| Opponents | 79 | 3167 | 40.1 | 14 | 64 |

### Punt Returns

| | No. | FC | Yds. | Avg. | LG | TD |
|---|---|---|---|---|---|---|
| Jenkins | 23 | 1 | 230 | 10.0 | 43 | 0 |
| Martin | 15 | 3 | 183 | 12.2 | 81t | 1 |
| Hall | 8 | 4 | 109 | 13.6 | 66 | 0 |
| Latimer | 0 | 1 | 0 | — | 0 | 0 |
| Detroit | 46 | 9 | 522 | 11.3 | 81t | 1 |
| Opponents | 39 | 4 | 302 | 7.7 | 33 | 0 |

### Kickoff Returns

| | No. | Yds. | Avg. | LG | TD |
|---|---|---|---|---|---|
| Hall | 23 | 492 | 21.4 | 32 | 0 |
| Jenkins | 22 | 459 | 20.9 | 30 | 0 |
| Martin | 8 | 140 | 17.5 | 51 | 0 |
| Caver | 4 | 71 | 17.8 | 33 | 0 |
| Curley | 1 | 7 | 7.0 | 7 | 0 |
| King | 1 | 11 | 11.0 | 11 | 0 |
| E. Lee | 1 | 11 | 11.0 | 11 | 0 |
| Norris | 1 | 0 | 0.0 | 0 | 0 |
| Detroit | 61 | 1191 | 19.5 | 51 | 0 |
| Opponents | 71 | 1146 | 16.1 | 49 | 0 |

### Scoring

| | TD | TD R | TD P | TD Rt | PAT | FG | TP |
|---|---|---|---|---|---|---|---|
| Murray | | | | | 38/38 | 25/32 | 113 |
| Jones | 7 | 6 | 1 | 0 | | | 42 |
| Norris | 7 | 0 | 7 | 0 | | | 42 |
| Sims | 7 | 7 | 0 | 0 | | | 42 |
| Chadwick | 4 | 0 | 4 | 0 | | | 24 |
| L. Thompson | 4 | 1 | 3 | 0 | | | 24 |
| Hipple | 3 | 3 | 0 | 0 | | | 18 |
| Bussey | 1 | 0 | 1 | 0 | | | 6 |
| Martin | 1 | 0 | 0 | 1 | | | 6 |
| Nichols | 1 | 0 | 1 | 0 | | | 6 |
| Rubick | 1 | 0 | 1 | 0 | | | 6 |
| Scott | 1 | 0 | 1 | 0 | | | 6 |
| V. Thompson | 1 | 1 | 0 | 0 | | | 6 |
| English | (2 Safeties) | | | | | | 4 |
| Fanning | (Safety) | | | | | | 2 |
| Detroit | 38 | 18 | 19 | 1 | 38/38 | 25/32 | 347 |
| Opponents | 33 | 11 | 21 | 1 | 32/33 | 18/26 | 286 |

## FIRST-ROUND SELECTIONS

(If Club had no first-round selection, first player drafted is listed with round in parentheses.)

| Year | Player, College, Position |
|---|---|
| 1936 | Sid Wagner, Michigan State, G |
| 1937 | Lloyd Cardwell, Nebraska, B |
| 1938 | Alex Wojciechowicz, Fordham, C |
| 1939 | John Pingel, Michigan State, B |
| 1940 | Doyle Nave, Southern California, B |
| 1941 | Jim Thomason, Texas A&M, B |
| 1942 | Bob Westfall, Michigan, B |
| 1943 | Frank Sinkwich, Georgia, B |
| 1944 | Otto Graham, Northwestern, B |
| 1945 | Frank Szymanski, Notre Dame, C |
| 1946 | Bill Dellastatious, Missouri, B |
| 1947 | Glenn Davis, Army, B |
| 1948 | Y. A. Tittle, Louisiana State, B |
| 1949 | John Rauch, Georgia, B |
| 1950 | Leon Hart, Notre Dame, E |
| | Joe Watson, Rice, C |
| 1951 | Dick Stanfel, San Francisco, G (2) |
| 1952 | Yale Lary, Texas A&M, B (3) |
| 1953 | Harley Sewell, Texas, G |
| 1954 | Dick Chapman, Rice, T |
| 1955 | Dave Middleton, Auburn, B |
| 1956 | Hopalong Cassady, Ohio State, B |
| 1957 | Bill Glass, Baylor, G |
| 1958 | Alex Karras, Iowa, T |
| 1959 | Nick Pietrosante, Notre Dame, B |
| 1960 | John Robinson, Louisiana State, S |
| 1961 | Danny LaRose, Missouri, T (2) |
| 1962 | John Hadl, Kansas, QB |
| 1963 | Daryl Sanders, Ohio State, T |
| 1964 | Pete Beathard, Southern California, QB |
| 1965 | Tom Nowatzke, Indiana, RB |
| 1966 | Nick Eddy, Notre Dame, RB (2) |
| 1967 | Mel Farr, UCLA, RB |
| 1968 | Greg Landry, Massachusetts, QB |
| | Earl McCullouch, USC, WR |
| 1969 | Altie Taylor, Utah State, RB (2) |
| 1970 | Steve Owens, Oklahoma, RB |
| 1971 | Bob Bell, Cincinnati, DT |
| 1972 | Herb Orvis, Colorado, DE |
| 1973 | Ernie Price, Texas A&I, DE |
| 1974 | Ed O'Neil, Penn State, LB |
| 1975 | Lynn Boden, South Dakota State, G |
| 1976 | James Hunter, Grambling, DB |
| | Lawrence Gaines, Wyoming, RB |
| 1977 | Walt Williams, New Mexico State, DB (2) |
| 1978 | Luther Bradley, Notre Dame, DB |
| 1979 | Keith Dorney, Penn State, T |
| 1980 | Billy Sims, Oklahoma, RB |
| 1981 | Mark Nichols, San Jose State, WR |
| 1982 | Jimmy Williams, Nebraska, LB |
| 1983 | James Jones, Florida, RB |
| 1984 | David Lewis, California, TE |

## DETROIT LIONS 1984 VETERAN ROSTER

| No. | Name | Pos. | Ht. | Wt. | Birth-date | NFL Exp. | College | Birthplace | Residence | Games in '83 |
|---|---|---|---|---|---|---|---|---|---|---|
| 54 | Barnes, Roosevelt | LB | 6-2 | 222 | 8/3/58 | 3 | Purdue | Ft. Wayne, Ind. | Ft. Wayne, Ind. | 16 |
| 11 | Black, Mike | P | 6-1 | 197 | 1/18/61 | 2 | Arizona State | Glendale, Calif. | Glendale, Calif. | 16 |
| 24 | Bussey, Dexter | RB | 5-11 | 210 | 3/11/52 | 11 | Texas-Arlington | Dallas, Tex. | Birmingham, Mich. | 15 |
| 89 | Chadwick, Jeff | WR | 6-3 | 185 | 12/16/60 | 2 | Grand Valley State | Detroit, Mich. | Dearborn Heights, Mich. | 16 |
| 53 | Cobb, Garry | LB | 6-2 | 227 | 3/16/57 | 6 | Southern California | Stamford, Conn. | West Bloomfield, Mich. | 15 |
| 66 | Cofer, Mike | DE | 6-5 | 245 | 4/7/60 | 2 | Tennessee | Knoxville, Tenn. | Knoxville, Tenn. | 16 |
| 50 | Curley, August | LB | 6-3 | 222 | 1/24/60 | 2 | Southern California | Little Rock, Ark. | Pontiac, Mich. | 10 |
| 16 | Danielson, Gary | QB | 6-2 | 196 | 9/10/51 | 8 | Purdue | Detroit, Mich. | Troy, Mich. | 10 |
| 73 | †Dawson, Mike | DT | 6-3 | 254 | 10/16/53 | 9 | Arizona | Dorking, England | Manchester, Mo. | 16 |
| 72 | Dieterich, Chris | T | 6-3 | 255 | 7/27/58 | 5 | North Carolina State | Freeport, N.Y. | Raleigh, N.C. | 16 |
| 58 | Doig, Steve | LB | 6-2 | 242 | 3/28/60 | 3 | New Hampshire | Melrose, Mass. | North Reading, Mass. | 9 |
| 70 | Dorney, Keith | T | 6-5 | 265 | 12/3/57 | 6 | Penn State | Macungie, Pa. | Capistrano, Calif. | 13 |
| 61 | Elias, Homer | G | 6-2 | 255 | 5/1/55 | 7 | Tennessee State | Ft. Benning, Ga. | Rochester, Mich. | 14 |
| 78 | English, Doug | DT | 6-5 | 258 | 8/25/53 | 9 | Texas | Dallas, Tex. | Austin, Tex. | 15 |
| 57 | Fantetti, Ken | LB | 6-2 | 232 | 4/7/57 | 6 | Wyoming | Toledo, Ore. | Rochester, Mich. | 16 |
| 65 | Fowler, Amos | C | 6-3 | 253 | 2/11/56 | 7 | Southern Mississippi | Pensacola, Fla. | Rochester, Mich. | 16 |
| 79 | Gay, William | DE | 6-5 | 255 | 5/28/55 | 7 | Southern California | San Francisco, Calif. | Rochester, Mich. | 15 |
| 33 | Graham, William | S | 5-11 | 191 | 9/27/59 | 3 | Texas | Greenwood, Miss. | Silsbee, Tex. | 14 |
| 67 | Greco, Don | G | 6-3 | 255 | 4/1/59 | 3 | Western Illinois | St. Louis, Mo. | St. Louis, Mo. | 12 |
| 62 | Green, Curtis | DE | 6-3 | 252 | 6/3/57 | 4 | Alabama State | Quincy, Fla. | Quincy, Fla. | 16 |
| 35 | Hall, Alvin | S-KR | 5-10 | 184 | 8/12/58 | 4 | Miami, Ohio | Dayton, Ohio | Rochester, Mich. | 16 |
| 23 | Harvey, Maurice | S | 5-9 | 187 | 1/14/56 | 6 | Ball State | Cincinnati, Ohio | Cincinnati, Ohio | 13* |
| 17 | Hipple, Eric | QB | 6-2 | 196 | 9/16/57 | 5 | Utah State | Lubbock, Tex. | Bloomfield Hills, Mich. | 16 |
| 31 | Jenkins, Ken | RB-KR | 5-8 | 184 | 5/8/59 | 2 | Bucknell | Washington, D.C. | Bensalem, Pa. | 12 |
| 21 | Johnson, Demetrious | CB-S | 5-11 | 190 | 7/21/61 | 2 | Missouri | St. Louis, Mo. | St. Louis, Mo. | 14 |
| 30 | Jones, James | FB | 6-2 | 228 | 3/21/61 | 2 | Florida | Pompano Beach, Fla. | Bloomfield Hills, Mich. | 14 |
| 32 | Kane, Rick | RB | 6-0 | 200 | 11/12/54 | 8 | San Jose State | Concord, Calif. | Pontiac, Mich. | 14 |
| 25 | †King, Horace | RB | 5-11 | 205 | 3/5/53 | 10 | Georgia | Athens, Ga. | Rochester, Mich. | 16 |
| 43 | Latimer, Al | CB | 5-11 | 177 | 10/14/57 | 5 | Clemson | Winter Park, Fla. | Farmington Hills, Mich. | 8 |
| 82 | Lee, Edward | WR | 5-11 | 182 | 12/8/59 | 2 | South Carolina State | Washington, D.C. | Troy, Mich. | 0* |
| 64 | Lee, Larry | G | 6-2 | 260 | 9/10/59 | 4 | UCLA | Dayton, Ohio | Rochester, Mich. | 16 |
| 14 | Machurek, Mike | QB | 6-1 | 205 | 7/22/60 | 3 | Idaho State | Las Vegas, Nev. | Rochester, Mich. | 0* |
| 83 | Martin, Robbie | WR-KR | 5-8 | 177 | 12/3/58 | 4 | Cal Poly-SLO | Los Angeles, Calif. | San Luis Obispo, Calif. | 10 |
| 81 | †McCall, Reese | TE | 6-6 | 232 | 6/15/56 | 7 | Auburn | Bessemer, Ala. | Randallstown, Md. | 16 |
| 29 | McNorton, Bruce | CB | 5-11 | 175 | 2/28/59 | 3 | Georgetown, Ky. | Daytona Beach, Fla. | Daytona Beach, Fla. | 16 |
| 63 | Moss, Martin | DT | 6-4 | 252 | 12/16/58 | 3 | UCLA | San Diego, Calif. | Van Nuys, Calif. | 15 |
| 52 | Mott, Steve | C | 6-3 | 260 | 3/24/61 | 2 | Alabama | New Orleans, La. | Rochester, Mich. | 13 |
| 3 | Murray, Ed | K | 5-10 | 175 | 8/29/56 | 5 | Tulane | Halifax, Nova Scotia | Southfield, Mich. | 16 |
| 86 | Nichols, Mark | WR | 6-2 | 208 | 10/29/59 | 4 | San Jose State | Bakersfield, Calif. | Rochester, Mich. | 16 |
| 80 | Norris, Ulysses | TE | 6-4 | 232 | 1/15/57 | 6 | Georgia | Monticello, Ga. | Rochester, Mich. | 15 |
| 84 | †Rubick, Rob | TE | 6-2 | 228 | 9/27/60 | 3 | Grand Valley State | Newberry, Mich. | Pontiac, Mich. | 16 |
| 20 | Sims, Billy | RB | 6-0 | 212 | 9/18/55 | 5 | Oklahoma | St. Louis, Mo. | Hooks, Tex. | 13 |
| 71 | Strenger, Rich | T | 6-7 | 269 | 3/10/60 | 2 | Michigan | Port Washington, Wis. | Rochester, Mich. | 16 |
| 39 | Thompson, Leonard | WR | 5-11 | 192 | 7/28/52 | 10 | Oklahoma State | Tucson, Ariz. | Scottsdale, Ariz. | 13 |
| 38 | Thompson, Vince | FB | 6-0 | 225 | 2/21/57 | 3 | Villanova | Trenton, N.J. | Rochester, Mich. | 10 |
| 55 | †Turnure, Tom | C | 6-4 | 253 | 7/9/57 | 3 | Washington | Seattle, Wash. | Seattle, Wash. | 16 |
| 34 | Wagoner, Dan | CB-S | 5-10 | 180 | 12/12/59 | 3 | Kansas | High Point, N.C. | High Point, N.C. | 14 |
| 27 | Watkins, Bobby | CB | 5-10 | 184 | 5/31/60 | 3 | Southwest Texas State | Cottonwood, Idaho | Dallas, Tex. | 16 |
| 59 | Williams, Jimmy | LB | 6-2 | 222 | 11/19/59 | 3 | Nebraska | Washington, D.C. | Rochester, Mich. | 16 |

\* Harvey played 4 games with Green Bay, 9 with Detroit in '83; E. Lee missed '83 season due to injury; Machurek active for 16 games with Detroit in '83, but did not play.

†Option playout; subject to developments.

Also played with Lions in '83—S James Caver (2 games), CB Hector Gray (1), LB James Harrell (16), WR Fred Scott (15).

## COACHING STAFF

### Head Coach, Monte Clark

**Pro Career:** Starts his seventh season as Lions head coach. Directed Lions to 9-7 mark in 1983 and NFC Central Title. Was head coach of San Francisco 49ers in 1976, guiding them to 8-6 record. Was an assistant under Don Shula in Miami 1970-75 as offensive line coach. Drafted fourth by 49ers in 1959. Played defensive tackle until 1962 when he was traded to Dallas and switched to offensive tackle. Clark was traded to Cleveland and played for the Browns from 1963-69. Career record: 47-58.

**Background:** Three-year letterman who played offense and defense at Southern California 1956-58, co-captain of the 1958 squad.

**Personal:** Born January 24, 1937 in Fillmore, Calif. Monte and his wife, Charlotte, live in Bloomfield Township, Mich. and have three children—Bryan, Randy, and Eric.

### Assistant Coaches

**Ed Beard,** defensive coordinator; born December 9, 1939, Chesapeake, Va., lives in Pontiac, Mich. Linebacker Tennessee 1960-63. Pro linebacker San Francisco 49ers 1965-72. Pro coach: San Francisco 49ers 1973-77, New Orleans Saints 1978-80, joined Lions in 1983.

**Don Doll,** special assignments; born August 29, 1926, Los Angeles, Calif., lives in Detroit. Defensive back Southern California 1944, 1946-48. Pro defensive back Detroit Lions 1949-52, Washington Redskins 1953, Los Angeles Rams 1954. College coach: Washington 1955, Contra Costa, Calif., J.C. 1956, Southern California 1957-58, Notre Dame 1959-62. Pro coach: Detroit Lions 1963-64, Los Angeles Rams 1965, Washington Redskins 1966-70, Green Bay Packers 1971-73, Baltimore Colts 1974, Miami Dolphins 1975-76, rejoined Lions in 1978.

**Fred Hoaglin,** offensive line; born January 28, 1944, Alliance, Ohio, lives in Detroit. Center Pittsburgh 1965-67. Pro center Cleveland Browns 1966-72, Baltimore Colts 1973, Houston Oilers 1974-75, Seattle Seahawks 1976. Pro coach: Joined Lions in 1978.

**Bill Johnson,** offensive backfield; born July 14, 1926, Tyler, Tex., lives in Pontiac, Mich. Center Texas A&M 1944-46. Pro center San Francisco 49ers 1948-55. Pro coach: San Francisco 49ers 1956-67, Cincinnati Bengals 1968-78 (head coach 1976-78), Tampa Bay Buccaneers 1979-82, joined Lions in 1983.

**Ed Khayat,** defensive line; born September 14, 1935, Moss Point, Miss., lives in Detroit. Lineman Millsaps 1953, Perkinston J.C. 1954, Tulane 1955-56. Pro lineman Washington Redskins 1957, 1962-63, Philadelphia Eagles 1958-61, 1964-65, Boston Patriots 1966. Pro coach: New Orleans Saints 1967-70, Philadelphia Eagles 1971-72 (head coach), Detroit Lions 1973-74, Atlanta Falcons 1975-76, Baltimore Colts 1977-81, rejoined Lions in 1982.

**Joe Madden,** special teams; born March 5, 1935, Washington, D.C., lives in Pontiac, Mich. Back Maryland 1954-56. No pro playing experience. College coach: Mississippi State 1962, Morehead State 1963, Wake Forest 1964-67, Iowa State 1968-71, Kansas State 1972, Pittsburgh 1973-76, Tennessee 1977-79. Pro coach: Joined Lions in 1980.

**Bill Nelsen,** offensive coordinator; born January 29, 1941, Los Angeles, Calif., lives in Pontiac, Mich. Quarterback Southern California 1959-62. Pro quarterback Pittsburgh Steelers 1963-67, Cleveland Browns 1968-72. Pro coach: New England Patriots 1973-74, Atlanta Falcons 1975-76, Tampa Bay Buccaneers 1977-82, first year with Lions.

**Mel Phillips,** defensive backfield; born January 6, 1942, Shelby, N.C., lives in Pontiac, Mich. Defensive back North Carolina A&T 1963-65. Pro defensive back San Francisco 49ers 1966-76. Pro coach: Joined Lions in 1980.

**Larry Seiple,** receivers; born February 14, 1945, Allentown, Pa., lives in Pontiac, Mich. Punter-tight end Kentucky 1964-66. Pro punter Miami Dolphins 1967-77. College coach: Miami 1979. Pro coach: Joined Lions in 1980.

## DETROIT LIONS 1984 FIRST-YEAR ROSTER

| Name | Pos. | Ht. | Wt. | Birth-date | College | Birthplace | Residence | How Acq. |
|---|---|---|---|---|---|---|---|---|
| Atkins, Renwick | T | 6-3 | 269 | 4/10/61 | Kansas | Chicago, Ill. | Chicago, Ill. | D7a |
| Baack, Steve | DE-DT | 6-4 | 252 | 11/16/60 | Oregon | Ames, Iowa | John Day, Ore. | D3b |
| Carter, Jimmy | LB | 6-1 | 220 | 7/26/61 | New Mexico | Reimar, Tex. | Austin, Tex. | D7 |
| Caver, James (1) | KR-WR | 5-10 | 179 | 9/28/60 | Missouri | Birmingham, Ala. | Columbia, Mo. | FA |
| D'Addio, Dave | FB | 6-2 | 235 | 2/23/63 | Maryland | Union, N.J. | Union, N.J. | D4 |
| Frizzell, William | CB-S | 6-2 | 195 | 9/8/62 | N. Carolina Central | Greenville, N.C. | Greenville, N.C. | D10 |
| Hollins, Rich | WR | 6-0 | 195 | 7/26/62 | West Virginia | Zanesville, Ohio | Zanesville, Ohio | D9 |
| Jones, David | C | 6-3 | 266 | 10/25/61 | Texas | Taiwan | San Angelo, Tex. | D8 |
| Lewis, David | TE | 6-4 | 230 | 6/8/61 | California | Portland, Ore. | Portland, Ore. | D1 |
| Mandley, Pete | WR-KR | 5-10 | 183 | 7/29/61 | Northern Arizona | Mesa, Ariz. | Flagstaff, Ariz. | D2 |
| Menas, Tom (1) | G | 6-4 | 230 | 4/26/60 | Kansas State | Highland Park, Mich. | Warren, Mich. | FA |
| Saxon, Mike | P | 6-2 | 183 | 7/10/62 | San Diego State | Whittier, Calif. | Arcadia, Calif. | D11 |
| Streno, Glenn | C | 6-2 | 265 | 2/1/62 | Tennessee | Pittsburgh, Pa. | Pittsburgh, Pa. | D12 |
| Thaxton, James | CB-S | 5-10 | 177 | 3/16/62 | Louisiana Tech | Monroe, La. | Oak Ridge, La. | D10a |
| Williams, Eric | DT | 6-4 | 265 | 2/24/62 | Washington State | Stockton, Calif. | Stockton, Calif. | D3 |
| Witkowski, John | QB | 6-2 | 200 | 6/18/62 | Columbia | Lindenhurst, N.J. | Lindenhurst, N.J. | D6 |

Players who report to an NFL team for the first time are designated on rosters as rookies (R). If a player reported to an NFL training camp in a previous year but was not on the active squad for three or more regular season or postseason games, he is listed on the first-year roster and designated by a (1). Thereafter, a player who is on the active squad for three or more regular season or postseason games is credited with an additional year of playing experience.

## NOTES

# GREEN BAY PACKERS

**National Football Conference
Central Division**

**Team Colors:** Dark Green, Gold, and White

**1265 Lombardi Avenue
Green Bay, Wisconsin 54303
Telephone: (414) 494-2351**

**Club Officials**

Chairman of the Board: Dominic Olejniczak
President, CEO: Robert Parins
Vice President: Tony Canadeo
Secretary: John Torinus
Treasurer: John S. Stiles
Assistant to the President: Bob Harlan
Assistant to the President: Tom Miller
Green Bay Ticket Director: Mark Wagner
Public Relations Director: Lee Remmel
Director of Player Personnel: Dick Corrick
Director of Pro Personnel: Burt Gustafson
Film Director: Al Treml
Trainer: Domenic Gentile
Equipment Manager: Bob Noel

**Stadium:** Lambeau Field • **Capacity:** 56,155
1265 Lombardi Avenue
Green Bay, Wisconsin 54303

Milwaukee County Stadium •
**Capacity:** 55,958
Highway I-94
Milwaukee, Wisconsin 53214

**Playing Surfaces:** Grass

**Training Camp:** St. Norbert College
DePere, Wisconsin 54115

## 1984 SCHEDULE

**Preseason**

| | | |
|---|---|---|
| Aug. 4 | at Dallas | 8:00 |
| Aug. 11 | **Chicago** at Milwaukee | 7:00 |
| Aug. 18 | at Los Angeles Rams | 7:00 |
| Aug. 25 | **Colts** | 7:00 |

**Regular Season**

| | | |
|---|---|---|
| Sept. 2 | **St. Louis** | 12:00 |
| Sept. 9 | at Los Angeles Raiders | 1:00 |
| Sept. 16 | **Chicago** | 12:00 |
| Sept. 23 | at Dallas | 3:00 |
| Sept. 30 | at Tampa Bay | 4:00 |
| Oct. 7 | **San Diego** | 3:00 |
| Oct. 15 | at Denver (Monday) | 7:00 |
| Oct. 21 | **Seattle** at Milwaukee | 12:00 |
| Oct. 28 | **Detroit** | 12:00 |
| Nov. 4 | at New Orleans | 12:00 |
| Nov. 11 | **Minnesota** at Milwaukee | 12:00 |
| Nov. 18 | **L.A. Rams** at Milwaukee | 12:00 |
| Nov. 22 | at Detroit (Thanksgiving) | 12:30 |
| Dec. 2 | **Tampa Bay** | 12:00 |
| Dec. 9 | at Chicago | 12:00 |
| Dec. 16 | at Minnesota | 12:00 |

## PACKERS COACHING HISTORY

**(444-336-36)**

| | | |
|---|---|---|
| 1921-49 | Earl (Curly) Lambeau | 216-106-22 |
| 1950-53 | Gene Ronzani | 14-33-1 |
| 1954-57 | Lisle Blackbourn | 17-31-0 |
| 1958 | Ray (Scooter) McLean | 1-10-1 |
| 1959-67 | Vince Lombardi | 98-30-4 |
| 1968-70 | Phil Bengtson | 20-21-1 |
| 1971-74 | Dan Devine | 25-28-4 |
| 1975-83 | Bart Starr | 53-77-3 |

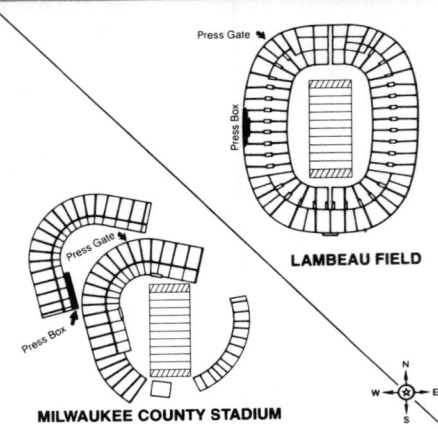

**LAMBEAU FIELD**

**MILWAUKEE COUNTY STADIUM**

## RECORD HOLDERS

### Individual Records — Career

| Category | Name | Performance |
|---|---|---|
| Rushing (Yds.) | Jim Taylor, 1958-1966 | 8,207 |
| Passing (Yds.) | Bart Starr, 1956-1971 | 23,718 |
| Passing (TDs) | Bart Starr, 1956-1971 | 152 |
| Receiving (No.) | Don Hutson, 1935-1945 | 488 |
| Receiving (Yds.) | Don Hutson, 1935-1945 | 8,010 |
| Interceptions | Bobby Dillon, 1952-59 | 52 |
| Punt Return (Avg.) | Billy Grimes, 1950-52 | 13.2 |
| Kickoff Return (Avg.) | Dave Hampton, 1970-71 | 28.9 |
| Field Goals | Chester Marcol, 1972-1980 | 120 |
| Touchdowns (Tot.) | Don Hutson, 1935-1945 | 105 |
| Points | Don Hutson, 1935-1945 | 823 |

### Individual Records — Single Season

| Category | Name | Performance |
|---|---|---|
| Rushing (Yds.) | Jim Taylor, 1962 | 1,407 |
| Passing (Yds.) | Lynn Dickey, 1983 | 4,458 |
| Passing (TDs) | Lynn Dickey, 1983 | 32 |
| Receiving (No.) | Don Hutson, 1942 | 74 |
| Receiving (Yds.) | James Lofton, 1983 | 1,300 |
| Interceptions | Irv Comp, 1943 | 10 |
| Punting (Avg.) | Jerry Norton, 1963 | 44.7 |
| Punt Return (Avg.) | Billy Grimes, 1950 | 19.1 |
| Kickoff Return (Avg.) | Travis Williams, 1967 | 41.1 |
| Field Goals | Chester Marcol, 1972 | 33 |
| Touchdowns (Tot.) | Jim Taylor, 1962 | 19 |
| Points | Paul Hornung, 1960 | 176 |

### Individual Records — Single Game

| Category | Name | Performance |
|---|---|---|
| Rushing (Yds.) | Jim Taylor, 12-3-61 | 186 |
| Passing (Yds.) | Lynn Dickey, 10-12-80 | 418 |
| Passing (TDs) | Many times | 5 |
| | Last time by Lynn Dickey, 9-4-83 | |
| Receiving (No.) | Don Hutson, 11-22-42 | 14 |
| Receiving (Yds.) | Bill Howton, 10-21-56 | 257 |
| Interceptions | Bobby Dillon, 11-26-53 | 4 |
| | Willie Buchanon, 9-24-78 | 4 |
| Field Goals | Many times | 4 |
| | Last time by Jan Stenerud, 12-12-83 | |
| Touchdowns (Tot.) | Paul Hornung, 12-12-65 | 5 |
| Points | Paul Hornung, 10-8-61 | 33 |

## 1983 TEAM STATISTICS

| | Green Bay | Opp. |
|---|---|---|
| Total First Downs | 340 | 366 |
| Rushing | 99 | 171 |
| Passing | 214 | 187 |
| Penalty | 27 | 8 |
| Third Down Efficiency | 72/189 | 111/239 |
| Third Down Percentage | 38.1 | 46.4 |
| Total Net Yards | 6172 | 6403 |
| Total Offensive Plays | 1007 | 1156 |
| Avg. Gain per Play | 6.1 | 5.5 |
| Avg. Gain per Game | 385.8 | 400.2 |
| Net Yards Rushing | 1807 | 2641 |
| Total Rushing Plays | 439 | 597 |
| Avg. Gain per Rush | 4.1 | 4.4 |
| Avg. Gain Rushing per Game | 112.9 | 165.1 |
| Net Yards Passing | 4365 | 3762 |
| Lost Attempting to Pass | 42/323 | 41/271 |
| Gross Yards Passing | 4688 | 4033 |
| Attempts/Completions | 526/311 | 518/300 |
| Percent Completed | 59.1 | 57.9 |
| Had Intercepted | 32 | 19 |
| Avg. Net Passing per Game | 272.8 | 235.1 |
| Punts/Avg. | 70/41.0 | 78/39.1 |
| Punt Returns/Avg. | 41/8.0 | 43/8.9 |
| Kickoff Returns/Avg. | 79/16.9 | 78/18.3 |
| Interceptions/Avg. Ret. | 19/11.9 | 32/10.5 |
| Penalties/Yards | 80/648 | 110/965 |
| Fumbles/Ball Lost | 37/18 | 32/12 |
| Total Points | 429 | 439 |
| Avg. Points per Game | 26.8 | 27.4 |
| Touchdowns | 52 | 55 |
| Rushing | 15 | 28 |
| Passing | 33 | 20 |
| Returns and Recoveries | 4 | 7 |
| Field Goals | 21/26 | 19/29 |
| Conversions | 52/52 | 50/55 |
| Safeties | 1 | 1 |
| Avg. Time of Possession | 27:01 | 32:59 |

## 1983 TEAM RECORD
### Preseason (1-3)

| Date | Green Bay | | Opponents |
|---|---|---|---|
| 8/6 | 20 | *Cleveland | 21 |
| 8/12 | 21 | Seattle | 38 |
| 8/20 | 14 | *Philadelphia | 27 |
| 8/27 | 39 | St. Louis | 27 |
| | 94 | | 113 |

### Regular Season (8-8)

| Date | Green Bay | | Opp. | Att. |
|---|---|---|---|---|
| 9/4 | 41 | Houston (OT) | 38 | 44,073 |
| 9/11 | 21 | *Pittsburgh | 25 | 55,204 |
| 9/18 | 27 | *L.A. Rams (Mil.) | 24 | 54,037 |
| 9/26 | 3 | New York Giants | 27 | 75,308 |
| 10/2 | 55 | *Tampa Bay | 14 | 54,272 |
| 10/9 | 14 | Detroit | 38 | 67,738 |
| 10/17 | 48 | *Washington | 47 | 55,255 |
| 10/23 | 17 | *Minnesota (OT) | 20 | 55,236 |
| 10/30 | 14 | Cincinnati | 34 | 53,349 |
| 11/6 | 35 | *Cleveland (Mil.) | 21 | 54,089 |
| 11/13 | 29 | Minnesota | 21 | 60,113 |
| 11/20 | 20 | *Detroit (OT) (Mil.) | 23 | 50,050 |
| 11/27 | 41 | Atlanta (OT) | 47 | 35,688 |
| 12/4 | 31 | *Chicago | 28 | 51,244 |
| 12/12 | 12 | Tampa Bay (OT) | 9 | 50,763 |
| 12/18 | 21 | Chicago | 23 | 35,807 |
| | 429 | | 439 | 852,226 |

*Home Game    (OT) Overtime

### Score by Periods

| | | | | | | | |
|---|---|---|---|---|---|---|---|
| Green Bay | 120 | 147 | 44 | 112 | 6 | — | 429 |
| Opponents | 74 | 105 | 109 | 139 | 12 | — | 439 |

### Attendance

Home 429,387    Away 422,839    Total 852,226
Single game home record, 56,267 (11-28-76;
Lambeau Field) 56,258 (9-28-80; Milwaukee
County Stadium)
Single season home record, 435,521 (1980)

## 1983 INDIVIDUAL STATISTICS

### Rushing

| | Att. | Yds. | Avg. | LG | TD |
|---|---|---|---|---|---|
| Ellis | 141 | 696 | 4.9 | 71 | 4 |
| Ivery | 86 | 340 | 4.0 | 21 | 2 |
| J. Clark | 71 | 328 | 4.6 | 42 | 0 |
| Meade | 55 | 201 | 3.7 | 15 | 1 |
| Huckleby | 50 | 182 | 3.6 | 20 | 4 |
| Lofton | 9 | 36 | 4.0 | 13 | 0 |
| G. Lewis | 4 | 16 | 4.0 | 11 | 1 |
| Dickey | 21 | 12 | 0.6 | 4 | 3 |
| Whitehurst | 2 | −4 | −2.0 | 0 | 0 |
| Green Bay | 439 | 1807 | 4.1 | 71 | 15 |
| Opponents | 597 | 2641 | 4.4 | 43 | 28 |

### Passing

| | Att. | Comp. | Pct. | Yds. | TD | Int. | Tkld. | Rate |
|---|---|---|---|---|---|---|---|---|
| Dickey | 484 | 289 | 59.7 | 4458 | 32 | 29 | 40/307 | 87.3 |
| Whitehurst | 35 | 18 | 51.4 | 149 | 0 | 2 | 2/16 | 38.9 |
| Ellis | 5 | 2 | 40.0 | 31 | 1 | 1 | 0/0 | 61.3 |
| Ivery | 2 | 2 | 100.0 | 50 | 0 | 0 | 0/0 | 118.8 |
| Green Bay | 526 | 311 | 59.1 | 4688 | 33 | 32 | 42/323 | 84.1 |
| Opponents | 518 | 300 | 57.9 | 4033 | 20 | 19 | 41/271 | 80.4 |

### Receiving

| | No. | Yds. | Avg. | LG | TD |
|---|---|---|---|---|---|
| Lofton | 58 | 1300 | 22.4 | 74t | 8 |
| Jefferson | 57 | 830 | 14.6 | 36 | 7 |
| Coffman | 54 | 814 | 15.1 | 74 | 11 |
| Ellis | 52 | 603 | 11.6 | 56 | 2 |
| Epps | 18 | 313 | 17.4 | 45 | 0 |
| J. Clark | 18 | 279 | 15.5 | 75t | 1 |
| Ivery | 16 | 139 | 8.7 | 17 | 1 |
| Meade | 16 | 110 | 6.9 | 31t | 2 |
| G. Lewis | 11 | 204 | 18.5 | 49 | 1 |
| Huckleby | 10 | 87 | 8.7 | 14 | 0 |
| Kitson | 1 | 9 | 9.0 | 9 | 0 |
| Green Bay | 311 | 4688 | 15.1 | 75t | 33 |
| Opponents | 300 | 4033 | 13.4 | 87t | 20 |

### Interceptions

| | No. | Yds. | Avg. | LG | TD |
|---|---|---|---|---|---|
| T. Lewis | 5 | 111 | 22.2 | 46 | 0 |
| Anderson | 5 | 54 | 10.8 | 27t | 1 |
| Lee | 4 | 23 | 5.8 | 15 | 0 |
| Gray | 2 | 5 | 2.5 | 5 | 0 |
| Laughlin | 1 | 22 | 22.0 | 22 | 0 |
| Scott | 1 | 12 | 12.0 | 12 | 0 |
| Jolly | 1 | 0 | 0.0 | 0 | 0 |
| Green Bay | 19 | 227 | 11.9 | 46 | 1 |
| Opponents | 32 | 337 | 10.5 | 58 | 4 |

### Punting

| | No. | Yds. | Avg. | In 20 | LG |
|---|---|---|---|---|---|
| Scribner | 69 | 2869 | 41.6 | 11 | 70 |
| Green Bay | 70 | 2869 | 41.0 | 11 | 70 |
| Opponents | 78 | 3052 | 39.1 | 19 | 59 |

### Punt Returns

| | No. | FC | Yds. | Avg. | LG | TD |
|---|---|---|---|---|---|---|
| Epps | 36 | 13 | 324 | 9.0 | 90t | 1 |
| Gray | 2 | 0 | 9 | 4.5 | 5 | 0 |
| Hood | 1 | 0 | 0 | 0.0 | 0 | 0 |
| C. Lewis | 1 | 0 | 0 | 0.0 | 0 | 0 |
| Lee | 1 | 0 | −4 | −4.0 | −4 | 0 |
| Green Bay | 41 | 13 | 329 | 8.0 | 90t | 1 |
| Opponents | 43 | 8 | 384 | 8.9 | 59t | 1 |

### Kickoff Returns

| | No. | Yds. | Avg. | LG | TD |
|---|---|---|---|---|---|
| Huckleby | 41 | 757 | 18.5 | 57 | 0 |
| T. Lewis | 20 | 358 | 17.9 | 30 | 0 |
| Gray | 11 | 178 | 16.2 | 26 | 0 |
| Winters | 3 | 28 | 9.3 | 12 | 0 |
| Drechsler | 1 | 1 | 1.0 | 1 | 0 |
| Ivery | 1 | 17 | 17.0 | 17 | 0 |
| Kitson | 1 | 0 | 0.0 | 0 | 0 |
| Lee | 1 | 0 | 0.0 | 0 | 0 |
| Green Bay | 79 | 1339 | 16.9 | 57 | 0 |
| Opponents | 78 | 1429 | 18.3 | 41 | 0 |

### Scoring

| | TD | TD R | TD P | TD Rt | PAT | FG | TP |
|---|---|---|---|---|---|---|---|
| Stenerud | | | | | 52/52 | 21/26 | 115 |
| Coffman | 11 | 0 | 11 | 0 | | | 66 |
| Lofton | 8 | 0 | 8 | 0 | | | 48 |
| Jefferson | 7 | 0 | 7 | 0 | | | 42 |
| Ellis | 6 | 4 | 2 | 0 | | | 36 |
| Huckleby | 4 | 4 | 0 | 0 | | | 24 |
| Dickey | 3 | 3 | 0 | 0 | | | 18 |
| Ivery | 3 | 2 | 1 | 0 | | | 18 |
| Meade | 3 | 1 | 2 | 0 | | | 18 |
| Douglass | 2 | 0 | 0 | 2 | | | 12 |
| G. Lewis | 2 | 1 | 1 | 0 | | | 12 |
| Anderson | 1 | 0 | 0 | 1 | | | 6 |
| J. Clark | 1 | 0 | 1 | 0 | | | 6 |
| Epps | 1 | 0 | 0 | 1 | | | 6 |
| Boyd | (Safety) | | | | | | 2 |
| Green Bay | 52 | 15 | 33 | 4 | 52/52 | 21/26 | 429 |
| Opponents | 55 | 28 | 20 | 7 | 50/54 | 19/29 | 439 |

## FIRST-ROUND SELECTIONS

(If Club had no first-round selection, first player
drafted is listed with round in parentheses.)

## GREEN BAY PACKERS 1984 VETERAN ROSTER

| No. | Name | Pos. | Ht. | Wt. | Birth-date | NFL Exp. | College | Birthplace | Residence | Games in '83 |
|---|---|---|---|---|---|---|---|---|---|---|
| 59 | Anderson, John | LB | 6-3 | 229 | 2/14/56 | 7 | Michigan | Waukesha, Wis. | Elm Grove, Wis. | 16 |
| 76 | Bishop, Richard | NT | 6-1 | 283 | 3/23/50 | 8 | Louisville | Cleveland, Ohio | Miami, Fla. | 2* |
| 72 | Boyd, Greg | DE | 6-6 | 280 | 9/15/53 | 7 | San Diego State | Merced, Calif. | Denver, Colo. | 12 |
| 73 | Braggs, Byron | DE | 6-4 | 270 | 10/10/59 | 4 | Alabama | Los Angeles, Calif. | Montgomery, Ala. | 16 |
| 93 | Brown, Robert | DE | 6-2 | 250 | 5/21/60 | 3 | Virginia Tech | Edenton, N.C. | Alexandria, Va. | 16 |
| 19 | Campbell, Rich | QB | 6-4 | 219 | 12/21/58 | 4 | California | Miami, Fla. | Green Bay, Wis. | 1 |
| 88 | Cassidy, Ron | WR | 6-0 | 180 | 7/23/57 | 5 | Utah State | Ventura, Calif. | Green Bay, Wis. | 16 |
| 33 | Clark, Jessie | FB | 6-2 | 233 | 1/3/60 | 2 | Arkansas | Thebes, Ark. | Fayetteville, Ark. | 16 |
| 82 | Coffman, Paul | TE | 6-3 | 225 | 3/29/56 | 7 | Kansas State | St. Louis, Mo. | Wichita, Kan. | 16 |
| 52 | Cumby, George | LB | 6-1 | 224 | 7/5/56 | 5 | Oklahoma | Gorman, Tex. | Green Bay, Wis. | 15 |
| 57 | Curcio, Mike | LB | 6-1 | 232 | 1/24/57 | 4 | Temple | Hudson, N.Y. | Miami, Fla. | 14 |
| 12 | Dickey, Lynn | QB | 6-4 | 203 | 10/19/49 | 14 | Kansas State | Osawawatomie, Kan. | Lenexa, Kan. | 16 |
| 53 | Douglass, Mike | LB | 6-0 | 214 | 3/15/55 | 7 | San Diego State | St. Louis, Mo. | El Cajon, Calif. | 15 |
| 61 | Drechsler, Dave | G | 6-3 | 264 | 7/18/60 | 2 | North Carolina | Cleveland, N.C. | Green Bay, Wis. | 16 |
| 31 | Ellis, Gerry | FB | 5-11 | 225 | 11/12/57 | 5 | Missouri | Columbia, Mo. | Green Bay, Wis. | 15 |
| 85 | Epps, Phillip | WR | 5-10 | 155 | 11/11/59 | 3 | Texas Christian | Atlanta, Tex. | Fort Worth, Tex. | 16 |
| 60 | Favron, Calvin | LB | 6-2 | 230 | 7/3/57 | 5 | Southeast Louisiana | New Orleans, La. | Baton Rouge, La. | 0* |
| 11 | Garcia, Eddie | K | 5-8 | 178 | 4/15/59 | 2 | Southern Methodist | New Orleans, La. | Green Bay, Wis. | 12 |
| 24 | Gray, Johnnie | S | 5-11 | 202 | 12/18/53 | 9 | Cal State-Fullerton | Lake Charles, La. | Green Bay, Wis. | 16 |
| 65 | Hallstrom, Ron | T | 6-6 | 283 | 6/11/59 | 3 | Iowa | Holden, Mass. | Green Bay, Wis. | 16 |
| 69 | Harris, Leotis | G | 6-1 | 265 | 6/28/55 | 6 | Arkansas | Little Rock, Ark. | Little Rock, Ark. | 6 |
| 38 | Hood, Estus | CB-S | 5-11 | 189 | 11/14/55 | 7 | Illinois | Hattiesburg, Miss. | Green Bay, Wis. | 16 |
| 25 | Huckleby, Harlan | RB | 6-1 | 201 | 12/30/57 | 5 | Michigan | Detroit, Mich. | Detroit, Mich. | 16 |
| 74 | Huffman, Tim | G | 6-5 | 282 | 8/31/59 | 4 | Notre Dame | Canton, Ohio | Green Bay, Wis. | 15 |
| 40 | Ivery, Eddie Lee | RB | 6-1 | 214 | 7/30/57 | 5 | Georgia Tech | McDuffie, Ga. | Decatur, Ga. | 8 |
| 83 | Jefferson, John | WR | 6-1 | 204 | 2/3/56 | 7 | Arizona State | Dallas, Tex. | Dallas, Tex. | 16 |
| 99 | Johnson, Charles | NT | 6-2 | 265 | 6/29/57 | 4 | Maryland | Baltimore, Md. | Baltimore, Md. | 15 |
| 90 | Johnson, Ezra | DE | 6-4 | 259 | 10/2/55 | 7 | Morris Brown | Shreveport, La. | Shreveport, La. | 16 |
| 21 | Jolly, Mike | CB-S | 6-3 | 185 | 3/19/58 | 4 | Michigan | Detroit, Mich. | Green Bay, Wis. | 12 |
| 63 | Jones, Terry | DT | 6-2 | 253 | 11/8/56 | 6 | Alabama | Sandersville, Ga. | Tuscaloosa, Ala. | 1 |
| 64 | Kitson, Syd | G | 6-4 | 264 | 9/27/58 | 4 | Wake Forest | Orange, N.J. | Bedminster, N.J. | 14 |
| 86 | Knafelc, Greg | TE | 6-4 | 230 | 2/20/59 | 2 | Notre Dame | Green Bay, Wis. | Green Bay, Wis. | 6* |
| 68 | Koch, Greg | T | 6-4 | 276 | 6/14/55 | 6 | Arkansas | Bethesda, Md. | Green Bay, Wis. | 15 |
| 98 | Lapka, Myron | NT | 6-4 | 260 | 5/10/56 | 3 | Southern California | Van Nuys, Calif. | Chatsworth, Calif. | 4* |
| 62 | Laughlin, Jim | LB | 6-1 | 222 | 7/5/58 | 5 | Ohio State | Euclid, Ohio | Roswell, Ga. | 15 |
| 22 | Lee, Mark | CB | 5-11 | 188 | 3/20/58 | 5 | Washington | Hanford, Calif. | Bellevue, Wash. | 16 |
| 56 | Lewis, Cliff | LB | 6-1 | 224 | 11/9/59 | 4 | Southern Mississippi | Brewton, Ala. | Ft. Walton Beach, Fla. | 16 |
| 26 | Lewis, Tim | CB-S | 5-11 | 191 | 12/18/61 | 2 | Pittsburgh | Perkasie, Pa. | Green Bay, Wis. | 16 |
| 80 | Lofton, James | WR | 6-3 | 197 | 7/5/56 | 7 | Stanford | Los Angeles, Calif. | Milwaukee, Wis. | 16 |
| 54 | McCarren, Larry | C | 6-3 | 251 | 11/9/51 | 12 | Illinois | Chicago, Ill. | Green Bay, Wis. | 16 |
| 29 | McCoy, Mike | CB-S | 5-11 | 190 | 8/16/53 | 9 | Colorado | Memphis, Ark. | Green Bay, Wis. | 9 |
| 39 | Meade, Mike | FB | 5-10 | 224 | 2/12/60 | 3 | Penn State | Dover, Del. | Newark, Del. | 16 |
| 37 | Murphy, Mark | S | 6-2 | 201 | 4/22/58 | 4 | West Liberty State | Canton, Ohio | North Canton, Ohio | 16 |
| 44 | O'Steen, Dwayne | CB | 6-1 | 195 | 12/20/54 | 7 | San Jose State | Los Angeles, Calif. | Tampa, Fla. | 10* |
| 51 | Prather, Guy | LB | 6-2 | 229 | 3/28/58 | 4 | Grambling | Olney, Md. | Reston, Va. | 16 |
| 35 | Rodgers, Del | RB | 5-10 | 202 | 6/22/60 | 2 | Utah | Tacoma, Wash. | Salinas, Calif. | 0* |
| 58 | Rubens, Larry | C | 6-1 | 250 | 1/25/59 | 3 | Montana State | Spokane, Wash. | Green Bay, Wis. | 5 |
| 70 | Sams, Ron | G | 6-3 | 269 | 4/12/61 | 2 | Pittsburgh | Bridgeville, Pa. | Green Bay, Wis. | 5 |
| 55 | Scott, Randy | LB | 6-1 | 222 | 1/31/59 | 4 | Alabama | Atlanta, Ga. | Decatur, Ga. | 6 |
| 13 | Scribner, Bucky | P | 6-0 | 202 | 7/11/60 | 2 | Kansas | Lawrence, Kan. | Lawrence, Kan. | 16 |
| 91 | Skaugstad, Daryle | NT | 6-5 | 268 | 4/8/57 | 4 | California | Prosser, Wash. | Missouri City, Tex. | 12* |
| 79 | Spears, Ron | DE | 6-6 | 255 | 11/23/59 | 3 | San Diego State | Los Angeles, Calif. | Los Angeles, Calif. | 14* |
| 10 | †Stenerud, Jan | K | 6-2 | 190 | 11/26/43 | 18 | Montana State | Fetsund, Norway | Overland Park, Kan. | 16 |
| 67 | Swanke, Karl | T-C | 6-6 | 262 | 12/29/57 | 5 | Boston College | Elmhurst, Ill. | Green Bay, Wis. | 16 |
| 34 | Thomaselli, Rich | FB | 6-1 | 205 | 2/26/57 | 3 | West Virginia Wesleyan | Follansbee, W. Va. | Sugarland, Tex. | 0* |
| 75 | Turner, Rich | NT | 6-2 | 261 | 2/14/59 | 4 | Oklahoma | Hugo, Okla. | Norman, Okla. | 6 |
| 17 | Whitehurst, David | QB | 6-2 | 205 | 4/27/55 | 8 | Furman | Baumholder, Germany | Roswell, Ga. | 4 |
| 50 | Wingo, Rich | LB | 6-1 | 227 | 7/16/56 | 5 | Alabama | Elkhart, Ind. | Green Bay, Wis. | 16 |
| 20 | Winters, Chet | RB | 5-11 | 204 | 10/22/61 | 2 | Oklahoma | Chicago, Ill. | Sacramento, Calif. | 4 |

* Bishop played 2 games with L.A. Rams in '83; Favron and Rodgers missed '83 season due to injuries; Knafelc played 6 games with New Orleans in '83; Lapka played 4 games with L.A. Rams in '83; O'Steen played 3 games with Tampa Bay, 7 with Green Bay in '83; Skaugstad played 3 games with San Francisco, 9 with Green Bay in '83; Spears played 1 game with New England, 13 with Green Bay in '83; Thomaselli last active with Houston in '82.

†Option playout; subject to developments.

Retired—Charlie Getty, 10-year offensive tackle, 16 games in '83.

Also played with Packers in '83—S Maurice Harvey (4 games), TE Gary Lewis (16), DE Casey Merrill (5), LB Chet Parlavecchio (3).

## COACHING STAFF

### Head Coach, Forrest Gregg

**Pro Career:** Named Packers head coach on December 26, 1983 after compiling 34-27 record as Cincinnati's coach from 1980-83, including 1981 AFC Central title and Super Bowl XVI appearance. Was previously head coach of Cleveland Browns, where he compiled an 18-23 record from 1975-77, including 9-5 record in 1976. Also was head coach of Toronto Argonauts (CFL) in 1979 before signing to take over Bengals. Served as an NFL assistant coach from 1972-74. He was offensive line coach with San Diego Chargers before joining Browns in same capacity in 1974. Had outstanding 15-year playing career in NFL as a guard-tackle with Green Bay Packers 1956-70 (he played in the Packers' two Super Bowl wins) and as a player-coach with Dallas Cowboys in Super Bowl championship season of 1971. Inducted into the Pro Football Hall of Fame in 1977. Career record: 52-50.

**Background:** Tackle at Southern Methodist 1953-55. Twice named to the All-Southwest Conference team. Captain of the SMU team his senior year. Spent 1957 in military service.

**Personal:** Born October 18, 1933 in Birthright, Tex. Attended Sulphur Springs (Tex.) High School. He and his wife, Barbara, live in Green Bay and have two children—Forrest Jr. and Karen.

### Assistant Coaches

**Lew Carpenter,** receivers; born January 12, 1932, Hayti, Mo., lives in Green Bay. Running back-end Arkansas 1950-52. Pro running back-defensive back-end Detroit Lions 1953-55, Cleveland Browns 1957-58, Green Bay Packers 1959-63. Pro coach: Minnesota Vikings 1964-66, Atlanta Falcons 1967-68, Washington Redskins 1969-70, St. Louis Cardinals 1971-72, Houston Oilers 1973-74, joined Packers in 1975.

**Virgil Knight,** strength-conditioning; born January 30, 1948, Clarksville, Ark., lives in Green Bay. Tight end Northeastern Oklahoma 1968-70. No pro playing experience. College coach: Arkansas Tech 1975-78, Florida 1979-80, Auburn 1981-83. Pro coach: First year with Packers.

**Dick Modzelewski,** defensive coordinator-defensive line; born January 16, 1931, West Natrona, Pa., lives in Green Bay. Tackle Maryland 1950-52. Pro defensive tackle Washington Redskins 1953-54, Pittsburgh Steelers 1955, New York Giants 1956-63, Cleveland Browns 1964-66. Pro coach: Cleveland Browns 1968-77, New York Giants 1978, Cincinnati Bengals 1979-83, first year with Packers.

**Herb Paterra,** linebackers-special teams; born November 8, 1940, Grassport, Pa., lives in Green Bay. Offensive guard-linebacker Michigan State 1960-62. Pro linebacker Buffalo Bills 1963-64, Hamilton Tiger Cats (CFL) 1965-68. College coach: Michigan State 1969-71, Wyoming 1972-74. Pro coach: Charlotte Hornets (WFL) 1975, Hamilton Tiger Cats (CFL) 1978-79, Los Angeles Rams 1980-82, Edmonton Eskimos (CFL) 1983, first year with Packers.

**Ken Riley,** secondary; born August 6, 1947, Bartow, Fla., lives in Green Bay. Defensive back Florida A&M 1966-68. Pro cornerback Cincinnati Bengals 1969-83. Pro coach: First year with Packers.

**George Sefcik,** offensive backfield; born December 27, 1939, Cleveland Ohio, lives in Green Bay. Halfback Notre Dame 1959-61. No pro playing experience. College coach: Notre Dame 1963-68, Kentucky 1969-72. Pro coach: Baltimore Colts 1973-74, Cleveland Browns 1975-77, Cincinnati Bengals 1978-83, first year with Packers.

**Bob Schnelker,** offensive coordinator; born October 17, 1928, Galion, Ohio, lives in Green Bay. End Bowling Green 1946-50. Pro end Cleveland Browns 1953, New York Giants 1954-60, Minnesota Vikings 1961. Pro coach: Los Angeles Rams 1963-64, Green Bay Packers 1965-71, San Diego Chargers 1972-73, Miami Dolphins 1974, Kansas City Chiefs 1975-77, Detroit Lions 1978-81, rejoined Packers in 1982.

**Jerry Wampfler,** offensive line; born August 6, 1932, New Philadelphia, Ohio, lives in Green Bay. Tackle Miami, Ohio 1951-54. No pro playing experience. College coach: Presbyterian 1955, Miami, Ohio 1963-65, Notre Dame 1966-69, Colorado State 1970-72 (head coach). Pro coach: Philadelphia Eagles 1973-75, 1979-83, Buffalo Bills 1976-77, New York Giants 1978, first year with Packers.

## GREEN BAY PACKERS 1984 FIRST-YEAR ROSTER

| Name | Pos. | Ht. | Wt. | Birth-date | College | Birthplace | Residence | How Acq. |
|------|------|-----|-----|-----------|---------|------------|-----------|----------|
| Bethune, Darryel | G-C | 6-2 | 250 | 3/6/62 | Bethune-Cookman | Miami Beach, Fla. | Miami, Fla. | FA |
| Cannon, Mark | C | 6-3 | 258 | 6/14/62 | Texas-Arlington | Austin, Tex. | Arlington, Tex. | D11 |
| Carreker, Alphonso | DE | 6-6 | 260 | 5/25/62 | Florida State | Columbus, Ohio | Tallahassee, Fla. | D1 |
| Casanova, John (1) | TE | 6-3 | 233 | 1/30/61 | Northern Michigan | Crystal Falls, Mich. | East Lansing, Mich. | FA |
| Christopher, John (1) | P | 6-3 | 200 | 12/10/60 | Morehead State | Sandusky, Ohio | Norwalk, Ohio | FA |
| Dorsey, John | LB | 6-2 | 235 | 8/31/60 | Connecticut | Leonardtown, Md. | Storrs, Conn. | D4 |
| Emans, Mark | LB | 6-3 | 235 | 11/2/61 | Bowling Green | Luckey, Ohio | Bowling Green, Ohio | D12a |
| Feraday, Dan (1) | QB | 6-2 | 211 | 6/30/56 | Toronto | Toronto, Canada | Toronto, Canada | FA |
| Flynn, Tom | S | 6-0 | 195 | 3/24/62 | Pittsburgh | Verona, Pa. | Pittsburgh, Pa. | D5 |
| Forsythe, Steve (1) | WR | 6-0 | 188 | 2/24/61 | Frostburg State | Williamsport, Md. | Williamsport, Md. | FA |
| Fuller, Daniel (1) | LB | 6-2 | 255 | 9/20/61 | Ashland | Honolulu, Hawaii | Broadview Hgts., Ohio | FA |
| Gamble, Shelby | RB | 5-11 | 196 | 11/21/59 | Boston College | South Haven, Mich. | South Haven, Mich. | FA |
| Gordon, Carl | NT-DE | 6-3 | 264 | 7/7/60 | Alcorn State | Birmingham, Ala. | Birmingham, Ala. | FA |
| Hardville, Drew | CB-S | 6-1 | 192 | 3/16/58 | Arizona | Racine, Wis. | Racine, Wis. | FA |
| Hayes, Gary (1) | CB-S | 5-10 | 180 | 8/19/57 | Fresno State | Tucson, Ariz. | Richmond, Calif. | FA |
| Hoffman, Gary | T-G | 6-7 | 282 | 9/28/61 | Santa Clara | Sacramento, Calif. | Santa Clara, Calif. | D10 |
| Humphrey, Donnie | DE | 6-3 | 275 | 4/20/61 | Auburn | Huntsville, Ala. | Auburn, Ala. | D3 |
| Jones, Boyd | T | 6-3 | 265 | 5/30/61 | Texas Southern | Galveston, Tex. | Houston, Tex. | FA |
| Jones, Daryll | S | 6-0 | 190 | 3/23/62 | Georgia | Columbus, Ga. | Athens, Ga. | D7 |
| Krieg, Kevin | G | 6-2 | 270 | 3/4/62 | Eastern Michigan | South Bend, Ind. | Mishawaka, Ind. | FA |
| Mireski, Bob | TE | 6-5 | 235 | 5/19/60 | Kutztown State | Scranton, Pa. | Peapack, N.J. | FA |
| Pointer, John | LB | 6-2 | 230 | 1/16/58 | Vanderbilt | Columbia, Tenn. | Columbia, Tenn. | FA |
| Richard, Donald Ray (1) | NT | 6-1 | 254 | 3/8/60 | Utah | Austin, Tex. | Austin, Tex. | FA |
| Schliem, Daryl | LB | 6-3 | 235 | 9/17/61 | Wis.-Whitewater | Darlington, Wis. | South Wayne, Wis. | FA |
| Stransky, David | WR | 6-1 | 190 | 7/10/61 | Washington | Sedro Woolley, Wash. | Bellevue, Wash. | FA |
| Taylor, Lenny | WR | 5-10 | 173 | 2/15/61 | Tenn.-Knoxville | Miami, Fla. | Knoxville, Tenn. | D12 |
| Viaene, Jim | NT-DE | 6-2 | 270 | 3/19/62 | Wisconsin-Superior | Tacoma, Wash. | Appleton, Wis. | FA |
| Viaene, Tom | NT | 6-1 | 265 | 3/19/62 | Wisconsin-Superior | Tacoma, Wash. | Appleton, Wis. | FA |
| Walter, Ken | C-G | 6-4 | 260 | 3/2/58 | Texas Tech | Corsicana, Tex. | Richardson, Tex. | FA |
| Wright, Randy | QB | 6-2 | 194 | 1/12/61 | Wisconsin | St. Charles, Ill. | Madison, Wis. | D6 |

Players who report to an NFL team for the first time are designated on rosters as rookies (R). If a player reported to an NFL training camp in a previous year but was not on the active squad for three or more regular season or postseason games, he is listed on the first-year roster and designated by a (1). Thereafter, a player who is on the active squad for three or more regular season or postseason games is credited with an additional year of playing experience.

## NOTES

**National Football Conference**
**Western Division**

**Team Colors:** Royal Blue, Gold, and White

**Business Address:**
2327 West Lincoln Ave.
Anaheim, California 92801

**Ticket Office:**
Anaheim Stadium
1900 State College Blvd.
Anaheim, California 92806
**Telephone:** (714) 535-7267
or (213) 585-5400

**Club Officials**

President: Georgia Frontiere
Vice President, Finance: John Shaw
Legal Counsel: Jay Zygmunt
Administrator, Football Operations: Jack Faulkner
Director of Operations: Dick Beam
Director of Player Personnel: John Math
Director of Public Relations: Pete Donovan
Assistant Director of Public Relations:
John Oswald
Director of Community Relations: Marshall Klein
Trainers: Gary Tuthill, George Menefee
Equipment Manager: Don Hewitt

**Stadium:** Anaheim Stadium • **Capacity:** 69,007
Anaheim, California 92806

**Playing Surface:** Grass

**Training Camp:** California State University
Fullerton, California 92634

## 1984 SCHEDULE

**Preseason**

| | | |
|---|---|---|
| Aug. 4 | at San Diego | 6:00 |
| Aug. 13 | **Cleveland** | 7:00 |
| Aug. 18 | **Green Bay** | 7:00 |
| Aug. 23 | **San Diego** | 7:00 |

**Regular Season**

| | | |
|---|---|---|
| Sept. 3 | **Dallas** (Monday) | 6:00 |
| Sept. 9 | **Cleveland** | 1:00 |
| Sept. 16 | at Pittsburgh | 4:00 |
| Sept. 23 | at Cincinnati | 1:00 |
| Sept. 30 | **New York Giants** | 1:00 |
| Oct. 7 | **Atlanta** | 1:00 |
| Oct. 14 | at New Orleans | 12:00 |
| Oct. 22 | at Atlanta (Monday) | 9:00 |
| Oct. 28 | **San Francisco** | 1:00 |
| Nov. 4 | at St. Louis | 12:00 |
| Nov. 11 | **Chicago** | 1:00 |
| Nov. 18 | vs. Green Bay at Milw. | 12:00 |
| Nov. 25 | at Tampa Bay | 1:00 |
| Dec. 2 | **New Orleans** | 1:00 |
| Dec. 9 | **Houston** | 1:00 |
| Dec. 14 | at San Francisco (Friday) | 6:00 |

## RAMS COACHING HISTORY

**Cleveland 1937-45**
**(325-270-20)**

| | | |
|---|---|---|
| 1937-38 | Hugo Bezdek* | 1-13-0 |
| 1938 | Art Lewis | 4-4-0 |
| 1939-42 | Earl (Dutch) Clark | 16-26-2 |
| 1944 | Aldo (Buff) Donelli | 4-6-0 |
| 1945-46 | Adam Walsh | 15-5-1 |
| 1947 | Bob Snyder | 6-6-0 |
| 1948-49 | Clark Shaughnessy | 14-8-3 |
| 1950-52 | Joe Stydahar** | 18-9-0 |
| 1952-54 | Hamp Pool | 23-11-2 |
| 1955-59 | Sid Gillman | 28-32-1 |
| 1960-62 | Bob Waterfield*** | 9-24-1 |
| 1962-65 | Harland Svare | 14-31-3 |
| 1966-70 | George Allen | 49-19-4 |
| 1971-72 | Tommy Prothro | 14-12-2 |
| 1973-77 | Chuck Knox | 57-20-1 |
| 1978-82 | Ray Malavasi | 43-36-0 |
| 1983 | John Robinson | 10-8-0 |

*Resigned after three games in 1938
**Resigned after one game in 1952
***Resigned after eight games in 1962

## RECORD HOLDERS
### Individual Records — Career

| Category | Name | Performance |
|---|---|---|
| Rushing (Yds.) | Lawrence McCutcheon, 1973-79 | 6,186 |
| Passing (Yds.) | Roman Gabriel, 1962-1972 | 22,223 |
| Passing (TDs) | Roman Gabriel, 1962-1972 | 154 |
| Receiving (No.) | Tom Fears, 1948-1956 | 400 |
| Receiving (Yds.) | Elroy Hirsch, 1949-1957 | 6,289 |
| Interceptions | Ed Meador, 1959-1970 | 46 |
| Punting (Avg.) | Danny Villanueva, 1960-64 | 45.5 |
| Punt Return (Avg.) | Verda (Vitamin T) Smith, 1949-1953 | 10.9 |
| Kickoff Return (Avg.) | Drew Hill, 1979-1982 | 20.0 |
| Field Goals | Bruce Gossett, 1964-69 | 120 |
| Touchdowns (Tot.) | Elroy Hirsch, 1949-1957 | 55 |
| Points | Bob Waterfield, 1946-1952 | 573 |

### Individual Records — Single Season

| Category | Name | Performance |
|---|---|---|
| Rushing (Yds.) | Eric Dickerson, 1983 | 1,808 |
| Passing (Yds.) | Vince Ferragamo, 1983 | 3,276 |
| Passing (TDs) | Vince Ferragamo, 1980 | 30 |
| Receiving (No.) | Tom Fears, 1950 | 84 |
| Receiving (Yds.) | Elroy Hirsch, 1951 | 1,425 |
| Interceptions | Dick (Night Train) Lane, 1952 | 14 |
| Punting (Avg.) | Danny Villanueva, 1962 | 45.5 |
| Punt Return (Avg.) | Woodley Lewis, 1952 | 18.5 |
| Kickoff Return (Avg.) | Verda (Vitamin T) Smith, 1950 | 33.7 |
| Field Goals | David Ray, 1973 | 30 |
| Touchdowns | Eric Dickerson, 1983 | 20 |
| Points | David Ray, 1973 | 130 |

### Individual Records — Single Game

| Category | Name | Performance |
|---|---|---|
| Rushing (Yds.) | Willie Ellison, 12-5-71 | 247 |
| Passing (Yds.) | Norm Van Brocklin, 9-28-51 | 554 |
| Passing (TDs) | Many times | 5 |
| | Last time by Vince Ferragamo, 10-23-83 | |
| Receiving (No.) | Tom Fears, 12-3-50 | 18 |
| Receiving (Yds.) | Jim Benton, 11-22-45 | 303 |
| Interceptions | Many times | 3 |
| | Last time by Pat Thomas, 10-7-79 | |
| Field Goals | Bob Waterfield, 12-9-51 | 5 |
| Touchdowns | Bob Shaw, 12-11-49 | 4 |
| | Elroy Hirsch, 9-28-51 | 4 |
| | Harold Jackson, 10-14-73 | 4 |
| Points | Bob Shaw, 12-11-49 | 24 |
| | Elroy Hirsch, 9-28-51 | 24 |
| | Harold Jackson, 10-14-73 | 24 |

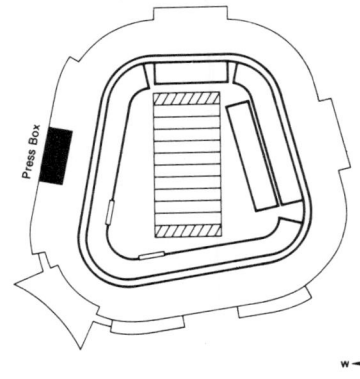

Press Box

N
W — S E

**ANAHEIM STADIUM**

## 1983 TEAM STATISTICS

| | L.A. Rams | Opp. |
|---|---|---|
| Total First Downs | 316 | 311 |
| Rushing | 148 | 118 |
| Passing | 150 | 179 |
| Penalty | 18 | 14 |
| Third Down Efficiency | 77/200 | 87/219 |
| Third Down Percentage | 38.5 | 39.7 |
| Total Net Yards | 5474 | 5392 |
| Total Offensive Plays | 1023 | 1078 |
| Avg. Gain per Play | 5.4 | 5.0 |
| Avg. Gain per Game | 342.1 | 337.0 |
| Net Yards Rushing | 2253 | 1781 |
| Total Rushing Plays | 511 | 489 |
| Avg. Gain per Rush | 4.4 | 3.6 |
| Avg. Gain Rushing per Game | 140.8 | 111.3 |
| Net Yards Passing | 3221 | 3611 |
| Lost Attempting to Pass | 23/190 | 33/258 |
| Gross Yards Passing | 3411 | 3869 |
| Attempts/Completions | 489/286 | 556/319 |
| Percent Completed | 58.5 | 57.4 |
| Had Intercepted | 23 | 24 |
| Avg. Net Passing per Game | 201.3 | 225.7 |
| Punts/Avg. | 83/39.8 | 83/41.7 |
| Punt Returns/Avg. | 55/9.8 | 39/6.4 |
| Kickoff Returns/Avg. | 52/18.2 | 71/18.7 |
| Interceptions/Avg. Ret. | 24/21.5 | 23/13.2 |
| Penalties/Yards | 96/748 | 89/804 |
| Fumbles/Ball Lost | 38/24 | 38/20 |
| Total Points | 361 | 344 |
| Avg. Points per Game | 22.6 | 21.5 |
| Touchdowns | 47 | 42 |
| Rushing | 20 | 21 |
| Passing | 23 | 18 |
| Returns and Recoveries | 4 | 3 |
| Field Goals | 11/20 | 17/28 |
| Conversions | 42/47 | 39/42 |
| Safeties | 2 | 1 |
| Avg. Time of Possession | 29:16 | 30:44 |

## 1983 TEAM RECORD

### Preseason (2-2)

| Date | Los Angeles Rams | | Opponents |
|---|---|---|---|
| 8/6 | *San Diego | 34 | 20 |
| 8/15 | *Dallas | 7 | 30 |
| 8/20 | *New England | 13 | 7 |
| 8/26 | San Diego | 17 | 27 |
| | | 71 | 84 |

### Regular Season (9-7)

| Date | Los Angeles Rams | | Opp. | Att. |
|---|---|---|---|---|
| 9/4 | New York Giants | 16 | 6 | 75,281 |
| 9/11 | *New Orleans | 30 | 27 | 45,662 |
| 9/18 | Green Bay | 24 | 27 | 54,037 |
| 9/25 | New York Jets (OT) | 24 | 27 | 52,070 |
| 10/2 | *Detroit | 21 | 10 | 49,403 |
| 10/9 | San Francisco | 10 | 7 | 59,119 |
| 10/16 | *Atlanta | 27 | 21 | 50,404 |
| 10/23 | *San Francisco | 35 | 45 | 66,070 |
| 10/30 | Miami | 14 | 30 | 72,175 |
| 11/6 | *Chicago | 21 | 14 | 53,010 |
| 11/14 | Atlanta | 36 | 13 | 31,203 |
| 11/20 | *Washington | 20 | 42 | 63,031 |
| 11/27 | *Buffalo | 41 | 17 | 48,246 |
| 12/4 | Philadelphia | 9 | 13 | 32,867 |
| 12/11 | *New England | 7 | 21 | 46,503 |
| 12/18 | New Orleans | 26 | 24 | 70,148 |
| | | 361 | 344 | 869,229 |

*Home Game     (OT) Overtime

### Score by Periods

| | | | | | | | |
|---|---|---|---|---|---|---|---|
| L.A. Rams | 46 | 114 | 91 | 110 | 0 | — | 361 |
| Opponents | 63 | 98 | 75 | 105 | 3 | — | 344 |

### Attendance

Home 422,329     Away 446,900     Total 869,229
Single game home record, 102,368 (11-10-57; L.A. Coliseum), 66,070 (10-23-83; Anaheim Stadium)
Single season home record, 519,175 (1973; L.A. Coliseum) 500,403 (1980; Anaheim Stadium)

## 1983 INDIVIDUAL STATISTICS

### Rushing

| | Att. | Yds. | Avg. | LG | TD |
|---|---|---|---|---|---|
| Dickerson | 390 | 1808 | 4.6 | 85t | 18 |
| Redden | 75 | 372 | 5.0 | 40t | 2 |
| Guman | 7 | 42 | 6.0 | 11 | 0 |
| Alexander | 7 | 28 | 4.0 | 15 | 0 |
| Ferragamo | 22 | 17 | 0.8 | 8 | 0 |
| Ellard | 3 | 7 | 2.3 | 12 | 0 |
| Cromwell | 1 | 0 | 0 | 0 | 0 |
| Kemp | 3 | −2 | −0.7 | 0 | 0 |
| Farmer | 1 | −9 | −9.0 | −9 | 0 |
| Grant | 2 | −10 | −5.0 | 1 | 0 |
| L.A. Rams | 511 | 2253 | 4.4 | 85t | 20 |
| Opponents | 489 | 1781 | 3.6 | 44 | 21 |

### Passing

| | Att. | Comp. | Pct. | Yds. | TD | Int. | Tkld. | Rate |
|---|---|---|---|---|---|---|---|---|
| Ferragamo | 464 | 274 | 59.1 | 3276 | 22 | 23 | 21/178 | 75.9 |
| Kemp | 25 | 12 | 48.0 | 135 | 1 | 0 | 2/12 | 77.9 |
| L.A. Rams | 489 | 286 | 58.5 | 3411 | 23 | 23 | 23/190 | 76.0 |
| Opponents | 556 | 319 | 57.4 | 3869 | 18 | 24 | 33/258 | 71.7 |

### Receiving

| | No. | Yds. | Avg. | LG | TD |
|---|---|---|---|---|---|
| Barber | 55 | 657 | 11.9 | 42t | 3 |
| Dickerson | 51 | 404 | 7.9 | 37t | 2 |
| Farmer | 40 | 556 | 13.9 | 46t | 5 |
| Guman | 34 | 347 | 10.2 | 60 | 4 |
| Dennard | 33 | 465 | 14.1 | 61t | 5 |
| Da. Hill | 28 | 280 | 10.0 | 34 | 2 |
| Ellard | 16 | 268 | 16.8 | 44 | 0 |
| Grant | 12 | 221 | 18.4 | 57 | 1 |
| G. Jones | 11 | 172 | 15.6 | 46 | 0 |
| Redden | 4 | 30 | 7.5 | 9 | 0 |
| Alexander | 1 | 10 | 10.0 | 10 | 0 |
| McDonald | 1 | 1 | 1.0 | 1t | 1 |
| L.A. Rams | 286 | 3411 | 11.9 | 61t | 23 |
| Opponents | 319 | 3869 | 12.1 | 48 | 18 |

### Interceptions

| | No. | Yds. | Avg. | LG | TD |
|---|---|---|---|---|---|
| K. Collins | 5 | 113 | 22.6 | 58 | 0 |
| Johnson | 4 | 115 | 28.8 | 60t | 2 |
| Harris | 4 | 100 | 25.0 | 45 | 0 |
| Irvin | 4 | 42 | 10.5 | 22 | 0 |
| Cromwell | 3 | 76 | 25.3 | 43t | 1 |
| J. Collins | 2 | 46 | 23.0 | 29 | 0 |
| Andrews | 1 | 22 | 22.0 | 22 | 0 |
| Ekern | 1 | 1 | 1.0 | 1 | 0 |
| L.A. Rams | 24 | 515 | 21.5 | 60t | 3 |
| Opponents | 23 | 303 | 13.2 | 45 | 0 |

### Punting

| | No. | Yds. | Avg. | In 20 | LG |
|---|---|---|---|---|---|
| Misko | 82 | 3301 | 40.3 | 18 | 67 |
| L.A. Rams | 83 | 3301 | 39.8 | 18 | 67 |
| Opponents | 83 | 3465 | 41.7 | 15 | 61 |

### Punt Returns

| | No. | FC | Yds. | Avg. | LG | TD |
|---|---|---|---|---|---|---|
| Ellard | 16 | 4 | 217 | 13.6 | 72t | 1 |
| Irvin | 25 | 3 | 212 | 8.5 | 20 | 0 |
| Johnson | 14 | 1 | 109 | 7.8 | 26 | 0 |
| L.A. Rams | 55 | 8 | 538 | 9.8 | 72t | 1 |
| Opponents | 39 | 12 | 251 | 6.4 | 27 | 0 |

### Kickoff Returns

| | No. | Yds. | Avg. | LG | TD |
|---|---|---|---|---|---|
| Redden | 19 | 358 | 18.8 | 43 | 0 |
| Ellard | 15 | 314 | 20.9 | 44 | 0 |
| Alexander | 13 | 222 | 17.1 | 30 | 0 |
| Guman | 2 | 30 | 15.0 | 21 | 0 |
| Barnett | 1 | 0 | 0.0 | 0 | 0 |
| Irvin | 1 | 22 | 22.0 | 22 | 0 |
| Simmons | 1 | 0 | 0.0 | 0 | 0 |
| L.A. Rams | 52 | 946 | 18.2 | 44 | 0 |
| Opponents | 71 | 1325 | 18.7 | 46 | 0 |

### Scoring

| | TD | TD R | TD P | TD Rt | PAT | FG | TP |
|---|---|---|---|---|---|---|---|
| Dickerson | 20 | 18 | 2 | 0 | | | 120 |
| Nelson | | | | | 33/37 | 5/11 | 48 |
| Dennard | 5 | 0 | 5 | 0 | | | 30 |
| Farmer | 5 | 0 | 5 | 0 | | | 30 |
| Lansford | | | | | 9/9 | 6/9 | 27 |
| Guman | 4 | 0 | 4 | 0 | | | 24 |
| Barber | 3 | 0 | 3 | 0 | | | 18 |
| Da. Hill | 2 | 0 | 2 | 0 | | | 12 |
| Johnson | 2 | 0 | 0 | 2 | | | 12 |
| Redden | 2 | 2 | 0 | 0 | | | 12 |
| Cromwell | 1 | 0 | 0 | 1 | | | 6 |
| Ellard | 1 | 0 | 0 | 1 | | | 6 |
| Grant | 1 | 0 | 1 | 0 | | | 6 |
| McDonald | 1 | 0 | 1 | 0 | | | 6 |
| Ja. Youngblood | (Safety) | | | | | | 2 |
| L.A. Rams | 47 | 20 | 23 | 4 | 42/47 | 11/20 | 361 |
| Opponents | 42 | 21 | 18 | 3 | 39/42 | 17/28 | 344 |

## FIRST-ROUND SELECTIONS

(If Club had no first-round selection, first player drafted is listed with round in parentheses.)

| Year | Player, College, Position |
|---|---|
| 1937 | Johnny Drake, Purdue, B |
| 1938 | Corbett Davis, Indiana, B |
| 1939 | Parker Hall, Mississippi, B |
| 1940 | Ollie Cordill, Rice, B |
| 1941 | Rudy Mucha, Washington, C |
| 1942 | Jack Wilson, Baylor, B |
| 1943 | Mike Holovak, Boston College, B |
| 1944 | Tony Butkovich, Illinois, B |
| 1945 | Elroy (Crazylegs) Hirsch, Wisconsin, B |
| 1946 | Emil Sitko, Notre Dame, B |
| 1947 | Herman Wedemeyer, St. Mary's, Cal., B |
| 1948 | Tom Keane, West Virginia, B (2) |
| 1949 | Bobby Thomason, Virginia Military, B |
| 1950 | Ralph Pasquariello, Villanova, B |
| | Stan West, Oklahoma, G |
| 1951 | Bud McFadin, Texas, G |
| 1952 | Bill Wade, Vanderbilt, QB |
| | Bob Carey, Michigan State, E |
| 1953 | Donn Moomaw, UCLA, C |
| | Ed Barker, Washington State, E |
| 1954 | Ed Beatty, Cincinnati, C |
| 1955 | Larry Morris, Georgia Tech, C |
| 1956 | Joe Marconi, West Virginia, B |
| | Charles Horton, Vanderbilt, B |
| 1957 | Jon Arnett, Southern California, B |
| | Del Shofner, Baylor, E |
| 1958 | Lou Michaels, Kentucky, T |
| | Jim Phillips, Auburn, E |
| 1959 | Dick Bass, Pacific, B |
| | Paul Dickson, Baylor, T |
| 1960 | Billy Cannon, Louisiana State, RB |
| 1961 | Marlin McKeever, Southern California, E-LB |
| 1962 | Roman Gabriel, North Carolina State, QB |
| | Merlin Olsen, Utah State, DT |
| 1963 | Terry Baker, Oregon State, QB |
| | Rufus Guthrie, Georgia Tech, G |
| 1964 | Bill Munson, Utah State, QB |
| 1965 | Clancy Williams, Washington State, CB |
| 1966 | Tom Mack, Michigan, G |
| 1967 | Willie Ellison, Texas Southern, RB (2) |
| 1968 | Gary Beban, UCLA, QB (2) |
| 1969 | Larry Smith, Florida, RB |
| | Jim Seymour, Notre Dame, WR |
| | Bob Klein, Southern California, TE |
| 1970 | Jack Reynolds, Tennessee, LB |
| 1971 | Isiah Robertson, Southern, LB |
| | Jack Youngblood, Florida, DE |
| 1972 | Jim Bertelsen, Texas, RB (2) |
| 1973 | Cullen Bryant, Colorado, DB (2) |
| 1974 | John Cappelletti, Penn State, RB |
| 1975 | Mike Fanning, Notre Dame, DT |
| | Dennis Harrah, Miami, T |
| | Doug France, Ohio State, T |
| 1976 | Kevin McLain, Colorado State, LB |
| 1977 | Bob Brudzinski, Ohio State, LB |
| 1978 | Elvis Peacock, Oklahoma, RB |
| 1979 | George Andrews, Nebraska, LB |
| | Kent Hill, Georgia Tech, T |
| 1980 | Johnnie Johnson, Texas, DB |
| 1981 | Mel Owens, Michigan, LB |
| 1982 | Barry Redden, Richmond, RB |
| 1983 | Eric Dickerson, Southern Methodist, RB |
| 1984 | Hal Stephens, East Carolina, DE (5) |

# LOS ANGELES RAMS 1984 VETERAN ROSTER

| No. | Name | Pos. | Ht. | Wt. | Birth-date | NFL Exp. | College | Birthplace | Residence | Games in '83 |
|---|---|---|---|---|---|---|---|---|---|---|
| 35 | Alexander, Robert | RB | 6-0 | 185 | 4/21/58 | 3 | West Virginia | Charleston, W. Va. | Anaheim, Calif. | 15 |
| 52 | Andrews, George | LB | 6-3 | 225 | 11/28/55 | 6 | Nebraska | Omaha, Neb. | Anaheim, Calif. | 16 |
| 62 | Bain, Bill | T | 6-4 | 290 | 8/9/52 | 10 | Southern California | Pico Rivera, Calif. | Westminster, Calif. | 16 |
| 86 | †Barber, Mike | TE | 6-3 | 237 | 6/4/53 | 9 | Louisiana Tech | White Oak, Tex. | Houston, Tex. | 16 |
| 96 | Barnett, Doug | DE | 6-3 | 250 | 4/12/60 | 3 | Azusa Pacific | Montebello, Calif. | Lake Arrowhead, Calif. | 16 |
| 73 | Bolinger, Russ | G | 6-5 | 255 | 9/10/54 | 8 | Long Beach State | Wichita, Kan. | Newport Beach, Calif. | 16 |
| 50 | Collins, Jim | LB | 6-2 | 230 | 6/11/58 | 4 | Syracuse | Orange, N.J. | Huntington Beach, Calif. | 16 |
| 21 | Cromwell, Nolan | S | 6-1 | 200 | 1/30/55 | 8 | Kansas | Smith Center, Kan. | Mission Viejo, Calif. | 16 |
| | t-Crutchfield, Dwayne | RB | 6-0 | 235 | 9/30/59 | 3 | Iowa State | Cincinnati, Ohio | Cincinnati, Ohio | 13* |
| 70 | †DeJurnett, Charles | NT | 6-4 | 260 | 6/17/52 | 8 | San Jose State | Picayune, Miss. | San Diego, Calif. | 10 |
| 88 | †Dennard, Preston | WR | 6-1 | 183 | 11/28/55 | 7 | New Mexico | Cordele, Ga. | Fountain Valley, Calif. | 14 |
| 29 | Dickerson, Eric | RB | 6-3 | 220 | 9/2/60 | 2 | Southern Methodist | Sealy, Tex. | Sealy, Tex. | 16 |
| 71 | Doss, Reggie | DE | 6-4 | 263 | 12/7/56 | 7 | Hampton Institute | Mobile, Ala. | Huntington Beach, Calif. | 16 |
| 55 | Ekern, Carl | LB | 6-3 | 222 | 5/27/54 | 8 | San Jose State | Richland, Wash. | Fountain Valley, Calif. | 16 |
| 80 | Ellard, Henry | WR | 5-11 | 170 | 7/21/61 | 2 | Fresno State | Fresno, Calif. | Fresno, Calif. | 12 |
| 84 | †Farmer, George | WR | 5-10 | 175 | 12/5/58 | 3 | Southern | Los Angeles, Calif. | Los Angeles, Calif. | 16 |
| 15 | Ferragamo, Vince | QB | 6-3 | 212 | 4/24/54 | 7 | Nebraska | Torrance, Calif. | Irvine, Calif. | 16 |
| 82 | Grant, Otis | WR | 6-3 | 197 | 8/13/61 | 2 | Michigan State | Atlanta, Ga. | Atlanta, Ga. | 16 |
| | t-Green, Gary | CB | 5-11 | 191 | 10/2/55 | 8 | Baylor | San Antonio, Tex. | San Antonio, Tex. | 16 |
| 44 | Guman, Mike | RB | 6-2 | 218 | 4/21/58 | 5 | Penn State | Allentown, Pa. | Tustin, Calif. | 16 |
| 60 | Harrah, Dennis | G | 6-5 | 265 | 3/9/53 | 10 | Miami | Charleston, W. Va. | Long Beach, Calif. | 15 |
| 26 | Harris, Eric | CB | 6-3 | 202 | 8/11/55 | 5 | Memphis State | Memphis, Tenn. | Memphis, Tenn. | 16 |
| 81 | †Hill, David | TE | 6-2 | 228 | 1/1/54 | 9 | Texas A&I | San Antonio, Tex. | Bloomfield Hills, Mich. | 16 |
| 87 | Hill, Drew | WR | 5-9 | 170 | 10/5/56 | 6 | Georgia Tech | Newnan, Ga. | Newnan, Ga. | 0* |
| 72 | Hill, Kent | G | 6-5 | 260 | 3/7/57 | 6 | Georgia Tech | Americus, Ga. | Americus, Ga. | 16 |
| 47 | Irvin, LeRoy | CB | 5-11 | 184 | 9/15/57 | 5 | Kansas | Fort Dix, N.J. | Fullerton, Calif. | 15 |
| 59 | Jerue, Mark | LB | 6-3 | 229 | 1/15/60 | 2 | Washington | Seattle, Wash. | Seattle, Wash. | 16 |
| 77 | Jeter, Gary | DE | 6-4 | 260 | 3/24/55 | 8 | Southern California | Weirton, W. Va. | Secaucus, N.J. | 16 |
| 20 | Johnson, Johnnie | S | 6-1 | 183 | 10/8/56 | 5 | Texas | La Grange, Tex. | Huntington Beach, Calif. | 16 |
| 24 | Jones, A.J. | RB | 6-1 | 202 | 5/30/59 | 3 | Texas | Youngstown, Ohio | Youngstown, Ohio | 9 |
| 25 | †Jones, Gordon | WR | 6-0 | 190 | 7/25/57 | 6 | Pittsburgh | Buffalo, N.Y. | Tampa, Fla. | 11 |
| 9 | Kemp, Jeff | QB | 6-0 | 201 | 7/11/59 | 4 | Dartmouth | Santa Ana, Calif. | Laguna Hills, Calif. | 4 |
| 76 | Kowalski, Gary | T | 6-5 | 275 | 7/2/60 | 2 | Boston College | New Haven, Conn. | Anaheim, Calif. | 16 |
| 1 | Lansford, Mike | K | 6-0 | 183 | 7/20/58 | 3 | Washington | Monterey Park, Calif. | Huntington Beach, Calif. | 4 |
| 51 | Lewis, David | LB | 6-4 | 245 | 10/15/54 | 8 | Southern California | Houston, Tex. | Tampa, Fla. | 13 |
| 83 | McDonald, James | TE | 6-5 | 230 | 3/29/61 | 2 | Southern California | Long Beach, Calif. | Long Beach, Calif. | 16 |
| 69 | Meisner, Greg | NT | 6-3 | 253 | 4/23/59 | 4 | Pittsburgh | New Kensington, Pa. | Huntington Beach, Calif. | 16 |
| 6 | Misko, John | P | 6-5 | 207 | 10/1/54 | 3 | Oregon State | Highland Park, Mich. | Strathmore, Calif. | 16 |
| 13 | Nelson, Chuck | K | 5-11 | 175 | 2/23/60 | 2 | Washington | Seattle, Wash. | Everett, Wash. | 12 |
| 22 | Newsome, Vince | S | 6-1 | 179 | 1/22/61 | 2 | Washington | Braintree, England | Seattle, Wash. | 16 |
| 58 | Owens, Mel | LB | 6-2 | 224 | 12/7/58 | 4 | Michigan | Detroit, Mich. | Balboa, Calif. | 16 |
| 75 | Pankey, Irv | T | 6-4 | 267 | 12/15/58 | 4 | Penn State | Aberdeen, Md. | Diamond Bar, Calif. | 0* |
| 30 | Redden, Barry | RB | 5-10 | 205 | 7/21/60 | 3 | Richmond | Sarasota, Fla. | Anaheim, Calif. | 15 |
| 57 | Reilly, Mike | LB | 6-4 | 220 | 2/14/59 | 2 | Oklahoma | Miami, Fla. | Miami, Fla. | 0* |
| 64 | Shearin, Joe | G | 6-4 | 250 | 4/16/60 | 2 | Texas | Dallas, Tex. | Austin, Tex. | 16 |
| 78 | Slater, Jackie | T | 6-4 | 271 | 5/27/54 | 9 | Jackson State | Jackson, Miss. | Anaheim, Calif. | 16 |
| 56 | Smith, Doug | C | 6-3 | 253 | 11/25/56 | 7 | Bowling Green | Columbus, Ohio | Laguna Hills, Calif. | 14 |
| 37 | Sully, Ivory | S | 6-0 | 200 | 6/20/57 | 6 | Delaware | Salisbury, Md. | Fullerton, Calif. | 16 |
| 54 | Wilcher, Mike | LB | 6-3 | 235 | 3/20/60 | 2 | North Carolina | Washington, D.C. | Washington, D.C. | 15 |
| 53 | †Williams, Eric | LB | 6-2 | 235 | 6/17/55 | 8 | Southern California | Sacramento, Calif. | St. Charles, Mo. | 11* |
| 85 | Youngblood, Jack | DE | 6-4 | 242 | 1/26/50 | 14 | Florida | Jacksonville, Fla. | Orange, Calif. | 16 |

* Crutchfield played 11 games with N.Y. Jets, 2 games with Houston in '83; Drew Hill and Pankey missed '83 season due to injuries; Reilly missed '83 season due to suspension; E. Williams played 3 games with Pittsburgh, 11 with Los Angeles.

†Option playout; subject to developments.

t-Rams traded for Crutchfield (Houston), Green (Kansas City).

Traded—Quarterback Steve Fuller to Chicago.

Also played with Rams in '83—NT Richard Bishop (2 games), LB Howard Carson (16), CB Kirk Collins (4), CB Monte Jackson (6), NT Myron Lapka (4), CB Henry Williams (6), CB Mike Williams (2), LB Jim Youngblood (7).

## COACHING STAFF

### Head Coach, John Robinson

**Pro Career:** Guided Rams to 9-7 record and first playoff berth in three seasons as rookie coach last year. Became seventeenth head coach in Rams history on February 14, 1983. Arrived with 23 years of coaching experience, including one on the professional level with the Raiders in 1975. No pro playing experience.

**Background:** Played with Oregon 1955-58. Began coaching career at his alma mater from 1960-71. Became an assistant at Southern California from 1972-74. Returned as head coach in 1976 before resigning after the 1982 season. Compiled seven-year .819 winning percentage at Southern California with 67 wins, 14 losses, and 2 ties.

**Personal:** Born July 25, 1935 in Chicago. John and his wife, Barbara, live in Pasadena and have four children—Teresa, Lynn, David, and Christopher.

### Assistant Coaches

**Bob Baker,** quarterbacks; born November 28, 1927, Bluffton, Ind., lives in Anaheim. Quarterback Ball State 1947-51. No pro playing experience. College coach: Indiana 1966-72, Illinois 1973, Michigan State 1977-79, Arizona State 1980-82. Pro coach: Calgary (CFL) 1974-76 (1976 head coach), joined Rams in 1983.

**Marv Goux,** defensive line; born September 8, 1932, Santa Barbara, Calif., lives in Long Beach. Linebacker Southern California 1952, 1954-55. No pro playing experience. College coach: Southern California 1957-82. Pro coach: Joined Rams in 1983.

**Gil Haskell,** special teams; born September 24, 1943, San Francisco, Calif., lives in Diamond Bar. Defensive back San Francisco State 1961, 1963-65. No pro playing experience. College coach: Southern California 1978-82. Pro coach: Joined Rams in 1983.

**Hudson Houck,** offensive line; born January 7, 1943, Los Angeles, Calif., lives in Long Beach. Center Southern California 1962-64. No pro playing experience. College coach: Southern California 1970-72, 1976-82, Stanford 1973-75. Pro coach: Joined Rams in 1983.

**Jimmy Raye,** wide receivers-passing game coordinator; born July 3, 1945, Fayetteville, N.C., lives in Anaheim. Quarterback Michigan State 1965-67. Pro defensive back Philadelphia Eagles 1969. College coach: Michigan State 1971-75, Wyoming 1976. Pro coach: San Francisco 49ers 1977, Detroit Lions 1978-79, Atlanta Falcons 1980-82, joined Rams in 1983.

**Steve Shafer,** defensive backs; born December 8, 1940, Glendale, Calif., lives in Anaheim. Quarterback-defensive back Utah State 1961-62. Pro defensive back British Columbia (CFL) 1963-67. College coach: San Mateo J.C. 1968-74 (1973-74 head coach), San Diego State 1975-82. Pro coach: Joined Rams in 1983.

**Fritz Shurmur,** inside linebackers; born July 15, 1932, Riverview, Mich., lives in Diamond Bar. Center Albion 1951-53. No pro playing experience. College coach: Albion 1956-61, Wyoming 1962-74 (1971-74 head coach). Pro coach: Detroit Lions 1975-77, New England Patriots 1978-81, joined Rams in 1982.

**Bruce Snyder,** running backs-running game coordinator; born March 14, 1940, Santa Monica, Calif., lives in Anaheim. Fullback Oregon 1960-62. No pro playing experience. College coach: Oregon 1966-72, Utah State 1973, Southern California 1974-75, Utah State 1976-82 (head coach). Pro coach: Joined Rams in 1983.

**Fred Whittingham,** outside linebackers; born February 4, 1939, Boston, Mass., lives in Anaheim. Linebacker Brigham Young 1957-58, Cal Poly-SLO 1961-62. Pro linebacker Los Angeles Rams 1964, Philadelphia Eagles 1965-66, 1971, New Orleans Saints 1967-68, Dallas Cowboys 1969-70. College coach: Brigham Young 1973-81. Pro coach: Joined Rams in 1982.

## LOS ANGELES RAMS 1984 FIRST-YEAR ROSTER

| Name | Pos. | Ht. | Wt. | Birth-date | College | Birthplace | Residence | How Acq. |
|------|------|-----|-----|-----------|---------|-----------|-----------|----------|
| Bias, Moe | LB | 6-1 | 220 | 9/1/61 | Illinois | Los Angeles, Calif. | Los Angeles, Calif. | D12a |
| Brady, Ed | LB | 6-2 | 228 | 6/17/60 | Illinois | Morris, Ill. | Morris, Ill. | D8 |
| Brafford, Todd | G | 6-5 | 265 | 9/2/60 | Utah State | Concord, N.C. | El Monte, Calif. | FA |
| t-Brown, Ron | WR | 5-11 | 181 | 3/31/61 | Arizona State | Los Angeles, Calif. | Tempe, Ariz. | D2('83) |
| Byers, Scott (1) | CB | 5-11 | 170 | 7/3/58 | Long Beach State | Bayonne, N.J. | Fullerton, Calif. | FA |
| Caldwell, Ralph | LB | 6-2 | 227 | 1/18/61 | Indiana | Inglewood, Calif. | Westchester, Calif. | FA |
| Croudip, David | CB-S | 5-9 | 183 | 1/25/59 | San Diego State | Indianapolis, Ind. | San Diego, Calif. | FA |
| Deluca, Tony | NT | 6-4 | 250 | 11/16/60 | Rhode Island | Cos Cob, Conn. | Cos Cob, Conn. | FA |
| Dooley, Joe | C | 6-5 | 270 | 3/1/62 | Ohio State | Cincinnati, Ohio | Cincinnati, Ohio | D10a |
| Dumont, Bob | LB | 6-1 | 210 | 7/16/61 | Rutgers | Levittown, Pa. | Levittown, Pa. | FA |
| Emanuel, Vince | RB | 6-0 | 215 | 2/13/60 | San Diego State | Palmdale, Calif. | San Diego, Calif. | FA |
| Faulkner, Chris (1) | G | 6-4 | 260 | 4/13/60 | Florida | Tipton, Ind. | Arcadia, Calif. | FA |
| Fisher, Roderick | CB | 5-10 | 190 | 11/23/61 | Oklahoma State | Dallas, Tex. | Dallas, Tex. | D12 |
| Ford, Kerry (1) | LB | 6-1 | 225 | 12/30/60 | San Jose State | Los Angeles, Calif. | Culver City, Calif. | FA |
| Greene, Marcellus | CB | 6-0 | 183 | 12/12/57 | Arizona | Indianapolis, Ind. | Indianapolis, Ind. | D11('81) |
| Harper, Michael | WR | 5-11 | 185 | 5/11/61 | Southern California | Kansas City, Kan. | Kansas City, Kan. | D11 |
| Johnson, John | T | 6-5 | 265 | 2/9/61 | Idaho State | Zaragoza, Spain | Rainier, Ore. | FA |
| Kamana, John | RB | 6-2 | 215 | 12/3/61 | Southern California | Honolulu, Hawaii | Honolulu, Hawaii | FA |
| Love, Dwyane | RB | 6-1 | 205 | 11/18/61 | Houston | Garland, Tex. | Garland, Tex. | D11a |
| McDonald, Mike (1) | LB | 6-1 | 235 | 6/22/58 | Southern California | Burbank, Calif. | Burbank, Calif. | FA |
| McQuaid, Dan | LB | 6-6 | 255 | 10/4/60 | Nevada-Las Vegas | Cortland, Calif. | Cortland, Calif. | FA |
| Miller, Shawn (1) | NT | 6-4 | 255 | 3/14/61 | Utah State | Ogden, Utah | Ogden, Utah | FA |
| Martin, Ricky (1) | WR | 6-3 | 200 | 10/26/58 | New Mexico | Los Angeles, Calif. | Los Angeles, Calif. | FA |
| Peters, Ken (1) | TE | 6-4 | 238 | 9/30/60 | Houston | Dallas, Tex. | Dallas, Tex. | FA |
| Radachowsky, George | S | 5-11 | 178 | 9/7/62 | Boston College | Danbury, Conn. | Danbury, Conn. | D7 |
| Reed, Doug | DE | 6-3 | 250 | 7/16/60 | San Diego State | San Diego, Calif. | San Diego, Calif. | D4 |
| Reynolds, George | P | 6-0 | 188 | 8/31/61 | Penn State | Walnut Creek, Pa. | University Park, Pa. | D9 |
| Stephens, Hal | DE | 6-4 | 252 | 4/14/61 | East Carolina | Whiteville, N.C. | Greenville, N.C. | D5 |
| Taylor, Tom | G | 6-3 | 267 | 9/14/62 | Georgia Tech | Acton, Calif. | Acton, Calif. | FA |
| Thompson, Broderick (1) | T | 6-5 | 280 | 8/14/60 | Kansas | Cerritos, Calif. | Cerritos, Calif. | FA |
| Tinsley, Scott (1) | QB | 6-2 | 195 | 11/14/59 | Southern California | Oklahoma City, Okla. | Oklahoma City, Okla. | FA |
| Torretta, Gary | QB | 6-2 | 205 | 7/13/61 | St. Mary's, Calif. | San Pablo, Calif. | Pinole, Calif. | FA |
| Uperesa, Kevin | T | 6-6 | 270 | 7/8/59 | California | Honolulu, Hawaii | Punahou, Hawaii | FA |
| Vann, Norwood | RB | 6-2 | 225 | 2/18/62 | East Carolina | Philadelphia, Pa. | Magnolia, N.C. | D10 |

t-Rams traded for Brown (Cleveland).

Players who report to an NFL team for the first time are designated on rosters as rookies (R). If a player reported to an NFL training camp in a previous year but was not on the active squad for three or more regular season or postseason games, he is listed on the first-year roster and designated by a (1). Thereafter, a player who is on the active squad for three or more regular season or postseason games is credited with an additional year of playing experience.

## NOTES

_____
_____
_____
_____
_____
_____
_____
_____
_____
_____
_____
_____
_____
_____
_____
_____
_____
_____

# MINNESOTA VIKINGS

## VIKINGS COACHING HISTORY
**(190-150-9)**

| | | |
|---|---|---|
| 1961-66 | Norm Van Brocklin | 29-51-4 |
| 1967-83 | Bud Grant | 161-99-5 |

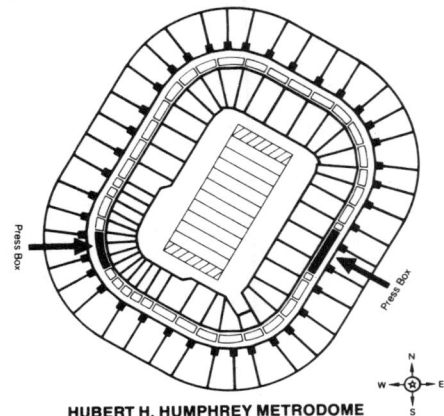

**HUBERT H. HUMPHREY METRODOME**

**National Football Conference
Central Division**

**Team Colors:** Purple, Gold, and White

**9520 Viking Drive
Eden Prairie, Minnesota 55344
Telephone: 612-828-6500**

**Club Officials**

Board of Directors: Max Winter, Mike Lynn,
  John Skoglund, Jack Steele, Sheldon Kaplan
President: Max Winter
Executive Vice President-General Manager:
  Mike Lynn
Assistant to the General Manager/
  Director of Operations: Jeff Diamond
Director of Administration: Harley Peterson
Ticket Manager: Harry Randolph
Director of Football Operations: Jerry Reichow
Director of Player Personnel: Frank Gilliam
Head Scout: Ralph Kohl
Assistant Head Scout: Don Deisch
Scout: John Carson
Director of Public Relations: Merrill Swanson
Director of Communications and Community
  Relations: Kernal Buhler
Public Relations Assistant: Katie Hogan
Trainer: Fred Zamberletti
Equipment Manager: Dennis Ryan

**Stadium:** Hubert H. Humphrey Metrodome •
  **Capacity:** 62,212
  500 11th Avenue, So.,
  Minneapolis, Minn. 55415

**Playing Surface:** SuperTurf

**Training Camp:** Mankato State University
  Mankato, Minnesota 56001

## 1984 SCHEDULE

**Preseason**

| | | |
|---|---|---|
| Aug. 4 | **Atlanta** | 7:00 |
| Aug. 11 | **Miami** | 7:00 |
| Aug. 18 | **Philadelphia** | 7:00 |
| Aug. 24 | at St. Louis | 7:30 |

**Regular Season**

| | | |
|---|---|---|
| Sept. 2 | **San Diego** | 12:00 |
| Sept. 9 | at Philadelphia | 1:00 |
| Sept. 16 | **Atlanta** | 12:00 |
| Sept. 23 | at Detroit | 1:00 |
| Sept. 30 | **Seattle** | 12:00 |
| Oct. 7 | at Tampa Bay | 1:00 |
| Oct. 14 | at Los Angeles Raiders | 1:00 |
| Oct. 21 | **Detroit** | 12:00 |
| Oct. 28 | at Chicago | 12:00 |
| Nov. 4 | **Tampa Bay** | 12:00 |
| Nov. 11 | vs. Green Bay at Milwaukee | 12:00 |
| Nov. 18 | at Denver | 2:00 |
| Nov. 25 | **Chicago** | 3:00 |
| Nov. 29 | **Washington** (Thursday) | 8:00 |
| Dec. 8 | at San Francisco (Saturday) | 1:00 |
| Dec. 16 | **Green Bay** | 12:00 |

## RECORD HOLDERS
### Individual Records—Career

| Category | Name | Performance |
|---|---|---|
| Rushing (Yds.) | Chuck Foreman, 1973-79 | 5,879 |
| Passing (Yds.) | Fran Tarkenton, 1961-66, 1972-78 | 33,098 |
| Passing (TDs) | Fran Tarkenton, 1961-66, 1972-78 | 239 |
| Receiving (No.) | Ahmad Rashad, 1976-1982 | 400 |
| Receiving (Yds.) | Sammy White, 1976-1983 | 5,925 |
| Interceptions | Paul Krause, 1968-1979 | 53 |
| Punting (Avg.) | Bobby Walden, 1964-67 | 42.9 |
| Punt Return (Avg.) | Tommy Mason, 1961-66 | 10.5 |
| Kickoff Return (Avg.) | Bob Reed, 1962-63 | 27.1 |
| Field Goals | Fred Cox, 1963-1977 | 282 |
| Touchdowns (Tot.) | Bill Brown, 1962-1974 | 76 |
| Points | Fred Cox, 1963-1977 | 1,365 |

### Individual Records—Single Season

| Category | Name | Performance |
|---|---|---|
| Rushing (Yds.) | Chuck Foreman, 1976 | 1,155 |
| Passing (Yds.) | Tommy Kramer, 1981 | 3,912 |
| Passing (TDs) | Tommy Kramer, 1981 | 26 |
| Receiving (No.) | Rickey Young, 1978 | 88 |
| Receiving (Yds.) | Ahmad Rashad, 1979 | 1,156 |
| Interceptions | Paul Krause, 1975 | 10 |
| Punting (Avg.) | Bobby Walden, 1964 | 46.4 |
| Punt Return (Avg.) | Billy Butler, 1963 | 10.5 |
| Kickoff Return (Avg.) | John Gilliam, 1972 | 26.3 |
| Field Goals | Fred Cox, 1970 | 30 |
| Touchdowns (Tot.) | Chuck Foreman, 1975 | 22 |
| Points | Chuck Foreman, 1975 | 132 |

### Individual Records—Single Game

| Category | Name | Performance |
|---|---|---|
| Rushing (Yds.) | Chuck Foreman, 10-24-76 | 200 |
| Passing (Yds.) | Tommy Kramer, 12-14-80 | 456 |
| Passing (TDs) | Joe Kapp, 9-28-69 | 7 |
| Receiving (No.) | Rickey Young, 12-16-79 | 15 |
| Receiving (Yds.) | Sammy White, 11-7-76 | 210 |
| Interceptions | Many times | 3 |
| | Last time by Willie Teal, 11-28-82 | |
| Field Goals | Fred Cox, 9-23-73 | 5 |
| Touchdowns (Tot.) | Chuck Foreman, 12-20-75 | 4 |
| | Ahmad Rashad, 9-2-79 | 4 |
| Points | Chuck Foreman, 12-20-75 | 24 |
| | Ahmad Rashad, 9-2-79 | 24 |

MINNESOTA VIKINGS

# MINNESOTA VIKINGS

## 1983 TEAM STATISTICS

| | Minnesota | Opp. |
|---|---|---|
| Total First Downs | 303 | 318 |
| Rushing | 112 | 147 |
| Passing | 169 | 150 |
| Penalty | 22 | 21 |
| Third Down Efficiency | 65/220 | 97/235 |
| Third Down Percentage | 29.5 | 41.3 |
| Total Net Yards | 5019 | 5487 |
| Total Offensive Plays | 1068 | 1104 |
| Avg. Gain per Play | 4.7 | 5.0 |
| Avg. Gain per Game | 313.7 | 342.9 |
| Net Yards Rushing | 1808 | 2584 |
| Total Rushing Plays | 470 | 579 |
| Avg. Gain per Rush | 3.8 | 4.5 |
| Avg. Gain Rushing per Game | 113.0 | 161.5 |
| Net Yards Passing | 3211 | 2903 |
| Lost Attempting to Pass | 43/303 | 47/326 |
| Gross Yards Passing | 3514 | 3229 |
| Attempts/Completions | 555/310 | 478/263 |
| Percent Completed | 55.9 | 55.0 |
| Had Intercepted | 22 | 25 |
| Avg. Net Passing per Game | 200.7 | 181.4 |
| Punts/Avg. | 91/41.5 | 77/39.3 |
| Punt Returns/Avg. | 24/8.8 | 40/7.4 |
| Kickoff Returns/Avg. | 68/21.6 | 70/19.9 |
| Interceptions/Avg. Ret. | 25/6.7 | 22/14.0 |
| Penalties/Yards | 90/748 | 92/759 |
| Fumbles/Ball Lost | 33/10 | 33/23 |
| Total Points | 316 | 348 |
| Avg. Points per Game | 19.8 | 21.8 |
| Touchdowns | 34 | 42 |
| Rushing | 17 | 16 |
| Passing | 15 | 23 |
| Returns and Recoveries | 2 | 3 |
| Field Goals | 25/33 | 18/27 |
| Conversions | 33/34 | 40/42 |
| Safeties | 2 | 1 |
| Avg. Time of Possession | 28:47 | 31:13 |

## 1983 TEAM RECORD
### Preseason (3-1)

| Date | Minnesota | | Opponents |
|---|---|---|---|
| 8/6 | 28 | St. Louis | 10 |
| 8/13 | 7 | *Baltimore | 10 |
| 8/19 | 19 | Seattle | 17 |
| 8/26 | 34 | *Denver | 3 |
| | 88 | | 40 |

### Regular Season (8-8)

| Date | Minnesota | | Opp. | Att. |
|---|---|---|---|---|
| 9/4 | 27 | Cleveland | 21 | 70,087 |
| 9/8 | 17 | *San Francisco | 48 | 58,167 |
| 9/18 | 19 | Tampa Bay (OT) | 16 | 57,567 |
| 9/25 | 20 | *Detroit | 17 | 58,254 |
| 10/2 | 24 | *Dallas | 37 | 60,774 |
| 10/9 | 23 | Chicago | 14 | 59,632 |
| 10/16 | 34 | *Houston | 14 | 58,910 |
| 10/23 | 20 | Green Bay (OT) | 17 | 55,236 |
| 10/30 | 31 | St. Louis | 41 | 38,796 |
| 11/6 | 2 | *Tampa Bay | 17 | 59,239 |
| 11/13 | 21 | *Green Bay | 29 | 60,113 |
| 11/20 | 17 | Pittsburgh | 14 | 58,417 |
| 11/27 | 16 | New Orleans | 17 | 59,502 |
| 12/5 | 2 | Detroit | 13 | 79,169 |
| 12/11 | 13 | *Chicago | 19 | 57,880 |
| 12/17 | 20 | *Cincinnati | 14 | 51,565 |
| | 316 | | 348 | 943,308 |

*Home Game  (OT) Overtime

### Score by Periods

| | | | | | | | |
|---|---|---|---|---|---|---|---|
| Minnesota | 85 | 85 | 68 | 72 | 6 | — | 316 |
| Opponents | 71 | 119 | 72 | 86 | 0 | — | 348 |

### Attendance
Home 464,902  Away 478,406  Total 943,308
Single game home record, 60,774 (10-2-83)
Single season home record, 464,902 (1983)

## 1983 INDIVIDUAL STATISTICS
### Rushing

| | Att. | Yds. | Avg. | LG | TD |
|---|---|---|---|---|---|
| Nelson | 154 | 642 | 4.2 | 56t | 1 |
| T. Brown | 120 | 476 | 4.0 | 43 | 10 |
| Galbreath | 113 | 474 | 4.2 | 52t | 4 |
| Young | 39 | 90 | 2.3 | 9 | 2 |
| Redwine | 10 | 48 | 4.8 | 21 | 0 |
| LeCount | 2 | 42 | 21.0 | 40 | 0 |
| Dils | 16 | 28 | 1.8 | 8 | 0 |
| Jones | 1 | 9 | 9.0 | 9 | 0 |
| S. White | 1 | 7 | 7.0 | 7 | 0 |
| Kramer | 8 | 3 | 0.4 | 8 | 0 |
| Lewis | 1 | 2 | 2.0 | 2 | 0 |
| Manning | 1 | -1 | -1.0 | -1 | 0 |
| Wilson | 3 | -3 | -1.0 | 2 | 0 |
| Coleman | 1 | -9 | -9.0 | -9 | 0 |
| Minnesota | 470 | 1808 | 3.8 | 56t | 17 |
| Opponents | 579 | 2584 | 4.5 | 75t | 16 |

### Passing

| | Att. | Comp. | Pct. | Yds. | TD | Int. | Tkld. | Rate |
|---|---|---|---|---|---|---|---|---|
| Dils | 444 | 239 | 53.8 | 2840 | 11 | 16 | 37/254 | 66.8 |
| Kramer | 82 | 55 | 67.1 | 550 | 3 | 4 | 3/27 | 77.8 |
| Wilson | 28 | 16 | 57.1 | 124 | 1 | 2 | 3/22 | 50.3 |
| LeCount | 1 | 0 | 0.0 | 0 | 0 | 0 | 0/0 | 39.6 |
| Minnesota | 555 | 310 | 55.9 | 3514 | 15 | 22 | 43/303 | 67.5 |
| Opponents | 478 | 263 | 55.0 | 3229 | 23 | 25 | 47/326 | 70.3 |

### Receiving

| | No. | Yds. | Avg. | LG | TD |
|---|---|---|---|---|---|
| Nelson | 51 | 618 | 12.1 | 68 | 0 |
| Galbreath | 45 | 348 | 7.7 | 23 | 2 |
| T. Brown | 41 | 357 | 8.7 | 25 | 1 |
| Bruer | 31 | 315 | 10.2 | 26 | 2 |
| S. White | 29 | 412 | 14.2 | 43t | 4 |
| LeCount | 21 | 318 | 15.1 | 49 | 2 |
| McCullum | 21 | 314 | 15.0 | 49t | 2 |
| Young | 21 | 193 | 9.2 | 48 | 0 |
| Jordan | 15 | 212 | 14.1 | 28 | 2 |
| Casper | 13 | 172 | 13.2 | 34 | 0 |
| Lewis | 12 | 127 | 10.6 | 18 | 0 |
| Jones | 6 | 95 | 15.8 | 47 | 0 |
| McDole | 3 | 29 | 9.7 | 10 | 0 |
| Redwine | 1 | 4 | 4.0 | 4 | 0 |
| Minnesota | 310 | 3514 | 11.3 | 68 | 15 |
| Opponents | 263 | 3229 | 12.3 | 74t | 23 |

### Interceptions

| | No. | Yds. | Avg. | LG | TD |
|---|---|---|---|---|---|
| Turner | 6 | 37 | 6.2 | 14 | 0 |
| Swain | 6 | 12 | 2.0 | 11 | 0 |
| Bess | 3 | 38 | 12.7 | 19 | 0 |
| Teal | 3 | 26 | 8.7 | 12 | 0 |
| Browner | 2 | 0 | 0.0 | 0 | 0 |
| Lee | 1 | 31 | 31.0 | 31 | 0 |
| J. White | 1 | 22 | 22.0 | 22 | 0 |
| C. Johnson | 1 | 2 | 2.0 | 2 | 0 |
| Blair | 1 | 0 | 0.0 | 0 | 0 |
| Nord | 1 | 0 | 0.0 | 0 | 0 |
| Minnesota | 25 | 168 | 6.7 | 31 | 0 |
| Opponents | 22 | 308 | 14.0 | 60t | 2 |

### Punting

| | No. | Yds. | Avg. | In 20 | LG |
|---|---|---|---|---|---|
| Coleman | 91 | 3780 | 41.5 | 28 | 65 |
| Minnesota | 91 | 3780 | 41.5 | 28 | 65 |
| Opponents | 77 | 3027 | 39.3 | 17 | 64 |

### Punt Returns

| | No. | FC | Yds. | Avg. | LG | TD |
|---|---|---|---|---|---|---|
| Bess | 21 | 10 | 158 | 7.5 | 17 | 0 |
| Lewis | 3 | 3 | 52 | 17.3 | 34 | 0 |
| Bell | 0 | 2 | 0 | — | 0 | 0 |
| Minnesota | 24 | 15 | 210 | 8.8 | 34 | 0 |
| Opponents | 40 | 10 | 297 | 7.4 | 37 | 0 |

### Kickoff Returns

| | No. | Yds. | Avg. | LG | TD |
|---|---|---|---|---|---|
| Nelson | 18 | 445 | 24.7 | 50 | 0 |
| Redwine | 38 | 838 | 22.1 | 41 | 0 |
| Huffman | 3 | 42 | 14.0 | 15 | 0 |
| Young | 3 | 27 | 9.0 | 15 | 0 |
| Bess | 2 | 44 | 22.0 | 30 | 0 |
| Jones | 2 | 31 | 15.5 | 16 | 0 |
| Bell | 1 | 14 | 14.0 | 14 | 0 |
| Lewis | 1 | 25 | 25.0 | 25 | 0 |
| Minnesota | 68 | 1466 | 21.6 | 50 | 0 |
| Opponents | 70 | 1392 | 19.9 | 53 | 0 |

### Scoring

| | TD | TD R | TD P | TD Rt | PAT | FG | TP |
|---|---|---|---|---|---|---|---|
| Ricardo | | | | | 33/34 | 25/33 | 108 |
| T. Brown | 11 | 10 | 1 | 0 | | | 66 |
| Galbreath | 6 | 4 | 2 | 0 | | | 36 |
| S. White | 4 | 0 | 4 | 0 | | | 24 |
| Bruer | 2 | 0 | 2 | 0 | | | 12 |
| Jordan | 2 | 0 | 2 | 0 | | | 12 |
| LeCount | 2 | 0 | 2 | 0 | | | 12 |
| McCullum | 2 | 0 | 2 | 0 | | | 12 |
| Young | 2 | 2 | 0 | 0 | | | 12 |
| Huffman | 1 | 0 | 0 | 1 | | | 6 |
| C. Johnson | 1 | 0 | 0 | 1 | | | 6 |
| Nelson | 1 | 1 | 0 | 0 | | | 6 |
| Minnesota | 34 | 17 | 15 | 2 | 33/34 | 25/33 | 316 |
| Opponents | 42 | 16 | 23 | 3 | 40/42 | 18/27 | 348 |

## FIRST-ROUND SELECTIONS

(If Club had no first-round selection, first player drafted is listed with round in parentheses.)

| Year | Player, College, Position |
|---|---|
| 1961 | Tommy Mason, Tulane, RB |
| 1962 | Bill Miller, Miami, WR (3) |
| 1963 | Jim Dunaway, Mississippi, T |
| 1964 | Carl Eller, Minnesota, DE |
| 1965 | Jack Snow, Notre Dame, WR |
| 1966 | Jerry Shay, Purdue, DT |
| 1967 | Clinton Jones, Michigan State, RB |
| | Gene Washington, Michigan State, WR |
| | Alan Page, Notre Dame, DT |
| 1968 | Ron Yary, Southern California, T |
| 1969 | Ed White, California, G (2) |
| 1970 | John Ward, Oklahoma State, DT |
| 1971 | Leo Hayden, Ohio State, RB |
| 1972 | Jeff Siemon, Stanford, LB |
| 1973 | Chuck Foreman, Miami, RB |
| 1974 | Fred McNeill, UCLA, LB |
| | Steve Riley, Southern California, T |
| 1975 | Mark Mullaney, Colorado State, DE |
| 1976 | James White, Oklahoma State, DT |
| 1977 | Tommy Kramer, Rice, QB |
| 1978 | Randy Holloway, Pittsburgh, DE |
| 1979 | Ted Brown, North Carolina State, RB |
| 1980 | Doug Martin, Washington, DT |
| 1981 | Mardye McDole, Mississippi State, WR (2) |
| 1982 | Darrin Nelson, Stanford, RB |
| 1983 | Joey Browner, Southern California, DB |
| 1984 | Keith Millard, Washington State, DE |

## MINNESOTA VIKINGS 1984 VETERAN ROSTER

| No. | Name | Pos. | Ht. | Wt. | Birth-date | NFL Exp. | College | Birthplace | Residence | Games in '83 |
|-----|------|------|-----|-----|-----------|----------|---------|-----------|-----------|--------------|
| 58 | Ashley, Walker Lee | LB | 6-0 | 240 | 7/28/60 | 2 | Penn State | Bayonne, N.J. | Edina, Minn. | 15 |
| 33 | Bell, Rick | RB | 6-0 | 205 | 10/18/60 | 2 | St. John's, Minn. | St. Cloud, Minn. | Rochester, Minn. | 14 |
| 21 | Bess, Rufus | CB | 5-9 | 185 | 3/13/56 | 6 | South Carolina State | Hartsville, S.C. | Hartsville, S.C. | 14 |
| 59 | Blair, Matt | LB | 6-5 | 235 | 9/20/50 | 11 | Iowa State | Honolulu, Hawaii | Prior Lake, Minn. | 16 |
| 62 | Boyd, Brent | G | 6-3 | 275 | 3/23/57 | 5 | UCLA | La Habra, Calif. | Leucadia, Calif. | 16 |
| 23 | Brown, Ted | RB | 5-10 | 210 | 2/2/57 | 6 | North Carolina State | High Point, N.C. | Burnsville, Minn. | 10 |
| 47 | Browner, Joey | CB-S | 6-2 | 205 | 5/15/60 | 2 | Southern California | Warren, Ohio | Burnsville, Minn. | 16 |
| 82 | †Bruer, Bob | TE | 6-5 | 240 | 5/22/54 | 6 | Mankato State | Madison, Wis. | Waconia, Minn. | 13* |
| 44 | Casper, Dave | TE | 6-4 | 241 | 2/2/52 | 11 | Notre Dame | Bemidji, Minn. | Burnsville, Minn. | 16 |
| 8 | Coleman, Greg | P | 6-0 | 185 | 9/9/54 | 8 | Florida A&M | Jacksonville, Fla. | Edina, Minn. | 16 |
| 7 | Danmeier, Rick | K | 6-0 | 200 | 4/8/52 | 6 | Sioux Falls | White Bear Lake, Minn. | Edina, Minn. | 0* |
| 12 | Dils, Steve | QB | 6-1 | 195 | 12/8/55 | 5 | Stanford | Vancouver, Wash. | Richfield, Minn. | 16 |
| 73 | Elshire, Neil | DE | 6-6 | 260 | 3/8/58 | 4 | Oregon | Albany, Ore. | Lake Oswego, Ore. | 16 |
| 50 | Fowlkes, Dennis | LB | 6-2 | 230 | 3/11/61 | 2 | West Virginia | Columbus, Ohio | Columbus, Ohio | 11 |
| 32 | Galbreath, Tony | RB | 6-0 | 228 | 1/29/54 | 9 | Missouri | Fulton, Mo. | Jefferson City, Mo. | 13 |
| 61 | †Hamilton, Wes | G | 6-3 | 270 | 4/24/53 | 9 | Tulsa | Texas City, Tex. | Burnsville, Minn. | 15 |
| 45 | Hannon, Tom | S | 5-11 | 195 | 3/5/55 | 8 | Michigan State | Massillon, Ohio | Eden Prairie, Minn. | 16 |
| 75 | Holloway, Randy | DE | 6-5 | 255 | 8/26/55 | 7 | Pittsburgh | Sharon, Pa. | Burnsville, Minn. | 16 |
| 51 | Hough, Jim | G | 6-2 | 275 | 8/4/56 | 7 | Utah State | Lynwood, Calif. | Jordan, Minn. | 16 |
| 76 | Irwin, Tim | T | 6-6 | 285 | 12/13/58 | 4 | Tennessee | Memphis, Tenn. | Knoxville, Tenn. | 16 |
| 65 | Johnson, Charlie | NT | 6-3 | 275 | 2/17/52 | 8 | Colorado | West Columbia, Tex. | West Berlin, N.J. | 16 |
| 52 | †Johnson, Dennis | LB | 6-3 | 235 | 6/19/58 | 5 | Southern California | Flint, Mich. | Torrance, Calif. | 16 |
| 89 | Jones, Mike | WR | 5-11 | 176 | 4/14/60 | 2 | Tennessee State | Chattanooga, Tenn. | Apple Valley, Minn. | 16 |
| 83 | Jordan, Steve | TE | 6-3 | 230 | 1/10/61 | 3 | Brown | Phoenix, Ariz. | Eagan, Minn. | 13 |
| 9 | Kramer, Tommy | QB | 6-2 | 205 | 3/7/55 | 8 | Rice | San Antonio, Tex. | Bloomington, Minn. | 3 |
| 80 | LeCount, Terry | WR | 5-10 | 185 | 7/9/56 | 7 | Florida | Jacksonville, Fla. | Eden Prairie, Minn. | 11 |
| 39 | Lee, Carl | CB-S | 5-11 | 185 | 4/6/61 | 2 | Marshall | South Charleston, W. Va. | South Charleston, W. Va. | 16 |
| 87 | Lewis, Leo | WR | 5-8 | 170 | 9/17/56 | 4 | Missouri | Columbia, Mo. | Knoxville, Tenn. | 14 |
| 4 | Manning, Archie | QB | 6-3 | 211 | 5/9/49 | 14 | Mississippi | Drew, Miss. | New Orleans, La. | 5* |
| 79 | †Martin, Doug | DE | 6-3 | 255 | 5/22/57 | 5 | Washington | Greenville, S.C. | Kirkland, Wash. | 16 |
| 84 | †McCullum, Sam | WR | 6-2 | 195 | 11/30/52 | 11 | Montana State | McComb, Miss. | Mercer Island, Wash. | 10 |
| 88 | McDole, Mardye | WR | 5-11 | 205 | 5/5/59 | 3 | Mississippi State | Pensacola, Fla. | Ocean Springs, Miss. | 15 |
| 54 | †McNeill, Fred | LB | 6-2 | 230 | 5/6/52 | 11 | UCLA | Durham, Calif. | Edina, Minn. | 16 |
| 86 | Mularkey, Mike | TE | 6-4 | 245 | 11/19/61 | 2 | Florida | Miami, Fla. | Ft. Lauderdale, Fla. | 3 |
| 77 | Mullaney, Mark | DE | 6-6 | 245 | 4/30/53 | 10 | Colorado State | Denver, Colo. | Denver, Colo. | 7 |
| 20 | Nelson, Darrin | RB | 5-9 | 180 | 1/2/59 | 3 | Stanford | Sacramento, Calif. | Burnsville, Minn. | 15 |
| 49 | Nord, Keith | S | 6-0 | 195 | 3/13/57 | 6 | St. Cloud State | Minneapolis, Minn. | Minnetonka, Minn. | 3 |
| 22 | Redwine, Jarvis | RB | 5-10 | 205 | 5/16/57 | 4 | Nebraska | Los Angeles, Calif. | Rosemount, Minn. | 16 |
| 1 | Ricardo, Benny | K | 5-10 | 170 | 1/4/54 | 7 | San Diego State | Asuncion, Paraguay | Costa Mesa, Calif. | 16 |
| 78 | †Riley, Steve | T | 6-6 | 260 | 11/23/52 | 11 | Southern California | Chula Vista, Calif. | Tustin, Calif. | 16 |
| 68 | Rouse, Curtis | G | 6-3 | 305 | 7/13/60 | 3 | Tenn.-Chattanooga | Augusta, Ga. | Augusta, Ga. | 16 |
| 57 | Sendlein, Robin | LB | 6-3 | 225 | 12/1/58 | 4 | Texas | Las Vegas, Nev. | Minnetonka, Minn. | 16 |
| 81 | Senser, Joe | TE | 6-4 | 235 | 8/18/56 | 5 | West Chester State | Philadelphia, Pa. | Burnsville, Minn. | 0* |
| 55 | Studwell, Scott | LB | 6-2 | 230 | 8/27/54 | 8 | Illinois | Evansville, Ind. | Bloomington, Minn. | 16 |
| 29 | Swain, John | CB | 6-1 | 195 | 9/4/59 | 4 | Miami | Miami, Fla. | Miami, Fla. | 14 |
| 67 | Swilley, Dennis | C | 6-3 | 245 | 6/28/55 | 8 | Texas A&M | Bossier City, La. | Denton, Tex. | 16 |
| 66 | Tausch, Terry | T | 6-5 | 275 | 2/5/59 | 3 | Texas | New Braunfels, Tex. | Plano, Tex. | 10 |
| 37 | Teal, Willie | CB | 5-10 | 195 | 12/20/57 | 5 | Louisiana State | Texarkana, Tex. | Baton Rouge, La. | 16 |
| 27 | Turner, John | S | 6-0 | 200 | 2/22/56 | 7 | Miami | Miami, Fla. | Miami, Fla. | 16 |
| 42 | Waddy, Billy | WR | 5-11 | 190 | 2/19/54 | 7 | Colorado | Wharton, Tex. | Huntington Beach, Calif. | 0* |
| 72 | White, James | NT | 6-3 | 270 | 10/26/53 | 9 | Oklahoma State | Hot Springs, Ark. | Hot Springs, Ark. | 16 |
| 85 | White, Sammy | WR | 5-11 | 195 | 3/16/54 | 9 | Grambling | Winnsboro, La. | Monroe, La. | 11 |
| 11 | Wilson, Wade | QB | 6-3 | 210 | 2/1/59 | 4 | East Texas State | Greenville, Tex. | Rockwall, Tex. | 1 |
| 34 | †Young, Rickey | RB | 6-2 | 200 | 12/7/53 | 10 | Jackson State | Mobile, Ala. | Eden Prairie, Minn. | 16 |

\* Casper played 3 games with Houston, 10 with Minnesota in '83; Danmeier missed '83 season due to injury; Manning played 3 games with Houston, 2 with Minnesota; Senser active for 3 games but did not play; Waddy last active with L.A. Rams in '82.

†Option playout; subject to developments.

Also played with Vikings in '83—TE Norris Brown (2 games), C-G David Huffman (15), LB Henry Johnson (5), NT Ray Yakavonis (2).

## COACHING STAFF

### Head Coach, Les Steckel

**Pro Career:** Became only the third coach in the history of the Vikings when he was promoted to lead the Vikings, January 29, 1984. Had served as an assistant coach with the Vikings since 1979, working with quarterbacks, wide receivers, tight ends and special teams. Was an assistant coach with San Francisco (1978) before joining the Vikings. No pro playing experience.

**Background:** Attended Whitehall (Pa.) High School where he played basketball for four years, baseball for three, and football as a senior. Attended Kansas University in 1964 and played running back for four years, graduating in 1968 with degrees in social work, human relations, and political science. Won a regional Golden Glove title as a light heavyweight when he was 19. Enlisted in the Marine Corps in 1968. Spent one year in a combat unit in Vietnam as a Lieutenant, returning as a decorated Marine officer whose MOS (Military Occupational Specialty) was infantry. Played running back for the Quantico Marines (1970-71), leading the team in rushing and winning the first Leadership Award in Quantico history. Was an assistant coach at Colorado University (1972-76), and at the Naval Academy (1977).

**Personal:** Is active as a member of the Fellowship of Christian Athletes and as a Major in the Marine Corps Reserve. Earned a Master's degree in Sports Administration from the College of St. Thomas, St. Paul, Minn., in 1982. Les and his wife, Chris, have two children—a son, Christian and a daughter, Lesley—and live in Bloomington, Minn.

### Assistant Coaches

**Tom Batta,** defensive line; born October 6, 1942, Youngstown, Ohio, lives in Eden Prairie, Minn. Offensive-defensive line Kent State 1961-63. No pro playing experience. College coach: Akron 1973, Colorado 1974-78, Kansas 1979-82, North Carolina State 1983. Pro coach: First year with Vikings.

**Bud Bjornaraa,** strength; born August 23, 1938, Thief River Falls, Minn., lives in Apple Valley, Minn. Linebacker University of North Dakota 1958-60. No pro playing experience. Pro coach: First year with Vikings.

**Dean Brittenham,** conditioning; born June 25, 1931, Brady, Neb., lives in Eden Prairie, Minn. No college or pro playing experience. College coach: Nebraska 1967-70, Colorado 1971-76. Pro coach: New Orleans Saints 1977-78, Denver Broncos 1982-83, first year with Vikings.

**Jerry Burns,** offensive coordinator; born January 24, 1927, Detroit, lives in Eden Prairie, Minn. Quarterback Michigan 1947-50. No pro playing experience. College coach: Hawaii 1951, Whittier 1952, Iowa 1954-65 (head coach 1961-65). Pro coach: Green Bay Packers 1966-67, joined Vikings in 1968.

**Tom Cecchini,** outside linebackers; born September 12, 1944, Detroit, lives in Bloomington, Minn. Linebacker-center Michigan 1963-65. No pro playing experience. College coach: Michigan 1968-69, Xavier 1970-73, Iowa 1974-75, 1978-79, Tulane 1976-77. Pro coach: Joined Vikings in 1980.

**Ross Fichtner,** defensive backs; born October 26, 1938, McKeesport, Pa., lives in Eden Prairie, Minn. Quarterback Purdue 1957-59. Pro defensive back Cleveland Browns 1960-67, New Orleans Saints 1968. Pro coach: Florida Blazers (WFL) 1974, Chicago Bears 1975-77, Green Bay Packers 1980-83, first year with Vikings.

**Bob Hollway,** quality control; born January 29, 1926, Ann Arbor, Mich., lives in Edina, Minn. End Michigan 1947-49. No pro playing experience. College coach: Maine 1951-52, Eastern Michigan 1953, Michigan 1954-66. Pro coach: Minnesota Vikings 1967-70, St. Louis Cardinals 1971-72 (head coach), Detroit Lions 1973-74, San Francisco 49ers 1975, Seattle Seahawks 1976-77, rejoined Vikings in 1978.

**John Michels,** running backs; born February 15, 1931, Philadelphia, lives in Bloomington, Minn. Guard Tennessee 1949-52. Pro guard Philadelphia Eagles 1953, 1956, Winnipeg Blue Bombers (CFL) 1957. College coach: Texas A&M 1958. Pro coach: Winnipeg Blue Bombers (CFL) 1959-66, joined Vikings in 1967.

**Bus Mertes,** quality control; born October 6, 1923, Chicago, lives in Edina, Minn. Running back Iowa 1939-41. Pro running back Chicago Cardinals 1945, Los Angeles Dons (AAFC) 1946, Baltimore Colts (AAFC) 1947-48, New York Giants 1949-50. College coach: Bradley 1951-52, Kansas State 1953-59, Drake 1960-64. Pro coach: Denver Broncos 1965-66, joined Vikings in 1967.

**Dan Radakovich,** offensive line; born November 27, 1935, Duquesne, Pa., lives in Eden Prairie, Minn. Center-linebacker Penn State 1954-56. No pro playing experience. College coach: Penn State 1960-69, Cincinnati 1970, Colorado 1972-73, North Carolina State 1982. Pro coach: Pittsburgh Steelers 1971, 1974-77, San Francisco 49ers 1978, Los Angeles Rams 1979-81, Denver Broncos 1983, joined Vikings in 1984.

**Floyd Reese,** defensive coordinator; born August 8, 1948, Springfield, Mo., lives in Bloomington, Minn. Defensive tackle UCLA 1967-69. No pro playing experience. College coach: UCLA 1970-73, Georgia Tech 1974. Pro coach: Detroit Lions 1975-77, San Francisco 49ers 1978, joined Vikings in 1979.

**Mike Sweatman,** defensive assistant/special teams; born October 23, 1946, Kansas City, Mo., lives in Edina, Minn. Linebackers Kansas 1964-67. No pro playing experience. College coach: Kansas 1973-74, 1979-82, Tulsa 1977-78, Tennessee 1983. Pro coach: First year with Vikings.

## MINNESOTA VIKINGS 1984 FIRST-YEAR ROSTER

| Name | Pos. | Ht. | Wt. | Birth-date | College | Birthplace | Residence | How Acq. |
|---|---|---|---|---|---|---|---|---|
| Anderson, Alfred | RB | 6-0 | 214 | 8/4/61 | Baylor | Waco, Tex. | Waco, Tex. | D3 |
| Brown, Melvin (1) | CB | 5-11 | 187 | 10/25/58 | Mississippi | Biloxi, Miss. | Biloxi, Miss. | D10a |
| Brown, Melvin L. | WR | 6-4 | 198 | 11/29/59 | Alabama | Miami, Fla. | Florence, Ala. | FA |
| Butcher, Brian | G | 6-5 | 260 | 9/28/60 | Clemson | Knoxville, Tenn. | Clemson, S.C. | FA |
| Collins, Dwight | WR | 6-1 | 200 | 8/23/61 | Pittsburgh | Rochester, N.Y. | Beaver Falls, Pa. | D6 |
| Frye, Philip (1) | RB | 5-11 | 195 | 12/20/58 | Cal Lutheran | Washington, D.C. | Thousand Oaks, Calif. | FA |
| Grant, Bruce | QB | 6-2 | 205 | 12/31/60 | Minnesota-Duluth | Winnipeg, Canada | Bloomington, Minn. | FA |
| Gustafson, Jim (1) | WR | 6-1 | 185 | 3/16/61 | St. Thomas | Minneapolis, Minn. | St. Paul, Minn. | FA |
| Haines, John | NT | 6-6 | 263 | 12/16/61 | Texas | Ft. Worth, Tex. | Ft. Worth, Tex. | D7 |
| Hallstrom, Todd (1) | G | 6-6 | 280 | 4/7/60 | Minnesota | Mora, Minn. | Brook Park, Minn. | FA |
| Howard, Doug (1) | G | 6-5 | 270 | 6/14/59 | North Carolina | Washington, D.C. | Wayne, Pa. | FA |
| Keller, Jeffrey (1) | WR | 5-11 | 180 | 11/16/58 | Washington | Los Angeles, Calif. | Pullman, Wash. | FA |
| Kidd, Keith | WR | 6-1 | 198 | 9/10/62 | Arkansas | Crossett, Ark. | Fayetteville, Ark. | D9 |
| Millard, Keith | DE | 6-5 | 255 | 3/18/62 | Washington State | Pleasanton, Calif. | Pullman, Wash. | D1 |
| Noel, Dana | CB | 5-10 | 190 | 8/27/58 | Minnesota | Chicago, Ill. | Minneapolis, Minn. | FA |
| Pickett, Edgar | LB | 6-1 | 232 | 1/30/62 | Clemson | Lexington, N.C. | Lexington, N.C. | D11 |
| Rice, Allen | RB | 5-10 | 200 | 4/5/62 | Baylor | Houston, Tex. | Waco, Tex. | D5a |
| Smith, Gregory (1) | NT | 6-3 | 270 | 10/22/59 | Kansas | Chicago, Ill. | Lena, Miss. | FA |
| Spencer, James | LB | 6-2 | 236 | 11/22/61 | Oklahoma State | Dallas, Tex. | Stillwater, Okla. | D10 |
| Stewart, Mark (1) | LB | 6-2 | 230 | 10/13/59 | Washington | Palo Alto, Calif. | Mercer Island, Wash. | D5 |
| Sverchek, Paul | NT | 6-3 | 256 | 5/9/61 | Cal Poly-SLO | S. Luis Obispo, Calif. | San Luis Obispo, Calif. | D8 |
| Thompson, Lawrence | WR | 5-11 | 167 | 1/6/61 | Miami | Wauchula, Fla. | Miami, Fla. | D11a |
| Wagner, Vince (1) | K | 5-11 | 175 | 7/16/59 | Northwestern, Minn. | Bozeman, Mont. | St. Paul, Minn. | FA |

Players who report to an NFL team for the first time are designated on rosters as rookies (R). If a player reported to an NFL training camp in a previous year but was not on the active squad for three or more regular season or postseason games, he is listed on the first-year roster and designated by a (1). Thereafter, a player who is on the active squad for three or more regular season or postseason games is credited with an additional year of playing experience.

## NOTES

# NEW ORLEANS SAINTS

**National Football Conference
Western Division**

**Team Colors:** Old Gold, Black, and White

**1500 Poydras Street
New Orleans, Louisiana 70112
Telephone: (504) 522-1500**

### Club Officials

Owner: John W. Mecom, Jr.
President: Eddie Jones
Vice President-Administration: Fred Williams
Director of Football Operations: Pat Peppler
Head Coach-General Manager:
   O.A. (Bum) Phillips
Business Manager-Controller: Bob Landry
Director of Public Relations: Greg Suit
Assistant Director of Public Relations:
   Rusty Kasmiersky
Public Relations Assistant: Sylvia Alfortish
Ticket Manager: Bruce Broussard
Marketing Director: Barra Birrcher
Administrative Assistant: Jack Cherry
Trainer: Dean Kleinschmidt
Equipment Manager: Dan Simmons

**Stadium:** Louisiana Superdome •
     **Capacity: 71,647**
     1500 Poydras Street
     New Orleans, Louisiana 70112

**Playing Surface:** AstroTurf

**Training Camp:** Dodgertown
              Vero Beach, Florida 32960

## 1984 SCHEDULE

### Preseason
| | | |
|---|---|---|
| Aug. 4 | at Kansas City | 7:30 |
| Aug. 11 | **Atlanta** | 7:00 |
| Aug. 18 | at Houston | 8:00 |
| Aug. 25 | **Washington** | 12:00 |

### Regular Season
| | | |
|---|---|---|
| Sept. 2 | **Atlanta** | 12:00 |
| Sept. 9 | **Tampa Bay** | 12:00 |
| Sept. 16 | at San Francisco | 1:00 |
| Sept. 23 | **St. Louis** | 12:00 |
| Sept. 30 | at Houston | 3:00 |
| Oct. 7 | at Chicago | 12:00 |
| Oct. 14 | **Los Angeles Rams** | 12:00 |
| Oct. 21 | at Dallas | 8:00 |
| Oct. 28 | at Cleveland | 1:00 |
| Nov. 4 | **Green Bay** | 12:00 |
| Nov. 11 | at Atlanta | 1:00 |
| Nov. 19 | **Pittsburgh** (Monday) | 8:00 |
| Nov. 25 | **San Francisco** | 3:00 |
| Dec. 2 | at Los Angeles Rams | 1:00 |
| Dec. 9 | **Cincinnati** | 12:00 |
| Dec. 15 | at N.Y. Giants (Saturday) | 12:30 |

## SAINTS COACHING HISTORY

### (71-167-5)
| | | |
|---|---|---|
| 1967-70 | Tom Fears* | 13-34-2 |
| 1970-72 | J.D. Roberts | 7-25-3 |
| 1973-75 | John North** | 11-23-0 |
| 1975 | Ernie Hefferle | 1-7-0 |
| 1976-77 | Hank Stram | 7-21-0 |
| 1978-80 | Dick Nolan*** | 15-29-0 |
| 1980 | Dick Stanfel | 1-3-0 |
| 1981-83 | O.A. (Bum) Phillips | 16-25-0 |

 *Released after seven games in 1970
 **Released after six games in 1975
 ***Released after 12 games in 1980

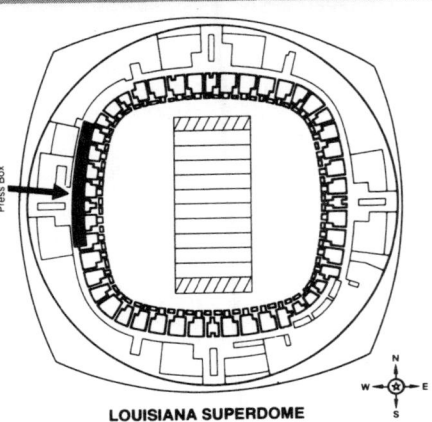

**LOUISIANA SUPERDOME**

## RECORD HOLDERS

### Individual Records — Career
| Category | Name | Performance |
|---|---|---|
| Rushing (Yds.) | Chuck Muncie, 1976-1980 | 3,386 |
| Passing (Yds.) | Archie Manning, 1971-1982 | 21,734 |
| Passing (TDs) | Archie Manning, 1971-1982 | 115 |
| Receiving (No.) | Dan Abramowicz, 1967-1973 | 309 |
| Receiving (Yds.) | Dan Abramowicz, 1967-1973 | 4,875 |
| Interceptions | Tommy Myers, 1972-1982 | 36 |
| Punting (Avg.) | Tom McNeill, 1967-69 | 42.3 |
| Punt Return (Avg.) | Gil Chapman, 1975 | 12.2 |
| Kickoff Return (Avg.) | Walt Roberts, 1967 | 26.3 |
| Field Goals | Charlie Durkee, 1967-68, 1971-72 | 52 |
| Touchdowns (Tot.) | Dan Abramowicz, 1967-1973 | 37 |
| Points | Charlie Durkee, 1967-68, 1971-72 | 243 |

### Individual Records — Single Season
| Category | Name | Performance |
|---|---|---|
| Rushing (Yds.) | George Rogers, 1981 | 1,674 |
| Passing (Yds.) | Archie Manning, 1980 | 3,716 |
| Passing (TDs) | Archie Manning, 1980 | 23 |
| Receiving (No.) | Tony Galbreath, 1978 | 74 |
| Receiving (Yds.) | Wes Chandler, 1979 | 1,069 |
| Interceptions | Dave Whitsell, 1967 | 10 |
| Punting (Avg.) | Russell Erxleben, 1982 | 43.0 |
| Punt Return (Avg.) | Gil Chapman, 1975 | 12.2 |
| Kickoff Return (Avg.) | Don Shy, 1969 | 27.9 |
| Field Goals | Tom Dempsey, 1969 | 22 |
| Touchdowns (Tot.) | George Rogers, 1981 | 13 |
| Points | Tom Dempsey, 1969 | 99 |

### Individual Records — Single Game
| Category | Name | Performance |
|---|---|---|
| Rushing (Yds.) | George Rogers, 9-4-83 | 206 |
| Passing (Yds.) | Archie Manning, 12-7-80 | 377 |
| Passing (TDs) | Bill Kilmer, 11-2-69 | 6 |
| Receiving (No.) | Tony Galbreath, 9-10-78 | 14 |
| Receiving (Yds.) | Wes Chandler, 9-2-79 | 205 |
| Interceptions | Tommy Myers, 9-3-78 | 3 |
| Field Goals | Garo Yepremian, 10-14-79 | 6 |
| Touchdowns (Tot.) | Many times | 3 |
| | Last time by Wayne Wilson, 1-2-83 | |
| Points | Many times | 18 |
| | Last time by Wayne Wilson, 1-2-83 | |

## 1983 TEAM STATISTICS

| | New Orleans | Opp. |
|---|---|---|
| Total First Downs | 286 | 289 |
| Rushing | 135 | 108 |
| Passing | 136 | 159 |
| Penalty | 15 | 22 |
| Third Down Efficiency | 89/226 | 87/225 |
| Third Down Percentage | 39.4 | 38.7 |
| Total Net Yards | 4938 | 4691 |
| Total Offensive Plays | 1055 | 1024 |
| Avg. Gain per Play | 4.7 | 4.6 |
| Avg. Gain per Game | 308.6 | 293.2 |
| Net Yards Rushing | 2461 | 2000 |
| Total Rushing Plays | 595 | 472 |
| Avg. Gain per Rush | 4.1 | 4.2 |
| Avg. Gain Rushing per Game | 153.8 | 125.0 |
| Net Yards Passing | 2477 | 2691 |
| Lost Attempting to Pass | 35/305 | 56/437 |
| Gross Yards Passing | 2782 | 3128 |
| Attempts/Completions | 425/243 | 496/271 |
| Percent Completed | 57.2 | 54.6 |
| Had Intercepted | 25 | 23 |
| Avg. Net Passing per Game | 154.8 | 168.2 |
| Punts/Avg. | 78/40.7 | 83/41.8 |
| Punt Returns/Avg. | 39/7.1 | 51/11.2 |
| Kickoff Returns/Avg. | 66/20.3 | 44/21.3 |
| Interceptions/Avg. Ret. | 23/17.9 | 25/17.0 |
| Penalties/Yards | 91/802 | 96/814 |
| Fumbles/Ball Lost | 37/22 | 33/16 |
| Total Points | 319 | 337 |
| Avg. Points per Game | 19.9 | 21.1 |
| Touchdowns | 38 | 39 |
| Rushing | 19 | 11 |
| Passing | 14 | 20 |
| Returns and Recoveries | 5 | 8 |
| Field Goals | 18/24 | 20/34 |
| Conversions | 37/38 | 37/39 |
| Safeties | 0 | 3 |
| Avg. Time of Possession | 30:24 | 29:36 |

## 1983 TEAM RECORD
### Preseason (3-2)

| Date | New Orleans | | Opponents |
|---|---|---|---|
| 7/30 | 14 | Pittsburgh | 27 |
| 8/6 | 17 | Tampa Bay | 20 |
| 8/13 | 19 | Miami | 17 |
| 8/20 | 20 | *Houston | 13 |
| 8/27 | 17 | *New York Jets | 10 |
| | 87 | | 87 |

### Regular Season (8-8)

| Date | New Orleans | | Opp. | Att. |
|---|---|---|---|---|
| 9/4 | 28 | *St. Louis | 17 | 65,225 |
| 9/11 | 27 | Los Angeles Rams | 30 | 45,662 |
| 9/18 | 34 | *Chicago (OT) | 31 | 64,692 |
| 9/25 | 20 | Dallas | 21 | 62,136 |
| 10/2 | 17 | *Miami | 7 | 66,489 |
| 10/9 | 19 | Atlanta | 17 | 51,654 |
| 10/16 | 13 | *San Francisco | 32 | 68,154 |
| 10/23 | 24 | Tampa Bay | 21 | 48,242 |
| 10/30 | 21 | Buffalo | 27 | 49,413 |
| 11/6 | 27 | *Atlanta | 10 | 67,062 |
| 11/13 | 0 | San Francisco | 27 | 40,022 |
| 11/21 | 28 | *New York Jets | 31 | 68,606 |
| 11/27 | 17 | *Minnesota | 16 | 59,502 |
| 12/4 | 0 | New England | 7 | 24,579 |
| 12/11 | 20 | Philadelphia (OT) | 17 | 45,182 |
| 12/18 | 24 | *Los Angeles Rams | 26 | 70,148 |
| | 319 | | 337 | 896,768 |

*Home Game        (OT) Overtime

### Score by Periods

| | | | | | | | |
|---|---|---|---|---|---|---|---|
| New Orleans | 41 | 81 | 103 | 88 | 6 | — | 319 |
| Opponents | 74 | 86 | 61 | 116 | 0 | — | 337 |

### Attendance
Home 529,878    Away 366,890    Total 896,768
Single game home record, 76,490 (11-4-79)
Single season home record, 557,530 (1979)

## 1983 INDIVIDUAL STATISTICS

### Rushing

| | Att. | Yds. | Avg. | LG | TD |
|---|---|---|---|---|---|
| G. Rogers | 256 | 1144 | 4.5 | 76t | 5 |
| W. Wilson | 199 | 787 | 4.0 | 29 | 9 |
| Gajan | 81 | 415 | 5.1 | 58 | 4 |
| J. Rogers | 26 | 80 | 3.1 | 13 | 0 |
| T. Wilson | 8 | 21 | 2.6 | 7 | 0 |
| Austin | 4 | 16 | 4.0 | 5 | 0 |
| Merkens | 1 | 16 | 16.0 | 16 | 0 |
| Groth | 1 | 15 | 15.0 | 15 | 0 |
| Goodlow | 1 | 3 | 3.0 | 3 | 0 |
| D. Wilson | 5 | 3 | 0.6 | 5 | 1 |
| Erxleben | 2 | −9 | −4.5 | 1 | 0 |
| Stabler | 9 | −14 | −1.6 | 0 | 0 |
| Duckett | 2 | −16 | −8.0 | 2 | 0 |
| New Orleans | 595 | 2461 | 4.1 | 76t | 19 |
| Opponents | 472 | 2000 | 4.2 | 71 | 11 |

### Passing

| | Att. | Comp. | Pct. | Yds. | TD | Int. | Tkld. | Rate |
|---|---|---|---|---|---|---|---|---|
| Stabler | 311 | 176 | 56.6 | 1988 | 9 | 18 | 18/159 | 61.4 |
| D. Wilson | 112 | 66 | 58.9 | 770 | 5 | 7 | 17/146 | 68.7 |
| Erxleben | 1 | 1 | 100.0 | 24 | 0 | 0 | 0/0 | 118.8 |
| Gajan | 1 | 0 | 0.0 | 0 | 0 | 0 | 0/0 | 39.6 |
| New Orleans | 425 | 243 | 57.2 | 2782 | 14 | 25 | 35/305 | 63.5 |
| Opponents | 496 | 271 | 54.6 | 3128 | 20 | 23 | 56/437 | 68.0 |

### Receiving

| | No. | Yds. | Avg. | LG | TD |
|---|---|---|---|---|---|
| Groth | 49 | 585 | 11.9 | 42 | 1 |
| Brenner | 41 | 574 | 14.0 | 38t | 3 |
| Goodlow | 41 | 487 | 11.9 | 26 | 2 |
| Scott | 24 | 274 | 11.4 | 35 | 0 |
| W. Wilson | 20 | 178 | 8.9 | 24 | 2 |
| Duckett | 19 | 283 | 14.9 | 48 | 2 |
| Gajan | 17 | 130 | 7.6 | 26 | 0 |
| G. Rogers | 12 | 69 | 5.8 | 22 | 0 |
| Young | 7 | 85 | 12.1 | 32 | 3 |
| Tice | 7 | 33 | 4.7 | 12t | 1 |
| Mauti | 2 | 30 | 15.0 | 23 | 0 |
| Hardy | 2 | 29 | 14.5 | 22 | 0 |
| Austin | 2 | 25 | 12.5 | 18 | 0 |
| New Orleans | 243 | 2782 | 11.4 | 48 | 14 |
| Opponents | 271 | 3128 | 11.5 | 60 | 20 |

### Interceptions

| | No. | Yds. | Avg. | LG | TD |
|---|---|---|---|---|---|
| Poe | 7 | 146 | 20.9 | 31t | 1 |
| Gary | 3 | 70 | 23.3 | 26 | 0 |
| Winston | 3 | 21 | 7.0 | 15 | 0 |
| Johnson | 2 | 80 | 40.0 | 70t | 1 |
| Wattelet | 2 | 33 | 16.5 | 24 | 0 |
| Paul | 2 | 3 | 1.5 | 3 | 0 |
| Re. Lewis | 1 | 27 | 27.0 | 27t | 1 |
| Stemrick | 1 | 26 | 26.0 | 26 | 0 |
| Warren | 1 | 6 | 6.0 | 6 | 0 |
| Jackson | 1 | 0 | 0.0 | 0 | 0 |
| New Orleans | 23 | 412 | 17.9 | 70t | 3 |
| Opponents | 25 | 424 | 17.0 | 69t | 5 |

### Punting

| | No. | Yds. | Avg. | In 20 | LG |
|---|---|---|---|---|---|
| Erxleben | 74 | 3034 | 41.0 | 10 | 60 |
| Merkens | 4 | 144 | 36.0 | 0 | 45 |
| New Orleans | 78 | 3178 | 40.7 | 10 | 60 |
| Opponents | 83 | 3473 | 41.8 | 22 | 70 |

### Punt Returns

| | No. | FC | Yds. | Avg. | LG | TD |
|---|---|---|---|---|---|---|
| Groth | 39 | 15 | 275 | 7.1 | 30 | 0 |
| New Orleans | 39 | 15 | 275 | 7.1 | 30 | 0 |
| Opponents | 51 | 10 | 573 | 11.2 | 76t | 2 |

### Kickoff Returns

| | No. | Yds. | Avg. | LG | TD |
|---|---|---|---|---|---|
| Duckett | 33 | 719 | 21.8 | 61 | 0 |
| W. Wilson | 9 | 239 | 26.6 | 52 | 0 |
| Mauti | 8 | 147 | 18.4 | 35 | 0 |
| Austin | 7 | 112 | 16.0 | 27 | 0 |
| J. Rogers | 7 | 103 | 14.7 | 25 | 0 |
| Brock | 1 | 15 | 15.0 | 15 | 0 |
| Wattelet | 1 | 4 | 4.0 | 4 | 0 |
| New Orleans | 66 | 1339 | 20.3 | 61 | 0 |
| Opponents | 44 | 938 | 21.3 | 53 | 0 |

### Scoring

| | TD | TD R | TD P | TD Rt | PAT | FG | TP |
|---|---|---|---|---|---|---|---|
| Andersen | | | | | 37/38 | 18/24 | 91 |
| W. Wilson | 11 | 9 | 2 | 0 | | | 66 |
| G. Rogers | 5 | 5 | 0 | 0 | | | 30 |
| Gajan | 4 | 4 | 0 | 0 | | | 24 |
| Brenner | 3 | 0 | 3 | 0 | | | 18 |
| Young | 3 | 0 | 3 | 0 | | | 18 |
| Duckett | 2 | 0 | 2 | 0 | | | 12 |
| Goodlow | 2 | 0 | 2 | 0 | | | 12 |
| K. Clark | 1 | 0 | 0 | 1 | | | 6 |
| Groth | 1 | 0 | 1 | 0 | | | 6 |
| Johnson | 1 | 0 | 0 | 1 | | | 6 |
| Korte | 1 | 0 | 0 | 1 | | | 6 |
| Re. Lewis | 1 | 0 | 0 | 1 | | | 6 |
| Poe | 1 | 0 | 0 | 1 | | | 6 |
| Tice | 1 | 0 | 1 | 0 | | | 6 |
| D. Wilson | 1 | 1 | 0 | 0 | | | 6 |
| New Orleans | 38 | 19 | 14 | 5 | 37/38 | 18/24 | 319 |
| Opponents | 39 | 11 | 20 | 8 | 37/39 | 20/34 | 337 |

## FIRST-ROUND SELECTIONS

(If Club had no first-round selection, first player drafted is listed with round in parentheses.)

| Year | Player, College, Position |
|---|---|
| 1967 | Les Kelley, Alabama, RB |
| 1968 | Kevin Hardy, Notre Dame, DE |
| 1969 | John Shinners, Xavier, G |
| 1970 | Ken Burrough, Texas Southern, WR |
| 1971 | Archie Manning, Mississippi, QB |
| 1972 | Royce Smith, Georgia, G |
| 1973 | Derland Moore, Oklahoma, DE (2) |
| 1974 | Rick Middleton, Ohio State, LB |
| 1975 | Larry Burton, Purdue, WR |
| | Kurt Schumacher, Ohio State, T |
| 1976 | Chuck Muncie, California, RB |
| 1977 | Joe Campbell, Maryland, DE |
| 1978 | Wes Chandler, Florida, WR |
| 1979 | Russell Erxleben, Texas, P-K |
| 1980 | Stan Brock, Colorado, T |
| 1981 | George Rogers, South Carolina, RB |
| 1982 | Lindsay Scott, Georgia, WR |
| 1983 | Steve Korte, Arkansas, G (2) |
| 1984 | James Geathers, Wichita State, DE |

# NEW ORLEANS SAINTS 1984 VETERAN ROSTER

| No. | Name | Pos. | Ht. | Wt. | Birth-date | NFL Exp. | College | Birthplace | Residence | Games in '83 |
|---|---|---|---|---|---|---|---|---|---|---|
| 7 | Andersen, Morten | K | 6-2 | 210 | 8/19/60 | 3 | Michigan State | Struer, Denmark | New Orleans, La. | 16 |
| 47 | Austin, Cliff | RB | 6-0 | 190 | 3/2/60 | 2 | Clemson | Atlanta, Ga. | Lithonia, Ga. | 11 |
| 50 | †Bordelon, Ken | LB | 6-4 | 226 | 8/26/54 | 7 | Louisiana State | New Orleans, La. | Kenner, La. | 0* |
| 85 | Brenner, Hoby | TE | 6-4 | 240 | 6/2/59 | 4 | Southern California | Lynwood, Calif. | San Clemente, Calif. | 16 |
| 67 | Brock, Stan | T | 6-6 | 285 | 6/8/58 | 5 | Colorado | Portland, Ore. | Mandeville, La. | 16 |
| 75 | Clark, Bruce | DE | 6-3 | 275 | 3/31/58 | 3 | Penn State | New Castle, Pa. | Kenner, La. | 15 |
| 68 | Clark, Kelvin | G | 6-3 | 265 | 1/30/56 | 6 | Nebraska | Odessa, Tex. | Mandeville, La. | 16 |
| 83 | Duckett, Kenny | WR | 6-0 | 187 | 10/1/59 | 3 | Wake Forest | Winston-Salem, N.C. | Kenner, La. | 14 |
| 63 | Edelman, Brad | G | 6-6 | 265 | 9/3/60 | 3 | Missouri | Jacksonville, Fla. | Kenner, La. | 16 |
| 99 | Elliott, Tony | NT | 6-2 | 265 | 4/23/59 | 3 | North Texas State | New York, N.Y. | Kenner, La. | 12 |
| 14 | Erxleben, Russell | P | 6-4 | 221 | 1/13/57 | 5 | Texas | Seguin, Tex. | Kenner, La. | 16 |
| 77 | Fields, Angelo | T | 6-6 | 314 | 9/15/57 | 4 | Michigan State | Washington, D.C. | Washington, D.C. | 0* |
| 46 | Gajan, Hokie | FB | 5-11 | 220 | 9/6/59 | 3 | Louisiana State | Baton Rouge, La. | Mandeville, La. | 16 |
| 20 | Gary, Russell | S | 5-11 | 195 | 7/31/59 | 4 | Nebraska | Minneapolis, Minn. | New Orleans, La. | 14 |
| 88 | Goodlow, Eugene | WR | 6-2 | 190 | 12/19/58 | 2 | Kansas State | St. Louis, Mo. | Miami, Fla. | 16 |
| 72 | Gray, Leon | T | 6-3 | 270 | 11/15/51 | 12 | Jackson State | Olive Branch, Miss. | Westwood, Mass. | 11 |
| 86 | Groth, Jeff | WR | 5-10 | 175 | 7/2/57 | 6 | Bowling Green | Mankato, Minn. | Destrehan, La. | 16 |
| 87 | †Hardy, Larry | TE | 6-3 | 230 | 7/9/56 | 7 | Jackson State | Mendenhall, Miss. | Jackson, Miss. | 6 |
| 62 | Hill, John | C | 6-2 | 260 | 4/16/50 | 13 | Lehigh | East Orange, N.J. | Destrehan, La. | 16 |
| 57 | Jackson, Rickey | LB | 6-2 | 240 | 3/20/58 | 4 | Pittsburgh | Pahokee, Fla. | Kenner, La. | 16 |
| 34 | Johnson, Bobby | CB-S | 6-0 | 191 | 9/1/60 | 2 | Texas | La Grange, Tex. | Kenner, La. | 16 |
| 60 | Korte, Steve | G | 6-2 | 270 | 1/15/60 | 2 | Arkansas | Denver, Colo. | Mandeville, La. | 16 |
| 52 | Kovach, Jim | LB | 6-2 | 225 | 5/1/56 | 6 | Kentucky | Parma Heights, Ohio | Lexington, Ky. | 16 |
| 21 | Krimm, John | S | 6-2 | 190 | 5/30/60 | 2 | Notre Dame | Philadelphia, Pa. | River Ridge, La. | 0* |
| 64 | Lafary, Dave | T | 6-7 | 280 | 1/13/55 | 8 | Purdue | Cincinnati, Ohio | Mandeville, La. | 16 |
| 93 | Lewis, Gary | NT | 6-3 | 260 | 1/14/61 | 2 | Oklahoma State | Oklahoma City, Okla. | Stillwater, Okla. | 6 |
| 98 | Lewis, Reggie | DE | 6-2 | 260 | 1/20/54 | 3 | San Diego State | New Orleans, La. | New Orleans, La. | 12 |
| 29 | Lewis, Rodney | CB | 5-11 | 190 | 4/2/59 | 2 | Nebraska | Minneapolis, Minn. | New Orleans, La. | 2 |
| 59 | Martin, Chris | LB | 6-2 | 220 | 12/19/60 | 2 | Auburn | Huntsville, Ala. | Auburn, Ala. | 15 |
| 84 | †Mauti, Rich | WR | 6-0 | 195 | 5/25/54 | 7 | Penn State | Hollis Place, N.Y. | Mandeville, La. | 16 |
| 19 | Merkens, Guido | QB | 6-1 | 195 | 8/14/55 | 7 | Sam Houston State | San Antonio, Tex. | Destrehan, La. | 16 |
| 74 | Moore, Derland | NT | 6-4 | 270 | 10/7/51 | 12 | Oklahoma | Poplar Bluff, Mo. | Covington, La. | 16 |
| 55 | Nairne, Rob | LB | 6-4 | 227 | 3/24/54 | 8 | Oregon State | Redding, Calif. | Corvallis, Ore. | 16 |
| 66 | Oubre, Louis | G | 6-4 | 262 | 5/15/58 | 3 | Oklahoma | New Orleans, La. | Kenner, La. | 16 |
| 51 | Paul, Whitney | LB | 6-3 | 220 | 10/8/55 | 9 | Colorado | Galveston, Tex. | Kansas City, Mo. | 16 |
| 53 | Pelluer, Scott | LB | 6-2 | 220 | 4/28/59 | 4 | Washington State | Yakima, Wash. | Kenner, La. | 16 |
| 32 | †Perry, Vernon | S | 6-2 | 210 | 9/22/53 | 6 | Jackson State | Jackson, Miss. | Jackson, Miss. | 12 |
| 76 | †Pietrzak, Jim | C | 6-5 | 260 | 2/21/53 | 10 | Eastern Michigan | Hamtramck, Mich. | Kenner, La. | 16 |
| 25 | Poe, Johnnie | CB | 6-1 | 185 | 8/29/59 | 4 | Missouri | St. Louis, Mo. | Metairie, La. | 16 |
| 58 | Redd, Glen | LB | 6-1 | 225 | 6/17/58 | 3 | Brigham Young | Ogden, Utah | Ogden, Utah | 16 |
| 38 | Rogers, George | RB | 6-2 | 229 | 12/8/58 | 4 | South Carolina | Duluth, Ga. | Kenner, La. | 13 |
| 41 | Rogers, Jimmy | RB | 5-10 | 190 | 6/29/55 | 5 | Oklahoma | Earle, Ark. | New Orleans, La. | 16 |
| 80 | Scott, Lindsay | WR | 6-1 | 190 | 12/6/60 | 3 | Georgia | Jesup, Ga. | Kenner, La. | 16 |
| 16 | †Stabler, Ken | QB | 6-3 | 210 | 12/25/45 | 15 | Alabama | Foley, Ala. | Gulf Shores, Ala. | 14 |
| 27 | Stemrick, Greg | CB | 5-11 | 185 | 10/25/51 | 10 | Colorado State | Cincinnati, Ohio | Kenner, La. | 11 |
| 82 | Tice, John | TE | 6-5 | 242 | 6/22/60 | 2 | Maryland | Bayshore, N.Y. | Kenner, La. | 16 |
| 11 | t-Todd, Richard | QB | 6-2 | 206 | 11/19/53 | 9 | Alabama | Birmingham, Ala. | Jericho, N.Y. | 16 |
| 73 | Warren, Frank | DE | 6-4 | 275 | 9/14/59 | 4 | Auburn | Birmingham, Ala. | Kenner, La. | 16 |
| 49 | Wattelet, Frank | S | 6-0 | 185 | 10/25/58 | 4 | Kansas | Paola, Kan. | Kenner, La. | 16 |
| 44 | Waymer, Dave | CB | 6-1 | 195 | 7/1/58 | 5 | Notre Dame | Brooklyn, N.Y. | Los Angeles, Calif. | 16 |
| 94 | Wilks, Jim | DE | 6-5 | 260 | 3/12/58 | 4 | San Diego State | Los Angeles, Calif. | Altadena, Calif. | 16 |
| 18 | Wilson, Dave | QB | 6-3 | 210 | 4/27/59 | 3 | Illinois | Anaheim, Calif. | Anaheim, Calif. | 8 |
| 45 | †Wilson, Tim | FB | 6-3 | 235 | 1/14/55 | 8 | Maryland | New Castle, Del. | Richmond, Tex. | 6 |
| 30 | Wilson, Wayne | RB | 6-3 | 220 | 9/4/57 | 6 | Shepherd | Montgomery County, Md. | Columbia, Md. | 14 |
| 56 | Winston, Dennis | LB | 6-0 | 230 | 10/25/55 | 8 | Arkansas | Marianna, Ark. | Fayetteville, Ark. | 16 |
| 89 | Young, Tyrone | WR | 6-6 | 190 | 4/29/60 | 2 | Florida | Ocala, Fla. | Metairie, La. | 16 |

* Bordelon and Krimm missed '83 season due to injuries; Fields last active with Green Bay in '82.

†Option playout; subject to developments.

t-Saints traded for Todd (New York Jets).

Also played with Saints in '83—S Bill Hurley (4 games), QB Greg Knafelc (6).

## COACHING STAFF

### Head Coach,
### O. A. (Bum) Phillips

**Pro Career:** Starts tenth season in the NFL and fourth with the Saints after signing with New Orleans as head coach on January 22, 1981. He had a career 59-38 record with the Oilers and twice played the AFC bridesmaid role with championship game losses to the Steelers in 1978 and 1979. Joined the Oilers on January 25, 1975 as head coach and general manager after serving as assistant coach with the San Diego Chargers 1967-71 and as defensive coordinator with Oilers in 1974 prior to being named head coach. Career record: 75-63.

**Background:** Guard at Lamar Junior College 1941, 1946-47, Stephen F. Austin 1948-49. College assistant coach at Texas A&M 1957, Houston 1963-66, Southern Methodist 1971-72, and Oklahoma State 1973. Head coach at Texas-El Paso 1962.

**Personal:** Born September 29, 1923 in Orange, Tex. Bum and his wife, Helen, live in Destrehan, La., and have six children—Wade, Susan, Cicely, Dee Jean, Andrea, and Kim Ann.

### Assistant Coaches

**Andy Everest,** tight ends; born October 27, 1924, Wichita Falls, Tex., lives in Destrehan, La. Guard Texas-El Paso 1947-50. No pro playing experience. College coach: Foot Hills College 1963-64, U.C.-Santa Barbara 1965-71, Southern Methodist 1972, North Texas State 1973-76. Pro coach: Joined Saints in 1981.

**King Hill,** offensive coordinator; born November 8, 1936, Freeport, Tex., lives in Destrehan, La. Quarterback Rice, 1954-58. Pro quarterback St. Louis Cardinals 1958-60, 1969, Philadelphia Eagles 1961-67, Minnesota Vikings 1968. Pro coach: Houston Oilers 1972-80, joined Saints in 1981.

**John Levra,** offensive backfield; born October 2, 1937, Arma, Kan., lives in Destrehan, La. Guard-linebacker Pittsburgh (Kan.) State 1963-65. No pro playing experience. College coach: Stephen F. Austin 1971-74, Kansas 1975-78, North Texas State 1979. Pro coach: British Columbia Lions (CFL) 1979, joined Saints in 1981.

**Carl Mauck,** offensive line; born July 7, 1947, McLeansboro, Ill., lives in New Orleans. Center Southern Illinois 1965-68. Pro center San Diego Chargers 1969-74, Houston Oilers 1975-80. Pro coach: Joined Saints in 1982.

**Lamar McHan,** receivers; born December 16, 1932, Lake Village Ark., lives in Metairie, La. Offensive back Arkansas 1951-53. Pro quarterback Chicago Cardinals 1954-58, Green Bay Packers 1959-60, Baltimore Colts 1961-62, San Francisco 49ers 1963. College coach: Northern Arizona 1969-70, Texas-Arlington 1971-73. Pro coach: New Orleans Saints 1974-75, rejoined Saints in 1978.

**Russell Paternostro,** strength and conditioning; born July 21, 1940, New Orleans, lives in Jefferson, La. Pro coach: Joined Saints in 1981.

**Wade Phillips,** defensive coordinator; born June 21, 1947, Orange, Tex., lives in Destrehan, La. Linebacker Houston 1966-69. No pro playing experience. College coach: Oklahoma State 1973-75. Pro coach: Houston Oilers 1976-80, joined Saints in 1981.

**Harold Richardson,** special teams; born September 27, 1944, Houston, lives in Destrehan, La. Tight end Southern Methodist 1964-67. No pro playing experience. College coach: Southern Methodist 1971-72, Oklahoma State 1973-76, Texas Christian 1977-78, North Texas State 1979-80. Pro coach: Joined Saints in 1981.

**Joe Spencer,** quality control; born August 15, 1923, Cleveland County, Okla., lives in Destrehan, La. Tackle Oklahoma State 1942-47. Pro tackle Brooklyn Dodgers (AAFC) 1948, Cleveland Browns 1949, Green Bay Packers 1950-52. College coach: Austin (Tex.) College 1952-60, Kansas 1972-73. Pro coach: Houston Oilers 1961-65, Edmonton Eskimos (CFL) 1966-67, New York Jets 1968-70, St. Louis Cardinals 1971, Chicago Fire (WFL) 1974, Kansas City Chiefs 1975-80, joined Saints in 1981.

**Lance Van Zandt,** defensive backfield; born January 19, 1939, Amarillo, Tex., lives in Destrehan, La. Attended Lamar University. College coach: New Mexico Highlands 1966-67, West Texas State 1968-69, Texas A&M 1970-71, Rice 1972, Oklahoma State 1973-74, Nebraska 1976-80. Pro coach: Joined Saints in 1981.

**John Paul Young,** linebackers; born December 31, 1939, Dallas, Tex., lives in Destrehan, La. Linebacker Texas-El Paso 1959-61. No pro playing experience. College coach: Texas-El Paso 1962-63, Southern Methodist 1967-68, Oklahoma State 1969, Texas A&M 1970-77. Pro coach: Houston Oilers 1978-80, joined Saints in 1981.

**Willie Zapalac,** defensive line; born December 11, 1922, Sealy, Tex., lives in Destrehan, La. Fullback Texas A&M 1941-42, 1946. No pro playing experience. College coach: Texas A&M 1953-60, Texas Tech 1961-62, Oklahoma State 1963, Texas 1964-75. Pro coach: St. Louis Cardinals 1976-77, Buffalo Bills 1978-80, joined Saints in 1981.

## NEW ORLEANS SAINTS 1984 FIRST-YEAR ROSTER

| Name | Pos. | Ht. | Wt. | Birth-date | College | Birthplace | Residence | How Acq. |
|------|------|-----|-----|-----------|---------|-----------|-----------|----------|
| Anthony, Tyrone | RB | 5-11 | 200 | 3/3/62 | North Carolina | Winston-Salem, N.C. | Pfafftown, N.C. | D3a |
| Bourgeau, Michel | DE | 6-4 | 249 | 6/28/60 | Boise State | Montreal, Can. | Montreal, Can. | D11 |
| Faggett, Mack | LB | 6-0 | 210 | 1/9/61 | North Texas State | Longview, Tex. | Longview, Tex. | FA |
| Fields, Jitter | CB | 5-8 | 185 | 8/16/62 | Texas | Dallas, Tex. | Dallas, Tex. | D5 |
| Geathers, James | NT | 6-7 | 263 | 6/26/60 | Wichita State | Georgetown, S.C. | Georgetown, S.C. | D2 |
| Gray, Paul | LB | 6-2 | 231 | 6/21/62 | Western Kentucky | Gilbertsville, Ky. | Owensboro, Ky. | D10 |
| Harding, Greg | S | 6-2 | 202 | 7/31/60 | Nicholls State | New Orleans, La. | Houma, La. | FA |
| Hansen, Brian | P | 6-3 | 207 | 10/26/60 | Sioux Falls | Hawarden, Iowa | Hawarden, Iowa | D9 |
| Hilgenberg, Joel | C | 6-3 | 250 | 7/10/62 | Iowa | Iowa City, Iowa | Iowa City, Iowa | D4 |
| Hoage, Terry | S | 6-3 | 197 | 4/11/62 | Georgia | Ames, Iowa | Huntsville, Tex. | D3 |
| Nelson, Byron | T | 6-5 | 286 | 5/8/62 | Arizona | San Diego, Calif. | Glendale, Ariz. | D12 |
| Terrell, Clemon | RB | 6-2 | 225 | 12/19/62 | So. Mississippi | Hattiesburg, Miss. | Hattiesburg, Miss. | D8 |
| Thorp, Don | NT | 6-4 | 248 | 7/10/62 | Illinois | Chicago, Ill. | Arlington Heights, Ill. | D6 |

Players who report to an NFL team for the first time are designated on rosters as rookies (R). If a player reported to an NFL training camp in a previous year but was not on the active squad for three or more regular season or postseason games, he is listed on the first-year roster and designated by a (1). Thereafter, a player who is on the active squad for three or more regular season or postseason games is credited with an additional year of playing experience.

# NOTES

_____
_____
_____
_____
_____
_____
_____
_____
_____
_____
_____
_____
_____
_____
_____
_____

## GIANTS COACHING HISTORY

**(399-350-32)**

| | | |
|---|---|---|
| 1925 | Bob Folwell | 8-4-0 |
| 1926 | Joe Alexander | 8-4-1 |
| 1927-28 | Earl Potteiger | 15-8-3 |
| 1929-30 | LeRoy Andrews | 26-5-1 |
| 1931-53 | Steve Owen | 154-108-17 |
| 1954-60 | Jim Lee Howell | 54-29-4 |
| 1961-68 | Allie Sherman | 57-54-4 |
| 1969-73 | Alex Webster | 29-40-1 |
| 1974-76 | Bill Arnsparger* | 7-28-0 |
| 1976-78 | John McVay | 14-23-0 |
| 1979-82 | Ray Perkins | 24-35-0 |
| 1983 | Bill Parcells | 3-12-1 |

*Released after seven games in 1976

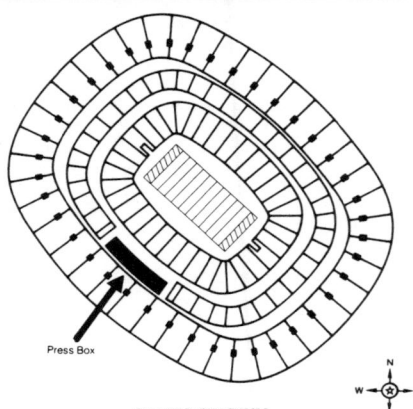

Press Box

**GIANTS STADIUM**

W E N S

**National Football Conference
Eastern Division**

**Team Colors:** Blue, Red, and White

**Giants Stadium
East Rutherford, New Jersey 07073
Telephone: (201) 935-8111**

**Club Officials**

President: Wellington T. Mara
Vice President-Treasurer: Timothy J. Mara
Vice President-Secretary: Raymond J. Walsh
Vice President-General Manager: George Young
Assistant General Manager: Harry Hulmes
Controller: John Pasquali
Director of Player Personnel: Tom Boisture
Director of Pro Personnel: Ernie Adams
Director of Media Services: Ed Croke
Director of Promotions: Tom Power
Director of Special Projects: Victor Del Guercio
Box Office Treasurer: Jim Gleason
Trainer Emeritus: John Dziegiel
Head Trainer: Ronnie Barnes
Assistant Trainers: Dave Barringer, John Johnson
Equipment Manager: Ed Wagner, Jr.

**Stadium:** Giants Stadium • **Capacity:** 76,891
East Rutherford, N.J. 07073

**Playing Surface:** AstroTurf

**Training Camp:** Pace University
Pleasantville, New York 10570

## 1984 SCHEDULE

**Preseason**

| Aug. 3 | at New England | 7:30 |
|---|---|---|
| Aug. 11 | at Colts | 7:00 |
| Aug. 18 | **New York Jets** | 8:00 |
| Aug. 25 | **Pittsburgh** | 8:00 |

**Regular Season**

| Sept. 2 | **Philadelphia** | 1:00 |
|---|---|---|
| Sept. 9 | **Dallas** | 1:00 |
| Sept. 16 | at Washington | 4:00 |
| Sept. 23 | **Tampa Bay** | 4:00 |
| Sept. 30 | at Los Angeles Rams | 1:00 |
| Oct. 8 | **San Francisco** (Monday) | 9:00 |
| Oct. 14 | at Atlanta | 1:00 |
| Oct. 21 | at Philadelphia | 1:00 |
| Oct. 28 | **Washington** | 4:00 |
| Nov. 4 | at Dallas | 12:00 |
| Nov. 11 | at Tampa Bay | 4:00 |
| Nov. 18 | **St. Louis** | 1:00 |
| Nov. 25 | **Kansas City** | 1:00 |
| Dec. 2 | at New York Jets | 1:00 |
| Dec. 9 | at St. Louis | 12:00 |
| Dec. 15 | **New Orleans** (Saturday) | 12:30 |

## RECORD HOLDERS

**Individual Records—Career**

| Category | Name | Performance |
|---|---|---|
| Rushing (Yds.) | Alex Webster, 1955-1964 | 4,638 |
| Passing (Yds.) | Charlie Conerly, 1948-1961 | 19,488 |
| Passing (TDs) | Charlie Conerly, 1948-1961 | 173 |
| Receiving (No.) | Joe Morrison, 1959-1972 | 395 |
| Receiving (Yds.) | Frank Gifford, 1952-1960, 1962-64 | 5,434 |
| Interceptions | Emlen Tunnell, 1948-1958 | 74 |
| Punting (Avg.) | Don Chandler, 1956-1964 | 43.8 |
| Punt Return (Avg.) | Bob Hammond, 1976-78 | 9.1 |
| Kickoff Return (Avg.) | Rocky Thompson, 1971-72 | 27.2 |
| Field Goals | Pete Gogolak, 1966-1974 | 126 |
| Touchdowns (Tot.) | Frank Gifford, 1952-1960, 1962-64 | 78 |
| Points | Pete Gogolak, 1966-1974 | 646 |

**Individual Records—Single Season**

| Category | Name | Performance |
|---|---|---|
| Rushing (Yds.) | Ron Johnson, 1972 | 1,182 |
| Passing (Yds.) | Y.A. Tittle, 1962 | 3,224 |
| Passing (TDs) | Y.A. Tittle, 1963 | 36 |
| Receiving (No.) | Earnest Gray, 1983 | 78 |
| Receiving (Yds.) | Homer Jones, 1967 | 1,209 |
| Interceptions | Otto Schnellbacher, 1951 | 11 |
| | Jim Patton, 1958 | 11 |
| Punting (Avg.) | Don Chandler, 1959 | 46.6 |
| Punt Return (Avg.) | Merle Hapes, 1942 | 15.5 |
| Kickoff Return (Avg.) | John Salscheider, 1949 | 31.6 |
| Field Goals | Ali Haji-Sheikh, 1983 | 35 |
| Touchdowns (Tot.) | Gene Roberts, 1949 | 17 |
| Points | Ali Haji-Sheikh, 1983 | 127 |

**Individual Records—Single Game**

| Category | Name | Performance |
|---|---|---|
| Rushing (Yds.) | Gene Roberts, 11-12-50 | 218 |
| Passing (Yds.) | Y.A. Tittle, 10-28-62 | 505 |
| Passing (TDs) | Y.A. Tittle, 10-28-62 | 7 |
| Receiving (No.) | Many times | 11 |
| | Last time by Gary Shirk, 9-20-81 | |
| Receiving (Yds.) | Del Shofner, 10-28-62 | 269 |
| Interceptions | Many times | 3 |
| | Last time by Carl Lockhart, 12-4-66 | |
| Field Goals | Joe Danelo, 10-18-81 | 6 |
| Touchdowns (Tot.) | Ron Johnson, 10-2-72 | 4 |
| | Earnest Gray, 9-7-80 | 4 |
| Points | Ron Johnson, 10-2-72 | 24 |
| | Earnest Gray, 9-7-80 | 24 |

## 1983 TEAM STATISTICS

| | N.Y. Giants | Opp. |
|---|---|---|
| Total First Downs | 296 | 289 |
| Rushing | 104 | 98 |
| Passing | 164 | 167 |
| Penalty | 28 | 24 |
| Third Down Efficiency | 87/250 | 66/218 |
| Third Down Percentage | 34.8 | 30.3 |
| Total Net Yards | 5285 | 4994 |
| Total Offensive Plays | 1130 | 1039 |
| Avg. Gain per Play | 4.7 | 4.8 |
| Avg. Gain per Game | 330.3 | 312.1 |
| Net Yards Rushing | 1794 | 1733 |
| Total Rushing Plays | 506 | 502 |
| Avg. Gain per Rush | 3.5 | 3.5 |
| Avg. Gain Rushing per Game | 112.1 | 108.3 |
| Net Yards Passing | 3491 | 3261 |
| Lost Attempting to Pass | 49/363 | 44/323 |
| Gross Yards Passing | 3854 | 3584 |
| Attempts/Completions | 575/284 | 493/283 |
| Percent Completed | 49.4 | 57.4 |
| Had Intercepted | 31 | 23 |
| Avg. Net Passing per Game | 218.2 | 203.8 |
| Punts/Avg. | 85/39.8 | 99/39.2 |
| Punt Returns/Avg. | 55/6.9 | 47/6.0 |
| Kickoff Returns/Avg. | 71/18.8 | 67/19.3 |
| Interceptions/Avg. Ret. | 23/9.1 | 31/14.1 |
| Penalties/Yards | 113/1020 | 114/927 |
| Fumbles/Ball Lost | 39/27 | 31/13 |
| Total Points | 267 | 347 |
| Avg. Points per Game | 16.7 | 21.7 |
| Touchdowns | 23 | 40 |
| Rushing | 9 | 10 |
| Passing | 12 | 26 |
| Returns and Recoveries | 2 | 4 |
| Field Goals | 35/42 | 22/32 |
| Conversions | 22/23 | 39/40 |
| Safeties | 1 | 1 |
| Avg. Time of Possession | 30:37 | 29:23 |

## 1983 TEAM RECORD

### Preseason (3-1)

| Date | New York Giants | | Opponents |
|---|---|---|---|
| 8/7 | 23 | *New York Jets | 16 |
| 8/12 | 22 | Pittsburgh | 13 |
| 8/20 | 27 | *Baltimore | 14 |
| 8/26 | 3 | *Miami | 24 |
| | 75 | | 67 |

### Regular Season (3-12-1)

| Date | New York Giants | | Opp. | Att. |
|---|---|---|---|---|
| 9/4 | 6 | *Los Angeles Rams | 16 | 75,281 |
| 9/11 | 16 | Atlanta (OT) | 13 | 52,850 |
| 9/18 | 13 | Dallas | 28 | 62,347 |
| 9/26 | 27 | *Green Bay | 3 | 75,308 |
| 10/2 | 34 | *San Diego | 41 | 73,892 |
| 10/9 | 13 | *Philadelphia | 17 | 73,291 |
| 10/16 | 17 | Kansas City | 38 | 55,449 |
| 10/24 | 20 | St. Louis (OT) | 20 | 45,630 |
| 10/30 | 20 | *Dallas | 38 | 76,142 |
| 11/7 | 9 | Detroit | 15 | 68,985 |
| 11/13 | 17 | *Washington | 33 | 71,482 |
| 11/20 | 23 | Philadelphia | 0 | 57,977 |
| 11/27 | 12 | Los Angeles Raiders | 27 | 41,473 |
| 12/4 | 6 | *St. Louis | 10 | 25,156 |
| 12/11 | 12 | *Seattle | 17 | 48,942 |
| 12/17 | 22 | Washington | 31 | 53,874 |
| | 267 | | 347 | 958,079 |

*Home Game    (OT) Overtime

### Score by Periods

| | | | | | | | |
|---|---|---|---|---|---|---|---|
| New York Giants | 46 | 99 | 62 | 57 | 3 | — | 267 |
| Opponents | 56 | 117 | 75 | 99 | 0 | — | 347 |

### Attendance

Home 519,494    Away 438,585    Total 958,079
Single game home record, 76,490 (11-4-79)
Single season home record, 557,530 (1979)

## 1983 INDIVIDUAL STATISTICS

### Rushing

| | Att. | Yds. | Avg. | LG | TD |
|---|---|---|---|---|---|
| Woolfolk | 246 | 857 | 3.5 | 22 | 4 |
| Carpenter | 170 | 624 | 3.7 | 37 | 4 |
| Morris | 35 | 145 | 4.1 | 16 | 0 |
| Brunner | 26 | 64 | 2.5 | 12 | 0 |
| Tuggle | 17 | 49 | 2.9 | 7t | 1 |
| Rutledge | 7 | 27 | 3.9 | 14 | 0 |
| Campfield | 2 | 21 | 10.5 | 13 | 0 |
| Eddings | 1 | 3 | 3.0 | 3 | 0 |
| Bright | 1 | 2 | 2.0 | 2 | 0 |
| Miller | 1 | 2 | 2.0 | 2 | 0 |
| N.Y. Giants | 506 | 1794 | 3.5 | 37 | 9 |
| Opponents | 502 | 1733 | 3.5 | 44 | 10 |

### Passing

| | Att. | Comp. | Pct. | Yds. | TD | Int. | Tkld. | Rate |
|---|---|---|---|---|---|---|---|---|
| Brunner | 386 | 190 | 49.2 | 2516 | 9 | 22 | 31/218 | 54.3 |
| Rutledge | 174 | 87 | 50.0 | 1208 | 3 | 8 | 15/110 | 59.3 |
| Simms | 13 | 7 | 53.8 | 130 | 0 | 1 | 3/35 | 56.6 |
| Jennings | 1 | 0 | 0.0 | 0 | 0 | 0 | 0/0 | 39.6 |
| Mistler | 1 | 0 | 0.0 | 0 | 0 | 0 | 0/0 | 39.6 |
| N.Y. Giants | 575 | 284 | 49.4 | 3854 | 12 | 31 | 49/363 | 55.7 |
| Opponents | 493 | 283 | 57.4 | 3584 | 26 | 23 | 44/323 | 78.4 |

### Receiving

| | No. | Yds. | Avg. | LG | TD |
|---|---|---|---|---|---|
| Gray | 78 | 1139 | 14.6 | 62 | 5 |
| Mistler | 45 | 422 | 9.4 | 24 | 0 |
| Woolfolk | 28 | 368 | 13.1 | 44 | 0 |
| Carpenter | 26 | 258 | 9.9 | 38 | 2 |
| Mowatt | 21 | 280 | 13.3 | 46t | 1 |
| B. Williams | 20 | 346 | 17.3 | 43t | 1 |
| Scott | 17 | 206 | 12.1 | 24 | 0 |
| Eddings | 14 | 231 | 16.5 | 33 | 0 |
| Mullady | 13 | 184 | 14.2 | 35 | 1 |
| Miller | 7 | 170 | 24.3 | 54 | 0 |
| Pittman | 7 | 154 | 22.0 | 40t | 1 |
| Tuggle | 3 | 50 | 16.7 | 27 | 0 |
| Bright | 2 | 33 | 16.5 | 19 | 0 |
| Morris | 2 | 1 | 0.5 | 6t | 1 |
| Campfield | 1 | 12 | 12.0 | 12 | 0 |
| N.Y. Giants | 284 | 3854 | 13.6 | 62 | 12 |
| Opponents | 283 | 3584 | 12.7 | 61t | 26 |

### Interceptions

| | No. | Yds. | Avg. | LG | TD |
|---|---|---|---|---|---|
| Jackson | 6 | 20 | 3.3 | 17 | 0 |
| Kinard | 3 | 49 | 16.3 | 25 | 0 |
| Haynes | 3 | 18 | 6.0 | 23 | 0 |
| Currier | 2 | 37 | 18.5 | 30t | 1 |
| Reece | 2 | 33 | 16.5 | 22 | 0 |
| Taylor | 2 | 10 | 5.0 | 10 | 0 |
| Van Pelt | 2 | 7 | 3.5 | 6 | 0 |
| Flowers | 1 | 19 | 19.0 | 19 | 0 |
| Kelley | 1 | 17 | 17.0 | 17 | 0 |
| Dennis | 1 | 0 | 0.0 | 0 | 0 |
| N.Y. Giants | 23 | 210 | 9.1 | 30t | 1 |
| Opponents | 31 | 436 | 14.1 | 68t | 2 |

### Punting

| | No. | Yds. | Avg. | In 20 | LG |
|---|---|---|---|---|---|
| Jennings | 84 | 3386 | 40.3 | 29 | 66 |
| N.Y. Giants | 85 | 3386 | 39.8 | 29 | 66 |
| Opponents | 99 | 3884 | 39.2 | 25 | 60 |

### Punt Returns

| | No. | FC | Yds. | Avg. | LG | TD |
|---|---|---|---|---|---|---|
| Shaw | 29 | 4 | 234 | 8.1 | 27 | 0 |
| Bright | 17 | 0 | 117 | 6.9 | 20 | 0 |
| Reece | 9 | 2 | 26 | 2.9 | 7 | 0 |
| Pittman | 0 | 1 | 0 | — | 0 | 0 |
| N.Y. Giants | 55 | 7 | 377 | 6.9 | 27 | 0 |
| Opponents | 47 | 9 | 283 | 6.0 | 21 | 0 |

### Kickoff Returns

| | No. | Yds. | Avg. | LG | TD |
|---|---|---|---|---|---|
| Bright | 21 | 475 | 22.6 | 36 | 0 |
| Morris | 14 | 255 | 18.2 | 26 | 0 |
| Campfield | 9 | 154 | 17.1 | 23 | 0 |
| Tuggle | 9 | 156 | 17.3 | 28 | 0 |
| Pittman | 6 | 107 | 17.8 | 24 | 0 |
| Heater | 5 | 71 | 14.2 | 26 | 0 |
| Miller | 2 | 31 | 15.5 | 26 | 0 |
| Woolfolk | 2 | 13 | 6.5 | 11 | 0 |
| Dennis | 1 | 54 | 54.0 | 54 | 0 |
| Mayock | 1 | 9 | 9.0 | 9 | 0 |
| McLaughlin | 1 | 8 | 8.0 | 8 | 0 |
| N.Y. Giants | 71 | 1333 | 18.8 | 54 | 0 |
| Opponents | 67 | 1296 | 19.3 | 58 | 0 |

### Scoring

| | TD | TD R | TD P | TD Rt | PAT | FG | TP |
|---|---|---|---|---|---|---|---|
| Haji-Sheikh | | | | | 22/23 | 35/42 | 127 |
| Carpenter | 6 | 4 | 2 | 0 | | | 36 |
| Gray | 5 | 0 | 5 | 0 | | | 30 |
| Woolfolk | 4 | 4 | 0 | 0 | | | 24 |
| Currier | 1 | 0 | 0 | 1 | | | 6 |
| Jackson | 1 | 0 | 0 | 1 | | | 6 |
| Morris | 1 | 0 | 1 | 0 | | | 6 |
| Mowatt | 1 | 0 | 1 | 0 | | | 6 |
| Mullady | 1 | 0 | 1 | 0 | | | 6 |
| Pittman | 1 | 0 | 1 | 0 | | | 6 |
| Tuggle | 1 | 1 | 0 | 0 | | | 6 |
| B. Williams | 1 | 0 | 1 | 0 | | | 6 |
| Marshall | | (Safety) | | | | | 2 |
| N.Y. Giants | 23 | 9 | 12 | 2 | 22/23 | 35/42 | 267 |
| Opponents | 40 | 10 | 26 | 4 | 39/40 | 22/32 | 347 |

## FIRST-ROUND SELECTIONS

(If Club had no first-round selection, first player drafted is listed with round in parentheses.)

| Year | Player, College, Position |
|---|---|
| 1936 | Art Lewis, Ohio U., T |
| 1937 | Ed Widseth, Minnesota, T |
| 1938 | George Karamatic, Gonzaga, B |
| 1939 | Walt Neilson, Arizona, B |
| 1940 | Grenville Lansdell, Southern California, B |
| 1941 | George Franck, Minnesota, B |
| 1942 | Merle Hapes, Mississippi, B |
| 1943 | Steve Filipowicz, Fordham, B |
| 1944 | Billy Hillenbrand, Indiana, B |
| 1945 | Elmer Barbour, Wake Forest, B |
| 1946 | George Connor, Notre Dame, T |
| 1947 | Vic Schwall, Northwestern, B |
| 1948 | Tony Minisi, Pennsylvania, B |
| 1949 | Paul Page, Southern Methodist, B |
| 1950 | Travis Tidwell, Auburn, B |
| 1951 | Kyle Rote, Southern Methodist, B |
| | Jim Spavital, Oklahoma A&M, B |
| 1952 | Frank Gifford, Southern California, B |
| 1953 | Bobby Marlow, Alabama, B |
| 1954 | Ken Buck, Pacific, C (2) |
| 1955 | Joe Heap, Notre Dame, B |
| 1956 | Henry Moore, Arkansas, B (2) |
| 1957 | Sam DeLuca, South Carolina, T (2) |
| 1958 | Phil King, Vanderbilt, B |
| 1959 | Lee Grosscup, Utah, B |
| 1960 | Lou Cordileone, Clemson, G |
| 1961 | Bruce Tarbox, Syracuse, G (2) |
| 1962 | Jerry Hillebrand, Colorado, LB |
| 1963 | Frank Lasky, Florida, T (2) |
| 1964 | Joe Don Looney, Oklahoma, RB |
| 1965 | Tucker Frederickson, Auburn, RB |
| 1966 | Francis Peay, Missouri, T |
| 1967 | Louis Thompson, Alabama, DT (4) |
| 1968 | Dick Buzin, Penn State, T (2) |
| 1969 | Fred Dryer, San Diego State, DE |
| 1970 | Jim Files, Oklahoma, LB |
| 1971 | Rocky Thompson, West Texas State, WR |
| 1972 | Eldridge Small, Texas A&I, DB |
| | Larry Jacobson, Nebraska, DT |
| 1973 | Brad Van Pelt, Michigan State, LB (2) |
| 1974 | John Hicks, Ohio State, G |
| 1975 | Al Simpson, Colorado State, T (2) |
| 1976 | Troy Archer, Colorado, DE |
| 1977 | Gary Jeter, Southern California, DT |
| 1978 | Gordon King, Stanford, T |
| 1979 | Phil Simms, Morehead State, QB |
| 1980 | Mark Haynes, Colorado, DB |
| 1981 | Lawrence Taylor, North Carolina, LB |
| 1982 | Butch Woolfolk, Michigan, RB |
| 1983 | Terry Kinard, Clemson, DB |
| 1984 | Carl Banks, Michigan State, LB |
| | Bill Roberts, Ohio State, T |

# NEW YORK GIANTS 1984 VETERAN ROSTER

| No. | Name | Pos. | Ht. | Wt. | Birth- date | NFL Exp. | College | Birthplace | Residence | Games in '83 |
|---|---|---|---|---|---|---|---|---|---|---|
| 67 | Ard, Billy | G | 6-3 | 250 | 3/12/59 | 4 | Wake Forest | East Orange, N.J. | Westfield, N.J. | 16 |
| 73 | Belcher, Kevin | G | 6-3 | 255 | 2/23/61 | 2 | Texas-El Paso | Detroit, Mich. | Montclair, N.J. | 16 |
| 60 | Benson, Brad | T | 6-3 | 258 | 11/25/55 | 7 | Penn State | Altoona, Pa. | Tuxedo, N.Y. | 16 |
| 45 | Bright, Leon | RB | 5-9 | 192 | 5/19/55 | 7 | Florida State | Merritt Island, Fla. | Rockledge, Fla. | 7 |
| 64 | Burt, Jim | NT | 6-1 | 255 | 6/7/59 | 4 | Miami | Buffalo, N.Y. | Waldwick, N.J. | 7 |
| 26 | Carpenter, Rob | RB | 6-1 | 230 | 4/20/55 | 8 | Miami, Ohio | Lancaster, Ohio | Missouri City, Tex. | 10 |
| 53 | Carson, Harry | LB | 6-2 | 235 | 11/26/53 | 9 | South Carolina State | Florence, S.C. | Wash. Township, N.J. | 10 |
| 74 | Cook, Charles | NT | 6-3 | 255 | 5/13/59 | 2 | Miami | Miami, Fla. | Houston, Tex. | 4 |
| 29 | Currier, Bill | CB-S | 6-0 | 202 | 1/5/55 | 8 | South Carolina | Richmond, Va. | Missouri City, Tex. | 15 |
| 46 | Dennis, Mike | CB | 5-10 | 190 | 6/6/58 | 5 | Wyoming | Los Angeles, Calif. | Pasadena, Calif. | 16 |
| 88 | Eddings, Floyd | WR | 5-11 | 177 | 2/15/58 | 3 | California | Birmingham, Ala. | Pomona, Calif. | 9 |
| 37 | Flowers, Larry | S | 6-1 | 190 | 4/19/58 | 4 | Texas Tech | Temple, Tex. | Temple, Tex. | 14 |
| 83 | Gray, Earnest | WR | 6-3 | 195 | 3/2/57 | 6 | Memphis State | Greenwood, Miss. | Memphis, Tenn. | 16 |
| 6 | Haji-Sheikh, Ali | K | 6-0 | 172 | 1/11/61 | 2 | Michigan | Ann Arbor, Mich. | Paramus, N.J. | 16 |
| 79 | Hardison, Dee | DE | 6-4 | 269 | 5/2/56 | 7 | North Carolina | Jacksonville, N.C. | Fayetteville, N.C. | 16 |
| 36 | Haynes, Mark | CB | 5-11 | 198 | 11/6/58 | 5 | Colorado | Kansas City, Kan. | Woodridge, N.J. | 15 |
| 54 | Headen, Andy | LB | 6-5 | 230 | 7/8/60 | 2 | Clemson | Asheboro, N.C. | Liberty, N.C. | 16 |
| 27 | †Heater, Larry | RB | 5-11 | 205 | 1/9/58 | 5 | Arizona | Cincinnati, Ohio | Las Vegas, Nev. | 6 |
| 82 | Hugger, Keith | WR | 5-11 | 175 | 5/18/61 | 2 | Connecticut | Elizabeth, N.J. | Rahway, N.J. | 0* |
| 61 | Hughes, Ernie | C | 6-3 | 265 | 1/24/55 | 6 | Notre Dame | Boise, Idaho | Mt. Lakes, N.J. | 12 |
| 57 | Hunt, Byron | LB | 6-5 | 230 | 12/17/58 | 4 | Southern Methodist | Longview, Tex. | Dallas, Tex. | 16 |
| 13 | Jennings, Dave | P | 6-4 | 205 | 6/8/52 | 11 | St. Lawrence | New York, N.Y. | Upper Saddle River, N.J. | 16 |
| 43 | Kinard, Terry | S | 6-1 | 190 | 11/24/59 | 2 | Clemson | Bitburg, Germany | Sumter, S.C. | 16 |
| 72 | King, Gordon | T | 6-6 | 275 | 2/3/56 | 7 | Stanford | Madison, Wis. | Park Ridge, N.J. | 14 |
| 70 | Marshall, Leonard | DE | 6-3 | 285 | 10/22/61 | 2 | Louisiana State | Franklin, La. | Jersey City, N.J. | 14 |
| 75 | Martin, George | DE | 6-4 | 245 | 2/16/53 | 10 | Oregon | Greenville, S.C. | Vacaville, Calif. | 14 |
| 39 | Mayock, Mike | S | 6-2 | 195 | 8/14/58 | 3 | Boston College | Philadelphia, Pa. | Haverford, Pa. | 6 |
| 33 | McDaniel, LeCharls | CB | 5-9 | 170 | 10/15/58 | 4 | Cal Poly-SLO | Ft. Bragg, N.C. | Lake Hiawatha, N.J. | 9 |
| 76 | McGriff, Curtis | DE | 6-5 | 265 | 5/17/58 | 5 | Alabama | Donaldsville, Ga. | Gordon, Ala. | 8 |
| 52 | McLaughlin, Joe | LB | 6-1 | 235 | 7/1/57 | 6 | Massachusetts | Springfield, Mass. | Stoneham, Mass. | 7 |
| 71 | Merrill, Casey | DE | 6-4 | 255 | 7/16/57 | 6 | Cal-Davis | Oakland, Calif. | Palm Desert, Calif. | 15* |
| 89 | Miller, Mike | WR | 5-11 | 182 | 12/29/59 | 2 | Tennessee | Flint, Mich. | Flint, Mich. | 13 |
| 85 | Mistler, John | WR | 6-2 | 186 | 10/28/58 | 4 | Arizona State | Columbia, Md. | East Brunswick, N.J. | 16 |
| 20 | Morris, Joe | RB | 5-7 | 190 | 9/15/60 | 3 | Syracuse | Ft. Bragg, N.C. | Wash. Township, N.J. | 15 |
| 84 | Mowatt, Zeke | TE | 6-3 | 238 | 3/5/61 | 2 | Florida State | Wauchula, Fla. | Tallahassee, Fla. | 16 |
| 81 | Mullady, Tom | TE | 6-3 | 232 | 1/30/57 | 5 | Southwestern Memphis | Dayton, Ohio | Park Ridge, N.J. | 16 |
| 77 | Neill, Bill | NT | 6-4 | 255 | 3/15/59 | 3 | Pittsburgh | Norristown, Pa. | Wayne, N.J. | 1 |
| 9 | †Owen, Tom | QB | 6-1 | 194 | 9/1/52 | 11 | Wichita State | Shreveport, La. | Wichita, Kan. | 0* |
| 86 | Perkins, Johnny | WR | 6-2 | 205 | 4/21/53 | 7 | Abilene Christian | Franklin, Tex. | Granbury, Tex. | 1 |
| 17 | Rutledge, Jeff | QB | 6-1 | 190 | 1/22/57 | 6 | Alabama | Birmingham, Ala. | Mission Viejo, Calif. | 4 |
| 78 | Sally, Jerome | NT | 6-3 | 260 | 2/24/59 | 3 | Missouri | Chicago, Ill. | Columbia, Mo. | 16 |
| 80 | Scott, Malcolm | TE | 6-4 | 240 | 7/10/61 | 2 | Louisiana State | New Orleans, La. | New Orleans, La. | 16 |
| 44 | †Shaw, Pete | S | 5-10 | 183 | 8/25/54 | 8 | Northwestern | Newark, N.J. | Rancho La Costa, Calif. | 15 |
| 11 | Simms, Phil | QB | 6-3 | 216 | 11/3/56 | 6 | Morehead State | Louisville, Ky. | Wyckoff, N.J. | 2 |
| 63 | Steinfeld, Al | C | 6-5 | 256 | 10/28/56 | 4 | C.W. Post | Brooklyn, N.Y. | Brooklyn, N.Y. | 13* |
| 65 | Tautolo, John | G | 6-3 | 260 | 5/29/59 | 3 | UCLA | Long Beach, Calif. | Bellflower, Calif. | 6 |
| 56 | Taylor, Lawrence | LB | 6-3 | 237 | 2/4/59 | 4 | North Carolina | Williamsburg, Va. | Upper Saddle River, N.J. | 16 |
| 38 | Tuggle, John | RB | 6-1 | 210 | 1/31/61 | 2 | California | Honolulu, Hawaii | San Jose, Calif. | 16 |
| 68 | Turner, J.T. | G | 6-3 | 250 | 4/17/53 | 8 | Duke | Moultrie, Ga. | Wash. Township, N.J. | 16 |
| 59 | Umphrey, Rich | C | 6-3 | 255 | 12/13/58 | 3 | Colorado | Garden Grove, Calif. | Santa Ana, Calif. | 10 |
| 10 | Van Pelt, Brad | LB | 6-5 | 235 | 4/5/51 | 12 | Michigan State | Owosso, Mich. | Owosso, Mich. | 16 |
| 58 | †Whittington, Mike | LB | 6-2 | 220 | 8/9/58 | 5 | Notre Dame | Miami, Fla. | Miami, Fla. | 8 |
| 87 | Williams, Byron | WR | 6-2 | 180 | 10/31/60 | 2 | Texas-Arlington | Texarkana, Tex. | Duncanville, Tex. | 5 |
| 25 | Woolfolk, Butch | RB | 6-1 | 207 | 3/1/60 | 3 | Michigan | Milwaukee, Wis. | Secaucus, N.J. | 16 |

* Hugger active for 2 games in '83, but did not play; Merrill played 5 games with Green Bay, 10 with N.Y. Giants in '83; Owen active for 7 games but did not play; Steinfeld played 8 games with Houston, 5 with N.Y. Giants in '83.

†Option playout; subject to developments.

Retired—Frank Marion, 7-year linebacker, 10 games in '83.

Traded—Quarterback Scott Brunner to Denver; cornerback Terry Jackson to Seattle; linebacker Brian Kelley to San Diego.

Also played with Giants in '83—T Rich Baldinger (2 games), RB Billy Campfield (4), LB Paul Davis (3), C Chris Foote (11), S Beasley Reece (7).

## COACHING STAFF

### Head Coach,
### Bill Parcells

**Pro Career:** Became twelfth head coach in New York Giants history on December 15, 1982. Parcells begins second campaign as head coach after spending two seasons as the Giants' defensive coordinator and linebacker coach. Started pro coaching career in 1980 as linebacker coach with New England. Career record: 3-12-1

**Background:** Linebacker at Wichita State 1961-63. College assistant Hastings (Neb.) 1964, Wichita State 1965, Army 1966-69, Florida State 1970-72, Vanderbilt 1973-74, Texas Tech 1975-77. Air Force 1978 (head coach).

**Personal:** Born August 22, 1941, Englewood, N.J. Bill and his wife, Judy, live in Upper Saddle River, N.J., and have three daughters—Suzy, Jill, and Dallas.

## ASSISTANT COACHES

**Bill Belichick,** linebackers; born April 16, 1952, Nashville, Tenn., lives in East Rutherford, N.J. Center-tight end Wesleyan 1972-74. No pro playing experience. Pro coach: Baltimore Colts 1975, Detroit Lions 1976-77, Denver Broncos 1978, joined Giants in 1979.

**Tom Bresnahan,** offensive line; born January 21, 1935, Springfield, Mass., lives in East Rutherford, N.J. Tackle Holy Cross 1953-55. No pro playing experience. College coach: Williams 1963-67, Columbia 1968-72, Navy 1973-80. Pro coach: Kansas City Chiefs 1981-82, joined Giants in 1983.

**Romeo Crennel,** special teams; born June 18, 1947, Lynchburg, Va., lives in East Rutherford, N.J., Defensive lineman Western Kentucky 1966-69. No pro playing experience. College coach: Western Kentucky 1970-74, Texas Tech 1975-77, Mississippi 1978-79, Georgia Tech 1980. Pro coach: Joined Giants in 1981.

**Ron Erhardt,** offensive coordinator; born February 27, 1932, Mandan, N.D., lives in East Rutherford, N.J. Quarterback Jamestown (N.D.) College 1951-54. No pro playing experience. College coach: North Dakota State 1963-72 (head coach 1966-72). Pro coach: New England Patriots 1973-81 (head coach 1979-81), joined Giants in 1982.

**Len Fontes,** defensive backfield; born March 8, 1938, New Bedford, Mass., lives in East Rutherford, N.J. Defensive back Ohio State 1958-59. No pro playing experience. College coach: Eastern Michigan 1968, Dayton 1969-72, Navy 1973-76, Miami 1977-79. Pro coach: Cleveland Browns 1980-82, joined Giants in 1983.

**Ray Handley,** running backs; born October 8, 1944, Artesia, N.M., lives in East Rutherford, N.J. Running back Stanford 1963-65. No pro playing experience. College coach: Stanford 1967, 1971-74, 1979-83, Army 1968-69, Air Force 1975-78. Pro coach: First year with Giants.

**Pat Hodgson,** receivers; born January 30, 1944, Columbus, Ga., lives in East Rutherford, N.J. Tight end Georgia 1963-65. Pro tight end Washington Redskins 1966, Minnesota Vikings 1967. College coach: Georgia 1968-70, 1972-77, Florida State 1971, Texas Tech 1978. Pro coach: San Diego Chargers 1978, joined Giants in 1979.

**Lamar Leachman,** defensive line; born August 7, 1934, Cartersville, Ga., lives in East Rutherford, N.J. Center-linebacker Tennessee 1952-55. No pro playing experience. College coach: Richmond 1966-67, Georgia Tech 1968-71, Memphis State 1972, South Carolina 1973. Pro coach: New York Stars (WFL) 1974, Toronto Argonauts (CFL) 1975-77, Montreal Alouettes (CFL) 1978-79, joined Giants in 1980.

**Johnny Parker,** strength and conditioning; born February 1, 1947, Greenville, S.C., lives in East Rutherford, N.J. No pro playing experience. Graduate of Mississippi, M.A., Delta State University. College coach: South Carolina 1974-76, Indiana 1977-79, Louisiana State 1980, Mississippi 1981-83. Pro coach: First year with Giants.

## NEW YORK GIANTS 1984 FIRST-YEAR ROSTER

| Name | Pos. | Ht. | Wt. | Birth-date | College | Birthplace | Residence | How Acq. |
|---|---|---|---|---|---|---|---|---|
| Banks, Carl | LB | 6-4 | 232 | 2/29/62 | Michigan State | Flint, Mich. | Flint, Mich. | D1 |
| Cephous, Frank | RB | 5-10 | 205 | 7/4/61 | UCLA | Philadelphia, Pa. | Newark, Del. | D11 |
| Golden, Heyward | CB-S | 6-0 | 192 | 11/5/60 | S. Carolina State | Sumter, S.C. | Sumter, S.C. | D10a |
| Goode, Conrad | T | 6-6 | 275 | 1/19/62 | Missouri | St. Louis, Mo. | St. Louis, Mo. | D4 |
| Green, Lawrence | LB | 6-2 | 230 | 5/15/62 | Tenn.-Chattanooga | Florence, Ala. | Florence, Ala. | D12 |
| Harris, Clint | CB-S | 6-0 | 205 | 8/19/62 | East Carolina | Chesapeake, Va. | Chesapeake, Va. | D5 |
| Hostetler, Jeff | QB | 6-3 | 215 | 4/22/61 | West Virginia | Hollsopple, Pa. | Hollsopple, Pa. | D3 |
| Jones, Robbie (1) | LB | 6-2 | 230 | 12/25/59 | Alabama | Demopolis, Ala. | Demopolis, Ala. | D12('83) |
| Jordan, David | G | 6-6 | 267 | 7/14/62 | Auburn | Birmingham, Ala. | Birmingham, Ala. | D10 |
| Magwood, Frank (1) | WR | 6-0 | 188 | 7/7/61 | Clemson | Charleston, S.C. | Johns-Is., S.C. | D12a('83) |
| Manuel, Lionel | WR | 5-11 | 175 | 4/13/62 | Pacific | Cucamonga, Calif. | Cucamonga, Calif. | D7 |
| Nelson, Karl (1) | T | 6-6 | 272 | 6/14/60 | Iowa State | De Kalb, Ill. | De Kalb, Ill. | D3('83) |
| Reasons, Gary | LB | 6-4 | 235 | 2/18/62 | N.W. Louisiana | Crowley, Tex. | Crowley, Tex. | D4a |
| Roberts, Bill | T | 6-5 | 275 | 8/5/62 | Ohio State | Miami, Fla. | Miami, Fla. | D1a |
| Scott, James | DE | 6-5 | 260 | 4/14/62 | Clemson | Alexandria, Va. | Alexandria, Va. | D6 |
| Thomas, Rodney (1) | RB | 5-11 | 210 | 9/20/58 | Western Illinois | New Orleans, La. | New Orleans, La. | FA |
| Williams, Perry (1) | CB | 6-2 | 195 | 5/12/61 | N. Carolina State | Hamlet, N.C. | Hamlet, N.C. | D7('83) |

Players who report to an NFL team for the first time are designated on rosters as rookies (R). If a player reported to an NFL training camp in a previous year but was not on the active squad for three or more regular season or postseason games, he is listed on the first-year roster and designated by a (1). Thereafter, a player who is on the active squad for three or more regular season or postseason games is credited with an additional year of playing experience.

# NOTES

_____
_____
_____
_____
_____
_____
_____
_____
_____
_____
_____
_____
_____
_____
_____
_____
_____
_____
_____
_____

**Mike Pope,** assistant special teams; born March 15, 1942, Monroe, N.C., lives in River Vale, N.J. Quarterback Lenoir Rhyne 1962-64. No pro playing experience. College coach: Florida State 1970-74, Texas Tech 1975-77, Mississippi 1978-82. Pro coach: Joined Giants in 1983.

**Steve Schnall,** offensive assistant, administrative assistant; born January 20, 1944, Rockaway Beach, N.Y., lives in Mercerville, N.J. Defensive back Springfield College 1961-65. No pro playing experience. College coach: Widener 1969-70, Lafayette 1971-77, William and Mary 1978, East Carolina 1979, Princeton 1980-82. Pro coach: Joined Giants in 1983.

# PHILADELPHIA EAGLES

## National Football Conference Eastern Division

**Team Colors:** Kelly Green, Silver, and White

**Veterans Stadium**
**Broad Street and Pattison Avenue**
**Philadelphia, Pennsylvania 19148**
Telephone: (215) 463-2500

### Club Officials

Owner and President: Leonard H. Tose
Vice President-Legal Counsel: Susan Fletcher
Executive Director of Player Personnel:
    Lynn Stiles
Director of Football Administration: Harry Gamble
Director of Communications: Ed Wisneski
Director of Public Relations: Jim Gallagher
Assistant Director of Public Relations:
    Ron Howard
Director of Sales and Marketing: Bob Caesar
Assistant Director of Sales and Marketing:
    Sherry Lewis
Ticket Manager: Hugh Ortman
Business Manager: Mimi Box
Controller: Dave Toner
Assistant Director of Player Personnel:
    Jackie Graves
Talent Scouts: Ken Blair, Jim Katcavage, Phil Neri
Trainer: Otho Davis
Strength and Conditioning Coordinator:
    Tim Jorgensen
Equipment Manager: Rusty Sweeney
Film Director: Mike Dougherty

**Stadium:** Veterans Stadium •
    **Capacity:** 73,484
    Broad Street and Pattison Avenue
    Philadelphia, Pennsylvania 19148

**Playing Surface:** AstroTurf

**Training Camp:** West Chester University
    West Chester, Pennsylvania
    19380

## 1984 SCHEDULE

### Preseason
| | | |
|---|---|---|
| Aug. 4 | at Detroit | 7:00 |
| Aug. 11 | at Pittsburgh | 6:00 |
| Aug. 18 | at Minnesota | 7:00 |
| Aug. 23 | **Cleveland** | 7:00 |

### Regular Season
| | | |
|---|---|---|
| Sept. 2 | at New York Giants | 1:00 |
| Sept. 9 | **Minnesota** | 1:00 |
| Sept. 16 | at Dallas | 3:00 |
| Sept. 23 | **San Francisco** | 1:00 |
| Sept. 30 | at Washington | 4:00 |
| Oct. 7 | at Buffalo | 1:00 |
| Oct. 14 | **Colts** | 1:00 |
| Oct. 21 | **New York Giants** | 1:00 |
| Oct. 28 | **St. Louis** | 1:00 |
| Nov. 4 | at Detroit | 1:00 |
| Nov. 11 | at Miami | 1:00 |
| Nov. 18 | **Washington** | 1:00 |
| Nov. 25 | at St. Louis | 12:00 |
| Dec. 2 | **Dallas** | 1:00 |
| Dec. 9 | **New England** | 1:00 |
| Dec. 16 | at Atlanta | 4:00 |

## EAGLES COACHING HISTORY

**(277-358-22)**

| | | |
|---|---|---|
| 1933-35 | Lud Wray | 9-21-1 |
| 1936-40 | Bert Bell | 10-44-2 |
| 1941-50 | Earle (Greasy) Neale* | 66-44-5 |
| 1951 | Alvin (Bo) McMillin** | 2-0-0 |
| 1951 | Wayne Millner | 2-8-0 |
| 1952-55 | Jim Trimble | 25-20-3 |
| 1956-57 | Hugh Devore | 7-16-1 |
| 1958-60 | Lawrence (Buck) Shaw | 20-16-1 |
| 1961-63 | Nick Skorich | 15-24-3 |
| 1964-68 | Joe Kuharich | 28-41-1 |
| 1969-71 | Jerry Williams*** | 7-22-2 |
| 1971-72 | Ed Khayat | 8-15-2 |
| 1973-75 | Mike McCormack | 16-25-1 |
| 1976-82 | Dick Vermeil | 57-51-0 |
| 1983 | Marion Campbell | 5-11-0 |

*Co-coach with Walt Kiesling in Philadelphia-Pittsburgh merger in 1943
**Retired after two games in 1951
***Released after three games in 1971

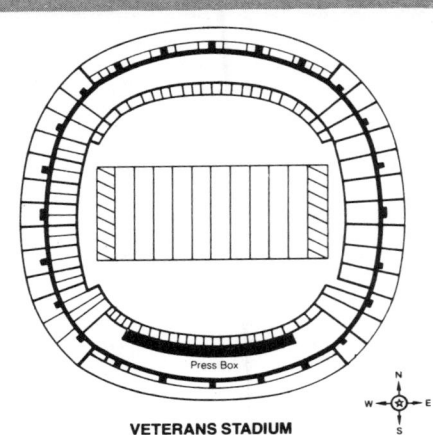

**VETERANS STADIUM**

## RECORD HOLDERS
### Individual Records—Career
| Category | Name | Performance |
|---|---|---|
| Rushing (Yds.) | Steve Van Buren, 1944-1951 | 5,860 |
| Passing (Yds.) | Ron Jaworski, 1977-1983 | 19,354 |
| Passing (TDs) | Ron Jaworski, 1977-1983 | 134 |
| Receiving (No.) | Harold Carmichael, 1971-1983 | 589 |
| Receiving (Yds.) | Harold Carmichael, 1971-1983 | 8,978 |
| Interceptions | Bill Bradley, 1969-1976 | 34 |
| Field Goals | Sam Baker, 1964-69 | 90 |
| Touchdowns (Tot.) | Harold Carmichael, 1971-1983 | 79 |
| Points | Bobby Walston, 1951-1962 | 881 |

### Individual Records—Single Season
| Category | Name | Performance |
|---|---|---|
| Rushing (Yds.) | Wilbert Montgomery, 1979 | 1,512 |
| Passing (Yds.) | Sonny Jurgensen, 1961 | 3,723 |
| Passing (TDs) | Sonny Jurgensen, 1961 | 32 |
| Receiving (No.) | Mike Quick, 1983 | 69 |
| Receiving (Yds.) | Mike Quick, 1983 | 1,409 |
| Interceptions | Bill Bradley, 1971 | 11 |
| Field Goals | Tom Dempsey, 1973 | 24 |
| Touchdowns (Tot.) | Steve Van Buren, 1945 | 18 |
| Points | Bobby Walston, 1954 | 114 |

### Individual Records—Single Game
| Category | Name | Performance |
|---|---|---|
| Rushing (Yds.) | Steve Van Buren, 11-27-49 | 205 |
| Passing (Yds.) | Bobby Thomason, 11-18-53 | 437 |
| Passing (TDs) | Adrian Burk, 10-17-54 | 7 |
| Receiving (No.) | Don Looney, 12-1-40 | 14 |
| Receiving (Yds.) | Tommy McDonald, 12-10-60 | 237 |
| Interceptions | Russ Craft, 9-24-50 | 4 |
| Field Goals | Tom Dempsey, 11-12-72 | 6 |
| Touchdowns (Tot.) | Many times | 4 |
| | Last time by Wilbert Montgomery, 10-7-79 | |
| Points | Bobby Walston, 10-17-54 | 25 |

## 1983 TEAM STATISTICS

| | Philadelphia | Opp. |
|---|---|---|
| Total First Downs | 253 | 310 |
| Rushing | 91 | 144 |
| Passing | 150 | 149 |
| Penalty | 12 | 17 |
| Third Down Efficiency | 68/203 | 100/241 |
| Third Down Percentage | 33.5 | 41.5 |
| Total Net Yards | 4534 | 5447 |
| Total Offensive Plays | 945 | 1099 |
| Avg. Gain per Play | 4.8 | 5.0 |
| Avg. Gain per Game | 283.4 | 340.4 |
| Net Yards Rushing | 1417 | 2655 |
| Total Rushing Plays | 402 | 633 |
| Avg. Gain per Rush | 3.5 | 4.2 |
| Avg. Gain Rushing per Game | 88.6 | 165.9 |
| Net Yards Passing | 3117 | 2792 |
| Lost Attempting to Pass | 57/415 | 36/256 |
| Gross Yards Passing | 3532 | 3048 |
| Attempts/Completions | 486/252 | 430/247 |
| Percent Completed | 51.9 | 57.4 |
| Had Intercepted | 18 | 8 |
| Avg. Net Passing per Game | 194.8 | 174.5 |
| Punts/Avg. | 86/40.9 | 80/37.8 |
| Punt Returns/Avg. | 45/5.8 | 57/9.0 |
| Kickoff Returns/Avg. | 62/18.8 | 45/17.9 |
| Interceptions/Avg. Ret. | 8/9.9 | 18/8.6 |
| Penalties/Yards | 79/637 | 94/755 |
| Fumbles/Ball Lost | 37/18 | 30/15 |
| Total Points | 233 | 322 |
| Avg. Points per Game | 14.6 | 20.1 |
| Touchdowns | 27 | 34 |
| Rushing | 5 | 14 |
| Passing | 22 | 20 |
| Returns and Recoveries | 0 | 0 |
| Field Goals | 15/26 | 28/37 |
| Conversions | 24/27 | 34/34 |
| Safeties | 1 | 0 |
| Avg. Time of Possession | 27:07 | 32:53 |

## 1983 TEAM RECORD

### Preseason (3-1)

| Date | Philadelphia | | Opponents |
|---|---|---|---|
| 8/5 | 21 | *Detroit | 17 |
| 8/13 | 21 | San Diego | 20 |
| 8/20 | 27 | Green Bay | 14 |
| 8/25 | 3 | *Pittsburgh | 10 |
| | 72 | | 61 |

### Regular Season (5-11)

| Date | Philadelphia | | Opp. | Att. |
|---|---|---|---|---|
| 9/3 | 22 | San Francisco | 17 | 55,775 |
| 9/11 | 13 | *Washington | 23 | 69,544 |
| 9/18 | 13 | Denver | 10 | 74,202 |
| 9/25 | 11 | *St. Louis | 14 | 64,465 |
| 10/2 | 28 | Atlanta | 24 | 50,621 |
| 10/9 | 17 | New York Giants | 13 | 73,291 |
| 10/16 | 7 | Dallas | 37 | 63,070 |
| 10/23 | 6 | *Chicago | 7 | 45,263 |
| 10/30 | 21 | *Baltimore | 22 | 59,150 |
| 11/6 | 20 | *Dallas | 27 | 71,236 |
| 11/13 | 14 | Chicago | 17 | 47,524 |
| 11/20 | 0 | *New York Giants | 23 | 57,977 |
| 11/27 | 24 | Washington | 28 | 54,324 |
| 12/4 | 13 | *Los Angeles Rams | 9 | 32,867 |
| 12/11 | 17 | *New Orleans (OT) | 20 | 45,182 |
| 12/18 | 7 | St. Louis | 31 | 21,902 |
| | 233 | | 322 | 886,393 |

*Home Game     (OT) Overtime

### Score by Periods

| | | | | | | | |
|---|---|---|---|---|---|---|---|
| Philadelphia | 58 | 54 | 61 | 60 | 0 | — | 233 |
| Opponents | 47 | 128 | 53 | 91 | 3 | — | 322 |

### Attendance

Home 445,684     Away 440,709     Total 886,393
Single game home record, 72,111 (11-1-81)
Single season home record, 557,325 (1980)

## 1983 INDIVIDUAL STATISTICS

### Rushing

| | Att. | Yds. | Avg. | LG | TD |
|---|---|---|---|---|---|
| Oliver | 121 | 434 | 3.6 | 24 | 1 |
| M. Williams | 103 | 385 | 3.7 | 32 | 0 |
| Haddix | 91 | 220 | 2.4 | 11 | 2 |
| Montgomery | 29 | 139 | 4.8 | 32 | 0 |
| Jaworski | 25 | 129 | 5.2 | 29 | 1 |
| Harrington | 23 | 98 | 4.3 | 35 | 1 |
| Everett | 5 | 7 | 1.4 | 7 | 0 |
| Runager | 1 | 6 | 6.0 | 6 | 0 |
| Pastorini | 1 | 0 | 0.0 | 0 | 0 |
| Pisarcik | 3 | −1 | −0.3 | 0 | 0 |
| Philadelphia | 402 | 1417 | 3.5 | 35 | 5 |
| Opponents | 633 | 2655 | 4.2 | 39t | 14 |

### Passing

| | Att. | Comp. | Pct. | Yds. | TD | Int. | Tkld. | Rate |
|---|---|---|---|---|---|---|---|---|
| Jaworski | 446 | 235 | 52.7 | 3315 | 20 | 18 | 53/385 | 75.1 |
| Pisarcik | 34 | 16 | 47.1 | 172 | 1 | 0 | 4/30 | 72.2 |
| Pastorini | 5 | 0 | 0.0 | 0 | 0 | 0 | 0/0 | 39.6 |
| Carmichael | 1 | 1 | 100.0 | 45 | 1 | 0 | 0/0 | 158.3 |
| Phil. | 486 | 252 | 51.9 | 3532 | 22 | 18 | 57/415 | 75.2 |
| Opponents | 430 | 247 | 57.4 | 3048 | 20 | 8 | 36/256 | 87.2 |

### Receiving

| | No. | Yds. | Avg. | LG | TD |
|---|---|---|---|---|---|
| Quick | 69 | 1409 | 20.4 | 83t | 13 |
| Oliver | 49 | 421 | 8.6 | 25 | 2 |
| Carmichael | 38 | 515 | 13.6 | 35 | 3 |
| Haddix | 23 | 254 | 11.0 | 34 | 0 |
| Kab | 18 | 195 | 10.8 | 25 | 1 |
| M. Williams | 17 | 142 | 8.4 | 29 | 0 |
| Hoover | 10 | 221 | 22.1 | 68 | 0 |
| Montgomery | 9 | 53 | 5.9 | 13 | 0 |
| Woodruff | 6 | 70 | 11.7 | 29t | 2 |
| Dixon | 4 | 54 | 13.5 | 22 | 0 |
| G. Young | 3 | 125 | 41.7 | 71t | 1 |
| Sampleton | 2 | 28 | 14.0 | 19 | 0 |
| Everett | 2 | 18 | 9.0 | 11 | 0 |
| Harrington | 1 | 19 | 19.0 | 19 | 0 |
| Smith | 1 | 8 | 8.0 | 8 | 0 |
| Philadelphia | 252 | 3532 | 14.0 | 83t | 22 |
| Opponents | 247 | 3048 | 12.3 | 75t | 20 |

### Interceptions

| | No. | Yds. | Avg. | LG | TD |
|---|---|---|---|---|---|
| Griggs | 3 | 61 | 20.3 | 32 | 0 |
| Ellis | 1 | 18 | 18.0 | 18 | 0 |
| Edwards | 1 | 0 | 0.0 | 0 | 0 |
| Foules | 1 | 0 | 0.0 | 0 | 0 |
| Logan | 1 | 0 | 0.0 | 0 | 0 |
| R. Young | 1 | 0 | 0.0 | 0 | 0 |
| Philadelphia | 8 | 79 | 9.9 | 32 | 0 |
| Opponents | 18 | 155 | 8.6 | 29 | 0 |

### Punting

| | No. | Yds. | Avg. | In 20 | LG |
|---|---|---|---|---|---|
| Runager | 59 | 2459 | 41.7 | 12 | 55 |
| Skladany | 27 | 1062 | 39.3 | 5 | 51 |
| Philadelphia | 86 | 3521 | 40.9 | 17 | 55 |
| Opponents | 80 | 3020 | 37.8 | 20 | 59 |

### Punt Returns

| | No. | FC | Yds. | Avg. | LG | TD |
|---|---|---|---|---|---|---|
| Sciarra | 22 | 3 | 115 | 5.2 | 14 | 0 |
| G. Young | 14 | 3 | 93 | 6.6 | 23 | 0 |
| Hoover | 7 | 4 | 44 | 6.3 | 13 | 0 |
| Foules | 1 | 0 | 7 | 7.0 | 7 | 0 |
| Logan | 1 | 0 | 0 | 0.0 | 0 | 0 |
| Philadelphia | 45 | 10 | 259 | 5.8 | 23 | 0 |
| Opponents | 57 | 4 | 511 | 9.0 | 25 | 0 |

### Kickoff Returns

| | No. | Yds. | Avg. | LG | TD |
|---|---|---|---|---|---|
| G. Young | 26 | 547 | 21.0 | 52 | 0 |
| Everett | 14 | 275 | 19.6 | 46 | 0 |
| Ellis | 7 | 119 | 17.0 | 26 | 0 |
| Harrington | 4 | 79 | 19.8 | 26 | 0 |
| Haddix | 3 | 51 | 17.0 | 24 | 0 |
| M. Williams | 3 | 59 | 19.7 | 25 | 0 |
| Darby | 2 | 3 | 1.5 | 3 | 0 |
| Fritzsche | 2 | 17 | 8.5 | 15 | 0 |
| R. Young | 1 | 18 | 18.0 | 18 | 0 |
| Philadelphia | 62 | 1168 | 18.8 | 52 | 0 |
| Opponents | 45 | 804 | 17.9 | 30 | 0 |

### Scoring

| | TD | TD R | TD P | TD Rt | PAT | FG | TP |
|---|---|---|---|---|---|---|---|
| Quick | 13 | 0 | 13 | 0 | | | 78 |
| Franklin | | | | | 24/27 | 15/26 | 69 |
| Carmichael | 3 | 0 | 3 | 0 | | | 18 |
| Oliver | 3 | 1 | 2 | 0 | | | 18 |
| Haddix | 2 | 2 | 0 | 0 | | | 12 |
| Woodruff | 2 | 0 | 2 | 0 | | | 12 |
| Harrington | 1 | 1 | 0 | 0 | | | 6 |
| Jaworski | 1 | 1 | 0 | 0 | | | 6 |
| Kab | 1 | 0 | 1 | 0 | | | 6 |
| G. Young | 1 | 0 | 1 | 0 | | | 6 |
| Philadelphia | 27 | 5 | 22 | 0 | 24/27 | 15/26 | 233 |
| Opponents | 34 | 14 | 20 | 0 | 34/34 | 28/37 | 322 |

## FIRST-ROUND SELECTIONS

(If Club had no first-round selection, first player drafted is listed with round in parentheses.)

| Year | Player, College, Position |
|---|---|
| 1936 | Jay Berwanger, Chicago, B |
| 1937 | Sam Francis, Nebraska, B |
| 1938 | Jim McDonald, Ohio State, B |
| 1939 | Davey O'Brien, Texas Christian, B |
| 1940 | George McAfee, Duke, B |
| 1941 | Art Jones, Richmond, B (2) |
| 1942 | Pete Kmetovic, Stanford, B |
| 1943 | Joe Muha, Virginia Military, B |
| 1944 | Steve Van Buren, Louisiana State, B |
| 1945 | John Yonaker, Notre Dame, E |
| 1946 | Leo Riggs, Southern California, B |
| 1947 | Neill Armstrong, Oklahoma A&M, E |
| 1948 | Clyde (Smackover) Scott, Arkansas, B |
| 1949 | Chuck Bednarik, Pennsylvania, C |
| | Frank Tripucka, Notre Dame, B |
| 1950 | Harry (Bud) Grant, Minnesota, E |
| 1951 | Ebert Van Buren, Louisiana State, B |
| | Chet Mutryn, Xavier, B |
| 1952 | Johnny Bright, Drake, B |
| 1953 | Al Conway, Army, B (2) |
| 1954 | Neil Worden, Notre Dame, B |
| 1955 | Dick Bielski, Maryland, B |
| 1956 | Bob Pellegrini, Maryland, C |
| 1957 | Clarence Peaks, Michigan State, B |
| 1958 | Walt Kowalczyk, Michigan State, B |
| 1959 | J.D. Smith, Rice, T (2) |
| 1960 | Ron Burton, Northwestern, RB |
| 1961 | Art Baker, Syracuse, RB |
| 1962 | Pete Case, Georgia, G (2) |
| 1963 | Ed Budde, Michigan State, G |
| 1964 | Bob Brown, Nebraska, B |
| 1965 | Ray Rissmiller, Georgia, T (2) |
| 1966 | Randy Beisler, Indiana, DE |
| 1967 | Harry Jones, Arkansas, RB |
| 1968 | Tim Rossovich, Southern California, DE |
| 1969 | Leroy Keyes, Purdue, RB |
| 1970 | Steve Zabel, Oklahoma, TE |
| 1971 | Richard Harris, Grambling, DE |
| 1972 | John Reaves, Florida, QB |
| 1973 | Jerry Sisemore, Texas, T |
| | Charle Young, Southern California, TE |
| 1974 | Mitch Sutton, Kansas, DT (3) |
| 1975 | Bill Capraun, Miami, T (7) |
| 1976 | Mike Smith, Florida, DE (4) |
| 1977 | Skip Sharp, Kansas, DB (5) |
| 1978 | Reggie Wilkes, Georgia Tech, LB (3) |
| 1979 | Jerry Robinson, UCLA, LB |
| 1980 | Roynell Young, Alcorn State, DB |
| 1981 | Leonard Mitchell, Houston, DE |
| 1982 | Mike Quick, North Carolina State, WR |
| 1983 | Michael Haddix, Mississippi State, RB |
| 1984 | Kenny Jackson, Penn State, WR |

## PHILADELPHIA EAGLES 1984 VETERAN ROSTER

| No. | Name | Pos. | Ht. | Wt. | Birth-date | NFL Exp. | College | Birthplace | Residence | Games in '83 |
|---|---|---|---|---|---|---|---|---|---|---|
| 96 | Armstrong, Harvey | NT | 6-2 | 255 | 12/29/59 | 3 | Southern Methodist | Houston, Tex. | Houston, Tex. | 16 |
| 63 | Baker, Ron | G | 6-4 | 250 | 11/19/54 | 7 | Oklahoma State | Gary, Ind. | Stillwater, Okla. | 16 |
| 98 | Brown, Greg | DE | 6-5 | 240 | 1/5/57 | 4 | Kansas State | Washington, D.C. | Clementon, N.J. | 16 |
| 71 | Clarke, Ken | NT | 6-2 | 255 | 8/28/56 | 7 | Syracuse | Savannah, Ga. | Sewell, N.J. | 16 |
| 57 | Cowher, Bill | LB | 6-3 | 225 | 5/8/57 | 4 | North Carolina State | Pittsburgh, Pa. | Olmstead Falls, Ohio | 16 |
| 94 | Darby, Byron | DE | 6-4 | 250 | 6/4/60 | 2 | Southern California | Los Angeles, Calif. | Philadelphia, Pa. | 16 |
| 65 | t-Dennard, Mark | C | 6-1 | 252 | 11/2/55 | 6 | Texas A&M | Bay City, Tex. | Bryan, Tex. | 8 |
| 25 | DeVaughn, Dennis | CB | 5-10 | 175 | 10/28/60 | 3 | Bishop | Los Angeles, Calif. | Dallas, Tex. | 9 |
| 46 | Edwards, Herman | CB | 6-0 | 190 | 4/27/54 | 8 | San Diego State | Fort Monmouth, N.J. | Seaside, Calif. | 16 |
| 24 | Ellis, Ray | S | 6-1 | 192 | 4/27/59 | 4 | Ohio State | Canton, Ohio | Philadelphia, Pa. | 16 |
| 39 | Everett, Major | FB | 5-10 | 207 | 1/4/60 | 2 | Mississippi College | Monticello, Miss. | New Hebron, Miss. | 16 |
| 67 | Feehery, Gerry | C-G | 6-2 | 268 | 3/9/60 | 2 | Syracuse | Philadelphia, Pa. | Springfield, Pa. | 2 |
| 29 | Foules, Elbert | CB | 5-11 | 185 | 7/4/61 | 2 | Alcorn State | Greenville, Miss. | Greenville, Miss. | 16 |
| 72 | Fritzsche, Jim | T-G | 6-8 | 265 | 10/11/60 | 2 | Purdue | Berea, Ohio | Lindenwold, N.J. | 15 |
| 58 | Griggs, Anthony | LB | 6-3 | 230 | 2/12/60 | 3 | Ohio State | Lawton, Okla. | Sicklerville, N.J. | 16 |
| 26 | Haddix, Michael | FB | 6-2 | 225 | 12/27/61 | 2 | Mississippi State | Tippah County, Miss. | Walnut, Miss. | 14 |
| 35 | †Harrington, Perry | RB | 5-11 | 210 | 3/13/58 | 5 | Jackson State | Bentonia, Miss. | Jackson, Miss. | 15 |
| 68 | Harrison, Dennis | DE | 6-8 | 275 | 7/31/56 | 7 | Vanderbilt | Cleveland, Ohio | Nashville, Tenn. | 16 |
| 85 | Hoover, Melvin | WR | 6-0 | 185 | 8/21/59 | 3 | Arizona State | Charlotte, N.C. | Charlotte, N.C. | 11 |
| 48 | Hopkins, Wes | S | 6-1 | 205 | 9/26/81 | 2 | Southern Methodist | Birmingham, Ala. | Dallas, Tex. | 14 |
| 7 | Jaworski, Ron | QB | 6-2 | 196 | 3/23/51 | 11 | Youngstown State | Lackawanna, N.Y. | West Berlin, N.J. | 16 |
| 84 | Kab, Vyto | TE | 6-5 | 240 | 12/23/59 | 3 | Penn State | Albany, Ga. | Sicklerville, N.J. | 14 |
| 73 | †Kenney, Steve | G | 6-4 | 262 | 12/26/55 | 5 | Clemson | Wilmington, N.C. | Raleigh, N.C. | 16 |
| 52 | Kraynak, Rich | LB | 6-1 | 221 | 1/20/60 | 2 | Pittsburgh | Phoenixville, Pa. | Phoenixville, Pa. | 16 |
| 41 | Logan, Randy | S | 6-1 | 195 | 5/1/51 | 12 | Michigan | Detroit, Mich. | Detroit, Mich. | 16 |
| 64 | Miraldi, Dean | T-G | 6-5 | 254 | 4/8/58 | 2 | Utah | Culver City, Calif. | Newport Beach, Calif. | 13 |
| 74 | Mitchell, Leonard | T | 6-7 | 272 | 10/12/58 | 4 | Houston | Houston, Tex. | Houston, Tex. | 10 |
| 31 | Montgomery, Wilbert | RB | 5-10 | 195 | 9/16/54 | 8 | Abilene Christian | Greenville, Miss. | West Berlin, N.J. | 5 |
| 34 | Oliver, Hubie | FB | 5-10 | 212 | 11/12/57 | 3 | Arizona | Elyria, Ohio | Elyria, Ohio | 16 |
| 62 | Perot, Petey | G | 6-2 | 261 | 4/18/57 | 5 | Northwestern Louisiana | Natchitoches, La. | Natchitoches, La. | 0* |
| 9 | Pisarcik, Joe | QB | 6-4 | 220 | 7/2/52 | 8 | New Mexico State | Wilkes-Barre, Pa. | Bradenton, Fla. | 5 |
| 82 | Quick, Mike | WR | 6-2 | 190 | 5/14/59 | 3 | North Carolina State | Hamlet, N.C. | Sicklerville, N.J. | 16 |
| 56 | Robinson, Jerry | LB | 6-2 | 225 | 12/18/56 | 6 | UCLA | San Francisco, Calif. | West Chester, Pa. | 16 |
| 4 | Runager, Max | P | 6-1 | 189 | 3/24/56 | 6 | South Carolina | Greenwood, S.C. | West Chester, Pa. | 12 |
| •87 | Sampleton, Lawrence | TE | 6-5 | 233 | 9/25/59 | 3 | Texas | Waelder, Tex. | Seguin, Tex. | 7 |
| 53 | Schulz, Jody | LB | 6-4 | 235 | 8/17/60 | 2 | East Carolina | Easton, Md. | Chester, Md. | 6 |
| 76 | Sisemore, Jerry | T | 6-4 | 265 | 7/16/51 | 12 | Texas | Olton, Tex. | Sicklerville, N.J. | 14 |
| 88 | Spagnola, John | TE | 6-4 | 240 | 8/1/57 | 5 | Yale | Stroudsburg, Pa. | Cherry Hill, N.J. | 0* |
| 93 | Strauthers, Thomas | DE | 6-4 | 255 | 4/6/61 | 2 | Jackson State | Wesson, Miss. | Brookhaven, Miss. | 4 |
| 54 | Valentine, Zack | LB | 6-2 | 220 | 5/29/57 | 5 | East Carolina | Edenton, N.C. | Swedesboro, N.J. | 0* |
| 51 | Wilkes, Reggie | LB | 6-4 | 230 | 5/27/56 | 7 | Georgia Tech | Pine Bluff, Ark. | Philadelphia, Pa. | 14 |
| 59 | Williams, Joel | LB | 6-1 | 220 | 12/12/56 | 6 | Wisconsin-LaCrosse | Miami, Fla. | Norcross, Ga. | 16 |
| 32 | Williams, Michael | RB | 6-2 | 217 | 7/16/61 | 2 | Mississippi College | Atmore, Ala. | Atmore, Ala. | 15 |
| 22 | †Wilson, Brenard | S | 6-0 | 175 | 8/15/55 | 6 | Vanderbilt | Daytona Beach, Fla. | Nashville, Tenn. | 16 |
| 83 | Woodruff, Tony | WR | 6-0 | 175 | 11/12/58 | 3 | Fresno State | Hazen, Ark. | Fresno, Calif. | 6 |
| 89 | Young, Glen | WR | 6-2 | 205 | 10/11/60 | 2 | Mississippi State | Greenwood, Miss. | Greenwood, Miss. | 16 |
| 43 | Young, Roynell | CB | 6-1 | 181 | 12/1/57 | 5 | Alcorn State | New Orleans, La. | New Orleans, La. | 16 |

* Perot, Spagnola, and Valentine missed '83 season due to injuries.

†Option playout; subject to developments.

t-Eagles traded for Dennard (Miami).

Traded—Kicker Tony Franklin to New England; defensive end Carl Hairston to Cleveland; linebacker Frank LeMaster to San Francisco.

Retired—John Sciarra, 6-year safety, 10 games in '83; Stan Walters, 12-year tackle, 12 in '83.

Also played with Eagles in '83—WR Harold Carmichael (15 games), TE Al Dixon (9), C Guy Morriss (16), QB Dan Pastorini (3), P Tom Skladany (4), C Mark Slater (16), WR Byron Williams (2).

## COACHING STAFF

### Head Coach, Marion Campbell

**Pro Career:** Campbell was named head coach of the Eagles on January 10, 1983 after six seasons as the club's defensive coordinator. Campbell's first association with the Eagles came in 1956 when, as a defensive lineman, he was traded to Philadelphia by San Francisco. He was the 49ers' fourth-round draft choice in 1951 but spent three years in the Army before he joined the 49ers. During his six-year playing career with the Eagles, Campbell played defensive tackle on the Eagles' 1960 NFL championship team and played in the 1960 and 1961 Pro Bowls. His pro coaching career began in 1962 as an assistant with the Boston Patriots. Two years later he moved into the NFL coaching ranks where he developed outstanding defensive lines at Minnesota (1964-66) and Los Angeles (1967-68). He joined Atlanta in 1969 and was the Falcons' head coach from November of 1974 to October of 1976. His head coaching record was 6-19, including a 4-10 mark in 1975, his only full season as a head coach. He was released by the Falcons after nine games in 1976 and joined the Eagles in 1977. Career record: 11-30.

**Background:** At the University of Georgia, where he played tackle, he was an All-Southeastern Conference selection three times and the team's most valuable player his senior year.

**Personal:** Born May 25, 1929 in Chester, S.C., Marion and his wife, June, live in Medford, N.J. and have two children—Scott and Alicia.

### Assistant Coaches

**Fred Bruney,** assistant head coach-defensive backfield; born December 30, 1931, Martins Ferry, Ohio, lives in Medford, N.J. Back Ohio State 1949-52. Pro defensive back San Francisco 49ers 1953-56, Pittsburgh Steelers 1957, Washington Redskins 1958, Boston Patriots 1960-62. College coach: Ohio State 1959. Pro coach: Boston Patriots 1963, Philadelphia Eagles 1964-68, Atlanta Falcons 1969-76, rejoined Eagles in 1977.

**Chuck Clausen,** defensive line; born June 23, 1940, Anamosa, Iowa, lives in Mount Laurel, N.J. Defensive lineman New Mexico 1961-63. No pro playing experience. College coach: William & Mary 1969-70, Ohio State 1971-75. Pro coach: Joined Eagles in 1976.

**Tom Coughlin,** wide receivers; born August 31, 1946, Waterloo, N.Y., lives in Medford, N.J. Wingback Syracuse 1965-67. No pro playing experience. College coach: Syracuse 1968, 1974-1980, Rochester Institute of Technology 1969-73 (head coach 1970-73), Boston College 1981-83. Pro coach: First year with Eagles.

**Frank Gansz,** tight ends-special teams; born November 22, 1938, Altoona, Pa., lives in Cherry Hill, N.J. Center Navy 1957-59. No pro playing experience. College coach: Air Force 1964-66, Colgate 1968, Navy 1969-72, Oklahoma State 1973, 1975, Army 1974, UCLA 1976-77. Pro coach: San Francisco 49ers 1978, Cincinnati Bengals 1979-80, Kansas City Chiefs 1981-82, joined Eagles in 1983.

**George Hill,** linebackers; born April 28, 1933, Bay Village, Ohio, lives in Mount Laurel, N.J. Tackle-fullback Denison 1954-57. No pro playing experience. College coach: Findlay 1959, Denison 1960-64, Cornell 1965, Duke 1966-70, Ohio State 1971-78. Pro coach: Joined Eagles in 1979.

**Ken Iman,** offensive line; born February 8, 1939, St. Louis, Mo., lives in Springfield, Pa. Center-linebacker Southeast Missouri State 1956-59. Pro center Green Bay Packers 1960-63, Los Angeles Rams 1964-74. Pro coach: Joined Eagles in 1976.

**Ted Marchibroda,** offensive coordinator; born March 15, 1931, Franklin, Pa., lives in Philadelphia. Quarterback St. Bonaventure 1950-51, Detroit 1952. Pro quarterback Pittsburgh Steelers 1953, 1955-56, Chicago Cardinals 1957. Pro coach: Washington Redskins 1961-65, 1971-74, Los Angeles Rams 1966-1970, Baltimore Colts (head coach) 1975-79, Chicago Bears 1981, Detroit Lions 1982-83, first year with Eagles.

**Billie Matthews,** running backs; born March 15, 1930, Houston, Tex., lives in Medford, N.J. Quarterback Southern University 1954-57. No pro playing experience. College coach: Kansas 1970, UCLA 1971-78. Pro coach: San Francisco 49ers 1979-82, joined Eagles in 1983.

## PHILADELPHIA EAGLES 1984 FIRST-YEAR ROSTER

| Name | Pos. | Ht. | Wt. | Birth-date | College | Birthplace | Residence | How Acq. |
|------|------|-----|-----|-----------|---------|-----------|-----------|----------|
| Asmus, Jim (1) | K | 6-2 | 195 | 12/2/58 | Hawaii | Meppal, Holland | La Puente, Calif. | FA |
| Cooper, Evan | CB-S-KR | 5-11 | 180 | 6/28/62 | Michigan | Miami, Fla. | Miami, Fla. | D4 |
| Evans, Leon (1) | DE | 6-6 | 265 | 10/12/61 | Miami | Washington, D.C. | Silver Spring, Md. | FA |
| Hardy, Andre | RB-KR | 6-1 | 233 | 11/28/61 | St. Mary's, Calif. | San Diego, Calif. | San Diego, Calif. | D5 |
| Hayes, Joe | RB-KR | 5-9 | 185 | 9/15/60 | Central State, Okla. | Dallas, Tex. | Dallas, Tex. | D7 |
| Gaynor, Ronald (1) | QB | 6-2 | 207 | 12/15/59 | West Chester State | Akron, Ohio | Jacobus, Pa. | FA |
| Gross, Lynnard (1) | G | 6-3 | 275 | 8/1/60 | Delaware State | Philadelphia, Pa. | Philadelphia, Pa. | FA |
| Horan, Michael (1) | P | 5-11 | 190 | 2/1/59 | Long Beach State | Orange, Calif. | Anaheim, Calif. | FA |
| Jackson, Kenny | WR | 6-0 | 180 | 2/15/62 | Penn State | Neptune, N.J. | South River, N.J. | D1 |
| Jelesky, Tom (1) | T | 6-6 | 290 | 10/4/60 | Purdue | Gary, Ind. | Philadelphia, Pa. | FA |
| Mangrum, David (1) | QB | 6-4 | 196 | 10/14/59 | Baylor | Harlinger, Tex. | Waco, Tex. | D12('83) |
| Matsakis, Manny | K | 5-10 | 200 | 4/16/62 | Capital | New Britain, Conn. | Shadyside, Ohio | D8 |
| McFadden, Paul | K | 5-11 | 160 | 9/24/61 | Youngstown State | Cleveland, Ohio | Euclid, Ohio | D12 |
| Polonz, Mark (1) | G | 6-5 | 265 | 6/3/61 | Central Michigan | Lansing, Mich. | New Boston, Mich. | FA |
| Raridon, Scott | T-G | 6-3 | 288 | 2/22/61 | Nebraska | Newton, Iowa | Mason City, Iowa | D6 |
| Robertson, John | G-T | 6-5 | 270 | 9/26/61 | East Carolina | Eden, N.C. | Eden, N.C. | D11 |
| Russell, Rusty | T | 6-5 | 295 | 8/16/63 | South Carolina | Orangeburg, S.C. | Orangeburg, S.C. | D3 |
| Sperbeck, Marshall (1) | QB | 6-3 | 210 | 5/19/60 | Nevada-Reno | Sacramento, Calif. | Sacramento, Calif. | FA |
| Thomas, John | CB-S-KR | 6-0 | 200 | 1/7/62 | Texas Christian | Paris, Tex. | Paris, Tex. | D10 |
| Tolbert, Willie (1) | RB | 6-2 | 212 | 8/1/59 | Cheyney State | Hastings, Fla. | West Chester, Pa. | FA |
| Woetzel, Keith (1) | LB | 6-2 | 223 | 11/15/60 | Rutgers | Ridgewood, N.J. | Waldwick, N.J. | FA |

Players who report to an NFL team for the first time are designated on rosters as rookies (R). If a player reported to an NFL training camp in a previous year but was not on the active squad for three or more regular season or postseason games, he is listed on the first-year roster and designated by a (1). Thereafter, a player who is on the active squad for three or more regular season or postseason games is credited with an additional year of playing experience.

## NOTES

**National Football Conference
Eastern Division**

**Team Colors:** Cardinal Red, Black,
and White

**Busch Stadium, Box 888
St. Louis, Missouri 63188
Telephone: (314) 421-0777**

### Club Officials

Chairman of the Board, CEO: William V. Bidwill
President: Bing Devine
Vice President/Administration: Curt Mosher
Secretary and General Counsel: Thomas J.
Guilfoil
Treasurer: Charley Schlegel
Director of Pro Personnel: Larry Wilson
Director of Player Personnel: George Boone
Public Relations Director: Michael Menchel
Media Coordinator: Greg Gladysiewski
Director of Community Relations: Adele Harris
Ticket Manager: Steve Walsh
Trainer: John Omohundro
Assistant Trainers: Jim Shearer, Ed Fleming
Equipment Manager: Bill Simmons
Assistant Equipment Managers: Mark Ahlmeier,
Eric Youngstrom

**Stadium:** Busch Memorial Stadium •
**Capacity:** 51,392
200 Stadium Plaza
St. Louis, Missouri 63102

**Playing Surface:** AstroTurf

**Training Camp:** Eastern Illinois University
Charleston, Illinois 61920

## 1984 SCHEDULE

### Preseason

| | | |
|---|---|---|
| Aug. 4 | at Chicago | 6:00 |
| Aug. 10 | **Kansas City** | 7:30 |
| Aug. 17 | at Seattle | 7:30 |
| Aug. 24 | **Minnesota** | 7:30 |

### Regular Season

| | | |
|---|---|---|
| Sept. 2 | at Green Bay | 12:00 |
| Sept. 9 | **Buffalo** | 12:00 |
| Sept. 16 | at Colts | 12:00 |
| Sept. 23 | at New Orleans | 12:00 |
| Sept. 30 | **Miami** | 12:00 |
| Oct. 7 | at Dallas | 12:00 |
| Oct. 14 | **Chicago** | 12:00 |
| Oct. 21 | **Washington** | 12:00 |
| Oct. 28 | at Philadelphia | 1:00 |
| Nov. 4 | **Los Angeles Rams** | 12:00 |
| Nov. 11 | **Dallas** | 12:00 |
| Nov. 18 | at New York Giants | 1:00 |
| Nov. 25 | **Philadelphia** | 12:00 |
| Dec. 2 | at New England | 1:00 |
| Dec. 9 | **New York Giants** | 12:00 |
| Dec. 16 | at Washington | 1:00 |

## CARDINALS COACHING HISTORY

### Chicago 1920-59
### (327-427-38)

| | | |
|---|---|---|
| 1920 | Marshall Smith | 5-2-1 |
| 1921-22 | John (Paddy) Driscoll | 12-6-3 |
| 1923-24 | Arnold Horween | 13-8-1 |
| 1925-26 | Norman Barry | 16-8-2 |
| 1927 | Fred Gillies | 3-7-1 |
| 1928 | Guy Chamberlin | 1-5-0 |
| 1929-30 | Ernie Nevers | 11-12-3 |
| 1931 | LeRoy Andrews* | 0-2-0 |
| 1931 | Ernie Nevers | 5-2-0 |
| 1932 | Jack Chevigny | 2-6-2 |
| 1933-34 | Paul Schissler | 6-15-1 |
| 1935-38 | Milan Creighton | 16-26-4 |
| 1939 | Ernie Nevers | 1-10-0 |
| 1940-42 | Jimmy Conzelman | 8-22-3 |
| 1943-45 | Phil Handler** | 1-29-0 |
| 1946-48 | Jimmy Conzelman | 27-10-0 |
| 1949 | Phil Handler-Buddy Parker*** | 6-5-1 |
| 1950-51 | Earl (Curly) Lambeau | 8-16-0 |
| 1952 | Joe Kuharich | 4-8-0 |
| 1953-54 | Joe Stydahar | 3-20-1 |
| 1955-57 | Ray Richards | 14-21-1 |
| 1958-61 | Frank (Pop) Ivy | 17-31-2 |
| 1962-65 | Wally Lemm | 27-26-3 |
| 1966-70 | Charley Winner | 35-30-5 |
| 1971-72 | Bob Hollway | 8-18-2 |
| 1973-77 | Don Coryell | 42-29-1 |
| 1978-79 | Bud Wilkinson**** | 9-20-0 |
| 1979 | Larry Wilson | 2-1-0 |
| 1980-83 | Jim Hanifan | 25-32-1 |

*Resigned after two games in 1931
**Co-coach with Walt Kiesling of 1944 Card-Pitt team
***Co-coaches
****Released after 13 games in 1979

## RECORD HOLDERS
### Individual Records—Career

| Category | Name | Performance |
|---|---|---|
| Rushing (Yds.) | Ottis Anderson, 1979-1983 | 6,190 |
| Passing (Yds.) | Jim Hart, 1966-1983 | 34,639 |
| Passing (TDs) | Jim Hart, 1966-1983 | 209 |
| Receiving (No.) | Jackie Smith, 1963-1977 | 480 |
| Receiving (Yds.) | Jackie Smith, 1963-1977 | 7,918 |
| Interceptions | Larry Wilson, 1960-1972 | 52 |
| Punting (Avg.) | Jerry Norton, 1959-1961 | 44.9 |
| Punt Return (Avg.) | Charley Trippi, 1947-1955 | 13.7 |
| Kickoff Return (Avg.) | Ollie Matson, 1952, 1954-58 | 28.5 |
| Field Goals | Jim Bakken, 1962-1978 | 282 |
| Touchdowns (Tot.) | Sonny Randle, 1959-1966 | 60 |
| Points | Jim Bakken, 1962-1978 | 1,380 |

### Individual Records—Single Season

| Category | Name | Performance |
|---|---|---|
| Rushing (Yds.) | Ottis Anderson, 1979 | 1,605 |
| Passing (Yds.) | Charley Johnson, 1963 | 3,280 |
| Passing (TDs) | Charley Johnson, 1963 | 28 |
| Receiving (No.) | Roy Green, 1983 | 78 |
| Receiving (Yds.) | Roy Green, 1983 | 1,227 |
| Interceptions | Bob Nussbaumer, 1949 | 12 |
| Punting (Avg.) | Jerry Norton, 1960 | 45.6 |
| Punt Return (Avg.) | John (Red) Cochran, 1949 | 20.9 |
| Kickoff Return (Avg.) | Ollie Matson, 1958 | 35.5 |
| Field Goals | Jim Bakken, 1967 | 27 |
| Touchdowns (Tot.) | John David Crow, 1962 | 17 |
| Points | Jim Bakken, 1967 | 117 |

### Individual Records—Single Game

| Category | Name | Performance |
|---|---|---|
| Rushing (Yds.) | John David Crow, 12-18-60 | 203 |
| Passing (Yds.) | Charley Johnson, 10-13-63 | 428 |
| Passing (TDs) | Jim Hardy, 10-2-50 | 6 |
| | Charley Johnson, 9-26-65, 11-2-69 | 6 |
| Receiving (No.) | Sonny Randle, 11-4-62 | 16 |
| Receiving (Yds.) | Sonny Randle, 11-4-62 | 256 |
| Interceptions | Bob Nussbaumer, 11-13-49 | 4 |
| | Jerry Norton, 11-20-60 | 4 |
| Field Goals | Jim Bakken, 9-24-67 | 7 |
| Touchdowns (Tot.) | Ernie Nevers, 11-28-29 | 6 |
| Points | Ernie Nevers, 11-28-29 | 40 |

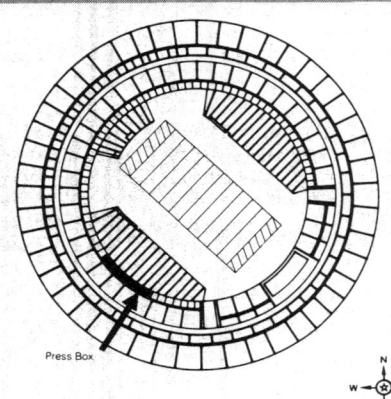

**BUSCH MEMORIAL STADIUM**

Press Box

## 1983 TEAM STATISTICS

| | St. Louis | Opp. |
|---|---|---|
| Total First Downs | 296 | 286 |
| Rushing | 123 | 107 |
| Passing | 147 | 161 |
| Penalty | 26 | 18 |
| Third Down Efficiency | 84/224 | 66/207 |
| Third Down Percentage | 37.5 | 31.9 |
| Total Net Yards | 5145 | 5005 |
| Total Offensive Plays | 1044 | 1021 |
| Avg. Gain per Play | 4.9 | 4.9 |
| Avg. Gain per Game | 321.6 | 312.8 |
| Net Yards Rushing | 2277 | 1838 |
| Total Rushing Plays | 525 | 443 |
| Avg. Gain per Rush | 4.3 | 4.1 |
| Avg. Gain Rushing per Game | 142.3 | 114.9 |
| Net Yards Passing | 2868 | 3167 |
| Lost Attempting to Pass | 59/441 | 59/468 |
| Gross Yards Passing | 3309 | 3635 |
| Attempts/Completions | 460/267 | 519/290 |
| Percent Completed | 58.0 | 55.9 |
| Had Intercepted | 21 | 28 |
| Avg. Net Passing per Game | 179.3 | 197.9 |
| Punts/Avg. | 85/41.5 | 88/40.3 |
| Punt Returns/Avg. | 58/7.9 | 47/6.5 |
| Kickoff Returns/Avg. | 72/20.3 | 66/19.7 |
| Interceptions/Avg. Ret. | 28/9.5 | 21/18.3 |
| Penalties/Yards | 89/770 | 102/819 |
| Fumbles/Ball Lost | 50/27 | 32/20 |
| Total Points | 374 | 428 |
| Avg. Points per Game | 23.4 | 26.8 |
| Touchdowns | 47 | 56 |
| Rushing | 15 | 23 |
| Passing | 29 | 24 |
| Returns and Recoveries | 3 | 9 |
| Field Goals | 15/28 | 12/15 |
| Conversions | 45/47 | 54/56 |
| Safeties | 1 | 1 |
| Avg. Time of Possession | 31:20 | 28:40 |

## 1983 TEAM RECORD
### Preseason (1-3)

| Date | St. Louis | | Opponents |
|---|---|---|---|
| 8/6 | 10 | Minnesota | 28 |
| 8/13 | 27 | *Chicago (OT) | 24 |
| 8/20 | 16 | Kansas City | 17 |
| 8/27 | 27 | *Green Bay | 39 |
| | 80 | | 108 |

### Regular Season (8-7-1)

| Date | St. Louis | | Opp. | Att. |
|---|---|---|---|---|
| 9/4 | 17 | New Orleans | 28 | 65,225 |
| 9/11 | 17 | *Dallas | 34 | 48,532 |
| 9/18 | 27 | *San Francisco | 42 | 38,130 |
| 9/25 | 14 | Philadelphia | 11 | 64,465 |
| 10/2 | 14 | Kansas City | 38 | 58,975 |
| 10/9 | 14 | *Washington | 38 | 42,698 |
| 10/16 | 34 | Tampa Bay | 27 | 48,244 |
| 10/24 | 20 | *New York Giants (OT) | 20 | 45,630 |
| 10/30 | 41 | *Minnesota | 31 | 38,796 |
| 11/6 | 7 | Washington | 45 | 51,380 |
| 11/13 | 33 | *Seattle | 28 | 33,280 |
| 11/20 | 44 | *San Diego | 14 | 40,644 |
| 11/24 | 17 | Dallas | 35 | 60,764 |
| 12/4 | 10 | New York Giants | 6 | 25,156 |
| 12/11 | 34 | Los Angeles Raiders | 24 | 32,111 |
| 12/18 | 31 | *Philadelphia | 7 | 21,902 |
| | 374 | | 428 | 715,932 |

*Home Game       (OT) Overtime

### Score by Periods

| | | | | | | | |
|---|---|---|---|---|---|---|---|
| St. Louis | 79 | 128 | 86 | 81 | 0 | — | 374 |
| Opponents | 88 | 124 | 105 | 111 | 0 | — | 428 |

### Attendance
Home 309,612    Away 406,320    Total 715,932
Single game home record, 50,885 (9-2-79)
Single season home record, 384,375 (1981)

## 1983 INDIVIDUAL STATISTICS

### Rushing

| | Att. | Yds. | Avg. | LG | TD |
|---|---|---|---|---|---|
| Anderson | 296 | 1270 | 4.3 | 43 | 5 |
| Mitchell | 68 | 373 | 5.5 | 46 | 3 |
| Morris | 75 | 257 | 3.4 | 17 | 2 |
| Lomax | 27 | 127 | 4.7 | 35 | 2 |
| Love | 35 | 103 | 2.9 | 16 | 2 |
| Ferrell | 7 | 53 | 7.6 | 21 | 1 |
| Green | 4 | 49 | 12.3 | 25 | 0 |
| Harrell | 4 | 13 | 3.3 | 8 | 0 |
| Hart | 5 | 12 | 2.4 | 13 | 0 |
| Sharpe | 1 | 11 | 11.0 | 11 | 0 |
| Lisch | 2 | 9 | 4.5 | 5 | 0 |
| Perrin | 1 | 0 | 0.0 | 0 | 0 |
| St. Louis | 525 | 2277 | 4.3 | 46 | 15 |
| Opponents | 443 | 1838 | 4.1 | 76t | 23 |

### Passing

| | Att. | Comp. | Pct. | Yds. | TD | Int. | Tkld. | Rate |
|---|---|---|---|---|---|---|---|---|
| Lomax | 354 | 209 | 59.0 | 2636 | 24 | 11 | 43/315 | 92.0 |
| Hart | 91 | 50 | 54.9 | 592 | 4 | 8 | 13/99 | 53.0 |
| Lisch | 13 | 6 | 46.2 | 66 | 1 | 2 | 3/27 | 47.8 |
| Birdsong | 1 | 1 | 100.0 | 11 | 0 | 0 | 0/0 | 112.5 |
| Perrin | 1 | 1 | 100.0 | 4 | 0 | 0 | 0/0 | 83.3 |
| St. Louis | 460 | 267 | 58.0 | 3309 | 29 | 21 | 59/441 | 82.4 |
| Opponents | 519 | 290 | 55.9 | 3635 | 24 | 28 | 59/468 | 70.8 |

### Receiving

| | No. | Yds. | Avg. | LG | TD |
|---|---|---|---|---|---|
| Green | 78 | 1227 | 15.7 | 71t | 14 |
| Anderson | 54 | 459 | 8.5 | 40 | 1 |
| Tilley | 44 | 690 | 15.7 | 71t | 5 |
| Marsh | 32 | 421 | 13.2 | 38 | 8 |
| Morris | 14 | 55 | 3.9 | 11 | 0 |
| LaFleur | 12 | 99 | 8.3 | 21 | 0 |
| Shumann | 11 | 154 | 14.0 | 33 | 0 |
| Mitchell | 7 | 54 | 7.7 | 17 | 0 |
| Love | 6 | 58 | 9.7 | 16 | 1 |
| Harrell | 3 | 25 | 8.3 | 13 | 0 |
| Thompson | 2 | 31 | 15.5 | 22 | 0 |
| Pittman | 2 | 21 | 10.5 | 11 | 0 |
| McGill | 1 | 11 | 11.0 | 11 | 0 |
| Ahrens | 1 | 4 | 4.0 | 4 | 0 |
| St. Louis | 267 | 3309 | 12.4 | 71t | 29 |
| Opponents | 290 | 3635 | 12.5 | 69t | 24 |

### Interceptions

| | No. | Yds. | Avg. | LG | TD |
|---|---|---|---|---|---|
| Washington | 8 | 92 | 11.5 | 26 | 0 |
| Perrin | 4 | 50 | 12.5 | 30 | 0 |
| Junior | 3 | 27 | 9.0 | 19 | 0 |
| Mack | 3 | 25 | 8.3 | 13 | 0 |
| Harris | 3 | 10 | 3.3 | 10 | 0 |
| A. Baker | 2 | 24 | 12.0 | 19 | 0 |
| W. Smith | 2 | 3 | 1.5 | 3 | 0 |
| Galloway | 1 | 17 | 17.0 | 17 | 0 |
| Grooms | 1 | 10 | 10.0 | 10 | 0 |
| Nelson | 1 | 8 | 8.0 | 8 | 0 |
| St. Louis | 28 | 266 | 9.5 | 30 | 0 |
| Opponents | 21 | 385 | 18.3 | 70t | 5 |

### Punting

| | No. | Yds. | Avg. | In 20 | LG |
|---|---|---|---|---|---|
| Birdsong | 85 | 3529 | 41.5 | 14 | 59 |
| St. Louis | 85 | 3529 | 41.5 | 14 | 59 |
| Opponents | 88 | 3545 | 40.3 | 21 | 56 |

### Punt Returns

| | No. | FC | Yds. | Avg. | LG | TD |
|---|---|---|---|---|---|---|
| Mitchell | 38 | 1 | 337 | 8.9 | 34 | 0 |
| Bird | 14 | 2 | 76 | 5.4 | 16 | 0 |
| Harrell | 5 | 1 | 31 | 6.2 | 11 | 0 |
| Ferrell | 1 | 0 | 17 | 17.0 | 17 | 0 |
| St. Louis | 58 | 4 | 461 | 7.9 | 34 | 0 |
| Opponents | 47 | 13 | 307 | 6.5 | 19 | 0 |

### Kickoff Returns

| | No. | Yds. | Avg. | LG | TD |
|---|---|---|---|---|---|
| Mitchell | 36 | 778 | 21.6 | 66 | 0 |
| Ferrell | 13 | 257 | 19.8 | 28 | 0 |
| Bird | 9 | 194 | 21.6 | 33 | 0 |
| Schmitt | 4 | 41 | 10.3 | 19 | 0 |
| Harrell | 3 | 62 | 20.7 | 26 | 0 |
| Love | 3 | 71 | 23.7 | 23 | 0 |
| Allerman | 1 | 11 | 11.0 | 11 | 0 |
| Duda | 1 | 12 | 12.0 | 12 | 0 |
| Green | 1 | 14 | 14.0 | 14 | 0 |
| L. Smith | 1 | 19 | 19.0 | 19 | 0 |
| St. Louis | 72 | 1459 | 20.3 | 66 | 0 |
| Opponents | 66 | 1300 | 19.7 | 94t | 1 |

### Scoring

| | TD | TD R | TD P | TD Rt | PAT | FG | TP |
|---|---|---|---|---|---|---|---|
| O'Donoghue | | | | | 45/47 | 15/28 | 90 |
| Green | 14 | 0 | 14 | 0 | | | 84 |
| Marsh | 8 | 0 | 8 | 0 | | | 48 |
| Anderson | 6 | 5 | 1 | 0 | | | 36 |
| Tilley | 5 | 0 | 5 | 0 | | | 30 |
| Love | 3 | 2 | 1 | 0 | | | 18 |
| Mitchell | 3 | 3 | 0 | 0 | | | 18 |
| Lomax | 2 | 2 | 0 | 0 | | | 12 |
| Morris | 2 | 2 | 0 | 0 | | | 12 |
| Ferrell | 1 | 1 | 0 | 0 | | | 6 |
| Grooms | 1 | 0 | 0 | 1 | | | 6 |
| Nelson | 1 | 0 | 0 | 1 | | | 6 |
| Perrin | 1 | 0 | 0 | 1 | | | 6 |
| Galloway | | | (Safety) | | | | 2 |
| St. Louis | 47 | 15 | 29 | 3 | 45/47 | 15/28 | 374 |
| Opponents | 56 | 23 | 24 | 9 | 54/56 | 12/15 | 428 |

## FIRST-ROUND SELECTIONS

(If Club had no first-round selection, first player drafted is listed with round in parentheses.)

| Year | Player, College, Position |
|---|---|
| 1936 | Jim Lawrence, Texas Christian, B |
| 1937 | Ray Buivid, Marquette, B |
| 1938 | Jack Robbins, Arkansas, B |
| 1939 | Charles (Ki) Aldrich, Texas Christian, C |
| 1940 | George Cafego, Tennessee, B |
| 1941 | John Kimbrough, Texas A&M, B |
| 1942 | Steve Lach, Duke, B |
| 1943 | Glenn Dobbs, Tulsa, B |
| 1944 | Pat Harder, Wisconsin, B |
| 1945 | Charley Trippi, Georgia, B |
| 1946 | Dub Jones, Louisiana State, B |
| 1947 | DeWitt (Tex) Coulter, Army, T |
| 1948 | Jim Spavital, Oklahoma A&M, B |
| 1949 | Bill Fischer, Notre Dame, G |
| 1950 | Jack Jennings, Ohio State, T (2) |
| 1951 | Jerry Groom, Notre Dame, C |
| 1952 | Ollie Matson, San Francisco, B |
| 1953 | Johnny Olszewski, California, B |
| 1954 | Lamar McHan, Arkansas, B |
| 1955 | Max Boydston, Oklahoma, E |
| 1956 | Joe Childress, Auburn, B |
| 1957 | Jerry Tubbs, Oklahoma, C |
| 1958 | King Hill, Rice, B |
| | John David Crow, Texas A&M, B |
| 1959 | Bill Stacy, Mississippi State, B |
| 1960 | George Izo, Notre Dame, QB |
| 1961 | Ken Rice, Auburn, T |
| 1962 | Fate Echols, Northwestern, DT |
| | Irv Goode, Kentucky, B |
| 1963 | Jerry Stovall, Louisiana State, S |
| | Don Brumm, Purdue, DE |
| 1964 | Ken Kortas, Louisville, DT |
| 1965 | Joe Namath, Alabama, QB |
| 1966 | Carl McAdams, Oklahoma, LB |
| 1967 | Dave Williams, Washington, WR |
| 1968 | MacArthur Lane, Utah State, RB |
| 1969 | Roger Wehrli, Missouri, DB |
| 1970 | Larry Stegent, Texas A&M, RB |
| 1971 | Norm Thompson, Utah, CB |
| 1972 | Bobby Moore, Oregon, RB-WR |
| 1973 | Dave Butz, Purdue, DT |
| 1974 | J. V. Cain, Colorado, TE |
| 1975 | Tim Gray, Texas A&M, DB |
| 1976 | Mike Dawson, Arizona, DT |
| 1977 | Steve Pisarkiewicz, Missouri, QB |
| 1978 | Steve Little, Arkansas, K |
| | Ken Greene, Washington State, DB |
| 1979 | Ottis Anderson, Miami, RB |
| 1980 | Curtis Greer, Michigan, DE |
| 1981 | E. J. Junior, Alabama, LB |
| 1982 | Luis Sharpe, UCLA, T |
| 1983 | Leonard Smith, McNeese State, DB |
| 1984 | Clyde Duncan, Tennessee, WR |

## ST. LOUIS CARDINALS 1984 VETERAN ROSTER

| No. | Name | Pos. | Ht. | Wt. | Birth-date | NFL Exp. | College | Birthplace | Residence | Games in '83 |
|-----|------|------|-----|-----|-----------|----------|---------|------------|-----------|--------------|
| 58 | Ahrens, Dave | LB | 6-3 | 228 | 12/5/58 | 4 | Wisconsin | Cedar Falls, Iowa | St. Louis, Mo. | 16 |
| 51 | Allerman, Kurt | LB | 6-2 | 222 | 8/30/50 | 8 | Penn State | Glenridge, N.J. | Ballwin, Mo. | 16 |
| 32 | Anderson, Ottis | RB | 6-2 | 220 | 1/19/57 | 6 | Miami | West Palm Beach, Fla. | St. Louis, Mo. | 15 |
| 61 | Audick, Dan | G-T | 6-3 | 253 | 11/15/54 | 7 | Hawaii | San Bernardino, Calif. | San Diego, Calif. | 12 |
| 60 | Baker, Al | DE | 6-6 | 260 | 12/9/56 | 7 | Colorado State | Jacksonville, Fla. | St. Louis, Mo. | 16 |
| 52 | Baker, Charlie | LB | 6-2 | 217 | 9/26/57 | 5 | New Mexico | Mt. Pleasant, Tex. | St. Louis, Mo. | 16 |
| 82 | Bird, Steve | WR | 5-11 | 171 | 10/20/60 | 2 | Eastern Kentucky | Indianapolis, Ind. | Corbin, Ky. | 14 |
| 18 | Birdsong, Carl | P | 6-0 | 192 | 1/1/59 | 4 | S.W. Oklahoma State | Kaufman, Tex. | Amarillo, Tex. | 16 |
| 71 | Bostic, Joe | G | 6-3 | 265 | 4/20/57 | 6 | Clemson | Greensboro, N.C. | St. Louis, Mo. | 14 |
| 69 | †Brown, Rush | DT | 6-2 | 260 | 6/27/54 | 5 | Ball State | Laurinburg, N.C. | Chesterfield, Mo. | 6 |
| 64 | Clark, Randy | C | 6-3 | 254 | 7/27/57 | 5 | Northern Illinois | Chicago, Ill. | St. Ann, Mo. | 14 |
| 59 | Davis, Paul | LB | 6-3 | 210 | 7/10/58 | 4 | North Carolina | Wise, Va. | Norcross, Ga. | 9* |
| 73 | Duda, Mark | DT | 6-3 | 263 | 2/4/61 | 2 | Maryland | Wilkes-Barre, Pa. | Plymouth, Pa. | 14 |
| 31 | Ferrell, Earl | RB | 6-0 | 215 | 3/27/58 | 3 | East Tennessee State | Halifax, Va. | South Boston, Va. | 16 |
| 65 | Galloway, David | DT | 6-3 | 277 | 2/16/59 | 3 | Florida | Tampa, Fla. | Creve Coeur, Mo. | 16 |
| 81 | Green, Roy | WR | 6-0 | 195 | 6/30/57 | 6 | Henderson State | Magnolia, Ark. | St. Louis, Mo. | 16 |
| 75 | Greer, Curtis | DE | 6-4 | 252 | 11/10/57 | 5 | Michigan | Detroit, Mich. | St. Louis, Mo. | 16 |
| 35 | Griffin, Jeff | CB | 6-0 | 185 | 7/19/58 | 4 | Utah | Carson, Calif. | University City, Mo. | 3 |
| 78 | †Grooms, Elois | DT | 6-4 | 250 | 5/20/53 | 9 | Tennessee Tech | Tomkinsville, Ky. | Mandeville, La. | 11 |
| 39 | Harrell, Willard | RB | 5-8 | 182 | 9/16/52 | 10 | Pacific | Stockton, Calif. | St. Louis, Mo. | 14 |
| 50 | Harris, Bob | LB | 6-2 | 205 | 11/11/60 | 2 | Auburn | Everett, Wash. | Stone Mountain, Ga. | 8 |
| 46 | Heflin, Victor | CB | 6-0 | 184 | 7/7/60 | 2 | Delaware State | Springfield, Mass. | Dayton, Ohio | 8 |
| 54 | Junior, E.J. | LB | 6-3 | 235 | 12/8/59 | 4 | Alabama | Sallsburg, N.C. | Florissant, Mo. | 12 |
| 89 | LaFleur, Greg | TE | 6-4 | 236 | 9/16/58 | 4 | Louisiana State | Lafayette, La. | Baton Rouge, La. | 16 |
| 16 | Lisch, Rusty | QB | 6-3 | 213 | 12/21/56 | 5 | Notre Dame | Belleville, Ill. | Belleville, Ill. | 4 |
| 15 | Lomax, Neil | QB | 6-3 | 215 | 2/17/59 | 4 | Portland State | Portland, Ore. | West Linn, Ore. | 13 |
| 40 | †Love, Randy | FB | 6-1 | 205 | 9/30/56 | 6 | Houston | Wylie. Tex. | Garland, Tex. | 16 |
| 47 | Mack, Cedric | CB | 6-0 | 190 | 9/14/60 | 2 | Baylor | Freeport, Tex. | Freeport, Tex. | 16 |
| 80 | Marsh, Doug | TE | 6-3 | 240 | 6/18/58 | 5 | Michigan | Akron, Ohio | St. Louis, Mo. | 16 |
| 76 | †Mays, Stafford | DE | 6-2 | 250 | 3/13/58 | 5 | Washington | Lawrence, Kan. | Tacoma, Wash. | 16 |
| 87 | McGill, Eddie | TE | 6-6 | 225 | 7/5/60 | 2 | Western Carolina | Asheville, N.C. | Candler, N.C. | 2 |
| 30 | Mitchell, Stump | RB | 5-9 | 188 | 3/15/59 | 4 | Citadel | St. Mary's, Ga. | St. Louis, Mo. | 15 |
| 24 | Morris, Wayne | FB | 6-0 | 210 | 5/3/54 | 9 | Southern Methodist | Dallas, Tex. | Dallas, Tex. | 15 |
| 38 | †Nelson, Lee | S | 5-10 | 185 | 1/30/54 | 9 | Florida State | Kissimee, Fla. | Tallahassee, Fla. | 16 |
| 11 | O'Donoghue, Neil | K | 6-6 | 210 | 6/18/53 | 8 | Auburn | Dublin, Ireland | Indian Rocks, Fla. | 16 |
| 57 | †Parlavecchio, Chet | LB | 6-2 | 225 | 2/14/60 | 2 | Penn State | Newark, N.J. | West Orange, N.J. | 12* |
| 23 | Perrin, Benny | S | 6-2 | 178 | 10/20/59 | 3 | Alabama | Orange County, Calif. | Decatur, Ga. | 16 |
| 85 | Pittman, Danny | WR | 6-2 | 205 | 4/3/58 | 5 | Wyoming | Memphis, Tenn. | Pasadena, Calif. | 12* |
| 70 | Plunkett, Art | T | 6-7 | 270 | 3/8/59 | 4 | Nevada-Las Vegas | Chicago, Ill. | Henderson, Nev. | 16 |
| 63 | Robbins, Tootie | T | 6-4 | 278 | 6/2/58 | 3 | East Carolina | Windsor, N.C. | St. Louis, Mo. | 13 |
| 26 | Schmitt, George | S | 5-11 | 193 | 3/6/61 | 2 | Delaware | Bryn Mawr, Pa. | Broomall, Pa. | 16 |
| 56 | Scott, Carlos | C | 6-4 | 300 | 7/2/60 | 2 | Texas-El Paso | Hempstead, Tex. | Hempstead, Tex. | 13 |
| 53 | Shaffer, Craig | LB | 6-0 | 230 | 3/31/59 | 3 | Indiana State | Terre Haute, Ind. | St. Louis, Mo. | 9 |
| 67 | Sharpe, Luis | T | 6-4 | 260 | 6/16/60 | 3 | UCLA | Havana, Cuba | Maryland Heights, Mo. | 16 |
| 84 | Shumann, Mike | WR | 6-1 | 185 | 10/13/55 | 7 | Florida State | Louisville, Ky. | Woodside, Calif. | 16 |
| 45 | Smith, Leonard | S | 5-11 | 190 | 9/2/60 | 2 | McNeese State | New Orleans, La. | Chesterfield, Mo. | 16 |
| 44 | Smith, Wayne | CB | 6-0 | 175 | 5/9/57 | 5 | Purdue | Chicago, Ill. | St. Louis, Mo. | 16 |
| 68 | †Stieve, Terry | G | 6-2 | 265 | 3/10/54 | 8 | Wisconsin | Baraboo, Wis. | St. Louis, Mo. | 16 |
| 83 | Tilley, Pat | WR | 5-10 | 178 | 2/15/53 | 9 | Louisiana Tech | Marshall, Tex. | Shreveport, La. | 16 |
| 48 | Washington, Lionel | CB | 6-0 | 184 | 10/21/60 | 2 | Tulane | New Orleans, La. | Lutcher, La. | 16 |
| 55 | Whitaker, Bill | LB | 6-0 | 182 | 11/18/59 | 4 | Missouri | Kansas City, Mo. | Columbia, Mo. | 7 |

* Davis played 3 games with New York Giants in '83, 6 with St. Louis; Parlavecchio played 3 games with Green Bay, 9 with St. Louis; Pittman played 8 games with New York Giants, 4 with St. Louis.

†Option playout; subject to developments.

Retired—Dan Dierdorf, 12-year center, 7 games in '83.

Also played with Cardinals in '83—DE Russ Brown (6 games), LB Jim Eliopulos (4), QB Jim Hart (5), CB-S Monty Hunter (5), WR Kenny Thompson (5), TE Jamie Williams (1).

## COACHING STAFF

### Head Coach, Jim Hanifan

**Pro Career:** Named head coach on January 30, 1980 and posted 5-11 mark in 1980 followed by 7-9 in 1981, 5-4 in 1982, and 8-7-1 in 1983. No stranger to city of St. Louis, where he began his pro coaching career in 1973 as offensive line coach. Served Cardinals in that capacity until 1979 when he left to become assistant head coach of San Diego Chargers. During his first tenure at St. Louis, his offensive lines allowed fewest quarterback sacks in NFL for three straight years (1974-76), including an NFL record low of eight in 1975. Played end for the Toronto Argonauts (CFL) in 1955. Career record: 25-32-1.

**Background:** Played end for California 1952-54 and led the nation in receiving as a senior. Began coaching career at Charter Oak High School in Covina, Calif., in 1962. Was a college assistant for 14 years: Yuba, Calif., J.C. 1959-61, Glendale, Calif., J.C. 1964-65, Utah 1966-69, California 1970-71, San Diego State 1972.

**Personal:** Born September 21, 1933 in Compton, Calif. He and his wife, Mariana, live in St. Louis and have two children — Kathleen and James.

### Assistant Coaches

**Chuck Banker,** special teams-defensive assistant; born March 12, 1941, Prescott Ariz., lives in St. Louis. Linebacker-tight end Pasadena C.C. 1959-60. No pro playing experience. College coach: Glendale, Calif., J.C. 1962-65, Utah 1966-67, 1974-75, Westminster 1968-70, Boise State 1976-79. Pro coach: Joined Cardinals in 1980.

**Tom Bettis,** defensive coordinator; born March 17, 1933, Chicago, lives in St. Louis. Guard Purdue 1951-54. Pro linebacker Green Bay Packers 1955-61, Pittsburgh Steelers 1962, Chicago Bears 1963. Pro coach: Kansas City Chiefs 1966-77 (head coach for final seven games of 1977), joined Cardinals in 1978.

**Don Brown,** strength and conditioning; born February 2, 1951, Butler, Pa., lives in St. Louis. Linebacker Wake Forest 1970-72. No pro playing experience. College coach: Wake Forest 1973, 1975-77. Pro coach: Joined Cardinals in 1978.

**Rod Dowhower,** offensive coordinator; born April 15, 1943, Ord., Neb., lives in St. Louis. Quarterback San Diego State 1963-64. No pro playing experience. College coach: San Diego State 1968-72, UCLA 1974-75, Boise State 1976, Stanford 1977-79 (head coach 1979). Pro coach: St. Louis Cardinals 1973, Denver Broncos 1980-82, rejoined Cardinals in 1983.

**Rudy Feldman,** linebackers; born May 18, 1932, San Francisco, lives in St. Louis. Guard UCLA 1950-53. No pro playing experience. College coach: Iowa State 1957, Oklahoma 1963-67, New Mexico 1968-73 (head coach). Pro coach: San Diego Chargers 1974-77, joined Cardinals in 1978.

**Dick Jamieson,** offensive backfield; born November 13, 1937, Streator, Ill., lives in St. Louis. Quarterback Bradley 1955-58. Pro quarterback Baltimore Colts 1959, New York Titans 1960, Houston Oilers 1965. College coach: Bradley 1962-64, Missouri 1972-79. Pro coach: Joined Cardinals in 1980.

**Tom Lovat,** offensive line; born December 28, 1938, Bingham, Utah, lives in St. Louis. Guard-linebacker Utah 1958-60. No pro playing experience. College coach: Utah 1967, 1972-76 (head coach 1974-76), Idaho State 1968-70, Stanford 1977-79. Pro coach: Saskatchewan Roughriders (CFL) 1971, Green Bay Packers 1980, joined Cardinals in 1981.

**Leon McLaughlin,** special assistant; born May 30, 1925, San Diego, Calif., lives in St. Louis. Center-linebacker UCLA 1946-49. Pro center Los Angeles Rams 1951-55. College coach: Washington State 1956, Stanford 1959-65, San Fernando Valley State 1969-70 (head coach). Pro coach: Pittsburgh Steelers 1966-68, Los Angeles Rams 1971-72, Detroit Lions 1973-74, Green Bay Packers 1975-76, New England Patriots 1977, joined Cardinals in 1978.

**Floyd Peters,** assistant head coach-defensive line; born May 21, 1936, Council Bluffs, Iowa, lives in St. Louis. Defensive tackle San Francisco State 1954-57. Pro defensive tackle Baltimore Colts 1958, Cleveland Browns 1959-62, Detroit Lions 1963, Philadelphia Eagles 1964-69, Washington Redskins 1970. Pro coach: Washington Redskins 1970, New York Giants 1974-75, San Francisco 49ers 1976-77, Detroit Lions 1978-81, joined Cardinals in 1982.

**Emmitt Thomas,** receivers; born June 4, 1943, Angleton, Tex., lives in St. Louis. Quarterback-wide receiver Bishop College 1963-65. Pro defensive back Kansas City Chiefs 1966-78. College coach: Central Missouri State 1979-80. Pro coach: Joined Cardinals in 1981.

## ST. LOUIS CARDINALS 1984 FIRST-YEAR ROSTER

| Name | Pos. | Ht. | Wt. | Birth-date | College | Birthplace | Residence | How Acq. |
|------|------|-----|-----|-----------|---------|-----------|-----------|----------|
| Bayless, Martin | S | 6-2 | 195 | 10/11/62 | Bowling Green | Dayton, Ohio | Dayton, Ohio | D4 |
| Clark, Rod | LB | 6-2 | 228 | 1/14/62 | S.W. Texas State | San Marcos, Tex. | Prairie View, Tex. | D6 |
| Dawson, Doug | G | 6-3 | 267 | 12/27/61 | Texas | Houston, Tex. | Houston, Tex. | D2 |
| Duncan, Clyde | WR | 6-1 | 192 | 2/5/61 | Tennessee | Oxon Hill, Md. | Knoxville, Tenn. | D1 |
| Goode, John | TE | 6-2 | 222 | 11/5/62 | Youngstown State | Cleveland Hts., Ohio | Youngstown, Ohio | D5a |
| Leiding, Jeff | LB | 6-4 | 240 | 10/28/61 | Texas | Kansas City, Mo. | Tulsa, Okla. | D5 |
| Mackey, Kyle | QB | 6-2 | 220 | 3/2/62 | East Texas State | Alpine, Tex. | Commerce, Tex. | D11 |
| McIvor, Rick | QB | 6-4 | 210 | 9/26/60 | Texas | Ft. Davis, Tex. | Austin, Tex. | D3 |
| Noga, Falaniko | LB | 6-1 | 230 | 3/1/62 | Hawaii | American Samoa | Honolulu, Hawaii | D8 |
| Parker, Paul | G | 6-3 | 280 | 2/1/61 | Oklahoma | Tulsa, Okla. | Norman, Okla. | D12 |
| Paulling, Bob | K | 6-2 | 188 | 5/21/61 | Clemson | St. Matthews, S.C. | St. Matthews, S.C. | D8a |
| Smythe, Mark | DT | 6-3 | 265 | 12/12/59 | Indiana | Bloomington, Ind. | Bloomington, Ind. | D10 |
| Walker, John | RB | 6-0 | 205 | 8/31/61 | Texas | Killeen, Tex. | Killeen, Tex. | D9 |
| Walker, Quentin | RB | 6-1 | 200 | 8/27/61 | Virginia | Teaneck, N.J. | Charlottesville, Va. | D7 |

Players who report to an NFL team for the first time are designated on rosters as rookies (R). If a player reported to an NFL training camp in a previous year but was not on the active squad for three or more regular season or postseason games, he is listed on the first-year roster and designated by a (1). Thereafter, a player who is on the active squad for three or more regular season or postseason games is credited with an additional year of playing experience.

## NOTES

# SAN FRANCISCO 49ERS

**National Football Conference
Western Division**

**Team Colors:** Forty Niners Gold
and Scarlet

**711 Nevada Street
Redwood City, California 94061
Telephone (415) 365-3420**

**Club Officials**

Owner, Chairman of the Board: Edward J.
DeBartolo, Jr.
President, Head Coach: Bill Walsh
General Manager: John McVay
Vice President of Marketing and Community
Affairs: Ken Flower
Director of Pro Scouting: Alan Webb
Director of College Scouting: Tony Razzano
Director of Publicity and Media Relations:
Jerry Walker
Publications Coordinator: Rodney Knox
Business Manager: Keith Simon
Ticket Manager: Ken Dargel
Trainer: Lindsy McLean
Assistant Trainer: John Miller
Equipment Manager: Chico Norton
Equipment Assistant: Bronco Hinek

**Stadium:** Candlestick Park • **Capacity:** 61,185
San Francisco, California 94124

**Playing Surface:** Grass

**Training Camp:** Sierra Community College
Rocklin, California 95677

## 1984 SCHEDULE

**Preseason**

| | | |
|---|---|---|
| Aug. 4 | **Los Angeles Raiders** | 6:00 |
| Aug. 11 | at Denver | 7:00 |
| Aug. 18 | at San Diego | 6:00 |
| Aug. 24 | **Seattle** | 6:00 |

**Regular Season**

| | | |
|---|---|---|
| Sept. 2 | at Detroit | 1:00 |
| Sept. 10 | **Washington** (Monday) | 6:00 |
| Sept. 16 | **New Orleans** | 1:00 |
| Sept. 23 | at Philadelphia | 1:00 |
| Sept. 30 | **Atlanta** | 1:00 |
| Oct. 8 | at N.Y. Giants (Monday) | 9:00 |
| Oct. 14 | **Pittsburgh** | 1:00 |
| Oct. 21 | at Houston | 3:00 |
| Oct. 28 | at Los Angeles Rams | 1:00 |
| Nov. 4 | **Cincinnati** | 1:00 |
| Nov. 11 | at Cleveland | 1:00 |
| Nov. 18 | **Tampa Bay** | 1:00 |
| Nov. 25 | at New Orleans | 3:00 |
| Dec. 2 | at Atlanta | 1:00 |
| Dec. 8 | **Minnesota** (Saturday) | 1:00 |
| Dec. 14 | **L.A. Rams** (Friday) | 6:00 |

## 49ERS COACHING HISTORY

**(218-240-12)**

| | | |
|---|---|---|
| 1950-54 | Lawrence (Buck) Shaw | 33-25-2 |
| 1955 | Norman (Red) Strader | 4-8-0 |
| 1956-58 | Frankie Albert | 19-17-1 |
| 1959-63 | Howard (Red) Hickey* | 27-27-1 |
| 1963-67 | Jack Christiansen | 26-38-3 |
| 1968-75 | Dick Nolan | 56-56-5 |
| 1976 | Monte Clark | 8-6-0 |
| 1977 | Ken Meyer | 5-9-0 |
| 1978 | Pete McCulley** | 1-8-0 |
| 1978 | Fred O'Connor | 1-6-0 |
| 1979-83 | Bill Walsh | 38-40-0 |

*Resigned after three games in 1963
**Released after nine games in 1978

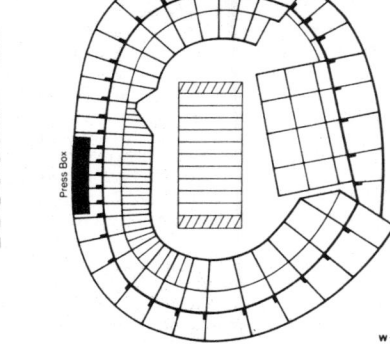

**CANDLESTICK PARK**

## RECORD HOLDERS

### Individual Records—Career

| Category | Name | Performance |
|---|---|---|
| Rushing (Yds.) | Joe Perry, 1950-1960, 1963 | 7,344 |
| Passing (Yds.) | John Brodie, 1957-1973 | 31,548 |
| Passing (TDs) | John Brodie, 1957-1973 | 214 |
| Receiving (No.) | Billy Wilson, 1951-1960 | 407 |
| Receiving (Yds.) | Gene Washington, 1969-1977 | 6,664 |
| Interceptions | Jimmy Johnson, 1961-1976 | 47 |
| Punting (Avg.) | Tommy Davis, 1959-1969 | 44.7 |
| Punt Return (Avg.) | Manfred Moore, 1974-75 | 14.7 |
| Kickoff Return (Avg.) | Abe Woodson, 1958-1964 | 29.4 |
| Field Goals | Tommy Davis, 1959-1969 | 130 |
| Touchdowns (Tot.) | Ken Willard, 1965-1973 | 61 |
| Points | Tommy Davis, 1959-1969 | 738 |

### Individual Records—Single Season

| Category | Name | Performance |
|---|---|---|
| Rushing (Yds.) | Delvin Williams, 1976 | 1,203 |
| Passing (Yds.) | Joe Montana, 1983 | 3,910 |
| Passing (TDs) | John Brodie, 1965 | 30 |
| Receiving (No.) | Dwight Clark, 1981 | 85 |
| Receiving (Yds.) | Dave Parks, 1965 | 1,344 |
| Interceptions | Dave Baker, 1960 | 10 |
| Punting (Avg.) | Tommy Davis, 1965 | 45.8 |
| Punt Return (Avg.) | Dana McLemore, 1982 | 22.3 |
| Kickoff Return (Avg.) | Joe Arenas, 1953 | 34.4 |
| Field Goals | Bruce Gossett, 1973 | 26 |
| Touchdowns (Tot.) | Joe Perry, 1953 | 13 |
| Points | Ray Wersching, 1983 | 126 |

### Individual Records—Single Game

| Category | Name | Performance |
|---|---|---|
| Rushing (Yds.) | Delvin Williams, 10-31-76 | 194 |
| Passing (Yds.) | Joe Montana, 11-21-82 | 408 |
| Passing (TDs) | John Brodie, 11-23-65 | 5 |
| | Steve Spurrier, 11-19-72 | 5 |
| Receiving (No.) | Bernie Casey, 11-13-66 | 12 |
| | Dwight Clark, 12-11-82 | 12 |
| Receiving (Yds.) | Dave Parks, 10-3-65 | 231 |
| Interceptions | Dave Baker, 12-4-60 | 4 |
| Field Goals | Ray Wersching, 10-16-83 | 6 |
| Touchdowns (Tot.) | Billy Kilmer, 10-15-61 | 4 |
| Points | Gordy Soltau, 10-27-51 | 26 |

## 1983 TEAM STATISTICS

| | San Francisco | Opp. |
|---|---|---|
| Total First Downs | 344 | 302 |
| Rushing | 129 | 98 |
| Passing | 199 | 181 |
| Penalty | 16 | 23 |
| Third Down Efficiency | 96/215 | 83/216 |
| Third Down Percentage | 44.7 | 38.4 |
| Total Net Yards | 6054 | 5189 |
| Total Offensive Plays | 1072 | 1032 |
| Avg. Gain per Play | 5.6 | 5.0 |
| Avg. Gain per Game | 378.4 | 324.3 |
| Net Yards Rushing | 2257 | 1936 |
| Total Rushing Plays | 511 | 449 |
| Avg. Gain per Rush | 4.4 | 4.3 |
| Avg. Gain Rushing per Game | 141.1 | 121.0 |
| Net Yards Passing | 3797 | 3253 |
| Lost Attempting to Pass | 33/224 | 57/448 |
| Gross Yards Passing | 4021 | 3701 |
| Attempts/Completions | 528/339 | 526/322 |
| Percent Completed | 64.2 | 61.2 |
| Had Intercepted | 12 | 24 |
| Avg. Net Passing per Game | 237.3 | 203.3 |
| Punts/Avg. | 66/38.7 | 74/40.4 |
| Punt Returns/Avg. | 36/10.1 | 38/7.3 |
| Kickoff Returns/Avg. | 52/18.4 | 78/21.5 |
| Interceptions/Avg. Ret. | 24/18.2 | 12/14.0 |
| Penalties/Yards | 89/695 | 91/793 |
| Fumbles/Ball Lost | 27/19 | 39/18 |
| Total Points | 432 | 293 |
| Avg. Points per Game | 27.0 | 18.3 |
| Touchdowns | 51 | 35 |
| Rushing | 17 | 10 |
| Passing | 27 | 23 |
| Returns and Recoveries | 7 | 2 |
| Field Goals | 25/30 | 17/27 |
| Conversions | 51/51 | 32/35 |
| Safeties | 0 | 0 |
| Avg. Time of Possession | 30:12 | 29:48 |

## 1983 TEAM RECORD
### Preseason (1-3)

| Date | San Francisco | | Opponents |
|---|---|---|---|
| 8/6 | 23 | L.A. Raiders (OT) | 26 |
| 8/14 | 17 | *New England | 15 |
| 8/20 | 7 | San Diego | 24 |
| 8/27 | 6 | *Seattle | 20 |
| | 53 | | 85 |

### Regular Season (10-6)

| Date | San Francisco | | Opp. | Att. |
|---|---|---|---|---|
| 9/3 | 17 | *Philadelphia | 22 | 55,775 |
| 9/8 | 48 | Minnesota | 17 | 58,167 |
| 9/18 | 42 | St. Louis | 27 | 38,130 |
| 9/25 | 24 | *Atlanta | 20 | 57,814 |
| 10/2 | 33 | New England | 13 | 54,293 |
| 10/9 | 7 | *Los Angeles Rams | 10 | 59,119 |
| 10/16 | 32 | New Orleans | 13 | 68,154 |
| 10/23 | 45 | Los Angeles Rams | 35 | 66,070 |
| 10/30 | 13 | *New York Jets | 27 | 54,796 |
| 11/6 | 17 | *Miami | 20 | 57,832 |
| 11/13 | 27 | *New Orleans | 0 | 40,022 |
| 11/20 | 24 | Atlanta | 28 | 32,782 |
| 11/27 | 3 | Chicago | 13 | 40,483 |
| 12/4 | 35 | *Tampa Bay | 21 | 49,773 |
| 12/11 | 23 | Buffalo | 10 | 38,039 |
| 12/19 | 42 | *Dallas | 17 | 59,957 |
| | 432 | | 293 | 831,206 |

*Home Game   (OT) Overtime

### Score by Periods

| | | | | | | |
|---|---|---|---|---|---|---|
| San Francisco | 88 | 134 | 104 | 106 | — | 432 |
| Opponents | 33 | 119 | 69 | 72 | — | 293 |

### Attendance
Home 435,088   Away 396,118   Total 831,206
Single game home record, 61,214 (4 times, 1972)
Single season home record, 442,067 (1972)

## 1983 INDIVIDUAL STATISTICS

### Rushing

| | Att. | Yds. | Avg. | LG | TD |
|---|---|---|---|---|---|
| Tyler | 176 | 856 | 4.9 | 39 | 4 |
| Craig | 176 | 725 | 4.1 | 71 | 8 |
| Montana | 61 | 284 | 4.7 | 18 | 2 |
| Ring | 64 | 254 | 4.0 | 25 | 2 |
| Moore | 15 | 43 | 2.9 | 14 | 1 |
| Orosz | 2 | 39 | 19.5 | 23 | 0 |
| Monroe | 10 | 23 | 2.3 | 5 | 0 |
| D. Clark | 3 | 18 | 6.0 | 9 | 0 |
| Cavanaugh | 1 | 8 | 8.0 | 8 | 0 |
| Ramson | 1 | 3 | 3.0 | 3 | 0 |
| Solomon | 1 | 3 | 3.0 | 3 | 0 |
| Benjamin | 1 | 1 | 1.0 | 1 | 0 |
| San Francisco | 511 | 2257 | 4.4 | 71 | 17 |
| Opponents | 449 | 1936 | 4.3 | 49 | 10 |

### Passing

| | Att. | Comp. | Pct. | Yds. | TD | Int. | Tkld. | Rate |
|---|---|---|---|---|---|---|---|---|
| Montana | 515 | 332 | 64.5 | 3910 | 26 | 12 | 33/224 | 94.6 |
| Benjamin | 12 | 7 | 58.3 | 111 | 1 | 0 | 0/0 | 117.0 |
| D. Clark | 1 | 0 | 0.0 | 0 | 0 | 0 | 0/0 | 39.6 |
| San Fran. | 528 | 339 | 64.2 | 4021 | 27 | 12 | 33/224 | 94.9 |
| Opponents | 526 | 322 | 61.2 | 3701 | 23 | 24 | 57/448 | 78.0 |

### Receiving

| | No. | Yds. | Avg. | LG | TD |
|---|---|---|---|---|---|
| D. Clark | 70 | 840 | 12.0 | 46t | 8 |
| Craig | 48 | 427 | 8.9 | 23 | 4 |
| Tyler | 34 | 285 | 8.4 | 26 | 2 |
| Francis | 33 | 357 | 10.8 | 25 | 4 |
| Solomon | 31 | 662 | 21.4 | 77t | 3 |
| Wilson | 30 | 433 | 14.4 | 49 | 0 |
| Ring | 23 | 182 | 7.9 | 24 | 0 |
| Moore | 19 | 206 | 10.8 | 34 | 0 |
| Nehemiah | 17 | 236 | 13.9 | 27 | 1 |
| Ramson | 17 | 125 | 7.4 | 16 | 1 |
| Cooper | 15 | 207 | 13.8 | 73t | 3 |
| Monroe | 2 | 61 | 30.5 | 50 | 0 |
| San Francisco | 339 | 4021 | 11.9 | 77t | 27 |
| Opponents | 322 | 3701 | 11.5 | 76t | 23 |

### Interceptions

| | No. | Yds. | Avg. | LG | TD |
|---|---|---|---|---|---|
| Wright | 7 | 164 | 23.4 | 60t | 2 |
| Williamson | 4 | 51 | 12.8 | 26 | 0 |
| Lott | 4 | 22 | 5.5 | 22 | 0 |
| Collier | 3 | 32 | 10.7 | 32t | 1 |
| Hicks | 2 | 102 | 51.0 | 62t | 2 |
| Leopold | 2 | 13 | 6.5 | 9 | 0 |
| Harper | 1 | 37 | 37.0 | 37 | 0 |
| Pillers | 1 | 16 | 16.0 | 16 | 0 |
| San Francisco | 24 | 437 | 18.2 | 62t | 5 |
| Opponents | 12 | 168 | 14.0 | 43t | 1 |

### Punting

| | No. | Yds. | Avg. | In 20 | LG |
|---|---|---|---|---|---|
| Orosz | 65 | 2552 | 39.3 | 16 | 61 |
| San Francisco | 66 | 2552 | 38.7 | 16 | 61 |
| Opponents | 74 | 2993 | 40.4 | 16 | 60 |

### Punt Returns

| | No. | FC | Yds. | Avg. | LG | TD |
|---|---|---|---|---|---|---|
| McLemore | 31 | 6 | 331 | 10.7 | 56t | 1 |
| Solomon | 5 | 3 | 34 | 6.8 | 11 | 0 |
| San Francisco | 36 | 9 | 365 | 10.1 | 56t | 1 |
| Opponents | 38 | 7 | 278 | 7.3 | 19 | 0 |

### Kickoff Returns

| | No. | Yds. | Avg. | LG | TD |
|---|---|---|---|---|---|
| McLemore | 30 | 576 | 19.2 | 39 | 0 |
| Monroe | 8 | 152 | 19.0 | 32 | 0 |
| Moore | 7 | 117 | 16.7 | 46 | 0 |
| Ring | 4 | 68 | 17.0 | 18 | 0 |
| Cooper | 3 | 45 | 15.0 | 20 | 0 |
| San Francisco | 52 | 958 | 18.4 | 46 | 0 |
| Opponents | 78 | 1675 | 21.5 | 50 | 0 |

### Scoring

| | TD | TD R | TD P | TD Rt | PAT | FG | TP |
|---|---|---|---|---|---|---|---|
| Wersching | | | | | 51/51 | 25/30 | 126 |
| Craig | 12 | 8 | 4 | 0 | | | 72 |
| D. Clark | 8 | 0 | 8 | 0 | | | 48 |
| Tyler | 6 | 4 | 2 | 0 | | | 36 |
| Francis | 4 | 0 | 4 | 0 | | | 24 |
| Solomon | 4 | 0 | 4 | 0 | | | 24 |
| Cooper | 3 | 0 | 3 | 0 | | | 18 |
| Hicks | 2 | 0 | 0 | 2 | | | 12 |
| Montana | 2 | 2 | 0 | 0 | | | 12 |
| Ring | 2 | 2 | 0 | 0 | | | 12 |
| Wright | 2 | 0 | 0 | 2 | | | 12 |
| Board | 1 | 0 | 0 | 1 | | | 6 |
| Collier | 1 | 0 | 0 | 1 | | | 6 |
| McLemore | 1 | 0 | 0 | 1 | | | 6 |
| Moore | 1 | 1 | 0 | 0 | | | 6 |
| Nehemiah | 1 | 0 | 1 | 0 | | | 6 |
| Ramson | 1 | 0 | 1 | 0 | | | 6 |
| San Fran. | 51 | 17 | 27 | 7 | 51/51 | 25/30 | 432 |
| Opponents | 35 | 10 | 23 | 2 | 32/35 | 17/27 | 293 |

## FIRST-ROUND SELECTIONS

(If Club had no first-round selection, first player drafted is listed with round in parentheses.)

| Year | Player, College, Position |
|---|---|
| 1950 | Leo Nomellini, Minnesota, T |
| 1951 | Y. A. Tittle, Louisiana State, B |
| 1952 | Hugh McElhenny, Washington, B |
| 1953 | Harry Babcock, Georgia, E |
| | Tom Stolhandske, Texas, E |
| 1954 | Bernie Faloney, Maryland, B |
| 1955 | Dickie Moegle, Rice, B |
| 1956 | Earl Morrall, Michigan State, B |
| 1957 | John Brodie, Stanford, B |
| 1958 | Jim Pace, Michigan, B |
| | Charlie Krueger, Texas A&M, T |
| 1959 | Dave Baker, Oklahoma, B |
| | Dan James, Ohio State, C |
| 1960 | Monty Stickles, Notre Dame, E |
| 1961 | Jimmy Johnson, UCLA, CB |
| | Bernie Casey, Bowling Green, WR |
| | Bill Kilmer, UCLA, QB |
| 1962 | Lance Alworth, Arkansas, WR |
| 1963 | Kermit Alexander, UCLA, CB |
| 1964 | Dave Parks, Texas Tech, WR |
| 1965 | Ken Willard, North Carolina, RB |
| | George Donnelly, Illinois, DB |
| 1966 | Stan Hindman, Mississippi, DE |
| 1967 | Steve Spurrier, Florida, QB |
| | Cas Banaszek, Northwestern, T |
| 1968 | Forrest Blue, Auburn, C |
| 1969 | Ted Kwalick, Penn State, TE |
| | Gene Washington, Stanford, WR |
| 1970 | Cedrick Hardman, North Texas State, DE |
| | Bruce Taylor, Boston U., DB |
| 1971 | Tim Anderson, Ohio State, DB |
| 1972 | Terry Beasley, Auburn, WR |
| 1973 | Mike Holmes, Texas Southern, DB |
| 1974 | Wilbur Jackson, Alabama, RB |
| | Bill Sandifer, UCLA, DT |
| 1975 | Jimmy Webb, Mississippi State, DT |
| 1976 | Randy Cross, UCLA, C (2) |
| 1977 | Elmo Boyd, Eastern Kentucky, WR (3) |
| 1978 | Ken MacAfee, Notre Dame, TE |
| | Dan Bunz, Cal State-Long Beach, LB |
| 1979 | James Owens, UCLA, WR (2) |
| 1980 | Earl Cooper, Rice, RB |
| | Jim Stuckey, Clemson, DT |
| 1981 | Ronnie Lott, Southern California, DB |
| 1982 | Bubba Paris, Michigan, T (2) |
| 1983 | Roger Craig, Nebraska, RB (2) |
| 1984 | Todd Shell, Brigham Young, LB |

# SAN FRANCISCO 49ERS 1984 VETERAN ROSTER

| No. | Name | Pos. | Ht. | Wt. | Birth-date | NFL Exp. | College | Birthplace | Residence | Games in '83 |
|---|---|---|---|---|---|---|---|---|---|---|
| 68 | Ayers, John | G | 6-5 | 265 | 4/14/53 | 8 | West Texas State | Carrizo Springs, Tex. | Canyon, Tex. | 16 |
| 7 | Benjamin, Guy | QB | 6-3 | 210 | 6/27/55 | 7 | Stanford | Hollywood, Calif. | Montara, Calif. | 4 |
| 44 | †Blackmore, Richard | CB | 5-10 | 174 | 8/14/56 | 6 | Mississippi State | Vicksburg, Miss. | Senatobia, Miss. | 11 |
| 76 | Board, Dwaine | DE | 6-5 | 248 | 11/29/56 | 5 | North Carolina A&T | Union Hall, Va. | Redwood City, Calif. | 16 |
| 57 | †Bunz, Dan | LB | 6-4 | 225 | 10/7/55 | 6 | Long Beach State | Roseville, Calif. | Loomis, Calif. | 9 |
| 6 | Cavanaugh, Matt | QB | 6-2 | 212 | 10/27/56 | 7 | Pittsburgh | Youngstown, Ohio | Foxboro, Mass. | 5 |
| 15 | Clark, Bryan | QB | 6-2 | 196 | 7/27/60 | 2 | Michigan State | Redwood City, Calif. | San Mateo, Calif. | 0* |
| 87 | Clark, Dwight | WR | 6-4 | 210 | 1/8/57 | 6 | Clemson | Kinston, N.C. | Redwood Shores, Calif. | 16 |
| 47 | Collier, Tim | CB | 6-0 | 176 | 5/31/54 | 9 | East Texas State | Dallas, Tex. | Dallas, Tex. | 10 |
| 89 | Cooper, Earl | TE-RB | 6-2 | 227 | 9/17/57 | 5 | Rice | Lexington, Tex. | Houston, Tex. | 16 |
| 33 | Craig, Roger | FB | 6-0 | 222 | 7/10/60 | 2 | Nebraska | Preston, Miss. | Bettendorf, Iowa | 16 |
| 51 | Cross, Randy | G | 6-3 | 265 | 4/25/54 | 9 | UCLA | New York, N.Y. | Redwood City, Calif. | 16 |
| 74 | Dean, Fred | DE | 6-2 | 236 | 2/24/52 | 10 | Louisiana Tech | Arcadia, La. | San Diego, Calif. | 16 |
| 84 | Durham, Darius | WR | 6-2 | 185 | 5/27/61 | 2 | San Diego State | Long Beach, Calif. | Garden Grove, Calif. | 0* |
| 50 | Ellison, Riki | LB | 6-2 | 220 | 8/15/60 | 2 | Southern California | Christchurch, New Zealand | Foster City, Calif. | 16 |
| 71 | Fahnhorst, Keith | T | 6-6 | 273 | 2/6/52 | 11 | Minnesota | St. Cloud, Minn. | St. Paul, Minn. | 16 |
| 54 | Ferrari, Ron | LB | 6-0 | 212 | 7/30/59 | 3 | Illinois | Springfield, Ill. | San Mateo, Calif. | 16 |
| 81 | Francis, Russ | TE | 6-6 | 242 | 4/3/53 | 9 | Oregon | Seattle, Wash. | Wallingford, Ver. | 16 |
| 24 | Gervais, Rick | S | 5-11 | 190 | 11/4/59 | 4 | Stanford | Bend, Ore. | Redwood City, Calif. | 5 |
| 75 | Harty, John | DT | 6-4 | 263 | 12/17/58 | 4 | Iowa | Sioux City, Iowa | Sioux City, Iowa | 5 |
| 22 | Hicks, Dwight | S | 6-1 | 192 | 4/5/56 | 6 | Michigan | Mt. Holly, N.J. | Foster City, Calif. | 15 |
| 28 | Holmoe, Tom | CB-S | 6-2 | 180 | 3/7/60 | 2 | Brigham Young | Los Angeles, Calif. | Foster City, Calif. | 16 |
|  | t-Kelcher, Louie | NT | 6-5 | 310 | 8/23/53 | 10 | Southern Methodist | Beaumont Tex. | Olivenhain, Calif. | 8 |
| 66 | Kennedy, Allan | T | 6-7 | 275 | 1/8/58 | 3 | Washington State | Vancouver, Canada | San Mateo, Calif. | 16 |
|  | t-LeMaster, Frank | LB | 6-2 | 238 | 3/12/52 | 10 | Kentucky | Lexington, Ky. | West Chester, Pa. | 0* |
| 42 | Lott, Ronnie | S-CB | 6-0 | 199 | 5/8/59 | 4 | Southern California | Albuquerque, N.M. | Santa Clara, Calif. | 15 |
| 53 | †McColl, Milt | LB | 6-6 | 230 | 8/28/59 | 4 | Stanford | Oak Park, Ill. | Menlo Park, Calif. | 12 |
| 43 | McLemore, Dana | KR-CB | 5-10 | 183 | 7/1/60 | 3 | Hawaii | Los Angeles, Calif. | Milpitas, Calif. | 14 |
| 32 | Monroe, Carl | RB-KR | 5-8 | 166 | 2/20/60 | 2 | Utah | Pittsburgh, Pa. | Mountain View, Calif. | 5 |
| 16 | Montana, Joe | QB | 6-2 | 195 | 6/11/56 | 6 | Notre Dame | Monongahela, Pa. | San Francisco, Calif. | 16 |
| 60 | Montgomery, Blanchard | LB | 6-2 | 236 | 2/17/61 | 2 | UCLA | Los Angeles, Calif. | Foster City, Calif. | 11 |
| 25 | Moore, Jeff | RB | 6-0 | 196 | 8/20/56 | 5 | Jackson State | Kosciusko, Miss. | Jackson, Miss. | 15 |
| 63 | Moten, Gary | LB | 6-1 | 210 | 4/3/61 | 2 | Southern Methodist | Galveston, Tex. | Clute, Tex. | 6 |
| 83 | Nehemiah, Renaldo | WR | 6-1 | 183 | 3/24/59 | 3 | Maryland | Newark, N.J. | Gaithersburg, Md. | 16 |
| 3 | Orosz, Tom | P | 6-1 | 204 | 9/26/59 | 4 | Ohio State | Painesville, Ohio | Worthington, Ohio | 16 |
| 77 | Paris, Bubba | T | 6-6 | 295 | 10/6/60 | 2 | Michigan | Louisville, Ky. | Redwood City, Calif. | 16 |
| 65 | Pillers, Lawrence | DT-DE | 6-4 | 250 | 11/4/52 | 9 | Alcorn A&M | Hazlehurst, Miss. | San Carlos, Calif. | 16 |
| 56 | Quillan, Fred | C | 6-5 | 266 | 1/27/56 | 7 | Oregon | West Palm Beach, Fla. | San Mateo, Calif. | 14 |
| 64 | Reynolds, Jack | LB | 6-1 | 232 | 11/22/47 | 15 | Tennessee | Cincinnati, Ohio | San Salvador, Bahamas | 13 |
| 30 | Ring, Bill | RB | 5-10 | 205 | 12/13/56 | 4 | Brigham Young | Des Moines, Iowa | Redwood City, Calif. | 16 |
| 61 | Sapolu, Jesse | G | 6-4 | 260 | 3/10/61 | 2 | Hawaii | Laie, Western Samoa | Honolulu, Hawaii | 16 |
| 88 | †Solomon, Freddie | WR | 5-11 | 188 | 1/11/53 | 10 | Tampa | Sumter, N.C. | Temple Terrace, Fla. | 13 |
| 72 | Stover, Jeff | NT | 6-5 | 275 | 5/22/58 | 3 | Oregon | Corning, Calif. | Chico, Calif. | 16 |
| 79 | Stuckey, Jim | DE | 6-4 | 253 | 6/21/58 | 5 | Clemson | Cayce, S.C. | Clemson, S.C. | 16 |
|  | t-Tuiasosopo, Manu | NT | 6-3 | 250 | 8/30/57 | 6 | UCLA | Los Angeles, Calif. | Woodinville, Wash. | 16 |
| 58 | Turner, Keena | LB | 6-2 | 219 | 10/22/58 | 5 | Purdue | Chicago, Ill. | San Carlos, Calif. | 15 |
| 26 | Tyler, Wendell | RB | 5-10 | 200 | 5/20/55 | 7 | UCLA | Shreveport, La. | West Covina, Calif. | 14 |
| 14 | †Wersching, Ray | K | 5-11 | 210 | 8/21/50 | 12 | California | Mondsee, Austria | Vista, Calif. | 16 |
| 27 | Williamson, Carlton | S | 6-0 | 204 | 6/12/58 | 4 | Pittsburgh | Atlanta, Ga. | Atlanta, Ga. | 9 |
| 85 | Wilson, Mike | WR | 6-3 | 210 | 12/19/58 | 4 | Washington State | Los Angeles, Calif. | Foster City, Calif. | 15 |
|  | Wood, Mike | K | 5-11 | 205 | 9/3/54 | 5 | S.E. Missouri State | St. Louis, Mo. | St. Louis, Mo. | 0* |
| 21 | Wright, Eric | CB | 6-1 | 180 | 4/18/59 | 4 | Missouri | St. Louis, Mo. | San Carlos, Calif. | 16 |

\* B. Clark and LeMaster missed '83 season due to injury; Durham active for three games in '83, but did not play; Wood last active with the Colts in '82.

†Option playout; subject to developments.

t-49ers traded for Kelcher (San Diego), LeMaster (Philadelphia), Tuiasosopo (Seattle).

Traded—Center-guard Walt Downing to San Diego, tight end Eason Ramson to Denver.

Also played with 49ers in '83—G John Choma (6 games), LB Willie Harper (16), LB Bob Horn (8), LB Ed Judie (4), NT Pete Kugler (16), LB Bobby Leopold (16), LB Ken McAlister (4), NT Daryle Skaugstad (3), RB Vince Williams (1).

## COACHING STAFF

### Head Coach, Bill Walsh

**Pro Career:** Begins sixth season as an NFL head coach. Directed 49ers to NFC championship in 1981 and Super Bowl XVI victory over Cincinnati, 26-21. Started pro coaching career in 1966 as offensive backfield coach for the Oakland Raiders. He then spent eight seasons (1967-75) in Cincinnati, where he was responsible for coaching the Bengals' quarterbacks and receivers. His tenure in Cincinnati was followed by a season with the San Diego Chargers as offensive coordinator. While at Cincinnati he tutored Ken Anderson, who became the first NFL quarterback to lead the league in passing two straight years. At San Diego, he helped develop the talents of quarterback Dan Fouts. No pro playing experience. Career record: 38-40.

**Background:** End at San Jose State in 1953-54. Started college coaching career at California, where he served under Marv Levy from 1960-62. In 1963, he joined John Ralston's Stanford staff and worked with the defensive backfield for three seasons. Returned to Stanford as head coach in 1977 .and directed Cardinals to a two-year record of 17-7, including wins in the Sun and Bluebonnet Bowls. Received his master's degree in history from San Jose State in 1959.

**Personal:** Born November 30, 1931, in Los Angeles. He and his wife, Geri, live in Menlo Park and have three children—Steve, Craig, and Elizabeth.

### Assistant Coaches

**Jerry Attaway,** conditioning; born January 3, 1946, Susanville, Calif., lives in San Carlos. Defensive back Yuba J.C. 1964-65, Cal-Davis 1967. No pro playing experience. College coach: Cal-Davis 1970-71, Idaho 1972-74, Utah State 1975-77, Southern California 1978-82. Pro coach: Joined 49ers in 1983.

**Paul Hackett,** quarterbacks-receivers; born July 5, 1947, Burlington, Vt., lives in Redwood City. Quarterback Cal-Davis 1965-68. No pro playing experience. College coach: Cal-Davis 1970-71, California 1972-75, Southern California 1976-80. Pro coach: Cleveland Browns 1981-82, joined 49ers in 1983.

**Norb Hecker,** linebackers; born May 26, 1927, Berea, Ohio, lives in San Francisco. End Baldwin-Wallace 1947-50. Pro end-defensive back Los Angeles Rams 1951-53, Toronto Argonauts (CFL) 1954, Washington Redskins 1955-57. College coach: Stanford 1972-78. Pro coach: Hamilton Tiger-Cats (CFL) 1958, Green Bay Packers 1959-65, Atlanta Falcons 1966-68 (head coach), New York Giants 1969-71, joined 49ers in 1979.

**Sherman Lewis,** running backs, born June 29, 1942, Louisville, Ky., lives in Redwood City. Running back Michigan State 1961-63. Pro running back Toronto Argonauts (CFL) 1964-65, New York Jets 1966. College coach: Michigan State 1969-82. Pro coach: Joined 49ers in 1983.

**Bobb McKittrick,** offensive line; born December 29, 1935, Baker, Ore., lives in San Mateo. Guard Oregon State 1955-57. No pro playing experience. College coach: Oregon State 1961-64, UCLA 1965-70. Pro coach: Los Angeles Rams 1971-72, San Diego Chargers 1974-78, joined 49ers in 1979.

**Bill McPherson,** defensive line; born October 24, 1931, Santa Clara, Calif., lives in San Jose. Tackle Santa Clara 1950-52. No pro playing experience. College coach: Santa Clara 1963-74, UCLA 1975-77. Pro coach: Philadelphia Eagles 1978, joined 49ers in 1979.

**Ray Rhodes,** defensive backfield; born October 20, 1950, Mexia, Tex., lives in Fremont. Running back-receiver Texas Christian 1969-70, Tulsa 1972-73. Pro defensive back New York Giants 1974-79, San Francisco 49ers 1980. Pro coach: Joined 49ers in 1981.

**George Siefert,** defensive coordinator; born January 22, 1940, San Francisco, Calif., lives in Sunnyvale. Linebacker Utah 1960-62. No pro playing experience. College coach: Westminster 1965 (head coach), Iowa 1966, Oregon 1967-71, Stanford 1972-74, 1977-79, Cornell 1975-76 (head coach). Pro coach: Joined 49ers in 1980.

## SAN FRANCISCO 49ERS 1984 FIRST-YEAR ROSTER

| Name | Pos. | Ht. | Wt. | Birth-date | College | Birthplace | Residence | How Acq. |
|------|------|-----|-----|-----------|---------|-----------|-----------|----------|
| Awbrey, John (1) | NT | 6-3 | 257 | 9/11/59 | Stanford | Berkeley, Calif. | Redwood City, Calif. | FA |
| Bonner, Mark (1) | C-G | 6-5 | 260 | 10/19/59 | Oregon State | Sacramento, Calif. | Sacramento, Calif. | FA |
| Bouier, Lorenzo (1) | RB | 6-1 | 198 | 2/27/61 | Maine | Hartford, Conn. | Hartford, Conn. | FA |
| Carr, Gary (1) | RB | 5-10 | 205 | 9/15/58 | Fresno State | Phoenix, Ariz. | Pomona, Calif. | FA |
| Carter, Michael | NT | 6-2 | 281 | 10/29/60 | Southern Methodist | Dallas, Tex. | Dallas, Tex. | D5 |
| Durham, James (1) | CB-S | 6-0 | 195 | 11/12/59 | Houston | Lufkin, Tex. | Lufkin, Tex. | FA |
| Fontes, Kevin | WR | 5-10 | 173 | 7/18/60 | Sacramento State | Sacramento, Calif. | Sacramento, Calif. | FA |
| Foster, Frank (1) | G-T | 6-4 | 275 | 11/24/60 | San Diego State | Taft, Calif. | Taft, Calif. | FA |
| Frank, John | TE | 6-3 | 225 | 4/17/62 | Ohio State | Mt. Lebanon, Pa. | Mt. Lebanon, Pa. | D2 |
| Fuller, Jeff | LB | 6-2 | 216 | 8/8/62 | Texas A&M | Dallas, Tex. | Dallas, Tex. | D5a |
| Harmon, Derrick | RB | 5-10 | 202 | 4/26/63 | Cornell | New York, N.Y. | Ithaca, N.Y. | D9a |
| Hodge, Davis (1) | LB | 6-3 | 226 | 1/16/57 | Houston | Freeport, Tex. | Clute, Tex. | FA |
| Jackson, Dwaine (1) | DE | 6-5 | 260 | 6/27/60 | S. Carolina State | Atlanta, Ga. | Atlanta, Ga. | FA |
| McIntyre, Guy | G | 6-3 | 271 | 2/17/61 | Georgia | Thomasville, Ga. | Thomasville, Ga. | D3 |
| Miller, Lee | CB-S | 6-1 | 186 | 1/25/61 | Cal State-Fullerton | Los Angeles, Calif. | Los Angeles, Calif. | D9 |
| Moritz, Dave | WR | 6-0 | 181 | 6/12/62 | Iowa | Evergreen, Ill. | Iowa City, Iowa | D10 |
| Pendleton, Kirk | WR | 6-3 | 191 | 4/4/62 | Brigham Young | Salt Lake City, Utah | Richfield, Utah | D11 |
| Phillips, Scott (1) | RB | 6-2 | 185 | 11/11/58 | Brigham Young | Provo, Utah | Springville, Utah | FA |
| Shell, Todd | LB | 6-4 | 225 | 6/26/62 | Brigham Young | Mesa, Ariz. | Mesa, Ariz. | D1 |
| Washington, Ron (1) | WR | 6-0 | 190 | 1/6/58 | Arizona State | Phoenix, Ariz. | Tempe, Ariz. | FA |
| Wilson, Mark (1) | WR | 6-3 | 205 | 3/8/60 | Louisville | Youngstown, Ohio | Youngstown, Ohio | FA |
| Young, Reggie (1) | RB | 6-1 | 210 | 3/10/60 | Hawaii | Springfield, Mass. | Sacramento, Calif. | FA |

Players who report to an NFL team for the first time are designated on rosters as rookies (R). If a player reported to an NFL training camp in a previous year but was not on the active squad for three or more regular season or postseason games, he is listed on the first-year roster and designated by a (1). Thereafter, a player who is on the active squad for three or more regular season or postseason games is credited with an additional year of playing experience.

## NOTES

127

# TAMPA BAY BUCCANEERS

## National Football Conference Central Division

**Team Colors:** Florida Orange, White, and Red

**One Buccaneer Place**
**Tampa, Florida 33607**
**Telephone: (813) 870-2700**

### Club Officials
Owner: Hugh F. Culverhouse
President: Hugh F. Culverhouse
Vice President: Joy Culverhouse
Vice President-Head Coach: John H. McKay
Secretary/Treasurer: Ward Holland
Director of Administration: Herbert M. Gold
Assistant to the President: Phil Krueger
Director of Player Personnel: Jim Gruden
Director of Ticket Operations: Terry Wooten
Director of Public Relations: Rick Odioso
Director of Marketing & Advertising:
  Bob Passwaters
Assistant Director-Community Relations:
  Sandy Cottrell
Assistant Director-Media Relations: John Gerdes
Pro Personnel: Gary Horton
College Personnel: Bill Baker, George Saimes,
  Erik Widmark
Controller: Ed Easom
Trainer: Tom Oxley
Assistant Trainer: Scott Anderson
Equipment Manager: Frank Pupello
Assistant Equipment Manager: Yoshimi Core

**Stadium:** Tampa Stadium • **Capacity:** 74,270
    North Dale Mabry
    Tampa, Florida 33607

**Playing Surface:** Grass

**Training Camp:** One Buccaneer Place
    Tampa, Florida 33607

## 1984 SCHEDULE
### Preseason
| | | |
|---|---|---|
| July 28 | vs. Seattle at Canton, Ohio. | 3:00 |
| Aug. 4 | **Houston** | 8:00 |
| Aug. 11 | **Cincinnati** | 8:00 |
| Aug. 18 | at Atlanta | 8:00 |
| Aug. 24 | **Miami** | 8:00 |

### Regular Season
| | | |
|---|---|---|
| Sept. 2 | at Chicago | 12:00 |
| Sept. 9 | at New Orleans | 12:00 |
| Sept. 16 | **Detroit** | 4:00 |
| Sept. 23 | at New York Giants | 4:00 |
| Sept. 30 | **Green Bay** | 4:00 |
| Oct. 7 | **Minnesota** | 1:00 |
| Oct. 14 | at Detroit | 1:00 |
| Oct. 21 | **Chicago** | 1:00 |
| Oct. 28 | at Kansas City | 12:00 |
| Nov. 4 | at Minnesota | 12:00 |
| Nov. 11 | **New York Giants** | 4:00 |
| Nov. 18 | at San Francisco | 1:00 |
| Nov. 25 | **Los Angeles Rams** | 1:00 |
| Dec. 2 | at Green Bay | 12:00 |
| Dec. 9 | **Atlanta** | 1:00 |
| Dec. 16 | **New York Jets** | 1:00 |

## BUCCANEERS COACHING HISTORY
### (39-81-1)
1976-83   John McKay . . . . . . . . . . . . . . . . 39-81-1

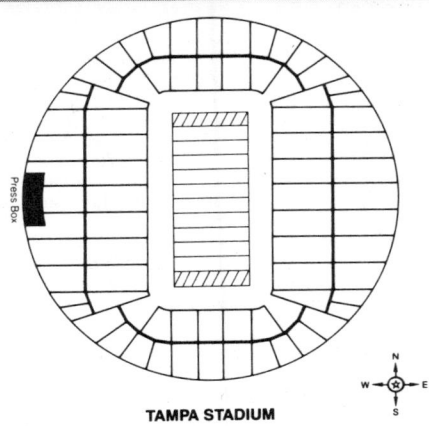

**TAMPA STADIUM**

## RECORD HOLDERS
### Individual Records—Career
| Category | Name | Performance |
|---|---|---|
| Rushing (Yds.) | Ricky Bell, 1977-1981 | 3,057 |
| Passing (Yds.) | Doug Williams, 1978-1982 | 12,648 |
| Passing (TDs) | Doug Williams, 1978-1982 | 73 |
| Receiving (No.) | Jimmie Giles, 1978-1983 | 194 |
| Receiving (Yds.) | Jimmie Giles, 1978-1983 | 3,139 |
| Interceptions | Mike Washington, 1976-1983 | 28 |
| | Cedric Brown, 1977-1983 | 28 |
| Punting (Avg.) | Tom Blanchard, 1979-1981 | 40.9 |
| Punt Return (Avg.) | John Holt, 1981-83 | 7.5 |
| Kickoff Return (Avg.) | Isaac Hagins, 1976-1980 | 21.9 |
| Field Goals | Bill Capece, 1981-83 | 43 |
| Touchdowns (Tot.) | Jimmie Giles, 1978-1983 | 23 |
| Points | Bill Capece, 1981-83 | 196 |

### Individual Records—Single Season
| Category | Name | Performance |
|---|---|---|
| Rushing (Yds.) | Ricky Bell, 1979 | 1,263 |
| Passing (Yds.) | Doug Williams, 1981 | 3,563 |
| Passing (TDs) | Doug Williams, 1980 | 20 |
| Receiving (No.) | James Wilder, 1983 | 57 |
| Receiving (Yds.) | Kevin House, 1981 | 1,176 |
| Interceptions | Cedric Brown, 1981 | 9 |
| Punting (Avg.) | Larry Swider, 1981 | 42.7 |
| Punt Return (Avg.) | Danny Reece, 1978 | 8.9 |
| Kickoff Return (Avg.) | Isaac Hagins, 1977 | 23.5 |
| Field Goals | Bill Capece, 1982 | 18 |
| Touchdowns (Tot.) | Ricky Bell, 1979 | 9 |
| | Kevin House, 1981 | 9 |
| Points | Garo Yepremian, 1980 | 79 |

### Individual Records—Single Game
| Category | Name | Performance |
|---|---|---|
| Rushing (Yds.) | James Wilder, 11-6-83 | 219 |
| Passing (Yds.) | Doug Williams, 11-16-80 | 486 |
| Passing (TDs) | Doug Williams, 11-16-80, 10-4-81 | 4 |
| | Jack Thompson, 11-27-83 | 4 |
| Receiving (No.) | James Wilder, 12-12-82, 9-25-83 | 11 |
| Receiving (Yds.) | Kevin House, 10-18-81 | 178 |
| Interceptions | Many times | 2 |
| | Last time by Beasley Reece, 11-27-83 | |
| Field Goals | Bill Capece, 10-30-83, 1-2-83 | 4 |
| Touchdowns | Morris Owens, 10-24-76 | 3 |
| Points | Morris Owens, 10-24-76 | 18 |

## 1983 TEAM STATISTICS

| | Tampa Bay | Opp. |
|---|---|---|
| Total First Downs | 249 | 320 |
| Rushing | 72 | 124 |
| Passing | 157 | 172 |
| Penalty | 20 | 24 |
| Third Down Efficiency | 74/226 | 91/230 |
| Third Down Percentage | 32.7 | 39.6 |
| Total Net Yards | 4477 | 5397 |
| Total Offensive Plays | 1005 | 1093 |
| Avg. Gain per Play | 4.5 | 4.9 |
| Avg. Gain per Game | 279.8 | 337.3 |
| Net Yards Rushing | 1353 | 2082 |
| Total Rushing Plays | 428 | 561 |
| Avg. Gain per Rush | 3.2 | 3.7 |
| Avg. Gain Rushing per Game | 84.6 | 130.1 |
| Net Yards Passing | 3124 | 3315 |
| Lost Attempting to Pass | 49/366 | 42/309 |
| Gross Yards Passing | 3490 | 3624 |
| Attempts/Completions | 528/300 | 490/300 |
| Percent Completed | 56.8 | 61.2 |
| Had Intercepted | 24 | 23 |
| Avg. Net Passing per Game | 195.3 | 207.2 |
| Punts/Avg. | 96/41.8 | 79/40.7 |
| Punt Returns/Avg. | 42/7.1 | 59/10.2 |
| Kickoff Returns/Avg. | 68/19.3 | 50/20.8 |
| Interceptions/Avg. Ret. | 23/16.0 | 24/13.2 |
| Penalties/Yards | 94/832 | 105/799 |
| Fumbles/Ball Lost | 39/13 | 43/18 |
| Total Points | 241 | 380 |
| Avg. Points per Game | 15.1 | 23.8 |
| Touchdowns | 31 | 42 |
| Rushing | 9 | 19 |
| Passing | 18 | 15 |
| Returns and Recoveries | 4 | 8 |
| Field Goals | 10/24 | 28/34 |
| Conversions | 25/31 | 40/42 |
| Safeties | 0 | 2 |
| Avg. Time of Possession | 27:55 | 32:05 |

## 1983 TEAM RECORD

### Preseason (4-0)

| Date | Tampa Bay | | Opponents |
|---|---|---|---|
| 8/6 | 20 | *New Orleans | 17 |
| 8/13 | 23 | Houston | 17 |
| 8/20 | 17 | *Atlanta | 6 |
| 8/26 | 41 | *New England | 21 |
| | 101 | | 61 |

### Regular Season (2-14)

| Date | Tampa Bay | | Opp. | Att. |
|---|---|---|---|---|
| 9/4 | 0 | *Detroit | 11 | 62,154 |
| 9/11 | 10 | Chicago | 17 | 58,186 |
| 9/18 | 16 | *Minnesota (OT) | 19 | 57,567 |
| 9/25 | 17 | *Cincinnati | 23 | 56,023 |
| 10/2 | 14 | Green Bay | 55 | 54,272 |
| 10/9 | 24 | Dallas (OT) | 27 | 63,308 |
| 10/16 | 27 | *St. Louis | 34 | 48,224 |
| 10/23 | 21 | *New Orleans | 24 | 48,242 |
| 10/30 | 12 | Pittsburgh | 17 | 57,648 |
| 11/6 | 17 | Minnesota | 12 | 59,239 |
| 11/13 | 0 | Cleveland | 20 | 56,091 |
| 11/20 | 0 | *Chicago | 27 | 36,816 |
| 11/27 | 33 | *Houston | 24 | 38,625 |
| 12/4 | 21 | San Francisco | 35 | 49,773 |
| 12/12 | 9 | *Green Bay (OT) | 12 | 50,763 |
| 12/18 | 20 | Detroit | 23 | 78,553 |
| | 241 | | 380 | 875,484 |

*Home Game       (OT) Overtime

### Score by Periods

| | | | | | | | |
|---|---|---|---|---|---|---|---|
| Tampa Bay | 43 | 68 | 65 | 65 | 0 | — | 241 |
| Opponents | 70 | 127 | 70 | 104 | 9 | — | 380 |

### Attendance

Home 398,414      Away 477,070      Total 875,484
Single game home record, 71,733 (10-4-81)
Single season home record, 545,980 (1979)

## 1983 INDIVIDUAL STATISTICS

### Rushing

| | Att. | Yds. | Avg. | LG | TD |
|---|---|---|---|---|---|
| Wilder | 161 | 640 | 4.0 | 75t | 4 |
| Carver | 114 | 348 | 3.1 | 16 | 0 |
| Owens | 96 | 266 | 2.8 | 15 | 5 |
| Armstrong | 7 | 30 | 4.3 | 7 | 0 |
| Morton | 13 | 28 | 2.2 | 5 | 0 |
| J. Thompson | 26 | 27 | 1.0 | 10 | 0 |
| Komlo | 2 | 11 | 5.5 | 11 | 0 |
| Middleton | 2 | 4 | 2.0 | 2 | 0 |
| Golsteyn | 5 | 3 | 0.6 | 2 | 0 |
| Carter | 1 | 0 | 0.0 | 0 | 0 |
| House | 1 | −4 | −4.0 | −4 | 0 |
| Tampa Bay | 428 | 1353 | 3.2 | 75t | 9 |
| Opponents | 561 | 2082 | 3.7 | 39 | 19 |

### Passing

| | Att. | Comp. | Pct. | Yds. | TD | Int. | Tkld. | Rate |
|---|---|---|---|---|---|---|---|---|
| J. Thompson | 423 | 249 | 58.9 | 2906 | 18 | 21 | 39/289 | 73.3 |
| Golsteyn | 97 | 47 | 48.5 | 535 | 0 | 2 | 7/52 | 56.9 |
| Komlo | 8 | 4 | 50.0 | 49 | 0 | 1 | 3/25 | 29.7 |
| Tampa Bay | 528 | 300 | 56.8 | 3490 | 18 | 24 | 49/366 | 69.4 |
| Opponents | 490 | 300 | 61.2 | 3624 | 15 | 23 | 42/309 | 74.6 |

### Receiving

| | No. | Yds. | Avg. | LG | TD |
|---|---|---|---|---|---|
| Wilder | 57 | 380 | 6.7 | 31 | 2 |
| Carter | 48 | 694 | 14.5 | 56t | 2 |
| House | 47 | 769 | 16.4 | 74t | 5 |
| Carver | 32 | 262 | 8.2 | 20 | 1 |
| T. Bell | 25 | 410 | 16.4 | 52 | 2 |
| Giles | 25 | 349 | 14.0 | 80 | 1 |
| J. Bell | 18 | 200 | 11.1 | 33 | 1 |
| Armstrong | 15 | 173 | 11.5 | 41 | 2 |
| Owens | 15 | 81 | 5.4 | 11 | 1 |
| Obradovich | 9 | 71 | 7.9 | 19 | 1 |
| Tyler | 6 | 77 | 12.8 | 21 | 0 |
| Witte | 2 | 15 | 7.5 | 10 | 0 |
| Morton | 1 | 9 | 9.0 | 9 | 0 |
| Tampa Bay | 300 | 3490 | 11.6 | 80 | 18 |
| Opponents | 300 | 3624 | 12.1 | 80t | 15 |

### Interceptions

| | No. | Yds. | Avg. | LG | TD |
|---|---|---|---|---|---|
| Reece | 6 | 70 | 11.7 | 29 | 0 |
| Brown | 4 | 78 | 19.5 | 36 | 0 |
| Holt | 3 | 43 | 14.3 | 25 | 0 |
| Green | 2 | 54 | 27.0 | 33t | 2 |
| Washington | 2 | 41 | 20.5 | 25 | 0 |
| Reese | 2 | 11 | 5.5 | 11 | 0 |
| Cotney | 2 | 1 | 0.5 | 1 | 0 |
| Castille | 1 | 69 | 69.0 | 69t | 1 |
| Brantley | 1 | 0 | 0.0 | 0 | 0 |
| Tampa Bay | 23 | 367 | 16.0 | 69t | 3 |
| Opponents | 24 | 316 | 13.2 | 70t | 4 |

### Punting

| | No. | Yds. | Avg. | In 20 | LG |
|---|---|---|---|---|---|
| Garcia | 95 | 4008 | 42.2 | 16 | 64 |
| Tampa Bay | 96 | 4008 | 41.8 | 16 | 64 |
| Opponents | 79 | 3217 | 40.7 | 11 | 65 |

### Punt Returns

| | No. | FC | Yds. | Avg. | LG | TD |
|---|---|---|---|---|---|---|
| Tyler | 27 | 5 | 208 | 7.7 | 16 | 0 |
| T. Bell | 10 | 2 | 48 | 4.8 | 11 | 0 |
| Holt | 5 | 0 | 43 | 8.6 | 17 | 0 |
| Tampa Bay | 42 | 7 | 299 | 7.1 | 17 | 0 |
| Opponents | 59 | 11 | 603 | 10.2 | 90t | 1 |

### Kickoff Returns

| | No. | Yds. | Avg. | LG | TD |
|---|---|---|---|---|---|
| Morton | 30 | 689 | 23.0 | 50 | 0 |
| Owens | 20 | 380 | 19.0 | 31 | 0 |
| Smith | 8 | 136 | 17.0 | 43 | 0 |
| Spradlin | 3 | 35 | 11.7 | 24 | 0 |
| Carver | 2 | 24 | 12.0 | 13 | 0 |
| O'Steen | 2 | 30 | 15.0 | 16 | 0 |
| Armstrong | 1 | 10 | 10.0 | 10 | 0 |
| Middleton | 1 | 10 | 10.0 | 10 | 0 |
| Obradovich | 1 | 0 | 0.0 | 0 | 0 |
| Tampa Bay | 68 | 1314 | 19.3 | 50 | 0 |
| Opponents | 50 | 1039 | 20.8 | 81 | 0 |

### Scoring

| | TD | TD R | TD P | TD Rt | PAT | FG | TP |
|---|---|---|---|---|---|---|---|
| Capece | | | | | 23/26 | 10/23 | 53 |
| Owens | 6 | 5 | 1 | 0 | | | 36 |
| Wilder | 6 | 4 | 2 | 0 | | | 36 |
| House | 5 | 0 | 5 | 0 | | | 30 |
| Armstrong | 2 | 0 | 2 | 0 | | | 12 |
| T. Bell | 2 | 0 | 2 | 0 | | | 12 |
| Carter | 2 | 0 | 2 | 0 | | | 12 |
| Green | 2 | 0 | 0 | 2 | | | 12 |
| J. Bell | 1 | 0 | 1 | 0 | | | 6 |
| Carver | 1 | 0 | 1 | 0 | | | 6 |
| Castille | 1 | 0 | 0 | 1 | | | 6 |
| Giles | 1 | 0 | 1 | 0 | | | 6 |
| Logan | 1 | 0 | 0 | 1 | | | 6 |
| Obradovich | 1 | 0 | 1 | 0 | | | 6 |
| Warnke | | | | | 1/2 | 0/1 | 1 |
| Yarno | | | | | 1/1 | 0/0 | 1 |
| Tampa Bay | 31 | 9 | 18 | 4 | 25/31 | 10/24 | 241 |
| Opponents | 42 | 19 | 15 | 8 | 40/42 | 28/34 | 380 |

## FIRST-ROUND SELECTIONS

(If Club had no first-round selection, first player drafted is listed with round in parentheses.)

| Year | Player, College, Position |
|---|---|
| 1976 | Lee Roy Selmon, Oklahoma, DT |
| 1977 | Ricky Bell, Southern California, RB |
| 1978 | Doug Williams, Grambling, QB |
| 1979 | Greg Roberts, Oklahoma, G (2) |
| 1980 | Ray Snell, Wisconsin, G |
| 1981 | Hugh Green, Pittsburgh, LB |
| 1982 | Sean Farrell, Penn State, G |
| 1983 | Randy Grimes, Baylor, C (2) |
| 1984 | Keith Browner, Southern California, LB (2) |

# TAMPA BAY BUCCANEERS 1984 VETERAN ROSTER

| No. | Name | Pos. | Ht. | Wt. | Birth-date | NFL Exp. | College | Birthplace | Residence | Games in '83 |
|-----|------|------|-----|-----|------------|----------|---------|------------|------------|--------------|
| 69 | Arbubakrr, Hasson | DE | 6-4 | 250 | 12/9/60 | 2 | Texas Tech | Newark, N.J. | Newark, N.J. | 16 |
| 46 | Armstrong, Adger | RB | 6-0 | 225 | 6/21/57 | 5 | Texas A&M | Houston, Tex. | Houston, Tex. | 11 |
| 30 | Barrett, David | RB | 6-0 | 235 | 9/9/59 | 2 | Houston | Corpus Christi, Tex. | Corpus Christi, Tex. | 0* |
| 82 | Bell, Jerry | TE | 6-5 | 225 | 3/7/59 | 3 | Arizona State | Derby, Conn. | Tampa, Fla. | 16 |
| 83 | †Bell, Theo | WR | 6-0 | 190 | 12/21/53 | 8 | Arizona | Bakersfield, Calif. | Tampa, Fla. | 16 |
| 52 | Brantley, Scot | LB | 6-1 | 230 | 2/24/58 | 5 | Florida | Chester, S.C. | Lutz, Fla. | 16 |
| 34 | Brown, Cedric | S | 6-2 | 200 | 5/6/54 | 7 | Kent State | Columbus, Ohio | Tampa, Fla. | 8 |
| 77 | Bujnoch, Glenn | G | 6-6 | 265 | 12/20/53 | 9 | Texas A&M | Houston, Tex. | Cincinnati, Ohio | 6 |
| 78 | Cannon, John | DE | 6-5 | 260 | 7/30/60 | 3 | William & Mary | Long Branch, N.J. | Tampa, Fla. | 14 |
| 3 | Capece, Bill | K | 5-7 | 170 | 4/1/59 | 4 | Florida State | Miami, Fla. | Tampa, Fla. | 15 |
| 87 | Carter, Gerald | WR | 6-1 | 190 | 6/19/57 | 5 | Texas A&M | Bryan, Tex. | Bryan, Tex. | 16 |
| 28 | Carver, Melvin | RB | 5-11 | 215 | 7/14/59 | 3 | Nevada-Las Vegas | Pensacola, Fla. | Tampa, Fla. | 16 |
| 23 | Castille, Jeremiah | CB | 5-10 | 175 | 1/15/61 | 2 | Alabama | Columbus, Ga. | Phenix City, Ala. | 15 |
| 20 | Colzie, Neal | S | 6-2 | 205 | 2/28/53 | 10 | Ohio State | Fitzgerald, Ga. | Tampa, Fla. | 5 |
| 33 | Cotney, Mark | S | 6-0 | 205 | 6/26/52 | 9 | Cameron State | Altus, Okla. | Tampa, Fla. | 12 |
| 58 | Davis, Jeff | LB | 6-0 | 230 | 1/26/60 | 3 | Clemson | Greensboro, N.C. | Greensboro, N.C. | 15 |
| | t-DeBerg, Steve | QB | 6-3 | 205 | 1/19/54 | 8 | San Jose State | Oakland, Calif. | Littleton, Colo. | 10 |
| | t-Dierking, Scott | RB | 5-10 | 220 | 5/24/55 | 8 | Purdue | Great Lakes, Ill. | West Chicago, Ill. | 16 |
| 62 | Farrell, Sean | G | 6-3 | 260 | 5/25/60 | 3 | Penn State | Southampton, N.Y. | Tampa, Fla. | 10 |
| 5 | Garcia, Frank | P | 6-0 | 205 | 6/5/57 | 2 | Arizona | Tucson, Ariz. | Tucson, Ariz. | 16 |
| 88 | Giles, Jimmie | TE | 6-3 | 240 | 11/8/54 | 8 | Alcorn State | Greenville, Miss. | Tampa, Fla. | 11 |
| 53 | Green, Hugh | LB | 6-2 | 225 | 7/27/59 | 4 | Pittsburgh | Natchez, Miss. | Tampa, Fla. | 16 |
| 60 | Grimes, Randy | G-C | 6-4 | 265 | 7/20/60 | 2 | Baylor | Tyler, Tex. | Tyler, Tex. | 15 |
| 8 | Hewko, Bob | QB | 6-3 | 195 | 6/8/60 | 2 | Florida | Abington, Pa. | Tampa, Fla. | 2 |
| 21 | †Holt, John | CB | 5-11 | 175 | 5/14/59 | 4 | West Texas State | Lawton, Okla. | Tampa, Fla. | 16 |
| 89 | House, Kevin | WR | 6-1 | 175 | 12/20/57 | 5 | Southern Illinois | St. Louis, Mo. | Tampa, Fla. | 16 |
| 59 | Johnson, Cecil | LB | 6-2 | 235 | 8/19/55 | 8 | Pittsburgh | Miami, Fla. | Tampa, Fla. | 5 |
| 51 | Judie, Ed | LB | 6-2 | 235 | 7/6/59 | 3 | Northern Arizona | Tyler, Tex. | Mesa, Ariz. | 15* |
| 7 | Komlo, Jeff | QB | 6-2 | 195 | 7/30/56 | 6 | Delaware | Cleverly, Md. | Radnor, Pa. | 2 |
| 29 | LaBeaux, Sandy | S | 6-3 | 210 | 8/22/61 | 2 | Cal State-Hayward | San Antonio, Tex. | San Ramon, Calif. | 3 |
| 76 | †Logan, David | NT | 6-2 | 250 | 10/25/56 | 6 | Pittsburgh | Pittsburgh, Pa. | Pittsburgh, Pa. | 16 |
| 64 | Lowry, Quentin | LB | 6-2 | 235 | 11/11/57 | 4 | Youngstown State | Shaker Heights, Ohio | Shaker Heights, Ohio | 9* |
| 24 | †Morris, Thomas | CB-S | 5-11 | 175 | 4/2/60 | 3 | Michigan State | Anniston, Ala. | Tampa, Fla. | 12 |
| 1 | Morton, Michael | KR-RB | 5-8 | 180 | 2/6/60 | 3 | Nevada-Las Vegas | Birmingham, Ala. | Tampa, Fla. | 16 |
| 86 | Obradovich, Jim | TE | 6-2 | 225 | 4/2/53 | 10 | Southern California | Los Angeles, Calif. | Hermosa Beach, Calif. | 16 |
| 26 | Owens, James | RB | 5-11 | 200 | 7/5/55 | 6 | UCLA | Sacramento, Calif. | Tampa, Fla. | 12 |
| | t-Phillips, Irvin | CB | 6-1 | 190 | 1/23/60 | 3 | Arkansas Tech | Leesburg, Fla. | San Diego, Calif. | 5 |
| 75 | Reavis, Dave | T | 6-5 | 265 | 6/19/50 | 10 | Arkansas | Nashville, Tenn. | Tampa, Fla. | 15 |
| 43 | Reece, Beasley | S | 6-1 | 195 | 3/18/54 | 9 | North Texas State | Waco, Tex. | Tampa, Fla. | 16* |
| 66 | Reese, Booker | DE | 6-6 | 260 | 9/20/59 | 3 | Bethune-Cookman | Jacksonville, Fla. | Tampa, Fla. | 16 |
| 74 | Sanders, Gene | T | 6-3 | 280 | 11/10/56 | 6 | Texas A&M | New Orleans, La. | Tampa, Fla. | 12 |
| 63 | Selmon, Lee Roy | DE | 6-3 | 250 | 10/20/54 | 9 | Oklahoma | Eufaula, Okla. | Tampa, Fla. | 14 |
| 22 | Smith, Johnny Ray | CB-S | 5-9 | 185 | 9/7/57 | 3 | Lamar | Crockett, Tex. | Cleveland, Tex. | 16 |
| 72 | Snell, Ray | G | 6-4 | 265 | 2/2/58 | 5 | Wisconsin | Baltimore, Md. | Tampa, Fla. | 9 |
| 55 | Spradlin, Danny | LB | 6-1 | 235 | 3/3/59 | 4 | Tennessee | Maryville, Tenn. | Maryville, Tenn. | 16 |
| 70 | Thomas, Kelly | T | 6-6 | 270 | 9/9/60 | 2 | Southern California | Lynwood, Calif. | La Mirada, Calif. | 14 |
| 41 | Thomas, Norris | CB | 6-0 | 180 | 5/3/54 | 8 | Southern Mississippi | Inverness, Miss. | Pascagoula, Miss. | 10 |
| 14 | Thompson, Jack | QB | 6-3 | 220 | 5/18/56 | 5 | Washington State | Pago Pago, Amer. Samoa | Seattle, Wash. | 14 |
| 56 | Thompson, Robert | LB | 6-3 | 225 | 2/4/60 | 2 | Michigan | Chicago, Ill. | Chicago, Ill. | 10 |
| 81 | Tyler, Andre | WR | 6-0 | 180 | 7/17/59 | 3 | Stanford | Tucson, Ariz. | Tampa, Fla. | 14 |
| 40 | Washington, Mike | CB-S | 6-2 | 200 | 7/1/53 | 9 | Alabama | Montgomery, Ala. | Montgomery, Ala. | 14 |
| 90 | White, Brad | NT | 6-2 | 255 | 10/18/58 | 4 | Tennessee | Rexburg, Idaho | Knoxville, Tenn. | 16 |
| 32 | Wilder, James | RB | 6-3 | 220 | 5/12/58 | 4 | Missouri | Sikeston, Mo. | Tampa, Fla. | 10 |
| 50 | Wilson, Steve | C | 6-4 | 270 | 5/19/54 | 9 | Georgia | Fort Sill, Okla. | Tampa, Fla. | 10 |
| 85 | Witte, Mark | TE | 6-3 | 235 | 12/3/59 | 2 | North Texas State | Corpus Christi, Tex. | San Marcos, Tex. | 16 |
| 54 | Wood, Richard | LB | 6-2 | 230 | 5/31/53 | 10 | Southern California | Elizabeth, N.J. | Tampa, Fla. | 16 |

\* Barrett missed '83 season due to injury; Judie played 4 games with San Francisco, 11 with Tampa Bay in '83; Lowry played 3 games with Washington, 6 with Tampa Bay; Reece played 7 games with New York Giants, 9 with Tampa Bay.

†Option playout; subject to developments.

t-Buccaneers traded for Dierking (N.Y. Jets), DeBerg (Denver), Phillips (L.A. Raiders).

Traded—Quarterback Jerry Golsteyn to L.A. Raiders.

Also played with Buccaneers in '83—WR Gene Branton (1 game), LB Andy Hawkins (6), C-G Jim Leonard (15), RB Terdell Middleton (7), CB Dwayne O'Steen (3), DE Dave Stalls (6), K Dave Warnke (1), G-T George Yarno (14).

## COACHING STAFF

### Head Coach, John McKay

**Pro Career:** Starts ninth season as Buccaneers head coach. Led Tampa Bay to division championship in 1981. In 1979, guided Tampa Bay to NFC Central title and first playoff berth. Under his direction, Buccaneers became the second expansion team to qualify for the playoffs in one of its first four seasons and the first expansion team to win 10 games in one of its first four seasons. Drafted by the New York Yankees (AAFC) in 1950 but turned down pro playing career. Career record: 39-81-1.

**Background:** Defensive back Purdue 1946, transferred to Oregon and played both ways 1947-49. Holds Oregon records for most touchdowns rushing in a game and highest career average per carry. Assistant coach at Oregon 1950-58 and Southern California 1959. Head coach at Southern California 1960-75. Directed Southern California teams to four national championships and nine Bowl appearances (Rose 8, Liberty 1). Southern California coaching record: 127-40-8.

**Personal:** Born July 5, 1923, Everettsville, West Virginia. John and his wife, Corky, live in Tampa and have four children — Michele, John Jr., Richard, and Terri.

### Assistant Coaches

**John Brunner,** offensive moderator; born September 6, 1937, Perkesie, Pa. lives in Clearwater Beach. Running back East Stroudsburg State 1957-59. No pro playing experience. College coach: Villanova 1967-69, Temple 1970-73, 1976-79, Princeton 1974-75. Pro coach: Detroit Lions 1980-82, Green Bay Packers 1983, first year with Buccaneers.

**Joe Diange,** strength; born April 24, 1956, Massapequa Park, N.Y., lives in Tampa. Linebacker Penn State 1976-77. No pro playing experience. College coach: Penn State 1978-81; Navy 1982-83. Pro coach: First year with Buccaneers.

**Boyd Dowler,** quarterbacks; born October 18, 1937, Rock Springs, Wyo., lives in Tampa. Quarterback Colorado 1955-58. Pro wide receiver Green Bay Packers 1959-69, Washington Redskins 1971. Pro coach: Los Angeles Rams 1970, Washington Redskins 1971-72, Philadelphia Eagles 1973-75, Cincinnati Bengals 1976-79, joined Buccaneers in 1980.

**Wayne Fontes,** assistant head coach-defensive coordinator-defensive secondary; born February 17, 1940, New Bedford, Mass., lives in Tampa. Defensive back Michigan State 1959-62. Pro defensive back New York Titans (AFL) 1963-64. College coach: Dayton 1968, Iowa 1969-71, Southern California 1972-75. Pro coach: Joined Buccaneers in 1976.

**Abe Gibron,** defensive line; born September 22, 1925, Michigan City, Ind., lives in Tampa. Guard Purdue 1945-47. Pro guard Buffalo Bills (AAFC) 1949, Cleveland Browns 1950-55, Philadelphia Eagles 1956-57, Chicago Bears 1958-59. Pro coach: Washington Redskins 1960-64, Chicago Bears 1965-74 (head coach 1972-74), Chicago Wind (WFL) 1975 (head coach), joined Buccaneers in 1976.

**Kim Helton,** offensive line, born July 28, 1948, Pensacola, Fla., lives in Tampa. Center Florida 1967-69. No pro playing experience. College coach: Florida 1972-78, Miami 1979-82. Pro coach: Joined Buccaneers in 1983.

**Chip Myers,** receivers, born July 9, 1945, Panama City, Fla., lives in Tampa. Receiver Northwest Oklahoma 1964-66. Pro receiver San Francisco 49ers 1967, Cincinnati Bengals 1969-76. College coach: Illinois 1980-82. Pro coach: Joined Buccaneers in 1983.

## TAMPA BAY BUCCANEERS 1984 FIRST-YEAR ROSTER

| Name | Pos. | Ht. | Wt. | Birth-date | College | Birthplace | Residence | How Acq. |
|---|---|---|---|---|---|---|---|---|
| Acorn, Fred | CB | 5-10 | 185 | 3/17/61 | Texas | Rotan, Tex. | Rotan, Tex. | D3 |
| Arriri, Obed (1) | K | 5-8 | 170 | 4/4/56 | Clemson | Owerri, Nigeria | Washington, D.C. | FA |
| Bailey, Don (1) | C | 6-3 | 250 | 3/24/61 | Miami | Miami, Fla. | N. Miami Beach, Fla. | FA |
| Branton, Gene (1) | WR | 6-4 | 215 | 11/23/60 | Texas Southern | Tampa, Fla. | Tampa, Fla. | D6('83) |
| Browner, Keith | LB | 6-5 | 225 | 1/24/62 | Southern California | Warren, Ohio | Atlanta, Ga. | D2 |
| Burtness, Richard (1) | G | 6-5 | 265 | 6/25/60 | Montana | Anacortes, Wash. | Anacortes, Wash. | FA |
| Carroll, Jay | TE | 6-4 | 230 | 11/8/61 | Minnesota | Winona, Minn. | Winona, Minn. | D7 |
| Chickillo, Tony (1) | NT | 6-3 | 255 | 7/8/60 | Miami | Miami, Fla. | Tampa, Fla. | D5('83) |
| Gallery, Jim | K | 6-1 | 200 | 9/15/61 | Minnesota | Redwood Falls, Minn. | Morton, Minn. | D10 |
| Gunter, Michael | RB | 5-11 | 205 | 1/18/61 | Tulsa | Gladewater, Tex. | Gladewater, Tex. | D4 |
| Heller, Ron | T | 6-6 | 265 | 8/25/62 | Penn State | Farmingdale, N.Y. | Farmingdale, N.Y. | D4a |
| Jemison, Thad | WR | 6-2 | 195 | 12/24/61 | Ohio State | Cincinnati, Ohio | Cincinnati, Ohio | D12 |
| Kaplan, Ken (1) | T | 6-4 | 275 | 1/12/60 | New Hampshire | Boston, Mass. | Tampa, Fla. | D6('83) |
| Kiel, Blair | QB | 6-0 | 200 | 11/29/61 | Notre Dame | Columbus, Ind. | Columbus, Ind. | D11 |
| Mallory, Rick | G | 6-2 | 265 | 8/25/62 | Washington | Seattle, Wash. | Renton, Wash. | D9 |
| Natividad, Frank (1) | P | 6-3 | 205 | 1/11/61 | Hawaii | Los Angeles, Calif. | Hacienda Hts., Calif. | FA |
| Richardson, Al (1) | LB | 6-0 | 225 | 11/15/60 | Louisiana State | New Orleans, La. | Baton Rouge, La. | FA |
| Robinson, Fred | DE | 6-4 | 240 | 10/22/61 | Miami | Miami, Fla. | Miami, Fla. | D8 |
| Vernon, Skip (1) | K | 5-10 | 175 | 10/12/56 | New Mexico State | Inglewood, Calif. | Albuquerque, N.M. | FA |
| Washington, Chris | LB | 6-4 | 220 | 3/6/62 | Iowa State | Jackson, Miss. | Chicago, Ill. | D6 |

Players who report to an NFL team for the first time are designated on rosters as rookies (R). If a player reported to an NFL training camp in a previous year but was not on the active squad for three or more regular season or postseason games, he is listed on the first-year roster and designated by a (1). Thereafter, a player who is on the active squad for three or more regular season or postseason games is credited with an additional year of playing experience.

# NOTES

_____
_____
_____
_____
_____
_____
_____
_____
_____
_____
_____
_____
_____
_____
_____
_____
_____
_____
_____
_____
_____

**Howard Tippett,** linebackers; born September 23, 1938, Tallassee, Ala., lives in Tampa. Quarterback-safety East Tennessee State 1955-57. No pro playing experience. College coach: Tulane 1963-65, West Virginia 1966, 1971, Houston 1967-70, Mississippi State 1972-73, 1979, Washington State 1976, Oregon 1977-78, UCLA 1980. Pro coach: Jacksonville Sharks (WFL) 1974-75, joined Buccaneers in 1981.

# WASHINGTON REDSKINS

**National Football Conference
Eastern Division**

**Team Colors:** Burgundy and Gold

**Redskin Park,
P.O. Box 17247
Dulles International Airport,
Washington, D.C. 20041
Telephone: (703) 471-9100**

## Club Officials

Chairman of the Board-Chief Operating Executive:
Jack Kent Cooke
President: Edward Bennett Williams
Executive Vice President: John Kent Cooke
Senior Vice President: Gerard T. Gabrys
Board of Directors: Jack Kent Cooke, John Kent
Cooke, Lawrence Lucchino, Esq., W. Jarvis
Moody, Robert A. Schulman, Esq., William A.
Shea, Esq., The Honorable John W. Warner,
Edward Bennett Williams, Esq.
General Manager: Bobby Beathard
Assistant General Managers: Bobby Mitchell,
Charles Casserly
Director of Pro Scouting: Kirk Mee
Talent Scout: Billy Devaney
Director of Public Relations: Charles M. Taylor
Assistant Public Relations Directors: Ronn Levine,
John C. Konoza
Director of Stadium Operations: Joel Margolis
Ticket Manager: Sue Barton
Head Trainer: Lamar (Bubba) Tyer
Assistant Trainers: Joe Kuczo, Keoki Kamau
Equipment Manager: Jay Brunetti

**Stadium:** Robert F. Kennedy Stadium •
**Capacity:** 55,363
East Capitol Street
Washington, D.C. 20003
**Playing Surface:** Grass (PAT)
**Training Camp:** Dickinson College
Carlisle, Pennsylvania 17013

## 1984 SCHEDULE

### Preseason
| | | |
|---|---|---|
| Aug. 4 | at Denver | 7:00 |
| Aug. 10 | **Los Angeles Raiders** | 8:00 |
| Aug. 17 | **New England** | 8:00 |
| Aug. 25 | at New Orleans | 12:00 |

### Regular Season
| | | |
|---|---|---|
| Sept. 2 | **Miami** | 1:00 |
| Sept. 10 | at San Francisco (Monday) | 6:00 |
| Sept. 16 | **New York Giants** | 4:00 |
| Sept. 23 | at New England | 1:00 |
| Sept. 30 | **Philadelphia** | 4:00 |
| Oct. 7 | at Colts | 12:00 |
| Oct. 14 | **Dallas** | 4:00 |
| Oct. 21 | at St. Louis | 12:00 |
| Oct. 28 | at New York Giants | 4:00 |
| Nov. 5 | **Atlanta** (Monday) | 9:00 |
| Nov. 11 | **Detroit** | 1:00 |
| Nov. 18 | at Philadelphia | 1:00 |
| Nov. 25 | **Buffalo** | 1:00 |
| Nov. 29 | at Minnesota (Thursday) | 8:00 |
| Dec. 9 | at Dallas | 3:00 |
| Dec. 16 | **St. Louis** | 1:00 |

## REDSKINS COACHING HISTORY
### Boston 1932-36
### (342-312-26)
| | | |
|---|---|---|
| 1932 | Lud Wray | 4-4-2 |
| 1933-34 | William (Lone Star) Dietz | 11-11-2 |
| 1935 | Eddie Casey | 2-8-1 |
| 1936-42 | Ray Flaherty* | 56-23-3 |
| 1943 | Arthur (Dutch) Bergman | 7-4-1 |
| 1944-45 | Dudley DeGroot | 14-6-1 |
| 1946-48 | Glen (Turk) Edwards | 16-18-1 |
| 1949 | John (Billick) Whelchel** | 2-4-1 |
| 1949-51 | Herman Ball*** | 5-15-0 |
| 1951 | Dick Todd | 5-4-0 |
| 1952-53 | Earl (Curly) Lambeau | 10-13-1 |
| 1954-58 | Joe Kuharich | 26-32-2 |
| 1959-60 | Mike Nixon | 4-18-2 |
| 1961-65 | Bill McPeak | 21-46-3 |
| 1966-68 | Otto Graham | 17-22-3 |
| 1969 | Vince Lombardi | 7-5-2 |
| 1970 | Bill Austin | 6-8-0 |
| 1971-77 | George Allen | 69-35-1 |
| 1978-80 | Jack Pardee | 24-24-0 |
| 1981-83 | Joe Gibbs | 36-12-0 |

*Retired to enter Navy
**Released after seven games in 1949
***Released after three games in 1951

## RECORD HOLDERS
### Individual Records—Career
| Category | Name | Performance |
|---|---|---|
| Rushing (Yds.) | Larry Brown, 1969-1976 | 5,875 |
| Passing (Yds.) | Sonny Jurgensen, 1964-1974 | 22,585 |
| Passing (TDs) | Sonny Jurgensen, 1964-1974 | 209 |
| Receiving (No.) | Charley Taylor, 1964-1977 | 649 |
| Receiving (Yds.) | Charley Taylor, 1964-1977 | 9,140 |
| Interceptions | Brig Owens, 1966-1977 | 36 |
| Punting (Avg.) | Sammy Baugh, 1937-1952 | 45.1 |
| Punt Return (Avg.) | Johnny Williams, 1952-53 | 12.8 |
| Kickoff Return (Avg.) | Bobby Mitchell, 1962-68 | 28.5 |
| Field Goals | Mark Moseley, 1974-1983 | 211 |
| Touchdowns (Tot.) | Charley Taylor, 1964-1977 | 90 |
| Points | Mark Moseley, 1974-1983 | 959 |

### Individual Records—Single Season
| Category | Name | Performance |
|---|---|---|
| Rushing (Yds.) | John Riggins, 1983 | 1,347 |
| Passing (Yds.) | Sonny Jurgensen, 1967 | 3,747 |
| Passing (TDs) | Sonny Jurgensen, 1967 | 31 |
| Receiving (No.) | Charlie Brown, 1983 | 78 |
| Receiving (Yds.) | Bobby Mitchell, 1963 | 1,436 |
| Interceptions | Dan Sandifer, 1948 | 13 |
| Punting (Avg.) | Sammy Baugh, 1940 | 51.4 |
| Punt Return (Avg.) | Johnny Williams, 1952 | 15.3 |
| Kickoff Return (Avg.) | Mike Nelms, 1981 | 29.7 |
| Field Goals | Mark Moseley, 1983 | 33 |
| Touchdowns (Tot.) | John Riggins, 1983 | 24 |
| Points | Mark Moseley, 1983 | 161 |

### Individual Records—Single Game
| Category | Name | Performance |
|---|---|---|
| Rushing (Yds.) | Mike Thomas, 11-21-76 | 195 |
| Passing (Yds.) | Sammy Baugh, 10-31-48 | 446 |
| Passing (TDs) | Sammy Baugh, 10-31-43, 11-23-47 | 6 |
| Receiving (No.) | Clarence Harmon, 12-7-80 | 12 |
| Receiving (Yds.) | Bobby Mitchell, 11-7-63 | 218 |
| Interceptions | Sammy Baugh, 11-14-43 | 4 |
| | Dan Sandifer, 10-31-48 | 4 |
| Field Goals | Curt Knight, 10-10-71, 11-14-71, 11-18-73 | 5 |
| | Mark Moseley, 10-26-80 | 5 |
| Touchdowns (Tot.) | Dick James, 12-17-61 | 4 |
| | Larry Brown, 12-4-73 | 4 |
| Points | Dick James, 12-17-61 | 24 |
| | Larry Brown, 12-4-73 | 24 |

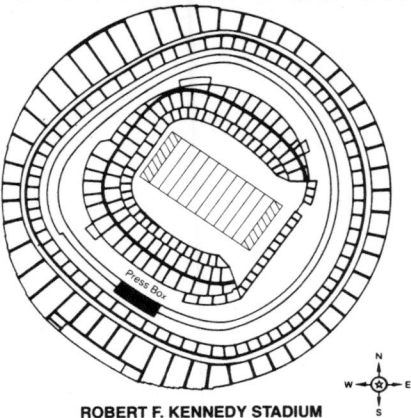

**ROBERT F. KENNEDY STADIUM**

## 1983 TEAM STATISTICS

| | Washington | Opp. |
|---|---|---|
| Total First Downs | 353 | 290 |
| Rushing | 165 | 76 |
| Passing | 173 | 196 |
| Penalty | 15 | 18 |
| Third Down Efficiency | 99/234 | 82/202 |
| Third Down Percentage | 42.3 | 40.6 |
| Total Net Yards | 6139 | 5264 |
| Total Offensive Plays | 1127 | 970 |
| Avg. Gain per Play | 5.4 | 5.4 |
| Avg. Gain per Game | 383.7 | 329.0 |
| Net Yards Rushing | 2625 | 1289 |
| Total Rushing Plays | 629 | 349 |
| Avg. Gain per Rush | 4.2 | 3.7 |
| Avg. Gain Rushing per Game | 164.1 | 80.6 |
| Net Yards Passing | 3514 | 3975 |
| Lost Attempting to Pass | 35/251 | 51/402 |
| Gross Yards Passing | 3765 | 4377 |
| Attempts/Completions | 463/278 | 570/301 |
| Percent Completed | 60.0 | 52.8 |
| Had Intercepted | 11 | 34 |
| Avg. Net Passing per Game | 219.6 | 248.4 |
| Punts/Avg. | 72/38.8 | 66/41.6 |
| Punt Returns/Avg. | 49/7.9 | 41/9.9 |
| Kickoff Returns/Avg. | 63/20.7 | 91/19.5 |
| Interceptions/Avg. Ret. | 34/12.9 | 11/8.2 |
| Penalties/Yards | 90/776 | 80/710 |
| Fumbles/Ball Lost | 13/7 | 46/27 |
| Total Points | 541 | 332 |
| Avg. Points per Game | 33.8 | 20.8 |
| Touchdowns | 63 | 39 |
| Rushing | 30 | 9 |
| Passing | 29 | 28 |
| Returns and Recoveries | 4 | 2 |
| Field Goals | 33/47 | 20/28 |
| Conversions | 62/63 | 38/39 |
| Safeties | 1 | 0 |
| Avg. Time of Possession | 33:44 | 26:16 |

## 1983 TEAM RECORD
### Preseason (2-2)

| Date | Washington | | Opponents |
|---|---|---|---|
| 8/6 | 10 | Atlanta (OT) | 13 |
| 8/12 | 27 | *Cincinnati | 23 |
| 8/19 | 7 | *Miami | 38 |
| 8/27 | 27 | Buffalo | 19 |
| | 71 | | 93 |

### Regular Season (14-2)

| Date | Washington | | Opp. | Att. |
|---|---|---|---|---|
| 9/5 | 30 | *Dallas | 31 | 55,045 |
| 9/11 | 23 | Philadelphia | 13 | 69,544 |
| 9/18 | 27 | *Kansas City | 12 | 52,610 |
| 9/25 | 27 | Seattle | 17 | 60,718 |
| 10/2 | 37 | *Los Angeles Raiders | 35 | 54,016 |
| 10/9 | 38 | St. Louis | 14 | 42,698 |
| 10/17 | 47 | Green Bay | 48 | 55,255 |
| 10/23 | 38 | *Detroit | 17 | 43,189 |
| 10/31 | 27 | San Diego | 24 | 46,414 |
| 11/6 | 45 | *St. Louis | 7 | 51,380 |
| 11/13 | 33 | New York Giants | 17 | 71,482 |
| 11/20 | 42 | Los Angeles Rams | 20 | 63,031 |
| 11/27 | 28 | *Philadelphia | 24 | 54,324 |
| 12/4 | 37 | *Atlanta | 21 | 52,074 |
| 12/11 | 31 | Dallas | 10 | 65,074 |
| 12/17 | 31 | *New York Giants | 22 | 53,874 |
| | 541 | | 332 | 890,728 |

*Home Game     (OT) Overtime

### Score by Periods

| | | | | | | |
|---|---|---|---|---|---|---|
| Washington | 127 | 153 | 129 | 132 | — | 541 |
| Opponents | 42 | 86 | 73 | 131 | — | 332 |

### Attendance

Home 416,512     Away 474,216     Total 890,728
Single game home record, 55,045
(9-8-80, 9-6-81, 9-5-83)
Single season home record, 427,651 (1979)

## 1983 INDIVIDUAL STATISTICS

### Rushing

| | Att. | Yds. | Avg. | LG | TD |
|---|---|---|---|---|---|
| Riggins | 375 | 1347 | 3.6 | 44 | 24 |
| J. Washington | 145 | 772 | 5.3 | 41 | 0 |
| Theismann | 37 | 234 | 6.3 | 22 | 1 |
| Wonsley | 25 | 88 | 3.5 | 9 | 0 |
| Hayes | 2 | 63 | 31.5 | 48 | 0 |
| Brown | 4 | 53 | 13.3 | 17 | 0 |
| Giaquinto | 14 | 53 | 3.8 | 11 | 1 |
| Holly | 4 | 13 | 3.3 | 13 | 0 |
| Evans | 16 | 11 | 0.7 | 5 | 4 |
| Walker | 2 | 10 | 5.0 | 11 | 0 |
| Garrett | 2 | 0 | 0.0 | 4 | 0 |
| Monk | 3 | −19 | −6.3 | 2 | 0 |
| Washington | 629 | 2625 | 4.2 | 48 | 30 |
| Opponents | 349 | 1289 | 3.7 | 77 | 9 |

### Passing

| | Att. | Comp. | Pct. | Yds. | TD | Int. | Tkld. | Rate |
|---|---|---|---|---|---|---|---|---|
| Theismann | 459 | 276 | 60.1 | 3714 | 29 | 11 | 34/242 | 97.0 |
| Holly | 1 | 1 | 100.0 | 5 | 0 | 0 | 1/9 | 87.5 |
| Monk | 1 | 1 | 100.0 | 46 | 0 | 0 | 0/0 | 118.8 |
| Riggins | 1 | 0 | 0.0 | 0 | 0 | 0 | 0/0 | 39.6 |
| J. Washington | 1 | 0 | 0.0 | 0 | 0 | 0 | 0/0 | 39.6 |
| Washington | 463 | 278 | 60.0 | 3765 | 29 | 11 | 35/251 | 97.0 |
| Opponents | 570 | 301 | 52.8 | 4377 | 28 | 34 | 51/402 | 69.6 |

### Receiving

| | No. | Yds. | Avg. | LG | TD |
|---|---|---|---|---|---|
| Brown | 78 | 1225 | 15.7 | 75t | 8 |
| Monk | 47 | 746 | 15.9 | 43t | 5 |
| J. Washington | 47 | 454 | 9.7 | 67 | 6 |
| Giaquinto | 27 | 372 | 13.8 | 35 | 0 |
| Garrett | 25 | 332 | 13.3 | 84 | 1 |
| Warren | 20 | 225 | 11.3 | 33 | 2 |
| Walker | 17 | 168 | 9.9 | 29 | 2 |
| Didier | 9 | 153 | 17.0 | 40t | 4 |
| Riggins | 5 | 29 | 5.8 | 14 | 0 |
| Seay | 2 | 55 | 27.5 | 39t | 1 |
| McGrath | 1 | 6 | 6.0 | 6 | 0 |
| Washington | 278 | 3765 | 13.5 | 84 | 29 |
| Opponents | 301 | 4377 | 14.5 | 99t | 28 |

### Interceptions

| | No. | Yds. | Avg. | LG | TD |
|---|---|---|---|---|---|
| Murphy | 9 | 127 | 14.1 | 48 | 0 |
| Dean | 5 | 54 | 10.8 | 26 | 0 |
| Coffey | 4 | 62 | 15.5 | 29 | 0 |
| A. Washington | 4 | 12 | 3.0 | 8 | 0 |
| Kaufman | 2 | 93 | 46.5 | 70t | 1 |
| G. Williams | 2 | 25 | 12.5 | 25 | 0 |
| Milot | 2 | 20 | 10.0 | 20 | 0 |
| Green | 2 | 7 | 3.5 | 7 | 0 |
| Jordan | 1 | 20 | 20.0 | 20 | 0 |
| Olkewicz | 1 | 14 | 14.0 | 14 | 0 |
| Carpenter | 1 | 2 | 2.0 | 2 | 0 |
| Manley | 1 | 1 | 1.0 | 1 | 0 |
| Washington | 34 | 437 | 12.9 | 70t | 1 |
| Opponents | 11 | 90 | 8.2 | 33 | 0 |

### Punting

| | No. | Yds. | Avg. | In 20 | LG |
|---|---|---|---|---|---|
| Hayes | 72 | 2796 | 38.8 | 29 | 56 |
| Washington | 72 | 2796 | 38.8 | 29 | 56 |
| Opponents | 66 | 2748 | 41.6 | 7 | 60 |

### Punt Returns

| | No. | FC | Yds. | Avg. | LG | TD |
|---|---|---|---|---|---|---|
| Nelms | 38 | 0 | 289 | 7.6 | 35 | 0 |
| Seay | 5 | 1 | 57 | 11.4 | 42 | 0 |
| Green | 4 | 0 | 29 | 7.3 | 18 | 0 |
| Giaquinto | 2 | 4 | 12 | 6.0 | 12 | 0 |
| Washington | 49 | 5 | 387 | 7.9 | 42 | 0 |
| Opponents | 41 | 11 | 407 | 9.9 | 97t | 1 |

### Kickoff Returns

| | No. | Yds. | Avg. | LG | TD |
|---|---|---|---|---|---|
| Nelms | 35 | 802 | 22.9 | 41 | 0 |
| Evans | 10 | 141 | 14.1 | 28 | 0 |
| Seay | 9 | 218 | 24.2 | 50 | 0 |
| Garrett | 2 | 50 | 25.0 | 28 | 0 |
| Wonsley | 2 | 36 | 18.0 | 20 | 0 |
| Cronan | 1 | 17 | 17.0 | 17 | 0 |
| Giaquinto | 1 | 0 | 0.0 | 0 | 0 |
| Sawyer | 1 | 15 | 15.0 | 15 | 0 |
| G. Williams | 1 | 6 | 6.0 | 6 | 0 |
| J. Washington | 1 | 16 | 16.0 | 16 | 0 |
| Washington | 63 | 1301 | 20.7 | 58 | 0 |
| Opponents | 91 | 1772 | 19.5 | 57 | 0 |

### Scoring

| | TD | TD R | TD P | TD Rt | PAT | FG | TP |
|---|---|---|---|---|---|---|---|
| Moseley | | | | | 62/63 | 33/47 | 161 |
| Riggins | 24 | 24 | 0 | 0 | | | 144 |
| Brown | 8 | 0 | 8 | 0 | | | 48 |
| J. Washington | 6 | 0 | 6 | 0 | | | 36 |
| Didier | 5 | 0 | 4 | 1 | | | 30 |
| Monk | 5 | 0 | 5 | 0 | | | 30 |
| Evans | 4 | 4 | 0 | 0 | | | 24 |
| Kaufman | 2 | 0 | 0 | 2 | | | 12 |
| Walker | 2 | 0 | 2 | 0 | | | 12 |
| Warren | 2 | 0 | 2 | 0 | | | 12 |
| Dean | 1 | 0 | 0 | 1 | | | 6 |
| Garrett | 1 | 0 | 1 | 0 | | | 6 |
| Giaquinto | 1 | 1 | 0 | 0 | | | 6 |
| Seay | 1 | 0 | 1 | 0 | | | 6 |
| Theismann | 1 | 1 | 0 | 0 | | | 6 |
| Mann | | | (Safety) | | | | 2 |
| Washington | 63 | 30 | 29 | 4 | 62/63 | 33/47 | 541 |
| Opponents | 39 | 9 | 28 | 2 | 38/39 | 20/28 | 332 |

## FIRST-ROUND SELECTIONS

(If Club had no first-round selection, first player drafted is listed with round in parentheses.)

| Year | Player, College, Position |
|---|---|
| 1936 | Riley Smith, Alabama, B |
| 1937 | Sammy Baugh, Texas Christian, B |
| 1938 | Andy Farkas, Detroit, B |
| 1939 | I.B. Hale, Texas Christian, T |
| 1940 | Ed Boell, New York U., B |
| 1941 | Forest Evashevski, Michigan, B |
| 1942 | Orban (Spec) Sanders, Texas, B |
| 1943 | Jack Jenkins, Missouri, B |
| 1944 | Mike Micka, Colgate, B |
| 1945 | Jim Hardy, Southern California, B |
| 1946 | Cal Rossi, UCLA, B* |
| 1947 | Cal Rossi, UCLA, B* |
| 1948 | Harry Gilmer, Alabama, B |
| | Lowell Tew, Alabama, B |
| 1949 | Rob Goode, Texas A&M, B |
| 1950 | George Thomas, Oklahoma, B |
| 1951 | Leon Heath, Oklahoma, B |
| 1952 | Larry Isbell, Baylor, B |
| 1953 | Jack Scarbath, Maryland, B |
| 1954 | Steve Meilinger, Kentucky, E |
| 1955 | Ralph Guglielmi, Notre Dame, B |
| 1956 | Ed Vereb, Maryland, B |
| 1957 | Don Bosseler, Miami, B |
| 1958 | M. Sommer, George Washington, B (2) |
| 1959 | Don Allard, Boston College, B |
| 1960 | Richie Lucas, Penn State, QB |
| 1961 | Norman Snead, Wake Forest, QB |
| | Joe Rutgens, Illinois, DT |
| 1962 | Ernie Davis, Syracuse, RB |
| 1963 | Pat Richter, Wisconsin, TE |
| 1964 | Charley Taylor, Arizona State, RB-WR |
| 1965 | Bob Breitenstein, Tulsa, T (2) |
| 1966 | Charlie Gogolak, Princeton, K |
| 1967 | Ray McDonald, Idaho, RB |
| 1968 | Jim Smith, Oregon, DB |
| 1969 | Eugene Epps, Texas-El Paso, DB (2) |
| 1970 | Bill Brundige, Colorado, DT (2) |
| 1971 | Cotton Speyrer, Texas, WR (2) |
| 1972 | Moses Denson, Maryland State, RB (8) |
| 1973 | Charles Cantrell, Lamar, G (5) |
| 1974 | Jon Keyworth, Colorado, TE (6) |
| 1975 | Mike Thomas, Nevada-Las Vegas, RB (6) |
| 1976 | Mike Hughes, Baylor, G (5) |
| 1977 | Duncan McColl, Stanford, DE (4) |
| 1978 | Tony Green, Florida, RB (6) |
| 1979 | Don Warren, San Diego State, TE (4) |
| 1980 | Art Monk, Syracuse, WR |
| 1981 | Mark May, Pittsburgh, T |
| 1982 | Vernon Dean, San Diego State, DB (2) |
| 1983 | Darrell Green, Texas A&I, DB |
| 1984 | Bob Slater, Oklahoma, DT (2) |

*Choice lost due to ineligibility.

# WASHINGTON REDSKINS 1984 VETERAN ROSTER

| No. | Name | Pos. | Ht. | Wt. | Birth-date | NFL Exp. | College | Birthplace | Residence | Games in '83 |
|-----|------|------|-----|-----|-----------|----------|---------|-----------|-----------|--------------|
| 58 | Anderson, Stuart | LB | 6-1 | 224 | 12/25/59 | 3 | Virginia | Mathews, Va. | Herndon, Va. | 16 |
| 53 | Bostic, Jeff | C | 6-2 | 250 | 9/18/58 | 5 | Clemson | Greensboro, N.C. | Oakton, Va. | 16 |
| 69 | Brooks, Perry | DT | 6-3 | 270 | 12/4/54 | 7 | Southern | Bogalousa, La. | Fairfax, Va. | 16 |
| 87 | Brown, Charlie | WR | 5-10 | 179 | 10/29/58 | 3 | South Carolina State | John's Island, S.C. | Herndon, Va. | 15 |
| 65 | Butz, Dave | DT | 6-7 | 295 | 6/23/50 | 12 | Purdue | Lafayette, Ala. | Belleville, Ill. | 16 |
| 41 | Carpenter, Brian | CB-S | 5-10 | 167 | 11/27/60 | 3 | Michigan | Flint, Mich. | Reston, Va. | 15 |
| 48 | Coffey, Ken | S | 6-0 | 190 | 7/11/60 | 2 | Southwest Texas State | Rantoul, Ill. | Reston, Va. | 13 |
| 51 | †Coleman, Monte | LB | 6-2 | 230 | 11/4/57 | 6 | Central Arkansas | Pine Bluff, Ark. | Reston, Va. | 10 |
| 54 | †Cronan, Peter | LB | 6-2 | 238 | 1/13/55 | 7 | Boston College | Bourue, Mass. | Framingham, Mass. | 16 |
| 32 | Dean, Vernon | CB | 5-11 | 178 | 5/5/59 | 3 | San Diego State | Los Angeles, Calif. | Los Angeles, Calif. | 16 |
| 86 | Didier, Clint | TE | 6-5 | 240 | 4/4/59 | 3 | Portland State | Pasco, Wash. | Eltopia, Wash. | 16 |
| 26 | †Evans, Reggie | RB | 5-11 | 201 | 1/5/59 | 2 | Richmond | Newport News, Va. | Reston, Va. | 16 |
| 89 | Garrett, Alvin | WR | 5-7 | 185 | 10/1/55 | 5 | Angelo State | Mineral Wells, Tex. | Reston, Va. | 15 |
| 77 | Grant, Darryl | DT | 6-1 | 275 | 11/22/59 | 4 | Rice | San Antonio, Tex. | Reston, Va. | 16 |
| 28 | Green, Darrell | CB-KR | 5-8 | 170 | 12/15/60 | 2 | Texas A&I | Houston, Tex. | Houston, Tex. | 16 |
| 68 | Grimm, Russ | G | 6-3 | 290 | 5/2/59 | 4 | Pittsburgh | Scottsdale, Pa. | Oakton, Va. | 16 |
|  | Hart, Jim | QB | 6-1 | 210 | 4/29/44 | 19 | Southern Illinois | Evanston, Ill. | St. Louis, Mo. | 5* |
| 5 | Hayes, Jeff | P | 5-11 | 175 | 8/19/55 | 3 | North Carolina | Elkin, N.C. | Centerville, Ill. | 16 |
| 8 | †Holly, Bob | QB | 6-2 | 196 | 6/1/60 | 3 | Princeton | Clifton, N.J. | Vienna, Va. | 5 |
| 61 | †Huff, Ken | G | 6-4 | 265 | 2/21/53 | 10 | North Carolina | Hutchinson, Kan. | Glen Arm, Md. | 13 |
|  | Hunter, Monty | S | 6-0 | 202 | 1/21/59 | 3 | Salem, W. Va. | Dover, Ohio | Dallas, Tex. | 5* |
| 66 | Jacoby, Joe | T | 6-7 | 300 | 7/6/59 | 4 | Louisville | Louisville, Ky. | Vienna, Va. | 16 |
| 22 | Jordan, Curtis | S | 6-2 | 205 | 1/25/54 | 8 | Texas Tech | Lubbock, Tex. | Oakton, Va. | 15 |
| 55 | Kaufman, Mel | LB | 6-2 | 220 | 2/24/58 | 4 | Cal Poly-SLO | Los Angeles, Calif. | Culver City, Calif. | 16 |
| 67 | Kimball, Bruce | G | 6-2 | 260 | 8/19/56 | 3 | Massachusetts | Beverly, Mass. | Old Bridge, N.J. | 16 |
| 50 | Kubin, Larry | LB | 6-2 | 238 | 2/26/59 | 3 | Penn State | Union, N.J. | Reston, Va. | 12 |
| 62 | Laster, Donald | T | 6-5 | 285 | 12/13/58 | 2 | Tennessee State | Albany, N.J. | Steubenville, Ohio | 0* |
| 12 | Laufenberg, Babe | QB | 6-2 | 195 | 12/5/59 | 2 | Indiana | Burbank, Calif. | Canoga Park, Calif. | 0* |
| 79 | Liebenstein, Todd | DE | 6-6 | 255 | 1/9/60 | 3 | Nevada-Las Vegas | Las Vegas, Nev. | Salem, Ore. | 15 |
| 72 | Manley, Dexter | DE | 6-3 | 250 | 2/2/59 | 4 | Oklahoma State | Houston, Tex. | Reston, Va. | 16 |
| 71 | Mann, Charles | DE | 6-6 | 250 | 4/12/61 | 2 | Nevada-Reno | Sacramento, Calif. | Reston, Va. | 16 |
| 73 | May, Mark | G | 6-6 | 288 | 11/2/59 | 4 | Pittsburgh | Oneonta, N.Y. | Oakton, Va. | 15 |
| 78 | †McGee, Tony | DE | 6-3 | 249 | 1/18/49 | 14 | Bishop, Tex. | Battle Creek, Mich. | Centerville, Va. | 16 |
| 83 | McGrath, Mark | WR | 5-11 | 175 | 12/17/57 | 3 | Montana State | San Diego, Calif. | Seattle, Wash. | 2 |
| 76 | Mendenhall, Mat | DE | 6-6 | 255 | 5/14/57 | 3 | Brigham Young | Salt Lake City, Utah | Alpine, Utah | 0* |
| 57 | Milot, Rich | LB | 6-4 | 237 | 5/28/57 | 6 | Penn State | Coraopolis, Pa. | Herndon, Va. | 16 |
| 81 | Monk, Art | WR | 6-3 | 209 | 12/5/57 | 5 | Syracuse | White Plains, N.Y. | Arlington, Va. | 12 |
| 3 | Moseley, Mark | K | 6-0 | 204 | 3/12/48 | 13 | Stephen F. Austin | Laneville, Tex. | Haymarket, Va. | 16 |
| 29 | Murphy, Mark | S | 6-4 | 210 | 7/13/55 | 8 | Colgate | Fulton, N.Y. | Vienna, Va. | 15 |
| 21 | Nelms, Mike | WR-KR | 6-1 | 185 | 4/8/55 | 5 | Baylor | Ft. Worth, Tex. | Herndon, Va. | 12 |
| 52 | Olkewicz, Neal | LB | 6-0 | 233 | 1/30/57 | 6 | Maryland | Phoenixville, Pa. | Rockville, Md. | 16 |
| 23 | Peters, Tony | S | 6-1 | 190 | 4/28/53 | 9 | Oklahoma | Oklahoma City, Okla. | Chantilly, Va. | 0* |
| 44 | Riggins, John | RB | 6-2 | 235 | 8/4/49 | 13 | Kansas | Senaca, Kan. | Vienna, Va. | 15 |
| 80 | Seay, Virgil | WR | 5-9 | 175 | 1/1/58 | 4 | Troy State | Moultrie, Ga. | Fairfax, Va. | 14 |
| 60 | Simmons, Roy | G-T | 6-3 | 264 | 11/8/56 | 5 | Georgia Tech | Savannah, Ga. | Reston, Va. | 10 |
| 74 | Starke, George | T | 6-5 | 260 | 7/18/48 | 12 | Columbia | New York, N.Y. | Washington, D.C. | 16 |
| 7 | Theismann, Joe | QB | 6-0 | 198 | 9/9/49 | 11 | Notre Dame | New Brunswick, N.J. | Vienna, Va. | 16 |
| 88 | Walker, Rick | TE | 6-4 | 235 | 5/28/55 | 8 | UCLA | Santa Ana, Calif. | Arlington, Va. | 16 |
| 85 | Warren, Don | TE | 6-4 | 242 | 5/5/56 | 6 | San Diego State | Bellingham, Wash. | Huntington Beach, Calif. | 13 |
| 24 | Washington, Anthony | CB | 6-1 | 204 | 2/4/58 | 4 | Fresno State | San Francisco, Calif. | Fresno, Calif. | 16 |
| 25 | Washington, Joe | RB | 5-10 | 179 | 9/24/53 | 8 | Oklahoma | Crockett, Tex. | Reistertown, Md. | 15 |
| 47 | Williams, Greg | S | 5-11 | 185 | 8/1/59 | 3 | Mississippi State | Greenville, Miss. | Centerville, Va. | 16 |
| 84 | Williams, Mike | TE | 6-4 | 251 | 8/27/59 | 3 | Alabama A&M | Lafayette, Ala. | Reston, Va. | 7 |
| 39 | †Wonsley, Otis | RB | 5-10 | 214 | 8/13/57 | 4 | Alcorn State | Pascagoula, Miss. | Moss Point, Miss. | 16 |

* Hart played five games with St. Louis in '83; Hunter played 5 games with St. Louis in '83; Laster missed '83 season due to injury; Laufenberg active with Washington for 16 games in '83 but did not play; Mendenhall missed '83 season due to non-football illness; Peters missed '83 season due to suspension.

†Option playout; subject to developments.

Retired—Nick Giaquinto, 4-year running back, 16 games in '83.

Also played with Redskins in '83—LB Quentin Lowry (3 games), TE John Sawyer (7), WR Dave Stief (3).

## COACHING STAFF

### Head Coach, Joe Gibbs

**Pro Career:** Enters fourth year as Redskins coach. Led Washington to an 14-2 record in 1983 and second straight trip to Super Bowl. Named head coach on January 13, 1981 after spending eight years as an NFL assistant coach and nine years on the college level. Came to Redskins from the San Diego Chargers where he was offensive coordinator in 1979 and 1980. Prior to that, he was offensive coordinator for the Tampa Bay Buccaneers in 1978 and offensive backfield coach for the St. Louis Cardinals from 1973-77. While he was with San Diego, the Chargers won the AFC West title and led the NFL in passing two straight years. No pro playing experience. Career record: 36-12.

**Background:** Played tight end, linebacker, and guard under Don Coryell at San Diego State in 1961 and 1962 after spending two years at Cerritos (Calif.) J.C. (1959-60). Started his college coaching career at San Diego State (1964-66) followed by stints at Florida State (1967-68), Southern California (1969-70), and Arkansas (1971-72).

**Personal:** Born November 25, 1940, in Mocksville, N.C. Graduated from Santa Fe Springs, California, high school. Two-time national racquetball champion and ranked second in the over-35 category in 1978. He and his wife, Pat, live in Washington, D.C. and have two sons—J.D. and Coy.

### Assistant Coaches

**Don Breaux,** offensive backs; born August 3, 1940, Jennings, La., lives in Washington, D.C. Quarterback McNeese State 1959-61. Pro quarterback Denver Broncos 1963, San Diego Chargers 1964-65. College coach: Florida State 1966-67, Arkansas 1968-71, 1977-80, Florida 1973-74, Texas 1975-76. Pro coach: Joined Redskins in 1981.

**Joe Bugel,** assistant head coach-offense; born March 10, 1940, Pittsburgh, Pa., lives in Washington, D.C. Guard Western Kentucky 1960-62. No pro playing experience. College coach: Western Kentucky 1964-68, Navy 1969-72, Iowa State 1973, Ohio State 1974. Pro coach: Detroit Lions 1975-76, Houston Oilers 1977-80, joined Redskins in 1981.

**Bill Hickman,** administrative assistant; born June 21, 1923, Baltimore, Md., lives in Washington, D.C. Halfback Virginia 1946-48. No pro playing experience. College coach: Virginia 1949, Duke 1950, North Carolina State 1951, Vanderbilt 1953, North Carolina 1966-72. Pro coach: Washington Redskins 1973-77, Los Angeles Rams 1978-80, rejoined Redskins in 1981.

**Larry Peccatiello,** defensive coordinator; born December 21, 1935, Newark, N.J., lives in Washington, D.C. Receiver William & Mary 1955-58. No pro playing experience. College coach: William & Mary 1961-68, Navy 1969-70, Rice 1971. Pro coach: Houston Oilers 1972-75, Seattle Seahawks 1976-80, joined Redskins in 1981.

**Richie Petitbon,** assistant head coach-defense; born April 18, 1938, New Orleans, lives in Washington, D.C. Back Tulane 1955-58. Pro defensive back Chicago Bears 1959-67, Los Angeles Rams 1969-70, Washington Redskins 1971-73. Pro coach: Houston Oilers 1974-77, joined Redskins in 1978.

**Jerry Rhome,** quarterbacks; born March 6, 1942, Dallas, Tex., lives in Washington, D.C. Quarterback Southern Methodist 1960-61, Tulsa 1963-64. Pro quarterback Dallas Cowboys 1965-68, Cleveland Browns 1969, Houston Oilers 1970, Los Angeles Rams 1971-72. College coach: Tulsa 1973-75. Pro coach: Seattle Seahawks 1976-82, joined Redskins in 1983.

**Dan Riley,** conditioning; born October 19, 1949, Syracuse, N.Y., lives in Chantilly, Va. No college or pro playing experience. College coach: Army 1973-76, Penn State 1977-81. Pro coach: Joined Redskins in 1982.

**Wayne Sevier,** special teams; born July 3, 1941, San Diego, lives in Washington, D.C. Quarterback Chaffey, Calif., J.C. 1960, San Diego State 1961-62. No pro playing experience. College coach: California Western 1968-69. Pro coach: St. Louis Cardinals 1974-75, Atlanta Falcons 1976, San Diego Chargers 1979-80, joined Redskins in 1981.

**Warren Simmons,** tight ends; born February 25, 1942, Poughkeepsie, N.Y., lives in Washington, D.C. Center San Diego State 1963-65. No pro playing experience. College coach: Cal State-Fullerton 1972-75, Cerritos, Calif., J.C. 1976-80. Pro coach: Joined Redskins in 1981.

**Charley Taylor,** wide receivers; born September 28, 1942, Grand Prairie, Tex., lives in Reston, Va. Running back Arizona State 1962-64. Pro wide receiver Washington Redskins 1964-76. Pro coach: Joined Redskins in 1982.

**LaVern Torgeson,** defensive line; born February 28, 1929, LaCrosse, Wash., lives in Washington, D.C. Center-linebacker Washington State 1948-50. Pro linebacker Detroit Lions 1951-54, Washington Redskins 1955-58. Pro coach: Washington Redskins 1959-61, 1971-77, Pittsburgh Steelers 1962-68, Los Angeles Rams 1969-70, 1978-80, rejoined Redskins in 1981.

## WASHINGTON REDSKINS 1984 FIRST-YEAR ROSTER

| Name | Pos. | Ht. | Wt. | Birth-date | College | Birthplace | Residence | How Acq. |
|------|------|-----|-----|-----------|---------|------------|-----------|----------|
| Baldwin, Clarence | CB | 6-0 | 198 | 9/20/62 | Maryland | Roanoke Rapids, N.C. | Hyattsville, Md. | FA |
| Ellerbe, Jeff | WR | 6-0 | 187 | 9/26/60 | Virginia Union | Washington, D.C. | Washington, D.C. | FA |
| Gandy, Geff (1) | LB | 6-1 | 230 | 5/1/60 | Baylor | Dallas, Tex. | San Antonio, Tex. | D10('83) |
| Goodman, Don | RB | 5-11 | 215 | 4/23/59 | Cincinnati | Los Angeles, Calif. | Cincinnati, Ohio | FA |
| Goosby, Rodney (1) | WR | 6-2 | 190 | 5/20/58 | Washington State | Detroit, Mich. | Los Angeles, Calif. | FA |
| Griffin, Keith | RB | 5-8 | 185 | 10/26/61 | Miami | Columbus, Ohio | Columbus, Ohio | D10 |
| Gross, James | LB | 6-1 | 230 | 11/7/61 | Maryland | Landover, Md. | Palmer Park, Md. | FA |
| Hamilton, Steve | DE | 6-4 | 253 | 9/28/61 | East Carolina | Niagara Falls, N.Y. | Williamsville, N.Y. | D2a |
| Harris, Willie | S | 6-1 | 185 | 4/6/62 | North Carolina | Wilson, N.C. | Wilson N.C. | FA |
| Hornof, Tom | G | 6-4 | 270 | 7/31/61 | Missouri | Evanston, Ill. | St. Louis, Mo. | FA |
| Jones, Anthony | TE | 6-3 | 248 | 5/16/60 | Wichita State | Baltimore, Md. | Wichita, Kan. | D11 |
| Kent, Aaron | RB | 6-0 | 214 | 11/7/60 | Southern | New Orleans, La. | Gretna, La. | FA |
| Lowry, Orlando | LB | 6-4 | 226 | 8/14/61 | Ohio State | Cleveland, Ohio | Columbus, Ohio | FA |
| McCloyne, Henry | CB | 5-11 | 180 | 11/14/60 | Utah | Los Angeles, Calif. | Salt Lake City, Utah | FA |
| Parker, Steve (1) | WR | 5-11 | 185 | 5/19/59 | Abilene Christian | Athens, Ala. | Abilene, Tex. | FA |
| Pegues, Jeff | LB | 6-2 | 236 | 1/19/62 | East Carolina | Laurinburg, N.C. | Fayetteville, N.C. | D5 |
| Pennison, Jay | C | 6-2 | 255 | 9/9/61 | Nicholls State | Houma, La. | Houma, La. | FA |
| Poist, Bob | LB | 6-2 | 210 | 3/7/62 | Towson State | Baltimore, Md. | Sykesville, Md. | FA |
| Rubeling, Gary | S | 5-11 | 200 | 10/13/62 | Towson State | Baltimore, Md. | Frederick, Md. | FA |
| Schroeder, Jay | QB | 6-4 | 215 | 6/28/61 | UCLA | Milwaukee, Wis. | Thousand Oaks, Calif. | D3 |
| Singer, Curt | T | 6-5 | 264 | 11/4/61 | Tennessee | Aliquippa, Pa. | Aliquippa, Pa. | D6 |
| Slater, Bob | DT | 6-4 | 265 | 11/14/60 | Oklahoma | Pawhuska, Okla. | Tulsa, Okla. | D2 |
| Smith, James | RB | 6-0 | 205 | 9/25/60 | Elon | Kankakee, Ill. | Kankakee, Ill. | D4 |
| Smith, Jeff | CB | 6-0 | 189 | 5/12/61 | Missouri | Kansas City, Kan. | Kansas City, Kan. | D8 |
| Smith, Mark | WR | 6-0 | 180 | 4/4/62 | North Carolina | Fayetteville, N.C. | Fayetteville, N.C. | D7 |
| Thomas, Curtland | WR | 5-11 | 182 | 2/19/62 | Missouri | St. Louis, Mo. | Columbia, Mo. | D12 |
| Vines, Vic (1) | S | 6-0 | 189 | 12/28/60 | Baylor | Odessa, Tex. | Odessa, Tex. | FA |
| Wiley, Roger (1) | RB | 5-10 | 240 | 9/17/59 | Texas A&M | Houston, Tex. | Houston, Tex. | FA |
| Winckler, Bob (1) | G | 6-3 | 290 | 4/14/61 | Wisconsin | West Bend, Wis. | Madison, Wis. | D6('83) |

Players who report to an NFL team for the first time are designated on rosters as rookies (R). If a player reported to an NFL training camp in a previous year but was not on the active squad for three or more regular season or postseason games, he is listed on the first-year roster and designated by a (1). Thereafter, a player who is on the active squad for three or more regular season or postseason games is credited with an additional year of playing experience.

## NOTES

_____

_____

_____

_____

_____

_____

_____

_____

_____

_____

_____

_____

_____

_____

# 1983 SEASON IN REVIEW

Trades

Preseason Standings and Results

Regular Season Standings and Results

Week by Week Game Summaries

Paid Attendance Breakdown

Pro Football Awards

All-Star Teams

Rushing, Passing, and Receiving Leaders

Team and Individual Statistics

# Trades

## 1983 Interconference Trades

Tackle **Doug France** from L.A. Rams to Houston for past consideration (7/14).

Defensive end **Tyrone Keys** from New York Jets to Chicago for a draft choice (7/14).

Defensive back **Jeff Allen** from San Diego to San Francisco for a draft choice (7/18).

Tackle **Charley Hannah** from Tampa Bay to L.A. Raiders for defensive end **Dave Browning** and a draft choice (7/18).

Defensive back **Pat Thomas** from L.A. Rams to L.A. Raiders for defensive back **Monte Jackson** (7/25).

Tackle **Karl Baldischwiler** from Detroit to Baltimore for a draft choice (7/28).

Guard **Derrel Gofourth** from Green Bay to San Diego for a draft choice (7/28).

Linebacker **Ed Simonini** from New Orleans to Miami for past consideration (8/3).

Defensive back **Tommy Myers** from New Orleans to Buffalo for past consideration (8/4).

Defensive back **Bo Scott Metcalf** from Pittsburgh to Washington for a draft choice (8/9).

Quarterback **Matt Cavanaugh** from New England to San Francisco for a draft choice (8/11).

Defensive end **Greg Boyd** from Denver to Green Bay for a draft choice (8/17).

Defensive back **Anthony Washington** from Pittsburgh to Washington for a draft choice (8/18).

Tight end **Reese McCall** from Baltimore to Tampa Bay for a draft choice (8/18).

Defensive back **Eric Harris** from Kansas City to L.A. Rams for running back **Jewerl Thomas** (8/20).

Quarterback **Steve Fuller** from Kansas City to L.A. Rams for defensive back **Lucious Smith** and a draft choice (8/20).

Linebacker **Bill Cowher** from Cleveland to Philadelphia for a draft choice (8/22).

Center **Chris Foote** from New York Giants to New York Jets for a draft choice (8/23).

Running back **Lawrence Ricks** from Dallas to Kansas City for a draft choice (8/24).

Running back **John De Gruttola** from New York Giants to Kansas City for a draft choice (8/24).

Tackle **Steve Wright** from Dallas to Baltimore for a draft choice (8/27).

Wide receiver **Tracy Porter** from Detroit to Baltimore for a draft choice (8/29).

Kicker **Raul Allegre** from Dallas to Baltimore for a draft choice (8/29).

Tackle **Charlie Getty** from Kansas City to Green Bay for a draft choice (8/29).

Punter **Tom Orosz** from Miami to San Francisco for a draft choice (8/29).

Center **Les Studdard** from Kansas City to Philadelphia for a draft choice (8/29).

Tight end **Al Dixon** from Kansas City to Philadelphia for a draft choice (8/30).

Quarterback **Mark Reed** from L.A. Rams to Baltimore for linebacker **Mark Jerue** (8/31).

Quarterback **Archie Manning** and tight end **Dave Casper** from Houston to Minnesota for draft choices (9/21).

## 1984 Interconference Trades

Defensive end **Carl Hairston** from Philadelphia to Cleveland for a draft choice (2/9).

Quarterback **Richard Todd** from New York Jets to New Orleans for a draft choice (2/21).

Kicker **Tony Franklin** from Philadelphia to New England for a draft choice (2/22).

Center **Mark Dennard** from Miami to Philadelphia for a draft choice (3/6).

Defensive back **Terry Jackson** from New York Giants to Seattle for draft choices (3/12).

Linebacker **Brian Kelley** from New York Giants to San Diego for a draft choice (3/30).

Nose tackle **Louie Kelcher** from San Diego to San Francisco for draft choices (3/30).

Nose tackle **Manu Tuiasosopo** from Seattle to San Francisco for a draft choice (4/5).

Tight end **Eason Ramson** from San Francisco to Denver for a draft choice (4/9).

Running back **Dwayne Crutchfield** from Houston to L.A. Rams for a draft choice (4/11).

Running back **Scott Dierking** from New York Jets to Tampa Bay for a draft choice (4/17).

Wide receiver **Mike Renfro** and two draft choices from Houston to Dallas for wide receiver **Butch Johnson** and a draft choice in 1984 (4/19).

Quarterback **Steve DeBerg** from Denver to Tampa Bay for a draft choice (4/25).

Quarterback **Scott Brunner** from New York Giants to Denver for a draft choice (4/26).

Kansas City traded cornerback **Gary Green** to L.A. Rams for Rams' first- and fifth-round choices in 1984. Kansas City selected tackle **John Alt** (Iowa) and linebacker **Jeff Paine** (Texas A&M) (5/1).

L.A. Rams traded its second-round choice in 1984 to Cleveland for the negotiation rights to wide receiver **Ron Brown** (Arizona State) who was selected by Cleveland in 1983. Cleveland selected defensive back **Chris Rockins** (Oklahoma State) (5/1).

San Francisco traded its second-round choice in 1984 to L.A. Raiders for the Raiders' second-round choice and Washington's fifth-round choice, previously acquired by the Raiders, both in 1984. Raiders selected defensive end **Sean Jones** (Northeastern). San Francisco selected tight end **John Frank** (Ohio State) and linebacker **Jeff Fuller** (Texas A&M) (5/1).

Houston traded the fourth-round choice of L.A. Rams previously acquired by the Oilers in 1984, to Washington for the Redskins' third-round choice in 1985. Washington selected running back **Jimmy Smith** (Elon) (5/1).

New Orleans traded its seventh-round choice in 1984 to L.A. Raiders for past considerations. The Raiders selected defensive end **Mitch Willis** (Southern Methodist) (5/1).

Atlanta traded its fifth-round choice in 1984 to San Francisco for Denver's fifth-round choice, previously acquired by San Francisco, and the 49ers' sixth-round choice, both in 1984. San Francisco selected defensive tackle **Michael Carter** (Southern Methodist). Atlanta selected tight end **Cliff Benson** (Purdue) and defensive tackle **Dan Ralph** (Oregon) (5/1).

Houston traded its twelfth-round choice in 1984 to L.A. Rams for past considerations. The Rams selected defensive back **Rod Fisher** (Oklahoma State) (5/2).

Cleveland traded its ninth-, tenth-, eleventh-, and twelfth-round choices in 1984 to Chicago for the Bears three choices in the 1984 Supplemental Draft. Chicago selected quarterback **Mark Casale** (Montclair State), defensive back **Shaun Gayle** (Ohio State), defensive tackle **Mark Butkus** (Illinois), and running back **Donald Jordan** (Houston) (5/2).

Center **Walt Downing** from San Francisco to San Diego for a draft choice (5/4).

## 1983 AFC Trades

Center **Bob Rush** from San Diego to Kansas City for draft choices (7/11).

Wide receiver **Bobby Jones** from New York Jets to Cleveland for a draft choice (7/20).

Running back **Sherman Smith** from Seattle to Kansas City for a draft choice (8/10).

Defensive back **Mike Williams** from San Diego to Buffalo for wide receiver **Lou Piccone** (8/15).

Linebacker **Larry Evans** from Denver to Miami for a draft choice (8/16).

Running back **Curtis Brown** from Buffalo to Pittsburgh for a draft choice (8/17).

Wide receiver **Roger Carr** from Seattle to San Diego for draft choices (8/24).

Tackle **Shelby Jordan** from New England to L.A. Raiders for a draft choice (9/6).

Tight end **Derrick Ramsey** from L.A. Raiders to New England for tight end **Don Hasselbeck** (9/13).

## 1984 AFC Trades

Defensive end-defensive tackle **Kenny Neil** and defensive tackle **Abdul Salaam** from New York Jets to San Diego for draft choices (2/13).

Linebacker **Stan Blinka** from New York Jets to Denver for a draft choice (2/16).

Quarterback **David Woodley** from Miami to Pittsburgh for a draft choice (2/21).

Wide receiver **Duriel Harris** from Miami to Cleveland for a draft choice (3/28).

Wide receiver **Dave Logan** from Cleveland to Denver for a draft choice (4/26).

Buffalo traded its first-round choice in 1984 to Miami for the Dolphins' first- and third-round choices in 1984 and Pittsburgh's third-round choice in 1984, previously acquired by Miami. Miami selected linebacker **Jackie Shipp** (Oklahoma). Buffalo selected running back **Greg Bell** (Notre Dame), defensive end **Sean McNanie** (San Diego State), and running back **Speedy Neal** (Miami) (5/1).

Kansas City traded running back **Jewerl Thomas** to San Diego for a draft choice (5/1).

L.A. Raiders traded their ninth-round choice in 1984, plus past considerations, to Houston for the Oilers' eleventh-round choice in 1984. Houston selected linebacker **Mike Russell** (Toledo). The Raiders selected defensive back **Gardner Williams** (St. Mary's, California) (5/2).

## 1983 NFC Trades

Defensive tackle **Mike Dawson** from St. Louis to Detroit for a draft choice (7/18).

Defensive end **Al Baker** from Detroit to St. Louis for draft choices (7/18).

Tight end **David Hill** from Detroit to L.A. Rams for a draft choice (8/19).

Linebacker **Joel Williams** from Atlanta to Philadelphia for a draft choice (8/22).

Linebacker **Danny Spradlin** from Dallas to Tampa Bay for a draft choice (8/24).

## 1984 NFC Trades

Linebacker **Frank LeMaster** from Philadelphia to San Francisco for a draft choice (3/16).

Washington traded its first-round choice in 1984 to New York Giants for the Giants' second-round choice and Chicago's fifth-round choice, previously obtained by New York, both in 1984. The Giants selected tackle **Bill Roberts** (Ohio State). Washington selected defensive tackle **Bob Slater** (Oklahoma) and linebacker **Jeff Pegues** (East Carolina) (5/1).

St. Louis traded its third-round choice in 1984 to San Francisco for the 49ers' third- and fifth-round choices in 1984. San Francisco selected guard **Guy McIntyre** (Georgia). St. Louis selected quarterback **Rick McIvor** (Texas) and tight end **John Goode** (Youngstown) (5/1).

L.A. Rams traded quarterback **Steve Fuller** to Chicago for the Bears' eleventh-round choice in 1984 and a 1985 draft choice. The Rams selected running back **Michael Harper** (Southern California) (5/1).

# 1983 PRESEASON STANDINGS

## American Football Conference

### EASTERN DIVISION
|  | W | L | T | Pct. | Pts. | OP |
|---|---|---|---|---|---|---|
| Baltimore | 2 | 2 | 0 | .500 | 46 | 44 |
| Miami | 2 | 2 | 0 | .500 | 96 | 49 |
| N.Y. Jets | 2 | 2 | 0 | .500 | 66 | 74 |
| Buffalo | 1 | 3 | 0 | .250 | 63 | 97 |
| New England | 0 | 4 | 0 | .000 | 59 | 98 |

### CENTRAL DIVISION
|  | W | L | T | Pct. | Pts. | OP |
|---|---|---|---|---|---|---|
| Pittsburgh* | 4 | 1 | 0 | .800 | 101 | 62 |
| Cleveland | 3 | 1 | 0 | .750 | 78 | 66 |
| Cincinnati | 0 | 4 | 0 | .000 | 54 | 105 |
| Houston | 0 | 4 | 0 | .000 | 61 | 92 |

### WESTERN DIVISION
|  | W | L | T | Pct. | Pts. | OP |
|---|---|---|---|---|---|---|
| Denver | 3 | 1 | 0 | .750 | 53 | 61 |
| Kansas City | 2 | 2 | 0 | .500 | 71 | 60 |
| San Diego | 2 | 2 | 0 | .500 | 91 | 79 |
| Seattle | 2 | 2 | 0 | .500 | 82 | 56 |
| L.A. Raiders | 1 | 3 | 0 | .250 | 81 | 90 |

*Includes Hall of Fame Game

## National Football Conference

### EASTERN DIVISION
|  | W | L | T | Pct. | Pts. | OP |
|---|---|---|---|---|---|---|
| Dallas | 3 | 1 | 0 | .750 | 91 | 79 |
| N.Y. Giants | 3 | 1 | 0 | .750 | 75 | 67 |
| Philadelphia | 3 | 1 | 0 | .750 | 72 | 61 |
| Washington | 2 | 2 | 0 | .500 | 71 | 93 |
| St. Louis | 1 | 3 | 0 | .250 | 80 | 108 |

### CENTRAL DIVISION
|  | W | L | T | Pct. | Pts. | OP |
|---|---|---|---|---|---|---|
| Tampa Bay | 4 | 0 | 0 | 1.000 | 101 | 61 |
| Chicago | 3 | 1 | 0 | .750 | 98 | 82 |
| Minnesota | 3 | 1 | 0 | .750 | 88 | 40 |
| Detroit | 2 | 2 | 0 | .500 | 84 | 58 |
| Green Bay | 1 | 3 | 0 | .250 | 94 | 113 |

### WESTERN DIVISION
|  | W | L | T | Pct. | Pts. | OP |
|---|---|---|---|---|---|---|
| New Orleans* | 3 | 2 | 0 | .600 | 87 | 87 |
| Atlanta | 2 | 2 | 0 | .500 | 39 | 55 |
| L.A. Rams | 2 | 2 | 0 | .500 | 71 | 84 |
| San Francisco | 1 | 3 | 0 | .250 | 53 | 85 |

## AFC Preseason Records —Team By Team

### EASTERN DIVISION

**BALTIMORE (2-2)**
| 15 | Houston | 0 |
|---|---|---|
| 10 | Minnesota | 7 |
| 14 | N.Y. Giants | 27 |
| 7 | Atlanta | 10 |
| 46 | | 44 |

**MIAMI (2-2)**
| 17 | Dallas | 20 |
|---|---|---|
| 17 | *New Orleans | 19 |
| 38 | Washington | 7 |
| 24 | N.Y. Giants | 3 |
| 96 | | 49 |

**N.Y. JETS (2-2)**
| 16 | N.Y. Giants | 23 |
|---|---|---|
| 20 | *L.A. Raiders | 17 |
| 20 | Cincinnati (OT) | 17 |
| 10 | New Orleans | 17 |
| 66 | | 74 |

**BUFFALO (1-3)**
| 17 | Chicago | 27 |
|---|---|---|
| 10 | *Cleveland | 27 |
| 17 | Detroit | 16 |
| 19 | *Washington | 27 |
| 63 | | 97 |

**NEW ENGLAND (0-4)**
| 16 | Pittsburgh | 27 |
|---|---|---|
| 15 | San Francisco | 17 |
| 7 | L.A. Rams | 13 |
| 21 | Tampa Bay | 41 |
| 59 | | 98 |

### CENTRAL DIVISION

**PITTSBURGH (4-1)**
| 27 | Saints (HOF) | 14 |
|---|---|---|
| 27 | New England | 16 |
| 13 | *N.Y. Giants | 22 |
| 24 | Dallas | 7 |
| 10 | Philadelphia | 3 |
| 101 | | 62 |

**CLEVELAND (3-1)**
| 21 | Green Bay | 20 |
|---|---|---|
| 27 | Buffalo | 10 |
| 10 | Denver | 19 |
| 20 | *L.A. Raiders | 17 |
| 78 | | 66 |

**CINCINNATI (0-4)**
| 7 | *Kansas City | 24 |
|---|---|---|
| 23 | Washington | 27 |
| 17 | *N.Y. Jets (OT) | 20 |
| 7 | Detroit | 34 |
| 54 | | 105 |

**HOUSTON (0-4)**
| 0 | *Baltimore | 15 |
|---|---|---|
| 17 | *Tampa Bay | 23 |
| 13 | New Orleans | 20 |
| 31 | Dallas | 34 |
| 61 | | 92 |

### WESTERN DIVISION

**DENVER (3-1)**
| 10 | *Seattle | 7 |
|---|---|---|
| 21 | *Atlanta | 10 |
| 19 | *Cleveland | 10 |
| 3 | Minnesota | 34 |
| 53 | | 61 |

**KANSAS CITY (2-2)**
| 24 | Cincinnati | 7 |
|---|---|---|
| 13 | *Detroit | 17 |
| 17 | *St. Louis | 16 |
| 17 | Chicago (OT) | 20 |
| 71 | | 60 |

**SAN DIEGO (2-2)**
| 20 | L.A. Rams | 34 |
|---|---|---|
| 20 | *Philadelphia | 21 |
| 24 | *San Francisco | 7 |
| 27 | *L.A. Rams | 17 |
| 91 | | 79 |

**SEATTLE (2-2)**
| 7 | Denver | 10 |
|---|---|---|
| 38 | *Green Bay | 21 |
| 17 | *Minnesota | 19 |
| 20 | San Francisco | 6 |
| 82 | | 56 |

**L.A. RAIDERS (1-3)**
| 26 | *San Fran. (OT) | 23 |
|---|---|---|
| 17 | N.Y. Jets | 20 |
| 21 | *Chicago | 27 |
| 17 | Cleveland | 20 |
| 81 | | 90 |

## NFC Preseason Records —Team By Team

### EASTERN DIVISION

**DALLAS (3-1)**
| 20 | *Miami | 17 |
|---|---|---|
| 30 | L.A. Rams | 7 |
| 7 | *Pittsburgh | 24 |
| 34 | *Houston | 31 |
| 91 | | 79 |

**N.Y. GIANTS (3-1)**
| 23 | *N.Y. Jets | 16 |
|---|---|---|
| 22 | Pittsburgh | 13 |
| 27 | *Baltimore | 14 |
| 3 | *Miami | 24 |
| 75 | | 67 |

**PHILADELPHIA (3-1)**
| 21 | *Detroit | 17 |
|---|---|---|
| 21 | San Diego | 20 |
| 27 | Green Bay | 14 |
| 3 | *Pittsburgh | 10 |
| 72 | | 61 |

**WASHINGTON (2-2)**
| 10 | Atlanta (OT) | 13 |
|---|---|---|
| 27 | *Cincinnati | 23 |
| 7 | *Miami | 38 |
| 27 | Buffalo | 19 |
| 71 | | 93 |

**ST. LOUIS (1-3)**
| 10 | Minnesota | 28 |
|---|---|---|
| 27 | *Chicago (OT) | 24 |
| 16 | Kansas City | 17 |
| 27 | *Green Bay | 39 |
| 80 | | 108 |

### CENTRAL DIVISION

**TAMPA BAY (4-0)**
| 20 | *New Orleans | 17 |
|---|---|---|
| 23 | Houston | 17 |
| 17 | *Atlanta | 6 |
| 41 | *New England | 21 |
| 101 | | 61 |

**MINNESOTA (3-1)**
| 28 | St. Louis | 10 |
|---|---|---|
| 7 | *Baltimore | 10 |
| 19 | Seattle | 17 |
| 34 | *Denver | 3 |
| 88 | | 40 |

**CHICAGO (3-1)**
| 27 | *Buffalo | 17 |
|---|---|---|
| 24 | St. Louis (OT) | 27 |
| 27 | L.A. Raiders | 21 |
| 20 | *Kansas City (OT) | 17 |
| 98 | | 82 |

**DETROIT (2-2)**
| 17 | Philadelphia | 21 |
|---|---|---|
| 17 | Kansas City | 13 |
| 16 | *Buffalo | 17 |
| 34 | *Cincinnati | 7 |
| 84 | | 58 |

**GREEN BAY (1-3)**
| 20 | *Cleveland | 21 |
|---|---|---|
| 21 | Seattle | 38 |
| 14 | *Philadelphia | 27 |
| 39 | St. Louis | 27 |
| 94 | | 113 |

### WESTERN DIVISION

**NEW ORLEANS (3-2)**
| 14 | Pitt. (HOF) | 27 |
|---|---|---|
| 17 | Tampa Bay | 20 |
| 19 | Miami | 17 |
| 20 | *Houston | 13 |
| 17 | *N.Y. Jets | 10 |
| 87 | | 87 |

**ATLANTA (2-2)**
| 13 | *Washington (OT) | 10 |
|---|---|---|
| 10 | Denver | 21 |
| 6 | Tampa Bay | 17 |
| 10 | *Baltimore | 7 |
| 39 | | 55 |

**L.A. RAMS (2-2)**
| 34 | *San Diego | 20 |
|---|---|---|
| 7 | *Dallas | 30 |
| 13 | *New England | 7 |
| 17 | San Diego | 27 |
| 71 | | 84 |

**SAN FRANCISCO (1-3)**
| 23 | L.A. Raiders (OT) | 26 |
|---|---|---|
| 17 | *New England | 15 |
| 7 | San Diego | 24 |
| 6 | *Seattle | 20 |
| 53 | | 85 |

*Denotes Home Game
(OT) Denotes Overtime
(HOF) Denotes Hall of Fame Game

# 1983 NFL STANDINGS

## American Football Conference

### EASTERN DIVISION

|  | W | L | T | Pct. | Pts. | OP |
|---|---|---|---|---|---|---|
| Miami | 12 | 4 | 0 | .750 | 389 | 250 |
| New England | 8 | 8 | 0 | .500 | 274 | 289 |
| Buffalo | 8 | 8 | 0 | .500 | 283 | 351 |
| Baltimore | 7 | 9 | 0 | .438 | 264 | 354 |
| N.Y. Jets | 7 | 9 | 0 | .438 | 313 | 331 |

### CENTRAL DIVISION

|  | W | L | T | Pct. | Pts. | OP |
|---|---|---|---|---|---|---|
| Pittsburgh | 10 | 6 | 0 | .625 | 355 | 303 |
| Cleveland | 9 | 7 | 0 | .563 | 356 | 342 |
| Cincinnati | 7 | 9 | 0 | .438 | 346 | 302 |
| Houston | 2 | 14 | 0 | .125 | 288 | 460 |

### WESTERN DIVISION

|  | W | L | T | Pct. | Pts. | OP |
|---|---|---|---|---|---|---|
| L.A. Raiders | 12 | 4 | 0 | .750 | 442 | 338 |
| Seattle* | 9 | 7 | 0 | .563 | 403 | 397 |
| Denver* | 9 | 7 | 0 | .563 | 302 | 327 |
| San Diego | 6 | 10 | 0 | .375 | 358 | 462 |
| Kansas City | 6 | 10 | 0 | .375 | 386 | 367 |

*Wild Card qualifiers for playoffs
New England finished ahead of Buffalo based on sweep of the Bills. Baltimore finished ahead of the New York Jets based on a better conference record (5-9 to 4-8). Seattle finished ahead of Denver based on a better division record (5-3 to 3-5). Seattle and Denver won Wild Card playoff berths over Cleveland on the basis of their victories versus the Browns. San Diego swept Kansas City to finish ahead of the Chiefs. Green Bay won common games tie-breaker with Chicago (4-4 to 3-5) after Minnesota was eliminated from a three-way tie based on conference record (Green Bay 6-6, Chicago 7-7 vs. Minnesota 4-8).

**FIRST-ROUND PLAYOFFS**
AFC............................Seattle 31, Denver 7, December 24 at Seattle
NFC......................Los Angeles Rams 24, Dallas 17, December 26 at Dallas
**DIVISIONAL PLAYOFFS**
AFC.................................Seattle 27, Miami 20, December 31 at Miami
Los Angeles Raiders 38, Pittsburgh 10, January 1 at Los Angeles
NFC.................San Francisco 24, Detroit 23, December 31 at San Francisco
Washington 51, Los Angeles Rams 7, January 1 at Washington
**CHAMPIONSHIP GAMES**
AFC....................Los Angeles Raiders 30, Seattle 14, January 8 at Los Angeles
NFC.......................Washington 24, San Francisco 21, January 8 at Washington
**SUPER BOWL XVIII**....Los Angeles Raiders (AFC) 38, Washington (NFC) 9, January 22 at Tampa Stadium, Tampa, Florida
**AFC-NFC PRO BOWL**..NFC 45, AFC 3, January 29 at Aloha Stadium, Honolulu, Hawaii

## National Football Conference

### EASTERN DIVISION

|  | W | L | T | Pct. | Pts. | OP |
|---|---|---|---|---|---|---|
| Washington | 14 | 2 | 0 | .875 | 541 | 332 |
| Dallas* | 12 | 4 | 0 | .750 | 479 | 360 |
| St. Louis | 8 | 7 | 1 | .531 | 374 | 428 |
| Philadelphia | 5 | 11 | 0 | .313 | 233 | 322 |
| N.Y. Giants | 3 | 12 | 1 | .219 | 267 | 347 |

### CENTRAL DIVISION

|  | W | L | T | Pct. | Pts. | OP |
|---|---|---|---|---|---|---|
| Detroit | 9 | 7 | 0 | .563 | 347 | 286 |
| Green Bay | 8 | 8 | 0 | .500 | 429 | 439 |
| Chicago | 8 | 8 | 0 | .500 | 311 | 301 |
| Minnesota | 8 | 8 | 0 | .500 | 316 | 348 |
| Tampa Bay | 2 | 14 | 0 | .125 | 241 | 380 |

### WESTERN DIVISION

|  | W | L | T | Pct. | Pts. | OP |
|---|---|---|---|---|---|---|
| San Francisco | 10 | 6 | 0 | .625 | 432 | 293 |
| L.A. Rams* | 9 | 7 | 0 | .563 | 361 | 344 |
| New Orleans | 8 | 8 | 0 | .500 | 319 | 337 |
| Atlanta | 7 | 9 | 0 | .438 | 370 | 389 |

## AFC Season Records—Team By Team

### BALTIMORE (7-9)

| | | |
|---|---|---|
| 29 | New England (OT) | 23 |
| 10 | *Denver | 17 |
| 23 | Buffalo | 28 |
| 22 | *Chicago (OT) | 19 |
| 34 | Cincinnati | 31 |
| 12 | *New England | 7 |
| 7 | *Buffalo | 30 |
| 7 | *Miami | 21 |
| 22 | Philadelphia | 21 |
| 17 | N.Y. Jets | 14 |
| 13 | *Pittsburgh | 24 |
| 0 | Miami | 37 |
| 23 | Cleveland | 41 |
| 6 | *N.Y. Jets | 10 |
| 19 | Denver | 21 |
| 20 | *Houston | 10 |
| **264** | | **354** |

### BUFFALO (8-8)

| | | |
|---|---|---|
| 0 | *Miami | 12 |
| 10 | Cincinnati | 6 |
| 28 | *Baltimore | 23 |
| 30 | *Houston | 13 |
| 10 | *N.Y. Jets | 34 |
| 38 | Miami (OT) | 35 |
| 30 | Baltimore | 7 |
| 0 | *New England | 31 |
| 27 | *New Orleans | 3 |
| 7 | New England | 21 |
| 24 | N.Y. Jets | 17 |
| 24 | *L.A. Raiders | 27 |
| 17 | L.A. Rams | 41 |
| 9 | Kansas City | 14 |
| 10 | *San Francisco | 23 |
| 14 | Atlanta | 31 |
| **283** | | **351** |

### CINCINNATI (7-9)

| | | |
|---|---|---|
| 10 | *L.A. Raiders | 20 |
| 6 | *Buffalo | 10 |
| 7 | Cleveland | 17 |
| 23 | Tampa Bay | 17 |
| 31 | *Baltimore | 34 |
| 14 | *Pittsburgh | 24 |
| 17 | Denver | 24 |
| 28 | *Cleveland | 21 |
| 34 | *Green Bay | 14 |
| 55 | Houston | 14 |
| 15 | Kansas City | 20 |
| 38 | *Houston | 10 |
| 14 | Miami | 38 |
| 23 | Pittsburgh | 10 |
| 17 | *Detroit | 9 |
| 14 | Minnesota | 20 |
| **346** | | **302** |

### CLEVELAND (9-7)

| | | |
|---|---|---|
| 21 | *Minnesota | 27 |
| 31 | Detroit | 26 |
| 17 | *Cincinnati | 7 |
| 30 | San Diego (OT) | 24 |
| 9 | *Seattle | 24 |
| 10 | *N.Y. Jets | 7 |
| 17 | Pittsburgh | 44 |
| 21 | Cincinnati | 28 |
| 25 | *Houston (OT) | 19 |
| 21 | Green Bay | 35 |
| 20 | *Tampa Bay | 0 |
| 30 | New England | 0 |
| 41 | *Baltimore | 23 |
| 6 | Denver | 27 |
| 27 | Houston | 34 |
| 30 | *Pittsburgh | 17 |
| **356** | | **342** |

### DENVER (9-7)

| | | |
|---|---|---|
| 14 | Pittsburgh | 10 |
| 17 | Baltimore | 10 |
| 10 | *Philadelphia | 13 |
| 7 | *L.A. Raiders | 22 |
| 14 | Chicago | 31 |
| 26 | Houston | 14 |
| 24 | *Cincinnati | 17 |
| 14 | *San Diego | 6 |
| 27 | *Kansas City | 24 |
| 19 | Seattle | 27 |
| 20 | L.A. Raiders | 22 |
| 38 | *Seattle | 27 |
| 7 | San Diego | 31 |
| 27 | *Cleveland | 6 |
| 21 | *Baltimore | 19 |
| 17 | Kansas City | 48 |
| **302** | | **327** |

### HOUSTON (2-14)

| | | |
|---|---|---|
| 38 | *Green Bay (OT) | 41 |
| 6 | L.A. Raiders | 20 |
| 28 | *Pittsburgh | 40 |
| 13 | Buffalo | 30 |
| 10 | Pittsburgh | 17 |
| 14 | *Denver | 26 |
| 14 | Minnesota | 34 |
| 10 | *Kansas City (OT) | 13 |
| 19 | Cleveland (OT) | 25 |
| 14 | *Cincinnati | 55 |
| 27 | *Detroit | 17 |
| 24 | Tampa Bay | 33 |
| 17 | *Miami | 24 |
| 34 | *Cleveland | 27 |
| 10 | Baltimore | 20 |
| **288** | | **460** |

### KANSAS CITY (6-10)

| | | |
|---|---|---|
| 17 | *Seattle | 13 |
| 14 | *San Diego | 17 |
| 12 | Washington | 27 |
| 6 | Miami | 14 |
| 38 | *St. Louis | 14 |
| 20 | L.A. Raiders | 21 |
| 38 | *N.Y. Giants | 17 |
| 13 | Houston (OT) | 10 |
| 24 | Denver | 27 |
| 20 | *Cincinnati | 15 |
| 21 | Dallas | 41 |
| 48 | Seattle (OT) | 51 |
| 9 | *Buffalo | 14 |
| 38 | San Diego | 41 |
| 48 | *Denver | 17 |
| **386** | | **367** |

### L.A. RAIDERS (12-4)

| | | |
|---|---|---|
| 20 | Cincinnati | 10 |
| 20 | *Houston | 6 |
| 27 | *Miami | 14 |
| 22 | Denver | 7 |
| 35 | Washington | 37 |
| 21 | *Kansas City | 20 |
| 36 | Seattle | 38 |
| 40 | Dallas | 38 |
| 21 | *Seattle | 34 |
| 28 | Kansas City | 20 |
| 22 | *Denver | 20 |
| 27 | Buffalo | 24 |
| 27 | *N.Y. Giants | 12 |
| 42 | San Diego | 10 |
| 24 | *St. Louis | 34 |
| 30 | *San Diego | 14 |
| **442** | | **338** |

### MIAMI (12-4)

| | | |
|---|---|---|
| 12 | Buffalo | 0 |
| 34 | *New England | 24 |
| 14 | L.A. Raiders | 27 |
| 14 | *Kansas City | 6 |
| 7 | New Orleans | 17 |
| 35 | *Buffalo (OT) | 38 |
| 32 | N.Y. Jets | 14 |
| 21 | Baltimore | 7 |
| 30 | *L.A. Rams | 14 |
| 20 | San Francisco | 17 |
| 6 | New England | 17 |
| 37 | *Baltimore | 0 |
| 38 | *Cincinnati | 14 |
| 24 | Houston | 17 |
| 31 | *Atlanta | 24 |
| 34 | *N.Y. Jets | 14 |
| **389** | | **250** |

### NEW ENGLAND (8-8)

| | | |
|---|---|---|
| 23 | **Baltimore (OT) | 29 |
| 24 | Miami | 34 |
| 23 | *N.Y. Jets | 13 |
| 28 | Pittsburgh | 23 |
| 13 | *San Francisco | 33 |
| 7 | Baltimore | 12 |
| 37 | *San Diego | 21 |
| 31 | Buffalo | 0 |
| 13 | Atlanta | 24 |
| 21 | *Buffalo | 7 |
| 17 | *Miami | 6 |
| 0 | *Cleveland | 30 |
| 3 | N.Y. Jets | 26 |
| 7 | *New Orleans | 0 |
| 21 | L.A. Rams | 7 |
| 6 | Seattle | 24 |
| **274** | | **289** |

### N.Y. JETS (7-9)

| | | |
|---|---|---|
| 41 | San Diego | 29 |
| 10 | *Seattle | 17 |
| 13 | New England | 23 |
| 27 | *L.A. Rams (OT) | 24 |
| 34 | Buffalo | 10 |
| 7 | Cleveland | 10 |
| 14 | *Miami | 32 |
| 21 | *Atlanta | 27 |
| 27 | San Francisco | 13 |
| 14 | *Baltimore | 17 |
| 17 | *Buffalo | 24 |
| 31 | New Orleans | 28 |
| 26 | *New England | 3 |
| 10 | Baltimore | 6 |
| 7 | *Pittsburgh | 34 |
| 14 | Miami | 34 |
| **313** | | **331** |

### PITTSBURGH (10-6)

| | | |
|---|---|---|
| 10 | *Denver | 14 |
| 25 | Green Bay | 21 |
| 40 | Houston | 28 |
| 23 | *New England | 28 |
| 17 | Houston | 10 |
| 24 | Cincinnati | 14 |
| 44 | *Cleveland | 17 |
| 27 | Seattle | 21 |
| 17 | *Tampa Bay | 12 |
| 26 | *San Diego | 3 |
| 24 | Baltimore | 13 |
| 14 | *Minnesota | 17 |
| 3 | Detroit | 45 |
| 10 | *Cincinnati | 23 |
| 34 | N.Y. Jets | 7 |
| 17 | Cleveland | 30 |
| **355** | | **303** |

### SAN DIEGO (6-10)

| | | |
|---|---|---|
| 29 | *N.Y. Jets | 41 |
| 17 | Kansas City | 14 |
| 31 | Seattle | 34 |
| 24 | *Cleveland (OT) | 30 |
| 41 | N.Y. Giants | 34 |
| 28 | *Seattle | 21 |
| 21 | New England | 37 |
| 6 | Denver | 14 |
| 24 | *Washington | 27 |
| 3 | Pittsburgh | 26 |
| 24 | *Dallas | 23 |
| 14 | St. Louis | 44 |
| 31 | *Denver | 7 |
| 10 | *L.A. Raiders | 42 |
| 41 | Kansas City | 38 |
| 14 | L.A. Raiders | 30 |
| **358** | | **462** |

### SEATTLE (9-7)

| | | |
|---|---|---|
| 13 | Kansas City | 17 |
| 17 | N.Y. Jets | 10 |
| 34 | *San Diego | 31 |
| 17 | *Washington | 27 |
| 24 | Cleveland | 9 |
| 21 | San Diego | 28 |
| 38 | *L.A. Raiders | 36 |
| 21 | *Pittsburgh | 27 |
| 34 | L.A. Raiders | 21 |
| 27 | *Denver | 19 |
| 28 | St. Louis | 33 |
| 27 | Denver | 38 |
| 51 | *Kansas City (OT) | 48 |
| 10 | *Dallas | 35 |
| 17 | N.Y. Giants | 12 |
| 24 | *New England | 6 |
| **403** | | **397** |

*Denotes Home Game
(OT) Denotes Overtime

# NFC Season Records—Team by Team

**ATLANTA (7-9)**

| | | |
|---|---|---|
| 20 | Chicago | 17 |
| 13 | *N.Y. Giants (OT) | 16 |
| 30 | Detroit | 14 |
| 20 | San Francisco | 24 |
| 24 | *Philadelphia | 28 |
| 17 | *New Orleans | 19 |
| 21 | L.A. Rams | 27 |
| 27 | N.Y. Jets | 21 |
| 24 | *New England | 13 |
| 10 | New Orleans | 27 |
| 13 | *L.A. Rams | 36 |
| 28 | *San Francisco | 24 |
| 47 | *Green Bay (OT) | 41 |
| 21 | Washington | 37 |
| 24 | Miami | 31 |
| 31 | *Buffalo | 14 |
| 370 | | 389 |

**CHICAGO (8-8)**

| | | |
|---|---|---|
| 17 | *Atlanta | 20 |
| 17 | *Tampa Bay | 10 |
| 31 | New Orleans (OT) | 34 |
| 19 | Baltimore (OT) | 22 |
| 31 | *Denver | 14 |
| 14 | *Minnesota | 23 |
| 17 | Detroit | 31 |
| 7 | Philadelphia | 6 |
| 17 | *Detroit | 38 |
| 14 | L.A. Rams | 21 |
| 17 | *Philadelphia | 14 |
| 27 | Tampa Bay | 0 |
| 13 | *San Francisco | 3 |
| 28 | Green Bay | 31 |
| 19 | Minnesota | 13 |
| 23 | *Green Bay | 21 |
| 311 | | 301 |

**DALLAS (12-4)**

| | | |
|---|---|---|
| 31 | Washington | 30 |
| 34 | St. Louis | 17 |
| 28 | *N.Y. Giants | 13 |
| 21 | *New Orleans | 20 |
| 37 | Minnesota | 24 |
| 27 | *Tampa Bay (OT) | 24 |
| 37 | *Philadelphia | 7 |
| 38 | *L.A. Raiders | 40 |
| 38 | N.Y. Giants | 20 |
| 27 | Philadelphia | 20 |
| 23 | San Diego | 24 |
| 41 | *Kansas City | 21 |
| 35 | *St. Louis | 17 |
| 35 | Seattle | 10 |
| 10 | *Washington | 31 |
| 17 | San Francisco | 42 |
| 479 | | 360 |

**DETROIT (9-7)**

| | | |
|---|---|---|
| 11 | Tampa Bay | 0 |
| 26 | *Cleveland | 31 |
| 14 | *Atlanta | 30 |
| 17 | Minnesota | 20 |
| 10 | L.A. Rams | 21 |
| 38 | *Green Bay | 14 |
| 31 | *Chicago | 17 |
| 17 | Washington | 38 |
| 38 | Chicago | 17 |
| 15 | *N.Y. Giants | 9 |
| 17 | Houston | 27 |
| 23 | Green Bay (OT) | 20 |
| 45 | *Pittsburgh | 3 |
| 13 | *Minnesota | 2 |
| 9 | Cincinnati | 17 |
| 23 | *Tampa Bay | 20 |
| 347 | | 286 |

**GREEN BAY (8-8)**

| | | |
|---|---|---|
| 41 | Houston (OT) | 38 |
| 21 | *Pittsburgh | 25 |
| 27 | *L.A. Rams | 24 |
| 3 | N.Y. Giants | 27 |
| 55 | *Tampa Bay | 14 |
| 14 | Detroit | 38 |
| 48 | *Washington | 47 |
| 17 | *Minnesota (OT) | 20 |
| 14 | Cincinnati | 34 |
| 35 | *Cleveland | 21 |
| 29 | Minnesota | 21 |
| 20 | *Detroit (OT) | 23 |
| 41 | Atlanta (OT) | 47 |
| 31 | *Chicago | 28 |
| 12 | Tampa Bay (OT) | 9 |
| 21 | Chicago | 23 |
| 429 | | 439 |

**L.A. RAMS (9-7)**

| | | |
|---|---|---|
| 16 | N.Y. Giants | 6 |
| 30 | *New Orleans | 27 |
| 24 | Green Bay | 27 |
| 24 | N.Y. Jets (OT) | 27 |
| 21 | *Detroit | 10 |
| 10 | San Francisco | 7 |
| 27 | *Atlanta | 21 |
| 35 | *San Francisco | 45 |
| 14 | Miami | 30 |
| 21 | *Chicago | 14 |
| 36 | Atlanta | 13 |
| 20 | *Washington | 42 |
| 41 | *Buffalo | 17 |
| 9 | Philadelphia | 13 |
| 7 | *New England | 21 |
| 26 | New Orleans | 24 |
| 361 | | 344 |

**MINNESOTA (8-8)**

| | | |
|---|---|---|
| 27 | Cleveland | 21 |
| 17 | *San Francisco | 48 |
| 19 | Tampa Bay (OT) | 16 |
| 20 | *Detroit | 17 |
| 24 | *Dallas | 37 |
| 23 | Chicago | 14 |
| 34 | *Houston | 14 |
| 20 | Green Bay (OT) | 17 |
| 31 | St. Louis | 41 |
| 12 | *Tampa Bay | 17 |
| 21 | *Green Bay | 29 |
| 17 | Pittsburgh | 14 |
| 16 | New Orleans | 17 |
| 2 | Detroit | 13 |
| 13 | *Chicago | 19 |
| 20 | *Cincinnati | 14 |
| 316 | | 348 |

**NEW ORLEANS (8-8)**

| | | |
|---|---|---|
| 28 | *St. Louis | 17 |
| 27 | L.A. Rams | 30 |
| 34 | *Chicago (OT) | 31 |
| 20 | Dallas | 21 |
| 17 | *Miami | 7 |
| 19 | Atlanta | 17 |
| 13 | *San Francisco | 32 |
| 24 | Tampa Bay | 21 |
| 21 | Buffalo | 27 |
| 27 | *Atlanta | 10 |
| 0 | San Francisco | 27 |
| 28 | *N.Y. Jets | 31 |
| 17 | *Minnesota | 16 |
| 0 | New England | 7 |
| 20 | Philadelphia (OT) | 17 |
| 24 | *L.A. Rams | 26 |
| 319 | | 337 |

**N.Y. GIANTS (3-12-1)**

| | | |
|---|---|---|
| 6 | *L.A. Rams | 16 |
| 16 | Atlanta (OT) | 13 |
| 13 | Dallas | 28 |
| 27 | *Green Bay | 3 |
| 34 | *San Diego | 41 |
| 13 | *Philadelphia | 17 |
| 17 | Kansas City | 38 |
| 20 | St. Louis (OT) | 20 |
| 20 | *Dallas | 38 |
| 9 | Detroit | 15 |
| 17 | *Washington | 33 |
| 23 | Philadelphia | 0 |
| 12 | L.A. Raiders | 27 |
| 6 | *St. Louis | 10 |
| 12 | *Seattle | 17 |
| 22 | Washington | 31 |
| 267 | | 347 |

**PHILADELPHIA (5-11)**

| | | |
|---|---|---|
| 22 | San Francisco | 17 |
| 13 | *Washington | 23 |
| 13 | Denver | 10 |
| 11 | *St. Louis | 14 |
| 28 | Atlanta | 24 |
| 17 | N.Y. Giants | 13 |
| 7 | Dallas | 37 |
| 6 | *Chicago | 7 |
| 21 | *Baltimore | 22 |
| 20 | *Dallas | 27 |
| 14 | Chicago | 17 |
| 0 | *N.Y. Giants | 23 |
| 24 | Washington | 28 |
| 13 | *L.A. Rams | 9 |
| 17 | *N. Orleans (OT) | 20 |
| 7 | St. Louis | 31 |
| 233 | | 322 |

**ST. LOUIS (8-7-1)**

| | | |
|---|---|---|
| 17 | New Orleans | 28 |
| 17 | *Dallas | 34 |
| 27 | *San Francisco | 42 |
| 14 | Philadelphia | 11 |
| 14 | Kansas City | 38 |
| 14 | *Washington | 38 |
| 34 | Tampa Bay | 27 |
| 20 | *N.Y. Giants (OT) | 20 |
| 41 | *Minnesota | 31 |
| 7 | Washington | 45 |
| 33 | *Seattle | 28 |
| 44 | *San Diego | 14 |
| 17 | Dallas | 35 |
| 10 | N.Y. Giants | 6 |
| 34 | L.A. Raiders | 24 |
| 31 | *Philadelphia | 7 |
| 374 | | 428 |

**SAN FRANCISCO (10-6)**

| | | |
|---|---|---|
| 17 | *Philadelphia | 22 |
| 48 | Minnesota | 17 |
| 42 | St. Louis | 27 |
| 24 | *Atlanta | 20 |
| 33 | New England | 13 |
| 7 | *L.A. Rams | 10 |
| 32 | New Orleans | 13 |
| 45 | L.A. Rams | 35 |
| 13 | *N.Y. Jets | 27 |
| 17 | *Miami | 20 |
| 27 | *New Orleans | 0 |
| 24 | Atlanta | 28 |
| 3 | Chicago | 13 |
| 35 | *Tampa Bay | 21 |
| 23 | Buffalo | 10 |
| 42 | *Dallas | 17 |
| 432 | | 293 |

**TAMPA BAY (2-14)**

| | | |
|---|---|---|
| 0 | *Detroit | 11 |
| 10 | Chicago | 17 |
| 16 | *Minnesota (OT) | 19 |
| 17 | *Cincinnati | 23 |
| 14 | Green Bay | 55 |
| 24 | Dallas (OT) | 27 |
| 27 | *St. Louis | 34 |
| 21 | *New Orleans | 24 |
| 12 | Pittsburgh | 17 |
| 17 | Minnesota | 12 |
| 0 | Cleveland | 20 |
| 0 | *Chicago | 27 |
| 33 | *Houston | 24 |
| 21 | San Francisco | 35 |
| 9 | *Green Bay (OT) | 12 |
| 20 | Detroit | 23 |
| 241 | | 380 |

**WASHINGTON (14-2)**

| | | |
|---|---|---|
| 30 | *Dallas | 31 |
| 23 | Philadelphia | 13 |
| 27 | *Kansas City | 12 |
| 27 | Seattle | 17 |
| 37 | *L.A. Raiders | 35 |
| 38 | St. Louis | 14 |
| 47 | Green Bay | 48 |
| 38 | *Detroit | 17 |
| 27 | San Diego | 24 |
| 45 | *St. Louis | 7 |
| 33 | N.Y. Giants | 17 |
| 42 | L.A. Rams | 20 |
| 28 | Philadelphia | 24 |
| 37 | *Atlanta | 21 |
| 31 | Dallas | 10 |
| 31 | *N.Y. Giants | 22 |
| 541 | | 332 |

*Denotes Home Game
(OT) Denotes Overtime

**Attendances as they appear in the following, and in the club-by-club sections starting on page 22, are turnstile counts and not paid attendance. Paid attendance totals are on page 162.**

## FIRST WEEK SUMMARY

Opening the season on the road was unusually kind to 12 of 14 teams as the National Football League began its sixty-fourth year. Only two teams, New Orleans and Kansas City, were winners at home. George Rogers gained a club-record 206 yards and scored two touchdowns to lead the Saints to their first opening-day victory in three seasons under Bum Phillips. In Kansas City, John Mackovic posted his first NFL head coaching win as the Chiefs downed the Seahawks. Three other rookie head coaches were victorious. Atlanta's Dan Henning used a pair of Steve Bartkowski touchdown passes to beat Chicago. Freeman McNeil rushed for 120 yards to help Joe Walton secure his initial victory, a 41-29 win over the Chargers. John Robinson made the transition from college to the pros an easy one as the Rams defeated the Giants. Frank Kush, beginning his second season in Baltimore following the Colts 0-8-1 mark in 1982, got his first win as Baltimore beat New England after 30 seconds of overtime. Green Bay also needed an extra period to defeat Houston. Jan Stenerud's second field goal followed five touchdown passes by Lynn Dickey to give the Packers a 41-38 win. Two teams were shutout winners. Detroit blanked Tampa Bay 11-0 as William Gay recorded 5½ sacks for the Lions and Miami shutout Buffalo 12-0 on four Uwe von Schamann field goals. Dallas and Washington renewed their NFC East rivalry with the Cowboys prevailing by a point. Danny White brought the Cowboys back from a 23-3 halftime deficit by throwing for three touchdowns in the second half. Steve DeBerg's touchdown pass finished the Broncos comeback win over the Steelers. Running back Ted Brown's three touchdowns helped the Vikings over the Browns. Matt Millen's interception led to the Raiders' second touchdown as Los Angeles defeated Cincinnati 20-10.

**SATURDAY, SEPTEMBER 3**

**Philadelphia 22, San Francisco 17**—At Candlestick Park, attendance 55,775. Reserve quarterback Joe Pisarcik ignited a 16-point third-quarter outburst to help Marion Campbell secure his first head coaching win with the Eagles. Pisarcik came on for Ron Jaworski, who had suffered a concussion in the second period, and completed 8 of 10 passes for 101 yards, including a 17-yard scoring pass to Hubie Oliver, that gave the Eagles a 19-10 advantage. The 49ers led 10-3 at the half, but Michael Haddix scored on a one-yard run early in the third period to tie the score and Tony Franklin's second of three field goals (a 30-yarder) put the Eagles ahead to stay. Roynell Young's fumble recovery in Philadelphia's end zone with just over a minute to play sent the 49ers to their third consecutive opening-day loss.

| | | | | | |
|---|---|---|---|---|---|
| Philadelphia | 0 | 3 | 16 | 3 | — 22 |
| San Francisco | 0 | 10 | 0 | 7 | — 17 |

Phil — FG Franklin 32
SF — Tyler 32 run (Wersching kick)
SF — FG Wersching 23
Phil — Haddix 1 run (kick failed)
Phil — FG Franklin 30
Phil — Oliver 17 pass from Pisarcik (Franklin kick)
Phil — FG Franklin 47
SF — Cooper 73 pass from Benjamin (Wersching kick)

**SUNDAY, SEPTEMBER 4**

**Atlanta 20, Chicago 17**—At Soldier Field, attendance 60,165. Steve Bartkowski fired two touchdown passes, including a 21-yarder to Alfred Jenkins in the fourth quarter, to lift the Falcons to a 20-17 win. Bartkowski (14 of 23 for 201 yards) opened the scoring with a 23-yard pass to running back William Andrews. After Chicago took a 10-6 advantage, Alfred Jackson's 25-yard reception set up Gerald Riggs' one-yard scoring plunge. The Bears regained the lead 17-13 but Bartkowski guided the Falcons 81 yards in seven plays for the winning touchdown and Dan Henning's first head coaching victory.

| | | | | | |
|---|---|---|---|---|---|
| Atlanta | 6 | 0 | 7 | 7 | — 20 |
| Chicago | 0 | 10 | 7 | 0 | — 17 |

Atl — Andrews 23 pass from Bartkowski (kick blocked)
Chi — Margerum 8 pass from McMahon (B. Thomas kick)
Chi — FG B. Thomas 29
Atl — Riggs 1 run (Luckhurst kick)
Chi — Hutchison 2 run (B. Thomas kick)
Atl — Jenkins 21 pass from Bartkowski (Luckhurst kick)

**Baltimore 29, New England 23**—At Sullivan Stadium, attendance 45,526. With 30 seconds gone in overtime, linebacker Johnie Cooks recovered a fumble and ran 52 yards for a touchdown to give the Colts their first victory since 1981. Raul Allegre's third field goal of the game, a 33-yarder with no time remaining, sent the game into the extra period. Baltimore trailed 13-3 in the second period but fought back behind the passing of second-year quarterback Mike Pagel, who threw for 292 yards and a pair of touchdowns to Bernard Henry. The win gave Colts head coach Frank Kush his first NFL victory.

| | | | | | | |
|---|---|---|---|---|---|---|
| Baltimore | 3 | 10 | 7 | 3 | 6 | — 29 |
| New England | 0 | 13 | 3 | 7 | 0 | — 23 |

Balt — FG Allegre 25
NE — Starring 73 pass from Grogan (kick failed)
NE — Morgan 50 pass from Grogan (J. Smith kick)
Balt — Henry 16 pass from Pagel (Allegre kick)
Balt — FG Allegre 52
NE — FG J. Smith 39
Balt — Henry 5 pass from Pagel (Allegre kick)
NE — R. Weathers 9 run (J. Smith kick)
Balt — FG Allegre 33
Balt — Cooks 52 fumble recovery return

**Denver 14, Pittsburgh 10**—At Three Rivers Stadium, attendance 58,233. Steve DeBerg passed two yards to Ron Egloff with 2:54 to play to lift the Broncos over the Steelers 14-10. DeBerg replaced John Elway in the second half and guided Denver 56 yards in 10 plays for the winning score. Pittsburgh dominated the game statistically, gaining 314 total yards to Denver's 139 (1 yard net passing). But Steelers turnovers (four fumbles, three interceptions) proved the difference.

| | | | | | |
|---|---|---|---|---|---|
| Denver | 0 | 7 | 0 | 7 | — 14 |
| Pittsburgh | 0 | 7 | 3 | 0 | — 10 |

Den — Winder 1 run (Karlis kick)
Pitt — F. Harris 4 run (Anderson kick)
Pitt — FG Anderson 31
Den — Egloff 2 pass from DeBerg (Karlis kick)

**Detroit 11, Tampa Bay 0**—At Tampa Stadium, attendance 62,154. Three field goals by Eddie Murray and William Gay's 5½ sacks highlighted the Lions' fourth consecutive opening-day win. Doug English sacked Tampa quarterback Jerry Golsteyn in the end zone for a safety, and Murray booted a 29-yard field goal four minutes later to give the Lions a 5-0 halftime lead. Murray added field goals of 48 and 38 yards in the second half as the Buccaneers suffered their first shutout since October 6, 1980 against the Bears.

| | | | | | |
|---|---|---|---|---|---|
| Detroit | 5 | 0 | 3 | 3 | — 11 |
| Tampa Bay | 0 | 0 | 0 | 0 | — 0 |

Det — Safety, English tackled Golsteyn in end zone
Det — FG Murray 29
Det — FG Murray 48
Det — FG Murray 38

**Green Bay 41, Houston 38**—At Astrodome, attendance 44,073. Seventeen-year veteran Jan Stenerud kicked a 42-yard field goal with 5:55 elapsed in overtime to down the Oilers 41-38. Packers quarterback Lynn Dickey completed a club-record 18 passes in a row and finished with 27 of 31 for 333 yards. His four touchdown passes in the first half (25, 5, 13, and 11 yards) gave Green Bay a 28-10 halftime lead but Houston running back Earl Campbell's three second-half scores (7, 1, 8 yards) deadlocked the game 31-31. Dickey broke the tie, connecting on a 74-yard scoring bomb to James Lofton, but rookie Larry Moriarty's two-yard run with 48 seconds left in regulation time forced the overtime period.

| | | | | | | |
|---|---|---|---|---|---|---|
| Green Bay | 7 | 21 | 3 | 7 | 3 | — 41 |
| Houston | 10 | 0 | 7 | 21 | 0 | — 38 |

GB — Coffman 25 pass from Dickey (Stenerud kick)
Hou — FG Kempf 49
Hou — Smith 47 pass from Manning (Kempf kick)
GB — Jefferson 5 pass from Dickey (Stenerud kick)
GB — Jefferson 13 pass from Dickey (Stenerud kick)
GB — Ellis 11 pass from Dickey (Stenerud kick)
Hou — Campbell 7 run (Kempf kick)
GB — FG Stenerud 46
Hou — Campbell 8 run (Kempf kick)
Hou — Campbell 1 run (Kempf kick)
GB — Lofton 74 pass from Dickey (Stenerud kick)
Hou — Moriarty 2 run (Kempf kick)
GB — FG Stenerud 42

**Los Angeles Raiders 20, Cincinnati 10**—At Riverfront Stadium, attendance 50,956. A pair of one-yard touchdown runs by Marcus Allen helped lead the Raiders to a 20-10 triumph. Los Angeles took the opening kickoff and marched 84 yards in 15 plays for a 7-0 lead. The Raiders made it 14-0 when linebacker Matt Millen's interception set up a 77-yard scoring drive. Chris Bahr kicked two field goals (38 and 39 yards), and Lyle Alzado and Bill Pickel each had a pair of sacks.

| | | | | | |
|---|---|---|---|---|---|
| L.A. Raiders | 7 | 10 | 0 | 3 | — 20 |
| Cincinnati | 0 | 0 | 3 | 7 | — 10 |

Raiders — Allen 1 run (Bahr kick)
Raiders — Allen 1 run (Bahr kick)
Raiders — FG Bahr 38
Cin — FG Breech 36
Raiders — FG Bahr 39
Cin — Harris 9 pass from Anderson (Breech kick)

**Los Angeles Rams 16, New York Giants 6**—At Giants Stadium, attendance 75,281. Vince Ferragamo passed for 279 yards and two touchdowns to help make John Robinson's NFL coaching debut a successful one. Ferragamo completed 17 of 28 passes, including scoring strikes of 8 and 42 yards to Mike Barber, who had seven receptions for 93 yards. LeRoy Irvin had two interceptions and Jack Youngblood contributed two of the Rams' five sacks. Rob Carpenter gained 113 of the Giants' 122 yards rushing.

| | | | | | |
|---|---|---|---|---|---|
| L.A. Rams | 3 | 7 | 6 | 0 | — 16 |
| New York Giants | 0 | 6 | 0 | 0 | — 6 |

Rams — FG Nelson 36
NYG — Carpenter 4 run (kick failed)
Rams — Barber 8 pass from Ferragamo (Nelson kick)
Rams — Barber 42 pass from Ferragamo (kick blocked)

**Miami 12, Buffalo 0**—At Rich Stadium, attendance 78,715. Four field goals by Uwe von Schamann (33, 23, 36, and 50 yards) helped lead Miami to its first regular-season shutout victory since November 11, 1979 (19-0 against Baltimore). Von Schamann's first and last field goals were set up by interceptions by Glenn and Lyle Blackwood, respectively. Defensive end Doug Betters (four sacks) led the Dolphins' defense, which held the Bills to 258 total yards.

| | | | | | |
|---|---|---|---|---|---|
| Miami | 0 | 6 | 3 | 3 | — 12 |
| Buffalo | 0 | 0 | 0 | 0 | — 0 |

Mia — FG von Schamann 33
Mia — FG von Schamann 23
Mia — FG von Schamann 36
Mia — FG von Schamann 50

**Minnesota 27, Cleveland 21**—At Cleveland Stadium, attendance 70,087. Ted Brown ran for two touchdowns and caught a pass for another to lead the Vikings over the Browns. Brown's scoring bursts of one and five yards, sandwiched around Benny Ricardo's 23-yard field goal, gave Minnesota a 17-7 halftime lead. Tommy Kramer, who completed 22 of 33 passes for 198 yards, hit Brown on a 10-yarder for a 24-14 edge late in the third quarter. Brown ended the day with 74 yards rushing on 19 carries and 63 yards on six receptions. Rufus Bess' interception at the Vikings' 31-yard line with 32 seconds remaining preserved the victory.

| | | | | | |
|---|---|---|---|---|---|
| Minnesota | 7 | 10 | 10 | 0 | — 27 |
| Cleveland | 0 | 7 | 7 | 7 | — 21 |

Minn — T. Brown 1 run (Ricardo kick)
Minn — FG Ricardo 23
Cle — Feacher 18 pass from Sipe (Bahr kick)
Minn — T. Brown 5 run (Ricardo kick)
Cle — Pruitt 6 pass from Sipe (Bahr kick)
Minn — T. Brown 10 pass from Kramer (Ricardo kick)
Minn — FG Ricardo 38
Cle — Adams 23 pass from Sipe (Bahr kick)

**New York Jets 41, San Diego 29**—At San Diego Jack Murphy Stadium, attendance 51,004. Kirk Springs' 64-yard kickoff return set up Richard Todd's decisive 18-yard touchdown pass to Freeman McNeil with 6:43 remaining to give the Jets their first opening-day win since 1978. Trailing 7-0, Todd culminated a 74-yard drive with a 26-yard scoring pass to Wesley Walker. Pat Leahy booted field goals from 32 and 27 yards for a 13-7 halftime lead. McNeil, who gained 120 yards, scored on a nine-yard run in the third quarter. Dwayne Crutchfield's one-yard plunge put the Jets up 27-16. Johnny Lynn's interception at the New York 23-yard line with two minutes left led to Mike Augustyniak's one-yard touchdown and sealed Joe Walton's first head coaching victory.

| | | | | | |
|---|---|---|---|---|---|
| New York Jets | 0 | 13 | 7 | 21 | — 41 |
| San Diego | 7 | 0 | 9 | 13 | — 29 |

SD — Muncie 1 run (Benirschke kick)
NYJ — Walker 26 pass from Todd (Leahy kick)
NYJ — FG Leahy 32
NYJ — FG Leahy 27
SD — FG Benirschke 23
NYJ — McNeil 9 run (Leahy kick)
SD — Muncie 2 run (kick failed)
NYJ — Crutchfield 1 run (Leahy kick)
SD — Duckworth 29 pass from Fouts (kick failed)
NYJ — McNeil 18 pass from Todd (Leahy kick)
SD — Joiner 33 pass from Fouts (Benirschke kick)
NYJ — Augustyniak 1 run (Leahy kick)

**New Orleans 28, St. Louis 17**—At Louisiana Superdome, attendance 60,430. George Rogers ran for a club-record 206 yards and two touchdowns to lead the Saints to their first opening-day victory in three seasons under coach Bum Phillips. Rogers' 76-yard touchdown run, followed by a 1-yard score three minutes later, gave New Orleans a 21-10 third-quarter lead. Dave Wilson, who relieved Ken Stabler (knee injury) three plays into the game, fired a 35-yard scoring pass to Kenny Duckett to finish the Saints' scoring.

| | | | | | |
|---|---|---|---|---|---|
| St. Louis | 7 | 3 | 0 | 7 | — 17 |
| New Orleans | 0 | 7 | 14 | 7 | — 28 |

StL — Marsh 11 pass from Lomax (O'Donoghue kick)
NO — W. Wilson 9 run (Andersen kick)
StL — FG O'Donoghue 47
NO — G. Rogers 76 run (Andersen kick)
NO — G. Rogers 1 run (Andersen kick)
NO — Duckett 35 pass from D. Wilson (Andersen kick)
StL — Tilley 16 pass from Hart (O'Donoghue kick)

**Kansas City 17, Seattle 13**—At Arrowhead Stadium, attendance 42,531. Touchdown passes by quarterback Bill Kenney and running back Jewerl Thomas helped John

Mackovic notch his first NFL coaching win. Kenney, who completed 19 of 32 for 247 yards, connected with Henry Marshall on a nine-yard scoring pass midway through the first quarter to put the Chiefs ahead to stay 7-3. Thomas, running to his right, lofted an 18-yard strike to Carlos Carson to cap a 67-yard third-period drive. Carson finished the day with seven receptions for 104 yards. Curt Warner, making his rookie debut, carried the ball 12 times for 93 yards and scored Seattle's only touchdown on an 18-yard pass from Jim Zorn with 3:16 left.

| | | | | | |
|---|---|---|---|---|---|
| Seattle | 3 | 0 | 3 | 7 | — 13 |
| Kansas City | 7 | 0 | 7 | 3 | — 17 |

Sea — FG N. Johnson 34
KC — Marshall 9 pass from Kenney (Lowery kick)
Sea — FG N. Johnson 48
KC — Carson 18 pass from J. Thomas (Lowery kick)
KC — FG Lowery 19
Sea — Warner 18 pass from Zorn (N. Johnson kick)

**MONDAY, SEPTEMBER 5**

**Dallas 31, Washington 30**—At Robert F. Kennedy Stadium, attendance 55,045. Danny White passed for three second-half touchdowns and ran for another to rally the Cowboys from a 23-3 halftime deficit and post a 31-30 comeback win. Dallas compiled only 85 first-half yards but exploded for 271 in the final two quarters. White, who completed 9 of 20 passes for 193 yards, threw third-period bombs of 75 and 51 yards to Tony Hill to put the Cowboys within striking distance of the Redskins. Dallas took the lead 24-23 on White's one-yard run two and a half minutes into the final period. Joe Theismann (28 of 38 for 325 yards) tried to rally Washington, but Ron Fellows' 33-yard interception return set up Doug Cosbie's one-yard touchdown catch two plays later to complete the Cowboys' scoring.

| | | | | | |
|---|---|---|---|---|---|
| Dallas | 0 | 3 | 14 | 14 | — 31 |
| Washington | 10 | 13 | 0 | 7 | — 30 |

Wash — FG Moseley 23
Wash — Riggins 1 run (Moseley kick)
Dall — FG Septien 26
Wash — FG Moseley 30
Wash — FG Moseley 39
Wash — Brown 41 pass from Theismann (Moseley kick)
Dall — Hill 75 pass from D. White (Septien kick)
Dall — Hill 51 pass from D. White (Septien kick)
Dall — D. White 1 run (Septien kick)
Dall — Cosbie 1 pass from D. White (Septien kick)
Wash — Warren 1 pass from Theismann (Moseley kick)

## SECOND WEEK SUMMARY

After two weeks of the season, only five teams remained undefeated. For the second consecutive game, Steve DeBerg replaced John Elway and rallied the Broncos to a victory, 17-10 over the Colts. Miami defeated New England for the sixteenth straight time in the Orange Bowl 34-24. Jim Plunkett directed a pair of 80-yard scoring drives as the Raiders beat the Oilers 20-6. Ron Springs ran for two touchdowns in Dallas' 34-17 comeback win over NFC East rival St. Louis. Rams rookie running back Eric Dickerson scored three times to lead Los Angeles over the Saints. Three other running backs turned in big games to lead their team's victories. Franco Harris rushed for 118 yards to become the third NFL player to gain over 11,000 yards in a career as Pittsburgh defeated Green Bay 25-21. Seattle's Curt Warner broke loose for 128 yards rushing and two touchdowns to help the Seahawks to their seventh consecutive win over the Jets. Outstanding efforts by San Diego's Chuck Muncie and Rolf Benirschke cast a shadow on Kansas City's first Monday night appearance in six years. Muncie ran for 110 yards and one touchdown while Benirschke kicked a 51-yard field goal in the Chargers 17-14 win. Benirschke converted one of two field goal attempts to become the NFL's leader in career field goal accuracy with a 72.9% rating. Ali Haji-Sheikh's 30-yard field goal 3:38 into overtime brought the Giants a 16-13 victory and Bill Parcells his first NFL head coaching win. Kay Stephenson got his initial win as the Buffalo head coach with a 10-6 defeat of Cincinnati. San Francisco's Joe Montana and Cleveland's Brian Sipe each threw four touchdown passes for their respective teams as the 49ers sank the Vikings 48-17 on Thursday night and the Browns edged the Lions 31-26. Running back Walter Payton showed he could be a dangerous receiver by catching six passes for 115 yards, including a 73-yard touchdown bomb, to lead the Bears over Tampa Bay 17-10. Washington won for the first time with a 23-13 win over Philadelphia, while five teams—New England, Cincinnati, Houston, St. Louis, and Tampa Bay—still remained winless.

**THURSDAY, SEPTEMBER 8**

**San Francisco 48, Minnesota 17**—At Metrodome, attendance 58,162. Joe Montana fired a career-high four touchdown passes in the first half as the 49ers cruised to a 48-17 victory. Montana's (17 of 24 for 230 yards) scoring passes to Dwight Clark (21 yards), Earl Cooper (2), Freddie Solomon (14), and Wendell Tyler (6), plus Eric Wright's 60-yard interception return for a score, helped San Francisco build an insurmountable 41-10 halftime lead. Wright had three of San Francisco's five interceptions and Fred Dean two of the team's four sacks. Tyler rushed for 107 yards (19 carries), his first 100-yard effort as a 49er.

| | | | | | |
|---|---|---|---|---|---|
| San Francisco | 13 | 28 | 0 | 7 | — 48 |
| Minnesota | 7 | 3 | 7 | 0 | — 17 |

SF — FG Wersching 38
SF — Clark 21 pass from Montana (Wersching kick)
Minn — T. Brown 1 run (Ricardo kick)
SF — FG Wersching 32
SF — Cooper 2 pass from Montana (Wersching kick)
SF — Wright 60 interception return (Wersching kick)
SF — Solomon 14 pass from Montana (Wersching kick)
SF — Tyler 6 pass from Montana (Wersching kick)
Minn — FG Ricardo 32
Minn — LeCount 30 pass from Kramer (Ricardo kick)
SF — Craig 1 run (Wersching kick)

**SUNDAY, SEPTEMBER 11**

**Buffalo 10, Cincinnati 6**—At Riverfront Stadium, attendance 46,839. Joe Ferguson hit Jerry Butler with a 14-yard pass for the game's only touchdown to help coach Kay Stephenson celebrate his first NFL coaching victory. The teams traded field goals in the first half but Buffalo took the second-half kickoff and marched 81 yards for the winning score. The Bills' defense saved the win, stopping the Bengals on Buffalo's 1-yard line with 2:00 left in the game.

| | | | | | |
|---|---|---|---|---|---|
| Buffalo | 0 | 3 | 7 | 0 | — 10 |
| Cincinnati | 0 | 3 | 0 | 3 | — 6 |

Buff — FG Steinfort 28
Cin — FG Breech 30
Buff — Butler 14 pass from Ferguson (Steinfort kick)
Cin — FG Breech 47

**Cleveland 31, Detroit 26**—At Pontiac Silverdome, attendance 60,095. Brian Sipe fired four touchdown passes and Mike Pruitt ran for 137 yards on 24 carries as the Browns recorded their first win. Sipe completed scoring passes of 42 yards to Ricky Feacher and 6 yards to Mike Pruitt in the first half and came back in the second half with touchdowns of 15 yards to Ozzie Newsome and 22 yards to Dave Logan. Matt Bahr's 25-yard field goal with less than two minutes to play added some insurance after Detroit's Doug English cut the lead to 28-26 by sacking Sipe in the end zone for a safety. The Cleveland defense had two fumble recoveries, three interceptions, and three sacks.

| | | | | | |
|---|---|---|---|---|---|
| Cleveland | 7 | 7 | 7 | 10 | — 31 |
| Detroit | 7 | 7 | 3 | 9 | — 26 |

Det — L. Thompson 80 pass from Hipple (Murray kick)
Cle — Feacher 42 pass from Sipe (Bahr kick)
Cle — Pruitt 6 pass from Sipe (Bahr kick)
Det — Norris 5 pass from Hipple (Murray kick)
Det — FG Murray 43
Cle — Newsome 15 pass from Sipe (Bahr kick)
Cle — Logan 22 pass from Sipe (Bahr kick)
Det — Norris 15 pass from Danielson (Murray kick)
Det — Safety, English tackled Sipe in end zone
Cle — FG Bahr 25

**Dallas 34, St. Louis 17**—At Busch Memorial Stadium, attendance 48,532. Ron Springs ran for two touchdowns and Rafael Septien kicked a pair of field goals (45 and 24 yards) to pace the Cowboys' win. St. Louis led 10-0 before Danny White, who completed 19 of 27 for 234 yards, set up Springs' one-yard touchdown run and threw a 10-yard scoring pass to Drew Pearson. Springs added a 19-yard touchdown run in the third quarter. The Dallas defense had five sacks, four interceptions, and two fumble recoveries, including Dennis Thurman's recovery in the end zone for a score.

| | | | | | |
|---|---|---|---|---|---|
| Dallas | 0 | 17 | 7 | 10 | — 34 |
| St. Louis | 10 | 0 | 0 | 7 | — 17 |

StL — Green 39 pass from Hart (O'Donoghue kick)
StL — FG O'Donoghue 23
Dall — Springs 1 run (Septien kick)
Dall — Pearson 10 pass from D. White (Septien kick)
Dall — FG Septien 45
Dall — Springs 19 run (Septien kick)
Dall — Thurman recovered fumble in end zone (Septein kick)
StL — Mitchell 5 run (O'Donoghue kick)
Dall — FG Septien 24

**Denver 17, Baltimore 10**—At Memorial Stadium, attendance 52,613. Steve DeBerg came off the bench to throw for one touchdown and run for another to lead the Broncos past the Colts. DeBerg's 54-yard pass to Steve Watson (six receptions, 161 yards) set up his two-yard scoring run, which put Denver ahead 17-10 with less than a minute to play. Earlier, Watson and DeBerg, who completed 9 of 11 passes for 158 yards, teamed up on a 24-yard touchdown with 5:55 remaining to deadlock the game 10-10. DeBerg replaced starter John Elway, who injured his shoulder in the third quarter.

| | | | | | |
|---|---|---|---|---|---|
| Denver | 0 | 3 | 0 | 14 | — 17 |
| Baltimore | 3 | 0 | 0 | 7 | — 10 |

Balt — FG Allegre 32
Den — FG Karlis 42
Balt — Anderson 41 fumble recovery return (Allegre kick)
Den — Watson 24 pass from DeBerg (Karlis kick)
Den — DeBerg 2 run (Karlis kick)

**Los Angeles Raiders 20, Houston 6**—At Memorial Coliseum, attendance 37,526. Jim Plunkett completed 19 of 28 passes for 229 yards, including a two-yard touchdown pass to Todd Christensen, to lift the Raiders to a 20-6 win. Los Angeles scored on its first possession as Kenny King's two-yard run culminated a 49-yard drive. Plunkett then engineered a pair of 80-yard touchdown drives climaxed by Greg Pruitt's 10-yard run and Christensen's scoring catch. The Raiders' defense limited the Oilers to seven first downs and 223 total yards.

| | | | | | |
|---|---|---|---|---|---|
| Houston | 0 | 3 | 3 | 0 | — 6 |
| L.A. Raiders | 6 | 7 | 0 | 7 | — 20 |

Raiders — King 2 run (kick failed)
Raiders — Pruitt 10 run (Bahr kick)
Hou — FG Kempf 40
Hou — FG Kempf 38
Raiders — Christensen 2 pass from Plunkett (Bahr kick)

**Miami 34, New England 24**—At Orange Bowl, attendance 59,343. David Woodley passed for two touchdowns, Andra Franklin ran for two more, and Uwe von Schamann kicked a pair of field goals as the Dolphins defeated the Patriots for the sixteenth consecutive time in the Orange Bowl. Franklin's six-yard run in the first quarter gave Miami the lead 7-3. His seven-yard scoring run in the final period followed Woodley touchdown passes of 1 yard to Dan Johnson and 64 yards to Duriel Harris, who had four receptions for 109 yards. The Miami defense recorded five sacks.

| | | | | | |
|---|---|---|---|---|---|
| New England | 3 | 0 | 0 | 21 | — 24 |
| Miami | 7 | 10 | 10 | 7 | — 34 |

NE — FG J. Smith 22
Mia — Franklin 6 run (von Schamann kick)
Mia — FG von Schamann 28
Mia — D. Johnson 1 pass from Woodley (von Schamann kick)
Mia — FG von Schamann 23
Mia — Harris 64 pass from Woodley (von Schamann kick)
NE — Dawson 12 pass from Grogan (J. Smith kick)
NE — C. Weathers 36 pass from Grogan (J. Smith kick)
Mia — Franklin 7 run (von Schamann kick)
NE — Tatupu 5 run (J. Smith kick)

**Los Angeles Rams 30, New Orleans 27**—At Anaheim Stadium, attendance 45,572. Rookie Eric Dickerson's third touchdown of the game, a three-yard run with 1:22 to play, helped the Rams break a two-game losing streak against the Saints. New Orleans led 10-0, but touchdowns by Dickerson and David Hill gave Los Angeles a 21-20 edge. Ken Stabler's 15-yard scoring pass to Eugene Goodlow put the Saints back on top 27-21. Rams rookie wide receiver Ottis Grant set up Dickerson's winning touchdown with a 57-yard pass reception.

| | | | | | |
|---|---|---|---|---|---|
| New Orleans | 3 | 7 | 10 | 7 | — 27 |
| L.A. Rams | 0 | 7 | 7 | 16 | — 30 |

NO — FG Andersen 27
NO — W. Wilson 1 run (Andersen kick)
Rams — Dickerson 3 run (Nelson kick)
NO — Gajan 4 run (Andersen kick)
Rams — D. Hill 11 pass from Ferragamo (Nelson kick)
NO — FG Andersen 30
Rams — Dickerson 1 run (Nelson kick)
NO — Goodlow 15 pass from Stabler (Andersen kick)
Rams — Safety, Erxleben ran out of end zone
Rams — Dickerson 3 run (Nelson kick)

**New York Giants 16, Atlanta 13**—At Atlanta-Fulton County Stadium, attendance 52,850. Ali Haji-Sheikh's 30-yard field goal 3:38 into overtime gave Giants head coach Bill Parcells his first NFL win. New York took a 13-6 lead on Haji-Sheikh field goals from 37 and 31 yards and Scott Brunner's eight-yard scoring pass to Earnest Gray. But Atlanta deadlocked the score 13-13 on Steve Bartkowski's 11-yard scoring toss to Alfred Jackson with 3:06 left in regulation time. Rob Carpenter rushed for 100 yards for the second week in a row, gaining 111 on 28 carries.

| | | | | | | |
|---|---|---|---|---|---|---|
| New York Giants | 3 | 7 | 0 | 3 | 3 | — 16 |
| Atlanta | 0 | 3 | 3 | 7 | 0 | — 13 |

NYG — FG Haji-Sheikh 37
NYG — Gray 8 pass from Brunner (Haji-Sheikh kick)
Atl — FG Luckhurst 42
Atl — FG Luckhurst 39
NYG — FG Haji-Sheikh 31
Atl — Jackson 11 pass from Bartkowski (Luckhurst kick)
NYG — FG Haji-Sheikh 30

**Pittsburgh 25, Green Bay 21**—At Lambeau Field, attendance 55,154. Franco Harris gained 118 yards to become only the third player to top the 11,000-yard career rushing mark as the Steelers edged the Packers 25-21. Harris topped the milestone with a three-yard scoring run in the first quarter, but Pittsburgh trailed at halftime 14-13. Frank Pollard (90 yards on 20 carries) blasted for the go-ahead touchdown from one-yard on the first play of the fourth period. Bob Kohrs sacked Packers quarterback Lynn Dickey in the end zone for a safety, the Steelers' fourth sack of the game, to finish the scoring. Pittsburgh's victory overshadowed the performance of Dickey (14 of 20 for 290 yards), who teamed with James Lofton (five receptions for 169 yards) on scoring passes of 71, 73, and 12 yards.

| | | | | | |
|---|---|---|---|---|---|
| Pittsburgh | 7 | 6 | 3 | 9 | — 25 |
| Green Bay | 7 | 7 | 0 | 7 | — 21 |

Pitt — F. Harris 3 run (Anderson kick)
GB — Lofton 71 pass from Dickey (Stenerud kick)

Pitt — Stoudt 1 run (kick blocked)
GB — Lofton 73 pass from Dickey (Stenerud kick)
Pitt — FG Anderson 30
Pitt — Pollard 1 run (Anderson kick)
GB — Lofton 12 pass from Dickey (Stenerud kick)
Pitt — Safety, Kohrs tackled Dickey in end zone

**Seattle 17, New York Jets 10**—At Shea Stadium, attendance 54,972. Curt Warner rushed for 128 yards on 24 carries and scored two touchdowns to lead the Seahawks over the Jets for the seventh time in as many meetings. Warner's seven-yard run helped give Seattle a 10-3 halftime lead, and his one-yard plunge with 3:54 remaining clinched the win. The Seahawks' defense recovered four fumbles and had three interceptions, the last by Gene Williams with 18 seconds left. Harold Jackson caught one pass for 21 yards to move into second place on the NFL's all-time list with 10,286 yards.

| | | | | | |
|---|---|---|---|---|---|
| Seattle | 0 | 10 | 0 | 7 | — 17 |
| New York Jets | 0 | 3 | 0 | 7 | — 10 |

Sea — Warner 7 run (N. Johnson kick)
Sea — FG N. Johnson 40
NYJ — FG Leahy 18
Sea — Warner 1 run (N. Johnson kick)
NYJ — Walker 46 pass from Todd (Leahy kick)

**Chicago 17, Tampa Bay 10**—At Soldier Field, attendance 58,186. Terry Schmidt's 32-yard interception return for a touchdown early in the fourth quarter led the Bears to their first win. Chicago held the Buccaneers on their own 1-yard line and one minute later Jim McMahon hit Walter Payton on a 73-yard scoring bomb for a 7-3 second-quarter lead. Bob Thomas' 50-yard field goal with one second left in the first half extended the Bears' lead to 10-3, but Tampa Bay evened the score on its opening drive of the second half. Payton had six receptions for 115 yards, the third 100-yard receiving day of his career.

| | | | | | |
|---|---|---|---|---|---|
| Tampa Bay | 0 | 3 | 7 | 0 | — 10 |
| Chicago | 0 | 10 | 0 | 7 | — 17 |

TB — FG Capece 20
Chi — Payton 73 pass from McMahon (B. Thomas kick)
Chi — FG B. Thomas 50
TB — Owens 1 run (Capece kick)
Chi — Schmidt 32 interception return (B. Thomas kick)

**Washington 23, Philadelphia 13**—At Veterans Stadium, attendance 69,542. John Riggins ran for 100 yards on 27 carries and scored on a 14-yard run two minutes into the fourth quarter to help the Redskins notch their first victory. Joe Theismann completed a 12-yard touchdown pass to Charlie Brown and Mark Moseley converted all three of his field goal attempts (36, 24 and 23 yards). Dave Butz and Dexter Manley each had two quarterback sacks.

| | | | | | |
|---|---|---|---|---|---|
| Washington | 7 | 0 | 3 | 13 | — 23 |
| Philadelphia | 0 | 3 | 7 | 3 | — 13 |

Wash — Brown 12 pass from Theismann (Moseley kick)
Phil — FG Franklin 27
Phil — Quick 27 pass from Jaworski (Franklin kick)
Wash — FG Moseley 36
Wash — Riggins 14 run (Moseley kick)
Wash — FG Moseley 24
Phil — FG Franklin 33
Wash — FG Moseley 23

**MONDAY, SEPTEMBER 12**

**San Diego 17, Kansas City 14**—At Arrowhead Stadium, attendance 62,150. Dan Fouts' 12-yard touchdown pass to Wes Chandler with 1:44 to play lifted the Chargers to a 17-14 win. Chuck Muncie (110 yards rushing) gave San Diego a 10-7 lead with a 10-yard scoring burst in the third quarter. Wide receiver Carlos Carson put the Chiefs back on top 14-10 when he completed a 48-yard touchdown pass to Henry Marshall, but the lead was short-lived as Fouts marched the Chargers 80 yards in five plays for the winning score. Rolf Benirschke kicked a 51-yard field goal to become the NFL's all-time career leader for field goal accuracy (100 of 137, 72.9 percent). It was Kansas City's first Monday night appearance in six years.

| | | | | | |
|---|---|---|---|---|---|
| San Diego | 3 | 0 | 7 | 7 | — 17 |
| Kansas City | 0 | 7 | 0 | 7 | — 14 |

SD — FG Benirschke 51
KC — Hancock 45 pass from Kenney (Lowery kick)
SD — Muncie 10 run (Benirschke kick)
KC — Marshall 48 pass from Carson (Lowery kick)
SD — Chandler 12 pass from Fouts (Benirschke kick)

## THIRD WEEK SUMMARY

Home teams were victorious more often than not for the first time this season, winning 9 of 14 games. The Cowboys and the Raiders remained the only clubs with undefeated records. Dextor Clinkscale and Michael Downs scored touchdowns 12 seconds apart to cap Dallas' 28-13 comeback win over the New York Giants. Meanwhile, the Raiders easily beat the Dolphins in the Coliseum. Los Angeles, led by Marcus Allen's 105 yards rushing, capitalized on Miami turnovers to open a 27-0 lead and improve their Monday night record to 20-2-1. Two touchdown passes in the final three minutes by rookie Dan Marino, who was playing for the first time in the NFL, were all the Dolphins could muster against the league's number-one ranked defense. Two other teams were first-time losers. The Rams fell to Green Bay 27-24 as Jan Stenerud kicked a 36-yard field goal with one second remaining. Tony Franklin's 43-yard field goal with 57 seconds left helped the Eagles to a 13-10 victory over the Broncos. New England won for the first time as Tony Collins ran for 212 yards and three touchdowns to help the Patriots christen newly dedicated Sullivan Stadium with a 23-13 win over the Jets. Curt Warner became the first Seattle running back to rush for over 100 yards (109) in consecutive games as the Seahawks defeated San Diego 34-31. Morten Andersen's 41-yard field goal after 10:57 of overtime gave New Orleans a 34-31 win over Chicago. The Saints' victory overshadowed a remarkable performance by the Bears' Walter Payton. Payton ran for 161 yards and completed two touchdown passes to rookie Willie Gault, including a 21-yarder that sent the game into overtime. Benny Ricardo's fourth field goal of the game provided Minnesota with a 19-16 overtime win in Tampa. Washington trailed Kansas City 12-0 at halftime but mounted a second-half assault to beat the Chiefs 27-12. In Buffalo, the Bills gave up their first touchdown at home in 20 quarters and had to rely on Joe Ferguson's three scoring passes to complete a 28-23 comeback win over Baltimore. Joe Montana threw two touchdown passes in San Francisco's 42-27 win over St. Louis.

**THURSDAY, SEPTEMBER 15**

**Cleveland 17, Cincinnati 7**—At Cleveland Stadium, attendance 79,700. Brian Sipe completed his first nine passes, including a 19-yard touchdown to Ozzie Newsome, to help lead the Browns over the Bengals. Matt Bahr kicked a 19-yard field goal for a 10-7 halftime edge and Mike Pruitt's one-yard plunge in the third quarter extended Cleveland's lead to 17-7. Clarence Scott's interception in the end zone sealed the win. Sipe finished the day with 201 yards on 21 completions in 31 attempts.

| | | | | | |
|---|---|---|---|---|---|
| Cincinnati | 0 | 7 | 0 | 0 | — 7 |
| Cleveland | 7 | 3 | 7 | 0 | — 17 |

Cle — Newsome 19 pass from Sipe (Bahr kick)
Cle — FG Bahr 19
Cin — Kinnebrew 1 run (Breech kick)
Cle — Pruitt 1 run (Bahr kick)

**SUNDAY, SEPTEMBER 18**

**Atlanta 30, Detroit 14**—At Pontiac Silverdome, attendance 54,622. Steve Bartkowski fired three touchdown passes and William Andrews ran for 150 yards on a club record 32 carries as the Falcons beat the Lions 30-14. Bartkowski led Atlanta's 535-yard offensive explosion, completing 24 of 34 passes for 366 yards and touchdowns of 54 and 36 yards to Alfred Jackson and 11 yards to Ben Young. Jackson caught five passes for 123 yards and Mick Luckhurst chipped in with field goals of 28, 42, and 45 yards.

| | | | | | |
|---|---|---|---|---|---|
| Atlanta | 3 | 21 | 0 | 6 | — 30 |
| Detroit | 0 | 7 | 7 | 0 | — 14 |

Atl — FG Luckhurst 28
Atl — Jackson 54 pass from Bartkowski (Luckhurst kick)
Atl — Young 11 pass from Bartkowski (Luckhurst kick)
Det — Jones 1 run (Murray kick)
Atl — Jackson 36 pass from Bartkowski (Luckhurst kick)
Det — Rubick 6 pass from Danielson (Murray kick)
Atl — FG Luckhurst 42
Atl — FG Luckhurst 45

**Buffalo 28, Baltimore 23**—At Rich Stadium, attendance 40,937. Joe Ferguson's two-yard touchdown pass to Joe Cribbs with 4:44 to play clinched the Bills' comeback win. Ferguson's scoring tosses of 3 yards to Cribbs and 27 yards to Frank Lewis, plus Cribbs' one-yard plunge put the Bills ahead 21-16. But Curtis Dickey's 33-yard run gave the Colts a 23-21 edge with 10:20 to play. Chris Keating's fumble recovery at the Colts' 14-yard line set up the winning score. Buffalo's streak of 20 straight quarters without yielding a touchdown at home was snapped by Mike Pagel's 72-yard scoring bomb to Dickey in the third quarter.

| | | | | | |
|---|---|---|---|---|---|
| Baltimore | 6 | 3 | 7 | 7 | — 23 |
| Buffalo | 0 | 7 | 7 | 14 | — 28 |

Balt — FG Allegre 28
Balt — FG Allegre 49
Buff — Cribbs 3 pass from Ferguson (Danelo kick)
Balt — FG Allegre 45
Buff — Cribbs 1 run (Danelo kick)
Balt — Dickey 72 pass from Pagel (Allegre kick)
Buff — Lewis 27 pass from Ferguson (Danelo kick)
Balt — Dickey 33 run (Allegre kick)
Buff — Cribbs 2 pass from Ferguson (Danelo kick)

**New Orleans 34, Chicago 31**—At Louisiana Superdome, attendance 64,692. Morten Andersen's 41-yard field goal 10:57 into overtime gave the Saints a 34-31 win. Ken Stabler completed all four of his passes for 36 yards (25 of 39 for 279 yards overall) in the winning drive, which began on New Orleans' 2-yard line. The Saints' defense compiled a team-record eight sacks for 73 yards, recovered two fumbles, and intercepted two passes, but yielded 493 yards. The victory overshadowed the performance of Walter Payton, who rushed 28 times for 161 yards and completed two touchdown passes to Willie Gault, including a 21-yarder that sent the game into overtime.

| | | | | | | |
|---|---|---|---|---|---|---|
| Chicago | 7 | 3 | 7 | 14 | 0 | — 31 |
| New Orleans | 7 | 3 | 14 | 7 | 3 | — 34 |

Chi — Gault 8 pass from McMahon (B. Thomas kick)
NO — Gajan 3 run (Andersen kick)
NO — FG Andersen 21
Chi — FG B. Thomas 27
NO — Brenner 15 pass from Stabler (Andersen kick)
NO — Duckett 25 pass from Stabler (Andersen kick)
Chi — Payton 49 run (B. Thomas kick)
Chi — Gault 56 pass from Payton (B. Thomas kick)
NO — Poe 31 interception return (Andersen kick)
Chi — Gault 21 pass from Payton (B. Thomas kick)
NO — FG Andersen 41

**Washington 27, Kansas City 12**—At Robert F. Kennedy Stadium, attendance 55,045. Joe Theismann threw for two touchdowns to rally the Redskins to a 27-12 win. Kansas City jumped to a 12-0 lead on field goals of 58 (the third longest in NFL history), 21, 32 and 22 yards by Nick Lowery. Washington scored 17 unanswered points in the third period on Mark Moseley's 35-yard field goal, John Riggins' two-yard run, and Don Warren's 12-yard touchdown reception. The Redskins registered five quarterback sacks and held their opponent under 100 yards rushing (33) for the eighth time in the last 10 games.

| | | | | | |
|---|---|---|---|---|---|
| Kansas City | 3 | 9 | 0 | 0 | — 12 |
| Washington | 0 | 0 | 17 | 10 | — 27 |

KC — FG Lowery 58
KC — FG Lowery 21
KC — FG Lowery 32
KC — FG Lowery 22
Wash — FG Moseley 35
Wash — Riggins 2 run (Moseley kick)
Wash — Warren 12 pass from Theismann (Moseley kick)
Wash — Didier 39 pass from Theismann (Moseley kick)
Wash — FG Moseley 34

**Green Bay 27, Los Angeles Rams 24**—At Milwaukee County Stadium, attendance 54,037. Byron Braggs recovered Eric Dickerson's fumble on the Rams' 19-yard line to set up Jan Stenerud's 36-yard field goal with one second remaining, as the Packers edged the Rams. Green Bay jumped to a 17-0 lead on Stenerud's 38-yard field goal and touchdowns by Eddie Lee Ivery (one-yard run) and John Jefferson (23-yard reception), but Los Angeles bounced back to take a 24-17 lead with three touchdowns in the third quarter. The Packers knotted the score with 11:10 to play when Ivery scored on a four-yard run following a Mark Lee interception.

| | | | | | |
|---|---|---|---|---|---|
| L.A. Rams | 0 | 3 | 21 | 0 | — 24 |
| Green Bay | 10 | 7 | 0 | 10 | — 27 |

GB — FG Stenerud 38
GB — Ivery 1 run (Stenerud kick)
GB — Jefferson 23 pass from Dickey (Stenerud kick)
Rams — FG Nelson 31
Rams — Grant 23 pass from Ferragamo (Nelson kick)
Rams — Dickerson 3 run (Nelson kick)
Rams — Farmer 8 pass from Ferragamo (Nelson kick)
GB — Ivery 4 run (Stenerud kick)
GB — FG Stenerud 36

**Minnesota 19, Tampa Bay 16**—At Tampa Stadium, attendance 57,567. Benny Ricardo connected on a 42-yard field goal 9:27 into overtime to give the Vikings a 19-16 win. Ricardo earlier kicked field goals of 29, 37, and 38 yards, the last with 24 seconds left in regulation time to tie the score at 16-16. Tommy Kramer completed his first eight passes of the game, including an eight-yard touchdown to Terry LeCount, but was replaced by Steve Dils in the first half after a knee injury forced him to the sidelines. Dils completed 16 of 33 for 205 yards, including a 48-yarder to Rickey Young to set up Ricardo's winning field goal.

| | | | | | | |
|---|---|---|---|---|---|---|
| Minnesota | 7 | 6 | 0 | 3 | 3 | — 19 |
| Tampa Bay | 0 | 6 | 3 | 7 | 0 | — 16 |

Minn — LeCount 8 pass from Kramer (Ricardo kick)
Minn — FG Ricardo 29
TB — Owens 1 run (run failed)
Minn — FG Ricardo 37
TB — FG Capece 40
TB — Wilder 5 pass from Thompson (Capece kick)
Minn — FG Ricardo 38
Minn — FG Ricardo 42

**Dallas 28, New York Giants 13**—At Texas Stadium, attendance 62,347. Fourth-quarter touchdowns by Dextor Clinkscale and Michael Downs 12 seconds apart secured the Cowboys' comeback win. Clinkscale's 68-yard interception return for a score was followed by Downs' 10-yard fumble recovery touchdown on the ensuing kickoff. New York took a 3-0 lead on Ali Haji-Sheikh's 31-yard field goal, but a pair of second-quarter Danny White to Doug Cosbie scoring passes from four and two yards put Dallas ahead to stay 14-3.

| | | | | | |
|---|---|---|---|---|---|
| New York Giants | 3 | 0 | 10 | 0 | — 13 |
| Dallas | 0 | 14 | 0 | 14 | — 28 |

NYG — FG Haji-Sheikh 31
Dall — Cosbie 4 pass from D. White (Septien kick)
Dall — Cosbie 2 pass from D. White (Septien kick)
NYG — Woolfolk 1 run (Haji-Sheikh kick)
NYG — FG Haji-Sheikh 27
Dall — Clinkscale 68 interception return (Septien kick)
Dall — Downs 10 fumble recovery return (Septien kick)

**New England 23, New York Jets 13**—At Sullivan Stadium, attendance 43,182. Tony Collins ran for a club-record 212 yards on 23 carries and scored three touchdowns to lead the Patriots over the Jets. New England led 16-13 at halftime on scoring runs by Collins of 39 and 7 yards and John Smith's 43-yard field goal. Collins added a 23-yard touchdown late in the third quarter, and the defense held New York scoreless in the second half and limited Freeman McNeil to 33 yards in 12 attempts. Jim Nance held the previous Patriots mark of 208 yards rushing, set on October 30, 1966 against the Raiders.

| | | | | | |
|---|---|---|---|---|---|
| New York Jets | 0 | 13 | 0 | 0 — | 13 |
| New England | 13 | 3 | 7 | 0 — | 23 |

NE — Collins 39 run (J. Smith kick)
NE — Collins 7 run (kick failed)
NYJ — Crutchfield 1 run (Leahy kick)
NE — FG J. Smith 43
NYJ — Walker 13 pass from Todd (kick blocked)
NE — Collins 23 run (J. Smith kick)

**Philadelphia 13, Denver 10**—At Mile High Stadium, attendance 74,202. Tony Franklin kicked a 43-yard field goal with 57 seconds remaining as the Eagles edged the Cardinals. Ron Jaworski led the Philadelphia offense, which gained 407 total yards, completing 18 of 28 passes for 284 yards, including a 38-yard scoring toss to Mike Quick (six catches, 152 yards). Franklin's 20-yard field goal gave the Eagles a 10-3 edge but John Elway, making his home debut, connected with Rick Parros on a 33-yard touchdown pass with 1:54 left to tie the score 10-10. Rick Upchurch returned two punts for 23 yards to become the first NFL player to reach the 3,000-yard mark on career punt returns.

| | | | | | |
|---|---|---|---|---|---|
| Philadelphia | 7 | 0 | 0 | 6 — | 13 |
| Denver | 0 | 0 | 3 | 7 — | 10 |

Phil — Quick 38 pass from Jaworski (Franklin kick)
Den — FG Karlis 34
Phil — FG Franklin 20
Den — Parros 33 pass from Elway (Karlis kick)
Phil — FG Franklin 43

**Pittsburgh 40, Houston 28**—At Astrodome, attendance 44,150. Gary Anderson kicked field goals of 49, 35, 20, and 22 yards, and Walter Abercrombie added a pair of touchdowns to highlight the Steelers' win. After Anderson staked Pittsburgh to a 12-7 halftime lead, Abercrombie scored on a 30-yard pass from Cliff Stoudt and a 50-yard run. Franco Harris compiled 115 yards on 26 carries (including a six-yard touchdown run), and linebacker Bryan Hinkle returned an interception 14 yards for another score. Pittsburgh's defense had four interceptions, one fumble recovery, and six sacks. Carl Roaches scored the Oilers' first touchdown on an electrifying 97-yard kickoff return.

| | | | | | |
|---|---|---|---|---|---|
| Pittsburgh | 6 | 6 | 14 | 14 — | 40 |
| Houston | 7 | 0 | 0 | 21 — | 28 |

Pitt — FG Anderson 49
Hou — Roaches 97 kickoff return (Kempf kick)
Pitt — FG Anderson 35
Pitt — FG Anderson 20
Pitt — FG Anderson 22
Pitt — F. Harris 6 run (Anderson kick)
Pitt — Abercrombie 30 pass from Stoudt (Anderson kick)
Pitt — Hinkle 14 interception return (Anderson kick)
Hou — Moriarty 1 run (Kempf kick)
Hou — Campbell 1 run (Kempf kick)
Pitt — Abercrombie 50 run (Anderson kick)
Hou — Walls 28 pass from Manning (Kempf kick)

**Seattle 34, San Diego 31**—At Kingdome, attendance 61,714. Seattle opened a 34-17 lead on a pair of Jim Zorn to Steve Largent touchdown passes and fought off a furious Chargers' rally for the win. Dan Fouts, who completed 21 of 41 passes for 338 yards, fired three of his four touchdown passes within a nine-minute span of the final period to bring San Diego back from a 27-10 deficit. Seattle intercepted three Fouts passes, including Paul Moyer's 19-yard return for a score. Curt Warner became the first Seahawk to rush for over 100 yards in two straight games, gaining 109 yards on 22 carries.

| | | | | | |
|---|---|---|---|---|---|
| San Diego | 7 | 3 | 0 | 21 — | 31 |
| Seattle | 14 | 3 | 10 | 7 — | 34 |

Sea — Doornink 2 run (N. Johnson kick)
SD — Joiner 25 pass from Fouts (Benirschke kick)
Sea — Largent 5 pass from Zorn (N. Johnson kick)
Sea — FG N. Johnson 33
SD — FG Benirschke 26
Sea — FG N. Johnson 43
Sea — Moyer 19 interception return (N. Johnson kick)
SD — Sievers 26 pass from Fouts (Benirschke kick)
Sea — Largent 41 pass from Zorn (N. Johnson kick)
SD — Duckworth 44 pass from Fouts (Benirschke kick)
SD — Sievers 27 pass from Fouts (Benirschke kick)

**San Francisco 42, St. Louis 27**—At Busch Memorial Stadium, attendance 38,132. Joe Montana completed 20 of 32 passes for 341 yards to lead the 49ers over the Cardinals. Montana and Freddie Solomon connected on a pair of touchdowns of 69 and 28 yards, and Dwight Hicks' 40-yard interception return for a score gave San Francisco a 21-10 lead at the half. The 49ers, who compiled 527 yards total offense, added three touchdowns in the third quarter to put the game out of reach. Montana found Russ Francis on an 11-yard scoring pass and Wendell Tyler's 15-yard touchdown run followed former Cardinal Tim Collier's 32-yard interception return for a touchdown.

| | | | | | |
|---|---|---|---|---|---|
| San Francisco | 7 | 14 | 21 | 0 — | 42 |
| St. Louis | 7 | 3 | 10 | 7 — | 27 |

SF — Solomon 69 pass from Montana (Wersching kick)
StL — Tilley 8 pass from Lomax (O'Donoghue kick)
SF — Solomon 28 pass from Montana (Wersching kick)
SF — Hicks 40 interception return (Wersching kick)
StL — FG O'Donoghue 43
SF — Francis 11 pass from Montana (Wersching kick)
StL — Morris 1 run (O'Donoghue kick)
SF — Collier 32 interception return (Wersching kick)
StL — FG O'Donoghue 48
SF — Tyler 15 run (Wersching kick)
StL — Love 12 pass from Lomax (O'Donoghue kick)

**MONDAY, SEPTEMBER 19**

**Los Angeles Raiders 27, Miami 14**—At Memorial Coliseum, attendance 57,796. Greg Townsend's 66-yard fumble recovery return for a touchdown and Greg Pruitt's five-yard run helped the Raiders to an insurmountable 27-0 lead over the Dolphins. Frank Hawkins opened the scoring with a two-yard run. Jim Plunkett's 14-yard scoring pass to Todd Christensen put Los Angeles up 13-0 at halftime. Two touchdown passes by Dan Marino in the final three minutes helped Miami avert a shutout. Marcus Allen carried 22 times for 105 yards as the Raiders ran their Monday night record to 20-2-1.

| | | | | | |
|---|---|---|---|---|---|
| Miami | 0 | 0 | 0 | 14 — | 14 |
| L.A. Raiders | 7 | 6 | 7 | 7 — | 27 |

Raiders — Hawkins 2 run (Bahr kick)
Raiders — Christensen 14 pass from Plunkett (kick failed)
Raiders — Townsend 66 fumble recovery return (Bahr kick)
Raiders — Pruitt 5 run (Bahr kick)
Mia — Rose 6 pass from Marino (von Schamann kick)
Mia — Duper 2 pass from Marino (von Schamann kick)

## FOURTH WEEK SUMMARY

Buffalo, Miami, Baltimore, New England, and New York pulled off a rare five-game sweep for the AFC East. The Bills got 166 yards rushing from Joe Cribbs and seven sacks from their defense to down the Oilers 30-13. In Miami, the Dolphins won despite themselves. Miami committed a club-record-tying five fumbles and was intercepted twice but the Dolphins' defense came through, holding Kansas City to 155 total yards and winning 14-6. The Colts accumulated 461 total yards but needed Raul Allegre's 33-yard overtime field goal to edge the Bears 22-19. The Patriots defeated the Steelers for only the second time in their history 28-23. Pittsburgh dominated New England, running 86 plays to the Patriots' 45 and outgaining them 448 to 296, but Steve Grogan's 76-yard scoring bomb to Stephen Starring evened New England's record at 2-2. The Steelers' Franco Harris gained 106 yards to move ahead of O.J. Simpson into second place on the all-time rushing list with 11,309 yards. At Shea Stadium, a veteran quarterback and a rookie running back shared the spotlight. Richard Todd of the Jets completed 37 of 50 passes for 446 yards and Los Angeles' Eric Dickerson rushed for 192 yards to take over the NFL rushing lead with 645 yards. Pat Leahy's 26-yard field goal, following 8:22 of overtime, enabled the Jets to defeat the Rams 27-24. Cincinnati won for the first time in 1983 with a 23-17 victory over Tampa Bay. Cleveland needed Brian Sipe's 48-yard touchdown pass to Harry Holt to beat San Diego 30-24 in overtime and gain the top spot in the AFC Central. The Raiders scored on three consecutive second-half possessions to defeat Denver 22-7 and remain the only unbeaten team (4-0) in the AFC. Undefeated Dallas came away with the most improbable win of the day. The Cowboys were victimized by seven quarterback sacks, four interceptions, and two lost fumbles, yet only trailed the Saints by a point with two minutes to play. Anthony Dickerson found himself in the hero's role, sacking New Orleans quarterback Ken Stabler in the end zone for a safety with 1:58 remaining to give Dallas a 21-20 win. Jim Hart replaced Neil Lomax in the starting lineup and completed a 26-yard touchdown pass to Roy Green with 29 seconds left to lift the Cardinals to a 14-11 win over the Eagles. Joe Theismann's three touchdown passes helped make the Redskins first game in the Kingdome a successful one as Washington downed Seattle 27-17. San Francisco's Joe Montana threw for three scores as the 49ers beat the Falcons 24-20 to snap a six-game winless streak at Candlestick Park. Minnesota survived five interceptions to post a 20-17 win over Detroit and move into first place in the NFC Central Division. Ali Haji-Sheikh kicked a team-record 56-yard field goal in the Giants' 27-3 victory over the Packers.

**SUNDAY, SEPTEMBER 25**

**San Francisco 24, Atlanta 20**—At Candlestick Park, attendance 57,814. Joe Montana directed a 418-yard offensive attack, throwing for 261 yards and three touchdowns, as the 49ers halted a six-game losing streak at home. Montana fired touchdowns of 21 and 12 yards to Dwight Clark for a 14-0 advantage and added a one-yard pass to Earl Cooper in the fourth quarter. Freddie Solomon caught six passes for 103 yards. The 49ers' defense sacked Steve Bartkowski eight times.

| | | | | | |
|---|---|---|---|---|---|
| Atlanta | 0 | 7 | 6 | 7 — | 20 |
| San Francisco | 7 | 7 | 3 | 7 — | 24 |

SF — Clark 21 pass from Montana (Wersching kick)
SF — Clark 12 pass from Montana (Wersching kick)
Atl — B. Johnson 20 pass from Bartkowski (Luckhurst kick)
Atl — Hodge 76 pass from Bartkowski (kicked failed)
SF — FG Wersching 24
Atl — Bartkowski 3 run (Luckhurst kick)
SF — Cooper 1 pass from Montana (Wersching kick)

**Baltimore 22, Chicago 19**—At Memorial Stadium, attendance 34,350. Raul Allegre's 33-yard field goal with 4:51 elapsed in overtime lifted the Colts to a 22-19 win. Baltimore dominated the first half 13-3 by allowing Chicago to cross mid-field only once. Vince Evans brought Chicago back in the game by engineering two fourth-period scoring drives to send the game into overtime. Allegre also converted field goals of 37 and 47 yards. The Colts' offense generated 461 total yards.

| | | | | | | |
|---|---|---|---|---|---|---|
| Chicago | 0 | 3 | 3 | 13 | 0 — | 19 |
| Baltimore | 0 | 13 | 0 | 6 | 3 — | 22 |

Balt — McMillan 1 run (Allegre kick)
Chi — FG B. Thomas 45
Balt — Henry 19 pass from Pagel (kick failed)
Chi — FG B. Thomas 21
Balt — FG Allegre 37
Chi — Gault 57 pass from Evans (kick failed)
Balt — FG Allegre 47
Chi — Evans 8 run (B. Thomas kick)
Balt — FG Allegre 33

**Cincinnati 23, Tampa Bay 17**—At Tampa Stadium, attendance 56,023. The Bengals opened a 20-0 lead on touchdowns by Ken Riley (34-yard interception return), Stanley Wilson (four-yard run), and Charles Alexander (two-yard run) and held on for their first win. Buccaneers quarterback Jack Thompson completed a club-record 75 percent (30 of 40) of his passes for 316 yards and brought Tampa Bay to within 23-17 following a 15-yard touchdown pass to Kevin House. But Robert Jackson intercepted a pass in the end zone to kill a late Buccaneers threat.

| | | | | | |
|---|---|---|---|---|---|
| Cincinnati | 14 | 6 | 0 | 3 — | 23 |
| Tampa Bay | 0 | 7 | 3 | 7 — | 17 |

Cin — Riley 34 interception return (Breech kick)
Cin — S. Wilson 4 pass from Anderson (Breech kick)
Cin — Alexander 2 run (pass failed)
TB — Owens 1 run (Capece kick)
TB — FG Capece 20
Cin — FG Breech 24
TB — House 15 pass from Thompson (Capece kick)

**Cleveland 30, San Diego 24**—At San Diego Jack Murphy Stadium, attendance 49,482. Brian Sipe's 48-yard touchdown pass to tight end Harry Holt 1:53 into overtime lifted the Browns over the Chargers. Matt Bahr's 32-yard field goal with 18 seconds remaining tied the game. Dwight Walker's 33-yard return of the overtime kickoff set up the winning score four plays later. San Diego rallied from a 21-10 deficit to take a 24-21 lead on a pair of scoring passes by Dan Fouts 2:08 apart. Sipe finished with 327 yards on 27 completions in 44 attempts and three touchdowns. Fouts hit on 24 of 38 for 351 yards and three scores.

| | | | | | | |
|---|---|---|---|---|---|---|
| Cleveland | 7 | 7 | 7 | 3 | 6 — | 30 |
| San Diego | 3 | 7 | 14 | 0 | 0 — | 24 |

SD — FG Benirschke 37
Cle — Pruitt 1 run (Bahr kick)
Cle — Newsome 11 pass from Sipe (Bahr kick)
SD — Sievers 15 pass from Fouts (Benirschke kick)
Cle — B. Jones 27 pass from Sipe (Bahr kick)
SD — Chandler 25 pass from Fouts (Benirschke kick)
SD — Chandler 34 pass from Fouts (Benirschke kick)
Cle — FG Bahr 32
Cle — Holt 48 pass from Sipe

**Minnesota 20, Detroit 17**—At Metrodome, attendance 58,254. Benny Ricardo's 24-yard field goal midway through the fourth quarter gave the Vikings a 20-17 win and first place in the NFC Central Division. Minnesota jumped to a 17-0 lead on Ricardo's 27-yard field goal, Steve Dils' three-yard pass to Bob Bruer, and Dave Huffman's recovery of a blocked punt in the end zone. Detroit tied the game as Eric Hipple ran for one touchdown and passed for another, but five interceptions and eight sacks did in the Lions. Detroit outgained Minnesota 371 yards to 181.

| | | | | | |
|---|---|---|---|---|---|
| Detroit | 0 | 7 | 10 | 0 — | 17 |
| Minnesota | 3 | 14 | 0 | 3 — | 20 |

Minn — FG Ricardo 27
Minn — Bruer 3 pass from Dils (Ricardo kick)
Minn — Huffman recovered blocked punt in end zone (Ricardo kick)
Det — Nichols 41 pass from Hipple (Murray kick)
Det — FG Murray 24
Det — Hipple 1 run (Murray kick)
Minn — FG Ricardo 24

**Buffalo 30, Houston 13**—At Rich Stadium, attendance 60,070. Joe Cribbs ran for a career-high 166 yards on 22 carries to lead the Bills to a 30-13 win. Cribbs' one-yard touchdown plunge and Joe Ferguson's seven-yard pass to Jerry Butler gave Buffalo a 13-6 halftime advantage. But Houston tied the score 13-13 on Earl Campbell's (142 yards, 30 carries) one-yard run midway through the third quarter. The Bills pulled away on Joe Danelo's 48-yard field goal and touchdowns by Frank Lewis (19-yard reception) and David Kilson (87-yard fumble return). Fred Smerlas had three of Buffalo's seven sacks.

| | | | | | |
|---|---|---|---|---|---|
| Houston | 3 | 3 | 7 | 0 — | 13 |

| | | | | | |
|---|---|---|---|---|---|
| Buffalo | 7 | 6 | 3 | 14 — | 30 |

Hou — FG Kempf 31
Buff — Cribbs 1 run (Danelo kick)
Buff — Butler 7 pass from Ferguson (kick failed)
Hou — FG Kempf 26
Hou — Campbell 1 run (Kempf kick)
Buff — FG Danelo 48
Buff — Lewis 19 pass from Ferguson (Danelo kick)
Buff — Kilson 87 fumble recovery return (Danelo kick)

**Miami 14, Kansas City 6**—At Orange Bowl, attendance 50,785. Andra Franklin's one-yard touchdown run and David Woodley's one-yard scoring pass to Dan Johnson helped the Dolphins upend the Chiefs 14-6. Miami suffered five first-half turnovers (one interception, four fumbles), but Woodley engineered an 85-yard, 14-play march culminated by Johnson's touchdown in the third quarter. The Dolphins top-rated defense (249.5 yards per game) held the Chiefs to 155 total yards and had four interceptions and a fumble recovery. Miami committed seven turnovers, including a club-record-tying five fumbles.

| | | | | | |
|---|---|---|---|---|---|
| Kansas City | 3 | 3 | 0 | 0 — | 6 |
| Miami | 0 | 7 | 7 | 0 — | 14 |

KC — FG Lowery 45
KC — FG Lowery 46
Mia — Franklin 1 run (von Schamann kick)
Mia — Johnson 1 pass from Woodley (von Schamann kick)

**Los Angeles Raiders 22, Denver 7**—At Mile High Stadium, attendance 74,289. The Raiders scored on three consecutive second-half possessions to notch their fourth straight win. Leading 7-0 at halftime on Jim Plunkett's 35-yard touchdown pass to Cliff Branch, Los Angeles added a pair of Chris Bahr field goals (from 27 and 29 yards) and Plunkett's 17-yard toss to Branch for a 20-0 third-period edge. The Raiders' defense limited the Broncos to 268 total yards, and held Denver scoreless until Zack Thomas returned a punt 70 yards for a score with 1:42 to play.

| | | | | | |
|---|---|---|---|---|---|
| L.A. Raiders | 0 | 7 | 13 | 2 — | 22 |
| Denver | 0 | 0 | 0 | 7 — | 7 |

Raiders — Branch 35 pass from Plunkett (Bahr kick)
Raiders — FG Bahr 27
Raiders — FG Bahr 29
Raiders — Branch 17 pass from Plunkett (Bahr kick)
Den — Thomas 70 punt return (Karlis kick)
Raiders — Safety, Townsend tackled DeBerg in end zone

**New York Jets 27, Los Angeles Rams 24**—At Shea Stadium, attendance 52,070. Pat Leahy kicked a 26-yard field goal after 8:22 of overtime to give the Jets the win. Richard Todd, who completed 37 of 50 passes for 446 yards, fired touchdown passes of 15 and 37 yards to Wesley Walker (eight receptions, 135 yards) for a 21-17 lead. After Leahy's 22-yard field goal put New York ahead 24-17, Vince Ferragamo hit Mike Guman with a two-yard scoring pass with 32 seconds left to send the game into overtime. Jerry Holmes, who scored on a 57-yard blocked field goal return, set up the decisive field goal with a 30-yard interception return. Eric Dickerson gained 192 yards on 28 carries and scored on runs of 85 and 5 yards.

| | | | | | | |
|---|---|---|---|---|---|---|
| L.A. Rams | 14 | 0 | 3 | 7 | 0 — | 24 |
| New York Jets | 7 | 7 | 7 | 3 | 3 — | 27 |

Rams — Dickerson 85 run (Nelson kick)
NYJ — Walker 15 pass from Todd (Leahy kick)
Rams — Dickerson 5 run (Nelson kick)
NYJ — Holmes 57 blocked field goal return (Leahy kick)
Rams — FG Nelson 34
NYJ — Walker 37 pass from Todd (Leahy kick)
NYJ — FG Leahy 22
Rams — Guman 2 pass from Ferragamo (Nelson kick)
NYJ — FG Leahy 26

**New England 28, Pittsburgh 23**—At Three Rivers Stadium, attendance 58,282. Steve Grogan and Stephen Starring connected on a 76-yard touchdown pass with 3:59 remaining to give the Patriots a 28-23 win. New England converted two interceptions into a 14-13 halftime lead. Clayton Weishuhn ran 27 yards with an interception after taking a lateral from Steve Nelson, and Grogan fired a four-yard pass to Derrick Ramsey following Rick Sanford's first of two thefts. The Steelers dominated the Patriots, outgaining New England 448 yards to 296, accumulating 30 first downs to the Patriots' 12, and running 86 plays to New England's 45. Franco Harris rushed for over 100 yards for the third straight week (106 on 25 carries) to move ahead of O.J. Simpson (11,236) on the all-time NFL rushing list with 11,309 career yards.

| | | | | | |
|---|---|---|---|---|---|
| New England | 7 | 7 | 7 | 7 — | 28 |
| Pittsburgh | 7 | 6 | 0 | 10 — | 23 |

Pitt — Sweeney 3 pass from Stoudt (Anderson kick)
NE — Weishuhn 27 run with lateral of interception from Nelson (J. Smith kick)
Pitt — FG Anderson 20
NE — Ramsey 4 pass from Grogan (J. Smith kick)
Pitt — FG Anderson 34
NE — Collins 4 run (J. Smith kick)
Pitt — FG Anderson 28
Pitt — Abercrombie 26 pass from Stoudt (Anderson kick)
NE — Starring 76 pass from Grogan (J. Smith kick)

**Dallas 21, New Orleans 20**—At Texas Stadium, attendance 62,136. Anthony Dickerson sacked Ken Stabler in the end zone for a safety with 1:58 to play to keep the Cowboys' unbeaten record intact. The Saints took a 20-13 lead when Frank Warren's interception of a Drew Pearson pass set up Wayne Wilson's (108 yards on 31 carries) one-yard scoring run. Ron Fellows returned a blocked field goal 62 yards for a score with 7:05 left, but Tyrone Young blocked the extra point to keep New Orleans in front 20-19. Tony Dorsett gained 124 yards on 16 carries. The Saints' defense had seven quarterback sacks.

| | | | | | |
|---|---|---|---|---|---|
| New Orleans | 0 | 10 | 3 | 7 — | 20 |
| Dallas | 7 | 6 | 0 | 8 — | 21 |

Dall — Pearson 4 pass from D. White (Septien kick)
Dall — FG Septien 41
NO — FG Andersen 19
NO — W. Wilson 2 run (Andersen kick)
Dall — FG Septien 34
NO — FG Andersen 42
NO — W. Wilson 1 run (Andersen kick)
Dall — Fellows 62 blocked field goal return (kick blocked)
Dall — Safety, Dickerson tackled Stabler in end zone

**St. Louis 14, Philadelphia 11**—At Veterans Stadium, attendance 64,465. Jim Hart, replacing injured Neil Lomax, threw a 26-yard touchdown pass to Roy Green with 29 seconds remaining to lead the Cardinals to their first win. Hart completed 12 of 19 passes for 123 yards, including an eight-yard scoring pass to Doug Marsh for a 7-3 halftime edge. Ottis Anderson ran for 133 yards on 29 carries, his twenty-third career 100-yard game.

| | | | | | |
|---|---|---|---|---|---|
| St. Louis | 0 | 7 | 0 | 7 — | 14 |
| Philadelphia | 3 | 0 | 8 | 0 — | 11 |

Phil — FG Franklin 32
StL — Marsh 8 pass from Hart (O'Donoghue kick)
Phil — Safety, Ferrell fumbled out of end zone
Phil — Haddix 2 run (kick failed)
StL — Green 26 pass from Hart (O'Donoghue kick)

**Washington 27, Seattle 17**—At Kingdome, attendance 60,718. Joe Theismann passed for three touchdowns to lead the Redskins to a 27-17 win in their first visit ever to the Kingdome. Theismann, who threw only 16 passes, completed 9, including scoring bombs of 64 yards to Charlie Brown and 47 yards to Alvin Garrett. He also hooked up with Rick Walker on a four-yard touchdown pass late in the fourth quarter to put the game away. John Riggins ran for 83 yards to move into sixth place on the NFL career rushing list with 8,445 yards.

| | | | | | |
|---|---|---|---|---|---|
| Washington | 7 | 13 | 0 | 7 — | 27 |
| Seattle | 3 | 7 | 0 | 7 — | 17 |

Wash — Riggins 1 run (Moseley kick)
Sea — FG N. Johnson 27
Wash — Brown 64 pass from Theismann (Moseley kick)
Sea — Largent 13 pass from Zorn (N. Johnson kick)
Wash — Garrett 47 pass from Theismann (kick failed)
Wash — Walker 4 pass from Theismann (Moseley kick)
Sea — Largent 7 pass from Zorn (N. Johnson kick)

**MONDAY, SEPTEMBER 26**

**New York Giants 27, Green Bay 3**—At Giants Stadium, attendance 75,308. New York's defense registered four sacks, three fumble recoveries, and an interception, and Rob Carpenter rushed for 116 yards on 28 carries to lead the Giants over the Packers. Carpenter's 14-yard touchdown run and Ali Haji-Sheikh's team-record 56-yard field goal gave New York a 10-3 halftime lead. The Giants put the game out of reach in the third quarter when Terry Jackson returned a fumble 35 yards for a score and Jerome Sally's fumble recovery set up Haji-Sheikh's 32-yard field goal. Scott Brunner's 27-yard pass to Earnest Gray finished the scoring. Mark Haynes turned in the play of the game, tackling Packer tight end Gary Lewis for no gain inches short of the New York goal line with the Giants leading 7-3 in the second quarter.

| | | | | | |
|---|---|---|---|---|---|
| Green Bay | 3 | 0 | 0 | 0 — | 3 |
| New York Giants | 0 | 10 | 17 | 0 — | 27 |

GB — FG Stenerud 20
NYG — Carpenter 14 run (Haji-Sheikh kick)
NYG — FG Haji-Sheikh 56
NYG — Jackson 35 fumble recovery return (Haji-Sheikh kick)
NYG — FG Haji-Sheikh 32
NYG — Gray 27 pass from Brunner (Haji-Sheikh kick)

## FIFTH WEEK SUMMARY

The Redskins scored 17 points in the final 7:31 to cap a 37-35 comeback and knock the Raiders from the unbeaten ranks. Los Angeles had built a 35-20 lead on Jim Plunkett's 99-yard bomb to Cliff Branch and Greg Pruitt's 97-yard punt return for a touchdown. Washington quarterback Joe Theismann had his finest day as a pro to lead the comeback. Theismann completed 23 of 39 passes for 417 yards and his six-yard touchdown pass to Joe Washington with 33 seconds left proved decisive. Meanwhile, Dallas retained the only unbeaten record (5-0) in the NFL . . . but it wasn't easy. The Cowboys trailed the Vikings 24-13 at halftime before Ron Fellows returned an interception 58 yards for a score early in the fourth quarter to put Dallas in command. The Bears and Rams both snapped two-game losing streaks. Chicago's Willie Gault scored twice, and the defense recorded nine quarterback sacks in a 31-14 win over Denver. Eric Dickerson rushed for 199 yards and three touchdowns to lead Los Angeles over Detroit 21-10. San Francisco extended its unbeaten string to four games by scoring on six of its first eight possessions in defeating New England 33-13. Seattle handed Cleveland its first loss in three games, 24-9, while New Orleans defeated Miami for the first time ever 17-7. Wayne Wilson, playing in place of injured George Rogers, rushed for 160 yards to lead the Saints' victory. Ron Jaworski rushed for one touchdown and threw for three more (the last a 53-yarder to Mike Quick with 1:45 remaining) to give the Eagles a 28-24 come-from-behind win over the Falcons. San Diego held off the New York Giants' 17-point rally to win 41-34. Kansas City captured the "Battle of Missouri" by scoring 21 points in the fourth quarter to down St. Louis 38-14. There was no comeback possible at Lambeau Field however, where the Packers scored an NFL record 49 points in the first half to dominate the Buccaneers 55-14. Green Bay gained 519 total yards and Jan Stenerud totaled 13 points to move past Jim Turner into second place among kick scorers with 1,447 points. The Jets defeated the Bills 34-10 by holding Joe Cribbs to 28 yards rushing while New York's Bruce Harper ran for 118 yards, the first 100-yard rushing game of his career. Pittsburgh contained Earl Campbell (69 yards on 26 carries) to defeat Houston 17-10.

**SUNDAY, OCTOBER 2**

**Baltimore 34, Cincinnati 31**—At Riverfront Stadium, attendance 48,104. Leo Wisniewski's fumble recovery set up Curtis Dickey's three-yard touchdown run with 7:10 remaining to lift the Colts over the Bengals. Randy McMillan's eight-yard scoring run in the third quarter cut Cincinnati's lead to 24-21. Following Cris Collinsworth's 20-yard touchdown reception from Ken Anderson, Baltimore's Raul Allegre kicked field goals of 29 and 53 yards to keep the Colts within striking distance at 31-27. Derrick Hatchett's interception as time ran out preserved the victory. Baltimore's win overshadowed the performance of Anderson, whose 21 completions in 31 attempts for 330 yards and three touchdowns included 8 to Collinsworth for a club-record 206 yards.

| | | | | | |
|---|---|---|---|---|---|
| Baltimore | 7 | 7 | 10 | 10 — | 34 |
| Cincinnati | 10 | 14 | 7 | 0 — | 31 |

Cin — FG Breech 19
Balt — Moore 9 run (Allegre kick)
Cin — Harris 3 pass from Anderson (Breech kick)
Cin — Curtis 20 pass from Anderson (Breech kick)
Balt — McMillan 1 run (Allegre kick)
Cin — Anderson 3 run (Breech kick)
Balt — McMillan 8 run (Allegre kick)
Cin — Collinsworth 20 pass from Anderson (Breech kick)
Balt — FG Allegre 29
Balt — FG Allegre 53
Balt — Dickey 3 run (Allegre kick)

**Dallas 37, Minnesota 24**—At Metrodome, attendance 60,774. Ron Fellows returned an interception 58 yards for a score and Rafael Septien kicked three field goals as the Cowboys registered a 37-24 comeback win. Dallas reversed a 24-13 halftime deficit on Ron Springs' five-yard run and Fellows' interception to take a 27-24 lead early in the fourth quarter. Danny White's 11-yard touchdown pass to Drew Pearson capped an 84-yard drive and increased the Cowboys margin to 34-24. Septien kicked field goals of 45, 45, and 35 yards and had three extra points to become the first Dallas player to score over 500 career points (503). Tony Dorsett gained 141 yards on 26 carries.

| | | | | | |
|---|---|---|---|---|---|
| Dallas | 3 | 10 | 14 | 10 — | 37 |
| Minnesota | 7 | 17 | 0 | 0 — | 24 |

Minn — S. White 43 pass from Dils (Ricardo kick)
Dall — FG Septien 45
Minn — S. White 36 pass from Dils (Ricardo kick)
Minn — FG Ricardo 41
Dall — D. White 2 run (Septien kick)
Minn — Brown 5 run (Ricardo kick)
Dall — FG Septien 45
Dall — Springs 5 run (Septien kick)
Dall — Fellows 58 interception return (Septien kick)
Dall — Pearson 11 pass from D. White (Septien kick)
Dall — FG Septien 35

**Chicago 31, Denver 14**—At Soldier Field, attendance 58,210. Willie Gault caught a pair of touchdown passes to help the Bears end a two-game losing streak. Chicago led 24-0 at halftime on Jim McMahon's 15-yard scoring pass to Gault, Matt Suhey's 13-yard run, Leslie Frazier's 11-yard interception return, and Bob Thomas' 19-yard field goal. Denver capitalized on two interceptions to close the score to 24-14. But Vince Evans came off the bench to replace McMahon in the fourth quarter and combined with Gault on a 72-yard touchdown pass on his first play of the game. Safety Todd Bell had three of the Bears' nine sacks. Chicago's offense gained 423 total yards.

| | | | | | |
|---|---|---|---|---|---|
| Denver | 0 | 0 | 7 | 7 — | 14 |
| Chicago | 14 | 10 | 0 | 7 — | 31 |

Chi — Suhey 13 run (B. Thomas kick)
Chi — Gault 15 pass from McMahon (B. Thomas kick)
Chi — Frazier 11 interception return (B. Thomas kick)
Chi — FG B. Thomas 19
Den — Poole 15 run (Karlis kick)
Den — Upchurch 15 pass from DeBerg (Karlis kick)
Chi — Gault 72 pass from Evans (B. Thomas kick)

**Los Angeles Rams 21, Detroit 10**—At Anaheim Stadium, attendance 49,403. Eric Dickerson ran for 199 yards on 30 carries and scored three touchdowns as the Rams halted a two-game losing streak. Los Angeles built a 14-3 lead on scores of eight and one yards by Dickerson and never looked back. The Rams' defense contained the Lions in the second half while Dickerson added his third touchdown, a four-yard blast, with 6:25 left. Los Angeles gained 355 total yards to Detroit's 265.

| | | | | | |
|---|---|---|---|---|---|
| Detroit | 3 | 7 | 0 | 0 | — 10 |
| L.A. Rams | 0 | 14 | 0 | 7 | — 21 |

Det — FG Murray 51
Rams — Dickerson 8 run (Nelson kick)
Rams — Dickerson 1 run (Nelson kick)
Det — Norris 5 pass from Hipple (Murray kick)
Rams — Dickerson 4 run (Nelson kick)

**Pittsburgh 17, Houston 10**—At Three Rivers Stadium, attendance 56,901. Cliff Stoudt and Walter Abercrombie hooked up on a 51-yard scoring pass, and Gary Anderson added an 18-yard field goal to cap the Steelers' fourth-quarter rally that gave Pittsburgh its first home victory. Frank Pollard's one-yard touchdown plunge gave Pittsburgh a 7-3 halftime lead, but Houston went ahead 10-7 on Florian Kempf's 34-yard field goal and Earl Campbell's one-yard run. The Oilers outgained the Steelers 270 total yards to 225, but suffered three interceptions.

| | | | | | |
|---|---|---|---|---|---|
| Houston | 0 | 3 | 7 | 0 | — 10 |
| Pittsburgh | 0 | 7 | 0 | 10 | — 17 |

Pitt — Pollard 1 run (Anderson kick)
Hou — FG Kempf 34
Hou — Campbell 1 run (Kempf kick)
Pitt — Abercrombie 51 pass from Stoudt (Anderson kick)
Pitt — FG Anderson 18

**Washington 37, Los Angeles Raiders 35**—At Robert F. Kennedy Stadium, attendance 54,016. Joe Theismann's six-yard touchdown pass to Joe Washington with 33 seconds left lifted the Redskins over the Raiders. Theismann completed 23 of 39 passes for 417 yards and rallied Washington from a 35-20 deficit with 7:31 to play by firing an 11-yard scoring pass to Charlie Brown (11 receptions, 180 yards) and setting up Mark Moseley's 34-yard field goal. The Redskins led 20-7 in the third quarter, but the Raiders scored 28 consecutive points on Jim Plunkett's touchdown passes to Calvin Muhammad (35 and 22 yards) and Todd Christensen (2 yards), and Greg Pruitt's club-record 97-yard punt return. Plunkett's 16 completions in 29 attempts for 372 yards included an NFL record-tying 99-yard scoring bomb to Cliff Branch in the second period.

| | | | | | |
|---|---|---|---|---|---|
| L.A. Raiders | 0 | 7 | 14 | 14 | — 35 |
| Washington | 7 | 10 | 3 | 17 | — 37 |

Wash — Riggins 2 run (Moseley kick)
Wash — FG Moseley 28
Raiders — Branch 99 pass from Plunkett (Bahr kick)
Wash — J. Washington 5 pass from Theismann (Moseley kick)
Wash — FG Moseley 29
Raiders — Muhammad 35 pass from Plunkett (Bahr kick)
Raiders — Muhammad 22 pass from Plunkett (Bahr kick)
Raiders — Christensen 2 pass from Plunkett (Bahr kick)
Raiders — Pruitt 97 punt return (Bahr kick)
Wash — Brown 11 pass from Theismann (Moseley kick)
Wash — FG Moseley 34
Wash — J. Washington 6 pass from Theismann (Moseley kick)

**New Orleans 17, Miami 7**—At Louisiana Superdome, attendance 66,489. Wayne Wilson, subbing for injured George Rogers, rushed for 160 yards on 34 carries to help the Saints capture their first win ever against the Dolphins. New Orleans opened a 17-0 lead on Ken Stabler's 16-yard pass to Tyrone Young, Morten Andersen's 32-yard field goal, and Reggie Lewis' 27-yard interception return. Miami, limited to 244 total yards, didn't get on the board until there was 6:16 left in the game, when Dan Marino, in relief of starter David Woodley, hit Mark Duper on a 10-yard scoring pass.

| | | | | | |
|---|---|---|---|---|---|
| Miami | 0 | 0 | 0 | 7 | — 7 |
| New Orleans | 0 | 7 | 10 | 0 | — 17 |

NO — Young 16 pass from Stabler (Andersen kick)
NO — FG Andersen 32
NO — Lewis 27 interception return (Andersen kick)
Mia — Duper 10 pass from Marino (von Schamann kick)

**Philadelphia 28, Atlanta 24**—At Atlanta-Fulton County Stadium, attendance 50,621. Ron Jaworski's third touchdown pass of the day, a 53-yarder to Mike Quick with 1:45 remaining, capped the Eagles' comeback. Philadelphia led 21-7 at the half on Jaworski's eight-yard scoring run and touchdown receptions by Vyto Kab (5 yards) and Harold Carmichael (29). Atlanta took a 24-21 lead with 2:31 left, but Hubie Oliver's four-yard gain on a fourth-and-one play preceded the decisive score. Jaworski completed 16 of 28 passes for 239 yards, including 4 to Quick, who registered his fourth consecutive 100-yard game with 122 yards.

| | | | | | |
|---|---|---|---|---|---|
| Philadelphia | 14 | 7 | 0 | 7 | — 28 |
| Atlanta | 0 | 7 | 7 | 10 | — 24 |

Phil — Jaworski 8 run (Franklin kick)
Phil — Kab 5 pass from Jaworski (Franklin kick)
Atl — Hodge 6 pass from Bartkowski (Luckhurst kick)
Phil — Carmichael 29 pass from Jaworski (Franklin kick)
Atl — Bailey 41 pass from Bartkowski (Luckhurst kick)
Atl — Bailey 8 pass from Bartkowski (Luckhurst kick)
Atl — FG Luckhurst 44
Phil — Quick 53 pass from Jaworski (Franklin kick)

**Kansas City 38, St. Louis 14**—At Arrowhead Stadium, attendance 58,975. The Chiefs capitalized on nine Cardinal's turnovers to register a 38-14 win. Kansas City had five interceptions and four fumble recoveries, which included Charles Jackson's 37-yard touchdown return. Bill Kenney's 10-yard pass to Henry Marshall gave the Chiefs the lead for good, 14-7 at the half. Touchdown runs by Billy Jackson (six-yards) and Theotis Brown (one) put the game out of reach, 31-7. Jackson's score was Kansas City's first rushing touchdown this season. Deron Cherry picked off two passes to grab a share of the AFC interception lead with four.

| | | | | | |
|---|---|---|---|---|---|
| St. Louis | 7 | 0 | 0 | 7 | — 14 |
| Kansas City | 14 | 0 | 3 | 21 | — 38 |

StL — Nelson 36 fumble recovery return (O'Donoghue kick)
KC — C. Jackson 37 fumble recovery return (Lowery kick)
KC — Marshall 10 pass from Kenney (Lowery kick)
KC — FG Lowery 45
KC — B. Jackson 6 run (Lowery kick)
KC — Brown 1 run (Lowery kick)
KC — Scott 15 pass from Blackledge (Lowery kick)
StL — Anderson 39 run (O'Donoghue kick)

**San Diego 41, New York Giants 34**—At Giants Stadium, attendance 73,892. Chuck Muncie's third touchdown of the game, a 34-yard run with 4:32 remaining, lifted the Chargers to a 41-34 win. Muncie, who rushed for 87 yards, also had scoring runs of one and two yards. Dan Fouts, who was replaced by Ed Luther after leaving the game with a bruised shoulder in the third quarter, fired touchdown passes to Charlie Joiner (13 yards) and Kellen Winslow (16) for a 27-17 halftime advantage. Billy Ray Smith's fumble recovery at the Chargers' 12-yard line with 52 seconds left preserved the win. Scott Brunner highlighted the Giants 441-yard attack, completing 31 of 51 passes for 395 yards and three touchdowns.

| | | | | | |
|---|---|---|---|---|---|
| San Diego | 13 | 14 | 7 | 7 | — 41 |
| New York Giants | 0 | 17 | 7 | 10 | — 34 |

SD — FG Benirschke 40
SD — FG Benirschke 37
SD — Muncie 1 run (Benirschke kick)
NYG — FG Haji-Sheikh 20
SD — Joiner 13 pass from Fouts (Benirschke kick)
NYG — Gray 51 pass from Brunner (Haji-Sheikh kick)
SD — Winslow 16 pass from Fouts (Benirschke kick)
NYG — Pittman 40 pass from Brunner (Haji-Sheikh kick)
NYG — Carpenter 1 run (Haji-Sheikh kick)
SD — Muncie 2 run (Benirschke kick)
NYG — Mullady 21 pass from Brunner (Haji-Sheikh kick)
NYG — FG Haji-Sheikh 37
SD — Muncie 34 run (Benirschke kick)

**San Francisco 33, New England 13**—At Sullivan Stadium, attendance 54,293. The 49ers opened a 30-6 lead by scoring on six of their first eight possessions and won their fourth straight game. Joe Montana connected on 25 of 38 passes for 288 yards and completed touchdowns of 8 yards to Russ Francis and 13 yards to Dwight Clark. Ray Wersching was perfect on four field goal attempts (45, 35, 36, and 24 yards) and Jeff Moore added a two-yard touchdown run. The 49ers gained 426 yards total offense and limited the Patriots to 295.

| | | | | | |
|---|---|---|---|---|---|
| San Francisco | 7 | 10 | 13 | 3 | — 33 |
| New England | 6 | 0 | 0 | 7 | — 13 |

NE — Ramsey 30 pass from Grogan (kick failed)
SF — Francis 8 pass from Montana (Wersching kick)
SF — Moore 2 run (Wersching kick)
SF — FG Wersching 45
SF — FG Wersching 35
SF — FG Wersching 36
SF — Clark 13 pass from Montana (Wersching kick)
NE — Morgan 32 pass from Grogan (J. Smith kick)
SF — FG Wersching 24

**Seattle 24, Cleveland 9**—At Cleveland Stadium, attendance 75,446. Curt Warner scored on a pair of one-yard runs to help the Seahawks snap the Browns' three-game win streak. Shelton Robinson's interception early in the third quarter set up Warner's first score and Jeff Bryant's fumble recovery midway through the fourth period led to the second. Defensive end Jacob Green's 73-yard interception return for a touchdown with 1:49 left ended Cleveland's final threat. The Browns had 405 yards total offense compared to the Seahawks' 259.

| | | | | | |
|---|---|---|---|---|---|
| Seattle | 3 | 0 | 7 | 14 | — 24 |
| Cleveland | 0 | 3 | 0 | 6 | — 9 |

Sea — FG N. Johnson 24
Cle — FG Bahr 40
Sea — Warner 1 run (N. Johnson kick)
Cle — Green 5 pass from Sipe (kick failed)
Sea — Warner 1 run (N. Johnson kick)
Sea — Green 73 interception return (N. Johnson kick)

**Green Bay 55, Tampa Bay 14**—At Lambeau Field, attendance 54,272. The Packers scored an NFL record 49 points in the first half to rout the Buccaneers 55-14. Lynn Dickey completed 10 of 15 passes for 267 yards, including touchdowns of 75 yards to Jessie Clark, 1 yard to Paul Coffman, and 57 yards to James Lofton (four catches, 112 yards). Jan Stenerud kicked a pair of field goals (19 and 27 yards) and had seven extra points to pass Jim Turner and move into second place on the NFL's all-time scoring list with 1,447 points. The Packers gained 519 yards and broke their own NFL record for points scored in the first half (45), which was set on November 12, 1967 against Cleveland.

| | | | | | |
|---|---|---|---|---|---|
| Tampa Bay | 0 | 7 | 0 | 7 | — 14 |
| Green Bay | 14 | 35 | 0 | 6 | — 55 |

GB — Epps 90 punt return (Stenerud kick)
GB — Clark 75 pass from Dickey (Stenerud kick)
GB — Huckleby 1 run (Stenerud kick)
TB — Green 21 interception return (Capece kick)
GB — Coffman 1 pass from Dickey (Stenerud kick)
GB — Douglass 35 fumble recovery return (Stenerud kick)
GB — Anderson 27 interception return (Stenerud kick)
GB — Lofton 57 pass from Dickey (Stenerud kick)
GB — FG Stenerud 19
GB — FG Stenerud 27
TB — Owens 2 run (Capece kick)

**MONDAY, OCTOBER 3**

**New York Jets 34, Buffalo 10**—At Rich Stadium, attendance 79,933. Richard Todd threw two touchdown passes and Bruce Harper ran for 118 yards (the first 100-yard rushing game of his career) to lead the Jets over the Bills. Todd opened the scoring with an 11-yard scoring pass to Harper and added a 22-yarder to Johnny Hector in the fourth quarter. Mark Gastineau had three of New York's seven sacks and also recovered a fumble in the end zone for a touchdown.

| | | | | | |
|---|---|---|---|---|---|
| New York Jets | 0 | 7 | 10 | 17 | — 34 |
| Buffalo | 0 | 0 | 0 | 10 | — 10 |

NYJ — Harper 11 pass from Todd (Leahy kick)
NYJ — FG Leahy 19
NYJ — Gastineau fumble recovery in end zone (Leahy kick)
Buff — FG Danelo 38
NYJ — Hector 22 pass from Todd (Leahy kick)
Buff — Cribbs 12 pass from Kofler (Danelo kick)
NYJ — Dierking 1 run (Leahy kick)
NYJ — FG Leahy 42

## SIXTH WEEK SUMMARY

Buffalo's Joe Danelo kicked a 36-yard field goal 13:58 into overtime to give the Bills a 38-35 win, their first in the Orange Bowl since 1966. Joe Ferguson had his best day in the NFL, completing 38 of 55 passes for 419 yards and five touchdowns, including a one-yarder to Joe Cribbs with 23 seconds left in regulation to tie the score 35-35. Dallas captured its sixth straight comeback win to remain undefeated when Rafael Septien kicked a 42-yard field goal after 4:58 of overtime to down Tampa Bay 27-24. Morten Andersen's fourth field goal of the game, a 35-yarder with no time left, gave the Saints a 19-17 victory over the Falcons. New Orleans' record improved to 4-2, good enough for a share of the lead in the NFC West and marked the Saints' fastest start in their 17-year history. The Browns' Matt Bahr also was cast as the hero after he kicked a 44-yard field goal as time expired to defeat the Jets 10-7. Eric Dickerson rushed for 142 yards but Chuck Nelson's 41-yard field goal proved decisive in the Rams' 10-7 win over the 49ers. Baltimore continued winning, defeating New England 12-7 to improve its record to 4-2 and keep pace with Buffalo in the AFC East. Denver got four field goals from Rich Karlis and a pair of touchdown passes from Steve DeBerg, who was making his first start of the season, to defeat Houston 26-14 and halt the Broncos' three-game losing streak. It was the Oilers' thirteenth consecutive loss, prompting coach Ed Biles to call it quits after the game. Mike Quick scored two touchdowns to lead the Eagles to a 17-13 win over the Giants. Defenses held the upper hand in two games. San Diego's Andre Young returned an interception 40 yards for a touchdown with 2:04 to play to lead the Chargers to a 28-21 victory over the Seahawks. Pittsburgh got three touchdowns from its defense to secure its first win in Riverfront Stadium since 1978, 24-14 over Cincinnati. Tony Galbreath and Darrin Nelson combined for 182 yards rushing and two touchdowns to help the Vikings down the Bears 23-14 and gain sole possession of first place in the NFC Central. James Jones rushed for three touchdowns and Eric Hipple passed for two more as the Lions took to heart a pre-game pep talk by owner William Clay Ford to defeat the Packers 38-14 and snap a four-game losing streak.

**SUNDAY, OCTOBER 9**

**Buffalo 38, Miami 35**—At Orange Bowl, attendance 59,948. Joe Danelo's 36-yard field goal after 13:58 of overtime gave the Bills their first win in Miami since 1966. Joe Ferguson set Buffalo game records for completions (38), attempts (55), yards (419), and tied the mark for touchdown passes (5). His one-yard pass to Joe Cribbs with 23 seconds left sent the game into the extra period. Ferguson earlier completed touchdown passes to Byron Franklin (9 and 30 yards), Booker Moore (11), and Cribbs (4). Miami had chances to win the game in overtime but Uwe von Schamann's 52- and 43-yard field goal attempts were wide. Dan Marino completed 19 of 29 passes for 322 yards in his first start for the Dolphins.

| | | | | | | |
|---|---|---|---|---|---|---|
| Buffalo | 7 | 7 | 7 | 14 | 3 | — 38 |

| | | | | | | |
|---|---|---|---|---|---|---|
| Miami | 0 | 7 | 14 | 14 | 0 — | 35 |

Buff — Franklin 9 pass from Ferguson (Danelo kick)
Buff — Franklin 30 pass from Ferguson (Danelo kick)
Mia — Bennett 1 run (von Schamann kick)
Mia — Duper 63 pass from Marino (von Schamann kick)
Buff — Moore 11 pass from Ferguson (Danelo kick)
Mia — Duper 48 pass from Clayton (von Schamann kick)
Buff — Cribbs 4 pass from Ferguson (Danelo kick)
Mia — Moore 2 pass from Marino (von Schamann kick)
Mia — Clayton 14 pass from Marino (von Schamann kick)
Buff — Cribbs 1 pass from Ferguson (Danelo kick)
Buff — FG Danelo 36

**Denver 26, Houston 14**—At Astrodome, attendance 44,209. Steve DeBerg threw two touchdown passes in his first start of the season and Rich Karlis kicked four field goals (45, 39, 49, and 35 yards) to help the Broncos snap a three-game losing streak. DeBerg passed Denver to a 20-14 halftime lead with scoring tosses of 7 yards to Ron Egloff and 24 yards to Steve Watson. The Broncos generated 401 yards total offense, including 165 yards rushing by Sammy Winder. It was Ed Biles' last game as Oilers head coach.

| | | | | | |
|---|---|---|---|---|---|
| Denver | 7 | 13 | 3 | 3 — | 26 |
| Houston | 0 | 14 | 0 | 0 — | 14 |

Den — Egloff 7 pass from DeBerg (Karlis kick)
Hou — Smith 40 pass from Nielsen (Kempf kick)
Den — FG Karlis 45
Den — Watson 24 pass from DeBerg (Karlis kick)
Den — FG Karlis 39
Hou — Campbell 1 run (Kempf kick)
Den — FG Karlis 49
Den — FG Karlis 35

**Detroit 38, Green Bay 14**—At Pontiac Silverdome, attendance 67,738. James Jones ran for three touchdowns and Eric Hipple passed for two more to help the Lions snap a four-game losing streak. Detroit jumped to a 24-0 halftime lead on Jones' scoring runs of 1 and 13 yards, Hipple's 18-yard pass to Leonard Thompson, and Eddie Murray's 29-yard field goal. Hipple, who had a 37-yard touchdown pass to Thompson in the fourth quarter, finished with 21 completions in 29 attempts for 235 yards. Jones' one-yard scoring run in the third quarter gave him a share of the club record for rushing touchdowns in a game.

| | | | | | |
|---|---|---|---|---|---|
| Green Bay | 0 | 0 | 7 | 7 — | 14 |
| Detroit | 10 | 14 | 7 | 7 — | 38 |

Det — Jones 1 run (Murray kick)
Det — FG Murray 29
Det — Jones 13 run (Murray kick)
Det — L. Thompson 18 pass from Hipple (Murray kick)
GB — Ivery 2 pass from Dickey (Stenerud kick)
Det — Jones 1 run (Murray kick)
Det — L. Thompson 37 pass from Hipple (Murray kick)
GB — Huckleby 1 run (Stenerud kick)

**Los Angeles Raiders 21, Kansas City 20**—At Memorial Coliseum, attendance 40,492. Marcus Allen recovered Frank Hawkins' fourth-quarter fumble in the end zone and Chris Bahr kicked the extra point to give the Raiders a 21-20 win. Kansas City scored twice within 40 seconds to take a 14-0 first-quarter lead, but Los Angeles closed the gap to 14-7 on Jim Plunkett's three-yard pass to Todd Christensen. Allen's 21-yard halfback option pass to rookie Dokie Williams to open the second half capped a 75-yard drive and cut the Chiefs' lead to 17-14. Nick Lowery's 48-yard field goal attempt in the closing seconds was blocked by Ted Hendricks to preserve the victory.

| | | | | | |
|---|---|---|---|---|---|
| Kansas City | 14 | 3 | 0 | 3 — | 20 |
| L.A. Raiders | 0 | 7 | 7 | 7 — | 21 |

KC — Paige 36 pass from Kenney (Lowery kick)
KC — Brown 1 run (Lowery kick)
Raiders — Christensen 3 pass from Plunkett (Bahr kick)
KC — FG Lowery 32
Raiders — Williams 21 pass from Allen (Bahr kick)
KC — FG Lowery 39
Raiders — Allen fumble recovery in end zone (Bahr kick)

**Los Angeles Rams 10, San Francisco 7**—At Candlestick Park, attendance 59,119. Eric Dickerson ran for 142 yards and one touchdown as the Rams defeated the 49ers 10-7. Following a scoreless first half, Dickerson scored on a 15-yard run and Chuck Nelson added a 41-yard field goal for a 10-0 lead with 4:50 to play. Roger Craig's three-yard run cut the Rams' lead to 10-7, but Ivory Sully blocked Ray Wersching's 51-yard field goal attempt with three seconds remaining to preserve the victory.

| | | | | | |
|---|---|---|---|---|---|
| L.A. Rams | 0 | 0 | 10 | 0 — | 10 |
| San Francisco | 0 | 0 | 0 | 7 — | 7 |

Rams — Dickerson 15 run (Nelson kick)
Rams — FG Nelson 41
SF — Craig 3 run (Wersching kick)

**Minnesota 23, Chicago 14**—At Soldier Field, attendance 59,632. Darrin Nelson and Tony Galbreath each scored on long touchdown runs to spark the Vikings' win. Nelson ran 56 yards for a score on Minnesota's first possession and Rufus Bess' interception set up Benny Ricardo's 22-yard goal, which put the Vikings ahead at halftime 10-7. Galbreath's (16 carries, 104 yards) 52-yard touchdown run midway through the third period put the game out of reach. Ricardo added field goals of 32 and 30 yards for a club-record 13 straight. Walter Payton scored both Chicago touchdowns and totaled 102 yards rushing, his fifty-first 100-yard rushing game. Chicago compiled 425 total yards to Minnesota's 368.

| | | | | | |
|---|---|---|---|---|---|
| Minnesota | 7 | 3 | 10 | 3 — | 23 |
| Chicago | 0 | 7 | 0 | 7 — | 14 |

Minn — Nelson 56 run (Ricardo kick)
Chi — Payton 1 run (B. Thomas kick)
Minn — FG Ricardo 22
Minn — FG Ricardo 32
Minn — Galbreath 52 run (Ricardo kick)
Chi — Payton 6 run (B. Thomas kick)
Minn — FG Ricardo 30

**Baltimore 12, New England 7**—At Memorial Stadium, attendance 37,013. Raul Allegre's 52-yard field goal broke a 7-7 tie and helped the Colts notch their third straight win. Steve Grogan's nine-yard touchdown pass to Cedric Jones following the opening kickoff gave New England a 7-0 lead, but Mike Pagel's 68-yard touchdown pass to Curtis Dickey tied the score at 7-7. Donnell Thompson sacked Grogan in the end zone for Baltimore's final points with two minutes to play. Jeff Delaney had a pair of interceptions and Barry Krauss and Vernon Maxwell each had a fumble recovery for the Colts.

| | | | | | |
|---|---|---|---|---|---|
| New England | 7 | 0 | 0 | 0 — | 7 |
| Baltimore | 0 | 0 | 7 | 5 — | 12 |

NE — Jones 9 pass from Grogan (Steinfort kick)
Balt — Dickey 68 pass from Pagel (Allegre kick)
Balt — FG Allegre 52
Balt — Safety, Thompson tackled Grogan in end zone.

**New Orleans 19, Atlanta 17**—At Atlanta-Fulton County Stadium, attendance 51,654. Morten Andersen kicked four field goals, including a 35-yarder with no time remaining, to lift the Saints over the Falcons 19-17. Wayne Wilson, who rushed for more than 100 yards for the third consecutive week (103), scored on a 23-yard pass from Ken Stabler to cap a 90-yard drive that gave New Orleans a 13-10 lead. Atlanta recaptured the lead 17-16 on William Andrews' two-yard run with 1:16 to play. The victory gave the Saints a 4-2 record, the best start in their 17-year history.

| | | | | | |
|---|---|---|---|---|---|
| New Orleans | 3 | 0 | 3 | 13 — | 19 |
| Atlanta | 0 | 3 | 7 | 7 — | 17 |

NO — FG Andersen 23
Atl — FG Luckhurst 49
Atl — Bailey 20 pass from Bartkowski (Luckhurst kick)
NO — FG Andersen 27
NO — W. Wilson 23 pass from Stabler (Andersen kick)
NO — FG Andersen 19
Atl — Andrews 2 run (Luckhurst kick)
NO — FG Andersen 35

**Cleveland 10, New York Jets 7**—At Cleveland Stadium, attendance 78,235. Matt Bahr's 44-yard field goal as time expired enabled the Browns to edge the Jets 10-7. Cleveland led 7-0 on Brian Sipe's (21 of 34 for 294 yards) 32-yard scoring pass to ex-Jet Bobby Jones. New York tied the score with 1:28 left to play as Richard Todd completed a 15-yard touchdown pass to Bruce Harper to climax an 83-yard drive. Sipe drove the Browns 39 yards in six plays to set up the winning kick. Tom Cousineau had eight tackles and thwarted two New York scoring opportunities with a fumble recovery (on the Browns' 9-yard line) and an interception (on the 5).

| | | | | | |
|---|---|---|---|---|---|
| New York Jets | 0 | 0 | 0 | 7 — | 7 |
| Cleveland | 0 | 7 | 0 | 3 — | 10 |

Cle — Jones 32 pass from Sipe (Bahr kick)
NYJ — Harper 15 pass from Todd (Leahy kick)
Cle — FG Bahr 44

**Philadelphia 17, New York Giants 13**—At Giants Stadium, attendance 73,291. Mike Quick caught two touchdown passes to help the Eagles edge the Giants 17-13. Quarterback Ron Jaworski and Quick connected on scoring passes of 5 and 18 yards. Quick caught six passes for 72 yards, but ended his four-game streak of 100 or more yards receiving. Tony Franklin added a 25-yard field goal with 2:38 to play for the Eagles' final points. The Giants lost quarterback Phil Simms for the season with a fractured thumb, which he suffered in the fourth quarter.

| | | | | | |
|---|---|---|---|---|---|
| Philadelphia | 0 | 7 | 7 | 3 — | 17 |
| New York Giants | 3 | 3 | 0 | 7 — | 13 |

NYG — FG Haji-Sheikh 21
Phil — Quick 5 pass from Jaworski (Franklin kick)
NYG — FG Haji-Sheikh 37
Phil — Quick 18 pass from Jaworski (Franklin kick)
NYG — Woolfolk 7 run (Haji-Sheikh kick)
Phil — FG Franklin 25

**San Diego 28, Seattle 21**—At San Diego Jack Murphy Stadium, attendance 49,132. Andre Young returned an interception 40 yards for a touchdown with 2:04 remaining to clinch the comeback victory. Ed Luther relieved Dan Fouts for two plays in the second quarter and fired a 12-yard touchdown pass to Kellen Winslow to cut Seattle's lead to 21-7. Fouts (28 of 36 for 331 yards) returned and threw a 59-yard scoring bomb to Bobby Duckworth. Chuck Muncie's one-yard scoring run 40 seconds into the fourth quarter capped an 87-yard drive and tied the game 21-21. The Chargers' defense shut out the Seahawks for the final 32:50 of the game.

| | | | | | |
|---|---|---|---|---|---|
| Seattle | 7 | 14 | 0 | 0 — | 21 |
| San Diego | 0 | 7 | 7 | 14 — | 28 |

Sea — H. Jackson 7 pass from Zorn (N. Johnson kick)
Sea — Warner 2 run (N. Johnson kick)
Sea — Warner 2 run (N. Johnson kick)
SD — Winslow 12 pass from Luther (Benirschke kick)
SD — Duckworth 59 pass from Fouts (Benirschke kick)
SD — Muncie 1 run (Benirschke kick)
SD — Young 40 interception return (Benirschke kick)

**Dallas 27, Tampa Bay 24**—At Texas Stadium, attendance 63,308. Rafael Septien's 42-yard field goal 4:38 into overtime brought the Cowboys their sixth straight comeback win. The lead changed hands five times before Danny White and Timmy Newsome combined on a 52-yard pass play to tie the game 24-24 with 47 seconds remaining. White completed 29 of 44 passes for 377 yards, including an 80-yard bomb to Ron Springs (11 receptions for 126 yards). Septien missed a 50-yard field goal in overtime, but a roughing the kicker penalty on Tampa Bay provided him a second chance at the game-winner.

| | | | | | | |
|---|---|---|---|---|---|---|
| Tampa Bay | 10 | 0 | 7 | 7 | 0 — | 24 |
| Dallas | 7 | 7 | 3 | 7 | 3 — | 27 |

TB — FG Capece 48
Dall — Springs 80 pass from D. White (Septien kick)
TB — Owens 9 pass from Thompson (Capece kick)
Dall — Newsome 1 run (Septien kick)
TB — Carter 56 pass from Thompson (Capece kick)
Dall — FG Septien 41
TB — Wilder 23 run (Capece kick)
Dall — Newsome 52 pass from D. White (Septien kick)
Dall — FG Septien 42

**Washington 38, St. Louis 14**—At Busch Memorial Stadium, attendance 42,698. John Riggins ran for three touchdowns and Joe Theismann threw for two more to lead the Redskins to their fifth consecutive victory and ninth straight on the road. Theismann's 20-yard scoring pass to Art Monk was sandwiched between touchdown runs of 17 and 1 yards by Riggins for a 24-7 halftime edge. Rick Walker teamed with Theismann on a 10-yard touchdown pass, and Riggins' (115 yards on 22 carries) 15-yard run finished the scoring.

| | | | | | |
|---|---|---|---|---|---|
| Washington | 7 | 17 | 14 | 0 — | 38 |
| St. Louis | 0 | 7 | 7 | 0 — | 14 |

Wash — Riggins 17 run (Moseley kick)
StL — Green 35 pass from Lomax (O'Donoghue kick)
Wash — Monk 20 pass from Theismann (Moseley kick)
Wash — Riggins 1 run (Moseley kick)
Wash — FG Moseley 22
Wash — Walker 10 pass from Theismann (Moseley kick)
StL — Marsh 1 pass from Lisch (O'Donoghue kick)
Wash — Riggins 15 run (Moseley kick)

**MONDAY, OCTOBER 10**

**Pittsburgh 24, Cincinnati 14**—At Riverfront Stadium, attendance 56,086. The Pittsburgh defense scored three touchdowns, including two in the fourth quarter, to lift the Steelers to their first win at Riverfront Stadium since 1978. Cincinnati led 14-10 going into the fourth quarter, but interception returns for touchdowns by Ron Johnson (34 yards) and Harvey Clayton (70) clinched the win. Rick Woods' 38-yard fumble return for a score gave the Steelers a 7-0 lead. Pittsburgh recorded a team-record nine quarterback sacks for 77 yards and held Cincinnati to 281 total yards.

| | | | | | |
|---|---|---|---|---|---|
| Pittsburgh | 7 | 3 | 0 | 14 — | 24 |
| Cincinnati | 0 | 14 | 0 | 0 — | 14 |

Pitt — Woods 38 fumble recovery return (Anderson kick)
Pitt — FG Anderson 35
Cin — Johnson 1 run (Breech kick)
Cin — J. Griffin 41 interception return (Breech kick)
Pitt — Johnson 34 interception return (Anderson kick)
Pitt — Clayton 70 interception return (Anderson kick)

## SEVENTH WEEK SUMMARY

The Washington Redskins, the NFL's highest scoring team, took their scoring machine on the road for the second straight week but met their match in Green Bay. The Packers, ranked third in scoring, edged the Redskins 48-47 on Jan Stenerud's 20-yard field goal with 54 seconds left, climaxing the highest scoring game in Monday night history. The game produced five lead changes in the fourth quarter and would have had a sixth, but Mark Moseley's 39-yard field goal sailed wide on the game's final play. The loss, which snapped Washington's nine-game winning streak on the road, enabled Dallas, 37-7 winners over Philadelphia, to take a two-game lead in the NFC East. In Detroit, Billy Sims returned from a broken wrist which had sidelined him since September 11, and gained 77 yards and a touchdown to lead the Lions over the Bears 31-17. Minnesota capitalized on seven Houston turnovers to down the Oilers 34-14 and remain atop the NFC Central. Meanwhile, San Francisco and the Los Angeles Rams overcame divisional opponents New Orleans and Atlanta, respectively, to remain in a first-place tie in the NFC West. The 49ers relied on a team-record six field goals by Ray Wersching to defeat the Saints 32-13. The Falcons held Eric Dickerson to 64 yards rushing but Vince Ferragamo's two-yard touchdown pass to Mike Guman with 17 seconds remaining lifted the Rams to a 27-21 victory. Buffalo gained control of the top spot in the AFC East, relying on three Joe Ferguson touchdown passes and three field goals by Joe Danelo to beat the Colts 30-7. The Dolphins remained one game behind the Bills by defeating the Jets 32-14 on three Dan Marino touchdown passes and a club-record six interceptions. Pittsburgh took control of first place in the AFC Central by getting a pair of touchdowns from its defense (which intercepted six passes and recovered a fumble) in the Steelers' 44-17 win over the Browns. The Raiders had their AFC West lead cut to a single game as they lost in Seattle. The Seahawks capitalized on eight Raiders turnovers (five fumbles and three interceptions) and registered eight sacks to defeat Los Angeles 38-36. The Raiders dominated the Seahawks statistically, outgaining them 382 to 153 and allowing just two yards passing. NFL teams combined to score 761 points in Week Seven (54.4 points per game), the highest single weekend total on record.

**SUNDAY, OCTOBER 16**

**Los Angeles Rams 27, Atlanta 21**—At Anaheim Stadium, attendance 50,404. Vince Ferragamo fired a two-yard touchdown pass to Mike Guman with 17 seconds remaining to rally the Rams to a 27-21 win. Trailing 21-7, Los Angeles tied the score on Ferragamo's 10-yard pass to Preston Dennard and Eric Dickerson's second one-yard touchdown run of the game. The winning score climaxed a 47-yard drive and was set up by a pass interference penalty at the Falcons' 2-yard line.

| | | | | | |
|---|---|---|---|---|---|
| Atlanta | 7 | 7 | 7 | 0 | — 21 |
| L.A. Rams | 0 | 7 | 7 | 13 | — 27 |

Atl — Bailey 25 pass from Bartkowski (Luckhurst kick)
Atl — Hodge 1 pass from Bartkowski (Luckhurst kick)
Rams — Dickerson 1 run (Nelson kick)
Atl — Riggs 6 run (Luckhurst kick)
Rams — Dennard 10 pass from Ferragamo (Nelson kick)
Rams — Dickerson 1 run (Nelson kick)
Rams — Guman 2 pass from Ferragamo (kick blocked)

**Buffalo 30, Baltimore 7**—At Memorial Stadium, attendance 38,565. Joe Ferguson passed for three touchdowns and Joe Danelo added three field goals as the Bills won 30-7. Ferguson completed 21 of 30 passes for 230 yards, including touchdown passes of 4 yards to Mark Brammer and 20 yards to Frank Lewis for a 24-7 halftime lead. Danelo converted field goal attempts of 23, 40, and 30 yards. Buffalo gained 401 total yards, including 105 yards rushing by Joe Cribbs, who also scored on a 14-yard pass.

| | | | | | |
|---|---|---|---|---|---|
| Buffalo | 7 | 17 | 3 | 3 | — 30 |
| Baltimore | 7 | 0 | 0 | 0 | — 7 |

Balt — Butler 52 pass from Pagel (Allegre kick)
Buff — Cribbs 14 pass from Ferguson (Danelo kick)
Buff — Brammer 4 pass from Ferguson (Danelo kick)
Buff — Lewis 20 pass from Ferguson (Danelo kick)
Buff — FG Danelo 23
Buff — FG Danelo 40
Buff — FG Danelo 30

**Detroit 31, Chicago 17**—At Pontiac Silverdome, attendance 66,709. Eric Hipple passed for one touchdown and ran for another and Billy Sims scored his first touchdown of the season to lead the Lions over the Bears 31-17. Sims, in his first action since a broken wrist sidelined him September 11, scored on a three-yard run in the first quarter. Hipple hit Dexter Bussey on a 14-yard scoring pass and scored on an eight-yard run with 1:18 left to finish the scoring. Vince Evans made his first start for the Bears, completing 28 of 45 for 336 yards and two touchdowns.

| | | | | | |
|---|---|---|---|---|---|
| Chicago | 0 | 10 | 0 | 7 | — 17 |
| Detroit | 7 | 10 | 7 | 7 | — 31 |

Det — Sims 3 run (Murray kick)
Det — Bussey 14 pass from Hipple (Murray kick)
Chi — FG B. Thomas 23
Det — FG Murray 35
Chi — Margerum 12 pass from Evans (B. Thomas kick)
Det — Norris 20 pass from Danielson (Murray kick)
Chi — Suhey 10 pass from Evans (B. Thomas kick)
Det — Hipple 8 run (Murray kick)

**Denver 24, Cincinnati 17**—At Mile High Stadium, attendance 74,305. Steve DeBerg's game-winning seven-yard touchdown pass to Rick Parros with 6:57 remaining snapped the Broncos' five-game losing streak at home. Parros' third period three-yard run put Denver on top 17-10, but cornerback Ray Horton's 55-yard interception return for a touchdown tied the score at 17-17. Turk Schonert, making his first NFL start (in place of injured Ken Anderson), completed 20 of 33 for 290 yards. DeBerg hit on 25 of 37 for 284 yards.

| | | | | | |
|---|---|---|---|---|---|
| Cincinnati | 7 | 3 | 7 | 0 | — 17 |
| Denver | 7 | 3 | 7 | 7 | — 24 |

Den — Preston 3 pass from DeBerg (Karlis kick)
Cin — Alexander 3 run (Breech kick)
Cin — FG Breech 35
Den — FG Karlis 31
Den — Parros 3 run (Karlis kick)
Cin — Horton 55 interception return (Breech kick)
Den — Parros 7 pass from DeBerg (Karlis kick)

**Pittsburgh 44, Cleveland 17**—At Three Rivers Stadium, attendance 59,263. Cliff Stoudt completed 13 consecutive passes (14 of 18 for 194 yards for the game) and the defense forced seven turnovers (six interceptions, one fumble recovery) as the Steelers downed the Browns for the fourteenth straight time in Three Rivers Stadium. Pittsburgh led 17-0 six minutes into the game after Mike Merriweather returned one interception 31 yards for a score and set up Gary Anderson's 18-yard field goal with another. Rick Woods' interception of a Brian Sipe pass led to Walter Abercrombie's one-yard touchdown run. Safety Greg Best returned a fumble 94 yards for the game's final score. Boyce Green scored both Cleveland touchdowns and rushed for 137 yards on 28 carries.

| | | | | | |
|---|---|---|---|---|---|
| Cleveland | 3 | 7 | 7 | 0 | — 17 |
| Pittsburgh | 20 | 14 | 0 | 10 | — 44 |

Pitt — FG Anderson 18
Pitt — Abercrombie 1 run (Anderson kick)
Pitt — Merriweather 31 interception return (Anderson kick)
Cle — FG Bahr 27
Pitt — FG Anderson 29
Cle — Green 23 run (Bahr kick)
Pitt — Harris 1 run (Anderson kick)
Pitt — Sweeney 40 pass from Stoudt (Anderson kick)
Cle — Green 1 run (Bahr kick)
Pitt — FG Anderson 26
Pitt — Best 94 fumble recovery return (Anderson kick)

**Dallas 37, Philadelphia 7**—At Texas Stadium, attendance 63,070. Dallas, after trailing 7-3 in the first quarter, scored 34 unanswered points to post its seventh consecutive come-from-behind win. Danny White completed 24 of 37 passes for 266 yards and threw touchdowns to Doug Cosbie (14 yards) and Timmy Newsome (2). Ron Springs' one-yard run put the Cowboys in front 10-7 late in the first quarter. Tony Dorsett scored his first touchdown of the season on a seven-yard run early in the third period. Rafael Septien connected on field goals of 31, 46, and 34 yards. Dallas had the ball for 43:43 and accumulated 522 yards total offense in handing Philadelphia its worst defeat since a 31-0 loss to Cincinnati in 1975.

| | | | | | |
|---|---|---|---|---|---|
| Philadelphia | 7 | 0 | 0 | 0 | — 7 |
| Dallas | 10 | 13 | 7 | 7 | — 37 |

Dall — FG Septien 31
Phil — Quick 83 pass from Jaworski (Franklin kick)
Dall — Springs 1 run (Septien kick)
Dall — Cosbie 14 pass from D. White (Septien kick)
Dall — FG Septien 46
Dall — FG Septien 34
Dall — Dorsett 7 run (Septien kick)
Dall — Newsome 2 pass from D. White (Septien kick)

**Minnesota 34, Houston 14**—At Metrodome, attendance 58,910. Defensive end Neil Elshire had 11 tackles, three sacks, one fumble recovery, and forced one fumble, to spearhead the defense as the Vikings topped the Oilers 34-14. Elshire jarred the ball loose from Houston's Gifford Nielsen and nose tackle Charlie Johnson returned it 50 yards for the Vikings' first score. Ted Brown scored on runs of four and seven yards and Steve Dils completed a 23-yard scoring pass to Steve Jordan. Benny Ricardo kicked a 44-yard field goal but missed from 48 to end his streak at a club-record 15 in a row.

| | | | | | |
|---|---|---|---|---|---|
| Houston | 7 | 0 | 7 | 0 | — 14 |
| Minnesota | 17 | 3 | 0 | 14 | — 34 |

Minn — FG Ricardo 44
Minn — Johnson 50 fumble recovery return (Ricardo kick)
Hou — Campbell 13 run (Kempf kick)
Minn — Jordan 23 pass from Dils (Ricardo kick)
Minn — FG Ricardo 28
Hou — Dressel 35 pass from Nielsen (Kempf kick)
Minn — Brown 4 run (Ricardo kick)
Minn — Brown 7 run (Ricardo kick)

**Seattle 38, Los Angeles Raiders 36**—At Kingdome, attendance 60,967. Seattle capitalized on eight Raiders turnovers (five fumble recoveries, three interceptions) and registered a club-record eight sacks to down Los Angeles 38-36. With the Seahawks leading 24-22 in the third quarter, linebacker Shelton Robinson returned a fumble nine yards for a score. Jacob Green's fumble recovery 14 seconds later set up Curt Warner's six-yard scoring run for a 38-22 edge. Marc Wilson replaced Jim Plunkett and threw two touchdown passes in the final 4:32. The Raiders had 382 yards total offense while holding the Seahawks to 153, including just 2 net yards passing. Green set a Seattle club record with 3½ sacks.

| | | | | | |
|---|---|---|---|---|---|
| L.A. Raiders | 7 | 10 | 5 | 14 | — 36 |
| Seattle | 7 | 0 | 17 | 14 | — 38 |

Raiders — Christensen 19 pass from Allen (Bahr kick)
Sea — Doornink 1 run (N. Johnson kick)
Raiders — FG Bahr 32
Raiders — Christensen 12 pass from Plunkett (Bahr kick)
Sea — Zorn 18 run (N. Johnson kick)
Sea — Johns 75 punt return (N. Johnson kick)
Sea — FG N. Johnson 22
Raiders — FG Bahr 42
Raiders — Safety, Alzado tackled Pratt in end zone
Sea — Robinson 9 fumble recovery return (N. Johnson kick)
Sea — Warner 6 run (N. Johnson kick)
Raiders — Allen 1 pass from Wilson (Bahr kick)
Raiders — Christensen 22 pass from Wilson (Bahr kick)

**Miami 32, New York Jets 14**—At Shea Stadium, attendance 58,615. Dan Marino fired three touchdown passes and the defense came up with six interceptions as the Dolphins won their fourth straight from the Jets 32-14. Miami never trailed as Marino's 66-yard bomb to Nat Moore with just 2:56 gone in the game put the Dolphins up 7-0. Scoring receptions by Joe Rose (24 yards) and Dan Johnson (5), and Kim Bokamper's 24-yard interception return for a touchdown gave Miami an insurmountable 30-7 advantage. Marino finished with 17 of 30 completions for 225 yards. William Judson intercepted three passes for Miami.

| | | | | | |
|---|---|---|---|---|---|
| Miami | 7 | 13 | 10 | 2 | — 32 |
| New York Jets | 7 | 0 | 0 | 7 | — 14 |

Mia — Moore 66 pass from Marino (von Schamann kick)
NYJ — Augustyniak 2 pass from Todd (Leahy kick)
Mia — Bokamper 24 interception return (kick blocked)
Mia — Rose 24 pass from Marino (von Schamann kick)
Mia — FG von Schamann 35
Mia — Johnson 5 pass from Marino (von Schamann kick)
NYJ — Shuler 9 pass from Ryan (Leahy kick)
Mia — Safety, Charles tackled Ryan in end zone.

**Kansas City 38, New York Giants 17**—At Arrowhead Stadium, attendance 55,449. Bill Kenney threw for 342 yards (25 of 36 completions) and four touchdowns to lead the Chiefs to a 38-17 victory. Kansas City trailed New York 17-10 but erupted for 28 points in the second half. Kenney's 46-yard touchdown pass to Henry Marshall (seven receptions for 131 yards) was followed 1:10 later by Durwood Roquemore's 42-yard interception for a score. Albert Lewis' fumble recovery set up Kenney's 21-yard scoring strike to Marshall in the fourth quarter. Gary Green's interception led to Kenney's two-yard touchdown pass to Theotis Brown, capping an 86-yard drive. The Chiefs gained 432 yards to the Giants' 324.

| | | | | | |
|---|---|---|---|---|---|
| New York Giants | 0 | 14 | 3 | 0 | — 17 |
| Kansas City | 0 | 10 | 14 | 14 | — 38 |

KC — FG Lowery 23
NYG — Carpenter 15 pass from Brunner (Haji-Sheikh kick)
KC — Scott 4 pass from Kenney (Lowery kick)
NYG — Woolfolk 8 run (Haji-Sheikh kick)
NYG — FG Haji-Sheikh 21
KC — Marshall 46 pass from Kenney (Lowery kick)
KC — Roquemore 42 interception return (Lowery kick)
KC — Marshall 21 pass from Kenney (Lowery kick)
KC — Brown 2 pass from Kenney (Lowery kick)

**St. Louis 34, Tampa Bay 27**—At Tampa Stadium, attendance 48,224. Neil Lomax passed for three touchdowns to lead the Cardinals to a 34-27 win. Lomax scoring passes of 6 yards to Roy Green and 16 yards to Doug Marsh 26 seconds apart gave St. Louis a commanding 27-6 lead in the third quarter. Benny Perrin's interception set up Randy Love's one-yard run with 1:07 remaining to put the game away.

| | | | | | |
|---|---|---|---|---|---|
| St. Louis | 3 | 10 | 14 | 7 | — 34 |
| Tampa Bay | 6 | 0 | 14 | 7 | — 27 |

StL — FG O'Donoghue 52
TB — Wilder 11 pass from Thompson (kick failed)
StL — FG O'Donoghue 43
StL — Marsh 5 pass from Lomax (O'Donoghue kick)
StL — Green 6 pass from Lomax (O'Donoghue kick)
StL — Marsh 16 pass from Lomax (O'Donoghue kick)
TB — T. Bell 23 pass from Thompson (Capece kick)
TB — Green 33 interception return (Capece kick)
StL — Love 1 run (O'Donoghue kick)
TB — Giles 11 pass from Thompson (Capece kick)

**New England 37, San Diego 21**—At Sullivan Stadium, attendance 59,016. Safety Rick Sanford's fumble recovery and interception ignited a second-half rally and helped the Patriots win 37-21. New England trailed San Diego 21-10 at halftime but Sanford's interception led to Fred Steinfort's 20-yard field goal and his 26-yard fumble return set up Mark van Eeghen's one-yard scoring run to give New England a 23-21 lead. Fourth-quarter touchdown runs by Tony Collins (10 yards) and Steve Grogan (1 yard) put the game out of reach. Dan Fouts threw for 357 yards as the Chargers notched their NFL-record eleventh straight game of more than 400 yards total offense (427).

| | | | | | |
|---|---|---|---|---|---|
| San Diego | 7 | 14 | 0 | 0 | — 21 |
| New England | 3 | 7 | 3 | 24 | — 37 |

SD — Brooks 1 run (Benirschke kick)
NE — FG Steinfort 35
SD — Duckworth 40 pass from Fouts (Benirschke kick)
NE — Collins 7 run (Steinfort kick)
SD — Brooks 1 run (Benirschke kick)
NE — FG Steinfort 20
NE — FG Steinfort 32
NE — Van Eeghen 1 run (Steinfort kick)
NE — Collins 10 run (Steinfort kick)
NE — Grogan 1 run (Steinfort kick)

**San Francisco 32, New Orleans 13**—At Louisiana Superdome, attendance 68,154. Ray Wersching kicked a team-record six field goals as the 49ers snapped the Saints' two-game win streak. Wersching had a personal-best 52-yarder to go with field goals of 23, 32, 47, 24, and 23 yards. Dwight Hicks' 62-yard interception return for a score capped a 16-point explosion in a 5:01 span of the third period. Wendell Tyler added San Francisco's only offensive touchdown when he broke loose on a 34-yard run with 1:28 remaining.

| | | | | | |
|---|---|---|---|---|---|
| San Francisco | 6 | 0 | 16 | 10 | — 32 |
| New Orleans | 0 | 13 | 0 | 0 | — 13 |

SF — FG Wersching 23
SF — FG Wersching 32
NO — FG Andersen 28
NO — FG Andersen 26
NO — W. Wilson 1 run (Andersen kick)
SF — FG Wersching 47
SF — FG Wersching 52
SF — FG Wersching 24
SF — Hicks 62 interception return (Wersching kick)
SF — FG Wersching 23
SF — Tyler 34 run (Wersching kick)

**MONDAY, OCTOBER 17**

**Green Bay 48, Washington 47**—At Lambeau Field, attendance 55,255. Jan Stenerud's 20-yard field goal with 54 seconds left lifted the Packers over the Redskins in the highest-scoring Monday night game ever. Green Bay trailed 47-45 with 1:50 left, but Lynn Dickey's 56-yard pass to Gerry Ellis set up Stenerud's winning kick. Dickey completed 22 of 31 passes for 387 yards, including scoring passes of 36 and 9 yards to Paul Coffman and 31 yards to Mike Meade. Joe Theismann passed for 398 yards and two touchdowns but saw Washington's nine-game road win streak and six-game unbeaten string come to a halt. The two teams combined for 1,025 total yards (Washington 552, Green Bay 473). Mark Moseley kicked four field goals and five extra points to become the eleventh player to exceed 1,000-career points (1,016), but his 39-yard game-winning field goal attempt with three seconds left went wide.

| | | | | | | |
|---|---|---|---|---|---|---|
| Washington | 10 | 10 | 13 | 14 | — | 47 |
| Green Bay | 10 | 14 | 7 | 17 | — | 48 |

GB — Douglass 22 fumble recovery return (Stenerud kick)
Wash — Didier recovered fumble in end zone (Moseley kick)
GB — FG Stenerud 47
Wash — FG Moseley 42
GB — Coffman 36 pass from Dickey (Stenerud kick)
Wash — Riggins 1 run (Moseley kick)
GB — Coffman 9 pass from Dickey (Stenerud kick)
Wash — FG Moseley 28
GB — Ellis 24 run (Stenerud kick)
Wash — FG Moseley 31
Wash — J. Washington 6 pass from Theismann (Moseley kick)
Wash — FG Moseley 28
GB — G. Lewis 2 run (Stenerud kick)
Wash — Riggins 1 run (Moseley kick)
GB — Meade 31 pass from Dickey (Stenerud kick)
Wash — J. Washington 5 pass from Theismann (Moseley kick)
GB — FG Stenerud 20

## EIGHTH WEEK SUMMARY

For the first time this season Dallas ran out of comebacks. The Raiders handed the Cowboys their first defeat of the year, 40-38, when Chris Bahr's 26-yard field goal with 20 seconds to play was good. Six Los Angeles turnovers kept Dallas within striking distance but the Raiders effectively shut down the Cowboys' offense, allowing just 319 total yards, including only 81 rushing. Only three home teams won this weekend. Among them were the Redskins, who downed the Lions 38-17 to close to only one game back of the NFC East-leading Cowboys. Ken Riley returned his sixtieth career interception 42 yards for the winning touchdown in the Bengals' 28-21 win over the Browns. The victory helped snap Cincinnati's three-game losing streak. In Denver, Steve DeBerg directed two fourth-quarter touchdown drives as the Broncos beat the Chargers 14-6. San Diego, playing without Dan Fouts and Chuck Muncie, generated 299 yards, thus ending its streak of 11 straight games with 400-or-more yards total offense. The Steelers opened a 24-0 lead at the half and held on to defeat the Seahawks 27-21 and take a two-game lead in the AFC Central. Miami's win gave it a share of first place with Buffalo in the AFC East. The Dolphins, despite a heavy rain, scored on three first-half possessions to beat the Colts 21-7. Meanwhile, the Bills were shutout by the Patriots 31-0 as Roland James intercepted three passes to help New England score 24 points in the final period. San Francisco avenged an earlier loss to the Rams by upending Los Angeles 45-35 to take sole possession of first place in the NFC West. The Saints posted a 24-21 comeback win over the Buccaneers to stay one game back (along with the Rams) of the 49ers. Atlanta climbed back into the hunt, snapping a four-game losing streak by defeating the Jets 27-21. New York led 21-0 before Billy "White Shoes" Johnson took control. Johnson scored on a 71-yard punt return and a 15-yard touchdown reception and set up two more scores on punt returns of 41 and 36 yards. Minnesota grabbed a two-game lead in the NFC Central as Benny Ricardo's 32-yard field goal 5:05 into overtime helped beat Green Bay 20-17. Kansas City was also victorious in overtime, 13-10 over Houston, while the Giants and Cardinals played to the seventh tie, 20-20, since the NFL instituted the overtime period in 1974. The three overtime contests brought the season total to 13, matching the season record set in 1980.

**SUNDAY, OCTOBER 23**

**Atlanta 27, New York Jets 21**—At Shea Stadium, attendance 46,878. Billy Johnson's 71-yard punt return for a touchdown climaxed a 27-point second-half rally as the Falcons ended a four-game losing streak. Trailing 21-0, Atlanta's Steve Bartkowski (25 of 36 for 313 yards) fired a 15-yard touchdown pass to Johnson with four seconds left in the third quarter and added a 25-yard scoring pass to William Andrews three minutes later. Johnson's punt return touchdown tied the game at 21-21 and Mick Luckhurst kicked field goals of 32 and 40 yards for the winning margin.

| | | | | | | |
|---|---|---|---|---|---|---|
| Atlanta | 0 | 0 | 7 | 20 | — | 27 |
| New York Jets | 0 | 7 | 14 | 0 | — | 21 |

NYJ — Harper 78 run (Leahy kick)
NYJ — Dierking 4 run (Leahy kick)
NYJ — Augustyniak 3 run (Leahy kick)
Atl — Johnson 15 pass from Bartkowski (Luckhurst kick)
Atl — Andrews 25 pass from Bartkowski (Luckhurst kick)
Atl — Johnson 71 punt return (Luckhurst kick)
Atl — FG Luckhurst 32
Atl — FG Luckhurst 40

**Chicago 7, Philadelphia 6**—At Veterans Stadium, attendance 45,263. Vince Evans' 20-yard touchdown pass to Dennis McKinnon in the first quarter led the Bears to a 7-6 win. The Chicago defense held Philadelphia to 24 first-half yards and only allowed field goals of 24 and 38 yards by Tony Franklin. The key play in the Bears' touchdown drive was Evans' 10-yard scramble on a fourth-and-four at the Eagles' 33-yard line.

| | | | | | | |
|---|---|---|---|---|---|---|
| Chicago | 7 | 0 | 0 | 0 | — | 7 |
| Philadelphia | 0 | 0 | 3 | 3 | — | 6 |

Chi — McKinnon 20 pass from Evans (B. Thomas kick)
Phil — FG Franklin 24
Phil — FG Franklin 38

**Cincinnati 28, Cleveland 21**—At Riverfront Stadium, attendance 50,047. Ken Riley returned his sixtieth career interception 42 yards for the winning score to lead the Bengals' comeback and snap a three-game losing streak. Cincinnati rebounded to tie the game 14-14 on Turk Schonert's one-yard run in the third quarter and 21-21 on Charles Alexander's four-yard run in the final period. Brian Sipe threw three touchdown passes for the Browns but Riley's fifth career touchdown proved to be the winning points.

| | | | | | | |
|---|---|---|---|---|---|---|
| Cleveland | 0 | 14 | 7 | 0 | — | 21 |
| Cincinnati | 0 | 7 | 7 | 14 | — | 28 |

Cin — Johnson 1 run (Breech kick)
Cle — Newsome 5 pass from Sipe (Bahr kick)
Cle — Jones 8 pass from Sipe (Bahr kick)
Cin — Schonert 1 run (Breech kick)
Cle — Newsome 17 pass from Sipe (Bahr kick)
Cin — Alexander 4 run (Breech kick)
Cin — Riley 42 interception return (Breech kick)

**Washington 38, Detroit 17**—At Robert F. Kennedy Stadium, attendance 43,189. Rookie Reggie Evans, filling in for the injured John Riggins, scored three touchdowns and Joe Washington rushed for a career-high 147 yards as the Redskins ended the Lions' two-game winning streak. Evans scored on runs of two, two, and one yards, and Joe Theismann, despite playing in a steady downpour, threw for 247 yards and had scoring passes of 8 yards to Washington and 13 yards to Art Monk. The Redskins gained 441 yards total offense while limiting Detroit to 176.

| | | | | | | |
|---|---|---|---|---|---|---|
| Detroit | 0 | 3 | 7 | 7 | — | 17 |
| Washington | 14 | 14 | 3 | 7 | — | 38 |

Wash — Monk 13 pass from Theismann (Moseley kick)
Wash — Evans 2 run (Moseley kick)
Det — FG Murray 37
Wash — J. Washington 8 pass from Theismann (Moseley kick)
Wash — Evans 2 run (Moseley kick)
Det — Sims 13 run (Murray kick)
Wash — FG Moseley
Wash — Evans 1 run (Moseley kick)
Det — Norris 2 pass from Danielson (Murray kick)

**Kansas City 13, Houston 10**—At Astrodome, attendance 39,462. Nick Lowery's 41-yard field goal 7:41 into overtime lifted the Chiefs over the Oilers. The Chiefs won the overtime toss and Bill Kenney drove them 60 yards to set up the winning kick. Kenney finished the day with 25 completions in 43 attempts for 264 yards and one touchdown. He had a four-yard touchdown pass to Willie Scott. Both teams missed game-winning fourth-quarter field goal opportunities. Lowery's 52-yard attempt fell short with 4:04 to play and Houston's Florian Kempf's 41-yard attempt sailed wide with four seconds left in regulation.

| | | | | | | | |
|---|---|---|---|---|---|---|---|
| Kansas City | 0 | 10 | 0 | 0 | 3 | — | 13 |
| Houston | 7 | 0 | 0 | 3 | 0 | — | 10 |

Hou — Edwards 3 pass from Nielsen (Kempf kick)
KC — Scott 4 pass from Kenney (Lowery kick)
KC — FG Lowery 31
Hou — FG Kempf 32
KC — FG Lowery 41

**Los Angeles Raiders 40, Dallas 38**—At Texas Stadium, attendance 64,991. Chris Bahr's fourth field goal of the game, a 26-yarder with 20 seconds remaining, handed the Cowboys their first loss of the season. Marc Wilson, making his first start for the Raiders since 1981, completed 26 of 49 passes for 318 yards and threw touchdown passes to Derrick Jensen (2 yards), Frank Hawkins (17), and Todd Christensen (1) for a 31-24 halftime lead. The Cowboys tied the game 31-31 on Danny White's 17-yard touchdown pass to Doug Donley. Dallas went ahead 38-31 on Mike Hegman's nine-yard fumble recovery return for a touchdown 1:44 later. Hawkins collected 118 yards on 17 carries, and Los Angeles outgained Dallas 519 yards to 319.

| | | | | | | |
|---|---|---|---|---|---|---|
| L.A. Raiders | 10 | 21 | 3 | 6 | — | 40 |
| Dallas | 7 | 17 | 0 | 14 | — | 38 |

Dall — D. White 15 pass from Springs (Septien kick)
Raiders — FG Bahr 37
Raiders — Jensen 2 pass from Wilson (Bahr kick)
Dall — Springs 2 run (Septien kick)
Dall — FG Septien 23
Raiders — Hawkins 23 run (Bahr kick)
Dall — Johnson 15 pass from D. White (Septien kick)
Raiders — Hawkins 17 pass from Wilson (Bahr kick)
Raiders — Christensen 1 pass from Wilson (Bahr kick)
Raiders — FG Bahr 24
Dall — Donley 17 pass from D. White (Septien kick)
Dall — Hegman 9 fumble recovery return (Septien kick)
Raiders — FG Bahr 26
Raiders — FG Bahr 26

**Miami 21, Baltimore 7**—At Memorial Stadium, attendance 32,343. Dan Marino directed scoring drives on three consecutive first-half possessions as the Dolphins rolled to a 21-7 win. Playing in a driving rain, Marino followed Bob Baumhower's fumble recovery with an eight-yard touchdown pass to Nat Moore. On Miami's next possession, Marino set up Andra Franklin's one-yard scoring run with a 64-yard completion to Mark Duper. Paul Lankford's interception set up Marino's 28-yard touchdown pass to Duper that completed Miami's scoring. The Colts outgained the Dolphins 311 to 272 yards.

| | | | | | | |
|---|---|---|---|---|---|---|
| Miami | 7 | 14 | 0 | 0 | — | 21 |
| Baltimore | 0 | 0 | 0 | 7 | — | 7 |

Mia — Moore 8 pass from Marino (von Schamann kick)
Mia — Franklin 1 run (von Schamann kick)
Mia — Duper 28 pass from Marino (von Schamann kick)
Balt — Butler 20 pass from Pagel (Allegre kick)

**Minnesota 20, Green Bay 17**—At Lambeau Field, attendance 55,236. Benny Ricardo's 32-yard field goal 5:05 into overtime lifted the Vikings over the Packers 20-17. Minnesota led 17-3 late in the third quarter but Lynn Dickey's (23 of 41 for 383 yards) five-yard scoring pass to John Jefferson and his four-yard touchdown pass to Mike Meade tied the game with two seconds left. Ted Brown rushed 29 times for 179 yards for the Vikings and Doug Martin registered four of Minnesota's six sacks. Green Bay won the overtime coin toss but punted after four downs.

| | | | | | | | |
|---|---|---|---|---|---|---|---|
| Minnesota | 7 | 3 | 7 | 0 | 3 | — | 20 |
| Green Bay | 0 | 3 | 0 | 14 | 0 | — | 17 |

Minn — S. White 13 pass from Dils (Ricardo kick)
Minn — FG Ricardo 44
GB — FG Stenerud 48
Minn — Brown 1 run (Ricardo kick)
GB — Jefferson 5 pass from Dickey (Stenerud kick)
GB — Meade 4 pass from Dickey (Stenerud kick)
Minn — FG Ricardo 32

**New England 31, Buffalo 0**—At Rich Stadium, attendance 60,424. Steve Grogan threw two touchdown passes, Tony Collins rushed for 147 yards, Roland James had three interceptions, and the Patriots exploded for 24 fourth quarter points in evening their record at 4-4. Grogan combined with Derrick Ramsey on two scoring passes—from 35 yards 1:53 before halftime and from 2 yards 54 seconds into the fourth quarter. Touchdown runs by Collins (50 yards) and Mark van Eeghen (2), sandwiched around Fred Steinfort's 22-yard field goal, completed the offensive assault.

| | | | | | | |
|---|---|---|---|---|---|---|
| New England | 0 | 7 | 0 | 24 | — | 31 |
| Buffalo | 0 | 0 | 0 | 0 | — | 0 |

NE — Ramsey 35 pass from Grogan (Steinfort kick)
NE — Ramsey 2 pass from Grogan (Steinfort kick)
NE — Collins 50 run (Steinfort kick)
NE — FG Steinfort 22
NE — van Eeghen 2 run (Steinfort kick)

**New Orleans 24, Tampa Bay 21**—At Tampa Stadium, attendance 48,242. Rookie Bobby Johnson's 70-yard interception return for a touchdown with 50 seconds left in the third quarter gave the Saints the comeback victory. New Orleans rebounded from a 14-0 deficit on Kelvin Clark's fumble recovery in the end zone and Morten Andersen's 50-yard field goal. After Tampa Bay went ahead 21-10, Ken Stabler cut the Buccaneers' lead to 21-17 with a 12-yard touchdown pass to Eugene Goodlow. The Saints' defense had seven sacks and held Tampa Bay to 74 yards rushing and 67 passing.

| | | | | | | |
|---|---|---|---|---|---|---|
| New Orleans | 0 | 10 | 14 | 0 | — | 24 |
| Tampa Bay | 14 | 7 | 0 | 0 | — | 21 |

TB — Wilder 2 run (Capece kick)
TB — Castille 69 interception return (Capece kick)
NO — K. Clark recovered fumble in end zone (Andersen kick)
NO — FG Andersen 50
TB — Wilder 7 run (Capece kick)
NO — Goodlow 12 pass from Stabler (Andersen kick)
NO — Johnson 70 interception return (Andersen kick)

**Pittsburgh 27, Seattle 21**—At Kingdome, attendance 61,615. The Steelers built a 24-0 halftime lead and withstood the Seahawks' furious second-half rally to win 27-21.

Franco Harris carried 31 times for 132 yards and opened the scoring with a nine-yard run. Cliff Stoudt and Frank Pollard added one-yard runs and Gary Anderson's 20-yard field goal 12 seconds before intermission completed Pittsburgh's first-half onslaught. Dave Krieg replaced Jim Zorn in the second half and completed 13 of 20 passes for 214 yards and two touchdowns, but the Steelers' defense stopped the Seahawks on the Pittsburgh 42 with 1:13 left to secure the win.

| | | | | | | |
|---|---|---|---|---|---|---|
| Pittsburgh | 7 | 17 | 0 | 3 | — | 27 |
| Seattle | 0 | 0 | 7 | 14 | — | 21 |

Pitt — F. Harris 9 run (Anderson kick)
Pitt — Stoudt 1 run (Anderson kick)
Pitt — Pollard 1 run (Anderson kick)
Pitt — FG Anderson 20
Sea — Warner 1 run (N. Johnson kick)
Sea — Largent 21 pass from Krieg (N. Johnson kick)
Pitt — FG Anderson 32
Sea — Johns 26 pass from Krieg (N. Johnson kick)

**Denver 14, San Diego 6**—At Mile High Stadium, attendance 74,581. Steve DeBerg engineered two fourth-quarter touchdown drives to rally the Broncos over the Chargers. It was a defensive struggle for three periods before DeBerg hit Rick Upchurch on a 30-yard touchdown pass for a 7-6 lead. Dave Preston added a two-yard scoring run with 1:42 remaining to secure the victory. San Diego's NFL-record 11 straight 400-yard total offense games was halted by the Broncos, who yielded 299 yards.

| | | | | | | |
|---|---|---|---|---|---|---|
| San Diego | 0 | 3 | 3 | 0 | — | 6 |
| Denver | 0 | 0 | 0 | 14 | — | 14 |

SD — FG Benirschke 29
SD — FG Benirschke 30
Den — Upchurch 30 pass from DeBerg (Karlis kick)
Den — Preston 2 run (Karlis kick)

**San Francisco 45, Los Angeles Rams 35**—At Anaheim Stadium, attendance 66,070. Joe Montana completed a pair of fourth-quarter touchdown passes and Dwaine Board's fumble recovery for a touchdown proved to be the decisive points as the 49ers gained sole possession of first place in the NFC West. San Francisco trailed 35-24 midway through the fourth period when Montana (25 of 39 for 358 yards and three touchdowns) threw a 46-yard scoring pass to Dwight Clark to cut the Rams' lead to 35-31. Board followed 1:11 later by stripping the ball from Vince Ferragamo in the Rams' end zone and making the recovery for the winning points. Ferragamo completed 26 of 35 passes for 327 yards and five touchdowns and Eric Dickerson ran for 144 yards on 25 carries. The 49ers gained 460 total yards while giving up 441.

| | | | | | | |
|---|---|---|---|---|---|---|
| San Francisco | 0 | 14 | 3 | 28 | — | 45 |
| L.A. Rams | 0 | 21 | 7 | 7 | — | 35 |

Rams — Farmer 13 pass from Ferragamo (Nelson kick)
SF — Craig 4 run (Wersching kick)
Rams — McDonald 1 pass from Ferragamo (Nelson kick)
SF — Clark 15 pass from Montana (Wersching kick)
Rams — Dickerson 37 pass from Ferragamo (Nelson kick)
SF — FG Wersching 30
Rams — Dickerson 10 pass from Ferragamo (Nelson kick)
SF — Nehemiah 11 pass from Montana (Wersching kick)
Rams — Barber 17 pass from Ferragamo (Nelson kick)
SF — Clark 46 pass from Montana (Wersching kick)
SF — Board fumble recovery in end zone (Wersching kick)
SF — Ring 4 run (Wersching kick)

**MONDAY, OCTOBER 24**

**New York Giants 20, St. Louis 20**—At Busch Memorial Stadium, attendance 45,630. The Giants and Cardinals played to the seventh tie since the overtime period was introduced in regular-season play in 1974. Neil O'Donoghue kicked a 22-yard field goal with 54 seconds left to send the game into the extra period but missed 44-, 19-, and 42-yard tries in overtime. New York built a 14-10 halftime lead on Bill Currier's 30-yard interception return and Rob Carpenter's one-yard run. Ali Haji-Sheikh's 40-yard field goal extended the Giants' lead to 17-10, but Benny Perrin ran 32 yards for a touchdown after recovering a fumble to tie the score 17-17. Haji-Sheikh's 66-yard attempt with no time remaining in the fourth quarter fell short and snapped the rookie's club record 14 straight field goals. Stump Mitchell, playing for the injured Ottis Anderson, rushed for 108 yards. Roy Green added 100 yards on six receptions.

| | | | | | | | |
|---|---|---|---|---|---|---|---|
| N.Y. Giants | 7 | 7 | 3 | 3 | 0 | — | 20 |
| St. Louis | 3 | 7 | 7 | 3 | 0 | — | 20 |

StL — FG O' Donoghue 34
NYG — Currier 30 interception return (Haji-Sheikh kick)
StL — Mitchell 7 run (O'Donoghue kick)
NYG — Carpenter 1 run (Haji-Sheikh kick)
NYG — FG Haji-Sheikh 40
StL — Perrin 32 fumble recovery return (O'Donoghue kick)
NYG — FG Haji-Sheikh 28
StL — FG O'Donoghue 22

## NINTH WEEK SUMMARY

The AFC East won three of four games from the NFC West to take a 15-13 lead in the 52-game AFC-NFC interconference series. Eric Dickerson became the seventeenth rookie to rush for over a 1,000 yards in a season (1,096), but that didn't stop another rookie standout, Dan Marino, from contributing three touchdown passes to the Dolphins' 30-14 win over the Rams. Buffalo's Joe Ferguson threw four touchdown passes and the Bills held on to defeat the Saints 27-21. The Jets limited San Francisco's Wendell Tyler to nine yards on eight carries as New York snapped a three-game losing streak by beating the 49ers 23-13. Atlanta capitalized on four New England fumbles to defeat the Patriots 24-13. In other interconference matchups, Baltimore got five field goals from rookie Raul Allegre to edge Philadelphia 22-21, while the Redskins' Mark Moseley, after missing four field goal attempts, connected on a 37-yarder with four seconds left to give Washington a 27-24 victory over San Diego. Pete Johnson, in his first start of the season, rushed for 112 yards and scored twice to help Cincinnati post a 34-14 win over Green Bay. The Steelers retained a two-game cushion in the AFC Central by defeating the Buccaneers 17-12. Pittsburgh scored all 17 points in the fourth quarter to overshadow the running of Tampa Bay's James Wilder, who carried an NFL-record 42 times for 126 yards. The Seahawks completed a season-sweep of the Raiders with a 34-21 victory, marking Chuck Knox's one-hundredth NFL head coaching win. The Raiders' loss, coupled with the Broncos' 27-24 come-from-behind victory over the Chiefs, gave Denver a share of the lead in the AFC West. Cleveland handed Houston its second consecutive overtime loss, 25-19, as Boyce Green scored on a 20-yard run after 6:34 of the extra period. The game was the fourteenth overtime contest of the season, an NFL record.

**SUNDAY, OCTOBER 30**

**Baltimore 22, Philadelphia 21**—At Veterans Stadium, attendance 59,150. Five field goals by Raul Allegre, including a 30-yarder with 2:07 remaining, lifted the Colts over the Eagles. In a game in which the lead changed hands six times, Allegre also connected from 38, 39, 37, and 42 yards to tie Lou Michaels' club record of five field goals in a game. Randy McMillan gained 109 yards on 19 carries and scored on a 39-yard run to give the Colts a 13-7 lead. Philadelphia took a 14-13 edge and later went ahead 21-19, but Steve Parker's fumble recovery at the Eagles' 41-yard line with 8:10 left set up Allegre's winning kick.

| | | | | | | |
|---|---|---|---|---|---|---|
| Baltimore | 3 | 13 | 3 | 3 | — | 22 |
| Philadelphia | 7 | 7 | 7 | 0 | — | 21 |

Balt — FG Allegre 38
Phil — Quick 45 pass from Carmichael (Franklin kick)
Balt — FG Allegre 39
Balt — McMillan 39 run (Allegre kick)
Phil — Harrington 1 run (Franklin kick)
Balt — FG Allegre 37
Balt — FG Allegre 42
Phil — Carmichael 6 pass from Jaworski (Franklin kick)
Balt — FG Allegre 30

**Dallas 38, New York Giants 20**—At Giants Stadium, attendance 76,142. Danny White tied a club record with a career-high five touchdown passes as the Cowboys defeated the Giants 38-20. White completed 15 of 33 passes for 304 yards and capped scoring drives of 80, 81, and 76 yards with scoring passes to Tony Hill (21 yards), Tony Dorsett (14), and Drew Pearson (7), respectively. Hill, whose 58-yard touchdown reception finished the scoring, caught five passes for 106 yards for the day. Doug Cosbie had a career-long 61-yard scoring reception among his three catches for 93 yards. The Dallas defense had three interceptions, three fumble recoveries, and six sacks.

| | | | | | | |
|---|---|---|---|---|---|---|
| Dallas | 7 | 10 | 7 | 14 | — | 38 |
| New York Giants | 7 | 7 | 6 | 0 | — | 20 |

NYG — Mowatt 46 pass from Rutledge (Haji-Sheikh kick)
Dall — T. Hill 21 pass from D. White (Septien kick)
Dall — Dorsett 14 pass from D. White (Septien kick)
Dall — FG Septien 36
NYG — Carpenter 15 pass from Rutledge (Haji-Sheikh kick)
NYG — FG Haji-Sheikh 27
Dall — Cosbie 61 pass from D. White (Septien kick)
NYG — FG Haji-Sheikh 29
Dall — Pearson 7 pass from D. White (Septien kick)
Dall — T. Hill 58 pass from D. White (Septien kick)

**Detroit 38, Chicago 17**—At Soldier Field, attendance 58,764. Eric Hipple's passing helped the Lions open a 31-3 fourth-quarter lead on the way to a 38-17 win and season sweep of the Bears. Hipple (12 of 19 for 216 yards) had completions of 46, 39, and 37 yards to set up touchdown runs by Vince Thompson (1 yard), James Jones (8), and Leonard Thompson (40). He also combined with Jeff Chadwick on a 21-yard touchdown pass late in the first quarter for a 14-0 lead. Bob Thomas kicked his one-hundredth career field goal (45 yards) for the Bears in the second quarter.

| | | | | | | |
|---|---|---|---|---|---|---|
| Detroit | 14 | 3 | 14 | 7 | — | 38 |
| Chicago | 0 | 3 | 0 | 14 | — | 17 |

Det — V. Thompson 1 run (Murray kick)
Det — Chadwick 21 pass from Hipple (Murray kick)
Chi — FG B. Thomas 45
Det — FG Murray 29
Det — Jones 8 run (Murray kick)
Det — L. Thompson 40 run (Murray kick)
Chi — Payton 1 run (B. Thomas kick)
Chi — Moorehead 18 pass from McMahon (B. Thomas kick)
Det — Jones 1 run (Murray kick)

**Cincinnati 34, Green Bay 14**—At Riverfront Stadium, attendance 53,349. Pete Johnson, making his first start of the season, ran for 112 yards and two touchdowns and Turk Schonert ran and passed for three more scores as the Bengals defeated the Packers 34-14. Cincinnati scored on four of six first-half possessions. Johnson had touchdown runs of one and five yards. Schonert followed with a four-yard touchdown run and a two-yard scoring pass to Cris Collinsworth for a 27-7 third-quarter lead. Schonert, who completed 20 of 29 passes for 244 yards, finished the scoring with a 10-yard touchdown pass to Steve Kreider.

| | | | | | | |
|---|---|---|---|---|---|---|
| Green Bay | 7 | 0 | 7 | 0 | — | 14 |
| Cincinnati | 6 | 21 | 0 | 7 | — | 34 |

Cin — Johnson 1 run (kick failed)
GB — Dickey 1 run (Stenerud kick)
Cin — Johnson 5 run (Breech kick)
Cin — Schonert 4 run (Breech kick)
Cin — Collinsworth 2 pass from Schonert (Breech kick)
GB — Coffman 11 pass from Ellis (Stenerud kick)
Cin — Kreider 10 pass from Schonert (Breech kick)

**Cleveland 25, Houston 19**—At Cleveland Stadium, attendance 66,955. Rookie running back Boyce Green's 20-yard touchdown run after 6:34 of overtime clinched the Browns' victory and sent the Oilers to their second straight overtime defeat. Cleveland tied the score twice, at 10-10 on tackle Doug Dieken's 14-yard scoring reception on a fake field goal and later at 19-19 on Matt Bahr's fourth field goal of the game, a 30-yarder with 49 seconds left in regulation play. The two teams traded punts to open the overtime, but Mike Whitwell's 15-yard interception return to the Houston 20-yard line set up Green's decisive score.

| | | | | | | | |
|---|---|---|---|---|---|---|---|
| Houston | 7 | 3 | 9 | 0 | 0 | — | 19 |
| Cleveland | 3 | 7 | 3 | 6 | 6 | — | 25 |

Cle — FG Bahr 37
Hou — Renfro 19 pass from Nielsen (Kempf kick)
Hou — FG Kempf 19
Cle — Dieken 14 pass from McDonald (Bahr kick)
Hou — Renfro 38 pass from Nielsen (kick failed)
Cle — FG Bahr 37
Hou — FG Kempf 24
Cle — FG Bahr 29
Cle — FG Bahr 30
Cle — Green 20 run

**Denver 27, Kansas City 24**—At Mile High Stadium, attendance 74,640. Steve DeBerg passed for 350 yards (completing 21 of 41 passes) and one touchdown, and Nathan Poole had a pair of one-yard touchdown runs to help the Broncos gain a share of first place in the AFC West. Trailing 7-0, Denver scored 17 points in a span of four and a half minutes. Mike Harden's fumble recovery set up Poole's first score and Louis Wright's interception led to Rich Karlis' 31-yard field goal. DeBerg capped the scoring with a 46-yard touchdown pass to Steve Watson, who had six catches for 121 yards. Rick Upchurch also had six receptions for 143 yards. Bill Kenney completed 27 of a club-record 52 passes for 365 yards and one touchdown for the Chiefs.

| | | | | | | |
|---|---|---|---|---|---|---|
| Kansas City | 7 | 0 | 3 | 14 | — | 24 |
| Denver | 0 | 17 | 3 | 7 | — | 27 |

KC — Brown 1 run (Lowery kick)
Den — Poole 1 run (Karlis kick)
Den — FG Karlis 31
Den — Watson 46 pass from DeBerg (Karlis kick)
KC — FG Lowery 21
Den — FG Karlis 27
Den — Poole 1 run (Karlis kick)
KC — B. Jackson 9 run (Lowery kick)
KC — Carson 8 pass from Kenney (Lowery kick)

**Miami 30, Los Angeles Rams 14**—At Orange Bowl, attendance 72,175. Dan Marino passed for two touchdowns and ran for a third to help lead the Dolphins over the Rams. Marino opened the scoring with a two-yard run and put Miami ahead 14-7 with a 46-yard touchdown pass to Mark Duper (seven receptions for 134 yards). Uwe von Schamann's 32-yard field goal broke a 14-14 tie and Tony Nathan's 18-yard scoring run with 2:53 remaining in the third quarter put the Dolphins in front 24-14. Marino completed 25 of 38 passes for 279 yards, including a three-yard touchdown pass to David Overstreet to close out the scoring. Eric Dickerson rushed for 101 yards (14 carries) to become the seventeenth rookie in league history to gain more than 1,000 yards (1,096) in a season.

| | | | | | | |
|---|---|---|---|---|---|---|
| L.A. Rams | 7 | 7 | 0 | 0 | — | 14 |
| Miami | 7 | 7 | 10 | 6 | — | 30 |

Mia — Marino 2 run (von Schamann kick)
Rams — Guman 2 pass from Ferragamo (Nelson kick)
Mia — Duper 46 pass from Marino (von Schamann kick)
Rams — Dickerson 2 run (Nelson kick)
Mia — FG von Schamann 32
Mia — Nathan 18 run (von Schamann kick)
Mia — Overstreet 3 pass from Marino (kick blocked)

**St. Louis 41, Minnesota 31**—At Busch Memorial Stadium, attendance 38,796. Neil Lomax threw three touchdown passes and Ottis Anderson ran for 136 yards on 24 carries to lead the Cardinals over the Vikings. St. Louis jumped out to a 14-0 first-quarter lead and never trailed. Lionel Washington's interception set up Lomax's nine-yard scoring pass to Pat Tilley and Neil O'Donoghue followed Stump Mitchell's four-yard touchdown run with field goals of 52 and 47 yards to give the Cardinals a 20-10 lead at halftime. Anderson's 10-yard scoring run gave St. Louis a 34-10 margin. Roy Green had touchdown receptions of four and five yards. Lomax completed 19 of 28 for 241 yards while Minnesota quarterback Steve Dils (27 of 38 for 314 yards) made the game close with three fourth-quarter touchdowns.

| | | | | | | |
|---|---|---|---|---|---|---|
| Minnesota | 0 | 10 | 0 | 21 | — | 31 |
| St. Louis | 14 | 6 | 14 | 7 | — | 41 |

StL — Tilley 9 pass from Lomax (O'Donoghue kick)
StL — Mitchell 4 run (O'Donoghue kick)
Minn — Brown 1 run (Ricardo kick)
StL — FG O'Donoghue 52
StL — FG O'Donoghue 47
Minn — FG Ricardo 39
StL — Green 4 pass from Lomax (O'Donoghue kick)
StL — Anderson 10 run (O'Donoghue kick)
Minn — McCullum 49 pass from Dils (Ricardo kick)
Minn — Bruer 2 pass from Dils (Ricardo kick)
StL — Green 5 pass from Lomax (O'Donoghue kick)
Minn — S. White 5 pass from Dils (Ricardo kick)

**Atlanta 24, New England 13**—At Atlanta-Fulton County Stadium, attendance 47,546. The Falcons' defense recovered four fumbles to halt New England drives (at Atlanta's 11-, 7-, and 4-yard lines, and John Rade returned a fourth 16 yards for a touchdown) to help snap a four-game home losing streak. Steve Bartkowski completed 22 of 33 passes for 252 yards, including a 22-yard touchdown pass to Billy Johnson. William Andrews gained 125 yards on 25 carries as the Falcons gained 430 yards total offense.

| | | | | | | |
|---|---|---|---|---|---|---|
| New England | 0 | 0 | 0 | 13 | — | 13 |
| Atlanta | 3 | 14 | 7 | 0 | — | 24 |

Atl — FG Luckhurst 23
Atl — Riggs 1 run (Luckhurst kick)
Atl — Rade 16 fumble recovery return (Luckhurst kick)
Atl — B. Johnson 22 pass from Bartkowski (Luckhurst kick)
NE — Ramsey 4 pass from Grogan (Steinfort kick)
NE — Tatupu 12 pass from Grogan (kick blocked)

**Buffalo 27, New Orleans 21**—At Rich Stadium, attendance 49,413. Joe Ferguson passed for four touchdowns and the Bills survived the Saints' fourth-quarter rally to hold on and win 27-21. Buffalo scored on its first three possessions as Ferguson threw scoring passes to Jerry Butler (15 yards), Tony Hunter (40), and Mike Mosley (22) for a 20-0 lead midway through the second quarter. Ferguson added an eight-yard scoring toss to Mosley in the third period before New Orleans quarterback Dave Wilson, in relief of Ken Stabler (who had injured his ribs) fired touchdown passes to Hoby Brenner (two yards) and Tyrone Young (five). George Rogers rushed for 114 yards. The Saints had 389 total yards while the Bills gained 301.

| | | | | | | |
|---|---|---|---|---|---|---|
| New Orleans | 0 | 7 | 0 | 14 | — | 21 |
| Buffalo | 7 | 13 | 7 | 0 | — | 27 |

Buff — Butler 15 pass from Ferguson (Danelo kick)
Buff — Hunter 40 pass from Ferguson (Danelo kick)
Buff — Mosley 22 pass from Ferguson (kick failed)
NO — Tice 12 pass from W. Wilson (Andersen kick)
Buff — Mosley 8 pass from Ferguson (Danelo kick)
NO — Brenner 2 pass from D. Wilson (Andersen kick)
NO — Young 5 pass from D. Wilson (Andersen kick)

**New York Jets 27, San Francisco 13**—At Candlestick Park, attendance 54,796. Richard Todd completed 20 of 28 passes for 201 yards and one touchdown and Jerry Holmes returned an interception 43 yards for a score in the final minute as the Jets snapped a three-game losing streak. After Ray Wersching's second-quarter field goal, New York jumped in front 14-3 on Scott Dierking's one-yard run and Lam Jones' 28-yard touchdown reception. Pat Leahy kicked a pair of field goals (49 and 46 yards) before Holmes' interception sealed the win.

| | | | | | | |
|---|---|---|---|---|---|---|
| New York Jets | 0 | 17 | 0 | 10 | — | 27 |
| San Francisco | 0 | 10 | 3 | 0 | — | 13 |

SF — FG Wersching 45
NYJ — Dierking 1 run (Leahy kick)
NYJ — Jones 28 pass from Todd (Leahy kick)
SF — Craig 6 pass from Montana (Wersching kick)
NYJ — FG Leahy 49
SF — FG Wersching 24
NYJ — FG Leahy 46
NYJ — Holmes 43 interception return (Leahy kick)

**Seattle 34, Los Angeles Raiders 21**—At Memorial Coliseum, attendance 49,708. Seattle capitalized on four interceptions and a fumble recovery to complete its first season sweep of the Raiders since 1979. The Seahawks were held to only 13 yards in the first quarter, but in the second period Seattle's Shelton Robinson returned a Marcus Allen fumble 12 yards for a touchdown to tie the game 7-7. Dave Krieg, who started his first game of the season at quarterback for the Seahawks, followed Norm Johnson's 37-yard field goal with a five-yard scoring pass to Charle Young and a 17-7 halftime lead. Los Angeles closed the gap to 17-14 in the third quarter, but the Seahawks opened a 17-point lead on Curt Warner's (23 carries, 101 yards) one-yard run and Jim Zorn's 33-yard touchdown pass to David Hughes on a fake field goal. The win was Chuck Knox's 100th career NFL victory.

| | | | | | | |
|---|---|---|---|---|---|---|
| Seattle | 0 | 17 | 7 | 10 | — | 34 |
| L.A. Raiders | 0 | 7 | 7 | 7 | — | 21 |

Raiders — Allen 1 run (Bahr kick)
Sea — Robinson 12 fumble recovery return (N. Johnson kick)
Sea — FG N. Johnson 37
Sea — Young 5 pass from Krieg (N. Johnson kick)
Raiders — Hasselbeck 4 pass from Wilson (Bahr kick)
Sea — Warner 1 run (N. Johnson kick)
Sea — Hughes 33 pass from Zorn (N. Johnson kick)
Raiders — Williams 50 pass from Wilson (Bahr kick)
Sea — FG N. Johnson 44

**Pittsburgh 17, Tampa Bay 12**—At Three Rivers Stadium, attendance 57,648. Frank Pollard's two-yard touchdown run with 31 seconds remaining gave the Steelers a come-from-behind 17-12 win. Pittsburgh scored all 17 points in the fourth quarter. Cliff Stoudt passed 11 yards to Wayne Capers with 8:42 left to cut the Buccaneers' lead to 12-7. Paul Skansi's 57-yard punt return set up Gary Anderson's 42-yard field goal with 5:49 to play to put Pittsburgh within striking distance, 12-10. The Steelers survived three interceptions, four lost fumbles, and five sacks to post their seventh win. Tampa Bay's James Wilder set an NFL record with 42 rushes (for 126 yards).

| | | | | | | |
|---|---|---|---|---|---|---|
| Tampa Bay | 6 | 3 | 3 | 0 | — | 12 |
| Pittsburgh | 0 | 0 | 0 | 17 | — | 17 |

TB — FG Capece 26
TB — FG Capece 49
TB — FG Capece 27
TB — FG Capece 28
Pitt — Capers 11 pass from Stoudt (Anderson kick)
Pitt — FG Anderson 42
Pitt — Pollard 2 run (Anderson kick)

**MONDAY, OCTOBER 31**

**Washington 27, San Diego 24**—At San Diego Jack Murphy Stadium, attendance 46,114. Mark Moseley's 37-yard field goal with four seconds remaining gave the Redskins a 27-24 win. Washington built a 24-7 lead on Moseley's 43-yard field goal and John Riggins' touchdown runs of two and one yards, but San Diego tied the score with 1:52 to play. Joe Theismann completed 25 of 46 passes for 324 yards, including 8 to Charlie Brown for 101 yards and 7 to Art Monk for 106. Mark Murphy had three of the Redskins' six interceptions. Washington gained 482 yards and yielded 428.

| | | | | | | |
|---|---|---|---|---|---|---|
| Washington | 7 | 3 | 7 | 10 | — | 27 |
| San Diego | 7 | 0 | 0 | 17 | — | 24 |

Wash — Seay 39 pass from Theismann (Moseley kick)
SD — Muncie 5 run (Benirschke kick)
Wash — FG Moseley 43
Wash — Riggins 2 run (Moseley kick)
Wash — Riggins 1 run (Moseley kick)
SD — Holohan 23 pass from Luther (Benirschke kick)
SD — Chandler 27 pass from Luther (Benirschke kick)
SD — FG Benirschke 43
Wash — FG Moseley 37

## TENTH WEEK SUMMARY

For the first time in their history, the Chicago Bears played a game without their patriarch George Halas, who died on October 31. The result was a 21-14 loss to the Rams, who once again turned Eric Dickerson loose for 127 yards rushing and two scores. Chicago's Walter Payton gained 62 yards on the ground to become the fourth player in NFL history to rush for over 11,000 yards in a career. The Rams joined New Orleans and San Francisco in a three-way tie for first place in the NFC West, thanks to Miami's 20-17 win at San Francisco. The Cowboys' 27-20 comeback victory over the Eagles insured Dallas of an NFL-record eighteenth winning season and helped the Cowboys keep a one-game lead in the NFC East over Washington, which defeated St. Louis 45-7. James Wilder gained a Tampa Bay record 219 yards rushing and scored on a club-record 75-yard run to lead the Buccaneers to their first win, a 17-12 victory over the Vikings. Despite the loss, Minnesota retained a one-game advantage in the NFC's Central Division over Green Bay and Detroit. Pittsburgh extended its lead in the AFC Central to three games by defeating San Diego 26-3. The Steelers limited the Chargers, who were playing without Dan Fouts, to 218 total yards in winning their sixth straight game. Returning quarterbacks were the difference in two games. Ken Anderson came back after a three-game layoff and guided the Bengals to a 55-14 victory over the Oilers. Jim Plunkett relieved injured Marc Wilson in the third quarter and directed scoring drives of 85 and 75 yards to lead the Raiders over the Chiefs 28-20. Staying just one game back of Los Angeles in the AFC West were Seattle and Denver. The Seahawks beat the Broncos 27-19 thanks to Curt Warner's 134 yards rushing and Dave Krieg's pair of touchdown passes. A tight race also developed in the AFC East where Baltimore and New England were one game behind. The Colts surprised the Jets 17-14 to end a three-game losing streak to New York. Meanwhile, in Foxboro, the Patriots used two touchdown receptions from rookie Clarence Weathers to ignite a 21-7 victory over the Bills and complete their first season-sweep over Buffalo since 1978.

**SUNDAY, NOVEMBER 6**

**New Orleans 27, Atlanta 10**—At Louisiana Superdome, attendance 67,062. Hokie Gajan ran for a pair of touchdowns and George Rogers carried 20 times for 137 yards to power the Saints over the Falcons. Gajan's nine-yard scoring run followed Wayne Wilson's five-yard touchdown and put New Orleans ahead for good, 14-10. Dave Wilson started in place of injured Ken Stabler and fired a 19-yard touchdown pass to Tyrone Young. Rickey Jackson's fumble recovery set up Gajan's second score, an 11-yard run late in the fourth quarter. The Saints recorded five sacks in snapping the Falcons' two-game win streak.

| | | | | | | |
|---|---|---|---|---|---|---|
| Atlanta | 0 | 10 | 0 | 0 | — | 10 |
| New Orleans | 0 | 7 | 7 | 13 | — | 27 |

Atl — Andrews 1 run (Luckhurst kick)
Atl — FG Luckhurst 43
NO — W. Wilson 5 run (Andersen kick)
NO — Gajan 9 run (Andersen kick)
NO — Young 19 pass from D. Wilson (kick failed)
NO — Gajan 11 run (Andersen kick)

**Baltimore 17, New York Jets 14**—At Shea Stadium, attendance 53,323. Curtis Dickey scored a pair of touchdowns 3:46 apart to help the Colts halt a three-game losing streak to the Jets. New York took a 7-3 lead early in the third quarter but Johnny Hector's second fumble of the day set up Dickey's one-yard scoring run to give Baltimore a 10-7 edge. Dickey added the clinching touchdown, a 25-yard reception, when Mike Pagel's pass was deflected by the Jets' Bobby Jackson into Dickey's hands. Mark Gastineau tied a personal best with four sacks.

| | | | | | | |
|---|---|---|---|---|---|---|
| Baltimore | 3 | 0 | 7 | 7 | — | 17 |
| New York Jets | 0 | 0 | 7 | 7 | — | 14 |

Balt — FG Allegre 42
NYJ — Jones 50 pass from Todd (Leahy kick)
Balt — Dickey 1 run (Allegre kick)
Balt — Dickey 25 pass from Pagel (Allegre kick)
NYJ — Jones 10 pass from Todd (Leahy kick)

**New England 21, Buffalo 7**—At Sullivan Stadium, attendance 42,604. Steve Grogan and Clarence Weathers combined for two touchdowns as the Patriots swept the Bills for the first time since 1978. Grogan's 40-yard scoring pass to Weathers capped an 80-yard drive and helped the Patriots to a 14-0 halftime lead. Weathers and Grogan hooked-up on a 58-yard bomb on New England's first possession of the third quarter to put the game out of reach. Rick Sanford had a pair of interceptions, the first of which set up Tony Collins' four-yard scoring run in the first quarter. The Patriots gained 450 total yards compared to the Bills' 263.

| | | | | | | |
|---|---|---|---|---|---|---|
| Buffalo | 0 | 0 | 0 | 7 | — | 7 |
| New England | 0 | 14 | 7 | 0 | — | 21 |

NE — Collins 4 run (Steinfort kick)
NE — C. Weathers 40 pass from Grogan (Steinfort kick)
NE — C. Weathers 58 pass from Grogan (Steinfort kick)
Buff — Brammer 1 pass from Ferguson (Danelo kick)

**Los Angeles Rams 21, Chicago 14**—At Anaheim Stadium, attendance 53,010. Eric Dickerson's club-record 34 carries for 127 yards and two touchdowns overshadowed a pair of milestones by the Bears' Walter Payton and helped the Rams snap a two-game losing streak. Dickerson's seven-yard run and Preston Dennard's 21-yard touchdown reception (1:06 apart) gave Los Angeles a 14-0 halftime lead, which they never relinquished. Payton ran for 62 yards to become the fourth player in NFL history to top 11,000 yards (11,020) in a career, and caught four passes for 32 yards to total 14,440 combined yards, second only to Jim Brown's 15,459. Both Chicago touchdowns were scored by Bears quarterback Jim McMahon—on an 18-yard pass reception from Payton and a four-yard run.

| | | | | | | |
|---|---|---|---|---|---|---|
| Chicago | 0 | 0 | 0 | 14 | — | 14 |
| L.A. Rams | 0 | 14 | 0 | 7 | — | 21 |

Rams — Dickerson 7 run (Nelson kick)
Rams — Dennard 21 pass from Ferragamo (Nelson kick)
Chi — McMahon 18 pass from Payton (B. Thomas kick)
Rams — Dickerson 1 run (Nelson kick)
Chi — McMahon 4 run (B. Thomas kick)

**Cincinnati 55, Houston 14**—At Astrodome, attendance 39,706. Pete Johnson ran for three touchdowns and Ken Anderson returned to the starting lineup after a three-week layoff to guide the Bengals to their third straight win. Cincinnati opened a 34-0 halftime lead on Johnson's three scoring runs (five, one, and one yards), Anderson's 14-yard pass to Cris Collinsworth, and Jim Breech's two field goals (44 and 29 yards). The Bengals recorded four sacks, had three interceptions, and recovered four fumbles, including Reggie Williams' 59-yard return for a score.

| | | | | | | |
|---|---|---|---|---|---|---|
| Cincinnati | 24 | 10 | 14 | 7 | — | 55 |
| Houston | 0 | 0 | 0 | 14 | — | 14 |

Cin — Johnson 5 run (Breech kick)
Cin — Collinsworth 14 pass from Anderson (Breech kick)
Cin — FG Breech 44
Cin — Johnson 1 run (Breech kick)
Cin — Johnson 1 run (Browner pass from Kreider)
Cin — FG Breech 29
Cin — Wilson 1 run (Breech kick)
Cin — Williams 59 fumble recovery return (Breech kick)
Hou — Smith 21 pass from Luck (Kempf kick)
Cin — Kinnebrew 3 run (Breech kick)
Hou — Brown 1 run (Kempf kick)

**Green Bay 35, Cleveland 21**—At Milwaukee County Stadium, attendance 54,089. Lynn Dickey completed 20 of 33 passes for 228 yards and four touchdowns to help the Packers end a two-game losing streak and even their record at 5-5. Dickey's scoring passes of 18 yards to John Jefferson and 4 yards to Paul Coffman gave Green Bay a 14-7 lead. Cornerback Tim Lewis, making his first start, intercepted two passes to set up Dickey's next two touchdowns, a 10-yarder to Gary Lewis and a 2-yarder to Gerry Ellis. Jefferson caught seven passes for 102 yards, the twenty-third 100-yard game of his career.

| | | | | | |
|---|---|---|---|---|---|
| Cleveland | 7 | 0 | 0 | 14 | — 21 |
| Green Bay | 7 | 14 | 7 | 7 | — 35 |

GB — Jefferson 18 pass from Dickey (Stenerud kick)
Cle — Golic 7 interception return (Bahr kick)
GB — Coffman 4 pass from Dickey (Stenerud kick)
GB — G. Lewis 10 pass from Dickey (Stenerud kick)
GB — Ellis 2 pass from Dickey (Stenerud kick)
Cle — Jones 20 pass from Sipe (Bahr kick)
Cle — Walker 19 pass from Sipe (Bahr kick)
GB — Ellis 25 run (Stenerud kick)

**Seattle 27, Denver 19**—At Kingdome, attendance 61,189. Dave Krieg accounted for three touchdowns and Curt Warner rushed for 134 yards on 25 carries as the Seahawks downed the Broncos 27-19. Following a pair of Norm Johnson field goals (42, 18 yards), Krieg hit Steve Largent on a 14-yard touchdown pass and added a 30-yarder to Paul Johns for a 20-3 third-quarter lead. After Denver closed to 20-12, Krieg scrambled 10 yards for a score to give Seattle a 27-12 advantage. Largent's fifty-sixth career touchdown gave him 336 points, surpassing Efren Herrera's club record of 331.

| | | | | | |
|---|---|---|---|---|---|
| Denver | 0 | 3 | 6 | 10 | — 19 |
| Seattle | 6 | 0 | 14 | 7 | — 27 |

Sea — FG N. Johnson 42
Sea — FG N. Johnson 18
Den — FG Karlis 38
Sea — Largent 14 pass from Krieg (N. Johnson kick)
Sea — Johns 30 pass from Krieg (N. Johnson kick)
Den — Winder 1 run (kick failed)
Den — FG Karlis 43
Sea — Krieg 10 run (N. Johnson kick)
Den — Watson 25 pass from Elway (Karlis kick)

**Los Angeles Raiders 28, Kansas City 20**—At Arrowhead Stadium, attendance 75,497. Jim Plunkett came off the bench to direct two long scoring drives and rally the Raiders over the Chiefs 28-20. Plunkett replaced injured starter Marc Wilson in the third quarter and guided Los Angeles on an 85-yard march capped by Marcus Allen's one-yard touchdown run for a 14-13 lead. The Raiders increased their lead to 21-13 as Plunkett fired a 19-yard pass to Dokie Williams with 3:49 left. Rod Martin's 40-yard interception return for a touchdown with three seconds remaining ended Kansas City's final hope.

| | | | | | |
|---|---|---|---|---|---|
| L.A. Raiders | 7 | 0 | 0 | 21 | — 28 |
| Kansas City | 0 | 6 | 7 | 7 | — 20 |

Raiders — Hawkins 15 pass from Wilson (Bahr kick)
KC — FG Lowery 54
KC — FG Lowery 48
KC — Brown 1 run (Lowery kick)
Raiders — Allen 1 run (Bahr kick)
KC — K. Thomas 2 pass from Kenney (Lowery kick)
Raiders — Williams 19 pass from Plunkett (Bahr kick)
Raiders — Martin 40 interception return (Bahr kick)

**Miami 20, San Francisco 17**—At Candlestick Park, attendance 57,832. Dan Marino passed for two touchdowns and Doug Betters recovered two fumbles in the closing minutes to help the Dolphins extend their unbeaten streak to four games. Marino teamed with Nat Moore on first-half scoring passes of 24 and 19 yards to tie the game 14-14 at halftime. Uwe von Schamann kicked a pair of field goals (35 and 23 yards); the last, 6:26 into the fourth quarter, proved decisive. Betters also had 1 sack to increase his NFL lead to 14.

| | | | | | |
|---|---|---|---|---|---|
| Miami | 7 | 7 | 3 | 3 | — 20 |
| San Francisco | 7 | 7 | 0 | 3 | — 17 |

SF — Clark 39 pass from Montana (Wersching kick)
Mia — Moore 24 pass from Marino (von Schamann kick)
SF — Craig 10 run (Wersching kick)
Mia — Moore 19 pass from Marino (von Schamann kick)
Mia — FG von Schamann 35
SF — FG Wersching 36
Mia — FG von Schamann 23

**Dallas 27, Philadelphia 20**—At Veterans Stadium, attendance 71,236. Danny White completed 21 of 24 passes (268 yards, two touchdowns) for 87.5 percent, third-highest in NFL history, to assure the Cowboys of their NFL-record eighteenth straight winning season. Dallas rebounded from a 10-0 deficit by scoring 20 unanswered points on Rafael Septien field goals of 39 and 23 yards, White's 12-yard scoring pass to Timmy Newsome, and Tony Dorsett's 29-yard run. Tony Hill's 18-yard touchdown reception put the Cowboys ahead 27-13 with 2:51 to play. Dallas matched its previous best start (9-1 in 1976) with the victory.

| | | | | | |
|---|---|---|---|---|---|
| Dallas | 0 | 10 | 10 | 7 | — 27 |
| Philadelphia | 7 | 3 | 3 | 7 | — 20 |

Phil — Quick 20 pass from Jaworski (Franklin kick)
Phil — FG Franklin 19
Dall — FG Septien 39
Dall — Newsome 12 pass from D. White (Septien kick)
Dall — FG Septien 23
Dall — Dorsett 29 run (Septien kick)
Phil — FG Franklin 37
Dall — T. Hill 18 pass from D. White (Septien kick)
Phil — Young 71 pass from Jaworski (Franklin kick)

**Washington 45, St. Louis 7**—At Robert F. Kennedy Stadium, attendance 51,380. Mel Kaufman's 70-yard interception return for a score and Vernon Dean's fumble recovery in the end zone for another touchdown helped the Redskins register a 45-7 win over the Cardinals. Washington gained 209 yards rushing, including 99 by Joe Washington and 58 by John Riggins, who scored on a pair of two-yard runs. The Redskins sacked Cardinals quarterback Neil Lomax five times and limited St. Louis to 267 total yards.

| | | | | | |
|---|---|---|---|---|---|
| St. Louis | 0 | 0 | 7 | 0 | — 7 |
| Washington | 7 | 10 | 21 | 7 | — 45 |

Wash — Dean recovered fumble in end zone (Moseley kick)
Wash — Riggins 2 run (Moseley kick)
Wash — FG Moseley 42
Wash — Kaufman 70 interception return (Moseley kick)
StL — Green 23 pass from Lomax (O'Donoghue kick)
Wash — Riggins 2 run (Moseley kick)
Wash — Evans 1 run (Moseley kick)
Wash — Giaquinto 1 run (Moseley kick)

**Pittsburgh 26, San Diego 3**—At Three Rivers Stadium, attendance 58,191. Mel Blount scored the third touchdown of his 14-year career and the Pittsburgh defense set up two of Gary Anderson's four field goals as the Steelers extended their lead in the AFC Central to three games. Walter Abercrombie scored on a six-yard run 2:17 into the game and Blount followed an Anderson field goal (45 yards) with a three-yard fumble recovery for a score. Mike Merriweather's interception and Keith Gary's fumble recovery later set up Anderson field goals from 49 and 42 yards. Anderson also had a 30-yarder in the second period.

| | | | | | |
|---|---|---|---|---|---|
| San Diego | 0 | 3 | 0 | 0 | — 3 |
| Pittsburgh | 17 | 3 | 3 | 3 | — 26 |

Pitt — Abercrombie 6 run (Anderson kick)
Pitt — FG Anderson 45
Pitt — Blount 3 fumble recovery return (Anderson kick)
SD — FG Benirschke 39
Pitt — FG Anderson 30
Pitt — FG Anderson 49
Pitt — FG Anderson 42

**Tampa Bay 17, Minnesota 12**—At Metrodome, attendance 59,239. James Wilder rushed for a team-record 219 yards on 31 carries and scored the winning touchdown to lead the Buccaneers to their first win. Wilder's decisive 75-yard scoring run in the third quarter was also a club record. Minnesota jumped to a 9-0 lead but Dave Logan's 54-yard fumble recovery return for a touchdown cut the score to 9-7 at halftime. The Vikings' first loss to an NFC Central foe cut their division lead to one game.

| | | | | | |
|---|---|---|---|---|---|
| Tampa Bay | 0 | 7 | 7 | 3 | — 17 |
| Minnesota | 7 | 2 | 0 | 3 | — 12 |

Minn — Brown 1 run (Ricardo kick)
Minn — Safety, blocked punt out of end zone
TB — Logan 54 fumble recovery return (Capece kick)
TB — Wilder 75 run (Capece kick)
TB — FG Capece 29
Minn — FG Ricardo 21

**MONDAY, NOVEMBER 7**

**Detroit 15, New York Giants 9**—At Pontiac Silverdome, attendance 68,985. Billy Sims scored the game's only touchdown, a two-yard run in the first quarter, and rushed for 86 yards as the Lions won for the fourth time in their last five games. Detroit's defense recovered one fumble, intercepted three passes (including two by Bruce McNorton in the final five minutes), and recorded a safety when Mike Fanning tackled Rich Umphrey in the end zone. Rookie Ali Haji-Sheikh kicked three field goals for the Giants, including his second 56-yarder of the year.

| | | | | | |
|---|---|---|---|---|---|
| New York Giants | 3 | 3 | 3 | 0 | — 9 |
| Detroit | 7 | 5 | 0 | 3 | — 15 |

NYG — FG Haji-Sheikh 27
Det — Sims 2 run (Murray kick)
Det — FG Murray 35
Det — Safety, Fanning tackled Umphrey in end zone
NYG — FG Haji-Sheikh 56
NYG — FG Haji-Sheikh 35
Det — FG Murray 32

## ELEVENTH WEEK SUMMARY

With five weeks remaining there were ties for first place in all three NFC divisions as well as in the AFC East. The Chargers opened a 24-6 lead and held on to defeat the Cowboys 24-23. The Redskins seized the opportunity to gain a first-place tie with Dallas in the NFC East by easily beating the Giants 33-17. The Packers, going up against NFC Central-leading Minnesota, gave themselves a share of the division lead by outlasting the Vikings 29-21. In the NFC West, the Saints fell victim to the 49ers 27-0, and dropped from a three-way tie for the lead with San Francisco and the Rams. Los Angeles kept pace with the 49ers with a 36-13 victory over the Falcons on Monday night as both Eric Dickerson (146) and Barry Redden (110) ran for over 100 yards. Joe Ferguson's third scoring pass of the game, a 33-yarder to Joe Cribbs with 22 seconds remaining, brought the Bills a 24-17 win over the Jets and a share of the AFC East lead with the Dolphins. Miami was beaten by the Patriots 17-6. Pittsburgh, victorious for the seventh straight time with a 24-13 win over Baltimore, extended its lead to three games in the AFC Central. Cleveland, a distant second in that division, claimed its first shutout since 1974 by blanking Tampa Bay 20-0. The Raiders stretched their AFC West advantage to two games with a 22-20 defeat of the Broncos and with a little help from the NFC. Chris Bahr's 39-yard field goal with four seconds left helped the Raiders gain their eighth win. Meanwhile, Neil Lomax and Roy Green teamed up on four touchdown passes as the Cardinals defeated the Seahawks 33-28. Starting his first NFL game at quarterback for Houston, second-year man Oliver Luck threw two touchdown passes to lead the Oilers to a 27-17 win over the Lions. The victory was Houston's first of the season and snapped a 17-game losing streak. Kansas City ended a two-game losing streak with a 20-15 victory over Cincinnati, while the Bears did the same by downing the Eagles 17-14.

**SUNDAY, NOVEMBER 13**

**Buffalo 24, New York Jets 17**—At Shea Stadium, attendance 48,513. Joe Ferguson threw three touchdown passes, including a 33-yarder to Joe Cribbs with 22 seconds remaining, to conclude the Bills' comeback. Ferguson, who completed 24 of 41 for 262 yards, brought Buffalo back from a 14-0 deficit to tie the game with scoring passes to Mike Mosley (10 yards) and Byron Franklin (19). The teams exchanged field goals before Ferguson guided the Bills 75 yards in five plays for the game-winner.

| | | | | | |
|---|---|---|---|---|---|
| Buffalo | 0 | 0 | 14 | 10 | — 24 |
| New York Jets | 0 | 14 | 3 | 0 | — 17 |

NYJ — Crutchfield 1 run (Leahy kick)
NYJ — Lynn 42 interception return (Leahy kick)
Buff — Mosley 10 pass from Ferguson (Danelo kick)
Buff — Franklin 19 pass from Ferguson (Danelo kick)
NYJ — FG Leahy 48
Buff — FG Danelo 30
Buff — Cribbs 33 pass from Ferguson (Danelo kick)

**Kansas City 20, Cincinnati 15**—At Arrowhead Stadium, attendance 44,711. Bill Kenney accounted for two touchdowns and Nick Lowery kicked a pair of field goals as the Chiefs ended a two-game losing streak. Kenney's one-yard scoring run, sandwiched between Lowery field goals of 36 and 43 yards, gave Kansas City a 13-6 halftime lead. He added a 21-yard touchdown pass to Willie Scott in the third quarter to complete an 80-yard drive. Mike Bell had three of the Chiefs' seven sacks.

| | | | | | |
|---|---|---|---|---|---|
| Cincinnati | 3 | 3 | 3 | 6 | — 15 |
| Kansas City | 3 | 10 | 7 | 0 | — 20 |

KC — FG Lowery 36
Cin — FG Breech 23
KC — Kenney 1 run (Lowery kick)
Cin — FG Breech 31
KC — FG Lowery 43
Cin — FG Breech 23
KC — Scott 21 pass from Kenney (Lowery kick)
Cin — Collinsworth 5 pass from Anderson (kick blocked)

**San Diego 24, Dallas 23**—At San Diego Jack Murphy Stadium, attendance 46,192. Derrie Nelson returned a blocked punt for a score and Ed Luther passed for 340 yards to help the Chargers end a four-game losing streak. Nelson's 21-yard touchdown return after Miles McPherson blocked a Danny White punt was San Diego's first off a blocked kick since 1961. Luther completed 26 of 43 passes, including an 18-yard touchdown to Pete Holohan that put the Chargers on top 24-6. Dallas came back on a pair of Danny White (31 of 47 for 300 yards) scoring passes, but Rafael Septien's missed extra point following the Cowboys' first touchdown proved to be the difference.

| | | | | | |
|---|---|---|---|---|---|
| Dallas | 0 | 6 | 3 | 14 | — 23 |
| San Diego | 7 | 10 | 7 | 0 | — 24 |

SD — Nelson 21 return of blocked punt (Benirschke kick)
SD — Muncie 2 run (Benirschke kick)
Dall — Pearson 16 pass from D. White (kick failed)
SD — FG Benirschke 37
SD — Holohan 18 pass from Luther (Benirschke kick)
Dall — FG Septien 37
Dall — T. Hill 35 pass from D. White (Septien kick)
Dall — DuPree 4 pass from D. White (Septien kick)

**Los Angeles Raiders 22, Denver 20**—At Memorial Coliseum, attendance 51,945. Chris Bahr's 39-yard field goal with four seconds remaining gave the Raiders a 22-20 win and two-game lead in the AFC West. Denver opened a 10-0 first-quarter lead but Los Angeles countered with 19 consecutive points. Bahr connected from 28 and 42 yards and Frank Hawkins' 17-yard touchdown run followed Marcus Allen's seven-yard score for a 19-10 Raiders advantage. The Broncos regained the lead, 20-19 with 58 seconds left, on John Elways' four-yard run, but Jim Plunkett completed three straight passes to Todd Christensen (eight receptions for 114 yards) for 44 yards to set up Bahr's winning kick.

| | | | | | |
|---|---|---|---|---|---|
| Denver | 10 | 0 | 0 | 10 | — 20 |
| L.A. Raiders | 0 | 6 | 7 | 9 | — 22 |

Den — FG Karlis 23
Den — Chavous recovered fumble in end zone (Karlis kick)

Raiders — FG Bahr 28
Raiders — FG Bahr 42
Raiders — Allen 7 run (Bahr kick)
Raiders — Hawkins 17 run (kick failed)
Den — FG Karlis 22
Den — Elway 4 run (Karlis kick)
Raiders — FG Bahr 39

**Houston 27, Detroit 17**—At Astrodome, attendance 40,660. Oliver Luck, making his first NFL start, passed for two touchdowns to help the Oilers snap a 17-game losing streak. Luck completed 18 of 26 for 189 yards and directed three consecutive second-half scoring drives to rally Houston from a 17-10 deficit. Luck's 13-yard scoring pass to Chris Dressel tied the score, and Larry Moriarty's four-yard touchdown run gave the Oilers the lead for good, 24-17. Florian Kempf added a 21-yard field goal to finish the scoring. Billy Sims rushed for 105 yards and scored his thirty-ninth career touchdown to break Terry Barr's previous Detroit record of 38. It was the Oilers' first win since they defeated Seattle 23-21 on September 19, 1982.

| | | | | | | |
|---|---|---|---|---|---|---|
| Detroit | 0 | 10 | 7 | 0 | — | 17 |
| Houston | 3 | 7 | 14 | 3 | — | 27 |

Hou — FG Kempf 47
Det — Sims 1 run (Murray kick)
Det — FG Murray 35
Hou — McCloskey 13 pass from Luck (Kempf kick)
Det — Jones 3 pass from Danielson (Murray kick)
Hou — Dressel 13 pass from Luck (Kempf kick)
Hou — Moriarty 4 run (Kempf kick)
Hou — FG Kempf 21

**Green Bay 29, Minnesota 21**—At Metrodome, attendance 60,113. Lynn Dickey's 19-yard touchdown pass to James Lofton with 2:12 to play ensured the victory and gave the Packers a share of the NFC Central lead. Green Bay opened a 19-0 lead on touchdowns by Mike Meade (one-yard run) and John Jefferson (five-yard pass), Jan Stenerud's 46-yard field goal, and Greg Boyd's safety. Stenerud's second field goal, from 40 yards, gave the Packers a 22-7 lead, but the Vikings closed the score to 22-21. Darrin Nelson became the fourteenth NFL player to rush for 100 yards (119) and catch passes for 100 yards (137) in the same game. Nelson's 278 total yards broke Chuck Foreman's previous club record of 265 set in 1976.

| | | | | | | |
|---|---|---|---|---|---|---|
| Green Bay | 10 | 9 | 3 | 7 | — | 29 |
| Minnesota | 0 | 0 | 14 | 7 | — | 21 |

GB — FG Stenerud 46
GB — Meade 1 run (Stenerud kick)
GB — Jefferson 5 pass from Dickey (Stenerud kick)
GB — Safety, Boyd tackled Dils in end zone
Minn — Young 1 run (Ricardo kick)
GB — FG Stenerud 40
Minn — Young 4 run (Ricardo kick)
Minn — Galbreath 4 run (Ricardo kick)
GB — Lofton 19 pass from Dickey (Ricardo kick)

**New England 17, Miami 6**—At Sullivan Stadium, attendance 60,771. Steve Grogan and Tony Collins ran for touchdowns, and the New England defense held Miami to 207 total yards as the Patriots ended the Dolphins' four-game win streak. Grogan's first-quarter score capped a 64-yard march and Collins' four-yard run in the second period completed a 74-yard drive. New England controlled the ball for 13:05 of the third quarter and added Fred Steinfort's 20-yard field goal to finish the scoring. The Patriots gained 386 total yards.

| | | | | | | |
|---|---|---|---|---|---|---|
| Miami | 0 | 6 | 0 | 0 | — | 6 |
| New England | 7 | 7 | 3 | 0 | — | 17 |

NE — Grogan 1 run (Steinfort kick)
Mia — FG von Schamann 52
Mia — FG von Schamann 29
NE — Collins 4 run (Steinfort kick)
NE — FG Steinfort 20

**San Francisco 27, New Orleans 0**—At Candlestick Park, attendance 40,022. Joe Montana completed three touchdown passes and Fred Dean had six of San Francisco's nine quarterback sacks as the 49ers shut out the Saints 27-0. Montana (26 of 43 for 283 yards) threw scoring strikes to Eason Ramson (1 yard), Dwight Clark (14), and Russ Francis (2). Ray Wersching connected on field goals from 33 and 25 yards to complete the scoring. San Francisco stopped a two-game losing streak by holding New Orleans to 129 total yards, 74 rushing and 55 passing.

| | | | | | | |
|---|---|---|---|---|---|---|
| New Orleans | 0 | 0 | 0 | 0 | — | 0 |
| San Francisco | 7 | 10 | 7 | 3 | — | 27 |

SF — Ramson 1 pass from Montana (Wersching kick)
SF — Clark 14 pass from Montana (Wersching kick)
SF — FG Wersching 33
SF — Francis 2 pass from Montana (Wersching kick)
SF — FG Wersching 25

**Chicago 17, Philadelphia 14**—At Soldier Field, attendance 47,524. Bob Thomas' 22-yard field goal early in the fourth quarter proved decisive as the Bears defeated the Eagles 17-14. Jim McMahon's 43-yard scoring pass to Dennis McKinnon and 2-yarder to Emery Moorehead gave Chicago a 14-7 halftime lead. Philadelphia took the second-half kickoff and drove 79 yards for the tying score—a five-yard touchdown pass from Ron Jaworski to Tony Woodruff. Walter Payton rushed for 131 yards on 23 carries for the Bears.

| | | | | | | |
|---|---|---|---|---|---|---|
| Philadelphia | 7 | 0 | 7 | 0 | — | 14 |
| Chicago | 0 | 14 | 0 | 3 | — | 17 |

Phil — Quick 47 pass from Jaworski (Franklin kick)
Chi — McKinnon 43 pass from McMahon (B. Thomas kick)
Chi — Moorehead 2 pass from McMahon (B. Thomas kick)
Phil — Woodruff 5 pass from Jaworski (Franklin kick)
Chi — FG B. Thomas 22

**Pittsburgh 24, Baltimore 13**—At Memorial Stadium, attendance 57,319. A pair of Cliff Stoudt touchdown passes helped the Steelers record their seventh consecutive win. Stoudt completed 13 of 23 passes for 173 yards, including 6 to Calvin Sweeney for 104 yards and a seven-yard touchdown. Donnie Shell's fourth-quarter interception set up Bennie Cunningham's two-yard touchdown reception to finish the scoring. Curtis Dickey's five-yard touchdown run was the first allowed by Pittsburgh in 11 quarters.

| | | | | | | |
|---|---|---|---|---|---|---|
| Pittsburgh | 7 | 10 | 0 | 7 | — | 24 |
| Baltimore | 3 | 3 | 7 | 0 | — | 13 |

Pitt — Abercrombie 11 run (Anderson kick)
Balt — FG Allegre 46
Balt — FG Allegre 37
Pitt — FG Anderson 42
Pitt — Sweeney 7 pass from Stoudt (Anderson kick)
Balt — Dickey 5 run (Allegre kick)
Pitt — Cunningham 2 pass from Stoudt (Anderson kick)

**St. Louis 33, Seattle 28**—At Busch Memorial Stadium, attendance 33,280. Neil Lomax and Roy Green combined for four touchdown passes to lead the Cardinals over the Seahawks 33-28. Lomax completed 21 of 27 for 253 yards, including scoring passes to Green of 15, 23, 7, and 63 yards in the first half for a 28-21 halftime edge. Seattle quarterback Dave Krieg's third touchdown pass of the game, a 45-yarder to Steve Largent, tied the score, but Neil O'Donoghue's 33-yard field goal was the clincher. Dave Galloway had three of the Cardinals' six sacks and tackled Krieg in the end zone for a safety. Zack Dixon scored the Seahawks' first touchdown on a 94-yard kickoff return, the first in Seattle history.

| | | | | | | |
|---|---|---|---|---|---|---|
| Seattle | 7 | 14 | 0 | 7 | — | 28 |
| St. Louis | 7 | 21 | 0 | 5 | — | 33 |

StL — Green 15 pass from Lomax (O'Donoghue kick)
Sea — Dixon 94 kickoff return (N. Johnson kick)
StL — Green 23 pass from Lomax (O'Donoghue kick)
StL — Green 7 pass from Lomax (O'Donoghue kick)
Sea — Largent 15 pass from Krieg (N. Johnson kick)
StL — Green 63 pass from Lomax (O'Donoghue kick)
Sea — Largent 14 pass from Krieg (N. Johnson kick)
Sea — Largent 45 pass from Krieg (N. Johnson kick)
StL — FG O'Donoghue 33
StL — Safety, Galloway tackled Krieg in end zone

**Cleveland 20, Tampa Bay 0**—At Cleveland Stadium, attendance 56,091. Mike Pruitt ran for two touchdowns and Matt Bahr added a pair of field goals as the Browns recorded their first shutout since 1974. Bahr connected from 27 and 42 yards, while Pruitt's pair of one-yard runs came in the first and fourth quarters. Cleveland's last shutout was a 7-0 victory over San Francisco on December 1, 1974. James Wilder, the Buccaneers' leading rusher, was lost for the remainder of the season with broken ribs.

| | | | | | | |
|---|---|---|---|---|---|---|
| Tampa Bay | 0 | 0 | 0 | 0 | — | 0 |
| Cleveland | 10 | 0 | 3 | 7 | — | 20 |

Cle — FG Bahr 27
Cle — Pruitt 1 run (Bahr kick)
Cle — FG Bahr 42
Cle — Pruitt 1 run (Bahr kick)

**Washington 33, New York Giants 17**—At Giants Stadium, attendance 71,482. John Riggins ran for two touchdowns and Mark Moseley kicked four field goals as the Redskins gained a share of first place in the NFC East. Dexter Manley's interception set up Riggins' first of two two-yard scoring runs and Moseley followed with field goals of 47, 33, 38, and 32 yards for a 19-3 lead. Washington's 33 points broke a 17-year-old club record for points in a season (351 in 1966). Earnest Gray caught eight passes for 145 yards and two touchdowns for the Giants.

| | | | | | | |
|---|---|---|---|---|---|---|
| Washington | 13 | 3 | 10 | 7 | — | 33 |
| New York Giants | 3 | 0 | 0 | 14 | — | 17 |

Wash — Riggins 2 run (Moseley kick)
Wash — FG Moseley 47
NYG — FG Haji-Sheikh 45
Wash — FG Moseley 33
Wash — FG Moseley 38
Wash — FG Moseley 32
Wash — Brown 18 pass from Theismann (Moseley kick)
Wash — Riggins 2 run (Moseley kick)
NYG — Gray 6 pass from Brunner (Haji-Sheikh kick)
NYG — Gray 22 pass from Brunner (Haji-Sheikh kick)

**MONDAY, NOVEMBER 14**
**Los Angeles Rams 36, Atlanta 13**—At Atlanta-Fulton County Stadium, attendance 31,202. Eric Dickerson rushed for 146 yards and two scores, and Barry Redden added 110 yards and one touchdown to become the first Rams to go over 100 yards rushing in the same game in 1983. Dickerson's runs of one and seven yards gave him a club-record 19 touchdowns for the season. Vince Ferragamo completed 15 of 22 passes for 173 yards and had scoring passes of 61 yards to Preston Dennard and 9 yards to George Farmer. Atlanta's William Andrews gained 52 yards on 14 carries to go over the 1,000-yard mark for the season (1,007).

| | | | | | | |
|---|---|---|---|---|---|---|
| L.A. Rams | 7 | 7 | 13 | 9 | — | 36 |
| Atlanta | 3 | 3 | 0 | 7 | — | 13 |

Atl — FG Luckhurst 31
Rams — Dennard 61 pass from Ferragamo (Nelson kick)
Rams — Dickerson 1 run (Nelson kick)
Atl — FG Luckhurst 23
Rams — Dickerson 7 run (run failed)
Rams — Farmer 9 pass from Ferragamo (Nelson kick)
Rams — FG Nelson 27
Atl — Riggs 1 run (Luckhurst kick)
Rams — Redden 40 run (kicked failed)

## TWELFTH WEEK SUMMARY

Four shutouts and a last-second miracle win marked the three-quarter point in the season. Dan Marino and Mark Duper connected on a 85-yard scoring bomb and Mark Clayton scored on a 60-yard punt return 42 seconds later as the Dolphins beat the Colts 37-0. Walter Payton rushed for 106 yards to pass O.J. Simpson for third place on the all-time rushing chart and help lead the Bears to a 27-0 blanking of the Buccaneers. Cleveland got two interceptions from Tom Cousineau and 136 yards rushing from Mike Pruitt to record its second straight shutout, 30-0 over New England. The Patriots, who suffered their first scoreless game since 1975, also lost quarterback Steve Grogan with a broken leg. The Giants ended a seven-game winless streak with a 23-0 victory over the Eagles. New York's defense held Philadelphia to 79 yards total offense and let the Eagles cross midfield only once. Steve Bartkowski's 47-yard desperation pass to Billy "White Shoes" Johnson proved miraculous when Johnson stretched over the goal line, with no time remaining, to give Atlanta a 28-24 win. Dallas became the first team to clinch a playoff berth, its ninth straight, by downing Kansas City 41-21. The Redskins beat the Rams 42-20 by holding NFL rushing leader Eric Dickerson to just 37 yards. Green Bay opened a 20-3 lead over Detroit but could not hold on and lost 23-20 in overtime after Lynn Dickey left the game with a concussion. The loss dropped the Packers out of first place in the NFC Central. San Diego's Don Coryell hoped his return to St. Louis, where he was head coach from 1973-77, would be a winning one, but Cardinals quarterback Neil Lomax had other plans. Lomax passed for two touchdowns and ran for two more to lead St. Louis to a 44-14 win over the Chargers. Minnesota brought Pittsburgh's seven-game win streak to an end 17-14. The Jets, led by the return of Freeman McNeil after a seven-week layoff, edged the Saints 31-28. Chris Bahr's 36-yard field goal on the final play of the game rescued the Raiders from the Bills 27-24. In Cincinnati, Ken Anderson threw for three scores and Pete Johnson rushed for 137 yards as the Bengals scored on their first six possessions to defeat the Oilers 38-10. Rich Karlis' five field goals helped make Gary Kubiak's first NFL start a winning one, as Denver beat division-rival Seattle 38-27.

**SUNDAY, NOVEMBER 20**
**Miami 37, Baltimore 0**—At Orange Bowl, attendance 54,482. Dan Marino and Mark Duper combined on an 85-yard scoring bomb and Mark Clayton scored on a 60-yard punt return 42 seconds later as the Dolphins blanked the Colts 37-0. Following a scoreless first quarter, Marino (14 of 21 for 240 yards) drove Miami 70 yards, culminating in Andra Franklin's eight-yard touchdown run. Marino added a one-yard run and Woody Bennett's one-yard plunge finished the scoring. Kim Bokamper had two of Miami's six sacks as the Dolphins limited Baltimore to 89 yards rushing and 70 passing.

| | | | | | | |
|---|---|---|---|---|---|---|
| Baltimore | 0 | 0 | 0 | 0 | — | 0 |
| Miami | 0 | 24 | 7 | 6 | — | 37 |

Mia — Franklin 8 run (von Schamann kick)
Mia — FG von Schamann 42
Mia — Duper 85 pass from Marino (von Schamann kick)
Mia — Clayton 60 punt return (von Schamann kick)
Mia — Marino 1 run (von Schamann kick)
Mia — Bennett 1 run (kick blocked)

**Chicago 27, Tampa Bay 0**—At Tampa Stadium, attendance 36,816. Torrential rains didn't hinder Walter Payton as he rushed for 106 yards and scored two touchdowns to lead the Bears to a 27-0 shutout victory. Payton passed the 1,000-yard rushing mark for the seventh time in his career on an eight-yard scoring run in the second quarter. He became the NFL's third-leading career rusher (11,257), passing O.J. Simpson's career mark on a three-yard run in the third period. Matt Suhey added a career-high 112 yards rushing as Chicago gained a total of 273 yards on the ground.

| | | | | | | |
|---|---|---|---|---|---|---|
| Chicago | 0 | 14 | 6 | 7 | — | 27 |
| Tampa Bay | 0 | 0 | 0 | 0 | — | 0 |

Chi — Suhey 2 run (B. Thomas kick)
Chi — Payton 8 run (B. Thomas kick)
Chi — Payton 3 run (kick failed)
Chi — Hartenstine 10 fumble recovery return (B. Thomas kick)

**Cleveland 30, New England 0**—At Sullivan Stadium, attendance 40,987. Mike Pruitt broke loose for 136 yards on 24 carries as the Browns notched their second consecutive shutout for the first time since 1951. Cleveland exploded for 17 points in the second quarter on Chip Banks' 65-yard interception return, Rocky Belk's two-yard touchdown reception from Brian Sipe, and Matt Bahr's 20-yard field goal. Pruitt scored the Browns' final touchdown on a six-yard run. Hanford Dixon and Tom Cousineau each had a pair of interceptions. The Patriots suffered their first shutout in 125 regular season games.

| | | | | | |
|---|---|---|---|---|---|
| Cleveland | 3 | 17 | 3 | 7 | — 30 |
| New England | 0 | 0 | 0 | 0 | — 0 |

Cle — FG Bahr 22
Cle — Banks 65 interception return (Bahr kick)
Cle — Belk 2 pass from Sipe (Bahr kick)
Cle — FG Bahr 20
Cle — FG Bahr 20
Cle — Pruitt 6 run (Bahr kick)

**Detroit 23, Green Bay 20**—At Milwaukee County Stadium, attendance 50,050. Eddie Murray's third field goal of the game, a 37-yarder with 8:30 gone in overtime, helped the Lions even their record at 6-6. The loss knocked the Packers out of first place in the NFC Central. Green Bay opened up a 20-3 lead on a pair of Lynn Dickey touchdown passes and two Jan Stenerud field goals, but Detroit closed to within seven points on Murray's 30-yard field goal and Eric Hipple's 11-yard scoring run. Hipple's nine-yard touchdown pass to Freddie Scott with 6:55 remaining sent the game into overtime. Billy Sims rushed a club-record 36 times for a personal-best 189 yards.

| | | | | | | |
|---|---|---|---|---|---|---|
| Detroit | 3 | 0 | 10 | 7 | 3 | — 23 |
| Green Bay | 7 | 13 | 0 | 0 | 0 | — 20 |

GB — Jefferson 6 pass from Dickey (Stenerud kick)
Det — FG Murray 31
GB — FG Stenerud 36
GB — FG Stenerud 34
GB — Coffman 1 pass from Dickey (Stenerud kick)
Det — Hipple 11 run (Murray kick)
Det — FG Murray 30
Det — Scott 9 pass from Hipple (Murray kick)
Det — FG Murray 37

**Cincinnati 38, Houston 10**—At Riverfront Stadium, attendance 46,375. Ken Anderson threw three touchdown passes and Pete Johnson ran for 137 yards and two touchdowns on 30 carries to lead the Bengals to a 38-10 win. Cincinnati scored on its first six possessions to lead 38-3 at halftime. Anderson's 10 completions in 15 attempts for 177 yards included touchdowns of 16 and 1 yards to Dan Ross and 45 yards to Cris Collinsworth. Johnson added second-quarter scores on runs of 12 and 10 yards and Jim Breech added a 26-yard field goal as the Bengals downed the Oilers for the second time in three weeks.

| | | | | | |
|---|---|---|---|---|---|
| Houston | 3 | 0 | 0 | 7 | — 10 |
| Cincinnati | 17 | 21 | 0 | 0 | — 38 |

Cin — Ross 16 pass from Anderson (Breech kick)
Hou — FG Kempf 34
Cin — Collinsworth 45 pass from Anderson (Breech kick)
Cin — FG Breech 26
Cin — Johnson 12 run (Breech kick)
Cin — Johnson 10 run (Breech kick)
Cin — Ross 1 pass from Anderson (Breech kick)
Hou — Arnold 14 pass from Luck (Kempf kick)

**Dallas 41, Kansas City 21**—At Texas Stadium, attendance 64,103. Tony Dorsett became the ninth NFL player to gain more than 8,000 yards rushing in a career (8,051) as the Cowboys clinched an NFL-record ninth straight playoff berth. Dorsett gained 108 yards on 18 carries for his sixth 1,000-yard season (1,036) and scored on runs of 28 and 32 yards to help Dallas open a 27-0 lead. After the Chiefs closed to 27-14, Timmy Newsome's seven-yard run and Gary Allen's 68-yard punt return for a score put the game out of reach.

| | | | | | |
|---|---|---|---|---|---|
| Kansas City | 0 | 0 | 14 | 7 | — 21 |
| Dallas | 10 | 10 | 7 | 14 | — 41 |

Dall — Springs 1 run (Septien kick)
Dall — FG Septien 25
Dall — Dorsett 28 run (Septien kick)
Dall — FG Septien 40
Dall — Dorsett 32 run (Septien kick)
KC — Carson 13 pass from Kenney (Lowery kick)
KC — Carson 48 pass from Kenney (Lowery kick)
Dall — Newsome 7 run (Septien kick)
Dall — Allen 68 punt return (Septien kick)
KC — Paige 7 pass from Blackledge (Lowery kick)

**Los Angeles Raiders 27, Buffalo 24**—At Rich Stadium, attendance 72,393. Chris Bahr's 36-yard field goal on the game's final play lifted the Raiders over the Bills. Touchdowns by Marcus Allen (four-yard run) and Todd Christensen (15-yard pass) helped Los Angeles to a 24-3 lead, but Buffalo rallied with 21 fourth-quarter points. Matt Kofler replaced injured Bills quarterback Joe Ferguson and led three touchdown drives in a span of 4:13 to tie the score 24-24. Christensen caught seven passes for 86 yards to raise his total to 66 receptions for the season, the most ever by a Raiders tight end. Los Angeles generated 401 yards total offense compared to Buffalo's 184.

| | | | | | |
|---|---|---|---|---|---|
| L.A. Raiders | 7 | 3 | 7 | 10 | — 27 |
| Buffalo | 0 | 3 | 0 | 21 | — 24 |

Raiders — Hawkins 2 run (Bahr kick)
Buff — FG Danelo 48
Raiders — FG Bahr 41
Raiders — Allen 4 run (Bahr kick)
Raiders — Christensen 15 pass from Plunkett (Bahr kick)
Buff — Hunter 23 pass from Kofler (Danelo kick)
Buff — Cribbs 1 run (Danelo kick)
Buff — Tuttle 28 pass from Kofler (Danelo kick)
Raiders — FG Bahr 36

**Minnesota 17, Pittsburgh 14**—At Three Rivers Stadium, attendance 58,417. Steve Dils passed for two touchdowns to help the Vikings halt a three-game losing streak. Pittsburgh scored on the game's opening possession, but Minnesota's defense shut them out on their next 10 series. Dils connected on scoring passes to Sam McCullum (30 yards) and Tony Galbreath (6), and Benny Ricardo kicked a 39-yard field goal to put the Vikings on top 17-7 late in the third quarter. The Steelers cut the margin to 17-14 on Cliff Stoudt's four-yard run, which capped a 96-yard drive. Minnesota had 338 total yards (despite the absence of injured running backs Darrin Nelson and Ted Brown) in halting Pittsburgh's seven-game win streak.

| | | | | | |
|---|---|---|---|---|---|
| Minnesota | 7 | 0 | 10 | 0 | — 17 |
| Pittsburgh | 7 | 0 | 0 | 7 | — 14 |

Pitt — Cunningham 3 pass from Stoudt (Anderson kick)
Minn — McCullum 30 pass from Dils (Ricardo kick)
Minn — Galbreath 6 pass from Dils (Ricardo kick)
Minn — FG Ricardo 39
Pitt — Stoudt 4 run (Anderson kick)

**New York Giants 23, Philadelphia 0**—At Veterans Stadium, attendance 57,977. Butch Woolfolk rushed an NFL-record 43 times for 159 yards and the Giants' defense held Philadelphia to 79 yards total offense (10 rushing, 69 passing) as New York ended a seven-game winless streak. Ali Haji-Sheikh kicked field goals of 25 and 48 yards and Woolfolk scored on an 11-yard touchdown run to give New York a 13-0 halftime lead. Haji-Sheikh kicked a 27-yarder in the third quarter and John Tuggle collected his first NFL touchdown on a seven-yard run to finish the scoring. The Giants controlled the ball for 45:43 and gained 332 yards total offense.

| | | | | | |
|---|---|---|---|---|---|
| New York Giants | 3 | 10 | 3 | 7 | — 23 |
| Philadelphia | 0 | 0 | 0 | 0 | — 0 |

NYG — FG Haji-Sheikh 25
NYG — Woolfolk 11 run (Haji-Sheikh kick)
NYG — FG Haji-Sheikh 48
NYG — FG Haji-Sheikh 27
NYG — Tuggle 7 run (Haji-Sheikh kick)

**St. Louis 44, San Diego 14**—At Busch Memorial Stadium, attendance 40,644. Ottis Anderson rushed for 113 yards on 28 carries and Neil Lomax threw for two touchdowns and ran for two more to lead the Cardinals over the Chargers. The loss spoiled San Diego coach Don Coryell's St. Louis homecoming. Following Lomax's 71-yard touchdown bomb to Pat Tilley, St. Louis capitalized on four San Diego turnovers, all in the second quarter, to open up a 37-0 lead. Fumble recoveries by George Schmitt and Al Baker led to Neil O'Donoghue's 39-yard field goal and Lomax's 11-yard bootleg for a touchdown. The Cardinals also converted interceptions by Baker and Lionel Washington into Doug Marsh's 10-yard scoring reception and a one-yard run by Lomax. Lomax finished the day with 247 yards on 12 of 20 completions while San Diego counterpart Ed Luther hit on 24 of 50 for 338 yards.

| | | | | | |
|---|---|---|---|---|---|
| San Diego | 0 | 7 | 0 | 7 | — 14 |
| St. Louis | 7 | 30 | 7 | 0 | — 44 |

StL — Tilley 71 pass from Lomax (O'Donoghue kick)
StL — FG O'Donoghue 39
StL — Ferrell 11 run (O'Donoghue kick)
StL — Marsh 10 pass from Lomax (O'Donoghue kick)
StL — Lomax 1 run (O'Donoghue kick)
StL — Lomax 11 run (kick failed)
SD — Muncie 1 run (Benirschke kick)
StL — Anderson 1 run (O'Donoghue kick)
SD — Wilson 24 pass from Luther (Benirschke kick)

**Atlanta 28, San Francisco 24**—At Atlanta-Fulton County Stadium, attendance 32,782. Steve Bartkowski's 47-yard desperation pass to Billy Johnson on the game's final play lifted the Falcons over the 49ers 28-24. Johnson (six receptions, 104 yards) caught the tipped pass on the 7-yard line and fought his way into the end zone for the game-winning score. Bartkowski completed 28 of 39 for 301 yards to surpass the 20,000-yard career mark (20,240).

| | | | | | |
|---|---|---|---|---|---|
| San Francisco | 7 | 7 | 3 | 7 | — 24 |
| Atlanta | 0 | 14 | 0 | 14 | — 28 |

SF — Craig 6 run (Wersching kick)
SF — Tyler 8 pass from Montana (Wersching kick)
Atl — Bailey 18 pass from Bartkowski (Luckhurst kick)
Atl — Gaison 64 fumble recovery return (Luckhurst kick)
SF — FG Wersching 25
Atl — Riggs 40 run (Luckhurst kick)
SF — Montana 11 run (Wersching kick)
Atl — Johnson 47 pass from Bartkowski (Luckhurst kick)

**Denver 38, Seattle 27**—At Mile High Stadium, attendance 74,710. Gary Kubiak, making his first NFL start, accounted for two touchdowns and Rich Karlis kicked five field goals (42, 25, 21, 38, and 40 yards) enabling the Broncos to beat the Seahawks. Steve Wilson's first of three interceptions set up Kubiak's 78-yard scoring bomb to Steve Watson to cap a 99-yard drive. And Randy Gradishar's interception led to Kubiak's seven-yard scoring run. Curt Warner rushed for 70 yards to become the first 1,000-yard rusher in Seattle history (1,042). Dave Krieg completed 31 of 42 for a Seahawks record 418 yards. Seattle had eight turnovers and was sacked five times.

| | | | | | |
|---|---|---|---|---|---|
| Seattle | 0 | 7 | 13 | 7 | — 27 |
| Denver | 10 | 10 | 7 | 11 | — 38 |

Den — FG Karlis 42
Den — Watson 78 pass from Kubiak (Karlis kick)
Den — FG Karlis 25
Den — Willhite 24 run (Karlis kick)
Sea — Walker 50 pass from Krieg (N. Johnson kick)
Den — Kubiak 7 run (Karlis kick)
Sea — Hughes 1 run (N. Johnson kick)
Sea — Metzelaars 17 pass from Krieg (kick failed)
Den — FG Karlis 21
Den — FG Karlis 38
Sea — Young 11 pass from Krieg (N. Johnson kick)
Den — Safety, Jones tackled Krieg in end zone
Den — FG Karlis 40

**Washington 42, Los Angeles Rams 20**—At Anaheim Stadium, attendance 63,031. John Riggins scored three rushing touchdowns, Mark Moseley kicked four field goals, and the Redskins' defense held Eric Dickerson to 37 yards rushing as the Redskins beat the Rams 42-20. Washington opened up a 29-6 halftime advantage on two touchdowns by Riggins, Moseley field goals of 42 and 33 yards, Joe Theismann's 26-yard touchdown pass to Charlie Brown (eight receptions, 140 yards), and Charles Mann's safety. The Redskins' offense generated 467 total yards and the defense intercepted four passes in holding the Rams to 191 yards total offense. Riggins' twelfth straight game with a rushing touchdown eclipsed Lenny Moore's previous NFL record of 11.

| | | | | | |
|---|---|---|---|---|---|
| Washington | 10 | 19 | 10 | 3 | — 42 |
| L.A. Rams | 6 | 0 | 0 | 14 | — 20 |

Wash — FG Moseley 42
Rams — D. Hill 12 pass from Ferragamo (kick failed)
Wash — Riggins 1 run (Moseley kick)
Wash — Brown 26 pass from Theismann (Moseley kick)
Wash — Safety, Mann tackled Ferragamo in end zone
Wash — Riggins 1 run (Moseley kick)
Wash — FG Moseley 33
Wash — Riggins 1 run (Moseley kick)
Wash — FG Moseley 32
Wash — FG Moseley 19
Rams — Redden 1 run (Nelson kick)
Rams — Guman 3 pass from Kemp (Nelson kick)

**MONDAY, NOVEMBER 21**

**New York Jets 31, New Orleans 28**—At Louisiana Superdome, attendance 68,606. Kirk Springs' 76-yard punt return for a touchdown with 2:11 remaining lifted the Jets over the Saints. New York trailed 28-14 before Pat Leahy's 37-yard field goal and Richard Todd's 11-yard touchdown pass to Jerome Barkum cut the deficit to 28-24. Morten Andersen's 51-yard field goal attempt that would have sent the game into overtime was wide with 19 seconds left. Lance Mehl led the Jets' defense with a sack, fumble recovery, and 34-yard interception return for a score. Freeman McNeil returned to action after a seven-week layoff and rushed for 86 yards on 20 carries.

| | | | | | |
|---|---|---|---|---|---|
| New York Jets | 7 | 7 | 0 | 17 | — 31 |
| New Orleans | 14 | 0 | 14 | 0 | — 28 |

NO — G. Rogers 14 run (Andersen kick)
NYJ — Mehl 34 interception return (Leahy kick)
NO — Brenner 38 pass from Stabler (Andersen kick)
NYJ — Barber 1 run (Leahy kick)
NO — W. Wilson 1 run (Andersen kick)
NO — G. Rogers 2 run (Andersen kick)
NYJ — FG Leahy 37
NYJ — Barkum 11 pass from Todd (Leahy kick)
NYJ — Springs 76 punt return (Leahy kick)

## THIRTEENTH WEEK SUMMARY

There was no place like home in Week 13 as the 14 home-winners will attest. The Lions surprisingly defeated the Steelers on Thanksgiving Day 45-3, to post their fourth victory in the last five games and gain a share of the lead in the NFC Central. Dallas, in characteristic fashion, fell behind 7-0 to St. Louis, but rebounded to win 35-17 and record its twelfth Thanksgiving Day victory. Washington's 28-24 victory over Philadelphia guaranteed the Redskins a trip to the playoffs. John Riggins ran for two touchdowns to increase his season total to an NFL-record 21 rushing scores. Two overtime games helped produce the second-highest scoring weekend in history (725 points). Seattle beat Kansas City 51-48 on Norm Johnson's 42-yard field goal 1:46 into overtime. The win featured the Seahawk's 531-yard offensive attack led by Curt Warner's club-record 207 rushing yards on 32 carries. The 99 points scored by both teams were the third-highest total in NFL history. Atlanta grabbed its second comeback win in as many weeks. Kenny Johnson returned an interception 31 yards for a touchdown (his second scoring interception of the game), 2:13 into overtime, to give the Falcons a 47-41 victory. Brian Sipe threw three touchdown passes to power the Browns 41-23 victory over the Colts. The win helped Cleveland remain a game back in the AFC Central. Pat Leahy kicked four field goals and the Jets scored 23 unanswered points to avenge their earlier season loss to the Patriots 26-3. Miami took a two-game lead in the AFC East as Dan Marino passed for three touchdowns in the Dolphins' 38-14 victory over the Bengals. Cincinnati's Ken Anderson passed for 342 yards in that game to become the eighth quarterback in NFL history to throw for over 30,000 yards in a career. Dan Fouts made his first appearance since Week Seven and passed for a pair of scores to help the Chargers defeat the Broncos 31-7. The Raiders lengthened their lead to three games in the AFC West by downing the Giants 27-12. Eric Dickerson and Vince Ferragamo led the Rams past the Bills 41-17, while New Orleans survived five turnovers to edge Minnesota 17-16. The Bears won their third straight, 13-3 over the 49ers. The Buccaneers snapped a 10-quarter scoreless streak as Jack Thompson completed four touchdown passes enroute to a 33-24 win over the Oilers. In all, 24 teams remained in contention for Super Bowl XVIII.

**THURSDAY, NOVEMBER 24**

**Detroit 45, Pittsburgh 3**—At Pontiac Silverdome, attendance 77,724. Detroit built a 24-3 halftime lead over Pittsburgh and coasted to its fourth win in the last five games to gain a share of the lead in the NFC Central. The Lions scored on their first four possessions. Detroit took the opening kickoff and drove 83 yards with Billy Sims scoring on a two-yard run 5:17 into the game. Following Eddie Murray's 27-yard field goal, Eric Hipple threw a pair of touchdown passes to Ulysses Norris (13 and 4 yards). Robbie Martin's 81-yard punt return for a score put the Lions ahead 31-7. Roosevelt Barnes' 70-yard interception return (Detroit's fifth interception of the game) set up Gary Danielson's five-yard touchdown pass to Jeff Chadwick to complete the scoring. Sims rushed for 106 yards on 26 carries.

| | | | | | |
|---|---|---|---|---|---|
| Pittsburgh | 0 | 3 | 0 | 0 | — 3 |
| Detroit | 17 | 7 | 7 | 14 | — 45 |

Det — Sims 2 run (Murray kick)
Det — FG Murray 27
Det — Norris 13 pass from Hipple (Murray kick)
Pitt — FG Anderson 38
Det — Norris 4 pass from Hipple (Murray kick)
Det — Sims 2 run (Murray kick)
Det — Martin 81 punt return (Murray kick)
Det — Chadwick 5 pass from Danielson (Murray kick)

**Dallas 35, St. Louis 17**—At Texas Stadium, attendance 60,974. Tony Dorsett moved into eighth place on the all-time career rushing list (8,153 yards) by gaining 102 yards as the Cowboys beat the Cardinals. Dorsett followed Ron Springs' one-yard touchdown run with a five-yard scoring run to give Dallas the lead 14-7. Danny White (24 of 31 for 237 yards) increased the lead to 21-7 by hitting Butch Johnson on a 15-yard scoring pass for a 21-7 lead at the half. Dorsett (55 yards) and White (4) added fourth-quarter touchdown runs to close out the Cowboys' scoring. The Dallas defense recorded a season-high seven sacks.

| | | | | | |
|---|---|---|---|---|---|
| St. Louis | 7 | 0 | 3 | 7 | — 17 |
| Dallas | 7 | 14 | 0 | 14 | — 35 |

StL — Green 71 pass from Lomax (O'Donoghue kick)
Dall — Springs 1 run (Septien kick)
Dall — Dorsett 5 run (Septien kick)
Dall — Johnson 15 pass from D. White (Septien kick)
StL — FG O'Donoghue 42
Dall — Dorsett 55 run (Septien kick)
Dall — D. White 4 run (Septien kick)
StL — Anderson 14 pass from Lomax (O'Donoghue kick)

**SUNDAY, NOVEMBER 27**

**Cleveland 41, Baltimore 23**—At Cleveland Stadium, attendance 65,812. Brian Sipe completed 20 of 33 passes for 313 yards and three first-half touchdowns and Mike Pruitt ran for 110 yards and two scores to lead the Browns past the Colts. Following Pruitt's four-yard touchdown run, Sipe threw touchdown passes of 15 yards to Willis Adams, 66 yards to Ozzie Newsome, and 9 yards to Dave Logan for a 28-17 lead. Pruitt's two-yard scoring run and Matt Bahr field goals of 26 and 27 yards put the game out of reach. Newsome's eight receptions (for 108 yards) gave him a Browns career-record total 332.

| | | | | | |
|---|---|---|---|---|---|
| Baltimore | 3 | 14 | 0 | 6 | — 23 |
| Cleveland | 14 | 14 | 10 | 3 | — 41 |

Cle — Pruitt 4 run (Bahr kick)
Balt — FG Allegre 31
Cle — Adams 15 pass from Sipe (Bahr kick)
Balt — McMillan 4 pass from Pagel (Allegre kick)
Cle — Newsome 66 pass from Sipe (Bahr kick)
Balt — McMillan 2 run (Allegre kick)
Cle — Logan 9 pass from Sipe (Bahr kick)
Cle — FG Bahr 26
Cle — Pruitt 2 run (Bahr kick)
Balt — Butler 7 pass from Pagel (kick failed)
Cle — FG Bahr 27

**Los Angeles Rams 41, Buffalo 17**—At Anaheim Stadium, attendance 48,246. Eric Dickerson rushed for 125 yards, Vince Ferragamo threw three touchdowns passes, and the Rams' defense intercepted five passes to lead the victory. Ferragamo opened the scoring with a 45-yard touchdown pass to George Farmer and connected with Preston Dennard on 11- and 15-yard scoring tosses. Dickerson had a two-yard touchdown run and Johnnie Johnson returned his second interception of the game 60 yards for the Rams' final touchdown. Buffalo's Joe Ferguson passed for 233 yards to reach the 25,000-yard mark (25,148).

| | | | | | |
|---|---|---|---|---|---|
| Buffalo | 0 | 7 | 7 | 3 | — 17 |
| L.A. Rams | 0 | 14 | 10 | 17 | — 41 |

Rams — Farmer 45 pass from Ferragamo (Lansford kick)
Buff — Hunter 15 pass from Ferguson (Danelo kick)
Rams — Dennard 11 pass from Ferragamo (Lansford kick)
Rams — Dickerson 2 run (Lansford kick)
Buff — Franklin 43 pass from Ferguson (Danelo kick)
Rams — FG Lansford 37
Buff — FG Danelo 20
Rams — Dennard 15 pass from Ferragamo (Lansford kick)
Rams — FG Lansford 49
Rams — Johnson 60 interception return (Lansford kick)

**San Diego 31, Denver 7**—At San Diego Jack Murphy Stadium, attendance 43,650. Dan Fouts came off a five-week layoff because of an injured shoulder and completed 24 of 33 passes for 299 yards and two touchdowns to lead the Chargers to a 31-7 win. Fouts threw scoring passes of nine and two yards to Kellen Winslow in the first quarter to put San Diego ahead 14-7. Danny Walters had two interceptions; the first set up Winslow's second score and the second (1:53 before halftime) halted the Broncos' last serious scoring threat. James Brooks (three yards) and Chuck Muncie (one) added rushing touchdowns. Winslow caught six passes for 103 yards.

| | | | | | |
|---|---|---|---|---|---|
| Denver | 7 | 0 | 0 | 0 | — 7 |
| San Diego | 14 | 7 | 0 | 10 | — 31 |

Den — Poole 1 run (Karlis kick)
SD — Winslow 9 pass from Fouts (Benirschke kick)
SD — Winslow 2 pass from Fouts (Benirschke kick)
SD — Brooks 3 run (Benirschke kick)
SD — Muncie 1 run (Benirschke kick)
SD — FG Benirschke 20

**Atlanta 47, Green Bay 41**—At Atlanta-Fulton County Stadium, attendance 35,688. Kenny Johnson's 31-yard interception return for a touchdown 2:13 into overtime gave the Falcons a 47-41 comeback win and sent the Packers to their second consecutive overtime loss. Johnson also scored on a 26-yard interception return with 1:57 left in regulation to give Atlanta a 41-34 edge, but Green Bay tied the score on Gerry Ellis' four-yard run with three seconds remaining. The Falcons overcame a 21-0 deficit on the running of William Andrews (20 carries for 129 yards and two touchdowns) and the passing of Mike Moroski (22 of 35 for 303 yards and two touchdowns), who was making his first NFL start. Lynn Dickey, who completed 25 of 37 passes, accounted for 366 of the Packers' 500 total yards. The Falcons generated 445 yards total offense.

| | | | | | | |
|---|---|---|---|---|---|---|
| Green Bay | 14 | 10 | 7 | 10 | 0 | — 41 |
| Atlanta | 0 | 21 | 3 | 17 | 6 | — 47 |

GB — Lofton 14 pass from Dickey (Stenerud kick)
GB — Dickey 1 run (Stenerud kick)
GB — Coffman 7 pass from Dickey (Stenerud kick)
Atl — Andrews 6 pass from Moroski (Luckhurst kick)
Atl — Andrews 20 run (Luckhurst kick)
GB — FG Stenerud 23
Atl — Bailey 50 pass from Moroski (Luckhurst kick)
GB — Coffman 20 pass from Dickey (Stenerud kick)
Atl — FG Luckhurst 44
GB — FG Stenerud 33
Atl — Andrews 1 run (Luckhurst kick)
Atl — FG Luckhurst 22
Atl — K. Johnson 26 interception return (Luckhurst kick)
GB — Ellis 4 run (Stenerud kick)
Atl — K. Johnson 31 interception return

**Tampa Bay 33, Houston 24**—At Tampa Stadium, attendance 38,625. Jack Thompson threw four touchdown passes, including a pair to Kevin House, to lead the Buccaneers over the Oilers 33-24. Thompson, who completed 17 of 29 passes for 224 yards, had second-quarter scoring passes of 6 yards to Adger Armstrong and 25 yards to House to give Tampa Bay a 12-3 halftime lead. After Houston closed to 12-10, Thompson hit House on a 41-yard touchdown pass in the third period and added a 3-yard scoring pass to Jim Obradovich in the fourth quarter. Tampa Bay generated 345 yards total offense and snapped a 10-quarter scoreless streak.

| | | | | | |
|---|---|---|---|---|---|
| Houston | 0 | 3 | 7 | 14 | — 24 |
| Tampa Bay | 0 | 12 | 14 | 7 | — 33 |

TB — Armstrong 6 pass from Thompson (kick failed)
TB — House 25 pass from Thompson (run failed)
Hou — FG Kempf 51
Hou — Campbell 1 run (Kempf kick)
TB — House 41 pass from Thompson (Capece kick)
TB — Owens 4 run (Capece kick)
Hou — Campbell 2 run (Kempf kick)
TB — Obradovich 3 pass from Thompson (Capece kick)
Hou — Dressel 7 pass from Luck (Kempf kick)

**Seattle 51, Kansas City 48**—At Kingdome, attendance 56,793. Norm Johnson kicked three 42-yard field goals, the second to tie the game at 48-48 with two seconds left in regulation and the third to clinch the Seahawks' 51-48 win after 1:46 of overtime. Curt Warner spearheaded Seattle's 531-yard attack, rushing for 207 yards on 32 carries (both club records) and two touchdowns (28 and 1 yards). Dave Krieg also fired three touchdown passes. Zachary Dixon returned the overtime kickoff 47 yards and Warner had rushes of 17, 5, and 2 yards to set up Johnson's winning kick. The combined 99 points scored was the third-highest total in NFL history. Seattle and Kansas City also combined for an NFL-record 59 first downs.

| | | | | | | |
|---|---|---|---|---|---|---|
| Kansas City | 7 | 21 | 7 | 13 | 0 | — 48 |
| Seattle | 7 | 7 | 17 | 17 | 3 | — 51 |

KC — Marshall 11 pass from Kenney (Lowery kick)
Sea — Warner 28 run (N. Johnson kick)
KC — Paige 17 pass from Kenney (Lowery kick)
KC — Kenney 1 run (Lowery kick)
Sea — Walker 18 pass from Krieg (N. Johnson kick)
KC — Brown 13 run (Lowery kick)
Sea — Doornink 27 pass from Krieg (N. Johnson kick)
Sea — Warner 1 run (N. Johnson kick)
Sea — FG N. Johnson 42
KC — Kenney 1 run (Lowery kick)
KC — Carson 18 pass from Kenney (Lowery kick)
Sea — Warner 1 run (N. Johnson kick)
Sea — Johns 14 pass from Krieg (N. Johnson kick)
KC — Brown 21 pass from Kenney (kick failed)
Sea — FG N. Johnson 42
Sea — FG N. Johnson 42

**New Orleans 17, Minnesota 16**—At Louisiana Superdome, attendance 59,502. Wayne Wilson had two touchdowns and the Saints survived five turnovers to edge the Vikings. Benny Ricardo's second of three field goals, a 27-yarder, put Minnesota in front 13-10 late in the third quarter but Wilson's second touchdown (a one-yard run) opened the fourth quarter and gave New Orleans the lead for good, 17-13. The Saints recorded two quarterback sacks, bringing their season total to a team-record 48.

| | | | | | |
|---|---|---|---|---|---|
| Minnesota | 3 | 7 | 3 | 3 | — 16 |
| New Orleans | 7 | 3 | 0 | 7 | — 17 |

Minn — FG Ricardo 31
NO — W. Wilson 2 run (Andersen kick)
Minn — Galbreath 5 pass from Dils (Ricardo kick)
NO — FG Andersen 25
Minn — FG Ricardo 27
NO — W. Wilson 1 run (Andersen kick)
Minn — FG Ricardo 32

**New York Jets 26, New England 3**—At Shea Stadium, attendance 48,620. New York scored 23 unanswered points in the second half to split the season series with New England. After the Patriots tied the score 3-3 early in the third quarter, Richard Todd and Wesley Walker teamed on a 64-yard touchdown pass to give the Jets a 10-3 lead. Todd and Walker combined again on an eight-yard scoring pass 2:20 into the final period and Pat Leahy kicked his fourth field goal of the game (from 19 yards) to finish the scoring. Leahy had earlier hit from 18, 34, and 35 yards. New York had 421 total yards while limiting New England to 208. Tony Eason, the Patriots' number-one draft pick, made his first NFL start but was sacked five times for 47 yards.

| | | | | | |
|---|---|---|---|---|---|
| New England | 0 | 0 | 3 | 0 | — 3 |
| New York Jets | 0 | 3 | 13 | 10 | — 26 |

NYJ — FG Leahy 18
NE — FG Steinfort 33
NYJ — Walker 64 pass from Todd (Leahy kick)
NYJ — FG Leahy 34
NYJ — FG Leahy 35
NYJ — Walker 8 pass from Todd (Leahy kick)
NYJ — FG Leahy 19

**Los Angeles Raiders 27, New York Giants 12**—At Memorial Coliseum, attendance 41,473. Jim Plunkett concluded two long scoring drives with touchdown passes and Chris Bahr kicked a pair of field goals to help the Raiders down the Giants 27-12. Plunkett completed 19 of 32 passes for 243 yards and finished drives of 80 and 70 yards with scoring passes of 13 yards to Don Hasselbeck and 36 yards to Malcolm Barnwell. Bahr's 47- and 38-yard field goals gave Los Angeles a 13-5 lead at the half. Greg Townsend had three of the Raiders' seven quarterback sacks. Scott Brunner threw for 346 yards, and Earnest Gray and Byron Williams each caught five passes, for 134 and 119 yards respectively.

| | | | | | |
|---|---|---|---|---|---|
| New York Giants | 2 | 3 | 0 | 7 | — 12 |
| L.A. Raiders | 0 | 13 | 7 | 7 | — 27 |

NYG — Safety, Marshall tackled Plunkett in end zone
Raiders — Hasselbeck 13 pass from Plunkett (Bahr kick)
Raiders — FG Bahr 47
NYG — FG Haji-Sheikh 31
NYG — FG Bahr 38
Raiders — Barnwell 36 pass from Plunkett (Bahr kick)
NYG — Allen 11 run (Bahr kick)
NYG — Williams 43 pass from Brunner (Haji-Sheikh kick)

**Washington 28, Philadelphia 24**—At Robert F. Kennedy Stadium, attendance 54,324. John Riggins scored on a pair of two-yard runs and Joe Theismann threw touchdown passes of 75 yards to Charlie Brown and 17 yards to Art Monk as the Redskins clinched a playoff berth. Riggins gained 99 yards on 26 carries to go over the 1,000-yard mark (1,049) for the fourth time in his career. His two touchdowns gave him an NFL-record 21 rushing scores. Philadelphia's Mike Quick had a team-record sixth 100-yard game of the season, catching five passes for 104 yards.

| | | | | | |
|---|---|---|---|---|---|
| Philadelphia | 0 | 21 | 3 | 0 | — 24 |
| Washington | 7 | 21 | 0 | 0 | — 28 |

Wash — Monk 17 pass from Theismann (Moseley kick)
Phil — Oliver 2 pass from Jaworski (Franklin kick)
Wash — Riggins 2 run (Moseley kick)

Phil — Quick 17 pass from Jaworski (Franklin kick)
Wash — Riggins 2 run (Moseley kick)
Wash — Brown 75 pass from Theismann (Moseley kick)
Phil — Quick 3 pass from Jaworski (Franklin kick)
Phil — FG Franklin 52

**Chicago 13, San Francisco 3**—At Soldier Field, attendance 40,483. Jim McMahon passed for one touchdown and Bob Thomas kicked a pair of field goals to lead the Bears to their third straight win. McMahon, the leading rusher in the game with 74 yards on nine carries, also completed 11 of 19 passes for 159 yards, including a 49-yard touchdown pass to Dennis McKinnon to snap a 3-3 tie. Thomas, despite kicking in a steady rain, connected from 29 and 23 yards. Chicago had two interceptions and two fumble recoveries, one of which stopped San Francisco at the Bears' 1-yard line in the first half.

| | | | | | |
|---|---|---|---|---|---|
| San Francisco | 3 | 0 | 0 | 0 | — 3 |
| Chicago | 3 | 7 | 3 | 0 | — 13 |

Chi — FG B. Thomas 29
SF — FG Wersching 24
Chi — McKinnon 49 pass from McMahon (B. Thomas kick)
Chi — FG B. Thomas 23

**MONDAY, NOVEMBER 28**

**Miami 38, Cincinnati 14**—At Orange Bowl, attendance 74,506. Dan Marino completed three touchdown passes, including a pair to Mark Duper, to lead the Dolphins over the Bengals. Miami scored 21 unanswered points in the second half to win the game and take a two-game lead in the AFC East. Marino threw Duper scoring passes of 7 and 15 yards and Dan Johnson added a three-yard touchdown catch. Tony Nathan (one yard) and Andra Franklin (five) added rushing touchdowns for Miami. Cincinnati's Ken Anderson threw for 342 yards to become the eighth NFL quarterback to reach the 30,000-yard mark (30,010).

| | | | | | |
|---|---|---|---|---|---|
| Cincinnati | 0 | 14 | 0 | 0 | — 14 |
| Miami | 7 | 10 | 7 | 14 | — 38 |

Mia — Duper 7 pass from Marino (von Schamann kick)
Mia — Nathan 1 run (von Schamann kick)
Cin — Curtis 80 pass from Anderson (Breech kick)
Mia — FG von Schamann 47
Cin — Johnson 1 run (Breech kick)
Mia — Duper 15 pass from Marino (von Schamann kick)
Mia — Johnson 3 pass from Marino (von Schamann kick)
Mia — Franklin 5 run (von Schamann kick)

## FOURTEENTH WEEK SUMMARY

After 14 weeks of play, 19 teams remained in the Super Bowl XVIII race and only two divisions had crowned champions. The Raiders exploded for three touchdowns in two-and-a-half minutes to sack the Chargers 42-10 and capture their first AFC West title since 1976. Miami rallied from a 17-7 deficit to clinch the AFC Eastern Division championship with a 24-17 win over Houston. In the AFC Central, the Steelers' losing streak continued. Pete Johnson gained 126 yards on 38 carries and scored twice, and the Cincinnati offense outgained Pittsburgh's 350-154 as the Steelers lost their third consecutive game, 23-10 to the Bengals. Despite the loss, Pittsburgh still maintained a one-game advantage over Cleveland, which lost 27-6 to Denver. The Broncos' win kept them in the Wild Card hunt even though they trailed the Raiders by three games. Buffalo's Joe Cribbs rushed for a career-high 185 yards but it was Mike Kennedy's interception return for a score that proved decisive in the Bills' 14-9 victory over the Chiefs. The Jets celebrated their third straight win, 10-6 over the Colts, while the Patriots scored their first touchdown in 11 quarters to defeat the Saints 7-0 in a game played in snow and sleet at Sullivan Stadium. Washington and Dallas both won to keep the NFC Eastern Division top spot deadlocked. Joe Theismann completed three touchdown passes as the Redskins opened a 34-0 lead enroute to a 37-21 defeat of the Falcons. The Cowboys shut down the Seahawks' Curt Warner (22 yards rushing) and turned Tony Dorsett loose for 117 yards and two touchdowns to beat Seattle 35-10. Billy Sims helped Detroit take sole possession of first place in the NFC Central by rushing for over 100 yards for the fourth straight week to lead the Lions' 13-2 Monday night win over the Vikings. Meanwhile, the NFC West continued to be the league's most unpredictable division. Philadelphia beat the Rams 13-9 on Ron Jaworski's 29-yard touchdown pass to Tony Woodruff with 21 seconds left. San Francisco regained its share of the division lead, thanks in part to Roger Craig's three touchdowns, which helped defeat Tampa Bay 35-21.

**THURSDAY, DECEMBER 1**

**Los Angeles Raiders 42, San Diego 10**—At San Diego Jack Murphy Stadium, attendance 47,760. The Raiders overcame a sluggish start to beat the Chargers and capture their first AFC West title since 1976. After gaining only 72 yards in the game's first 28 minutes and trailing 10-0, Todd Christensen (eight catches for 140 yards and three touchdowns) caught a 43-yard touchdown pass from Marcus Allen and a 25-yarder from Jim Plunkett 1:24 later to put Los Angeles ahead at halftime 14-10. The Raiders blew the game open in the third quarter with three touchdowns in two and a half minutes. Frank Hawkins scored on a 20-yard run and added a 1-yard plunge following Dave Stall's fumble recovery. On the Chargers' next play, Rod Martin returned an interception 29 yards for a score and a 35-10 edge. Jim Plunkett, undefeated since returning to action in Week Ten, suffered his first interception in four games.

| | | | | | |
|---|---|---|---|---|---|
| L.A. Raiders | 0 | 14 | 28 | 0 | — 42 |
| San Diego | 7 | 3 | 0 | 0 | — 10 |

SD — Muncie 5 pass from Fouts (Benirschke kick)
SD — FG Benirschke 24
Raiders — Christensen 43 pass from Allen (Bahr kick)
Raiders — Christensen 25 pass from Plunkett (Bahr kick)
Raiders — Hawkins 20 run (Bahr kick)
Raiders — Hawkins 1 run (Bahr kick)
Raiders — Martin 29 interception return (Bahr kick)
Raiders — Christensen 14 pass from Plunkett (Bahr kick)

**SUNDAY, DECEMBER 4**

**Washington 37, Atlanta 21**—At Robert F. Kennedy Stadium, attendance 52,074. Joe Theismann threw three touchdown passes as the Redskins opened a 34-0 lead and cruised to a 37-21 win. Theismann completed 17 of 28 passes for 221 yards and had touchdowns of 18, 11, and 10 yards to Clint Didier, Joe Washington and Art Monk, respectively. Mark Moseley kicked three field goals (26, 51, and 43 yards) and added four extra points to set an NFL record for kick scoring in a season with 147 points (the previous record was 145). Washington converted four of six Atlanta turnovers into scores, including Mel Kaufman's 30-yard fumble return for a touchdown. John Riggins' NFL-record string of 13 consecutive games with a rushing touchdown came to an end.

| | | | | | |
|---|---|---|---|---|---|
| Atlanta | 0 | 0 | 0 | 21 | — 21 |
| Washington | 7 | 13 | 14 | 3 | — 37 |

Wash — Didier 18 pass from Theismann (Moseley kick)
Wash — FG Moseley 26
Wash — J. Washington 11 pass from Theismann (Moseley kick)
Wash — FG Moseley 51
Wash — Kaufman 30 fumble recovery return (Moseley kick)
Wash — Monk 10 pass from Theismann (Moseley kick)
Atl — Riggs 7 run (Luckhurst kick)
Wash — FG Moseley 43
Atl — Riggs 4 run (Luckhurst kick)
Atl — Cain 2 run (Luckhurst kick)

**Buffalo 14, Kansas City 9**—At Arrowhead Stadium, attendance 27,104. Mike Kennedy's 22-yard interception return for a touchdown early in the fourth quarter clinched the Bills' win. Buffalo entered the final period holding on to a 7-6 lead thanks to Joe Ferguson's 17-yard touchdown pass to Perry Tuttle and the Bills' defense, which held Kansas City scoreless on five plays on a first-and-goal opportunity. Joe Cribbs carried 36 times for 185 yards (both career highs) to top the 1,000-yard mark for the third time in his career (1,009).

| | | | | | |
|---|---|---|---|---|---|
| Buffalo | 0 | 7 | 0 | 7 | — 14 |
| Kansas City | 0 | 3 | 3 | 3 | — 9 |

Buff — Tuttle 17 pass from Ferguson (Danelo kick)
KC — FG Lowery 48
KC — FG Lowery 25
Buff — Kennedy 22 interception return (Danelo kick)
KC — FG Lowery 42

**Green Bay 31, Chicago 28**—At Lambeau Field, attendance 51,147. Green Bay gained 522 yards total offense but it was Jan Stenerud's 19-yard field goal with three seconds left that beat Chicago 31-28. Gerry Ellis rushed for a career-high 141 yards on 18 carries. His 71-yard run set up the Packers' first score, a nine-yard run by Harlan Huckleby. Lynn Dickey (16 of 34 for 355 yards) followed with a five-yard touchdown pass to Paul Coffman for a 14-0 lead. Second-half scoring runs by Ellis (12 yards) and Huckleby (10) put Green Bay on top 28-14, but Chicago's Dennis McKinnon returned a punt 59 yards for a touchdown to tie the game with 1:50 left. Dickey's 67-yard completion to James Lofton (six receptions for 120 yards) set up Stenerud's winning kick.

| | | | | | |
|---|---|---|---|---|---|
| Chicago | 7 | 7 | 0 | 14 | — 28 |
| Green Bay | 14 | 7 | 0 | 10 | — 31 |

GB — Huckleby 9 run (Stenerud kick)
GB — Coffman 5 pass from Dickey (Stenerud kick)
Chi — Gault 87 pass from McMahon (B. Thomas kick)
GB — Ellis 12 run (Stenerud kick)
Chi — Suhey 1 run (B. Thomas kick)
GB — Huckleby 10 run (Stenerud kick)
Chi — Suhey 1 run (B. Thomas kick)
Chi — McKinnon 59 punt return (B. Thomas kick)
GB — FG Stenerud 19

**Cincinnati 23, Pittsburgh 10**—At Three Rivers Stadium, attendance 55,832. Pete Johnson ran for two scores and Jim Breech kicked field goals from 19, 27, and 32 yards as the Bengals sent the Steelers to their third straight defeat. Cincinnati capitalized on two of Pittsburgh's five turnovers to take a 14-0 first-quarter lead. Reggie Williams' fumble recovery and Bobby Kemp's interception led to Johnson's touchdown runs of 1 and 16 yards just 1:14 apart. Johnson carried the ball a team-record 38 times for 126 yards as the Bengals generated 350 yards total offense while holding the Steelers to 154.

| | | | | | |
|---|---|---|---|---|---|
| Cincinnati | 14 | 3 | 3 | 3 | — 23 |
| Pittsburgh | 0 | 3 | 0 | 7 | — 10 |

Cin — Johnson 1 run (Breech kick)
Cin — Johnson 16 run (Breech kick)
Cin — FG Breech 19
Pitt — FG Anderson 48
Cin — FG Breech 27
Pitt — F. Harris 29 pass from Stoudt (Anderson kick)
Cin — FG Breech 32

**Denver 27, Cleveland 6**—At Mile High Stadium, attendance 70,912. Rookies John Elway and Clinton Sampson combined for two touchdowns to lead the Broncos over the Browns. Elway completed 16 of 24 passes for 284 yards and threw scoring passes of 39 and 49 yards to Sampson (three receptions for 101 yards) for a 21-6 halftime lead. Denver took a 7-3 lead when Steve Wilson's 36-yard interception return set up Sammy Winder's three-yard touchdown run early in the second quarter. Rich Karlis' 20- and 50-yard field goals in the second half closed out the scoring. Cleveland's points came on Matt Bahr's 47-yard field goal and Steve Cox's team-record 58-yarder.

| | | | | | |
|---|---|---|---|---|---|
| Cleveland | 3 | 3 | 0 | 0 | — 6 |
| Denver | 0 | 21 | 3 | 3 | — 27 |

Cle — FG Bahr 47
Den — Winder 3 run (Karlis kick)
Den — Sampson 39 pass from Elway (Karlis kick)
Den — Sampson 49 pass from Elway (Karlis kick)
Cle — FG Cox 58
Den — FG Karlis 20
Den — FG Karlis 50

**Dallas 35, Seattle 10**—At Kingdome, attendance 63,352. Tony Dorsett ran for two first-half touchdowns and Danny White threw for two more in the second half to power the Cowboys over the Seahawks. Dorsett gained 117 yards on 26 carries and scored on runs of eight and seven yards to give Dallas a 14-3 halftime advantage. White completed 19 of 26 passes for 233 yards and threw touchdown passes to Doug Donley (35 yards) and Butch Johnson (16). Randy White had three and a half of the Cowboys' eight sacks. Dallas held Seattle to 216 total yards (just 28 on the ground) while accumulating 418.

| | | | | | |
|---|---|---|---|---|---|
| Dallas | 7 | 7 | 7 | 14 | — 35 |
| Seattle | 0 | 3 | 0 | 7 | — 10 |

Dall — Dorsett 8 run (Septien kick)
Dall — Dorsett 7 run (Septien kick)
Sea — FG N. Johnson 54
Dall — Donley 35 pass from D. White (Septien kick)
Dall — Johnson 16 pass from D. White (Septien kick)
Sea — Warner 2 run (N. Johnson kick)
Dall — Newsome 15 pass from Hogeboom (Septien kick)

**Philadelphia 13, Los Angeles Rams 9**—At Veterans Stadium, attendance 32,867. Ron Jaworski completed a 29-yard touchdown pass to Tony Woodruff with 21 seconds remaining to edge the Rams and snap the Eagles' seven-game losing streak. Philadelphia took a 6-0 lead when Jerry Robinson's fumble recovery set up Hubie Oliver's two-yard scoring run. Mike Lansford countered with field goals from 27, 28, and 28 yards to give Los Angeles a 9-6 advantage with 1:46 to play. Jaworski drove the Eagles 71 yards in six plays for their first home win of the season. Eric Dickerson (103 yards on 28 carries) tied an NFL rookie record with his ninth 100-yard game.

| | | | | | |
|---|---|---|---|---|---|
| L.A. Rams | 0 | 6 | 0 | 3 | — 9 |
| Philadelphia | 6 | 0 | 0 | 7 | — 13 |

Phil — Oliver 2 run (kick failed)
Rams — FG Lansford 27
Rams — FG Lansford 28
Rams — FG Lansford 28
Phil — Woodruff 29 pass from Jaworski (Franklin kick)

**Miami 24, Houston 17**—At Astrodome, attendance 39,434. Miami rallied from a 17-7 deficit with two fourth-quarter touchdowns to clinch the AFC Eastern Division crown. Uwe von Schamann's 19-yard field goal and Dan Marino's 28-yard touchdown pass to Nat Moore with 11:46 to play tied the score 17-17. Tony Nathan scored the decisive touchdown on a five-yard run with 3:51 left. Earl Campbell gained 138 yards to top the 1,000-yard mark (1,078) for the fifth time and become the tenth player to crack the 8,000-yard barrier (8,073).

| | | | | | |
|---|---|---|---|---|---|
| Miami | 0 | 7 | 3 | 14 | — 24 |
| Houston | 7 | 7 | 3 | 0 | — 17 |

Hou — Smith 5 pass from Luck (Kempf kick)
Hou — Campbell 1 run (Kempf kick)
Mia — Franklin 1 run (von Schamann kick)
Hou — FG Kempf 23
Mia — FG von Schamann 19
Mia — Moore 28 pass from Marino (von Schamann kick)
Mia — Nathan 5 run (von Schamann kick)

**New England 7, New Orleans 0**—At Sullivan Stadium, attendance 24,579. New England scored on the game's opening drive and overcame snow, sleet, and heavy rain to even its record at 7-7. Ricky Smith returned the opening kickoff 53 yards and nine plays later Tony Collins scored from three yards out. It was the Patriots' first touchdown in 11 quarters. Mosi Tatapu carried 21 times for a career-high 128 yards to help the Patriots control the game. The Saints allowed just 207 total yards to remain the NFC's number-one ranked defense.

| | | | | | |
|---|---|---|---|---|---|
| New Orleans | 0 | 0 | 0 | 0 | — 0 |
| New England | 7 | 0 | 0 | 0 | — 7 |

NE — Collins 3 run (Steinfort kick)

**New York Jets 10, Baltimore 6**—At Memorial Stadium, attendance 29,431. Richard Todd's second-quarter eight-yard touchdown pass to Freeman McNeil broke a 3-3 tie and helped the Jets win their third straight game. The Colts threatened twice in the final period but came up empty. Bob Crable intercepted a pass in the end zone with 7:59 left to end the first threat and Baltimore's second march stalled at the Jets' 23-yard line with 19 seconds remaining. McNeil rushed for 102 yards on 24 carries and Joe Klecko had three of New York's five sacks.

| | | | | | |
|---|---|---|---|---|---|
| New York Jets | 0 | 10 | 0 | 0 | — 10 |
| Baltimore | 0 | 3 | 3 | 0 | — 6 |

NYJ — FG Leahy 31
Balt — FG Allegre 26
NYJ — McNeil 8 pass from Todd (Leahy kick)
Balt — FG Allegre 41

**St. Louis 10, New York Giants 6**—At Giants Stadium, attendance 25,156. Neil Lomax completed a 20-yard touchdown pass to Roy Green and Neil O'Donoghue added a 25-yard field goal in a steady downpour as the Cardinals defeated the Giants. St. Louis cornerback Lionel Washington recovered a fumble and had two interceptions to end New York scoring drives. David Galloway also intercepted a Scott Brunner pass, this one with 1:18 to play, to preserve the Cardinals' win. The Giants' Ali Haji-Sheikh kicked a pair of 44-yard field goals to total 26 for the season, 1 better than Pete Gogolak's previous club record set in 1970.

| | | | | | |
|---|---|---|---|---|---|
| St. Louis | 0 | 7 | 0 | 3 | — 10 |
| New York Giants | 6 | 0 | 0 | 0 | — 6 |

NYG — FG Haji-Sheikh 44
NYG — FG Haji-Sheikh 44
StL — Green 20 pass from Lomax (O'Donoghue kick)
StL — FG O'Donoghue 25

**San Fransicso 35, Tampa Bay 21**—At Candlestick Park, attendance 49,773. Wendell Tyler rushed for 102 yards and rookie Roger Craig scored three touchdowns rushing as the 49ers regained a first-place tie in the NFC West. Craig scored twice in the second quarter (10- and 1-yard runs) and San Francisco never looked back. Joe Montana (12-yard run) and Bill Ring (3-yard run) added touchdowns in the third period to put the 49ers ahead 28-14. Craig's 14-yard fourth-quarter run finished the scoring. Tampa Bay's Jack Thompson completed 25 of 46 for 337 yards and three touchdowns.

| | | | | | |
|---|---|---|---|---|---|
| Tampa Bay | 0 | 7 | 7 | 7 | — 21 |
| San Francisco | 0 | 14 | 14 | 7 | — 35 |

SF — Craig 10 run (Wersching kick)
SF — Craig 1 run (Wersching kick)
TB — T. Bell 9 pass from Thompson (Capece kick)
SF — Montana 12 run (Wersching kick)
TB — House 74 pass from Thompson (Capece kick)
SF — Ring 3 run (Wersching kick)
SF — Craig 14 run (Wersching kick)
TB — Carver 3 pass from Thompson (Capece kick)

**MONDAY, DECEMBER 5**

**Detroit 13, Minnesota 2**—At Pontiac Silverdome, attendance 79,169. Billy Sims (137 yards on 23 carries) rushed for more than 100 yards for the fourth straight week and the defense mounted a key goal-line stand in the fourth quarter to help the Lions win their third straight game. Detroit did all its scoring in the second quarter as Eddie Murray kicked field goals of 50 and 42 yards and Eric Hipple threw a 10-yard touchdown pass to Jeff Chadwick. Minnesota's only points came when Detroit punter Mike Black ran out of the end zone for a deliberate safety with 2:43 to play. Doug English had two of the Lions' seven sacks. Bruce McNorton's interception stopped a Minnesota first-half scoring threat.

| | | | | | |
|---|---|---|---|---|---|
| Minnesota | 0 | 0 | 0 | 2 | — 2 |
| Detroit | 0 | 13 | 0 | 0 | — 13 |

Det — FG Murray 50
Det — Chadwick 10 pass from Hipple (Murray kick)
Det — FG Murray 42
Minn — Safety, Black ran out of end zone

## FIFTEENTH WEEK SUMMARY

With a week to play, all three AFC division titles were claimed, while all three NFC crowns remained undecided. Six of 10 playoff berths were filled as 15 teams remained in contention for Super Bowl XVIII. The Steelers clinched the AFC Central title for the first time since 1979. Terry Bradshaw's initial start of the season inspired Pittsburgh to a 34-7 victory over the Jets who were eliminated from the playoff picture. Denver gained a postseason berth for the first time in four years as John Elway threw for three fourth-quarter touchdowns to rally the Broncos over the Colts 21-19. Still in contention for the AFC's remaining Wild Card berth were Seattle, 17-12 winners over the New York Giants, and New England, which defeated the Los Angeles Rams 21-7. Cleveland and Buffalo still held a glimmer of hope despite losses. The Browns got 153 yards rushing and three touchdowns from Mike Pruitt but came up short against the Oilers 34-27, while the Bills were beaten by the 49ers 23-10. San Francisco reclaimed first place in the NFC West with the win combined with the Rams loss to the Patriots. New Orleans renewed its Wild Card chances thanks to Morten Andersen's 50-yard field goal, 5:30 into overtime, which defeated Philadelphia 20-17. Green Bay took advantage of Cincinnati's 17-9 win over Detroit to deadlock the NFC Central Division race. The Packers, playing in a record fifth overtime game this season, came away with a 12-9 win over the Buccaneers as Jan Stenerud's 23-yard field goal was good after 4:07 of the extra period. Stenerud kicked four field goals to become the NFL's all-time career leader with 338, topping George Blanda's mark of 335. Lynn Dickey passed for 278 yards to become the first NFC quarterback to pass for over 4,000 yards in a season. Chicago removed Minnesota from playoff contention with a 19-13 win, the Bears' first victory in Minnesota since 1971. The battle for the NFC East leadership, a dead heat between Dallas and Washington the past four weeks, gained some stability. The Redskins overwhelmed the Cowboys 31-10 to assume possession of first place, as well as being able to hold their own destiny heading into the final week of the season. A victory would assure Washington the division title for the second straight season and the home field advantage throughout the playoffs.

**SATURDAY, DECEMBER 10**

**Miami 31, Atlanta 24**—At Orange Bowl, attendance 56,725. Don Strock, starting in place of injured Dan Marino, passed for two touchdowns to lead the Dolphins over the Falcons. Strock completed 18 of 22 passes for 229 yards in his nineteenth career start. He threw scoring passes of 7 yards to Joe Rose and 15 yards to Tony Nathan for a 17-3 halftime lead. Atlanta pulled to within 17-10, but third-quarter touchdown runs by Andra Franklin (1) and David Overstreet (13) put the game out of reach. William Andrews led all rushers with 161 yards on 21 carries to boost his season total to 1,409 yards, a Falcons record.

| | | | | | |
|---|---|---|---|---|---|
| Atlanta | 0 | 3 | 7 | 14 | — 24 |
| Miami | 7 | 10 | 14 | 0 | — 31 |

Mia — Rose 7 pass from Strock (von Schamann kick)
Atl — FG Luckhurst 35
Mia — FG von Schamann 18
Mia — Nathan 15 pass from Strock (von Schamann kick)
Atl — Riggs 2 run (Luckhurst kick)
Mia — Franklin 1 run (von Schamann kick)
Mia — Overstreet 13 run (von Schamann kick)
Atl — Andrews 24 run (Luckhurst kick)
Atl — Hodge 4 pass from Bartkowski (Luckhurst kick)

**Pittsburgh 34, New York Jets 7**—At Shea Stadium, attendance 53,996. Terry Bradshaw, starting his first game of the season, threw for two touchdowns and Cliff Stoudt completed two more in relief, as the Steelers clinched their first AFC Central Division title since 1979. Bradshaw (five of eight for 77 yards) had scoring passes of 17 yards to Gregg Garrity to conclude a 77-yard drive, and 10 yards to Calvin Sweeney to complete a 72-yard march on the Steelers' next possession. Stoudt replaced Bradshaw 2:30 into the second quarter and hit Bennie Cunningham on a 13-yard scoring pass and Sweeney on an 18-yarder to snap the Steelers' three-game losing streak. Franco Harris gained 103 yards on 26 carries in the Jets' last game at Shea Stadium, where they compiled a 70-70-3 record in 20 seasons.

| | | | | | |
|---|---|---|---|---|---|
| Pittsburgh | 7 | 13 | 7 | 7 | — 34 |
| New York Jets | 0 | 0 | 7 | 0 | — 7 |

Pitt — Garrity 17 pass from Bradshaw (Anderson kick)
Pitt — Sweeney 10 pass from Bradshaw (Anderson kick)
Pitt — FG Anderson 29
Pitt — FG Anderson 40
Pitt — Cunningham 13 pass from Stoudt (Anderson kick)
NYJ — Jones 27 pass from Ryan (Leahy kick)
Pitt — Sweeney 18 pass from Stoudt (Anderson kick)

**SUNDAY, DECEMBER 11**

**Denver 21, Baltimore 19**—At Mile High Stadium, attendance 74,864. John Elway threw three fourth-quarter touchdown passes to lead the Broncos to a 21-19 come-from-behind win and put them into the playoffs for the first time since 1979. Baltimore led 19-0 going into the fourth quarter before Elway completed touchdown passes of 21 yards to Clinton Sampson and 26 yards to Jesse Myles and Gerald Willhite, the latter with 44 seconds left to play. Elway completed 23 of 44 for 345 yards.

| | | | | | |
|---|---|---|---|---|---|
| Baltimore | 3 | 13 | 3 | 0 | — 19 |
| Denver | 0 | 0 | 0 | 21 | — 21 |

Balt — FG Allegre 42
Balt — FG Allegre 55
Balt — FG Allegre 41
Balt — Henry 40 pass from Pagel (Allegre kick)
Balt — FG Allegre 26
Den — Sampson 21 pass from Elway (Karlis kick)
Den — Myles 26 pass from Elway (Karlis kick)
Den — Willhite 26 pass from Elway (Karlis kick)

**Chicago 19, Minnesota 13**—At Metrodome, attendance 57,880. Matt Suhey rushed for 101 yards on 17 carries and threw a 74-yard touchdown pass to Walter Payton as the Bears captured their first win in Minnesota since 1971. Payton's scoring reception put Chicago in front 7-6. Bob Thomas kicked field goals of 42 and 22 yards and Jim McMahon's two-yard touchdown pass to Emery Moorehead gave the Bears a 16-6 lead. Payton finished with 94 yards rushing on 17 carries and had 95 yards on five receptions.

| | | | | | |
|---|---|---|---|---|---|
| Chicago | 10 | 6 | 0 | 3 | — 19 |
| Minnesota | 6 | 0 | 7 | 0 | — 13 |

Minn — FG Ricardo 30
Minn — FG Ricardo 29
Chi — Payton 74 pass from Suhey (B. Thomas kick)
Chi — FG B. Thomas 42
Chi — Moorehead 2 pass from McMahon (kick failed)
Minn — T. Brown 1 run (Ricardo kick)
Chi — FG B. Thomas 22

**Houston 34, Cleveland 27**—At Astrodome, attendance 29,746. Tim Smith's second touchdown catch of the game, a 43-yarder with 6:17 remaining, led the Oilers past the Browns. Houston converted fumble recoveries by Robert Brazile and Carter Hartwig into touchdowns by Smith (24-yard reception) and Earl Campbell (three-yard run). Steve Browns's 93-yard kickoff return gave the Oilers a 24-6 lead. Cleveland rebounded on three touchdown runs by Mike Pruitt (two, one, six yards) to grab a 27-24 edge. Smith gained 150 yards on seven receptions to total 1,107 yards for the season while Campbell added 130 yards rushing on 32 carries. Pruitt gained 153 yards (30 carries) to crack the 1,000-yard mark for the fourth time in five seasons (1,141).

| | | | | | |
|---|---|---|---|---|---|
| Cleveland | 3 | 10 | 14 | 0 | — 27 |
| Houston | 10 | 14 | 3 | 7 | — 34 |

Cle — FG Bahr 44
Hou — FG Kempf 40
Hou — Smith 24 pass from Bryant (Kempf kick)
Hou — Campbell 2 run (Kempf kick)
Cle — FG Bahr 45
Hou — Brown 93 kickoff return (Kempf kick)
Cle — Pruitt 2 run (Bahr kick)
Cle — Pruitt 1 run (Bahr kick)
Cle — Pruitt 4 run (Bahr kick)
Hou — Smith 43 pass from Luck (Kempf kick)

**Cincinnati 17, Detroit 9**—At Riverfront Stadium, attendance 45,728. Pete Johnson ran for more than 100 yards for the second straight week and scored two touchdowns to lead the Bengals over the Lions. Ken Riley's fumble recovery in the first quarter set up Johnson's one-yard scoring run and Louis Breeden's interception led to a 74-yard second-quarter scoring drive completed by Johnson's two-yard scoring burst. Johnson totaled 118 yards on 26 carries. Detroit's Eddie Murray kicked three field goals, including a career-best 54-yarder.

| | | | | | |
|---|---|---|---|---|---|
| Detroit | 0 | 6 | 3 | 0 | — 9 |
| Cincinnati | 7 | 7 | 3 | 0 | — 17 |

Cin — Johnson 1 run (Breech kick)
Cin — Johnson 2 run (Breech kick)
Det — FG Murray 54
Det — FG Murray 37
Cin — FG Breech 28
Det — FG Murray 29

**San Diego 41, Kansas City 38**—At San Diego Jack Murphy Stadium, attendance 35,510. Rolf Benirschke's 28-yard field goal with two seconds remaining helped the Chargers edge the Chiefs. The game was a passing duel between Kansas City's Bill Kenney and San Diego's Dan Fouts. Kenney completed 31 of 41 passes for 411 yards and four touchdowns, the last a three-yarder to Willie Scott with 1:34 left to tie the score 38-38. Fouts completed 25 of 36 for 285 yards and three scores, all to Kellen Winslow (14 catches for 162 yards). Kenney's performance gave him 4,187 yards for the season while Fouts joined the NFL's elite who have passed for over 30,000 yards in a career (30,114).

| | | | | | |
|---|---|---|---|---|---|
| Kansas City | 7 | 7 | 10 | 14 | — 38 |
| San Diego | 10 | 14 | 14 | 3 | — 41 |

SD — FG Benirschke 27
SD — Winslow 37 pass from Fouts (Benirschke kick)
KC — Carson 50 pass from Kenney (Lowery kick)
SD — Winslow 18 pass from Fouts (Benirschke kick)
KC — Paige 20 pass from Kenney (Lowery kick)
SD — Winslow 5 pass from Fouts (Benirschke kick)
KC — Brown 49 run (Lowery kick)
SD — Fouts 1 run (Benirschke kick)
KC — FG Lowery 49
SD — Chandler 44 pass from Luther (Benirschke kick)
KC — Paige 16 pass from Kenney (Lowery kick)
KC — Scott 3 pass from Kenney (Lowery kick)
SD — FG Benirschke 28

**New England 21, Los Angeles Rams 7**—At Anaheim Stadium, attendance 46,503. Mosi Tatupu ran for three touchdowns to lead the Patriots over the Rams. New England capitalized on three of Los Angeles' seven turnovers (six fumbles, one interception). Fumble recoveries by Andre Tippett and Clayton Weishuhn set up Tatupu scoring runs of four and seven yards and Don Blackmon's interception led to Tatupu's five-yard touchdown run. Tony Collins gained 42 yards to become the third Patriots' player to go over the 1,000-yard mark (1,001). Eric Dickerson had 94 yards on 27 carries to total 1,728 yards for the season and surpass George Rogers' 1981 rookie rushing record of 1,674 yards. The Rams outgained the Patriots 370 to 275 total yards.

| | | | | | |
|---|---|---|---|---|---|
| New England | 0 | 7 | 7 | 7 | — 21 |
| L.A. Rams | 7 | 0 | 0 | 0 | — 7 |

Rams — Farmer 46 pass from Ferragamo (Lansford kick)
NE — Tatupu 4 run (Zendejas kick)
NE — Tatupu 5 run (Zendejas kick)
NE — Tatupu 7 run (Zendejas kick)

**New Orleans 20, Philadelphia 17**—At Veterans Stadium, attendance 45,182. Morten Andersen's 50-yard field goal 5:30 into overtime lifted the Saints over the Eagles. New Orleans had opened a 17-3 lead but Philadelphia tied the score on Ron Jaworski's touchdown passes to Mike Quick (17 yards) and Harold Carmichael (7), the latter coming with 3:57 to play. Ken Stabler connected with Eugene Goodlow on two passes for 33 yards in overtime to set up Andersen's winning kick, the longest field goal in the history of overtime play. George Rogers ran for 76 yards on 22 carries to top the 1,000-yard mark for the season (1,020).

| | | | | | | | |
|---|---|---|---|---|---|---|---|
| New Orleans | 0 | 7 | 7 | 3 | 3 | — | 20 |
| Philadelphia | 0 | 3 | 0 | 14 | 0 | — | 17 |

NO — W. Wilson 21 pass from Stabler (Andersen kick)
Phil — FG Franklin 23
NO — G. Rogers 4 run (Andersen kick)
NO — FG Andersen 52
Phil — Quick 17 pass from Jaworski (Franklin kick)
Phil — Carmichael 7 pass from Jaworski (Franklin kick)
NO — FG Andersen 50

**St. Louis 34, Los Angeles Raiders 24**—At Memorial Coliseum, attendance 32,111. The Cardinals scored four touchdowns in a 17-minute span to down the Raiders 34-24. Neil Lomax, who completed 17 of 24 for 227 yards, fired a one-yard touchdown pass to Doug Marsh 21 seconds before halftime. Fifteen seconds later, defensive tackle Elois Grooms dashed 40-yards with a fumble recovery to cut the Raiders' lead to 24-20. Wayne Morris burst three-yards for a score in the third period and Lomax passed 15 yards to Pat Tilley 1:09 into the fourth quarter to complete the scoring. Ottis Anderson rushed 24 times for 119 yards to top the 1,000 yard mark (1,114) and scored the Cardinals' first touchdown, a one-yard run.

| | | | | | | |
|---|---|---|---|---|---|---|
| St. Louis | 0 | 20 | 7 | 7 | — | 34 |
| L.A. Raiders | 17 | 7 | 0 | 0 | — | 24 |

Raiders — King 34 pass from Plunkett (Bahr kick)
Raiders — FG Bahr 22
Raiders — Branch 5 pass from Plunkett (Bahr kick)
StL — Anderson 1 run (O'Donoghue kick)
Raiders — Allen 20 pass from Plunkett (Bahr kick)
StL — Marsh 1 pass from Lomax (kick blocked)
StL — Grooms 40 fumble recovery return (O'Donoghue kick)
StL — Morris 3 run (O'Donoghue kick)
StL — Tilley 15 pass from Lomax (O'Donoghue kick)

**San Francisco 23, Buffalo 10**—At Rich Stadium, attendance 38,039. Roger Craig and Wendell Tyler scored third-quarter touchdowns to give the 49ers a 23-10 comeback win. San Francisco trailed 10-6 at the half before a Buffalo fumble gave the 49ers the ball at the Bills' 41-yard line. Seven plays later, Joe Montana hit Craig on a four-yard touchdown pass for a 13-10 lead. Six minutes later, Tyler scored on a one-yard run. Ray Wersching kicked field goals of 37, 30, and 29 yards and Fred Dean registered a sack to give him an NFC-leading 17½.

| | | | | | | |
|---|---|---|---|---|---|---|
| San Francisco | 3 | 3 | 14 | 3 | — | 23 |
| Buffalo | 0 | 10 | 0 | 0 | — | 10 |

SF — FG Wersching 37
Buff — Leaks 1 run (Danelo kick)
SF — FG Wersching 29
Buff — FG Danelo 33
SF — Craig 4 pass from Montana (Wersching kick)
SF — Tyler 1 run (Wersching kick)
SF — FG Wersching 30

**Seattle 17, New York Giants 12**—At Giants Stadium, attendance 48,942. Dave Krieg threw for two touchdowns and the Seattle defense forced five turnovers as the Seahawks downed the Giants 17-12. Krieg followed Jacob Green's fumble recovery with a 12-yard touchdown pass to Steve Largent. Dave Brown's interception led to a six-yard scoring pass from Krieg to Paul Johns. Norm Johnson added a 31-yard field goal for a 17-6 halftime lead. Ali Haji-Sheikh provided all the Giants' scoring with four field goals (48, 44, 25, and 32 yards) to total 111 points for the season, breaking Pete Gogolak's 1970 club record of 107. New York outgained Seattle 440 to 183 total yards as the Giants' Jeff Rutledge completed 29 of 52 for 349 yards.

| | | | | | | |
|---|---|---|---|---|---|---|
| Seattle | 7 | 10 | 0 | 0 | — | 17 |
| New York Giants | 3 | 3 | 3 | 3 | — | 12 |

Sea — Largent 12 pass from Krieg (N. Johnson kick)
NYG — FG Haji-Sheikh 48
Sea — Johns 6 pass from Krieg (N. Johnson kick)
NYG — FG Haji-Sheikh 44
Sea — FG N. Johnson 31
NYG — FG Haji-Sheikh 25
NYG — FG Haji-Sheikh 32

**Washington 31, Dallas 10**—At Texas Stadium, attendance 65,074. Washington took over first place in the NFC East as Joe Theismann and John Riggins each contributed two touchdowns to help defeat Dallas 31-10. The Redskins scored on their first two possessions. Riggins had a three-yard run and Theismann hit Clint Didier on a 40-yard touchdown pass. Dallas trailed only 14-10 at halftime, but a pair of second-half interceptions by Greg Williams and one by Darrell Green ended the Dallas chances. Meanwhile, Theismann teamed with Art Monk (six receptions, 119 yards) on a 43-yard scoring pass and Riggins added a one-yard run. Dave Butz (2½ sacks) led a tenacious defense that held Tony Dorsett to only 34 yards rushing and allowed the Cowboys only 205 total yards. The Washington victory snapped the Cowboys' three-game winning streak.

| | | | | | | |
|---|---|---|---|---|---|---|
| Washington | 14 | 0 | 7 | 10 | — | 31 |
| Dallas | 7 | 3 | 0 | 0 | — | 10 |

Wash — Riggins 3 run (Moseley kick)
Wash — Didier 40 pass from Theismann (Moseley kick)
Dall — Cosbie 29 pass from D. White (Septien kick)
Dall — FG Septien 35
Wash — Monk 43 pass from Theismann (Moseley kick)
Wash — Riggins 1 run (Moseley kick)
Wash — FG Moseley 38

**MONDAY, DECEMBER 12**

**Green Bay 12, Tampa Bay 9**—At Tampa Stadium, attendance 50,763. Jan Stenerud kicked four field goals, including a 23-yarder with 28 seconds left to send the game into overtime, and followed with the deciding 23-yarder 4:07 into the overtime period. It was the Packers' NFL-record fifth overtime game of the season. Tampa Bay took a 9-6 lead on Adger Armstrong's four-yard touchdown reception with 7:33 left but could not hold on. Combined with his earlier field goals of 35 and 32 yards, Stenerud increased his career total to 338, bettering George Blanda's NFL mark of 335.

| | | | | | | | |
|---|---|---|---|---|---|---|---|
| Green Bay | 3 | 0 | 3 | 3 | 3 | — | 12 |
| Tampa Bay | 0 | 3 | 0 | 6 | 0 | — | 9 |

GB — FG Stenerud 35
TB — FG Capece 22
GB — FG Stenerud 32
TB — Armstrong 4 pass from Thompson (kick failed)
GB — FG Stenerud 23
GB — FG Stenerud 23

## SIXTEENTH WEEK SUMMARY

The Detroit Lions ended a 26-year title drought by defeating Tampa Bay 23-20 to clinch the NFC Central Division championship, their first of any kind since 1957. Washington needed 17 fourth-quarter points to beat the New York Giants 31-22, and claim the NFC East crown. The victory also helped the Redskins become the first NFC team ever to win 14 games in the regular season. The win overshadowed the effort of New York's Ali Haji-Sheikh, who kicked five field goals to total an NFL-record 35 for the season. Joe Montana's four touchdown passes helped the 49ers win 42-17 over Dallas and gave San Francisco the NFC West title. The Rams kept their playoff hopes alive by downing the Saints 26-24 on Mike Lansford's 42-yard field goal with two seconds left. Los Angeles captured the remaining NFC Wild Card berth when Chicago's Bob Thomas kicked a 22-yard field goal with 10 seconds left to defeat Green Bay 23-21. The win evened Chicago's record at 8-8, its best finish since 1979. Seattle gained entrance to the postseason tournament for the first time in its eight-year history with a 24-6 win over New England. Dave Krieg passed for two scores and Curt Warner added 116 yards rushing to lead the Seahawks' historic victory. Seattle's win eliminated Cleveland from the Wild Card picture despite the Browns 30-17 victory over the Steelers. Pittsburgh's Franco Harris gained 56 yards rushing to total 1,007, thus becoming the first player in NFL history to gain over 1,000 yards rushing in eight different seasons. The Raiders clinched the AFC home field advantage in the playoffs with a 30-14 win over the Chargers. Bill Kenney passed for two touchdowns to help the Chiefs past the Broncos 48-17. Miami's Mike Kozlowski returned two interceptions for touchdowns, just 61 seconds apart, in the Dolphins' 34-14 triumph over the Jets. The Cardinals' 31-7 win over the Eagles brought St. Louis its second winning season (8-7-1) in a row. Baltimore ended the season on a winning note, 20-10 over Houston, to snap a five-game losing streak. The 52-game AFC-NFC interconference series ended in a 26-26 tie as a result of Atlanta's 31-14 win over Buffalo and Minnesota's 20-14 defeat of Cincinnati.

**FRIDAY, DECEMBER 16**

**Miami 34, New York Jets 14**—At Orange Bowl, attendance 59,975. Safety Mike Kozlowski returned two fourth-quarter interceptions for touchdowns and Don Strock threw for two first-half scoring passes as the Dolphins beat the Jets 34-14. Strock's passes of 29 yards to Mark Duper and 2 yards to David Overstreet gave Miami a 14-7 half-time edge. New York tied the score 14-14 midway through the third period, but Uwe von Schamann's 49- and 20-yard field goals put the Dolphins ahead for good. Kozlowski's 35- and 38-yard interception returns for touchdowns just 61 seconds apart put the game out of reach. Bob Baumhower had three sacks to lead the defense.

| | | | | | | |
|---|---|---|---|---|---|---|
| New York Jets | 7 | 0 | 7 | 0 | — | 14 |
| Miami | 7 | 7 | 3 | 17 | — | 34 |

Mia — Duper 29 pass from Strock (von Schamann kick)
NYJ — McNeil 20 pass from Todd (Leahy kick)
Mia — Overstreet 2 pass from Strock (von Schamann kick)
NYJ — Barber 5 pass from McNeil (Ryan run)
Mia — FG von Schamann 49
Mia — FG von Schamann 20
Mia — Kozlowski 35 interception return (von Schamann kick)
Mia — Kozlowski 38 interception return (von Schamann kick)

**SATURDAY, DECEMBER 17**

**Minnesota 20, Cincinnati 14**—At Metrodome, attendance 51,565. Tony Galbreath scored a pair of fourth-quarter touchdowns to give the Vikings a 20-14 win in what turned out to be Bud Grant's last game as Minnesota's head coach. Galbreath's scores, both on fourth down and inches, tied the game 14-14 and put the Vikings in front 20-14. John Swain intercepted Ken Anderson's pass in the end zone with 4:20 remaining to seal the win. Cincinnati's Ken Riley finished his 15-year career in the NFL with his sixty-fourth and sixty-fifth interceptions. Grant resigned as the Vikings' head coach on January 28, 1984.

| | | | | | | |
|---|---|---|---|---|---|---|
| Cincinnati | 0 | 7 | 7 | 0 | — | 14 |
| Minnesota | 0 | 7 | 0 | 13 | — | 20 |

Minn — Jordan 2 pass from Wilson (Ricardo kick)
Cin — Ross 7 pass from Anderson (Breech kick)
Cin — Kinnebrew 2 run (Breech kick)
Minn — Galbreath 1 run (Ricardo kick)
Minn — Galbreath 1 run (kick blocked)

**Washington 31, New York Giants 22**—At Robert F. Kennedy Stadium, attendance 53,874. The Redskins scored 17 points in the fourth quarter to defeat the Giants and clinch the NFC Eastern Division title. New York led 19-7 midway through the third period on four Ali Haji-Sheikh field goals and Jeff Rutledge's six-yard touchdown pass to Joe Morris. Washington cut the deficit to 19-17 on Joe Theismann's three-yard run and Mark Moseley's 46-yard field goal. Theismann gave the Redskins the lead by throwing a seven-yard touchdown pass to Clint Didier. John Riggins (122 yards on 30 attempts) converted Dave Butz's fumble recovery into a two-yard scoring run with 1:37 to play to complete the comeback. Riggins' scoring run was his twenty-fourth rushing touchdown this season, an NFL record.

| | | | | | | |
|---|---|---|---|---|---|---|
| New York Giants | 3 | 9 | 7 | 3 | — | 22 |
| Washington | 0 | 7 | 7 | 17 | — | 31 |

NYG — FG Haji-Sheikh 20
Wash — Brown 17 pass from Theismann (Moseley kick)
NYG — FG Haji-Sheikh 39
NYG — FG Haji-Sheikh 19
NYG — FG Haji-Sheikh 45
NYG — Morris 6 pass from Rutledge (Haji-Sheikh kick)
Wash — Theismann 3 run (Moseley kick)
Wash — FG Moseley 46
NYG — FG Haji-Sheikh 28
Wash — Didier 7 pass from Theismann (Moseley kick)
Wash — Riggins 2 run (Moseley kick)

**SUNDAY, DECEMBER 18**

**Atlanta 31, Buffalo 14**—At Atlanta-Fulton County Stadium, attendance 31,015. William Andrews ran for 158 yards on 28 carries and scored three touchdowns to help the Falcons beat the Bills. Andrews scored on runs of 10 and 1 yards and caught a six-yard touchdown pass from Steve Bartkowski. He had seven receptions for 49 yards to bring his season rushing-receiving yardage total to 2,176 yards and become the first player since O.J. Simpson to total more than 2,000 yards in a season twice in a career. Buffalo, plagued by penalties (15 for 123 yards) and six quarterback sacks, could never get on track.

| | | | | | | |
|---|---|---|---|---|---|---|
| Buffalo | 0 | 7 | 0 | 7 | — | 14 |
| Atlanta | 3 | 14 | 7 | 7 | — | 31 |

Atl — FG Luckhurst 40
Atl — Cox 7 pass from Bartkowski (Luckhurst kick)
Atl — Andrews 10 run (Luckhurst kick)
Buff — Tuttle 13 pass from Ferguson (Danelo kick)
Atl — Andrews 1 run (Luckhurst kick)
Atl — Andrews 6 pass from Bartkowski (Luckhurst kick)
Buff — Dawkins 28 pass from Kofler (Danelo kick)

**Kansas City 48, Denver 17**—At Arrowhead Stadium, attendance 11,377. Bill Kenney overcame a wind-chill factor of minus-30 to throw two touchdown passes and lead the Chiefs over the Broncos. Lucious Smith intercepted a John Elway pass on the third play of the game and returned it 58 yards for a touchdown and Kenney followed with first-quarter scoring passes of 48 yards to Carlos Carson and 17 yards to Willie Scott. Theotis Brown added scoring runs of one and six yards and backup quarterback Todd Blackledge finished the scoring with a 23-yard touchdown pass to Stephon Paige. It was the most points scored against the Broncos since the Chargers totaled 55 in 1968.

| | | | | | | |
|---|---|---|---|---|---|---|
| Denver | 0 | 3 | 0 | 14 | — | 17 |
| Kansas City | 21 | 7 | 10 | 10 | — | 48 |

KC — Smith 58 interception return (Lowery kick)
KC — Carson 48 pass from Kenney (Lowery kick)
KC — Scott 17 pass from Kenney (Lowery kick)
Den — FG Karlis 24
KC — Brown 1 run (Lowery kick)
KC — FG Lowery 38
KC — Brown 6 run (Lowery kick)
KC — FG Lowery 43
Den — Willhite 1 run (Karlis kick)
Den — Willhite 2 run (Karlis kick)
KC — Paige 23 pass from Blackledge (Lowery kick)

**Chicago 23, Green Bay 21**—At Soldier Field, attendance 35,807. Bob Thomas kicked a 22-yard field goal with 10 seconds remaining to give the Bears a 23-21 victory and an 8-8 season record, their best since 1979. Chicago capitalized on seven Green Bay turnovers (three fumbles, four interceptions). Al Harris' fumble recovery set up Jim McMahon's 35-yard scoring pass to Willie Gault for a 7-0 advantage. The Packers led 14-7 at halftime but McMahon converted Dan Rains' fumble recovery into a 22-yard scoring pass to Dennis McKinnon to tie the score. McMahon's six-yard touchdown run put the Bears up 20-14 but Lynn Dickey threw a five-yard pass to Paul Coffman with 3:08

left for a 21-20 Packers edge. Walter Payton gained 148 yards on 30 carries.

| | | | | | |
|---|---|---|---|---|---|
| Green Bay | 7 | 7 | 0 | 7 | — 21 |
| Chicago | 7 | 0 | 7 | 9 | — 23 |

Chi — Gault 35 pass from McMahon (B. Thomas kick)
GB — Dickey 1 run (Stenerud kick)
GB — Lofton 31 pass from Dickey (Stenerud kick)
Chi — McKinnon 22 pass from McMahon (B. Thomas kick)
Chi — McMahon 6 run (run failed)
GB — Coffman 5 pass from Dickey (Stenerud kick)
Chi — FG B. Thomas 22

**Baltimore 20, Houston 10**—At Memorial Stadium, attendance 20,418. Kim Anderson returned an interception 71 yards for a touchdown and Curtis Dickey ran for 110 yards on 23 carries to help the Colts snap a five-game losing streak. The teams traded field goals before Anderson's second-quarter score gave Baltimore the lead for good, 10-3. Vernon Maxwell's interception set up Mike Pagel's 12-yard touchdown pass to Pat Beach with 1:56 left and James Burroughs' interception in the end zone with 54 seconds remaining sealed the win. Raul Allegre kicked field goals of 48 and 37 yards to set a Colts season-record (30).

| | | | | | |
|---|---|---|---|---|---|
| Houston | 3 | 0 | 0 | 7 | — 10 |
| Baltimore | 3 | 7 | 3 | 7 | — 20 |

Hou — FG Kempf 34
Balt — FG Allegre 48
Balt — K. Anderson 71 interception return (Allegre kick)
Balt — FG Allegre 37
Hou — Dressel 7 pass from Luck (Kempf kick)
Balt — Beach 12 pass from Pagel (Allegre kick)

**Los Angeles Rams 26, New Orleans 24**—At Louisiana Superdome, attendance 70,148. Mike Lansford's 42-yard field goal with two seconds to play gave the Rams the win and earned them a spot in the playoffs as a Wild Card entry. Los Angeles' defense provided most of the team's scoring punch. Jack Youngblood tackled Ken Stabler in the end zone for a safety and safeties Johnnie Johnson and Nolan Cromwell returned interceptions for touchdowns of 31 and 43 yards. Henry Ellard's 72-yard punt return for a touchdown put Los Angeles ahead 23-17 in the fourth quarter. Steve Korte's fumble recovery in the end zone with 3:47 left gave New Orleans a 24-23 edge, but Vince Ferragamo guided the Rams from their own 20-yard line to the Saints' 27 to set up Lansford's decisive kick with six seconds remaining.

| | | | | | |
|---|---|---|---|---|---|
| L.A. Rams | 2 | 7 | 7 | 10 | — 26 |
| New Orleans | 7 | 0 | 7 | 10 | — 24 |

NO — Groth 11 pass from Stabler (Andersen kick)
Rams — Safety, Jack Youngblood tackled Stabler in end zone
Rams — Ellard 72 punt return (Lansford kick)
Rams — Johnson 31 interception return (Lansford kick)
NO — D. Wilson 1 run (Andersen kick)
NO — FG Andersen 20
Rams — Cromwell 43 interception return (Lansford kick)
NO — Korte fumble recovery in end zone (Andersen kick)
Rams — FG Lansford 42

**Seattle 24, New England 6**—At Kingdome, attendance 59,688. Dave Krieg threw for two touchdowns and ran for a third to lead the Seahawks into the playoffs for the first time in their eight-year history. Seattle led from the start on Norm Johnson's 29-yard field goal and Krieg's 46-yard touchdown pass to Steve Largent for a 10-6 halftime lead. Krieg (13 of 21 for 230 yards) added a 16-yard scoring pass to Dan Doornink in the third period and ran two yards for the Seahawks' final points in the fourth quarter. Curt Warner gained 116 yards on 26 carries and Jacob Green led the defense with three sacks.

| | | | | | |
|---|---|---|---|---|---|
| New England | 0 | 6 | 0 | 0 | — 6 |
| Seattle | 3 | 7 | 7 | 7 | — 24 |

Sea — FG N. Johnson 29
Sea — Largent 46 pass from Krieg (N. Johnson kick)
NE — Ramsey 33 pass from Eason (kick failed)
Sea — Doornink 16 pass from Krieg (N. Johnson kick)
Sea — Krieg 2 run (N. Johnson kick)

**St. Louis 31, Philadelphia 7**—At Busch Memorial Stadium, attendance 21,902. Ottis Anderson gained 156 yards rushing on 23 carries and Neil Lomax threw for two touchdowns, despite playing on a frozen, snow-covered field, to lead the Cardinals over the Eagles. Lionel Washington's pair of interceptions led to St. Louis' first two scores, a 12-yard run by Anderson and a 10-yard pass from Lomax to Roy Green. Randy Love scored on a one-yard run to complete an 83-yard third quarter drive and Doug Marsh's 29-yard touchdown reception finished the scoring. Green caught 6 passes for 64 yards to raise his season total to a team-record 78.

| | | | | | |
|---|---|---|---|---|---|
| Philadelphia | 0 | 0 | 0 | 7 | — 7 |
| St. Louis | 7 | 7 | 10 | 7 | — 31 |

StL — Anderson 12 run (O'Donoghue kick)
StL — Green 10 pass from Lomax (O'Donoghue kick)
StL — FG O'Donoghue 28
StL — Love 1 run (O'Donoghue kick)
StL — Marsh 29 pass from Lomax (O'Donoghue kick)
Phil — Quick 20 pass from Jaworski (Franklin kick)

**Cleveland 30, Pittsburgh 17**—At Cleveland Stadium, attendance 72,313. Brian Sipe threw for four touchdowns, including a pair to Harry Holt, as the Browns beat the Steelers 30-17. Sipe completed 14 of 22 passes for 199 yards and had touchdown passes to Rocky Belk, (64 yards), Ricky Feacher (4), and Holt (3, 1). Franco Harris rushed for 56 yards, bringing his season total to 1,007 and marking the first time in NFL history a running back has rushed for over 1,000 yards in eight different seasons.

| | | | | | |
|---|---|---|---|---|---|
| Pittsburgh | 3 | 7 | 0 | 7 | — 17 |
| Cleveland | 9 | 14 | 7 | 0 | — 30 |

Pitt — FG Anderson 34
Cle — Belk 64 pass from Sipe (kick failed)
Cle — FG Bahr 30
Cle — Holt 3 pass from Sipe (Bahr kick)
Pitt — Stoudt 3 run (Anderson kick)
Cle — Feacher 4 pass from Sipe (Bahr kick)
Cle — Holt 1 pass from Sipe (Bahr kick)
Pitt — F. Harris 2 pass from Malone (Anderson kick)

**Los Angeles Raiders 30, San Diego 14**—At Memorial Coliseum, attendance 57,325. Jim Plunkett completed 21 of 30 passes for 332 yards, Marcus Allen scored two touchdowns, and Chris Bahr kicked three field goals (21, 32, and 28 yards) as the Raiders defeated the Chargers 30-14 to clinch the home-field advantage in the playoffs. Allen touchdown runs of eight and five yards opened and closed the Raiders' scoring, and Plunkett's four-yard touchdown pass to Cliff Branch completed a 90-yard drive that gave Los Angeles a 23-14 lead. Todd Christensen caught 8 passes for 136 yards to give him the NFL pass receiving championship with 92 receptions for 1,247 yards. Allen gained 72 yards to total 1,014 for the year.

| | | | | | |
|---|---|---|---|---|---|
| San Diego | 7 | 0 | 7 | 0 | — 14 |
| L.A. Raiders | 7 | 6 | 3 | 14 | — 30 |

SD — Duckworth 40 pass from Luther (Benirschke kick)
Raiders — Allen 8 run (Bahr kick)
Raiders — FG Bahr 21
Raiders — FG Bahr 32
Raiders — FG Bahr 28
SD — Muncie 2 run (Benirschke kick)
Raiders — Branch 4 pass from Plunkett (Bahr kick)
Raiders — Allen 5 run (Bahr kick)

**Detroit 23, Tampa Bay 20**—At Pontiac Silverdome, attendance 78,392. Touchdowns by Billy Sims and Jeff Chadwick, and three Eddie Murray field goals lifted the Lions to their first title since 1957. Sims' three-yard run tied the score 7-7 early in the second quarter and Murray field goals of 34 and 36 yards tied the game 13-13 in the third period. Murray's 38-yarder and Gary Danielson's six-yard touchdown pass to Chadwick gave the Lions a commanding 23-13 lead with 2:32 to play. Sims gained 56 yards rushing to total 1,040 yards on the season. The win overshadowed the performance of Tampa Bay's Jack Thompson, who completed 28 of 42 passes for 373 yards and three touchdowns.

| | | | | | |
|---|---|---|---|---|---|
| Tampa Bay | 7 | 6 | 0 | 7 | — 20 |
| Detroit | 0 | 10 | 3 | 10 | — 23 |

TB — J. Bell 4 pass from Thompson (Warnke kick)
Det — Sims 3 run (Murray kick)
Det — FG Murray 34
TB — House 20 pass from Thompson (kick failed)
Det — FG Murray 36
Det — FG Murray 38
Det — Chadwick 6 pass from Danielson (Murray kick)
TB — Carter 13 pass from Thompson (Yarno kick)

**MONDAY, DECEMBER 19**

**San Francisco 42, Dallas 17**—At Candlestick Park, attendance 59,957. Joe Montana completed 14 of 26 passes for 223 yards and four touchdowns to lead the 49ers to a 42-17 victory and the NFC West title. Lawrence Pillers' 16-yard interception return 90 seconds into the game set up Montana's six-yard scoring pass to Roger Craig. The 49ers built a 21-3 lead after the first quarter on Dana McLemore's punt return and Freddie Solomon's 77-yard touchdown on a screen pass. San Francisco extended its 21-10 halftime lead, marching 75 yards with the second-half kickoff. Montana hit Russ Francis on an 18-yard scoring pass. Eric Wright's 48-yard interception return for a touchdown preceded Montana's final scoring pass, a 16-yarder to Craig.

| | | | | | |
|---|---|---|---|---|---|
| Dallas | 3 | 7 | 0 | 7 | — 17 |
| San Francisco | 21 | 0 | 7 | 14 | — 42 |

SF — Craig 6 pass from Montana (Wersching kick)
SF — McLemore 56 punt return (Wersching kick)
Dall — FG Septien 47
SF — Solomon 77 pass from Montana (Wersching kick)
Dall — D. White 1 run (Septien kick)
SF — Francis 18 pass from Montana (Wersching kick)
Dall — Hill 13 pass from D. White (Septien kick)
SF — Wright 48 interception return (Wersching kick)
SF — Craig 16 pass from Montana (Wersching kick)

## SEVENTEENTH WEEK

**SATURDAY, DECEMBER 24, 1983**
**AFC FIRST-ROUND PLAYOFF GAME**

**Seattle 31, Denver 7**—At Kingdome, attendance 64,275. Quarterback Dave Krieg and running back Curt Warner provided the offensive spark that carried Seattle to victory in the first playoff game in the Seahawks' eight-year history. Krieg completed 12 of 13 passes for 200 yards, including his last 10 in a row. Warner rushed 23 times for 99 yards. On its first possession of the third period, Seattle drove 73 yards in five plays for a touchdown that gave the Seahawks a 17-7 lead. The score came on a five-yard pass from Krieg to tight end Pete Metzelaars. Seattle put the game out of reach early in the final period when Krieg hit wide receiver Paul Johns with an 18-yard touchdown pass.

| | | | | | |
|---|---|---|---|---|---|
| Denver | 7 | 0 | 0 | 0 | — 7 |
| Seattle | 7 | 3 | 7 | 14 | — 31 |

Sea — Largent 17 pass from Krieg (N. Johnson kick)
Den — Myles 13 pass from DeBerg (Karlis kick)
Sea — FG N. Johnson 37
Sea — Metzelaars 5 pass from Krieg (N. Johnson kick)
Sea — Johns 18 pass from Krieg (N. Johnson kick)
Sea — Hughes 2 run (N. Johnson kick)

**MONDAY, DECEMBER 26, 1983**
**NFC FIRST-ROUND PLAYOFF GAME**

**Los Angeles Rams 24, Dallas 17**—At Texas Stadium, attendance 62,118. The Rams, under first-year head coach John Robinson, advanced to the NFC divisional playoffs with a 24-17 victory over Dallas. Rams rookie running back Eric Dickerson rushed 23 times for 99 yards and quarterback Vince Ferragamo threw three touchdown passes while completing 15 of 30 for 162 yards to lead the victory. The Los Angeles defense also contributed with interceptions by Mel Owens, Jim Collins, and LeRoy Irvin. George Farmer paced the Rams' receivers with five catches for 47 yards, including an eight-yard touchdown. Cowboys quarterback Danny White completed 32 of 53 passes for 330 yards and two touchdowns, but threw three interceptions. Tony Hill of the Cowboys caught nine passes for 115 yards, including a 14-yard touchdown in the second period.

| | | | | | |
|---|---|---|---|---|---|
| L.A. Rams | 7 | 0 | 7 | 10 | — 24 |
| Dallas | 0 | 7 | 3 | 7 | — 17 |

Rams — D. Hill 18 pass from Ferragamo (Lansford kick)
Dall — T. Hill 14 pass from D. White (Septien kick)
Dall — FG Septien 41
Rams — Dennard 16 pass from Ferragamo (Lansford kick)
Rams — Farmer 8 pass from Ferragamo (Lansford kick)
Rams — FG Lansford 20
Dall — Cosbie 2 pass from D. White (Septien kick)

## EIGHTEENTH WEEK

**SATURDAY, DECEMBER 31, 1983**
**AFC DIVISIONAL PLAYOFF GAME**

**Seattle 27, Miami 20**—At Orange Bowl, attendance 74,136. Running back Curt Warner's two-yard scoring run with 1:48 remaining clinched the Seahawks' playoff victory over the Dolphins. Warner's touchdown came at the end of a 66-yard, five-play drive that included a 40-yard pass from quarterback Dave Krieg to wide receiver Steve Largent. Kicker Norm Johnson added a 37-yard field goal 33 seconds later after Miami's Fulton Walker fumbled the ensuing kickoff. The Dolphins had led 13-7, but four Miami turnovers in the second half led to their downfall. Warner rushed for 113 yards on 29 carries to lead the Seahawks. Krieg completed 15 of 28 passes for 192 yards and had one touchdown with one interception. Miami quarterback Dan Marino completed 15 of 25 for 193 yards and threw two touchdowns with two interceptions. Dolphins wide receiver Mark Duper had nine catches for 117 yards.

| | | | | | |
|---|---|---|---|---|---|
| Seattle | 0 | 7 | 7 | 13 | — 27 |
| Miami | 0 | 13 | 0 | 7 | — 20 |

Mia — Johnson 19 pass from Marino (kick failed)
Sea — C. Bryant 6 pass from Krieg (N. Johnson kick)
Mia — Duper 32 pass from Marino (von Schamann kick)
Sea — Warner 1 run (N. Johnson kick)
Sea — FG N. Johnson 27
Mia — Bennett 3 run (von Schamann kick)
Sea — Warner 2 run (N. Johnson kick)
Sea — FG N. Johnson 37

**SATURDAY, DECEMBER 31, 1983**
**NFC DIVISIONAL PLAYOFF GAME**

**San Francisco 24, Detroit 23**—At Candlestick Park, attendance 59,979. The NFC West champion 49ers gained their second NFC Championship Game berth in the last three seasons with a 24-23 win over the NFC Central titlist Lions. San Francisco took a 7-3 first-period lead on running back Roger Craig's one-yard run. Detroit's Eddie Murray kicked his third field goal of the first half (54 yards) to narrow the 49ers' halftime edge to 14-9. Ray Wersching's 19-yard field goal was the only scoring in the third period, and gave San Francisco a 17-9 lead. Detroit running back Billy Sims, who rushed 20 times for 114 yards, scored with 13:32 remaining in the game on an 11-yard run and again with 4:54 left on a three-yard run to help give the Lions a 23-17 advantage. San Francisco then drove 70 yards in nine plays for the game-winning score on a 13-yard pass from quarterback Joe Montana (18 of 33 for 201 yards, one touchdown, one interception) to wide receiver Freddie Solomon. The Lions then drove into position for the possible winning field goal of 43 yards, but Murray's try was wide right.

Detroit     3   6   0   14  — 23
San Francisco   7   7   3   7  — 24
Det — FG Murray 37
SF — Craig 1 run (Wersching kick)
SF — Tyler 2 run (Wersching kick)
Det — FG Murray 21
Det — FG Murray 54
SF — FG Wersching 19
Det — Sims 11 run (Murray kick)
Det — Sims 3 run (Murray kick)
SF — Solomon 14 pass from Montana (Wersching kick)

## SUNDAY, JANUARY 1, 1984
### AFC DIVISIONAL PLAYOFF GAME

**Los Angeles Raiders 38, Pittsburgh 10**—At Memorial Coliseum, attendance 90,380. A 21-point outburst by the Raiders in the third period put the game out of reach and the Raiders into the AFC Championship Game against the Seattle Seahawks. The Raiders' three touchdowns in the third period came on runs of 9 yards by Kenny King, 49 yards by Marcus Allen, and 2 yards by Frank Hawkins. Quarterback Jim Plunkett directed the Raiders' offense to 413 total yards, consisting of 188 on the ground and 225 through the air. Plunkett completed 21 of 34 for 225 yards. Allen rushed 13 times for 121 yards. Tight end Todd Christensen had seven receptions for 88 yards. The Raiders recorded five sacks, including two-and-a-half by defensive end Lyle Alzado.

Pittsburgh    3   0   7   0  — 10
L.A. Raiders   7   10   21   0  — 38
Pitt — FG Anderson 17
Raiders — Hayes 18 interception return (Bahr kick)
Raiders — Allen 4 run (Bahr kick)
Raiders — FG Bahr 45
Raiders — King 9 run (Bahr kick)
Raiders — Allen 49 run (Bahr kick)
Pitt — Stallworth 58 pass from Stoudt (Anderson kick)
Raiders — Hawkins 2 run (Bahr kick)

## SUNDAY, JANUARY 1, 1984
### NFC DIVISIONAL PLAYOFF GAME

**Washington 51, Los Angeles Rams 7**—At Robert F. Kennedy Stadium, attendance 54,440. Running back John Riggins rushed 25 times for 119 yards and three touchdowns (his fifth straight 100-yard rushing effort in postseason play) to lead the NFC East champion Redskins to a 51-7 win over the Los Angeles Rams. Riggins' three-yard scoring run 6:11 into the first period completed an eight-play, 65-yard drive for the Redskins. Quarterback Joe Theismann completed 18 of 23 for 302 yards, including 40- and 21-yard touchdowns to wide receiver Art Monk. Wide receiver Charlie Brown caught six passes for 171 yards. Washington built a 24-0 lead before Los Angeles scored on a 32-yard touchdown catch by wide receiver Preston Dennard. The Redskins' 38 first-half points set an NFL playoff record. Rookie cornerback Darrell Green completed Washington's scoring with a 72-yard interception return for a touchdown. Mark Moseley made 42-, 36-, and 41-yard field goals.

L.A. Rams    0   7   0   0  — 7
Washington   17   21   6   7  — 51
Wash — Riggins 3 run (Moseley kick)
Wash — Monk 40 pass from Theismann (Moseley kick)
Wash — FG Moseley 42
Wash — Riggins 1 run (Moseley kick)
Rams — Dennard 32 pass from Ferragamo (Lansford kick)
Wash — Monk 21 pass from Theismann (Moseley kick)
Wash — Riggins 1 run (Moseley kick)
Wash — FG Moseley 36
Wash — FG Moseley 41
Wash — Green 72 interception return (Moseley kick)

## NINETEENTH WEEK
SUNDAY, JANUARY 8, 1984
### AFC CHAMPIONSHIP GAME

**Los Angeles Raiders 30, Seattle 14**—At Memorial Coliseum, attendance 88,734. Los Angeles rolled up 401 yards offense and limited Seattle to 167 (65 rushing, 102 passing) as the Raiders advanced to Super Bowl XVIII. Raiders running back Marcus Allen carried 25 times for 154 yards and scored on a three-yard touchdown pass from quarterback Jim Plunkett, who completed 17 of 24 for 214 yards with two interceptions. The Raiders built a 20-0 halftime lead as running back Frank Hawkins scored on touchdown runs of one and five yards. The Raiders capitalized on five interceptions and four sacks. Safety Mike Davis had two of the Raiders' interceptions. Wide receiver Malcolm Barnwell had five catches for 116 yards while Allen caught seven for 62.

Seattle    0   0   7   7  — 14
L.A. Raiders   3   17   7   3  — 30
Raiders — FG Bahr 20
Raiders — Hawkins 1 run (Bahr kick)
Raiders — Hawkins 5 run (Bahr kick)
Raiders — FG Bahr 45
Raiders — Allen 3 pass from Plunkett (Bahr kick)
Seattle — Doornink 11 pass from Zorn (N. Johnson kick)

Raiders — FG Bahr 35
Seattle — Young 9 pass from Zorn (N. Johnson kick)

## SUNDAY, JANUARY 8, 1984
### NFC CHAMPIONSHIP GAME

**Washington 24, San Francisco 21**—At Robert F. Kennedy Stadium, attendance 55,363. The Washington Redskins gained their second consecutive NFC title and Super Bowl trip by defeating NFC West champion San Francisco 24-21. After a scoreless first quarter, the Redskins drove 64 yards in five plays to take a 7-0 lead on running back John Riggins' four-yard run. Riggins, who carried 36 times for 123 yards (his sixth straight 100-yard playoff game), raised Washington's lead to 14-0 on a one-yard run with 3:45 remaining in the third period. After the 49ers punted, the Redskins took over on their own 20-yard line. Following a 10-yard gain by Riggins, quarterback Joe Theismann completed a 70-yard touchdown pass to wide receiver Charlie Brown with 1:02 remaining in the third period. The 49ers scored in the fourth period by completing a nine-play, 79-yard drive with a five-yard touchdown pass from quarterback Joe Montana to wide receiver Mike Wilson. With 9:58 remaining, Montana completed a 76-yard touchdown pass to wide receiver Freddie Solomon to narrow the Redskins' lead to 21-14. After holding Washington on four downs, San Francisco tied the game on a four-play, 53-yard drive which ended in a 12-yard touchdown catch by Wilson from Montana. The Redskins got the ball back with 6:52 remaining in the game on their own 14-yard line. They drove to the 49ers' 8-yard line in 13 plays and Mark Moseley kicked the decisive 25-yard field goal with 40 seconds left.

San Francisco   0   0   0   21  — 21
Washington    0   7   14   3  — 24
Wash — Riggins 4 run (Moseley kick)
Wash — Riggins 1 run (Moseley kick)
Wash — Brown 70 pass from Theismann (Moseley kick)
SF — Wilson 5 pass from Montana (Wersching kick)
SF — Solomon 76 pass from Montana (Wersching kick)
SF — Wilson 12 pass from Montana (Wersching kick)
Wash — FG Moseley 25

## TWENTIETH WEEK
SUPER BOWL XVIII
SUNDAY, JANUARY 22, 1984
TAMPA, FLORIDA

**Los Angeles Raiders 38, Washington 9**—At Tampa Stadium, attendance 72,920. The Los Angeles Raiders dominated the Washington Redskins from the beginning in Super Bowl XVIII and achieved the most lopsided victory in Super Bowl history, surpassing Green Bay's 35-10 win over Kansas City in Super Bowl I. The Raiders took a 7-0 lead 4:52 into the game when Derrick Jensen blocked a Jeff Hayes punt and recovered it in the end zone for a touchdown. With 9:14 remaining in the first half, Raiders quarterback Jim Plunkett threw a 12-yard touchdown pass to wide receiver Cliff Branch to complete a three-play, 65-yard drive. Washington cut the Raiders' lead to 14-3 on a 24-yard field goal by Mark Moseley. With seven seconds left in the first half, Raiders linebacker Jack Squirek intercepted a Joe Theismann pass at the Redskins' 5-yard line and ran it in for a touchdown to give Los Angeles a 21-3 halftime lead. In the third period, running back Marcus Allen, who rushed for a Super Bowl-record 191 yards on 20 carries, increased the Raiders' lead to 35-3 on touchdown runs of 5 and 74 yards, the latter erasing the previous Super Bowl record of 58 yards set by Baltimore's Tom Matte in Game III. Allen was named the game's most valuable player. The victory over Washington raised Raiders coach Tom Flores' playoff record to 8-1, including a 27-10 win against Philadelphia in Super Bowl XV. The 38 points scored by the Raiders against Washington was the highest point total by a Super Bowl team. The previous high was 35 points by Green Bay in Game I.

Washington    0   3   6   0  — 9
L.A. Raiders   7   14   14   3  — 38
Raiders — Jensen recovered blocked punt in end zone (Bahr kick)
Raiders — Branch 12 pass from Plunkett (Bahr kick)
Wash — FG Moseley 24
Raiders — Squirek 5 interception return (Bahr kick)
Wash — Riggins 1 run (kick blocked)
Raiders — Allen 5 run (Bahr kick)
Raiders — Allen 74 run (Bahr kick)
Raiders — FG Bahr 21

## TWENTY-FIRST WEEK
AFC-NFC PRO BOWL
SUNDAY, JANUARY 29, 1984
HONOLULU, HAWAII

**NFC 45, AFC 3**—At Aloha Stadium, attendance 50,445. The NFC won its sixth Pro Bowl in the last seven seasons 45-3 over the AFC. The NFC was led by most valuable player Joe Theismann of Washington, who completed 21 of 27 passes for 242 yards and three touchdowns. Theismann set Pro Bowl records for completions and touchdown passes. The NFC established Pro Bowl marks for most

points scored and fewest points allowed. Running back William Andrews of Atlanta had six carries for 43 yards and caught four passes for 49 yards, including scoring receptions of 16 and 2 yards. Los Angeles Rams rookie Eric Dickerson gained 46 yards on 11 carries, including a 14-yard touchdown run, and had five catches for 45 yards. Rams safety Nolan Cromwell had a 44-yard interception return for a touchdown 1:39 into the third period, to give the NFC a commanding 24-3 lead. Green Bay wide receiver James Lofton caught an eight-yard touchdown, while Packer tight end Paul Coffman had a six-yard scoring catch.

NFC   3   14   14   14  — 45
AFC   0   3   0   0  — 3
NFC — FG Haji-Sheikh 23
NFC — Andrews 16 pass from Theismann (Haji-Sheikh kick)
NFC — Andrews 2 pass from Montana (Haji-Sheikh kick)
AFC — FG Anderson 43
NFC — Cromwell 44 interception return (Haji-Sheikh kick)
NFC — Lofton 8 pass from Theismann (Haji-Sheikh kick)
NFC — Coffman 6 pass from Theismann (Haji-Sheikh kick)
NFC — Dickerson 14 run (Haji-Sheikh kick)

# 1983 Paid Attendance Breakdown

|  | Games | Attendance | Average |
|---|---|---|---|
| AFC Preseason | 9 | 402,996 | |
| NFC Preseason | 8 | 459,296 | |
| AFC-NFC Preseason, Interconference | 40 | 2,002,043 | |
| **NFL Preseason Total** | **57** | **2,864,335** | **50,251** |
| AFC Regular Season | 86 | 4,948,776 | |
| NFC Regular Season | 86 | 5,326,091 | |
| AFC-NFC Regular Season, Interconference | 52 | 3,002,355 | |
| **NFL Regular Season Total** | **224** | **13,277,222** | **59,273** |
| AFC First-Round Playoff | 1 | | |
| (Denver at Seattle) | | 64,275 | |
| AFC Divisional Playoffs | 2 | | |
| (Seattle at Miami) | | 74,136 | |
| (Pittsburgh at Los Angeles Raiders) | | 90,380 | |
| AFC Championship | 1 | | |
| (Seattle at Los Angeles Raiders) | | 91,445 | |
| NFC First-Round Playoff | 1 | | |
| (Los Angeles Rams at Dallas) | | 62,118 | |
| NFC Divisional Playoffs | 2 | | |
| (Detroit at San Francisco) | | 59,979 | |
| (Los Angeles Rams at Washington) | | 54,440 | |
| NFC Championship | 1 | | |
| (San Francisco at Washington) | | 55,363 | |
| Super Bowl XVIII at Tampa, Fla. | 1 | | |
| (Washington vs. Los Angeles Raiders) | | 72,932 | |
| AFC-NFC Pro Bowl at Honolulu, Hawaii | 1 | 50,445 | |
| **NFL Postseason Total** | **10** | **675,513** | **67,551** |
| **NFL All Games** | **291** | **16,817,070** | **57,791** |

# 1983 Professional Football Awards

| | NFL | AFC | NFC |
|---|---|---|---|
| **Professional Football Writers Association** | | | |
| Most Valuable Player | Joe Theismann | | |
| Rookie of the Year | Eric Dickerson | | |
| Coach of the Year | | Chuck Noll | Joe Gibbs |
| **Associated Press** | | | |
| Most Valuable Player | Joe Theismann | | |
| Offensive Player-of-the-Year | Joe Theismann | | |
| Defensive Player-of-the-Year | Doug Betters | | |
| Rookie of the Year—Offense | Eric Dickerson | | |
| Rookie of the Year—Defense | Vernon Maxwell | | |
| Coach of the Year | Joe Gibbs | | |
| **United Press International** | | | |
| Player of the Year | | Curt Warner | Eric Dickerson |
| Rookie of the Year | | Curt Warner | Eric Dickerson |
| Coach of the Year | | Chuck Knox | John Robinson |
| **Newspaper Enterprise Association** | | | |
| Jim Thorpe Trophy—MVP | Joe Theismann | | |
| Bert Bell Trophy-Rookie of the Year | Eric Dickerson | | |
| George Halas Trophy—Defensive Player of the Year | Jack Lambert | | |
| **The Sporting News** | | | |
| Player of the Year | Eric Dickerson | | |
| Rookie of the Year | Dan Marino | | |
| Coach of the Year | Joe Gibbs | | |
| **Pro Football Weekly** | | | |
| Offensive Most Valuable Player | Joe Theismann | | |
| Defensive Most Valuable Player | Bob Baumhower | | |
| Offensive Rookie of the Year | Eric Dickerson | | |
| Defensive Rookie of the Year | Vernon Maxwell | | |
| Comeback Player of the Year | Billy Johnson | | |
| Coach of the Year | Joe Gibbs | | |
| **Football News** | | | |
| Coach of the Year | | Chuck Knox | John Robinson |
| Rookie of the Year | Eric Dickerson | | |
| **AFC-NFC Pro Bowl** | | | |
| Player of the Game | Joe Theismann | | |
| **Maxwell Club** | | | |
| Player of the Year | John Riggins | | |
| **College and Pro Football Newsweekly** | | | |
| Player of the Year | Eric Dickerson | | |
| Rookie of the Year | Eric Dickerson | | |
| Coach of the Year | Joe Gibbs | | |
| **Football Digest** | | | |
| Player of the Year | Joe Theismann | | |
| Coach of the Year | Joe Gibbs | | |
| Rookie of the Year | Eric Dickerson | | |

| **Past Super Bowl Most Valuable Players** (Selected by Sport Magazine) | |
|---|---|
| SB I | —Bart Starr, Green Bay |
| SB II | —Bart Starr, Green Bay |
| SB III | —Joe Namath, N.Y. Jets |
| SB IV | —Len Dawson, Kansas City |
| SB V | —Chuck Howley, Dallas |
| SB VI | —Roger Staubach, Dallas |
| SB VII | —Jake Scott, Miami |
| SB VIII | —Larry Csonka, Miami |
| SB IX | —Franco Harris, Pittsburgh |
| SB X | —Lynn Swann, Pittsburgh |
| SB XI | —Fred Biletnikoff, Oakland |
| SB XII | —Randy White and Harvey Martin, Dallas |
| SB XIII | —Terry Bradshaw, Pittsburgh |
| SB XIV | —Terry Bradshaw, Pittsburgh |
| SB XV | —Jim Plunkett, Oakland |
| SB XVI | —Joe Montana, San Francisco |
| SB XVII | —John Riggins, Washington |
| SB XVIII | —Marcus Allen, Los Angeles Raiders |

# ALL-PRO TEAMS

## 1983 PFWA ALL-PRO TEAM
Selected by Professional Football Writers Association.

### OFFENSE

James Lofton, Green Bay . . . . . . . . . . . . . . . . . . . . . . . . . . . Wide Receiver
Roy Green, St. Louis . . . . . . . . . . . . . . . . . . . . . . . . . . . . . Wide Receiver
Todd Christensen, Los Angeles Raiders . . . . . . . . . . . . . . . . . Tight End
Anthony Muñoz, Cincinnati . . . . . . . . . . . . . . . . . . . . . . . . . . . . Tackle
Joe Jacoby, Washington . . . . . . . . . . . . . . . . . . . . . . . . . . . . . . Tackle
Russ Grimm, Washington . . . . . . . . . . . . . . . . . . . . . . . . . . . . . Guard
John Hannah, New England . . . . . . . . . . . . . . . . . . . . . . . . . . . Guard
Dwight Stephenson, Miami . . . . . . . . . . . . . . . . . . . . . . . . . . . Center
Joe Theismann, Washington . . . . . . . . . . . . . . . . . . . . . Quarterback
Eric Dickerson, Los Angeles Rams . . . . . . . . . . . . . . . . Running Back
John Riggins, Washington . . . . . . . . . . . . . . . . . . . . . . Running Back
Ali Haji-Sheikh, New York Giants . . . . . . . . . . . . . . . . . . . . . . Kicker
Billy Johnson, Atlanta . . . . . . . . . . . . . . . . . . . . . . . . . . Punt Returner
Fulton Walker, Miami . . . . . . . . . . . . . . . . . . . . . . . . . . Kick Returner

### DEFENSE

Doug Betters, Miami . . . . . . . . . . . . . . . . . . . . . . . . . . . Defensive End
Howie Long, Los Angeles Raiders . . . . . . . . . . . . . . . . . Defensive End
Doug English, Detroit . . . . . . . . . . . . . . . . . . . . . . . . . Defensive Tackle
Randy White, Dallas . . . . . . . . . . . . . . . . . . . . . . . . . . Defensive Tackle
Jack Lambert, Pittsburgh . . . . . . . . . . . . . . . . . . . . . Middle Linebacker
Chip Banks, Cleveland . . . . . . . . . . . . . . . . . . . . . . . Outside Linebacker
Lawrence Taylor, New York Giants . . . . . . . . . . . . . . . Outside Linebacker
Gary Green, Kansas City . . . . . . . . . . . . . . . . . . . . . . . . . . Cornerback
Ronnie Lott, San Francisco . . . . . . . . . . . . . . . . . . . . . . . . Cornerback
Kenny Easley, Seattle . . . . . . . . . . . . . . . . . . . . . . . . . . . . . . . Safety
Mark Murphy, Washington . . . . . . . . . . . . . . . . . . . . . . . . . . . Safety
Rich Camarillo, New England . . . . . . . . . . . . . . . . . . . . . . . . . Punter

## 1983 NEA ALL-PRO TEAM
Selected by Newspaper Enterprise Association.

### OFFENSE

Roy Green, St. Louis . . . . . . . . . . . . . . . . . . . . . . . . . . . Wide Receiver
Mike Quick, Philadelphia . . . . . . . . . . . . . . . . . . . . . . . . Wide Receiver
Todd Christensen, Los Angeles Raiders . . . . . . . . . . . . . . . . . Tight End
Joe Jacoby, Washington . . . . . . . . . . . . . . . . . . . . . . . . . . . . . . Tackle
Keith Fahnhorst, San Francisco . . . . . . . . . . . . . . . . . . . . . . . Tackle
Russ Grimm, Washington . . . . . . . . . . . . . . . . . . . . . . . . . . . . . Guard
John Hannah, New England . . . . . . . . . . . . . . . . . . . . . . . . . . Guard
Dwight Stephenson, Miami . . . . . . . . . . . . . . . . . . . . . . . . . . . Center
Joe Theismann, Washington . . . . . . . . . . . . . . . . . . . . . Quarterback
Eric Dickerson, Los Angeles Rams . . . . . . . . . . . . . . . . Running Back
William Andrews, Atlanta . . . . . . . . . . . . . . . . . . . . . . Running Back
Ali Haji-Sheikh, New York Giants . . . . . . . . . . . . . . . . . . . . . . Kicker

### DEFENSE

Doug Betters, Miami . . . . . . . . . . . . . . . . . . . . . . . . . . . Defensive End
Howie Long, Los Angeles Raiders . . . . . . . . . . . . . . . . . Defensive End
Dave Butz, Washington . . . . . . . . . . . . . . . . . . . . . . . . Defensive Tackle
Fred Smerlas, Buffalo . . . . . . . . . . . . . . . . . . . . . . . . . . . Nose Tackle
Jack Lambert, Pittsburgh . . . . . . . . . . . . . . . . . . . . . . Inside Linebacker
Mike Singletary, Chicago . . . . . . . . . . . . . . . . . . . . . . Inside Linebacker
Lawrence Taylor, New York Giants . . . . . . . . . . . . . . . Outside Linebacker
Rod Martin, Los Angeles Raiders . . . . . . . . . . . . . . . . Outside Linebacker
Gary Green, Kansas City . . . . . . . . . . . . . . . . . . . . . . . . . . Cornerback
Louis Wright, Denver . . . . . . . . . . . . . . . . . . . . . . . . . . . . Cornerback
Kenny Easley, Seattle . . . . . . . . . . . . . . . . . . . . . . . . . . . . . . . Safety
Johnnie Johnson, Los Angeles Rams . . . . . . . . . . . . . . . . . . . . Safety
Rich Camarillo, New England . . . . . . . . . . . . . . . . . . . . . . . . . Punter

## 1983 ASSOCIATED PRESS ALL-PRO TEAM

### OFFENSE

Roy Green, St. Louis . . . . . . . . . . . . . . . . . . . . . . . . . . . Wide Receiver
Mike Quick, Philadelphia . . . . . . . . . . . . . . . . . . . . . . . . Wide Receiver
Todd Christensen, Los Angeles Raiders . . . . . . . . . . . . . . . . . Tight End
Joe Jacoby, Washington . . . . . . . . . . . . . . . . . . . . . . . . . . . . . . Tackle
Anthony Muñoz, Cincinnati . . . . . . . . . . . . . . . . . . . . . . . . . . . Tackle
Russ Grimm, Washington . . . . . . . . . . . . . . . . . . . . . . . . . . . . . Guard
John Hannah, New England . . . . . . . . . . . . . . . . . . . . . . . . . . Guard
Mike Webster, Pittsburgh . . . . . . . . . . . . . . . . . . . . . . . . . . . . Center
Joe Theismann, Washington . . . . . . . . . . . . . . . . . . . . . Quarterback
Eric Dickerson, Los Angeles Rams . . . . . . . . . . . . . . . . Running Back
John Riggins, Washington . . . . . . . . . . . . . . . . . . . . . . Running Back
Ali Haji-Sheikh, New York Giants . . . . . . . . . . . . . . . . . . . . . . Kicker
Mike Nelms, Washington . . . . . . . . . . . . . . . . . . . . . . . . Kick Returner

### DEFENSE

Doug Betters, Miami . . . . . . . . . . . . . . . . . . . . . . . . . . . Defensive End
Mark Gastineau, New York Jets . . . . . . . . . . . . . . . . . . . Defensive End
Dave Butz, Washington . . . . . . . . . . . . . . . . . . . . . . . . Defensive Tackle
Randy White, Dallas . . . . . . . . . . . . . . . . . . . . . . . . . . Defensive Tackle
Bob Baumhower, Miami . . . . . . . . . . . . . . . . . . . . . . . . . . . Nose Tackle
Jack Lambert, Pittsburgh . . . . . . . . . . . . . . . . . . . . . . Inside Linebacker
Chip Banks, Cleveland . . . . . . . . . . . . . . . . . . . . . . . Outside Linebacker
Lawrence Taylor, New York Giants . . . . . . . . . . . . . . . Outside Linebacker
Ken Riley, Cincinnati . . . . . . . . . . . . . . . . . . . . . . . . . . . . Cornerback
Everson Walls, Dallas . . . . . . . . . . . . . . . . . . . . . . . . . . . Cornerback
Kenny Easley, Seattle . . . . . . . . . . . . . . . . . . . . . . . . . . . . . . . Safety
Mark Murphy, Washington . . . . . . . . . . . . . . . . . . . . . . . . . . . Safety
Rohn Stark, Baltimore . . . . . . . . . . . . . . . . . . . . . . . . . . . . . . Punter

## 1983 ALL-NFL TEAM
Selected by Associated Press, Newspaper Enterprise Association,
and Professional Football Writers Association.

### OFFENSE

Roy Green, St. Louis (AP, NEA, PFWA) . . . . . . . . . . . . . . . Wide Receiver
Mike Quick, Philadelphia (AP, NEA) . . . . . . . . . . . . . . . . Wide Receiver
James Lofton, Green Bay (PFWA) . . . . . . . . . . . . . . . . . . Wide Receiver
Todd Christensen, Los Angeles Raiders (AP, NEA, PFWA) . . . . . . . Tight End
Joe Jacoby, Washington (AP, NEA, PFWA) . . . . . . . . . . . . . . . . . Tackle
Anthony Muñoz, Cincinnati (AP, PFWA) . . . . . . . . . . . . . . . . . . . Tackle
Keith Fahnhorst, San Francisco (NEA) . . . . . . . . . . . . . . . . . . . Tackle
Russ Grimm, Washington (AP, NEA, PFWA) . . . . . . . . . . . . . . . . Guard
John Hannah, New England (AP, NEA, PFWA) . . . . . . . . . . . . . . Guard
Dwight Stephenson, Miami (NEA, PFWA) . . . . . . . . . . . . . . . . . . Center
Mike Webster, Pittsburgh (AP) . . . . . . . . . . . . . . . . . . . . . . . . . Center
Joe Theismann, Washington (AP, NEA, PFWA) . . . . . . . . . . . Quarterback
Eric Dickerson, Los Angeles Rams (AP, NEA, PFWA) . . . . . . . . Running Back
John Riggins, Washington (AP, PFWA) . . . . . . . . . . . . . . Running Back
William Andrews, Atlanta (NEA) . . . . . . . . . . . . . . . . . . . Running Back
Ali Haji-Sheikh, New York Giants (AP, NEA, PFWA) . . . . . . . . . . . Kicker
Mike Nelms, Washington (AP) . . . . . . . . . . . . . . . . . . . . . Kick Returner
Fulton Walker, Miami (PFWA) . . . . . . . . . . . . . . . . . . . . . Kick Returner
Billy Johnson, Atlanta (PFWA) . . . . . . . . . . . . . . . . . . . . . Punt Returner

### DEFENSE

Doug Betters, Miami (AP, NEA, PFWA) . . . . . . . . . . . . . . . Defensive End
Howie Long, Los Angeles Raiders (NEA, PFWA) . . . . . . . . . . . Defensive End
Mark Gastineau, New York Jets (AP) . . . . . . . . . . . . . . . . Defensive End
Dave Butz, Washington (AP, NEA) . . . . . . . . . . . . . . . . . Defensive Tackle
Randy White, Dallas (AP, PFWA) . . . . . . . . . . . . . . . . . . Defensive Tackle
Doug English, Detroit (PFWA) . . . . . . . . . . . . . . . . . . . . Defensive Tackle
Bob Baumhower, Miami (AP) . . . . . . . . . . . . . . . . . . . . . . . . Nose Tackle
Fred Smerlas, Buffalo (NEA) . . . . . . . . . . . . . . . . . . . . . . . Nose Tackle
Jack Lambert, Pittsburgh (AP, NEA, PFWA) . . . . . . . . . . Inside Linebacker
Mike Singletary, Chicago (NEA) . . . . . . . . . . . . . . . . . . Inside Linebacker
Lawrence Taylor, New York Giants (AP, NEA, PFWA) . . . . Outside Linebacker
Chip Banks, Cleveland (AP, PFWA) . . . . . . . . . . . . . . . . Outside Linebacker
Rod Martin, Los Angeles Raiders (NEA) . . . . . . . . . . . . . Outside Linebacker
Gary Green, Kansas City (NEA, PFWA) . . . . . . . . . . . . . . . . . Cornerback
Ronnie Lott, San Francisco (PFWA) . . . . . . . . . . . . . . . . . . . Cornerback
Ken Riley, Cincinnati (AP) . . . . . . . . . . . . . . . . . . . . . . . . . Cornerback
Everson Walls, Dallas (AP) . . . . . . . . . . . . . . . . . . . . . . . . Cornerback
Louis Wright, Denver (NEA) . . . . . . . . . . . . . . . . . . . . . . . . Cornerback
Kenny Easley, Seattle (AP, NEA, PFWA) . . . . . . . . . . . . . . . . . . Safety
Mark Murphy, Washington (AP, PFWA) . . . . . . . . . . . . . . . . . . . Safety
Johnnie Johnson, Los Angeles Rams (NEA) . . . . . . . . . . . . . . . . Safety
Rich Camarillo, New England (NEA, PFWA) . . . . . . . . . . . . . . . . Punter
Rohn Stark, Baltimore (AP) . . . . . . . . . . . . . . . . . . . . . . . . . . Punter

## 1983 ALL-AFC TEAM
Selected by United Press International.

### OFFENSE

Carlos Carson, Kansas City . . . . . . . . . . . . . . . . . . . . . . . . . . . . . Wide Receiver
Cris Collinsworth, Cincinnati. . . . . . . . . . . . . . . . . . . . . . . . . . . Wide Receiver
Todd Christensen, Los Angeles Raiders . . . . . . . . . . . . . . . . . . . . Tight End
Anthony Muñoz, Cincinnati . . . . . . . . . . . . . . . . . . . . . . . . . . . . . . . . Tackle
Cody Risien, Cleveland . . . . . . . . . . . . . . . . . . . . . . . . . . . . . . . . . . . Tackle
John Hannah, New England . . . . . . . . . . . . . . . . . . . . . . . . . . . . . . . . Guard
Ed Newman, Miami . . . . . . . . . . . . . . . . . . . . . . . . . . . . . . . . . . . . . . . Guard
Dwight Stephenson, Miami. . . . . . . . . . . . . . . . . . . . . . . . . . . . . . . . Center
Dan Marino, Miami. . . . . . . . . . . . . . . . . . . . . . . . . . . . . . . . Quarterback
Joe Cribbs, Buffalo . . . . . . . . . . . . . . . . . . . . . . . . . . . . . . . Running Back
Curt Warner, Seattle . . . . . . . . . . . . . . . . . . . . . . . . . . . . . . Running Back
Gary Anderson, Pittsburgh . . . . . . . . . . . . . . . . . . . . . . . . . . . . . . . Kicker

### DEFENSE

Doug Betters, Miami . . . . . . . . . . . . . . . . . . . . . . . . . . . . . . Defensive End
Mark Gastineau, New York Jets . . . . . . . . . . . . . . . . . . . . . . . Defensive End
Bob Baumhower, Miami. . . . . . . . . . . . . . . . . . . . . . . . . . . . . Nose Tackle
Chip Banks, Cleveland. . . . . . . . . . . . . . . . . . . . . . . . . . Outside Linebacker
Rod Martin, Los Angeles Raiders . . . . . . . . . . . . . . . . . . . Outside Linebacker
Tom Cousineau, Cleveland. . . . . . . . . . . . . . . . . . . . . . . Inside Linebacker
Jack Lambert, Pittsburgh . . . . . . . . . . . . . . . . . . . . . . . . Inside Linebacker
Gary Green, Kansas City . . . . . . . . . . . . . . . . . . . . . . . . . . . Cornerback
Lester Hayes, Los Angeles Raiders. . . . . . . . . . . . . . . . . . . . . Cornerback
Kenny Easley, Seattle . . . . . . . . . . . . . . . . . . . . . . . . . . . . . . . . . Safety
Deron Cherry, Kansas City. . . . . . . . . . . . . . . . . . . . . . . . . . . . . . Safety
Rich Camarillo, New England. . . . . . . . . . . . . . . . . . . . . . . . . . . . Punter

## 1983 ALL-NFC TEAM
Selected by United Press International.

### OFFENSE

Roy Green, St. Louis . . . . . . . . . . . . . . . . . . . . . . . . . . . . . Wide Receiver
Mike Quick, Philadelphia. . . . . . . . . . . . . . . . . . . . . . . . . . Wide Receiver
Paul Coffman, Green Bay . . . . . . . . . . . . . . . . . . . . . . . . . . . . . Tight End
Joe Jacoby, Washington . . . . . . . . . . . . . . . . . . . . . . . . . . . . . . . Tackle
Jackie Slater, Los Angeles Rams . . . . . . . . . . . . . . . . . . . . . . . . Tackle
Russ Grimm, Washington. . . . . . . . . . . . . . . . . . . . . . . . . . . . . . Guard
Kent Hill, Los Angeles Rams . . . . . . . . . . . . . . . . . . . . . . . . . . . . Guard
Jeff Bostic, Washington. . . . . . . . . . . . . . . . . . . . . . . . . . . . . . . Center
Joe Theismann, Washington . . . . . . . . . . . . . . . . . . . . . . Quarterback
Eric Dickerson, Los Angeles Rams . . . . . . . . . . . . . . . . . Running Back
John Riggins, Washington . . . . . . . . . . . . . . . . . . . . . . . Running Back
Ali Haji-Sheikh, New York Giants . . . . . . . . . . . . . . . . . . . . . . . Kicker

### DEFENSE

William Gay, Detroit . . . . . . . . . . . . . . . . . . . . . . . . . . . . Defensive End
Ed Jones, Dallas. . . . . . . . . . . . . . . . . . . . . . . . . . . . . . . Defensive End
Randy White, Dallas. . . . . . . . . . . . . . . . . . . . . . . . . . . . . Nose Tackle
Hugh Green, Tampa Bay . . . . . . . . . . . . . . . . . . . . . . Outside Linebacker
Lawrence Taylor, New York Giants . . . . . . . . . . . . . . . . Outside Linebacker
Bob Bruenig, Dallas. . . . . . . . . . . . . . . . . . . . . . . . . . . Inside Linebacker
Mike Singletary, Chicago. . . . . . . . . . . . . . . . . . . . . . . Inside Linebacker
Johnnie Poe, New Orleans. . . . . . . . . . . . . . . . . . . . . . . . . . Cornerback
Eric Wright, San Francisco. . . . . . . . . . . . . . . . . . . . . . . . . . Cornerback
Russell Gary, New Orleans . . . . . . . . . . . . . . . . . . . . . . . . . . . . Safety
Mark Murphy, Washington . . . . . . . . . . . . . . . . . . . . . . . . . . . . . Safety
Carl Birdsong, St. Louis . . . . . . . . . . . . . . . . . . . . . . . . . . . . . . Punter

## 1983 ALL-ROOKIE TEAM
Selected by Professional Football Writers Association.

### OFFENSE

Jeff Chadwick, Detroit . . . . . . . . . . . . . . . . . . . . . . . . . . . . Wide Receiver
Willie Gault, Chicago . . . . . . . . . . . . . . . . . . . . . . . . . . . . Wide Receiver
Tony Hunter, Buffalo . . . . . . . . . . . . . . . . . . . . . . . . . . . . . . . Tight End
Jim Covert, Chicago . . . . . . . . . . . . . . . . . . . . . . . . . . . . . . . . Tackle
Harvey Salem, Houston . . . . . . . . . . . . . . . . . . . . . . . . . . . . . . Tackle
Chris Hinton, Baltimore . . . . . . . . . . . . . . . . . . . . . . . . . . . . . . . Guard
Bruce Matthews, Houston . . . . . . . . . . . . . . . . . . . . . . . . . . . . Guard
Dave Rimington, Cincinnati . . . . . . . . . . . . . . . . . . . . . . . . . . . Center
Dan Marino, Miami. . . . . . . . . . . . . . . . . . . . . . . . . . . . . Quarterback
Eric Dickerson, Los Angeles Rams . . . . . . . . . . . . . . . . . Running Back
Curt Warner, Seattle . . . . . . . . . . . . . . . . . . . . . . . . . . . Running Back
Ali Haji-Sheikh, New York Giants . . . . . . . . . . . . . . . . . . . . . . . Kicker

### DEFENSE

Mike Pitts, Atlanta. . . . . . . . . . . . . . . . . . . . . . . . . . . . . . Defensive End
Greg Townsend, Los Angeles Raiders . . . . . . . . . . . . . . . . Defensive End
Bill Pickel, Los Angeles Raiders . . . . . . . . . . . . . . . . . . Defensive Tackle
Andrew Provence, Atlanta . . . . . . . . . . . . . . . . . . . . . . Defensive Tackle
Mike Green, San Diego . . . . . . . . . . . . . . . . . . . . . . . Middle Linebacker
Vernon Maxwell, Baltimore . . . . . . . . . . . . . . . . . . . . Outside Linebacker
John Rade, Atlanta . . . . . . . . . . . . . . . . . . . . . . . . . . . Outside Linebacker
Darrell Green, Washington . . . . . . . . . . . . . . . . . . . . . . . . . Cornerback
Danny Walters, San Diego. . . . . . . . . . . . . . . . . . . . . . . . . . Cornerback
Terry Kinard, New York Giants. . . . . . . . . . . . . . . . . . . . . . . . . . Safety
Bill Bates, Dallas . . . . . . . . . . . . . . . . . . . . . . . . . . . . . . . . . . . Safety
Reggie Roby, Miami . . . . . . . . . . . . . . . . . . . . . . . . . . . . . . . . . Punter

## Ten Best Rushing Performances, 1983

| | Attempts | Yards | TD |
|---|---|---|---|
| 1. James Wilder<br>Tampa Bay vs. Minnesota, November 6 | 31 | 219 | 1 |
| 2. Tony Collins<br>New England vs. N.Y. Jets, September 18 | 23 | 212 | 3 |
| 3. Curt Warner<br>Seattle vs. Kansas City, November 27 | 32 | 207 | 3 |
| 4. George Rogers<br>New Orleans vs. St. Louis, September 4 | 24 | 206 | 2 |
| 5. Eric Dickerson<br>L.A. Rams vs. Detroit, October 2 | 30 | 199 | 3 |
| 6. Eric Dickerson<br>L.A. Rams vs. N.Y. Jets, September 25 | 28 | 192 | 2 |
| 7. Billy Sims<br>Detroit vs. Green Bay, November 20 | 36 | 189 | 0 |
| 8. Joe Cribbs<br>Buffalo vs. Kansas City, December 4 | 36 | 185 | 0 |
| 9. Ted Brown<br>Minnesota vs. Green Bay, October 23 | 29 | 179 | 1 |
| 10. Joe Cribbs<br>Buffalo vs. Houston, September 25 | 22 | 166 | 1 |

## 100-Yard Rushing Performances, 1983

### First Week
| | |
|---|---|
| George Rogers, New Orleans | 206 yards vs. St. Louis |
| Tony Dorsett, Dallas | 151 yards vs. Washington |
| Earl Campbell, Houston | 123 yards vs. Green Bay |
| Freeman McNeil, N.Y. Jets | 120 yards vs. San Diego |
| Rob Carpenter, N.Y. Giants | 113 yards vs. L.A. Rams |
| Walter Payton, Chicago | 103 yards vs. Atlanta |
| Robert Weathers, New England | 100 yards vs. Baltimore |

### Second Week
| | |
|---|---|
| Freeman McNeil, N.Y. Jets | 140 yards vs. Seattle |
| Mike Pruitt, Cleveland | 137 yards vs. Detroit |
| Curt Warner, Seattle | 128 yards vs. N.Y. Jets |
| Franco Harris, Pittsburgh | 118 yards vs. Green Bay |
| Rob Carpenter, N.Y. Giants | 111 yards vs. Atlanta |
| Chuck Muncie, San Diego | 110 yards vs. Kansas City |
| Wendell Tyler, San Francisco | 107 yards vs. Minnesota |
| John Riggins, Washington | 100 yards vs. Philadelphia |

### Third Week
| | |
|---|---|
| Tony Collins, New England | 212 yards vs. N.Y. Jets |
| Walter Payton, Chicago | 161 yards vs. New Orleans |
| William Andrews, Atlanta | 150 yards vs. Detroit |
| Stump Mitchell, St. Louis | 123 yards vs. San Francisco |
| Franco Harris, Pittsburgh | 115 yards vs. Houston |
| Curt Warner, Seattle | 109 yards vs. San Diego |
| Wendell Tyler, San Francisco | 108 yards vs. St. Louis |
| Marcus Allen, L.A. Raiders | 105 yards vs. Miami |

### Fourth Week
| | |
|---|---|
| Eric Dickerson, L.A. Rams | 192 yards vs. N.Y. Jets |
| Joe Cribbs, Buffalo | 166 yards vs. Houston |
| Earl Campbell, Houston | 142 yards vs. Buffalo |
| Ottis Anderson, St. Louis | 133 yards vs. Philadelphia |
| William Andrews, Atlanta | 126 yards vs. San Francisco |
| Tony Dorsett, Dallas | 124 yards vs. New Orleans |
| Sammy Winder, Denver | 119 yards vs. L.A. Raiders |
| Rob Carpenter, N.Y. Giants | 116 yards vs. Green Bay |
| Wayne Wilson, New Orleans | 108 yards vs. Dallas |
| Franco Harris, Pittsburgh | 106 yards vs. New England |

### Fifth Week
| | |
|---|---|
| Eric Dickerson, L.A. Rams | 199 yards vs. Detroit |
| Wayne Wilson, New Orleans | 160 yards vs. Miami |
| William Andrews, Atlanta | 150 yards vs. Philadelphia |
| Tony Dorsett, Dallas | 141 yards vs. Minnesota |
| Bruce Harper, N.Y. Jets | 118 yards vs. Buffalo |
| Mike Pruitt, Cleveland | 107 yards vs. Seattle |
| Ottis Anderson, St. Louis | 106 yards vs. Kansas City |

### Sixth Week
| | |
|---|---|
| Sammy Winder, Denver | 165 yards vs. Houston |
| Eric Dickerson, L.A. Rams | 142 yards vs. San Francisco |
| John Riggins, Washington | 115 yards vs. St. Louis |
| Tony Galbreath, Minnesota | 104 yards vs. Chicago |
| Wayne Wilson, New Orleans | 103 yards vs. Atlanta |
| Walter Payton, Chicago | 102 yards vs. Minnesota |
| Earl Campbell, Houston | 101 yards vs. Denver |

### Seventh Week
| | |
|---|---|
| Boyce Green, Cleveland | 137 yards vs. Pittsburgh |
| Earl Campbell, Houston | 130 yards vs. Minnesota |
| Joe Cribbs, Buffalo | 105 yards vs. Baltimore |

### Eighth Week
| | |
|---|---|
| Ted Brown, Minnesota | 179 yards vs. Green Bay |
| Tony Collins, New England | 147 yards vs. Buffalo |
| Joe Washington, Washington | 147 yards vs. Detroit |
| Eric Dickerson, L.A. Rams | 144 yards vs. San Francisco |
| Franco Harris, Pittsburgh | 132 yards vs. Seattle |
| Frank Hawkins, L.A. Raiders | 118 yards vs. Dallas |
| Stump Mitchell, St. Louis | 108 yards vs. N.Y. Giants |

### Ninth Week
| | |
|---|---|
| Ottis Anderson, St. Louis | 136 yards vs. Minnesota |
| James Wilder, Tampa Bay | 126 yards vs. Pittsburgh |
| William Andrews, Atlanta | 125 yards vs. New England |
| George Rogers, New Orleans | 114 yards vs. Buffalo |
| Pete Johnson, Cincinnati | 112 yards vs. Green Bay |
| Randy McMillan, Baltimore | 109 yards vs. Philadelphia |
| Boyce Green, Cleveland | 107 yards vs. Houston |
| Eric Dickerson, L.A. Rams | 101 yards vs. Miami |
| Curt Warner, Seattle | 101 yards vs. L.A. Raiders |

### Tenth Week
| | |
|---|---|
| James Wilder, Tampa Bay | 219 yards vs. Minnesota |
| George Rogers, New Orleans | 137 yards vs. Atlanta |
| Curt Warner, Seattle | 134 yards vs. Denver |
| Eric Dickerson, L.A. Rams | 127 yards vs. Chicago |
| Tony Collins, New England | 100 yards vs. Buffalo |

### Eleventh Week
| | |
|---|---|
| Eric Dickerson, L.A. Rams | 146 yards vs. Atlanta |
| Walter Payton, Chicago | 131 yards vs. Philadelphia |
| Ottis Anderson, St. Louis | 130 yards vs. Seattle |
| Darrin Nelson, Minnesota | 119 yards vs. Green Bay |
| Barry Redden, L.A. Rams | 110 yards vs. Atlanta |
| Earl Campbell, Houston | 107 yards vs. Detroit |
| Billy Sims, Detroit | 105 yards vs. Houston |

### Twelfth Week
| | |
|---|---|
| Billy Sims, Detroit | 189 yards vs. Green Bay |
| Butch Woolfolk, N.Y. Giants | 159 yards vs. Philadelphia |
| Pete Johnson, Cincinnati | 137 yards vs. Houston |
| Mike Pruitt, Cleveland | 136 yards vs. New England |
| Ottis Anderson, St. Louis | 113 yards vs. San Diego |
| Hokie Gajan, New Orleans | 113 yards vs. N.Y. Jets |
| Matt Suhey, Chicago | 112 yards vs. Tampa Bay |
| Tony Dorsett, Dallas | 108 yards vs. Kansas City |
| Walter Payton, Chicago | 106 yards vs. Tampa Bay |

### Thirteenth Week
| | |
|---|---|
| Curt Warner, Seattle | 207 yards vs. Kansas City |
| William Andrews, Atlanta | 129 yards vs. Green Bay |
| Eric Dickerson, L.A. Rams | 125 yards vs. Buffalo |
| Mike Pruitt, Cleveland | 110 yards vs. Baltimore |
| Billy Sims, Detroit | 106 yards vs. Pittsburgh |
| Tony Dorsett, Dallas | 102 yards vs. St. Louis |

### Fourteenth Week
| | |
|---|---|
| Joe Cribbs, Buffalo | 185 yards vs. Kansas City |
| Gerry Ellis, Green Bay | 141 yards vs. Chicago |
| Earl Campbell, Houston | 138 yards vs. Miami |
| Billy Sims, Detroit | 137 yards vs. Minnesota |
| Mosi Tatupu, New England | 128 yards vs. New Orleans |
| Pete Johnson, Cincinnati | 126 yards vs. Pittsburgh |
| Curtis Dickey, Baltimore | 123 yards vs. N.Y. Jets |
| Tony Dorsett, Dallas | 117 yards vs. Seattle |
| Eric Dickerson, L.A. Rams | 103 yards vs. Philadelphia |
| Freeman McNeil, N.Y. Jets | 102 yards vs. Baltimore |
| Wendell Tyler, San Francisco | 102 yards vs. Tampa Bay |

### Fifteenth Week
| | |
|---|---|
| William Andrews, Atlanta | 161 yards vs. Miami |
| Mike Pruitt, Cleveland | 153 yards vs. Houston |
| Earl Campbell, Houston | 130 yards vs. Cleveland |
| Ottis Anderson, St. Louis | 119 yards vs. L.A. Raiders |
| Pete Johnson, Cincinnati | 118 yards vs. Detroit |
| Franco Harris, Pittsburgh | 103 yards vs. N.Y. Jets |
| Matt Suhey, Chicago | 101 yards vs. Minnesota |
| Joe Cribbs, Buffalo | 100 yards vs. San Francisco |

### Sixteenth Week
| | |
|---|---|
| William Andrews, Atlanta | 158 yards vs. Buffalo |
| Ottis Anderson, St. Louis | 156 yards vs. Philadelphia |

| | | |
|---|---|---|
| Walter Payton, Chicago | 148 yards vs. Green Bay | |
| George Rogers, New Orleans | 124 yards vs. L.A. Rams | |
| John Riggins, Washington | 122 yards vs. N.Y. Giants | |
| Curt Warner, Seattle | 116 yards vs. New England | |
| Curtis Dickey, Baltimore | 110 yards vs. Houston | |

**Times 100 or More**
Dickerson 9; Anderson, Andrews, Campbell 7; Dorsett, Payton, Warner 6; Harris, Pruitt 5; Cribbs, Johnson, Rogers, Sims 4; Carpenter, Collins, McNeil, Riggins, Tyler, Wilson 3; Dickey, Green, Mitchell, Suhey, Wilder, Winder 2.

## Ten Best Passing Yardage Performances, 1983

| | Att. | Comp. | Yards | TD |
|---|---|---|---|---|
| 1. Richard Todd<br>N.Y. Jets vs. L.A. Rams, September 25 | 50 | 37 | 446 | 2 |
| 2. Joe Ferguson<br>Buffalo vs. Miami, October 9 | 55 | 38 | 419 | 5 |
| 3. Dave Krieg<br>Seattle vs. Denver, November 20 | 42 | 31 | 418 | 3 |
| 4. Joe Theismann<br>Washington vs. L.A. Raiders, October 2 | 39 | 23 | 417 | 3 |
| 5. Bill Kenney<br>Kansas City vs. San Diego, December 11 | 41 | 31 | 411 | 4 |
| 6. Joe Theismann<br>Washington vs. Green Bay, October 17 | 39 | 27 | 398 | 2 |
| 7. Scott Brunner<br>N.Y. Giants vs. San Diego, October 2 | 51 | 31 | 395 | 3 |
| 8. Lynn Dickey<br>Green Bay vs. Washington, October 17 | 31 | 22 | 387 | 3 |
| 9. Lynn Dickey<br>Green Bay vs. Minnesota, October 23 | 41 | 23 | 383 | 2 |
| 10. Danny White<br>Dallas vs. Tampa Bay, October 9 | 44 | 29 | 377 | 2 |

## 300-Yard Passing Performances, 1983

**First Week**
| | |
|---|---|
| Dan Fouts, San Diego | 354 yards vs. N.Y. Jets |
| Archie Manning, Houston | 348 yards vs. Green Bay |
| Lynn Dickey, Green Bay | 333 yards vs. Houston |
| Joe Theismann, Washington | 325 yards vs. Dallas |

**Second Week**
| | |
|---|---|
| Ron Jaworski, Philadelphia | 326 yards vs. Washington |

**Third Week**
| | |
|---|---|
| Steve Bartkowski, Atlanta | 366 yards vs. Detroit |
| Joe Montana, San Francisco | 341 yards vs. St. Louis |
| Dan Fouts, San Diego | 338 yards vs. Seattle |
| Bill Kenney, Kansas City | 330 yards vs. Washington |
| Archie Manning, Houston | 300 yards vs. Pittsburgh |

**Fourth Week**
| | |
|---|---|
| Richard Todd, N.Y. Jets | 446 yards vs. L.A. Rams |
| Dan Fouts, San Diego | 351 yards vs. Cleveland |
| Brian Sipe, Cleveland | 327 yards vs. San Diego |
| Jack Thompson, Tampa Bay | 316 yards vs. Cincinnati |

**Fifth Week**
| | |
|---|---|
| Joe Theismann, Washington | 417 yards vs. L.A. Raiders |
| Scott Brunner, N.Y. Giants | 395 yards vs. San Diego |
| Jim Plunkett, L.A. Raiders | 372 yards vs. Washington |
| Ken Anderson, Cincinnati | 330 yards vs. Baltimore |
| Brian Sipe, Cleveland | 310 yards vs. Seattle |

**Sixth Week**
| | |
|---|---|
| Joe Ferguson, Buffalo | 419 yards vs. Miami |
| Danny White, Dallas | 377 yards vs. Tampa Bay |
| Dan Fouts, San Diego | 331 yards vs. Seattle |
| Dan Marino, Miami | 322 yards vs. Buffalo |
| Joe Montana, San Francisco | 316 yards vs. L.A. Rams |

**Seventh Week**
| | |
|---|---|
| Joe Theismann, Washington | 398 yards vs. Green Bay |
| Lynn Dickey, Green Bay | 387 yards vs. Washington |
| Dan Fouts, San Diego | 357 yards vs. New England |
| Bill Kenney, Kansas City | 342 yards vs. N.Y. Giants |
| Vince Evans, Chicago | 336 yards vs. Detroit |
| Brian Sipe, Cleveland | 310 yards vs. Pittsburgh |

**Eighth Week**
| | |
|---|---|
| Lynn Dickey, Green Bay | 383 yards vs. Minnesota |
| Joe Montana, San Francisco | 358 yards vs. L.A. Rams |
| Vince Ferragamo, L.A. Rams | 327 yards vs. San Francisco |
| Marc Wilson, L.A. Raiders | 318 yards vs. Dallas |
| Steve Bartkowski, Atlanta | 313 yards vs. N.Y. Jets |

**Ninth Week**
| | |
|---|---|
| Bill Kenney, Kansas City | 365 yards vs. Denver |
| Steve DeBerg, Denver | 350 yards vs. Kansas City |
| Jeff Rutledge, N.Y. Giants | 325 yards vs. Dallas |
| Joe Theismann, Washington | 324 yards vs. San Diego |
| Steve Dils, Minnesota | 314 yards vs. St. Louis |
| Ed Luther, San Diego | 314 yards vs. Washington |
| Danny White, Dallas | 304 yards vs. N.Y. Giants |

**Tenth Week**
None

**Eleventh Week**
| | |
|---|---|
| Ed Luther, San Diego | 340 yards vs. Dallas |
| Steve Dils, Minnesota | 303 yards vs. Green Bay |
| Danny White, Dallas | 300 yards vs. San Diego |

**Twelfth Week**
| | |
|---|---|
| Dave Krieg, Seattle | 418 yards vs. Denver |
| Ed Luther, San Diego | 338 yards vs. St. Louis |
| Bill Kenney, Kansas City | 337 yards vs. Dallas |
| Steve Bartkowski, Atlanta | 301 yards vs. San Francisco |

**Thirteenth Week**
| | |
|---|---|
| Lynn Dickey, Green Bay | 366 yards vs. Atlanta |
| Scott Brunner, N.Y. Giants | 346 yards vs. L.A. Raiders |
| Ken Anderson, Cincinnati | 342 yards vs. Miami |
| Ron Jaworski, Philadelphia | 333 yards vs. Washington |
| Brian Sipe, Cleveland | 313 yards vs. Baltimore |
| Bill Kenney, Kansas City | 311 yards vs. Seattle |
| Richard Todd, N.Y. Jets | 305 yards vs. New England |
| Mike Moroski, Atlanta | 303 yards vs. Green Bay |

**Fourteenth Week**
| | |
|---|---|
| Lynn Dickey, Green Bay | 345 yards vs. Chicago |
| Jack Thompson, Tampa Bay | 337 yards vs. San Francisco |
| Bill Kenney, Kansas City | 306 yards vs. Buffalo |

**Fifteenth Week**
| | |
|---|---|
| Bill Kenney, Kansas City | 411 yards vs. San Diego |
| Jeff Rutledge, N.Y. Giants | 349 yards vs. Seattle |
| John Elway, Denver | 345 yards vs. Baltimore |

**Sixteenth Week**
| | |
|---|---|
| Jack Thompson, Tampa Bay | 373 yards vs. Detroit |
| Jim Plunkett, L.A. Raiders | 332 yards vs. San Diego |
| Jeff Rutledge, N.Y. Giants | 324 yards vs. Washington |

**Times 300 or more**
Kenney 7; Dickey, Fouts 5; Sipe, Theismann 4; Bartkowski, Luther, Montana, Rutledge, Thompson, White 3; Anderson, Brunner, Dils, Jaworski, Manning, Plunkett, Todd 2.

## Ten Best Receiving Yardage Performances, 1983

| | Yards | No. | TD |
|---|---|---|---|
| 1. Cris Collinsworth<br>Cincinnati vs. Baltimore, October 2 | 206 | 8 | 1 |
| 2. Mark Duper<br>Miami vs. Buffalo, October 9 | 202 | 7 | 2 |
| 3. Tim Smith<br>Houston vs. Green Bay, September 4 | 197 | 8 | 1 |
| 4. Charlie Brown<br>Washington vs. L.A. Raiders, October 2 | 180 | 11 | 1 |
| 5. Leonard Thompson<br>Detroit vs. Cleveland, September 11 | 179 | 8 | 1 |
| 6. Bernard Henry<br>Baltimore vs. Denver, December 11 | 169 | 8 | 1 |
| James Lofton<br>Green Bay vs. Pittsburgh, September 11 | 169 | 5 | 3 |
| 8. Carlos Carson<br>Kansas City vs. San Diego, December 11 | 165 | 7 | 1 |
| 9. Kellen Winslow<br>San Diego vs. Kansas City, December 11 | 162 | 14 | 3 |
| 10. James Lofton<br>Green Bay vs. Atlanta, November 27 | 161 | 7 | 1 |
| Steve Watson<br>Denver vs. Baltimore, September 11 | 161 | 6 | 1 |

## 100-Yard Receiving Performances, 1983
**(Number in parentheses is receptions.)**

### First Week
| | | |
|---|---|---|
| Tim Smith, Houston | 197 yards (8) | vs. Green Bay |
| James Lofton, Green Bay | 154 yards (8) | vs. Houston |
| Tony Hill, Dallas | 133 yards (3) | vs. Washington |
| Bobby Duckworth, San Diego | 110 yards (4) | vs. N.Y. Jets |
| Charlie Joiner, San Diego | 106 yards (5) | vs. N.Y. Jets |
| Carlos Carson, Kansas City | 104 yards (7) | vs. Seattle |
| Alvin Garrett, Washington | 101 yards (10) | vs. Dallas |

### Second Week
| | | |
|---|---|---|
| Leonard Thompson, Detroit | 179 yards (8) | vs. Cleveland |
| James Lofton, Green Bay | 169 yards (5) | vs. Pittsburgh |
| Steve Watson, Denver | 161 yards (6) | vs. Baltimore |
| Wesley Walker, N.Y. Jets | 116 yards (3) | vs. Seattle |
| Walter Payton, Chicago | 115 yards (6) | vs. Tampa Bay |
| Duriel Harris, Miami | 109 yards (4) | vs. New England |
| Harold Carmichael, Philadelphia | 108 yards (9) | vs. Washington |
| Terry LeCount, Minnesota | 107 yards (5) | vs. San Francisco |
| Mike Quick, Philadelphia | 106 yards (4) | vs. Washington |
| Pat Tilley, St. Louis | 105 yards (7) | vs. Dallas |

### Third Week
| | | |
|---|---|---|
| Mike Quick, Philadelphia | 152 yards (6) | vs. Denver |
| Roy Green, St. Louis | 133 yards (8) | vs. San Francisco |
| Earnest Gray, N.Y. Giants | 124 yards (4) | vs. Dallas |
| Alfred Jackson, Atlanta | 123 yards (5) | vs. Detroit |
| Freddie Solomon, San Francisco | 121 yards (3) | vs. St. Louis |
| Steve Largent, Seattle | 116 yards (8) | vs. San Diego |
| Eric Sievers, San Diego | 115 yards (6) | vs. Seattle |
| Carlos Carson, Kansas City | 109 yards (6) | vs. Washington |
| Hoby Brenner, New Orleans | 105 yards (6) | vs. Chicago |
| Willie Gault, Chicago | 103 yards (4) | vs. New Orleans |

### Fourth Week
| | | |
|---|---|---|
| Tim Smith, Houston | 147 yards (11) | vs. Buffalo |
| Wesley Walker, N.Y. Jets | 135 yards (8) | vs. L.A. Rams |
| Wes Chandler, San Diego | 134 yards (6) | vs. Cleveland |
| Mike Quick, Philadelphia | 133 yards (6) | vs. St. Louis |
| Willie Gault, Chicago | 130 yards (5) | vs. Baltimore |
| Steve Largent, Seattle | 130 yards (8) | vs. Washington |
| James Wilder, Tampa Bay | 126 yards (11) | vs. Cincinnati |
| Dave Logan, Cleveland | 121 yards (8) | vs. San Diego |
| Stephen Starring, New England | 108 yards (2) | vs. Pittsburgh |
| Kellen Winslow, San Diego | 108 yards (8) | vs. Cleveland |
| Freddie Solomon, San Francisco | 103 yards (6) | vs. Atlanta |
| Mark Nichols, Detroit | 100 yards (5) | vs. Minnesota |

### Fifth Week
| | | |
|---|---|---|
| Cris Collinsworth, Cincinnati | 206 yards (8) | vs. Baltimore |
| Charlie Brown, Washington | 180 yards (11) | vs. L.A. Raiders |
| Earnest Gray, N.Y. Giants | 159 yards (9) | vs. San Diego |
| Mike Quick, Philadelphia | 122 yards (4) | vs. Atlanta |
| James Lofton, Green Bay | 112 yards (4) | vs. Tampa Bay |
| Calvin Muhammad, L.A. Raiders | 112 yards (5) | vs. Washington |
| Sammy White, Minnesota | 107 yards (3) | vs. Dallas |
| Stacey Bailey, Atlanta | 106 yards (7) | vs. Philadelphia |

### Sixth Week
| | | |
|---|---|---|
| Mark Duper, Miami | 202 yards (7) | vs. Buffalo |
| Charle Young, Seattle | 140 yards (7) | vs. San Diego |
| Stanley Morgan, New England | 136 yards (9) | vs. Baltimore |
| Ron Springs, Dallas | 126 yards (11) | vs. Tampa Bay |
| Stacey Bailey, Atlanta | 109 yards (7) | vs. New Orleans |

### Seventh Week
| | | |
|---|---|---|
| Todd Christensen, L.A. Raiders | 152 yards (11) | vs. Seattle |
| Cris Collinsworth, Cincinnati | 149 yards (7) | vs. Denver |
| Henry Marshall, Kansas City | 131 yards (7) | vs. N.Y. Giants |
| Paul Coffman, Green Bay | 124 yards (6) | vs. Washington |
| Steve Watson, Denver | 119 yards (8) | vs. Cincinnati |
| Earnest Gray, N.Y. Giants | 111 yards (8) | vs. Kansas City |
| Stacey Bailey, Atlanta | 106 yards (6) | vs. L.A. Rams |
| Gerry Ellis, Green Bay | 105 yards (4) | vs. Washington |
| Art Monk, Washington | 105 yards (5) | vs. Green Bay |
| Ozzie Newsome, Cleveland | 103 yards (9) | vs. Pittsburgh |

### Eighth Week
| | | |
|---|---|---|
| Paul Johns, Seattle | 118 yards (6) | vs. Pittsburgh |
| Frank Lewis, Buffalo | 116 yards (7) | vs. New England |
| Mike Barber, L.A. Rams | 113 yards (8) | vs. San Francisco |
| Roy Green, St. Louis | 100 yards (6) | vs. N.Y. Giants |

### Ninth Week
| | | |
|---|---|---|
| Rick Upchurch, Denver | 143 yards (6) | vs. Kansas City |
| Butch Woolfolk, N.Y. Giants | 135 yards (4) | vs. Dallas |
| Mark Duper, Miami | 134 yards (7) | vs. L.A. Rams |
| Steve Watson, Denver | 121 yards (6) | vs. Kansas City |
| Tony Hill, Dallas | 106 yards (5) | vs. N.Y. Giants |
| Art Monk, Washington | 106 yards (7) | vs. San Diego |
| Marcus Allen, L.A. Raiders | 104 yards (8) | vs. Seattle |
| Wes Chandler, San Diego | 103 yards (4) | vs. Washington |
| Charlie Brown, Washington | 101 yards (8) | vs. San Diego |

### Tenth Week
| | | |
|---|---|---|
| Mike Quick, Philadelphia | 120 yards (7) | vs. Dallas |
| Tony Galbreath, Minnesota | 110 yards (11) | vs. Tampa Bay |
| Steve Watson, Denver | 110 yards (7) | vs. Seattle |
| Carlos Carson, Kansas City | 103 yards (5) | vs. L.A. Raiders |
| John Jefferson, Green Bay | 102 yards (7) | vs. Cleveland |

### Eleventh Week
| | | |
|---|---|---|
| Steve Largent, Seattle | 155 yards (8) | vs. St. Louis |
| Earnest Gray, N.Y. Giants | 145 yards (8) | vs. Washington |
| Darrin Nelson, Minnesota | 137 yards (7) | vs. Green Bay |
| Roy Green, St. Louis | 130 yards (6) | vs. Seattle |
| Cris Collinsworth, Cincinnati | 118 yards (7) | vs. Kansas City |
| Todd Christensen, L.A. Raiders | 114 yards (8) | vs. Denver |
| Kevin House, Tampa Bay | 110 yards (5) | vs. Cleveland |
| Calvin Sweeney, Pittsburgh | 104 yards (6) | vs. Baltimore |
| Bruce Harper, N.Y. Jets | 102 yards (10) | vs. Buffalo |

### Twelfth Week
| | | |
|---|---|---|
| Charlie Brown, Washington | 140 yards (8) | vs. L.A. Rams |
| Carlos Carson, Kansas City | 135 yards (7) | vs. Dallas |
| Mark Duper, Miami | 121 yards (5) | vs. Baltimore |
| Steve Watson, Denver | 119 yards (4) | vs. Seattle |
| Kellen Winslow, San Diego | 117 yards (5) | vs. St. Louis |
| Paul Johns, Seattle | 116 yards (9) | vs. Denver |
| Henry Marshall, Kansas City | 115 yards (8) | vs. Dallas |
| Wesley Walker, N.Y. Jets | 110 yards (7) | vs. New Orleans |
| Billy Johnson, Atlanta | 104 yards (6) | vs. San Francisco |

### Thirteenth Week
| | | |
|---|---|---|
| James Lofton, Green Bay | 161 yards (7) | vs. Atlanta |
| Carlos Carson, Kansas City | 149 yards (7) | vs. Seattle |
| Charlie Brown, Washington | 147 yards (7) | vs. Philadelphia |
| Earnest Gray, N.Y. Giants | 134 yards (5) | vs. L.A. Raiders |
| Melvin Hoover, Philadelphia | 128 yards (4) | vs. Washington |
| Cris Collinsworth, Cincinnati | 127 yards (8) | vs. Miami |
| Byron Williams, N.Y. Giants | 119 yards (5) | vs. L.A. Raiders |
| Isaac Curtis, Cincinnati | 114 yards (4) | vs. Miami |
| Ozzie Newsome, Cleveland | 108 yards (8) | vs. Baltimore |
| Byron Franklin, Buffalo | 106 yards (4) | vs. L.A. Rams |
| Mike Quick, Philadelphia | 104 yards (5) | vs. Washington |
| Kellen Winslow, San Diego | 103 yards (6) | vs. Denver |
| Charlie Joiner, San Diego | 102 yards (7) | vs. Denver |

### Fourteenth Week
| | | |
|---|---|---|
| Stacey Bailey, Atlanta | 159 yards (9) | vs. Washington |
| Kevin House, Tampa Bay | 156 yards (6) | vs. San Francisco |
| Todd Christensen, L.A. Raiders | 140 yards (8) | vs. San Diego |
| Willie Gault, Chicago | 129 yards (4) | vs. Green Bay |
| James Lofton, Green Bay | 120 yards (6) | vs. Chicago |
| Clinton Sampson, Denver | 101 yards (3) | vs. Cleveland |

### Fifteenth Week
| | | |
|---|---|---|
| Bernard Henry, Baltimore | 169 yards (8) | vs. Denver |
| Carlos Carson, Kansas City | 165 yards (7) | vs. San Diego |
| Kellen Winslow, San Diego | 162 yards (14) | vs. Kansas City |
| Tim Smith, Houston | 150 yards (7) | vs. Cleveland |
| Lam Jones, N.Y. Jets | 146 yards (7) | vs. Pittsburgh |
| George Farmer, L.A. Rams | 122 yards (6) | vs. New England |
| Art Monk, Washington | 119 yards (6) | vs. Dallas |
| Byron Williams, N.Y. Giants | 103 yards (7) | vs. Seattle |

### Sixteenth Week
| | | |
|---|---|---|
| Todd Christensen, L.A. Raiders | 136 yards (8) | vs. San Diego |
| Kevin House, Tampa Bay | 136 yards (8) | vs. Detroit |
| Steve Largent, Seattle | 133 yards (7) | vs. New England |
| Byron Williams, N.Y. Giants | 124 yards (8) | vs. Washington |
| Paul Coffman, Green Bay | 122 yards (4) | vs. Chicago |
| Steve Kreider, Cincinnati | 109 yards (9) | vs. Minnesota |
| Perry Tuttle, Buffalo | 103 yards (6) | vs. Atlanta |
| Harold Carmichael, Philadelphia | 102 yards (5) | vs. St. Louis |

> **Times 100 or More**
> Carson, Quick 6; Gray, Lofton, Watson 5; Bailey, Brown, Christensen, Collinsworth, Largent, Winslow 4; Duper, Gault, Green, House, Monk, Smith, Walker, Williams 3; Carmichael, Chandler, Coffman, Hill, Johns, Joiner, Marshall, Newsome, Solomon 2.

| | Balt. | Buff. | Cin. | Clev. | Den. | Hou. | K.C. | Raid. | Mia. | N.E. | N.Y.J. | Pitt. | S.D. | Sea. |
|---|---|---|---|---|---|---|---|---|---|---|---|---|---|---|
| **First Downs** | 272 | 309 | 327 | 327 | 292 | 295 | 314 | 356 | 314 | 284 | 313 | 312 | 361 | 300 |
| Rushing | 146 | 100 | 127 | 113 | 99 | 120 | 83 | 143 | 132 | 130 | 126 | 156 | 106 | 131 |
| Passing | 110 | 171 | 179 | 186 | 155 | 155 | 208 | 181 | 151 | 138 | 171 | 141 | 230 | 153 |
| Penalty | 16 | 38 | 21 | 28 | 38 | 20 | 23 | 32 | 31 | 16 | 16 | 15 | 25 | 16 |
| **Rushes** | 601 | 415 | 542 | 465 | 471 | 502 | 387 | 542 | 568 | 538 | 474 | 614 | 423 | 546 |
| Net Yds. Gained | 2695 | 1736 | 2104 | 1922 | 1784 | 1998 | 1254 | 2240 | 2150 | 2605 | 2068 | 2610 | 1536 | 2119 |
| Avg. Gain | 4.5 | 4.2 | 3.9 | 4.1 | 3.8 | 4.0 | 3.2 | 4.1 | 3.8 | 4.8 | 4.4 | 4.3 | 3.6 | 3.9 |
| Avg. Yds. per Game | 168.4 | 108.5 | 131.5 | 120.1 | 111.5 | 124.9 | 78.4 | 140.0 | 134.4 | 162.8 | 129.3 | 163.1 | 96.0 | 132.4 |
| **Passes Attempted** | 377 | 571 | 454 | 567 | 499 | 482 | 641 | 504 | 442 | 412 | 559 | 409 | 635 | 449 |
| Completed | 188 | 317 | 290 | 324 | 254 | 260 | 369 | 301 | 254 | 220 | 330 | 211 | 369 | 251 |
| % Completed | 49.9 | 55.5 | 63.9 | 57.1 | 50.9 | 53.9 | 57.6 | 59.7 | 57.5 | 53.3 | 59.0 | 51.6 | 58.1 | 55.9 |
| Total Yds. Gained | 2663 | 3438 | 3492 | 3932 | 3466 | 3286 | 4684 | 3910 | 3235 | 3040 | 3742 | 2754 | 4891 | 3316 |
| Times Sacked | 47 | 37 | 40 | 33 | 55 | 49 | 46 | 55 | 23 | 45 | 43 | 52 | 28 | 47 |
| Yds. Lost | 340 | 351 | 309 | 271 | 439 | 384 | 343 | 464 | 190 | 334 | 317 | 350 | 230 | 343 |
| Net Yds. Gained | 2323 | 3087 | 3183 | 3661 | 3027 | 2902 | 4341 | 3446 | 3045 | 2706 | 3425 | 2404 | 4661 | 2973 |
| Avg. Yds. per Game | 145.2 | 192.9 | 198.9 | 228.8 | 189.2 | 181.4 | 271.3 | 215.4 | 190.3 | 169.1 | 214.1 | 150.3 | 291.3 | 185.8 |
| Net Yds. per Pass Play | 5.48 | 5.08 | 6.44 | 6.10 | 5.46 | 5.47 | 6.32 | 6.16 | 6.55 | 5.92 | 5.69 | 5.21 | 7.03 | 5.99 |
| Yds. Gained per Comp. | 14.16 | 10.85 | 12.04 | 12.14 | 13.65 | 12.64 | 12.69 | 12.99 | 12.74 | 13.82 | 11.34 | 13.05 | 13.25 | 13.21 |
| **Combined Net Yds. Gained** | 5018 | 4823 | 5287 | 5583 | 4811 | 4900 | 5595 | 5686 | 5195 | 5311 | 5493 | 5014 | 6197 | 5092 |
| % Total Yds., Rushing | 53.71 | 35.99 | 39.80 | 34.43 | 37.08 | 40.78 | 22.41 | 39.40 | 41.39 | 49.05 | 37.65 | 52.05 | 24.79 | 41.61 |
| % Total Yds., Passing | 46.29 | 64.01 | 60.20 | 65.57 | 62.92 | 59.22 | 77.59 | 60.60 | 58.61 | 50.95 | 62.35 | 47.95 | 75.21 | 58.39 |
| Avg. Yds. per Game | 313.6 | 301.4 | 330.4 | 348.9 | 300.7 | 306.3 | 349.7 | 355.4 | 324.7 | 331.9 | 343.3 | 313.4 | 387.3 | 318.3 |
| **Ball Control Plays** | 1025 | 1023 | 1036 | 1065 | 1025 | 1033 | 1074 | 1101 | 1033 | 995 | 1076 | 1075 | 1086 | 1042 |
| Avg. Yds. per Play | 4.9 | 4.7 | 5.1 | 5.2 | 4.7 | 4.7 | 5.2 | 5.2 | 5.0 | 5.3 | 5.1 | 4.7 | 5.7 | 4.9 |
| Avg. Time of Poss. | 29:26 | 28:24 | 31:29 | 30:50 | 29:31 | 29:40 | 28:53 | 30:58 | 31:20 | 29:21 | 29:23 | 30:40 | 28:04 | 29:52 |
| **Third Down Efficiency** | 34.5 | 33.5 | 45.8 | 44.4 | 31.9 | 39.0 | 39.9 | 44.8 | 38.2 | 39.8 | 37.4 | 42.9 | 43.3 | 43.8 |
| **Had Intercepted** | 22 | 28 | 18 | 28 | 22 | 29 | 19 | 24 | 11 | 18 | 28 | 23 | 33 | 18 |
| Yds. Opp. Returned | 117 | 330 | 298 | 508 | 281 | 392 | 323 | 381 | 203 | 361 | 372 | 252 | 377 | 279 |
| Ret. by Opp. for TD | 0 | 2 | 2 | 3 | 3 | 2 | 2 | 0 | 1 | 1 | 3 | 2 | 2 | 1 |
| **Punts** | 91 | 89 | 69 | 70 | 87 | 80 | 93 | 78 | 75 | 81 | 82 | 80 | 63 | 79 |
| Yds. Punted | 4124 | 3533 | 2804 | 2854 | 3620 | 3136 | 3710 | 3336 | 3189 | 3615 | 3218 | 3352 | 2763 | 3118 |
| Avg. Yds. per Punt | 45.3 | 39.7 | 40.6 | 40.8 | 41.6 | 39.2 | 39.9 | 42.8 | 42.5 | 44.6 | 39.2 | 41.9 | 43.9 | 39.5 |
| **Punt Returns** | 44 | 44 | 49 | 42 | 38 | 20 | 40 | 58 | 55 | 44 | 38 | 51 | 33 | 34 |
| Yds. Returned | 294 | 241 | 410 | 310 | 420 | 159 | 291 | 666 | 581 | 399 | 420 | 421 | 213 | 366 |
| Avg. Yds. per Return | 6.7 | 5.5 | 8.4 | 7.4 | 11.1 | 8.0 | 7.3 | 11.5 | 10.6 | 9.1 | 11.1 | 8.3 | 6.5 | 10.8 |
| Returned for TD | 0 | 0 | 0 | 0 | 1 | 0 | 0 | 1 | 1 | 0 | 1 | 0 | 0 | 1 |
| **Kickoff Returns** | 62 | 64 | 54 | 63 | 56 | 83 | 54 | 61 | 47 | 57 | 66 | 59 | 74 | 71 |
| Yds. Returned | 1198 | 1363 | 1097 | 1290 | 1077 | 1676 | 929 | 1175 | 1085 | 1155 | 1375 | 1068 | 1377 | 1575 |
| Avg. Yds. per Return | 19.3 | 21.3 | 20.3 | 20.5 | 19.2 | 20.2 | 17.2 | 19.3 | 23.1 | 20.3 | 20.8 | 18.1 | 18.6 | 22.2 |
| Returned for TD | 0 | 0 | 0 | 0 | 0 | 2 | 0 | 0 | 0 | 0 | 0 | 0 | 0 | 1 |
| **Penalties** | 120 | 144 | 99 | 115 | 100 | 84 | 113 | 121 | 64 | 90 | 110 | 99 | 115 | 102 |
| Yds. Penalized | 986 | 1094 | 837 | 991 | 804 | 784 | 911 | 992 | 567 | 815 | 1059 | 836 | 961 | 890 |
| **Fumbles** | 32 | 24 | 35 | 21 | 34 | 26 | 31 | 46 | 30 | 47 | 29 | 42 | 42 | 36 |
| Lost | 11 | 12 | 15 | 10 | 19 | 18 | 19 | 25 | 16 | 20 | 19 | 20 | 22 | 20 |
| Out of Bounds | 6 | 1 | 1 | 1 | 3 | 1 | 2 | 4 | 3 | 3 | 0 | 2 | 5 | 0 |
| Own Rec. for TD | 0 | 0 | 0 | 0 | 0 | 0 | 0 | 1 | 0 | 0 | 0 | 0 | 0 | 0 |
| Opp. Rec. by | 16 | 17 | 16 | 10 | 20 | 15 | 21 | 16 | 17 | 19 | 14 | 17 | 17 | 28 |
| Opp. Rec. for TD | 2 | 1 | 1 | 0 | 1 | 0 | 1 | 1 | 0 | 0 | 1 | 3 | 0 | 2 |
| **Total Points Scored** | 264 | 283 | 346 | 356 | 302 | 288 | 386 | 442 | 389 | 274 | 313 | 355 | 358 | 403 |
| Total TDs | 25 | 36 | 43 | 42 | 34 | 34 | 45 | 54 | 48 | 36 | 38 | 39 | 45 | 50 |
| TDs Rushing | 10 | 4 | 24 | 13 | 15 | 16 | 13 | 18 | 16 | 19 | 11 | 17 | 16 | 19 |
| TDs Passing | 12 | 30 | 14 | 27 | 17 | 16 | 29 | 31 | 28 | 16 | 21 | 15 | 27 | 25 |
| TDs on Ret. and Rec. | 3 | 2 | 5 | 2 | 2 | 2 | 3 | 5 | 4 | 1 | 6 | 7 | 2 | 6 |
| Extra Points | 22 | 34 | 40 | 38 | 33 | 33 | 44 | 51 | 45 | 31 | 37 | 38 | 43 | 49 |
| Safeties | 1 | 0 | 0 | 0 | 1 | 0 | 0 | 2 | 1 | 0 | 0 | 1 | 0 | 0 |
| Field Goals Made | 30 | 11 | 16 | 22 | 21 | 17 | 24 | 21 | 18 | 9 | 16 | 27 | 15 | 18 |
| Field Goals Attempted | 35 | 26 | 23 | 25 | 25 | 21 | 30 | 27 | 27 | 22 | 24 | 31 | 24 | 25 |
| % Successful | 85.7 | 42.3 | 69.6 | 88.0 | 84.0 | 81.0 | 80.0 | 77.8 | 66.7 | 40.9 | 66.7 | 87.1 | 62.5 | 72.0 |

## AMERICAN FOOTBALL CONFERENCE DEFENSE

| | Balt. | Buff. | Cin. | Clev. | Den. | Hou. | K.C. | Raid. | Mia. | N.E. | N.Y.J. | Pitt. | S.D. | Sea. |
|---|---|---|---|---|---|---|---|---|---|---|---|---|---|---|
| **First Downs** | 321 | 332 | 276 | 309 | 321 | 332 | 319 | 285 | 288 | 326 | 298 | 278 | 347 | 351 |
| Rushing | 123 | 148 | 96 | 138 | 119 | 161 | 136 | 86 | 122 | 129 | 126 | 100 | 137 | 128 |
| Passing | 166 | 148 | 156 | 155 | 185 | 150 | 158 | 170 | 147 | 172 | 151 | 151 | 187 | 195 |
| Penalty | 32 | 36 | 24 | 16 | 17 | 21 | 25 | 29 | 19 | 25 | 21 | 27 | 23 | 28 |
| **Rushes** | 516 | 566 | 430 | 528 | 509 | 576 | 554 | 436 | 460 | 549 | 547 | 509 | 552 | 511 |
| Net Yds. Gained | 2118 | 2503 | 1499 | 2065 | 1938 | 2787 | 2275 | 1586 | 2037 | 2281 | 2378 | 1833 | 2173 | 2198 |
| Avg. Gain | 4.1 | 4.4 | 3.5 | 3.9 | 3.8 | 4.8 | 4.1 | 3.6 | 4.4 | 4.2 | 4.3 | 3.6 | 3.9 | 4.3 |
| Avg. Yds. per Game | 132.4 | 156.4 | 93.7 | 129.1 | 121.1 | 174.2 | 142.2 | 99.1 | 127.3 | 142.6 | 148.6 | 114.6 | 135.8 | 137.4 |
| **Passes Attempted** | 488 | 480 | 502 | 469 | 552 | 424 | 500 | 531 | 480 | 514 | 463 | 447 | 544 | 521 |
| Completed | 281 | 286 | 288 | 280 | 307 | 252 | 261 | 282 | 277 | 277 | 269 | 238 | 330 | 311 |
| % Completed | 57.6 | 59.6 | 57.4 | 59.7 | 55.6 | 59.4 | 52.2 | 53.1 | 57.7 | 53.9 | 58.1 | 53.2 | 60.7 | 59.7 |
| Total Yds. Gained | 3832 | 3553 | 3163 | 3316 | 3988 | 3095 | 3361 | 3646 | 3365 | 3565 | 3301 | 3260 | 4051 | 4182 |
| Times Sacked | 41 | 32 | 41 | 32 | 38 | 31 | 35 | 57 | 49 | 39 | 48 | 50 | 31 | 43 |
| Yds. Lost | 310 | 247 | 335 | 239 | 317 | 250 | 250 | 484 | 363 | 270 | 378 | 361 | 269 | 351 |
| Net Yds. Gained | 3522 | 3306 | 2828 | 3077 | 3671 | 2845 | 3111 | 3162 | 3002 | 3295 | 2923 | 2899 | 3782 | 3831 |
| Avg. Yds. per Game | 220.1 | 206.6 | 176.8 | 192.3 | 229.4 | 177.8 | 194.4 | 197.6 | 187.6 | 205.9 | 182.7 | 181.2 | 236.4 | 239.4 |
| Net Yds. per Pass Play | 6.66 | 6.46 | 5.21 | 6.14 | 6.22 | 6.25 | 5.81 | 5.38 | 5.67 | 5.96 | 5.72 | 5.83 | 6.58 | 6.79 |
| Yds. Gained per Comp. | 13.64 | 12.42 | 10.98 | 11.84 | 12.99 | 12.28 | 12.88 | 12.93 | 12.15 | 12.87 | 12.27 | 13.70 | 12.28 | 13.45 |
| **Combined Net Yds. Gained** | 5640 | 5809 | 4327 | 5142 | 5609 | 5632 | 5386 | 4748 | 5039 | 5576 | 5301 | 4732 | 5955 | 6029 |
| % Total Yds., Rushing | 37.55 | 43.09 | 34.64 | 40.16 | 34.55 | 49.49 | 42.24 | 33.40 | 40.42 | 40.91 | 44.86 | 38.74 | 36.49 | 36.46 |
| % Total Yds., Passing | 62.45 | 56.91 | 65.36 | 59.84 | 65.45 | 50.51 | 57.76 | 66.60 | 59.58 | 59.09 | 55.14 | 61.26 | 63.51 | 63.54 |
| Avg. Yds. per Game | 352.5 | 363.1 | 270.4 | 321.4 | 350.6 | 352.0 | 336.6 | 296.8 | 314.9 | 348.5 | 331.3 | 295.8 | 372.2 | 376.8 |
| **Ball Control Plays** | 1045 | 1078 | 973 | 1029 | 1099 | 1031 | 1089 | 1024 | 989 | 1102 | 1058 | 1006 | 1127 | 1075 |
| Avg. Yds. per Play | 5.4 | 5.4 | 4.4 | 5.0 | 5.1 | 5.5 | 4.9 | 4.6 | 5.1 | 5.1 | 5.0 | 4.7 | 5.3 | 5.6 |
| **Third Down Efficiency** | 39.7 | 36.7 | 43.5 | 40.2 | 39.1 | 41.5 | 38.5 | 32.0 | 38.0 | 43.4 | 37.7 | 35.2 | 47.2 | 44.4 |
| **Intercepted by** | 20 | 13 | 23 | 22 | 27 | 14 | 30 | 20 | 26 | 17 | 22 | 28 | 16 | 26 |
| Yds. Returned by | 314 | 154 | 369 | 296 | 355 | 135 | 482 | 238 | 345 | 202 | 342 | 435 | 153 | 363 |
| Returned for TD | 1 | 1 | 4 | 2 | 0 | 0 | 2 | 2 | 3 | 1 | 3 | 4 | 1 | 2 |
| **Punts** | 80 | 78 | 76 | 73 | 77 | 65 | 85 | 100 | 90 | 78 | 85 | 88 | 70 | 68 |
| Yds. Punted | 3329 | 3344 | 3211 | 2954 | 3406 | 2567 | 3500 | 4060 | 3674 | 3273 | 3491 | 3615 | 2780 | 2754 |
| Avg. Yds. per Punt | 41.6 | 42.9 | 42.3 | 40.5 | 44.2 | 39.5 | 41.2 | 40.6 | 40.8 | 42.0 | 41.1 | 41.1 | 39.7 | 40.5 |
| **Punt Returns** | 55 | 42 | 41 | 30 | 55 | 47 | 54 | 35 | 32 | 48 | 47 | 44 | 35 | 36 |
| Yds. Returned | 642 | 403 | 310 | 309 | 524 | 354 | 559 | 334 | 229 | 392 | 367 | 418 | 299 | 185 |
| Avg. Yds. per Return | 11.7 | 9.6 | 7.6 | 10.3 | 9.5 | 7.5 | 10.4 | 9.5 | 7.2 | 8.2 | 7.8 | 9.5 | 8.5 | 5.1 |
| Returned for TD | 1 | 0 | 0 | 0 | 0 | 0 | 1 | 2 | 0 | 0 | 1 | 1 | 0 | 0 |
| **Kickoff Returns** | 61 | 53 | 68 | 61 | 46 | 61 | 75 | 68 | 54 | 55 | 50 | 65 | 70 | 59 |
| Yds. Returned | 1138 | 949 | 1298 | 1155 | 824 | 1280 | 1528 | 1227 | 1024 | 1082 | 1063 | 1507 | 1426 | 952 |
| Avg. Yds. per Return | 18.7 | 17.9 | 19.1 | 18.9 | 17.9 | 21.0 | 20.4 | 18.0 | 19.0 | 19.7 | 21.3 | 23.2 | 20.4 | 16.1 |
| Returned for TD | 0 | 0 | 0 | 0 | 1 | 0 | 0 | 0 | 0 | 0 | 0 | 1 | 0 | 0 |
| **Penalties** | 82 | 128 | 100 | 105 | 138 | 104 | 105 | 109 | 95 | 84 | 96 | 96 | 111 | 91 |
| Yds. Penalized | 666 | 1298 | 871 | 940 | 1097 | 825 | 837 | 947 | 837 | 674 | 784 | 782 | 953 | 725 |
| **Fumbles** | 29 | 32 | 35 | 30 | 46 | 34 | 35 | 31 | 38 | 30 | 29 | 34 | 26 | 44 |
| Lost | 16 | 18 | 16 | 10 | 20 | 15 | 21 | 16 | 17 | 19 | 14 | 17 | 17 | 28 |
| Out of Bounds | 4 | 0 | 3 | 1 | 4 | 4 | 3 | 0 | 0 | 2 | 1 | 2 | 1 | 5 |
| Own Rec. for TD | 0 | 0 | 0 | 0 | 0 | 0 | 1 | 0 | 0 | 0 | 0 | 0 | 0 | 0 |
| Opp. Rec. | 10 | 12 | 15 | 10 | 19 | 18 | 19 | 25 | 16 | 20 | 19 | 20 | 21 | 20 |
| Opp. Rec. for TD | 0 | 1 | 1 | 1 | 1 | 3 | 1 | 5 | 1 | 2 | 0 | 0 | 1 | 0 |
| **Total Points Scored** | 354 | 351 | 302 | 342 | 327 | 460 | 367 | 338 | 250 | 289 | 331 | 303 | 462 | 397 |
| Total TDs | 45 | 39 | 36 | 42 | 36 | 54 | 44 | 40 | 32 | 31 | 39 | 37 | 57 | 48 |
| TDs Rushing | 13 | 14 | 16 | 15 | 14 | 23 | 18 | 13 | 11 | 9 | 13 | 14 | 26 | 14 |
| TDs Passing | 31 | 22 | 17 | 22 | 18 | 26 | 21 | 20 | 19 | 19 | 22 | 19 | 28 | 33 |
| TDs on Ret. and Rec. | 1 | 3 | 3 | 5 | 4 | 5 | 5 | 7 | 2 | 3 | 4 | 4 | 3 | 1 |
| Extra Points | 42 | 39 | 35 | 40 | 34 | 49 | 43 | 39 | 31 | 29 | 35 | 36 | 54 | 43 |
| Safeties | 0 | 0 | 0 | 1 | 1 | 0 | 0 | 1 | 0 | 1 | 1 | 0 | 0 | 3 |
| Field Goals Made | 14 | 26 | 17 | 16 | 25 | 29 | 20 | 19 | 9 | 24 | 20 | 15 | 22 | 20 |
| Field Goals Attempted | 23 | 39 | 22 | 22 | 33 | 36 | 26 | 25 | 15 | 31 | 28 | 20 | 29 | 26 |
| % Successful | 60.9 | 66.7 | 77.3 | 72.7 | 75.8 | 80.6 | 76.9 | 76.0 | 60.0 | 77.4 | 71.4 | 75.0 | 75.9 | 76.9 |

# NATIONAL FOOTBALL CONFERENCE OFFENSE

| | Atl. | Chi. | Dall. | Det. | G.B. | Rams | Minn. | N.O. | N.Y.G. | Phil. | St.L. | S.F. | T.B. | Wash. |
|---|---|---|---|---|---|---|---|---|---|---|---|---|---|---|
| **First Downs** | 325 | 308 | 342 | 315 | 340 | 316 | 303 | 286 | 296 | 253 | 296 | 344 | 249 | 353 |
| Rushing | 118 | 154 | 109 | 136 | 99 | 148 | 112 | 135 | 104 | 91 | 123 | 129 | 72 | 165 |
| Passing | 190 | 136 | 205 | 156 | 214 | 150 | 169 | 136 | 164 | 150 | 147 | 199 | 157 | 173 |
| Penalty | 17 | 18 | 28 | 23 | 27 | 18 | 22 | 15 | 28 | 12 | 26 | 16 | 20 | 15 |
| **Rushes** | 492 | 583 | 519 | 513 | 439 | 511 | 470 | 595 | 506 | 402 | 525 | 511 | 428 | 629 |
| Net Yds. Gained | 2224 | 2727 | 2117 | 2181 | 1807 | 2253 | 1808 | 2461 | 1794 | 1417 | 2277 | 2257 | 1353 | 2625 |
| Avg. Gain | 4.5 | 4.7 | 4.1 | 4.3 | 4.1 | 4.4 | 3.8 | 4.1 | 3.5 | 3.5 | 4.3 | 4.4 | 3.2 | 4.2 |
| Avg. Yds. per Game | 139.0 | 170.4 | 132.3 | 136.3 | 112.9 | 140.8 | 113.0 | 153.8 | 112.1 | 88.6 | 142.3 | 141.1 | 84.6 | 164.1 |
| **Passes Attempted** | 507 | 447 | 554 | 503 | 526 | 489 | 555 | 425 | 575 | 486 | 460 | 528 | 528 | 463 |
| Completed | 321 | 255 | 346 | 263 | 311 | 286 | 310 | 243 | 284 | 252 | 267 | 339 | 300 | 278 |
| % Completed | 63.3 | 57.0 | 62.5 | 52.3 | 59.1 | 58.5 | 55.9 | 57.2 | 49.4 | 51.9 | 58.0 | 64.2 | 56.8 | 60.0 |
| Total Yds. Gained | 3793 | 3461 | 4156 | 3297 | 4688 | 3411 | 3514 | 2782 | 3854 | 3532 | 3309 | 4021 | 3490 | 3765 |
| Times Sacked | 55 | 53 | 37 | 45 | 42 | 23 | 43 | 35 | 49 | 57 | 59 | 33 | 49 | 35 |
| Yds. Lost | 389 | 358 | 314 | 342 | 323 | 190 | 303 | 305 | 363 | 415 | 441 | 224 | 366 | 251 |
| Net Yds. Gained | 3404 | 3103 | 3842 | 2955 | 4365 | 3221 | 3211 | 2477 | 3491 | 3117 | 2868 | 3797 | 3124 | 3514 |
| Avg. Yds. per Game | 212.8 | 193.9 | 240.1 | 184.7 | 272.8 | 201.3 | 200.7 | 154.8 | 218.2 | 194.8 | 179.3 | 237.3 | 195.3 | 219.6 |
| Net Yds. per Pass Play | 6.06 | 6.21 | 6.50 | 5.39 | 7.68 | 6.29 | 5.37 | 5.38 | 5.59 | 5.74 | 5.53 | 6.77 | 5.41 | 7.06 |
| Yds. Gained per Comp. | 11.82 | 13.57 | 12.01 | 12.54 | 15.07 | 11.93 | 11.34 | 11.45 | 13.57 | 14.02 | 12.39 | 11.86 | 11.63 | 13.54 |
| **Combined Net Yds. Gained** | 5628 | 5830 | 5959 | 5136 | 6172 | 5474 | 5019 | 4938 | 5285 | 4534 | 5145 | 6054 | 4477 | 6139 |
| % Total Yds., Rushing | 39.52 | 46.78 | 35.53 | 42.46 | 29.28 | 41.16 | 36.02 | 49.84 | 33.95 | 31.25 | 44.26 | 37.28 | 30.22 | 42.76 |
| % Total Yds., Passing | 60.48 | 53.22 | 64.47 | 57.54 | 70.72 | 58.84 | 63.98 | 50.16 | 66.05 | 68.75 | 55.74 | 62.72 | 69.78 | 57.24 |
| Avg. Yds. per Game | 351.8 | 364.4 | 372.4 | 321.0 | 385.8 | 342.1 | 313.7 | 308.6 | 330.3 | 283.4 | 321.6 | 378.4 | 279.8 | 383.7 |
| **Ball Control Plays** | 1054 | 1083 | 1110 | 1061 | 1007 | 1023 | 1068 | 1055 | 1130 | 945 | 1044 | 1072 | 1005 | 1127 |
| Avg. Yds. per Play | 5.3 | 5.4 | 5.4 | 4.8 | 6.1 | 5.4 | 4.7 | 4.7 | 4.7 | 4.8 | 4.9 | 5.6 | 4.5 | 5.4 |
| Avg. Time of Poss. | 30:12 | 32:11 | 33:08 | 30:08 | 27:01 | 29:16 | 28:47 | 30:24 | 30:37 | 27:07 | 31:20 | 30:12 | 27:55 | 33:44 |
| **Third Down Efficiency** | 48.4 | 34.5 | 43.0 | 43.3 | 38.1 | 38.5 | 29.5 | 39.4 | 34.8 | 33.5 | 37.5 | 44.7 | 32.7 | 42.3 |
| **Had Intercepted** | 10 | 22 | 25 | 23 | 32 | 23 | 22 | 25 | 31 | 18 | 21 | 12 | 24 | 11 |
| Yds. Opp. Returned | 94 | 291 | 358 | 241 | 337 | 303 | 308 | 424 | 436 | 155 | 385 | 168 | 316 | 90 |
| Ret. by Opp. for TD | 0 | 1 | 1 | 0 | 4 | 0 | 2 | 5 | 2 | 0 | 5 | 1 | 4 | 0 |
| **Punts** | 71 | 94 | 83 | 72 | 70 | 83 | 91 | 78 | 85 | 86 | 85 | 66 | 96 | 72 |
| Yds. Punted | 2823 | 3399 | 3272 | 2911 | 2869 | 3301 | 3780 | 3178 | 3386 | 3521 | 3529 | 2552 | 4008 | 2796 |
| Avg. Yds. per Punt | 39.8 | 36.2 | 39.4 | 40.4 | 41.0 | 39.8 | 41.5 | 40.7 | 39.8 | 40.9 | 41.5 | 38.7 | 41.8 | 38.8 |
| **Punt Returns** | 46 | 56 | 51 | 46 | 41 | 55 | 24 | 39 | 55 | 45 | 58 | 36 | 42 | 49 |
| Yds. Returned | 489 | 447 | 461 | 522 | 329 | 538 | 210 | 275 | 377 | 259 | 461 | 365 | 299 | 387 |
| Avg. Yds. per Return | 10.6 | 8.0 | 9.0 | 11.3 | 8.0 | 9.8 | 8.8 | 7.1 | 6.9 | 5.8 | 7.9 | 10.1 | 7.1 | 7.9 |
| Returned for TD | 1 | 1 | 1 | 1 | 1 | 1 | 0 | 0 | 0 | 0 | 0 | 1 | 0 | 0 |
| **Kickoff Returns** | 67 | 58 | 71 | 61 | 79 | 52 | 68 | 66 | 71 | 62 | 72 | 52 | 68 | 63 |
| Yds. Returned | 1258 | 953 | 1351 | 1191 | 1339 | 946 | 1466 | 1339 | 1333 | 1168 | 1459 | 958 | 1314 | 1301 |
| Avg. Yds. per Return | 18.8 | 16.4 | 19.0 | 19.5 | 16.9 | 18.2 | 21.6 | 20.3 | 18.8 | 18.8 | 20.3 | 18.4 | 19.3 | 20.7 |
| Returned for TD | 0 | 0 | 0 | 0 | 0 | 0 | 0 | 0 | 0 | 0 | 0 | 0 | 0 | 0 |
| **Penalties** | 90 | 107 | 99 | 118 | 80 | 96 | 90 | 91 | 113 | 79 | 89 | 89 | 94 | 90 |
| Yds. Penalized | 806 | 869 | 847 | 988 | 648 | 748 | 748 | 802 | 1020 | 637 | 770 | 695 | 832 | 776 |
| **Fumbles** | 36 | 25 | 30 | 41 | 37 | 38 | 33 | 37 | 39 | 37 | 50 | 27 | 39 | 13 |
| Lost | 19 | 14 | 14 | 16 | 18 | 24 | 10 | 22 | 27 | 18 | 27 | 19 | 13 | 7 |
| Out of Bounds | 5 | 1 | 2 | 4 | 3 | 2 | 2 | 0 | 1 | 3 | 5 | 2 | 3 | 1 |
| Own Rec. for TD | 0 | 0 | 1 | 0 | 0 | 0 | 0 | 2 | 0 | 0 | 0 | 0 | 0 | 1 |
| Opp. Rec. by | 15 | 17 | 21 | 15 | 12 | 20 | 23 | 16 | 13 | 15 | 20 | 18 | 18 | 26 |
| Opp. Rec. for TD | 2 | 1 | 2 | 0 | 2 | 0 | 1 | 0 | 1 | 0 | 3 | 1 | 1 | 2 |
| **Total Points Scored** | 370 | 311 | 479 | 347 | 429 | 361 | 316 | 319 | 267 | 233 | 374 | 432 | 241 | 541 |
| Total TDs | 46 | 39 | 59 | 38 | 52 | 47 | 34 | 38 | 23 | 27 | 47 | 51 | 31 | 63 |
| TDs Rushing | 17 | 14 | 21 | 18 | 15 | 20 | 17 | 19 | 9 | 5 | 15 | 17 | 9 | 30 |
| TDs Passing | 24 | 21 | 31 | 19 | 33 | 23 | 15 | 14 | 12 | 22 | 29 | 27 | 18 | 29 |
| TDs on Ret. and Rec. | 5 | 4 | 7 | 1 | 4 | 4 | 2 | 5 | 2 | 0 | 3 | 7 | 4 | 4 |
| Extra Points | 43 | 35 | 57 | 38 | 52 | 42 | 33 | 37 | 22 | 24 | 45 | 51 | 25 | 62 |
| Safeties | 0 | 0 | 1 | 3 | 1 | 2 | 2 | 0 | 1 | 1 | 1 | 0 | 0 | 1 |
| Field Goals Made | 17 | 14 | 22 | 25 | 21 | 11 | 25 | 18 | 35 | 15 | 15 | 25 | 10 | 33 |
| Field Goals Attempted | 22 | 25 | 27 | 32 | 26 | 20 | 33 | 24 | 42 | 26 | 28 | 30 | 24 | 47 |
| % Successful | 77.3 | 56.0 | 81.5 | 78.1 | 80.8 | 55.0 | 75.8 | 75.0 | 83.3 | 57.7 | 53.6 | 83.3 | 41.7 | 70.2 |

## NATIONAL FOOTBALL CONFERENCE DEFENSE

| | Atl. | Chi. | Dall. | Det. | G.B. | Rams | Minn. | N.O. | N.Y.G. | Phil. | St.L. | S.F. | T.B. | Wash. |
|---|---|---|---|---|---|---|---|---|---|---|---|---|---|---|
| **First Downs** | 342 | 286 | 286 | 324 | 366 | 311 | 318 | 289 | 289 | 310 | 286 | 302 | 320 | 290 |
| Rushing | 139 | 113 | 82 | 133 | 171 | 118 | 147 | 108 | 98 | 144 | 107 | 98 | 124 | 76 |
| Passing | 187 | 154 | 181 | 161 | 187 | 179 | 150 | 159 | 167 | 149 | 161 | 181 | 172 | 196 |
| Penalty | 16 | 19 | 23 | 30 | 8 | 14 | 21 | 22 | 24 | 17 | 18 | 23 | 24 | 18 |
| **Rushes** | 499 | 482 | 410 | 503 | 597 | 489 | 579 | 472 | 502 | 633 | 443 | 449 | 561 | 349 |
| Net Yds. Gained | 2309 | 2000 | 1499 | 2104 | 2641 | 1781 | 2584 | 2000 | 1733 | 2655 | 1838 | 1936 | 2082 | 1289 |
| Avg. Gain | 4.6 | 4.1 | 3.7 | 4.2 | 4.4 | 3.6 | 4.5 | 4.2 | 3.5 | 4.2 | 4.1 | 4.3 | 3.7 | 3.7 |
| Avg. Yds. per Game | 144.3 | 125.0 | 93.7 | 131.5 | 165.1 | 111.3 | 161.5 | 125.0 | 108.3 | 165.9 | 114.9 | 121.0 | 130.1 | 80.6 |
| **Passes Attempted** | 493 | 490 | 558 | 515 | 518 | 556 | 478 | 496 | 493 | 430 | 519 | 526 | 490 | 570 |
| Completed | 313 | 249 | 299 | 297 | 300 | 319 | 263 | 271 | 283 | 247 | 290 | 322 | 300 | 301 |
| % Completed | 63.5 | 50.8 | 53.6 | 57.7 | 57.9 | 57.4 | 55.0 | 54.6 | 57.4 | 57.4 | 55.9 | 61.2 | 61.2 | 52.8 |
| Total Yds. Gained | 3734 | 3516 | 4365 | 3401 | 4033 | 3869 | 3229 | 3128 | 3584 | 3048 | 3635 | 3701 | 3624 | 4377 |
| Times Sacked | 31 | 51 | 57 | 43 | 41 | 33 | 47 | 56 | 44 | 36 | 59 | 57 | 42 | 51 |
| Yds. Lost | 217 | 384 | 437 | 289 | 271 | 258 | 326 | 437 | 323 | 256 | 468 | 448 | 309 | 402 |
| Net Yds. Gained | 3517 | 3132 | 3928 | 3112 | 3762 | 3611 | 2903 | 2691 | 3261 | 2792 | 3167 | 3253 | 3315 | 3975 |
| Avg. Yds. per Game | 219.8 | 195.8 | 245.5 | 194.5 | 235.1 | 225.7 | 181.4 | 168.2 | 203.8 | 174.5 | 197.9 | 203.3 | 207.2 | 248.4 |
| Net Yds. per Pass Play | 6.71 | 5.79 | 6.39 | 5.58 | 6.73 | 6.13 | 5.53 | 4.88 | 6.07 | 5.99 | 5.48 | 5.58 | 6.23 | 6.40 |
| Yds. Gained per Comp. | 11.93 | 14.12 | 14.60 | 11.45 | 13.44 | 12.13 | 12.28 | 11.54 | 12.66 | 12.34 | 12.53 | 11.49 | 12.08 | 14.54 |
| **Combined Net Yds. Gained** | 5826 | 5132 | 5427 | 5216 | 6403 | 5392 | 5487 | 4691 | 4994 | 5447 | 5005 | 5189 | 5397 | 5264 |
| % Total Yds., Rushing | 39.63 | 38.97 | 27.62 | 40.34 | 41.25 | 33.03 | 47.09 | 42.63 | 34.70 | 48.74 | 36.72 | 37.31 | 38.58 | 24.49 |
| % Total Yds., Passing | 60.37 | 61.03 | 72.38 | 59.66 | 58.75 | 66.97 | 52.91 | 57.37 | 65.30 | 51.26 | 63.28 | 62.69 | 61.42 | 75.51 |
| Avg. Yds. per Game | 364.1 | 320.8 | 339.2 | 326.0 | 400.2 | 337.0 | 342.9 | 293.2 | 312.1 | 340.4 | 312.8 | 324.3 | 337.3 | 329.0 |
| **Ball Control Plays** | 1023 | 1023 | 1025 | 1061 | 1156 | 1078 | 1104 | 1024 | 1039 | 1099 | 1021 | 1032 | 1093 | 970 |
| Avg. Yds. per Play | 5.7 | 5.0 | 5.3 | 4.9 | 5.5 | 5.0 | 5.0 | 4.6 | 4.8 | 5.0 | 4.9 | 5.0 | 4.9 | 5.4 |
| **Third Down Efficiency** | 47.0 | 33.6 | 35.3 | 37.6 | 46.4 | 39.7 | 41.3 | 38.7 | 30.3 | 41.5 | 31.9 | 38.4 | 39.6 | 40.6 |
| **Intercepted by** | 15 | 21 | 27 | 22 | 19 | 24 | 25 | 23 | 23 | 8 | 28 | 24 | 23 | 34 |
| Yds. Returned by | 212 | 215 | 467 | 185 | 227 | 515 | 168 | 412 | 210 | 79 | 266 | 437 | 367 | 437 |
| Returned for TD | 2 | 2 | 2 | 0 | 1 | 3 | 0 | 3 | 1 | 0 | 0 | 5 | 3 | 1 |
| **Punts** | 67 | 99 | 84 | 79 | 78 | 83 | 77 | 83 | 99 | 80 | 88 | 74 | 79 | 66 |
| Yds. Punted | 2812 | 3821 | 3515 | 3167 | 3052 | 3465 | 3027 | 3473 | 3884 | 3020 | 3545 | 2993 | 3217 | 2748 |
| Avg. Yds. per Punt | 42.0 | 38.6 | 41.8 | 40.1 | 39.1 | 41.7 | 39.3 | 41.8 | 39.2 | 37.8 | 40.3 | 40.4 | 40.7 | 41.6 |
| **Punt Returns** | 34 | 44 | 53 | 39 | 43 | 39 | 40 | 51 | 47 | 57 | 47 | 38 | 59 | 41 |
| Yds. Returned | 179 | 322 | 588 | 302 | 384 | 251 | 297 | 573 | 283 | 511 | 307 | 278 | 603 | 407 |
| Avg. Yds. per Return | 5.3 | 7.3 | 11.1 | 7.7 | 8.9 | 6.4 | 7.4 | 11.2 | 6.0 | 9.0 | 6.5 | 7.3 | 10.2 | 9.9 |
| Returned for TD | 0 | 0 | 1 | 0 | 1 | 0 | 0 | 2 | 0 | 0 | 0 | 0 | 1 | 1 |
| **Kickoff Returns** | 60 | 66 | 78 | 71 | 78 | 71 | 70 | 44 | 67 | 45 | 66 | 78 | 50 | 91 |
| Yds. Returned | 1212 | 1229 | 1806 | 1146 | 1429 | 1325 | 1392 | 938 | 1296 | 804 | 1300 | 1675 | 1039 | 1772 |
| Avg. Yds. per Return | 20.2 | 18.6 | 23.2 | 16.1 | 18.3 | 18.7 | 19.9 | 21.3 | 19.3 | 17.9 | 19.7 | 21.5 | 20.8 | 19.5 |
| Returned for TD | 0 | 0 | 0 | 0 | 0 | 0 | 0 | 0 | 0 | 0 | 1 | 0 | 0 | 0 |
| **Penalties** | 81 | 86 | 100 | 117 | 110 | 89 | 92 | 96 | 114 | 94 | 102 | 91 | 105 | 80 |
| Yds. Penalized | 710 | 687 | 873 | 1062 | 965 | 804 | 759 | 814 | 927 | 755 | 819 | 793 | 799 | 710 |
| **Fumbles** | 26 | 37 | 31 | 33 | 32 | 38 | 33 | 33 | 31 | 30 | 32 | 39 | 43 | 46 |
| Lost | 15 | 17 | 21 | 15 | 12 | 20 | 23 | 16 | 13 | 15 | 20 | 18 | 18 | 27 |
| Out of Bounds | 0 | 5 | 0 | 0 | 2 | 3 | 2 | 1 | 3 | 3 | 5 | 4 | 4 | 4 |
| Own Rec. for TD | 0 | 0 | 0 | 0 | 1 | 1 | 0 | 0 | 0 | 0 | 1 | 0 | 1 | 0 |
| Opp. Rec. | 19 | 14 | 14 | 16 | 18 | 24 | 10 | 22 | 27 | 18 | 27 | 19 | 13 | 7 |
| Opp. Rec. for TD | 1 | 0 | 0 | 0 | 1 | 1 | 1 | 0 | 2 | 0 | 2 | 1 | 2 | 1 |
| **Total Points Scored** | 389 | 301 | 360 | 286 | 439 | 344 | 348 | 337 | 347 | 322 | 428 | 293 | 380 | 332 |
| Total TDs | 49 | 36 | 42 | 33 | 55 | 42 | 42 | 39 | 40 | 34 | 56 | 35 | 42 | 39 |
| TDs Rushing | 20 | 20 | 12 | 11 | 28 | 21 | 16 | 11 | 10 | 14 | 23 | 10 | 19 | 9 |
| TDs Passing | 28 | 15 | 27 | 21 | 20 | 18 | 23 | 20 | 26 | 20 | 24 | 23 | 15 | 28 |
| TDs on Ret. and Rec. | 1 | 1 | 3 | 1 | 7 | 3 | 3 | 8 | 4 | 0 | 9 | 2 | 8 | 2 |
| Extra Points | 44 | 34 | 42 | 32 | 50 | 39 | 40 | 37 | 39 | 34 | 54 | 32 | 40 | 38 |
| Safeties | 0 | 0 | 0 | 1 | 1 | 1 | 1 | 3 | 1 | 0 | 1 | 0 | 2 | 0 |
| Field Goals Made | 17 | 17 | 22 | 18 | 19 | 17 | 18 | 20 | 22 | 28 | 12 | 17 | 28 | 20 |
| Field Goals Attempted | 26 | 23 | 30 | 26 | 29 | 28 | 27 | 34 | 32 | 37 | 15 | 27 | 34 | 28 |
| % Successful | 65.4 | 73.9 | 73.3 | 69.2 | 65.5 | 60.7 | 66.7 | 58.8 | 68.8 | 75.7 | 80.0 | 63.0 | 82.4 | 71.4 |

## AFC, NFC, AND NFL SUMMARY

| | AFC Offense Total | AFC Offense Average | AFC Defense Total | AFC Defense Average | NFC Offense Total | NFC Offense Average | NFC Defense Total | NFC Defense Average | NFL Total | NFL Average |
|---|---|---|---|---|---|---|---|---|---|---|
| **First Downs** | 4376 | 312.6 | 4383 | 313.1 | 4326 | 309.0 | 4319 | 308.5 | 8702 | 310.8 |
| Rushing | 1712 | 122.3 | 1749 | 124.9 | 1695 | 121.1 | 1658 | 118.4 | 3407 | 121.7 |
| Passing | 2329 | 166.4 | 2291 | 163.6 | 2346 | 167.6 | 2384 | 170.3 | 4675 | 167.0 |
| Penalty | 335 | 23.9 | 343 | 24.5 | 285 | 20.4 | 277 | 19.8 | 620 | 22.1 |
| **Rushes** | 7088 | 506.3 | 7243 | 517.4 | 7123 | 508.8 | 6968 | 497.7 | 14,211 | 507.5 |
| Net Yds. Gained | 28,821 | 2058.6 | 29,671 | 2119.4 | 29,301 | 2092.9 | 28,451 | 2032.2 | 58,122 | 2075.8 |
| Avg. Gain | — | 4.1 | — | 4.1 | — | 4.1 | — | 4.1 | — | 4.1 |
| Avg. Yds. per Game | — | 128.7 | — | 132.5 | — | 130.8 | — | 127.0 | — | 129.7 |
| **Passes Attempted** | 7001 | 500.1 | 6915 | 493.9 | 7046 | 503.3 | 7132 | 509.4 | 14,047 | 501.7 |
| Completed | 3938 | 281.3 | 3939 | 281.4 | 4055 | 289.6 | 4054 | 289.6 | 7993 | 285.5 |
| % Completed | — | 56.2 | — | 57.0 | — | 57.6 | — | 56.8 | — | 56.9 |
| Total Yds. Gained | 49,849 | 3560.6 | 49,678 | 3548.4 | 51,073 | 3648.1 | 51,244 | 3660.3 | 100,922 | 3604.4 |
| Times Sacked | 600 | 42.9 | 567 | 40.5 | 615 | 43.9 | 648 | 46.3 | 1215 | 43.4 |
| Yds. Lost | 4665 | 333.2 | 4424 | 316.0 | 4584 | 327.4 | 4825 | 344.6 | 9249 | 330.3 |
| Net Yds. Gained | 45,184 | 3227.4 | 45,254 | 3232.4 | 46,489 | 3220.6 | 46,419 | 3315.6 | 91,673 | 3274.0 |
| Avg. Yds. per Game | — | 201.7 | — | 202.0 | — | 207.5 | — | 207.2 | — | 204.6 |
| Net Yds. per Pass Play | — | 5.94 | — | 6.05 | — | 6.07 | — | 5.97 | — | 6.01 |
| Yds. Gained per Comp. | — | 12.66 | — | 12.61 | — | 12.60 | — | 12.64 | — | 12.63 |
| **Combined Net Yds. Gained** | 74,005 | 5286.1 | 74,925 | 5351.8 | 75,790 | 5413.6 | 74,870 | 5347.9 | 149,795 | 5349.8 |
| % Total Yds., Rushing | — | 38.94 | — | 39.60 | — | 38.66 | — | 38.00 | — | 38.80 |
| % Total Yds., Passing | — | 61.06 | — | 60.40 | — | 61.34 | — | 62.00 | — | 61.20 |
| Avg. Yds. per Game | — | 330.4 | — | 334.5 | — | 338.3 | — | 334.2 | — | 334.4 |
| **Ball Control Plays** | 14,689 | 1049.2 | 14,725 | 1051.8 | 14,784 | 1056.0 | 14,748 | 1053.4 | 29,473 | 1052.6 |
| Avg. Yds. per Play | — | 5.0 | — | 5.1 | — | 5.1 | — | 5.1 | — | 5.1 |
| **Third Down Efficiency** | — | 40.0 | — | 39.8 | — | 38.6 | — | 38.8 | — | 39.3 |
| **Interceptions** | 304 | 21.7 | 321 | 22.9 | 316 | 22.6 | 299 | 21.4 | 620 | 22.1 |
| Yds. Returned | 4183 | 298.8 | 4474 | 319.6 | 4197 | 299.8 | 3906 | 279.0 | 8380 | 299.3 |
| Returned for TD | 26 | 1.9 | 24 | 1.7 | 23 | 1.6 | 25 | 1.8 | 49 | 1.8 |
| **Punts** | 1117 | 79.8 | 1113 | 79.5 | 1132 | 80.9 | 1136 | 81.1 | 2249 | 80.3 |
| Yds. Punted | 46,372 | 3312.3 | 45,958 | 3282.7 | 45,325 | 3237.5 | 45,739 | 3267.1 | 91,697 | 3274.9 |
| Avg. Yds. per Punt | — | 41.5 | — | 41.3 | — | 40.0 | — | 40.3 | — | 40.8 |
| **Punt Returns** | 590 | 42.1 | 601 | 42.9 | 643 | 45.9 | 632 | 45.1 | 1233 | 44.0 |
| Yds. Returned | 5191 | 370.8 | 5325 | 380.4 | 5419 | 387.1 | 5285 | 377.5 | 10,610 | 378.9 |
| Avg. Yds. per Return | — | 8.8 | — | 8.9 | — | 8.4 | — | 8.4 | — | 8.6 |
| Returned for TD | 5 | 0.4 | 6 | 0.4 | 7 | 0.5 | 6 | 0.4 | 12 | 0.4 |
| **Kickoff Returns** | 871 | 62.2 | 846 | 60.4 | 910 | 65.0 | 935 | 66.8 | 1781 | 63.6 |
| Yds. Returned | 17,440 | 1245.7 | 16,453 | 1175.2 | 17,376 | 1241.1 | 18,363 | 1311.6 | 34,816 | 1243.4 |
| Avg. Yds. per Return | — | 20.0 | — | 19.4 | — | 19.1 | — | 19.6 | — | 19.5 |
| Returned for TD | 3 | 0.2 | 2 | 0.1 | 0 | 0.0 | 1 | 0.1 | 3 | 0.1 |
| **Penalties** | 1476 | 105.4 | 1444 | 103.1 | 1325 | 94.6 | 1357 | 96.9 | 2801 | 100.0 |
| Yds. Penalized | 12,527 | 894.8 | 12,236 | 874.0 | 11,186 | 799.0 | 11,477 | 819.8 | 23,713 | 846.9 |
| **Fumbles** | 475 | 33.9 | 473 | 33.8 | 482 | 34.4 | 484 | 34.6 | 957 | 34.2 |
| Lost | 246 | 17.6 | 244 | 17.4 | 248 | 17.7 | 250 | 17.9 | 494 | 17.6 |
| Out of Bounds | 32 | 2.3 | 30 | 2.1 | 34 | 2.4 | 36 | 2.6 | 66 | 2.4 |
| Own Rec. for TD | 1 | 0.1 | 1 | 0.1 | 4 | 0.3 | 4 | 0.3 | 5 | 0.2 |
| Opp. Rec. | 243 | 17.4 | 244 | 17.4 | 249 | 17.8 | 248 | 17.7 | 492 | 17.6 |
| Opp. Rec. for TD | 13 | 0.9 | 17 | 1.2 | 16 | 1.1 | 12 | 0.9 | 29 | 1.0 |
| **Total Points Scored** | 4759 | 339.9 | 4873 | 348.1 | 5020 | 358.6 | 4906 | 350.4 | 9779 | 349.3 |
| Total TDs | 569 | 40.6 | 580 | 41.4 | 595 | 42.5 | 584 | 41.7 | 1164 | 41.6 |
| TDs Rushing | 211 | 15.1 | 213 | 15.2 | 226 | 16.1 | 224 | 16.0 | 437 | 15.6 |
| TDs Passing | 308 | 22.0 | 317 | 22.6 | 317 | 22.6 | 308 | 22.0 | 625 | 22.3 |
| TDs on Ret. and Rec. | 50 | 3.6 | 50 | 3.6 | 52 | 3.7 | 52 | 3.7 | 102 | 3.6 |
| Extra Points | 538 | 38.4 | 549 | 39.2 | 566 | 40.4 | 555 | 39.6 | 1104 | 39.4 |
| Safeties | 6 | 0.4 | 8 | 0.6 | 13 | 0.9 | 11 | 0.8 | 19 | 0.7 |
| Field Goals Made | 265 | 18.9 | 276 | 19.7 | 286 | 20.4 | 275 | 19.6 | 551 | 19.7 |
| Field Goals Attempted | 365 | 26.1 | 375 | 26.8 | 406 | 29.0 | 396 | 28.3 | 771 | 27.5 |
| % Successful | — | 72.6 | — | 73.6 | — | 70.4 | — | 69.4 | — | 71.5 |

## CLUB LEADERS

**First Downs**

| | Offense | Defense |
|---|---|---|
| | S.D. 361 | Cin. 276 |
| Rushing | Wash. 165 | Wash. 76 |
| Passing | S.D. 230 | Mia. 147 |
| Penalty | Buff. & Den. 38 | G.B. 8 |

**Rushes**

| | Offense | Defense |
|---|---|---|
| | Wash. 629 | Wash. 349 |
| Net Yds. Gained | Chi. 2727 | Wash. 1289 |
| Avg. Gain | N.E. 4.8 | N.Y.G. 3.5 |

**Passes Attempted**

| | Offense | Defense |
|---|---|---|
| | K.C. 641 | Hou. 424 |
| Completed | K.C. & S.D. 369 | Pitt. 238 |
| % Completed | S.F. 64.2 | Chi. 50.8 |
| Total Yds. Gained | S.D. 4891 | Phil. 3048 |
| Times Sacked | Rams & Mia. 23 | St.L. 59 |
| Yds. Lost | Rams & Mia. 190 | Raid. 484 |
| Net Yds. Gained | S.D. 4661 | N.O. 2691 |
| Net Yds. per Pass Play | G.B. 7.68 | N.O. 4.88 |
| Yds. Gained per Comp. | G.B. 15.07 | Cin. 10.98 |

**Combined Net Yds. Gained**

| | Offense | Defense |
|---|---|---|
| | S.D. 6197 | Cin. 4327 |
| % Total Yds., Rushing | Balt. 53.71 | Wash. 24.49 |
| % Total Yds., Passing | K.C. 77.59 | Hou. 50.51 |

**Ball Control Plays**

| | Offense | Defense |
|---|---|---|
| | N.Y.G. 1130 | Wash. 970 |
| Avg. Yds. per Play | G.B. 6.1 | Cin. 4.4 |
| Avg. Time of Poss. | Wash. 33:44 | — |

**Third Down Efficiency**

| | Offense | Defense |
|---|---|---|
| | Atl. 48.4 | N.Y.G. 30.3 |

**Interceptions**

| | Offense | Defense |
|---|---|---|
| | — | Wash. 34 |
| Yds. Returned | — | Rams 515 |
| Returned for TD | — | S.F. 5 |

**Punts**

| | Offense | Defense |
|---|---|---|
| | T.B. 96 | — |
| Yds. Punted | Balt. 4124 | — |
| Avg. Yds. per Punt | Balt. 45.3 | — |

**Punt Returns**

| | Offense | Defense |
|---|---|---|
| | Raid. & St.L. 58 | Clev. 30 |
| Yds. Returned | Raid. 666 | Atl. 179 |
| Avg. Yds. per Return | Raid. 11.5 | Sea. 5.1 |
| Returned for TD | By 12 teams 1 | — |

**Kickoff Returns**

| | Offense | Defense |
|---|---|---|
| | Hou. 83 | N.O. 44 |
| Yds. Returned | Hou. 1676 | Phil. 804 |
| Avg. Yds. per Return | Mia. 23.1 | Sea. 16.1 |
| Returned for TD | Hou. 2 | — |

**Total Points Scored**

| | Offense | Defense |
|---|---|---|
| | Wash. 541 | Mia. 250 |
| Total TDs | Wash. 63 | N.E. 31 |
| TDs Rushing | Wash. 30 | N.E. & Wash. 9 |
| TDs Passing | G.B. 33 | Chi. & T.B. 15 |
| TDs on Ret. and Rec. | Three with 7 | Phil. 0 |
| Extra Points | Wash. 62 | N.E. 29 |
| Safeties | Det. 3 | — |
| Field Goals Made | N.Y.G. 35 | Mia. 9 |
| Field Goals Attempted | Wash. 47 | Mia. & St.L. 15 |
| % Successful | Clev. 88.0 | N.O. 58.8 |

## CLUB RANKINGS BY YARDS

| Team | Offense Total | Offense Rush | Offense Pass | Defense Total | Defense Rush | Defense Pass |
|---|---|---|---|---|---|---|
| Atlanta | 8 | 11 | 11 | 25 | 22 | 20 |
| Baltimore | 21 | 2 | 28 | 23 | 17 | 21 |
| Buffalo | 25 | 24 | 18 | 24 | 24 | 18 |
| Chicago | 6 | 1 | 17 | 8 | 11t | 12 |
| Cincinnati | 14 | 16 | 14 | 1 | 2t | 3 |
| Cleveland | 10 | 19 | 6 | 9 | 14 | 9 |
| Dallas | 5 | 15 | 4 | 17 | 2t | 27 |
| Denver | 26 | 23 | 20 | 21 | 10 | 23 |
| Detroit | 18 | 12 | 22 | 11 | 16 | 11 |
| Green Bay | 2 | 21 | 2 | 28 | 26 | 24 |
| Houston | 24 | 18 | 23 | 22 | 28 | 4 |
| Kansas City | 9 | 28 | 3 | 14 | 20 | 10 |
| Los Angeles Raiders | 7 | 10 | 9 | 4 | 4 | 13 |
| Los Angeles Rams | 12 | 9 | 12 | 15 | 6 | 22 |
| Miami | 16 | 13 | 19 | 7 | 13 | 8 |
| Minnesota | 20 | 20 | 13 | 19 | 25 | 6 |
| New England | 13 | 5 | 25 | 20 | 21 | 17 |
| New Orleans | 23 | 6 | 26 | 2 | 11t | 1 |
| New York Giants | 15 | 22 | 8 | 5 | 5 | 16 |
| New York Jets | 11 | 17 | 10 | 13 | 23 | 7 |
| Philadelphia | 27 | 26 | 16 | 18 | 27 | 2 |
| Pittsburgh | 22 | 4 | 27 | 3 | 7 | 5 |
| St. Louis | 17 | 7 | 24 | 6 | 8 | 14 |
| San Diego | 1 | 25 | 1 | 26 | 18 | 25 |
| San Francisco | 4 | 8 | 5 | 10 | 9 | 15 |
| Seattle | 19 | 14 | 21 | 27 | 19 | 26 |
| Tampa Bay | 28 | 27 | 15 | 16 | 15 | 19 |
| Washington | 3 | 3 | 7 | 12 | 1 | 28 |

t—Tie for position

## SCORING

**POINTS**
**Kickers**
**NFC:** 161—Mark Moseley, Washington
**AFC:** 119—Gary Anderson, Pittsburgh
**Non-kickers**
**NFC:** 144—John Riggins, Washington
**AFC:** 84—Pete Johnson, Cincinnati
Curt Warner, Seattle
**TOUCHDOWNS**
**NFC:** 24—John Riggins, Washington (24-rush)
**AFC:** 14—Pete Johnson, Cincinnati (14-rush)
Curt Warner, Seattle (13-rush, 1-pass)
**EXTRA POINTS**
**NFC:** 62—Mark Moseley, Washington (63 attempts)
**AFC:** 51—Chris Bahr, Los Angeles Raiders (53 attempts)
**FIELD GOALS**
**NFC:** 35—Ali Haji-Sheikh, New York Giants (42 attempts)
**AFC:** 30—Raul Allegre, Baltimore (35 attempts)
**MOST POINTS, GAME**
**NFC:** 24—Roy Green, St. Louis vs. Seattle, November 13 (4 TD)
**AFC:** 18—Earl Campbell, Houston vs. Green Bay, September 4 (3 TD)
Todd Christensen, Raiders vs. Seattle, October 16 (3 TD); vs. San Diego, December 1 (3 TD)
Anthony Collins, New England vs. Jets, September 18 (3 TD)
Joe Cribbs, Buffalo vs. Baltimore, September 18 (3 TD)
Pete Johnson, Cincinnati vs. Houston, November 6 (3 TD)
Rich Karlis, Denver vs. Seattle, November 20 (3 XP, 5 FG)
Steve Largent, Seattle vs. St. Louis, November 13 (3 TD)
Chuck Muncie, San Diego vs. Giants, October 2 (3 TD)
Mike Pruitt, Cleveland vs. Houston, December 11 (3 TD)
Mosi Tatupu, New England vs. Rams, December 11 (3 TD)
Curt Warner, Seattle vs. Kansas City, November 27 (3 TD)
Kellen Winslow, San Diego vs. Kansas City, December 11 (3 TD)
**TEAM LEADERS**
**AFC:** BALTIMORE: 112, Raul Allegre; BUFFALO: 63, Joe Danelo; CINCINNATI: 87, Jim Breech; CLEVELAND: 101, Matt Bahr; DENVER: 96, Rich Karlis; HOUSTON: 84, Florian Kempf; KANSAS CITY: 116, Nick Lowery; LOS ANGELES RAIDERS: 114, Chris Bahr; MIAMI: 99, Uwe von Schamann; NEW ENGLAND: 60, Anthony Collins; NEW YORK JETS: 84, Pat Leahy; PITTSBURGH: 119, Gary Anderson; SAN DIEGO: 88, Rolf Benirschke; SEATTLE: 103, Norm Johnson.
**NFC:** ATLANTA: 94, Mick Luckhurst; CHICAGO: 77, Bob Thomas; DALLAS: 123, Rafael Septien; DETROIT: 113, Ed Murray; GREEN BAY: 115, Jan Stenerud; LOS ANGELES RAMS: 120, Eric Dickerson; MINNESOTA: 108, Benny Ricardo; NEW ORLEANS: 91, Morten Andersen; NEW YORK GIANTS: 127, Ali Haji-Sheikh; PHILADELPHIA: 78, Mike Quick; ST. LOUIS: 90, Neil O'Donoghue; SAN FRANCISCO: 126, Ray Wersching; TAMPA BAY: 53, Bill Capece; WASHINGTON: 161, Mark Moseley.
**TEAM CHAMPIONS**
**NFC:** 541—Washington
**AFC:** 442—Los Angeles Raiders

### AFC SCORING—TEAM

| | TD | TDR | TDP | TD Misc. | PAT | PAT Att. | FG | FG Att. | SAF | TP |
|---|---|---|---|---|---|---|---|---|---|---|
| L.A. Raiders | 54 | 18 | 31 | 5 | 51 | 54 | 21 | 27 | 2 | 442 |
| Seattle | 50 | 19 | 25 | 6 | 49 | 50 | 18 | 25 | 0 | 403 |
| Miami | 48 | 16 | 28 | 4 | 45 | 48 | 18 | 27 | 1 | 389 |
| Kansas City | 45 | 13 | 29 | 3 | 44 | 45 | 24 | 30 | 0 | 386 |
| San Diego | 45 | 16 | 27 | 2 | 43 | 45 | 15 | 24 | 0 | 358 |
| Cleveland | 42 | 13 | 27 | 2 | 38 | 40 | 22 | 25 | 0 | 356 |
| Pittsburgh | 39 | 17 | 15 | 7 | 38 | 39 | 27 | 31 | 1 | 355 |
| Cincinnati | 43 | 24 | 14 | 5 | 40 | 43 | 16 | 23 | 0 | 346 |
| N.Y. Jets | 38 | 11 | 21 | 6 | 37 | 38 | 16 | 24 | 0 | 313 |
| Denver | 34 | 15 | 17 | 2 | 33 | 34 | 21 | 25 | 1 | 302 |
| Houston | 34 | 16 | 16 | 2 | 33 | 34 | 17 | 21 | 0 | 288 |
| Buffalo | 36 | 4 | 30 | 2 | 34 | 36 | 11 | 26 | 0 | 283 |
| New England | 36 | 19 | 16 | 1 | 31 | 36 | 9 | 22 | 0 | 274 |
| Baltimore | 25 | 10 | 12 | 3 | 22 | 24 | 30 | 35 | 1 | 264 |
| AFC Total | 569 | 211 | 308 | 50 | 538 | 566 | 265 | 365 | 6 | 4,759 |
| AFC Average | 40.6 | 15.1 | 22.0 | 3.6 | 38.4 | 40.4 | 18.9 | 26.1 | 0.4 | 339.9 |

### NFC SCORING—TEAM

| | TD | TDR | TDP | TD Misc. | PAT | PAT Att. | FG | FG Att. | SAF | TP |
|---|---|---|---|---|---|---|---|---|---|---|
| Washington | 63 | 30 | 29 | 4 | 62 | 63 | 33 | 47 | 1 | 541 |
| Dallas | 59 | 21 | 31 | 7 | 57 | 59 | 22 | 27 | 1 | 479 |
| San Francisco | 51 | 17 | 27 | 7 | 51 | 51 | 25 | 30 | 0 | 432 |
| Green Bay | 52 | 15 | 33 | 4 | 52 | 52 | 21 | 26 | 1 | 429 |
| St. Louis | 47 | 15 | 29 | 3 | 45 | 47 | 15 | 28 | 1 | 374 |
| Atlanta | 46 | 17 | 24 | 5 | 43 | 45 | 17 | 22 | 0 | 370 |
| L.A. Rams | 47 | 20 | 23 | 4 | 42 | 47 | 11 | 20 | 2 | 361 |
| Detroit | 38 | 18 | 19 | 1 | 38 | 38 | 25 | 32 | 3 | 347 |
| New Orleans | 38 | 19 | 14 | 5 | 37 | 38 | 18 | 24 | 0 | 319 |
| Minnesota | 34 | 17 | 15 | 2 | 33 | 34 | 25 | 33 | 2 | 316 |
| Chicago | 39 | 14 | 21 | 4 | 35 | 39 | 14 | 25 | 0 | 311 |
| N.Y. Giants | 23 | 9 | 12 | 2 | 22 | 23 | 35 | 42 | 1 | 267 |
| Tampa Bay | 31 | 9 | 18 | 4 | 25 | 31 | 10 | 24 | 0 | 241 |
| Philadelphia | 27 | 5 | 22 | 0 | 24 | 27 | 15 | 26 | 1 | 233 |
| NFC Total | 595 | 226 | 317 | 52 | 566 | 594 | 286 | 406 | 13 | 5,020 |
| NFC Average | 42.5 | 16.1 | 22.6 | 3.7 | 40.4 | 42.4 | 20.4 | 29.0 | 0.9 | 358.6 |
| League Total | 1164 | 437 | 625 | 102 | 1104 | 1160 | 551 | 771 | 19 | 9,779 |
| League Avg. | 41.6 | 15.6 | 22.3 | 3.6 | 39.4 | 41.4 | 19.7 | 27.5 | 0.7 | 349.3 |

### NFL TOP 10 SCORERS —TOUCHDOWNS

| | TD | TDR | TDP | TD Misc. | TP |
|---|---|---|---|---|---|
| Riggins, John, Washington | 24 | 24 | 0 | 0 | 144 |
| Dickerson, Eric, L.A. Rams | 20 | 18 | 2 | 0 | 120 |
| Green, Roy, St. Louis | 14 | 0 | 14 | 0 | 84 |
| Johnson, Pete, Cincinnati | 14 | 14 | 0 | 0 | 84 |
| Warner, Curt, Seattle | 14 | 13 | 1 | 0 | 84 |
| Muncie, Chuck, San Diego | 13 | 12 | 1 | 0 | 78 |
| Quick, Mike, Philadelphia | 13 | 0 | 13 | 0 | 78 |
| Allen, Marcus, L.A. Raiders | 12 | 9 | 2 | 1 | 72 |
| Campbell, Earl, Houston | 12 | 12 | 0 | 0 | 72 |
| Christensen, Todd, L.A. Raiders | 12 | 0 | 12 | 0 | 72 |
| Craig, Roger, San Francisco | 12 | 8 | 4 | 0 | 72 |
| Pruitt, Mike, Cleveland | 12 | 10 | 2 | 0 | 72 |

### NFL TOP 10 SCORERS — KICKING

| | PAT | PAT Att. | FG | FG Att. | TP |
|---|---|---|---|---|---|
| Moseley, Mark, Washington | 62 | 63 | 33 | 47 | 161 |
| Haji-Sheikh, Ali, N.Y. Giants | 22 | 23 | 35 | 42 | 127 |
| Wersching, Ray, San Francisco | 51 | 51 | 25 | 30 | 126 |
| Septien, Rafael, Dallas | 57 | 59 | 22 | 27 | 123 |
| Anderson, Gary, Pittsburgh | 38 | 39 | 27 | 31 | 119 |
| Lowery, Nick, Kansas City | 44 | 45 | 24 | 30 | 116 |
| Stenerud, Jan, Green Bay | 52 | 52 | 21 | 26 | 115 |
| Bahr, Chris, Raiders | 51 | 53 | 21 | 27 | 114 |
| Murray, Ed, Detroit | 38 | 38 | 25 | 32 | 113 |
| Allegre, Raul, Baltimore | 22 | 24 | 30 | 35 | 112 |

### AFC SCORING—INDIVIDUAL

| KICKERS | PAT | PAT Att. | FG | FG Att. | TP |
|---|---|---|---|---|---|
| Anderson, Gary, Pittsburgh | 38 | 39 | 27 | 31 | 119 |
| Lowery, Nick, Kansas City | 44 | 45 | 24 | 30 | 116 |
| Bahr, Chris, L.A. Raiders | 51 | 53 | 21 | 27 | 114 |
| Allegre, Raul, Baltimore | 22 | 24 | 30 | 35 | 112 |
| Johnson, Norm, Seattle | 49 | 50 | 18 | 25 | 103 |
| Bahr, Matt, Cleveland | 38 | 40 | 21 | 24 | 101 |
| von Schamann, Uwe, Miami | 45 | 48 | 18 | 27 | 99 |
| Karlis, Rich, Denver | 33 | 34 | 21 | 25 | 96 |
| Benirschke, Rolf, San Diego | 43 | 45 | 15 | 24 | 88 |
| Breech, Jim, Cincinnati | 39 | 41 | 16 | 23 | 87 |
| Kempf, Florian, Houston | 33 | 34 | 17 | 21 | 84 |
| Leahy, Pat, New York Jets | 36 | 37 | 16 | 24 | 84 |
| Danelo, Joe, Buffalo | 33 | 34 | 10 | 20 | 63 |
| Steinfort, Fred, Buff-NE | 17 | 18 | 7 | 21 | 38 |
| Smith, John, New England | 12 | 15 | 3 | 6 | 21 |
| Cox, Steve, Cleveland | 0 | 0 | 1 | 1 | 3 |
| Zendejas, Joaquin, New England | 3 | 4 | 0 | 1 | 3 |

| NON-KICKERS | TD | TDR | TDP | TD Misc. | TP |
|---|---|---|---|---|---|
| Johnson, Pete, Cincinnati | 14 | 14 | 0 | 0 | 84 |
| Warner, Curt, Seattle | 14 | 13 | 1 | 0 | 84 |
| Muncie, Chuck, San Diego | 13 | 12 | 1 | 0 | 78 |
| Allen, Marcus, L.A. Raiders | 12 | 9 | 2 | 1 | 72 |
| Campbell, Earl, Houston | 12 | 12 | 0 | 0 | 72 |
| Christensen, Todd, L.A. Raiders | 12 | 0 | 12 | 0 | 72 |
| Pruitt, Mike, Cleveland | 12 | 10 | 2 | 0 | 72 |
| Largent, Steve, Seattle | 11 | 0 | 11 | 0 | 66 |
| Brown, Theotis, Kansas City | 10 | 8 | 2 | 0 | 60 |
| Collins, Anthony, New England | 10 | 10 | 0 | 0 | 60 |
| Cribbs, Joe, Buffalo | 10 | 3 | 7 | 0 | 60 |
| Duper, Mark, Miami | 10 | 0 | 10 | 0 | 60 |
| Franklin, Andra, Miami | 8 | 8 | 0 | 0 | 48 |
| Hawkins, Frank, L.A. Raiders | 8 | 6 | 2 | 0 | 48 |
| Winslow, Kellen, San Diego | 8 | 0 | 8 | 0 | 48 |
| Abercrombie, Walter, Pittsburgh | 7 | 4 | 3 | 0 | 42 |
| Carson, Carlos, Kansas City | 7 | 0 | 7 | 0 | 42 |
| Dickey, Curtis, Baltimore | 7 | 4 | 3 | 0 | 42 |
| Harris, Franco, Pittsburgh | 7 | 5 | 2 | 0 | 42 |
| Walker, Wesley, New York Jets | 7 | 0 | 7 | 0 | 42 |

| | TD | TDR | TDP | TD Misc. | TP |
|---|---|---|---|---|---|
| Marshall, Henry, Kansas City | 6 | 0 | 6 | 0 | 36 |
| McMillan, Randy, Baltimore | 6 | 5 | 1 | 0 | 36 |
| Moore, Nat, Miami | 6 | 0 | 6 | 0 | 36 |
| Newsome, Ozzie, Cleveland | 6 | 0 | 6 | 0 | 36 |
| Paige, Stephon, Kansas City | 6 | 0 | 6 | 0 | 36 |
| Ramsey, Derrick, New England | 6 | 0 | 6 | 0 | 36 |
| Scott, Willie, Kansas City | 6 | 0 | 6 | 0 | 36 |
| Smith, Tim, Houston | 6 | 0 | 6 | 0 | 36 |
| Branch, Cliff, Los Angeles Raiders | 5 | 0 | 5 | 0 | 30 |
| Chandler, Wes, San Diego | 5 | 0 | 5 | 0 | 30 |
| Collinsworth, Cris, Cincinnati | 5 | 0 | 5 | 0 | 30 |
| Duckworth, Bobby, San Diego | 5 | 0 | 5 | 0 | 30 |
| Johns, Paul, Seattle | 5 | 0 | 4 | 1 | 30 |
| Sweeney, Calvin, Pittsburgh | 5 | 0 | 5 | 0 | 30 |
| Tatupu, Mosi, New England | 5 | 4 | 1 | 0 | 30 |
| Watson, Steve, Denver | 5 | 0 | 5 | 0 | 30 |
| Doornink, Dan, Seattle | 4 | 2 | 2 | 0 | 24 |
| Dressel, Chris, Houston | 4 | 0 | 4 | 0 | 24 |
| Franklin, Byron, Buffalo | 4 | 0 | 4 | 0 | 24 |
| Green, Boyce, Cleveland | 4 | 3 | 1 | 0 | 24 |
| Henry, Bernard, Baltimore | 4 | 0 | 4 | 0 | 24 |
| Johnson, Dan, Miami | 4 | 0 | 4 | 0 | 24 |
| Jones, Bobby, Cleveland | 4 | 0 | 4 | 0 | 24 |
| Jones, Lam, New York Jets | 4 | 0 | 4 | 0 | 24 |
| McNeil, Freeman, New York Jets | 4 | 1 | 3 | 0 | 24 |
| Nathan, Tony, Miami | 4 | 3 | 1 | 0 | 24 |
| Pollard, Frank, Pittsburgh | 4 | 4 | 0 | 0 | 24 |
| Poole, Nathan, Denver | 4 | 4 | 0 | 0 | 24 |
| Stoudt, Cliff, Pittsburgh | 4 | 4 | 0 | 0 | 24 |
| Willhite, Gerald, Denver | 4 | 3 | 1 | 0 | 24 |
| Alexander, Charles, Cincinnati | 3 | 3 | 0 | 0 | 18 |
| Augustyniak, Mike, New York Jets | 3 | 2 | 1 | 0 | 18 |
| Brooks, James, San Diego | 3 | 3 | 0 | 0 | 18 |
| Butler, Jerry, Buffalo | 3 | 0 | 3 | 0 | 18 |
| Butler, Raymond, Baltimore | 3 | 0 | 3 | 0 | 18 |
| Crutchfield, Dwayne, Jets-Hou. | 3 | 3 | 0 | 0 | 18 |
| Cunningham, Bennie, Pittsburgh | 3 | 0 | 3 | 0 | 18 |
| Dierking, Scott, New York Jets | 3 | 3 | 0 | 0 | 18 |
| Feacher, Ricky, Cleveland | 3 | 0 | 3 | 0 | 18 |
| Harper, Bruce, New York Jets | 3 | 1 | 2 | 0 | 18 |
| Holt, Harry, Cleveland | 3 | 0 | 3 | 0 | 18 |
| Hunter, Tony, Buffalo | 3 | 0 | 3 | 0 | 18 |
| Joiner, Charlie, San Diego | 3 | 0 | 3 | 0 | 18 |
| Kenney, Bill, Kansas City | 3 | 3 | 0 | 0 | 18 |
| Kinnebrew, Larry, Cincinnati | 3 | 3 | 0 | 0 | 18 |
| Lewis, Frank, Buffalo | 3 | 0 | 3 | 0 | 18 |
| Moriarty, Larry, Houston | 3 | 3 | 0 | 0 | 18 |
| Mosley, Mike, Buffalo | 3 | 0 | 3 | 0 | 18 |
| Overstreet, David, Miami | 3 | 1 | 2 | 0 | 18 |
| Parros, Rick, Denver | 3 | 1 | 2 | 0 | 18 |
| Pruitt, Greg, Los Angeles Raiders | 3 | 2 | 0 | 1 | 18 |
| Rose, Joe, Miami | 3 | 0 | 3 | 0 | 18 |
| Ross, Dan, Cincinnati | 3 | 0 | 3 | 0 | 18 |
| Sampson, Clinton, Denver | 3 | 0 | 3 | 0 | 18 |
| Sievers, Eric, San Diego | 3 | 0 | 3 | 0 | 18 |
| Tuttle, Perry, Buffalo | 3 | 0 | 3 | 0 | 18 |
| Weathers, Clarence, New England | 3 | 0 | 3 | 0 | 18 |
| Williams, Dokie, L.A. Raiders | 3 | 0 | 3 | 0 | 18 |
| Winder, Sammy, Denver | 3 | 3 | 0 | 0 | 18 |
| Adams, Willis, Cleveland | 2 | 0 | 2 | 0 | 12 |
| Barber, Marion, N.Y. Jets | 2 | 1 | 1 | 0 | 12 |
| Belk, Rocky, Cleveland | 2 | 0 | 2 | 0 | 12 |
| Bennett, Woody, Miami | 2 | 2 | 0 | 0 | 12 |
| Brammer, Mark, Buffalo | 2 | 0 | 2 | 0 | 12 |
| Clayton, Mark, Miami | 2 | 0 | 1 | 1 | 12 |
| Curtis, Isaac, Cincinnati | 2 | 0 | 2 | 0 | 12 |
| Egloff, Ron, Denver | 2 | 0 | 2 | 0 | 12 |
| Grogan, Steve, New England | 2 | 2 | 0 | 0 | 12 |
| Harris, M.L., Cincinnati | 2 | 0 | 2 | 0 | 12 |
| Hasselbeck, Don, L.A. Raiders | 2 | 0 | 2 | 0 | 12 |
| Holmes, Jerry, New York Jets | 2 | 0 | 0 | 2 | 12 |
| Holohan, Pete, San Diego | 2 | 0 | 2 | 0 | 12 |
| Hughes, David, Seattle | 2 | 1 | 1 | 0 | 12 |
| Jackson, Billy, Kansas City | 2 | 2 | 0 | 0 | 12 |
| King, Kenny, Los Angeles Raiders | 2 | 1 | 1 | 0 | 12 |
| Kozlowski, Mike, Miami | 2 | 0 | 0 | 2 | 12 |
| Krieg, Dave, Seattle | 2 | 2 | 0 | 0 | 12 |
| Logan, Dave, Cleveland | 2 | 0 | 2 | 0 | 12 |
| Marino, Dan, Miami | 2 | 2 | 0 | 0 | 12 |
| Martin, Rod, Los Angeles Raiders | 2 | 0 | 0 | 2 | 12 |
| Morgan, Stanley, New England | 2 | 0 | 2 | 0 | 12 |
| Muhammad, Calvin, L.A. Raiders | 2 | 0 | 2 | 0 | 12 |
| Preston, Dave, Denver | 2 | 1 | 1 | 0 | 12 |
| Renfro, Mike, Houston | 2 | 0 | 2 | 0 | 12 |
| Riley, Ken, Cincinnati | 2 | 0 | 0 | 2 | 12 |
| Robinson, Shelton, Seattle | 2 | 0 | 0 | 2 | 12 |
| Schonert, Turk, Cincinnati | 2 | 2 | 0 | 0 | 12 |
| Starring, Stephen, New England | 2 | 0 | 2 | 0 | 12 |
| Upchurch, Rick, Denver | 2 | 0 | 2 | 0 | 12 |
| van Eeghan, Mark, New England | 2 | 2 | 0 | 0 | 12 |
| Walker, Byron, Seattle | 2 | 0 | 2 | 0 | 12 |
| Wilson, Stanley, Cincinnati | 2 | 1 | 1 | 0 | 12 |
| Young, Charle, Seattle | 2 | 0 | 2 | 0 | 12 |
| Townsend, Greg, L.A. Raiders | 1 | 0 | 0 | 1 | *8 |
| Anderson, Ken, Cincinnati | 1 | 1 | 0 | 0 | 6 |
| Anderson, Kim, Baltimore | 1 | 0 | 0 | 1 | 6 |
| Anderson, Larry, Baltimore | 1 | 0 | 0 | 1 | 6 |
| Arnold, Walt, Houston | 1 | 0 | 1 | 0 | 6 |
| Banks, Chip, Cleveland | 1 | 0 | 0 | 1 | 6 |
| Barkum, Jerome, New York Jets | 1 | 0 | 1 | 0 | 6 |
| Barnwell, Malcolm, L.A. Raiders | 1 | 0 | 1 | 0 | 6 |
| Beach, Pat, Baltimore | 1 | 0 | 1 | 0 | 6 |
| Best, Greg, Pittsburgh | 1 | 0 | 0 | 1 | 6 |
| Blount, Mel, Pittsburgh | 1 | 0 | 0 | 1 | 6 |
| Bokamper, Kim, Miami | 1 | 0 | 0 | 1 | 6 |
| Brown, Curtis, Houston | 1 | 1 | 0 | 0 | 6 |
| Brown, Steve, Houston | 1 | 0 | 0 | 1 | 6 |
| Capers, Wayne, Pittsburgh | 1 | 0 | 1 | 0 | 6 |
| Chavous, Barney, Denver | 1 | 0 | 0 | 1 | 6 |
| Clayton, Harvey, Pittsburgh | 1 | 0 | 0 | 1 | 6 |
| Cooks, Johnie, Baltimore | 1 | 0 | 0 | 1 | 6 |
| Dawkins, Julius, Buffalo | 1 | 0 | 1 | 0 | 6 |
| Dawson, Lin, New England | 1 | 0 | 1 | 0 | 6 |
| DeBerg, Steve, Denver | 1 | 1 | 0 | 0 | 6 |
| Dieken, Doug, Cleveland | 1 | 0 | 1 | 0 | 6 |
| Dixon, Zachary, Seattle | 1 | 0 | 1 | 0 | 6 |
| Edwards, Stan, Houston | 1 | 0 | 1 | 0 | 6 |
| Elway, John, Denver | 1 | 1 | 0 | 0 | 6 |
| Fouts, Dan, San Diego | 1 | 1 | 0 | 0 | 6 |
| Garrity, Gregg, Pittsburgh | 1 | 0 | 1 | 0 | 6 |
| Gastineau, Mark, New York Jets | 1 | 0 | 0 | 1 | 6 |
| Golic, Bob, Cleveland | 1 | 0 | 0 | 1 | 6 |
| Green, Jacob, Seattle | 1 | 0 | 0 | 1 | 6 |
| Griffin, James, Cincinnati | 1 | 0 | 0 | 1 | 6 |
| Hancock, Anthony, Kansas City | 1 | 0 | 1 | 0 | 6 |
| Harris, Duriel, Miami | 1 | 0 | 1 | 0 | 6 |
| Hector, Johnny, New York Jets | 1 | 0 | 1 | 0 | 6 |
| Hinkle, Bryan, Pittsburgh | 1 | 0 | 0 | 1 | 6 |
| Horton, Ray, Cincinnati | 1 | 0 | 0 | 1 | 6 |
| Jackson, Charles, Kansas City | 1 | 0 | 0 | 1 | 6 |
| Jackson, Harold, Seattle | 1 | 0 | 1 | 0 | 6 |
| Jensen, Derrick, L.A. Raiders | 1 | 0 | 1 | 0 | 6 |
| Johnson, Ron, Pittsburgh | 1 | 0 | 0 | 1 | 6 |
| Jones, Cedric, New England | 1 | 0 | 1 | 0 | 6 |
| Kennedy, Mike, Buffalo | 1 | 0 | 0 | 1 | 6 |
| Kilson, David, Buffalo | 1 | 0 | 0 | 1 | 6 |
| Kreider, Steve, Cincinnati | 1 | 0 | 1 | 0 | 6 |
| Kubiak, Gary, Denver | 1 | 1 | 0 | 0 | 6 |
| Leaks, Roosevelt, Buffalo | 1 | 1 | 0 | 0 | 6 |
| Lynn, Johnny, New York Jets | 1 | 0 | 0 | 1 | 6 |
| McCloskey, Mike, Houston | 1 | 0 | 1 | 0 | 6 |
| Mehl, Lance, New York Jets | 1 | 0 | 0 | 1 | 6 |
| Merriweather, Mike, Pittsburgh | 1 | 0 | 0 | 1 | 6 |
| Metzelaars, Pete, Seattle | 1 | 0 | 1 | 0 | 6 |
| Moore, Alvin, Baltimore | 1 | 1 | 0 | 0 | 6 |
| Moore, Booker, Buffalo | 1 | 0 | 1 | 0 | 6 |
| Moyer, Paul, Seattle | 1 | 0 | 0 | 1 | 6 |
| Myles, Jesse, Denver | 1 | 0 | 1 | 0 | 6 |
| Nelson, Derrie, San Diego | 1 | 0 | 0 | 1 | 6 |
| Roaches, Carl, Houston | 1 | 0 | 0 | 1 | 6 |
| Roquemore, Durwood, Kansas City | 1 | 0 | 0 | 1 | 6 |
| Shuler, Mickey, New York Jets | 1 | 0 | 1 | 0 | 6 |
| Smith, Lucious, Kansas City | 1 | 0 | 0 | 1 | 6 |
| Springs, Kirk, New York Jets | 1 | 0 | 0 | 1 | 6 |
| Thomas, Ken, Kansas City | 1 | 0 | 1 | 0 | 6 |
| Thomas, Zack, Denver | 1 | 0 | 0 | 1 | 6 |
| Walker, Dwight, Cleveland | 1 | 0 | 1 | 0 | 6 |
| Walls, Herkie, Houston | 1 | 0 | 1 | 0 | 6 |
| Weathers, Robert, New England | 1 | 1 | 0 | 0 | 6 |
| Weishuhn, Clayton, New England | 1 | 0 | 0 | 1 | 6 |
| Williams, Reggie, Cincinnati | 1 | 0 | 0 | 1 | 6 |
| Woods, Rick, Pittsburgh | 1 | 0 | 0 | 1 | 6 |
| Young, Andre, San Diego | 1 | 0 | 0 | 1 | 6 |
| Zorn, Jim, Seattle | 1 | 1 | 0 | 0 | 6 |
| Alzado, Lyle, Los Angeles Raiders | 0 | 0 | 0 | 0 | *2 |
| Charles, Mike, Miami | 0 | 0 | 0 | 0 | *2 |
| Jones, Rulon, Denver | 0 | 0 | 0 | 0 | *2 |
| Kohrs, Bob, Pittsburgh | 0 | 0 | 0 | 0 | *2 |
| Thompson, Donnell, Baltimore | 0 | 0 | 0 | 0 | *2 |
| Browner, Ross, Cincinnati | 0 | 0 | 0 | 0 | #1 |
| Ryan, Pat, New York Jets | 0 | 0 | 0 | 0 | #1 |

*indicates safety.

#indicates scored extra point.

## NFC SCORING—INDIVIDUAL

| KICKERS | PAT | PAT Att. | FG | FG Att. | TP |
|---|---|---|---|---|---|
| Moseley, Mark, Washington | 62 | 63 | 33 | 47 | 161 |
| Haji-Sheikh, Ali, New York Giants | 22 | 23 | 35 | 42 | 127 |
| Wersching, Ray, San Francisco | 51 | 51 | 25 | 30 | 126 |
| Septien, Rafael, Dallas | 57 | 59 | 22 | 27 | 123 |
| Stenerud, Jan, Green Bay | 52 | 52 | 21 | 26 | 115 |
| Murray, Ed, Detroit | 38 | 38 | 25 | 32 | 113 |
| Ricardo, Benny, Minnesota | 33 | 34 | 25 | 33 | 108 |
| Luckhurst, Mick, Atlanta | 43 | 45 | 17 | 22 | 94 |
| Andersen, Morten, New Orleans | 37 | 38 | 18 | 24 | 91 |
| O'Donoghue, Neil, St. Louis | 45 | 47 | 15 | 28 | 90 |
| Thomas, Bob, Chicago | 35 | 38 | 14 | 25 | 77 |
| Franklin, Tony, Philadelphia | 24 | 27 | 15 | 26 | 69 |
| Capece, Bill, Tampa Bay | 23 | 26 | 10 | 23 | 53 |
| Nelson, Chuck, L.A. Rams | 33 | 37 | 5 | 11 | 48 |
| Lansford, Mike, L.A. Rams | 9 | 9 | 6 | 9 | 27 |
| Warnke, David, Tampa Bay | 1 | 2 | 0 | 1 | 1 |

| NON-KICKERS | TD | TDR | TDP | TD Misc. | TP |
|---|---|---|---|---|---|
| Riggins, John, Washington | 24 | 24 | 0 | 0 | 144 |
| Dickerson, Eric, L.A. Rams | 20 | 18 | 2 | 0 | 120 |
| Green, Roy, St. Louis | 14 | 0 | 14 | 0 | 84 |
| Quick, Mike, Philadelphia | 13 | 0 | 13 | 0 | 78 |
| Craig, Roger, San Francisco | 12 | 8 | 4 | 0 | 72 |
| Andrews, William, Atlanta | 11 | 7 | 4 | 0 | 66 |
| Brown, Ted, Minnesota | 11 | 10 | 1 | 0 | 66 |
| Coffman, Paul, Green Bay | 11 | 0 | 11 | 0 | 66 |
| Wilson, Wayne, New Orleans | 11 | 9 | 2 | 0 | 66 |
| Dorsett, Tony, Dallas | 9 | 8 | 1 | 0 | 54 |
| Brown, Charlie, Washington | 8 | 0 | 8 | 0 | 48 |
| Clark, Dwight, San Francisco | 8 | 0 | 8 | 0 | 48 |
| Gault, Willie, Chicago | 8 | 0 | 8 | 0 | 48 |
| Lofton, James, Green Bay | 8 | 0 | 8 | 0 | 48 |
| Marsh, Doug, St. Louis | 8 | 0 | 8 | 0 | 48 |
| Payton, Walter, Chicago | 8 | 6 | 2 | 0 | 48 |
| Riggs, Gerald, Atlanta | 8 | 8 | 0 | 0 | 48 |
| Springs, Ron, Dallas | 8 | 7 | 1 | 0 | 48 |
| Hill, Tony, Dallas | 7 | 0 | 7 | 0 | 42 |
| Jefferson, John, Green Bay | 7 | 0 | 7 | 0 | 42 |
| Jones, James, Detroit | 7 | 6 | 1 | 0 | 42 |
| Norris, Ulysses, Detroit | 7 | 0 | 7 | 0 | 42 |
| Sims, Billy, Detroit | 7 | 7 | 0 | 0 | 42 |
| Anderson, Ottis, St. Louis | 6 | 5 | 1 | 0 | 36 |
| Bailey, Stacey, Atlanta | 6 | 0 | 6 | 0 | 36 |
| Carpenter, Rob, New York Giants | 6 | 4 | 2 | 0 | 36 |
| Cosbie, Doug, Dallas | 6 | 0 | 6 | 0 | 36 |
| Ellis, Gerry, Green Bay | 6 | 4 | 2 | 0 | 36 |
| Galbreath, Tony, Minnesota | 6 | 4 | 2 | 0 | 36 |
| Newsome, Tim, Dallas | 6 | 2 | 4 | 0 | 36 |
| Owens, James, Tampa Bay | 6 | 5 | 1 | 0 | 36 |
| Tyler, Wendell, San Francisco | 6 | 4 | 2 | 0 | 36 |
| Washington, Joe, Washington | 6 | 0 | 6 | 0 | 36 |
| Wilder, James, Tampa Bay | 6 | 4 | 2 | 0 | 36 |
| Dennard, Preston, L.A. Rams | 5 | 0 | 5 | 0 | 30 |
| Didier, Clint, Washington | 5 | 0 | 4 | 1 | 30 |
| Farmer, George, L.A. Rams | 5 | 0 | 5 | 0 | 30 |
| Gray, Earnest, New York Giants | 5 | 0 | 5 | 0 | 30 |
| House, Kevin, Tampa Bay | 5 | 0 | 5 | 0 | 30 |
| Johnson, Billy, Atlanta | 5 | 0 | 4 | 1 | 30 |
| McKinnon, Dennis, Chicago | 5 | 0 | 4 | 1 | 30 |
| Monk, Art, Washington | 5 | 0 | 5 | 0 | 30 |
| Pearson, Drew, Dallas | 5 | 0 | 5 | 0 | 30 |
| Rogers, George, New Orleans | 5 | 5 | 0 | 0 | 30 |
| Suhey, Matt, Chicago | 5 | 4 | 1 | 0 | 30 |
| Tilley, Pat, St. Louis | 5 | 0 | 5 | 0 | 30 |
| White, Danny, Dallas | 5 | 4 | 1 | 0 | 30 |
| Chadwick, Jeff, Detroit | 4 | 0 | 4 | 0 | 24 |
| Evans, Reggie, Washington | 4 | 4 | 0 | 0 | 24 |
| Francis, Russ, San Francisco | 4 | 0 | 4 | 0 | 24 |
| Gajan, Hokie, New Orleans | 4 | 4 | 0 | 0 | 24 |
| Guman, Mike, Los Angeles Rams | 4 | 0 | 4 | 0 | 24 |
| Hodge, Floyd, Atlanta | 4 | 0 | 4 | 0 | 24 |
| Huckleby, Harlan, Green Bay | 4 | 4 | 0 | 0 | 24 |
| Solomon, Freddie, San Francisco | 4 | 0 | 4 | 0 | 24 |
| Thompson, Leonard, Detroit | 4 | 1 | 3 | 0 | 24 |
| White, Sammy, Minnesota | 4 | 0 | 4 | 0 | 24 |
| Woolfolk, Butch, New York Giants | 4 | 4 | 0 | 0 | 24 |
| Barber, Mike, Los Angeles Rams | 3 | 0 | 3 | 0 | 18 |
| Brenner, Hoby, New Orleans | 3 | 0 | 3 | 0 | 18 |
| Carmichael, Harold, Philadelphia | 3 | 0 | 3 | 0 | 18 |
| Cooper, Earl, San Francisco | 3 | 0 | 3 | 0 | 18 |
| Dickey, Lynn, Green Bay | 3 | 3 | 0 | 0 | 18 |
| Hipple, Eric, Detroit | 3 | 3 | 0 | 0 | 18 |
| Ivery, Eddie Lee, Green Bay | 3 | 2 | 1 | 0 | 18 |
| Jackson, Alfred, Atlanta | 3 | 0 | 3 | 0 | 18 |
| Johnson, Butch, Dallas | 3 | 0 | 3 | 0 | 18 |
| Love, Randy, St. Louis | 3 | 2 | 1 | 0 | 18 |
| McMahon, Jim, Chicago | 3 | 2 | 1 | 0 | 18 |
| Meade, Mike, Green Bay | 3 | 1 | 2 | 0 | 18 |
| Mitchell, Stump, St. Louis | 3 | 3 | 0 | 0 | 18 |
| Moorehead, Emery, Chicago | 3 | 0 | 3 | 0 | 18 |
| Oliver, Hubert, Philadelphia | 3 | 1 | 2 | 0 | 18 |
| Young, Tyrone, New Orleans | 3 | 0 | 3 | 0 | 18 |
| Armstrong, Adger, Tampa Bay | 2 | 0 | 2 | 0 | 12 |
| Bell, Theo, Tampa Bay | 2 | 0 | 2 | 0 | 12 |
| Bruer, Bob, Minnesota | 2 | 0 | 2 | 0 | 12 |
| Carter, Gerald, Tampa Bay | 2 | 0 | 2 | 0 | 12 |
| Donley, Doug, Dallas | 2 | 0 | 2 | 0 | 12 |
| Douglass, Mike, Green Bay | 2 | 0 | 0 | 2 | 12 |
| Duckett, Kenny, New Orleans | 2 | 0 | 2 | 0 | 12 |
| Fellows, Ron, Dallas | 2 | 0 | 0 | 2 | 12 |
| Goodlow, Eugene, New Orleans | 2 | 0 | 2 | 0 | 12 |
| Green, Hugh, Tampa Bay | 2 | 0 | 0 | 2 | 12 |
| Haddix, Michael, Philadelphia | 2 | 2 | 0 | 0 | 12 |
| Hicks, Dwight, San Francisco | 2 | 0 | 0 | 2 | 12 |
| Hill, David, Los Angeles Rams | 2 | 0 | 2 | 0 | 12 |
| Johnson, Johnnie, L.A. Rams | 2 | 0 | 0 | 2 | 12 |
| Johnson, Kenny, Atlanta | 2 | 0 | 0 | 2 | 12 |
| Jordan, Steve, Minnesota | 2 | 0 | 2 | 0 | 12 |
| Kaufman, Mel, Washington | 2 | 0 | 0 | 2 | 12 |
| LeCount, Terry, Minnesota | 2 | 0 | 2 | 0 | 12 |
| Lewis, Gary, Green Bay | 2 | 1 | 1 | 0 | 12 |
| Lomax, Neil, St. Louis | 2 | 2 | 0 | 0 | 12 |
| Margerum, Ken, Chicago | 2 | 0 | 2 | 0 | 12 |
| McCullum, Sam, Minnesota | 2 | 0 | 2 | 0 | 12 |
| Montana, Joe, San Francisco | 2 | 2 | 0 | 0 | 12 |
| Morris, Wayne, St. Louis | 2 | 2 | 0 | 0 | 12 |
| Redden, Barry, Los Angeles Rams | 2 | 2 | 0 | 0 | 12 |
| Ring, Bill, San Francisco | 2 | 2 | 0 | 0 | 12 |
| Walker, Rick, Washington | 2 | 0 | 2 | 0 | 12 |
| Warren, Don, Washington | 2 | 0 | 2 | 0 | 12 |
| Woodruff, Tony, Philadelphia | 2 | 0 | 2 | 0 | 12 |
| Wright, Eric, San Francisco | 2 | 0 | 0 | 2 | 12 |
| Young, Rickey, Minnesota | 2 | 2 | 0 | 0 | 12 |
| Allen, Gary, Dallas | 1 | 0 | 0 | 1 | 6 |
| Anderson, John, Green Bay | 1 | 0 | 0 | 1 | 6 |
| Bartkowski, Steve, Atlanta | 1 | 1 | 0 | 0 | 6 |
| Bell, Jerry, Tampa Bay | 1 | 0 | 1 | 0 | 6 |
| Board, Dwaine, San Francisco | 1 | 0 | 0 | 1 | 6 |
| Bussey, Dexter, Detroit | 1 | 0 | 1 | 0 | 6 |
| Cain, Lynn, Atlanta | 1 | 1 | 0 | 0 | 6 |
| Carver, Mel, Tampa Bay | 1 | 0 | 1 | 0 | 6 |
| Castille, Jeremiah, Tampa Bay | 1 | 0 | 0 | 1 | 6 |
| Clark, Jessie, Green Bay | 1 | 0 | 1 | 0 | 6 |
| Clark, Kelvin, New Orleans | 1 | 0 | 0 | 1 | 6 |
| Clinkscale, Dextor, Dallas | 1 | 0 | 0 | 1 | 6 |
| Collier, Tim, San Francisco | 1 | 0 | 0 | 1 | 6 |
| Cox, Arthur, Atlanta | 1 | 0 | 1 | 0 | 6 |
| Cromwell, Nolan, L.A. Rams | 1 | 0 | 0 | 1 | 6 |
| Currier, Bill, New York Giants | 1 | 0 | 0 | 1 | 6 |
| Dean, Vernon, Washington | 1 | 0 | 0 | 1 | 6 |
| Downs, Mike, Dallas | 1 | 0 | 0 | 1 | 6 |
| DuPree, Billy Joe, Dallas | 1 | 0 | 1 | 0 | 6 |
| Ellard, Henry, Los Angeles Rams | 1 | 0 | 0 | 1 | 6 |
| Epps, Phillip, Green Bay | 1 | 0 | 0 | 1 | 6 |
| Evans, Vince, Chicago | 1 | 1 | 0 | 0 | 6 |
| Ferrell, Earl, St. Louis | 1 | 1 | 0 | 0 | 6 |
| Frazier, Leslie, Chicago | 1 | 0 | 0 | 1 | 6 |
| Gaison, Blane, Atlanta | 1 | 0 | 0 | 1 | 6 |
| Garrett, Alvin, Washington | 1 | 0 | 1 | 0 | 6 |
| Giaquinto, Nick, Washington | 1 | 1 | 0 | 0 | 6 |
| Giles, Jimmie, Tampa Bay | 1 | 0 | 1 | 0 | 6 |
| Grant, Otis, Los Angeles Rams | 1 | 0 | 1 | 0 | 6 |
| Grooms, Elois, St. Louis | 1 | 0 | 0 | 1 | 6 |
| Groth, Jeff, New Orleans | 1 | 0 | 1 | 0 | 6 |
| Harrington, Perry, Philadelphia | 1 | 1 | 0 | 0 | 6 |
| Hartenstine, Mike, Chicago | 1 | 0 | 0 | 1 | 6 |
| Hegman, Mike, Dallas | 1 | 0 | 0 | 1 | 6 |
| Huffman, Dave, Minnesota | 1 | 0 | 0 | 1 | 6 |
| Hutchison, Anthony, Chicago | 1 | 1 | 0 | 0 | 6 |
| Jackson, Terry, New York Giants | 1 | 0 | 0 | 1 | 6 |
| Jaworski, Ron, Philadelphia | 1 | 1 | 0 | 0 | 6 |
| Jenkins, Alfred, Atlanta | 1 | 0 | 1 | 0 | 6 |
| Johnson, Bobby, New Orleans | 1 | 0 | 0 | 1 | 6 |
| Johnson, Charlie, Minnesota | 1 | 0 | 0 | 1 | 6 |
| Kab, Vyto, Philadelphia | 1 | 0 | 1 | 0 | 6 |
| Korte, Steve, New Orleans | 1 | 0 | 0 | 1 | 6 |
| Lewis, Reggie, New Orleans | 1 | 0 | 0 | 1 | 6 |
| Logan, Dave, Tampa Bay | 1 | 0 | 0 | 1 | 6 |
| Martin, Robbie, Detroit | 1 | 0 | 1 | 0 | 6 |
| McDonald, James, L.A. Rams | 1 | 0 | 1 | 0 | 6 |
| McLemore, Dana, San Francisco | 1 | 0 | 0 | 1 | 6 |
| Moore, Jeff, San Francisco | 1 | 1 | 0 | 0 | 6 |
| Morris, Joe, New York Giants | 1 | 0 | 1 | 0 | 6 |
| Mowatt, Zeke, New York Giants | 1 | 0 | 1 | 0 | 6 |
| Mullady, Tom, New York Giants | 1 | 0 | 1 | 0 | 6 |

| | TD | TDR | TDP | TD Misc. | TP |
|---|---|---|---|---|---|
| Nehemiah, Renaldo, San Fran. | 1 | 0 | 1 | 0 | 6 |
| Nelson, Darrin, Minnesota | 1 | 1 | 0 | 0 | 6 |
| Nelson, Lee, St. Louis | 1 | 0 | 0 | 1 | 6 |
| Nichols, Mark, Detroit | 1 | 0 | 1 | 0 | 6 |
| Obradovich, Jim, Tampa Bay | 1 | 0 | 1 | 0 | 6 |
| Perrin, Benny, St. Louis | 1 | 0 | 0 | 1 | 6 |
| Pittman, Danny, New York Giants | 1 | 0 | 1 | 0 | 6 |
| Poe, Johnnie, New Orleans | 1 | 0 | 0 | 1 | 6 |
| Rade, John, Atlanta | 1 | 0 | 0 | 1 | 6 |
| Ramson, Eason, San Francisco | 1 | 0 | 1 | 0 | 6 |
| Rubick, Rob, Detroit | 1 | 0 | 1 | 0 | 6 |
| Schmidt, Terry, Chicago | 1 | 0 | 0 | 1 | 6 |
| Scott, Fred, Detroit | 1 | 0 | 1 | 0 | 6 |
| Seay, Virgil, Washington | 1 | 0 | 1 | 0 | 6 |
| Theismann, Joe, Washington | 1 | 1 | 0 | 0 | 6 |
| Thompson, Vince, Detroit | 1 | 1 | 0 | 0 | 6 |
| Thurman, Dennis, Dallas | 1 | 0 | 0 | 1 | 6 |
| Tice, John, New Orleans | 1 | 0 | 1 | 0 | 6 |
| Tuggle, John, New York Giants | 1 | 1 | 0 | 0 | 6 |
| Williams, Byron, New York Giants | 1 | 0 | 1 | 0 | 6 |
| Wilson, Dave, New Orleans | 1 | 1 | 0 | 0 | 6 |
| Young, Benjamin, Atlanta | 1 | 0 | 1 | 0 | 6 |
| Young, Glen, Philadelphia | 1 | 0 | 1 | 0 | 6 |
| English, Doug, Detroit | 0 | 0 | 0 | 0 | *4 |
| Boyd, Greg, Green Bay | 0 | 0 | 0 | 0 | *2 |
| Dickerson, Anthony, Dallas | 0 | 0 | 0 | 0 | *2 |
| Fanning, Mike, Detroit | 0 | 0 | 0 | 0 | *2 |
| Galloway, David, St. Louis | 0 | 0 | 0 | 0 | *2 |
| Mann, Charles, Washington | 0 | 0 | 0 | 0 | *2 |
| Marshall, Leonard, N.Y. Giants | 0 | 0 | 0 | 0 | *2 |
| Youngblood, Jack, L.A. Rams | 0 | 0 | 0 | 0 | *2 |
| Yarno, George, Tampa Bay | 0 | 0 | 0 | 0 | #1 |

*indicates safety (also 2 Minn., 1 each Rams, Phil.)
#indicates scored extra point.

## FIELD GOALS

**BEST PERCENTAGE**
**AFC:** .875—Matt Bahr, Cleveland (21 made, 24 attempts)
**NFC:** .833—Ali Haji-Sheikh, New York Giants (35 made, 42 attempts)
Ray Wersching, San Francisco (25 made, 30 attempts)
**MADE**
**NFC:** 35—Ali Haji-Sheikh, New York Giants
**AFC:** 30—Raul Allegre, Baltimore
**ATTEMPTS**
**NFC:** 47—Mark Moseley, Washington
**AFC:** 35—Raul Allegre, Baltimore
**AVERAGE YARDS MADE**
**AFC:** 39.1—Raul Allegre, Baltimore
**NFC:** 38.5—Neil O'Donoghue, St. Louis

**LONGEST**
**AFC:** 58—Nick Lowery, Kansas City vs. Washington, September 18
Steve Cox, Cleveland vs. Denver, December 4
**NFC:** 56—Ali Haji-Sheikh, New York Giants vs. Green Bay, September 26
Ali Haji-Sheikh, New York Giants vs. Detroit, November 7

## AFC FIELD GOALS—TEAM

| | Made | Att. | Pct. | Long |
|---|---|---|---|---|
| Cleveland | 22 | 25 | .880 | 58 |
| Pittsburgh | 27 | 31 | .871 | 49 |
| Baltimore | 30 | 35 | .857 | 55 |
| Denver | 21 | 25 | .840 | 50 |
| Houston | 17 | 21 | .810 | 51 |
| Kansas City | 24 | 30 | .800 | 58 |
| Los Angeles Raiders | 21 | 27 | .778 | 47 |
| Seattle | 18 | 25 | .720 | 54 |
| Cincinnati | 16 | 23 | .696 | 47 |
| Miami | 18 | 27 | .667 | 52 |
| New York Jets | 16 | 24 | .667 | 49 |
| San Diego | 15 | 24 | .625 | 51 |
| Buffalo | 11 | 26 | .423 | 48 |
| New England | 9 | 22 | .409 | 43 |
| AFC Totals | 265 | 365 | — | 58 |
| AFC Average | 18.9 | 26.1 | .726 | — |

## NFC FIELD GOALS—TEAM

| | Made | Att. | Pct. | Long |
|---|---|---|---|---|
| New York Giants | 35 | 42 | .833 | 56 |
| San Francisco | 25 | 30 | .833 | 52 |
| Dallas | 22 | 27 | .815 | 47 |
| Green Bay | 21 | 26 | .808 | 48 |
| Detroit | 25 | 32 | .781 | 54 |
| Atlanta | 17 | 22 | .773 | 49 |
| Minnesota | 25 | 33 | .758 | 47 |
| New Orleans | 18 | 24 | .750 | 52 |
| Washington | 33 | 47 | .702 | 51 |
| Philadelphia | 15 | 26 | .577 | 52 |
| Chicago | 14 | 25 | .560 | 50 |
| Los Angeles Rams | 11 | 20 | .550 | 49 |
| St. Louis | 15 | 28 | .536 | 52 |
| Tampa Bay | 10 | 24 | .417 | 49 |
| NFC Totals | 286 | 406 | — | 56 |
| NFC Average | 20.4 | 29.0 | .704 | — |
| League Totals | 551 | 771 | — | 58 |
| League Average | 19.7 | 27.5 | .715 | — |

## AFC FIELD GOALS—INDIVIDUAL

| | 1-19 | 20-29 | 30-39 | 40-49 | 50 & Over | Totals | Avg. Yds. Att. | Avg. Yds. Made | Avg. Yds. Miss | Long |
|---|---|---|---|---|---|---|---|---|---|---|
| Bahr, Matt, Cleveland | 1-1 1.000 | 9-9 1.000 | 5-6 .833 | 6-7 .857 | 0-1 .000 | 21-24 .875 | 33.2 | 31.9 | 42.3 | 47 |
| Anderson, Gary, Pittsburgh | 2-2 1.000 | 8-9 .889 | 9-10 .900 | 8-10 .800 | 0-0 — | 27-31 .871 | 33.4 | 32.8 | 37.3 | 49 |
| Allegre, Raul, Baltimore | 0-0 — | 5-6 .833 | 11-12 .917 | 10-12 .833 | 4-5 .800 | 30-35 .857 | 39.7 | 39.1 | 43.6 | 55 |
| Karlis, Rich, Denver | 0-0 — | 7-8 .875 | 7-9 .778 | 6-7 .875 | 1-1 1.000 | 21-25 .840 | 34.2 | 34.2 | 34.0 | 50 |
| Kempf, Florian, Houston | 1-1 1.000 | 4-4 1.000 | 7-8 .875 | 4-6 .667 | 1-2 .500 | 17-21 .810 | 36.3 | 34.2 | 45.0 | 51 |
| Lowery, Nick, Kansas City | 1-1 1.000 | 5-5 1.000 | 6-6 1.000 | 10-14 .714 | 2-4 .500 | 24-30 .800 | 39.5 | 37.5 | 47.2 | 58 |
| Bahr, Chris, Los Angeles Raiders | 0-0 — | 9-11 .818 | 8-9 .889 | 4-6 .667 | 0-1 .000 | 21-27 .778 | 34.0 | 33.0 | 37.3 | 47 |
| Johnson, Norm, Seattle | 1-1 1.000 | 4-4 1.000 | 4-7 .571 | 8-10 .800 | 1-3 .333 | 18-25 .720 | 38.2 | 36.2 | 43.3 | 54 |
| Breech, Jim, Cincinnati | 2-2 1.000 | 7-7 1.000 | 5-7 .714 | 2-5 .400 | 0-2 .000 | 16-23 .696 | 33.7 | 29.6 | 43.0 | 47 |
| Leahy, Pat, New York Jets | 4-4 1.000 | 3-4 .750 | 5-7 .714 | 4-8 .500 | 0-1 .000 | 16-24 .667 | 35.1 | 31.4 | 42.5 | 49 |
| von Schamann, Uwe, Miami | 2-2 1.000 | 6-6 1.000 | 5-8 .625 | 3-6 .500 | 2-5 .400 | 18-27 .667 | 36.8 | 33.0 | 44.4 | 52 |
| Benirschke, Rolf, San Diego | 0-0 — | 7-7 1.000 | 5-7 .714 | 2-7 .286 | 1-3 .333 | 15-24 .625 | 37.2 | 32.7 | 44.6 | 51 |
| Danelo, Joe, Buffalo | 0-0 — | 2-4 .500 | 5-6 .833 | 3-6 .500 | 0-4 .000 | 10-20 .500 | 39.0 | 34.6 | 43.3 | 48 |
| Steinfort, Fred, Buff.-N.E. | 0-0 — | 4-5 .800 | 3-7 .429 | 0-9 .000 | 0-0 — | 7-21 .333 | 36.7 | 27.1 | 41.4 | 35 |
| **Non-Qualifiers** | | | | | | | | | | |
| Cox, Steve, Cleveland | 0-0 — | 0-0 — | 0-0 — | 0-0 — | 1-1 1.000 | 1-1 1.000 | 58.0 | 58.0 | 0.0 | 58 |
| Smith, John, New England | 0-0 — | 1-1 1.000 | 1-4 .250 | 1-1 1.000 | 0-0 — | 3-6 .500 | 35.0 | 34.7 | 35.3 | 43 |
| Zendejas, Joaquin, New England | 0-0 — | 0-0 — | 0-0 — | 0-1 .000 | 0-0 — | 0-1 .000 | 41.0 | 0.0 | 41.0 | 0 |
| AFC Totals | 14-14 1.000 | 81-90 .900 | 86-113 .761 | 71-115 .617 | 13-33 .394 | 265-365 .726 | 36.3 | 34.1 | 42.2 | 58 |
| League Totals | 22-23 .957 | 182-199 .915 | 181-239 .757 | 139-239 .582 | 27-71 .380 | 551-771 .715 | 36.4 | 33.9 | 42.5 | 58 |

## NFC FIELD GOALS — INDIVIDUAL

| | 1-19 | 20-29 | 30-39 | 40-49 | 50 & Over | Totals | Avg. Yds. Att. | Avg. Yds. Made | Avg. Yds. Miss | Long |
|---|---|---|---|---|---|---|---|---|---|---|
| Haji-Sheikh, Ali, | 1-1 | 13-13 | 11-12 | 8-11 | 2-5 | 35-42 | 36.5 | 33.9 | 49.9 | 56 |
| New York Giants | 1.000 | 1.000 | .917 | .727 | .400 | .833 | | | | |
| Wersching, Ray, | 0-0 | 11-11 | 10-10 | 3-5 | 1-4 | 25-30 | 34.7 | 31.8 | 48.8 | 52 |
| San Francisco | — | 1.000 | 1.000 | .600 | .250 | .833 | | | | |
| Septien, Rafael, | 0-0 | 5-5 | 8-8 | 9-12 | 0-2 | 22-27 | 38.3 | 36.1 | 47.8 | 47 |
| Dallas | — | 1.000 | 1.000 | .750 | .000 | .815 | | | | |
| Stenerud, Jan, | 2-2 | 6-6 | 7-9 | 6-9 | 0-0 | 21-26 | 34.3 | 32.7 | 41.2 | 48 |
| Green Bay | 1.000 | 1.000 | .778 | .667 | — | .808 | | | | |
| Murray, Ed, | 0-0 | 6-6 | 13-15 | 3-7 | 3-4 | 25-32 | 38.0 | 36.4 | 43.7 | 54 |
| Detroit | — | 1.000 | .867 | .429 | .750 | .781 | | | | |
| Luckhurst, Mick, | 0-0 | 4-5 | 4-5 | 9-11 | 0-1 | 17-22 | 37.7 | 36.6 | 41.4 | 49 |
| Atlanta | — | .800 | .800 | .818 | .000 | .773 | | | | |
| Ricardo, Benny, | 0-0 | 9-10 | 12-14 | 4-9 | 0-0 | 25-33 | 34.5 | 32.4 | 40.8 | 44 |
| Minnesota | — | .900 | .857 | .444 | — | .758 | | | | |
| Andersen, Morten, | 2-2 | 8-8 | 3-4 | 2-6 | 3-4 | 18-24 | 34.6 | 31.5 | 43.8 | 52 |
| New Orleans | 1.000 | 1.000 | .750 | .333 | .750 | .750 | | | | |
| Moseley, Mark, | 1-1 | 10-10 | 14-19 | 7-14 | 1-3 | 33-47 | 36.3 | 33.6 | 42.5 | 51 |
| Washington | 1.000 | 1.000 | .737 | .500 | .333 | .702 | | | | |
| Franklin, Tony, | 1-1 | 5-5 | 6-9 | 2-8 | 1-3 | 15-26 | 37.5 | 32.1 | 44.7 | 52 |
| Philadelphia | 1.000 | 1.000 | .667 | .250 | .333 | .577 | | | | |
| Thomas, Bob, | 1-1 | 9-9 | 0-4 | 3-6 | 1-5 | 14-25 | 36.8 | 29.9 | 45.5 | 50 |
| Chicago | 1.000 | 1.000 | .000 | .500 | .200 | .560 | | | | |
| O'Donoghue, Neil, | 0-1 | 4-6 | 3-8 | 6-10 | 2-3 | 15-28 | 37.5 | 38.5 | 36.4 | 52 |
| St. Louis | .000 | .667 | .375 | .600 | .667 | .536 | | | | |
| Capece, Bill, | 0-0 | 7-8 | 0-4 | 3-8 | 0-3 | 10-23 | 37.0 | 30.9 | 41.8 | 49 |
| Tampa Bay | — | .875 | .000 | .375 | .000 | .435 | | | | |
| **Non-Qualifiers** | | | | | | | | | | |
| Lansford, Mike, | 0-0 | 3-3 | 1-1 | 2-4 | 0-1 | 6-9 | 39.6 | 35.2 | 48.3 | 49 |
| Los Angeles Rams | — | 1.000 | 1.000 | .500 | .000 | .667 | | | | |
| Nelson, Chuck, | 0-0 | 1-3 | 3-4 | 1-4 | 0-0 | 5-11 | 34.5 | 33.8 | 35.2 | 41 |
| Los Angeles Rams | — | .333 | .750 | .250 | — | .455 | | | | |
| Warnke, David, | 0-0 | 0-1 | 0-0 | 0-0 | 0-0 | 0-1 | 29.0 | 0.0 | 29.0 | 0 |
| Tampa Bay | — | .000 | — | — | — | .000 | | | | |
| NFC Totals | 8-9 | 101-109 | 95-126 | 68-124 | 14-38 | 286-406 | 36.4 | 33.8 | 42.7 | 56 |
| | .889 | .927 | .754 | .548 | .368 | .704 | | | | |
| League Totals | 22-23 | 182-199 | 181-239 | 139-239 | 27-71 | 551-771 | 36.4 | 33.9 | 42.5 | 58 |
| | .957 | .915 | .757 | .582 | .380 | .715 | | | | |

## RUSHING

**INDIVIDUAL CHAMPIONS**
**NFC:** 1,808—Eric Dickerson, Los Angeles Rams
**AFC:** 1,449—Curt Warner, Seattle

**YARDS PER ATTEMPT**
**AFC:** 5.5—Mosi Tatupu, New England (106 attempts, 578 yards)
**NFC:** 5.3—Joe Washington, Washington (145 attempts, 772 yards)

**TOUCHDOWNS**
**NFC:** 24—John Riggins, Washington
**AFC:** 14—Pete Johnson, Cincinnati

**ATTEMPTS**
**NFC:** 390—Eric Dickerson, Los Angeles Rams
**AFC:** 335—Curt Warner, Seattle

**LONGEST**
**NFC:** 85 yards—Eric Dickerson, Los Angeles Rams vs. New York Jets, September 25 (TD)
**AFC:** 80 yards—Larry Moriarty, Houston vs. Los Angeles Raiders, September 11

**MOST YARDS, GAME**
**NFC:** 219 yards—James Wilder, Tampa Bay vs. Minnesota, November 6 (31 attempts)
**AFC:** 212 yards—Anthony Collins, New England vs. New York Jets, September 18 (23 attempts)

**TEAM LEADERS**
**AFC:** BALTIMORE: 1122, Curtis Dickey; BUFFALO: 1131, Joe Cribbs; CINCINNATI: 763, Pete Johnson; CLEVELAND: 1184, Mike Pruitt; DENVER: 757, Sammy Winder; HOUSTON: 1301, Earl Campbell; KANSAS CITY: 499, Billy Jackson; L.A. RAIDERS: 1014, Marcus Allen; MIAMI: 746, Andra Franklin; NEW ENGLAND: 1049, Anthony Collins; N.Y. JETS: 654, Freeman McNeil; PITTSBURGH: 1007, Franco Harris; SAN DIEGO: 886, Chuck Muncie; SEATTLE: 1449, Curt Warner.
**NFC:** ATLANTA: 1567, Williams Andrews; CHICAGO: 1421, Walter Payton; DALLAS: 1321, Tony Dorsett; DETROIT: 1040, Billy Sims; GREEN BAY: 696, Gerry Ellis; L.A. RAMS: 1808, Eric Dickerson; MINNESOTA: 642, Darrin Nelson; NEW ORLEANS: 1144, George Rogers; N.Y. GIANTS: 857, Butch Woolfolk; PHILADELPHIA: 434, Hubert Oliver; ST. LOUIS: 1270, Ottis Anderson; SAN FRANCISCO: 856, Wendell Tyler; TAMPA BAY: 640, James Wilder; WASHINGTON: 1347, John Riggins.

**TEAM CHAMPIONS (NET YARDS)**
**NFC:** 2,727—Chicago
**AFC:** 2,695—Baltimore

## AFC RUSHING—TEAM

| | Att. | Yards | Avg. | Long | TD |
|---|---|---|---|---|---|
| Baltimore | 601 | 2695 | 4.5 | 56 | 10 |
| Pittsburgh | 614 | 2610 | 4.3 | 50t | 17 |
| New England | 538 | 2605 | 4.8 | 77 | 19 |
| Los Angeles Raiders | 542 | 2240 | 4.1 | 32 | 18 |
| Miami | 568 | 2150 | 3.8 | 44 | 16 |
| Seattle | 546 | 2119 | 3.9 | 60 | 19 |
| Cincinnati | 542 | 2104 | 3.9 | 29 | 24 |
| New York Jets | 474 | 2068 | 4.4 | 78t | 11 |
| Houston | 502 | 1998 | 4.0 | 80 | 16 |
| Cleveland | 465 | 1922 | 4.1 | 29 | 13 |
| Denver | 471 | 1784 | 3.8 | 52 | 15 |
| Buffalo | 415 | 1736 | 4.2 | 45 | 4 |
| San Diego | 423 | 1536 | 3.6 | 61 | 16 |
| Kansas City | 387 | 1254 | 3.2 | 49t | 13 |
| AFC Total | 7088 | 28821 | — | 80 | 211 |
| AFC Average | 506.3 | 2058.6 | 4.1 | — | 15.1 |

## NFC RUSHING—TEAM

| | Att. | Yards | Avg. | Long | TD |
|---|---|---|---|---|---|
| Chicago | 583 | 2727 | 4.7 | 49t | 14 |
| Washington | 629 | 2625 | 4.2 | 48 | 30 |
| New Orleans | 595 | 2461 | 4.1 | 76t | 19 |
| St. Louis | 525 | 2277 | 4.3 | 46 | 15 |
| San Francisco | 511 | 2257 | 4.4 | 71 | 17 |
| Los Angeles Rams | 511 | 2253 | 4.4 | 85t | 20 |
| Atlanta | 492 | 2224 | 4.5 | 40t | 17 |
| Detroit | 513 | 2181 | 4.3 | 41 | 18 |
| Dallas | 519 | 2117 | 4.1 | 77 | 21 |
| Minnesota | 470 | 1808 | 3.8 | 56t | 17 |
| Green Bay | 439 | 1807 | 4.1 | 71 | 15 |
| New York Giants | 506 | 1794 | 3.5 | 37 | 9 |
| Philadelphia | 402 | 1417 | 3.5 | 35 | 5 |
| Tampa Bay | 428 | 1353 | 3.2 | 75t | 9 |
| NFC Total | 7123 | 29301 | — | 85t | 226 |
| NFC Average | 508.8 | 2092.9 | 4.1 | — | 16.1 |
| League Total | 14211 | 58122 | — | 85t | 437 |
| League Average | 507.5 | 2075.8 | 4.1 | — | 15.6 |

## NFL TOP 10 RUSHERS

| | Att. | Yards | Avg. | Long | TD |
|---|---|---|---|---|---|
| Dickerson, Eric, L.A. Rams | 390 | 1808 | 4.6 | 85t | 18 |
| Andrews, William, Atlanta | 331 | 1567 | 4.7 | 27 | 7 |
| Warner, Curt, Seattle | 335 | 1449 | 4.3 | 60 | 13 |
| Payton, Walter, Chicago | 314 | 1421 | 4.5 | 49t | 6 |
| Riggins, John, Washington | 375 | 1347 | 3.6 | 44 | 24 |
| Dorsett, Tony, Dallas | 289 | 1321 | 4.6 | 77 | 8 |
| Campbell, Earl, Houston | 322 | 1301 | 4.0 | 42 | 12 |
| Anderson, Ottis, St. Louis | 296 | 1270 | 4.3 | 43 | 5 |
| Pruitt, Mike, Cleveland | 293 | 1184 | 4.0 | 27 | 10 |
| Rogers, George, New Orleans | 256 | 1144 | 4.5 | 76t | 5 |

## AFC RUSHING—INDIVIDUAL

| | Att. | Yards | Avg. | Long | TD |
|---|---|---|---|---|---|
| Warner, Curt, Seattle | 335 | 1449 | 4.3 | 60 | 13 |
| Campbell, Earl, Houston | 322 | 1301 | 4.0 | 42 | 12 |
| Pruitt, Mike, Cleveland | 293 | 1184 | 4.0 | 27 | 10 |
| Cribbs, Joe, Buffalo | 263 | 1131 | 4.3 | 45 | 3 |
| Dickey, Curtis, Baltimore | 254 | 1122 | 4.4 | 56 | 4 |
| Collins, Anthony, New England | 219 | 1049 | 4.8 | 50t | 10 |
| Allen, Marcus, L.A. Raiders | 266 | 1014 | 3.8 | 19 | 9 |
| Harris, Franco, Pittsburgh | 279 | 1007 | 3.6 | 19 | 5 |
| Muncie, Chuck, San Diego | 235 | 886 | 3.8 | 34t | 12 |
| McMillan, Randy, Baltimore | 198 | 802 | 4.1 | 39t | 5 |
| Johnson, Pete, Cincinnati | 210 | 763 | 3.6 | 16t | 14 |
| Winder, Sammy, Denver | 196 | 757 | 3.9 | 52 | 3 |
| Franklin, Andra, Miami | 224 | 746 | 3.3 | 18 | 8 |
| Nathan, Tony, Miami | 151 | 685 | 4.5 | 40 | 3 |
| McNeil, Freeman, New York Jets | 160 | 654 | 4.1 | 19 | 1 |
| Pollard, Frank, Pittsburgh | 135 | 608 | 4.5 | 32 | 4 |
| Crutchfield, Dwayne, Jets-Hou. | 140 | 578 | 4.1 | 17 | 3 |
| Tatupu, Mosi, New England | 106 | 578 | 5.5 | 55 | 4 |
| Hawkins, Frank, L.A. Raiders | 110 | 526 | 4.8 | 32 | 6 |
| Alexander, Charles, Cincinnati | 153 | 523 | 3.4 | 12 | 3 |
| Brooks, James, San Diego | 127 | 516 | 4.1 | 61 | 3 |
| Jackson, Billy, Kansas City | 152 | 499 | 3.3 | 19 | 2 |
| Green, Boyce, Cleveland | 104 | 497 | 4.8 | 29 | 3 |
| Brown, Theotis, Sea.-K.C. | 130 | 481 | 3.7 | 49t | 8 |
| Stoudt, Cliff, Pittsburgh | 77 | 479 | 6.2 | 23 | 4 |
| Abercrombie, Walter, Pittsburgh | 112 | 446 | 4.0 | 50t | 4 |
| Pagel, Mike, Baltimore | 54 | 441 | 8.2 | 33 | 0 |
| Weathers, Robert, New England | 73 | 418 | 5.7 | 77 | 1 |
| Overstreet, David, Miami | 85 | 392 | 4.6 | 44 | 1 |
| van Eeghen, Mark, New England | 95 | 358 | 3.8 | 11 | 2 |
| Harper, Bruce, New York Jets | 51 | 354 | 6.9 | 78t | 1 |
| Moriarty, Larry, Houston | 65 | 321 | 4.9 | 80 | 3 |
| Hughes, David, Seattle | 83 | 313 | 3.8 | 26 | 1 |
| King, Kenny, Los Angeles Raiders | 82 | 294 | 3.6 | 16 | 1 |
| Moore, Booker, Buffalo | 60 | 275 | 4.6 | 21 | 0 |
| Wilson, Stanley, Cincinnati | 56 | 267 | 4.8 | 18 | 1 |
| Poole, Nathan, Denver | 81 | 246 | 3.0 | 19 | 4 |
| Preston, Dave, Denver | 57 | 222 | 3.9 | 28 | 1 |
| Moore, Alvin, Baltimore | 57 | 205 | 3.6 | 13 | 1 |
| Bennett, Woody, Miami | 49 | 197 | 4.0 | 25 | 2 |
| Willhite, Gerald, Denver | 43 | 188 | 4.4 | 24t | 3 |
| Leaks, Roosevelt, Buffalo | 58 | 157 | 2.7 | 12 | 1 |
| Kinnebrew, Larry, Cincinnati | 39 | 156 | 4.0 | 17 | 3 |
| Pruitt, Greg, Los Angeles Raiders | 26 | 154 | 5.9 | 18 | 2 |
| Anderson, Ken, Cincinnati | 22 | 147 | 6.7 | 29 | 1 |
| Craft, Donald, Houston | 55 | 147 | 2.7 | 8 | 0 |
| Elway, John, Denver | 28 | 146 | 5.2 | 23 | 1 |
| Wilson, Marc, L.A. Raiders | 13 | 122 | 9.4 | 23 | 0 |
| Schonert, Turk, Cincinnati | 29 | 117 | 4.0 | 15 | 2 |
| Thomas, Jewerl, Kansas City | 44 | 115 | 2.6 | 11 | 0 |
| Dierking, Scott, New York Jets | 28 | 113 | 4.0 | 31 | 3 |
| Grogan, Steve, New England | 23 | 108 | 4.7 | 17 | 2 |
| Todd, Richard, New York Jets | 35 | 101 | 2.9 | 17 | 0 |
| Walker, Dwight, Cleveland | 19 | 100 | 5.3 | 15 | 0 |
| Doornink, Dan, Seattle | 40 | 99 | 2.5 | 9 | 2 |
| Parros, Rick, Denver | 30 | 96 | 3.2 | 13 | 1 |
| Smith, Sherman, San Diego | 24 | 91 | 3.8 | 20 | 0 |
| Ferguson, Joe, Buffalo | 20 | 88 | 4.4 | 19 | 0 |
| Bryant, Cullen, Seattle | 27 | 87 | 3.2 | 9 | 0 |
| Hector, Johnny, New York Jets | 16 | 85 | 5.3 | 42 | 0 |
| Plunkett, Jim, L.A. Raiders | 26 | 78 | 3.0 | 20 | 0 |
| Woodley, David, Miami | 19 | 78 | 4.1 | 15 | 0 |
| Barber, Marion, New York Jets | 15 | 77 | 5.1 | 13 | 1 |
| Tate, Rodney, Cincinnati | 25 | 77 | 3.1 | 13 | 0 |
| Williams, Newton, Baltimore | 28 | 77 | 2.8 | 13 | 0 |
| Zorn, Jim, Seattle | 30 | 71 | 2.4 | 18t | 1 |
| Kenney, Bill, Kansas City | 23 | 59 | 2.6 | 11 | 3 |
| Sipe, Brian, Cleveland | 26 | 56 | 2.2 | 9 | 0 |
| Krieg, Dave, Seattle | 16 | 55 | 3.4 | 10t | 2 |
| Luck, Oliver, Houston | 17 | 55 | 3.2 | 17 | 0 |
| Thomas, Ken, Kansas City | 15 | 55 | 3.7 | 28 | 0 |
| Myles, Jesse, Denver | 8 | 52 | 6.5 | 16 | 0 |
| Augustyniak, Mike, New York Jets | 18 | 50 | 2.8 | 6 | 2 |
| Hawthorne, Greg, Pittsburgh | 5 | 47 | 9.4 | 20 | 0 |

| | Att. | Yards | Avg. | Long | TD |
|---|---|---|---|---|---|
| Marino, Dan, Miami | 28 | 45 | 1.6 | 15 | 2 |
| Walls, Herkie, Houston | 5 | 44 | 8.8 | 14 | 0 |
| Nielsen, Gifford, Houston | 8 | 43 | 5.4 | 20 | 0 |
| Davis, Johnny, Cleveland | 13 | 42 | 3.2 | 16 | 0 |
| Edwards, Stan, Houston | 16 | 40 | 2.5 | 9 | 0 |
| Eason, Tony, New England | 19 | 39 | 2.1 | 12 | 0 |
| Jackson, Ernest, San Diego | 11 | 39 | 3.5 | 6 | 0 |
| Dixon, Zachary, Balt.-Sea. | 9 | 32 | 3.6 | 7 | 0 |
| Verser, David, Cincinnati | 2 | 31 | 15.5 | 29 | 0 |
| DeBerg, Steve, Denver | 13 | 28 | 2.2 | 11 | 1 |
| Hunter, Tony, Buffalo | 2 | 28 | 14.0 | 24 | 0 |
| Ricks, Lawrence, Kansas City | 21 | 28 | 1.3 | 10 | 0 |
| Weathers, Clarence, New England | 1 | 28 | 28.0 | 28 | 0 |
| Reed, Mark, Baltimore | 2 | 27 | 13.5 | 18 | 0 |
| Chandler, Wes, San Diego | 2 | 25 | 12.5 | 23 | 0 |
| Kofler, Matt, Buffalo | 4 | 25 | 6.3 | 11 | 0 |
| Lewis, Kenny, New York Jets | 5 | 25 | 5.0 | 7 | 0 |
| Ryan, Pat, New York Jets | 4 | 23 | 5.8 | 25 | 0 |
| Berns, Rick, Los Angeles Raiders | 6 | 22 | 3.7 | 13 | 0 |
| Martin, Mike, Cincinnati | 2 | 21 | 10.5 | 15 | 0 |
| Branch, Cliff, Los Angeles Raiders | 1 | 20 | 20.0 | 20 | 0 |
| Carson, Carlos, Kansas City | 2 | 20 | 10.0 | 18 | 0 |
| Jones, Bobby, Cleveland | 1 | 19 | 19.0 | 19 | 0 |
| Upchurch, Rick, Denver | 6 | 19 | 3.2 | 9 | 0 |
| Riddick, Robb, Buffalo | 4 | 18 | 4.5 | 12 | 0 |
| Kubiak, Gary, Denver | 4 | 17 | 4.3 | 8 | 1 |
| McDonald, Paul, Cleveland | 3 | 17 | 5.7 | 10 | 0 |
| Watson, Steve, Denver | 3 | 17 | 5.7 | 10 | 0 |
| Smith, Tim, Houston | 2 | 16 | 8.0 | 9 | 0 |
| Harris, Tim, Pittsburgh | 2 | 15 | 7.5 | 10 | 0 |
| Kerrigan, Mike, New England | 1 | 14 | 14.0 | 14 | 0 |
| Morgan, Stanley, New England | 1 | 13 | 13.0 | 13 | 0 |
| Barnwell, Malcolm, L.A. Raiders | 1 | 12 | 12.0 | 12 | 0 |
| Hill, Eddie, Miami | 2 | 12 | 6.0 | 10 | 0 |
| Johns, Paul, Seattle | 2 | 12 | 6.0 | 26 | 0 |
| Williams, Van, Buffalo | 3 | 11 | 3.7 | 5 | 0 |
| Hadnot, James, Kansas City | 4 | 10 | 2.5 | 7 | 0 |
| Jones, Lam, New York Jets | 4 | 10 | 2.5 | 9 | 0 |
| Clayton, Mark, Miami | 2 | 9 | 4.5 | 9 | 0 |
| Holt, Harry, Cleveland | 3 | 8 | 2.7 | 4 | 0 |
| Stark, Rohn, Baltimore | 1 | 8 | 8.0 | 8 | 0 |
| Montgomery, Cle, L.A. Raiders | 2 | 7 | 3.5 | 5 | 0 |
| Odom, Henry, Pittsburgh | 2 | 7 | 3.5 | 4 | 0 |
| Prestridge, Luke, Denver | 1 | 7 | 7.0 | 7 | 0 |
| Allen, Gary, Houston | 1 | 5 | 5.0 | 5 | 0 |
| Cappelletti, John, San Diego | 1 | 5 | 5.0 | 5 | 0 |
| Crosby, Ron, New York Jets | 1 | 5 | 5.0 | 5 | 0 |
| Jensen, Derrick, L.A. Raiders | 1 | 5 | 5.0 | 5 | 0 |
| Bradshaw, Terry, Pittsburgh | 1 | 3 | 3.0 | 3 | 0 |
| Dressel, Chris, Houston | 1 | 3 | 3.0 | 3 | 0 |
| Franklin, Bryon, Buffalo | 1 | 3 | 3.0 | 3 | 0 |
| Renfro, Mike, Houston | 1 | 3 | 3.0 | 3 | 0 |
| Adams, Willis, Cleveland | 1 | 2 | 2.0 | 2 | 0 |
| Collinsworth, Cris, Cincinnati | 2 | 2 | 1.0 | 8 | 0 |
| Hall, Dino, Cleveland | 1 | 2 | 2.0 | 2 | 0 |
| Hardy, Bruce, Miami | 1 | 2 | 2.0 | 2 | 0 |
| Kreider, Steve, Cincinnati | 1 | 2 | 2.0 | 2 | 0 |
| Lane, Eric, Seattle | 3 | 1 | 0.3 | 7 | 0 |
| Scott, Willie, Kansas City | 1 | 1 | 1.0 | 1 | 0 |
| Blackledge, Todd, Kansas City | 1 | 0 | 0.0 | 0 | 0 |
| Brown, Curtis, Houston | 3 | 0 | 0.0 | 1t | 1 |
| Harris, Duriel, Miami | 1 | 0 | 0.0 | 0 | 0 |
| Herrmann, Mark, Baltimore | 1 | 0 | 0.0 | 0 | 0 |
| James, John, Houston | 1 | 0 | 0.0 | 0 | 0 |
| Mathison, Bruce, San Diego | 1 | 0 | 0.0 | 0 | 0 |
| Willis, Chester, L.A. Raiders | 5 | 0 | 0.0 | 4 | 0 |
| Humm, David, Los Angeles Raiders | 1 | −1 | −1.0 | −1 | 0 |
| Krauss, Barry, Baltimore | 1 | −1 | −1.0 | −1 | 0 |
| Christensen, Jeff, Cincinnati | 1 | −2 | −2.0 | −2 | 0 |
| Sweeney, Calvin, Pittsburgh | 1 | −2 | −2.0 | −2 | 0 |
| Belk, Rocky, Cleveland | 1 | −5 | −5.0 | −5 | 0 |
| Fouts, Dan, San Diego | 12 | −5 | −0.4 | 3 | 1 |
| Sievers, Eric, San Diego | 1 | −7 | −7.0 | −7 | 0 |
| Wright, James, Denver | 1 | −11 | −11.0 | −11 | 0 |
| Guy, Ray, Los Angeles Raiders | 2 | −13 | −6.5 | −3 | 0 |
| Luther, Ed, San Diego | 9 | −14 | −1.6 | 8 | 0 |
| Strock, Don, Miami | 6 | −16 | −2.7 | 0 | 0 |

*t indicates touchdown*
*Leader based on most yards gained.*

## NFC RUSHING—INDIVIDUAL

| | Att. | Yards | Avg. | Long | TD |
|---|---|---|---|---|---|
| Dickerson, Eric, L.A. Rams | 390 | 1808 | 4.6 | 85t | 18 |
| Andrews, William, Atlanta | 331 | 1567 | 4.7 | 27 | 7 |
| Payton, Walter, Chicago | 314 | 1421 | 4.5 | 49t | 6 |
| Riggins, John, Washington | 375 | 1347 | 3.6 | 44 | 24 |
| Dorsett, Tony, Dallas | 289 | 1321 | 4.6 | 77 | 8 |

| | Att. | Yards | Avg. | Long | TD |
|---|---|---|---|---|---|
| Anderson, Ottis, St. Louis | 296 | 1270 | 4.3 | 43 | 5 |
| Rogers, George, New Orleans | 256 | 1144 | 4.5 | 76t | 5 |
| Sims, Billy, Detroit | 220 | 1040 | 4.7 | 41 | 7 |
| Woolfolk, Butch, N.Y. Giants | 246 | 857 | 3.5 | 22 | 4 |
| Tyler, Wendell, San Francisco | 176 | 856 | 4.9 | 39 | 4 |
| Wilson, Wayne, New Orleans | 199 | 787 | 4.0 | 29 | 9 |
| Washington, Joe, Washington | 145 | 772 | 5.3 | 41 | 0 |
| Craig, Roger, San Francisco | 176 | 725 | 4.1 | 71 | 8 |
| Ellis, Gerry, Green Bay | 141 | 696 | 4.9 | 71 | 4 |
| Suhey, Matt, Chicago | 149 | 681 | 4.6 | 39 | 4 |
| Nelson, Darrin, Minnesota | 154 | 642 | 4.2 | 56t | 1 |
| Wilder, James, Tampa Bay | 161 | 640 | 4.0 | 75t | 4 |
| Carpenter, Rob, N.Y. Giants | 170 | 624 | 3.7 | 37 | 4 |
| Springs, Ron, Dallas | 149 | 541 | 3.6 | 19t | 7 |
| Brown, Ted, Minnesota | 120 | 476 | 4.0 | 43 | 10 |
| Jones, James, Detroit | 135 | 475 | 3.5 | 18 | 6 |
| Galbreath, Tony, Minnesota | 113 | 474 | 4.2 | 52t | 4 |
| Riggs, Gerald, Atlanta | 100 | 437 | 4.4 | 40t | 8 |
| Oliver, Hubert, Philadelphia | 121 | 434 | 3.6 | 24 | 1 |
| Gajan, Hokie, New Orleans | 81 | 415 | 5.1 | 58 | 4 |
| Williams, Mike, Philadelphia | 103 | 385 | 3.7 | 32 | 0 |
| Mitchell, Stump, St. Louis | 68 | 373 | 5.5 | 46 | 3 |
| Redden, Barry, L.A. Rams | 75 | 372 | 5.0 | 40t | 2 |
| Carver, Mel, Tampa Bay | 114 | 348 | 3.1 | 16 | 0 |
| Ivery, Eddie Lee, Green Bay | 86 | 340 | 4.0 | 21 | 2 |
| Clark, Jessie, Green Bay | 71 | 328 | 4.6 | 42 | 0 |
| McMahon, Jim, Chicago | 55 | 307 | 5.6 | 32 | 2 |
| Montana, Joe, San Francisco | 61 | 284 | 4.7 | 18 | 2 |
| Owens, James, Tampa Bay | 96 | 266 | 2.8 | 15 | 5 |
| Morris, Wayne, St. Louis | 75 | 257 | 3.4 | 17 | 2 |
| Ring, Bill, San Francisco | 64 | 254 | 4.0 | 25 | 2 |
| Bussey, Dexter, Detroit | 57 | 249 | 4.4 | 26 | 0 |
| Theismann, Joe, Washington | 37 | 234 | 6.3 | 22 | 1 |
| Haddix, Michael, Philadelphia | 91 | 220 | 2.4 | 11 | 2 |
| Meade, Mike. Green Bay | 55 | 201 | 3.7 | 15 | 1 |
| Newsome, Tim, Dallas | 44 | 185 | 4.2 | 20 | 2 |
| Huckleby, Harlan, Green Bay | 50 | 182 | 3.6 | 20 | 4 |
| Hipple, Eric, Detroit | 41 | 171 | 4.2 | 27 | 3 |
| Morris, Joe, New York Giants | 35 | 145 | 4.1 | 16 | 0 |
| Evans, Vince, Chicago | 22 | 142 | 6.5 | 27 | 1 |
| Montgomery, Wilbert, Philadelphia | 29 | 139 | 4.8 | 32 | 0 |
| Thompson, Vince, Detroit | 40 | 138 | 3.5 | 10 | 1 |
| Jaworski, Ron, Philadelphia | 25 | 129 | 5.2 | 29 | 1 |
| Lomax, Neil, St. Louis | 27 | 127 | 4.7 | 35 | 2 |
| Love, Randy, St. Louis | 35 | 103 | 2.9 | 16 | 2 |
| Harrington, Perry, Philadelphia | 23 | 98 | 4.3 | 35 | 1 |
| Young, Rickey, Minnesota | 39 | 90 | 2.3 | 9 | 2 |
| Wonsley, Otis, Washington | 25 | 88 | 3.5 | 9 | 0 |
| Johnson, Billy, Atlanta | 15 | 83 | 5.5 | 36 | 0 |
| Rogers, Jimmy, New Orleans | 26 | 80 | 3.1 | 13 | 0 |
| Thompson, Leonard, Detroit | 4 | 72 | 18.0 | 40t | 1 |
| Gentry, Dennis, Chicago | 16 | 65 | 4.1 | 17 | 0 |
| Brunner, Scott, New York Giants | 26 | 64 | 2.5 | 12 | 0 |
| Cain, Lynn, Atlanta | 19 | 63 | 3.3 | 10 | 1 |
| Hayes, Jeff, Washington | 2 | 63 | 31.5 | 48 | 0 |
| Brown, Charlie, Washington | 4 | 53 | 13.3 | 17 | 0 |
| Ferrell, Earl, St. Louis | 7 | 53 | 7.6 | 21 | 1 |
| Giaquinto, Nick, Washington | 14 | 53 | 3.8 | 11 | 1 |
| Green, Roy, St. Louis | 4 | 49 | 12.3 | 25 | 0 |
| Tuggle, John, New York Giants | 17 | 49 | 2.9 | 7t | 1 |
| Redwine, Jarvis, Minnesota | 10 | 48 | 4.8 | 21 | 0 |
| Moore, Jeff, San Francisco | 15 | 43 | 2.9 | 14 | 1 |
| Guman, Mike, Los Angeles Rams | 7 | 42 | 6.0 | 11 | 0 |
| LeCount, Terry, Minnesota | 2 | 42 | 21.0 | 40 | 0 |
| Orosz, Tom, San Francisco | 2 | 39 | 19.5 | 23 | 0 |
| Bartkowski, Steve, Atlanta | 16 | 38 | 2.4 | 10 | 1 |
| Lofton, James, Green Bay | 9 | 36 | 4.0 | 13 | 0 |
| Newhouse, Robert, Dallas | 9 | 34 | 3.8 | 8 | 0 |
| Gault, Willie, Chicago | 4 | 31 | 7.8 | 22 | 0 |
| White, Danny, Dallas | 18 | 31 | 1.7 | 22 | 4 |
| Armstrong, Adger, Tampa Bay | 7 | 30 | 4.3 | 7 | 0 |
| Alexander, Robert, L.A. Rams | 7 | 28 | 4.0 | 15 | 0 |
| Dils, Steve, Minnesota | 16 | 28 | 1.8 | 8 | 0 |
| Morton, Michael, Tampa Bay | 13 | 28 | 2.2 | 5 | 0 |
| Parsons, Bob, Chicago | 1 | 27 | 27.0 | 27 | 0 |
| Rutledge, Jeff, New York Giants | 7 | 27 | 3.9 | 14 | 0 |
| Thompson, Jack, Tampa Bay | 26 | 27 | 1.0 | 10 | 0 |
| Thomas, Calvin, Chicago | 8 | 25 | 3.1 | 9 | 0 |
| Monroe, Carl, San Francisco | 10 | 23 | 2.3 | 5 | 0 |
| Campfield, Billy, New York Giants | 2 | 21 | 10.5 | 13 | 0 |
| Wilson, Tim, New Orleans | 8 | 21 | 2.6 | 7 | 0 |
| Kane, Rick, Detroit | 4 | 19 | 4.8 | 9 | 0 |
| Clark, Dwight, San Francisco | 3 | 18 | 6.0 | 9 | 0 |
| Ferragamo, Vince, L.A. Rams | 22 | 17 | 0.8 | 8 | 0 |
| Austin, Cliff, New Orleans | 4 | 16 | 4.0 | 5 | 0 |
| Lewis, Gary, Green Bay | 4 | 16 | 4.0 | 11 | 1 |
| Merkens, Guido, New Orleans | 1 | 16 | 16.0 | 16 | 0 |
| Groth, Jeff, New Orleans | 1 | 15 | 15.0 | 15 | 0 |
| Giacomarro, Ralph, Atlanta | 2 | 13 | 6.5 | 13 | 0 |
| Harrell, Willard, St. Louis | 4 | 13 | 3.3 | 8 | 0 |
| Holly, Bob, Washington | 4 | 13 | 3.3 | 13 | 0 |
| Hutchison, Anthony, Chicago | 6 | 13 | 2.2 | 5 | 1 |
| Nichols, Mark, Detroit | 1 | 13 | 13.0 | 13 | 0 |
| Pearson, Drew, Dallas | 2 | 13 | 6.5 | 10 | 0 |
| Dickey, Lynn, Green Bay | 21 | 12 | 0.6 | 4 | 3 |
| Hart, Jim, St. Louis | 5 | 12 | 2.4 | 13 | 0 |
| Manning, Archie, Hou.-Minn. | 3 | 12 | 4.0 | 11 | 0 |
| Moroski, Mike, Atlanta | 2 | 12 | 6.0 | 7 | 0 |
| Evans, Reggie, Washington | 16 | 11 | 0.7 | 5 | 4 |
| Komlo, Jeff, Tampa Bay | 2 | 11 | 5.5 | 11 | 0 |
| Sharpe, Luis, St. Louis | 1 | 11 | 11.0 | 11 | 0 |
| Walker, Rick, Washington | 2 | 10 | 5.0 | 11 | 0 |
| Jones, Mike, Minnesota | 1 | 9 | 9.0 | 9 | 0 |
| Lisch, Rusty, St. Louis | 2 | 9 | 4.5 | 5 | 0 |
| Robinson, Bo, Atlanta | 3 | 9 | 3.0 | 7 | 0 |
| Cavanaugh, Matt, San Francisco | 1 | 8 | 8.0 | 8 | 0 |
| Danielson, Gary, Detroit | 6 | 8 | 1.3 | 8 | 0 |
| Ellard, Henry, Los Angeles Rams | 3 | 7 | 2.3 | 12 | 0 |
| Everett, Major, Philadelphia | 5 | 7 | 1.4 | 7 | 0 |
| Margerum, Ken, Chicago | 1 | 7 | 7.0 | 7 | 0 |
| White, Sammy, Minnesota | 1 | 7 | 7.0 | 7 | 0 |
| King, Horace, Detroit | 3 | 6 | 2.0 | 4 | 0 |
| Moorehead, Emery, Chicago | 5 | 6 | 1.2 | 5 | 0 |
| Runager, Max, Philadelphia | 1 | 6 | 6.0 | 6 | 0 |
| Williams, Richard, Atlanta | 1 | 5 | 5.0 | 5 | 0 |
| Middleton, Terdell, Tampa Bay | 2 | 4 | 2.0 | 2 | 0 |
| Eddings, Floyd, New York Giants | 1 | 3 | 3.0 | 3 | 0 |
| Golsteyn, Jerry, Tampa Bay | 5 | 3 | 0.6 | 2 | 0 |
| Goodlow, Eugene, New Orleans | 1 | 3 | 3.0 | 3 | 0 |
| Kramer, Tommy, Minnesota | 8 | 3 | 0.4 | 8 | 0 |
| Ramson, Eason, San Francisco | 1 | 3 | 3.0 | 3 | 0 |
| Solomon, Freddie, San Francisco | 1 | 3 | 3.0 | 3 | 0 |
| Wilson, Dave, New Orleans | 5 | 3 | 0.6 | 5 | 1 |
| Baschnagel, Brian, Chicago | 2 | 2 | 1.0 | 2 | 0 |
| Bright, Leon, New York Giants | 1 | 2 | 2.0 | 2 | 0 |
| Hill, Tony, Dallas | 1 | 2 | 2.0 | 2 | 0 |
| Lewis, Leo, Minnesota | 1 | 2 | 2.0 | 2 | 0 |
| Miller, Junior, Atlanta | 1 | 2 | 2.0 | 2 | 0 |
| Miller, Mike, New York Giants | 1 | 2 | 2.0 | 2 | 0 |
| Benjamin, Guy, San Francisco | 1 | 1 | 1.0 | 1 | 0 |
| Carter, Gerald, Tampa Bay | 1 | 0 | 0.0 | 0 | 0 |
| Cromwell, Nolan, L.A. Rams | 1 | 0 | 0.0 | 0 | 0 |
| Garrett, Alvin, Washington | 2 | 0 | 0.0 | 4 | 0 |
| Johnson, Butch, Dallas | 1 | 0 | 0.0 | 0 | 0 |
| Pastorini, Dan, Philadelphia | 1 | 0 | 0.0 | 0 | 0 |
| Perrin, Benny, St. Louis | 1 | 0 | 0.0 | 0 | 0 |
| Pisarcik, Joe, Philadelphia | 3 | −1 | −0.3 | 0 | 0 |
| Kemp, Jeff, Los Angeles Rams | 3 | −2 | −0.7 | 0 | 0 |
| Wilson, Wade, Minnesota | 3 | −3 | −1.0 | 2 | 0 |
| House, Kevin, Tampa Bay | 1 | −4 | −4.0 | −4 | 0 |
| Whitehurst, David, Green Bay | 2 | −4 | −2.0 | 0 | 0 |
| Bailey, Stacey, Atlanta | 2 | −5 | −2.5 | 0 | 0 |
| Coleman, Greg, Minnesota | 1 | −9 | −9.0 | −9 | 0 |
| Erxleben, Russell, New Orleans | 2 | −9 | −4.5 | 1 | 0 |
| Farmer, George, L.A. Rams | 1 | −9 | −9.0 | −9 | 0 |
| Black, Mike, Detroit | 2 | −10 | −5.0 | 0 | 0 |
| Grant, Otis, Los Angeles Rams | 2 | −10 | −5.0 | 1 | 0 |
| Hogeboom, Gary, Dallas | 6 | −10 | −1.7 | −1 | 0 |
| Stabler, Ken, New Orleans | 9 | −14 | −1.6 | 0 | 0 |
| Duckett, Kenny, New Orleans | 2 | −16 | −8.0 | 2 | 0 |
| Monk, Art, Washington | 3 | −19 | −6.3 | 2 | 0 |

*t indicates touchdown*
*Leader based on most yards gained.*

# PASSING

## INDIVIDUAL CHAMPIONS (RATING POINTS)
**NFC:** 97.6—Steve Bartkowski, Atlanta
**AFC:** 96.0—Dan Marino, Miami

## ATTEMPTS
**AFC:** 603—Bill Kenney, Kansas City
**NFC:** 533—Danny White, Dallas

## COMPLETIONS
**AFC:** 346—Bill Kenney, Kansas City
**NFC:** 334—Danny White, Dallas

## COMPLETION PERCENTAGE
**AFC:** 66.7—Ken Anderson, Cincinnati (297 attempts, 198 completions)
**NFC:** 64.5—Joe Montana, San Francisco (515 attempts, 332 completions)

## YARDS
**NFC:** 4,458—Lynn Dickey, Green Bay
**AFC:** 4,348—Bill Kenney, Kansas City

## YARDS PER ATTEMPT
**NFC:** 9.21—Lynn Dickey, Green Bay (484 attempts, 4,458 yards)
**AFC:** 8.80—Dave Krieg, Seattle (243 attempts, 2,139 yards)

## TOUCHDOWN PASSES
**NFC:** 32—Lynn Dickey, Green Bay
**AFC:** 26—Joe Ferguson, Buffalo
Brian Sipe, Cleveland

## TOUCHDOWN PERCENTAGE
**AFC:** 7.4—Dave Krieg, Seattle (243 attempts, 18 touchdowns)
**NFC:** 6.8—Neil Lomax, St. Louis (354 attempts, 24 touchdowns)

## MOST INTERCEPTIONS
**NFC:** 29—Lynn Dickey, Green Bay (484 attempts)
**AFC:** 26—Richard Todd, New York Jets (518 attempts)

## LOWEST PERCENTAGE INTERCEPTED
**NFC:** 1.2—Steve Bartkowski, Atlanta (432 attempts, 5 intercepted)
**AFC:** 2.0—Dan Marino, Miami (296 attempts, 6 intercepted)

## LONGEST
**AFC:** 99 yards—Jim Plunkett, Los Angeles Raiders vs. Washington, October 2 (to Cliff Branch)—TD
**NFC:** 87 yards—Jim McMahon, Chicago vs. Green Bay, December 4 (to Willie Gault)—TD

## TEAM CHAMPIONS
**AFC:** 4,661—San Diego
**NFC:** 4,365—Green Bay

## AFC PASSING—TEAM

| | Att. | Comp. | Pct. Comp. | Gross Yards | Tkd. | Yards Lost | Net Yards | TD | Pct. TD | Long | Had Int. | Pct. Int. | Avg. Yds. Att. | Avg. Yds. Comp. |
|---|---|---|---|---|---|---|---|---|---|---|---|---|---|---|
| San Diego | 635 | 369 | 58.1 | 4891 | 28 | 230 | 4661 | 27 | 4.3 | 59t | 33 | 5.2 | 7.70 | 13.25 |
| Kansas City | 641 | 369 | 57.6 | 4684 | 46 | 343 | 4341 | 29 | 4.5 | 53 | 19 | 3.0 | 7.31 | 12.69 |
| Cleveland | 567 | 324 | 57.1 | 3932 | 33 | 271 | 3661 | 27 | 4.8 | 66t | 28 | 4.9 | 6.93 | 12.14 |
| Los Angeles Raiders | 504 | 301 | 59.7 | 3910 | 55 | 464 | 3446 | 31 | 6.2 | 99t | 24 | 4.8 | 7.76 | 12.99 |
| New York Jets | 559 | 330 | 59.0 | 3742 | 43 | 317 | 3425 | 21 | 3.8 | 64t | 28 | 5.0 | 6.69 | 11.34 |
| Cincinnati | 454 | 290 | 63.9 | 3492 | 40 | 309 | 3183 | 14 | 3.1 | 80t | 18 | 4.0 | 7.69 | 12.04 |
| Buffalo | 571 | 317 | 55.5 | 3438 | 37 | 351 | 3087 | 30 | 5.3 | 43t | 28 | 4.9 | 6.02 | 10.85 |
| Miami | 442 | 254 | 57.5 | 3235 | 23 | 190 | 3045 | 28 | 6.3 | 85t | 11 | 2.5 | 7.32 | 12.74 |
| Denver | 499 | 254 | 50.9 | 3466 | 55 | 439 | 3027 | 17 | 3.4 | 78t | 22 | 4.4 | 6.95 | 13.65 |
| Seattle | 449 | 251 | 55.9 | 3316 | 47 | 343 | 2973 | 25 | 5.6 | 50t | 18 | 4.0 | 7.39 | 13.21 |
| Houston | 482 | 260 | 53.9 | 3286 | 49 | 384 | 2902 | 16 | 3.3 | 66 | 29 | 6.0 | 6.82 | 12.64 |
| New England | 412 | 220 | 53.4 | 3040 | 45 | 334 | 2706 | 16 | 3.9 | 76t | 18 | 4.4 | 7.38 | 13.82 |
| Pittsburgh | 409 | 211 | 51.6 | 2754 | 52 | 350 | 2404 | 15 | 3.7 | 52 | 23 | 5.6 | 6.73 | 13.05 |
| Baltimore | 377 | 188 | 49.9 | 2663 | 47 | 340 | 2323 | 12 | 3.2 | 72t | 22 | 5.8 | 7.06 | 14.16 |
| **AFC Total** | 7001 | 3938 | — | 49,849 | 600 | 4,665 | 45,184 | 308 | — | 99t | 321 | — | — | — |
| **AFC Average** | 500.1 | 281.3 | 56.2 | 3,560.6 | 42.9 | 333.2 | 3,227.4 | 22.0 | 4.4 | — | 22.9 | 4.6 | 7.12 | 12.66 |

## NFC PASSING—TEAM

| | Att. | Comp. | Pct. Comp. | Gross Yards | Tkd. | Yards Lost | Net Yards | TD | Pct. TD | Long | Had Int. | Pct. Int. | Avg. Yds. Att. | Avg. Yds. Comp. |
|---|---|---|---|---|---|---|---|---|---|---|---|---|---|---|
| Green Bay | 526 | 311 | 59.1 | 4688 | 42 | 323 | 4365 | 33 | 6.3 | 75t | 32 | 6.1 | 8.91 | 15.07 |
| Dallas | 554 | 346 | 62.5 | 4156 | 37 | 314 | 3842 | 31 | 5.6 | 80t | 25 | 4.5 | 7.50 | 12.01 |
| San Francisco | 528 | 339 | 64.2 | 4021 | 33 | 224 | 3797 | 27 | 5.1 | 77t | 12 | 2.3 | 7.62 | 11.86 |
| Washington | 463 | 278 | 60.0 | 3765 | 35 | 251 | 3514 | 29 | 6.3 | 84 | 11 | 2.4 | 8.13 | 13.54 |
| New York Giants | 575 | 284 | 49.4 | 3854 | 49 | 363 | 3491 | 12 | 2.1 | 62 | 31 | 5.4 | 6.70 | 13.57 |
| Atlanta | 507 | 321 | 63.3 | 3793 | 55 | 389 | 3404 | 24 | 4.7 | 76t | 10 | 2.0 | 7.48 | 11.82 |
| Los Angeles Rams | 489 | 286 | 58.5 | 3411 | 23 | 190 | 3221 | 23 | 4.7 | 61t | 23 | 4.7 | 6.98 | 11.93 |
| Minnesota | 555 | 310 | 55.9 | 3514 | 43 | 303 | 3211 | 15 | 2.7 | 68 | 22 | 4.0 | 6.33 | 11.34 |
| Tampa Bay | 528 | 300 | 56.8 | 3490 | 49 | 366 | 3124 | 18 | 3.4 | 80 | 24 | 4.5 | 6.61 | 11.63 |
| Philadelphia | 486 | 252 | 51.9 | 3532 | 57 | 415 | 3117 | 22 | 4.5 | 83t | 18 | 3.7 | 7.27 | 14.02 |
| Chicago | 447 | 255 | 57.0 | 3461 | 53 | 358 | 3103 | 21 | 4.7 | 87t | 22 | 4.9 | 7.74 | 13.57 |
| Detroit | 503 | 263 | 52.3 | 3297 | 45 | 342 | 2955 | 19 | 3.8 | 80t | 23 | 4.6 | 6.55 | 12.54 |
| St. Louis | 460 | 267 | 58.0 | 3309 | 59 | 441 | 2868 | 29 | 6.3 | 71t | 21 | 4.6 | 7.19 | 12.39 |
| New Orleans | 425 | 243 | 57.2 | 2782 | 35 | 305 | 2477 | 14 | 3.3 | 48 | 25 | 5.9 | 6.55 | 11.45 |
| **NFC Total** | 7046 | 4055 | — | 51,073 | 615 | 4584 | 46,489 | 317 | — | 87t | 299 | — | — | — |
| **NFC Average** | 503.3 | 289.6 | 57.6 | 3,648.1 | 43.9 | 327.4 | 3,320.6 | 22.6 | 4.5 | — | 21.4 | 4.2 | 7.25 | 12.60 |
| **League Total** | 14047 | 7993 | — | 100,922 | 1215 | 9249 | 91,673 | 625 | — | 99t | 620 | — | — | — |
| **League Average** | 501.7 | 285.5 | 56.9 | 3,604.4 | 43.4 | 330.3 | 3,274.0 | 22.3 | 4.4 | — | 22.1 | 4.4 | 7.18 | 12.63 |

*Leader based on net yards.*

## NFL TOP 10 INDIVIDUAL QUALIFIERS

| | Att. | Comp. | Pct. Comp. | Yards | Avg. Gain | TD | Pct. TD | Long | Int. | Pct. Int. | Rating Points |
|---|---|---|---|---|---|---|---|---|---|---|---|
| Bartkowski, Steve, Atlanta | 432 | 274 | 63.4 | 3167 | 7.33 | 22 | 5.1 | 76t | 5 | 1.2 | 97.6 |
| Theismann, Joe, Washington | 459 | 276 | 60.1 | 3714 | 8.09 | 29 | 6.3 | 84 | 11 | 2.4 | 97.0 |
| Marino, Dan, Miami | 296 | 173 | 58.4 | 2210 | 7.47 | 20 | 6.8 | 85t | 6 | 2.0 | 96.0 |
| Krieg, Dave, Seattle | 243 | 147 | 60.5 | 2139 | 8.80 | 18 | 7.4 | 50t | 11 | 4.5 | 95.0 |
| Montana, Joe, San Francisco | 515 | 332 | 64.5 | 3910 | 7.59 | 26 | 5.0 | 77t | 12 | 2.3 | 94.6 |
| Fouts, Dan, San Diego | 340 | 215 | 63.2 | 2975 | 8.75 | 20 | 5.9 | 59t | 15 | 4.4 | 92.5 |
| Lomax, Neil, St. Louis | 354 | 209 | 59.0 | 2636 | 7.45 | 24 | 6.8 | 71t | 11 | 3.1 | 92.0 |
| Dickey, Lynn, Green Bay | 484 | 289 | 59.7 | 4458 | 9.21 | 32 | 6.6 | 75t | 29 | 6.0 | 87.3 |
| Anderson, Ken, Cincinnati | 297 | 198 | 66.7 | 2333 | 7.86 | 12 | 4.0 | 80t | 13 | 4.4 | 85.6 |
| White, Danny, Dallas | 533 | 334 | 62.7 | 3980 | 7.47 | 29 | 5.4 | 80t | 23 | 4.3 | 85.6 |

## AFC PASSING — INDIVIDUAL QUALIFIERS

| | Att. | Comp. | Pct. Comp. | Yards | Avg. Gain | TD | Pct. TD | Long | Int. | Pct. Int. | Rating Points |
|---|---|---|---|---|---|---|---|---|---|---|---|
| Marino, Dan, Miami | 296 | 173 | 58.4 | 2210 | 7.47 | 20 | 6.8 | 85t | 6 | 2.0 | 96.0 |
| Krieg, Dave, Seattle | 243 | 147 | 60.5 | 2139 | 8.80 | 18 | 7.4 | 50t | 11 | 4.5 | 95.0 |
| Fouts, Dan, San Diego | 340 | 215 | 63.2 | 2975 | 8.75 | 20 | 5.9 | 59t | 15 | 4.4 | 92.5 |
| Anderson, Ken, Cincinnati | 297 | 198 | 66.7 | 2333 | 7.86 | 12 | 4.0 | 80t | 13 | 4.4 | 85.6 |
| Plunkett, Jim, L.A. Raiders | 379 | 230 | 60.7 | 2935 | 7.74 | 20 | 5.3 | 99t | 18 | 4.7 | 82.7 |
| Grogan, Steve, New England | 303 | 168 | 55.4 | 2411 | 7.96 | 15 | 5.0 | 76t | 12 | 4.0 | 81.4 |
| Kenney, Bill, Kansas City | 603 | 346 | 57.4 | 4348 | 7.21 | 24 | 4.0 | 53 | 18 | 3.0 | 80.8 |
| DeBerg, Steve, Denver | 215 | 119 | 55.3 | 1617 | 7.52 | 9 | 4.2 | 54 | 7 | 3.3 | 79.9 |
| Sipe, Brian, Cleveland | 496 | 291 | 58.7 | 3566 | 7.19 | 26 | 5.2 | 66t | 23 | 4.6 | 79.1 |
| Todd, Richard, N.Y. Jets | 518 | 308 | 59.5 | 3478 | 6.71 | 18 | 3.5 | 64t | 26 | 5.0 | 70.3 |
| Ferguson, Joe, Buffalo | 508 | 281 | 55.3 | 2995 | 5.90 | 26 | 5.1 | 43t | 25 | 4.9 | 69.3 |
| Zorn, Jim, Seattle | 205 | 103 | 50.2 | 1166 | 5.69 | 7 | 3.4 | 43 | 7 | 3.4 | 64.8 |
| Pagel, Mike, Baltimore | 328 | 163 | 49.7 | 2353 | 7.17 | 12 | 3.7 | 72t | 17 | 5.2 | 64.0 |
| Luck, Oliver, Houston | 217 | 124 | 57.1 | 1375 | 6.34 | 8 | 3.7 | 66 | 13 | 6.0 | 63.4 |
| Stoudt, Cliff, Pittsburgh | 381 | 197 | 51.7 | 2553 | 6.70 | 12 | 3.1 | 52 | 21 | 5.5 | 60.6 |
| Luther, Ed, San Diego | 287 | 151 | 52.6 | 1875 | 6.53 | 7 | 2.4 | 46 | 17 | 5.9 | 56.6 |
| Elway, John, Denver | 259 | 123 | 47.5 | 1663 | 6.42 | 7 | 2.7 | 49t | 14 | 5.4 | 54.9 |

| Non-Qualifiers | Att. | Comp. | Pct. Comp. | Yards | Avg. Gain | TD | Pct. TD | Long | Int. | Pct. Int. | Rating Points |
|---|---|---|---|---|---|---|---|---|---|---|---|
| Blackledge, Todd, Kansas City | 34 | 20 | 58.8 | 259 | 7.62 | 3 | 8.8 | 43 | 0 | 0.0 | 112.3 |
| Strock, Don, Miami | 52 | 34 | 65.4 | 403 | 7.75 | 4 | 7.7 | 47 | 1 | 1.9 | 106.5 |
| Wilson, Marc, Los Angeles Raiders | 117 | 67 | 57.3 | 864 | 7.38 | 8 | 6.8 | 50t | 6 | 5.1 | 82.0 |
| Kofler, Matt, Buffalo | 61 | 35 | 57.4 | 440 | 7.21 | 4 | 6.6 | 28t | 3 | 4.9 | 81.3 |
| Kubiak, Gary, Denver | 22 | 12 | 54.5 | 186 | 8.45 | 1 | 4.5 | 78t | 1 | 4.5 | 79.0 |
| Schonert, Turk, Cincinnati | 156 | 92 | 59.0 | 1159 | 7.43 | 2 | 1.3 | 54 | 5 | 3.2 | 73.1 |
| Ryan, Pat, New York Jets | 40 | 21 | 52.5 | 259 | 6.48 | 2 | 5.0 | 36 | 2 | 5.0 | 68.6 |
| Nielsen, Gifford, Houston | 175 | 90 | 51.4 | 1125 | 6.43 | 5 | 2.9 | 48 | 8 | 4.6 | 62.2 |
| Woodley, David, Miami | 89 | 43 | 48.3 | 528 | 5.93 | 3 | 3.4 | 64t | 4 | 4.5 | 59.6 |
| Manning, Archie, Houston | 88 | 44 | 50.0 | 755 | 8.58 | 2 | 2.3 | 47t | 8 | 9.1 | 49.2 |
| Eason, Tony, New England | 95 | 46 | 48.4 | 557 | 5.86 | 1 | 1.1 | 35 | 5 | 5.3 | 48.4 |
| McDonald, Paul, Cleveland | 68 | 32 | 47.1 | 341 | 5.01 | 1 | 1.5 | 27 | 4 | 5.9 | 42.6 |
| Malone, Mark, Pittsburgh | 20 | 9 | 45.0 | 124 | 6.20 | 1 | 5.0 | 38 | 2 | 10.0 | 42.5 |
| Herrmann, Mark, Baltimore | 36 | 18 | 50.0 | 256 | 7.11 | 0 | 0.0 | 35 | 3 | 8.3 | 38.7 |
| Kerrigan, Mike, New England | 14 | 6 | 42.9 | 72 | 5.14 | 0 | 0.0 | 19 | 1 | 7.1 | 29.5 |
| Reed, Mark, Baltimore | 10 | 6 | 60.0 | 34 | 3.40 | 0 | 0.0 | 16 | 1 | 10.0 | 26.7 |

| Less than 10 attempts | Att. | Comp. | Pct. Comp. | Yards | Avg. Gain | TD | Pct. TD | Long | Int. | Pct. Int. | |
|---|---|---|---|---|---|---|---|---|---|---|---|
| Allen, Marcus, Los Angeles Raiders | 7 | 4 | 57.1 | 111 | 15.86 | 3 | 42.9 | 43t | 0 | 0.0 | |
| Bradshaw, Terry, Pittsburgh | 8 | 5 | 62.5 | 77 | 9.63 | 2 | 25.0 | 24 | 0 | 0.0 | |
| Brown, Theotis, Kansas City | 1 | 1 | 100.0 | 11 | 11.00 | 0 | 0.0 | 11 | 0 | 0.0 | |
| Bryant, Steve, Houston | 1 | 1 | 100.0 | 24 | 24.00 | 1 | 100.0 | 24t | 0 | 0.0 | |
| Buford, Maury, San Diego | 1 | 0 | 0.0 | 0 | 0.00 | 0 | 0.0 | 0 | 0 | 0.0 | |
| Carson, Carlos, Kansas City | 1 | 1 | 100.0 | 48 | 48.00 | 1 | 100.0 | 48t | 0 | 0.0 | |
| Chandler, Wes, San Diego | 0 | 0 | — | 0 | — | 0 | — | 0 | 0 | — | |
| Clayton, Mark, Miami | 1 | 1 | 100.0 | 48 | 48.00 | 1 | 100.0 | 48t | 0 | 0.0 | |
| Cribbs, Joe, Buffalo | 2 | 1 | 50.0 | 3 | 1.50 | 0 | 0.0 | 3 | 0 | 0.0 | |
| Holohan, Pete, San Diego | 1 | 0 | 0.0 | 0 | 0.00 | 0 | 0.0 | 0 | 0 | 0.0 | |
| James, John, Houston | 1 | 1 | 100.0 | 7 | 7.00 | 0 | 0.0 | 7 | 0 | 0.0 | |
| Kreider, Steve, Cincinnati | 1 | 0 | 0.0 | 0 | 0.00 | 0 | 0.0 | 0 | 0 | 0.0 | |
| Largent, Steve, Seattle | 1 | 1 | 100.0 | 11 | 11.00 | 0 | 0.0 | 11 | 0 | 0.0 | |
| Marshall, Henry, Kansas City | 0 | 0 | — | 0 | — | 0 | — | 0 | 0 | — | |
| Mathison, Bruce, San Diego | 5 | 3 | 60.0 | 41 | 8.20 | 0 | 0.0 | 25 | 1 | 20.0 | |
| McNeil, Freeman, New York Jets | 1 | 1 | 100.0 | 5 | 5.00 | 1 | 100.0 | 5t | 0 | 0.0 | |
| Nathan, Tony, Miami | 4 | 3 | 75.0 | 46 | 11.50 | 0 | 0.0 | 22 | 0 | 0.0 | |
| Pruitt, Greg, Los Angeles Raiders | 1 | 0 | 0.0 | 0 | 0.00 | 0 | 0.0 | 0 | 0 | 0.0 | |
| Smith, Sherman, San Diego | 1 | 0 | 0.0 | 0 | 0.00 | 0 | 0.0 | 0 | 0 | 0.0 | |
| Stark, Rohn, Baltimore | 1 | 0 | 0.0 | 0 | 0.00 | 0 | 0.0 | 0 | 0 | 0.0 | |
| Taylor, Jim Bob, Baltimore | 2 | 1 | 50.0 | 20 | 10.00 | 0 | 0.0 | 20 | 1 | 50.0 | |
| Thomas, Jewerl, Kansas City | 2 | 1 | 50.0 | 18 | 9.00 | 1 | 50.0 | 18t | 1 | 50.0 | |
| Upchurch, Rick, Denver | 2 | 0 | 0.0 | 0 | 0.00 | 0 | 0.0 | 0 | 0 | 0.0 | |
| Walker, Dwight, Cleveland | 3 | 1 | 33.3 | 25 | 8.33 | 0 | 0.0 | 25 | 1 | 33.3 | |
| Willhite, Gerald, Denver | 1 | 0 | 0.0 | 0 | 0.00 | 0 | 0.0 | 0 | 0 | 0.0 | |

*t indicates touchdown.*

## NFC PASSING—INDIVIDUAL QUALIFIERS

| | Att. | Comp. | Pct. Comp. | Yards | Avg. Gain | TD | Pct. TD | Long | Int. | Pct. Int. | Rating Points |
|---|---|---|---|---|---|---|---|---|---|---|---|
| Bartkowski, Steve, Atlanta | 432 | 274 | 63.4 | 3167 | 7.33 | 22 | 5.1 | 76t | 5 | 1.2 | 97.6 |
| Theismann, Joe, Washington | 459 | 276 | 60.1 | 3714 | 8.09 | 29 | 6.3 | 84 | 11 | 2.4 | 97.0 |
| Montana, Joe, San Francisco | 515 | 332 | 64.5 | 3910 | 7.59 | 26 | 5.0 | 77t | 12 | 2.3 | 94.6 |
| Lomax, Neil, St. Louis | 354 | 209 | 59.0 | 2636 | 7.45 | 24 | 6.8 | 71t | 11 | 3.1 | 92.0 |
| Dickey, Lynn, Green Bay | 484 | 289 | 59.7 | 4458 | 9.21 | 32 | 6.6 | 75t | 29 | 6.0 | 87.3 |
| White, Danny, Dallas | 533 | 334 | 62.7 | 3980 | 7.47 | 29 | 5.4 | 80t | 23 | 4.3 | 85.6 |
| McMahon, Jim, Chicago | 295 | 175 | 59.3 | 2184 | 7.40 | 12 | 4.1 | 87t | 13 | 4.4 | 77.6 |
| Ferragamo, Vince, Los Angeles Rams | 464 | 274 | 59.1 | 3276 | 7.06 | 22 | 4.7 | 61t | 23 | 5.0 | 75.9 |
| Jaworski, Ron, Philadelphia | 446 | 235 | 52.7 | 3315 | 7.43 | 20 | 4.5 | 83t | 18 | 4.0 | 75.1 |
| Thompson, Jack, Tampa Bay | 423 | 249 | 58.9 | 2906 | 6.87 | 18 | 4.3 | 80 | 21 | 5.0 | 73.3 |
| Dils, Steve, Minnesota | 444 | 239 | 53.8 | 2840 | 6.40 | 11 | 2.5 | 68 | 16 | 3.6 | 66.8 |
| Hipple, Eric, Detroit | 387 | 204 | 52.7 | 2577 | 6.66 | 12 | 3.1 | 80t | 18 | 4.7 | 64.7 |
| Stabler, Ken, New Orleans | 311 | 176 | 56.6 | 1988 | 6.39 | 9 | 2.9 | 48 | 18 | 5.8 | 61.4 |
| Brunner, Scott, New York Giants | 386 | 190 | 49.2 | 2516 | 6.52 | 9 | 2.3 | 62 | 22 | 5.7 | 54.3 |

| Non-Qualifiers | Att. | Comp. | Pct. Comp. | Yards | Avg. Gain | TD | Pct. TD | Long | Int. | Pct. Int. | Rating Points |
|---|---|---|---|---|---|---|---|---|---|---|---|
| Benjamin, Guy, San Francisco | 12 | 7 | 58.3 | 111 | 9.25 | 1 | 8.3 | 73t | 0 | 0.0 | 117.0 |
| Hogeboom, Gary, Dallas | 17 | 11 | 64.7 | 161 | 9.47 | 1 | 5.9 | 24 | 1 | 5.9 | 90.6 |
| Danielson, Gary, Detroit | 113 | 59 | 52.2 | 720 | 6.37 | 7 | 6.2 | 54 | 4 | 3.5 | 78.0 |

| | Att. | Comp. | Pct. Comp. | Yards | Avg. Gain | TD | Pct. TD | Long | Int. | Pct. Int. | Rating Points |
|---|---|---|---|---|---|---|---|---|---|---|---|
| Kemp, Jeff, Los Angeles Rams | 25 | 12 | 48.0 | 135 | 5.40 | 1 | 4.0 | 21 | 0 | 0.0 | 77.9 |
| Kramer, Tommy, Minnesota | 82 | 55 | 67.1 | 550 | 6.71 | 3 | 3.7 | 49 | 4 | 4.9 | 77.8 |
| Moroski, Mike, Atlanta | 70 | 45 | 64.3 | 575 | 8.21 | 2 | 2.9 | 50t | 4 | 5.7 | 75.6 |
| Pisarcik, Joe, Philadelphia | 34 | 16 | 47.1 | 172 | 5.06 | 1 | 2.9 | 33 | 0 | 0.0 | 72.2 |
| Evans, Vince, Chicago | 145 | 76 | 52.4 | 1108 | 7.64 | 5 | 3.4 | 72t | 7 | 4.8 | 69.0 |
| Wilson, Dave, New Orleans | 112 | 66 | 58.9 | 770 | 6.88 | 5 | 4.5 | 42 | 7 | 6.3 | 68.7 |
| Rutledge, Jeff, New York Giants | 174 | 87 | 50.0 | 1208 | 6.94 | 3 | 1.7 | 54 | 8 | 4.6 | 59.3 |
| Golsteyn, Jerry, Tampa Bay | 97 | 47 | 48.5 | 535 | 5.52 | 0 | 0.0 | 52 | 2 | 2.1 | 56.9 |
| Simms, Phil, New York Giants | 13 | 7 | 53.8 | 130 | 10.00 | 0 | 0.0 | 36 | 1 | 7.7 | 56.6 |
| Hart, Jim, St. Louis | 91 | 50 | 54.9 | 592 | 6.51 | 4 | 4.4 | 39t | 8 | 8.8 | 53.0 |
| Wilson, Wade, Minnesota | 28 | 16 | 57.1 | 124 | 4.43 | 1 | 3.6 | 36 | 2 | 7.1 | 50.3 |
| Lisch, Rusty, St. Louis | 13 | 6 | 46.2 | 66 | 5.08 | 1 | 7.7 | 26 | 2 | 15.4 | 47.8 |
| Whitehurst, David, Green Bay | 35 | 18 | 51.4 | 149 | 4.26 | 0 | 0.0 | 19 | 2 | 5.7 | 38.9 |
| **Less than 10 attempts** | | | | | | | | | | | |
| Andrews, William, Atlanta | 1 | 0 | 0.0 | 0 | 0.00 | 0 | 0.0 | 0 | 0 | 0.0 | |
| Birdsong, Carl, St. Louis | 1 | 1 | 100.0 | 11 | 11.00 | 0 | 0.0 | 11 | 0 | 0.0 | |
| Black, Mike, Detroit | 1 | 0 | 0.0 | 0 | 0.00 | 0 | 0.0 | 0 | 1 | 100.0 | |
| Carmichael, Harold, Philadelphia | 1 | 1 | 100.0 | 45 | 45.00 | 1 | 100.0 | 45t | 0 | 0.0 | |
| Clark, Dwight, San Francisco | 1 | 0 | 0.0 | 0 | 0.00 | 0 | 0.0 | 0 | 0 | 0.0 | |
| Dorsett, Tony, Dallas | 1 | 0 | 0.0 | 0 | 0.00 | 0 | 0.0 | 0 | 0 | 0.0 | |
| Ellis, Gerry, Green Bay | 5 | 2 | 40.0 | 31 | 6.20 | 1 | 20.0 | 20 | 1 | 20.0 | |
| Erxleben, Russell, New Orleans | 1 | 1 | 100.0 | 24 | 24.00 | 0 | 0.0 | 24 | 0 | 0.0 | |
| Gajan, Hokie, New Orleans | 1 | 0 | 0.0 | 0 | 0.00 | 0 | 0.0 | 0 | 0 | 0.0 | |
| Giacomarro, Ralph, Atlanta | 1 | 1 | 100.0 | 23 | 23.00 | 0 | 0.0 | 23 | 0 | 0.0 | |
| Hodge, Floyd, Atlanta | 2 | 1 | 50.0 | 28 | 14.00 | 0 | 0.0 | 28 | 1 | 50.0 | |
| Holly, Bob, Washington | 1 | 1 | 100.0 | 5 | 5.00 | 0 | 0.0 | 5 | 0 | 0.0 | |
| Ivery, Eddie Lee, Green Bay | 2 | 2 | 100.0 | 50 | 25.00 | 0 | 0.0 | 35 | 0 | 0.0 | |
| Jennings, Dave, New York Giants | 1 | 0 | 0.0 | 0 | 0.00 | 0 | 0.0 | 0 | 0 | 0.0 | |
| Johnson, Billy, Atlanta | 1 | 0 | 0.0 | 0 | 0.00 | 0 | 0.0 | 0 | 0 | 0.0 | |
| Jones, James, Detroit | 2 | 0 | 0.0 | 0 | 0.00 | 0 | 0.0 | 0 | 0 | 0.0 | |
| Komlo, Jeff, Tampa Bay | 8 | 4 | 50.0 | 49 | 6.13 | 0 | 0.0 | 17 | 1 | 12.5 | |
| LeCount, Terry, Minnesota | 1 | 0 | 0.0 | 0 | 0.00 | 0 | 0.0 | 0 | 0 | 0.0 | |
| Mistler, John, New York Giants | 1 | 0 | 0.0 | 0 | 0.00 | 0 | 0.0 | 0 | 0 | 0.0 | |
| Monk, Art, Washington | 1 | 1 | 100.0 | 46 | 46.00 | 0 | 0.0 | 46 | 0 | 0.0 | |
| Pastorini, Dan, Philadelphia | 5 | 0 | 0.0 | 0 | 0.00 | 0 | 0.0 | 0 | 0 | 0.0 | |
| Payton, Walter, Chicago | 6 | 3 | 50.0 | 95 | 15.83 | 3 | 50.0 | 56t | 2 | 33.3 | |
| Pearson, Drew, Dallas | 1 | 0 | 0.0 | 0 | 0.00 | 0 | 0.0 | 0 | 1 | 100.0 | |
| Perrin, Benny, St. Louis | 1 | 1 | 100.0 | 4 | 4.00 | 0 | 0.0 | 4 | 0 | 0.0 | |
| Riggins, John, Washington | 1 | 0 | 0.0 | 0 | 0.00 | 0 | 0.0 | 0 | 0 | 0.0 | |
| Springs, Ron, Dallas | 2 | 1 | 50.0 | 15 | 7.50 | 1 | 50.0 | 15t | 0 | 0.0 | |
| Suhey, Matt, Chicago | 1 | 1 | 100.0 | 74 | 74.00 | 1 | 100.0 | 74t | 0 | 0.0 | |
| Washington, Joe, Washington | 1 | 0 | 0.0 | 0 | 0.00 | 0 | 0.0 | 0 | 0 | 0.0 | |

*t indicates touchdown.*

## PASS RECEIVING

**INDIVIDUAL CHAMPIONS**
**AFC:** 92—Todd Christensen, Los Angeles Raiders
**NFC:** 78—Charlie Brown, Washington
78—Earnest Gray, New York Giants
78—Roy Green, St. Louis
**YARDS**
**NFC:** 1,409—Mike Quick, Philadelphia
**AFC:** 1,351—Carlos Carson, Kansas City
**YARDS PER RECEPTION**
**NFC:** 22.4—James Lofton, Green Bay (58 receptions, 1300 yards)
**AFC:** 19.7—Mark Duper, Miami (51 receptions, 1003 yards)
**TOUCHDOWNS**
**NFC:** 14—Roy Green, St. Louis
**AFC:** 12—Todd Christensen, Los Angeles Raiders
**MOST RECEPTIONS, GAME**
**AFC:** 14—Kellen Winslow, San Diego vs. Kansas City, December 11 (162 yards)
**NFC:** 11—Charlie Brown, Washington vs. Los Angeles Raiders, October 2 (180 yards)
11—Tony Galbreath, Minnesota vs. Tampa Bay, November 6 (110 yards)
11—Ron Springs, Dallas vs. Tampa Bay, October 9 (126 yards)
11—James Wilder, Tampa Bay vs. Cincinnati, September 25 (126 yards)
**MOST YARDS, GAME**
**AFC:** 206—Cris Collinsworth, Cincinnati vs. Baltimore, October 2 (8 receptions)
**NFC:** 180—Charlie Brown, Washington vs. Los Angeles Raiders, October 2 (11 receptions)
**LONGEST**
**AFC:** 99 yards—Cliff Branch, Los Angeles Raiders vs. Washington, October 2 (from Jim Plunkett)—TD
**NFC:** 87 yards—Willie Gault, Chicago vs. Green Bay, December 4 (from Jim McMahon)—TD
**TEAM LEADERS**
**AFC:** BALTIMORE: 30, Bernard Henry; BUFFALO: 57, Joe Cribbs; CINCINNATI: 66, Cris Collinsworth; CLEVELAND: 89, Ozzie Newsome; DENVER: 59, Steve Watson; HOUSTON: 83, Tim Smith; KANSAS CITY: 80, Carlos Carson; LOS ANGELES RAIDERS: 92, Todd Christensen; MIAMI: 52, Tony Nathan; NEW ENGLAND: 58, Stanley Morgan; NEW YORK JETS: 61, Wesley Walker; PITTSBURGH: 39, Calvin Sweeney; SAN DIEGO: 88, Kellen Winslow; SEATTLE: 72, Steve Largent.
**NFC:** ATLANTA: 64, Billy Johnson; CHICAGO: 53, Walter Payton; DALLAS: 73, Ron Springs; DETROIT: 46, James Jones; GREEN BAY: 58, James Lofton; LOS ANGELES RAMS: 55, Mike Barber; MINNESOTA: 51, Darrin Nelson; NEW ORLEANS: 49, Jeff Groth; NEW YORK GIANTS: 78, Earnest Gray; PHILADELPHIA: 69, Mike Quick; ST. LOUIS: 78, Roy Green; SAN FRANCISCO: 70, Dwight Clark; TAMPA BAY: 57, James Wilder; WASHINGTON: 78, Charlie Brown.

## NFL TOP 10 PASS RECEIVERS

| | No. | Yards | Avg. | Long | TD |
|---|---|---|---|---|---|
| Christensen, Todd, L.A. Raiders | 92 | 1247 | 13.6 | 45 | 12 |
| Newsome, Ozzie, Cleveland | 89 | 970 | 10.9 | 66t | 6 |
| Winslow, Kellen, San Diego | 88 | 1172 | 13.3 | 46 | 8 |
| Smith, Tim, Houston | 83 | 1176 | 14.2 | 47t | 6 |
| Carson, Carlos, Kansas City | 80 | 1351 | 16.9 | 50t | 7 |
| Green, Roy, St. Louis | 78 | 1227 | 15.7 | 71t | 14 |
| Brown, Charlie, Washington | 78 | 1225 | 15.7 | 75t | 8 |
| Gray, Earnest, New York Giants | 78 | 1139 | 14.6 | 62 | 5 |
| Springs, Ron, Dallas | 73 | 589 | 8.1 | 80t | 1 |
| Largent, Steve, Seattle | 72 | 1074 | 14.9 | 46t | 11 |

## NFL TOP 10 PASS RECEIVERS BY YARDS

| | Yards | No. | Avg. | Long | TD |
|---|---|---|---|---|---|
| Quick, Mike, Philadelphia | 1409 | 69 | 20.4 | 83t | 13 |
| Carson, Carlos, Kansas City | 1351 | 80 | 16.9 | 50t | 7 |
| Lofton, James, Green Bay | 1300 | 58 | 22.4 | 74t | 8 |
| Christensen, Todd, L.A. Raiders | 1247 | 92 | 13.6 | 45 | 12 |
| Green, Roy, St. Louis | 1227 | 78 | 15.7 | 71t | 14 |
| Brown, Charlie, Washington | 1225 | 78 | 15.7 | 75t | 8 |
| Smith, Tim, Houston | 1176 | 83 | 14.2 | 47t | 6 |
| Winslow, Kellen, San Diego | 1172 | 88 | 13.3 | 46 | 8 |
| Gray, Earnest, New York Giants | 1139 | 78 | 14.6 | 62 | 5 |
| Watson, Steve, Denver | 1133 | 59 | 19.2 | 78t | 5 |

## AFC PASS RECEIVING—INDIVIDUAL

| | No. | Yards | Avg. | Long | TD |
|---|---|---|---|---|---|
| Christensen, Todd, L.A. Raiders | 92 | 1247 | 13.6 | 45 | 12 |
| Newsome, Ozzie, Cleveland | 89 | 970 | 10.9 | 66t | 6 |
| Winslow, Kellen, San Diego | 88 | 1172 | 13.3 | 46 | 8 |
| Smith, Tim, Houston | 83 | 1176 | 14.2 | 47t | 6 |
| Carson, Carlos, Kansas City | 80 | 1351 | 16.9 | 50t | 7 |
| Largent, Steve, Seattle | 72 | 1074 | 14.9 | 46t | 11 |
| Allen, Marcus, L.A. Raiders | 68 | 590 | 8.7 | 36 | 2 |
| Collinsworth, Cris, Cincinnati | 66 | 1130 | 17.1 | 63 | 5 |
| Joiner, Charlie, San Diego | 65 | 960 | 14.8 | 33t | 3 |
| Walker, Wesley, New York Jets | 61 | 868 | 14.2 | 64t | 7 |
| Watson, Steve, Denver | 59 | 1133 | 19.2 | 78t | 5 |
| Morgan, Stanley, New England | 58 | 863 | 14.9 | 50t | 2 |
| Chandler, Wes, San Diego | 58 | 845 | 14.6 | 44t | 5 |
| Cribbs, Joe, Buffalo | 57 | 524 | 9.2 | 33t | 7 |
| Nathan, Tony, Miami | 52 | 461 | 8.9 | 25 | 1 |
| Duper, Mark, Miami | 51 | 1003 | 19.7 | 85t | 10 |
| Marshall, Henry, Kansas City | 50 | 788 | 15.8 | 52 | 6 |
| Harper, Bruce, New York Jets | 48 | 413 | 8.6 | 33 | 2 |
| Brown, Theotis, Seattle | 47 | 418 | 8.9 | 53 | 2 |
| Jones, Lam, New York Jets | 43 | 734 | 17.1 | 50t | 4 |
| Curtis, Isaac, Cincinnati | 42 | 571 | 13.6 | 80t | 2 |
| Kreider, Steve, Cincinnati | 42 | 554 | 13.2 | 54 | 1 |
| Ross, Dan, Cincinnati | 42 | 483 | 11.5 | 30 | 3 |
| Muncie, Chuck, San Diego | 42 | 396 | 9.4 | 27 | 1 |
| Warner, Curt, Seattle | 42 | 325 | 7.7 | 28 | 1 |
| Upchurch, Rick, Denver | 40 | 639 | 16.0 | 40 | 2 |
| Branch, Cliff, Los Angeles Raiders | 39 | 696 | 17.8 | 99t | 5 |
| Sweeney, Calvin, Pittsburgh | 39 | 577 | 14.8 | 42 | 5 |
| Moore, Nat, Miami | 39 | 558 | 14.3 | 66t | 6 |
| Logan, Dave, Cleveland | 37 | 627 | 16.9 | 34 | 2 |
| Hancock, Anthony, Kansas City | 37 | 584 | 15.8 | 50 | 1 |
| Young, Charle, Seattle | 36 | 529 | 14.7 | 47 | 2 |
| Jones, Bobby, Cleveland | 36 | 507 | 14.1 | 32t | 4 |
| Lewis, Frank, Buffalo | 36 | 486 | 13.5 | 27t | 3 |
| Hunter, Tony, Buffalo | 36 | 402 | 11.2 | 40t | 3 |
| Butler, Jerry, Buffalo | 36 | 385 | 10.7 | 25 | 3 |
| Barnwell, Malcolm, L.A. Raiders | 35 | 513 | 14.7 | 41 | 1 |
| Cunningham, Bennie, Pittsburgh | 35 | 442 | 12.6 | 29 | 3 |
| Johns, Paul, Seattle | 34 | 486 | 14.3 | 30t | 4 |
| Harris, Franco, Pittsburgh | 34 | 278 | 8.2 | 29t | 2 |
| Moore, Booker, Buffalo | 34 | 199 | 5.9 | 21 | 1 |
| Sievers, Eric, San Diego | 33 | 452 | 13.7 | 28 | 3 |
| Dierking, Scott, New York Jets | 33 | 275 | 8.3 | 19 | 0 |
| Barkum, Jerome, New York Jets | 32 | 385 | 12.0 | 34 | 1 |
| Dressel, Chris, Houston | 32 | 316 | 9.9 | 35t | 4 |
| Jackson, Billy, Kansas City | 32 | 243 | 7.6 | 29 | 0 |
| Alexander, Charles, Cincinnati | 32 | 187 | 5.8 | 14 | 0 |
| Paige, Stephon, Kansas City | 30 | 528 | 17.6 | 43 | 6 |
| Franklin, Byron, Buffalo | 30 | 452 | 15.1 | 43t | 4 |
| Henry, Bernard, Baltimore | 30 | 416 | 13.9 | 40t | 4 |
| Pruitt, Mike, Cleveland | 30 | 157 | 5.2 | 21 | 2 |
| Holt, Harry, Cleveland | 29 | 420 | 14.5 | 48t | 3 |
| Rose, Joe, Miami | 29 | 345 | 11.9 | 37 | 3 |
| Walker, Dwight, Cleveland | 29 | 273 | 9.4 | 35 | 1 |
| Scott, Willie, Kansas City | 29 | 247 | 8.5 | 22 | 6 |
| Porter, Tracy, Baltimore | 28 | 384 | 13.7 | 38 | 0 |
| Thomas, Ken, Kansas City | 28 | 236 | 8.4 | 25 | 1 |
| Collins, Anthony, New England | 27 | 257 | 9.5 | 20 | 0 |
| Abercrombie, Walter, Pittsburgh | 26 | 391 | 15.0 | 51t | 3 |
| Shuler, Mickey, New York Jets | 26 | 272 | 10.5 | 28 | 1 |
| Bouza, Matt, Baltimore | 25 | 385 | 15.4 | 26 | 0 |
| Sherwin, Tim, Baltimore | 25 | 358 | 14.3 | 30 | 0 |
| Brammer, Mark, Buffalo | 25 | 215 | 8.6 | 21 | 2 |
| Brooks, James, San Diego | 25 | 215 | 8.6 | 36 | 0 |
| Green, Boyce, Cleveland | 25 | 167 | 6.7 | 33 | 1 |
| Dickey, Curtis, Baltimore | 24 | 483 | 20.1 | 72t | 3 |
| Ramsey, Derrick, New England | 24 | 335 | 14.0 | 39 | 6 |
| Doornink, Dan, Seattle | 24 | 328 | 13.7 | 47 | 2 |
| McMillan, Randy, Baltimore | 24 | 195 | 8.1 | 27 | 1 |
| Johnson, Dan, Miami | 24 | 189 | 7.9 | 33 | 4 |
| Renfro, Mike, Houston | 23 | 316 | 13.7 | 38t | 2 |
| Holohan, Pete, San Diego | 23 | 272 | 11.8 | 35 | 2 |
| Weathers, Robert, New England | 23 | 212 | 9.2 | 19 | 0 |
| Winder, Sammy, Denver | 23 | 150 | 6.5 | 17 | 0 |
| Hardy, Bruce, Miami | 22 | 202 | 9.2 | 25 | 0 |
| McNeil, Freeman, New York Jets | 21 | 172 | 8.2 | 21 | 3 |
| Duckworth, Bobby, San Diego | 20 | 422 | 21.1 | 59t | 5 |
| Adams, Willis, Cleveland | 20 | 374 | 18.7 | 59 | 2 |
| Jones, Cedric, New England | 20 | 323 | 16.2 | 30 | 1 |
| Egloff, Ron, Denver | 20 | 205 | 10.3 | 32 | 2 |
| Poole, Nathan, Denver | 20 | 184 | 9.2 | 23 | 0 |
| Hawkins, Frank, L.A. Raiders | 20 | 150 | 7.5 | 28 | 2 |
| Weathers, Clarence, New England | 19 | 379 | 19.9 | 58t | 3 |
| Hawthorne, Greg, Pittsburgh | 19 | 300 | 15.8 | 52 | 0 |
| Garrity, Gregg, Pittsburgh | 19 | 279 | 14.7 | 38 | 1 |
| Campbell, Earl, Houston | 19 | 216 | 11.4 | 66 | 0 |
| Crutchfield, Dwayne, Jets-Hou. | 19 | 133 | 7.0 | 15 | 0 |
| Tate, Rodney, Cincinnati | 18 | 142 | 7.9 | 25 | 0 |
| Starring, Stephen, New England | 17 | 389 | 22.9 | 76t | 2 |
| Tuttle, Perry, Buffalo | 17 | 261 | 15.4 | 38 | 3 |
| Gaffney, Derrick, New York Jets | 17 | 243 | 14.3 | 35 | 0 |
| Preston, Dave, Denver | 17 | 137 | 8.1 | 25 | 1 |
| Bryant, Steve, Houston | 16 | 211 | 13.2 | 26 | 0 |
| McCloskey, Mike, Houston | 16 | 137 | 8.6 | 20 | 1 |
| Pollard, Frank, Pittsburgh | 16 | 127 | 7.9 | 17 | 0 |
| Harris, Duriel, Miami | 15 | 260 | 17.3 | 64t | 1 |
| Johnson, Pete, Cincinnati | 15 | 129 | 8.6 | 18 | 0 |
| Williams, Dokie, L.A. Raiders | 14 | 259 | 18.5 | 50t | 3 |
| Holston, Michael, Houston | 14 | 205 | 14.6 | 43 | 0 |
| Mosley, Mike, Buffalo | 14 | 180 | 12.9 | 35 | 3 |
| Willhite, Gerald, Denver | 14 | 153 | 10.9 | 26t | 1 |
| King, Kenny, Los Angeles Raiders | 14 | 149 | 10.6 | 34t | 1 |
| Muhammad, Calvin, L.A. Raiders | 13 | 252 | 19.4 | 45 | 2 |
| Feacher, Ricky, Cleveland | 13 | 217 | 16.7 | 42t | 3 |
| Wright, James, Denver | 13 | 134 | 10.3 | 23 | 0 |
| Beckman, Ed, Kansas City | 13 | 130 | 10.0 | 20 | 0 |
| Walls, Herkie, Houston | 12 | 276 | 23.0 | 48 | 1 |
| Walker, Byron, Seattle | 12 | 248 | 20.7 | 50t | 2 |
| Thomas, Zack, Denver | 12 | 182 | 15.2 | 44 | 0 |
| Arnold, Walt, Houston | 12 | 137 | 11.4 | 37 | 1 |
| Parros, Rick, Denver | 12 | 126 | 10.5 | 33t | 2 |
| Wilson, Stanley, Cincinnati | 12 | 107 | 8.9 | 19 | 1 |
| Craft, Donald, Houston | 12 | 99 | 8.3 | 14 | 0 |
| Dawkins, Julius, Buffalo | 11 | 123 | 11.2 | 28t | 1 |
| Butler, Raymond, Baltimore | 10 | 207 | 20.7 | 60 | 3 |
| Sampson, Clinton, Denver | 10 | 200 | 20.0 | 49t | 3 |
| Capers, Wayne, Pittsburgh | 10 | 185 | 18.5 | 36 | 1 |
| van Eeghen, Mark, New England | 10 | 102 | 10.2 | 23 | 0 |
| Hughes, David, Seattle | 10 | 100 | 10.0 | 33t | 1 |
| Tatupu, Mosi, New England | 10 | 97 | 9.7 | 17 | 1 |
| Barnett, Buster, Buffalo | 10 | 94 | 9.4 | 14 | 0 |
| Augustyniak, Mike, New York Jets | 10 | 71 | 7.1 | 17 | 1 |
| Thomas, Jewerl, Kansas City | 10 | 51 | 5.1 | 9 | 0 |
| Dawson, Lin, New England | 9 | 84 | 9.3 | 14 | 1 |
| Edwards, Stan, Houston | 9 | 79 | 8.8 | 20 | 1 |
| Jackson, Harold, Seattle | 8 | 126 | 15.8 | 29 | 1 |
| Stallworth, John, Pittsburgh | 8 | 100 | 12.5 | 20 | 0 |
| Leaks, Roosevelt, Buffalo | 8 | 74 | 9.3 | 12 | 0 |
| Harris, M.L., Cincinnati | 8 | 66 | 8.3 | 14 | 2 |
| Overstreet, David, Miami | 8 | 55 | 6.9 | 20 | 2 |
| Myles, Jesse, Denver | 7 | 119 | 17.0 | 33 | 1 |
| Smith, J.T., Kansas City | 7 | 85 | 12.1 | 18 | 0 |
| Verser, David, Cincinnati | 7 | 82 | 11.7 | 22 | 0 |
| Metzelaars, Pete, Seattle | 7 | 72 | 10.3 | 17t | 1 |
| Barber, Marion, New York Jets | 7 | 48 | 6.9 | 12 | 1 |
| Clayton, Mark, Miami | 6 | 114 | 19.0 | 39 | 1 |
| Oatis, Victor, Baltimore | 6 | 93 | 15.5 | 25 | 0 |
| Lewis, Kenny, New York Jets | 6 | 62 | 10.3 | 23 | 0 |
| Smith, Sherman, San Diego | 6 | 51 | 8.5 | 21 | 0 |
| Moore, Alvin, Baltimore | 6 | 38 | 6.3 | 16 | 0 |
| Bennett, Woody, Miami | 6 | 35 | 5.8 | 9 | 0 |
| Belk, Rocky, Cleveland | 5 | 141 | 28.2 | 64t | 1 |
| Hector, Johnny, New York Jets | 5 | 61 | 12.2 | 22t | 1 |
| Beach, Pat, Baltimore | 5 | 56 | 11.2 | 16 | 1 |
| Jackson, Ernest, San Diego | 5 | 42 | 8.4 | 10 | 0 |
| Davis, Johnny, Cleveland | 5 | 20 | 4.0 | 10 | 0 |
| Odoms, Riley, Denver | 4 | 62 | 15.5 | 21 | 0 |
| Williams, Newton, Baltimore | 4 | 46 | 11.5 | 19 | 0 |
| Hall, Dino, Cleveland | 4 | 33 | 8.3 | 18 | 0 |
| Moriarty, Larry, Houston | 4 | 32 | 8.0 | 12 | 0 |
| Riddick, Robb, Buffalo | 3 | 43 | 14.3 | 24 | 0 |
| Sawyer, John, Denver | 3 | 42 | 14.0 | 17 | 0 |
| Skansi, Paul, Pittsburgh | 3 | 39 | 13.0 | 21 | 0 |
| Hasselbeck, Don, N.E.-Raiders | 3 | 24 | 8.0 | 13t | 2 |
| Bryant, Cullen, Seattle | 3 | 8 | 2.7 | 3 | 0 |
| Ricks, Lawrence, Kansas City | 3 | 5 | 1.7 | 7 | 0 |
| Carr, Roger, San Diego | 2 | 36 | 18.0 | 23 | 0 |
| Rodgers, John, Pittsburgh | 2 | 36 | 18.0 | 25 | 0 |
| Montgomery, Cleotha, L.A. Raiders | 2 | 29 | 14.5 | 15 | 0 |
| Scales, Dwight, San Diego | 2 | 28 | 14.0 | 14 | 0 |
| Martin, Mike, Cincinnati | 2 | 22 | 11.0 | 12 | 0 |
| Hadnot, James, Kansas City | 2 | 18 | 9.0 | 16 | 0 |
| Holman, Rodney, Cincinnati | 2 | 15 | 7.5 | 10 | 0 |
| Lane, Eric, Seattle | 2 | 9 | 4.5 | 7 | 0 |
| Kinnebrew, Larry, Cincinnati | 2 | 4 | 2.0 | 2 | 0 |
| Dieken, Doug, Cleveland | 1 | 14 | 14.0 | 14t | 1 |
| Stracka, Tim, Cleveland | 1 | 12 | 12.0 | 12 | 0 |
| Krieg, Dave, Seattle | 1 | 11 | 11.0 | 11 | 0 |
| Kempf, Florian, Houston | 1 | 7 | 7.0 | 7 | 0 |
| Vigorito, Tom, Miami | 1 | 7 | 7.0 | 7 | 0 |
| Pruitt, Greg, Los Angeles Raiders | 1 | 6 | 6.0 | 6 | 0 |
| Woodley, David, Miami | 1 | 6 | 6.0 | 6 | 0 |
| Harmon, Mike, New York Jets | 1 | 4 | 4.0 | 4 | 0 |
| Dixon, Zachary, Baltimore | 1 | 2 | 2.0 | 2 | 0 |
| Jensen, Derrick, L.A. Raiders | 1 | 2 | 2.0 | 2t | 1 |

| | No. | Yards | Avg. | Long | TD |
|---|---|---|---|---|---|
| Coombs, Tom, New York Jets | 1 | 1 | 1.0 | 1 | 0 |
| Kenney, Bill, Kansas City | 1 | 0 | 0.0 | 0 | 0 |
| Williams, Brooks, New England | 1 | 0 | 0.0 | 0 | 0 |
| Grogan, Steve, New England | 1 | −8 | −8.0 | −8 | 0 |

*t indicates touchdown*
*Leader based on most passes caught.*

## AFC TOP 25 PASS RECEIVERS BY YARDS

| | Yards | No. | Avg. | Long | TD |
|---|---|---|---|---|---|
| Carson, Carlos, Kansas City | 1351 | 80 | 16.9 | 50t | 7 |
| Christensen, Todd, Los Angeles Raiders | 1247 | 92 | 13.6 | 45 | 12 |
| Smith, Tim, Houston | 1176 | 83 | 14.2 | 47t | 6 |
| Winslow, Kellen, San Diego | 1172 | 88 | 13.3 | 46 | 8 |
| Watson, Steve, Denver | 1133 | 59 | 19.2 | 78t | 5 |
| Collinsworth, Cris, Cincinnati | 1130 | 66 | 17.1 | 63 | 5 |
| Largent, Steve, Seattle | 1074 | 72 | 14.9 | 46t | 11 |
| Duper, Mark, Miami | 1003 | 51 | 19.7 | 85t | 10 |
| Newsome, Ozzie, Cleveland | 970 | 89 | 10.9 | 66t | 6 |
| Joiner, Charlie, San Diego | 960 | 65 | 14.8 | 33t | 3 |
| Walker, Wesley, New York Jets | 868 | 61 | 14.2 | 64t | 7 |
| Morgan, Stanley, New England | 863 | 58 | 14.9 | 50t | 2 |
| Chandler, Wes, San Diego | 845 | 58 | 14.6 | 44t | 5 |
| Marshall, Henry, Kansas City | 788 | 50 | 15.8 | 52 | 6 |
| Jones, Lam, New York Jets | 734 | 43 | 17.1 | 50t | 4 |
| Branch, Cliff, Los Angeles Raiders | 696 | 39 | 17.8 | 99t | 5 |
| Upchurch, Rick, Denver | 639 | 40 | 16.0 | 40 | 2 |
| Logan, Dave, Cleveland | 627 | 37 | 16.9 | 34 | 2 |
| Allen, Marcus, Los Angeles Raiders | 590 | 68 | 8.7 | 36 | 2 |
| Hancock, Anthony, Kansas City | 584 | 37 | 15.8 | 50 | 1 |
| Sweeney, Calvin, Pittsburgh | 577 | 39 | 14.8 | 42 | 5 |
| Curtis, Isaac, Cincinnati | 571 | 42 | 13.6 | 80t | 2 |
| Moore, Nat, Miami | 558 | 39 | 14.3 | 66t | 6 |
| Kreider, Steve, Cincinnati | 554 | 42 | 13.2 | 54 | 1 |
| Young, Charle, Seattle | 529 | 36 | 14.7 | 47 | 2 |

## NFC PASS RECEIVING — INDIVIDUAL

| | No. | Yards | Avg. | Long | TD |
|---|---|---|---|---|---|
| Green, Roy, St. Louis | 78 | 1227 | 15.7 | 71t | 14 |
| Brown, Charlie, Washington | 78 | 1225 | 15.7 | 75t | 8 |
| Gray, Earnest, New York Giants | 78 | 1139 | 14.6 | 62 | 5 |
| Springs, Ron, Dallas | 73 | 589 | 8.1 | 80t | 1 |
| Clark, Dwight, San Francisco | 70 | 840 | 12.0 | 46t | 8 |
| Quick, Mike, Philadelphia | 69 | 1409 | 20.4 | 83t | 13 |
| Johnson, Billy, Atlanta | 64 | 709 | 11.1 | 47t | 4 |
| Andrews, William, Atlanta | 59 | 609 | 10.3 | 40 | 4 |
| Lofton, James, Green Bay | 58 | 1300 | 22.4 | 74t | 8 |
| Jefferson, John, Green Bay | 57 | 830 | 14.6 | 36 | 7 |
| Wilder, James, Tampa Bay. | 57 | 380 | 6.7 | 31 | 2 |
| Bailey, Stacey, Atlanta | 55 | 881 | 16.0 | 53 | 6 |
| Barber, Mike, Los Angeles Rams | 55 | 657 | 11.9 | 42t | 3 |
| Coffman, Paul, Green Bay | 54 | 814 | 15.1 | 74 | 11 |
| Anderson, Ottis, St. Louis | 54 | 459 | 8.5 | 40 | 1 |
| Payton, Walter, Chicago | 53 | 607 | 11.5 | 74t | 2 |
| Ellis, Gerry, Green Bay | 52 | 603 | 11.6 | 56 | 2 |
| Nelson, Darrin, Minnesota | 51 | 618 | 12.1 | 68 | 0 |
| Dickerson, Eric, L.A. Rams | 51 | 404 | 7.9 | 37t | 2 |
| Hill, Tony, Dallas | 49 | 801 | 16.3 | 75t | 7 |
| Groth, Jeff, New Orleans | 49 | 585 | 11.9 | 42 | 1 |
| Suhey, Matt, Chicago | 49 | 429 | 8.8 | 52 | 1 |
| Oliver, Hubert, Philadelphia | 49 | 421 | 8.6 | 25 | 2 |
| Carter, Gerald, Tampa Bay | 48 | 694 | 14.5 | 56t | 2 |
| Craig, Roger, San Francisco | 48 | 427 | 8.9 | 23 | 4 |
| House, Kevin, Tampa Bay | 47 | 769 | 16.4 | 74t | 5 |
| Monk, Art, Washington | 47 | 746 | 15.9 | 43t | 5 |
| Pearson, Drew, Dallas | 47 | 545 | 11.6 | 32 | 5 |
| Washington, Joe, Washington | 47 | 454 | 9.7 | 67 | 6 |
| Cosbie, Doug, Dallas | 46 | 588 | 12.8 | 61t | 6 |
| Jones, James, Detroit | 46 | 467 | 10.2 | 46 | 1 |
| Mistler, John, New York Giants | 45 | 422 | 9.4 | 24 | 0 |
| Galbreath, Tony, Minnesota | 45 | 348 | 7.7 | 23 | 2 |
| Tilley, Pat, St. Louis | 44 | 690 | 15.7 | 71t | 5 |
| Moorehead, Emery, Chicago | 42 | 597 | 14.2 | 36 | 3 |
| Sims, Billy, Detroit | 42 | 419 | 10.0 | 54 | 0 |
| Thompson, Leonard, Detroit | 41 | 752 | 18.3 | 80t | 3 |
| Brenner, Hoby, New Orleans | 41 | 574 | 14.0 | 38t | 3 |
| Johnson, Butch, Dallas | 41 | 561 | 13.7 | 46 | 3 |
| Goodlow, Eugene, New Orleans | 41 | 487 | 11.9 | 26 | 2 |
| Brown, Ted, Minnesota | 41 | 357 | 8.7 | 25 | 1 |
| Gault, Willie, Chicago | 40 | 836 | 20.9 | 87t | 8 |
| Chadwick, Jeff, Detroit | 40 | 617 | 15.4 | 45 | 4 |
| Farmer, George, L.A. Rams | 40 | 556 | 13.9 | 46t | 5 |
| Dorsett, Tony, Dallas | 40 | 287 | 7.2 | 24 | 1 |
| Carmichael, Harold, Philadelphia | 38 | 515 | 13.6 | 35 | 3 |
| Jenkins, Alfred, Atlanta | 38 | 487 | 12.8 | 26 | 1 |
| Guman, Mike, Los Angeles Rams | 34 | 347 | 10.2 | 60 | 4 |
| Tyler, Wendell, San Francisco | 34 | 285 | 8.4 | 26 | 2 |
| Dennard, Preston, L.A. Rams | 33 | 465 | 14.1 | 61t | 5 |
| Francis, Russ, San Francisco | 33 | 357 | 10.8 | 25 | 4 |
| Marsh, Doug, St. Louis | 32 | 421 | 13.2 | 38 | 8 |
| Carver, Mel, Tampa Bay | 32 | 262 | 8.2 | 20 | 1 |
| Solomon, Freddie, San Francisco | 31 | 662 | 21.4 | 77t | 4 |
| Bruer, Bob, Minnesota | 31 | 315 | 10.2 | 26 | 2 |
| Wilson, Mike, San Francisco | 30 | 433 | 14.4 | 49 | 0 |
| Nichols, Mark, Detroit | 29 | 437 | 15.1 | 46t | 1 |
| White, Sammy, Minnesota | 29 | 412 | 14.2 | 43t | 4 |
| Woolfolk, Butch, New York Giants | 28 | 368 | 13.1 | 44 | 0 |
| Hill, David, Los Angeles Rams | 28 | 280 | 10.0 | 34 | 2 |
| Giaquinto, Nick, Washington | 27 | 372 | 13.8 | 35 | 0 |
| Norris, Ulysses, Detroit | 26 | 291 | 11.2 | 41 | 7 |
| Carpenter, Rob, New York Giants | 26 | 258 | 9.9 | 38 | 2 |
| Bell, Theo, Tampa Bay | 25 | 410 | 16.4 | 52 | 2 |
| Giles, Jimmie, Tampa Bay | 25 | 349 | 14.0 | 80 | 1 |
| Garrett, Alvin, Washington | 25 | 332 | 13.3 | 84 | 1 |
| Hodge, Floyd, Atlanta | 25 | 280 | 11.2 | 76t | 4 |
| Scott, Lindsay, New Orleans | 24 | 274 | 11.4 | 35 | 0 |
| Haddix, Michael, Philadelphia | 23 | 254 | 11.0 | 34 | 0 |
| Ring, Bill, San Francisco | 23 | 182 | 7.9 | 24 | 1 |
| Margerum, Ken, Chicago | 21 | 336 | 16.0 | 60 | 2 |
| LeCount, Terry, Minnesota | 21 | 318 | 15.1 | 49 | 2 |
| McCullum, Sam, Minnesota | 21 | 314 | 15.0 | 49t | 2 |
| Mowatt, Zeke, New York Giants | 21 | 280 | 13.3 | 46t | 1 |
| Young, Rickey, Minnesota | 21 | 193 | 9.2 | 48 | 0 |
| Williams, Byron, New York Giants | 20 | 346 | 17.3 | 43t | 1 |
| McKinnon, Dennis, Chicago | 20 | 326 | 16.3 | 49t | 4 |
| Casper, Dave, Hou.-Minn. | 20 | 251 | 12.6 | 34 | 0 |
| Warren, Don, Washington | 20 | 225 | 11.3 | 33 | 2 |
| Wilson, Wayne, New Orleans | 20 | 178 | 8.9 | 24 | 2 |
| Duckett, Kenny, New Orleans | 19 | 283 | 14.9 | 48 | 2 |
| Moore, Jeff, San Francisco | 19 | 206 | 10.8 | 34 | 0 |
| Donley, Doug, Dallas | 18 | 370 | 20.6 | 47 | 2 |
| Epps, Phillip, Green Bay | 18 | 313 | 17.4 | 45 | 0 |
| Clark, Jessie, Green Bay | 18 | 279 | 15.5 | 75t | 1 |
| Newsome, Tim, Dallas | 18 | 250 | 13.9 | 52t | 4 |
| Bell, Jerry, Tampa Bay | 18 | 200 | 11.1 | 33 | 1 |
| Kab, Vyto, Philadelphia | 18 | 195 | 10.8 | 25 | 1 |
| Nehemiah, Renaldo, S.F. | 17 | 236 | 13.9 | 27 | 1 |
| Scott, Malcolm, New York Giants | 17 | 206 | 12.1 | 24 | 0 |
| Walker, Rick, Washington | 17 | 168 | 9.9 | 29 | 2 |
| Riggs, Gerald, Atlanta | 17 | 149 | 8.8 | 25 | 0 |
| Williams, Mike, Philadelphia | 17 | 142 | 8.4 | 29 | 0 |
| Gajan, Hokie, New Orleans | 17 | 130 | 7.6 | 26 | 0 |
| Ramson, Eason, San Francisco | 17 | 125 | 7.4 | 16 | 1 |
| Ellard, Henry, Los Angeles Rams | 16 | 268 | 16.8 | 44 | 0 |
| Ivery, Eddie Lee, Green Bay | 16 | 139 | 8.7 | 17 | 1 |
| Miller, Junior, Atlanta | 16 | 125 | 7.8 | 19 | 0 |
| Meade, Mike, Green Bay | 16 | 110 | 6.9 | 31t | 2 |
| Jordan, Steve, Minnesota | 15 | 212 | 14.1 | 28 | 2 |
| Cooper, Earl, San Francisco | 15 | 207 | 13.8 | 73t | 3 |
| Armstrong, Adger, Tampa Bay | 15 | 173 | 11.5 | 41 | 2 |
| Owens, James, Tampa Bay | 15 | 81 | 5.4 | 11 | 1 |
| Eddings, Floyd, New York Giants | 14 | 231 | 16.5 | 33 | 0 |
| Morris, Wayne, St. Louis | 14 | 55 | 3.9 | 11 | 0 |
| Jackson, Alfred, Atlanta | 13 | 220 | 16.9 | 54t | 3 |
| Mullady, Tom, New York Giants | 13 | 184 | 14.2 | 35 | 1 |
| Grant, Otis, Los Angeles Rams | 12 | 221 | 18.4 | 57 | 1 |
| DuPree, Billy Joe, Dallas | 12 | 142 | 11.8 | 28 | 1 |
| Lewis, Leo, Minnesota | 12 | 127 | 10.6 | 18 | 0 |
| Saldi, Jay, Chicago | 12 | 119 | 9.9 | 16 | 0 |
| Robinson, Bo, Atlanta | 12 | 100 | 8.3 | 15 | 0 |
| LaFleur, Greg, St. Louis | 12 | 99 | 8.3 | 21 | 0 |
| Rogers, George, New Orleans | 12 | 69 | 5.8 | 22 | 0 |
| Lewis, Gary, Green Bay | 11 | 204 | 18.5 | 49 | 1 |
| Jones, Gordon, L.A. Rams | 11 | 172 | 15.6 | 46 | 0 |
| Shumann, Mike, St. Louis | 11 | 154 | 14.0 | 33 | 0 |
| Hoover, Mel, Philadelphia | 10 | 221 | 22.1 | 68 | 0 |
| Huckleby, Harlan, Green Bay | 10 | 87 | 8.7 | 14 | 0 |
| Rubick, Rob, Detroit | 10 | 81 | 8.1 | 15 | 1 |
| Pittman, Danny, Giants-St. Louis | 9 | 175 | 19.4 | 40t | 1 |
| Didier, Clint, Washington | 9 | 153 | 17.0 | 40t | 4 |
| Cox, Arthur, Atlanta | 9 | 83 | 9.2 | 19 | 1 |
| King, Horace, Detroit | 9 | 76 | 8.4 | 14 | 0 |
| Obradovich, Jim, Tampa Bay | 9 | 71 | 7.9 | 19 | 1 |
| Montgomery, Wilbert, Philadelphia | 9 | 53 | 5.9 | 13 | 0 |
| Dunsmore, Pat, Chicago | 8 | 102 | 12.8 | 24 | 0 |
| Bussey, Dexter, Detroit | 8 | 49 | 6.1 | 14t | 1 |
| Miller, Mike, New York Giants | 7 | 170 | 24.3 | 54 | 0 |
| Young, Tyrone, New Orleans | 7 | 85 | 12.1 | 32 | 3 |
| Mitchell, Stump, St. Louis | 7 | 54 | 7.7 | 17 | 0 |
| Tice, John, New Orleans | 7 | 33 | 4.7 | 12t | 1 |
| Jones, Mike, Minnesota | 6 | 95 | 15.8 | 47 | 0 |
| Tyler, Andre, Tampa Bay | 6 | 77 | 12.8 | 21 | 0 |
| Young, Benjamin, Atlanta | 6 | 74 | 12.3 | 19 | 1 |
| Woodruff, Tony, Philadelphia | 6 | 70 | 11.7 | 29t | 2 |
| Love, Randy, St. Louis | 6 | 58 | 9.7 | 16 | 1 |
| Scott, Fred, Detroit | 5 | 71 | 14.2 | 25 | 1 |
| Baschnagel, Brian, Chicago | 5 | 70 | 14.0 | 24 | 0 |

| | No. | Yards | Avg. | Long | TD |
|---|---|---|---|---|---|
| Riggins, John, Washington | 5 | 29 | 5.8 | 14 | 0 |
| Dixon, Al, Philadelphia | 4 | 54 | 13.5 | 22 | 0 |
| Redden, Barry, Los Angeles Rams | 4 | 30 | 7.5 | 9 | 0 |
| Thompson, Vince, Detroit | 4 | 16 | 4.0 | 8 | 0 |
| Young, Glen, Philadelphia | 3 | 125 | 41.7 | 71t | 1 |
| Tuggle, John, New York Giants | 3 | 50 | 16.7 | 27 | 0 |
| Matthews, Allama, Atlanta | 3 | 37 | 12.3 | 23 | 0 |
| McDole, Mardye, Minnesota | 3 | 29 | 9.7 | 10 | 0 |
| Harrell, Willard, St. Louis | 3 | 25 | 8.3 | 13 | 0 |
| Cain, Lynn, Atlanta | 3 | 24 | 8.0 | 11 | 0 |
| Monroe, Carl, San Francisco | 2 | 61 | 30.5 | 50 | 0 |
| Seay, Virgil, Washington | 2 | 55 | 27.5 | 39t | 1 |
| Bright, Leon, New York Giants | 2 | 33 | 16.5 | 19 | 0 |
| Thompson, Kenny, St. Louis | 2 | 31 | 15.5 | 22 | 0 |
| Mauti, Rich, New Orleans | 2 | 30 | 15.0 | 23 | 0 |
| Hardy, Larry, New Orleans | 2 | 29 | 14.5 | 22 | 0 |
| Sampleton, Lawrence, Philadelphia | 2 | 28 | 14.0 | 19 | 0 |
| Austin, Cliff, New Orleans | 2 | 25 | 12.5 | 18 | 0 |
| Everett, Major, Philadelphia | 2 | 18 | 9.0 | 11 | 0 |
| Kane, Rick, Detroit | 2 | 15 | 7.5 | 9 | 0 |
| Witte, Mark, Tampa Bay | 2 | 15 | 7.5 | 10 | 0 |
| Thomas, Calvin, Chicago | 2 | 13 | 6.5 | 7 | 0 |
| Gentry, Dennis, Chicago | 2 | 8 | 4.0 | 6 | 0 |
| Morris, Joe, New York Giants | 2 | 1 | 0.5 | 6t | 1 |
| Harrington, Perry, Philadelphia | 1 | 19 | 19.0 | 19 | 0 |
| McMahon, Jim, Chicago | 1 | 18 | 18.0 | 18t | 1 |
| Curran, Willie, Atlanta | 1 | 15 | 15.0 | 15 | 0 |
| White, Danny, Dallas | 1 | 15 | 15.0 | 15t | 1 |
| Campfield, Billy, New York Giants | 1 | 12 | 12.0 | 12 | 0 |
| McGill, Eddie, St. Louis | 1 | 11 | 11.0 | 11 | 0 |
| Alexander, Robert, L.A. Rams | 1 | 10 | 10.0 | 10 | 0 |
| Kitson, Syd, Green Bay | 1 | 9 | 9.0 | 9 | 0 |
| Morton, Michael, Tampa Bay | 1 | 9 | 9.0 | 9 | 0 |
| Rafferty, Tom, Dallas | 1 | 8 | 8.0 | 8 | 0 |
| Smith, Ron, Philadelphia | 1 | 8 | 8.0 | 8 | 0 |
| McCall, Reese, Detroit | 1 | 6 | 6.0 | 6 | 0 |
| McGrath, Mark, Washington | 1 | 6 | 6.0 | 6 | 0 |
| Ahrens, Dave, St. Louis | 1 | 4 | 4.0 | 4 | 0 |
| Redwine, Jarvis, Minnesota | 1 | 4 | 4.0 | 4 | 0 |
| McDonald, James, L.A. Rams | 1 | 1 | 1.0 | 1t | 1 |

t indicates touchdown.
Leader based on most passes caught.

## NFC TOP 25 PASS RECEIVERS BY YARDS

| | Yards | No. | Avg. | Long | TD |
|---|---|---|---|---|---|
| Quick, Mike, Philadelphia | 1409 | 69 | 20.4 | 83t | 13 |
| Lofton, James, Green Bay | 1300 | 58 | 22.4 | 74t | 8 |
| Green, Roy, St. Louis | 1227 | 78 | 15.7 | 71t | 14 |
| Brown, Charlie, Washington | 1225 | 78 | 15.7 | 75t | 8 |
| Gray, Earnest, New York Giants | 1139 | 78 | 14.6 | 62 | 5 |
| Bailey, Stacey, Atlanta | 881 | 55 | 16.0 | 53 | 6 |
| Clark, Dwight, San Francisco | 840 | 70 | 12.0 | 46t | 8 |
| Gault, Willie, Chicago | 836 | 40 | 20.9 | 87t | 8 |
| Jefferson, John, Green Bay | 830 | 57 | 14.6 | 36 | 7 |
| Coffman, Paul, Green Bay | 814 | 54 | 15.1 | 74 | 11 |
| Hill, Tony, Dallas | 801 | 49 | 16.3 | 75t | 7 |
| House, Kevin, Tampa Bay | 769 | 47 | 16.4 | 74t | 5 |
| Thompson, Leonard, Detroit | 752 | 41 | 18.3 | 80t | 3 |
| Monk, Art, Washington | 746 | 47 | 15.9 | 43t | 5 |
| Johnson, Billy, Atlanta | 709 | 64 | 11.1 | 47t | 4 |
| Carter, Gerald, Tampa Bay | 694 | 48 | 14.5 | 56t | 2 |
| Tilley, Pat, St. Louis | 690 | 44 | 15.7 | 71t | 5 |
| Solomon, Freddie, San Francisco | 662 | 31 | 21.4 | 77t | 4 |
| Barber, Mike, Los Angeles Rams | 657 | 55 | 11.9 | 42t | 3 |
| Nelson, Darrin, Minnesota | 618 | 51 | 12.1 | 68 | 0 |
| Chadwick, Jeff, Detroit | 617 | 40 | 15.4 | 45 | 4 |
| Andrews, William, Atlanta | 609 | 59 | 10.3 | 40 | 4 |
| Payton, Walter, Chicago | 607 | 53 | 11.5 | 74t | 2 |
| Ellis, Gerry, Green Bay | 603 | 52 | 11.6 | 56 | 2 |
| Moorehead, Emery, Chicago | 597 | 42 | 14.2 | 36 | 3 |

## INTERCEPTIONS

**INDIVIDUAL CHAMPIONS**
**NFC:** 9—Mark Murphy, Washington
**AFC:** 8—Vann McElroy, Los Angeles Raiders
    8—Ken Riley, Cincinnati
**YARDAGE**
**NFC:** 164—Eric Wright, San Francisco (7 interceptions)
**AFC:** 127—Mike Harden, Denver (4 interceptions)
**LONGEST**
**AFC:** 73—Jacob Green, Seattle vs. Cleveland, October 2 (TD)
**NFC:** 70—Roosevelt Barnes, Detroit vs. Pittsburgh, November 24
    70—Bobby Johnson, New Orleans vs. Tampa Bay, October 23 (TD)
    70—Mel Kaufman, Washington vs. St. Louis, November 6 (TD)
**TOUCHDOWNS**
**AFC:** 2—Mike Kozlowski, Miami
    2—Rod Martin, Los Angeles Raiders
    2—Ken Riley, Cincinnati

**NFC:** 2—Hugh Green, Tampa Bay
    2—Dwight Hicks, San Francisco
    2—Johnnie Johnson, Los Angeles Rams
    2—Kenny Johnson, Atlanta
    2—Eric Wright, San Francisco
**MOST INTERCEPTIONS, GAME**
**AFC:** 3—Roland James, New England vs. Buffalo, October 23 (63 yards)
    3—William Judson, Miami vs. N.Y. Jets, October 16 (23 yards)
    3—Steve Wilson, Denver vs. Seattle, November 20 (55 yards)
**NFC:** 3—Mark Murphy, Washington vs. San Diego, October 31 (65 yards)
    3—Eric Wright, San Francisco vs. Minnesota, September 8 (78 yards)
**MOST TOUCHDOWNS, GAME**
**AFC:** 2—Mike Kozlowski, Miami vs. New York Jets, December 16
**NFC:** 2—Kenny Johnson, Atlanta vs. Green Bay, November 27
**TEAM LEADERS**
**AFC:** BALTIMORE: 4, Derrick Hatchett; BUFFALO: 3, Steve Freeman & Chris Williams; CINCINNATI: 8, Ken Riley; CLEVELAND: 4, Tom Cousineau; DENVER: 6, Louis Wright; HOUSTON: 5, Willie Tullis; KANSAS CITY: 7, Deron Cherry; LOS ANGELES RAIDERS: 8, Vann McElroy; MIAMI: 6, William Judson; NEW ENGLAND: 7, Rick Sanford; NEW YORK JETS: 7, Lance Mehl; PITTSBURGH: 5, Donnie Shell & Rick Woods; SAN DIEGO: 7, Danny Walters; SEATTLE: 7, Ken Easley.
**NFC:** ATLANTA: 4, Bobby Butler & Tom Pridemore; CHICAGO: 7, Leslie Frazier; DALLAS: 6, Dennis Thurman; DETROIT: 7, Bruce McNorton; GREEN BAY: 5, John Anderson & Tim Lewis; LOS ANGELES RAMS: 5, Kirk Collins; MINNESOTA: 6, John Swain & John Turner; NEW ORLEANS: 7, Johnnie Poe; NEW YORK GIANTS: 6, Terry Jackson; PHILADELPHIA: 3, Anthony Griggs; ST. LOUIS: 8, Lionel Washington; SAN FRANCISCO: 7, Eric Wright; TAMPA BAY: 6, Beasley Reece; WASHINGTON: 9, Mark Murphy.
**TEAM CHAMPIONS**
**NFC:** 34—Washington
**AFC:** 30—Kansas City

## AFC INTERCEPTIONS—TEAM

| | No. | Yards | Avg. | Long | TD |
|---|---|---|---|---|---|
| Kansas City | 30 | 482 | 16.1 | 58t | 2 |
| Pittsburgh | 28 | 435 | 15.5 | 70t | 4 |
| Denver | 27 | 355 | 13.1 | 48 | 0 |
| Miami | 26 | 345 | 13.3 | 45 | 3 |
| Seattle | 26 | 363 | 14.0 | 73t | 2 |
| Cincinnati | 23 | 369 | 16.0 | 55t | 4 |
| Cleveland | 22 | 296 | 13.5 | 65t | 2 |
| New York Jets | 22 | 342 | 15.5 | 43t | 3 |
| Baltimore | 20 | 314 | 15.7 | 71t | 1 |
| Los Angeles Raiders | 20 | 238 | 11.9 | 40t | 2 |
| New England | 17 | 202 | 11.9 | 46 | 1 |
| San Diego | 16 | 153 | 9.6 | 40t | 1 |
| Houston | 14 | 135 | 9.6 | 44 | 0 |
| Buffalo | 13 | 154 | 11.8 | 29 | 1 |
| AFC Total | 304 | 4183 | — | 73t | 26 |
| AFC Average | 21.7 | 298.8 | 13.8 | — | 1.9 |

## NFC INTERCEPTIONS—TEAM

| | No. | Yards | Avg. | Long | TD |
|---|---|---|---|---|---|
| Washington | 34 | 437 | 12.9 | 70t | 1 |
| St. Louis | 28 | 266 | 9.5 | 30 | 0 |
| Dallas | 27 | 467 | 17.3 | 68t | 2 |
| Minnesota | 25 | 168 | 6.7 | 31 | 0 |
| Los Angeles Rams | 24 | 515 | 21.5 | 60t | 3 |
| San Francisco | 24 | 437 | 18.2 | 62t | 5 |
| New Orleans | 23 | 412 | 17.9 | 70t | 3 |
| New York Giants | 23 | 210 | 9.1 | 30t | 1 |
| Tampa Bay | 23 | 367 | 16.0 | 69t | 3 |
| Detroit | 22 | 185 | 8.4 | 70 | 0 |
| Chicago | 21 | 215 | 10.2 | 58 | 2 |
| Green Bay | 19 | 227 | 11.9 | 46 | 1 |
| Atlanta | 15 | 212 | 14.1 | 38 | 2 |
| Philadelphia | 8 | 79 | 9.9 | 32 | 0 |
| NFC Total | 316 | 4197 | — | 70t | 23 |
| NFC Average | 22.6 | 299.8 | 13.3 | — | 1.6 |
| League Total | 620 | 8380 | — | 73t | 49 |
| League Average | 22.1 | 299.3 | 13.5 | — | 1.8 |

## NFL TOP 10 INTERCEPTORS

| | No. | Yards | Avg. | Long | TD |
|---|---|---|---|---|---|
| Murphy, Mark, Washington | 9 | 127 | 14.1 | 48 | 0 |
| Reece, Beasley, N.Y.G.-Tampa Bay | 8 | 103 | 12.9 | 29 | 0 |
| Washington, Lionel, St. Louis | 8 | 92 | 11.5 | 26 | 0 |
| Riley, Ken, Cincinnati | 8 | 89 | 11.1 | 42t | 2 |
| McElroy, Vann, L.A. Raiders | 8 | 68 | 8.5 | 28 | 0 |
| Wright, Eric, San Francisco | 7 | 164 | 23.4 | 60t | 2 |
| Poe, Johnnie, New Orleans | 7 | 146 | 20.9 | 31t | 1 |
| Frazier, Leslie, Chicago | 7 | 135 | 19.3 | 58 | 1 |
| Easley, Ken, Seattle | 7 | 106 | 15.1 | 48 | 0 |

|  | No. | Yards | Avg. | Long | TD |
|---|---|---|---|---|---|
| Cherry, Deron, Kansas City | 7 | 100 | 14.3 | 41 | 0 |
| Mehl, Lance, New York Jets | 7 | 57 | 8.1 | 34t | 1 |
| Walters, Danny, San Diego | 7 | 55 | 7.9 | 33 | 0 |
| McNorton, Bruce, Detroit | 7 | 30 | 4.3 | 15 | 0 |
| Sanford, Rick, New England | 7 | 24 | 3.4 | 16 | 0 |

## AFC INTERCEPTIONS—INDIVIDUAL

|  | No. | Yards | Avg. | Long | TD |
|---|---|---|---|---|---|
| Riley, Ken, Cincinnati | 8 | 89 | 11.1 | 42t | 2 |
| McElroy, Vann, L.A. Raiders | 8 | 68 | 8.5 | 28 | 0 |
| Easley, Ken, Seattle | 7 | 106 | 15.1 | 48 | 0 |
| Cherry, Deron, Kansas City | 7 | 100 | 14.3 | 41 | 0 |
| Mehl, Lance, New York Jets | 7 | 57 | 8.1 | 34t | 1 |
| Walters, Danny, San Diego | 7 | 55 | 7.9 | 33 | 0 |
| Sanford, Rick, New England | 7 | 24 | 3.4 | 16 | 0 |
| Brown, Dave, Seattle | 6 | 83 | 13.8 | 37 | 0 |
| Judson, William, Miami | 6 | 60 | 10.0 | 29 | 0 |
| Green, Gary, Kansas City | 6 | 59 | 9.8 | 25 | 0 |
| Wright, Louis, Denver | 6 | 50 | 8.3 | 34 | 0 |
| Horton, Ray, Cincinnati | 5 | 121 | 24.2 | 55t | 1 |
| James, Roland, New England | 5 | 99 | 19.8 | 46 | 0 |
| Wilson, Steve, Denver | 5 | 91 | 18.2 | 36 | 0 |
| Tullis, Willie, Houston | 5 | 65 | 13.0 | 44 | 0 |
| Small, Gerald, Miami | 5 | 60 | 12.0 | 28 | 0 |
| Woods, Rick, Pittsburgh | 5 | 53 | 10.6 | 31 | 0 |
| Foley, Steve, Denver | 5 | 28 | 5.6 | 16 | 0 |
| Shell, Donnie, Pittsburgh | 5 | 18 | 3.6 | 18 | 0 |
| Harden, Mike, Denver | 4 | 127 | 31.8 | 48 | 0 |
| Roquemore, Durwood, K.C. | 4 | 117 | 29.3 | 42t | 1 |
| Martin, Rod, Los Angeles Raiders | 4 | 81 | 20.3 | 40t | 2 |
| Blackwood, Lyle, Miami | 4 | 77 | 19.3 | 45 | 0 |
| Cousineau, Tom, Cleveland | 4 | 47 | 11.8 | 15 | 0 |
| Burruss, Lloyd, Kansas City | 4 | 46 | 11.5 | 27 | 0 |
| Lewis, Albert, Kansas City | 4 | 42 | 10.5 | 34 | 0 |
| Simpson, Keith, Seattle | 4 | 39 | 9.8 | 14 | 0 |
| Smith, Dennis, Denver | 4 | 39 | 9.8 | 23 | 0 |
| Hatchett, Derrick, Baltimore | 4 | 36 | 9.0 | 25 | 0 |
| Blount, Mel, Pittsburgh | 4 | 32 | 8.0 | 21 | 0 |
| Holmes, Jerry, New York Jets | 3 | 107 | 35.7 | 43t | 1 |
| Smith, Lucious, Kansas City | 3 | 99 | 33.0 | 58t | 1 |
| Banks, Chip, Cleveland | 3 | 95 | 31.7 | 65t | 1 |
| Woodruff, Dwayne, Pittsburgh | 3 | 85 | 28.3 | 47 | 0 |
| Johnson, Ron, Pittsburgh | 3 | 84 | 28.0 | 34t | 1 |
| Ray, Darrol, New York Jets | 3 | 77 | 25.7 | 42 | 0 |
| Lynn, Johnny, New York Jets | 3 | 70 | 23.3 | 42t | 1 |
| Whitwell, Mike, Cleveland | 3 | 67 | 22.3 | 28 | 0 |
| Merriweather, Mike, Pittsburgh | 3 | 55 | 18.3 | 31t | 1 |
| Dixon, Hanford, Cleveland | 3 | 41 | 13.7 | 35 | 0 |
| Freeman, Steve, Buffalo | 3 | 40 | 13.3 | 29 | 0 |
| Glasgow, Nesby, Baltimore | 3 | 35 | 11.7 | 18 | 0 |
| Kemp, Bobby, Cincinnati | 3 | 26 | 8.7 | 26 | 0 |
| Williams, Chris, Buffalo | 3 | 6 | 2.0 | 4 | 0 |
| Blackwood, Glenn, Miami | 3 | 0 | 0.0 | 0 | 0 |
| Anderson, Kim, Baltimore | 2 | 81 | 40.5 | 71t | 1 |
| Kozlowski, Mike, Miami | 2 | 73 | 36.5 | 38t | 2 |
| Hayes, Lester, L.A. Raiders | 2 | 49 | 24.5 | 28 | 0 |
| Young, Andre, San Diego | 2 | 49 | 24.5 | 40t | 1 |
| Breeden, Louis, Cincinnati | 2 | 47 | 23.5 | 39 | 0 |
| Bokamper, Kim, Miami | 2 | 43 | 21.5 | 24t | 1 |
| Sanford, Lucius, Buffalo | 2 | 39 | 19.5 | 20 | 0 |
| Kay, Bill, Houston | 2 | 31 | 15.5 | 27 | 0 |
| Romes, Charles, Buffalo | 2 | 27 | 13.5 | 27 | 0 |
| Griffin, Ray, Cincinnati | 2 | 24 | 12.0 | 24 | 0 |
| Jackson, Robert, Cincinnati | 2 | 21 | 10.5 | 15 | 0 |
| Keating, Chris, Buffalo | 2 | 20 | 10.0 | 17 | 0 |
| Bracelin, Greg, Baltimore | 2 | 19 | 9.5 | 19 | 0 |
| Delaney, Jeff, Baltimore | 2 | 16 | 8.0 | 11 | 0 |
| Harris, John, Seattle | 2 | 15 | 7.5 | 10 | 0 |
| Fox, Tim, San Diego | 2 | 14 | 7.0 | 14 | 0 |
| Burroughs, Jim, Baltimore | 2 | 8 | 4.0 | 8 | 0 |
| Jackson, Bobby, New York Jets | 2 | 8 | 4.0 | 8 | 0 |
| Schroy, Ken, New York Jets | 2 | 6 | 3.0 | 4 | 0 |
| Marion, Fred, New England | 2 | 4 | 2.0 | 4 | 0 |
| Bostic, Keith, Houston | 2 | 0 | 0.0 | 0 | 0 |
| Burrell, Clinton, Cleveland | 2 | 0 | 0.0 | 0 | 0 |
| Johnson, Lawrence, Cleveland | 2 | 0 | 0.0 | 0 | 0 |
| Scott, Clarence, Cleveland | 2 | 0 | 0.0 | 0 | 0 |
| Lambert, Jack, Pittsburgh | 2 | −1 | −0.5 | 0 | 0 |
| Green, Jacob, Seattle | 1 | 73 | 73.0 | 73t | 1 |
| Clayton, Harvey, Pittsburgh | 1 | 70 | 70.0 | 70t | 1 |
| Griffin, James, Cincinnati | 1 | 41 | 41.0 | 41t | 1 |
| Randle, Tate, Baltimore | 1 | 41 | 41.0 | 41 | 0 |
| Blackmon, Don, New England | 1 | 39 | 39.0 | 39 | 0 |
| Williams, Kendall, Baltimore | 1 | 32 | 32.0 | 18 | 0 |
| Maxwell, Vernon, Baltimore | 1 | 31 | 31.0 | 31 | 0 |
| Washington, Sam, Pittsburgh | 1 | 25 | 25.0 | 25 | 0 |
| Kennedy, Mike, Buffalo | 1 | 22 | 22.0 | 22t | 1 |
| Perry, Rod, Cleveland | 1 | 21 | 21.0 | 21 | 0 |

|  | No. | Yards | Avg. | Long | TD |
|---|---|---|---|---|---|
| Bryant, Trent, Kansas City | 1 | 19 | 19.0 | 19 | 0 |
| King, Linden, San Diego | 1 | 19 | 19.0 | 19 | 0 |
| Moyer, Paul, Seattle | 1 | 19 | 19.0 | 19t | 1 |
| Reinfeldt, Mike, Houston | 1 | 19 | 19.0 | 19 | 0 |
| Gross, Al, Cleveland | 1 | 18 | 18.0 | 18 | 0 |
| Robinson, Shelton, Seattle | 1 | 18 | 18.0 | 18 | 0 |
| Buttle, Greg, New York Jets | 1 | 17 | 17.0 | 17 | 0 |
| Brown, Steve, Houston | 1 | 16 | 16.0 | 16 | 0 |
| Cooks, Johnie, Baltimore | 1 | 15 | 15.0 | 15 | 0 |
| Jackson, Roger, Denver | 1 | 15 | 15.0 | 15 | 0 |
| Rhone, Earnest, Miami | 1 | 15 | 15.0 | 15 | 0 |
| Hinkle, Bryan, Pittsburgh | 1 | 14 | 14.0 | 14t | 1 |
| Millen, Matt, Los Angeles Raiders | 1 | 14 | 14.0 | 14 | 0 |
| Preston, Ray, San Diego | 1 | 13 | 13.0 | 13 | 0 |
| Watts, Ted, Los Angeles Raiders | 1 | 13 | 13.0 | 13 | 0 |
| Davis, James, L.A. Raiders | 1 | 10 | 10.0 | 10 | 0 |
| Lankford, Paul, Miami | 1 | 10 | 10.0 | 10 | 0 |
| Scholtz, Bruce, Seattle | 1 | 8 | 8.0 | 8 | 0 |
| Golic, Bob, Cleveland | 1 | 7 | 7.0 | 7t | 1 |
| Walker, Fulton, Miami | 1 | 7 | 7.0 | 7 | 0 |
| Nelson, Steve, New England | 1 | 6 | 6.0 | 6 | 0 |
| Gradishar, Randy, Denver | 1 | 5 | 5.0 | 5 | 0 |
| Bingham, Gregg, Houston | 1 | 4 | 4.0 | 4 | 0 |
| Davis, Mike, Los Angeles Raiders | 1 | 3 | 3.0 | 3 | 0 |
| Green, Mike, San Diego | 1 | 3 | 3.0 | 3 | 0 |
| McGrew, Larry, New England | 1 | 3 | 3.0 | 3 | 0 |
| Justin, Kerry, Seattle | 1 | 2 | 2.0 | 2 | 0 |
| Abraham, Robert, Houston | 1 | 0 | 0.0 | 0 | 0 |
| Anderson, Larry, Baltimore | 1 | 0 | 0.0 | 0 | 0 |
| Brown, Mark, Miami | 1 | 0 | 0.0 | 0 | 0 |
| Butler, Keith, Seattle | 1 | 0 | 0.0 | 0 | 0 |
| Byrd, Gill, San Diego | 1 | 0 | 0.0 | 0 | 0 |
| Crable, Bob, New York Jets | 1 | 0 | 0.0 | 0 | 0 |
| Haynes, Mike, L.A. Raiders | 1 | 0 | 0.0 | 0 | 0 |
| Jackson, Tom, Denver | 1 | 0 | 0.0 | 0 | 0 |
| McKinney, Odis, L.A. Raiders | 1 | 0 | 0.0 | 0 | 0 |
| McPherson, Miles, San Diego | 1 | 0 | 0.0 | 0 | 0 |
| Potter, Steve, Kansas City | 1 | 0 | 0.0 | 0 | 0 |
| Riley, Avon, Houston | 1 | 0 | 0.0 | 0 | 0 |
| Williams, Eugene, Seattle | 1 | 0 | 0.0 | 0 | 0 |
| Weishuhn, Clayton, New England | 0 | 27 | — | 27t | 1 |

*t indicates touchdown*
*Leader based on most interceptions.*

## NFC INTERCEPTIONS—INDIVIDUAL

|  | No. | Yards | Avg. | Long | TD |
|---|---|---|---|---|---|
| Murphy, Mark, Washington | 9 | 127 | 14.1 | 48 | 0 |
| Reece, Beasley, Giants-T.B. | 8 | 103 | 12.9 | 29 | 0 |
| Washington, Lionel, St. Louis | 8 | 92 | 11.5 | 26 | 0 |
| Wright, Eric, San Francisco | 7 | 164 | 23.4 | 60t | 2 |
| Poe, Johnnie, New Orleans | 7 | 146 | 20.9 | 31t | 1 |
| Frazier, Leslie, Chicago | 7 | 135 | 19.3 | 58 | 1 |
| McNorton, Bruce, Detroit | 7 | 30 | 4.3 | 15 | 0 |
| Thurman, Dennis, Dallas | 6 | 49 | 8.2 | 34 | 0 |
| Turner, John, Minnesota | 6 | 37 | 6.2 | 14 | 0 |
| Jackson, Terry, New York Giants | 6 | 20 | 3.3 | 17 | 0 |
| Swain, John, Minnesota | 6 | 12 | 2.0 | 11 | 0 |
| Fellows, Ron, Dallas | 5 | 139 | 27.8 | 58t | 1 |
| Collins, Kirk, Los Angeles Rams | 5 | 113 | 22.6 | 58 | 0 |
| Lewis, Tim, Green Bay | 5 | 111 | 22.2 | 46 | 0 |
| Anderson, John, Green Bay | 5 | 54 | 10.8 | 27t | 1 |
| Dean, Vernon, Washington | 5 | 54 | 10.8 | 26 | 0 |
| Schmidt, Terry, Chicago | 5 | 31 | 6.2 | 32t | 1 |
| Richardson, Mike, Chicago | 5 | 9 | 1.8 | 6 | 0 |
| Johnson, Johnnie, L.A. Rams | 4 | 115 | 28.8 | 60t | 2 |
| Harris, Eric, Los Angeles Rams | 4 | 100 | 25.0 | 45 | 0 |
| Downs, Mike, Dallas | 4 | 80 | 20.0 | 28 | 0 |
| Brown, Cedric, Tampa Bay | 4 | 78 | 19.5 | 36 | 0 |
| Walls, Everson, Dallas | 4 | 70 | 17.5 | 37 | 0 |
| Coffey, Ken, Washington | 4 | 62 | 15.5 | 29 | 0 |
| Pridemore, Tom, Atlanta | 4 | 56 | 14.0 | 25 | 0 |
| Williamson, Carlton, San Francisco | 4 | 51 | 12.8 | 26 | 0 |
| Perrin, Benny, St. Louis | 4 | 50 | 12.5 | 30 | 0 |
| Watkins, Bobby, Detroit | 4 | 48 | 12.0 | 31 | 0 |
| Irvin, LeRoy, Los Angeles Rams | 4 | 42 | 10.5 | 22 | 0 |
| Lee, Mark, Green Bay | 4 | 23 | 5.8 | 15 | 0 |
| Lott, Ronnie, San Francisco | 4 | 22 | 5.5 | 22 | 0 |
| Cobb, Garry, Detroit | 4 | 19 | 4.8 | 13 | 0 |
| Butler, Bobby, Atlanta | 4 | 12 | 3.0 | 12 | 0 |
| Washington, Anthony, Washington | 4 | 12 | 3.0 | 8 | 0 |
| Cromwell, Nolan, L.A. Rams | 3 | 76 | 25.3 | 43t | 1 |
| Gary, Russell, New Orleans | 3 | 70 | 23.3 | 26 | 0 |
| Griggs, Anthony, Philadelphia | 3 | 61 | 20.3 | 32 | 0 |
| Kinard, Terry, New York Giants | 3 | 49 | 16.3 | 25 | 0 |
| Holt, John, Tampa Bay | 3 | 43 | 14.3 | 25 | 0 |
| Bess, Rufus, Minnesota | 3 | 38 | 12.7 | 19 | 0 |
| Collier, Tim, San Francisco | 3 | 32 | 10.7 | 32t | 1 |
| Glazebrook, Bob, Atlanta | 3 | 30 | 10.0 | 25 | 0 |

| | No. | Yards | Avg. | Long | TD |
|---|---|---|---|---|---|
| Junior, E.J., St. Louis | 3 | 27 | 9.0 | 19 | 0 |
| Teal, Willie, Minnesota | 3 | 26 | 8.7 | 12 | 0 |
| Mack, Cedric, St. Louis | 3 | 25 | 8.3 | 13 | 0 |
| Winston, Dennis, New Orleans | 3 | 21 | 7.0 | 15 | 0 |
| Haynes, Mark, New York Giants | 3 | 18 | 6.0 | 23 | 0 |
| Harris, Bob, St. Louis | 3 | 10 | 3.3 | 10 | 0 |
| Hicks, Dwight, San Francisco | 2 | 102 | 51.0 | 62t | 2 |
| Kaufman, Mel, Washington | 2 | 93 | 46.5 | 70t | 1 |
| Johnson, Bobby, New Orleans | 2 | 80 | 40.0 | 70t | 1 |
| Barnes, Roosevelt, Detroit | 2 | 70 | 35.0 | 70 | 0 |
| Clinkscale, Dextor, Dallas | 2 | 68 | 34.0 | 68t | 1 |
| Johnson, Kenny, Atlanta | 2 | 57 | 28.5 | 31t | 2 |
| Green, Hugh, Tampa Bay | 2 | 54 | 27.0 | 33t | 2 |
| Collins, Jim, Los Angeles Rams | 2 | 46 | 23.0 | 29 | 0 |
| Washington, Mike, Tampa Bay | 2 | 41 | 20.5 | 25 | 0 |
| Currier, Bill, New York Giants | 2 | 37 | 18.5 | 30t | 1 |
| Fencik, Gary, Chicago | 2 | 34 | 17.0 | 20 | 0 |
| Wattelet, Frank, New Orleans | 2 | 33 | 16.5 | 24 | 0 |
| Williams, Greg, Washington | 2 | 25 | 12.5 | 25 | 0 |
| Baker, Al, St. Louis | 2 | 24 | 12.0 | 19 | 0 |
| Milot, Rich, Washington | 2 | 20 | 10.0 | 20 | 0 |
| Hall, Alvin, Detroit | 2 | 18 | 9.0 | 18 | 0 |
| Leopold, Bobby, San Francisco | 2 | 13 | 6.5 | 9 | 0 |
| Hill, Rod, Dallas | 2 | 12 | 6.0 | 12 | 0 |
| Reese, Booker, Tampa Bay | 2 | 11 | 5.5 | 11 | 0 |
| Taylor, Lawrence, N.Y. Giants | 2 | 10 | 5.0 | 10 | 0 |
| Green, Darrell, Washington | 2 | 7 | 3.5 | 7 | 0 |
| Van Pelt, Brad, New York Giants | 2 | 7 | 3.5 | 6 | 0 |
| Gray, Johnnie, Green Bay | 2 | 5 | 2.5 | 5 | 0 |
| Paul, Whitney, New Orleans | 2 | 3 | 1.5 | 3 | 0 |
| Smith, Wayne, St. Louis | 2 | 3 | 1.5 | 3 | 0 |
| Cotney, Mark, Tampa Bay | 2 | 1 | 0.5 | 1 | 0 |
| Browner, Joey, Minnesota | 2 | 0 | 0.0 | 0 | 0 |
| Fantetti, Ken, Detroit | 2 | 0 | 0.0 | 0 | 0 |
| Castille, Jeremiah, Tampa Bay | 1 | 69 | 69.0 | 69t | 1 |
| Richardson, Al, Atlanta | 1 | 38 | 38.0 | 38 | 0 |
| Harper, Willie, San Francisco | 1 | 37 | 37.0 | 37 | 0 |
| Lee, Carl, Minnesota | 1 | 31 | 31.0 | 31 | 0 |
| Bates, Bill, Dallas | 1 | 29 | 29.0 | 29 | 0 |
| Lewis, Reggie, New Orleans | 1 | 27 | 27.0 | 27t | 1 |
| Stemrick, Greg, New Orleans | 1 | 26 | 26.0 | 26 | 0 |
| Andrews, George, L.A. Rams | 1 | 22 | 22.0 | 22 | 0 |
| Laughlin, Jim, Green Bay | 1 | 22 | 22.0 | 22 | 0 |
| White, James, Minnesota | 1 | 22 | 22.0 | 22 | 0 |
| Jordan, Curtis, Washington | 1 | 20 | 20.0 | 20 | 0 |
| Flowers, Larry, New York Giants | 1 | 19 | 19.0 | 19 | 0 |
| Jones, Earl, Atlanta | 1 | 19 | 19.0 | 19 | 0 |
| Ellis, Ray, Philadelphia | 1 | 18 | 18.0 | 18 | 0 |
| Galloway, David, St. Louis | 1 | 17 | 17.0 | 17 | 0 |
| Kelley, Brian, New York Giants | 1 | 17 | 17.0 | 17 | 0 |
| Pillers, Lawrence, San Francisco | 1 | 16 | 16.0 | 16 | 0 |
| Olkewicz, Neal, Washington | 1 | 14 | 14.0 | 14 | 0 |
| Jones, Ed, Dallas | 1 | 12 | 12.0 | 12 | 0 |
| Scott, Randy, Green Bay | 1 | 12 | 12.0 | 12 | 0 |
| Grooms, Elois, St. Louis | 1 | 10 | 10.0 | 10 | 0 |
| Dickerson, Anthony, Dallas | 1 | 8 | 8.0 | 8 | 0 |
| Nelson, Lee, St. Louis | 1 | 8 | 8.0 | 8 | 0 |
| Warren, Frank, New Orleans | 1 | 6 | 6.0 | 6 | 0 |
| Wilson, Otis, Chicago | 1 | 6 | 6.0 | 6 | 0 |
| Carpenter, Brian, Washington | 1 | 2 | 2.0 | 2 | 0 |
| Johnson, Charlie, Minnesota | 1 | 2 | 2.0 | 2 | 0 |
| Ekern, Carl, Los Angeles Rams | 1 | 1 | 1.0 | 1 | 0 |
| Manley, Dexter, Washington | 1 | 1 | 1.0 | 1 | 0 |
| Blair, Matt, Minnesota | 1 | 0 | 0.0 | 0 | 0 |
| Brantley, Scot, Tampa Bay | 1 | 0 | 0.0 | 0 | 0 |
| Breunig, Bob, Dallas | 1 | 0 | 0.0 | 0 | 0 |
| Dennis, Mike, New York Giants | 1 | 0 | 0.0 | 0 | 0 |
| Edwards, Herman, Philadelphia | 1 | 0 | 0.0 | 0 | 0 |
| Foules, Elbert, Philadelphia | 1 | 0 | 0.0 | 0 | 0 |
| Jackson, Rickey, New Orleans | 1 | 0 | 0.0 | 0 | 0 |
| Jolly, Mike, Green Bay | 1 | 0 | 0.0 | 0 | 0 |

| | No. | Yards | Avg. | Long | TD |
|---|---|---|---|---|---|
| Latimer, Al, Detroit | 1 | 0 | 0.0 | 0 | 0 |
| Logan, Randy, Philadelphia | 1 | 0 | 0.0 | 0 | 0 |
| Nord, Keith, Minnesota | 1 | 0 | 0.0 | 0 | 0 |
| Singletary, Mike, Chicago | 1 | 0 | 0.0 | 0 | 0 |
| Young, Roynell, Philadelphia | 1 | 0 | 0.0 | 0 | 0 |

*t indicates touchdown.*
*Leader based on most interceptions.*

## PUNTING

**INDIVIDUAL CHAMPIONS (AVERAGE)**
AFC: 45.3 — Rohn Stark, Baltimore (91 punts, 4,124 yards)
NFC: 42.2 — Frank Garcia, Tampa Bay (95 punts, 4,008 yards)
**NET AVERAGE**
AFC: 37.1 — Rich Camarillo, New England (81 punts, 3,003 net yards)
NFC: 36.5 — Greg Coleman, Minnesota (91 punts, 3,323 net yards)
**LONGEST**
AFC: 70 — Rich Camarillo, New England vs. New Orleans, December 4
NFC: 70 — Bucky Scribner, Green Bay vs. Cincinnati, October 30
**MOST PUNTS**
NFC: 95 — Frank Garcia, Tampa Bay
AFC: 93 — Jim Arnold, Kansas City
**MOST PUNTS, GAME**
NFC: 11 — Max Runager, Philadelphia vs. N.Y. Giants, November 20
AFC: 10 — John James, Houston vs. Cleveland, October 30
10 — Luke Prestridge, Denver vs. Baltimore, September 11
10 — Rohn Stark, Baltimore vs. Denver, September 11
**TEAM CHAMPIONS (AVERAGE)**
AFC: 45.3 — Baltimore
NFC: 41.8 — Tampa Bay

### AFC PUNTING — TEAM

| | Total Punts | Gross Yards | Long | Gross Avg. | TB | Blk. | Opp. Ret. | Ret. Yards | In 20 | Net Avg. |
|---|---|---|---|---|---|---|---|---|---|---|
| Baltimore | 91 | 4124 | 68 | 45.3 | 9 | 0 | 55 | 642 | 20 | 36.3 |
| New England | 81 | 3615 | 70 | 44.6 | 11 | 0 | 48 | 392 | 25 | 37.1 |
| San Diego | 63 | 2763 | 60 | 43.9 | 8 | 0 | 35 | 299 | 13 | 36.6 |
| Los Angeles Raiders | 78 | 3336 | 67 | 42.8 | 10 | 0 | 35 | 334 | 17 | 35.9 |
| Miami | 75 | 3189 | 64 | 42.5 | 11 | 1 | 32 | 229 | 26 | 36.5 |
| Pittsburgh | 80 | 3352 | 58 | 41.9 | 7 | 0 | 44 | 418 | 20 | 34.9 |
| Denver | 87 | 3620 | 60 | 41.6 | 7 | 0 | 55 | 524 | 19 | 34.0 |
| Cleveland | 70 | 2854 | 60 | 40.8 | 8 | 0 | 30 | 309 | 17 | 34.1 |
| Cincinnati | 69 | 2804 | 60 | 40.6 | 9 | 2 | 41 | 310 | 13 | 33.5 |
| Kansas City | 93 | 3710 | 64 | 39.9 | 6 | 0 | 54 | 559 | 21 | 32.6 |
| Buffalo | 89 | 3533 | 60 | 39.7 | 7 | 0 | 42 | 403 | 24 | 33.6 |
| Seattle | 79 | 3118 | 56 | 39.5 | 10 | 0 | 36 | 185 | 25 | 34.6 |
| New York Jets | 82 | 3218 | 56 | 39.2 | 5 | 1 | 47 | 367 | 17 | 33.5 |
| Houston | 80 | 3136 | 53 | 39.2 | 8 | 1 | 47 | 354 | 12 | 32.8 |
| AFC Total | 1117 | 46372 | 70 | — | 116 | 5 | 601 | 5325 | 269 | — |
| AFC Average | 79.8 | 3312.3 | — | 41.5 | 8.3 | 0.4 | 42.9 | 380.4 | 19.2 | 34.7 |

### NFC PUNTING — TEAM

| | Total Punts | Gross Yards | Long | Gross Avg. | TB | Blk. | Opp. Ret. | Ret. Yards | In 20 | Net Avg. |
|---|---|---|---|---|---|---|---|---|---|---|
| Tampa Bay | 96 | 4008 | 64 | 41.8 | 12 | 1 | 59 | 603 | 16 | 33.0 |
| Minnesota | 91 | 3780 | 65 | 41.5 | 8 | 0 | 40 | 297 | 28 | 36.5 |
| St. Louis | 85 | 3529 | 59 | 41.5 | 7 | 0 | 47 | 307 | 14 | 36.3 |
| Green Bay | 70 | 2869 | 70 | 41.0 | 7 | 1 | 43 | 384 | 11 | 33.5 |
| Philadelphia | 86 | 3521 | 55 | 40.9 | 7 | 0 | 57 | 511 | 17 | 33.4 |
| New Orleans | 78 | 3178 | 60 | 40.7 | 10 | 0 | 51 | 573 | 10 | 30.8 |
| Detroit | 72 | 2911 | 60 | 40.4 | 9 | 1 | 39 | 302 | 17 | 33.7 |
| New York Giants | 85 | 3386 | 66 | 39.8 | 5 | 1 | 47 | 283 | 29 | 35.3 |
| Los Angeles Rams | 83 | 3301 | 67 | 39.8 | 12 | 1 | 39 | 251 | 18 | 33.9 |
| Atlanta | 71 | 2823 | 57 | 39.8 | 8 | 1 | 34 | 179 | 18 | 35.0 |
| Dallas | 83 | 3272 | 54 | 39.4 | 4 | 1 | 53 | 588 | 14 | 31.4 |
| Washington | 72 | 2796 | 56 | 38.8 | 2 | 0 | 41 | 407 | 29 | 32.6 |
| San Francisco | 66 | 2552 | 61 | 38.7 | 6 | 1 | 38 | 278 | 16 | 32.6 |
| Chicago | 94 | 3399 | 54 | 36.2 | 5 | 2 | 44 | 322 | 21 | 31.7 |
| NFC Total | 1132 | 45325 | 70 | — | 102 | 10 | 632 | 5285 | 258 | — |
| NFC Average | 80.9 | 3237.5 | — | 40.0 | 7.3 | 0.7 | 45.1 | 377.5 | 18.4 | 33.6 |
| League Total | 2249 | 91697 | 70 | — | 218 | 15 | 1233 | 10610 | 527 | — |
| League Average | 80.3 | 3274.9 | — | 40.8 | 7.8 | 0.5 | 44.0 | 378.9 | 18.8 | 34.1 |

## NFL TOP 10 PUNTERS

| | Net Punts | Gross Yards | Long | Gross Avg. | Total Punts | TB | Blk. | Opp. Ret. | Ret. Yds. | In 20 | Net Avg. |
|---|---|---|---|---|---|---|---|---|---|---|---|
| Stark, Rohn, Baltimore | 91 | 4124 | 68 | 45.3 | 91 | 9 | 0 | 55 | 642 | 20 | 36.3 |
| Camarillo, Rich, New England | 81 | 3615 | 70 | 44.6 | 81 | 11 | 0 | 48 | 392 | 25 | 37.1 |
| Buford, Maury, San Diego | 63 | 2763 | 60 | 43.9 | 63 | 8 | 0 | 35 | 299 | 13 | 36.6 |
| Roby, Reggie, Miami | 74 | 3189 | 64 | 43.1 | 75 | 11 | 1 | 32 | 229 | 26 | 36.5 |
| Guy, Ray, Los Angeles Raiders | 78 | 3336 | 67 | 42.8 | 78 | 10 | 0 | 35 | 334 | 17 | 35.9 |
| Garcia, Frank, Tampa Bay | 95 | 4008 | 64 | 42.2 | 96 | 12 | 1 | 59 | 603 | 16 | 33.0 |
| Colquitt, Craig, Pittsburgh | 80 | 3352 | 58 | 41.9 | 80 | 7 | 0 | 44 | 418 | 20 | 34.9 |
| McInally, Pat, Cincinnati | 67 | 2804 | 60 | 41.9 | 69 | 9 | 2 | 41 | 310 | 13 | 33.5 |
| Runager, Max, Philadelphia | 59 | 2459 | 55 | 41.7 | 59 | 5 | 0 | 37 | 339 | 12 | 34.2 |
| Prestridge, Luke, Denver | 87 | 3620 | 60 | 41.6 | 87 | 7 | 0 | 55 | 524 | 19 | 34.0 |
| Scribner, Bucky, Green Bay | 69 | 2869 | 70 | 41.6 | 70 | 7 | 1 | 43 | 384 | 11 | 33.5 |

## AFC PUNTING — INDIVIDUAL

| | Net Punts | Gross Yards | Long | Gross Avg. | Total Punts | TB | Blk. | Opp. Ret. | Ret. Yds. | In 20 | Net Avg. |
|---|---|---|---|---|---|---|---|---|---|---|---|
| Stark, Rohn, Baltimore | 91 | 4124 | 68 | 45.3 | 91 | 9 | 0 | 55 | 642 | 20 | 36.3 |
| Camarillo, Rich, New England | 81 | 3615 | 70 | 44.6 | 81 | 11 | 0 | 48 | 392 | 25 | 37.1 |
| Buford, Maury, San Diego | 63 | 2763 | 60 | 43.9 | 63 | 8 | 0 | 35 | 299 | 13 | 36.6 |
| Roby, Reggie, Miami | 74 | 3189 | 64 | 43.1 | 75 | 11 | 1 | 32 | 229 | 26 | 36.5 |
| Guy, Ray, Los Angeles Raiders | 78 | 3336 | 67 | 42.8 | 78 | 10 | 0 | 35 | 334 | 17 | 35.9 |
| Colquitt, Craig, Pittsburgh | 80 | 3352 | 58 | 41.9 | 80 | 7 | 0 | 44 | 418 | 20 | 34.9 |
| McInally, Pat, Cincinnati | 67 | 2804 | 60 | 41.9 | 69 | 9 | 2 | 41 | 310 | 13 | 33.5 |
| Prestridge, Luke, Denver | 87 | 3620 | 60 | 41.6 | 87 | 7 | 0 | 55 | 524 | 19 | 34.0 |
| Gossett, Jeff, Cleveland | 70 | 2854 | 60 | 40.8 | 70 | 8 | 0 | 30 | 309 | 17 | 34.1 |
| Arnold, Jim, Kansas City | 93 | 3710 | 64 | 39.9 | 93 | 6 | 0 | 54 | 559 | 21 | 32.6 |
| Ramsey, Chuck, New York Jets | 81 | 3218 | 56 | 39.7 | 82 | 5 | 1 | 47 | 367 | 17 | 33.5 |
| Cater, Greg, Buffalo | 89 | 3533 | 60 | 39.7 | 89 | 7 | 0 | 42 | 403 | 24 | 33.6 |
| James, John, Houston | 79 | 3136 | 53 | 39.7 | 80 | 8 | 1 | 47 | 354 | 12 | 32.8 |
| West, Jeff, Seattle | 79 | 3118 | 56 | 39.5 | 79 | 10 | 0 | 36 | 185 | 25 | 34.6 |

*Leader based on gross average, minimum 40 punts.*

## NFC PUNTING — INDIVIDUAL

| | Net Punts | Gross Yards | Long | Gross Avg. | Total Punts | TB | Blk. | Opp. Ret. | Ret. Yds. | In 20 | Net Avg. |
|---|---|---|---|---|---|---|---|---|---|---|---|
| Garcia, Frank, Tampa Bay | 95 | 4008 | 64 | 42.2 | 96 | 12 | 1 | 59 | 603 | 15 | 33.0 |
| Runager, Max, Philadelphia | 59 | 2459 | 55 | 41.7 | 59 | 5 | 0 | 37 | 339 | 12 | 34.2 |
| Scribner, Bucky, Green Bay | 69 | 2869 | 70 | 41.6 | 70 | 7 | 1 | 43 | 384 | 11 | 33.5 |
| Coleman, Greg, Minnesota | 91 | 3780 | 65 | 41.5 | 91 | 8 | 0 | 40 | 297 | 28 | 36.5 |
| Birdsong, Carl, St. Louis | 85 | 3529 | 59 | 41.5 | 85 | 7 | 0 | 47 | 307 | 14 | 36.3 |
| Black, Mike, Detroit | 71 | 2911 | 60 | 41.0 | 72 | 9 | 1 | 39 | 302 | 17 | 33.7 |
| Erxleben, Russell, New Orleans | 74 | 3034 | 60 | 41.0 | 74 | 9 | 0 | 49 | 571 | 10 | 30.9 |
| Giacomarro, Ralph, Atlanta | 70 | 2823 | 57 | 40.3 | 71 | 8 | 1 | 34 | 179 | 18 | 35.0 |
| Jennings, Dave, New York Giants | 84 | 3386 | 66 | 40.3 | 85 | 5 | 1 | 47 | 283 | 29 | 35.3 |
| Misko, John, Los Angeles Rams | 82 | 3301 | 67 | 40.3 | 83 | 12 | 1 | 39 | 251 | 18 | 33.9 |
| Orosz, Tom, San Francisco | 65 | 2552 | 61 | 39.3 | 66 | 6 | 1 | 38 | 278 | 16 | 32.6 |
| Hayes, Jeff, Washington | 72 | 2796 | 56 | 38.8 | 72 | 2 | 0 | 41 | 407 | 29 | 32.6 |
| Parsons, Bob, Chicago | 79 | 2916 | 54 | 36.9 | 79 | 5 | 0 | 37 | 261 | 21 | 32.3 |
| **Non-Qualifiers** | | | | | | | | | | | |
| Warren, John, Dallas | 39 | 1551 | 54 | 39.8 | 39 | 1 | 0 | 24 | 283 | 7 | 32.0 |
| White, Danny, Dallas | 38 | 1543 | 50 | 40.6 | 39 | 3 | 1 | 26 | 233 | 6 | 32.1 |
| Skladany, Tom, Philadelphia | 27 | 1062 | 51 | 39.3 | 27 | 2 | 0 | 20 | 172 | 5 | 31.5 |
| Stachowicz, Ray, Chicago | 12 | 447 | 48 | 37.3 | 14 | 0 | 2 | 7 | 61 | 0 | 27.6 |
| Miller, Jim, Dallas | 5 | 178 | 43 | 35.6 | 5 | 0 | 0 | 3 | 72 | 1 | 21.2 |
| Merkens, Guido, New Orleans | 4 | 144 | 45 | 36.0 | 4 | 1 | 0 | 2 | 2 | 0 | 30.5 |
| McMahon, Jim, Chicago | 1 | 36 | 36 | 36.0 | 1 | 0 | 0 | 0 | 0 | 0 | 36.0 |

*Leader based on gross average, minimum 40 punts.*

## PUNT RETURNS

**INDIVIDUAL CHAMPIONS (AVERAGE)**
**NFC:** 13.6—Henry Ellard, Los Angeles Rams (16 returns, 217 yards)
**AFC:** 12.5—Kirk Springs, New York Jets (23 returns, 287 yards)
**YARDAGE**
**AFC:** 666—Greg Pruitt, Los Angeles Raiders (58 returns)
**NFC:** 489—Billy Johnson, Atlanta (46 returns)
**RETURNS**
**AFC:** 58—Greg Pruitt, Los Angeles Raiders (666 yards)
**NFC:** 46—Billy Johnson, Atlanta (489 yards)
**FAIR CATCHES**
**AFC:** 18—Greg Pruitt, Los Angeles Raiders
**NFC:** 15—Jeff Groth, New Orleans
**LONGEST**
**AFC:** 97—Greg Pruitt, Los Angeles Raiders vs. Washington, October 2 (TD)
**NFC:** 90—Phillip Epps, Green Bay vs. Tampa Bay, October 2 (TD)
**TOUCHDOWNS**
**AFC:** Mark Clayton, Miami vs. Baltimore, November 20 (60 yards)
Paul Johns, Seattle vs. Los Angeles Raiders, October 16 (75 yards)
Greg Pruitt, Los Angeles Raiders vs. Washington, October 2 (97 yards)
Kirk Springs, New York Jets vs. New Orleans, November 21 (76 yards)
Zack Thomas, Denver vs. Los Angeles Raiders, September 25 (70 yards)
**NFC:** Gary Allen, Dallas vs. Kansas City, November 20 (68 yards)
Henry Ellard, Los Angeles Rams vs. New Orleans, December 18 (72 yards)
Phillip Epps, Green Bay vs. Tampa Bay, October 2 (90 yards)
Billy Johnson, Atlanta vs. New York Jets, October 23 (71 yards)
Robbie Martin, Detroit vs. Pittsburgh, November 24 (81 yards)
Dennis McKinnon, Chicago vs. Green Bay, December 4 (59 yards)
Dana McLemore, San Francisco vs. Dallas, December 19 (56 yards)
**MOST YARDS, GAME**
**NFC:** 140—Robbie Martin, Detroit vs. Pittsburgh, November 24 (6 returns)
**AFC:** 128—Kirk Springs, New York Jets vs. New Orleans, November 21 (3 returns)
**MOST RETURNS, GAME**
**NFC:** 9—Pete Shaw, Giants vs. Philadelphia, November 20 (96 yards)
**AFC:** 8—Paul Skansi, Pittsburgh vs. Tampa Bay, October 30 (100 yards)
**TEAM CHAMPIONS (AVERAGE)**
**AFC:** 11.5—Los Angeles Raiders (58 returns, 666 yards)
**NFC:** 11.3—Detroit (46 returns, 522 yards)

## AFC PUNT RETURNS—TEAM

| | No. | FC | Yards | Avg. | Long | TD |
|---|---|---|---|---|---|---|
| Los Angeles Raiders | 58 | 18 | 666 | 11.5 | 97t | 1 |
| Denver | 38 | 10 | 420 | 11.1 | 70t | 1 |
| New York Jets | 38 | 15 | 420 | 11.1 | 76t | 1 |
| Seattle | 34 | 6 | 366 | 10.8 | 75t | 1 |
| Miami | 55 | 23 | 581 | 10.6 | 62 | 1 |
| New England | 44 | 14 | 399 | 9.1 | 55 | 0 |
| Cincinnati | 49 | 6 | 410 | 8.4 | 43 | 0 |
| Pittsburgh | 51 | 9 | 421 | 8.3 | 57 | 0 |
| Houston | 20 | 9 | 159 | 8.0 | 23 | 0 |
| Cleveland | 42 | 12 | 310 | 7.4 | 19 | 0 |
| Kansas City | 40 | 14 | 291 | 7.3 | 19 | 0 |
| Baltimore | 44 | 14 | 294 | 6.7 | 50 | 0 |
| San Diego | 33 | 10 | 213 | 6.5 | 30 | 0 |
| Buffalo | 44 | 5 | 241 | 5.5 | 24 | 0 |
| AFC Total | 590 | 165 | 5191 | — | 97t | 5 |
| AFC Average | 42.1 | 11.8 | 370.8 | 8.8 | — | 0.4 |

## NFC PUNT RETURNS—TEAM

| | No. | FC | Yards | Avg. | Long | TD |
|---|---|---|---|---|---|---|
| Detroit | 46 | 9 | 522 | 11.3 | 81t | 1 |
| Atlanta | 46 | 4 | 489 | 10.6 | 71t | 1 |
| San Francisco | 36 | 9 | 365 | 10.1 | 56t | 1 |
| Los Angeles Rams | 55 | 8 | 538 | 9.8 | 72t | 1 |
| Dallas | 51 | 6 | 461 | 9.0 | 68t | 1 |
| Minnesota | 24 | 15 | 210 | 8.8 | 34 | 0 |
| Green Bay | 41 | 13 | 329 | 8.0 | 90t | 1 |
| Chicago | 56 | 7 | 447 | 8.0 | 59t | 1 |
| St. Louis | 58 | 4 | 461 | 7.9 | 34 | 0 |
| Washington | 49 | 5 | 387 | 7.9 | 42 | 0 |
| Tampa Bay | 42 | 7 | 299 | 7.1 | 17 | 0 |
| New Orleans | 39 | 15 | 275 | 7.1 | 30 | 0 |
| New York Giants | 55 | 7 | 377 | 6.9 | 27 | 0 |
| Philadelphia | 45 | 10 | 259 | 5.8 | 23 | 0 |
| NFC Total | 643 | 119 | 5419 | — | 90t | 7 |
| NFC Average | 45.9 | 8.5 | 387.1 | 8.4 | — | 0.5 |
| League Total | 1233 | 284 | 10610 | — | 97t | 12 |
| League Average | 44.0 | 10.1 | 378.9 | 8.6 | — | 0.4 |

## NFL TOP 10 PUNT RETURNERS

| | No. | FC | Yards | Avg. | Long | TD |
|---|---|---|---|---|---|---|
| Ellard, Henry, Los Angeles Rams | 16 | 4 | 217 | 13.6 | 72t | 1 |
| Springs, Kirk, New York Jets | 23 | 4 | 287 | 12.5 | 76t | 1 |
| Pruitt, Greg, Los Angeles Raiders | 58 | 18 | 666 | 11.5 | 97t | 1 |
| Johns, Paul, Seattle | 28 | 5 | 316 | 11.3 | 75t | 1 |
| Thomas, Zack, Denver | 33 | 9 | 368 | 11.2 | 70t | 1 |
| McLemore, Dana, San Francisco | 31 | 6 | 331 | 10.7 | 56t | 1 |
| Johnson, Billy, Atlanta | 46 | 4 | 489 | 10.6 | 71t | 1 |
| Smith, Ricky, New England | 38 | 12 | 398 | 10.5 | 55 | 0 |
| Jenkins, Ken, Detroit | 23 | 1 | 230 | 10.0 | 43 | 0 |
| Martin, Mike, Cincinnati | 23 | 3 | 227 | 9.9 | 19 | 0 |

## AFC PUNT RETURNS—INDIVIDUAL

| | No. | FC | Yards | Avg. | Long | TD |
|---|---|---|---|---|---|---|
| Springs, Kirk, New York Jets | 23 | 4 | 287 | 12.5 | 76t | 1 |
| Pruitt, Greg, Los Angeles Raiders | 58 | 18 | 666 | 11.5 | 97t | 1 |
| Johns, Paul, Seattle | 28 | 5 | 316 | 11.3 | 75t | 1 |
| Thomas, Zack, Denver | 33 | 9 | 368 | 11.2 | 70t | 1 |
| Smith, Ricky, New England | 38 | 12 | 398 | 10.5 | 55 | 0 |
| Martin, Mike, Cincinnati | 23 | 3 | 227 | 9.9 | 19 | 0 |
| Clayton, Mark, Miami | 41 | 11 | 392 | 9.6 | 60t | 1 |
| Skansi, Paul, Pittsburgh | 43 | 9 | 363 | 8.4 | 57 | 0 |
| Smith, J.T., Kansas City | 26 | 5 | 210 | 8.1 | 19 | 0 |
| Roaches, Carl, Houston | 20 | 9 | 159 | 8.0 | 23 | 0 |
| Brooks, James, San Diego | 18 | 4 | 137 | 7.6 | 30 | 0 |
| Hall, Dino, Cleveland | 39 | 12 | 284 | 7.3 | 19 | 0 |
| Simmons, John, Cincinnati | 25 | 2 | 173 | 6.9 | 43 | 0 |
| Anderson, Larry, Baltimore | 20 | 4 | 138 | 6.9 | 20 | 0 |
| Riddick, Robb, Buffalo | 42 | 5 | 241 | 5.7 | 24 | 0 |
| **Non-Qualifiers** | | | | | | |
| Porter, Ricky, Baltimore | 14 | 5 | 104 | 7.4 | 50 | 0 |
| Hancock, Anthony, Kansas City | 14 | 9 | 81 | 5.8 | 18 | 0 |
| Harmon, Mike, New York Jets | 12 | 8 | 109 | 9.1 | 21 | 0 |
| Williams, Kendall, Baltimore | 9 | 4 | 43 | 4.8 | 13 | 0 |
| Walker, Fulton, Miami | 8 | 0 | 86 | 10.8 | 23 | 0 |
| Chandler, Wes, San Diego | 8 | 6 | 26 | 3.3 | 11 | 0 |
| Woods, Rick, Pittsburgh | 5 | 0 | 46 | 9.2 | 13 | 0 |
| Upchurch, Rick, Denver | 4 | 1 | 52 | 13.0 | 17 | 0 |
| Fortune, Hosea, San Diego | 4 | 0 | 16 | 4.0 | 9 | 0 |
| Weathers, Clarence, New England | 4 | 0 | 1 | 0.3 | 3 | 0 |
| Walker, Dwight, Cleveland | 3 | 0 | 26 | 8.7 | 13 | 0 |
| Johnson, Gregg, Seattle | 3 | 1 | 17 | 5.7 | 10 | 0 |
| Harris, Tim, Pittsburgh | 3 | 0 | 12 | 4.0 | 8 | 0 |
| Scales, Dwight, San Diego | 2 | 0 | 34 | 17.0 | 30 | 0 |
| Harris, John, Seattle | 2 | 0 | 27 | 13.5 | 14 | 0 |
| Mullen, Davlin, New York Jets | 2 | 3 | 13 | 6.5 | 9 | 0 |
| Kozlowski, Mike, Miami | 2 | 10 | 12 | 6.0 | 11 | 0 |
| Vigorito, Tom, Miami | 1 | 0 | 62 | 62.0 | 62 | 0 |
| Heflin, Vince, Miami | 1 | 0 | 19 | 19.0 | 19 | 0 |
| Schroy, Ken, New York Jets | 1 | 0 | 11 | 11.0 | 11 | 0 |
| Blackwood, Glenn, Miami | 1 | 2 | 10 | 10.0 | 10 | 0 |
| Horton, Ray, Cincinnati | 1 | 1 | 10 | 10.0 | 10 | 0 |
| Glasgow, Nesby, Baltimore | 1 | 1 | 9 | 9.0 | 9 | 0 |
| Easley, Ken, Seattle | 1 | 0 | 6 | 6.0 | 6 | 0 |
| Hurley, Bill, Buffalo | 1 | 0 | 0 | 0.0 | 0 | 0 |
| Laird, Bruce, San Diego | 1 | 0 | 0 | 0.0 | 0 | 0 |
| Lee, Keith, New England | 1 | 0 | 0 | 0.0 | 0 | 0 |
| Sanford, Rick, New England | 1 | 2 | 0 | 0.0 | 0 | 0 |
| Sowell, Robert, Miami | 1 | 0 | 0 | 0.0 | 0 | 0 |
| Williams, Van, Buffalo | 1 | 0 | 0 | 0.0 | 0 | 0 |
| Wright, Louis, Denver | 1 | 0 | 0 | 0.0 | 0 | 0 |

*t indicates touchdown*
*Leader based on average return, minimum 16 returns.*

## NFC PUNT RETURNS—INDIVIDUAL

| | No. | FC | Yards | Avg. | Long | TD |
|---|---|---|---|---|---|---|
| Ellard, Henry, Los Angeles Rams | 16 | 4 | 217 | 13.6 | 72t | 1 |
| McLemore, Dana, San Francisco | 31 | 6 | 331 | 10.7 | 56t | 1 |
| Johnson, Billy, Atlanta | 46 | 4 | 489 | 10.6 | 71t | 1 |
| Jenkins, Ken, Detroit | 23 | 1 | 230 | 10.0 | 43 | 0 |
| McKinnon, Dennis, Chicago | 34 | 3 | 316 | 9.3 | 59t | 1 |
| Epps, Phillip, Green Bay | 36 | 13 | 324 | 9.0 | 90t | 1 |
| Mitchell, Stump, St. Louis | 38 | 1 | 337 | 8.9 | 34 | 0 |
| Irvin, LeRoy, Los Angeles Rams | 25 | 3 | 212 | 8.5 | 20 | 0 |
| Shaw, Pete, New York Giants | 29 | 4 | 234 | 8.1 | 27 | 0 |
| Hill, Rod, Dallas | 30 | 2 | 232 | 7.7 | 37 | 0 |
| Tyler, Andre, Tampa Bay | 27 | 5 | 208 | 7.7 | 16 | 0 |
| Nelms, Mike, Washington | 38 | 0 | 289 | 7.6 | 35 | 0 |
| Bess, Rufus, Minnesota | 21 | 10 | 158 | 7.5 | 17 | 0 |
| Groth, Jeff, New Orleans | 39 | 15 | 275 | 7.1 | 30 | 0 |
| Bright, Leon, New York Giants | 17 | 0 | 117 | 6.9 | 20 | 0 |
| Sciarra, John, Philadelphia | 22 | 3 | 115 | 5.2 | 14 | 0 |
| **Non-Qualifiers** | | | | | | |
| Martin, Robbie, Detroit | 15 | 3 | 183 | 12.2 | 81t | 1 |
| Johnson, Johnnie, L.A. Rams | 14 | 1 | 109 | 7.8 | 26 | 0 |
| Young, Glen, Philadelphia | 14 | 3 | 93 | 6.6 | 23 | 0 |
| Bird, Steve, St. Louis | 14 | 2 | 76 | 5.4 | 16 | 0 |

| | No. | FC | Yards | Avg. | Long | TD |
|---|---|---|---|---|---|---|
| Fisher, Jeff, Chicago | 13 | 3 | 71 | 5.5 | 11 | 0 |
| Fellows, Ron, Dallas | 10 | 3 | 75 | 7.5 | 14 | 0 |
| Bell, Theo, Tampa Bay | 10 | 2 | 48 | 4.8 | 11 | 0 |
| Allen, Gary, Dallas | 9 | 1 | 153 | 17.0 | 68t | 1 |
| Gault, Willie, Chicago | 9 | 1 | 60 | 6.7 | 12 | 0 |
| Reece, Beasley, New York Giants | 9 | 2 | 26 | 2.9 | 7 | 0 |
| Hall, Alvin, Detroit | 8 | 4 | 109 | 13.6 | 66 | 0 |
| Hoover, Mel, Philadelphia | 7 | 4 | 44 | 6.3 | 13 | 0 |
| Seay, Virgil, Washington | 5 | 1 | 57 | 11.4 | 42 | 0 |
| Holt, John, Tampa Bay | 5 | 0 | 43 | 8.6 | 17 | 0 |
| Solomon, Freddie, San Francisco | 5 | 3 | 34 | 6.8 | 11 | 0 |
| Harrell, Willard, St. Louis | 5 | 1 | 31 | 6.2 | 11 | 0 |
| Green, Darrell, Washington | 4 | 0 | 29 | 7.3 | 18 | 0 |
| Lewis, Leo, Minnesota | 3 | 3 | 52 | 17.3 | 34 | 0 |
| Giaquinto, Nick, Washington | 2 | 4 | 12 | 6.0 | 12 | 0 |
| Gray, Johnnie, Green Bay | 2 | 0 | 9 | 4.5 | 5 | 0 |
| Ferrell, Earl, St. Louis | 1 | 0 | 17 | 17.0 | 17 | 0 |
| Foules, Elbert, Philadelphia | 1 | 0 | 7 | 7.0 | 7 | 0 |
| Donley, Doug, Dallas | 1 | 0 | 1 | 1.0 | 1 | 0 |
| Hood, Estus, Green Bay | 1 | 0 | 0 | 0.0 | 0 | 0 |
| Lewis, Cliff, Green Bay | 1 | 0 | 0 | 0.0 | 0 | 0 |
| Logan, Randy, Philadelphia | 1 | 0 | 0 | 0.0 | 0 | 0 |
| Newhouse, Robert, Dallas | 1 | 0 | 0 | 0.0 | 0 | 0 |
| Lee, Mark, Green Bay | 1 | 0 | −4 | −4.0 | −4 | 0 |
| Bell, Rick, Minnesota | 0 | 2 | 0 | — | 0 | 0 |
| Latimer, Al, Detroit | 0 | 1 | 0 | — | 0 | 0 |
| Pittman, Danny, New York Giants | 0 | 1 | 0 | — | 0 | 0 |

*t indicates touchdown*
*Leader based on average return, minimum 16 returns.*

## KICKOFF RETURNS

**INDIVIDUAL CHAMPIONS (AVERAGE)**
**AFC:** 26.7—Fulton Walker, Miami (36 returns, 962 yards)
**NFC:** 24.7—Darrin Nelson, Minnesota (18 returns, 445 yards)
**YARDAGE**
**AFC:** 1,171—Zachary Dixon, Baltimore-Seattle (51 returns)
**NFC:** 855—Ron Fellows, Dallas (43 returns)
**RETURNS**
**AFC:** 51—Zachary Dixon, Baltimore-Seattle (1,171 yards)
**NFC:** 43—Ron Fellows, Dallas (855 yards)
**LONGEST**
**AFC:** 97—Carl Roaches, Houston vs. Pittsburgh, September 18 (TD)
**NFC:** 66—Stump Mitchell, St. Louis vs. Dallas, September 11
**TOUCHDOWNS**
**AFC:** 1—Steve Brown, Houston vs. Cleveland, December 11 (93 yards)
Zachary Dixon, Seattle vs. St. Louis, November 13 (94 yards)
Carl Roaches, Houston vs. Pittsburgh, September 18 (97 yards)
**MOST YARDS, GAME**
**NFC:** 208—Harlan Huckleby, Green Bay vs. Washington, October 17 (8 returns)
**AFC:** 173—Zachary Dixon, Seattle vs. St. Louis, November 13 (5 returns)
**MOST RETURNS, GAME**
**NFC:** 8—Harlan Huckleby, Green Bay vs. Washington, October 17 (208 yards)
**AFC:** 7—James Brooks, San Diego vs. New York Giants, October 2 (123 yards)
Preston Brown, New York Jets vs. Pittsburgh, December 10 (134 yards)
**TEAM CHAMPIONS (AVERAGE)**
**AFC:** 23.1—Miami (47 returns, 1,085 yards)
**NFC:** 21.6—Minnesota (68 returns, 1,466 yards)

## AFC KICKOFF RETURNS — TEAM

| | No. | Yards | Avg. | Long | TD |
|---|---|---|---|---|---|
| Miami | 47 | 1085 | 23.1 | 78 | 0 |
| Seattle | 71 | 1575 | 22.2 | 94t | 1 |
| Buffalo | 64 | 1363 | 21.3 | 60 | 0 |
| New York Jets | 66 | 1375 | 20.8 | 64 | 0 |
| Cleveland | 63 | 1290 | 20.5 | 38 | 0 |
| Cincinnati | 54 | 1097 | 20.3 | 49 | 0 |
| New England | 57 | 1155 | 20.3 | 53 | 0 |
| Houston | 83 | 1676 | 20.2 | 97t | 2 |
| Baltimore | 62 | 1198 | 19.3 | 90 | 0 |
| Los Angeles Raiders | 61 | 1175 | 19.3 | 48 | 0 |
| Denver | 56 | 1077 | 19.2 | 42 | 0 |
| San Diego | 74 | 1377 | 18.6 | 41 | 0 |
| Pittsburgh | 59 | 1068 | 18.1 | 35 | 0 |
| Kansas City | 54 | 929 | 17.2 | 46 | 0 |
| AFC Total | 871 | 17440 | — | 97t | 3 |
| AFC Average | 62.2 | 1245.7 | 20.0 | — | 0.2 |

## NFC KICKOFF RETURNS—TEAM

| | No. | Yards | Avg. | Long | TD |
|---|---|---|---|---|---|
| Minnesota | 68 | 1466 | 21.6 | 50 | 0 |
| Washington | 63 | 1301 | 20.7 | 58 | 0 |
| New Orleans | 66 | 1339 | 20.3 | 61 | 0 |
| St. Louis | 72 | 1459 | 20.3 | 66 | 0 |

| | No. | Yards | Avg. | Long | TD |
|---|---|---|---|---|---|
| Detroit | 61 | 1191 | 19.5 | 51 | 0 |
| Tampa Bay | 68 | 1314 | 19.3 | 50 | 0 |
| Dallas | 71 | 1351 | 19.0 | 53 | 0 |
| Philadelphia | 62 | 1168 | 18.8 | 52 | 0 |
| Atlanta | 67 | 1258 | 18.8 | 35 | 0 |
| New York Giants | 71 | 1333 | 18.8 | 54 | 0 |
| San Francisco | 52 | 958 | 18.4 | 46 | 0 |
| Los Angeles Rams | 52 | 946 | 18.2 | 44 | 0 |
| Green Bay | 79 | 1339 | 16.9 | 57 | 0 |
| Chicago | 58 | 953 | 16.4 | 38 | 0 |
| NFC Total | 910 | 17376 | — | 66 | 0 |
| NFC Average | 65.0 | 1241.1 | 19.1 | — | 0.0 |
| League Total | 1781 | 34816 | — | 97t | 3 |
| League Average | 63.6 | 1243.4 | 19.5 | — | 0.1 |

## NFL TOP 10 KICKOFF RETURNERS

| | No. | Yards | Avg. | Long | TD |
|---|---|---|---|---|---|
| Walker, Fulton, Miami | 36 | 962 | 26.7 | 78 | 0 |
| Brown, Steve, Houston | 31 | 795 | 25.6 | 93t | 1 |
| Nelson, Darrin, Minnesota | 18 | 445 | 24.7 | 50 | 0 |
| Williams, Kendall, Baltimore | 20 | 490 | 24.5 | 90 | 0 |
| Morton, Michael, Tampa Bay | 30 | 689 | 23.0 | 50 | 0 |
| Dixon, Zachary, Baltimore-Seattle | 51 | 1171 | 23.0 | 94t | 1 |
| Nelms, Mike, Washington | 35 | 802 | 22.9 | 41 | 0 |
| Springs, Kirk, New York Jets | 16 | 364 | 22.8 | 64 | 0 |
| Bright, Leon, New York Giants | 21 | 475 | 22.6 | 36 | 0 |
| Williams, Van, Buffalo | 22 | 494 | 22.5 | 60 | 0 |

## AFC KICKOFF RETURNS—INDIVIDUAL

| | No. | Yards | Avg. | Long | TD |
|---|---|---|---|---|---|
| Walker, Fulton, Miami | 36 | 962 | 26.7 | 78 | 0 |
| Brown, Steve, Houston | 31 | 795 | 25.6 | 93t | 1 |
| Williams, Kendall, Baltimore | 20 | 490 | 24.5 | 90 | 0 |
| Dixon, Zachary, Baltimore-Seattle | 51 | 1171 | 23.0 | 94t | 1 |
| Springs, Kirk, New York Jets | 16 | 364 | 22.8 | 64 | 0 |
| Williams, Van, Buffalo | 22 | 494 | 22.5 | 60 | 0 |
| Brown, Preston, New York Jets | 29 | 645 | 22.2 | 46 | 0 |
| Montgomery, Cleotha, L.A. Raiders | 21 | 464 | 22.1 | 48 | 0 |
| Smith, Ricky, New England | 42 | 916 | 21.8 | 53 | 0 |
| Walker, Dwight, Cleveland | 29 | 627 | 21.6 | 38 | 0 |
| Green, Boyce, Cleveland | 17 | 350 | 20.6 | 30 | 0 |
| Thomas, Zack, Denver | 28 | 573 | 20.5 | 42 | 0 |
| Riddick, Robb, Buffalo | 28 | 568 | 20.3 | 49 | 0 |
| Wilson, Steve, Denver | 24 | 485 | 20.2 | 32 | 0 |
| Pruitt, Greg, Los Angeles Raiders | 31 | 604 | 19.5 | 42 | 0 |
| Odom, Henry, Pittsburgh | 39 | 756 | 19.4 | 35 | 0 |
| Brooks, James, San Diego | 32 | 607 | 19.0 | 34 | 0 |
| Porter, Ricky, Baltimore | 18 | 340 | 18.9 | 28 | 0 |
| Roaches, Carl, Houston | 34 | 641 | 18.9 | 97t | 1 |
| Hancock, Anthony, Kansas City | 29 | 515 | 17.8 | 33 | 0 |
| Anderson, Larry, Baltimore | 18 | 309 | 17.2 | 26 | 0 |
| Harris, Tim, Pittsburgh | 18 | 289 | 16.1 | 32 | 0 |
| **Non-Qualifiers** | | | | | |
| Laird, Bruce, San Diego | 15 | 342 | 22.8 | 41 | 0 |
| Brown, Theotis, Kansas City | 15 | 301 | 20.1 | 46 | 0 |
| Simmons, John, Cincinnati | 14 | 317 | 22.6 | 36 | 0 |
| Hector, Johnny, New York Jets | 14 | 274 | 19.6 | 45 | 0 |
| Verser, David, Cincinnati | 13 | 253 | 19.5 | 29 | 0 |
| Tate, Rodney, Cincinnati | 13 | 218 | 16.8 | 23 | 0 |
| Hughes, David, Seattle | 12 | 282 | 23.5 | 35 | 0 |
| Hall, Dino, Cleveland | 11 | 237 | 21.5 | 28 | 0 |
| Jackson, Ernest, San Diego | 11 | 201 | 18.3 | 32 | 0 |
| Mosley, Mike, Buffalo | 9 | 236 | 26.2 | 33 | 0 |
| Walls, Herkie, Houston | 9 | 110 | 12.2 | 25 | 0 |
| Wilson, Stanley, Cincinnati | 7 | 161 | 23.0 | 32 | 0 |
| Horton, Ray, Cincinnati | 5 | 128 | 25.6 | 49 | 0 |
| Williams, Dokie, L.A. Raiders | 5 | 88 | 17.6 | 19 | 0 |
| McPherson, Miles, San Diego | 5 | 77 | 15.4 | 19 | 0 |
| Jones, Cedric, New England | 4 | 63 | 15.8 | 23 | 0 |
| Lane, Eric, Seattle | 4 | 58 | 14.5 | 18 | 0 |
| Kozlowski, Mike, Miami | 4 | 50 | 12.5 | 23 | 0 |
| Dressel, Chris, Houston | 4 | 40 | 10.0 | 13 | 0 |
| Lee, Keith, New England | 4 | 40 | 10.0 | 19 | 0 |
| Weathers, Robert, New England | 3 | 68 | 22.7 | 29 | 0 |
| McAlister, Ken, Seattle | 3 | 59 | 19.7 | 22 | 0 |
| Weathers, Clarence, New England | 3 | 58 | 19.3 | 33 | 0 |
| Mullen, Davlin, New York Jets | 3 | 57 | 19.0 | 26 | 0 |
| Williams, Ben, Buffalo | 3 | 56 | 18.7 | 23 | 0 |
| Jodat, Jim, San Diego | 3 | 45 | 15.0 | 18 | 0 |
| Young, Andre, San Diego | 3 | 41 | 13.7 | 19 | 0 |
| Roquemore, Durwood, Kansas City | 3 | 36 | 12.0 | 13 | 0 |
| Nathan, Tony, Miami | 3 | 15 | 5.0 | 12 | 0 |
| Cherry, Deron, Kansas City | 2 | 54 | 27.0 | 31 | 0 |
| Moore, Alvin, Baltimore | 2 | 40 | 20.0 | 23 | 0 |
| Ferguson, Vagas, Cleveland | 2 | 36 | 18.0 | 27 | 0 |
| Smith, Sherman, San Diego | 2 | 32 | 16.0 | 21 | 0 |

| | No. | Yards | Avg. | Long | TD |
|---|---|---|---|---|---|
| Nicolas, Scott, Cleveland | 2 | 29 | 14.5 | 15 | 0 |
| Tice, Mike, Seattle | 2 | 28 | 14.0 | 19 | 0 |
| Moriarty, Larry, Houston | 2 | 25 | 12.5 | 16 | 0 |
| Millen, Matt, Los Angeles Raiders | 2 | 19 | 9.5 | 10 | 0 |
| Talley, Darryl, Buffalo | 2 | 9 | 4.5 | 5 | 0 |
| Studdard, Dave, Denver | 2 | 8 | 4.0 | 8 | 0 |
| Heflin, Vince, Miami | 1 | 27 | 27.0 | 27 | 0 |
| Clayton, Mark, Miami | 1 | 25 | 25.0 | 25 | 0 |
| Martin, Mike, Cincinnati | 1 | 19 | 19.0 | 19 | 0 |
| Harper, Bruce, New York Jets | 1 | 16 | 16.0 | 16 | 0 |
| Scales, Dwight, San Diego | 1 | 16 | 16.0 | 16 | 0 |
| Tullis, Willie, Houston | 1 | 16 | 16.0 | 16 | 0 |
| Bingham, Craig, Pittsburgh | 1 | 15 | 15.0 | 15 | 0 |
| Carson, Carlos, Kansas City | 1 | 12 | 12.0 | 12 | 0 |
| Hunt, Daryl, Houston | 1 | 12 | 12.0 | 12 | 0 |
| McCloskey, Mike, Houston | 1 | 11 | 11.0 | 11 | 0 |
| Golden, Tim, New England | 1 | 10 | 10.0 | 10 | 0 |
| Smith, Billy Ray, San Diego | 1 | 10 | 10.0 | 10 | 0 |
| Barber, Marion, New York Jets | 1 | 9 | 9.0 | 9 | 0 |
| Harden, Mike, Denver | 1 | 9 | 9.0 | 9 | 0 |
| Davis, Johnny, Cleveland | 1 | 8 | 8.0 | 8 | 0 |
| McElroy, Reggie, New York Jets | 1 | 7 | 7.0 | 7 | 0 |
| Bennett, Woody, Miami | 1 | 6 | 6.0 | 6 | 0 |
| Kohrs, Bob, Pittsburgh | 1 | 6 | 6.0 | 6 | 0 |
| Sievers, Eric, San Diego | 1 | 6 | 6.0 | 6 | 0 |
| Thomas, Ken, Kansas City | 1 | 6 | 6.0 | 6 | 0 |
| Smith, J.T., Kansas City | 1 | 5 | 5.0 | 5 | 0 |
| Contz, Bill, Cleveland | 1 | 3 | 3.0 | 3 | 0 |
| Shuler, Mickey, New York Jets | 1 | 3 | 3.0 | 3 | 0 |
| Jackson, Tom, Denver | 1 | 2 | 2.0 | 2 | 0 |
| Dinkel, Tom, Cincinnati | 1 | 1 | 1.0 | 1 | 0 |
| Beach, Pat, Baltimore | 1 | 0 | 0.0 | 0 | 0 |
| Brown, Mark, Miami | 1 | 0 | 0.0 | 0 | 0 |
| Daniels, Calvin, Kansas City | 1 | 0 | 0.0 | 0 | 0 |
| Jensen, Derrick, L.A. Raiders | 1 | 0 | 0.0 | 0 | 0 |
| Lindstrom, Dave, Kansas City | 1 | 0 | 0.0 | 0 | 0 |
| Martin, Rod, Los Angeles Raiders | 1 | 0 | 0.0 | 0 | 0 |
| Metzelaars, Pete, Seattle | 1 | 0 | 0.0 | 0 | 0 |
| Bouza, Matt, Baltimore | 1 | −4 | −4.0 | −4 | 0 |
| Riley, Avon, Houston | 0 | 26 | — | 26 | 0 |
| Donnalley, Rick, Pittsburgh | 0 | 2 | — | 2 | 0 |
| Burruss, Lloyd, Kansas City | 0 | 0 | — | 0 | 0 |

*FAIR CATCHES: Burruss, Kansas City and Jones, New England*
*t indicates touchdown*
*Leader based on average return, minimum 16 returns.*

## NFC KICKOFF RETURNS—INDIVIDUAL

| | No. | Yards | Avg. | Long | TD |
|---|---|---|---|---|---|
| Nelson, Darrin, Minnesota | 18 | 445 | 24.7 | 50 | 0 |
| Morton, Michael, Tampa Bay | 30 | 689 | 23.0 | 50 | 0 |
| Nelms, Mike, Washington | 35 | 802 | 22.9 | 41 | 0 |
| Bright, Leon, New York Giants | 21 | 475 | 22.6 | 36 | 0 |
| Redwine, Jarvis, Minnesota | 38 | 838 | 22.1 | 41 | 0 |
| Duckett, Kenny, New Orleans | 33 | 719 | 21.8 | 61 | 0 |
| Mitchell, Stump, St. Louis | 36 | 778 | 21.6 | 66 | 0 |
| Hall, Alvin, Detroit | 23 | 492 | 21.4 | 32 | 0 |
| Young, Glen, Philadelphia | 26 | 547 | 21.0 | 52 | 0 |
| Jenkins, Ken, Detroit | 22 | 459 | 20.9 | 30 | 0 |
| Williams, Richard, Atlanta | 23 | 461 | 20.0 | 34 | 0 |
| Fellows, Ron, Dallas | 43 | 855 | 19.9 | 53 | 0 |
| Riggs, Gerald, Atlanta | 17 | 330 | 19.4 | 35 | 0 |
| McLemore, Dana, San Francisco | 30 | 576 | 19.2 | 39 | 0 |
| Owens, James, Tampa Bay | 20 | 380 | 19.0 | 31 | 0 |
| Redden, Barry, Los Angeles Rams | 19 | 358 | 18.8 | 43 | 0 |
| Huckleby, Harlan, Green Bay | 41 | 757 | 18.5 | 57 | 0 |
| Lewis, Tim, Green Bay | 20 | 358 | 17.9 | 30 | 0 |
| Hutchison, Anthony, Chicago | 17 | 259 | 15.2 | 28 | 0 |
| **Non-Qualifiers** | | | | | |
| Ellard, Henry, Los Angeles Rams | 15 | 314 | 20.9 | 44 | 0 |
| Everett, Major, Philadelphia | 14 | 275 | 19.6 | 46 | 0 |
| Morris, Joe, New York Giants | 14 | 255 | 18.2 | 26 | 0 |
| Hill, Rod, Dallas | 14 | 243 | 17.4 | 40 | 0 |
| Gault, Willie, Chicago | 13 | 276 | 21.2 | 38 | 0 |
| Ferrell, Earl, St. Louis | 13 | 257 | 19.8 | 28 | 0 |
| Alexander, Robert, L.A. Rams | 13 | 222 | 17.1 | 30 | 0 |
| Johnson, Kenny, Atlanta | 11 | 224 | 20.4 | 28 | 0 |
| Cain, Lynn, Atlanta | 11 | 200 | 18.2 | 24 | 0 |
| Gray, Johnnie, Green Bay | 11 | 178 | 16.2 | 26 | 0 |
| Evans, Reggie, Washington | 10 | 141 | 14.1 | 28 | 0 |
| Wilson, Wayne, New Orleans | 9 | 239 | 26.6 | 52 | 0 |
| Seay, Virgil, Washington | 9 | 218 | 24.2 | 50 | 0 |
| Bird, Steve, St. Louis | 9 | 194 | 21.6 | 33 | 0 |
| Tuggle, John, New York Giants | 9 | 156 | 17.3 | 28 | 0 |
| Campfield, Billy, New York Giants | 9 | 154 | 17.1 | 23 | 0 |
| Allen, Gary, Dallas | 8 | 178 | 22.3 | 31 | 0 |
| Monroe, Carl, San Francisco | 8 | 152 | 19.0 | 32 | 0 |
| Mauti, Rich, New Orleans | 8 | 147 | 18.4 | 35 | 0 |
| Martin, Robbie, Detroit | 8 | 140 | 17.5 | 51 | 0 |

| | No. | Yards | Avg. | Long | TD |
|---|---|---|---|---|---|
| Smith, Johnny Ray, Tampa Bay | 8 | 136 | 17.0 | 43 | 0 |
| Gentry, Dennis, Chicago | 7 | 130 | 18.6 | 28 | 0 |
| Ellis, Ray, Philadelphia | 7 | 119 | 17.0 | 25 | 0 |
| Moore, Jeff, San Francisco | 7 | 117 | 16.7 | 46 | 0 |
| Austin, Cliff, New Orleans | 7 | 112 | 16.0 | 27 | 0 |
| Rogers, Jimmy, New Orleans | 7 | 103 | 14.7 | 25 | 0 |
| Pittman, Danny, New York Giants | 6 | 107 | 17.8 | 24 | 0 |
| Watts, Rickey, Chicago | 5 | 79 | 15.8 | 21 | 0 |
| Heater, Larry, New York Giants | 5 | 71 | 14.2 | 26 | 0 |
| Harrington, Perry, Philadelphia | 4 | 79 | 19.8 | 26 | 0 |
| Caver, Jim, Detroit | 4 | 71 | 17.8 | 33 | 0 |
| Ring, Bill, San Francisco | 4 | 68 | 17.0 | 18 | 0 |
| Schmitt, George, St. Louis | 4 | 41 | 10.3 | 19 | 0 |
| Love, Randy, St. Louis | 3 | 71 | 23.7 | 23 | 0 |
| Duerson, Dave, Chicago | 3 | 66 | 22.0 | 24 | 0 |
| Harrell, Willard, St. Louis | 3 | 62 | 20.7 | 26 | 0 |
| Williams, Mike, Philadelphia | 3 | 59 | 19.7 | 25 | 0 |
| Haddix, Michael, Philadelphia | 3 | 51 | 17.0 | 24 | 0 |
| Cooper, Earl, San Francisco | 3 | 45 | 15.0 | 20 | 0 |
| Baschnagel, Brian, Chicago | 3 | 42 | 14.0 | 19 | 0 |
| Huffman, Dave, Minnesota | 3 | 42 | 14.0 | 15 | 0 |
| Spradlin, Danny, Tampa Bay | 3 | 35 | 11.7 | 24 | 0 |
| Winters, Chet, Green Bay | 3 | 28 | 9.3 | 12 | 0 |
| Young, Rickey, Minnesota | 3 | 27 | 9.0 | 15 | 0 |
| Garrett, Alvin, Washington | 2 | 50 | 25.0 | 28 | 0 |
| Bess, Rufus, Minnesota | 2 | 44 | 22.0 | 30 | 0 |
| McKinnon, Dennis, Chicago | 2 | 42 | 21.0 | 25 | 0 |
| Wonsley, Otis, Washington | 2 | 36 | 18.0 | 20 | 0 |
| Jones, Mike, Minnesota | 2 | 31 | 15.5 | 16 | 0 |
| Miller, Mike, New York Giants | 2 | 31 | 15.5 | 26 | 0 |
| Guman, Mike, Los Angeles Rams | 2 | 30 | 15.0 | 21 | 0 |
| O'Steen, Dwayne, Tampa Bay | 2 | 30 | 15.0 | 16 | 0 |
| Curran, Willie, Atlanta | 2 | 26 | 13.0 | 16 | 0 |
| Carver, Mel, Tampa Bay | 2 | 24 | 12.0 | 13 | 0 |
| Bell, Todd, Chicago | 2 | 18 | 9.0 | 18 | 0 |
| Cosbie, Doug, Dallas | 2 | 17 | 8.5 | 10 | 0 |
| Fitzsche, Jim, Philadelphia | 2 | 17 | 8.5 | 15 | 0 |
| Woolfolk, Butch, New York Giants | 2 | 13 | 6.5 | 11 | 0 |
| Cabral, Brian, Chicago | 2 | 11 | 5.5 | 6 | 0 |
| Rains, Dan, Chicago | 2 | 11 | 5.5 | 11 | 0 |
| Darby, Byron, Philadelphia | 2 | 3 | 1.5 | 3 | 0 |
| Glazebrook, Bob, Atlanta | 2 | 0 | 0.0 | 0 | 0 |
| Dennis, Mike, New York Giants | 1 | 54 | 54.0 | 54 | 0 |
| Newsome, Tim, Dallas | 1 | 28 | 28.0 | 28 | 0 |
| Lewis, Leo, Minnesota | 1 | 25 | 25.0 | 25 | 0 |
| Irvin, LeRoy, Los Angeles Rams | 1 | 22 | 22.0 | 22 | 0 |
| Smith, Leonard, St. Louis | 1 | 19 | 19.0 | 19 | 0 |
| Young, Roynell, Philadelphia | 1 | 18 | 18.0 | 18 | 0 |
| Butler, Bobby, Atlanta | 1 | 17 | 17.0 | 17 | 0 |
| Cronan, Pete, Washington | 1 | 17 | 17.0 | 17 | 0 |
| Ivery, Eddie Lee, Green Bay | 1 | 17 | 17.0 | 17 | 0 |
| McSwain, Chuck, Dallas | 1 | 17 | 17.0 | 17 | 0 |
| Richardson, Mike, Chicago | 1 | 17 | 17.0 | 17 | 0 |
| Washington, Joe, Washington | 1 | 16 | 16.0 | 16 | 0 |
| Brock, Stan, New Orleans | 1 | 15 | 15.0 | 15 | 0 |
| Sawyer, John, Washington | 1 | 15 | 15.0 | 15 | 0 |
| Bell, Rick, Minnesota | 1 | 14 | 14.0 | 14 | 0 |
| Green, Roy, St. Louis | 1 | 14 | 14.0 | 14 | 0 |
| Springs, Ron, Dallas | 1 | 13 | 13.0 | 13 | 0 |
| Duda, Mark, St. Louis | 1 | 12 | 12.0 | 12 | 0 |
| Allerman, Kurt, St. Louis | 1 | 11 | 11.0 | 11 | 0 |
| King, Horace, Detroit | 1 | 11 | 11.0 | 11 | 0 |
| Lee, Larry, Detroit | 1 | 11 | 11.0 | 11 | 0 |
| Armstrong, Adger, Tampa Bay | 1 | 10 | 10.0 | 10 | 0 |
| Middleton, Terdell, Tampa Bay | 1 | 10 | 10.0 | 10 | 0 |
| Mayock, Mike, New York Giants | 1 | 9 | 9.0 | 9 | 0 |
| McLaughlin, Joe, New York Giants | 1 | 8 | 8.0 | 8 | 0 |
| Curley, August, Detroit | 1 | 7 | 7.0 | 7 | 0 |
| Williams, Greg, Washington | 1 | 6 | 6.0 | 6 | 0 |
| Wattelet, Frank, New Orleans | 1 | 4 | 4.0 | 4 | 0 |
| Janata, John, Chicago | 1 | 2 | 2.0 | 2 | 0 |
| Drechsler, Dave, Green Bay | 1 | 1 | 1.0 | 1 | 0 |
| Barnett, Doug, Los Angeles Rams | 1 | 0 | 0.0 | 0 | 0 |
| Giaquinto, Nick, Washington | 1 | 0 | 0.0 | 0 | 0 |
| Huther, Bruce, Dallas | 1 | 0 | 0.0 | 0 | 0 |
| Kitson, Syd, Green Bay | 1 | 0 | 0.0 | 0 | 0 |
| Lee, Mark, Green Bay | 1 | 0 | 0.0 | 0 | 0 |
| Norris, Ulysses, Detroit | 1 | 0 | 0.0 | 0 | 0 |
| Obradovich, Jim, Tampa Bay | 1 | 0 | 0.0 | 0 | 0 |
| Simmons, Jeff, Los Angeles Rams | 1 | 0 | 0.0 | 0 | 0 |

FAIR CATCHES: Bates, Dallas and Giaquinto, Washington.
t indicates touchdown
Leader based on average return, minimum 16 returns.

## AFC FUMBLES — TEAM

| | Fum. | Own Rec. | Fum. *O.B. | TD | Opp. Rec. | Yds. | TD | Tot. Rec. |
|---|---|---|---|---|---|---|---|---|
| Cleveland | 21 | 10 | 1 | 0 | 10 | 20 | 0 | 20 |
| Buffalo | 24 | 11 | 1 | 0 | 17 | 125 | 1 | 28 |
| Houston | 26 | 7 | 1 | 0 | 15 | 4 | 0 | 22 |
| New York Jets | 29 | 10 | 0 | 0 | 14 | 27 | 1 | 24 |
| Miami | 30 | 11 | 3 | 0 | 17 | 9 | 0 | 28 |
| Kansas City | 31 | 10 | 2 | 0 | 21 | 114 | 1 | 31 |
| Baltimore | 32 | 15 | 6 | 0 | 16 | 93 | 2 | 31 |
| Denver | 34 | 12 | 3 | 0 | 20 | 78 | 1 | 32 |
| Cincinnati | 35 | 19 | 1 | 0 | 16 | 77 | 1 | 35 |
| Seattle | 36 | 16 | 0 | 0 | 28 | 112 | 2 | 44 |
| Pittsburgh | 42 | 20 | 2 | 0 | 17 | 181 | 3 | 37 |
| San Diego | 42 | 15 | 5 | 0 | 17 | 15 | 0 | 32 |
| Los Angeles Raiders | 46 | 17 | 4 | 1 | 16 | 71 | 1 | 33 |
| New England | 47 | 24 | 3 | 0 | 19 | 30 | 0 | 43 |
| AFC Totals | 475 | 197 | 32 | 1 | 243 | 956 | 13 | 440 |
| AFC Average | 33.9 | 14.1 | 2.3 | 0.1 | 17.4 | 68.3 | 0.9 | 31.4 |

## NFC FUMBLES — TEAM

| | Fum. | Own Rec. | Fum. *O.B. | TD | Opp. Rec. | Yds. | TD | Tot. Rec. |
|---|---|---|---|---|---|---|---|---|
| Washington | 13 | 5 | 1 | 1 | 26 | 59 | 2 | 31 |
| Chicago | 25 | 10 | 1 | 0 | 17 | 45 | 1 | 27 |
| San Francisco | 27 | 6 | 2 | 0 | 18 | 5 | 1 | 24 |
| Dallas | 30 | 14 | 2 | 1 | 21 | 19 | 2 | 35 |
| Minnesota | 33 | 21 | 2 | 0 | 23 | 112 | 1 | 44 |
| Atlanta | 36 | 12 | 5 | 0 | 15 | 132 | 2 | 27 |
| Green Bay | 37 | 16 | 3 | 0 | 12 | 72 | 2 | 28 |
| New Orleans | 37 | 15 | 0 | 2 | 16 | 4 | 0 | 31 |
| Philadelphia | 37 | 16 | 3 | 0 | 15 | 29 | 0 | 31 |
| Los Angeles Rams | 38 | 12 | 2 | 0 | 20 | 15 | 0 | 32 |
| New York Giants | 39 | 11 | 1 | 0 | 13 | 52 | 1 | 24 |
| Tampa Bay | 39 | 23 | 3 | 0 | 18 | 69 | 1 | 41 |
| Detroit | 41 | 21 | 4 | 0 | 15 | 17 | 0 | 36 |
| St. Louis | 50 | 18 | 5 | 0 | 20 | 122 | 3 | 38 |
| NFC Totals | 482 | 200 | 34 | 4 | 249 | 752 | 16 | 449 |
| NFC Average | 34.4 | 14.3 | 2.4 | 0.3 | 17.8 | 53.7 | 1.1 | 32.1 |
| League Totals | 957 | 397 | 66 | 5 | 492 | 1708 | 29 | 889 |
| League Average | 34.2 | 14.2 | 2.4 | 0.2 | 17.6 | 61.0 | 1.0 | 31.8 |

*Fumbled out of bounds.
Fumbled through the end zone, ball awarded to opponents: Baltimore (awarded to Buffalo), San Diego (awarded to Washington).

## AFC FUMBLES — INDIVIDUAL

| | Fum. | Own Rec. | Opp. Rec. | Yds. | Tot. Rec. |
|---|---|---|---|---|---|
| Abercrombie, Walter, Pittsburgh | 2 | 0 | 0 | 0 | 0 |
| Ackerman, Rick, San Diego | 0 | 0 | 2 | 0 | 2 |
| Adams, Julius, New England | 0 | 0 | 1 | 0 | 1 |
| Adams, Willis, Cleveland | 1 | 0 | 1 | 0 | 1 |
| Alexander, Charles, Cincinnati | 1 | 0 | 0 | 0 | 0 |
| Allen, Marcus, Los Angeles Raiders | 14 | 2 | 0 | 0 | 2 |
| Alzado, Lyle, Los Angeles Raiders | 0 | 0 | 1 | 0 | 1 |
| Ambrose, Dick, Cleveland | 0 | 0 | 1 | 0 | 1 |
| Anderson, Ken, Cincinnati | 4 | 1 | 0 | 0 | 1 |
| Anderson, Kim, Baltimore | 0 | 1 | 0 | 0 | 1 |
| Anderson, Larry, Baltimore | 1 | 1 | 2 | 41 | 3 |
| Banks, Chip, Cleveland | 0 | 0 | 1 | 0 | 1 |
| Barber, Marion, New York Jets | 0 | 1 | 1 | 0 | 2 |
| Barkum, Jerome, New York Jets | 2 | 0 | 0 | 0 | 0 |
| Baumhower, Bob, Miami | 0 | 0 | 1 | 0 | 1 |
| Beasley, Tom, Pittsburgh | 0 | 0 | 2 | 0 | 2 |
| Beckman, Ed, Kansas City | 1 | 0 | 0 | 0 | 0 |
| Bell, Mike, Kansas City | 0 | 0 | 1 | 0 | 1 |
| Bennett, Woody, Miami | 1 | 1 | 0 | 0 | 1 |
| Best, Greg, Pittsburgh | 0 | 0 | 1 | 94 | 1 |
| Betters, Doug, Miami | 0 | 0 | 4 | 0 | 4 |
| Bingham, Gregg, Houston | 0 | 0 | 2 | 0 | 2 |
| Bishop, Keith, Denver | 0 | 1 | 0 | 0 | 1 |
| Blackledge, Todd, Kansas City | 1 | 0 | 0 | 0 | 0 |
| Blackwood, Glenn, Miami | 0 | 0 | 4 | 0 | 4 |
| Blount, Mel, Pittsburgh | 0 | 0 | 1 | 3 | 1 |
| Bokamper, Kim, Miami | 1 | 0 | 1 | 0 | 1 |
| Boures, Emil, Pittsburgh | 1 | 0 | 0 | 0 | 0 |
| Bouza, Matt, Baltimore | 1 | 0 | 0 | 0 | 0 |
| Bowyer, Walt, Denver | 0 | 0 | 1 | 0 | 1 |
| Bradley, Carlos, San Diego | 0 | 0 | 1 | 0 | 1 |
| Brazile, Robert, Houston | 0 | 0 | 3 | 0 | 3 |
| Breech, Jim, Cincinnati | 1 | 0 | 0 | 0 | 0 |
| Breeden, Louis, Cincinnati | 0 | 0 | 1 | 0 | 1 |
| Brooks, James, San Diego | 8 | 3 | 0 | 0 | 3 |
| Brown, Dave, Seattle | 1 | 1 | 2 | 0 | 3 |
| Brown, Mark, Miami | 0 | 0 | 1 | 0 | 1 |
| Brown, Preston, New York Jets | 3 | 1 | 0 | 0 | 1 |
| Brown, Steve, Houston | 2 | 0 | 0 | 0 | 0 |
| Brown, Theotis, Seattle-Kansas City | 4 | 1 | 0 | 0 | 1 |
| Brudzinski, Bob, Miami | 0 | 0 | 1 | 0 | 1 |
| Bryant, Jeff, Seattle | 0 | 0 | 1 | 0 | 1 |

193

| Name | Fum. | Own Rec. | Opp. Rec. | Yds. | Tot. Rec. |
|---|---|---|---|---|---|
| Burrell, Clinton, Cleveland | 0 | 0 | 1 | 0 | 1 |
| Burroughs, Jim, Baltimore | 0 | 0 | 1 | 0 | 1 |
| Burruss, Lloyd, Kansas City | 0 | 0 | 2 | 26 | 2 |
| Butler, Jerry, Buffalo | 1 | 0 | 0 | 0 | 0 |
| Caldwell, Darryl, Buffalo | 0 | 0 | 1 | 0 | 1 |
| Caldwell, Tony, Los Angeles Raiders | 0 | 0 | 1 | 0 | 1 |
| Cameron, Glenn, Cincinnati | 0 | 0 | 1 | 1 | 1 |
| Campbell, Earl, Houston | 4 | 0 | 0 | 0 | 0 |
| Carson, Carlos, Kansas City | 2 | 0 | 0 | 0 | 0 |
| Carter, David, Houston | 1 | 0 | 0 | 0 | 0 |
| Carter, Rubin, Denver | 0 | 0 | 3 | 0 | 3 |
| Chandler, Wes, San Diego | 3 | 1 | 0 | 0 | 1 |
| Charles, Mike, Miami | 0 | 0 | 1 | 0 | 1 |
| Chavous, Barney, Denver | 0 | 0 | 1 | 0 | 1 |
| Cherry, Deron, Kansas City | 2 | 0 | 2 | 4 | 2 |
| Christensen, Todd, Los Angeles Raiders | 1 | 1 | 0 | 0 | 1 |
| Clayton, Mark, Miami | 3 | 1 | 0 | 0 | 1 |
| Cole, Robin, Pittsburgh | 0 | 0 | 2 | 20 | 2 |
| Collins, Anthony, New England | 10 | 2 | 0 | 0 | 2 |
| Collins, Glen, Cincinnati | 0 | 0 | 1 | 0 | 1 |
| Collinsworth, Cris, Cincinnati | 2 | 1 | 0 | 0 | 1 |
| Cooks, Johnie, Baltimore | 1 | 1 | 1 | 52 | 2 |
| Cousineau, Tom, Cleveland | 0 | 0 | 2 | 14 | 2 |
| Craft, Donald, Houston | 0 | 1 | 0 | 0 | 1 |
| Cribbs, Joe, Buffalo | 6 | 1 | 0 | 0 | 1 |
| Crosby, Ron, New York Jets | 0 | 0 | 1 | 0 | 1 |
| Cross, Justin, Buffalo | 0 | 0 | 1 | 0 | 1 |
| Crutchfield, Dwayne, Jets-Hou. | 2 | 0 | 0 | 0 | 0 |
| Cryder, Bob, New England | 0 | 2 | 1 | 0 | 3 |
| Cunningham, Bennie, Pittsburgh | 4 | 1 | 0 | 0 | 1 |
| Curtis, Isaac, Cincinnati | 1 | 0 | 0 | 0 | 0 |
| Dalby, Dave, Los Angeles Raiders | 0 | 1 | 0 | 0 | 1 |
| Daniels, Calvin, Kansas City | 0 | 0 | 1 | 0 | 1 |
| Davis, Bruce, Los Angeles Raiders | 0 | 1 | 0 | 0 | 1 |
| Davis, James, Los Angeles Raiders | 0 | 0 | 1 | 0 | 1 |
| Davis, Mike, Los Angeles Raiders | 0 | 0 | 2 | 0 | 2 |
| DeBerg, Steve, Denver | 5 | 0 | 0 | 0 | 0 |
| Delaney, Jeff, Baltimore | 0 | 0 | 1 | 0 | 1 |
| DeLeone, Tom, Cleveland | 1 | 0 | 0 | 0 | 0 |
| Dickey, Curtis, Baltimore | 9 | 1 | 0 | 0 | 1 |
| Dinkel, Tom, Cincinnati | 0 | 0 | 2 | 4 | 2 |
| Dixon, Zachary, Seattle | 1 | 1 | 0 | 0 | 1 |
| Donaldson, Ray, Baltimore | 1 | 0 | 0 | 0 | 0 |
| Doornink, Dan, Seattle | 1 | 1 | 0 | 0 | 1 |
| Dufek, Don, Seattle | 0 | 1 | 0 | 0 | 1 |
| Duhe, A.J., Miami | 0 | 0 | 1 | 0 | 1 |
| Easley, Ken, Seattle | 0 | 0 | 3 | 29 | 3 |
| Eason, Tony, New England | 5 | 1 | 0 | 0 | 1 |
| Edwards, Eddie, Cincinnati | 0 | 0 | 1 | 0 | 1 |
| Eliopulos, Jim, New York Jets | 0 | 0 | 1 | 0 | 1 |
| Elko, Bill, San Diego | 0 | 0 | 1 | 0 | 1 |
| Elway, John, Denver | 6 | 3 | 0 | 0 | 3 |
| Essink, Ron, Seattle | 0 | 1 | 0 | 0 | 1 |
| Feacher, Ricky, Cleveland | 1 | 0 | 0 | 0 | 0 |
| Ferguson, Joe, Buffalo | 3 | 3 | 0 | 0 | 3 |
| Ferguson, Keith, San Diego | 0 | 0 | 2 | 0 | 2 |
| Foley, Steve, Denver | 1 | 0 | 1 | 0 | 1 |
| Fortune, Hosea, San Diego | 1 | 1 | 0 | 0 | 1 |
| Fouts, Dan, San Diego | 5 | 1 | 1 | 0 | 2 |
| France, Doug, Houston | 0 | 1 | 0 | 0 | 1 |
| Franklin, Andra, Miami | 6 | 1 | 0 | 0 | 1 |
| Franks, Elvis, Cleveland | 0 | 0 | 1 | 0 | 1 |
| Freeman, Steve, Buffalo | 0 | 0 | 2 | 31 | 2 |
| Gaines, Greg, Seattle | 0 | 0 | 4 | 0 | 4 |
| Garrity, Gregg, Pittsburgh | 1 | 1 | 0 | 0 | 1 |
| Gary, Keith, Pittsburgh | 0 | 0 | 2 | 17 | 2 |
| Gastineau, Mark, New York Jets | 0 | 0 | 2 | 0 | 2 |
| Golden, Tim, New England | 0 | 1 | 1 | 0 | 2 |
| Gradishar, Randy, Denver | 0 | 0 | 3 | 1 | 3 |
| Green, Boyce, Cleveland | 4 | 0 | 0 | 0 | 0 |
| Green, Gary, Kansas City | 0 | 0 | 2 | 0 | 2 |
| Green, Jacob, Seattle | 0 | 0 | 2 | 0 | 2 |
| Greene, Ken, San Diego | 0 | 0 | 1 | 0 | 1 |
| Griffin, Ray, Cincinnati | 0 | 1 | 1 | 13 | 2 |
| Grogan, Steve, New England | 4 | 1 | 0 | 0 | 1 |
| Gross, Al, Cleveland | 0 | 0 | 1 | 4 | 1 |
| Hancock, Anthony, Kansas City | 2 | 0 | 0 | 0 | 0 |
| Hannah, John, New England | 0 | 3 | 0 | 0 | 3 |
| Harden, Mike, Denver | 0 | 1 | 2 | 0 | 3 |
| Harmon, Mike, New York Jets | 3 | 2 | 0 | 0 | 2 |
| Harper, Bruce, New York Jets | 1 | 0 | 0 | 0 | 0 |
| Harris, Franco, Pittsburgh | 10 | 0 | 0 | 0 | 0 |
| Harris, John, Seattle | 0 | 0 | 3 | 62 | 3 |
| Harris, Tim, Pittsburgh | 2 | 1 | 0 | 0 | 1 |
| Hart, Jeff, Baltimore | 0 | 1 | 0 | 0 | 1 |
| Hartwig, Carter, Houston | 0 | 0 | 2 | 0 | 2 |
| Hawkins, Frank, Los Angeles Raiders | 2 | 1 | 0 | 0 | 1 |
| Hawthorne, Greg, Pittsburgh | | | | | |
| Haynes, Louis, Kansas City | 0 | 0 | 1 | 0 | 1 |
| Hector, Johnny, New York Jets | 2 | 0 | 0 | 0 | 0 |
| Hendricks, Ted, Los Angeles Raiders | 0 | 0 | 1 | 0 | 1 |
| Herrmann, Mark, Baltimore | 2 | 1 | 0 | 0 | 1 |
| Hill, Eddie, Miami | 0 | 1 | 0 | 0 | 1 |
| Hinkle, Bryan, Pittsburgh | 0 | 1 | 1 | 4 | 2 |
| Hinton, Chris, Baltimore | 0 | 1 | 0 | 0 | 1 |
| Holmes, Jerry, New York Jets | 0 | 0 | 1 | 3 | 1 |
| Holston, Michael, Houston | 0 | 0 | 1 | 0 | 1 |
| Holt, Harry, Cleveland | 1 | 1 | 0 | 0 | 1 |
| Horton, Ray, Cincinnati | 1 | 1 | 0 | 0 | 1 |
| Hughes, David, Seattle | 2 | 0 | 0 | 0 | 0 |
| Hunter, Tony, Buffalo | 1 | 1 | 0 | 0 | 1 |
| Hurley, Bill, New Orleans-Buffalo | 1 | 1 | 1 | 0 | 2 |
| Ilkin, Tunch, Pittsburgh | 0 | 1 | 0 | 0 | 1 |
| Jackson, Billy, Kansas City | 3 | 2 | 0 | 0 | 2 |
| Jackson, Charles, Kansas City | 0 | 0 | 4 | 47 | 4 |
| Jackson, Ernest, San Diego | 1 | 1 | 0 | 0 | 1 |
| Jackson, Harold, San Diego | 1 | 0 | 0 | 0 | 0 |
| Jackson, Michael, Seattle | 0 | 0 | 1 | 0 | 1 |
| Jackson, Roger, Denver | 1 | 0 | 0 | 0 | 0 |
| Jackson, Tom, Denver | 0 | 0 | 2 | 34 | 2 |
| James, Roland, New England | 0 | 1 | 3 | 0 | 4 |
| Jensen, Derrick, Los Angeles Raiders | 1 | 0 | 0 | 0 | 0 |
| Jodat, Jim, San Diego | 0 | 0 | 1 | 0 | 1 |
| Johns, Paul, Seattle | 1 | 2 | 0 | 0 | 2 |
| Johnson, Dan, Miami | 1 | 0 | 0 | 0 | 0 |
| Johnson, Gary, San Diego | 0 | 0 | 2 | 0 | 2 |
| Johnson, Gregg, Seattle | 1 | 1 | 0 | 0 | 1 |
| Johnson, Ken, Buffalo | 0 | 0 | 1 | 0 | 1 |
| Johnson, Pete, Cincinnati | 2 | 1 | 0 | 0 | 1 |
| Johnson, Ron, Pittsburgh | 0 | 0 | 1 | 5 | 1 |
| Joiner, Charlie, San Diego | 2 | 0 | 0 | 0 | 0 |
| Jones, Cedric, New England | 1 | 0 | 0 | 0 | 0 |
| Jones, Ken, Buffalo | 0 | 1 | 0 | 0 | 1 |
| Jones, Lam, New York Jets | 2 | 0 | 0 | 0 | 0 |
| Jones, Leroy, San Diego | 0 | 0 | 1 | 15 | 1 |
| Jones, Rulon, Denver | 0 | 0 | 2 | 4 | 2 |
| Junkin, Trey, Buffalo | 0 | 1 | 0 | 0 | 1 |
| Keating, Chris, Buffalo | 0 | 0 | 1 | 0 | 1 |
| Kemp, Bobby, Cincinnati | 0 | 0 | 1 | 0 | 1 |
| Kennedy, Mike, Buffalo | 0 | 0 | 1 | 0 | 1 |
| Kenney, Bill, Kansas City | 7 | 4 | 0 | 0 | 4 |
| Kilson, David, Buffalo | 0 | 0 | 3 | 88 | 3 |
| King, Kenny, Los Angeles Raiders | 1 | 0 | 0 | 0 | 0 |
| King, Linden, San Diego | 0 | 0 | 2 | 0 | 2 |
| Kinnebrew, Larry, Cincinnati | 3 | 1 | 0 | 0 | 1 |
| Klecko, Joe, New York Jets | 0 | 0 | 1 | 0 | 1 |
| Kohrs, Bob, Pittsburgh | 0 | 0 | 1 | 0 | 1 |
| Kozlowski, Mike, Miami | 2 | 1 | 0 | 0 | 1 |
| Krauss, Barry, Baltimore | 0 | 0 | 2 | 0 | 2 |
| Kremer, Ken, Kansas City | 0 | 0 | 1 | 0 | 1 |
| Krieg, Dave, Seattle | 10 | 2 | 0 | 0 | 2 |
| Krumrie, Tim, Cincinnati | 0 | 0 | 1 | 0 | 1 |
| Kuechenberg, Bob, Miami | 1 | 0 | 0 | 0 | 0 |
| Laird, Bruce, San Diego | 1 | 0 | 0 | 0 | 0 |
| Lambert, Jack, Pittsburgh | 0 | 0 | 2 | 0 | 2 |
| Lane, Eric, Seattle | 2 | 0 | 1 | 0 | 1 |
| Lapham, Dave, Cincinnati | 0 | 3 | 0 | 0 | 3 |
| Largent, Steve, Seattle | 3 | 0 | 0 | 0 | 0 |
| Lee, Keith, New England | 1 | 1 | 1 | 0 | 2 |
| Lewis, Albert, Kansas City | 0 | 0 | 2 | 0 | 2 |
| Lippett, Ronnie, New England | 0 | 0 | 1 | 0 | 1 |
| Logan, Dave, Cleveland | 1 | 2 | 0 | 0 | 2 |
| Long, Howie, Los Angeles Raiders | 0 | 0 | 2 | 0 | 2 |
| Lowe, Woodrow, San Diego | 0 | 0 | 1 | 0 | 1 |
| Luck, Oliver, Houston | 5 | 1 | 0 | 0 | 1 |
| Lumpkin, Joey, Buffalo | 0 | 0 | 1 | 0 | 1 |
| Luther, Ed, San Diego | 6 | 0 | 0 | 0 | 0 |
| Macek, Don, San Diego | 0 | 1 | 0 | 0 | 1 |
| Malone, Mark, Pittsburgh | 0 | 1 | 0 | 0 | 1 |
| Mangiero, Dino, Kansas City | 0 | 0 | 1 | 32 | 1 |
| Manning, Archie, Houston | 2 | 2 | 0 | 0 | 2 |
| Manor, Brison, Denver | 0 | 0 | 1 | 0 | 1 |
| Marino, Dan, Miami | 5 | 2 | 0 | 0 | 2 |
| Martin, Mike, Cincinnati | 2 | 0 | 0 | 0 | 0 |
| Mathison, Bruce, San Diego | 1 | 0 | 0 | 0 | 0 |
| Maxwell, Vernon, Baltimore | 0 | 0 | 2 | 0 | 2 |
| McDonald, Paul, Cleveland | 1 | 1 | 0 | 0 | 1 |
| McElroy, Vann, Los Angeles Raiders | 0 | 0 | 3 | 5 | 3 |
| McGrew, Larry, New England | 0 | 0 | 1 | 0 | 1 |
| McKnight, Dennis, San Diego | 0 | 2 | 0 | 0 | 2 |
| McMillan, Randy, Baltimore | 5 | 3 | 0 | 0 | 3 |
| McNeil, Freeman, New York Jets | 4 | 1 | 0 | 0 | 1 |
| McPherson, Miles, San Diego | 1 | 0 | 0 | 0 | 0 |
| Mehl, Lance, New York Jets | 0 | 0 | 1 | 0 | 1 |
| Merriman, Sam, Seattle | 0 | 1 | 0 | 0 | 1 |
| Merriweather, Mike, Pittsburgh | 0 | 2 | 0 | 0 | 2 |

| | Fum. | Own Rec. | Opp. Rec. | Yds. | Tot. Rec. |
|---|---|---|---|---|---|
| Montgomery, Cleotha, Los Angeles Raiders | 1 | 0 | 0 | 0 | 0 |
| Moore, Booker, Buffalo | 1 | 1 | 0 | 0 | 1 |
| Moore, Nat, Miami | 1 | 0 | 0 | 0 | 0 |
| Morgan, Stanley, New England | 5 | 2 | 0 | 0 | 2 |
| Moriarty, Larry, Houston | 1 | 0 | 1 | 0 | 1 |
| Mosley, Mike, Buffalo | 1 | 0 | 0 | 0 | 0 |
| Moyer, Paul, Seattle | 0 | 0 | 3 | 0 | 3 |
| Muhammad, Calvin, Los Angeles Raiders | 2 | 0 | 0 | 0 | 0 |
| Mullen, Davlin, New York Jets | 1 | 0 | 0 | 0 | 0 |
| Muncie, Chuck, San Diego | 8 | 1 | 0 | 0 | 1 |
| Nathan, Tony, Miami | 2 | 0 | 0 | 0 | 0 |
| Nelson, Bob, Los Angeles Raiders | 0 | 0 | 1 | 0 | 1 |
| Nelson, Steve, New England | 0 | 0 | 1 | 0 | 1 |
| Nielsen, Gifford, Houston | 6 | 1 | 0 | 0 | 1 |
| Odom, Henry, Pittsburgh | 2 | 1 | 0 | 0 | 1 |
| Overstreet, David, Miami | 2 | 1 | 0 | 0 | 1 |
| Owens, Dennis, New England | 0 | 0 | 1 | 4 | 1 |
| Padjen, Gary, Baltimore | 0 | 0 | 1 | 0 | 1 |
| Pagel, Mike, Baltimore | 4 | 0 | 0 | 0 | 0 |
| Paige, Stephon, Kansas City | 1 | 1 | 0 | 0 | 1 |
| Parker, Steve, Baltimore | 0 | 0 | 3 | 0 | 3 |
| Parros, Rick, Denver | 3 | 1 | 0 | 0 | 1 |
| Pellegrini, Joe, New York Jets | 0 | 1 | 0 | 0 | 1 |
| Peoples, George, New England | 0 | 1 | 0 | 0 | 1 |
| Perry, Rod, Cleveland | 0 | 0 | 1 | 0 | 1 |
| Petersen, Ted, Pittsburgh | 0 | 2 | 0 | 0 | 2 |
| Pickel, Bill, Los Angeles Raiders | 0 | 0 | 1 | 0 | 1 |
| Plunkett, Jim, Los Angeles Raiders | 7 | 3 | 0 | 0 | 3 |
| Pollard, Frank, Pittsburgh | 5 | 1 | 0 | 0 | 1 |
| Poole, Nathan, Denver | 1 | 0 | 1 | −1 | 1 |
| Porter, Ricky, Baltimore | 6 | 4 | 0 | 0 | 4 |
| Prater, Dean, Kansas City | 0 | 0 | 1 | 0 | 1 |
| Pratt, Bob, Seattle | 0 | 1 | 0 | 0 | 1 |
| Preston, Dave, Denver | 0 | 1 | 0 | 0 | 1 |
| Pruitt, Greg, Los Angeles Raiders | 10 | 7 | 0 | 0 | 7 |
| Pruitt, Mike, Cleveland | 4 | 2 | 0 | 0 | 2 |
| Puzzuoli, Dave, Cleveland | 0 | 0 | 1 | 2 | 1 |
| Ray, Darrol, New York Jets | 0 | 0 | 1 | 0 | 1 |
| Razzano, Rick, Cincinnati | 0 | 0 | 1 | 0 | 1 |
| Reinfeldt, Mike, Houston | 0 | 0 | 2 | 0 | 2 |
| Rembert, Johnny, New England | 0 | 0 | 1 | 0 | 1 |
| Renfro, Mike, Houston | 1 | 0 | 0 | 0 | 0 |
| Reynolds, Ed, New England | 0 | 1 | 1 | 0 | 2 |
| Ricks, Lawrence, Kansas City | 1 | 0 | 0 | 0 | 0 |
| Rhone, Earnest, Miami | 0 | 0 | 2 | 9 | 2 |
| Riddick, Robb, Buffalo | 7 | 1 | 0 | 0 | 1 |
| Riley, Avon, Houston | 0 | 0 | 3 | 4 | 3 |
| Riley, Ken, Cincinnati | 0 | 0 | 1 | 0 | 1 |
| Rimington, Dave, Cincinnati | 1 | 1 | 0 | 0 | 1 |
| Roaches, Carl, Houston | 3 | 1 | 0 | 0 | 1 |
| Robinson, Shelton, Seattle | 0 | 0 | 4 | 21 | 4 |
| Rudolph, Ben, New York Jets | 0 | 1 | 0 | 0 | 1 |
| Rush, Bob, Kansas City | 2 | 1 | 0 | 0 | 1 |
| Ryan, Jim, Denver | 0 | 0 | 1 | 0 | 1 |
| Ryan, Pat, New York Jets | 2 | 1 | 0 | 0 | 1 |
| Sanford, Lucius, Buffalo | 0 | 0 | 1 | 0 | 1 |
| Sanford, Rick, New England | 1 | 0 | 1 | 26 | 1 |
| Sawyer, John, Denver | 1 | 0 | 0 | 0 | 0 |
| Scholtz, Bruce, Seattle | 0 | 0 | 1 | 0 | 1 |
| Schonert, Turk, Cincinnati | 6 | 4 | 0 | 0 | 4 |
| Schroy, Ken, New York Jets | 0 | 0 | 1 | 24 | 1 |
| Shell, Donnie, Pittsburgh | 0 | 0 | 1 | 0 | 1 |
| Simmons, John, Cincinnati | 4 | 3 | 0 | 0 | 3 |
| Simpkins, Ron, Cincinnati | 0 | 0 | 1 | 0 | 1 |
| Simpson, Keith, Seattle | 1 | 0 | 2 | 0 | 2 |
| Sipe, Brian, Cleveland | 6 | 1 | 0 | 0 | 1 |
| Skansi, Paul, Pittsburgh | 5 | 2 | 0 | 0 | 2 |
| Smith, Billy Ray, San Diego | 0 | 0 | 1 | 0 | 1 |
| Smith, Lucious, Kansas City | 0 | 0 | 1 | 0 | 1 |
| Smith, Ricky, New England | 11 | 6 | 0 | 0 | 6 |
| Smith, Sherman, San Diego | 2 | 1 | 0 | 0 | 1 |
| Smith, Tim, Houston | 1 | 0 | 0 | 0 | 0 |
| Sowell, Robert, Miami | 0 | 1 | 0 | 0 | 1 |
| Spani, Gary, Kansas City | 0 | 0 | 1 | 5 | 1 |
| Springs, Kirk, New York Jets | 2 | 1 | 0 | 0 | 1 |
| Stalls, Dave, Tampa Bay-Los Angeles Raiders | 0 | 0 | 2 | 0 | 2 |
| Starring, Stephen, New England | 1 | 0 | 0 | 0 | 0 |
| Stensrud, Mike, Houston | 0 | 0 | 1 | 0 | 1 |
| Still, Art, Kansas City | 0 | 0 | 1 | 0 | 1 |
| Stoudt, Cliff, Pittsburgh | 10 | 2 | 0 | 0 | 2 |
| Strock, Don, Miami | 0 | 1 | 0 | 0 | 1 |
| Studdard, Dave, Denver | 0 | 1 | 0 | 0 | 1 |
| Talley, Darryl, Buffalo | 0 | 1 | 1 | 6 | 2 |
| Tate, Rodney, Cincinnati | 3 | 0 | 0 | 0 | 0 |
| Tatupu, Mosi, New England | 1 | 0 | 1 | 0 | 1 |
| Thomas, Jewerl, Kansas City | 4 | 1 | 0 | 0 | 1 |
| Thomas, Ken, Kansas City | 2 | 1 | 0 | 0 | 1 |
| Thomas, Rodell, Miami | 0 | 0 | 1 | 0 | 1 |
| Thomas, Zack, Denver | 4 | 3 | 0 | 0 | 3 |
| Tice, Mike, Seattle | 0 | 0 | 1 | 0 | 1 |
| Tippett, Andre, New England | 0 | 0 | 1 | 0 | 1 |
| Todd, Richard, New York Jets | 5 | 1 | 0 | 0 | 1 |
| Townsend, Greg, Los Angeles Raiders | 0 | 0 | 1 | 66 | 1 |
| Tuttle, Perry, Buffalo | 1 | 0 | 0 | 0 | 0 |
| van Eeghen, Mark, New England | 1 | 1 | 0 | 0 | 1 |
| Walker, Dwight, Cleveland | 1 | 3 | 0 | 0 | 3 |
| Walker, Fulton, Miami | 1 | 1 | 0 | 0 | 1 |
| Warner, Curt, Seattle | 6 | 2 | 0 | 0 | 2 |
| Watson, Steve, Denver | 1 | 0 | 0 | 0 | 0 |
| Watts, Ted, Los Angeles Raiders | 0 | 0 | 1 | 0 | 1 |
| Weathers, Clarence, New England | 2 | 1 | 0 | 0 | 1 |
| Weathers, Robert, New England | 4 | 0 | 0 | 0 | 0 |
| Webster, Mike, Pittsburgh | 0 | 2 | 0 | 0 | 2 |
| Weishuhn, Clayton, New England | 0 | 0 | 3 | 0 | 3 |
| White, Ed, San Diego | 0 | 1 | 0 | 0 | 1 |
| Williams, Ben, Buffalo | 0 | 0 | 2 | 0 | 2 |
| Williams, Chris, Buffalo | 0 | 0 | 1 | 0 | 1 |
| Williams, Dokie, Los Angeles Raiders | 2 | 0 | 0 | 0 | 0 |
| Williams, Kendall, Baltimore | 2 | 1 | 1 | 0 | 2 |
| Williams, Reggie, Cincinnati | 0 | 0 | 4 | 59 | 4 |
| Williams, Van, Buffalo | 2 | 0 | 1 | 0 | 1 |
| Willis, Chester, Los Angeles Raiders | 1 | 0 | 0 | 0 | 0 |
| Willis, Keith, Pittsburgh | 0 | 0 | 1 | 0 | 1 |
| Wilson, Marc, Los Angeles Raiders | 4 | 1 | 0 | 0 | 1 |
| Wilson, Stanley, Cincinnati | 4 | 2 | 0 | 0 | 2 |
| Wilson, Steve, Denver | 1 | 1 | 0 | 0 | 1 |
| Winder, Sammy, Denver | 7 | 0 | 0 | 0 | 0 |
| Winslow, Kellen, San Diego | 3 | 2 | 0 | 0 | 2 |
| Wisniewski, Leo, Baltimore | 0 | 0 | 2 | 0 | 2 |
| Wolfley, Craig, Pittsburgh | 0 | 1 | 0 | 0 | 1 |
| Woodard, Kenneth, Denver | 0 | 0 | 1 | 0 | 1 |
| Woodley, David, Miami | 4 | 0 | 0 | 0 | 0 |
| Woodring, John, New York Jets | 0 | 0 | 4 | 0 | 4 |
| Woods, Rick, Pittsburgh | 0 | 0 | 2 | 38 | 2 |
| Wright, James, Denver | 2 | 0 | 0 | 0 | 0 |
| Wright, Louis, Denver | 1 | 0 | 1 | 40 | 1 |
| Young, Andre, San Diego | 0 | 0 | 1 | 0 | 1 |
| Young, Charle, Seattle | 1 | 1 | 0 | 0 | 1 |
| Zorn, Jim, Seattle | 4 | 0 | 0 | 0 | 0 |

*Touchdowns: Shelton Robinson, Seattle, 2; Marcus Allen, Los Angeles Raiders; Larry Anderson, Baltimore; Greg Best, Pittsburgh; Mel Blount, Pittsburgh; Barney Chavous, Denver; Johnie Cooks, Baltimore; Mark Gastineau, New York Jets; Charles Jackson, Kansas City; David Kilson, Buffalo; Greg Townsend, Los Angeles Raiders; Reggie Williams, Cincinnati; and Rick Woods, Pittsburgh, 1 each.*

## NFC FUMBLES—INDIVIDUAL

| | Fum. | Own Rec. | Opp. Rec. | Yds. | Tot. Rec. |
|---|---|---|---|---|---|
| Alexander, Robert, Los Angeles Rams | 2 | 2 | 0 | 0 | 2 |
| Anderson, John, Green Bay | 0 | 0 | 1 | 0 | 1 |
| Anderson, Ottis, St. Louis | 10 | 3 | 0 | 0 | 3 |
| Andrews, William, Atlanta | 6 | 2 | 0 | 0 | 2 |
| Armstrong, Adger, Tampa Bay | 0 | 1 | 0 | 0 | 1 |
| Armstrong, Harvey, Philadelphia | 0 | 0 | 2 | 0 | 2 |
| Bailey, Stacey, Atlanta | 1 | 1 | 0 | 0 | 1 |
| Baker, Al, St. Louis | 0 | 0 | 2 | 0 | 2 |
| Baker, Ron, Philadelphia | 0 | 1 | 0 | 0 | 1 |
| Barber, Mike, Los Angeles Rams | 1 | 0 | 0 | 0 | 0 |
| Barnes, Roosevelt, Detroit | 0 | 0 | 1 | 0 | 1 |
| Barnett, Doug, Los Angeles Rams | 0 | 0 | 1 | 0 | 1 |
| Bartkowski, Steve, Atlanta | 7 | 1 | 0 | 0 | 1 |
| Baschnagel, Brian, Chicago | 1 | 0 | 0 | 0 | 0 |
| Bates, Bill, Dallas | 1 | 0 | 2 | 0 | 2 |
| Bell, Jerry, Tampa Bay | 2 | 1 | 0 | 0 | 1 |
| Bell, Theo, Tampa Bay | 0 | 1 | 0 | 0 | 1 |
| Bell, Todd, Chicago | 0 | 0 | 1 | 10 | 1 |
| Benjamin, Guy, San Francisco | 1 | 1 | 0 | 0 | 1 |
| Bess, Rufus, Minnesota | 2 | 0 | 0 | 0 | 0 |
| Bethea, Larry, Dallas | 0 | 0 | 1 | 0 | 1 |
| Bird, Steve, St. Louis | 1 | 1 | 0 | 0 | 1 |
| Black, Mike, Detroit | 1 | 0 | 0 | 0 | 0 |
| Blair, Matt, Minnesota | 0 | 0 | 2 | 0 | 2 |
| Board, Dwaine, San Francisco | 0 | 0 | 5 | 0 | 5 |
| Bostic, Jeff, Washington | 0 | 1 | 2 | 0 | 3 |
| Bostic, Joe, St. Louis | 0 | 0 | 1 | 0 | 1 |
| Bragg, Byron, Green Bay | 0 | 0 | 2 | 0 | 2 |
| Breunig, Bob, Dallas | 0 | 0 | 1 | 0 | 1 |
| Bright, Leon, New York Giants | 2 | 0 | 0 | 0 | 0 |
| Brock, Stan, New Orleans | 0 | 1 | 0 | 0 | 1 |
| Brown, Charlie, Washington | 0 | 1 | 0 | 0 | 1 |
| Brown, Rush, St. Louis | 0 | 0 | 1 | 8 | 1 |
| Brown, Ted, Minnesota | 2 | 1 | 0 | 0 | 1 |
| Browner, Joey, Minnesota | 1 | 2 | 2 | 4 | 4 |
| Brunner, Scott, New York Giants | 8 | 3 | 0 | 0 | 3 |
| Bunz, Dan, San Francisco | 0 | 0 | 1 | 0 | 1 |

| | Fum. | Own Rec. | Opp. Rec. | Yds. | Tot. Rec. |
|---|---|---|---|---|---|
| Burt, Jim, New York Giants | 0 | 0 | 1 | 0 | 1 |
| Bussey, Dexter, Detroit | 1 | 0 | 0 | 0 | 0 |
| Butler, Bobby, Atlanta | 0 | 0 | 1 | 0 | 1 |
| Butz, Dave, Washington | 0 | 0 | 1 | 0 | 1 |
| Cain, Lynn, Atlanta | 1 | 0 | 0 | 0 | 0 |
| Campfield, Billy, New York Giants | 1 | 0 | 0 | 0 | 0 |
| Cannon, John, Tampa Bay | 0 | 0 | 1 | 0 | 1 |
| Carpenter, Rob, New York Giants | 2 | 0 | 0 | 0 | 0 |
| Carter, Gerald, Tampa Bay | 3 | 0 | 0 | 0 | 0 |
| Carver, Mel, Tampa Bay | 6 | 2 | 0 | 0 | 2 |
| Casper, Dave, Minnesota | 0 | 1 | 0 | 0 | 1 |
| Caver, Jim, Detroit | 1 | 0 | 0 | 0 | 0 |
| Clark, Bruce, New Orleans | 0 | 0 | 1 | 0 | 1 |
| Clark, Jessie, Green Bay | 2 | 1 | 0 | 0 | 1 |
| Clark, Kelvin, New Orleans | 0 | 1 | 0 | 0 | 1 |
| Clark, Randy, St. Louis | 1 | 0 | 0 | 0 | 0 |
| Clarke, Ken, Philadelphia | 0 | 0 | 3 | 5 | 3 |
| Clinkscale, Dextor, Dallas | 0 | 0 | 4 | 0 | 4 |
| Cobb, Garry, Detroit | 0 | 0 | 2 | 0 | 2 |
| Cofer, Mike, Detroit | 0 | 0 | 1 | 0 | 1 |
| Coffey, Ken, Washington | 0 | 0 | 1 | 0 | 1 |
| Coffman, Paul, Green Bay | 1 | 0 | 0 | 0 | 0 |
| Coleman, Monte, Washington | 0 | 0 | 2 | 0 | 2 |
| Collins, Jim, Los Angeles Rams | 0 | 0 | 1 | 0 | 1 |
| Colzie, Neal, Tampa Bay | 0 | 0 | 1 | 0 | 1 |
| Cooper, Earl, San Francisco | 1 | 0 | 0 | 0 | 0 |
| Cotney, Mark, Tampa Bay | 0 | 0 | 1 | 0 | 1 |
| Covert, Jimbo, Chicago | 0 | 1 | 0 | 0 | 1 |
| Cowher, Bill, Philadelphia | 0 | 0 | 1 | 0 | 1 |
| Cox, Arthur, Atlanta | 1 | 0 | 0 | 0 | 0 |
| Craig, Roger, San Francisco | 6 | 1 | 0 | 0 | 1 |
| Cromwell, Nolan, Los Angeles Rams | 0 | 1 | 1 | 0 | 2 |
| Curran, Willie, Atlanta | 1 | 0 | 0 | 0 | 0 |
| Currier, Bill, New York Giants | 0 | 1 | 0 | 0 | 1 |
| Curry, Buddy, Atlanta | 0 | 0 | 1 | 0 | 1 |
| Danielson, Gary, Detroit | 2 | 1 | 0 | 0 | 1 |
| Darby, Byron, Philadelphia | 1 | 0 | 0 | 0 | 0 |
| Dean, Vernon, Washington | 0 | 0 | 3 | 0 | 3 |
| Dickerson, Anthony, Dallas | 0 | 0 | 3 | 0 | 3 |
| Dickerson, Eric, Los Angeles Rams | 13 | 1 | 0 | 0 | 1 |
| Dickey, Lynn, Green Bay | 9 | 6 | 0 | 0 | 6 |
| Didier, Clint, Washington | 1 | 1 | 0 | 0 | 1 |
| Dieterich, Chris, Detroit | 0 | 1 | 0 | 0 | 1 |
| Dils, Steve, Minnesota | 13 | 6 | 0 | 0 | 6 |
| Dorsett, Tony, Dallas | 5 | 1 | 0 | 0 | 1 |
| Doss, Reggie, Los Angeles Rams | 0 | 0 | 1 | 0 | 1 |
| Douglass, Mike, Green Bay | 0 | 0 | 4 | 57 | 4 |
| Downs, Mike, Dallas | 0 | 0 | 2 | 10 | 2 |
| Duckett, Kenny, New Orleans | 1 | 0 | 0 | 0 | 0 |
| Duda, Mark, St. Louis | 0 | 0 | 2 | 0 | 2 |
| Dutton, John, Dallas | 0 | 0 | 1 | 0 | 1 |
| Ekern, Carl, Los Angeles Rams | 0 | 0 | 2 | 0 | 2 |
| Elias, Homer, Detroit | 0 | 1 | 0 | 0 | 1 |
| Ellard, Henry, Los Angeles Rams | 2 | 2 | 0 | 0 | 2 |
| Ellis, Gerry, Green Bay | 7 | 1 | 0 | 0 | 1 |
| Ellis, Ray, Philadelphia | 0 | 0 | 1 | 0 | 1 |
| Elshire, Neil, Minnesota | 0 | 0 | 3 | 0 | 3 |
| Epps, Phillip, Green Bay | 2 | 0 | 0 | 0 | 0 |
| Evans, Vince, Chicago | 4 | 0 | 0 | 0 | 0 |
| Everett, Major, Philadelphia | 0 | 1 | 0 | 0 | 1 |
| Fahnhorst, Keith, San Francisco | 0 | 1 | 0 | 0 | 1 |
| Fantetti, Ken, Detroit | 0 | 0 | 1 | 0 | 1 |
| Ferrell, Sean, Tampa Bay | 0 | 1 | 0 | 0 | 1 |
| Fellows, Ron, Dallas | 4 | 2 | 1 | 0 | 3 |
| Fencik, Gary, Chicago | 0 | 0 | 1 | 0 | 1 |
| Ferragamo, Vince, Los Angeles Rams | 8 | 2 | 0 | 0 | 2 |
| Ferrell, Earl, St. Louis | 2 | 0 | 0 | 0 | 0 |
| Flowers, Larry, New York Giants | 0 | 1 | 0 | 0 | 1 |
| Fowlkes, Dennis, Minnesota | 0 | 0 | 2 | 5 | 2 |
| Francis, Russ, San Francisco | 2 | 0 | 0 | 0 | 0 |
| Frazier, Leslie, Chicago | 0 | 0 | 1 | 3 | 1 |
| Frye, David, Atlanta | 0 | 0 | 2 | 0 | 2 |
| Gaison, Blane, Atlanta | 0 | 0 | 1 | 64 | 1 |
| Gajan, Hokie, New Orleans | 3 | 1 | 0 | 0 | 1 |
| Galbreath, Tony, Minnesota | 4 | 2 | 0 | 0 | 2 |
| Galloway, David, St. Louis | 0 | 0 | 1 | 0 | 1 |
| Gary, Russell, New Orleans | 1 | 0 | 0 | 0 | 0 |
| Gault, Willie, Chicago | 1 | 1 | 0 | 0 | 1 |
| Gay, William, Detroit | 0 | 0 | 1 | 11 | 1 |
| Gentry, Dennis, Chicago | 1 | 0 | 0 | 0 | 0 |
| Gervais, Rick, San Francisco | 0 | 0 | 1 | 0 | 1 |
| Giacomarro, Ralph, Atlanta | 1 | 1 | 0 | 0 | 1 |
| Giles, Jimmie, Tampa Bay | 1 | 0 | 0 | 0 | 0 |
| Glazebrook, Bob, Atlanta | 1 | 0 | 1 | 0 | 1 |
| Golsteyn, Jerry, Tampa Bay | 3 | 3 | 0 | 0 | 3 |
| Graham, William, Detroit | 0 | 0 | 3 | 0 | 3 |
| Grant, Darryl, Washington | 0 | 0 | 2 | 0 | 2 |
| Grant, Otis, Los Angeles Rams | 1 | 1 | 0 | 0 | 1 |
| Gray, Johnnie, Green Bay | 2 | 1 | 0 | 0 | 1 |
| Gray, Leon, New Orleans | 0 | 2 | 0 | 0 | 2 |
| Greco, Don, Detroit | 0 | 1 | 0 | 0 | 1 |
| Green, Darrell, Washington | 1 | 0 | 1 | 0 | 1 |
| Green, Hugh, Tampa Bay | 1 | 0 | 2 | 11 | 2 |
| Green, Roy, St. Louis | 3 | 1 | 0 | 0 | 1 |
| Greer, Curtis, St. Louis | 0 | 0 | 1 | 5 | 1 |
| Grimes, Randy, Tampa Bay | 0 | 1 | 0 | 0 | 1 |
| Grooms, Elois, St. Louis | 0 | 0 | 1 | 40 | 1 |
| Groth, Jeff, New Orleans | 3 | 2 | 0 | 0 | 2 |
| Haddix, Michael, Philadelphia | 4 | 0 | 0 | 0 | 0 |
| Hairston, Carl, Philadelphia | 0 | 0 | 2 | 0 | 2 |
| Hall, Alvin, Detroit | 1 | 0 | 2 | 0 | 2 |
| Hannon, Tom, Minnesota | 0 | 0 | 2 | 17 | 2 |
| Hardison, Dee, New York Giants | 0 | 0 | 1 | 0 | 1 |
| Harrell, Willard, St. Louis | 1 | 0 | 0 | 0 | 0 |
| Harrington, Perry, Philadelphia | 1 | 0 | 0 | 0 | 0 |
| Harris, Al, Chicago | 0 | 0 | 2 | 0 | 2 |
| Harris, Eric, Los Angeles Rams | 0 | 1 | 0 | 0 | 1 |
| Harrison, Dennis, Philadelphia | 0 | 0 | 1 | 16 | 1 |
| Hart, Jim, St. Louis | 5 | 2 | 0 | 0 | 2 |
| Hartenstine, Mike, Chicago | 0 | 0 | 1 | 10 | 1 |
| Haynes, Mark, New York Giants | 0 | 0 | 2 | 4 | 2 |
| Hegman, Mike, Dallas | 0 | 0 | 1 | 9 | 1 |
| Hicks, Dwight, San Francisco | 0 | 0 | 2 | 5 | 2 |
| Hilgenberg, Jay, Chicago | 0 | 1 | 0 | 0 | 1 |
| Hill, David, Los Angeles Rams | 1 | 1 | 0 | 0 | 1 |
| Hill, Rod, Dallas | 2 | 1 | 1 | 0 | 2 |
| Hill, Tony, Dallas | 1 | 0 | 0 | 0 | 0 |
| Hipple, Eric, Detroit | 12 | 6 | 0 | 0 | 6 |
| Holloway, Randy, Minnesota | 0 | 0 | 1 | 7 | 1 |
| Holly, Bob, Washington | 2 | 0 | 0 | 0 | 0 |
| Holmoe, Tom, San Francisco | 0 | 0 | 1 | 0 | 1 |
| Holt, John, Tampa Bay | 1 | 0 | 1 | 0 | 1 |
| Hoover, Mel, Philadelphia | 3 | 0 | 0 | 0 | 0 |
| Huckleby, Harlan, Green Bay | 4 | 1 | 0 | 0 | 1 |
| Huffman, Dave, Minnesota | 0 | 1 | 1 | 0 | 2 |
| Hughes, Ernie, New York Giants | 1 | 0 | 0 | 0 | 0 |
| Hutchison, Anthony, Chicago | 1 | 0 | 0 | 0 | 0 |
| Irvin, LeRoy, Los Angeles Rams | 4 | 1 | 1 | 0 | 2 |
| Irwin, Tim, Minnesota | 0 | 1 | 0 | 0 | 1 |
| Ivery, Eddie Lee, Green Bay | 1 | 0 | 0 | 0 | 0 |
| Jackson, Rickey, New Orleans | 1 | 0 | 2 | −2 | 2 |
| Jackson, Terry, New York Giants | 0 | 0 | 1 | 35 | 1 |
| Janata, John, Chicago | 0 | 1 | 0 | 0 | 1 |
| Jaworski, Ron, Philadelphia | 11 | 4 | 0 | 0 | 4 |
| Jefferson, John, Green Bay | 1 | 0 | 0 | 0 | 0 |
| Jenkins, Ken, Detroit | 2 | 1 | 0 | 0 | 1 |
| Johnson, Billy, Atlanta | 4 | 2 | 0 | 0 | 2 |
| Johnson, Bobby, New Orleans | 1 | .1 | 0 | 0 | 0 |
| Johnson, Charlie, Minnesota | 0 | 0 | 1 | 50 | 1 |
| Johnson, Demetrious, Detroit | 0 | 0 | 1 | 0 | 1 |
| Johnson, Ezra, Green Bay | 0 | 0 | 2 | 0 | 2 |
| Johnson, Johnnie, Los Angeles Rams | 1 | 0 | 4 | 2 | 4 |
| Johnson, Kenny, Atlanta | 1 | 1 | 0 | 0 | 1 |
| Jones, Earl, Atlanta | 0 | 0 | 1 | 0 | 1 |
| Jones, Ed, Dallas | 0 | 0 | 2 | 0 | 2 |
| Jones, James, Detroit | 4 | 1 | 0 | 0 | 1 |
| Jordan, Curtis, Washington | 0 | 0 | 2 | 20 | 2 |
| Judie, Ed, Tampa Bay | 0 | 0 | 2 | 0 | 2 |
| Junior, E.J., St. Louis | 0 | 0 | 1 | 1 | 1 |
| Kaufman, Mel, Washington | 0 | 0 | 1 | 30 | 1 |
| Kelley, Brian, New York Giants | 0 | 0 | 2 | 0 | 2 |
| Kemp, Jeff, Los Angeles Rams | 2 | 0 | 0 | 0 | 0 |
| Kenn, Mike, Atlanta | 0 | 1 | 0 | 0 | 1 |
| Kinard, Terry, New York Giants | 0 | 0 | 1 | 10 | 1 |
| King, Horace, Detroit | 0 | 1 | 0 | 0 | 1 |
| Komlo, Jeff, Tampa Bay | 2 | 0 | 0 | 0 | 0 |
| Korte, Steve, New Orleans | 0 | 1 | 0 | 0 | 1 |
| Kramer, Tommy, Minnesota | 2 | 1 | 0 | 0 | 1 |
| Kraynak, Rich, Philadelphia | 0 | 1 | 0 | 0 | 1 |
| Kuykendall, Fulton, Atlanta | 0 | 0 | 1 | 0 | 1 |
| Lafary, Dave, New Orleans | 0 | 1 | 0 | 0 | 1 |
| LaFleur, Greg, St. Louis | 3 | 0 | 0 | 0 | 0 |
| LeCount, Terry, Minnesota | 1 | 1 | 0 | 0 | 1 |
| Lee, Mark, Green Bay | 1 | 0 | 1 | 15 | 1 |
| Leonard, Jim, Tampa Bay | 0 | 1 | 0 | 0 | 1 |
| Leopold, Bobby, San Francisco | 0 | 0 | 1 | 0 | 1 |
| Lewis, David, Los Angeles Rams | 0 | 0 | 1 | 0 | 1 |
| Lewis, Gary, Green Bay | 0 | 1 | 0 | 0 | 1 |
| Lewis, Rodney, New Orleans | 0 | 1 | 0 | 0 | 1 |
| Lewis, Tim, Green Bay | 3 | 1 | 0 | 0 | 1 |
| Liebenstein, Todd, Washington | 0 | 0 | 2 | 5 | 2 |
| Lisch, Rusty, St. Louis | 1 | 0 | 0 | 0 | 0 |
| Logan, Dave, Tampa Bay | 0 | 0 | 1 | 54 | 1 |
| Logan, Randy, Philadelphia | 1 | 0 | 1 | 8 | 1 |
| Lomax, Neil, St. Louis | 9 | 3 | 0 | 0 | 3 |
| Lott, Ronnie, San Francisco | 0 | 0 | 1 | 0 | 1 |
| Love, Randy, St. Louis | 4 | 1 | 0 | 0 | 1 |
| Margerum, Ken, Chicago | 1 | 0 | 0 | 0 | 0 |

| | Fum. | Own Rec. | Opp. Rec. | Yds. | Tot. Rec. |
|---|---|---|---|---|---|
| Marsh, Doug, St. Louis | 1 | 0 | 0 | 0 | 0 |
| Martin, Doug, Minnesota | 0 | 0 | 2 | 0 | 2 |
| Martin, Robbie, Detroit | 3 | 1 | 0 | 0 | 1 |
| Matthews, Allama, Atlanta | 0 | 1 | 0 | 0 | 1 |
| May, Mark, Washington | 0 | 1 | 0 | 0 | 1 |
| Mayock, Mike, New York Giants | 1 | 0 | 0 | 0 | 0 |
| Mays, Stafford, St. Louis | 0 | 1 | 1 | 0 | 2 |
| McCullum, Sam, Minnesota | 0 | 1 | 0 | 0 | 1 |
| McDole, Mardye, Minnesota | 1 | 0 | 0 | 0 | 0 |
| McGee, Tony, Washington | 0 | 0 | 2 | 0 | 2 |
| McKinnon, Dennis, Chicago | 2 | 1 | 0 | 0 | 1 |
| McMahon, Jim, Chicago | 4 | 3 | 0 | 0 | 3 |
| McMichael, Steve. Chicago | 0 | 0 | 2 | 0 | 2 |
| Meade, Mike, Green Bay | 2 | 1 | 0 | 0 | 1 |
| Merrow, Jeff, Atlanta | 0 | 0 | 1 | 0 | 1 |
| Miller, Junior, Atlanta | 1 | 0 | 0 | 0 | 0 |
| Mistler, John, New York Giants | 1 | 0 | 0 | 0 | 0 |
| Mitchell, Stump, St. Louis | 5 | 1 | 0 | 0 | 1 |
| Montana, Joe, San Francisco | 3 | 0 | 0 | 0 | 0 |
| Montgomery, Wilbert, Philadelphia | 1 | 0 | 0 | 0 | 0 |
| Moroski, Mike, Atlanta | 2 | 0 | 0 | 0 | 0 |
| Morris, Joe, New York Giants | 2 | 1 | 0 | 0 | 1 |
| Morris, Tom, Tampa Bay | 0 | 0 | 1 | 0 | 1 |
| Morris, Wayne, St. Louis | 2 | 0 | 0 | 0 | 0 |
| Morriss, Guy, Philadelphia | 1 | 0 | 0 | 0 | 0 |
| Morton, Michael, Tampa Bay | 5 | 2 | 0 | 0 | 2 |
| Mott, Steve, Detroit | 1 | 0 | 0 | 0 | 0 |
| Mullady, Tom, New York Giants | 0 | 1 | 0 | 0 | 1 |
| Mullaney, Mark, Minnesota | 0 | 0 | 1 | 0 | 1 |
| Murphy, Mark. Green Bay | 0 | 0 | 1 | 0 | 1 |
| Nehemiah, Renaldo, San Francisco | 1 | 0 | 0 | 0 | 0 |
| Nelson, Chuck, Los Angeles Rams | 0 | 0 | 1 | 0 | 1 |
| Nelson, Darrin, Minnesota | 5 | 1 | 0 | 0 | 1 |
| Nelson, Lee, St. Louis | 0 | 0 | 4 | 36 | 4 |
| Newhouse, Robert, Dallas | 3 | 1 | 0 | 0 | 1 |
| Nichols, Mark, Detroit | 2 | 0 | 0 | 0 | 0 |
| Norris, Ulysses, Detroit | 0 | 1 | 0 | 0 | 1 |
| Obradovich, Jim, Tampa Bay | 1 | 1 | 0 | 0 | 1 |
| O'Donoghue, Neil, St. Louis | 0 | 0 | 1 | 0 | 1 |
| Oliver, Hubert, Philadelphia | 5 | 2 | 0 | 0 | 2 |
| Olkewicz, Neal, Washington | 0 | 0 | 2 | 0 | 2 |
| Orosz, Tom, San Francisco | 1 | 0 | 0 | 0 | 0 |
| Osborne, Jim, Chicago | 0 | 0 | 1 | 0 | 1 |
| Owens, James, Tampa Bay | 0 | 1 | 0 | 0 | 1 |
| Owens, Mel, Los Angeles Rams | 0 | 0 | 2 | 0 | 2 |
| Pastorini, Dan, Philadelphia | 1 | 1 | 0 | 0 | 1 |
| Payton, Walter, Chicago | 5 | 2 | 0 | 0 | 2 |
| Pearson, Drew, Dallas | 1 | 0 | 0 | 0 | 0 |
| Perrin, Benny, St. Louis | 0 | 1 | 1 | 32 | 2 |
| Pisarcik, Joe, Philadelphia | 1 | 1 | 0 | 0 | 1 |
| Pitts, Mike, Atlanta | 0 | 0 | 1 | 26 | 1 |
| Poe, Johnnie, New Orleans | 0 | 0 | 2 | 0 | 2 |
| Provence, Andrew, Atlanta | 0 | 0 | 1 | 26 | 1 |
| Quick, Mike, Philadelphia | 1 | 0 | 0 | 0 | 0 |
| Quillan, Fred, San Francisco | 0 | 1 | 0 | 0 | 1 |
| Rade, John, Atlanta | 0 | 0 | 2 | 16 | 2 |
| Rains, Dan, Chicago | 0 | 0 | 1 | 0 | 1 |
| Ramson, Eason, San Francisco | 2 | 0 | 0 | 0 | 0 |
| Redden, Barry, Los Angeles Rams | 2 | 0 | 0 | 0 | 0 |
| Redwine, Jarvis, Minnesota | 1 | 0 | 0 | 0 | 0 |
| Reece, Beasley, N.Y. Giants-Tampa Bay | 1 | 1 | 3 | 0 | 4 |
| Reynolds, Jack, San Francisco | 0 | 0 | 2 | 0 | 2 |
| Richardson, Mike, Chicago | 0 | 0 | 2 | 7 | 2 |
| Riggins, John, Washington | 5 | 0 | 0 | 0 | 0 |
| Riggs, Gerald, Atlanta | 7 | 1 | 0 | 0 | 1 |
| Riley, Steve, Minnesota | 0 | 1 | 0 | 0 | 1 |
| Ring, Bill, San Francisco | 1 | 1 | 1 | 0 | 2 |
| Robbins, Tootie, St. Louis | 0 | 1 | 0 | 0 | 1 |
| Robinson, Bo, Atlanta | 1 | 0 | 0 | 0 | 0 |
| Robinson, Jerry, Philadelphia | 0 | 0 | 2 | 0 | 2 |
| Rogers, George, New Orleans | 8 | 2 | 0 | 0 | 2 |
| Rogers, Jimmy, New Orleans | 2 | 0 | 1 | 0 | 1 |
| Rouse, Curtis, Minnesota | 0 | 2 | 0 | 0 | 2 |
| Rubens, Larry, Green Bay | 0 | 0 | 1 | 0 | 1 |
| Rutledge, Jeff, New York Giants | 6 | 0 | 0 | 0 | 0 |
| Sally, Jerome, New York Giants | 0 | 0 | 1 | 0 | 1 |
| Sanders, Eugene, Tampa Bay | 0 | 1 | 0 | 0 | 1 |
| Schmitt, George, St. Louis | 1 | 0 | 1 | 0 | 1 |
| Sciarra, John, Philadelphia | 2 | 0 | 0 | 0 | 0 |
| Scott, Fred, Detroit | 1 | 0 | 0 | 0 | 0 |
| Scott, Herbert, Dallas | 0 | 1 | 0 | 0 | 1 |
| Scott, Lindsay, New Orleans | 1 | 0 | 0 | 0 | 0 |
| Selmon, Lee Roy, Tampa Bay | 0 | 0 | 1 | 4 | 1 |
| Sharpe, Luis, St. Louis | 0 | 2 | 0 | 0 | 2 |
| Shaw, Pete, New York Giants | 4 | 0 | 0 | 0 | 0 |
| Simmons, Dave, Chicago | 0 | 0 | 1 | 0 | 1 |
| Sims, Billy, Detroit | 6 | 4 | 0 | 0 | 4 |
| Singletary, Mike, Chicago | 0 | 0 | 4 | 15 | 4 |
| Slater, Jackie, Los Angeles Rams | 0 | 0 | 1 | 13 | 1 |
| Smith, Doug, Los Angeles Rams | 1 | 0 | 0 | 0 | 0 |
| Smith, Johnny Ray, Tampa Bay | 2 | 2 | 1 | 0 | 3 |
| Smith, Wayne, St. Louis | 0 | 0 | 1 | 0 | 1 |
| Solomon, Freddie, San Francisco | 1 | 1 | 0 | 0 | 1 |
| Spradlin, Danny, Tampa Bay | 0 | 0 | 1 | 0 | 1 |
| Springs, Ron, Dallas | 3 | 3 | 0 | 0 | 3 |
| Stabler, Ken, New Orleans | 4 | 0 | 0 | 0 | 0 |
| Steinfeld, Al, New York Giants | 0 | 1 | 0 | 0 | 1 |
| Stover, Jeff, San Francisco | 0 | 0 | 1 | 0 | 1 |
| Studwell, Scott, Minnesota | 0 | 0 | 1 | 0 | 1 |
| Suhey, Matt, Chicago | 5 | 0 | 0 | 0 | 0 |
| Sully, Ivory, Los Angeles Rams | 0 | 0 | 1 | 0 | 1 |
| Swanke, Karl, Green Bay | 0 | 2 | 0 | 0 | 2 |
| Taylor, Lawrence, New York Giants | 1 | 0 | 2 | 3 | 2 |
| Teal, Willie, Minnesota | 0 | 0 | 3 | 5 | 3 |
| Theismann, Joe, Washington | 1 | 0 | 0 | 0 | 0 |
| Thielemann, R.C., Atlanta | 0 | 0 | 1 | 0 | 1 |
| Thompson, Jack, Tampa Bay | 10 | 5 | 0 | 0 | 5 |
| Thompson, Leonard, Detroit | 2 | 1 | 0 | 0 | 1 |
| Thompson, Robert, Tampa Bay | 0 | 0 | 2 | 0 | 2 |
| Thompson, Vince, Detroit | 1 | 0 | 0 | 0 | 0 |
| Thurman, Dennis, Dallas | 0 | 1 | 1 | 0 | 2 |
| Tice, John, New Orleans | 0 | 1 | 1 | 0 | 2 |
| Tilley, Pat, St. Louis | 1 | 1 | 0 | 0 | 1 |
| Turner, John, Minnesota | 0 | 0 | 2 | 24 | 2 |
| Turner, Keena, San Francisco | 0 | 0 | 1 | 0 | 1 |
| Tyler, Andre, Tampa Bay | 1 | 0 | 0 | 0 | 0 |
| Tyler, Wendell, San Francisco | 7 | 0 | 0 | 0 | 0 |
| Umphrey, Rich, New York Giants | 0 | 1 | 0 | 0 | 1 |
| Walters, Stan, Philadelphia | 0 | 2 | 0 | 0 | 2 |
| Warren, Frank, New Orleans | 0 | 0 | 1 | 0 | 1 |
| Washington, Anthony, Washington | 1 | 1 | 0 | 0 | 1 |
| Washington, Joe, Washington | 2 | 0 | 0 | 0 | 0 |
| Washington, Lionel, St. Louis | 0 | 0 | 1 | 0 | 1 |
| Watkins, Bobby, Detroit | 1 | 1 | 2 | 6 | 3 |
| Wattelet, Frank, New Orleans | 0 | 0 | 3 | 6 | 3 |
| Waymer, Dave, New Orleans | 0 | 1 | 2 | 0 | 3 |
| White, Danny, Dallas | 10 | 4 | 0 | 0 | 4 |
| White, Randy, Dallas | 0 | 0 | 1 | 0 | 1 |
| Whitehurst, David, Green Bay | 2 | 1 | 0 | 0 | 1 |
| Whittington, Mike, New York Giants | 0 | 0 | 1 | 0 | 1 |
| Wilder, James, Tampa Bay | 1 | 0 | 0 | 0 | 0 |
| Wilks, Jim, New Orleans | 0 | 0 | 1 | 0 | 1 |
| Williams, Byron, New York Giants | 1 | 0 | 0 | 0 | 0 |
| Williams, Eric, Los Angeles Rams | 0 | 0 | 1 | 0 | 1 |
| Williams, Greg, Washington | 0 | 0 | 4 | 4 | 4 |
| Williams, Jimmy, Detroit | 0 | 0 | 1 | 0 | 1 |
| Williams, Joel, Philadelphia | 0 | 0 | 1 | 0 | 1 |
| Williams, Mike, Philadelphia | 1 | 0 | 0 | 0 | 0 |
| Williams, Richard, Atlanta | 1 | 1 | 0 | 0 | 1 |
| Wilson, Dave, New Orleans | 5 | 0 | 0 | 0 | 0 |
| Wilson, Mike, San Francisco | 1 | 0 | 0 | 0 | 0 |
| Wilson, Wade, Minnesota | 1 | 0 | 0 | 0 | 0 |
| Wilson, Wayne, New Orleans | 6 | 0 | 0 | 0 | 0 |
| Winston, Dennis, New Orleans | 1 | 0 | 1 | 0 | 1 |
| Wonsley, Otis, Washington | 0 | 0 | 1 | 0 | 1 |
| Woodruff, Tony, Philadelphia | 1 | 1 | 0 | 0 | 1 |
| Woolfolk, Butch, New York Giants | 8 | 1 | 0 | 0 | 1 |
| Wright, Eric, San Francisco | 0 | 0 | 1 | 0 | 1 |
| Yeates, Jeff, Atlanta | 0 | 0 | 1 | 0 | 1 |
| Young, Glen, Philadelphia | 2 | 1 | 0 | 0 | 1 |
| Young, Roynell, Philadelphia | 0 | 1 | 1 | 0 | 2 |
| Youngblood, Jack, Los Angeles Rams | 0 | 0 | 2 | 0 | 2 |

*Touchdowns:* Mike Douglass, Green Bay, 2; Dwaine Board, San Francisco; Kelvin Clark, New Orleans; Vernon Dean, Washington; Clint Didier, Washington; Michael Downs, Dallas; Blane Gaison, Atlanta; Elois Grooms, St. Louis; Mike Hartenstine, Chicago; Mike Hegman, Dallas; Terry Jackson, New York Giants; Charlie Johnson, Minnesota; Mel Kaufman, Washington; Steve Korte, New Orleans; Dave Logan, Tampa Bay; Lee Nelson, St. Louis; Benny Perrin, St. Louis; John Rade, Atlanta; and Dennis Thurman, Dallas; 1 each.

# SACKS

## INDIVIDUAL CHAMPIONS
**AFC: 19** —Mark Gastineau, New York Jets
**NFC: 17.5**—Fred Dean, San Francisco

## TEAM CHAMPIONS
**NFC: 59**—St. Louis
**AFC: 57**—Los Angeles Raiders

## AFC SACKS—TEAM

| | Sacks | Yards |
|---|---|---|
| Los Angeles Raiders | 57 | 484 |
| Pittsburgh | 50 | 361 |
| Miami | 49 | 363 |
| New York Jets | 48 | 378 |
| Seattle | 43 | 351 |
| Baltimore | 41 | 310 |
| Cincinnati | 41 | 335 |
| New England | 39 | 270 |
| Denver | 38 | 317 |
| Kansas City | 35 | 250 |
| Buffalo | 32 | 247 |
| Cleveland | 32 | 239 |
| Houston | 31 | 250 |
| San Diego | 31 | 269 |
| AFC Total | 567 | 4424 |
| AFC Average | 40.5 | 316.0 |

## NFC SACKS—TEAM

| | Sacks | Yards |
|---|---|---|
| St. Louis | 59 | 468 |
| Dallas | 57 | 437 |
| San Francisco | 57 | 448 |
| New Orleans | 56 | 437 |
| Chicago | 51 | 384 |
| Washington | 51 | 402 |
| Minnesota | 47 | 326 |
| New York Giants | 44 | 323 |
| Detroit | 43 | 289 |
| Tampa Bay | 42 | 309 |
| Green Bay | 41 | 271 |
| Philadelphia | 36 | 256 |
| Los Angeles Rams | 33 | 258 |
| Atlanta | 31 | 217 |
| NFC Total | 648 | 4825 |
| NFC Average | 46.3 | 344.6 |
| League Total | 1215 | 9249 |
| League Average | 43.4 | 330.3 |

## NFL TOP 10 INDIVIDUAL LEADERS IN SACKS

| | Total | | Total |
|---|---|---|---|
| Gastineau, Mark, N.Y. Jets | 19 | Gay, William, Detroit | 13.5 |
| Dean, Fred, San Francisco | 17.5 | Baker, Al, St. Louis | 13 |
| Betters, Doug, Miami | 16 | Board, Dwaine, San Fran. | 13 |
| Green, Jacob, Seattle | 16 | Edwards, Eddie, Cincinnati | 13 |
| Greer, Curtis, St. Louis | 16 | English, Doug, Detroit | 13 |
| Johnson, Ezra, Green Bay | 14.5 | Long, Howie, L.A. Raiders | 13 |
| Willis, Keith, Pittsburgh | 14 | Martin, Doug, Minnesota | 13 |

## AFC SACKS—INDIVIDUAL

| | | | |
|---|---|---|---|
| Gastineau, Mark, N.Y. Jets | 19.0 | Duhe, A.J., Miami | 5.5 |
| Betters, Doug, Miami | 16.0 | Jackson, Tom, Denver | 5.5 |
| Green, Jacob, Seattle | 16.0 | Neil, Kenny, N.Y. Jets | 5.5 |
| Willis, Keith, Pittsburgh | 14.0 | Cole, Robin, Pittsburgh | 5.0 |
| Edwards, Eddie, Cincinnati | 13.0 | Collins, Glen, Cincinnati | 5.0 |
| Long, Howie, L.A. Raiders | 13.0 | Cooks, Johnie, Baltimore | 5.0 |
| Maxwell, Vernon, Baltimore | 11.0 | Ferguson, Keith, San Diego | 5.0 |
| Townsend, Greg, L.A. Raiders | 10.5 | Franks, Elvis, Cleveland | 5.0 |
| Bell, Mike, Kansas City | 10.0 | Mangiero, Dino, Kansas City | 5.0 |
| Williams, Ben, Buffalo | 10.0 | Smith, Dennis, Denver | 5.0 |
| Tippett, Andre, New England | 8.5 | Talley, Darryl, Buffalo | 5.0 |
| Adams, Julius, New England | 8.0 | Wisniewski, Leo, Baltimore | 5.0 |
| Baumhower, Bob, Miami | 8.0 | Camp, Reggie, Cleveland | 4.5 |
| Bryant, Jeff, Seattle | 8.0 | Chavous, Barney, Denver | 4.5 |
| King, Linden, San Diego | 8.0 | Lowe, Woodrow, San Diego | 4.5 |
| Gary, Keith, Pittsburgh | 7.5 | Taylor, Malcolm, Houston | 4.5 |
| Williams, Reggie, Cincinnati | 7.5 | Banks, Chip, Cleveland | 4.0 |
| Alzado, Lyle, L.A. Raiders | 7.0 | Cousineau, Tom, Cleveland | 4.0 |
| Bowser, Charles, Miami | 6.5 | Jackson, Charles, Kansas City | 4.0 |
| Klecko, Joe, N.Y. Jets | 6.5 | Jones, Rulon, Denver | 4.0 |
| Dunn, Gary, Pittsburgh | 6.0 | Lambert, Jack, Pittsburgh | 4.0 |
| Martin, Rod, L.A. Raiders | 6.0 | Lyons, Marty, N.Y. Jets | 4.0 |
| Matthews, Clay, Cleveland | 6.0 | Owens, Dennis, New England | 4.0 |
| Pickel, Bill, L.A. Raiders | 6.0 | Parker, Ervin, Buffalo | 4.0 |
| Smerlas, Fred, Buffalo | 6.0 | Reese, Archie, L.A. Raiders | 4.0 |
| Baker, Jesse, Houston | 5.5 | Still, Art, Kansas City | 4.0 |
| Bracelin, Greg, Baltimore | 5.5 | Thompson, Donnell, Baltimore | 4.0 |

| | | | |
|---|---|---|---|
| Blackmon, Don, New England | 3.5 | Kohrs, Bob, Pittsburgh | 1.5 |
| Foster, Jerome, Houston | 3.5 | Krumrie, Tim, Cincinnati | 1.5 |
| Golic, Bob, Cleveland | 3.5 | Parker, Steve, Baltimore | 1.5 |
| Bostic, Keith, Houston | 3.0 | Robinson, Shelton, Seattle | 1.5 |
| Browner, Ross, Cincinnati | 3.0 | Scholtz, Bruce, Seattle | 1.5 |
| Charles, Mike, Miami | 3.0 | Waechter, Henry, Baltimore | 1.5 |
| Easley, Ken, Seattle | 3.0 | Abraham, Robert, Houston | 1.0 |
| Hamm, Bob, Houston | 3.0 | Baldwin, Keith, Cleveland | 1.0 |
| Jackson, Michael, Seattle | 3.0 | Bennett, Barry, N.Y. Jets | 1.0 |
| Johnson, Gary, San Diego | 3.0 | Blackwood, Glenn, Miami | 1.0 |
| Manor, Brison, Denver | 3.0 | Breeden, Louis, Cincinnati | 1.0 |
| Nash, Joe, Seattle | 3.0 | Brudzinski, Bob, Miami | 1.0 |
| Nelson, Edmund, Pittsburgh | 3.0 | Carter, Rubin, Denver | 1.0 |
| Rhone, Earnest, Miami | 3.0 | Dixon, Hanford, Cleveland | 1.0 |
| Smith, Billy Ray, San Diego | 3.0 | Frazier, Guy, Cincinnati | 1.0 |
| Spani, Gary, Kansas City | 3.0 | Gaines, Greg, Seattle | 1.0 |
| White, Sherman, Buffalo | 3.0 | Glasgow, Nesby, Baltimore | 1.0 |
| Beasley, Tom, Pittsburgh | 2.5 | Goodman, John, Pittsburgh | 1.0 |
| Brazile, Robert, Houston | 2.5 | Green, Mike, San Diego | 1.0 |
| Gradishar, Randy, Denver | 2.5 | Griffin, Ray, Cincinnati | 1.0 |
| Hicks, Mark, Seattle | 2.5 | Guilbeau, Rusty, N.Y. Jets | 1.0 |
| Mehl, Lance, N.Y. Jets | 2.5 | Hartwig, Carter, Houston | 1.0 |
| Sochia, Brian, Houston | 2.5 | Henderson, Reuben, San Diego | 1.0 |
| Ballard, Quinton, Baltimore | 2.0 | Howard, Thomas, Kansas City | 1.0 |
| Bokamper, Kim, Miami | 2.0 | Hunt, Daryl, Houston | 1.0 |
| Bowyer, Walt, Denver | 2.0 | Jackson, Roger, Denver | 1.0 |
| Brown, Mark, Miami | 2.0 | Kemp, Bobby, Cincinnati | 1.0 |
| Browning, Dave, New England | 2.0 | Kinlaw, Reggie, L.A. Raiders | 1.0 |
| Burley, Gary, Cincinnati | 2.0 | Kozlowski, Mike, Miami | 1.0 |
| Busick, Steve, Denver | 2.0 | Krauss, Barry, Baltimore | 1.0 |
| Cameron, Glenn, Cincinnati | 2.0 | LeClair, Jim, Cincinnati | 1.0 |
| Clayton, Harvey, Pittsburgh | 2.0 | Lindstrom, Dave, Kansas City | 1.0 |
| Crable, Bob, N.Y. Jets | 2.0 | McPherson, Miles, San Diego | 1.0 |
| Daniels, Calvin, Kansas City | 2.0 | Nelson, Steve, New England | 1.0 |
| Davis, Mike, L.A. Raiders | 2.0 | Odom, Clifton, Baltimore | 1.0 |
| Dufek, Don, Seattle | 2.0 | Shiver, Sanders, Baltimore | 1.0 |
| Hendricks, Ted, L.A. Raiders | 2.0 | Simpson, Keith, Seattle | 1.0 |
| James, Roland, New England | 2.0 | Squirek, Jack, L.A. Raiders | 1.0 |
| Johnson, Ken, Buffalo | 2.0 | Stalls, Dave, Tampa Bay-Raiders | 1.0 |
| Kremer, Ken, Kansas City | 2.0 | Thompson, Ted, Houston | 1.0 |
| Marve, Eugene, Buffalo | 2.0 | Whitwell, Mike, Cleveland | 1.0 |
| McGrew, Larry, New England | 2.0 | Williams, Kendall, Baltimore | 1.0 |
| Mecklenburg, Karl, Denver | 2.0 | Williams, Lester, New England | 1.0 |
| Millen, Matt, L.A. Raiders | 2.0 | Woodring, John, N.Y. Jets | 1.0 |
| Nelson, Bob, L.A. Raiders | 2.0 | Woodruff, Dwayne, Pittsburgh | 1.0 |
| Puzzuoli, Dave, Cleveland | 2.0 | Wright, Louis, Denver | 1.0 |
| Rembert, Johnny, New England | 2.0 | Young, Andre, San Diego | 1.0 |
| Rivera, Gabriel, Pittsburgh | 2.0 | Anderson, Kim, Baltimore | 0.5 |
| Rudolph, Ben, N.Y. Jets | 2.0 | Bradley, Carlos, San Diego | 0.5 |
| Schroy, Ken, N.Y. Jets | 2.0 | Burruss, Lloyd, Kansas City | 0.5 |
| Stensrud, Mike, Houston | 2.0 | Dinkel, Tom, Cincinnati | 0.5 |
| Weishuhn, Clayton, New Eng. | 2.0 | Elko, Bill, San Diego | 0.5 |
| Williams, Toby, New England | 2.0 | Harris, Marshall, New England | 0.5 |
| Woodard, Kenneth, Denver | 2.0 | Latimer, Don, Denver | 0.5 |
| Ackerman, Rick, San Diego | 1.5 | Merriweather, Mike, Pittsburgh | 0.5 |
| Boyarsky, Jerry, Cincinnati | 1.5 | Riley, Avon, Houston | 0.5 |
| Buttle, Greg, N.Y. Jets | 1.5 | Rogers, Doug, New England | 0.5 |
| Cherry, Deron, Kansas City | 1.5 | Tuiasosopo, Manu, Seattle | 0.5 |

## NFC SACKS—INDIVIDUAL

| | | | |
|---|---|---|---|
| Dean, Fred, San Francisco | 17.5 | Jeter, Gary, L.A. Rams | 6.5 |
| Greer, Curtis, St. Louis | 16.0 | Lewis, Reggie, New Orleans | 6.5 |
| Johnson, Ezra, Green Bay | 14.5 | Harris, Al, Chicago | 6.0 |
| Gay, William, Detroit | 13.5 | Moore, Derland, New Orleans | 6.0 |
| Baker, Al, St. Louis | 13.0 | Smerek, Don, Dallas | 6.0 |
| Board, Dwaine, San Francisco | 13.0 | Smith, Don, Atlanta | 6.0 |
| English, Doug, Detroit | 13.0 | Braggs, Byron, Green Bay | 5.5 |
| Martin, Doug, Minnesota | 13.0 | Douglass, Mike, Green Bay | 5.5 |
| White, Randy, Dallas | 12.5 | Elliott, Tony, New Orleans | 5.5 |
| Galloway, David, St. Louis | 12.0 | Paul, Whitney, New Orleans | 5.5 |
| Hartenstine, Mike, Chicago | 12.0 | Cannon, John, Tampa Bay | 5.0 |
| Jackson, Rickey, New Orleans | 12.0 | Doss, Reggie, L.A. Rams | 5.0 |
| Butz, Dave, Washington | 11.5 | Hairston, Carl, Philadelphia | 5.0 |
| Harrison, Dennis, Philadelphia | 11.5 | Hampton, Dan, Chicago | 5.0 |
| Manley, Dexter, Washington | 11.0 | Headen, Andy, N.Y. Giants | 5.0 |
| Selmon, Lee Roy, Tampa Bay | 11.0 | Osborne, Jim, Chicago | 5.0 |
| Dickerson, Anthony, Dallas | 10.5 | Anderson, John, Green Bay | 4.5 |
| Youngblood, Jack, L.A. Rams | 10.5 | Blair, Matt, Minnesota | 4.5 |
| McGee, Tony, Washington | 10.0 | Clark, Bruce, New Orleans | 4.5 |
| Elshire, Neil, Minnesota | 9.5 | Cofer, Mike, Detroit | 4.5 |
| Logan, Dave, Tampa Bay | 9.5 | Dutton, John, Dallas | 4.5 |
| Martin, George, N.Y. Giants | 9.0 | Green, Curtis, Detroit | 4.5 |
| Taylor, Lawrence, N.Y. Giants | 9.0 | Sally, Jerome, N.Y. Giants | 4.5 |
| Brown, Greg, Philadelphia | 8.5 | Bates, Bill, Dallas | 4.0 |
| McMichael, Steve, Chicago | 8.5 | Curry, Buddy, Atlanta | 4.0 |
| Wilks, Jim, New Orleans | 8.0 | Owens, Mel, L.A. Rams | 4.0 |
| Holloway, Randy, Minnesota | 7.5 | Pillers, Lawrence, San Fran. | 4.0 |
| Junior, E.J., St. Louis | 7.5 | Yeates, Jeff, Atlanta | 4.0 |
| Jones, Ed, Dallas | 7.0 | Armstrong, Harvey, Philadelphia | 3.5 |
| Pitts, Mike, Atlanta | 7.0 | Green, Hugh, Tampa Bay | 3.5 |

198

Johnson, Charles, Green Bay . 3.5
Singletary, Mike, Chicago...... 3.5
Turner, Keena, San Francisco . 3.5
Andrews, George, L.A. Rams . 3.0
Bell, Todd, Chicago.......... 3.0
Bethea, Larry, Dallas......... 3.0
Dent, Richard, Chicago ....... 3.0
Ferrari, Ron, San Francisco .... 3.0
Harper, Willie, San Francisco .. 3.0
Hawkins, Andy, Tampa Bay ... 3.0
Kovach, Jim, New Orleans..... 3.0
Kugler, Pete, San Francisco.... 3.0
Mann, Charles, Washington.... 3.0
Merrill, Casey, N.Y. Giants ..... 3.0
Merrow, Jeff, Atlanta.......... 3.0
Van Pelt, Brad, N.Y. Giants..... 3.0
Brooks, Perry, Washington..... 2.5
Grant, Darryl, Washington ..... 2.5
Hardison, Dee, N.Y. Giants .... 2.5
Mays, Stafford, St. Louis....... 2.5
Mullaney, Mark, Minnesota .... 2.5
Stover, Jeff, San Francisco..... 2.5
Stuckey, Jim, San Francisco ... 2.5
Williams, Joel, Philadelphia.... 2.5
Boyd, Greg, Green Bay ....... 2.0
Brantley, Scot, Tampa Bay..... 2.0
Browner, Joey, Minnesota...... 2.0
Clinkscale, Dextor, Dallas ..... 2.0
Coleman, Monte, Washington . 2.0
Cumby, George, Green Bay.... 2.0
Jeffcoat, Jim, Dallas.......... 2.0
Lewis, Cliff, Green Bay........ 2.0
Martin, Harvey, Dallas......... 2.0
Nairne, Rob, New Orleans..... 2.0
Nelson, Lee, St. Louis........ 2.0
Olkewicz, Neal, Washington ... 2.0
Studwell, Scott, Minnesota..... 2.0
Warren, Frank, New Orleans ... 2.0
Wilson, Otis, Chicago......... 2.0
Davis, Jeff, Tampa Bay........ 1.5
Downs, Mike, Dallas.......... 1.5
Kaufman, Mel, Washington .... 1.5
Kelley, Brian, N.Y. Giants ...... 1.5
Liebenstein, Todd, Washington 1.5
Milot, Rich, Washington ....... 1.5
Provence, Andrew, Atlanta..... 1.5
Rade, John, Atlanta........... 1.5
Arbubakrr, Hasson, Tampa Bay 1.0
Barnes, Roosevelt, Detroit..... 1.0
Benish, Dan, Atlanta.......... 1.0
Brown, Rush, St. Louis ........ 1.0
Cabral, Brian, Chicago........ 1.0
Campbell, Gary, Chicago...... 1.0
Carson, Harry, N.Y. Giants ..... 1.0
Clarke, Ken, Philadelphia...... 1.0
Cobb, Garry, Detroit .......... 1.0
Coffey, Ken, Washington ...... 1.0
Collins, Jim, L.A. Rams........ 1.0
Cotney, Mark, Tampa Bay ..... 1.0
Currier, Bill, N.Y. Giants........ 1.0
Darby, Byron, Philadelphia..... 1.0
Dawson, Mike, Detroit......... 1.0
Duda, Mark, St. Louis ........ 1.0
Fanning, Mike, Detroit......... 1.0
Fantetti, Ken, Detroit.......... 1.0
Flowers, Larry, N.Y. Giants ..... 1.0
Frye, David, Atlanta........... 1.0
Gervais, Rick, San Francisco... 1.0
Griggs, Anthony, Philadelphia.. 1.0
Grooms, Elois, St. Louis ....... 1.0
Harrell, James, Detroit ........ 1.0
Harris, Bob, St. Louis ......... 1.0
Hegman, Mike, Dallas ........ 1.0
Holt, John, Tampa Bay ........ 1.0
Hopkins, Wes, Philadelphia.... 1.0
Hunt, Byron, N.Y. Giants....... 1.0
Irvin, LeRoy, L.A. Rams........ 1.0
Johnson, Charlie, Minnesota... 1.0
Johnson, Dennis, Minnesota ... 1.0
Johnson, Johnnie, L.A. Rams . 1.0
Judie, Ed, Tampa Bay......... 1.0
Keys, Tyrone, Chicago ........ 1.0
Kinard, Terry, N.Y. Giants ...... 1.0
Kuykendall, Fulton, Atlanta .... 1.0
Leopold, Bobby, San Francisco 1.0
Lott, Ronnie, San Francisco.... 1.0
McColl, Milt, San Francisco .... 1.0
Murphy, Mark, Washington..... 1.0
Nord, Keith, Minnesota........ 1.0
Perrin, Benny, St. Louis........ 1.0

Reese, Booker, Tampa Bay .... 1.0
Reynolds, Jack, San Francisco 1.0
Robinson, Jerry, Philadelphia .. 1.0
Shaw, Pete, N.Y. Giants ....... 1.0
Spradlin, Danny, Tampa Bay ... 1.0
Sully, Ivory, L.A. Rams......... 1.0
Thurman, Dennis, Dallas ...... 1.0
Turner, John, Minnesota ....... 1.0
Turner, Richard, Green Bay .... 1.0
White, James, Minnesota...... 1.0
Williams, Jimmy, Detroit ....... 1.0
Winston, Dennis, New Orleans 1.0
Zele, Mike, Atlanta............ 1.0
Hannon, Tom, Minnesota ...... 0.5
Marshall, Leonard, N.Y. Giants 0.5
McNeill, Fred, Minnesota...... 0.5
Moss, Martin, Detroit.......... 0.5
Spears, Ron, Green Bay....... 0.5

# HISTORY

# PRO FOOTBALL HALL OF FAME

The Professional Football Hall of Fame is located in Canton, Ohio, site of the organizational meeting on September 17, 1920, from which the National Football League evolved. The NFL recognized Canton as the Hall of Fame site on April 27, 1961. Canton area individuals, foundations, and companies donated almost $400,000 in cash and services to provide funds for the construction of the original two-building complex, which was dedicated on September 7, 1963. The original Hall of Fame complex was almost doubled in size with the completion of a $620,000 expansion project that was dedicated on May 10, 1971. A second expansion project was completed on November 20, 1978. It features three exhibition areas and a theater twice the size of the original one.

The Hall represents the sport of pro football in many ways—through three large and colorful exhibition galleries, in the twin enshrinement halls, with numerous fan-participation electronic devices, a research library, and an NFL gift shop.

In recent years, the Pro Football Hall of Fame has become an extremely popular tourist attraction. At the end of 1983, a total of 3,531,544 fans had visited the Pro Football Hall of Fame.

New members of the Pro Football Hall of Fame are elected annually by a 29-member National Board of Selectors, made up of media representatives from every league city and the president of the Pro Football Writers Association. Between three and six new members are elected each year. An affirmative vote of approximately 80 percent is needed for election.

Any fan may nominate any eligible player or contributor simply by writing to the Pro Football Hall of Fame. Players must be retired five years to be eligible, while a coach need only be retired with no time limit specified. Contributors (administrators, owners, et al.) may be elected while they are still active.

The charter class of 17 enshrinees was elected in 1963 and the honor roll now stands at 123 with the election of a four-man class in 1984. That class consists of Willie Brown, Mike McCormack, Charley Taylor, and Arnie Weinmeister.

## Roster of Members

**HERB ADDERLEY**
Defensive back. 6-1, 200. Born in Philadelphia, Pennsylvania, June 8, 1939. Michigan State. Inducted in 1980. 1961-69 Green Bay Packers, 1970-72 Dallas Cowboys.

**LANCE ALWORTH**
Wide receiver. 6-0, 184. Born in Houston, Texas, August 3, 1940. Arkansas. Inducted in 1978. 1962-1970 San Diego Chargers, 1971-72 Dallas Cowboys.

**DOUG ATKINS**
Defensive end. 6-8, 275. Born in Humboldt, Tennessee, May 8, 1930. Tennessee. Inducted in 1982. 1953-54 Cleveland Browns, 1955-1966 Chicago Bears, 1967-69 New Orleans Saints.

**MORRIS (RED) BADGRO**
End. 6-0, 190. Born in Orilla, Washington, December 1, 1902. USC. Inducted in 1981. 1927 New York Yankees, 1930-1935 New York Giants, 1936 Brooklyn Dodgers.

**CLIFF BATTLES**
Halfback. 6-1, 201. Born in Akron, Ohio, May 1, 1910. Died April 27, 1981. West Virginia Wesleyan. Inducted in 1968. 1932 Boston Braves, 1933-36 Boston Redskins, 1937 Washington Redskins.

**SAMMY BAUGH**
Quarterback. 6-2, 180. Born in Temple, Texas, March 17, 1914. Texas Christian. Inducted in 1963. 1937-1952 Washington Redskins.

**CHUCK BEDNARIK**
Center-linebacker. 6-3, 230. Born in Bethlehem, Pennsylvania, May 1, 1925. Pennsylvania. Inducted in 1967. 1949-1962 Philadelphia Eagles.

**BERT BELL**
Commissioner. Team owner. Born in Philadelphia, Pennsylvania, February 25, 1895. Died October 11, 1959. Pennsylvania. Inducted in 1963. 1933-1940 Philadelphia Eagles, 1941-42 Pittsburgh Steelers, 1943 Phil-Pitt, 1944-46 Pittsburgh Steelers.

**BOBBY BELL**
Linebacker. 6-4, 225. Born in Shelby, North Carolina, June 17, 1940. Minnesota. Inducted in 1983. 1963-1974 Kansas City Chiefs.

**RAYMOND BERRY**
End. 6-2, 187. Born in Corpus Christi, Texas, February 27, 1933. Southern Methodist. Inducted in 1973. 1955-1967 Baltimore Colts.

**CHARLES W. BIDWILL, SR.**
Team owner. Born in Chicago, Illinois, September 16, 1895. Died April 19, 1947. Loyola of Chicago. Inducted in 1967. 1933-1943 Chicago Cardinals, 1944 Card-Pitt, 1945-47 Chicago Cardinals.

**GEORGE BLANDA**
Quarterback-kicker. 6-2, 215. Born in Youngwood, Pennsylvania, September 17, 1927. Kentucky. Inducted in 1981. 1949-1958 Chicago Bears, 1960-66 Houston Oilers, 1967-1975 Oakland Raiders.

**JIM BROWN**
Fullback. 6-2, 232. Born in St. Simons, Georgia, February 17, 1936. Syracuse. Inducted in 1971. 1957-1965 Cleveland Browns.

**PAUL BROWN**
Coach. Born in Norwalk, Ohio, September 7, 1908. Miami, Ohio. Inducted in 1967. 1946-49 Cleveland Browns (AAFC), 1950-1962 Cleveland Browns, 1968-1975 Cincinnati Bengals.

**ROOSEVELT BROWN**
Offensive tackle. 6-3, 255. Born in Charlottesville, Virginia, October 20, 1932. Morgan State. Inducted in 1975. 1953-1965 New York Giants.

**WILLIE BROWN**
Defensive back. 6-1, 210. Born in Yazoo City, Mississippi, December 2, 1940. Grambling. Inducted in 1984. 1963-66 Denver Broncos, 1967-1978 Oakland Raiders.

**DICK BUTKUS**
Linebacker. 6-3, 245. Born in Chicago, Illinois, December 9, 1942. Illinois. Inducted in 1979. 1965-1973 Chicago Bears.

**TONY CANADEO**
Halfback. 5-11, 195. Born in Chicago, Illinois, May 5, 1919. Gonzaga. Inducted in 1974. 1941-44 Green Bay Packers, 1946-1952 Green Bay Packers.

**JOE CARR**
NFL president. Born in Columbus, Ohio, October 22, 1880. Died May 20, 1939. Did not attend college. Inducted in 1963. President, 1921-1939 National Football League.

**GUY CHAMBERLIN**
End. Coach. 6-2, 210. Born in Blue Springs, Nebraska, January 16, 1894. Died April 4, 1967. Nebraska. Inducted in 1965. 1920 Decatur Staleys, 1921 Chicago Staleys, 1922-23 Canton Bulldogs, 1924 Cleveland Bulldogs, 1925-26 Frankford Yellowjackets, 1927-28 Chicago Cardinals.

**JACK CHRISTIANSEN**
Defensive back. 6-1, 185. Born in Sublette, Kansas, December 20, 1928. Colorado State. Inducted in 1970. 1951-58 Detroit Lions.

**EARL (DUTCH) CLARK**
Quarterback. 6-0, 185. Born in Fowler, Colorado, October 11, 1906. Died August 5, 1978. Colorado College. Inducted in 1963. 1931-32 Portsmouth Spartans, 1934-38 Detroit Lions.

**GEORGE CONNOR**
Tackle-linebacker. 6-3, 240. Born in Chicago, Illinois, January 1, 1925. Holy Cross, Notre Dame. Inducted in 1975. 1948-1955 Chicago Bears.

**JIMMY CONZELMAN**
Quarterback. Coach. Team owner. 6-0, 180. Born in St. Louis, Missouri, March 6, 1898. Died July 31, 1970. Washington, Missouri. Inducted in 1964. 1920 Decatur Staleys, 1921-22 Rock Island, Ill., Independents, 1923-24 Milwaukee Badgers; owner-coach, 1925-26 Detroit Panthers; player-coach 1927-29, coach 1930 Providence Steamroller; coach, 1940-42 Chicago Cardinals, 1946-48 Chicago Cardinals.

**WILLIE DAVIS**
Defensive end. 6-3, 245. Born in Lisbon, Louisiana, July 24, 1934. Grambling. Inducted in 1981. 1958-59 Cleveland Browns, 1960-69 Green Bay Packers.

**ART DONOVAN**
Defensive tackle. 6-3, 265. Born in Bronx, New York, June 5, 1925. Boston College. Inducted in 1968. 1950 Baltimore Colts, 1951 New York Yanks, 1952 Dallas Texans, 1953-1961 Baltimore Colts.

**JOHN (PADDY) DRISCOLL**
Quarterback. 5-11, 160. Born in Evanston, Illinois, January 11, 1896. Died June 29, 1968. Northwestern. Inducted in 1965. 1920 Decatur Staleys, 1920-25 Chicago Cardinals, 1926-29 Chicago Bears. Head coach, 1956-57 Chicago Bears.

**BILL DUDLEY**
Halfback. 5-10, 176. Born in Bluefield, Virginia, December 24, 1921. Virginia. Inducted in 1966. 1942 Pittsburgh Steelers, 1945-46 Pittsburgh Steelers, 1947-49 Detroit Lions, 1950-51, 1953 Washington Redskins.

**GLEN (TURK) EDWARDS**
Tackle. 6-2, 260. Born in Mold, Washington, September 28, 1907. Died January 10, 1973. Washington State. Inducted in 1969. 1932 Boston Braves, 1933-36 Washington Redskins, 1937-1940 Washington Redskins.

**WEEB EWBANK**
Coach. Born in Richmond, Indiana, May 6, 1907. Miami, Ohio. Inducted in 1978. 1954-1962 Baltimore Colts, 1963-1973 New York Jets.

**TOM FEARS**
End. 6-2, 215. Born in Los Angeles, California, December 3, 1923. Santa Clara, UCLA. Inducted in 1970. 1948-1956 Los Angeles Rams.

**RAY FLAHERTY**
Coach. Born in Spokane, Washington, September 1, 1904. Gonzaga. Inducted in 1976. 1926 Los Angeles Wildcats (AFL), 1927 New York Yankees, 1928-29, 1931-35 New York Giants. Coach, 1936 Boston Redskins, 1937-1942 Washington Redskins, 1946-48 New York Yankees (AAFC), 1949 Chicago Hornets (AAFC).

**LEN FORD**
End. 6-5, 260. Born in Washington, D.C., February 18, 1926. Died March 14, 1972. Michigan. Inducted in 1976. 1948-49 Los Angeles Dons (AAFC), 1950-57 Cleveland Browns, 1958 Green Bay Packers.

**DAN FORTMANN**
Guard. 6-0, 207. Born in Pearl River, New York, April 11, 1916. Colgate. Inducted in 1965. 1936-1943 Chicago Bears.

**BILL GEORGE**
Linebacker. 6-2, 230. Born in Waynesburg, Pennsylvania, October 27, 1930. Wake Forest. Inducted in 1974. 1952-1965 Chicago Bears, 1966 Los Angeles Rams.

**FRANK GIFFORD**
Halfback. 6-1, 195. Born in Santa Monica, California, August 16, 1930. USC. Inducted in 1977. 1952-1960, 1962-64 New York Giants.

**SID GILLMAN**
Coach. Born in Minneapolis, Minnesota, October 26, 1911. Ohio State. Inducted in 1983. 1955-59 Los Angeles Rams, 1960-69 San Diego Chargers, 1973-74 Houston Oilers.

**OTTO GRAHAM**
Quarterback. 6-1, 195. Born in Waukegan, Illinois, December 6, 1921. Northwestern. Inducted in 1965. 1946-49 Cleveland Browns (AAFC), 1950-55 Cleveland Browns.

**RED GRANGE**
Halfback. 6-0, 185. Born in Forksville, Pennsylvania, June 13, 1903. Illinois. Inducted in 1963. 1925 Chicago Bears, 1926 New York Yankees (AFL), 1927 New York Yankees, 1929-1934 Chicago Bears.

**FORREST GREGG**
Tackle. 6-4, 250. Born in Sulphur Springs, Texas, October 18, 1933. Southern Methodist. Inducted in 1977. 1956, 1958-1970 Green Bay Packers, 1971 Dallas Cowboys.

**LOU GROZA**
Tackle-kicker. 6-3, 250. Born in Martin's Ferry, Ohio, January 25, 1924. Ohio State. Inducted in 1974. 1946-49 Cleveland Browns (AAFC), 1950-59, 1961-67 Cleveland Browns.

**JOE GUYON**
Halfback. 6-1, 180. Born in Mahnomen, Minnesota, November 26, 1892. Died November 27, 1971. Carlisle, Georgia Tech. Inducted in 1966. 1920 Canton Bulldogs, 1921 Cleveland Indians, 1922-23 Oorang Indians, 1924 Rock Island, Ill., Independents, 1924-25 Kansas City Cowboys, 1927 New York Giants.

**GEORGE HALAS**
End. Coach. Team Owner. Born in Chicago, Illinois, February 2, 1895. Died October 31, 1983. Illinois. Inducted in 1963. 1920 Decatur Staleys, 1921 Chicago Staleys, 1922-29 Chicago Bears; coach, 1933-1942, 1946-1955, 1958-1967 Chicago Bears.

**ED HEALEY**
Tackle. 6-3, 220. Born in Indian Orchard, Massachusetts, December 28, 1894. Died December 9, 1978. Dartmouth. Inducted in 1964. 1920-22 Rock Island, Ill., Independents, 1922-27 Chicago Bears.

**MEL HEIN**
Center. 6-2, 225. Born in Redding, California. August 22, 1909. Washington State. Inducted in 1963. 1931-1945 New York Giants.

**WILBUR (PETE) HENRY**
Tackle. 6-0, 250. Born in Mansfield, Ohio, October 31, 1897. Died February 7, 1952. Washington & Jefferson. Inducted in 1963. 1920-23 Canton Bulldogs, 1925-26 Canton Bulldogs, 1927 New York Giants, 1927-28 Pottsville Maroons.

**ARNIE HERBER**
Quarterback. 6-1, 200. Born in Green Bay, Wisconsin, April 2, 1910. Died October 14, 1969. Wisconsin, Regis College. Inducted in 1966. 1930-1940 Green Bay Packers, 1944-45 New York Giants.

**BILL HEWITT**
End. 5-11, 191. Born in Bay City, Michigan, October 8, 1909. Died January 14, 1947. Michigan. Inducted in 1971. 1932-36 Chicago Bears, 1937-39 Philadelphia Eagles, 1943 Phil-Pitt.

**CLARKE HINKLE**
Fullback. 5-11, 201. Born in Toronto, Ohio, April 10, 1912. Bucknell. Inducted in 1964. 1932-1941 Green Bay Packers.

**ELROY (CRAZYLEGS) HIRSCH**
Halfback-end. 6-2, 190. Born in Wau-

sau, Wisconsin, June 17, 1923. Wisconsin, Michigan. Inducted in 1968. 1946-48 Chicago Rockets (AAFC), 1949-1957 Los Angeles Rams.

**CAL HUBBARD**
Tackle. 6-5, 250. Born in Keytesville, Missouri, October 11, 1900. Died October 17, 1977. Centenary, Geneva. Inducted in 1963. 1927-28 New York Giants, 1929-1933 Green Bay Packers, 1935 Green Bay Packers, 1936 New York Giants, 1936 Pittsburgh Pirates.

**SAM HUFF**
Linebacker. 6-1, 230. Born in Morgantown, West Virginia, October 4, 1934. West Virginia. Inducted in 1982. 1956-1963 New York Giants, 1964-67, 1969 Washington Redskins.

**LAMAR HUNT**
Team owner. Born in El Dorado, Arkansas, August 2, 1932. Southern Methodist. Inducted in 1972. 1960-62 Dallas Texans, 1963-1984 Kansas City Chiefs.

**DON HUTSON**
End. 6-1, 180. Born in Pine Bluff, Arkansas, January 31, 1913. Alabama. Inducted in 1963. 1935-1945 Green Bay Packers.

**DAVID (DEACON) JONES**
Defensive end. 6-5, 250. Born in Eatonville, Florida, December 9, 1938. South Carolina State. Inducted 1980. 1961-1971 Los Angeles Rams, 1972-73 San Diego Chargers, 1974 Washington Redskins.

**SONNY JURGENSEN**
Quarterback. 6-0, 203. Born in Wilmington, North Carolina, August 23, 1934. Duke. Inducted in 1983. 1957-1963 Philadelphia Eagles, 1964-1974 Washington Redskins.

**WALT KIESLING**
Guard. Coach. 6-2, 245. Born in St. Paul, Minnesota, March 27, 1903. Died March 2, 1962. St. Thomas (Minnesota). Inducted in 1966. 1926-27 Duluth Eskimos, 1928 Pottsville Maroons, 1929-1933 Chicago Cardinals, 1934 Chicago Bears, 1935-36 Green Bay Packers, 1937-38 Pittsburgh Pirates; coach, 1939-1942 Pittsburgh Steelers; co-coach, 1943 Phil-Pitt, 1944 Card-Pitt; coach, 1954-56 Pittsburgh Steelers.

**FRANK (BRUISER) KINARD**
Tackle. 6-1, 210. Born in Pelahatchie, Mississippi, October 23, 1914. Mississippi. Inducted in 1971. 1938-1944 Brooklyn Dodgers-Tigers, 1946-47 New York Yankees (AAFC).

**EARL (CURLY) LAMBEAU**
Coach. Born in Green Bay, Wisconsin, April 9, 1898. Died June 1, 1965. Notre Dame. Inducted in 1963. 1919-1949 Green Bay Packers, 1950-51 Chicago Cardinals, 1952-53 Washington Redskins.

**DICK (NIGHT TRAIN) LANE**
Defensive back. 6-2, 210. Born in Austin, Texas, April 16, 1928. Scottsbluff Junior College. Inducted in 1974. 1952-53 Los Angeles Rams, 1954-59 Chicago Cardinals, 1960-65 Detroit Lions.

**YALE LARY**
Defensive back-punter. 5-11, 189. Born in Fort Worth, Texas, November

24, 1930. Texas A&M. Inducted in 1979. 1952-53, 1956-1964 Detroit Lions.

**DANTE LAVELLI**
End. 6-0, 199. Born in Hudson, Ohio, February 23, 1923. Ohio State. Inducted in 1975. 1946-49 Cleveland Browns (AAFC), 1950-56 Cleveland Browns.

**BOBBY LAYNE**
Quarterback. 6-2, 190. Born in Santa Anna, Texas, December 19, 1926. Texas. Inducted in 1967. 1948 Chicago Bears, 1949 New York Bulldogs, 1950-58 Detroit Lions, 1958-1962 Pittsburgh Steelers.

**ALPHONSE (TUFFY) LEEMANS**
Fullback. 6-0, 200. Born in Superior, Wisconsin, November 12, 1912. Died January 19, 1979. George Washington. Inducted in 1978. 1936-1943 New York Giants.

**BOB LILLY**
Defensive tackle. 6-5, 260. Born in Olney, Texas, July 24, 1939. Texas Christian. Inducted in 1980. 1961-1974 Dallas Cowboys.

**VINCE LOMBARDI**
Coach. Born in Brooklyn, New York, June 11, 1913. Died September 3, 1970. Fordham. Inducted in 1971. 1959-1967 Green Bay Packers, 1969 Washington Redskins.

**SID LUCKMAN**
Quarterback. 6-0, 195. Born in Brooklyn, New York, November 21, 1916. Columbia. Inducted in 1965. 1939-1950 Chicago Bears.

**ROY (LINK) LYMAN**
Tackle. 6-2, 252. Born in Table Rock, Nebraska, November 30, 1898. Died December 28, 1972. Nebraska. Inducted in 1964. 1922-23, 1925 Canton Bulldogs, 1924 Cleveland Bulldogs, 1925 Frankford Yellowjackets, 1926-28, 1930-31, 1933-34 Chicago Bears.

**TIM MARA**
Team owner. Born in New York, New York, July 29, 1887. Died February 17, 1959. Did not attend college. Inducted in 1963. 1925-1959 New York Giants.

**GINO MARCHETTI**
Defensive end. 6-4, 245. Born in Antioch, California, January 2, 1927. San Francisco. Inducted in 1972. 1952 Dallas Texans, 1953-1964, 1966 Baltimore Colts.

**GEORGE PRESTON MARSHALL**
Team owner. Born in Grafton, West Virginia, October 11, 1897. Died August 9, 1969. Randolph-Macon. Inducted in 1963. 1932 Boston Braves, 1933-36 Boston Redskins, 1937-1969 Washington Redskins.

**OLLIE MATSON**
Halfback. 6-2, 220. Born in Trinity, Texas, May 1, 1930. San Francisco. Inducted in 1972. 1952, 1954-58 Chicago Cardinals, 1959-1962 Los Angeles Rams, 1963 Detroit Lions, 1964-66 Philadelphia Eagles.

**GEORGE McAFEE**
Halfback. 6-0, 177. Born in Ironton, Ohio, March 13, 1918. Duke. Inducted in 1966. 1940-41, 1945-1950 Chicago Bears.

**MIKE McCORMACK**
Offensive tackle. 6-4, 248. Born in Chicago, Illinois, June 21, 1930. Kansas. Inducted in 1984. 1951 New York Yankees, 1954-1962 Cleveland Browns.

**HUGH McELHENNY**
Halfback. 6-1, 198. Born in Los Angeles, California, December 31, 1928. Washington. Inducted in 1970. 1952-1960 San Francisco 49ers, 1961-62 Minnesota Vikings, 1963 New York Giants, 1964 Detroit Lions.

**JOHNNY BLOOD (McNALLY)**
Halfback. 6-0, 185. Born in New Richmond, Wisconsin, November 27, 1903. St. John's (Minnesota). Inducted in 1963. 1925-26 Milwaukee Badgers, 1926-27 Duluth Eskimos, 1928 Pottsville Maroons, 1929-1933 Green Bay Packers, 1934 Pittsburgh Pirates, 1935-36 Green Bay Packers. Player-coach, 1937-39 Pittsburgh Pirates.

**MIKE MICHALSKE**
Guard. 6-0, 209. Born in Cleveland, Ohio, April 24, 1903. Penn State. Inducted in 1964. 1926 New York Yankees (AFL), 1927-28 New York Yankees, 1929-1935, 1937 Green Bay Packers.

**WAYNE MILLNER**
End. 6-0, 191. Born in Roxbury, Massachusetts, January 31, 1913. Died November 19, 1976. Notre Dame. Inducted in 1968. 1936 Boston Redskins, 1937-1941, 1945 Washington Redskins.

**BOBBY MITCHELL**
Running back-wide receiver. 6-0, 195. Born in Hot Springs, Arkansas, June 6, 1935. Illinois. Inducted in 1983. 1958-1961 Cleveland Browns, 1962-68 Washington Redskins.

**RON MIX**
Tackle. 6-4, 250. Born in Los Angeles, California, March 10, 1938. USC. Inducted in 1979. 1960-69 San Diego Chargers, 1971 Oakland Raiders.

**LENNY MOORE**
Back. 6-1, 198. Born in Reading, Pennsylvania, November 25, 1933. Penn State. Inducted in 1975. 1956-1967 Baltimore Colts.

**MARION MOTLEY**
Fullback. 6-1, 238. Born in Leesburg, Georgia, June 5, 1920. South Carolina State, Nevada. Inducted in 1968. 1946-49 Cleveland Browns (AAFC), 1950-53 Cleveland Browns, 1955 Pittsburgh Steelers.

**GEORGE MUSSO**
Defensive and offensive guard. 6-2, 270. Born in Collinsville, Illinois. April 8, 1910. Milliken. Inducted in 1982. 1933-1944 Chicago Bears.

**BRONKO NAGURSKI**
Fullback. 6-2, 225. Born in Rainy River, Ontario, Canada, November 3, 1908. Minnesota. Inducted in 1963. 1930-37, 1943 Chicago Bears.

**EARLE (GREASY) NEALE**
Coach. Born in Parkersburg, West Virginia, November 5, 1891. Died November 2, 1973. West Virginia Wesleyan. Inducted in 1969. 1941-42, 1944-1950 Philadelphia Eagles, co-coach Phil-Pitt 1943.

203

**ERNIE NEVERS**
Fullback. 6-1, 205. Born in Willow River, Minnesota, June 11, 1903. Died May 3, 1976. Stanford. Inducted in 1963. 1926-27 Duluth Eskimos, 1929-1931 Chicago Cardinals.

**RAY NITSCHKE**
Linebacker. 6-3, 235. Born in Elmwood Park, Illinois, December 29, 1936. Illinois. Inducted in 1978. 1958-1972 Green Bay Packers.

**LEO NOMELLINI**
Defensive tackle. 6-3, 264. Born in Lucca, Italy, June 19, 1924. Minnesota. Inducted in 1969. 1950-1963 San Francisco 49ers.

**MERLIN OLSEN**
Defensive tackle. 6-5, 270. Born in Logan, Utah, September 14, 1940. Utah State. Inducted in 1982. 1962-1976 Los Angeles Rams.

**JIM OTTO**
Center. 6-2, 255. Born in Wausau, Wisconsin, January 5, 1938. Miami. Inducted in 1980. 1960-1974 Oakland Raiders.

**STEVE OWEN**
Tackle. Coach. 6-0, 235. Born in Cleo Springs, Oklahoma, April 21, 1898. Died May 17, 1964. Phillips. Inducted in 1966. 1924-25 Kansas City Cowboys, 1926-1930 New York Giants; coach, 1931-1953 New York Giants.

**CLARENCE (ACE) PARKER**
Quarterback. 5-11, 168. Born in Portsmouth, Virginia, May 17, 1912. Duke. Inducted in 1972. 1937-1941 Brooklyn Dodgers, 1945 Boston Yanks, 1946 New York Yankees (AAFC).

**JIM PARKER**
Guard-tackle. 6-3, 273. Born in Macon, Georgia, April 3, 1934. Ohio State. Inducted in 1973. 1957-1967 Baltimore Colts.

**JOE PERRY**
Fullback. 6-0, 200. Born in Stevens, Arkansas, January 27, 1927. Compton Junior College. Inducted in 1969. 1948-49 San Francisco 49ers (AAFC), 1950-1960, 1963 San Francisco 49ers, 1961-62 Baltimore Colts.

**PETE PIHOS**
End. 6-1, 210. Born in Orlando, Florida, October 22, 1923. Indiana. Inducted in 1970. 1947-1955 Philadelphia Eagles.

**HUGH (SHORTY) RAY**
Supervisor of officials. Born in Highland Park, Illinois, September 21, 1884. Died September 16, 1956. Illinois. Inducted in 1966.

**DAN REEVES**
Team owner. Born in New York, New York, June 30, 1912. Died April 15, 1971. Georgetown. Inducted in 1967. 1941-45 Cleveland Rams, 1946-1971 Los Angeles Rams.

**JIM RINGO**
Center. 6-1, 235. Born in Orange, New Jersey, November 21, 1932. Syracuse. Inducted in 1981. 1953-1963 Green Bay Packers, 1964-67 Philadelphia Eagles.

**ANDY ROBUSTELLI**
Defensive end. 6-0, 230. Born in Stamford, Connecticut, December 6, 1925. Arnold College. Inducted in 1971. 1951-55 Los Angeles Rams, 1956-1964 New York Giants.

**ART ROONEY**
Team owner. Born in Coulterville, Pennsylvania, January 27, 1901. Georgetown, Duquesne. Inducted in 1964. 1933-1940 Pittsburgh Pirates, 1941-42, 1949-1984 Pittsburgh Steelers, 1943 Phil-Pitt, 1944 Card-Pitt.

**GALE SAYERS**
Running back. 6-0, 200. Born in Wichita, Kansas, May 30, 1943. Kansas. Inducted in 1977. 1965-1971 Chicago Bears.

**JOE SCHMIDT**
Linebacker. 6-0, 222. Born in Pittsburgh, Pennsylvania, January 19, 1932. Pittsburgh. Inducted in 1973. 1953-1965 Detroit Lions.

**BART STARR**
Quarterback. 6-1, 200. Born in Montgomery, Alabama, January 9, 1934. Alabama. Inducted in 1977. 1956-1971 Green Bay Packers; coach, 1975-1983 Green Bay Packers.

**ERNIE STAUTNER**
Defensive tackle. 6-2, 235. Born in Calm, Bavaria, Germany, April 20, 1925. Boston College. Inducted in 1969. 1950-1963 Pittsburgh Steelers.

**KEN STRONG**
Halfback. 5-11, 210. Born in New Haven, Connecticut, August 6, 1906. Died October 5, 1979. New York University. Inducted in 1967. 1929-1932 Staten Island Stapletons, 1936-37 New York Yanks (AFL), 1933-35, 1939, 1944-47 New York Giants.

**JOE STYDAHAR**
Tackle. 6-4, 230. Born in Kaylor, Pennsylvania, March 3, 1912. Died March 23, 1977. West Virginia. Inducted in 1967. 1936-1942, 1945-46 Chicago Bears.

**CHARLEY TAYLOR**
Wide receiver-running back. 6-3, 210. Born in Grand Prairie, Texas, September 28, 1941. Arizona State. Inducted in 1984. 1964-1975, 1977 Washington Redskins.

**JIM TAYLOR**
Fullback. 6-0, 216. Born in Baton Rouge, Louisiana, September 20, 1935. Louisiana State. Inducted in 1976. 1958-1966 Green Bay Packers, 1967 New Orleans Saints.

**JIM THORPE**
Halfback. 6-1, 190. Born in Prague, Oklahoma, May 28, 1888. Died March 28, 1953. Carlisle. Inducted in 1963. 1920 Canton Bulldogs, 1921 Cleveland Indians, 1922-23 Oorang Indians, 1923 Toledo Maroons, 1924 Rock Island, Ill., Independents, 1925 New York Giants, 1926 Canton Bulldogs, 1928 Chicago Cardinals.

**Y. A. TITTLE**
Quarterback. 6-0, 200. Born in Marshall, Texas, October 24, 1926. Louisiana State. Inducted in 1971. 1948-49 Baltimore Colts (AAFC), 1950 Baltimore Colts, 1951-1960 San Francisco 49ers, 1961-64 New York Giants.

**GEORGE TRAFTON**
Center. 6-2, 235. Born in Chicago, Illinois, December 6, 1896. Died September 5, 1971. Notre Dame. Inducted in 1964. 1920 Decatur Staleys, 1921 Chicago Staleys, 1922-1932 Chicago Bears.

**CHARLEY TRIPPI**
Halfback. 6-0, 185. Born in Pittston, Pennsylvania, December 14, 1922. Georgia. Inducted in 1968. 1947-1955 Chicago Cardinals.

**EMLEN TUNNELL**
Safety. 6-1, 200. Born in Bryn Mawr, Pennsylvania, March 29, 1925. Died July 23, 1975. Toledo, Iowa. Inducted in 1967. 1948-1958 New York Giants, 1959-1961 Green Bay Packers.

**CLYDE (BULLDOG) TURNER**
Center. 6-2, 235. Born in Sweetwater, Texas, November 10, 1919. Hardin-Simmons. Inducted in 1966. 1940-1952 Chicago Bears.

**JOHNNY UNITAS**
Quarterback. 6-1, 195. Born in Pittsburgh, Pennsylvania, May 7, 1933. Louisville. Inducted in 1979. 1956-1972 Baltimore Colts, 1973 San Diego Chargers.

**NORM VAN BROCKLIN**
Quarterback. 6-1, 190. Born in Eagle Butte, South Dakota, March 15, 1926. Died May 1, 1983. Oregon. Inducted in 1971. 1949-1957 Los Angeles Rams, 1958-1960 Philadelphia Eagles.

**STEVE VAN BUREN**
Halfback. 6-1, 200. Born in La Ceiba, Honduras, December 28, 1920. Louisiana State. Inducted in 1965. 1944-1951 Philadelphia Eagles.

**PAUL WARFIELD**
Wide receiver. 6-0, 188. Born in Warren, Ohio, November 28, 1942. Ohio State. Inducted in 1983. 1964-69, 1976-77 Cleveland Browns, 1970-74 Miami Dolphins, 1975 Memphis Grizzlies (WFL).

**BOB WATERFIELD**
Quarterback. 6-2, 200. Born in Elmira, New York, July 26, 1920. Died April 25, 1983. UCLA. Inducted in 1965. 1945 Cleveland Rams, 1946-1952 Los Angeles Rams.

**ARNIE WEINMEISTER**
Defensive tackle. 6-4, 235. Born in Rhein, Saskatchewan, Canada, March 23, 1923. Washington. Inducted in 1984. 1948-49 New York Yankees (AAFC), 1950-53 New York Giants.

**BILL WILLIS**
Guard. 6-2, 215. Born in Columbus, Ohio, October 5, 1921. Ohio State. Inducted in 1977. 1946-49 Cleveland Browns (AAFC), 1950-53 Cleveland Browns.

**LARRY WILSON**
Defensive back. 6-0, 190. Born in Rigby, Idaho, March 24, 1938. Utah. Inducted in 1978. 1960-1972 St. Louis Cardinals.

**ALEX WOJCIECHOWICZ**
Center. 6-0, 235. Born in South River, New Jersey, August 12, 1915. Fordham. Inducted in 1968. 1938-1946 Detroit Lions, 1946-1950 Philadelphia Eagles.

**1892** Rutgers and Princeton had played a college soccer football game, the first ever, in 1869. Rugby had gained favor over soccer, however, and from it rugby football, then football, had evolved among American colleges. It was also played by athletic clubs. Intense competition existed between two Pittsburgh clubs, Allegheny Athletic Association and Pittsburgh Athletic Club. William (Pudge) Heffelfinger, former star at Yale, brought in by AAA, paid $500 to play in game against PAC, becoming first person known to have been paid openly to play football, Nov. 12. AAA won 4–0 when Heffelfinger picked up PAC fumble and ran for touchdown, which then counted four points.

**1898** Morgan AC founded on Chicago's South Side, later became Chicago Normals, Racine (a Chicago street) Cardinals, Chicago Cardinals, and St. Louis Cardinals, oldest continuing operation in pro football.

**1899** Duquesne Country and Athletic Club, or Pittsburgh Duquesnes, incurred large payroll signing players returning from Spanish-American War, sought help from Pittsburgh Sportsman William C. Temple. He bought football team from athletic club, became first known individual club owner.

**1901** Temple and Barney Dreyfuss of baseball Pirates formed new team and urged cross-state rivalry with Philadelphia.

**1902** Philadelphia Athletics, managed by Connie Mack, and Nationals or Phillies formed football teams. Athletics won first night football game, 39–0 over Kanaweola AC at Elmira, N.Y., Nov. 21.

Athletics claimed pro championship after winning two, losing one against Phillies and going 1–1–1 against Pittsburgh Pros. Pitcher Rube Waddell played for Athletics, pitcher Christy Mathewson was fullback for Pittsburgh in one game.

"World Series," actually four-team tournament, played among Athletics, New York Knickerbockers, Watertown, N.Y., Red and Blacks, and Syracuse AC was played in Madison Square Garden. Philadelphia and Syracuse played first indoor football game before 3,000, Dec. 28. Syracuse, with Pop Warner at guard, won game 6–0, went on to win tournament.

**1903** Franklin (Pa.) AC won second and last "World Series" of pro football over Philadelphia, Watertown, and Orange, N.J. AC.

Pro football declined in Pittsburgh area. Some PAC players hired by Massillon, Ohio, Tigers, making Massillon first openly professional team in Ohio. Emphasis shifted there from Pennsylvania.

**1904** Ohio had at least eight pro teams. Attempt failed to form league to end cutthroat bidding for players, write rules for all.

**1905** Canton Bulldogs turned professional.

**1906** Arch-rivals Massillon and Canton played twice, Massillon won both. Because of betting scandal, Canton manager Blondy Wallace left in disgrace, interest in pro football in two cities declined.

**1913** Jim Thorpe, former football star for Carlisle Indian School and hero of 1912 Olympics, played season for Pine Village Pros in Indiana.

**1915** Canton revived name "Bulldogs." and signed Thorpe for $250 a game.

**1916** With Thorpe starring, Canton won 10 straight, most by lopsided scores, was acclaimed pro football champion of world.

**1919** George Calhoun, Curly Lambeau organized Green Bay Packers. Indian Packing Company provided equipment, name "Packers." They had 10–1 record against other company teams.

**1920** Pro football was in state of confusion, teams were loosely organized, players moved freely among teams, there was no system for recruiting players. A league in which all followed the same rules was needed. Meeting was held among interested teams in August, second meeting was held in Canton and American Professional Football Association, forerunner of National Football League, formed Sept. 17. Teams were from five states—Akron Pros, Canton Bulldogs, Cleveland Indians, Dayton Triangles, Massillon Tigers from Ohio; Hammond Pros, Muncie Flyers from Indiana; Racine Cardinals, Rock Island Independents, Decatur Staleys, represented by George Halas, from Illinois; Rochester, N.Y., Jeffersons; and "Wisconsin."

Capitalizing on his fame, Thorpe was chosen league president, Stan Cofall of Massillon vice-president. Membership fee of $100 arrived at to give aura of respectability. No team ever paid it. Massillon and Muncie did not field teams. Buffalo All-Americans, Chicago Tigers, Columbus, Ohio, Panhandles, and Detroit Tigers joined league later in year. League operated sporadically, teams played as many non-members as members, either no standings kept or have since been lost. Akron, Buffalo, Canton all claimed championship, hastily-arranged series of games, one of them between Buffalo and Canton at Polo Grounds, New York City, failed to settle issue of championship.

First recorded player deal sale of Bob Nash, tackle and end for Akron, to Buffalo for $300, five percent of gate receipts.

**1921** APFA reorganized at Akron, Joe Carr of Panhandles named president, Apr. 30. Carl Storck of Dayton named secretary-treasurer. Carr established league headquarters at Columbus.

Chicago Tigers, beaten by Racine Cardinals in 1920 game for "rights" to Chicago, dropped out, so did Hammond.

J.E. Clair of Acme Packing Company granted franchise for Green Bay Packers, Aug. 27. Cincinnati Celts also joined league.

Thorpe moved from Canton to Cleveland Indians.

A.E. Staley turned Decatur Staleys over to George Halas, who moved them to Cubs Park in Chicago, promising to keep the name "Staleys" one more year.

Five teams that dropped out had records stricken from standings—Evansville, Hammond, Louisville, Minneapolis, and Muncie.

Chicago Staleys claimed league championship with 10–1–1 record.

Buffalo, 9–1–2, claimed Chicago included nonleague games in record, but Carr ruled for Staleys.

**1922** Packers disciplined for using college players under assumed names, Clair turned franchise back to league, Jan. 28. Curly Lambeau promised to obey rules, used $50 of own money to buy back franchise, June 24. Bad weather, low attendance plagued Packers, merchants raised $2,500, public non-profit corporation set up to operate team with Lambeau as manager, coach.

APFA changed name to National Football League, June 24. Staleys became Chicago Bears.

Thorpe, other Indian players formed Oorang Indians in Marion, Ohio, sponsored by Oorang dog kennels.

**1923** Oorang folded with 1–10 record, Thorpe moved to Toledo Maroons. Player-coach Halas of Chicago recovered fumble by Thorpe in game against Oorang, ran 98 yards for touchdown.

**1924** Frankford Yellowjackets of Philadelphia awarded franchise, that city entered league for first time. League champion Canton moved to Cleveland to play before larger crowds to meet rising payroll.

**1925** Tim Mara and Billy Gibson awarded franchise for New York City for $500. Detroit Panthers, coached by Jimmy Conzelman, Pottsville, Pa., Maroons, Providence R.I., Steam Roller also entered league. New team in Canton took name "Bulldogs."

University of Illinois season ended and Red Grange signed contract to play for Chicago Bears immediately, Nov. 22. Crowd of 38,000 watched Grange and Bears in traditional Thanksgiving game against Cardinals. Barnstorming tour began in which Bears played seven games in 11 days in St. Louis, Philadelphia, New York, then cities in South and West. Crowd of 70,000 watched game against Giants at Polo Grounds, helping assure future of NFL franchise in New York.

Pottsville defeated Chicago Cardinals for what they thought was NFL championship, but week later played "Notre Dame All-Stars" in Philadelphia. Frankford protested, saying "territorial rights" had been impinged upon. Carr upheld protest, cancelled Pottsville franchise, ordered Cardinals to play two more games. They did, won both, were proclaimed NFL champions.

**1926** Grange's manager, C.C. Pyle, asked Bears for five-figure salary for Grange, one-third ownership of team. Bears refused, lost Grange. Pyle leased Yankee Stadium in New York City, petitioned for NFL franchise, was refused, started first American Football League. It lasted one season, included Grange's New York Yankees, eight other teams. AFL champion Philadelphia Quakers played postseason game against NFL New York Giants, lost 31–0.

Halas pushed through rule prohibiting any team from signing player whose college class had not graduated, Feb. 6.

NFL membership swelled to 22, frustrating AFL growth. Paddy Driscoll of Cardinals moved to rival Bears. Ole Haugsrud, operator of Duluth,

Minn., Eskimos, gained NFL franchise, signed Ernie Nevers of Stanford, giving NFL gate attraction to rival Grange. Thirteen-member Eskimos, "Iron Men of the North," played 28 exhibition or league games, 26 on road.

**1927** AFL folded, NFL shrank to 12 teams. Akron, Canton, Columbus left NFL. New York Yankees and Grange joined NFL. Grange suffered knee injury. New York Giants won first NFL championship, scoring five consecutive shutouts at one point.

**1928** Grange left football, appeared in movie and on vaudeville circuit. Duluth disbanded, Nevers quit pro football, played baseball, was assistant coach at Stanford.

**1929** Chris O'Brien sold Chicago Cardinals to David Jones, July 27. NFL added fourth official, field judge, July 28. Cardinals became first pro team to go to out-of-town training camp, Coldwater, Mich., Aug. 21. Dayton played final season, last of original Ohio teams to leave league.

Grange, Nevers returned to NFL. Nevers scored 40 points for Cardinals against Bears, Nov. 28, six touchdowns rushing, four extra points. Grange returned to Bears.

Packers signed back Johnny Blood (McNally), tackle Cal Hubbard, guard Mike Michalske, and won first NFL championship.

**1930** Portsmouth, Ohio, Spartans, joined NFL. Defunct Dayton franchise bought by John Dwyer, became Brooklyn Dodgers. Bears, Cardinals played exhibition for unemployment relief funds, indoors at Chicago Stadium, layer of dirt covering arena floor. New York Giants, "Notre Dame All-Stars" coached by Knute Rockne, played charity exhibition before 55,000 at Polo Grounds.

Halas retired as player, resigned as coach of Bears in favor of Ralph Jones.

Packers won second straight NFL championship.

**1931** Pro football shrank to 10 teams. Carr fined Bears, Packers, Portsmouth $1,000 each for using players whose college classes had not graduated, July 11.

Playing career of Al Nesser, last of six brothers to play in NFL, ended when Cleveland Indians disbanded.

Green Bay won third straight NFL championship.

**1932** George P. Marshall, Vincent Bendix, Jay O'Brien, M. Dorland Doyle awarded franchise for Boston, July 9. Named team "Braves" after baseball team using same park.

NFL membership dropped to eight, lowest in history. First playoff in NFL history arranged between Bears and Spartans. Moved indoors to Chicago Stadium because of blizzard conditions in city. Arena allowed only 80-yard field that came right to walls. For safety, goal posts moved from end to goal lines, inbounds lines or hashmarks drawn 10 yards from side lines for ball to be put in play. Bears won 9–0, Dec. 18, scoring touchdown disputed by Spartans who claimed Bronko Nagurski threw jump pass to Red Grange from point less than five yards behind line of scrimmage, violating existing passing rule.

**1933** NFL made significant changes in rules of football first time. Innovations of 1932 indoor playoffs—inbounds lines or hashmarks 10 yards from sidelines, goal posts on goal lines—became rules, Feb. 25. Following resolution by George P. Marshall, NFL divided into two five-team divisions, winners to meet in annual championship playoff, July, 8.

Franchise was awarded to Art Rooney and A. McCool for Pittsburgh, July 8; team was named "Pirates." Inactive Frankford franchise declared forfeited, Philadelphia franchise awarded to Bert Bell, Lud Wray, July 9; named team "Eagles." Boston changed name to "Redskins." George Halas bought out Ed (Dutch) Sternaman, became sole owner of Chicago Bears, reinstated himself as head coach. David Jones sold Cardinals to Charles W. Bidwill. Cincinnati Reds joined league.

Eastern Division champion New York Giants met Western Division champion Bears at Wrigley Field in first NFL championship game, Dec. 17. Bears won 23–21.

**1934** Bears played scoreless tie against collegians in first Chicago All-Star Game before 79,432 at Soldier Field, Aug. 31.

NFL legalized forward passes anywhere behind line of scrimmage.

G. A. (Dick) Richards purchased Portsmouth Spartans, moved them to Detroit, June 30; they took name "Lions." Cincinnati Reds franchise moved during season, became St. Louis Gunners.

Player waiver rule adopted, Dec. 10.

Grange retired from football.

**1935** Bell of Philadelphia proposed, NFL adopted annual draft of college players, to begin in 1936, with team finishing last in standings having first choice each round of draft, May 19.

Cincinnati Reds-St. Louis Gunners franchise died.

Inbounds lines or hashmarks moved nearer center of field, 15 yards from sidelines.

**1936** No franchise shifts for first time since formation of NFL and for first time all teams played same number of games.

Last-place previous year, Philadelphia Eagles made Jay Berwanger, University of Chicago back, first choice in first NFL draft, Feb. 8. Eagles later traded negotiation rights to him to Bears. He never played pro football.

Rival league was formed, became second to call itself American Football League. It included six teams, Boston Shamrocks won championship.

**1937** Cleveland returned to NFL. Homer Marshman was granted a franchise, Feb. 12; he named new team "Rams." Marshall moved Redskins to Washington, Feb. 13.

Los Angeles Bulldogs had 8–0 record in American Football League; six-team league folded.

**1938** Fifteen-yard penalty adopted for roughing passer.

Hugh (Shorty) Ray became technical advisor on rules and officiating to NFL. Marshall, Los Angeles newspaper officials established Pro Bowl game between NFL champion, team of all stars.

**1939** New York Giants defeated Pro All-Stars 13–10 in first Pro Bowl game at Wrigley Field, Los Angeles, Jan. 15.

Carr, NFL president since 1921, died at Columbus, May 20. Carl Storck named successor, May 25.

National Broadcasting Company camera beamed Brooklyn Dodgers-Philadelphia Eagles game from Ebbets Field back to studios of network, handful of sets then in New York City, first NFL game to be televised.

**1940** Clipping penalty reduced from 25 to 15 yards, all distance penalties enforced from spot on field of play limited to half distance to goal, Apr. 12.

Pittsburgh changed nickname from Pirates to Steelers.

Rival league formed, became third to call itself American Football League. It included six teams, Columbus, Ohio, Bullies won championship.

Art Rooney sold Pittsburgh to Alexis Thompson, Dec. 9, and later purchased part-interest in Philadelphia.

Bears, playing T-formation with man-in-motion, defeated Washington 73–0 in NFL championship, Dec. 8. It was first championship carried on network radio, broadcast by Red Barber to 120 stations of Mutual Broadcasting System, which paid $2,500 for rights.

**1941** Elmer Layden, head coach, athletic director at Notre Dame, named first commissioner of NFL, March 1. Moved league headquarters to Chicago. Carl Storck resigned as president-secretary, Apr. 5.

Co-owners Bell, Rooney of Eagles transferred them to Alexis Thompson in exchange for Pittsburgh franchise. Homer Marshman, associates sold Cleveland Rams to Daniel F. Reeves, Fred Levy, Jr., June 1.

Playoffs were provided for in case of ties in division races. Sudden death overtime provided for in case playoff was tied after four quarters.

Columbus won championship of five-team American Football League; it folded.

Bears defeated Green Bay 33–14 in first divisional playoff in NFL history, winning Western Division championship, Dec. 14.

**1942** Players departing for service in World War II reduced rosters of NFL teams. Halas left Bears for armed forces, was replaced by co-coaches Hunk Anderson, Luke Johnsos.

**1943** Cleveland Rams, with co-owners Lt. Daniel F. Reeves, Maj. Fred Levy, Jr. in service, granted permission to suspend operations for one season, Apr. 6. Levy transferred his stock in team to Reeves, Apr. 16.

NFL adopted free substitution, Apr. 7. Abbreviated wartime rosters, however, prevented its effects from taking place immediately.

Philadelphia, Pittsburgh granted permission to merge, became Phil-Pitt, June 19. They divided home games between two cities, Greasy Neale, Walt Kiesling were co-coaches. Merger automatically dissolved last day of season, Dec. 5.

Ted Collins granted franchise for Boston to become active in 1944.

**1944** Collins, who had wanted franchise in Yankee Stadium in New York, named new team in Boston "Yanks." Cleveland resumed operations. Brooklyn Dodgers changed name to "Tigers."

Cardinals, Pittsburgh requested by league to merge for one year under name, Card-Pitt, Apr. 21. Merger automatically dissolved last day of season, Dec. 3.

Coaching from bench legalized, Apr. 20.

**1945** Inbounds lines or hashmarks moved nearer center of field, 20 yards from side lines. Players required to wear long stockings, Apr. 9.

Boston Yanks, Brooklyn Tigers merged as "Yanks," Apr. 10.

Halas rejoined Bears after service with U.S. Navy in Pacific. Returned to head coaching.

After Japanese surrender ending World War II count showed NFL service roster, limited to men who played in league games, totaled 638, 21 of whom had died.

**1946** Layden resigned as commissioner, replaced by Bell, co-owner of Pittsburgh Steelers, Jan. 11. Bell moved league headquarters from Chicago to Philadelphia suburb of Bala Cynwyd.

Free substitution withdrawn, substitutions limited to no more than three men at time. Forward passes made automatically incomplete upon striking goal posts, Jan. 11.

NFL champion Cleveland given permission to transfer to Los Angeles, Jan. 12. NFL became coast-to-coast league first time.

Rival league, All-America Football Conference, formed. Four of its eight teams were in same population centers as NFL teams—Brooklyn Dodgers, New York Yankees, Chicago Rockets, Los Angeles Dons. Cleveland Browns won AAFC championship.

Backs Frank Filchock and Merle Hapes of the Giants questioned about attempt by New York man to fix championship game vs. Chicago; Commissioner Bell suspended Hapes, permitted Filchock to play. He played well but Chicago won 24–14.

**1947** Bell's contract as commissioner was renewed for five years, Jan. 1; same day NFL Constitution amended imposing major penalty for anyone not reporting offer of bribe, attempt to fix game, or any other infraction of rules having to do with gambling.

NFL added fifth official, back judge. Sudden death readopted for championship games, Jan. 24.

"Bonus" draft choice made for first time; one team each year would get special bonus choice before first round began.

Halfback Fred Gehrke of Los Angeles Rams painted horns on Rams' helmets, first helmet emblems in pro football.

AAFC again had eight teams, Cleveland Browns won second championship.

**1948** Plastic head protectors prohibited. Flexible artificial tee permitted at kickoff. Officials besides referee equipped with whistles, not horns, Jan. 14.

Fred Mandel sold Lions to syndicate headed by D. Lyle Fife, Jan. 15.

Cleveland Browns won third straight championship of eight-team AAFC.

**1949** Thompson sold NFL champion Philadelphia Eagles to syndicate headed by James P. Clark, Jan. 15.

Commissioner Bell, vice-president and treasurer Dennis Shea, given 10-year contracts, Jan. 20.

Free substitution adopted for one year, Jan. 20.

Boston Yanks became New York Bulldogs, shared Polo Grounds with Giants.

Cleveland won fourth straight championship of AAFC, reduced to seven teams. Bell announced merger agreement Dec. 9 in which three

AAFC teams—Cleveland, San Francisco 49ers, Baltimore Colts—would enter NFL in 1950.

**1950** Free substitution restored, way opened for two-platoon era, specialization in pro football, Jan. 23.

Name "National Football League" returned after about three months as "National-American Football League." American, National Conferences replaced Eastern, Western Divisions, Mar. 3.

New York Bulldogs became "Yanks," divided players of former AAFC Yankees with Giants. Special allocation draft held in which 13 teams drafted remaining AAFC players, with special consideration for Baltimore, 15 choices compared to 10 for other teams.

Los Angeles Rams became first NFL team to contract to have all its games televised. Arrangement covered both home and away games, sponsor agreed to make up difference in home game income if lower than year before (cost sponsor $307,000). Washington also arranged to televise games, other teams made deals to put selected games on television.

For first time in history deadlocks occurred, playoffs were necessary in both conferences (divisions). Cleveland defeated Giants in American, Los Angeles defeated Bears in National. In one of most exciting championship games, Cleveland defeated Los Angeles 30–28, Dec. 24.

**1951** Pro Bowl game, dormant since 1942, revived under new format matching all-stars of each conference at Los Angeles Memorial Coliseum. American Conference defeated National 28–27, Jan. 14.

Abraham Watner returned Baltimore Colts franchise to league, was voted $50,000 for Colts' players, Jan. 18.

Rule passed that no tackle, guard, or center eligible for forward pass, Jan. 18.

DuMont Network paid $75,000 for rights to championship game, televised coast-to-coast for first time. Los Angeles defeated Cleveland 24–17, Dec. 23.

**1952** Ted Collins sold New York Yanks' franchise to NFL, Jan. 19. New franchise awarded to Dallas Texans, first NFL team in Texas, Jan. 24. Yanks had been, in order, Boston Yanks, New York Bulldogs, New York Yanks. Texans won 1, lost 11, folded, last NFL team to become extinct.

Pittsburgh Steelers abandoned single wing for T formation, last pro team to do so.

Los Angeles reversed television policy, aired only road games.

**1953** Baltimore re-entered NFL. League awarded holdings of defunct Dallas to group headed by Carroll Rosenbloom that formed team with name "Colts," same as former franchise, Jan. 23.

Names of American, National Conferences changed to Eastern, Western Conferences, Jan. 24.

Thorpe died, Mar. 28.

Arthur McBride sold Cleveland to syndicate headed by Dave R. Jones, June 10.

NFL policy of blacking out television of home games upheld by Judge Allan K. Grim of U.S. District Court in Philadelphia, Nov. 12.

**1954** Bell given new 12-year contract.

**1955** Sudden death overtime rule used for first time, on experimental basis in preseason game between Los Angeles, New York at Portland, Ore., Aug. 28. Los Angeles won 23–17 three minutes into overtime.

Runners could advance ball, even by crawling along ground, until stopped, sometimes leading to rough play. As result, rules changed so ball declared dead immediately if player touched ground with any part of body except hands or feet while in grasp of opponent.

Quarterback Otto Graham played last game for Cleveland, 38–14 victory over Los Angeles for NFL championship.

NBC replaced DuMont as network for title game, paying rights fee of $100,000.

**1956** Halas retired as coach of Bears, replaced by Paddy Driscoll. Giants moved from Polo Grounds to Yankee Stadium.

Grabbing opponent's facemask made illegal, with exception of ball carrier. "Loudspeaker coaching" from side line prohibited. Brown ball with white stripes replaced white with black stripes for night games. Language of "dead ball rule" improved, stipulating ball dead when runner contacted by defensive player and touched ground with any part of body except hands or feet.

CBS became first to broadcast some NFL regular season games to selected television markets across nation.

Hugh (Shorty) Ray, former NFL rules advisor and rules author, died.

**1957** Pete Rozelle named general manager of Los Angeles. Anthony J. Morabito, founder, co-owner of 49ers died of heart attack during game against Bears, Oct. 28. Then NFL record crowd, 102,368, saw 49ers-Rams game at Los Angeles Memorial Coliseum, Nov. 10. Detroit Lions came from 20 points down for playoff victory over 49ers 31–27, Dec. 22.

**1958** "Bonus" draft choice eliminated, Jan. 29.

Halas reinstated himself as Bears coach for third time; others were in 1933, 1946.

Jim Brown of Cleveland gained NFL record 1,527 yards rushing.

Baltimore, coached by Weeb Ewbank, defeated New York 23–17 in first sudden death NFL championship game, Alan Ameche scoring for Colts after 8 minutes, 15 seconds of overtime, Dec. 28.

**1959** Tim Mara, co-founder of Giants, died, Feb. 17.

Lamar Hunt announced intentions to form second pro football league. Hunt representing Dallas, others representing Denver, Houston, Los Angeles, Minneapolis-St. Paul, New York City held first meeting of league at Chicago, Aug. 14. Made plans to begin play in 1960. Eight days later at second meeting announced name of organization would be "American Football League." Buffalo became seventh AFL team, Oct. 28, Boston eighth, Nov. 22. First AFL draft held, Nov. 22. Joe Foss named AFL commissioner, Nov. 30. Second draft held, Dec. 2.

NFL commissioner Bell died of heart attack suffered at Franklin Field, Philadelphia, during last two minutes of game between Eagles, Pittsburgh, Oct. 11. Treasurer Austin Gunsel named President in office of Commissioner until January, 1960, annual meeting, Oct. 14.

**1960** Pete Rozelle elected NFL commissioner on 23rd ballot, succeeding Bell, Jan. 26.

Hunt, founder of AFL, elected president for 1960, Jan. 26. Oakland became eighth AFL team, Jan. 30. Eastern, Western Divisions set up, Jan. 30. Five-year contract signed with American Broadcasting Company for network televising of selected games, June 9.

AFL adopted two-point option on points after touchdown, one point if successful kick, two for successful run or pass across goal line from 2-yard line, Jan. 31.

NFL awarded Dallas 1960 franchise, Minnesota 1961 franchise, expanding to 14 teams, Jan. 28. They took nicknames "Cowboys," "Vikings."

"No-tampering" verbal pact, relative to players' contracts, agreed to between NFL, AFL, Feb. 9.

Chicago Cardinals transferred to St. Louis, Mar. 13.

Boston Patriots defeated Bills 28–7 at Buffalo in first AFL preseason game before 16,000, July 30. Denver Broncos defeated Patriots 13–10 at Boston in first AFL regular season game before 21,597, Sept. 9.

**1961** Houston Oilers defeated Los Angeles Chargers 24–16 for first AFL championship before 32,183 at Houston, Jan. 1.

Detroit defeated Cleveland 17–16 in first Playoff Bowl, or Bert Bell Benefit Bowl, between second-place teams in each conference in Miami, Jan. 7.

End Willard Dewveall of Bears played out his option, joined Houston of AFL, first player to deliberately move from one league to other, Jan. 14.

Ed McGah, Wayne Valley, Robert Osborne bought out their partners in ownership of Oakland Raiders, Jan. 17. Chargers transferred to San Diego, Feb. 10. Dave R. Jones sold Cleveland to group headed by Arthur B. Modell, Mar. 22. Howsam brothers sold Denver to group headed by Calvin Kunz, Gerry Phipps, May 26.

NBC awarded two-year contract for radio and television rights to NFL championship game for $615,000 annually, $300,000 of which was to go directly into NFL Player Benefit Plan, Apr. 5.

Canton, where league that became NFL had been formed in 1920, chosen site of Pro Football Hall of Fame, Apr. 27.

Bill legalizing single network television contracts by professional sports leagues introduced in Congress by Rep. Emanuel Celler passed House, Senate, signed into law by President John F. Kennedy, Sept. 30.

Green Bay won first NFL championship since 1944, defeating New York 37–0, Dec. 31.

**1962** West defeated East 47–27 in first AFL All-Star Game before 20,973 in San Diego, Jan. 7.

NFL prohibited grabbing any player's facemask, Jan. 9.

Commissioners Rozelle of NFL, Foss of AFL given new five-year contracts, Jan. 8, 9.

NFL entered into single network agreement with CBS for telecasting all regular season games for $4,650,000 annually, Jan. 10.

Judge Roszel Thompson of U.S. District Court, Baltimore, ruled against AFL in antitrust suit against NFL, May 21. AFL had charged monopoly, conspiracy in areas of expansion, television, player signings. Case lasted two and a half years, trial lasted two months.

McGah, Valley acquired controlling interest in Oakland, May 24. AFL assumed financial responsibility for New York Titans, Nov. 8. Dan Reeves purchased partners' stock in Los Angeles Rams, becoming majority owner, Dec. 27.

Dallas defeated Oilers 20–17 for AFL championship at Houston after 17 minutes, 54 seconds of sudden death overtime on 25-yard field goal by Tommy Brooker, Dec. 23. Game lasted record 77 minutes, 54 seconds.

Judge Edward Weinfeld of U.S. District Court, New York City, upheld legality of NFL's television blackout within 75-mile radius of home games, denied injunction sought by persons who had demanded championship between Giants, Green Bay be televised in New York City area, Dec. 23.

**1963** AFL's guarantee for visiting teams during regular season increased from $20,000 to $30,000, Jan. 10.

Hunt's Dallas Texans transferred to Kansas City, becoming "Chiefs," Feb. 8. New York Titans sold to five-member syndicate headed by David (Sonny) Werblin, name changed to "Jets," Mar. 28.

Commissioner Rozelle suspended indefinitely Paul Hornung, Green Bay halfback, Alex Karras, Detroit defensive tackle, for placing bets on their own teams and on other NFL games; also fined five other Detroit players $2,000 each for betting on one game in which they did not participate, and the Detroit Lions Football Co. $2,000 on each of two counts for failure to report promptly information and for lack of sideline supervision.

AFL allowed New York, Oakland to select players from other franchises in hopes of giving league more competitive balance, May 11.

NBC awarded exclusive network broadcasting rights for 1963 AFL championship game for $926,000, May 23.

U.S. Fourth Circuit Court of Appeals reaffirmed lower court's finding for NFL in $10 million suit brought by AFL, ending three and a half years of litigation, Nov. 21.

Boston defeated Buffalo 26–8 in first divisional playoff in AFL history before 33,044 in Buffalo, Dec. 28.

Chicago defeated New York 14–10 for NFL championship, record sixth and last title for Halas in his thirty-sixth season as Bears' coach, Dec. 29.

**1964** William Clay Ford, their president since 1961, purchased Detroit, Jan. 10. Group representing late James P. Clark sold Philadelphia to group headed by Jerry Wolman, Jan. 21. Carroll Rosenbloom, majority owner since 1953, acquired complete ownership of Baltimore, Jan. 23.

CBS submitted winning bid of $14.1 million per year for NFL regular season television rights for 1964, 1965, Jan. 24. CBS acquired rights to 1964, 1965 NFL championship games for $1.8 million per game, Apr. 17. AFL signed five-year, $36 million television contract with NBC to begin with 1965 season, assuring each team approximately $900,000 a year from television rights, Jan. 29.

Paul Hornung of Green Bay, Alex Karras of Detroit reinstated by Rozelle, Mar. 16.

Paul Brown departed Cleveland after 17 years as their head coach, Blanton Collier replaced him.

AFL commissioner Foss given new three-year contract commencing in 1965, May 22.

New York defeated Denver 30–6 before then AFL record crowd of 45,665 in first game at Shea Stadium, Sept. 12.

Pete Gogolak of Cornell signed contract with Buffalo, becoming first soccer-style kicker in pro football.

**1965** NFL teams pledged not to sign college seniors until completion of all their games, including bowl games, empowered commissioner to discipline club up to as much as loss of entire draft list for violation of pledge, Feb. 15.

NFL added sixth official, line judge, Feb. 19. Color of officials' penalty flags changed from white to bright gold, Apr. 5.

Atlanta awarded NFL franchise for 1966, with Rankin Smith owner, June 30. Miami awarded AFL franchise for 1966, with Joe Robbie, Danny Thomas as owners, Aug. 16.

Green Bay defeated Baltimore 13–10 in sudden death Western Conference playoff game, Don Chandler kicking 25-yard field goal for Packers after 13 minutes, 39 seconds of overtime, Dec. 26.

CBS acquired rights to NFL regular season games in 1966, 1967, plus option for 1968, for $18.8 million per year, Dec. 29.

**1966** AFL-NFL war reached its peak, leagues spent combined total of $7 million to sign 1966 draft choices. NFL signed 75 percent of its 232 draftees, AFL 46 percent of its 181. Of 111 common draft choices, 79 joined NFL, 28 joined AFL, four went unsigned.

Rights to NFL 1966, 1967 championship games sold to CBS for $2 million per game, Feb. 14.

Joe Foss resigned as AFL commissioner, Apr. 7. Al Davis, head coach, general manager of Oakland Raiders, named to replace him, Apr. 8.

Goal posts offset from goal line, colored bright gold, with uprights 20 feet above crossbar made standard in NFL, May 16.

Merger announced; NFL, AFL entered into agreement to form combined league of 24 teams, expanding to 26 in 1968, June 8. Rozelle named commissioner. Leagues agreed to play separate schedules until 1970 but would meet, starting in 1967, in world championship game (Super Bowl) and play each other in preseason games.

Davis rejoined Oakland Raiders, Milt Woodard named president of AFL, July 25.

Barron Hilton sold San Diego to group headed by Eugene Klein, Sam Schulman, Aug. 25.

Congress approved merger, passing special legislation exempting agreement itself from anti-trust action, Oct. 21.

New Orleans awarded NFL franchise to begin play in 1967, Nov. 1.

NFL realigned for 1967–69 seasons into Capitol, Century Divisions in Eastern Conference, Central, Coastal Divisions in Western Conference, Dec. 2. New Orleans, New York agreed to switch divisions in 1968, return to 1967 alignment in 1969.

Rights to Super Bowl for four years sold to CBS and NBC for $9.5 million, Dec. 13.

**1967** Green Bay Packers of NFL defeated Kansas City of AFL 35–10 at Los Angeles in first Super Bowl, Jan. 15. Winning share for Packers was $15,000 each, losing share for Chiefs $7,500 each.

"Sling-shot" goal posts, six-foot-wide border around field made standard in NFL, Feb. 22.

Baltimore made Bubba Smith, Michigan State defensive lineman, first choice in first combined AFL-NFL draft, Mar. 14.

AFL awarded franchise to Cincinnati, to begin play in 1968, with Paul Brown as part-owner, general manager, head coach, May 24.

Arthur B. Modell, president of the Cleveland Browns, elected president of the NFL, May 28.

AFL team defeated NFL team for first time, Denver beat Detroit 13–7 in preseason game, Aug. 5.

Green Bay defeated Dallas 21–17 for NFL championship on last minute one-yard quarterback sneak by Bart Starr in 13-below temperature at Green Bay, Dec. 31.

George Halas retired fourth and last time as head coach of Chicago Bears at age 73.

**1968** Green Bay defeated Oakland 33–14 in Super Bowl II at Miami, game had first $3 million gate in pro football history, Jan. 14.

Lombardi resigned as head coach of Packers, remained as general manager.

Sonny Werblin sold his shares in New York Jets to partners Don Lillis, Leon Hess, Townsend Martin, Phil Iselin; Lillis assumed presidency of Jets, May 21. Lillis died, July 23. Iselin appointed president, Aug. 6.

Ewbank became first coach to win titles in both NFL, AFL, his Jets defeated Oakland 27–23 for AFL championship, Dec. 29.

**1969** AFL established format of inter-division playoffs with winner in one division playing runner-up in other, for 1969 only, Jan. 11.

AFL team won Super Bowl for first time; Jets defeated Baltimore 16–7 at Miami, Jan. 12.

Lombardi became part-owner, executive vice-president, head coach of Washington Redskins.

NFL and AFL scrapped preseason experiment "Pressure Point" run or pass one-point conversion tried in 1969, Mar. 20.

Wolman sold Philadelphia Eagles to Leonard Tose, May 1.

Baltimore, Cleveland, Pittsburgh agreed to join AFL teams to form 13-team American Football Conference, remaining NFL teams to form National Football Conference in NFL in 1970, May 17. AFC teams voted to realign in Eastern, Central, Western Divisions.

Monday night football set for 1970; ABC acquired rights to televise 13 NFL regular season Monday night games in 1970, 1971, 1972.

George P. Marshall, president-emeritus of Redskins, died at 72, Aug. 9.

**1970** Kansas City defeated Minnesota 23–7 in Super Bowl IV at New Orleans, Jan. 11. Gross receipts of approximately $3.8 million largest ever for one-day team sports event, television audience largest ever for one-day sports events.

NFC realigned into Eastern, Central, Western Divisions, Jan. 16.

CBS acquired rights to televise all NFC games, except Monday night games, in 1970–73, including divisional playoffs and NFC cham-

pionship, also rights to Super Bowl in 1972, 1974, AFC-NFC Pro Bowl in 1971, 1973, Jan. 26.

NBC acquired rights to televise all AFC games, except Monday night games, in 1970–73, including divisional playoffs and AFC championship, also rights to Super Bowl in 1971, 1973, AFC-NFC Pro Bowl in 1972, 1974, Jan. 26.

Art Modell resigned as president of NFL, Mar. 12. Milt Woodard resigned as president of AFL, Mar. 13. Lamar Hunt elected president of AFC, George S. Halas, Sr. elected president of NFC, Mar. 19.

Merged league adopted rules changes putting names on backs of players' jerseys, making Wilson brand official football of league, making point after touchdown worth one point, making scoreboard clock official timing device of game, Mar. 18.

Players Negotiating Committee, NFL Players Association announced four-year agreement guaranteeing approximately $4,535,000 annually to player pension, insurance benefits, Aug. 3. Owners also agreed to contribute $250,000 annually to improve or implement such items as disability payments, widows' benefits, maternity benefits, dental benefits. Agreement also provided for increased preseason game and per diem payments averaging approximately $2,600,000 annually.

Lombardi, executive vice-president, head coach of Redskins, died at 57, Sept. 3.

Tom Dempsey of New Orleans Saints kicked game-winning NFL record 63-yard field goal against Detroit Lions, Nov. 8.

**1971** Baltimore defeated Dallas 16–13 on Jim O'Brien's 32-yard field goal with five seconds to go in Super Bowl V at Miami, Jan. 17. NBC telecast was viewed in estimated 23,980,000 homes, largest audience ever for one-day sports event.

NFC defeated AFC 27–6 in first AFC-NFC Pro Bowl at Los Angeles, Jan. 24.

Boston Patriots changed name to New England Patriots, Mar. 25.

Rules change adopted making sole criteria for determining intentional grounding whether passer was making deliberate attempt to prevent loss of yardage, Mar. 25.

Reeves, president, general manager of Rams, died at 58, Apr. 15.

Miami defeated Kansas City 27–24 in sudden death in AFC divisional playoff game, Garo Yepremian kicking 37-yard field goal for Dolphins after 22 minutes, 40 seconds of overtime, game lasting 82 minutes, 40 seconds in all, longest in history, Dec. 25.

**1972** Dallas defeated Miami 24–3 in Super Bowl VI at Miami, Jan. 16. CBS telecast was viewed in estimated 27,450,000 homes, top-rated one-day telecast ever.

Inbounds lines or hashmarks moved nearer center of field, 23 yards, 1 foot, 9 inches from side lines, Mar. 23. Exception made to the rule allowing team in possession on its own 15 yard line or within would put ball in play at spot 20 yards from nearest sideline so it could punt without direct conflict with goal post, May 24.

Method of determining won-lost percentage in standings changed, May 24. Tie games, previously not counted in standings, made equal to

half-game won and half-game lost.

Hunt, Halas, reelected presidents of AFC, NFC, May 25.

Robert Irsay purchased Los Angeles, transferred ownership to Carroll Rosenbloom in exchange for Baltimore, July 13.

William V. Bidwill purchased stock of brother Charles (Stormy) Bidwill, became sole owner, president of St. Louis Cardinals, Sept. 2.

National District Attorneys Association endorsed position of professional leagues in opposing proposed legalization of gambling in professional team sports, Sept. 28.

**1973** Rozelle announced all Super Bowl VII tickets sold, game would be telecast in Los Angeles, site of game, on experimental basis, Jan. 3.

Miami defeated Washington 14–7 in Super Bowl VII at Los Angeles, completing undefeated 17–0 record for 1972 season, Jan. 14. NBC telecast viewed by approximately 75,000,000 people. Although all 90,182 tickets had been sold and temperature reached 84 degrees on clear, sunny day, 8,476 ticket buyers did not attend game that was first ever televised locally.

AFC defeated NFC 33–28 in Pro Bowl at Dallas, first time since 1951 game played outside Los Angeles, Jan. 21.

Jersey numbering system adopted, 1–19 for quarterbacks, specialists; 20–49, running, defensive backs; 50–59, centers, linebackers; 60–79, defensive linemen, interior offensive linemen except centers; 80–89, wide receivers, tight ends, Apr. 5. Players who had been in NFL in 1972 could continue to use old numbers.

Dan Rooney of Pittsburgh appointed chairman of Expansion Committee, Apr. 6.

NFL Charities non-profit organization created to derive income from monies generated by licensing of NFL trademarks and names, June 26; would support education, charitable activities, supply economic support to persons formerly associated with professional football no longer able to support themselves.

Congress adopted for three years experimental legislation requiring any NFL game that had been declared a sellout 72 hours prior to kick-off to be made available for local telecast, Sept. 14. Legislation provided for annual review to be made by Federal Communications Commission.

**1974** Miami defeated Minnesota 24–7 in Super Bowl VIII at Houston, second straight Super Bowl championship for Miami, Jan. 13. CBS telecast viewed by approximately 75 million people.

Rival league formed; World Football League held organizational meeting, Jan. 14.

Rozelle given 10-year contract effective January 1, 1973, Feb. 27.

Tampa awarded franchise to begin play in 1976, Apr. 24. NFL announced one more franchise would be awarded to become operative in 1976.

Sweeping rules changes adopted as recommended by Competition Committee to add action, tempo to game: sudden death for preseason, regular season games, limited to one 15-minute overtime; goal posts moved from goal lines to end lines; kickoffs to be made from 35 not 40 yard line; after missed field goals ball to be returned to line of scrimmage or

20 yard line, whichever is farthest from goal line; restrictions placed on members of punting team to open up return possibilities; roll-blocking, cutting of wide receivers eliminated; extent of downfield contact defender can have with eligible receivers restricted; penalty for offensive holding, illegal use of hands, tripping reduced from 15 to 10 yards when occurs within three yards of line of scrimmage; wide receivers blocking back toward ball within three yards of line of scrimmage prevented from blocking below the waist, Apr. 25.

Toronto Northmen of World Football League signed Larry Csonka, Jim Kiick, Paul Warfield of Miami, Mar. 31.

Seattle awarded NFL franchise to begin play in 1976, June 4. Lloyd W. Nordstrom, president of Seattle Seahawks, Hugh F. Culverhouse, president of Tampa Bay Buccaneers, sign franchise agreement, Dec. 5.

Birmingham Americans defeated Florida Blazers 22–21 in WFL World Bowl, winning championship of the 12-team league, Dec. 5.

**1975** Pittsburgh defeated Minnesota 16–6 in Super Bowl IX at New Orleans, Steelers' first championship since entering NFL in 1933. NBC telecast was viewed by approximately 78 million people.

Rules changed making incomplete pass into end zone on fourth down with line of scrimmage inside 20 returned to line of scrimmage instead of 20; double shift on or inside opponent's 20 permitted provided it has been shown three times in game instead of three times in quarter; penalty for ineligible receiver downfield reduced from 15 to 10 yards, Mar. 19.

Divisional winners with highest won-lost percentage made home teams for playoffs, surviving winners with highest percentage made home teams for championship games, June 26.

World Football League folded, Sept. 22.

**1976** Pittsburgh defeated Dallas 21–17 in Super Bowl X in Miami; Steelers joined Green Bay, Miami as two-time winners of Super Bowl. CBS telecast viewed by estimated 80 million people, largest television audience in history.

Lloyd Nordstrom, president of Seattle, died at 66, Jan. 20. His brother Elmer succeeded him as majority representative of the team.

Veteran player allocation held to stock Seattle, Tampa Bay franchises with 39 players each, Mar. 30–31. College draft held, with Seattle, Tampa Bay getting eight extra choices each, Apr. 8–9.

Steelers defeated College All-Stars 24–0 in storm-shortened final Chicago All-Star game, July 23. St. Louis defeated San Diego 20–10 in preseason game before 38,000 in Korakuen Stadium, Tokyo, in first NFL game outside North America Aug. 16.

**1977** Oakland defeated Minnesota 32–14 before record crowd of 100,421 in Super Bowl XI at Pasadena, Jan. 9. Paid attendance was pro record 103,438. NBC telecast was viewed by 81.9 million people, largest ever to view sports event. Victory was fifth straight for AFC in Super Bowl.

Players Association, NFL Management Council ratified collective bargaining agreement extending until July 15, 1982, covering five football seasons while continuing pension plan—including years 1974,

1975, and 1976—with contributions totaling more than $55 million. Total cost of agreement estimated at $107 million. Agreement called for college draft at least through 1986, contained no-strike, no-suit clause, established 43-man active player limit, reducing pension vesting to four years, provided for increases in minimum salaries, preseason and postseason pay, improved insurance, medical, dental benefits, modified previous previous practices in player movement and control. Reaffirmed NFL commissioner's disciplinary authority. Additionally, agreement called for NFL member clubs to make payments totaling $16 million the next 10 years to settle various legal disputes, Feb. 25.

NFL regular season paid attendance was record 11,070.543.

San Francisco 49ers sold to Edward J. DeBartolo, Jr., Mar. 28.

Sixteen-game regular season, four-game preseason adopted to begin in 1978, Mar. 29. Second wild card team adopted for playoffs beginning in 1978, wild card teams to play each other with winners advancing to round of eight postseason series along with six division winners.

Defender permitted to contact eligible receiver either in three-yard zone at or beyond line of scrimmage or once beyond that zone, but not both, Mar. 31. Wide receivers prohibited from clipping anywhere, even in legal clipping zone. Penalty of loss of coin toss option in addition to 15-yard penalty provided if team does not arrive on field for warmup at least 15 minutes prior to scheduled kickoff.

Seattle Seahawks permanently aligned in AFC Western Division, Tampa Bay in NFC Central Division, Mar. 31.

NFL decided to experiment with seventh official in selected preseason games, Apr. 1.

Rules changes made it illegal to strike an opponent above shoulders (head slap) during initial charge of a defensive lineman, made it illegal for an offensive lineman to thrust his hands to an opponent's neck, face, or head; made it illegal for a back who lines up inside the tight end to break to the outside and then cut back inside to deliver a block below the waist of an opponent. Also, if a punting team commits a foul before its opponent takes possession and the receiving team subsequently commits a foul, the penalties offset each other and the down is replayed, June 14–15.

Commissioner Rozelle confirmed that agreements were negotiated with the three television networks—ABC, CBS, and NBC—to televise all NFL regular season and postseason games, plus selected preseason games, for four years beginning with the 1978 season. ABC was awarded rights to 16 Monday night, four prime time (with possible expansion to six during the last three years of the contract), the AFC-NFC Pro Bowl, and the AFC-NFC Hall of Fame games. CBS received rights to all NFC regular season and postseason games (except those in the ABC package) and Super Bowls XIV (1980) and XVI (1982). NBC received rights to all AFC regular season and postseason games (except those in the ABC package) and Super Bowls XIII (1979) and XV (1981). Industry sources considered it the largest single television package ever negotiated, October.

Chicago's Walter Payton set a single game rushing record with 275 yards (40 carries) against Minnesota, Nov. 20.

Cincinnati defeated Kansas City 27–7 at Arrowhead Stadium in the NFL's 5,000th game in recorded history, Dec. 4.

**1978** Dallas defeated Denver 27–10 in Super Bowl XII, held indoors for the first time, at the Louisiana Superdome in New Orleans, Jan. 15. CBS telecast viewed by 102,010,000 people, meaning the game was watched by more viewers than any other show of any kind in the history of television. Dallas's win was first NFC victory in last six Super Bowls.

According to Harris Sports Survey, 70 percent of the nation's sports fans say they follow football, compared to 54 percent who follow baseball. As far as fans' favorite sport, football increased its lead as the country's favorite sport to 26 to 16 percent over baseball, Jan. 19.

NFL regular season paid attendance was 11,018,632. In addition, during five years of TV blackout legislation, percent of capacity in NFL attendance has declined from record level of 95.5 percent in 1973 to 87.8 percent in 1977. NFL had over 1.5 million unsold seats in 1977, compared to fewer than one-half million in 1973. Added seventh official, side judge, Mar. 14.

Study on the use of instant replay as an officiating aid to be made during seven nationally televised preseason games in 1978, Mar. 16.

Rules changes adopted permitting defender to maintain contact on receivers within a five-yard zone beyond scrimmage line, but restricted contact on receivers beyond that point; further clarified the pass blocking rule interpretation to permit extended arms and open hands, Mar. 17.

The NFL played for the first time in Mexico City with the Saints defeating the Eagles, 14–7, in a preseason game before a sellout crowd, Aug. 5.

**1979** Pittsburgh defeated Dallas 35–31 in Super Bowl XIII to become the first team ever to win three Super Bowls, Jan. 21. Super Bowl XIII was the top ranked TV sporting event of all time, according to figures compiled by A. C. Nielsen Co. The NBC telecast was viewed in 35,090,000 homes, which bettered the previous record of Super Bowl XII with 34,410,000.

Bolstered by the expansion of the regular season schedule from 14 to 16 weeks, the NFL paid attendance exceeded 12 million (12,771,800) for the first time. The per-game average of 57,017 was the third highest in league history and best since 1973.

Rules changes emphasized additional player safety: prohibited players on the receiving team from blocking below the waist during kickoffs, punts, and field goal attempts; prohibited wearing of torn or altered equipment and exposed pads that may be hazardous; extended the zone in which there can be no crackback blocks from three yards on either side of the line of scrimmage to five yards in order to provide a greater measure of protection; permit free activation of three players from the injured reserve list after the final cutdown to 45 players, Mar. 16.

Commissioner Pete Rozelle announced that the 1980 AFC-NFC Pro Bowl Game will be played at Aloha Stadium in Honolulu, Hawaii. This will mark the first time in the 30-year history of the Pro Bowl that the game will be played in a non-NFL city.

Carroll D. Rosenbloom, president of the Rams, died at 72, April 2.

**1980** Nielsen figures show that the CBS telecast of SB XIV between Pittsburgh and Los Angeles was the most watched sports event of all time. It was viewed in 35,330,000 homes.

Rule changes adopted placed greater restrictions on contact in the area of the head, neck, and face. Under the heading of "Personal Foul," players have been prohibited from directly striking, swinging, or clubbing on the head, neck, or face. Starting in 1980, a penalty may be called for such contact to the head, neck, or face whether or not the initial contact is made below the neck area.

The NFL entered into an agreement with the National Athletic Injury/Illness Reporting System (NAIRS) to proceed with developing a program to study injuries.

CBS, with a record bid of $12 million, won the national radio rights to 26 National Football League regular season games and all 10 postseason games for the 1980 through 1983 seasons.

NFL regular season attendance of nearly 13.4 million set a record for the second year in a row; 1979's total was 13.2 million. Average paid attendance for the 224-game 1980 regular season was 59,787, highest in the league's 61-year history. The previous high was 58,961 for 182 games in 1973. NFL games in 1980 were played before 92.4 percent of total stadium capacity.

Television ratings in 1980 were the second best in NFL history, trailing only the combined ratings of the 1976 season.

**1981** The Oakland Raiders became the first Wild Card team to win the Super Bowl by defeating Philadelphia 27–10 at the Louisiana Superdome in New Orleans, Jan. 25. The Raiders finished second to San Diego in the AFC Western Division. In the playoffs they beat Houston at Oakland and Cleveland and San Diego on the road to advance to the Super Bowl.

The 1980 season concluded with a record Aloha Stadium crowd viewing the NFC's win over the AFC in the annual AFC-NFC Pro Bowl game in Honolulu, Feb. 1. It was the second straight sellout of the game in Honolulu.

Industrialist Edgar F. Kaiser, Jr. purchased the Denver Broncos from Gerald and Allan Phipps, Feb. 26.

**1982** The 1981 NFL regular season paid attendance of 13,606,990 for an average of 60,745 was the highest in the league's 62-year history. It also was the first time the season average exceeded 60,000. NFL games in 1981 were played before 93.8 percent of total stadium capacity.

NFL signed a five-year contract with the three TV networks (ABC, CBS, NBC) to televise all NFL regular and postseason games starting with the 1982 season.

The San Francisco-Cincinnati Super Bowl game on January 24 achieved the highest rating of any televised sports event. The game was watched by a record 110,230,000 viewers in this country for a rating of 49.1.

**1983** The 1982 season was reduced from a 16-game schedule to 9 as the result of the 57-day players' strike. Because of the shortened season, the league adopted for the 1982 playoffs a format of 16 teams competing in a Super Bowl Tournament. NFC number-one seed Washington eventually defeated AFC number-two seed Miami, 27-17, in Super Bowl XVII at the Rose Bowl to mark only the second time the NFC had won consecutive Super Bowls.

Despite the players' strike, the average paid attendance in 1982 was 58,472, the fifth highest in league history, compared to 1981's record average of 60,745.

Super Bowl XVII was the second-highest rated live television program of all time and gave the NFL a sweep of the top 10 live programs in TV history. Super Bowl XVII was viewed in over 40 million homes, the largest total ever for a live telecast.

**1984** The Los Angeles Raiders-Washington Redskins Super Bowl XVIII game on Jan. 22 achieved a 46.4 television rating to become the eleventh highest-rated TV program of all time and fifth-highest Super Bowl.

An 11-man group headed by H. R. Bright purchased the Dallas Cowboys from Clint Murchison, Jr., March 20. Club President Tex Schramm was designated as managing general partner.

Businessman Patrick Bowlen purchased a majority interest in the Denver Broncos from Edgar Kaiser, March 21.

## 1983

### AMERICAN CONFERENCE
#### EASTERN DIVISION

|  | W | L | T | Pct. | Pts. | OP |
|---|---|---|---|---|---|---|
| Miami | 12 | 4 | 0 | .750 | 389 | 250 |
| New England | 8 | 8 | 0 | .500 | 274 | 289 |
| Buffalo | 8 | 8 | 0 | .500 | 283 | 351 |
| Baltimore | 7 | 9 | 0 | .438 | 264 | 354 |
| N.Y. Jets | 7 | 9 | 0 | .438 | 313 | 331 |

#### CENTRAL DIVISION

|  | W | L | T | Pct. | Pts. | OP |
|---|---|---|---|---|---|---|
| Pittsburgh | 10 | 6 | 0 | .625 | 355 | 303 |
| Cleveland | 9 | 7 | 0 | .563 | 356 | 342 |
| Cincinnati | 7 | 9 | 0 | .438 | 346 | 302 |
| Houston | 2 | 14 | 0 | .125 | 288 | 460 |

#### WESTERN DIVISION

|  | W | L | T | Pct. | Pts. | OP |
|---|---|---|---|---|---|---|
| L.A. Raiders | 12 | 4 | 0 | .750 | 442 | 338 |
| Seattle* | 9 | 7 | 0 | .563 | 403 | 397 |
| Denver* | 9 | 7 | 0 | .563 | 302 | 327 |
| San Diego | 6 | 10 | 0 | .375 | 358 | 462 |
| Kansas City | 6 | 10 | 0 | .375 | 386 | 367 |

### NATIONAL CONFERENCE
#### EASTERN DIVISION

|  | W | L | T | Pct. | Pts. | OP |
|---|---|---|---|---|---|---|
| Washington | 14 | 2 | 0 | .875 | 541 | 332 |
| Dallas* | 12 | 4 | 0 | .750 | 479 | 360 |
| St. Louis | 8 | 7 | 1 | .531 | 374 | 428 |
| Philadelphia | 5 | 11 | 0 | .313 | 233 | 322 |
| N.Y. Giants | 3 | 12 | 1 | .219 | 267 | 347 |

#### CENTRAL DIVISION

|  | W | L | T | Pct. | Pts. | OP |
|---|---|---|---|---|---|---|
| Detroit | 9 | 7 | 0 | .563 | 347 | 286 |
| Green Bay | 8 | 8 | 0 | .500 | 429 | 439 |
| Chicago | 8 | 8 | 0 | .500 | 311 | 301 |
| Minnesota | 8 | 8 | 0 | .500 | 316 | 348 |
| Tampa Bay | 2 | 14 | 0 | .125 | 241 | 380 |

#### WESTERN DIVISION

|  | W | L | T | Pct. | Pts. | OP |
|---|---|---|---|---|---|---|
| San Francisco | 10 | 6 | 0 | .625 | 432 | 293 |
| L.A. Rams* | 9 | 7 | 0 | .563 | 361 | 344 |
| New Orleans | 8 | 8 | 0 | .500 | 319 | 337 |
| Atlanta | 7 | 9 | 0 | .438 | 370 | 389 |

*Wild Card qualifiers for playoffs

*Seattle and Denver gained Wild Card berths over Cleveland because of their victories over the Browns.*

First round playoff: SEATTLE 31, Denver 7
Divisional playoffs: Seattle 27, MIAMI 20, L.A. RAIDERS 38, Pittsburgh 10
AFC championship: L.A. RAIDERS 30, Seattle 14
First round playoff: Los Angeles Rams 24, DALLAS 17
Divisional playoffs: SAN FRANCISCO 24, Detroit 23, WASHINGTON 51, L.A. Rams 7
NFC championship: WASHINGTON 24, San Francisco 17
Super Bowl XVIII: Los Angeles Raiders (AFC) 38, Washington (NFC) 9 at Tampa Stadium, Tampa, Florida.

## 1982

### AMERICAN CONFERENCE

|  | W | L | T | Pct. | Pts. | OP |
|---|---|---|---|---|---|---|
| L.A. Raiders | 8 | 1 | 0 | .889 | 260 | 200 |
| Miami | 7 | 2 | 0 | .778 | 198 | 131 |
| Cincinnati | 7 | 2 | 0 | .778 | 232 | 177 |
| Pittsburgh | 6 | 3 | 0 | .667 | 204 | 146 |
| San Diego | 6 | 3 | 0 | .667 | 288 | 221 |
| N.Y. Jets | 6 | 3 | 0 | .667 | 245 | 166 |
| New England | 5 | 4 | 0 | .556 | 143 | 157 |
| Cleveland | 4 | 5 | 0 | .444 | 140 | 182 |
| Buffalo | 4 | 5 | 0 | .444 | 150 | 154 |
| Seattle | 4 | 5 | 0 | .444 | 127 | 147 |
| Kansas City | 3 | 6 | 0 | .333 | 176 | 184 |
| Denver | 2 | 7 | 0 | .222 | 148 | 226 |
| Houston | 1 | 8 | 0 | .111 | 136 | 245 |
| Baltimore | 0 | 8 | 1 | .056 | 113 | 236 |

### NATIONAL CONFERENCE

|  | W | L | T | Pct. | Pts. | OP |
|---|---|---|---|---|---|---|
| Washington | 8 | 1 | 0 | .889 | 190 | 128 |
| Dallas | 6 | 3 | 0 | .667 | 226 | 145 |
| Green Bay | 5 | 3 | 1 | .611 | 226 | 169 |
| Minnesota | 5 | 4 | 0 | .556 | 187 | 198 |
| Atlanta | 5 | 4 | 0 | .556 | 183 | 199 |
| St. Louis | 5 | 4 | 0 | .556 | 135 | 170 |
| Tampa Bay | 5 | 4 | 0 | .556 | 158 | 178 |
| Detroit | 4 | 5 | 0 | .444 | 181 | 176 |
| New Orleans | 4 | 5 | 0 | .444 | 129 | 160 |
| N.Y. Giants | 4 | 5 | 0 | .444 | 164 | 160 |
| San Francisco | 3 | 6 | 0 | .333 | 209 | 206 |
| Chicago | 3 | 6 | 0 | .333 | 141 | 174 |
| Philadelphia | 3 | 6 | 0 | .333 | 191 | 195 |
| L.A. Rams | 2 | 7 | 0 | .222 | 200 | 250 |

*As the result of a 57-day players' strike, the 1982 NFL regular season schedule was reduced from 16 weeks to 9. At the conclusion of the regular season, the NFL conducted a 16-team postseason Super Bowl Tournament. Eight teams from each conference were seeded 1-8 based on their records during the season.*

*Miami finished ahead of Cincinnati based on better conference record (6-1 to 6-2). Pittsburgh won common games tie-breaker with San Diego (3-1 to 2-1) after Jets were eliminated from three-way tie based on conference record (Pittsburgh and San Diego 5-3 vs. Jets 2-3). Cleveland finished ahead of Buffalo and Seattle based on better conference record (4-3 to 3-3 to 3-5). Minnesota (4-1), Atlanta (4-3), St. Louis (5-4), Tampa Bay (3-3) seeds were determined by best won-lost record in conference games. Detroit finished ahead of New Orleans and the New York Giants based on better conference record (4-4 to 3-5 to 3-5).*

First round playoff: MIAMI 28, New England 13
LOS ANGELES RAIDERS 27, Cleveland 10
New York Jets 44, CINCINNATI 17
San Diego 31, PITTSBURGH 28
Second round playoff: New York Jets 17, LOS ANGELES RAIDERS 14
MIAMI 34, San Diego 13
AFC championship: MIAMI 14, New York Jets 0
First round playoff: WASHINGTON 31, Detroit 7
GREEN BAY 41, St. Louis 16
MINNESOTA 30, Atlanta 24
DALLAS 30, Tampa Bay 17
Second round playoff: WASHINGTON 21, Minnesota 7
DALLAS 37, Green Bay 26
NFC championship: WASHINGTON 31, Dallas 17
Super Bowl XVII: Washington (NFC) 27, Miami (AFC) 17 at Rose Bowl, Pasadena, Calif.

*In the Past Standings section, home teams in playoff games are indicated by capital letters.*

## 1981

### AMERICAN CONFERENCE
#### EASTERN DIVISION

|  | W | L | T | Pct. | Pts. | OP |
|---|---|---|---|---|---|---|
| Miami | 11 | 4 | 1 | .719 | 345 | 275 |
| N.Y. Jets* | 10 | 5 | 1 | .656 | 355 | 287 |
| Buffalo* | 10 | 6 | 0 | .625 | 311 | 276 |
| Baltimore | 2 | 14 | 0 | .125 | 259 | 533 |
| New England | 2 | 14 | 0 | .125 | 322 | 370 |

#### CENTRAL DIVISION

|  | W | L | T | Pct. | Pts. | OP |
|---|---|---|---|---|---|---|
| Cincinnati | 12 | 4 | 0 | .750 | 421 | 304 |
| Pittsburgh | 8 | 8 | 0 | .500 | 356 | 297 |
| Houston | 7 | 9 | 0 | .438 | 281 | 355 |
| Cleveland | 5 | 11 | 0 | .313 | 276 | 375 |

#### WESTERN DIVISION

|  | W | L | T | Pct. | Pts. | OP |
|---|---|---|---|---|---|---|
| San Diego | 10 | 6 | 0 | .625 | 478 | 390 |
| Denver | 10 | 6 | 0 | .625 | 321 | 289 |
| Kansas City | 9 | 7 | 0 | .563 | 343 | 290 |
| Oakland | 7 | 9 | 0 | .438 | 273 | 343 |
| Seattle | 6 | 10 | 0 | .375 | 322 | 388 |

### NATIONAL CONFERENCE
#### EASTERN DIVISION

|  | W | L | T | Pct. | Pts. | OP |
|---|---|---|---|---|---|---|
| Dallas | 12 | 4 | 0 | .750 | 367 | 277 |
| Philadelphia* | 10 | 6 | 0 | .625 | 368 | 221 |
| N.Y. Giants* | 9 | 7 | 0 | .563 | 295 | 257 |
| Washington | 8 | 8 | 0 | .500 | 347 | 349 |
| St. Louis | 7 | 9 | 0 | .438 | 315 | 408 |

#### CENTRAL DIVISION

|  | W | L | T | Pct. | Pts. | OP |
|---|---|---|---|---|---|---|
| Tampa Bay | 9 | 7 | 0 | .563 | 315 | 268 |
| Detroit | 8 | 8 | 0 | .500 | 397 | 322 |
| Green Bay | 8 | 8 | 0 | .500 | 324 | 361 |
| Minnesota | 7 | 9 | 0 | .438 | 325 | 369 |
| Chicago | 6 | 10 | 0 | .375 | 253 | 324 |

#### WESTERN DIVISION

|  | W | L | T | Pct. | Pts. | OP |
|---|---|---|---|---|---|---|
| San Francisco | 13 | 3 | 0 | .813 | 357 | 250 |
| Atlanta | 7 | 9 | 0 | .438 | 426 | 355 |
| Los Angeles | 6 | 10 | 0 | .375 | 303 | 351 |
| New Orleans | 4 | 12 | 0 | .250 | 207 | 378 |

*Wild Card qualifiers for playoffs

*San Diego won AFC Western title over Denver on the basis of a better division record (6-2 to 5-3). Buffalo won a Wild Card playoff berth over Denver as the result of a 9-7 victory in head-to-head competition.*

First round playoff: Buffalo 31, NEW YORK JETS 27
Divisional playoffs: San Diego 41, MIAMI 38 (OT, 13:52), CINCINNATI 28, Buffalo 21
AFC championship: CINCINNATI 27, San Diego 7
First round playoff: New York Giants 27, PHILADELPHIA 21
Divisional playoffs: DALLAS 38, Tampa Bay 0, SAN FRANCISCO 38, New York Giants 24
NFC championship: SAN FRANCISCO 28, Dallas 27
Super Bowl XVI: San Francisco (NFC) 26, Cincinnati (AFC) 21, at Silverdome, Pontiac, Mich.

## 1980

### AMERICAN CONFERENCE
#### EASTERN DIVISION

|  | W | L | T | Pct. | Pts. | OP |
|---|---|---|---|---|---|---|
| Buffalo | 11 | 5 | 0 | .688 | 320 | 260 |
| New England | 10 | 6 | 0 | .625 | 441 | 325 |
| Miami | 8 | 8 | 0 | .500 | 266 | 305 |
| Baltimore | 7 | 9 | 0 | .438 | 355 | 387 |
| N.Y. Jets | 4 | 12 | 0 | .250 | 302 | 395 |

#### CENTRAL DIVISION

|  | W | L | T | Pct. | Pts. | OP |
|---|---|---|---|---|---|---|
| Cleveland | 11 | 5 | 0 | .688 | 357 | 310 |
| Houston* | 11 | 5 | 0 | .688 | 295 | 251 |
| Pittsburgh | 9 | 7 | 0 | .563 | 352 | 313 |
| Cincinnati | 6 | 10 | 0 | .375 | 244 | 312 |

#### WESTERN DIVISION

|  | W | L | T | Pct. | Pts. | OP |
|---|---|---|---|---|---|---|
| San Diego | 11 | 5 | 0 | .688 | 418 | 327 |
| Oakland* | 11 | 5 | 0 | .688 | 364 | 306 |
| Kansas City | 8 | 8 | 0 | .500 | 319 | 336 |
| Denver | 8 | 8 | 0 | .500 | 310 | 323 |
| Seattle | 4 | 12 | 0 | .250 | 291 | 408 |

### NATIONAL CONFERENCE
#### EASTERN DIVISION

|  | W | L | T | Pct. | Pts. | OP |
|---|---|---|---|---|---|---|
| Philadelphia | 12 | 4 | 0 | .750 | 384 | 222 |
| Dallas* | 12 | 4 | 0 | .750 | 454 | 311 |
| Washington | 6 | 10 | 0 | .375 | 261 | 293 |
| St. Louis | 5 | 11 | 0 | .313 | 299 | 350 |
| N.Y. Giants | 4 | 12 | 0 | .250 | 249 | 425 |

#### CENTRAL DIVISION

|  | W | L | T | Pct. | Pts. | OP |
|---|---|---|---|---|---|---|
| Minnesota | 9 | 7 | 0 | .563 | 317 | 308 |
| Detroit | 9 | 7 | 0 | .563 | 334 | 272 |
| Chicago | 7 | 9 | 0 | .438 | 304 | 264 |
| Tampa Bay | 5 | 10 | 1 | .344 | 271 | 341 |
| Green Bay | 5 | 10 | 1 | .344 | 231 | 371 |

#### WESTERN DIVISION

|  | W | L | T | Pct. | Pts. | OP |
|---|---|---|---|---|---|---|
| Atlanta | 12 | 4 | 0 | .750 | 405 | 272 |
| Los Angeles* | 11 | 5 | 0 | .688 | 424 | 289 |
| San Francisco | 6 | 10 | 0 | .375 | 320 | 415 |
| New Orleans | 1 | 15 | 0 | .063 | 291 | 487 |

*Wild Card qualifiers for playoffs

*Philadelphia won division title over Dallas on the basis of best net points in division games (plus 84 net points to plus 50). Minnesota won division title because of a better conference record than Detroit (8-4 to 9-5). Cleveland won division title because of a better conference record than Houston (8-4 to 7-5). San Diego won division title over Oakland on the basis of best net points in division games (plus 60 net points to plus 37).*

First round playoff: OAKLAND 27, Houston 7
Divisional playoffs: SAN DIEGO 20, Buffalo 14: Oakland 14, CLEVELAND 12
AFC championship: Oakland 34, SAN DIEGO 27
First round playoff: DALLAS 34, Los Angeles 13
Divisional playoffs: PHILADELPHIA 31, Minnesota 16: Dallas 30, ATLANTA 27
NFC championship: PHILADELPHIA 20, Dallas 7
Super Bowl XV: Oakland (AFC) 27, Philadelphia (NFC) 10, at Louisiana Superdome, New Orleans, La.

## 1979

### AMERICAN CONFERENCE
#### EASTERN DIVISION
| | W | L | T | Pct. | Pts. | OP |
|---|---|---|---|---|---|---|
| Miami | 10 | 6 | 0 | .625 | 341 | 257 |
| New England | 9 | 7 | 0 | .563 | 411 | 326 |
| N.Y. Jets | 8 | 8 | 0 | .500 | 337 | 383 |
| Buffalo | 7 | 9 | 0 | .438 | 268 | 279 |
| Baltimore | 5 | 11 | 0 | .313 | 271 | 351 |

#### CENTRAL DIVISION
| | W | L | T | Pct. | Pts. | OP |
|---|---|---|---|---|---|---|
| Pittsburgh | 12 | 4 | 0 | .750 | 416 | 262 |
| Houston* | 11 | 5 | 0 | .688 | 362 | 331 |
| Cleveland | 9 | 7 | 0 | .563 | 359 | 352 |
| Cincinnati | 4 | 12 | 0 | .250 | 337 | 421 |

#### WESTERN DIVISION
| | W | L | T | Pct. | Pts. | OP |
|---|---|---|---|---|---|---|
| San Diego | 12 | 4 | 0 | .750 | 411 | 246 |
| Denver* | 10 | 6 | 0 | .625 | 289 | 262 |
| Seattle | 9 | 7 | 0 | .563 | 378 | 372 |
| Oakland | 9 | 7 | 0 | .563 | 365 | 337 |
| Kansas City | 7 | 9 | 0 | .438 | 238 | 262 |

### NATIONAL CONFERENCE
#### EASTERN DIVISION
| | W | L | T | Pct. | Pts. | OP |
|---|---|---|---|---|---|---|
| Dallas | 11 | 5 | 0 | .688 | 371 | 313 |
| Philadelphia* | 11 | 5 | 0 | .688 | 339 | 282 |
| Washington | 10 | 6 | 0 | .625 | 348 | 295 |
| N.Y. Giants | 6 | 10 | 0 | .375 | 237 | 323 |
| St. Louis | 5 | 11 | 0 | .313 | 307 | 358 |

#### CENTRAL DIVISION
| | W | L | T | Pct. | Pts. | OP |
|---|---|---|---|---|---|---|
| Tampa Bay | 10 | 6 | 0 | .625 | 273 | 237 |
| Chicago* | 10 | 6 | 0 | .625 | 306 | 249 |
| Minnesota | 7 | 9 | 0 | .438 | 259 | 337 |
| Green Bay | 5 | 11 | 0 | .313 | 246 | 316 |
| Detroit | 2 | 14 | 0 | .125 | 219 | 365 |

#### WESTERN DIVISION
| | W | L | T | Pct. | Pts. | OP |
|---|---|---|---|---|---|---|
| Los Angeles | 9 | 7 | 0 | .563 | 323 | 309 |
| New Orleans | 8 | 8 | 0 | .500 | 370 | 360 |
| Atlanta | 6 | 10 | 0 | .375 | 300 | 388 |
| San Francisco | 2 | 14 | 0 | .125 | 308 | 416 |

*Wild Card qualifier for playoffs
*Dallas won division title because of a better conference record than Philadelphia (10-2 to 9-3). Tampa Bay won division title because of a better division record than Chicago (6-2 to 5-3). Chicago won a wild card berth over Washington on the basis of best net points in all games (plus 57 net points to plus 53).*
First round playoff: HOUSTON 13, Denver 7
Divisional playoffs: Houston 17, SAN DIEGO 14; PITTSBURGH 34, Miami 14
AFC championship: PITTSBURGH 27, Houston 13
First round playoff: PHILADELPHIA 27, Chicago 17
Divisional playoffs: TAMPA BAY 24, Philadelphia 17; Los Angeles 21, DALLAS 19
NFC championship: Los Angeles 9, TAMPA BAY 0
Super Bowl XIV: Pittsburgh (AFC) 31, Los Angeles (NFC) 19, at Rose Bowl, Pasadena, Calif.

## 1978

### AMERICAN CONFERENCE
#### EASTERN DIVISION
| | W | L | T | Pct. | Pts. | OP |
|---|---|---|---|---|---|---|
| New England | 11 | 5 | 0 | .688 | 358 | 286 |
| Miami* | 11 | 5 | 0 | .688 | 372 | 254 |
| N.Y. Jets | 8 | 8 | 0 | .500 | 359 | 364 |
| Buffalo | 5 | 11 | 0 | .313 | 302 | 354 |
| Baltimore | 5 | 11 | 0 | .313 | 239 | 421 |

#### CENTRAL DIVISION
| | W | L | T | Pct. | Pts. | OP |
|---|---|---|---|---|---|---|
| Pittsburgh | 14 | 2 | 0 | .875 | 356 | 195 |
| Houston* | 10 | 6 | 0 | .625 | 283 | 298 |
| Cleveland | 8 | 8 | 0 | .500 | 334 | 356 |
| Cincinnati | 4 | 12 | 0 | .250 | 252 | 284 |

#### WESTERN DIVISION
| | W | L | T | Pct. | Pts. | OP |
|---|---|---|---|---|---|---|
| Denver | 10 | 6 | 0 | .625 | 282 | 198 |
| Oakland | 9 | 7 | 0 | .563 | 311 | 283 |
| Seattle | 9 | 7 | 0 | .563 | 345 | 358 |
| San Diego | 9 | 7 | 0 | .563 | 355 | 309 |
| Kansas City | 4 | 12 | 0 | .250 | 243 | 327 |

### NATIONAL CONFERENCE
#### EASTERN DIVISION
| | W | L | T | Pct. | Pts. | OP |
|---|---|---|---|---|---|---|
| Dallas | 12 | 4 | 0 | .750 | 384 | 208 |
| Philadelphia* | 9 | 7 | 0 | .563 | 270 | 250 |
| Washington | 8 | 8 | 0 | .500 | 273 | 283 |
| St. Louis | 6 | 10 | 0 | .375 | 248 | 296 |
| N.Y. Giants | 6 | 10 | 0 | .375 | 264 | 298 |

#### CENTRAL DIVISION
| | W | L | T | Pct. | Pts. | OP |
|---|---|---|---|---|---|---|
| Minnesota | 8 | 7 | 1 | .531 | 294 | 306 |
| Green Bay | 8 | 7 | 1 | .531 | 249 | 269 |
| Detroit | 7 | 9 | 0 | .438 | 290 | 300 |
| Chicago | 7 | 9 | 0 | .438 | 253 | 274 |
| Tampa Bay | 5 | 11 | 0 | .313 | 241 | 259 |

#### WESTERN DIVISION
| | W | L | T | Pct. | Pts. | OP |
|---|---|---|---|---|---|---|
| Los Angeles | 12 | 4 | 0 | .750 | 316 | 245 |
| Atlanta* | 9 | 7 | 0 | .563 | 240 | 290 |
| New Orleans | 7 | 9 | 0 | .438 | 281 | 298 |
| San Francisco | 2 | 14 | 0 | .125 | 219 | 350 |

*Wild Card qualifiers for playoffs
*New England won division title on the basis of a better division record than Miami (6-2 to 5-3). Minnesota won division title because of a better head-to-head record against Green Bay (1-0-1).*
First round playoff: Houston 17, MIAMI 9
Divisional playoffs: Houston 31, NEW ENGLAND 14; PITTSBURGH 33, Denver 10
AFC Championship: PITTSBURGH 34, Houston 5
First round playoff: ATLANTA 14, Philadelphia 13
Divisional playoffs: DALLAS 27, Atlanta 20; LOS ANGELES 34, Minnesota 10
NFC championship: Dallas 28, LOS ANGELES 0
Super Bowl XIII: Pittsburgh (AFC) 35, Dallas (NFC) 31, at Orange Bowl, Miami, Fla.

## 1977

### AMERICAN CONFERENCE
#### EASTERN DIVISION
| | W | L | T | Pct. | Pts. | OP |
|---|---|---|---|---|---|---|
| Baltimore | 10 | 4 | 0 | .714 | 295 | 221 |
| Miami | 10 | 4 | 0 | .714 | 313 | 197 |
| New England | 9 | 5 | 0 | .643 | 278 | 217 |
| N.Y. Jets | 3 | 11 | 0 | .214 | 191 | 300 |
| Buffalo | 3 | 11 | 0 | .214 | 160 | 313 |

#### CENTRAL DIVISION
| | W | L | T | Pct. | Pts. | OP |
|---|---|---|---|---|---|---|
| Pittsburgh | 9 | 5 | 0 | .643 | 283 | 243 |
| Houston | 8 | 6 | 0 | .571 | 299 | 230 |
| Cincinnati | 8 | 6 | 0 | .571 | 238 | 235 |
| Cleveland | 6 | 8 | 0 | .429 | 269 | 267 |

#### WESTERN DIVISION
| | W | L | T | Pct. | Pts. | OP |
|---|---|---|---|---|---|---|
| Denver | 12 | 2 | 0 | .857 | 274 | 148 |
| Oakland* | 11 | 3 | 0 | .786 | 351 | 230 |
| San Diego | 7 | 7 | 0 | .500 | 222 | 205 |
| Seattle | 5 | 9 | 0 | .357 | 282 | 373 |
| Kansas City | 2 | 12 | 0 | .143 | 225 | 349 |

### NATIONAL CONFERENCE
#### EASTERN DIVISION
| | W | L | T | Pct. | Pts. | OP |
|---|---|---|---|---|---|---|
| Dallas | 12 | 2 | 0 | .857 | 345 | 212 |
| Washington | 9 | 5 | 0 | .643 | 196 | 189 |
| St. Louis | 7 | 7 | 0 | .500 | 272 | 287 |
| Philadelphia | 5 | 9 | 0 | .357 | 220 | 207 |
| N.Y. Giants | 5 | 9 | 0 | .357 | 181 | 265 |

#### CENTRAL DIVISION
| | W | L | T | Pct. | Pts. | OP |
|---|---|---|---|---|---|---|
| Minnesota | 9 | 5 | 0 | .643 | 231 | 227 |
| Chicago* | 9 | 5 | 0 | .643 | 255 | 253 |
| Detroit | 6 | 8 | 0 | .429 | 183 | 252 |
| Green Bay | 4 | 10 | 0 | .286 | 134 | 219 |
| Tampa Bay | 2 | 12 | 0 | .143 | 103 | 223 |

#### WESTERN DIVISION
| | W | L | T | Pct. | Pts. | OP |
|---|---|---|---|---|---|---|
| Los Angeles | 10 | 4 | 0 | .714 | 302 | 146 |
| Atlanta | 7 | 7 | 0 | .500 | 179 | 129 |
| San Francisco | 5 | 9 | 0 | .357 | 220 | 260 |
| New Orleans | 3 | 11 | 0 | .214 | 232 | 336 |

*Wild Card qualifier for playoffs
*Baltimore won division title on the basis of a better conference record than Miami (9-3 to 8-4). Chicago won a wild card berth over Washington on the basis of best net points in conference games (plus 48 net points to plus 4).*
Divisional playoffs: DENVER 34, Pittsburgh 21; Oakland 37, BALTIMORE 31 sudden death overtime
AFC championship: DENVER 20, Oakland 17
Divisional playoffs: DALLAS 37, Chicago 7, Minnesota 14, LOS ANGELES 7
NFC championship: DALLAS 23, Minnesota 6.
Super Bowl XII: Dallas (NFC) 27, Denver (AFC) 10, at Louisiana Superdome, New Orleans, La.

## 1976

### AMERICAN CONFERENCE
#### EASTERN DIVISION
| | W | L | T | Pct. | Pts. | OP |
|---|---|---|---|---|---|---|
| Baltimore | 11 | 3 | 0 | .786 | 417 | 246 |
| New England* | 11 | 3 | 0 | .786 | 376 | 236 |
| Miami | 6 | 8 | 0 | .429 | 263 | 264 |
| N.Y. Jets | 3 | 11 | 0 | .214 | 169 | 383 |
| Buffalo | 2 | 12 | 0 | .143 | 245 | 363 |

#### CENTRAL DIVISION
| | W | L | T | Pct. | Pts. | OP |
|---|---|---|---|---|---|---|
| Pittsburgh | 10 | 4 | 0 | .714 | 342 | 138 |
| Cincinnati | 10 | 4 | 0 | .714 | 335 | 210 |
| Cleveland | 9 | 5 | 0 | .643 | 267 | 287 |
| Houston | 5 | 9 | 0 | .357 | 222 | 273 |

#### WESTERN DIVISION
| | W | L | T | Pct. | Pts. | OP |
|---|---|---|---|---|---|---|
| Oakland | 13 | 1 | 0 | .929 | 350 | 237 |
| Denver | 9 | 5 | 0 | .643 | 315 | 206 |
| San Diego | 6 | 8 | 0 | .429 | 248 | 285 |
| Kansas City | 5 | 9 | 0 | .357 | 290 | 376 |
| Tampa Bay | 0 | 14 | 0 | .000 | 125 | 412 |

### NATIONAL CONFERENCE
#### EASTERN DIVISION
| | W | L | T | Pct. | Pts. | OP |
|---|---|---|---|---|---|---|
| Dallas | 11 | 3 | 0 | .786 | 296 | 194 |
| Washington* | 10 | 4 | 0 | .714 | 291 | 217 |
| St. Louis | 10 | 4 | 0 | .714 | 309 | 267 |
| Philadelphia | 4 | 10 | 0 | .286 | 165 | 286 |
| N.Y. Giants | 3 | 11 | 0 | .214 | 170 | 250 |

#### CENTRAL DIVISION
| | W | L | T | Pct. | Pts. | OP |
|---|---|---|---|---|---|---|
| Minnesota | 11 | 2 | 1 | .821 | 305 | 176 |
| Chicago | 7 | 7 | 0 | .500 | 253 | 216 |
| Detroit | 6 | 8 | 0 | .429 | 262 | 220 |
| Green Bay | 5 | 9 | 0 | .357 | 218 | 299 |

#### WESTERN DIVISION
| | W | L | T | Pct. | Pts. | OP |
|---|---|---|---|---|---|---|
| Los Angeles | 10 | 3 | 1 | .750 | 351 | 190 |
| San Francisco | 8 | 6 | 0 | .571 | 270 | 190 |
| Atlanta | 4 | 10 | 0 | .286 | 172 | 312 |
| New Orleans | 4 | 10 | 0 | .286 | 253 | 346 |
| Seattle | 2 | 12 | 0 | .143 | 229 | 429 |

*Wild Card qualifier for playoffs
*Baltimore won division title on the basis of a better division record than New England (7-1 to 6-2). Pittsburgh won division title because of a two-game sweep over Cincinnati. Washington won wild card berth over St. Louis because of a two-game sweep over Cardinals.*
Divisional playoffs: OAKLAND 24, New England 21; Pittsburgh 40, BALTIMORE 14
AFC championship: OAKLAND 24, Pittsburgh 7
Divisional playoffs: MINNESOTA 35, Washington 20; Los Angeles 14, DALLAS 12
NFC championship: MINNESOTA 24, Los Angeles 13
Super Bowl XI: Oakland (AFC) 32, Minnesota (NFC) 14, at Rose Bowl, Pasadena, Calif.

## 1975

### AMERICAN CONFERENCE
#### EASTERN DIVISION
| | W | L | T | Pct. | Pts. | OP |
|---|---|---|---|---|---|---|
| Baltimore | 10 | 4 | 0 | .714 | 395 | 269 |
| Miami | 10 | 4 | 0 | .714 | 357 | 222 |
| Buffalo | 8 | 6 | 0 | .571 | 420 | 355 |
| New England | 3 | 11 | 0 | .214 | 258 | 358 |
| N.Y. Jets | 3 | 11 | 0 | .214 | 258 | 433 |

#### CENTRAL DIVISION
| | W | L | T | Pct. | Pts. | OP |
|---|---|---|---|---|---|---|
| Pittsburgh | 12 | 2 | 0 | .857 | 373 | 162 |
| Cincinnati | 11 | 3 | 0 | .786 | 340 | 246 |
| Houston | 10 | 4 | 0 | .714 | 293 | 226 |
| Cleveland | 3 | 11 | 0 | .214 | 218 | 372 |

#### WESTERN DIVISION
| | W | L | T | Pct. | Pts. | OP |
|---|---|---|---|---|---|---|
| Oakland | 11 | 3 | 0 | .786 | 375 | 255 |
| Denver | 6 | 8 | 0 | .429 | 254 | 307 |
| Kansas City | 5 | 9 | 0 | .357 | 282 | 341 |
| San Diego | 2 | 12 | 0 | .143 | 189 | 345 |

### NATIONAL CONFERENCE
#### EASTERN DIVISION
| | W | L | T | Pct. | Pts. | OP |
|---|---|---|---|---|---|---|
| St. Louis | 11 | 3 | 0 | .786 | 356 | 276 |
| Dallas* | 10 | 4 | 0 | .714 | 350 | 268 |
| Washington | 8 | 6 | 0 | .571 | 325 | 276 |
| N.Y. Giants | 5 | 9 | 0 | .357 | 216 | 306 |
| Philadelphia | 4 | 10 | 0 | .286 | 225 | 302 |

#### CENTRAL DIVISION
| | W | L | T | Pct. | Pts. | OP |
|---|---|---|---|---|---|---|
| Minnesota | 12 | 2 | 0 | .857 | 377 | 180 |
| Detroit | 7 | 7 | 0 | .500 | 245 | 262 |
| Chicago | 4 | 10 | 0 | .286 | 191 | 379 |
| Green Bay | 4 | 10 | 0 | .286 | 226 | 285 |

#### WESTERN DIVISION
| | W | L | T | Pct. | Pts. | OP |
|---|---|---|---|---|---|---|
| Los Angeles | 12 | 2 | 0 | .857 | 312 | 135 |
| San Francisco | 5 | 9 | 0 | .357 | 255 | 286 |
| Atlanta | 4 | 10 | 0 | .286 | 240 | 289 |
| New Orleans | 2 | 12 | 0 | .143 | 165 | 360 |

*Wild Card qualifier for playoffs
*Baltimore won division title on the basis of a two-game sweep over Miami.*
Divisional playoffs: PITTSBURGH 28, Baltimore 10; OAKLAND 31, Cincinnati 28
AFC championship: PITTSBURGH 16, Oakland 10
Divisional playoffs: LOS ANGELES 35, St. Louis 23; Dallas 17, MINNESOTA 14
NFC championship: Dallas 37, LOS ANGELES 7
Super Bowl X: Pittsburgh (AFC) 21, Dallas (NFC) 17, at Orange Bowl, Miami, Fla.

## 1974

### AMERICAN CONFERENCE

#### EASTERN DIVISION

| | W | L | T | Pct. | Pts. | OP |
|---|---|---|---|---|---|---|
| Miami | 11 | 3 | 0 | .786 | 327 | 216 |
| Buffalo* | 9 | 5 | 0 | .643 | 264 | 244 |
| New England | 7 | 7 | 0 | .500 | 348 | 289 |
| N.Y. Jets | 7 | 7 | 0 | .500 | 279 | 300 |
| Baltimore | 2 | 12 | 0 | .143 | 190 | 329 |

#### CENTRAL DIVISION

| | W | L | T | Pct. | Pts. | OP |
|---|---|---|---|---|---|---|
| Pittsburgh | 10 | 3 | 1 | .750 | 305 | 189 |
| Cincinnati | 7 | 7 | 0 | .500 | 283 | 259 |
| Houston | 7 | 7 | 0 | .500 | 236 | 282 |
| Cleveland | 4 | 10 | 0 | .286 | 251 | 344 |

#### WESTERN DIVISION

| | W | L | T | Pct. | Pts. | OP |
|---|---|---|---|---|---|---|
| Oakland | 12 | 2 | 0 | .857 | 355 | 228 |
| Denver | 7 | 6 | 1 | .536 | 302 | 294 |
| Kansas City | 5 | 9 | 0 | .357 | 233 | 293 |
| San Diego | 5 | 9 | 0 | .357 | 212 | 285 |

### NATIONAL CONFERENCE

#### EASTERN DIVISION

| | W | L | T | Pct. | Pts. | OP |
|---|---|---|---|---|---|---|
| St. Louis | 10 | 4 | 0 | .714 | 285 | 218 |
| Washington* | 10 | 4 | 0 | .714 | 320 | 196 |
| Dallas | 8 | 6 | 0 | .571 | 297 | 235 |
| Philadelphia | 7 | 7 | 0 | .500 | 242 | 217 |
| N.Y. Giants | 2 | 12 | 0 | .143 | 195 | 299 |

#### CENTRAL DIVISION

| | W | L | T | Pct. | Pts. | OP |
|---|---|---|---|---|---|---|
| Minnesota | 10 | 4 | 0 | .714 | 310 | 195 |
| Detroit | 7 | 7 | 0 | .500 | 256 | 270 |
| Green Bay | 6 | 8 | 0 | .429 | 210 | 206 |
| Chicago | 4 | 10 | 0 | .286 | 152 | 279 |

#### WESTERN DIVISION

| | W | L | T | Pct. | Pts. | OP |
|---|---|---|---|---|---|---|
| Los Angeles | 10 | 4 | 0 | .714 | 263 | 181 |
| San Francisco | 6 | 8 | 0 | .429 | 226 | 236 |
| New Orleans | 5 | 9 | 0 | .357 | 166 | 263 |
| Atlanta | 3 | 11 | 0 | .214 | 111 | 271 |

*Wild Card qualifier for playoffs
St. Louis won division title because of a two-game sweep over Washington.
Divisional playoffs: OAKLAND 28, Miami 26; PITTSBURGH 32, Buffalo 14
AFC championship: Pittsburgh 24, OAKLAND 13
Divisional playoffs: MINNESOTA 30, St. Louis 14; LOS ANGELES 19, Washington 10
NFC championship: MINNESOTA 14, Los Angeles 10
Super Bowl IX: Pittsburgh (AFC) 16, Minnesota (NFC) 6, at Tulane Stadium, New Orleans, La

## 1973

### AMERICAN CONFERENCE

#### EASTERN DIVISION

| | W | L | T | Pct. | Pts. | OP |
|---|---|---|---|---|---|---|
| Miami | 12 | 2 | 0 | .857 | 343 | 150 |
| Buffalo | 9 | 5 | 0 | .643 | 259 | 230 |
| New England | 5 | 9 | 0 | .357 | 258 | 300 |
| Baltimore | 4 | 10 | 0 | .286 | 226 | 341 |
| N.Y. Jets | 4 | 10 | 0 | .286 | 240 | 306 |

#### CENTRAL DIVISION

| | W | L | T | Pct. | Pts. | OP |
|---|---|---|---|---|---|---|
| Cincinnati | 10 | 4 | 0 | .714 | 286 | 231 |
| Pittsburgh* | 10 | 4 | 0 | .714 | 347 | 210 |
| Cleveland | 7 | 5 | 2 | .571 | 234 | 255 |
| Houston | 1 | 13 | 0 | .071 | 199 | 447 |

#### WESTERN DIVISION

| | W | L | T | Pct. | Pts. | OP |
|---|---|---|---|---|---|---|
| Oakland | 9 | 4 | 1 | .679 | 292 | 175 |
| Denver | 7 | 5 | 2 | .571 | 354 | 296 |
| Kansas City | 7 | 5 | 2 | .571 | 231 | 192 |
| San Diego | 2 | 11 | 1 | .179 | 188 | 386 |

### NATIONAL CONFERENCE

#### EASTERN DIVISION

| | W | L | T | Pct. | Pts. | OP |
|---|---|---|---|---|---|---|
| Dallas | 10 | 4 | 0 | .714 | 382 | 203 |
| Washington* | 10 | 4 | 0 | .714 | 325 | 198 |
| Philadelphia | 5 | 8 | 1 | .393 | 310 | 393 |
| St. Louis | 4 | 9 | 1 | .321 | 286 | 365 |
| N.Y. Giants | 2 | 11 | 1 | .179 | 226 | 362 |

#### CENTRAL DIVISION

| | W | L | T | Pct. | Pts. | OP |
|---|---|---|---|---|---|---|
| Minnesota | 12 | 2 | 0 | .857 | 296 | 168 |
| Detroit | 6 | 7 | 1 | .464 | 271 | 247 |
| Green Bay | 5 | 7 | 2 | .429 | 202 | 259 |
| Chicago | 3 | 11 | 0 | .214 | 195 | 334 |

#### WESTERN DIVISION

| | W | L | T | Pct. | Pts. | OP |
|---|---|---|---|---|---|---|
| Los Angeles | 12 | 2 | 0 | .857 | 388 | 178 |
| Atlanta | 9 | 5 | 0 | .643 | 318 | 224 |
| New Orleans | 5 | 9 | 0 | .357 | 163 | 312 |
| San Francisco | 5 | 9 | 0 | .357 | 262 | 319 |

*Wild Card qualifier for playoffs
Cincinnati won division title on the basis of a better conference record than Pittsburgh (8-3 to 7-4). Dallas won division title on the basis of a better point differential vs. Washington (net 13 points).
Divisional playoffs: OAKLAND 33, Pittsburgh 14; MIAMI 34, Cincinnati 16
AFC championship: MIAMI 27, Oakland 10
Divisional playoffs: MINNESOTA 27, Washington 20; DALLAS 27, Los Angeles 16
NFC championship: Minnesota 27, DALLAS 10
Super Bowl VIII: Miami (AFC) 24, Minnesota (NFC) 7, at Rice Stadium, Houston, Tex.

## 1972

### AMERICAN CONFERENCE

#### EASTERN DIVISION

| | W | L | T | Pct. | Pts. | OP |
|---|---|---|---|---|---|---|
| Miami | 14 | 0 | 0 | 1.000 | 385 | 171 |
| N.Y. Jets | 7 | 7 | 0 | .500 | 367 | 324 |
| Baltimore | 5 | 9 | 0 | .357 | 235 | 252 |
| Buffalo | 4 | 9 | 1 | .321 | 257 | 377 |
| New England | 3 | 11 | 0 | .214 | 192 | 446 |

#### CENTRAL DIVISION

| | W | L | T | Pct. | Pts. | OP |
|---|---|---|---|---|---|---|
| Pittsburgh | 11 | 3 | 0 | .786 | 343 | 175 |
| Cleveland* | 10 | 4 | 0 | .714 | 268 | 249 |
| Cincinnati | 8 | 6 | 0 | .571 | 299 | 229 |
| Houston | 1 | 13 | 0 | .071 | 164 | 380 |

#### WESTERN DIVISION

| | W | L | T | Pct. | Pts. | OP |
|---|---|---|---|---|---|---|
| Oakland | 10 | 3 | 1 | .750 | 365 | 248 |
| Kansas City | 8 | 6 | 0 | .571 | 287 | 254 |
| Denver | 5 | 9 | 0 | .357 | 325 | 350 |
| San Diego | 4 | 9 | 1 | .321 | 264 | 344 |

### NATIONAL CONFERENCE

#### EASTERN DIVISION

| | W | L | T | Pct. | Pts. | OP |
|---|---|---|---|---|---|---|
| Washington | 11 | 3 | 0 | .786 | 336 | 218 |
| Dallas* | 10 | 4 | 0 | .714 | 319 | 240 |
| N.Y. Giants | 8 | 6 | 0 | .571 | 331 | 247 |
| St. Louis | 4 | 9 | 1 | .321 | 193 | 303 |
| Philadelphia | 2 | 11 | 1 | .179 | 145 | 352 |

#### CENTRAL DIVISION

| | W | L | T | Pct. | Pts. | OP |
|---|---|---|---|---|---|---|
| Green Bay | 10 | 4 | 0 | .714 | 304 | 226 |
| Detroit | 8 | 5 | 1 | .607 | 339 | 290 |
| Minnesota | 7 | 7 | 0 | .500 | 301 | 252 |
| Chicago | 4 | 9 | 1 | .321 | 225 | 275 |

#### WESTERN DIVISION

| | W | L | T | Pct. | Pts. | OP |
|---|---|---|---|---|---|---|
| San Francisco | 8 | 5 | 1 | .607 | 353 | 249 |
| Atlanta | 7 | 7 | 0 | .500 | 269 | 274 |
| Los Angeles | 6 | 7 | 1 | .464 | 291 | 286 |
| New Orleans | 2 | 11 | 1 | .179 | 215 | 361 |

*Wild Card qualifier for playoffs
Divisional playoffs: PITTSBURGH 13, Oakland 7; MIAMI 20, Cleveland 14
AFC championship: Miami 21, PITTSBURGH 17
Divisional playoffs: Dallas 30, SAN FRANCISCO 28; WASHINGTON 16, Green Bay 3
NFC championship: WASHINGTON 26, Dallas 3
Super Bowl VII: Miami (AFC) 14, Washington (NFC) 7, at Memorial Coliseum, Los Angeles, Calif.

## 1971

### AMERICAN CONFERENCE

#### EASTERN DIVISION

| | W | L | T | Pct. | Pts. | OP |
|---|---|---|---|---|---|---|
| Miami | 10 | 3 | 1 | .769 | 315 | 174 |
| Baltimore* | 10 | 4 | 0 | .714 | 313 | 140 |
| New England | 6 | 8 | 0 | .429 | 238 | 325 |
| N.Y. Jets | 6 | 8 | 0 | .429 | 212 | 299 |
| Buffalo | 1 | 13 | 0 | .071 | 184 | 394 |

#### CENTRAL DIVISION

| | W | L | T | Pct. | Pts. | OP |
|---|---|---|---|---|---|---|
| Cleveland | 9 | 5 | 0 | .643 | 285 | 273 |
| Pittsburgh | 6 | 8 | 0 | .429 | 246 | 292 |
| Houston | 4 | 9 | 1 | .308 | 251 | 330 |
| Cincinnati | 4 | 10 | 0 | .286 | 284 | 265 |

#### WESTERN DIVISION

| | W | L | T | Pct. | Pts. | OP |
|---|---|---|---|---|---|---|
| Kansas City | 10 | 3 | 1 | .769 | 302 | 208 |
| Oakland | 8 | 4 | 2 | .667 | 344 | 278 |
| San Diego | 6 | 8 | 0 | .429 | 311 | 341 |
| Denver | 4 | 9 | 1 | .308 | 203 | 275 |

### NATIONAL CONFERENCE

#### EASTERN DIVISION

| | W | L | T | Pct. | Pts. | OP |
|---|---|---|---|---|---|---|
| Dallas | 11 | 3 | 0 | .786 | 406 | 222 |
| Washington* | 9 | 4 | 1 | .692 | 276 | 190 |
| Philadelphia | 6 | 7 | 1 | .462 | 221 | 302 |
| St. Louis | 4 | 9 | 1 | .308 | 231 | 279 |
| N.Y. Giants | 4 | 10 | 0 | .286 | 228 | 362 |

#### CENTRAL DIVISION

| | W | L | T | Pct. | Pts. | OP |
|---|---|---|---|---|---|---|
| Minnesota | 11 | 3 | 0 | .786 | 245 | 139 |
| Detroit | 7 | 6 | 1 | .538 | 341 | 286 |
| Chicago | 6 | 8 | 0 | .429 | 185 | 276 |
| Green Bay | 4 | 8 | 2 | .333 | 274 | 298 |

#### WESTERN DIVISION

| | W | L | T | Pct. | Pts. | OP |
|---|---|---|---|---|---|---|
| San Francisco | 9 | 5 | 0 | .643 | 300 | 216 |
| Los Angeles | 8 | 5 | 1 | .615 | 313 | 260 |
| Atlanta | 7 | 6 | 1 | .538 | 274 | 277 |
| New Orleans | 4 | 8 | 2 | .333 | 266 | 347 |

*Wild Card qualifier for playoffs
Divisional playoffs: Miami 27, KANSAS CITY 24, sudden death overtime; Baltimore 20, CLEVELAND 3
AFC championship: MIAMI 21, Baltimore 0
Divisional playoffs: Dallas 20, MINNESOTA 12; SAN FRANCISCO 24, Washington 20
NFC championship: DALLAS 14, San Francisco 3
Super Bowl VI: Dallas (NFC) 24, Miami (AFC) 3, at Tulane Stadium, New Orleans, La.

## 1970

### AMERICAN CONFERENCE

#### EASTERN DIVISION

| | W | L | T | Pct. | Pts. | OP |
|---|---|---|---|---|---|---|
| Baltimore | 11 | 2 | 1 | .846 | 321 | 234 |
| Miami* | 10 | 4 | 0 | .714 | 297 | 228 |
| N.Y. Jets | 4 | 10 | 0 | .286 | 255 | 286 |
| Buffalo | 3 | 10 | 1 | .231 | 204 | 337 |
| Boston Patriots | 2 | 12 | 0 | .143 | 149 | 361 |

#### CENTRAL DIVISION

| | W | L | T | Pct. | Pts. | OP |
|---|---|---|---|---|---|---|
| Cincinnati | 8 | 6 | 0 | .571 | 312 | 255 |
| Cleveland | 7 | 7 | 0 | .500 | 286 | 265 |
| Pittsburgh | 5 | 9 | 0 | .357 | 210 | 272 |
| Houston | 3 | 10 | 1 | .231 | 217 | 352 |

#### WESTERN DIVISION

| | W | L | T | Pct. | Pts. | OP |
|---|---|---|---|---|---|---|
| Oakland | 8 | 4 | 2 | .667 | 300 | 293 |
| Kansas City | 7 | 5 | 2 | .583 | 272 | 244 |
| San Diego | 5 | 6 | 3 | .455 | 282 | 278 |
| Denver | 5 | 8 | 1 | .385 | 253 | 264 |

### NATIONAL CONFERENCE

#### EASTERN DIVISION

| | W | L | T | Pct. | Pts. | OP |
|---|---|---|---|---|---|---|
| Dallas | 10 | 4 | 0 | .714 | 299 | 221 |
| N.Y. Giants | 9 | 5 | 0 | .643 | 301 | 270 |
| St. Louis | 8 | 5 | 1 | .615 | 325 | 228 |
| Washington | 6 | 8 | 0 | .429 | 297 | 314 |
| Philadelphia | 3 | 10 | 1 | .231 | 241 | 332 |

#### CENTRAL DIVISION

| | W | L | T | Pct. | Pts. | OP |
|---|---|---|---|---|---|---|
| Minnesota | 12 | 2 | 0 | .857 | 335 | 143 |
| Detroit* | 10 | 4 | 0 | .714 | 347 | 202 |
| Chicago | 6 | 8 | 0 | .429 | 256 | 261 |
| Green Bay | 6 | 8 | 0 | .429 | 196 | 293 |

#### WESTERN DIVISION

| | W | L | T | Pct. | Pts. | OP |
|---|---|---|---|---|---|---|
| San Francisco | 10 | 3 | 1 | .769 | 352 | 267 |
| Los Angeles | 9 | 4 | 1 | .692 | 325 | 202 |
| Atlanta | 4 | 8 | 2 | .333 | 206 | 261 |
| New Orleans | 2 | 11 | 1 | .154 | 172 | 347 |

*Wild Card qualifier for playoffs
Divisional playoffs: BALTIMORE 17, Cincinnati 0; OAKLAND 21, Miami 14
AFC championship: BALTIMORE 27, Oakland 17
Divisional playoffs: DALLAS 5, Detroit 0; San Francisco 17, MINNESOTA 14
NFC championship: Dallas 17, SAN FRANCISCO 10
Super Bowl V: Baltimore (AFC) 16, Dallas (NFC) 13, at Orange Bowl, Miami, Fla.

## 1969 NFL

### EASTERN CONFERENCE

#### Capitol Division

| | W | L | T | Pct. | Pts. | OP |
|---|---|---|---|---|---|---|
| Dallas | 11 | 2 | 1 | .846 | 369 | 223 |
| Washington | 7 | 5 | 2 | .583 | 307 | 319 |
| New Orleans | 5 | 9 | 0 | .357 | 311 | 393 |
| Philadelphia | 4 | 9 | 1 | .308 | 279 | 377 |

#### Century Division

| | W | L | T | Pct. | Pts. | OP |
|---|---|---|---|---|---|---|
| Cleveland | 10 | 3 | 1 | .769 | 351 | 300 |
| N.Y. Giants | 6 | 8 | 0 | .429 | 264 | 298 |
| St. Louis | 4 | 9 | 1 | .308 | 314 | 389 |
| Pittsburgh | 1 | 13 | 0 | .071 | 218 | 404 |

### WESTERN CONFERENCE

#### Coastal Division

| | W | L | T | Pct. | Pts. | OP |
|---|---|---|---|---|---|---|
| Los Angeles | 11 | 3 | 0 | .786 | 320 | 243 |
| Baltimore | 8 | 5 | 1 | .615 | 279 | 268 |
| Atlanta | 6 | 8 | 0 | .429 | 276 | 268 |
| San Francisco | 4 | 8 | 2 | .333 | 277 | 319 |

#### Central Division

| | W | L | T | Pct. | Pts. | OP |
|---|---|---|---|---|---|---|
| Minnesota | 12 | 2 | 0 | .857 | 379 | 133 |
| Detroit | 9 | 4 | 1 | .692 | 259 | 188 |
| Green Bay | 8 | 6 | 0 | .571 | 269 | 221 |
| Chicago | 1 | 13 | 0 | .071 | 210 | 339 |

Conference championships: Cleveland 38, DALLAS 14; MINNESOTA 23, Los Angeles 20
NFL championship: MINNESOTA 27, Cleveland 7
Super Bowl IV: Kansas City (AFL) 23, Minnesota (NFL) 7, at Tulane Stadium, New Orleans, La.

## 1969 AFL

### EASTERN DIVISION

| | W | L | T | Pct. | Pts. | OP |
|---|---|---|---|---|---|---|
| N.Y. Jets | 10 | 4 | 0 | .714 | 353 | 269 |
| Houston | 6 | 6 | 2 | .500 | 278 | 279 |
| Boston Patriots | 4 | 10 | 0 | .286 | 266 | 316 |
| Buffalo | 4 | 10 | 0 | .286 | 230 | 359 |
| Miami | 3 | 10 | 1 | .231 | 233 | 332 |

### WESTERN DIVISION

| | W | L | T | Pct. | Pts. | OP |
|---|---|---|---|---|---|---|
| Oakland | 12 | 1 | 1 | .923 | 377 | 242 |
| Kansas City | 11 | 3 | 0 | .786 | 359 | 177 |
| San Diego | 8 | 6 | 0 | .571 | 288 | 276 |
| Denver | 5 | 8 | 1 | .385 | 297 | 344 |
| Cincinnati | 4 | 9 | 1 | .308 | 280 | 367 |

Divisional Playoffs: Kansas City 13, N.Y. JETS 6; OAKLAND 56, Houston 7
AFL championship: Kansas City 17, OAKLAND 7

## 1968 NFL

### EASTERN CONFERENCE
**Capitol Division**

|  | W | L | T | Pct. | Pts. | OP |
|---|---|---|---|---|---|---|
| Dallas | 12 | 2 | 0 | .857 | 431 | 186 |
| N.Y. Giants | 7 | 7 | 0 | .500 | 294 | 325 |
| Washington | 5 | 9 | 0 | .357 | 249 | 358 |
| Philadelphia | 2 | 12 | 0 | .143 | 202 | 351 |

**Century Division**

|  | W | L | T | Pct. | Pts. | OP |
|---|---|---|---|---|---|---|
| Cleveland | 10 | 4 | 0 | .714 | 394 | 273 |
| St. Louis | 9 | 4 | 1 | .692 | 325 | 289 |
| New Orleans | 4 | 9 | 1 | .308 | 246 | 327 |
| Pittsburgh | 2 | 11 | 1 | .154 | 244 | 397 |

### WESTERN CONFERENCE
**Coastal Division**

|  | W | L | T | Pct. | Pts. | OP |
|---|---|---|---|---|---|---|
| Baltimore | 13 | 1 | 0 | .929 | 402 | 144 |
| Los Angeles | 10 | 3 | 1 | .769 | 312 | 200 |
| San Francisco | 7 | 6 | 1 | .538 | 303 | 310 |
| Atlanta | 2 | 12 | 0 | .143 | 170 | 389 |

**Central Division**

|  | W | L | T | Pct. | Pts. | OP |
|---|---|---|---|---|---|---|
| Minnesota | 8 | 6 | 0 | .571 | 282 | 242 |
| Chicago | 7 | 7 | 0 | .500 | 250 | 333 |
| Green Bay | 6 | 7 | 1 | .462 | 281 | 227 |
| Detroit | 4 | 8 | 2 | .333 | 207 | 241 |

Conference championships: CLEVELAND 31, Dallas 20; BALTIMORE 24, Minnesota 14
NFL championship: Baltimore 34, CLEVELAND 0
Super Bowl III: N.Y. Jets (AFL) 16, Baltimore (NFL) 7, at Orange Bowl, Miami, Fla.

## 1968 AFL

### EASTERN DIVISION

|  | W | L | T | Pct. | Pts. | OP |
|---|---|---|---|---|---|---|
| N.Y. Jets | 11 | 3 | 0 | .786 | 419 | 280 |
| Houston | 7 | 7 | 0 | .500 | 303 | 248 |
| Miami | 5 | 8 | 1 | .385 | 276 | 355 |
| Boston Patriots | 4 | 10 | 0 | .286 | 229 | 406 |
| Buffalo | 1 | 12 | 1 | .077 | 199 | 367 |

### WESTERN DIVISION

|  | W | L | T | Pct. | Pts. | OP |
|---|---|---|---|---|---|---|
| Oakland | 12 | 2 | 0 | .857 | 453 | 233 |
| Kansas City | 12 | 2 | 0 | .857 | 371 | 170 |
| San Diego | 9 | 5 | 0 | .643 | 382 | 310 |
| Denver | 5 | 9 | 0 | .357 | 255 | 404 |
| Cincinnati | 3 | 11 | 0 | .214 | 215 | 329 |

Western Division playoff: OAKLAND 41, Kansas City 6
AFL championship: N.Y. JETS 27, Oakland 23

## 1967 NFL

### EASTERN CONFERENCE
**Capitol Division**

|  | W | L | T | Pct. | Pts. | OP |
|---|---|---|---|---|---|---|
| Dallas | 9 | 5 | 0 | .643 | 342 | 268 |
| Philadelphia | 6 | 7 | 1 | .462 | 351 | 409 |
| Washington | 5 | 6 | 3 | .455 | 347 | 353 |
| New Orleans | 3 | 11 | 0 | .214 | 233 | 379 |

**Century Division**

|  | W | L | T | Pct. | Pts. | OP |
|---|---|---|---|---|---|---|
| Cleveland | 9 | 5 | 0 | .643 | 334 | 297 |
| N.Y. Giants | 7 | 7 | 0 | .500 | 369 | 379 |
| St. Louis | 6 | 7 | 1 | .462 | 333 | 356 |
| Pittsburgh | 4 | 9 | 1 | .308 | 281 | 320 |

### WESTERN CONFERENCE
**Coastal Division**

|  | W | L | T | Pct. | Pts. | OP |
|---|---|---|---|---|---|---|
| Los Angeles | 11 | 1 | 2 | .917 | 398 | 196 |
| Baltimore | 11 | 1 | 2 | .917 | 394 | 198 |
| San Francisco | 7 | 7 | 0 | .500 | 273 | 337 |
| Atlanta | 1 | 12 | 1 | .077 | 175 | 422 |

**Central Division**

|  | W | L | T | Pct. | Pts. | OP |
|---|---|---|---|---|---|---|
| Green Bay | 9 | 4 | 1 | .692 | 332 | 209 |
| Chicago | 7 | 6 | 1 | .538 | 239 | 218 |
| Detroit | 5 | 7 | 2 | .417 | 260 | 259 |
| Minnesota | 3 | 8 | 3 | .273 | 233 | 294 |

*Los Angeles won division title on the basis of advantage in points (58-34) in two games vs. Baltimore.*
Conference championships: DALLAS 52, Cleveland 14; GREEN BAY 28, Los Angeles 7
NFL championship: GREEN BAY 21, Dallas 17
Super Bowl II: Green Bay (NFL) 33, Oakland (AFL) 14, at Orange Bowl, Miami, Fla.

## 1967 AFL

### EASTERN DIVISION

|  | W | L | T | Pct. | Pts. | OP |
|---|---|---|---|---|---|---|
| Houston | 9 | 4 | 1 | .692 | 258 | 199 |
| N.Y. Jets | 8 | 5 | 1 | .615 | 371 | 329 |
| Buffalo | 4 | 10 | 0 | .286 | 237 | 285 |
| Miami | 4 | 10 | 0 | .286 | 219 | 407 |
| Boston Patriots | 3 | 10 | 1 | .231 | 280 | 389 |

### WESTERN DIVISION

|  | W | L | T | Pct. | Pts. | OP |
|---|---|---|---|---|---|---|
| Oakland | 13 | 1 | 0 | .929 | 468 | 233 |
| Kansas City | 9 | 5 | 0 | .643 | 408 | 254 |
| San Diego | 8 | 5 | 1 | .615 | 360 | 352 |
| Denver | 3 | 11 | 0 | .214 | 256 | 409 |

AFL championship: OAKLAND 40, Houston 7

## 1966 NFL

### EASTERN CONFERENCE

|  | W | L | T | Pct. | Pts. | OP |
|---|---|---|---|---|---|---|
| Dallas | 10 | 3 | 1 | .769 | 445 | 239 |
| Cleveland | 9 | 5 | 0 | .643 | 403 | 259 |
| Philadelphia | 9 | 5 | 0 | .643 | 326 | 340 |
| St. Louis | 8 | 5 | 1 | .615 | 264 | 265 |
| Washington | 7 | 7 | 0 | .500 | 351 | 355 |
| Pittsburgh | 5 | 8 | 1 | .385 | 316 | 347 |
| Atlanta | 3 | 11 | 0 | .214 | 204 | 437 |
| N.Y. Giants | 1 | 12 | 1 | .077 | 263 | 501 |

### WESTERN CONFERENCE

|  | W | L | T | Pct. | Pts. | OP |
|---|---|---|---|---|---|---|
| Green Bay | 12 | 2 | 0 | .857 | 335 | 163 |
| Baltimore | 9 | 5 | 0 | .643 | 314 | 226 |
| Los Angeles | 8 | 6 | 0 | .571 | 289 | 212 |
| San Francisco | 6 | 6 | 2 | .500 | 320 | 325 |
| Chicago | 5 | 7 | 2 | .417 | 234 | 272 |
| Detroit | 4 | 9 | 1 | .308 | 206 | 317 |
| Minnesota | 4 | 9 | 1 | .308 | 292 | 304 |

NFL championship: Green Bay 34, DALLAS 27
Super Bowl I: Green Bay (NFL) 35, Kansas City (AFL) 10, at Memorial Coliseum, Los Angeles, Calif.

## 1966 AFL

### EASTERN DIVISION

|  | W | L | T | Pct. | Pts. | OP |
|---|---|---|---|---|---|---|
| Buffalo | 9 | 4 | 1 | .692 | 358 | 255 |
| Boston Patriots | 8 | 4 | 2 | .677 | 315 | 283 |
| N.Y. Jets | 6 | 6 | 2 | .500 | 322 | 312 |
| Houston | 3 | 11 | 0 | .214 | 355 | 396 |
| Miami | 3 | 11 | 0 | .214 | 213 | 362 |

### WESTERN DIVISION

|  | W | L | T | Pct. | Pts. | OP |
|---|---|---|---|---|---|---|
| Kansas City | 11 | 2 | 1 | .846 | 448 | 276 |
| Oakland | 8 | 5 | 1 | .615 | 315 | 288 |
| San Diego | 7 | 6 | 1 | .538 | 335 | 284 |
| Denver | 4 | 10 | 0 | .286 | 196 | 381 |

AFL championship: Kansas City 31, BUFFALO 7

## 1965 NFL

### EASTERN CONFERENCE

|  | W | L | T | Pct. | Pts. | OP |
|---|---|---|---|---|---|---|
| Cleveland | 11 | 3 | 0 | .786 | 363 | 325 |
| Dallas | 7 | 7 | 0 | .500 | 325 | 280 |
| N.Y. Giants | 7 | 7 | 0 | .500 | 270 | 338 |
| Washington | 6 | 8 | 0 | .429 | 257 | 301 |
| Philadelphia | 5 | 9 | 0 | .357 | 363 | 359 |
| St. Louis | 5 | 9 | 0 | .357 | 296 | 309 |
| Pittsburgh | 2 | 12 | 0 | .143 | 202 | 397 |

### WESTERN CONFERENCE

|  | W | L | T | Pct. | Pts. | OP |
|---|---|---|---|---|---|---|
| Green Bay | 10 | 3 | 1 | .769 | 316 | 224 |
| Baltimore | 10 | 3 | 1 | .769 | 389 | 284 |
| Chicago | 9 | 5 | 0 | .643 | 409 | 275 |
| San Francisco | 7 | 6 | 1 | .538 | 421 | 402 |
| Minnesota | 7 | 7 | 0 | .500 | 383 | 403 |
| Detroit | 6 | 7 | 1 | .462 | 257 | 295 |
| Los Angeles | 4 | 10 | 0 | .286 | 269 | 328 |

Western Conference playoff: GREEN BAY 13, Baltimore 10, sudden death overtime
NFL championship: GREEN BAY 23, Cleveland 12

## 1965 AFL

### EASTERN DIVISION

|  | W | L | T | Pct. | Pts. | OP |
|---|---|---|---|---|---|---|
| Buffalo | 10 | 3 | 1 | .769 | 313 | 226 |
| N.Y. Jets | 5 | 8 | 1 | .385 | 285 | 303 |
| Boston Patriots | 4 | 8 | 2 | .333 | 244 | 302 |
| Houston | 4 | 10 | 0 | .286 | 298 | 429 |

### WESTERN DIVISION

|  | W | L | T | Pct. | Pts. | OP |
|---|---|---|---|---|---|---|
| San Diego | 9 | 2 | 3 | .818 | 340 | 227 |
| Oakland | 8 | 5 | 1 | .615 | 298 | 239 |
| Kansas City | 7 | 5 | 2 | .583 | 322 | 285 |
| Denver | 4 | 10 | 0 | .286 | 303 | 392 |

AFL championship: Buffalo 23, SAN DIEGO 0

## 1964 NFL

### EASTERN CONFERENCE

|  | W | L | T | Pct. | Pts. | OP |
|---|---|---|---|---|---|---|
| Cleveland | 10 | 3 | 1 | .769 | 415 | 293 |
| St. Louis | 9 | 3 | 2 | .750 | 357 | 331 |
| Philadelphia | 6 | 8 | 0 | .429 | 312 | 313 |
| Washington | 6 | 8 | 0 | .429 | 307 | 305 |
| Dallas | 5 | 8 | 1 | .385 | 250 | 289 |
| Pittsburgh | 5 | 9 | 0 | .357 | 253 | 315 |
| N.Y. Giants | 2 | 10 | 2 | .167 | 241 | 399 |

### WESTERN CONFERENCE

|  | W | L | T | Pct. | Pts. | OP |
|---|---|---|---|---|---|---|
| Baltimore | 12 | 2 | 0 | .857 | 428 | 225 |
| Green Bay | 8 | 5 | 1 | .615 | 342 | 245 |
| Minnesota | 8 | 5 | 1 | .615 | 355 | 296 |
| Detroit | 7 | 5 | 2 | .583 | 280 | 260 |
| Los Angeles | 5 | 7 | 2 | .417 | 283 | 339 |
| Chicago | 5 | 9 | 0 | .357 | 260 | 379 |
| San Francisco | 4 | 10 | 0 | .286 | 236 | 330 |

NFL championship: CLEVELAND 27, Baltimore 0

## 1964 AFL

### EASTERN DIVISION

|  | W | L | T | Pct. | Pts. | OP |
|---|---|---|---|---|---|---|
| Buffalo | 12 | 2 | 0 | .857 | 400 | 242 |
| Boston Patriots | 10 | 3 | 1 | .769 | 365 | 297 |
| N.Y. Jets | 5 | 8 | 1 | .385 | 278 | 315 |
| Houston | 4 | 10 | 0 | .286 | 310 | 355 |

### WESTERN DIVISION

|  | W | L | T | Pct. | Pts. | OP |
|---|---|---|---|---|---|---|
| San Diego | 8 | 5 | 1 | .615 | 341 | 300 |
| Kansas City | 7 | 7 | 0 | .500 | 366 | 306 |
| Oakland | 5 | 7 | 2 | .417 | 303 | 350 |
| Denver | 2 | 11 | 1 | .154 | 240 | 438 |

AFL championship: BUFFALO 20, San Diego 7

## 1963 NFL

### EASTERN CONFERENCE

|  | W | L | T | Pct. | Pts. | OP |
|---|---|---|---|---|---|---|
| N.Y. Giants | 11 | 3 | 0 | .786 | 448 | 280 |
| Cleveland | 10 | 4 | 0 | .714 | 343 | 262 |
| St. Louis | 9 | 5 | 0 | .643 | 341 | 283 |
| Pittsburgh | 7 | 4 | 3 | .636 | 321 | 295 |
| Dallas | 4 | 10 | 0 | .286 | 305 | 378 |
| Washington | 3 | 11 | 0 | .214 | 279 | 398 |
| Philadelphia | 2 | 10 | 2 | .167 | 242 | 381 |

### WESTERN CONFERENCE

|  | W | L | T | Pct. | Pts. | OP |
|---|---|---|---|---|---|---|
| Chicago | 11 | 1 | 2 | .917 | 301 | 144 |
| Green Bay | 11 | 2 | 1 | .846 | 369 | 206 |
| Baltimore | 8 | 6 | 0 | .571 | 316 | 285 |
| Detroit | 5 | 8 | 1 | .385 | 326 | 265 |
| Minnesota | 5 | 8 | 1 | .385 | 309 | 390 |
| Los Angeles | 5 | 9 | 0 | .357 | 210 | 350 |
| San Francisco | 2 | 12 | 0 | .143 | 198 | 391 |

NFL championship: CHICAGO 14, N.Y. Giants 10

## 1963 AFL

### EASTERN DIVISION

|  | W | L | T | Pct. | Pts. | OP |
|---|---|---|---|---|---|---|
| Boston Patriots | 7 | 6 | 1 | .538 | 317 | 257 |
| Buffalo | 7 | 6 | 1 | .538 | 304 | 291 |
| Houston | 6 | 8 | 0 | .429 | 302 | 372 |
| N.Y. Jets | 5 | 8 | 1 | .385 | 249 | 399 |

### WESTERN DIVISION

|  | W | L | T | Pct. | Pts. | OP |
|---|---|---|---|---|---|---|
| San Diego | 11 | 3 | 0 | .786 | 399 | 255 |
| Oakland | 10 | 4 | 0 | .714 | 363 | 282 |
| Kansas City | 5 | 7 | 2 | .417 | 347 | 263 |
| Denver | 2 | 11 | 1 | .154 | 301 | 473 |

Eastern Division playoff: Boston 26, BUFFALO 8
AFL championship: SAN DIEGO 51, Boston 10

## 1962 NFL

### EASTERN CONFERENCE

|  | W | L | T | Pct. | Pts. | OP |
|---|---|---|---|---|---|---|
| N.Y. Giants | 12 | 2 | 0 | .857 | 398 | 283 |
| Pittsburgh | 9 | 5 | 0 | .643 | 312 | 363 |
| Cleveland | 7 | 6 | 1 | .538 | 291 | 257 |
| Washington | 5 | 7 | 2 | .417 | 305 | 376 |
| Dallas Cowboys | 5 | 8 | 1 | .385 | 398 | 402 |
| St. Louis | 4 | 9 | 1 | .308 | 287 | 361 |
| Philadelphia | 3 | 10 | 1 | .231 | 282 | 356 |

### WESTERN CONFERENCE

|  | W | L | T | Pct. | Pts. | OP |
|---|---|---|---|---|---|---|
| Green Bay | 13 | 1 | 0 | .929 | 415 | 148 |
| Detroit | 11 | 3 | 0 | .786 | 315 | 177 |
| Chicago | 9 | 5 | 0 | .643 | 321 | 287 |
| Baltimore | 7 | 7 | 0 | .500 | 293 | 288 |
| San Francisco | 6 | 8 | 0 | .429 | 282 | 331 |
| Minnesota | 2 | 11 | 1 | .154 | 254 | 410 |
| Los Angeles | 1 | 12 | 1 | .077 | 220 | 334 |

NFL championship: Green Bay 16, N.Y. GIANTS 7

## 1962 AFL

### EASTERN DIVISION

|  | W | L | T | Pct. | Pts. | OP |
|---|---|---|---|---|---|---|
| Houston | 11 | 3 | 0 | .786 | 387 | 270 |
| Boston Patriots | 9 | 4 | 1 | .692 | 346 | 295 |
| Buffalo | 7 | 6 | 1 | .538 | 309 | 272 |
| N.Y. Titans | 5 | 9 | 0 | .357 | 278 | 423 |

### WESTERN DIVISION

|  | W | L | T | Pct. | Pts. | OP |
|---|---|---|---|---|---|---|
| Dallas Texans | 11 | 3 | 0 | .786 | 389 | 233 |
| Denver | 7 | 7 | 0 | .500 | 353 | 334 |
| San Diego | 4 | 10 | 0 | .286 | 314 | 392 |
| Oakland | 1 | 13 | 0 | .071 | 213 | 370 |

AFL championship: Dallas Texans 20, HOUSTON 17, sudden death overtime

## 1961 NFL

**EASTERN CONFERENCE**

| | W | L | T | Pct. | Pts. | OP |
|---|---|---|---|---|---|---|
| N.Y. Giants | 10 | 3 | 1 | .769 | 368 | 220 |
| Philadelphia | 10 | 4 | 0 | .714 | 361 | 297 |
| Cleveland | 8 | 5 | 1 | .615 | 319 | 270 |
| St. Louis | 7 | 7 | 0 | .500 | 279 | 267 |
| Pittsburgh | 6 | 8 | 0 | .429 | 295 | 287 |
| Dallas Cowboys | 4 | 9 | 1 | .308 | 236 | 380 |
| Washington | 1 | 12 | 1 | .077 | 174 | 392 |

**WESTERN CONFERENCE**

| | W | L | T | Pct. | Pts. | OP |
|---|---|---|---|---|---|---|
| Green Bay | 11 | 3 | 0 | .786 | 391 | 223 |
| Detroit | 8 | 5 | 1 | .615 | 270 | 258 |
| Baltimore | 8 | 6 | 0 | .571 | 302 | 307 |
| Chicago Bears | 8 | 6 | 0 | .571 | 326 | 302 |
| San Francisco | 7 | 6 | 1 | .538 | 346 | 272 |
| Los Angeles | 4 | 10 | 0 | .286 | 263 | 333 |
| Minnesota | 3 | 11 | 0 | .214 | 285 | 407 |

NFL championship: GREEN BAY 37, N.Y. Giants 0

## 1961 AFL

**EASTERN DIVISION**

| | W | L | T | Pct. | Pts. | OP |
|---|---|---|---|---|---|---|
| Houston | 10 | 3 | 1 | .769 | 513 | 242 |
| Boston Patriots | 9 | 4 | 1 | .692 | 413 | 313 |
| N.Y. Titans | 7 | 7 | 0 | .500 | 301 | 390 |
| Buffalo | 6 | 8 | 0 | .429 | 294 | 342 |

**WESTERN DIVISION**

| | W | L | T | Pct. | Pts. | OP |
|---|---|---|---|---|---|---|
| San Diego | 12 | 2 | 0 | .857 | 396 | 219 |
| Dallas Texans | 6 | 8 | 0 | .429 | 334 | 343 |
| Denver | 3 | 11 | 0 | .214 | 251 | 432 |
| Oakland | 2 | 12 | 0 | .143 | 237 | 458 |

AFL championship: Houston 10, SAN DIEGO 3

## 1960 NFL

**EASTERN CONFERENCE**

| | W | L | T | Pct. | Pts. | OP |
|---|---|---|---|---|---|---|
| Philadelphia | 10 | 2 | 0 | .833 | 321 | 246 |
| Cleveland | 8 | 3 | 1 | .727 | 362 | 217 |
| N.Y. Giants | 6 | 4 | 2 | .600 | 271 | 261 |
| St. Louis | 6 | 5 | 1 | .545 | 288 | 230 |
| Pittsburgh | 5 | 6 | 1 | .455 | 240 | 275 |
| Washington | 1 | 9 | 2 | .100 | 178 | 309 |

**WESTERN CONFERENCE**

| | W | L | T | Pct. | Pts. | OP |
|---|---|---|---|---|---|---|
| Green Bay | 8 | 4 | 0 | .667 | 332 | 209 |
| Detroit | 7 | 5 | 0 | .583 | 239 | 212 |
| San Francisco | 7 | 5 | 0 | .583 | 208 | 205 |
| Baltimore | 6 | 6 | 0 | .500 | 288 | 234 |
| Chicago | 5 | 6 | 1 | .455 | 194 | 299 |
| L.A. Rams | 4 | 7 | 1 | .364 | 265 | 297 |
| Dall. Cowboys | 0 | 11 | 1 | .000 | 177 | 369 |

NFL championship: PHILADELPHIA 17, Green Bay 13

## 1960 AFL

**EASTERN CONFERENCE**

| | W | L | T | Pct. | Pts. | OP |
|---|---|---|---|---|---|---|
| Houston | 10 | 4 | 0 | .714 | 379 | 285 |
| N.Y. Titans | 7 | 7 | 0 | .500 | 382 | 399 |
| Buffalo | 5 | 8 | 1 | .385 | 296 | 303 |
| Boston | 5 | 9 | 0 | .357 | 286 | 349 |

**WESTERN CONFERENCE**

| | W | L | T | Pct. | Pts. | OP |
|---|---|---|---|---|---|---|
| L.A. Chargers | 10 | 4 | 0 | .714 | 373 | 336 |
| Dall. Texans | 8 | 6 | 0 | .571 | 362 | 253 |
| Oakland | 6 | 8 | 0 | .429 | 319 | 388 |
| Denver | 4 | 9 | 1 | .308 | 309 | 393 |

AFL championship: HOUSTON 24, L.A. Chargers 16

## 1959

**EASTERN CONFERENCE**

| | W | L | T | Pct. | Pts. | OP |
|---|---|---|---|---|---|---|
| N.Y. Giants | 10 | 2 | 0 | .833 | 284 | 170 |
| Cleveland | 7 | 5 | 0 | .583 | 270 | 214 |
| Philadelphia | 7 | 5 | 0 | .583 | 268 | 278 |
| Pittsburgh | 6 | 5 | 1 | .545 | 257 | 216 |
| Washington | 3 | 9 | 0 | .250 | 185 | 350 |
| Chi. Cardinals | 2 | 10 | 0 | .167 | 234 | 324 |

**WESTERN CONFERENCE**

| | W | L | T | Pct. | Pts. | OP |
|---|---|---|---|---|---|---|
| Baltimore | 9 | 3 | 0 | .750 | 374 | 251 |
| Chi. Bears | 8 | 4 | 0 | .667 | 252 | 196 |
| Green Bay | 7 | 5 | 0 | .583 | 248 | 246 |
| San Francisco | 7 | 5 | 0 | .583 | 255 | 237 |
| Detroit | 3 | 8 | 1 | .273 | 203 | 275 |
| Los Angeles | 2 | 10 | 0 | .167 | 242 | 315 |

NFL championship: BALTIMORE 31, N.Y. Giants 16

## 1958

**EASTERN CONFERENCE**

| | W | L | T | Pct. | Pts. | OP |
|---|---|---|---|---|---|---|
| N.Y. Giants | 9 | 3 | 0 | .750 | 246 | 183 |
| Cleveland | 9 | 3 | 0 | .750 | 302 | 217 |
| Pittsburgh | 7 | 4 | 1 | .636 | 261 | 230 |
| Washington | 4 | 7 | 1 | .364 | 214 | 268 |
| Chi. Cardinals | 2 | 9 | 1 | .182 | 261 | 356 |
| Philadelphia | 2 | 9 | 1 | .182 | 235 | 306 |

**WESTERN CONFERENCE**

| | W | L | T | Pct. | Pts. | OP |
|---|---|---|---|---|---|---|
| Baltimore | 9 | 3 | 0 | .750 | 381 | 203 |
| Chi. Bears | 8 | 4 | 0 | .667 | 298 | 230 |
| Los Angeles | 8 | 4 | 0 | .667 | 344 | 278 |
| San Francisco | 6 | 6 | 0 | .500 | 257 | 324 |
| Detroit | 4 | 7 | 1 | .364 | 261 | 276 |
| Green Bay | 1 | 10 | 1 | .091 | 193 | 382 |

Eastern Conference playoff: N.Y. GIANTS 10, Cleveland 0
NFL championship: Baltimore 23, N.Y. GIANTS 17, sudden death overtime

## 1957

**EASTERN CONFERENCE**

| | W | L | T | Pct. | Pts. | OP |
|---|---|---|---|---|---|---|
| Cleveland | 9 | 2 | 1 | .818 | 269 | 172 |
| N.Y. Giants | 7 | 5 | 0 | .583 | 254 | 211 |
| Pittsburgh | 6 | 6 | 0 | .500 | 161 | 178 |
| Washington | 5 | 6 | 1 | .455 | 251 | 230 |
| Philadelphia | 4 | 8 | 0 | .333 | 173 | 230 |
| Chi. Cardinals | 3 | 9 | 0 | .250 | 200 | 299 |

**WESTERN CONFERENCE**

| | W | L | T | Pct. | Pts. | OP |
|---|---|---|---|---|---|---|
| Detroit | 8 | 4 | 0 | .667 | 251 | 231 |
| San Francisco | 8 | 4 | 0 | .667 | 260 | 264 |
| Baltimore | 7 | 5 | 0 | .583 | 303 | 235 |
| Los Angeles | 6 | 6 | 0 | .500 | 307 | 278 |
| Chi. Bears | 5 | 7 | 0 | .417 | 203 | 211 |
| Green Bay | 3 | 9 | 0 | .250 | 218 | 311 |

Western Conference playoff: Detroit 31, SAN FRANCISCO 27
NFL championship: DETROIT 59, Cleveland 14

## 1956

**EASTERN CONFERENCE**

| | W | L | T | Pct. | Pts. | OP |
|---|---|---|---|---|---|---|
| N.Y. Giants | 8 | 3 | 1 | .727 | 264 | 197 |
| Chi. Cardinals | 7 | 5 | 0 | .583 | 240 | 182 |
| Washington | 6 | 6 | 0 | .500 | 183 | 225 |
| Cleveland | 5 | 7 | 0 | .417 | 167 | 177 |
| Pittsburgh | 5 | 7 | 0 | .417 | 217 | 250 |
| Philadelphia | 3 | 8 | 1 | .273 | 143 | 215 |

**WESTERN CONFERENCE**

| | W | L | T | Pct. | Pts. | OP |
|---|---|---|---|---|---|---|
| Chi. Bears | 9 | 2 | 1 | .818 | 363 | 246 |
| Detroit | 9 | 3 | 0 | .750 | 300 | 188 |
| San Francisco | 5 | 6 | 1 | .455 | 233 | 284 |
| Baltimore | 5 | 7 | 0 | .417 | 270 | 322 |
| Green Bay | 4 | 8 | 0 | .333 | 264 | 342 |
| Los Angeles | 4 | 8 | 0 | .333 | 291 | 307 |

NFL championship: N.Y. GIANTS 47, Chi. Bears 7

## 1955

**EASTERN CONFERENCE**

| | W | L | T | Pct. | Pts. | OP |
|---|---|---|---|---|---|---|
| Cleveland | 9 | 2 | 1 | .818 | 349 | 218 |
| Washington | 8 | 4 | 0 | .667 | 246 | 222 |
| N.Y. Giants | 6 | 5 | 1 | .545 | 267 | 223 |
| Chi. Cardinals | 4 | 7 | 1 | .364 | 224 | 252 |
| Philadelphia | 4 | 7 | 1 | .364 | 248 | 231 |
| Pittsburgh | 4 | 8 | 0 | .333 | 195 | 285 |

**WESTERN CONFERENCE**

| | W | L | T | Pct. | Pts. | OP |
|---|---|---|---|---|---|---|
| Los Angeles | 8 | 3 | 1 | .727 | 260 | 231 |
| Chi. Bears | 8 | 4 | 0 | .667 | 294 | 251 |
| Green Bay | 6 | 6 | 0 | .500 | 258 | 276 |
| Baltimore | 5 | 6 | 1 | .455 | 214 | 239 |
| San Francisco | 4 | 8 | 0 | .333 | 216 | 298 |
| Detroit | 3 | 9 | 0 | .250 | 230 | 275 |

NFL championship: Cleveland 38, LOS ANGELES 14

## 1954

**EASTERN CONFERENCE**

| | W | L | T | Pct. | Pts. | OP |
|---|---|---|---|---|---|---|
| Cleveland | 9 | 3 | 0 | .750 | 336 | 162 |
| Philadelphia | 7 | 4 | 1 | .636 | 284 | 230 |
| N.Y. Giants | 7 | 5 | 0 | .583 | 293 | 184 |
| Pittsburgh | 5 | 7 | 0 | .417 | 219 | 263 |
| Washington | 3 | 9 | 0 | .250 | 207 | 432 |
| Chi. Cardinals | 2 | 10 | 0 | .167 | 183 | 347 |

**WESTERN CONFERENCE**

| | W | L | T | Pct. | Pts. | OP |
|---|---|---|---|---|---|---|
| Detroit | 9 | 2 | 1 | .818 | 337 | 189 |
| Chi. Bears | 8 | 4 | 0 | .667 | 301 | 279 |
| San Francisco | 7 | 4 | 1 | .636 | 313 | 251 |
| Los Angeles | 6 | 5 | 1 | .545 | 314 | 285 |
| Green Bay | 4 | 8 | 0 | .333 | 234 | 251 |
| Baltimore | 3 | 9 | 0 | .250 | 131 | 279 |

NFL championship: CLEVELAND 56, Detroit 10

## 1953

**EASTERN CONFERENCE**

| | W | L | T | Pct. | Pts. | OP |
|---|---|---|---|---|---|---|
| Cleveland | 11 | 1 | 0 | .917 | 348 | 162 |
| Philadelphia | 7 | 4 | 1 | .636 | 352 | 215 |
| Washington | 6 | 5 | 1 | .545 | 208 | 215 |
| Pittsburgh | 6 | 6 | 0 | .500 | 211 | 263 |
| N.Y. Giants | 3 | 9 | 0 | .250 | 179 | 277 |
| Chi. Cardinals | 1 | 10 | 1 | .091 | 190 | 337 |

**WESTERN CONFERENCE**

| | W | L | T | Pct. | Pts. | OP |
|---|---|---|---|---|---|---|
| Detroit | 10 | 2 | 0 | .833 | 271 | 205 |
| San Francisco | 9 | 3 | 0 | .750 | 372 | 237 |
| Los Angeles | 8 | 3 | 1 | .727 | 366 | 236 |
| Chi. Bears | 3 | 8 | 1 | .273 | 218 | 262 |
| Baltimore | 3 | 9 | 0 | .250 | 182 | 350 |
| Green Bay | 2 | 9 | 1 | .182 | 200 | 338 |

NFL championship: DETROIT 17, Cleveland 16

## 1952

**AMERICAN CONFERENCE**

| | W | L | T | Pct. | Pts. | OP |
|---|---|---|---|---|---|---|
| Cleveland | 8 | 4 | 0 | .667 | 310 | 213 |
| N.Y. Giants | 7 | 5 | 0 | .583 | 234 | 231 |
| Philadelphia | 7 | 5 | 0 | .583 | 252 | 271 |
| Pittsburgh | 5 | 7 | 0 | .417 | 300 | 273 |
| Chi. Cardinals | 4 | 8 | 0 | .333 | 172 | 221 |
| Washington | 4 | 8 | 0 | .333 | 240 | 287 |

**NATIONAL CONFERENCE**

| | W | L | T | Pct. | Pts. | OP |
|---|---|---|---|---|---|---|
| Detroit | 9 | 3 | 0 | .750 | 344 | 192 |
| Los Angeles | 9 | 3 | 0 | .750 | 349 | 234 |
| San Francisco | 7 | 5 | 0 | .583 | 285 | 221 |
| Green Bay | 6 | 6 | 0 | .500 | 295 | 312 |
| Chi. Bears | 5 | 7 | 0 | .417 | 245 | 326 |
| Dallas Texans | 1 | 11 | 0 | .083 | 182 | 427 |

National Conference playoff: DETROIT 31, Los Angeles 21
NFL championship: Detroit 17, CLEVELAND 7

## 1951

**AMERICAN CONFERENCE**

| | W | L | T | Pct. | Pts. | OP |
|---|---|---|---|---|---|---|
| Cleveland | 11 | 1 | 0 | .917 | 331 | 152 |
| N.Y. Giants | 9 | 2 | 1 | .818 | 254 | 161 |
| Washington | 5 | 7 | 0 | .417 | 183 | 296 |
| Pittsburgh | 4 | 7 | 1 | .364 | 183 | 235 |
| Philadelphia | 4 | 8 | 0 | .333 | 234 | 264 |
| Chi. Cardinals | 3 | 9 | 0 | .250 | 210 | 287 |

**NATIONAL CONFERENCE**

| | W | L | T | Pct. | Pts. | OP |
|---|---|---|---|---|---|---|
| Los Angeles | 8 | 4 | 0 | .667 | 392 | 261 |
| Detroit | 7 | 4 | 1 | .636 | 336 | 259 |
| San Francisco | 7 | 4 | 1 | .636 | 255 | 205 |
| Chi. Bears | 7 | 5 | 0 | .583 | 286 | 282 |
| Green Bay | 3 | 9 | 0 | .250 | 254 | 375 |
| N.Y. Yanks | 1 | 9 | 2 | .100 | 241 | 382 |

NFL championship: LOS ANGELES 24, Cleveland 17

## 1950

**AMERICAN CONFERENCE**

| | W | L | T | Pct. | Pts. | OP |
|---|---|---|---|---|---|---|
| Cleveland | 10 | 2 | 0 | .833 | 310 | 144 |
| N.Y. Giants | 10 | 2 | 0 | .833 | 268 | 150 |
| Philadelphia | 6 | 6 | 0 | .500 | 254 | 141 |
| Pittsburgh | 6 | 6 | 0 | .500 | 180 | 195 |
| Chi. Cardinals | 5 | 7 | 0 | .417 | 233 | 287 |
| Washington | 3 | 9 | 0 | .250 | 232 | 326 |

**NATIONAL CONFERENCE**

| | W | L | T | Pct. | Pts. | OP |
|---|---|---|---|---|---|---|
| Los Angeles | 9 | 3 | 0 | .750 | 466 | 309 |
| Chi. Bears | 9 | 3 | 0 | .750 | 279 | 207 |
| N.Y. Yanks | 7 | 5 | 0 | .583 | 366 | 367 |
| Detroit | 6 | 6 | 0 | .500 | 321 | 285 |
| Green Bay | 3 | 9 | 0 | .250 | 244 | 406 |
| San Francisco | 3 | 9 | 0 | .250 | 213 | 300 |
| Baltimore | 1 | 11 | 0 | .083 | 213 | 462 |

American Conference playoff: CLEVELAND 8, N.Y. Giants 3
National Conference playoff: LOS ANGELES 24, Chi. Bears 14
NFL championship: CLEVELAND 30, Los Angeles 28

## 1949

**EASTERN DIVISION**

| | W | L | T | Pct. | Pts. | OP |
|---|---|---|---|---|---|---|
| Philadelphia | 11 | 1 | 0 | .917 | 364 | 134 |
| Pittsburgh | 6 | 5 | 1 | .545 | 224 | 214 |
| N.Y. Giants | 6 | 6 | 0 | .500 | 287 | 298 |
| Washington | 4 | 7 | 1 | .364 | 268 | 339 |
| N.Y. Bulldogs | 1 | 10 | 1 | .091 | 153 | 365 |

**WESTERN DIVISION**

| | W | L | T | Pct. | Pts. | OP |
|---|---|---|---|---|---|---|
| Los Angeles | 8 | 2 | 2 | .800 | 360 | 239 |
| Chi. Bears | 9 | 3 | 0 | .750 | 332 | 218 |
| Chi. Cardinals | 6 | 5 | 1 | .545 | 360 | 301 |
| Detroit | 4 | 8 | 0 | .333 | 237 | 259 |
| Green Bay | 2 | 10 | 0 | .167 | 114 | 329 |

NFL championship: Philadelphia 14, LOS ANGELES 0

## 1948

**EASTERN DIVISION**

| | W | L | T | Pct. | Pts. | OP |
|---|---|---|---|---|---|---|
| Philadelphia | 9 | 2 | 1 | .818 | 376 | 156 |
| Washington | 7 | 5 | 0 | .583 | 291 | 287 |
| N.Y. Giants | 4 | 8 | 0 | .333 | 297 | 388 |
| Pittsburgh | 4 | 8 | 0 | .333 | 200 | 243 |
| Boston | 3 | 9 | 0 | .250 | 174 | 372 |

**WESTERN DIVISION**

| | W | L | T | Pct. | Pts. | OP |
|---|---|---|---|---|---|---|
| Chi. Cardinals | 11 | 1 | 0 | .917 | 395 | 226 |
| Chi. Bears | 10 | 2 | 0 | .833 | 375 | 151 |
| Los Angeles | 6 | 5 | 1 | .545 | 327 | 269 |
| Green Bay | 3 | 9 | 0 | .250 | 154 | 290 |
| Detroit | 2 | 10 | 0 | .167 | 200 | 407 |

NFL championship: PHILADELPHIA 7, Chi. Cardinals 0

## 1947

**EASTERN DIVISION**

| | W | L | T | Pct. | Pts. | OP |
|---|---|---|---|---|---|---|
| Philadelphia | 8 | 4 | 0 | .667 | 308 | 242 |
| Pittsburgh | 8 | 4 | 0 | .667 | 240 | 259 |
| Boston | 4 | 7 | 1 | .364 | 168 | 256 |
| Washington | 4 | 8 | 0 | .333 | 295 | 367 |
| N.Y. Giants | 2 | 8 | 2 | .200 | 190 | 309 |

**WESTERN DIVISION**

| | W | L | T | Pct. | Pts. | OP |
|---|---|---|---|---|---|---|
| Chi. Cardinals | 9 | 3 | 0 | .750 | 306 | 231 |
| Chi. Bears | 8 | 4 | 0 | .667 | 363 | 241 |
| Green Bay | 6 | 5 | 1 | .545 | 274 | 210 |
| Los Angeles | 6 | 6 | 0 | .500 | 259 | 214 |
| Detroit | 3 | 9 | 0 | .250 | 231 | 305 |

Eastern Division playoff: Philadelphia 21, PITTSBURGH 0
NFL championship: CHI. CARDINALS 28, Philadelphia 21

## 1946

**EASTERN DIVISION**

| | W | L | T | Pct. | Pts. | OP |
|---|---|---|---|---|---|---|
| N.Y. Giants | 7 | 3 | 1 | .700 | 236 | 162 |
| Philadelphia | 6 | 5 | 0 | .545 | 231 | 220 |
| Washington | 5 | 5 | 1 | .500 | 171 | 191 |
| Pittsburgh | 5 | 5 | 1 | .500 | 136 | 117 |
| Boston | 2 | 8 | 1 | .200 | 189 | 273 |

**WESTERN DIVISION**

| | W | L | T | Pct. | Pts. | OP |
|---|---|---|---|---|---|---|
| Chi. Bears | 8 | 2 | 1 | .800 | 289 | 193 |
| Los Angeles | 6 | 4 | 1 | .600 | 277 | 257 |
| Green Bay | 6 | 5 | 0 | .545 | 148 | 158 |
| Chi. Cardinals | 6 | 5 | 0 | .545 | 260 | 198 |
| Detroit | 1 | 10 | 0 | .091 | 142 | 310 |

NFL championship: Chi. Bears 24, N.Y. GIANTS 14

## 1945

**EASTERN DIVISION**

| | W | L | T | Pct. | Pts. | OP |
|---|---|---|---|---|---|---|
| Washington | 8 | 2 | 0 | .800 | 209 | 121 |
| Philadelphia | 7 | 3 | 0 | .700 | 272 | 133 |
| N.Y. Giants | 3 | 6 | 1 | .333 | 179 | 198 |
| Boston | 3 | 6 | 1 | .333 | 123 | 211 |
| Pittsburgh | 2 | 8 | 0 | .200 | 79 | 220 |

**WESTERN DIVISION**

| | W | L | T | Pct. | Pts. | OP |
|---|---|---|---|---|---|---|
| Cleveland | 9 | 1 | 0 | .900 | 244 | 136 |
| Detroit | 7 | 3 | 0 | .700 | 195 | 194 |
| Green Bay | 6 | 4 | 0 | .600 | 258 | 173 |
| Chi. Bears | 3 | 7 | 0 | .300 | 192 | 235 |
| Chi. Cardinals | 1 | 9 | 0 | .100 | 98 | 228 |

NFL championship: CLEVELAND 15, Washington 14

## 1944

**EASTERN DIVISION**

| | W | L | T | Pct. | Pts. | OP |
|---|---|---|---|---|---|---|
| N.Y. Giants | 8 | 1 | 1 | .889 | 206 | 75 |
| Philadelphia | 7 | 1 | 2 | .875 | 267 | 131 |
| Washington | 6 | 3 | 1 | .667 | 169 | 180 |
| Boston | 2 | 8 | 0 | .200 | 82 | 233 |
| Brooklyn | 0 | 10 | 0 | .000 | 69 | 166 |

**WESTERN DIVISION**

| | W | L | T | Pct. | Pts. | OP |
|---|---|---|---|---|---|---|
| Green Bay | 8 | 2 | 0 | .800 | 238 | 141 |
| Chi. Bears | 6 | 3 | 1 | .667 | 258 | 172 |
| Detroit | 6 | 3 | 1 | .667 | 216 | 151 |
| Cleveland | 4 | 6 | 0 | .400 | 188 | 224 |
| Card-Pitt | 0 | 10 | 0 | .000 | 108 | 328 |

NFL championship: Green Bay 14, N.Y. GIANTS 7

## 1943

**EASTERN DIVISION**

| | W | L | T | Pct. | Pts. | OP |
|---|---|---|---|---|---|---|
| Washington | 6 | 3 | 1 | .667 | 229 | 137 |
| N.Y. Giants | 6 | 3 | 1 | .667 | 197 | 170 |
| Phil-Pitt | 5 | 4 | 1 | .556 | 225 | 230 |
| Brooklyn | 2 | 8 | 0 | .200 | 65 | 234 |

**WESTERN DIVISION**

| | W | L | T | Pct. | Pts. | OP |
|---|---|---|---|---|---|---|
| Chi. Bears | 8 | 1 | 1 | .889 | 303 | 157 |
| Green Bay | 7 | 2 | 1 | .778 | 264 | 172 |
| Detroit | 3 | 6 | 1 | .333 | 178 | 218 |
| Chi. Cardinals | 0 | 10 | 0 | .000 | 95 | 238 |

Eastern Division playoff: Washington 28, N.Y. GIANTS 0
NFL championship: CHI. BEARS 41, Washington 21

## 1942

**EASTERN DIVISION**

| | W | L | T | Pct. | Pts. | OP |
|---|---|---|---|---|---|---|
| Washington | 10 | 1 | 0 | .909 | 227 | 102 |
| Pittsburgh | 7 | 4 | 0 | .636 | 167 | 119 |
| N.Y. Giants | 5 | 5 | 1 | .500 | 155 | 139 |
| Brooklyn | 3 | 8 | 0 | .273 | 100 | 168 |
| Philadelphia | 2 | 9 | 0 | .182 | 134 | 239 |

**WESTERN DIVISION**

| | W | L | T | Pct. | Pts. | OP |
|---|---|---|---|---|---|---|
| Chi. Bears | 11 | 0 | 0 | 1.000 | 376 | 84 |
| Green Bay | 8 | 2 | 1 | .800 | 300 | 215 |
| Cleveland | 5 | 6 | 0 | .455 | 150 | 207 |
| Chi. Cardinals | 3 | 8 | 0 | .273 | 98 | 209 |
| Detroit | 0 | 11 | 0 | .000 | 38 | 263 |

NFL championship: WASHINGTON 14, Chi. Bears 6

## 1941

**EASTERN DIVISION**

| | W | L | T | Pct. | Pts. | OP |
|---|---|---|---|---|---|---|
| N.Y. Giants | 8 | 3 | 0 | .727 | 238 | 114 |
| Brooklyn | 7 | 4 | 0 | .636 | 158 | 127 |
| Washington | 6 | 5 | 0 | .545 | 176 | 174 |
| Philadelphia | 2 | 8 | 1 | .200 | 119 | 218 |
| Pittsburgh | 1 | 9 | 1 | .100 | 103 | 276 |

**WESTERN DIVISION**

| | W | L | T | Pct. | Pts. | OP |
|---|---|---|---|---|---|---|
| Chi. Bears | 10 | 1 | 0 | .909 | 396 | 147 |
| Green Bay | 10 | 1 | 0 | .909 | 258 | 120 |
| Detroit | 4 | 6 | 1 | .400 | 121 | 195 |
| Chi. Cardinals | 3 | 7 | 1 | .300 | 127 | 197 |
| Cleveland | 2 | 9 | 0 | .182 | 116 | 244 |

Western Division playoff: CHI. BEARS 33, Green Bay 14
NFL championship: CHI. BEARS 37, N.Y. Giants 9

## 1940

**EASTERN DIVISION**

| | W | L | T | Pct. | Pts. | OP |
|---|---|---|---|---|---|---|
| Washington | 9 | 2 | 0 | .818 | 245 | 142 |
| Brooklyn | 8 | 3 | 0 | .727 | 186 | 120 |
| N.Y. Giants | 6 | 4 | 1 | .600 | 131 | 133 |
| Pittsburgh | 2 | 7 | 2 | .222 | 60 | 178 |
| Philadelphia | 1 | 10 | 0 | .091 | 111 | 211 |

**WESTERN DIVISION**

| | W | L | T | Pct. | Pts. | OP |
|---|---|---|---|---|---|---|
| Chi. Bears | 8 | 3 | 0 | .727 | 238 | 152 |
| Green Bay | 6 | 4 | 1 | .600 | 238 | 155 |
| Detroit | 5 | 5 | 1 | .500 | 138 | 153 |
| Cleveland | 4 | 6 | 1 | .400 | 171 | 191 |
| Chi. Cardinals | 2 | 7 | 2 | .222 | 139 | 222 |

NFL championship: Chi. Bears 73, WASHINGTON 0

## 1939

**EASTERN DIVISION**

| | W | L | T | Pct. | Pts. | OP |
|---|---|---|---|---|---|---|
| N.Y. Giants | 9 | 1 | 1 | .900 | 168 | 85 |
| Washington | 8 | 2 | 1 | .800 | 242 | 94 |
| Brooklyn | 4 | 6 | 1 | .400 | 108 | 219 |
| Philadelphia | 1 | 9 | 1 | .100 | 105 | 200 |
| Pittsburgh | 1 | 9 | 1 | .100 | 114 | 216 |

**WESTERN DIVISION**

| | W | L | T | Pct. | Pts. | OP |
|---|---|---|---|---|---|---|
| Green Bay | 9 | 2 | 0 | .818 | 233 | 153 |
| Chi. Bears | 8 | 3 | 0 | .727 | 298 | 157 |
| Detroit | 6 | 5 | 0 | .545 | 145 | 150 |
| Cleveland | 5 | 5 | 1 | .500 | 195 | 164 |
| Chi. Cardinals | 1 | 10 | 0 | .091 | 84 | 254 |

NFL championship: GREEN BAY 27, N.Y. Giants 0

## 1938

**EASTERN DIVISION**

| | W | L | T | Pct. | Pts. | OP |
|---|---|---|---|---|---|---|
| N.Y. Giants | 8 | 2 | 1 | .800 | 194 | 79 |
| Washington | 6 | 3 | 2 | .667 | 148 | 154 |
| Brooklyn | 4 | 4 | 3 | .500 | 131 | 161 |
| Philadelphia | 5 | 6 | 0 | .455 | 154 | 164 |
| Pittsburgh | 2 | 9 | 0 | .182 | 79 | 169 |

**WESTERN DIVISION**

| | W | L | T | Pct. | Pts. | OP |
|---|---|---|---|---|---|---|
| Green Bay | 8 | 3 | 0 | .727 | 223 | 118 |
| Detroit | 7 | 4 | 0 | .636 | 119 | 108 |
| Chi. Bears | 6 | 5 | 0 | .545 | 194 | 148 |
| Cleveland | 4 | 7 | 0 | .364 | 131 | 215 |
| Chi. Cardinals | 2 | 9 | 0 | .182 | 111 | 168 |

NFL championship: N.Y. GIANTS 23, Green Bay 17

## 1937

**EASTERN DIVISION**

| | W | L | T | Pct. | Pts. | OP |
|---|---|---|---|---|---|---|
| Washington | 8 | 3 | 0 | .727 | 195 | 120 |
| N.Y. Giants | 6 | 3 | 2 | .667 | 128 | 109 |
| Pittsburgh | 4 | 7 | 0 | .364 | 122 | 145 |
| Brooklyn | 3 | 7 | 1 | .300 | 82 | 174 |
| Philadelphia | 2 | 8 | 1 | .200 | 86 | 177 |

**WESTERN DIVISION**

| | W | L | T | Pct. | Pts. | OP |
|---|---|---|---|---|---|---|
| Chi. Bears | 9 | 1 | 1 | .900 | 201 | 100 |
| Green Bay | 7 | 4 | 0 | .636 | 220 | 122 |
| Detroit | 7 | 4 | 0 | .636 | 180 | 105 |
| Chi. Cardinals | 5 | 5 | 1 | .500 | 135 | 165 |
| Cleveland | 1 | 10 | 0 | .091 | 75 | 207 |

NFL championship: Washington 28, CHI. BEARS 21

## 1936

**EASTERN DIVISION**

| | W | L | T | Pct. | Pts. | OP |
|---|---|---|---|---|---|---|
| Boston | 7 | 5 | 0 | .583 | 149 | 110 |
| Pittsburgh | 6 | 6 | 0 | .500 | 98 | 187 |
| N.Y. Giants | 5 | 6 | 1 | .455 | 115 | 163 |
| Brooklyn | 3 | 8 | 1 | .273 | 92 | 161 |
| Philadelphia | 1 | 11 | 0 | .083 | 51 | 206 |

**WESTERN DIVISION**

| | W | L | T | Pct. | Pts. | OP |
|---|---|---|---|---|---|---|
| Green Bay | 10 | 1 | 1 | .909 | 248 | 118 |
| Chi. Bears | 9 | 3 | 0 | .750 | 222 | 94 |
| Detroit | 8 | 4 | 0 | .667 | 235 | 102 |
| Chi. Cardinals | 3 | 8 | 1 | .273 | 74 | 143 |

NFL championship: Green Bay 21, Boston 6, at Polo Grounds, N.Y.

## 1935

**EASTERN DIVISION**

| | W | L | T | Pct. | Pts. | OP |
|---|---|---|---|---|---|---|
| N. Y. Giants | 9 | 3 | 0 | .750 | 180 | 96 |
| Brooklyn | 5 | 6 | 1 | .455 | 90 | 141 |
| Pittsburgh | 4 | 8 | 0 | .333 | 100 | 209 |
| Boston | 2 | 8 | 1 | .200 | 65 | 123 |
| Philadelphia | 2 | 9 | 0 | .182 | 60 | 179 |

**WESTERN DIVISION**

| | W | L | T | Pct. | Pts. | OP |
|---|---|---|---|---|---|---|
| Detroit | 7 | 3 | 2 | .700 | 191 | 111 |
| Green Bay | 8 | 4 | 0 | .667 | 181 | 96 |
| Chi. Bears | 6 | 4 | 2 | .600 | 192 | 106 |
| Chi. Cardinals | 6 | 4 | 2 | .600 | 99 | 97 |

NFL championship: DETROIT 26, N.Y. Giants 7
One game between Boston and Philadelphia was canceled.

## 1934

**EASTERN DIVISION**

| | W | L | T | Pct. | Pts. | OP |
|---|---|---|---|---|---|---|
| N.Y. Giants | 8 | 5 | 0 | .615 | 147 | 107 |
| Boston | 6 | 6 | 0 | .500 | 107 | 94 |
| Brooklyn | 4 | 7 | 0 | .364 | 61 | 153 |
| Philadelphia | 4 | 7 | 0 | .364 | 127 | 85 |
| Pittsburgh | 2 | 10 | 0 | .167 | 51 | 206 |

**WESTERN DIVISION**

| | W | L | T | Pct. | Pts. | OP |
|---|---|---|---|---|---|---|
| Chi. Bears | 13 | 0 | 0 | 1.000 | 286 | 86 |
| Detroit | 10 | 3 | 0 | .769 | 238 | 59 |
| Green Bay | 7 | 6 | 0 | .538 | 156 | 112 |
| Chi. Cardinals | 5 | 6 | 0 | .455 | 80 | 84 |
| St. Louis | 1 | 2 | 0 | .333 | 27 | 61 |
| Cincinnati | 0 | 8 | 0 | .000 | 10 | 243 |

NFL championship: N.Y. GIANTS 30, Chi. Bears 13

## 1933

**EASTERN DIVISION**

| | W | L | T | Pct. | Pts. | OP |
|---|---|---|---|---|---|---|
| N.Y. Giants | 11 | 3 | 0 | .786 | 244 | 101 |
| Brooklyn | 5 | 4 | 1 | .556 | 93 | 54 |
| Boston | 5 | 5 | 2 | .500 | 103 | 97 |
| Philadelphia | 3 | 5 | 1 | .375 | 77 | 158 |
| Pittsburgh | 3 | 6 | 2 | .333 | 67 | 208 |

**WESTERN DIVISION**

| | W | L | T | Pct. | Pts. | OP |
|---|---|---|---|---|---|---|
| Chi. Bears | 10 | 2 | 1 | .833 | 133 | 82 |
| Portsmouth | 6 | 5 | 0 | .545 | 128 | 87 |
| Green Bay | 5 | 7 | 1 | .417 | 170 | 107 |
| Cincinnati | 3 | 6 | 1 | .333 | 38 | 110 |
| Chi. Cardinals | 1 | 9 | 1 | .100 | 52 | 101 |

NFL championship: CHI. BEARS 23, N.Y. Giants 21

## 1932

| | W | L | T | Pct. |
|---|---|---|---|---|
| Chicago Bears | 7 | 1 | 6 | .875 |
| Green Bay Packers | 10 | 3 | 1 | .769 |
| Portsmouth, O., Spartans | 6 | 2 | 4 | .750 |
| Boston Braves | 4 | 4 | 2 | .500 |
| New York Giants | 4 | 6 | 2 | .400 |
| Brooklyn Dodgers | 3 | 9 | 0 | .250 |
| Chicago Cardinals | 2 | 6 | 2 | .250 |
| Stapleton Stapes | 2 | 7 | 3 | .222 |

## 1931

| | W | L | T | Pct. |
|---|---|---|---|---|
| Green Bay Packers | 12 | 2 | 0 | .857 |
| Portsmouth, O., Spartans | 11 | 3 | 0 | .786 |
| Chicago Bears | 8 | 5 | 0 | .615 |
| Chicago Cardinals | 5 | 4 | 0 | .556 |
| N.Y. Giants | 7 | 6 | 1 | .538 |
| Providence Steamroller | 4 | 4 | 3 | .500 |
| Stapleton Stapes | 4 | 6 | 1 | .400 |
| Cleveland Indians | 2 | 8 | 0 | .200 |
| Brooklyn Dodgers | 2 | 12 | 0 | .143 |
| Frankford Yellowjackets | 1 | 6 | 1 | .143 |

## 1930

| | W | L | T | Pct. |
|---|---|---|---|---|
| Green Bay Packers | 10 | 3 | 1 | .769 |
| New York Giants | 13 | 4 | 0 | .765 |
| Chicago Bears | 9 | 4 | 1 | .692 |
| Brooklyn Dodgers | 7 | 4 | 1 | .636 |
| Providence Steamroller | 6 | 4 | 1 | .600 |
| Stapleton Stapes | 5 | 5 | 2 | .500 |
| Chicago Cardinals | 5 | 6 | 2 | .455 |
| Portsmouth, O., Spartans | 5 | 6 | 3 | .455 |
| Frankford Yellowjackets | 4 | 14 | 1 | .222 |
| Minneapolis Red Jackets | 1 | 7 | 1 | .125 |
| Newark Tornadoes | 1 | 10 | 1 | .091 |

## 1929

| | W | L | T | Pct. |
|---|---|---|---|---|
| Green Bay Packers | 12 | 0 | 1 | 1.000 |
| New York Giants | 13 | 1 | 1 | .929 |
| Frankford Yellowjackets | 9 | 4 | 5 | .692 |
| Chicago Cardinals | 6 | 6 | 1 | .500 |
| Boston Bulldogs | 4 | 4 | 0 | .500 |
| Orange, N.J., Tornadoes | 3 | 4 | 4 | .429 |
| Stapleton Stapes | 3 | 4 | 3 | .429 |
| Providence Steamroller | 4 | 6 | 2 | .400 |
| Chicago Bears | 4 | 9 | 2 | .308 |
| Buffalo Bisons | 1 | 7 | 1 | .125 |
| Minneapolis Red Jackets | 1 | 9 | 0 | .100 |
| Dayton Triangles | 0 | 6 | 0 | .000 |

## 1928

| | W | L | T | Pct. |
|---|---|---|---|---|
| Providence Steamroller | 8 | 1 | 2 | .889 |
| Frankford Yellowjackets | 11 | 3 | 2 | .786 |
| Detroit Wolverines | 7 | 2 | 1 | .778 |
| Green Bay Packers | 6 | 4 | 3 | .600 |
| Chicago Bears | 7 | 5 | 1 | .583 |
| New York Giants | 4 | 7 | 2 | .364 |
| New York Yankees | 4 | 8 | 1 | .333 |
| Pottsville, Pa., Maroons | 2 | 8 | 0 | .200 |
| Chicago Cardinals | 1 | 5 | 0 | .167 |
| Dayton Triangles | 0 | 7 | 0 | .000 |

## 1927

| | W | L | T | Pct. |
|---|---|---|---|---|
| New York Giants | 11 | 1 | 1 | .917 |
| Green Bay Packers | 7 | 2 | 1 | .778 |
| Chicago Bears | 9 | 3 | 2 | .750 |
| Cleveland Bulldogs | 8 | 4 | 1 | .667 |
| Providence Steamroller | 8 | 5 | 1 | .615 |
| New York Yankees | 7 | 8 | 1 | .467 |
| Frankford Yellowjackets | 6 | 9 | 0 | .400 |
| Pottsville, Pa., Maroons | 5 | 8 | 0 | .385 |
| Chicago Cardinals | 3 | 7 | 1 | .300 |
| Dayton Triangles | 1 | 6 | 1 | .143 |
| Duluth Eskimos | 1 | 8 | 0 | .111 |
| Buffalo Bisons | 0 | 5 | 0 | .000 |

## 1926

| | W | L | T | Pct. |
|---|---|---|---|---|
| Frankford Yellowjackets | 14 | 1 | 1 | .933 |
| Chicago Bears | 12 | 1 | 3 | .923 |
| Pottsville, Pa., Maroons | 10 | 2 | 1 | .833 |
| Kansas City Cowboys | 8 | 3 | 1 | .727 |
| Green Bay Packers | 7 | 3 | 3 | .700 |
| Los Angeles Buccaneers | 6 | 3 | 1 | .667 |
| New York Giants | 8 | 4 | 1 | .667 |
| Duluth Eskimos | 6 | 5 | 2 | .545 |
| Buffalo Rangers | 4 | 4 | 2 | .500 |
| Chicago Cardinals | 5 | 6 | 1 | .455 |
| Providence Steamroller | 5 | 7 | 0 | .417 |
| Detroit Panthers | 4 | 6 | 2 | .400 |
| Hartford Blues | 3 | 7 | 0 | .300 |
| Brooklyn Lions | 3 | 8 | 0 | .273 |
| Milwaukee Badgers | 2 | 7 | 0 | .222 |
| Akron, Ohio, Indians | 1 | 4 | 3 | .200 |
| Dayton Triangles | 1 | 4 | 1 | .200 |
| Racine, Wis., Legion | 1 | 4 | 0 | .200 |
| Columbus Tigers | 1 | 6 | 0 | .143 |
| Canton, Ohio, Bulldogs | 1 | 9 | 3 | .100 |
| Hammond, Ind., Pros | 0 | 4 | 0 | .000 |
| Louisville Colonels | 0 | 4 | 0 | .000 |

## 1925

| | W | L | T | Pct. |
|---|---|---|---|---|
| Chicago Cardinals | 11 | 2 | 1 | .846 |
| Pottsville, Pa., Maroons | 10 | 2 | 0 | .833 |
| Detroit Panthers | 8 | 2 | 2 | .800 |
| New York Giants | 8 | 4 | 0 | .667 |
| Akron, Ohio, Indians | 4 | 2 | 2 | .667 |
| Frankford Yellowjackets | 13 | 7 | 0 | .650 |
| Chicago Bears | 9 | 5 | 3 | .643 |
| Rock Island Independents | 5 | 3 | 3 | .625 |
| Green Bay Packers | 8 | 5 | 0 | .615 |
| Providence Steamroller | 6 | 5 | 1 | .545 |
| Canton, Ohio, Bulldogs | 4 | 4 | 0 | .500 |
| Cleveland Bulldogs | 5 | 8 | 1 | .385 |
| Kansas City Cowboys | 2 | 5 | 1 | .286 |
| Hammond, Ind., Pros | 1 | 3 | 0 | .250 |
| Buffalo Bisons | 1 | 6 | 2 | .143 |
| Duluth Kelleys | 0 | 3 | 0 | .000 |
| Rochester Jeffersons | 0 | 6 | 1 | .000 |
| Milwaukee Badgers | 0 | 6 | 0 | .000 |
| Dayton Triangles | 0 | 7 | 1 | .000 |
| Columbus Tigers | 0 | 9 | 0 | .000 |

## 1924

| | W | L | T | Pct. |
|---|---|---|---|---|
| Cleveland Bulldogs | 7 | 1 | 1 | .875 |
| Chicago Bears | 6 | 1 | 4 | .857 |
| Frankford Yellowjackets | 11 | 2 | 1 | .846 |
| Duluth Kelleys | 5 | 1 | 0 | .833 |
| Rock Island Independents | 6 | 2 | 2 | .750 |
| Green Bay Packers | 8 | 4 | 0 | .667 |
| Buffalo Bisons | 6 | 4 | 0 | .600 |
| Racine, Wis., Legion | 4 | 3 | 3 | .571 |
| Chicago Cardinals | 5 | 4 | 1 | .556 |
| Columbus Tigers | 4 | 4 | 0 | .500 |
| Hammond, Ind., Pros | 2 | 2 | 1 | .500 |
| Milwaukee Badgers | 5 | 8 | 0 | .385 |
| Dayton Triangles | 2 | 7 | 0 | .222 |
| Kansas City Cowboys | 2 | 7 | 0 | .222 |
| Akron, Ohio, Indians | 1 | 6 | 0 | .143 |
| Kenosha, Wis., Maroons | 0 | 5 | 1 | .000 |
| Minneapolis Marines | 0 | 6 | 0 | .000 |
| Rochester Jeffersons | 0 | 7 | 0 | .000 |

## 1923

| | W | L | T | Pct. |
|---|---|---|---|---|
| Canton, Ohio, Bulldogs | 11 | 0 | 1 | 1.000 |
| Chicago Bears | 9 | 2 | 1 | .818 |
| Green Bay Packers | 7 | 2 | 1 | .778 |
| Milwaukee Badgers | 7 | 2 | 3 | .778 |
| Cleveland Indians | 3 | 1 | 3 | .750 |
| Chicago Cardinals | 8 | 4 | 0 | .667 |
| Duluth Kelleys | 4 | 3 | 0 | .571 |
| Buffalo All-Americans | 5 | 4 | 3 | .556 |
| Columbus Tigers | 5 | 4 | 1 | .556 |
| Racine, Wis., Legion | 4 | 4 | 2 | .500 |
| Toledo Maroons | 2 | 3 | 2 | .400 |
| Rock Island Independents | 2 | 3 | 3 | .400 |
| Minneapolis Marines | 2 | 5 | 2 | .286 |
| St. Louis All-Stars | 1 | 4 | 2 | .200 |
| Hammond, Ind., Pros | 1 | 5 | 1 | .167 |
| Dayton Triangles | 1 | 6 | 1 | .143 |
| Akron, Ohio, Indians | 1 | 6 | 0 | .143 |
| Oorang Indians | 1 | 10 | 0 | .091 |
| Rochester Jeffersons | 0 | 2 | 0 | .000 |
| Louisville Brecks | 0 | 3 | 0 | .000 |

## 1922

| | W | L | T | Pct. |
|---|---|---|---|---|
| Canton, Ohio, Bulldogs | 10 | 0 | 2 | 1.000 |
| Chicago Bears | 9 | 3 | 0 | .750 |
| Chicago Cardinals | 8 | 3 | 0 | .727 |
| Toledo Maroons | 5 | 2 | 2 | .714 |
| Rock Island Independents | 4 | 2 | 1 | .667 |
| Dayton Triangles | 4 | 3 | 1 | .571 |
| Green Bay Packers | 4 | 3 | 3 | .571 |
| Racine, Wis., Legion | 5 | 4 | 1 | .556 |
| Akron, Ohio, Pros | 3 | 4 | 2 | .429 |
| Buffalo All-Americans | 3 | 4 | 1 | .429 |
| Milwaukee Badgers | 2 | 4 | 3 | .333 |
| Oorang Indians | 2 | 6 | 0 | .250 |
| Minneapolis Marines | 1 | 3 | 0 | .250 |
| Evansville Crimson Giants | 0 | 2 | 0 | .000 |
| Louisville Brecks | 0 | 3 | 0 | .000 |
| Rochester Jeffersons | 0 | 3 | 1 | .000 |
| Hammond, Ind., Pros | 0 | 4 | 1 | .000 |
| Columbus Panhandles | 0 | 7 | 0 | .000 |

## 1921

| | W | L | T | Pct. |
|---|---|---|---|---|
| Chicago Staleys | 10 | 1 | 1 | .909 |
| Buffalo All-Americans | 9 | 1 | 2 | .900 |
| Akron, Ohio, Pros | 7 | 2 | 1 | .778 |
| Green Bay Packers | 6 | 2 | 2 | .750 |
| Canton, Ohio, Bulldogs | 4 | 3 | 3 | .571 |
| Dayton Triangles | 4 | 3 | 1 | .571 |
| Rock Island Independents | 5 | 4 | 1 | .556 |
| Chicago Cardinals | 2 | 3 | 2 | .400 |
| Cleveland Indians | 2 | 6 | 0 | .250 |
| Rochester Jeffersons | 2 | 6 | 0 | .250 |
| Detroit Heralds | 1 | 7 | 1 | .125 |
| Columbus Panhandles | 0 | 6 | 0 | .000 |
| Cincinnati Celts | 0 | 8 | 0 | .000 |

**ATLANTA vs. BALTIMORE**
Colts lead series, 8-0
1966—Colts, 19-7 (A)
1967—Colts, 38-31 (B)
    Colts, 49-7 (A)
1968—Colts, 28-20 (A)
    Colts, 44-0 (B)
1969—Colts, 21-14 (A)
    Colts, 13-6 (B)
1974—Colts, 17-7 (A)
(Points—Colts 229, Falcons 92)

**ATLANTA vs. BUFFALO**
Series tied, 2-2
1973—Bills, 17-6 (A)
1977—Bills, 3-0 (B)
1980—Falcons, 30-14 (B)
1983—Falcons, 31-14 (A)
(Points—Falcons 67, Bills 48)

**ATLANTA vs. CHICAGO**
Falcons lead series, 9-4
1966—Bears, 23-6 (C)
1967—Bears, 23-14 (A)
1968—Falcons, 16-13 (C)
1969—Falcons, 48-31 (A)
1970—Bears, 23-14 (A)
1972—Falcons, 37-21 (A)
1973—Falcons, 46-6 (A)
1974—Falcons, 13-10 (A)
1976—Falcons, 10-0 (C)
1977—Falcons, 16-10 (A)
1978—Bears, 13-7 (C)
1980—Falcons, 28-17 (A)
1983—Falcons, 20-17 (C)
(Points—Falcons 275, Bears 207)

**ATLANTA vs. CINCINNATI**
Bengals lead series, 3-1
1971—Falcons, 9-6 (A)
1975—Bengals, 21-14 (A)
1978—Bengals, 37-7 (C)
1981—Bengals, 30-28 (A)
(Points—Bengals 94, Falcons 58)

**ATLANTA vs. CLEVELAND**
Browns lead series, 5-1
1966—Browns, 49-17 (A)
1968—Browns, 30-7 (C)
1971—Falcons, 31-14 (C)
1976—Browns, 20-17 (A)
1978—Browns, 24-16 (A)
1981—Browns, 28-17 (C)
(Points—Browns 165, Falcons 105)

**ATLANTA vs. DALLAS**
Cowboys lead series, 7-1
1966—Cowboys, 47-14 (A)
1967—Cowboys, 37-7 (D)
1969—Cowboys, 24-17 (A)
1970—Cowboys, 13-0 (D)
1974—Cowboys, 24-0 (A)
1976—Falcons, 17-10 (A)
1978—*Cowboys, 27-20 (D)
1980—*Cowboys, 30-27 (A)
(Points—Cowboys 212, Falcons 102)
*NFC Divisional Playoff

**ATLANTA vs. DENVER**
Falcons lead series, 3-2
1970—Broncos, 24-10 (D)
1972—Falcons, 23-20 (A)
1975—Falcons, 35-21 (A)
1979—Broncos, 20-17 (A) OT
1982—Falcons, 34-27 (D)
(Points—Falcons 119, Broncos 112)

**ATLANTA vs. DETROIT**
Lions lead series, 10-4
1966—Lions, 28-10 (D)
1967—Lions, 24-3 (D)
1968—Lions, 24-7 (A)
1969—Lions, 27-21 (D)
1971—Lions, 41-38 (D)
1972—Lions, 26-23 (A)
1973—Lions, 31-6 (D)
1975—Lions, 17-14 (A)
1976—Lions, 24-10 (D)
1977—Falcons, 17-6 (A)
1978—Falcons, 14-0 (A)
1979—Lions, 24-23 (D)
1980—Falcons, 43-28 (A)
1983—Falcons, 30-14 (D)
(Points—Lions 314, Falcons 259)

**ATLANTA vs. GREEN BAY**
Packers lead series, 8-6
1966—Packers, 56-3 (Mil)
1967—Packers, 23-0 (Mil)
1968—Packers, 38-7 (A)
1969—Packers, 28-10 (GB)
1970—Packers, 27-24 (GB)
1971—Falcons, 28-21 (A)
1972—Falcons, 10-9 (Mil)
1974—Falcons, 10-3 (A)
1975—Packers, 22-13 (GB)
1976—Packers, 24-20 (A)

1979—Falcons, 25-7 (A)
1981—Falcons, 31-17 (GB)
1982—Packers, 38-7 (A)
1983—Falcons, 47-41 (A) OT
(Points—Packers 354, Falcons 235)

**ATLANTA vs. HOUSTON**
Falcons lead series, 3-1
1972—Falcons, 20-10 (A)
1976—Oilers, 20-14 (H)
1978—Falcons, 20-14 (A)
1981—Falcons, 31-27 (H)
(Points—Falcons 85, Oilers 71)

**ATLANTA vs. KANSAS CITY**
Chiefs lead series, 1-0
1972—Chiefs, 17-14 (A)

**ATLANTA vs. *L.A. RAIDERS**
Raiders lead series, 3-1
1971—Falcons, 24-13 (A)
1975—Raiders, 37-34 (O) OT
1979—Raiders, 50-19 (O)
1982—Falcons, 38-14 (A)
(Points—Raiders 138, Falcons 91)
*Franchise in Oakland prior to 1982

**ATLANTA vs. L.A. RAMS**
Rams lead series, 26-6-2
1966—Rams, 19-14 (A)
1967—Rams, 31-3 (A)
    Rams, 20-3 (LA)
1968—Rams, 27-14 (LA)
    Rams, 17-10 (A)
1969—Rams, 17-7 (LA)
    Rams, 38-6 (A)
1970—Tie, 10-10 (LA)
    Rams, 17-7 (A)
1971—Tie, 20-20 (LA)
    Rams, 24-16 (A)
1972—Rams, 31-3 (A)
    Rams, 20-7 (LA)
1973—Rams, 31-0 (LA)
    Falcons, 15-13 (A)
1974—Rams, 21-0 (LA)
    Rams, 30-7 (A)
1975—Rams, 22-7 (LA)
    Rams, 16-7 (A)
1976—Rams, 30-14 (A)
    Rams, 59-0 (LA)
1977—Falcons, 17-6 (A)
    Rams, 23-7 (LA)
1978—Rams, 10-0 (LA)
    Falcons, 15-7 (A)
1979—Falcons, 20-14 (LA)
    Rams, 34-13 (A)
1980—Falcons, 13-10 (A)
    Rams, 20-17 (LA) OT
1981—Rams, 37-35 (A)
    Rams, 21-16 (LA)
1982—Rams, 34-17 (A)
1983—Rams, 27-21 (LA)
    Rams, 36-13 (A)
(Points—Rams 753, Falcons 413)

**ATLANTA vs. MIAMI**
Dolphins lead series, 4-0
1970—Dolphins, 20-7 (A)
1974—Dolphins, 42-7 (M)
1980—Dolphins, 20-17 (A)
1983—Dolphins, 31-24 (M)
(Points—Dolphins 113, Falcons 55)

**ATLANTA vs. MINNESOTA**
Vikings lead series, 8-5
1966—Falcons, 20-13 (M)
1967—Falcons, 21-20 (A)
1968—Vikings, 47-7 (M)
1969—Falcons, 10-3 (A)
1970—Vikings, 37-7 (A)
1971—Vikings, 24-7 (M)
1973—Falcons, 20-14 (A)
1974—Vikings, 23-10 (M)
1975—Vikings, 38-0 (M)
1977—Vikings, 14-7 (A)
1980—Vikings, 24-23 (A)
1981—Falcons, 31-30 (A)
1982—*Vikings, 30-24 (M)
(Points—Vikings 317, Falcons 187)
*NFC First Round Playoff

**ATLANTA vs. NEW ENGLAND**
Series tied, 2-2
1972—Patriots, 21-20 (NE)
1977—Patriots, 16-10 (A)
1980—Falcons, 37-21 (NE)
1983—Falcons, 24-13 (A)
(Points—Falcons 91, Patriots 71)

**ATLANTA vs. NEW ORLEANS**
Falcons lead series, 20-10
1967—Saints, 27-24 (NO)
1969—Falcons, 45-17 (A)
1970—Falcons, 14-3 (NO)
    Falcons, 32-14 (A)
1971—Falcons, 28-6 (A)
    Falcons, 24-20 (NO)

1972—Falcons, 21-14 (NO)
    Falcons, 36-20 (A)
1973—Falcons, 62-7 (NO)
    Falcons, 14-10 (A)
1974—Saints, 14-13 (NO)
    Saints, 13-3 (A)
1975—Falcons, 14-7 (A)
    Saints, 23-7 (NO)
1976—Saints, 30-0 (NO)
    Falcons, 23-20 (A)
1977—Saints, 21-20 (NO)
    Falcons, 35-7 (A)
1978—Falcons, 20-17 (NO)
    Falcons, 20-17 (A)
1979—Falcons, 40-34 (NO) OT
    Saints, 37-6 (A)
1980—Falcons, 41-14 (NO)
    Falcons, 31-13 (A)
1981—Falcons, 27-0 (A)
    Falcons, 41-10 (NO)
1982—Falcons, 35-0 (A)
    Saints, 35-6 (NO)
1983—Saints, 19-17 (A)
    Saints, 27-10 (NO)
(Points—Falcons 709, Saints 496)

**ATLANTA vs. N.Y. GIANTS**
Falcons lead series, 6-4
1966—Falcons, 27-16 (NY)
1968—Falcons, 24-21 (A)
1971—Giants, 21-17 (A)
1974—Falcons, 14-7 (New Haven)
1977—Falcons, 17-3 (A)
1978—Falcons, 23-20 (A)
1979—Giants, 24-3 (NY)
1981—Giants, 27-24 (A) OT
1982—Falcons, 16-14 (NY)
1983—Giants, 16-13 (A) OT
(Points—Falcons 178, Giants 169)

**ATLANTA vs. N.Y. JETS**
Falcons lead series, 2-1
1973—Falcons, 28-20 (NY)
1980—Jets, 14-7 (A)
1983—Falcons, 27-21 (NY)
(Points—Falcons 62, Jets 55)

**ATLANTA vs. PHILADELPHIA**
Series tied, 5-5-1
1966—Eagles, 23-10 (P)
1967—Eagles, 38-7 (A)
1969—Falcons, 27-3 (P)
1970—Tie, 13-13 (P)
1973—Falcons, 44-27 (P)
1976—Eagles, 14-13 (A)
1978—*Falcons, 14-13 (A)
1979—Falcons, 14-10 (P)
1980—Falcons, 20-17 (P)
1981—Eagles, 16-13 (P)
1983—Eagles, 28-24 (A)
(Points—Eagles 202, Falcons 199)
*NFC First Round Playoff

**ATLANTA vs. PITTSBURGH**
Steelers lead series, 5-1
1966—Steelers, 57-33 (A)
1968—Steelers, 41-21 (A)
1970—Falcons, 27-16 (A)
1974—Steelers, 24-17 (P)
1978—Steelers, 31-7 (P)
1981—Steelers, 34-20 (A)
(Points—Steelers 203, Falcons 125)

**ATLANTA vs. ST. LOUIS**
Cardinals lead series, 6-3
1966—Falcons, 16-10 (A)
1968—Cardinals, 17-12 (StL)
1971—Cardinals, 26-9 (A)
1973—Cardinals, 32-10 (A)
1975—Cardinals, 23-20 (StL)
1978—Cardinals, 42-21 (StL)
1980—Falcons, 33-27 (StL) OT
1981—Falcons, 41-20 (A)
1982—Cardinals, 23-20 (A)
(Points—Cardinals 220, Falcons 182)

**ATLANTA vs. SAN DIEGO**
Falcons lead series, 2-0
1973—Falcons, 41-0 (SD)
1979—Falcons, 28-26 (SD)
(Points—Falcons 69, Chargers 26)

**ATLANTA vs. SAN FRANCISCO**
Series tied, 17-17
1966—49ers, 44-7 (A)
1967—49ers, 38-7 (SF)
    49ers, 34-28 (A)
1968—49ers, 28-13 (SF)
    49ers, 14-12 (A)
1969—Falcons, 24-12 (A)
    Falcons, 21-7 (SF)
1970—Falcons, 21-20 (A)
    49ers, 24-20 (SF)
1971—Falcons, 20-17 (A)
    49ers, 24-3 (SF)
1972—49ers, 49-14 (A)

49ers, 20-0 (SF)
1973—49ers, 13-9 (A)
    Falcons, 17-3 (SF)
1974—49ers, 16-10 (A)
    49ers, 27-0 (SF)
1975—Falcons, 17-3 (SF)
    Falcons, 31-9 (A)
1976—Falcons, 15-0 (SF)
    Falcons, 21-16 (A)
1977—Falcons, 7-0 (SF)
    49ers, 10-3 (A)
1978—Falcons, 20-17 (SF)
    Falcons, 21-10 (A)
1979—Falcons, 20-15 (SF)
    Falcons, 31-21 (A)
1980—Falcons, 20-17 (SF)
    Falcons, 35-10 (A)
1981—Falcons, 34-17 (A)
    49ers, 17-14 (SF)
1982—Falcons, 17-7 (SF)
1983—49ers, 24-20 (SF)
    Falcons, 28-24 (A)
(Points—49ers 627, Falcons 560)

**ATLANTA vs. SEATTLE**
Seahawks lead series, 2-0
1976—Seahawks, 30-13 (S)
1979—Seahawks, 31-28 (A)
(Points—Seahawks 61, Falcons 41)

**ATLANTA vs. TAMPA BAY**
Series tied, 2-2
1977—Falcons, 17-0 (TB)
1978—Buccaneers, 14-9 (TB)
1979—Falcons, 17-14 (A)
1981—Buccaneers, 24-23 (TB)
(Points—Falcons 66, Buccaneers 52)

**ATLANTA vs. WASHINGTON**
Redskins lead series, 7-2-1
1966—Redskins, 33-20 (W)
1967—Tie, 20-20 (W)
1969—Redskins, 27-20 (W)
1972—Redskins, 24-13 (W)
1975—Redskins, 30-27 (A)
1977—Falcons, 10-6 (W)
1978—Falcons, 20-17 (A)
1979—Redskins, 16-7 (A)
1980—Falcons, 10-6 (A)
1983—Redskins, 37-21 (W)
(Points—Redskins 220, Falcons 164)

---

**BALTIMORE vs. ATLANTA**
Colts lead series, 8-0;
See Atlanta vs. Baltimore

**BALTIMORE vs. BUFFALO**
Series tied, 13-13-1
1970—Tie, 17-17 (Balt)
    Colts, 20-14 (Buff)
1971—Colts, 43-0 (Buff)
    Colts, 24-0 (Balt)
1972—Colts, 17-0 (Buff)
    Colts, 35-7 (Balt)
1973—Bills, 31-13 (Buff)
    Bills, 24-17 (Balt)
1974—Bills, 27-14 (Balt)
    Bills, 6-0 (Buff)
1975—Bills, 38-31 (Balt)
    Colts, 42-35 (Buff)
1976—Colts, 31-13 (Balt)
    Colts, 58-20 (Buff)
1977—Colts, 17-14 (Balt)
    Colts, 31-13 (Buff)
1978—Bills, 24-17 (Buff)
    Bills, 21-14 (Balt)
1979—Bills, 31-13 (Balt)
    Colts, 14-13 (Buff)
1980—Colts, 17-12 (Buff)
    Colts, 28-24 (Balt)
1981—Bills, 35-3 (Balt)
    Bills, 23-17 (Buff)
1982—Bills, 20-0 (Buff)
1983—Bills, 28-23 (Buff)
    Bills, 30-7 (Balt)
(Points—Colts 563, Bills 520)

**BALTIMORE vs. CHICAGO**
Colts lead series, 21-13
1953—Colts, 13-9 (B)
    Colts, 16-14 (C)
1954—Bears, 28-9 (C)
    Bears, 28-13 (B)
1955—Colts, 23-17 (B)
    Bears, 38-10 (C)
1956—Colts, 28-21 (B)
    Bears, 58-27 (C)
1957—Colts, 21-10 (B)
    Colts, 29-14 (C)
1958—Colts, 51-38 (B)
    Colts, 17-0 (C)
1959—Bears, 26-21 (B)
    Colts, 21-7 (C)
1960—Colts, 42-7 (B)

Colts, 24-20 (C)
1961—Bears, 24-10 (C)
Bears, 21-20 (B)
1962—Bears, 35-15 (C)
Bears, 57-0 (B)
1963—Bears, 10-3 (C)
Bears, 17-7 (B)
1964—Colts, 52-0 (B)
Colts, 40-24 (C)
1965—Colts, 26-21 (C)
Bears, 13-0 (B)
1966—Bears. 27-17 (C)
Colts, 21-16 (B)
1967—Colts, 24-3 (C)
1968—Colts, 28-7 (B)
1969—Colts, 24-21 (C)
1970—Colts, 21-20 (B)
1975—Colts, 35-7 (B)
1983—Colts, 22-19 (B) OT
(Points—Colts 730, Bears 677)

**BALTIMORE vs. CINCINNATI**
Colts lead series, 5-4
1970—*Colts, 17-0 (B)
1972—Colts, 20-19 (C)
1974—Bengals, 24-14 (B)
1976—Colts, 28-27 (B)
1979—Colts, 38-28 (B)
1980—Bengals, 34-33 (C)
1981—Bengals, 41-19 (B)
1982—Bengals, 20-17 (B)
1983—Colts, 34-31 (C)
(Points—Bengals 224, Colts 220)
*AFC Divisional Playoff

**BALTIMORE vs. CLEVELAND**
Browns lead series, 10-5
1956—Colts, 21-7 (C)
1959—Browns, 38-31 (B)
1962—Colts, 36-14 (C)
1964—*Browns, 27-0 (C)
1968—Browns, 30-20 (B)
*Colts, 34-0 (C)
1971—Browns, 14-13 (B)
**Colts, 20-3 (C)
1973—Browns, 24-14 (C)
1975—Colts, 21-7 (B)
1978—Browns, 45-24 (B)
1979—Browns, 13-10 (C)
1980—Browns, 28-27 (B)
1981—Browns, 42-28 (C)
1983—Browns, 41-23 (C)
(Points—Browns 333, Colts 322)
*NFL Championship
**AFC Divisional Playoff

**BALTIMORE vs. DALLAS**
Cowboys lead series, 5-3
1960—Colts, 45-7 (D)
1967—Colts, 23-17 (B)
1969—Cowboys, 27-10 (D)
1970—*Colts, 16-13 (Miami)
1972—Cowboys, 21-0 (B)
1976—Cowboys, 30-27 (D)
1978—Cowboys, 38-0 (D)
1981—Cowboys, 37-13 (B)
(Points—Cowboys 190, Colts 134)
*Super Bowl V

**BALTIMORE vs. DENVER**
Broncos lead series, 5-1
1974—Broncos, 17-6 (B)
1977—Broncos, 27-13 (D)
1978—Colts, 7-6 (B)
1981—Broncos, 28-10 (D)
1983—Broncos, 17-10 (B)
Broncos, 21-19 (D)
(Points—Broncos 116, Colts 65)

**BALTIMORE vs. DETROIT**
Series tied, 16-16-2
1953—Lions, 27-17 (B)
Lions, 17-7 (D)
1954—Lions, 35-0 (D)
Lions, 27-3 (B)
1955—Colts, 28-13 (B)
Lions, 24-14 (D)
1956—Colts, 31-14 (B)
Lions, 27-3 (D)
1957—Colts, 34-14 (B)
Lions, 31-27 (D)
1958—Colts, 28-15 (B)
Colts, 40-14 (D)
1959—Colts, 21-9 (B)
Colts, 31-24 (D)
1960—Lions, 30-17 (D)
Lions, 20-15 (B)
1961—Colts, 16-15 (B)
Colts, 17-14 (D)
1962—Colts, 29-20 (B)
Lions, 21-14 (D)
1963—Colts, 25-21 (D)
Colts, 24-21 (B)
1964—Colts, 34-0 (D)
Lions, 31-14 (B)
1965—Colts, 31-7 (B)
Tie, 24-24 (D)
1966—Colts, 45-14 (B)

Lions, 20-14 (D)
1967—Colts, 41-7 (B)
1968—Colts, 27-10 (D)
1969—Tie, 17-17 (B)
1973—Colts, 29-27 (D)
1977—Lions, 13-10 (B)
1980—Colts, 10-9 (D)
(Points—Colts 710, Lions 659)

**BALTIMORE vs. GREEN BAY**
Packers lead series, 18-16-1
1953—Packers, 37-14 (GB)
Packers, 35-24 (B)
1954—Packers, 7-6 (B)
Packers, 24-13 (Mil)
1955—Colts, 24-20 (Mil)
Colts, 14-10 (B)
1956—Packers, 38-33 (Mil)
Colts, 28-21 (B)
1957—Colts, 45-17 (Mil)
Packers, 24-21 (B)
1958—Colts, 24-17 (Mil)
Colts, 56-0 (B)
1959—Colts, 38-21 (B)
Colts, 28-24 (Mil)
1960—Packers, 35-21 (GB)
Colts, 38-24 (B)
1961—Packers, 45-7 (GB)
Colts, 45-21 (B)
1962—Packers, 17-6 (B)
Packers, 17-13 (GB)
1963—Packers, 31-20 (GB)
Packers, 34-20 (B)
1964—Colts, 21-20 (GB)
Colts, 24-21 (B)
1965—Packers, 20-17 (Mil)
Packers, 42-27 (B)
*Packers, 13-10 (GB) OT
1966—Packers, 24-3 (Mil)
Packers, 14-10 (B)
1967—Colts, 13-10 (B)
1968—Colts, 16-3 (GB)
1969—Colts, 14-6 (B)
1970—Colts, 13-10 (GB)
1974—Packers, 20-13 (B)
1982—Tie, 20-20 (B) OT
(Points—Packers 742, Colts 739)
*Conference Playoff

**BALTIMORE vs. HOUSTON**
Series tied, 3-3
1970—Colts, 24-20 (H)
1973—Oilers, 31-27 (B)
1976—Colts, 38-14 (B)
1979—Oilers, 28-16 (B)
1980—Oilers, 21-16 (H)
1983—Colts, 20-10 (B)
(Points—Colts 141, Oilers 124)

**BALTIMORE vs. KANSAS CITY**
Chiefs lead series, 5-3
1970—Chiefs, 44-24 (B)
1972—Chiefs, 24-10 (KC)
1975—Colts, 28-14 (B)
1977—Colts, 17-6 (KC)
1979—Chiefs, 14-0 (KC)
Chiefs, 10-7 (B)
1980—Colts, 31-24 (KC)
Chiefs, 38-28 (B)
(Points—Chiefs 174, Colts 145)

**BALTIMORE vs. *L.A. RAIDERS**
Raiders lead series, 3-2
1970—**Colts, 27-17 (B)
1971—Colts, 37-14 (O)
1973—Raiders, 34-21 (B)
1975—Raiders, 31-20 (B)
1977—***Raiders, 37-31 (B) OT
(Points—Colts 136, Raiders 133)
*Franchise in Oakland prior to 1982
**AFC Championship
***AFC Divisional Playoff

**BALTIMORE vs. L.A. RAMS**
Colts lead series, 20-14-2
1953—Rams, 21-13 (B)
Rams, 45-2 (LA)
1954—Rams, 48-0 (B)
Colts, 22-21 (LA)
1955—Tie, 17-17 (B)
Rams, 20-14 (LA)
1956—Colts, 56-21 (B)
Rams, 31-7 (LA)
1957—Colts, 31-14 (B)
Rams, 37-21 (LA)
1958—Colts, 34-7 (B)
Rams, 30-28 (LA)
1959—Colts, 35-21 (B)
Colts, 45-26 (LA)
1960—Colts, 31-17 (B)
Rams, 10-3 (LA)
1961—Colts, 27-24 (B)
Rams, 34-17 (LA)
1962—Colts, 30-27 (B)
Colts, 14-2 (LA)
1963—Rams, 17-16 (LA)
Colts, 19-16 (B)
1964—Colts, 35-20 (B)

Colts, 24-7 (LA)
1965—Colts, 35-20 (B)
Colts, 20-17 (LA)
1966—Colts, 17-3 (LA)
Rams, 23-7 (B)
1967—Tie, 24-24 (B)
Rams, 34-10 (LA)
1968—Colts, 27-10 (B)
Colts, 28-24 (LA)
1969—Rams, 27-20 (B)
Colts, 13-7 (LA)
1971—Colts, 24-17 (B)
1975—Rams, 24-13 (LA)
(Points—Colts 779, Rams 763)

**BALTIMORE vs. MIAMI**
Dolphins lead series, 20-9
1970—Colts, 35-0 (B)
Dolphins, 34-17 (M)
1971—Dolphins, 17-14 (M)
Colts, 14-3 (B)
*Dolphins, 21-0 (M)
1972—Dolphins, 23-0 (B)
Dolphins, 16-0 (M)
1973—Dolphins, 44-0 (M)
Colts, 16-3 (B)
1974—Dolphins, 17-7 (M)
Dolphins, 17-16 (B)
1975—Colts, 33-17 (M)
Colts, 10-7 (B) OT
1976—Colts, 28-14 (B)
Colts, 17-16 (M)
1977—Colts, 45-28 (B)
Dolphins, 17-6 (M)
1978—Dolphins, 42-0 (M)
Dolphins, 26-8 (M)
1979—Dolphins, 19-0 (M)
Dolphins, 28-24 (B)
1980—Colts, 30-17 (M)
Dolphins, 24-14 (B)
1981—Dolphins, 31-28 (B)
Dolphins, 27-10 (M)
1982—Dolphins, 24-20 (M)
Dolphins, 34-7 (B)
1983—Dolphins, 21-7 (B)
Dolphins, 37-0 (M)
(Points—Dolphins 624, Colts 406)
*AFC Championship

**BALTIMORE vs. MINNESOTA**
Colts lead series, 12-5-1
1961—Colts, 34-33 (B)
Vikings, 28-20 (M)
1962—Colts, 34-7 (M)
Colts, 42-17 (B)
1963—Colts, 37-34 (M)
Colts, 41-10 (B)
1964—Vikings, 34-24 (M)
Colts, 17-14 (B)
1965—Colts, 35-16 (B)
Colts, 41-21 (M)
1966—Colts, 38-23 (M)
Colts, 20-17 (B)
1967—Tie, 20-20 (M)
1968—Colts, 21-9 (B)
*Colts, 24-14 (B)
1969—Vikings, 52-14 (M)
1971—Vikings, 10-3 (M)
1982—Vikings, 13-10 (M)
(Points—Colts 475, Vikings 372)
*Conference Championship

**BALTIMORE vs. *NEW ENGLAND**
Colts lead series, 15-12
1970—Colts, 14-6 (Bos)
Colts, 27-3 (Balt)
1971—Colts, 23-3 (NE)
Patriots, 21-17 (Balt)
1972—Colts, 24-17 (NE)
Colts, 31-0 (Balt)
1973—Patriots, 24-16 (NE)
Colts, 18-13 (Balt)
1974—Patriots, 42-3 (NE)
Patriots, 27-17 (Balt)
1975—Patriots, 21-10 (NE)
Colts, 34-21 (Balt)
1976—Colts, 27-13 (NE)
Patriots, 21-14 (Balt)
1977—Patriots, 17-3 (NE)
Colts, 30-24 (Balt)
1978—Colts, 34-27 (NE)
Patriots, 35-14 (Balt)
1979—Colts, 31-26 (Balt)
Patriots, 50-21 (NE)
1980—Patriots, 37-21 (Balt)
Patriots, 47-21 (NE)
1981—Colts, 29-28 (NE)
Colts, 23-21 (Balt)
1982—Patriots, 24-13 (Balt)
1983—Colts, 29-23 (NE) OT
Colts, 12-7 (B)
(Points—Patriots 598, Colts 556)
*Franchise in Boston prior to 1971

**BALTIMORE vs. NEW ORLEANS**
Colts lead series, 3-0
1967—Colts, 30-10 (B)

1969—Colts, 30-10 (NO)
1973—Colts, 14-10 (B)
(Points—Colts 74, Saints 30)

**BALTIMORE vs. N. Y. GIANTS**
Colts lead series, 7-3
1954—Colts, 20-14 (B)
1955—Giants, 17-7 (NY)
1958—Giants, 24-21 (NY)
*Colts, 23-17 (NY) OT
1959—*Colts, 31-16 (B)
1963—Giants, 37-28 (B)
1968—Colts, 26-0 (NY)
1971—Colts, 31-7 (NY)
1975—Colts, 21-0 (NY)
1979—Colts, 31-7 (NY)
(Points—Colts 239, Giants 139)
*NFL Championship

**BALTIMORE vs. N. Y. JETS**
Colts lead series, 15-13
1968—*Jets, 16-7 (Miami)
1970—Colts, 29-22 (NY)
Colts, 35-20 (B)
1971—Colts, 22-0 (B)
Colts, 14-13 (NY)
1972—Jets, 44-34 (B)
Jets, 24-20 (NY)
1973—Jets, 34-10 (B)
Jets, 20-17 (NY)
1974—Colts, 35-20 (NY)
Jets, 45-38 (B)
1975—Colts, 45-28 (NY)
Colts, 52-19 (B)
1976—Colts, 20-0 (NY)
Colts, 33-16 (B)
1977—Colts, 20-12 (NY)
Colts, 33-12 (B)
1978—Jets, 33-10 (B)
Jets, 24-16 (NY)
1979—Colts, 10-8 (B)
Jets, 30-17 (NY)
1980—Colts, 17-14 (NY)
Colts, 35-21 (B)
1981—Jets, 41-14 (B)
Jets, 25-0 (NY)
1982—Jets, 37-0 (NY)
1983—Colts, 17-14 (NY)
Jets, 10-6 (B)
(Points—Colts 606, Jets 602)
*Super Bowl III

**BALTIMORE vs. PHILADELPHIA**
Colts lead series, 5-4
1953—Eagles, 45-14 (P)
1965—Colts, 34-24 (B)
1967—Colts, 38-6 (P)
1969—Colts, 24-20 (B)
1970—Colts, 29-10 (B)
1974—Eagles, 30-10 (P)
1978—Eagles, 17-14 (B)
1981—Eagles, 38-13 (P)
1983—Colts, 22-21 (B)
(Points—Eagles 211, Colts 198)

**BALTIMORE vs. PITTSBURGH**
Steelers lead series, 8-3
1957—Steelers, 19-13 (B)
1968—Colts, 41-7 (P)
1971—Colts, 10-3 (B)
1974—Steelers, 30-0 (B)
1975—*Steelers, 28-10 (P)
1976—*Steelers, 40-14 (B)
1977—Colts, 31-21 (B)
1978—Steelers, 35-13 (P)
1979—Steelers, 17-13 (P)
1980—Steelers, 20-17 (B)
1983—Steelers, 24-13 (B)
(Points—Steelers 262, Colts 199)
*AFC Divisional Playoff

**BALTIMORE vs. ST. LOUIS**
Series tied, 4-4
1961—Colts, 16-0 (B)
1964—Colts, 47-27 (B)
1968—Colts, 27-0 (B)
1972—Cardinals, 10-3 (B)
1976—Cardinals, 24-17 (StL)
1978—Colts, 30-17 (StL)
1980—Cardinals, 17-10 (B)
1981—Cardinals, 35-24 (B)
(Points—Colts 174, Cardinals 130)

**BALTIMORE vs. SAN DIEGO**
Chargers lead series, 3-2
1970—Colts, 16-14 (SD)
1972—Chargers, 23-20 (B)
1976—Colts, 37-21 (SD)
1981—Chargers, 43-14 (B)
1982—Chargers, 44-26 (SD)
(Points—Chargers 145, Colts 113)

**BALTIMORE vs. SAN FRANCISCO**
Colts lead series, 21-14
1953—49ers, 38-21 (B)
49ers, 45-14 (SF)
1954—Colts, 17-13 (B)
49ers, 10-7 (SF)
1955—Colts, 26-14 (B)
49ers, 35-24 (SF)

1956—49ers, 20-17 (B)
49ers, 30-17 (SF)
1957—Colts, 27-21 (B)
49ers, 17-13 (SF)
1958—Colts, 35-27 (B)
49ers, 21-12 (SF)
1959—49ers, 45-14 (B)
Colts, 34-14 (SF)
1960—49ers, 30-22 (B)
49ers, 34-10 (SF)
1961—Colts, 20-17 (B)
Colts, 27-24 (SF)
1962—49ers, 21-13 (B)
Colts, 22-3 (SF)
1963—Colts, 20-14 (SF)
Colts, 20-3 (B)
1964—Colts, 37-7 (B)
Colts, 14-3 (SF)
1965—Colts, 27-24 (B)
Colts, 34-28 (SF)
1966—Colts, 36-14 (B)
Colts, 30-14 (SF)
1967—Colts, 41-7 (B)
Colts, 26-9 (SF)
1968—Colts, 27-10 (B)
Colts, 42-14 (SF)
1969—49ers, 24-21 (B)
49ers, 20-17 (SF)
1972—49ers, 24-21 (SF)
(Points—Colts 836, 49ers 663)

**BALTIMORE vs. SEATTLE**
Colts lead series, 2-0
1977—Colts, 29-14 (S)
1978—Colts, 17-14 (S)
(Points—Colts 46, Seahawks 28)

**BALTIMORE vs. TAMPA BAY**
Series tied, 1-1
1976—Colts, 42-17 (B)
1979—Buccaneers, 29-26 (B) OT
(Points—Colts 68, Buccaneers 46)

**BALTIMORE vs. WASHINGTON**
Colts lead series, 15-5
1953—Colts, 27-17 (B)
1954—Redskins, 24-21 (W)
1955—Redskins, 14-13 (B)
1956—Colts, 19-17 (B)
1957—Colts, 21-17 (W)
1958—Colts, 35-10 (B)
1959—Redskins, 27-24 (W)
1960—Colts, 20-0 (B)
1961—Colts, 27-6 (W)
1962—Colts, 34-21 (B)
1963—Colts, 36-20 (W)
1964—Colts, 45-17 (B)
1965—Colts, 38-7 (W)
1966—Colts, 37-10 (B)
1967—Colts, 17-13 (W)
1969—Colts, 41-17 (B)
1973—Redskins, 22-14 (W)
1977—Colts, 10-3 (B)
1978—Colts, 21-17 (B)
1981—Redskins, 38-14 (W)
(Points—Colts 514, Redskins 317)

**BUFFALO vs. ATLANTA**
Series tied, 2-2;
See Atlanta vs. Buffalo
**BUFFALO vs. BALTIMORE**
Series tied, 13-13-1;
See Baltimore vs. Buffalo
**BUFFALO vs. CHICAGO**
Bears lead series, 2-1
1970—Bears, 31-13 (C)
1974—Bills, 16-6 (B)
1979—Bears, 7-0 (B)
(Points—Bears 44, Bills 29)
**BUFFALO vs. CINCINNATI**
Bengals lead series, 6-5
1968—Bengals, 34-23 (C)
1969—Bills, 16-13 (B)
1970—Bengals, 43-14 (B)
1973—Bengals, 16-13 (B)
1975—Bengals, 33-24 (C)
1978—Bills, 5-0 (B)
1979—Bills, 51-24 (B)
1980—Bills, 14-0 (C)
1981—Bengals, 27-24 (C) OT
*Bengals, 28-21 (C)
1983—Bills, 10-6 (C)
(Points—Bengals 224, Bills 215)
*AFC Divisional Playoff
**BUFFALO vs. CLEVELAND**
Browns lead series, 3-2
1972—Browns, 27-10 (C)
1974—Bills, 15-10 (C)
1977—Browns, 27-16 (B)
1978—Browns, 41-20 (C)
1981—Bills, 22-13 (B)
(Points—Browns 118, Bills 83)
**BUFFALO vs. DALLAS**
Cowboys lead series, 3-0
1971—Cowboys, 49-37 (B)
1976—Cowboys, 17-10 (D)

1981—Cowboys, 27-14 (D)
(Points—Cowboys 93, Bills 61)
**BUFFALO vs. DENVER**
Bills lead series, 13-8-1
1960—Broncos, 27-21 (B)
Tie, 38-38 (D)
1961—Broncos, 22-10 (B)
Bills, 23-10 (D)
1962—Broncos, 23-20 (B)
Bills, 45-38 (D)
1963—Bills, 30-28 (D)
Bills, 27-17 (B)
1964—Bills, 30-13 (B)
Bills, 30-19 (D)
1965—Bills, 30-15 (D)
Bills, 31-13 (B)
1966—Bills, 38-21 (B)
1967—Bills, 17-16 (D)
Broncos, 21-20 (B)
1968—Broncos, 34-32 (D)
1969—Bills, 41-28 (B)
1970—Broncos, 25-10 (B)
1977—Broncos, 26-6 (D)
1979—Broncos, 19-16 (B)
1981—Bills, 9-7 (B)
(Points—Bills 562, Broncos 474)
**BUFFALO vs. DETROIT**
Series tied, 1-1-1
1972—Tie, 21-21 (B)
1976—Lions, 27-14 (D)
1979—Lions, 20-17 (D)
(Points—Lions 65, Bills 55)
**BUFFALO vs. GREEN BAY**
Bills lead series, 2-1
1974—Bills, 27-7 (GB)
1979—Bills, 19-12 (B)
1982—Packers, 33-21 (Mil)
(Points—Bills 67, Packers 52)
**BUFFALO vs. HOUSTON**
Oilers lead series, 17-8
1960—Bills, 25-24 (B)
Oilers, 31-23 (H)
1961—Bills, 22-12 (H)
Oilers, 28-16 (B)
1962—Oilers, 28-23 (B)
Oilers, 17-14 (H)
1963—Oilers, 31-20 (H)
Oilers, 28-14 (H)
1964—Bills, 48-17 (H)
Bills, 24-10 (B)
1965—Oilers, 19-17 (B)
Bills, 29-18 (H)
1966—Bills, 27-20 (B)
Bills, 42-20 (H)
1967—Oilers, 20-3 (B)
Oilers, 10-3 (H)
1968—Oilers, 30-7 (B)
Oilers, 35-6 (H)
1969—Oilers, 17-3 (B)
Oilers, 28-14 (H)
1971—Oilers, 20-14 (B)
1974—Oilers, 21-9 (B)
1976—Oilers, 13-3 (B)
1978—Oilers, 17-10 (H)
1983—Bills, 30-13 (B)
(Points—Oilers 527, Bills 446)
**BUFFALO vs. *KANSAS CITY**
Bills lead series, 14-11-1
1960—Texans, 45-28 (B)
Texans, 24-7 (D)
1961—Bills, 27-24 (B)
Bills, 30-20 (D)
1962—Texans, 41-21 (D)
Bills, 23-14 (B)
1963—Tie, 27-27 (B)
Bills, 35-26 (KC)
1964—Bills, 34-17 (B)
Bills, 35-22 (KC)
1965—Bills, 23-7 (KC)
Bills, 34-25 (B)
1966—Chiefs, 42-20 (B)
Bills, 29-14 (KC)
**Chiefs, 31-7 (B)
1967—Chiefs, 23-13 (KC)
1968—Chiefs, 18-7 (B)
1969—Chiefs, 29-7 (B)
Chiefs, 22-19 (KC)
1971—Chiefs, 22-9 (KC)
1973—Bills, 23-14 (B)
1976—Bills, 50-17 (B)
1978—Bills, 28-13 (B)
Chiefs, 14-10 (KC)
1982—Bills, 14-9 (B)
1983—Bills, 14-9 (KC)
(Points—Chiefs 574, Bills 569)
*Franchise in Dallas prior to 1963 and
known as Texans
**AFL Championship
**BUFFALO vs. *L.A. RAIDERS**
Raiders lead series, 12-11
1960—Bills, 38-9 (B)
Raiders, 20-7 (O)

1961—Raiders, 31-22 (B)
Bills, 26-21 (O)
1962—Bills, 14-6 (O)
Bills, 10-6 (O)
1963—Raiders, 35-17 (O)
Bills, 12-0 (B)
1964—Bills, 23-20 (B)
Raiders, 16-13 (O)
1965—Bills, 17-12 (B)
Bills, 17-14 (O)
1966—Bills, 31-10 (O)
1967—Raiders, 24-20 (B)
Raiders, 28-21 (O)
1968—Raiders, 48-6 (B)
Raiders, 13-10 (O)
1969—Raiders, 50-21 (O)
1972—Raiders, 28-16 (O)
1974—Bills, 21-20 (B)
1977—Raiders, 34-13 (O)
1980—Bills, 24-7 (B)
1983—Raiders, 27-24 (B)
(Points—Raiders 479, Bills 423)
*Franchise in Oakland prior to 1982
**BUFFALO vs. L.A. RAMS**
Rams lead series, 3-1
1970—Rams, 19-0 (B)
1974—Rams, 19-14 (B)
1980—Bills, 10-7 (B) OT
1983—Rams, 41-17 (LA)
(Points—Rams 86, Bills 41)
**BUFFALO vs. MIAMI**
Dolphins lead series, 28-7-1
1966—Bills, 58-24 (B)
Bills, 29-0 (M)
1967—Bills, 35-13 (B)
Dolphins, 17-14 (M)
1968—Tie, 14-14 (M)
Dolphins, 21-17 (B)
1969—Dolphins, 24-6 (M)
Bills, 28-3 (B)
1970—Dolphins, 33-14 (B)
Dolphins, 45-7 (M)
1971—Dolphins, 29-14 (B)
Dolphins, 34-0 (M)
1972—Dolphins, 24-23 (B)
Dolphins, 30-16 (M)
1973—Dolphins, 27-6 (M)
Dolphins, 17-0 (B)
1974—Dolphins, 24-16 (B)
Dolphins, 35-28 (M)
1975—Dolphins, 35-30 (B)
Dolphins, 31-21 (M)
1976—Dolphins, 30-21 (B)
Dolphins, 45-27 (M)
1977—Dolphins, 13-0 (B)
Dolphins, 31-14 (M)
1978—Dolphins, 31-24 (B)
Dolphins, 25-24 (M)
1979—Dolphins, 9-7 (B)
Dolphins, 17-7 (M)
1980—Bills, 17-7 (B)
Dolphins, 17-14 (M)
1981—Bills, 31-21 (B)
Dolphins, 16-6 (M)
1982—Dolphins, 9-7 (B)
Dolphins, 27-10 (M)
1983—Dolphins, 12-0 (B)
Bills, 38-35 (M) OT
(Points—Dolphins 825, Bills 623)
**BUFFALO vs. MINNESOTA**
Vikings lead series, 3-1
1971—Vikings, 19-0 (M)
1975—Vikings, 35-13 (M)
1979—Vikings, 10-3 (M)
1982—Bills, 23-22 (B)
(Points—Vikings 86, Bills 39)
**BUFFALO vs. *NEW ENGLAND**
Patriots lead series, 24-23-1
1960—Bills, 13-0 (B)
Bills, 38-14 (Buff)
1961—Patriots, 23-21 (Buff)
Patriots, 52-21 (B)
1962—Tie, 28-28 (Buff)
Patriots, 21-10 (B)
1963—Bills, 28-21 (Buff)
Patriots, 17-7 (B)
**Patriots, 26-8 (Buff)
1964—Patriots, 36-28 (Buff)
Bills, 24-14 (B)
1965—Bills, 24-7 (Buff)
Bills, 23-7 (B)
1966—Patriots, 20-10 (Buff)
Patriots, 14-3 (B)
1967—Patriots, 23-0 (Buff)
Bills, 44-16 (B)
1968—Patriots, 16-7 (Buff)
Patriots, 23-6 (B)
1969—Bills, 23-16 (Buff)
Patriots, 35-21 (B)
1970—Bills, 45-10 (B)
Patriots, 14-10 (Buff)
1971—Patriots, 38-33 (NE)
Bills, 27-20 (Buff)

1972—Bills, 38-14 (Buff)
Bills, 27-24 (NE)
1973—Bills, 31-13 (NE)
Bills, 37-13 (Buff)
1974—Bills, 30-28 (Buff)
Bills, 29-28 (NE)
1975—Bills, 45-31 (Buff)
Bills, 34-14 (NE)
1976—Patriots, 26-22 (Buff)
Patriots, 20-10 (NE)
1977—Bills, 24-14 (NE)
Patriots, 20-7 (Buff)
1978—Patriots, 14-10 (Buff)
Patriots, 26-24 (NE)
1979—Patriots, 26-6 (Buff)
Bills, 16-13 (NE) OT
1980—Bills, 31-13 (Buff)
Patriots, 24-2 (NE)
1981—Bills, 20-17 (Buff)
Bills, 19-10 (NE)
1982—Patriots, 30-19 (NE)
1983—Patriots, 31-0 (Buff)
Patriots, 21-7 (NE)
(Points—Bills 990, Patriots 981)
*Franchise in Boston prior to 1971
**Division Playoff
**BUFFALO vs. NEW ORLEANS**
Bills lead series, 2-1
1973—Saints, 13-0 (NO)
1980—Bills, 35-26 (NO)
1983—Bills, 27-21 (B)
(Points—Bills 62, Saints 60)
**BUFFALO vs. N.Y. GIANTS**
Giants lead series, 2-1
1970—Giants, 20-6 (NY)
1975—Giants, 17-14 (B)
1978—Bills, 41-17 (B)
(Points—Bills 61, Giants 54)
**BUFFALO vs. *N.Y. JETS**
Bills lead series, 26-21
1960—Titans, 27-3 (NY)
Titans, 17-13 (NY)
1961—Bills, 41-31 (B)
Titans, 21-14 (NY)
1962—Titans, 17-6 (B)
Bills, 20-3 (NY)
1963—Bills, 45-14 (B)
Bills, 19-10 (NY)
1964—Bills, 34-24 (B)
Bills, 20-7 (NY)
1965—Bills, 33-21 (B)
Jets, 14-12 (NY)
1966—Bills, 33-23 (NY)
Bills, 14-3 (B)
1967—Bills, 20-17 (B)
Jets, 20-10 (NY)
1968—Bills, 37-35 (B)
Jets, 25-21 (NY)
1969—Jets, 33-19 (B)
Jets, 16-6 (NY)
1970—Jets, 34-31 (B)
Bills, 10-6 (NY)
1971—Jets, 28-17 (B)
Jets, 20-7 (B)
1972—Jets, 41-24 (B)
Jets, 41-3 (NY)
1973—Bills, 9-7 (B)
Bills, 34-14 (NY)
1974—Bills, 16-12 (B)
Jets, 20-10 (NY)
1975—Bills, 42-14 (B)
Bills, 24-23 (NY)
1976—Jets, 17-14 (NY)
Jets, 19-14 (B)
1977—Jets, 24-19 (B)
Bills, 14-10 (NY)
1978—Jets, 21-20 (B)
Jets, 45-14 (NY)
1979—Bills, 46-31 (B)
Bills, 14-12 (NY)
1980—Bills, 20-10 (B)
Bills, 31-24 (NY)
1981—Bills, 31-0 (B)
Jets, 33-14 (NY)
**Bills, 31-27 (NY)
1983—Jets, 34-10 (B)
Bills, 24-17 (NY)
(Points—Bills 966, Jets 959)
*Jets known as Titans prior to 1963
**AFC First Round Playoff
**BUFFALO vs. PHILADELPHIA**
Series tied, 1-1
1973—Bills, 27-26 (B)
1981—Eagles, 20-14 (B)
(Points—Eagles 46, Bills 41)
**BUFFALO vs. PITTSBURGH**
Steelers lead series, 5-3
1970—Steelers, 23-10 (P)
1972—Steelers, 38-21 (B)
1974—*Steelers, 32-14 (P)
1975—Bills, 30-21 (P)
1978—Steelers, 28-17 (B)
1979—Steelers, 28-0 (P)

**1980**—Bills, 28-13 (B)
**1982**—Bills, 13-0 (B)
(Points—Steelers 183, Bills 133)
*AFC Divisional Playoff
**BUFFALO vs. ST. LOUIS**
Cardinals lead series, 2-1
**1971**—Cardinals, 28-23 (B)
**1975**—Bills, 32-14 (StL)
**1981**—Cardinals, 24-0 (StL)
(Points—Cardinals 66, Bills 55)
**BUFFALO vs. *SAN DIEGO**
Chargers lead series, 15-9-2
**1960**—Chargers, 24-10 (B)
　　　　Bills, 32-3 (LA)
**1961**—Chargers, 19-11 (B)
　　　　Chargers, 28-10 (SD)
**1962**—Bills, 35-10 (B)
　　　　Bills, 40-20 (SD)
**1963**—Chargers, 14-10 (SD)
　　　　Chargers, 23-13 (B)
**1964**—Bills, 30-3 (B)
　　　　Bills, 27-24 (SD)
　　　　**Bills, 20-7 (B)
**1965**—Chargers, 34-3 (B)
　　　　Tie, 20-20 (SD)
　　　　**Bills, 23-0 (SD)
**1966**—Chargers, 27-7 (SD)
　　　　Tie, 17-17 (B)
**1967**—Chargers, 37-17 (B)
**1968**—Chargers, 21-6 (B)
**1969**—Chargers, 45-6 (B)
**1971**—Chargers, 20-3 (SD)
**1973**—Chargers, 34-7 (SD)
**1976**—Chargers, 34-13 (B)
**1979**—Chargers, 27-19 (SD)
**1980**—Bills, 26-24 (SD)
　　　　***Chargers, 20-14 (SD)
**1981**—Bills, 28-27 (SD)
(Points—Chargers 562, Bills 447)
*Franchise in Los Angeles prior to 1961
**AFL Championship
***AFC Divisional Playoff
**BUFFALO vs. SAN FRANCISCO**
Bills lead series, 2-1
**1972**—Bills, 27-20 (B)
**1980**—Bills, 18-13 (SF)
**1983**—49ers, 23-10 (B)
(Points—49ers 56, Bills 55)
**BUFFALO vs. SEATTLE**
Seahawks lead series, 1-0
**1977**—Seahawks, 56-17 (S)
**BUFFALO vs. TAMPA BAY**
Buccaneers lead series, 2-1
**1976**—Bills, 14-9 (TB)
**1978**—Buccaneers, 31-10 (TB)
**1982**—Buccaneers, 24-23 (TB)
(Points—Buccaneers 64, Bills 47)
**BUFFALO vs. WASHINGTON**
Bills lead series, 2-1
**1972**—Bills, 24-17 (W)
**1977**—Redskins, 10-0 (B)
**1981**—Bills, 21-14 (B)
(Points—Bills 45, Redskins 41)

**CHICAGO vs. ATLANTA**
Falcons lead series, 9-4;
See Atlanta vs. Chicago
**CHICAGO vs. BALTIMORE**
Colts lead series, 21-13;
See Baltimore vs. Chicago
**CHICAGO vs. BUFFALO**
Bears lead series, 2-1;
See Buffalo vs. Chicago
**CHICAGO vs. CINCINNATI**
Bengals lead series, 2-0;
**1972**—Bengals, 13-3 (Chi)
**1980**—Bengals, 17-14 (Chi) OT
(Points—Bengals 30, Bears 17)
**CHICAGO vs. CLEVELAND**
Browns lead series, 6-2
**1951**—Browns, 42-21 (Cle)
**1954**—Browns, 39-10 (Chi)
**1960**—Browns, 42-0 (Cle)
**1961**—Bears, 17-14 (Chi)
**1967**—Browns, 24-0 (Cle)
**1969**—Browns, 28-24 (Chi)
**1972**—Bears, 17-0 (Cle)
**1980**—Browns, 27-21 (Cle)
(Points—Browns 216, Bears 110)
**CHICAGO vs. DALLAS**
Cowboys lead series, 7-3
**1960**—Bears, 17-7 (C)
**1962**—Bears, 34-33 (D)
**1964**—Cowboys, 24-10 (C)
**1968**—Cowboys, 34-3 (C)
**1971**—Bears, 23-19 (C)
**1973**—Cowboys, 20-17 (C)
**1976**—Cowboys, 31-21 (D)
**1977**—*Cowboys, 37-7 (D)
**1979**—Cowboys, 24-20 (D)
**1981**—Cowboys, 10-9 (C)
(Points—Cowboys 239, Bears 161)
*NFC Divisional Playoff

**CHICAGO vs. DENVER**
Series tied, 3-3
**1971**—Broncos, 6-3 (D)
**1973**—Bears, 33-14 (D)
**1976**—Broncos, 28-14 (D)
**1978**—Broncos, 16-7 (D)
**1981**—Bears, 35-24 (C)
**1983**—Bears, 31-14 (C)
(Points—Bears 123, Broncos 102)
**CHICAGO vs. *DETROIT**
Bears lead series, 60-44-5
**1930**—Spartans, 7-6 (P)
　　　　Bears, 14-6 (C)
**1931**—Bears, 9-6 (C)
　　　　Spartans, 3-0 (P)
**1932**—Tie, 13-13 (C)
　　　　Tie, 7-7 (P)
　　　　**Bears, 9-0 (C)
**1933**—Bears, 17-14 (C)
　　　　Bears, 17-7 (P)
**1934**—Bears, 19-16 (D)
　　　　Bears, 10-7 (C)
**1935**—Tie, 20-20 (C)
　　　　Lions, 14-2 (D)
**1936**—Bears, 12-10 (C)
　　　　Lions, 13-7 (D)
**1937**—Bears, 28-20 (C)
　　　　Bears, 13-0 (D)
**1938**—Lions, 13-7 (C)
　　　　Lions, 14-7 (D)
**1939**—Bears, 10-0 (C)
　　　　Bears, 23-13 (D)
**1940**—Bears, 7-0 (C)
　　　　Lions, 17-14 (D)
**1941**—Bears, 49-0 (C)
　　　　Bears, 24-7 (D)
**1942**—Bears, 16-0 (C)
　　　　Bears, 42-0 (D)
**1943**—Bears, 27-21 (C)
　　　　Bears, 35-14 (C)
**1944**—Tie, 21-21 (C)
　　　　Lions, 41-21 (D)
**1945**—Lions, 16-10 (D)
　　　　Lions, 35-28 (C)
**1946**—Bears, 42-6 (C)
　　　　Bears, 45-24 (D)
**1947**—Bears, 33-24 (C)
　　　　Bears, 34-14 (D)
**1948**—Bears, 28-0 (C)
　　　　Bears, 42-14 (D)
**1949**—Bears, 27-24 (C)
　　　　Bears, 28-7 (D)
**1950**—Bears, 35-21 (D)
　　　　Bears, 6-3 (C)
**1951**—Bears, 28-23 (D)
　　　　Lions, 41-28 (C)
**1952**—Bears, 24-23 (C)
　　　　Lions, 45-21 (D)
**1953**—Lions, 20-16 (C)
　　　　Lions, 13-7 (D)
**1954**—Lions, 48-23 (C)
　　　　Bears, 28-24 (C)
**1955**—Bears, 24-14 (D)
　　　　Bears, 21-20 (C)
**1956**—Lions, 42-10 (D)
　　　　Bears, 38-21 (C)
**1957**—Bears, 27-7 (D)
　　　　Lions, 21-13 (C)
**1958**—Bears, 20-7 (D)
　　　　Bears, 21-16 (C)
**1959**—Bears, 24-14 (D)
　　　　Bears, 25-14 (C)
**1960**—Bears, 28-7 (C)
　　　　Lions, 36-0 (D)
**1961**—Bears, 31-17 (D)
　　　　Lions, 16-15 (C)
**1962**—Lions, 11-3 (D)
　　　　Bears, 3-0 (C)
**1963**—Bears, 37-21 (D)
　　　　Bears, 24-14 (C)
**1964**—Lions, 10-0 (C)
　　　　Bears, 27-24 (D)
**1965**—Bears, 38-10 (C)
　　　　Bears, 17-10 (D)
**1966**—Lions, 14-3 (D)
　　　　Tie, 10-10 (C)
**1967**—Bears, 14-3 (C)
　　　　Bears, 27-13 (D)
**1968**—Lions, 42-0 (D)
　　　　Bears, 28-10 (C)
**1969**—Lions, 13-7 (D)
　　　　Lions, 20-3 (C)
**1970**—Lions, 28-14 (D)
　　　　Lions, 16-10 (C)
**1971**—Bears, 28-23 (D)
　　　　Lions, 28-3 (C)
**1972**—Lions, 38-24 (D)
　　　　Lions, 14-0 (C)
**1973**—Lions, 30-7 (C)
　　　　Lions, 40-7 (D)
**1974**—Lions, 17-9 (C)
　　　　Lions, 34-17 (D)
**1975**—Lions, 27-7 (D)

**1976**—Bears, 10-3 (C)
　　　　Lions, 14-10 (D)
**1977**—Bears, 30-20 (C)
　　　　Bears, 31-14 (D)
**1978**—Bears, 19-0 (D)
　　　　Lions, 21-17 (C)
**1979**—Bears, 35-7 (C)
　　　　Lions, 20-0 (D)
**1980**—Bears, 24-7 (C)
　　　　Bears, 23-17 (D) OT
**1981**—Lions, 48-17 (D)
　　　　Lions, 23-7 (C)
**1982**—Lions, 17-10 (D)
　　　　Bears, 20-17 (C)
**1983**—Lions, 31-17 (D)
　　　　Lions, 38-17 (C)
(Points—Bears 1,995, Lions 1,859)
*Franchise in Portsmouth prior to 1934
and known as the Spartans
**Championship
**CHICAGO vs. GREEN BAY**
Bears lead series, 67-54-6
**1921**—Staleys, 20-0 (C)
**1923**—Bears, 3-0 (GB)
**1924**—Bears, 3-0 (C)
**1925**—Packers, 14-10 (GB)
　　　　Bears, 21-0 (C)
**1926**—Tie, 6-6 (GB)
　　　　Bears, 19-13 (C)
　　　　Tie, 3-3 (C)
**1927**—Bears, 7-6 (GB)
　　　　Bears, 14-6 (C)
**1928**—Tie, 12-12 (GB)
　　　　Packers, 16-6 (C)
　　　　Packers, 6-0 (C)
**1929**—Packers, 23-0 (GB)
　　　　Packers, 14-0 (C)
　　　　Packers, 25-0 (C)
**1930**—Packers, 7-0 (GB)
　　　　Packers, 13-12 (C)
　　　　Bears, 21-0 (C)
**1931**—Packers, 7-0 (GB)
　　　　Packers, 6-2 (C)
　　　　Bears, 7-6 (C)
**1932**—Tie, 0-0 (GB)
　　　　Packers, 2-0 (C)
　　　　Bears, 9-0 (C)
**1933**—Bears, 14-7 (GB)
　　　　Bears, 10-7 (C)
　　　　Bears, 7-6 (C)
**1934**—Bears, 24-10 (GB)
　　　　Bears, 27-14 (C)
**1935**—Packers, 7-0 (GB)
　　　　Packers, 17-14 (C)
**1936**—Bears, 30-3 (GB)
　　　　Packers, 21-10 (C)
**1937**—Bears, 14-2 (GB)
　　　　Packers, 24-14 (C)
**1938**—Bears, 2-0 (GB)
　　　　Packers, 24-17 (C)
**1939**—Packers, 21-16 (GB)
　　　　Bears, 30-27 (C)
**1940**—Bears, 41-10 (GB)
　　　　Bears, 14-7 (C)
**1941**—Bears, 25-17 (GB)
　　　　Packers, 16-14 (C)
　　　　**Bears, 33-14 (C)
**1942**—Bears, 44-28 (GB)
　　　　Bears, 38-7 (C)
**1943**—Tie, 21-21 (GB)
　　　　Bears, 21-7 (C)
**1944**—Packers, 42-28 (GB)
　　　　Bears, 21-0 (C)
**1945**—Packers, 31-21 (GB)
　　　　Bears, 28-24 (C)
**1946**—Bears, 30-7 (GB)
　　　　Bears, 10-7 (C)
**1947**—Packers, 29-20 (GB)
　　　　Bears, 20-17 (C)
**1948**—Bears, 45-7 (GB)
　　　　Bears, 7-6 (C)
**1949**—Bears, 17-0 (GB)
　　　　Bears, 24-3 (C)
**1950**—Packers, 31-21 (GB)
　　　　Bears, 28-14 (C)
**1951**—Bears, 31-20 (GB)
　　　　Bears, 24-13 (C)
**1952**—Bears, 24-14 (GB)
　　　　Packers, 41-28 (C)
**1953**—Bears, 17-13 (GB)
　　　　Tie, 21-21 (C)
**1954**—Bears, 10-3 (GB)
　　　　Bears, 28-23 (C)
**1955**—Packers, 24-3 (GB)
　　　　Bears, 52-31 (C)
**1956**—Bears, 37-21 (GB)
　　　　Bears, 38-14 (C)
**1957**—Packers, 21-17 (GB)
　　　　Bears, 21-14 (C)
**1958**—Bears, 34-20 (GB)
　　　　Bears, 24-10 (C)
**1959**—Packers, 9-6 (GB)

**1960**—Bears, 17-14 (GB)
　　　　Packers, 41-13 (C)
**1961**—Packers, 24-0 (GB)
　　　　Packers, 31-28 (C)
**1962**—Packers, 49-0 (GB)
　　　　Packers, 38-7 (C)
**1963**—Bears, 10-3 (GB)
　　　　Bears, 26-7 (C)
**1964**—Packers, 23-12 (GB)
　　　　Packers, 17-3 (C)
**1965**—Packers, 23-14 (GB)
　　　　Bears, 31-10 (C)
**1966**—Packers, 17-0 (C)
　　　　Packers, 13-6 (GB)
**1967**—Packers, 13-10 (GB)
　　　　Packers, 17-13 (C)
**1968**—Bears, 13-10 (C)
　　　　Packers, 28-27 (C)
**1969**—Packers, 17-0 (C)
　　　　Packers, 21-3 (C)
**1970**—Packers, 20-19 (GB)
　　　　Bears, 35-17 (C)
**1971**—Packers, 17-14 (GB)
　　　　Packers, 31-10 (C)
**1972**—Packers, 20-17 (GB)
　　　　Bears, 23-17 (C)
**1973**—Bears, 31-17 (GB)
　　　　Packers, 21-0 (C)
**1974**—Bears, 10-9 (C)
　　　　Packers, 20-3 (Mil)
**1975**—Bears, 27-14 (C)
　　　　Packers, 28-7 (GB)
**1976**—Bears, 24-13 (C)
　　　　Bears, 16-10 (GB)
**1977**—Bears, 26-0 (C)
　　　　Bears, 21-10 (GB)
**1978**—Packers, 24-14 (GB)
　　　　Bears, 14-0 (C)
**1979**—Bears, 6-3 (C)
　　　　Bears, 15-14 (GB)
**1980**—Packers, 12-6 (GB) OT
　　　　Bears, 61-7 (C)
**1981**—Packers, 16-9 (C)
　　　　Packers, 21-17 (GB)
**1983**—Packers, 31-28 (GB)
　　　　Bears, 23-21 (C)
(Points—Bears 2,121, Packers 1,884)
*Bears known as Staleys prior to 1922
**Division Playoff
**CHICAGO vs. HOUSTON**
Oilers lead series, 2-1
**1973**—Bears, 35-14 (C)
**1977**—Oilers, 47-0 (H)
**1980**—Oilers, 10-6 (C)
(Points—Oilers 71, Bears 41)
**CHICAGO vs. KANSAS CITY**
Bears lead series, 2-1
**1973**—Chiefs, 19-7 (KC)
**1977**—Bears, 28-27 (C)
**1981**—Bears, 16-13 (KC) OT
(Points—Chiefs 59, Bears 51)
**CHICAGO vs. *L.A. RAIDERS**
Raiders lead series, 3-1
**1972**—Raiders, 28-21 (O)
**1976**—Raiders, 28-27 (C)
**1978**—Raiders, 25-19 (C) OT
**1981**—Bears, 23-6 (O)
(Points—Raiders 90, Bears 87)
*Franchise in Oakland prior to 1982
**CHICAGO vs. *L.A. RAMS**
Bears lead series, 42-26-3
**1937**—Bears, 20-2 (Clev)
　　　　Bears, 15-7 (C)
**1938**—Rams, 14-7 (C)
　　　　Rams, 23-21 (Clev)
**1939**—Bears, 30-21 (Clev)
　　　　Bears, 35-21 (C)
**1940**—Bears, 21-14 (Clev)
　　　　Bears, 47-25 (C)
**1941**—Bears, 48-21 (Clev)
　　　　Bears, 31-13 (C)
**1942**—Bears, 21-7 (Clev)
　　　　Bears, 47-0 (C)
**1944**—Rams, 19-7 (Clev)
　　　　Bears, 28-21 (C)
**1945**—Rams, 17-0 (Clev)
　　　　Rams, 41-21 (C)
**1946**—Tie, 28-28 (C)
　　　　Bears, 27-21 (LA)
**1947**—Bears, 41-21 (LA)
　　　　Rams, 17-14 (C)
**1948**—Bears, 42-21 (C)
　　　　Bears, 21-6 (LA)
**1949**—Rams, 31-16 (C)
　　　　Rams, 27-24 (LA)
**1950**—Bears, 24-20 (LA)
　　　　Bears, 24-14 (C)
　　　　**Rams, 24-14 (LA)
**1951**—Rams, 42-17 (C)
**1952**—Rams, 31-7 (LA)
　　　　Rams, 40-24 (C)
**1953**—Rams, 38-24 (LA)

Bears, 24-21 (C)
1954—Rams, 42-38 (LA)
　　　Bears, 24-13 (C)
1955—Bears, 31-20 (LA)
　　　Bears, 24-3 (C)
1956—Bears, 35-24 (LA)
　　　Bears, 30-21 (C)
1957—Bears, 34-26 (C)
　　　Bears, 16-10 (LA)
1958—Bears, 31-10 (C)
　　　Rams, 41-35 (LA)
1959—Rams, 28-21 (C)
　　　Bears, 26-21 (LA)
1960—Bears, 34-27 (C)
　　　Tie, 24-24 (LA)
1961—Bears, 21-17 (LA)
　　　Bears, 28-24 (C)
1962—Bears, 27-23 (LA)
　　　Bears, 30-14 (C)
1963—Bears, 52-14 (LA)
　　　Bears, 6-0 (C)
1964—Bears, 38-17 (C)
　　　Bears, 34-24 (LA)
1965—Rams, 30-28 (LA)
　　　Bears, 31-6 (C)
1966—Rams, 31-17 (LA)
　　　Bears, 17-10 (C)
1967—Rams, 28-17 (LA)
1968—Rams, 17-16 (LA)
1969—Rams, 9-7 (C)
1971—Rams, 17-3 (LA)
1972—Tie, 13-13 (C)
1973—Rams, 26-0 (C)
1975—Rams, 38-10 (LA)
1976—Rams, 20-12 (LA)
1977—Bears, 24-23 (C)
1979—Bears, 27-23 (C)
1981—Rams, 24-7 (C)
1982—Bears, 34-26 (LA)
1983—Rams, 21-14 (LA)
(Points—Bears 1,687, Rams 1,472)
*Franchise in Cleveland prior to 1946
**Conference Playoff

## CHICAGO vs. MIAMI
Dolphins lead series, 3-0
1971—Dolphins, 34-3 (M)
1975—Dolphins, 46-13 (C)
1979—Dolphins, 31-16 (M)
(Points—Dolphins 111, Bears 32)

## CHICAGO vs. MINNESOTA
Vikings lead series, 25-18-2
1961—Vikings, 37-13 (C)
　　　Bears, 52-35 (C)
1962—Bears, 13-0 (M)
　　　Bears, 31-30 (C)
1963—Bears, 28-7 (M)
　　　Tie, 17-17 (C)
1964—Bears, 34-28 (M)
　　　Vikings, 41-14 (C)
1965—Bears, 45-37 (M)
　　　Vikings, 24-17 (C)
1966—Bears, 13-10 (M)
　　　Bears, 41-28 (C)
1967—Bears, 17-7 (M)
　　　Tie, 10-10 (C)
1968—Bears, 27-17 (M)
　　　Bears, 26-24 (C)
1969—Vikings, 31-0 (C)
　　　Vikings, 31-14 (M)
1970—Vikings, 24-0 (C)
　　　Vikings, 16-13 (M)
1971—Bears, 20-17 (M)
　　　Vikings, 27-10 (C)
1972—Bears, 13-10 (C)
　　　Vikings, 23-10 (M)
1973—Vikings, 22-13 (C)
　　　Vikings, 31-13 (M)
1974—Vikings, 11-7 (M)
　　　Vikings, 17-0 (C)
1975—Vikings, 28-3 (C)
　　　Vikings, 13-9 (M)
1976—Vikings, 20-19 (M)
　　　Bears, 14-13 (C)
1977—Vikings, 22-16 (M) OT
　　　Bears, 10-7 (C)
1978—Vikings, 24-20 (C)
　　　Vikings, 17-14 (M)
1979—Bears, 26-7 (C)
　　　Vikings, 30-27 (M)
1980—Bears, 34-14 (C)
　　　Vikings, 13-7 (M)
1981—Vikings, 24-21 (M)
　　　Bears, 10-9 (C)
1982—Vikings, 35-7 (M)
1983—Vikings, 23-14 (C)
　　　Bears, 19-13 (M)
(Points—Vikings 944, Bears 761)

## CHICAGO vs. NEW ENGLAND
Patriots lead series, 2-1
1973—Patriots, 13-10 (C)
1979—Patriots, 27-7 (C)
1982—Bears, 26-13 (C)
(Points—Patriots 53, Bears 43)

## CHICAGO vs. NEW ORLEANS
Bears lead series, 6-4
1968—Bears, 23-17 (NO)
1970—Bears, 24-3 (NO)
1971—Bears, 35-14 (C)
1973—Saints, 21-16 (NO)
1974—Bears, 24-10 (C)
1975—Bears, 42-17 (NO)
1977—Saints, 42-24 (C)
1980—Bears, 22-3 (C)
1982—Saints, 10-0 (C)
1983—Saints, 34-31 (NO) OT
(Points—Bears 241, Saints 171)

## CHICAGO vs. N.Y. GIANTS
Bears lead series, 26-16-2
1925—Bears, 19-7 (NY)
　　　Giants, 9-0 (C)
1926—Bears, 7-0 (C)
1927—Giants, 13-7 (NY)
1928—Bears, 13-0 (C)
1929—Giants, 26-14 (C)
　　　Giants, 34-0 (NY)
　　　Giants, 14-9 (C)
1930—Giants, 12-0 (C)
　　　Bears, 12-0 (NY)
1931—Bears, 6-0 (C)
　　　Bears, 12-6 (NY)
　　　Giants, 25-6 (C)
1932—Bears, 28-8 (NY)
　　　Bears, 6-0 (C)
1933—Bears, 14-10 (C)
　　　Giants, 3-0 (NY)
　　　*Bears, 23-21 (C)
1934—Bears, 27-7 (C)
　　　Bears, 10-9 (NY)
　　　*Giants, 30-13 (NY)
1935—Bears, 20-3 (NY)
　　　Giants, 3-0 (C)
1936—Bears, 25-7 (NY)
1937—Tie, 3-3 (NY)
1939—Giants, 16-13 (NY)
1940—Giants, 37-21 (NY)
1941—*Bears, 37-9 (C)
1942—Bears, 26-7 (NY)
1943—Bears, 56-7 (NY)
1946—*Bears, 14-0 (NY)
1948—Bears, 35-14 (C)
1949—Bears, 35-28 (C)
1956—Tie, 17-17 (NY)
　　　*Giants, 47-7 (NY)
1962—Giants, 26-24 (C)
1963—*Bears, 14-10 (C)
1965—Bears, 35-14 (NY)
1967—Bears, 34-7 (C)
1969—Giants, 28-24 (NY)
1970—Bears, 24-16 (NY)
1974—Bears, 16-13 (C)
1977—Bears, 12-9 (NY) OT
(Points—Bears 737, Giants 574)
*NFL Championship

## CHICAGO vs. N.Y. JETS
Series tied, 1-1
1974—Jets, 23-21 (C)
1979—Bears, 23-13 (C)
(Points—Bears 44, Jets 36)

## CHICAGO vs. PHILADELPHIA
Bears lead series, 19-4-1
1933—Tie, 3-3 (P)
1935—Bears, 39-0 (P)
1936—Bears, 17-0 (P)
　　　Bears, 28-7 (P)
1938—Bears, 28-6 (P)
1939—Bears, 27-14 (C)
1941—Bears, 49-14 (P)
1942—Bears, 45-14 (C)
1944—Bears, 28-7 (P)
1946—Bears, 21-14 (C)
1947—Bears, 40-7 (C)
1948—Eagles, 12-7 (P)
1949—Bears, 38-21 (C)
1955—Bears, 17-10 (C)
1961—Eagles, 16-14 (P)
1963—Bears, 16-7 (C)
1968—Bears, 29-16 (P)
1970—Bears, 20-16 (C)
1972—Bears, 21-12 (P)
1975—Bears, 15-13 (C)
1979—*Eagles, 27-17 (P)
1980—Eagles, 17-14 (P)
1983—Bears, 7-6 (P)
　　　Bears, 17-14 (C)
(Points—Bears 557, Eagles 273)
*NFC First Round Playoff

## CHICAGO vs. *PITTSBURGH
Bears lead series, 13-4-1
1934—Bears, 28-0 (P)
1935—Bears, 23-7 (P)
1936—Bears, 27-9 (P)
　　　Bears, 26-6 (P)
1937—Bears, 7-0 (P)
1939—Bears, 32-0 (C)
1941—Bears, 34-7 (C)

1945—Bears, 28-7 (P)
1947—Bears, 49-7 (C)
1949—Bears, 30-21 (C)
1958—Steelers, 24-10 (P)
1959—Bears, 27-21 (C)
1963—Tie, 17-17 (P)
1967—Steelers, 41-13 (P)
1969—Bears, 38-7 (C)
1971—Bears, 17-15 (C)
1975—Steelers, 34-3 (P)
1980—Steelers, 38-3 (P)
(Points—Bears 412, Steelers 261)
*Steelers known as Pirates prior to 1941

## *CHICAGO vs. **ST. LOUIS
Bears lead series, 50-24-6
(NP denotes Normal Park;
Wr denotes Wrigley Field;
Co denotes Comiskey Park;
So denotes Soldier Field;
all Chicago)
1920—Cardinals, 7-6 (NP)
　　　Staleys, 10-0 (Wr)
1921—Tie, 0-0 (Wr)
1922—Cardinals, 6-0 (Co)
　　　Cardinals, 9-0 (Co)
1923—Bears, 3-0 (Wr)
1924—Bears, 6-0 (Wr)
　　　Bears, 21-0 (Co)
1925—Cardinals, 9-0 (Co)
　　　Tie, 0-0 (Wr)
1926—Bears, 16-0 (Wr)
　　　Bears, 10-0 (So)
　　　Tie, 0-0 (Wr)
1927—Bears, 9-0 (NP)
　　　Cardinals, 3-0 (Wr)
1928—Bears, 15-0 (NP)
　　　Bears, 34-0 (Wr)
1929—Tie, 0-0 (Wr)
　　　Cardinals, 40-6 (Co)
1930—Bears, 32-6 (Co)
　　　Bears, 6-0 (Wr)
1931—Bears, 26-13 (Wr)
　　　Bears, 18-7 (Wr)
1932—Tie, 0-0 (Wr)
　　　Bears, 34-0 (Wr)
1933—Bears, 12-9 (Wr)
　　　Bears, 22-6 (Co)
1934—Bears, 20-0 (Wr)
　　　Bears, 17-6 (Wr)
1935—Tie, 7-7 (Wr)
　　　Bears, 13-0 (Wr)
1936—Bears, 7-3 (Wr)
　　　Cardinals, 14-7 (Wr)
1937—Bears, 16-7 (Wr)
　　　Bears, 42-28 (Wr)
1938—Bears, 16-13 (So)
　　　Bears, 34-28 (Wr)
1939—Bears, 44-7 (Wr)
　　　Bears, 48-7 (Co)
1940—Cardinals, 21-7 (Co)
　　　Bears, 31-23 (Wr)
1941—Bears, 53-7 (Wr)
　　　Bears, 34-24 (Co)
1942—Bears, 41-14 (Wr)
　　　Bears, 21-7 (Co)
1943—Bears, 20-0 (Wr)
　　　Bears, 35-24 (Co)
1945—Cardinals, 16-7 (Wr)
　　　Bears, 28-20 (Co)
1946—Bears, 34-17 (Co)
　　　Cardinals, 35-28 (Wr)
1947—Cardinals, 31-7 (Co)
　　　Cardinals, 30-21 (Wr)
1948—Bears, 28-17 (Co)
　　　Cardinals, 24-21 (Wr)
1949—Bears, 17-7 (Co)
　　　Bears, 52-21 (Wr)
1950—Bears, 27-6 (Wr)
　　　Cardinals, 20-10 (Co)
1951—Cardinals, 28-14 (Co)
　　　Cardinals, 24-14 (Wr)
1952—Cardinals, 21-10 (Co)
　　　Bears, 10-7 (Wr)
1953—Cardinals, 24-17 (Wr)
1954—Bears, 29-7 (Co)
1955—Cardinals, 53-14 (Co)
1956—Bears, 10-3 (Wr)
1957—Bears, 14-6 (Co)
1958—Bears, 30-14 (Wr)
1959—Bears, 31-7 (So)
1965—Bears, 34-13 (Wr)
1966—Cardinals, 24-17 (Wr)
1967—Bears, 30-3 (Wr)
1969—Cardinals, 20-17 (StL)
1972—Bears, 27-10 (StL)
1975—Cardinals, 34-20 (So)
1977—Cardinals, 16-13 (StL)
1978—Bears, 17-10 (So)
1979—Bears, 42-6 (So)
1982—Cardinals, 10-7 (So)
(Points—Bears 1,496, Cardinals 939)
*Franchise in Decatur prior to 1921; Bears known as Staleys prior to 1922

**Franchise in Chicago prior to 1960

## CHICAGO vs. SAN DIEGO
Chargers lead series, 3-1
1970—Chargers, 20-7 (C)
1974—Chargers, 28-21 (SD)
1978—Chargers, 40-7 (SD)
1981—Bears, 20-17 (C) OT
(Points—Chargers 105, Bears 55)

## CHICAGO vs. SAN FRANCISCO
Bears lead series, 23-22-1
1950—Bears, 32-20 (SF)
　　　Bears, 17-0 (C)
1951—Bears, 13-7 (C)
1952—49ers, 40-16 (C)
　　　Bears, 20-17 (SF)
1953—49ers, 35-28 (C)
　　　49ers, 24-14 (SF)
1954—49ers, 31-24 (C)
　　　Bears, 31-27 (SF)
1955—49ers, 20-19 (C)
　　　Bears, 34-23 (SF)
1956—Bears, 31-7 (C)
　　　Bears, 38-21 (SF)
1957—49ers, 21-17 (C)
　　　49ers, 21-17 (SF)
1958—Bears, 28-6 (C)
　　　Bears, 27-14 (SF)
1959—49ers, 20-17 (SF)
　　　Bears, 14-3 (C)
1960—Bears, 27-10 (C)
　　　49ers, 25-7 (SF)
1961—Bears, 31-0 (C)
　　　49ers, 41-31 (SF)
1962—Bears, 30-14 (SF)
　　　49ers, 34-27 (C)
1963—49ers, 20-14 (SF)
　　　Bears, 27-7 (C)
1964—49ers, 31-21 (C)
　　　Bears, 23-21 (C)
1965—49ers, 52-24 (SF)
　　　Bears, 61-20 (C)
1966—Tie, 30-30 (C)
　　　49ers, 41-14 (SF)
1967—Bears, 28-14 (SF)
1968—Bears, 27-19 (C)
1969—49ers, 42-21 (SF)
1970—Bears, 37-16 (C)
1971—49ers, 13-0 (SF)
1972—49ers, 34-21 (C)
1974—49ers, 34-0 (C)
1975—49ers, 31-3 (SF)
1976—Bears, 19-12 (C)
1978—Bears, 16-13 (SF)
1979—Bears, 28-27 (SF)
1981—Bears, 28-17 (C)
1983—Bears, 13-3 (C)
(Points—Bears 1,013, 49ers 1,010)

## CHICAGO vs. SEATTLE
Seahawks lead series, 2-1
1976—Bears, 34-7 (S)
1978—Seahawks, 31-29 (C)
1982—Seahawks, 20-14 (S)
(Points—Bears 77, Seahawks 58)

## CHICAGO vs. TAMPA BAY
Bears lead series, 8-4
1977—Bears, 10-0 (C)
1978—Buccaneers, 33-19 (TB)
　　　Bears, 14-3 (C)
1979—Buccaneers, 17-13 (C)
　　　Bears, 14-0 (TB)
1980—Bears, 23-0 (C)
　　　Bears, 14-13 (TB)
1981—Bears, 28-17 (C)
　　　Buccaneers, 20-10 (TB)
1982—Buccaneers, 26-23 (TB) OT
1983—Bears, 17-10 (C)
　　　Bears, 27-0 (TB)
(Points—Bears 212, Buccaneers 139)

## CHICAGO vs. *WASHINGTON
Bears lead series, 18-11-1
1932—Tie, 7-7 (B)
1933—Bears, 7-0 (C)
　　　Redskins, 10-0 (B)
1934—Bears, 21-0 (B)
1935—Bears, 30-14 (B)
1936—Bears, 26-0 (B)
1937—**Redskins, 28-21 (C)
1938—Bears, 31-7 (C)
1940—Redskins, 7-3 (W)
　　　**Bears, 73-0 (W)
1941—Bears, 35-21 (C)
1942—**Redskins, 14-6 (W)
1943—Redskins, 21-7 (W)
　　　**Bears, 41-21 (W)
1945—Redskins, 28-21 (W)
1946—Bears, 24-20 (C)
1947—Bears, 56-20 (W)
1948—Bears, 48-13 (C)
1949—Bears, 31-21 (W)
1951—Bears, 27-0 (C)
1953—Bears, 27-24 (W)
1957—Redskins, 14-3 (C)
1964—Redskins, 27-20 (W)

1968—Redskins, 38-28 (C)
1971—Bears, 16-15 (C)
1974—Redskins, 42-0 (W)
1976—Bears, 33-7 (C)
1978—Bears, 14-10 (W)
1980—Bears, 35-21 (C)
1981—Redskins, 24-7 (C)
(Points—Bears 698, Redskins 474)
*Franchise in Boston prior to 1937 and known as Braves prior to 1933
**NFL Championship

**CINCINNATI vs. ATLANTA**
Bengals lead series, 3-1;
See Atlanta vs. Cincinnati
**CINCINNATI vs. BALTIMORE**
Colts lead series, 5-4;
See Baltimore vs. Cincinnati
**CINCINNATI vs. BUFFALO**
Bengals lead series, 6-5;
See Buffalo vs. Cincinnati
**CINCINNATI vs. CHICAGO**
Bengals lead series, 2-0;
See Chicago vs. Cincinnati
**CINCINNATI vs. CLEVELAND**
Browns lead series, 14-13
1970—Browns, 30-27 (Cle)
        Bengals, 14-10 (Cin)
1971—Browns, 27-24 (Cin)
        Browns, 31-27 (Cle)
1972—Browns, 27-6 (Cle)
        Browns, 27-24 (Cin)
1973—Browns, 17-10 (Cle)
        Bengals, 34-17 (Cin)
1974—Bengals, 33-7 (Cin)
        Bengals, 34-24 (Cle)
1975—Bengals, 24-17 (Cin)
        Browns, 35-23 (Cle)
1976—Bengals, 45-24 (Cin)
        Bengals, 21-6 (Cin)
1977—Browns, 13-3 (Cin)
        Bengals, 10-7 (Cle)
1978—Browns, 13-10 (Cle) OT
        Bengals, 48-16 (Cin)
1979—Browns, 28-27 (Cle)
        Bengals, 16-12 (Cin)
1980—Browns, 31-7 (Cin)
        Browns, 27-24 (Cin)
1981—Browns, 20-17 (Cin)
        Bengals, 41-21 (Cle)
1982—Bengals, 23-10 (Cin)
1983—Browns, 17-7 (Cle)
        Bengals, 28-21 (Cin)
(Points—Bengals 607, Browns 535)
**CINCINNATI vs. DALLAS**
Cowboys lead series, 2-0
1973—Cowboys, 38-10 (D)
1979—Cowboys, 38-13 (D)
(Points—Cowboys 76, Bengals 23)
**CINCINNATI vs. DENVER**
Broncos lead series, 7-6
1968—Bengals, 24-10 (C)
        Broncos, 10-7 (D)
1969—Broncos, 30-23 (C)
        Broncos, 27-16 (D)
1971—Bengals, 24-10 (D)
1972—Bengals, 21-10 (C)
1973—Broncos, 28-10 (D)
1975—Bengals, 17-16 (D)
1976—Bengals, 17-7 (C)
1977—Broncos, 24-13 (C)
1979—Broncos, 10-0 (D)
1981—Bengals, 38-21 (C)
1983—Broncos, 24-17 (D)
(Points—Bengals 227, Broncos 227)
**CINCINNATI vs. DETROIT**
Lions lead series, 2-1
1970—Lions, 38-3 (D)
1974—Lions, 23-19 (C)
1983—Bengals, 17-9 (C)
(Points—Lions 70, Bengals 39)
**CINCINNATI vs. GREEN BAY**
Bengals lead series, 3-2
1971—Packers, 20-17 (GB)
1976—Bengals, 28-7 (C)
1977—Bengals, 17-7 (Mil)
1980—Packers, 14-9 (GB)
1983—Bengals, 34-14 (C)
(Points—Bengals 105, Packers 62)
**CINCINNATI vs. HOUSTON**
Bengals lead series, 17-12-1
1968—Oilers, 27-17 (C)
1969—Tie, 31-31 (H)
1970—Oilers, 20-13 (C)
        Bengals, 30-20 (H)
1971—Oilers, 10-6 (H)
        Bengals, 28-13 (C)
1972—Bengals, 30-7 (C)
        Bengals, 61-17 (H)
1973—Bengals, 24-10 (C)
        Bengals, 27-24 (H)
1974—Oilers, 34-21 (C)
        Oilers, 20-3 (H)

1975—Bengals, 21-19 (H)
        Bengals, 23-19 (C)
1976—Bengals, 27-7 (H)
        Bengals, 31-27 (C) ✓
1977—Bengals, 13-10 (C) OT
        Oilers, 21-16 (H)
1978—Bengals, 28-13 (C)
        Oilers, 17-10 (H)
1979—Oilers, 30-27 (C) OT
        Oilers, 42-21 (H)
1980—Bengals, 13-10 (C)
        Oilers, 23-3 (H)
1981—Oilers, 17-10 (H)
        Bengals, 34-21 (C)
1982—Bengals, 27-6 (C)
        Bengals, 35-27 (C)
1983—Bengals, 55-14 (H)
        Bengals, 38-10 (C)
(Points—Bengals 720, Oilers 569)
**CINCINNATI vs. KANSAS CITY**
Series tied, 7-7
1968—Chiefs, 13-3 (KC)
        Chiefs, 16-9 (C)
1969—Bengals, 24-19 (C)
        Chiefs, 42-22 (KC)
1970—Chiefs, 27-19 (C)
1972—Bengals, 23-16 (KC)
1973—Bengals, 14-6 (C)
1974—Bengals, 33-6 (C)
1976—Bengals, 27-24 (KC)
1977—Bengals, 27-7 (KC)
1978—Chiefs, 24-23 (C)
1979—Chiefs, 10-7 (C)
1980—Bengals, 20-6 (KC)
1983—Chiefs, 20-15 (KC)
(Points—Bengals 266, Chiefs 236)
**CINCINNATI vs. *L.A. RAIDERS**
Raiders lead series, 11-4
1968—Raiders, 31-10 (O)
        Raiders, 34-0 (C)
1969—Bengals, 31-17 (C)
        Raiders, 37-17 (O)
1970—Bengals, 31-21 (O)
1971—Raiders, 31-27 (O)
1972—Raiders, 20-14 (O)
1974—Raiders, 30-27 (O)
1975—Bengals, 14-10 (C)
        **Raiders, 31-28 (O)
1976—Raiders, 35-20 (O)
1978—Raiders, 34-21 (C)
1980—Raiders, 28-17 (O)
1982—Raiders, 31-17 (C)
1983—Raiders, 20-10 (C)
(Points—Raiders 396, Bengals 298)
*Franchise in Oakland prior to 1982
**AFC Divisional Playoff
**CINCINNATI vs. L.A. RAMS**
Bengals lead series, 3-1
1972—Rams, 15-12 (LA)
1976—Bengals, 20-12 (C)
1978—Bengals, 20-19 (LA)
1981—Bengals, 24-10 (C)
(Points—Bengals 76, Rams 56)
**CINCINNATI vs. MIAMI**
Dolphins lead series, 7-3
1968—Dolphins, 24-22 (C)
        Bengals, 38-21 (M)
1969—Bengals, 27-21 (C)
1971—Bengals, 23-13 (C)
1973—*Dolphins, 34-16 (M)
1974—Dolphins, 24-3 (M)
1977—Bengals, 23-17 (C)
1978—Dolphins, 21-0 (M)
1980—Dolphins, 17-16 (M)
1983—Dolphins, 38-14 (M)
(Points—Dolphins 240, Bengals 172)
*AFC Divisional Playoff
**CINCINNATI vs. MINNESOTA**
Series tied, 2-2
1973—Bengals, 27-0 (C)
1977—Vikings, 42-10 (M)
1980—Bengals, 14-0 (C)
1983—Vikings, 20-14 (M)
(Points—Bengals 65, Vikings 62)
**CINCINNATI vs. *NEW ENGLAND**
Patriots lead series, 4-3
1968—Patriots, 33-14 (B)
1969—Patriots, 25-14 (C)
1970—Bengals, 45-7 (C)
1972—Bengals, 31-7 (NE)
1975—Bengals, 27-10 (C)
1978—Patriots, 10-3 (C)
1979—Bengals, 20-14 (C)
(Points—Bengals 148, Patriots 112)
*Franchise in Boston prior to 1971
**CINCINNATI vs. NEW ORLEANS**
Series tied, 2-2
1970—Bengals, 26-6 (C)
1975—Bengals, 21-0 (NO)
1978—Saints, 20-18 (C)
1981—Saints, 17-7 (NO)
(Points—Bengals 72, Saints 43)

**CINCINNATI vs. N.Y. GIANTS**
Bengals lead series, 2-0
1972—Bengals, 13-10 (C)
1977—Bengals, 30-13 (C)
(Points—Bengals 43, Giants 23)
**CINCINNATI vs. N.Y. JETS**
Jets lead series, 5-3
1968—Jets, 27-14 (NY)
1969—Jets, 21-7 (C)
        Jets, 40-7 (NY)
1971—Jets, 35-21 (NY)
1973—Bengals, 20-14 (C)
1976—Bengals, 42-3 (NY)
1981—Bengals, 31-30 (NY)
1982—*Jets, 44-17 (C)
(Points—Jets 214, Bengals 159)
*AFC First Round Playoff
**CINCINNATI vs. PHILADELPHIA**
Bengals lead series, 4-0
1971—Bengals, 37-14 (C)
1975—Bengals, 31-0 (C)
1979—Bengals, 37-13 (C)
1982—Bengals, 18-14 (P)
(Points—Bengals 123, Eagles 41)
**CINCINNATI vs. PITTSBURGH**
Steelers lead series, 16-11
1970—Steelers, 21-10 (P)
        Bengals, 34-7 (C)
1971—Steelers, 21-10 (P)
        Steelers, 21-13 (C)
1972—Bengals, 15-10 (C)
        Steelers, 40-17 (P)
1973—Bengals, 19-7 (C)
        Steelers, 20-13 (P)
1974—Bengals, 17-10 (C)
        Steelers, 27-3 (P)
1975—Steelers, 30-24 (C)
        Steelers, 35-14 (P)
1976—Steelers, 23-6 (P)
        Steelers, 7-3 (C)
1977—Bengals, 20-14 (P)
        Bengals, 17-10 (C)
1978—Steelers, 28-3 (C)
        Steelers, 7-6 (P)
1979—Bengals, 34-10 (C)
        Steelers, 37-17 (P)
1980—Bengals, 30-28 (C)
        Bengals, 17-16 (P)
1981—Bengals, 34-7 (C)
        Bengals, 17-10 (P)
1982—Steelers, 26-20 (P) OT
1983—Steelers, 24-14 (C)
        Bengals, 23-10 (P)
(Points—Steelers 512, Bengals 444)
**CINCINNATI vs. ST. LOUIS**
Bengals lead series, 2-0
1973—Bengals, 42-24 (C)
1979—Bengals, 34-28 (C)
(Points—Bengals 76, Cardinals 52)
**CINCINNATI vs. SAN DIEGO**
Chargers lead series, 9-7
1968—Chargers, 29-13 (SD)
        Chargers, 31-10 (C)
1969—Bengals, 34-20 (C)
        Chargers, 21-14 (SD)
1970—Chargers, 17-14 (SD)
1971—Bengals, 31-0 (C)
1973—Bengals, 20-13 (SD)
1974—Chargers, 20-17 (C)
1975—Bengals, 47-17 (C)
1977—Chargers, 24-3 (SD)
1978—Chargers, 22-13 (SD)
1979—Chargers, 26-24 (C)
1980—Chargers, 31-14 (C)
1981—Bengals, 40-17 (SD)
        *Bengals, 27-7 (C)
1982—Chargers, 50-34 (SD)
(Points—Bengals 358, Chargers 342)
*AFC Championship
**CINCINNATI vs. SAN FRANCISCO**
49ers lead series, 3-1
1974—Bengals, 21-3 (SF)
1978—49ers, 28-12 (SF)
1981—49ers, 21-3 (C)
        *49ers, 26-21 (Detroit)
(Points—49ers 78, Bengals 57)
*Super Bowl XVI
**CINCINNATI vs. SEATTLE**
Bengals lead series, 3-0
1977—Bengals, 42-20 (C)
1981—Bengals, 27-21 (C)
1982—Bengals, 24-10 (C)
(Points—Bengals 93, Seahawks 51)
**CINCINNATI vs. TAMPA BAY**
Bengals lead series, 2-1
1976—Bengals, 21-0 (C)
1980—Buccaneers, 17-12 (C)
1983—Bengals, 23-17 (TB)
(Points—Bengals 56, Buccaneers 34)
**CINCINNATI vs. WASHINGTON**
Redskins lead series, 2-1
1970—Redskins, 20-0 (W)
1974—Bengals, 28-17 (C)

1979—Redskins, 28-14 (W)
(Points—Redskins 65, Bengals 42)

**CLEVELAND vs. ATLANTA**
Browns lead series, 5-1;
See Atlanta vs. Cleveland
**CLEVELAND vs. BALTIMORE**
Browns lead series, 10-5;
See Baltimore vs. Cleveland
**CLEVELAND vs. BUFFALO**
Browns lead series, 3-2;
See Buffalo vs. Cleveland
**CLEVELAND vs. CHICAGO**
Browns lead series, 6-2;
See Chicago vs. Cleveland
**CLEVELAND vs. CINCINNATI**
Browns lead series, 14-13;
See Cincinnati vs. Cleveland
**CLEVELAND vs. DALLAS**
Browns lead series, 15-8
1960—Browns, 48-7 (D)
1961—Browns, 25-7 (C)
        Browns, 38-17 (D)
1962—Browns, 19-10 (C)
        Cowboys, 45-21 (D)
1963—Browns, 41-24 (D)
        Browns, 27-17 (C)
1964—Browns, 27-6 (C)
        Browns, 20-16 (D)
1965—Browns, 23-17 (C)
        Browns, 24-17 (D)
1966—Browns, 30-21 (C)
        Cowboys, 26-14 (D)
1967—Cowboys, 21-14 (C)
        *Cowboys, 52-14 (D)
1968—Cowboys, 28-7 (C)
        *Browns, 31-20 (C)
1969—Browns, 42-10 (C)
        *Browns, 38-14 (D)
1970—Cowboys, 6-2 (C)
1974—Cowboys, 41-17 (D)
1979—Browns, 26-7 (C)
1982—Cowboys, 31-14 (D)
(Points—Browns 562, Cowboys 460)
*Conference Championship
**CLEVELAND vs. DENVER**
Broncos lead series, 7-3
1970—Browns, 27-13 (D)
1971—Browns, 27-0 (C)
1972—Browns, 27-20 (D)
1974—Browns, 23-21 (C)
1975—Browns, 16-15 (C)
1976—Broncos, 44-13 (D)
1978—Broncos, 19-7 (C)
1980—Broncos, 19-16 (C)
1981—Broncos, 23-20 (D) OT
1983—Broncos, 27-6 (D)
(Points—Broncos 229, Browns 154)
**CLEVELAND vs. DETROIT**
Lions lead series, 12-3
1952—Lions, 17-6 (D)
        *Lions, 17-7 (C)
1953—*Lions, 17-16 (D)
1954—Lions, 14-10 (C)
        *Browns, 56-10 (C)
1957—Lions, 20-7 (D)
        *Lions, 59-14 (D)
1958—Lions, 30-10 (C)
1963—Lions, 38-10 (D)
1964—Browns, 37-21 (C)
1967—Lions, 31-14 (D)
1969—Lions, 28-21 (C)
1970—Lions, 41-24 (C)
1975—Lions, 21-10 (D)
1983—Browns, 31-26 (D)
(Points—Lions 390, Browns 273)
*NFL Championship
**CLEVELAND vs. GREEN BAY**
Packers lead series, 7-5
1953—Browns, 27-0 (Mil)
1955—Browns, 41-10 (C)
1956—Browns, 24-7 (Mil)
1961—Packers, 49-17 (C)
1964—Browns, 28-21 (Mil)
1965—*Packers, 23-12 (GB)
1966—Packers, 21-20 (C)
1967—Packers, 55-7 (Mil)
1969—Browns, 20-7 (C)
1972—Packers, 26-10 (C)
1980—Browns, 26-21 (C)
1983—Packers, 35-21 (Mil)
(Points—Packers 282, Browns 246)
*NFL Championship
**CLEVELAND vs. HOUSTON**
Browns lead series, 16-11
1970—Browns, 28-14 (C)
        Browns, 21-10 (H)
1971—Browns, 31-0 (C)
        Browns, 37-24 (H)
1972—Browns, 23-17 (C)
        Browns, 20-0 (H)
1973—Browns, 42-13 (C)
        Browns, 23-13 (H)

1974—Browns, 20-7 (C)
       Oilers, 28-24 (H)
1975—Oilers, 40-10 (C)
       Oilers, 21-10 (H)
1976—Browns, 21-7 (H)
       Browns, 13-10 (C)
1977—Browns, 24-23 (H)
       Oilers, 19-15 (C)
1978—Oilers, 16-13 (C)
       Oilers, 14-10 (H)
1979—Oilers, 31-10 (H)
       Browns, 14-7 (C)
1980—Oilers, 16-7 (C)
       Browns, 17-14 (H)
1981—Oilers, 9-3 (C)
       Oilers, 17-13 (H)
1982—Browns, 20-14 (H)
1983—Browns, 25-19 (C) OT
       Oilers, 34-27 (H)
(Points—Browns 521, Oilers 437)

**CLEVELAND vs. KANSAS CITY**
Series tied, 4-4-1
1971—Chiefs, 13-7 (KC)
1972—Chiefs, 31-7 (C)
1973—Tie, 20-20 (KC)
1975—Browns, 40-14 (C)
1976—Chiefs, 39-14 (KC)
1977—Browns, 44-7 (C)
1978—Chiefs, 17-3 (KC)
1979—Browns, 27-24 (KC)
1980—Browns, 20-13 (C)
(Points—Browns 182, Chiefs 178)

**CLEVELAND vs. *L.A.RAIDERS**
Raiders lead series, 8-1
1970—Raiders, 23-20 (O)
1971—Raiders, 34-20 (C)
1973—Raiders, 7-3 (O)
1974—Raiders, 40-24 (C)
1975—Raiders, 38-17 (O)
1977—Raiders, 26-10 (C)
1979—Raiders, 19-14 (O)
1980—**Raiders, 14-12 (C)
1982—***Raiders, 27-10 (LA)
(Points—Raiders 224, Browns 134)
*Franchise in Oakland prior to 1982
**AFC Divisional Playoff
***AFC First Round Playoff

**CLEVELAND vs. L.A. RAMS**
Browns lead series, 8-6
1950—*Browns, 30-28 (C)
1951—Browns, 38-23 (LA)
       *Rams, 24-17 (LA)
1952—Browns, 37-7 (C)
1955—*Browns, 38-14 (LA)
1957—Browns, 45-31 (C)
1958—Browns, 30-27 (LA)
1963—Browns, 20-6 (C)
1965—Rams, 42-7 (LA)
1968—Rams, 24-6 (C)
1973—Rams, 30-17 (LA)
1977—Rams, 9-0 (C)
1978—Rams, 30-19 (C)
1981—Rams, 27-16 (LA)
(Points—Browns 331, Rams 311)
*NFL Championship

**CLEVELAND vs. MIAMI**
Browns lead series, 3-2
1970—Browns, 28-0 (M)
1972—*Dolphins, 20-14 (M)
1973—Dolphins, 17-9 (C)
1976—Browns, 17-13 (C)
1979—Browns, 30-24 (C) OT
(Points—Browns 98, Dolphins 74)
*AFC Divisional Playoff

**CLEVELAND vs. MINNESOTA**
Vikings lead series, 7-1
1965—Vikings, 27-17 (C)
1967—Browns, 14-10 (C)
1969—Vikings, 51-3 (M)
       *Vikings, 27-7 (M)
1973—Vikings, 26-3 (M)
1975—Vikings, 42-10 (C)
1980—Vikings, 28-23 (M)
1983—Vikings, 27-21 (C)
(Points—Vikings 238, Browns 98)
*NFL Championship

**CLEVELAND vs. NEW ENGLAND**
Browns lead series, 5-1
1971—Browns, 27-7 (C)
1974—Browns, 21-14 (NE)
1977—Browns, 30-27 (C) OT
1980—Patriots, 34-17 (NE)
1982—Browns, 10-7 (C)
1983—Browns, 30-0 (NE)
(Points—Browns 135, Patriots 89)

**CLEVELAND vs. NEW ORLEANS**
Browns lead series, 8-0
1967—Browns, 42-7 (NO)
1968—Browns, 24-10 (NO)
       Browns, 35-17 (C)
1969—Browns, 27-17 (NO)
1971—Browns, 21-17 (NO)
1975—Browns, 17-16 (C)

1978—Browns, 24-16 (NO)
1981—Browns, 20-17 (C)
(Points—Browns 210, Saints 117)

**CLEVELAND vs. N.Y. GIANTS**
Browns lead series, 25-16-2
1950—Giants, 6-0 (C)
       Giants, 17-13 (NY)
       *Browns, 8-3 (C)
1951—Browns, 14-13 (C)
       Browns, 10-0 (NY)
1952—Giants, 17-9 (C)
       Giants, 37-34 (NY)
1953—Browns, 7-0 (NY)
       Browns, 62-14 (C)
1954—Browns, 24-14 (C)
       Browns, 16-7 (NY)
1955—Browns, 24-14 (C)
       Tie, 35-35 (NY)
1956—Giants, 21-9 (C)
       Browns, 24-7 (NY)
1957—Browns, 6-3 (C)
       Browns, 34-28 (NY)
1958—Giants, 21-17 (C)
       Giants, 13-10 (NY)
       *Giants, 10-0 (NY)
1959—Giants, 10-6 (C)
       Giants, 48-7 (NY)
1960—Giants, 17-13 (C)
       Browns, 48-34 (NY)
1961—Giants, 37-21 (C)
       Tie, 7-7 (NY)
1962—Browns, 17-7 (C)
       Giants, 17-13 (NY)
1963—Browns, 35-24 (NY)
       Giants, 33-6 (C)
1964—Browns, 42-20 (C)
       Browns, 52-20 (NY)
1965—Browns, 38-14 (NY)
       Browns, 34-21 (C)
1966—Browns, 28-7 (NY)
       Browns, 49-40 (C)
1967—Giants, 38-34 (NY)
       Browns, 24-14 (C)
1968—Browns, 45-10 (C)
1969—Browns, 28-17 (C)
       Giants, 27-14 (NY)
1973—Browns, 12-10 (C)
1977—Browns, 21-7 (NY)
(Points—Browns 950, Giants 759)
*Conference Playoff

**CLEVELAND vs. N.Y. JETS**
Browns lead series, 7-1
1970—Browns, 31-21 (C)
1972—Browns, 26-10 (NY)
1976—Browns, 38-17 (C)
1978—Browns, 37-34 (C) OT
1979—Browns, 25-22 (NY) OT
1980—Browns, 17-14 (C)
1981—Jets, 14-13 (C)
1983—Browns, 10-7 (C)
(Points—Browns 197, Jets 139)

**CLEVELAND vs. PHILADELPHIA**
Browns lead series, 29-11-1
1950—Browns, 35-10 (P)
       Browns, 13-7 (C)
1951—Browns, 20-17 (C)
       Browns, 24-9 (NY)
1952—Browns, 49-7 (P)
       Eagles, 28-20 (C)
1953—Browns, 37-13 (C)
       Eagles, 42-27 (P)
1954—Eagles, 28-10 (P)
       Browns, 6-0 (C)
1955—Browns, 21-17 (C)
       Eagles, 33-17 (P)
1956—Browns, 16-0 (P)
       Browns, 17-14 (C)
1957—Browns, 24-7 (C)
       Eagles, 17-7 (P)
1958—Browns, 28-14 (C)
       Browns, 21-14 (P)
1959—Browns, 28-7 (C)
       Browns, 28-21 (P)
1960—Browns, 41-24 (P)
       Eagles, 31-29 (C)
1961—Eagles, 27-20 (P)
       Browns, 45-24 (C)
1962—Eagles, 35-7 (P)
       Tie, 14-14 (C)
1963—Browns, 37-7 (P)
       Browns, 23-17 (C)
1964—Browns, 28-20 (P)
       Browns, 38-24 (C)
1965—Browns, 35-17 (P)
       Browns, 38-34 (C)
1966—Browns, 27-7 (C)
       Eagles, 33-21 (P)
1967—Eagles, 28-24 (P)
1968—Browns, 47-13 (C)
1969—Browns, 27-20 (P)
1972—Browns, 27-17 (P)
1976—Browns, 24-3 (C)
1979—Browns, 24-19 (P)

1982—Eagles, 24-21 (C)
(Points—Browns 1,045, Eagles 743)

**CLEVELAND vs. PITTSBURGH**
Browns lead series, 39-29
1950—Browns, 30-17 (C)
       Browns, 45-7 (C)
1951—Browns, 17-0 (C)
       Browns, 28-0 (P)
1952—Browns, 21-20 (P)
       Browns, 29-28 (C)
1953—Browns, 34-16 (C)
       Browns, 20-16 (P)
1954—Steelers, 55-27 (P)
       Browns, 42-7 (C)
1955—Browns, 41-14 (C)
       Browns, 30-7 (P)
1956—Browns, 14-10 (P)
       Steelers, 24-16 (C)
1957—Browns, 23-12 (P)
       Browns, 24-0 (C)
1958—Browns, 45-12 (P)
       Browns, 27-10 (C)
1959—Steelers, 17-7 (P)
       Steelers, 21-20 (C)
1960—Browns, 28-20 (C)
       Steelers, 14-10 (P)
1961—Browns, 30-28 (P)
       Steelers, 17-13 (C)
1962—Browns, 41-14 (P)
       Browns, 35-14 (C)
1963—Browns, 35-23 (C)
       Steelers, 9-7 (P)
1964—Steelers, 23-7 (C)
       Browns, 30-17 (P)
1965—Browns, 24-19 (C)
       Browns, 42-21 (P)
1966—Browns, 41-10 (C)
       Steelers, 16-6 (P)
1967—Browns, 21-10 (C)
       Browns, 34-14 (P)
1968—Browns, 31-24 (C)
       Browns, 45-24 (P)
1969—Browns, 42-31 (C)
       Browns, 24-3 (P)
1970—Browns, 15-7 (C)
       Steelers, 28-9 (P)
1971—Browns, 27-17 (C)
       Steelers, 26-9 (P)
1972—Browns, 26-24 (C)
       Steelers, 30-0 (P)
1973—Steelers, 33-6 (P)
       Browns, 21-16 (C)
1974—Steelers, 20-16 (P)
       Steelers, 26-16 (C)
1975—Steelers, 42-6 (C)
       Steelers, 31-17 (P)
1976—Steelers, 31-14 (P)
       Browns, 18-16 (C)
1977—Steelers, 28-14 (C)
       Steelers, 35-31 (P)
1978—Steelers, 15-9 (P) OT
       Steelers, 34-14 (C)
1979—Steelers, 51-35 (P)
       Steelers, 33-30 (P) OT
1980—Browns, 27-26 (C)
       Steelers, 16-13 (P)
1981—Steelers, 13-7 (P)
       Steelers, 32-10 (C)
1982—Browns, 10-9 (C)
       Steelers, 37-21 (P)
1983—Steelers, 44-17 (P)
       Browns, 30-17 (C)
(Points—Browns 1,554, Steelers 1,381)

**CLEVELAND vs. *ST. LOUIS**
Browns lead series, 30-9-3
1950—Browns, 34-24 (Cle)
       Browns, 10-7 (Chi)
1951—Browns, 34-17 (Chi)
       Browns, 49-28 (Cle)
1952—Browns, 28-13 (Cle)
       Browns, 10-0 (Chi)
1953—Browns, 27-7 (Chi)
       Browns, 27-16 (Cle)
1954—Browns, 31-7 (Cle)
       Browns, 35-3 (Chi)
1955—Browns, 26-20 (Chi)
       Browns, 35-24 (Cle)
1956—Cardinals, 9-7 (Chi)
       Cardinals, 24-7 (Cle)
1957—Browns, 17-7 (Chi)
       Browns, 31-0 (Cle)
1958—Browns, 35-28 (Chi)
       Browns, 38-24 (Chi)
1959—Browns, 34-7 (Cle)
       Browns, 17-7 (Cle)
1960—Browns, 28-27 (C)
       Tie, 17-17 (StL)
1961—Browns, 20-17 (C)
       Browns, 21-10 (StL)
1962—Browns, 34-7 (StL)
       Browns, 38-14 (C)
1963—Cardinals, 20-14 (C)
       Browns, 24-10 (StL)

1964—Tie, 33-33 (C)
       Cardinals, 28-19 (StL)
1965—Cardinals, 49-13 (C)
       Browns, 27-24 (StL)
1966—Cardinals, 34-28 (C)
       Browns, 38-10 (StL)
1967—Browns, 20-16 (C)
       Browns, 20-16 (StL)
1968—Cardinals, 27-21 (C)
       Cardinals, 27-16 (StL)
1969—Tie, 21-21 (C)
       Browns, 27-21 (StL)
1974—Cardinals, 29-7 (StL)
1979—Browns, 38-20 (StL)
(Points—Browns 1,056, Cardinals 749)
*Franchise in Chicago prior to 1960

**CLEVELAND vs. SAN DIEGO**
Chargers lead series, 5-3-1
1970—Chargers, 27-10 (C)
1972—Browns, 21-17 (SD)
1973—Tie, 16-16 (C)
1974—Chargers, 36-35 (SD)
1976—Browns, 21-17 (C)
1977—Chargers, 37-14 (SD)
1981—Chargers, 44-14 (C)
1982—Chargers, 30-13 (C)
1983—Browns, 30-24 (SD) OT
(Points—Chargers 248, Browns 174)

**CLEVELAND vs. SAN FRANCISCO**
Browns lead series, 8-3
1950—Browns, 34-14 (C)
1951—49ers, 24-10 (SF)
1953—Browns, 23-21 (C)
1955—Browns, 38-3 (SF)
1959—49ers, 21-20 (C)
1962—Browns, 13-10 (SF)
1968—Browns, 33-21 (SF)
1970—49ers, 34-31 (SF)
1974—Browns, 7-0 (C)
1978—Browns, 24-7 (C)
1981—Browns, 15-12 (SF)
(Points—Browns 248, 49ers 167)

**CLEVELAND vs. SEATTLE**
Seahawks lead series, 5-2
1977—Seahawks, 20-19 (S)
1978—Seahawks, 47-24 (S)
1979—Seahawks, 29-24 (C)
1980—Browns, 27-3 (S)
1981—Seahawks, 42-21 (S)
1982—Browns, 21-7 (S)
1983—Seahawks, 24-9 (C)
(Points—Seahawks 172, Browns 145)

**CLEVELAND vs. TAMPA BAY**
Browns lead series, 3-0
1976—Browns, 24-7 (TB)
1980—Browns, 34-27 (TB)
1983—Browns, 20-0 (C)
(Points—Browns 78, Buccaneers 34)

**CLEVELAND vs. WASHINGTON**
Browns lead series, 31-7-1
1950—Browns, 20-14 (C)
       Browns, 45-21 (W)
1951—Browns, 45-0 (C)
1952—Browns, 19-15 (C)
       Browns, 48-24 (W)
1953—Browns, 30-14 (W)
       Browns, 27-3 (C)
1954—Browns, 62-3 (C)
       Browns, 34-14 (W)
1955—Redskins, 27-17 (C)
       Browns, 24-14 (W)
1956—Redskins, 20-9 (W)
       Redskins, 20-17 (C)
1957—Browns, 21-17 (C)
       Tie, 30-30 (W)
1958—Browns, 20-10 (W)
       Browns, 21-14 (C)
1959—Browns, 34-7 (C)
       Browns, 31-17 (W)
1960—Browns, 31-10 (W)
       Browns, 27-16 (C)
1961—Browns, 31-7 (C)
       Browns, 17-6 (W)
1962—Redskins, 17-16 (C)
       Redskins, 17-9 (W)
1963—Browns, 37-14 (W)
       Browns, 27-20 (W)
1964—Browns, 27-13 (W)
       Browns, 34-24 (C)
1965—Browns, 17-7 (W)
       Browns, 24-16 (C)
1966—Browns, 38-14 (W)
       Browns, 14-3 (C)
1967—Browns, 42-37 (C)
1968—Browns, 24-21 (W)
1969—Browns, 27-23 (C)
1971—Browns, 20-13 (W)
1975—Redskins, 23-7 (C)
1979—Redskins, 13-9 (C)
(Points—Browns 1,032, Redskins 598)

**DALLAS vs. ATLANTA**
Cowboys lead series, 7-1;
See Atlanta vs. Dallas

**DALLAS vs. BALTIMORE**
Cowboys lead series, 5-3;
See Baltimore vs. Dallas
**DALLAS vs. BUFFALO**
Cowboys lead series, 3-0;
See Buffalo vs. Dallas
**DALLAS vs. CHICAGO**
Cowboys lead series, 7-3;
See Chicago vs. Dallas
**DALLAS vs. CINCINNATI**
Cowboys lead series, 2-0;
See Cincinnati vs. Dallas
**DALLAS vs. CLEVELAND**
Browns lead series, 15-8;
See Cleveland vs. Dallas
**DALLAS vs. DENVER**
Cowboys lead series, 3-1
1973—Cowboys, 22-10 (Den)
1977—Cowboys, 14-6 (Dal)
    *Cowboys, 27-10 (New Orleans)
1980—Broncos, 41-20 (Den)
(Points—Cowboys 83, Broncos 67)
*Super Bowl XII
**DALLAS vs. DETROIT**
Cowboys lead series, 6-2
1960—Lions, 23-14 (Det)
1963—Cowboys, 17-14 (Dal)
1968—Cowboys, 59-13 (Dal)
1970—*Cowboys, 5-0 (Dal)
1972—Cowboys, 28-24 (Dal)
1975—Cowboys, 36-10 (Det)
1977—Cowboys, 37-0 (Dal)
1981—Lions, 27-24 (Det)
(Points—Cowboys 220, Lions 111)
*NFC Divisional Playoff
**DALLAS vs. GREEN BAY**
Packers lead series, 8-4
1960—Packers, 41-7 (GB)
1964—Packers, 45-21 (D)
1965—Packers, 13-3 (Mil)
1966—*Packers, 34-27 (D)
1967—*Packers, 21-17 (GB)
1968—Packers, 28-17 (D)
1970—Cowboys, 16-3 (D)
1972—Packers, 16-13 (Mil)
1975—Cowboys, 19-17 (D)
1978—Cowboys, 42-14 (Mil)
1980—Cowboys, 28-7 (Mil)
1982—**Cowboys, 37-26 (D)
(Points—Packers 267, Cowboys 245)
*NFL Championship
**NFL Second Round Playoff
**DALLAS vs. HOUSTON**
Cowboys lead series, 3-1
1970—Cowboys, 52-10 (D)
1974—Cowboys, 10-0 (H)
1979—Oilers, 30-24 (D)
1982—Cowboys, 37-7 (H)
(Points—Cowboys 123, Oilers 47)
**DALLAS vs. KANSAS CITY**
Cowboys lead series, 2-1
1970—Cowboys, 27-16 (KC)
1975—Chiefs, 34-31 (D)
1983—Cowboys, 41-21 (D)
(Points—Cowboys 99, Chiefs 71)
**DALLAS vs. *L.A. RAIDERS**
Raiders lead series, 2-1
1974—Raiders, 27-23 (O)
1980—Cowboys, 19-13 (O)
1983—Raiders, 40-38 (D)
(Points—Raiders 80, Cowboys 80)
*Franchise in Oakland prior to 1982
**DALLAS vs. L.A. RAMS**
Series tied, 9-9
1960—Rams, 38-13 (D)
1962—Cowboys, 27-17 (LA)
1967—Rams, 35-13 (D)
1969—Rams, 24-23 (LA)
1971—Cowboys, 28-21 (D)
1973—Rams, 37-31 (LA)
    *Cowboys, 27-16 (D)
1975—Cowboys, 18-7 (D)
    **Cowboys, 37-7 (LA)
1976—*Rams, 14-12 (D)
1978—Rams, 27-14 (LA)
    **Cowboys, 28-0 (LA)
1979—Cowboys, 30-6 (D)
    *Rams, 21-19 (D)
1980—Rams, 38-14 (LA)
    ***Cowboys, 34-13 (D)
1981—Cowboys, 29-17 (D)
1983—***Rams, 24-17 (D)
(Points—Cowboys 414, Rams 362)
*NFC Divisional Playoff
**NFC Championship
***NFC First Round Playoff
**DALLAS vs. MIAMI**
Series tied, 2-2
1971—*Cowboys, 24-3 (New Orleans)
1973—Dolphins, 14-7 (D)
1978—Dolphins, 23-16 (M)
1981—Cowboys, 28-27 (D)
(Points—Cowboys 75, Dolphins 67)

*Super Bowl VI
**DALLAS vs. MINNESOTA**
Cowboys lead series, 10-5
1961—Cowboys, 21-7 (D)
    Cowboys, 28-0 (M)
1966—Cowboys, 28-17 (D)
1968—Cowboys, 20-7 (M)
1970—Vikings, 54-13 (M)
1971—*Cowboys, 20-12 (M)
1973—**Vikings, 27-10 (D)
1974—Vikings, 23-21 (D)
1975—*Cowboys, 17-14 (M)
1977—Cowboys, 16-10 (M) OT
    **Cowboys, 23-6 (D)
1978—Vikings, 21-10 (D)
1979—Cowboys, 36-20 (M)
1982—Vikings, 31-27 (M)
1983—Cowboys, 37-24 (M)
(Points—Cowboys 327, Vikings 273)
*NFC Divisional Playoff
**NFC Championship
**DALLAS vs. NEW ENGLAND**
Cowboys lead series, 4-0
1971—Cowboys, 44-21 (D)
1975—Cowboys, 34-31 (NE)
1978—Cowboys, 17-10 (D)
1981—Cowboys, 35-21 (NE)
(Points—Cowboys 130, Patriots 83)
**DALLAS vs. NEW ORLEANS**
Cowboys lead series, 10-1
1967—Cowboys, 14-10 (D)
    Cowboys, 27-10 (NO)
1968—Cowboys, 17-3 (NO)
1969—Cowboys, 21-17 (NO)
    Cowboys, 33-17 (D)
1971—Saints, 24-14 (NO)
1973—Cowboys, 40-3 (D)
1976—Cowboys, 24-6 (NO)
1978—Cowboys, 27-7 (D)
1982—Cowboys, 21-7 (D)
1983—Cowboys, 21-20 (D)
(Points—Cowboys 259, Saints 124)
**DALLAS vs. N.Y. GIANTS**
Cowboys lead series, 30-11-2
1960—Tie, 31-31 (NY)
1961—Giants, 31-10 (D)
    Cowboys, 17-16 (NY)
1962—Giants, 41-10 (D)
    Giants, 41-31 (NY)
1963—Giants, 37-21 (NY)
    Giants, 34-27 (D)
1964—Tie, 13-13 (D)
    Cowboys, 31-21 (NY)
1965—Cowboys, 31-2 (D)
    Cowboys, 38-20 (NY)
1966—Cowboys, 52-7 (D)
    Cowboys, 17-7 (NY)
1967—Cowboys, 38-24 (D)
    Cowboys, 28-10 (NY)
1968—Giants, 27-21 (D)
    Cowboys, 28-10 (NY)
1969—Cowboys, 25-3 (D)
1970—Cowboys, 28-10 (NY)
    Giants, 23-20 (NY)
1971—Cowboys, 20-13 (D)
    Cowboys, 42-14 (NY)
1972—Cowboys, 23-14 (NY)
    Giants, 23-3 (D)
1973—Cowboys, 45-28 (D)
    Cowboys, 23-10 (New Haven)
1974—Giants, 14-6 (D)
    Cowboys, 21-7 (New Haven)
1975—Cowboys, 13-7 (NY)
    Cowboys, 14-3 (D)
1976—Cowboys, 24-14 (NY)
    Cowboys, 9-3 (D)
1977—Cowboys, 41-21 (D)
    Cowboys, 24-10 (NY)
1978—Cowboys, 34-24 (NY)
    Cowboys, 24-3 (D)
1979—Cowboys, 16-14 (NY)
    Cowboys, 28-7 (D)
1980—Cowboys, 24-3 (D)
    Giants, 38-35 (NY)
1981—Cowboys, 18-10 (D)
    Giants, 13-10 (NY) OT
1983—Cowboys, 28-13 (D)
    Cowboys, 38-20 (NY)
(Points—Cowboys 1,052, Giants 724)
**DALLAS vs. N.Y. JETS**
Cowboys lead series, 3-0
1971—Cowboys, 52-10 (D)
1975—Cowboys, 31-21 (NY)
1978—Cowboys, 30-7 (NY)
(Points—Cowboys 113, Jets 38)
**DALLAS vs. PHILADELPHIA**
Cowboys lead series, 31-16
1960—Eagles, 27-25 (D)
1961—Eagles, 43-7 (D)
    Eagles, 35-13 (P)
1962—Cowboys, 41-19 (D)
    Eagles, 28-14 (P)
1963—Eagles, 24-21 (P)
    Cowboys, 27-20 (D)

1964—Eagles, 17-14 (D)
    Eagles, 24-14 (P)
1965—Eagles, 35-24 (D)
    Cowboys, 21-19 (P)
1966—Cowboys, 56-7 (D)
    Eagles, 24-23 (P)
1967—Eagles, 21-14 (P)
    Cowboys, 38-17 (D)
1968—Cowboys, 45-13 (P)
    Cowboys, 34-14 (D)
1969—Cowboys, 38-7 (P)
    Cowboys, 49-14 (D)
1970—Cowboys, 17-7 (P)
    Cowboys, 21-17 (D)
1971—Cowboys, 42-7 (P)
    Cowboys, 20-7 (D)
1972—Cowboys, 28-6 (D)
    Cowboys, 28-7 (P)
1973—Eagles, 30-16 (P)
    Cowboys, 31-10 (D)
1974—Eagles, 13-10 (P)
    Cowboys, 31-24 (D)
1975—Cowboys, 20-17 (P)
    Cowboys, 27-17 (D)
1976—Cowboys, 27-7 (D)
    Cowboys, 26-7 (P)
1977—Cowboys, 16-10 (P)
    Cowboys, 24-14 (D)
1978—Cowboys, 14-7 (D)
    Cowboys, 31-13 (P)
1979—Eagles, 31-21 (D)
    Cowboys, 24-17 (P)
1980—Eagles, 17-10 (P)
    Cowboys, 35-27 (D)
    *Eagles, 20-7 (P)
1981—Cowboys, 17-14 (P)
    Cowboys, 21-10 (D)
1982—Eagles, 24-20 (D)
1983—Cowboys, 37-7 (D)
    Cowboys, 27-20 (P)
(Points—Cowboys 1,166, Eagles 815)
*NFC Championship
**DALLAS vs. PITTSBURGH**
Steelers lead series, 12-10
1960—Steelers, 35-28 (D)
1961—Cowboys, 27-24 (D)
    Steelers, 37-7 (P)
1962—Steelers, 30-28 (D)
    Cowboys, 42-27 (P)
1963—Steelers, 27-21 (P)
    Steelers, 24-19 (D)
1964—Steelers, 23-17 (P)
    Cowboys, 17-14 (D)
1965—Steelers, 22-13 (P)
    Cowboys, 24-17 (D)
1966—Cowboys, 52-21 (D)
    Cowboys, 20-7 (P)
1967—Cowboys, 24-21 (P)
1968—Cowboys, 28-7 (D)
1969—Cowboys, 10-7 (P)
1972—Cowboys, 17-13 (D)
1975—*Steelers, 21-17 (Miami)
1977—Steelers, 28-13 (P)
1978—**Steelers, 35-31 (Miami)
1979—Steelers, 14-3 (P)
1982—Steelers, 36-28 (P)
(Points—Steelers 490, Cowboys 486)
*Super Bowl X
**Super Bowl XIII
**DALLAS vs. ST. LOUIS**
Cowboys lead series, 27-15-1
1960—Cardinals, 12-10 (StL)
1961—Cardinals, 31-17 (D)
    Cardinals, 31-13 (StL)
1962—Cardinals, 28-24 (D)
    Cardinals, 52-20 (StL)
1963—Cardinals, 34-7 (D)
    Cowboys, 28-24 (StL)
1964—Cardinals, 16-6 (D)
    Cowboys, 31-13 (StL)
1965—Cardinals, 20-13 (D)
    Cowboys, 27-13 (D)
1966—Tie, 10-10 (StL)
    Cowboys, 31-17 (D)
1967—Cowboys, 46-21 (D)
1968—Cowboys, 27-10 (StL)
1969—Cowboys, 24-3 (D)
1970—Cowboys, 20-7 (StL)
    Cardinals, 38-0 (D)
1971—Cowboys, 16-13 (StL)
    Cowboys, 31-12 (D)
1972—Cowboys, 33-24 (D)
    Cowboys, 27-6 (StL)
1973—Cowboys, 45-10 (D)
    Cowboys, 30-3 (StL)
1974—Cardinals, 31-28 (StL)
    Cowboys, 17-14 (D)
1975—Cowboys, 37-31 (D) OT
    Cardinals, 31-17 (StL)
1976—Cardinals, 21-17 (StL)
    Cowboys, 19-14 (D)
1977—Cowboys, 30-24 (StL)
    Cardinals, 24-17 (D)

1978—Cowboys, 21-12 (D)
    Cowboys, 24-21 (StL) OT
1979—Cowboys, 22-21 (D)
    Cowboys, 22-13 (D)
1980—Cowboys, 27-24 (StL)
    Cowboys, 31-21 (D)
1981—Cowboys, 30-17 (D)
    Cardinals, 20-17 (StL)
1982—Cowboys, 24-7 (StL)
1983—Cowboys, 34-17 (StL)
    Cowboys, 35-17 (D)
(Points—Cowboys 992, Cardinals 841)
**DALLAS vs. SAN DIEGO**
Cowboys lead series, 2-1
1972—Cowboys, 34-28 (SD)
1980—Cowboys, 42-31 (D)
1983—Chargers, 24-23 (SD)
(Points—Cowboys 99, Chargers 83)
**DALLAS vs. SAN FRANCISCO**
Cowboys lead series, 8-7-1
1960—49ers, 26-14 (D)
1963—49ers, 31-24 (SF)
1965—49ers, 39-31 (D)
1967—49ers, 24-16 (SF)
1969—Tie, 24-24 (D)
1970—*Cowboys, 17-10 (SF)
1971—*Cowboys, 14-3 (D)
1972—49ers, 31-10 (D)
    **Cowboys, 30-28 (SF)
1974—Cowboys, 20-14 (D)
1977—Cowboys, 42-35 (SF)
1979—Cowboys, 21-13 (SF)
1980—Cowboys, 59-14 (D)
1981—49ers, 45-14 (SF)
    *49ers, 28-27 (SF)
1983—49ers, 42-17 (SF)
(Points—49ers 399, Cowboys 388)
*NFC Championship
**NFC Divisional Playoff
**DALLAS vs. SEATTLE**
Cowboys lead series, 3-0
1976—Cowboys, 28-13 (S)
1980—Cowboys, 51-7 (D)
1983—Cowboys, 35-10 (S)
(Points—Cowboys 114, Seahawks 30)
**DALLAS vs. TAMPA BAY**
Cowboys lead series, 6-0
1977—Cowboys, 23-7 (D)
1980—Cowboys, 28-17 (D)
1981—*Cowboys, 38-0 (D)
1982—Cowboys, 14-9 (D)
    **Cowboys, 30-17 (D)
1983—Cowboys, 27-24 (D) OT
(Points—Cowboys 160, Buccaneers 74)
*NFC Divisional Playoff
**NFC First Round Playoff
**DALLAS vs. WASHINGTON**
Cowboys lead series, 28-18-2
1960—Redskins, 26-14 (W)
1961—Tie, 28-28 (D)
    Redskins, 34-24 (W)
1962—Tie, 35-35 (W)
    Cowboys, 38-10 (W)
1963—Redskins, 21-17 (D)
    Cowboys, 35-20 (D)
1964—Cowboys, 24-18 (D)
    Redskins, 28-16 (W)
1965—Cowboys, 27-7 (D)
    Redskins, 34-31 (W)
1966—Cowboys, 31-30 (D)
    Redskins, 34-31 (D)
1967—Cowboys, 17-14 (W)
    Redskins, 27-20 (D)
1968—Cowboys, 44-24 (W)
    Cowboys, 29-20 (D)
1969—Cowboys, 41-28 (W)
    Cowboys, 20-10 (D)
1970—Cowboys, 45-21 (W)
    Cowboys, 34-0 (D)
1971—Redskins, 20-16 (D)
    Cowboys, 13-0 (W)
1972—Redskins, 24-20 (D)
    Cowboys, 34-24 (D)
    *Redskins, 26-3 (W)
1973—Redskins, 14-7 (D)
    Cowboys, 27-7 (D)
1974—Redskins, 28-21 (D)
    Cowboys, 24-23 (D)
1975—Redskins, 30-24 (W) OT
    Cowboys, 31-10 (D)
1976—Cowboys, 20-7 (D)
    Redskins, 27-14 (D)
1977—Cowboys, 34-16 (D)
    Cowboys, 14-7 (W)
1978—Redskins, 9-5 (W)
    Cowboys, 37-10 (D)
1979—Redskins, 34-20 (D)
    Cowboys, 35-34 (D)
1980—Cowboys, 17-3 (W)
    Cowboys, 14-10 (D)
1981—Cowboys, 26-10 (W)
    Cowboys, 24-10 (D)
1982—Cowboys, 24-10 (W)
    *Redskins, 31-17 (W)

1983—Cowboys, 31-30 (W)
Redskins, 31-10 (D)
(Points—Cowboys 1,163, Redskins 954)
*NFC Championship

**DENVER vs. ATLANTA**
Falcons lead series, 3-2;
See Atlanta vs. Denver
**DENVER vs. BALTIMORE**
Broncos lead series, 5-1;
See Baltimore vs. Denver
**DENVER vs. BUFFALO**
Bills lead series, 13-8-1;
See Buffalo vs. Denver
**DENVER vs. CHICAGO**
Series tied, 3-3;
See Chicago vs. Denver
**DENVER vs. CINCINNATI**
Broncos lead series, 7-6;
See Cincinnati vs. Denver
**DENVER vs. CLEVELAND**
Broncos lead series 7-3;
See Cleveland vs. Denver
**DENVER vs. DALLAS**
Cowboys lead series, 3-1;
See Dallas vs. Denver
**DENVER vs. DETROIT**
Series tied, 2-2
1971—Lions, 24-20 (Den)
1974—Broncos, 31-27 (Det)
1978—Lions, 17-14 (Det)
1981—Broncos, 27-21 (Den)
(Points—Broncos 92. Lions 89)
**DENVER vs. GREEN BAY**
Broncos lead series, 2-1
1971—Packers, 34-13 (Mil)
1975—Broncos, 23-13 (D)
1978—Broncos, 16-3 (D)
(Points—Broncos 52, Packers 50)
**DENVER vs. HOUSTON**
Oilers lead series, 18-9-1
1960—Oilers, 45-25 (D)
Oilers, 20-10 (H)
1961—Oilers, 55-14 (D)
Oilers, 45-14 (H)
1962—Broncos, 20-10 (D)
Oilers, 34-17 (H)
1963—Oilers, 20-14 (H)
Oilers, 33-24 (D)
1964—Oilers, 38-17 (D)
Oilers, 34-15 (H)
1965—Broncos, 28-17 (D)
Broncos, 31-21 (H)
1966—Oilers, 45-7 (H)
Broncos, 40-38 (D)
1967—Oilers, 10-6 (H)
Oilers, 20-18 (D)
1968—Oilers, 38-17 (H)
1969—Oilers, 24-21 (H)
Tie, 20-20 (D)
1970—Oilers, 31-21 (H)
1972—Broncos, 30-17 (D)
1973—Broncos, 48-20 (H)
1974—Broncos, 37-14 (D)
1976—Oilers, 17-3 (H)
1977—Broncos, 24-14 (H)
1979—*Oilers, 13-7 (H)
1980—Oilers, 20-16 (D)
1983—Broncos, 26-14 (H)
(Points—Oilers 727, Broncos 570)
*AFC First Round Playoff
**DENVER vs. *KANSAS CITY**
Chiefs lead series, 32-15
1960—Texans, 17-14 (D)
Texans, 34-7 (Da)
1961—Texans, 19-12 (D)
Texans, 49-21 (Da)
1962—Texans, 24-3 (D)
Texans, 17-10 (Da)
1963—Chiefs, 59-7 (D)
Chiefs, 52-21 (KC)
1964—Broncos, 33-27 (D)
Chiefs, 49-39 (KC)
1965—Chiefs, 31-23 (D)
Chiefs, 45-35 (KC)
1966—Chiefs, 37-10 (KC)
Chiefs, 56-10 (D)
1967—Chiefs, 52-9 (KC)
Chiefs, 38-24 (D)
1968—Chiefs, 34-2 (KC)
Chiefs, 30-7 (D)
1969—Chiefs, 26-13 (D)
Chiefs, 31-17 (KC)
1970—Broncos, 26-13 (D)
Chiefs, 16-0 (KC)
1971—Chiefs, 16-3 (D)
Chiefs, 28-10 (KC)
1972—Chiefs, 45-24 (D)
Chiefs, 24-21 (KC)
1973—Chiefs, 16-14 (KC)
Broncos, 14-10 (D)
1974—Broncos, 17-14 (KC)
Chiefs, 42-34 (D)

1975—Broncos, 37-33 (D)
Chiefs, 26-13 (KC)
1976—Broncos, 35-26 (KC)
Broncos, 17-16 (D)
1977—Broncos, 23-7 (D)
Broncos, 14-7 (KC)
1978—Broncos, 23-17 (KC) OT
Broncos, 24-3 (D)
1979—Broncos, 24-10 (KC)
Broncos, 20-3 (D)
1980—Chiefs, 23-17 (D)
Chiefs, 31-14 (KC)
1981—Chiefs, 28-14 (KC)
Broncos, 16-13 (D)
1982—Chiefs, 37-16 (D)
1983—Broncos, 27-24 (D)
Chiefs, 48-17 (KC)
(Points—Chiefs 1,303, Broncos 831)
*Franchise in Dallas prior to 1963 and known as Texans
**DENVER vs. *L.A. RAIDERS**
Raiders lead series, 34-12-2
1960—Broncos, 31-14 (D)
Raiders, 48-10 (O)
1961—Raiders, 33-19 (O)
Broncos, 27-24 (D)
1962—Broncos, 44-7 (D)
Broncos, 23-6 (O)
1963—Raiders, 26-10 (D)
Raiders, 35-31 (O)
1964—Raiders, 40-7 (O)
Tie, 20-20 (D)
1965—Raiders, 28-20 (D)
Raiders, 24-13 (O)
1966—Raiders, 17-3 (D)
Raiders, 28-10 (O)
1967—Raiders, 51-0 (O)
Raiders, 21-17 (D)
1968—Raiders, 43-7 (D)
Raiders, 33-27 (O)
1969—Raiders, 24-14 (D)
Raiders, 41-10 (O)
1970—Raiders, 35-23 (O)
Raiders, 24-19 (D)
1971—Raiders, 27-16 (D)
Raiders, 21-13 (O)
1972—Broncos, 30-23 (O)
Raiders, 37-20 (D)
1973—Tie, 23-23 (D)
Raiders, 21-17 (O)
1974—Raiders, 28-17 (D)
Broncos, 20-17 (O)
1975—Raiders, 42-17 (D)
Raiders, 17-10 (O)
1976—Raiders, 17-10 (D)
Raiders, 19-6 (O)
1977—Broncos, 30-7 (D)
Raiders, 24-14 (D)
**Broncos, 20-17 (D)
1978—Broncos, 14-6 (D)
Broncos, 21-6 (O)
1979—Broncos, 27-3 (D)
Raiders, 14-10 (O)
1980—Raiders, 9-3 (O)
Raiders, 24-21 (D)
1981—Broncos, 9-7 (D)
Broncos, 17-0 (O)
1982—Raiders, 27-10 (LA)
1983—Raiders, 22-7 (D)
Raiders, 22-20 (LA)
(Points—Raiders 1,126, Broncos 783)
*Franchise in Oakland prior to 1982
**AFC Championship
**DENVER vs. L.A. RAMS**
Series tied, 2-2
1972—Broncos, 16-10 (LA)
1974—Rams, 17-10 (D)
1979—Rams, 13-9 (D)
1982—Broncos, 27-24 (LA)
(Points—Rams 64, Broncos 62)
**DENVER vs. MIAMI**
Dolphins lead series, 4-2-1
1966—Dolphins, 24-7 (M)
Broncos, 17-7 (D)
1967—Dolphins, 35-21 (M)
1968—Broncos, 21-14 (D)
1969—Broncos, 27-24 (M)
1971—Tie, 10-10 (D)
1975—Dolphins, 14-13 (M)
(Points—Dolphins 131, Broncos 113)
**DENVER vs. MINNESOTA**
Vikings lead series, 2-1
1972—Vikings, 23-20 (D)
1978—Vikings, 12-9 (M) OT
1981—Broncos, 19-17 (D)
(Points—Vikings 52, Broncos 48)
**DENVER vs. *NEW ENGLAND**
Patriots lead series, 12-10
1960—Broncos, 13-10 (B)
Broncos, 31-24 (D)
1961—Patriots, 45-17 (B)
Patriots, 28-24 (D)
1962—Patriots, 41-16 (B)

Patriots, 33-29 (D)
1963—Broncos, 14-10 (D)
Patriots, 40-21 (B)
1964—Patriots, 39-10 (D)
Patriots, 12-7 (B)
1965—Broncos, 27-10 (B)
Patriots, 28-20 (D)
1966—Patriots, 24-10 (D)
Broncos, 17-10 (B)
1967—Broncos, 26-21 (D)
1968—Patriots, 20-17 (D)
Broncos, 35-14 (B)
1969—Broncos, 35-7 (D)
1972—Broncos, 45-21 (D)
1976—Patriots, 38-14 (NE)
1979—Patriots, 45-10 (D)
1980—Patriots, 23-14 (NE)
(Points—Patriots 508, Broncos 487)
*Franchise in Boston prior to 1971
**DENVER vs. NEW ORLEANS**
Broncos lead series, 3-0
1970—Broncos, 31-6 (NO)
1974—Broncos, 33-17 (D)
1979—Broncos, 10-3 (D)
(Points—Broncos 74, Saints 26)
**DENVER vs. N. Y. GIANTS**
Broncos lead series, 2-1
1972—Giants, 29-17 (NY)
1976—Broncos, 14-13 (D)
1980—Broncos, 14-9 (NY)
(Points—Giants 51, Broncos 45)
**DENVER vs. *N.Y. JETS**
Series tied, 10-10-1
1960—Titans, 28-24 (NY)
Titans, 30-27 (D)
1961—Titans, 35-28 (NY)
Broncos, 27-10 (D)
1962—Broncos, 32-10 (NY)
Titans, 46-45 (D)
1963—Jets, 35-35 (NY)
Jets, 14-9 (D)
1964—Jets, 30-6 (NY)
Broncos, 20-16 (D)
1965—Broncos, 16-13 (D)
Jets, 45-10 (NY)
1966—Jets, 16-7 (D)
1967—Jets, 38-24 (D)
Broncos, 33-24 (NY)
1968—Broncos, 21-13 (NY)
1969—Broncos, 21-19 (D)
1973—Broncos, 40-28 (NY)
1976—Broncos, 46-3 (D)
1978—Jets, 31-28 (D)
1980—Broncos, 31-24 (D)
(Points—Broncos 530, Jets 508)
*Jets known as Titans prior to 1963
**DENVER vs. PHILADELPHIA**
Eagles lead series, 3-1
1971—Eagles, 17-16 (P)
1975—Broncos, 25-10 (D)
1980—Eagles, 27-6 (P)
1983—Eagles, 13-10 (D)
(Points—Eagles 67, Broncos 57)
**DENVER vs. PITTSBURGH**
Broncos lead series, 6-4-1
1970—Broncos, 16-13 (P)
1971—Broncos, 22-10 (P)
1973—Broncos, 23-13 (P)
1974—Tie, 35-35 (D) OT
1975—Steelers, 20-9 (P)
1977—Broncos, 21-7 (D)
*Broncos, 34-21 (D)
1978—Steelers, 21-17 (D)
*Steelers, 33-10 (P)
1979—Steelers, 42-7 (P)
1983—Broncos, 14-10 (P)
(Points—Steelers 225, Broncos 208)
*AFC Divisional Playoff
**DENVER vs. ST. LOUIS**
Broncos lead series, 1-0-1
1973—Tie, 17-17 (StL)
1977—Broncos, 7-0 (D)
(Points—Broncos 24, Cardinals 17)
**DENVER vs. *SAN DIEGO**
Chargers lead series, 26-21-1
1960—Chargers, 23-19 (D)
Chargers, 41-33 (LA)
1961—Chargers, 37-0 (SD)
Chargers, 19-16 (D)
1962—Broncos, 30-21 (D)
Broncos, 23-20 (SD)
1963—Broncos, 50-34 (D)
Chargers, 58-20 (SD)
1964—Chargers, 42-14 (SD)
Chargers, 31-20 (D)
1965—Chargers, 34-31 (SD)
Chargers, 33-21 (D)
1966—Chargers, 24-17 (SD)
Chargers, 20-17 (D)
1967—Chargers, 38-21 (D)
Chargers, 24-20 (SD)
1968—Chargers, 55-24 (SD)
Chargers, 47-23 (D)

1969—Broncos, 13-0 (D)
Chargers, 45-24 (SD)
1970—Chargers, 24-21 (SD)
Tie, 17-17 (D)
1971—Broncos, 20-16 (D)
Chargers, 45-17 (SD)
1972—Chargers, 37-14 (SD)
Broncos, 38-13 (D)
1973—Broncos, 30-19 (D)
Broncos, 42-28 (SD)
1974—Broncos, 27-7 (D)
Chargers, 17-0 (SD)
1975—Broncos, 27-17 (SD)
Broncos, 13-10 (D) OT
1976—Broncos, 26-0 (D)
Broncos, 17-0 (SD)
1977—Broncos, 17-14 (D)
Broncos, 17-9 (SD)
1978—Broncos, 27-14 (D)
Chargers, 23-0 (SD)
1979—Broncos, 7-0 (D)
Chargers, 17-7 (SD)
1980—Chargers, 30-13 (D)
Broncos, 20-13 (SD)
1981—Broncos, 42-24 (D)
Chargers, 34-17 (SD)
1982—Chargers, 23-3 (D)
Chargers, 30-20 (SD)
1983—Broncos, 14-6 (D)
Chargers, 31-7 (SD)
(Points—Chargers 1,161, Broncos 959)
*Franchise in Los Angeles prior to 1961
**DENVER vs. SAN FRANCISCO**
Series tied, 2-2
1970—49ers, 19-14 (SF)
1973—49ers, 36-34 (D)
1979—Broncos, 38-28 (SF)
1982—Broncos, 24-21 (D)
(Points—Broncos 110, 49ers 104)
**DENVER vs. SEATTLE**
Broncos lead series, 8-6
1977—Broncos, 24-13 (S)
1978—Broncos, 28-7 (D)
Broncos, 20-17 (S) OT
1979—Broncos, 37-34 (D)
Seahawks, 28-23 (S)
1980—Broncos, 36-20 (D)
Broncos, 25-17 (S)
1981—Seahawks, 13-10 (S)
Broncos, 23-13 (D)
1982—Seahawks, 17-10 (D)
Seahawks, 13-11 (S)
1983—Seahawks, 27-19 (S)
Broncos, 38-27 (D)
*Seahawks, 31-7 (S)
(Points—Broncos 311, Seahawks 277)
*AFC First Round Playoff
**DENVER vs. TAMPA BAY**
Broncos lead series, 2-0
1976—Broncos, 48-13 (D)
1981—Broncos, 24-7 (TB)
(Points—Broncos 72, Buccaneers 20)
**DENVER vs. WASHINGTON**
Redskins lead series, 2-1
1970—Redskins, 19-3 (D)
1974—Redskins, 30-3 (W)
1980—Broncos, 20-17 (D)
(Points—Redskins 66, Broncos 26)

**DETROIT vs. ATLANTA**
Lions lead series, 10-4;
See Atlanta vs. Detroit
**DETROIT vs. BALTIMORE**
Series tied, 16-16-2;
See Baltimore vs. Detroit
**DETROIT vs. BUFFALO**
Series tied, 1-1-1;
See Buffalo vs. Detroit
**DETROIT vs. CHICAGO**
Bears lead series, 60-44-5;
See Chicago vs. Detroit
**DETROIT vs. CINCINNATI**
Lions lead series, 2-1;
See Cincinnati vs. Detroit
**DETROIT vs. CLEVELAND**
Lions lead series, 12-3;
See Cleveland vs. Detroit
**DETROIT vs. DALLAS**
Cowboys lead series, 6-2;
See Dallas vs. Detroit
**DETROIT vs. DENVER**
Series tied, 2-2;
See Denver vs. Detroit
**\*DETROIT vs. GREEN BAY**
Packers lead series, 54-46-7
1930—Packers, 47-13 (GB)
Tie, 6-6 (P)
1932—Packers, 15-10 (GB)
Spartans, 19-0 (P)
1933—Packers, 17-0 (GB)
Spartans, 7-0 (P)
1934—Lions, 3-0 (GB)
Packers, 3-0 (D)

1935—Packers, 13-9 (GB)
    Packers, 31-7 (GB)
    Lions, 20-10 (D)
1936—Packers, 20-18 (GB)
    Packers, 26-17 (D)
1937—Packers, 26-6 (GB)
    Packers, 14-13 (D)
1938—Lions, 17-7 (GB)
    Packers, 28-7 (D)
1939—Packers, 26-7 (GB)
    Packers, 12-7 (D)
1940—Lions, 23-14 (GB)
    Packers, 50-7 (D)
1941—Packers, 23-0 (GB)
    Packers, 24-7 (D)
1942—Packers, 38-7 (Mil)
    Packers, 28-7 (D)
1943—Packers, 35-14 (GB)
    Packers, 27-6 (D)
1944—Packers, 27-6 (GB)
    Packers, 14-0 (D)
1945—Packers, 57-21 (Mil)
    Lions, 14-3 (D)
1946—Packers, 10-7 (Mil)
    Packers, 9-0 (D)
1947—Packers, 34-17 (GB)
    Packers, 35-14 (D)
1948—Packers, 33-21 (GB)
    Lions, 24-20 (D)
1949—Packers, 16-14 (GB)
    Lions, 21-7 (D)
1950—Packers, 45-7 (GB)
    Lions, 24-21 (D)
1951—Lions, 24-17 (GB)
    Lions, 52-35 (D)
1952—Lions, 52-17 (GB)
    Lions, 48-24 (D)
1953—Lions, 14-7 (GB)
    Lions, 34-15 (D)
1954—Lions, 21-17 (GB)
    Lions, 28-24 (D)
1955—Packers, 20-17 (GB)
    Lions, 24-10 (D)
1956—Lions, 20-16 (GB)
    Packers, 24-20 (D)
1957—Lions, 24-14 (GB)
    Lions, 18-6 (D)
1958—Tie, 13-13 (GB)
    Lions, 24-14 (D)
1959—Packers, 28-10 (GB)
    Packers, 24-17 (D)
1960—Packers, 28-9 (GB)
    Lions, 23-10 (D)
1961—Lions, 17-13 (Mil)
    Packers, 17-9 (D)
1962—Packers, 9-7 (GB)
    Lions, 26-14 (D)
1963—Packers, 31-10 (Mil)
    Tie, 13-13 (D)
1964—Lions, 14-10 (D)
    Packers, 30-7 (GB)
1965—Packers, 31-21 (D)
    Lions, 12-7 (GB)
1966—Packers, 23-14 (GB)
    Packers, 31-7 (D)
1967—Tie, 17-17 (GB)
    Packers, 27-17 (D)
1968—Packers, 23-17 (GB)
    Tie, 14-14 (D)
1969—Packers, 28-17 (GB)
    Lions, 16-10 (GB)
1970—Lions, 40-0 (GB)
    Lions, 20-0 (D)
1971—Lions, 31-28 (D)
    Tie, 14-14 (Mil)
1972—Packers, 24-23 (D)
    Packers, 33-7 (GB)
1973—Tie, 13-13 (GB)
    Lions, 34-0 (D)
1974—Packers, 21-19 (Mil)
    Lions, 19-17 (D)
1975—Lions, 30-16 (Mil)
    Lions, 13-10 (D)
1976—Packers, 24-14 (GB)
    Lions, 27-6 (D)
1977—Lions, 10-6 (D)
    Packers, 10-9 (GB)
1978—Packers, 13-7 (D)
    Packers, 35-14 (Mil)
1979—Packers, 24-16 (Mil)
    Packers, 18-13 (D)
1980—Lions, 29-7 (Mil)
    Lions, 24-3 (D)
1981—Lions, 31-27 (D)
    Packers, 31-17 (GB)
1982—Lions, 30-10 (GB)
    Lions, 27-24 (D)
1983—Lions, 38-14 (D)
    Lions, 23-20 (Mil) OT
(Points—Packers 1,990, Lions 1,826)
*Franchise in Portsmouth prior to 1934
and known as the Spartans

## DETROIT vs. HOUSTON

Oilers lead series, 2-1
1971—Lions, 31-7 (H)
1975—Oilers, 24-8 (H)
1983—Oilers, 27-17 (H)
(Points—Oilers 58, Lions 56)

## DETROIT vs. KANSAS CITY

Series tied, 2-2
1971—Lions, 32-21 (D)
1975—Chiefs, 24-21 (KC) OT
1980—Chiefs, 20-17 (KC)
1981—Lions, 27-10 (D)
(Points—Lions 97, Chiefs 75)

## DETROIT vs. *L.A. RAIDERS

Series tied, 2-2
1970—Lions, 28-14 (D)
1974—Raiders, 35-13 (O)
1978—Raiders, 29-17 (O)
1981—Lions, 16-0 (D)
(Points—Raiders 78, Lions 74)
*Franchise in Oakland prior to 1982

## DETROIT vs. *L.A. RAMS

Rams lead series, 36-34-1
1937—Lions, 28-0 (C)
    Lions, 27-7 (D)
1938—Rams, 21-17 (C)
    Lions, 6-0 (D)
1939—Lions, 15-7 (D)
    Rams, 14-3 (C)
1940—Lions, 6-0 (D)
    Rams, 24-0 (C)
1941—Lions, 17-7 (D)
    Lions, 14-0 (C)
1942—Rams, 14-0 (D)
    Rams, 27-7 (C)
1944—Rams, 20-17 (D)
    Lions, 26-14 (C)
1945—Lions, 28-21 (D)
1946—Rams, 35-14 (LA)
    Rams, 41-20 (D)
1947—Rams, 27-13 (D)
    Rams, 28-17 (LA)
1948—Rams, 44-7 (LA)
    Rams, 34-27 (D)
1949—Rams, 27-24 (LA)
    Rams, 21-10 (D)
1950—Rams, 30-28 (D)
    Rams, 65-24 (LA)
1951—Rams, 27-21 (D)
    Lions, 24-22 (LA)
1952—Lions, 17-14 (LA)
    Lions, 24-16 (D)
1953—Rams, 31-19 (D)
    Rams, 37-24 (LA)
1954—Lions, 21-3 (D)
    Lions, 27-24 (LA)
1955—Rams, 17-10 (D)
    Rams, 24-13 (LA)
1956—Lions, 24-21 (D)
    Lions, 16-7 (LA)
1957—Lions, 10-7 (D)
    Rams, 35-17 (LA)
1958—Rams, 42-28 (D)
    Lions, 41-24 (LA)
1959—Lions, 17-7 (LA)
    Lions, 23-17 (D)
1960—Rams, 48-35 (LA)
    Lions, 12-10 (D)
1961—Lions, 14-13 (D)
    Lions, 28-10 (LA)
1962—Lions, 13-10 (D)
    Lions, 12-3 (LA)
1963—Lions, 23-2 (LA)
    Rams, 28-21 (D)
1964—Tie, 17-17 (LA)
    Lions, 37-17 (D)
1965—Lions, 20-0 (D)
    Lions, 31-7 (LA)
1966—Rams, 14-7 (D)
    Rams, 23-3 (LA)
1967—Rams, 31-7 (D)
1968—Rams, 10-7 (LA)
1969—Lions, 28-0 (D)
1970—Lions, 28-23 (LA)
1971—Lions, 21-13 (D)
1972—Lions, 34-17 (LA)
1974—Rams, 16-13 (LA)
1975—Lions, 20-0 (D)
1976—Rams, 20-17 (D)
1980—Lions, 41-20 (LA)
1981—Rams, 20-13 (LA)
1982—Lions, 19-14 (LA)
1983—Lions, 21-10 (LA)
(Points—Rams 1,366, Lions 1,298)
*Franchise in Cleveland prior to 1946
**Conference Playoff

## DETROIT vs. MIAMI

Dolphins lead series, 2-0
1973—Dolphins, 34-7 (M)
1979—Dolphins, 28-10 (D)
(Points—Dolphins 62, Lions 17)

## DETROIT vs. MINNESOTA

Vikings lead series, 28-15-2
1961—Lions, 37-10 (M)
    Lions, 13-7 (D)
1962—Lions, 17-6 (M)
    Lions, 37-23 (D)
1963—Lions, 28-10 (D)
    Vikings, 34-31 (M)
1964—Lions, 24-20 (M)
    Tie, 23-23 (D)
1965—Lions, 31-29 (M)
    Vikings, 29-7 (D)
1966—Lions, 32-31 (M)
    Vikings, 28-16 (D)
1967—Tie, 10-10 (M)
    Lions, 14-3 (D)
1968—Vikings, 24-10 (M)
    Vikings, 13-6 (D)
1969—Vikings, 24-10 (M)
    Vikings, 27-0 (D)
1970—Vikings, 30-17 (D)
    Vikings, 24-20 (M)
1971—Vikings, 16-13 (D)
    Vikings, 29-10 (M)
1972—Vikings, 34-10 (D)
    Vikings, 16-14 (M)
1973—Vikings, 23-9 (D)
    Vikings, 28-7 (M)
1974—Vikings, 7-6 (D)
    Lions, 20-16 (M)
1975—Vikings, 25-19 (M)
    Lions, 17-10 (D)
1976—Vikings, 10-9 (D)
    Vikings, 31-23 (M)
1977—Vikings, 14-7 (M)
    Vikings, 30-21 (D)
1978—Vikings, 17-7 (M)
    Lions, 45-14 (D)
1979—Vikings, 13-10 (D)
    Vikings, 14-7 (M)
1980—Lions, 27-7 (D)
    Vikings, 34-0 (M)
1981—Vikings, 26-24 (M)
    Lions, 45-7 (D)
1982—Vikings, 34-31 (M)
    Vikings, 20-17 (M)
1983—Vikings, 20-17 (M)
    Lions, 13-2 (D)
(Points—Vikings 882, Lions 794)

## DETROIT vs. NEW ENGLAND

Lions lead series, 2-1
1971—Lions, 34-7 (NE)
1976—Lions, 30-10 (D)
1979—Patriots, 24-17 (NE)
(Points—Lions 81, Patriots 41)

## DETROIT vs. NEW ORLEANS

Series tied, 4-4-1
1968—Tie, 20-20 (D)
1970—Saints, 19-17 (NO)
1972—Lions, 27-14 (D)
1973—Saints, 20-13 (NO)
1974—Lions, 19-14 (D)
1976—Saints, 17-16 (NO)
1977—Lions, 23-19 (D)
1979—Saints, 17-7 (NO)
1980—Lions, 24-13 (D)
(Points—Lions 166, Saints 153)

## *DETROIT vs. N.Y. GIANTS

Lions lead series, 18-11-1
1930—Giants, 19-6 (P)
1931—Spartans, 14-6 (P)
    Giants, 14-0 (NY)
1932—Spartans, 7-0 (P)
    Spartans, 6-0 (NY)
1933—Spartans, 17-7 (P)
    Giants, 13-10 (NY)
1934—Lions, 9-0 (D)
1935—**Lions, 26-7 (D)
1936—Giants, 14-7 (NY)
    Lions, 38-0 (D)
1937—Lions, 17-0 (NY)
1939—Lions, 18-14 (D)
1941—Giants, 20-13 (NY)
1943—Tie, 0-0 (D)
1945—Giants, 35-14 (NY)
1947—Giants, 35-7 (D)
1949—Lions, 45-21 (NY)
1953—Lions, 27-16 (NY)
1955—Giants, 24-19 (D)
1958—Giants, 19-17 (D)
1962—Lions, 17-14 (NY)
1964—Lions, 26-3 (D)
1967—Lions, 30-7 (NY)
1969—Lions, 24-0 (D)
1972—Lions, 30-16 (D)
1974—Lions, 20-19 (D)
1976—Giants, 24-10 (NY)
1982—Giants, 13-6 (D)
1983—Lions, 15-9 (D)
(Points—Lions 520, Giants 344)
*Franchise in Portsmouth prior to 1934 and
known as the Spartans
**NFL Championship

## DETROIT vs. N.Y. JETS

Jets lead series, 2-1
1972—Lions, 37-20 (D)
1979—Jets, 31-10 (NY)
1982—Jets, 28-13 (D)
(Points—Jets 79, Lions 60)

## *DETROIT vs. PHILADELPHIA

Lions lead series, 11-9-1
1933—Spartans, 25-0 (P)
1934—Lions, 10-0 (D)
1935—Lions, 35-0 (D)
1936—Lions, 23-0 (D)
1938—Eagles, 21-7 (D)
1940—Lions, 21-0 (D)
1941—Lions, 21-17 (D)
1945—Lions, 28-24 (D)
1948—Eagles, 45-21 (P)
1949—Eagles, 22-14 (D)
1951—Lions, 28-10 (P)
1954—Tie, 13-13 (D)
1957—Lions, 27-16 (P)
1960—Eagles, 28-10 (P)
1961—Eagles, 27-24 (D)
1965—Lions, 35-28 (P)
1968—Eagles, 12-0 (D)
1971—Eagles, 23-20 (P)
1974—Eagles, 28-17 (P)
1977—Lions, 17-13 (D)
1979—Eagles, 44-7 (P)
(Points—Lions 403, Eagles 371)
*Franchise in Portsmouth prior to 1934 and
known as the Spartans

## DETROIT vs. *PITTSBURGH

Lions lead series, 13-8-1
1934—Lions, 40-7 (D)
1936—Lions, 28-3 (D)
1937—Lions, 7-3 (D)
1938—Lions, 16-7 (D)
1940—Pirates, 10-7 (D)
1942—Steelers, 35-7 (D)
1946—Lions, 17-7 (D)
1947—Steelers, 17-10 (P)
1948—Lions, 17-14 (D)
1949—Steelers, 14-7 (P)
1950—Lions, 10-7 (D)
1952—Lions, 31-6 (P)
1953—Lions, 38-21 (D)
1955—Lions, 31-28 (P)
1956—Lions, 45-7 (D)
1959—Tie, 10-10 (P)
1962—Lions, 45-7 (D)
1966—Steelers, 17-3 (P)
1967—Steelers, 24-14 (D)
1969—Steelers, 16-13 (P)
1973—Steelers, 24-10 (P)
1983—Lions, 45-3 (D)
(Points—Lions 451, Steelers 287)
*Steelers known as Pirates prior to 1941

## *DETROIT vs. **ST. LOUIS

Lions lead series, 25-15-5
1930—Tie, 0-0 (P)
    Cardinals, 23-0 (C)
1931—Cardinals, 20-19 (C)
1932—Tie, 7-7 (P)
1933—Spartans, 7-6 (P)
1934—Lions, 6-0 (D)
    Lions, 17-13 (C)
1935—Tie, 10-10 (D)
    Lions, 7-6 (C)
1936—Lions, 39-0 (D)
    Lions, 14-7 (C)
1937—Lions, 16-7 (C)
    Lions, 16-7 (D)
1938—Lions, 10-0 (C)
    Lions, 7-3 (D)
1939—Lions, 21-3 (D)
    Lions, 17-3 (C)
1940—Tie, 0-0 (Buffalo)
    Lions, 43-14 (C)
1941—Tie, 14-14 (C)
    Lions, 21-3 (D)
1942—Cardinals, 13-0 (C)
    Cardinals, 7-0 (D)
1943—Lions, 35-17 (D)
    Lions, 7-0 (C)
1945—Lions, 10-0 (C)
    Lions, 26-0 (D)
1946—Cardinals, 34-14 (C)
    Cardinals, 36-14 (D)
1947—Cardinals, 45-21 (C)
    Cardinals, 17-7 (D)
1948—Cardinals, 56-20 (C)
    Cardinals, 28-14 (D)
1949—Lions, 24-7 (C)
    Cardinals, 42-19 (D)
1959—Lions, 45-21 (D)
1961—Lions, 45-14 (StL)
1967—Cardinals, 38-28 (StL)
1969—Lions, 20-0 (D)
1970—Lions, 16-3 (D)
1973—Lions, 20-16 (StL)
1975—Cardinals, 24-13 (D)
1978—Cardinals, 21-14 (StL)
1980—Lions, 20-7 (D)
    Cardinals, 24-23 (StL)
(Points—Lions 746, Cardinals 626)

*Franchise in Portsmouth prior to 1934 and known as the Spartans
**Franchise in Chicago prior to 1960
**DETROIT vs. SAN DIEGO**
Lions lead series, 3-1
1972—Lions, 34-20 (D)
1977—Lions, 20-0 (D)
1978—Lions, 31-14 (D)
1981—Chargers, 28-23 (SD)
(Points—Lions 108, Chargers 62)
**DETROIT vs. SAN FRANCISCO**
Lions lead series, 25-22-1
1950—Lions, 24-7 (D)
    49ers, 28-27 (SF)
1951—Lions, 20-10 (D)
    49ers, 21-17 (SF)
1952—49ers, 17-3 (SF)
    49ers, 28-0 (SF)
1953—Lions, 24-21 (D)
    Lions, 14-10 (SF)
1954—49ers, 37-31 (SF)
    Lions, 48-7 (D)
1955—Lions, 27-24 (D)
    49ers, 38-21 (SF)
1956—Lions, 20-17 (D)
    Lions, 17-13 (SF)
1957—49ers, 35-31 (SF)
    Lions, 31-10 (D)
    *Lions, 31-27 (SF)
1958—49ers, 24-21 (SF)
    Lions, 35-21 (D)
1959—49ers, 34-13 (SF)
    49ers, 33-7 (SF)
1960—49ers, 14-10 (D)
    Lions, 24-0 (SF)
1961—49ers, 49-0 (D)
    Tie, 20-20 (SF)
1962—Lions, 45-24 (D)
    Lions, 38-24 (SF)
1963—Lions, 26-3 (D)
    Lions, 45-7 (SF)
1964—Lions, 26-17 (SF)
    Lions, 24-7 (D)
1965—49ers, 27-21 (D)
    49ers, 17-14 (SF)
1966—49ers, 27-24 (D)
    49ers, 41-14 (D)
1967—Lions, 45-3 (SF)
1968—49ers, 14-7 (D)
1969—Lions, 26-14 (SF)
1970—Lions, 28-7 (D)
1971—49ers, 31-27 (SF)
1973—Lions, 30-20 (D)
1974—Lions, 17-13 (D)
1975—Lions, 28-17 (SF)
1977—49ers, 28-7 (SF)
1978—Lions, 33-14 (D)
1980—Lions, 17-13 (D)
1981—Lions, 24-17 (D)
1983—**49ers, 24-23 (SF)
(Points—Lions 1,092, 49ers 967)
*Conference Playoff
**NFC Divisional Playoff
**DETROIT vs. SEATTLE**
Series tied, 1-1
1976—Lions, 41-14 (S)
1978—Seahawks, 28-16 (S)
(Points—Lions 57, Seahawks 42)
**DETROIT vs. TAMPA BAY**
Lions lead series, 7-5
1977—Lions, 16-7 (D)
1978—Lions, 15-7 (TB)
    Lions, 34-23 (D)
1979—Buccaneers, 31-16 (TB)
    Buccaneers, 16-14 (D)
1980—Lions, 24-10 (TB)
    Lions, 27-14 (D)
1981—Buccaneers, 28-10 (TB)
    Buccaneers, 20-17 (D)
1982—Buccaneers, 23-21 (TB)
1983—Lions, 11-0 (TB)
    Lions, 23-20 (D)
(Points—Lions 228, Buccaneers 199)
***DETROIT vs. **WASHINGTON**
Redskins lead series, 17-8
1932—Spartans, 10-0 (P)
1933—Spartans, 13-0 (B)
1934—Lions, 24-0 (D)
1935—Lions, 17-7 (B)
    Lions, 14-0 (D)
1938—Redskins, 7-5 (D)
1939—Redskins, 31-7 (W)
1940—Redskins, 20-14 (D)
1942—Redskins, 15-3 (D)
1943—Redskins, 42-20 (W)
1946—Redskins, 17-16 (W)
1947—Lions, 38-21 (D)
1948—Redskins, 46-21 (D)
1951—Lions, 35-17 (D)
1956—Redskins, 18-17 (W)
1965—Lions, 14-10 (D)
1968—Redskins, 14-3 (W)
1970—Redskins, 31-10 (W)

1973—Redskins, 20-0 (D)
1976—Redskins, 20-7 (W)
1978—Redskins, 21-19 (D)
1979—Redskins, 27-24 (D)
1981—Redskins, 33-31 (W)
1982—***Redskins, 31-7 (W)
1983—Redskins, 38-17 (W)
(Points—Redskins 486, Lions 386)
*Franchise in Portsmouth prior to 1934 and known as the Spartans
**Franchise in Boston prior to 1937
***NFC First Round Playoff

---

**GREEN BAY vs. ATLANTA**
Packers lead series, 8-6;
See Atlanta vs. Green Bay
**GREEN BAY vs. BALTIMORE**
Packers lead series, 18-16-1
See Baltimore vs. Green Bay
**GREEN BAY vs. BUFFALO**
Bills lead series, 2-1;
See Buffalo vs. Green Bay
**GREEN BAY vs. CHICAGO**
Bears lead series, 67-54-6;
See Chicago vs. Green Bay
**GREEN BAY vs. CINCINNATI**
Bengals lead series, 3-2;
See Cincinnati vs. Green Bay
**GREEN BAY vs. CLEVELAND**
Packers lead series, 7-5
See Cleveland vs. Green Bay
**GREEN BAY vs. DALLAS**
Packers lead series, 8-4;
See Dallas vs. Green Bay
**GREEN BAY vs. DENVER**
Broncos lead series, 2-1;
See Denver vs. Green Bay
**GREEN BAY vs. DETROIT**
Packers lead series, 54-46-7;
See Detroit vs. Green Bay
**GREEN BAY vs. HOUSTON**
Series tied, 2-2
1972—Packers, 23-10 (H)
1977—Oilers, 16-10 (GB)
1980—Oilers, 22-3 (GB)
1983—Packers, 41-38 (H) OT
(Points—Oilers 86, Packers 77)
**GREEN BAY vs. KANSAS CITY**
Series tied, 1-1-1
1966—*Packers, 35-10 (Los Angeles)
1973—Tie, 10-10 (Mil)
1977—Chiefs, 20-10 (KC)
(Points—Packers 55, Chiefs 40)
*Super Bowl I
**GREEN BAY vs. *L.A. RAIDERS**
Raiders lead series, 3-1
1967—**Packers, 33-14 (Miami)
1972—Raiders, 20-14 (GB)
1976—Raiders, 18-14 (O)
1978—Raiders, 28-3 (GB)
(Points—Raiders 80, Packers 64)
*Franchise in Oakland prior to 1982
**Super Bowl II
**GREEN BAY vs. *L.A. RAMS**
Rams lead series, 38-33-2
1937—Packers, 35-10 (C)
    Packers, 35-7 (GB)
1938—Packers, 26-17 (GB)
    Packers, 28-7 (C)
1939—Rams, 27-24 (GB)
    Packers, 7-6 (C)
1940—Packers, 31-14 (GB)
    Tie, 13-13 (C)
1941—Packers, 24-7 (Mil)
    Packers, 17-14 (C)
1942—Packers, 45-28 (GB)
    Packers, 30-12 (C)
1944—Packers, 30-21 (GB)
    Packers, 42-7 (C)
1945—Rams, 27-14 (GB)
    Rams, 20-7 (C)
1946—Rams, 21-17 (Mil)
    Rams, 38-17 (LA)
1947—Packers, 17-14 (Mil)
    Packers, 30-10 (LA)
1948—Packers, 16-0 (GB)
    Rams, 24-10 (LA)
1949—Rams, 48-7 (GB)
    Rams, 35-7 (LA)
1950—Rams, 45-14 (Mil)
    Rams, 51-14 (LA)
1951—Rams, 28-0 (Mil)
    Rams, 42-14 (LA)
1952—Rams, 30-28 (Mil)
    Rams, 45-27 (LA)
1953—Rams, 38-20 (Mil)
    Rams, 33-17 (LA)
1954—Packers, 35-17 (Mil)
    Rams, 35-27 (LA)
1955—Packers, 30-28 (Mil)
    Rams, 31-17 (LA)
1956—Packers, 42-17 (Mil)
    Rams, 49-21 (LA)

1957—Rams, 31-27 (Mil)
    Rams, 42-17 (LA)
1958—Rams, 20-7 (GB)
    Rams, 34-20 (LA)
1959—Rams, 45-6 (Mil)
    Packers, 38-20 (LA)
1960—Rams, 33-31 (Mil)
    Packers, 35-2 (LA)
1961—Packers, 35-17 (GB)
    Packers, 24-17 (LA)
1962—Packers, 41-10 (Mil)
    Packers, 20-17 (LA)
1963—Packers, 42-10 (Mil)
    Packers, 31-14 (LA)
1964—Packers, 27-17 (Mil)
    Tie, 24-24 (LA)
1965—Packers, 6-3 (Mil)
    Rams, 21-10 (LA)
1966—Packers, 24-13 (GB)
    Packers, 27-23 (LA)
1967—Rams, 27-24 (LA)
    **Packers, 28-7 (Mil)
1968—Rams, 16-14 (Mil)
1969—Rams, 34-21 (LA)
1970—Rams, 31-21 (GB)
1971—Rams, 30-13 (LA)
1973—Rams, 24-7 (LA)
1974—Packers, 17-6 (Mil)
1975—Rams, 22-5 (LA)
1977—Rams, 24-6 (Mil)
1978—Rams, 31-14 (LA)
1980—Rams, 51-21 (LA)
1981—Rams, 35-23 (LA)
1982—Packers, 35-23 (Mil)
1983—Packers, 27-24 (Mil)
(Points—Rams 1,743, Packers 1,593)
*Franchise in Cleveland prior to 1946
**Conference Championship
**GREEN BAY vs. MIAMI**
Dolphins lead series, 3-0
1971—Dolphins, 27-6 (Mia)
1975—Dolphins, 31-7 (GB)
1979—Dolphins, 27-7 (Mia)
(Points—Dolphins 85, Packers 20)
**GREEN BAY vs. MINNESOTA**
Vikings lead series, 24-20-1
1961—Packers, 33-7 (Minn)
    Packers, 28-10 (GB)
1962—Packers, 34-7 (GB)
    Packers, 48-21 (Minn)
1963—Packers, 37-28 (Minn)
    Packers, 28-7 (GB)
1964—Vikings, 24-23 (GB)
    Packers, 42-13 (Minn)
1965—Packers, 38-13 (Minn)
    Packers, 24-19 (GB)
1966—Vikings, 20-17 (GB)
    Packers, 28-16 (Minn)
1967—Vikings, 10-7 (Mil)
    Packers, 30-27 (Minn)
1968—Vikings, 26-13 (Mil)
    Vikings, 14-10 (Minn)
1969—Vikings, 19-7 (Minn)
    Vikings, 9-7 (Mil)
1970—Packers, 13-10 (Mil)
    Vikings, 10-3 (Minn)
1971—Vikings, 24-13 (GB)
    Vikings, 3-0 (Minn)
1972—Vikings, 27-13 (GB)
    Packers, 23-7 (Minn)
1973—Vikings, 11-3 (Minn)
    Vikings, 31-7 (GB)
1974—Vikings, 32-17 (GB)
    Packers, 19-7 (Minn)
1975—Vikings, 28-17 (GB)
    Vikings, 24-3 (Minn)
1976—Vikings, 17-10 (Minn)
    Vikings, 20-9 (Minn)
1977—Vikings, 19-7 (GB)
    Vikings, 13-6 (GB)
1978—Vikings, 21-7 (Minn)
    Tie, 10-10 (GB) OT
1979—Vikings, 27-21 (Minn) OT
    Packers, 19-7 (Mil)
1980—Packers, 16-3 (GB)
    Packers, 25-13 (Minn)
1981—Vikings, 30-13 (Mil)
    Packers, 35-23 (Minn)
1982—Packers, 26-7 (Mil)
1983—Vikings, 20-17 (GB) OT
(Points—Packers 835, Vikings 755)
**GREEN BAY vs. NEW ENGLAND**
Series tied, 1-1
1973—Patriots, 33-24 (NE)
1979—Packers, 27-14 (GB)
(Points—Packers 51, Patriots 47)
**GREEN BAY vs. NEW ORLEANS**
Packers lead series, 8-2
1968—Packers, 29-7 (Mil)
1971—Saints, 29-21 (Mil)
1972—Packers, 30-20 (NO)
1973—Packers, 30-10 (Mil)

1975—Saints, 20-19 (NO)
1976—Packers, 32-27 (Mil)
1977—Packers, 24-20 (NO)
1978—Packers, 28-17 (NO)
1979—Packers, 28-19 (Mil)
1981—Packers, 35-7 (NO)
(Points—Packers 276, Saints 176)
**GREEN BAY vs. N.Y. GIANTS**
Packers lead series, 24-18-2
1928—Giants, 6-0 (NY)
    Packers, 7-0 (NY)
1929—Packers, 20-6 (NY)
1930—Packers, 14-7 (GB)
    Giants, 13-6 (NY)
1931—Packers, 27-7 (GB)
    Packers, 14-10 (NY)
1932—Packers, 13-0 (GB)
    Giants, 6-0 (NY)
1933—Giants, 10-7 (Mil)
    Giants, 17-6 (NY)
1934—Packers, 20-6 (Mil)
    Giants, 17-3 (NY)
1935—Packers, 16-7 (GB)
1936—Packers, 26-14 (NY)
1937—Giants, 10-0 (NY)
1938—Packers, 15-3 (NY)
    *Giants, 23-17 (NY)
1939—*Packers, 27-0 (Mil)
1940—Giants, 7-3 (NY)
1942—Tie, 21-21 (NY)
1943—Packers, 35-21 (NY)
1944—Packers, 24-0 (NY)
    *Packers, 14-7 (NY)
1945—Packers, 23-14 (NY)
1947—Tie, 24-24 (NY)
1948—Giants, 49-3 (Mil)
1949—Giants, 30-10 (GB)
1952—Packers, 17-3 (NY)
1957—Giants, 31-17 (GB)
1959—Giants, 20-3 (NY)
1961—Packers, 20-17 (NY)
    *Packers, 37-0 (GB)
1962—*Packers, 16-7 (NY)
1967—Packers, 48-21 (NY)
1969—Packers, 20-10 (Mil)
1971—Giants, 42-40 (GB)
1973—Packers, 16-14 (New Haven)
1975—Packers, 40-14 (NY)
1980—Giants, 27-21 (NY)
1981—Packers, 27-14 (NY)
    Packers, 26-24 (NY)
1982—Packers, 27-19 (NY)
1983—Giants, 27-3 (NY)
(Points—Packers 737, Giants 661)
*NFL Championship
**GREEN BAY vs. N.Y. JETS**
Jets lead series, 3-1
1973—Packers, 23-7 (Mil)
1979—Jets, 27-22 (GB)
1981—Jets, 28-3 (NY)
1982—Jets, 15-13 (NY)
(Points—Jets 77, Packers 61)
**GREEN BAY vs. PHILADELPHIA**
Packers lead series, 17-5
1933—Packers, 35-9 (GB)
    Packers, 10-0 (P)
1934—Packers, 19-6 (GB)
1935—Packers, 13-6 (P)
1937—Packers, 37-7 (Mil)
1939—Packers, 23-16 (P)
1940—Packers, 27-20 (GB)
1942—Packers, 7-0 (P)
1946—Packers, 19-7 (P)
1947—Eagles, 28-14 (P)
1951—Packers, 37-24 (GB)
1952—Packers, 12-10 (Mil)
1954—Packers, 37-14 (P)
1958—Packers, 38-35 (GB)
1960—*Eagles, 17-13 (P)
1962—Packers, 49-0 (P)
1968—Packers, 30-13 (GB)
1970—Packers, 30-17 (Mil)
1974—Eagles, 36-14 (P)
1976—Packers, 28-13 (GB)
1978—Eagles, 10-3 (P)
1979—Eagles, 21-10 (GB)
(Points—Packers 505, Eagles 309)
*NFL Championship
**GREEN BAY vs. *PITTSBURGH**
Packers lead series, 16-10
1933—Packers, 47-0 (GB)
1935—Packers, 27-0 (GB)
    Packers, 34-14 (P)
1936—Packers, 42-10 (GB)
1938—Packers, 20-0 (GB)
1940—Packers, 24-3 (Mil)
1941—Packers, 54-7 (P)
1942—Packers, 24-21 (Mil)
1946—Packers, 17-7 (GB)
1947—Steelers, 18-17 (Mil)
1948—Steelers, 38-7 (P)
1949—Steelers, 30-7 (P)
1951—Packers, 35-33 (Mil)
    Steelers, 28-7 (P)

1953—Steelers, 31-14 (P)
1954—Steelers, 21-20 (GB)
1957—Packers, 27-10 (P)
1960—Packers, 19-13 (P)
1963—Packers, 33-14 (Mil)
1965—Packers, 41-9 (P)
1967—Steelers, 24-17 (GB)
1969—Packers, 38-34 (P)
1970—Packers, 20-12 (P)
1975—Steelers, 16-13 (Mil)
1980—Steelers, 22-20 (P)
1983—Steelers, 25-21 (GB)
(Points—Packers 645, Steelers 440)
*Steelers known as Pirates prior to 1941

**GREEN BAY vs. *ST. LOUIS**
Packers lead series, 37-20-4
1921—Tie, 3-3 (C)
1922—Cardinals, 16-3 (C)
1924—Cardinals, 3-0 (C)
1925—Cardinals, 9-6 (C)
1926—Cardinals, 13-7 (GB)
　　　Packers, 3-0 (C)
1927—Packers, 13-0 (GB)
　　　Tie, 6-6 (C)
1928—Packers, 20-0 (GB)
1929—Packers, 9-2 (GB)
　　　Packers, 7-6 (C)
　　　Packers, 12-0 (C)
1930—Packers, 14-0 (GB)
　　　Cardinals, 13-6 (C)
1931—Packers, 26-7 (GB)
　　　Cardinals, 21-13 (C)
1932—Packers, 15-7 (GB)
　　　Packers, 19-9 (C)
1933—Packers, 14-6 (C)
1934—Packers, 15-0 (GB)
　　　Cardinals, 9-0 (Mil)
　　　Cardinals, 6-0 (C)
1935—Cardinals, 7-6 (GB)
　　　Cardinals, 3-0 (Mil)
　　　Cardinals, 9-7 (C)
1936—Packers, 10-7 (GB)
　　　Packers, 24-0 (Mil)
　　　Tie, 0-0 (C)
1937—Cardinals, 14-7 (GB)
　　　Packers, 34-13 (Mil)
1938—Packers, 28-7 (Mil)
　　　Packers, 24-22 (Buffalo)
1939—Packers, 14-10 (GB)
　　　Packers, 27-20 (Mil)
1940—Packers, 31-6 (Mil)
　　　Packers, 28-7 (C)
1941—Packers, 14-13 (Mil)
　　　Packers, 17-9 (GB)
1942—Packers, 17-13 (C)
　　　Packers, 55-24 (GB)
1943—Packers, 28-7 (C)
　　　Packers, 35-14 (Mil)
1945—Packers, 33-14 (GB)
1946—Packers, 19-7 (C)
　　　Cardinals, 24-6 (GB)
1947—Cardinals, 14-10 (GB)
　　　Cardinals, 21-20 (C)
1948—Cardinals, 17-7 (Mil)
　　　Cardinals, 42-7 (C)
1949—Cardinals, 39-17 (Mil)
　　　Cardinals, 41-21 (C)
1955—Packers, 31-14 (GB)
1956—Packers, 24-21 (C)
1962—Packers, 17-0 (Mil)
1963—Packers, 30-7 (StL)
1967—Packers, 31-23 (StL)
1969—Packers, 45-28 (GB)
1971—Tie, 16-16 (StL)
1973—Packers, 25-21 (GB)
1976—Cardinals, 29-0 (StL)
1982—**Packers, 41-16 (GB)
(Points—Packers 1,017, Cardinals 735)
*Franchise in Chicago prior to 1960
**NFC First Round Playoff

**GREEN BAY vs. SAN DIEGO**
Packers lead series, 3-0
1970—Packers, 22-20 (SD)
1974—Packers, 34-0 (GB)
1978—Packers, 24-3 (SD)
(Points—Packers 80, Chargers 23)

**GREEN BAY vs. SAN FRANCISCO**
49ers lead series, 22-20-1
1950—Packers, 25-21 (GB)
　　　49ers, 30-14 (SF)
1951—49ers, 31-19 (SF)
1952—49ers, 24-14 (SF)
1953—49ers, 37-7 (Mil)
　　　49ers, 48-14 (SF)
1954—49ers, 23-17 (Mil)
　　　49ers, 35-0 (SF)
1955—Packers, 27-21 (Mil)
　　　Packers, 28-7 (SF)
1956—49ers, 17-16 (GB)
　　　49ers, 38-20 (SF)
1957—49ers, 24-14 (Mil)
　　　49ers, 27-20 (SF)
1958—49ers, 33-12 (Mil)

---

　　　49ers, 48-21 (SF)
1959—Packers, 21-20 (GB)
　　　Packers, 36-14 (SF)
1960—Packers, 41-14 (Mil)
　　　Packers, 13-0 (SF)
1961—Packers, 30-10 (GB)
　　　49ers, 22-21 (SF)
1962—Packers, 31-13 (Mil)
　　　Packers, 31-21 (SF)
1963—Packers, 28-10 (Mil)
　　　Packers, 21-17 (SF)
1964—Packers, 24-14 (Mil)
　　　49ers, 24-14 (SF)
1965—Packers, 27-10 (GB)
　　　Tie, 24-24 (SF)
1966—49ers, 21-20 (SF)
　　　Packers, 20-7 (Mil)
1967—Packers, 13-0 (GB)
1968—49ers, 27-20 (SF)
1969—Packers, 14-7 (Mil)
1970—49ers, 26-10 (SF)
1972—Packers, 34-24 (Mil)
1973—49ers, 20-6 (SF)
1974—49ers, 7-6 (SF)
1976—49ers, 26-14 (GB)
1977—Packers, 16-14 (Mil)
1980—49ers, 23-16 (GB)
1981—49ers, 13-3 (Mil)
(Points—49ers 885, Packers 829)

**GREEN BAY vs. SEATTLE**
Packers lead series, 3-0
1976—Packers, 27-20 (Mil)
1978—Packers, 45-28 (Mil)
1981—Packers, 34-24 (GB)
(Points—Packers 106, Seahawks 72)

**GREEN BAY vs. TAMPA BAY**
Series tied, 5-5-1
1977—Packers, 13-0 (TB)
1978—Packers, 9-7 (GB)
　　　Packers, 17-7 (TB)
1979—Buccaneers, 21-10 (GB)
　　　Buccaneers, 21-3 (TB)
1980—Tie, 14-14 (TB) OT
　　　Buccaneers, 20-17 (Mil)
1981—Buccaneers, 21-10 (GB)
　　　Buccaneers, 37-3 (TB)
1983—Packers, 55-14 (GB)
　　　Packers, 12-9 (TB) OT
(Points—Buccaneers 171, Packers 163)

**GREEN BAY vs. *WASHINGTON**
Packers lead series, 14-11-1
1932—Packers, 21-0 (B)
1933—Tie, 7-7 (GB)
　　　Redskins, 20-7 (B)
1934—Packers, 10-0 (B)
1936—Packers, 31-2 (GB)
　　　Packers, 7-3 (B)
　　　**Packers, 21-6 (New York)
1937—Redskins, 14-6 (W)
1939—Redskins, 24-14 (W)
1941—Packers, 22-17 (W)
1943—Redskins, 33-7 (Mil)
1946—Packers, 20-7 (W)
1947—Packers, 27-10 (Mil)
1948—Redskins, 23-7 (Mil)
1949—Redskins, 30-0 (W)
1950—Packers, 35-21 (Mil)
1952—Packers, 35-20 (Mil)
1958—Redskins, 37-21 (W)
1959—Packers, 21-0 (GB)
1968—Packers, 27-7 (W)
1972—Redskins, 21-16 (W)
　　　***Redskins, 16-3 (W)
1974—Redskins, 17-6 (GB)
1977—Redskins, 10-9 (W)
1979—Redskins, 38-21 (W)
1983—Packers, 48-47 (GB)
(Points—Packers 459, Redskins 420)
*Franchise in Boston prior to 1937 and known as Braves prior to 1933
**NFL Championship
***NFC Divisional Playoff

---

See Dallas vs. Houston
**HOUSTON vs. DENVER**
Oilers lead series, 18-9-1;
See Denver vs. Houston
**HOUSTON vs. DETROIT**
Oilers lead series, 2-1;
See Detroit vs. Houston
**HOUSTON vs. GREEN BAY**
Series tied, 2-2;
See Green Bay vs. Houston
**HOUSTON vs. *KANSAS CITY**
Chiefs lead series, 20-10
1960—Oilers, 20-10 (H)
　　　Texans, 24-0 (D)
1961—Texans, 26-21 (D)
　　　Oilers, 38-7 (H)
1962—Texans, 31-7 (H)
　　　Oilers, 14-6 (D)
　　　**Texans, 20-17 (H) OT
1963—Chiefs, 28-7 (KC)
　　　Oilers, 28-7 (H)
1964—Chiefs, 28-7 (KC)
　　　Chiefs, 28-19 (H)
1965—Chiefs, 52-21 (KC)
　　　Oilers, 38-36 (H)
1966—Chiefs, 48-23 (KC)
1967—Chiefs, 25-20 (H)
　　　Oilers, 24-19 (KC)
1968—Chiefs, 26-21 (H)
　　　Chiefs, 24-10 (KC)
1969—Chiefs, 24-0 (KC)
1970—Chiefs, 24-9 (KC)
1971—Chiefs, 20-16 (H)
1973—Chiefs, 38-14 (KC)
1974—Chiefs, 17-7 (H)
1975—Oilers, 17-13 (KC)
1977—Oilers, 34-20 (H)
1978—Oilers, 20-17 (KC)
1979—Oilers, 20-6 (H)
1980—Chiefs, 21-20 (KC)
1981—Chiefs, 23-10 (KC)
1983—Chiefs, 13-10 (H) OT
(Points—Chiefs 681, Oilers 512)
*Franchise in Dallas prior to 1963 and known as Texans
**AFL Championship
**HOUSTON vs. *L.A. RAIDERS**
Raiders lead series, 20-10
1960—Oilers, 37-22 (O)
　　　Raiders, 14-13 (H)
1961—Oilers, 55-0 (H)
　　　Oilers, 47-16 (O)
1962—Oilers, 28-20 (O)
　　　Oilers, 32-17 (H)
1963—Oilers, 24-13 (H)
　　　Raiders, 52-49 (O)
1964—Oilers, 42-28 (H)
　　　Raiders, 20-10 (O)
1965—Raiders, 21-17 (O)
　　　Raiders, 33-21 (H)
1966—Oilers, 31-0 (H)
　　　Raiders, 38-23 (O)
1967—Oilers, 19-7 (H)
　　　**Raiders, 40-7 (O)
1968—Raiders, 24-15 (H)
1969—Raiders, 21-17 (O)
　　　***Raiders, 56-7 (O)
1971—Raiders, 41-21 (O)
1972—Raiders, 34-0 (H)
1973—Raiders, 17-6 (H)
1975—Oilers, 27-26 (O)
1976—Raiders, 14-13 (H)
1977—Raiders, 34-29 (O)
1978—Raiders, 21-17 (O)
1979—Oilers, 31-17 (H)
1980—****Raiders, 27-7 (O)
1981—Oilers, 17-16 (H)
1983—Raiders, 20-6 (LA)
(Points—Raiders 732, Oilers 645)
*Franchise in Oakland prior to 1982
**AFL Championship
***Inter-Divisional Playoff
****AFC First Round Playoff
**HOUSTON vs. L.A. RAMS**
Rams lead series, 2-1
1973—Rams, 31-26 (H)
1978—Rams, 10-6 (H)
1981—Oilers, 27-20 (LA)
(Points—Rams 61, Oilers 59)
**HOUSTON vs. MIAMI**
Oilers lead series, 9-8
1966—Dolphins, 20-13 (H)
　　　Dolphins, 29-28 (M)
1967—Oilers, 17-14 (H)
　　　Oilers, 41-10 (M)
1968—Oilers, 24-10 (M)
　　　Dolphins, 24-7 (H)
1969—Oilers, 22-10 (H)
　　　Oilers, 32-7 (M)
1970—Dolphins, 20-10 (H)
1972—Dolphins, 34-13 (M)
1975—Oilers, 20-19 (H)
1977—Dolphins, 27-7 (M)

---

1978—Oilers, 35-30 (H)
　　　*Oilers, 17-9 (M)
1979—Oilers, 9-6 (M)
1981—Dolphins, 16-10 (H)
1983—Dolphins, 24-17 (H)
(Points—Oilers 322, Dolphins 309)
*AFC First Round Playoff
**HOUSTON vs. MINNESOTA**
Vikings lead series, 2-1
1974—Vikings, 51-10 (H)
1980—Oilers, 20-16 (H)
1983—Vikings, 34-14 (M)
(Points—Vikings 101, Oilers 44)
**HOUSTON vs. *NEW ENGLAND**
Patriots lead series 14-13-1
1960—Oilers, 24-10 (B)
　　　Oilers, 37-21 (H)
1961—Tie, 31-31 (H)
　　　Oilers, 27-15 (H)
1962—Patriots, 34-21 (B)
　　　Oilers, 21-17 (H)
1963—Patriots, 45-3 (B)
　　　Patriots, 46-28 (H)
1964—Patriots, 25-24 (B)
　　　Patriots, 34-17 (H)
1965—Oilers, 31-10 (H)
　　　Patriots, 42-14 (B)
1966—Patriots, 27-21 (B)
　　　Patriots, 38-14 (H)
1967—Patriots, 18-7 (B)
　　　Oilers, 27-6 (H)
1968—Oilers, 16-0 (B)
　　　Oilers, 45-17 (H)
1969—Patriots, 24-0 (B)
　　　Oilers, 27-23 (H)
1971—Patriots, 28-20 (NE)
1973—Patriots, 32-0 (H)
1975—Oilers, 7-0 (NE)
1978—Oilers, 26-23 (NE)
　　　**Oilers, 31-14 (NE)
1980—Oilers, 38-34 (H)
1981—Patriots, 38-10 (NE)
1982—Patriots, 29-21 (NE)
(Points—Patriots 681, Oilers 588)
*Franchise in Boston prior to 1971
**AFC Divisional Playoff
**HOUSTON vs. NEW ORLEANS**
Oilers lead series, 2-1-1
1971—Tie, 13-13 (H)
1976—Oilers, 31-26 (NO)
1978—Oilers, 17-12 (NO)
1981—Saints, 27-24 (H)
(Points—Oilers 85, Saints 78)
**HOUSTON vs. N.Y. GIANTS**
Giants lead series, 2-0
1973—Giants, 34-14 (NY)
1982—Giants, 17-14 (NY)
(Points—Giants 51, Oilers 28)
**HOUSTON vs. *N.Y. JETS**
Oilers lead series, 14-10-1
1960—Oilers, 27-21 (H)
　　　Oilers, 42-28 (NY)
1961—Oilers, 49-13 (H)
　　　Oilers, 48-21 (NY)
1962—Oilers, 56-17 (H)
　　　Oilers, 44-10 (NY)
1963—Jets, 24-17 (NY)
　　　Oilers, 31-27 (H)
1964—Jets, 24-21 (NY)
　　　Oilers, 33-17 (H)
1965—Oilers, 27-21 (H)
　　　Jets, 41-14 (NY)
1966—Jets, 52-13 (NY)
　　　Oilers, 24-0 (H)
1967—Tie, 28-28 (NY)
1968—Jets, 20-14 (H)
　　　Jets, 26-7 (NY)
1969—Jets, 26-17 (NY)
　　　Jets, 34-26 (H)
1972—Oilers, 26-20 (H)
1974—Oilers, 27-22 (NY)
1977—Oilers, 20-0 (H)
1979—Oilers, 27-24 (H) OT
1980—Jets, 31-28 (NY) OT
1981—Jets, 33-17 (NY)
(Points—Oilers 683, Jets 580)
*Jets known as Titans prior to 1963
**HOUSTON vs. PHILADELPHIA**
Eagles lead series, 3-0
1972—Eagles, 18-17 (H)
1979—Eagles, 26-20 (H)
1982—Eagles, 35-14 (P)
(Points—Eagles 79, Oilers 51)
**HOUSTON vs. PITTSBURGH**
Steelers lead series, 21-8
1970—Oilers, 19-7 (P)
　　　Steelers, 7-3 (H)
1971—Steelers, 23-16 (P)
　　　Oilers, 29-3 (H)
1972—Steelers, 24-7 (P)
　　　Steelers, 9-3 (H)
1973—Steelers, 36-7 (H)
　　　Steelers, 33-7 (P)

---

**HOUSTON vs. ATLANTA**
Falcons lead series, 3-1;
See Atlanta vs. Houston
**HOUSTON vs. BALTIMORE**
Series tied, 3-3;
See Baltimore vs. Houston
**HOUSTON vs. BUFFALO**
Oilers lead series, 17-8;
See Buffalo vs. Houston
**HOUSTON vs. CHICAGO**
Oilers lead series, 2-1;
See Chicago vs. Houston
**HOUSTON vs. CINCINNATI**
Bengals lead series, 17-12-1;
See Cincinnati vs. Houston
**HOUSTON vs. CLEVELAND**
Browns lead series, 16-11;
See Cleveland vs. Houston
**HOUSTON vs. DALLAS**
Cowboys lead series, 3-1;

1974—Steelers, 13-7 (H)
Oilers, 13-10 (P)
1975—Steelers, 24-17 (P)
Steelers, 32-9 (H)
1976—Steelers, 32-16 (P)
Steelers, 21-0 (H)
1977—Oilers, 27-10 (H)
Steelers, 27-10 (P)
1978—Oilers, 24-17 (P)
Steelers, 13-3 (H)
*Steelers, 34-5 (P)
1979—Steelers, 38-7 (P)
Oilers, 20-17 (H)
*Steelers, 27-13 (P)
1980—Steelers, 31-17 (P)
Oilers, 6-0 (H)
1981—Steelers, 26-13 (P)
Oilers, 21-20 (H)
1982—Steelers, 24-10 (H)
1983—Steelers, 40-28 (H)
Steelers, 17-10 (P)
(Points—Steelers 615, Oilers 367)
*AFC Championship
**HOUSTON vs. ST. LOUIS**
Cardinals lead series, 3-0
1970—Cardinals, 44-0 (StL)
1974—Cardinals, 31-27 (H)
1979—Cardinals, 24-17 (H)
(Points—Cardinals 99, Oilers 44)
**HOUSTON vs. *SAN DIEGO**
Chargers lead series, 15-11-1
1960—Oilers, 38-28 (H)
Chargers, 24-21 (LA)
**Oilers, 24-16 (H)
1961—Chargers, 34-24 (SD)
Oilers, 33-13 (H)
**Oilers, 10-3 (SD)
1962—Oilers, 42-17 (SD)
Oilers, 33-27 (H)
1963—Oilers, 27-0 (H)
Chargers 20-14 (H)
1964—Chargers, 27-21 (SD)
Oilers, 20-17 (H)
1965—Chargers, 31-14 (SD)
Chargers, 37-26 (H)
1966—Chargers, 28-22 (H)
Chargers, 24-17 (H)
1967—Chargers, 13-3 (SD)
Oilers, 24-17 (H)
1968—Chargers, 30-14 (SD)
1969—Chargers, 21-17 (H)
1970—Oilers, 31-31 (SD)
1971—Oilers, 49-33 (H)
1972—Chargers, 34-20 (SD)
1974—Oilers, 21-14 (H)
1975—Oilers, 33-17 (H)
1976—Chargers, 30-27 (SD)
1978—Chargers, 45-24 (H)
1979—***Oilers, 17-14 (SD)
(Points—Chargers 651, Oilers 619)
*Franchise in Los Angeles prior to 1961
**AFL Championship
***AFC Divisional Playoff
**HOUSTON vs. SAN FRANCISCO**
Series tied, 2-2
1970—49ers, 30-20 (H)
1975—Oilers, 27-13 (SF)
1978—Oilers, 20-19 (H)
1981—49ers, 28-6 (SF)
(Points—49ers 90, Oilers 73)
**HOUSTON vs. SEATTLE**
Oilers lead series, 3-2
1977—Oilers, 22-10 (S)
1979—Seahawks, 34-14 (S)
1980—Seahawks, 26-7 (H)
1981—Oilers, 35-17 (H)
1982—Oilers, 23-21 (H)
(Points—Seahawks 108, Oilers 101)
**HOUSTON vs. TAMPA BAY**
Oilers lead series, 2-1
1976—Oilers, 20-0 (H)
1980—Oilers, 20-14 (H)
1983—Buccaneers, 33-24 (TB)
(Points—Oilers 64, Buccaneers 47)
**HOUSTON vs. WASHINGTON**
Oilers lead series, 2-1
1971—Redskins, 22-13 (W)
1975—Oilers, 13-10 (H)
1979—Oilers, 29-27 (W)
(Points—Redskins 59, Oilers 55)

**KANSAS CITY vs. ATLANTA**
Chiefs lead series, 1-0;
See Atlanta vs. Kansas City
**KANSAS CITY vs. BALTIMORE**
Chiefs lead series, 5-3;
See Baltimore vs. Kansas City
**KANSAS CITY vs. BUFFALO**
Bills lead series, 14-11-1;
See Buffalo vs. Kansas City
**KANSAS CITY vs. CHICAGO**
Bears lead series, 2-1;
See Chicago vs. Kansas City
**KANSAS CITY vs. CINCINNATI**

Series tied, 7-7;
See Cincinnati vs. Kansas City
**KANSAS CITY vs. CLEVELAND**
Series tied, 4-4-1;
See Cleveland vs. Kansas City
**KANSAS CITY vs. DALLAS**
Cowboys lead series, 2-1;
See Dallas vs. Kansas City
**KANSAS CITY vs. DENVER**
Chiefs lead series, 32-15;
See Denver vs. Kansas City
**KANSAS CITY vs. DETROIT**
Series tied, 2-2;
See Detroit vs. Kansas City
**KANSAS CITY vs. GREEN BAY**
Series tied, 1-1-1;
See Green Bay vs. Kansas City
**KANSAS CITY vs. HOUSTON**
Chiefs lead series, 20-10;
See Houston vs. Kansas City
**\*KANSAS CITY vs. \*\*L.A. RAIDERS**
Raiders lead series, 27-20-2
1960—Texans, 34-16 (O)
Raiders, 20-19 (D)
1961—Texans, 42-35 (O)
Texans, 43-11 (D)
1962—Texans, 26-16 (O)
Texans, 35-7 (D)
1963—Chiefs, 10-7 (O)
Raiders, 22-7 (KC)
1964—Chiefs, 21-9 (O)
Chiefs, 42-7 (KC)
1965—Raiders, 37-10 (O)
Chiefs, 14-7 (KC)
1966—Chiefs, 32-10 (O)
Raiders, 34-13 (KC)
1967—Raiders, 23-21 (O)
Raiders, 44-22 (KC)
1968—Chiefs, 24-10 (KC)
Raiders, 38-21 (O)
***Raiders, 41-6 (O)
1969—Raiders, 27-24 (KC)
Raiders, 10-6 (O)
****Chiefs, 17-7 (O)
1970—Tie, 17-17 (KC)
Raiders, 20-6 (O)
1971—Tie, 20-20 (O)
Chiefs, 16-14 (KC)
1972—Chiefs, 27-14 (KC)
Raiders, 26-3 (O)
1973—Chiefs, 16-3 (KC)
Raiders, 37-7 (O)
1974—Raiders, 27-7 (O)
Raiders, 7-6 (KC)
1975—Chiefs, 42-10 (KC)
Raiders, 28-20 (O)
1976—Raiders, 24-21 (KC)
Raiders, 21-10 (O)
1977—Raiders, 37-28 (KC)
Raiders, 21-20 (O)
1978—Raiders, 28-6 (O)
Raiders, 20-10 (KC)
1979—Chiefs, 35-7 (KC)
Chiefs, 24-21 (O)
1980—Raiders, 27-14 (KC)
Chiefs, 31-17 (O)
1981—Chiefs, 27-0 (KC)
Chiefs, 28-17 (O)
1982—Raiders, 21-16 (KC)
1983—Raiders, 21-20 (LA)
Raiders, 28-20 (O)
(Points—Chiefs 983, Raiders 974)
*Franchise in Dallas prior to 1963 and known as Texans
**Franchise in Oakland prior to 1982
***Division Playoff
****AFL Championship
**KANSAS CITY vs. L.A. RAMS**
Rams lead series, 2-0
1973—Rams, 23-13 (KC)
1982—Rams, 20-14 (LA)
(Points—Rams 43, Chiefs 27)
**KANSAS CITY vs. MIAMI**
Chiefs lead series, 7-5
1966—Chiefs, 34-16 (KC)
Chiefs, 19-18 (M)
1967—Chiefs, 24-0 (M)
Chiefs, 41-0 (KC)
1968—Chiefs, 48-3 (M)
1969—Chiefs, 17-10 (KC)
1971—*Dolphins, 27-24 (KC) OT
1972—Dolphins, 20-10 (KC)
1974—Dolphins, 9-3 (M)
1976—Chiefs, 20-17 (M) OT
1981—Dolphins, 17-7 (KC)
1983—Dolphins, 14-6 (M)
(Points—Chiefs 253, Dolphins 151)
*AFC Divisional Playoff
**KANSAS CITY vs. MINNESOTA**
Series tied, 2-2
1969—*Chiefs, 23-7 (New Orleans)
1970—Vikings, 27-10 (M)
1974—Vikings, 35-15 (KC)

1981—Chiefs, 10-6 (M)
(Points—Vikings 75, Chiefs 58)
*Super Bowl IV
**\*KANSAS CITY vs. \*\*NEW ENGLAND**
Chiefs lead series, 11-7-3
1960—Patriots, 42-14 (B)
Texans, 34-0 (D)
1961—Patriots, 18-17 (D)
Patriots, 28-21 (B)
1962—Texans, 42-28 (D)
Texans, 27-7 (B)
1963—Tie, 24-24 (B)
Chiefs, 35-3 (KC)
1964—Patriots, 24-7 (B)
Patriots, 31-24 (KC)
1965—Chiefs, 27-17 (KC)
Tie, 10-10 (B)
1966—Chiefs, 43-24 (B)
Tie, 27-27 (KC)
1967—Chiefs, 33-10 (B)
1968—Chiefs, 31-17 (KC)
1969—Chiefs, 31-0 (B)
1970—Chiefs, 23-10 (KC)
1973—Chiefs, 10-7 (NE)
1977—Patriots, 21-17 (NE)
1981—Patriots, 33-17 (NE)
(Points—Chiefs 514, Patriots 381)
*Franchise located in Dallas prior to 1963 and known as Texans
**Franchise in Boston prior to 1971
**KANSAS CITY vs. NEW ORLEANS**
Saints lead series 2-1
1972—Chiefs, 20-17 (NO)
1976—Saints, 27-17 (KC)
1982—Saints, 27-17 (NO)
(Points—Saints 71, Chiefs 54)
**KANSAS CITY vs. N.Y. GIANTS**
Giants lead series, 3-1
1974—Giants, 33-27 (KC)
1978—Giants, 26-10 (NY)
1979—Giants, 21-17 (KC)
1983—Chiefs, 38-17 (KC)
(Points—Giants 97, Chiefs 92)
**\*KANSAS CITY vs. \*\*N.Y. JETS**
Chiefs lead series, 13-9
1960—Titans, 37-35 (D)
Titans, 41-35 (NY)
1961—Titans, 28-7 (NY)
Texans, 35-24 (D)
1962—Texans, 20-17 (D)
Texans, 52-31 (NY)
1963—Jets, 17-0 (NY)
Chiefs, 48-0 (KC)
1964—Jets, 27-14 (NY)
Chiefs, 24-7 (KC)
1965—Chiefs, 14-10 (NY)
Jets, 13-10 (KC)
1966—Chiefs, 32-24 (NY)
1967—Chiefs, 42-18 (KC)
Chiefs, 21-7 (NY)
1968—Jets, 20-19 (KC)
1969—Chiefs, 34-16 (NY)
***Chiefs, 13-6 (NY)
1971—Jets, 13-10 (NY)
1974—Chiefs, 24-16 (KC)
1975—Jets, 30-24 (KC)
1982—Chiefs, 37-13 (KC)
(Points—Chiefs 550, Jets 415)
*Franchise in Dallas prior to 1963 and known as Texans
**Jets known as Titans prior to 1963
***Inter-Divisional Playoff
**KANSAS CITY vs. PHILADELPHIA**
Eagles lead series, 1-0
1972—Eagles, 21-20 (KC)
**KANSAS CITY vs. PITTSBURGH**
Steelers lead series, 8-3
1970—Chiefs, 31-14 (P)
1971—Chiefs, 38-16 (KC)
1972—Steelers, 16-7 (P)
1974—Steelers, 34-24 (KC)
1975—Steelers, 28-3 (P)
1976—Steelers, 45-0 (KC)
1978—Steelers, 27-24 (P)
1979—Steelers, 30-3 (KC)
1980—Steelers, 21-16 (P)
1981—Chiefs, 37-33 (P)
1982—Steelers, 35-14 (P)
(Points—Steelers 299, Chiefs 197)
**KANSAS CITY vs. ST. LOUIS**
Chiefs lead series, 3-0-1
1970—Tie, 6-6 (KC)
1974—Chiefs, 17-13 (StL)
1980—Chiefs, 21-13 (StL)
1983—Chiefs, 38-14 (KC)
(Points—Chiefs 82, Cardinals 46)
**\*KANSAS CITY vs. \*\*SAN DIEGO**
Chargers lead series, 25-21-1
1960—Chargers, 21-20 (LA)
Texans, 17-0 (D)
1961—Chargers, 26-10 (D)
Chargers, 24-14 (SD)
1962—Chargers, 32-28 (SD)

Texans, 26-17 (D)
1963—Chargers, 24-10 (SD)
Chargers, 38-17 (KC)
1964—Chargers, 28-14 (KC)
Chiefs, 49-6 (SD)
1965—Tie, 10-10 (SD)
Chiefs, 31-7 (KC)
1966—Chiefs, 24-14 (KC)
Chiefs, 27-17 (SD)
1967—Chargers, 45-31 (SD)
Chargers, 17-16 (KC)
1968—Chiefs, 27-20 (SD)
Chiefs, 40-3 (KC)
1969—Chiefs, 27-9 (SD)
Chiefs, 27-3 (KC)
1970—Chiefs, 26-14 (KC)
Chargers, 31-13 (SD)
1971—Chargers, 21-14 (SD)
Chiefs, 31-10 (KC)
1972—Chiefs, 26-14 (SD)
Chargers, 27-17 (KC)
1973—Chiefs, 19-0 (SD)
Chiefs, 33-6 (KC)
1974—Chiefs, 24-14 (SD)
Chargers, 14-7 (KC)
1975—Chiefs, 12-10 (SD)
Chargers, 28-20 (KC)
1976—Chargers, 30-16 (KC)
Chiefs, 23-20 (SD)
1977—Chargers, 23-7 (KC)
Chiefs, 21-16 (SD)
1978—Chargers, 29-23 (SD) OT
Chiefs, 23-0 (KC)
1979—Chargers, 20-14 (KC)
Chargers, 28-7 (SD)
1980—Chargers, 24-7 (KC)
Chargers, 20-7 (SD)
1981—Chargers, 42-31 (KC)
Chargers, 22-20 (SD)
1982—Chiefs, 19-12 (KC)
1983—Chargers, 17-14 (KC)
Chargers, 41-38 (SD)
(Points—Chiefs 977, Chargers 894)
*Franchise in Dallas prior to 1963 and known as Texans
**Franchise in Los Angeles prior to 1961
**KANSAS CITY vs. SAN FRANCISCO**
49ers lead series, 2-1
1971—Chiefs, 26-17 (SF)
1975—49ers, 20-3 (KC)
1982—49ers, 26-13 (KC)
(Points—49ers 63, Chiefs 42)
**KANSAS CITY vs. SEATTLE**
Chiefs lead series, 6-5
1977—Seahawks, 34-31 (KC)
1978—Seahawks, 13-10 (KC)
Seahawks, 23-19 (S)
1979—Chiefs, 24-6 (S)
Chiefs, 37-21 (KC)
1980—Seahawks, 17-16 (KC)
Chiefs, 31-30 (S)
1981—Chiefs, 20-14 (S)
Chiefs, 40-13 (KC)
1983—Chiefs, 17-13 (KC)
Seahawks, 51-48 (S) OT
(Points—Chiefs 293, Seahawks 235)
**KANSAS CITY vs. TAMPA BAY**
Series tied, 2-2
1976—Chiefs, 28-19 (TB)
1978—Buccaneers, 30-13 (KC)
1979—Buccaneers, 3-0 (TB)
1981—Chiefs, 19-10 (KC)
(Points—Buccaneers 62, Chiefs 60)
**KANSAS CITY vs. WASHINGTON**
Chiefs lead series, 2-1
1971—Chiefs, 27-20 (KC)
1976—Chiefs, 33-30 (W)
1983—Redskins, 27-12 (W)
(Points—Redskins 77, Chiefs 72)

**L.A. RAIDERS vs. ATLANTA**
Raiders lead series, 3-1;
See Atlanta vs. L.A. Raiders
**L.A. RAIDERS vs. BALTIMORE**
Raiders lead series, 3-2;
See Baltimore vs. L.A. Raiders
**L.A. RAIDERS vs. BUFFALO**
Raiders lead series, 12-11;
See Buffalo vs. L.A. Raiders
**L.A. RAIDERS vs. CHICAGO**
Raiders lead series, 3-1;
See Chicago vs. L.A. Raiders
**L.A. RAIDERS vs. CINCINNATI**
Raiders lead series, 11-4;
See Cincinnati vs. L.A. Raiders
**L.A. RAIDERS vs. CLEVELAND**
Raiders lead series, 8-1;
See Cleveland vs. L.A. Raiders
**L.A. RAIDERS vs. DALLAS**
Raiders lead series, 2-1;
See Dallas vs. L.A. Raiders
**L.A. RAIDERS vs. DENVER**
Raiders lead series, 34-12-2;

See Denver vs. L.A. Raiders
**L.A. RAIDERS vs. DETROIT**
Series tied, 2-2;
See Detroit vs. L.A. Raiders
**L.A. RAIDERS vs. GREEN BAY**
Raiders lead series, 3-1;
See Green Bay vs. L.A. Raiders
**L.A. RAIDERS vs. HOUSTON**
Raiders lead series, 20-10;
See Houston vs. L.A. Raiders
**L.A. RAIDERS vs. KANSAS CITY**
Raiders lead series, 27-20-2;
See Kansas City vs. L.A. Raiders
**\*L.A. RAIDERS vs. L.A. RAMS**
Raiders lead series, 3-1
1972—Raiders, 45-17 (O)
1977—Rams, 20-14 (LA)
1979—Raiders, 24-17 (LA)
1982—Raiders, 37-31 (LA Raiders)
(Points—Raiders 120, Rams 85)
*Franchise in Oakland prior to 1982*
**\*L.A. RAIDERS vs. MIAMI**
Raiders lead series, 13-3-1
1966—Raiders, 23-14 (M)
       Raiders, 21-10 (O)
1967—Raiders, 31-17 (O)
1968—Raiders, 47-21 (M)
1969—Raiders, 20-17 (O)
       Tie, 20-20 (M)
1970—Dolphins, 20-13 (M)
       **Raiders, 21-14 (O)
1973—Raiders, 12-7 (O)
       ***Dolphins, 27-10 (M)
1974—**Raiders, 28-26 (O)
1975—Raiders, 31-21 (M)
1978—Dolphins, 23-6 (M)
1979—Raiders, 13-3 (O)
1980—Raiders, 16-10 (O)
1981—Raiders, 33-17 (M)
1983—Raiders, 27-14 (LA)
(Points—Raiders 372, Dolphins 281)
*Franchise in Oakland prior to 1982*
**AFC Divisional Playoff*
***AFC Championship*
**\*L.A. RAIDERS vs. MINNESOTA**
Raiders lead series, 4-1
1973—Vikings, 24-16 (M)
1976—**Raiders, 32-14 (Pasadena)
1977—Raiders, 35-13 (O)
1978—Raiders, 27-20 (O)
1981—Raiders, 36-10 (M)
(Points—Raiders 146, Vikings 81)
*Franchise in Oakland prior to 1982*
**Super Bowl XI*
**\*L.A. RAIDERS vs. **NEW ENGLAND**
Series tied, 11-11-1
1960—Raiders, 27-14 (O)
       Patriots, 34-28 (B)
1961—Patriots, 20-17 (B)
       Patriots, 35-21 (O)
1962—Patriots, 26-16 (B)
       Raiders, 20-0 (O)
1963—Patriots, 20-14 (O)
       Patriots, 20-14 (B)
1964—Patriots, 17-14 (O)
       Tie, 43-43 (B)
1965—Raiders, 24-10 (B)
       Raiders, 30-21 (O)
1966—Patriots, 24-21 (B)
1967—Raiders, 35-7 (O)
       Raiders, 48-14 (B)
1968—Raiders, 41-10 (O)
1969—Raiders, 38-23 (B)
1971—Patriots, 20-6 (NE)
1974—Raiders, 41-26 (O)
1976—Patriots, 48-17 (NE)
       ***Raiders, 24-21 (O)
1978—Patriots, 21-14 (O)
1981—Raiders, 27-17 (O)
(Points—Raiders 580, Patriots 491)
*Franchise in Oakland prior to 1982*
**Franchise in Boston prior to 1971*
***AFC Divisional Playoff*
**\*L.A. RAIDERS vs. NEW ORLEANS**
Raiders lead series, 2-0-1
1971—Tie, 21-21 (NO)
1975—Raiders, 48-10 (O)
1979—Raiders, 42-35 (NO)
(Points—Raiders 111, Saints 66)
*Franchise in Oakland prior to 1982*
**\*L.A. RAIDERS vs. N.Y. GIANTS**
Raiders lead series, 3-0
1973—Raiders, 42-0 (O)
1980—Raiders, 33-17 (NY)
1983—Raiders, 27-12 (LA)
(Points—Raiders 102, Giants 29)
*Franchise in Oakland prior to 1982*
**\*L.A. RAIDERS vs. **N.Y. JETS**
Series tied, 11-11-2
1960—Raiders, 28-27 (NY)
       Titans, 31-28 (O)
1961—Titans, 14-6 (NY)
       Titans, 23-12 (NY)

1962—Titans, 28-17 (O)
       Titans, 31-21 (NY)
1963—Jets, 10-7 (NY)
       Raiders, 49-26 (O)
1964—Jets, 35-13 (NY)
       Raiders, 35-26 (O)
1965—Tie, 24-24 (NY)
       Raiders, 24-14 (O)
1966—Raiders, 24-21 (NY)
       Tie, 28-28 (O)
1967—Jets, 27-14 (NY)
       Raiders, 38-29 (O)
1968—Raiders, 43-32 (O)
       ***Jets, 27-23 (NY)
1969—Raiders, 27-14 (NY)
1970—Raiders, 14-13 (NY)
1972—Raiders, 24-16 (O)
1977—Raiders, 28-27 (NY)
1979—Jets, 28-19 (NY)
1982—****Jets, 17-14 (LA)
(Points—Jets 568, Raiders 560)
*Franchise in Oakland prior to 1982*
**Jets known as Titans prior to 1963*
***AFL Championship*
****AFC Second Round Playoff*
**\*L.A. RAIDERS vs. PHILADELPHIA**
Raiders lead series, 3-1
1971—Raiders, 34-10 (O)
1976—Raiders, 26-7 (P)
1980—Eagles, 10-7 (P)
       **Raiders, 27-10 (NO)
(Points—Raiders 94, Eagles 27)
*Franchise in Oakland prior to 1982*
**Super Bowl XV*
**\*L.A. RAIDERS vs. PITTSBURGH**
Raiders lead series, 9-5
1970—Raiders, 31-14 (O)
1972—Steelers, 34-28 (P)
       **Steelers, 13-7 (P)
1973—Steelers, 17-9 (O)
       ***Raiders, 33-14 (O)
1974—Raiders, 17-0 (P)
       ***Steelers, 24-13 (O)
1975—***Steelers, 16-10 (P)
1976—Raiders, 31-28 (O)
       ***Raiders, 24-7 (O)
1977—Raiders, 16-7 (P)
1980—Raiders, 45-34 (P)
1981—Raiders, 30-27 (O)
1983—**Raiders, 38-10 (LA)
(Points—Raiders 332, Steelers 245)
*Franchise in Oakland prior to 1982*
**AFC Divisional Playoff*
***AFC Championship*
**\*L.A. RAIDERS vs. ST. LOUIS**
Series tied, 1-1
1973—Raiders, 17-10 (StL)
1983—Cardinals, 34-24 (LA)
(Points—Cardinals 44, Raiders 41)
*Franchise in Oakland prior to 1982*
**\*L.A. RAIDERS vs. **SAN DIEGO**
Raiders lead series, 30-17-2
1960—Chargers, 52-28 (LA)
       Chargers, 41-17 (O)
1961—Chargers, 44-0 (SD)
       Chargers, 41-10 (O)
1962—Chargers, 42-33 (O)
       Chargers, 31-21 (SD)
1963—Raiders, 34-33 (SD)
       Raiders, 41-27 (O)
1964—Chargers, 31-17 (O)
       Raiders, 21-20 (SD)
1965—Chargers, 17-6 (O)
       Chargers, 24-14 (SD)
1966—Chargers, 29-20 (O)
       Raiders, 41-19 (SD)
1967—Raiders, 51-10 (O)
       Raiders, 41-21 (SD)
1968—Chargers, 23-14 (O)
       Raiders, 34-27 (SD)
1969—Raiders, 24-12 (SD)
       Raiders, 21-16 (O)
1970—Tie, 27-27 (SD)
       Raiders, 20-17 (O)
1971—Raiders, 34-0 (SD)
       Raiders, 34-33 (O)
1972—Tie, 17-17 (O)
       Raiders, 21-19 (SD)
1973—Raiders, 27-17 (SD)
       Raiders, 31-3 (O)
1974—Raiders, 14-10 (SD)
       Raiders, 17-10 (O)
1975—Raiders, 6-0 (SD)
       Raiders, 25-0 (O)
1976—Raiders, 27-17 (SD)
       Raiders, 24-0 (O)
1977—Raiders, 24-0 (O)
       Chargers, 12-7 (SD)
1978—Raiders, 21-20 (SD)
       Chargers, 27-23 (O)
1979—Chargers, 30-10 (SD)
       Raiders, 45-22 (O)
1980—Chargers, 30-24 (SD) OT

Raiders, 38-24 (O)
       ***Raiders, 34-27 (SD)
1981—Chargers, 55-21 (O)
       Chargers, 23-10 (SD)
1982—Raiders, 28-24 (LA)
       Raiders, 41-34 (SD)
1983—Raiders, 42-10 (SD)
       Raiders, 30-14 (LA)
(Points—Raiders 1,210, Chargers 1,082)
*Franchise in Oakland prior to 1982*
**Franchise in Los Angeles prior to 1961*
***AFC Championship*
**\*L.A. RAIDERS vs. SAN FRANCISCO**
Raiders lead series, 3-1
1970—49ers, 38-7 (O)
1974—Raiders, 35-24 (SF)
1979—Raiders, 23-10 (O)
1982—Raiders, 23-17 (SF)
(Points—49ers 89, Raiders 88)
*Franchise in Oakland prior to 1982*
**\*L.A. RAIDERS vs. SEATTLE**
Raiders lead series, 7-6
1977—Raiders, 44-7 (O)
1978—Seahawks, 27-7 (S)
       Seahawks, 17-16 (O)
1979—Seahawks, 27-10 (S)
       Seahawks, 29-24 (O)
1980—Raiders, 33-14 (O)
       Raiders, 19-17 (S)
1981—Raiders, 20-10 (O)
       Raiders, 32-31 (S)
1982—Raiders, 28-23 (LA)
1983—Seahawks, 38-36 (S)
       Seahawks, 34-21 (LA)
       **Raiders, 30-14 (LA)
(Points—Raiders 320, Seahawks 288)
*Franchise in Oakland prior to 1982*
**AFC Championship*
**\*L.A. RAIDERS vs. TAMPA BAY**
Raiders lead series, 2-0
1976—Raiders, 49-16 (O)
1981—Raiders, 18-16 (O)
(Points—Raiders 67, Buccaneers 32)
*Franchise in Oakland prior to 1982*
**\*L.A. RAIDERS vs. WASHINGTON**
Raiders lead series, 4-1
1970—Raiders, 34-20 (O)
1975—Raiders, 26-23 (W) OT
1980—Raiders, 24-21 (O)
1983—Redskins, 37-35 (W)
       **Raiders, 38-9 (Tampa)
(Points—Raiders 157, Redskins 110)
*Franchise in Oakland prior to 1982*
**Super Bowl XVIII*

---

**L.A. RAMS vs. ATLANTA**
Rams lead series, 26-6-2;
See Atlanta vs. L.A. Rams
**L.A. RAMS vs. BALTIMORE**
Colts lead series, 20-14-2;
See Baltimore vs. L.A. Rams
**L.A. RAMS vs. BUFFALO**
Rams lead series, 3-1;
See Buffalo vs. L.A. Rams
**L.A. RAMS vs. CHICAGO**
Bears lead series, 42-26-3;
See Chicago vs. L.A. Rams
**L.A. RAMS vs. CINCINNATI**
Bengals lead series, 3-1;
See Cincinnati vs. L.A. Rams
**L.A. RAMS vs. CLEVELAND**
Browns lead series, 8-6;
See Cleveland vs. L.A. Rams
**L.A. RAMS vs. DALLAS**
Series tied, 9-9;
See Dallas vs. L.A. Rams
**L.A. RAMS vs. DENVER**
Series tied 2-2;
See Denver vs. L.A. Rams
**L.A. RAMS vs. DETROIT**
Rams lead series, 36-34-1;
See Detroit vs. L.A. Rams
**L.A. RAMS vs. GREEN BAY**
Rams lead series, 38-33-2;
See Green Bay vs. L.A. Rams
**L.A. RAMS vs. HOUSTON**
Rams lead series, 2-1;
See Houston vs. L.A. Rams
**L.A. RAMS vs. KANSAS CITY**
Rams lead series, 2-0;
See Kansas City vs. L.A. Rams
**L.A. RAMS VS. L.A. RAIDERS**
Raiders lead series, 3-1;
See L.A. Raiders vs. L.A. Rams
**L.A. RAMS vs. MIAMI**
Dolphins lead series, 3-1
1971—Dolphins, 20-14 (LA)
1976—Rams, 31-28 (M)
1980—Dolphins, 35-14 (LA)
1983—Dolphins, 30-14 (M)
(Points—Dolphins 113, Rams 73)
**L.A. RAMS vs. MINNESOTA**
Vikings lead series, 15-11-2

1961—Rams, 31-17 (LA)
       Vikings, 42-21 (M)
1962—Vikings, 38-14 (LA)
       Tie, 24-24 (M)
1963—Rams, 27-24 (LA)
       Vikings, 21-13 (M)
1964—Rams, 22-13 (LA)
       Vikings, 34-13 (M)
1965—Vikings, 38-35 (LA)
       Vikings, 24-13 (M)
1966—Vikings, 35-7 (M)
       Rams, 21-6 (LA)
1967—Rams, 39-3 (LA)
1968—Rams, 31-3 (M)
1969—Vikings, 20-13 (LA)
       *Vikings, 23-20 (M)
1970—Vikings, 13-3 (M)
1972—Vikings, 45-41 (LA)
1973—Vikings, 10-9 (M)
1974—Rams, 20-17 (LA)
       **Vikings, 14-10 (M)
1976—Tie, 10-10 (M) OT
       **Vikings, 24-13 (M)
1977—Rams, 35-3 (LA)
       ***Vikings, 14-7 (LA)
1978—Rams, 34-17 (M)
       ***Rams, 34-10 (LA)
1979—Rams, 27-21 (LA) OT
(Points—Rams 587, Vikings 563)
*Conference Championship*
**NFC Championship*
***NFC Divisional Playoff*
**L.A. RAMS vs. NEW ENGLAND**
Patriots lead series, 2-1
1974—Patriots, 20-14 (NE)
1980—Rams, 17-14 (NE)
1983—Patriots, 21-7 (LA)
(Points—Patriots 55, Rams 38)
**L.A. RAMS vs. NEW ORLEANS**
Rams lead series, 20-8
1967—Rams, 27-13 (LA)
1969—Rams, 36-17 (LA)
1970—Rams, 30-17 (NO)
       Rams, 34-16 (LA)
1971—Saints, 24-20 (NO)
       Rams, 45-28 (LA)
1972—Rams, 34-14 (LA)
       Saints, 19-16 (NO)
1973—Rams, 29-7 (LA)
       Rams, 24-13 (NO)
1974—Rams, 24-0 (LA)
       Saints, 20-7 (NO)
1975—Rams, 38-14 (LA)
       Rams, 14-7 (NO)
1976—Rams, 16-10 (NO)
       Rams, 33-14 (LA)
1977—Rams, 14-7 (LA)
       Saints, 27-26 (NO)
1978—Rams, 26-20 (NO)
       Saints, 10-3 (LA)
1979—Rams, 35-17 (NO)
       Saints, 29-14 (LA)
1980—Rams, 45-31 (LA)
       Rams, 27-7 (NO)
1981—Saints, 23-17 (NO)
       Saints, 21-13 (LA)
1983—Rams, 30-27 (LA)
       Rams, 26-24 (NO)
(Points—Rams 703, Saints 476)
**\*L.A. RAMS vs. N.Y. GIANTS**
Rams lead series, 15-6
1938—Giants, 28-0 (NY)
1940—Rams, 13-0 (NY)
1941—Giants, 49-14 (NY)
1945—Rams, 21-17 (NY)
1946—Rams, 31-21 (NY)
1947—Rams, 34-10 (LA)
1948—Rams, 52-37 (NY)
1953—Rams, 21-7 (LA)
1954—Rams, 17-16 (NY)
1959—Giants, 23-21 (LA)
1961—Giants, 24-14 (NY)
1966—Rams, 55-14 (LA)
1968—Rams, 24-21 (M)
1970—Rams, 31-3 (NY)
1973—Rams, 40-6 (LA)
1976—Rams, 24-10 (LA)
1978—Rams, 20-17 (NY)
1979—Giants, 20-14 (LA)
1980—Rams, 28-7 (NY)
1981—Giants, 10-7 (NY)
1983—Rams, 16-6 (NY)
(Points—Rams 497, Giants 346)
*Franchise in Cleveland prior to 1946*
**L.A. RAMS vs. N.Y. JETS**
Series tied, 2-2
1970—Jets, 31-20 (LA)
1974—Rams, 20-13 (NY)
1980—Rams, 38-13 (LA)
1983—Jets, 27-24 (NY) OT
(Points—Rams 102, Jets 84)
**\*L.A. RAMS vs. PHILADELPHIA**
Rams lead series, 14-9-1

1937—Rams, 21-3 (P)
1939—Rams, 35-13 (Colorado Springs)
1940—Rams, 21-13 (C)
1942—Rams, 24-14 (Akron)
1944—Eagles, 26-13 (P)
1945—Eagles, 28-14 (P)
1946—Eagles, 25-14 (LA)
1947—Eagles, 14-7 (P)
1948—Tie, 28-28 (LA)
1949—Eagles, 38-14 (P)
    **Eagles, 14-0 (LA)
1950—Eagles, 56-20 (P)
1955—Rams, 23-21 (P)
1956—Rams, 27-7 (LA)
1957—Rams, 17-13 (LA)
1959—Eagles, 23-20 (P)
1964—Rams, 20-10 (LA)
1967—Rams, 33-17 (LA)
1969—Rams, 23-17 (P)
1972—Rams, 34-3 (P)
1975—Rams, 42-3 (P)
1977—Rams, 20-0 (LA)
1978—Rams, 16-14 (LA)
1983—Eagles, 13-9 (P)
(Points—Rams 495, Eagles 413)
*Franchise in Cleveland prior to 1946
**NFL Championship

**\*L.A. RAMS vs. \*\*PITTSBURGH**
Rams lead series, 12-3-2
1938—Rams, 13-7 (New Orleans)
1939—Tie, 14-14 (C)
1941—Rams, 17-14 (Akron)
1947—Rams, 48-7 (P)
1948—Rams, 31-14 (LA)
1949—Tie, 7-7 (P)
1952—Rams, 28-14 (LA)
1955—Rams, 27-26 (LA)
1956—Steelers, 30-13 (P)
1961—Rams, 24-14 (LA)
1964—Rams, 26-14 (P)
1968—Rams, 45-10 (LA)
1971—Rams, 23-14 (P)
1975—Rams, 10-3 (LA)
1978—Rams, 10-7 (LA)
1979—***Steelers, 31-19 (Pasadena)
1981—Steelers, 24-0 (P)
(Points—Rams 355, Steelers 250)
*Franchise in Cleveland prior to 1946
**Steelers known as Pirates prior to 1941
***Super Bowl XIV

**\*L.A. RAMS vs. \*\*ST. LOUIS**
Rams lead series, 18-15-2
1937—Cardinals, 6-0 (Clev)
    Cardinals, 13-7 (Chi)
1938—Cardinals, 7-6 (Clev)
    Cardinals, 31-17 (Chi)
1939—Rams, 24-0 (Chi)
    Rams, 14-0 (Clev)
1940—Cardinals, 26-14 (Clev)
    Cardinals, 17-7 (Chi)
1941—Rams, 10-6 (Clev)
    Cardinals, 7-0 (Chi)
1942—Cardinals, 7-0 (Chi)
    Rams, 7-3 (Clev)
1945—Rams, 21-0 (Clev)
    Rams, 35-21 (Chi)
1946—Cardinals, 34-10 (Chi)
    Rams, 17-14 (LA)
1947—Rams, 27-7 (LA)
    Cardinals, 17-10 (Chi)
1948—Cardinals, 27-22 (LA)
    Cardinals, 27-24 (Chi)
1949—Tie, 28-28 (Chi)
    Cardinals, 31-27 (LA)
1951—Rams, 45-21 (LA)
1953—Tie, 24-24 (Chi)
1954—Rams, 28-17 (LA)
1958—Rams, 20-14 (Chi)
1960—Cardinals, 43-21 (LA)
1965—Rams, 27-3 (StL)
1968—Rams, 24-13 (LA)
1970—Rams, 34-13 (LA)
1972—Cardinals, 24-14 (StL)
1975—***Rams, 35-23 (LA)
1976—Cardinals, 30-28 (LA)
1979—Rams, 21-0 (LA)
1980—Rams, 21-13 (StL)
(Points—Rams 681, Cardinals 555)
*Franchise in Cleveland prior to 1946
**Franchise in Chicago prior to 1960
***NFC Divisional Playoff

**L.A. RAMS vs. SAN DIEGO**
Rams lead series, 2-1
1970—Rams, 37-10 (LA)
1975—Rams, 13-10 (SD) OT
1979—Chargers, 40-16 (LA)
(Points—Rams 66, Chargers 60)

**L.A. RAMS vs. SAN FRANCISCO**
Rams lead series, 43-23-2
1950—Rams, 35-14 (SF)
    Rams, 28-21 (LA)
1951—49ers, 44-17 (SF)
    Rams, 23-16 (LA)

1952—Rams, 35-9 (LA)
    Rams, 34-21 (SF)
1953—49ers, 31-30 (SF)
    49ers, 31-27 (LA)
1954—Tie, 24-24 (LA)
    Rams, 42-34 (SF)
1955—Rams, 23-14 (SF)
    Rams, 27-14 (LA)
1956—49ers, 33-30 (SF)
    Rams, 30-6 (LA)
1957—49ers, 23-20 (SF)
    Rams, 37-24 (LA)
1958—Rams, 33-3 (SF)
    Rams, 56-7 (LA)
1959—49ers, 34-0 (SF)
    49ers, 24-16 (LA)
1960—49ers, 13-9 (SF)
    49ers, 23-7 (LA)
1961—49ers, 35-0 (SF)
    Rams, 17-7 (LA)
1962—Rams, 28-14 (SF)
    49ers, 24-17 (LA)
1963—Rams, 28-21 (SF)
    Rams, 21-17 (LA)
1964—Rams, 42-14 (LA)
    49ers, 28-7 (SF)
1965—Rams, 45-21 (LA)
    49ers, 30-27 (SF)
1966—Rams, 34-3 (LA)
    49ers, 21-13 (SF)
1967—49ers, 27-24 (LA)
    Rams, 17-7 (SF)
1968—Rams, 24-10 (LA)
    Tie, 20-20 (SF)
1969—49ers, 27-21 (SF)
    Rams, 41-30 (LA)
1970—49ers, 20-6 (LA)
    Rams, 30-13 (SF)
1971—Rams, 20-13 (SF)
    Rams, 17-6 (LA)
1972—Rams, 31-7 (LA)
    Rams, 26-16 (SF)
1973—Rams, 40-20 (LA)
    Rams, 31-13 (LA)
1974—Rams, 37-14 (LA)
    Rams, 15-13 (SF)
1975—Rams, 23-14 (SF)
    49ers, 24-23 (LA)
1976—49ers, 16-0 (LA)
    Rams, 23-3 (SF)
1977—Rams, 34-14 (LA)
    Rams, 23-10 (SF)
1978—Rams, 27-10 (LA)
    Rams, 31-28 (SF)
1979—Rams, 27-24 (SF)
    Rams, 26-20 (LA)
1980—Rams, 48-26 (LA)
    Rams, 31-17 (SF)
1981—49ers, 20-17 (SF)
    49ers, 33-31 (LA)
1982—49ers, 30-24 (LA)
    Rams, 21-20 (SF)
1983—Rams, 10-7 (SF)
    49ers, 45-35 (LA)
(Points—Rams 1,698, 49ers 1,333)

**L.A. RAMS vs. SEATTLE**
Rams lead series, 2-0
1976—Rams, 45-6 (LA)
1979—Rams, 24-0 (S)
(Points—Rams 69, Seahawks 6)

**L.A. RAMS vs. TAMPA BAY**
Rams lead series, 3-2
1977—Rams, 31-0 (LA)
1978—Rams, 26-23 (LA)
1979—Buccaneers, 21-6 (TB)
    *Rams, 9-0 (TB)
1980—Buccaneers, 10-9 (TB)
(Points—Rams 81, Buccaneers 54)
*NFC Championship

**\*L.A. RAMS vs. WASHINGTON**
Redskins lead series, 14-5-1
1937—Redskins, 16-7 (C)
1938—Redskins, 37-13 (W)
1941—Redskins, 17-13 (W)
1942—Redskins, 33-14 (W)
1944—Redskins, 14-10 (W)
1945—**Rams, 15-14 (C)
1948—Rams, 41-13 (W)
1949—Rams, 53-27 (LA)
1951—Redskins, 31-21 (W)
1962—Redskins, 20-14 (W)
1963—Redskins, 37-14 (LA)
1967—Tie, 28-28 (LA)
1969—Rams, 24-13 (W)
1971—Redskins, 38-24 (LA)
1974—Redskins, 23-17 (LA)
    ***Rams, 19-10 (LA)
1977—Redskins, 17-14 (W)
1981—Redskins, 30-7 (LA)
1983—Redskins, 42-20 (LA)
    ***Redskins, 51-7 (W)
(Points—Redskins 511, Rams 375)
*Franchise in Cleveland prior to 1946

**NFL Championship
***NFC Divisional Playoff

**MIAMI vs. ATLANTA**
Dolphins lead series, 4-0;
See Atlanta vs. Miami

**MIAMI vs. BALTIMORE**
Dolphins lead series, 20-9;
See Baltimore vs. Miami

**MIAMI vs. BUFFALO**
Dolphins lead series, 28-7-1;
See Buffalo vs. Miami

**MIAMI vs. CHICAGO**
Dolphins lead series, 3-0;
See Chicago vs. Miami

**MIAMI vs. CINCINNATI**
Dolphins lead series, 7-3;
See Cincinnati vs. Miami

**MIAMI vs. CLEVELAND**
Browns lead series, 3-2;
See Cleveland vs. Miami

**MIAMI vs. DALLAS**
Series tied, 2-2;
See Dallas vs. Miami

**MIAMI vs. DENVER**
Dolphins lead series, 4-2-1;
See Denver vs. Miami

**MIAMI vs. DETROIT**
Dolphins lead series, 2-0;
See Detroit vs. Miami

**MIAMI vs. GREEN BAY**
Dolphins lead series, 3-0;
See Green Bay vs. Miami

**MIAMI vs. HOUSTON**
Oilers lead series, 9-8;
See Houston vs. Miami

**MIAMI vs. KANSAS CITY**
Chiefs lead series, 7-5;
See Kansas City vs. Miami

**MIAMI vs. L.A. RAIDERS**
Raiders lead series, 13-3-1;
See L.A. Raiders vs. Miami

**MIAMI vs. L.A. RAMS**
Dolphins lead series, 3-1;
See L.A. Rams vs. Miami

**MIAMI vs. MINNESOTA**
Dolphins lead series, 4-1
1972—Dolphins, 16-14 (Minn)
1973—*Dolphins, 24-7 (Houston)
1976—Vikings, 29-7 (Mia)
1979—Dolphins, 27-12 (Minn)
1982—Dolphins, 22-14 (Mia)
(Points—Dolphins 96, Vikings 76)
*Super Bowl VIII

**MIAMI vs. \*NEW ENGLAND**
Dolphins lead series, 22-13
1966—Patriots, 20-14 (M)
1967—Patriots, 41-10 (B)
    Dolphins, 41-32 (M)
1968—Dolphins, 34-10 (B)
    Dolphins, 38-7 (M)
1969—Dolphins, 17-16 (B)
    Patriots, 38-23 (Tampa)
1970—Patriots, 27-14 (B)
    Dolphins, 37-20 (M)
1971—Dolphins, 41-3 (M)
    Patriots, 34-13 (NE)
1972—Dolphins, 52-0 (M)
    Dolphins, 37-21 (NE)
1973—Dolphins, 44-23 (M)
    Dolphins, 30-14 (NE)
1974—Patriots, 34-24 (NE)
    Dolphins, 34-27 (M)
1975—Dolphins, 22-14 (NE)
    Dolphins, 20-7 (M)
1976—Patriots, 30-14 (NE)
    Dolphins, 10-3 (M)
1977—Dolphins, 17-5 (M)
    Patriots, 14-10 (NE)
1978—Patriots, 33-24 (NE)
    Dolphins, 23-3 (M)
1979—Patriots, 28-13 (NE)
    Dolphins, 39-24 (M)
1980—Patriots, 34-0 (NE)
    Dolphins, 16-13 (M) OT
1981—Dolphins, 30-27 (NE) OT
    Dolphins, 24-14 (M)
1982—Patriots, 3-0 (NE)
    **Dolphins, 28-13 (M)
1983—Dolphins, 34-24 (M)
    Patriots, 17-6 (NE)
(Points—Dolphins 833, Patriots 673)
*Franchise in Boston prior to 1971
**AFC First Round Playoff

**MIAMI vs. NEW ORLEANS**
Dolphins lead series, 3-1
1970—Dolphins, 21-10 (M)
1974—Dolphins, 21-0 (NO)
1980—Dolphins, 21-16 (M)
1983—Saints, 17-7 (NO)
(Points—Dolphins 70, Saints 43)

**MIAMI vs. N.Y. GIANTS**
Dolphins lead series, 1-0
1972—Dolphins, 23-13 (NY)

**MIAMI vs. N.Y. JETS**
Dolphins lead series, 19-17-1
1966—Jets, 19-14 (M)
    Jets, 30-13 (M)
1967—Jets, 29-7 (NY)
    Jets, 33-14 (M)
1968—Jets, 35-17 (NY)
    Jets, 31-7 (M)
1969—Jets, 34-31 (NY)
    Jets, 27-9 (M)
1970—Dolphins, 20-6 (NY)
    Dolphins, 16-10 (M)
1971—Jets, 14-10 (NY)
    Dolphins, 30-14 (NY)
1972—Jets, 27-17 (NY)
    Dolphins, 28-24 (M)
1973—Dolphins, 31-3 (M)
    Dolphins, 24-14 (NY)
1974—Dolphins, 21-17 (M)
    Jets, 17-14 (NY)
1975—Dolphins, 43-0 (M)
    Dolphins, 27-7 (M)
1976—Dolphins, 16-0 (M)
    Dolphins, 27-7 (NY)
1977—Dolphins, 21-17 (NY)
    Dolphins, 14-10 (NY)
1978—Jets, 33-20 (NY)
    Jets, 24-13 (M)
1979—Jets, 33-27 (NY)
    Jets, 27-24 (M)
1980—Jets, 17-14 (NY)
    Jets, 24-17 (M)
1981—Tie, 28-28 (M) OT
    Jets, 16-15 (NY)
1982—Dolphins, 45-28 (NY)
    Dolphins, 20-19 (NY)
    *Dolphins, 14-0 (M)
1983—Dolphins, 32-14 (NY)
    Dolphins, 34-14 (M)
(Points—Dolphins 784, Jets 692)
*AFC Championship

**MIAMI vs. PHILADELPHIA**
Series tied, 2-2
1970—Eagles, 24-17 (P)
1975—Dolphins, 24-16 (M)
1978—Eagles, 17-3 (P)
1981—Dolphins, 13-10 (M)
(Points—Eagles 67, Dolphins 57)

**MIAMI vs. PITTSBURGH**
Dolphins lead series, 4-3
1971—Dolphins, 24-21 (M)
1972—*Dolphins, 21-17 (P)
1973—Dolphins, 30-26 (M)
1976—Steelers, 14-3 (P)
1979—**Steelers, 34-14 (P)
1980—Steelers, 23-10 (P)
1981—Dolphins, 30-10 (M)
(Points—Steelers 145, Dolphins 132)
*AFC Championship
**AFC Divisional Playoff

**MIAMI vs. ST. LOUIS**
Dolphins lead series, 4-0
1972—Dolphins, 31-10 (M)
1977—Dolphins, 55-14 (StL)
1978—Dolphins, 24-10 (M)
1981—Dolphins, 20-7 (StL)
(Points—Dolphins 130, Cardinals 41)

**MIAMI vs. SAN DIEGO**
Chargers lead series, 7-5
1966—Chargers, 44-10 (SD)
1967—Chargers, 24-0 (SD)
    Dolphins, 41-24 (M)
1968—Chargers, 34-28 (SD)
1969—Chargers, 21-14 (M)
1972—Dolphins, 24-10 (M)
1974—Dolphins, 28-21 (SD)
1977—Chargers, 14-13 (M)
1978—Dolphins, 28-21 (SD)
1980—Chargers, 27-24 (M) OT
1981—*Chargers, 41-38 (M) OT
1982—**Dolphins, 34-13 (M)
(Points—Chargers 294, Dolphins 282)
*AFC Divisional Playoff
**AFC Second Round Playoff

**MIAMI vs. SAN FRANCISCO**
Dolphins lead series, 4-0
1973—Dolphins, 21-13 (M)
1977—Dolphins, 19-15 (SF)
1980—Dolphins, 17-13 (M)
1983—Dolphins, 20-17 (SF)
(Points—Dolphins 77, 49ers 58)

**MIAMI vs. SEATTLE**
Dolphins lead series, 2-1
1977—Dolphins, 31-13 (M)
1979—Dolphins, 19-10 (M)
1983—*Seahawks, 27-20 (M)
(Points—Dolphins 70, Seahawks 50)
*AFC Divisional Playoff

**MIAMI vs. TAMPA BAY**
Series tied, 1-1
1976—Dolphins, 23-20 (TB)
1982—Buccaneers, 23-17 (TB)
(Points—Buccaneers 43, Dolphins 40)

**MIAMI vs. WASHINGTON**
Dolphins lead series, 3-2
1972—*Dolphins, 14-7 (Los Angeles)
1974—Redskins, 20-17 (W)
1978—Dolphins, 16-0 (W)
1981—Dolphins, 13-10 (M)
1982—**Redskins, 27-17 (Pasadena)
(Points—Dolphins 77, Redskins 64)
*Super Bowl VII
**Super Bowl XVII
_____

**MINNESOTA vs. ATLANTA**
Vikings lead series, 8-5;
See Atlanta vs. Minnesota
**MINNESOTA vs. BALTIMORE**
Colts lead series, 12-5-1;
See Baltimore vs. Minnesota
**MINNESOTA vs. BUFFALO**
Vikings lead series, 3-1;
See Buffalo vs. Minnesota
**MINNESOTA vs. CHICAGO**
Vikings lead series, 25-18-2;
See Chicago vs. Minnesota
**MINNESOTA vs. CINCINNATI**
Series tied, 2-2;
See Cincinnati vs. Minnesota
**MINNESOTA vs. CLEVELAND**
Vikings lead series, 7-1;
See Cleveland vs. Minnesota
**MINNESOTA vs. DALLAS**
Cowboys lead series, 10-5;
See Dallas vs. Minnesota
**MINNESOTA vs. DENVER**
Vikings lead series, 2-1;
See Denver vs. Minnesota
**MINNESOTA vs. DETROIT**
Vikings lead series, 28-15-2;
See Detroit vs. Minnesota
**MINNESOTA vs. GREEN BAY**
Vikings lead series, 24-20-1;
See Green Bay vs. Minnesota
**MINNESOTA vs. HOUSTON**
Vikings lead series, 2-1;
See Houston vs. Minnesota
**MINNESOTA vs. KANSAS CITY**
Series tied, 2-2;
See Kansas City vs. Minnesota
**MINNESOTA vs. L.A. RAIDERS**
Raiders lead series, 4-1;
See L.A. Raiders vs. Minnesota
**MINNESOTA vs. L.A. RAMS**
Vikings lead series, 15-11-2;
See L.A. Rams vs. Minnesota
**MINNESOTA vs. MIAMI**
Dolphins lead series, 4-1;
See Miami vs. Minnesota
**MINNESOTA vs. *NEW ENGLAND**
Patriots lead series, 2-1
1970—Vikings, 35-14 (B)
1974—Patriots, 17-14 (M)
1979—Patriots, 27-23 (NE)
(Points—Vikings 72, Patriots 58)
*Franchise in Boston prior to 1971
**MINNESOTA vs. NEW ORLEANS**
Vikings lead series, 8-3
1968—Saints, 20-17 (NO)
1970—Vikings, 26-0 (M)
1971—Vikings, 23-10 (NO)
1972—Vikings, 37-6 (M)
1974—Vikings, 29-9 (M)
1975—Vikings, 20-7 (NO)
1976—Vikings, 40-9 (NO)
1978—Saints, 31-24 (NO)
1980—Vikings, 23-20 (NO)
1981—Vikings, 20-10 (M)
1983—Saints, 17-16 (NO)
(Points—Vikings 275, Saints 139)
**MINNESOTA vs. N.Y. GIANTS**
Vikings lead series, 6-1
1964—Vikings, 30-21 (NY)
1965—Vikings, 40-14 (M)
1967—Vikings, 27-24 (M)
1969—Giants, 24-23 (NY)
1971—Vikings, 17-10 (NY)
1973—Vikings, 31-7 (New Haven)
1976—Vikings, 24-7 (M)
(Points—Vikings 192, Giants 107)
**MINNESOTA vs. N.Y. JETS**
Jets lead series, 3-1
1970—Jets, 20-10 (NY)
1975—Vikings, 29-21 (M)
1979—Jets, 14-7 (NY)
1982—Jets, 42-14 (M)
(Points—Jets 97, Vikings 60)
**MINNESOTA vs. PHILADELPHIA**
Vikings lead series, 8-2
1962—Vikings, 31-21 (M)
1963—Vikings, 34-13 (P)
1968—Vikings, 24-17 (P)
1971—Vikings, 13-0 (P)
1973—Vikings, 28-21 (M)
1976—Vikings, 31-12 (P)
1978—Vikings, 28-27 (M)

1980—Eagles, 42-7 (M)
*Eagles, 31-16 (P)
1981—Vikings, 35-23 (M)
(Points—Vikings 247, Eagles 207)
*NFC Divisional Playoff
**MINNESOTA vs. PITTSBURGH**
Vikings lead series, 5-4
1962—Steelers, 39-31 (P)
1964—Vikings, 30-10 (M)
1967—Vikings, 41-27 (P)
1969—Vikings, 52-14 (M)
1972—Steelers, 23-10 (P)
1974—*Steelers, 16-6 (New Orleans)
1976—Vikings, 17-6 (M)
1980—Steelers, 23-17 (M)
1983—Vikings, 17-14 (P)
(Points—Vikings 221, Steelers 172)
*Super Bowl IX
**MINNESOTA vs. ST. LOUIS**
Cardinals lead series, 7-3
1963—Cardinals, 56-14 (M)
1967—Cardinals, 34-24 (M)
1969—Vikings, 27-10 (StL)
1972—Cardinals, 19-17 (M)
1974—Vikings, 28-24 (StL)
*Vikings, 30-14 (M)
1977—Cardinals, 27-7 (M)
1979—Cardinals, 37-7 (StL)
1981—Cardinals, 30-17 (StL)
1983—Cardinals, 41-31 (StL)
(Points—Cardinals 292, Vikings 202)
*NFC Divisional Playoff
**MINNESOTA vs. SAN DIEGO**
Series tied, 2-2
1971—Chargers, 30-14 (SD)
1975—Vikings, 28-13 (M)
1978—Chargers, 13-7 (M)
1981—Vikings, 33-31 (SD)
(Points—Chargers 87, Vikings 82)
**MINNESOTA vs. SAN FRANCISCO**
Vikings lead series, 12-11-1
1961—49ers, 38-24 (M)
49ers, 38-28 (SF)
1962—Vikings, 21-7 (SF)
49ers, 35-12 (M)
1963—Vikings, 24-20 (SF)
Vikings, 45-14 (M)
1964—Vikings, 27-22 (SF)
Vikings, 24-7 (M)
1965—Vikings, 42-41 (SF)
49ers, 45-24 (M)
1966—Tie, 20-20 (SF)
Vikings, 28-3 (SF)
1967—49ers, 27-21 (M)
1968—Vikings, 30-20 (SF)
1969—Vikings, 10-7 (M)
1970—*49ers, 17-14 (M)
1971—Vikings, 13-9 (M)
1972—49ers, 20-17 (SF)
1973—Vikings, 17-13 (SF)
1975—Vikings, 27-17 (M)
1976—49ers, 20-16 (SF)
1977—Vikings, 28-27 (M)
1979—Vikings, 28-22 (M)
1983—49ers, 48-17 (M)
(Points—49ers 555, Vikings 539)
*NFC Divisional Playoff
**MINNESOTA vs. SEATTLE**
Series tied, 1-1
1976—Vikings, 27-21 (M)
1978—Seahawks, 29-28 (S)
(Points—Vikings 55, Seahawks 50)
**MINNESOTA vs. TAMPA BAY**
Vikings lead series, 8-4
1977—Vikings, 9-3 (TB)
1978—Buccaneers, 16-10 (M)
Vikings, 24-7 (TB)
1979—Buccaneers, 12-10 (M)
Vikings, 23-22 (TB)
1980—Vikings, 38-30 (M)
Vikings, 21-10 (TB)
1981—Buccaneers, 21-13 (TB)
Vikings, 25-10 (M)
1982—Vikings, 17-10 (M)
1983—Vikings, 19-16 (TB) OT
Buccaneers, 17-12 (M)
(Points—Vikings 221, Buccaneers 174)
**MINNESOTA vs. WASHINGTON**
Vikings lead series, 5-3
1968—Vikings, 27-14 (M)
1970—Vikings, 19-10 (W)
1972—Redskins, 24-21 (M)
1973—*Vikings, 27-20 (M)
1975—Redskins, 31-30 (W)
1976—*Vikings, 35-20 (M)
1980—Vikings, 39-14 (W)
1982—**Redskins, 21-7 (W)
(Points—Vikings 205, Redskins 154)
*NFC Divisional Playoff
**NFC Second Round Playoff
_____

**NEW ENGLAND vs. ATLANTA**
Series tied, 2-2;

See Atlanta vs. New England
**NEW ENGLAND vs. BALTIMORE**
Colts lead series, 15-12;
See Baltimore vs. New England
**NEW ENGLAND vs. BUFFALO**
Patriots lead series, 24-23-1;
See Buffalo vs. New England
**NEW ENGLAND vs. CHICAGO**
Patriots lead series, 2-1;
See Chicago vs. New England
**NEW ENGLAND vs. CINCINNATI**
Patriots lead series, 4-3;
See Cincinnati vs. New England
**NEW ENGLAND vs. CLEVELAND**
Browns lead series, 5-1;
See Cleveland vs. New England
**NEW ENGLAND vs. DALLAS**
Cowboys lead series, 4-0;
See Dallas vs. New England
**NEW ENGLAND vs. DENVER**
Patriots lead series, 12-10;
See Denver vs. New England
**NEW ENGLAND vs. DETROIT**
Lions lead series, 2-1;
See Detroit vs. New England
**NEW ENGLAND vs. GREEN BAY**
Series tied, 1-1;
See Green Bay vs. New England
**NEW ENGLAND vs. HOUSTON**
Patriots lead series, 14-13-1;
See Houston vs. New England
**NEW ENGLAND vs. KANSAS CITY**
Chiefs lead series, 11-7-3;
See Kansas City vs. New England
**NEW ENGLAND vs. L.A. RAIDERS**
Series tied, 11-11-1;
See L.A. Raiders vs. New England
**NEW ENGLAND vs. L.A. RAMS**
Patriots lead series, 2-1;
See L.A. Rams vs. New England
**NEW ENGLAND vs. MIAMI**
Dolphins lead series, 22-13;
See Miami vs. New England
**NEW ENGLAND vs. MINNESOTA**
Patriots lead series, 2-1;
See Minnesota vs. New England
**NEW ENGLAND vs. NEW ORLEANS**
Patriots lead series, 4-0
1972—Patriots, 17-10 (NO)
1976—Patriots, 27-6 (NE)
1980—Patriots, 38-27 (NO)
1983—Patriots, 7-0 (NE)
(Points—Patriots 89, Saints 43)
***NEW ENGLAND vs. N.Y. GIANTS**
Series tied, 1-1
1970—Giants, 16-0 (B)
1974—Patriots, 28-20 (New Haven)
(Points—Giants 36, Patriots 28)
*Franchise in Boston prior to 1971
***NEW ENGLAND vs. **N.Y. JETS**
Jets lead series, 28-18-1
1960—Patriots, 28-24 (NY)
Patriots, 38-21 (B)
1961—Titans, 21-20 (B)
Titans, 37-30 (NY)
1962—Patriots, 43-14 (NY)
Patriots, 24-17 (B)
1963—Patriots, 38-14 (B)
Jets, 31-24 (NY)
1964—Patriots, 26-10 (B)
Jets, 35-14 (NY)
1965—Jets, 30-20 (B)
Patriots, 27-23 (NY)
1966—Tie, 24-24 (B)
Jets, 38-28 (NY)
1967—Jets, 30-23 (NY)
Jets, 29-24 (B)
1968—Jets, 47-31 (Birmingham)
Jets, 48-14 (NY)
1969—Jets, 23-14 (B)
Jets, 23-17 (NY)
1970—Jets, 31-21 (B)
Jets, 17-3 (NY)
1971—Patriots, 20-0 (NE)
Jets, 13-6 (NY)
1972—Jets, 41-13 (NE)
Jets, 34-10 (NY)
1973—Jets, 9-7 (NE)
Jets, 33-13 (NY)
1974—Patriots, 24-0 (NY)
Jets, 21-16 (NE)
1975—Jets, 36-7 (NY)
Jets, 30-28 (NE)
1976—Patriots, 41-7 (NE)
Patriots, 38-24 (NY)
1977—Jets, 30-27 (NY)
Patriots, 24-13 (NE)
1978—Patriots, 55-21 (NE)
Patriots, 19-17 (NY)
1979—Jets, 56-3 (NE)
Jets, 27-26 (NY)
1980—Patriots, 21-11 (NY)
Patriots, 34-21 (NE)

1981—Jets, 28-24 (NY)
Jets, 17-6 (NE)
1982—Jets, 31-7 (NE)
1983—Patriots, 23-13 (NE)
Jets, 26-3 (NY)
(Points—Jets 1,093, Patriots 1,079)
*Franchise in Boston prior to 1971
**Jets known as Titans prior to 1963
**NEW ENGLAND vs. PHILADELPHIA**
Series tied, 2-2
1973—Eagles, 24-23 (P)
1977—Patriots, 14-6 (NE)
1978—Patriots, 24-14 (NE)
1981—Eagles, 13-3 (P)
(Points—Patriots 64, Eagles 57)
**NEW ENGLAND vs. PITTSBURGH**
Steelers lead series, 5-2
1972—Steelers, 33-3 (P)
1974—Steelers, 21-17 (NE)
1976—Patriots, 30-27 (P)
1979—Steelers, 16-13 (NE) OT
1981—Steelers, 27-21 (P) OT
1982—Steelers, 37-14 (P)
1983—Patriots, 28-23 (P)
(Points—Steelers 184, Patriots 126)
***NEW ENGLAND vs. ST. LOUIS**
Cardinals lead series, 3-1
1970—Cardinals, 31-0 (StL)
1975—Cardinals, 24-17 (StL)
1978—Patriots, 16-6 (StL)
1981—Cardinals, 27-20 (NE)
(Points—Cardinals 88, Patriots 53)
*Franchise in Boston prior to 1971
***NEW ENGLAND vs. **SAN DIEGO**
Patriots lead series, 13-12-2
1960—Patriots, 35-0 (LA)
Chargers, 45-16 (B)
1961—Chargers, 38-27 (B)
Patriots, 41-0 (SD)
1962—Patriots, 24-20 (B)
Patriots, 20-14 (SD)
1963—Chargers, 17-13 (SD)
Chargers, 7-6 (B)
***Chargers, 51-10 (SD)
1964—Chargers, 33-28 (SD)
Chargers, 26-17 (B)
1965—Tie, 10-10 (B)
Patriots, 22-6 (SD)
1966—Chargers, 24-0 (SD)
Patriots, 35-17 (B)
1967—Chargers, 28-14 (SD)
Tie, 31-31 (B)
1968—Chargers, 27-17 (B)
1969—Chargers, 13-10 (B)
Chargers, 28-18 (SD)
1970—Chargers, 16-14 (B)
1973—Chargers, 30-14 (NE)
1975—Chargers, 33-19 (SD)
1977—Patriots, 24-20 (SD)
1978—Patriots, 28-23 (NE)
1979—Patriots, 27-21 (NE)
1983—Patriots, 37-21 (NE)
(Points—Patriots 592, Chargers 564)
*Franchise in Boston prior to 1971
**Franchise in Los Angeles prior to 1961
***AFL Championship
**NEW ENGLAND vs. SAN FRANCISCO**
49ers lead series, 3-1
1971—49ers, 27-10 (SF)
1975—Patriots, 24-16 (M)
1980—49ers, 21-17 (SF)
1983—49ers, 33-13 (NE)
(Points—49ers 97, Patriots 64)
**NEW ENGLAND vs. SEATTLE**
Patriots lead series, 3-1
1977—Patriots, 31-0 (NE)
1980—Patriots, 37-31 (S)
1982—Patriots, 16-0 (S)
1983—Seahawks, 24-6 (S)
(Points—Patriots 90, Seahawks 55)
**NEW ENGLAND vs. TAMPA BAY**
Patriots lead series, 1-0
1976—Patriots, 31-14 (NE)
**NEW ENGLAND vs. WASHINGTON**
Redskins lead series, 2-1
1972—Patriots, 24-23 (NE)
1978—Redskins, 16-14 (NE)
1981—Redskins, 24-22 (W)
(Points—Redskins 63, Patriots 60)
_____

**NEW ORLEANS vs. ATLANTA**
Falcons lead series, 20-10;
See Atlanta vs. New Orleans
**NEW ORLEANS vs. BALTIMORE**
Colts lead series, 3-0;
See Baltimore vs. New Orleans
**NEW ORLEANS vs. BUFFALO**
Bills lead series, 2-1;
See Buffalo vs. New Orleans
**NEW ORLEANS vs. CHICAGO**
Bears lead series, 6-4;
See Chicago vs. New Orleans
**NEW ORLEANS vs. CINCINNATI**

**NEW ENGLAND vs. ATLANTA**
Series tied, 2-2;

Series tied, 2-2;
See Cincinnati vs. New Orleans
**NEW ORLEANS vs. CLEVELAND**
Browns lead series, 8-0;
See Cleveland vs. New Orleans
**NEW ORLEANS vs. DALLAS**
Cowboys lead series, 10-1;
See Dallas vs. New Orleans
**NEW ORLEANS vs. DENVER**
Broncos lead series, 3-0;
See Denver vs. New Orleans
**NEW ORLEANS vs. DETROIT**
Series tied, 4-4-1;
See Detroit vs. New Orleans
**NEW ORLEANS vs. GREEN BAY**
Packers lead series, 8-2;
See Green Bay vs. New Orleans
**NEW ORLEANS vs. HOUSTON**
Oilers lead series, 2-1-1;
See Houston vs. New Orleans
**NEW ORLEANS vs. KANSAS CITY**
Saints lead series, 2-1;
See Kansas City vs. New Orleans
**NEW ORLEANS vs. L.A. RAIDERS**
Raiders lead series, 2-0-1;
See L.A. Raiders vs. New Orleans
**NEW ORLEANS vs. L.A. RAMS**
Rams lead series, 20-8;
See L.A. Rams vs. New Orleans
**NEW ORLEANS vs. MIAMI**
Dolphins lead series, 3-1;
See Miami vs. New Orleans
**NEW ORLEANS vs. MINNESOTA**
Vikings lead series, 8-3;
See Minnesota vs. New Orleans
**NEW ORLEANS vs. NEW ENGLAND**
Patriots lead series, 4-0;
See New England vs. New Orleans
**NEW ORLEANS vs. N.Y. GIANTS**
Giants lead series, 5-4
1967—Giants, 27-21 (NY)
1968—Giants, 38-21 (NY)
1969—Saints, 25-24 (NY)
1970—Saints, 14-10 (NO)
1972—Saints, 45-21 (NY)
1975—Giants, 28-14 (NY)
1978—Saints, 28-17 (NO)
1979—Saints, 24-14 (NO)
1981—Giants, 20-7 (NY)
(Points—Giants 223, Saints 175)
**NEW ORLEANS vs. N.Y. JETS**
Jets lead series, 3-1
1972—Jets, 18-17 (NY)
1977—Jets, 16-13 (NO)
1980—Saints, 21-20 (NY)
1983—Jets, 31-28 (NO)
(Points—Jets 85, Saints 79)
**NEW ORLEANS vs. PHILADELPHIA**
Eagles lead series, 8-5
1967—Saints, 31-24 (NO)
Eagles, 48-21 (P)
1968—Eagles, 29-17 (P)
1969—Eagles, 13-10 (P)
Saints, 26-17 (NO)
1972—Saints, 21-3 (NO)
1974—Saints, 14-10 (NO)
1977—Eagles, 28-7 (P)
1978—Eagles, 24-17 (NO)
1979—Eagles, 26-14 (NO)
1980—Eagles, 34-21 (NO)
1981—Eagles, 31-14 (NO)
1983—Saints, 20-17 (P) OT
(Points—Eagles 304, Saints 233)
**NEW ORLEANS vs. PITTSBURGH**
Steelers lead series, 4-3
1967—Steelers, 14-10 (NO)
1968—Saints, 16-12 (P)
Saints, 24-14 (NO)
1969—Steelers, 27-24 (NO)
1974—Steelers, 28-7 (NO)
1978—Steelers, 20-14 (P)
1981—Steelers, 20-6 (NO)
(Points—Steelers 132, Saints 104)
**NEW ORLEANS vs. ST. LOUIS**
Cardinals lead series, 8-3
1967—Cardinals, 31-20 (StL)
1968—Cardinals, 21-20 (NO)
Cardinals, 31-17 (StL)
1969—Saints, 51-42 (StL)
1970—Cardinals, 24-17 (StL)
1974—Saints, 14-0 (NO)
1977—Cardinals, 49-31 (StL)
1980—Cardinals, 40-7 (NO)
1981—Cardinals, 30-3 (StL)
1982—Cardinals, 21-7 (NO)
1983—Cardinals, 28-17 (NO)
(Points—Cardinals 306, Saints 215)
**NEW ORLEANS vs. SAN DIEGO**
Chargers lead series, 3-0
1973—Chargers, 17-14 (SD)
1977—Chargers, 14-0 (NO)
1979—Chargers, 35-0 (NO)
(Points—Chargers 66, Saints 14)

**NEW ORLEANS vs. SAN FRANCISCO**
49ers lead series, 19-8-2
1967—49ers, 27-13 (SF)
1969—Saints, 43-38 (NO)
1970—Tie, 20-20 (SF)
49ers, 38-27 (NO)
1971—49ers, 38-20 (NO)
Saints, 26-20 (SF)
1972—49ers, 37-2 (NO)
Tie, 20-20 (SF)
1973—49ers, 40-0 (SF)
Saints, 16-10 (NO)
1974—49ers, 17-13 (NO)
49ers, 35-21 (SF)
1975—49ers, 35-21 (SF)
49ers, 16-6 (NO)
1976—49ers, 33-3 (SF)
49ers, 27-7 (NO)
1977—49ers, 10-7 (NO) OT
49ers, 20-17 (SF)
1978—Saints, 14-7 (SF)
Saints, 24-13 (NO)
1979—Saints, 30-21 (SF)
Saints, 31-20 (NO)
1980—49ers, 26-23 (NO)
49ers, 38-35 (SF) OT
1981—49ers, 21-14 (SF)
49ers, 21-17 (NO)
1982—Saints, 23-20 (SF)
1983—49ers, 32-13 (NO)
49ers, 27-0 (SF)
(Points—49ers 727, Saints 506)
**NEW ORLEANS vs. SEATTLE**
Series tied, 1-1
1976—Saints, 51-27 (S)
1979—Seahawks, 38-24 (S)
(Points—Saints 75, Seahawks 65)
**NEW ORLEANS vs. TAMPA BAY**
Series tied, 3-3
1977—Buccaneers, 33-14 (NO)
1978—Saints, 17-10 (TB)
1979—Saints, 42-14 (TB)
1981—Buccaneers, 31-14 (NO)
1982—Buccaneers, 13-10 (NO)
1983—Saints, 24-21 (TB)
(Points—Buccaneers 122, Saints 121)
**NEW ORLEANS vs. WASHINGTON**
Redskins lead series, 7-4
1967—Redskins, 30-10 (NO)
Saints, 30-14 (W)
1968—Saints, 37-17 (NO)
1969—Redskins, 26-20 (NO)
Redskins, 17-14 (W)
1971—Redskins, 24-14 (W)
1973—Saints, 19-3 (NO)
1975—Redskins, 41-3 (W)
1979—Saints, 14-10 (W)
1980—Redskins, 22-14 (W)
1982—Redskins, 27-10 (NO)
(Points—Redskins 231, Saints 185)

---

**N.Y. GIANTS vs. ATLANTA**
Falcons lead series, 6-4;
See Atlanta vs. N.Y. Giants
**N.Y. GIANTS vs. BALTIMORE**
Colts lead series, 7-3;
See Baltimore vs. N.Y. Giants
**N.Y. GIANTS vs. BUFFALO**
Giants lead series, 2-1;
See Buffalo vs. N.Y. Giants
**N.Y. GIANTS vs. CHICAGO**
Bears lead series, 26-16-2;
See Chicago vs. N.Y. Giants
**N.Y. GIANTS vs. CINCINNATI**
Bengals lead series, 2-0;
See Cincinnati vs. N.Y. Giants
**N.Y. GIANTS vs. CLEVELAND**
Browns lead series, 25-16-2;
See Cleveland vs. N.Y. Giants
**N.Y. GIANTS vs. DALLAS**
Cowboys lead series, 30-11-2;
See Dallas vs. N.Y. Giants
**N.Y. GIANTS vs. DENVER**
Broncos lead series, 2-1;
See Denver vs. N.Y. Giants
**N.Y. GIANTS VS. DETROIT**
Lions lead series, 18-11-1;
See Detroit vs. N.Y. Giants
**N.Y. GIANTS vs. GREEN BAY**
Packers lead series, 24-18-2;
See Green Bay vs. N.Y. Giants
**N.Y. GIANTS vs. HOUSTON**
Giants lead series, 2-0;
See Houston vs. N.Y. Giants
**N.Y. GIANTS vs. KANSAS CITY**
Giants lead series, 3-1;
See Kansas City vs. N.Y. Giants
**N.Y. GIANTS vs. L.A. RAIDERS**
Raiders lead series, 3-0;
See L.A. Raiders vs. N.Y. Giants
**N.Y. GIANTS vs. L.A. RAMS**
Rams lead series, 15-6;
See L.A. Rams vs. N.Y. Giants

**N.Y. GIANTS vs. MIAMI**
Dolphins lead series, 1-0;
See Miami vs. N.Y. Giants
**N.Y. GIANTS vs. MINNESOTA**
Vikings lead series, 6-1;
See Minnesota vs. N.Y. Giants
**N.Y. GIANTS vs. NEW ENGLAND**
Series tied, 1-1;
See New England vs. N.Y. Giants
**N.Y. GIANTS vs. NEW ORLEANS**
Giants lead series, 5-4;
See New Orleans vs. N.Y. Giants
**N.Y. GIANTS vs. N.Y. JETS**
Jets lead series, 2-1
1970—Giants, 22-10 (NYJ)
1974—Jets, 26-20 (New Haven) OT
1981—Jets, 26-7 (NYG)
(Points—Jets 62, Giants 49)
**N.Y. GIANTS vs. PHILADELPHIA**
Giants lead series, 53-44-2
1933—Giants, 56-0 (NY)
Giants, 20-14 (P)
1934—Giants, 17-0 (NY)
Eagles, 6-0 (P)
1935—Giants, 10-0 (NY)
Giants, 21-14 (P)
1936—Eagles, 10-7 (P)
Giants, 21-17 (NY)
1937—Giants, 16-7 (P)
Giants, 21-0 (NY)
1938—Eagles, 14-10 (P)
Giants, 17-7 (NY)
1939—Giants, 13-3 (P)
Giants, 27-10 (NY)
1940—Giants, 20-14 (P)
Giants, 17-7 (NY)
1941—Giants, 24-0 (P)
Giants, 16-0 (NY)
1942—Giants, 35-17 (NY)
Giants, 14-0 (P)
1944—Eagles, 24-17 (NY)
Tie, 21-21 (P)
1945—Eagles, 38-17 (P)
Giants, 28-21 (NY)
1946—Eagles, 24-14 (P)
Giants, 45-17 (NY)
1947—Eagles, 23-0 (P)
Eagles, 41-24 (NY)
1948—Eagles, 45-0 (P)
Giants, 35-14 (NY)
1949—Eagles, 24-3 (NY)
Eagles, 17-3 (P)
1950—Giants, 7-3 (NY)
Giants, 9-7 (P)
1951—Giants, 26-24 (NY)
Giants, 23-7 (P)
1952—Giants, 31-7 (P)
Eagles, 14-10 (NY)
1953—Eagles, 30-7 (P)
Giants, 37-28 (NY)
1954—Giants, 27-14 (NY)
Eagles, 29-14 (P)
1955—Eagles, 27-17 (P)
Giants, 31-7 (NY)
1956—Giants, 20-3 (NY)
Giants, 21-7 (P)
1957—Giants, 24-20 (P)
Giants, 13-0 (NY)
1958—Eagles, 27-24 (P)
Giants, 24-10 (NY)
1959—Eagles, 49-21 (P)
Giants, 24-7 (NY)
1960—Eagles, 17-10 (NY)
Eagles, 31-23 (P)
1961—Giants, 38-21 (NY)
Giants, 28-24 (P)
1962—Giants, 29-13 (P)
Giants, 19-14 (NY)
1963—Giants, 37-14 (P)
Giants, 42-14 (NY)
1964—Eagles, 38-7 (P)
Eagles, 23-17 (NY)
1965—Eagles, 16-14 (P)
Giants, 35-27 (NY)
1966—Giants, 35-17 (P)
Eagles, 31-3 (NY)
1967—Giants, 44-7 (NY)
1968—Giants, 34-25 (P)
Giants, 7-6 (NY)
1969—Eagles, 23-20 (NY)
Giants, 30-23 (NY)
Eagles, 23-20 (P)
1971—Eagles, 23-7 (P)
Eagles, 41-28 (NY)
1972—Giants, 27-12 (NY)
Giants, 62-10 (NY)
1973—Tie, 23-23 (NY)
Eagles, 20-16 (P)
1974—Eagles, 35-7 (P)
Eagles, 20-7 (New Haven)
1975—Giants, 23-14 (P)
Eagles, 13-10 (NY)
1976—Eagles, 20-7 (P)

Eagles, 10-0 (NY)
1977—Eagles, 28-10 (NY)
Eagles, 17-14 (P)
1978—Eagles, 19-17 (NY)
Eagles, 20-3 (P)
1979—Eagles, 23-17 (P)
Eagles, 17-13 (NY)
1980—Eagles, 35-3 (P)
Eagles, 31-16 (NY)
1981—Eagles, 24-10 (NY)
Giants, 20-10 (P)
*Giants, 27-21 (P)
1982—Giants, 23-7 (NY)
Eagles, 26-24 (P)
1983—Eagles, 17-13 (NY)
Giants, 23-0 (P)
(Points—Giants 1,906, Eagles 1,747)
*NFC First Round Playoff
**N.Y. GIANTS vs. \*PITTSBURGH**
Giants lead series, 40-26-3
1933—Giants, 23-2 (P)
Giants, 27-3 (NY)
1934—Giants, 14-12 (P)
Giants, 17-7 (NY)
1935—Giants, 42-7 (P)
Giants, 13-0 (NY)
1936—Pirates, 10-7 (P)
1937—Giants, 10-7 (P)
Giants, 17-0 (NY)
1938—Giants, 27-14 (P)
Pirates, 13-10 (NY)
1939—Giants, 14-7 (P)
Giants, 23-7 (NY)
1940—Tie, 10-10 (P)
Giants, 12-0 (NY)
1941—Giants, 37-10 (P)
Giants, 28-7 (NY)
1942—Steelers, 13-10 (P)
Steelers, 17-9 (NY)
1945—Giants, 34-6 (P)
Steelers, 21-7 (NY)
1946—Giants, 17-14 (P)
Giants, 7-0 (NY)
1947—Steelers, 38-21 (NY)
Steelers, 24-7 (P)
1948—Giants, 34-27 (NY)
Steelers, 38-28 (P)
1949—Steelers, 28-7 (P)
Steelers, 21-17 (NY)
1950—Giants, 18-7 (P)
Steelers, 17-6 (NY)
1951—Tie, 13-13 (P)
Giants, 14-0 (NY)
1952—Steelers, 63-7 (P)
1953—Steelers, 24-14 (P)
Steelers, 14-10 (NY)
1954—Giants, 30-6 (P)
Giants, 24-3 (NY)
1955—Steelers, 30-23 (P)
Steelers, 19-17 (NY)
1956—Giants, 38-10 (NY)
Giants, 17-14 (P)
1957—Giants, 35-0 (NY)
Steelers, 21-10 (P)
1958—Giants, 17-6 (NY)
Steelers, 31-10 (P)
1959—Giants, 21-16 (P)
Steelers, 14-9 (NY)
1960—Giants, 19-17 (NY)
Giants, 27-24 (NY)
1961—Giants, 17-14 (P)
Giants, 42-21 (NY)
1962—Giants, 31-27 (P)
Steelers, 20-17 (NY)
1963—Steelers, 31-0 (P)
Giants, 33-17 (NY)
1964—Steelers, 27-24 (P)
Steelers, 44-17 (NY)
1965—Giants, 23-13 (P)
Giants, 35-10 (NY)
1966—Tie, 34-34 (P)
Steelers, 47-28 (NY)
1967—Giants, 27-24 (P)
Giants, 28-20 (NY)
1968—Giants, 34-20 (P)
1969—Giants, 10-7 (NY)
Giants, 21-17 (P)
1971—Steelers, 17-13 (P)
1976—Steelers, 27-0 (NY)
(Points—Giants 1,342, Steelers 1,149)
*Steelers known as Pirates prior to 1941
**N.Y. GIANTS vs. \*ST. LOUIS**
Giants lead series, 50-30-2
1926—Giants, 20-0 (NY)
1927—Giants, 28-7 (NY)
1929—Giants, 24-21 (NY)
1930—Giants, 25-12 (NY)
Giants, 13-7 (C)
1935—Cardinals, 14-13 (NY)
1936—Giants, 14-6 (NY)
1938—Giants, 6-0 (NY)
1939—Giants, 17-7 (NY)
1941—Cardinals, 10-7 (NY)

1942—Giants, 21-7 (NY)
1943—Giants, 24-13 (NY)
1946—Giants, 28-24 (NY)
1947—Giants, 35-31 (NY)
1948—Cardinals, 63-35 (NY)
1949—Giants, 41-38 (C)
1950—Cardinals, 17-3 (C)
      Giants, 51-21 (NY)
1951—Giants, 28-17 (NY)
      Giants, 10-0 (C)
1952—Cardinals, 24-23 (NY)
      Giants, 28-6 (C)
1953—Giants, 21-7 (NY)
      Giants, 23-20 (C)
1954—Giants, 41-10 (C)
      Giants, 31-17 (NY)
1955—Cardinals, 28-17 (C)
      Giants, 10-0 (NY)
1956—Cardinals, 35-27 (C)
      Giants, 23-10 (NY)
1957—Giants, 27-14 (NY)
      Giants, 28-21 (C)
1958—Giants, 37-7 (Buffalo)
      Cardinals, 23-6 (NY)
1959—Giants, 9-3 (NY)
      Giants, 30-20 (Minn)
1960—Giants, 35-14 (NY)
      Cardinals, 20-13 (NY)
1961—Giants, 21-10 (NY)
      Giants, 24-9 (StL)
1962—Giants, 31-14 (StL)
      Giants, 31-28 (NY)
1963—Giants, 38-21 (StL)
      Cardinals, 24-17 (NY)
1964—Giants, 34-17 (NY)
      Tie, 10-10 (StL)
1965—Giants, 14-10 (NY)
      Giants, 28-15 (StL)
1966—Cardinals, 24-19 (StL)
      Cardinals, 20-17 (NY)
1967—Giants, 37-20 (StL)
      Giants, 37-14 (NY)
1968—Cardinals, 28-21 (NY)
1969—Cardinals, 42-17 (StL)
      Giants, 49-6 (NY)
1970—Giants, 35-17 (NY)
      Giants, 34-17 (StL)
1971—Giants, 21-20 (StL)
      Cardinals, 24-7 (NY)
1972—Giants, 27-21 (NY)
      Giants, 13-7 (StL)
1973—Cardinals, 35-27 (StL)
      Giants, 24-13 (New Haven)
1974—Cardinals, 23-21 (New Haven)
      Cardinals, 26-14 (StL)
1975—Cardinals, 26-14 (StL)
      Cardinals, 20-13 (NY)
1976—Cardinals, 27-21 (StL)
      Cardinals, 17-14 (NY)
1977—Cardinals, 28-0 (StL)
      Giants, 27-7 (NY)
1978—Cardinals, 20-10 (StL)
      Giants, 17-0 (NY)
1979—Cardinals, 27-14 (NY)
      Cardinals, 29-20 (StL)
1980—Cardinals, 41-35 (StL)
      Cardinals, 23-7 (NY)
1981—Giants, 34-14 (NY)
      Giants, 20-10 (StL)
1982—Cardinals, 24-21 (StL)
1983—Tie, 20-20 (StL) OT
      Cardinals, 10-6 (NY)
(Points—Giants 1,828, Cardinals 1,457)
*Franchise in Chicago prior to 1960
**N.Y. GIANTS vs. SAN DIEGO**
Series tied, 2-2
1971—Giants, 35-17 (NY)
1975—Giants, 35-24 (NY)
1980—Chargers, 44-7 (SD)
1983—Chargers, 41-34 (NY)
(Points—Chargers 126, Giants 111)
**N.Y. GIANTS vs. SAN FRANCISCO**
Giants lead series, 9-5
1952—Giants, 23-14 (NY)
1956—Giants, 38-21 (SF)
1957—49ers, 27-17 (NY)
1960—Giants, 21-19 (SF)
1963—Giants, 48-14 (NY)
1968—49ers, 26-10 (NY)
1972—Giants, 23-17 (SF)
1975—Giants, 26-23 (SF)
1977—Giants, 20-17 (NY)
1978—Giants, 27-10 (NY)
1979—Giants, 32-16 (NY)
1980—49ers, 12-0 (SF)
1981—Giants, 17-10 (SF)
    *49ers, 38-24 (SF)
(Points—Giants 319, 49ers 271)
*NFC Divisional Playoff
**N.Y. GIANTS vs. SEATTLE**
Giants lead series, 3-1
1976—Giants, 28-16 (NY)
1980—Giants, 27-21 (S)

1981—Giants, 32-0 (S)
1983—Seahawks, 17-12 (NY)
(Points—Giants 99, Seahawks 54)
**N.Y. GIANTS vs. TAMPA BAY**
Giants lead series, 4-2
1977—Giants, 10-0 (TB)
1978—Giants, 19-13 (TB)
      Giants, 17-14 (NY)
1979—Giants, 17-14 (NY)
      Buccaneers, 31-3 (TB)
1980—Buccaneers, 30-13 (TB)
(Points—Buccaneers 102, Giants 79)
**N.Y. GIANTS vs. *WASHINGTON**
Giants lead series, 56-44-3
1932—Braves, 14-6 (B)
      Tie, 0-0 (NY)
1933—Redskins, 21-20 (B)
      Giants, 7-0 (NY)
1934—Giants, 16-13 (B)
      Giants, 3-0 (NY)
1935—Giants, 20-12 (B)
      Giants, 17-6 (NY)
1936—Giants, 7-0 (B)
      Redskins, 14-0 (NY)
1937—Redskins, 13-3 (N)
      Redskins, 49-14 (NY)
1938—Giants, 10-7 (W)
      Giants, 36-0 (NY)
1939—Tie, 0-0 (W)
      Giants, 9-7 (NY)
1940—Redskins, 21-7 (W)
      Giants, 21-7 (NY)
1941—Giants, 17-10 (W)
      Giants, 20-13 (NY)
1942—Giants, 14-7 (W)
      Redskins, 14-7 (NY)
1943—Giants, 14-10 (NY)
      Giants, 31-7 (W)
      **Redskins, 28-0 (NY)
1944—Giants, 16-13 (NY)
      Giants, 31-0 (W)
1945—Redskins, 24-14 (NY)
      Redskins, 17-0 (NY)
1946—Redskins, 24-14 (NY)
      Giants, 31-0 (NY)
1947—Redskins, 28-20 (W)
      Giants, 35-10 (NY)
1948—Giants, 41-10 (W)
      Redskins, 28-21 (NY)
1949—Giants, 45-35 (W)
      Giants, 23-7 (NY)
1950—Giants, 21-17 (W)
      Giants, 24-21 (NY)
1951—Giants, 35-14 (W)
      Giants, 28-14 (NY)
1952—Giants, 14-10 (W)
      Redskins, 27-17 (NY)
1953—Redskins, 13-9 (W)
      Redskins, 24-21 (NY)
1954—Giants, 51-21 (W)
      Giants, 24-7 (NY)
1955—Giants, 35-7 (W)
      Giants, 27-20 (W)
1956—Redskins, 33-7 (W)
      Giants, 28-14 (NY)
1957—Giants, 24-20 (W)
      Redskins, 31-14 (NY)
1958—Giants, 21-14 (W)
      Giants, 30-0 (NY)
1959—Giants, 45-14 (NY)
      Giants, 24-10 (W)
1960—Tie, 24-24 (NY)
      Giants, 17-3 (W)
1961—Giants, 24-21 (W)
      Giants, 53-0 (NY)
1962—Giants, 49-34 (NY)
      Giants, 42-24 (W)
1963—Giants, 24-14 (W)
      Giants, 44-14 (NY)
1964—Giants, 13-10 (NY)
      Redskins, 36-21 (W)
1965—Redskins, 23-7 (NY)
      Giants, 27-10 (W)
1966—Giants, 13-10 (NY)
      Redskins, 72-41 (W)
1967—Redskins, 38-34 (W)
      Giants, 13-10 (NY)
1968—Giants, 48-21 (NY)
      Giants, 13-10 (W)
1969—Giants, 20-14 (W)
      Giants, 27-24 (NY)
1970—Giants, 35-33 (NY)
      Giants, 27-24 (W)
1971—Redskins, 30-3 (NY)
      Redskins, 23-7 (W)
1972—Redskins, 23-16 (NY)
      Redskins, 27-13 (W)
1973—Redskins, 21-3 (New Haven)
      Redskins, 27-24 (W)
1974—Redskins, 13-10 (New Haven)
      Redskins, 24-3 (W)
1975—Redskins, 49-13 (W)
      Redskins, 21-13 (NY)
1976—Redskins, 19-17 (W)
      Giants, 12-9 (NY)

1977—Giants, 20-17 (NY)
      Giants, 17-6 (W)
1978—Giants, 17-6 (NY)
      Redskins, 16-13 (W) OT
1979—Redskins, 27-0 (W)
      Giants, 14-6 (W)
1980—Redskins, 23-21 (NY)
      Redskins, 16-13 (W)
1981—Giants, 17-7 (W)
      Redskins, 30-27 (NY) OT
1982—Redskins, 27-17 (NY)
      Redskins, 15-14 (W)
1983—Redskins, 33-17 (NY)
      Redskins, 31-22 (W)
(Points—Giants 1,991, Redskins 1,818)
*Franchise in Boston prior to 1937 and known as Braves prior to 1933
**Division Playoff

---

**N.Y. JETS vs. ATLANTA**
Falcons lead series, 2-1;
See Atlanta vs. N.Y. Jets
**N.Y. JETS vs. BALTIMORE**
Colts lead series, 15-13;
See Baltimore vs. N.Y. Jets
**N.Y. JETS vs. BUFFALO**
Bills lead series, 26-21;
See Buffalo vs. N.Y. Jets
**N.Y. JETS vs. CHICAGO**
Series tied, 1-1;
See Chicago vs. N.Y. Jets
**N.Y. JETS vs. CINCINNATI**
Jets lead series, 5-3;
See Cincinnati vs. N.Y. Jets
**N.Y. JETS vs. CLEVELAND**
Browns lead series, 7-1;
See Cleveland vs. N.Y. Jets
**N.Y. JETS vs. DALLAS**
Cowboys lead series, 3-0;
See Dallas vs. N.Y. Jets
**N.Y. JETS vs. DENVER**
Series tied, 10-10-1;
See Denver vs. N.Y. Jets
**N.Y. JETS vs. DETROIT**
Jets lead series, 2-1;
See Detroit vs. N.Y. Jets
**N.Y. JETS vs. GREEN BAY**
Jets lead series, 3-1;
See Green Bay vs. N.Y. Jets
**N.Y. JETS vs. HOUSTON**
Oilers lead series, 14-10-1;
See Houston vs. N.Y. Jets
**N.Y. JETS vs. KANSAS CITY**
Chiefs lead series, 13-9;
See Kansas City vs. N.Y. Jets
**N.Y. JETS vs. L.A. RAIDERS**
Series tied, 11-11-2;
See L.A. Raiders vs. N.Y. Jets
**N.Y. JETS vs. L.A. RAMS**
Series tied, 2-2;
See L.A. Rams vs. N.Y. Jets
**N.Y. JETS vs. MIAMI**
Dolphins lead series, 19-17-1;
See Miami vs. N.Y. Jets
**N.Y. JETS vs. MINNESOTA**
Jets lead series, 3-1;
See Minnesota vs. N.Y. Jets
**N.Y. JETS vs. NEW ENGLAND**
Jets lead series, 28-18-1;
See New England vs. N.Y. Jets
**N.Y. JETS vs. NEW ORLEANS**
Jets lead series, 3-1;
See New Orleans vs. N.Y. Jets
**N.Y. JETS vs. N.Y. GIANTS**
Jets lead series, 2-1;
See N.Y. Giants vs. N.Y. Jets
**N.Y. JETS vs. PHILADELPHIA**
Eagles lead series, 3-0
1973—Eagles, 24-23 (P)
1977—Eagles, 27-0 (P)
1978—Eagles, 17-9 (P)
(Points—Eagles 68, Jets 32)
**N.Y. JETS vs. PITTSBURGH**
Steelers lead series, 7-0
1970—Steelers, 21-17 (P)
1973—Steelers, 26-14 (P)
1975—Steelers, 20-7 (NY)
1977—Steelers, 23-20 (NY)
1978—Steelers, 28-17 (NY)
1981—Steelers, 38-10 (P)
1983—Steelers, 34-7 (NY)
(Points—Steelers 190, Jets 92)
**N.Y. JETS vs. ST. LOUIS**
Cardinals lead series, 2-1
1971—Cardinals, 17-10 (StL)
1975—Cardinals, 37-6 (NY)
1978—Jets, 23-10 (NY)
(Points—Cardinals 64, Jets 39)
**N.Y. JETS vs. **SAN DIEGO**
Chargers lead series, 14-7-1
1960—Chargers, 21-7 (NY)
      Chargers, 50-43 (LA)
1961—Chargers, 25-10 (NY)

Chargers, 48-13 (SD)
1962—Chargers, 40-14 (SD)
      Titans, 23-3 (NY)
1963—Chargers, 24-20 (SD)
      Chargers, 53-7 (NY)
1964—Tie, 17-17 (NY)
      Chargers, 38-3 (SD)
1965—Chargers, 34-9 (NY)
      Chargers, 38-7 (SD)
1966—Jets, 17-16 (NY)
      Chargers, 42-27 (SD)
1967—Jets, 42-31 (SD)
1968—Jets, 23-20 (NY)
      Jets, 37-15 (SD)
1969—Chargers, 34-27 (SD)
1971—Chargers, 49-21 (SD)
1974—Jets, 27-14 (NY)
1975—Chargers, 24-16 (SD)
1983—Jets, 41-29 (SD)
(Points—Chargers 665, Jets 451)
*Jets known as Titans prior to 1963
**Franchise in Los Angeles prior to 1961
**N.Y. JETS vs. SAN FRANCISCO**
49ers lead series, 3-1
1971—49ers, 24-21 (NY)
1976—49ers, 17-6 (SF)
1980—49ers, 37-27 (NY)
1983—Jets, 27-13 (SF)
(Points—49ers 91, Jets 81)
**N.Y. JETS vs. SEATTLE**
Seahawks lead series, 7-0
1977—Seahawks, 17-0 (NY)
1978—Seahawks, 24-17 (NY)
1979—Seahawks, 30-7 (S)
1980—Seahawks, 27-17 (NY)
1981—Seahawks, 19-3 (NY)
      Seahawks, 27-23 (S)
1983—Seahawks, 17-10 (NY)
(Points—Seahawks 161, Jets 77)
**N.Y. JETS vs. TAMPA BAY**
Jets lead series, 2-0
1976—Jets, 34-0 (NY)
1982—Jets, 32-17 (NY)
(Points—Jets 66, Buccaneers 17)
**N.Y. JETS vs. WASHINGTON**
Redskins lead series, 3-0
1972—Redskins, 35-17 (NY)
1976—Redskins, 37-16 (NY)
1978—Redskins, 23-3 (W)
(Points—Redskins 95, Jets 36)

---

**PHILADELPHIA vs. ATLANTA**
Series tied, 5-5-1;
See Atlanta vs. Philadelphia
**PHILADELPHIA vs. BALTIMORE**
Colts lead series, 5-4;
See Baltimore vs. Philadelphia
**PHILADELPHIA vs. BUFFALO**
Series tied, 1-1;
See Buffalo vs. Philadelphia
**PHILADELPHIA vs. CHICAGO**
Bears lead series, 19-4-1;
See Chicago vs. Philadelphia
**PHILADELPHIA vs. CINCINNATI**
Bengals lead series, 4-0;
See Cincinnati vs. Philadelphia
**PHILADELPHIA vs. CLEVELAND**
Browns lead series, 29-11-1;
See Cleveland vs. Philadelphia
**PHILADELPHIA vs. DALLAS**
Cowboys lead series, 31-16;
See Dallas vs. Philadelphia
**PHILADELPHIA vs. DENVER**
Eagles lead series, 3-1;
See Denver vs. Philadelphia
**PHILADELPHIA vs. DETROIT**
Lions lead series, 12-9-1;
See Detroit vs. Philadelphia
**PHILADELPHIA vs. GREEN BAY**
Packers lead series, 17-5;
See Green Bay vs. Philadelphia
**PHILADELPHIA vs. HOUSTON**
Eagles lead series, 3-0;
See Houston vs. Philadelphia
**PHILADELPHIA vs. KANSAS CITY**
Eagles lead series, 1-0;
See Kansas City vs. Philadelphia
**PHILADELPHIA vs. L.A. RAIDERS**
Raiders lead series, 3-1;
See L.A. Raiders vs. Philadelphia
**PHILADELPHIA vs. L.A. RAMS**
Rams lead series, 14-9-1;
See L.A. Rams vs. Philadelphia
**PHILADELPHIA vs. MIAMI**
Series tied, 2-2;
See Miami vs. Philadelphia
**PHILADELPHIA vs. MINNESOTA**
Vikings lead series, 8-2;
See Minnesota vs. Philadelphia
**PHILADELPHIA vs. NEW ENGLAND**
Series tied, 2-2;
See New England vs. Philadelphia

**PHILADELPHIA vs. NEW ORLEANS**
Eagles lead series, 8-5;
See New Orleans vs. Philadelphia
**PHILADELPHIA vs. N.Y. GIANTS**
Giants lead series, 53-44-2;
See N.Y. Giants vs. Philadelphia
**PHILADELPHIA vs. N.Y. JETS**
Eagles lead series, 3-0;
See N.Y. Jets vs. Philadelphia
**PHILADELPHIA vs. \*PITTSBURGH**
Eagles lead series, 42-25-3
1933—Eagles, 25-6 (Phila)
1934—Eagles, 17-0 (Pitt)
　　　Pirates, 9-7 (Phila)
1935—Eagles, 17-7 (Phila)
　　　Eagles, 17-6 (Pitt)
1936—Eagles, 17-0 (Pitt)
　　　Pirates, 6-0 (Johnstown, Pa.)
1937—Pirates, 27-14 (Pitt)
　　　Pirates, 16-7 (Pitt)
1938—Eagles, 27-7 (Buffalo)
　　　Eagles, 14-7 (Charleston, W. Va)
1939—Eagles, 17-14 (Phila)
　　　Pirates, 24-12 (Pitt)
1940—Pirates, 7-3 (Pitt)
　　　Eagles, 7-0 (Phila)
1941—Eagles, 10-7 (Pitt)
　　　Tie, 7-7 (Phila)
1942—Eagles, 24-14 (Pitt)
　　　Steelers, 14-0 (Phila)
1945—Eagles, 45-3 (Pitt)
　　　Eagles, 30-6 (Phila)
1946—Steelers, 10-7 (Pitt)
　　　Eagles, 10-7 (Phila)
1947—Steelers, 35-24 (Pitt)
　　　Eagles, 21-0 (Phila)
　　　\*\*Eagles, 21-0 (Pitt)
1948—Eagles, 34-7 (Pitt)
　　　Eagles, 17-0 (Phila)
1949—Eagles, 38-7 (Pitt)
　　　Eagles, 34-17 (Phila)
1950—Eagles, 17-10 (Pitt)
　　　Steelers, 9-7 (Phila)
1951—Eagles, 34-13 (Pitt)
　　　Steelers, 17-13 (Phila)
1952—Eagles, 31-25 (Pitt)
　　　Eagles, 26-21 (Phila)
1953—Eagles, 23-17 (Phila)
　　　Eagles, 35-7 (Pitt)
1954—Eagles, 24-22 (Phila)
　　　Steelers, 17-7 (Pitt)
1955—Steelers, 13-7 (Pitt)
　　　Eagles, 24-0 (Phila)
1956—Eagles, 35-21 (Pitt)
　　　Eagles, 14-7 (Phila)
1957—Steelers, 6-0 (Pitt)
　　　Eagles, 7-6 (Phila)
1958—Steelers, 24-3 (Pitt)
　　　Steelers, 31-24 (Phila)
1959—Eagles, 28-24 (Phila)
　　　Eagles, 31-0 (Pitt)
1960—Eagles, 34-7 (Phila)
　　　Steelers, 27-21 (Pitt)
1961—Eagles, 21-16 (Phila)
　　　Eagles, 35-24 (Pitt)
1962—Steelers, 13-7 (Pitt)
　　　Steelers, 26-17 (Phila)
1963—Tie, 21-21 (Phila)
　　　Tie, 20-20 (Pitt)
1964—Eagles, 21-7 (Phila)
　　　Eagles, 34-10 (Pitt)
1965—Steelers, 20-14 (Phila)
　　　Eagles, 47-13 (Pitt)
1966—Eagles, 31-14 (Pitt)
　　　Eagles, 27-23 (Phila)
1967—Eagles, 34-24 (Pitt)
1968—Steelers, 6-3 (Pitt)
1969—Eagles, 41-27 (Phila)
1970—Eagles, 30-20 (Phila)
1974—Steelers, 27-0 (Pitt)
1979—Eagles, 17-14 (Phila)
(Points—Eagles 1,330, Steelers 967)
\*Steelers known as Pirates prior to 1941
\*\*Division Playoff
**PHILADELPHIA vs. \*ST. LOUIS**
Cardinals lead series, 38-32-4
1935—Cardinals, 12-3 (C)
1936—Cardinals, 13-0 (C)
1937—Tie, 6-6 (P)
1938—Eagles, 7-0 (Erie, Pa.)
1941—Eagles, 21-14 (P)
1945—Eagles, 21-6 (P)
1947—Cardinals, 45-21 (P)
　　　\*\*Cardinals, 28-21 (C)
1948—Cardinals, 21-14 (C)
　　　\*\*Eagles, 7-0 (P)
1949—Eagles, 28-3 (P)
1950—Eagles, 45-7 (C)
　　　Cardinals, 14-10 (P)
1951—Eagles, 17-14 (C)
1952—Eagles, 10-7 (P)
　　　Cardinals, 28-22 (C)
1953—Eagles, 56-17 (C)

Eagles, 38-0 (P)
1954—Eagles, 35-16 (C)
　　　Eagles, 30-14 (P)
1955—Tie, 24-24 (C)
　　　Eagles, 27-3 (P)
1956—Cardinals, 20-6 (P)
　　　Cardinals, 28-17 (C)
1957—Eagles, 38-21 (C)
　　　Cardinals, 31-27 (P)
1958—Tie, 21-21 (C)
　　　Eagles, 49-21 (P)
1959—Eagles, 28-24 (Minn)
　　　Eagles, 27-17 (P)
1960—Eagles, 31-27 (P)
　　　Eagles, 20-6 (StL)
1961—Cardinals, 30-27 (P)
　　　Eagles, 20-7 (StL)
1962—Cardinals, 27-21 (P)
　　　Cardinals, 45-35 (StL)
1963—Cardinals, 28-24 (P)
　　　Cardinals, 38-14 (StL)
1964—Cardinals, 38-13 (P)
　　　Cardinals, 36-34 (StL)
1965—Eagles, 34-27 (P)
　　　Eagles, 28-24 (StL)
1966—Eagles, 16-13 (StL)
　　　Cardinals, 41-10 (P)
1967—Cardinals, 48-14 (StL)
1968—Cardinals, 45-17 (P)
1969—Eagles, 34-30 (StL)
1970—Eagles, 35-20 (P)
　　　Cardinals, 23-14 (StL)
1971—Eagles, 37-20 (StL)
　　　Eagles, 19-7 (P)
1972—Tie, 6-6 (P)
　　　Cardinals, 24-23 (StL)
1973—Cardinals, 34-23 (P)
　　　Eagles, 27-24 (StL)
1974—Cardinals, 7-3 (StL)
　　　Cardinals, 13-3 (P)
1975—Cardinals, 31-20 (StL)
　　　Cardinals, 24-23 (P)
1976—Cardinals, 33-14 (StL)
　　　Cardinals, 17-14 (P)
1977—Cardinals, 21-17 (P)
　　　Cardinals, 21-16 (StL)
1978—Cardinals, 16-10 (P)
　　　Eagles, 14-10 (StL)
1979—Eagles, 24-20 (StL)
　　　Eagles, 16-13 (P)
1980—Cardinals, 24-14 (StL)
　　　Eagles, 17-3 (P)
1981—Eagles, 52-10 (StL)
　　　Eagles, 38-0 (P)
1982—Cardinals, 23-20 (P)
1983—Cardinals, 14-11 (P)
　　　Cardinals, 31-7 (StL)
(Points—Eagles 1,567, Cardinals 1,492)
\*Franchise in Chicago prior to 1960
\*\*NFL Championship
**PHILADELPHIA vs. SAN DIEGO**
Series tied, 1-1
1974—Eagles, 13-7 (SD)
1980—Chargers, 22-21 (SD)
(Points—Eagles 34, Chargers 29)
**PHILADELPHIA vs. SAN FRANCISCO**
49ers lead series, 8-4-1
1951—Eagles, 21-14 (P)
1953—49ers, 31-21 (SF)
1956—Tie, 10-10 (P)
1958—49ers, 30-24 (P)
1959—49ers, 24-14 (SF)
1964—49ers, 28-24 (P)
1966—Eagles, 35-34 (SF)
1967—49ers, 28-27 (P)
1969—49ers, 14-13 (SF)
1971—Eagles, 31-3 (P)
1973—49ers, 38-28 (SF)
1975—Eagles, 27-17 (P)
1983—Eagles, 22-17 (SF)
(Points—49ers 316, Eagles 269)
**PHILADELPHIA vs. SEATTLE**
Eagles lead series, 2-0
1976—Eagles, 27-10 (P)
1980—Eagles, 27-20 (S)
(Points—Eagles 54, Seahawks 30)
**PHILADELPHIA vs. TAMPA BAY**
Eagles lead series, 2-1
1977—Eagles, 13-3 (P)
1979—\*Buccaneers, 24-17 (TB)
1981—Eagles, 20-10 (P)
(Points—Eagles 50, Buccaneers 37)
\*NFC Divisional Playoff
**PHILADELPHIA vs. \*WASHINGTON**
Redskins lead series, 55-37-5
1934—Redskins, 6-0 (B)
　　　Redskins, 14-7 (P)
1935—Eagles, 7-6 (B)
1936—Redskins, 26-3 (P)
　　　Redskins, 17-7 (B)
1937—Eagles, 14-0 (W)
　　　Redskins, 10-7 (P)
1938—Redskins, 26-23 (P)

Redskins, 20-14 (W)
1939—Redskins, 7-0 (P)
　　　Redskins, 7-6 (W)
1940—Redskins, 34-17 (P)
　　　Redskins, 13-6 (W)
1941—Redskins, 21-17 (P)
　　　Redskins, 20-14 (W)
1942—Redskins, 14-10 (P)
　　　Redskins, 30-27 (W)
1944—Tie, 31-31 (P)
　　　Eagles, 37-7 (W)
1945—Redskins, 24-14 (W)
　　　Eagles, 16-0 (P)
1946—Eagles, 28-24 (W)
　　　Redskins, 27-10 (P)
1947—Eagles, 45-42 (P)
　　　Eagles, 38-14 (W)
1948—Eagles, 45-0 (W)
　　　Eagles, 42-21 (P)
1949—Eagles, 49-14 (P)
　　　Eagles, 44-21 (W)
1950—Eagles, 35-3 (P)
　　　Eagles, 33-0 (W)
1951—Redskins, 27-23 (P)
　　　Eagles, 35-21 (W)
1952—Eagles, 38-20 (P)
　　　Redskins, 27-21 (W)
1953—Tie, 21-21 (P)
　　　Redskins, 10-0 (W)
1954—Eagles, 49-21 (W)
　　　Eagles, 41-33 (P)
1955—Redskins, 31-30 (P)
　　　Redskins, 34-21 (W)
1956—Eagles, 13-9 (P)
　　　Redskins, 19-17 (W)
1957—Eagles, 21-12 (P)
　　　Redskins, 42-7 (W)
1958—Redskins, 24-14 (P)
　　　Redskins, 20-0 (W)
1959—Eagles, 30-23 (P)
　　　Eagles, 34-14 (W)
1960—Eagles, 19-13 (P)
　　　Eagles, 38-28 (W)
1961—Eagles, 14-7 (P)
　　　Eagles, 27-24 (W)
1962—Redskins, 27-21 (P)
　　　Eagles, 37-14 (W)
1963—Eagles, 37-24 (W)
　　　Redskins, 13-10 (P)
1964—Redskins, 35-20 (W)
　　　Redskins, 21-10 (P)
1965—Redskins, 23-21 (W)
　　　Eagles, 21-14 (P)
1966—Redskins, 27-13 (P)
　　　Eagles, 37-28 (W)
1967—Eagles, 35-24 (P)
　　　Tie, 35-35 (W)
1968—Redskins, 17-14 (W)
　　　Redskins, 16-10 (P)
1969—Tie, 28-28 (W)
　　　Redskins, 34-29 (P)
1970—Redskins, 33-21 (P)
　　　Redskins, 24-6 (W)
1971—Tie, 7-7 (W)
　　　Redskins, 20-13 (P)
1972—Redskins, 14-0 (W)
　　　Redskins, 23-7 (P)
1973—Redskins, 28-7 (P)
　　　Redskins, 38-20 (W)
1974—Redskins, 27-20 (W)
　　　Redskins, 26-7 (P)
1975—Eagles, 26-10 (P)
　　　Eagles, 26-3 (W)
1976—Redskins, 20-17 (P) OT
　　　Redskins, 24-0 (W)
1977—Redskins, 23-17 (P)
　　　Redskins, 17-14 (W)
1978—Redskins, 35-30 (W)
　　　Eagles, 17-10 (P)
1979—Eagles, 28-17 (P)
　　　Redskins, 17-7 (W)
1980—Eagles, 24-14 (P)
　　　Eagles, 24-0 (W)
1981—Eagles, 36-13 (P)
　　　Redskins, 15-13 (W)
1982—Redskins, 37-34 (P) OT
　　　Redskins, 13-9 (W)
1983—Redskins, 23-13 (P)
　　　Redskins, 28-24 (W)
(Points—Eagles 2,004, Redskins 1,918)
\*Franchise in Boston prior to 1937

────────────

**PITTSBURGH vs. ATLANTA**
Steelers lead series, 5-1;
See Atlanta vs. Pittsburgh
**PITTSBURGH vs. BALTIMORE**
Steelers lead series, 8-3;
See Baltimore vs. Pittsburgh
**PITTSBURGH vs. BUFFALO**
Steelers lead series, 5-3;
See Buffalo vs. Pittsburgh
**PITTSBURGH vs. CHICAGO**
Bears lead series, 13-4-1;

See Chicago vs. Pittsburgh
**PITTSBURGH vs. CINCINNATI**
Steelers lead series, 16-11;
See Cincinnati vs. Pittsburgh
**PITTSBURGH vs. CLEVELAND**
Browns lead series, 39-29;
See Cleveland vs. Pittsburgh
**PITTSBURGH vs. DALLAS**
Steelers lead series, 12-10;
See Dallas vs. Pittsburgh
**PITTSBURGH vs. DENVER**
Broncos lead series, 6-4-1;
See Denver vs. Pittsburgh
**PITTSBURGH vs. DETROIT**
Lions lead series, 13-8-1;
See Detroit vs. Pittsburgh
**PITTSBURGH vs. GREEN BAY**
Packers lead series, 16-10;
See Green Bay vs. Pittsburgh
**PITTSBURGH vs. HOUSTON**
Steelers lead series, 21-8;
See Houston vs. Pittsburgh
**PITTSBURGH vs. KANSAS CITY**
Steelers lead series, 8-3;
See Kansas City vs. Pittsburgh
**PITTSBURGH vs. L.A. RAIDERS**
Raiders lead series, 9-5;
See L.A. Raiders vs. Pittsburgh
**PITTSBURGH vs. L.A. RAMS**
Rams lead series, 12-3-2;
See L.A. Rams vs. Pittsburgh
**PITTSBURGH vs. MIAMI**
Dolphins lead series, 4-3;
See Miami vs. Pittsburgh
**PITTSBURGH vs. MINNESOTA**
Vikings lead series, 5-4;
See Minnesota vs. Pittsburgh
**PITTSBURGH vs. NEW ENGLAND**
Steelers lead series, 5-2;
See New England vs. Pittsburgh
**PITTSBURGH vs. NEW ORLEANS**
Steelers lead series, 4-3;
See New Orleans vs. Pittsburgh
**PITTSBURGH vs. N.Y. GIANTS**
Giants lead series, 40-26-3;
See N.Y. Giants vs. Pittsburgh
**PITTSBURGH vs. N.Y. JETS**
Steelers lead series, 7-0;
See N.Y. Jets vs. Pittsburgh
**PITTSBURGH vs. PHILADELPHIA**
Eagles lead series, 42-25-3;
See Philadelphia vs. Pittsburgh
**\*PITTSBURGH vs. \*\*ST. LOUIS**
Steelers lead series, 28-20-3
1933—Pirates, 14-13 (C)
1935—Pirates, 17-13 (P)
1936—Cardinals, 14-6 (C)
1937—Cardinals, 13-7 (P)
1939—Cardinals, 10-0 (P)
1940—Tie, 7-7 (P)
1942—Steelers, 19-3 (P)
1945—Steelers, 23-0 (P)
1946—Steelers, 14-7 (P)
1948—Cardinals, 24-7 (P)
1950—Steelers, 28-17 (C)
　　　Steelers, 28-7 (P)
1951—Steelers, 28-14 (C)
1952—Steelers, 34-28 (C)
　　　Steelers, 17-14 (P)
1953—Steelers, 31-28 (P)
　　　Steelers, 21-17 (C)
1954—Cardinals, 17-14 (C)
　　　Steelers, 20-17 (P)
1955—Steelers, 14-7 (P)
　　　Cardinals, 27-13 (C)
1956—Steelers, 14-7 (P)
　　　Cardinals, 38-27 (C)
1957—Steelers, 29-20 (P)
　　　Steelers, 27-2 (C)
1958—Steelers, 27-20 (C)
　　　Steelers, 38-21 (P)
1959—Cardinals, 45-24 (C)
　　　Steelers, 35-20 (P)
1960—Steelers, 27-14 (P)
　　　Cardinals, 38-7 (StL)
1961—Steelers, 30-27 (P)
　　　Cardinals, 20-0 (StL)
1962—Steelers, 26-17 (StL)
　　　Steelers, 19-7 (P)
1963—Steelers, 23-10 (P)
　　　Cardinals, 24-23 (StL)
1964—Cardinals, 34-30 (StL)
　　　Cardinals, 21-20 (P)
1965—Cardinals, 20-7 (P)
　　　Cardinals, 21-17 (P)
1966—Steelers, 30-9 (P)
　　　Cardinals, 6-3 (StL)
1967—Cardinals, 28-14 (P)
　　　Tie, 14-14 (StL)
1968—Tie, 28-28 (StL)
　　　Cardinals, 20-10 (P)
1969—Cardinals, 27-14 (P)
　　　Cardinals, 47-10 (StL)

235

1972—Steelers, 25-19 (StL)
1979—Steelers, 24-21 (StL)
(Points—Steelers 984, Cardinals 942)
*Steelers known as Pirates prior to 1941
**Franchise in Chicago prior to 1960

**PITTSBURGH vs. SAN DIEGO**
Steelers lead series, 7-3
1971—Steelers, 21-17 (P)
1972—Steelers, 24-2 (SD)
1973—Steelers, 38-21 (P)
1975—Steelers, 37-0 (SD)
1976—Steelers, 23-0 (P)
1977—Steelers, 10-9 (SD)
1979—Chargers, 35-7 (SD)
1980—Chargers, 26-17 (SD)
1982—*Chargers, 31-28 (P)
1983—Steelers, 26-3 (P)
(Points—Steelers 231, Chargers 144)
*AFC First Round Playoff

**PITTSBURGH vs. SAN FRANCISCO**
49ers lead series, 6-5
1951—49ers, 28-24 (P)
1952—Steelers, 24-7 (SF)
1954—49ers, 31-3 (SF)
1958—49ers, 23-20 (SF)
1961—Steelers, 20-10 (P)
1965—49ers, 27-17 (SF)
1968—49ers, 45-28 (P)
1973—Steelers, 37-14 (SF)
1977—Steelers, 27-0 (P)
1978—Steelers, 24-7 (SF)
1981—49ers, 17-14 (P)
(Points—Steelers 238, 49ers 209)

**PITTSBURGH vs. SEATTLE**
Steelers lead series, 3-2
1977—Steelers, 30-20 (P)
1978—Steelers, 21-10 (P)
1981—Seahawks, 24-21 (S)
1982—Seahawks, 16-0 (S)
1983—Steelers, 27-21 (S)
(Points—Steelers 99, Seahawks 91)

**PITTSBURGH vs. TAMPA BAY**
Steelers lead series, 3-0
1976—Steelers, 42-0 (P)
1980—Steelers, 24-21 (TB)
1983—Steelers, 17-12 (P)
(Points—Steelers 83, Buccaneers 33)

**\*PITTSBURGH vs. \*\*WASHINGTON**
Redskins lead series, 39-27-3
1933—Redskins, 21-6 (P)
         Pirates, 16-14 (B)
1934—Redskins, 7-0 (P)
         Redskins, 39-0 (B)
1935—Pirates, 6-0 (P)
         Redskins, 13-3 (B)
1936—Pirates, 10-0 (P)
         Redskins, 30-0 (B)
1937—Redskins, 34-20 (W)
         Pirates, 21-13 (P)
1938—Redskins, 7-0 (P)
         Redskins, 15-0 (W)
1939—Redskins, 44-14 (W)
         Redskins, 21-14 (P)
1940—Redskins, 40-10 (P)
         Redskins, 37-10 (W)
1941—Redskins, 24-20 (P)
         Redskins, 23-3 (W)
1942—Redskins, 28-14 (W)
         Redskins, 14-0 (P)
1945—Redskins, 14-0 (P)
         Redskins, 24-0 (W)
1946—Tie, 14-14 (W)
         Steelers, 14-7 (P)
1947—Redskins, 27-26 (W)
         Steelers, 21-14 (P)
1948—Redskins, 17-14 (W)
         Steelers, 10-7 (P)
1949—Redskins, 27-14 (P)
         Redskins, 24-14 (W)
1950—Steelers, 26-7 (W)
         Redskins, 24-7 (P)
1951—Redskins, 22-7 (P)
         Steelers, 20-10 (W)
1952—Redskins, 28-24 (P)
         Steelers, 24-23 (W)
1953—Redskins, 17-9 (P)
         Steelers, 14-13 (W)
1954—Steelers, 37-7 (P)
         Redskins, 17-14 (W)
1955—Redskins, 23-14 (P)
         Redskins, 28-17 (W)
1956—Steelers, 30-13 (P)
         Steelers, 23-0 (W)
1957—Steelers, 28-7 (P)
         Redskins, 10-3 (W)
1958—Steelers, 24-16 (P)
         Tie, 14-14 (W)
1959—Redskins, 23-17 (P)
         Steelers, 27-6 (W)
1960—Tie, 27-27 (W)
         Steelers, 22-10 (P)
1961—Steelers, 20-0 (P)
         Steelers, 30-14 (P)

---

1962—Steelers, 23-21 (P)
         Steelers, 27-24 (W)
1963—Steelers, 38-27 (P)
         Steelers, 34-28 (W)
1964—Redskins, 30-0 (P)
         Steelers, 14-7 (W)
1965—Redskins, 31-3 (P)
         Redskins, 35-14 (W)
1966—Redskins, 33-27 (P)
         Redskins, 24-10 (W)
1967—Redskins, 15-10 (P)
1968—Redskins, 16-13 (W)
1969—Redskins, 14-7 (P)
1973—Steelers, 21-16 (P)
1979—Redskins, 38-7 (P)
(Points—Redskins 1,289, Steelers 1,051)
*Steelers known as Pirates prior to 1941
**Franchise in Boston prior to 1937

---

**ST. LOUIS vs. ATLANTA**
Cardinals lead series, 6-3
See Atlanta vs. St. Louis
**ST. LOUIS vs. BALTIMORE**
Series tied, 4-4;
See Baltimore vs. St. Louis
**ST. LOUIS vs. BUFFALO**
Cardinals lead series, 2-1;
See Buffalo vs. St. Louis
**ST. LOUIS vs. CHICAGO**
Bears lead series, 50-24-6;
See Chicago vs. St. Louis
**ST. LOUIS vs. CINCINNATI**
Bengals lead series, 2-0;
See Cincinnati vs. St. Louis
**ST. LOUIS vs. CLEVELAND**
Browns lead series, 30-9-3;
See Cleveland vs. St. Louis
**ST. LOUIS vs. DALLAS**
Cowboys lead series, 27-15-1;
See Dallas vs. St. Louis
**ST. LOUIS vs. DENVER**
Broncos lead series, 1-0-1;
See Denver vs. St. Louis
**ST. LOUIS vs. DETROIT**
Lions lead series, 25-15-5;
See Detroit vs. St. Louis
**ST. LOUIS vs. GREEN BAY**
Packers lead series, 37-20-4;
See Green Bay vs. St. Louis
**ST. LOUIS vs. HOUSTON**
Cardinals lead series, 3-0;
See Houston vs. St. Louis
**ST. LOUIS vs. KANSAS CITY**
Chiefs lead series, 3-0-1;
See Kansas City vs. St. Louis
**ST. LOUIS vs. L.A. RAIDERS**
Series tied, 1-1;
See L.A. Raiders vs. St. Louis
**ST. LOUIS vs. L.A. RAMS**
Rams lead series, 18-15-2;
See L.A. Rams vs. St. Louis
**ST. LOUIS vs. MIAMI**
Dolphins lead series, 4-0;
See Miami vs. St. Louis
**ST. LOUIS vs. MINNESOTA**
Cardinals lead series, 7-3;
See Minnesota vs. St. Louis
**ST. LOUIS vs. NEW ENGLAND**
Cardinals lead series, 3-1;
See New England vs. St. Louis
**ST. LOUIS vs. NEW ORLEANS**
Cardinals lead series, 8-3;
See New Orleans vs. St. Louis
**ST. LOUIS vs. N.Y. GIANTS**
Giants lead series, 50-30-2;
See N.Y. Giants vs. St. Louis
**ST. LOUIS vs. N.Y. JETS**
Cardinals lead series, 2-1;
See N.Y. Jets vs. St. Louis
**ST. LOUIS vs. PHILADELPHIA**
Cardinals lead series, 38-32-4;
See Philadelphia vs. St. Louis
**ST. LOUIS vs. PITTSBURGH**
Steelers lead series, 28-20-3;
See Pittsburgh vs. St. Louis
**ST. LOUIS vs. SAN DIEGO**
Chargers lead series, 2-1;
1971—Chargers, 20-17 (SD)
1976—Chargers, 43-24 (SD)
1983—Cardinals, 44-14 (StL)
(Points—Cardinals 85, Chargers 77)
**\*ST. LOUIS vs. SAN FRANCISCO**
Cardinals lead series, 7-6
1951—Cardinals, 27-21 (SF)
1957—Cardinals, 20-10 (SF)
1962—49ers, 24-17 (StL)
1964—Cardinals, 23-13 (SF)
1968—49ers, 35-17 (SF)
1971—49ers, 26-14 (StL)
1974—Cardinals, 34-9 (SF)
1976—Cardinals, 23-20 (StL) OT
1978—Cardinals, 16-10 (SF)
1979—Cardinals, 13-10 (StL)

---

1980—49ers, 24-21 (SF) OT
1982—49ers, 31-20 (StL)
1983—49ers, 42-27 (StL)
(Points—49ers 275, Cardinals 272)
*Team in Chicago prior to 1960
**ST. LOUIS vs. SEATTLE**
Cardinals lead series, 2-0
1976—Cardinals, 30-24 (S)
1983—Cardinals, 33-28 (StL)
(Points—Cardinals 63, Seahawks 52)
**ST. LOUIS vs. TAMPA BAY**
Buccaneers lead series, 2-1
1977—Buccaneers, 17-7 (TB)
1981—Buccaneers, 20-10 (TB)
1983—Cardinals, 34-27 (StL)
(Points—Buccaneers 64, Cardinals 51)
**\*ST. LOUIS vs. \*\*WASHINGTON**
Redskins lead series, 46-31-2
1932—Cardinals, 9-0 (C)
         Braves, 8-6 (C)
1933—Redskins, 10-0 (C)
         Tie, 0-0 (B)
1934—Redskins, 9-0 (B)
1935—Cardinals, 6-0 (B)
1936—Redskins, 13-10 (B)
1937—Cardinals, 21-14 (W)
1939—Redskins, 28-7 (W)
1940—Redskins, 28-21 (W)
1942—Redskins, 28-0 (W)
1943—Redskins, 13-7 (W)
1945—Redskins, 24-21 (W)
1947—Redskins, 45-21 (W)
1949—Cardinals, 38-7 (C)
1950—Cardinals, 38-28 (W)
1951—Cardinals, 7-3 (C)
         Redskins, 20-17 (W)
1952—Cardinals, 23-7 (C)
         Cardinals, 17-6 (W)
1953—Redskins, 24-13 (C)
         Redskins, 28-17 (W)
1954—Cardinals, 38-16 (C)
         Redskins, 37-20 (W)
1955—Cardinals, 24-10 (W)
         Redskins, 31-0 (C)
1956—Cardinals, 31-3 (W)
         Redskins, 17-14 (C)
1957—Redskins, 37-14 (C)
         Cardinals, 44-14 (W)
1958—Cardinals, 37-10 (C)
         Redskins, 45-31 (W)
1959—Cardinals, 49-21 (C)
         Redskins, 23-14 (W)
1960—Cardinals, 44-7 (StL)
         Cardinals, 26-14 (W)
1961—Cardinals, 24-0 (W)
         Cardinals, 38-24 (StL)
1962—Cardinals, 24-14 (W)
         Tie, 17-17 (StL)
1963—Cardinals, 21-7 (W)
         Cardinals, 24-20 (StL)
1964—Cardinals, 23-17 (W)
         Cardinals, 38-24 (StL)
1965—Cardinals, 37-16 (W)
         Redskins, 24-20 (StL)
1966—Cardinals, 23-7 (W)
         Redskins, 26-20 (StL)
1967—Cardinals, 27-21 (W)
1968—Cardinals, 41-14 (W)
1969—Redskins, 33-17 (W)
1970—Cardinals, 27-17 (StL)
         Redskins, 28-27 (W)
1971—Redskins, 24-17 (StL)
         Redskins, 20-0 (W)
1972—Cardinals, 24-10 (W)
         Redskins, 33-3 (StL)
1973—Cardinals, 34-27 (StL)
         Redskins, 31-13 (W)
1974—Cardinals, 17-10 (W)
         Cardinals, 23-20 (StL)
1975—Cardinals, 27-17 (W)
         Cardinals, 20-17 (StL) OT
1976—Redskins, 20-10 (W)
         Redskins, 16-10 (StL)
1977—Redskins, 24-14 (W)
         Redskins, 26-20 (StL)
1978—Redskins, 28-10 (StL)
         Cardinals, 27-17 (W)
1979—Redskins, 17-7 (StL)
         Redskins, 30-28 (W)
1980—Redskins, 23-0 (W)
         Redskins, 31-7 (StL)
1981—Cardinals, 40-30 (StL)
         Redskins, 42-21 (W)
1982—Cardinals, 12-7 (StL)
         Redskins, 28-0 (W)
1983—Redskins, 38-14 (StL)
         Redskins, 45-7 (W)
(Points—Redskins 1,627, Cardinals 1,479)
*Team in Chicago prior to 1960
**Team in Boston prior to 1937 and known
as Braves prior to 1933

---

**SAN DIEGO vs. ATLANTA**
Falcons lead series, 2-0;
See Atlanta vs. San Diego
**SAN DIEGO vs. BALTIMORE**
Chargers lead series, 3-2;
See Baltimore vs. San Diego
**SAN DIEGO vs. BUFFALO**
Chargers lead series, 15-9-2;
See Buffalo vs. San Diego
**SAN DIEGO vs. CHICAGO**
Chargers lead series, 3-1;
See Chicago vs. San Diego
**SAN DIEGO vs. CINCINNATI**
Chargers lead series, 9-7;
See Cincinnati vs. San Diego
**SAN DIEGO vs. CLEVELAND**
Chargers lead series, 5-3-1;
See Cleveland vs. San Diego
**SAN DIEGO vs. DALLAS**
Cowboys lead series, 2-1;
See Dallas vs. San Diego
**SAN DIEGO vs. DENVER**
Chargers lead series, 26-21-1;
See Denver vs. San Diego
**SAN DIEGO vs. DETROIT**
Lions lead series, 3-1;
See Detroit vs. San Diego
**SAN DIEGO vs. GREEN BAY**
Packers lead series, 3-0;
See Green Bay vs. San Diego
**SAN DIEGO vs. HOUSTON**
Chargers lead series, 15-11-1;
See Houston vs. San Diego
**SAN DIEGO vs. KANSAS CITY**
Chargers lead series, 25-21-1;
See Kansas City vs. San Diego
**SAN DIEGO vs. L.A. RAIDERS**
Raiders lead series, 30-17-2;
See L.A. Raiders vs. San Diego
**SAN DIEGO vs. L.A. RAMS**
Rams lead series, 2-1;
See L.A. Rams vs. San Diego
**SAN DIEGO vs. MIAMI**
Chargers lead series, 7-5;
See Miami vs. San Diego
**SAN DIEGO vs. MINNESOTA**
Series tied, 2-2;
See Minnesota vs. San Diego
**SAN DIEGO vs. NEW ENGLAND**
Patriots lead series, 13-12-2;
See New England vs. San Diego
**SAN DIEGO vs. NEW ORLEANS**
Chargers lead series, 3-0;
See New Orleans vs. San Diego
**SAN DIEGO vs. N.Y. GIANTS**
Series tied, 2-2;
See N.Y. Giants vs. San Diego
**SAN DIEGO vs. N.Y. JETS**
Chargers lead series, 14-7-1;
See N.Y. Jets vs. San Diego
**SAN DIEGO vs. PHILADELPHIA**
Series tied, 1-1;
See Philadelphia vs. San Diego
**SAN DIEGO vs. PITTSBURGH**
Steelers lead series, 7-3;
See Pittsburgh vs. San Diego
**SAN DIEGO vs. ST. LOUIS**
Chargers lead series, 2-1;
See St. Louis vs. San Diego
**SAN DIEGO vs. SAN FRANCISCO**
Chargers lead series, 3-1
1972—49ers, 34-3 (SF)
1976—Chargers, 13-7 (SD) OT
1979—Chargers, 31-9 (SD)
1982—Chargers, 41-37 (SF)
(Points—Chargers, 88, 49ers 87)
**SAN DIEGO vs. SEATTLE**
Chargers lead series, 9-2
1977—Chargers, 30-28 (S)
1978—Chargers, 24-20 (S)
         Chargers, 37-10 (SD)
1979—Chargers, 33-16 (S)
         Chargers, 20-10 (SD)
1980—Chargers, 34-13 (S)
         Chargers, 21-14 (SD)
1981—Chargers, 24-10 (SD)
         Seahawks, 44-23 (S)
1983—Seahawks, 34-31 (SD)
         Chargers, 28-21 (SD)
(Points—Chargers 305, Seahawks 220)
**SAN DIEGO vs. TAMPA BAY**
Chargers lead series, 2-0
1976—Chargers, 23-0 (TB)
1981—Chargers, 24-23 (TB)
(Points—Chargers 47, Buccaneers 23)
**SAN DIEGO vs. WASHINGTON**
Redskins lead series, 3-0
1973—Redskins, 38-0 (W)
1980—Redskins, 40-17 (W)
1983—Redskins, 27-24 (D)
(Points—Redskins 105, Chargers 41)

236

**SAN FRANCISCO vs. ATLANTA**
Series tied, 17-17;
See Atlanta vs. San Francisco
**SAN FRANCISCO vs. BALTIMORE**
Colts lead series, 21-14;
See Baltimore vs. San Francisco
**SAN FRANCISCO vs. BUFFALO**
Bills lead series, 2-1;
See Buffalo vs. San Francisco
**SAN FRANCISCO vs. CHICAGO**
Bears lead series, 23-22-1;
See Chicago vs. San Francisco
**SAN FRANCISCO vs. CINCINNATI**
49ers lead series, 3-1;
See Cincinnati vs. San Francisco
**SAN FRANCISCO vs. CLEVELAND**
Browns lead series, 8-3;
See Cleveland vs. San Francisco
**SAN FRANCISCO vs. DALLAS**
Cowboys lead series, 8-7-1;
See Dallas vs. San Francisco
**SAN FRANCISCO vs. DENVER**
Series tied, 2-2;
See Denver vs. San Francisco
**SAN FRANCISCO vs. DETROIT**
Lions lead series, 25-22-1;
See Detroit vs. San Francisco
**SAN FRANCISCO vs. GREEN BAY**
49ers lead series, 22-20-1;
See Green Bay vs. San Francisco
**SAN FRANCISCO vs. HOUSTON**
Series tied, 2-2;
See Houston vs. San Francisco
**SAN FRANCISCO vs. KANSAS CITY**
49ers lead series, 2-1;
See Kansas City vs. San Francisco
**SAN FRANCISCO vs. L.A. RAIDERS**
Raiders lead series, 3-1;
See L.A. Raiders vs. San Francisco
**SAN FRANCISCO vs. L.A. RAMS**
Rams lead series, 43-23-2;
See L.A. Rams vs. San Francisco
**SAN FRANCISCO vs. MIAMI**
Dolphins lead series, 4-0;
See Miami vs. San Francisco
**SAN FRANCISCO vs. MINNESOTA**
Vikings lead series, 12-11-1;
See Minnesota vs. San Francisco
**SAN FRANCISCO vs. NEW ENGLAND**
49ers lead series, 3-1;
See New England vs. San Francisco
**SAN FRANCISCO vs. NEW ORLEANS**
49ers lead series, 19-8-2;
See New Orleans vs. San Francisco
**SAN FRANCISCO vs. N.Y. GIANTS**
Giants lead series, 9-5;
See N.Y. Giants vs. San Francisco
**SAN FRANCISCO vs. N.Y. JETS**
49ers lead series, 3-1;
See N.Y. Jets vs. San Francisco
**SAN FRANCISCO vs. PHILADELPHIA**
49ers lead series, 8-4-1;
See Philadelphia vs. San Francisco
**SAN FRANCISCO vs. PITTSBURGH**
49ers lead series, 6-5;
See Pittsburgh vs. San Francisco
**SAN FRANCISCO vs. ST. LOUIS**
Cardinals lead series, 7-6;
See St. Louis vs. San Francisco
**SAN FRANCISCO vs. SAN DIEGO**
Chargers lead series, 3-1;
See San Diego vs. San Francisco
**SAN FRANCISCO vs. SEATTLE**
Series tied, 1-1
1976—49ers, 37-21 (S)
1979—Seahawks, 35-24 (SF)
(Points—49ers 61, Seahawks 56)
**SAN FRANCISCO vs. TAMPA BAY**
49ers lead series, 4-1
1977—49ers, 20-10 (SF)
1978—49ers, 6-3 (SF)
1979—49ers, 23-7 (SF)
1980—Buccaneers, 24-23 (SF)
1983—49ers, 35-21 (SF)
(Points—49ers 107, Buccaneers 65)
**SAN FRANCISCO vs. WASHINGTON**
Series tied, 6-6-1
1952—49ers, 23-17 (W)
1954—49ers, 41-7 (SF)
1955—Redskins, 7-0 (W)
1961—49ers, 35-3 (SF)
1967—Redskins, 31-28 (W)
1969—Tie, 17-17 (SF)
1970—49ers, 26-17 (SF)
1971—*49ers, 24-20 (SF)
1973—Redskins, 33-9 (W)
1976—Redskins, 24-21 (SF)
1978—Redskins, 38-20 (W)
1981—49ers, 30-17 (W)
1983—**Redskins, 24-21 (W)
(Points—49ers 295, Redskins 255)
*NFC Divisional Playoff
**NFC Championship

**SEATTLE vs. ATLANTA**
Seahawks lead series, 2-0;
See Atlanta vs. Seattle
**SEATTLE vs. BALTIMORE**
Colts lead series, 2-0;
See Baltimore vs. Seattle
**SEATTLE vs. BUFFALO**
Seahawks lead series, 1-0;
See Buffalo vs. Seattle
**SEATTLE vs. CHICAGO**
Seahawks lead series, 2-1;
See Chicago vs. Seattle
**SEATTLE vs. CINCINNATI**
Bengals lead series, 3-0;
See Cincinnati vs. Seattle
**SEATTLE vs. CLEVELAND**
Seahawks lead series, 5-2;
See Cleveland vs. Seattle
**SEATTLE vs. DALLAS**
Cowboys lead series, 3-0;
See Dallas vs. Seattle
**SEATTLE vs. DENVER**
Broncos lead series, 8-6;
See Denver vs. Seattle
**SEATTLE vs. DETROIT**
Series tied, 1-1;
See Detroit vs. Seattle
**SEATTLE vs. GREEN BAY**
Packers lead series, 3-0;
See Green Bay vs. Seattle
**SEATTLE vs. HOUSTON**
Oilers lead series, 3-2;
See Houston vs. Seattle
**SEATTLE vs. KANSAS CITY**
Chiefs lead series, 6-5;
See Kansas City vs. Seattle
**SEATTLE vs. L.A. RAIDERS**
Raiders lead series, 7-6;
See L.A. Raiders vs. Seattle
**SEATTLE vs. L.A. RAMS**
Rams lead series, 2-0;
See L.A. Rams vs. Seattle
**SEATTLE vs. MIAMI**
Dolphins lead series, 2-1;
See Miami vs. Seattle
**SEATTLE vs. MINNESOTA**
Series tied, 1-1;
See Minnesota vs. Seattle
**SEATTLE vs. NEW ENGLAND**
Patriots lead series, 3-1;
See New England vs. Seattle
**SEATTLE vs. NEW ORLEANS**
Series tied, 1-1;
See New Orleans vs. Seattle
**SEATTLE vs. N.Y. GIANTS**
Giants lead series, 3-1;
See N.Y. Giants vs. Seattle
**SEATTLE vs. N.Y. JETS**
Seahawks lead series, 7-0;
See N.Y. Jets vs. Seattle
**SEATTLE vs. PHILADELPHIA**
Eagles lead series, 2-0;
See Philadelphia vs. Seattle
**SEATTLE vs. PITTSBURGH**
Steelers lead series, 3-2;
See Pittsburgh vs. Seattle
**SEATTLE vs. ST. LOUIS**
Cardinals lead series, 2-0;
See St. Louis vs. Seattle
**SEATTLE vs. SAN DIEGO**
Chargers lead series, 9-2;
See San Diego vs. Seattle
**SEATTLE vs. SAN FRANCISCO**
Series tied, 1-1;
See San Francisco vs. Seattle
**SEATTLE vs. TAMPA BAY**
Seahawks lead series, 2-0
1976—Seahawks, 13-10 (TB)
1977—Seahawks, 30-23 (S)
(Points—Seahawks 43, Buccaneers 33)
**SEATTLE vs. WASHINGTON**
Redskins lead series, 2-1
1976—Redskins, 31-7 (W)
1980—Seahawks, 14-0 (W)
1983—Redskins, 27-17 (S)
(Points—Redskins 58, Seahawks 38)

**TAMPA BAY vs. ATLANTA**
Series tied, 2-2;
See Atlanta vs. Tampa Bay
**TAMPA BAY vs. BALTIMORE**
Series tied, 1-1;
See Baltimore vs. Tampa Bay
**TAMPA BAY vs. BUFFALO**
Buccaneers lead series, 2-1;
See Buffalo vs. Tampa Bay
**TAMPA BAY vs. CHICAGO**
Bears lead series, 8-4;
See Chicago vs. Tampa Bay
**TAMPA BAY vs. CINCINNATI**
Bengals lead series, 2-1;
See Cincinnati vs. Tampa Bay
**TAMPA BAY vs. CLEVELAND**

Browns lead series, 3-0;
See Cleveland vs. Tampa Bay
**TAMPA BAY vs. DALLAS**
Cowboys lead series, 6-0;
See Dallas vs. Tampa Bay
**TAMPA BAY vs. DENVER**
Broncos lead series, 2-0;
See Denver vs. Tampa Bay
**TAMPA BAY vs. DETROIT**
Lions lead series, 7-5;
See Detroit vs. Tampa Bay
**TAMPA BAY vs. GREEN BAY**
Series tied, 5-5-1;
See Green Bay vs. Tampa Bay
**TAMPA BAY vs. HOUSTON**
Oilers lead series, 2-1;
See Houston vs. Tampa Bay
**TAMPA BAY vs. KANSAS CITY**
Series tied, 2-2;
See Kansas City vs. Tampa Bay
**TAMPA BAY vs. L.A. RAIDERS**
Raiders lead series, 2-0;
See L.A. Raiders vs. Tampa Bay
**TAMPA BAY vs. L.A. RAMS**
Rams lead series, 3-2;
See L.A. Rams vs. Tampa Bay
**TAMPA BAY vs. MIAMI**
Series tied, 1-1;
See Miami vs. Tampa Bay
**TAMPA BAY vs. MINNESOTA**
Vikings lead series, 8-4;
See Minnesota vs. Tampa Bay
**TAMPA BAY vs. NEW ENGLAND**
Patriots lead series, 1-0;
See New England vs. Tampa Bay
**TAMPA BAY vs. NEW ORLEANS**
Series tied, 3-3;
See New Orleans vs. Tampa Bay
**TAMPA BAY vs. N.Y. GIANTS**
Giants lead series, 4-2;
See N.Y. Giants vs. Tampa Bay
**TAMPA BAY vs. N.Y. JETS**
Jets lead series, 2-0;
See N.Y. Jets vs. Tampa Bay
**TAMPA BAY vs. PHILADELPHIA**
Eagles lead series, 2-1;
See Philadelphia vs. Tampa Bay
**TAMPA BAY vs. PITTSBURGH**
Steelers lead series, 3-0;
See Pittsburgh vs. Tampa Bay
**TAMPA BAY vs. ST. LOUIS**
Buccaneers lead series, 2-1;
See St. Louis vs. Tampa Bay
**TAMPA BAY vs. SAN DIEGO**
Chargers lead series, 2-0;
See San Diego vs. Tampa Bay
**TAMPA BAY vs. SAN FRANCISCO**
49ers lead series, 4-1;
See San Francisco vs. Tampa Bay
**TAMPA BAY vs. SEATTLE**
Seahawks lead series, 2-0;
See Seattle vs. Tampa Bay
**TAMPA BAY vs. WASHINGTON**
Redskins lead series, 2-0
1977—Redskins, 10-0 (TB)
1982—Redskins, 21-13 (TB)
(Points—Redskins 31, Buccaneers 13)

**WASHINGTON vs. ATLANTA**
Redskins lead series, 7-2-1;
See Atlanta vs. Washington
**WASHINGTON vs. BALTIMORE**
Colts lead series, 15-5;
See Baltimore vs. Washington
**WASHINGTON vs. BUFFALO**
Bills lead series, 2-1;
See Buffalo vs. Washington
**WASHINGTON vs. CHICAGO**
Bears lead series, 18-11-1;
See Chicago vs. Washington
**WASHINGTON vs. CINCINNATI**
Redskins lead series, 2-1;
See Cincinnati vs. Washington
**WASHINGTON vs. CLEVELAND**
Browns lead series, 31-7-1;
See Cleveland vs. Washington
**WASHINGTON vs. DALLAS**
Cowboys lead series, 28-18-2;
See Dallas vs. Washington
**WASHINGTON vs. DENVER**
Redskins lead series, 2-1;
See Denver vs. Washington
**WASHINGTON vs. DETROIT**
Redskins lead series, 17-8;
See Detroit vs. Washington
**WASHINGTON vs. GREEN BAY**
Packers lead series, 14-11-1;
See Green Bay vs. Washington
**WASHINGTON vs. HOUSTON**
Oilers lead series, 2-1;
See Houston vs. Washington
**WASHINGTON vs. KANSAS CITY**
Chiefs lead series, 2-1;

See Kansas City vs. Washington
**WASHINGTON vs. L.A. RAIDERS**
Raiders lead series, 4-1;
See L.A. Raiders vs. Washington
**WASHINGTON vs. L.A. RAMS**
Redskins lead series, 14-5-1;
See L.A. Rams vs. Washington
**WASHINGTON vs. MIAMI**
Dolphins lead series, 3-2;
See Miami vs. Washington
**WASHINGTON vs. MINNESOTA**
Vikings lead series, 5-3;
See Minnesota vs. Washington
**WASHINGTON vs. NEW ENGLAND**
Redskins lead series, 2-1;
See New England vs. Washington
**WASHINGTON vs. NEW ORLEANS**
Redskins lead series, 7-4;
See New Orleans vs. Washington
**WASHINGTON vs. N.Y. GIANTS**
Giants lead series, 56-44-3;
See N.Y. Giants vs. Washington
**WASHINGTON vs. N.Y. JETS**
Redskins lead series, 3-0;
See N.Y. Jets vs. Washington
**WASHINGTON vs. PHILADELPHIA**
Redskins lead series, 55-37-5;
See Philadelphia vs. Washington
**WASHINGTON vs. PITTSBURGH**
Redskins lead series, 39-27-3;
See Pittsburgh vs. Washington
**WASHINGTON vs. ST. LOUIS**
Redskins lead series, 46-31-2;
See St. Louis vs. Washington
**WASHINGTON vs. SAN DIEGO**
Redskins lead series, 3-0;
See San Diego vs. Washington
**WASHINGTON vs. SAN FRANCISCO**
Series tied, 6-6-1;
See San Francisco vs. Washington
**WASHINGTON vs. SEATTLE**
Redskins lead series, 2-1;
See Seattle vs. Washington
**WASHINGTON vs. TAMPA BAY**
Redskins lead series, 2-0;
See Tampa Bay vs. Washington

## RESULTS

| Game | Date | Winner | Loser | Site | Attendance |
|------|------|--------|-------|------|-----------|
| XVIII | 1-22-84 | L.A. Raiders (AFC) 38 | Washington (NFC) 9 | Tampa | 72,920 |
| XVII | 1-30-83 | Washington (NFC) 27 | Miami (AFC) 17 | Pasadena | 103,667 |
| XVI | 1-24-82 | San Francisco (NFC) 26 | Cincinnati (AFC) 21 | Pontiac | 81,270 |
| XV | 1-25-81 | Oakland (AFC) 27 | Philadelphia (NFC) 10 | New Orleans | 76,135 |
| XIV | 1-20-80 | Pittsburgh (AFC) 31 | Los Angeles (NFC) 19 | Pasadena | 103,985 |
| XIII | 1-21-79 | Pittsburgh (AFC) 35 | Dallas (NFC) 31 | Miami | 79,484 |
| XII | 1-15-78 | Dallas (NFC) 27 | Denver (AFC) 10 | New Orleans | 75,583 |
| XI | 1- 9-77 | Oakland (AFC) 32 | Minnesota (NFC) 14 | Pasadena | 103,438 |
| X | 1-18-76 | Pittsburgh (AFC) 21 | Dallas (NFC) 17 | Miami | 80,187 |
| IX | 1-12-75 | Pittsburgh (AFC) 16 | Minnesota (NFC) 6 | New Orleans | 80,997 |
| VIII | 1-13-74 | Miami (AFC) 24 | Minnesota (NFC) 7 | Houston | 71,882 |
| VII | 1-14-73 | Miami (AFC) 14 | Washington (NFC) 7 | Los Angeles | 90,182 |
| VI | 1-16-72 | Dallas (NFC) 24 | Miami (AFC) 3 | New Orleans | 81,023 |
| V | 1-17-71 | Baltimore (AFC) 16 | Dallas (NFC) 13 | Miami | 79,204 |
| IV | 1-11-70 | Kansas City (AFL) 23 | Minnesota (NFL) 7 | New Orleans | 80,562 |
| III | 1-12-69 | N.Y. Jets (AFL) 16 | Baltimore (NFL) 7 | Miami | 75,389 |
| II | 1-14-68 | Green Bay (NFL) 33 | Oakland (AFL) 14 | Miami | 75,546 |
| I | 1-15-67 | Green Bay (NFL) 35 | Kansas City (AFL) 10 | Los Angeles | 61,946 |

## SUPER BOWL COMPOSITE STANDINGS

| | W | L | Pct | Pts. | OP |
|---|---|---|-----|------|-----|
| Pittsburgh Steelers | 4 | 0 | 1.000 | 103 | 73 |
| Green Bay Packers | 2 | 0 | 1.000 | 68 | 24 |
| New York Jets | 1 | 0 | 1.000 | 16 | 7 |
| San Francisco 49ers | 1 | 0 | 1.000 | 26 | 21 |
| Oakland/L.A. Raiders | 3 | 1 | .750 | 111 | 66 |
| Baltimore Colts | 1 | 1 | .500 | 23 | 29 |
| Kansas City Chiefs | 1 | 1 | .500 | 33 | 42 |
| Miami Dolphins | 2 | 2 | .500 | 58 | 65 |
| Dallas Cowboys | 2 | 3 | .400 | 112 | 85 |
| Washington Redskins | 1 | 2 | .333 | 43 | 69 |
| Cincinnati Bengals | 0 | 1 | .000 | 21 | 26 |
| Denver Broncos | 0 | 1 | .000 | 10 | 27 |
| Los Angeles Rams | 0 | 1 | .000 | 19 | 31 |
| Philadelphia Eagles | 0 | 1 | .000 | 10 | 27 |
| Minnesota Vikings | 0 | 4 | .000 | 34 | 95 |

## SUPER BOWL XVIII

Tampa Stadium, Tampa, Florida — January 22, 1984
Attendance: 72,920

**LOS ANGELES RAIDERS 38, WASHINGTON 9**—The Los Angeles Raiders dominated the Washington Redskins from the beginning in Super Bowl XVIII and achieved the most lopsided victory in Super Bowl history, surpassing Green Bay's 35-10 win over Kansas City in Super Bowl I. The Raiders took a 7-0 lead 4:52 into the game when Derrick Jensen blocked a Jeff Hayes punt and recovered it in the end zone for a touchdown. With 9:14 remaining in the first half, Raiders quarterback Jim Plunkett threw a 12-yard touchdown pass to wide receiver Cliff Branch to complete a three-play, 65-yard drive. Washington cut the Raiders' lead to 14-3 on a 24-yard field goal by Mark Moseley. With seven seconds left in the first half, Raiders linebacker Jack Squirek intercepted a Joe Theismann pass at the Redskins' 5-yard line and ran it in for a touchdown to give Los Angeles a 21-3 halftime lead. In the third period, running back Marcus Allen, who rushed for a Super Bowl record 191 yards on 20 carries, increased the Raiders' lead to 35-3 on touchdown runs of 5 and 74 yards, the latter erasing the previous Super Bowl record of 58 yards set by Baltimore's Tom Matte in Super Bowl III. Allen was named the game's most valuable player. The victory over Washington raised Raiders coach Tom Flores' playoff record to 8-1, including a 27-10 win against Philadelphia in Super Bowl XV. The 38 points scored by the Raiders was the highest point total by a Super Bowl team. The previous high was 35 points by Green Bay in Game I.

| Washington (9) | Offense | Los Angeles Raiders (38) |
|---|---|---|
| Charlie Brown | WR | Cliff Branch |
| Joe Jacoby | LT | Bruce Davis |
| Russ Grimm | LG | Charley Hannah |
| Jeff Bostic | C | Dave Dalby |
| Mark May | RG | Mickey Marvin |
| George Starke | RT | Henry Lawrence |
| Don Warren | TE | Todd Christensen |
| Art Monk | WR | Malcolm Barnwell |
| Joe Theismann | QB | Jim Plunkett |
| John Riggins | RB | Marcus Allen |
| Rick Walker | TE-RB | Kenny King |
| | **Defense** | |
| Todd Liebenstein | LE | Howie Long |
| Dave Butz | LT-NT | Reggie Kinlaw |
| Darryl Grant | RT-RE | Lyle Alzado |
| Dexter Manley | RE-LOLB | Ted Hendricks |
| Mel Kaufman | LLB-LILB | Matt Millen |
| Neal Olkewicz | MLB-LILB | Bob Nelson |
| Rich Milot | RLB-ROLB | Rod Martin |
| Darrell Green | LCB | Lester Hayes |
| Anthony Washington | RCB | Mike Haynes |
| Ken Coffey | SS | Mike Davis |
| Mark Murphy | FS | Vann McElroy |

## SUBSTITUTIONS

**Washington**—Offense: K—Mark Moseley. P—Jeff Hayes. RB—Reggie Evans, Nick Giaquinto, Joe Washington, Otis Wonsley. TE—Clint Didier, Mike Williams. WR—Alvin Garrett. T/G—Roy Simmons. G—Ken Huff, Bruce Kimball. Defense: E—Charles Mann, Tony McGee. T—Perry Brooks. LB—Stuart Anderson, Monte Coleman, Peter Cronan, Larry Kubin. CB—Brian Carpenter, Vernon Dean. S—Curtis Jordan, Greg Williams. DNP—Bob Holly (QB), Babe Laufenberg (QB), Mark McGrath (WR), Virgil Seay (WR).
**L.A. Raiders**—Offense: K—Chris Bahr. P—Ray Guy. QB—David Humm, Marc Wilson. RB—Frank Hawkins, Greg Pruitt, Chester Willis. TE—Don Hasselbeck, Derrick Jensen. WR—Cle Montgomery, Calvin Muhammad, Dokie Williams. T—Shelby Jordan, Don Mosebar. G—Steve Sylvester. Defense: E—Johnny Robinson, Greg Townsend. T—Bill Pickel, Dave Stalls. LB—Jeff Barnes, Darryl Byrd, Tony Caldwell, Jack Squirek. CB—James Davis, Ted Watts. S—Kenny Hill, Odis McKinney. DNP—None.

## OFFICIALS

Referee—Gene Barth. Umpire—Gordon Wells. Head Linesman—Jerry Bergman. Line Judge—Bob Beeks. Back Judge—Ben Tompkins. Side Judge—Gil Mace. Field Judge—Fritz Graf.

## SCORING

| | | | | | |
|---|---|---|---|---|---|
| **Washington (NFC)** | 0 | 3 | 6 | 0 | — 9 |
| **L.A. Raiders (AFC)** | 7 | 14 | 14 | 3 | — 38 |

Raiders —Jensen recovered blocked punt in end zone (Bahr kick)
Raiders —Branch 12 pass from Plunkett (Bahr kick)
Wash —FG Moseley 24
Raiders —Squirek 5 interception return (Bahr kick)
Wash —Riggins 1 run (kick blocked)
Raiders —Allen 5 run (Bahr kick)
Raiders —Allen 74 run (Bahr kick)
Raiders —FG Bahr 21

## TEAM STATISTICS

| | Washington | Raiders |
|---|---|---|
| Total First Downs | 19 | 18 |
| First Downs Rushing | 7 | 8 |
| First Downs Passing | 10 | 9 |
| First Downs Penalty | 2 | 1 |
| Total Net Yardage | 283 | 385 |
| Total Offensive Plays | 73 | 60 |
| Average Gain per Offensive Play | 3.9 | 6.4 |
| Rushes | 32 | 33 |
| Yards Gained Rushing (net) | 90 | 231 |
| Average Yards per Rush | 2.8 | 7.0 |
| Passes Attempted | 35 | 25 |
| Passes Completed | 16 | 16 |
| Had Intercepted | 2 | 0 |
| Times Tackled Attempting to Pass | 6 | 2 |
| Yards Lost Attempting to Pass | 50 | 18 |
| Yards Gained Passing (net) | 193 | 154 |
| Punts | 8 | 7 |
| Average Distance | 32.4 | 42.7 |
| Punt Returns | 2 | 2 |
| Punt Return Yardage | 35 | 8 |
| Kickoff Returns | 7 | 1 |
| Kickoff Return Yardage | 132 | 17 |
| Interception Return Yardage | 0 | 5 |
| Total Return Yardage | 167 | 30 |
| Fumbles | 1 | 3 |
| Own Fumbles Recovered | 0 | 1 |
| Opponent Fumbles Recovered | 2 | 1 |
| Penalties | 4 | 7 |
| Yards Penalized | 62 | 56 |
| Total Points Scored | 9 | 38 |
| Touchdowns | 1 | 5 |
| Touchdowns Rushing | 1 | 2 |
| Touchdowns Passing | 0 | 1 |
| Touchdown Returns | 0 | 2 |
| Extra Points | 0 | 5 |
| Field Goals | 1 | 1 |
| Field Goals Attempted | 2 | 1 |
| 3rd Down Efficiency | 6/17 | 5/13 |
| 4th Down Efficiency | 0/1 | 0/0 |
| Time of Possession | 30:38 | 29:22 |

## INDIVIDUAL STATISTICS

### RUSHING

| Washington | Att. | Yds. | LG | TD |
|---|---|---|---|---|
| Riggins | 26 | 64 | 8 | 1 |
| Theismann | 3 | 18 | 3 | 0 |
| J. Washington | 3 | 8 | 5 | 0 |

| Raiders | Att. | Yds. | LG | TD |
|---|---|---|---|---|
| Allen | 20 | 191 | 74t | 2 |
| Pruitt | 5 | 17 | 11 | 0 |
| King | 3 | 12 | 10 | 0 |
| Willis | 1 | 7 | 7 | 0 |
| Hawkins | 3 | 6 | 3 | 0 |
| Plunkett | 1 | -2 | -2 | 0 |

### PASSING

| Wash. | Att. | Comp. | Yds. | TD | Int. |
|---|---|---|---|---|---|
| Theismann | 35 | 16 | 243 | 0 | 2 |

| Raiders | Att. | Comp. | Yds. | TD | Int. |
|---|---|---|---|---|---|
| Plunkett | 25 | 16 | 172 | 1 | 0 |

### RECEIVING

| Washington | No. | Yds. | LG | TD |
|---|---|---|---|---|
| Didier | 5 | 65 | 20 | 0 |
| Brown | 3 | 93 | 60 | 0 |
| J. Washington | 3 | 20 | 10 | 0 |
| Giaquinto | 2 | 21 | 14 | 0 |
| Monk | 1 | 26 | 26 | 0 |
| Garrett | 1 | 17 | 17 | 0 |
| Riggins | 1 | 1 | 1 | 0 |
| **Raiders** | **No.** | **Yds.** | **LG** | **TD** |
| Branch | 6 | 94 | 50 | 1 |
| Christensen | 4 | 32 | 14 | 0 |
| Hawkins | 2 | 20 | 14 | 0 |
| Allen | 2 | 18 | 12 | 0 |
| King | 2 | 8 | 7 | 0 |

**INTERCEPTIONS**

| Washington | No. | Yds. | LG | TD |
|---|---|---|---|---|
| None | | | | |
| **Raiders** | **No.** | **Yds.** | **LG** | **TD** |
| Squirek | 1 | 5 | 5t | 1 |
| Haynes | 1 | 0 | 0 | 0 |

**PUNTING**

| Washington | No. | Avg. | LG | Blk. |
|---|---|---|---|---|
| Hayes | 7 | 37.0 | 48 | 1 |
| **Raiders** | **No.** | **Avg.** | **LG** | **Blk.** |
| Guy | 7 | 42.7 | 47 | 0 |

**PUNT RETURNS**

| Washington | No. | FC | Yds. | LG | TD |
|---|---|---|---|---|---|
| Green | 1 | 0 | 34 | 34 | 0 |
| Giaquinto | 1 | 2 | 1 | 1 | 0 |
| **Raiders** | **No.** | **FC** | **Yds.** | **LG** | **TD** |
| Pruitt | 1 | 3 | 8 | 8 | 0 |
| Watts | 1 | 0 | 0 | 0 | 0 |

**KICKOFF RETURNS**

| Washington | No. | Yds. | LG | TD |
|---|---|---|---|---|
| Garrett | 5 | 100 | 35 | 0 |
| Grant | 1 | 32 | 32 | 0 |
| Kimball | 1 | 0 | 0 | 0 |
| **Raiders** | **No.** | **Yds.** | **LG** | **TD** |
| Pruitt | 1 | 17 | 17 | 0 |

## SUPER BOWL XVII

Rose Bowl, Pasadena, California          January 30, 1983
Attendance: 103,667

**WASHINGTON 27, MIAMI 17**—Fullback John Riggins' Super Bowl record 166 yards on 38 carries sparked Washington to a 27-17 victory over AFC champion Miami. It was Riggins' fourth straight 100-yard rushing game during the play-offs, also a record. The win marked Washington's first NFL title since 1942, and was only the second time in Super Bowl history NFC teams scored consecutive wins (Green Bay did it in Super Bowls I and II and San Francisco won Super Bowl XVI). The Redskins, under second-year head coach Joe Gibbs, presented a balanced offense that accounted for 400 total yards (a Super Bowl record 276 yards rushing and 124 passing), second in Super Bowl history to 429 yards by Oakland in Super Bowl XI. The Dolphins built a 17-10 halftime lead on a 76-yard touchdown pass from quarterback David Woodley to wide receiver Jimmy Cefalo 6:49 into the first period, a 20-yard field goal by Uwe von Schamann with 6:00 left in the half, and a Super Bowl record 98-yard kickoff return by Fulton Walker with 1:38 remaining. Washington had tied the score at 10-10 with 1:51 left on a four-yard touchdown pass from Joe Theismann to wide receiver Alvin Garrett. Mark Moseley started the Redskins' scoring with a 31-yard field goal late in the first period, and added a 20-yard field goal midway through the third period to cut the Dolphins' lead to 17-13. Riggins, who was voted the game's most valuable player, gave Washington its first lead of the game with 10:01 left when he ran 43 yards off left tackle for a touchdown on a fourth-and-one situation. Wide receiver Charlie Brown caught a six-yard scoring pass from Theismann with 1:55 left to complete the scoring. The Dolphins managed only 176 yards (142 in first half). Theismann completed 15 of 23 for 143 yards, two touchdowns, and had two interceptions. For Miami, Woodley was 4 of 14 for 97 yards, with one touchdown and one interception. Don Strock was 0 for 3 in relief.

**SCORING**

| | | | | | | |
|---|---|---|---|---|---|---|
| **Miami (AFC)** | 7 | 10 | 0 | 0 | — | 17 |
| **Washington (NFC)** | 0 | 10 | 3 | 14 | — | 27 |

Mia —Cefalo 76 pass from Woodley (von Schamann kick)
Wash—FG Moseley 31
Mia —FG von Schamann 20
Wash—Garrett 4 pass from Theismann (Moseley kick)
Mia —Walker 98 kickoff return (von Schamann kick)
Wash—FG Moseley 20
Wash—Riggins 43 run (Moseley kick)
Wash—Brown 6 pass from Theismann (Moseley kick)

## SUPER BOWL XVI

Pontiac Silverdome, Pontiac Michigan          January 24, 1982
Attendance: 81,270

**SAN FRANCISO 26, CINCINNATI 21**—Ray Wersching's Super Bowl record-tying four field goals and Joe Montana's controlled passing helped lift the San Francisco 49ers to their first NFL championship with a 26-21 victory over Cincinnati. The 49ers built a game-record 20-0 halftime lead via Montana's one-yard touchdown run, which capped an 11-play, 68-yard drive; fullback Earl Cooper's 11-yard scoring pass from Montana, which climaxed a Super Bowl record 92-yard drive on 12 plays; and Wersching's 22- and 26-yard field goals. The Bengals rebounded in the second half, closing the gap to 20-14 on quarterback Ken Anderson's five-yard run and Dan Ross's four-yard catch from Anderson, who established Super Bowl passing records for completions (25) and completion percentage (73.5 percent on 25 of 34). Wersching added early fourth-period field goals of 40 and 23 yards to increase the 49ers' lead to 26-14. The Bengals managed to score on an Anderson-to-Ross three-yard pass with only 16 seconds remaining. Ross set a Super Bowl record with 11 receptions for 104 yards. Montana, the game's most valuable player, completed 14 of 22 passes for 157 yards. Cincinnati compiled 356 yards to San Francisco's 275, which marked the first time in Super Bowl history that the team that gained the most yards from scrimmage lost the game.

| | | | | | | |
|---|---|---|---|---|---|---|
| **San Francisco (NFC)** | 7 | 13 | 0 | 6 | — | 26 |
| **Cincinnati (AFC)** | 0 | 0 | 7 | 14 | — | 21 |

SF —Montana 1 run (Wersching kick)
SF —Cooper 11 pass from Montana (Wersching kick)
SF —FG Wersching 22
SF —FG Wersching 26
Cin—Anderson 5 run (Breech kick)

Cin—Ross 4 pass from Anderson (Breech kick)
SF —FG Wersching 40
SF —FG Wersching 23
Cin—Ross 3 pass from Anderson (Breech kick)

## SUPER BOWL XV

Louisiana Superdome, New Orleans, Louisiana          January 25, 1981
Attendance: 76,135

**OAKLAND 27, PHILADELPHIA 10**—Jim Plunkett threw three touchdown passes, including an 80-yarder to Kenny King, as the Raiders became the first wild card team to win the Super Bowl. Plunkett's touchdown bomb to King—the longest play in Super Bowl history—gave Oakland a decisive 14-0 lead with nine seconds left in the first period. Linebacker Rod Martin had set up Oakland's first touchdown, a two-yard reception by Cliff Branch, with a 16-yard interception return to the Eagles' 32 yard line. The Eagles never recovered from that early deficit, managing only a Tony Franklin field goal (30 yards) and an eight-yard touchdown pass from Ron Jaworski to Keith Krepfle the rest of the game. Plunkett, who became a starter in the sixth game of the season, completed 13 of 21 for 261 yards and was named the game's most valuable player. Oakland won 9 of 11 games with Plunkett starting, but that was good enough only for second place in the AFC West, although they tied division winner San Diego with an 11-5 record. The Raiders, who had previously won Super Bowl XI over Minnesota, had to win three playoff games to get to the championship game. Oakland defeated Houston 27-7 at home followed by road victories over Cleveland, 14-12 and San Diego, 34-27. Oakland's Mark van Eeghen was the game's leading rusher with 80 yards on 19 carries. Philadelphia's Wilbert Montgomery led all receivers with six receptions for 91 yards. Branch had five for 67 and Harold Carmichael of Philadelphia five for 83. Martin finished the game with three interceptions, a Super Bowl record.

| | | | | | | |
|---|---|---|---|---|---|---|
| **Oakland (AFC)** | 14 | 0 | 10 | 3 | — | 27 |
| **Philadelphia (NFC)** | 0 | 3 | 0 | 7 | — | 10 |

Oak—Branch 2 pass from Plunkett (Bahr kick)
Oak—King 80 pass from Plunkett (Bahr kick)
Phil—FG Franklin 30
Oak—Branch 29 pass from Plunkett (Bahr kick)
Oak—FG Bahr 46
Phil—Krepfle 8 pass from Jaworski (Franklin kick)
Oak—FG Bahr 35

## SUPER BOWL XIV

Rose Bowl, Pasadena, California          January 20, 1980
Attendance: 103,985

**PITTSBURGH 31, LOS ANGELES 19**—Terry Bradshaw completed 14 of 21 passes for 309 yards and set two passing records as the Steelers became the first team to win four Super Bowls. Despite three interceptions by the Rams, Bradshaw kept his poise and brought the Steelers from behind twice in the second half. Trailing 13-10 at halftime, Pittsburgh went ahead 17-13 when Bradshaw hit Lynn Swann on a 47-yard touchdown pass after 2:48 of the third quarter. On the Rams' next possession Vince Ferragamo, who completed 15 of 25 passes for 212 yards, responded with a 50-yard pass to Billy Waddy that moved Los Angeles from its own 26 to the Steelers' 24. On the following play, Lawrence McCutcheon connected with Ron Smith on a halfback option pass that gave the Rams a 19-17 lead. On Pittsburgh's initial possession of the final period, Bradshaw lofted a 73-yard scoring pass to John Stallworth to put the Steelers in front to stay, 24-19. Franco Harris scored on a one-yard run later in the quarter to seal the verdict. A 45-yard pass from Bradshaw to Stallworth was the key play in the drive to Harris's score. Bradshaw, the game's most valuable player for the second straight year, set career Super Bowl records for most touchdown passes (nine) and most passing yards (932). Larry Anderson gave the Steelers excellent field position throughout the game with five kickoff returns for a record 162 yards.

| | | | | | | |
|---|---|---|---|---|---|---|
| **Los Angeles (NFC)** | 7 | 6 | 6 | 0 | — | 19 |
| **Pittsburgh (AFC)** | 3 | 7 | 7 | 14 | — | 31 |

Pitt—FG Bahr 41
LA —Bryant 1 run (Corral kick)
Pitt—Harris 1 run (Bahr kick)
LA —FG Corral 31
LA —FG Corral 45
Pitt—Swann 47 pass from Bradshaw (Bahr kick)
LA —Smith 24 pass from McCutcheon (kick failed)
Pitt—Stallworth 73 pass from Bradshaw (Bahr kick)
Pitt—Harris 1 run (Bahr kick)

## SUPER BOWL XIII

Orange Bowl, Miami, Florida          January 21, 1979
Attendance: 79,484

**PITTSBURGH 35, DALLAS 31**—Terry Bradshaw threw a record four touchdown passes to lead the Steelers to victory. The Steelers became the first team to win three Super Bowls, mostly because of Bradshaw's accurate arm. Bradshaw, voted the game's most valuable player, completed 17 of 30 passes for 318 yards, a personal high. Three of those passes went for touchdowns—two to John Stallworth and the third, with 26 seconds remaining in the second period, to Rocky Bleier. The Cowboys scored twice before intermission on Roger Staubach's 39-yard pass to Tony Hill and a 37-yard run by linebacker Mike Hegman, who stole the ball from Bradshaw. The Steelers broke open the contest with two touchdowns in a span of 19 seconds midway through the final period. Franco Harris rambled 22 yards up the middle to give the Steelers a 28-17 lead with 7:10 left. Pittsburgh got the ball right back when Randy White fumbled the kickoff and Dennis Winston recovered for the Steelers. On first down, Bradshaw hit Lynn Swann with an 18-yard scoring pass to boost the Steelers' lead to 35-17 with 6:51 to play. The Cowboys refused to let the Steelers run away with the contest. Staubach connected with Billy Joe DuPree on an eight-yard scoring pass with 2:23 left. Then the Cowboys recovered an onside kick and Staubach took them in for another score, passing four yards to Butch Johnson with 22 seconds remaining. Bleier recovered another onside kick with 17 seconds left to seal the victory for the Steelers.

| Pittsburgh (AFC) | 7 | 14 | 0 | 14 — 35 |
|---|---|---|---|---|
| Dallas (NFC) | 7 | 7 | 3 | 14 — 31 |

Pitt —Stallworth 28 pass from Bradshaw (Gerela kick)
Dall—Hill 39 pass from Staubach (Septien kick)
Dall—Hegman 37 fumble recovery return (Septien kick)
Pitt —Stallworth 75 pass from Bradshaw (Gerela kick)
Pitt —Bleier 7 pass from Bradshaw (Gerela kick)
Dall—FG Septien 27
Pitt —Harris 22 run (Gerela kick)
Pitt —Swann 18 pass from Bradshaw (Gerela kick)
Dall—DuPree 7 pass from Staubach (Septien kick)
Dall—B. Johnson 4 pass from Staubach (Septien kick)

## SUPER BOWL XII

Louisiana Superdome, New Orleans, Louisiana          January 15, 1978
Attendance: 75,583

**DALLAS 27, DENVER 10**—The Cowboys evened their Super Bowl record at 2-2 by defeating Denver before a sellout crowd of 75,583, plus 102,010,000 television viewers, the largest audience ever to watch a sporting event. Dallas converted two interceptions into 10 points and Efren Herrera added a 35-yard field goal for a 13-0 halftime advantage. In the third period Craig Morton engineered a drive to the Cowboys' 30 and Jim Turner's 47-yard field goal made the score 13-3. After an exchange of punts, Butch Johnson made a spectacular diving catch in the end zone to complete a 45-yard pass from Roger Staubach and put the Cowboys ahead 20-3. Following Rick Upchurch's 67-yard kickoff return, Norris Weese guided the Broncos to a touchdown to cut the Dallas lead to 20-10. Dallas clinched the victory when running back Robert Newhouse threw a 29-yard touchdown pass to Golden Richards with 7:04 remaining in the game. It was the first pass thrown by Newhouse since 1975. Harvey Martin and Randy White, who were named co-most valuable players, led the Cowboys' defense, which recovered four fumbles and intercepted four passes.

| Dallas (NFC) | 10 | 3 | 7 | 7 — 27 |
|---|---|---|---|---|
| Denver (AFC) | 0 | 0 | 10 | 0 — 10 |

Dall—Dorsett 3 run (Herrera kick)
Dall—FG Herrera 35
Dall—FG Herrera 43
Den—FG Turner 47
Dall—Johnson 45 pass from Staubach (Herrera kick)
Den—Lytle 1 run (Turner kick)
Dall—Richards 29 pass from Newhouse (Herrera kick)

## SUPER BOWL XI

Rose Bowl, Pasadena, California          January 9, 1977
Attendance: 103,438

**OAKLAND 32, MINNESOTA 14**—The Raiders won their first NFL championship before a record Super Bowl crowd plus 81 million television viewers, the largest audience ever to watch a sporting event. The Raiders gained a record-breaking 429 yards, including running back Clarence Davis's 137 yards rushing, and wide receiver Fred Biletnikoff made four key receptions, which earned him the game's most valuable player trophy. Oakland scored on three successive possessions in the second quarter to build a 16-0 halftime lead. Errol Mann's 24-yard field goal opened the scoring, then the AFC champions put together drives of 64 and 35 yards, scoring on a one-yard pass from Ken Stabler to Dave Casper and a one-yard run by Pete Banaszak. The Raiders increased their lead to 19-0 on a 40-yard field goal in the third quarter, but Minnesota responded with a 12-play, 58-yard drive late in the period, with Fran Tarkenton passing eight yards to wide receiver Sammy White to cut the deficit to 19-7. Two fourth quarter interceptions clinched the title for the Raiders. One set up Banaszak's second touchdown run, the other resulted in cornerback Willie Brown's Super Bowl record 75-yard interception return.

| Oakland (AFC) | 0 | 16 | 3 | 13 — 32 |
|---|---|---|---|---|
| Minnesota (NFC) | 0 | 0 | 7 | 7 — 14 |

Oak —FG Mann 24
Oak —Casper 1 pass from Stabler (Mann kick)
Oak —Banaszak 1 run (kick failed)
Oak —FG Mann 40
Minn—S. White 8 pass from Tarkenton (Cox kick)
Oak —Banaszak 2 run (Mann kick)
Oak —Brown 75 interception return (kick failed)
Minn—Voigt 13 pass from Lee (Cox kick)

## SUPER BOWL X

Orange Bowl, Miami, Florida          January 18, 1976
Attendance: 80,187

**PITTSBURGH 21, DALLAS 17**—The Steelers won the Super Bowl for the second year in a row on Terry Bradshaw's 64-yard touchdown pass to Lynn Swann and an aggressive defense that snuffed out a late rally by the Cowboys with an end zone interception on the final play of the game. In the fourth quarter Pittsburgh ran on fourth down and gave up the ball on the Cowboys' 39 with 1:22 to play. Staubach ran and passed for two first downs but his last desperation pass was picked off by Glen Edwards. Dallas's scoring was the result of two touchdown passes by Staubach, one to Drew Pearson for 29 yards and the other to

Percy Howard for 34 yards. Toni Fritsch had a 36-yard field goal. The Steelers scored on two touchdown passes by Bradshaw, one to Randy Grossman for seven yards and the long bomb to Swann. Roy Gerela had 36- and 18-yard field goals. Reggie Harrison blocked a punt through the end zone for a safety. Swann set a Super Bowl record by gaining 161 yards on his four receptions.

| Dallas (NFC) | 7 | 3 | 0 | 7 — 17 |
|---|---|---|---|---|
| Pittsburgh (AFC) | 7 | 0 | 0 | 14 — 21 |

Dall—D. Pearson 29 pass from Staubach (Fritsch kick)
Pitt —Grossman 7 pass from Bradshaw (Gerela kick)
Dall—FG Fritsch 36
Pitt —Safety, Harrison blocked Hoopes's punt through end zone
Pitt —FG Gerela 36
Pitt —FG Gerela 18
Pitt —Swann 64 pass from Bradshaw (kick failed)
Dall—P. Howard 34 pass from Staubach (Fritsch kick)

## SUPER BOWL IX

Tulane Stadium, New Orleans, Louisiana          January 12, 1975
Attendance: 80,997

**PITTSBURGH 16, MINNESOTA 6**—AFC champion Pittsburgh, in its initial Super Bowl appearance, and NFC champion Minnesota, making a third bid for its first Super Bowl title, struggled through a first half in which the only score was produced by the Steelers' defense when Dwight White downed Vikings' quarterback Fran Tarkenton in the end zone for a safety 7:49 into the second period. The Steelers forced another break and took advantage on the second half kickoff when Minnesota's Bill Brown fumbled and Marv Kellum recovered for Pittsburgh on the Vikings' 30. After Rocky Bleier failed to gain on first down, Franco Harris carried three consecutive times for 24 yards, a loss of 3, and a 12-yard touchdown and a 9-0 lead. Though its offense was completely stymied by Pittsburgh's defense, Minnesota managed to move into a threatening position after 4:27 of the final period when Matt Blair blocked Bobby Walden's punt and Terry Brown recovered the ball in the end zone for a touchdown. Fred Cox's kick failed and the Steelers led 9-6. Pittsburgh wasted no time putting the victory away. The Steelers took the ensuing kickoff and marched 66 yards in 11 plays, climaxed by Terry Bradshaw's four-yard scoring pass to Larry Brown with 3:31 left. Pittsburgh's defense permitted Minnesota only 119 yards total offense, including a Super Bowl low of 17 yards rushing. The Steelers, meanwhile, gained 333 yards, including Harris's record 158 yards on 34 carries.

| Pittsburgh (AFC) | 0 | 2 | 7 | 7 — 16 |
|---|---|---|---|---|
| Minnesota (NFC) | 0 | 0 | 0 | 6 — 6 |

Pitt —Safety, White downed Tarkenton in end zone
Pitt —Harris 12 run (Gerela kick)
Minn—T. Brown recovered blocked punt in end zone (kick failed)
Pitt —L. Brown 4 pass from Bradshaw (Gerela kick)

## SUPER BOWL VIII

Rice Stadium, Houston, Texas          January 13, 1974
Attendance: 71,882

**MIAMI 24, MINNESOTA 7**—The defending NFL champion Dolphins, representing the AFC for the third straight year, scored the first two times they had possession on marches of 62 and 56 yards in the first period while the Miami defense limited the Vikings to only seven plays. Larry Csonka climaxed the initial 10-play drive with a five-yard touchdown bolt through right guard after 5:27 had elapsed. Four plays later, Miami began another 10-play scoring drive, which ended with Jim Kiick bursting one yard through the middle for another touchdown after 13:38 of the period. Garo Yepremian added a 28-yard field goal midway in the second period for a 17-0 Miami lead. Minnesota then drove from its 20 to a second-and-two situation on the Miami 7 yard line with 1:18 left in the half. But on two plays, Miami limited Oscar Reed to one yard. On fourth-and-one from the 6, Reed went over right tackle, but Dolphins middle linebacker Nick Buoniconti jarred the ball loose and Jake Scott recovered for Miami to halt the Minnesota threat. The Vikings were unable to muster enough offense in the second half to threaten the Dolphins. Csonka rushed 33 times for a Super Bowl record 145 yards. Bob Griese of Miami completed six of seven passes for 73 yards.

| Minnesota (NFC) | 0 | 0 | 0 | 7 — 7 |
|---|---|---|---|---|
| Miami (AFC) | 14 | 3 | 7 | 0 — 24 |

Mia —Csonka 5 run (Yepremian kick)
Mia —Kiick 1 run (Yepremian kick)
Mia —FG Yepremian 28
Mia —Csonka 2 run (Yepremian kick)
Minn—Tarkenton 4 run (Cox kick)

## SUPER BOWL VII

Memorial Coliseum, Los Angeles, California          January 14, 1973
Attendance: 90,182

**MIAMI 14, WASHINGTON 7**—The Dolphins played virtually perfect football in the first half as their defense permitted the Redskins to cross midfield only once and their offense turned good field position into two touchdowns. On its third possession, Miami opened its first scoring drive from the Dolphins' 37 yard line. An 18-yard pass from Bob Griese to Paul Warfield preceded by three plays Griese's 28-yard touchdown pass to Howard Twilley. After Washington moved from its 17 to the Miami 48 with two minutes remaining in the first half, Dolphins linebacker Nick Buoniconti intercepted a Billy Kilmer pass at the Miami 41 and returned it to the Washington 27. Jim Kiick ran for three yards, Larry Csonka for three, Griese passed to Jim Mandich for 19, and Kiick gained one to the 1 yard line. With 18 seconds left until intermission, Kiick scored from the 1. Washington's only touchdown came with 7:07 left in the game and resulted from a misplayed field goal attempt and fumble by Garo Yepremian, with the

Redskins' Mike Bass picking the ball out of the air and running 49 yards for the score.

| | | | | | |
|---|---|---|---|---|---|
| **Miami (AFC)** | 7 | 7 | 0 | 0 — | 14 |
| **Washington (NFC)** | 0 | 0 | 0 | 7 — | 7 |

Mia —Twilley 28 pass from Griese (Yepremian kick)
Mia —Kiick 1 run (Yepremian kick)
Wash—Bass 49 fumble recovery return (Knight kick)

## SUPER BOWL VI

Tulane Stadium, New Orleans, Louisiana     January 16, 1972
Attendance: 81,023

**DALLAS 24, MIAMI 3**—The Cowboys rushed for a record 252 yards and their defense limited the Dolphins to a low of 185 yards while not permitting a touchdown for the first time in Super Bowl history. Dallas converted Chuck Howley's recovery of Larry Csonka's first fumble of the season into a 3-0 advantage and led at halftime 10-3. After Dallas received the second half kickoff, Duane Thomas ran a 71-yard march in eight plays for a 17-3 margin. Howley intercepted Bob Griese's pass at the 50 and returned it to the Miami 9 early in the fourth period, and three plays later Roger Staubach passed seven yards to Mike Ditka for the final touchdown. Thomas rushed for 95 yards and Walt Garrison gained 74. Staubach, voted the game's most valuable player, completed 12 of 19 passes for 119 yards and two touchdowns.

| | | | | | |
|---|---|---|---|---|---|
| **Dallas (NFC)** | 3 | 7 | 7 | 7 — | 24 |
| **Miami (AFC)** | 0 | 3 | 0 | 0 — | 3 |

Dall—FG Clark 9
Dall—Alworth 7 pass from Staubach (Clark kick)
Mia—FG Yepremian 31
Dall—D. Thomas 3 run (Clark kick)
Dall—Ditka 7 pass from Staubach (Clark kick)

## SUPER BOWL V

Orange Bowl, Miami, Florida     January 17, 1971
Attendance: 79,204

**BALTIMORE 16, DALLAS 13**—A 32-yard field goal by first-year kicker Jim O'Brien brought the Baltimore Colts a victory over the Dallas Cowboys in the final five seconds of Super Bowl V. The game between the champions of the AFC and NFC was played on artificial turf for the first time. Dallas led 13-6 at the half but interceptions by Rick Volk and Mike Curtis set up a Baltimore touchdown and O'Brien's decisive kick in the fourth period. Earl Morrall relieved an injured Johnny Unitas late in the first half, although Unitas completed the Colts' only scoring pass. It caromed off receiver Eddie Hinton's finger tips, off Dallas defensive back Mel Renfro, and finally settled into the grasp of John Mackey, who went 45 yards to score on a 75-yard play.

| | | | | | |
|---|---|---|---|---|---|
| **Baltimore (AFC)** | 0 | 6 | 0 | 10 — | 16 |
| **Dallas (NFC)** | 3 | 10 | 0 | 0 — | 13 |

Dall—FG Clark 14
Dall—FG Clark 30
Balt—Mackey 75 pass from Unitas (kick blocked)
Dall—Thomas 7 pass from Morton (Clark kick)
Balt—Nowatzke 2 run (O'Brien kick)
Balt—FG O'Brien 32

## SUPER BOWL IV

Tulane Stadium, New Orleans, Louisiana     January 11, 1970
Attendance: 80,562

**KANSAS CITY 23, MINNESOTA 7**—The AFL squared the Super Bowl at two games apiece with the NFL, building a 16-0 halftime lead behind Len Dawson's superb quarterbacking and a powerful defense. Dawson, the fourth consecutive quarterback to be chosen the Super Bowl's top player, called an almost flawless game, completing 12 of 17 passes and hitting Otis Taylor on a 46-yard play for the final Chiefs touchdown. The Kansas City defense limited Minnesota's strong rushing game to 67 yards and made three interceptions and two fumble recoveries. The crowd of 80,562 set a Super Bowl record, as did the gross receipts of $3,817,872.69.

| | | | | | |
|---|---|---|---|---|---|
| **Minnesota (NFL)** | 0 | 0 | 7 | 0 — | 7 |
| **Kansas City (AFL)** | 3 | 13 | 7 | 0 — | 23 |

KC —FG Stenerud 48
KC —FG Stenerud 32
KC —FG Stenerud 25
KC —Garrett 5 run (Stenerud kick)
Minn—Osborn 4 run (Cox kick)
KC —Taylor 46 pass from Dawson (Stenerud kick)

## SUPER BOWL III

Orange Bowl, Miami, Florida     January 12, 1969
Attendance: 75,389

**NEW YORK JETS 16, BALTIMORE 7**—Jets quarterback Joe Namath "guaranteed" victory on the Thursday before the game, then went out and led the AFL to its first Super Bowl victory over a Baltimore team that had lost only once in 16 games all season. Namath, chosen the outstanding player, completed 17 of 28 passes for 206 yards and directed a steady attack that dominated the NFL champions after the Jets' defense had intercepted Colts quarterback Earl Morrall three times in the first half. The Jets had 337 total yards, including 121 yards rushing by Matt Snell. Johnny Unitas, who had missed most of the season with a sore elbow, came off the bench and led Baltimore to its only touchdown late in the fourth quarter after New York led 16-0.

| | | | | | |
|---|---|---|---|---|---|
| **New York Jets (AFL)** | 0 | 7 | 6 | 3 — | 16 |
| **Baltimore (NFL)** | 0 | 0 | 0 | 7 — | 7 |

NYJ—Snell 4 run (Turner kick)

NYJ—FG Turner 32
NYJ—FG Turner 30
NYJ—FG Turner 9
Balt—Hill 1 run (Michaels kick)

## SUPER BOWL II

Orange Bowl, Miami, Florida     January 14, 1968
Attendance: 75,546

**GREEN BAY 33, OAKLAND 14**—Green Bay, after winning its third consecutive NFL championship, won the Super Bowl title for the second straight year 33-14 over the AFL champion Raiders in a game that drew the first $3 million dollar gate in football history. Bart Starr again was chosen the game's most valuable player as he completed 13 of 24 passes for 202 yards and one touchdown and directed a Packers attack that was in control all the way after building a 16-7 halftime lead. Don Chandler kicked four field goals and all-pro cornerback Herb Adderley capped the Green Bay scoring with a 60-yard run with an interception. The game marked the last for Vince Lombardi as Packers coach, ending nine years at Green Bay in which he won six Western Conference championships, five NFL championships, and two Super Bowls.

| | | | | | |
|---|---|---|---|---|---|
| **Green Bay (NFL)** | 3 | 13 | 10 | 7 — | 33 |
| **Oakland (AFL)** | 0 | 7 | 0 | 7 — | 14 |

GB —FG Chandler 39
GB —FG Chandler 20
GB —Dowler 62 pass from Starr (Chandler kick)
Oak—Miller 23 pass from Lamonica (Blanda kick)
GB —FG Chandler 43
GB —Anderson 2 run (Chandler kick)
GB —FG Chandler 31
GB —Adderley 60 interception return (Chandler kick)
Oak—Miller 23 pass from Lamonica (Blanda kick)

## SUPER BOWL I

Memorial Coliseum, Los Angeles, California     January 15, 1967
Attendance: 61,946

**GREEN BAY 35, KANSAS CITY 10**—The Green Bay Packers opened the Super Bowl series by defeating Kansas City's American Football League champions 35-10 behind the passing of Bart Starr, the receiving of Max McGee, and a key interception by all-pro safety Willie Wood. Green Bay broke open the game with three second-half touchdowns, the first of which was set up by Wood's 40-yard return of an interception to the Chiefs' 5 yard line. McGee, filling in for ailing Boyd Dowler after having caught only three passes all season, caught seven from Starr for 138 yards and two touchdowns. Elijah Pitts ran for two other scores. The Chiefs' 10 points came in the second quarter, the only touchdown on a seven-yard pass from Len Dawson to Curtis McClinton. Starr completed 16 of 23 passes for 250 yards and two touchdowns and was chosen the most valuable player. The Packers collected $15,000 per man and the Chiefs $7,500—the largest single-game shares in the history of team sports.

| | | | | | |
|---|---|---|---|---|---|
| **Kansas City (AFL)** | 0 | 10 | 0 | 0 — | 10 |
| **Green Bay (NFL)** | 7 | 7 | 14 | 7 — | 35 |

GB—McGee 37 pass from Starr (Chandler kick)
KC—McClinton 7 pass from Dawson (Mercer kick)
GB—Taylor 14 run (Chandler kick)
KC—FG Mercer 31
GB—Pitts 5 run (Chandler kick)
GB—McGee 13 pass from Starr (Chandler kick)
GB—Pitts 1 run (Chandler kick)

## AFC Championship Game

Includes AFL Championship Games (1960-69)

### RESULTS

| Season | Date | Winner (Share) | Loser (Share) | Score | Site | Attendance |
|--------|------|----------------|---------------|-------|------|------------|
| 1983 | Jan. 8 | L.A. Raiders ($18,000) | Seattle ($18,000) | 30-14 | Los Angeles | 91,445 |
| 1982 | Jan. 23 | Miami ($18,000) | N.Y. Jets ($18,000) | 14-0 | Miami | 67,396 |
| 1981 | Jan. 10 | Cincinnati ($9,000) | San Diego ($9,000) | 27-7 | Cincinnati | 46,302 |
| 1980 | Jan. 11 | Oakland ($9,000) | San Diego ($9,000) | 34-27 | San Diego | 52,675 |
| 1979 | Jan. 6 | Pittsburgh ($9,000) | Houston ($9,000) | 27-13 | Pittsburgh | 50,475 |
| 1978 | Jan. 7 | Pittsburgh ($9,000) | Houston ($9,000) | 34-5 | Pittsburgh | 50,725 |
| 1977 | Jan. 1 | Denver ($9,000) | Oakland ($9,000) | 20-17 | Denver | 75,044 |
| 1976 | Dec. 26 | Oakland ($8,500) | Pittsburgh ($5,500) | 24-7 | Oakland | 53,821 |
| 1975 | Jan. 4 | Pittsburgh ($8,500) | Oakland ($5,500) | 16-10 | Pittsburgh | 50,609 |
| 1974 | Dec. 29 | Pittsburgh ($8,500) | Oakland ($5,500) | 24-13 | Oakland | 53,800 |
| 1973 | Dec. 30 | Miami ($8,500) | Oakland ($5,500) | 27-10 | Miami | 79,325 |
| 1972 | Dec. 31 | Miami ($8,500) | Pittsburgh ($5,500) | 21-17 | Pittsburgh | 50,845 |
| 1971 | Jan. 2 | Miami ($8,500) | Baltimore ($5,500) | 21-0 | Miami | 76,622 |
| 1970 | Jan. 3 | Baltimore ($8,500) | Oakland ($5,500) | 27-17 | Baltimore | 54,799 |
| 1969 | Jan. 4 | Kansas City ($7,755) | Oakland ($6,252) | 17-7 | Oakland | 53,564 |
| 1968 | Dec. 29 | N.Y. Jets ($7,007) | Oakland ($5,349) | 27-23 | New York | 62,627 |
| 1967 | Dec. 31 | Oakland ($6,321) | Houston ($4,996) | 40-7 | Oakland | 53,330 |
| 1966 | Jan. 1 | Kansas City ($5,309) | Buffalo ($3,799) | 31-7 | Buffalo | 42,080 |
| 1965 | Dec. 26 | Buffalo ($5,189) | San Diego ($3,447) | 23-0 | San Diego | 30,361 |
| 1964 | Dec. 26 | Buffalo ($2,668) | San Diego ($1,738) | 20-7 | Buffalo | 40,242 |
| 1963 | Jan. 5 | San Diego ($2,498) | Boston ($1,596) | 51-10 | San Diego | 30,127 |
| 1962 | Dec. 23 | Dallas ($2,206) | Houston ($1,471) | 20-17* | Houston | 37,981 |
| 1961 | Dec. 24 | Houston ($1,792) | San Diego ($1,111) | 10-3 | San Diego | 29,556 |
| 1960 | Jan. 1 | Houston ($1,025) | Los Angeles ($718) | 24-16 | Houston | 32,183 |

*Sudden death overtime.

## AFC CHAMPIONSHIP GAME COMPOSITE STANDINGS

| | W | L | Pct. | Pts. | OP |
|---|---|---|------|------|-----|
| Miami Dolphins | 4 | 0 | 1.000 | 83 | 27 |
| Kansas City Chiefs* | 3 | 0 | 1.000 | 68 | 31 |
| Cincinnati Bengals | 1 | 0 | 1.000 | 27 | 7 |
| Denver Broncos | 1 | 0 | 1.000 | 20 | 17 |
| Buffalo Bills | 2 | 1 | .667 | 50 | 38 |
| Pittsburgh Steelers | 4 | 2 | .667 | 125 | 86 |
| Baltimore Colts | 1 | 1 | .500 | 27 | 38 |
| New York Jets | 1 | 1 | .500 | 27 | 37 |
| Oakland/L.A. Raiders | 4 | 7 | .364 | 225 | 213 |
| Houston Oilers | 2 | 4 | .333 | 76 | 140 |
| San Diego Chargers** | 1 | 6 | .143 | 111 | 148 |
| New England Patriots*** | 0 | 1 | .000 | 10 | 51 |
| Seattle Seahawks | 0 | 1 | .000 | 14 | 30 |

*One game played when franchise was in Dallas (Texans). (Won 20-17)
**One game played when franchise was in Los Angeles. (Lost 24-16)
***Game played when franchise was in Boston. (Lost 51-10)

## 1983 AMERICAN FOOTBALL CONFERENCE CHAMPIONSHIP GAME

Memorial Coliseum, Los Angeles, California  
January 8, 1984  
Attendance: 91,445

**LOS ANGELES RAIDERS 30, SEATTLE 14**—Los Angeles rolled up 401 yards offense and limited Seattle to 167 (65 rushing, 102 passing) as the Raiders advanced to Super Bowl XVIII. Raiders running back Marcus Allen carried 25 times for 154 yards and scored on a three-yard touchdown pass from quarterback Jim Plunkett, who completed 17 of 24 for 214 yards with two interceptions. The Raiders built a 20-0 halftime lead as running back Frank Hawkins scored on touchdown runs of one and five yards. The Raiders capitalized on five interceptions and four sacks. Safety Mike Davis had two of the Raiders' interceptions. Wide receiver Malcolm Barnwell had five catches for 116 yards while Allen caught seven for 62.

| Seattle Seahawks (14) | Offense | Los Angeles Raiders (30) |
|-----------------------|---------|--------------------------|
| Pete Metzelaars | TE | Don Hasselbeck |
| Ron Essink | LT | Bruce Davis |
| Edwin Bailey | LG | Charley Hannah |
| Blair Bush | C | Dave Dalby |
| Robert Pratt | RG | Mickey Marvin |
| Steve August | RT | Henry Lawrence |
| Charle Young | TE | Todd Christensen |
| Steve Largent | WR | Cliff Branch |
| Dave Krieg | QB | Jim Plunkett |
| Curt Warner | RB | Marcus Allen |
| Cullen Bryant | RB-WR | Malcolm Barnwell |
| | **Defense** | |
| Jacob Green | LE | Howie Long |
| Joe Nash | NT | Reggie Kinlaw |
| Jeff Bryant | RE | Lyle Alzado |
| Bruce Scholtz | LOLB | Ted Hendricks |
| Joe Norman | LILB | Matt Millen |
| Keith Butler | RILB | Bob Nelson |
| Greg Gaines | ROLB | Rod Martin |
| Kerry Justin | LCB | Lester Hayes |
| Dave Brown | RCB | Mike Haynes |
| Kenny Easley | SS | Mike Davis |
| John Harris | FS | Vann McElroy |

## SUBSTITUTIONS

**Seattle**—Offense: K—Norm Johnson. P—Jeff West. QB—Jim Zorn. RB—Zachary Dixon, Dan Doornink, David Hughes, Eric Lane. TE—Mike Tice. WR—Chris Castor, Harold Jackson, Paul Johns, Byron Walker. T—Matt Hernandez. G—Bill Dugan. Defense: E—Sam Clancy, Darrell Irvin. NT—Manu Tuiasosopo. LB—Mark Hicks, Michael Jackson, Sam Merriman, Shelton Robinson. CB—Greggory Johnson, Keith Simpson. S—Don Dufek, Paul Moyer. DNP—Kani Kauahi (C), Reggie McKenzie (G).

**Raiders**—Offense: K—Chris Bahr. P—Ray Guy. QB—David Humm, Marc Wilson. RB—Frank Hawkins, Kenny King, Greg Pruitt, Chester Willis. TE—Derrick Jensen. WR—Cle Montgomery, Calvin Muhammad. T—Shelby Jordan, Don Mosebar. G—Steve Sylvester. Defense: E—Johnny Robinson, Greg Townsend. T—Bill Pickel, Dave Stalls. LB—Jeff Barnes, Darryl Byrd, Tony Caldwell, Jack Squirek. CB—James Davis, Ted Watts. S—Kenny Hill, Odis McKinney. DNP—Dokie Williams (WR).

## OFFICIALS

Referee—Dick Jorgensen. Umpire—Bob Boylston. Head Linesman—Leo Miles. Line Judge—Ray Dodez. Back Judge—Pat Knight. Side Judge—Bill Quimby. Field Judge—Johnny Grier.

## SCORING

| | | | | | |
|---|---|---|---|---|---|
| **Seattle** | 0 | 0 | 7 | 7 | — 14 |
| **L.A. Raiders** | 3 | 17 | 7 | 3 | — 30 |

Raiders—FG Bahr 20  
Raiders—Hawkins 1 run (Bahr kick)  
Raiders—Hawkins 5 run (Bahr kick)  
Raiders—FG Bahr 45  
Raiders—Allen 3 pass from Plunkett (Bahr kick)  
Sea —Doornink 11 pass from Zorn (N. Johnson kick)  
Raiders—FG Bahr 35  
Sea —Young 9 pass from Zorn (N. Johnson kick)

## TEAM STATISTICS

| | Seattle | Raiders |
|---|---------|---------|
| Total First Downs | 16 | 21 |
| First Downs Rushing | 4 | 10 |
| First Downs Passing | 10 | 11 |
| First Downs Penalty | 2 | 0 |
| Total Net Yardage | 167 | 401 |
| Total Offensive Plays | 58 | 72 |
| Average Gain per Offensive Play | 2.9 | 5.6 |
| Rushes | 18 | 46 |
| Yards Gained Rushing (net) | 65 | 205 |
| Average Yards per Rush | 3.6 | 4.5 |
| Passes Attempted | 36 | 24 |
| Passes Completed | 17 | 17 |
| Had Intercepted | 5 | 2 |
| Times Tackled Attempting to Pass | 4 | 2 |
| Yards Lost Attempting to Pass | 44 | 18 |
| Yards Gained Passing (net) | 102 | 196 |
| Punts | 5 | 2 |
| Average Distance | 32.0 | 34.0 |
| Punt Returns | 0 | 1 |
| Punt Return Yardage | 0 | 1 |
| Kickoff Returns | 7 | 2 |
| Kickoff Return Yardage | 136 | 46 |
| Interception Return Yardage | 8 | 53 |
| Total Return Yardage | 144 | 100 |
| Fumbles | 1 | 3 |
| Own Fumbles Recovered | 1 | 1 |
| Opponent Fumbles Recovered | 2 | 0 |
| Penalties | 2 | 7 |
| Yards Penalized | 20 | 53 |
| Total Points Scored | 14 | 30 |
| Touchdowns | 2 | 3 |
| Touchdowns Rushing | 0 | 2 |
| Touchdowns Passing | 2 | 1 |
| Touchdown Returns | 0 | 0 |
| Extra Points | 2 | 3 |
| Field Goals | 0 | 3 |
| Field Goals Attempted | 0 | 3 |
| 3rd Down Efficiency | 2/12 | 9/16 |
| 4th Down Efficiency | 1/2 | 0/1 |
| Time of Possession | 22:54 | 37:06 |

## INDIVIDUAL STATISTICS
### RUSHING

| Seattle | Att. | Yds. | LG | TD |
|---|---|---|---|---|
| Warner | 11 | 26 | 7 | 0 |
| Dixon | 3 | 24 | 10 | 0 |
| Hughes | 3 | 14 | 8 | 0 |
| C. Bryant | 1 | 1 | 1 | 0 |
| **Raiders** | **Att.** | **Yds.** | **LG** | **TD** |
| Allen | 25 | 154 | 43 | 0 |
| Plunkett | 7 | 26 | 10 | 0 |
| Hawkins | 10 | 24 | 8 | 2 |
| Pruitt | 1 | 4 | 4 | 0 |
| King | 2 | 0 | 0 | 0 |
| Wilson | 1 | −3 | −3 | 0 |

### PASSING

| Seattle | Att. | Comp. | Yds. | TD | Int. |
|---|---|---|---|---|---|
| Zorn | 27 | 14 | 134 | 2 | 2 |
| Krieg | 9 | 3 | 12 | 0 | 3 |
| **Raiders** | **Att.** | **Comp.** | **Yds.** | **TD** | **Int.** |
| Plunkett | 24 | 17 | 214 | 1 | 2 |

### RECEIVING

| Seattle | No. | Yds. | LG | TD |
|---|---|---|---|---|
| Doornink | 6 | 48 | 12 | 1 |
| Johns | 5 | 49 | 14 | 0 |
| Largent | 2 | 25 | 14 | 0 |
| Warner | 2 | 10 | 12 | 0 |
| Young | 1 | 9 | 9t | 1 |
| H. Jackson | 1 | 5 | 5 | 0 |
| **Raiders** | **No.** | **Yds.** | **LG** | **TD** |
| Allen | 7 | 62 | 16 | 1 |
| Barnwell | 5 | 116 | 49 | 0 |
| Christensen | 3 | 14 | 6 | 0 |
| Branch | 2 | 22 | 11 | 0 |

### INTERCEPTIONS

| Seattle | No. | Yds. | LG | TD |
|---|---|---|---|---|
| Scholtz | 1 | 8 | 8 | 0 |
| G. Johnson | 1 | 0 | 0 | 0 |
| **Raiders** | **No.** | **Yds.** | **LG** | **TD** |
| M. Davis | 2 | 2 | 2 | 0 |
| Hayes | 1 | 44 | 44 | 0 |
| Millen | 1 | 13 | 13 | 0 |
| McElroy | 1 | −6 | −6 | 0 |

# NFC Championship Game
Includes NFL Championship Games (1933-69)

## RESULTS

| Season | Date | Winner (Share) | Loser (Share) | Score | Site | Attendance |
|---|---|---|---|---|---|---|
| 1983 | Jan. 8 | Washington ($18.000) | San Francisco ($18.000) | 24-21 | Washington | 55.363 |
| 1982 | Jan. 22 | Washington ($18.000) | Dallas ($18.000) | 31-17 | Washington | 55.045 |
| 1981 | Jan. 10 | San Francisco ($9.000) | Dallas ($9.000) | 28-27 | San Francisco | 60.525 |
| 1980 | Jan. 11 | Philadelphia ($9.000) | Dallas ($9.000) | 20-7 | Philadelphia | 71.522 |
| 1979 | Jan. 6 | Los Angeles ($9.000) | Tampa Bay ($9.000) | 9-0 | Tampa Bay | 72.033 |
| 1978 | Jan. 7 | Dallas ($9.000) | Los Angeles ($9.000) | 28-0 | Los Angeles | 71.086 |
| 1977 | Jan. 1 | Dallas ($9.000) | Minnesota ($9.000) | 23-6 | Dallas | 64.293 |
| 1976 | Dec. 26 | Minnesota ($8.500) | Los Angeles ($5.500) | 24-13 | Minnesota | 48.379 |
| 1975 | Jan. 4 | Dallas ($8.500) | Los Angeles ($5.500) | 37-7 | Los Angeles | 88.919 |
| 1974 | Dec. 29 | Minnesota ($8.500) | Los Angeles ($5.500) | 14-10 | Minnesota | 48.444 |
| 1973 | Dec. 30 | Minnesota ($8.500) | Dallas ($5.500) | 27-10 | Dallas | 64.422 |
| 1972 | Dec. 31 | Washington ($8.500) | Dallas ($5.500) | 26-3 | Washington | 53.129 |
| 1971 | Jan. 2 | Dallas ($8.500) | San Francisco ($5.500) | 14-3 | Dallas | 63.409 |
| 1970 | Jan. 3 | Dallas ($8.500) | San Francisco ($5.500) | 17-10 | San Francisco | 59.364 |
| 1969 | Jan. 4 | Minnesota ($7.930) | Cleveland ($5.118) | 27-7 | Minnesota | 46.503 |
| 1968 | Dec. 29 | Baltimore ($9.306) | Cleveland ($5.963) | 34-0 | Cleveland | 78.410 |
| 1967 | Dec. 31 | Green Bay ($7.950) | Dallas ($5.299) | 21-17 | Green Bay | 50.861 |
| 1966 | Jan. 1 | Green Bay ($9.813) | Dallas ($6.527) | 34-27 | Dallas | 74.152 |
| 1965 | Jan. 2 | Green Bay ($7.819) | Cleveland ($5.288) | 23-12 | Green Bay | 50.777 |
| 1964 | Dec. 27 | Cleveland ($8.052) | Baltimore ($5.571) | 27-0 | Cleveland | 79.544 |
| 1963 | Dec. 29 | Chicago ($5.899) | New York ($4.218) | 14-10 | Chicago | 45.801 |
| 1962 | Dec. 30 | Green Bay ($5.888) | New York ($4.166) | 16-7 | New York | 64.892 |
| 1961 | Dec. 31 | Green Bay ($5.195) | New York ($3.339) | 37-0 | Green Bay | 39.029 |
| 1960 | Dec. 26 | Philadelphia ($5.116) | Green Bay ($3.105) | 17-13 | Philadelphia | 67.325 |
| 1959 | Dec. 27 | Baltimore ($4.674) | New York ($3.083) | 31-16 | Baltimore | 57.545 |
| 1958 | Dec. 28 | Baltimore ($4.718) | New York ($3.111) | 23-17* | New York | 64.185 |
| 1957 | Dec. 29 | Detroit ($4.295) | Cleveland ($2.750) | 59-14 | Detroit | 55.263 |
| 1956 | Dec. 30 | New York ($3.779) | Chi. Bears ($2.485) | 47-7 | New York | 56.836 |
| 1955 | Dec. 26 | Cleveland ($3.508) | Los Angeles ($2.316) | 38-14 | Los Angeles | 85.693 |
| 1954 | Dec. 26 | Cleveland ($2.478) | Detroit ($1.585) | 56-10 | Cleveland | 43.827 |
| 1953 | Dec. 27 | Detroit ($2.424) | Cleveland ($1.654) | 17-16 | Detroit | 54.577 |
| 1952 | Dec. 28 | Detroit ($2.274) | Cleveland ($1.712) | 17-7 | Cleveland | 50.934 |
| 1951 | Dec. 23 | Los Angeles ($2.108) | Cleveland ($1.483) | 24-17 | Los Angeles | 57.522 |
| 1950 | Dec. 24 | Cleveland ($1.113) | Los Angeles ($686) | 30-28 | Cleveland | 29.751 |
| 1949 | Dec. 18 | Philadelphia ($1.094) | Los Angeles ($739) | 14-0 | Los Angeles | 27.980 |
| 1948 | Dec. 19 | Philadelphia ($1.540) | Chi. Cardinals ($874) | 7-0 | Philadelphia | 36.309 |
| 1947 | Dec. 28 | Chi. Cardinals ($1.132) | Philadelphia ($754) | 28-21 | Chicago | 30.759 |
| 1946 | Dec. 15 | Chi. Bears ($1.975) | New York ($1.295) | 24-14 | New York | 58.346 |
| 1945 | Dec. 16 | Cleveland ($1.469) | Washington ($902) | 15-14 | Cleveland | 32.178 |
| 1944 | Dec. 17 | Green Bay ($1.449) | New York ($814) | 14-7 | New York | 46.016 |
| 1943 | Dec. 26 | Chi. Bears ($1.146) | Washington ($765) | 41-21 | Chicago | 34.320 |
| 1942 | Dec. 13 | Washington ($965) | Chi. Bears ($637) | 14-6 | Washington | 36.006 |
| 1941 | Dec. 21 | Chi. Bears ($430) | New York ($288) | 37-9 | Chicago | 13.341 |
| 1940 | Dec. 8 | Chi. Bears ($873) | Washington ($606) | 73-0 | Washington | 36.034 |
| 1939 | Dec. 10 | Green Bay ($703.97) | New York ($455.57) | 27-0 | Milwaukee | 32.279 |
| 1938 | Dec. 11 | New York ($504.45) | Green Bay ($368.81) | 23-17 | New York | 48.120 |
| 1937 | Dec. 12 | Washington ($225.90) | Chi. Bears ($127.78) | 28-21 | Chicago | 15.870 |
| 1936 | Dec. 13 | Green Bay ($250) | Boston ($180) | 21-6 | New York | 29.545 |
| 1935 | Dec. 15 | Detroit ($313.35) | New York ($200.20) | 26-7 | Detroit | 15.000 |
| 1934 | Dec. 9 | New York ($621) | Chi. Bears ($414.02) | 30-13 | New York | 35.059 |
| 1933 | Dec. 17 | Chi. Bears ($210.34) | New York ($140.22) | 23-21 | Chicago | 26.000 |

*Sudden death overtime.

## NFC CHAMPIONSHIP GAME COMPOSITE STANDINGS

| | W | L | Pct. | Pts. | OP |
|---|---|---|---|---|---|
| Green Bay Packers | 8 | 2 | .800 | 223 | 116 |
| Detroit Lions | 4 | 1 | .800 | 129 | 100 |
| Minnesota Vikings | 4 | 1 | .800 | 98 | 63 |
| Philadelphia Eagles | 4 | 1 | .800 | 79 | 48 |
| Baltimore Colts | 3 | 1 | .750 | 88 | 60 |
| Chicago Bears | 6 | 4 | .600 | 259 | 194 |
| Washington Redskins* | 5 | 4 | .556 | 164 | 218 |
| St. Louis Cardinals** | 1 | 1 | .500 | 28 | 28 |
| Dallas Cowboys | 5 | 7 | .417 | 227 | 213 |
| Cleveland Browns | 4 | 7 | .364 | 224 | 253 |
| Los Angeles Rams*** | 3 | 7 | .300 | 120 | 216 |
| San Francisco 49ers | 1 | 3 | .250 | 62 | 82 |
| New York Giants | 3 | 11 | .214 | 208 | 309 |
| Tampa Bay Buccaneers | 0 | 1 | .000 | 0 | 9 |

*One game played when franchise was in Boston. (Lost 21-6)
**Both games played when franchise was in Chicago. (Won 28-21, lost 7-0)
***One game played when franchise was in Cleveland. (Won 15-14)

## 1983 NATIONAL FOOTBALL CONFERENCE CHAMPIONSHIP GAME

Robert F. Kennedy Stadium, Washington, D.C.  January 8, 1984
Attendance: 55,363

**WASHINGTON 24, SAN FRANCISCO 21** — The Washington Redskins gained their second consecutive NFC title and Super Bowl trip by defeating NFC West champion San Francisco 24-21. After a scoreless first quarter, the Redskins drove 64 yards in five plays to take a 7-0 lead on running back John Riggins' four-yard run. Riggins, who carried 36 times for 123 yards (his sixth straight 100-yard playoff game), raised Washington's lead to 14-0 on a one-yard run with 3:45 remaining in the third period. After the 49ers punted, the Redskins took over on their own 20-yard line. Following a 10-yard gain by Riggins, quarterback Joe Theismann completed a 70-yard touchdown pass to wide receiver Charlie Brown with 1:02 remaining in the third period. The 49ers scored in the fourth period by completing a nine-play, 79-yard touchdown drive with a five-yard touchdown pass from quarterback Joe Montana to wide receiver Mike Wilson. With 9:58 remaining, Montana completed a 76-yard touchdown pass to wide receiver Freddie Solomon to narrow the Redskins' lead to 21-14. After holding Washington on four downs, San Francisco tied the game on a four-play, 53-yard drive ending in a 12-yard touchdown catch by Wilson from Montana. The Redskins got the ball back with 6:52 remaining in the game on their own 14-yard line. They drove to the 49ers' 8-yard line in 13 plays and Mark Moseley kicked the decisive 25-yard field goal with 40 seconds left.

| San Francisco (21) | Offense | Washington (24) |
|---|---|---|
| Mike Wilson | WR | Charlie Brown |
| Bubba Paris | LT | Joe Jacoby |
| John Ayers | LG | Russ Grimm |
| Fred Quillan | C | Jeff Bostic |
| Randy Cross | RG | Mark May |
| Keith Fahnhorst | RT | George Starke |
| Russ Francis | TE | Don Warren |
| Freddie Solomon | WR | Art Monk |
| Joe Montana | QB | Joe Theismann |
| Roger Craig | RB | John Riggins |
| Wendell Tyler | RB-TE | Rick Walker |
| | **Defense** | |
| Lawrence Pillers | LE | Todd Liebenstein |
| Pete Kugler | NT-LT | Dave Butz |
| Dwaine Board | RE-RT | Darryl Grant |
| Willie Harper | LOLB-RE | Dexter Manley |
| Riki Ellison | LILB-LLB | Mel Kaufman |
| Jack Reynolds | RILB-MLB | Neal Olkewicz |
| Keena Turner | ROLB-RLB | Rich Milot |
| Ronnie Lott | LCB | Darrell Green |
| Eric Wright | RCB | Anthony Washington |
| Carlton Williamson | SS | Ken Coffey |
| Dwight Hicks | FS | Mark Murphy |

## SUBSTITUTIONS

**San Francisco**—Offense: K—Ray Wersching. P—Tom Orosz. RB—Carl Monroe, Jeff Moore, Bill Ring. TE—Earl Cooper, Eason Ramson. WR—Renaldo Nehemiah. T—Allan Kennedy. G—Walt Downing. C—Jesse Sapolu. Defense: E—Fred Dean, Jeff Stover, Jim Stuckey. LB—Dan Bunz, Ron Ferrari, Bobby Leopold, Gary Moten. CB—Richard Blackmore, Tim Collier, Dana McLemore. S—Tom Holmoe. DNP—Guy Benjamin (QB), Matt Cavanaugh (QB), Darius Durham (WR), Chris Lindstrom (T), Milt McColl (LB).

**Washington**—Offense: K—Mark Moseley. P—Jeff Hayes. RB—Reggie Evans, Nick Giaquinto, Joe Washington, Otis Wonsley. TE—Clint Didier. WR—Alvin Garrett. G—Bruce Kimball, Roy Simmons. Defense: E—Charles Mann, Tony McGee. T—Perry Brooks. LB—Stuart Anderson, Monte Coleman, Peter Cronan, Larry Kubin. CB—Brian Carpenter, Vernon Dean. S—Curtis Jordan, Greg Williams. DNP—Bob Holly (QB), Ken Huff (G), Babe Laufenberg (QB), Mark McGrath (WR), Virgil Seay (WR), Mike Williams (TE).

## OFFICIALS

Referee—Jerry Markbreit. Umpire—Tom Hensley. Head Linesman—Burl Toler. Line Judge—Walt Peters. Back Judge—Tom Kelleher. Side Judge—Dave Hawk. Field Judge—Ed Merrifield.

## SCORING

| | | | | | |
|---|---|---|---|---|---|
| **San Francisco** | 0 | 0 | 0 | 21 | — 21 |
| **Washington** | 0 | 7 | 14 | 3 | — 24 |

Wash—Riggins 4 run (Moseley kick)
Wash—Riggins 1 run (Moseley kick)
Wash—Brown 70 pass from Theismann (Moseley kick)
SF   —Wilson 5 pass from Montana (Wersching kick)
SF   —Solomon 76 pass from Montana (Wersching kick)
SF   —Wilson 12 pass from Montana (Wersching kick)
Wash—FG Moseley 25

## TEAM STATISTICS

| | San Francisco | Washington |
|---|---|---|
| Total First Downs | 19 | 24 |
| First Downs Rushing | 3 | 11 |
| First Downs Passing | 16 | 10 |
| First Downs Penalty | 0 | 3 |
| Total Net Yardage | 434 | 410 |
| Total Offensive Plays | 64 | 75 |
| Average Gain per Offensive Play | 6.6 | 5.5 |
| Rushes | 16 | 45 |
| Yards Gained Rushing (net) | 87 | 172 |
| Average Yards per Rush | 5.4 | 3.8 |
| Passes Attempted | 48 | 27 |
| Passes Completed | 27 | 15 |
| Had Intercepted | 1 | 1 |
| Times Tackled Attempting to Pass | 0 | 3 |
| Yards Lost Attempting to Pass | 0 | 27 |
| Yards Gained Passing (net) | 347 | 238 |
| Punts | 7 | 5 |
| Average Distance | 33.5 | 40.2 |
| Punt Returns | 2 | 4 |
| Punt Return Yardage | 7 | 31 |
| Kickoff Returns | 5 | 4 |
| Kickoff Return Yardage | 98 | 48 |
| Interception Return Yardage | 0 | 5 |
| Total Return Yardage | 105 | 84 |
| Fumbles | 4 | 2 |
| Own Fumbles Recovered | 2 | 1 |
| Opponents Fumbles Recovered | 1 | 2 |
| Penalties | 6 | 4 |
| Yards Penalized | 72 | 35 |
| Total Points Scored | 21 | 24 |
| Touchdowns | 3 | 3 |
| Touchdowns Rushing | 0 | 2 |
| Touchdowns Passing | 3 | 1 |
| Touchdown Returns | 0 | 0 |
| Extra Points | 3 | 3 |
| Field Goals | 0 | 1 |
| Field Goals Attempted | 2 | 5 |
| 3rd Down Efficiency | 3/13 | 5/16 |
| 4th Down Efficiency | 0/0 | 1/1 |
| Time of Possession | 21.53 | 38.07 |

## INDIVIDUAL STATISTICS

### RUSHING

| San Fran. | Att. | Yds. | LG | TD |
|---|---|---|---|---|
| Tyler | 8 | 44 | 10 | 0 |
| Montana | 5 | 40 | 18 | 0 |
| Craig | 3 | 3 | 2 | 0 |
| **Washington** | **Att.** | **Yds.** | **LG** | **TD** |
| Riggins | 36 | 123 | 23 | 2 |
| J.Washington | 6 | 23 | 8 | 0 |
| Hayes | 1 | 14 | 14 | 0 |
| Theismann | 2 | 12 | 6 | 0 |

### PASSING

| San Fran. | Att. | Comp. | Yds. | TD | Int. |
|---|---|---|---|---|---|
| Montana | 48 | 27 | 347 | 3 | 1 |
| **Wash.** | **Att.** | **Comp.** | **Yds.** | **TD** | **Int.** |
| Theismann | 26 | 14 | 229 | 1 | 1 |
| Riggins | 1 | 1 | 36 | 0 | 0 |

### RECEIVING

| San Francisco | No. | Yds. | LG | TD |
|---|---|---|---|---|
| Wilson | 8 | 57 | 22 | 2 |
| Solomon | 4 | 106 | 76t | 1 |
| Francis | 4 | 48 | 13 | 0 |
| Ramson | 3 | 47 | 23 | 0 |
| Nehemiah | 3 | 46 | 21 | 0 |
| Craig | 3 | 15 | 13 | 0 |
| Tyler | 1 | 17 | 17 | 0 |
| Cooper | 1 | 11 | 11 | 0 |
| **Washington** | **No.** | **Yds.** | **LG** | **TD** |
| Brown | 5 | 137 | 70t | 1 |
| Didier | 3 | 61 | 46 | 0 |
| Monk | 3 | 35 | 13 | 0 |
| J. Washington | 3 | 21 | 9 | 0 |
| Walker | 1 | 11 | 11 | 0 |

### INTERCEPTIONS

| San Francisco | No. | Yds. | LG | TD |
|---|---|---|---|---|
| Wright | 1 | 0 | 0 | 0 |
| **Washington** | **No.** | **Yds.** | **LG** | **TD** |
| Dean | 1 | 5 | 5 | 0 |

## AFC Divisional Playoffs

Includes Second-Round Playoff Games (1982), AFL Inter-Divisional Playoff Games (1969), and special playoff games to break ties for AFL Division Championships (1963, 1968)

### RESULTS

| Season | Date | Winner | Loser | Site | Attendance |
|---|---|---|---|---|---|
| 1983 | Jan. 1 | L.A. Raiders 38 | Pittsburgh 10 | Los Angeles | 90,380 |
| | Dec. 31 | Seattle 27 | Miami 20 | Miami | 74,136 |
| 1982 | Jan. 16 | Miami 34 | San Diego 13 | Miami | 71,383 |
| | Jan. 15 | N.Y. Jets 17 | L.A. Raiders 14 | Los Angeles | 90,038 |
| 1981 | Jan. 3 | Cincinnati 28 | Buffalo 21 | Cincinnati | 55,420 |
| | Jan. 2 | *San Diego 41 | Miami 38 | Miami | 73,735 |
| 1980 | Jan. 4 | Oakland 14 | Cleveland 12 | Cleveland | 78,245 |
| | Jan. 3 | San Diego 20 | Buffalo 14 | San Diego | 52,253 |
| 1979 | Dec. 30 | Pittsburgh 34 | Miami 14 | Pittsburgh | 50,214 |
| | Dec. 29 | Houston 17 | San Diego 14 | San Diego | 51,192 |
| 1978 | Dec. 31 | Houston 31 | New England 14 | New England | 60,735 |
| | Dec. 30 | Pittsburgh 33 | Denver 10 | Pittsburgh | 50,230 |
| 1977 | Dec. 24 | *Oakland 37 | Baltimore 31 | Baltimore | 59,925 |
| | Dec. 24 | Denver 34 | Pittsburgh 21 | Denver | 75,059 |
| 1976 | Dec. 19 | Pittsburgh 40 | Baltimore 14 | Baltimore | 59,296 |
| | Dec. 18 | Oakland 24 | New England 21 | Oakland | 53,050 |
| 1975 | Dec. 28 | Oakland 31 | Cincinnati 28 | Oakland | 53,030 |
| | Dec. 27 | Pittsburgh 28 | Baltimore 10 | Pittsburgh | 49,557 |
| 1974 | Dec. 22 | Pittsburgh 32 | Buffalo 14 | Pittsburgh | 49,841 |
| | Dec. 21 | Oakland 28 | Miami 26 | Oakland | 53,023 |
| 1973 | Dec. 23 | Miami 34 | Cincinnati 16 | Miami | 78,928 |
| | Dec. 22 | Oakland 33 | Pittsburgh 14 | Oakland | 52,646 |
| 1972 | Dec. 24 | Miami 20 | Cleveland 14 | Miami | 78,916 |
| | Dec. 23 | Pittsburgh 13 | Oakland 7 | Pittsburgh | 50,327 |
| 1971 | Dec. 26 | Baltimore 20 | Cleveland 3 | Cleveland | 70,734 |
| | Dec. 25 | *Miami 27 | Kansas City 24 | Kansas City | 45,822 |
| 1970 | Dec. 27 | Oakland 21 | Miami 14 | Oakland | 52,594 |
| | Dec. 26 | Baltimore 17 | Cincinnati 0 | Baltimore | 49,694 |
| 1969 | Dec. 21 | Oakland 56 | Houston 7 | Oakland | 53,539 |
| | Dec. 20 | Kansas City 13 | N.Y. Jets 6 | New York | 62,977 |
| 1968 | Dec. 22 | Oakland 41 | Kansas City 6 | Oakland | 53,605 |
| 1963 | Dec. 28 | Boston 26 | Buffalo 8 | Buffalo | 33,044 |

*Sudden death overtime.

### 1983 AFC DIVISIONAL PLAYOFFS

Orange Bowl, Miami, Florida — December 31, 1983
Attendance: 74,136

**SEATTLE 27, MIAMI 20**—Running back Curt Warner's two-yard scoring run with 1:48 remaining clinched the Seahawks' playoff victory over the Dolphins. Warner's touchdown came at the end of a 66-yard, five-play drive, that included a 40-yard pass from quarterback Dave Krieg to wide receiver Steve Largent. Kicker Norm Johnson added a 37-yard field goal 33 seconds later after Miami's Fulton Walker fumbled the ensuing kickoff. The Dolphins led 13-7, but four Miami turn-overs in the second half led to their downfall. Warner rushed for 113 yards on 29 carries to lead the Seahawks. Krieg completed 15 of 28 passes for 192 yards and had one touchdown with one interception. Miami quarterback Dan Marino completed 15 of 25 for 193 yards and threw two touchdowns with two interceptions. Dolphins wide receiver Mark Duper had nine catches for 117 yards.

| Seattle | 0 | 7 | 7 | 13 | — | 27 |
|---|---|---|---|---|---|---|
| Miami | 0 | 13 | 0 | 7 | — | 20 |

Mia—Johnson 19 pass from Marino (kick failed)
Sea—C. Bryant 6 pass from Krieg (N. Johnson kick)
Mia—Duper 32 pass from Marino (von Schamann kick)
Sea—Warner 1 run (N. Johnson kick)
Sea—FG N. Johnson 27
Mia—Bennett 3 run (von Schmann kick)
Sea—Warner 2 run (N. Johnson kick)
Sea—FG N. Johnson 37

Memorial Coliseum, Los Angeles, California — January 1, 1984
Attendance: 90,380

**LOS ANGELES RAIDERS 38, PITTSBURGH 10**—A 21-point outburst by the Raiders in the third period put the game out of reach and the Raiders into the AFC Championship Game against the Seattle Seahawks. The Raiders' three touchdowns in the third period came on runs of 9 yards by Kenny King, 49 by Marcus Allen, and 2 by Frank Hawkins. Quarterback Jim Plunkett directed the Raiders' offense to 413 total yards, consisting of 188 on the ground and 225 in the air. Plunkett completed 21 of 34 for 232 yards. Allen rushed 13 times for 121 yards. Tight end Todd Christensen had seven receptions for 88 yards. The Raiders recorded five sacks, including two-and-a-half by defensive end Lyle Alzado.

| Pittsburgh | 3 | 0 | 7 | 0 | — | 10 |
|---|---|---|---|---|---|---|
| L.A. Raiders | 7 | 10 | 21 | 0 | — | 38 |

Pitt—FG Anderson 17
Raiders—Hayes 18 interception return (Bahr kick)
Raiders—Allen 4 run (Bahr kick)
Raiders—FG Bahr 45
Raiders—King 9 run (Bahr kick)
Raiders—Allen 49 run (Bahr kick)
Pitt—Stallworth 58 pass from Stoudt (Anderson kick)
Raiders—Hawkins 2 run (Bahr kick)

## NFC Divisional Playoffs

Includes Second-Round Playoff Games (1982), NFL Conference Championship Games (1967-69), and special playoff games to break ties for NFL Division or Conference Championships (1941, 1943, 1947, 1950, 1952, 1957, 1958, 1965)

### RESULTS

| Season | Date | Winner | Loser | Site | Attendance |
|---|---|---|---|---|---|
| 1983 | Jan.1 | Washington 51 | L.A. Rams 7 | Washington | 54,440 |
| | Dec. 31 | San Francisco 24 | Detroit 23 | San Francisco | 59,979 |
| 1982 | Jan. 16 | Dallas 37 | Green Bay 26 | Dallas | 63,972 |
| | Jan. 15 | Washington 21 | Minnesota 7 | Washington | 54,593 |
| 1981 | Jan. 3 | San Francisco 38 | N.Y. Giants 24 | San Francisco | 58,360 |
| | Jan. 2 | Dallas 38 | Tampa Bay 0 | Dallas | 64,848 |
| 1980 | Jan. 4 | Dallas 30 | Atlanta 27 | Atlanta | 59,793 |
| | Jan. 3 | Philadelphia 31 | Minnesota 16 | Philadelphia | 70,178 |
| 1979 | Dec. 30 | Los Angeles 21 | Dallas 19 | Dallas | 64,792 |
| | Dec. 29 | Tampa Bay 24 | Philadelphia 17 | Tampa Bay | 71,402 |
| 1978 | Dec. 31 | Los Angeles 34 | Minnesota 10 | Los Angeles | 70,436 |
| | Dec. 30 | Dallas 27 | Atlanta 20 | Dallas | 63,406 |
| 1977 | Dec. 26 | Dallas 37 | Chicago 7 | Dallas | 63,260 |
| | Dec. 26 | Minnesota 14 | Los Angeles 7 | Los Angeles | 70,203 |
| 1976 | Dec. 19 | Los Angeles 14 | Dallas 12 | Dallas | 63,283 |
| | Dec. 18 | Minnesota 35 | Washington 20 | Minnesota | 47,466 |
| 1975 | Dec. 28 | Dallas 17 | Minnesota 14 | Minnesota | 48,050 |
| | Dec. 27 | Los Angeles 35 | St. Louis 23 | Los Angeles | 73,459 |
| 1974 | Dec. 22 | Los Angeles 19 | Washington 10 | Los Angeles | 77,925 |
| | Dec. 21 | Minnesota 30 | St. Louis 14 | Minnesota | 48,150 |
| 1973 | Dec. 23 | Dallas 27 | Los Angeles 16 | Dallas | 63,272 |
| | Dec. 22 | Minnesota 27 | Washington 20 | Minnesota | 48,040 |
| 1972 | Dec. 24 | Washington 16 | Green Bay 3 | Washington | 52,321 |
| | Dec. 23 | Dallas 30 | San Francisco 28 | San Francisco | 59,746 |
| 1971 | Dec. 26 | San Francisco 24 | Washington 20 | San Francisco | 45,327 |
| | Dec. 25 | Dallas 20 | Minnesota 12 | Minnesota | 47,307 |
| 1970 | Dec. 27 | San Francisco 17 | Minnesota 14 | Minnesota | 45,103 |
| | Dec. 26 | Dallas 5 | Detroit 0 | Dallas | 69,613 |
| 1969 | Dec. 28 | Cleveland 38 | Dallas 14 | Dallas | 69,321 |
| | Dec. 27 | Minnesota 23 | Los Angeles 20 | Minnesota | 47,900 |
| 1968 | Dec. 22 | Baltimore 24 | Minnesota 14 | Baltimore | 60,238 |
| | Dec. 21 | Cleveland 31 | Dallas 20 | Cleveland | 81,497 |
| 1967 | Dec. 24 | Dallas 52 | Cleveland 14 | Dallas | 70,786 |
| | Dec. 23 | Green Bay 28 | Los Angeles 7 | Milwaukee | 49,861 |
| 1965 | Dec. 26 | *Green Bay 13 | Baltimore 10 | Green Bay | 50,484 |
| 1958 | Dec. 21 | N.Y. Giants 10 | Cleveland 0 | New York | 61,274 |
| 1957 | Dec. 22 | Detroit 31 | San Francisco 27 | San Francisco | 60,118 |
| 1952 | Dec. 21 | Detroit 31 | Los Angeles 21 | Detroit | 47,645 |
| 1950 | Dec. 17 | Los Angeles 24 | Chi. Bears 14 | Los Angeles | 83,501 |
| | Dec. 17 | Cleveland 8 | N.Y. Giants 3 | Cleveland | 33,054 |
| 1947 | Dec. 21 | Philadelphia 21 | Pittsburgh 0 | Pittsburgh | 35,729 |
| 1943 | Dec. 19 | Washington 28 | N.Y. Giants 10 | New York | 42,800 |
| 1941 | Dec. 14 | Chi. Bears 33 | Green Bay 14 | Chicago | 43,425 |

*Sudden death overtime.

### 1983 NFC DIVISIONAL PLAYOFFS

Candlestick Park, San Francisco, California — December 31, 1983
Attendance: 59,979

**SAN FRANCISCO 24, DETROIT 23**—The NFC West champion 49ers gained their second NFC Championship Game berth in the last three seasons with a 24-23 win over Detroit. San Francisco took a 7-3 first-period lead on running back Roger Craig's one-yard run. The Lions' Eddie Murray kicked his third field goal of the first half (54 yards) to narrow the 49ers' halftime edge to 14-9. Ray Wersching's 19-yard field goal was the only scoring in the third period. Detroit running back Billy Sims, who rushed 20 times for 114 yards, scored with 13:32 remaining in the game on an 11-yard run and again with 4:54 left on a three-yard run to give the Lions a 23-17 advantage. San Francisco then drove 70 yards in nine plays for the game-winning score on a 13-yard pass from quarterback Joe Montana (18 of 33 for 201 yards, one touchdown, one interception) to wide receiver Freddie Solomon. The Lions then drove into position for the possible winning field goal of 43 yards but Murray's try was wide right.

| Detroit | 3 | 6 | 0 | 14 | — | 23 |
|---|---|---|---|---|---|---|
| San Francisco | 7 | 7 | 3 | 7 | — | 24 |

Det—FG Murray 37
SF—Craig 1 run (Wersching kick)
SF—Tyler 2 run (Wersching kick)
Det—FG Murray 21
Det—FG Murray 54
SF—FG Wersching 19
Det—Sims 11 run (Murray kick)
Det—Sims 3 run (Murray kick)
SF—Solomon 14 pass from Montana (Wersching kick)

Robert F. Kennedy Stadium, Washington, D.C. — January 1, 1984
Attendance: 54,440

**WASHINGTON 51, LOS ANGELES RAMS 7**—Running back John Riggins rushed 25 times for 119 yards and three touchdowns (his fifth straight 100-yard rushing effort in postseason play) in leading the NFC East champion Redskins to a 51-7 win over the Los Angeles Rams. Riggins' three-yard scoring run 6:11 into the first period completed an eight-play, 65-yard opening drive for the Redskins. Quarterback Joe Theismann completed 18 of 23 for 302 yards, including 40- and 21-yard touchdowns to wide receiver Art Monk. Wide receiver Charlie Brown caught six passes for 171 yards. Washington built a 24-0 lead before Los Angeles scored on a 32-yard touchdown catch by wide receiver Preston Dennard. The Redskins' 38 first-half points set an NFL playoff record. Rookie cornerback Darrell Green completed Washington's scoring with a 72-yard interception return for a touchdown with 50 seconds gone in the fourth period. Mark Moseley made 42-, 36-, and 41-yard field goals to finish out the Redskins' scoring.

| | | | | | |
|---|---|---|---|---|---|
| **L.A. Rams** | 0 | 7 | 0 | 0 — | 7 |
| **Washington** | 17 | 21 | 6 | 7 — | 51 |

Wash— Riggins 3 run (Moseley kick)
Wash— Monk 40 pass from Theismann (Moseley kick)
Wash— FG Moseley 42
Wash— Riggins 1 run (Moseley kick)
Rams— Dennard 32 pass from Ferragamo (Lansford kick)
Wash— Monk 21 pass from Theismann (Moseley kick)
Wash— Riggins 1 run (Moseley kick)
Wash— FG Moseley 36
Wash— FG Moseley 41
Wash— Green 72 interception return (Moseley kick)

# AFC First-Round Playoff Games
## RESULTS

| Season | Date | Winner | Loser | Site | Attendance |
|---|---|---|---|---|---|
| 1983 | Dec. 24 | Seattle 31 | Denver 7 | Seattle | 64,275 |
| 1982 | Jan. 9 | N.Y. Jets 44 | Cincinnati 17 | Cincinnati | 57,560 |
| | Jan. 9 | San Diego 31 | Pittsburgh 28 | Pittsburgh | 53,546 |
| | Jan. 8 | L.A. Raiders 27 | Cleveland 10 | Los Angeles | 56,555 |
| | Jan. 8 | Miami 28 | New England 13 | Miami | 68,842 |
| 1981 | Dec. 27 | Buffalo 31 | N.Y. Jets 27 | New York | 57,050 |
| 1980 | Dec. 28 | Oakland 27 | Houston 7 | Oakland | 53,333 |
| 1979 | Dec. 23 | Houston 13 | Denver 7 | Houston | 48,776 |
| 1978 | Dec. 24 | Houston 17 | Miami 9 | Miami | 72,445 |

### 1983 AFC FIRST-ROUND PLAYOFF GAME

Kingdome, Seattle, Washington                    December 24, 1983
Attendance: 64,275

**SEATTLE 31, DENVER 7**—Quarterback Dave Krieg and running back Curt Warner provided the offensive spark that carried Seattle to victory in the first playoff game in the Seahawks' eight-year history. Krieg completed 12 of 13 passes for 200 yards, including his last 10 in a row. Warner rushed 23 times for 99 yards. On its first possession of the third period, Seattle drove 73 yards in five plays for a touchdown that gave the Seahawks a 17-7 lead. The score came on a five-yard pass from Krieg to tight end Pete Metzelaars. Seattle put the game out of reach early in the final period when Krieg hit wide receiver Paul Johns with an 18-yard touchdown pass.

| | | | | | |
|---|---|---|---|---|---|
| **Denver** | 7 | 0 | 0 | 0 — | 7 |
| **Seattle** | 7 | 3 | 7 | 14 — | 31 |

Sea —Largent 17 pass from Krieg (N. Johnson kick)
Den —Myles 13 pass from DeBerg (Karlis kick)
Sea —FG N. Johnson 37
Sea —Metzelaars 5 pass from Krieg (N. Johnson kick)
Sea —Johns 18 pass from Krieg (N. Johnson kick)
Sea —Hughes 2 run (N. Johnson kick)

# NFC First-Round Playoff Games
## RESULTS

| Season | Date | Winner | Loser | Site | Attendance |
|---|---|---|---|---|---|
| 1983 | Dec. 26 | L.A. Rams 24 | Dallas 17 | Dallas | 62,118 |
| 1982 | Jan. 9 | Dallas 30 | Tampa Bay 17 | Dallas | 65,042 |
| | Jan. 9 | Minnesota 30 | Atlanta 24 | Minnesota | 60,560 |
| | Jan. 8 | Green Bay 41 | St. Louis 16 | Green Bay | 54,282 |
| | Jan. 8 | Washington 31 | Detroit 7 | Washington | 55,045 |
| 1981 | Dec. 27 | N.Y. Giants 27 | Philadelphia 21 | Philadelphia | 71,611 |
| 1980 | Dec. 28 | Dallas 34 | Los Angeles 13 | Dallas | 63,052 |
| 1979 | Dec. 23 | Philadelphia 27 | Chicago 17 | Philadelphia | 69,397 |
| 1978 | Dec. 24 | Atlanta 14 | Philadelphia 13 | Atlanta | 59,403 |

### 1983 NFC FIRST-ROUND PLAYOFF GAME

Texas Stadium, Irving, Texas                    December 26, 1983
Attendance: 62,118

**LOS ANGELES RAMS 24, DALLAS 17**—The Rams, under first-year head coach John Robinson, advanced to the NFC divisional playoffs with a 24-17 victory over Dallas. Rams rookie running back Eric Dickerson rushed 23 times for 99 yards and quarterback Vince Ferragamo completed 15 of 30 passes for 162 yards and three touchdowns to lead the victory. The Los Angeles defense also contributed interceptions by Mel Owens, Jim Collins, and LeRoy Irvin. George Farmer paced the Rams' receivers with five catches for 47 yards, including an eight-yard touchdown. Cowboys' quarterback Danny White completed 32 of 53 passes for 330 yards and two touchdowns, but threw three interceptions. Receiver Tony Hill caught nine passes for 115 yards, including a 14-yard touchdown in the second period.

| | | | | | |
|---|---|---|---|---|---|
| **L.A. Rams** | 7 | 0 | 7 | 10 — | 24 |
| **Dallas** | 0 | 7 | 3 | 7 — | 17 |

Rams—D. Hill 18 pass from Ferragamo (Lansford kick)
Dall —T. Hill 14 pass from D. White (Septien kick)
Dall —FG Septien 41
Rams—Dennard 16 pass from Ferragamo (Lansford kick)
Rams—Farmer 8 pass from Ferragamo (Lansford kick)
Rams—FG Lansford 20
Dall —Cosbie 2 pass from D. White (Septien kick)

## RESULTS

NFC leads series, 9-5

| Year | Date | Winner | Loser | Site | Attendance |
|------|------|--------|-------|------|-----------|
| 1984 | Jan. 29 | NFC 45 | AFC 3 | Honolulu | 50,445 |
| 1983 | Feb. 6 | NFC 20 | AFC 19 | Honolulu | 47,201 |
| 1982 | Jan. 31 | AFC 16 | NFC 13 | Honolulu | 49,521 |
| 1981 | Feb. 1 | NFC 21 | AFC 7 | Honolulu | 47,879 |
| 1980 | Jan. 27 | NFC 37 | AFC 27 | Honolulu | 48,060 |
| 1979 | Jan. 29 | NFC 13 | AFC 7 | Los Angeles | 46,281 |
| 1978 | Jan. 23 | NFC 14 | AFC 13 | Tampa | 51,337 |
| 1977 | Jan. 17 | AFC 24 | NFC 14 | Seattle | 64,151 |
| 1976 | Jan. 26 | NFC 23 | AFC 20 | New Orleans | 30,546 |
| 1975 | Jan. 20 | NFC 17 | AFC 10 | Miami | 26,484 |
| 1974 | Jan. 20 | AFC 15 | NFC 13 | Kansas City | 66,918 |
| 1973 | Jan. 21 | AFC 33 | NFC 28 | Dallas | 37,091 |
| 1972 | Jan. 23 | AFC 26 | NFC 13 | Los Angeles | 53,647 |
| 1971 | Jan. 24 | NFC 27 | AFC 6 | Los Angeles | 48,222 |

## 1984 AFC-NFC PRO BOWL

Aloha Stadium, Honolulu, Hawaii  January 29, 1984
Attendance: 50,445

**NFC 45, AFC 3**—The NFC won its sixth Pro Bowl in the last seven seasons, 45-3 over the AFC behind the passing of most valuable player Joe Theismann of Washington, who completed 21 of 27 for 242 yards and three touchdowns. Theismann set Pro Bowl records for completions and touchdown passes. The NFC established Pro Bowl marks for most points scored and fewest points allowed. Running back William Andrews of Atlanta had six carries for 43 yards and caught four passes for 49 yards, including scoring receptions of 16 and 2 yards. Los Angeles Rams rookie Eric Dickerson gained 46 yards on 11 carries, including a 14-yard touchdown run, and had 45 yards on five catches. Rams safety Nolan Cromwell had a 44-yard interception return for a touchdown 1:39 into the third period to give the NFC a commanding 24-3 lead. Green Bay wide receiver James Lofton caught an eight-yard touchdown pass, while tight end teammate Paul Coffman had a six-yard scoring catch.

| NFC (45) | Offense | AFC (3) |
|----------|---------|---------|
| James Lofton (Green Bay) | WR | Carlos Carson (Kansas City) |
| Mike Kenn (Atlanta) | LT | Anthony Muñoz (Cincinnati) |
| Kent Hill (L.A. Rams) | LG | Chris Hinton (Baltimore) |
| Jeff Bostic (Washington) | C | Dwight Stephenson (Miami) |
| Russ Grimm (Washington) | RG | Ed Newman (Miami) |
| Joe Jacoby (Washington) | RT | Brian Holloway (New England) |
| Paul Coffman (Green Bay) | TE | Todd Christensen (L.A. Raiders) |
| Mike Quick (Philadelphia) | WR | Cris Collinsworth (Cincinnati) |
| Joe Theismann (Washington) | QB | Dan Fouts (San Diego) |
| Eric Dickerson (L.A. Rams) | RB | Curt Warner (Seattle) |
| William Andrews (Atlanta) | RB | Earl Campbell (Houston) |
| | **Defense** | |
| Ed Jones (Dallas) | LE | Doug Betters (Miami) |
| Doug English (Detroit) | LT | Fred Smerlas (Buffalo) |
| Randy White (Dallas) | RT | Bob Baumhower (Miami) |
| Lee Roy Selmon (Tampa Bay) | RE | Howie Long (L.A. Raiders) |
| Hugh Green (Tampa Bay) | LLB | Chip Banks (Cleveland) |
| Mike Singletary (Chicago) | MLB | Jack Lambert (Pittsburgh) |
| Lawrence Taylor (N.Y. Giants) | RLB | Rod Martin (L.A. Raiders) |
| Ronnie Lott (San Francisco) | LCB | Lester Hayes (L.A. Raiders) |
| Everson Walls (Dallas) | RCB | Gary Green (Kansas City) |
| Nolan Cromwell (L.A. Rams) | SS | Kenny Easley (Seattle) |
| Mark Murphy (Washington) | FS | Deron Cherry (Kansas City) |

### HEAD COACHES

**NFC**—Bill Walsh (San Francisco)
**AFC**—Chuck Knox (Seattle)

### SUBSTITUTIONS

**NFC**—Offense: K—Ali Haji-Sheikh (N.Y. Giants). P—Carl Birdsong (St. Louis). QB—Joe Montana (San Francisco). RB—Tony Dorsett (Dallas), Walter Payton (Chicago). TE—Doug Cosbie (Dallas). WR—Charlie Brown (Washington), Roy Green (St. Louis). KR—Billy Johnson (Atlanta). C—Larry McCarren (Green Bay). T—Jackie Slater (L.A. Rams). G—R.C. Theielmann (Atlanta). Defense: E—William Gay (Detroit). T—Dave Butz (Washington). OLB—Rickey Jackson (New Orleans). MLB—Harry Carson (N.Y. Giants). CB—Mark Haynes (N.Y. Giants). S—Dwight Hicks (San Francisco).
**AFC**—Offense: K—Gary Anderson (Pittsburgh). P—Rich Camarillo (New England). QB—Bill Kenney (Kansas City). RB—Tony Collins (New England). Joe Cribbs (Buffalo). TE—Kellen Winslow (San Diego). WR—Wes Chandler (San Diego), Mark Duper (Miami). KR—Greg Pruitt (L.A. Raiders). C—Mike Webster (Pittsburgh). T—Henry Lawrence (L.A. Raiders). G—Bob Kuechenberg (Miami). Defense: E—Mark Gastineau (N.Y. Jets). T—Joe Klecko (N.Y. Jets). OLB—Ted Hendricks (L.A. Raiders). MLB—Randy Gradishar (Denver). CB—Ray Clayborn (New England). S—Vann McElroy (L.A. Raiders).

### OFFICIALS

Referee: Jerry Seeman. Umpire: Frank Sinkovitz. Head Linesman: Tony Veteri. Line Judge: Dale Orem. Back Judge: Al Jury. Field Judge: Bill O'Brien. Side Judge: Gerald Austin.

### SCORING

| | | | | | |
|---|---|---|---|---|---|
| NFC | 3 | 14 | 14 | 14 — | 45 |
| AFC | 0 | 3 | 0 | 0 — | 3 |

NFC—FG Haji-Sheikh 23
NFC—Andrews 16 pass from Theismann (Haji-Sheikh kick)
NFC—Andrews 2 pass from Montana (Haji-Sheikh kick)
AFC—FG Anderson 43
NFC—Cromwell 44 interception return (Haji-Sheikh kick)
NFC—Lofton 8 pass from Theismann (Haji-Sheikh kick)
NFC—Coffman 6 pass from Theismann (Haji-Sheikh kick)
NFC—Dickerson 14 run (Haji-Sheikh kick)

### TEAM STATISTICS

| | NFC | AFC |
|---|-----|-----|
| Total First Downs | 26 | 15 |
| First Downs Rushing | 10 | 6 |
| First Downs Passing | 14 | 9 |
| First Downs Penalty | 2 | 0 |
| Total Net Yardage | 423 | 209 |
| Total Offensive Plays | 77 | 67 |
| Average Gain per Offensive Play | 5.5 | 3.1 |
| Rushes | 36 | 18 |
| Net Yards Gained Rushing | 164 | 78 |
| Average Yards per Rush | 4.6 | 4.3 |
| Passes Attempted | 38 | 41 |
| Passes Completed | 28 | 14 |
| Net Yards Gained Passing | 259 | 131 |
| Times Tackled Attempting to Pass | 3 | 8 |
| Yards Lost Attempting to Pass | 28 | 52 |
| Had Intercepted | 1 | 3 |
| Punts | 2 | 4 |
| Average Distance per Punt | 42.5 | 40.3 |
| Punt Returns | 3 | 0 |
| Punt Return Yardage | 16 | 0 |
| Kickoff Returns | 1 | 7 |
| Kickoff Return Yardage | 29 | 215 |
| Interception Return Yardage | 63 | 3 |
| Fumbles | 2 | 3 |
| Own Fumbles Recovered | 1 | 1 |
| Opponent Fumbles Recovered | 2 | 1 |
| Penalties | 3 | 4 |
| Yards Penalized | 20 | 30 |
| Total Points Scored | 45 | 3 |
| Touchdowns | 6 | 0 |
| Touchdowns Rushing | 1 | 0 |
| Touchdowns Passing | 4 | 0 |
| Touchdowns Returns | 1 | 0 |
| Extra Points | 6 | 0 |
| Field Goals | 1 | 1 |
| Field Goals Attempted | 1 | 2 |
| Safeties | 0 | 0 |
| Third Down Efficiency | 6/12 | 3/14 |
| Fourth Down Efficiency | 2/4 | 1/3 |
| Time of Possession | 35:34 | 24:26 |

### INDIVIDUAL STATISTICS

**RUSHING**

| NFC | Att. | Yds. | LG | TD |
|-----|------|------|----|----|
| Dickerson | 11 | 46 | 14t | 1 |
| Andrews | 6 | 43 | 19 | 0 |
| Payton | 11 | 40 | 9 | 0 |
| Dorsett | 5 | 17 | 10 | 0 |
| Theismann | 1 | 12 | 12 | 0 |
| Montana | 2 | 6 | 6 | 0 |

| AFC | Att. | Yds. | LG | TD |
|-----|------|------|----|----|
| Cribbs | 4 | 32 | 12 | 0 |
| Collins | 3 | 25 | 13 | 0 |
| Warner | 4 | 12 | 6 | 0 |
| Campbell | 5 | 9 | 7 | 0 |
| Camarillo | 1 | 0 | 0 | 0 |
| Fouts | 1 | 0 | 0 | 0 |

| | No. | Yds. | LG | TD |
|--|-----|------|----|----|
| Coffman | 5 | 37 | 10 | 1 |
| Andrews | 4 | 49 | 22 | 2 |
| Payton | 3 | 11 | 5 | 0 |
| Brown | 2 | 26 | 14 | 0 |
| Lofton | 2 | 23 | 15 | 1 |
| R. Green | 2 | 21 | 12 | 0 |
| Cosbie | 2 | 19 | 11 | 0 |
| Dorsett | 2 | 5 | 4 | 0 |
| Quick | 1 | 51 | 51 | 0 |

| AFC | No. | Yds. | LG | TD |
|-----|-----|------|----|----|
| Collinsworth | 5 | 73 | 21 | 0 |
| Christensen | 2 | 18 | 13 | 0 |
| Cribbs | 2 | 10 | 5 | 0 |
| Chandler | 1 | 25 | 25 | 0 |
| Carson | 1 | 20 | 20 | 0 |
| Duper | 1 | 19 | 19 | 0 |
| Warner | 1 | 9 | 9 | 0 |
| Winslow | 1 | 9 | 9 | 0 |

**PASSING**

| NFC | Att. | Comp. | Yds. | TD | Int. |
|-----|------|-------|------|----|----|
| Theismann | 27 | 21 | 242 | 3 | 0 |
| Montana | 10 | 7 | 45 | 1 | 1 |
| Payton | 1 | 0 | 0 | 0 | 0 |

| AFC | Att. | Comp. | Yds. | TD | Int. |
|-----|------|-------|------|----|----|
| Fouts | 9 | 7 | 103 | 0 | 1 |
| Kenney | 32 | 7 | 80 | 0 | 2 |

**INTERCEPTIONS**

| NFC | No. | Yds. | LG | TD |
|-----|-----|------|----|----|
| Cromwell | 1 | 44 | 44t | 1 |
| Haynes | 1 | 22 | 22 | 0 |
| Hicks | 1 | −3 | −3 | 0 |

| AFC | No. | Yds. | LG | TD |
|-----|-----|------|----|----|
| Banks | 1 | 3 | 3 | 0 |

**RECEIVING**

| NFC | No. | Yds. | LG | TD |
|-----|-----|------|----|----|
| Dickerson | 5 | 45 | 15 | 0 |

## 1983 AFC-NFC PRO BOWL

Aloha Stadium, Honolulu, Hawaii      Sunday, February 6, 1983
Attendance: 47,201

**NFC 20, AFC 19**—Danny White threw an 11-yard touchdown pass to John Jefferson with 35 seconds remaining to give the NFC a 20-19 victory over the AFC. White, who completed 14 of 26 passes for 162 yards, kept the winning 65-yard drive alive with a 14-yard completion to Jefferson on a fourth-and-seven play at the AFC 25. The AFC was ahead 12-10 at halftime and increased the lead to 19-10, in the third period when Marcus Allen scored on a one-yard run. Dan Fouts, who attempted 30 passes, set Pro Bowl records for most completions (17) and yards (274). John Stallworth was the AFC's leading receiver with seven catches for 67 yards. William Andrews topped the NFC with five receptions for 48 yards. Fouts and Jefferson were voted co-winners of the player of the game award.

| | | | | | |
|---|---|---|---|---|---|
| **AFC** | 9 | 3 | 7 | 0 | — 19 |
| **NFC** | 0 | 10 | 0 | 10 | — 20 |

AFC—Walker 34 pass from Fouts (Benirschke kick)
AFC—Safety, Still tackled Theismann in end zone
NFC—Andrews 3 run (Moseley kick)
NFC—FG Moseley 35
AFC—FG Benirschke 29
AFC—Allen 1 run (Benirschke kick)
NFC—FG Moseley 41
NFC—Jefferson 11 pass from D. White (Moseley kick)

## 1982 AFC-NFC PRO BOWL

Aloha Stadium, Honolulu, Hawaii      Sunday, January 31, 1982
Attendance: 50,402

**AFC 16, NFC 13**—Nick Lowery kicked a 23-yard field goal with three seconds remaining to give the AFC a 16-13 victory over the NFC. Lowery's kick climaxed a 69-yard drive directed by quarterback Dan Fouts. The NFC gained a 13-13 tie with 2:43 to go when Tony Dorsett ran four yards for a touchdown. In the drive to the game-winning field goal, Fouts completed three passes, including a 23-yarder to San Diego teammate Kellen Winslow that put the ball on the NFC's 5 yard line. Two plays later, Lowery kicked the field goal. Winslow, who caught six passes for 86 yards, was named co-player of the game along with NFC defensive end Lee Roy Selmon.

| | | | | | |
|---|---|---|---|---|---|
| **NFC** | 0 | 6 | 0 | 7 | — 13 |
| **AFC** | 0 | 0 | 13 | 3 | — 16 |

NFC—Giles 4 pass from Montana (kick blocked)
AFC—Muncie 2 run (kick failed)
AFC—Campbell 1 run (Lowery kick)
NFC—Dorsett 4 run (Septien kick)
AFC—FG Lowery 23

## 1981 AFC-NFC PRO BOWL

Aloha Stadium, Honolulu, Hawaii      February 1, 1981
Attendance: 47,879

**NFC 21, AFC 7**—Ed Murray kicked four field goals and Steve Bartkowski fired a 55-yard scoring pass to Alfred Jenkins to lead the NFC to its fourth straight victory over the AFC and a 7-4 edge in the series. Murray was named the game's most valuable player and missed tying Garo Yepremian's Pro Bowl record of five goals when a 37-yard attempt hit the crossbar with 22 seconds remaining. The AFC's only score came on a nine-yard pass from Brian Sipe to Stanley Morgan in the second period. Bartkowski completed 9 of 21 for 173 yards, while Sipe connected on 10 of 15 for 142 yards. Ottis Anderson led all rushers with 70 yards on 10 carries. Earl Campbell, the NFL's leading rusher in 1980, was limited to 24 yards on eight attempts.

| | | | | | |
|---|---|---|---|---|---|
| **AFC** | 0 | 7 | 0 | 0 | — 7 |
| **NFC** | 3 | 6 | 0 | 12 | — 21 |

NFC—FG Murray 31
AFC—Morgan 9 pass from Sipe (J. Smith kick)
NFC—FG Murray 31
NFC—FG Murray 34
NFC—Jenkins 55 pass from Bartkowski (Murray kick)
NFC—FG Murray 36
NFC—Safety (Team)

## 1980 AFC-NFC PRO BOWL

Aloha Stadium, Honolulu, Hawaii      January 27, 1980
Attendance: 48,060

**NFC 37, AFC 27**—Running back Chuck Muncie ran for two touchdowns and threw a 25-yard option pass for another score to give the NFC its third consecutive victory over the AFC. Muncie, who was selected the game's most valuable player, snapped a 3-3 tie on a one-yard touchdown run at 1:41 of the second quarter, then scored on an 11-yard run in the fourth quarter for the NFC's final touchdown. Two scoring records were set in the game—37 points by the NFC, eclipsing the 33 by the AFC in 1973, and the 64 points by both teams, surpassing the 61 scored in 1973.

| | | | | | |
|---|---|---|---|---|---|
| **NFC** | 3 | 20 | 7 | 7 | — 37 |
| **AFC** | 3 | 7 | 10 | 7 | — 27 |

NFC—FG Moseley 37
AFC—FG Fritsch 19
NFC—Muncie 1 run (Moseley kick)
AFC—Pruitt 1 pass from Bradshaw (Fritsch kick)
NFC—D. Hill 13 pass from Manning (kick failed)
NFC—T. Hill 25 pass from Muncie (Moseley kick)
NFC—Henry 86 punt return (Moseley kick)
AFC—Campbell 2 run (Fritsch kick)
AFC—FG Fritsch 29
NFC—Muncie 11 run (Moseley kick)
AFC—Campbell 1 run (Fritsch kick)

## 1979 AFC-NFC PRO BOWL

Memorial Coliseum, Los Angeles, California      January 29, 1979
Attendance: 46,281

**NFC 13, AFC 7**—Roger Staubach completed 9 of 15 passes for 125 yards, including the winning touchdown on a 19-yard strike to Dallas Cowboys teammate Tony Hill in the third period. The winning drive began at the AFC's 45 yard line after a shanked punt. Staubach hit Ahmad Rashad with passes of 15 and 17 yards to set up Hill's decisive catch. The victory gave the NFC a 5-4 advantage in Pro Bowl games. Rashad, who accounted for 89 yards on five receptions, was named the player of the game. The AFC led 7-6 at halftime on Bob Griese's eight-yard scoring toss to Steve Largent late in the second quarter. Largent finished the game with five receptions for 75 yards. The NFC scored first as Archie Manning marched his team 70 yards in 11 plays, capped by Wilbert Montgomery's two-yard touchdown run. The AFC's Earl Campbell was the game's leading rusher with 66 yards on 12 carries.

| | | | | | |
|---|---|---|---|---|---|
| **AFC** | 0 | 7 | 0 | 0 | — 7 |
| **NFC** | 0 | 6 | 7 | 0 | — 13 |

NFC—Montgomery 2 run (kick failed)
AFC—Largent 8 pass from Griese (Yepremian kick)
NFC—T. Hill 19 pass from Staubach (Corral kick)

## 1978 AFC-NFC PRO BOWL

Tampa Stadium, Tampa, Florida      January 23, 1978
Attendance: 51,337

**NFC 14, AFC 13**—Walter Payton, the NFL's leading rusher in 1977, sparked a second half comeback to give the NFC a 14-13 win and tie the series between the two conferences at four victories each. Payton, who was the game's most valuable player, gained 77 yards on 13 carries and scored the tying touchdown on a one-yard burst with 7:37 left in the game. Efren Herrera kicked the winning extra point. The AFC dominated the first half of the game, taking a 13-0 lead on field goals of 21 and 39 yards by Toni Linhart and a 10-yard touchdown pass from Ken Stabler to Oakland teammate Cliff Branch. On the NFC's first possession of the second half, Pat Haden put together the first touchdown drive after Eddie Brown returned Ray Guy's punt to the AFC 46 yard line. Haden connected on all four of his passes on that drive, finally hitting Terry Metcalf with a four-yard scoring toss. The NFC continued to rally and, with Jim Hart at quarterback, moved 63 yards in 12 plays for the go-ahead score. During the winning drive Hart completed five of six passes for 38 yards and Payton picked up 20 more on the ground.

| | | | | | |
|---|---|---|---|---|---|
| **AFC** | 3 | 10 | 0 | 0 | — 13 |
| **NFC** | 0 | 0 | 7 | 7 | — 14 |

AFC—FG Linhart 21
AFC—Branch 10 pass from Stabler (Linhart kick)
AFC—FG Linhart 39
NFC—Metcalf 4 pass from Haden (Herrera kick)
NFC—Payton 1 run (Herrera kick)

## 1977 AFC-NFC PRO BOWL

Kingdome, Seattle, Washington      January 17, 1977
Attendance: 64,752

**AFC 24, NFC 14**—O. J. Simpson's three-yard touchdown burst at 7:03 of the first quarter gave the AFC a lead it would not surrender, the victory breaking a two-game NFC win streak and giving the American Conference stars a 4-3 series lead. The AFC took a 17-7 lead midway through the second period on the first of two Ken Anderson touchdown passes, a 12-yarder to Charlie Joiner. But the NFC mounted a 73-yard scoring drive capped by Lawrence McCutcheon's one-yard touchdown plunge to pull within three of the AFC, 17-14, at the half. Following a scoreless third quarter, player of the game Mel Blount thwarted a possible NFC score when he intercepted Jim Hart's pass in the end zone. Less than three minutes later, Blount again picked off a Hart pass, returning it 16 yards to the NFC 27. That set up Anderson's 27-yard touchdown strike to Cliff Branch for the final score.

| | | | | |
|---|---|---|---|---|
| NFC | 0 | 14 | 0 | 0 — 14 |
| AFC | 10 | 7 | 0 | 7 — 24 |

AFC—Simpson 3 run (Linhart kick)
AFC—FG Linhart 31
NFC—Thomas 15 run (Bakken kick)
AFC—Joiner 12 pass from Anderson (Linhart kick)
NFC—McCutcheon 1 run (Bakken kick)
AFC—Branch 27 pass from Anderson (Linhart kick)

## 1976 AFC-NFC PRO BOWL

Superdome, New Orleans, Louisiana      January 26, 1976
Attendance: 30,546

**NFC 23, AFC 20**—Mike Boryla, a late substitute who did not enter the game until 5:39 remained, lifted the National Football Conference to a 23-20 victory over the American Football Conference with two touchdown passes in the final minutes. It was the second straight NFC win, squaring the series at 3-3. Until Boryla started firing the ball the AFC was in control, leading 13-0 at the half. Boryla entered the game after Billy Johnson had raced 90 yards with a punt to make the score 20-9 in favor of the AFC. He floated a 14-yard pass to Terry Metcalf and later fired an eight-yarder to Mel Gray for the winner.

| | | | | |
|---|---|---|---|---|
| AFC | 0 | 13 | 0 | 7 — 20 |
| NFC | 0 | 0 | 9 | 14 — 23 |

AFC—FG Stenerud 20
AFC—FG Stenerud 35
AFC—Burrough 64 pass from Pastorini (Stenerud kick)
NFC—FG Bakken 42
NFC—Foreman 4 pass from Hart (kick blocked)
AFC—Johnson 90 punt return (Stenerud kick)
NFC—Metcalf 14 pass from Boryla (Bakken kick)
NFC—Gray 8 pass from Boryla (Bakken kick)

## 1975 AFC-NFC PRO BOWL

Orange Bowl, Miami, Florida      January 20, 1975
Attendance: 26,484

**NFC 17, AFC 10**—Los Angeles quarterback James Harris, who took over the NFC offense after Jim Hart of St. Louis suffered a laceration above his right eye in the second period, threw a pair of touchdown passes early in the fourth period to pace the NFC to its second victory in the five-game Pro Bowl series. The NFC win snapped a three-game AFC victory string. Harris, who was named the player of the game, connected with St. Louis's Mel Gray for an eight-yard touchdown 2:03 into the final period. One minute and 24 seconds later, following a recovery by Washington's Ken Houston of a fumble by Franco Harris of Pittsburgh, Harris tossed another eight-yard scoring pass to Washington's Charley Taylor for the decisive points.

| | | | | |
|---|---|---|---|---|
| NFC | 0 | 3 | 0 | 14 — 17 |
| AFC | 0 | 0 | 10 | 0 — 10 |

NFC—FG Marcol 33
AFC—Warfield 32 pass from Griese (Gerela kick)
AFC—FG Gerela 33
NFC—Gray 8 pass from J. Harris (Marcol kick)
NFC—Taylor 8 pass from J. Harris (Marcol kick)

## 1974 AFC-NFC PRO BOWL

Arrowhead, Kansas City, Missouri      January 20, 1974
Attendance: 66,918

**AFC 15, NFC 13**—Miami's Garo Yepremian kicked his fifth consecutive field goal without a miss from the 42 yard line with 21 seconds remaining to give the AFC its third straight victory since the NFC won the inaugural game following the 1970 season. The field goal by Yepremian, who was voted the game's outstanding player, offset a 21-yard field goal by Atlanta's Nick Mike-Mayer that had given the NFC a 13-12 advantage with 1:41 remaining. The only touchdown in the game was scored by the NFC on a 14-yard pass from Roman Gabriel to Lawrence McCutcheon.

| | | | | |
|---|---|---|---|---|
| NFC | 0 | 10 | 0 | 3 — 13 |
| AFC | 3 | 3 | 3 | 6 — 15 |

AFC—FG Yepremian 16
NFC—FG Mike-Mayer 27
NFC—McCutcheon 14 pass from Gabriel (Mike-Mayer kick)
AFC—FG Yepremian 37
AFC—FG Yepremian 27
AFC—FG Yepremian 41
NFC—FG Mike-Mayer 21
AFC—FG Yepremian 42

## 1973 AFC-NFC PRO BOWL

Texas Stadium, Irving, Texas      January 21, 1973
Attendance: 37,091

**AFC 33, NFC 28**—Paced by the rushing and receiving of player of the game O.J. Simpson, the AFC erased a 14-0 first period deficit and built a commanding 33-14 lead midway through the fourth period before the NFC managed two touchdowns in the final minute of play. Simpson rushed for 112 yards and caught three passes for 58 more to gain unanimous recognition in the balloting for player of the game. John Brockington scored three touchdowns for the NFC.

| | | | | |
|---|---|---|---|---|
| AFC | 0 | 10 | 10 | 13 — 33 |
| NFC | 14 | 0 | 0 | 14 — 28 |

NFC—Brockington 1 run (Marcol kick)
NFC—Brockington 3 pass from Kilmer (Marcol kick)
AFC—Simpson 7 run (Gerela kick)
AFC—FG Gerela 18
AFC—FG Gerela 22
AFC—Hubbard 11 run (Gerela kick)
AFC—O. Taylor 5 pass from Lamonica (kick failed)
AFC—Bell 12 interception return (Gerela kick)
NFC—Brockington 1 run (Marcol kick)
NFC—Kwalick 12 pass from Snead (Marcol kick)

## 1972 AFC-NFC PRO BOWL

Memorial Coliseum, Los Angeles, California      January 23, 1972
Attendance: 53,647

**AFC 26, NFC 13**—Four field goals by Jan Stenerud of Kansas City, including a 6-6 tie-breaker from 48 yards, helped lift the AFC from a 6-0 deficit to a 19-6 advantage early in the fourth period. The AFC defense picked off three interceptions. Stenerud was selected as the outstanding offensive player and his Kansas City teammate, linebacker Willie Lanier, was the game's outstanding defensive player.

| | | | | |
|---|---|---|---|---|
| AFC | 0 | 3 | 13 | 10 — 26 |
| NFC | 0 | 6 | 0 | 7 — 13 |

NFC—Grim 50 pass from Landry (kick failed)
AFC—FG Stenerud 25
AFC—FG Stenerud 23
AFC—FG Stenerud 48
AFC—Morin 5 pass from Dawson (Stenerud kick)
AFC—FG Stenerud 42
NFC—V. Washington 2 run (Knight kick)
AFC—F. Little 6 run (Stenerud kick)

## 1971 AFC-NFC PRO BOWL

Memorial Coliseum, Los Angeles, California      January 24, 1971
Attendance: 48,222

**NFC 27, AFC 6**—Mel Renfro of Dallas broke open the first meeting between the American Football Conference and National Football Conference all-pro teams as he returned a pair of punts 82 and 56 yards for touchdowns in the final period to provide the NFC with a 26-6 victory over the AFC. Renfro was voted the game's outstanding back and linebacker Fred Carr of Green Bay the outstanding lineman.

| | | | | |
|---|---|---|---|---|
| AFC | 0 | 3 | 3 | 0 — 6 |
| NFC | 0 | 3 | 10 | 14 — 27 |

AFC—FG Stenerud 37
NFC—FG Cox 13
NFC—Osborn 23 pass from Brodie (Cox kick)
NFC—FG Cox 35
AFC—FG Stenerud 16
NFC—Renfro 82 punt return (Cox kick)
NFC—Renfro 56 punt return (Cox kick)

# Monday Night Football, 1970–1983

(Home Team in capitals, games listed in chronological order.)

## 1983
Dallas 31, WASHINGTON 30
San Diego 17, KANSAS CITY 14
LOS ANGELES RAIDERS 27, Miami 14
NEW YORK GIANTS 27, Green Bay 3
New York Jets 34, BUFFALO 10
Pittsburgh 24, CINCINNATI 14
GREEN BAY 48, Washington 47
ST. LOUIS 20, New York Giants 20 (OT)
Washington 27, SAN DIEGO 24
DETROIT 15, New York Giants 9
Los Angeles Rams 36, ATLANTA 13
New York Jets 31, NEW ORLEANS 28
MIAMI 38, Cincinnati 14
DETROIT 13, Minnesota 2
Green Bay 12, TAMPA BAY 9 (OT)
SAN FRANCISCO 42, Dallas 17

## 1982
Pittsburgh 36, DALLAS 28
Green Bay 27, NEW YORK GIANTS 19
LOS ANGELES RAIDERS 28, San Diego 24
TAMPA BAY 23, Miami 17
New York Jets 28, DETROIT 13
Dallas 37, HOUSTON 7
SAN DIEGO 50, Cincinnati 34
MIAMI 27, Buffalo 10
MINNESOTA 31, Dallas 27

## 1981
San Diego 44, CLEVELAND 14
Oakland 36, MINNESOTA 10
Dallas 35, NEW ENGLAND 21
Los Angeles 24, CHICAGO 7
PHILADELPHIA 16, Atlanta 13
BUFFALO 31, Miami 21
DETROIT 48, Chicago 17
PITTSBURGH 26, Houston 13
DENVER 19, Minnesota 17
DALLAS 27, Buffalo 14
SEATTLE 44, San Diego 23
ATLANTA 31, Minnesota 30
MIAMI 13, Philadelphia 10
OAKLAND 30, Pittsburgh 27
LOS ANGELES 21, Atlanta 16
SAN DIEGO 23, Oakland 10

## 1980
Dallas 17, WASHINGTON 3
Houston 16, CLEVELAND 7
PHILADELPHIA 35, New York Giants 3
NEW ENGLAND 23, Denver 14
CHICAGO 23, Tampa Bay 0
DENVER 20, Washington 17
Oakland 45, PITTSBURGH 34
NEW YORK JETS 17, Miami 14
CLEVELAND 27, Chicago 21
HOUSTON 38, New England 34
Oakland 19, SEATTLE 17
Los Angeles 27, NEW ORLEANS 7
OAKLAND 9, Denver 3
MIAMI 16, New England 13 (OT)
LOS ANGELES 38, Dallas 14
SAN DIEGO 26, Pittsburgh 17

## 1979
Pittsburgh 16, NEW ENGLAND 13 (OT)
Atlanta 14, PHILADELPHIA 10
WASHINGTON 27, New York Giants 0
CLEVELAND 26, Dallas 7
GREEN BAY 27, New England 14
OAKLAND 13, Miami 3
NEW YORK JETS 14, Minnesota 7
PITTSBURGH 42, Denver 7
Seattle 31, ATLANTA 28
Houston 9, MIAMI 6
Philadelphia 31, DALLAS 21
LOS ANGELES 20, Atlanta 14
SEATTLE 30, New York Jets 7
Oakland 42, NEW ORLEANS 35
HOUSTON 20, Pittsburgh 17
SAN DIEGO 17, Denver 7

## 1978
DALLAS 38, Baltimore 0
MINNESOTA 12, Denver 9 (OT)
Baltimore 34, NEW ENGLAND 27
Minnesota 24, CHICAGO 20
WASHINGTON 9, Dallas 5
MIAMI 21, Cincinnati 0
DENVER 16, Chicago 7
Houston 24, PITTSBURGH 17
ATLANTA 15, Los Angeles 7
BALTIMORE 21, Washington 17
Oakland 34, CINCINNATI 21
HOUSTON 35, Miami 30
Pittsburgh 24, SAN FRANCISCO 7
SAN DIEGO 40, Chicago 7
Cincinnati 20, LOS ANGELES 19
MIAMI 23, New England 3

## 1977
PITTSBURGH 27, San Francisco 0
CLEVELAND 30, New England 27 (OT)
Oakland 37, KANSAS CITY 28
CHICAGO 24, Los Angeles 23
PITTSBURGH 20, Cincinnati 14
LOS ANGELES 35, Minnesota 3
ST. LOUIS 28, New York Giants 0
BALTIMORE 10, Washington 3
St. Louis 24, DALLAS 17
WASHINGTON 10, Green Bay 9
OAKLAND 34, Buffalo 13
MIAMI 16, Baltimore 6
Dallas 42, SAN FRANCISCO 35

## 1976
Miami 30, BUFFALO 21
Oakland 24, KANSAS CITY 21
Washington 20, PHILADELPHIA 17 (OT)
MINNESOTA 17, Pittsburgh 6
San Francisco 16, LOS ANGELES 0
NEW ENGLAND 41, New York Jets 7
WASHINGTON 20, St. Louis 10
BALTIMORE 38, Houston 14
CINCINNATI 20, Los Angeles 12
DALLAS 17, Buffalo 10
Baltimore 17, MIAMI 16
SAN FRANCISCO 20, Minnesota 16
OAKLAND 35, Cincinnati 20

## 1975
Oakland 31, MIAMI 21
DENVER 23, Green Bay 13
Dallas 36, DETROIT 10
WASHINGTON 27, St. Louis 17
New York Giants 17, BUFFALO 14
Minnesota 13, CHICAGO 9
Los Angeles 42, PHILADELPHIA 3
Kansas City 34, DALLAS 31
CINCINNATI 33, Buffalo 24
Pittsburgh 32, HOUSTON 9
MIAMI 20, New England 7
OAKLAND 17, Denver 10
SAN DIEGO 24, New York Jets 16

## 1974
BUFFALO 21, Oakland 20
PHILADELPHIA 13, Dallas 10
WASHINGTON 30, Denver 3
MIAMI 21, New York Jets 17
DETROIT 17, San Francisco 13
CHICAGO 10, Green Bay 9
PITTSBURGH 24, Atlanta 17
Los Angeles 15, SAN FRANCISCO 13
Minnesota 28, ST. LOUIS 24
Kansas City 42, DENVER 34
Pittsburgh 28, NEW ORLEANS 7
MIAMI 24, Cincinnati 3
Washington 23, LOS ANGELES 17

## 1973
GREEN BAY 23, New York Jets 7
DALLAS 40, New Orleans 3
DETROIT 31, Atlanta 6
WASHINGTON 14, Dallas 7
Miami 17, CLEVELAND 9
DENVER 23, Oakland 23
BUFFALO 23, Kansas City 14
PITTSBURGH 21, Washington 16
KANSAS CITY 19, Chicago 7
ATLANTA 20, Minnesota 14
SAN FRANCISCO 20, Green Bay 6
MIAMI 30, Pittsburgh 26
LOS ANGELES 40, New York Giants 6

## 1972
Washington 24, MINNESOTA 21
Kansas City 20, NEW ORLEANS 17
New York Giants 27, PHILADELPHIA 12
Oakland 34, HOUSTON 0
Green Bay 24, DETROIT 23
CHICAGO 13, Minnesota 10
DALLAS 28, Detroit 24
Baltimore 24, NEW ENGLAND 17
Cleveland 21, SAN DIEGO 17
WASHINGTON 24, Atlanta 13
MIAMI 31, St. Louis 10
Los Angeles 26, SAN FRANCISCO 16
OAKLAND 24, New York Jets 16

## 1971
Minnesota 16, DETROIT 13
ST. LOUIS 17, New York Jets 10
Oakland 34, CLEVELAND 20
DALLAS 20, New York Giants 13
KANSAS CITY 38, Pittsburgh 16
MINNESOTA 10, Baltimore 3
GREEN BAY 14, Detroit 14
BALTIMORE 24, Los Angeles 17
SAN DIEGO 20, St. Louis 17
ATLANTA 28, Green Bay 21
MIAMI 34, Chicago 3
Kansas City 26, SAN FRANCISCO 17
Washington 38, LOS ANGELES 24

## 1970
CLEVELAND 31, New York Jets 21
Kansas City 44, BALTIMORE 24
DETROIT 28, Chicago 14
Green Bay 22, SAN DIEGO 20
OAKLAND 34, Washington 20
MINNESOTA 13, Los Angeles 3
PITTSBURGH 21, Cincinnati 10
Baltimore 13, GREEN BAY 10
St. Louis 38, DALLAS 0
PHILADELPHIA 23, New York Giants 20
Miami 20, ATLANTA 7
Cleveland 21, HOUSTON 10
Detroit 28, LOS ANGELES 23

## Monday Night Won-Loss Records, 1970-1983

| | Total | 1983 | 1982 | 1981 | 1980 | 1979 | 1978 | 1977 | 1976 | 1975 | 1974 | 1973 | 1972 | 1971 | 1970 |
|---|---|---|---|---|---|---|---|---|---|---|---|---|---|---|---|
| Baltimore | 8-4 | | | | | | 2-1 | 1-1 | 2-0 | | | | 1-0 | 1-1 | 1-1 |
| Buffalo | 3-8 | 0-1 | 0-1 | 1-1 | | | | 0-1 | 0-2 | 0-2 | 1-0 | 1-0 | | | |
| Cincinnati | 3-9 | 0-2 | 0-1 | | | | 1-2 | 0-1 | 1-1 | 1-0 | 0-1 | | | | 0-1 |
| Cleveland | 6-4 | | | 0-1 | 1-1 | 1-0 | | 1-0 | | | | 0-1 | 1-0 | 0-1 | 2-0 |
| Denver | 4-8-1 | | | 1-0 | 1-2 | 0-2 | 1-1 | | | 1-1 | 0-2 | 0-0-1 | | | |
| Houston | 6-6 | | 0-1 | 0-1 | 2-0 | 2-0 | 2-0 | | 0-1 | 0-1 | | | 0-1 | | 0-1 |
| Kansas City | 7-4 | 0-1 | | | | | | 0-1 | 0-1 | 1-0 | 1-0 | 1-1 | 1-0 | 2-0 | 1-0 |
| L.A. Raiders | 20-2-1 | 1-0 | 1-0 | 2-1 | 3-0 | 2-0 | 1-0 | 2-0 | 2-0 | 2-0 | 0-1 | 0-0-1 | 2-0 | 1-0 | 1-0 |
| Miami | 16-9 | 1-1 | 1-1 | 1-1 | 1-1 | 0-2 | 2-1 | 1-0 | 1-1 | 1-1 | 2-0 | 2-0 | 1-0 | 1-0 | 1-0 |
| New England | 2-10 | | | 0-1 | 1-2 | 0-2 | 0-2 | 0-1 | 1-0 | 0-1 | | | 0-1 | | |
| New York Jets | 5-8 | 2-0 | 1-0 | | 1-0 | 1-1 | | | | 0-1 | 0-1 | 0-1 | 0-1 | 0-1 | 0-1 |
| Pittsburgh | 13-8 | 1-0 | 1-0 | 1-1 | 0-2 | 2-1 | 1-1 | | 2-0 | 0-1 | 1-0 | 2-0 | | 0-1 | 1-0 |
| San Diego | 9-5 | 1-1 | 1-1 | 2-1 | 1-0 | 1-0 | 1-0 | | | 1-0 | | | 0-1 | 1-0 | 0-1 |
| Seattle | 3-1 | | | 1-0 | 0-1 | 2-0 | | | | | | | | | |
| Atlanta | 5-9 | 0-1 | | 1-2 | | 1-2 | 1-0 | | | | 0-1 | 1-1 | 0-1 | 1-0 | 0-1 |
| Chicago | 4-10 | | | 0-2 | 1-1 | | 0-3 | 1-0 | | 0-1 | 1-0 | 0-1 | 1-0 | 0-1 | 0-1 |
| Dallas | 12-12 | 1-1 | 1-2 | 2-0 | 1-1 | 0-2 | 1-1 | 1-1 | 1-0 | 1-1 | 0-1 | 1-1 | 1-0 | 1-0 | 0-1 |
| Detroit | 7-5-1 | 2-0 | 0-1 | 1-0 | | | | | | 0-1 | 1-0 | 1-0 | 0-2 | 0-1-1 | 2-0 |
| Green Bay | 7-7-1 | 2-1 | 1-0 | | | 1-0 | | 0-1 | | 0-1 | 0-1 | 1-1 | 1-0 | 0-1-1 | 1-1 |
| L.A. Rams | 11-10 | 1-0 | | 2-0 | 2-0 | 1-0 | 0-2 | 1-1 | 0-2 | 1-0 | 1-1 | 1-0 | 1-0 | 0-2 | 0-2 |
| Minnesota | 9-10 | 0-1 | 1-0 | 0-3 | | | 0-1 | 2-0 | 0-1 | 1-1 | 1-0 | 0-1 | 0-2 | 2-0 | 1-0 |
| New Orleans | 0-6 | 0-1 | | | 0-1 | 0-1 | | | | | | 0-1 | 0-1 | 0-1 | |
| New York Giants | 3-8-1 | 1-1-1 | 0-1 | | 0-1 | 0-1 | | 0-1 | | 1-0 | | 0-1 | 1-0 | 0-1 | 0-1 |
| Philadelphia | 5-5 | | | 1-1 | 1-0 | 1-1 | | | 0-1 | 0-1 | 1-0 | | 0-1 | | 1-0 |
| St. Louis | 4-5-1 | 0-0-1 | | | | | | 2-0 | 0-1 | 0-1 | 0-1 | | 0-1 | 1-1 | 1-0 |
| San Francisco | 4-7 | 1-0 | | | | 0-1 | | 0-2 | 2-0 | | | 0-2 | 1-0 | 0-1 | 0-1 |
| Tampa Bay | 1-2 | 0-1 | 1-0 | | 0-1 | | | | | | | | | | |
| Washington | 13-8 | 1-2 | | 0-2 | 1-0 | 1-1 | 1-1 | 2-0 | 1-0 | 2-0 | 1-0 | 2-0 | 1-1 | 2-0 | 1-0 |

## Monday Night Syndrome

**1983**

| Of the 14 winning teams: | 6 won the next week<br>8 lost the next week<br>0 tied the next week | Of the 30 NFL teams: | 15 won the next week<br>15 lost the next week<br>0 tied the next week |
|---|---|---|---|
| Of the 14 losing teams: | 8 won the next week<br>6 lost the next week<br>0 tied the next week | | |
| Of the 2 tying teams: | 1 won the next week<br>1 lost the next week<br>0 tied the next week | | |

**1970-83**

| Of the 184 winning teams: | 103 won the next week<br>78 lost the next week<br>3 tied the next week | Of the 374 NFL teams: | 203 won the next week<br>167 lost the next week<br>4 tied the next week |
|---|---|---|---|
| Of the 184 losing teams: | 95 won the next week<br>88 lost the next week<br>1 tied the next week | | |
| Of the 6 tying teams: | 5 won the next week<br>1 lost the next week<br>0 tied the next week | | |

## Thursday-Sunday Night Football, 1978-1983

(Home Team in capitals, games listed in chronological order.)

**1983**
San Francisco 48, MINNESOTA 17 (Thur.)
CLEVELAND 17, Cincinnati 7 (Thur.)
L.A. Raiders 40, DALLAS 38 (Sun.)
L.A. Raiders 42, SAN DIEGO 10 (Thur.)

**1982**
BUFFALO 23, Minnesota 22 (Thur.)
SAN FRANCISCO 30, L.A. Rams 24 (Thur.)
ATLANTA 17, San Francisco 7 (Sun.)

**1981**
MIAMI 30, Pittsburgh 10 (Thur.)
Philadelphia 20, BUFFALO 14 (Thur.)
DALLAS 29, Los Angeles 17 (Sun.)
HOUSTON 17, Cleveland 13 (Thur.)

**1980**
TAMPA BAY 10, Los Angeles 9 (Thur.)
DALLAS 42, San Diego 31 (Sun.)
San Diego 27, MIAMI 24 (OT) (Thur.)
HOUSTON 6, Pittsburgh 0 (Thur.)

**1979**
Los Angeles 13, DENVER 9 (Thur.)
DALLAS 30, Los Angeles 6 (Sun.)
OAKLAND 45, San Diego 22 (Thur.)
MIAMI 39, New England 24 (Thur.)

**1978**
New England 21, OAKLAND 14 (Sun.)
Minnesota 21, DALLAS 10 (Thur.)
LOS ANGELES 10, Pittsburgh 7 (Sun.)
Denver 21, OAKLAND 6 (Sun.)

## History of Overtime Games

### Preseason

| | |
|---|---|
| Aug. 28, 1955 | Los Angeles 23, New York Giants 17, at Portland, Oregon |
| Aug. 24, 1962 | Denver 27, Dallas Texans 24, at Fort Worth, Texas |
| Aug. 10, 1974 | San Diego 20, New York Jets 14, at San Diego |
| Aug. 17, 1974 | Pittsburgh 33, Philadelphia 30, at Philadelphia |
| Aug. 17, 1974 | Dallas 19, Houston 13, at Dallas |
| Aug. 17, 1974 | Cincinnati 13, Atlanta 7, at Atlanta |
| Sept. 6, 1974 | Buffalo 23, New York Giants 17, at Buffalo |
| Aug. 9, 1975 | Baltimore 23, Denver 20, at Denver |
| Aug. 30, 1975 | New England 20, Green Bay 17, at Milwaukee |
| Sept. 13, 1975 | Minnesota 14, San Diego 14, at San Diego |
| Aug. 1, 1976 | New England 13, New York Giants 7, at New England |
| Aug. 2, 1976 | Kansas City 9, Houston 3, at Kansas City |
| Aug. 20, 1976 | New Orleans 26, Baltimore 20, at Baltimore |
| Sept. 4, 1976 | Dallas 26, Houston 20, at Dallas |
| Aug. 13, 1977 | Seattle 23, Dallas 17, at Seattle |
| Aug. 28, 1977 | New England 13, Pittsburgh 10, at New England |
| Aug. 28, 1977 | New York Giants 24, Buffalo 21, at East Rutherford, N.J. |
| Aug. 2, 1979 | Seattle 12, Minnesota 9, at Minnesota |
| Aug. 4, 1979 | Los Angeles 20, Oakland 14, at Los Angeles |
| Aug. 24, 1979 | Denver 20, New England 17, at Denver |
| Aug. 23, 1980 | Tampa Bay 20, Cincinnati 14, at Tampa Bay |
| Aug. 5, 1981 | San Francisco 27, Seattle 24, at Seattle |
| Aug. 29, 1981 | New Orleans 20, Detroit 17, at New Orleans |
| Aug. 28, 1982 | Miami 17, Kansas City 17, at Kansas City |
| Sept. 3, 1982 | Miami 16, New York Giants 13, at Miami |
| Aug. 6, 1983 | L.A. Raiders 26, San Francisco 23, at Los Angeles |
| Aug. 6, 1983 | Atlanta 13, Washington 10, at Atlanta |
| Aug. 13, 1983 | St. Louis 27, Chicago 24, at St. Louis |
| Aug. 18, 1983 | New York Jets 20, Cincinnati 17, at Cincinnati |
| Aug. 27, 1983 | Chicago 20, Kansas City 17, at Chicago |

### Regular Season

**Sept. 22, 1974—Pittsburgh 35, Denver 35,** at Denver; Steelers win toss. Gilliam's pass intercepted and returned by Rowser to Denver's 42. Turner misses 41-yard field goal. Walden punts and Greer returns to Broncos' 39. Van Heusen punts and Edwards returns to Steelers' 16. Game ends with Steelers on own 26.

**Nov. 10, 1974—New York Jets 26, New York Giants 20,** at New Haven, Conn.; Giants win toss. Gogolak misses 42-yard field goal. Namath passes to Boozer for five yards and touchdown at 6:53.

**Sept. 28, 1975—Dallas 37, St. Louis 31,** at Dallas; Cardinals win toss. Hart's pass intercepted and returned by Jordan to Cardinals' 37. Staubach passes to DuPree for three yards and touchdown at 7:53.

**Oct. 12, 1975—Los Angeles 13, San Diego 10,** at San Diego; Chargers win toss. Partee punts to Rams' 14. Dempsey kicks 22-yard field goal at 9:27.

**Nov. 2, 1975—Washington 30, Dallas 24,** at Washington; Cowboys win toss. Staubach's pass intercepted and returned by Houston to Cowboys' 35. Kilmer runs one yard for touchdown at 6:34.

**Nov. 16, 1975—St. Louis 20, Washington 17,** at St. Louis; Cardinals win toss. Bakken kicks 37-yard field goal at 7:00.

**Nov. 23, 1975—Kansas City 24, Detroit 21,** at Kansas City; Lions win toss. Chiefs take over on downs at own 38. Stenerud kicks 26-yard field goal at 6:44.

**Nov. 23, 1975—Oakland 26, Washington 23,** at Washington; Redskins win toss. Bragg punts to Raiders' 42. Blanda kicks 27-yard field goal at 7:13.

**Nov. 30, 1975—Denver 13, San Diego 10,** at Denver; Broncos win toss. Turner kicks 25-yard field goal at 4:13.

**Nov. 30, 1975—Oakland 37, Atlanta 34,** at Oakland; Falcons win toss. James punts to Raiders' 16. Guy punts and Herron returns to Falcons' 41. Nick Mike-Mayer misses 45-yard field goal. Guy punts into Falcons' end zone. James punts to Raiders' 39. Blanda kicks 36-yard field goal at 15:00.

**Dec. 14, 1975—Baltimore 10, Miami 7,** at Baltimore; Dolphins win toss. Seiple punts to Colts' 4. Linhart kicks 31-yard field goal at 12:44.

**Sept. 19, 1976—Minnesota 10, Los Angeles 10,** at Minnesota; Vikings win toss. Tarkenton's pass intercepted by Monte Jackson and returned to Minnesota 16. Allen blocks Dempsey's 30-yard field goal attempt, ball rolls into end zone for touchback. Clabo punts and Scribner returns to Rams' 20. Rusty Jackson punts to Vikings' 35. Tarkenton's pass intercepted by Kay at Rams' 1, no return. Game ends with Rams on own 3.

**Sept. 27, 1976—Washington 20, Philadelphia 17,** at Philadelphia; Eagles win toss. Jones punts and Eddie Brown loses one yard on return to Redskins' 40. Bragg punts 51 yards into end zone for touchback. Jones punts and Brown returns to Redskins' 42. Bragg punts and Marshall returns to Eagles' 41. Boryla's pass intercepted by Dusek at Redskins' 37, no return. Bragg punts and Bradley returns. Philadelphia holding penalty moves ball back to Eagles' 8. Boryla pass intercepted by Eddie Brown and returned to Eagles' 22. Moseley kicks 29-yard field goal at 12:49.

**Oct. 17, 1976—Kansas City 20, Miami 17,** at Miami; Chiefs win toss. Wilson punts into end zone for touchback. Bulaich fumbles into Kansas City end zone, Collier recovers for touchback. Stenerud kicks 34-yard field goal at 14:48.

**Oct. 31, 1976—St. Louis 23, San Francisco 20,** at St. Louis; Cardinals win toss. Joyce punts and Leonard fumbles on return, Jones recovers at 49ers' 43. Bakken kicks 21-yard field goal at 6:42.

**Dec. 5, 1976—San Diego 13, San Francisco 7,** at San Diego; Chargers win toss. Morris runs 13 yards for touchdown at 5:12.

**Sept. 18, 1977—Dallas 16, Minnesota 10,** at Minnesota; Vikings win toss. Dallas starts on Vikings' 47 after a punt early in the overtime period. Staubach scores seven plays later on a four-yard run at 6:14.

**Sept. 26, 1977—Cleveland 30, New England 27,** at Cleveland; Browns win toss. Sipe throws a 22-yard pass to Logan at Patriots' 19. Cockroft kicks 35-yard field goal at 4:45.

**Oct. 16, 1977—Minnesota 22, Chicago 16,** at Minnesota; Bears win toss. Parsons punts 53 yards to Vikings' 18. Minnesota drives to Bears' 11. On a first-and-10, Vikings fake a field goal and holder Krause hits Voigt with a touchdown pass at 6:45.

**Oct. 30, 1977—Cincinnati 13, Houston 10,** at Cincinnati; Bengals win toss. Bahr kicks a 22-yard field goal at 5:51.

**Nov. 13, 1977—San Francisco 10, New Orleans 7,** at New Orleans; Saints win toss. Saints fail to move ball and Blanchard punts to 49ers' 41. Wersching kicks a 33-yard field goal at 6:33.

**Dec. 18, 1977—Chicago 12, New York Giants 9,** at East Rutherford, N.J.; Giants win toss. The ball changes hands eight times before Thomas kicks a 28-yard field goal at 14:51.

**Sept. 10, 1978—Cleveland 13, Cincinnati 10,** at Cleveland; Browns win toss. Collins returns kickoff 41 yards to the Browns' 47. Cockroft kicks 27-yard field goal at 4:30.

**Sept. 11, 1978—Minnesota 12, Denver 9,** at Minnesota; Vikings win toss. Danmeier kicks 44-yard field goal at 2:56.

**Sept. 24, 1978—Pittsburgh 15, Cleveland 9,** at Pittsburgh; Steelers win toss. Cunningham scores on a 37-yard "gadget" pass from Bradshaw at 3:43. Steelers start winning drive on their 21.

**Sept. 24, 1978—Denver 23, Kansas City 17,** at Kansas City; Broncos win toss. Dilts punts to Kansas City. Chiefs advance to Broncos' 40 where Reed fails to make first down on fourth-and-one situation. Broncos march downfield. Preston scores two-yard touchdown at 10:28.

**Oct. 1, 1978—Oakland 25, Chicago 19,** at Chicago; Bears win toss. Both teams punt on first possession. On Chicago's second offensive series, Colzie intercepts Avellini's pass and returns it to Bears' 3. Three plays later, Whittington runs two yards for a touchdown at 5:19.

**Oct. 15, 1978—Dallas 24, St. Louis 21,** at St. Louis; Cowboys win toss. Dallas drives from its 23 into field goal range. Septien kicks 27-yard field goal at 3:28.

**Oct. 29, 1978—Denver 20, Seattle 17,** at Seattle; Broncos win toss. Ball changes hands four times before Turner kicks 18-yard field goal at 12:59.

**Nov. 12, 1978—San Diego 29, Kansas City 23,** at San Diego; Chiefs win toss. Fouts hits Jefferson for decisive 14-yard touchdown pass on the last play (15:00) of overtime period.

**Nov. 12, 1978—Washington 16, New York Giants 13,** at Washington; Redskins win toss. Moseley kicks winning 45-yard field goal at 8:32 after missing first down field goal attempt of 35 yards at 4:50.

**Nov. 26, 1978—Green Bay 10, Minnesota 10,** at Green Bay; Packers win toss. Both teams have possession of the ball four times.

**Dec. 9, 1978—Cleveland 37, New York Jets 34,** at Cleveland; Browns win toss. Cockroft kicks 22-yard field goal at 3:07.

**Sept. 2, 1979—Atlanta 40, New Orleans 34,** at New Orleans; Falcons win toss. Bartkowski's pass intercepted by Myers and returned to Falcons' 46. Erxleben punts to Falcons' 4. James punts to Chandler on Saints' 43. Erxleben punts and Ryckman returns to Falcons' 28. James punts and Chandler returns to Saints' 36. Erxleben retrieves punt snap on Saints' 1 and attempts pass. Mayberry intercepts and returns six yards for touchdown at 8:22.

**Sept. 2, 1979—Cleveland 25, New York Jets 22,** at New York; Jets win toss. Leahy's 43-yard field goal attempt goes wide right at 4:41. Evans's punt blocked by Dykes is recovered by Newton. Ramsey punts into end zone for touchback. Evans punts and Harper returns to Jets' 24. Robinson's pass intercepted by Davis and returned 33 yards to Jets' 31. Cockroft kicks 27-yard field goal at 14:45.

**Sept. 3, 1979—Pittsburgh 16, New England 13,** at Foxboro; Patriots win toss. Hare punts to Swann at Steelers' 31. Bahr kicks 41-yard field goal at 5:10.

**Sept. 9, 1979—Tampa Bay 29, Baltimore 26,** at Baltimore; Colts win toss. Landry fumbles, recovered by Kollar at Colts' 14. O'Donoghue kicks 31-yard, first-down field goal at 1:41.

**Sept. 15, 1979—Denver 20, Atlanta 17,** at Atlanta; Broncos win toss. Broncos march 65 yards to Falcons' 7. Turner kicks 24-yard field goal at 6:15.

**Sept. 23, 1979—Houston 30, Cincinnati 27,** at Cincinnati; Oilers win toss. Parsley punts and Lusby returns to Bengals' 33. Bahr's 32-yard field goal attempt is wide right at 8:05. Parsley's punt downed on Bengals' 5. McInally punts and Ellender returns to Bengals' 42. Fritsch's third down, 29-yard field goal attempt hits left upright and bounces through at 14:28.

**Sept. 23, 1979—Minnesota 27, Green Bay 21,** at Minnesota; Vikings win toss. Kramer throws 50-yard touchdown pass to Rashad at 3:18.

**Oct. 28, 1979—Houston 27, New York Jets 24,** at Houston; Oilers win toss. Oilers march 58 yards to Jets' 18. Fritsch kicks 35-yard field goal at 5:10.

**Nov. 18, 1979—Cleveland 30, Miami 24,** at Cleveland; Browns win toss. Sipe passes 39 yards to Rucker for touchdown at 1:59.

**Nov. 25, 1979—Pittsburgh 33, Cleveland 30,** at Pittsburgh; Browns win toss. Sipe's pass intercepted by Blount on Steelers' 4. Bradshaw pass intercepted by Bolton on Browns' 12. Evans punts and Bell returns to Steelers' 17. Bahr kicks 37-yard field goal at 14:51.

**Nov. 25, 1979—Buffalo 16, New England 13,** at Foxboro; Patriots win toss. Hare's punt downed on Bills' 38. Jackson punts and Morgan returns to Patriots' 20. Grogan's pass intercepted by Haslett and returned to Bills' 42. Ferguson's 51-yard pass to Butler sets up N. Mike-Mayer's 29-yard field goal at 9:15.

**Dec. 2, 1979—Los Angeles 27, Minnesota 21,** at Los Angeles; Rams win toss. Clark punts and Miller returns to Vikings' 25. Kramer's pass intercepted by Brown and returned to Rams' 40. Cromwell, holding for 22-yard field goal attempt, runs around left end untouched for winning score at 6:53.

**Sept. 7, 1980—Green Bay 12, Chicago 6,** at Green Bay; Bears win toss. Parsons punts and Nixon returns 16 yards. Five plays later, Marcol returns own blocked field goal attempt 24 yards for touchdown at 6:00.

**Sept. 14, 1980—San Diego 30, Oakland 24,** at San Diego; Raiders win toss. Pastorini's first-down pass intercepted by Edwards. Millen intercepts Fouts' first-down pass and returns to San Diego 46. Bahr's 50-yard field goal attempt partially blocked by Williams and recovered on Chargers' 32. Eight plays later, Fouts throws 24-yard touchdown pass to Jefferson at 8:09.

**Sept. 14, 1980—San Francisco 24, St. Louis 21,** at San Francisco; Cardinals win toss. Swider punts and Robinson returns to 49ers' 32. San Francisco drives 52 yards to St. Louis 16, where Wersching kicks 33-yard field goal at 4:12.

**Oct. 12, 1980—Green Bay 14, Tampa Bay 14,** at Tampa Bay; Packers win toss. Teams trade punts twice. Lee returns second Tampa Bay punt to Green Bay 42. Dickey completes three passes to Buccaneers' 18, where Birney's 36-yard field goal attempt is wide right as time expires.

**Nov. 9, 1980—Atlanta 33, St. Louis 27,** at St. Louis; Falcons win toss. Strong runs 21 yards for touchdown at 4:20.

**Nov. 20, 1980—San Diego 27, Miami 24,** at Miami; Chargers win toss. Partridge punts into end zone, Dolphins take over on their own 20. Woodley's pass for Nathan intercepted by Lowe and returned 28 yards to Dolphins' 12. Benirschke kicks 28-yard field goal at 7:14.

**Nov. 23, 1980—New York Jets 31, Houston 28,** at New York; Jets win toss. Leahy kicks 38-yard field goal at 3:58.

**Nov. 27, 1980—Chicago 23, Detroit 17,** at Detroit; Bears win toss. Williams returns kickoff 95 yards for touchdown at 0:21.

**Dec. 7, 1980—Buffalo 10, Los Angeles 7,** at Buffalo; Rams win toss. Corral punts and Hooks returns to Bills' 34. Ferguson's 30-yard pass to Lewis sets up N. Mike-Mayer's 30-yard field goal at 5:14.

**Dec. 7, 1980—San Francisco 38, New Orleans 35,** at San Francisco; Saints win toss. Erxleben's punt downed by Hardy on 49ers' 27. Wersching kicks 36-yard field goal at 7:40.

**Dec. 8, 1980—Miami 16, New England 13,** at Miami; Dolphins win toss. Von Schamann kicks 23-yard field goal at 3:20.

**Dec. 14, 1980—Cincinnati 17, Chicago 14,** at Chicago; Bengals win toss. Breech kicks 28-yard field goal at 4:23.

**Dec. 21, 1980—Los Angeles 20, Atlanta 17,** at Los Angeles; Rams win toss. Corral's punt downed at Rams' 37. James punts into end zone for touchback. Corral's punt downed on Falcons' 17. Bartkowski fumbles when hit by Harris, recovered by Delaney. Corral kicks 23-yard field goal on first play of possession at 7:00.

**Sept. 27, 1981—Cincinnati 27, Buffalo 24,** at Cincinnati; Bills win toss. Cater punts into end zone for touchback. Bengals drive to the Bills' 10 yard line where Breech kicks 28-yard field goal at 9:33.

**Sept. 27, 1981—Pittsburgh 27, New England 21,** at Pittsburgh; Patriots win toss. Hubach punts and Smith returns five yards to midfield. Four plays later Bradshaw throws 24-yard touchdown pass to Swann at 3:19.

**Oct. 4, 1981—Miami 28, New York Jets 28,** at Miami; Jets win toss. Teams trade punts twice. Leahy's 48-yard field goal attempt is wide right as time expires.

**Oct. 25, 1981—New York Giants 27, Atlanta 24,** at Atlanta; Giants win toss. Jennings' punt goes out of bounds at New York 47. Bright returns Atlanta punt to Giants' 14. Woerner fair catches punt at own 28. Andrews fumbles on first play, recovered by Van Pelt. Danelo kicks 40-yard field goal four plays later at 9:20.

**Oct. 25, 1981—Chicago 20, San Diego 17,** at Chicago; Bears win toss. Teams trade punts. Bears' second punt returned by Brooks to Chargers' 33. Fouts pass intercepted by Fencik and returned 32 yards to San Diego 27. Roveto kicks 27-yard field goal seven plays later at 9:30.

**Nov. 8, 1981—Chicago 16, Kansas City 13,** at Kansas City; Bears win toss. Teams trade punts. Kansas City takes over on downs on its own 38. Fuller's fumble recovered by Harris on Chicago 36. Roveto's 37-yard field goal wide, but Chiefs penalized for leverage. Roveto's 22-yard field goal attempt three plays later is good at 13:07.

**Nov. 8, 1981—Denver 23, Cleveland 20,** at Denver; Browns win toss. D. Smith recovers Hill's fumble at Denver 48. Morton's 33-yard pass to Upchurch and six-yard run by Preston set up Steinfort's 30-yard field goal at 4:10.

**Nov. 8, 1981—Miami 30, New England 27,** at New England; Dolphins win toss. Orosz punts and Morgan returns six yards to New England 26. Grogan's pass intercepted by Brudzinski who returns 19 yards to Patriots' 26. Von Schamann kicks 30-yard field goal on first down at 7:09.

**Nov. 15, 1981—Washington 30, New York Giants 27,** at New York; Giants win toss. Nelms returns Giants' punt 26 yards to New York 47. Five plays later Moseley kicks 48-yard field goal at 3:44.

**Dec. 20, 1981—New York Giants 13, Dallas 10,** at New York; Cowboys win toss and kick off. Jennings punts to Dallas 40. Taylor recovers Dorsett's fumble on second down. Danelo's 33-yard field goal attempt hits right upright and bounces back. White's pass for Pearson intercepted by Hunt and returned seven yards to Dallas 24. Four plays later Danelo kicks 35-yard field goal at 6:19.

**Sept. 12, 1982—Washington 37, Philadelphia 34,** at Philadelphia; Redskins win toss. Theismann completes five passes for 63 yards to set up Moseley's 26-yard field goal at 4:47.

**Sept. 19, 1982—Pittsburgh 26, Cincinnati 20,** at Pittsburgh; Bengals win toss. Anderson's pass intended for Kreider intercepted by Woodruff and returned 30 yards to Cincinnati 2. Bradshaw completes two-yard touchdown pass to Stallworth on first down at 1:08.

**Dec. 19, 1982—Baltimore 20, Green Bay 20,** at Baltimore; Packers win toss. K. Anderson intercepts Dickey's first-down pass and returns to Packers' 42. Miller's 44-yard field goal attempt blocked by G. Lewis. Teams trade punts before Stenerud's 47-yard field goal attempt is wide right. Teams trade punts again before time expires in Colts possession.

**Jan. 2, 1983—Tampa Bay 26, Chicago 23,** at Tampa Bay; Bears win toss. Parsons punts to T. Bell at Buccaneers' 40. Capece kicks 33-yard field goal at 3:14.

**Sept. 4, 1983—Baltimore 29, New England 23,** at New England; Patriots win toss. Cooks runs 52 yards with fumble recovery three plays into overtime at 0:30.

**Sept. 4, 1983—Green Bay 41, Houston 38,** at Houston; Packers win toss. Stenerud kicks 42-yard field goal at 5:55.

**Sept. 11, 1983—New York Giants 16, Atlanta 13,** at Atlanta; Giants win toss. Dennis returns kickoff 54 yards to Atlanta 41. Haji-Sheikh kicks 30-yard field goal at 3:38.

**Sept. 18, 1983—New Orleans 34, Chicago 31,** at New Orleans; Bears win toss. Parsons punts and Groth returns five yards to New Orleans 34. Stabler pass intercepted by Schmidt at Chicago 47. Parsons punt downed by Gentry at New Orleans 2. Stabler gains 36 yards in four passes; Wilson 38 in six carries. Andersen kicks 41-yard field goal at 10:57.

**Sept. 18, 1983—Minnesota 19, Tampa Bay 16,** at Tampa; Vikings win toss. Coleman punts and Bell returns eight yards to Tampa Bay 47. Capece's 33-yard field goal attempt sails wide at 7:26. Dils and Young combine for 48-yard gain to Tampa Bay 27. Ricardo kicks 42-yard field goal at 9:27.

**Sept. 25, 1983—Baltimore 22, Chicago 19,** at Baltimore; Colts win toss. Allegre kicks 33-yard field goal nine plays later at 4:51.

**Sept. 25, 1983—Cleveland 30, San Diego 24,** at San Diego; Browns win toss. Walker returns kickoff 33 yards to Cleveland 37. Sipe completes 48-yard touchdown pass to Holt four plays later at 1:53.

**Sept. 25, 1983—New York Jets 27, Los Angeles Rams 24,** at New York; Jets win toss. Ramsey punts to Irvin who returns to 25 but penalty puts Rams on own 13. Holmes 30-yard interception return sets up Leahy's 26-yard field goal at 3:22.

**Oct. 9, 1983—Buffalo 38, Miami 35,** at Miami; Dolphins win toss. Von Schamann's 52-yard field goal attempt goes wide at 12:36. Cater punts to Clayton who loses 11 to own 13. Von Schamann's 43-yard field goal attempt sails wide at 5:15. Danelo kicks 36-yard field goal nine plays later at 13:58.

**Oct. 9, 1983—Dallas 27, Tampa Bay 24,** at Dallas; Cowboys win toss. Septien's 51-yard field goal attempt goes wide but Buccaneers penalized for roughing kicker. Septien kicks 42-yard field goal at 4:38.

**Oct. 23, 1983—Kansas City 13, Houston 10,** at Houston; Chiefs win toss. Lowery kicks 41-yard field goal 13 plays later at 7:41.

**Oct. 23, 1983—Minnesota 20, Green Bay 17,** at Green Bay; Packers win toss. Scribner's punt downed on Vikings' 42. Ricardo kicks 32-yard field goal eight plays later at 5:05.

**Oct. 24, 1983—N.Y. Giants 20, St. Louis 20,** at St. Louis; Cardinals win toss. Teams trade punts before O'Donoghue's 44-yard field goal attempt is wide left. Jennings' punt returned by Bird to St. Louis 21. Lomax pass intercepted by Haynes who loses six yards to New York 33. Jennings' punt downed on St. Louis 17. O'Donoghue's 19-yard field goal attempt is wide right. Rutledge's pass intercepted by L. Washington who returns 25 yards to New York 25. O'Donoghue's 42-yard field goal attempt is wide right. Rutledge's pass intercepted by W. Smith at St. Louis 33 to end game.

**Oct. 30, 1983—Cleveland 25, Houston 19,** at Cleveland; Oilers win toss. Teams trade punts. Nielsen pass intercepted by Whitwell who returns to Houston 20. Green runs 20 yards for touchdown on first down at 6:34.

**Nov. 20, 1983—Detroit 23, Green Bay 20,** at Milwaukee; Packers win toss. Scribner punts and Jenkins returns 14 yards to Green Bay 45. Murray's 33-yard field goal attempt is wide left at 9:32. Whitehurst's pass intercepted by Watkins and returned to Green Bay 27. Murray kicks 37-yard field goal four plays later at 8:30.

**Nov. 27, 1983—Atlanta 47, Green Bay 41,** at Atlanta; Packers win toss. K. Johnson returns interception 31 yards for touchdown at 2:13.

**Nov. 27, 1983—Seattle 51, Kansas City 48,** at Seattle; Seahawks win toss. Dixon's 47-yard kickoff return sets up N. Johnson's 42-yard field goal at 1:36.

**Dec. 11, 1983—New Orleans 20, Philadelphia 17,** at Philadelphia; Eagles win toss. Runager punts to Groth who fair catches on New Orleans 32. Stabler completes two passes for 36 yards to Goodlow to set up Andersen's 50-yard field goal at 5:30.

**Dec. 12, 1983—Green Bay 12, Tampa Bay 9,** at Tampa; Packers win toss. Stenerud kicks 23-yard field goal 11 plays later at 4:07.

## Postseason

**Dec. 28, 1958—Baltimore 23, New York Giants 17,** at New York; Giants win toss. Maynard returns kickoff to Giants' 20. Chandler punts and Taseff returns one yard to Colts' 20. Colts win at 8:15 on a one-yard run by Ameche.

**Dec. 23, 1962—Dallas Texans 20, Houston Oilers 17,** at Houston; Texans win toss and kick off. Jancik returns kickoff to Oilers' 33. Norton punts and Jackson makes fair catch on Texans' 22. Wilson punts and Jancik makes fair catch on Oilers' 45. Robinson intercepts Blanda's pass and returns 13 yards to Oilers' 47. Wilson's punt rolls dead at Oilers' 12. Hull intercepts Blanda's pass and returns 23 yards to midfield. Texans win at 17:54 on a 25-yard field goal by Brooker.

**Dec. 26, 1965—Green Bay 13, Baltimore 10,** at Green Bay; Packers win toss. Moore returns kickoff to Packers' 22. Chandler punts and Haymond returns nine yards to Colts' 41. Gilburg punts and Wood makes fair catch at Packers' 21. Chandler punts and Haymond returns one yard to Colts' 41. Michaels misses 47-yard field goal. Packers win at 13:39 on a 25-yard field goal by Chandler.

**Dec. 25, 1971—Miami 27, Kansas City 24,** at Kansas City; Chiefs win toss. Podolak, after a lateral from Buchanan, returns kickoff to Chiefs' 46. Stenerud's 42-yard field goal is blocked. Seiple punts and Podolak makes fair catch on Chiefs' 17. Wilson punts and Scott returns 18 yards to Dolphins' 39. Yepremian misses 62-yard field goal. Scott intercepts Dawson's pass and returns 13 yards to Dolphins' 46. Seiple punts and Podolak loses one yard to Chiefs' 15. Wilson punts and Scott makes fair catch on Dolphins' 30. Dolphins win at 22:40 on a 37-yard field goal by Yepremian.

**Dec. 24, 1977—Oakland 37, Baltimore 31,** at Baltimore; Colts win toss. Raiders start on own 42 following a punt late in the first overtime. Oakland works way into a threatening position on Stabler's 19-yard pass to Branch at the Colts' 26. Four plays later, on the second play of the second overtime, Stabler hits Casper with a 10-yard touchdown pass at 15:43.

**Jan. 2, 1982—San Diego 41, Miami 38** at Miami; Chargers win toss. San Diego drives from its 13 to Miami 8. On second-and-goal, Benirschke misses 27-yard field goal attempt wide to left at 9:15. Miami has the ball twice and San Diego twice more before the Dolphins get their third possession. Miami drives from the San Diego 46 to Chargers' 17 and on fourth-and-two, von Schamann's 34-yard field goal attempt is blocked by San Diego's Winslow after 11:27. Fouts then completes four of five passes including a 29-yarder to Joiner that puts the ball on Dolphins' 10. On first down, Benirschke kicks a 20-yard field goal at 13:52. San Diego's winning drive covered 74 yards in six plays.

## Overtime Won-Lost Records, 1974—1983 (Regular Season)

| | W | L | T |
|---|---|---|---|
| Atlanta | 3 | 5 | 0 |
| Baltimore | 3 | 1 | 1 |
| Buffalo | 3 | 1 | 0 |
| Chicago | 4 | 7 | 0 |
| Cincinnati | 3 | 3 | 0 |
| Cleveland | 7 | 3 | 0 |
| Dallas | 4 | 2 | 0 |
| Denver | 5 | 1 | 1 |
| Detroit | 1 | 2 | 0 |
| Green Bay | 3 | 4 | 3 |
| Houston | 2 | 5 | 0 |
| Kansas City | 3 | 4 | 0 |
| Los Angeles Raiders | 3 | 1 | 0 |
| Los Angeles Rams | 3 | 2 | 1 |
| Miami | 2 | 5 | 1 |
| Minnesota | 5 | 2 | 2 |
| New England | 0 | 7 | 0 |
| New Orleans | 2 | 3 | 0 |
| New York Giants | 3 | 4 | 1 |
| New York Jets | 3 | 3 | 1 |
| Philadelphia | 0 | 3 | 0 |
| Pittsburgh | 5 | 0 | 1 |
| St. Louis | 2 | 4 | 1 |
| San Diego | 4 | 4 | 0 |
| San Francisco | 3 | 2 | 0 |
| Seattle | 1 | 1 | 0 |
| Tampa Bay | 2 | 3 | 1 |
| Washington | 5 | 2 | 0 |

# Regular Season Interconference Records, 1970-1983

## American Football Conference

### Eastern Division

| | W | L | T | Pct. |
|---|---|---|---|---|
| Miami | 36 | 8 | 0 | .818 |
| New England | 20 | 23 | 0 | .465 |
| Baltimore | 17 | 20 | 1 | .461 |
| New York Jets | 20 | 24 | 0 | .455 |
| Buffalo | 17 | 25 | 1 | .407 |

### Central Division

| | | | | |
|---|---|---|---|---|
| Pittsburgh | 30 | 13 | 0 | .698 |
| Cincinnati | 27 | 17 | 0 | .614 |
| Cleveland | 24 | 21 | 0 | .533 |
| Houston | 17 | 27 | 1 | .389 |

### Western Division

| | | | | |
|---|---|---|---|---|
| Los Angeles Raiders | 34 | 11 | 1 | .750 |
| Denver | 24 | 23 | 1 | .510 |
| Seattle | 10 | 10 | 0 | .500 |
| San Diego | 20 | 23 | 0 | .465 |
| Kansas City | 16 | 21 | 2 | .436 |

## National Football Conference

### Eastern Division

| | W | L | T | Pct. |
|---|---|---|---|---|
| Dallas | 33 | 12 | 0 | .733 |
| Philadelphia | 24 | 19 | 0 | .558 |
| Washington | 22 | 20 | 0 | .524 |
| St. Louis | 18 | 20 | 2 | .475 |
| New York Giants | 14 | 23 | 0 | .378 |

### Central Division

| | | | | |
|---|---|---|---|---|
| Minnesota | 25 | 22 | 0 | .532 |
| Detroit | 20 | 21 | 1 | .488 |
| Green Bay | 17 | 25 | 2 | .409 |
| Tampa Bay | 8 | 12 | 0 | .400 |
| Chicago | 14 | 29 | 0 | .326 |

### Western Division

| | | | | |
|---|---|---|---|---|
| Los Angeles Rams | 25 | 21 | 0 | .543 |
| San Francisco | 20 | 27 | 0 | .426 |
| Atlanta | 18 | 27 | 0 | .400 |
| New Orleans | 8 | 34 | 2 | .205 |

# Interconference Victories, 1970-1983

## Regular Season

| | AFC | NFC | Tie |
|---|---|---|---|
| 1970 | 12 | 27 | 1 |
| 1971 | 15 | 23 | 2 |
| 1972 | 20 | 19 | 1 |
| 1973 | 19 | 19 | 2 |
| 1974 | 23 | 17 | 0 |
| 1975 | 23 | 17 | 0 |
| 1976 | 16 | 12 | 0 |
| 1977 | 19 | 9 | 0 |
| 1978 | 31 | 21 | 0 |
| 1979 | 36 | 16 | 0 |
| 1980 | 33 | 19 | 0 |
| 1981 | 24 | 28 | 0 |
| 1982 | 15 | 14 | 1 |
| 1983 | 26 | 26 | 0 |
| Total | 312 | 267 | 7 |

## Preseason

| | AFC | NFC | Tie |
|---|---|---|---|
| 1970 | 21 | 28 | 1 |
| 1971 | 28 | 28 | 3 |
| 1972 | 27 | 25 | 4 |
| 1973 | 23 | 35 | 2 |
| 1974 | 35 | 25 | 0 |
| 1975 | 30 | 26 | 1 |
| 1976 | 30 | 31 | 0 |
| 1977 | 38 | 25 | 0 |
| 1978 | 20 | 19 | 0 |
| 1979 | 25 | 18 | 0 |
| 1980 | 22 | 20 | 1 |
| 1981 | 18 | 19 | 0 |
| 1982 | 25 | 16 | 0 |
| 1983 | 15 | 24 | 0 |
| Total | 357 | 339 | 12 |

## AFC VS. NFC (REGULAR SEASON), 1970-1983

| | 1970 | 1971 | 1972 | 1973 | 1974 | 1975 | 1976 | 1977 | 1978 | 1979 | 1980 | 1981 | 1982 | 1983 | Totals |
|---|---|---|---|---|---|---|---|---|---|---|---|---|---|---|---|
| Miami | 2-1 | 3-0 | 3-0 | 3-0 | 2-1 | 3-0 | 0-2 | 2-0 | 3-1 | 4-0 | 4-0 | 3-1 | 1-1 | 3-1 | 36-8 |
| L.A. Raiders | 1-2 | 1-1-1 | 3-0 | 2-1 | 3-0 | 3-0 | 3-0 | 1-1 | 4-0 | 4-0 | 2-2 | 2-2 | 3-0 | 2-2 | 34-11-1 |
| Pittsburgh | 0-3 | 1-2 | 2-1 | 3-0 | 3-0 | 2-1 | 1-1 | 2-0 | 3-1 | 3-1 | 4-0 | 3-1 | 1-0 | 2-2 | 30-13 |
| Cincinnati | 1-2 | 1-2 | 2-1 | 2-1 | 2-1 | 3-0 | 2-0 | 2-1 | 2-2 | 2-2 | 2-2 | 1-2 | 1-0 | 3-1 | 27-17 |
| Cleveland | 0-3 | 2-1 | 1-2 | 1-2 | 1-2 | 1-3 | 2-0 | 1-1 | 4-0 | 3-1 | 3-1 | 3-1 | 0-2 | 2-2 | 24-21 |
| Denver | 2-2 | 1-3 | 1-3 | 0-3-1 | 2-2 | 2-1 | 2-0 | 1-1 | 2-2 | 3-1 | 3-1 | 3-1 | 2-1 | 0-2 | 24-23-1 |
| New England | 0-3 | 0-3 | 3-0 | 2-1 | 3-0 | 1-2 | 1-1 | 2-0 | 2-2 | 3-1 | 1-3 | 0-4 | 0-1 | 2-2 | 20-23 |
| San Diego | 1-2 | 2-1 | 0-3 | 1-2 | 1-2 | 0-3 | 2-0 | 1-1 | 2-2 | 3-1 | 2-2 | 2-2 | 1-0 | 2-2 | 20-23 |
| N.Y. Jets | 2-1 | 0-3 | 1-2 | 0-3 | 2-1 | 0-3 | 0-2 | 1-1 | 1-3 | 3-1 | 1-3 | 2-0 | 4-0 | 3-1 | 20-24 |
| Baltimore | 3-0 | 2-1 | 0-3 | 2-1 | 1-2 | 2-1 | 0-2 | 1-1 | 2-2 | 1-1 | 1-1 | 0-4 | 0-1-1 | 2-0 | 17-20-1 |
| Buffalo | 0-3 | 0-3 | 2-0-1 | 2-1 | 2-1 | 1-2 | 0-2 | 1-1 | 1-1 | 2-2 | 3-1 | 1-3 | 1-2 | 1-3 | 17-25-1 |
| Houston | 0-3 | 0-2-1 | 0-3 | 0-3 | 0-3 | 3-0 | 2-0 | 2-0 | 2-2 | 4-0 | 1-3 | 0-3 | 1-3 | 1-3 | 17-27-1 |
| Kansas City | 0-2-1 | 2-1 | 2-1 | 1-1-1 | 1-2 | 2-1 | 1-1 | 1-1 | 0-2 | 0-2 | 2-0 | 2-2 | 0-3 | 2-2 | 16-21-2 |
| Seattle | | | | | | | | | 1-0 | 3-1 | 3-1 | 0-2 | 1-0 | 1-3 | 10-10 |
| Tampa Bay | | | | | | 0-1 | | | | | | | | | 0-1 |
| TOTALS | 12-27-1 | 15-23-2 | 20-19-1 | 19-19-2 | 23-17 | 23-17 | 16-12 | 19-9 | 31-21 | 36-16 | 33-19 | 24-28 | 15-14-1 | 26-26 | 312-267-7 |

## NFC VS. AFC (REGULAR SEASON), 1970-1983

| | 1970 | 1971 | 1972 | 1973 | 1974 | 1975 | 1976 | 1977 | 1978 | 1979 | 1980 | 1981 | 1982 | 1983 | Totals |
|---|---|---|---|---|---|---|---|---|---|---|---|---|---|---|---|
| Dallas | 3-0 | 3-0 | 3-0 | 2-1 | 2-1 | 2-1 | 2-0 | 1-1 | 3-1 | 1-3 | 3-1 | 4-0 | 2-1 | 2-2 | 33-12 |
| L.A. Rams | 2-1 | 1-2 | 3-0 | 3-0 | 3-1 | 3-0 | 1-1 | 2-0 | 2-2 | 2-2 | 2-2 | 1-3 | 1-2 | 1-3 | 25-21 |
| Minnesota | 2-1 | 2-1 | 1-2 | 2-1 | 2-1 | 4-0 | 2-0 | 1-1 | 1-3 | 1-3 | 1-3 | 1-3 | 4-0 | | 25-22 |
| Philadelphia | 2-1 | 1-2 | 2-1 | 2-1 | 2-1 | 0-3 | 0-2 | 1-1 | 3-1 | 2-2 | 3-1 | 2-1 | 1-1 | 1-1 | 24-19 |
| Washington | 2-1 | 1-2 | 1-2 | 2-1 | 2-1 | 1-2 | 1-1 | 1-1 | 2-2 | 2-2 | 1-3 | 2-2 | | 4-0 | 22-20 |
| Detroit | 3-0 | 4-0 | 2-0-1 | 0-3 | 1-2 | 1-2 | 2-0 | 2-0 | 2-2 | 0-4 | 0-2 | 2-2 | 0-1 | 1-3 | 20-21-1 |
| San Francisco | 4-0 | 2-1 | 2-1 | 1-2 | 0-3 | 1-2 | 1-1 | 0-2 | 1-3 | 0-4 | 2-2 | 3-1 | 1-3 | 2-2 | 20-27 |
| St. Louis | 2-0-1 | 2-1 | 2-1 | 0-2-1 | 2-1 | 2-1 | 1-1 | 0-2 | 0-4 | 1-3 | 1-1 | 3-1 | | 3-1 | 18-20-2 |
| Atlanta | 1-2 | 3-0 | 2-2 | 2-1 | 0-3 | 1-2 | 0-2 | 0-2 | 1-3 | 1-3 | 2-2 | | 1-1 | 3-1 | 18-27 |
| Green Bay | 2-1 | 2-1 | 2-1 | 1-1-1 | 2-1 | 0-3 | 0-2 | 0-3 | 2-2 | 1-3 | 1-1 | 1-1 | 1-1-2 | 2-2 | 17-25-2 |
| N.Y. Giants | 3-0 | 1-2 | 1-2 | 1-2 | 1-2 | 2-1 | 0-2 | 1-1 | 1-1 | 1-3 | 1-1 | 1-0 | 0-4 | | 14-23 |
| Chicago | 1-2 | 1-2 | 1-2 | 2-2 | 0-3 | 0-3 | 0-2 | 1-1 | 0-4 | 2-2 | 0-4 | 4-0 | 1-1 | 1-1 | 14-29 |
| New Orleans | 0-3 | 0-1-2 | 0-3 | 1-2 | 0-3 | 0-3 | 1-2 | 0-2 | 1-3 | 0-4 | 1-3 | 2-2 | 1-0 | 1-3 | 8-34-2 |
| Tampa Bay | | | | | | | | 0-1 | 2-0 | 2-0 | 1-3 | 0-4 | 2-1 | 1-3 | 8-12 |
| Seattle | | | | | | 1-0 | | | | | | | | | 1-0 |
| TOTALS | 27-12-1 | 23-15-2 | 19-20-1 | 19-19-2 | 17-23 | 17-23 | 12-16 | 9-19 | 21-31 | 16-36 | 19-33 | 28-24 | 14-15-1 | 26-26 | 267-312-7 |

# 1983 Interconference Games

(Home Team in capital letters)

## AFC 26, NFC 26

### AFC Victories

Cleveland 31, DETROIT 26
Pittsburgh 25, GREEN BAY 21
BALTIMORE 22, Chicago 19 (OT)
Cincinnati 23, TAMPA BAY 17
N.Y. JETS 27, L.A. Rams 24 (OT)
KANSAS CITY 38, St. Louis 14
San Diego 41, N.Y. GIANTS 34
KANSAS CITY 38, N.Y. Giants 17
L.A. Raiders 40, DALLAS 38
Baltimore 22, PHILADELPHIA 21
CINCINNATI 34, Green Bay 14
MIAMI 30, L.A. Rams 14
BUFFALO 27, New Orleans 21
N.Y. Jets 27, SAN FRANCISCO 13
PITTSBURGH 17, Tampa Bay 12
Miami 20, SAN FRANCISCO 17
SAN DIEGO 24, Dallas 23
HOUSTON 27, Detroit 17
CLEVELAND 20, Tampa Bay 0
N.Y. Jets 31, NEW ORLEANS 28
L.A. RAIDERS 27, N.Y. Giants 12
NEW ENGLAND 7, New Orleans 0
MIAMI 31, Atlanta 24
CINCINNATI 17, Detroit 9
New England 21, L.A. RAMS 7
Seattle 17, N.Y. GIANTS 12

### NFC Victories

Green Bay 41, HOUSTON 38 (OT)
Minnesota 27, CLEVELAND 21
WASHINGTON 27, Kansas City 12
Philadelphia 13, DENVER 10
Washington 27, SEATTLE 17
CHICAGO 31, Denver 14
WASHINGTON 37, L.A. Raiders 35
NEW ORLEANS 17, Miami 7
San Francisco 33, NEW ENGLAND 13
MINNESOTA 34, Houston 14
Atlanta 27, N.Y. JETS 21
ATLANTA 24, New England 13
Washington 27, SAN DIEGO 24
GREEN BAY 35, Cleveland 21
ST. LOUIS 33, Seattle 28
DALLAS 41, Kansas City 21
Minnesota 17, PITTSBURGH 14
ST. LOUIS 44, San Diego 14
DETROIT 45, Pittsburgh 3
L.A. RAMS 41, Buffalo 17
TAMPA BAY 33, Houston 24
Dallas 35, SEATTLE 10
St. Louis 34, L.A. RAIDERS 24
San Francisco 23, BUFFALO 10
MINNESOTA 20, Cincinnati 14
ATLANTA 31, Buffalo 14

# NUMBER-ONE DRAFT CHOICES

| Season | Team | Player | Position | College |
|---|---|---|---|---|
| 1984 | New England | Irving Fryar | WR | Nebraska |
| 1983 | Baltimore | John Elway | QB | Stanford |
| 1982 | New England | Kenneth Sims | DT | Texas |
| 1981 | New Orleans | George Rogers | RB | South Carolina |
| 1980 | Detroit | Billy Sims | RB | Oklahoma |
| 1979 | Buffalo | Tom Cousineau | LB | Ohio State |
| 1978 | Houston | Earl Campbell | RB | Texas |
| 1977 | Tampa Bay | Ricky Bell | RB | Southern California |
| 1976 | Tampa Bay | Lee Roy Selmon | DE | Oklahoma |
| 1975 | Atlanta | Steve Bartkowski | QB | California |
| 1974 | Dallas | Ed Jones | DE | Tennessee State |
| 1973 | Houston | John Matuszak | DE | Tampa |
| 1972 | Buffalo | Walt Patulski | DE | Notre Dame |
| 1971 | New England | Jim Plunkett | QB | Stanford |
| 1970 | Pittsburgh | Terry Bradshaw | QB | Louisiana Tech |
| 1969 | Buffalo (AFL) | O. J. Simpson | RB | Southern California |
| 1968 | Minnesota | Ron Yary | T | Southern California |
| 1967 | Baltimore | Bubba Smith | DT | Michigan State |
| 1966 | Atlanta | Tommy Nobis | LB | Texas |
| | Miami (AFL) | Jim Grabowski | RB | Illinois |
| 1965 | New York Giants | Tucker Frederickson | RB | Auburn |
| | Houston (AFL) | Lawrence Elkins | E | Baylor |
| 1964 | San Francisco | Dave Parks | E | Texas Tech |
| | Boston (AFL) | Jack Concannon | QB | Boston College |
| 1963 | Los Angeles | Terry Baker | QB | Oregon State |
| | Kansas City (AFL) | Buck Buchanan | DT | Grambling |
| 1962 | Washington | Ernie Davis | RB | Syracuse |
| | Oakland (AFL) | Roman Gabriel | QB | North Carolina State |
| 1961 | Minnesota | Tommy Mason | RB | Tulane |
| | Buffalo (AFL) | Ken Rice | G | Auburn |
| 1960 | Los Angeles | Billy Cannon | RB | Louisiana State |
| | (AFL had no formal first pick) | | | |
| 1959 | Green Bay | Randy Duncan | QB | Iowa |
| 1958 | Chicago Cardinals | King Hill | QB | Rice |
| 1957 | Green Bay | Paul Hornung | HB | Notre Dame |
| 1956 | Pittsburgh | Gary Glick | DB | Colorado A&M |
| 1955 | Baltimore | George Shaw | QB | Oregon |
| 1954 | Cleveland | Bobby Garrett | QB | Stanford |
| 1953 | San Francisco | Harry Babcock | E | Georgia |
| 1952 | Los Angeles | Bill Wade | QB | Vanderbilt |
| 1951 | New York Giants | Kyle Rote | HB | Southern Methodist |
| 1950 | Detroit | Leon Hart | E | Notre Dame |
| 1949 | Philadelphia | Chuck Bednarik | C | Pennsylvania |
| 1948 | Washington | Harry Gilmer | QB | Alabama |
| 1947 | Chicago Bears | Bob Fenimore | HB | Oklahoma A&M |
| 1946 | Boston | Frank Dancewicz | QB | Notre Dame |
| 1945 | Chicago Cardinals | Charley Trippi | HB | Georgia |
| 1944 | Boston | Angelo Bertelli | QB | Notre Dame |
| 1943 | Detroit | Frank Sinkwich | HB | Georgia |
| 1942 | Pittsburgh | Bill Dudley | HB | Virginia |
| 1941 | Chicago Bears | Tom Harmon | HB | Michigan |
| 1940 | Chicago Cardinals | George Cafego | HB | Tennessee |
| 1939 | Chicago Cardinals | Ki Aldrich | C | Texas Christian |
| 1938 | Cleveland | Corbett Davis | FB | Indiana |
| 1937 | Philadelphia | Sam Francis | FB | Nebraska |
| 1936 | Philadelphia | Jay Berwanger | HB | Chicago |

## NFL Paid Attendance

| Year | Regular Season | Average | Postseason | Super Bowl |
|------|----------------|---------|------------|------------|
| 1983 | 13,277,222 (224 games) | 59,273 | 675,513 (10) | 72,932 |
| 1982* | 7,367,438 (126 games) | 58,472 | 1,033,153 (16) | 103,667 |
| 1981 | 13,606,990 (224 games) | 60,745 | 637,763 (10) | 81,270 |
| 1980 | 13,392,230 (224 games) | 59,787 | 624,430 (10) | 75,500 |
| 1979 | 13,182,039 (224 games) | 58,848 | 630,326 (10) | 103,985 |
| 1978 | 12,771,800 (224 games) | 57,017 | 624,388 (10) | 79,641 |
| 1977 | 11,018,632 (196 games) | 56,218 | 534,925 (8) | 75,804 |
| 1976 | 11,070,543 (196 games) | 56,482 | 492,884 (8) | 103,438 |
| 1975 | 10,213,193 (182 games) | 56,116 | 475,919 (8) | 80,187 |
| 1974 | 10,236,322 (182 games) | 56,244 | 438,664 (8) | 80,997 |
| 1973 | 10,730,933 (182 games) | 58,961 | 525,433 (8) | 71,882 |
| 1972 | 10,445,827 (182 games) | 57,395 | 483,345 (8) | 90,182 |
| 1971 | 10,076,035 (182 games) | 55,363 | 483,891 (8) | 81,023 |
| 1970 | 9,533,333 (182 games) | 52,381 | 458,493 (8) | 79,204 |
| 1969 | 6,096,127 (127 games) NFL | 54,430 | 162,279 (3) | 80,562 |
|      | 2,843,373 (70 games) AFL | 40,620 | 167,088 (3) | |
| 1968 | 5,882,313 (112 games) NFL | 52,521 | 215,902 (3) | 75,377 |
|      | 2,635,004 (70 games) AFL | 37,643 | 114,438 (2) | |
| 1967 | 5,938,924 (112 games) NFL | 53,026 | 166,208 (3) | 75,546 |
|      | 2,295,697 (63 games) AFL | 36,439 | 53,330 (1) | |
| 1966 | 5,337,044 (105 games) NFL | 50,829 | 74,152 (1) | 61,946** |
|      | 2,160,369 (63 games) AFL | 34,291 | 42,080 (1) | |
| 1965 | 4,634,021 (98 games) NFL | 47,286 | 100,304 (2) | |
|      | 1,782,384 (56 games) AFL | 31,828 | 30,361 (1) | |
| 1964 | 4,563,049 (98 games) NFL | 46,562 | 79,544 (1) | |
|      | 1,447,875 (56 games) AFL | 25,855 | 40,242 (1) | |
| 1963 | 4,163,643 (98 games) NFL | 42,486 | 45,801 (1) | |
|      | 1,208,697 (56 games) AFL | 21,584 | 63,171 (2) | |
| 1962 | 4,003,421 (98 games) NFL | 40,851 | 64,892 (1) | |
|      | 1,147,302 (56 games) AFL | 20,487 | 37,981 (1) | |
| 1961 | 3,986,159 (98 games) NFL | 40,675 | 39,029 (1) | |
|      | 1,002,657 (56 games) AFL | 17,904 | 29,556 (1) | |
| 1960 | 3,128,296 (78 games) NFL | 40,106 | 67,325 (1) | |
|      | 926,156 (56 games) AFL | 16,538 | 32,183 (1) | |
| 1959 | 3,140,000 (72 games) | 43,617 | 57,545 (1) | |
| 1958 | 3,006,124 (72 games) | 41,752 | 123,659 (2) | |
| 1957 | 2,836,318 (72 games) | 39,393 | 119,579 (2) | |
| 1956 | 2,551,263 (72 games) | 35,434 | 56,836 (1) | |
| 1955 | 2,521,836 (72 games) | 35,026 | 85,693 (1) | |
| 1954 | 2,190,571 (72 games) | 30,425 | 43,827 (1) | |
| 1953 | 2,164,585 (72 games) | 30,064 | 54,577 (1) | |
| 1952 | 2,052,126 (72 games) | 28,502 | 97,507 (2) | |
| 1951 | 1,913,019 (72 games) | 26,570 | 57,522 (1) | |
| 1950 | 1,977,753 (78 games) | 25,356 | 136,647 (3) | |
| 1949 | 1,391,735 (60 games) | 23,196 | 27,980 (1) | |
| 1948 | 1,525,243 (60 games) | 25,421 | 36,309 (1) | |
| 1947 | 1,837,437 (60 games) | 30,624 | 66,268 (2) | |
| 1946 | 1,732,135 (55 games) | 31,493 | 58,346 (1) | |
| 1945 | 1,270,401 (50 games) | 25,408 | 32,178 (1) | |
| 1944 | 1,019,649 (50 games) | 20,393 | 46,016 (1) | |
| 1943 | 969,128 (50 games) | 19,383 | 71,315 (2) | |
| 1942 | 887,920 (55 games) | 16,144 | 36,006 (1) | |
| 1941 | 1,108,615 (55 games) | 20,157 | 55,870 (2) | |
| 1940 | 1,063,025 (55 games) | 19,328 | 36,034 (1) | |
| 1939 | 1,071,200 (55 games) | 19,476 | 32,279 (1) | |
| 1938 | 937,197 (55 games) | 17,040 | 48,120 (1) | |
| 1937 | 963,039 (55 games) | 17,510 | 15,878 (1) | |
| 1936 | 816,007 (54 games) | 15,111 | 29,545 (1) | |
| 1935 | 638,178 (53 games) | 12,041 | 15,000 (1) | |
| 1934 | 492,684 (60 games) | 8,211 | 35,059 (1) | |

*Players 57-day strike reduced 224-game schedule to 126 games.

**Only Super Bowl that did not sell out.

## NFL's 10 Biggest Weekends

(Turnstile Count)

| Weekend | Games | Attendance |
|---------|-------|------------|
| October 12, 1980 | 14 | 875,466 |
| September 6, 1981 | 14 | 865,699 |
| September 12, 1982 | 14 | 862,954 |
| September 19, 1982 | 14 | 850,358 |
| September 23, 1979 | 14 | 848,777 |
| November 2, 1980 | 14 | 844,884 |
| November 1, 1981 | 14 | 842,978 |
| September 27, 1981 | 14 | 841,514 |
| October 2, 1983 | 14 | 841,329 |
| October 4, 1981 | 14 | 839,776 |

# RECORDS

All-Time Records

Outstanding Performers

Yearly Statistical Leaders

Super Bowl Records

Postseason Game Records

AFC-NFC Pro Bowl Records

Compiled by Elias Sports Bureau

The following records reflect all available official information on the National Football League from its formation in 1920 to date. Also included are all applicable records from the American Football League, 1960-69.

## INDIVIDUAL RECORDS

### SERVICE

**Most Seasons**
- 26 George Blanda, Chi. Bears, 1949, 1950-58; Baltimore, 1950; Houston, 1960-66; Oakland, 1967-75
- 21 Earl Morrall, San Francisco, 1956; Pittsburgh, 1957-58; Detroit, 1958-64; N.Y. Giants, 1965-67; Baltimore, 1968-71; Miami, 1972-76
- 20 Jim Marshall, Cleveland, 1960; Minnesota, 1961-79

**Most Seasons, One Club**
- 19 Jim Marshall, Minnesota, 1961-79
- 18 Jim Hart, St. Louis, 1966-83
- 17 Lou Groza, Cleveland, 1950-59, 1961-67
  Johnny Unitas, Baltimore, 1956-72
  John Brodie, San Francisco, 1957-73
  Jim Bakken, St. Louis, 1962-78
  Mick Tingelhoff, Minnesota, 1962-78

**Most Games Played, Career**
- 340 George Blanda, Chi. Bears, 1949, 1950-58; Baltimore, 1950; Houston, 1960-66; Oakland, 1967-75
- 282 Jim Marshall, Cleveland, 1960; Minnesota, 1961-79
- 255 Earl Morrall, San Francisco, 1956; Pittsburgh, 1957-58; Detroit, 1958-64; N.Y. Giants, 1965-67; Baltimore, 1968-71; Miami, 1972-76

**Most Consecutive Games Played, Career**
- 282 Jim Marshall, Cleveland, 1960; Minnesota, 1961-79
- 240 Mick Tingelhoff, Minnesota, 1962-78
- 234 Jim Bakken, St. Louis, 1962-78

**Most Seasons, Coach**
- 40 George Halas, Chi. Bears, 1920-29, 1933-42, 1946-55, 1958-67
- 33 Earl (Curly) Lambeau, Green Bay, 1921-49; Chi. Cardinals, 1950-51; Washington, 1952-53
- 24 Tom Landry, Dallas, 1960-83

### SCORING

**Most Seasons Leading League**
- 5 Don Hutson, Green Bay, 1940-44
  Gino Cappelletti, Boston, 1961, 1963-66
- 3 Earl (Dutch) Clark, Portsmouth, 1932; Detroit, 1935-36
  Pat Harder, Chi. Cardinals, 1947-49
  Paul Hornung, Green Bay, 1959-61
- 2 Jack Manders, Chi. Bears, 1934, 1937
  Gordy Soltau, San Francisco, 1952-53
  Doak Walker, Detroit, 1950, 1955
  Gene Mingo, Denver, 1960, 1962
  Jim Turner, N.Y. Jets, 1968-69
  Fred Cox, Minnesota, 1969-70
  Chester Marcol, Green Bay, 1972, 1974
  John Smith, New England, 1979-80

**Most Consecutive Seasons Leading League**
- 5 Don Hutson, Green Bay, 1940-44
- 4 Gino Cappelletti, Boston, 1963-66
- 3 Pat Harder, Chi. Cardinals, 1947-49
  Paul Hornung, Green Bay, 1959-61

#### POINTS

**Most Points, Career**
- 2,002 George Blanda, Chi. Bears, 1949, 1950-58; Baltimore, 1950; Houston, 1960-66; Oakland, 1967-75 (9-td, 943-pat, 335-fg)
- 1,523 Jan Stenerud, Kansas City, 1967-79; Green Bay, 1980-83 (509-pat, 338-fg)
- 1,439 Jim Turner, N.Y. Jets, 1964-70; Denver, 1971-79 (1-td, 521-pat, 304-fg)

**Most Points, Season**
- 176 Paul Hornung, Green Bay, 1960 (15-td, 41-pat, 15-fg)
- 161 Mark Moseley, Washington, 1983 (62-pat, 33-fg)
- 155 Gino Cappelletti, Boston, 1964 (7-td, 38-pat, 25-fg)

**Most Points, No Touchdowns, Season**
- 161 Mark Moseley, Washington, 1983 (62-pat, 33-fg)
- 145 Jim Turner, N.Y. Jets, 1968 (43-pat, 34-fg)
- 130 David Ray, Los Angeles, 1973 (40-pat, 30-fg)

**Most Seasons, 100 or More Points**
- 7 Jan Stenerud, Kansas City, 1967-71; Green Bay, 1981, 1983
- 6 Gino Cappelletti, Boston, 1961-66
  George Blanda, Houston, 1960-61; Oakland, 1967-69, 1973
  Bruce Gossett, Los Angeles, 1966-67, 1969; San Francisco, 1970-71, 1973
- 5 Lou Michaels, Pittsburgh, 1962; Baltimore, 1964-65, 1967-68

**Most Points, Rookie, Season**
- 132 Gale Sayers, Chicago, 1965 (22-td)
- 128 Doak Walker, Detroit, 1950 (11-td, 38-pat, 8-fg)
  Cookie Gilchrist, Buffalo, 1962 (15-td, 14-pat, 8-fg)
  Chester Marcol, Green Bay, 1972 (29-pat, 33-fg)
- 127 Ali Haji-Sheikh, N.Y. Giants, 1983 (22-pat, 35-fg)

**Most Points, Game**
- 40 Ernie Nevers, Chi. Cardinals vs. Chi. Bears, Nov. 28, 1929 (6-td, 4-pat)
- 36 Dub Jones, Cleveland vs. Chi. Bears, Nov. 25, 1951 (6-td)
  Gale Sayers, Chicago vs. San Francisco, Dec. 12, 1965 (6-td)
- 33 Paul Hornung, Green Bay vs. Baltimore, Oct. 8, 1961 (4-td, 6-pat, 1-fg)

**Most Consecutive Games Scoring**
- 151 Fred Cox, Minnesota, 1963-73
- 133 Garo Yepremian, Miami, 1970-78; New Orleans, 1979
- 118 Jim Turner, N.Y. Jets, 1966-70; Denver, 1971-74

#### TOUCHDOWNS

**Most Seasons Leading League**
- 8 Don Hutson, Green Bay, 1935-38, 1941-44

---

- 3 Jim Brown, Cleveland, 1958-59, 1963
  Lance Alworth, San Diego, 1964-66
- 2 By many players

**Most Consecutive Seasons Leading League**
- 4 Don Hutson, Green Bay, 1935-38, 1941-44
- 3 Lance Alworth, San Diego, 1964-66
- 2 By many players

**Most Touchdowns, Career**
- 126 Jim Brown, Cleveland, 1957-65 (106-r, 20-p)
- 113 Lenny Moore, Baltimore, 1956-67 (63-r, 48-p, 2-ret)
- 105 Don Hutson, Green Bay, 1935-45 (3-r, 99-p, 3-ret)

**Most Touchdowns, Season**
- 24 John Riggins, Washington, 1983 (24-r)
- 23 O.J. Simpson, Buffalo, 1975 (16-r, 7-p)
- 22 Gale Sayers, Chicago, 1965 (14-r, 6-p, 2-ret)
  Chuck Foreman, Minnesota, 1975 (13-r, 9-p)

**Most Touchdowns, Rookie, Season**
- 22 Gale Sayers, Chicago, 1965 (14-r, 6-p, 2-ret)
- 20 Eric Dickerson, L.A. Rams, 1983 (18-r, 2-p)
- 16 Billy Sims, Detroit, 1980 (13-r, 3-p)

**Most Touchdowns, Game**
- 6 Ernie Nevers, Chi. Cardinals vs. Chi. Bears, Nov. 28, 1929 (6-r)
  Dub Jones, Cleveland vs. Chi. Bears, Nov. 25, 1951 (4-r, 2-p)
  Gale Sayers, Chicago vs. San Francisco, Dec. 12, 1965 (4-r, 1-p, 1-ret)
- 5 Bob Shaw, Chi. Cardinals vs. Baltimore, Oct. 2, 1950 (5-p)
  Jim Brown, Cleveland vs. Baltimore, Nov. 1, 1959 (5-r)
  Abner Haynes, Dall. Texans vs. Oakland, Nov. 26, 1961 (4-r, 1-p)
  Billy Cannon, Houston vs. N.Y. Titans, Dec. 10, 1961 (3-r, 2-p)
  Cookie Gilchrist, Buffalo vs. N.Y. Jets, Dec. 8, 1963 (5-r)
  Paul Hornung, Green Bay vs. Baltimore, Dec. 12, 1965 (3-r, 2-p)
  Kellen Winslow, San Diego vs. Oakland, Nov. 22, 1981 (5-p)
- 4 By many players

**Most Consecutive Games Scoring Touchdowns**
- 18 Lenny Moore, Baltimore, 1963-65
- 14 O.J. Simpson, Buffalo, 1975
- 13 John Riggins, Washington, 1982-83

---

#### POINTS AFTER TOUCHDOWN

**Most Seasons Leading League**
- 8 George Blanda, Chi. Bears, 1956; Houston, 1961-62; Oakland, 1967-69, 1972, 1974
- 4 Bob Waterfield, Cleveland, 1945; Los Angeles, 1946, 1950, 1952
- 3 Earl (Dutch) Clark, Portsmouth, 1932; Detroit, 1935-36
  Jack Manders, Chi. Bears, 1933-35
  Don Hutson, Green Bay, 1941-42, 1945

**Most Points After Touchdown Attempted, Career**
- 959 George Blanda, Chi. Bears, 1949, 1950-58; Baltimore, 1950; Houston, 1960-66; Oakland, 1967-75
- 657 Lou Groza, Cleveland, 1950-59, 1961-67
- 553 Jim Bakken, St. Louis, 1962-78

**Most Points After Touchdown Attempted, Season**
- 65 George Blanda, Houston, 1961
- 63 Mark Moseley, Washington, 1983
- 61 Rolf Benirschke, San Diego, 1981

**Most Points After Touchdown Attempted, Game**
- 10 Charlie Gogolak, Washington vs. N.Y. Giants, Nov. 27, 1966
- 9 Pat Harder, Chi. Cardinals vs. N.Y. Giants, Oct. 17, 1948; vs. N.Y. Bulldogs, Nov. 13, 1949
  Bob Waterfield, Los Angeles vs. Baltimore, Oct. 22, 1950
  Bob Thomas, Chicago vs. Green Bay, Dec. 7, 1980
- 8 By many players

**Most Points After Touchdown, Career**
- 943 George Blanda, Chi. Bears, 1949, 1950-58; Baltimore, 1950; Houston, 1960-66; Oakland, 1967-75
- 641 Lou Groza, Cleveland, 1950-59, 1961-67
- 534 Jim Bakken, St. Louis, 1962-78

**Most Points After Touchdown, Season**
- 64 George Blanda, Houston, 1961
- 62 Mark Moseley, Washington, 1983
- 59 Rafael Septien, Dallas, 1980

**Most Points After Touchdown, Game**
- 9 Pat Harder, Chi. Cardinals vs. N.Y. Giants, Oct. 17, 1948
  Bob Waterfield, Los Angeles vs. Baltimore, Oct. 22, 1950
  Charlie Gogolak, Washington vs. N.Y. Giants, Nov. 27, 1966
- 8 By many players

**Most Consecutive Points After Touchdown**
- 234 Tommy Davis, San Francisco, 1959-65
- 221 Jim Turner, N.Y. Jets, 1967-70; Denver, 1971-74
- 201 George Blanda, Oakland, 1967-71

**Highest Points After Touchdown Percentage, Career (200 points after touchdown)**
- 99.43 Tommy Davis, San Francisco, 1959-69 (350-348)
- 98.33 George Blanda, Chi. Bears, 1949, 1950-58; Baltimore, 1950; Houston, 1960-66; Oakland, 1967-75 (959-943)
- 97.93 Danny Villanueva, L.A. Rams, 1960-64; Dallas, 1965-67 (241-236)

**Most Points After Touchdown, No Misses, Season**
- 56 Danny Villanueva, Dallas, 1966
- 54 Mike Clark, Dallas, 1968
  George Blanda, Oakland, 1968
- 53 Pat Harder, Chi. Cardinals, 1948

**Most Points After Touchdown, No Misses, Game**
- 9 Pat Harder, Chi. Cardinals vs. N.Y. Giants, Oct. 17, 1948
  Bob Waterfield, Los Angeles vs. Baltimore, Oct. 22, 1950
- 8 By many players

---

#### FIELD GOALS

**Most Seasons Leading League**
- 5 Lou Groza, Cleveland, 1950, 1952-54, 1957
- 4 Jack Manders, Chi. Bears, 1933-34, 1936-37
  Ward Cuff, N.Y. Giants, 1938-39, 1943; Green Bay, 1947

Mark Moseley, Washington, 1976-77, 1979, 1982
3  Bob Waterfield, Los Angeles, 1947, 1949, 1951
Gino Cappelletti, Boston, 1961, 1963-64
Fred Cox, Minnesota, 1965, 1969-70
Jan Stenerud, Kansas City, 1967, 1970, 1975

**Most Consecutive Seasons Leading League**
3  Lou Groza, Cleveland, 1952-54
2  By many players

**Most Field Goals Attempted, Career**
638  George Blanda, Chi. Bears, 1949, 1950-58; Baltimore, 1950; Houston, 1960-66; Oakland, 1967-75
509  Jan Stenerud, Kansas City, 1967-79; Green Bay, 1980-83
488  Jim Turner, N.Y. Jets, 1964-70; Denver, 1971-79

**Most Field Goals Attempted, Season**
49  Bruce Gossett, Los Angeles, 1966
     Curt Knight, Washington, 1971
48  Chester Marcol, Green Bay, 1972
47  Jim Turner, N.Y. Jets, 1969
     David Ray, Los Angeles, 1973
     Mark Moseley, Washington, 1983

**Most Field Goals Attempted, Game**
9  Jim Bakken, St. Louis vs. Pittsburgh, Sept. 24, 1967
8  Lou Michaels, Pittsburgh vs. St. Louis, Dec. 2, 1962
     Garo Yepremian, Detroit vs. Minnesota, Nov. 13, 1966
     Jim Turner, N.Y. Jets vs. Buffalo, Nov. 3, 1968
7  By many players

**Most Field Goals, Career**
338  Jan Stenerud, Kansas City, 1967-79; Green Bay, 1980-83
335  George Blanda, Chi. Bears, 1949, 1950-58; Baltimore, 1950; Houston, 1960-66; Oakland, 1967-75
304  Jim Turner, N.Y. Jets, 1964-70; Denver, 1971-79

**Most Field Goals, Season**
35  Ali Haji-Sheikh, N.Y. Giants, 1983
34  Jim Turner, N.Y. Jets, 1968
33  Chester Marcol, Green Bay, 1972
     Mark Moseley, Washington, 1983

**Most Field Goals, Rookie, Season**
35  Ali Haji-Sheikh, N.Y. Giants, 1983
33  Chester Marcol, Green Bay, 1972
30  Raul Allegre, Baltimore, 1983

**Most Field Goals, Game**
7  Jim Bakken, St. Louis vs. Pittsburgh, Sept. 24, 1967
6  Gino Cappelletti, Boston vs. Denver, Oct. 4, 1964
     Garo Yepremian, Detroit vs. Minnesota, Nov. 13, 1966
     Jim Turner, N.Y. Jets vs. Buffalo, Nov. 3, 1968
     Tom Dempsey, Philadelphia vs. Houston, Nov. 12, 1972
     Bobby Howfield, N.Y. Jets vs. New Orleans, Dec. 3, 1972
     Jim Bakken, St. Louis vs. Atlanta, Dec. 9, 1973
     Joe Danelo, N.Y. Giants vs. Seattle, Oct. 18, 1981
     Ray Wersching, San Francisco vs. New Orleans, Oct. 16, 1983
5  By many players

**Most Field Goals, One Quarter**
4  Garo Yepremian, Detroit vs. Minnesota, Nov. 13, 1966 (second quarter)
     Curt Knight, Washington vs. N.Y. Giants, Nov. 15, 1970 (second quarter)
3  By many players

**Most Consecutive Games Scoring Field Goals**
31  Fred Cox, Minnesota, 1968-70
28  Jim Turner, N.Y. Jets, 1970; Denver, 1971-72
21  Bruce Gossett, San Francisco, 1970-72

**Most Consecutive Field Goals**
23  Mark Moseley, Washington, 1981-82
20  Garo Yepremian, Miami, 1978; New Orleans, 1979
16  Jan Stenerud, Kansas City, 1969
     Don Cockroft, Cleveland, 1974-75
     Rolf Benirschke, San Diego, 1978-80
     Benny Ricardo, New Orleans, 1981; Minnesota, 1983

**Longest Field Goal**
63  Tom Dempsey, New Orleans vs. Detroit, Nov. 8, 1970
59  Tony Franklin, Philadelphia vs. Dallas, Nov. 12, 1979
58  Dan Miller, Baltimore vs. San Diego, Dec. 26, 1982
     Nick Lowery, Kansas City vs. Washington, Sept. 18, 1983
     Steve Cox, Cleveland vs. Denver, Dec. 4, 1983

**Highest Field Goal Percentage, Career (100 field goals)**
71.97  Rolf Benirschke, San Diego, 1977-83 (157-113)
69.10  Rafael Septien, Los Angeles, 1977; Dallas, 1978-83 (178-123)
67.97  Toni Fritsch, Dallas, 1971-73, 1975; San Diego, 1976; Houston, 1977-81; New Orleans, 1982 (231-157)

**Highest Field Goal Percentage, Season (14 attempts)**
95.24  Mark Moseley, Washington, 1982 (21-20)
91.67  Jan Stenerud, Green Bay, 1981 (24-22)
88.46  Lou Groza, Cleveland, 1953 (26-23)

**Most Field Goals, No Misses, Game**
6  Gino Cappelletti, Boston vs. Denver, Oct. 4, 1964
     Joe Danelo, N.Y. Giants vs. Seattle, Oct. 18, 1981
     Ray Wersching, San Francisco vs. Cincinnati, Oct. 16, 1983
5  Roger LeClerc, Chicago vs. Detroit, Dec. 3, 1961
     Lou Michaels, Baltimore vs. San Francisco, Sept. 25, 1966
     Mac Percival, Chicago vs. Philadelphia, Oct. 20, 1968
     Roy Gerela, Houston vs. Miami, Sept. 28, 1969
     Jan Stenerud, Kansas City vs. Buffalo, Nov. 2, 1969; vs. Buffalo, Dec. 7, 1969
     Horst Muhlmann, Cincinnati vs. Buffalo, Nov. 8, 1970; vs. Pittsburgh, Sept. 24, 1972
     Bruce Gossett, San Francisco vs. Denver, Sept. 23, 1973
     Nick Mike-Mayer, Atlanta vs. Los Angeles, Nov. 4, 1973
     Curt Knight, Washington vs. Baltimore, Nov. 18, 1973
     Tim Mazzetti, Atlanta vs. Los Angeles, Oct. 30, 1978
     Ed Murray, Detroit vs. Green Bay, Sept. 14, 1980
     Rich Karlis, Denver vs. Seattle, Nov. 20, 1983

**SAFETIES**

**Most Safeties, Career**
4  Ted Hendricks, Baltimore, 1969-73; Green Bay, 1974; Oakland, 1975-81; L.A. Raiders, 1982-83

Doug English, Detroit, 1975-79, 1981-83
3  Bill McPeak, Pittsburgh, 1949-57
Charlie Krueger, San Francisco, 1959-73
Ernie Stautner, Pittsburgh, 1950-63
Jim Katcavage, N.Y. Giants, 1956-68
Roger Brown, Detroit, 1960-66; Los Angeles, 1967-69
Bruce Maher, Detroit, 1960-67; N.Y. Giants, 1968-69
Ron McDole, St. Louis, 1961; Houston, 1962; Buffalo, 1963-70; Washington, 1971-78
Alan Page, Minnesota, 1967-78; Chicago, 1979-81
2  By many players

**Most Safeties, Season**
2  Tom Nash, Green Bay, 1932
Roger Brown, Detroit, 1962
Ron McDole, Buffalo, 1964
Alan Page, Minnesota, 1971
Fred Dryer, Los Angeles, 1973
Benny Barnes, Dallas, 1973
James Young, Houston, 1977
Tom Hannon, Minnesota, 1981
Doug English, Detroit, 1983

**Most Safeties, Game**
2  Fred Dryer, Los Angeles vs. Green Bay, Oct. 21, 1973

# RUSHING

**Most Seasons Leading League**
8  Jim Brown, Cleveland, 1957-61, 1963-65
4  Steve Van Buren, Philadelphia, 1945, 1947-49
     O.J. Simpson, Buffalo, 1972-73, 1975-76
3  Earl Campbell, Houston, 1978-80

**Most Consecutive Seasons Leading League**
5  Jim Brown, Cleveland, 1957-61
3  Steve Van Buren, Philadelphia, 1947-49
     Jim Brown, Cleveland, 1963-65
     Earl Campbell, Houston, 1978-80
2  Bill Paschal, N.Y. Giants, 1943-44
     Joe Perry, San Francisco, 1953-54
     Jim Nance, Boston, 1966-67
     Leroy Kelly, Cleveland, 1967-68
     O.J. Simpson, Buffalo, 1972-73; 1975-76

**ATTEMPTS**

**Most Seasons Leading League**
6  Jim Brown, Cleveland, 1958-59, 1961, 1963-65
4  Steve Van Buren, Philadelphia, 1947-50
     Walter Payton, Chicago, 1976-79
3  Cookie Gilchrist, Buffalo, 1963-64; Denver, 1965
     Jim Nance, Boston, 1966-67, 1969
     O. J. Simpson, Buffalo, 1973-75

**Most Consecutive Seasons Leading League**
4  Steve Van Buren, Philadelphia, 1947-50
     Walter Payton, Chicago, 1976-79
3  Jim Brown, Cleveland, 1963-65
     Cookie Gilchrist, Buffalo, 1963-64; Denver, 1965
     O.J. Simpson, Buffalo, 1973-75
2  By many players

**Most Attempts, Career**
2,881  Franco Harris, Pittsburgh, 1972-83
2,666  Walter Payton, Chicago, 1975-83
2,413  John Riggins, N.Y. Jets, 1971-75; Washington, 1976-79, 1981-83

**Most Attempts, Season**
390  Eric Dickerson, L.A. Rams, 1983
378  George Rogers, New Orleans, 1981
375  John Riggins, Washington, 1983

**Most Attempts, Rookie, Season**
390  Eric Dickerson, L.A. Rams, 1983
378  George Rogers, New Orleans, 1981
335  Curt Warner, Seattle, 1983

**Most Attempts, Game**
43  Butch Woolfolk, N.Y. Giants vs. Philadelphia, Nov. 20, 1983
42  James Wilder, Tampa Bay vs. Pittsburgh, Oct. 30, 1983
41  Franco Harris, Pittsburgh vs. Cincinnati, Oct. 17, 1976

**YARDS GAINED**

**Most Yards Gained, Career**
12,312  Jim Brown, Cleveland, 1957-65
11,950  Franco Harris, Pittsburgh, 1972-83
11,625  Walter Payton, Chicago, 1975-83

**Most Seasons, 1,000 or More Yards Rushing**
8  Franco Harris, Pittsburgh, 1972, 1974-79, 1983
7  Jim Brown, Cleveland, 1958-61, 1963-65
     Walter Payton, Chicago, 1976-81, 1983
6  Tony Dorsett, Dallas, 1977-81, 1983

**Most Yards Gained, Season**
2,003  O.J. Simpson, Buffalo, 1973
1,934  Earl Campbell, Houston, 1980
1,863  Jim Brown, Cleveland, 1963

**Most Yards Gained, Rookie, Season**
1,808  Eric Dickerson, L.A. Rams, 1983
1,674  George Rogers, New Orleans, 1981
1,605  Ottis Anderson, St. Louis, 1979

**Most Yards Gained, Game**
275  Walter Payton, Chicago vs. Minnesota, Nov. 20, 1977
273  O.J. Simpson, Buffalo vs. Detroit, Nov. 25, 1976
250  O.J. Simpson, Buffalo vs. New England, Sept. 16, 1973

**Most Games, 200 or More Yards Rushing, Career**
6  O.J. Simpson, Buffalo, 1969-77; San Francisco, 1978-79
4  Jim Brown, Cleveland, 1957-65
     Earl Campbell, Houston, 1978-83
2  Walter Payton, Chicago, 1975-83

**Most Games, 200 or More Yards Rushing, Season**
4  Earl Campbell, Houston, 1980
3  O.J. Simpson, Buffalo, 1973

2 Jim Brown, Cleveland, 1963
O.J. Simpson, Buffalo, 1976
Walter Payton, Chicago, 1977

**Most Consecutive Games, 200 or More Yards Rushing**
2 O.J. Simpson, Buffalo, 1973, 1976
Earl Campbell, Houston, 1980

**Most Games, 100 or More Yards Rushing, Career**
58 Jim Brown, Cleveland, 1957-65
54 Walter Payton, Chicago, 1975-83
47 Franco Harris, Pittsburgh, 1972-83

**Most Games, 100 or More Yards Rushing, Season**
11 O.J. Simpson, Buffalo, 1973
Earl Campbell, Houston, 1979
10 Walter Payton, Chicago, 1977
Earl Campbell, Houston, 1980
9 Jim Brown, Cleveland, 1958, 1963
Ottis Anderson, St. Louis, 1979
Tony Dorsett, Dallas, 1981
George Rogers, New Orleans, 1981
Eric Dickerson, L.A. Rams, 1983

**Most Consecutive Games, 100 or More Yards Rushing**
7 O.J. Simpson, Buffalo, 1972-73
Earl Campbell, Houston, 1979
6 Jim Brown, Cleveland, 1958
Franco Harris, Pittsburgh, 1972
Earl Campbell, Houston, 1980
5 Rob Goode, Washington, 1951
Jim Brown, Cleveland, 1961
Jim Nance, Boston, 1966
O.J. Simpson, Buffalo, 1973, 1975
Walter Payton, Chicago, 1977

**Longest Run From Scrimmage**
99 Tony Dorsett, Dallas vs. Minnesota, Jan. 3, 1983 (TD)
97 Andy Uram, Green Bay vs. Chi. Cardinals, Oct. 8, 1939 (TD)
Bob Gage, Pittsburgh vs. Chi. Bears, Dec. 4, 1949 (TD)
96 Jim Spavital, Baltimore vs. Green Bay, Nov. 5, 1950 (TD)
Bob Hoernschemeyer, Detroit vs. N.Y. Yanks, Nov. 23, 1950 (TD)

---

## AVERAGE GAIN
**Highest Average Gain, Career (700 attempts)**
5.22 Jim Brown, Cleveland, 1957-65 (2,359-12,312)
5.14 Eugene (Mercury) Morris, Miami, 1969-75; San Diego, 1976 (804-4,133)
5.00 Gale Sayers, Chicago, 1965-71 (991-4,956)

**Highest Average Gain, Season (Qualifiers)**
9.94 Beattie Feathers, Chi. Bears, 1934 (101-1,004)
6.87 Bobby Douglass, Chicago, 1972 (141-968)
6.78 Dan Towler, Los Angeles, 1951 (126-854)

**Highest Average Gain, Game (10 attempts)**
17.09 Marion Motley, Cleveland vs. Pittsburgh, Oct. 29, 1950 (11-188)
16.70 Bill Grimes, Green Bay vs. N.Y. Yanks, Oct. 8, 1950 (10-167)
16.57 Bobby Mitchell, Cleveland vs. Washington, Nov. 15, 1959 (14-232)

## TOUCHDOWNS
**Most Seasons Leading League**
5 Jim Brown, Cleveland, 1957-59, 1963, 1965
4 Steve Van Buren, Philadelphia, 1945, 1947-49
3 Abner Haynes, Dall. Texans, 1960-62
Cookie Gilchrist, Buffalo, 1962-64
Paul Lowe, L.A. Chargers, 1960; San Diego, 1961, 1965
Leroy Kelly, Cleveland, 1966-68

**Most Consecutive Seasons Leading League**
3 Steve Van Buren, Philadelphia, 1947-49
Jim Brown, Cleveland, 1957-59
Abner Haynes, Dall. Texans, 1960-62
Cookie Gilchrist, Buffalo, 1962-64
Leroy Kelly, Cleveland, 1966-68

**Most Touchdowns, Career**
106 Jim Brown, Cleveland, 1957-65
91 Franco Harris, Pittsburgh, 1972-83
83 Jim Taylor, Green Bay, 1958-66; New Orleans, 1967

**Most Touchdowns, Season**
24 John Riggins, Washington, 1983
19 Jim Taylor, Green Bay, 1962
Earl Campbell, Houston, 1979
Chuck Muncie, San Diego, 1981
18 Eric Dickerson, L.A. Rams, 1983

**Most Touchdowns, Rookie, Season**
18 Eric Dickerson, L.A. Rams, 1983
14 Gale Sayers, Chicago, 1965
13 Cookie Gilchrist, Buffalo, 1962
Earl Campbell, Houston, 1978
Billy Sims, Detroit, 1980
George Rogers, New Orleans, 1981
Curt Warner, Seattle, 1983

**Most Touchdowns, Game**
6 Ernie Nevers, Chi. Cardinals vs. Chi. Bears, Nov. 28, 1929
5 Jim Brown, Cleveland vs. Baltimore, Nov. 1, 1959
Cookie Gilchrist, Buffalo vs. N.Y. Jets, Dec. 8, 1963
4 By many players

**Most Consecutive Games Rushing for Touchdowns**
13 John Riggins, Washington, 1982-83
11 Lenny Moore, Baltimore, 1963-64
9 Leroy Kelly, Cleveland, 1968

---

# PASSING

**Most Seasons Leading League**
6 Sammy Baugh, Washington, 1937, 1940, 1943, 1945, 1947, 1949
4 Len Dawson, Dall. Texans, 1962; Kansas City, 1964, 1966, 1968
Roger Staubach, Dallas, 1971, 1973, 1978-79
Ken Anderson, Cincinnati, 1974-75, 1981-82
3 Arnie Herber, Green Bay, 1932, 1934, 1936
Norm Van Brocklin, Los Angeles, 1950, 1952, 1954
Bart Starr, Green Bay, 1962, 1964, 1966

**Most Consecutive Seasons Leading League**
2 Cecil Isbell, Green Bay, 1941-42
Milt Plum, Cleveland, 1960-61
Ken Anderson, Cincinnati, 1974-75; 1981-82
Roger Staubach, Dallas, 1978-79

---

## ATTEMPTS
**Most Seasons Leading League**
4 Sammy Baugh, Washington, 1937, 1943, 1947-48
Johnny Unitas, Baltimore, 1957, 1959-61
George Blanda, Chi. Bears, 1953; Houston, 1963-65
3 Arnie Herber, Green Bay, 1932, 1934, 1936
Sonny Jurgensen, Washington, 1966-67, 1969
2 By many players

**Most Consecutive Seasons Leading League**
3 Johnny Unitas, Baltimore, 1959-61
George Blanda, Houston, 1963-65
2 By many players

**Most Passes Attempted, Career**
6,467 Fran Tarkenton, Minnesota, 1961-66, 1972-78; N.Y. Giants, 1967-71
5,186 Johnny Unitas, Baltimore, 1956-72; San Diego, 1973
5,069 Jim Hart, St. Louis, 1966-83

**Most Passes Attempted, Season**
609 Dan Fouts, San Diego, 1981
603 Bill Kenney, Kansas City, 1983
593 Tommy Kramer, Minnesota, 1981

**Most Passes Attempted, Rookie, Season**
439 Jim Zorn, Seattle, 1976
392 Butch Songin, Boston, 1960
375 Norm Snead, Washington, 1961

**Most Passes Attempted, Game**
68 George Blanda, Houston vs. Buffalo, Nov. 1, 1964
62 Joe Namath, N.Y. Jets vs. Baltimore, Oct. 18, 1970
Steve Dils, Minnesota vs. Tampa Bay, Sept. 5, 1981
61 Tommy Kramer, Minnesota vs. Buffalo, Dec. 16, 1979

---

## COMPLETIONS
**Most Seasons Leading League**
5 Sammy Baugh, Washington, 1937, 1943, 1945, 1947-48
4 George Blanda, Chi. Bears, 1953; Houston, 1963-65
Sonny Jurgensen, Philadelphia, 1961; Washington, 1966-67, 1969
3 Arnie Herber, Green Bay, 1932, 1934, 1936
Johnny Unitas, Baltimore, 1959-60, 1963
John Brodie, San Francisco, 1965, 1968, 1970
Fran Tarkenton, Minnesota, 1975-76, 1978

**Most Consecutive Seasons Leading League**
3 George Blanda, Houston, 1963-65
2 By many players

**Most Passes Completed, Career**
3,686 Fran Tarkenton, Minnesota, 1961-66, 1972-78; N.Y. Giants, 1967-71
2,830 Johnny Unitas, Baltimore, 1956-72; San Diego, 1973
2,590 Jim Hart, St. Louis, 1966-83

**Most Passes Completed, Season**
360 Dan Fouts, San Diego, 1981
348 Dan Fouts, San Diego, 1980
347 Steve DeBerg, San Francisco, 1979

**Most Passes Completed, Rookie, Season**
208 Jim Zorn, Seattle, 1976
187 Butch Songin, Boston, 1960
183 Jeff Komlo, Detroit, 1979

**Most Passes Completed, Game**
42 Richard Todd, N.Y. Jets vs. San Francisco, Sept. 21, 1980
40 Ken Anderson, Cincinnati vs. San Diego, Dec. 20, 1982
38 Tommy Kramer, Minnesota vs. Cleveland, Dec. 14, 1980
Tommy Kramer, Minnesota vs. Green Bay, Nov. 29, 1981
Joe Ferguson, Buffalo vs. Miami, Oct. 9, 1983 (OT)

**Most Consecutive Passes Completed**
20 Ken Anderson, Cincinnati vs. Houston, Jan. 2, 1983
18 Steve DeBerg, Denver vs. L.A. Rams (17), Dec. 12, 1982; vs. Kansas City (1), Dec. 19, 1982
17 Bert Jones, Baltimore vs. N.Y. Jets, Dec. 15, 1974

---

## COMPLETION PERCENTAGE
**Most Seasons Leading League**
8 Len Dawson, Dall. Texans, 1962; Kansas City, 1964-69, 1975
7 Sammy Baugh, Washington, 1940, 1942-43, 1945, 1947-49
4 Bart Starr, Green Bay, 1962, 1966, 1968-69

**Most Consecutive Seasons Leading League**
6 Len Dawson, Kansas City, 1964-69
3 Sammy Baugh, Washington, 1947-49
Otto Graham, Cleveland, 1953-55
Milt Plum, Cleveland, 1959-61
2 By many players

**Highest Completion Percentage, Career (1,500 attempts)**
63.52 Joe Montana, San Francisco, 1979-83 (1,645-1,045)
60.18 Danny White, Dallas, 1976-83 (1,710-1,029)
60.09 Ken Stabler, Oakland, 1970-79; Houston, 1980-81; New Orleans, 1982-83 (3,723-2,237)

**Highest Completion Percentage, Season (Qualifiers)**
70.55 Ken Anderson, Cincinnati, 1982 (309-218)
70.33 Sammy Baugh, Washington, 1945 (182-128)
66.67 Ken Stabler, Oakland, 1976 (291-194)
Ken Anderson, Cincinnati, 1983 (297-198)

**Highest Completion Percentage, Rookie, Season (Qualifiers)**
58.45 Dan Marino, Miami, 1983 (296-173)
57.14 Jim McMahon, Chicago, 1982 (210-120)
56.07 Fran Tarkenton, Minnesota, 1961 (280-157)

**Highest Completion Percentage, Game (20 attempts)**
90.91 Ken Anderson, Cincinnati vs. Pittsburgh, Nov. 10, 1974 (22-20)
90.48 Lynn Dickey, Green Bay vs. New Orleans, Dec. 13, 1981 (21-19)
87.50 Dan Marino, Miami vs. Baltimore, Nov. 20, 1983 (24-21)

## YARDS GAINED
**Most Seasons Leading League**
- 5   Sonny Jurgensen, Philadelphia, 1961-62; Washington, 1966-67, 1969
- 4   Sammy Baugh, Washington, 1937, 1940, 1947-48
  - Johnny Unitas, Baltimore, 1957, 1959-60, 1963
  - Dan Fouts, San Diego, 1979-82
- 3   Arnie Herber, Green Bay, 1932, 1934, 1936
  - Sid Luckman, Chi. Bears, 1943, 1945-46
  - John Brodie, San Francisco, 1965, 1968, 1970
  - John Hadl, San Diego, 1965, 1968, 1971
  - Joe Namath, N.Y. Jets, 1966-67, 1972

**Most Consecutive Seasons Leading League**
- 4   Dan Fouts, San Diego, 1979-82
- 2   By many players

**Most Yards Gained, Career**
- 47,003   Fran Tarkenton, Minnesota, 1961-66, 1972-78; N.Y. Giants, 1967-71
- 40,239   Johnny Unitas, Baltimore, 1956-72; San Diego, 1973
- 34,639   Jim Hart, St. Louis, 1966-83

**Most Seasons, 3,000 or More Yards Passing**
- 5   Sonny Jurgensen, Philadelphia, 1961-62; Washington, 1966-67, 1969
- 4   Brian Sipe, Cleveland, 1979-81, 1983
- 3   By many players

**Most Yards Gained, Season**
- 4,802   Dan Fouts, San Diego, 1981
- 4,715   Dan Fouts, San Diego, 1980
- 4,458   Lynn Dickey, Green Bay, 1983

**Most Yards Gained, Rookie, Season**
- 2,571   Jim Zorn, Seattle, 1976
- 2,507   Dennis Shaw, Buffalo, 1970
- 2,476   Butch Songin, Boston, 1960

**Most Yards Gained, Game**
- 554   Norm Van Brocklin, Los Angeles vs. N.Y. Yanks, Sept. 28, 1951
- 509   Vince Ferragamo, L.A. Rams vs. Chicago, Dec. 26, 1982
- 505   Y.A. Tittle, N.Y. Giants vs. Washington, Oct. 28, 1962

**Most Games, 300 or More Yards Passing, Career**
- 35   Dan Fouts, San Diego, 1973-83
- 26   Johnny Unitas, Baltimore, 1956-72; San Diego, 1973
- 25   Sonny Jurgensen, Philadelphia, 1957-63; Washington, 1964-74

**Most Games, 300 or More Yards Passing, Season**
- 8   Dan Fouts, San Diego, 1980
- 7   Dan Fouts, San Diego, 1981
  - Bill Kenney, Kansas City, 1983
- 6   Joe Namath, N.Y. Jets, 1967
  - Dan Fouts, San Diego, 1979
  - Archie Manning, New Orleans, 1980
  - Brian Sipe, Cleveland, 1980

**Most Consecutive Games, 300 or More Yards, Passing, Season**
- 5   Joe Montana, San Francisco, 1982
- 4   Dan Fouts, San Diego, 1979
  - Bill Kenney, Kansas City, 1983
- 3   Frank Tripucka, Denver, 1960
  - Johnny Unitas, Baltimore, 1963
  - George Blanda, Houston, 1964
  - Cotton Davidson, Oakland, 1964
  - John Hadl, San Diego, 1967
  - Sonny Jurgensen, Washington, 1967
  - Dan Fouts, San Diego, 1980

**Longest Pass Completion (All TDs except as noted)**
- 99   Frank Filchock (to Farkas), Washington vs. Pittsburgh, Oct. 15, 1939
  - George Izo (to Mitchell), Washington vs. Cleveland, Sept. 15, 1963
  - Karl Sweetan (to Studstill), Detroit vs. Baltimore, Oct. 16, 1966
  - Sonny Jurgensen (to Allen), Washington vs. Chicago, Sept. 15, 1968
  - Jim Plunkett (to Branch), L.A. Raiders vs. Washington, Oct. 2, 1983
- 98   Doug Russell (to Tinsley), Chi. Cardinals vs. Cleveland, Nov. 27, 1938
  - Ogden Compton (to Lane), Chi. Cardinals vs. Green Bay, Nov. 13, 1955
  - Bill Wade (to Farrington), Chicago Bears vs. Detroit, Oct. 8, 1961
  - Jacky Lee (to Dewveall), Houston vs. San Diego, Nov. 25, 1962
  - Earl Morrall (to Jones), N.Y. Giants vs. Pittsburgh, Sept. 11, 1966
  - Jim Hart (to Moore), St. Louis vs. Los Angeles, Dec. 10, 1972 (no TD)
- 97   Pat Coffee (to Tinsley), Chi. Cardinals vs. Chi. Bears, Dec. 5, 1937
  - Bobby Layne (to Box), Detroit vs. Green Bay, Nov. 26, 1953
  - George Shaw (to Tarr), Denver vs. Boston, Sept. 21, 1962

## AVERAGE GAIN
**Most Seasons Leading League**
- 7   Sid Luckman, Chi. Bears, 1939-43, 1946-47
- 3   Arnie Herber, Green Bay, 1932, 1934, 1936
  - Norm Van Brocklin, Los Angeles, 1950, 1952, 1954
  - Len Dawson, Dall. Texans, 1962; Kansas City, 1966, 1968
  - Bart Starr, Green Bay, 1966-68

**Most Consecutive Seasons Leading League**
- 5   Sid Luckman, Chi. Bears, 1939-43
- 3   Bart Starr, Green Bay, 1966-68
- 2   Bernie Masterson, Chi. Bears, 1937-38
  - Sid Luckman, Chi. Bears, 1946-47
  - Johnny Unitas, Baltimore, 1964-65
  - Terry Bradshaw, Pittsburgh, 1977-78
  - Steve Grogan, New England, 1980-81

**Highest Average Gain, Career (1,500 attempts)**
- 8.63   Otto Graham, Cleveland, 1950-55 (1,565-13,499)
- 8.42   Sid Luckman, Chi. Bears, 1939-50 (1,744-14,686)
- 8.16   Norm Van Brocklin, Los Angeles, 1949-57; Philadelphia, 1958-60 (2,895-23,611)

**Highest Average Gain, Season (Qualifiers)**
- 11.17   Tommy O'Connell, Cleveland, 1957 (110-1,229)
- 10.86   Sid Luckman, Chi. Bears, 1943 (202-2,194)
- 10.55   Otto Graham, Cleveland, 1953 (258-2,722)

**Highest Average Gain, Rookie, Season (Qualifiers)**
- 9.411   Greg Cook, Cincinnati, 1969 (197-1,854)
- 9.409   Bob Waterfield, Cleveland, 1945 (171-1,609)
- 8.36   Zeke Bratkowski, Chi. Bears, 1954 (130-1,087)

---

**Highest Average Gain, Game (20 attempts)**
- 18.58   Sammy Baugh, Washington vs. Boston, Oct. 31, 1948 (24-446)
- 18.50   Johnny Unitas, Baltimore vs. Atlanta, Nov. 12, 1967 (20-370)
- 17.71   Joe Namath, N.Y. Jets vs. Baltimore, Sept. 24, 1972 (28-496)

## TOUCHDOWNS
**Most Seasons Leading League**
- 4   Johnny Unitas, Baltimore, 1957-60
  - Len Dawson, Dall. Texans, 1962; Kansas City, 1963, 1965-66
- 3   Arnie Herber, Green Bay, 1932, 1934, 1936
  - Sid Luckman, Chi. Bears, 1943, 1945-46
  - Y.A. Tittle, San Francisco, 1955; N.Y. Giants, 1962-63
- 2   By many players

**Most Consecutive Seasons Leading League**
- 4   Johnny Unitas, Baltimore, 1957-60
- 2   By many players

**Most Touchdown Passes, Career**
- 342   Fran Tarkenton, Minnesota, 1961-66, 1972-78; N.Y. Giants, 1967-71
- 290   Johnny Unitas, Baltimore, 1956-72; San Diego, 1973
- 255   Sonny Jurgensen, Philadelphia, 1957-63; Washington, 1964-74

**Most Touchdown Passes, Season**
- 36   George Blanda, Houston, 1961
  - Y.A. Tittle, N.Y. Giants, 1963
- 34   Daryle Lamonica, Oakland, 1969
- 33   Y.A. Tittle, N.Y. Giants, 1962
  - Dan Fouts, San Diego, 1981

**Most Touchdown Passes, Rookie, Season**
- 22   Charlie Conerly, N.Y. Giants, 1948
  - Butch Songin, Boston, 1960
- 20   Dan Marino, Miami, 1983
- 19   Jim Plunkett, New England, 1971

**Most Touchdown Passes, Game**
- 7   Sid Luckman, Chi. Bears vs. N.Y. Giants, Nov. 14, 1943
  - Adrian Burk, Philadelphia vs. Washington, Oct. 17, 1954
  - George Blanda, Houston vs. N.Y. Titans, Nov. 19, 1961
  - Y.A. Tittle, N.Y. Giants vs. Washington, Oct. 28, 1962
  - Joe Kapp, Minnesota vs. Baltimore, Sept. 28, 1969
- 6   By many players. Last time: Dan Fouts, San Diego vs. Oakland, Nov. 22, 1981

**Most Consecutive Games, Touchdown Passes**
- 47   Johnny Unitas, Baltimore, 1956-60
- 25   Daryle Lamonica, Oakland, 1968-70
- 23   Frank Ryan, Cleveland, 1965-67
  - Sonny Jurgensen, Washington, 1966-68

## HAD INTERCEPTED
**Most Consecutive Passes Attempted, None Intercepted**
- 294   Bart Starr, Green Bay, 1964-65
- 208   Milt Plum, Cleveland, 1959-60
- 206   Roman Gabriel, Los Angeles, 1968-69

**Most Passes Had Intercepted, Career**
- 277   George Blanda, Chi. Bears, 1949, 1950-58; Baltimore, 1950; Houston, 1960-66; Oakland, 1967-75
- 268   John Hadl, San Diego, 1962-72; Los Angeles, 1973-74; Green Bay, 1974-75; Houston, 1976-77
- 266   Fran Tarkenton, Minnesota, 1961-66, 1972-78; N.Y. Giants, 1967-71

**Most Passes Had Intercepted, Season**
- 42   George Blanda, Houston, 1962
- 34   Frank Tripucka, Denver, 1960
- 32   John Hadl, San Diego, 1968
  - Fran Tarkenton, Minnesota, 1978

**Most Passes Had Intercepted, Game**
- 8   Jim Hardy, Chi. Cardinals vs. Philadelphia, Sept. 24, 1950
- 7   Parker Hall, Cleveland vs. Green Bay, Nov. 8, 1942
  - Frank Sinkwich, Detroit vs. Green Bay, Oct. 24, 1943
  - Bob Waterfield, Los Angeles vs. Green Bay, Oct. 17, 1948
  - Zeke Bratkowski, Chicago vs. Baltimore, Oct. 2, 1960
  - Tommy Wade, Pittsburgh vs. Philadelphia, Dec. 12, 1965
  - Ken Stabler, Oakland vs. Denver, Oct. 16, 1977
- 6   By many players

**Most Attempts, No Interceptions, Game**
- 51   Scott Brunner, N.Y. Giants vs. St. Louis, Dec. 26, 1982
- 49   Greg Landry, Baltimore vs. N.Y. Jets, Dec. 2, 1979
  - Tommy Kramer, Minnesota vs. Cleveland, Dec. 14, 1980
- 48   Dan Fouts, San Diego vs. San Francisco, Dec. 11, 1982

## LOWEST PERCENTAGE, PASSES HAD INTERCEPTED
**Most Seasons Leading League, Lowest Percentage, Passes Had Intercepted**
- 5   Sammy Baugh, Washington, 1940, 1942, 1944-45, 1947
- 3   Charlie Conerly, N.Y. Giants, 1950, 1956, 1959
  - Bart Starr, Green Bay, 1962, 1964, 1966
  - Roger Staubach, Dallas, 1971, 1977, 1979
  - Ken Anderson, Cincinnati, 1972, 1981-82
- 2   By many players

**Lowest Percentage, Passes Had Intercepted, Career (1,500 attempts)**
- 2.67   Joe Montana, San Francisco, 1979-83 (1,645-44)
- 3.31   Roman Gabriel, Los Angeles, 1962-72; Philadelphia, 1973-77 (4,498-149)
- 3.52   Ken Anderson, Cincinnati, 1971-83 (4,145-146)

**Lowest Percentage, Passes Had Intercepted, Season (Qualifiers)**
- 0.66   Joe Ferguson, Buffalo, 1976 (151-1)
- 1.16   Steve Bartkowski, Atlanta, 1983 (432-5)
- 1.20   Bart Starr, Green Bay, 1966 (251-3)

**Lowest Percentage, Passes Had Intercepted, Rookie, Season (Qualifiers)**
- 2.03   Dan Marino, Miami, 1983 (296-6)
- 2.10   Gary Wood, N.Y. Giants, 1964 (143-3)
- 3.17   Mike Pagel, Baltimore, 1982 (221-7)

---

# PASS RECEIVING
**Most Seasons Leading League**
- 8   Don Hutson, Green Bay, 1936-37, 1939, 1941-45
- 5   Lionel Taylor, Denver, 1960-63, 1965

    3  Tom Fears, Los Angeles, 1948-50
       Pete Pihos, Philadelphia, 1953-55
       Billy Wilson, San Francisco, 1954, 1956-57
       Raymond Berry, Baltimore, 1958-60
       Lance Alworth, San Diego, 1966, 1968-69

**Most Consecutive Seasons Leading League**
    5  Don Hutson, Green Bay, 1941-45
    4  Lionel Taylor, Denver, 1960-63
    3  Tom Fears, Los Angeles, 1948-50
       Pete Pihos, Philadelphia, 1953-55
       Raymond Berry, Baltimore, 1958-60

**Most Pass Receptions, Career**
  649  Charley Taylor, Washington, 1964-75, 1977
  633  Don Maynard, N.Y. Giants, 1958; N.Y. Jets, 1960-72; St. Louis, 1973
  631  Raymond Berry, Baltimore, 1955-67

**Most Seasons, 50 or More Pass Receptions**
    7  Raymond Berry, Baltimore, 1958-62, 1965-66
       Art Powell, N.Y. Titans, 1960-62; Oakland, 1963-66
       Lance Alworth, San Diego, 1963-69
       Charley Taylor, Washington, 1964, 1966-67, 1969, 1973-75
    6  Lionel Taylor, Denver, 1960-65
       Bobby Mitchell, Washington, 1962-67
       Ahmad Rashad, Minnesota, 1976-81
       Steve Largent, Seattle, 1976, 1978-81, 1983
    5  Billy Wilson, San Francisco, 1953-57
       Pete Retzlaff, Philadelphia, 1958, 1961, 1963-65
       Bernie Casey, San Francisco, 1962, 1964-66; Los Angeles, 1967
       Don Maynard, N.Y. Jets, 1960, 1962, 1965, 1967-68
       Lydell Mitchell, Baltimore, 1974-77; San Diego, 1978
       Harold Carmichael, Philadelphia, 1973-74, 1978-79, 1981
       Charlie Joiner, San Diego, 1976, 1979-81, 1983

**Most Pass Receptions, Season**
  101  Charley Hennigan, Houston, 1964
  100  Lionel Taylor, Denver, 1961
   93  Johnny Morris, Chicago, 1964

**Most Pass Receptions, Rookie, Season**
   83  Earl Cooper, San Francisco, 1980
   72  Bill Groman, Houston, 1960
   67  Jack Clancy, Miami, 1967
       Cris Collinsworth, Cincinnati, 1981

**Most Pass Receptions, Game**
   18  Tom Fears, Los Angeles vs. Green Bay, Dec. 3, 1950
   17  Clark Gaines, N.Y. Jets vs. San Francisco, Sept. 21, 1980
   16  Sonny Randle, St. Louis vs. N.Y. Giants, Nov. 4, 1962

**Most Consecutive Games, Pass Receptions**
  127  Harold Carmichael, Philadelphia, 1972-80
  121  Mel Gray, St. Louis, 1973-82
  105  Dan Abramowicz, New Orleans, 1967-73; San Francisco, 1973-74

---

## YARDS GAINED
**Most Seasons Leading League**
    7  Don Hutson, Green Bay, 1936, 1938-39, 1941-44
    3  Raymond Berry, Baltimore, 1957, 1959-60
       Lance Alworth, San Diego, 1965-66, 1968
    2  By many players

**Most Consecutive Seasons Leading League**
    4  Don Hutson, Green Bay, 1941-44
    2  By many players

**Most Yards Gained, Career**
  11,834  Don Maynard, N.Y. Giants, 1958; N.Y. Jets, 1960-72; St. Louis, 1973
  10,372  Harold Jackson, Los Angeles, 1968, 1973-77; Philadelphia, 1969-72; New England, 1978-81; Minnesota, 1982; Seattle, 1983
  10,266  Lance Alworth, San Diego, 1962-70; Dallas, 1971-72

**Most Seasons, 1,000 or More Yards, Pass Receiving**
    7  Lance Alworth, San Diego, 1963-69
    5  Art Powell, N.Y. Titans, 1960, 1962; Oakland, 1963-64, 1966
       Don Maynard, N.Y. Jets, 1960, 1962, 1965, 1967-68
       Steve Largent, Seattle, 1978-81, 1983
    4  Del Shofner, Los Angeles, 1958; N.Y. Giants, 1961-63
       Lionel Taylor, Denver, 1960-61, 1963, 1965
       Charlie Joiner, San Diego, 1976, 1979-81

**Most Yards Gained, Season**
  1,746  Charley Hennigan, Houston, 1961
  1,602  Lance Alworth, San Diego, 1965
  1,546  Charley Hennigan, Houston, 1964

**Most Yards Gained, Rookie, Season**
  1,473  Bill Groman, Houston, 1960
  1,231  Bill Howton, Green Bay, 1952
  1,124  Harlon Hill, Chi. Bears, 1954

**Most Yards Gained, Game**
  303  Jim Benton, Cleveland vs. Detroit, Nov. 22, 1945
  302  Cloyce Box, Detroit vs. Baltimore, Dec. 3, 1950
  272  Charley Hennigan, Houston vs. Boston, Oct. 13, 1961

**Most Games, 100 or More Yards Pass Receiving, Career**
   50  Don Maynard, N.Y. Giants, 1958; N.Y. Jets, 1960-72; St. Louis, 1973
   41  Lance Alworth, San Diego, 1962-70; Dallas, 1971-72
   31  Art Powell, Philadelphia, 1959; N.Y. Titans, 1960-62; Oakland, 1963-66; Buffalo, 1967; Minnesota, 1968

**Most Games, 100 or More Yards Pass Receiving, Season**
   10  Charley Hennigan, Houston, 1961
    9  Elroy (Crazylegs) Hirsch, Los Angeles, 1951
       Bill Groman, Houston, 1960
       Lance Alworth, San Diego, 1965
       Don Maynard, N.Y. Jets, 1967
    8  Charley Hennigan, Houston, 1964
       Lance Alworth, San Diego, 1967

**Most Consecutive Games, 100 or More Yards Pass Receiving**
    7  Charley Hennigan, Houston, 1961
       Bill Groman, Houston, 1961
    6  Raymond Berry, Baltimore, 1960
       Pat Studstill, Detroit, 1966

    5  Elroy (Crazylegs) Hirsch, Los Angeles, 1951
       Bob Boyd, Los Angeles, 1954
       Terry Barr, Detroit, 1963
       Lance Alworth, San Diego, 1966

**Longest Pass Reception (All TDs except as noted)**
  99  Andy Farkas (from Filchock), Washington vs. Pittsburgh, Oct. 15, 1939
       Bobby Mitchell (from Izo), Washington vs. Cleveland, Sept. 15, 1963
       Pat Studstill (from Sweetan), Detroit vs. Baltimore, Oct. 16, 1966
       Gerry Allen (from Jurgensen), Washington vs. Chicago, Sept. 15, 1968
       Cliff Branch (from Plunkett), L.A. Raiders vs. Washington, Oct. 2, 1983
  98  Gaynell Tinsley (from Russell), Chi. Cardinals vs. Cleveland, Nov. 17, 1938
       Dick (Night Train) Lane (from Compton), Chi. Cardinals vs. Green Bay, Nov. 13, 1955
       John Farrington (from Wade), Chicago vs. Detroit, Oct. 8, 1961
       Willard Dewveall (from Lee), Houston vs. San Diego, Nov. 25, 1962
       Homer Jones (from Morrall), N.Y. Giants vs. Pittsburgh, Sept. 11, 1966
       Bobby Moore (from Hart), St. Louis vs. Los Angeles, Dec. 10, 1972 (no TD)
  97  Gaynell Tinsley (from Coffee), Chi. Cardinals vs. Chi. Bears, Dec. 5, 1937
       Cloyce Box (from Layne), Detroit vs. Green Bay, Nov. 26, 1953
       Jerry Tarr (from Shaw), Denver vs. Boston, Sept. 21, 1962

---

## TOUCHDOWNS
**Most Seasons Leading League**
    9  Don Hutson, Green Bay, 1935-38, 1940-44
    3  Lance Alworth, San Diego, 1964-66
    2  By many players

**Most Consecutive Seasons Leading League**
    5  Don Hutson, Green Bay, 1940-44
    4  Don Hutson, Green Bay, 1935-38
    3  Lance Alworth, San Diego, 1964-66

**Most Touchdowns, Career**
  99  Don Hutson, Green Bay, 1935-45
  88  Don Maynard, N.Y. Giants, 1958; N.Y. Jets, 1960-72; St. Louis, 1973
  85  Lance Alworth, San Diego, 1962-70; Dallas, 1971-72
       Paul Warfield, Cleveland, 1964-69, 1976-77; Miami, 1970-74

**Most Touchdowns, Season**
   17  Don Hutson, Green Bay, 1942
       Elroy (Crazylegs) Hirsch, Los Angeles, 1951
       Bill Groman, Houston, 1961
   16  Art Powell, Oakland, 1963
   15  Cloyce Box, Detroit, 1952
       Sonny Randle, St. Louis, 1960

**Most Touchdowns, Rookie, Season**
   13  Bill Howton, Green Bay, 1952
       John Jefferson, San Diego, 1979
   12  Harlon Hill, Chi. Bears, 1954
       Bill Groman, Houston, 1960
       Mike Ditka, Chicago, 1961
       Bob Hayes, Dallas, 1965
   10  Bill Swiacki, N.Y. Giants, 1948
       Bucky Pope, Los Angeles, 1964
       Sammy White, Minnesota, 1976

**Most Touchdowns, Game**
    5  Bob Shaw, Chi. Cardinals vs. Baltimore, Oct. 2, 1950
       Kellen Winslow, San Diego vs. Oakland, Nov. 22, 1981
    4  By many players

**Most Consecutive Games, Touchdowns**
   11  Elroy (Crazylegs) Hirsch, Los Angeles, 1950-51
       Buddy Dial, Pittsburgh, 1959-60
    9  Lance Alworth, San Diego, 1963
    8  Bill Groman, Houston, 1961
       Dave Parks, San Francisco, 1965

---

# INTERCEPTIONS BY
**Most Seasons Leading League**
    2  Dick (Night Train) Lane, Los Angeles, 1952; Chi. Cardinals, 1954
       Jack Christiansen, Detroit, 1953, 1957
       Milt Davis, Baltimore, 1957, 1959
       Dick Lynch, N.Y. Giants, 1961, 1963
       Johnny Robinson, Kansas City, 1966, 1970
       Bill Bradley, Philadelphia, 1971-72
       Emmitt Thomas, Kansas City, 1969, 1974
       Everson Walls, Dallas, 1981-82

**Most Interceptions By, Career**
  81  Paul Krause, Washington, 1964-67; Minnesota, 1968-79
  79  Emlen Tunnell, N.Y. Giants, 1948-58; Green Bay, 1959-61
  68  Dick (Night Train) Lane, Los Angeles, 1952-53; Chi. Cardinals, 1954-59; Detroit, 1960-65

**Most Interceptions By, Season**
  14  Dick (Night Train) Lane, Los Angeles, 1952
  13  Dan Sandifer, Washington, 1948
       Orban (Spec) Sanders, N.Y. Yanks, 1950
       Lester Hayes, Oakland, 1980
  12  By nine players

**Most Interceptions By, Rookie, Season**
  14  Dick (Night Train) Lane, Los Angeles, 1952
  13  Dan Sandifer, Washington, 1948
  12  Woodley Lewis, Los Angeles, 1950
       Paul Krause, Washington, 1964

**Most Interceptions By, Game**
    4  Sammy Baugh, Washington vs. Detroit, Nov. 14, 1943
       Dan Sandifer, Washington vs. Boston, Oct. 31, 1948
       Don Doll, Detroit vs. Chi. Cardinals, Oct. 23, 1949
       Bob Nussbaumer, Chi. Cardinals vs. N.Y. Bulldogs, Nov. 13, 1949
       Russ Craft, Philadelphia vs. Chi. Cardinals, Sept. 24, 1950
       Bobby Dillon, Green Bay vs. Detroit, Nov. 26, 1953
       Jack Butler, Pittsburgh vs. Washington, Dec. 13, 1953
       Austin (Goose) Gonsoulin, Denver vs. Buffalo, Sept. 18, 1960
       Jerry Norton, St. Louis vs. Washington, Nov. 20, 1960; vs. Pittsburgh, Nov. 26, 1961
       Dave Baker, San Francisco vs. L.A. Rams, Dec. 4, 1960
       Bobby Ply, Dall. Texans vs. San Diego, Dec. 16, 1962
       Bobby Hunt, Kansas City vs. Houston, Oct. 4, 1964

Willie Brown, Denver vs. N.Y. Jets, Nov. 15, 1964
Dick Anderson, Miami vs. Pittsburgh, Dec. 3, 1973
Willie Buchanon, Green Bay vs. San Diego, Sept. 24, 1978

**Most Consecutive Games, Passes Intercepted By**
- 8 Tom Morrow, Oakland, 1962-63
- 7 Paul Krause, Washington, 1964
  Larry Wilson, St. Louis, 1966
  Ben Davis, Cleveland, 1968
- 6 Dick (Night Train) Lane, Chi. Cardinals, 1954-55
  Will Sherman, Los Angeles, 1954-55
  Jim Shofner, Cleveland, 1960
  Paul Krause, Minnesota, 1968
  Willie Williams, N.Y. Giants, 1968
  Kermit Alexander, San Francisco, 1968-69
  Eric Harris, Kansas City, 1980
  Lester Hayes, Oakland, 1980

## YARDS GAINED
**Most Seasons Leading League**
- 2 Dick (Night Train) Lane, Los Angeles, 1952; Chi. Cardinals, 1954
  Herb Adderley, Green Bay, 1965, 1969
  Dick Anderson, Miami, 1968, 1970

**Most Yards Gained, Career**
- 1,282 Emlen Tunnell, N.Y. Giants, 1948-58; Green Bay, 1959-61
- 1,207 Dick (Night Train) Lane, Los Angeles, 1952-53; Chi. Cardinals, 1954-59; Detroit, 1960-65
- 1,185 Paul Krause, Washington, 1964-67; Minnesota, 1968-79

**Most Yards Gained, Season**
- 349 Charley McNeil, San Diego, 1961
- 301 Don Doll, Detroit, 1949
- 298 Dick (Night Train) Lane, Los Angeles, 1952

**Most Yards Gained, Rookie, Season**
- 301 Don Doll, Detroit, 1949
- 298 Dick (Night Train) Lane, Los Angeles, 1952
- 275 Woodley Lewis, Los Angeles, 1950

**Most Yards Gained, Game**
- 177 Charley McNeil, San Diego vs. Houston, Sept. 24, 1961
- 167 Dick Jauron, Detroit vs. Chicago, Nov. 18, 1973
- 151 Tom Myers, New Orleans vs. Minnesota, Sept. 3, 1978

**Longest Return (All TDs)**
- 102 Bob Smith, Detroit vs. Chi. Bears, Nov. 24, 1949
  Erich Barnes, N.Y. Giants vs. Dall. Cowboys, Oct. 22, 1961
  Gary Barbaro, Kansas City vs. Seattle, Dec. 11, 1977
  Louis Breeden, Cincinnati vs. San Diego, Nov. 8, 1981
- 101 Richie Petitbon, Chicago vs Los Angeles, Dec. 9, 1962
  Henry Carr, N.Y. Giants vs. Los Angeles, Nov. 13, 1966
  Tony Greene, Buffalo vs. Kansas City, Oct. 3, 1976
  Tom Pridemore, Atlanta vs. San Francisco, Sept. 20, 1981
- 100 Vern Huffman, Detroit vs. Brooklyn, Oct. 17, 1937
  Mike Gaechter, Dall. Cowboys vs. Philadelphia, Oct. 14, 1962
  Les (Speedy) Duncan, San Diego vs. Kansas City, Oct. 15, 1967
  Tom Janik, Buffalo vs. N.Y. Jets, Sept. 29, 1968
  Tim Collier, Kansas City vs. Oakland, Dec. 18, 1977

## TOUCHDOWNS
**Most Touchdowns, Career**
- 9 Ken Houston, Houston, 1967-72; Washington, 1973-80
- 7 Herb Adderley, Green Bay, 1961-69; Dallas, 1970-72
  Erich Barnes, Chi. Bears, 1958-60; N.Y. Giants, 1961-64; Cleveland, 1965-70
  Lem Barney, Detroit, 1967-77
- 6 Tom Janik, Denver, 1963-64; Buffalo, 1965-68; Boston, 1969-70; New England, 1971
  Miller Farr, Denver, 1965; San Diego, 1965-66; Houston, 1967-69; St. Louis, 1970-72; Detroit, 1973
  Bobby Bell, Kansas City, 1963-74

**Most Touchdowns, Season**
- 4 Ken Houston, Houston, 1971
  Jim Kearney, Kansas City, 1972
- 3 Dick Harris, San Diego, 1961
  Dick Lynch, N.Y. Giants, 1963
  Herb Adderley, Green Bay, 1965
  Lem Barney, Detroit, 1967
  Miller Farr, Houston, 1967
  Monte Jackson, Los Angeles, 1976
  Rod Perry, Los Angeles, 1978
  Ronnie Lott, San Francisco, 1981
- 2 By many players

**Most Touchdowns, Rookie, Season**
- 3 Lem Barney, Detroit, 1967
  Ronnie Lott, San Francisco, 1981
- 2 By many players

**Most Touchdowns, Game**
- 2 Bill Blackburn, Chi. Cardinals vs. Boston, Oct. 24, 1948
  Dan Sandifer, Washington vs. Boston, Oct. 31, 1948
  Bob Franklin, Cleveland vs. Chicago, Dec. 11, 1960
  Bill Stacy, St. Louis vs. Dall. Cowboys, Nov. 5, 1961
  Jerry Norton, St. Louis vs. Pittsburgh, Nov. 26, 1961
  Miller Farr, Houston vs. Buffalo, Dec. 7, 1968
  Ken Houston, Houston vs. San Diego, Dec. 19, 1971
  Jim Kearney, Kansas City vs. Denver, Oct. 1, 1972
  Lemar Parrish, Cincinnati vs. Houston, Dec. 17, 1972
  Dick Anderson, Miami vs. Pittsburgh, Dec. 3, 1973
  Prentice McCray, New England vs. N.Y. Jets, Nov. 21, 1976
  Kenny Johnson, Atlanta vs. Green Bay, Nov. 27, 1983 (OT)
  Mike Kozlowski, Miami vs. N.Y. Jets, Dec. 16, 1983

# PUNTING
**Most Seasons Leading League**
- 4 Sammy Baugh, Washington, 1940-43
  Jerrel Wilson, Kansas City, 1965, 1968, 1972-73
- 3 Yale Lary, Detroit, 1959, 1961, 1963
  Jim Fraser, Denver, 1962-64
  Ray Guy, Oakland, 1974-75, 1977

---

- 2 By many players

**Most Consecutive Seasons Leading League**
- 4 Sammy Baugh, Washington, 1940-43
- 3 Jim Fraser, Denver, 1962-64
- 2 By many players

## PUNTS
**Most Punts, Career**
- 1,072 Jerrel Wilson, Kansas City, 1963-77; New England, 1978
- 995 John James, Atlanta, 1972-81; Detroit, 1982; Houston, 1982-83
- 978 Mike Bragg, Washington, 1968-79; Baltimore, 1980

**Most Punts, Season**
- 114 Bob Parsons, Chicago, 1981
- 109 John James, Atlanta, 1978
- 106 David Beverly, Green Bay, 1978

**Most Punts, Rookie, Season**
- 96 Mike Connell, San Francisco, 1978
- 93 Wilbur Summers, Detroit, 1977
  Ken Clark, Los Angeles, 1979
  Jim Arnold, Kansas City, 1983
- 90 Bucky Dilts, Denver, 1977

**Most Punts, Game**
- 14 Dick Nesbitt, Chi. Cardinals vs. Chi. Bears, Nov. 30, 1933
  Keith Molesworth, Chi. Bears vs. Green Bay, Dec. 10, 1933
  Sammy Baugh, Washington vs. Philadelphia, Nov. 5, 1939
  Carl Kinscherf, N.Y. Giants vs. Detroit, Nov. 7, 1943
  George Taliaferro, N.Y. Yanks vs. Los Angeles, Sept. 28, 1951
- 12 Parker Hall, Cleveland vs. Green Bay, Nov. 26, 1939
  Beryl Clark, Chi. Cardinals vs. Detroit, Sept. 15, 1940
  Len Barnum, Philadelphia vs. Washington, Oct. 4, 1942
  Horace Gillom, Cleveland vs. Philadelphia, Dec. 3, 1950
  Adrian Burk, Philadelphia vs. Green Bay, Nov. 2, 1952; vs. N.Y. Giants, Dec. 12, 1954
  Bob Scarpitto, Denver vs. Oakland, Sept. 10, 1967
  Bill Van Heusen, Denver vs. Cincinnati, Oct. 6, 1968
  Tom Blanchard, New Orleans vs. Minnesota, Nov. 16, 1975
  Rusty Jackson, Los Angeles vs. San Francisco, Nov. 21, 1976
  Wilbur Summers, Detroit vs. San Francisco, Oct. 23, 1977
  John James, Atlanta vs. Washington, Dec. 10, 1978
  Luke Prestridge, Denver vs. Buffalo, Oct. 25, 1981
  Greg Coleman, Minnesota vs. Green Bay, Nov. 21, 1982
- 11 By many players

**Longest Punt**
- 98 Steve O'Neal, N.Y. Jets vs. Denver, Sept. 21, 1969
- 94 Joe Lintzenich, Chi. Bears vs. N.Y. Giants, Nov. 16, 1931
- 90 Don Chandler, Green Bay vs. San Francisco, Oct. 10, 1965

## AVERAGE YARDAGE
**Highest Average, Punting, Career (300 punts)**
- 45.10 Sammy Baugh, Washington, 1937-52 (338-15,245)
- 44.68 Tommy Davis, San Francisco, 1959-69 (511-22,833)
- 44.29 Yale Lary, Detroit, 1952-53, 1956-64 (503-22,279)

**Highest Average, Punting, Season (Qualifiers)**
- 51.40 Sammy Baugh, Washington, 1940 (35-1,799)
- 48.94 Yale Lary, Detroit, 1963 (35-1,713)
- 48.73 Sammy Baugh, Washington, 1941 (30-1,462)

**Highest Average, Punting, Rookie, Season (Qualifiers)**
- 46.40 Bobby Walden, Minnesota, 1964 (72-3,341)
- 46.22 Dave Lewis, Cincinnati, 1970 (79-3,651)
- 45.92 Frank Sinkwich, Detroit, 1943 (12-551)

**Highest Average, Punting, Game (4 punts)**
- 61.75 Bob Cifers, Detroit vs. Chi. Bears, Nov. 24, 1946 (4-247)
- 61.60 Roy McKay, Green Bay vs. Chi. Cardinals, Oct. 28, 1945 (5-308)
- 59.40 Sammy Baugh, Washington vs. Detroit, Oct. 27, 1940 (5-297)

# PUNT RETURNS
**Most Seasons Leading League**
- 3 Les (Speedy) Duncan, San Diego, 1965-66; Washington, 1971
  Rick Upchurch, Denver, 1976, 1978, 1982
- 2 Dick Christy, N.Y. Titans, 1961-62
  Claude Gibson, Oakland, 1963-64
  Billy Johnson, Houston, 1975, 1977

## PUNT RETURNS
**Most Punt Returns, Career**
- 258 Emlen Tunnell, N.Y. Giants, 1948-58; Green Bay, 1959-61
- 253 Alvin Haymond, Baltimore, 1964-67; Philadelphia, 1968; Los Angeles, 1969-71; Washington, 1972; Houston, 1973
- 252 Mike Fuller, San Diego, 1975-80; Cincinnati, 1981-82

**Most Punt Returns, Season**
- 70 Danny Reece, Tampa Bay, 1979
- 58 J. T. Smith, Kansas City, 1979
  Greg Pruitt, L.A. Raiders, 1983
- 57 Eddie Brown, Washington, 1977
  Danny Reece, Tampa Bay, 1980

**Most Punt Returns, Rookie, Season**
- 54 James Jones, Dallas, 1980
- 52 Leon Bright, N.Y. Giants, 1981
  Robbie Martin, Detroit, 1981
- 48 Neal Colzie, Oakland, 1975
  Kevin Miller, Minnesota, 1978
  Mike Nelms, Washington, 1980

**Most Punt Returns, Game**
- 11 Eddie Brown, Washington vs. Tampa Bay, Oct. 9, 1977
- 10 Theo Bell, Pittsburgh vs. Buffalo, Dec. 16, 1979
  Mike Nelms, Washington vs. New Orleans, Dec. 26, 1982
- 9 Rodger Bird, Oakland vs. Denver, Sept. 10, 1967
  Ralph McGill, San Francisco vs. Atlanta, Oct. 29, 1972
  Ed Podolak, Kansas City vs. San Diego, Nov. 10, 1974
  Anthony Leonard, San Francisco vs. New Orleans, Oct. 17, 1976
  Butch Johnson, Dallas vs. Buffalo, Nov. 15, 1976
  Larry Marshall, Philadelphia vs. Tampa Bay, Sept. 18, 1977
  Nesby Glasgow, Baltimore vs. Kansas City, Sept. 2, 1979

Mike Nelms, Washington vs. St. Louis, Dec. 21, 1980
Leon Bright, N.Y. Giants vs. Philadelphia, Dec. 11, 1982
Pete Shaw, N.Y. Giants vs. Philadelphia, Nov. 20, 1983

## FAIR CATCHES
### Most Fair Catches, Season
24  Ken Graham, San Diego, 1969
22  Lem Barney, Detroit, 1976
21  Ed Podolak, Kansas City, 1970
    Steve Schubert, Chicago, 1978
    Stanley Morgan, New England, 1979
### Most Fair Catches, Game
7  Lem Barney, Detroit vs. Chicago, Nov. 21, 1976
6  Jake Scott, Miami vs. Buffalo, Dec. 20, 1970
5  By many players

## YARDS GAINED
### Most Seasons Leading League
3  Alvin Haymond, Baltimore, 1965-66; Los Angeles, 1969
2  Bill Dudley, Pittsburgh, 1942, 1946
   Emlen Tunnell, N.Y. Giants, 1951-52
   Dick Christy, N.Y. Titans, 1961-62
   Claude Gibson, Oakland, 1963-64
   Rodger Bird, Oakland, 1966-67
   J. T. Smith, Kansas City, 1979-80
### Most Yards Gained, Career
3,008  Rick Upchurch, Denver, 1975-83
2,802  Billy Johnson, Houston, 1974-80; Atlanta, 1982-83
2,660  Mike Fuller, San Diego, 1975-80; Cincinnati, 1981-82
### Most Yards Gained, Season
666  Greg Pruitt, L.A. Raiders, 1983
655  Neal Colzie, Oakland, 1975
653  Rick Upchurch, Denver, 1977
### Most Yards Gained, Rookie, Season
655  Neal Colzie, Oakland, 1975
608  Mike Haynes, New England, 1976
577  Lynn Swann, Pittsburgh, 1974
### Most Yards Gained, Game
207  LeRoy Irvin, Los Angeles vs. Atlanta, Oct. 11, 1981
205  George Atkinson, Oakland vs. Buffalo, Sept. 15, 1968
184  Tom Watkins, Detroit vs. San Francisco, Oct. 6, 1963
### Longest Punt Return (All TDs)
98  Gil LeFebvre, Cincinnati vs. Brooklyn, Dec. 3, 1933
    Charlie West, Minnesota vs. Washington, Nov. 3, 1968
    Dennis Morgan, Dallas vs. St. Louis, Oct. 13, 1974
97  Greg Pruitt, L.A. Raiders vs. Washington, Oct. 2, 1983
96  Bill Dudley, Washington vs. Pittsburgh, Dec. 3, 1950

## AVERAGE YARDAGE
### Highest Average, Career (75 returns)
12.78  George McAfee, Chi. Bears, 1940-41, 1945-50 (112-1,431)
12.75  Jack Christiansen, Detroit, 1951-58 (85-1,084)
12.55  Claude Gibson, San Diego, 1961-62; Oakland, 1963-65 (110-1,381)
### Highest Average, Season (Qualifiers)
23.00  Herb Rich, Baltimore, 1950 (12-276)
21.47  Jack Christiansen, Detroit, 1952 (15-322)
21.28  Dick Christy, N.Y. Titans, 1961 (18-383)
### Highest Average, Rookie, Season (Qualifiers)
23.00  Herb Rich, Baltimore, 1950 (12-276)
20.88  Jerry Davis, Chi. Cardinals, 1948 (16-334)
20.73  Frank Sinkwich, Detroit, 1943 (11-228)
### Highest Average, Game (3 returns)
47.67  Chuck Latourette, St. Louis vs. New Orleans, Sept. 29, 1968 (3-143)
47.33  Johnny Roland, St. Louis vs. Philadelphia, Oct. 2, 1966 (3-142)
45.67  Dick Christy, N.Y. Titans vs. Denver, Sept. 24, 1961 (3-137)

## TOUCHDOWNS
### Most Touchdowns, Career
8  Jack Christiansen, Detroit, 1951-58
   Rick Upchurch, Denver, 1975-83
6  Billy Johnson, Houston, 1974-80; Atlanta, 1982-83
5  Emlen Tunnell, N.Y. Giants, 1948-58; Green Bay, 1959-61
### Most Touchdowns, Season
4  Jack Christiansen, Detroit, 1951
   Rick Upchurch, Denver, 1976
3  Emlen Tunnell, N.Y. Giants, 1951
   Billy Johnson, Houston, 1975
   LeRoy Irvin, Los Angeles, 1981
2  By many players
### Most Touchdowns, Rookie, Season
4  Jack Christiansen, Detroit, 1951
2  By five players
### Most Touchdowns, Game
2  Jack Christiansen, Detroit vs. Los Angeles, Oct. 14, 1951; vs. Green Bay, Nov. 22, 1951
   Dick Christy, N.Y. Titans vs. Denver, Sept. 24, 1961
   Rick Upchurch, Denver vs. Cleveland, Sept. 26, 1976
   LeRoy Irvin, Los Angeles vs. Atlanta, Oct. 11, 1981

# KICKOFF RETURNS
### Most Seasons Leading League
3  Abe Woodson, San Francisco, 1959, 1962-63
2  Lynn Chandnois, Pittsburgh, 1951-52
   Bobby Jancik, Houston, 1962-63
   Travis Williams, Green Bay, 1967; Los Angeles, 1971

## KICKOFF RETURNS
### Most Kickoff Returns, Career
275  Ron Smith, Chicago, 1965, 1970-72; Atlanta, 1966-67; Los Angeles, 1968-69; San Diego, 1973; Oakland, 1974
243  Bruce Harper, N.Y. Jets, 1977-83
193  Abe Woodson, San Francisco, 1958-64; St. Louis, 1965-66

### Most Kickoff Returns, Season
60  Drew Hill, Los Angeles, 1981
55  Bruce Harper, N.Y. Jets, 1978, 1979
    David Turner, Cincinnati, 1979
    Stump Mitchell, St. Louis, 1981
53  Eddie Payton, Minnesota, 1980
### Most Kickoff Returns, Rookie, Season
55  Stump Mitchell, St. Louis, 1981
50  Nesby Glasgow, Baltimore, 1979
    Dino Hall, Cleveland, 1979
47  Odell Barry, Denver, 1964
### Most Kickoff Returns, Game
9  Noland Smith, Kansas City vs. Oakland, Nov. 23, 1967
   Dino Hall, Cleveland vs. Pittsburgh, Oct. 7, 1979
8  George Taliaferro, N.Y. Yanks vs. N.Y. Giants, Dec. 3, 1950
   Bobby Jancik, Houston vs. Boston, Dec. 8, 1963; vs. Oakland, Dec. 22, 1963
   Mel Renfro, Dallas vs. Green Bay, Nov. 29, 1964
   Willie Porter, Boston vs. N.Y. Jets, Sept. 22, 1968
   Keith Moody, Buffalo vs. Seattle, Oct. 30, 1977
   Brian Baschnagel, Chicago vs. Houston, Nov. 6, 1977
   Bruce Harper, N.Y. Jets vs. New England, Oct. 29, 1978; vs. New England, Sept. 9, 1979
   Dino Hall, Cleveland vs. Pittsburgh, Nov. 25, 1979
   Terry Metcalf, Washington vs. St. Louis, Sept. 20, 1981
   Harlan Huckleby, Green Bay vs. Washington, Oct. 17, 1983
7  By many players

## YARDS GAINED
### Most Seasons Leading League
3  Bruce Harper, N.Y. Jets, 1977-79
2  Marshall Goldberg, Chi. Cardinals, 1941-42
   Woodley Lewis, Los Angeles, 1953-54
   Al Carmichael, Green Bay, 1956-57
   Timmy Brown, Philadelphia, 1961, 1963
   Bobby Jancik, Houston, 1963, 1966
   Ron Smith, Atlanta, 1966-67
### Most Yards Gained, Career
6,922  Ron Smith, Chicago, 1965, 1970-72; Atlanta, 1966-67; Los Angeles, 1968-69; San Diego, 1973; Oakland, 1974
5,538  Abe Woodson, San Francisco, 1958-64; St. Louis, 1965-66
5,407  Bruce Harper, N.Y. Jets, 1977-83
### Most Yards Gained, Season
1,317  Bobby Jancik, Houston, 1963
1,314  Dave Hampton, Green Bay, 1971
1,292  Stump Mitchell, St. Louis, 1981
### Most Yards Gained, Rookie, Season
1,292  Stump Mitchell, St. Louis, 1981
1,245  Odell Barry, Denver, 1964
1,148  Noland Smith, Kansas City, 1967
### Most Yards Gained, Game
294  Wally Triplett, Detroit vs. Los Angeles, Oct. 29, 1950
247  Timmy Brown, Philadelphia vs. Dallas, Nov. 6, 1966
244  Noland Smith, Kansas City vs. San Diego, Oct. 15, 1967
### Longest Kickoff Return (All TDs)
106  Al Carmichael, Green Bay vs. Chi. Bears, Oct. 7, 1956
     Noland Smith, Kansas City vs. Denver, Dec. 17, 1967
     Roy Green, St. Louis vs. Dallas, Oct. 21, 1979
105  Frank Seno, Chi. Cardinals vs. N.Y. Giants, Oct. 20, 1946
     Ollie Matson, Chi. Cardinals vs. Washington, Oct. 14, 1956
     Abe Woodson, San Francisco vs. Los Angeles, Nov. 8, 1959
     Timmy Brown, Philadelphia vs. Cleveland, Sept. 17, 1961
     Jon Arnett, Los Angeles vs. Detroit, Oct. 29, 1961
     Eugene (Mercury) Morris, Miami vs. Cincinnati, Sept. 14, 1969
     Travis Williams, Los Angeles vs. New Orleans, Dec. 5, 1971
104  By many players

## AVERAGE YARDAGE
### Highest Average, Career (75 returns)
30.56  Gale Sayers, Chicago, 1965-71 (91-2,781)
29.57  Lynn Chandnois, Pittsburgh, 1950-56 (92-2,720)
28.69  Abe Woodson, San Francisco, 1958-64; St. Louis, 1965-66 (193-5,538)
### Highest Average, Season (Qualifiers)
41.06  Travis Williams, Green Bay, 1967 (18-739)
37.69  Gale Sayers, Chicago, 1967 (16-603)
35.50  Ollie Matson, Chi. Cardinals, 1958 (14-497)
### Highest Average, Rookie, Season (Qualifiers)
41.06  Travis Williams, Green Bay, 1967 (18-739)
33.08  Tom Moore, Green Bay, 1960 (12-397)
32.88  Duriel Harris, Miami, 1976 (17-559)
### Highest Average, Game (3 returns)
73.50  Wally Triplett, Detroit vs. Los Angeles, Oct. 29, 1950 (4-294)
67.33  Lenny Lyles, San Francisco vs. Baltimore, Dec. 18, 1960 (3-202)
65.33  Ken Hall, Houston vs. N.Y. Titans, Oct. 23, 1960 (3-196)

## TOUCHDOWNS
### Most Touchdowns, Career
6  Ollie Matson, Chi. Cardinals, 1952, 1954-58; L.A. Rams, 1959-62; Detroit, 1963; Philadelphia, 1964
   Gale Sayers, Chicago, 1965-71
   Travis Williams, Green Bay, 1967-70; Los Angeles, 1971
5  Bobby Mitchell, Cleveland, 1958-61; Washington, 1962-68
   Abe Woodson, San Francisco, 1958-64; St. Louis, 1965-66
   Timmy Brown, Green Bay, 1959; Philadelphia, 1960-67; Baltimore, 1968
4  Cecil Turner, Chicago, 1968-73
### Most Touchdowns, Season
4  Travis Williams, Green Bay, 1967
   Cecil Turner, Chicago, 1970
3  Verda (Vitamin T) Smith, Los Angeles, 1950
   Abe Woodson, San Francisco, 1963
   Gale Sayers, Chicago, 1967
   Raymond Clayborn, New England, 1977
2  By many players

**Most Touchdowns, Rookie, Season**
    4  Travis Williams, Green Bay, 1967
    3  Raymond Clayborn, New England, 1977
    2  By six players
**Most Touchdowns, Game**
    2  Timmy Brown, Philadelphia vs. Dallas, Nov. 6, 1966
       Travis Williams, Green Bay vs. Cleveland, Nov. 12, 1967

## COMBINED KICK RETURNS

**Most Combined Kick Returns, Career**
  510  Ron Smith, Chicago, 1965, 1970-72; Atlanta, 1966-67; Los Angeles, 1968-69; San Diego, 1973; Oakland, 1974 (p-235, k-275)
  426  Bruce Harper, N.Y. Jets, 1977-83 (p-183, k-243)
  423  Alvin Haymond, Baltimore, 1964-67; Philadelphia, 1968; Los Angeles, 1969-71; Washington, 1972; Houston, 1973 (p-253, k-170)
**Most Combined Kick Returns, Season**
  100  Larry Jones, Washington, 1975 (p-53, k-47)
   97  Stump Mitchell, St. Louis, 1981 (p-42, k-55)
   94  Nesby Glasgow, Baltimore, 1979 (k-50, p-44)
**Most Combined Kick Returns, Game**
   13  Stump Mitchell, St. Louis vs. Atlanta, Oct. 18, 1981 (p-6, k-7)
   12  Mel Renfro, Dallas vs. Green Bay, Nov. 29, 1964 (p-4, k-8)
       Larry Jones, Washington vs. Dallas, Dec. 13, 1975 (p-6, k-6)
       Eddie Brown, Washington vs. Tampa Bay, Oct. 9, 1977 (p-11, k-1)
       Nesby Glasgow, Baltimore vs. Denver, Sept. 2, 1979 (p-9, k-3)
   11  By many players

**YARDS GAINED**
**Most Yards Returned, Career**
 8,710  Ron Smith, Chicago, 1965, 1970-72; Atlanta, 1966-67; Los Angeles, 1968-69; San Diego, 1973; Oakland, 1974 (p-1,788, k-6,922)
 7,191  Bruce Harper, N.Y. Jets, 1977-83 (p-1,784, k-5,407)
 6,740  Les (Speedy) Duncan, San Diego, 1964-70; Washington, 1971-74 (p-2,201, k-4,539)
**Most Yards Returned, Season**
 1,737  Stump Mitchell, St. Louis, 1981 (p-445, k-1,292)
 1,658  Bruce Harper, N.Y. Jets, 1978 (p-378, k-1,280)
 1,591  Mike Nelms, Washington, 1981 (p-492, k-1,099)
**Most Yards Returned, Game**
  294  Wally Triplett, Detroit vs. Los Angeles, Oct. 29, 1950 (k-294)
       Woodley Lewis, Los Angeles vs. Detroit, Oct. 18, 1953 (p-120, k-174)
  289  Eddie Payton, Detroit vs. Minnesota, Dec. 17, 1977 (p-105, k-184)
  282  Les (Speedy) Duncan, San Diego vs. N.Y. Jets, Nov. 24, 1968 (p-102, k-180)

**TOUCHDOWNS**
**Most Touchdowns, Career**
    9  Ollie Matson, Chi. Cardinals, 1952, 1954-58; Los Angeles, 1959-62; Detroit, 1963; Philadelphia, 1964-66 (p-3, k-6)
    8  Jack Christiansen, Detroit, 1951-58 (p-8)
       Bobby Mitchell, Cleveland, 1958-61; Washington, 1962-68 (p-3, k-5)
       Gale Sayers, Chicago, 1965-71 (p-2, k-6)
       Rick Upchurch, Denver, 1975-83 (p-8)
       Billy Johnson, Houston, 1974-80; Atlanta, 1982-83 (p-6, k-2)
    7  Abe Woodson, San Francisco, 1958-64; St. Louis, 1965-66 (p-2, k-5)
**Most Touchdowns, Season**
    4  Jack Christiansen, Detroit, 1951 (p-4)
       Emlen Tunnell, N.Y. Giants, 1951 (p-3, k-1)
       Gale Sayers, Chicago, 1967 (p-1, k-3)
       Travis Williams, Green Bay, 1967 (k-4)
       Cecil Turner, Chicago, 1970 (k-4)
       Billy Johnson, Houston, 1975 (p-3, k-1)
       Rick Upchurch, Denver, 1976 (p-4)
    3  Verda (Vitamin T) Smith, Los Angeles, 1950 (k-3)
       Abe Woodson, San Francisco, 1963 (k-3)
       Raymond Clayborn, New England, 1977 (k-3)
       Billy Johnson, Houston, 1977 (p-2, k-1)
       LeRoy Irvin, Los Angeles, 1981 (p-3)
    2  By many players
**Most Touchdowns, Game**
    2  Jack Christiansen, Detroit vs. Los Angeles, Oct. 14, 1951 (p-2); vs. Green Bay, Nov. 22, 1951 (p-2)
       Jim Patton, N.Y. Giants vs. Washington, Oct. 30, 1955 (p-1, k-1)
       Bobby Mitchell, Cleveland vs. Philadelphia, Nov. 23, 1958 (p-1, k-1)
       Dick Christy, N.Y. Titans vs. Denver, Sept. 24, 1961 (p-2)
       Al Frazier, Denver vs. Boston, Dec. 3, 1961 (p-1, k-1)
       Timmy Brown, Philadelphia vs. Dallas, Nov. 6, 1966 (k-2)
       Travis Williams, Green Bay vs. Cleveland, Nov. 12, 1967 (k-2); vs. Pittsburgh, Nov. 2, 1969 (p-1, k-1)
       Gale Sayers, Chicago vs. San Francisco, Dec. 3, 1967 (p-1, k-1)
       Rick Upchurch, Denver vs. Cleveland, Sept. 26, 1976 (p-2)
       Eddie Payton, Detroit vs. Minnesota, Dec. 17, 1977 (p-1, k-1)
       LeRoy Irvin, Los Angeles vs. Atlanta, Oct. 11, 1981 (p-2)

## FUMBLES

**Most Fumbles, Career**
  105  Roman Gabriel, Los Angeles, 1962-72; Philadelphia, 1973-77
   95  Johnny Unitas, Baltimore, 1956-72; San Diego, 1973
   90  Franco Harris, Pittsburgh, 1972-83
**Most Fumbles, Season**
   17  Dan Pastorini, Houston, 1973
   16  Don Meredith, Dallas, 1964
       Joe Cribbs, Buffalo, 1980
       Steve Fuller, Kansas City, 1980
   15  Paul Christman, Chi. Cardinals, 1946
       Sammy Baugh, Washington, 1947
       Sam Etcheverry, St. Louis, 1961
       Len Dawson, Kansas City, 1964
       Terry Metcalf, St. Louis, 1976
**Most Fumbles, Game**
    7  Len Dawson, Kansas City vs. San Diego, Nov. 15, 1964
    6  Sam Etcheverry, St. Louis vs. N.Y. Giants, Sept. 17, 1961

    5  Paul Christman, Chi. Cardinals vs. Green Bay, Nov. 10, 1946
       Charlie Conerly, N.Y. Giants vs San Francisco, Dec. 1, 1957
       Jack Kemp, Buffalo vs. Houston, Oct. 29, 1967
       Roman Gabriel, Philadelphia vs. Oakland, Nov. 21, 1976

**FUMBLES RECOVERED**
**Most Fumbles Recovered, Career, Own and Opponents'**
   43  Fran Tarkenton, Minnesota, 1961-66, 1972-78; N.Y. Giants, 1967-71 (43 own)
   38  Jack Kemp, Pittsburgh, 1957; L.A. Chargers, 1960; San Diego, 1961-62; Buffalo, 1962-67, 1969 (38 own)
   37  Roman Gabriel, Los Angeles, 1962-72; Philadelphia, 1973-77 (37 own)
**Most Fumbles Recovered, Season, Own and Opponents'**
    9  Don Hultz, Minnesota, 1963 (9 opp)
    8  Paul Christman, Chi. Cardinals, 1945 (8 own)
       Joe Schmidt, Detroit, 1955 (8 opp)
       Bill Butler, Minnesota, 1963 (8 own)
       Kermit Alexander, San Francisco, 1965 (4 own, 4 opp)
       Jack Lambert, Pittsburgh, 1976 (1 own, 7 opp)
       Danny White, Dallas, 1981 (8 own)
    7  By many players
**Most Fumbles Recovered, Game, Own and Opponents'**
    4  Otto Graham, Cleveland vs. N.Y. Giants, Oct. 25, 1953 (4 own)
       Sam Etcheverry, St. Louis vs. N.Y. Giants, Sept. 17, 1961 (4 own)
       Roman Gabriel, Los Angeles vs. San Francisco, Oct. 12, 1969 (4 own)
       Joe Ferguson, Buffalo vs. Miami, Sept. 18, 1977 (4 own)
    3  By many players

**OWN FUMBLES RECOVERED**
**Most Own Fumbles Recovered, Career**
   43  Fran Tarkenton, Minnesota, 1961-66, 1972-78; N.Y. Giants, 1967-71
   38  Jack Kemp, Pittsburgh, 1957; L.A. Chargers, 1960; San Diego, 1961-62; Buffalo, 1962-67, 1969
   37  Roman Gabriel, Los Angeles, 1962-72; Philadelphia, 1973-77
**Most Own Fumbles Recovered, Season**
    8  Paul Christman, Chi. Cardinals, 1945
       Bill Butler, Minnesota, 1963
       Danny White, Dallas, 1981
    7  Sammy Baugh, Washington, 1947
       Tommy Thompson, Philadelphia, 1947
       John Roach, St. Louis, 1960
       Jack Larscheid, Oakland, 1960
       Gary Huff, Chicago, 1974
       Terry Metcalf, St. Louis, 1974
       Joe Ferguson, Buffalo, 1977
       Fran Tarkenton, Minnesota, 1978
       Greg Pruitt, L.A. Raiders, 1983
    6  By many players
**Most Own Fumbles Recovered, Game**
    4  Otto Graham, Cleveland vs. N.Y. Giants, Oct. 25, 1953
       Sam Etcheverry, St. Louis vs. N.Y. Giants, Sept. 17, 1961
       Roman Gabriel, Los Angeles vs. San Francisco, Oct. 12, 1969
       Joe Ferguson, Buffalo vs. Miami, Sept. 18, 1977
    3  By many players

**OPPONENTS' FUMBLES RECOVERED**
**Most Opponents' Fumbles Recovered, Career**
   29  Jim Marshall, Cleveland, 1960; Minnesota, 1961-79
   25  Dick Butkus, Chicago, 1965-73
   23  Carl Eller, Minnesota, 1964-78; Seattle, 1979
**Most Opponents' Fumbles Recovered, Season**
    9  Don Hultz, Minnesota, 1963
    8  Joe Schmidt, Detroit, 1955
    7  Alan Page, Minnesota, 1970
       Jack Lambert, Pittsburgh, 1976
**Most Opponents' Fumbles Recovered, Game**
    3  Corwin Clatt, Chi. Cardinals vs. Detroit, Nov. 6, 1949
       Vic Sears, Philadelphia vs. Green Bay, Nov. 2, 1952
       Ed Beatty, San Francisco vs. Los Angeles, Oct. 7, 1956
       Ron Carroll, Houston vs. Cincinnati, Oct. 27, 1974
       Maurice Spencer, New Orleans vs. Atlanta, Oct. 10, 1976
       Steve Nelson, New England vs. Philadelphia, Oct. 8, 1978
       Charles Jackson, Kansas City vs. Pittsburgh, Sept. 6, 1981
       Willie Buchanon, San Diego vs. Denver, Sept. 27, 1981
    2  By many players

**YARDS RETURNING FUMBLES**
**Longest Fumble Run (All TDs)**
  104  Jack Tatum, Oakland vs. Green Bay, Sept. 24, 1972 (opp)
   98  George Halas, Chi. Bears vs. Oorang Indians, Marion, Ohio, Nov. 4, 1923 (opp)
   97  Chuck Howley, Dallas vs. Atlanta, Oct. 2, 1966 (opp)

**TOUCHDOWNS**
**Most Touchdowns, Career (Total)**
    4  Bill Thompson, Denver, 1969-81
    3  Ralph Heywood, Detroit, 1947-48; Boston, 1948; N.Y. Bulldogs, 1949
       Leo Sugar, Chi. Cardinals, 1954-59; St. Louis, 1960; Philadelphia, 1961; Detroit, 1962
       Bud McFadin, Los Angeles, 1952-56; Denver, 1960-63; Houston, 1964-65
       Doug Cline, Houston, 1960-66; San Diego, 1966
       Bob Lilly, Dall. Cowboys, 1961-74
       Chris Hanburger, Washington, 1965-78
       Lemar Parrish, Cincinnati, 1970-77; Washington, 1978-81; Buffalo, 1982
       Paul Krause, Washington, 1964-67; Minnesota, 1968-79
       Brad Dusek, Washington, 1974-81
       David Logan, Tampa Bay, 1979-83
    2  By many players

**Most Touchdowns, Season (Total)**
2  Harold McPhail, Boston, 1934
Harry Ebding, Detroit, 1937
John Morelli, Boston, 1944
Frank Maznicki, Boston, 1947
Fred (Dippy) Evans, Chi. Bears, 1948
Ralph Heywood, Boston, 1948
Art Tait, N.Y. Yanks, 1951
John Dwyer, Los Angeles, 1952
Leo Sugar, Chi. Cardinals, 1957
Doug Cline, Houston, 1961
Jim Bradshaw, Pittsburgh, 1964
Royce Berry, Cincinnati, 1970
Ahmad Rashad, Buffalo, 1974
Tim Gray, Kansas City, 1977
Charles Phillips, Oakland, 1978
Kenny Johnson, Atlanta, 1981
George Martin, N.Y. Giants, 1981
Del Rodgers, Green Bay, 1982
Mike Douglass, Green Bay, 1983
Shelton Robinson, Seattle, 1983

**Most Touchdowns, Career (Own recovered)**
2  Ken Kavanaugh, Chi. Bears, 1940-41, 1945-50
Mike Ditka, Chicago, 1961-66; Philadelphia, 1967-68; Dallas, 1969-72
Gail Cogdill, Detroit, 1960-68; Baltimore, 1968; Atlanta, 1969-70
Ahmad Rashad, St. Louis, 1972-73; Buffalo, 1974; Minnesota, 1976-82
Jim Mitchell, Atlanta, 1969-79
Drew Pearson, Dallas, 1973-83
Del Rodgers, Green Bay, 1982

**Most Touchdowns, Season (Own recovered)**
2  Ahmad Rashad, Buffalo, 1974
Del Rodgers, Green Bay, 1982
1  By many players

**Most Touchdowns, Career (Opponents' recovered)**
3  Leo Sugar, Chi. Cardinals, 1954-59; St. Louis, 1960; Philadelphia, 1961; Detroit, 1962
Doug Cline, Houston, 1960-66; San Diego, 1966
Bud McFadin, Los Angeles, 1952-56; Denver, 1960-63; Houston, 1964-65
Bob Lilly, Dall. Cowboys, 1961-74
Chris Hanburger, Washington, 1965-78
Paul Krause, Washington, 1964-67; Minnesota, 1968-79
Lemar Parrish, Cincinnati, 1970-77; Washington, 1978-81; Buffalo, 1982
Bill Thompson, Denver, 1969-81
Brad Dusek, Washington, 1974-81
David Logan, Tampa Bay, 1979-83
2  By many players

**Most Touchdowns, Season (Opponents' recovered)**
2  Harold McPhail, Boston, 1934
Harry Ebding, Detroit, 1937
John Morelli, Boston, 1944
Frank Maznicki, Boston, 1947
Fred Evans, Chi. Bears, 1948
Ralph Heywood, Boston, 1948
Art Tait, N.Y. Yanks, 1951
John Dwyer, Los Angeles, 1952
Leo Sugar, Chi. Cardinals, 1957
Doug Cline, Houston, 1961
Jim Bradshaw, Pittsburgh, 1964
Royce Berry, Cincinnati, 1970
Tim Gray, Kansas City, 1977
Charles Phillips, Oakland, 1978
Kenny Johnson, Atlanta, 1981
George Martin, N.Y. Giants, 1981
Mike Douglass, Green Bay, 1983
Shelton Robinson, Seattle, 1983

**Most Touchdowns, Game (Opponents' recovered)**
2  Fred (Dippy) Evans, Chi. Bears vs. Washington, Nov. 28, 1948

## COMBINED NET YARDS GAINED
Rushing, receiving, interception returns, punt returns, kickoff returns, and fumble returns

**Most Seasons Leading League**
5  Jim Brown, Cleveland, 1958-61, 1964
3  Cliff Battles, Boston, 1932-33; Washington, 1937
Gale Sayers, Chicago, 1965-67
2  By many players

**Most Consecutive Seasons Leading League**
4  Jim Brown, Cleveland, 1958-61
3  Gale Sayers, Chicago, 1965-67
2  Cliff Battles, Boston, 1932-33
Charley Trippi, Chi. Cardinals, 1948-49
Timmy Brown, Philadelphia, 1962-63
Floyd Little, Denver, 1967-68
James Brooks, San Diego, 1981-82

### ATTEMPTS
**Most Attempts, Career**
3,212  Franco Harris, Pittsburgh, 1972-83
3,030  Walter Payton, Chicago, 1975-83
2,658  Jim Brown, Cleveland, 1957-65
John Riggins, N.Y. Jets, 1971-75; Washington, 1976-79, 1981-83

**Most Attempts, Season**
442  Eric Dickerson, L.A. Rams, 1983
402  Walter Payton, Chicago, 1979
399  Earl Campbell, Houston, 1981

**Most Attempts, Rookie, Season**
442  Eric Dickerson, L.A. Rams, 1983
395  George Rogers, New Orleans, 1981
390  Joe Cribbs, Buffalo, 1980

**Most Attempts, Game**
48  James Wilder, Tampa Bay vs. Pittsburgh, Oct. 30, 1983
43  Lydell Mitchell, Baltimore vs. N.Y. Jets, Oct. 20, 1974
Butch Woolfolk, N.Y. Giants vs. Philadelphia, Nov. 20, 1983

42  Walter Payton, Chicago vs. Minnesota, Nov. 20, 1977
Earl Campbell, Houston vs. Seattle, Oct. 11, 1981

### YARDS GAINED
**Most Yards Gained, Career**
15,459  Jim Brown, Cleveland, 1957-65
15,252  Walter Payton, Chicago, 1975-83
14,449  Franco Harris, Pittsburgh, 1972-83

**Most Yards Gained, Season**
2,462  Terry Metcalf, St. Louis, 1975
2,444  Mack Herron, New England, 1974
2,440  Gale Sayers, Chicago, 1966

**Most Yards Gained, Rookie, Season**
2,272  Gale Sayers, Chicago, 1965
2,212  Eric Dickerson, L.A. Rams, 1983
2,100  Abner Haynes, Dall. Texans, 1960

**Most Yards Gained, Game**
373  Billy Cannon, Houston vs. N.Y. Titans, Dec. 10, 1961
341  Timmy Brown, Philadelphia vs. St. Louis, Dec. 16, 1962
339  Gale Sayers, Chicago vs. Minnesota, Dec. 18, 1966

## MISCELLANEOUS
**Longest Return of Missed Field Goal (All TDs)**
101  Al Nelson, Philadelphia vs. Dallas, Sept. 26, 1971
100  Al Nelson, Philadelphia vs. Cleveland, Dec. 11, 1966
Ken Ellis, Green Bay vs. N.Y. Giants, Sept. 19, 1971
99  Jerry Williams, Los Angeles vs. Green Bay, Dec. 16, 1951
Carl Taseff, Baltimore vs. Los Angeles, Dec. 12, 1959
Timmy Brown, Philadelphia vs. St. Louis, Sept. 16, 1962

## TEAM RECORDS

## CHAMPIONSHIPS
**Most Seasons League Champion**
11  Green Bay, 1929-31, 1936, 1939, 1944, 1961-62, 1965-67
8  Chi. Bears, 1921, 1932-33, 1940-41, 1943, 1946, 1963
4  N.Y. Giants, 1927, 1934, 1938, 1956
Detroit, 1935, 1952-53, 1957
Clev. Browns, 1950, 1954-55, 1964
Baltimore, 1958-59, 1968, 1970
Pittsburgh, 1974-75, 1978-79
Oakland/L.A. Raiders, 1967, 1976, 1980, 1983

**Most Consecutive Seasons League Champion**
3  Green Bay, 1929-31, 1965-67
2  Canton, 1922-23
Chi. Bears, 1932-33, 1940-41
Philadelphia, 1948-49
Detroit, 1952-53
Cleveland, 1954-55
Baltimore, 1958-59
Houston, 1960-61
Green Bay, 1961-62
Buffalo, 1964-65
Miami, 1972-73
Pittsburgh, 1974-75, 1978-79

**Most Times Finishing First, Regular Season (Since 1933)**
14  N.Y. Giants, 1933-35, 1938-39, 1941, 1944, 1946, 1956, 1958-59, 1961-63
Clev./L.A. Rams, 1945, 1949-51, 1955, 1967, 1969, 1973-79
Clev. Browns, 1950-55, 1957, 1964-65, 1967-69, 1971, 1980
12  Dallas, 1966-71, 1973, 1976-79, 1981
11  Green Bay, 1936, 1938-39, 1944, 1960-62, 1965-67, 1972
Minnesota 1968-71, 1973-78, 1980

**Most Consecutive Times Finishing First, Regular Season (Since 1933)**
7  Los Angeles, 1973-79
6  Cleveland, 1950-55
Dallas, 1966-71
Minnesota, 1973-78
Pittsburgh, 1974-79
5  Oakland, 1972-76

## GAMES WON
**Most Consecutive Games Won (Incl. postseason games)**
18  Chi. Bears, 1933-34, 1941-42
Miami, 1972-73
17  Oakland, 1976-77
14  Washington, 1942-43

**Most Consecutive Games Won (Regular season)**
17  Chi. Bears, 1933-34
16  Chi. Bears, 1941-42
Miami, 1971-73
15  L.A. Chargers/San Diego, 1960-61

**Most Consecutive Games Without Defeat (Incl. postseason games)**
24  Canton, 1922-23 (won 21, tied 3)
23  Green Bay, 1928-30 (won 21, tied 2)
18  Chi. Bears, 1933-34 (won 18); 1941-42 (won 18)
Miami, 1972-73 (won 18)

**Most Consecutive Games Without Defeat (Regular season)**
24  Canton, 1922-23 (won 21, tied 3)
Chi. Bears, 1941-43 (won 23, tied 1)
23  Green Bay, 1928-30 (won 21, tied 2)
17  Chi. Bears, 1933-34 (won 17)

**Most Games Won, One Season (Incl. postseason games)**
17  Miami, 1972
Pittsburgh, 1978
16  Oakland, 1976
San Francisco, 1981
Washington, 1983
15  Miami, 1973
Baltimore, 1968
Pittsburgh, 1975, 1979
Dallas, 1977
Oakland, 1980
L.A. Raiders, 1983

**Most Games Won, Season (Since 1932)**
14 Miami, 1972
   Pittsburgh, 1978
   Washington, 1983
13 Chi. Bears, 1934
   Green Bay, 1962
   Oakland, 1967, 1976
   Baltimore, 1968
   San Francisco, 1981
12 By many teams

**Most Consecutive Games Won, One Season (Incl. postseason games)**
17 Miami, 1972
13 Chi. Bears, 1934
   Oakland, 1976
12 Minnesota, 1969

**Most Consecutive Games Won, One Season**
14 Miami, 1972
13 Chi. Bears, 1934
12 Minnesota, 1969

**Most Consecutive Games Won, Start of Season**
14 Miami, 1972, entire season
13 Chi. Bears, 1934, entire season
11 Chi. Bears, 1942, entire season
   Cleveland, 1953
   San Diego, 1961
   Los Angeles, 1969

**Most Consecutive Games Won, End of Season**
14 Miami, 1972, entire season
13 Chi. Bears, 1934, entire season
11 Chi. Bears, 1942, entire season
   Cleveland, 1951

**Most Consecutive Games Without Defeat, One Season (Incl. postseason games)**
17 Miami, 1972
13 Chi. Bears, 1926, 1934
   Green Bay, 1929
   Baltimore, 1967
   Oakland, 1976
12 Canton, 1922, 1923
   Minnesota, 1969

**Most Consecutive Games Without Defeat, One Season**
14 Miami, 1972
13 Chi. Bears, 1926; 1934
   Green Bay, 1929
   Baltimore, 1967
12 Canton, 1922, 1923
   Minnesota, 1969

**Most Consecutive Games Without Defeat, Start of Season**
14 Miami, 1972, entire season
13 Chi. Bears, 1926; 1934, entire season
   Green Bay, 1929, entire season
   Baltimore, 1967
12 Canton, 1922, 1923, entire seasons

**Most Consecutive Games Without Defeat, End of Season**
14 Miami, 1972, entire season
13 Green Bay, 1929, entire season
   Chi. Bears, 1934, entire season
12 Canton, 1922, 1923, entire seasons

**Most Consecutive Home Games Won**
27 Miami, 1971-74
20 Green Bay, 1929-32
18 Oakland, 1968-70
   Dallas, 1979-81

**Most Consecutive Home Games Without Defeat**
30 Green Bay, 1928-33 (won 27, tied 3)
27 Miami, 1971-74 (won 27)
18 Chi. Bears, 1932-35 (won 17, tied 1); 1941-44 (won 17, tied 1)
   Oakland, 1968-70 (won 18)
   Dallas, 1979-81 (won 18)

**Most Consecutive Road Games Won**
11 L.A. Chargers/San Diego, 1960-61
10 Chi. Bears, 1941-42
   Dallas, 1968-69
 9 Chi. Bears, 1933-34
   Kansas City, 1966-67
   Oakland, 1967-68, 1974-75, 1976-77
   Pittsburgh, 1974-75
   Washington, 1981-83

**Most Consecutive Road Games Without Defeat**
13 Chi. Bears, 1941-43 (won 12, tied 1)
12 Green Bay, 1928-30 (won 10, tied 2)
11 L.A. Chargers/San Diego, 1960-61 (won 11)
   Los Angeles, 1966-68 (won 10, tied 1)

**Most Shutout Games Won or Tied, Season (Since 1932)**
 7 Chi. Bears, 1932 (won 4, tied 3)
   Green Bay, 1932 (won 6, tied 1)
   Detroit, 1934 (won 7)
 5 Chi. Cardinals, 1934 (won 5)
   N.Y. Giants, 1944 (won 5)
   Pittsburgh, 1976 (won 5)
 4 By many teams

**Most Consecutive Shutout Games Won or Tied (Since 1932)**
 7 Detroit, 1934 (won 7)
 3 Chi. Bears, 1932 (tied 3)
   Green Bay, 1932 (won 3)
   New York, 1935 (won 3)
   St. Louis, 1970 (won 3)
   Pittsburgh, 1976 (won 3)
 2 By many teams

# GAMES LOST

**Most Consecutive Games Lost**
26 Tampa Bay, 1976-77
19 Chi. Cardinals, 1942-43, 1945

Oakland, 1961-62
18 Houston, 1972-73

**Most Consecutive Games Without Victory**
26 Tampa Bay, 1976-77 (lost 26)
23 Washington, 1960-61 (lost 20, tied 3)

**Most Games Lost, Season (Since 1932)**
15 New Orleans, 1980
14 Tampa Bay, 1976, 1983
   San Francisco, 1978, 1979
   Detroit, 1979
   Baltimore, 1981
   New England, 1981
   Houston, 1983
13 Oakland, 1962
   Chicago, 1969
   Pittsburgh, 1969
   Buffalo, 1971
   Houston, 1972, 1973

**Most Consecutive Games Lost, One Season**
14 Tampa Bay, 1976
   New Orleans, 1980
   Baltimore, 1981
13 Oakland, 1962
12 Tampa Bay, 1977

**Most Consecutive Games Lost, Start of Season**
14 Tampa Bay, 1976, entire season
   New Orleans, 1980
13 Oakland, 1962
12 Tampa Bay, 1977

**Most Consecutive Games Lost, End of Season**
14 Tampa Bay, 1976, entire season
13 Pittsburgh, 1969
11 Philadelphia, 1936
   Detroit, 1942, entire season
   Houston, 1972

**Most Consecutive Games Without Victory, One Season**
14 Tampa Bay, 1976, entire season
   New Orleans, 1980
   Baltimore, 1981
13 Washington, 1961
   Oakland, 1962
12 Dall. Cowboys, 1960, entire season
   Tampa Bay, 1977

**Most Consecutive Games Without Victory, Start of Season**
14 Tampa Bay, 1976, entire season
   New Orleans, 1980
13 Washington, 1961
   Oakland, 1962
12 Dall. Cowboys, 1960, entire season
   Tampa Bay, 1977

**Most Consecutive Games Without Victory, End of Season**
14 Tampa Bay, 1976, entire season
13 Pittsburgh, 1969
12 Dall. Cowboys, 1960, entire season

**Most Consecutive Home Games Lost**
13 Houston, 1972-73
   Tampa Bay, 1976-77
11 Oakland, 1961-62
   Los Angeles, 1961-63
10 Pittsburgh, 1937-39, 1943-45
   Washington, 1960-61
   N.Y. Giants, 1973-75
   New Orleans, 1979-80

**Most Consecutive Home Games Without Victory**
13 Houston, 1972-73 (lost 13)
   Tampa Bay, 1976-77 (lost 13)
12 Philadelphia, 1936-38 (lost 11, tied 1)
11 Washington, 1960-61 (lost 10, tied 1)
   Oakland, 1961-62 (lost 11)
   Los Angeles, 1961-63 (lost 11)

**Most Consecutive Road Games Lost**
18 San Francisco, 1977-79
   Houston, 1981-83 (current)
16 Chicago, 1973-75
14 Brooklyn, 1942-44
   Chi. Cardinals, 1942-45
   New Orleans, 1972-74

**Most Consecutive Road Games Without Victory**
18 Washington, 1959-62 (lost 15, tied 3)
   New Orleans, 1971-74 (lost 17, tied 1)
   San Francisco, 1977-79 (lost 18)
   Houston, 1981-83 (lost 18, current)
17 Denver, 1962-65 (lost 16, tied 1)
16 Chicago, 1973-75 (lost 16)

**Most Shutout Games Lost or Tied, Season (Since 1932)**
 6 Cincinnati, 1934 (lost 6)
   Pittsburgh, 1934 (lost 6)
   Philadelphia, 1936 (lost 6)
   Tampa Bay, 1977 (lost 6)
 5 Boston, 1932 (lost 4, tied 1), 1933 (lost 4, tied 1)
   N.Y. Giants, 1932 (lost 4, tied 1)
   Cincinnati, 1933 (lost 4, tied 1)
   Brooklyn, 1934 (lost 5), 1942 (lost 5)
   Detroit, 1942 (lost 5)
   Tampa Bay, 1976 (lost 5)
 4 By many teams

**Most Consecutive Shutout Games Lost or Tied (Since 1932)**
 6 Brooklyn, 1942-43 (lost 6)
 4 Chi. Bears, 1932 (lost 1, tied 3)
   Philadelphia, 1936 (lost 4)
 3 Chi. Cardinals, 1934 (lost 3), 1938 (lost 3)
   Brooklyn, 1935 (lost 3), 1937 (lost 3)
   Oakland, 1981 (lost 3)

# TIE GAMES

**Most Tie Games, Season**
- 6 Chi. Bears, 1932
- 5 Frankford, 1929
- 4 Chi. Bears, 1924
  - Orange, 1929
  - Portsmouth, 1929

**Most Consecutive Tie Games**
- 3 Chi. Bears, 1932
- 2 By many teams

# SCORING

**Most Seasons Leading League**
- 9 Chi. Bears, 1934-35, 1939, 1941-43, 1946-47, 1956
- 6 Green Bay, 1932, 1936-38, 1961-62
  - L.A. Rams, 1950-52, 1957, 1967, 1973
- 5 Oakland, 1967-69, 1974, 1977
  - Dall. Cowboys, 1966, 1968, 1971, 1978, 1980

**Most Consecutive Seasons Leading League**
- 3 Green Bay, 1936-38
  - Chi. Bears, 1941-43
  - Los Angeles, 1950-52
  - Oakland, 1967-69

## POINTS

**Most Points, Season**
- 541 Washington, 1983
- 513 Houston, 1961
- 479 Dallas, 1983

**Fewest Points, Season (Since 1932)**
- 37 Cincinnati/St. Louis, 1934
- 38 Cincinnati, 1933
  - Detroit, 1942
- 51 Pittsburgh, 1934
  - Philadelphia, 1936

**Most Points, Game**
- 72 Washington vs. N.Y. Giants, Nov. 27, 1966
- 70 Los Angeles vs. Baltimore, Oct. 22, 1950
- 65 Chi. Cardinals vs. N.Y. Bulldogs, Nov. 13, 1949
  - Los Angeles vs. Detroit, Oct. 29, 1950

**Most Points, Both Teams, Game**
- 113 Washington (72) vs. N.Y. Giants (41), Nov. 27, 1966
- 101 Oakland (52) vs. Houston (49), Dec. 22, 1963
- 99 Seattle (51) vs. Kansas City (48), Nov. 27, 1983 (OT)

**Fewest Points, Both Teams, Game**
- 0 In many games. Last time: N.Y. Giants vs. Detroit, Nov. 7, 1943

**Most Points, Shutout Victory, Game**
- 64 Philadelphia vs. Cincinnati, Nov. 6, 1934
- 59 Los Angeles vs. Atlanta, Dec. 4, 1976
- 57 Chicago vs. Baltimore, Nov. 25, 1962

**Fewest Points, Shutout Victory, Game**
- 2 Green Bay vs. Chi. Bears, Oct. 16, 1932
  - Chi. Bears vs. Green Bay, Sept. 18, 1938

**Most Points Overcome to Win Game**
- 28 San Francisco vs. New Orleans, Dec. 7, 1980 (OT) (trailed 7-35, won 38-35)
- 24 Philadelphia vs. Washington, Oct. 27, 1946 (trailed 0-24, won 28-24)
  - Denver vs. Boston, Oct. 23, 1960 (trailed 0-24, won 31-24)
  - Miami vs. New England, Dec. 15, 1974 (trailed 0-24, won 34-27)
  - Minnesota vs. San Francisco, Dec. 4, 1977 (trailed 0-24, won 28-27)
  - Denver vs. Seattle, Sept. 23, 1979 (trailed 10-34, won 37-34)
  - L.A. Raiders vs. San Diego, Nov. 22, 1982 (trailed 0-24, won 28-24)

**Most Points Overcome to Tie Game**
- 31 Denver vs. Buffalo, Nov. 27, 1960 (trailed 7-38, tied 38-38)
- 28 Los Angeles vs. Philadelphia, Oct. 3, 1948 (trailed 0-28, tied 28-28)

**Most Points, Each Half**
- 1st: 49 Green Bay vs. Tampa Bay, Oct. 2, 1983
  - 45 Green Bay vs. Cleveland, Nov. 12, 1967
- 2nd: 49 Chi. Bears vs. Philadelphia, Nov. 30, 1941
  - 48 Chi. Cardinals vs. Baltimore, Oct. 2, 1950
  - N.Y. Giants vs. Baltimore, Nov. 19, 1950

**Most Points, Both Teams, Each Half**
- 1st: 70 Houston (35) vs. Oakland (35), Dec. 22, 1963
- 2nd: 65 Washington (38) vs. N.Y. Giants (27), Nov. 27, 1966

**Most Points, One Quarter**
- 41 Green Bay vs. Detroit, Oct. 7, 1945 (second quarter)
  - Los Angeles vs. Detroit, Oct. 29, 1950 (third quarter)
- 37 Los Angeles vs. Green Bay, Sept. 21, 1980 (second quarter)
- 35 Chi. Cardinals vs. Boston, Oct. 24, 1948 (third quarter)
  - Green Bay vs. Cleveland, Nov. 12, 1967 (first quarter); vs. Tampa Bay, Oct. 2, 1983 (second quarter)

**Most Points, Both Teams, One Quarter**
- 49 Oakland (28) vs. Houston (21), Dec. 22, 1963 (second quarter)
- 48 Green Bay (41) vs. Detroit (7), Oct. 7, 1945 (second quarter)
  - Los Angeles (41) vs. Detroit (7), Oct. 29, 1950 (third quarter)
- 47 St. Louis (27) vs. Philadelphia (20), Dec. 13, 1964 (second quarter)

**Most Points, Each Quarter**
- 1st: 35 Green Bay vs. Cleveland, Nov. 12, 1967
- 2nd: 41 Green Bay vs. Detroit, Oct. 7, 1945
- 3rd: 41 Los Angeles vs. Detroit, Oct. 29, 1950
- 4th: 31 Oakland vs. Denver, Dec. 17, 1960; vs. San Diego, Dec. 8, 1963
  - Atlanta vs. Green Bay, Sept. 13, 1981

**Most Points, Both Teams, Each Quarter**
- 1st: 42 Green Bay (35) vs. Cleveland (7), Nov. 12, 1967
- 2nd: 49 Oakland (28) vs. Houston (21), Dec. 22, 1963
- 3rd: 48 Los Angeles (41) vs. Detroit (7), Oct. 29, 1950
- 4th: 42 Chi. Cardinals (28) vs. Philadelphia (14), Dec. 7, 1947
  - Green Bay (28) vs. Chi. Bears (14), Nov. 6, 1955
  - N.Y. Jets (28) vs. Boston (14), Oct. 27, 1968
  - Pittsburgh (21) vs. Cleveland (21), Oct. 18, 1969

## GAMES

**Most Consecutive Games Scoring**
- 274 Cleveland, 1950-71

---

- 217 Oakland, 1966-81
- 192 Dallas, 1970-83 (current)

## TOUCHDOWNS

**Most Seasons Leading League, Touchdowns**
- 13 Chi. Bears, 1932, 1934-35, 1939, 1941-44, 1946-48, 1956, 1965
- 7 Dall. Cowboys, 1966, 1968, 1971, 1973, 1977-78, 1980
- 6 Oakland, 1967-69, 1972, 1974, 1977

**Most Consecutive Seasons Leading League, Touchdowns**
- 4 Chi. Bears, 1941-44
  - Los Angeles, 1949-52
- 3 Chi. Bears, 1946-48
  - Baltimore, 1957-59
  - Oakland, 1967-69
- 2 By many teams

**Most Touchdowns, Season**
- 66 Houston, 1961
- 64 Los Angeles, 1950
- 63 Washington, 1983

**Fewest Touchdowns, Season (Since 1932)**
- 3 Cincinnati, 1933
- 4 Cincinnati/St. Louis, 1934
- 5 Detroit, 1942

**Most Touchdowns, Game**
- 10 Philadelphia vs. Cincinnati, Nov. 6, 1934
  - Los Angeles vs. Baltimore, Oct. 22, 1950
  - Washington vs. N.Y. Giants, Nov. 27, 1966
- 9 Chi. Cardinals vs. Rochester, Oct. 7, 1923; vs. N.Y. Giants, Oct. 17, 1948; vs. N.Y. Bulldogs, Nov. 13, 1949
  - Los Angeles vs. Detroit, Oct. 29, 1950
  - Pittsburgh vs. N.Y. Giants, Nov. 30, 1952
  - Chicago vs. San Francisco, Dec. 12, 1965; vs. Green Bay, Dec. 7, 1980
- 8 By many teams.

**Most Touchdowns, Both Teams, Game**
- 16 Washington (10) vs. N.Y. Giants (6), Nov. 27, 1966
- 14 Chi. Cardinals (9) vs. N.Y. Giants (5), Oct. 17, 1948
  - Los Angeles (10) vs. Baltimore (4), Oct. 22, 1950
  - Houston (7) vs. Oakland (7), Dec. 22, 1963
- 13 New Orleans (7) vs. St. Louis (6), Nov. 2, 1969
  - Kansas City (7) vs. Seattle (6), Nov. 27, 1983 (OT)

**Most Consecutive Games Scoring Touchdowns**
- 166 Cleveland, 1957-69
- 97 Oakland, 1966-73
- 96 Kansas City, 1963-70

## POINTS AFTER TOUCHDOWN

**Most Points After Touchdown, Season**
- 65 Houston, 1961
- 62 Washington, 1983
- 59 Los Angeles, 1950
  - Dallas, 1980

**Fewest Points After Touchdown, Season**
- 2 Chi. Cardinals, 1933
- 3 Cincinnati, 1933
  - Pittsburgh, 1934
- 4 Cincinnati/St. Louis, 1934

**Most Points After Touchdown, Game**
- 10 Los Angeles vs. Baltimore, Oct. 22, 1950
- 9 Chi. Cardinals vs. N.Y. Giants, Oct. 17, 1948
  - Pittsburgh vs. N.Y. Giants, Nov. 30, 1952
  - Washington vs. N.Y. Giants, Nov. 27, 1966
- 8 By many teams

**Most Points After Touchdown, Both Teams, Game**
- 14 Chi. Cardinals (9) vs. N.Y. Giants (5), Oct. 17, 1948
  - Houston (7) vs. Oakland (7), Dec. 22, 1963
  - Washington (9) vs. N.Y. Giants (5), Nov. 27, 1966
- 13 Los Angeles (10) vs. Baltimore (3), Oct. 22, 1950
- 12 In many games

## FIELD GOALS

**Most Seasons Leading League, Field Goals**
- 11 Green Bay, 1935-36, 1940-43, 1946-47, 1955, 1972, 1974
- 7 Washington, 1945, 1956, 1971, 1976-77, 1979, 1982
  - N.Y. Giants, 1933, 1937, 1939, 1941, 1944, 1959, 1983
- 5 Portsmouth/Detroit, 1932-33, 1937-38, 1980

**Most Consecutive Seasons Leading League, Field Goals**
- 4 Green Bay, 1940-43
- 3 Cleveland, 1952-54
- 2 By many teams

**Most Field Goals Attempted, Season**
- 49 Los Angeles, 1966
  - Washington, 1971
- 48 Green Bay, 1972
- 47 N.Y. Jets, 1969
  - Los Angeles, 1973
  - Washington, 1983

**Fewest Field Goals Attempted, Season (Since 1938)**
- 0 Chi. Bears, 1944
- 2 Cleveland, 1939
  - Card-Pitt, 1944
  - Boston, 1946
  - Chi. Bears, 1947
- 3 Chi. Bears, 1945
  - Cleveland, 1945

**Most Field Goals Attempted, Game**
- 9 St. Louis vs. Pittsburgh, Sept. 24, 1967
- 8 Pittsburgh vs. St. Louis, Dec. 2, 1962
  - Detroit vs. Minnesota, Nov. 13, 1966
  - N.Y. Jets vs. Buffalo, Nov. 3, 1968
- 7 By many teams

**Most Field Goals Attempted, Both Teams, Game**
- 11 St. Louis (6) vs. Pittsburgh (5), Nov. 13, 1966
  - Washington (6) vs. Chicago (5), Nov. 14, 1971

Green Bay (6) vs. Detroit (5), Sept. 29, 1974
Washington (6) vs. N.Y. Giants (5), Nov. 14, 1976
10 Denver (5) vs. Boston (5), Nov. 11, 1962
Boston (7) vs. San Diego (3), Sept. 20, 1964
Buffalo (7) vs. Houston (3), Dec. 5, 1965
St. Louis (7) vs. Atlanta (3), Dec. 11, 1966
Boston (7) vs. Buffalo (3), Sept. 24, 1967
Detroit (7) vs. Minnesota (3), Sept. 20, 1971
Washington (7) vs. Houston (3), Oct. 10, 1971
Green Bay (5) vs. St. Louis (5), Dec. 5, 1971
Kansas City (7) vs. Buffalo (3), Dec. 19, 1971
Kansas City (5) vs. San Diego (5), Oct. 29, 1972
Minnesota (6) vs. Chicago (4), Sept. 23, 1973
Cleveland (7) vs. Denver (3), Oct. 19, 1975
Cleveland (5) vs. Denver (5), Oct. 5, 1980
9 In many games

**Most Field Goals, Season**
35 N.Y. Giants, 1983
34 N.Y. Jets, 1968
33 Green Bay, 1972
Washington, 1983

**Fewest Field Goals, Season (Since 1932)**
0 Boston, 1932, 1935
Chi. Cardinals, 1932, 1945
Green Bay, 1932, 1944
New York, 1932
Brooklyn, 1944
Card-Pitt, 1944
Chi. Bears, 1944, 1947
Boston, 1946
Baltimore, 1950
Dallas, 1952

**Most Field Goals, Game**
7 St. Louis vs. Pittsburgh, Sept. 24, 1967
6 Boston vs. Denver, Oct. 4, 1964
Detroit vs. Minnesota, Nov. 13, 1966
N.Y. Jets vs. Buffalo, Nov. 3, 1968; vs. New Orleans, Dec. 3, 1972
Philadelphia vs. Houston, Nov. 12, 1972
St. Louis vs. Atlanta, Dec. 9, 1973
N.Y. Giants vs. Seattle, Oct. 18, 1981
San Francisco vs. New Orleans, Oct. 16, 1983
5 By many teams

**Most Field Goals, Both Teams, Game**
8 Cleveland (4) vs. St. Louis (4), Sept. 20, 1964
Chicago (5) vs. Philadelphia (3), Oct. 20, 1968
Washington (5) vs. Chicago (3), Nov. 14, 1971
Kansas City (5) vs. Buffalo (3), Dec. 19, 1971
Detroit (4) vs. Green Bay (4), Sept. 29, 1974
Cleveland (5) vs. Denver (3), Oct. 19, 1975
New England (4) vs. San Diego (4), Nov. 9, 1975
San Francisco (6) vs. New Orleans (2), Oct. 16, 1983
7 In many games

**Most Consecutive Games Scoring Field Goals**
31 Minnesota, 1968-70
21 San Francisco, 1970-72
20 Los Angeles, 1970-71
Miami, 1970-72

**SAFETIES**
**Most Safeties, Season**
4 Detroit, 1962
3 Green Bay, 1932, 1975
Pittsburgh, 1947
N.Y. Yanks, 1950
Detroit, 1960
St. Louis, 1960
Buffalo, 1964
Minnesota, 1965, 1981
Cleveland, 1970
Los Angeles, 1973
Houston, 1977
Dallas, 1981
Oakland, 1981
2 By many teams

**Most Safeties, Game**
2 Cincinnati vs. Chi. Cardinals, Nov. 19, 1933
Detroit vs. Brooklyn, Dec. 1, 1935
N.Y. Giants vs. Pittsburgh, Sept. 17, 1950; vs. Washington, Nov. 5, 1961
Chicago vs. Pittsburgh, Nov. 9, 1969
Dallas vs. Philadelphia, Nov. 19, 1972
Los Angeles vs. Green Bay, Oct. 21, 1973
Oakland vs. San Diego, Oct. 26, 1975
Denver vs. Seattle, Jan. 2, 1983

**Most Safeties, Both Teams, Game**
2 Chi. Bears (1) vs. San Francisco (1), Oct. 19, 1952
Cincinnati (1) vs. Los Angeles (1), Oct. 22, 1972
Atlanta (1) vs. Detroit (1), Oct. 5, 1980
(Also see previous record)

# FIRST DOWNS
**Most Seasons Leading League**
9 Chi. Bears, 1935, 1939, 1941, 1943, 1945, 1947-49, 1955
6 L.A. Rams, 1946, 1950-51, 1954, 1957, 1973
San Diego, 1965, 1969, 1980-83
5 Green Bay, 1940, 1942, 1944, 1960, 1962

**Most Consecutive Seasons Leading League**
4 San Diego, 1980-83
3 Chi. Bears, 1947-49
2 By many teams

**Most First Downs, Season**
379 San Diego, 1981
372 San Diego, 1980
364 Cleveland, 1981

**Fewest First Downs, Season**
51 Cincinnati, 1933
64 Pittsburgh, 1935
67 Philadelphia, 1937

**Most First Downs, Game**
38 Los Angeles vs. N.Y. Giants, Nov. 13, 1966
37 Green Bay vs. Philadelphia, Nov. 11, 1962
36 Pittsburgh vs. Cleveland, Nov. 25, 1979 (OT)

**Fewest First Downs, Game**
0 N.Y. Giants vs. Green Bay, Oct. 1, 1933; vs. Washington, Sept. 27, 1942
Pittsburgh vs. Boston, Oct. 29, 1933
Philadelphia vs. Detroit, Sept. 20, 1935
Denver vs. Houston, Sept. 3, 1966

**Most First Downs, Both Teams, Game**
59 Miami (31) vs. Buffalo (28), Oct. 9, 1983 (OT)
Seattle (33) vs. Kansas City (26), Nov. 27, 1983 (OT)
58 Los Angeles (30) vs. Chi. Bears (28), Oct. 24, 1954
Denver (34) vs. Kansas City (24), Nov. 18, 1974
Atlanta (35) vs. New Orleans (23), Sept. 2, 1979 (OT)
Pittsburgh (36) vs. Cleveland (22), Nov. 25, 1979 (OT)
57 Los Angeles (32) vs. N.Y. Yanks (25), Nov. 19, 1950
Baltimore (33) vs. N.Y. Jets (24), Dec. 15, 1974
San Francisco (29) vs. San Diego (28), Dec. 11, 1982
Green Bay (32) vs. Atlanta (25), Nov. 27, 1983 (OT)

**Fewest First Downs, Both Teams, Game**
5 N.Y. Giants (0) vs. Green Bay (5), Oct. 1, 1933

**Most First Downs, Rushing, Season**
181 New England, 1978
177 Los Angeles, 1973
170 Miami, 1972

**Fewest First Downs, Rushing, Season**
36 Cleveland, 1942
Boston, 1944
39 Brooklyn, 1943
40 Philadelphia, 1940
Detroit, 1945

**Most First Downs, Rushing, Game**
25 Philadelphia vs. Washington, Dec. 2, 1951
21 Cleveland vs. Philadelphia, Dec. 13, 1959
Los Angeles vs. New Orleans, Nov. 25, 1973
Pittsburgh vs. Kansas City, Nov. 7, 1976
New England vs. Denver, Nov. 28, 1976
Oakland vs. Green Bay, Sept. 17, 1978
20 By eight teams

**Fewest First Downs, Rushing, Game**
0 By many teams

**Most First Downs, Passing, Season**
244 San Diego, 1980
230 San Diego, 1983
224 San Diego, 1981

**Fewest First Downs, Passing, Season**
18 Pittsburgh, 1941
23 Brooklyn, 1942
N.Y. Giants, 1944
24 N.Y. Giants, 1943

**Most First Downs, Passing, Game**
25 Denver vs. Kansas City, Nov. 18, 1974
N.Y Jets vs. San Francisco, Sept. 21, 1980
24 Houston vs. Buffalo, Nov. 1, 1964
Minnesota vs. Baltimore, Sept. 28, 1969
23 Dallas vs. San Francisco, Nov. 10, 1963
Denver vs. Houston, Dec. 20, 1964
San Diego vs. N.Y. Giants, Oct. 19, 1980; vs. Cincinnati, Dec. 20, 1982

**Fewest First Downs, Passing, Game**
0 By many teams

**Most First Downs, Penalty, Season**
39 Seattle, 1978
38 Buffalo, 1983
Denver, 1983
37 Cleveland, 1981

**Fewest First Downs, Penalty, Season**
2 Brooklyn, 1940
4 Chi. Cardinals, 1940
N.Y. Giants, 1942, 1944
Washington, 1944
Cleveland, 1952
Kansas City, 1969
5 Brooklyn, 1939
Chi. Bears, 1939
Detroit, 1953
Los Angeles, 1953
Houston, 1982

**Most First Downs, Penalty, Game**
9 Chi. Bears vs. Cleveland, Nov. 25, 1951
Baltimore vs. Pittsburgh, Oct. 30, 1977
8 Philadelphia vs. Detroit, Dec. 2, 1979
7 Boston vs. Houston, Sept. 19, 1965
Baltimore vs. Detroit, Nov. 19, 1967; vs. Buffalo, Dec. 17, 1978;
vs. Pittsburgh, Sept. 14, 1980
Oakland vs. Boston, Oct. 6, 1968
Cleveland vs. Buffalo, Oct. 23, 1977; vs. Pittsburgh, Sept. 24, 1978;
vs. Atlanta, Sept. 27, 1981
Buffalo vs. Cleveland, Oct. 29, 1978
Cincinnati vs. Oakland, Nov. 9, 1980
Miami vs. Buffalo, Oct. 9, 1983 (OT)

**Fewest First Downs, Penalty, Game**
0 By many teams

## NET YARDS GAINED RUSHING AND PASSING

**Most Seasons Leading League**
12  Chi. Bears, 1932, 1934-35, 1939, 1941-44, 1947, 1949, 1955-56
6  L.A. Rams, 1946, 1950-51, 1954, 1957, 1973
   Baltimore, 1958-60, 1964, 1967, 1976
   Dall. Cowboys, 1966, 1968-69, 1971, 1974, 1977
   San Diego, 1963, 1965, 1980-83
3  Green Bay, 1937-38, 1940
   Houston, 1960-62
   N.Y. Giants, 1933, 1962-63
   Oakland, 1968-70

**Most Consecutive Seasons Leading League**
4  Chi. Bears, 1941-44
   San Diego, 1980-83
3  Baltimore, 1958-60
   Houston, 1960-62
   Oakland, 1968-70
2  By many teams

**Most Yards Gained, Season**
6,744  San Diego, 1981
6,410  San Diego, 1980
6,288  Houston, 1961

**Fewest Yards Gained, Season**
1,150  Cincinnati, 1933
1,443  Chi. Cardinals, 1934
1,486  Chi. Cardinals, 1933

**Most Yards Gained, Game**
735  Los Angeles vs. N.Y. Yanks, Sept. 28, 1951
683  Pittsburgh vs. Chi. Cardinals, Dec. 13, 1958
682  Chi. Bears vs. N.Y. Giants, Nov. 14, 1943

**Fewest Yards Gained, Game**
-7  Seattle vs. Los Angeles, Nov. 4, 1979
-5  Denver vs. Oakland, Sept. 10, 1967
14  Chi. Cardinals vs. Detroit, Sept. 15, 1940

**Most Yards Gained, Both Teams, Game**
1,133  Los Angeles (636) vs. N.Y. Yanks (497), Nov. 19, 1950
1,102  San Diego (661) vs. Cincinnati (441), Dec. 20, 1982
1,087  St. Louis (589) vs. Philadelphia (498), Dec. 16, 1962

**Fewest Yards Gained, Both Teams, Game**
30  Chi. Cardinals (14) vs. Detroit (16), Sept. 15, 1940

**Most Consecutive Games, 400 or More Yards Gained**
11  San Diego, 1982-83
6  Houston, 1961-62
   San Diego, 1981
5  Chi. Bears, 1947, 1955
   Los Angeles, 1950
   Philadelphia, 1953
   Oakland, 1968
   New England, 1981

**Most Consecutive Games, 300 or More Yards Gained**
29  Los Angeles, 1949-51
20  Chi. Bears, 1948-50
19  Cleveland, 1978-79
   San Diego, 1980-82

---

## RUSHING

**Most Seasons Leading League**
13  Chi. Bears, 1932, 1934-35, 1939-42, 1951, 1955-56, 1968, 1977, 1983
6  Clev. Browns, 1958-59, 1963, 1965-67
5  Buffalo, 1962, 1964, 1973, 1975, 1982

**Most Consecutive Seasons Leading League**
4  Chi. Bears, 1939-42
3  Detroit, 1936-38
   San Francisco, 1952-54
   Cleveland, 1965-67
2  By many teams

**Most Rushing Attempts, Season**
681  Oakland, 1977
671  New England, 1978
659  Los Angeles, 1973

**Fewest Rushing Attempts, Season**
211  Philadelphia, 1982
219  San Francisco, 1982
225  Houston, 1982

**Most Rushing Attempts, Game**
72  Chi. Bears vs. Brooklyn, Oct. 20, 1935
70  Chi. Cardinals vs. Green Bay, Nov. 25, 1951
69  Chi. Cardinals vs. Green Bay, Dec. 6, 1936
   Kansas City vs. Cincinnati, Sept. 3, 1978

**Fewest Rushing Attempts, Game**
6  Chi. Cardinals vs. Boston, Oct. 29, 1933
7  Oakland vs. Buffalo, Oct. 15, 1963
8  Denver vs. Oakland, Dec. 17, 1960

**Most Rushing Attempts, Both Teams, Game**
108  Chi. Cardinals (70) vs. Green Bay (38), Dec. 5, 1948
105  Oakland (62) vs. Atlanta (43), Nov. 30, 1975 (OT)
103  Kansas City (53) vs. San Diego (50), Nov. 12, 1978 (OT)

**Fewest Rushing Attempts, Both Teams, Game**
36  Cincinnati (16) vs. Chi. Bears (20), Sept. 30, 1934
38  N.Y. Jets (13) vs. Buffalo (25), Nov. 8, 1964
39  Denver (16) vs. N.Y. Titans (23), Sept. 24, 1961
   Denver (14) vs. Boston (25), Sept. 21, 1962
   Denver (14) vs. Houston (25), Dec. 2, 1962

### YARDS GAINED

**Most Yards Gained Rushing, Season**
3,165  New England, 1978
3,088  Buffalo, 1973
2,986  Kansas City, 1978

**Fewest Yards Gained Rushing, Season**
298  Philadelphia, 1940
467  Detroit, 1946
471  Boston, 1944

**Most Yards Gained Rushing, Game**
426  Detroit vs. Pittsburgh, Nov. 4, 1934
423  N.Y. Giants vs. Baltimore, Nov. 19, 1950
420  Boston vs. N.Y. Giants, Oct. 8, 1933

**Fewest Yards Gained Rushing, Game**
-53  Detroit vs. Chi. Cardinals, Oct. 17, 1943
-36  Philadelphia vs. Chi. Bears, Nov. 19, 1939
-33  Phil-Pitt vs. Brooklyn, Oct. 2, 1943

**Most Yards Gained Rushing, Both Teams, Game**
595  Los Angeles (371) vs. N.Y. Yanks (224), Nov. 18, 1951
574  Chi. Bears (396) vs. Pittsburgh (178), Oct. 10, 1934
557  Chi. Bears (406) vs. Green Bay (151), Nov. 6, 1955

**Fewest Yards Gained Rushing, Both Teams, Game**
-15  Detroit (-53) vs. Chi. Cardinals (38), Oct. 17, 1943
4  Detroit (-10) vs. Chi. Cardinals (14), Sept. 15, 1940
63  Chi. Cardinals (-1) vs. N.Y. Giants (64), Oct. 18, 1953

---

### AVERAGE GAIN

**Highest Average Gain, Rushing, Season**
5.74  Cleveland, 1963
5.65  San Francisco, 1954
5.56  San Diego, 1963

**Lowest Average Gain, Rushing, Season**
0.94  Philadelphia, 1940
1.45  Boston, 1944
1.55  Pittsburgh, 1935

---

### TOUCHDOWNS

**Most Touchdowns, Rushing, Season**
36  Green Bay, 1962
33  Pittsburgh, 1976
30  Chi. Bears, 1941
   New England, 1978
   Washington, 1983

**Fewest Touchdowns, Rushing, Season**
1  Brooklyn, 1934
2  Chi. Cardinals, 1933
   Cincinnati, 1933
   Pittsburgh, 1934, 1940
   Philadelphia, 1935, 1936, 1937, 1938, 1972
3  By many teams

**Most Touchdowns, Rushing, Game**
7  Los Angeles vs. Atlanta, Dec. 4, 1976
6  By many teams

**Most Touchdowns, Rushing, Both Teams, Game**
8  Los Angeles (6) vs. N.Y. Yanks (2), Nov. 18, 1951
   Cleveland (6) vs. Los Angeles (2), Nov. 24, 1957
7  In many games

---

## PASSING

### ATTEMPTS

**Most Passes Attempted, Season**
709  Minnesota, 1981
641  Kansas City, 1983
635  San Diego, 1983

**Fewest Passes Attempted, Season**
102  Cincinnati, 1933
106  Boston, 1933
120  Detroit, 1937

**Most Passes Attempted, Game**
68  Houston vs. Buffalo, Nov 1, 1964
63  Minnesota vs. Tampa Bay, Sept. 5, 1981
62  N.Y. Jets vs. Denver, Dec. 3, 1967; vs Baltimore, Oct. 18, 1970

**Fewest Passes Attempted, Game**
0  Green Bay vs. Portsmouth, Oct. 8, 1933
   Detroit vs. Cleveland, Sept. 10, 1937
   Pittsburgh vs. Brooklyn, Nov. 16, 1941; vs. Los Angeles, Nov. 13, 1949
   Cleveland vs. Philadelphia, Dec. 3, 1950

**Most Passes Attempted, Both Teams, Game**
98  Minnesota (56) vs. Baltimore (42), Sept. 28, 1969
97  Denver (53) vs. Houston (44), Dec. 2, 1962
   Cincinnati (56) vs. San Diego (41), Dec. 20, 1982
96  Tampa Bay (56) vs. Minnesota (40), Nov. 16, 1980

**Fewest Passes Attempted, Both Teams, Game**
4  Chi. Cardinals (1) vs. Detroit (3), Nov. 3, 1935
   Detroit (0) vs. Cleveland (4), Sept. 10, 1937
6  Chi. Cardinals (2) vs. Detroit (4), Sept 15, 1940
8  Brooklyn (2) vs. Philadelphia (6), Oct. 1, 1939

---

### COMPLETIONS

**Most Passes Completed, Season**
382  Minnesota, 1981
369  Kansas City, 1983
   San Diego, 1983
368  San Diego, 1981

**Fewest Passes Completed, Season**
25  Cincinnati, 1933
33  Boston, 1933
34  Chi. Cardinals, 1934
   Detroit, 1934

**Most Passes Completed, Game**
42  N.Y. Jets vs. San Francisco, Sept. 21, 1980
40  Cincinnati vs. San Diego, Dec. 20, 1982
38  Minnesota vs. Cleveland, Dec. 14, 1980; vs. Green Bay, Nov. 29, 1981
   Buffalo vs. Miami, Oct. 9, 1983 (OT)

**Most Passes Completed, Both Teams, Game**
66  Cincinnati (40) vs. San Diego (26), Dec. 20, 1982
65  San Diego (33) vs. San Francisco (32), Dec. 11, 1982
63  N.Y. Jets (42) vs. San Francisco (21), Sept. 21, 1980

**Fewest Passes Completed, Both Teams, Game**
1  Chi. Cardinals (0) vs. Philadelphia (1), Nov. 8, 1936
   Detroit (0) vs. Cleveland (1), Sept. 10, 1937
   Chi. Cardinals (0) vs. Detroit (1), Sept. 15, 1940

Brooklyn (C) vs. Pittsburgh (1), Nov. 29, 1942
   2  Chi. Cardinals (0) vs. Detroit (2), Nov. 3, 1935
      Buffalo (0) vs. N.Y. Jets (2), Sept. 29, 1974
   3  Brooklyn (1) vs. Philadelphia (2), Oct. 1, 1939

## YARDS GAINED
### Most Seasons Leading League, Passing Yardage
   9  San Diego, 1965, 1968, 1971, 1978-83
   8  Chi. Bears, 1932, 1939, 1941, 1943, 1945, 1949, 1954, 1964
   7  Washington, 1938, 1940, 1944, 1947-48, 1967, 1974
### Most Consecutive Seasons Leading League, Passing Yardage
   6  San Diego, 1978-83
   4  Green Bay, 1934-37
   2  By many teams
### Most Yards Gained, Passing, Season
4,739  San Diego, 1981
4,661  San Diego, 1983
4,531  San Diego, 1980
### Fewest Yards Gained, Passing, Season
  302  Chi. Cardinals, 1934
  357  Cincinnati, 1933
  459  Boston, 1934
### Most Yards Gained, Passing, Game
  554  Los Angeles vs. N.Y. Yanks, Sept. 28, 1951
  530  Minnesota vs. Baltimore, Sept. 28, 1969
  506  L.A. Rams vs. Chicago, Dec. 26, 1982
### Fewest Yards Gained, Passing, Game
 −53  Denver vs. Oakland, Sept. 10, 1967
 −52  Cincinnati vs. Houston, Oct. 31, 1971
 −39  Atlanta vs. San Francisco, Oct. 23, 1976
### Most Yards Gained, Passing, Both Teams, Game
 883  San Diego (486) vs. Cincinnati (397), Dec. 20, 1982
 834  Philadelphia (419) vs. St. Louis (415), Dec. 16, 1962
 822  N.Y. Jets (490) vs. Baltimore (332), Sept. 24, 1972
### Fewest Yards Gained, Passing, Both Teams, Game
−11  Green Bay (−10) vs. Dallas (−1), Oct. 24, 1965
  1  Chi. Cardinals (0) vs. Philadelphia (1), Nov. 8, 1936
  7  Brooklyn (0) vs. Pittsburgh (7), Nov. 29, 1942

## TIMES SACKED
### Most Times Sacked, Season
  70  Atlanta, 1968
  68  Dallas, 1964
  67  Detroit, 1976
### Fewest Times Sacked, Season
   8  San Francisco, 1970
      St. Louis, 1975
   9  N.Y. Jets, 1966
  10  N.Y. Giants, 1972
### Most Times Sacked, Game
  12  Pittsburgh vs. Dallas, Nov. 20, 1966
      Baltimore vs. St. Louis, Oct. 26, 1980
  11  St. Louis vs. N.Y. Giants, Nov. 1, 1964
      Los Angeles vs. Baltimore, Nov. 22, 1964
      Denver vs Buffalo, Dec. 13, 1964; vs. Oakland, Nov. 5, 1967
      Green Bay vs. Detroit, Nov. 7, 1965
      Buffalo vs. Oakland, Oct. 15, 1967
      Atlanta vs. St. Louis, Nov. 24, 1968
      Detroit vs. Dallas, Oct. 6, 1975
      Philadelphia vs. St. Louis, Dec. 18, 1983
  10  By many teams
### Most Times Sacked, Both Teams, Game
  18  Green Bay (10) vs. San Diego (8), Sept. 24, 1978
  17  Buffalo (10) vs. N.Y. Titans (7), Nov. 23, 1961
      Pittsburgh (12) vs. Dallas (5), Nov. 20, 1966
  16  Los Angeles (11) vs. Baltimore (5), Nov. 22, 1964
      Buffalo (11) vs. Oakland (5), Oct. 15, 1967

## COMPLETION PERCENTAGE
### Most Seasons Leading League, Completion Percentage
  11  Washington, 1937, 1939-40, 1942-45, 1947-48, 1969-70
   7  Green Bay, 1936, 1941, 1961-62, 1964, 1966, 1968
   6  Clev. Browns, 1951, 1953-55, 1959-60
      Dall. Texans/Kansas City, 1962, 1964, 1966-69
      San Francisco, 1952, 1957-58, 1965, 1981, 1983
### Most Consecutive Seasons Leading League, Completion Percentage
   4  Washington, 1942-45
      Kansas City, 1966-69
   3  Cleveland, 1953-55
   2  By many teams
### Highest Completion Percentage, Season
 70.6  Cincinnati, 1982 (310-219)
 64.3  Oakland, 1976 (361-232)
 64.2  San Francisco, 1983 (528-339)
### Lowest Completion Percentage, Season
 22.9  Philadelphia, 1936 (170-39)
 24.5  Cincinnati, 1933 (102-25)
 25.0  Pittsburgh, 1941 (168-42)

## TOUCHDOWNS
### Most Touchdowns, Passing, Season
  48  Houston, 1961
  39  N.Y. Giants, 1963
  36  Oakland, 1969
### Fewest Touchdowns, Passing, Season
   0  Cincinnati, 1933
      Pittsburgh, 1945
   1  Boston, 1932, 1933
      Chi. Cardinals, 1934
      Cincinnati/St. Louis, 1934
      Detroit, 1942

   2  Chi. Cardinals, 1932, 1935
      Stapleton, 1932
      Brooklyn, 1936
      Pittsburgh, 1942
### Most Touchdowns, Passing, Game
   7  Chi. Bears vs. N.Y. Giants, Nov. 14, 1943
      Philadelphia vs. Washington, Oct. 17, 1954
      Houston vs. N.Y. Titans, Nov. 19, 1961; vs. N.Y. Titans, Oct. 14, 1962
      N.Y. Giants vs. Washington, Oct. 28, 1962
      Minnesota vs. Baltimore, Sept. 28, 1969
      San Diego vs. Oakland, Nov. 22, 1981
   6  By many teams.
### Most Touchdowns, Passing, Both Teams, Game
  12  New Orleans (6) vs. St. Louis (6), Nov. 2, 1969
  11  N.Y. Giants (7) vs. Washington (4), Oct. 28, 1962
      Oakland (6) vs. Houston (5), Dec. 22, 1963
   9  In many games

## PASSES HAD INTERCEPTED
### Most Passes Had Intercepted, Season
  48  Houston, 1962
  45  Denver, 1961
  41  Card-Pitt, 1944
### Fewest Passes Had Intercepted, Season
   5  Cleveland, 1960
      Green Bay, 1966
   6  Green Bay, 1964
      St. Louis, 1982
   7  Los Angeles, 1969
### Most Passes Had Intercepted, Game
   9  Detroit vs. Green Bay, Oct. 24, 1943
      Pittsburgh vs. Philadelphia, Dec. 12, 1965
   8  Green Bay vs. N.Y. Giants, Nov. 21, 1948
      Chi. Cardinals vs. Philadelphia, Sept. 24, 1950
      N.Y. Yanks vs. N.Y. Giants, Dec. 16, 1951
      Denver vs. Houston, Dec. 2, 1962
      Chi. Bears vs. Detroit, Sept. 22, 1968
      Baltimore vs. N.Y. Jets, Sept. 23, 1973
   7  By many teams
### Most Passes Had Intercepted, Both Teams, Game
  13  Denver (8) vs. Houston (5), Dec. 2, 1962
  11  Philadelphia (7) vs. Boston (4), Nov. 3, 1935
      Boston (6) vs. Pittsburgh (5), Dec. 1, 1935
      Cleveland (7) vs. Green Bay (4), Oct. 30, 1938
      Green Bay (7) vs. Detroit (4), Oct. 20, 1940
      Detroit (7) vs. Chi. Bears (4), Nov. 22, 1942
      Detroit (7) vs. Cleveland (4), Nov. 26, 1944
      Chi. Cardinals (8) vs. Philadelphia (3), Sept. 24, 1950
      Washington (7) vs. N.Y. Giants (4), Dec. 8, 1963
      Pittsburgh (9) vs. Philadelphia (2), Dec 12, 1965
  10  In many games

# PUNTING
### Most Seasons Leading League (Average Distance)
   6  Washington, 1940-43, 1945, 1958
      Denver, 1962-64, 1966-67, 1982
   5  Kansas City, 1968, 1971-73, 1979
   4  L.A. Rams, 1946, 1949, 1955-56
### Most Consecutive Seasons Leading League (Average Distance)
   4  Washington, 1940-43
   3  Cleveland, 1950-52
      Denver, 1962-64
      Kansas City, 1971-73
### Most Punts, Season
 114  Chicago, 1981
 113  Boston, 1934
      Brooklyn, 1934
 112  Boston, 1935
### Fewest Punts, Season
  23  San Diego, 1982
  31  Cincinnati, 1982
  32  Chi. Bears, 1941
### Most Punts, Game
  17  Chi. Bears vs. Green Bay, Oct. 22, 1933
      Cincinnati vs. Pittsburgh, Oct. 22, 1933
  16  Cincinnati vs. Portsmouth, Sept. 17, 1933
      Chi. Cardinals vs. Chi. Bears, Nov. 30, 1933; vs. Detroit, Sept. 15, 1940
### Fewest Punts, Game
   0  By many teams. Last time: New Orleans vs. Atlanta, Jan. 2, 1983
### Most Punts, Both Teams, Game
  31  Chi. Bears (17) vs. Green Bay (14), Oct. 22, 1933
      Cincinnati (17), vs. Pittsburgh (14), Oct. 22, 1933
  29  Chi. Cardinals (15) vs. Cincinnati (14), Nov. 12, 1933
      Chi. Cardinals (16) vs. Chi. Bears (13), Nov. 30, 1933
      Chi. Cardinals (16) vs. Detroit (13), Sept. 15, 1940
### Fewest Punts, Both Teams, Game
   1  Dall. Cowboys (0) vs. Cleveland (1), Dec. 3, 1961
      Chicago (0) vs. Detroit (1), Oct. 1, 1972
      San Francisco (0) vs. N.Y. Giants (1), Oct. 15, 1972
      Green Bay (0) vs. Buffalo (1), Dec. 5, 1982
   2  In many games

## AVERAGE YARDAGE
### Highest Average Distance, Punting, Season
 47.6  Detroit, 1961 (56-2,664)
 47.0  Pittsburgh, 1961 (73-3,431)
 46.9  Pittsburgh, 1953 (80-3.752)
### Lowest Average Distance, Punting, Season
 32.7  Card-Pitt, 1944 (60-1,964)
 33.9  Detroit, 1969 (74-2,510)
 34.4  Phil-Pitt, 1943 (62-2,132)

# PUNT RETURNS

**Most Seasons Leading League (Average Return)**
- 8 Detroit, 1943-45, 1951-52, 1962, 1966, 1969
- 5 Chi. Cardinals, 1948-49, 1955-56, 1959
  - Clev. Browns, 1958, 1960, 1964-65, 1967
  - Green Bay, 1950, 1953-54, 1961, 1972
  - Dall. Texans/Kansas City, 1960, 1968, 1970, 1979-80
- 4 Denver, 1963, 1967, 1969, 1982

**Most Consecutive Seasons Leading League (Average Return)**
- 3 Detroit, 1943-45
- 2 By many teams

**Most Punt Returns, Season**
- 71 Pittsburgh, 1976
  - Tampa Bay, 1979
- 67 Pittsburgh, 1974
  - Los Angeles, 1978
- 65 San Francisco, 1976

**Fewest Punt Returns, Season**
- 12 Baltimore, 1981
  - San Diego, 1982
- 14 Los Angeles, 1961
  - Philadelphia, 1962
  - Baltimore, 1982
- 15 Houston, 1960
  - Washington, 1960
  - Oakland, 1961
  - N.Y. Giants, 1969
  - Philadelphia, 1973
  - Kansas City, 1982

**Most Punt Returns, Game**
- 12 Philadelphia vs. Cleveland, Dec. 3, 1950
- 11 Chi. Bears vs. Chi. Cardinals, Oct. 8, 1950
  - Washington vs. Tampa Bay, Oct. 9, 1977
- 10 Philadelphia vs. N.Y. Giants, Nov. 26, 1950
  - Philadelphia vs. Tampa Bay, Sept. 18, 1977
  - Pittsburgh vs. Buffalo, Dec. 16, 1979
  - Washington vs. New Orleans, Dec. 26, 1982

**Most Punt Returns, Both Teams, Game**
- 17 Philadelphia (12) vs. Cleveland (5), Dec. 3, 1950
- 16 N.Y. Giants (9) vs. Philadelphia (7), Dec. 12, 1954
  - Washington (11) vs. Tampa Bay (5), Oct. 9, 1977
- 15 Detroit (8) vs. Cleveland (7), Sept. 27, 1942
  - Los Angeles (8) vs. Baltimore (7), Nov. 27, 1966
  - Pittsburgh (8) vs. Houston (7), Dec. 1, 1974
  - Philadelphia (10) vs. Tampa Bay (5), Sept. 18, 1977
  - Baltimore (9) vs. Kansas City (6), Sept. 2, 1979
  - Washington (10) vs. New Orleans (5), Dec. 26, 1982

## FAIR CATCHES

**Most Fair Catches, Season**
- 34 Baltimore, 1971
- 32 San Diego, 1969
- 30 St. Louis, 1967
  - Minnesota, 1971

**Fewest Fair Catches, Season**
- 0 San Diego, 1975
  - New England, 1976
  - Tampa Bay, 1976
  - Pittsburgh, 1977
  - Dallas, 1982
- 1 Cleveland, 1974
  - San Francisco, 1975
  - Kansas City, 1976
  - St. Louis, 1976, 1982
  - San Diego, 1976
  - L.A. Rams, 1982
  - Tampa Bay, 1982
- 2 By many teams

**Most Fair Catches, Game**
- 7 Minnesota vs. Dallas, Sept. 25, 1966
  - Detroit vs. Chicago, Nov. 21, 1976
- 6 By many teams

## YARDS GAINED

**Most Yards, Punt Returns, Season**
- 781 Chi. Bears, 1948
- 774 Pittsburgh, 1974
- 729 Green Bay, 1950

**Fewest Yards, Punt Returns, Season**
- 27 St. Louis, 1965
- 35 N.Y. Giants, 1965
- 37 New England, 1972

**Most Yards, Punt Returns, Game**
- 231 Detroit vs. San Francisco, Oct. 6, 1963
- 225 Oakland vs. Buffalo, Sept. 15, 1968
- 219 Los Angeles vs. Atlanta, Oct. 11, 1981

**Most Yards, Punt Returns, Both Teams, Game**
- 282 Los Angeles (219) vs. Atlanta (63), Oct. 11, 1981
- 245 Detroit (231) vs. San Francisco (14), Oct. 6, 1963
- 244 Oakland (225) vs. Buffalo (19), Sept. 15, 1968

## AVERAGE YARDS RETURNING PUNTS

**Highest Average, Punt Returns, Season**
- 20.2 Chi. Bears, 1941 (27-546)
- 19.1 Chi. Cardinals, 1948 (35-669)
- 18.2 Chi. Cardinals, 1949 (30-546)

**Lowest Average, Punt Returns, Season**
- 1.2 St. Louis, 1965 (23-27)
- 1.5 N.Y. Giants, 1965 (24-35)
- 1.7 Washington, 1970 (27-45)

## TOUCHDOWNS RETURNING PUNTS

**Most Touchdowns, Punt Returns, Season**
- 5 Chi. Cardinals, 1959
- 4 Chi. Cardinals, 1948
  - Detroit, 1951
  - N.Y. Giants, 1951
  - Denver, 1976
- 3 Washington, 1941
  - Detroit, 1952
  - Pittsburgh, 1952
  - Houston, 1975
  - Los Angeles, 1981

**Most Touchdowns, Punt Returns, Game**
- 2 Detroit vs. Los Angeles, Oct. 14, 1951; vs. Green Bay, Nov. 22, 1951
  - Chi. Cardinals vs. Pittsburgh, Nov. 1, 1959; vs. N.Y. Giants, Nov. 22, 1959
  - N.Y. Titans vs. Denver, Sept. 24, 1961
  - Denver vs. Cleveland, Sept. 26, 1976
  - Los Angeles vs. Atlanta, Oct. 11, 1981

**Most Touchdowns, Punt Returns, Both Teams, Game**
- 2 Philadelphia (1) vs. Washington (1), Nov. 9, 1952
  - Kansas City (1) vs. Buffalo (1), Sept. 11, 1966
  - Baltimore (1) vs. New England (1), Nov. 18, 1979
  - (Also see previous record)

# KICKOFF RETURNS

**Most Seasons Leading League (Average Return)**
- 7 Washington, 1942, 1947, 1962-63, 1973-74, 1981
- 5 N.Y. Giants, 1944, 1946, 1949, 1951, 1953
  - Chi. Bears, 1943, 1948, 1958, 1966, 1972
- 4 Houston, 1960, 1962-63, 1968

**Most Consecutive Seasons Leading League (Average Return)**
- 3 Denver, 1965-67
- 2 By many teams

**Most Kickoff Returns, Season**
- 88 New Orleans, 1980
- 84 Baltimore, 1981
- 83 Houston, 1983

**Fewest Kickoff Returns, Season**
- 17 N.Y. Giants, 1944
- 20 N.Y. Giants, 1941, 1943
  - Chi. Bears, 1942
- 23 Washington, 1942

**Most Kickoff Returns, Game**
- 12 N.Y. Giants vs. Washington, Nov. 27, 1966
- 10 By many teams

**Most Kickoff Returns, Both Teams, Game**
- 19 N.Y. Giants (12) vs. Washington (7), Nov. 27, 1966
- 18 Houston (10) vs. Oakland (8), Dec. 22, 1963
- 17 Washington (9) vs. Green Bay (8), Oct. 17, 1983

## YARDS GAINED

**Most Yards, Kickoff Returns, Season**
- 1,973 New Orleans, 1980
- 1,824 Houston, 1963
- 1,801 Denver, 1963

**Fewest Yards, Kickoff Returns, Season**
- 282 N.Y. Giants, 1940
- 381 Green Bay, 1940
- 424 Chicago, 1963

**Most Yards, Kickoff Returns, Game**
- 362 Detroit vs. Los Angeles, Oct. 29, 1950
- 304 Chi. Bears vs. Green Bay, Nov. 9, 1952
- 295 Denver vs. Boston, Oct. 4, 1964

**Most Yards, Kickoff Returns, Both Teams, Game**
- 560 Detroit (362) vs. Los Angeles (198), Oct. 29, 1950
- 453 Washington (236) vs. Philadelphia (217), Sept. 28, 1947
- 447 N.Y. Giants (236) vs. Cleveland (211), Dec. 4, 1966

## AVERAGE YARDAGE

**Highest Average, Kickoff Returns, Season**
- 29.4 Chicago, 1972 (52-1,528)
- 28.9 Pittsburgh, 1952 (39-1,128)
- 28.2 Washington, 1962 (61-1,720)

**Lowest Average, Kickoff Returns, Season**
- 16.3 Chicago, 1963 (26-424)
- 16.4 Chicago, 1983 (58-953)
- 16.5 San Diego, 1961 (51-642)

## TOUCHDOWNS

**Most Touchdowns, Kickoff Returns, Season**
- 4 Green Bay, 1967
  - Chicago, 1970
- 3 Los Angeles, 1950
  - Chi. Cardinals, 1954
  - San Francisco, 1963
  - Denver, 1966
  - Chicago, 1967
  - New England, 1977
- 2 By many teams

**Most Touchdowns, Kickoff Returns, Game**
- 2 Chi. Bears vs. Green Bay, Sept. 22, 1940; vs. Green Bay, Nov. 9, 1952
  - Philadelphia vs. Dallas, Nov. 6, 1966
  - Green Bay vs. Cleveland, Nov. 12, 1967

**Most Touchdowns, Kickoff Returns, Both Teams, Game**
- 2 Washington (1) vs. Philadelphia (1), Nov. 1, 1942
  - Washington (1) vs. Philadelphia (1), Sept. 28, 1947
  - Los Angeles (1) vs. Detroit (1), Oct. 29, 1950
  - N.Y. Yanks (1) vs. N.Y. Giants (1), Nov. 4, 1951 (consecutive)
  - Baltimore (1) vs. Chi. Bears (1), Oct. 4, 1958
  - Buffalo (1) vs. Boston (1), Nov. 3, 1962
  - Pittsburgh (1) vs. Dallas (1), Oct. 30, 1966
  - St. Louis (1) vs. Washington (1), Sept. 23, 1973 (consecutive)
  - (Also see previous record)

# FUMBLES

**Most Fumbles, Season**
- 56 Chi. Bears, 1938
  - San Francisco, 1978
- 54 Philadelphia, 1946
- 51 New England, 1973

**Fewest Fumbles, Season**
- 8 Cleveland, 1959
- 11 Green Bay, 1944
- 12 Brooklyn, 1934
  - Detroit, 1943
  - Cincinnati, 1982
  - Minnesota, 1982

**Most Fumbles, Game**
- 10 Phil-Pitt vs. New York, Oct. 9, 1943
  - Detroit vs. Minnesota, Nov. 12, 1967
  - Kansas City vs. Houston, Oct. 12, 1969
  - San Francisco vs. Detroit, Dec. 17, 1978
- 9 Philadelphia vs. Green Bay, Oct. 13, 1946
  - Kansas City vs. San Diego, Nov. 15, 1964
  - N.Y. Giants vs. Buffalo, Oct. 20, 1975
  - St. Louis vs. Washington, Oct. 25, 1976
  - San Diego vs. Green Bay, Sept. 24, 1978
  - Pittsburgh vs. Cincinnati, Oct. 14, 1979
  - Cleveland vs. Seattle, Dec. 20, 1981
- 8 By many teams. Last time: Tampa Bay vs. New York Jets, Dec. 12, 1982

**Most Fumbles, Both Teams, Game**
- 14 Chi. Bears (7) vs. Cleveland (7), Nov. 24, 1940
  - St. Louis (8) vs. N.Y. Giants (6), Sept. 17, 1961
  - Kansas City (10) vs. Houston (4), Oct. 12, 1969
- 13 Washington (8) vs. Pittsburgh (5), Nov. 14, 1937
  - Philadelphia (7) vs. Boston (6), Dec. 8, 1946
  - N.Y. Giants (7) vs. Washington (6), Nov. 5, 1950
  - Kansas City (9) vs. San Diego (4), Nov. 15, 1964
  - Buffalo (7) vs. Denver (6), Dec. 13, 1964
  - N.Y. Jets (7) vs. Houston (6), Sept. 12, 1965
  - Houston (8) vs. Pittsburgh (5), Dec. 9, 1973
  - St. Louis (9) vs. Washington (4), Oct. 25, 1976
  - Cleveland (9) vs. Seattle (4), Dec. 20, 1981
- 12 In many games

## FUMBLES LOST

**Most Fumbles Lost, Season**
- 36 Chi. Cardinals, 1959
- 31 Green Bay, 1952
- 29 Chi. Cardinals, 1946
  - Pittsburgh, 1950

**Fewest Fumbles Lost, Season**
- 3 Philadelphia, 1938
  - Minnesota, 1980
- 4 San Francisco, 1960
  - Kansas City, 1982
- 5 Chi. Cardinals, 1943
  - Detroit, 1943
  - N.Y. Giants, 1943
  - Cleveland, 1959
  - Minnesota, 1982

**Most Fumbles Lost, Game**
- 8 St. Louis vs. Washington, Oct. 25, 1976
- 7 Cincinnati vs. Buffalo, Nov. 30, 1969
  - Cleveland vs. Seattle, Dec. 20, 1981
- 6 By many teams. Last time: L.A. Rams vs. New England, Dec. 11, 1983

## FUMBLES RECOVERED

**Most Fumbles Recovered, Season, Own and Opponents'**
- 58 Minnesota, 1963 (27 own, 31 opp)
- 51 Chi. Bears, 1938 (37 own, 14 opp)
  - San Francisco, 1978 (24 own, 27 opp)
- 47 Atlanta, 1978 (22 own, 25 opp)

**Fewest Fumbles Recovered, Season, Own and Opponents'**
- 9 San Francisco, 1982 (5 own, 4 opp)
- 11 Cincinnati, 1982 (5 own, 6 opp)
- 13 Baltimore, 1967 (5 own, 8 opp)
  - N.Y. Jets, 1967 (7 own, 6 opp)
  - Philadelphia, 1968 (6 own, 7 opp)
  - Miami, 1973 (5 own, 8 opp)
  - Chicago, 1982 (6 own, 7 opp)
  - Denver, 1982 (6 own, 7 opp)
  - Miami, 1982 (5 own, 8 opp)
  - N.Y. Giants, 1982 (7 own, 6 opp)

**Most Fumbles Recovered, Game, Own and Opponents'**
- 10 Denver vs. Buffalo, Dec. 13, 1964 (5 own, 5 opp)
  - Pittsburgh vs. Houston, Dec. 9, 1973 (5 own, 5 opp)
  - Washington vs. St. Louis, Oct. 25, 1976 (2 own, 8 opp)
- 9 St. Louis vs. N.Y. Giants, Sept. 17, 1961 (6 own, 3 opp)
  - Houston vs. Cincinnati, Oct. 27, 1974 (4 own, 5 opp)
  - Kansas City vs. Dallas, Nov. 10, 1975 (4 own, 5 opp)
- 8 By many teams

**Most Own Fumbles Recovered, Season**
- 37 Chi. Bears, 1938
- 27 Philadelphia, 1946
  - Minnesota, 1963
- 26 Washington, 1940
  - Pittsburgh, 1948

**Fewest Own Fumbles Recovered, Season**
- 2 Washington, 1958
- 3 Detroit, 1956
  - Cleveland, 1959
  - Houston, 1982
- 4 By many teams

**Most Opponents' Fumbles Recovered, Season**
- 31 Minnesota, 1963
- 29 Cleveland, 1951

**Most Opponents' Fumbles Recovered, Season** *(continued)*
- 28 Green Bay, 1946
  - Houston, 1977
  - Seattle, 1983

**Fewest Opponents' Fumbles Recovered, Season**
- 3 Los Angeles, 1974
- 4 Philadelphia, 1944
  - San Francisco, 1982
- 5 Baltimore, 1982

**Most Opponents' Fumbles Recovered, Game**
- 8 Washington vs. St. Louis, Oct. 25, 1976
- 7 Buffalo vs. Cincinnati, Nov. 30, 1969
  - Seattle vs. Cleveland, Dec. 20, 1981
- 6 By many teams. Last time: New England vs. L.A. Rams, Dec. 11, 1983

## TOUCHDOWNS

**Most Touchdowns, Fumbles Recovered, Season, Own and Opponents'**
- 5 Chi. Bears, 1942 (1 own, 4 opp)
  - Los Angeles, 1952 (1 own, 4 opp)
  - San Francisco, 1965 (1 own, 4 opp)
  - Oakland, 1978 (2 own, 3 opp)
- 4 Chi. Bears, 1948 (1 own, 3 opp)
  - Boston, 1948 (4 opp)
  - Denver, 1979 (1 own, 3 opp)
  - Atlanta, 1981 (1 own, 3 opp)
- 3 By many teams

**Most Touchdowns, Own Fumbles Recovered, Season**
- 2 Chi. Bears, 1953
  - New England, 1973
  - Buffalo, 1974
  - Denver, 1975
  - Oakland, 1978
  - Green Bay, 1982
  - New Orleans, 1983

**Most Touchdowns, Opponents' Fumbles Recovered, Season**
- 4 Detroit, 1937
  - Chi. Bears, 1942
  - Boston, 1948
  - Los Angeles, 1952
  - San Francisco, 1965
- 3 By many teams

**Most Touchdowns, Fumbles Recovered, Game, Own and Opponents'**
- 2 Detroit vs. Cleveland, Nov. 7, 1937 (2 opp); vs. Los Angeles, Sept. 17, 1950 (1 own, 1 opp); vs. Chi. Cardinals, Dec. 6, 1959 (1 own, 1 opp); vs. Minnesota, Dec. 9, 1962 (1 own, 1 opp)
  - Philadelphia vs. New York, Sept. 25, 1938 (2 opp); vs. St. Louis, Nov. 21, 1971 (1 own, 1 opp)
  - Chi. Bears vs. Washington, Nov. 28, 1948 (2 opp)
  - N.Y. Giants vs. Pittsburgh, Sept. 17, 1950 (2 opp); vs. Green Bay, Sept. 19, 1971 (2 opp)
  - Cleveland vs. Dall. Cowboys, Dec. 3, 1961 (2 opp); vs. N.Y. Giants, Oct. 25, 1964 (2 opp)
  - Green Bay vs. Dallas, Nov. 26, 1964 (2 opp)
  - San Francisco vs. Detroit, Nov. 14, 1965 (2 opp)
  - Oakland vs. Buffalo, Dec. 24, 1967 (2 opp)
  - Washington vs. San Diego, Sept. 16, 1973 (2 opp)
  - New Orleans vs. San Francisco, Oct 19, 1975 (2 opp)
  - Cincinnati vs. Pittsburgh, Oct. 14, 1979 (2 opp)
  - Atlanta vs. Detroit, Oct. 5, 1980 (2 opp)
  - Kansas City vs. Oakland, Oct. 5, 1980 (2 opp)
  - New England vs. Baltimore, Nov. 23, 1980 (2 opp)

**Most Touchdowns, Own Fumbles Recovered, Game**
- 1 By many teams

**Most Touchdowns, Opponents' Fumbles Recovered, Game**
- 2 Detroit vs. Cleveland, Nov. 7, 1937
  - Philadelphia vs. N.Y. Giants, Sept. 25, 1938
  - Chi. Bears vs. Washington, Nov. 28, 1948
  - N.Y. Giants vs. Pittsburgh, Sept. 17, 1950; vs. Green Bay, Sept. 19, 1971
  - Cleveland vs. Dall. Cowboys, Dec. 3, 1961; vs. N.Y. Giants, Oct. 25, 1964
  - Green Bay vs. Dallas, Nov. 26, 1964
  - San Francisco vs. Detroit, Nov. 14, 1965
  - Oakland vs. Buffalo, Dec. 24, 1967
  - Washington vs. San Diego, Sept. 16, 1973
  - New Orleans vs. San Francisco, Oct. 19, 1975
  - Cincinnati vs. Pittsburgh, Oct. 14, 1979
  - Atlanta vs. Detroit, Oct. 5, 1980
  - Kansas City vs. Oakland, Oct. 5, 1980
  - New England vs. Baltimore, Nov. 23, 1980

# TURNOVERS
(Number of times losing the ball on interceptions and fumbles.)

**Most Turnovers, Season**
- 63 San Francisco, 1978
- 58 Chi. Bears, 1947
  - Pittsburgh, 1950
  - N.Y. Giants, 1983
- 57 Green Bay, 1950
  - Houston, 1962, 1963
  - Pittsburgh, 1965

**Fewest Turnovers, Season**
- 12 Kansas City, 1982
- 14 N.Y. Giants, 1943
  - Cleveland, 1959
- 16 San Francisco, 1960
  - Cincinnati, 1982
  - St. Louis, 1982
  - Washington, 1982

**Most Turnovers, Game**
- 12 Detroit vs. Chi. Bears, Nov. 22, 1942
  - Chi. Cardinals vs. Philadelphia, Sept. 24, 1950
  - Pittsburgh vs. Philadelphia, Dec. 12, 1965
- 11 San Diego vs. Green Bay, Sept. 24, 1978

10  Washington vs. N.Y. Giants, Dec. 4, 1938; vs. N.Y. Giants, Dec. 8, 1963
    Pittsburgh vs. Green Bay, Nov. 23, 1941
    Detroit vs. Green Bay, Oct. 24, 1943
    Chi. Cardinals vs. Green Bay, Nov. 10, 1946; vs. N.Y. Giants, Nov. 2, 1952
    Minnesota vs. Detroit, Dec. 9, 1962
    Houston vs. Oakland, Sept. 7, 1963
    Chicago vs. Detroit, Sept. 22, 1968
    St. Louis vs. Washington, Oct. 25, 1976
    N.Y. Jets vs. New England, Nov. 21, 1976
    San Francisco vs. Dallas, Oct. 12, 1980
    Cleveland vs. Seattle, Dec. 20, 1981

**Most Turnovers, Both Teams, Game**
17  Detroit (12) vs. Chi. Bears (5), Nov. 22, 1942
    Boston (9) vs. Philadelphia (8), Dec. 8, 1946
16  Chi. Cardinals (12) vs. Philadelphia (4), Sept. 24, 1950
    Chi. Cardinals (8) vs. Chi. Bears (8), Dec. 7, 1958
    Minnesota (10) vs. Detroit (6), Dec. 9, 1962
    Houston (9) vs. Kansas City (7), Oct. 12, 1969
15  Philadelphia (8) vs. Chi. Cardinals (7), Oct. 3, 1954
    Denver (9) vs. Houston (6), Dec. 2, 1962
    Washington (10) vs. N.Y. Giants (5), Dec. 8, 1963
    St. Louis (9) vs. Kansas City (6), Oct. 2, 1983

## PENALTIES

**Most Seasons Leading League, Fewest Penalties**
9  Pittsburgh, 1946-47, 1950-52, 1954, 1963, 1965, 1968
   Miami, 1968, 1976-83
5  Green Bay, 1955-56, 1966-67, 1974
4  Boston/New England, 1962, 1964-65, 1973

**Most Consecutive Seasons Leading League, Fewest Penalties**
8  Miami, 1976-83
3  Pittsburgh, 1950-52
2  By many teams

**Most Seasons Leading League, Most Penalties**
16  Chi. Bears, 1941-44, 1946-49, 1951, 1959-61, 1963, 1965, 1968, 1976
6   L.A. Rams, 1950, 1952, 1962, 1969, 1978, 1980
    Oakland/L.A. Raiders, 1963, 1966, 1968-69, 1975, 1982
4   San Diego, 1962, 1964-65, 1981

**Most Consecutive Seasons Leading League, Most Penalties**
4  Chi. Bears, 1941-44, 1946-49
3  Chi. Cardinals, 1954-56
   Chi. Bears, 1959-61

**Fewest Penalties, Season**
19  Detroit, 1937
21  Boston, 1935
24  Philadelphia, 1936

**Most Penalties, Season**
144  Buffalo, 1983
137  Baltimore, 1979
133  Los Angeles, 1978

**Fewest Penalties, Game**
0  By many teams. Last time: Tampa Bay vs. Detroit, Dec. 18, 1983

**Most Penalties, Game**
22  Brooklyn vs. Green Bay, Sept. 17, 1944
    Chi. Bears vs. Philadelphia, Nov. 26, 1944
21  Cleveland vs. Chi. Bears, Nov. 25, 1951
20  Tampa Bay vs. Seattle, Oct. 17, 1976

**Fewest Penalties, Both Teams, Game**
0  Brooklyn vs. Pittsburgh, Oct. 28, 1934
   Brooklyn vs. Boston, Sept. 28, 1936
   Cleveland vs. Chi. Bears, Oct. 9, 1938
   Pittsburgh vs. Philadelphia, Nov. 10, 1940

**Most Penalties, Both Teams, Game**
37  Cleveland (21) vs. Chi. Bears (16), Nov. 25, 1951
35  Tampa Bay (20) vs. Seattle (15), Oct. 17, 1976
33  Brooklyn (22) vs. Green Bay (11), Sept. 17, 1944

### YARDS PENALIZED

**Most Seasons Leading League, Fewest Yards Penalized**
10  Miami, 1967-68, 1973, 1977-83
7   Pittsburgh, 1946-47, 1950, 1952, 1962, 1965, 1968
    Boston/Washington, 1935, 1953-54, 1956-58, 1970
4   Philadelphia, 1936, 1940, 1951, 1964
    Boston, 1962, 1964-66

**Most Consecutive Seasons Leading League, Fewest Yards Penalized**
7  Miami, 1977-83
3  Washington, 1956-58
   Boston, 1964-66
2  By many teams

**Most Seasons Leading League, Most Yards Penalized**
15  Chi. Bears, 1935, 1937, 1939-44, 1946-47, 1949, 1951, 1961-62, 1968
6   Oakland/L.A. Raiders, 1963-64, 1968-69, 1975, 1982
    Buffalo, 1962, 1967, 1970, 1972, 1981, 1983
5   Cleveland, 1965, 1976-78, 1980

**Most Consecutive Seasons Leading League, Most Yards Penalized**
6  Chi. Bears, 1939-44
3  Cleveland, 1976-78
2  By many teams

**Fewest Yards Penalized, Season**
139  Detroit, 1937
146  Philadelphia, 1937
159  Philadelphia, 1936

**Most Yards Penalized, Season**
1,274  Oakland, 1969
1,239  Baltimore, 1979
1,194  Chicago, 1968

**Fewest Yards Penalized, Game**
0  By many teams. Last time: Tampa Bay vs. Detroit, Dec. 18, 1983

**Most Yards Penalized, Game**
209  Cleveland vs. Chi. Bears, Nov. 25, 1951
190  Tampa Bay vs. Seattle, Oct. 17, 1976
189  Houston vs. Buffalo, Oct. 31, 1965

**Fewest Yards Penalized, Both Teams, Game**
0  Brooklyn vs. Pittsburgh, Oct. 28, 1934
   Brooklyn vs. Boston, Sept. 28, 1936
   Cleveland vs. Chi. Bears, Oct. 9, 1938
   Pittsburgh vs. Philadelphia, Nov. 10, 1940

**Most Yards Penalized, Both Teams, Game**
374  Cleveland (209) vs. Chi. Bears (165), Nov. 25, 1951
310  Tampa Bay (190) vs. Seattle (120), Oct. 17, 1976
309  Green Bay (184) vs. Boston (125), Oct. 21, 1945

# DEFENSE

## SCORING

**Most Seasons Leading League, Fewest Points Allowed**
8  N.Y. Giants, 1935, 1938-39, 1941, 1944, 1958-59, 1961
6  Cleveland, 1951, 1953-57
   Chi. Bears, 1932, 1936-37, 1942, 1948, 1963
5  Green Bay, 1935, 1947, 1962, 1965-66

**Most Consecutive Seasons Leading League, Fewest Points Allowed**
5  Cleveland, 1953-57
3  Buffalo, 1964-66
   Minnesota, 1969-71
2  By many teams

**Fewest Points Allowed, Season (Since 1932)**
44  Chi. Bears, 1932
54  Brooklyn, 1933
59  Detroit, 1934

**Most Points Allowed, Season**
533  Baltimore, 1981
501  N.Y. Giants, 1966
487  New Orleans, 1980

**Fewest Touchdowns Allowed, Season (Since 1932)**
6  Chi. Bears, 1932
   Brooklyn, 1933
7  Detroit, 1934
8  Green Bay, 1932

**Most Touchdowns Allowed, Season**
68  Baltimore, 1981
66  N.Y. Giants, 1966
63  Baltimore, 1950

## FIRST DOWNS

**Fewest First Downs Allowed, Season**
77  Detroit, 1935
79  Boston, 1935
82  Washington, 1937

**Most First Downs Allowed, Season**
406  Baltimore, 1981
371  Seattle, 1981
366  Green Bay, 1983

**Fewest First Downs Allowed, Rushing, Season**
35  Chi. Bears, 1942
40  Green Bay, 1939
41  Brooklyn, 1944

**Most First Downs Allowed, Rushing, Season**
178  New Orleans, 1980
175  Seattle, 1981
171  Buffalo, 1978
     Green Bay, 1983

**Fewest First Downs Allowed, Passing, Season**
33  Chi. Bears, 1943
34  Pittsburgh, 1941
    Washington, 1943
35  Detroit, 1940
    Philadelphia, 1940, 1944

**Most First Downs Allowed, Passing, Season**
216  San Diego, 1981
214  Baltimore, 1981
198  N.Y. Jets, 1979, 1980

**Fewest First Downs Allowed, Penalty, Season**
1  Boston, 1944
3  Philadelphia, 1940
   Pittsburgh, 1945
   Washington, 1957
4  Cleveland, 1940
   Green Bay, 1943
   N.Y. Giants, 1943

**Most First Downs Allowed, Penalty, Season**
41  Detroit, 1979
40  Pittsburgh, 1978
38  Cleveland, 1978, 1980

## NET YARDS ALLOWED RUSHING AND PASSING

**Most Seasons Leading League, Fewest Yards Allowed**
6  N.Y. Giants, 1938, 1940-41, 1951, 1956, 1959
5  Boston/Washington, 1935-37, 1939, 1946
   Chi. Bears, 1942-43, 1948, 1958, 1963
   Philadelphia, 1944-45, 1949, 1953, 1981
4  Cleveland, 1950, 1952, 1954-55

**Most Consecutive Seasons Leading League, Fewest Yards Allowed**
3  Boston/Washington, 1935-37
2  By many teams

**Fewest Yards Allowed, Season**
1,539  Chi. Cardinals, 1934
1,703  Chi. Bears, 1942
1,789  Brooklyn, 1933

**Most Yards Allowed, Season**
6,793  Baltimore, 1981
6,403  Green Bay, 1983
6,218  New Orleans, 1980

## RUSHING

**Most Seasons Leading League, Fewest Yards Allowed**
- 7 Detroit, 1938, 1950, 1952, 1962, 1970, 1980-81
- 6 Chi. Bears, 1937, 1939, 1942, 1946, 1949, 1963
- Dallas, 1966-69, 1972, 1978
- 5 Philadelphia, 1944-45, 1947-48, 1953

**Most Consecutive Seasons Leading League, Fewest Yards Allowed**
- 4 Dallas, 1966-69
- 2 By many teams

**Fewest Yards Allowed, Rushing, Season**
- 519 Chi. Bears, 1942
- 558 Philadelphia, 1944
- 762 Pittsburgh, 1982

**Most Yards Allowed, Rushing, Season**
- 3,228 Buffalo, 1978
- 3,106 New Orleans, 1980
- 3,010 Baltimore, 1978

**Fewest Touchdowns Allowed, Rushing, Season**
- 2 Detroit, 1934
- Dallas, 1968
- Minnesota, 1971
- 3 By many teams

**Most Touchdowns Allowed, Rushing, Season**
- 36 Oakland, 1961
- 31 N.Y. Giants, 1980
- 30 Baltimore, 1981

## PASSING

**Most Seasons Leading League, Fewest Yards Allowed**
- 8 Green Bay, 1947-48, 1962, 1964-68
- 6 Chi. Bears, 1938, 1943-44, 1958, 1960, 1963
- Washington, 1939, 1942, 1945, 1952-53, 1980
- 5 Pittsburgh, 1941, 1946, 1951, 1955, 1974
- Minnesota, 1969-70, 1972, 1975-76
- Philadelphia, 1934, 1936, 1940, 1949, 1981

**Most Consecutive Seasons Leading League, Fewest Yards Allowed**
- 5 Green Bay, 1964-68
- 2 By many teams

**Fewest Yards Allowed, Passing, Season**
- 545 Philadelphia, 1934
- 558 Portsmouth, 1933
- 585 Chi. Cardinals, 1934

**Most Yards Allowed, Passing, Season**
- 4,311 San Diego, 1981
- 4,128 Baltimore, 1981
- 4,115 N.Y. Jets, 1979

**Most Sacks, Season**
- 67 Oakland, 1967
- 66 N.Y. Jets, 1981
- 61 San Francisco, 1976

**Fewest Sacks, Season**
- 11 Baltimore, 1982
- 12 Buffalo, 1982
- 13 Baltimore, 1981

**Most Sacks, Game**
- 12 Dallas vs. Pittsburgh, Nov. 20, 1966
- St. Louis vs. Baltimore, Oct. 26, 1980
- 11 N.Y. Giants vs. St. Louis, Nov. 1, 1964
- Baltimore vs. Los Angeles, Nov. 22, 1964
- Buffalo vs. Denver, Dec. 13, 1964
- Detroit vs. Green Bay, Nov. 7, 1965
- Oakland vs. Buffalo, Oct. 15, 1967; vs. Denver, Nov. 5, 1967
- St. Louis vs. Atlanta, Nov. 24, 1968
- Dallas vs. Detroit, Oct. 6, 1975
- St. Louis vs. Philadelphia, Dec. 18, 1983
- 10 By many teams

**Most Opponents Yards Lost Attempting to Pass, Season**
- 666 Oakland, 1967
- 573 San Francisco, 1976
- 526 Boston, 1963

**Fewest Opponents Yards Lost Attempting to Pass, Season**
- 75 Green Bay, 1956
- 77 N.Y. Bulldogs, 1949
- 78 Green Bay, 1958

**Fewest Touchdowns Allowed, Passing, Season**
- 1 Portsmouth, 1932
- Philadelphia, 1934
- 2 Brooklyn, 1933
- Chi. Bears, 1934
- 3 Chi. Bears, 1932, 1936
- Green Bay, 1932, 1934
- N.Y. Giants, 1939, 1944

**Most Touchdowns Allowed, Passing, Season**
- 40 Denver, 1963
- 38 St. Louis, 1969
- 37 Washington, 1961
- Baltimore, 1981

## INTERCEPTIONS BY

**Most Seasons Leading League**
- 9 N.Y. Giants, 1933, 1937-39, 1944, 1948, 1951, 1954, 1961
- 8 Green Bay, 1940, 1942-43, 1947, 1955, 1957, 1962, 1965
- 6 Chi. Bears, 1935-36, 1941-42, 1946, 1963
- Kansas City, 1966-70, 1974

**Most Consecutive Seasons Leading League**
- 5 Kansas City, 1966-70
- 3 N.Y. Giants, 1937-39
- 2 By many teams

**Most Passes Intercepted By, Season**
- 49 San Diego, 1961
- 42 Green Bay, 1943
- 41 N.Y. Giants, 1951

**Fewest Passes Intercepted By, Season**
- 3 Houston, 1982
- 5 Baltimore, 1982
- 6 Houston, 1972
- St. Louis, 1982

**Most Passes Intercepted By, Game**
- 9 Green Bay vs. Detroit, Oct. 24, 1943
- Philadelphia vs. Pittsburgh, Dec. 12, 1965
- 8 N.Y. Giants vs. Green Bay, Nov. 21, 1948; vs. N.Y. Yanks, Dec. 16, 1951
- Philadelphia vs. Chi. Cardinals, Sept. 24, 1950
- Houston vs. Denver, Dec. 2, 1962
- Detroit vs. Chicago, Sept. 22, 1968
- N.Y. Jets vs. Baltimore, Sept. 23, 1973
- 7 By many teams

**Most Consecutive Games, One or More Interceptions By**
- 46 L.A. Chargers/San Diego, 1960-63
- 37 Detroit, 1960-63
- 36 Boston, 1944-47
- Washington, 1962-65

**Most Yards Returning Interceptions, Season**
- 929 San Diego, 1961
- 712 Los Angeles, 1952
- 676 Houston, 1967

**Fewest Yards Returning Interceptions, Season**
- 5 Los Angeles, 1959
- 42 Philadelphia, 1982
- 47 Houston, 1982

**Most Yards Returning Interceptions, Game**
- 314 Los Angeles vs. San Francisco, Oct. 18, 1964
- 245 Houston vs. N.Y. Jets, Oct. 15, 1967
- 235 Buffalo vs. N.Y. Jets, Sept. 29, 1968

**Most Touchdowns, Returning Interceptions, Season**
- 9 San Diego, 1961
- 6 Cleveland, 1960
- Green Bay, 1966
- Detroit, 1967
- Houston, 1967
- 5 By 11 teams

**Most Touchdowns Returning Interceptions, Game**
- 3 Baltimore vs. Green Bay, Nov. 5, 1950
- Cleveland vs. Chicago, Dec. 11, 1960
- Philadelphia vs. Pittsburgh, Dec. 12, 1965
- Baltimore vs. Pittsburgh, Sept. 29, 1968
- Buffalo vs. N.Y. Jets, Sept. 29, 1968
- Houston vs. San Diego, Dec. 19, 1971
- Cincinnati vs. Houston, Dec. 17, 1972
- Tampa Bay vs. New Orleans, Dec. 11, 1977
- 2 By many teams

**Most Touchdowns Returning Interceptions, Both Teams, Game**
- 4 Philadelphia (3) vs. Pittsburgh (1), Dec. 12, 1965
- 3 Los Angeles (2) vs. Detroit (1), Nov. 1, 1953
- Cleveland (2) vs. N.Y. Giants (1), Dec. 18, 1960
- Pittsburgh (2) vs. Cincinnati (1), Oct. 10, 1983
- (Also see previous record)

## PUNT RETURNS

**Fewest Opponents Punt Returns, Season**
- 7 Washington, 1962
- San Diego, 1982
- 10 Buffalo, 1982
- 11 Boston, 1962

**Most Opponents Punt Returns, Season**
- 71 Tampa Bay, 1976, 1977
- 69 N.Y. Giants, 1953
- 68 Cleveland, 1974

**Fewest Yards Allowed, Punt Returns, Season**
- 22 Green Bay, 1967
- 34 Washington, 1962
- 39 Cleveland, 1959
- Washington, 1972

**Most Yards Allowed, Punt Returns, Season**
- 932 Green Bay, 1949
- 913 Boston, 1947
- 906 New Orleans, 1974

**Lowest Average Allowed, Punt Returns, Season**
- 1.20 Chi. Cardinals, 1954 (46-55)
- 1.22 Cleveland, 1959 (32-39)
- 1.55 Chi. Cardinals, 1953 (44-68)

**Highest Average Allowed, Punt Returns, Season**
- 18.6 Green Bay, 1949 (50-932)
- 18.0 Cleveland, 1977 (31-558)
- 17.9 Boston, 1960 (20-357)

**Most Touchdowns Allowed, Punt Returns, Season**
- 4 New York, 1959
- 3 Green Bay, 1949
- Chi. Cardinals, 1951
- Los Angeles, 1951
- Washington, 1952
- Dallas, 1952
- Pittsburgh, 1959
- N.Y. Jets, 1968
- Cleveland, 1977
- 2 By many teams

## KICKOFF RETURNS

**Fewest Opponents Kickoff Returns, Season**
- 10 Brooklyn, 1943
- 15 Detroit, 1942
- Brooklyn, 1944
- 18 Cleveland, 1941
- Boston, 1944

**Most Opponents Kickoff Returns, Season**
- 91 Washington, 1983
- 89 New England, 1980
- 88 San Diego, 1981

**Fewest Yards Allowed, Kickoff Returns, Season**
- 225 Brooklyn, 1943
- 293 Brooklyn, 1944
- 361 Seattle, 1982

**Most Yards Allowed, Kickoff Returns, Season**
- 2,045 Kansas City, 1966
- 1,816 N.Y. Giants, 1963
- 1,806 Dallas, 1983

**Lowest Average Allowed, Kickoff Returns, Season**
- 14.3 Cleveland, 1980 (71-1,018)
- 15.0 Seattle, 1982 (24-361)
- 15.8 Oakland, 1977 (63-997)

**Highest Average Allowed, Kickoff Returns, Season**
- 29.5 N.Y. Jets, 1972 (47-1,386)
- 29.4 Los Angeles, 1950 (48-1,411)
- 29.1 New England, 1971 (49-1,427)

**Most Touchdowns Allowed, Kickoff Returns, Season**
- 3 Minnesota, 1963, 1970
  - Dallas, 1966
  - Detroit, 1980
- 2 By many teams

## FUMBLES

**Fewest Opponents Fumbles, Season**
- 11 Cleveland, 1956
  - Baltimore, 1982
- 13 Los Angeles, 1956
  - Chicago, 1960
  - Cleveland, 1963, 1965
  - Detroit, 1967
  - San Diego, 1969
- 14 Baltimore, 1970
  - Oakland, 1975
  - Buffalo, 1982
  - St. Louis, 1982
  - San Francisco, 1982

**Most Opponents Fumbles, Season**
- 50 Minnesota, 1963
  - San Francisco, 1978
- 48 N.Y. Giants, 1980
- 47 N.Y. Giants, 1977

## TURNOVERS
(Number of times losing the ball on interceptions and fumbles.)

**Fewest Opponents Turnovers, Season**
- 11 Baltimore, 1982
- 13 San Francisco, 1982
- 15 St. Louis, 1982

**Most Opponents Turnovers, Season**
- 68 Denver, 1961
- 66 San Diego, 1961
- 61 Washington, 1983

**Most Opponents Turnovers, Game**
- 12 Chi. Bears vs. Detroit, Nov. 22, 1942
  - Philadelphia vs. Chi. Cardinals, Sept. 24, 1950; vs. Pittsburgh, Dec. 12, 1965
- 11 Green Bay vs. San Diego, Sept. 24, 1978
- 10 N.Y. Giants vs. Washington, Dec. 4, 1938; vs. Chi. Cardinals, Nov. 2, 1952;
  - vs. Washington, Dec. 8, 1963
  - Green Bay vs. Pittsburgh, Nov. 23, 1941; vs. Detroit, Oct. 24, 1943;
  - vs. Chi. Cardinals, Nov. 10, 1946
  - Detroit vs. Minnesota, Dec. 9, 1962; vs. Chicago, Sept. 22, 1968
  - Oakland vs. Houston, Sept. 7, 1963
  - Washington vs. St. Louis, Oct. 25, 1976
  - New England vs. N.Y. Jets, Nov. 21, 1976
  - Dallas vs. San Francisco, Oct. 12, 1980
  - Seattle vs. Cleveland, Dec. 20, 1981

# OUTSTANDING PERFORMERS

## 1,000 YARDS RUSHING IN A SEASON

| Year | Player, Team | Att. | Yards | Avg. | Long | TD |
|---|---|---|---|---|---|---|
| 1983 | *Eric Dickerson, L.A. Rams | 390 | 1,808 | 4.6 | 85 | 18 |
| | William Andrews, Atlanta[4] | 331 | 1,567 | 4.7 | 27 | 7 |
| | *Curt Warner, Seattle | 335 | 1,449 | 4.3 | 60 | 13 |
| | Walter Payton, Chicago[7] | 314 | 1,421 | 4.5 | 49 | 6 |
| | John Riggins, Washington[4] | 375 | 1,347 | 3.6 | 44 | 24 |
| | Tony Dorsett, Dallas[6] | 289 | 1,321 | 4.6 | 77 | 8 |
| | Earl Campbell, Houston[5] | 322 | 1,301 | 4.0 | 42 | 12 |
| | Ottis Anderson, St. Louis[4] | 296 | 1,270 | 4.3 | 43 | 5 |
| | Mike Pruitt, Cleveland[4] | 293 | 1,184 | 4.0 | 27 | 10 |
| | George Rogers, New Orleans[2] | 256 | 1,144 | 4.5 | 76 | 5 |
| | Joe Cribbs, Buffalo[3] | 263 | 1,131 | 4.3 | 45 | 3 |
| | Curtis Dickey, Baltimore | 254 | 1,122 | 4.4 | 56 | 4 |
| | Tony Collins, New England | 219 | 1,049 | 4.8 | 50 | 10 |
| | Billy Sims, Detroit[3] | 220 | 1,040 | 4.7 | 41 | 7 |
| | Marcus Allen, L.A. Raiders | 266 | 1,014 | 3.8 | 19 | 9 |
| | Franco Harris, Pittsburgh[8] | 279 | 1,007 | 3.6 | 19 | 5 |
| 1981 | *George Rogers, New Orleans | 378 | 1,674 | 4.4 | 79 | 13 |
| | Tony Dorsett, Dallas[5] | 342 | 1,646 | 4.8 | 75 | 4 |
| | Billy Sims, Detroit[2] | 296 | 1,437 | 4.9 | 51 | 13 |
| | Wilbert Montgomery, Philadelphia[3] | 286 | 1,402 | 4.9 | 41 | 8 |
| | Ottis Anderson, St. Louis[3] | 328 | 1,376 | 4.2 | 28 | 9 |
| | Earl Campbell, Houston[4] | 361 | 1,376 | 3.8 | 43 | 10 |
| | William Andrews, Atlanta[3] | 289 | 1,301 | 4.5 | 29 | 10 |
| | Walter Payton, Chicago[6] | 339 | 1,222 | 3.6 | 39 | 6 |
| | Chuck Muncie, San Diego[2] | 251 | 1,144 | 4.6 | 73 | 19 |
| | *Joe Delaney, Kansas City | 234 | 1,121 | 4.8 | 82 | 3 |
| | Mike Pruitt, Cleveland[3] | 247 | 1,103 | 4.5 | 21 | 7 |
| | Joe Cribbs, Buffalo[2] | 257 | 1,097 | 4.3 | 35 | 3 |
| | Pete Johnson, Cincinnati | 274 | 1,077 | 3.9 | 39 | 12 |
| | Wendell Tyler, Los Angeles[2] | 260 | 1,074 | 4.1 | 69 | 12 |
| | Ted Brown, Minnesota | 274 | 1,063 | 3.9 | 34 | 6 |
| 1980 | Earl Campbell, Houston[3] | 373 | 1,934 | 5.2 | 55 | 13 |
| | Walter Payton, Chicago[5] | 317 | 1,460 | 4.6 | 69 | 6 |
| | Ottis Anderson, St. Louis[2] | 301 | 1,352 | 4.5 | 52 | 9 |
| | William Andrews, Atlanta[2] | 265 | 1,308 | 4.9 | 33 | 4 |
| | *Billy Sims, Detroit | 313 | 1,303 | 4.2 | 52 | 13 |
| | Tony Dorsett, Dallas[4] | 278 | 1,185 | 4.3 | 56 | 11 |
| | *Joe Cribbs, Buffalo | 306 | 1,185 | 3.9 | 48 | 11 |
| | Mike Pruitt, Cleveland[2] | 249 | 1,034 | 4.2 | 56 | 6 |
| 1979 | Earl Campbell, Houston[2] | 368 | 1,697 | 4.6 | 61 | 19 |
| | Walter Payton, Chicago[4] | 369 | 1,610 | 4.4 | 43 | 14 |
| | *Ottis Anderson, St. Louis | 331 | 1,605 | 4.8 | 76 | 8 |
| | Wilbert Montgomery, Philadelphia[2] | 338 | 1,512 | 4.5 | 62 | 9 |
| | Mike Pruitt, Cleveland | 264 | 1,294 | 4.9 | 77 | 9 |
| | Ricky Bell, Tampa Bay | 283 | 1,263 | 4.5 | 49 | 7 |
| | Chuck Muncie, New Orleans | 238 | 1,198 | 5.0 | 69 | 11 |
| | Franco Harris, Pittsburgh[7] | 267 | 1,186 | 4.4 | 71 | 11 |
| | John Riggins, Washington[3] | 260 | 1,153 | 4.4 | 66 | 9 |
| | Wendell Tyler, Los Angeles | 218 | 1,109 | 5.1 | 63 | 9 |
| | Tony Dorsett, Dallas[3] | 250 | 1,107 | 4.4 | 41 | 6 |
| | *William Andrews, Atlanta | 239 | 1,023 | 4.3 | 23 | 3 |
| 1978 | *Earl Campbell, Houston | 302 | 1,450 | 4.8 | 81 | 13 |
| | Walter Payton, Chicago[3] | 333 | 1,395 | 4.2 | 76 | 11 |
| | Tony Dorsett, Dallas[2] | 290 | 1,325 | 4.6 | 63 | 7 |
| | Delvin Williams, Miami[2] | 272 | 1,258 | 4.6 | 58 | 8 |
| | Wilbert Montgomery, Philadelphia | 259 | 1,220 | 4.7 | 47 | 9 |
| | Terdell Middleton, Green Bay | 284 | 1,116 | 3.9 | 76 | 11 |
| | Franco Harris, Pittsburgh[6] | 310 | 1,082 | 3.5 | 37 | 8 |
| | Mark van Eeghen, Oakland[3] | 270 | 1,080 | 4.0 | 34 | 9 |
| | *Terry Miller, Buffalo | 238 | 1,060 | 4.5 | 60 | 7 |
| | Tony Reed, Kansas City | 206 | 1,053 | 5.1 | 62 | 5 |
| | John Riggins, Washington[2] | 248 | 1,014 | 4.1 | 31 | 5 |
| 1977 | Walter Payton, Chicago[2] | 339 | 1,852 | 5.5 | 73 | 14 |
| | Mark van Eeghen, Oakland[2] | 324 | 1,273 | 3.9 | 27 | 7 |
| | Lawrence McCutcheon, Los Angeles[4] | 294 | 1,238 | 4.2 | 48 | 7 |
| | Franco Harris, Pittsburgh[5] | 300 | 1,162 | 3.9 | 61 | 11 |
| | Lydell Mitchell, Baltimore[3] | 301 | 1,159 | 3.9 | 64 | 3 |
| | Chuck Foreman, Minnesota[3] | 270 | 1,112 | 4.1 | 51 | 6 |
| | Greg Pruitt, Cleveland[3] | 236 | 1,086 | 4.6 | 78 | 3 |
| | Sam Cunningham, New England | 270 | 1,015 | 3.8 | 31 | 4 |
| | *Tony Dorsett, Dallas | 208 | 1,007 | 4.8 | 84 | 12 |
| 1976 | O.J. Simpson, Buffalo[5] | 290 | 1,503 | 5.2 | 75 | 8 |
| | Walter Payton, Chicago | 311 | 1,390 | 4.5 | 60 | 13 |
| | Delvin Williams, San Francisco | 248 | 1,203 | 4.9 | 80 | 7 |
| | Lydell Mitchell, Baltimore[2] | 289 | 1,200 | 4.2 | 43 | 5 |
| | Lawrence McCutcheon, Los Angeles[3] | 291 | 1,168 | 4.0 | 40 | 9 |
| | Chuck Foreman, Minnesota[2] | 278 | 1,155 | 4.2 | 46 | 13 |
| | Franco Harris, Pittsburgh[4] | 289 | 1,128 | 3.9 | 30 | 14 |
| | Mike Thomas, Washington | 254 | 1,101 | 4.3 | 28 | 5 |
| | Rocky Bleier, Pittsburgh | 220 | 1,036 | 4.7 | 28 | 5 |
| | Mark van Eeghen, Oakland | 233 | 1,012 | 4.3 | 21 | 3 |
| | Otis Armstrong, Denver[2] | 247 | 1,008 | 4.1 | 31 | 5 |
| | Greg Pruitt, Cleveland[2] | 209 | 1,000 | 4.8 | 64 | 4 |
| 1975 | O.J. Simpson, Buffalo[4] | 329 | 1,817 | 5.5 | 88 | 16 |
| | Franco Harris, Pittsburgh[3] | 262 | 1,246 | 4.8 | 36 | 10 |
| | Lydell Mitchell, Baltimore | 289 | 1,193 | 4.1 | 70 | 11 |
| | Jim Otis, St. Louis | 269 | 1,076 | 4.0 | 30 | 5 |
| | Chuck Foreman, Minnesota | 280 | 1,070 | 3.8 | 31 | 13 |
| | Greg Pruitt, Cleveland | 217 | 1,067 | 4.9 | 50 | 8 |
| | John Riggins, N.Y. Jets | 238 | 1,005 | 4.2 | 42 | 8 |
| | Dave Hampton, Atlanta | 250 | 1,002 | 4.0 | 22 | 5 |
| 1974 | Otis Armstrong, Denver | 263 | 1,407 | 5.3 | 43 | 9 |
| | *Don Woods, San Diego | 227 | 1,162 | 5.1 | 56 | 7 |
| | O.J. Simpson, Buffalo[3] | 270 | 1,125 | 4.2 | 41 | 3 |
| | Lawrence McCutcheon, Los Angeles[2] | 236 | 1,109 | 4.7 | 23 | 3 |
| | Franco Harris, Pittsburgh[2] | 208 | 1,006 | 4.8 | 54 | 5 |
| 1973 | O.J. Simpson, Buffalo[2] | 332 | 2,003 | 6.0 | 80 | 12 |
| | John Brockington, Green Bay[3] | 265 | 1,144 | 4.3 | 53 | 3 |
| | Calvin Hill, Dallas[2] | 273 | 1,142 | 4.2 | 21 | 6 |
| | *Lawrence McCutcheon, Los Angeles | 210 | 1,097 | 5.2 | 37 | 2 |
| | Larry Csonka, Miami[3] | 219 | 1,003 | 4.6 | 25 | 5 |
| 1972 | O.J. Simpson, Buffalo | 292 | 1,251 | 4.3 | 94 | 6 |
| | Larry Brown, Washington[2] | 285 | 1,216 | 4.3 | 38 | 8 |
| | Ron Johnson, N.Y. Giants[2] | 298 | 1,182 | 4.0 | 35 | 9 |
| | Larry Csonka, Miami[2] | 213 | 1,117 | 5.2 | 45 | 6 |
| | Marv Hubbard, Oakland | 219 | 1,100 | 5.0 | 39 | 4 |
| | *Franco Harris, Pittsburgh | 188 | 1,055 | 5.6 | 75 | 10 |
| | Calvin Hill, Dallas | 245 | 1,036 | 4.2 | 26 | 6 |
| | Mike Garrett, San Diego[2] | 272 | 1,031 | 3.8 | 41 | 6 |
| | John Brockington, Green Bay[2] | 274 | 1,027 | 3.7 | 30 | 8 |
| | Eugene (Mercury) Morris, Miami | 190 | 1,000 | 5.3 | 33 | 12 |
| 1971 | Floyd Little, Denver | 284 | 1,133 | 4.0 | 40 | 6 |
| | *John Brockington, Green Bay | 216 | 1,105 | 5.1 | 52 | 4 |
| | Larry Csonka, Miami | 195 | 1,051 | 5.4 | 28 | 7 |
| | Steve Owens, Detroit | 246 | 1,035 | 4.2 | 23 | 8 |
| | Willie Ellison, Los Angeles | 211 | 1,000 | 4.7 | 80 | 4 |
| 1970 | Larry Brown, Washington | 237 | 1,125 | 4.7 | 75 | 5 |
| | Ron Johnson, N.Y. Giants | 263 | 1,027 | 3.9 | 68 | 8 |
| 1969 | Gale Sayers, Chicago[2] | 236 | 1,032 | 4.4 | 28 | 8 |
| 1968 | Leroy Kelly, Cleveland[3] | 248 | 1,239 | 5.0 | 65 | 16 |
| | *Paul Robinson, Cincinnati | 238 | 1,023 | 4.3 | 87 | 8 |
| 1967 | Jim Nance, Boston[2] | 269 | 1,216 | 4.5 | 53 | 7 |
| | Leroy Kelly, Cleveland[2] | 235 | 1,205 | 5.1 | 42 | 11 |
| | Hoyle Granger, Houston | 236 | 1,194 | 5.1 | 67 | 6 |
| | Mike Garrett, Kansas City | 236 | 1,087 | 4.6 | 58 | 9 |
| 1966 | Jim Nance, Boston | 299 | 1,458 | 4.9 | 65 | 11 |
| | Gale Sayers, Chicago | 229 | 1,231 | 5.4 | 58 | 8 |
| | Leroy Kelly, Cleveland | 209 | 1,141 | 5.5 | 70 | 15 |
| | Dick Bass, Los Angeles[2] | 248 | 1,090 | 4.4 | 50 | 8 |
| 1965 | Jim Brown, Cleveland[7] | 289 | 1,544 | 5.3 | 67 | 17 |
| | Paul Lowe, San Diego[2] | 222 | 1,121 | 5.0 | 59 | 7 |
| 1964 | Jim Brown, Cleveland[6] | 280 | 1,446 | 5.2 | 71 | 7 |
| | Jim Taylor, Green Bay[5] | 235 | 1,169 | 5.0 | 84 | 12 |
| | John Henry Johnson, Pittsburgh[2] | 235 | 1,048 | 4.5 | 45 | 7 |
| 1963 | Jim Brown, Cleveland[5] | 291 | 1,863 | 6.4 | 80 | 12 |
| | Clem Daniels, Oakland | 215 | 1,099 | 5.1 | 74 | 3 |
| | Jim Taylor, Green Bay[4] | 248 | 1,018 | 4.1 | 40 | 9 |
| | Paul Lowe, San Diego | 177 | 1,010 | 5.7 | 66 | 8 |
| 1962 | Jim Taylor, Green Bay[3] | 272 | 1,474 | 5.4 | 51 | 19 |
| | John Henry Johnson, Pittsburgh | 251 | 1,141 | 4.5 | 40 | 7 |
| | *Cookie Gilchrist, Buffalo | 214 | 1,096 | 5.1 | 44 | 13 |
| | Abner Haynes, Dall. Texans | 221 | 1,049 | 4.7 | 71 | 13 |
| | Dick Bass, Los Angeles | 196 | 1,033 | 5.3 | 57 | 6 |
| | Charlie Tolar, Houston | 244 | 1,012 | 4.1 | 25 | 7 |
| 1961 | Jim Brown, Cleveland[4] | 305 | 1,408 | 4.6 | 38 | 8 |
| | Jim Taylor, Green Bay[2] | 243 | 1,307 | 5.4 | 53 | 15 |
| 1960 | Jim Brown, Cleveland[3] | 215 | 1,257 | 5.8 | 71 | 9 |
| | Jim Taylor, Green Bay | 230 | 1,101 | 4.8 | 32 | 11 |
| | John David Crow, St. Louis | 183 | 1,071 | 5.9 | 57 | 6 |
| 1959 | Jim Brown, Cleveland[2] | 290 | 1,329 | 4.6 | 70 | 14 |
| | J. D. Smith, San Francisco | 207 | 1,036 | 5.0 | 73 | 10 |
| 1958 | Jim Brown, Cleveland | 257 | 1,527 | 5.9 | 65 | 17 |
| 1956 | Rick Casares, Chi. Bears | 234 | 1,126 | 4.8 | 68 | 12 |
| 1954 | Joe Perry, San Francisco[2] | 173 | 1,049 | 6.1 | 58 | 8 |
| 1953 | Joe Perry, San Francisco | 192 | 1,018 | 5.3 | 51 | 10 |
| 1949 | Steve Van Buren, Philadelphia[2] | 263 | 1,146 | 4.4 | 41 | 11 |
| | Tony Canadeo, Green Bay | 208 | 1,052 | 5.1 | 54 | 4 |
| 1947 | Steve Van Buren, Philadelphia | 217 | 1,008 | 4.6 | 45 | 13 |
| 1934 | *Beattie Feathers, Chi. Bears | 101 | 1,004 | 9.9 | 82 | 8 |

*First year in the league.*

## 200 YARDS RUSHING IN A GAME

| Date | Player, Team, Opponent | Att. | Yards | TD |
|---|---|---|---|---|
| Nov. 27, 1983 | *Curt Warner, Seattle vs. Kansas City (OT) | 32 | 207 | 3 |
| Nov. 6, 1983 | James Wilder, Tampa Bay vs. Minnesota | 31 | 219 | 1 |
| Sept. 18, 1983 | Tony Collins, New England vs. N.Y. Jets | 23 | 212 | 3 |
| Sept. 4, 1983 | George Rogers, New Orleans vs. St. Louis | 24 | 206 | 2 |
| Dec. 21, 1980 | Earl Campbell, Houston vs. Minnesota | 29 | 203 | 1 |
| Nov. 16, 1980 | Earl Campbell, Houston vs. Chicago | 31 | 206 | 0 |
| Oct. 26, 1980 | Earl Campbell, Houston vs. Cincinnati | 27 | 202 | 2 |
| Oct. 19, 1980 | Earl Campbell, Houston vs. Tampa Bay | 33 | 203 | 0 |
| Nov. 26, 1978 | *Terry Miller, Buffalo vs. N.Y. Giants | 21 | 208 | 2 |
| Dec. 4, 1977 | *Tony Dorsett, Dallas vs. Philadelphia | 23 | 206 | 2 |
| Nov. 20, 1977 | Walter Payton, Chicago vs. Minnesota | 40 | 275 | 1 |
| Oct. 30, 1977 | Walter Payton, Chicago vs. Green Bay | 23 | 205 | 2 |
| Dec. 5, 1976 | O.J. Simpson, Buffalo vs. Miami | 24 | 203 | 1 |
| Nov. 25, 1976 | O.J. Simpson, Buffalo vs. Detroit | 29 | 273 | 2 |
| Oct. 24, 1976 | Chuck Foreman, Minnesota vs. Philadelphia | 28 | 200 | 2 |
| Dec. 14, 1975 | Greg Pruitt, Cleveland vs. Kansas City | 26 | 214 | 3 |
| Sept. 28, 1975 | O.J. Simpson, Buffalo vs. Pittsburgh | 28 | 227 | 1 |
| Dec. 16, 1973 | O.J. Simpson, Buffalo vs. N.Y. Jets | 34 | 200 | 1 |
| Dec. 9, 1973 | O.J. Simpson, Buffalo vs. New England | 22 | 219 | 1 |
| Sept. 16, 1973 | O.J. Simpson, Buffalo vs. New England | 29 | 250 | 2 |
| Dec. 5, 1971 | Willie Ellison, Los Angeles vs. New Orleans | 26 | 247 | 1 |
| Dec. 20, 1970 | John (Frenchy) Fuqua, Pittsburgh vs. Philadelphia | 20 | 218 | 2 |
| Nov. 3, 1968 | Gale Sayers, Chicago vs. Green Bay | 24 | 205 | 0 |
| Oct. 30, 1966 | Jim Nance, Boston vs. Oakland | 38 | 208 | 2 |
| Oct. 10, 1964 | John Henry Johnson, Pittsburgh vs. Cleveland | 30 | 200 | 3 |
| Dec. 8, 1963 | Cookie Gilchrist, Buffalo vs. N.Y. Jets | 36 | 243 | 5 |
| Nov. 3, 1963 | Jim Brown, Cleveland vs. Philadelphia | 28 | 223 | 1 |
| Oct. 20, 1963 | Clem Daniels, Oakland vs. N.Y. Jets | 27 | 200 | 2 |
| Sept. 22, 1963 | Jim Brown, Cleveland vs. Dallas | 20 | 232 | 2 |
| Dec. 10, 1961 | Billy Cannon, Houston vs. N.Y. Titans | 25 | 216 | 3 |
| Nov. 19, 1961 | Jim Brown, Cleveland vs. Philadelphia | 34 | 237 | 4 |
| Dec. 18, 1960 | John David Crow, St. Louis vs. Pittsburgh | 24 | 203 | 0 |

| | | | | |
|---|---|---|---|---|
| Nov. 15, 1959 | Bobby Mitchell, Cleveland vs. Washington | 14 | 232 | 3 |
| Nov. 24, 1957 | *Jim Brown, Cleveland vs. Los Angeles | 31 | 237 | 4 |
| Dec. 16, 1956 | *Tom Wilson, Los Angeles vs. Green Bay | 23 | 223 | 0 |
| Nov. 22, 1953 | Dan Towler, Los Angeles vs. Baltimore | 14 | 205 | 1 |
| Nov. 12, 1950 | Gene Roberts, N.Y. Giants vs. Chi. Cardinals | 26 | 218 | 2 |
| Nov. 27, 1949 | Steve Van Buren, Philadelphia vs. Pittsburgh | 27 | 205 | 0 |
| Oct. 8, 1933 | Cliff Battles, Boston vs. N.Y. Giants | 16 | 215 | 1 |

*First year in the league.*

## 400 YARDS PASSING IN A GAME

| Date | Player, Team, Opponent | Att. | Comp. | Yards | TD |
|---|---|---|---|---|---|
| Dec. 11, 1983 | Bill Kenney, Kansas City vs. San Diego | 41 | 31 | 411 | 4 |
| Nov. 20, 1983 | Dave Krieg, Seattle vs. Denver | 42 | 31 | 418 | 3 |
| Oct. 9, 1983 | Joe Ferguson, Buffalo vs. Miami (OT) | 55 | 38 | 419 | 5 |
| Oct. 2, 1983 | Joe Theismann, Washington vs. L.A. Raiders | 39 | 23 | 417 | 3 |
| Sept. 25, 1983 | Richard Todd, N.Y. Jets vs. L.A. Rams (OT) | 50 | 37 | 446 | 2 |
| Dec. 26, 1982 | Vince Ferragamo, L.A. Rams vs. Chicago | 46 | 30 | 509 | 3 |
| Dec. 20, 1982 | Dan Fouts, San Diego vs. Cincinnati | 40 | 25 | 435 | 1 |
| Dec. 20, 1982 | Ken Anderson, Cincinnati vs. San Diego | 56 | 40 | 416 | 2 |
| Dec. 11, 1982 | Dan Fouts, San Diego vs. San Francisco | 48 | 33 | 444 | 5 |
| Nov. 21, 1982 | Joe Montana, San Francisco vs. St. Louis | 39 | 26 | 408 | 3 |
| Nov. 15, 1981 | Steve Bartkowski, Atlanta vs. Pittsburgh | 50 | 33 | 416 | 2 |
| Oct. 25, 1981 | Brian Sipe, Cleveland vs. Baltimore | 41 | 30 | 444 | 4 |
| Oct. 25, 1981 | David Woodley, Miami vs. Dallas | 37 | 21 | 408 | 3 |
| Oct. 11, 1981 | Tommy Kramer, Minnesota vs. San Diego | 43 | 27 | 444 | 4 |
| Dec. 14, 1980 | Tommy Kramer, Minnesota vs. Cleveland | 49 | 38 | 456 | 4 |
| Nov. 16, 1980 | Doug Williams, Tampa Bay vs. Minnesota | 55 | 30 | 486 | 4 |
| Oct. 19, 1980 | Dan Fouts, San Diego vs. N.Y. Giants | 41 | 26 | 444 | 3 |
| Oct. 12, 1980 | Lynn Dickey, Green Bay vs. Tampa Bay (OT) | 51 | 35 | 418 | 1 |
| Sept. 21, 1980 | Richard Todd, N.Y. Jets vs. San Francisco | 60 | 42 | 447 | 3 |
| Oct. 3, 1976 | James Harris, Los Angeles vs. Miami | 29 | 17 | 436 | 2 |
| Nov. 17, 1975 | Ken Anderson, Cincinnati vs. Buffalo | 46 | 30 | 447 | 2 |
| Nov. 18, 1974 | Charley Johnson, Denver vs. Kansas City | 42 | 28 | 445 | 2 |
| Dec. 11, 1972 | Joe Namath, N.Y. Jets vs. Oakland | 46 | 25 | 403 | 1 |
| Sept. 24, 1972 | Joe Namath, N.Y. Jets vs. Baltimore | 28 | 15 | 496 | 6 |
| Dec. 21, 1969 | Don Horn, Green Bay vs. St. Louis | 31 | 22 | 410 | 5 |
| Sept. 28, 1969 | Joe Kapp, Minnesota vs. Baltimore | 43 | 28 | 449 | 7 |
| Sept. 9, 1968 | Pete Beathard, Houston vs. Kansas City | 48 | 23 | 413 | 2 |
| Nov. 26, 1967 | Sonny Jurgensen, Washington vs. Cleveland | 50 | 32 | 418 | 3 |
| Oct. 1, 1967 | Joe Namath, N.Y. Jets vs. Miami | 39 | 23 | 415 | 3 |
| Sept. 17, 1967 | Johnny Unitas, Baltimore vs. Atlanta | 32 | 22 | 401 | 2 |
| Nov. 13, 1966 | Don Meredith, Dallas vs. Washington | 29 | 21 | 406 | 2 |
| Nov. 28, 1965 | Sonny Jurgensen, Washington vs. Dallas | 43 | 26 | 411 | 3 |
| Oct. 24, 1965 | Fran Tarkenton, Minnesota vs. San Francisco | 35 | 21 | 407 | 3 |
| Nov. 1, 1964 | Len Dawson, Kansas City vs. Denver | 38 | 23 | 435 | 6 |
| Oct. 25, 1964 | Cotton Davidson, Oakland vs. Denver | 36 | 23 | 427 | 5 |
| Oct. 16, 1964 | Babe Parilli, Boston vs. Oakland | 47 | 25 | 422 | 4 |
| Dec. 22, 1963 | Tom Flores, Oakland vs. Houston | 29 | 17 | 407 | 6 |
| Nov. 17, 1963 | Norm Snead, Washington vs. Pittsburgh | 40 | 23 | 424 | 2 |
| Nov. 10, 1963 | Don Meredith, Dallas vs. San Francisco | 48 | 30 | 460 | 3 |
| Oct. 13, 1963 | Charley Johnson, St. Louis vs. Pittsburgh | 41 | 20 | 428 | 2 |
| Dec. 16, 1962 | Sonny Jurgensen, Philadelphia vs. St. Louis | 34 | 15 | 419 | 5 |
| Nov. 18, 1962 | Bill Wade, Chicago vs. Dall. Cowboys | 46 | 28 | 466 | 2 |
| Oct. 28, 1962 | Y.A. Tittle, N.Y. Giants vs. Washington | 39 | 27 | 505 | 7 |
| Sept. 15, 1962 | Frank Tripucka, Denver vs. Buffalo | 56 | 29 | 447 | 2 |
| Dec. 17, 1961 | Sonny Jurgensen, Philadelphia vs. Detroit | 42 | 27 | 403 | 3 |
| Nov. 19, 1961 | George Blanda, Houston vs. N.Y. Titans | 32 | 20 | 418 | 7 |
| Oct. 29, 1961 | Sonny Jurgensen, Philadelphia vs. Washington | 41 | 27 | 436 | 3 |
| Oct. 29, 1961 | George Blanda, Houston vs. Buffalo | 32 | 18 | 464 | 4 |
| Oct. 13, 1961 | Jacky Lee, Houston vs. Boston | 41 | 27 | 457 | 2 |
| Dec. 13, 1958 | Bobby Layne, Pittsburgh vs. Chi. Cardinals | 49 | 23 | 409 | 2 |
| Nov. 8, 1953 | Bobby Thomason, Philadelphia vs. N.Y. Giants | 44 | 22 | 437 | 4 |
| Oct. 4, 1952 | Otto Graham, Cleveland vs. Pittsburgh | 49 | 21 | 401 | 3 |
| Sept. 28, 1951 | Norm Van Brocklin, Los Angeles vs. N.Y. Yanks | 41 | 27 | 554 | 5 |
| Dec. 11, 1949 | Johnny Lujack, Chi. Bears vs. Chi. Cardinals | 39 | 24 | 468 | 6 |
| Oct. 31, 1948 | Jim Hardy, Los Angeles vs. Chi. Cardinals | 53 | 28 | 406 | 3 |
| Oct. 31, 1948 | Sammy Baugh, Washington vs. Boston | 24 | 17 | 446 | 4 |
| Nov. 14, 1943 | Sid Luckman, Chi. Bears vs. N.Y. Giants | 32 | 21 | 433 | 7 |

## 1,000 YARDS PASS RECEIVING IN A SEASON

| Year | Player, Team | No. | Yards | Avg. | Long | TD |
|---|---|---|---|---|---|---|
| 1983 | Mike Quick, Philadelphia | 69 | 1,409 | 20.4 | 83 | 13 |
| | Carlos Carson, Kansas City | 80 | 1,351 | 16.9 | 50 | 7 |
| | James Lofton, Green Bay[3] | 58 | 1,300 | 22.4 | 74 | 8 |
| | Todd Christensen, L.A. Raiders | 92 | 1,247 | 13.6 | 45 | 12 |
| | Roy Green, St. Louis | 78 | 1,227 | 15.7 | 71 | 14 |
| | Charlie Brown, Washington | 78 | 1,225 | 15.7 | 75 | 8 |
| | Tim Smith, Houston | 83 | 1,176 | 14.2 | 47 | 6 |
| | Kellen Winslow, San Diego[3] | 88 | 1,172 | 13.3 | 46 | 8 |
| | Earnest Gray, N.Y. Giants | 78 | 1,139 | 14.6 | 62 | 5 |
| | Steve Watson, Denver[2] | 59 | 1,133 | 19.2 | 78 | 5 |
| | Cris Collinsworth, Cincinnati[2] | 66 | 1,130 | 17.1 | 63 | 5 |
| | Steve Largent, Seattle[5] | 72 | 1,074 | 14.9 | 46 | 11 |
| | Mark Duper, Miami | 51 | 1,003 | 19.7 | 85 | 10 |
| 1982 | Wes Chandler, San Diego[3] | 49 | 1,032 | 21.1 | 66 | 9 |
| 1981 | Alfred Jenkins, Atlanta[2] | 70 | 1,358 | 19.4 | 67 | 13 |
| | James Lofton, Green Bay[2] | 71 | 1,294 | 18.2 | 75 | 8 |
| | Frank Lewis, Buffalo[2] | 70 | 1,244 | 17.8 | 33 | 4 |
| | Steve Watson, Denver | 60 | 1,244 | 20.7 | 95 | 13 |
| | Steve Largent, Seattle[4] | 75 | 1,224 | 16.3 | 57 | 9 |
| | Charlie Joiner, San Diego[4] | 70 | 1,188 | 17.0 | 57 | 7 |
| | Kevin House, Tampa Bay | 56 | 1,176 | 21.0 | 84 | 9 |
| | Wes Chandler, N.O.-San Diego[2] | 69 | 1,142 | 16.6 | 51 | 6 |
| | Dwight Clark, San Francisco | 85 | 1,105 | 13.0 | 78 | 4 |
| | John Stallworth, Pittsburgh[2] | 63 | 1,098 | 17.4 | 55 | 5 |
| | Kellen Winslow, San Diego[2] | 88 | 1,075 | 12.2 | 67 | 10 |
| | Pat Tilley, St. Louis | 66 | 1,040 | 15.8 | 75 | 3 |
| | Stanley Morgan, New England[2] | 44 | 1,029 | 23.4 | 76 | 6 |
| | Harold Carmichael, Philadelphia[3] | 61 | 1,028 | 16.9 | 85 | 6 |
| | Freddie Scott, Detroit | 53 | 1,022 | 19.3 | 48 | 5 |
| | *Cris Collinsworth, Cincinnati | 67 | 1,009 | 15.1 | 74 | 8 |
| | Joe Senser, Minnesota | 79 | 1,004 | 12.7 | 53 | 8 |
| | Ozzie Newsome, Cleveland | 69 | 1,002 | 14.5 | 62 | 6 |
| | Sammy White, Minnesota | 66 | 1,001 | 15.2 | 53 | 3 |
| 1980 | John Jefferson, San Diego[2] | 82 | 1,340 | 16.3 | 58 | 13 |
| | Kellen Winslow, San Diego | 89 | 1,290 | 14.5 | 65 | 9 |
| | James Lofton, Green Bay | 71 | 1,226 | 17.3 | 47 | 4 |
| | Charlie Joiner, San Diego[3] | 71 | 1,132 | 15.9 | 51 | 4 |
| | Ahmad Rashad, Minnesota[2] | 69 | 1,095 | 15.9 | 76 | 5 |
| | Steve Largent, Seattle[3] | 66 | 1,064 | 16.1 | 67 | 6 |
| | Tony Hill, Dallas[2] | 60 | 1,055 | 17.6 | 58 | 8 |
| | Alfred Jenkins, Atlanta | 57 | 1,026 | 18.0 | 57 | 6 |
| 1979 | Steve Largent, Seattle[2] | 66 | 1,237 | 18.7 | 55 | 9 |
| | John Stallworth, Pittsburgh | 70 | 1,183 | 16.9 | 65 | 8 |
| | Ahmad Rashad, Minnesota | 80 | 1,156 | 14.5 | 52 | 9 |
| | John Jefferson, San Diego[2] | 61 | 1,090 | 17.9 | 65 | 10 |
| | Frank Lewis, Buffalo | 54 | 1,082 | 20.0 | 55 | 2 |
| | Wes Chandler, New Orleans | 65 | 1,069 | 16.4 | 85 | 6 |
| | Tony Hill, Dallas | 60 | 1,062 | 17.7 | 75 | 10 |
| | Drew Pearson, Dallas[2] | 55 | 1,026 | 18.7 | 56 | 8 |
| | Wallace Francis, Atlanta | 74 | 1,013 | 13.7 | 42 | 8 |
| | Harold Jackson, New England[3] | 45 | 1,013 | 22.5 | 59 | 7 |
| | Charlie Joiner, San Diego[2] | 72 | 1,008 | 14.0 | 39 | 4 |
| | Stanley Morgan, New England | 44 | 1,002 | 22.8 | 63 | 12 |
| 1978 | Wesley Walker, N.Y. Jets | 48 | 1,169 | 24.4 | 77 | 8 |
| | Steve Largent, Seattle | 71 | 1,168 | 16.5 | 57 | 8 |
| | Harold Carmichael, Philadelphia[2] | 55 | 1,072 | 19.5 | 56 | 8 |
| | *John Jefferson, San Diego | 56 | 1,001 | 17.9 | 46 | 13 |
| 1976 | Roger Carr, Baltimore | 43 | 1,112 | 25.9 | 79 | 11 |
| | Cliff Branch, Oakland[2] | 46 | 1,111 | 24.2 | 88 | 12 |
| | Charlie Joiner, San Diego | 50 | 1,056 | 21.1 | 81 | 7 |
| 1975 | Ken Burrough, Houston | 53 | 1,063 | 20.1 | 77 | 8 |
| 1974 | Cliff Branch, Oakland | 60 | 1,092 | 18.2 | 67 | 13 |
| | Drew Pearson, Dallas | 62 | 1,087 | 17.5 | 50 | 2 |
| 1973 | Harold Carmichael, Philadelphia | 67 | 1,116 | 16.7 | 73 | 9 |
| 1972 | Harold Jackson, Philadelphia[2] | 62 | 1,048 | 16.9 | 77 | 4 |
| | John Gilliam, Minnesota | 47 | 1,035 | 22.0 | 66 | 7 |
| 1971 | Otis Taylor, Kansas City[2] | 57 | 1,110 | 19.5 | 82 | 7 |
| 1970 | Gene Washington, San Francisco | 53 | 1,100 | 20.8 | 79 | 12 |
| | Marlin Briscoe, Buffalo | 57 | 1,036 | 18.2 | 48 | 8 |
| | Dick Gordon, Chicago | 71 | 1,026 | 14.5 | 69 | 13 |
| | Gary Garrison, San Diego[2] | 44 | 1,006 | 22.9 | 67 | 12 |
| 1969 | Warren Wells, Oakland[2] | 47 | 1,260 | 26.8 | 80 | 14 |
| | Harold Jackson, Philadelphia | 65 | 1,116 | 17.2 | 65 | 9 |
| | Roy Jefferson, Pittsburgh[2] | 67 | 1,079 | 16.1 | 63 | 9 |
| | Dan Abramowicz, New Orleans | 73 | 1,015 | 13.9 | 49 | 7 |
| | Lance Alworth, San Diego[7] | 64 | 1,003 | 15.7 | 76 | 4 |
| 1968 | Lance Alworth, San Diego[6] | 68 | 1,312 | 19.3 | 80 | 10 |
| | Don Maynard, N.Y. Jets[5] | 57 | 1,297 | 22.8 | 87 | 10 |
| | George Sauer, N.Y. Jets[3] | 66 | 1,141 | 17.3 | 43 | 3 |
| | Warren Wells, Oakland | 53 | 1,137 | 21.5 | 94 | 11 |
| | Gary Garrison, San Diego | 52 | 1,103 | 21.2 | 84 | 10 |
| | Roy Jefferson, Pittsburgh | 58 | 1,074 | 18.5 | 62 | 11 |
| | Paul Warfield, Cleveland | 50 | 1,067 | 21.3 | 65 | 12 |
| | Homer Jones, N.Y. Giants[3] | 45 | 1,057 | 23.5 | 84 | 7 |
| | Fred Biletnikoff, Oakland | 61 | 1,037 | 17.0 | 82 | 6 |
| | Lance Rentzel, Dallas | 54 | 1,009 | 18.7 | 65 | 6 |
| 1967 | Don Maynard, N.Y. Jets[4] | 71 | 1,434 | 20.2 | 75 | 10 |
| | Ben Hawkins, Philadelphia | 59 | 1,265 | 21.4 | 87 | 10 |
| | Homer Jones, N.Y. Giants[2] | 49 | 1,209 | 24.7 | 70 | 13 |
| | Jackie Smith, St. Louis | 56 | 1,205 | 21.5 | 76 | 9 |
| | George Sauer, N.Y. Jets[2] | 75 | 1,189 | 15.9 | 61 | 6 |
| | Lance Alworth, San Diego[5] | 52 | 1,010 | 19.4 | 71 | 9 |
| 1966 | Lance Alworth, San Diego[4] | 73 | 1,383 | 18.9 | 78 | 13 |
| | Otis Taylor, Kansas City | 58 | 1,297 | 22.4 | 89 | 8 |
| | Pat Studstill, Detroit | 67 | 1,266 | 18.9 | 99 | 5 |
| | Bob Hayes, Dallas[2] | 64 | 1,232 | 19.3 | 95 | 13 |
| | Charlie Frazier, Houston | 57 | 1,129 | 19.8 | 79 | 12 |
| | Charley Taylor, Washington | 72 | 1,119 | 15.5 | 86 | 12 |
| | George Sauer, N.Y. Jets | 63 | 1,081 | 17.2 | 77 | 5 |
| | Homer Jones, N.Y. Giants | 48 | 1,044 | 21.8 | 98 | 8 |
| | Art Powell, Oakland[5] | 53 | 1,026 | 19.4 | 46 | 11 |
| 1965 | Lance Alworth, San Diego[3] | 69 | 1,602 | 23.2 | 85 | 14 |
| | Dave Parks, San Francisco | 80 | 1,344 | 16.8 | 53 | 12 |
| | Don Maynard, N.Y. Jets[3] | 68 | 1,218 | 17.9 | 56 | 14 |
| | Pete Retzlaff, Philadelphia | 66 | 1,190 | 18.0 | 78 | 10 |
| | Lionel Taylor, Denver[4] | 85 | 1,131 | 13.3 | 63 | 6 |
| | Tommy McDonald, Los Angeles[3] | 67 | 1,036 | 15.5 | 51 | 9 |
| | *Bob Hayes, Dallas | 46 | 1,003 | 21.8 | 82 | 12 |
| 1964 | Charley Hennigan, Houston[3] | 101 | 1,546 | 15.3 | 53 | 8 |
| | Art Powell, Oakland[4] | 76 | 1,361 | 17.9 | 77 | 11 |
| | Lance Alworth, San Diego[2] | 61 | 1,235 | 20.2 | 82 | 13 |
| | Johnny Morris, Chicago | 93 | 1,200 | 12.9 | 63 | 10 |
| | Elbert Dubenion, Buffalo | 42 | 1,139 | 27.1 | 72 | 10 |
| | Terry Barr, Detroit[2] | 57 | 1,030 | 18.1 | 58 | 9 |
| 1963 | Bobby Mitchell, Washington[2] | 69 | 1,436 | 20.8 | 99 | 7 |
| | Art Powell, Oakland[3] | 73 | 1,304 | 17.9 | 85 | 16 |
| | Buddy Dial, Pittsburgh[2] | 60 | 1,295 | 21.6 | 83 | 9 |
| | Lance Alworth, San Diego | 61 | 1,205 | 19.8 | 85 | 11 |
| | Del Shofner, N.Y. Giants[4] | 64 | 1,181 | 18.5 | 70 | 9 |
| | Lionel Taylor, Denver[3] | 78 | 1,101 | 14.1 | 72 | 10 |
| | Terry Barr, Detroit | 66 | 1,086 | 16.5 | 75 | 13 |
| | Charley Hennigan, Houston[2] | 61 | 1,051 | 17.2 | 83 | 10 |
| | Sonny Randle, St. Louis[2] | 51 | 1,014 | 19.9 | 68 | 12 |
| | Bake Turner, N.Y. Jets | 71 | 1,009 | 14.2 | 53 | 6 |
| 1962 | Bobby Mitchell, Washington | 72 | 1,384 | 19.2 | 81 | 11 |
| | Sonny Randle, St. Louis | 63 | 1,158 | 18.4 | 86 | 7 |
| | Tommy McDonald, Philadelphia[2] | 58 | 1,146 | 19.8 | 60 | 10 |
| | Del Shofner, N.Y. Giants[3] | 53 | 1,133 | 21.4 | 69 | 12 |
| | Art Powell, N.Y. Titans[2] | 64 | 1,130 | 17.7 | 80 | 8 |
| | Frank Clarke, Dall. Cowboys | 47 | 1,043 | 22.2 | 66 | 14 |
| | Don Maynard, N.Y. Titans[2] | 56 | 1,041 | 18.6 | 86 | 8 |
| 1961 | Charley Hennigan, Houston | 82 | 1,746 | 21.3 | 80 | 12 |
| | Lionel Taylor, Denver[2] | 100 | 1,176 | 11.8 | 52 | 4 |
| | Bill Groman, Houston[2] | 50 | 1,175 | 23.5 | 80 | 17 |
| | Tommy McDonald, Philadelphia | 64 | 1,144 | 17.9 | 66 | 13 |
| | Del Shofner, N.Y. Giants[2] | 68 | 1,125 | 16.5 | 46 | 11 |

| | No. | Yards | Avg. | Long | TD |
|---|---|---|---|---|---|
| Jim Phillips, Los Angeles | 78 | 1,092 | 14.0 | 69 | 5 |
| *Mike Ditka, Chicago | 56 | 1,076 | 19.2 | 76 | 12 |
| Dave Kocourek, San Diego | 55 | 1,055 | 19.2 | 76 | 4 |
| Buddy Dial, Pittsburgh | 53 | 1,047 | 19.8 | 88 | 12 |
| R.C. Owens, San Francisco | 55 | 1,032 | 18.8 | 54 | 5 |
| 1960 *Bill Groman, Houston | 72 | 1,473 | 20.5 | 92 | 12 |
| Raymond Berry, Baltimore | 74 | 1,298 | 17.5 | 70 | 10 |
| Don Maynard, N.Y. Titans | 72 | 1,265 | 17.6 | 65 | 6 |
| Lionel Taylor, Denver | 92 | 1,235 | 13.4 | 80 | 12 |
| Art Powell, N.Y. Titans | 69 | 1,167 | 16.9 | 76 | 14 |
| 1958 Del Shofner, Los Angeles | 51 | 1,097 | 21.5 | 92 | 8 |
| 1956 Bill Howton, Green Bay[2] | 55 | 1,188 | 21.6 | 66 | 12 |
| Harlon Hill, Chi. Bears[2] | 47 | 1,128 | 24.0 | 79 | 11 |
| 1954 Bob Boyd, Los Angeles | 53 | 1,212 | 22.9 | 80 | 6 |
| *Harlon Hill, Chi. Bears | 45 | 1,124 | 25.0 | 76 | 12 |
| 1953 Pete Pihos, Philadelphia | 63 | 1,049 | 16.7 | 59 | 10 |
| 1952 *Bill Howton, Green Bay | 53 | 1,231 | 23.2 | 90 | 13 |
| 1951 Elroy (Crazylegs) Hirsch, Los Angeles | 66 | 1,495 | 22.7 | 91 | 17 |
| 1950 Tom Fears, Los Angeles[2] | 84 | 1,116 | 13.3 | 53 | 7 |
| Cloyce Box, Detroit | 50 | 1,009 | 20.2 | 82 | 11 |
| 1949 Bob Mann, Detroit | 66 | 1,014 | 15.4 | 64 | 4 |
| Tom Fears, Los Angeles | 77 | 1,013 | 13.2 | 51 | 9 |
| 1945 Jim Benton, Cleveland | 45 | 1,067 | 23.7 | 84 | 8 |
| 1942 Don Hutson, Green Bay | 74 | 1,211 | 16.4 | 73 | 17 |

*First year in the league.

## 250 YARDS PASS RECEIVING IN A GAME

| Date | Player, Team, Opponent | No. | Yards | TD |
|---|---|---|---|---|
| Dec. 20, 1982 | Wes Chandler, San Diego vs. Cincinnati | 10 | 260 | 2 |
| Sept. 23, 1979 | *Jerry Butler, Buffalo vs. N.Y. Jets | 10 | 255 | 4 |
| Nov. 4, 1962 | Sonny Randle, St. Louis vs. N.Y. Giants | 16 | 256 | 1 |
| Oct. 28, 1962 | Del Shofner, N.Y. Giants vs. Washington | 11 | 269 | 1 |
| Oct. 13, 1961 | Charley Hennigan, Houston vs. Boston | 13 | 272 | 1 |
| Oct. 21, 1956 | Billy Howton, Green Bay vs. Los Angeles | 7 | 257 | 2 |
| Dec. 3, 1950 | Cloyce Box, Detroit vs. Baltimore | 12 | 302 | 4 |
| Nov. 22, 1945 | Jim Benton, Cleveland vs. Detroit | 10 | 303 | 1 |

*First year in the league.

## 2,000 COMBINED NET YARDS GAINED IN A SEASON

| Year Player, Team | Rushing Att.-Yds. | Pass Rec. | Punt Ret. | Kickoff Ret. | Fum. Runs | Total Yds. |
|---|---|---|---|---|---|---|
| 1983 *Eric Dickerson, L.A. Rams | 390-1,808 | 51-404 | 0-0 | 0-0 | 1-0 | 442-2,212 |
| William Andrews, Atlanta | 331-1,567 | 59-609 | 0-0 | 0-0 | 2-0 | 392-2,176 |
| Walter Payton, Chicago | 314-1,421 | 53-607 | 0-0 | 0-0 | 2-0 | 369-2,028 |
| 1981 *James Brooks, San Diego | 109-525 | 46-329 | 22-290 | 40-949 | 2-0 | 219-2,093 |
| William Andrews, Atlanta | 289-1,301 | 81-735 | 0-0 | 0-0 | 2-0 | 370-2,036 |
| 1980 Bruce Harper, N.Y. Jets | 45-126 | 50-634 | 28-242 | 49-1,070 | 3-0 | 175-2,072 |
| 1979 Wilbert Montgomery, Phil. | 338-1,512 | 41-494 | 0-0 | 0-0 | 2-0 | 382-2,012 |
| 1978 Bruce Harper, N.Y. Jets | 58-303 | 13-196 | 30-378 | 55-1,280 | 1-0 | 157-2,157 |
| 1977 Walter Payton, Chicago | 339-1,852 | 27-269 | 0-0 | 2-95 | 5-0 | 373-2,216 |
| Terry Metcalf, St. Louis | 149-739 | 34-403 | 14-108 | 32-772 | 1-0 | 230-2,022 |
| 1975 Terry Metcalf, St. Louis | 165-816 | 43-378 | 23-285 | 35-960 | 2-23 | 268-2,462 |
| O.J. Simpson, Buffalo | 329-1,817 | 28-426 | 0-0 | 0-0 | 1-0 | 358-2,243 |
| 1974 Mack Herron, New England | 231-824 | 38-474 | 35-517 | 28-629 | 3-0 | 335-2,444 |
| Otis Armstrong, Denver | 263-1,407 | 38-405 | 0-0 | 16-386 | 1-0 | 318-2,198 |
| Terry Metcalf, St. Louis | 152-718 | 50-377 | 26-340 | 20-623 | 7-0 | 255-2,058 |
| 1973 O.J. Simpson, Buffalo | 332-2,003 | 6-70 | 0-0 | 0-0 | 0-0 | 338-2,073 |
| 1966 Gale Sayers, Chicago | 229-1,231 | 34-447 | 6-44 | 23-718 | 3-0 | 295-2,440 |
| Leroy Kelly, Cleveland | 209-1,141 | 32-366 | 13-104 | 19-403 | 0-0 | 273-2,014 |
| 1965 *Gale Sayers, Chicago | 166-867 | 29-507 | 16-238 | 21-660 | 0-0 | 236-2,272 |
| 1963 Timmy Brown, Philadelphia | 192-841 | 36-487 | 16-152 | 33-945 | 2-3 | 279-2,428 |
| Jim Brown, Cleveland | 291-1,863 | 24-268 | 0-0 | 0-0 | 0-0 | 315-2,131 |
| 1962 Timmy Brown, Philadelphia | 137-545 | 52-849 | 6-81 | 30-831 | 0-0 | 229-2,306 |
| Dick Christy, N.Y. Titans | 114-535 | 62-538 | 15-250 | 38-824 | 2-0 | 231-2,147 |
| 1961 Billy Cannon, Houston | 200-948 | 43-586 | 9-70 | 18-439 | 2-0 | 272-2,043 |
| 1960 *Abner Haynes, Dall. Texans | 156-875 | 55-576 | 14-215 | 19-434 | 4-0 | 248-2,100 |

*First year in the league.

## 300 COMBINED NET YARDS GAINED IN A GAME

| Date | Player, Team, Opponent | No. | Yards | TD |
|---|---|---|---|---|
| Dec. 21, 1975 | Walter Payton, Chicago vs. New Orleans | 32 | 300 | 1 |
| Nov. 23, 1975 | Greg Pruitt, Cleveland vs. Cincinnati | 28 | 304 | 2 |
| Nov. 1, 1970 | Eugene (Mercury) Morris, Miami vs. Baltimore | 17 | 302 | 0 |
| Oct. 4, 1970 | O.J. Simpson, Buffalo vs. N.Y. Jets | 26 | 303 | 2 |
| Dec. 6, 1969 | Jerry LeVias, Houston vs. N.Y. Jets | 18 | 329 | 1 |
| Nov. 2, 1969 | Travis Williams, Green Bay vs. Pittsburgh | 11 | 314 | 3 |
| Dec. 18, 1966 | Gale Sayers, Chicago vs. Minnesota | 20 | 339 | 2 |
| Dec. 12, 1965 | Gale Sayers, Chicago vs. San Francisco | 17 | 336 | 6 |
| Nov. 17, 1963 | Gary Ballman, Pittsburgh vs. Washington | 12 | 320 | 2 |
| Dec. 16, 1962 | Timmy Brown, Philadelphia vs. St. Louis | 19 | 341 | 2 |
| Dec. 10, 1961 | Billy Cannon, Houston vs. N.Y. Titans | 32 | 373 | 5 |
| Nov 19, 1961 | Jim Brown, Cleveland vs. Philadelphia | 38 | 313 | 4 |
| Dec. 3, 1950 | Cloyce Box, Detroit vs. Baltimore | 13 | 302 | 4 |
| Oct. 29, 1950 | Wally Triplett, Detroit vs. Los Angeles | 11 | 331 | 1 |
| Nov. 22, 1945 | Jim Benton, Cleveland vs. Detroit | 10 | 303 | 1 |

## TOP 10 SCORERS

| Player | Years | TD | FG | PAT | TP |
|---|---|---|---|---|---|
| George Blanda | 26 | 9 | 335 | 943 | 2,002 |
| Jan Stenerud | 17 | 0 | 338 | 509 | 1,523 |
| Jim Turner | 16 | 1 | 304 | 521 | 1,439 |
| Jim Bakken | 17 | 0 | 282 | 534 | 1,380 |
| Fred Cox | 15 | 0 | 282 | 519 | 1,365 |
| Lou Groza | 17 | 1 | 234 | 641 | 1,349 |
| Gino Cappelletti | 11 | 42 | 176 | 350 | 1,130 |
| Mark Moseley | 13 | 0 | 242 | 378 | 1,104 |
| Don Cockroft | 13 | 0 | 216 | 432 | 1,080 |
| Garo Yepremian | 14 | 0 | 210 | 444 | 1,074 |

*Cappelletti's total includes four two-point conversions.*

## TOP 10 TOUCHDOWN SCORERS

| Player | Years | Rush | Pass Rec. | Returns | Total TD |
|---|---|---|---|---|---|
| Jim Brown | 9 | 106 | 20 | 0 | 126 |
| Lenny Moore | 12 | 63 | 48 | 2 | 113 |
| Don Hutson | 11 | 3 | 99 | 3 | 105 |
| Franco Harris | 12 | 91 | 9 | 0 | 100 |
| John Riggins | 12 | 82 | 12 | 0 | 94 |
| Jim Taylor | 10 | 83 | 10 | 0 | 93 |
| Bobby Mitchell | 11 | 18 | 65 | 8 | 91 |
| Leroy Kelly | 10 | 74 | 13 | 3 | 90 |
| Charley Taylor | 13 | 11 | 79 | 0 | 90 |
| Don Maynard | 15 | 0 | 88 | 0 | 88 |

## TOP 10 RUSHERS

| Player | Years | Att. | Yards | Avg. | Long | TD |
|---|---|---|---|---|---|---|
| Jim Brown | 9 | 2,359 | 12,312 | 5.2 | 80 | 106 |
| Franco Harris | 12 | 2,881 | 11,950 | 4.1 | 75 | 91 |
| Walter Payton | 9 | 2,666 | 11,625 | 4.4 | 76 | 78 |
| O.J. Simpson | 11 | 2,404 | 11,236 | 4.7 | 94 | 61 |
| John Riggins | 12 | 2,413 | 9,436 | 3.9 | 66 | 82 |
| Jim Taylor | 10 | 1,941 | 8,597 | 4.4 | 84 | 83 |
| Joe Perry | 14 | 1,737 | 8,378 | 4.8 | 78 | 53 |
| Tony Dorsett | 7 | 1,834 | 8,336 | 4.5 | 99 | 53 |
| Earl Campbell | 6 | 1,883 | 8,296 | 4.4 | 81 | 69 |
| Larry Csonka | 11 | 1,891 | 8,081 | 4.3 | 54 | 64 |

## TOP 10 PASSERS

| Player | Years | Att. | Comp. | Pct. Comp. | Yards | TD | Pct. TD | Int. | Pct. Int. | Avg. Gain | Rating |
|---|---|---|---|---|---|---|---|---|---|---|---|
| Joe Montana | 5 | 1,645 | 1,045 | 63.5 | 11,979 | 78 | 4.7 | 44 | 2.7 | 7.28 | 90.0 |
| Danny White | 8 | 1,710 | 1,029 | 60.2 | 13,174 | 98 | 5.7 | 79 | 4.6 | 7.70 | 84.2 |
| Roger Staubach | 11 | 2,958 | 1,685 | 57.0 | 22,700 | 153 | 5.2 | 109 | 3.7 | 7.67 | 83.4 |
| Sonny Jurgensen | 18 | 4,262 | 2,433 | 57.1 | 32,224 | 255 | 6.0 | 189 | 4.4 | 7.56 | 82.6 |
| Len Dawson | 19 | 3,741 | 2,136 | 57.1 | 28,711 | 239 | 6.4 | 183 | 4.9 | 7.67 | 82.6 |
| Ken Anderson | 13 | 4,145 | 2,452 | 59.2 | 30,390 | 184 | 4.4 | 146 | 3.5 | 7.33 | 82.0 |
| Dan Fouts | 11 | 3,873 | 2,268 | 58.6 | 30,114 | 182 | 4.7 | 168 | 4.3 | 7.78 | 80.9 |
| Bart Starr | 16 | 3,149 | 1,808 | 57.4 | 24,718 | 152 | 4.8 | 138 | 4.4 | 7.85 | 80.5 |
| Fran Tarkenton | 18 | 6,467 | 3,686 | 57.0 | 47,003 | 342 | 5.3 | 266 | 4.1 | 7.27 | 80.4 |
| Bert Jones | 10 | 2,551 | 1,430 | 56.1 | 18,190 | 124 | 4.9 | 101 | 4.0 | 7.13 | 78.2 |

*1,500 or more attempts. The passing ratings are based on performance standards established for completion percentage, interception percentage, touchdown percentage, and average gain. Passers are allocated points according to how their marks compare with those standards.*

## TOP 10 PASS RECEIVERS

| Player | Years | No. | Yards | Avg. | Long | TD |
|---|---|---|---|---|---|---|
| Charley Taylor | 13 | 649 | 9,110 | 14.0 | 88 | 79 |
| Don Maynard | 15 | 633 | 11,834 | 18.7 | 87 | 88 |
| Raymond Berry | 13 | 631 | 9,275 | 14.7 | 70 | 68 |
| Charlie Joiner | 15 | 596 | 9,981 | 16.7 | 87 | 50 |
| Harold Carmichael | 13 | 589 | 8,978 | 15.2 | 85 | 79 |
| Fred Biletnikoff | 14 | 589 | 8,974 | 15.2 | 82 | 76 |
| Harold Jackson | 16 | 579 | 10,372 | 17.9 | 79 | 76 |
| Lionel Taylor | 10 | 567 | 7,195 | 12.7 | 80 | 45 |
| Lance Alworth | 11 | 542 | 10,266 | 18.9 | 85 | 85 |
| Bobby Mitchell | 11 | 521 | 7,954 | 15.3 | 99 | 65 |

## TOP 10 INTERCEPTORS

| Player | Years | No. | Yards | Avg. | Long | TD |
|---|---|---|---|---|---|---|
| Paul Krause | 16 | 81 | 1,185 | 14.6 | 81 | 3 |
| Emlen Tunnell | 14 | 79 | 1,282 | 16.2 | 55 | 4 |
| Dick (Night Train) Lane | 14 | 68 | 1,207 | 17.8 | 80 | 5 |
| Ken Riley | 15 | 65 | 596 | 9.2 | 66 | 5 |
| Dick LeBeau | 13 | 62 | 762 | 12.3 | 70 | 3 |
| Emmitt Thomas | 13 | 58 | 937 | 16.2 | 73 | 5 |
| Bobby Boyd | 9 | 57 | 994 | 17.4 | 74 | 4 |
| Johnny Robinson | 12 | 57 | 741 | 13.0 | 57 | 1 |
| Mel Blount | 14 | 57 | 736 | 12.9 | 52 | 2 |
| Lem Barney | 11 | 56 | 1,077 | 19.2 | 71 | 7 |
| Pat Fischer | 17 | 56 | 941 | 16.8 | 69 | 4 |

## TOP 10 PUNTERS

| Player | Years | No. | Yards | Avg. | Long | Blk. |
|---|---|---|---|---|---|---|
| Sammy Baugh | 16 | 338 | 15,245 | 45.1 | 85 | 9 |
| Tommy Davis | 11 | 511 | 22,833 | 44.7 | 82 | 2 |
| Yale Lary | 11 | 503 | 22,279 | 44.3 | 74 | 4 |
| Horace Gillom | 7 | 385 | 16,872 | 43.8 | 80 | 5 |
| Jerry Norton | 11 | 358 | 15,671 | 43.8 | 78 | 2 |
| Don Chandler | 12 | 660 | 28,678 | 43.5 | 90 | 4 |
| Jerrel Wilson | 16 | 1,072 | 46,139 | 43.0 | 72 | 12 |
| Ray Guy | 11 | 779 | 33,437 | 42.9 | 74 | 3 |
| Norm Van Brocklin | 12 | 523 | 22,413 | 42.9 | 72 | 3 |
| Danny Villanueva | 8 | 488 | 20,862 | 42.8 | 68 | 2 |

*300 or more punts.*

## TOP 10 PUNT RETURNERS

| Player | Years | No. | Yards | Avg. | Long | TD |
|---|---|---|---|---|---|---|
| George McAfee | 8 | 112 | 1,431 | 12.8 | 74 | 2 |
| Jack Christiansen | 8 | 85 | 1,084 | 12.8 | 89 | 8 |
| Claude Gibson | 5 | 110 | 1,381 | 12.6 | 85 | 3 |
| Billy Johnson | 9 | 225 | 2,802 | 12.5 | 87 | 6 |
| Bill Dudley | 9 | 124 | 1,515 | 12.2 | 96 | 3 |
| Rick Upchurch | 9 | 248 | 3,008 | 12.1 | 92 | 8 |
| Mack Herron | 3 | 84 | 982 | 11.7 | 66 | 0 |
| Bill Thompson | 13 | 157 | 1,814 | 11.6 | 60 | 0 |
| Rodger Bird | 3 | 94 | 1,063 | 11.3 | 78 | 0 |
| Bosh Pritchard | 6 | 95 | 1,072 | 11.3 | 81 | 2 |

*75 or more returns.*

## TOP 10 KICKOFF RETURNERS

| Player | Years | No. | Yards | Avg. | Long | TD |
|---|---|---|---|---|---|---|
| Gale Sayers | 7 | 91 | 2,781 | 30.6 | 103 | 6 |
| Lynn Chandnois | 7 | 92 | 2,720 | 29.6 | 93 | 3 |
| Abe Woodson | 9 | 193 | 5,538 | 28.7 | 105 | 5 |
| Claude (Buddy) Young | 6 | 90 | 2,514 | 27.9 | 104 | 2 |
| Travis Williams | 5 | 102 | 2,801 | 27.5 | 105 | 6 |
| Joe Arenas | 7 | 139 | 3,798 | 27.3 | 96 | 1 |
| Clarence Davis | 8 | 79 | 2,140 | 27.1 | 76 | 0 |
| Steve Van Buren | 8 | 76 | 2,030 | 26.7 | 98 | 3 |
| Lenny Lyles | 12 | 81 | 2,161 | 26.7 | 103 | 3 |
| Eugene (Mercury) Morris | 8 | 111 | 2,947 | 26.5 | 105 | 3 |

*75 or more returns.*

## ANNUAL SCORING LEADERS

| Year | Player, Team | TD | FG | PAT | TP |
|------|--------------|----|----|-----|-----|
| 1983 | Mark Moseley, Washington, NFC | 0 | 33 | 62 | 161 |
|  | Gary Anderson, Pittsburgh, AFC | 0 | 27 | 38 | 119 |
| 1982 | *Marcus Allen, L.A. Raiders, AFC | 14 | 0 | 0 | 84 |
|  | Wendell Tyler, L.A. Rams, NFC | 13 | 0 | 0 | 78 |
| 1981 | Ed Murray, Detroit, NFC | 0 | 25 | 46 | 121 |
|  | Rafael Septien, Dallas, NFC | 0 | 27 | 40 | 121 |
|  | Jim Breech, Cincinnati, AFC | 0 | 22 | 49 | 115 |
|  | Nick Lowery, Kansas City, AFC | 0 | 26 | 37 | 115 |
| 1980 | John Smith, New England, AFC | 0 | 26 | 51 | 129 |
|  | *Ed Murray, Detroit, NFC | 0 | 27 | 35 | 116 |
| 1979 | John Smith, New England, AFC | 0 | 23 | 46 | 115 |
|  | Mark Moseley, Washington, NFC | 0 | 25 | 39 | 114 |
| 1978 | *Frank Corral, Los Angeles, NFC | 0 | 29 | 31 | 118 |
|  | Pat Leahy, N.Y. Jets, AFC | 0 | 22 | 41 | 107 |
| 1977 | Errol Mann, Oakland, AFC | 0 | 20 | 39 | 99 |
|  | Walter Payton, Chicago, NFC | 16 | 0 | 0 | 96 |
| 1976 | Toni Linhart, Baltimore, AFC | 0 | 20 | 49 | 109 |
|  | Mark Moseley, Washington, NFC | 0 | 22 | 31 | 97 |
| 1975 | O.J. Simpson, Buffalo, AFC | 23 | 0 | 0 | 138 |
|  | Chuck Foreman, Minnesota, NFC | 22 | 0 | 0 | 132 |
| 1974 | Chester Marcol, Green Bay, NFC | 0 | 25 | 19 | 94 |
|  | Roy Gerela, Pittsburgh, AFC | 0 | 20 | 33 | 93 |
| 1973 | David Ray, Los Angeles, NFC | 0 | 30 | 40 | 130 |
|  | Roy Gerela, Pittsburgh, AFC | 0 | 29 | 36 | 123 |
| 1972 | *Chester Marcol, Green Bay, NFC | 0 | 33 | 29 | 128 |
|  | Bobby Howfield, N.Y. Jets, AFC | 0 | 27 | 40 | 121 |
| 1971 | Garo Yepremian, Miami, AFC | 0 | 28 | 33 | 117 |
|  | Curt Knight, Washington, NFC | 0 | 29 | 27 | 114 |
| 1970 | Fred Cox, Minnesota, NFC | 0 | 30 | 35 | 125 |
|  | Jan Stenerud, Kansas City, AFC | 0 | 30 | 26 | 116 |
| 1969 | Jim Turner, N.Y. Jets, AFL | 0 | 32 | 33 | 129 |
|  | Fred Cox, Minnesota, NFL | 0 | 26 | 43 | 121 |
| 1968 | Jim Turner, N.Y. Jets, AFL | 0 | 34 | 43 | 145 |
|  | Leroy Kelly, Cleveland, NFL | 20 | 0 | 0 | 120 |
| 1967 | Jim Bakken, St. Louis, NFL | 0 | 27 | 36 | 117 |
|  | George Blanda, Oakland, AFL | 0 | 20 | 56 | 116 |
| 1966 | Gino Cappelletti, Boston, AFL | 6 | 16 | 35 | 119 |
|  | Bruce Gossett, Los Angeles, NFL | 0 | 28 | 29 | 113 |
| 1965 | *Gale Sayers, Chicago, NFL | 22 | 0 | 0 | 132 |
|  | Gino Cappelletti, Boston, AFL | 9 | 17 | 27 | 132 |
| 1964 | Gino Cappelletti, Boston, AFL | 7 | 25 | 36 | 155 |
|  | Lenny Moore, Baltimore, NFL | 20 | 0 | 0 | 120 |
| 1963 | Gino Cappelletti, Boston, AFL | 2 | 22 | 35 | 113 |
|  | Don Chandler, N.Y. Giants, NFL | 0 | 18 | 52 | 106 |
| 1962 | Gene Mingo, Denver, AFL | 4 | 27 | 32 | 137 |
|  | Jim Taylor, Green Bay, NFL | 19 | 0 | 0 | 114 |
| 1961 | Gino Cappelletti, Boston, AFL | 8 | 17 | 48 | 147 |
|  | Paul Hornung, Green Bay, NFL | 10 | 15 | 41 | 146 |
| 1960 | Paul Hornung, Green Bay, NFL | 15 | 15 | 41 | 176 |
|  | *Gene Mingo, Denver, AFL | 6 | 18 | 33 | 123 |
| 1959 | Paul Hornung, Green Bay | 7 | 7 | 31 | 94 |
| 1958 | Jim Brown, Cleveland | 18 | 0 | 0 | 108 |
| 1957 | Sam Baker, Washington | 1 | 14 | 29 | 77 |
|  | Lou Groza, Cleveland | 0 | 15 | 32 | 77 |
| 1956 | Bobby Layne, Detroit | 5 | 12 | 33 | 99 |
| 1955 | Doak Walker, Detroit | 7 | 9 | 27 | 96 |
| 1954 | Bobby Walston, Philadelphia | 11 | 4 | 36 | 114 |
| 1953 | Gordy Soltau, San Francisco | 6 | 10 | 48 | 114 |
| 1952 | Gordy Soltau, San Francisco | 7 | 6 | 34 | 94 |
| 1951 | Elroy (Crazylegs) Hirsch, Los Angeles | 17 | 0 | 0 | 102 |
| 1950 | *Doak Walker, Detroit | 11 | 8 | 38 | 128 |
| 1949 | Pat Harder, Chi. Cardinals | 8 | 3 | 45 | 102 |
|  | Gene Roberts, N.Y. Giants | 17 | 0 | 0 | 102 |
| 1948 | Pat Harder, Chi. Cardinals | 6 | 7 | 53 | 110 |
| 1947 | Pat Harder, Chi. Cardinals | 7 | 7 | 39 | 102 |
| 1946 | Ted Fritsch, Green Bay | 10 | 9 | 13 | 100 |
| 1945 | Steve Van Buren, Philadelphia | 18 | 0 | 2 | 110 |
| 1944 | Don Hutson, Green Bay | 9 | 0 | 31 | 85 |
| 1943 | Don Hutson, Green Bay | 12 | 3 | 36 | 117 |
| 1942 | Don Hutson, Green Bay | 17 | 1 | 33 | 138 |
| 1941 | Don Hutson, Green Bay | 12 | 1 | 20 | 95 |
| 1940 | Don Hutson, Green Bay | 7 | 0 | 15 | 57 |
| 1939 | Andy Farkas, Washington | 11 | 0 | 2 | 68 |
| 1938 | Clarke Hinkle, Green Bay | 7 | 3 | 7 | 58 |
| 1937 | Jack Manders, Chi. Bears | 5 | 8 | 15 | 69 |
| 1936 | Earl (Dutch) Clark, Detroit | 7 | 4 | 19 | 73 |
| 1935 | Earl (Dutch) Clark, Detroit | 6 | 1 | 16 | 55 |
| 1934 | Jack Manders, Chi. Bears | 3 | 10 | 28 | 76 |
| 1933 | Ken Strong, N.Y. Giants | 6 | 5 | 13 | 64 |
|  | Glenn Presnell, Portsmouth | 6 | 6 | 10 | 64 |
| 1932 | Earl (Dutch) Clark, Portsmouth | 6 | 3 | 10 | 55 |

*First year in the league.

## ANNUAL LEADERS—MOST FIELD GOALS MADE

| Year | Player, Team | Att. | Made | Pct. |
|------|--------------|------|------|------|
| 1983 | *Ali Haji-Sheikh, N.Y. Giants, NFC | 42 | 35 | 83.3 |
|  | *Raul Allegre, Baltimore, AFC | 35 | 30 | 85.7 |
| 1982 | Mark Moseley, Washington, NFC | 21 | 20 | 95.2 |
|  | Nick Lowery, Kansas City, AFC | 24 | 19 | 79.2 |
| 1981 | Rafael Septien, Dallas, NFC | 35 | 27 | 77.1 |
|  | Nick Lowery, Kansas City, AFC | 36 | 26 | 72.2 |
| 1980 | *Ed Murray, Detroit, NFC | 42 | 27 | 64.3 |
|  | John Smith, New England, AFC | 34 | 26 | 76.5 |
|  | Fred Steinfort, Denver, AFC | 34 | 26 | 76.5 |
| 1979 | Mark Moseley, Washington, NFC | 33 | 25 | 75.8 |
|  | John Smith, New England, AFC | 33 | 23 | 69.7 |

| Year | Player, Team | Att. | Made | Pct. |
|------|--------------|------|------|------|
| 1978 | *Frank Corral, Los Angeles, NFC | 43 | 29 | 67.4 |
|  | Pat Leahy, N.Y. Jets, AFC | 30 | 22 | 73.3 |
| 1977 | Mark Moseley, Washington, NFC | 37 | 21 | 56.8 |
|  | Errol Mann, Oakland, AFC | 28 | 20 | 71.4 |
| 1976 | Mark Moseley, Washington, NFC | 34 | 22 | 64.7 |
|  | Jan Stenerud, Kansas City, AFC | 38 | 21 | 55.3 |
| 1975 | Jan Stenerud, Kansas City, AFC | 32 | 22 | 68.8 |
|  | Toni Fritsch, Dallas, NFC | 35 | 22 | 62.9 |
| 1974 | Chester Marcol, Green Bay, NFC | 39 | 25 | 64.1 |
|  | Roy Gerela, Pittsburgh, AFC | 29 | 20 | 69.0 |
| 1973 | David Ray, Los Angeles, NFC | 47 | 30 | 63.8 |
|  | Roy Gerela, Pittsburgh, AFC | 43 | 29 | 67.4 |
| 1972 | *Chester Marcol, Green Bay, NFC | 48 | 33 | 68.8 |
|  | Roy Gerela, Pittsburgh, AFC | 41 | 28 | 68.3 |
| 1971 | Curt Knight, Washington, NFC | 49 | 29 | 59.2 |
|  | Garo Yepremian, Miami, AFC | 40 | 28 | 70.0 |
| 1970 | Fred Cox, Minnesota, NFC | 46 | 30 | 65.2 |
|  | Jan Stenerud, Kansas City, AFC | 42 | 30 | 71.4 |
| 1969 | Jim Turner, N.Y. Jets, AFL | 47 | 32 | 68.1 |
|  | Fred Cox, Minnesota, NFL | 37 | 26 | 70.3 |
| 1968 | Jim Turner, N.Y. Jets, AFL | 46 | 34 | 73.9 |
|  | Mac Percival, Chicago, NFL | 36 | 25 | 69.4 |
| 1967 | Jim Bakken, St. Louis, NFL | 39 | 27 | 69.2 |
|  | Jan Stenerud, Kansas City, AFL | 36 | 21 | 58.3 |
| 1966 | Bruce Gossett, Los Angeles, NFL | 49 | 28 | 57.1 |
|  | Mike Mercer, Oakland-Kansas City, AFL | 30 | 21 | 70.0 |
| 1965 | Pete Gogolak, Buffalo, AFL | 46 | 28 | 60.9 |
|  | Fred Cox, Minnesota, NFL | 35 | 23 | 65.7 |
| 1964 | Jim Bakken, St. Louis, NFL | 38 | 25 | 65.8 |
|  | Gino Cappelletti, Boston, AFL | 39 | 25 | 64.1 |
| 1963 | Jim Martin, Baltimore, NFL | 39 | 24 | 61.5 |
|  | Gino Cappelletti, Boston, AFL | 38 | 22 | 57.9 |
| 1962 | Gene Mingo, Denver, AFL | 39 | 27 | 69.2 |
|  | Lou Michaels, Pittsburgh, NFL | 42 | 26 | 61.9 |
| 1961 | Steve Myhra, Baltimore, NFL | 39 | 21 | 53.8 |
|  | Gino Cappelletti, Boston, AFL | 32 | 17 | 53.1 |
| 1960 | Tommy Davis, San Francisco, NFL | 32 | 19 | 59.4 |
|  | *Gene Mingo, Denver, AFL | 28 | 18 | 64.3 |
| 1959 | Pat Summerall, New York Giants | 29 | 20 | 69.0 |
| 1958 | Paige Cothren, Los Angeles | 25 | 14 | 56.0 |
|  | *Tom Miner, Pittsburgh | 28 | 14 | 50.0 |
| 1957 | Lou Groza, Cleveland | 22 | 15 | 68.2 |
| 1956 | Sam Baker, Washington | 25 | 17 | 68.0 |
| 1955 | Fred Cone, Green Bay | 24 | 16 | 66.7 |
| 1954 | Lou Groza, Cleveland | 24 | 16 | 66.7 |
| 1953 | Lou Groza, Cleveland | 26 | 23 | 88.5 |
| 1952 | Lou Groza, Cleveland | 33 | 19 | 57.6 |
| 1951 | Bob Waterfield, Los Angeles | 23 | 13 | 56.5 |
| 1950 | *Lou Groza, Cleveland | 19 | 13 | 68.4 |
| 1949 | Cliff Patton, Philadelphia | 18 | 9 | 50.0 |
|  | Bob Waterfield, Los Angeles | 16 | 9 | 56.3 |
| 1948 | Cliff Patton, Philadelphia | 12 | 8 | 66.7 |
| 1947 | Ward Cuff, Green Bay | 16 | 7 | 43.8 |
|  | Pat Harder, Chi. Cardinals | 10 | 7 | 70.0 |
|  | Bob Waterfield, Los Angeles | 16 | 7 | 43.8 |
| 1946 | Ted Fritsch, Green Bay | 17 | 9 | 52.9 |
| 1945 | Joe Aguirre, Washington | 13 | 7 | 53.8 |
| 1944 | Ken Strong, N.Y. Giants | 12 | 6 | 50.0 |
| 1943 | Ward Cuff, N.Y. Giants | 9 | 3 | 33.3 |
|  | Don Hutson, Green Bay | 5 | 3 | 60.0 |
| 1942 | Bill Daddio, Chi. Cardinals | 10 | 5 | 50.0 |
| 1941 | Clarke Hinkle, Green Bay | 14 | 6 | 42.9 |
| 1940 | Clarke Hinkle, Green Bay | 14 | 9 | 64.3 |
| 1939 | Ward Cuff, N.Y. Giants | 16 | 7 | 43.8 |
| 1938 | Ward Cuff, N.Y. Giants | 9 | 5 | 55.6 |
|  | Ralph Kercheval, Brooklyn | 13 | 5 | 38.5 |
| 1937 | Jack Manders, Chi. Bears |  | 8 |  |
| 1936 | Jack Manders, Chi. Bears |  | 7 |  |
|  | Armand Niccolai, Pittsburgh |  | 7 |  |
| 1935 | Armand Niccolai, Pittsburgh |  | 6 |  |
|  | Bill Smith, Chi. Cardinals |  | 6 |  |
| 1934 | Jack Manders, Chi. Bears |  | 10 |  |
| 1933 | *Jack Manders, Chi. Bears |  | 6 |  |
|  | Glenn Presnell, Portsmouth |  | 6 |  |
| 1932 | Earl (Dutch) Clark, Portsmouth |  | 3 |  |

*First year in the league.

## ANNUAL RUSHING LEADERS

| Year | Player, Team | Att. | Yards | Avg. | TD |
|------|--------------|------|-------|------|-----|
| 1983 | *Eric Dickerson, L.A. Rams, NFC | 390 | 1,808 | 4.6 | 18 |
|  | *Curt Warner, Seattle, AFC | 335 | 1,449 | 4.3 | 13 |
| 1982 | Freeman McNeil, N.Y. Jets, AFC | 151 | 786 | 5.2 | 6 |
|  | Tony Dorsett, Dallas, NFC | 177 | 745 | 4.2 | 5 |
| 1981 | *George Rogers, New Orleans, NFC | 378 | 1,674 | 4.4 | 13 |
|  | Earl Campbell, Houston, AFC | 361 | 1,376 | 3.8 | 10 |
| 1980 | Earl Campbell, Houston, AFC | 373 | 1,934 | 5.2 | 13 |
|  | Walter Payton, Chicago, NFC | 317 | 1,460 | 4.6 | 6 |
| 1979 | Earl Campbell, Houston, AFC | 368 | 1,697 | 4.6 | 19 |
|  | Walter Payton, Chicago, NFC | 369 | 1,610 | 4.4 | 14 |
| 1978 | *Earl Campbell, Houston, AFC | 302 | 1,450 | 4.8 | 13 |
|  | Walter Payton, Chicago, NFC | 333 | 1,395 | 4.2 | 11 |
| 1977 | Walter Payton, Chicago, NFC | 339 | 1,852 | 5.5 | 14 |
|  | Mark van Eeghen, Oakland, AFC | 324 | 1,273 | 3.9 | 7 |
| 1976 | O.J. Simpson, Buffalo, AFC | 290 | 1,503 | 5.2 | 8 |
|  | Walter Payton, Chicago, NFC | 311 | 1,390 | 4.5 | 13 |
| 1975 | O.J. Simpson, Buffalo, AFC | 329 | 1,817 | 5.5 | 16 |
|  | Jim Otis, St. Louis, NFC | 269 | 1,076 | 4.0 | 5 |
| 1974 | Otis Armstrong, Denver, AFC | 263 | 1,407 | 5.3 | 9 |

| Year | Player, Team | Att. | Yards | Avg. | TD |
|---|---|---|---|---|---|
| | Lawrence McCutcheon, Los Angeles, NFC | 236 | 1,109 | 4.7 | 3 |
| 1973 | O.J. Simpson, Buffalo, AFC | 332 | 2,003 | 6.0 | 12 |
| | John Brockington, Green Bay, NFC | 265 | 1,144 | 4.3 | 3 |
| 1972 | O.J. Simpson, Buffalo, AFC | 292 | 1,251 | 4.3 | 6 |
| | Larry Brown, Washington, NFC | 285 | 1,216 | 4.3 | 8 |
| 1971 | Floyd Little, Denver, AFC | 284 | 1,133 | 4.0 | 6 |
| | *John Brockington, Green Bay, NFC | 216 | 1,105 | 5.1 | 4 |
| 1970 | Larry Brown, Washington, NFC | 237 | 1,125 | 4.7 | 5 |
| | Floyd Little, Denver, AFC | 209 | 901 | 4.3 | 3 |
| 1969 | Gale Sayers, Chicago, NFL | 236 | 1,032 | 4.4 | 8 |
| | Dickie Post, San Diego, AFL | 182 | 873 | 4.8 | 6 |
| 1968 | Leroy Kelly, Cleveland, NFL | 248 | 1,239 | 5.0 | 16 |
| | *Paul Robinson, Cincinnati, AFL | 238 | 1,023 | 4.3 | 8 |
| 1967 | Jim Nance, Boston, AFL | 269 | 1,216 | 4.5 | 7 |
| | Leroy Kelly, Cleveland, NFL | 235 | 1,205 | 5.1 | 11 |
| 1966 | Jim Nance, Boston, AFL | 299 | 1,458 | 4.9 | 11 |
| | Gale Sayers, Chicago, NFL | 229 | 1,231 | 5.4 | 8 |
| 1965 | Jim Brown, Cleveland, NFL | 289 | 1,544 | 5.3 | 17 |
| | Paul Lowe, San Diego, AFL | 222 | 1,121 | 5.0 | 7 |
| 1964 | Jim Brown, Cleveland, NFL | 280 | 1,446 | 5.2 | 7 |
| | Cookie Gilchrist, Buffalo, AFL | 230 | 981 | 4.3 | 6 |
| 1963 | Jim Brown, Cleveland, NFL | 291 | 1,863 | 6.4 | 12 |
| | Clem Daniels, Oakland, AFL | 215 | 1,099 | 5.1 | 3 |
| 1962 | Jim Taylor, Green Bay, NFL | 272 | 1,474 | 5.4 | 19 |
| | *Cookie Gilchrist, Buffalo, AFL | 214 | 1,096 | 5.1 | 13 |
| 1961 | Jim Brown, Cleveland, NFL | 305 | 1,408 | 4.6 | 8 |
| | Billy Cannon, Houston, AFL | 200 | 948 | 4.7 | 6 |
| 1960 | Jim Brown, Cleveland, NFL | 215 | 1,257 | 5.8 | 9 |
| | *Abner Haynes, Dall. Texans, AFL | 156 | 875 | 5.6 | 9 |
| 1959 | Jim Brown, Cleveland | 290 | 1,329 | 4.6 | 14 |
| 1958 | Jim Brown, Cleveland | 257 | 1,527 | 5.9 | 17 |
| 1957 | *Jim Brown, Cleveland | 202 | 942 | 4.7 | 9 |
| 1956 | Rick Casares, Chi. Bears | 234 | 1,126 | 4.8 | 12 |
| 1955 | *Alan Ameche, Baltimore | 213 | 961 | 4.5 | 9 |
| 1954 | Joe Perry, San Francisco | 173 | 1,049 | 6.1 | 8 |
| 1953 | Joe Perry, San Francisco | 192 | 1,018 | 5.3 | 10 |
| 1952 | Dan Towler, Los Angeles | 156 | 894 | 5.7 | 10 |
| 1951 | Eddie Price, N.Y. Giants | 271 | 971 | 3.6 | 7 |
| 1950 | *Marion Motley, Cleveland | 140 | 810 | 5.8 | 3 |
| 1949 | Steve Van Buren, Philadelphia | 263 | 1,146 | 4.4 | 11 |
| 1948 | Steve Van Buren, Philadelphia | 201 | 945 | 4.7 | 10 |
| 1947 | Steve Van Buren, Philadelphia | 217 | 1,008 | 4.6 | 13 |
| 1946 | Bill Dudley, Pittsburgh | 146 | 604 | 4.1 | 3 |
| 1945 | Steve Van Buren, Philadelphia | 143 | 832 | 5.8 | 15 |
| 1944 | Bill Paschal, N.Y. Giants | 196 | 737 | 3.8 | 9 |
| 1943 | *Bill Paschal, N.Y. Giants | 147 | 572 | 3.9 | 10 |
| 1942 | *Bill Dudley, Pittsburgh | 162 | 696 | 4.3 | 5 |
| 1941 | Clarence (Pug) Manders, Brooklyn | 111 | 486 | 4.4 | 5 |
| 1940 | Byron (Whizzer) White, Detroit | 146 | 514 | 3.5 | 5 |
| 1939 | *Bill Osmanski, Chicago | 121 | 699 | 5.8 | 7 |
| 1938 | *Byron (Whizzer) White, Pittsburgh | 152 | 567 | 3.7 | 4 |
| 1937 | Cliff Battles, Washington | 216 | 874 | 4.0 | 5 |
| 1936 | *Alphonse (Tuffy) Leemans, N.Y. Giants | 206 | 830 | 4.0 | 2 |
| 1935 | Doug Russell, Chi. Cardinals | 140 | 499 | 3.6 | 0 |
| 1934 | *Beattie Feathers, Chi. Bears | 101 | 1,004 | 9.9 | 8 |
| 1933 | Jim Musick, Boston | 173 | 809 | 4.7 | 5 |
| 1932 | *Cliff Battles, Boston | 148 | 576 | 3.9 | 3 |

**First year in the league.*

## ANNUAL PASSING LEADERS

| Year | Player, Team | Att. | Comp. | Yards | TD | Int. |
|---|---|---|---|---|---|---|
| 1983 | Steve Bartkowski, Atlanta, NFC | 432 | 274 | 3,167 | 22 | 5 |
| | *Dan Marino, Miami, AFC | 296 | 173 | 2,210 | 20 | 6 |
| 1982 | Ken Anderson, Cincinnati, AFC | 309 | 218 | 2,495 | 12 | 9 |
| | Joe Theismann, Washington, NFC | 252 | 161 | 2,033 | 13 | 9 |
| 1981 | Ken Anderson, Cincinnati, AFC | 479 | 300 | 3,754 | 29 | 10 |
| | Joe Montana, San Francisco, NFC | 488 | 311 | 3,565 | 19 | 12 |
| 1980 | Brian Sipe, Cleveland, AFC | 554 | 337 | 4,132 | 30 | 14 |
| | Ron Jaworski, Philadelphia, NFC | 451 | 257 | 3,529 | 27 | 12 |
| 1979 | Roger Staubach, Dallas, NFC | 461 | 267 | 3,586 | 27 | 11 |
| | Dan Fouts, San Diego, AFC | 530 | 332 | 4,082 | 24 | 24 |
| 1978 | Roger Staubach, Dallas, NFC | 413 | 231 | 3,190 | 25 | 16 |
| | Terry Bradshaw, Pittsburgh, AFC | 368 | 207 | 2,915 | 28 | 20 |
| 1977 | Bob Griese, Miami, AFC | 307 | 180 | 2,252 | 22 | 13 |
| | Roger Staubach, Dallas, NFC | 361 | 210 | 2,620 | 18 | 9 |
| 1976 | Ken Stabler, Oakland, AFC | 291 | 194 | 2,737 | 27 | 17 |
| | James Harris, Los Angeles, NFC | 158 | 91 | 1,460 | 8 | 6 |
| 1975 | Ken Anderson, Cincinnati, AFC | 377 | 228 | 3,169 | 21 | 11 |
| | Fran Tarkenton, Minnesota, NFC | 425 | 273 | 2,994 | 25 | 13 |
| 1974 | Ken Anderson, Cincinnati, AFC | 328 | 213 | 2,667 | 18 | 10 |
| | Sonny Jurgensen, Washington, NFC | 167 | 107 | 1,185 | 11 | 5 |
| 1973 | Roger Staubach, Dallas, NFC | 286 | 179 | 2,428 | 23 | 15 |
| | Ken Stabler, Oakland, AFC | 260 | 163 | 1,997 | 14 | 10 |
| 1972 | Norm Snead, N.Y. Giants, NFC | 325 | 196 | 2,307 | 17 | 12 |
| | Earl Morrall, Miami, AFC | 150 | 83 | 1,360 | 11 | 7 |
| 1971 | Roger Staubach, Dallas, NFC | 211 | 126 | 1,882 | 15 | 4 |
| | Bob Griese, Miami, AFC | 263 | 145 | 2,089 | 19 | 9 |
| 1970 | John Brodie, San Francisco, NFC | 378 | 223 | 2,941 | 24 | 10 |
| | Daryle Lamonica, Oakland, AFC | 356 | 179 | 2,516 | 22 | 15 |
| 1969 | Sonny Jurgensen, Washington, NFL | 442 | 274 | 3,102 | 22 | 15 |
| | *Greg Cook, Cincinnati, AFL | 197 | 106 | 1,854 | 15 | 11 |
| 1968 | Len Dawson, Kansas City, AFL | 224 | 131 | 2,109 | 17 | 9 |
| | Earl Morrall, Baltimore, NFL | 317 | 182 | 2,909 | 26 | 17 |
| 1967 | Sonny Jurgensen, Washington, NFL | 508 | 288 | 3,747 | 31 | 16 |
| | Daryle Lamonica, Oakland, AFL | 425 | 220 | 3,228 | 30 | 20 |
| 1966 | Bart Starr, Green Bay, NFL | 251 | 156 | 2,257 | 14 | 3 |
| | Len Dawson, Kansas City, AFL | 284 | 159 | 2,527 | 26 | 10 |
| 1965 | Rudy Bukich, Chicago, NFL | 312 | 176 | 2,641 | 20 | 9 |
| | John Hadl, San Diego, AFL | 348 | 174 | 2,798 | 20 | 21 |
| 1964 | Len Dawson, Kansas City, AFL | 354 | 199 | 2,879 | 30 | 18 |
| | Bart Starr, Green Bay, NFL | 272 | 163 | 2,144 | 15 | 4 |
| 1963 | Y.A. Tittle, N.Y. Giants, NFL | 367 | 221 | 3,145 | 36 | 14 |
| | Tobin Rote, San Diego, AFL | 286 | 170 | 2,510 | 20 | 17 |
| 1962 | Len Dawson, Dall. Texans, AFL | 310 | 189 | 2,759 | 29 | 17 |
| | Bart Starr, Green Bay, NFL | 285 | 178 | 2,438 | 12 | 9 |
| 1961 | George Blanda, Houston, AFL | 362 | 187 | 3,330 | 36 | 22 |
| | Milt Plum, Cleveland, NFL | 302 | 177 | 2,416 | 18 | 10 |
| 1960 | Milt Plum, Cleveland, NFL | 250 | 151 | 2,297 | 21 | 5 |
| | Jack Kemp, L.A. Chargers, AFL | 406 | 211 | 3,018 | 20 | 25 |
| 1959 | Charlie Conerly, N.Y. Giants | 194 | 113 | 1,706 | 14 | 4 |
| 1958 | Eddie LeBaron, Washington | 145 | 79 | 1,365 | 11 | 10 |
| 1957 | Tommy O'Connell, Cleveland | 110 | 63 | 1,229 | 9 | 8 |
| 1956 | Ed Brown, Chi. Bears | 168 | 96 | 1,667 | 11 | 12 |
| 1955 | Otto Graham, Cleveland | 185 | 98 | 1,721 | 15 | 8 |
| 1954 | Norm Van Brocklin, Los Angeles | 260 | 139 | 2,637 | 13 | 21 |
| 1953 | Otto Graham, Cleveland | 258 | 167 | 2,722 | 11 | 9 |
| 1952 | Norm Van Brocklin, Los Angeles | 205 | 113 | 1,736 | 14 | 17 |
| 1951 | Bob Waterfield, Los Angeles | 176 | 88 | 1,566 | 13 | 10 |
| 1950 | Norm Van Brocklin, Los Angeles | 233 | 127 | 2,061 | 18 | 14 |
| 1949 | Sammy Baugh, Washington | 255 | 145 | 1,903 | 18 | 14 |
| 1948 | Tommy Thompson, Philadelphia | 246 | 141 | 1,965 | 25 | 11 |
| 1947 | Sammy Baugh, Washington | 354 | 210 | 2,938 | 25 | 15 |
| 1946 | Bob Waterfield, Los Angeles | 251 | 127 | 1,747 | 18 | 17 |
| 1945 | Sammy Baugh, Washington | 182 | 128 | 1,669 | 11 | 4 |
| | Sid Luckman, Chi. Bears | 217 | 117 | 1,725 | 14 | 10 |
| 1944 | Frank Filchock, Washington | 147 | 84 | 1,139 | 13 | 9 |
| 1943 | Sammy Baugh, Washington | 239 | 133 | 1,754 | 23 | 19 |
| 1942 | Cecil Isbell, Green Bay | 268 | 146 | 2,021 | 24 | 14 |
| 1941 | Cecil Isbell, Green Bay | 206 | 117 | 1,479 | 15 | 11 |
| 1940 | Sammy Baugh, Washington | 177 | 111 | 1,367 | 12 | 10 |
| 1939 | *Parker Hall, Cleveland | 208 | 106 | 1,227 | 9 | 13 |
| 1938 | Ed Danowski, N.Y. Giants | 129 | 70 | 848 | 7 | 8 |
| 1937 | *Sammy Baugh, Washington | 171 | 81 | 1,127 | 8 | 14 |
| 1936 | Arnie Herber, Green Bay | 173 | 77 | 1,239 | 11 | 13 |
| 1935 | Ed Danowski, N.Y. Giants | 113 | 57 | 794 | 10 | 9 |
| 1934 | Arnie Herber, Green Bay | 115 | 42 | 799 | 8 | 12 |
| 1933 | *Harry Newman, N.Y. Giants | 136 | 53 | 973 | 11 | 17 |
| 1932 | Arnie Herber, Green Bay | 101 | 37 | 639 | 9 | 9 |

**First year in the league.*

## ANNUAL PASS RECEIVING LEADERS

| Year | Player, Team | No. | Yards | Avg. | TD |
|---|---|---|---|---|---|
| 1983 | Todd Christensen, L.A. Raiders, AFC | 92 | 1,247 | 13.6 | 12 |
| | Roy Green, St. Louis, NFC | 78 | 1,227 | 15.7 | 14 |
| | Charlie Brown, Washington, NFC | 78 | 1,225 | 15.7 | 8 |
| | Earnest Gray, N.Y. Giants, NFC | 78 | 1,139 | 14.6 | 5 |
| 1982 | Dwight Clark, San Francisco, NFC | 60 | 913 | 15.2 | 5 |
| | Kellen Winslow, San Diego, AFC | 54 | 721 | 13.4 | 6 |
| 1981 | Kellen Winslow, San Diego, AFC | 88 | 1,075 | 12.2 | 10 |
| | Dwight Clark, San Francisco, NFC | 85 | 1,105 | 13.0 | 4 |
| 1980 | Kellen Winslow, San Diego, AFC | 89 | 1,290 | 14.5 | 9 |
| | *Earl Cooper, San Francisco, NFC | 83 | 567 | 6.8 | 4 |
| 1979 | Joe Washington, Baltimore, AFC | 82 | 750 | 9.1 | 3 |
| | Ahmad Rashad, Minnesota, NFC | 80 | 1,156 | 14.5 | 9 |
| 1978 | Rickey Young, Minnesota, NFC | 88 | 704 | 8.0 | 5 |
| | Steve Largent, Seattle, AFC | 71 | 1,168 | 16.5 | 8 |
| 1977 | Lydell Mitchell, Baltimore, AFC | 71 | 620 | 8.7 | 4 |
| | Ahmad Rashad, Minnesota, NFC | 51 | 681 | 13.4 | 2 |
| 1976 | MacArthur Lane, Kansas City, AFC | 66 | 686 | 10.4 | 1 |
| | Drew Pearson, Dallas, NFC | 58 | 806 | 13.9 | 6 |
| 1975 | Chuck Foreman, Minnesota, NFC | 73 | 691 | 9.5 | 9 |
| | Reggie Rucker, Cleveland, AFC | 60 | 770 | 12.8 | 3 |
| | Lydell Mitchell, Baltimore, AFC | 60 | 544 | 9.1 | 4 |
| 1974 | Lydell Mitchell, Baltimore, AFC | 72 | 544 | 7.6 | 2 |
| | Charles Young, Philadelphia, NFC | 63 | 696 | 11.0 | 3 |
| 1973 | Harold Carmichael, Philadelphia, NFC | 67 | 1,116 | 16.7 | 9 |
| | Fred Willis, Houston, AFC | 57 | 371 | 6.5 | 1 |
| 1972 | Harold Jackson, Philadelphia, NFC | 62 | 1,048 | 16.9 | 4 |
| | Fred Biletnikoff, Oakland, AFC | 58 | 802 | 13.8 | 7 |
| 1971 | Fred Biletnikoff, Oakland, AFC | 61 | 929 | 15.2 | 9 |
| | Bob Tucker, N.Y. Giants, NFC | 59 | 791 | 13.4 | 4 |
| 1970 | Dick Gordon, Chicago, NFC | 71 | 1,026 | 14.5 | 13 |
| | Marlin Briscoe, Buffalo, AFC | 57 | 1,036 | 18.2 | 8 |
| 1969 | Dan Abramowicz, New Orleans, NFL | 73 | 1,015 | 13.9 | 7 |
| | Lance Alworth, San Diego, AFL | 64 | 1,003 | 15.7 | 4 |
| 1968 | Clifton McNeil, San Francisco, NFL | 71 | 994 | 14.0 | 7 |
| | Lance Alworth, San Diego, AFL | 68 | 1,312 | 19.3 | 10 |
| 1967 | George Sauer, N.Y. Jets, AFL | 75 | 1,189 | 15.9 | 6 |
| | Charley Taylor, Washington, NFL | 70 | 990 | 14.1 | 9 |
| 1966 | Lance Alworth, San Diego, AFL | 73 | 1,383 | 18.9 | 13 |
| | Charley Taylor, Washington, NFL | 72 | 1,119 | 15.5 | 12 |
| 1965 | Lionel Taylor, Denver, AFL | 85 | 1,131 | 13.3 | 6 |
| | Dave Parks, San Francisco, NFL | 80 | 1,344 | 16.8 | 12 |
| 1964 | Charley Hennigan, Houston, AFL | 101 | 1,546 | 15.3 | 8 |
| | Johnny Morris, Chicago, NFL | 93 | 1,200 | 12.9 | 10 |
| 1963 | Lionel Taylor, Denver, AFL | 78 | 1,101 | 14.1 | 10 |
| | Bobby Joe Conrad, St. Louis, NFL | 73 | 967 | 13.2 | 10 |
| 1962 | Lionel Taylor, Denver, AFL | 77 | 908 | 11.8 | 4 |
| | Bobby Mitchell, Washington, NFL | 72 | 1,384 | 19.2 | 11 |
| 1961 | Lionel Taylor, Denver, AFL | 100 | 1,176 | 11.8 | 4 |
| | Jim (Red) Phillips, Los Angeles, NFL | 78 | 1,092 | 14.0 | 5 |
| 1960 | Lionel Taylor, Denver, AFL | 92 | 1,235 | 13.4 | 12 |
| | Raymond Berry, Baltimore, NFL | 74 | 1,298 | 17.5 | 10 |
| 1959 | Raymond Berry, Baltimore | 66 | 959 | 14.5 | 14 |
| 1958 | Raymond Berry, Baltimore | 56 | 794 | 14.2 | 9 |
| | Pete Retzlaff, Philadelphia | 56 | 766 | 13.7 | 2 |
| 1957 | Billy Wilson, San Francisco | 52 | 757 | 14.6 | 6 |
| 1956 | Billy Wilson, San Francisco | 60 | 889 | 14.8 | 5 |
| 1955 | Pete Pihos, Philadelphia | 62 | 864 | 13.9 | 7 |
| 1954 | Pete Pihos, Philadelphia | 60 | 872 | 14.5 | 10 |
| | Billy Wilson, San Francisco | 60 | 830 | 13.8 | 5 |
| 1953 | Pete Pihos, Philadelphia | 63 | 1,049 | 16.7 | 10 |
| 1952 | Mac Speedie, Cleveland | 62 | 911 | 14.7 | 5 |
| 1951 | Elroy (Crazylegs) Hirsch, Los Angeles | 66 | 1,495 | 22.7 | 17 |
| 1950 | Tom Fears, Los Angeles | 84 | 1,116 | 13.3 | 7 |
| 1949 | Tom Fears, Los Angeles | 77 | 1,013 | 13.2 | 9 |

| 1948 | *Tom Fears, Los Angeles | 51 | 698 | 13.7 | 4 |
| 1947 | Jim Keane, Chi. Bears | 64 | 910 | 14.2 | 10 |
| 1946 | Jim Benton, Los Angeles | 63 | 981 | 15.6 | 6 |
| 1945 | Don Hutson, Green Bay | 47 | 834 | 17.7 | 9 |
| 1944 | Don Hutson, Green Bay | 58 | 866 | 14.9 | 9 |
| 1943 | Don Hutson, Green Bay | 47 | 776 | 16.5 | 11 |
| 1942 | Don Hutson, Green Bay | 74 | 1,211 | 16.4 | 17 |
| 1941 | Don Hutson, Green Bay | 58 | 738 | 12.7 | 10 |
| 1940 | *Don Looney, Philadelphia | 58 | 707 | 12.2 | 4 |
| 1939 | Don Hutson, Green Bay | 34 | 846 | 24.9 | 6 |
| 1938 | Gaynell Tinsley, Chi. Cardinals | 41 | 516 | 12.6 | 1 |
| 1937 | Don Hutson, Green Bay | 41 | 552 | 13.5 | 7 |
| 1936 | Don Hutson, Green Bay | 34 | 536 | 15.8 | 8 |
| 1935 | *Tod Goodwin, N.Y. Giants | 26 | 432 | 16.6 | 4 |
| 1934 | Joe Carter, Philadelphia | 16 | 238 | 14.9 | 4 |
|  | Morris (Red) Badgro, N.Y. Giants | 16 | 206 | 12.9 | 1 |
| 1933 | John (Shipwreck) Kelly, Brooklyn | 22 | 246 | 11.2 | 3 |
| 1932 | Ray Flaherty, N.Y. Giants | 21 | 350 | 16.7 | 3 |

*First year in the league.

## ANNUAL INTERCEPTION LEADERS

| Year | Player, Team | No. | Yards | TD |
|---|---|---|---|---|
| 1983 | Mark Murphy, Washington, NFC | 9 | 127 | 0 |
|  | Ken Riley, Cincinnati, AFC | 8 | 89 | 2 |
|  | Vann McElroy, L.A. Raiders, AFC | 8 | 68 | 0 |
| 1982 | Everson Walls, Dallas, NFC | 7 | 61 | 0 |
|  | Ken Riley, Cincinnati, AFC | 5 | 88 | 1 |
|  | Bobby Jackson, N.Y. Jets, AFC | 5 | 84 | 1 |
|  | Dwayne Woodruff, Pittsburgh, AFC | 5 | 53 | 0 |
|  | Donnie Shell, Pittsburgh, AFC | 5 | 27 | 0 |
| 1981 | *Everson Walls, Dallas, NFC | 11 | 133 | 0 |
|  | John Harris, Seattle, AFC | 10 | 155 | 2 |
| 1980 | Lester Hayes, Oakland, AFC | 13 | 273 | 1 |
|  | Nolan Cromwell, Los Angeles, NFC | 8 | 140 | 1 |
| 1979 | Mike Reinfeldt, Houston, AFC | 12 | 205 | 0 |
|  | Lemar Parrish, Washington, NFC | 9 | 65 | 0 |
| 1978 | Thom Darden, Cleveland, AFC | 10 | 200 | 0 |
|  | Ken Stone, St. Louis, NFC | 9 | 139 | 0 |
|  | Willie Buchanon, Green Bay, NFC | 9 | 93 | 1 |
| 1977 | Lyle Blackwood, Baltimore, AFC | 10 | 163 | 0 |
|  | Rolland Lawrence, Atlanta, NFC | 7 | 138 | 0 |
| 1976 | Monte Jackson, Los Angeles, NFC | 10 | 173 | 3 |
|  | Ken Riley, Cincinnati, AFC | 9 | 141 | 1 |
| 1975 | Mel Blount, Pittsburgh, AFC | 11 | 121 | 0 |
|  | Paul Krause, Minnesota, NFC | 10 | 201 | 0 |
| 1974 | Emmitt Thomas, Kansas City, AFC | 12 | 214 | 2 |
|  | Ray Brown, Atlanta, NFC | 8 | 164 | 1 |
| 1973 | Dick Anderson, Miami, AFC | 8 | 163 | 2 |
|  | Mike Wagner, Pittsburgh, AFC | 8 | 134 | 0 |
|  | Bobby Bryant, Minnesota, NFC | 7 | 105 | 1 |
| 1972 | Bill Bradley, Philadelphia, NFC | 9 | 73 | 0 |
|  | Mike Sensibaugh, Kansas City, AFC | 8 | 65 | 0 |
| 1971 | Bill Bradley, Philadelphia, NFC | 11 | 248 | 0 |
|  | Ken Houston, Houston, AFC | 9 | 220 | 4 |
| 1970 | Johnny Robinson, Kansas City, AFC | 10 | 155 | 0 |
|  | Dick LeBeau, Detroit, NFC | 9 | 96 | 0 |
| 1969 | Mel Renfro, Dallas, NFL | 10 | 118 | 0 |
|  | Emmitt Thomas, Kansas City, AFL | 9 | 146 | 1 |
| 1968 | Dave Grayson, Oakland, AFL | 10 | 195 | 1 |
|  | Willie Williams, N.Y. Giants, NFL | 10 | 103 | 0 |
| 1967 | Miller Farr, Houston, AFL | 10 | 264 | 3 |
|  | *Lem Barney, Detroit, NFL | 10 | 232 | 3 |
|  | Tom Janik, Buffalo AFL | 10 | 222 | 2 |
|  | Dave Whitsell, New Orleans, NFL | 10 | 178 | 2 |
|  | Dick Westmoreland, Miami, AFL | 10 | 127 | 1 |
| 1966 | Larry Wilson, St. Louis, NFL | 10 | 180 | 2 |
|  | Johnny Robinson, Kansas City, AFL | 10 | 136 | 1 |
|  | Bobby Hunt, Kansas City, AFL | 10 | 113 | 0 |
| 1965 | W.K. Hicks, Houston, AFL | 9 | 156 | 0 |
|  | Bobby Boyd, Baltimore, NFL | 9 | 78 | 1 |
| 1964 | Dainard Paulson, N.Y. Jets, AFL | 12 | 157 | 1 |
|  | *Paul Krause, Washington, NFL | 12 | 140 | 1 |
| 1963 | Fred Glick, Houston, AFL | 12 | 180 | 1 |
|  | Dick Lynch, N.Y. Giants, NFL | 9 | 251 | 3 |
|  | Roosevelt Taylor, Chicago, NFL | 9 | 172 | 1 |
| 1962 | Lee Riley, N.Y. Titans, AFL | 11 | 122 | 0 |
|  | Willie Wood, Green Bay, NFL | 9 | 132 | 0 |
| 1961 | Billy Atkins, Buffalo, AFL | 10 | 158 | 0 |
|  | Dick Lynch, N.Y. Giants, NFL | 9 | 60 | 0 |
| 1960 | *Austin (Goose) Gonsoulin, Denver, AFL | 11 | 98 | 0 |
|  | Dave Baker, San Francisco, NFL | 10 | 96 | 0 |
|  | Jerry Norton, St. Louis, NFL | 10 | 96 | 0 |
| 1959 | Dean Derby, Pittsburgh | 7 | 127 | 0 |
|  | Milt Davis Baltimore | 7 | 119 | 1 |
|  | Don Shinnick, Baltimore | 7 | 70 | 0 |
| 1958 | Jim Patton, N.Y. Giants | 11 | 183 | 0 |
| 1957 | *Milt Davis, Baltimore | 10 | 219 | 2 |
|  | Jack Christiansen, Detroit | 10 | 137 | 1 |
|  | Jack Butler, Pittsburgh | 10 | 85 | 0 |
| 1956 | Lindon Crow, Chi. Cardinals | 11 | 170 | 0 |
| 1955 | Will Sherman, Los Angeles | 11 | 101 | 0 |
| 1954 | Dick (Night Train) Lane, Chi. Cardinals | 10 | 181 | 0 |
| 1953 | Jack Christiansen, Detroit | 12 | 238 | 1 |
| 1952 | *Dick (Night Train) Lane, Los Angeles | 14 | 298 | 2 |
| 1951 | Otto Schnellbacher, N.Y. Giants | 11 | 194 | 2 |
| 1950 | *Orban (Spec) Sanders, N.Y. Yanks | 13 | 199 | 0 |
| 1949 | Bob Nussbaumer, Chi. Cardinals | 12 | 157 | 0 |
| 1948 | *Dan Sandifer, Washington | 13 | 258 | 2 |
| 1947 | Frank Reagan, N.Y. Giants | 10 | 203 | 1 |
|  | Frank Seno, Boston | 10 | 100 | 0 |
| 1946 | Bill Dudley, Pittsburgh | 10 | 242 | 1 |
| 1945 | Roy Zimmerman, Philadelphia | 7 | 90 | 0 |
| 1944 | *Howard Livingston, N.Y. Giants | 9 | 172 | 1 |

| 1943 | Sammy Baugh, Washington | 11 | 112 | 0 |
|---|---|---|---|---|
| 1942 | *Clyde (Bulldog) Turner, Chi. Bears | 8 | 96 | 1 |
| 1941 | Marshall Goldberg, Chi. Cardinals | 7 | 54 | 0 |
|  | *Art Jones, Pittsburgh | 7 | 35 | 0 |
| 1940 | Clarence (Ace) Parker, Brooklyn | 6 | 146 | 1 |
|  | Kent Ryan, Detroit | 6 | 65 | 0 |
|  | Don Hutson, Green Bay | 6 | 24 | 0 |

*First year in the league.

## ANNUAL PUNTING LEADERS

| Year | Player, Team | No. | Avg. | Long |
|---|---|---|---|---|
| 1983 | Rohn Stark, Baltimore, AFC | 91 | 45.3 | 68 |
|  | *Frank Garcia, Tampa Bay, NFC | 95 | 42.2 | 64 |
| 1982 | Luke Prestridge, Denver, AFC | 45 | 45.0 | 65 |
|  | Carl Birdsong, St. Louis, NFC | 54 | 43.8 | 65 |
| 1981 | Pat McInally, Cincinnati, AFC | 72 | 45.4 | 62 |
|  | Tom Skladany, Detroit, NFC | 64 | 43.5 | 74 |
| 1980 | Dave Jennings, N.Y. Giants, NFC | 94 | 44.8 | 63 |
|  | Luke Prestridge, Denver, AFC | 70 | 43.9 | 57 |
| 1979 | *Bob Grupp, Kansas City, AFC | 89 | 43.6 | 74 |
|  | Dave Jennings, N.Y. Giants, NFC | 104 | 42.7 | 72 |
| 1978 | Pat McInally, Cincinnati, AFC | 91 | 43.1 | 65 |
|  | *Tom Skladany, Detroit, NFC | 86 | 42.5 | 63 |
| 1977 | Ray Guy, Oakland, AFC | 59 | 43.3 | 74 |
|  | Tom Blanchard, New Orleans, NFC | 82 | 42.4 | 66 |
| 1976 | Marv Bateman, Buffalo, AFC | 86 | 42.8 | 78 |
|  | John James, Atlanta, NFC | 101 | 42.1 | 67 |
| 1975 | Ray Guy, Oakland, AFC | 68 | 43.8 | 64 |
|  | Herman Weaver, Detroit, NFC | 80 | 42.0 | 61 |
| 1974 | Ray Guy, Oakland, AFC | 74 | 42.2 | 66 |
|  | Tom Blanchard, New Orleans, NFC | 88 | 42.1 | 71 |
| 1973 | Jerrel Wilson, Kansas City, AFC | 80 | 45.5 | 68 |
|  | *Tom Wittum, San Francisco, NFC | 79 | 43.7 | 62 |
| 1972 | Jerrel Wilson, Kansas City, AFC | 66 | 44.8 | 69 |
|  | Dave Chapple, Los Angeles, NFC | 53 | 44.2 | 70 |
| 1971 | Dave Lewis, Cincinnati, AFC | 72 | 44.8 | 56 |
|  | Tom McNeill, Philadelphia, NFC | 73 | 42.0 | 64 |
| 1970 | *Dave Lewis, Cincinnati, AFC | 79 | 46.2 | 63 |
|  | *Julian Fagan, New Orleans, NFC | 77 | 42.5 | 64 |
| 1969 | David Lee, Baltimore, NFL | 57 | 45.3 | 66 |
|  | Dennis Partee, San Diego, AFL | 71 | 44.6 | 62 |
| 1968 | Jerrel Wilson, Kansas City, AFL | 63 | 45.1 | 70 |
|  | Billy Lothridge, Atlanta, NFL | 75 | 44.3 | 70 |
| 1967 | Bob Scarpitto, Denver, AFL | 105 | 44.9 | 73 |
|  | Billy Lothridge, Atlanta, NFL | 87 | 43.7 | 62 |
| 1966 | Bob Scarpitto, Denver, AFL | 76 | 45.8 | 70 |
|  | *David Lee, Baltimore, NFL | 49 | 45.6 | 64 |
| 1965 | Gary Collins, Cleveland, NFL | 65 | 46.7 | 71 |
|  | Jerrel Wilson, Kansas City, AFL | 69 | 45.4 | 64 |
| 1964 | *Bobby Walden, Minnesota, NFL | 72 | 46.4 | 73 |
|  | Jim Fraser, Denver, AFL | 73 | 44.2 | 67 |
| 1963 | Yale Lary, Detroit, NFL | 35 | 48.9 | 73 |
|  | Jim Fraser, Denver, AFL | 81 | 44.4 | 66 |
| 1962 | Tommy Davis, San Francisco, NFL | 48 | 45.6 | 82 |
|  | Jim Fraser, Denver, AFL | 55 | 43.6 | 75 |
| 1961 | Yale Lary, Detroit, NFL | 52 | 48.4 | 71 |
|  | Billy Atkins, Buffalo, AFL | 85 | 44.5 | 70 |
| 1960 | Jerry Norton, St. Louis, NFL | 39 | 45.6 | 62 |
|  | *Paul Maguire, L.A. Chargers, AFL | 43 | 40.5 | 61 |
| 1959 | Yale Lary, Detroit | 45 | 47.1 | 67 |
| 1958 | Sam Baker, Washington | 48 | 45.4 | 64 |
| 1957 | Don Chandler, N.Y. Giants | 60 | 44.6 | 61 |
| 1956 | Norm Van Brocklin, Los Angeles | 48 | 43.1 | 72 |
| 1955 | Norm Van Brocklin, Los Angeles | 60 | 44.6 | 61 |
| 1954 | Pat Brady, Pittsburgh | 66 | 43.2 | 72 |
| 1953 | Pat Brady, Pittsburgh | 80 | 46.9 | 64 |
| 1952 | Horace Gillom, Cleveland | 61 | 45.7 | 73 |
| 1951 | Horace Gillom, Cleveland | 73 | 45.5 | 66 |
| 1950 | *Fred (Curly) Morrison, Chi. Bears | 57 | 43.3 | 65 |
| 1949 | *Mike Boyda, N.Y. Bulldogs | 56 | 44.2 | 61 |
| 1948 | Joe Muha, Philadelphia | 57 | 47.3 | 82 |
| 1947 | Jack Jacobs, Green Bay | 57 | 43.5 | 74 |
| 1946 | Roy McKay, Green Bay | 64 | 42.7 | 64 |
| 1945 | Roy McKay, Green Bay | 44 | 41.2 | 73 |
| 1944 | Frank Sinkwich, Detroit | 45 | 41.0 | 73 |
| 1943 | Sammy Baugh, Washington | 50 | 45.9 | 81 |
| 1942 | Sammy Baugh, Washington | 37 | 48.2 | 74 |
| 1941 | Sammy Baugh, Washington | 30 | 48.7 | 75 |
| 1940 | Sammy Baugh, Washington | 35 | 51.4 | 85 |
| 1939 | *Parker Hall, Cleveland | 58 | 40.8 | 80 |

*First year in the league.

## ANNUAL PUNT RETURN LEADERS

| Year | Player, Team | No. | Yards | Avg. | Long | TD |
|---|---|---|---|---|---|---|
| 1983 | *Henry Ellard, L.A. Rams, NFC | 16 | 217 | 13.6 | 72 | 1 |
|  | Kirk Springs, N.Y. Jets, AFC | 23 | 287 | 12.5 | 76 | 1 |
| 1982 | Rick Upchurch, Denver, AFC | 15 | 242 | 16.1 | 78 | 2 |
|  | Billy Johnson, Atlanta, NFC | 24 | 273 | 11.4 | 71 | 0 |
| 1981 | LeRoy Irvin, Los Angeles, NFC | 46 | 615 | 13.4 | 84 | 3 |
|  | *James Brooks, San Diego, AFC | 22 | 290 | 13.2 | 42 | 0 |
| 1980 | J. T. Smith, Kansas City, AFC | 40 | 581 | 14.5 | 75 | 2 |
|  | *Kenny Johnson, Atlanta, NFC | 23 | 281 | 12.2 | 56 | 0 |
| 1979 | John Sciarra, Philadelphia, NFC | 16 | 182 | 11.4 | 38 | 0 |
|  | *Tony Nathan, Miami, AFC | 28 | 306 | 10.9 | 86 | 1 |
| 1978 | Rick Upchurch, Denver, AFC | 36 | 493 | 13.7 | 75 | 1 |
|  | Jackie Wallace, Los Angeles, NFC | 52 | 618 | 11.9 | 58 | 0 |
| 1977 | Billy Johnson, Houston, AFC | 35 | 539 | 15.4 | 87 | 2 |
|  | Larry Marshall, Philadelphia, NFC | 46 | 489 | 10.6 | 48 | 0 |
| 1976 | Rick Upchurch, Denver, AFC | 39 | 536 | 13.7 | 92 | 4 |
|  | Eddie Brown, Washington, NFC | 48 | 646 | 13.5 | 71 | 1 |
| 1975 | Billy Johnson, Houston, AFC | 40 | 612 | 15.3 | 83 | 3 |
|  | Terry Metcalf, St. Louis, NFC | 23 | 285 | 12.4 | 69 | 1 |
| 1974 | Lemar Parrish, Cincinnati, AFC | 18 | 338 | 18.8 | 90 | 2 |

| | | | | | | |
|---|---|---|---|---|---|---|
| | Dick Jauron, Detroit, NFC | 17 | 286 | 16.8 | 58 | 0 |
| 1973 | Bruce Taylor, San Francisco, NFC | 15 | 207 | 13.8 | 61 | 0 |
| | Ron Smith, San Diego, AFC | 27 | 352 | 13.0 | 84 | 2 |
| 1972 | *Ken Ellis, Green Bay, NFC | 14 | 215 | 15.4 | 80 | 1 |
| | Chris Farasopoulos, N.Y. Jets, AFC | 17 | 179 | 10.5 | 65 | 1 |
| 1971 | Les (Speedy) Duncan, Washington, NFC | 22 | 233 | 10.6 | 33 | 0 |
| | Leroy Kelly, Cleveland, AFC | 30 | 292 | 9.7 | 74 | 0 |
| 1970 | Ed Podolak, Kansas City, AFC | 23 | 311 | 13.5 | 60 | 0 |
| | *Bruce Taylor, San Francisco, NFC | 43 | 516 | 12.0 | 76 | 0 |
| 1969 | Alvin Haymond, Los Angeles, NFL | 33 | 435 | 13.2 | 52 | 0 |
| | *Bill Thompson, Denver, AFL | 25 | 288 | 11.5 | 40 | 0 |
| 1968 | Bob Hayes, Dallas, NFL | 15 | 312 | 20.8 | 90 | 2 |
| | Noland Smith, Kansas City, AFL | 18 | 270 | 15.0 | 80 | 1 |
| 1967 | Floyd Little, Denver, AFL | 16 | 270 | 16.9 | 72 | 1 |
| | Ben Davis, Cleveland, NFL | 18 | 229 | 12.7 | 52 | 1 |
| 1966 | Les (Speedy) Duncan, San Diego, AFL | 18 | 238 | 13.2 | 81 | 1 |
| | Johnny Roland, St. Louis, NFL | 20 | 221 | 11.1 | 86 | 1 |
| 1965 | Leroy Kelly, Cleveland, NFL | 17 | 265 | 15.6 | 67 | 2 |
| | Les (Speedy) Duncan, San Diego, AFL | 30 | 464 | 15.5 | 66 | 2 |
| 1964 | Bobby Jancik, Houston, AFL | 12 | 220 | 18.3 | 82 | 1 |
| | Tommy Watkins, Detroit, NFL | 16 | 238 | 14.9 | 68 | 2 |
| 1963 | Dick James, Washington, NFL | 16 | 214 | 13.4 | 39 | 0 |
| | Claude (Hoot) Gibson, Oakland, AFL | 26 | 307 | 11.8 | 85 | 2 |
| 1962 | Dick Christy, N.Y. Titans, AFL | 15 | 250 | 16.7 | 73 | 2 |
| | Pat Studstill, Detroit, NFL | 29 | 457 | 15.8 | 44 | 0 |
| 1961 | Dick Christy, N.Y. Titans, AFL | 18 | 383 | 21.3 | 70 | 2 |
| | Willie Wood, Green Bay, NFL | 14 | 225 | 16.1 | 72 | 2 |
| 1960 | *Abner Haynes, Dall. Texans, AFL | 14 | 215 | 15.4 | 46 | 0 |
| | Abe Woodson, San Francisco, NFL | 13 | 174 | 13.4 | 48 | 0 |
| 1959 | Johnny Morris, Chi. Bears | 14 | 171 | 12.2 | 78 | 1 |
| 1958 | Jon Arnett, Los Angeles | 18 | 223 | 12.4 | 58 | 0 |
| 1957 | Bert Zagers, Washington | 14 | 217 | 15.5 | 76 | 2 |
| 1956 | Ken Konz, Cleveland | 13 | 187 | 14.4 | 65 | 1 |
| 1955 | Ollie Matson, Chi. Cardinals | 13 | 245 | 18.8 | 78 | 2 |
| 1954 | *Veryl Switzer, Green Bay | 24 | 306 | 12.8 | 93 | 1 |
| 1953 | Charley Trippi, Chi. Cardinals | 21 | 239 | 11.4 | 38 | 0 |
| 1952 | Jack Christiansen, Detroit | 15 | 322 | 21.5 | 79 | 2 |
| 1951 | Claude (Buddy) Young, N.Y. Yanks | 12 | 231 | 19.3 | 79 | 1 |
| 1950 | *Herb Rich, Baltimore | 12 | 276 | 23.0 | 86 | 1 |
| 1949 | Verda (Vitamin T) Smith, Los Angeles | 27 | 427 | 15.8 | 85 | 1 |
| 1948 | George McAfee, Chi. Bears | 30 | 417 | 13.9 | 60 | 1 |
| 1947 | *Walt Slater, Pittsburgh | 28 | 435 | 15.5 | 33 | 0 |
| 1946 | Bill Dudley, Pittsburgh | 27 | 385 | 14.3 | 52 | 0 |
| 1945 | *Dave Ryan, Detroit | 15 | 220 | 14.7 | 56 | 0 |
| 1944 | *Steve Van Buren, Philadelphia | 15 | 230 | 15.3 | 55 | 1 |
| 1943 | Andy Farkas, Washington | 15 | 168 | 11.2 | 33 | 0 |
| 1942 | Merlyn Condit, Brooklyn | 21 | 210 | 10.0 | 23 | 0 |
| 1941 | Byron (Whizzer) White, Detroit | 19 | 262 | 13.8 | 64 | 0 |

**First year in the league.*

## ANNUAL KICKOFF RETURN LEADERS

| Year | Player, Team | No. | Yards | Avg. | Long | TD |
|---|---|---|---|---|---|---|
| 1983 | Fulton Walker, Miami, AFC | 36 | 962 | 26.7 | 78 | 0 |
| | Darrin Nelson, Minnesota, NFC | 18 | 445 | 24.7 | 50 | 0 |
| 1982 | *Mike Mosley, Buffalo, AFC | 18 | 487 | 27.1 | 66 | 0 |
| | Alvin Hall, Detroit, NFC | 16 | 426 | 26.6 | 96 | 1 |
| 1981 | Mike Nelms, Washington, NFC | 37 | 1,099 | 29.7 | 84 | 0 |
| | Carl Roaches, Houston, AFC | 28 | 769 | 27.5 | 96 | 1 |
| 1980 | Horace Ivory, New England, AFC | 36 | 992 | 27.6 | 98 | 1 |
| | Rich Mauti, New Orleans, NFC | 31 | 798 | 25.7 | 52 | 0 |
| 1979 | Larry Brunson, Oakland, AFC | 17 | 441 | 25.9 | 89 | 0 |
| | *Jimmy Edwards, Minnesota, NFC | 44 | 1,103 | 25.1 | 83 | 0 |
| 1978 | Steve Odom, Green Bay, NFC | 25 | 677 | 27.1 | 95 | 1 |
| | *Keith Wright, Cleveland, AFC | 30 | 789 | 26.3 | 86 | 0 |
| 1977 | *Raymond Clayborn, New England, AFC | 28 | 869 | 31.0 | 101 | 3 |
| | *Wilbert Montgomery, Philadelphia, NFC | 23 | 619 | 26.9 | 99 | 1 |
| 1976 | *Duriel Harris, Miami, AFC | 17 | 559 | 32.9 | 69 | 0 |
| | Cullen Bryant, Los Angeles, NFC | 16 | 459 | 28.7 | 90 | 1 |
| 1975 | *Walter Payton, Chicago, NFC | 14 | 444 | 31.7 | 70 | 0 |
| | Harold Hart, Oakland, AFC | 17 | 518 | 30.5 | 102 | 1 |
| 1974 | Terry Metcalf, St. Louis, NFC | 20 | 623 | 31.2 | 94 | 1 |
| | Greg Pruitt, Cleveland, AFC | 22 | 606 | 27.5 | 88 | 1 |
| 1973 | Carl Garrett, Chicago, NFC | 16 | 486 | 30.4 | 67 | 0 |
| | *Wallace Francis, Buffalo, AFC | 23 | 687 | 29.9 | 101 | 2 |
| 1972 | Ron Smith, Chicago, NFC | 30 | 924 | 30.8 | 94 | 1 |
| | *Bruce Laird, Baltimore, AFC | 29 | 843 | 29.1 | 73 | 0 |
| 1971 | Travis Williams, Los Angeles, NFC | 25 | 743 | 29.7 | 105 | 1 |
| | Eugene (Mercury) Morris, Miami, AFC | 15 | 423 | 28.2 | 94 | 1 |
| 1970 | Jim Duncan, Baltimore, AFC | 20 | 707 | 35.4 | 99 | 1 |
| | Cecil Turner, Chicago, NFC | 23 | 752 | 32.7 | 96 | 4 |
| 1969 | Bobby Williams, Detroit, NFL | 17 | 563 | 33.1 | 96 | 1 |
| | *Bill Thompson, Denver, AFL | 18 | 513 | 28.5 | 63 | 0 |
| 1968 | Preston Pearson, Baltimore, NFL | 15 | 527 | 35.1 | 102 | 2 |
| | *George Atkinson, Oakland, AFL | 32 | 802 | 25.1 | 60 | 0 |
| 1967 | *Travis Williams, Green Bay, NFL | 18 | 739 | 41.1 | 104 | 4 |
| | *Zeke Moore, Houston, AFL | 14 | 405 | 28.9 | 92 | 1 |
| 1966 | Gale Sayers, Chicago, NFL | 23 | 718 | 31.2 | 93 | 2 |
| | *Goldie Sellers, Denver, AFL | 19 | 541 | 28.5 | 100 | 2 |
| 1965 | Tommy Watkins, Detroit, NFL | 17 | 584 | 34.4 | 94 | 0 |
| | Abner Haynes, Denver, AFL | 34 | 901 | 26.5 | 60 | 0 |
| 1964 | *Clarence Childs, N.Y. Giants, NFL | 34 | 987 | 29.0 | 100 | 1 |
| | Bo Robertson, Oakland, AFL | 36 | 975 | 27.1 | 59 | 0 |
| 1963 | Abe Woodson, San Francisco, NFL | 29 | 935 | 32.2 | 103 | 3 |
| | Bobby Jancik, Houston, AFL | 45 | 1,317 | 29.3 | 53 | 0 |
| 1962 | Abe Woodson, San Francisco, NFL | 37 | 1,157 | 31.3 | 79 | 0 |
| | *Bobby Jancik, Houston, AFL | 24 | 826 | 30.3 | 61 | 0 |
| 1961 | Dick Bass, Los Angeles, NFL | 23 | 698 | 30.3 | 64 | 0 |
| | *Dave Grayson, Dall. Texans, AFL | 16 | 453 | 28.3 | 73 | 0 |
| 1960 | *Tom Moore, Green Bay, NFL | 12 | 397 | 33.1 | 84 | 0 |
| | Ken Hall, Houston, AFL | 19 | 594 | 31.3 | 104 | 1 |
| 1959 | Abe Woodson, San Francisco | 13 | 382 | 29.4 | 105 | 1 |
| 1958 | Ollie Matson, Chi. Cardinals | 14 | 497 | 35.5 | 101 | 2 |
| 1957 | *Jon Arnett, Los Angeles | 18 | 504 | 28.0 | 98 | 1 |
| 1956 | *Tom Wilson, Los Angeles | 15 | 477 | 31.8 | 103 | 1 |
| 1955 | Al Carmichael, Green Bay | 14 | 418 | 29.9 | 100 | 1 |
| 1954 | Billy Reynolds, Cleveland | 14 | 413 | 29.5 | 51 | 0 |
| 1953 | Joe Arenas, San Francisco | 16 | 551 | 34.4 | 82 | 0 |
| 1952 | Lynn Chandnois, Pittsburgh | 17 | 599 | 35.2 | 93 | 2 |
| 1951 | Lynn Chandnois, Pittsburgh | 12 | 390 | 32.5 | 55 | 0 |
| 1950 | Verda (Vitamin T) Smith, Los Angeles | 22 | 742 | 33.7 | 97 | 3 |
| 1949 | *Don Doll, Detroit | 21 | 536 | 25.5 | 56 | 0 |
| 1948 | *Joe Scott, N.Y. Giants | 20 | 569 | 28.5 | 99 | 1 |
| 1947 | Eddie Saenz, Washington | 29 | 797 | 27.5 | 94 | 2 |
| 1946 | Abe Karnofsky, Boston | 21 | 599 | 28.5 | 97 | 1 |
| 1945 | Steve Van Buren, Philadelphia | 13 | 373 | 28.7 | 98 | 1 |
| 1944 | Bob Thurbon, Card.-Pitt. | 12 | 291 | 24.3 | 55 | 0 |
| 1943 | Ken Heineman, Brooklyn | 16 | 444 | 27.8 | 69 | 0 |
| 1942 | Marshall Goldberg, Chi. Cardinals | 15 | 393 | 26.2 | 95 | 1 |
| 1941 | Marshall Goldberg, Chi. Cardinals | 12 | 290 | 24.2 | 41 | 0 |

**First year in the league.*

## POINTS SCORED — TEAM

| Year | Team | Points |
|---|---|---|
| 1983 | Washington, NFC | 541 |
| | L.A. Raiders, AFC | 442 |
| 1982 | San Diego, AFC | 288 |
| | Dallas, NFC | 226 |
| | Green Bay, NFC | 226 |
| 1981 | San Diego, AFC | 478 |
| | Atlanta, NFC | 426 |
| 1980 | Dallas, NFC | 454 |
| | New England, AFC | 441 |
| 1979 | Pittsburgh, AFC | 416 |
| | Dallas, NFC | 371 |
| 1978 | Dallas, NFC | 384 |
| | Miami, AFC | 372 |
| 1977 | Oakland, AFC | 351 |
| | Dallas, NFC | 345 |
| 1976 | Baltimore, AFC | 417 |
| | Los Angeles, NFC | 351 |
| 1975 | Buffalo, AFC | 420 |
| | Minnesota, NFC | 377 |
| 1974 | Oakland, AFC | 355 |
| | Washington, NFC | 320 |
| 1973 | Los Angeles, NFC | 388 |
| | Denver, AFC | 354 |
| 1972 | Miami, AFC | 385 |
| | San Francisco, NFC | 353 |
| 1971 | Dallas, NFC | 406 |
| | Oakland, AFC | 344 |
| 1970 | San Francisco, NFC | 352 |
| | Baltimore, AFC | 321 |
| 1969 | Minnesota, NFL | 379 |
| | Oakland, AFL | 377 |
| 1968 | Oakland, AFL | 453 |
| | Dallas, NFL | 431 |
| 1967 | Oakland, AFL | 468 |
| | Los Angeles, NFL | 398 |
| 1966 | Kansas City, AFL | 448 |
| | Dallas, NFL | 445 |
| 1965 | San Francisco, NFL | 421 |
| | San Diego, AFL | 340 |
| 1964 | Baltimore, NFL | 428 |
| | Buffalo, AFL | 400 |
| 1963 | N.Y. Giants, NFL | 448 |
| | San Diego, AFL | 399 |
| 1962 | Green Bay, NFL | 415 |
| | Dall. Texans, AFL | 389 |
| 1961 | Houston, AFL | 513 |
| | Green Bay, NFL | 391 |
| 1960 | N.Y. Titans, AFL | 382 |
| | Cleveland, NFL | 362 |
| 1959 | Baltimore | 374 |
| 1958 | Baltimore | 381 |
| 1957 | Los Angeles | 307 |
| 1956 | Chi. Bears | 363 |
| 1955 | Cleveland | 349 |
| 1954 | Detroit | 337 |
| 1953 | San Francisco | 372 |
| 1952 | Los Angeles | 349 |
| 1951 | Los Angeles | 392 |
| 1950 | Los Angeles | 466 |
| 1949 | Philadelphia | 364 |
| 1948 | Chi. Cardinals | 395 |
| 1947 | Chi. Bears | 363 |
| 1946 | Chi. Bears | 289 |
| 1945 | Philadelphia | 272 |
| 1944 | Philadelphia | 267 |
| 1943 | Chi. Bears | 303 |
| 1942 | Chi. Bears | 376 |
| 1941 | Chi. Bears | 396 |
| 1940 | Washington | 245 |
| 1939 | Chi. Bears | 298 |
| 1938 | Green Bay | 223 |
| 1937 | Green Bay | 220 |
| 1936 | Green Bay | 248 |
| 1935 | Chi. Bears | 192 |
| 1934 | Chi. Bears | 286 |
| 1933 | N.Y. Giants | 244 |
| 1932 | Green Bay | 152 |

## YARDS GAINED — TEAM

| Year | Team | Yards |
|---|---|---|
| 1983 | San Diego, AFC | 6,197 |
| | Green Bay, NFC | 6,172 |
| 1982 | San Diego, AFC | 4,048 |
| | San Francisco, NFC | 3,242 |
| 1981 | San Diego, AFC | 6,744 |
| | Detroit, NFC | 5,933 |
| 1980 | San Diego, AFC | 6,410 |
| | Los Angeles, NFC | 6,006 |
| 1979 | Pittsburgh, AFC | 6,258 |
| | Dallas, NFC | 5,968 |
| 1978 | New England, AFC | 5,965 |
| | Dallas, NFC | 5,959 |
| 1977 | Dallas, NFC | 4,812 |
| | Oakland, AFC | 4,736 |
| 1976 | Baltimore, AFC | 5,236 |
| | St. Louis, NFC | 5,136 |
| 1975 | Buffalo, AFC | 5,467 |
| | Dallas, NFC | 5,025 |
| 1974 | Dallas, NFC | 4,983 |
| | Oakland, AFC | 4,718 |
| 1973 | Los Angeles, NFC | 4,906 |
| | Oakland, AFC | 4,773 |
| 1972 | Miami, AFC | 5,036 |
| | N.Y. Giants, NFC | 4,483 |
| 1971 | Dallas, NFC | 5,035 |
| | San Diego, AFC | 4,738 |
| 1970 | Oakland, AFC | 4,829 |
| | San Francisco, NFC | 4,503 |
| 1969 | Dallas, NFL | 5,122 |
| | Oakland, AFL | 5,036 |
| 1968 | Oakland, AFL | 5,696 |
| | Dallas, NFL | 5,117 |
| 1967 | N.Y. Jets, AFL | 5,152 |
| | Baltimore, NFL | 5,008 |
| 1966 | Dallas, NFL | 5,145 |
| | Kansas City, AFL | 5,114 |
| 1965 | San Francisco, NFL | 5,270 |
| | San Diego, AFL | 5,188 |
| 1964 | Buffalo, AFL | 5,206 |
| | Baltimore, NFL | 4,779 |
| 1963 | San Diego, AFL | 5,153 |
| | N.Y. Giants, NFL | 5,024 |
| 1962 | N.Y. Giants, NFL | 5,005 |
| | Houston, AFL | 4,971 |
| 1961 | Houston, AFL | 6,288 |
| | Philadelphia, NFL | 5,112 |
| 1960 | Houston, AFL | 4,936 |
| | Baltimore, NFL | 4,245 |
| 1959 | Baltimore | 4,458 |
| 1958 | Baltimore | 4,539 |
| 1957 | Los Angeles | 4,143 |
| 1956 | Chi. Bears | 4,537 |
| 1955 | Chi. Bears | 4,316 |
| 1954 | Los Angeles | 5,187 |
| 1953 | Philadelphia | 4,811 |
| 1952 | Cleveland | 4,352 |
| 1951 | Los Angeles | 5,506 |
| 1950 | Los Angeles | 5,420 |
| 1949 | Chi. Bears | 4,873 |
| 1948 | Chi. Cardinals | 4,705 |
| 1947 | Chi. Bears | 5,053 |
| 1946 | Los Angeles | 3,793 |
| 1945 | Washington | 3,549 |
| 1944 | Chi. Bears | 3,239 |
| 1943 | Chi. Bears | 4,045 |
| 1942 | Chi. Bears | 3,900 |
| 1941 | Chi. Bears | 4,265 |
| 1940 | Green Bay | 3,400 |
| 1939 | Chi. Bears | 3,988 |
| 1938 | Green Bay | 3,037 |
| 1937 | Green Bay | 3,201 |
| 1936 | Detroit | 3,703 |
| 1935 | Chi. Bears | 3,454 |
| 1934 | Chi. Bears | 3,900 |
| 1933 | N.Y. Giants | 2,973 |
| 1932 | Chi. Bears | 2,755 |

## RUSHING

| Year | Team | Yards |
|---|---|---|
| 1983 | Chicago, NFC | 2,727 |
| | Baltimore, AFC | 2,695 |
| 1982 | Buffalo, AFC | 1,371 |
| | Dallas, NFC | 1,313 |
| 1981 | Detroit, NFC | 2,795 |
| | Kansas City, AFC | 2,633 |
| 1980 | Los Angeles, NFC | 2,799 |
| | Houston, AFC | 2,635 |
| 1979 | N.Y. Jets, AFC | 2,646 |

| Year | Team | |
|---|---|---|
| 1978 | St. Louis, NFC | 2,582 |
| | New England, AFC | 3,165 |
| 1977 | Dallas, NFC | 2,783 |
| | Chicago, NFC | 2,811 |
| 1976 | Oakland, AFC | 2,627 |
| | Pittsburgh, AFC | 2,971 |
| 1975 | Los Angeles, NFC | 2,528 |
| | Buffalo, AFC | 2,974 |
| 1974 | Dallas, NFC | 2,432 |
| | Dallas, NFC | 2,454 |
| | Pittsburgh, AFC | 2,417 |
| 1973 | Buffalo, AFC | 3,088 |
| | Los Angeles, NFC | 2,925 |
| 1972 | Miami, AFC | 2,960 |
| | Chicago, NFC | 2,360 |
| 1971 | Miami, AFC | 2,429 |
| | Detroit, NFC | 2,376 |
| 1970 | Dallas, NFC | 2,300 |
| | Miami, AFC | 2,082 |
| 1969 | Dallas, NFL | 2,276 |
| | Kansas City, AFL | 2,220 |
| 1968 | Chicago, NFL | 2,377 |
| | Kansas City, AFL | 2,227 |
| 1967 | Cleveland, NFL | 2,139 |
| | Houston, AFL | 2,122 |
| 1966 | Kansas City, AFL | 2,274 |
| | Cleveland, NFL | 2,166 |
| 1965 | Cleveland, NFL | 2,331 |
| | San Diego, AFL | 2,085 |
| 1964 | Green Bay, NFL | 2,276 |
| | Buffalo, AFL | 2,040 |
| 1963 | Cleveland, NFL | 2,639 |
| | San Diego, AFL | 2,203 |
| 1962 | Buffalo, AFL | 2,480 |
| | Green Bay, NFL | 2,460 |
| 1961 | Green Bay, NFL | 2,350 |
| | Dall. Texans, AFL | 2,189 |
| 1960 | St. Louis, NFL | 2,356 |
| | Oakland, AFL | 2,056 |
| 1959 | Cleveland | 2,149 |
| 1958 | Cleveland | 2,526 |
| 1957 | Los Angeles | 2,142 |
| 1956 | Chi. Bears | 2,468 |
| 1955 | Chi. Bears | 2,388 |
| 1954 | San Francisco | 2,498 |
| 1953 | San Francisco | 2,230 |
| 1952 | San Francisco | 1,905 |
| 1951 | Chi. Bears | 2,408 |
| 1950 | N.Y. Giants | 2,336 |
| 1949 | Philadelphia | 2,607 |
| 1948 | Chi. Cardinals | 2,560 |
| 1947 | Los Angeles | 2,171 |
| 1946 | Green Bay | 1,765 |
| 1945 | Cleveland | 1,714 |
| 1944 | Philadelphia | 1,661 |
| 1943 | Phil-Pitt | 1,730 |
| 1942 | Chi. Bears | 1,881 |
| 1941 | Chi. Bears | 2,263 |
| 1940 | Chi. Bears | 1,818 |
| 1939 | Chi. Bears | 2,043 |
| 1938 | Detroit | 1,893 |
| 1937 | Detroit | 2,074 |
| 1936 | Detroit | 2,885 |
| 1935 | Chi. Bears | 2,096 |
| 1934 | Chi. Bears | 2,847 |
| 1933 | Boston | 2,260 |
| 1932 | Chi. Bears | 1,770 |

## FEWEST POINTS ALLOWED

| Year | Team | Points |
|---|---|---|
| 1983 | Miami, AFC | 250 |
| | Detroit, NFC | 286 |
| 1982 | Washington, AFC | 128 |
| | Miami, AFC | 131 |
| 1981 | Philadelphia, NFC | 221 |
| | Miami, AFC | 275 |
| 1980 | Philadelphia, NFC | 222 |
| | Houston, AFC | 251 |
| 1979 | Tampa Bay, NFC | 237 |
| | San Diego, AFC | 246 |
| 1978 | Pittsburgh, AFC | 195 |
| | Dallas, NFC | 208 |
| 1977 | Atlanta, NFC | 129 |
| | Denver, AFC | 148 |
| 1976 | Pittsburgh, AFC | 138 |
| | Minnesota, NFC | 176 |
| 1975 | Los Angeles, NFC | 135 |
| | Pittsburgh, AFC | 162 |
| 1974 | Los Angeles, NFC | 181 |
| | Pittsburgh, AFC | 189 |
| 1973 | Miami, AFC | 150 |
| | Minnesota, NFC | 168 |
| 1972 | Miami, AFC | 171 |
| | Washington, NFC | 218 |
| 1971 | Minnesota, NFC | 139 |
| | Baltimore, AFC | 140 |
| 1970 | Minnesota, NFC | 143 |
| | Miami, AFC | 228 |
| 1969 | Minnesota, NFL | 133 |
| | Kansas City, AFL | 177 |
| 1968 | Baltimore, NFL | 144 |
| | Kansas City, AFL | 170 |
| 1967 | Los Angeles, NFL | 196 |
| | Houston, AFL | 199 |
| 1966 | Green Bay, NFL | 163 |
| | Buffalo, AFL | 255 |
| 1965 | Green Bay, NFL | 224 |
| | Buffalo, AFL | 226 |
| 1964 | Baltimore, NFL | 225 |
| | Buffalo, AFL | 242 |
| 1963 | Chicago, NFL | 144 |
| | San Diego, AFL | 255 |
| 1962 | Green Bay, NFL | 148 |
| | Dall. Texans, AFL | 233 |
| 1961 | San Diego, AFL | 219 |
| | New York Giants, NFL | 220 |
| 1960 | San Francisco, NFL | 205 |
| | Dall. Texans, AFL | 253 |
| 1959 | New York | 170 |
| 1958 | New York | 183 |
| 1957 | Cleveland | 172 |
| 1956 | Cleveland | 177 |
| 1955 | Cleveland | 218 |
| 1954 | Cleveland | 162 |
| 1953 | Cleveland | 162 |
| 1952 | Detroit | 192 |
| 1951 | Cleveland | 152 |
| 1950 | Philadelphia | 141 |
| 1949 | Philadelphia | 134 |
| 1948 | Chi. Bears | 151 |
| 1947 | Green Bay | 210 |
| 1946 | Pittsburgh | 117 |
| 1945 | Washington | 121 |
| 1944 | New York | 75 |
| 1943 | Washington | 137 |
| 1942 | Chi. Bears | 84 |
| 1941 | New York | 114 |
| 1940 | Brooklyn | 120 |
| 1939 | New York | 85 |
| 1938 | New York | 79 |
| 1937 | Chi. Bears | 100 |
| 1936 | Chi. Bears | 94 |
| 1935 | Green Bay | 96 |
| | New York | 96 |
| 1934 | Detroit | 59 |
| 1933 | Brooklyn | 54 |
| 1932 | Chi. Bears | 44 |

## FEWEST TOTAL YARDS ALLOWED

| Year | Team | Yards |
|---|---|---|
| 1983 | Cincinnati, AFC | 4,327 |
| | New Orleans, NFC | 4,691 |
| 1982 | Miami, AFC | 2,312 |
| | Tampa Bay, NFC | 2,442 |
| 1981 | Philadelphia, NFC | 4,447 |
| | N.Y. Jets, AFC | 4,871 |
| 1980 | Buffalo, AFC | 4,101 |
| | Philadelphia, NFC | 4,443 |
| 1979 | Tampa Bay, NFC | 3,949 |
| | Pittsburgh, AFC | 4,270 |
| 1978 | Los Angeles, NFC | 3,893 |
| | Pittsburgh, AFC | 4,168 |
| 1977 | Dallas, NFC | 3,213 |
| | New England, AFC | 3,638 |
| 1976 | Pittsburgh, AFC | 3,323 |
| | San Francisco, NFC | 3,562 |
| 1975 | Minnesota, NFC | 3,153 |
| | Oakland, AFC | 3,629 |
| 1974 | Pittsburgh, AFC | 3,074 |
| | Washington, NFC | 3,285 |
| 1973 | Los Angeles, NFC | 2,951 |
| | Oakland, AFC | 3,160 |
| 1972 | Miami, AFC | 3,297 |
| | Green Bay, NFC | 3,474 |
| 1971 | Baltimore, AFC | 2,852 |
| | Minnesota, NFC | 3,406 |
| 1970 | Minnesota, NFC | 2,803 |
| | N.Y. Jets, AFC | 3,655 |
| 1969 | Minnesota, NFL | 2,720 |
| | Kansas City, AFL | 3,163 |
| 1968 | Los Angeles, NFL | 3,118 |
| | N.Y. Jets, AFL | 3,363 |
| 1967 | Oakland, AFL | 3,294 |
| | Green Bay, NFL | 3,300 |
| 1966 | St. Louis, NFL | 3,492 |
| | Oakland, AFL | 3,910 |
| 1965 | San Diego, AFL | 3,262 |
| | Detroit, NFL | 3,557 |
| 1964 | Green Bay, NFL | 3,179 |
| | Buffalo, AFL | 3,878 |
| 1963 | Chicago, NFL | 3,176 |
| | Boston, AFL | 3,834 |
| 1962 | Detroit, NFL | 3,217 |
| | Dall. Texans, AFL | 3,951 |
| 1961 | San Diego, AFL | 3,726 |
| | Baltimore, NFL | 3,782 |
| 1960 | St. Louis, NFL | 3,029 |
| | Buffalo, AFL | 3,866 |
| 1959 | New York | 2,843 |
| 1958 | Chi. Bears | 3,066 |
| 1957 | Pittsburgh | 2,791 |
| 1956 | New York | 3,081 |
| 1955 | Cleveland | 2,841 |
| 1954 | Cleveland | 2,658 |
| 1953 | Philadelphia | 2,998 |
| 1952 | Cleveland | 3,075 |
| 1951 | New York | 3,250 |
| 1950 | Cleveland | 3,154 |
| 1949 | Philadelphia | 2,831 |
| 1948 | Chi. Bears | 2,931 |
| 1947 | Green Bay | 3,396 |
| 1946 | Washington | 2,451 |
| 1945 | Philadelphia | 2,073 |
| 1944 | Philadelphia | 1,943 |
| 1943 | Chi. Bears | 2,262 |
| 1942 | Chi. Bears | 1,703 |
| 1941 | New York | 2,368 |
| 1940 | New York | 2,219 |
| 1939 | Washington | 2,116 |
| 1938 | New York | 2,029 |
| 1937 | Washington | 2,123 |
| 1936 | Boston | 2,181 |
| 1935 | Boston | 1,996 |
| 1934 | Chi. Cardinals | 1,539 |
| 1933 | Brooklyn | 1,789 |

## FEWEST YARDS RUSHING ALLOWED

| Year | Team | Yards |
|---|---|---|
| 1983 | Washington, NFC | 1,289 |
| | Cincinnati, AFC | 1,499 |
| 1982 | Pittsburgh, AFC | 762 |
| | Detroit, NFC | 854 |
| 1981 | Detroit, NFC | 1,623 |
| | Kansas City, AFC | 1,747 |
| 1980 | Detroit, NFC | 1,599 |
| | Cincinnati, AFC | 1,680 |
| 1979 | Denver, AFC | 1,693 |
| | Tampa Bay, NFC | 1,873 |
| 1978 | Dallas, NFC | 1,721 |
| | Pittsburgh, AFC | 1,774 |
| 1977 | Denver, AFC | 1,531 |
| | Dallas, NFC | 1,651 |
| 1976 | Pittsburgh, AFC | 1,457 |
| | Los Angeles, NFC | 1,564 |
| 1975 | Minnesota, NFC | 1,532 |
| | Houston, AFC | 1,680 |
| 1974 | Los Angeles, NFC | 1,302 |
| | New England, AFC | 1,587 |
| 1973 | Los Angeles, NFC | 1,270 |
| | Oakland, AFC | 1,470 |
| 1972 | Dallas, NFC | 1,515 |
| | Miami, AFC | 1,548 |
| 1971 | Baltimore, AFC | 1,113 |
| | Dallas, NFC | 1,144 |
| 1970 | Detroit, NFC | 1,152 |
| | N.Y. Jets, AFC | 1,283 |
| 1969 | Dallas, NFL | 1,050 |
| | Kansas City, AFL | 1,091 |
| 1968 | Dallas, NFL | 1,195 |
| | N.Y. Jets, AFL | 1,195 |
| 1967 | Dallas, NFL | 1,081 |
| | Oakland, AFL | 1,129 |
| 1966 | Buffalo, AFL | 1,051 |
| | Dallas, NFL | 1,176 |
| 1965 | San Diego, AFL | 1,094 |
| | Los Angeles, NFL | 1,409 |
| 1964 | Buffalo, AFL | 913 |
| | Los Angeles, NFL | 1,501 |
| 1963 | Boston, AFL | 1,107 |
| | Chicago, NFL | 1,442 |
| 1962 | Detroit, NFL | 1,231 |
| | Dall. Texans, AFL | 1,250 |
| 1961 | Boston, AFL | 1,041 |
| | Pittsburgh, NFL | 1,463 |
| 1960 | St. Louis, NFL | 1,212 |
| | Dall. Texans, AFL | 1,338 |
| 1959 | New York | 1,261 |
| 1958 | Baltimore | 1,291 |
| 1957 | Baltimore | 1,174 |
| 1956 | New York | 1,443 |
| 1955 | Cleveland | 1,189 |
| 1954 | Cleveland | 1,050 |
| 1953 | Philadelphia | 1,117 |
| 1952 | Detroit | 1,145 |
| 1951 | New York | 913 |
| 1950 | Detroit | 1,367 |
| 1949 | Chi. Bears | 1,196 |
| 1948 | Philadelphia | 1,209 |
| 1947 | Philadelphia | 1,329 |
| 1946 | Chi. Bears | 1,060 |
| 1945 | Philadelphia | 817 |
| 1944 | Philadelphia | 558 |
| 1943 | Phil-Pitt | 793 |
| 1942 | Chi. Bears | 519 |
| 1941 | Washington | 1,042 |
| 1940 | New York | 977 |
| 1939 | Chi. Bears | 812 |
| 1938 | Detroit | 1,081 |
| 1937 | Chi. Bears | 933 |
| 1936 | Boston | 1,148 |
| 1935 | Boston | 998 |
| 1934 | Chi. Cardinals | 954 |
| 1933 | Brooklyn | 964 |

## FEWEST YARDS PASSING ALLOWED

Leadership in this category has been based on net yards since 1952.

| Year | Team | Yards |
|---|---|---|
| 1983 | New Orleans, NFC | 2,691 |
| | Cincinnati, AFC | 2,828 |
| 1982 | Miami, AFC | 1,027 |
| | Tampa Bay, NFC | 1,384 |
| 1981 | Philadelphia, NFC | 2,696 |
| | Buffalo, AFC | 2,870 |
| 1980 | Washington, NFC | 2,171 |
| | Buffalo, AFC | 2,282 |
| 1979 | Tampa Bay, NFC | 2,076 |
| | Buffalo, AFC | 2,530 |
| 1978 | Buffalo, AFC | 1,960 |
| | Los Angeles, NFC | 2,048 |
| 1977 | Atlanta, NFC | 1,384 |
| | San Diego, AFC | 1,725 |
| 1976 | Minnesota, NFC | 1,575 |
| | Cincinnati, AFC | 1,758 |
| 1975 | Minnesota, NFC | 1,621 |
| | Cincinnati, AFC | 1,729 |
| 1974 | Pittsburgh, AFC | 1,466 |
| | Atlanta, NFC | 1,572 |
| 1973 | Miami, AFC | 1,290 |
| | Atlanta, NFC | 1,430 |
| 1972 | Minnesota, NFC | 1,699 |
| | Cleveland, AFC | 1,736 |
| 1971 | Atlanta, NFC | 1,638 |
| | Baltimore, AFC | 1,739 |
| 1970 | Minnesota, NFC | 1,438 |
| | Kansas City, AFC | 2,010 |
| 1969 | Minnesota, NFL | 1,631 |
| | Kansas City, AFL | 2,072 |
| 1968 | Houston, AFL | 1,671 |
| | Green Bay, NFL | 1,796 |
| 1967 | Green Bay, NFL | 1,377 |
| | Buffalo, AFL | 1,825 |
| 1966 | Green Bay, NFL | 1,959 |
| | Oakland, AFL | 2,118 |
| 1965 | Green Bay, NFL | 1,981 |
| | San Diego, AFL | 2,168 |
| 1964 | Green Bay, NFL | 1,647 |
| | San Diego, AFL | 2,518 |
| 1963 | Chicago, NFL | 1,734 |
| | Oakland, AFL | 2,589 |
| 1962 | Green Bay, NFL | 1,746 |
| | Oakland, AFL | 2,306 |
| 1961 | Baltimore, NFL | 1,913 |
| | San Diego, AFL | 2,363 |
| 1960 | Chicago, NFL | 1,388 |
| | Buffalo, AFL | 2,124 |
| 1959 | New York | 1,582 |
| 1958 | Chi. Bears | 1,769 |
| 1957 | Cleveland | 1,300 |
| 1956 | Cleveland | 1,103 |
| 1955 | Pittsburgh | 1,295 |
| 1954 | Cleveland | 1,608 |
| 1953 | Washington | 1,751 |
| 1952 | Washington | 1,580 |
| 1951 | Pittsburgh | 1,687 |
| 1950 | Cleveland | 1,581 |
| 1949 | Philadelphia | 1,607 |
| 1948 | Green Bay | 1,626 |
| 1947 | Green Bay | 1,790 |
| 1946 | Pittsburgh | 939 |
| 1945 | Washington | 1,121 |
| 1944 | Chi. Bears | 1,052 |
| 1943 | Chi. Bears | 980 |
| 1942 | Washington | 1,093 |
| 1941 | Pittsburgh | 1,168 |
| 1940 | Philadelphia | 1,012 |
| 1939 | Washington | 1,116 |
| 1938 | Chi. Bears | 897 |
| 1937 | Detroit | 804 |
| 1936 | Philadelphia | 853 |
| 1935 | Chi. Cardinals | 793 |
| 1934 | Philadelphia | 545 |
| 1933 | Portsmouth | 558 |

Compiled by Elias Sports Bureau

| | | |
|---|---|---|
| 1967: Super Bowl I | 1973: Super Bowl VII | 1979: Super Bowl XIII |
| 1968: Super Bowl II | 1974: Super Bowl VIII | 1980: Super Bowl XIV |
| 1969: Super Bowl III | 1975: Super Bowl IX | 1981: Super Bowl XV |
| 1970: Super Bowl IV | 1976: Super Bowl X | 1982: Super Bowl XVI |
| 1971: Super Bowl V | 1977: Super Bowl XI | 1983: Super Bowl XVII |
| 1972: Super Bowl VI | 1978: Super Bowl XII | 1984: Super Bowl XVIII |

## INDIVIDUAL RECORDS

### SERVICE

**Most Games**
- 5 Marv Fleming, Green Bay, 1967-68; Miami, 1972-74
  Larry Cole, Dallas, 1971-72, 1976, 1978-79
  Cliff Harris, Dallas, 1971-72, 1976, 1978-79
  D.D. Lewis, Dallas, 1971-72, 1976, 1978-79
  Preston Pearson, Baltimore, 1969; Pittsburgh, 1975; Dallas, 1976, 1978-79
  Charlie Waters, Dallas, 1971-72, 1976, 1978-79
  Rayfield Wright, Dallas, 1971-72, 1976, 1978-79
- 4 By many players

**Most Games, Winning Team**
- 4 By many players

**Most Games, Coach**
- 5 Tom Landry, Dallas, 1971-72, 1976, 1978-79
  Don Shula, Baltimore, 1969; Miami, 1972-74, 1983
- 4 Bud Grant, Minnesota, 1970, 1974-75, 1977
  Chuck Noll, Pittsburgh, 1975-76, 1979-80
- 2 Vince Lombardi, Green Bay, 1967, 1968
  Hank Stram, Kansas City, 1967, 1970
  Joe Gibbs, Washington, 1983-84
  Tom Flores, Oakland, 1981; L.A. Raiders, 1984

**Most Games, Winning Team, Coach**
- 4 Chuck Noll, Pittsburgh, 1975-76, 1979-80
- 2 Vince Lombardi, Green Bay, 1967-68
  Tom Landry, Dallas, 1972, 1978
  Don Shula, Miami, 1973-74
  Tom Flores, Oakland, 1981; L.A. Raiders, 1984

### SCORING

**POINTS**

**Most Points, Career**
- 24 Franco Harris, Pittsburgh, 4 games (4-td)
- 20 Don Chandler, Green Bay, 2 games (8-pat, 4-fg)
- 18 John Stallworth, Pittsburgh, 4 games (3-td)
  Lynn Swann, Pittsburgh, 4 games (3-td)
  Cliff Branch, Oakland-L.A. Raiders, 3 games (3-td)

**Most Points, Game**
- 15 Don Chandler, Green Bay vs. Oakland, 1968 (3-pat, 4-fg)
- 14 Ray Wersching, San Francisco vs. Cincinnati, 1982 (2-pat, 4-fg)
- 12 By many players

**TOUCHDOWNS**

**Most Touchdowns, Career**
- 4 Franco Harris, Pittsburgh, 4 games (4-r)
- 3 John Stallworth, Pittsburgh, 4 games (3-p)
  Lynn Swann, Pittsburgh, 4 games (3-p)
  Cliff Branch, Oakland-L.A. Raiders, 3 games (3-p)
- 2 By many players

**Most Touchdowns, Game**
- 2 Max McGee, Green Bay vs. Kansas City, 1967 (2-p)
  Elijah Pitts, Green Bay vs. Kansas City, 1967 (2-r)
  Bill Miller, Oakland vs. Green Bay, 1968 (2-p)
  Larry Csonka, Miami vs. Minnesota, 1974 (2-r)
  Pete Banaszak, Oakland vs. Minnesota, 1977 (2-r)
  John Stallworth, Pittsburgh vs. Dallas, 1979 (2-p)
  Franco Harris, Pittsburgh vs. Los Angeles, 1980 (2-r)
  Cliff Branch, Oakland vs. Philadelphia, 1981 (2-p)
  Dan Ross, Cincinnati vs. San Francisco, 1982 (2-p)
  Marcus Allen, L.A. Raiders vs. Washington, 1984 (2-r)

**POINTS AFTER TOUCHDOWN**

**Most Points After Touchdown, Career**
- 8 Don Chandler, Green Bay, 2 games (8 att)
  Roy Gerela, Pittsburgh, 3 games (9 att)
  Chris Bahr, Oakland-L.A. Raiders, 2 games (8 att)
- 5 Garo Yepremian, Miami, 3 games (5 att)
- 4 By four players

**Most Points After Touchdown, Game**
- 5 Don Chandler, Green Bay vs. Kansas City, 1967 (5 att)
  Roy Gerela, Pittsburgh vs. Dallas, 1979 (5 att)
  Chris Bahr, L.A. Raiders vs. Washington, 1984 (5 att)
- 4 Rafael Septien, Dallas vs. Pittsburgh, 1979 (4 att)
  Matt Bahr, Pittsburgh vs. Los Angeles, 1980 (4 att)

**FIELD GOALS**

**Field Goals Attempted, Career**
- 7 Roy Gerela, Pittsburgh, 3 games
- 6 Jim Turner, N.Y. Jets-Denver, 2 games
- 5 Efren Herrera, Dallas, 1 game

**Most Field Goals Attempted, Game**
- 5 Jim Turner, N.Y. Jets vs. Baltimore, 1969
  Efren Herrera, Dallas vs. Denver, 1978
- 4 Don Chandler, Green Bay vs. Oakland, 1968
  Roy Gerela, Pittsburgh vs. Dallas, 1976
  Ray Wersching, San Francisco vs. Cincinnati, 1982

**Most Field Goals, Career**
- 4 Don Chandler, Green Bay, 2 games (4 att)
  Jim Turner, N.Y. Jets-Denver, 2 games (6 att)
  Ray Wersching, San Francisco, 1 game (4 att)

- 3 Mike Clark, Dallas, 2 games (3 att)
  Jan Stenerud, Kansas City, 1 game (3 att)
  Chris Bahr, Oakland-L.A. Raiders, 2 games (4 att)
  Mark Moseley, Washington, 2 games (4 att)

**Most Field Goals, Game**
- 4 Don Chandler, Green Bay vs. Oakland, 1968
  Ray Wersching, San Francisco vs. Cincinnati, 1982
- 3 Jim Turner, N.Y. Jets vs. Baltimore, 1969
  Jan Stenerud, Kansas City vs. Minnesota, 1970

**Longest Field Goal**
- 48 Jan Stenerud, Kansas City vs. Minnesota, 1970
- 47 Jim Turner, Denver vs. Dallas, 1978
- 46 Chris Bahr, Oakland vs. Philadelphia, 1981

**SAFETIES**

**Most Safeties, Game**
- 1 Dwight White, Pittsburgh vs. Minnesota, 1975
  Reggie Harrison, Pittsburgh vs. Dallas, 1976

### RUSHING

**ATTEMPTS**

**Most Attempts, Career**
- 101 Franco Harris, Pittsburgh, 4 games
- 64 John Riggins, Washington, 2 games
- 57 Larry Csonka, Miami, 3 games

**Most Attempts, Game**
- 38 John Riggins, Washington vs. Miami, 1983
- 34 Franco Harris, Pittsburgh vs. Minnesota, 1975
- 33 Larry Csonka, Miami vs. Minnesota, 1974

**YARDS GAINED**

**Most Yards Gained, Career**
- 354 Franco Harris, Pittsburgh, 4 games
- 297 Larry Csonka, Miami, 3 games
- 230 John Riggins, Washington, 2 games

**Most Yards Gained, Game**
- 191 Marcus Allen, L.A. Raiders vs. Washington, 1984
- 166 John Riggins, Washington vs. Miami, 1983
- 158 Franco Harris, Pittsburgh vs. Minnesota, 1975

**Longest Run From Scrimmage**
- 74 Marcus Allen, L.A. Raiders vs. Washington, 1984 (TD)
- 58 Tom Matte, Baltimore vs. N.Y. Jets, 1969
- 49 Larry Csonka, Miami vs. Washington, 1973

**AVERAGE GAIN**

**Highest Average Gain, Career (20 attempts)**
- 9.6 Marcus Allen, L.A. Raiders, 1 game (20-191)
- 5.3 Walt Garrison, Dallas, 2 games (26-139)
- 5.2 Tony Dorsett, Dallas, 2 games (31-162)

**Highest Average Gain, Game (10 attempts)**
- 10.5 Tom Matte, Baltimore vs. N.Y. Jets, 1969 (11-116)
- 9.6 Marcus Allen, L.A. Raiders vs. Washington, 1984 (20-191)
- 8.6 Clarence Davis, Oakland vs. Minnesota, 1977 (16-137)

**TOUCHDOWNS**

**Most Touchdowns, Career**
- 4 Franco Harris, Pittsburgh, 4 games
- 2 Elijah Pitts, Green Bay, 1 game
  Jim Kiick, Miami, 3 games
  Larry Csonka, Miami, 3 games
  Pete Banaszak, Oakland, 2 games
  Marcus Allen, L.A. Raiders, 1 game
  John Riggins, Washington, 2 games

**Most Touchdowns, Game**
- 2 Elijah Pitts, Green Bay vs. Kansas City, 1967
  Larry Csonka, Miami vs. Minnesota, 1974
  Pete Banaszak, Oakland vs. Minnesota, 1977
  Franco Harris, Pittsburgh vs. Los Angeles, 1980
  Marcus Allen, L.A. Raiders vs. Washington, 1984

### PASSING

**ATTEMPTS**

**Most Passes Attempted, Career**
- 98 Roger Staubach, Dallas, 4 games
- 89 Fran Tarkenton, Minnesota, 3 games
- 84 Terry Bradshaw, Pittsburgh, 4 games

**Most Passes Attempted, Game**
- 38 Ron Jaworski, Philadelphia vs. Oakland, 1981
- 35 Fran Tarkenton, Minnesota vs. Oakland, 1977
  Joe Theismann, Washington vs. L.A. Raiders, 1984
- 34 Daryle Lamonica, Oakland vs. Green Bay, 1968
  Ken Anderson, Cincinnati vs. San Francisco, 1982

**COMPLETIONS**

**Most Passes Completed, Career**
- 61 Roger Staubach, Dallas, 4 games
- 49 Terry Bradshaw, Pittsburgh, 4 games
- 46 Fran Tarkenton, Minnesota, 3 games

**Most Passes Completed, Game**
- 25 Ken Anderson, Cincinnati vs. San Francisco, 1982
- 18 Fran Tarkenton, Minnesota vs. Miami, 1974
  Ron Jaworski, Philadelphia vs. Oakland, 1981
- 17 By five players

**Most Consecutive Completions, Game**
- 8 Len Dawson, Kansas City vs. Green Bay, 1967
  Joe Theismann, Washington vs. Miami, 1983

## COMPLETION PERCENTAGE
**Highest Completion Percentage, Career (40 attempts)**
- 63.6 Len Dawson, Kansas City, 2 games (44-28)
- 63.4 Bob Griese, Miami, 3 games (41-26)
- 63.0 Jim Plunkett, Oakland-L.A. Raiders, 2 games (46-29)

**Highest Completion Percentage, Game (20 attempts)**
- 73.5 Ken Anderson, Cincinnati vs. San Francisco, 1982 (34-25)
- 69.6 Bart Starr, Green Bay vs. Kansas City, 1967 (23-16)
- 68.0 Roger Staubach, Dallas vs. Denver, 1978 (25-17)

## YARDS GAINED
**Most Yards Gained, Career**
- 932 Terry Bradshaw, Pittsburgh, 4 games
- 734 Roger Staubach, Dallas, 4 games
- 489 Fran Tarkenton, Minnesota, 3 games

**Most Yards Gained, Game**
- 318 Terry Bradshaw, Pittsburgh vs. Dallas, 1979
- 309 Terry Bradshaw, Pittsburgh vs. Los Angeles, 1980
- 300 Ken Anderson, Cincinnati vs. San Francisco, 1982

**Longest Pass Completion**
- 80 Jim Plunkett (to King), Oakland vs. Philadelphia, 1981 (TD)
- 76 David Woodley (to Cefalo), Miami vs. Washington, 1983 (TD)
- 75 John Unitas (to Mackey), Baltimore vs. Dallas, 1971 (TD)
  Terry Bradshaw (to Stallworth), Pittsburgh vs. Dallas, 1979 (TD)

## AVERAGE GAIN
**Highest Average Gain, Career (40 attempts)**
- 11.10 Terry Bradshaw, Pittsburgh, 4 games (84-932)
- 9.62 Bart Starr, Green Bay, 2 games (47-452)
- 9.41 Jim Plunkett, Oakland-L.A. Raiders, 2 games (46-433)

**Highest Average Gain, Game (20 attempts)**
- 14.71 Terry Bradshaw, Pittsburgh vs. Los Angeles, 1980 (21-309)
- 12.43 Jim Plunkett, Oakland vs. Philadelphia, 1981 (21-261)
- 10.87 Bart Starr, Green Bay vs. Kansas City, 1967 (23-250)

## TOUCHDOWNS
**Most Touchdown Passes, Career**
- 9 Terry Bradshaw, Pittsburgh, 4 games
- 8 Roger Staubach, Dallas, 4 games
- 4 Jim Plunkett, Oakland-L.A. Raiders, 2 games

**Most Touchdown Passes, Game**
- 4 Terry Bradshaw, Pittsburgh vs. Dallas, 1979
- 3 Roger Staubach, Dallas vs. Pittsburgh, 1979
  Jim Plunkett, Oakland vs. Philadelphia, 1981
- 2 By many players

## HAD INTERCEPTED
**Lowest Percentage, Passes Had Intercepted, Career (40 attempts)**
- 0.00 Jim Plunkett, Oakland-L.A. Raiders, 2 games (46-0)
- 2.13 Bart Starr, Green Bay, 2 games (47-1)
- 4.08 Roger Staubach, Dallas, 4 games (98-4)

**Most Attempts, Without Interception, Game**
- 28 Joe Namath, N.Y. Jets vs. Baltimore, 1969
- 25 Roger Staubach, Dallas vs. Denver, 1978
  Jim Plunkett, L.A. Raiders vs. Washington, 1984
- 24 Bart Starr, Green Bay vs. Oakland, 1968

**Most Passes Had Intercepted, Career**
- 7 Craig Morton, Dallas-Denver, 2 games
- 6 Fran Tarkenton, Minnesota, 3 games
- 4 Earl Morrall, Baltimore-Miami, 4 games
  Roger Staubach, Dallas, 4 games
  Terry Bradshaw, Pittsburgh, 4 games
  Joe Theismann, Washington, 2 games

**Most Passes Had Intercepted, Game**
- 4 Craig Morton, Denver vs. Dallas, 1978
- 3 By seven players

# PASS RECEIVING

## RECEPTIONS
**Most Receptions, Career**
- 16 Lynn Swann, Pittsburgh, 4 games
- 15 Chuck Foreman, Minnesota, 3 games
- 14 Cliff Branch, Oakland-L.A. Raiders, 3 games

**Most Receptions, Game**
- 11 Dan Ross, Cincinnati vs. San Francisco, 1982
- 8 George Sauer, N.Y. Jets vs. Baltimore, 1969
- 7 Max McGee, Green Bay vs. Kansas City, 1967
  John Henderson, Minnesota vs. Kansas City, 1970
  Lynn Swann, Pittsburgh vs. Dallas, 1979

## YARDS GAINED
**Most Yards Gained, Career**
- 364 Lynn Swann, Pittsburgh, 4 games
- 268 John Stallworth, Pittsburgh, 4 games
- 181 Cliff Branch, Oakland-L.A. Raiders, 3 games

**Most Yards Gained, Game**
- 161 Lynn Swann, Pittsburgh vs. Dallas, 1976
- 138 Max McGee, Green Bay vs. Kansas City, 1967
- 133 George Sauer, N.Y. Jets vs. Baltimore, 1969

**Longest Reception**
- 80 Kenny King (from Plunkett), Oakland vs. Philadelphia, 1981 (TD)
- 76 Jimmy Cefalo (from Woodley), Miami vs. Washington, 1983 (TD)
- 75 John Mackey (from Unitas), Baltimore vs. Dallas, 1971 (TD)
  John Stallworth (from Bradshaw), Pittsburgh vs. Dallas, 1979 (TD)

## AVERAGE GAIN
**Highest Average Gain, Career (8 receptions)**
- 24.4 John Stallworth, Pittsburgh, 4 games (11-268)
- 22.8 Lynn Swann, Pittsburgh, 4 games (16-364)
- 17.0 Charlie Brown, Washington, 2 games (9-153)

**Highest Average Gain, Game (3 receptions)**
- 40.33 John Stallworth, Pittsburgh vs. Los Angeles, 1980 (3-121)
- 40.25 Lynn Swann, Pittsburgh vs. Dallas, 1979 (4-161)

- 38.33 John Stallworth, Pittsburgh vs. Dallas, 1979 (3-115)

## TOUCHDOWNS
**Most Touchdowns, Career**
- 3 John Stallworth, Pittsburgh, 4 games
  Lynn Swann, Pittsburgh, 4 games
  Cliff Branch, Oakland-L.A. Raiders, 3 games
- 2 Max McGee, Green Bay, 2 games
  Bill Miller, Oakland, 1 game
  Butch Johnson, Dallas, 2 games
  Dan Ross, Cincinnati, 1 game

**Most Touchdowns, Game**
- 2 Max McGee, Green Bay vs. Kansas City, 1967
  Bill Miller, Oakland vs. Green Bay, 1968
  John Stallworth, Pittsburgh vs. Dallas, 1979
  Cliff Branch, Oakland vs. Philadelphia, 1981
  Dan Ross, Cincinnati vs. San Francisco, 1982

# INTERCEPTIONS BY
**Most Interceptions By, Career**
- 3 Chuck Howley, Dallas, 2 games
  Rod Martin, Oakland-L.A. Raiders, 2 games
- 2 Randy Beverly, N.Y. Jets, 1 game
  Jake Scott, Miami, 3 games
  Mike Wagner, Pittsburgh, 3 games
  Mel Blount, Pittsburgh, 4 games

**Most Interceptions By, Game**
- 3 Rod Martin, Oakland vs. Philadelphia, 1981
- 2 Randy Beverly, N.Y. Jets vs. Baltimore, 1969
  Chuck Howley, Dallas vs. Baltimore, 1971
  Jake Scott, Miami vs. Washington, 1973

## YARDS GAINED
**Most Yards Gained, Career**
- 75 Willie Brown, Oakland, 2 games
- 63 Chuck Howley, Dallas, 2 games
  Jake Scott, Miami, 3 games
- 60 Herb Adderley, Green Bay-Dallas, 4 games

**Most Yards Gained, Game**
- 75 Willie Brown, Oakland vs. Minnesota, 1977
- 63 Jake Scott, Miami vs. Washington, 1973
- 60 Herb Adderley, Green Bay vs. Oakland, 1968

**Longest Return**
- 75 Willie Brown, Oakland vs. Minnesota, 1977 (TD)
- 60 Herb Adderley, Green Bay vs. Oakland, 1968 (TD)
- 55 Jake Scott, Miami vs. Washington, 1973

## TOUCHDOWNS
**Most Touchdowns, Game**
- 1 Herb Adderley, Green Bay vs. Oakland, 1968
  Willie Brown, Oakland vs. Minnesota, 1977
  Jack Squirek, L.A. Raiders vs. Washington, 1984

# PUNTING
**Most Punts, Career**
- 17 Mike Eischeid, Oakland-Minnesota, 3 games
- 15 Larry Seiple, Miami, 3 games
- 14 Ron Widby, Dallas, 2 games
  Ray Guy, Oakland-L.A. Raiders, 3 games

**Most Punts, Game**
- 9 Ron Widby, Dallas vs. Baltimore, 1971
- 7 By seven players

**Longest Punt**
- 61 Jerrel Wilson, Kansas City vs. Green Bay, 1967
- 59 Jerrel Wilson, Kansas City vs. Minnesota, 1970
  Bobby Walden, Pittsburgh vs. Dallas, 1976
  Ken Clark, Los Angeles vs. Pittsburgh, 1980
- 57 Larry Seiple, Miami vs. Minnesota, 1974

## AVERAGE YARDAGE
**Highest Average, Punting, Career (10 punts)**
- 46.5 Jerrel Wilson, Kansas City, 2 games (11-151)
- 41.9 Ray Guy, Oakland-L.A. Raiders, 3 games (14-587)
- 41.3 Larry Seiple, Miami, 3 games (15-620)

**Highest Average, Punting, Game (4 punts)**
- 48.5 Jerrel Wilson, Kansas City vs. Minnesota, 1970 (4-194)
- 46.3 Jim Miller, San Francisco vs. Cincinnati, 1982 (4-185)
- 45.3 Jerrel Wilson, Kansas City vs. Green Bay, 1967 (7-317)

# PUNT RETURNS
**Most Punt Returns, Career**
- 6 Willie Wood, Green Bay, 2 games
  Jake Scott, Miami, 3 games
  Theo Bell, Pittsburgh, 2 games
  Mike Nelms, Washington, 1 game
- 4 By seven players

**Most Punt Returns, Game**
- 6 Mike Nelms, Washington vs. Miami, 1983
- 5 Willie Wood, Green Bay vs. Oakland, 1968
- 4 By six players

**Most Fair Catches, Game**
- 3 Ron Gardin, Baltimore vs. Dallas, 1971
  Golden Richards, Dallas vs. Pittsburgh, 1976
  Greg Pruitt, L.A. Raiders vs. Washington, 1984

## YARDS GAINED
**Most Yards Gained, Career**
- 52 Mike Nelms, Washington, 1 game
- 45 Jake Scott, Miami, 3 games
- 44 Theo Bell, Pittsburgh, 2 games

**Most Yards Gained, Game**
  52  Mike Nelms, Washington vs. Miami, 1983
  43  Neal Colzie, Oakland vs. Minnesota, 1977
  35  Willie Wood, Green Bay vs. Oakland, 1968
      Mike Fuller, Cincinnati vs. San Francisco, 1982
**Longest Return**
  34  Darrell Green, Washington vs. L.A. Raiders, 1984
  31  Willie Wood, Green Bay vs. Oakland, 1968
  25  Neal Colzie, Oakland vs. Minnesota, 1977

**AVERAGE YARDAGE**
**Highest Average, Career (4 returns)**
  10.8  Neal Colzie, Oakland, 1 game (4-43)
  8.8  Mike Fuller, Cincinnati, 1 game (4-35)
  8.7  Mike Nelms, Washington, 1 game (6-52)
**Highest Average, Game (3 returns)**
  11.3  Lynn Swann, Pittsburgh vs. Minnesota, 1975 (3-34)
  10.8  Neal Colzie, Oakland vs. Minnesota, 1977 (4-43)
  8.8  Mike Fuller, Cincinnati vs. San Francisco, 1982 (4-35)

**TOUCHDOWNS**
**Most Touchdowns, Game**
    None

# KICKOFF RETURNS

**Most Kickoff Returns, Career**
  8  Larry Anderson, Pittsburgh, 2 games
  7  Preston Pearson, Baltimore-Pittsburgh-Dallas, 5 games
  6  Eugene (Mercury) Morris, Miami, 3 games
**Most Kickoff Returns, Game**
  5  Larry Anderson, Pittsburgh vs. Los Angeles, 1980
     Billy Campfield, Philadelphia vs. Oakland, 1981
     David Verser, Cincinnati vs. San Francisco, 1982
     Alvin Garrett, Washington vs. L.A. Raiders, 1984
  4  By six players

**YARDS GAINED**
**Most Yards Gained, Career**
  207  Larry Anderson, Pittsburgh, 2 games
  190  Fulton Walker, Miami, 1 game
  123  Eugene (Mercury) Morris, Miami, 3 games
**Most Yards Gained, Game**
  190  Fulton Walker, Miami vs. Washington, 1983
  162  Larry Anderson, Pittsburgh vs. Los Angeles, 1980
  100  Alvin Garrett, Washington vs. L.A. Raiders, 1984
**Longest Return**
  98  Fulton Walker, Miami vs. Washington, 1983 (TD)
  67  Rick Upchurch, Denver vs. Dallas, 1978
  48  Thomas Henderson, Dallas vs. Pittsburgh, 1976 (lateral)

**AVERAGE YARDAGE**
**Highest Average, Career (4 returns)**
  47.5  Fulton Walker, Miami, 1 game (4-190)
  25.9  Larry Anderson, Pittsburgh, 2 games (8-207)
  22.5  Jim Duncan, Baltimore, 1 game (4-90)
**Highest Average, Game (3 returns)**
  47.5  Fulton Walker, Miami vs. Washington, 1983 (4-190)
  32.4  Larry Anderson, Pittsburgh vs. Los Angeles, 1980 (5-162)
  31.3  Rick Upchurch, Denver vs. Dallas, 1978 (3-94)

**TOUCHDOWNS**
**Most Touchdowns, Game**
  1  Fulton Walker, Miami vs. Washington, 1983

# FUMBLES

**Most Fumbles, Career**
  5  Roger Staubach, Dallas, 4 games
  3  Franco Harris, Pittsburgh, 4 games
     Terry Bradshaw, Pittsburgh, 4 games
  2  By five players
**Most Fumbles, Game**
  3  Roger Staubach, Dallas vs. Pittsburgh, 1976
  2  Franco Harris, Pittsburgh vs. Minnesota, 1975
     Butch Johnson, Dallas vs. Denver, 1978
     Terry Bradshaw, Pittsburgh vs. Dallas, 1979

**RECOVERIES**
**Most Fumbles Recovered, Career**
  2  Jake Scott, Miami, 3 games (1 own, 1 opp)
     Fran Tarkenton, Minnesota, 3 games (2 own)
     Franco Harris, Pittsburgh, 4 games (2 own)
     Roger Staubach, Dallas, 4 games (2 own)
     Bobby Walden, Pittsburgh, 2 games (2 own)
     John Fitzgerald, Dallas, 4 games (2 own)
     Randy Hughes, Dallas, 3 games (2 opp)
     Butch Johnson, Dallas, 2 games (2 own)
**Most Fumbles Recovered, Game**
  2  Jake Scott, Miami vs. Minnesota, 1974 (1 own, 1 opp)
     Roger Staubach, Dallas vs. Pittsburgh, 1976 (2 own)
     Randy Hughes, Dallas vs. Denver, 1978 (2 opp)
     Butch Johnson, Dallas vs. Denver, 1978 (2 own)

**YARDS GAINED**
**Most Yards Gained, Game**
  49  Mike Bass, Washington vs. Miami, 1973 (opp)
  37  Mike Hegman, Dallas vs. Pittsburgh, 1979 (opp)
  21  Randy Hughes, Dallas vs. Denver, 1978 (opp)
**Longest Return**
  49  Mike Bass, Washington vs. Miami, 1973 (TD)
  37  Mike Hegman, Dallas vs. Pittsburgh, 1979 (TD)
  19  Randy Hughes, Dallas vs. Denver, 1978

**TOUCHDOWNS**
**Most Touchdowns, Game**
  1  Mike Bass, Washington vs. Miami, 1973 (opp 49 yds)
     Mike Hegman, Dallas vs. Pittsburgh, 1979 (opp 37 yds)

# COMBINED NET YARDS GAINED

**ATTEMPTS**
**Most Attempts, Career**
  108  Franco Harris, Pittsburgh, 4 games
  66  John Riggins, Washington, 2 games
  60  Larry Csonka, Miami, 3 games
**Most Attempts, Game**
  39  John Riggins, Washington vs. Miami, 1983
  35  Franco Harris, Pittsburgh vs. Minnesota, 1975
  34  Matt Snell, N.Y. Jets vs. Baltimore, 1969

**YARDS GAINED**
**Most Yards Gained, Career**
  468  Franco Harris, Pittsburgh, 4 games
  391  Lynn Swann, Pittsburgh, 4 games
  314  Larry Csonka, Miami, 3 games
**Most Yards Gained, Game**
  209  Marcus Allen, L.A. Raiders vs. Washington, 1984
  190  Fulton Walker, Miami vs. Washington, 1983
  181  John Riggins, Washington vs. Miami, 1983

# TEAM RECORDS

## GAMES, VICTORIES, DEFEATS

**Most Games**
  5  Dallas, 1971-72, 1976, 1978-79
  4  Minnesota, 1970, 1974-75, 1977
     Pittsburgh, 1975-76, 1979-80
     Miami, 1972-74, 1983
     Oakland/L.A. Raiders, 1968, 1977, 1981, 1984
  3  Washington, 1973, 1983-84
**Most Consecutive Games**
  3  Miami, 1972-74
  2  Green Bay, 1967-68
     Dallas, 1971-72
     Minnesota, 1974-75
     Pittsburgh, 1975-76, 1979-80
     Washington, 1983-84
**Most Games Won**
  4  Pittsburgh, 1975-76, 1979-80
  3  Oakland/L.A. Raiders, 1977, 1981, 1984
  2  Green Bay, 1967-68
     Miami, 1973-74
     Dallas, 1972, 1978
**Most Consecutive Games Won**
  2  Green Bay, 1967-68
     Miami, 1973-74
     Pittsburgh, 1975-76, 1979-80
**Most Games Lost**
  4  Minnesota, 1970, 1974-75, 1977
  3  Dallas, 1971, 1976, 1979
  2  Miami, 1972, 1983
     Washington, 1973, 1984
**Most Consecutive Games Lost**
  2  Minnesota, 1974-75

## SCORING

**Most Points, Game**
  38  L.A. Raiders vs. Washington, 1984
  35  Green Bay vs. Kansas City, 1967
     Pittsburgh vs. Dallas, 1979
  33  Green Bay vs. Kansas City, 1967
**Fewest Points, Game**
  3  Miami vs. Dallas, 1972
  6  Minnesota vs. Pittsburgh, 1975
  7  By four teams
**Most Points, Both Teams, Game**
  66  Pittsburgh (35) vs. Dallas (31), 1979
  50  Pittsburgh (31) vs. Los Angeles (19), 1980
  47  Green Bay (33) vs. Oakland (14), 1968
     San Francisco (26) vs. Cincinnati (21), 1982
     L.A. Raiders (38) vs. Washington (9), 1984
**Fewest Points, Both Teams, Game**
  21  Washington (7) vs. Miami (14), 1973
  22  Minnesota (6) vs. Pittsburgh (16), 1975
  23  Baltimore (7) vs. N.Y. Jets (16), 1969
**Largest Margin of Victory, Game**
  29  L.A. Raiders vs. Washington, 1984 (38-9)
  25  Green Bay vs. Kansas City, 1967 (35-10)
  21  Dallas vs. Miami, 1972 (24-3)
**Most Points, Each Half**
 1st:  21  Pittsburgh vs. Dallas, 1979
         L.A. Raiders vs. Washington, 1984
 2nd:  21  Green Bay vs. Kansas City, 1967
         Pittsburgh vs. Los Angeles, 1980
         Cincinnati vs. San Francisco, 1982
**Most Points, Each Quarter**
 1st:  14  Miami vs. Minnesota, 1974
         Oakland vs. Philadelphia, 1981
 2nd:  16  Oakland vs. Minnesota, 1977
 3rd:  14  Green Bay vs. Kansas City, 1967
         L.A. Raiders vs. Washington, 1984
 4th:  14  Pittsburgh vs. Dallas, 1976; vs. Dallas, 1979; vs. Los Angeles, 1980
         Dallas vs. Pittsburgh, 1979
         Cincinnati vs. San Francisco, 1982
         Washington vs. Miami, 1983

**Most Points, Both Teams, Each Half**
1st: 35  Pittsburgh (21) vs. Dallas (14), 1979
2nd: 31  Dallas (17) vs. Pittsburgh (14), 1979
**Most Points, Both Teams, Each Quarter**
1st: 14  Miami (14) vs. Minnesota (0), 1974
          Dallas (7) vs. Pittsburgh (7), 1976, 1979
          Oakland (14) vs. Philadelphia (0), 1981
2nd: 21  Pittsburgh (14) vs. Dallas (7), 1979
3rd: 20  L.A. Raiders (14) vs. Washington (6), 1984
4th: 28  Dallas (14) vs. Pittsburgh (14), 1979

## TOUCHDOWNS
**Most Touchdowns, Game**
  5  Green Bay vs. Kansas City, 1967
     Pittsburgh vs. Dallas, 1979
     L.A. Raiders vs. Washington, 1984
  4  Oakland vs. Minnesota, 1977
     Dallas vs. Pittsburgh, 1979
     Pittsburgh vs. Los Angeles, 1980
  3  By many teams
**Fewest Touchdowns, Game**
  0  Miami vs. Dallas, 1972
  1  By 11 teams
**Most Touchdowns, Both Teams, Game**
  9  Pittsburgh (5) vs. Dallas (4), 1979
  6  Green Bay (5) vs. Kansas City (1), 1967
     Oakland (4) vs. Minnesota (2), 1977
     Pittsburgh (4) vs. Los Angeles (2), 1980
     L.A. Raiders (5) vs. Washington (1), 1984
**Fewest Touchdowns, Both Teams, Game**
  2  Baltimore (1) vs. N.Y. Jets (1), 1969
  3  In five games

## POINTS AFTER TOUCHDOWN
**Most Points After Touchdown, Game**
  5  Green Bay vs. Kansas City, 1967
     Pittsburgh vs. Dallas, 1979
     L.A. Raiders vs. Washington, 1984
  4  Dallas vs. Pittsburgh, 1979
     Pittsburgh vs. Los Angeles, 1980
**Most Points After Touchdown, Both Teams, Game**
  9  Pittsburgh (5) vs. Dallas (4), 1979
  6  Green Bay (5) vs. Kansas City (1), 1967
**Fewest Points After Touchdown, Both Teams, Game**
  2  Baltimore (1) vs. N.Y. Jets (1), 1969
     Baltimore (1) vs. Dallas (1), 1971
     Minnesota (0) vs. Pittsburgh (2), 1975

## FIELD GOALS
**Most Field Goals Attempted, Game**
  5  N.Y. Jets vs. Baltimore, 1969
     Dallas vs. Denver, 1978
  4  Green Bay vs. Oakland, 1968
     Pittsburgh vs. Dallas, 1976
     San Francisco vs. Cincinnati, 1982
**Most Field Goals Attempted, Both Teams, Game**
  7  N.Y. Jets (5) vs. Baltimore (2), 1969
  6  Dallas (5) vs. Denver (1), 1978
  5  Green Bay (4) vs. Oakland (1), 1968
     Pittsburgh (4) vs. Dallas (1), 1976
     Oakland (3) vs. Philadelphia (2), 1981
**Fewest Field Goals Attempted, Both Teams, Game**
  1  Minnesota (0) vs. Miami (1), 1974
  2  Green Bay (0) vs. Kansas City (2), 1967
     Miami (1) vs. Washington (1), 1973
     Dallas (1) vs. Pittsburgh (1), 1979
**Most Field Goals, Game**
  4  Green Bay vs. Oakland, 1968
     San Francisco vs. Cincinnati, 1982
  3  N.Y. Jets vs. Baltimore, 1969
     Kansas City vs. Minnesota, 1970
**Most Field Goals, Both Teams, Game**
  4  Green Bay (4) vs. Oakland (0), 1968
     San Francisco (4) vs. Cincinnati (0), 1982
  3  In seven games
**Fewest Field Goals, Both Teams, Game**
  0  Miami vs. Washington, 1973
     Pittsburgh vs. Minnesota, 1975
  1  Green Bay (0) vs. Kansas City (1), 1967
     Minnesota (0) vs. Miami (1), 1974
     Pittsburgh (0) vs. Dallas (1), 1979

## SAFETIES
**Most Safeties, Game**
  1  Pittsburgh vs. Minnesota, 1975; vs. Dallas, 1976

# FIRST DOWNS
**Most First Downs, Game**
 24  Cincinnati vs. San Francisco, 1982
    Washington vs. Miami, 1983
 23  Dallas vs. Miami, 1972
 21  By four teams
**Fewest First Downs, Game**
  9  Minnesota vs. Pittsburgh, 1975
    Miami vs. Washington, 1983
 10  Dallas vs. Baltimore, 1971
    Miami vs. Dallas, 1972
 11  Denver vs. Dallas, 1978
**Most First Downs, Both Teams, Game**
 44  Cincinnati (24) vs. San Francisco (20), 1982
 41  Oakland (21) vs. Minnesota (20), 1977
 39  N.Y. Jets (21) vs. Baltimore (18), 1969
    Dallas (20) vs. Pittsburgh (19), 1979

**Fewest First Downs, Both Teams, Game**
 24  Dallas (10) vs. Baltimore (14), 1971
 26  Minnesota (9) vs. Pittsburgh (17), 1975
 27  Pittsburgh (13) vs. Dallas (14), 1976

## RUSHING
**Most First Downs, Rushing, Game**
 15  Dallas vs. Miami, 1972
 14  Washington vs. Miami, 1983
 13  Miami vs. Minnesota, 1974
    Oakland vs. Minnesota, 1977
**Fewest First Downs, Rushing, Game**
  2  Minnesota vs. Kansas City, 1970; vs. Pittsburgh, 1975; vs. Oakland, 1977
    Pittsburgh vs. Dallas, 1979
  3  Miami vs. Dallas, 1972
    Philadelphia vs. Oakland, 1981
  4  Kansas City, vs. Green Bay, 1967
    Baltimore vs. Dallas, 1971
    Dallas vs. Baltimore, 1971
**Most First Downs, Rushing, Both Teams, Game**
 21  Washington (14) vs. Miami (7), 1983
 18  Dallas (15) vs. Miami (3), 1972
    Miami (13) vs. Minnesota (5), 1974
 17  N.Y. Jets (10) vs. Baltimore (7), 1969
**Fewest First Downs, Rushing, Both Teams, Game**
  8  Baltimore (4) vs. Dallas (4), 1971
    Pittsburgh (2) vs. Dallas (6), 1979
  9  Philadelphia (3) vs. Oakland (6), 1981
 10  Minnesota (2) vs. Kansas City (8), 1970

## PASSING
**Most First Downs, Passing, Game**
 15  Minnesota vs. Oakland, 1977
    Pittsburgh vs. Dallas, 1979
 14  Philadelphia vs. Oakland, 1981
 13  Dallas vs. Pittsburgh, 1979
    Cincinnati vs. San Francisco, 1982
**Fewest First Downs, Passing, Game**
  1  Denver vs. Dallas, 1978
  2  Miami vs. Washington, 1983
  4  Miami vs. Minnesota, 1974
**Most First Downs, Passing, Both Teams, Game**
 28  Pittsburgh (15) vs. Dallas (13), 1979
 24  Philadelphia (14) vs. Oakland (10), 1981
 23  Kansas City (12) vs. Green Bay (11), 1967
    Minnesota (15) vs. Oakland (8), 1977
**Fewest First Downs, Passing, Both Teams, Game**
  9  Denver (1) vs. Dallas (8), 1978
 10  Minnesota (5) vs. Pittsburgh (5), 1975
 11  Dallas (5) vs. Baltimore (6), 1971
    Miami (2) vs. Washington (9), 1983

## PENALTY
**Most First Downs, Penalty, Game**
  4  Baltimore vs. Dallas, 1971
    Miami vs. Minnesota, 1974
    Cincinnati vs. San Francisco, 1982
  3  Kansas City vs. Minnesota, 1970
    Minnesota vs. Oakland, 1977
**Most First Downs, Penalty, Both Teams, Game**
  6  Cincinnati (4) vs. San Francisco (2), 1982
  5  Baltimore (4) vs. Dallas (1), 1971
    Miami (4) vs. Minnesota (1), 1974
  4  Kansas City (3) vs. Minnesota (1), 1970
**Fewest First Downs, Penalty, Both Teams, Game**
  0  Dallas vs. Miami, 1972
    Miami vs. Washington, 1973
    Dallas vs. Pittsburgh, 1976
  1  Green Bay (0) vs. Kansas City (1), 1967
    Miami (0) vs. Washington (1), 1983

# NET YARDS GAINED RUSHING AND PASSING
**Most Yards Gained, Game**
 429  Oakland vs. Minnesota, 1977
 400  Washington vs. Miami, 1983
 393  Pittsburgh vs. Los Angeles, 1980
**Fewest Yards Gained, Game**
 119  Minnesota vs. Pittsburgh, 1975
 156  Denver vs. Dallas, 1978
 176  Miami vs. Washington, 1983
**Most Yards Gained, Both Teams, Game**
 782  Oakland (429) vs. Minnesota (353), 1977
 737  Oakland (377) vs. Philadelphia (360), 1981
 694  Pittsburgh (393) vs. Los Angeles (301), 1980
**Fewest Yards Gained, Both Teams, Game**
 452  Minnesota (119) vs. Pittsburgh (333), 1975
 481  Washington (228) vs. Miami (253), 1973
    Denver (156) vs. Dallas (325), 1978
 497  Minnesota (238) vs. Miami (259), 1974

# RUSHING
**ATTEMPTS**
**Most Attempts, Game**
 57  Pittsburgh vs. Minnesota, 1975
 53  Miami vs. Minnesota, 1974
 52  Oakland vs. Minnesota, 1977
    Washington vs. Miami, 1983
**Fewest Attempts, Game**
 19  Kansas City vs. Green Bay, 1967
    Minnesota vs. Kansas City, 1970
 20  Oakland vs. Green Bay, 1968
    Miami vs. Dallas, 1972
 21  Minnesota vs. Pittsburgh, 1975

**Most Attempts, Both Teams, Game**
81 Washington (52) vs. Miami (29), 1983
78 Pittsburgh (57) vs. Minnesota (21), 1975
Oakland (52) vs. Minnesota (26), 1977
77 Miami (53) vs. Minnesota (24), 1974
Pittsburgh (46) vs. Dallas (31), 1976
**Fewest Attempts, Both Teams, Game**
52 Kansas City (19) vs. Green Bay (33), 1967
56 Pittsburgh (24) vs. Dallas (32), 1979
60 Philadelphia (26) vs. Oakland (34), 1981

### YARDS GAINED
**Most Yards Gained, Game**
276 Washington vs. Miami, 1983
266 Oakland vs. Minnesota, 1977
252 Dallas vs. Miami, 1972
**Fewest Yards Gained, Game**
17 Minnesota vs. Pittsburgh, 1975
66 Pittsburgh vs. Dallas, 1979
67 Minnesota vs. Kansas City, 1970
**Most Yards Gained, Both Teams, Game**
372 Washington (276) vs. Miami (96), 1983
337 Oakland (266) vs. Minnesota (71), 1977
332 Dallas (252) vs. Miami (80), 1972
**Fewest Yards Gained, Both Teams, Game**
171 Baltimore (69) vs. Dallas (102), 1971
186 Philadelphia (69) vs. Oakland (117), 1981
191 Pittsburgh (84) vs. Los Angeles (107), 1980

### AVERAGE GAIN
**Highest Average Gain, Game**
7.00 L.A. Raiders vs. Washington, 1984 (33-231)
6.22 Baltimore vs. N.Y. Jets, 1969 (23-143)
5.35 Oakland vs. Green Bay, 1968 (20-107)
**Lowest Average Gain, Game**
0.81 Minnesota vs. Pittsburgh, 1975 (21-17)
2.23 Baltimore vs. Dallas, 1971 (31-69)
2.27 Pittsburgh vs. Los Angeles, 1980 (37-84)

### TOUCHDOWNS
**Most Touchdowns, Game**
3 Green Bay vs. Kansas City, 1967
Miami vs. Minnesota, 1974
2 Oakland vs. Minnesota, 1977
Pittsburgh vs. Los Angeles, 1980
L.A. Raiders vs. Washington, 1984
**Fewest Touchdowns, Game**
0 By 12 teams
**Most Touchdowns, Both Teams, Game**
4 Miami (3) vs. Minnesota (1), 1974
3 Green Bay (3) vs. Kansas City (0), 1967
Pittsburgh (2) vs. Los Angeles (1), 1980
L.A. Raiders (2) vs. Washington (1), 1984
**Fewest Touchdowns, Both Teams, Game**
0 Pittsburgh vs. Dallas, 1976
Oakland vs. Philadelphia, 1981
1 In seven games

# PASSING

## ATTEMPTS
**Most Passes Attempted, Game**
44 Minnesota vs. Oakland, 1977
41 Baltimore vs. N.Y. Jets, 1969
38 Philadelphia vs. Oakland, 1981
**Fewest Passes Attempted, Game**
7 Miami vs. Minnesota, 1974
11 Miami vs. Washington, 1973
14 Pittsburgh vs. Minnesota, 1975
**Most Passes Attempted, Both Teams, Game**
70 Baltimore (41) vs. N.Y. Jets (29), 1969
63 Minnesota (44) vs. Oakland (19), 1977
60 Dallas (30) vs. Pittsburgh (30), 1979
Washington (35) vs. L.A. Raiders (25), 1984
**Fewest Passes Attempted, Both Teams, Game**
35 Miami (7) vs. Minnesota (28), 1974
39 Miami (11) vs. Washington (28), 1973
40 Pittsburgh (14) vs. Minnesota (26), 1975
Miami (17) vs. Washington (23), 1983

## COMPLETIONS
**Most Passes Completed, Game**
25 Cincinnati vs. San Francisco, 1982
24 Minnesota vs. Oakland, 1977
19 Dallas vs. Denver, 1978
**Fewest Passes Completed, Game**
4 Miami vs. Washington, 1983
6 Miami vs. Minnesota, 1974
8 Miami vs. Washington, 1973
Denver vs. Dallas, 1978
**Most Passes Completed, Both Teams, Game**
39 Cincinnati (25) vs. San Francisco (14), 1982
36 Minnesota (24) vs. Oakland (12), 1977
34 Baltimore (17) vs. N.Y. Jets (17), 1969
Dallas (17) vs. Pittsburgh (17), 1979
**Fewest Passes Completed, Both Teams, Game**
19 Miami (4) vs. Washington (15), 1983
20 Pittsburgh (9) vs. Minnesota (11), 1975
22 Miami (8) vs. Washington (14), 1973

## COMPLETION PERCENTAGE
**Highest Completion Percentage, Game (20 attempts)**
73.5 Cincinnati vs. San Francisco, 1982 (34-25)
67.9 Dallas vs. Denver, 1978 (28-19)

66.7 Pittsburgh vs. Los Angeles, 1980 (21-14)
**Lowest Completion Percentage, Game (20 attempts)**
32.0 Denver vs. Dallas, 1978 (25-8)
41.5 Baltimore vs. N.Y. Jets, 1969 (41-17)
42.3 Minnesota vs. Pittsburgh, 1975 (26-11)

### YARDS GAINED
**Most Yards Gained, Game**
309 Pittsburgh vs. Los Angeles, 1980
291 Pittsburgh vs. Dallas, 1979
Philadelphia vs. Oakland, 1981
284 Cincinnati vs. San Francisco, 1982
**Fewest Yards Gained, Game**
35 Denver vs. Dallas, 1978
63 Miami vs. Minnesota, 1974
69 Miami vs. Washington, 1973
**Most Yards Gained, Both Teams, Game**
551 Philadelphia (291) vs. Oakland (260), 1981
503 Pittsburgh (309) vs. Los Angeles (194), 1980
467 Pittsburgh (291) vs. Dallas (176), 1979
**Fewest Yards Gained, Both Teams, Game**
156 Miami (69) vs. Washington (87), 1973
186 Pittsburgh (84) vs. Minnesota (102), 1975
205 Dallas (100) vs. Miami (105), 1972

### TIMES SACKED
**Most Times Sacked, Game**
7 Dallas vs. Pittsburgh, 1976
6 Kansas City vs. Green Bay, 1967
Washington vs. L.A. Raiders, 1984
5 Dallas vs. Denver, 1978; vs. Pittsburgh, 1979
Cincinnati vs. San Francisco, 1982
**Fewest Times Sacked, Game**
0 Baltimore vs. N.Y. Jets, 1969; vs. Dallas, 1971
Minnesota vs. Pittsburgh, 1975
Pittsburgh vs. Los Angeles, 1980
Philadelphia vs. Oakland, 1981
1 By six teams
**Most Times Sacked, Both Teams, Game**
9 Kansas City (6) vs. Green Bay (3), 1967
Dallas (7) vs. Pittsburgh (2), 1976
Dallas (5) vs. Denver (4), 1978
Dallas (5) vs. Pittsburgh (4), 1979
8 Washington (6) vs. L.A. Raiders (2), 1984
7 Green Bay (4) vs. Oakland (3), 1968
**Fewest Times Sacked, Both Teams, Game**
1 Philadelphia (0) vs. Oakland (1), 1981
2 Baltimore (0) vs. N.Y. Jets (2), 1969
Baltimore (0) vs. Dallas (2), 1971
Minnesota (0) vs. Pittsburgh (2), 1975
3 In three games

### TOUCHDOWNS
**Most Touchdowns, Game**
4 Pittsburgh vs. Dallas, 1979
3 Dallas vs. Pittsburgh, 1979
Oakland vs. Philadelphia, 1981
2 By 10 teams
**Fewest Touchdowns, Game**
0 By 10 teams
**Most Touchdowns, Both Teams, Game**
7 Pittsburgh (4) vs. Dallas (3), 1979
4 Dallas (2) vs. Pittsburgh (2), 1976
Oakland (3) vs. Philadelphia (1), 1981
3 In six games
**Fewest Touchdowns, Both Teams, Game**
0 N.Y. Jets vs. Baltimore, 1969
Miami vs. Minnesota, 1974
1 In four games

# INTERCEPTIONS BY

**Most Interceptions By, Game**
4 N.Y. Jets vs. Baltimore, 1969
Dallas vs. Denver, 1978
3 By eight teams
**Most Interceptions By, Both Teams, Game**
6 Baltimore (3) vs. Dallas (3), 1971
4 In five games

### YARDS GAINED
**Most Yards Gained, Game**
95 Miami vs. Washington, 1973
91 Oakland vs. Minnesota, 1977
89 Pittsburgh vs. Dallas, 1976
**Most Yards Gained, Both Teams, Game**
95 Miami (95) vs. Washington (0), 1973
91 Oakland (91) vs. Minnesota (0), 1977
89 Pittsburgh (89) vs. Dallas (0), 1976

### TOUCHDOWNS
**Most Touchdowns, Game**
1 Green Bay vs. Oakland, 1968
Oakland vs. Minnesota, 1977
L.A. Raiders vs. Washington, 1984

# PUNTING

**Most Punts, Game**
9 Dallas vs. Baltimore, 1971
8 Washington vs. L.A. Raiders, 1984
7 By six teams
**Fewest Punts, Game**
2 Pittsburgh vs. Los Angeles, 1980
3 By seven teams

**Most Punts, Both Teams, Game**
15 Washington (8) vs. L.A. Raiders (7), 1984
13 Dallas (9) vs. Baltimore (4), 1971
Pittsburgh (7) vs. Minnesota (6), 1975
12 In three games
**Fewest Punts, Both Teams, Game**
6 Oakland (3) vs. Philadelphia (3), 1981
7 In four games

## AVERAGE YARDAGE
**Highest Average, Game (4 punts)**
48.50 Kansas City vs. Minnesota, 1970 (4-194)
46.25 San Francisco vs. Cincinnati, 1982 (4-185)
45.29 Kansas City vs. Green Bay, 1967 (7-317)
**Lowest Average, Game (4 punts)**
31.20 Washington vs. Miami, 1973 (5-156)
32.38 Washington vs. L.A. Raiders, 1984 (8-259)
32.40 Oakland vs. Minnesota, 1977 (5-162)

# PUNT RETURNS

**Most Punt Returns, Game**
6 Washington vs. Miami, 1983
5 By four teams
**Fewest Punt Returns, Game**
0 Minnesota vs. Miami, 1974
1 By eight teams
**Most Punt Returns, Both Teams, Game**
9 Pittsburgh (5) vs. Minnesota (4), 1975
8 Green Bay (5) vs. Oakland (3), 1968
Baltimore (5) vs. Dallas (3), 1971
Washington (6) vs. Miami (2), 1983
7 Green Bay (4) vs. Kansas City (3), 1967
Oakland (4) vs. Minnesota (3), 1977
**Fewest Punt Returns, Both Teams, Game**
2 Dallas (1) vs. Miami (1), 1972
3 Kansas City (1) vs. Minnesota (2), 1970
Minnesota (0) vs. Miami (3), 1974
4 L.A. Raiders (2) vs. Washington (2), 1984

## YARDS GAINED
**Most Yards Gained, Game**
52 Washington vs. Miami, 1983
43 Oakland vs. Minnesota, 1977
36 Pittsburgh vs. Minnesota, 1975
**Fewest Yards Gained, Game**
−1 Dallas vs. Miami, 1972
0 By four teams
**Most Yards Gained, Both Teams, Game**
74 Washington (52) vs. Miami (22), 1983
60 Dallas (33) vs. Pittsburgh (27), 1979
57 Oakland (43) vs. Minnesota (14), 1977
**Fewest Yards Gained, Both Teams, Game**
13 Miami (4) vs. Washington (9), 1973
18 Kansas City (0) vs. Minnesota (18), 1970
20 Dallas (−1) vs. Miami (21), 1972
Minnesota (0) vs. Miami (20), 1974

## AVERAGE RETURN
**Highest Average, Game (3 returns)**
10.8 Oakland vs. Minnesota, 1977 (4-43)
8.8 Cincinnati vs. San Francisco, 1982 (4-35)
8.7 Washington vs. Miami, 1983 (6-52)

## TOUCHDOWNS
**Most Touchdowns, Game**
None

# KICKOFF RETURNS

**Most Kickoff Returns, Game**
7 Oakland vs. Green Bay, 1968
Minnesota vs. Oakland, 1977
Cincinnati vs. San Francisco, 1982
Washington vs. L.A. Raiders, 1984
6 By six teams
**Fewest Kickoff Returns, Game**
1 N.Y. Jets vs. Baltimore, 1969
L.A. Raiders vs. Washington, 1984
2 By six teams
**Most Kickoff Returns, Both Teams, Game**
11 Los Angeles (6) vs. Pittsburgh (5), 1980
10 Oakland (7) vs. Green Bay (3), 1968
9 In seven games
**Fewest Kickoff Returns, Both Teams, Game**
5 N.Y. Jets (1) vs. Baltimore (4), 1969
Miami (2) vs. Washington (3), 1973
6 In three games

## YARDS GAINED
**Most Yards Gained, Game**
222 Miami vs. Washington, 1983
173 Denver vs. Dallas, 1978
162 Pittsburgh vs. Los Angeles, 1980
**Fewest Yards Gained, Game**
17 L.A. Raiders vs. Washington, 1984
25 N.Y. Jets vs. Baltimore, 1969
32 Pittsburgh vs. Minnesota, 1975
**Most Yards Gained, Both Teams, Game**
279 Miami (222) vs. Washington (57), 1983
231 Pittsburgh (162) vs. Los Angeles (79), 1980
224 Denver (173) vs. Dallas (51), 1978
**Fewest Yards Gained, Both Teams, Game**
78 Miami (33) vs. Washington (45), 1973

82 Pittsburgh (32) vs. Minnesota (50), 1975
92 San Francisco (40) vs. Cincinnati (52), 1982

## AVERAGE GAIN
**Highest Average, Game (3 returns)**
37.0 Miami vs. Washington, 1983 (6-222)
32.4 Pittsburgh vs. Los Angeles, 1980 (5-162)
28.8 Denver vs. Dallas, 1978 (6-173)

## TOUCHDOWNS
**Most Touchdowns, Game**
1 Miami vs. Washington, 1983

# PENALTIES

**Most Penalties, Game**
12 Dallas vs. Denver, 1978
10 Dallas vs. Baltimore, 1971
9 Dallas vs. Pittsburgh, 1979
**Fewest Penalties, Game**
0 Miami vs. Dallas, 1972
Pittsburgh vs. Dallas, 1976
1 Green Bay vs. Oakland, 1968
Miami vs. Minnesota, 1974
2 In three games
**Most Penalties, Both Teams, Game**
20 Dallas (12) vs. Denver (8), 1978
16 Cincinnati (8) vs. San Francisco (8), 1982
14 Dallas (10) vs. Baltimore (4), 1971
Dallas (9) vs. Pittsburgh (5), 1979
**Fewest Penalties, Both Teams, Game**
2 Pittsburgh (0) vs. Dallas (2), 1976
3 Miami (0) vs. Dallas (3), 1972
5 Green Bay (1) vs. Oakland (4), 1968

## YARDS PENALIZED
**Most Yards Penalized, Game**
133 Dallas vs. Baltimore, 1971
122 Pittsburgh vs. Minnesota, 1975
94 Dallas vs. Denver, 1978
**Fewest Yards Penalized, Game**
0 Miami vs. Dallas, 1972
Pittsburgh vs. Dallas, 1976
4 Miami vs. Minnesota, 1974
12 Green Bay vs. Oakland, 1968
**Most Yards Penalized, Both Teams, Game**
164 Dallas (133) vs. Baltimore (31), 1971
154 Dallas (94) vs. Denver (60), 1978
140 Pittsburgh (122) vs. Minnesota (18), 1975
**Fewest Yards Penalized, Both Teams, Game**
15 Miami (0) vs. Dallas (15), 1972
20 Pittsburgh (0) vs. Dallas (20), 1976
43 Green Bay (12) vs. Oakland (31), 1968

# FUMBLES

**Most Fumbles, Game**
6 Dallas vs. Denver, 1978
5 Baltimore vs. Dallas, 1971
4 In four games
**Fewest Fumbles, Game**
0 In six games
**Most Fumbles, Both Teams, Game**
10 Dallas (6) vs. Denver (4), 1978
8 Dallas (4) vs. Pittsburgh (4), 1976
7 Pittsburgh (4) vs. Minnesota (3), 1975
**Fewest Fumbles, Both Teams, Game**
0 Los Angeles vs. Pittsburgh, 1980
1 Oakland (0) vs. Minnesota (1), 1977
Oakland (0) vs. Philadelphia (1), 1981
2 In three games
**Most Fumbles Lost, Game**
4 Baltimore vs. Dallas, 1971
Denver vs. Dallas, 1978
2 In many games
**Most Fumbles Recovered, Game**
8 Dallas vs. Denver, 1978 (4 own, 4 opp)
4 Pittsburgh vs. Minnesota, 1975 (2 own, 2 opp)
Dallas vs. Pittsburgh, 1976 (4 own)

# TURNOVERS
(Number of times losing the ball on interceptions and fumbles.)
**Most Turnovers, Game**
8 Denver vs. Dallas, 1978
7 Baltimore vs. Dallas, 1971
5 In three games
**Fewest Turnovers, Game**
0 Green Bay vs. Oakland, 1968
Miami vs. Minnesota, 1974
Pittsburgh vs. Dallas, 1976
Oakland vs. Minnesota, 1977; vs. Philadelphia, 1981
1 By many teams
**Most Turnovers, Both Teams, Game**
11 Baltimore (7) vs. Dallas (4), 1971
10 Denver (8) vs. Dallas (2), 1978
7 Minnesota (5) vs. Pittsburgh (2), 1975
**Fewest Turnovers, Both Teams, Game**
2 Green Bay (1) vs. Kansas City (1), 1967
Miami (0) vs. Minnesota (2), 1974
3 Green Bay (0) vs. Oakland (3), 1968
Pittsburgh (0) vs. Dallas (3), 1976
Oakland (0) vs. Minnesota (3), 1977
4 In four games

Compiled by Elias Sports Bureau

Throughout this all-time postseason record section, the following abbreviations are used to indicate various levels of postseason games:

SB    Super Bowl (1966 to date)
AFC    AFC Championship Game (1970 to date) or AFL Championship Game (1960-69)
NFC    NFC Championship Game (1970 to date) or NFL Championship Game (1933-69)
AFC-D    AFC Divisional Playoff Game (1970 to date), AFC Second-Round Playoff Game (1982), AFC Inter-Divisional Playoff Game (1969), or special playoff game to break tie for AFL Division Championship (1963, 1968)
NFC-D    NFC Divisional Playoff Game (1970 to date), NFC Second-Round Playoff Game (1982), NFL Conference Championship (1967-69), or special playoff game to break tie for NFL Division or Conference Championship (1941, 1943, 1947, 1950, 1952, 1957, 1958, 1965)
AFC-FR    AFC First-Round Playoff Game (1978 to date)
NFC-FR    NFC First-Round Playoff Game (1978 to date)

Year references are to the season following which the postseason game occurred, even if the game was in the next calendar year.

## POSTSEASON GAME COMPOSITE STANDINGS

| | W | L | Pct. | Pts. | OP |
|---|---|---|---|---|---|
| Green Bay Packers | 13 | 5 | .722 | 416 | 259 |
| Pittsburgh Steelers | 14 | 7 | .667 | 481 | 385 |
| Seattle Seahawks | 2 | 1 | .667 | 72 | 57 |
| Los Angeles Raiders* | 19 | 10 | .655 | 734 | 495 |
| Kansas City Chiefs** | 5 | 3 | .625 | 144 | 147 |
| Detroit Lions | 6 | 4 | .600 | 221 | 208 |
| Philadelphia Eagles | 7 | 5 | .583 | 219 | 173 |
| Miami Dolphins | 11 | 8 | .579 | 405 | 340 |
| Dallas Cowboys | 20 | 15 | .571 | 805 | 620 |
| New York Jets | 4 | 3 | .571 | 137 | 119 |
| San Francisco 49ers | 6 | 5 | .545 | 246 | 245 |
| Baltimore Colts | 8 | 7 | .533 | 264 | 262 |
| Washington Redskins*** | 11 | 10 | .524 | 424 | 426 |
| Chicago Bears | 7 | 7 | .500 | 330 | 296 |
| Houston Oilers | 6 | 6 | .500 | 168 | 267 |
| Minnesota Vikings | 10 | 12 | .455 | 378 | 427 |
| Los Angeles Rams**** | 10 | 15 | .400 | 401 | 560 |
| Buffalo Bills | 3 | 5 | .375 | 138 | 171 |
| Cleveland Browns | 7 | 13 | .350 | 354 | 433 |
| Denver Broncos | 2 | 4 | .333 | 88 | 142 |
| San Diego Chargers† | 4 | 8 | .333 | 230 | 279 |
| Cincinnati Bengals | 2 | 5 | .286 | 137 | 180 |
| New York Giants | 5 | 14 | .263 | 282 | 404 |
| Atlanta Falcons | 1 | 3 | .250 | 85 | 100 |
| Tampa Bay Buccaneers | 1 | 3 | .250 | 41 | 94 |
| New England Patriots†† | 1 | 4 | .200 | 84 | 142 |
| St. Louis Cardinals††† | 1 | 4 | .200 | 81 | 134 |

*24 games played when franchise was in Oakland. (Won 15, lost 9, 587 points scored, 435 points allowed)
**One game played when franchise was in Dallas (Texans). (Won 20-17)
***One game played when franchise was in Boston. (Lost 21-6)
****One game played when franchise was in Cleveland. (Won 15-14)
†One game played when franchise was in Los Angeles. (Lost 24-16)
††Two games played when franchise was in Boston. (Won 26-8, lost 51-10)
†††Two games played when franchise was in Chicago. (Won 28-21, lost 7-0)

## INDIVIDUAL RECORDS

### SERVICE

**Most Games, Career**
27    D. D. Lewis, Dallas (SB-5, NFC-9, NFC-D 12, NFC-FR 1)
26    Larry Cole, Dallas (SB-5, NFC-8, NFC-D-12, NFC-FR 1)
25    Charlie Waters, Dallas (SB-5, NFC-9, NFC-D 10, NFC-FR 1)

### SCORING

**POINTS**
**Most Points, Career**
115    George Blanda, Chi. Bears-Houston-Oakland, 19 games (49-pat, 22-fg)
102    Franco Harris, Pittsburgh, 19 games (17-td)
95    Rafael Septien, L.A. Rams-Dallas, 14 games (41-pat, 18-fg)
**Most Points, Game**
19    Pat Harder, NFC-D: Detroit vs. Los Angeles, 1952 (2-td, 4-pat, 1-fg)
      Paul Hornung, NFC: Green Bay vs. N.Y. Giants, 1961 (1-td, 4-pat, 3-fg)
18    By 14 players

**TOUCHDOWNS**
**Most Touchdowns, Career**
17    Franco Harris, Pittsburgh, 19 games (16-r, 1-p)
10    Fred Biletnikoff, Oakland, 19 games (10-p)
      Larry Csonka, Miami, 12 games (9-r, 1-p)
      Tony Dorsett, Dallas, 16 games (9-r, 1-p)
      John Riggins, Washington, 8 games (10-r)
      John Stallworth, Pittsburgh, 16 games (10-p)
9    Lynn Swann, Pittsburgh, 16 games (9-p)
**Most Touchdowns, Game**
3    Andy Farkas, NFC-D: Washington vs. N.Y. Giants, 1943 (3-r)
      Tom Fears, NFC-D: Los Angeles vs. Chi. Bears, 1950 (3-p)
      Otto Graham, NFC: Cleveland vs. Detroit, 1954 (3-r)
      Gary Collins, NFC: Cleveland vs. Baltimore, 1964 (3-p)

      Craig Baynham, NFC-D: Dallas vs. Cleveland, 1967 (2-r, 1-p)
      Fred Biletnikoff, AFC: Oakland vs. Kansas City, 1968 (3-p)
      Tom Matte, NFC: Baltimore vs. Cleveland, 1968 (3-r)
      Larry Schreiber, NFC-D: San Francisco vs. Dallas, 1972 (3-r)
      Larry Csonka, AFC: Miami vs. Oakland, 1973 (3-r)
      Franco Harris, AFC-D: Pittsburgh vs. Buffalo, 1974 (3-r)
      Preston Pearson, NFC: Dallas vs. Los Angeles, 1975 (3-p)
      Dave Casper, AFC-D: Oakland vs. Baltimore, 1977 (OT) (3-p)
      Alvin Garrett, NFC-FR: Washington vs. Detroit, 1982 (3-p)
      John Riggins, NFC-D: Washington vs. L.A. Rams, 1983 (3-r)
**Most Consecutive Games Scoring Touchdowns**
8    John Stallworth, Pittsburgh, 1978-83 (current)
6    John Riggins, Washington, 1982-83 (current)
5    Duane Thomas, Dallas, 1970-71
      Franco Harris, Pittsburgh, 1974-75
      Franco Harris, Pittsburgh, 1977-79

**POINTS AFTER TOUCHDOWN**
**Most Points After Touchdown, Career**
49    George Blanda, Chi. Bears-Houston-Oakland, 19 games (49 att)
41    Rafael Septien, L.A. Rams-Dallas, 14 games (41 att)
38    Fred Cox, Minnesota, 18 games (40 att)
**Most Points After Touchdown, Game**
8    Lou Groza, NFC: Cleveland vs. Detroit, 1954 (8 att)
      Jim Martin, NFC: Detroit vs. Cleveland, 1957 (8 att)
      George Blanda, AFC-D: Oakland vs. Houston, 1969 (8 att)
7    Danny Villanueva, NFC-D: Dallas vs. Cleveland, 1967 (7 att)
6    George Blair, AFC: San Diego vs. Boston, 1963 (6 att)
      Mark Moseley, NFC-D: Washington vs. L.A. Rams, 1983 (6 att)
**Most Points After Touchdown, No Misses, Career**
49    George Blanda, Chi. Bears-Houston-Oakland, 19 games
41    Rafael Septien, L.A. Rams-Dallas, 14 games
30    Chris Bahr, Oakland-L.A. Raiders, 9 games

**FIELD GOALS**
**Most Field Goals Attempted, Career**
39    George Blanda, Chi. Bears-Houston-Oakland, 19 games
27    Roy Gerela, Houston-Pittsburgh, 15 games
25    Toni Fritsch, Dallas-Houston, 14 games
**Most Field Goals Attempted, Game**
6    George Blanda, AFC: Oakland vs. Houston, 1967
      David Ray, NFC-D: Los Angeles vs. Dallas, 1973
5    Jerry Kramer, NFC: Green Bay vs. N.Y. Giants, 1962
      Gino Cappelletti, AFC-D: Boston vs. Buffalo, 1963
      Pete Gogolak, AFC: Buffalo vs. San Diego, 1965
      Jan Stenerud, AFC-D: Kansas City vs. N.Y. Jets, 1969
      George Blanda, AFC-D: Oakland vs. Pittsburgh, 1973
      Ed Murray, NFC-D: Detroit vs. San Francisco, 1983
      Mark Moseley, NFC: Washington vs. San Francisco, 1983
4    By many players
**Most Field Goals, Career**
22    George Blanda, Chi. Bears-Houston-Oakland, 19 games
20    Toni Fritsch, Dallas-Houston, 14 games
18    Rafael Septien, L.A. Rams-Dallas, 14 games
**Most Field Goals, Game**
4    Gino Cappelletti, AFC-D: Boston vs. Buffalo, 1963
      George Blanda, AFC: Oakland vs. Houston, 1967
      Don Chandler, SB: Green Bay vs. Oakland, 1967
      Curt Knight, NFC: Washington vs. Dallas, 1972
      George Blanda, AFC-D: Oakland vs. Pittsburgh, 1973
      Ray Wersching, SB: San Francisco vs. Cincinnati, 1981
3    By many players
**Most Consecutive Field Goals**
15    Rafael Septien, Dallas, 1978-82
**Longest Field Goal**
54    Ed Murray, NFC-D: Detroit vs. San Francisco, 1983
52    Lou Groza, NFC: Cleveland vs. Los Angeles, 1951
      Curt Knight, NFC-D: Washington vs. Minnesota, 1973
      Matt Bahr, AFC-FR: Cleveland vs. L.A. Raiders, 1982
50    Garo Yepremian, AFC-D: Miami vs. Cincinnati, 1973
      Rafael Septien, NFC-D: Dallas vs. Green Bay, 1982
**Highest Field Goal Percentage, Career (10 field goals)**
85.7    Rafael Septien, L.A. Rams-Dallas, 14 games (21-18)
81.3    Chris Bahr, Oakland-L.A. Raiders, 9 games (16-13)
80.0    Toni Fritsch, Dallas-Houston, 14 games (25-20)

**SAFETIES**
**Most Safeties, Game**
1    Bill Willis, NFC-D: Cleveland vs. N.Y. Giants, 1950
      Carl Eller, NFC-D: Minnesota vs. Los Angeles, 1969
      George Andrie, NFC-D: Dallas vs. Detroit, 1970
      Alan Page, NFC-D: Minnesota vs. Dallas, 1971
      Dwight White, SB: Pittsburgh vs. Minnesota, 1974
      Reggie Harrison, SB: Pittsburgh vs. Dallas, 1975
      Jim Jensen, NFC-D: Dallas vs. Los Angeles, 1976
      Ted Washington, AFC: Houston vs. Pittsburgh, 1978
      Randy White, NFC-D: Dallas vs. Los Angeles, 1979

### RUSHING

**ATTEMPTS**
**Most Attempts, Career**
400    Franco Harris, Pittsburgh, 19 games
285    Tony Dorsett, Dallas, 16 games
230    John Riggins, Washington, 8 games
**Most Attempts, Game**
38    Ricky Bell, NFC-D: Tampa Bay vs. Philadelphia, 1979
      John Riggins, SB: Washington vs. Miami, 1982

37 Lawrence McCutcheon, NFC-D: Los Angeles vs. St. Louis, 1975
   John Riggins, NFC-D: Washington vs. Minnesota, 1982
36 John Riggins, NFC: Washington vs. Dallas, 1982
   John Riggins, NFC: Washington vs. San Francisco, 1983

## YARDS GAINED
**Most Yards Gained, Career**
1,556 Franco Harris, Pittsburgh, 19 games
1,325 Tony Dorsett, Dallas, 16 games
  946 John Riggins, Washington, 8 games
**Most Yards Gained, Game**
206 Keith Lincoln, AFC: San Diego vs. Boston, 1963
202 Lawrence McCutcheon, NFC-D: Los Angeles vs. St. Louis, 1975
    Freeman McNeil, AFC-FR: N.Y. Jets vs. Cincinnati, 1982
196 Steve Van Buren, NFC: Philadelphia vs. Los Angeles, 1949
**Most Games, 100 or More Yards Rushing, Career**
6 John Riggins, Washington, 8 games
5 Franco Harris, Pittsburgh, 19 games
4 Larry Csonka, Miami, 12 games
  Chuck Foreman, Minnesota, 13 games
**Most Consecutive Games, 100 or More Yards Rushing**
6 John Riggins, Washington, 1982-83
3 Larry Csonka, Miami, 1973-74
  Franco Harris, Pittsburgh, 1974-75
  Marcus Allen, L.A. Raiders, 1983 (current)
**Longest Run From Scrimmage**
74 Marcus Allen SB: L.A. Raiders vs. Washington, 1983 (TD)
71 Hugh McElhenny, NFC-D: San Francisco vs. Detroit, 1957
   James Lofton, NFC-D: Green Bay vs. Dallas, 1982 (TD)
70 Elmer Angsman, NFC: Chi. Cardinals vs. Philadelphia, 1947 (twice, 2 TDs)

## AVERAGE GAIN
**Highest Average Gain, Career (50 attempts)**
6.67 Paul Lowe, L.A. Chargers / San Diego, 5 games (57-380)
6.34 Marcus Allen, L.A. Raiders, 5 games (90-574)
5.68 Roger Staubach, Dallas, 20 games (76-432)
**Highest Average Gain, Game (10 attempts)**
15.90 Elmer Angsman, NFC: Chi. Cardinals vs. Philadelphia, 1947 (10-159)
15.85 Keith Lincoln, AFC: San Diego vs. Boston, 1963 (13-206)
10.90 Bill Osmanski, NFC: Chi. Bears vs. Washington, 1940 (10-109)

## TOUCHDOWNS
**Most Touchdowns, Career**
16 Franco Harris, Pittsburgh, 19 games
10 John Riggins, Washington, 8 games
 9 Larry Csonka, Miami, 12 games
   Tony Dorsett, Dallas, 16 games
**Most Touchdowns, Game**
3 Andy Farkas, NFC-D: Washington vs. N.Y. Giants, 1943
  Otto Graham, NFC: Cleveland vs. Detroit, 1954
  Tom Matte, NFC: Baltimore vs. Cleveland, 1968
  Larry Schreiber, NFC-D: San Francisco vs. Dallas, 1972
  Larry Csonka, AFC: Miami vs. Oakland, 1973
  Franco Harris, AFC-D: Pittsburgh vs. Buffalo, 1974
  John Riggins, NFC-D: Washington vs. L.A. Rams, 1983
**Most Consecutive Games Rushing for Touchdowns**
6 John Riggins, Washington, 1982-83 (current)
5 Franco Harris, Pittsburgh, 1974-75
  Franco Harris, Pittsburgh, 1977-79
3 By many players

# PASSING

## ATTEMPTS
**Most Passes Attempted, Career**
456 Terry Bradshaw, Pittsburgh, 19 games
410 Roger Staubach, Dallas, 20 games
351 Ken Stabler, Oakland-Houston, 13 games
**Most Passes Attempted, Game**
53 Dan Fouts, AFC-D: San Diego vs. Miami, 1981 (OT)
   Danny White, NFC-FR: Dallas vs. L.A. Rams, 1983
51 Richard Todd, AFC-FR: N.Y. Jets vs. Buffalo, 1981
   Neil Lomax, NFC-FR: St. Louis vs. Green Bay, 1982
49 Joe Namath, AFC: N.Y. Jets vs. Oakland, 1968
   Billy Kilmer, NFC-D: Washington vs. Minnesota, 1976

## COMPLETIONS
**Most Passes Completed, Career**
261 Terry Bradshaw, Pittsburgh, 19 games
223 Roger Staubach, Dallas, 20 games
203 Ken Stabler, Oakland-Houston, 13 games
**Most Passes Completed, Game**
33 Dan Fouts, AFC-D: San Diego vs. Miami, 1981 (OT)
32 Neil Lomax, NFC-FR: St. Louis vs. Green Bay, 1982
   Danny White, NFC-FR: Dallas vs. L.A. Rams, 1983
29 Don Strock, AFC-D: Miami vs. San Diego, 1981 (OT)

## COMPLETION PERCENTAGE
**Highest Completion Percentage, Career (100 attempts)**
66.3 Ken Anderson, Cincinnati, 6 games (166-110)
62.7 Joe Theismann, Washington, 9 games (169-106)
61.2 Dan Pastorini, Houston, 5 games (116-71)
**Highest Completion Percentage, Game (15 completions)**
84.2 David Woodley, AFC-FR: Miami vs. New England, 1982 (19-16)
78.9 Norm Van Brocklin, NFC-D: Los Angeles vs. Detroit, 1952 (19-15)
78.3 Joe Theismann, NFC-D: Washington vs. L.A. Rams, 1983 (23-18)

## YARDS GAINED
**Most Yards Gained, Career**
3,833 Terry Bradshaw, Pittsburgh, 19 games
2,791 Roger Staubach, Dallas, 20 games
2,641 Ken Stabler, Oakland-Houston, 13 games

**Most Yards Gained, Game**
433 Dan Fouts, AFC-D: San Diego vs. Miami, 1981 (OT)
403 Don Strock, AFC-D: Miami vs. San Diego, 1981 (OT)
401 Daryle Lamonica, AFC: Oakland vs. N.Y. Jets, 1968
**Most Games, 300 or More Yards Passing, Career**
5 Dan Fouts, San Diego, 7 games
3 Terry Bradshaw, Pittsburgh, 19 games
  Danny White, Dallas, 17 games
2 Daryle Lamonica, Buffalo-Oakland, 13 games
  Ken Anderson, Cincinnati, 6 games
  Joe Montana, San Francisco, 5 games
**Most Consecutive Games, 300 or More Yards Passing**
4 Dan Fouts, San Diego, 1979-81
2 Daryle Lamonica, Oakland, 1968
  Ken Anderson, Cincinnati, 1981-82 (current)
  Terry Bradshaw, Pittsburgh, 1979-82 (current)
**Longest Pass Completion**
93 Daryle Lamonica (to Dubenion), AFC-D: Buffalo vs. Boston, 1963 (TD)
88 George Blanda (to Cannon), AFC: Houston vs. L.A. Chargers, 1960 (TD)
86 Don Meredith (to Hayes), NFC-D: Dallas vs. Cleveland, 1967 (TD)

## AVERAGE GAIN
**Highest Average Gain, Career (100 attempts)**
8.82 Joe Theismann, Washington, 9 games (169-1,490)
8.61 Jim Plunkett, Oakland-L.A. Raiders, 9 games (245-2,109)
8.41 Terry Bradshaw, Pittsburgh, 19 games (456-3,833)
**Highest Average Gain, Game (20 attempts)**
14.71 Terry Bradshaw, SB: Pittsburgh vs. Los Angeles, 1979 (21-309)
13.33 Bob Waterfield, NFC-D: Los Angeles vs. Chi. Bears, 1950 (21-280)
13.13 Joe Theismann, NFC-D: Washington vs. L.A. Rams, 1983 (23-302)

## TOUCHDOWNS
**Most Touchdown Passes, Career**
30 Terry Bradshaw, Pittsburgh, 19 games
24 Roger Staubach, Dallas, 20 games
19 Daryle Lamonica, Buffalo-Oakland, 13 games
   Ken Stabler, Oakland-Houston, 13 games
**Most Touchdown Passes, Game**
6 Daryle Lamonica, AFC-D: Oakland vs. Houston, 1969
5 Sid Luckman, NFC: Chi. Bears vs. Washington, 1943
  Daryle Lamonica, AFC-D: Oakland vs. Kansas City, 1968
4 Otto Graham, NFC: Cleveland vs. Los Angeles, 1950
  Tobin Rote, NFC: Detroit vs. Cleveland, 1957
  Bart Starr, NFC: Green Bay vs. Dallas, 1966
  Ken Stabler, AFC-D: Oakland vs. Miami, 1974
  Roger Staubach, NFC: Dallas vs. Los Angeles, 1975
  Terry Bradshaw, SB: Pittsburgh vs. Dallas, 1978
  Don Strock, AFC-D: Miami vs. San Diego, 1981 (OT)
  Lynn Dickey, NFC-FR: Green Bay vs. St. Louis, 1982
**Most Consecutive Games, Touchdown Passes**
10 Ken Stabler, Oakland, 1973-77
 8 Terry Bradshaw, Pittsburgh, 1977-82
 6 Bart Starr, Green Bay, 1965-67
   Terry Bradshaw, Pittsburgh, 1972-74
   Dan Fouts, San Diego, 1980-82 (current)
   Joe Theismann, Washington, 1982-83

## HAD INTERCEPTED
**Lowest Percentage, Passes Had Intercepted, Career (100 attempts)**
1.41 Bart Starr, Green Bay, 10 games (213-3)
3.42 Joe Namath, N.Y. Jets, 3 games (117-4)
3.55 Joe Theismann, Washington, 9 games (169-6)
**Most Attempts Without Interception, Game**
47 Daryle Lamonica, AFC: Oakland vs. N.Y. Jets, 1968
42 Dan Fouts, AFC-FR: San Diego vs. Pittsburgh, 1982
39 Daryle Lamonica, AFC-D: Oakland vs. Kansas City, 1968
   Ron Jaworski, NFC-D: Philadelphia vs. Tampa Bay, 1979
   Tommy Kramer, NFC-D: Minnesota vs. Washington, 1982
**Most Passes Had Intercepted, Career**
26 Terry Bradshaw, Pittsburgh, 19 games
19 Roger Staubach, Dallas, 20 games
17 George Blanda, Chi. Bears-Houston-Oakland, 19 games
   Fran Tarkenton, Minnesota, 11 games
**Most Passes Had Intercepted, Game**
6 Frank Filchock, NFC: N.Y. Giants vs. Chi. Bears, 1946
  Bobby Layne, NFC: Detroit vs. Cleveland, 1954
  Norm Van Brocklin, NFC: Los Angeles vs. Cleveland, 1955
5 Frank Filchock, NFC: Washington vs. Chi. Bears, 1940
  George Blanda, AFC: Houston vs. San Diego, 1961
  George Blanda, AFC: Houston vs. Dall. Texans, 1962 (OT)
  Y.A. Tittle, NFC: N.Y. Giants vs. Chicago, 1963
  Mike Phipps, AFC: Cleveland vs. Miami, 1972
  Dan Pastorini, AFC: Houston vs. Pittsburgh, 1978
  Dan Fouts, AFC-D: San Diego vs. Houston, 1979
  Tommy Kramer, NFC-D: Minnesota vs. Philadelphia, 1980
  Dan Fouts, AFC-D: San Diego vs. Miami, 1982
  Richard Todd, AFC: N.Y. Jets vs Miami, 1982
  Gary Danielson, NFC-D: Detroit vs. San Francisco, 1983
4 By many players

# PASS RECEIVING

## RECEPTIONS
**Most Receptions, Career**
73 Cliff Branch, Oakland-L.A. Raiders, 21 games
70 Fred Biletnikoff, Oakland, 19 games
67 Drew Pearson, Dallas, 22 games
**Most Receptions, Game**
13 Kellen Winslow, AFC-D: San Diego vs. Miami, 1981 (OT)
12 Raymond Berry, NFC: Baltimore vs. N.Y. Giants, 1958
11 Dante Lavelli, NFC: Cleveland vs. Los Angeles, 1950
   Dan Ross, SB: Cincinnati vs. San Francisco, 1981
   Franco Harris, AFC-FR: Pittsburgh vs. San Diego, 1982

**Most Consecutive Games, Pass Receptions**
22　Drew Pearson, Dallas, 1973-83 (current)
18　Paul Warfield, Cleveland-Miami, 1964-74
　　Cliff Branch, Oakland-L.A. Raiders, 1974-83 (current)
15　John Stallworth, Pittsburgh, 1974-83 (current)

**YARDS GAINED**
**Most Yards Gained, Career**
1,289　Cliff Branch, Oakland-L.A. Raiders, 21 games
1,167　Fred Biletnikoff, Oakland, 19 games
1,121　Paul Warfield, Cleveland-Miami, 18 games
**Most Yards Gained, Game**
198　Tom Fears, NFC-D: Los Angeles vs. Chi. Bears, 1950
190　Fred Biletnikoff, AFC: Oakland vs. N.Y. Jets, 1968
186　Cliff Branch, AFC: Oakland vs. Pittsburgh, 1974
**Longest Reception**
93　Elbert Dubenion (from Lamonica), AFC-D: Buffalo vs. Boston, 1963 (TD)
88　Billy Cannon (from Blanda), AFC: Houston vs. L.A. Chargers, 1960 (TD)
86　Bob Hayes (from Meredith), NFC: Dallas vs. Cleveland, 1967 (TD)

**AVERAGE GAIN**
**Highest Average Gain, Career (20 receptions)**
22.8　Harold Jackson, L.A. Rams-New England-Minnesota-Seattle, 14 games (24-548)
20.7　Charlie Brown, Washington, 7 games (31-643)
20.5　Frank Lewis, Pittsburgh-Buffalo, 12 games (27-553)
**Highest Average Gain, Game (3 receptions)**
46.3　Harold Jackson, NFC: Los Angeles vs. Minnesota, 1974 (3-139)
42.7　Billy Cannon, AFC: Houston vs. L.A. Chargers, 1960 (3-128)
42.0　Lenny Moore, NFC: Baltimore vs. N.Y. Giants, 1959 (3-126)

**TOUCHDOWNS**
**Most Touchdowns, Career**
10　Fred Biletnikoff, Oakland, 19 games
　　John Stallworth, Pittsburgh, 16 games
9　Lynn Swann, Pittsburgh, 16 games
8　Drew Pearson, Dallas, 22 games
**Most Touchdowns, Game**
3　Tom Fears, NFC-D: Los Angeles vs. Chi. Bears, 1950
　　Gary Collins, NFC: Cleveland vs. Baltimore, 1964
　　Fred Biletnikoff, AFC-D: Oakland vs. Kansas City, 1968
　　Preston Pearson, NFC: Dallas vs. Los Angeles, 1975
　　Dave Casper, AFC-D: Oakland vs. Baltimore, 1977 (OT)
　　Alvin Garrett, NFC-FR: Washington vs. Detroit, 1982

# INTERCEPTIONS BY

**Most Interceptions, Career**
9　Charlie Waters, Dallas, 25 games
　　Bill Simpson, Los Angeles-Buffalo, 11 games
8　Lester Hayes, Oakland-L.A. Raiders, 11 games
7　Willie Brown, Oakland, 17 games
　　Dennis Thurman, Dallas, 13 games
**Most Interceptions, Game**
4　Vernon Perry, AFC-D: Houston vs. San Diego, 1979
3　Joe Laws, NFC: Green Bay vs. N.Y. Giants, 1944
　　Charlie Waters, NFC-D: Dallas vs. Chicago, 1977
　　Rod Martin, SB: Oakland vs. Philadelphia, 1980
　　Dennis Thurman, NFC-D: Dallas vs. Green Bay, 1982
　　A.J. Duhe, AFC: Miami vs. N.Y. Jets, 1982
2　By many players

**YARDS GAINED**
**Most Yards Gained, Career**
196　Willie Brown, Oakland, 17 games
151　Glen Edwards, Pittsburgh-San Diego, 17 games
149　Bill Simpson, Los Angeles-Buffalo, 11 games
**Most Yards Gained, Game**
98　Darrol Ray, AFC-FR: N.Y. Jets vs. Cincinnati, 1982
94　LeRoy Irvin, NFC-FR: L.A. Rams vs. Dallas, 1983
88　Walt Sumner, NFC-D: Cleveland vs. Dallas, 1969
**Longest Return**
98　Darrol Ray, AFC-FR: N.Y. Jets vs. Cincinnati, 1982 (TD)
94　LeRoy Irvin, NFC-FR: L.A. Rams vs. Dallas, 1983
88　Walt Sumner, NFC-D: Cleveland vs. Dallas, 1969 (TD)

**TOUCHDOWNS**
**Most Touchdowns, Career**
3　Willie Brown, Oakland, 17 games
2　Lester Hayes, Oakland-L.A. Raiders, 11 games
**Most Touchdowns, Game**
1　By 36 players

# PUNTING

**Most Punts, Career**
101　Ray Guy, Oakland-L.A. Raiders, 20 games
84　Danny White, Dallas, 17 games
73　Mike Eischeid, Oakland-Minnesota, 14 games
**Most Punts, Game**
12　David Lee, AFC-D: Baltimore vs. Oakland, 1977 (OT)
11　Ken Strong, NFC: N.Y. Giants vs. Chi. Bears, 1933
　　Jim Norton, AFC: Houston vs. Oakland, 1967
10　Keith Molesworth, NFC: Chi. Bears vs. N.Y. Giants, 1933
　　Riley Smith, NFC: Boston vs. Green Bay, 1936
　　Len Younce, NFC: N.Y. Giants vs. Green Bay, 1944
　　Curley Johnson, AFC: N.Y. Jets vs. Oakland, 1968
　　Tom Orosz, AFC: Miami vs. N.Y. Jets, 1982
**Longest Punt**
76　Ed Danowski, NFC: N.Y. Giants vs. Detroit, 1935
72　Charlie Conerly, NFC-D: N.Y. Giants vs. Cleveland, 1950
71　Ray Guy, AFC: Oakland vs. San Diego, 1980

**AVERAGE YARDAGE**
**Highest Average, Career (20 punts)**
43.4　Jerrel Wilson, Kansas City-New England, 8 games (43-1,866)
43.1　Don Chandler, N.Y. Giants-Green Bay, 14 games (53-2,282)
42.6　Ray Guy, Oakland-L.A. Raiders, 20 games (101-4,302)
**Highest Average, Game (4 punts)**
56.0　Ray Guy, AFC: Oakland vs. San Diego, 1980 (4-224)
52.5　Sammy Baugh, NFC: Washington vs. Chi. Bears, 1942 (6-315)
51.4　John Hadl, AFC: San Diego vs. Buffalo, 1965 (5-257)

# PUNT RETURNS

**Most Punt Returns, Career**
25　Theo Bell, Pittsburgh-Tampa Bay, 10 games
19　Willie Wood, Green Bay, 10 games
　　Butch Johnson, Dallas, 17 games
18　Neal Colzie, Oakland-Miami-Tampa Bay, 10 games
**Most Punt Returns, Game**
7　Ron Gardin, AFC-D: Baltimore vs. Cincinnati, 1970
　　Carl Roaches, AFC-FR: Houston vs. Oakland, 1980
6　George McAfee, NFC-D: Chi. Bears vs. Los Angeles, 1950
　　Eddie Brown, NFC-D: Washington vs. Minnesota, 1976
　　Theo Bell, AFC: Pittsburgh vs. Houston, 1978
　　Eddie Brown, NFC: Los Angeles vs. Tampa Bay, 1979
　　John Sciarra, NFC: Philadelphia vs. Dallas, 1980
　　Kurt Sohn, AFC: N.Y. Jets vs. Miami, 1982
　　Mike Nelms, SB: Washington vs. Miami, 1982
5　By many players

**YARDS GAINED**
**Most Yards Gained, Career**
221　Neal Colzie, Oakland-Miami-Tampa Bay, 10 games
208　Butch Johnson, Dallas, 17 games
204　Theo Bell, Pittsburgh-Tampa Bay, 10 games
**Most Yards Gained, Game**
141　Bob Hayes, NFC-D: Dallas vs. Cleveland, 1967
102　Charley Trippi, NFC: Chi. Cardinals vs. Philadelphia, 1947
101　Bosh Pritchard, NFC-D: Philadelphia vs. Pittsburgh, 1947
**Longest Return**
81　Hugh Gallarneau, NFC-D: Chi. Bears vs. Green Bay, 1941 (TD)
79　Bosh Pritchard, NFC-D: Philadelphia vs. Pittsburgh, 1947 (TD)
75　Charley Trippi, NFC: Chi. Cardinals vs. Philadelphia, 1947 (TD)

**AVERAGE YARDAGE**
**Highest Average, Career (10 returns)**
12.6　Bob Hayes, Dallas, 15 games (12-151)
12.4　Mike Fuller, San Diego-Cincinnati, 7 games (13-161)
12.3　Neal Colzie, Oakland-Miami-Tampa Bay, 10 games (18-221)
**Highest Average Gain, Game (3 returns)**
47.0　Bob Hayes, NFC-D: Dallas vs. Cleveland, 1967 (3-141)
29.0　George (Butch) Byrd, AFC: Buffalo vs. San Diego, 1965 (3-87)
25.3　Bosh Pritchard, NFC-D: Philadelphia vs. Pittsburgh, 1947 (4-101)

**TOUCHDOWNS**
**Most Touchdowns**
1　Hugh Gallarneau, NFC-D: Chi. Bears vs. Green Bay, 1941
　　Bosh Pritchard, NFC: Philadelphia vs. Pittsburgh, 1947
　　Charley Trippi, NFC: Chi. Cardinals vs. Philadelphia, 1947
　　Verda (Vitamin T) Smith, NFC-D: Los Angeles vs. Detroit, 1952
　　George (Butch) Byrd, AFC: Buffalo vs. San Diego, 1965
　　Golden Richards, NFC: Dallas vs. Minnesota, 1973
　　Wes Chandler, AFC-D: San Diego vs. Miami, 1981 (OT)

# KICKOFF RETURNS

**Most Kickoff Returns, Career**
19　Preston Pearson, Baltimore-Pittsburgh-Dallas, 22 games
18　Charlie West, Minnesota, 9 games
17　David Verser, Cincinnati, 4 games
　　James Brooks, San Diego, 4 games
　　Fulton Walker, Miami, 6 games
**Most Kickoff Returns, Game**
7　Don Bingham, NFC: Chi. Bears vs. N.Y. Giants, 1956
　　Reggie Brown, NFC-FR: Atlanta vs. Minnesota, 1982
　　David Verser, AFC-FR: Cincinnati vs. N.Y. Jets, 1982
　　Del Rodgers, NFC-D: Green Bay vs. Dallas, 1982
　　Henry Ellard, NFC-D: L.A. Rams vs. Washington, 1983
6　Wallace Francis, AFC-D: Buffalo vs. Pittsburgh, 1974
　　Eddie Brown, NFC-D: Washington vs. Minnesota, 1976
　　Eddie Payton, NFC-D: Minnesota vs. Philadelphia, 1980
　　Alvin Hall, NFC-FR: Detroit vs. Washington, 1982
　　Fulton Walker, AFC-D: Miami vs. Seattle, 1983
5　By many players

**YARDS GAINED**
**Most Yards Gained, Career**
481　Carl Garrett, Oakland, 5 games
433　Fulton Walker, Miami, 6 games
391　Preston Pearson, Baltimore-Pittsburgh-Dallas, 22 games
**Most Yards Gained, Game**
190　Fulton Walker, SB: Miami vs. Washington, 1982
170　Les (Speedy) Duncan, NFC-D: Washington vs. San Francisco, 1971
169　Carl Garrett, AFC-D: Oakland vs. Baltimore, 1977 (OT)
**Longest Return**
98　Fulton Walker, SB: Miami vs. Washington, 1982 (TD)
97　Vic Washington, NFC-D: San Francisco vs. Dallas, 1972 (TD)
89　Nat Moore, AFC-D: Miami vs. Oakland, 1974 (TD)
　　Rod Hill, NFC-D: Dallas vs. Green Bay, 1982

**AVERAGE YARDAGE**
**Highest Average, Career (10 returns)**
30.1　Carl Garrett, Oakland, 5 games (16-481)
27.9　George Atkinson, Oakland, 16 games (12-335)
25.5　Fulton Walker, Miami, 6 games (17-433)

**Highest Average, Game (3 returns)**
  56.7  Les (Speedy) Duncan, NFC-D: Washington vs. San Francisco, 1971 (3-170)
  51.3  Ed Podolak, AFC-D: Kansas City vs. Miami, 1971 (OT) (3-154)
  49.0  Les (Speedy) Duncan, AFC: San Diego vs. Buffalo, 1964 (3-147)

## TOUCHDOWNS
**Most Touchdowns**
    1  Vic Washington, NFC-D: San Francisco vs. Dallas, 1972
      Nat Moore, AFC-D: Miami vs. Oakland, 1974
      Marshall Johnson, AFC-D: Baltimore vs. Oakland, 1977 (OT)
      Fulton Walker, SB: Miami vs. Washington, 1982

# FUMBLES
**Most Fumbles, Career**
  13  Tony Dorsett, Dallas, 16 games
  10  Franco Harris, Pittsburgh, 19 games
      Terry Bradshaw, Pittsburgh, 19 games
      Roger Staubach, Dallas, 20 games
   9  Chuck Foreman, Minnesota, 13 games
**Most Fumbles, Game**
   4  Brian Sipe, AFC-D: Cleveland vs. Oakland, 1980
   3  Y.A. Tittle, NFC-D: San Francisco vs. Detroit, 1957
      Bill Nelsen, AFC-D: Cleveland vs. Baltimore, 1972
      Chuck Foreman, NFC: Minnesota vs. Los Angeles, 1974
      Lawrence McCutcheon, NFC-D: Los Angeles vs. St. Louis, 1975
      Roger Staubach, SB: Dallas vs. Pittsburgh, 1975
      Terry Bradshaw, AFC: Pittsburgh vs. Houston, 1978
      Earl Campbell, AFC: Houston vs. Pittsburgh, 1978
      Franco Harris, AFC: Pittsburgh vs. Houston, 1978
      Chuck Muncie, AFC: San Diego vs. Cincinnati, 1981
      Andra Franklin, AFC-FR: Miami vs. New England, 1982
   2  By many players

## RECOVERIES
**Most Own Fumbles Recovered, Career**
   5  Roger Staubach, Dallas, 20 games
   4  Fran Tarkenton, Minnesota, 11 games
   3  Alex Webster, N.Y. Giants, 7 games
      Don Meredith, Dallas, 4 games
      Franco Harris, Pittsburgh, 19 games
      Gerry Mullins, Pittsburgh, 18 games
      Ron Jaworski, Los Angeles-Philadelphia, 10 games
      Lyle Blackwood, Cincinnati-Baltimore-Miami, 9 games
**Most Opponents' Fumbles Recovered, Career**
   4  Cliff Harris, Dallas, 21 games
      Harvey Martin, Dallas, 22 games
      Ted Hendricks, Baltimore-Oakland/L.A. Raiders, 21 games
   3  Paul Krause, Minnesota, 19 games
      Jack Lambert, Pittsburgh, 17 games
      Fred Dryer, Los Angeles, 14 games
      Charlie Waters, Dallas, 25 games
      Jack Ham, Pittsburgh, 16 games
      Mike Hegman, Dallas, 15 games
**Most Fumbles Recovered, Game, Own and Opponents'**
   3  Jack Lambert, AFC: Pittsburgh vs. Oakland, 1975 (3 opp)
      Ron Jaworski, NFC-FR: Philadelphia vs. N.Y. Giants, 1981 (3 own)

## YARDS GAINED
**Longest Return**
  93  Andy Russell, AFC-D: Pittsburgh vs. Baltimore, 1975 (opp, TD)
  60  Mike Curtis, NFC-D: Baltimore vs. Minnesota, 1968 (opp, TD)
      Hugh Green, NFC-FR: Tampa Bay vs. Dallas, 1982 (opp, TD)
  50  Lee Artoe, NFC: Chi. Bears vs. Washington, 1942 (opp, TD)

## TOUCHDOWNS
**Most Touchdowns**
   1  By 19 players

# TEAM RECORDS

## GAMES, VICTORIES, DEFEATS
**Most Consecutive Seasons Participating in Postseason Games**
   9  Dallas, 1975-83
   8  Dallas, 1966-73
      Pittsburgh, 1972-79
      Los Angeles, 1973-80
   6  Cleveland, 1950-55
      Oakland, 1972-77
      Minnesota, 1973-78
**Most Games**
  35  Dallas, 1966-73, 1975-83
  29  Oakland/L.A. Raiders, 1967-70, 1973-77, 1980, 1982-83
  25  Cleveland/L.A. Rams, 1945, 1949-52, 1955, 1967, 1969, 1973-80, 1983
**Most Games Won**
  20  Dallas, 1967, 1970-73, 1975, 1977-78, 1980-82
  19  Oakland/L.A. Raiders, 1967-70, 1973-77, 1980, 1982-83
  14  Pittsburgh, 1972, 1974-76, 1978-79
**Most Consecutive Games Won**
   9  Green Bay, 1961-62, 1965-67
   7  Pittsburgh, 1974-76
   6  Miami, 1972-73
      Pittsburgh, 1978-79
      Washington, 1982-83
**Most Games Lost**
  15  Dallas, 1966-70, 1972-73, 1975-76, 1978-83
      L.A. Rams, 1949-50, 1952, 1955, 1967, 1969, 1973-80, 1983
  14  N.Y. Giants, 1933, 1935, 1939, 1941, 1943-44, 1946, 1950, 1958-59, 1961-63, 1981
  13  Cleveland, 1951-53, 1957-58, 1965, 1967-69, 1971-72, 1980, 1982

**Most Consecutive Games Lost**
   6  N.Y. Giants, 1939, 1941, 1943-44, 1946, 1950
   5  N.Y. Giants, 1958-59, 1961-63
      Los Angeles, 1952, 1955, 1967, 1969, 1973
      Cleveland, 1969, 1971-72, 1980, 1982 (current)
   4  Washington, 1972-74, 1976
      Baltimore, 1971, 1975-77 (current)
      Miami, 1974, 1978-79, 1981
      Chi. Cards/St. Louis, 1948, 1974-75, 1982 (current)
      Boston/New England, 1963, 1976, 1978, 1982 (current)
      Denver, 1977-79, 1983 (current)

# SCORING
**Most Points, Game**
  73  NFC: Chi. Bears vs. Washington, 1940
  59  NFC: Detroit vs. Cleveland, 1957
  56  NFC: Cleveland vs. Detroit, 1954
      AFC-D: Oakland vs. Houston, 1969
**Most Points, Both Teams, Game**
  79  AFC-D: San Diego (41) vs. Miami (38), 1981 (OT)
  73  NFC: Chi. Bears (73) vs. Washington (0), 1940
      NFC: Detroit (59) vs. Cleveland (14), 1957
  68  AFC-D: Oakland (37) vs. Baltimore (31), 1977 (OT)
**Fewest Points, Both Teams, Game**
   5  NFC-D: Detroit (0) vs. Dallas (5), 1970
   7  NFC: Chi. Cardinals (0) vs. Philadelphia (7), 1948
   9  NFC: Tampa Bay (0) vs. Los Angeles (9), 1979
**Largest Margin of Victory, Game**
  73  NFC: Chi. Bears vs. Washington, 1940 (73-0)
  49  AFC-D: Oakland vs. Houston, 1969 (56-7)
  46  NFC: Cleveland vs. Detroit, 1954 (56-10)
**Most Points, Shutout Victory, Game**
  73  NFC: Chi. Bears vs. Washington, 1940
  38  NFC-D: Dallas vs. Tampa Bay, 1981
  37  NFC: Green Bay vs. N.Y. Giants, 1961

**Most Points, Each Half**

| | | |
|---|---|---|
| 1st: | 38 | NFC-D: Washington vs. L.A. Rams, 1983 |
| | 35 | NFC: Cleveland vs. Detroit, 1954 |
| | | AFC-D: Oakland vs. Houston, 1969 |
| | 34 | NFC: N.Y. Giants vs. Chi. Bears, 1956 |
| 2nd: | 45 | NFC: Chi. Bears vs. Washington, 1940 |
| | 28 | NFC: Chi. Bears vs. N.Y. Giants, 1941 |
| | | NFC: Detroit vs. Cleveland, 1957 |
| | | NFC-D: Dallas vs. Cleveland, 1967 |
| | | NFC-D: Dallas vs. Tampa Bay, 1981 |
| | 27 | NFC: N.Y. Giants vs. Chi. Bears, 1934 |
| | | NFC: Chi. Bears vs. Washington, 1943 |
| | | NFC: Cleveland vs. Baltimore, 1964 |

**Most Points, Each Quarter**

| | | |
|---|---|---|
| 1st: | 28 | AFC-D: Oakland vs. Houston, 1969 |
| | 24 | NFC-D: San Diego vs. Miami, 1981 (OT) |
| | 21 | NFC: Chi. Bears vs. Washington, 1940 |
| | | AFC: San Diego vs. Boston, 1963 |
| | | AFC-D: Oakland vs. Kansas City, 1968 |
| | | AFC: Oakland vs. San Diego, 1980 |
| 2nd: | 26 | AFC-D: Pittsburgh vs. Buffalo, 1974 |
| | 24 | NFC-D: Chi. Bears vs. Green Bay, 1941 |
| | | NFC: Green Bay vs. N.Y. Giants, 1961 |
| | 21 | NFC: Cleveland vs. Detroit, 1954 |
| | | NFC: N.Y. Giants vs. Chi. Bears, 1956 |
| | | AFC-D: Houston vs. New England, 1978 |
| | | NFC-FR: Green Bay vs. St. Louis, 1982 |
| | | NFC-D: Washington vs. L.A. Rams, 1983 |
| 3rd: | 26 | NFC: Chi. Bears vs. Washington, 1940 |
| | 21 | NFC-D: Dallas vs. Cleveland, 1967 |
| | | NFC-D: Dallas vs. Tampa Bay, 1981 |
| | | AFC-D: L.A. Raiders vs. Pittsburgh, 1983 |
| | 17 | NFC: Cleveland vs. Baltimore, 1964 |
| | | NFC-D: Dallas vs. Chicago, 1977 |
| 4th: | 27 | NFC: N.Y. Giants vs. Chi. Bears, 1934 |
| | 24 | NFC: Baltimore vs. N.Y. Giants, 1959 |
| | 21 | AFC: Pittsburgh vs. Oakland, 1974 |
| | | NFC: Dallas vs. Los Angeles, 1978 |
| | | AFC-FR: N.Y. Jets vs. Cincinnati, 1982 |
| | | NFC: San Francisco vs. Washington, 1983 |
| OT: | 6 | NFC: Baltimore vs. N.Y. Giants, 1958 |
| | | AFC-D: Oakland vs. Baltimore, 1977 |

## TOUCHDOWNS
**Most Touchdowns, Game**
  11  NFC: Chi. Bears vs. Washington, 1940
   8  NFC: Cleveland vs. Detroit, 1954
      NFC: Detroit vs. Cleveland, 1957
      AFC-D: Oakland vs. Houston, 1969
   7  AFC: San Diego vs. Boston, 1963
      NFC-D: Dallas vs. Cleveland, 1967
**Most Touchdowns, Both Teams, Game**
  11  NFC: Chi. Bears (11) vs. Washington (0), 1940
  10  NFC: Detroit (8) vs. Cleveland (2), 1957
      AFC-D: Miami (5) vs. San Diego (5), 1981 (OT)
   9  NFC: Chi. Bears (6) vs. Washington (3), 1943
      NFC: Cleveland (8) vs. Detroit (1), 1954
      NFC-D: Dallas (7) vs. Cleveland (2), 1967
      AFC-D: Oakland (8) vs. Houston (1), 1969
      AFC-D: Oakland (5) vs. Baltimore (4), 1977 (OT)
      SB: Pittsburgh (5) vs. Dallas (4), 1978
**Fewest Touchdowns, Both Teams, Game**
   0  NFC-D: N.Y. Giants vs. Cleveland, 1950
      NFC-D: Dallas vs. Detroit, 1970
      NFC: Los Angeles vs. Tampa Bay, 1979

1 NFC: Chi. Cardinals (0) vs. Philadelphia (1), 1948
AFC: San Diego (0) vs. Houston (1), 1961
AFC-D: N. Y. Jets (0) vs. Kansas City (1), 1969
NFC-D: Green Bay (0) vs. Washington (1), 1972
2 In many games

## POINTS AFTER TOUCHDOWN
**Most Points After Touchdown, Game**
8 NFC: Cleveland vs. Detroit, 1954
NFC: Detroit vs. Cleveland, 1957
AFC-D: Oakland vs. Houston, 1969
7 NFC: Chi. Bears vs. Washington, 1940
NFC-D: Dallas vs. Cleveland, 1967
6 AFC: San Diego vs. Boston, 1963
NFC-D: Washington vs. L.A. Rams, 1983
**Most Points After Touchdown, Both Teams, Game**
10 NFC: Detroit (8) vs. Cleveland (2), 1957
AFC-D: Miami (5) vs. San Diego (5), 1981 (OT)
9 NFC: Cleveland (8) vs. Detroit (1), 1954
NFC-D: Dallas (7) vs. Cleveland (2), 1967
AFC-D: Oakland (8) vs. Houston (1), 1969
8 In many games
**Fewest Points After Touchdown, Both Teams, Game**
0 NFC-D: N.Y. Giants vs. Cleveland, 1950
NFC-D: Dallas vs. Detroit, 1970
NFC: Los Angeles vs. Tampa Bay, 1979

## FIELD GOALS
**Most Field Goals, Game**
4 AFC-D: Boston vs. Buffalo, 1963
AFC: Oakland vs. Houston, 1967
SB: Green Bay vs. Oakland, 1967
NFC: Washington vs. Dallas, 1972
AFC-D: Oakland vs. Pittsburgh, 1973
SB: San Francisco vs. Cincinnati, 1981
3 By many teams
**Most Field Goals, Both Teams, Game**
5 NFC: Green Bay (3) vs. Cleveland (2), 1965
AFC: Oakland (3) vs. N.Y. Jets (2), 1968
NFC: Washington (4) vs. Dallas (1), 1972
AFC-D: Cincinnati (3) vs. Miami (2), 1973
NFC-D: Los Angeles (3) vs. Dallas (2), 1973
NFC-D: Dallas (3) vs. Green Bay (2), 1982
4 In many games
**Most Field Goals Attempted, Game**
6 AFC: Oakland vs. Houston, 1967
NFC-D: Los Angeles vs. Dallas, 1973
5 By many teams
**Most Field Goals Attempted, Both Teams, Game**
8 NFC-D: Los Angeles (6) vs. Dallas (2), 1973
NFC-D: Detroit (5) vs. San Francisco (3), 1983
7 In many games

## SAFETIES
**Most Safeties, Game**
1 By 11 teams

# FIRST DOWNS
**Most First Downs, Game**
34 AFC-D: San Diego vs. Miami, 1981 (OT)
29 AFC-D: Pittsburgh vs. Buffalo, 1974
AFC-D: Pittsburgh vs. Baltimore, 1976
NFC-FR: Dallas vs. Los Angeles, 1980
NFC-FR: Dallas vs. Tampa Bay, 1982
AFC-FR: San Diego vs. Pittsburgh, 1982
AFC-D: Miami vs. San Diego, 1982
28 AFC-D: Oakland vs. Baltimore, 1977 (OT)
NFC-FR: St. Louis vs. Green Bay, 1982
**Fewest First Downs, Game**
6 NFC: N.Y. Giants vs. Green Bay, 1961
7 NFC: Green Bay vs. Boston, 1936
NFC-D: Pittsburgh vs. Philadelphia, 1947
NFC: Chi. Cardinals vs. Philadelphia, 1948
NFC: Los Angeles vs. Philadelphia, 1949
NFC-D: Cleveland vs. N.Y. Giants, 1958
AFC-D: Cincinnati vs. Baltimore, 1970
NFC-D: Detroit vs. Dallas, 1970
8 By many teams
**Most First Downs, Both Teams, Game**
59 AFC-D: San Diego (34) vs. Miami (25), 1981 (OT)
55 AFC-FR: San Diego (29) vs. Pittsburgh (26), 1982
50 AFC: Oakland (28) vs. Baltimore (22), 1977 (OT)
NFC-FR: St. Louis (28) vs. Green Bay (22), 1982
AFC-FR: N.Y. Jets (27) vs. Cincinnati (23), 1982
**Fewest First Downs, Both Teams, Game**
15 NFC: Green Bay (7) vs. Boston (8), 1936
19 NFC: N.Y. Giants (9) vs. Green Bay (10), 1939
NFC: Washington (9) vs. Chi. Bears (10), 1942
20 NFC-D: Cleveland (9) vs. N.Y. Giants (11), 1950

## RUSHING
**Most First Downs, Rushing, Game**
19 NFC-FR: Dallas vs. Los Angeles, 1980
18 AFC-D: Miami vs. Cincinnati,1973
AFC-D: Pittsburgh vs. Buffalo, 1974
16 NFC: Philadelphia vs. Chi. Cardinals, 1948
NFC: Dallas vs. San Francisco, 1970
**Fewest First Downs, Rushing, Game**
0 NFC: Los Angeles vs. Philadelphia, 1949
AFC-D: Buffalo vs. Boston, 1963
AFC: Oakland vs. Pittsburgh, 1974

1 NFC: N.Y. Giants vs. Green Bay, 1961
AFC-D: Houston vs. Oakland, 1969
NFC: Los Angeles vs. Dallas, 1975
AFC-FR: Cleveland vs. L.A. Raiders, 1982
2 By many teams
**Most First Downs, Rushing, Both Teams, Game**
25 NFC-FR: Dallas (19) vs. Los Angeles (6), 1980
23 NFC: Cleveland (15) vs. Detroit (8), 1952
AFC-D: Miami (18) vs. Cincinnati (5), 1973
AFC-D: Pittsburgh (18) vs. Buffalo (5), 1974
22 AFC: Miami (18) vs. Oakland (4), 1973
AFC-D: Buffalo (11) vs. Cincinnati (11), 1981
AFC-D: L.A. Raiders (13) vs. Pittsburgh (9), 1983
**Fewest First Downs, Rushing, Both Teams, Game**
5 AFC-D: Buffalo (0) vs. Boston (5), 1963
6 NFC: Green Bay (2) vs. Boston (4), 1936
NFC-D: Baltimore (2) vs. Minnesota (4), 1968
AFC-D: Houston (1) vs. Oakland (5), 1969
7 NFC-D: Washington (2) vs. N.Y. Giants (5), 1943
NFC: Baltimore (3) vs. N.Y. Giants (4), 1959
NFC: Washington (3) vs: Dallas (4), 1972
AFC-FR: N.Y. Jets (3) vs. Buffalo (4), 1981

## PASSING
**Most First Downs, Passing, Game**
21 AFC-D: Miami vs. San Diego, 1981 (OT)
AFC-D: San Diego vs. Miami, 1981 (OT)
20 NFC-FR: Dallas vs. L.A. Rams, 1983
19 NFC-FR: St. Louis vs. Green Bay, 1982
NFC-FR: Dallas vs. Tampa Bay, 1982
AFC-FR: Pittsburgh vs. San Diego, 1982
AFC-FR: San Diego vs. Pittsburgh, 1982
NFC: Dallas vs. Washington, 1982
**Fewest First Downs, Passing, Game**
0 NFC: Philadelphia vs. Chi. Cardinals, 1948
1 NFC-D: N.Y. Giants vs. Washington, 1943
NFC: Cleveland vs. Detroit, 1953
SB: Denver vs. Dallas, 1977
2 By many teams
**Most First Downs, Passing, Both Teams, Game**
42 AFC-D: Miami (21) vs. San Diego (21), 1981 (OT)
38 AFC-FR: Pittsburgh (19) vs. San Diego (19), 1982
32 NFC-FR: St. Louis (19) vs. Green Bay (13), 1982
**Fewest First Downs, Passing, Both Teams, Game**
2 NFC: Philadelphia (0) vs. Chi. Cardinals (2), 1948
4 NFC-D: Cleveland (2) vs. N.Y. Giants (2), 1950
5 NFC: Detroit (2) vs. N.Y. Giants (3), 1935
NFC: Green Bay (2) vs. N.Y. Giants (3), 1939

## PENALTY
**Most First Downs, Penalty, Game**
7 AFC-D: New England vs. Oakland, 1976
5 AFC-FR: Cleveland vs. L.A. Raiders, 1982
4 By many teams
**Most First Downs, Penalty, Both Teams, Game**
9 AFC-D: New England (7) vs. Oakland (2), 1976
8 NFC-FR: Atlanta (4) vs. Minnesota (4), 1982
7 AFC-D: Baltimore (4) vs. Oakland (3), 1977 (OT)

# NET YARDS GAINED RUSHING AND PASSING
**Most Yards Gained, Game**
610 AFC: San Diego vs. Boston, 1963
564 AFC-D: San Diego vs. Miami, 1981 (OT)
528 NFC-FR: Dallas vs. Los Angeles, 1980
**Fewest Yards Gained, Game**
86 NFC-D: Cleveland vs. N.Y. Giants, 1958
99 NFC: Chi. Cardinals vs. Philadelphia, 1948
114 NFC-D: N.Y. Giants vs. Washington, 1943
**Most Yards Gained, Both Teams, Game**
1,036 AFC-D: San Diego (564) vs. Miami (472), 1981 (OT)
912 AFC-FR: N. Y. Jets (517) vs. Cincinnati (395), 1982
901 AFC-FR: San Diego (479) vs. Pittsburgh (422), 1982
**Fewest Yards Gained, Both Teams, Game**
331 NFC: Chi. Cardinals (99) vs. Philadelphia (232), 1948
332 NFC-D: N.Y. Giants (150) vs. Cleveland (182), 1950
336 NFC: Boston (116) vs. Green Bay (220), 1936

# RUSHING
## ATTEMPTS
**Most Attempts, Game**
65 NFC: Detroit vs. N.Y. Giants, 1935
61 NFC: Philadelphia vs. Los Angeles, 1949
57 NFC: Chi. Bears vs. Washington, 1940
NFC: Philadelphia vs. Chi. Cardinals, 1948
SB: Pittsburgh vs. Minnesota, 1974
**Fewest Attempts, Game**
12 AFC-D: Buffalo vs. Boston, 1963
13 NFC-D: Cleveland vs. N.Y. Giants, 1958
AFC: Buffalo vs. Kansas City, 1966
NFC-D: Minnesota vs. Philadelphia, 1980
14 NFC: Washington vs. Chi. Bears, 1940
NFC: N.Y. Giants vs. Green Bay, 1961
**Most Attempts, Both Teams, Game**
109 NFC: Detroit (65) vs. N.Y. Giants (44), 1935
97 AFC-D: Baltimore (50) vs. Oakland (47), 1977 (OT)
91 NFC: Philadelphia (57) vs. Chi. Cardinals (34), 1948
**Fewest Attempts, Both Teams, Game**
45 AFC-FR: N.Y. Jets (22) vs. Buffalo (23), 1981
46 AFC: Buffalo (13) vs. Kansas City (33), 1966
48 AFC-D: Buffalo (12) vs. Boston (36), 1963
AFC: Boston (16) vs. San Diego (32), 1963

## YARDS GAINED
**Most Yards Gained, Game**
- 382   NFC: Chi. Bears vs. Washington, 1940
- 338   NFC-FR: Dallas vs. Los Angeles, 1980
- 318   AFC: San Diego vs. Boston, 1963

**Fewest Yards Gained, Game**
- 7   AFC-D: Buffalo vs. Boston, 1963
- 17   SB: Minnesota vs. Pittsburgh, 1974
- 21   NFC: Los Angeles vs. Philadelphia, 1949

**Most Yards Gained, Both Teams, Game**
- 430   NFC-FR: Dallas (338) vs. Los Angeles (92), 1980
- 426   NFC: Cleveland (227) vs. Detroit (199), 1952
- 404   NFC: Chi. Bears (382) vs. Washington (22), 1940

**Fewest Yards Gained, Both Teams, Game**
- 90   AFC-D: Buffalo (7) vs. Boston (83), 1963
- 106   NFC: Boston (39) vs. Green Bay (67), 1936
- 128   NFC-FR: Philadelphia (53) vs. Atlanta (75), 1978

## AVERAGE GAIN
**Highest Average Gain, Game**
- 9.94   AFC: San Diego vs. Boston, 1963 (32-318)
- 9.29   NFC-D: Green Bay vs. Dallas, 1982 (17-158)
- 7.35   NFC-FR: Dallas vs. Los Angeles, 1980 (46-338)

**Lowest Average Gain, Game**
- 0.58   AFC-D: Buffalo vs. Boston, 1963 (12-7)
- 0.81   SB: Minnesota vs. Pittsburgh, 1974 (21-17)
- 0.88   NFC: Los Angeles vs. Philadelphia, 1949 (24-21)

## TOUCHDOWNS
**Most Touchdowns, Game**
- 7   NFC: Chi. Bears vs. Washington, 1940
- 5   NFC: Cleveland vs. Detroit, 1954
- 4   NFC: Detroit vs. N.Y. Giants, 1935
  - AFC: San Diego vs. Boston, 1963
  - NFC-D: Dallas vs. Cleveland, 1967
  - NFC: Baltimore vs. Cleveland, 1968
  - NFC-FR: Dallas vs. Los Angeles, 1980
  - AFC-D: L.A. Raiders vs. Pittsburgh, 1983

**Most Touchdowns, Both Teams, Game**
- 7   NFC: Chi. Bears (7) vs. Washington (0), 1940
- 6   NFC: Cleveland (5) vs. Detroit (1), 1954
- 5   NFC: Chi. Cardinals (3) vs. Philadelphia (2), 1947
  - AFC: San Diego (4) vs. Boston (1), 1963
  - AFC-D: Cincinnati (3) vs. Buffalo (2), 1981

# PASSING

## ATTEMPTS
**Most Attempts, Game**
- 54   AFC-D: San Diego vs. Miami, 1981 (OT)
- 53   NFC-FR: Dallas vs. L.A. Rams, 1983
- 51   NFC: Washington vs. Chi. Bears, 1940
  - AFC-FR: N.Y. Jets vs. Buffalo, 1981
  - NFC-FR: St. Louis vs. Green Bay, 1982

**Fewest Attempts, Game**
- 5   NFC: Detroit vs. N.Y. Giants, 1935
- 6   AFC: Miami vs. Oakland, 1973
- 7   SB: Miami vs. Minnesota, 1973

**Most Attempts, Both Teams, Game**
- 102   AFC-D: San Diego (54) vs. Miami (48), 1981 (OT)
- 96   AFC: N.Y. Jets (49) vs. Oakland (47), 1968
- 85   AFC-FR: N.Y. Jets (51) vs. Buffalo (34), 1981

**Fewest Attempts, Both Teams, Game**
- 18   NFC: Detroit (5) vs. N.Y. Giants (13), 1935
- 21   NFC: Chi. Bears (7) vs. N.Y. Giants (14), 1933
- 23   NFC: Chi. Cardinals (11) vs. Philadelphia (12), 1948

## COMPLETIONS
**Most Completions, Game**
- 33   AFC-D: San Diego vs. Miami, 1981 (OT)
- 32   NFC-FR: St. Louis vs. Green Bay, 1982
  - NFC-FR: Dallas vs. L.A. Rams, 1983
- 31   AFC-D: Miami vs. San Diego, 1981 (OT)

**Fewest Completions, Game**
- 2   NFC: Detroit vs. N.Y. Giants, 1935
  - NFC: Philadelphia vs. Chi. Cardinals, 1948
- 3   NFC: N.Y. Giants vs. Chi. Bears, 1941
  - NFC: Green Bay vs. N.Y. Giants, 1944
  - NFC: Chi. Cardinals vs. Philadelphia, 1947
  - NFC: Chi. Cardinals vs. Philadelphia, 1948
  - NFC-D: Cleveland vs. N.Y. Giants, 1950
  - NFC-D: N.Y. Giants vs. Cleveland, 1950
  - NFC: Cleveland vs. Detroit, 1953
  - AFC: Miami vs. Oakland, 1973
- 4   NFC-D: Dallas vs. Detroit, 1970
  - AFC: Miami vs. Baltimore, 1971
  - SB: Miami vs. Washington, 1982

**Most Completions, Both Teams, Game**
- 64   AFC-D: San Diego (33) vs. Miami (31), 1981 (OT)
- 55   AFC-FR: Pittsburgh (28) vs. San Diego (27), 1982
- 51   NFC-FR: St. Louis (32) vs. Green Bay (19), 1982

**Fewest Completions, Both Teams, Game**
- 5   NFC: Philadelphia (2) vs. Chi. Cardinals (3), 1948
- 6   NFC: Detroit (2) vs. N.Y. Giants (4), 1935
  - NFC-D: Cleveland (3) vs. N.Y. Giants (3), 1950
- 11   NFC: Green Bay (3) vs. N.Y. Giants (8), 1944
  - NFC-D: Dallas (4) vs. Detroit (7), 1970

## COMPLETION PERCENTAGE
**Highest Completion Percentage, Game (20 attempts)**
- 80.0   NFC-D: Washington vs. L.A. Rams, 1983 (25-20)
- 79.2   AFC-D: Pittsburgh vs. Baltimore, 1976 (24-19)
- 78.3   AFC-D: Miami vs. San Diego, 1982 (23-18)

**Lowest Completion Percentage, Game (20 attempts)**
- 18.5   NFC: Tampa Bay vs. Los Angeles, 1979 (27-5)
- 20.0   NFC-D: N.Y. Giants vs. Washington, 1943 (20-4)
- 25.8   NFC: Chi. Bears vs. Washington, 1937 (31-8)

## YARDS GAINED
**Most Yards Gained, Game**
- 415   AFC-D: San Diego vs. Miami, 1981 (OT)
- 394   AFC-D: Miami vs. San Diego, 1981 (OT)
- 393   AFC: Oakland vs. N.Y. Jets, 1968

**Fewest Yards Gained, Game**
- 3   NFC: Chi. Cardinals vs. Philadelphia, 1948
- 7   NFC: Philadelphia vs. Chi. Cardinals, 1948
- 9   NFC-D: N.Y. Giants vs. Cleveland, 1950
  - NFC: Cleveland vs. Detroit, 1953

**Most Yards Gained, Both Teams, Game**
- 809   AFC-D: San Diego (415) vs. Miami (394), 1981 (OT)
- 658   AFC-FR: San Diego (333) vs. Pittsburgh (325), 1982
- 649   AFC: Oakland (393) vs. N.Y. Jets (256), 1968

**Fewest Yards Gained, Both Teams, Game**
- 10   NFC: Chi. Cardinals (3) vs. Philadelphia (7), 1948
- 38   NFC-D: N.Y. Giants (9) vs. Cleveland (29), 1950
- 102   NFC-D: Dallas (22) vs. Detroit (80), 1970

## TIMES SACKED
**Most Times Sacked, Game**
- 9   AFC: Kansas City vs. Buffalo, 1966
- 8   NFC: Green Bay vs. Dallas, 1967
- 7   NFC-D: Dallas vs. Los Angeles, 1973
  - SB: Dallas vs. Pittsburgh, 1975
  - AFC-FR: Houston vs. Oakland, 1980

**Most Times Sacked, Both Teams, Game**
- 13   AFC: Kansas City (9) vs. Buffalo (4), 1966
- 12   NFC-D: Dallas (7) vs. Los Angeles (5), 1973
- 10   AFC-FR: Houston (7) vs. Oakland (3), 1980

**Fewest Times Sacked, Both Teams, Game**
- 0   AFC-D: Buffalo vs. Pittsburgh, 1974
  - AFC-FR: Pittsburgh vs. San Diego, 1982
- 1   In many games

## TOUCHDOWNS
**Most Touchdowns, Game**
- 6   AFC-D: Oakland vs. Houston, 1969
- 5   NFC: Chi. Bears vs. Washington, 1943
  - NFC: Detroit vs. Cleveland, 1957
  - AFC-D: Oakland vs. Kansas City, 1968
- 4   NFC: Cleveland vs. Los Angeles, 1950
  - NFC: Green Bay vs. Dallas, 1966
  - AFC-D: Oakland vs. Miami, 1974
  - NFC: Dallas vs. Los Angeles, 1975
  - SB: Pittsburgh vs. Dallas, 1978
  - AFC-D: Miami vs. San Diego, 1981 (OT)
  - NFC-FR: Green Bay vs. St. Louis, 1982

**Most Touchdowns, Both Teams, Game**
- 7   NFC: Chi. Bears (5) vs. Washington (2), 1943
  - AFC-D: Oakland (6) vs. Houston (1), 1969
  - SB: Pittsburgh (4) vs. Dallas (3), 1978
  - AFC-D: Miami (4) vs. San Diego (3), 1981 (OT)
- 6   NFC-FR: Green Bay (4) vs. St. Louis (2), 1982
- 5   In many games

# INTERCEPTIONS BY

**Most Interceptions By, Game**
- 8   NFC: Chi. Bears vs. Washington, 1940
- 7   NFC: Cleveland vs. Los Angeles, 1955
- 6   NFC: Green Bay vs. N.Y. Giants, 1939
  - NFC: Chi. Bears vs. N.Y. Giants, 1946
  - NFC: Cleveland vs. Detroit, 1954
  - AFC: San Diego vs. Houston, 1961

**Most Interceptions By, Both Teams, Game**
- 10   NFC: Cleveland (7) vs. Los Angeles (3), 1955
  - AFC: San Diego (6) vs. Houston (4), 1961
- 9   NFC: Green Bay (6) vs. N.Y. Giants (3), 1939
- 8   NFC: Chi. Bears (8) vs. Washington (0), 1940
  - NFC: Chi. Bears (6) vs. N.Y. Giants (2), 1946
  - NFC: Cleveland (6) vs. Detroit (2), 1954
  - AFC-FR: Buffalo (4) vs. N.Y. Jets (4), 1981
  - AFC: Miami (5) vs. N.Y. Jets (3), 1982

## YARDS GAINED
**Most Yards Gained, Game**
- 138   AFC-FR: N.Y. Jets vs. Cincinnati, 1982
- 136   AFC: Dall. Texans vs. Houston, 1962 (OT)
- 130   NFC-D: Los Angeles vs. St. Louis, 1975

**Most Yards Gained, Both Teams, Game**
- 156   NFC: Green Bay (123) vs. N.Y. Giants (33), 1939
- 149   NFC: Cleveland (103) vs. Los Angeles (46), 1955
- 141   AFC-FR: Buffalo (79) vs. N.Y. Jets (62), 1981

## TOUCHDOWNS
**Most Touchdowns, Game**
- 3   NFC: Chi. Bears vs. Washington, 1940
- 2   NFC-D: Los Angeles vs. St. Louis, 1975
- 1   In many games

# PUNTING

**Most Punts, Game**
- 13   NFC: N.Y. Giants vs. Chi. Bears, 1933
  - AFC-D: Baltimore vs. Oakland, 1977 (OT)
- 11   AFC: Houston vs. Oakland, 1967
  - AFC-D: Houston vs. Oakland, 1969
- 10   In many games

**Fewest Punts, Game**
- 0   NFC-FR: St. Louis vs. Green Bay, 1982
  - AFC-FR: N.Y. Jets vs. Cincinnati, 1982
- 1   NFC-D: Cleveland vs. Dallas, 1969
  - AFC: Miami vs. Oakland, 1973
  - AFC-D: Oakland vs. Cincinnati, 1975
  - AFC-D: Pittsburgh vs. Baltimore, 1976
  - AFC: Pittsburgh vs. Houston, 1978
  - NFC-FR: Green Bay vs. St. Louis, 1982
  - AFC-FR: Miami vs. New England, 1982
  - AFC-FR: San Diego vs. Pittsburgh, 1982
- 2   In many games

**Most Punts, Both Teams, Game**
- 23   NFC: N.Y. Giants (13) vs. Chi. Bears (10), 1933
- 21   AFC-D: Baltimore (13) vs. Oakland (8), 1977 (OT)
- 20   NFC: Green Bay (10) vs. N.Y. Giants (10), 1944
  - AFC: Miami (10) vs. N.Y. Jets (10), 1982

**Fewest Punts, Both Teams, Game**
- 1   NFC-FR: St. Louis (0) vs. Green Bay (1), 1982
- 2   AFC-FR: N.Y. Jets (0) vs. Cincinnati (2), 1982
- 3   AFC: Miami (1) vs. Oakland (2), 1973
  - AFC-FR: San Diego (1) vs. Pittsburgh (2), 1982

**AVERAGE YARDAGE**

**Highest Average, Punting, Game (4 punts)**
- 56.0   AFC: Oakland vs. San Diego, 1980
- 52.5   NFC: Washington vs. Chi. Bears, 1942
- 51.3   AFC: Pittsburgh vs. Miami, 1972

**Lowest Average, Punting, Game (4 punts)**
- 24.9   NFC: Washington vs. Chi. Bears, 1937
- 25.5   NFC: Green Bay vs. N.Y. Giants, 1962
- 27.8   AFC-D: San Diego vs. Buffalo, 1980

# PUNT RETURNS

**Most Punt Returns, Game**
- 8   NFC: Green Bay vs. N.Y. Giants, 1944
- 7   NFC-D: Washington vs. N.Y. Giants, 1943
  - NFC-D: Chi. Bears vs. Los Angeles, 1950
  - AFC-D: Baltimore vs. Cincinnati, 1970
  - NFC: Los Angeles vs. Minnesota, 1976
  - AFC-FR: Houston vs. Oakland, 1980
  - AFC-D: Cleveland vs. Oakland, 1980
- 6   By many teams

**Most Punt Returns, Both Teams, Game**
- 13   AFC-FR: Houston (7) vs. Oakland (6), 1980
- 11   NFC: Green Bay (8) vs. N.Y. Giants (3), 1944
  - NFC-D: Green Bay (6) vs. Baltimore (5), 1965
- 10   In many games

**Fewest Punt Returns, Both Teams, Game**
- 0   NFC: Chi. Bears vs. N.Y. Giants, 1941
  - AFC: Boston vs. San Diego, 1963
  - NFC-FR: Green Bay vs. St. Louis, 1982
- 1   AFC: Miami (0) vs. Pittsburgh (1), 1972
  - AFC: Cincinnati (0) vs. San Diego (1), 1981
  - AFC-FR: Cincinnati (0) vs. N.Y. Jets (1), 1982
  - AFC-FR: San Diego (0) vs. Pittsburgh (1), 1982
  - NFC-D: Minnesota (0) vs. Washington (1), 1982
  - AFC: Seattle (0) vs. L.A. Raiders (1), 1983
- 2   In many games

**YARDS GAINED**

**Most Yards Gained, Game**
- 155   NFC-D: Dallas vs. Cleveland, 1967
- 150   NFC: Chi. Cardinals vs. Philadelphia, 1947
- 112   NFC-D: Philadelphia vs. Pittsburgh, 1947

**Fewest Yards Gained, Game**
- −10   NFC: Green Bay vs. Cleveland, 1965
- −9   NFC: Dallas vs. Green Bay, 1966
  - AFC-D: Kansas City vs. Oakland, 1968
- −5   AFC-D: Miami vs. Oakland, 1970
  - NFC-D: San Francisco vs. Dallas, 1972
  - NFC: Dallas vs. Washington, 1972

**Most Yards Gained, Both Teams, Game**
- 166   NFC-D: Dallas (155) vs. Cleveland (11), 1967
- 160   NFC: Chi. Cardinals (150) vs. Philadelphia (10), 1947
- 146   NFC-D: Philadelphia (112) vs. Pittsburgh (34), 1947

**Fewest Yards Gained, Both Teams, Game**
- −9   NFC: Dallas (−9) vs. Green Bay (0), 1966
- −6   AFC-D: Miami (−5) vs. Oakland (−1), 1970
- −3   NFC-D: San Francisco (−5) vs. Dallas (2), 1972

**TOUCHDOWNS**

**Most Touchdowns, Game**
- 1   By seven teams

# KICKOFF RETURNS

**Most Kickoff Returns, Game**
- 10   NFC-D: L.A. Rams vs. Washington, 1983
- 9   NFC: Chi. Bears vs. N.Y. Giants, 1956
  - AFC: Boston vs. San Diego, 1963
  - AFC: Houston vs. Oakland, 1967
- 8   By many teams

**Most Kickoff Returns, Both Teams, Game**
- 13   NFC-D: Green Bay (7) vs. Dallas (6), 1982
- 12   AFC: Boston (9) vs. San Diego (3), 1963
  - NFC: Dallas (6) vs. Green Bay (6), 1966
  - AFC-D: Baltimore (6) vs. Oakland (6), 1977 (OT)
  - AFC: Oakland (6) vs. San Diego (6), 1980
  - AFC-D: Miami (6) vs. San Diego (6), 1981 (OT)
  - NFC-D: N.Y. Giants (7) vs. San Francisco (5), 1981
  - AFC-FR: Cincinnati (8) vs. N.Y. Jets (4), 1982
  - NFC-D: L.A. Rams (10) vs. Washington (2), 1983
- 11   In many games

**Fewest Kickoff Returns, Both Teams, Game**
- 1   NFC: Green Bay (0) vs. Boston (1), 1936
- 2   NFC-D: Los Angeles (0) vs. Chi. Bears (2), 1950
  - AFC: Houston (0) vs. San Diego (2), 1961
  - AFC-D: Oakland (1) vs. Pittsburgh (1), 1972
  - AFC-D: N.Y. Jets (0) vs. L.A. Raiders (2), 1982
  - AFC: Miami (1) vs. N.Y. Jets (1), 1982
- 3   In many games

**YARDS GAINED**

**Most Yards Gained, Game**
- 225   NFC: Washington vs. Chi. Bears, 1940
- 222   SB: Miami vs. Washington, 1982
- 215   AFC: Houston vs. Oakland, 1967

**Most Yards Gained, Both Teams, Game**
- 379   AFC-D: Baltimore (193) vs. Oakland (186), 1977 (OT)
- 321   NFC-D: Dallas (173) vs. Green Bay (148), 1982
- 318   AFC-D: Miami (183) vs. Oakland (135), 1974

**Fewest Yards Gained, Both Teams, Game**
- 31   NFC-D: Los Angeles (0) vs. Chi. Bears (31), 1950
- 32   NFC: Green Bay (0) vs. Boston (32), 1936
- 46   NFC-D: Philadelphia (15) vs. Pittsburgh (31), 1947
  - AFC-D: Baltimore (0) vs. Cincinnati (46), 1970

**TOUCHDOWNS**

**Most Touchdowns, Game**
- 1   NFC-D: San Francisco vs. Dallas, 1972
  - AFC-D: Miami vs. Oakland, 1974
  - AFC-D: Baltimore vs. Oakland, 1977 (OT)
  - SB: Miami vs. Washington, 1982

# PENALTIES

**Most Penalties, Game**
- 14   AFC-FR: Oakland vs. Houston, 1980
  - NFC-D: San Francisco vs. N.Y. Giants, 1981
- 12   NFC-D: Chi. Bears vs. Green Bay, 1941
  - AFC-D: Pittsburgh vs. Baltimore, 1976
  - SB: Dallas vs. Denver, 1977
  - AFC-FR: N.Y. Jets vs. Cincinnati, 1982
- 11   NFC: N.Y. Giants vs. Green Bay, 1944
  - AFC-D: Oakland vs. New England, 1976
  - AFC-D: Pittsburgh vs. Denver, 1978
  - NFC-FR: Dallas vs. Los Angeles, 1980

**Fewest Penalties, Game**
- 0   NFC: Philadelphia vs. Green Bay, 1960
  - NFC-D: Detroit vs. Dallas, 1970
  - AFC-D: Miami vs. Oakland, 1970
  - SB: Miami vs. Dallas, 1971
  - NFC-D: Washington vs. Minnesota, 1973
  - SB: Pittsburgh vs. Dallas, 1975
- 1   By many teams

**Most Penalties, Both Teams, Game**
- 22   AFC-FR: Oakland (14) vs. Houston (8), 1980
  - NFC-D: San Francisco (14) vs. N.Y. Giants (8), 1981
- 21   AFC-D: Oakland (11) vs. New England (10), 1976
- 20   SB: Dallas (12) vs. Denver (8), 1977

**Fewest Penalties, Both Teams, Game**
- 2   NFC: Washington (1) vs. Chi. Bears (1), 1937
  - NFC-D: Washington (0) vs. Minnesota (2), 1973
  - SB: Pittsburgh (0) vs. Dallas (2), 1975
- 3   AFC: Miami (1) vs. Baltimore (2), 1971
  - NFC: San Francisco (1) vs. Dallas (2), 1971
  - SB: Dallas (0) vs. Dallas (3), 1971
  - AFC-D: Pittsburgh (1) vs. Oakland (2), 1972
  - AFC-D: Miami (1) vs. Cincinnati (2), 1973
- 4   NFC-D: Cleveland (2) vs. Dallas (2), 1967
  - NFC-D: Minnesota (1) vs. San Francisco (3), 1970
  - AFC-D: Miami (0) vs. Oakland (4), 1970
  - NFC-D: Dallas (2) vs. Minnesota (2), 1971

**YARDS PENALIZED**

**Most Yards Penalized, Game**
- 145   NFC-D: San Francisco vs. N.Y. Giants, 1981
- 133   SB: Dallas vs. Baltimore, 1970
- 128   NFC-D: Chi. Bears vs. Green Bay, 1941

**Fewest Yards Penalized, Game**
- 0   By six teams

**Most Yards Penalized, Both Teams, Game**
- 206   NFC-D: San Francisco (145) vs. N.Y. Giants (61), 1981
- 192   AFC-D: Denver (104) vs. Pittsburgh (88), 1978
- 182   NFC-FR: Atlanta (98) vs. Minnesota (84), 1982

**Fewest Yards Penalized, Both Teams, Game**
- 9   NFC-D: Washington (0) vs. Minnesota (9), 1973
- 15   SB: Miami (0) vs. Dallas (15), 1971
- 20   NFC: Washington (5) vs. Chi. Bears (15), 1937
  - AFC-D: Pittsburgh (5) vs. Oakland (15), 1972
  - SB: Pittsburgh (0) vs. Dallas (20), 1975

# FUMBLES

**Most Fumbles, Game**
- 6   By nine teams

**Most Fumbles, Both Teams, Game**
- 12   AFC: Houston (6) vs. Pittsburgh (6), 1978
- 10   NFC: Chi. Bears (5) vs. N.Y. Giants (5), 1934
  - SB: Dallas (6) vs. Denver (4), 1977
- 9   NFC-D: San Francisco (6) vs. Detroit (3), 1957
  - NFC-D: San Francisco (5) vs. Dallas (4), 1972
  - NFC: Dallas (5) vs. Philadelphia (4), 1980

**Most Fumbles Lost, Game**
    4  NFC: N.Y. Giants vs. Baltimore, 1958 (OT)
        AFC: Kansas City vs. Oakland, 1969
        SB: Baltimore vs. Dallas, 1970
        AFC: Pittsburgh vs. Oakland, 1975
        SB: Denver vs. Dallas, 1977
        AFC: Houston vs. Pittsburgh, 1978
    3  By many teams

**Fewest Fumbles, Both Teams, Game**
    0  NFC: Green Bay vs. Cleveland, 1965
        AFC: Buffalo vs. San Diego, 1965
        AFC-D: Oakland vs. Miami, 1974
        AFC-D: Houston vs. San Diego, 1979
        NFC-D: Dallas vs. Los Angeles, 1979
        SB: Los Angeles vs. Pittsburgh, 1979
        AFC-D: Buffalo vs. Cincinnati, 1981
    1  In many games

**RECOVERIES**

**Most Total Fumbles Recovered, Game**
    8  SB: Dallas vs. Denver, 1977 (4 own, 4 opp)
    7  NFC: Chi. Bears vs. N.Y. Giants, 1934 (5 own, 2 opp)
        NFC-D: San Francisco vs. Detroit, 1957 (4 own, 3 opp)
        NFC-D: San Francisco vs. Dallas, 1972 (4 own, 3 opp)
        AFC: Pittsburgh vs. Houston, 1978 (3 own, 4 opp)
    6  AFC: Houston vs. San Diego, 1961 (4 own, 2 opp)
        AFC-D: Cleveland vs. Baltimore, 1971 (4 own, 2 opp)
        AFC-D: Cleveland vs. Oakland, 1980 (5 own, 1 opp)
        NFC: Philadelphia vs. Dallas, 1980 (3 own, 3 opp)

**Most Own Fumbles Recovered, Game**
    5  NFC: Chi. Bears vs. N.Y. Giants, 1934
        AFC-D: Cleveland vs. Oakland, 1980
    4  By many teams

# TURNOVERS
(Numbers of times losing the ball on interceptions and fumbles.)

**Most Turnovers, Game**
    9  NFC: Washington vs. Chi. Bears, 1940
        NFC: Detroit vs. Cleveland, 1954
        AFC: Houston vs. Pittsburgh, 1978
    8  NFC: N.Y. Giants vs. Chi. Bears, 1946
        NFC: Los Angeles vs. Cleveland, 1955
        NFC: Cleveland vs. Detroit, 1957
        SB: Denver vs. Dallas, 1977
        NFC-D: Minnesota vs. Philadelphia, 1980
    7  AFC: Houston vs. San Diego, 1961
        SB: Baltimore vs. Dallas, 1970
        AFC: Pittsburgh vs. Oakland, 1975
        NFC-D: Chicago vs. Dallas, 1977
        NFC: Los Angeles vs. Dallas, 1978
        AFC-D: San Diego vs. Miami, 1982

**Fewest Turnovers, Game**
    0  By many teams

**Most Turnovers, Both Teams, Game**
   14  AFC: Houston (9) vs. Pittsburgh (5), 1978
   13  NFC: Detroit (9) vs. Cleveland (4), 1954
        AFC: Houston (7) vs. San Diego (6), 1961
   12  AFC: Pittsburgh (7) vs. Oakland (5), 1975

**Fewest Turnovers, Both Teams, Game**
    1  AFC-D: Baltimore (0) vs. Cincinnati (1), 1970
        AFC-D: Pittsburgh (0) vs. Buffalo (1), 1974
        AFC: Oakland (0) vs. Pittsburgh (1), 1976
        NFC-D: Minnesota (0) vs. Washington (1), 1982
    2  In many games

Compiled by Elias Sports Bureau

## INDIVIDUAL RECORDS

### SERVICE

**Most Games**
- 9 Ken Houston, Houston, 1971-73; Washington, 1974-79
  Joe Greene, Pittsburgh, 1971-77, 1979-80
  Jack Lambert, Pittsburgh, 1976-84
- 8 Tom Mack, Los Angeles, 1971-76, 1978-79
  Franco Harris, Pittsburgh, 1973-76, 1978-81
  Lemar Parrish, Cincinnati, 1971-72, 1975-77; Washington, 1978, 1980-81
  Art Shell, Oakland, 1973-79, 1981
  Ted Hendricks, Baltimore, 1972-74; Green Bay, 1975, Oakland, 1981-82; L.A. Raiders, 1983-84
- 7 Ron Yary, Minnesota, 1972-78
  Elvin Bethea, Houston, 1972-76, 1979-80
  Roger Wehrli, St. Louis, 1971-72, 1975-78, 1980
  Jack Youngblood, Los Angeles, 1974-80
  Ray Guy, Oakland, 1974-76, 1981
  Robert Brazile, Houston, 1977-83
  Randy Gradishar, Denver, 1976, 1978-80, 1982-84

### SCORING

**POINTS**

**Most Points, Career**
- 28 Jan Stenerud, Kansas City, 1971-72, 1976 (4-pat, 8-fg)
- 18 John Brockington, Green Bay, 1972-74 (3-td)
  Earl Campbell, Houston, 1979-82, 1984 (3-td)
  Chuck Muncie, New Orleans, 1980; San Diego, 1982-83 (3-td)
  William Andrews, Atlanta, 1981-84 (3-td)
- 16 Garo Yepremian, Miami, 1974, 1979 (1-pat, 5-fg)

**Most Points, Game**
- 18 John Brockington, Green Bay, 1973 (3-td)
- 15 Garo Yepremian, Miami, 1974 (5-fg)
- 14 Jan Stenerud, Kansas City, 1972 (2-pat, 4-fg)

**TOUCHDOWNS**

**Most Touchdowns, Career**
- 3 John Brockington, Green Bay, 1972-74 (2-r, 1-p)
  Earl Campbell, Houston, 1979-82, 1984 (3-td)
  Chuck Muncie, New Orleans, 1980; San Diego, 1982-83 (3-r)
  William Andrews, Atlanta, 1981-84 (l-r, 2-p)
- 2 By seven players

**Most Touchdowns, Game**
- 3 John Brockington, Green Bay, 1973 (2-r, 1-p)
- 2 Mel Renfro, Dallas, 1971 (2-ret)
  Earl Campbell, Houston, 1980 (2-r)
  Chuck Muncie, New Orleans, 1980 (2-r)
  William Andrews, Atlanta, 1984 (2-p)

**POINTS AFTER TOUCHDOWN**

**Most Points After Touchdown, Career**
- 6 Chester Marcol, Green Bay, 1973, 1975 (6 att)
  Mark Moseley, Washington, 1980, 1983 (7 att)
  Ali Haji-Sheikh, N.Y. Giants, 1984 (6 att)

**Most Points After Touchdown, Game**
- 6 Ali Haji-Sheikh, N.Y. Giants, 1984 (6 att)
- 4 Chester Marcol, Green Bay, 1973 (4 att)
  Mark Moseley, Washington, 1980 (5 att)

**FIELD GOALS**

**Most Field Goals Attempted, Career**
- 13 Jan Stenerud, Kansas City, 1971-72, 1976
- 7 Garo Yepremian, Miami, 1974, 1979
  Mark Moseley, Washington, 1980, 1983
- 6 Ed Murray, Detroit, 1981

**Most Field Goals Attempted, Game**
- 6 Jan Stenerud, Kansas City, 1972
  Ed Murray, Detroit, 1981
  Mark Moseley, Washington, 1983
- 5 Garo Yepremian, Miami, 1974
- 4 Jan Stenerud, Kansas City, 1976

**Most Field Goals, Career**
- 8 Jan Stenerud, Kansas City, 1971-72, 1976
- 5 Garo Yepremian, Miami, 1974, 1979
- 4 Ed Murray, Detroit, 1981

**Most Field Goals, Game**
- 5 Garo Yepremian, Miami, 1974 (5 att)
- 4 Jan Stenerud, Kansas City, 1972 (6 att)
  Ed Murray, Detroit, 1981 (6 att)
- 2 By many players

**Longest Field Goal**
- 48 Jan Stenerud, Kansas City, 1972
- 43 Gary Anderson, Pittsburgh, 1984
- 42 Jim Bakken, St. Louis, 1976

### RUSHING

**ATTEMPTS**

**Most Attempts, Career**
- 68 O.J. Simpson, Buffalo, 1973-77
- 62 Walter Payton, Chicago, 1977-81, 1984
- 46 Franco Harris, Pittsburgh, 1973-76, 1978-81
  Earl Campbell, Houston, 1979-82, 1984

**Most Attempts, Game**
- 19 O.J. Simpson, Buffalo, 1973
- 17 Marv Hubbard, Oakland, 1974
- 16 O.J. Simpson, Buffalo, 1973

**YARDS GAINED**

**Most Yards Gained, Career**
- 356 O.J. Simpson, Buffalo, 1973-77
- 254 Walter Payton, Chicago, 1977-81, 1984
- 220 Earl Campbell, Houston, 1979-82, 1984

**Most Yards Gained, Game**
- 112 O.J. Simpson, Buffalo, 1973
- 104 Marv Hubbard, Oakland, 1974
- 77 Walter Payton, Chicago, 1978

**Longest Run From Scrimmage**
- 41 Lawrence McCutcheon, Los Angeles, 1976
- 30 O.J. Simpson, Buffalo, 1975
- 29 Franco Harris, Pittsburgh, 1973

**AVERAGE GAIN**

**Highest Average Gain, Career (20 attempts)**
- 5.81 Marv Hubbard, Oakland, 1972-74 (36-209)
- 5.71 Wilbert Montgomery, Philadelphia, 1979-80 (21-120)
- 5.36 Larry Csonka, Miami, 1971-72, 1975 (22-118)

**Highest Average Gain, Game (10 attempts)**
- 7.00 O.J. Simpson, Buffalo, 1973 (16-112)
  Ottis Anderson, St. Louis, 1981 (10-70)
- 6.90 Earl Campbell, Houston, 1980 (10-69)
- 6.12 Marv Hubbard, Oakland, 1974 (17-104)

**TOUCHDOWNS**

**Most Touchdowns, Career**
- 3 Earl Campbell, Houston, 1979-82, 1984
  Chuck Muncie, New Orleans, 1980; San Diego, 1982-83
- 2 John Brockington, Green Bay, 1972-74
  O.J. Simpson, Buffalo, 1973-77

**Most Touchdowns, Game**
- 2 John Brockington, Green Bay, 1973
  Earl Campbell, Houston, 1980
  Chuck Muncie, New Orleans, 1980

### PASSING

**ATTEMPTS**

**Most Attempts, Career**
- 93 Dan Fouts, San Diego, 1980-84
- 88 Bob Griese, Miami, 1971-72, 1974-75, 1977, 1979
- 56 Ken Anderson, Cincinnati, 1976-77, 1982-83

**Most Attempts, Game**
- 32 Bill Kenney, Kansas City, 1984
- 30 Dan Fouts, San Diego, 1983
- 28 Jim Hart, St. Louis, 1976

**COMPLETIONS**

**Most Completions, Career**
- 47 Dan Fouts, San Diego, 1980-84
- 44 Bob Griese, Miami, 1971-72, 1974-75, 1977, 1979
- 33 Ken Anderson, Cincinnati, 1976-77, 1982-83

**Most Completions, Game**
- 21 Joe Theismann, Washington, 1984
- 17 Dan Fouts, San Diego, 1983
- 14 Norm Snead, N.Y. Giants, 1973
  Ken Anderson, Cincinnati, 1983
  Danny White, Dallas, 1983

**COMPLETION PERCENTAGE**

**Highest Completion Percentage, Career (40 attempts)**
- 68.9 Joe Theismann, Washington, 1983-84 (45-31)
- 58.9 Ken Anderson, Cincinnati, 1976-77, 1982-83 (56-33)
- 50.5 Dan Fouts, San Diego, 1980-84 (93-47)

**Highest Completion Percentage, Game (10 attempts)**
- 90.0 Archie Manning, New Orleans, 1980 (10-9)
- 77.8 Joe Theismann, Washington, 1984 (27-21)
- 70.0 Ken Anderson, Cincinnati, 1977 (10-7)
  Ken Anderson, Cincinnati, 1983 (20-14)
  Joe Montana, San Francisco, 1984 (10-7)

**YARDS GAINED**

**Most Yards Gained, Career**
- 717 Dan Fouts, San Diego, 1980-84
- 554 Bob Griese, Miami, 1971-72, 1974-75, 1977, 1979
- 398 Ken Anderson, Cincinnati, 1976-77, 1982-83

**Most Yards Gained, Game**
- 274 Dan Fouts, San Diego, 1983
- 242 Joe Theismann, Washington, 1984
- 173 Steve Bartkowski, Atlanta, 1981

**Longest Completion**
- 64 Dan Pastorini, Houston (to Burrough, Houston), 1976 (TD)
- 57 James Harris, Los Angeles (to Gray, St. Louis), 1975
  Ken Anderson, Cincinnati (to G. Pruitt, Cleveland), 1977
- 55 Steve Bartkowski, Atlanta (to Jenkins, Atlanta), 1981 (TD)

**AVERAGE GAIN**

**Highest Average Gain, Career (40 attempts)**
- 7.71 Dan Fouts, San Diego, 1980-84 (93-717)
- 7.64 Joe Theismann, Washington, 1983-84 (45-344)
- 7.11 Ken Anderson, Cincinnati, 1976-77, 1982-83 (56-398)

**Highest Average Gain, Game (10 attempts)**
- 11.40 Ken Anderson, Cincinnati, 1977 (10-114)
- 11.20 Archie Manning, New Orleans, 1980 (10-112)
- 11.09 Greg Landry, Detroit, 1972 (11-122)

## TOUCHDOWNS
**Most Touchdowns, Career**
- 3 Joe Theismann, Washington, 1983-84
- 2 By four players

**Most Touchdowns, Game**
- 3 Joe Theismann, Washington, 1984
- 2 James Harris, Los Angeles, 1975
  Mike Boryla, Philadelphia, 1976
  Ken Anderson, Cincinnati, 1977

## HAD INTERCEPTED
**Most Passes Had Intercepted, Career**
- 6 Jim Hart, St. Louis, 1975-78
- 5 Ken Stabler, Oakland, 1974-75, 1978
  Dan Fouts, San Diego, 1980-84
- 4 Roger Staubach, Dallas, 1972, 1977, 1979-80

**Most Passes Had Intercepted, Game**
- 5 Jim Hart, St. Louis, 1977
- 4 Ken Stabler, Oakland, 1974
- 2 By many players

## PERCENTAGE, PASSES HAD INTERCEPTED
**Lowest Percentage, Passes Had Intercepted, Career (40 attempts)**
- 0.00 Joe Theismann, Washington, 1983-84 (45-0)
- 3.41 Bob Griese, Miami, 1971-72, 1974-75, 1977, 1979 (88-3)
- 5.36 Ken Anderson, Cincinnati, 1976-77, 1982-83 (56-3)

### Most Attempts, Without Interception, Game
- 27 Joe Theismann, Washington, 1984
- 26 John Brodie, San Francisco, 1971
  Danny White, Dallas, 1983
- 21 Roman Gabriel, Los Angeles, 1974

# PASS RECEIVING

## RECEPTIONS
**Most Receptions, Career**
- 13 John Stallworth, Pittsburgh, 1980, 1983
  William Andrews, Atlanta, 1981-84
- 12 Kellen Winslow, San Diego, 1981-84
- 11 John Jefferson, San Diego, 1979-81; Green Bay, 1983
  Walter Payton, Chicago, 1977-81, 1984

**Most Receptions, Game**
- 7 John Stallworth, Pittsburgh, 1983
- 6 John Stallworth, Pittsburgh, 1980
  Kellen Winslow, San Diego, 1982
- 5 By many players

## YARDS GAINED
**Most Yards Gained, Career**
- 179 Kellen Winslow, San Diego, 1981-84
- 169 John Jefferson, San Diego, 1979-81; Green Bay, 1983
- 163 Cliff Branch, Oakland, 1975-78

**Most Yards Gained, Game**
- 96 Ken Burrough, Houston, 1976
- 91 Alfred Jenkins, Atlanta, 1981
- 89 Ahmad Rashad, Minnesota, 1979

**Longest Reception**
- 64 Ken Burrough, Houston (from Pastorini, Houston), 1976 (TD)
- 57 Mel Gray, St. Louis (from Harris, Los Angeles), 1975
  Greg Pruitt, Cleveland (from Anderson, Cincinnati), 1977
- 55 Alfred Jenkins, Atlanta (from Bartkowski, Atlanta), 1981 (TD)

## TOUCHDOWNS
**Most Touchdowns, Career**
- 2 Mel Gray, St. Louis, 1975-78
  Cliff Branch, Oakland, 1975-78
  Terry Metcalf, St. Louis, 1975-76, 1978
  Tony Hill, Dallas, 1979-80
  William Andrews, Atlanta, 1981-84

**Most Touchdowns, Game**
- 2 William Andrews, Atlanta, 1984
- 1 By many players

# INTERCEPTIONS BY
**Most Interceptions, Career**
- 4 Everson Walls, Dallas, 1982-84
- 3 Ken Houston, Houston, 1971-73; Washington, 1975-79
  Jack Lambert, Pittsburgh, 1976-84
  Ted Hendricks, Baltimore, 1972-74; Green Bay, 1975; Oakland, 1981-82;
    L.A. Raiders, 1983-84
- 2 By five players

**Most Interceptions By, Game**
- 2 Mel Blount, Pittsburgh, 1977
  Everson Walls, Dallas, 1982, 1983

## YARDS GAINED
**Most Yards Gained, Career**
- 77 Ted Hendricks, Baltimore, 1972-74; Green Bay, 1975; Oakland, 1981-82;
    L.A. Raiders, 1983-84
- 44 Nolan Cromwell, L.A. Rams, 1981-84
- 40 Tom Myers, New Orleans, 1980
  Everson Walls, Dallas, 1982-84

**Most Yards Gained, Game**
- 65 Ted Hendricks, Baltimore, 1973
- 44 Nolan Cromwell, L.A. Rams, 1984
- 40 Tom Myers, New Orleans, 1980

**Longest Gain**
- 65 Ted Hendricks, Baltimore, 1973
- 44 Nolan Cromwell, L.A. Rams, 1984 (TD)
- 40 Tom Myers, New Orleans, 1980

## TOUCHDOWNS
**Most Touchdowns, Game**
- 1 Bobby Bell, Kansas City, 1973
  Nolan Cromwell, L.A. Rams, 1984

# PUNTING
**Most Punts, Career**
- 33 Ray Guy, Oakland, 1974-79, 1981
- 19 Dave Jennings, N.Y. Giants, 1979-81, 1983
- 16 Jerrel Wilson, Kansas City, 1971-73
  Tom Wittum, San Francisco, 1974-75

**Most Punts, Game**
- 9 Tom Wittum, San Francisco, 1974
- 8 Jerrel Wilson, Kansas City, 1971
  Tom Skladany, Detroit, 1982
- 7 Bobby Joe Green, Chicago, 1971
  Tom Wittum, San Francisco, 1975

**Longest Punt**
- 64 Tom Wittum, San Francisco, 1974
- 60 Ron Widby, Dallas, 1972
- 53 Pat McInally, Cincinnati, 1982

## AVERAGE YARDAGE
**Highest Average, Career (10 punts)**
- 45.25 Jerrel Wilson, Kansas City, 1971-73 (16-724)
- 44.64 Ray Guy, Oakland, 1974-79, 1981 (33-1,473)
- 44.63 Tom Wittum, San Francisco, 1974-75 (16-714)

**Highest Average, Game (4 punts)**
- 49.00 Ray Guy, Oakland, 1974 (4-196)
- 47.75 Bob Grupp, Kansas City, 1980 (4-191)
- 47.40 Ray Guy, Oakland, 1976 (5-237)

# PUNT RETURNS
**Most Punt Returns, Career**
- 13 Rick Upchurch, Denver, 1977, 1979-80, 1983
- 10 Mike Nelms, Washington, 1981-83
- 9 Greg Pruitt, Cleveland, 1974-75, 1977-78; L.A. Raiders, 1984

**Most Punt Returns, Game**
- 5 Rick Upchurch, Denver, 1980
  Mike Nelms, Washington, 1981
  Carl Roaches, Houston, 1982
- 4 By five players

**Most Fair Catches, Game**
- 2 Jerry Logan, Baltimore, 1971
  Dick Anderson, Miami, 1974

## YARDS GAINED
**Most Yards Gained, Career**
- 183 Billy Johnson, Houston, 1976, 1978; Atlanta, 1984
- 138 Rick Upchurch, Denver, 1977, 1979-80, 1983
- 119 Mike Nelms, Washington, 1981-83

**Most Yards Gained, Game**
- 159 Billy Johnson, Houston, 1976
- 138 Mel Renfro, Dallas, 1971
- 117 Wally Henry, Philadelphia, 1980

**Longest Punt Return**
- 90 Billy Johnson, Houston, 1976 (TD)
- 86 Wally Henry, Philadelphia, 1980 (TD)
- 82 Mel Renfro, Dallas, 1971 (TD)

## TOUCHDOWNS
**Most Touchdowns, Game**
- 2 Mel Renfro, Dallas, 1971
- 1 Billy Johnson, Houston, 1976
  Wally Henry, Philadelphia, 1980

# KICKOFF RETURNS
**Most Kickoff Returns, Career**
- 10 Rick Upchurch, Denver, 1977, 1979-80, 1983
  Greg Pruitt, Cleveland, 1974-75, 1977-78; L.A. Raiders, 1984
- 8 Mike Nelms, Washington, 1981-83
- 6 Terry Metcalf, St. Louis, 1975-76, 1978

**Most Kickoff Returns, Game**
- 6 Greg Pruitt, L.A. Raiders, 1984
- 5 Les (Speedy) Duncan, Washington, 1972
  Ron Smith, Chicago, 1973
  Herb Mul-Key, Washington, 1974
- 4 By three players

## YARDS GAINED
**Most Yards Gained, Career**
- 309 Greg Pruitt, Cleveland, 1974-75, 1977-78; L.A. Raiders, 1984
- 222 Rick Upchurch, Denver, 1977, 1979-80, 1983
- 175 Les (Speedy) Duncan, Washington, 1972

**Most Yards Gained, Game**
- 192 Greg Pruitt, L.A. Raiders, 1984
- 175 Les (Speedy) Duncan, Washington, 1972
- 152 Ron Smith, Chicago, 1973

**Longest Kickoff Return**
- 62 Greg Pruitt, L.A. Raiders, 1984
- 61 Mercury Morris, Miami, 1972
- 55 Ron Smith, Chicago, 1973

## TOUCHDOWNS
**Most Touchdowns, Game**
- None

# FUMBLES
**Most Fumbles, Career**
- 6 Dan Fouts, San Diego, 1980-84
- 4 Lawrence McCutcheon, Los Angeles, 1974-78
  Franco Harris, Pittsburgh, 1973-76, 1978-81
- 3 O.J. Simpson, Buffalo, 1973-77
  William Andrews, Atlanta, 1981-84

**Most Fumbles, Game**
   3   Dan Fouts, San Diego, 1982
   2   By seven players

**RECOVERIES**
**Most Fumbles Recovered, Career**
   3   Harold Jackson, Philadelphia, 1973; Los Angeles, 1974, 1976, 1978, (3-own)
      Dan Fouts, San Diego, 1980-84 (3-own)
   2   By many players
**Most Fumbles Recovered, Game**
   2   Dick Anderson, Miami, 1974 (1-own, 1-opp)
      Harold Jackson, Los Angeles, 1974 (2-own)
      Dan Fouts, San Diego, 1982 (2-own)

**YARDAGE**
**Longest Fumble Return**
   51   Phil Villapiano, Oakland, 1974 (opp)
   34   Rick Upchurch, Denver, 1980 (own)
   21   Mark Gastineau, N.Y. Jets, 1982 (opp)

**TOUCHDOWNS**
**Most Touchdowns, Game**
      None

# TEAM RECORDS
## SCORING

**Most Points, Game**
   45   NFC, 1984
**Fewest Points, Game**
   3   AFC, 1984
**Most Points, Both Teams, Game**
   64   NFC (37) vs. AFC (27), 1980
**Fewest Points, Both Teams, Game**
   20   AFC (7) vs. NFC (13), 1979

**TOUCHDOWNS**
**Most Touchdowns, Game**
   6   NFC, 1984
**Fewest Touchdowns, Game**
   0   AFC, 1971, 1974, 1984
**Most Touchdowns, Both Teams, Game**
   8   AFC (4) vs. NFC (4), 1973
      NFC (5) vs. AFC (3), 1980
**Fewest Touchdowns, Both Teams, Game**
   1   AFC (0) vs. NFC (1), 1974

**POINTS AFTER TOUCHDOWNS**
**Most Points After Touchdown, Game**
   6   NFC, 1984
**Most Points After Touchdown, Both Teams, Game**
   7   NFC (4) vs. AFC (3), 1973
      NFC (4) vs. AFC (3), 1980

**FIELD GOALS**
**Most Field Goals Attempted, Game**
   6   AFC, 1972
      NFC, 1981, 1983
**Most Field Goals Attempted, Both Teams, Game**
   9   NFC (6) vs. AFC (3), 1983
**Most Field Goals, Game**
   5   AFC, 1974
**Most Field Goals, Both Teams, Game**
   7   AFC (5) vs. NFC (2), 1974

## NET YARDS GAINED RUSHING AND PASSING
**Most Yards Gained, Game**
   466   AFC, 1983
**Fewest Yards Gained, Game**
   146   AFC, 1971
**Most Yards Gained, Both Teams, Game**
   811   AFC (466) vs. NFC (345), 1983
**Fewest Yards Gained, Both Teams, Game**
   468   NFC (159) vs. AFC (309), 1972

## RUSHING

**ATTEMPTS**
**Most Attempts, Game**
   50   AFC, 1974
**Fewest Attempts, Game**
   18   AFC, 1984
**Most Attempts, Both Teams, Game**
   80   AFC (50) vs. NFC (30), 1974
**Fewest Attempts, Both Teams, Game**
   54   AFC (27) vs. NFC (27), 1983
      AFC (18) vs. NFC (36), 1984

**YARDS GAINED**
**Most Yards Gained, Game**
   224   NFC, 1976
**Fewest Yards Gained, Game**
   64   NFC, 1974
**Most Yards Gained, Both Teams, Game**
   425   NFC (224) vs. AFC (201), 1976
**Fewest Yards Gained, Both Teams, Game**
   178   AFC (66) vs. NFC (112), 1971

**TOUCHDOWNS**
**Most Touchdowns, Game**
   2   AFC, 1973, 1980, 1982
      NFC, 1973, 1977, 1980

# PASSING

**ATTEMPTS**
**Most Attempts, Game**
   50   AFC, 1983
**Fewest Attempts, Game**
   17   NFC, 1972
**Most Attempts, Both Teams, Game**
   94   AFC (50) vs. NFC (44), 1983
**Fewest Attempts, Both Teams, Game**
   42   NFC (17) vs. AFC (25), 1972

**COMPLETIONS**
**Most Completions, Game**
   31   AFC, 1983
**Fewest Completions, Game**
   7   NFC, 1972, 1982
**Most Completions, Both Teams, Game**
   55   AFC (31) vs. NFC (24), 1983
**Fewest Completions, Both Teams, Game**
   18   NFC (7) vs. AFC (11), 1972

**YARDS GAINED**
**Most Yards Gained, Game**
   387   AFC, 1983
**Fewest Yards Gained, Game**
   42   NFC, 1982
**Most Yards Gained, Both Teams, Game**
   608   AFC (387) vs. NFC (221), 1983
**Fewest Yards Gained, Both Teams, Game**
   215   NFC (89) vs. AFC (126), 1972

**TIMES SACKED**
**Most Times Sacked, Game**
   8   AFC, 1984
**Fewest Times Sacked, Game**
   0   NFC, 1971
**Most Times Sacked, Both Teams, Game**
   11   AFC (8) vs. NFC (3), 1984
**Fewest Times Sacked, Both Teams, Game**
   4   AFC (2) vs. NFC (2), 1978

**TOUCHDOWNS**
**Most Touchdowns, Game**
   4   NFC, 1984
**Fewest Touchdowns, Game**
   0   AFC, 1971, 1974, 1982, 1984
      NFC, 1977
**Most Touchdowns, Both Teams, Game**
   4   NFC (3) vs. AFC (1), 1976
**Fewest Touchdowns, Both Teams, Game**
   1   AFC (0) vs. NFC (1), 1971
      AFC (0) vs. NFC (1), 1974
      AFC (0) vs. NFC (1), 1982

## INTERCEPTIONS BY
**Most Interceptions By, Game**
   6   AFC, 1977
**Most Interceptions By, Both Teams, Game**
   7   AFC (6) vs. NFC (1), 1977

**YARDS GAINED**
**Most Yards Gained, Game**
   77   AFC, 1973
**Most Yards Gained, Both Teams, Game**
   99   NFC (64) vs. AFC (35), 1975

**TOUCHDOWNS**
**Most Touchdowns, Game**
   1   AFC, 1973
      NFC, 1984

## PUNTING
**Most Punts, Game**
   9   NFC, 1974
**Fewest Punts, Game**
   2   NFC, 1984
**Most Punts, Both Teams, Game**
   15   AFC (8) vs. NFC (7), 1971
**Fewest Punts, Both Teams, Game**
   6   NFC (2) vs. AFC (4), 1984

**AVERAGE YARDAGE**
**Highest Average, Game**
   49.00   AFC, 1974 (4-196)

## PUNT RETURNS
**Most Punt Returns, Game**
   6   NFC, 1971
**Fewest Punt Returns, Game**
   0   AFC, 1984
**Most Punt Returns, Both Teams, Game**
   10   AFC (5) vs. NFC (5), 1981
**Fewest Punt Returns, Both Teams, Game**
   3   AFC (0) vs. NFC (3), 1984

**YARDS GAINED**
**Most Yards Gained, Game**
   177   AFC, 1976
**Fewest Yards Gained, Game**
   0   AFC, 1984
**Most Yards Gained, Both Teams, Game**
   263   AFC (177) vs. NFC (86), 1976

**Fewest Yards Gained, Both Teams, Game**
   16  AFC (0) vs. NFC (16), 1984

**TOUCHDOWNS**
**Most Touchdowns, Game**
   2  NFC, 1971

# KICKOFF RETURNS

**Most Kickoff Returns, Game**
   7  AFC, 1984
**Fewest Kickoff Returns, Game**
   1  NFC, 1971, 1984
**Most Kickoff Returns, Both Teams, Game**
   10  AFC (5) vs. NFC (5), 1976
**Fewest Kickoff Returns, Both Teams, Game**
   5  NFC (2) vs AFC (3), 1979

**YARDS GAINED**
**Most Yards Gained, Game**
   215  AFC, 1984
**Fewest Yards Gained, Game**
   6  NFC, 1971
**Most Yards Gained, Both Teams, Game**
   293  NFC (200) vs. AFC (93), 1972
**Fewest Yards Gained, Both Teams, Game**
   108  AFC (49) vs. NFC (59), 1979

**TOUCHDOWNS**
**Most Touchdowns, Game**
   None

# FUMBLES

**Most Fumbles, Game**
   10  NFC, 1974
**Most Fumbles, Both Teams, Game**
   15  NFC (10) vs. AFC (5), 1974

**RECOVERIES**
**Most Fumbles Recovered, Game**
   10  NFC, 1974 (6 own, 4 opp)
**Most Fumbles Lost, Game**
   4  AFC, 1974

**YARDS GAINED**
**Most Yards Gained, Game**
   60  AFC, 1974

**TOUCHDOWNS**
**Most Touchdowns, Game**
   None

# TURNOVERS
(Number of times losing the ball on interceptions and fumbles.)
**Most Turnovers, Game**
   8  AFC, 1974
**Fewest Turnovers, Game**
   1  AFC, 1972, 1976, 1978, 1979
      NFC, 1976, 1980, 1983
**Most Turnovers, Both Teams, Game**
   12  AFC (8) vs. NFC (4), 1974
**Fewest Turnovers, Both Teams, Game**
   2  AFC (1) vs. NFC (1), 1976

# RULES

1984 NFL Roster of Officials
Official Signals
Digest of Rules

# 1984 NFL Roster of Officials

**Art McNally,** Supervisor of Officials
**Jack Reader,** Assistant Supervisor of Officials
**Nick Skorich,** Assistant Supervisor of Officials
**Stu Kirkpatrick,** Officiating Assistant
**Mark Burns,** Officiating Assistant

| No. | Name | Position | College | No. | Name | Position | College |
|---|---|---|---|---|---|---|---|
| 115 | Ancich, Hendi | Umpire | Harbor College | 68 | Leimbach, John | Umpire | Missouri |
| 81 | Anderson, Dave | Head Linemen | Salem College | 18 | Lewis, Bob | Field Judge | No College |
| 34 | Austin, Gerald | Side Judge | Western Carolina | 21 | Liske, Pete | Back Judge | Penn State |
| 22 | Baetz, Paul | Back Judge | Heidelberg | 49 | Look, Dean | Side Judge | Michigan State |
| 14 | Barth, Gene | Referee | St. Louis | 90 | Mace, Gil | Side Judge | Westminster |
| 59 | Beeks, Bob | Line Judge | Lincoln | 82 | Mallette, Pat | Field Judge | Nebraska |
| 17 | Bergman, Jerry | Head Linesman | Duquesne | 26 | Marion, Ed | Head Linesman | Pennsylvania |
| 110 | Botchan, Ron | Umpire | Occidental | 9 | Markbreit, Jerry | Referee | Illinois |
| 101 | Boylston, Bob | Umpire | Alabama | 94 | Marshall, Vern | Line Judge | Linfield |
| 43 | Cashion, Red | Referee | Texas A&M | 116 | McCallum, Chuck | Field Judge | Michigan State |
| 16 | Cathcart, Royal | Side Judge | UC Santa Barbara | 48 | McCarter, Gordon | Referee | Western Reserve |
| 24 | Clymer, Roy | Back Judge | New Mexico State | 95 | McElwee, Bob | Referee | Navy |
| 27 | Conway, Al | Umpire | Army | 41 | McKenzie, Dick | Line Judge | Ashland |
| 61 | Creed, Dick | Side Judge | Louisville | 108 | McLaughlin, Bob | Head Linesman | Xavier |
| 78 | Demmas, Art | Umpire | Vanderbilt | 76 | Merrifield, Ed | Field Judge | Missouri |
| 45 | DeSouza, Ron | Line Judge | Morgan State | 35 | Miles, Leo | Head Linesman | Virginia State |
| 74 | Dodez, Ray | Head Linesman | Wooster | 117 | Montgomery, Ben | Umpire | Morehouse |
| 31 | Dolack, Dick | Field Judge | Ferris State | 36 | Moore, Bob | Back Judge | Dayton |
| 6 | Dooley, Tom | Referee | VMI | 88 | Moss, Dave | Umpire | Dartmouth |
| 102 | Douglas, Merrill | Side Judge | Utah | 55 | Musser, Charley | Field Judge | N. Carolina State |
| 12 | Dreith, Ben | Referee | Colorado State | 51 | Orem, Dale | Line Judge | Louisville |
| 87 | Ferguson, Dick | Side Judge | West Virginia | 77 | Orr, Don | Field Judge | Vanderbilt |
| 39 | Fette, Jack | Line Judge | No College | 64 | Parry, Dave | Side Judge | Wabash |
| 57 | Fiffick, Ed | Umpire | Marquette | 44 | Peters, Walt | Line Judge | Indiana State, Pa. |
| 47 | Fincken, Tom | Side Judge | Kan. St. Teachers | 92 | Poole, Jim | Back Judge | San Diego State |
| 111 | Frantz, Earnie | Head Linesman | No College | 58 | Quinby, Bill | Side Judge | Iowa State |
| 71 | Frederic, Bob | Referee | Colorado | 53 | Reynolds, Bill | Line Judge | West Chester State |
| 62 | Gandy, Duwayne | Side Judge | Tulsa | 80 | Rice, Bob | Side Judge | Denison |
| 50 | Gereb, Neil | Umpire | California | 33 | Roe, Howard | Line Judge | Wichita State |
| 72 | Gierke, Terry | Head Linesman | Portland State | 98 | Rosser, Jimmy | Back Judge | Auburn |
| 15 | Glass, Bama | Line Judge | Colorado | 29 | Sanders, J. W. | Back Judge | Southern Illinois |
| 85 | Glover, Frank | Head Linesman | Morris Brown | 56 | Shannon, Carver | Line Judge | Southern Illinois |
| 23 | Grier, Johnny | Field Judge | D.C. Teachers | 70 | Seeman, Jerry | Referee | Winona State |
| 75 | Habel, Don | Field Judge | Western Oregon | 109 | Semon, Sid | Head Linesman | So. California |
| 63 | Hagerty, Ligouri | Head Linesman | Syracuse | 7 | Silva, Fred | Referee | San Jose State |
| 40 | Haggerty, Pat | Referee | Colorado State | 3 | Smith, Boyce | Line Judge | Vanderbilt |
| 96 | Hakes, Don | Field Judge | Bradley | 119 | Spitler, Ron | Field Judge | Panhandle State |
| 104 | Hamer, Dale | Head Linesman | Calif. State, Pa. | 91 | Stanley, Bill | Field Judge | Redlands |
| 42 | Hamilton, Dave | Umpire | Utah | 103 | Stuart, Rex | Umpire | Appalachian State |
| 105 | Hantak, Dick | Back Judge | S.E. Missouri | 38 | Swanson, Bill | Back Judge | Lake Forest |
| 66 | Hawk, Dave | Side Judge | Southern Methodist | 37 | Toler, Burl | Head Linesman | San Francisco |
| 112 | Haynes, Joe | Line Judge | Alcorn State | 52 | Tompkins, Ben | Back Judge | Texas |
| 46 | Heberling, Chuck | Referee | Wash. & Jefferson | 32 | Tunney, Jim | Referee | Occidental |
| 19 | Hensley, Tommy | Umpire | Tennessee | 93 | Vaughan, Jack | Field Judge | Mississippi State |
| 54 | Johnson, Jack | Line Judge | Pacific Lutheran | 28 | Wedge, Don | Back Judge | Ohio Wesleyan |
| 114 | Johnson, Tom | Head Linesman | Miami, Ohio | 89 | Wells, Gordon | Umpire | Occidental |
| 97 | Jones, Nathan | Side Judge | Lewis & Clark | 30 | Wilford, Dan | Line Judge | Mississippi |
| 60 | Jorgensen, Dick | Referee | Wisconsin | 99 | Williams, Banks | Back Judge | Houston |
| 106 | Jury, Al | Back Judge | San Bernardino | 8 | Williams, Dale | Head Linesman | Cal-Northridge |
| 107 | Kearney, Jim | Back Judge | Pennsylvania | 84 | Wortman, Bob | Field Judge | Findlay |
| 67 | Keck, John | Umpire | Cornell College | 11 | Wyant, Fred | Referee | West Virginia |
| 25 | Kelleher, Tom | Back Judge | Holy Cross | | | | |
| 65 | Kragseth, Norm | Head Linesman | Northwestern | | | | |
| 86 | Kukar, Bernie | Field Judge | St. John's | | | | |
| 120 | Lane, Gary | Side Judge | Missouri | | | | |

## Numerical Roster

**Referees**

| No. | |
|---|---|
| 6 | Tom Dooley |
| 7 | Fred Silva |
| 9 | Jerry Markbreit |
| 11 | Fred Wyant |
| 12 | Ben Dreith |
| 14 | Gene Barth |
| 32 | Jim Tunney |
| 40 | Pat Haggerty |
| 43 | Red Cashion |
| 46 | Chuck Heberling |
| 48 | Gordon McCarter |
| 60 | Dick Jorgensen |
| 70 | Jerry Seeman |
| 71 | Bob Frederic |
| 95 | Bob McElwee |

**Umpires**

| No. | |
|---|---|
| 19 | Tommy Hensley |
| 27 | Al Conway |
| 42 | Dave Hamilton |
| 50 | Neil Gereb |
| 57 | Ed Fiffick |
| 67 | John Keck |
| 68 | John Leimbach |
| 78 | Art Demmas |
| 88 | Dave Moss |
| 89 | Gordon Wells |
| 101 | Bob Boylston |
| 103 | Rex Stuart |
| 110 | Ron Botchan |
| 115 | Hendi Ancich |
| 117 | Ben Montgomery |

**Head Linesmen**

| No. | |
|---|---|
| 8 | Dale Williams |
| 17 | Jerry Bergman |
| 26 | Ed Marion |
| 35 | Leo Miles |
| 37 | Burl Toler |
| 63 | Ligouri Hagerty |
| 65 | Norm Kragseth |
| 72 | Terry Gierke |
| 74 | Ray Dodez |
| 81 | Dave Anderson |
| 85 | Frank Glover |
| 104 | Dale Hamer |
| 108 | Bob McLaughlin |
| 109 | Sid Semon |
| 111 | Earnie Frantz |
| 114 | Tom Johnson |

**Line Judges**

| No. | |
|---|---|
| 3 | Boyce Smith |
| 15 | Bama Glass |
| 30 | Dan Wilford |
| 33 | Howard Roe |
| 39 | Jack Fette |
| 41 | Dick McKenzie |
| 44 | Walt Peters |
| 45 | Ron DeSouza |
| 51 | Dale Orem |
| 53 | Bill Reynolds |
| 54 | Jack Johnson |
| 56 | Carver Shannon |
| 59 | Bob Beeks |
| 94 | Vern Marshall |
| 112 | Joe Haynes |

**Back Judges**

| No. | |
|---|---|
| 21 | Pete Liske |
| 22 | Paul Baetz |
| 24 | Roy Clymer |
| 25 | Tom Kelleher |
| 28 | Don Wedge |
| 29 | J. W. Sanders |
| 36 | Bob Moore |
| 38 | Bill Swanson |
| 52 | Ben Tompkins |
| 92 | Jim Poole |
| 98 | Jimmy Rosser |
| 99 | Banks Williams |
| 105 | Dick Hantak |
| 106 | Al Jury |
| 107 | Jim Kearney |

**Side Judges**

| No. | |
|---|---|
| 16 | Royal Cathcart |
| 34 | Gerald Austin |
| 47 | Tom Fincken |
| 49 | Dean Look |
| 58 | Bill Quinby |
| 61 | Dick Creed |
| 62 | Duwayne Gandy |
| 64 | Dave Parry |
| 66 | Dave Hawk |
| 80 | Bob Rice |
| 87 | Dick Ferguson |
| 90 | Gil Mace |
| 97 | Nate Jones |
| 102 | Merrill Douglas |
| 120 | Gary Lane |

**Field Judges**

| No. | |
|---|---|
| 18 | Bob Lewis |
| 23 | Johnny Grier |
| 31 | Dick Dolack |
| 55 | Charley Musser |
| 75 | Don Habel |
| 76 | Ed Merrifield |
| 77 | Don Orr |
| 82 | Pat Mallette |
| 84 | Bob Wortman |
| 86 | Bernie Kukar |
| 91 | Bill Stanley |
| 93 | Jack Vaughan |
| 96 | Don Hakes |
| 116 | Chuck McCallum |
| 119 | Ron Spitler |

## 1984 Officials at a Glance

### Referees

**Gene Barth,** No. 14, St. Louis, president, oil company, 14th year.

**Red Cashion,** No. 43, Texas A&M, chairman of the board, insurance company, 13th year.

**Tom Dooley,** No. 6, VMI, general contractor, 7th year.

**Ben Dreith,** No. 12, Colorado State, teacher-counselor, 25th year.

**Bob Frederic,** No. 71, Colorado, president, printing and lithographing company, 17th year.

**Pat Haggerty,** No. 40, Colorado State, teacher-coach, 20th year.

**Chuck Heberling,** No. 46, Washington & Jefferson, executive administrator, state high school athletic program, 20th year.

**Dick Jorgensen,** No. 60, Wisconsin, president, commercial bank, 17th year.

**Jerry Markbreit,** No. 9, Illinois, national sales manager, 9th year.

**Gordon McCarter,** No. 48, Western Reserve, industrial sales, 18th year.

**Bob McElwee,** No. 95, U.S. Naval Academy, owner, construction company, 9th year.

**Jerry Seeman,** No. 70, Winona State, assistant superintendent, 10th year.

**Fred Silva,** No. 7, San Jose State, vice-president, director, chain store sales, 18th year.

**Jim Tunney,** No. 32, Occidental, president of motivation company, professional speaker, 25th year.

**Fred Wyant,** No. 11, West Virginia, executive insurance sales director, former NFL player, 19th year.

### Umpires

**Hendi Ancich,** No. 115, Harbor, longshoreman, 3rd year.

**Ron Botchan,** No. 110, Occidental, college professor, former AFL player, 5th year.

**Bob Boylston,** No. 101, Alabama, manufacturers representative, 7th year.

**Al Conway,** No. 27, Army, national director, industrial sales, 16th year.

**Art Demmas,** No. 78, Vanderbilt, investments and financial planning, insurance company, 17th year.

**Ed Fiffick,** No. 57, Marquette, podiatric physician, 6th year.

**Neil Gereb,** No. 50, California, supervisor, aircraft company, 4th year.

**Dave Hamilton,** No. 42, Utah, hospital administrator, 10th year.

**Tommy Hensley,** No. 19, Tennessee, owner, land development and management company, 18th year.

**John Keck,** No. 67, Cornell, petroleum distributor, 13th year.

**John Leimbach,** No. 68, Missouri, school teacher, 4th year.

**Ben Montgomery,** No. 117, Morehouse, assistant principal, 3rd year.

**Dave Moss,** No. 88, Dartmouth, insurance, 4th year.

**Rex Stuart,** No. 103, Appalachian State, agency manager, life and health insurance, 1st year.

**Gordon Wells,** No. 89, Occidental, college professor, physical education, 13th year.

### Head Linesmen

**Dave Anderson,** No. 81, Salem, district sales manager, health insurance, 1st year.

**Jerry Bergman,** No. 17, Duquesne, administrative assistant, 19th year.

**Ray Dodez,** No. 74, Wooster, communications consultant, 17th year.

**Ernie Frantz,** No. 111, vice-president and manager, land title company, 4th year.

**Terry Gierke,** No. 72, Portland State, real estate broker, 4th year.

**Frank Glover,** No. 85, Morris Brown, assistant area superintendent, 13th year.

**Ligouri Hagerty,** No. 63, Syracuse, manager, sporting goods company, 9th year.

**Dale Hamer,** No. 104, California State, Pa., senior planning specialist, 7th year.

**Tom Johnson,** No. 114, Miami, Ohio, teacher-coach, 3rd year.

**Norm Kragseth,** No. 65, Northwestern, chairman, physical education department, 11th year.

**Ed Marion,** No. 26, Pennsylvania, vice-president-pension marketing, insurance company, 25th year.

**Bob McLaughlin,** No. 108, Xavier, president, art sign company, 7th year.

**Leo Miles,** No. 35, Virginia State, university athletic director, former NFL player, 16th year.

**Sid Semon,** No. 109, Southern California, chairman, physical education department, 7th year.

**Burl Toler,** No. 37, University of San Francisco, director, certificated services, 20th year.

**Dale Williams,** No. 8, Cal State-Northridge, coordinator of athletic officials, 5th year.

### Line Judges

**Bob Beeks,** No. 59, Lincoln, law enforcement officer, 17th year.

**Ron DeSouza,** No. 45, Morgan State, vice-president, student affairs, 5th year.

**Jack Fette,** No. 39, district sales manager, sporting goods company, 20th year.

**Bama Glass,** No. 15, Colorado, owner, consumer products, 6th year.

**Joe Haynes,** No. 112, Alcorn State, administrative officer, school services, 1st year.

**Jack Johnson,** No. 54, Pacific Lutheran, fund raising consultant, 9th year.

**Vern Marshall,** No. 94, Linfield College, counseling coordinator, 9th year.

**Dick McKenzie,** No. 41, Ashland, vice-president, insurance agency, 7th year.

**Dale Orem,** No. 51, Louisville, owner, sporting goods company, 5th year.

**Walt Peters,** No. 44, Indiana State, insurance broker, 17th year.

**Bill Reynolds,** No. 53, West Chester State, teacher-athletic director, 10th year.

**Howard Roe,** No. 33, Wichita State, manager and administrator, employee benefits, 1st year.

**Carver Shannon,** No. 56, Southern Illinois, executive, aircraft corporation, former NFL player, 2nd year.

**Boyce Smith,** No. 3, Vanderbilt, president and general manager, steel company, 4th year.

**Dan Wilford,** No. 30, Mississippi, hospital executive, 2nd year.

### Back Judges

**Paul Baetz,** No. 22, Heidelberg, financial consultant, 7th year.

**Roy Clymer,** No. 24, New Mexico State, area manager, gas company, 5th year.

**Dick Hantak,** No. 105, Southeast Missouri, high school department chairman, 7th year.

**Al Jury,** No. 106, San Bernardino Valley, state traffic officer, 7th year.

**Jim Kearney,** No. 107, Pennsylvania, marketing manager, 7th year.

**Tom Kelleher,** No. 25, Holy Cross, president, marketing company, 25th year.

**Pete Liske,** No. 21, Penn State, general manager, manufacturer and sales company, former NFL player, 2nd year.

**Bob Moore,** No. 36, Dayton, attorney, 1st year.

**Jim Poole,** No. 92, San Diego State, college physical education professor, 10th year.

**Jimmy Rosser,** No. 98, Auburn, personnel director, 8th year.

**J. W. Sanders,** No. 29, Southern Illinois, physical education professor, 5th year.

**Bill Swanson,** No. 38, Lake Forest, real estate appraiser, 20th year.

**Ben Tompkins,** No. 52, Texas, attorney, 14th year.

**Don Wedge,** No. 28, Ohio Wesleyan, marketing executive, 13th year.

**Banks Williams,** No. 99, Houston, vice-president sales, concrete company, 7th year.

### Side Judges

**Gerald Austin,** No. 34, Western Carolina, high school principal, 3rd year.

**Royal Cathcart,** No. 16, UC Santa Barbara, real estate broker, former NFL player, 14th year.

**Dick Creed,** No. 61, Louisville, real estate management, 7th year.

**Merrill Douglas,** No. 102, Utah, deputy sheriff, former NFL player, 4th year.

**Dick Ferguson,** No. 87, West Virginia, commissioner of officials, 11th year.

**Tom Fincken,** No. 47, Kansas State Teachers College, high school teacher, 1st year.

**Duwayne Gandy,** No. 62, Tulsa, sales-public relations, oil field wireline service, 4th year.

**Dave Hawk,** No. 66, Southern Methodist, co-owner, warehousing company, 13th year.

**Nate Jones,** No. 97, Lewis and Clark, high school principal, 8th year.

**Gary Lane,** No. 120, Missouri, director, marketing, former NFL player, 3rd year.

**Dean Look,** No. 49, Michigan State, director, marketing and sales, former AFL player, 13th year.

**Gil Mace,** No. 90, Westminster, national accounts manager, 11th year.

**Dave Parry,** No. 64, Wabash, high school athletic director, 10th year.

**Bill Quinby,** No. 58, Iowa State, director, personnel services, 7th year.

**Bob Rice,** No. 80, Denison, chairman, physical education department, 16th year.

### Field Judges

**Dick Dolack,** No. 31, Ferris State, pharmacist, 19th year.

**Johnny Grier,** No. 23, D.C. Teachers, planning engineer, telephone company, 4th year.

**Don Habel,** No. 75, Western Oregon, auto claim superintendent, 1st year.

**Don Hakes,** No. 96, Bradley, high school dean of students, 8th year.

**Bernie Kukar,** No. 86, St. John's, health insurance representative, 1st year.

**Bob Lewis,** No. 18, supervisor, air force base, 9th year.

**Pat Mallette,** No. 82, Nebraska, real estate broker, 16th year.

**Chuck McCallum,** No. 116, Michigan State, executive director, physicians foundation, 3rd year.

**Ed Merrifield,** No. 76, Missouri, sales manager, heavy equipment, 10th year.

**Charley Musser,** No. 55, North Carolina State, vice-president and general manager, refining company, 20th year.

**Don Orr,** No. 77, Vanderbilt, president, machine company, 14th year.

**Ron Spitler,** No. 119, Panhandle State, transportation director, 3nd year.

**Bill Stanley,** No. 91, Redlands, college athletic director, 11th year.

**Jack Vaughan,** No. 93, Mississippi State, real estate broker, 9th year.

**Bob Wortman,** No. 84, Findlay, owner, insurance company, 19th year.

# Official Signals

**1**

**TOUCHDOWN, FIELD GOAL,
or SUCCESSFUL TRY**
Both arms extended above head.

**2**

**SAFETY**
Palms together above head.

**3**

**FIRST DOWN**
Arms pointed toward defensive
team's goal.

**4**

**DEAD BALL or NEUTRAL
ZONE ESTABLISHED**
One arm above head
with an open hand.
With fist closed: **Fourth Down.**

**5**

**BALL ILLEGALLY
TOUCHED, KICKED,
OR BATTED**
Fingertips tap both shoulders.

**6**

**TIME OUT**
Hands crisscrossed above head.
Same signal followed by placing one
hand on top of cap: **Referee's Time Out.**
Same signal followed by arm swung at
side: **Touchback.**

**7**

**NO TIME OUT or
TIME IN WITH WHISTLE**
Full arm circled to
simulate moving clock.

**8**

**DELAY OF GAME or
EXCESS TIME OUT**
Folded arms.

**9**

**FALSE START, ILLEGAL SHIFT, ILLEGAL PROCEDURE, ILLEGAL FORMATION, or KICKOFF OR SAFETY KICK OUT OF BOUNDS**
Forearms rotated over and over in front of body.

**10**

**PERSONAL FOUL**
One wrist striking the other above head.
Same signal followed by swinging leg: **Running Into or Roughing Kicker.**
Same signal followed by raised arm swinging forward: **Running Into or Roughing Passer.**
Same signal followed by hand striking back of calf: **Clipping.**

**11**

**HOLDING**
Grasping one wrist, the fist clenched, in front of chest.

**12**

**ILLEGAL USE OF HANDS, ARMS, OR BODY**
Grasping one wrist, the hand open and facing forward, in front of chest.

**13**

**PENALTY REFUSED, INCOMPLETE PASS, PLAY OVER or MISSED GOAL**
Hands shifted in horizontal plane.

**14**

**PASS JUGGLED INBOUNDS AND CAUGHT OUT OF BOUNDS**
Hands up and down in front of chest (following incomplete pass signal).

**15**

**ILLEGAL FORWARD PASS**
One hand waved behind back followed by loss of down signal.

**16**

**INTENTIONAL GROUNDING OF PASS**
Parallel arms waved in a diagonal plane across body.

**17**

**INTERFERENCE WITH FORWARD PASS or FAIR CATCH**
Hands open and extended forward from shoulders with hands vertical.

**18**

**INVALID FAIR CATCH SIGNAL**
One hand waved above head.

**19**

**INELIGIBLE RECEIVER or INELIGIBLE MEMBER OF KICKING TEAM DOWNFIELD**
Right hand touching top of cap.

**20**

**ILLEGAL CONTACT**
One open hand extended forward.

**21**

**OFFSIDE or ENCROACHING**
Hands on hips.

**22**

**ILLEGAL MOTION AT SNAP**
Horizontal arc with one hand.

**23**

**LOSS OF DOWN**
Both hands held behind head.

**24**

**CRAWLING, INTERLOCKING INTERFERENCE, PUSHING, or HELPING RUNNER**
Pushing movement of hands to front with arms downward.

**25**

**TOUCHING A FORWARD
PASS OR SCRIMMAGE KICK**
Diagonal motion of
one hand across another.

**26**

**UNSPORTSMANLIKE
CONDUCT (Non-contact fouls)**
Arms outstretched, palms down.
(Same signal means continuous
action fouls are disregarded.)

**27**

**ILLEGAL CUT or
BLOCKING BELOW
THE WAIST**
Hand striking front of knee.

**28**

**ILLEGAL CRACKBACK**
Strike of an open right hand
against the right mid thigh.

**29**

**PLAYER DISQUALIFIED**
Ejection signal.

**30**

**TRIPPING**
Repeated action of right foot
in back of left heel.

# NFL Digest of Rules

This Digest of Rules of the National Football League has been prepared to aid players, fans, and members of the press, radio, and television media in their understanding of the game.

It is not meant to be a substitute for the official rule book. In any case of conflict between these explanations and the official rules, the rules always have precedence.

In order to make it easier to coordinate the information in this digest the topics discussed generally follow the order of the rule book.

## Officials' Jurisdictions, Positions, and Duties

**Referee**—General oversight and control of game. Gives signals for all fouls and is final authority for rule interpretations. Takes a position in backfield 10 to 12 yards behind line of scrimmage, favors right side (if quarterback is right-handed passer). Determines legality of snap, observes deep back(s) for legal motion. On running play, observes quarterback during and after handoff, remains with him until action has cleared away, then proceeds downfield, checking on runner and contact behind him. When runner is downed, Referee determines forward progress from wing official and if necessary, adjusts final position of ball.

On pass plays, drops back as quarterback begins to fade back, picks up legality of blocks by near linemen. Changes to complete concentration on quarterback as defenders approach. Primarily responsible to rule on possible roughing action on passer and if ball becomes loose, rules whether ball is free on a fumble or dead on an incomplete pass.

During kicking situations, Referee has primary responsibility to rule on kicker's actions and whether or not any subsequent contact by a defender is legal.

**Umpire**—Primary responsibility to rule on players' equipment, as well as their conduct and actions on scrimmage line. Lines up approximately four to five yards downfield, varying position from in front of weakside tackle to strongside guard. Looks for possible false start by offensive linemen. Observes legality of contact by both offensive linemen while blocking and by defensive players while they attempt to ward off blockers. Is prepared to call rule infractions if they occur on offense or defense. Moves forward to line of scrimmage when pass play develops in order to insure that interior linemen do not move illegally downfield. If offensive linemen indicate screen pass is to be attempted, Umpire shifts his attention toward screen side, picks up potential receiver in order to insure that he will legally be permitted to run his pattern and continues to rule on action of blockers. Umpire is to assist in ruling on incomplete or trapped passes when ball is thrown overhead or short.

**Head Linesman**—Primarily responsible for ruling on offside, encroachment, and actions pertaining to scrimmage line prior to or at snap. Keys on closest setback on his side of the field. On pass plays, Linesman is responsible to clear this receiver approximately seven yards downfield as he moves to a point five yards beyond the line. Linesman's secondary responsibility is to rule on any illegal action taken by defenders on any delay receiver moving downfield. Has full responsibility for ruling on sideline plays on his side, e.g., pass receiver or runner in or out of bounds. Together with Referee, Linesman is responsible for keeping track of number of downs and is in charge of mechanics of his chain crew in connection with its duties.

Linesman must be prepared to assist in determining forward progress by a runner on play directed toward middle or into his side zone. He, in turn, is to signal Referee or Umpire what forward point ball has reached. Linesman is also responsible to rule on legality of action involving any receiver who approaches his side zone. He is to call pass interference when the infraction occurs and is to rule on legality of blockers and defenders on plays involving ball carriers, whether it is entirely a running play, a combination pass and run, or a play involving a kick.

**Line Judge**—Straddles line of scrimmage on side of field opposite Linesman. Keeps time of game as a backup for clock operator. Along with Linesman is responsible for offside, encroachment, and actions pertaining to scrimmage line prior to or at snap. Line Judge keys on closest setback on his side of field. Line Judge is to observe his receiver until he moves at least seven yards downfield. He then moves toward backfield side, being especially alert to rule on any back in motion and on flight of ball when pass is made (he must rule whether forward or backward). Line Judge has primary responsibility to rule whether or not passer is behind or beyond line of scrimmage when pass is made. He also assists in observing actions by blockers and defenders who are on his side of field. After pass is thrown, Line Judge directs attention toward activities that occur in back of Umpire. During punting situations, Line Judge remains at line of scrimmage to be sure that only the end men move downfield until kick has been made. He also rules whether or not the kick crossed line and then observes action by members of the kicking team who are moving downfield to cover the kick.

**Back Judge**—Operates on same side of field as Line Judge, 17 yards deep. Keys on wide receiver on his side. Concentrates on path of end or back, observing legality of his potential block(s) or of actions taken against him. Is prepared to rule from deep position on holding or illegal use of hands by end or back or on defensive infractions committed by player guarding him. Has primary responsibility to make decisions involving sideline on his side of field, e.g., pass receiver or runner in or out of bounds.

Back Judge makes decisions involving catching, recovery, or illegal touching of a loose ball beyond line of scrimmage; rules on plays involving pass receiver, including legality of catch or pass interference; assists in covering actions of runner, including blocks by teammates and that of defenders; calls clipping on punt returns; and, together with Field Judge, rules whether or not field goal attempts are successful.

**Side Judge**—Operates on same side of field as Linesman, 17 yards deep. Keys on wide receiver on his side. Concentrates on path of end or back, observing legality of his potential block(s) or of actions taken against him. Is prepared to rule from deep position on holding or illegal use of hands by end or back or on defensive infractions committed by player guarding him. Has primary responsibility to make decisions involving sideline on his side of field, e.g., pass receiver or runner in or out of bounds.

Side Judge makes decisions involving catching, recovery, or illegal touching of a loose ball beyond line of scrimmage; rules on plays involving pass receiver, including legality of catch or pass interference; assists in covering actions of runner, including blocks by teammates and that of defenders; and calls clipping on punt returns.

**Field Judge**—Takes a position 25 yards downfield. In general, favors the tight end's side of field. Keys on tight end, concentrates on his path and observes legality of tight end's potential block(s) or of actions taken against him. Is prepared to rule from deep position on holding or illegal use of hands by end or back or on defensive infractions committed by player guarding him.

Field Judge times interval between plays on 30-second clock plus intermission between two periods of each half; makes decisions involving catching, recovery, or illegal touching of a loose ball beyond line of scrimmage; is responsible to rule on plays involving end line; calls pass interference, fair catch infractions, and clipping on kick returns; and, together with Back Judge, rules whether or not field goals and conversions are successful.

## Definitions

1. **Chucking:** Warding off an opponent who is in front of a defender by contacting him with a quick extension of arm or arms, followed by the return of arm(s) to a flexed position, thereby breaking the original contact.
2. **Clipping:** Throwing the body across the back of an opponent's leg or hitting him from the back below the waist while moving up from behind unless the opponent is a runner or the action is in close line play.
3. **Close Line Play:** The area between the positions normally occupied by the offensive tackles, extending three yards on each side of the line of scrimmage.
4. **Crackback:** Eligible receivers who take or move to a position more than two yards outside the tackle may not block an opponent below the waist if they then move back inside to block.
5. **Dead Ball:** Ball not in play.
6. **Double Foul:** A foul by each team during the same down.
7. **Down:** The period of action that starts when the ball is put in play and ends when it is dead.
8. **Encroachment:** When a player enters the neutral zone and makes contact with an opponent before the ball is snapped.
9. **Fair Catch:** An unhindered catch of a kick by a member of the receiving team who must raise one arm a full length above his head while the kick is in flight.
10. **Foul:** Any violation of a playing rule.
11. **Free Kick:** A kickoff, kick after a safety, or kick after a fair catch. It may be a placekick, dropkick, or punt, except a punt may not be used on a kickoff.
12. **Fumble:** The loss of possession of the ball.
13. **Impetus:** The action of a player that gives momentum to the ball.
14. **Live Ball:** A ball legally free kicked or snapped. It continues in play until the down ends.
15. **Loose Ball:** A live ball not in possession of any player.
16. **Muff:** The touching of a loose ball by a player in an unsuccessful attempt to obtain possession.
17. **Neutral Zone:** The space the length of a ball between the two scrimmage lines. The offensive team and defensive team must remain behind their end of the ball.
    **Exception:** The offensive player who snaps the ball.
18. **Offside:** A player is offside when any part of his body is beyond his scrimmage or free kick line when the ball is snapped.
19. **Own Goal:** The goal a team is guarding.
20. **Pocket Area (Pass):** Applies from a point two yards outside of either offensive tackle and includes the tight end if he drops off the line of scrimmage to pass protect. Pocket extends longitudinally behind the line back to offensive team's own end line.
21. **Pocket Area (Run):** Applies from a point two yards outside of either offensive tackle (five normally spaced down linemen) and extends three yards beyond the line of scrimmage when contact is made. This area remains constant and could be shifted by an unbalanced line but cannot be expanded through use of an additional lineman.
22. **Possession:** When a player controls the ball throughout the act of clearly touching both feet, or any other part of his body other than his hand(s), to the ground inbounds.
23. **Punt:** A kick made when a player drops the ball and kicks it while it is in flight.
24. **Safety:** The situation in which the ball is dead on or behind a team's own goal if the impetus comes from a player on that team. Two points are scored for the opposing team.
25. **Shift:** The movement of two or more offensive players at the same time before the snap.
26. **Striking:** The act of swinging, clubbing, or propelling the arm or forearm in contacting an opponent.
27. **Sudden Death:** The continuation of a tied game into sudden death overtime in which the team scoring first (by safety, field goal, or touchdown) wins.
28. **Touchback:** When a ball is dead on or behind a team's own goal line, provided the impetus came from an opponent and provided it is not a touchdown or a missed field goal.

29. **Touchdown:** When any part of the ball, legally in possession of a player in-bounds, is on, above, or over the opponent's goal line, provided it is not a touchback.
30. **Unsportsmanlike Conduct:** Any act contrary to the generally understood principles of sportsmanship.

## Summary of Penalties
### Automatic First Down
1. Awarded to offensive team on all defensive fouls with these exceptions:
   (a) Offside.
   (b) Encroachment.
   (c) Delay of game.
   (d) Illegal substitution.
   (e) Excessive time out(s).
   (f) Incidental grasp of face mask.
   (g) Prolonged, excessive or premeditated celebrations by individual players or groups of players.

### Loss of Down (No yardage)
1. Second forward pass behind the line.
2. Forward pass strikes ground, goal post, or crossbar.
3. Forward pass goes out of bounds.
4. Forward pass is first touched by eligible receiver who has gone out of bounds and returned.
5. Forward pass touches or is caught by an ineligible receiver on or behind line.
6. Forward pass thrown from behind line of scrimmage after ball once crossed the line.

### Five Yards
1. Crawling.
2. Defensive holding or illegal use of hands (automatic first down).
3. Delay of game.
4. Encroachment.
5. Too many time outs.
6. False start.
7. Illegal formation.
8. Illegal shift.
9. Illegal motion.
10. Illegal substitution.
11. Kickoff out of bounds between goal lines and not touched.
12. Invalid fair catch signal.
13. More than 11 players on the field at snap for either team.
14. Less than seven men on offensive line at snap.
15. Offside.
16. Failure to pause one second after shift or huddle.
17. Running into kicker (automatic first down).
18. More than one man in motion at snap.
19. Grasping face mask of opponent.
20. Player out of bounds at snap.
21. Ineligible member(s) of kicking team going beyond line of scrimmage before ball is kicked.
22. Illegal return.
23. Failure to report change of eligibility.
24. Prolonged, excessive or premeditated celebrations by individual players or groups of players.

### 10 Yards
1. Offensive pass interference.
2. Ineligible player downfield during passing down.
3. Holding, illegal use of hands, arms or body by offense.
4. Tripping by a member of either team.
5. Helping the runner.
6. Illegal batting or punching a loose ball.
7. Deliberately kicking a loose ball.

### 15 Yards
1. Clipping below the waist.
2. Fair catch interference.
3. Illegal crackback block by offense.
4. Piling on (automatic first down).
5. Roughing the kicker (automatic first down).
6. Roughing the passer (automatic first down).
7. Twisting, turning, or pulling an opponent by the face mask.
8. Unnecessary roughness.
9. Unsportsmanlike conduct.
10. Delay of game at start of either half.
11. Illegal blocking below the waist.
12. A tackler using his helmet to butt, spear, or ram an opponent.
13. Any player who uses the top of his helmet unnecessarily.
14. A punter, placekicker or holder who simulates being roughed by a defensive player.
15. A defender who takes a running start from beyond the line of scrimmage in an attempt to block a field goal or point after touchdown.

### Five Yards and Loss of Down
1. Forward pass thrown from beyond line of scrimmage.

### 10 Yards and Loss of Down
1. Intentional grounding of forward pass (safety if passer is in own end zone). If foul occurs more than 10 yards behind line, play results in loss of down at spot of foul.

### 15 Yards and Loss of Coin Toss Option
1. Team's late arrival on the field prior to scheduled kickoff.

### 15 Yards (and disqualification if flagrant)
1. Striking opponent with fist.
2. Kicking or kneeing opponent.
3. Striking opponent on head or neck with forearm, elbow, or hands whether or not the initial contact is made below the neck area.
4. Roughing kicker.
5. Roughing passer.
6. Malicious unnecessary roughness.
7. Unsportsmanlike conduct.
8. Palpably unfair act. (Distance penalty determined by the Referee after consultation with other officials.)

### 15 Yards and Automatic Disqualification
1. Using a helmet that is not worn as a weapon.

### Suspension From Game
1. Illegal equipment. (Player may return after one down when legally equipped.)

### Touchdown
1. When Referee determines a palpably unfair act deprived a team of a touchdown. (Example: Player comes off bench and tackles runner apparently en route to touchdown.)

## Field
1. Sidelines and end lines are out of bounds. The goal line is actually in the end zone. A player with the ball in his possession scores when the ball is on, above, or over the goal line.
2. The field is rimmed by a white border, a minimum six feet wide, along the sidelines. All of this is out of bounds.
3. The hashmarks (inbound lines) are 70 feet, 9 inches from each sideline.
4. Goal posts must be single-standard type, offset from the end line and painted bright gold. The goal posts must be 18 feet, 6 inches wide and the top face of the crossbar must be 10 feet above the ground. Vertical posts extend at least 30 feet above the crossbar. A ribbon 4 inches by 42 inches long is to be attached to the top of each post. The actual goal is the plane extending indefinitely above the crossbar and between the outer edges of the posts.
5. The field is 360 feet long and 160 feet wide. The end zones are 30 feet deep. The line used in try-for-point plays is two yards out from the goal line.
6. Chain crew members and ball boys must be uniformly identifiable.
7. All clubs must use standardized sideline markers. Pylons must be used for goal line and end line markings.
8. End zone markings and club identification at 50 yard line must be approved by the Commissioner to avoid any confusion as to delineation of goal lines, sidelines, and end lines.

## Ball
1. The home club must have 24 balls available for testing by the Referee one hour before game time. In case of bad weather, a playable ball is to be substituted on request of the offensive team captain.

## Coin Toss
1. The toss of coin will take place within three minutes of kickoff in center of field. The toss will be called by the visiting captain. The winner may choose one of two privileges and the loser gets the other:
   (a) Receive or kick
   (b) Goal his team will defend
2. Immediately prior to the start of the second half, the captains of both teams must inform the officials of their respective choices. The loser of the original coin toss gets first choice.

## Timing
1. The stadium clock is official. In case it stops or is operating incorrectly, the Line Judge takes over the official timing on the field.
2. Each period is 15 minutes. The intermission between the periods is two minutes. Halftime is 15 minutes, unless otherwise specified.
3. On charged team time outs, the Field Judge starts watch and blows whistle after 1 minute 30 seconds. However, Referee may allow two minutes for injured player and three minutes for equipment repair.
4. Each team is allowed three time outs each half.
5. Offensive team has 30 seconds to put the ball in play. The time is displayed on two 30-second clocks, which are visible to the players, officials, and fans. Field Judge is to call a delay of game (five yards) when the time limit is exceeded. In case 30-second clocks are not operating, Field Judge takes over the official timing on the field.
6. Clock will start running when ball is snapped following all changes of team possession.

## Sudden Death
1. The sudden death system of determining the winner shall prevail when score is tied at the end of the regulation playing time of all NFL games. The team scoring first during overtime play shall be the winner and the game automatically ends upon any score (by safety, field goal, or touchdown) or when a score is awarded by Referee for a palpably unfair act.
2. At the end of regulation time the Referee will immediately toss coin at center of field in accordance with rules pertaining to the usual pregame toss. The captain of the visiting team will call the toss.
3. Following a three-minute intermission after the end of the regulation game, play will be continued in 15-minute periods or until there is a score. There is a two-minute intermission between subsequent periods. The teams change goals at the start of each period. Each team has three time outs and general provisions for play in the last two-minutes of a half shall prevail. Disqualified players are not allowed to return.
   **Exception:** In preseason and regular season games there shall be a maximum of 15 minutes of sudden death with two time outs instead of three. General provisions for play in the last two minutes of a half will be in force.

## Timing in Final Two Minutes of Each Half
1. On kickoff, clock does not start until the ball has been legally touched by

player of either team in the field of play. (In all other cases, clock starts with kickoff.)

2. A team cannot "buy" an excess time out for a penalty. However, a fourth time out is allowed without penalty for an injured player, who must be removed immediately. A fifth time out or more is allowed for an injury and a five-yard penalty is assessed if the clock was running. Additionally, if the clock was running and the score is tied or the team in possession is losing, the ball cannot be put in play for at least 10 seconds on the fourth or more time out. The half or game can end while those 10 seconds are run off on the clock.

3. If the defensive team is behind in the score and commits a foul when it has no time outs left in the final 30 seconds of either half, the offensive team can decline the penalty for the foul and have the time on the clock expire.

## Try-for-Point

1. After a touchdown, the scoring team is allowed a try-for-point during one scrimmage down. The ball may be spotted anywhere between the inbounds lines, two or more yards from the goal line. The successful conversion counts one point, whether by run, kick, or pass.

2. The defensive team never can score on a try-for-point. As soon as defense gets possession, or kick is blocked, ball is dead.

3. Any distance penalty for fouls committed by the defense that prevent the try from being attempted can be enforced on the succeeding kickoff. Any foul committed on a successful try will result in a distance penalty being assessed on the ensuing kickoff.

## Players-Substitutions

1. Each team is permitted 11 men on the field at the snap.

2. Unlimited substitution is permitted. However, players may enter the field only when the ball is dead. Players who have been substituted for are not permitted to linger on the field. Such lingering will be interpreted as unsportsmanlike conduct.

3. Players leaving the game must be out of bounds on their own side, clearing the field between the end lines, before a snap or free kick. If player crosses end line leaving field, it is delay of game (five-yard penalty).

## Kickoff

1. The kickoff shall be from the kicking team's 35 yard line at the start of each half and after a field goal and try-for-point. A kickoff is one type of free kick.

2. Either a one-, two-, or three-inch tee may be used (no tee permitted for field goal or try-for-point plays). The ball is put in play by a placekick or dropkick.

3. If kickoff clears the opponent's goal posts it is not a field goal.

4. A kickoff is illegal unless it travels 10 yards OR is touched by the receiving team. Once the ball is touched by the receiving team it is a free ball. Receivers may recover and advance. Kicking team may recover but NOT advance UNLESS receiver had possession and lost the ball.

5. When a kickoff goes out of bounds between the goal lines without being touched by the receiving team, it must be kicked again. There is a five-yard penalty for a short kick or an out-of-bounds kick.

6. If the kicking team either illegally kicks off out of bounds or is guilty of a short free kick on two or more consecutive kickoffs, receiving team shall have an option of either re-kick with a five-yard penalty, or they may take possession of the ball at the dead-ball spot, out-of-bounds spot, or spot of illegal touch.

7. When a kickoff goes out of bounds between the goal lines and is touched last by receiving team, it is receiver's ball at out-of-bounds spot.

## Free Kick

1. In addition to a kickoff, the other free kicks are a kick after a safety and a kick after a fair catch. In both cases, a dropkick, placekick, or punt may be used (a punt may not be used on a kickoff.)

2. On free kick after a fair catch, captain of receiving team has the option to put ball in play by punt, dropkick, or placekick without a tee, or by snap. If the placekick or dropkick goes between the uprights a field goal is scored.

3. On a free kick after a safety, the team scored upon puts ball in play by a punt, dropkick, or placekick without tee. No score can be made on a free kick following a safety, even if a series of penalties places team in position. (A field goal can be scored only on a play from scrimmage or a free kick after a fair catch.)

## Field Goal

1. All field goals attempted and missed from scrimmage line beyond the 20 yard line will result in the defensive team taking possession of the ball at the scrimmage line. On any field goal attempted and missed from scrimmage line inside the 20 yard line, ball will revert to defensive team at the 20 yard line.

## Safety

1. The important factor in a safety is impetus. Two points are scored for the opposing team when the ball is dead on or behind a team's own goal line if the impetus came from a player on that team.

**Examples of Safety:**

(a) Blocked punt goes out of kicking team's end zone. Impetus was provided by punting team. The block only changes direction of ball, not impetus.

(b) Ball carrier retreats from field of play into his own end zone and is downed. Ball carrier provides impetus.

(c) Offensive team commits a foul and spot of enforcement is behind its own goal line.

(d) Player on receiving team muffs punt and, trying to get ball, forces or illegally kicks it into end zone where he or a teammate recovers. He has given new impetus to the ball.

**Examples of Non-Safety:**

(a) Player intercepts a pass inside his own 5 yard line and his momentum car-

ries him into his own end zone. Ball is put in play at spot of interception.

(b) Player intercepts a pass in his own end zone and is downed. Impetus came from passing team, not from defense. (Touchback)

(c) Player passes from behind his own goal line. Opponent bats down ball in end zone. (Incomplete pass)

## Measuring

1. The forward point of the ball is used when measuring.

## Position of Players at Snap

1. Offensive team must have at least seven players on line.

2. Offensive players, not on line, must be at least one yard back at snap. (**Exception:** player who takes snap.)

3. No interior lineman may move after taking or simulating a three-point stance.

4. No player of either team may invade neutral zone before snap.

5. No player of offensive team may charge or move, after assuming set position, in such manner as to lead defense to believe snap has started.

6. If a player changes his eligibility, the Referee must alert the defensive captain after player has reported to him.

7. All players of offensive team must be stationary at snap, except one back who may be in motion parallel to scrimmage line or backward (not forward).

8. After a shift or huddle all players on offensive team must come to an absolute stop for at least one second with no movement of hands, feet, head, or swaying of body.

9. Linemen may lock legs only with the snapper.

10. Quarterbacks can be called for a false start penalty (five yards) if their actions are judged to be an obvious attempt to draw an opponent offside.

## Use of Hands, Arms, and Body

1. No player on offense may assist a runner except by blocking for him. There shall be no interlocking interference.

2. A runner may ward off opponents with his hands and arms but no other player on offense may use hands or arms to obstruct an opponent by grasping with hands, pushing, or encircling any part of his body during a block.

3. Pass blocking is the obstruction of an opponent by use of that part of the body above the knees. During a legal block, hands (open or closed) must be inside the blocker's elbows and can be thrust forward to contact an opponent as long as the contact is inside the frame. Hands cannot be thrust forward above the frame to contact an opponent on the neck, face, or head. (**Note:** The frame is defined as that part of the opponent's body below the neck that is presented to the blocker.) Blocker cannot use his hands or arms to push from behind, hang onto, or encircle an opponent in a manner that restricts his movements as the play develops. By use of up and down action of arm(s), the blocker is permitted to ward off the opponent's attempt to grasp his jersey or arm(s) and prevent legal contact to the head.

4. Run blocking is an aggressive action by a blocker to obstruct an opponent from the ball carrier. During a legal block, contact can be made with the head, shoulders, hands, and/or outer surface of the forearm, or any other part of the body. Hands with extended arms can be thrust forward to contact an opponent as long as the contact is inside the frame and inside the pocket area. [See Pocket Area (Run) Definitions, page 314.] As the play develops, a blocker is permitted to work for and maintain position on an opponent as long as he does not push from behind or clip (outside legal clip zone). A blocker who makes contact with extended arms within the pocket area may maintain such contact outside of the pocket area as long as the action is continuous. A blocker cannot make initial contact with extended arms outside the pocket area. A blocker lined up more than 2 yards outside the tackle is subject, also, to the crackback rule.

5. A defensive player may not tackle or hold an opponent other than a runner. Otherwise, he may use his hands, arms, or body only:

(a) To defend or protect himself against an obstructing opponent.
**Exception:** An eligible receiver is considered to be an obstructing opponent ONLY to a point five yards beyond the line of scrimmage unless the player who receives the snap clearly demonstrates no further intention to pass the ball. Within this five-yard zone, a defensive player may make contact with an eligible receiver that may be maintained as long as it is continuous and unbroken. The defensive player cannot use his hands or arms to push from behind, hang onto, or encircle an eligible receiver in a manner that restricts movement as the play develops. Beyond this five-yard limitation, a defender may use his hands or arms ONLY to defend or protect himself against impending contact caused by a receiver. In such reaction, the defender may not contact a receiver who attempts to take a path to evade him.

(b) To push or pull opponent out of the way on line of scrimmage.

(c) In actual attempt to get at or tackle runner.

(d) To push or pull opponent out of the way in a legal attempt to recover a loose ball.

(e) During a legal block on an opponent who is not an eligible pass receiver.

(f) When legally blocking an eligible pass receiver above the waist.
**Exception:** Eligible receivers lined up within two yards of the tackle, whether on or immediately behind the line, may be blocked below the waist at or behind the line of scrimmage. NO eligible receiver may be blocked below the waist after he goes beyond the line.
**Note:** Once the quarterback hands off or pitches the ball to a back, or if the quarterback leaves the pocket area, the restrictions on the defensive team relative to the offensive receivers will end, provided the ball is not in the air.

6. A defensive player must not contact an opponent above the shoulders with the palm of his hand except to ward him off on the line. This exception is permitted only if it is not a repeated act against the same opponent during any one contact. In all other cases the palms may be used on head, neck, or face only to ward off or push an opponent in legal attempt to get at the ball.

7. Any offensive player who pretends to possess the ball or to whom a teammate pretends to give the ball may be tackled provided he is crossing his scrimmage line between the ends of a normal tight offensive line.

8. An offensive player who lines up more than two yards outside his own tackle or a player who, at the snap, is in a backfield position and subsequently takes a position more than two yards outside a tackle may not clip an opponent anywhere nor may he contact an opponent below the waist if the blocker is moving toward the ball and if contact is made within an area five yards on either side of the line.

9. A player of either team may block at any time provided it is not pass interference, fair catch interference, or unnecessary roughness.

10. A player may not bat or punch:
    (a) A loose ball (in field of play) toward his opponent's goal line or in any direction in either end zone.
    (b) A ball in player possession or attempt to get possession.
    (c) A pass in flight forward toward opponent's goal line.
    **Exception:** A forward or backward pass may be batted in any direction at any time by the defense.

11. No player may deliberately kick any ball except as a punt, dropkick, or placekick.

## Forward Pass

1. A forward pass may be touched or caught by any eligible receiver. All members of the defensive team are eligible. Eligible receivers on the offensive team are players on either end of line (other than center, guard, or tackle) or players at least one yard behind the line at the snap. A T-formation quarterback is not eligible to receive a forward pass during a play from scrimmage.
   **Exception:** T-formation quarterback becomes eligible if pass is previously touched by an eligible receiver.

2. An offensive team may make only one forward pass during each play from scrimmage (Loss of down).

3. The passer must be behind his line of scrimmage (Loss of down and five yards, enforced from the spot of pass).

4. Any eligible offensive player may catch a forward pass. If a pass is touched by one offensive player and touched or caught by a second eligible offensive player, pass completion is legal. Further, all offensive players become eligible once a pass is touched by an eligible receiver or any defensive player.

5. The rules concerning a forward pass and ineligible receivers:
   (a) If ball is touched accidentally by an ineligible receiver on or behind his line: loss of down.
   (b) If ineligible receiver is illegally downfield: loss of 10 yards.
   (c) If touched or caught (intentionally or accidentally) by ineligible receiver beyond the line: loss of 10 yards.
   (d) If ineligible receiver is illegally downfield: loss of 10 yards.

6. If a forward pass is caught simultaneously by eligible players on opposing teams, possession goes to passing team.

7. Any forward pass becomes incomplete and ball is dead if:
   (a) Pass hits the ground or goes out of bounds.
   (b) Hits the goal post or the cross bar of either team.
   (c) Is caught by offensive player after touching ineligible receiver.
   (d) An illegal pass is caught by the passer.

8. A forward pass is complete when a receiver clearly touches the ground with both feet inbounds while in possession of the ball. If a receiver is carried out of bounds by an opponent while in possession in the air, pass is complete at the out-of-bounds spot.

9. If an eligible receiver goes out of bounds accidentally or is forced out by a defender and returns to catch a pass, the play is regarded as a pass caught out of bounds. (Loss of down, no yardage.)

10. On a fourth down pass—when the offensive team is inside the opposition's 20 yard line—an incomplete pass results in a loss of down at the line of scrimmage.

11. If a personal foul is committed by the defense prior to the completion of a pass, the penalty is 15 yards from the spot where ball becomes dead.

12. If a personal foul is committed by the offense prior to the completion of a pass, the penalty is 15 yards from the previous line of scrimmage.

## Intentional Grounding of Forward Pass

1. Intentional grounding of a forward pass is a foul: loss of down and 10 yards from previous spot if passer is in the field of play or loss of down at the spot of the foul if it occurs more than 10 yards behind the line or safety if passer is in his own end zone when ball is released.

2. It is considered intentional grounding of a forward pass when the ball strikes the ground after the passer throws, tosses, or lobs the ball to prevent a loss of yards by his team.

## Protection of Passer

1. By interpretation, a pass begins when the passer—with possession of ball—starts to bring his hand forward. If ball strikes ground after this action has begun, play is ruled an incomplete pass. If passer loses control of ball prior to his bringing his hand forward, play is ruled a fumble.

2. No defensive player may run into a passer of a legal forward pass after the ball has left his hand (15 yards). The Referee must determine whether opponent had a reasonable chance to stop his momentum during an attempt to block the pass or tackle the passer while he still had the ball.

---

3. Officials are to blow the play dead as soon as the quarterback is clearly in the grasp of any tackler.

## Pass Interference

1. There shall be no interference with a forward pass thrown from behind the line. The restriction for the passing team starts with the snap. The restriction on the defensive team starts when the ball leaves the passer's hand. Both restrictions end when the ball is touched by anyone.

2. The penalty for defensive pass interference is an automatic first down at the spot of the foul. If interference is in the end zone, it is first down for the offense on the defense's 1 yard line. If previous spot was inside the defense's 1 yard line, penalty is half the distance to the goal line.

3. The penalty for offensive pass interference is 10 yards from the previous spot.

4. It is interference when a player's movement beyond the passing team's line materially hinders the progress of an eligible opponent in his attempt to reach a pass.
   **Exception:** Such incidental movement or contact when two or more eligible players make a simultaneous and bona fide attempt to catch or bat the ball is permitted. "Simultaneous and bona fide" means the contact of an eligible receiver and a defensive player when each is playing the ball and contact is unavoidable and incidental to the act of trying to catch or bat the ball.

5. It must be remembered that defensive players have as much right to the path of the ball as eligible receivers. Any bodily contact, however severe, is not interference if a player is making a bona fide and simultaneous attempt to catch or bat the ball.

## Backward Pass

1. Any pass not a forward pass is regarded as a backward pass or lateral. A pass parallel to the line is a backward pass. A runner may pass backward at any time. Any player on either team may catch the pass or recover the ball after it touches the ground.

2. A backward pass that strikes the ground can be recovered and advanced by offensive team.

3. A backward pass that strikes the ground can be recovered but cannot be advanced by the defensive team.

4. A backward pass caught in the air can be advanced by the defensive team.

## Fumble

1. The distinction between a fumble and a muff should be kept in mind in considering rules about fumbles. A fumble is the loss of possession of the ball. A muff is the touching of a loose ball by a player in an unsuccessful attempt to obtain possession.

2. A fumble may be advanced by any player on either team regardless of whether recovered before or after ball hits the ground.

3. If an offensive player fumbles anywhere on the field during a fourth down play, or if a player fumbles on any down after the two-minute warning in a half, only the fumbling player is permitted to recover and/or advance the ball. If recovered by any other offensive player, the ball is dead at the spot of the fumble unless it is recovered behind the spot of the fumble. In that case, ball is dead at spot of recovery. Any defensive player may recover and/or advance any fumble.
   **Exception:** The fourth-down fumble rule does not apply if a player touches, but does not possess, a direct snap from center, i.e., a snap in flight as opposed to hand-to-hand exchange.

## Kicks From Scrimmage

1. Any punt or missed field goal that touches a goal post is dead.

2. During a kick from scrimmage, only the end men, as eligible receivers on the line of scrimmage at the time of the snap, are permitted to go beyond the line before the ball is kicked.
   **Exception:** An eligible receiver who, at the snap, is aligned or in motion behind the line and more than one yard outside the end man on his side of the line, clearly making him the outside receiver, REPLACES that end man as the player eligible to go downfield after the snap. All other members of the kicking team must remain at the line of scrimmage until the ball has been kicked.

3. Any punt that is blocked and does not cross the line of scrimmage can be recovered and advanced by either team. However, if offensive team recovers it must make the yardage necessary for its first down to retain possession if punt was on fourth down.

4. The kicking team may never advance its own kick even though legal recovery is made beyond the line of scrimmage. Possession only.

5. A member of the receiving team may not run into or rough a kicker who kicks from behind his line unless contact is:
   (a) Incidental to and after he had touched ball in flight.
   (b) Caused by kicker's own motions.
   (c) Occurs during a quick kick, or a kick made after a run, or after kicker recovers a loose ball. Ball is loose when kicker muffs snap or snap hits ground.
   (d) Defender is blocked into kicker.
   The penalty for running into the kicker is 5 yards and an automatic first down. For roughing the kicker: 15 yards and disqualification if flagrant.

6. If a member of the kicking team attempting to down the ball on or inside opponent's 5 yard line carries the ball into the end zone, it is a touchback.

7. Fouls during a punt are enforced from the previous spot (line of scrimmage).
   **Exception:** Illegal touching, illegal fair catch, invalid fair catch signal, and fouls by the receiving team during loose ball after ball is kicked.

8. While the ball is in the air or rolling on the ground following a punt or field goal attempt and receiving team commits a foul before gaining possession, receiving team will retain possession and will be penalized for its foul.

9. It will be illegal for a defensive player to jump or stand on any player, or be picked up by a teammate or to use a hand or hands on a teammate to gain additional height in an attempt to block a kick (Penalty 15 yards, unsportsmanlike conduct).

10. A punted ball remains a kicked ball until it is declared dead or in possession of either team.

11. Any member of the punting team may down the ball anywhere in the field of play. However, it is illegal touching (Official's time out and receiver's ball at spot of illegal touching). This foul does not offset any foul by receivers during the down.

12. Defensive team may advance all kicks from scrimmage (including unsuccessful field goal) whether or not ball crosses defensive team's goal line. Rules pertaining to kicks from scrimmage apply until defensive team gains possession.

## Fair Catch

1. The member of the receiving team must raise one arm full length above his head while kick is in flight. (Failure to give proper sign: receivers' ball five yards behind spot of signal.)

2. No opponent may interfere with the fair catcher, the ball, or his path to the ball. Penalty: 15 yards from spot of foul and fair catch is awarded.

3. A player who signals for a fair catch is not required to catch the ball. However, if a player signals for a fair catch, he may not block or initiate contact with any player on the kicking team until the ball touches a player. Penalty: snap 15 yards behind spot of foul.

4. If ball hits ground or is touched by member of kicking team in flight, fair catch signal is off and all rules for a kicked ball apply.

5. Any undue advance by a fair catch receiver is delay of game. No specific distance is specified for "undue advance" as ball is dead at spot of catch. If player comes to a reasonable stop, no penalty. For violation, five yards.

6. If time expires while ball is in play and a fair catch is awarded, receiving team may choose to extend the period with one free kick down. However, placekicker may not use tee.

## Foul on Last Play of Half or Game

1. On a foul by defense on last play of half or game, the down is replayed if penalty is accepted.

2. On a foul by the offense on last play of half or game, the down is not replayed and the play in which the foul is committed is nullified. Exception: Fair catch interference, foul following change of possession, illegal touching. No score by offense counts.

3. On double foul on last play of half or game, down is replayed.

## Spot of Enforcement of Foul

1. There are four basic spots at which a penalty for a foul is enforced:
   (a) Spot of foul: The spot where the foul is committed.
   (b) Previous spot: The spot where the ball was put in play.
   (c) Spot of snap, pass, fumble, return kick, or free kick: The spot where the act connected with the foul occurred.
   (d) Succeeding spot: The spot where the ball next would be put in play if no distance penalty were to be enforced.
   **Exception:** If foul occurs after a touchdown and before the whistle for a try-for-point, succeeding spot is spot of next kickoff.

2. All fouls committed by offensive team behind the line of scrimmage and in the field of play shall be penalized from the previous spot.

3. When spot of enforcement for fouls involving defensive holding or illegal use of hands by the defense is behind the line of scrimmage, any penalty yardage to be assessed on that play shall be measured from the line if the foul occurred beyond the line.

## Double Foul

1. If there is a double foul during a down in which there is a change of possession, the team last gaining possession may keep the ball unless its foul was committed prior to the change of possession.

2. If double foul occurs after a change of possession, the defensive team retains the ball at the spot of its foul or dead ball spot.

3. If one of the fouls of a double foul involves disqualification, that player must be removed, but no penalty yardage is to be assessed.

4. If the kickers foul during a punt before possession changes and the receivers foul after possession changes, penalties will be offset and the down is replayed.

## Penalty Enforced on Following Kickoff

1. When a team scores by touchdown, field goal, extra point, or safety and either team commits a personal foul, unsportsmanlike conduct, or obvious unfair act during the down, the penalty will be assessed on the following kickoff.

# NOTES